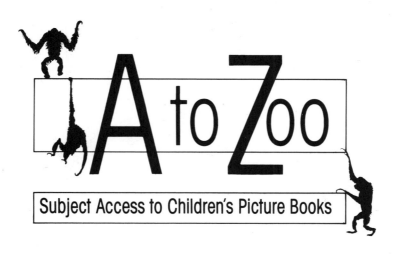

Subject Access to Children's Picture Books

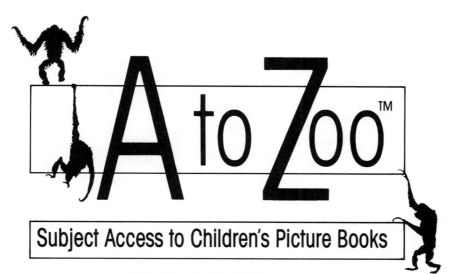

A to Zoo™

Subject Access to Children's Picture Books

Third Edition

Carolyn W. Lima   John A. Lima

R. R. BOWKER
New York

Published by R. R. Bowker Company
a division of Reed Publishing (USA) Inc.
Copyright © 1989 by Reed Publishing (USA) Inc.
All rights reserved
Printed and bound in the United States of America

Interior illustrations by Jean Catherine Lima

Library of Congress Cataloging-in-Publication Data

Lima, Carolyn W.
  A to zoo.

  Bibliography: p.
  Includes index.
  1. Picture-books for children—Bibliography.
2. Children's literature—Bibliography. 3. Catalogs,
Subject. 4. Libraries, Children's—Book lists.
5. Subject headings—Picture-books for children.
6. Subject headings—Children's literature. I. Lima,
John A. II. Title.
Z1037.L715 1989   011.62   89-15916
ISBN 0-8352-2599-2

ISBN 0-8352-2599-2

To the loving memory of our granddaughter
Carolyn Courtney Keyte
September 7, 1988

Contents

Preface

The picture book, long a source of delight and learning for young readers, has gained even more importance during the past few years with the increasing emphasis on early childhood education and the growing need for supervised child care for working mothers. Teachers, librarians, and parents are finding the picture book to be an important learning and entertainment tool. Choosing the right book for a particular situation is time-consuming and frustrating without some guidance. Many responsible professionals and parents do not have the time nor the materials to develop an intimate familiarity with the field. Rather than simply choosing the first title that appears to treat a specific subject from among the many thousands of books available, the user can now identify a book confident that it will cover the desired subject. This third edition of *A to Zoo: Subject Access to Children's Picture Books*, the only comprehensive guide of its kind, provides the necessary help making the task easier for the user. It has nearly 12,000 titles cataloged under 700 subjects.

Originally, the titles in *A to Zoo* (first edition) were based on the San Diego (California) Public Library's collection of picture books for children. This large and versatile collection remains typical of the best and most carefully chosen children's works acquired over a period of time. In the effort to ensure that the most up-to-date information is included in this third edition, the authors consulted many sources. Other public and university library collections, review copies from various publishers, published reviews, and the authors' personal searches of titles and literature provided an information base. Nearly every book was read by the authors to determine subject information and suitability. Out-of-print titles were included because school and public library collections consist mostly of out-of-print materials.

The picture book, as broadly defined within the scope of this book, is a fiction or nonfiction title with illustrations occupying as much or more space than the text and with text vocabulary or concepts suitable for preschool to grade two.

The Introduction: Genesis of the English-Language Picture Book has been updated, and recent sources and reference works were added to the list of suggested titles for further reading. Developments of historical proportion have not been discerned in the years since the second edition was published (1986). Some trends, however, seem evident: mechanical and "pop-up" books are becoming more prolific; attention to the very young reader is reflected in a large number of "board books"—books with cardboard pages designed for tiny tots; and, there is a continued trend toward picture books of a serious nature, bearing a message or lesson, designed to accomplish some social purpose other than mere entertainment of the young reader. Additionally, a large number of classics are being reissued, some with new illustrations, and a number of lengthy collections of an author's or illustrator's works are appearing.

HOW TO USE THIS BOOK

A to Zoo can be used to obtain information about children's picture books in two ways: to learn the titles, authors, and illustrators of books on a particular subject, such as farms or magic; or to ascertain the subject (or subjects) when only the title, author and title, or illustrator and title are known. For example, if the title *Midnight snowman* is known, this volume will enable the user to discover that *Midnight snowman* is written by Caroline Feller Bauer, illustrated by Catherine Stock, and published by Atheneum in 1987, and that it also concerns Seasons—winter, Snowmen, and Weather—snow.

For ease and convenience of reference use, *A to Zoo* is divided into five sections:

> Subject Headings
> Subject Guide
> Bibliographic Guide
> Title Index
> Illustrator Index

SUBJECT HEADINGS: This section contains an alphabetical list of the subjects cataloged in this book. The subject headings reflect the established terms used commonly in public libraries, originally based on questions asked by parents and teachers and then modified and adapted by librarians. To facilitate reference use, and because subjects are requested in a variety of terms, the list of subject headings contains numerous cross-references. Subheadings are arranged alphabetically under each general topic, for example:

> Animals (general topic)
> Animals—anteaters (subheading)
> Animals—antelopes (subheading)
> Animals—apes *see* Animals—gorillas; Animals—monkeys (cross-reference)

SUBJECT GUIDE: This subject-arranged guide to nearly 12,000 picture books for preschool children through second graders is cataloged under 700 subjects. The guide reflects the arrangement in the Subject Headings, alphabetically arranged by subject heading and subheading. Many books, of course, relate to more than one subject, and this comprehensive list provides a means of identifying all those books that may contain any information or material on a particular subject.

If, for example, the user wants books on crabs (crustacea), the Subject Headings section will show that Crustacea is a subject classification. A look in the Subject Guide reveals that under Crustacea there are 13 titles listed alphabetically by author.

BIBLIOGRAPHIC GUIDE: Each book is listed with full bibliographic information. This section is arranged alphabetically by author, or by title when the author is unknown, or by uniform (classic) title. Each entry contains bibliographic information in this order: author, title, illustrator, publisher and date of publication, miscellaneous notes when given, International Standard Book Number (ISBN), and subjects, listed according to the alphabetical classification in the Subject Headings section. Where ISBNs appear they indicate new entries and are the library binding edition or the next best quality edition available.

The user can consult the Bibliographic Guide to find complete data on each of the 13 titles listed in the Subject Guide under the subject of Crustacea, as for example:

> **Knutson, Barbara.** *Why the crab has no head: an African tale*
> ill. by author. Carolrhoda Books, 1987. ISBN 0-87614-
> 322-2. Subj: Behavior—boasting. Crustacea. Folk
> and fairy tales. Foreign lands—Africa. Foreign lands—Zaire.

In the case of joint authors, the second author is listed in alphabetical order, followed by the book title and the name of the primary author or main entry. The user can then locate the first-named author for complete bibliographic information. For example:

> **Stoker, Wayne.** *I can be a welder* (Lillegard, Dee)

Bibliographic information for this title will be found in the Bibliographic Guide section under Lillegard, Dee.

Titles for an author who is both a single author and a joint author are interfiled alphabetically.

Where the author is not known, the entry is listed alphabetically by title with complete bibliographic information following the same format as given above.

Library of Congress conventions regarding the cataloged name of the author(s) have been followed in this edition. Thus, books published under the name Aliki are listed in alphabetical order under Aliki; a cross-reference with the name Brandenberg, Aliki refers the user to the name preferred.

TITLE INDEX: This section contains an alphabetical list of all titles in the book with authors in parentheses, followed by the page number of the full listing in the Bibliographic Guide, such as:

> *Albert's story* (Long, Claudia), 549

If a title has no known author, the name of the illustrator is given if available.

When multiple versions of the same title are listed, the illustrator's name is given with the author's name (when known) in parentheses:

> *The night before Christmas*, ill. by Michael Foreman (Moore, Clement C.), 573
> *The night before Christmas*, ill. by Scott Gustafson (Moore, Clement C.), 573

ILLUSTRATOR INDEX: This section contains an alphabetical list of illustrators with titles and authors, followed by the page number of the full listing in the Bibliographic Guide, for example:

> **Glasser, Judy.** *Albert's story* (Long, Claudia), 549

Titles listed under an illustrator's name appear in alphabetical sequence. When the author is the same as the illustrator then the author's name is not repeated.

Introduction
Genesis of the English-Language Picture Book

Each year increasing numbers of children's books are published, with nearly twice as many titles appearing in 1986 as in 1984, and each one touched in some way by those that preceded it.[1] But how or by what path did the unique genre known as children's picture books arrive at this present and prolific state? Certainly, to imagine a time when children's books did not exist takes more than a little effort. Probably the roots of what we know as children's literature lie in the stories and folktales told and retold through the centuries in every civilization since human beings first learned to speak. These stories were narrated over and over as a sort of oral history, literature, and education.[2] But they were not intended, either primarily or exclusively, for children. It was only through the passing years, as the children who were at least part of any audience responded with interest and delight to these tales, and as adults found less leisure time to be entertained in an increasingly busy world, that the stories and folktales came to be regarded as belonging to the world of the child. These were repeated or retold often by traveling storytellers. Some tales were written down, printed, and spread throughout England and Europe. In the nineteenth century, the brothers Grimm, Jacob and Wilhelm, invited storytellers to their home to narrate the tales and folk stories of Germany, and to collect them and refine them. They altered stories to make them more acceptable for children, or for adults who were concerned about what children read and heard. Nevertheless, they created a stylistic ideal for the fairy tale, making them "more proper and prudent for bourgeois audiences."[3]

Book art or book illustration began with manuscripts—handwritten on parchment or other materials, rolled or scrolled, and later loosely bound into books—that were illuminated or "decorated in lively, vigorous and versatile styles."[4] In time, these decorations, some realistic, some intricate, some imaginative, took on the technological advances of other art forms, notably stained glass, and color was introduced to these illustrated texts.[5]

The children's books that existed in the Middle Ages, before the invention of movable type, were rarely intended to amuse the reader. They were, instead, mostly instructional and moralizing. Monastic teachers, writing essentially for the children of wealthy families, usually wrote in Latin and "began the tradition of didacticism that was to dominate children's books for hundreds of years."[6]

Children's books of that day frequently followed either the rhymed format or the question-and-answer form, both attributed to Aldhelm, abbot of Malmesbury.[7] An early encyclopedia, thought to be the work of Anselm (1033–1109), archbishop of Canterbury, addressed such subjects as "manners and customs, natural science, children's duties, morals, and religious precepts."[8] The books were intended for instruction and indoctrination in the principles of moral and religious belief and behavior,[9] an intent that persisted even after the invention of movable type. Indeed, "children were not born to live happy but to die holy, and true education lay in preparing the soul to meet its maker."[10]

Perhaps the first printed book that was truly intended for children, other than elementary Latin grammar texts, was the French *Les Contenances de la Table*, on the courtesies and manners of dining.[11] Printed and illustrated children's books in Europe followed the invention of printing in the fifteenth century. Those first books were printed in lowercase letters, and "blank spaces were left on the page for initials and marginal decorations to be added in color by hand. In general, the effect was the same as in manuscript."[12] Some well-known and important artists of the time did the illustrations, using woodcuts, engravings, and lithographic processes.[13]

This combination of pictures and printed text, still with the intent of teaching and incorporating the earlier, but persistent dedication to moral and religious education, finally resulted in what is often assumed to be the first real children's picture book in 1657—the *Orbis Pictus* of John Amos Comenius.[14] The simple idea by this Czechoslovakian author was that a child would learn most quickly by naming and showing the object at the same time, a seventeenth-century ABC! Noted for its many illustrations, the book contained the seeds of future children's publications, softening somewhat the earlier "harshness with which, in the unsympathetic age, the first steps of learning were always associated."[15]

In the English language, children's books followed a parallel pattern. William Caxton, England's first printer, was responsible for printing many books, which although intended for adults, were often adopted by children as their own. One, *Aesop's Fables* (about 1484), featured woodcut illustrations, and is an early "milestone" in the history of children's literature.[16] His stories, the first for English children in their own language, gave the lessons of "The Fox and the Grapes" and "The Tortoise and the Hare" to children of the fifteenth century and all who followed thereafter.

Nearly 200 years later, American authors and books for American children, in English, began to appear. Like English publications before them, these books reflected a basic profile of moral and religious education. American John Cotton's *Spiritual Milk for Boston Babes* (1646) was not an especially easy text for the young minds that had to master its Puritan lessons. Later came similar books such as *Pilgrim's Progress* by John Bunyan (1678), *The New England Primer* with its rhyming alphabet (1691), and *Divine and Moral Songs for Children* by Isaac Watts (1715).

In the early eighteenth century, a significant movement began in English children's books with the publication of *Robinson Crusoe* by Daniel Defoe (1715), a narrative that delighted children as well as adults. This innovation, utilizing children's books to carry more intricate messages, perhaps aimed at adults as well as older children, reflected a growing sophistication of society, and perhaps some shifting of purely religious or moral bases toward political morality. An all-time favorite with young readers, *Gulliver's Travels* by Jonathan Swift, published in 1726, illustrates this dual thrust. This work, embellished with a wit and rather pointed sarcasm that is sure to escape the young, nonetheless delighted children with the inhabitants of mythical lands and has managed to survive through the years. Perhaps the ultimate development of this trend is found in Lewis Carroll's *Alice's Adventures in Wonderland* (1865), which manages to be perfectly palatable and interesting to children, yet contains subtle lessons for adult society. Although based on earlier plays and vignettes that had been written only for the purpose of entertainment and use of imagination, *Alice*, and other books of the time, began to reflect a change in society's view of children and of reading materials suitable for children.

The English translation of *Tales of Mother Goose* by Charles Perrault in 1729 made moral lessons for young readers less didactic, but it was 1744 that "saw the real foundation of something today everywhere taken for granted— the production of books for children's enjoyment."[17] This book from a small bookstall in London was *A Little Pretty Pocket-Book*, "now famous as the first book for children published by John Newbery"[18] and may indeed be the first book recognizing children as people with intelligence and other human needs, notably the need for humor and entertainment.[19]

For the next 20 years or so, Newbery published well-illustrated and inexpensive little books for young readers. Soon other books designed especially for children followed this trend. Pictures became an essential and integral part of the book, somewhat downplaying the soul-saving educational harshness of earlier books and promoting amusement and enlightened education. Thomas Bewick's first book specifically intended for children, *A Pretty Book of Pictures for Little Masters and Misses, or Tommy Trip's History of Beasts and Birds*, was published in 1779; and its particular effort represented major strides in the refinement of woodcuts used for book illustration. Bewick "developed better tools for this work, made effective use of the white line, and carried the woodcut to a new level of beauty."[20] His efforts and those of his brother John not only achieved a high level of artistic achievement for woodcuts, but had a more lasting effect on illustrators and illustrations for children's books. "An interesting by-product of the Bewicks' contribution is that artists of established reputation began to sign their pictures for children's books."[21] Some talented artists lovingly produced children's books with special artistic achievement, although their principal skills may have been directed toward adults. For example, William Blake, an artist and poet of considerable renown, published *Songs-of-Innocence* in 1789.[22] An engraver, he produced this "first great original picture book" using etched plates in which the garlands and scrolls were lovingly engraved, of his own original designs, and hand-colored after printing.[23]

Such loving dedication did not long enjoy a singular place in publishing history. Before long commercialism entered the scene and, although some very dedicated people in America and England alike continued to develop books for children, some hackwork also appeared. "Publishers, realizing that children formed a new and somewhat undiscriminating market, were quick to take advantage of the fact. Having chosen a suitable title, and having available some spare woodcut blocks that might be sufficiently relevant for a juvenile book, a publisher would commission a story or series of tales to be woven around the illustrations. One of the results of this was that illustrations of different proportions might be used in the same story, while on other occasions it was clear that the pictures were by different hands. Sometimes the inclusion of a picture was obviously forced. A good example occurs in one of the editions of *Goody Two-Shoes*," attributed to Oliver Goldsmith.[24]

Fortunately, the "hacks" did not totally invade the field of children's picture books. Carefully designed works, crafted with an eye toward the complete and final unit, with special consideration for the means of reproduction, appeared under the guidance of innovative and bold publishers. Beautiful printing became the mark of publishers such as Edmund Evans, printer and artist in his own right, who with his special skill in color engraving published the works of Walter Crane, Randolph Caldecott, and Kate Greenaway. "The work of the three great English picture-book artists of the nineteenth century represents the best to be found in picture books for children in any era; the strength of design and richness of color and detail of Walter Crane's pictures; the eloquence, humor, vitality, and movement of Randolph Caldecott's art; and the tenderness, dignity, and grace of the very personal interpretation of Kate Greenaway's enchanted land of childhood."[25]

These three were indeed great names of the century in the history of children's picture books. The first nursery picture books of Walter Crane, an apprentice wood engraver, were *Sing a Song for Sixpence, The House That Jack Built, Dame Trot and Her Comical Cat,* and *The History of Cock Robin and Jenny Wren*, published by the firm of Warne in 1865 and 1866. Crane was one of the first of the modern illustrators who believed that text and illustrations should be in harmony, forming a complete unit.

Randolph Caldecott, who began drawing at age six, could make animals seemingly come alive on a page. During his short life (1846–1886), he illustrated numerous books for children with fine examples of fun and good humor such as *The Diverting History of John Gilpin, The Babes in the Wood*, and many others from about 1877 until near his death. His preeminence in the art of the children's picture book has been acknowledged by many more recent artists, and is certainly a seminal factor in the establishment of the English style as a standard from which to measure picture book art.[26]

Kate Greenaway's simple verses made an appropriate accompaniment to her lovely drawings. *Under the Window* was her first picture book published by Routledge in 1878. Everywhere in her books are the flowers she so loved. She is probably best known for her *Almanacs*, published between 1883 and 1897.

Like Crane, Caldecott, and Greenaway, the works of Beatrix Potter became as well known to American children as to English. Potter, a self-taught artist addicted to pets with charming characteristics, produced a number of tales for young children, the best known being *The Tale of Peter Rabbit* (1901), which presented the illustrations as an integral part of the story and marked a pivotal point in the development of the modern picture book in Europe.

The very excellence of the growing children's book field in England eclipsed the technologically inferior American product, virtually driving American efforts from the marketplace until nearly 15 years after World War I.[27] Meanwhile, the books of English artists such as L. Leslie Brooke, Arthur Rackham, Edmund Dulac, Charles Folkard, and others continued the tradition of excellence through the first three decades of the twentieth century.

Despite the superior English publications, "a self-conscious and systematic concern for children and the books they read had been growing in the United States."[28] Children's libraries and children's librarians appeared around the turn of the century. In 1916, the Bookshop for Boys and Girls was founded in Boston.[29] In 1924 the Bookshop published *The Horn Book Magazine*, "the first journal in the world to be devoted to the critical appraisal of children's books."[30] Another publication, *Junior Libraries*, made its appearance in 1954; this periodical later became *School Library Journal*, published by R. R. Bowker. In this area, the Americans were ten years ahead of Europeans.

Publishers and editors were becoming more and more oriented toward children's literature. In 1919, Macmillan established a Children's Book Department to be separate from its adult publishing line; other publishing houses began to do the same. Children's Book Week was instituted, an idea that started with Franklin K. Mathiews and was supported by Frederic G. Melcher. A landmark in children's book publishing was established in the United States in 1922 when Melcher, then chief editor of *Publishers Weekly*, proposed at the 1921 American Library Association meeting that a medal be awarded each year for the year's most distinguished contribution to American literature for children written by an American citizen or resident and published in the United States. Named for John Newbery, the medal was first awarded to Hendrik Willem van Loon for his book *The Story of Mankind*.

Melcher, who was always aware of the significance of books in the lives of children, later proposed the establishment of a similar award for picture books, named in honor of Randolph Caldecott whose pictures still delight today's children. Since 1938, the Caldecott Medal has been awarded annually by an awards committee of the American Library Association's Children's Services Division to the illustrator of the most distinguished American picture book for children published in the United States during the preceding year. Again, the recipient must reside in or be a citizen of the United States.

The end of the 1920s marked the newly emerging prominence of the modern children's picture book in America. Mainly imported from Europe until that time, children's picture books now began to be published in America. William Nicholson's *Clever Bill* (1927) was followed the next year by one of the most successful picture books of all time, *Millions of Cats* by Wanda Gág. The perfect marriage of the rhythmic prose and flowing movement of her dramatic black-and-white drawings tell a simple, direct story with a folk flavor. This title is still included in the repertoire of today's storytellers and continues to be taken from the shelves by young readers; it ushered in an explosion of children's book publishing.[31]

By 1930, many publishers had set up separate editing departments expressly for the purpose of publishing children's materials. The White House Conference on Child Health and Protection was held that year to study the plight of the child.[32] Improved technologies accelerated and economized book production. The stage was set for the modern picture book with its profuse illustration. Until this time there were only a few great children's books, illustrated with pictures that were largely an extension of the text. "Yet in a very few years, in respect to the books for the younger children, the artist has attained a place of equal importance with the writer."[33]

The period between World War I and World War II brought many foreign authors and illustrators to America to join and collaborate with American authors and artists. Their talents and varied backgrounds have contributed immensely to the changes in the picture book in America, which truly came into its own in this period of lower production costs. The years of the 1930s, known as the "Golden Thirties," and the years of the 1940s produced a spectacular number and variety of profusely illustrated books for young children.[34] The many new authors and illustrators then beginning their careers in this developing field of children's picture books have continued to keep their places in the hearts of children: such familiar names as Marjorie Flack, Maud and Miska Petersham, Ingri and Edgar d'Aulaire, Ludwig Bemelmans, Theodor Geisel (Dr. Seuss), Marcia Brown, Feodor Rojankovsky, James Daugherty, Robert Lawson, Marguerite de Angeli, Virginia Lee Burton, Robert McCloskey, and many, many more.

The war years of the mid-1940s affected the progress of children's picture books with shortages of materials, priorities, poor quality paper, narrow margins, inferior bindings, and less color and illustration. However, the postwar years began to boom in children's publishing, adding to the list of talented authors and illustrators such names as Maurice Sendak, Brian Wildsmith, Trina Schart Hyman, Paul Galdone, Leo Politi, Ezra Jack Keats, Gyo Fujikawa, Arnold Lobel, and so many more.

Through the years many factors have contributed to the growth, even explosion, of children's picture books—society's changing attitudes toward the child; the development of children's libraries, awards, councils, and studies; increasing interest in children's reading on the part of publishers, educators, and literary critics; changing technologies; and the development of American artists and authors. More recently, new directions in publishing, challenging the library as the principal outlet for children's books, seeking consumer markets and applying modern marketing strategies have affected the nature of the children's picture book.[35] Today the picture book is a part of growing up, a teaching tool, an entertainment medium, a memory to treasure. Perhaps only imagination and the talent of the artist and author can define its limits.

Emphasizing the need for quality materials, some proclaim the 1980s and 1990s as the "day of the artist" in children's books.[36] Significantly, others decry the lack of quality in children's materials and are critical of the abundance of "commercial fluff" published today.[37] Certainly, some of the modern trends give one pause. Spectacular color, shading, and texture are all very evident today, along with broader subject perspectives, picture books that are aimed more at older children (and adults?) than at the traditional audience, and a general sophistication of the product. More mechanical books (pop-ups) reminiscent of the Victorian age are reappearing, as are gimmicks and the trading on the familiarity of prior themes.[38] Many old favorites are being reissued, often showcasing a new illustrator's talents. Many collections or compendiums of an author's or illustrator's works are being published, often in large formats with 60 to 120 or more pages, straining the definition and concept of "picture book." At times, these appear in what can only be called a "coffee-table" format; impressive but hardly "child-friendly." Other trends include the large number of "board" books and other unusual formats, and the development of themes that emphasize reality, such as everyday situations, misbehavior or mischievous behavior, and multicultural or multiethnic experiences.

Professionalism, curiosity on all subjects, and freedom of expression have brought the children's picture book into the late twentieth century with a bewildering array of materials from which to choose. Imaginary animals of the past and future line the shelves with the cats, dogs, horses, and dolphins of the modern day. Fantasy lands compete with tales of spaceships and astronauts; dreams of the future can be found with the realities of the past; picture books of all kinds for all kinds of children—and adults—to enjoy!

For the teacher, librarian, or parent who wishes to open this fantastic world of color and imagination for the child, some tool is necessary to put oneself in touch with the great number of possibilities for enjoyment in the picture book field today. *A to Zoo: Subject Access to Children's Picture Books* is designed with just this purpose in mind.

For those interested in exploring more deeply the world of children's publishing and the children's picture book, a list of suggested titles for further reading begins on page xx.

Notes

1. Jill Rachlin, "Timeless Tales = Big Sales," *U.S. News & World Report,* 105: 5 (Aug. 1, 1988): 50.

2. Caroline M. Hewins, "The History of Children's Books (1888)," in *Children and Literature: Views and Reviews,* comp. Virginia Haviland (New York: Lothrop, 1974), p. 30.

3. Jack Zipes, tr. "Once There Were Two Brothers Named Grimm," in *The Complete Fairy Tales of the Brothers Grimm* (New York: Bantam, 1987), pp. xvii–xxxi.

4. Donnarae MacCann and Olga Richard, *The Child's First Books: A Critical Study of Pictures and Texts* (New York: Wilson, 1973), p. 11.

5. Ibid.

6. Zena Sutherland and May Hill Arbuthnot, *Children and Books,* 7th ed. (Glenview, Ill.: Scott, Foresman, 1986), p. 60.

7. Ibid.

8. Ibid.

9. Ibid.

10. Bettina Hürlimann, *Three Centuries of Children's Books in Europe,* tr. and ed. by Brian Alderson (London: Oxford Univ. Pr., 1967), p. xii.

11. Sutherland and Arbuthnot, *Children and Books,* p. 60.

12. MacCann and Richard, *The Child's First Books,* p. 11.

13. Ibid.

14. Hürlimann, *Three Centuries of Children's Books in Europe,* pp. 127–129.

15. Ruth Sunderlin Freeman, *Children's Picture Books, Yesterday and Today* (Watkins Glen, N.Y.: Century House, 1967), p. 12.

16. Sutherland and Arbuthnot, *Children and Books,* pp. 60, 77, 138.

17. John Newbery, *A Little Pretty Pocket-Book: A Facsimile* (London: Oxford Univ. Pr., 1966), p. 2.

18. Ibid., p. 3.

19. Ibid., p. 2.

20. Sutherland and Arbuthnot, *Children and Books,* p. 139.

21. Ibid., p. 139.

22. Ibid.

23. Brian, Alderson, *Sing a Song for Sixpence: The English Picture Book Tradition and Randolph Caldecott* (Cambridge, England: Cambridge Univ. Pr., 1986), p. 46.

24. Joyce Irene Whalley, *Cobwebs to Catch Flies: Illustrated Books for the Nursery and Schoolroom 1700–1900* (Berkeley: Univ. of California Pr., 1975), p. 14.

25. Alderson, *Sing a Song for Sixpence*, p. 8.

26. Ruth Hill Viguers, "Introduction," in Kate Greenaway, *The Kate Greenaway Treasury* (Cleveland: World, 1967), p. 13.

27. Barbara Bader, *American Picturebooks from Noah's Ark to the Beast Within* (New York: Macmillan, 1976), p. 7.

28. Viguers, "Introduction," p. 39.

29. Ibid.

30. Ibid.

31. Sutherland and Arbuthnot, *Children and Books*, p. 122.

32. Binnie Tate Wilkin, *Survival Themes in Fiction for Children and Young People* (Metuchen, N.J.: Scarecrow, 1978), p. 21.

33. Cornelia Meigs et al. *A Critical History of Children's Literature* (New York: Macmillan, 1953), p. 587.

34. Ibid., p. 438.

35. Barbara Elleman, "Current Trends in Literature for Children," *Library Trends* 35: 3 (Winter 1987): 421.

36. Sutherland and Arbuthnot, *Children and Books*, p. 161.

37. Rachlin, "Timeless Tales = Big Sales," p. 51.

38. Elleman, "Current Trends in Literature for Children," pp. 415, 421.

Further Reading

Alderson, Brian. *Looking at Picture Books 1973*. Chicago: Children's Book Council, 1974.

*———. *Sing a Song for Sixpence: The English Picture Book Tradition and Randolph Caldecott*. Cambridge, England: Cambridge Univ. Pr., 1986.

Andersson, Theodore. *A Guide to Family Reading in Two Languages: The Preschool Years*. Wheaton, Md.: National Clearinghouse for Bilingual Education, 1981.

Arbuthnot, May Hill et al. *The Arbuthnot Anthology of Children's Literature*, 4th ed. Glenview, Ill.: Scott, Foresman, 1976.

*Bader, Barbara. *American Picturebooks from Noah's Ark to the Beast Within*. New York: Macmillan, 1976.

Barchilon, Jacques, and Pettit, Henry. *The Authentic Mother Goose Fairy Tales and Nursery Rhymes*. Athens, Ohio: Swallow Pr., 1960.

Barry, Florence V. *A Century of Children's Books*. London: Methuen, 1922.

Bingham, Jane, ed. *Writers for Children*. New York: Scribner's, 1987.

*———, and Scholt, Grayce, eds. *Fifteen Centuries of Children's Literature: An Annotated Chronology of British and American Works in Historical Context*. Westport, Conn.: Greenwood Pr., 1980.

Bland, David. *A History of Book Illustration*, 2nd ed. London: Faber & Faber, 1969.

———. *The Illustration of Books*. London: Faber & Faber, 1962.

Bodger, Joan. *How the Heather Looks*. New York: Viking, 1965.

Bottigheimer, Ruth B. *Grimms' Bad Girls and Bold Boys*. New Haven, Conn.: Yale Univ. Pr., 1987.

Braun, Saul. "Sendak Raises the Shade on Childhood." *New York Times Magazine* (June 7, 1970): 34+.

Bush, Margaret A. *Children's Literature: A Guide to Reference Services and Monographs*. Englewood, Colo.: Libraries Unlimited, 1988.

Butler, Dorothy. *Babies Need Books*. New York: Atheneum, 1980.

Butler, Francelia, and Rotert, Richard W., eds. *Reflections on Literature for Children*. Hamden, Conn.: Shoe String Pr., 1984.

———. *Triumphs of the Spirit in Children's Literature*. Hamden, Conn.: Library Professional Publications, 1986.

Carroll, Frances Laverne, and Meacham, Mary. *Exciting, Funny, Scary, Short, Differ-*

*Indicates especially recommended titles in this reading list.

ent, and Sad Books Kids Like about Animals, Science, Sports, Families, Songs, and Other Things. Chicago: ALA, 1984.

Cianciola, Patricia. Illustrations in Children's Books, 2nd ed. Dubuque, Iowa: William C. Brown, 1976.

Clay, Marie. "Introduction." In Cushla and Her Books, by Dorothy Butler. Boston: Horn Book, 1980.

————, and Butler, Dorothy. Reading Begins at Home. 2nd ed. Exeter, N.H.: Heinemann, 1987.

Comenius, John Amos. The Orbis Pictus of John Amos Comenius. Detroit: Singing Tree, 1968.

Crouch, Marcus. Treasure Seekers and Borrowers: Children's Books in Britain 1900–1960. London: Library Association, 1962.

Daniel, Eloise. A Treasury of Books for Family Enjoyment: Books for Children from Infancy to Grade 2. Pontiac, Mich.: Blue Engine Pr., 1983.

Darling, Richard L. The Rise of Children's Book Reviewing in America, 1865–1881. New York: R. R. Bowker, 1968.

Darrell, Margery, ed. Once Upon a Time: The Fairy-Tale World of Arthur Rackham. New York: Viking, 1972.

*Darton, F. J. H. Children's Books in England: Five Centuries of Social Life, 3rd ed. Ed. by Brian Alderson. New York: Cambridge Univ. Pr., 1982.

*Delamar, Gloria T. Mother Goose: From Nursery to Literature. Jefferson, N.C.: McFarland, 1987.

Demers, Patricia, ed. A Garland from the Golden Age: Children's Literature from 1850–1900. New York: Oxford Univ. Pr., 1984.

————, and Moyles, Gordon, eds. From Instruction to Delight: An Anthology of Children's Literature to 1850. New York: Oxford Univ. Pr., 1982.

Duvoisin, Roger. "Children's Book Illustration: The Pleasure and Problems." Top of the News 22: 30 (Nov. 1965).

Earle, Alice Morse. Child Life in Colonial Days. New York: Macmillan, 1899.

Eckenstein, Lina. Comparative Studies in Nursery Rhymes. London: Duckworth, 1906; Detroit: Singing Tree, 1968.

Egoff, Sheila A.; Stubbs, G. T.; and Ashley, L. F., eds. Only Connect: Readings on Children's Literature, 2nd ed. New York: Oxford Univ. Pr., 1980.

————. Worlds Within: Children's Fantasy from the Middle Ages to Today. Chicago: ALA, 1988.

Ellis, Alec. A History of Children's Reading and Literature. Elmsford, N.Y.: Pergamon Pr., 1968.

Estes, Glenn, ed. American Writers for Children Since 1960. Detroit: Gale, 1987.

Ettlinger, John R. T., and Spirt, Diana L. Choosing Books for Young People, Vol. 2. Phoenix: Oryx, 1987.

Eyre, Frank. British Children's Books in the Twentieth Century. New York: Dutton, 1973.

————. Twentieth Century Children's Books. Cambridge, Mass.: Robert Bentley, 1953.

Fiction, Folklore, Fantasy and Poetry for Children, 1876–1985, 2 vols. New York: R. R. Bowker, 1986.

Field, Louise F. The Child and His Book: Some Account of the History and Progress of Children's Literature in England. Detroit: Singing Tree, 1968.

Fisher, Margery Turner. Intent upon Reading: A Critical Appraisal of Modern Fiction for Children. Leicester, England: Brockhampton Pr., 1961.

————. Who's Who in Children's Books: A Treasury of the Familiar Characters of Childhood. New York: Holt, 1975.

Fox, Geoffrey Percival et al., eds. Writers, Critics, and Children: Articles from Children's Literature in Education. New York: Agathon Pr., 1976.

*Freeman, Ruth Sunderlin. Children's Picture Books, Yesterday and Today. Watkins Glen, N.Y.: Century House, 1967.

Galinsky, Ellen, and David, Judy. The Preschool Years: Family Strategies That Work—From Experts and Parents. New York: Times Books, 1988.

*Gillespie, John T., and Gilbert, Christine B., eds. Best Books for Children: Preschool Through the Middle Grades, 3rd ed. New York: R. R. Bowker, 1985.

Gillespie, Margaret C., and Connor, John W. Creative Growth Through Literature for Children and Adolescents. Columbus, Ohio: Merrill, 1975.

Gottlieb, Gerald. Early Children's Books and Their Illustration. Boston: Godine, 1975.

Green, Percy B. A History of Nursery Rhymes. Detroit: Singing Tree, 1968.

Green, Roger Lancelyn. *Tellers of Tales: British Authors of Children's Books from 1800 to 1964*. New York: Watts, 1965.

*Greenaway, Kate. *The Kate Greenaway Treasury*. Cleveland: World 1967.

Halsey, Rosalie V. *Forgotten Books of the American Nursery*. Detroit: Singing Tree, 1969.

Harrison, Barbara G., and Maguire, Gregory. *Innocence and Experience: Essays and Conversations on Children's Literature*. New York: Lothrop, 1987.

*Haviland, Virginia, comp. *Children and Literature: Views and Reviews*. New York: Lothrop, 1974.

_____. *Children's Literature: A Guide to Reference Sources*. Washington, D.C.: Library of Congress, 1966; first supplement, 1972.

Hendrickson, Linnea. *Children's Literature: A Guide to the Criticism*. Boston: G. K. Hall, 1987.

Huber, Miriam Blanton. *Story and Verse for Children*, 3rd ed. New York: Macmillan, 1965.

*Hürlimann, Bettina. *Three Centuries of Children's Books in Europe*. Ed. and tr. by Brian Alderson. London: Oxford Univ. Pr., 1967; Cleveland: World, 1968.

Inglis, Fred. *The Promise of Happiness*. New York: Cambridge Univ. Pr., 1981.

James, Philip. *Children's Books of Yesterday*. Ed. by C. Geoffrey Holme. London and New York: Studio, 1933; Detroit: Gale, 1976.

Jan, Isabelle. *On Children's Literature*. Ed. by Catherine Storr. New York: Schocken Books, 1974.

Katz, Lillian G., ed. *Current Topics in Early Childhood Education*, Vol. 6. Norwood, N.J.: Ablex, 1986.

Kiefer, Monica. *American Children Through Their Books, 1700–1835*. Philadelphia: Univ. of Pennsylvania Pr., 1948, 1970.

Klemin, Diana. *The Art of Art for Children's Books*. Greenwich, Conn.: Murton Pr., 1966, 1982.

_____. *The Illustrated Book*. Greenwich, Conn.: Murton Pr., 1970, 1983.

Lanes, Selma G. "The Art of Maurice Sendak: A Diversity of Influences Inform an Art for Children," *Artforum* IX (May 1971): 70–73.

Leif, Irving P. *Children's Literature: A Historical and Contemporary Bibliography*. Troy, N.Y.: Whitston, 1977.

Lewis, John. *The Twentieth Century Book: Its Illustration and Design*. New York: Van Nostrand Reinhold, 1967.

Linder, Leslie L. *The Art of Beatrix Potter*, 6th rev. ed. London: Warne, 1972.

*Lipson, Eden Ross. *The New York Times Parent's Guide to the Best Books for Children*. New York: Times Books, 1989.

Lukens, Rebecca J. *A Critical Handbook of Children's Literature*, 2nd ed. Glenview, Ill: Scott, Foresman, 1981.

Lynn, Ruth Nadelman. *Fantasy Literature for Children and Young Adults: An Annotated Bibliography*, 3rd ed. New York: R. R. Bowker, 1989.

Lystad, Mary. *From Dr. Mather to Dr. Seuss: Two Hundred Years of American Books for Children*. Cambridge, Mass.: Schenkman, 1980.

*MacCann, Donnarae, and Richard, Olga. *The Child's First Books*. New York: Wilson, 1973.

MacCann, Donnarae, and Woodard, Gloria, eds. *The Black American in Books for Children: Readings in Racism*, 2nd ed. Metuchen, N.J.: Scarecrow Pr., 1985.

MacDonald, Margaret Read. *The Storyteller's Sourcebook: A Subject, Title, and Motif Index to Folklore Collections for Children*. Detroit: Neal-Schuman Publishers, Inc., in association with Gale Research Co., 1982.

MacDonald, Ruth K. *Dr. Seuss*. Boston: Twayne, 1988.

*McTigue, Bernard, ed. *A Child's Garden of Delights: Pictures, Poems, and Stories for Children from the Collection of the New York Public Library*. New York: Abrams, 1987.

Mahoney, Ellen, and Wilcox, Leah. *Ready, Set, Read: Best Books to Prepare Preschoolers*. Metuchen, N.J.: Scarecrow, 1985.

Mahony, Bertha E.; Latimer, Louise P.; and Folmsbee, Beulah, comps. *Illustrators of Children's Books, 1744–1945*. Boston: Horn Book, 1947.

Meacham, Mary. *Information Sources in Children's Literature*. Westport, Conn.: Greenwood Pr., 1978.

*Meigs, Cornelia et al. *A Critical History of Children's Literature*. New York: Macmillan, 1953; rev. ed., 1969.

Monson, Diane L., ed. *Adventuring with Books: A Booklist for Pre-K–Grade 6.* Urbana, Ill.: NCTE, 1985.

Moore, Anne Carroll. *My Roads to Childhood.* Boston: Horn Book, 1961.

Moransee, Jesse R., ed. *Children's Prize Books.* Ridgewood, N.J.: K. G. Saur, 1983.

Muir, Percy. *English Children's Books, 1600–1900.* New York: Praeger, 1969.

*Newbery, John. *A Little Pretty Pocket-Book: A Facsimile.* London: Oxford Univ. Pr., 1966.

*Nodelman, Perry. *Words about Pictures: The Narrative Art of Children's Picture Books.* Athens, Ga.: Univ. of Georgia Pr., 1989.

Opie, Iona, and Opie, Peter. *A Family Book of Nursery Rhymes.* New York: Oxford Univ. Pr., 1964.

_____. *A Nursery Companion.* New York: Oxford Univ. Pr., 1980.

_____. *The Oxford Dictionary of Nursery Rhymes.* New York: Oxford Univ. Pr., 1951.

Oppenheim, Joanne F. et al. *Choosing Books for Kids.* New York: Ballantine, 1986.

The Original Mother Goose's Melody, As First Issued by John Newbery, of London, about A.D. 1760. Reproduced in facsimile from the edition as reprinted by Isaiah Thomas of Worcester, Mass., about A.D. 1785, with introductory notes by William H. Whitmore. Detroit: Singing Tree, 1969.

Paterson, Katherine. *The Spying Heart: More Thoughts on Reading and Writing Books for Children.* New York: Dutton, 1988.

*Pellowski, Anne. *The Family Storytelling Handbook.* New York: Macmillan, 1987.

Pitz, Henry C. *Illustrating Children's Books: History, Technique, Production.* New York: Watson-Guptill, 1963.

Potter, Beatrix. *Beatrix Potter: The V and A Collection.* London: Warne, 1986.

Prentice, Jeffrey, and Bird, Bettina. *Dromkeen: A Journey into Children's Literature.* New York: Henry Holt, 1988.

Preschool Services and Parent Education Committee, Association for Library Service to Children. *Opening Doors for Preschool Children and Their Parents,* 2nd ed. Chicago: ALA, 1981.

Richard, Olga. "The Visual Language of the Picture Book." *Wilson Library Bulletin* (Dec. 1969).

Roback, Diane, ed. "Arnold Lobel's Three Years with Mother Goose." *Publishers Weekly* 230: 8 (Aug. 22, 1986).

Roberts, Ellen E. M. *The Children's Picture Book.* Cincinnati, Ohio: Writer's Digest, 1981, 1987.

Rosenbach, Abraham S. W. *Early American Children's Books with Bibliographical Descriptions of the Books in His Private Collection.* Foreword by A. Edward Newton. Portland, Maine: Southworth Pr., 1933.

Sadker, Myra, and Sadker, David Miller. *Now Upon a Time: A Contemporary View of Children's Literature.* New York: Harper, 1977.

Salway, Lance, ed. *A Peculiar Gift.* New York: Penguin, 1976.

San Diego Museum of Art Staff, eds. *Dr. Seuss from Then to Now.* New York: Random House, 1987.

Sendak, Maurice. *Caldecott & Co.: Notes on Books and Pictures.* New York: Farrar, Straus & Giroux, 1988.

_____. "Mother Goose's Garnishings." *Book Week.* Fall Children's Issue (Oct. 31, 1965): 5, 38–40; also printed in Haviland, *Children and Literature,* pp. 188–195.

Senick, Gerald J., ed. *Children's Literature Review,* Vols. 12, 13. Detroit: Gale, 1987.

Smith, Dora V. *Fifty Years of Children's Books, 1910–1960.* Urbana, Ill.: NCTE, 1963.

*Smith, Elva S. *The History of Children's Literature: A Syllabus with Selected Bibliographies,* rev. and enlarged by Margaret Hodges and Susan Steinfirst. Chicago: ALA, 1980.

Stott, Jon. *Children's Literature from A to Z: A Guide for Parents and Teachers.* New York: McGraw-Hill, 1984.

Sutherland, Zena, ed. *The Best in Children's Books: The University of Chicago Guide to Children's Literature, 1979–1984.* Chicago: Univ. of Chicago Pr., 1986.

*_____, and Arbuthnot, May Hill. *Children and Books,* 7th ed. Glenview, Ill.: Scott, Foresman, 1986.

Targ, William, ed. *Bibliophile in the Nursery.* Metuchen, N.J.: Scarecrow, 1969.

*Taylor, Judy. *Beatrix Potter: Artist, Storyteller and Countrywoman.* London: Warne, 1986.

_____ et al. *Beatrix Potter, 1866–1943: The Artist and Her World.* London: Warne, 1987.

Thomas, Katherine Elwes. *The Real Personages of Mother Goose.* New York: Lothrop, 1930.

Thomson, Susan Ruth, ed. *Kate Greenaway: A Catalogue of the Kate Greenaway Collection, Rare Book Room, Detroit Public Library.* Detroit: Wayne State Univ. Pr., 1977.

Thwaite, Mary. *From Primer to Pleasure in Reading,* 2nd ed. London: The Library Association, 1972.

Townsend, John Rowe. *Written for Children: An Outline of English-Language Children's Literature,* 3rd rev. ed. New York: Harper, 1988.

Viguers, Ruth Hill; Dalphin, Marcia; and Miller, Bertha Mahony, comps. *Illustrators of Children's Books, 1946–1956.* Boston: Horn Book, 1958.

Weitenkampf, Frank. *The Illustrated Book.* Cambridge, Mass.: Harvard Univ. Pr., 1938.

Welch, D'Alte A. *A Bibliography of American Children's Books Printed Prior to 1821.* Worcester, Mass.: American Antiquarian Society, 1972.

*Whalley, Joyce Irene. *Cobwebs to Catch Flies: Illustrated Books for the Nursery and Schoolroom 1700–1900.* Berkeley: Univ. of California Pr., 1975.

White, Burton L. *Educating the Infant and Toddler.* Lexington, Mass.: Lexington Bks., 1987.

White, Dorothy M. Neal. *Books Before Five.* New York: Oxford Univ. Pr., 1954.

White, Mary Lou. *Adventuring with Books: A Booklist for Pre-K–Grade 6.* Chicago: ALA, 1981.

————. *Children's Literature: Criticism and Response.* Columbus, Ohio: Merrill, 1976.

*Wilkin, Binnie Tate. *Survival Themes in Fiction for Children and Young People.* Metuchen, N.J.: Scarecrow, 1978.

Wilson, Elizabeth L. *Books Children Love.* Westchester, Ill.: Good News, 1987.

*Zipes, Jack, tr. *The Complete Fairy Tales of the Brothers Grimm.* New York: Bantam, 1987.

A to Zoo

Subject Access to Children's Picture Books

Subject Headings

Main headings, subheadings, and cross-references are arranged alphabetically and provide a quick reference to the subjects used in the Subject Guide section where author and title names appear under appropriate headings.

Aardvarks *see* Animals – aardvarks
ABC books
Abuse to children *see* Child abuse
Accordion books *see* Format, unusual
Activities
Activities – baby-sitting
Activities – ballooning
Activities – bathing
Activities – cooking
Activities – dancing
Activities – digging
Activities – flying
Activities – gardening
Activities – jumping
Activities – knitting
Activities – painting
Activities – photographing
Activities – picnicking
Activities – playing
Activities – reading
Activities – shopping *see* Shopping
Activities – swinging
Activities – trading
Activities – traveling
Activities – vacationing
Activities – walking
Activities – weaving
Activities – whistling
Activities – working
Activities – writing
Adoption
Africa *see* Foreign lands – Africa
Afro-Americans *see* Ethnic groups in the U.S. – Afro-Americans
Aged *see* Old age
Aggressiveness *see* Character traits – assertiveness
Airplane pilots *see* Careers – airplane pilots
Airplanes, airports
Albatrosses *see* Birds – albatrosses
Alligators *see* Reptiles – alligators, crocodiles
Alphabet books *see* ABC books
Alzheimer's *see* Illness – Alzheimer's

Ambition *see* Character traits – ambition
American Indians *see* Indians of North America
Amphibians *see* Frogs and toads; Reptiles
Anatomy
Angels
Anger *see* Emotions – anger
Animals
Animals – aardvarks
Animals – anteaters
Animals – apes *see* Animals – gorillas; Animals – monkeys
Animals – armadillos
Animals – badgers
Animals – bats
Animals – bears
Animals – beavers
Animals – bobcats
Animals – buffaloes
Animals – bulls, cows
Animals – camels
Animals – caribou *see* Animals – reindeer
Animals – cats
Animals – cheetahs
Animals – chipmunks
Animals – cougars
Animals – coyotes
Animals – deer
Animals, dislike of *see* Behavior – animals, dislike of
Animals – dogs
Animals – dolphins
Animals – donkeys
Animals – elephants
Animals – endangered animals
Animals – foxes
Animals – gerbils
Animals – giraffes
Animals – goats
Animals – gorillas
Animals – groundhogs
Animals – guinea pigs
Animals – hamsters
Animals – hedgehogs
Animals – hippopotami
Animals – horses
Animals – hyenas
Animals – kangaroos
Animals – kinkajous

Animals – koala bears
Animals – lemmings
Animals – leopards
Animals – lions
Animals – llamas
Animals – mice
Animals – minks
Animals – moles
Animals – mongooses
Animals – monkeys
Animals – moose
Animals – mules
Animals – muskrats
Animals – octopuses *see* Octopuses
Animals – otters
Animals – pack rats
Animals – pandas
Animals – pigs
Animals – polar bears
Animals – porcupines
Animals – possums
Animals – prairie dogs
Animals – rabbits
Animals – raccoons
Animals – rats
Animals – reindeer
Animals – rhinoceros
Animals – sea lions
Animals – seals
Animals – sheep
Animals – shrews
Animals – skunks
Animals – sloths
Animals – snails
Animals – squirrels
Animals – tapirs
Animals – tigers
Animals – walruses
Animals – water buffaloes
Animals – weasels
Animals – whales
Animals – wolves
Animals – wombats
Animals – worms
Animals – yaks
Animals – zebras
Antarctic *see* Foreign lands – Antarctic
Anteaters *see* Animals – anteaters
Anti-violence *see* Violence, anti-violence
Ants *see* Insects – ants

Apes *see* Animals – gorillas;
  Animals – monkeys
Appearance *see* Character
  traits – appearance
April Fools' Day *see* Holidays
  – April Fools' Day
Aquariums
Arabia *see* Foreign lands –
  Arabia
Architects *see* Careers –
  architects
Arctic *see* Foreign lands –
  Arctic
Arguing *see* Behavior –
  fighting, arguing
Arithmetic *see* Counting
Armadillos *see* Animals –
  armadillos
Armenia *see* Foreign lands –
  Armenia
Art
Artists *see* Careers – artists
Assertiveness *see* Character
  traits – assertiveness
Astrology *see* Zodiac
Astronauts *see* Careers –
  astronauts; Space and space
  ships
Astronomers *see* Careers –
  astronomers
Australia *see* Foreign lands –
  Australia
Austria *see* Foreign lands –
  Austria
Authors, children *see* Children
  as authors
Automobiles
Autumn *see* Seasons – fall

Babies
Baby-sitting *see* Activities –
  baby-sitting
Bad day *see* Behavior – bad
  day
Badgers *see* Animals – badgers
Bakers *see* Careers – bakers
Bali *see* Foreign lands – Bali
Ballooning *see* Activities –
  ballooning
Balloons *see* Toys – balloons
Balls *see* Toys – balls
Barbers *see* Careers – barbers
Barns
Barons *see* Royalty
Baseball *see* Sports – baseball
Basketball *see* Sports –
  basketball
Bathing *see* Activities –
  bathing
Bats *see* Animals – bats
Bavaria *see* Foreign lands –
  Austria; Foreign lands –
  Germany; Foreign lands –
  Tyrol
Beaches *see* Sea and seashore
Bears *see* Animals – bears;
  Animals – pandas; Animals
  – polar bears
Bears – toys *see* Toys – teddy
  bears
Beasts *see* Monsters

Beavers *see* Animals – beavers
Bedtime
Bees *see* Insects – bees
Beetles *see* Insects – beetles
Behavior
Behavior – aggressiveness *see*
  Character traits –
  assertiveness
Behavior – animals, dislike of
Behavior – bad day
Behavior – boasting
Behavior – boredom
Behavior – bullying
Behavior – carelessness
Behavior – collecting things
Behavior – disbelief
Behavior – dissatisfaction
Behavior – fighting, arguing
Behavior – forgetfulness
Behavior – gossip
Behavior – greed
Behavior – growing up
Behavior – hiding
Behavior – hiding things
Behavior – hurrying
Behavior – imitation
Behavior – indifference
Behavior – lateness *see*
  Behavior – tardiness
Behavior – losing things
Behavior – lost
Behavior – lying
Behavior – misbehavior
Behavior – mistakes
Behavior – misunderstanding
Behavior – nagging
Behavior – needing someone
Behavior – running away
Behavior – saving things
Behavior – secrets
Behavior – seeking better
  things
Behavior – sharing
Behavior – solitude
Behavior – stealing
Behavior – talking to
  strangers
Behavior – tardiness
Behavior – thumbsucking *see*
  Thumbsucking
Behavior – trickery
Behavior – unnoticed, unseen
Behavior – wishing
Behavior – worrying
Being different *see* Character
  traits – being different
Bicycling *see* Sports – bicycling
Bigotry *see* Prejudice
Birds
Birds – albatrosses
Birds – blackbirds
Birds – bluejays
Birds – buzzards
Birds – canaries
Birds – cardinals
Birds – chickens
Birds – cockatoos
Birds – cormorants
Birds – cranes
Birds – crows
Birds – doves
Birds – ducks

Birds – eagles
Birds – egrets
Birds – flamingos
Birds – geese
Birds – hawks
Birds – mockingbirds
Birds – nightingales
Birds – ostriches
Birds – owls
Birds – parakeets, parrots
Birds – peacocks, peahens
Birds – pelicans
Birds – penguins
Birds – pigeons
Birds – puffins
Birds – ravens
Birds – robins
Birds – sandpipers
Birds – sea gulls
Birds – sparrows
Birds – storks
Birds – swallows
Birds – swans
Birds – toucans
Birds – turkeys
Birds – vultures
Birds – woodpeckers
Birds – wrens
Birthdays
Black Americans *see* Ethnic
  groups in the U.S. –
  Afro-Americans
Blackbirds *see* Birds –
  blackbirds
Blackouts *see* Power failure
Blindness *see* Handicaps –
  blindness
Blocks *see* Toys – blocks
Bluejays *see* Birds – bluejays
Board books *see* Format,
  unusual – board books
Boasting *see* Behavior –
  boasting
Boats, ships
Bobcats *see* Animals – bobcats
Boogeyman *see* Monsters
Books *see* Activities – reading;
  Libraries
Boredom *see* Behavior –
  boredom
Bravery *see* Character traits –
  bravery
Bridges
Brothers *see* Family life –
  Brothers
Brownies *see* Elves and little
  people
Buffaloes *see* Animals –
  buffaloes
Bugs *see* Insects
Bulls *see* Animals – bulls, cows
Bullying *see* Behavior –
  bullying
Bumble bees *see* Insects – bees
Burglars *see* Crime
Burros *see* Animals – donkeys
Bus drivers *see* Careers – bus
  drivers
Buses
Butchers *see* Careers –
  butchers

Butterflies *see* Insects –
butterflies, caterpillars
Buzzards *see* Birds – buzzards

Cab drivers *see* Careers – taxi
drivers
Cable cars, trolleys
Cabs *see* Taxis
Caldecott award book
Caldecott award honor book
Camels *see* Animals – camels
Camping *see* Sports – camping
Canada *see* Foreign lands –
Canada
Canaries *see* Birds – canaries
Cardboard page books *see*
Format, unusual – board
books
Cardinals *see* Birds – cardinals
Careers
Careers – airplane pilots
Careers – architects
Careers – artists
Careers – astronauts
Careers – astronomers
Careers – bakers
Careers – barbers
Careers – bus drivers
Careers – butchers
Careers – cab drivers *see*
Careers – taxi drivers
Careers – carpenters
Careers – chefs
Careers – clockmakers
Careers – dentists
Careers – detectives
Careers – doctors
Careers – electricians
Careers – farmers
Careers – firefighters
Careers – fishermen
Careers – forest rangers *see*
Careers – park rangers
Careers – fortune tellers
Careers – garbage collectors
Careers – geologists
Careers – handyman
Careers – judges
Careers – librarians
Careers – maids
Careers – mail carriers
Careers – mechanics
Careers – military
Careers – miners
Careers – models
Careers – nuns
Careers – nurses
Careers – park rangers
Careers – peddlers
Careers – physicians *see*
Careers – doctors
Careers – pilots *see* Careers –
airplane pilots
Careers – police officers
Careers – race car drivers
Careers – railroad engineers
Careers – rangers *see* Careers
– park rangers
Careers – reporters
Careers – sailors *see* Careers –
military

Careers – seamstresses
Careers – shoemakers
Careers – soldiers *see* Careers
– military
Careers – storekeepers
Careers – tailors
Careers – taxi drivers
Careers – teachers
Careers – telephone operators
Careers – train engineers *see*
Careers – railroad engineers
Careers – truck drivers
Careers – veterinarians
Careers – waiters, waitresses
Careers – waitresses *see*
Careers – waiters, waitresses
Careers – welders
Careers – window cleaners
Careers – writers
Carelessness *see* Behavior –
carelessness
Caribbean Islands *see* Foreign
lands – Caribbean Islands
Carnivals *see* Fairs
Carousels *see* Merry-go-rounds
Carpenters *see* Careers –
carpenters
Cars *see* Automobiles
Caterpillars *see* Insects –
butterflies, caterpillars
Cats *see* Animals – cats
Cavemen
Caves
Chanukah *see* Holidays –
Hanukkah
Character traits
Character traits – ambition
Character traits – appearance
Character traits – assertiveness
Character traits – being
different
Character traits – bravery
Character traits – cleanliness
Character traits – cleverness
Character traits – completing
things
Character traits –
compromising
Character traits – conceit
Character traits – confidence
Character traits – cruelty to
animals *see* Character traits
– kindness to animals
Character traits – curiosity
Character traits – envy *see*
Emotions – envy, jealousy
Character traits – flattery
Character traits – foolishness
Character traits – fortune *see*
Character traits – luck
Character traits – freedom
Character traits – generosity
Character traits – helpfulness
Character traits – honesty
Character traits – incentive *see*
Character traits – ambition
Character traits – individuality
Character traits – jealousy *see*
Emotions – envy, jealousy
Character traits – kindness
Character traits – kindness to
animals

Character traits – laziness
Character traits – littleness *see*
Character traits – smallness
Character traits – loyalty
Character traits – luck
Character traits – meanness
Character traits – optimism
Character traits – ostracism *see*
Character traits – being
different
Character traits – patience
Character traits –
perseverance
Character traits – persistence
Character traits – practicality
Character traits – pride
Character traits – questioning
Character traits – selfishness
Character traits – shyness
Character traits – smallness
Character traits –
stubbornness
Character traits – vanity
Character traits – willfulness
Cheetahs *see* Animals –
cheetahs
Chefs *see* Careers – chefs
Chickens *see* Birds – chickens
Child abuse
Children as authors
Children as illustrators
China *see* Foreign lands –
China
Chinese-Americans *see* Ethnic
groups in the U.S. –
Chinese-Americans
Chinese New Year *see*
Holidays – Chinese New
Year
Chipmunks *see* Animals –
chipmunks
Christmas *see* Holidays –
Christmas
Cinco de Mayo *see* Holidays –
Cinco de Mayo
Circular tales
Circus
City
Cleanliness *see* Character traits
– cleanliness
Cleverness *see* Character traits
– cleverness
Clockmakers *see* Careers –
clockmakers
Clocks
Clothing
Clouds *see* Weather – clouds
Clowns, jesters
Clubs, gangs
Cockatoos *see* Birds –
cockatoos
Codes *see* Secret codes
Cold *see* Weather – cold
Collecting things *see* Behavior
– collecting things
Color *see* Concepts – color
Columbus Day *see* Holidays –
Columbus Day ·
Communication
Communities, neighborhoods
Competition *see* Sibling rivalry

Completing things *see*
Character traits –
completing things
Compromising *see* Character
traits – compromising
Computers *see* Machines
Conceit *see* Character traits –
conceit
Concepts
Concepts – color
Concepts – counting *see*
Counting
Concepts – distance
Concepts – in and out
Concepts – left and right
Concepts – measurement
Concepts – opposites
Concepts – perspective
Concepts – self *see*
Self-concept
Concepts – shape
Concepts – size
Concepts – speed
Concepts – up and down
Concepts – weight
Confidence *see* Character traits
– confidence
Conservation *see* Ecology
Cooking *see* Activities –
cooking
Cooks *see* Careers – bakers;
Careers – chefs
Copying *see* Behavior –
imitation
Coral Islands *see* Foreign
lands – South Sea Islands
Cormorants *see* Birds –
cormorants
Correspondence *see* Pen pals
Cougars *see* Animals – cougars
Counting
Countries, foreign *see* Foreign
lands
Country
Cowboys
Cows *see* Animals – bulls, cows
Coyotes *see* Animals – coyotes
Crabs *see* Crustacea
Cranes *see* Birds – cranes
Creatures *see* Goblins;
Monsters
Creeks *see* Rivers
Crickets *see* Insects – crickets
Crime
Criminals *see* Crime; Prisons
Crippled *see* Handicaps
Crocodiles *see* Reptiles –
alligators, crocodiles
Crows *see* Birds – crows
Cruelty to animals *see*
Character traits – kindness
to animals
Crustacea
Cumulative tales
Curiosity *see* Character traits –
curiosity
Currency *see* Money
Cycles *see* Motorcycles; Sports
– bicycling

Czechoslovakia *see* Foreign
lands – Czechoslovakia

Dancing *see* Activities –
dancing
Dark *see* Night
Darkness – fear *see* Emotions
– fear
Dawn *see* Morning
Days of the week, months of
the year
Deafness *see* Handicaps –
deafness
Death
Deer *see* Animals – deer
Demons *see* Devil; Monsters
Denmark *see* Foreign lands –
Denmark
Dentists *see* Careers – dentists
Department stores *see* Stores
Desert
Detective stories *see* Problem
solving
Detectives *see* Careers –
detectives
Devil
Dictionaries
Digging *see* Activities –
digging
Dinosaurs
Disbelief *see* Behavior –
disbelief
Dissatisfaction *see* Behavior –
dissatisfaction
Distance *see* Concepts –
distance
Diving *see* Sports – skin diving
Divorce
Doctors *see* Careers – doctors
Dogs *see* Animals – Dogs
Dolls *see* Toys – dolls
Dolphins *see* Animals –
dolphins
Donkeys *see* Animals –
donkeys
Doves *see* Birds – doves
Down and up *see* Concepts –
up and down
Dragonflies *see* Insects
Dragons
Drawing games *see* Games
Dreams
Droughts *see* Weather –
droughts
Ducks *see* Birds – ducks
Dwarfs *see* Elves and little
people
Dying *see* Death

Eagles *see* Birds – eagles
Ears *see* Anatomy
Earth
Easter *see* Holidays – Easter
Eating *see* Food
Ecology
Ecuador *see* Foreign lands –
Ecuador
Education *see* School

Eggs
Egrets *see* Birds – egrets
Egypt *see* Foreign lands –
Egypt
Egyptian language *see*
Hieroglyphics
Electricians *see* Careers –
electricians
Elephants *see* Animals –
elephants
Elves and little people
Embarrassment *see* Emotions –
embarrassment
Emergencies *see* Hospitals
Emotions
Emotions – anger
Emotions – embarrassment
Emotions – envy, jealousy
Emotions – fear
Emotions – happiness
Emotions – hate
Emotions – jealousy *see*
Emotions – envy, jealousy;
Sibling rivalry
Emotions – loneliness
Emotions – love
Emotions – sadness
Emotions – unhappiness *see*
Emotions – happiness;
Emotions – sadness
Emperors *see* Royalty
Endangered animals *see*
Animals – endangered
animals
Engineered books *see* Format,
unusual – toy and movable
books
England *see* Foreign lands –
England
Entertainment *see* Theater
Envy *see* Emotions – envy,
jealousy; Sibling rivalry
Eskimos
Ethnic groups in the U.S.
Ethnic groups in the U.S. –
Afro-Americans
Ethnic groups in the U.S. –
Black Americans *see* Ethnic
groups in the U.S. –
Afro-Americans
Ethnic groups in the U.S. –
Chinese-Americans
Ethnic groups in the U.S. –
Eskimos *see* Eskimos
Ethnic groups in the U.S. –
Indians *see* Indians of North
America
Ethnic groups in the U.S. –
Japanese-Americans
Ethnic groups in the U.S. –
Mexican-Americans
Ethnic groups in the U.S. –
Puerto Rican-Americans
Ethnic groups in the U.S. –
Vietnamese-Americans
Etiquette
Europe *see* Foreign lands –
Europe
Evening *see* Twilight
Experiments *see* Science
Eye glasses *see* Glasses
Eyes *see* Anatomy

Fables *see* Folk and fairy tales
Faces *see* Anatomy
Fairies
Fairs
Fairy tales *see* Folk and fairy tales
Fall *see* Seasons – fall
Families *see* Family life
Family life
Family life – brothers
Family life – fathers
Family life – grandfathers
Family life – grandmothers
Family life – grandparents
Family life – great-grandparents
Family life – mothers
Family life – only child
Family life – sibling rivalry *see* Sibling rivalry
Family life – sisters
Family life – step families
Family life – stepchildren *see* Divorce; Family life – step families
Family life – stepparents *see* Divorce; Family life – step families
Farmers *see* Careers – farmers
Farms
Fathers *see* Family life – fathers
Father's Day *see* Holidays – Father's Day
Fear *see* Emotions – fear
Feeling *see* Senses – touching
Feelings *see* Emotions
Feet *see* Anatomy
Fighting *see* Behavior – fighting, arguing
Fingers *see* Anatomy
Finishing things *see* Character traits – completing things
Finland *see* Foreign lands – Finland
Fire
Fire engines *see* Careers – firefighters; Trucks
Firefighters *see* Careers – firefighters
Fireflies *see* Insects – fireflies
Fish
Fish tanks *see* Aquariums
Fishermen *see* Careers – fishermen
Fishing *see* Sports – fishing
Flamingos *see* Birds – flamingos
Flattery *see* Character traits – flattery
Fleas *see* Insects – fleas
Flies *see* Insects – flies
Floods *see* Weather – floods
Flowers
Flying *see* Activities – flying
Fog *see* Weather – fog
Fold-out books *see* Format, unusual – toy and movable books
Folk and fairy tales
Food

Foolishness *see* Character traits – foolishness
Football *see* Sports – football
Foreign lands
Foreign lands – Africa
Foreign lands – Antarctic
Foreign lands – Arabia
Foreign lands – Arctic
Foreign lands – Armenia
Foreign lands – Australia
Foreign lands – Austria
Foreign lands – Bali
Foreign lands – Bavaria *see* Foreign lands – Austria; Foreign lands – Germany; Foreign lands – Tyrol
Foreign lands – Canada
Foreign lands – Caribbean Islands
Foreign lands – China
Foreign lands – Czechoslovakia
Foreign lands – Denmark
Foreign lands – Ecuador
Foreign lands – Egypt
Foreign lands – England
Foreign lands – Europe
Foreign lands – Finland
Foreign lands – France
Foreign lands – Germany
Foreign lands – Greece
Foreign lands – Greenland
Foreign lands – Guyana
Foreign lands – Holland
Foreign lands – Hungary
Foreign lands – India
Foreign lands – Ireland
Foreign lands – Israel
Foreign lands – Italy
Foreign lands – Japan
Foreign lands – Korea
Foreign lands – Lapland
Foreign lands – Latvia
Foreign lands – Lithuania
Foreign lands – Malaysia
Foreign lands – Mexico
Foreign lands – New Guinea
Foreign lands – Nicaragua
Foreign lands – Norway
Foreign lands – Pakistan
Foreign lands – Panama
Foreign lands – Persia
Foreign lands – Peru
Foreign lands – Philippines
Foreign lands – Poland
Foreign lands – Portugal
Foreign lands – Puerto Rico
Foreign lands – Russia
Foreign lands – Scotland
Foreign lands – Siam *see* Foreign lands – Thailand
Foreign lands – South Africa
Foreign lands – South America
Foreign lands – South Sea Islands
Foreign lands – Spain
Foreign lands – Sweden
Foreign lands – Switzerland
Foreign lands – Thailand
Foreign lands – Tibet
Foreign lands – Turkey

Foreign lands – Tyrol
Foreign lands – Ukraine
Foreign lands – Vatican City
Foreign lands – Vietnam
Foreign lands – Zaire
Foreign lands – Zanzibar
Foreign languages
Forest rangers *see* Careers – park rangers
Forest, woods
Forgetfulness *see* Behavior – forgetfulness
Format, unusual
Format, unusual – board books
Format, unusual – cardboard pages *see* Format, unusual – board books
Format, unusual – toy and movable books
Fortune *see* Character traits – luck
Fortune tellers *see* Careers – fortune tellers
Fourth of July *see* Holidays – Fourth of July
Foxes *see* Animals – foxes
France *see* Foreign lands – France
Freedom *see* Character traits – freedom
Friendship
Frogs and toads

Games
Gangs *see* Clubs, gangs
Garage sales
Garbage collectors *see* Careers – garbage collectors
Gardening *see* Activities – gardening
Geese *see* Birds – geese
Generosity *see* Character traits – generosity
Geologists *see* Careers – geologists
Gerbils *see* Animals – gerbils
Germany *see* Foreign lands – Germany
Ghosts
Giants
Gilbert Islands *see* Foreign lands – South Sea Islands
Giraffes *see* Animals – giraffes
Glasses
Gnats *see* Insects – gnats
Gnomes *see* Elves and little people
Goats *see* Animals – goats
Goblins
Gorillas *see* Animals – gorillas
Gossip *see* Behavior – gossip
Grammar *see* Language
Grandfathers *see* Family life – grandfathers; Family life – grandparents
Grandmothers *see* Family life – grandmothers; Family life – grandparents

Grandparents *see* Family life –
grandfathers; Family life –
grandmothers; Family life –
grandparents
Grasshoppers *see* Insects –
grasshoppers
Great-grandparents *see* Family
life – great-grandparents
Greece *see* Foreign lands –
Greece
Greed *see* Behavior – greed
Greenland *see* Foreign lands –
Greenland
Griffins *see* Mythical creatures
Grocery stores *see* Shopping;
Stores
Groundhog Day *see* Holidays
– Groundhog Day
Groundhogs *see* Animals –
groundhogs
Growing up *see* Behavior –
growing up
Guinea pigs *see* Animals –
guinea pigs
Guns *see* Weapons
Guyana *see* Foreign lands –
Guyana
Gymnastics *see* Sports –
gymnastics
Gypsies

Hair
Halloween *see* Holidays –
Halloween
Hamsters *see* Animals –
hamsters
Handicaps
Handicaps – blindness
Handicaps – deafness
Hands *see* Anatomy
Handyman *see* Careers –
handyman
Hanukkah *see* Holidays –
Hanukkah
Happiness *see* Emotions –
happiness
Hares *see* Animals – rabbits
Hate *see* Emotions – hate
Hawaii
Hawks *see* Birds – hawks
Health
Hearing *see* Handicaps –
deafness; Senses – hearing
Heavy equipment *see*
Machines
Hedgehogs *see* Animals –
hedgehogs
Helicopters
Helpfulness *see* Character
traits – helpfulness
Hens *see* Birds – chickens
Hibernation
Hiding *see* Behavior – hiding
Hiding things *see* Behavior –
hiding things
Hieroglyphics
Hiking *see* Sports – hiking
Hippopotami *see* Animals –
Hippopotami
Hobby horses *see* Toys –
rocking horses

Hockey *see* Sports – hockey
Holidays
Holidays – April Fools' Day
Holidays – Chanukah *see*
Holidays – Hanukkah
Holidays – Chinese New Year
Holidays – Christmas
Holidays – Cinco de Mayo
Holidays – Columbus Day
Holidays – Easter
Holidays – Father's Day
Holidays – Fourth of July
Holidays – Groundhog Day
Holidays – Halloween
Holidays – Hanukkah
Holidays – Independence Day
see Holidays – Fourth of
July
Holidays – Mardi Gras *see*
Mardi Gras
Holidays – May Day
Holidays – Memorial Day
Holidays – Mother's Day
Holidays – New Year's
Holidays – Passover
Holidays – Purim
Holidays – Rosh Hashanah
Holidays – St. Patrick's Day
Holidays – Thanksgiving
Holidays – Valentine's Day
Holidays – Washington's
Birthday
Holland *see* Foreign lands –
Holland
Homes *see* Houses
Honesty *see* Character traits –
honesty
Honey bees *see* Insects – bees
Horses *see* Animals – horses
Horses, rocking *see* Toys –
rocking horses
Hospitals
Hotels
Houses
Humor
Hungary *see* Foreign lands –
Hungary
Hunting *see* Sports – hunting
Hurrying *see* Behavior –
hurrying
Hyenas *see* Animals – hyenas

Ice skating *see* Sports – ice
skating
Iguanas *see* Reptiles – Iguanas
Illness
Illness – Alzheimer's
Illusions, optical *see* Optical
illusions
Illustrators, children *see*
Children as illustrators
Imaginary friends *see*
Imagination – imaginary
friends
Imagination
Imagination – imaginary
friends
Imitation *see* Behavior –
imitation
In and out *see* Concepts – in
and out

Incentive *see* Character traits –
ambition
Independence Day *see*
Holidays – Fourth of July
India *see* Foreign lands –
India
Indians, American *see* Indians
of North America
Indians of North America
Indifference *see* Behavior –
indifference
Individuality *see* Character
traits – individuality
Indonesian Archipelago *see*
Foreign lands – South Sea
Islands
Insects
Insects – ants
Insects – bees
Insects – beetles
Insects – butterflies,
caterpillars
Insects – caterpillars *see*
Insects – butterflies,
caterpillars
Insects – crickets
Insects – fireflies
Insects – fleas
Insects – flies
Insects – gnats
Insects – grasshoppers
Insects – lady birds *see* Insects
– ladybugs
Insects – ladybugs
Insects – lightning bugs *see*
Insects – fireflies
Insects – mosquitoes
Insects – moths
Insects – praying mantis
Insects – wasps
Interracial marriage *see*
Marriage, interracial
Ireland *see* Foreign lands –
Ireland
Islands
Israel *see* Foreign lands –
Israel
Italy *see* Foreign lands – Italy

Jail *see* Prisons
Japan *see* Foreign lands –
Japan
Japanese-Americans *see* Ethnic
groups in the U.S. –
Japanese-Americans
Jealousy *see* Emotions – envy,
jealousy; Sibling rivalry
Jesters *see* Clowns, jesters
Jewish culture
Jobs *see* Careers
Jokes *see* Riddles
Judges *see* Careers – judges
Jumping *see* Activities –
jumping
Jungle

Kangaroos *see* Animals –
kangaroos
Kindness *see* Character traits –
kindness

Kindness to animals *see* Character traits – kindness to animals
Kings *see* Royalty
Kinkajous *see* Animals – kinkajous
Kites
Knights
Knitting *see* Activities – knitting
Koala bears *see* Animals – koala bears
Korea *see* Foreign lands – Korea

Lady birds *see* Insects – ladybugs
Ladybugs *see* Insects – ladybugs
Language
Language, foreign *see* Foreign languages
Lapland *see* Foreign lands – Lapland
Lateness *see* Behavior – tardiness
Latvia *see* Foreign lands – Latvia
Laundry
Law *see* Careers – judges; Careers – police officers; Crime
Laziness *see* Character traits – laziness
Left and right *see* Concepts – left and right
Left-handedness
Legends *see* Folk and fairy tales
Lemmings *see* Animals – lemmings
Leopards *see* Animals – leopards
Leprechauns *see* Elves and little people
Letters
Librarians *see* Careers – librarians
Libraries
Lighthouses
Lightning bugs *see* Insects – fireflies
Lights
Lions *see* Animals – lions
Lithuania *see* Foreign lands – Lithuania
Little people *see* Elves and little people
Littleness *see* Character traits – smallness
Lizards *see* Reptiles – lizards
Llamas *see* Animals – llamas
Lobsters *see* Crustacea
Loneliness *see* Emotions – loneliness
Losing things *see* Behavior – losing things
Lost *see* Behavior – lost
Love *see* Emotions – love
Loyalty *see* Character traits – loyalty

Luck *see* Character traits – luck
Lying *see* Behavior – lying

Machines
Magic
Maids *see* Careers – maids
Mail *see* Letters
Mail carriers *see* Careers – mail carriers
Malaysia *see* Foreign lands – Malaysia
Manners *see* Etiquette
Mardi Gras
Marionettes *see* Puppets
Markets *see* Stores
Marriage, interracial
Marriages *see* Weddings
Math *see* Counting
May Day *see* Holidays – May Day
Meanness *see* Character traits – meanness
Measurement *see* Concepts – measurement
Mechanical books *see* Format, unusual – toy and movable books
Mechanical men *see* Robots
Mechanics *see* Careers – mechanics
Memorial Day *see* Holidays – Memorial Day
Mermaids *see* Mythical creatures
Merry-go-rounds
Mexican-Americans *see* Ethnic groups in the U.S. – Mexican-Americans
Mexico *see* Foreign lands – Mexico
Mice *see* Animals – mice
Middle ages
Military *see* Careers – military
Mimes *see* Clowns, jesters
Miners *see* Careers – miners
Minks *see* Animals – minks
Minorities *see* Ethnic groups in the U.S.
Mirages *see* Optical illusions
Misbehavior *see* Behavior – misbehavior
Missions
Mist *see* Weather – fog
Mistakes *see* Behavior – mistakes
Misunderstanding *see* Behavior – misunderstanding
Mockingbirds *see* Birds – mockingbirds
Models *see* Careers – models
Moles *see* Animals – moles
Money
Mongooses *see* Animals – mongooses
Monkeys *see* Animals – monkeys
Monsters

Months of the year *see* Days of the week, months of the year
Moon
Moose *see* Animals – moose
Mopeds *see* Motorcycles
Morning
Mosquitoes *see* Insects – mosquitoes
Mother Goose *see* Nursery rhymes
Mothers *see* Family life – mothers
Mother's Day *see* Holidays – Mother's Day
Moths *see* Insects – moths
Motorcycles
Movable books *see* Format, unusual – toy and movable books
Moving
Mules *see* Animals – mules
Multi-ethnic *see* Ethnic groups in the U.S.
Multiple birth childen *see* Triplets; Twins
Muppets *see* Puppets
Museums
Music
Musical instruments *see* Music
Muskrats *see* Animals – muskrats
Mysteries *see* Problem solving
Mythical creatures

Nagging *see* Behavior – nagging
Names
Napping *see* Sleep
Native Americans *see* Eskimos; Indians of North America
Nature
Needing someone *see* Behavior – needing someone
Neighborhoods *see* Communities, neighborhoods
New Guinea *see* Foreign lands – New Guinea
New Year's *see* Holidays – New Year's
Nicaragua *see* Foreign lands – Nicaragua
Night
Nightingales *see* Birds – nightingales
Nightmares *see* Bedtime; Goblins; Monsters; Night; Sleep
No text *see* Wordless
Noah *see* Religion – Noah
Noise, sounds
Norway *see* Foreign lands – Norway
Noses *see* Anatomy
Numbers *see* Counting
Nuns *see* Careers – nuns
Nursery rhymes

Nursery school *see* School
Nurses *see* Careers – nurses

Oceans *see* Sea and seashore
Octopuses
Oil
Old age
Olympics *see* Sports – Olympics
Only child *see* Family life – only child
Opossums *see* Animals – possums
Opposites *see* Concepts – opposites
Optical illusions
Optimism *see* Character traits – optimism
Orphans
Ostracism *see* Character traits – being different
Ostriches *see* Birds – ostriches
Otters *see* Animals – otters
Out and in *see* Concepts – in and out
Owls *see* Birds – owls

Pack rats *see* Animals – pack rats
Painters *see* Activities – painting; Careers – artists
Painting *see* Activities – painting
Pakistan *see* Foreign lands – Pakistan
Panama *see* Foreign lands – Panama
Pandas *see* Animals – pandas
Panthers *see* Animals – leopards
Paper
Parades
Parakeets *see* Birds – parakeets, parrots
Park rangers *see* Careers – park rangers
Parrots *see* Birds – parakeets, parrots
Participation
Parties
Passover *see* Holidays – Passover
Patience *see* Character traits – patience
Peacocks *see* Birds – peacocks, peahens
Peahens *see* Birds – peacocks, peahens
Peddlers *see* Careers – peddlers
Pelicans *see* Birds – pelicans
Pen pals
Penguins *see* Birds – penguins
Perseverance *see* Character traits – perseverance
Persia *see* Foreign lands – Persia
Persistence *see* Character traits – persistence
Perspective *see* Concepts – perspective

Peru *see* Foreign lands – Peru
Petroleum *see* Oil
Pets
Philippines *see* Foreign lands – Philippines
Phoenix *see* Mythical creatures
Photography *see* Activities – photographing
Physicians *see* Careers – doctors
Picnicking *see* Activities – picnicking
Pigeons *see* Birds – pigeons
Pigs *see* Animals – pigs
Pilots *see* Careers – airplane pilots
Pirates
Pixies *see* Elves and little people; Fairies
Planes *see* Airplanes, airports
Plants
Playing *see* Activities – playing
Plays *see* Theater
Poetry, rhyme
Poland *see* Foreign lands – Poland
Polar bears *see* Animals – polar bears
Police officers *see* Careers – police officers
Poltergeists *see* Ghosts
Poor *see* Poverty
Pop-up books *see* Format, unusual – toy and movable books
Porcupines *see* Animals – porcupines
Porpoise *see* Animals – dolphins
Portugal *see* Foreign lands – Portugal
Possums *see* Animals – possums
Poverty
Power failure
Practicality *see* Character traits – practicality
Prairie dogs *see* Animals – prairie dogs
Praying mantis *see* Insects – praying mantis
Prejudice
Pride *see* Character traits – pride
Princes *see* Royalty
Princesses *see* Royalty
Prisons
Problem solving
Progress
Puerto Rican-Americans *see* Ethnic groups in the U.S. – Puerto Rican-Americans
Puerto Rico *see* Foreign lands – Puerto Rico
Puffins *see* Birds – puffins
Pumas *see* Animals – cougars
Puppets
Purim *see* Holidays – Purim
Puzzles *see* Rebuses; Riddles

Queens *see* Royalty

Questioning *see* Character traits – questioning
Quicksand *see* Sand

Rabbits *see* Animals – rabbits
Raccoons *see* Animals – raccoons
Race *see* Ethnic groups in the U.S.
Race car drivers *see* Careers – race car drivers
Racing *see* Sports – racing
Railroad engineers *see* Careers – railroad engineers
Railroads *see* Trains
Rain *see* Weather – rain
Rainbows *see* Weather – rainbows
Rangers *see* Careers – park rangers
Rats *see* Animals – rats
Ravens *see* Birds – ravens
Reading *see* Activities – reading
Rebuses
Reindeer *see* Animals – reindeer
Religion
Religion – Noah
Repetitive stories *see* Circular tales; Cumulative tales
Reporters *see* Careers – reporters
Reptiles
Reptiles – alligators, crocodiles
Reptiles – crocodiles *see* Reptiles – alligators, crocodiles
Reptiles – iguanas
Reptiles – lizards
Reptiles – snakes
Reptiles – turtles, tortoises
Rest *see* Sleep
Rhinoceros *see* Animals – rhinoceros
Rhyming text *see* Poetry, rhyme
Riddles
Right and left *see* Concepts – left and right
Rivers
Roads
Robbers *see* Crime
Robins *see* Birds – robins
Robots
Rockets *see* Space and space ships
Rocking horses *see* Toys – rocking horses
Rocks
Roller skating *see* Sports – Roller skating
Roosters *see* Birds – chickens
Rosh Hashanah *see* Holidays – Rosh Hashanah
Round-robin tales *see* Circular tales
Royalty
Running *see* Sports – racing
Running away *see* Behavior – running away

Russia *see* Foreign lands –
  Russia

Sadness *see* Emotions –
  sadness
Safety
Sailors *see* Careers – military
St. Patrick's Day *see* Holidays
  – St. Patrick's Day
Sand
Sandcastles *see* Sand
Sandman
Sandpipers *see* Birds –
  sandpipers
Saving things *see* Behavior –
  saving things
Scarecrows
School
Science
Scotland *see* Foreign lands –
  Scotland
Scuba diving *see* Sports – skin
  diving
Sea and seashore
Sea gulls *see* Birds – sea gulls
Sea horses *see* Crustacea
Sea lions *see* Animals – sea
  lions
Sea serpents *see* Monsters;
  Mythical creatures
Seals *see* Animals – seals
Seamstresses *see* Careers –
  seamstresses
Seashore *see* Sea and seashore
Seasons
Seasons – autumn *see* Seasons
  – fall
Seasons – fall
Seasons – spring
Seasons – summer
Seasons – winter
Secret codes
Secrets *see* Behavior – secrets
Seeds
Seeing *see* Senses – seeing
Seeking better things *see*
  Behavior – seeking better
  things
Self-concept
Self-esteem *see* Self-concept
Self-image *see* Self-concept
Selfishness *see* Character traits
  – selfishness
Senility *see* Illness –
  Alzheimer's
Senses – hearing
Senses – seeing
Senses – smelling
Senses – tasting
Senses – touching
Shadows
Shakespeare
Shape *see* Concepts – shape
Shaped books *see* Format,
  unusual
Sharing *see* Behavior –
  sharing
Sheep *see* Animals – sheep
Ships *see* Boats, ships
Shoemakers *see* Careers –
  shoemakers

Shopping
Shops *see* Stores
Shows *see* Theaters
Shrews *see* Animals – shrews
Shyness *see* Character traits –
  shyness
Siam *see* Foreign lands –
  Thailand
Sibling rivalry
Sickness *see* Health; Illness
Sight *see* Handicaps –
  blindness; Senses – seeing
Signs *see* Traffic, traffic signs
Sisters *see* Family life – Sisters
Size *see* Concepts – size
Skating *see* Sports – ice
  skating; Sports – roller
  skating
Skiing *see* Sports – skiing
Skin diving *see* Sports – skin
  diving
Skunks *see* Animals – skunks
Sky
Sledding *see* Sports – sledding
Sleep
Sleight-of-hand *see* Magic
Sloths *see* Animals – sloths
Smallness *see* Character traits
  – smallness
Smelling *see* Senses – smelling
Snails *see* Animals – snails
Snakes *see* Reptiles – snakes
Snow *see* Weather – snow
Snowmen
Snowplows *see* Machines
Soccer *see* Sports – soccer
Society Islands *see* Foreign
  lands – South Sea Islands
Soldiers *see* Careers – military
Soldiers, toy *see* Toys –
  soldiers
Solitude *see* Behavior –
  solitude
Songs
Sounds *see* Noise, sounds
South Africa *see* Foreign lands
  – South Africa
South America *see* Foreign
  lands – South America
South Sea Islands *see* Foreign
  lands – South Sea Islands
Space and space ships
Spain *see* Foreign lands –
  Spain
Sparrows *see* Birds – sparrows
Spectacles *see* Glasses
Speech *see* Language
Speed *see* Concepts – speed
Spelunking *see* Caves
Spiders
Split-page books *see* Format,
  unusual
Spooks *see* Ghosts; Goblins
Sports
Sports – baseball
Sports – basketball
Sports – bicycling
Sports – camping
Sports – fishing
Sports – football
Sports – gymnastics
Sports – hiking

Sports – hockey
Sports – hunting
Sports – ice skating
Sports – Olympics
Sports – racing
Sports – roller skating
Sports – skiing
Sports – skin diving
Sports – sledding
Sports – soccer
Sports – surfing
Sports – swimming
Sports – T-ball
Sports – tennis
Sports – wrestling
Spring *see* Seasons – spring
Squirrels *see* Animals –
  squirrels
Stage *see* Theater
Stars
Stealing *see* Behavior –
  stealing
Steam shovels *see* Machines
Steamrollers *see* Machines
Step families *see* Divorce;
  Family life – step families
Stepchildren *see* Divorce;
  Family life – step families
Stepparents *see* Divorce;
  Family life – step families
Stones *see* Rocks
Storekeepers *see* Careers –
  storekeepers
Stores
Stories in the round *see*
  Circular tales
Storks *see* Birds – storks
Storms *see* Weather – storms
Streams *see* Rivers
Street signs *see* Traffic, traffic
  signs
Streets *see* Roads
String
Stubbornness *see* Character
  traits – stubbornness
Sucking of thumb *see*
  Thumbsucking
Sullivan Islands *see* Foreign
  lands – South Sea Islands
Summer *see* Seasons –
  summer
Sun
Surfing *see* Sports – surfing
Swallows *see* Birds – swallows
Swans *see* Birds – swans
Sweden *see* Foreign lands –
  Sweden
Swimming *see* Sports –
  swimming
Swinging *see* Activities –
  swinging
Switzerland *see* Foreign lands
  – Switzerland

T-ball *see* Sports – T-ball
Tailors *see* Careers – tailors
Talking to strangers *see*
  Behavior – talking to
  strangers; Safety
Tapirs *see* Animals – tapirs

Tardiness *see* Behavior – tardiness

Tasting *see* Senses – tasting

Taxi drivers *see* Careers – taxi drivers

Taxis

Teachers *see* Careers – teachers

Teddy bears *see* Toys – teddy bears

Teeth

Telephone

Telephone operators *see* Careers – telephone operators

Television

Telling time *see* Clocks; Time

Temper tantrums *see* Emotions – anger

Tennis *see* Sports – tennis

Textless *see* Wordless

Thailand *see* Foreign lands – Thailand

Thanksgiving *see* Holidays – Thanksgiving

Theater

Thumbsucking

Thunder *see* Weather – storms; Weather – thunder

Tibet *see* Foreign lands – Tibet

Tigers *see* Animals – tigers

Time

Tin soldiers *see* Toys – soldiers

Toads *see* Frogs and toads

Tongue twisters

Tools

Tortoises *see* Reptiles – turtles, tortoises

Toucans *see* Birds – toucans

Touching *see* Senses – touching

Towns *see* City

Toy and movable books *see* Format, unusual – toy and movable books

Toy books *see* Format, unusual – toy and movable books

Toys

Toys – balloons

Toys – balls

Toys – bears *see* Toys – teddy bears

Toys – blocks

Toys – dolls

Toys – hobby horses *see* Toys – rocking horses

Toys – pandas *see* Toys – teddy bears

Toys – rocking horses

Toys – soldiers

Toys – teddy bears

Toys – tin soldiers *see* Toys – soldiers

Toys – trains

Tractors *see* Machines

Trading *see* Activities – trading

Traffic, traffic signs

Train engineers *see* Careers – railroad engineers

Trains

Trains, toy *see* Toys – trains

Transportation

Traveling *see* Activities – traveling

Trees

Trickery *see* Behavior – trickery

Tricks *see* Magic

Triplets

Trolleys *see* Cable cars, trolleys

Trolls

Truck drivers *see* Careers – truck drivers

Trucks

Turkey *see* Foreign lands – Turkey

Turkeys *see* Birds – turkeys

Turtles *see* Reptiles – turtles, tortoises

TV *see* Television

Twilight

Twins

Tyrol *see* Foreign lands – Tyrol

Ukraine *see* Foreign lands – Ukraine

Umbrellas

Unhappiness *see* Emotions – happiness; Emotions – sadness

UNICEF

Unicorns *see* Mythical creatures

U.S. history

Unnoticed *see* Behavior – unnoticed, unseen

Unseen *see* Behavior – unnoticed, unseen

Unusual format *see* Format, unusual

Up and down *see* Concepts – up and down

Vacationing *see* Activities – vacationing

Vacuum cleaners *see* Machines

Valentine's Day *see* Holidays – Valentine's Day

Values

Vampires *see* Monsters

Vanity *see* Character traits – vanity

Vatican City *see* Foreign lands – Vatican City

Veterinarians *see* Careers – veterinarians

Vietnam *see* Foreign lands – Vietnam

Vietnamese-Americans *see* Ethnic groups in the U.S. – Vietnamese-Americans

Violence, anti-violence

Volcanoes

Vultures *see* Birds – vultures

Waiters *see* Careers – waiters, waitresses

Waitresses *see* Careers – waiters, waitresses

Walking *see* Activities – walking

Walruses *see* Animals – walruses

War

Washington's Birthday *see* Holidays – Washington's Birthday

Wasps *see* Insects – wasps

Watches *see* Clocks

Water buffaloes *see* Animals – water buffaloes

Weapons

Weasels *see* Animals – weasels

Weather

Weather – clouds

Weather – cold

Weather – droughts

Weather – floods

Weather – fog

Weather – mist *see* Weather – fog

Weather – rain

Weather – rainbows

Weather – snow

Weather – storms

Weather – thunder

Weather – wind

Weaving *see* Activities – weaving

Weddings

Weekdays *see* Days of the week, months of the year

Weight *see* Concepts – weight

Welders *see* Careers – welders

Werewolves *see* Monsters

Whales *see* Animals – whales

Wheels

Whistling *see* Activities – whistling

Willfulness *see* Character traits – willfulness

Wind *see* Weather – wind

Windmills

Window cleaners *see* Careers – window cleaners

Winter *see* Seasons – winter

Wishing *see* Behavior – wishing

Witches

Wizards

Wolves *see* Animals – wolves

Wombats *see* Animals – wombats

Woodchucks *see* Animals –
  groundhogs
Woodpeckers *see* Birds –
  woodpeckers
Woods *see* Forest, woods
Word games *see* Language
Wordless
Words *see* Language
Working *see* Activities –
  working
World

Worms *see* Animals – worms
Worrying *see* Behavior –
  worrying
Wrecking machines *see*
  Machines
Wrens *see* Birds – wrens
Wrestling *see* Sports –
  wrestling
Writers *see* Careers – writers
Writing *see* Activities – writing
Writing letters *see* Letters

Yaks *see* Animals – yaks

Zaire *see* Foreign lands –
  Zaire
Zanzibar *see* Foreign lands –
  Zanzibar
Zebras *see* Animals – zebras
Zodiac
Zoos

Subject Guide

This is a subject-arranged guide to picture books. Under appropriate subject headings and subheadings, titles appear alphabetically by author name, or by title when author is unknown. Complete bibliographic information for each title cited will be found in the Bibliographic Guide.

Aardvarks *see* Animals – aardvarks

ABC books

A is for alphabet
ABCDEF...
Abrons, Mary. *For Alice a palace*
Ackerman, Karen. *Flannery Row*
Alda, Arlene. *Arlene Alda's ABC*
Alexander, Anne. *ABC of cars and trucks*
Anglund, Joan Walsh. *A is for always*
Anno, Mitsumasa. *Anno's alphabet*
  Anno's magical ABC
Arnosky, Jim. *Mouse numbers and letters*
  Mouse writing
Asch, Frank. *Little Devil's ABC*
Azarian, Mary. *A farmer's alphabet*
Balian, Lorna. *Humbug potion*
Barry, Katharina. *A is for anything*
Barry, Robert E. *Animals around the world*
Base, Graeme. *Animalia*
Baskin, Leonard. *Hosie's alphabet*
Bayer, Jane. *A my name is Alice*
Beller, Janet. *A-B-C-ing*
Berenstain, Stan. *The Berenstains' B book*
Berger, Terry. *Ben's ABC day*
Bishop, Ann. *Riddle-iculous rid-alphabet book*
Black, Floyd. *Alphabet cat*
Bond, Jean Carey. *A is for Africa*
Bove, Linda. *Sign language ABC with Linda Bove*
Boxer, Deborah. *26 ways to be somebody else*
Boynton, Sandra. *A is for angry*
Bridwell, Norman. *Clifford's ABC*
Brown, Judith Gwyn. *Alphabet dreams*

Brown, Marcia. *All butterflies Peter Piper's alphabet*
Brown, Margaret Wise. *Sleepy ABC*
Bruna, Dick. *B is for bear*
Brunhoff, Laurent de. *Babar's ABC*
Budd, Lillian. *The pie wagon*
Budney, Blossom. *N is for nursery school*
Burningham, John. *John Burningham's ABC*
Burton, Marilee Robin. *Aaron awoke*
Chaplin, Susan Gibbons. *I can sign my ABCs*
Chardiet, Bernice. *C is for circus*
Charles, Donald. *Shaggy dog's animal alphabet*
Charlip, Remy. *Handtalk*
Chase, Catherine. *An alphabet book Baby mouse learns his ABC's*
Chess, Victoria. *Alfred's alphabet walk*
A child's picture English-Hebrew dictionary
Chouinard, Roger. *The amazing animal alphabet book*
Chwast, Seymour. *Still another alphabet book*
Cleary, Beverly. *The hullabaloo ABC*
Cleaver, Elizabeth. *ABC*
Clifton, Lucille. *The black B C's*
Cohen, Peter Zachary. *Authorized autumn charts of the Upper Red Canoe River country*
Coletta, Irene. *From A to Z*
Conran, Sebastian. *My first ABC book*
Cooney, Barbara. *A garland of games and other diversions*
Corbett, Scott. *The mysterious Zetabet*
Cremins, Robert. *My animal ABC*
Crews, Donald. *We read A to Z*
Crowther, Robert. *The most amazing hide-and-seek alphabet book*
Dauphin, Francine Legrand. *A French A. B. C.*
DeLage, Ida. *ABC Easter bunny ABC triplets at the zoo*
Delaunay, Sonia. *Sonia Delaunay's alphabet*
Demi. *Demi's find the animals A B C*
Doolittle, Eileen. *The ark in the attic*

Downie, Jill. *Alphabet puzzle*
Dragonwagon, Crescent. *Alligator arrived with apples*
Dreamer, Sue. *Circus ABC*
Duke, Kate. *The guinea pig ABC*
Duvoisin, Roger Antoine. *A for the ark*
Eichenberg, Fritz. *Ape in cape*
Elting, Mary. *Q is for duck*
Emberley, Ed. *Ed Emberley's ABC*
Falls, C. B. (Charles Buckles). *ABC book*
Farber, Norma. *As I was crossing Boston Common*
Feelings, Muriel. *Jambo means hello*
Fife, Dale. *Adam's ABC*
Floyd, Lucy. *Agatha's alphabet, with her very own dictionary*
Freeman, Don. *Add-a-line alphabet*
Fujikawa, Gyo. *Gyo Fujikawa's A to Z picture book*
Gág, Wanda. *ABC bunny*
Gantz, David. *The genie bear with the light brown hair word book*
Gardner, Beau. *Have you ever seen...?*
Garten, Jan. *The alphabet tale*
Geisert, Arthur. *Pigs from A to Z*
Greenaway, Kate. *A apple pie*
Gretz, Susanna. *Teddy bears ABC*
Grossbart, Francine. *A big city*
Gundersheimer, Karen. *A B C say with me*
Gunning, Monica. *The two Georges*
Hague, Kathleen. *Alphabears*
Harada, Joyce. *It's the ABC book*
Harrison, Ted. *A northern alphabet*
Hawkins, Colin. *Busy ABC*
Hillman, Priscilla. *A Merry-Mouse Christmas A B C*
Hoban, Tana. *A B See!*
26 letters and 99 cents
Hoberman, Mary Ann. *Nuts to you and nuts to me*
Hoguet, Susan Ramsay. *I unpacked my grandmother's trunk*
Holabird, Katharine. *The little mouse ABC*
Holl, Adelaide. *The ABC of cars, trucks and machines*
Hooper, Patricia. *A bundle of beasts*
Howard-Gibbon, Amelia Frances. *An illustrated comic alphabet*
Hughes, Shirley. *Lucy and Tom's A.B.C.*
Hyman, Trina Schart. *A little alphabet*
Ilsley, Velma. *A busy day for Chris*
M is for moving
Ipcar, Dahlov. *I love my anteater with an A*
Isadora, Rachel. *City seen from A to Z*
Jefferds, Vincent. *Disney's elegant ABC book*
Jewell, Nancy. *ABC cat*
Johnson, Crockett. *Harold's ABC*
Johnson, Jean. *Teachers A to Z*
Kellogg, Steven. *Aster Aardvark's alphabet adventures*

Kightley, Rosalinda. *ABC*
Kitamura, Satoshi. *What's inside?*
Kitchen, Bert. *Animal alphabet*
Kuskin, Karla. *ABCDEFGHIJKLMNOPQRSTUVW XYZ*
Lalicki, Barbara. *If there were dreams to sell*
Lalli, Judy. *Feelings alphabet*
Leander, Ed. *Q is for crazy*
Lear, Edward. *ABC*
An Edward Lear alphabet
Edward Lear's ABC
Nonsense alphabets
Lillie, Patricia. *One very, very quiet afternoon*
Lionni, Leo. *Letters to talk about*
A little ABC book
Little, Mary E. *ABC for the library*
Lobel, Arnold. *On Market Street*
Low, Joseph. *Adam's book of odd creatures*
Lyon, George Ella. *A B Cedar*
MacDonald, Suse. *Alphabatics*
McGinley, Phyllis. *All around the town*
McKissack, Patricia C. *Big bug book of the alphabet*
My Bible ABC book
McMillan, Bruce. *The alphabet symphony*
McPhail, David. *Animals A to Z*
Manson, Beverlie. *The fairies' alphabet book*
Margalit, Avishai. *The Hebrew alphabet book*
Mayer, Mercer. *Little Monster's alphabet book*
Mayers, Florence Cassen. *Egyptian art from the Brooklyn Museum ABC*
The Museum of Fine Arts, Boston ABC
The Museum of Modern Art, New York ABC
The National Air and Space Museum ABC
Mendoza, George. *The alphabet boat*
Alphabet sheep
Norman Rockwell's American ABC
Merriam, Eve. *Good night to Annie*
Halloween ABC
Miles, Miska. *Apricot ABC*
Miller, Edna. *Mousekin's ABC*
Miller, Jane. *Farm alphabet book*
Milne, A. A. (Alan Alexander). *Pooh's alphabet book*
Moak, Allan. *A big city ABC*
Montresor, Beni. *A for angel*
Morice, Dave. *A visit from St. Alphabet*
Morse, Samuel French. *All in a suitcase*
Moss, Jeffrey. *The Sesame Street ABC storybook*
Mother Goose. *ABC rhymes*, ill. by Lulu Delarce
In a pumpkin shell
Munari, Bruno. *ABC*
Musgrove, Margaret. *Ashanti to Zulu*
Neumeier, Marty. *Action alphabet*
Newberry, Clare Turlay. *The kittens' ABC*

Niland, Deborah. *ABC of monsters*
Obligado, Lilian. *Faint frogs feeling feverish and other terrifically tantalizing tongue twisters*
Ogle, Lucille. *A B See*
Oliver, Dexter. *I want to be...*
O'Shell, Marcia. *Alphabet Annie announces an all-American album*
Owens, Mary Beth. *A caribou alphabet*
Oxenbury, Helen. *Helen Oxenbury's ABC of things*
Peaceable kingdom
Pearson, Tracey Campbell. *A apple pie*
Peppé, Rodney. *The alphabet book*
Petersham, Maud. *An American ABC*
Piatti, Celestino. *Celestino Piatti's animal ABC*
Piers, Helen. *Puppy's ABC*
Potter, Beatrix. *Peter Rabbit's ABC*
Rey, Hans Augusto. *Curious George learns the alphabet*
Look for the letters
Roe, Richard. *Animal ABC*
Rojankovsky, Feodor. *ABC, an alphabet of many things*
Animals in the zoo
Rosario, Idalia. *Idalia's project ABC*
Ruben, Patricia. *Apples to zippers*
Rubin, Cynthia Elyce. *ABC Americana from the National Gallery of Art*
Scarry, Richard. *Richard Scarry's ABC word book*
Richard Scarry's great big schoolhouse
The Sea World alphabet book
Sendak, Maurice. *Alligators all around*
The Sesame Street book of letters
Seuss, Dr. *Dr. Seuss's ABC*
Hooper Humperdink...? Not him!
Shuttlesworth, Dorothy E. *ABC of buses*
Silverman, Maida. *Bunny's ABC*
Smith, William Jay. *Puptents and pebbles*
Steiner, Charlotte. *Charlotte Steiner's ABC*
Stevenson, James. *Grandpa's great city tour*
Stock, Catherine. *Alexander's midnight snack*
Van Allsburg, Chris. *The Z was zapped*
Waber, Bernard. *An anteater named Arthur*
Walters, Marguerite. *The city-country ABC*
Watson, Clyde. *Applebet*
Watson, Nancy Dingman. *What does A begin with?*
Wild, Robin. *The bears' ABC book*
Williams, Garth. *The big golden animal ABC*
Wilson, Barbara. *ABC et/and 123*
Wolf, Janet. *Adelaide to Zeke*
Yolen, Jane. *All in the woodland early*

Abuse to children *see* Child abuse

Accordion books *see* Format, unusual

Activities

Alderson, Sue Ann. *Bonnie McSmithers is at it again!*
Alexander, Sue. *Witch, Goblin and Ghost's book of things to do*
Aliki. *Overnight at Mary Bloom's*
Allington, Richard L. *Feelings*
  Hearing
  Looking
  Smelling
  Tasting
  Touching
Andre, Evelyn M. *Places I like to be*
Anno, Mitsumasa. *All in a day*
Arnold, Caroline. *How do we have fun?*
Azarian, Mary. *A farmer's alphabet*
Behrens, June. *Can you walk the plank?*
Beller, Janet. *A-B-C-ing*
Beni, Ruth. *Sir Baldergog the great*
Benjamin, Alan. *Busy bunnies*
Bennett, Jill. *Days are where we live and other poems*
Boyd, Lizi. *The not-so-wicked stepmother*
Brandenberg, Franz. *Otto is different*
Brann, Esther. *A book for baby*
Brown, Elinor. *The little story book*
Brown, Margaret Wise. *The little fur family*
Brown, Ruth. *Our cat Flossie*
Brunhoff, Jean de. *Babar's anniversary album*
Bryant, Dean. *Here am I*
Buck, Pearl S. (Pearl Sydenstricker). *Stories for little children*
Bulla, Clyde Robert. *Daniel's duck*
Burdekin, Harold. *A child's grace*
Burningham, John. *Skip trip*
  Sniff shout
  Wobble pop
Calmenson, Stephanie. *The kindergarten book*
Carlson, Nancy. *Bunnies and their hobbies*
Cartlidge, Michelle. *The bear's bazaar*
  A mouse's diary
Carton, Lonnie Caming. *Mommies*
Chernoff, Goldie Taub. *Clay-dough, play-dough*
  Just a box?
  Pebbles and pods
  Puppet party
Cole, Ann. *I saw a purple cow*
  Purple cow to the rescue
Crume, Marion W. *Let me see you try*
  Listen!
  What do you say?
Delton, Judy. *I'm telling you now*
Dinosaurs and monsters
Dunn, Phoebe. *Busy, busy toddlers*
Ehrlich, Amy. *Bunnies all day long*
Ernst, Lisa Campbell. *Sam Johnson and the blue ribbon quilt*

Erskine, Jim. *Bert and Susie's messy tale*
Facklam, Margery. *So can I*
Fair, Sylvia. *The bedspread*
Faunce-Brown, Daphne. *Snuffles' house*
Flournoy, Valerie. *The best time of day*
Freeman, Don. *The day is waiting*
Fujikawa, Gyo. *My favorite thing*
  Surprise! Surprise!
Gibbons, Gail. *The missing maple syrup sap mystery*
Gipson, Morrell. *Hello, Peter*
Goennel, Heidi. *My day*
Goor, Ron. *In the driver's seat*
Hallinan, P. K. (Patrick K.). *I'm glad to be me*
  Just being alone
Hawkins, Colin. *Busy ABC*
Holzenthaler, Jean. *My feet do*
  My hands can
Hynard, Julia. *Percival's party*
Hynard, Stephen. *Snowy the rabbit*
Jensen, Helen Zane. *When Panda came to our house*
Jonas, Ann. *When you were a baby*
Kaufman, Curt. *Hotel boy*
Kelley, True. *Look, baby! Listen, baby! Do, baby!*
Kilroy, Sally. *Busy babies*
Krementz, Jill. *Katherine goes to nursery school*
Kunnas, Mauri. *The nighttime book*
Leedy, Loreen. *A dragon Christmas*
Lester, Alison. *Clive eats alligators*
Le-Tan, Pierre. *The afternoon cat*
Lilly, Kenneth. *Animal builders*
  Animal climbers
  Animal jumpers
  Animal runners
  Animal swimmers
Lionni, Leo. *Let's make rabbits*
McKié, Roy. *Snow*
McMillan, Bruce. *Step by step*
McNaughton, Colin. *Autumn*
  Winter
Maestro, Betsy. *Busy day*
Mangin, Marie-France. *Suzette and Nicholas and the seasons clock*
Masks and puppets
Moncure, Jane Belk. *Now I am five!*
  Now I am four!
  Now I am three!
My day
Myers, Arthur. *Kids do amazing things*
Nelson, Brenda. *Mud for sale*
Neumeier, Marty. *Action alphabet*
Noble, Trinka Hakes. *The day Jimmy's boa ate the wash*
Noll, Sally. *Jiggle wiggle prance*
O'Brien, Anne S. *Come play with us*
Oxenbury, Helen. *I can*
  Tom and Pippo's day

Parish, Peggy. *I can - can you?*
Pelham, David. *Worms wiggle*
Peyo. *What do smurfs do all day?*
Pitcher, Caroline. *Animals*
  Cars and boats
Pizer, Abigail. *Harry's night out*
Rockwell, Anne F. *In our house*
Rockwell, Harlow. *I did it*
  Look at this
Ross, H. L. *Not counting monsters*
Rubel, Nicole. *Me and my kitty*
Rukeyser, Muriel. *More night*
Samuels, Barbara. *Duncan and Dolores*
Scarry, Richard. *Richard Scarry's busy busy world*
Simon, Norma. *I'm busy, too*
  What do I do?
Tafuri, Nancy. *Do not disturb*
Takeshita, Fumiko. *The park bench*
Thomson, Ruth. *My bear I can...can you?*
Thorne, Jenny. *My uncle*
Tudor, Tasha. *A time to keep*
Türk, Hanne. *The rope skips Max*
Vasiliu, Mircea. *What's happening?*
Voake, Charlotte. *First things first*
What we do
Winn, Chris. *Helping*
Winteringham, Victoria. *Penguin day*
Wood, Audrey. *King Bidgood's in the bathtub*
Zalben, Jane Breskin. *Oliver and Alison's week*
Ziefert, Harriet. *Baby Ben's busy book*
  Baby Ben's noisy book
  Bear's busy morning
  Piggety Pig from morn 'til night

Activities – baby-sitting

Abel, Ruth. *The new sitter*
Anderson, Peggy Perry. *Time for bed, the babysitter said*
Berenstain, Stan. *The Berenstain bears and the sitter*
Berman, Linda. *The goodbye painting*
Blaustein, Muriel. *Baby Mabu and Auntie Moose*
Brandenberg, Franz. *Leo and Emily and the dragon*
Carlson, Natalie Savage. *Marie Louise's heyday*
Carrick, Carol. *The climb*
Cazet, Denys. *Big shoe, little shoe*
Chalmers, Mary. *Be good, Harry*
Christelow, Eileen. *Jerome the babysitter*
Cole, William. *What's good for a three-year-old?*
Coombs, Patricia. *Dorrie and the goblin*
Crowley, Arthur. *Bonzo Beaver*
Finfer, Celentha. *Grandmother dear*
Gordon, Margaret. *Frogs' holiday*

Greenberg, Barbara. *The bravest babysitter*
Gretz, Susanna. *Roger takes charge!*
Harris, Robie H. *Don't forget to come back*
Hines, Anna Grossnickle. *Grandma gets grumpy*
Hughes, Shirley. *An evening at Alfie's*
George the babysitter
Hurd, Edith Thacher. *Hurry hurry!*
Stop, stop
Joyce, William. *George shrinks*
Lawson, Annetta. *The lucky yak*
McCully, Emily Arnold. *The grandma mix-up*
Martin, C. L. G. *The dragon nanny*
Moore, Lilian. *Little Raccoon and no trouble at all*
Mueller, Virginia. *Monster and the baby*
Newberry, Clare Turlay. *T-Bone, the baby-sitter*
Nilsson, Ulf. *Little sister rabbit*
Paterson, Bettina. *Bun and Mrs. Tubby*
Puner, Helen Walker. *The sitter who didn't sit*
Quackenbush, Robert M. *Henry babysits*
Rayner, Mary. *Mr. and Mrs. Pig's evening out*
Rubel, Nicole. *Uncle Henry and Aunt Henrietta's honeymoon*
Schick, Eleanor. *Peter and Mr. Brandon*
Sendak, Maurice. *Outside over there*
Standiford, Natalie. *The best little monkeys in the world*
Van den Honert, Dorry. *Demi the baby sitter*
Viorst, Judith. *The good-bye book*
Wahl, Jan. *Peter and the troll baby*
Watson, Jane Werner. *My friend the babysitter*
Watson, Pauline. *Curley Cat baby-sits*
Wells, Rosemary. *Shy Charles*
Stanley and Rhoda
Williams, Barbara. *Jeremy isn't hungry*
Winthrop, Elizabeth. *Bear and Mrs. Duck*
Young, Ruth. *My baby-sitter*
Zweifel, Frances. *Animal baby-sitters*

Activities – ballooning

Adams, Adrienne. *The great Valentine's Day balloon race*
Calhoun, Mary. *Hot-air Henry*
Coerr, Eleanor. *The big balloon race*
Geisert, Arthur. *Pa's balloon and other pig tales*
Gibbons, Gail. *Flying*
Goffe, Toni. *Toby's animal rescue service*
Peppé, Rodney. *The mice and the flying basket*
Quin-Harkin, Janet. *Benjamin's balloon*
Wegen, Ron. *The balloon trip*
Wildsmith, Brian. *Bear's adventure*

Activities – bathing

Alborough, Jez. *Bare bear*
Allen, Pamela. *Mr. Archimedes' bath*
Ambrus, Victor G. *The Sultan's bath*
Aulaire, Ingri Mortenson d'. *Children of the northlights*
Bethell, Jean. *Bathtime*
Blocksma, Mary. *Rub-a-dub-dub*
Burningham, John. *Time to get out of the bath, Shirley*
Buxbaum, Susan Kovacs. *Splash!*
Faulkner, Matt. *The amazing voyage of Jackie Grace*
Hall, Derek. *Elephant bathes*
Hazen, Barbara Shook. *The me I see*
Hedderwick, Mairi. *Katie Morag and the two grandmothers*
Henkes, Kevin. *Clean enough*
Hughes, Shirley. *Bathwater's hot*
Jackson, Ellen B. *The bear in the bathtub*
Kudrna, C. Imbior. *To bathe a boa*
Lindbloom, Steven. *Let's give kitty a bath!*
Lindgren, Barbro. *Sam's bath*
McLeod, Emilie Warren. *One snail and me*
McPhail, David. *Andrew's bath*
Manushkin, Fran. *Bubblebath!*
Paterson, Diane. *The bathtub ocean*
Pryor, Ainslie. *The baby blue cat and the dirty dog brothers*
Reavin, Sam. *Hurray for Captain Jane!*
Rudolph, Marguerita. *Sharp and shiny*
Slate, Joseph. *The mean, clean, giant canoe machine*
Stevens, Kathleen. *The beast in the bathtub*
Sutherland, Harry A. *Dad's car wash*
Wabbes, Marie. *Rose's bath*
Watanabe, Shigeo. *I can take a bath!*
Wells, Rosemary. *Max's bath*
Willis, Jeanne. *The tale of Georgie Grub*
Wood, Audrey. *King Bidgood's in the bathtub*
Yolen, Jane. *No bath tonight*
Ziefert, Harriet. *Harry takes a bath*
Zion, Gene. *Harry, the dirty dog*

Activities – cooking

Abolafia, Yossi. *A fish for Mrs. Gardenia*
Brown, Marcia. *Skipper John's cook*
Brunhoff, Laurent de. *Babar learns to cook*
Cauley, Lorinda Bryan. *The bake-off*
Pease porridge hot
Cunliffe, John. *The king's birthday cake*
Da Rif, Andrea. *The blueberry cake that little fox baked*
De Paola, Tomie. *Pancakes for breakfast*
The popcorn book
Things to make and do for Valentine's Day
De Regniers, Beatrice Schenk. *Sam and the impossible thing*

Devlin, Wende. *Old Black Witch*
Old Witch and the polka-dot ribbon
Old Witch rescues Halloween
Douglass, Barbara. *The chocolate chip cookie contest*
Gibbons, Gail. *The too-great bread bake book*
Gretz, Susanna. *Teddybears cookbook*
Hitte, Kathryn. *Mexicallie soup*
Hoban, Lillian. *Arthur's Christmas cookies*
Kahl, Virginia. *The Duchess bakes a cake*
Krasilovsky, Phyllis. *The man who entered a contest*
Lasker, Joe. *Lentil soup*
Lemerise, Bruce. *Sheldon's lunch*
Levitin, Sonia. *Nobody stole the pie*
Lindman, Maj. *Flicka, Ricka, Dicka bake a cake*
Lindsey, Treska. *When Batistine made bread*
Long, Earlene. *Johnny's egg*
Miller, Alice P. *The mouse family's blueberry pie*
Nixon, Joan Lowery. *Beats me, Claude*
O'Connor, Jane. *The Care Bears' party cookbook*
Parker, Nancy Winslow. *Love from Aunt Betty*
Petie, Haris. *The seed the squirrel dropped*
Rice, Eve. *Benny bakes a cake*
Rockwell, Anne F. *The Mother Goose cookie-candy book*
Schwalje, Marjory. *Mr. Angelo*
Tomchek, Ann Heinrichs. *I can be a chef*
Tornborg, Pat. *The Sesame Street cookbook*
Ungerer, Tomi. *Zeralda's ogre*
Young, Miriam Burt. *The sugar mouse cake*

Activities – dancing

Ackerman, Karen. *Song and dance man*
Allen, Pamela. *Bertie and the bear*
Ambrus, Victor G. *The seven skinny goats*
Ancona, George. *Dancing is*
Andersen, H. C. (Hans Christian). *The red shoes*, ill. by Chihiro Iwasaki
Asch, Frank. *Moongame*
Bell, Anthea. *Swan Lake*
Bianco, Margery Williams. *The hurdy-gurdy man*
Blocksma, Mary. *The best dressed bear*
Bornstein, Ruth Lercher. *The dancing man*
Bottner, Barbara. *Messy Myra*
Charlot, Martin. *Felisa and the magic tikling bird*
Cox, David. *Ayu and the perfect moon*
Craig, Janet. *Ballet dancer*
De Paola, Tomie. *Oliver Button is a sissy*
Edelman, Elaine. *Boom-de-boom*
Fern, Eugene. *Pepito's story*

Geringer, Laura. *Molly's new washing machine*
Getz, Arthur. *Humphrey, the dancing pig*
Goble, Paul. *Star boy*
Grimm, Jacob. *The twelve dancing princesses*, ill. by Dennis Hockerman
The twelve dancing princesses, ill. by Errol Le Cain
The twelve dancing princesses, ill. by Gerald McDermott
The twelve dancing princesses, ill. by Uri Shulevitz
Hoban, Russell. *Charlie Meadows*
The dancing tigers
Hoffmann, E. T. A. *The nutcracker*, ill. by Rachel Isadora
The nutcracker, ill. by Maurice Sendak
Holabird, Katharine. *Angelina and the princess*
Angelina ballerina
Angelina on stage
Hurd, Edith Thacher. *I dance in my red pajamas*
Isadora, Rachel. *Max*
My ballet class
Opening night
Jennings, Linda M. *Coppelia*
Crispin and the dancing piglet
The sleeping beauty: the story of the ballet
McKissack, Patricia C. *Mirandy and brother wind*
Maiorano, Robert. *A little interlude*
Marshall, James. *George and Martha encore*
Martin, Bill (William Ivan). *Barn dance!*
Mayer, Mercer. *The queen always wanted to dance*
Nelson, Esther L. *Holiday singing and dancing games*
Oxenbury, Helen. *The dancing class*
Quin-Harkin, Janet. *Peter Penny's dance*
Richardson, Jean. *Clara's dancing feet*
Schertle, Alice. *Bill and the google-eyed goblins*
Sorine, Stephanie Riva. *Our ballet class*
Sutton, Jane. *What should a hippo wear?*
Tallon, Robert. *Handella*
Wood, Audrey. *Three sisters*
Wright, Jill. *The old woman and the Willy Nilly Man*

Activities – digging

Aliki. *Digging up dinosaurs*
Ayres, Pam. *When dad fills in the garden pond*
Baynton, Martin. *Fifty gets the picture*
Cleary, Beverly. *The real hole*, ill. by DyAnne DiSalvo-Ryan
The real hole, ill. by Mary Stevens
Gibbons, Gail. *Tunnels*

Kumin, Maxine. *Speedy digs downside up*
Perkins, Al. *The digging-est dog*

Activities – flying

Abolafia, Yossi. *Yanosh's Island*
Adoff, Arnold. *Flamboyan*
Allen, Laura Jean. *Where is Freddy?*
Anderson, Lonzo. *Mr. Biddle and the birds*
Arabian Nights. *The flying carpet*
Arvetis, Chris. *Why does it fly?*
Aulaire, Ingri Mortenson d'. *Wings for Per*
Ayal, Ora. *The adventures of Chester the chest*
Benchley, Nathaniel. *The flying lessons of Gerald Pelican*
Bradfield, Roger. *The flying hockey stick*
Brenner, Barbara. *The flying patchwork quilt*
Brock, Emma Lillian. *Surprise balloon*
Brown, Marc. *Wings on things*
Brown, Margaret Wise. *Streamlined pig*
Buchanan, Heather S. *George Mouse learns to fly*
Coombs, Patricia. *Dorrie and the Halloween plot*
Corbalis, Judy. *Porcellus, the flying pig*
Crews, Donald. *Flying*
Duvoisin, Roger Antoine. *Petunia takes a trip*
Florian, Douglas. *Airplane ride*
Fort, Patrick. *Redbird*
Gay, Michel. *Bibi takes flight*
Gibbons, Gail. *Flying*
Gramatky, Hardie. *Loopy*
Hays, Hoffman Reynolds. *Charley sang a song*
Hill, Eric. *Up there*
Hoban, Russell. *Ace Dragon Ltd.*
Hughes, Shirley. *Up and up*
Jenny, Anne. *The fantastic story of King Brioche the First*
Jeschke, Susan. *Perfect the pig*
Kaufmann, John. *Flying giants of long ago*
King, Christopher. *The boy who ate the moon*
Kojima, Naomi. *The flying grandmother*
Kuskin, Karla. *Just like everyone else*
Le Guin, Ursula K. *Catwings*
McConnachie, Brian. *Flying boy*
McPhail, David. *First flight*
Mariana. *Miss Flora McFlimsey's birthday*
Peet, Bill. *The kweeks of Kookatumdee*
  Merle the high flying squirrel
Phleger, Fred B. *Ann can fly*
Provensen, Alice. *The glorious flight*
Ransome, Arthur. *The fool of the world and the flying ship*
Ross, Pat. *Your first airplane trip*
Schumacher, Claire. *Nutty's birthday*
Scruton, Clive. *Pig in the air*

Spurr, Elizabeth. *Mrs. Minetta's car pool*
Stadler, John. *Three cheers for hippo!*
Stevenson, James. *Grandpa's great city tour*
Taylor, Judy. *Dudley goes flying*
Testa, Fulvio. *The paper airplane*
Titus, Eve. *Anatole over Paris*
Trez, Denise. *Maila and the flying carpet*
Ungerer, Tomi. *The Mellops go flying*
Valens, Evans G. *Wingfin and Topple*
Walter, Mildred Pitts. *Brother to the wind*
Watson, Clyde. *Midnight moon*
Wende, Philip. *Bird boy*
West, Ian. *Silas, the first pig to fly*
Wheeling, Lynn. *When you fly*
Wolkstein, Diane. *The cool ride in the sky*
  The magic wings
Young, Miriam Burt. *If I flew a plane*

Activities – gardening

Aliki. *Corn is maize*
  The story of Johnny Appleseed
Balian, Lorna. *A garden for a groundhog*
Barrett, Judi. *Old MacDonald had an apartment house*
Berson, Harold. *Pop! goes the turnip*
Bishop, Gavin. *Mrs. McGinty and the bizarre plant*
Bjork, Christina. *Linnea's windowsill garden*
Bond, Michael. *Paddington's garden*
Boon, Emilie. *Peterkin's very own garden*
Boyle, Constance. *Little Owl and the weed*
Brown, Marc. *Your first garden book*
Browne, Caroline. *Mrs. Christie's farmhouse*
Buchanan, Heather S. *Emily Mouse's garden*
Cavagnaro, David. *The pumpkin people*
Collier, Ethel. *Who goes there in my garden?*
Craft, Ruth. *Carrie Hepple's garden*
DeJong, Meindert. *Nobody plays with a cabbage*
De Paola, Tomie. *Four stories for four seasons*
  Too many Hopkins
Domanska, Janina. *The best of the bargain*
Ehlert, Lois. *Growing vegetable soup*
  Planting a rainbow
Ernst, Lisa Campbell. *Hamilton's art show*
Farjeon, Eleanor. *Mr. Garden*
Fife, Dale. *Rosa's special garden*
Firmin, Peter. *Chicken stew*
Fontaine, Jan. *The spaghetti tree*
Fujikawa, Gyo. *Let's grow a garden*
Gage, Wilson. *Mrs. Gaddy and the fast-growing vine*
Goldin, Augusta. *Where does your garden grow?*
Griffith, Helen V. *Georgia music*
Hader, Berta Hoerner. *Mister Billy's gun*
Hall, Fergus. *Groundsel*

Himmelman, John. *Amanda and the magic garden*
Hurd, Thacher. *The pea patch jig*
Ichikawa, Satomi. *Suzanne and Nicholas in the garden*
Ipcar, Dahlov. *The land of flowers*
Johnson, Hannah Lyons. *From seed to jack-o'-lantern*
Keeping, Charles. *Joseph's yard*
Kemp, Anthea. *Mr. Percy's magic greenhouse*
Kilroy, Sally. *Grandpa's garden*
Krauss, Ruth. *The carrot seed*
Le Tord, Bijou. *Rabbit seeds*
Lord, John Vernon. *Mr. Mead and his garden*
Marino, Dorothy. *Buzzy Bear in the garden*
Moore, Inga. *The vegetable thieves*
Morgenstern, Elizabeth. *The little gardeners*
Muntean, Michaela. *Alligator's garden*
Musicant, Elke. *The night vegetable eater*
Oechsli, Helen. *In my garden*
Pike, Norman. *The peach tree*
Rockwell, Anne F. *How my garden grew*
Rockwell, Harlow. *The compost heap*
Rylant, Cynthia. *This year's garden*
Sharpe, Sara. *Gardener George goes to town*
Shecter, Ben. *Partouche plants a seed*
Sobol, Harriet Langsam. *A book of vegetables*
Taylor, Judy. *Sophie and Jack help out*
Titherington, Jeanne. *Pumpkin pumpkin*
Trimby, Elisa. *Mr. Plum's paradise*
Wabbes, Marie. *Little Rabbit's garden*
Westcott, Nadine Bernard. *The giant vegetable garden*

Activities – jumping

Bright, Robert. *My hopping bunny*
Cole, Joanna. *Norma Jean, jumping bean*
Easton, Violet. *Elephants never jump*
Stephens, Karen. *Jumping*

Activities – knitting

Holl, Adelaide. *Mrs. McGarrity's peppermint sweater*
Laurin, Anne. *Little things*
Storr, Catherine. *Hugo and his grandma*

Activities – painting

Adams, Adrienne. *The Easter egg artists*
Agee, Jon. *The incredible painting of Felix Clousseau*
Asch, Frank. *Bread and honey*
Baker, Alan. *Benjamin's portrait*
Bang, Molly. *Tye May and the magic brush*
Becker, Edna. *Nine hundred buckets of paint*
Beim, Jerrold. *Jay's big job*

Bond, Michael. *Paddington's art exhibit*
Bromhall, Winifred. *Mary Ann's first picture*
Carrick, Donald. *Morgan and the artist*
Coats, Laura Jane. *Marcella and the moon*
Craven, Carolyn. *What the mailman brought*
Decker, Dorothy W. *Stripe visits New York*
Demi. *Liang and the magic paintbrush*
De Paola, Tomie. *The legend of the Indian paintbrush*
Duvoisin, Roger Antoine. *The house of four seasons*
Ernst, Lisa Campbell. *Hamilton's art show*
Freeman, Don. *The chalk box story*
Johnston, Tony. *Pages of music*
Kessler, Leonard P. *Mr. Pine's purple house*
Leaf, Margaret. *Eyes of the dragon*
Lindsay, Elizabeth. *A letter for Maria*
McPhail, David. *Lorenzo Something special*
Martin, Charles E. *For rent*
Menter, Ian. *The Albany Road mural*
Miller, Warren. *Pablo paints a picture*
Morris, Jill. *The boy who painted the sun*
Pinkwater, Daniel Manus. *The big orange splot*
Rylant, Cynthia. *All I see*
Spier, Peter. *Oh, were they ever happy!*
Wabbes, Marie. *Rose's picture*
Walsh, Ellen Stoll. *Mouse paint*
Weisgard, Leonard. *Mr. Peaceable paints*

Activities – photographing

Levinson, Riki. *I go with my family to Grandma's*
McPhail, David. *Pig Pig and the magic photo album*
Manushkin, Fran. *The perfect Christmas picture*
Seguin-Fontes, Marthe. *A wedding book*
Tison, Annette. *Animal hide-and-seek*
Türk, Hanne. *Snapshot Max*
Villarejo, Mary. *The tiger hunt*
Vincent, Gabrielle. *Smile, Ernest and Celestine*
Watts, Mabel. *Weeks and weeks*
Willard, Nancy. *Simple pictures are best*

Activities – picnicking

Asch, Frank. *Sand cake*
Benjamin, Alan. *A change of plans*
Berger, Terry. *The turtles' picnic and other nonsense stories*
Bishop, Bonnie. *Ralph rides away*
Bowden, Joan Chase. *The Ginghams and the backward picnic*
Brandenberg, Franz. *A picnic, hurrah!*
Brunhoff, Laurent de. *Babar's picnic*
Chalmers, Mary. *Here comes the trolley Mr. Cat's wonderful surprise*

Christian, Mary Blount. *Go west, swamp monsters*
Claverie, Jean. *The picnic*
Coombs, Patricia. *Dorrie and the weather-box*
Daugherty, James Henry. *The picnic*
Delton, Judy. *On a picnic*
Denton, Kady MacDonald. *The picnic*
Dickinson, Mary. *Alex's outing*
Dubanevich, Arlene. *Pig William*
Dunham, Meredith. *Picnic: how do you say it?*
Ernst, Lisa Campbell. *Up to ten and down again*
Ets, Marie Hall. *In the forest*
Freschet, Berniece. *The ants go marching*
Garland, Sarah. *Having a picnic*
Goodall, John S. *The surprise picnic*
Gordon, Margaret. *Wilberforce goes on a picnic*
Graham, Bob. *Libby, Oscar and me*
Graham, Thomas. *Mr. Bear's boat*
Higham, Jon Atlas. *Aardvark's picnic*
Hill, Eric. *Spot's first picnic*
Hines, Anna Grossnickle. *Come to the meadow*
Hurd, Edith Thacher. *No funny business*
Kasza, Keiko. *The pigs' picnic*
Keller, Holly. *Henry's Fourth of July*
Kennedy, Jimmy. *The teddy bears' picnic*, ill. by Alexandra Day
The teddy bears' picnic, ill. by Prue Theobalds
Killingback, Julia. *Busy Bears' picnic*
Knox-Wagner, Elaine. *The oldest kid*
Kroll, Steven. *It's Groundhog Day!*
Lathrop, Dorothy Pulis. *Who goes there?*
McCully, Emily Arnold. *Picnic*
MacGregor, Marilyn. *Helen the hungry bear*
Maestro, Betsy. *The perfect picnic*
Maris, Ron. *In my garden*
Marshall, Edward. *Three by the sea*
Radlauer, Ruth Shaw. *Molly*
Molly goes hiking
Rappus, Gerhard. *When the sun was shining*
Robertson, Lilian. *Picnic woods*
Saunders, Susan. *Charles Rat's picnic*
Fish fry
Scarry, Richard. *My first word book*
Schroeder, Binette. *Tuffa and the picnic*
Taylor, Judy. *Sophie and Jack*
Tether, Graham. *Skunk and possum*
Tsutsui, Yoriko. *Before the picnic*
Vaës, Alain. *The porcelain pepper pot*
Van Stockum, Hilda. *A day on skates*
Vincent, Gabrielle. *Ernest and Celestine's picnic*
Wasmuth, Eleanor. *The picnic basket*
Watson, Clyde. *Hickory stick rag*
The weekend

Westcott, Nadine Bernard. *The giant vegetable garden*
Wheeler, Cindy. *Marmalade's picnic*
Wood, Joyce. *Grandmother Lucy goes on a picnic*
Yeoman, John. *The bear's water picnic*
Yolen, Jane. *Picnic with Piggins*

Activities – playing

Adam, Barbara. *The big big box*
Agee, Jon. *Ellsworth*
Ahlberg, Janet. *Funnybones*
Alexander, Martha G. *I'll be the horse if you'll play with me*
Aliki. *Overnight at Mary Bloom's*
Allen, Robert. *Ten little babies play*
Arnold, Caroline. *How do we have fun?*
Arnosky, Jim. *Watching foxes*
Artis, Vicki Kimmel. *Pajama walking*
Asch, Frank. *Rebecka*
Aulaire, Ingri Mortenson d'. *Children of the northlights*
Ayal, Ora. *Ugbu*
Bauer, Helen. *Good times in the park*
Baugh, Dolores M. *Slides*
Swings
Benét, William Rose. *Angels*
Bethell, Jean. *Playmates*
Blegvad, Lenore. *Rainy day Kate*
Bonsall, Crosby Newell. *And I mean it, Stanley*
Piggle
Bram, Elizabeth. *Saturday morning lasts forever*
Breinburg, Petronella. *Doctor Shawn*
Brinckloe, Julie. *Playing marbles*
Brown, Myra Berry. *First night away from home*
Brown, Ruth. *Our puppy's vacation*
Bruna, Dick. *Miffy at the playground*
Miffy's dream
Burningham, John. *Where's Julius?*
Burns, Maurice. *Go ducks, go!*
Carrier, Lark. *Scout and Cody*
Carroll, Ruth. *Where's the bunny?*
Cartlidge, Michelle. *Pippin and Pod*
Christian, Mary Blount. *The sand lot*
Clymer, Eleanor Lowenton. *The big pile of dirt*
Cole, William. *What's good for a four-year-old?*
What's good for a six-year-old?
Duke, Kate. *The playground*
Emecheta, Buchi. *Nowhere to play*
Ets, Marie Hall. *Play with me*
Fitzhugh, Louise. *Bang, bang, you're dead*
Fujikawa, Gyo. *That's not fair!*
Gebert, Warren. *The old ball and the sea*
Gelman, Rita Golden. *Dumb Joey*
Gibbons, Gail. *Playgrounds*

Goffstein, M. B. (Marilyn Brooke). *Our snowman*
Hann, Jacquie. *Follow the leader*
Haus, Felice. *Beep! Beep! I'm a jeep*
Hawkins, Colin. *Dip, dip, dip*
  One finger, one thumb
  Oops-a-Daisy
  Where's bear?
Hendrickson, Karen. *Baby and I can play*
  Fun with toddlers
Henkes, Kevin. *A weekend with Wendell*
Herz, Irene. *Hey! Don't do that!*
Hill, Eric. *Spot at play*
  Spot goes to the beach
Hillert, Margaret. *Play ball*
  What is it?
Hines, Anna Grossnickle. *Bethany for real*
  It's just me, Emily
  Keep your old hat
Hughes, Shirley. *Alfie's feet*
Ichikawa, Satomi. *Let's play*
  Suzette and Nicholas in the garden
Jewell, Nancy. *Try and catch me*
Johnson, Mildred D. *Wait, skates!*
Keats, Ezra Jack. *Skates*
  The snowy day
Keeping, Charles. *Willie's fire-engine*
Kent, Jack. *Joey*
Kline, Suzy. *Don't touch!*
Krahn, Fernando. *Robot-bot-bot*
Kraus, Robert. *Come out and play, little mouse*
Krementz, Jill. *Lily goes to the playground*
Krupp, Robin Rector. *Get set to wreck!*
Lenski, Lois. *Let's play house*
Lindgren, Barbro. *The wild baby goes to sea*
Lipkind, William. *Sleepyhead*
McCarthy, Ruth. *Katie and the smallest bear*
McCord, David. *Every time I climb a tree*
McCully, Emily Arnold. *First snow*
McNulty, Faith. *When a boy wakes up in the morning*
McPhail, David. *Pig Pig rides*
Maestro, Betsy. *Harriet at play*
Major, Beverly. *Playing sardines*
Manushkin, Fran. *Swinging and swinging*
Marino, Dorothy. *Edward and the boxes*
Marshall, James. *Three up a tree*
Mayers, Patrick. *Just one more block*
Meeks, Esther K. *The hill that grew*
Merriam, Eve. *Boys and girls, girls and boys*
Miranda, Anne. *Baby walk*
Mitchell, Cynthia. *Halloweena Hecatee*
  Playtime
Moss, Elaine. *Polar*
Mueller, Virginia. *A playhouse for Monster*
Oppenheim, Joanne. *James will never die*
Oram, Hiawyn. *In the attic*
Oxenbury, Helen. *All fall down*
  Clap hands
  Grandma and Grandpa
  Playing
  Say goodnight
  Tickle, tickle
Pearson, Susan. *That's enough for one day!*
Pollock, Penny. *Water is wet*
Raebeck, Lois. *Who am I?*
Rockwell, Anne F. *At the beach*
  I play in my room
  My back yard
Rogers, Fred. *Making friends*
Rosner, Ruth. *Arabba gah zee, Marissa and Me!*
Rudolph, Marguerita. *Sharp and shiny*
Russ, Lavinia. *Alec's sand castle*
Russo, Marisabina. *The line up book*
Sendak, Maurice. *Maurice Sendak's Really Rosie*
  The sign on Rosie's door
Snyder, Zilpha Keatley. *Come on, Patsy*
Standon, Anna. *Three little cats*
Steiner, Charlotte. *Kiki's play house*
  Look what Tracy found
Steptoe, John. *Baby says*
Stevenson, Suçie. *Do I have to take Violet?*
Thwaites, Lyndsay. *Super Adam and Rosie Wonder*
Todd, Kathleen. *Snow*
Turkle, Brinton. *Obadiah the Bold*
Udry, Janice May. *Mary Ann's mud day*
Van Leeuwen, Jean. *More tales of Amanda Pig*
Vasiliu, Mircea. *A day at the beach*
Vigna, Judith. *Boot weather*
Viorst, Judith. *Sunday morning*
Waber, Bernard. *Ira sleeps over*
Wahl, Jan. *Push Kitty*
Wasmuth, Eleanor. *An alligator day*
Watanabe, Shigeo. *Daddy, play with me!*
  I can build a house!
  I can ride it!
  I'm the king of the castle!
Wells, Rosemary. *A lion for Lewis*
Winn, Chris. *Playing*
Winthrop, Elizabeth. *Bunk beds*
  That's mine
Young, Miriam Burt. *Jellybeans for breakfast*
Ziefert, Harriet. *Baby Ben's go-go book*
  Lewis the fire fighter
  Strike four!
Zimelman, Nathan. *Walls are to be walked*
Ziner, Feenie. *Counting carnival*
Zinnemann-Hope, Pam. *Let's play ball, Ned*
Zolotow, Charlotte. *The park book*
  The white marble

Activities – reading

Aliki. *How a book is made*
Baker, Betty. *Worthington Botts and the steam machine*

Bank Street College of Education. *People read*
Bauer, Caroline Feller. *Too many books!*
Black, Irma Simonton. *The little old man who could not read*
Bruna, Dick. *I can read difficult words*
Cohen, Miriam. *When will I read?*
DiFiori, Lawrence. *My first book*
Duvoisin, Roger Antoine. *Petunia*
Friskey, Margaret. *Mystery of the gate sign*
Funk, Tom. *I read signs*
Furtado, Jo. *Sorry, Miss Folio!*
Giff, Patricia Reilly. *The beast in Ms. Rooney's room*
Gillham, Bill. *The early words picture book*
Goor, Ron. *Signs*
Hallinan, P. K. (Patrick K.). *Just open a book*
Hoban, Lillian. *Arthur's prize reader*
Hoban, Tana. *I read signs*
  I read symbols
  I walk and read
Holl, Adelaide. *Most-of-the-time Maxie*
Hurd, Edith Thacher. *Johnny Lion's book*
Hutchins, Pat. *The tale of Thomas Mead*
Kuskin, Karla. *Watson, the smartest dog in the U.S.A.*
Levinson, Nancy Smiler. *Clara and the bookwagon*
Lexau, Joan M. *Olaf reads*
McLenighan, Valjean. *One whole doughnut, one doughnut hole*
McPhail, David. *Fix-it*
Maestro, Betsy. *Harriet reads signs and more signs*
Marshall, James. *Wings*
Minsberg, David. *The book monster*
Most, Bernard. *There's an ant in Anthony*
O'Neill, Catharine. *Mrs. Dunphy's dog*
Ormerod, Jan. *Reading*
Ormondroyd, Edward. *Broderick*
Pearson, Susan. *That's enough for one day!*
Porazińska, Janina. *The enchanted book*
Purdy, Carol. *Least of all*
Radlauer, Ruth Shaw. *Molly at the library*
Ross, Pat. *M and M and the big bag*
Seuss, Dr. *I can read with my eyes shut*
Sharmat, Marjorie Weinman. *My mother never listens to me*
Viorst, Judith. *The good-bye book*
Wiesner, David. *Free fall*

Activities – shopping *see* Shopping

Activities – swinging

Anderson, Robin. *Sinabouda Lily*
Baugh, Dolores M. *Swings*
Manushkin, Fran. *Swinging and swinging*
Marks, Marcia Bliss. *Swing me, swing tree*

Activities – trading

Andersen, H. C. (Hans Christian). *The old man is always right*, ill. by Feodor Rojankovsky
Burdick, Margaret. *Bobby Otter and the blue boat*
Bushey, Jerry. *The barge book*
De Regniers, Beatrice Schenk. *Was it a good trade?*
Dick Whittington and his cat. *Dick Whittington*, ill. by Edward Ardizzone
  Dick Whittington, ill. by Antony Maitland
  Dick Whittington and his cat, ill. by Marcia Brown
  Dick Whittington and his cat, ill. by Kurt Werth
Gill, Bob. *A balloon for a blunderbuss*
Hale, Irina. *The lost toys*
Hirsh, Marilyn. *The pink suit*
Hughes, Shirley. *David and dog*
  Dogger
Langstaff, John M. *The swapping boy*
Shannon, George. *The Piney Woods peddler*
Stroyer, Poul. *It's a deal*
Watts, Mabel. *Something for you, something for me*

Activities – traveling

Aksakov, Sergei. *The scarlet flower*
Arnold, Caroline. *How do we travel?*
Austin, Margot. *Willamet way*
Barklem, Jill. *The high hills*
Bate, Lucy. *How Georgina drove the car very carefully from Boston to New York*
Baum, Louis. *JuJu and the pirate*
Beatty, Hetty Burlingame. *Moorland pony*
Bemelmans, Ludwig. *Quito express*
Billout, Guy. *By camel or by car*
Biro, Val. *The wind in the willows the open road*
Blech, Dietlind. *Hello Irina*
Bolognese, Don. *A new day*
Borchers, Elisabeth. *Dear Sarah*
Brandenberg, Franz. *Everyone ready?*
Brann, Esther. *'Round the world*
Bridgman, Elizabeth. *How to travel with grownups*
  Nanny bear's cruise
Bröger, Achim. *Bruno takes a trip*
Bromhall, Winifred. *Johanna arrives*
Brown, Laurene Krasny. *Dinosaurs travel*
Brown, Margaret Wise. *Three little animals*
Bruna, Dick. *The sailor*
Brunhoff, Jean de. *The travels of Babar*
Buchanan, Heather S. *George Mouse's covered wagon*
Buffett, Jimmy. *The jolly mon*
Bunting, Eve. *The traveling men of Ballycoo*
Caines, Jeannette. *Just us women*

Carle, Eric. *The rooster who set out to see the world*
  Rooster's off to see the world
Carmi, Giora. *And Shira imagined*
Chalmers, Mary. *Here comes the trolley*
Chwast, Seymour. *Tall city, wide country*
Coerr, Eleanor. *The Josefina story quilt*
Cooney, Barbara. *Miss Rumphius*
Davis, Maggie S. *The best way to Ripton*
Demi. *The adventures of Marco Polo*
Ekker, Ernest A. *What is beyond the hill?*
Fairclough, Chris. *Take a trip to China*
  Take a trip to England
  Take a trip to Holland
  Take a trip to Israel
  Take a trip to Italy
  Take a trip to West Germany
Fox, Mem. *Possum magic*
Gantschev, Ivan. *The train to Grandma's*
Gay, Michel. *Night ride*
Gikow, Louise. *Follow that Fraggle!*
Gomi, Taro. *Bus stop*
Goodall, John S. *Paddy goes traveling*
Grahame, Kenneth. *The open road*
Gray, Genevieve. *How far, Felipe?*
Greene, Carla. *A motor holiday*
Gretz, Susanna. *Teddy bears take the train*
Haley, Patrick. *The little person*
Handford, Martin. *Find Waldo now*
  Where's Waldo?
Heuck, Sigrid. *Who stole the apples?*
Howard, Elizabeth Fitzgerald. *The train to Lulu's*
Hurd, Thacher. *Hobo dog*
Isadora, Rachel. *No, Agatha!*
Isele, Elizabeth. *Pooks*
Janosch. *The trip to Panama*
Jonas, Ann. *Round trip*
Kellogg, Steven. *Johnny Appleseed*
Kesselman, Wendy. *There's a train going by my window*
Kessler, Leonard P. *Mrs. Pine takes a trip*
Kilroy, Sally. *On the road*
Krementz, Jill. *Jamie goes on an airplane*
  A visit to Washington, D.C.
Lenski, Lois. *Davy goes places*
Lewin, Hugh. *Jafta - the journey*
Lewis, Thomas P. *Clipper ship*
Locker, Thomas. *Sailing with the wind*
Loof, Jan. *Uncle Louie's fantastic sea voyage*
Lydon, Kerry Raines. *A birthday for Blue*
Lyon, George Ella. *A regular rolling Noah*
McCormack, John E. *Rabbit travels*
McKissack, Patricia C. *Big bug book of places to go*
McToots, Rudi. *The kid's book of games for cars, trains and planes*
Maestro, Betsy. *Ferryboat*
Marshak, Samuel. *The pup grew up!*
Martin, Charles E. *Sam saves the day*
May, Charles Paul. *High-noon rocket*

Meddaugh, Susan. *Maude and Claude go abroad*
Miller, Edna. *Mousekin takes a trip*
Munro, Roxie. *The inside-outside book of Washington, D.C.*
Nixon, Joan Lowery. *If you say so, Claude*
Nordqvist, Sven. *Willie in the big world*
Patz, Nancy. *Gina Farina and the Prince of Mintz*
Petty, Kate. *On a plane*
Rabe, Berniece. *A smooth move*
Robbins, Ken. *Citycountry*
Rose, Gerald. *PB takes a holiday*
Rylant, Cynthia. *The relatives came*
Schulz, Charles M. *Bon voyage, Charlie Brown (and don't come back!!)*
Seuss, Dr. *I had trouble getting to Solla Sollew*
Smyth, Gwenda. *A pet for Mrs. Arbuckle*
Steger, Hans-Ulrich. *Traveling to Tripiti*
Stevenson, James. *Are we almost there?*
Suben, Eric. *Pigeon takes a trip*
Tapio, Pat Decker. *The lady who saw the good side of everything*
Türk, Hanne. *Max packs*
Turner, Ann. *Nettie's trip south*
Ungerer, Tomi. *Adelaide*
Vevers, Gwynne. *Animals that travel*
Willard, Nancy. *The voyage of the Ludgate Hill*
Williams, Vera B. *Stringbean's trip to the shining sea*
Ziefert, Harriet. *Keeping daddy awake on the way home from the beach*

Activities – vacationing

Adams, Adrienne. *The Easter egg artists*
Bemelmans, Ludwig. *Hansi*
Bond, Michael. *Paddington at the seaside*
Bornstein, Ruth Lercher. *I'll draw a meadow*
Briggs, Raymond. *Father Christmas goes on holiday*
Bright, Robert. *Georgie and the noisy ghost*
Brown, Ruth. *Our puppy's vacation*
Brunhoff, Laurent de. *Babar's cousin, that rascal Arthur*
  Babar's mystery
Buchanan, Heather S. *George Mouse's covered wagon*
Carlstrom, Nancy White. *The moon came too*
Carrick, Carol. *The washout*
Cole, Joanna. *The Clown-Arounds go on vacation*
Du Bois, William Pène. *Otto and the magic potatoes*
Duvoisin, Roger Antoine. *Petunia takes a trip*
Everton, Macduff. *El circo magico modelo*

Fatio, Louise. *The happy lion's vacation*
Florian, Douglas. *A summer day*
Gili, Phillida. *Fanny and Charles*
Goodall, John S. *Paddy Pork's holiday*
Goyder, Alice. *Holiday in Catland*
Hale, Kathleen. *Orlando and the water cats*
Kellogg, Steven. *Ralph's secret weapon*
Kessler, Leonard P. *Are we lost, daddy?*
Khalsa, Dayal Kaur. *My family vacation*
Lazard, Naomi. *What Amanda saw*
Levy, Elizabeth. *Something queer on vacation*
Lindman, Maj. *Snipp, Snapp, Snurr and the red shoes*
Lippman, Peter. *The Know-It-Alls take a winter vacation*
McPhail, David. *Emma's pet*
Emma's vacation
Maestro, Betsy. *The pandas take a vacation*
Marshall, James. *George and Martha round and round*
Martin, Charles E. *Sam saves the day*
Neumeyer, Peter F. *The faithful fish*
Newton, Patricia Montgomery. *Vacation surprise*
Roffey, Maureen. *I spy on vacation*
Schick, Eleanor. *Summer at the sea*
Stevenson, James. *The Sea View Hotel*
Thomson, Ruth. *Peabody all at sea*
Tobias, Tobi. *At the beach*
Weiss, Nicki. *Weekend at Muskrat Lake*
Williams, Jay. *The city witch and the country witch*

Activities – walking

Arnosky, Jim. *Outdoors on foot*
Aylesworth, Jim. *Siren in the night*
Bax, Martin. *Edmond went far away*
Brown, Margaret Wise. *Four fur feet*
Buchanan, Joan. *It's a good thing*
Buckley, Helen Elizabeth. *Grandfather and I*
De Regniers, Beatrice Schenk. *Going for a walk*
Hill, Eric. *The park*
Spot's first walk
Hoban, Tana. *I walk and read*
Jonas, Ann. *The trek*
Kingman, Lee. *Peter's long walk*
Klein, Leonore. *Henri's walk to Paris*
Lenski, Lois. *I went for a walk*
Lobe, Mira. *The snowman who went for a walk*
McNaughton, Colin. *Walk rabbit walk*
Oxenbury, Helen. *Our dog*
Radlauer, Ruth Shaw. *Molly*
Molly goes hiking
Ray, Deborah Kogan. *The cloud*
Sarton, May. *A walk through the woods*

Sharmat, Marjorie Weinman. *Burton and Dudley*
Showers, Paul. *The listening walk*
Thomas, Ianthe. *Walk home tired, Billy Jenkins*
Tobias, Tobi. *The dawdlewalk*
Türk, Hanne. *Rainy day Max*
Tworkov, Jack. *The camel who took a walk*
Viorst, Judith. *Try it again, Sam*
Watanabe, Shigeo. *I can take a walk!*
Wood, Joyce. *Grandmother Lucy goes on a picnic*
Zolotow, Charlotte. *One step, two...*
Say it!
The summer night

Activities – weaving

Bang, Molly. *Dawn*
Blood, Charles L. *The goat in the rug*
Coombs, Patricia. *Tilabel*
Ernst, Lisa Campbell. *Nattie Parsons' good-luck lamb*
Le Tord, Bijou. *Picking and weaving*
San Souci, Robert D. *The enchanted tapestry*
Selsam, Millicent E. *Cotton*
Trân-Khánh-Tuyêt. *The little weaver of Thái-Yên Village*
Yagawa, Sumiko. *The crane wife*

Activities – whistling

Alexander, Anne. *I want to whistle*
Ambrus, Victor G. *The three poor tailors*
Avery, Kay. *Wee willow whistle*
Bason, Lillian. *Pick a raincoat, pick a whistle*
Blackwood, Gladys Rourke. *Whistle for Cindy*
Keats, Ezra Jack. *Whistle for Willie*

Activities – working

Abelson, Danny. *The Muppets take Manhattan*
Alda, Arlene. *Sonya's mommy works*
Allen, Jeffrey. *Mary Alice, operator number 9*
Ardizzone, Edward. *Paul, the hero of the fire*
Arkin, Alan. *Tony's hard work day*
Armstrong, Louise. *How to turn lemons into money*
Asch, Frank. *Good lemonade*
Aylesworth, Jim. *Shenandoah Noah*
Bach, Othello. *Lilly, Willy and the mail-order witch*
Baker, Betty. *Turkey girl*
Barton, Byron. *Machines at work*
Basso, Bill. *The top of the pizzas*
Beim, Jerrold. *Jay's big job*

Bethell, Jean. *Three cheers for Mother Jones!*
Blance, Ellen. *Monster gets a job*
Bond, Michael. *Paddington cleans up*
Burton, Virginia Lee. *Mike Mulligan and his steam shovel*
Caple, Kathy. *The purse*
Carle, Eric. *Walter the baker*
Civardi, Anne. *Things people do*
Clark, Ann Nolan. *The little Indian basket maker*
The little Indian pottery maker
Claverie, Jean. *Working*
Cole, Babette. *The trouble with dad*
Dahl, Roald. *The giraffe and the pelly and me*
Delaney, Ned. *Terrible things could happen*
Delton, Judy. *My mother lost her job today*
Duke, Kate. *Clean-up day*
Euvremer, Teryl. *Sun's up*
Fleischman, Paul. *The animal hedge*
Florian, Douglas. *People working*
Gág, Wanda. *Gone is gone*
Gallo, Giovanni. *The lazy beaver*
Gibbons, Gail. *Deadline!*
Zoo
Goffstein, M. B. (Marilyn Brooke). *An actor*
A writer
Goodall, John S. *Paddy Pork odd jobs*
Hall, Donald. *The ox-cart man*
Harper, Anita. *How we work*
Harvey, Brett. *My prairie year*
Hautzig, Deborah. *It's not fair!*
Heine, Helme. *Merry-go-round*
Hoban, Russell. *Charlie the tramp*
Horvath, Betty F. *Jasper makes music*
Kessler, Ethel. *Night story*
Killingback, Julia. *Monday is washing day*
Krahn, Fernando. *Robot-bot-bot*
Lasker, Joe. *Mothers can do anything*
Leiner, Katherine. *Both my parents work*
Lindsey, Treska. *When Batistine made bread*
Lyon, David. *The biggest truck*
McCunn, Ruthanne L. *Pie-Biter*
McGowen, Tom. *The only glupmaker in the U.S. Navy*
Maestro, Betsy. *Harriet at work*
Marshall, James. *Fox on the job*
Martini, Teri. *Cowboys*
Maynard, Joyce. *New house*
Merriam, Eve. *Mommies at work*
Mitchell, Joyce Slayton. *My mommy makes money*
Paterson, Diane. *Soap and suds*
Petrides, Heidrun. *Hans and Peter*
Puner, Helen Walker. *Daddys, what they do all day*
Purdy, Carol. *Least of all*
Quinlan, Patricia. *My dad takes care of me*

Ross, Jessica. *Ms. Klondike*
Sandberg, Inger. *Come on out, Daddy!*
Schick, Eleanor. *Home alone*
Simon, Norma. *I'm busy, too*
Skurzynski, Gloria. *Martin by himself*
Stolz, Mary Slattery. *Zekmet, the stone carver*
Türk, Hanne. *Raking leaves with Max*
Yeoman, John. *The wild washerwomen*

Activities – writing

Arnosky, Jim. *Mouse writing*
Felt, Sue. *Rosa-too-little*
Hoban, Lillian. *Arthur's pen pal*
Johnston, Johanna. *That's right, Edie*
Joslin, Sesyle. *Dear dragon*
Krauss, Ruth. *I write it*
Miles, Miska. *The pointed brush...*
Nixon, Joan Lowery. *If you were a writer*
Oakley, Graham. *The diary of a church mouse*
Seuss, Dr. *I can write!*

Adoption

Bawden, Nina. *Princess Alice*
Buck, Pearl S. (Pearl Sydenstricker). *Welcome child*
Bunin, Catherine. *Is that your sister?*
Caines, Jeannette. *Abby*
Chapman, Noralee. *The story of Barbara*
Fisher, Iris L. *Katie-Bo*
Freudberg, Judy. *Susan and Gordon adopt a baby*
Girard, Linda Walvoord. *Adoption is for always*
Greenberg, Judith E. *Adopted*
Hess, Edith. *Peter and Susie find a family*
Lapsley, Susan. *I am adopted*
Livingston, Carole. *"Why was I adopted?"*
MacKay, Jed. *The big secret*
Milgram, Mary. *Brothers are all the same*
Rondell, Florence. *The family that grew*
Rosenberg, Maxine B. *Being adopted*
Sobol, Harriet Langsam. *We don't look like our mom and dad*
Stanek, Muriel. *My little foster sister*
Stein, Sara Bonnett. *The adopted one*
Udry, Janice May. *Theodore's parents*
Wasson, Valentina Pavlovna. *The chosen baby*

Africa *see* Foreign lands – Africa

Afro-Americans *see* Ethnic groups in the U.S. – Afro-Americans

Aged *see* Old age

Aggressiveness *see* Character traits – assertiveness

Airplane pilots *see* Careers – airplane pilots

Airplanes, airports

Bagwell, Richard. *This is an airport*
Baker, Donna. *I want to be a pilot*
Barrett, N. S. *Airliners*
Barton, Byron. *Airplanes*
  Airport
Baumann, Kurt. *The paper airplane*
Brenner, Anita. *I want to fly*
Brown, Margaret Wise. *Streamlined pig*
Buchanan, Heather S. *George Mouse learns to fly*
Cave, Ron. *Airplanes*
Crews, Donald. *Flying*
Emberley, Ed. *Cars, boats, and planes*
Firmin, Peter. *Basil Brush goes flying*
Florian, Douglas. *Airplane ride*
Fort, Patrick. *Redbird*
Gay, Michel. *Bibi takes flight*
  Little plane
Gibbons, Gail. *Flying*
Gramatky, Hardie. *Loopy*
Ingoglia, Gina. *The big book of real airplanes*
Krementz, Jill. *Jamie goes on an airplane*
Lenski, Lois. *The little airplane*
McPhail, David. *First flight*
Nolan, Dennis. *Wizard McBean and his flying machine*
Olschewski, Alfred. *We fly*
Petty, Kate. *On a plane*
Phleger, Fred B. *Ann can fly*
Provensen, Alice. *The glorious flight*
Rockwell, Anne F. *Planes*
Ross, Pat. *Your first airplane trip*
Scarry, Richard. *Richard Scarry's great big air book*
Schulz, Charles M. *Snoopy's facts and fun book about planes*
Spier, Peter. *Bored - nothing to do!*
Testa, Fulvio. *The paper airplane*
Thompson, Brenda. *Famous planes*
Ungerer, Tomi. *The Mellops go flying*
Wheeling, Lynn. *When you fly*
Young, Miriam Burt. *If I flew a plane*
Zaffo, George J. *The big book of real airplanes*
  The giant nursery book of things that go

Airports *see* Airplanes, airports

Albatrosses *see* Birds – albatrosses

Alligators *see* Reptiles – alligators, crocodiles

Alphabet books *see* ABC books

Alzheimer's *see* Illness – Alzheimer's

Ambition *see* Character traits – ambition

American Indians *see* Indians of North America

Amphibians *see* Frogs and toads; Reptiles

Anatomy

Aliki. *My hands*
Bailey, Jill. *Eyes*
  Feet
  Mouths
  Noses
Bishop, Claire Huchet. *The man who lost his head*
Bolliger, Max. *The rabbit with the sky blue ears*
Boujon, Claude. *The fairy with the long nose*
Boynton, Sandra. *Horns to toes and in between*
Brenner, Barbara. *Faces, faces, faces*
Campbell, Rod. *It's mine*
Caple, Kathy. *The biggest nose*
Caputo, Robert. *More than just pets*
Carle, Eric. *My very first book of heads and tails*
Castle, Sue. *Face talk, hand talk, body talk*
Chase, Catherine. *Feet*
Cole, Brock. *The giant's toe*
Cole, Joanna. *A bird's body*
  A cat's body
  A dog's body
Dubov, Christine Salac. *Aleksandra, where are your toes?*
  Aleksandra, where is your nose?
Elkin, Benjamin. *Gillespie and the guards*
Emberley, Ed. *Ed Emberley's crazy mixed-up face game*
Facklam, Margery. *But not like mine*
Goor, Ron. *All kinds of feet*
Gross, Ruth Belov. *A book about your skeleton*
Hawkins, Colin. *This little pig*
Hazen, Barbara Shook. *The me I see*
Hirschmann, Linda. *In a lick of a flick of a tongue*
Holzenthaler, Jean. *My feet do*
  My hands can
Kilroy, Sally. *Babies' bodies*
Krauss, Ruth. *Eyes, nose, fingers, toes*
Martin, Bill (William Ivan). *Here are my hands*
Moncure, Jane Belk. *What your nose knows!*
My body
Ormerod, Jan. *This little nose*

Perkins, Al. *The ear book*
Hand, hand, fingers, thumb
The nose book
Rothman, Joel. *This can lick a lollipop*
Schertle, Alice. *My two feet*
Seuss, Dr. *The eye book*
The foot book
Sharmat, Marjorie Weinman. *Helga high-up*
Showers, Paul. *Look at your eyes*
You can't make a move without your muscles
Your skin and mine
Smallman, Clare. *Outside in*
Stinson, Kathy. *The bare naked book*
Thomson, Ruth. *Eyes*
Weiss, Leatie. *Funny feet!*
Yudell, Lynn Deena. *Make a face*

Angels

Andersen, H. C. (Hans Christian). *The red shoes*, ill. by Chihiro Iwasaki
Benét, William Rose. *Angels*
Brown, Abbie Farwell. *The Christmas angel*
Collington, Peter. *The angel and the soldier boy*
Kavanaugh, James J. *The crooked angel*
Knight, Hilary. *Angels and berries and candy canes*
Krahn, Fernando. *A funny friend from heaven*
Lathrop, Dorothy Pulis. *An angel in the woods*
Martin, Judith. *The tree angel*
Ness, Evaline. *Marcella's guardian angel*
Sawyer, Ruth. *The Christmas Anna angel*
Thomas, Kathy. *The angel's quest*
Wallace, Ian. *Morgan the magnificent*
Zimelman, Nathan. *The star of Melvin*

Anger *see* Emotions – anger

Animals

Aardema, Verna. *Princess Gorilla and a new kind of water*
Rabbit makes a monkey of lion
The vingananee and the tree toad
What's so funny, Ketu?
Who's in Rabbit's house?
Why mosquitoes buzz in people's ears
Abisch, Roz. *The clever turtle*
Adler, David A. *The carsick zebra and other riddles*
Æsop. *Seven fables from Æsop*, ill. by Robert W. Alley
Aitken, Amy. *Kate and Mona in the jungle*
Wanda's circus
Aldridge, Alan. *The butterfly ball and the grasshopper's feast*

Aldridge, Josephine Haskell. *The best of friends*
Alexander, Martha G. *Pigs say oink*
Aliki. *Wild and woolly mammoths*
Allamand, Pascale. *The animals who changed their colors*
Allan, Ted. *Willie the squowse*
Allard, Harry. *Bumps in the night*
Allen, Gertrude E. *Everyday animals*
Allen, Jeffrey. *Mary Alice, operator number 9*
Nosey Mrs. Rat
Allen, Jonathan. *A bad case of animal nonsense*
Allen, Linda. *Mrs. Simkin's bed*
Allen, Marjorie N. *One, two, three - ah-choo!*
Allen, Martha Dickson. *Real life monsters*
Allen, Pamela. *Mr. Archimedes' bath*
Who sank the boat?
Allen, Robert. *The zoo book*
Amery, H. *The farm picture book*
Amos, William H. *Exploring the seashore*
Anholt, Catherine. *Chaos at Cold Custard Farm*
Anno, Mitsumasa. *Anno's animals*
Applebaum, Stan. *Going my way?*
Ariane. *Animal stories*
Armour, Richard Willard. *Animals on the ceiling*
Have you ever wished you were something else?
Arnold, Caroline. *Five nests*
Pets without homes
Arnosky, Jim. *A kettle of hawks, and other wildlife groups*
Aruego, José. *Look what I can do*
We hide, you seek
Arvetis, Chris. *Why does it fly?*
Why is it dark?
Asch, Frank. *Bread and honey*
Asimov, Isaac. *Animals of the Bible*
Atwood, Margaret. *Anna's pet*
Aulaire, Ingri Mortenson d'. *Animals everywhere*
Children of the northlights
Aylesworth, Jim. *One crow*
B. B. *Blacksheep and Company*
Bahr, Robert. *Blizzard at the zoo*
Bailey, Jill. *Eyes*
Feet
Mouths
Noses
Baker, Betty. *Latki and the lightning lizard*
Sonny-Boy Sim
Baker, Eugene. *Bicycles*
Fire
Home
Outdoors
School
Water

Baker, Jeffrey J. W. *Patterns of nature*
Baker, Laura Nelson. *The friendly beasts*
Bang, Betsy. *The old woman and the red pumpkin*
The old woman and the rice thief
Bang, Molly. *Delphine*
Bannon, Laura. *The best house in the world*
Little people of the night
Red mittens
The scary thing
Barrett, Judi. *Animals should definitely not act like people*
Animals should definitely not wear clothing
Snake is totally tail
Barry, Robert E. *Animals around the world*
Baruch, Dorothy. *Kappa's tug-of-war with the big brown horse*
Base, Graeme. *Animalia*
My grandma lived in Gooligulch
Baskin, Leonard. *Hosie's zoo*
Bason, Lillian. *Castles and mirrors and cities of sand*
Bassett, Lisa. *A clock for Beany*
Batherman, Muriel. *Animals live here*
Battles, Edith. *What does the rooster say, Yoshio?*
Baugh, Dolores M. *Let's see the animals*
Baumann, Hans. *Chip has many brothers*
Bax, Martin. *Edmond went far away*
Bayer, Jane. *A my name is Alice*
Bayley, Nicola. *One old Oxford ox*
Baylor, Byrd. *Desert voices*
We walk in sandy places
Beach, Stewart. *Good morning, sun's up!*
Beim, Jerrold. *Eric on the desert*
Bellamy, David. *The forest*
The river
Belling the cat and other stories
Belloc, Hilaire. *The bad child's book of beasts*
The bad child's book of beasts, and more beasts for worse children
The bad child's pop-up book of beasts
More beasts for worse children
Bellville, Cheryl Walsh. *Rodeo*
Bellville, Rod. *Large animal veterinarians*
Belpré, Pura. *Dance of the animals*
Bemelmans, Ludwig. *Rosebud*
Benchley, Nathaniel. *Running Owl the hunter*
Bendick, Jeanne. *Why can't I?*
Berger, Melvin. *Prehistoric mammals*
Berger, Terry. *The turtles' picnic and other nonsense stories*
Bernstein, Joanne E. *Creepy crawly critter riddles*
Bernstein, Margery. *Coyote goes hunting for fire*
The first morning
Berson, Harold. *Why the jackal won't speak to the hedgehog*

Bester, Roger. *Guess what?*
Bethell, Jean. *Bathtime Playmates*
Bible, Charles. *Hamdaani*
Bierhorst, John. *Doctor Coyote*
The big Peter Rabbit book
Binzen, Bill. *Alfred goes house hunting*
Biro, Val. *The wind in the willows home sweet home*
The wind in the willows the open road
The wind in the willows the river bank
The wind in the willows the wild wood
Blough, Glenn O. *Who lives in this meadow?*
Bodsworth, Nan. *Monkey business*
Bograd, Larry. *Egon*
Bohdal, Susi. *Tom cat*
Bonino, Louise. *The cozy little farm*
Boon, Emilie. *1 2 3 how many animals can you see?*
Peterkin's very own garden
Peterkin's wet walk
Borden, Beatrice Brown. *Wild animals of Africa*
Borg, Inga. *Plupp builds a house*
Bottner, Barbara. *Zoo song*
Boyd, Selma. *I met a polar bear*
Boynton, Sandra. *A is for angry*
The going to bed book
Good night, good night
Moo, baa, lalala
Bradman, Tony. *See you later, alligator*
Brady, Irene. *A mouse named Mus*
Brandenberg, Franz. *Aunt Nina and her nephews and nieces*
Cock-a-doodle-doo
Leo and Emily's zoo
Branley, Franklyn M. *Big tracks, little tracks*
Brasch, Kate. *Prehistoric monsters*
Brenner, Barbara. *Ostrich feathers*
Brett, Jan. *Annie and the wild animals*
Brice, Tony. *Baby animals*
Brierley, Louise. *King Lion and his cooks*
Brister, Hope. *The cunning fox and other tales*
Bro, Marguerite H. *The animal friends of Peng-u*
Brock, Emma Lillian. *Nobody's mouse*
Surprise balloon
Brooke, L. Leslie (Leonard Leslie). *Johnny Crow's garden*
Johnny Crow's new garden
Johnny Crow's party
Brown, Marc. *Arthur goes to camp*
Arthur's April fool
Arthur's Christmas
Arthur's eyes
Arthur's Halloween
Arthur's teacher trouble
Arthur's Thanksgiving

Arthur's tooth
Arthur's Valentine
The bionic bunny show
D. W. flips!
The silly tail book
The true Francine
Brown, Marcia. *The blue jackal*
The bun
Once a mouse...
Brown, Margaret Wise. *Baby animals*
The big fur secret
Don't frighten the lion
The duck
Fox eyes
Once upon a time in pigpen and three other stories
Streamlined pig
They all saw it
Three little animals
Wait till the moon is full
Where have you been?
Brown, Richard Eric. *One hundred words about animals*
Browner, Richard. *Everyone has a name*
Brunhoff, Laurent de. *Babar's counting book*
Babar's little circus star
Buck, Frank. *Jungle animals*
Buff, Mary. *Forest folk*
Bunting, Eve. *Happy birthday, dear duck*
Terrible things
Burdick, Margaret. *Bobby Otter and the blue boat*
Burningham, John. *Cluck baa*
Mr. Gumpy's outing
Burton, Marilee Robin. *The elephant's nest*
Tail toes eyes ears nose
Byars, Betsy Cromer. *The groober*
Calhoun, Mary. *Euphonia and the flood*
Calmenson, Stephanie. *All aboard the goodnight train*
The kindergarten book
Where will the animals stay?
Campbell, Rod. *Dear zoo*
It's mine
Carle, Eric. *1, 2, 3 to the zoo*
The very busy spider
Carlson, Nancy. *Louanne Pig in making the team*
The talent show
Carlson, Natalie Savage. *Surprise in the mountains*
Carrick, Carol. *Patrick's dinosaurs*
Carrick, Malcolm. *I can squash elephants!*
Carrier, Lark. *A Christmas promise*
Cartwright, Ann. *Norah's ark*
Cassidy, Dianne. *Circus animals*
Castle, Caroline. *Herbert Binns and the flying tricycle*
Catchpole, Clive. *Deserts*
Grasslands

Jungles
Mountains
Cathon, Laura E. *Tot Botot and his little flute*
Cauley, Lorinda Bryan. *The animal kids*
The bake-off
The cock, the mouse and the little red hen
Causley, Charles. *"Quack!" said the billy-goat*
Cazet, Denys. *The duck with squeaky feet*
Frosted glass
Lucky me
Sunday
Chalmers, Audrey. *Hundreds and hundreds of pancakes*
Chalmers, Mary. *A Christmas story*
Easter parade
Charles, Donald. *Calico Cat at the zoo*
Shaggy dog's animal alphabet
Cherry, Lynne. *Who's sick today?*
Chicken Little. *Chicken Licken*, ill. by Jutta Ash
Chicken Licken, ill. by Gavin Bishop
Henny Penny, ill. by Paul Galdone
Henny Penny, ill. by William Stobbs
The story of Chicken Licken, adapt. and ill. by Jan Ormerod
Chorao, Kay. *Lemon moon*
Chouinard, Roger. *The amazing animal alphabet book*
Christelow, Eileen. *Olive and the magic hat*
The robbery at the diamond dog diner
Christensen, Gardell Dano. *Mrs. Mouse needs a house*
Clewes, Dorothy. *Henry Hare's boxing match*
The wild wood
Climo, Shirley. *The cobweb Christmas*
Clymer, Ted. *The horse and the bad morning*
Coatsworth, Elizabeth. *A peaceable kingdom, and other poems*
Cober, Alan E. *Cober's choice*
Colby, C. B. (Carroll Burleigh). *Who lives there?*
Who went there?
Cole, Joanna. *Animal sleepyheads*
Evolution
Large as life daytime animals
Large as life nighttime animals
Cole, Sheila. *When the tide is low*
Cole, William. *I went to the animal fair*
Colman, Hila. *Watch that watch*
Conklin, Gladys. *I caught a lizard*
Cooper, Gale. *Unicorn moon*
Corey, Dorothy. *A shot for baby bear*
Will it ever be my birthday?
Cormack, M. Grant. *Animal tales from Ireland*
Cortesi, Wendy W. *Explore a spooky swamp*
Cosgrove, Margaret. *Wintertime for animals*

Coville, Bruce. *Sarah's unicorn*
Cowcher, Helen. *Rain forest*
Craig, M. Jean. *Spring is like the morning*
Cremins, Robert. *My animal ABC*
  My animal Mother Goose
Cristini, Ermanno. *In the pond*
  In the woods
Cross, Genevieve. *A trip to the yard*
Crowe, Robert L. *Tyler Toad and the thunder*
Croxford, Vera. *All kinds of animals*
Crump, Donald J. *Creatures small and furry*
Curle, Jock. *The four good friends*
Curry, Peter. *Animals*
Cutler, Ivor. *The animal house*
  Herbert
Dahl, Roald. *The enormous crocodile*
  The giraffe and the pelly and me
Daly, Kathleen N. *Today's biggest animals*
  Unusual animals
Davis, Douglas F. *There's an elephant in the garage*
DeLage, Ida. *ABC triplets at the zoo*
Demi. *A Chinese zoo*
  Demi's count the animals 1-2-3
  Demi's find the animals A B C
Dennis, Suzanne E. *Answer me that*
Dennis, Wesley. *Flip*
De Paola, Tomie. *Country farm*
  The hunter and the animals
De Posadas Mane, Carmen. *Mister North Wind*
De Regniers, Beatrice Schenk. *It does not say meow!*
  May I bring a friend?
DiFiori, Lawrence. *Baby animals*
Dionetti, Michelle. *The day Eli went looking for bear*
Dodd, Lynley. *Wake up, bear*
Dodds, Siobhan. *Charles Tiger*
  Elizabeth Hen
Domanska, Janina. *What do you see?*
Domestic animals
Dragonwagon, Crescent. *Alligator arrived with apples*
Du Bois, William Pène. *Bear circus*
  Bear party
Duff, Maggie. *Dancing turtle*
Duncan, Riana. *A nutcracker in a tree*
Dunn, Judy. *The animals of Buttercup Farm*
Dunn, Phoebe. *Baby's animal friends*
Durrell, Julie. *Mouse tails*
Duvoisin, Roger Antoine. *A for the ark*
  The crocodile in the tree
  Jasmine
  Our Veronica goes to Petunia's farm
  Petunia
  Petunia and the song
  Petunia, beware!
  Petunia takes a trip

  Petunia, the silly goose
  Petunia's treasure
Easton, Violet. *Elephants never jump*
Eberle, Irmengarde. *Picture stories for children*
Eichenberg, Fritz. *Dancing in the moon*
Elborn, Andrew. *Noah and the ark and the animals*
Elkin, Benjamin. *Why the sun was late*
Elting, Mary. *Q is for duck*
Emberley, Barbara. *One wide river to cross*
Emberley, Ed. *Animals*
Erickson, Russell E. *Warton's Christmas eve adventure*
Ernst, Lisa Campbell. *Hamilton's art show*
Ets, Marie Hall. *Another day*
  Beasts and nonsense
  Elephant in a well
  In the forest
  Just me
  Mister Penny
  Mister Penny's circus
  Play with me
Evans, Eva Knox. *Sleepy time*
  Where do you live?
Facklam, Margery. *But not like mine*
  So can I
Farber, Norma. *As I was crossing Boston Common*
  How the hibernators came to Bethlehem
  How the left-behind beasts built Ararat
  How to ride a tiger
Farm animals
Farm house
Fay, Hermann. *My zoo*
Feczko, Kathy. *Umbrella parade*
Fiddle-i-fee
Fife, Dale. *The little park*
Fischer, Hans. *The birthday*
Fisher, Aileen. *Do bears have mothers too?*
  We went looking
  Where does everyone go?
Flack, Marjorie. *Ask Mr. Bear*
Flanders, Michael. *Creatures great and small*
Fletcher, Elizabeth. *What am I?*
Flora, James. *The day the cow sneezed*
Florian, Douglas. *A bird can fly*
Foreman, Michael. *Panda and the bushfire*
Fournier, Catharine. *The coconut thieves*
Fowler, Richard. *Mr. Little's noisy car*
Fox, Charles Philip. *Mr. Stripes the gopher*
Fox, Mem. *Hattie and the fox*
Francis, Frank. *The magic wallpaper*
Frascino, Edward. *My cousin the king*
Freedman, Russell. *Farm babies*
  Hanging on
  Tooth and claw
  When winter comes
Freeman, Don. *Add-a-line alphabet*

Freschet, Berniece. *Owl in the garden*
Where's Henrietta's hen?
Friedrich, Priscilla. *The wishing well in the woods*
Frith, Michael K. *Some of us walk, some fly, some swim*
A frog he would a-wooing go (folk-song). *Froggie went a-courting*, ill. by Chris Conovers
From King Boggen's hall to nothing-at-all
Fromm, Lilo. *Muffel and Plums*
Fussenegger, Gertrud. *Noah's ark*
Futamata, Eigorō. *How not to catch a mouse*
Gackenbach, Dick. *Supposes*
Galdone, Paul. *Cat goes fiddle-i-fee*
Gammell, Stephen. *Once upon MacDonald's farm*
Gantos, Jack. *The perfect pal*
Gardner, Beau. *Can you imagine...?*
Guess what?
Garelick, May. *Look at the moon*
Garten, Jan. *The alphabet tale*
Gay, Michel. *Bibi's birthday surprise*
Night ride
Gay, Zhenya. *Look!*
What's your name?
Gendel, Evelyn. *Tortoise and turtle*
Tortoise and turtle abroad
Geraghty, Paul. *Over the steamy swamp*
Gerstein, Mordicai. *William, where are you?*
Gibbons, Gail. *Prehistoric animals*
Zoo
Ginsburg, Mirra. *Four brave sailors*
The fox and the hare
Mushroom in the rain
Goffe, Toni. *Toby's animal rescue service*
Goffstein, M. B. (Marilyn Brooke). *Natural history*
Goodspeed, Peter. *A rhinoceros wakes me up in the morning*
Goor, Ron. *All kinds of feet*
Gordon, Shirley. *Grandma zoo*
Grabianski, Janusz. *Grabianski's wild animals*
Graham, Bob. *First there was Frances*
Graham, John. *A crowd of cows*
I love you, mouse
Grahame, Kenneth. *The open road*
The river bank
Greeley, Valerie. *Farm animals*
Field animals
Pets
Zoo animals
Greydanus, Rose. *Animals at the zoo*
Griffith, Helen V. *Grandaddy's place*
Grimm, Jacob. *The Bremen town musicians*, ill. by Donna Diamond
The Bremen town musicians, ill. by Janina Domanska
The Bremen town musicians, ill. by Paul Galdone

Bremen town musicians, ill. by Josef Paleček
The Bremen town musicians, ill. by Ilse Plume
Little Red Riding Hood, ill. by John S. Goodall
The musicians of Bremen, ill. by Svend Otto S.
The musicians of Bremen, ill. by Martin Ursell
Grosvenor, Donna. *Zoo babies*
Gundersheimer, Karen. *Colors to know*
Hadithi, Mwenye. *Crafty chameleon*
Tricky tortoise
Haley, Gail E. *Noah's ark*
Hall, Bill. *A year in the forest*
Hall, Malcolm. *CariCATures*
Hamberger, John. *The day the sun disappeared*
Hands, Hargrave. *Duckling sees*
Little lamb sees
Harris, Joel Chandler. *Jump!*
Jump again!
Harris, Susan. *Creatures that look alike*
Harrison, David Lee. *Wake up, sun!*
Harrison, Sarah. *In granny's garden*
Haseley, Dennis. *The cave of snores*
Hawkins, Colin. *Max and the magic word*
Where's my mommy?
Hawkinson, John. *Robins and rabbits*
Haywood, Carolyn. *Hello, star*
Hazen, Barbara Shook. *Where do bears sleep?*
Heine, Helme. *Friends*
Three little friends: the alarm clock
Three little friends: the racing cart
Three little friends: the visitor
Heller, Ruth. *Animals born alive and well*
How to hide a polar bear
How to hide an octopus
Helweg, Hans. *Farm animals*
Henley, Karyn. *Hatch!*
Herriot, James. *Only one woof*
Herz, Irene. *Hey! Don't do that!*
Heuck, Sigrid. *Who stole the apples?*
Hewitt, Kathryn. *The three sillies*
Higham, Jon Atlas. *Aardvark's picnic*
Hill, Eric. *Spot at play*
Spot at the fair
Spot goes to the farm
Spot on the farm
Himmelman, John. *Amanda and the magic garden*
Montigue on the high seas
Hines, Anna Grossnickle. *I'll tell you what they say*
Hirschi, Ron. *Who lives in... Alligator Swamp?*
Who lives in... the forest?
Hirschmann, Linda. *In a lick of a flick of a tongue*

Hoban, Lillian. *The case of the two masked robbers*

Hoban, Tana. *Big ones, little ones*
A children's zoo

Hoff, Carol. *The four friends*

Hogrogian, Nonny. *Billy Goat and his well-fed friends*

Holl, Adelaide. *The rain puddle*
Small Bear builds a playhouse

Holm, Mayling Mack. *A forest Christmas*

Hooper, Patricia. *A bundle of beasts*

Houston, John A. *A room full of animals*

Hurd, Edith Thacher. *Christmas eve*

Hurd, Thacher. *A night in the swamp*

Hurford, John. *The dormouse*

Hutchins, Pat. *1 hunter*
The silver Christmas tree
The surprise party

Ichikawa, Satomi. *Nora's castle*

Inkpen, Mick. *One bear at bedtime*

Ipcar, Dahlov. *Animal hide and seek*
Bright barnyard
Brown cow farm
The calico jungle
A flood of creatures
I like animals
I love my anteater with an A
Lost and found
Wild and tame animals

Irvine, Georgeanne. *The nursery babies*
Tully the tree kangaroo

Isenbart, Hans-Heinrich. *Baby animals on the farm*

Jacobs, Francine. *Sewer Sam*

Jacobs, Joseph. *Hereafterthis*

Janosch. *Tonight at nine*

Jaynes, Ruth M. *Tell me please! What's that?*

Joerns, Consuelo. *Oliver's escape*

Johnson, Crockett. *We wonder what will Walter be? When he grows up*

Jonas, Ann. *The trek*

Jones, Chuck. *William the backwards skunk*

Kalman, Benjamin. *Animals in danger*

Kamen, Gloria. *The ringdoves*

Kane, Henry B. *Wings, legs, or fins*

Kaufmann, John. *Flying giants of long ago*

Keats, Ezra Jack. *Pet show!*

Keller, Holly. *Too big*
Will it rain?

Kellogg, Steven. *Aster Aardvark's alphabet adventures*
Chicken Little

Kemp, Anthea. *Mr. Percy's magic greenhouse*

Kent, Jack. *Joey runs away*
Little Peep

Kepes, Juliet. *Five little monkeys*

Kessler, Ethel. *Are there hippos on the farm?*
Do baby bears sit in chairs?

Is there an elephant in your kitchen?
What's inside the box?

Kessler, Leonard P. *The big mile race*
Do you have any carrots?
Kick, pass, and run
Old Turtle's winter games
On your mark, get set, go!
Super bowl

Kherdian, David. *The animal*

Kilroy, Sally. *Animal noises*
Babies' zoo

Kingman, Lee. *Peter's long walk*

Kipling, Rudyard. *The elephant's child*, ill. by Louise Brierley
The elephant's child, ill. by Lorinda Bryan Cauley
The elephant's child, ill. by Tim Raglin
How the camel got his hump, ill. by Quentin Blake
Just so stories, ill. by Meg Rutherford
The miracle of the mountain

Kirn, Ann. *Beeswax catches a thief*

Kitchen, Bert. *Animal alphabet*
Animal numbers

Koelling, Caryl. *Animal mix and match*

Koide, Tan. *May we sleep here tonight?*

Komori, Atsushi. *Animal mothers*

Koralek, Jenny. *The friendly fox*

Korschunow, Irina. *Small fur*

Krahn, Fernando. *The biggest Christmas tree on earth*

Kramer, Anthony Penta. *Numbers on parade*

Krauze, Andrzej. *What's so special about today?*

Kroll, Steven. *It's Groundhog Day!*

Krüss, James. *3 X 3*

Kubler, Susanne. *The three friends*

Kuchalla, Susan. *Baby animals*

Kuklin, Susan. *Taking my dog to the vet*

Kuskin, Karla. *The animals and the ark*
James and the rain
Roar and more
Something sleeping in the hall

Kwitz, Mary DeBall. *When it rains*

Lady Eden's School. *Just how stories*

Langstaff, John M. *Over in the meadow*

Lapp, Eleanor. *The mice came in early this year*

Lathrop, Dorothy Pulis. *Who goes there?*

Laurencin, Geneviève. *I wish I were*

Lazard, Naomi. *What Amanda saw*

Lee, Jeanne M. *Toad is the uncle of heaven*

Leigh, Oretta. *The merry-go-round*

Lenski, Lois. *Animals for me*
Big little Davy

Lesser, Carolyn. *The goodnight circle*

Lester, Helen. *It wasn't my fault*

Lewin, Betsy. *Animal snackers*

Lewis, Naomi. *Hare and badger go to town*

Lewis, Stephen. *Zoo city*

Lilly, Kenneth. *Animal builders*
Animal climbers
Animal jumpers
Animal runners
Animal swimmers
Animals at the zoo
Animals in the country
Animals in the jungle
Animals on the farm
Lindberg, Reeve. *Midnight farm*
Lionni, Leo. *The biggest house in the world*
Frederick's fables
Lipkind, William. *The boy and the forest*
Lippman, Peter. *New at the zoo*
The little red hen. *The little red hen*, ill. by
Janina Domanska
The little red hen, ill. by Paul Galdone
The little red hen, ill. by Mel Pekarsky
The little red hen, ill. by William Stobbs
The little red hen, ill. by Margot Zemach
Livingston, Myra Cohn. *Valentine poems*
Lloyd, David. *Duck*
Hello, goodbye
Lobel, Anita. *King Rooster, Queen Hen*
Lobel, Arnold. *Fables*
A holiday for Mister Muster
A zoo for Mister Muster
Löfgren, Ulf. *One-two-three*
Lorenz, Lee. *Hugo and the spacedog*
Lorian, Nicole. *A birthday present for Mama*
Low, Joseph. *Adam's book of odd creatures*
Lüton, Mildred. *Little chicks' mothers and
all the others*
Luttrell, Ida. *Mattie and the chicken thief*
Lyfick, Warren. *Animal tales*
Lynn, Sara. *Big animals*
Farm animals
Garden animals
1 2 3
Small animals
Lyon, George Ella. *A regular rolling Noah*
McCauley, Jane. *The way animals sleep*
McClung, Robert. *How animals hide*
McConnachie, Brian. *Lily of the forest*
McCrea, Lilian. *Mother hen*
MacDonald, Elizabeth. *My aunt and the
animals*
McKissack, Patricia C. *The little red hen*, ill.
by Dennis Hockerman
McLeod, Emilie Warren. *One snail and me*
McNaught, Harry. *Baby animals*
McNeer, May Yonge. *Little Baptiste*
McPhail, David. *Andrew's bath*
Animals A to Z
Farm morning
Lorenzo
Where can an elephant hide?
Maestro, Giulio. *Leopard is sick*
One more and one less
Mahy, Margaret. *17 kings and 42 elephants*

Mann, Peggy. *King Laurence, the alarm
clock*
Mari, Iela. *Eat and be eaten*
Mariana. *Miss Flora McFlimsey's May Day*
Maris, Ron. *I wish I could fly*
In my garden
Marshall, Edward. *Fox all week*
Marshall, James. *Four little troubles*
Willis
Massie, Diane Redfield. *The baby beebee
bird*
Mayer, Marianna. *Beauty and the beast*
The little jewel box
Mayer, Mercer. *Appelard and Liverwurst*
What do you do with a kangaroo?
Mayne, William. *Come, come to my corner*
Meeks, Esther K. *Friendly farm animals*
Something new at the zoo
Mendoza, George. *Need a house? Call Ms.
Mouse*
Merriam, Eve. *The birthday cow*
Miklowitz, Gloria D. *The zoo that moved*
Miles, Miska. *Noisy gander*
Sylvester Jones and the voice in the forest
Miller, Edna. *Mousekin's Thanksgiving*
Miller, J. P. (John Parr). *Farmer John's
animals*
Miller, Jane. *Seasons on the farm*
Miller, Susanne Santoro. *Prehistoric
mammals*
*Whales and sharks and other creatures of
the deep*
Millhouse, Nicholas. *Blue-footed booby*
Mitchell, Adrian. *Our mammoth*
Mizumura, Kazue. *If I were a cricket...*
Moncure, Jane Belk. *Riddle me a riddle*
Monsell, Mary. *Underwear!*
Moore, Elaine. *Grandma's house*
Moore, John. *Granny Stickleback*
Mora, Emma. *Animals of the forest*
Morgan, Michaela. *Edward gets a pet*
Morrison, Sean. *Is that a happy
hippopotamus?*
Morse, Samuel French. *All in a suitcase*
Moser, Erwin. *The crow in the snow and
other bedtime stories*
Mullins, Edward S. *Animal limericks*
Munari, Bruno. *Animals for sale*
Bruno Munari's zoo
The elephant's wish
Who's there? Open the door
Murdocca, Sal. *Tuttle's shell*
Musicant, Elke. *The night vegetable eater*
My first book of baby animals
Nakano, Hirotaka. *Elephant blue*
Nakatani, Chiyoko. *The zoo in my garden*
Nash, Ogden. *Custard the dragon*
Nerlove, Miriam. *I made a mistake*
Newsham, Ian. *Lost in the jungle*
Newton, Patricia Montgomery. *The frog
who drank the waters of the world*

Nichol, B. P. *Once*
Noll, Sally. *Jiggle wiggle prance*
Norman, Charles. *The hornbean tree and other poems*
Nussbaum, Hedda. *Animals build amazing homes*
Obligado, Lilian. *Faint frogs feeling feverish and other terrifically tantalizing tongue twisters*
Old MacDonald had a farm. *Old MacDonald had a farm*, ill. by Mel Crawford
Old MacDonald had a farm, ill. by David Frankland
Old MacDonald had a farm, ill. by Abner Graboff
Old MacDonald had a farm, ill. by Tracey Campbell Pearson
Old MacDonald had a farm, ill. by Robert M. Quackenbush
Old MacDonald had a farm, ill. by William Stobbs
Oppenheim, Joanne. *You can't catch me!*
Over in the meadow, ill. by Paul Galdone
Over in the meadow, ill. by Ezra Jack Keats
Oxenbury, Helen. *Friends*
Monkey see, monkey do
729 curious creatures
729 merry mix-ups
Oxford Scientific Films. *Jellyfish and other sea creatures*
Pack, Robert. *Then what did you do?*
Palazzo, Tony. *Animal babies*
Animals 'round the mulberry bush
Palmer, Helen Marion. *I was kissed by a seal at the zoo*
Why I built the boogle house
Palmer, Mary Babcock. *No-sort-of-animal*
Park, W. B. *The costume party*
Parnall, Peter. *Alfalfa Hill*
Winter barn
Partridge, Jenny. *Colonel Grunt*
Grandma Snuffles
Hopfellow
Mr. Squint
Peterkin Pollensnuff
Paterson, Diane. *If I were a toad*
Paul, Jan S. *Hortense*
Payne, Joan Balfour. *The stable that stayed*
Peaceable kingdom
Peek, Merle. *The balancing act*
Mary wore her red dress and Henry wore his green sneakers
Peet, Bill. *The ant and the elephant*
Farewell to Shady Glade
The gnats of knotty pine
No such things
Pelham, David. *Worms wiggle*
Peppé, Rodney. *Little circus*
Peters, Sharon. *Animals at night*
Petersham, Maud. *The box with red wheels*

Peterson, Esther Allen. *Frederick's alligator*
Pevear, Richard. *Mister cat-and-a-half*
Peyo. *The Smurfs and their woodland friends*
Piatti, Celestino. *Celestino Piatti's animal ABC*
Pieńkowski, Jan. *Farm*
Homes
Zoo
Piers, Helen. *A Helen Piers animal book*
Pitcher, Caroline. *Animals*
Pittman, Helena Clare. *Once when I was scared*
Plante, Patricia. *The turtle and the two ducks*
Polushkin, Maria. *Who said meow?* ill. by Giulio Maestro
Potter, Beatrix. *Appley Dapply's nursery rhymes*
Beatrix Potter's nursery rhyme book
Cecily Parsley's nursery rhymes
Ginger and Pickles
More tales from Beatrix Potter
Peter Rabbit's ABC
The tale of Jemima Puddle-Duck and other farmyard tales
The tale of Peter Rabbit and other stories
A treasury of Peter Rabbit and other stories
Yours affectionately, Peter Rabbit
Pouyanne, Rési. *What I see hidden by the pond*
Powzyk, Joyce. *Tasmania*
Prelutsky, Jack. *The pack rat's day and other poems*
Price, Mathew. *Do you see what I see?*
Price-Thomas, Brian. *The magic ark*
Provensen, Alice. *Our animal friends*
The year at Maple Hill Farm
The pudgy book of farm animals
Purcell, John Wallace. *African animals*
Quackenbush, Robert M. *Calling Doctor Quack*
Detective Mole
Detective Mole and the haunted castle mystery
Detective Mole and the secret clues
Detective Mole and the Tip-Top mystery
Pete Pack Rat
Raskin, Ellen. *And it rained*
Who, said Sue, said whoo?
Rey, Hans Augusto. *Tit for tat*
Where's my baby?
Rey, Margaret Elisabeth Waldstein. *Billy's picture*
Rice, Eve. *Sam who never forgets*
Richter, Mischa. *Quack?*
Riddell, Chris. *Bird's new shoes*
Robinson, Irene Bowen. *Picture book of animal babies*
Robinson, W. W. (William Wilcox). *On the farm*

Rockwell, Anne F. *Big bad goat*
The good llama
Honk honk!
Poor Goose
Roe, Richard. *Animal ABC*
Roffey, Maureen. *I spy at the zoo*
Rojankovsky, Feodor. *Animals in the zoo*
Animals on the farm
The great big animal book
The great big wild animal book
Root, Phyllis. *Moon tiger*
Roscoe, William. *The butterfly's ball*
Rose, Anne. *Spider in the sky*
Rose, Gerald. *Trouble in the ark*
Roughsey, Dick. *The giant devil-dingo*
Rounds, Glen. *Washday on Noah's ark*
Rowan, James P. *I can be a zoo keeper*
Rusling, Albert. *The mouse and Mrs. Proudfoot*
Russell, Solveig Paulson. *What good is a tail?*
Ryder, Joanne. *Fog in the meadow*
The night flight
Rylant, Cynthia. *Night in the country*
Saleh, Harold J. *Even tiny ants must sleep*
San Diego Zoological Society. *Families*
A visit to the zoo
Sandberg, Inger. *Nicholas' favorite pet*
Scarry, Richard. *Is this the house of Mistress Mouse?*
Richard Scarry's animal nursery tales
Richard Scarry's great big mystery book
Richard Scarry's mix or match storybook
Richard Scarry's Postman Pig and his busy neighbors
Schatz, Letta. *The extraordinary tug-of-war*
Schick, Eleanor. *A surprise in the forest*
Schmid, Eleonore. *Farm animals*
Schongut, Emanuel. *Look kitten*
Schumacher, Claire. *King of the zoo*
Nutty's birthday
Tim and Jim
Schweitzer, Iris. *Hilda's restful chair*
Seignobosc, Françoise. *The big rain*
The story of Colette
Selberg, Ingrid. *Nature's hidden world*
Selkowe, Valrie M. *Spring green*
Selsam, Millicent E. *All kinds of babies*
Benny's animals and how he put them in order
A first look at kangaroos, koalas and other animals with pouches
A first look at seashells
Hidden animals
Keep looking!
Night animals
Strange creatures that really lived
When an animal grows
Sendak, Maurice. *Very far away*
Seuss, Dr. *Mr. Brown can moo! Can you?*
Would you rather be a bullfrog?

Sewall, Marcia. *Animal song*
Seymour, Peter. *Animals in disguise*
Sharmat, Marjorie Weinman. *Bartholomew the bossy*
Taking care of Melvin
Walter the wolf
Shecter, Ben. *Stone house stories*
Short, Mayo. *Andy and the wild ducks*
Simon, Mina Lewiton. *If you were an eel, how would you feel?*
Simon, Seymour. *Animal fact - animal fable*
Singer, Isaac Bashevis. *Why Noah chose the dove*
Skaar, Grace Marion. *What do the animals say?*
Skorpen, Liesel Moak. *All the Lassies*
Slate, Joseph. *Who is coming to our house?*
Slobodkin, Louis. *Friendly animals*
Melvin, the moose child
Our friendly friends
Slobodkina, Esphyr. *The wonderful feast*
Small, David. *Imogene's antlers*
Smith, Donald. *Who's wearing my baseball cap?*
Who's wearing my bow tie?
Who's wearing my sneakers?
Who's wearing my sunglasses?
Smith, Jim. *The frog band and the onion seller*
The frog band and the owlnapper
Nimbus the explorer
Smith, Roger. *How the animals saved the ark and put two and two together*
Snyder, Dick. *One day at the zoo*
Talk to me tiger
Solotareff, Grégoire. *Never trust an ogre*
Spier, Peter. *Gobble, growl, grunt*
The pet store
Spilka, Arnold. *Little birds don't cry*
Stadler, John. *Animal cafe*
Gorman and the treasure chest
Stehr, Frédéric. *Quack-quack*
Steig, William. *Sylvester and the magic pebble*
Steinmetz, Leon. *Clocks in the woods*
Stevens, Carla. *Hooray for pig!*
Pig and the blue flag
Stories from a snowy meadow
Stevens, Harry. *Fat mouse*
Parrot told snake
Stevens, Janet. *Animal fair*
Stevenson, James. *Clams can't sing*
Happy Valentine's Day, Emma!
No need for Monty
We can't sleep
Stevenson, Suçie. *I forgot*
Stobbs, William. *Animal pictures*
Stoddard, Sandol. *Bedtime mouse*
Stone, Lynn M. *Endangered animals*
Stratemeyer, Clara Georgeanna. *Pepper*
Struppi

·ks

r's baby
ctor Aardvark and the

Aardvark's picnic
'er Aardvark's alphabet

Schaller, Libor. *Arthur sets sail*

Animals – anteaters

Brown, Marc. *D. W. all wet*
Hall, Malcolm. *The friends of Charlie Ant Bear*
Waber, Bernard. *An anteater named Arthur*

Animals – apes *see* Animals – gorillas; Animals – monkeys

Animals – armadillos

Kipling, Rudyard. *The beginning of the armadillos*, ill. by Lorinda Bryan Cauley
The beginning of the armadillos, ill. by Charles Keeping
Lewis, Robin Baird. *Aunt Armadillo*
Saunders, Susan. *Charles Rat's picnic*
Simon, Sidney B. *The armadillo who had no shell*
Singer, Marilyn. *Archer Armadillo's secret room*

Animals – badgers

Baker, Betty. *Partners*
Hoban, Russell. *A baby sister for Frances*
A bargain for Frances
Bedtime for Frances
Best friends for Frances
A birthday for Frances
Bread and jam for Frances
Neal, Ernest. *Badgers*
Potter, Beatrix. *The tale of Mr. Tod*
Tompert, Ann. *Badger on his own*
Varley, Susan. *Badger's parting gifts*
Wells, Rosemary. *Hazel's amazing mother*

Animals – bats

Carlson, Natalie Savage. *Spooky and the wizard's bats*
Freeman, Don. *Hattie the backstage bat*
Hoban, Russell. *Lavina bat*
Jarrell, Randall. *A bat is born*
Ungerer, Tomi. *Rufus*

Animals – bears

Alexander, Martha G. *And my mean old mother will be sorry, Blackboard Bear*
Blackboard Bear
I sure am glad to see you, Blackboard Bear
We're in big trouble, Blackboard Bear

Allen, Pamela. *Bertie and the bear*
Amoit, Pierre. *Bijou the little bear*
Anglund, Joan Walsh. *Cowboy and his friend*
The cowboy's Christmas
Asch, Frank. *Bear shadow*
Bear's bargain
Bread and honey
Goodbye house
Happy birthday, moon!
Just like daddy
Moon bear
Mooncake
Moongame
Popcorn
Sand cake
Skyfire
Austin, Margot. *Growl Bear*
Bach, Alice. *Millicent the magnificent*
The smartest bear and his brother Oliver
Warren Weasel's worse than measles
Baker, Jill. *Basil of Bywater Hollow*
Barrett, John M. *The bear who slept through Christmas*
The Easter bear
Barto, Emily N. *Chubby bear*
Bartoli, Jennifer. *Snow on bear's nose*
Bassett, Lisa. *Beany and Scamp*
A clock for Beany
Benchley, Nathaniel. *Red Fox and his canoe*
Benton, Robert. *Don't ever wish for a 7-foot bear*
Berenstain, Stan. *After the dinosaurs*
The bear detectives
The bears' almanac
Bears in the night
Bears on wheels
The Berenstain bears and the bad dream
The Berenstain bears and the double dare
The Berenstain bears and the ghost of the forest
The Berenstain bears and the messy room
The Berenstain bears and the missing dinosaur bone
The Berenstain bears and the sitter
The Berenstain bears and the spooky old tree
The Berenstain bears and the truth
The Berenstain bears and too much TV
The Berenstain bears' Christmas tree
The Berenstain bears' counting book
The Berenstain bears forget their manners
The Berenstain bears get in a fight
The Berenstain bears get the gimmies
The Berenstain bears go to camp
The Berenstain bears go to school
The Berenstain bears go to the doctor
The Berenstain bears in the dark
The Berenstain bears learn about strangers
The Berenstain bears meet Santa Bear
The Berenstain bears' moving day

The Berenstain bears on the moon
The Berenstain bears ready, set, go!
The Berenstain bears' science fair
The Berenstain bears' trouble with money
The Berenstain bears visit the dentist
The Berenstains' B book
He bear, she bear
Inside outside upside down
Old hat, new hat
Bishop, Claire Huchet. *Twenty-two bears*
Blathwayt, Benedict. *Bear's adventure*
Blocksma, Mary. *The best dressed bear*
Boegehold, Betty. *Bear underground*
Bond, Michael. *Paddington and the knickerbocker rainbow*
Paddington at the circus
Paddington at the fair
Paddington at the palace
Paddington at the seaside
Paddington at the tower
Paddington at the zoo
Paddington cleans up
Paddington's art exhibit
Paddington's garden
Paddington's lucky day
Boon, Emilie. *Belinda's balloon*
Bowden, Joan Chase. *The bear's surprise party*
Bridgman, Elizabeth. *Nanny bear's cruise*
Bright, Robert. *Me and the bears*
Brimner, Larry Dane. *Country Bear's good neighbor*
Brinckloe, Julie. *Gordon's house*
Browne, Anthony. *Bear hunt*
Bucknall, Caroline. *One bear all alone*
One bear in the picture
Bunting, Eve. *The Valentine bears*
Carleton, Barbee Oliver. *Benny and the bear*
Carlstrom, Nancy White. *Better not get wet, Jesse Bear*
Jesse Bear, what will you wear?
Cartlidge, Michelle. *The bear's bazaar*
Teddy trucks
Chevalier, Christa. *The little bear who forgot*
Christian, Mary Blount. *Penrod again*
Penrod's pants
Crespi, Francesca. *Little Bear and the oompah-pah*
Dabcovich, Lydia. *Sleepy bear*
Day, Alexandra. *Frank and Ernest*
Degen, Bruce. *Jamberry*
Delton, Judy. *Bear and Duck on the run*
Brimhall comes to stay
Brimhall turns detective
Brimhall turns to magic
The elephant in Duck's garden
A pet for Duck and Bear
Dennis, Morgan. *Burlap*
Dodd, Lynley. *Wake up, bear*
Dorian, Marguerite. *When the snow is blue*

Dunbar, Joyce. *A cake for Barney*
Duvoisin, Roger Antoine. *Snowy and Woody*
Eberle, Irmengarde. *Bears live here*
Edwards, Roberta. *Anna Bear's first winter*
Fatio, Louise. *The happy lion and the bear*
Flack, Marjorie. *Ask Mr. Bear*
Fleishman, Seymour. *Too hot in Potzburg*
Flory, Jane. *The bear on the doorstep*
Foreman, Michael. *Moose*
Freeman, Don. *Bearymore*
Gage, Wilson. *Cully Cully and the bear*
Galdone, Joanna. *The little girl and the big bear*
Gantschev, Ivan. *Otto the bear*
RumpRump
Gantz, David. *The genie bear with the light brown hair word book*
George, Jean Craighead. *The grizzly bear with the golden ears*
Ginsburg, Mirra. *Two greedy bears*
Gordon, Margaret. *Wilberforce goes on a picnic*
Wilberforce goes to a party
Gordon, Sharon. *Christmas surprise*
Graham, Thomas. *Mr. Bear's boat*
Mr. Bear's chair
Greaves, Margaret. *Little Bear and the Papagini circus*
Grimm, Jacob. *The bear and the kingbird*
Snow White and Rose Red, ill. by Adrienne Adams
Snow-White and Rose-Red, ill. by Barbara Cooney
Snow White and Rose Red, ill. by John Wallner
Snow White and Rose Red, ill. by Bernadette Watts
Guilfoile, Elizabeth. *Nobody listens to Andrew*
Hamsa, Bobbie. *Your pet bear*
Hansen, Carla. *Barnaby Bear builds a boat*
Barnaby Bear visits the farm
Hawkins, Colin. *Dip, dip, dip*
I'm not sleepy!
One finger, one thumb
Oops-a-Daisy
Where's bear?
Hayes, Geoffrey. *Patrick and his grandpa*
Patrick and Ted
The secret inside
Hellsing, Lennart. *The wonderful pumpkin*
Hill, Eric. *At home*
Baby Bear's bedtime
Good morning, baby bear
My pets
Up there
Hillert, Margaret. *The three bears*
Hoff, Syd. *Grizzwold*

Holl, Adelaide. *Small Bear builds a playhouse*
Small Bear solves a mystery
Isenberg, Barbara. *The adventures of Albert, the running bear*
Albert the running bear gets the jitters
Albert the running bear's exercise book
Jackson, Ellen B. *The bear in the bathtub*
Janice. *Little Bear marches in the St. Patrick's Day parade*
Little Bear's Christmas
Little Bear's New Year's party
Little Bear's pancake party
Little Bear's Sunday breakfast
Little Bear's Thanksgiving
Jennings, Michael. *The bears who came to breakfix*
Jeschke, Susan. *Angela and Bear*
The devil did it
Jonas, Ann. *Two bear cubs*
Killingback, Julia. *Busy Bears at the fire station*
Busy Bears' picnic
Monday is washing day
What time is it, Mrs. Bear?
Kraus, Robert. *Milton the early riser*
Krauss, Ruth. *Bears*
Kuchalla, Susan. *Bears*
Kuratomi, Chizuko. *Mr. Bear and the robbers*
Lapp, Eleanor. *The blueberry bears*
Lemieux, Michèle. *What's that noise?*
Le Tord, Bijou. *Good wood bear*
Lipkind, William. *Nubber bear*
Lisowski, Gabriel. *Roncalli's magnificent circus*
Lucas, Barbara. *Sleeping over*
McCarthy, Ruth. *Katie and the smallest bear*
McCloskey, Robert. *Blueberries for Sal*
MacGregor, Marilyn. *Helen the hungry bear*
Mack, Stanley. *Ten bears in my bed*
McPhail, David. *The bear's toothache*
Emma's pet
Emma's vacation
Henry Bear's park
Stanley Henry Bear's friend
Margolis, Richard J. *Big bear, spare that tree*
Marino, Dorothy. *Buzzy Bear and the rainbow*
Buzzy Bear goes camping
Buzzy Bear in the garden
Buzzy Bear's busy day
Maris, Ron. *Hold tight, bear!*
Marshall, James. *What's the matter with Carruthers?*
Martin, Bill (William Ivan). *Brown bear, brown bear, what do you see?*
Mayer, Mercer. *Two moral tales*

Minarik, Else Holmelund. *Father Bear comes home*
A kiss for Little Bear
Little Bear
Little Bear's friend
Little Bear's visit
Monsell, Helen Albee. *Paddy's Christmas*
Muntean, Michaela. *Bicycle bear*
The house that bear built
Murphy, Jill. *Peace at last*
What next, baby bear!
Myers, Bernice. *Herman and the bears and the giants*
Naylor, Phyllis Reynolds. *Old Sadie and the Christmas bear*
Obrist, Jürg. *Bear business*
O'Connor, Jane. *The Care Bears' party cookbook*
Parker, Nancy Winslow. *The ordeal of Byron B. Blackbear*
Peek, Merle. *Mary wore her red dress and Henry wore his green sneakers*
Peet, Bill. *Big bad Bruce*
Phillips, Joan. *Peek-a-boo! I see you!*
Pinkwater, Daniel Manus. *The bear's picture*
Pluckrose, Henry. *Bears*
Polushkin, Maria. *Bubba and Babba*
Pomerantz, Charlotte. *Where's the bear?*
Raphael, Elaine. *Turnabout*
Ressner, Phil. *August explains*
Riddell, Chris. *Ben and the bear*
Rockwell, Anne F. *A bear, a bobcat and three ghosts*
Bear Child's book of hours
Boats
Come to town
First comes spring
In our house
Ruck-Pauquèt, Gina. *Mumble bear*
Shannon, George. *Lizard's song*
Sharmat, Marjorie Weinman. *I'm terrific*
Lucretia the unbearable
Siewert, Margaret. *Bear hunt*
Sivulich, Sandra Stroner. *I'm going on a bear hunt*
Skorpen, Liesel Moak. *Outside my window*
Stapler, Sarah. *Trilby's trumpet*
Steiner, Jörg. *The bear who wanted to be a bear*
Steptoe, John. *Jeffrey Bear cleans up his act*
Stevenson, James. *The bear who had no place to go*
Stoddard, Sandol. *Bedtime for bear*
Stubbs, Joanna. *Happy Bear's day*
Taylor, Mark. *Henry the explorer*
Tejima, Keizaburo. *The bears' autumn*
The three bears. *Goldilocks and the three bears*, ill. by Jan Brett
Goldilocks and the three bears, ill. by Lorinda Bryan Cauley

Goldilocks and the three bears, ill. by Jane Dyer

Goldilocks and the three bears, ill. by Lynn Bywaters Ferris

Goldilocks and the three bears, ill. by James Marshall

Goldilocks and the three bears, ill. by Janet Stevens

Goldilocks and the three bears, ill. by Bernadette Watts

The story of the three bears, ill. by L. Leslie Brooke

The story of the three bears, ill. by William Stobbs

The three bears, ill. Paul Galdone

The three bears, ill. by Feodor Rojankovsky

The three bears, ill. by Robin Spowart

Turkle, Brinton. *Deep in the forest*

Upham, Elizabeth. *Little brown bear loses his clothes*

Van Woerkom, Dorothy. *Becky and the bear*

Venable, Alan. *The checker players*

Vincent, Gabrielle. *Bravo, Ernest and Celestine!*
Breakfast time, Ernest and Celestine
Ernest and Celestine
Ernest and Celestine's patchwork quilt
Ernest and Celestine's picnic
Merry Christmas, Ernest and Celestine
Smile, Ernest and Celestine
Where are you, Ernest and Celestine?

Wahl, Jan. *Sylvester Bear overslept*

Ward, Andrew. *Baby bear and the long sleep*

Ward, Lynd. *The biggest bear*

Warren, Cathy. *Springtime bears*

Watanabe, Shigeo. *Daddy, play with me!*
How do I put it on?
I can build a house!
I can ride it!
I can take a bath!
I can take a walk!
I'm the king of the castle!
It's my birthday
What a good lunch!
Where's my daddy?

Weinberg, Lawrence. *The Forgetful Bears*
The Forgetful Bears meet Mr. Memory

Wild, Robin. *The bears' ABC book*
The bears' counting book

Wildsmith, Brian. *Bear's adventure*
The lazy bear

Williams, Leslie. *A bear in the air*

Winter, Paula. *The bear and the fly*

Winthrop, Elizabeth. *Bear and Mrs. Duck*

Wiseman, Bernard. *Morris and Boris at the circus*
Morris has a birthday party!

Yektai, Niki. *Bears in pairs*

Yeoman, John. *The bear's water picnic*

Ylla. *Two little bears*

Yolen, Jane. *The three bears rhyme book*

Yulya. *Bears are sleeping*

Zalben, Jane Breskin. *Beni's first Chanukah*

Ziefert, Harriet. *Bear all year*
Bear gets dressed
Bear goes shopping
Bear's busy morning

Zimnik, Reiner. *The bear on the motorcycle*

Zirbes, Laura. *How many bears?*

Animals – beavers

Barr, Cathrine. *Little Ben*

Bowen, Vernon. *The lazy beaver*

Crowley, Arthur. *Bonzo Beaver*

Dabcovich, Lydia. *Busy beavers*

Gallo, Giovanni. *The lazy beaver*

George, William T. *Beaver at Long Pond*

Hamsa, Bobbie. *Your pet beaver*

Hoban, Russell. *Charlie the tramp*

Kalas, Sybille. *The beaver family book*

Sheehan, Angela. *The beaver*

Tresselt, Alvin R. *The beaver pond*

Animals – bobcats

Rockwell, Anne F. *A bear, a bobcat and three ghosts*

Animals – buffaloes

Baker, Olaf. *Where the buffaloes begin*

Goble, Paul. *Her seven brothers*

McCarthy, Bobette. *Buffalo girls*

Animals – bulls, cows

Asch, Frank. *Oats and wild apples*

Barker, Melvern J. *Country fair*

Bellville, Cheryl Walsh. *Round-up*

Bulla, Clyde Robert. *Dandelion Hill*

Carlson, Natalie Savage. *Time for the white egret*

Carrick, Donald. *The deer in the pasture*
Milk

Coats, Belle. *Little maverick cow*

Cole, Joanna. *A calf is born*

Cushman, Jerome. *Marvella's hobby*

Dennis, Wesley. *Flip and the cows*

Drescher, Henrik. *Looking for Santa Claus*

Du Bois, William Pène. *Elisabeth the cow ghost*

Ets, Marie Hall. *The cow's party*

Forrester, Victoria. *The magnificent moo*

Glass, Andrew. *Chickpea and the talking cow*

Hader, Berta Hoerner. *The story of Pancho and the bull with the crooked tail*

Hancock, Sibyl. *Old Blue*

Herriot, James. *Blossom comes home*

Koch, Dorothy Clarke. *When the cows got out*
Krasilovsky, Phyllis. *The cow who fell in the canal*
Leaf, Munro. *The story of Ferdinand the bull*
Lent, Blair. *Pistachio*
Martin, Bill (William Ivan). *White Dynamite and Curly Kidd*
Meeks, Esther K. *The curious cow*
Merrill, Jean. *Tell about the cowbarn, Daddy*
Moers, Hermann. *Camomile heads for home*
Pellowski, Michael. *Clara joins the circus*
Scruton, Clive. *Circus cow*
Sewall, Marcia. *The wee, wee mannie and the big, big coo*
Thomas, Patricia. *"There are rocks in my socks!" said the ox to the fox*
Wildsmith, Brian. *Daisy*
Wiseman, Bernard. *Oscar is a mama*
Wright, Dare. *Look at a calf*

Animals – camels

Goodenow, Earle. *The last camel*
Hamsa, Bobbie. *Your pet camel*
Kipling, Rudyard. *How the camel got his hump*, ill. by Quentin Blake
McKee, David. *The day the tide went out and out and out*
Parker, Nancy Winslow. *The Christmas camel*
Peet, Bill. *Pamela Camel*
Tworkov, Jack. *The camel who took a walk*
Wells, Rosemary. *Abdul*

Animals – cats

Adam, Barbara. *The big big box*
Allen, Jonathan. *My cat*
Althea. *Jeremy Mouse and cat*
Ambrus, Victor G. *Grandma, Felix, and Mustapha Biscuit*
Anderson, Douglas. *Let's draw a story*
Arbeit, Eleanor Werner. *Mrs. cat hides something*
Asare, Meshack. *Cat... in search of a friend*
Aulaire, Ingri Mortenson d'. *Foxie, the singing dog*
Averill, Esther. *The fire cat*
Jenny and the cat club
Jenny's adopted brothers
Jenny's birthday book
Jenny's first party
Jenny's moonlight adventure
When Jenny lost her scarf
Baba, Noboru. *Eleven cats and a pig*
Eleven cats and albatrosses
Eleven cats in a bag
Eleven hungry cats
Baker, Barbara. *Digby and Kate*
Baker, Leslie A. *The third-story cat*

Balian, Lorna. *Amelia's nine lives*
Leprechauns never lie
Barbaresi, Nina. *Firemouse*
Bare, Colleen Stanley. *To love a cat*
Barrows, Marjorie Wescott. *Fraidy cat*
Bascom, Joe. *Malcolm Softpaws*
Malcolm's job
Bayley, Nicola. *Crab cat*
Elephant cat
Parrot cat
Polar bear cat
Spider cat
Beecroft, John. *What? Another cat!*
Berg, Jean Horton. *The O'Learys and friends*
The wee little man
Bernhard, Josephine Butkowska. *Lullaby*
Berson, Harold. *Raminagrobis and the mice*
Bible. Old Testament. Jonah. *Jonah*, ill. by Kurt Mitchell
Bingham, Mindy. *Minou*
Black, Floyd. *Alphabet cat*
Blegvad, Lenore. *Mr. Jensen and cat*
Mittens for kittens and other rhymes about cats
Boegehold, Betty. *In the castle of cats*
Pawpaw's run
Three to get ready
Bohdal, Susi. *Tom cat*
Bonsall, Crosby Newell. *The amazing the incredible super dog*
The case of the cat's meow
Listen, listen!
Boynton, Sandra. *Chloë and Maude*
Bradbury, Bianca. *The antique cat*
Muggins
One kitten too many
Brandenberg, Franz. *Aunt Nina and her nephews and nieces*
Aunt Nina's visit
No school today!
A picnic, hurrah!
A robber! A robber!
What's wrong with a van?
Brett, Jan. *Annie and the wild animals*
Brewster, Patience. *Ellsworth and the cats from Mars*
Bright, Robert. *Miss Pattie*
Brown, Marc. *The cloud over Clarence*
Brown, Marcia. *Felice*
Brown, Margaret Wise. *House of a hundred windows*
Night and day
Pussycat's Christmas
Sneakers
When the wind blew
Brown, Myra Berry. *Benjy's blanket*
Brown, Ruth. *Our cat Flossie*
Bruna, Dick. *Kitten Nell*
Bryan, Ashley. *The cat's purr*

Buck, Pearl S. (Pearl Sydenstricker). *The Chinese story teller*
Buckmaster, Henrietta. *Lucy and Loki*
Bulla, Clyde Robert. *Valentine cat*
Burch, Robert. *Joey's cat*
Byrd, Robert. *Marcella was bored*
Calhoun, Mary. *Audubon cat*
Cross-country cat
Hot-air Henry
The nine lives of Homer C. Cat
The witch of Hissing Hill
The witch who lost her shadow
Wobble the witch cat
Cameron, John. *If mice could fly*
Cameron, Polly. *The cat who thought he was a tiger*
Campbell, Rod. *Misty's mischief*
Carle, Eric. *Have you seen my cat?*
Carlson, Natalie Savage. *Spooky and the bad luck raven*
Spooky and the ghost cat
Spooky and the wizard's bats
Spooky night
Carroll, Ruth. *Old Mrs. Billups and the black cats*
Carter, Anne. *Bella's secret garden*
Cass, Joan E. *The cat thief*
The cats go to market
Cate, Rikki. *A cat's tale*
Chalmers, Audrey. *Fancy be good*
A kitten's tale
Chalmers, Mary. *Be good, Harry*
Boats finds a house
The cat who liked to pretend
Come to the doctor, Harry
George Appleton
Merry Christmas, Harry
Mr. Cat's wonderful surprise
Take a nap, Harry
Throw a kiss, Harry
Chapman, Jean. *Moon-Eyes*
Charles, Donald. *Calico Cat at school*
Calico Cat at the zoo
Calico Cat meets bookworm
Calico Cat's exercise book
Calico Cat's year
Time to rhyme with Calico Cat
Chenery, Janet. *Pickles and Jake*
Chittum, Ida. *The cat's pajamas*
Cleary, Beverly. *Two dog biscuits*, ill. by DyAnne DiSalvo-Ryan
Clymer, Eleanor Lowenton. *Horatio*
Horatio goes to the country
Coats, Laura Jane. *City cat*
Coatsworth, Elizabeth. *The giant golden book of cat stories*
Cohen, Caron Lee. *Whiffle Squeek*
Cohn, Norma. *Brother and sister*
Cole, Joanna. *A cat's body*
Collington, Peter. *My darling kitten*
Cook, Bernadine. *Looking for Susie*

Coombs, Patricia. *The magician and McTree*
Cooper, Jacqueline. *Angus and the Mona Lisa*
Costa, Nicoletta. *The birthday party*
Dressing up
A friend comes to play
The missing cat
Craft, Ruth. *Carrie Hepple's garden*
Crawford, Phyllis. *The blot*
Cretan, Gladys Yessayan. *Lobo and Brewster*
Damjan, Mischa. *The little prince and the tiger cat*
Dauer, Rosamond. *The 300 pound cat*
Daugherty, Charles Michael. *Wisher*
Davis, Douglas F. *There's an elephant in the garage*
Degen, Bruce. *Aunt Possum and the pumpkin man*
DeJong, David Cornel. *Looking for Alexander*
Dennis, Morgan. *Skit and Skat*
De Regniers, Beatrice Schenk. *Cats cats cats*
Everyone is good for something
Picture book theater
So many cats!
Dick Whittington and his cat. *Dick Whittington*, ill. by Edward Ardizzone
Dick Whittington, ill. by Antony Maitland
Dick Whittington and his cat, ill. by Marcia Brown
Dick Whittington and his cat, ill. by Kurt Werth
Dillon, Eilis. *The cats' opera*
Diska, Pat. *Andy says … Bonjour!*
Dodd, Lynley. *Hairy Maclary from Donaldson's dairy*
Hairy Maclary Scattercat
Doherty, Berlie. *Paddiwak and cozy*
Douglas, Michael. *Round, round world*
Duvoisin, Roger Antoine. *Veronica and the birthday present*
Eisler, Colin. *Cats know best*
Elzbieta. *Brave Babette and sly Tom*
Ernst, Lisa Campbell. *The rescue of Aunt Pansy*
Ets, Marie Hall. *Mr. T. W. Anthony Woo*
Evans, Eva Knox. *That lucky Mrs. Plucky*
The fat cat
Fatio, Louise. *Marc and Pixie and the walls in Mrs. Jones's garden*
Faunce-Brown, Daphne. *Snuffles' house*
Feder, Jane. *Beany*
Fischer-Nagel, Heiderose. *A kitten is born*
Fish, Hans. *Pitschi, the kitten who always wanted to do something else*
Flack, Marjorie. *Angus and the cat*
William and his kitten
Flory, Jane. *We'll have a friend for lunch*

Foreman, Michael. *Cat and canary*
Forrester, Victoria. *The magnificent moo*
Fowler, Richard. *Cat's story*
Frascino, Edward. *My cousin the king*
Nanny Noony and the magic spell
Fremlin, Robert. *Three friends*
Freschet, Berniece. *Furlie Cat*
Fujikawa, Gyo. *Shags finds a kitten*
Funakoshi, Canna. *One morning*
Gág, Flavia. *Chubby's first year*
Gág, Wanda. *Millions of cats*
Galdone, Paul. *King of the cats*
Gantos, Jack. *Rotten Ralph*
Rotten Ralph's rotten Christmas
Rotten Ralph's trick or treat
Worse than Rotten Ralph
Gay, Marie-Louise. *Moonbeam on a cat's ear*
Gay, Michel. *Rabbit express*
Gibbon, David. *Kittens*
Ginsburg, Mirra. *Kitten from one to ten*
Godden, Rumer. *A kindle of kittens*
Goodall, John S. *The surprise picnic*
Gordon, Margaret. *The supermarket mice*
Goyder, Alice. *Holiday in Catland*
Party in Catland
Grabianski, Janusz. *Cats*
Graham, Bob. *Libby, Oscar and me*
Griffith, Helen V. *Alex and the cat*
Alex remembers
More Alex and the cat
Grimm, Jacob. *Godfather Cat and Mousie*, ill. by Ann Schweninger
Hale, Kathleen. *Orlando and the water cats*
Orlando buys a farm
Orlando the frisky housewife
Haley, Gail E. *The post office cat*
Hasler, Eveline. *Winter magic*
Hausherr, Rosmarie. *My first kitten*
Hawkins, Colin. *Pat the cat*
Hawthorne, Julian. *Rumpty-Dudget's tower*
Hayes, Geoffrey. *Elroy and the witch's child*
Hazen, Barbara Shook. *The Fat Cats, Cousin Scraggs and the monster mice*
Tight times
Hearn, Michael Patrick. *The porcelain cat*
Heilbroner, Joan. *Tom the TV cat*
Henrie, Fiona. *Cats*
Herriot, James. *Christmas Day kitten*
Moses the kitten
Hess, Lilo. *A cat's nine lives*
Hiller, Catherine. *Abracatabby*
Hillert, Margaret. *The little runaway*
Hoban, Russell. *Flat cat*
Hoban, Tana. *One little kitten*
Hogrogian, Nonny. *The cat who loved to sing*
Holmes, Efner Tudor. *The Christmas cat*
Howell, Lynn. *Winifred's new bed*
Hulse, Gillian. *Morris, where are you?*

Hurd, Edith Thacher. *Come and have fun*
No funny business
The so-so cat
Hürlimann, Ruth. *The proud white cat*
Inkiow, Dimiter. *Me and Clara and Casimir the cat*
Ipcar, Dahlov. *The cat at night*
The cat came back
Jack Sprat. *The life of Jack Sprat, his wife and his cat*
Janice. *Minette*
Jenkin-Pearce, Susie. *Bad Boris and the new kitten*
Jeschke, Susan. *Lucky's choice*
Jewell, Nancy. *ABC cat*
Kahl, Virginia. *Whose cat is that?*
Kanao, Keiko. *Kitten up a tree*
Kay, Helen. *A stocking for a kitten*
Keats, Ezra Jack. *Hi, cat!*
Kitten for a day
Psst, doggie
Kellogg, Steven. *A rose for Pinkerton*
Tallyho, Pinkerton!
Kent, Lorna. *No, no, Charlie Rascal!*
Kerr, Judith. *Mog and bunny*
Mog's Christmas
Kherdian, David. *Country cat, city cat*
Kipling, Rudyard. *The cat that walked by himself*
Kitamura, Satoshi. *Captain Toby*
Knotts, Howard. *The summer cat*
The winter cat
Kočí, Marta. *Katie's kitten*
Koenig, Marion. *The tale of fancy Nancy*
The wonderful world of night
Komoda, Beverly. *Simon's soup*
Koontz, Robin Michal. *Pussycat ate the dumplings*
Krahn, Fernando. *Catch that cat!*
Krasilovsky, Phyllis. *Scaredy cat*
Kraus, Robert. *Come out and play, little mouse*
Kunhardt, Dorothy. *Kitty's new doll*
Kunhardt, Edith. *Pat the cat*
Kyte, Dennis. *Mattie and Cataragus*
Landshoff, Ursula. *Cats are good company*
Lansdown, Brenda. *Galumpf*
Larrick, Nancy. *Cats are cats*
Laskowski, Jerzy. *Master of the royal cats*
Lasson, Robert. *Orange Oliver*
Lawrence, John. *Rabbit and pork*
Lear, Edward. *The owl and the pussycat*, ill. by Lorinda Bryan Cauley
The owl and the pussy-cat, ill. by Barbara Cooney
The owl and the pussycat, ill. by Emma Crosby
The owl and the pussy-cat, ill. by William Pène Du Bois
The owl and the pussycat, ill. by Lori Farbanish

The owl and the pussy-cat, ill. by Gwen Fulton

The owl and the pussycat, ill. by Paul Galdone

The owl and the pussy-cat, ill. by Elaine Muis

The owl and the pussycat, ill. by Erica Rutherford

The owl and the pussycat, ill. by Janet Stevens

The owl and the pussycat, ill. by Colin West

The owl and the pussy-cat, ill. by Owen Wood

Le Guin, Ursula K. *Catwings*
A visit from Dr. Katz
Le-Tan, Pierre. *The afternoon cat*
Levitin, Sonia. *All the cats in the world*
Lewin, Betsy. *Cat count*
Lewis, Naomi. *The stepsister*
Lexau, Joan M. *Come here, cat*
Lindbloom, Steven. *Let's give kitty a bath!*
Lindgren, Barbro. *Sam's ball*
Lindman, Maj. *Flicka, Ricka, Dicka and the three kittens*
Lipkind, William. *Russet and the two reds*
The two reds
Livermore, Elaine. *Find the cat*
Three little kittens lost their mittens
Livingston, Myra Cohn. *Cat poems*
Lloyd, David. *Cat and dog*
Lobel, Arnold. *The rose in my garden*
Whiskers and rhymes
MacArthur-Onslow, Annette Rosemary. *Minnie*
McMillan, Bruce. *Kitten can...*
McPhail, David. *Great cat*
Mandry, Kathy. *The cat and the mouse and the mouse and the cat*
Mariana. *Miss Flora McFlimsey's Valentine*
Maris, Ron. *My book*
Marzollo, Jean. *Uproar on Hollercat Hill*
Maschler, Fay. *T. G. and Moonie go shopping*
T. G. and Moonie have a baby
T. G. and Moonie move out of town
Matthias, Catherine. *I love cats*
Mayer, Mercer. *The great cat chase*
Mayne, William. *The patchwork cat*
Tibber
Meddaugh, Susan. *Too short Fred*
Merriam, Eve. *The birthday door*
Minarik, Else Holmelund. *Cat and dog*
Modell, Frank. *Seen any cats?*
Moncure, Jane Belk. *The talking tabby cat*
Moore, Lilian. *See my lovely poison ivy, and other verses about witches, ghosts and things*
Mooser, Stephen. *The fat cat*
Moskin, Marietta D. *Lysbet and the fire kittens*

Mother Goose. *Cats by Mother Goose*, ill. by Carol Newsom
Kitten rhymes
The three little kittens, ill. by Lorinda Bryan Cauley
The three little kittens, ill. by Paul Galdone
The three little kittens, ill. by Dorothy Stott
The three little kittens, ill. by Shelley Thornton
The moving adventures of Old Dame Trot and her comical cat
Murphey, Sara. *The animal hat shop*
Newberry, Clare Turlay. *April's kittens*
The kittens' ABC
Marshmallow
Mittens
Pandora
Percy, Polly and Pete
Smudge
T-Bone, the baby-sitter
Widget
Nicoll, Helen. *Meg and Mog*
Meg at sea
Meg on the moon
Meg's eggs
Mog's box
Nordqvist, Sven. *The fox hunt*
Pancake pie
Northrup, Mili. *The watch cat*
Oakley, Graham. *The church cat abroad*
The church mice and the moon
The church mice at bay
The church mice spread their wings
The church mouse
The diary of a church mouse
Oana, Kay D. *Shasta and the shebang machine*
Obrist, Jürg. *Fluffy*
Otto, Margaret Glover. *The little brown horse*
Panek, Dennis. *Catastrophe Cat*
Catastrophe Cat at the zoo
Parish, Peggy. *The cat's burglar*
Scruffy
Parker, Nancy Winslow. *Puddums, the Cathcarts' orange cat*
Patterson, Francine. *Koko's kitten*
Pearson, Tracey Campbell. *The storekeeper*
Peet, Bill. *Jennifer and Josephine*
Peppé, Rodney. *Cat and mouse*
Perrault, Charles. *Puss in boots*, ill. by Marcia Brown
Puss in boots, ill. by Lorinda Bryan Cauley
Puss in boots, ill. by Jean Claverie
Puss in boots, ill. by Hans Fischer
Puss in boots, ill. by Paul Galdone
Puss in boots, ill. by Julia Noonan
Puss in boots, ill. by Tony Ross
Puss in boots, ill. by William Stobbs
Puss in boots, ill. by Barry Wilkinson

Pevear, Richard. *Mister cat-and-a-half*
Pfloog, Jan. *Kittens*
Pinkwater, Daniel Manus. *Roger's umbrella*
Pizer, Abigail. *Harry's night out*
  Nosey Gilbert
Politi, Leo. *Lito and the clown*
Polushkin, Maria. *Kitten in trouble*
  Who said meow? ill. by Ellen Weiss
Pomerantz, Charlotte. *The ballad of the
  long-tailed rat*
  Buffy and Albert
Potter, Beatrix. *The pie and the patty-pan*
  Rolly-polly pudding
  The sly old cat
  The story of Miss Moppet
  The tale of Tom Kitten
Poulin, Stephane. *Can you catch Josephine?*
  Have you seen Josephine?
Pryor, Ainslie. *The baby blue cat and the
  dirty dog brothers*
  The baby blue cat who said no
Puppies and kittens
Redies, Rainer. *The cats' party*
Ridlon, Marcia. *Kittens and more kittens*
Robinson, Thomas P. *Buttons*
Ross, George Maxim. *When Lucy went
  away*
Rubel, Nicole. *Me and my kitty*
  Sam and Violet are twins
  Sam and Violet go camping
Rylant, Cynthia. *Henry and Mudge in
  puddle trouble*
Samuels, Barbara. *Duncan and Dolores*
Schaffer, Marion. *I love my cat!*
Schatz, Letta. *Whiskers, my cat*
Schertle, Alice. *That Olive!*
Schilling, Betty. *Two kittens are born*
Scruton, Clive. *Scaredy cat*
Seguin-Fontes, Marthe. *The cat's surprise*
Seidler, Rosalie. *Grumpus and the Venetian
  cat*
Seignobosc, Françoise. *Minou*
Selsam, Millicent E. *A first look at cats*
  How kittens grow
Seuss, Dr. *The cat in the hat*
  The cat in the hat comes back!
Shaw, Richard. *The kitten in the pumpkin
  patch*
Siekkinen, Raija. *Mister King*
Simmonds, Posy. *Fred*
Simon, Norma. *Cats do, dogs don't*
  Oh, that cat!
  Where does my cat sleep?
Skaar, Grace Marion. *Nothing but (cats)
  and all about (dogs)*
  The very little dog
Slate, Joseph. *Lonely Lula cat*
Sloan, Carolyn. *Carter is a painter's cat*
Slobodkin, Louis. *Colette and the princess*

Slobodkina, Esphyr. *Billy, the condominium
  cat*
  Pinky and the petunias
Smart, Christopher. *For I will consider my
  cat Jeoffry*
Smyth, Gwenda. *A pet for Mrs. Arbuckle*
Spanner, Helmut. *I am a little cat*
Spier, Peter. *Little cats*
Standon, Anna. *Three little cats*
Stanley, Diane. *Captain Whiz-Bang*
  A country tale
Steig, William. *Solomon the rusty nail*
Stein, Sara Bonnett. *Cat*
Steiner, Charlotte. *Kiki and Muffy*
Stern, Peter. *Floyd, a cat's story*
Stevens, Cat. *Teaser and the firecat*
Stock, Catherine. *Sampson the Christmas cat*
Stoddard, Sandol. *My very own special
  particular private and personal cat*
Stone, Bernard. *The charge of the mouse
  brigade*
Stratemeyer, Clara Georgeanna. *Pepper*
Sumiko. *Kittymouse*
Sutton, Eve. *My cat likes to hide in boxes*
Taber, Anthony. *Cats' eyes*
Tapio, Pat Decker. *The lady who saw the
  good side of everything*
Taylor, Mark. *The case of the missing kittens*
Thayer, Jane. *The cat that joined the club*
Thompson, Harwood. *The witch's cat*
Titus, Eve. *Anatole and the cat*
Turkle, Brinton. *Do not open*
Uchida, Yoshiko. *The two foolish cats*
Udry, Janice May. *"Oh no, cat!"*
Ungerer, Tomi. *No kiss for mother*
Untermeyer, Louis. *The kitten who barked*
Vacheron, Edith. *Here is Henri!*
Van Horn, William. *Harry Hoyle's giant
  jumping bean*
Vesey, A. *Merry Christmas, Thomas!*
Viorst, Judith. *The tenth good thing about
  Barney*
Voake, Charlotte. *Tom's cat*
Waber, Bernard. *Mice on my mind*
  Rich cat, poor cat
Wagner, Jenny. *John Brown, Rose and the
  midnight cat*
Wahl, Jan. *Dracula's cat*
  Push Kitty
Ward, Cindy. *Cookie's week*
Watson, Pauline. *Curley Cat baby-sits*
Weihs, Erika. *Count the cats*
Welch, Martha McKeen. *Will that wake
  mother?*
Wezel, Peter. *The naughty bird*
Wheeler, Cindy. *Marmalade's Christmas
  present*
  Marmalade's nap
  Marmalade's picnic
  Marmalade's snowy day
  Marmalade's yellow leaf

Whitmore, Adam. *Max in America*
Max in Australia
Max in India
Max leaves home
Whitney, Alma Marshak. *Leave Herbert alone*
Wild, Robin. *Spot's dogs and the alley cats*
Wilson, Joyce Lancaster. *Tobi*
Withers, Carl. *The tale of a black cat*
Wolff, Ashley. *Only the cat saw*
Wright, Dare. *The doll and the kitten*
The lonely doll learns a lesson
Look at a kitten
Wright, Josephine Lord. *Cotton Cat and Martha Mouse*
Yashima, Mitsu. *Momo's kitten*
Yeoman, John. *Mouse trouble*
Ylla. *I'll show you cats*
Young, Ed. *Up a tree*
Ziefert, Harriet. *Nicky upstairs and down*
Nicky's Christmas surprise
Nicky's friends
No, no, Nicky!
Where's the cat?
Zimelman, Nathan. *Mean Murgatroyd and the ten cats*

Animals – cheetahs

Adamson, Joy. *Pippa the cheetah and her cubs*
Conklin, Gladys. *Cheetahs, the swift hunters*
Irvine, Georgeanne. *Sasha the cheetah*

Animals – chipmunks

Angelo, Valenti. *The acorn tree*
Conger, Marion. *The chipmunk that went to church*
Eberle, Irmengarde. *A chipmunk lives here*
Moore, Lilian. *Little Raccoon and no trouble at all*
Price, Dorothy E. *Speedy gets around*
Ryder, Joanne. *Chipmunk song*
Stevenson, James. *Wilfred the rat*
Williams, Barbara. *Chester Chipmunk's Thanksgiving*

Animals – cougars

Anderson, C. W. (Clarence Williams). *Blaze and the mountain lion*

Animals – coyotes

Baker, Betty. *And me, coyote!*
Partners
Baylor, Byrd. *Coyote cry*
Moon song
Bernstein, Margery. *Coyote goes hunting for fire*
Bierhorst, John. *Doctor Coyote*
Carrick, Carol. *Two coyotes*

Animals – deer

Aragon, Jane Chelsea. *Winter harvest*
Arnosky, Jim. *Deer at the brook*
Asch, Frank. *Oats and wild apples*
Bemelmans, Ludwig. *Parsley*
Boegehold, Betty. *Small Deer's magic tricks*
Buff, Mary. *Dash and Dart*
Forest folk
Carrick, Donald. *The deer in the pasture*
Harold and the great stag
Eberle, Irmengarde. *Fawn in the woods*
Frankel, Bernice. *Half-As-Big and the tiger*
Lindman, Maj. *Snipp, Snapp, Snurr and the reindeer*
Prusski, Jeffrey. *Bring back the deer*
Schlein, Miriam. *Deer in the snow*
Troughton, Joanna. *Mouse-Deer's market*

Animals, dislike of *see* Behavior – animals, dislike of

Animals – dogs

Adler, David A. *My dog and the birthday mystery*
My dog and the green sock mystery
My dog and the key mystery
My dog and the knock knock mystery
Agee, Jon. *Ellsworth*
Alexander, Martha G. *Bobo's dream*
Maggie's moon
The magic picture
Allen, Jeffrey. *The secret life of Mr. Weird*
Allen, Pamela. *Bertie and the bear*
Ambler, Christopher Gifford. *Ten little foxhounds.*
Anderson, Douglas. *Let's draw a story*
Annett, Cora. *The dog who thought he was a boy*
Ardizzone, Edward. *Tim's friend Towser*
Asch, Frank. *The last puppy*
Rebecka
Aulaire, Ingri Mortenson d'. *Foxie, the singing dog*
Austin, Margot. *Trumpet*
Willamet way
Aylesworth, Jim. *The bad dream*
Baker, Barbara. *Digby and Kate*
Baker, Charlotte. *Little brother*
Baker, Jeannie. *Home in the sky*
Baker, Margaret. *A puppy called Spinach*
Bannon, Laura. *Watchdog*
Bare, Colleen Stanley. *To love a dog*
Barr, Cathrine. *Hound dog's bone*
Barton, Byron. *Jack and Fred*
Where's Al?
Batherman, Muriel. *Some things you should know about my dog*
Battles, Edith. *The terrible terrier*
Baumann, Kurt. *Piro and the fire brigade*
Baylor, Byrd. *Coyote cry*

Baynes, Pauline. *How dog began*
Beim, Lorraine. *The little igloo*
Belting, Natalia Maree. *Verity Mullens and the Indian*
Bemelmans, Ludwig. *Madeline's rescue*
Benchley, Nathaniel. *Snip*
Benchley, Peter. *Jonathan visits the White House*
Berends, Polly Berrien. *Ladybug and dog and the night walk*
Berenstain, Stan. *The Berenstain bears on the moon*
Beresford, Elisabeth. *Snuffle to the rescue*
Bettina (Bettina Ehrlich). *Pantaloni*
Bingham, Mindy. *My way Sally*
Black, Irma Simonton. *Big puppy and little puppy*
Blackwood, Gladys Rourke. *Whistle for Cindy*
Blegvad, Lenore. *Hark! Hark! The dogs do bark, and other poems about dogs*
Bliss, Corinne Demas. *That dog Melly!*
Blocksma, Mary. *The pup went up*
Rub-a-dub-dub
Bolognese, Elaine. *The sleepy watchdog*
Bonsall, Crosby Newell. *The amazing the incredible super dog*
And I mean it, Stanley
Listen, listen!
Who's afraid of the dark?
Bontemps, Arna Wendell. *The fast sooner hound*
Bornstein, Ruth Lercher. *I'll draw a meadow*
Jim
Bottner, Barbara. *Horrible Hannah*
Bowden, Joan Chase. *Boo and the flying flews*
Boynton, Sandra. *Doggies*
Bradbury, Bianca. *Mutt*
Bradford, Ann. *The mystery of the blind writer*
The mystery of the missing dogs
Brenner, Barbara. *A dog I know*
Brett, Jan. *The first dog*
Bridgman, Elizabeth. *A new dog next door*
Bridwell, Norman. *Clifford goes to Hollywood*
Clifford's ABC
Clifford's good deeds
Clifford's Halloween
Bright, Robert. *Georgie and the little dog*
Bröger, Achim. *Francie's paper puppy*
Brown, Margaret Wise. *Big dog, little dog*
The country noisy book
Don't frighten the lion
The indoor noisy book
The quiet noisy book
The winter noisy book
Brown, Ruth. *Our puppy's vacation*

Bryan, Dorothy. *Friendly little Jonathan*
Just Tammie!
Buck, Pearl S. (Pearl Sydenstricker). *The Chinese story teller*
Buckley, Helen Elizabeth. *Josie's Buttercup*
Buckmaster, Henrietta. *Lucy and Loki*
Bunting, Eve. *Ghost's hour, spook's hour*
Jane Martin, dog detective
Burningham, John. *Cannonball Simp*
The dog
Calhoun, Mary. *Houn' dog*
Mrs. Dog's own house
Campbell, Rod. *Henry's busy day*
Carlson, Nancy. *Harriet and the garden*
Harriet and the roller coaster
Harriet and Walt
Harriet's Halloween candy
Harriet's recital
Poor Carl
Carrick, Carol. *The accident*
Ben and the porcupine
The foundling
Carrier, Lark. *Scout and Cody*
Carroll, Ruth. *What Whiskers did*
Carter, Debby L. *Clipper*
Cazet, Denys. *Frosted glass*
Saturday
Chalmers, Audrey. *Hector and Mr. Murfit*
Charles, Donald. *Shaggy dog's birthday*
Shaggy dog's Halloween
Shaggy dog's tall tale
Time to rhyme with Calico Cat
Chase, Catherine. *Pete, the wet pet*
Chenery, Janet. *Pickles and Jake*
Christian, Mary Blount. *No dogs allowed, Jonathan!*
Ciardi, John. *Scrappy the pup*
Cleary, Beverly. *Two dog biscuits*, ill. by DyAnne DiSalvo-Ryan
Cohen, Caron Lee. *Three yellow dogs*
Cohen, Miriam. *Jim's dog Muffins*
Cole, Joanna. *A dog's body*
My puppy is born
Cook, Marion B. *Waggles and the dog catcher*
Coontz, Otto. *The quiet house*
Costa, Nicoletta. *The naughty puppy*
The new puppy
Cretan, Gladys Yessayan. *Lobo and Brewster*
Cuyler, Margery. *Freckles and Willie*
Dale, Ruth Bluestone. *Benjamin — and Sylvester also*
Daly, Kathleen N. *The Giant little Golden Book of dogs*
Daly, Maureen. *Patrick visits the library*
Damjan, Mischa. *Atuk*
Delaney, Ned. *Bad dog!*
Delton, Judy. *I'll never love anything ever again*
Denison, Carol. *A part-time dog for Nick*

Dennis, Morgan. *Burlap*
  The pup himself
  The sea dog
  Skit and Skat
Dodd, Lynley. *Hairy Maclary from*
    Donaldson's dairy
  Hairy Maclary Scattercat
  Hairy Maclary's bone
Doughtie, Charles. *Gabriel Wrinkles, the*
    bloodhound who couldn't smell
Du Bois, William Pène. *Giant Otto*
  Otto and the magic potatoes
  Otto at sea
  Otto in Africa
  Otto in Texas
Dumas, Philippe. *Laura, Alice's new puppy*
  Laura and the bandits
  Laura loses her head
  Laura on the road
Dunn, Judy. *The little puppy*
Dunrea, Olivier. *Fergus and Bridey*
Dupré, Ramona Dorrel. *Too many dogs*
Duvoisin, Roger Antoine. *Day and night*
Eastman, P. D. (Philip D.) *Go, dog, go!*
Elkin, Benjamin. *The big jump and other*
    stories
Erickson, Phoebe. *Just follow me*
Ets, Marie Hall. *Mr. T. W. Anthony Woo*
Fechner, Amrei. *I am a little dog*
Fischer-Nagel, Heiderose. *A puppy is born*
Fisher, Aileen. *I like weather*
Flack, Marjorie. *Angus and the cat*
  Angus and the ducks
  Angus lost
Foster, Sally. *A pup grows up*
Freeman, Don. *Ski pup*
Frith, Michael K. *I'll teach my dog 100*
    words
Fujikawa, Gyo. *Millie's secret*
  Shags finds a kitten
Furchgott, Terry. *Phoebe and the hot water*
    bottles
Gackenbach, Dick. *A bag full of pups*
  Claude and Pepper
  Claude the dog
  The dog and the deep dark woods
  Dog for a day
  Pepper and all the legs
  What's Claude doing?
Gág, Wanda. *Nothing at all*
Gannett, Ruth S. *Katie and the sad noise*
Gerson, Corinne. *Good dog, bad dog*
Gikow, Louise. *Follow that Fraggle!*
Goldsmith, Howard. *Little lost dog*
Goodspeed, Peter. *Hugh and Fitzhugh*
Gordon, Sharon. *What a dog!*
Graham, Amanda. *Who wants Arthur?*
Graham, Bob. *Libby, Oscar and me*
Graham, Margaret Bloy. *Benjy and his*
    friend Fifi
  Benjy and the barking bird

  Benjy's boat trip
  Benjy's dog house
Green, Phyllis. *Bagdad ate it*
Gregory, Valiska. *Sunny side up*
  Terribly wonderful
Griffith, Helen V. *Alex and the cat*
  Alex remembers
  Mine will, said John
  More Alex and the cat
Grimm, Jacob. *The horse, the fox, and the*
    lion, ill. by Paul Galdone
Grindley, Sally. *Four black puppies*
Hamberger, John. *Hazel was an only pet*
  The lazy dog
Harriott, Ted. *Coming home*
Hausherr, Rosmarie. *My first puppy*
Hawkins, Colin. *Tog the dog*
Hazen, Barbara Shook. *Fang*
Heine, Helme. *Mr. Miller the dog*
Heller, Nicholas. *Happy birthday, Moe dog*
Henrie, Fiona. *Dogs*
Herriot, James. *Only one woof*
Hewett, Joan. *Rosalie*
Hill, Eric. *Spot at play*
  Spot at the fair
  Spot goes to school
  Spot goes to the beach
  Spot goes to the circus
  Spot goes to the farm
  Spot looks at colors
  Spot looks at shapes
  Spot on the farm
  Spot visits the hospital
  Spot's big book of words
  Spot's first Christmas
  Spot's first Easter
  Spot's first picnic
  Spot's first walk
  Spot's first words
Hillert, Margaret. *What is it?*
Himmelman, John. *The talking tree*
Hines, Anna Grossnickle. *I'll tell you what*
    they say
Hoban, Lillian. *The laziest robot in zone one*
Hoban, Russell. *The stone doll of Sister*
    Brute
Hoff, Syd. *Barkley*
  Lengthy
Holmes, Efner Tudor. *Carrie's gift*
Holt, Margaret. *David McCheever's*
    twenty-nine dogs
Hopkins, Lee Bennett. *A dog's life*
Howe, James. *The fright before Christmas*
Hurd, Edith Thacher. *The black dog who*
    went into the woods
  Little dog, dreaming
Hurd, Thacher. *Hobo dog*
Hürlimann, Bettina. *Barry*
Inkiow, Dimiter. *Me and Clara and Snuffy*
    the dog
Ipcar, Dahlov. *Black and white*

Isele, Elizabeth. *Pooks*
Iwamura, Kazuo. *Ton and Pon*
Iwasaki, Chihiro. *What's fun without a friend?*
Janice. *Angélique*
  Mr. and Mrs. Button's wonderful watchdogs
Joerns, Consuelo. *Oliver's escape*
Johnson, Crockett. *The blue ribbon puppies*
  Terrible terrifying Toby
Jones, Rebecca C. *The biggest, meanest, ugliest dog in the whole wide world*
Joosse, Barbara M. *Better with two*
Jordan, June. *Kimako's story*
Kahl, Virginia. *Away went Wolfgang*
  Maxie
Keats, Ezra Jack. *Kitten for a day*
  My dog is lost!
  Psst, doggie
  Skates
  Whistle for Willie
Keller, Holly. *Goodbye, Max*
Kelley, Anne. *Daisy's discovery*
Kellogg, Steven. *Best friends*
  Pinkerton, behave!
  Prehistoric Pinkerton
  A rose for Pinkerton
  Tallyho, Pinkerton!
Keyser, Marcia. *Roger on his own*
Khalsa, Dayal Kaur. *I want a dog*
Kimura, Yasuko. *Fergus and the sea monster*
King, Deborah. *Sirius and Saba*
Kitamura, Satoshi. *Lily takes a walk*
Kočí, Marta. *Blackie and Marie*
Kopczynski, Anna. *Jerry and Ami*
Kraus, Robert. *The detective of London*
Kroll, Steven. *Don't get me in trouble*
  Woof, woof!
Kumin, Maxine. *What color is Caesar?*
Kuskin, Karla. *Watson, the smartest dog in the U.S.A.*
Laskowski, Jerzy. *Master of the royal cats*
Lathrop, Dorothy Pulis. *Puppies for keeps*
Leaf, Munro. *Noodle*
Leichman, Seymour. *Shaggy dogs and spotty dogs and shaggy and spotty dogs*
Lenski, Lois. *Davy and his dog*
  Debbie and her dolls
  A dog came to school
Levy, Elizabeth. *Something queer at the library*
  Something queer in rock 'n' roll
  Something queer is going on
Lewis, Thomas P. *Call for Mr. Sniff*
  Mr. Sniff and the motel mystery
Lexau, Joan M. *The dog food caper*
  Go away, dog
  I'll tell on you
Lindgren, Barbro. *Sam's bath*
  Sam's wagon

Lindman, Maj. *Flicka, Ricka, Dicka and a little dog*
  Snipp, Snapp, Snurr and the seven dogs
  Snipp, Snapp, Snurr and the yellow sled
Lipkind, William. *Even Steven*
  Finders keepers
Lloyd, David. *Cat and dog*
Lopshire, Robert. *Put me in the zoo*
Lorenz, Lee. *Hugo and the spacedog*
Low, Joseph. *My dog, your dog*
Machetanz, Sara. *A puppy named Gia*
Marie, Geraldine. *The magic box*
Marshak, Samuel. *In the van*
  The pup grew up!
Marshall, James. *Miss Dog's Christmas*
  Speedboat
Martin, Charles E. *Dunkel takes a walk*
Martin, Sarah Catherine. *The comic adventures of Old Mother Hubbard and her dog*
  Old Mother Hubbard, ill. by Colin Hawkins
  Old Mother Hubbard and her dog, ill. by Lisa Amoroso
  Old Mother Hubbard and her dog, ill. by Paul Galdone
  Old Mother Hubbard and her dog, ill. by Evaline Ness
Mathers, Petra. *Theodor and Mr. Balbini*
Miles, Miska. *Show and tell...*
  Somebody's dog
Minarik, Else Holmelund. *Cat and dog*
Modell, Frank. *Skeeter and the computer*
  Tooley! Tooley!
Morris, Terry Nell. *Lucky puppy! Lucky boy!*
Myller, Rolf. *A very noisy day*
Nakatani, Chiyoko. *The day Chiro was lost*
Newberry, Clare Turlay. *Barkis*
O'Neill, Catharine. *Mrs. Dunphy's dog*
Otto, Svend. *Taxi dog*
Overbeck, Cynthia. *Rusty the Irish setter*
Oxenbury, Helen. *Our dog*
Pape, Donna Lugg. *Doghouse for sale*
Parker, Nancy Winslow. *Cooper, the McNallys' big black dog*
  Poofy loves company
Patent, Dorothy Hinshaw. *Maggie, a sheep dog*
Peet, Bill. *The Whingdingdilly*
Perkins, Al. *The digging-est dog*
Pfloog, Jan. *Puppies*
Phillips, Joan. *My new boy*
Piers, Helen. *Puppy's ABC*
Pinkwater, Daniel Manus. *Aunt Lulu*
Pizer, Abigail. *Nosey Gilbert*
Politi, Leo. *Emmet*
  The nicest gift
Polushkin, Maria. *Who said meow?* ill. by Ellen Weiss
Porte, Barbara Ann. *Harry's dog*

Potter, Beatrix. *The pie and the patty-pan*
Prather, Ray. *Double dog dare*
Pryor, Ainslie. *The baby blue cat and the dirty dog brothers*
Puppies and kittens
Rand, Gloria. *Salty dog*
Rey, Margaret Elisabeth Waldstein. *Pretzel*
Pretzel and the puppies
Rice, Eve. *Benny bakes a cake*
Papa's lemonade and other stories
Robins, Joan. *Addie meets Max*
Rockwell, Anne F. *Fire engines*
Hugo at the window
Willy runs away
Rose, Gerald. *Scruff*
Rose, Mitchell. *Norman*
Ross, Tony. *Towser and the terrible thing*
Round, Graham. *Hangdog*
Rowand, Phyllis. *George*
George goes to town
Ruby-Spears Enterprises. *The puppy's new adventures*
Rylant, Cynthia. *Henry and Mudge*
Henry and Mudge in puddle trouble
Henry and Mudge in the green time
Henry and Mudge in the sparkle days
Henry and Mudge under the yellow moon
Saltzberg, Barney. *Cromwell*
Sandberg, Inger. *Nicholas' favorite pet*
Sarrazin, Johan. *Tootle*
Saunders, Susan. *Wales' tale*
Saxon, Charles D. *Don't worry about Poopsie*
Schneider, Elisa. *The merry-go-round dog*
Schroeder, Binette. *Tuffa and her friends*
Tuffa and the bone
Tuffa and the ducks
Tuffa and the picnic
Tuffa and the snow
Schulman, Janet. *The great big dummy*
Schulz, Charles M. *Snoopy's facts and fun book about boats*
Snoopy's facts and fun book about farms
Snoopy's facts and fun book about houses
Snoopy's facts and fun book about nature
Snoopy's facts and fun book about planes
Snoopy's facts and fun book about seashores
Snoopy's facts and fun book about seasons
Snoopy's facts and fun book about trucks
Schwartz, Amy. *Oma and Bobo*
Scott, Sally. *Little Wiener*
There was Timmy!
Seligson, Susan. *Amos*
Selsam, Millicent E. *A first look at dogs*
How puppies grow
Sendak, Maurice. *Some swell pup*
Sewall, Marcia. *The little wee tyke*
Sewell, Helen Moore. *Birthdays for Robin*
Ming and Mehitable

Sharmat, Marjorie Weinman. *Nate the Great and the fishy prize*
Sasha the silly
Shibano, Tamizo. *The old man who made the trees bloom*
Shortall, Leonard W. *Andy, the dog walker*
Shyer, Marlene Fanta. *Stepdog*
Simon, Norma. *Cats do, dogs don't*
Singer, Marilyn. *The dog who insisted he wasn't*
Skaar, Grace Marion. *Nothing but (cats) and all about (dogs)*
The very little dog
Skorpen, Liesel Moak. *All the Lassies*
His mother's dog
Old Arthur
Snoopy on wheels
Spier, Peter. *Little dogs*
Stadler, John. *Hector, the accordion-nosed dog*
Steig, William. *Caleb and Kate*
Tiffky Doofky
Steiner, Charlotte. *Lulu*
Pete and Peter
Stern, Mark. *It's a dog's life*
Stevenson, James. *Are we almost there?*
Stevenson, Suçie. *Jessica the blue streak*
Stratemeyer, Clara Georgeanna. *Tuggy*
Sugita, Yutaka. *My friend Little John and me*
Surany, Anico. *Kati and Kormos*
Tabler, Judith. *The new puppy*
Tafuri, Nancy. *Who's counting?*
Tallon, Robert. *Latouse my moose*
Tanaka, Hideyuki. *The happy dog*
Taylor, Mark. *The case of the missing kittens*
Old Blue, you good dog you
Taylor, Sydney. *The dog who came to dinner*
Thaler, Mike. *My puppy*
Thayer, Jane. *The puppy who wanted a boy*, ill. by Seymour Fleishman
The puppy who wanted a boy, ill. by Lisa McCue
Thomson, Ruth. *Peabody all at sea*
Peabody's first case
Titus, Eve. *Anatole and the poodle*
Turkle, Brinton. *The sky dog*
Udry, Janice May. *Alfred*
What Mary Jo wanted
Untermeyer, Louis. *The kitten who barked*
Updike, David. *A winter's journey*
Van Allsburg, Chris. *The garden of Abdul Gasazi*
Van den Honert, Dorry. *Demi the baby sitter*
Waber, Bernard. *Bernard*
Wagner, Jenny. *John Brown, Rose and the midnight cat*
Wahl, Jan. *Frankenstein's dog*

Walt Disney Productions. *Tod and Copper*
Tod and Vixey
Ward, Lynd. *Nic of the woods*
Weiss, Harvey. *The sooner hound*
Whitney, Alex. *The tiger that barks*
Wiese, Kurt. *The dog, the fox and the fleas*
Wild, Robin. *Spot's dogs and the alley cats*
Wildsmith, Brian. *Give a dog a bone*
Hunter and his dog
Wilhelm, Hans. *I'll always love you*
A new home, a new friend
Williamson, Stan. *The no-bark dog*
Willoughby, Elaine Macmann. *Boris and the monsters*
Wirth, Beverly. *Margie and me*
Wold, Jo Anne. *Well! Why didn't you say so?*
Wood, Leslie. *A dog called Mischief*
Yorinks, Arthur. *Hey, Al*
Ziefert, Harriet. *A dozen dogs*
Sleepy dog
Where's the dog?
Zimelman, Nathan. *Mean Murgatroyd and the ten cats*
Zion, Gene. *Harry and the lady next door*
Harry by the sea
Harry, the dirty dog
No roses for Harry
Zolotow, Charlotte. *The poodle who barked at the wind*

Animals – dolphins

Anderson, Lonzo. *Arion and the dolphins*
Benchley, Nathaniel. *The several tricks of Edgar Dolphin*
Berger, Gilda. *Whales*
Gordon, Sharon. *Dolphins and porpoises*
Lilly, Kenneth. *Animals of the ocean*
Morris, Robert A. *Dolphin*
Nakatani, Chiyoko. *Fumio and the dolphins*

Animals – donkeys

Æsop. *The miller, his son and their donkey*, ill. by Roger Antoine Duvoisin
The miller, his son and their donkey, ill. by Eugen Sopko
Alexander, Lloyd. *The four donkeys*
Bates, H. E. *Achilles and Diana*
Achilles the donkey
Bettina (Bettina Ehrlich). *Cocolo comes to America*
Cocolo's home
Piccolo
Brown, Marcia. *Tamarindo!*
Bulla, Clyde Robert. *The donkey cart*
Calhoun, Mary. *Old man Whickutt's donkey*
Cohen, Barbara. *The donkey's story*
Daugherty, Sonia. *Vanka's donkey*
Dumas, Philippe. *Lucy, a tale of a donkey*
The story of Edward

Duvoisin, Roger Antoine. *Donkey-donkey*
Evans, Katherine. *The man, the boy and the donkey*
Gramatky, Hardie. *Bolivar*
Gray, Genevieve. *How far, Felipe?*
Grimm, Jacob. *The donkey prince*, ill. by Barbara Cooney
Hale, Irina. *Donkey's dreadful day*
Hurd, Edith Thacher. *Under the lemon tree*
La Fontaine, Jean de. *The miller, the boy and the donkey*
McCrea, James. *The king's procession*
Maris, Ron. *Hold tight, bear!*
Morpurgo, Michael. *Jo-Jo the melon donkey*
Ness, Evaline. *Josefina February*
Palazzo, Tony. *Bianco and the New World*
Raphael, Elaine. *Donkey and Carlo*
Donkey, it's snowing
Seignobosc, Françoise. *Chouchou*
Showalter, Jean B. *The donkey ride*
Silver, Jody. *Isadora*
Steig, William. *Farmer Palmer's wagon ride*
Sylvester and the magic pebble
Van Woerkom, Dorothy. *Donkey Ysabel*
Winter, Paula. *Sir Andrew*

Animals – elephants

Ambrus, Victor G. *Mishka*
Barner, Bob. *Elephant facts*
Bishop, Ann. *The Ella Fannie elephant riddle book*
Bohman, Nils. *Jim, Jock and Jumbo*
Boynton, Sandra. *If at first...*
Brunhoff, Jean de. *Babar and Father Christmas*
Babar and his children
Babar and Zephir
Babar the king
Babar's anniversary album
The story of Babar, the little elephant
The travels of Babar
Brunhoff, Laurent de. *Babar and the ghost*
Babar and the Wully-Wully
Babar comes to America
Babar learns to cook
Babar loses his crown
Babar the magician
Babar visits another planet
Babar's ABC
Babar's birthday surprise
Babar's book of color
Babar's castle
Babar's counting book
Babar's cousin, that rascal Arthur
Babar's fair will be opened next Sunday
Babar's little circus star
Babar's little girl
Babar's mystery
Babar's picnic
Babar's visit to Bird Island

Burns, Diane L. *Elephants never forget!*
Cantieni, Benita. *Little Elephant and Big Mouse*
Caple, Kathy. *The biggest nose*
Chorao, Kay. *George told Kate*
Kate's box
Kate's car
Kate's quilt
Kate's snowman
Clifford, Eth. *Why is an elephant called an elephant?*
Cole, Babette. *Nungu and the elephant*
Cole, Joanna. *Aren't you forgetting something, Fiona?*
Day, Alexandra. *Frank and Ernest*
Delacre, Lulu. *Nathan and Nicholas Alexander*
Nathan's fishing trip
Delton, Judy. *The elephant in Duck's garden*
Penny wise, fun foolish
Domanska, Janina. *Why so much noise?*
DuBois, Ivy. *Baby Jumbo*
Easton, Violet. *Elephants never jump*
Ets, Marie Hall. *Elephant in a well*
Fechner, Amrei. *I am a little elephant*
Fern, Eugene. *What's he been up to now?*
Foulds, Elfrida Vipont. *The elephant and the bad baby*
Freschet, Berniece. *Elephant and friends*
Greene, Carol. *The insignificant elephant*
Hall, Derek. *Elephant bathes*
Hamsa, Bobbie. *Your pet elephant*
Hawkins, Colin. *The elephant*
Hewett, Joan. *The mouse and the elephant*
Hoff, Syd. *Oliver*
Hoffman, Mary. *Animals in the wild*
Hogan, Inez. *About Nono, the baby elephant*
Irvine, Georgeanne. *Elmer the elephant*
Jenkin-Pearce, Susie. *Bad Boris and the new kitten*
Joslin, Sesyle. *Baby elephant and the secret wishes*
Baby elephant goes to China
Baby elephant's trunk
Brave Baby Elephant
Señor Baby Elephant, the pirate
Kipling, Rudyard. *The elephant's child*, ill. by Louise Brierley
The elephant's child, ill. by Lorinda Bryan Cauley
The elephant's child, ill. by Tim Raglin
Klein, Suzanne. *An elephant in my bed*
Kraus, Robert. *Boris bad enough*
Lawrence, John. *Pope Leo's elephant*
Lewin, Hugh. *An elephant came to swim*
Lipkind, William. *Chaga*
Lobel, Arnold. *Uncle Elephant*
Löfgren, Ulf. *The traffic stopper that became a grandmother visitor*

McKee, David. *Elmer, the story of a patchwork elephant*
Tusk tusk
McNulty, Faith. *The elephant who couldn't forget*
McPhail, David. *Where can an elephant hide?*
Maestro, Betsy. *Around the clock with Harriet*
Harriet at home
Harriet at play
Harriet at school
Harriet at work
Harriet goes to the circus
Harriet reads signs and more signs
On the go
On the town
Through the year with Harriet
Where is my friend?
Martin, Bill (William Ivan). *Smoky Poky*
Mayer, Mercer. *Ah-choo*
Moser, Erwin. *Wilma the elephant*
Murphy, Jill. *All in one piece*
Five minutes' peace
Nakano, Hirotaka. *Elephant blue*
Paterson, Bettina. *Bun and Mrs. Tubby*
Bun's birthday
Patz, Nancy. *Pumpernickel tickle and mean green cheese*
Pearce, Philippa. *Emily's own elephant*
Peek, Merle. *The balancing act*
Peet, Bill. *The ant and the elephant*
Ella
Encore for Eleanor
Perkins, Al. *Tubby and the lantern*
Tubby and the Poo-Bah
Petersham, Maud. *The circus baby*
Platt, Kin. *Big Max*
Pluckrose, Henry. *Elephants*
Quigley, Lillian Fox. *The blind men and the elephant*
Riddell, Chris. *The trouble with elephants*
Rogers, Edmund. *Elephants*
Sadler, Marilyn. *Alistair's elephant*
Saxe, John Godfrey. *The blind men and the elephant*
Schlein, Miriam. *Elephant herd*
Seuss, Dr. *Horton hatches the egg*
Horton hears a Who!
Simont, Marc. *How come elephants?*
Slobodkina, Esphyr. *Pezzo the peddler and the circus elephant*
Smath, Jerry. *But no elephants*
Elephant goes to school
Steig, William. *An eye for elephants*
Stock, Catherine. *Alexander's midnight snack*
Tresselt, Alvin R. *Smallest elephant in the world*
Wahl, Jan. *Hello, elephant*

Ward, Nanda Weedon. *The elephant that ga-lumphed*
Weinberg, Lawrence. *The Forgetful Bears meet Mr. Memory*
Weisgard, Leonard. *Silly Willy Nilly*
Weiss, Leatie. *My teacher sleeps in school*
Wells, H. G. (Herbert George). *The adventures of Tommy*
Westcott, Nadine Bernard. *Peanut butter and jelly*
Williamson, Hamilton. *Little elephant*
Ylla. *The little elephant*
Young, Miriam Burt. *If I rode an elephant*

Animals – endangered animals

Cromie, William J. *Steven and the green turtle*

Animals – foxes

Æsop. *The raven and the fox*, ill. by Gerald Rose
Three fox fables
Ambrus, Victor G. *Country wedding*
Anderson, Paul S. *Red fox and the hungry tiger*
Anno, Mitsumasa. *Anno's Æsop*
Arnosky, Jim. *Watching foxes*
Barr, Cathrine. *Hound dog's bone*
Baynton, Martin. *Fifty and the fox*
Bemelmans, Ludwig. *Welcome home*
Berson, Harold. *Henry Possum*
Joseph and the snake
Bingham, Mindy. *My way Sally*
Brown, Marcia. *The neighbors*
Brown, Margaret Wise. *Fox eyes*
Buck, Pearl S. (Pearl Sydenstricker). *The little fox in the middle*
Burningham, John. *Harquin*
Calhoun, Mary. *Houn' dog*
Carroll, Ruth. *What Whiskers did*
Carter, Anne. *Ruff leaves home*
Chaucer, Geoffrey. *Chanticleer and the fox*, ill. by Barbara Cooney
Christelow, Eileen. *Henry and the red stripes*
Cunningham, Julia. *The vision of Francois the fox*
Davis, Lavinia. *Roger and the fox*
Delton, Judy. *Duck goes fishing*
Domanska, Janina. *The best of the bargain*
DuBois, Ivy. *Mother fox*
Eberle, Irmengarde. *Foxes live here*
Fatio, Louise. *The red bantam*
Firmin, Peter. *Basil Brush and a dragon*
Basil Brush and the windmills
Basil Brush finds treasure
Basil Brush gets a medal
Basil Brush goes flying
Fox, Charles Philip. *A fox in the house*
The fox went out on a chilly night

Ginsburg, Mirra. *Across the stream*
The fox and the hare
Mushroom in the rain
Two greedy bears
Grimm, Jacob. *The horse, the fox, and the lion*, ill. by Paul Galdone
Mrs. Fox's wedding
Guzzo, Sandra E. *Fox and Heggie*
Hartley, Deborah. *Up north in the winter*
Hess, Lilo. *Foxes in the woodshed*
Hogrogian, Nonny. *One fine day*
Hurd, Edith Thacher. *Under the lemon tree*
Hutchins, Pat. *Rosie's walk*
Kent, Jack. *Silly goose*
Koralek, Jenny. *The friendly fox*
Leverich, Kathleen. *The hungry fox and the foxy duck*
Lifton, Betty Jean. *The many lives of Chio and Goro*
Lindgren, Astrid. *The tomten and the fox*
Lionni, Leo. *In the rabbitgarden*
Lipkind, William. *The Christmas bunny*
The little tiny rooster
Livermore, Elaine. *Follow the fox*
McKissack, Patricia C. *Flossie and the fox*
Marshall, Edward. *Fox all week*
Fox and his friends
Fox at school
Fox in love
Fox on wheels
Marshall, James. *Fox on the job*
Rapscallion Jones
Wings
Mayne, William. *A house in town*
Meddaugh, Susan. *Maude and Claude go abroad*
Miles, Miska. *The fox and the fire*
Miller, Edward. *Frederick Ferdinand Fox*
Nordqvist, Sven. *The fox hunt*
Pevear, Richard. *Mister cat-and-a-half*
Potter, Beatrix. *The tale of Mr. Tod*
Preston, Edna Mitchell. *Squawk to the moon, little goose*
Roach, Marilynne K. *Dune fox*
Rockwell, Anne F. *Big boss*
Schlein, Miriam. *The four little foxes*
Selsam, Millicent E. *A first look at dogs*
Sharmat, Marjorie Weinman. *The best Valentine in the world*
Small, David. *Eulalie and the hopping head*
Steig, William. *Doctor De Soto*
Roland, the minstrel pig
Tejima, Keizaburo. *Fox's dream*
Thomas, Patricia. *"There are rocks in my socks!" said the ox to the fox*
Tompert, Ann. *Little Fox goes to the end of the world*
Varga, Judy. *The mare's egg*
Walt Disney Productions. *Tod and Copper*
Tod and Vixey

Watson, Clyde. *Father Fox's feast of songs*
  Tom Fox and the apple pie
  Valentine foxes
Watson, Wendy. *Tales for a winter's eve*
Weil, Lisl. *Gillie and the flattering fox*
Wells, Rosemary. *Don't spill it again, James*
Westwood, Jennifer. *Going to Squintum's*
Wiese, Kurt. *The dog, the fox and the fleas*
Wilhelm, Hans. *More bunny trouble*

Animals – gerbils

Henrie, Fiona. *Gerbils*
Tobias, Tobi. *Petey*

Animals – giraffes

Arnold, Caroline. *Giraffe*
Brenner, Barbara. *Mr. Tall and Mr. Small*
Brunhoff, Laurent de. *Serafina the giraffe*
Cooke, Ann. *Giraffes at home*
Doughtie, Charles. *High Henry...the cowboy
  who was too tall to ride a horse*
Duvoisin, Roger Antoine. *Periwinkle*
Hamsa, Bobbie. *Your pet giraffe*
Irvine, Georgeanne. *Georgie the giraffe*
Le Guin, Ursula K. *Solomon Leviathan's
  nine hundred and thirty-first trip around
  the world*
Rey, Hans Augusto. *Cecily G and the nine
  monkeys*
Sharmat, Marjorie Weinman. *Helga
  high-up*

Animals – goats

Allamand, Pascale. *The little goat in the
  mountains*
Ambrus, Victor G. *The seven skinny goats*
  The three poor tailors
Asbjørnsen, P. C. (Peter Christen). *The three
  billy goats Gruff*, ill. by Marcia Brown
  Three billy goats Gruff, ill. by Tom
  Dunnington
  The three billy goats Gruff, ill. by Paul
  Galdone
  The three billy goats Gruff, ill. by Janet
  Stevens
  The three billy goats Gruff, ill. by William
  Stobbs
Berson, Harold. *Balarin's goat*
Blood, Charles L. *The goat in the rug*
Bornstein, Ruth Lercher. *Of course a goat*
Carigiet, Alois. *Anton the goatherd*
Chandoha, Walter. *A baby goat for you*
Chiefari, Janet. *Kids are baby goats*
Damjan, Mischa. *The wolf and the kid*
Daudet, Alphonse. *The brave little goat of
  Monsieur Séguin*
Dunn, Judy. *The little goat*
Fletcher, Elizabeth. *The little goat*

Gage, Wilson. *Mrs. Gaddy and the
  fast-growing vine*
Grimm, Jacob. *The wolf and the seven kids*,
  ill. by Kinuko Craft
  The wolf and the seven little kids, ill. by
  Martin Ursell
Hillert, Margaret. *The three goats*
Hoff, Syd. *Happy birthday, Henrietta!*
Hogrogian, Nonny. *Billy Goat and his
  well-fed friends*
Kroll, Steven. *The goat parade*
Leaf, Munro. *Gordon, the goat*
Lipkind, William. *Billy the kid*
Mills, Alan. *The hungry goat*
Rappus, Gerhard. *When the sun was
  shining*
Sattler, Helen Roney. *No place for a goat*
Seignobosc, Françoise. *Biquette, the white
  goat*
  Springtime for Jeanne-Marie
Sharmat, Mitchell. *Gregory, the terrible eater*
Siddiqui, Ashraf. *Bhombal Dass, the uncle
  of lion*
Slobodkin, Louis. *The polka-dot goat*
  Up high and down low
Suhl, Yuri. *The Purim goat*
Tudor, Tasha. *Corgiville fair*
Watson, Nancy Dingman. *The birthday goat*
Wildsmith, Brian. *Goat's trail*
Wolkstein, Diane. *The banza*

Animals – gorillas

Aardema, Verna. *Princess Gorilla and a
  new kind of water*
Browne, Anthony. *Gorilla*
  Willy the champ
  Willy the wimp
Conklin, Gladys. *Little apes*
Delton, Judy. *On a picnic*
Hall, Derek. *Gorilla builds*
Harrison, David Lee. *Detective Bob and the
  great ape escape*
Hazen, Barbara Shook. *The gorilla did it!*
  Gorilla wants to be the baby
Hoff, Syd. *Julius*
Howe, James. *The day the teacher went
  bananas*
Krahn, Fernando. *The great ape*
Meyers, Susan. *The truth about gorillas*
Most, Bernard. *There's an ape behind the
  drape*
Patterson, Francine. *Koko's kitten*
Schertle, Alice. *The gorilla in the hall*
Selsam, Millicent E. *A first look at monkeys*
Zimelman, Nathan. *Positively no pets
  allowed*

Animals – groundhogs

Balian, Lorna. *A garden for a groundhog*
Bond, Felicia. *Wake up, Vladimir*

Cauley, Lorinda Bryan. *The new house*
Cohen, Carol L. *Wake up, groundhog!*
Coombs, Patricia. *Tilabel*
Delton, Judy. *Groundhog's Day at the doctor*
Glass, Marvin. *What happened today, Freddy Groundhog?*
Hamberger, John. *This is the day*
Johnson, Crockett. *Will spring be early?*
Kesselman, Wendy. *Time for Jody*
McNulty, Faith. *Woodchuck*
Palazzo, Tony. *Waldo the woodchuck*
Stanovich, Betty Jo. *Hedgehog adventures*
Tompert, Ann. *Nothing sticks like a shadow*
Watson, Wendy. *Has winter come?*

Animals – guinea pigs

Bare, Colleen Stanley. *Guinea pigs don't read books*
Brooks, Andrea. *The guinea pigs' adventure*
Duke, Kate. *Bedtime*
  Clean-up day
  The guinea pig ABC
  Guinea pigs far and near
  The playground
  What bounces?
Mayne, William. *Barnabas walks*
Meshover, Leonard. *The guinea pigs that went to school*
Potter, Beatrix. *The tale of Tuppeny*
Pursell, Margaret Sanford. *Polly the guinea pig*
Ziefert, Harriet. *Where's the guinea pig?*

Animals – hamsters

Ambrus, Victor G. *Grandma, Felix, and Mustapha Biscuit*
Baker, Alan. *Benjamin and the box*
  Benjamin bounces back
  Benjamin's book
  Benjamin's dreadful dream
  Benjamin's portrait
Blegvad, Lenore. *The great hamster hunt*
Brandenberg, Franz. *The hit of the party*
Brook, Judy. *Hector and Harriet the night hamsters*
Claude-Lafontaine, Pascale. *Monsieur Bussy, the celebrated hamster*
Harris, Dorothy Joan. *The school mouse and the hamster*
Vaës, Alain. *The wild hamster*
Watts, Barrie. *Hamster*

Animals – hedgehogs

Berson, Harold. *Why the jackal won't speak to the hedgehog*
Brook, Judy. *Tim mouse goes down the stream*
  Tim mouse visits the farm
Domanska, Janina. *The best of the bargain*

Flot, Jeannette B. *Princess Kalina and the hedgehog*
Guzzo, Sandra E. *Fox and Heggie*
Holden, Edith. *The hedgehog feast*
McClure, Gillian. *Prickly pig*
Myller, Lois. *No! No!*
Potter, Beatrix. *The tale of Mrs. Tiggy-Winkle*
Ruck-Pauquèt, Gina. *Little hedgehog*
Stanovich, Betty Jo. *Hedgehog adventures*
Stott, Rowena. *The hedgehog feast*
Yeoman, John. *The bear's water picnic*

Animals – hippopotami

Allen, Frances Charlotte. *Little hippo*
Bennett, Rainey. *The secret hiding place*
Bohman, Nils. *Jim, Jock and Jumbo*
Boynton, Sandra. *But not the hippopotamus*
  Hester in the wild
  Hippos go berserk
Brown, Marcia. *How, hippo!*
Calmenson, Stephanie. *The birthday hat*
  Where is Grandma Potamus?
Chalmers, Audrey. *Parade of Obash*
Cole, Babette. *Nungu and the hippopotamus*
Croswell, Volney. *How to hide a hippopotamus*
Duvoisin, Roger Antoine. *Lonely Veronica*
  Our Veronica goes to Petunia's farm
  Veronica
  Veronica and the birthday present
  Veronica's smile
Hadithi, Mwenye. *Hot hippo*
The hippo
Kishida, Eriko. *The hippo boat*
Lasher, Faith B. *Hubert Hippo's world*
Lewin, Betsy. *Hip, hippo, hooray!*
Mahy, Margaret. *The boy who was followed home*
Marshall, James. *George and Martha*
  George and Martha back in town
  George and Martha encore
  George and Martha one fine day
  George and Martha rise and shine
  George and Martha round and round
  George and Martha, tons of fun
Mayer, Mercer. *Hiccup*
  Oops
Panek, Dennis. *Matilda Hippo has a big mouth*
Parker, Nancy Winslow. *Love from Uncle Clyde*
Scarry, Richard. *The adventures of Tinker and Tanker*
Slobodkin, Louis. *Hustle and bustle*
Stadler, John. *Three cheers for hippo!*
Sugita, Yutaka. *Helena the unhappy hippopotamus*
Sutton, Jane. *What should a hippo wear?*

Taylor, Judy. *Sophie and Jack*
  Sophie and Jack help out
Thaler, Mike. *Hippo lemonade*
  It's me, hippo!
  There's a hippopotamus under my bed
Tyler, Linda Wagner. *Waiting for mom*
  When daddy comes home
Waber, Bernard. *"You look ridiculous," said the rhinoceros to the hippopotamus*
Wahl, Jan. *Old Hippo's Easter egg*
Young, Miriam Burt. *Please don't feed Horace*
Ziefert, Harriet. *Harry takes a bath*

Animals – horses

Aarle, Thomas Van. *Don't put your cart before the horse race*
Anderson, C. W. (Clarence Williams). *Billy and Blaze*
  Blaze and the forest fire
  Blaze and the gray spotted pony
  Blaze and the gypsies
  Blaze and the Indian cave
  Blaze and the lost quarry
  Blaze and the mountain lion
  Blaze and Thunderbolt
  Blaze finds forgotten roads
  Blaze finds the trail
  Blaze shows the way
  The crooked colt
  Linda and the Indians
  Lonesome little colt
  A pony for Linda
  A pony for three
  The rumble seat pony
Arundel, Jocelyn. *Shoes for Punch*
Asch, Frank. *Goodnight horsey*
Baker, Betty. *Three fools and a horse*
Balet, Jan B. *Five Rollatinis*
Barr, Cathrine. *A horse for Sherry*
Barrett, Lawrence Louis. *Twinkle, the baby colt*
Beatty, Hetty Burlingame. *Bucking horse*
  Little Owl Indian
  Moorland pony
Bellville, Cheryl Walsh. *Round-up*
Bemelmans, Ludwig. *Madeline in London*
Blech, Dietlind. *Hello Irina*
Bowden, Joan Chase. *A new home for Snow Ball*
Brett, Jan. *Fritz and the beautiful horses*
Burningham, John. *Humbert, Mister Firkin and the Lord Mayor of London*
Burton, Virginia Lee. *Calico the wonder horse*
Chan, Chin-Yi. *Good luck horse*
Chandler, Edna Walker. *Pony rider*
Charmatz, Bill. *The Troy St. bus*
Climo, Lindee. *Clyde*
Coerr, Eleanor. *Chang's paper pony*

Cohen, Carol L. *The mud pony*
Cox, David. *Tin Lizzie and Little Nell*
Cretien, Paul D. *Sir Henry and the dragon*
Cummings, W. T. (Walter Thies). *The kid*
Demi. *The hallowed horse*
Dennis, Wesley. *Flip and the cows*
  Flip and the morning
  Tumble, the story of a mustang
Duncan, Lois. *Horses of dreamland*
Elborn, Andrew. *Noah and the ark and the animals*
Ets, Marie Hall. *Mr. Penny's race horse*
Fain, James W. *Rodeos*
Farley, Walter. *Black stallion*
  Little Black, a pony
  Little Black goes to the circus
Fatio, Louise. *Anna, the horse*
Felton, Harold W. *Pecos Bill and the mustang*
Fregosi, Claudia. *The happy horse*
Friskey, Margaret. *Indian Two Feet and his horse*
Garbutt, Bernard. *Roger, the rosin back*
Gaston, Susan. *New boots for Salvador*
Gay, Zhenya. *Wonderful things*
Goble, Paul. *The gift of the sacred dog*
  The girl who loved wild horses
Grabianski, Janusz. *Horses*
Greaves, Margaret. *A net to catch the wind*
Greydanus, Rose. *Horses*
Grimm, Jacob. *The horse, the fox, and the lion*, ill. by Paul Galdone
Gross, Ruth Belov. *The girl who wouldn't get married*
Hasler, Eveline. *Martin is our friend*
Hawkinson, John. *Where the wild apples grow*
Heilbroner, Joan. *Robert the rose horse*
Herriot, James. *Bonny's big day*
Hoban, Russell. *The rain door*
Hoberman, Mary Ann. *Mr. and Mrs. Muddle*
Hoff, Syd. *Chester*
  The horse in Harry's room
Inkiow, Dimiter. *Me and Clara and Baldwin the pony*
Ipcar, Dahlov. *One horse farm*
  World full of horses
Jeffers, Susan. *All the pretty horses*
Keeping, Charles. *Molly o' the moors*
Kraus, Robert. *Springfellow*
Krauss, Ruth. *Charlotte and the white horse*
Krum, Charlotte. *The four riders*
La Farge, Phyllis. *Joanna runs away*
Lasell, Fen. *Michael grows a wish*
Lobel, Arnold. *Lucille*
Locker, Thomas. *The mare on the hill*
Low, Alice. *David's windows*
McGinley, Phyllis. *The horse who lived upstairs*
Mayer, Marianna. *The black horse*

Meeks, Esther K. *Playland pony*
Miles, Miska. *Friend of Miguel*
Miller, Jane. *Birth of a foal*
Otsuka, Yuzo. *Suho and the white horse*
Otto, Margaret Glover. *The little brown horse*
Patent, Dorothy Hinshaw. *Baby horses*
Paterson, Andrew Barton. *Mulga Bill's bicycle*
Peet, Bill. *Cowardly Clyde*
Pender, Lydia. *Barnaby and the horses*
Peterson, Jeanne Whitehouse. *Sometimes I dream horses*
Pluckrose, Henry. *Horses*
Primavera, Elise. *Basil and Maggie*
Rabinowitz, Sandy. *A colt named mischief*
What's happening to Daisy?
Richard, Jane. *A horse grows up*
Rounds, Glen. *Once we had a horse*
The strawberry roan
Saville, Lynn. *Horses in the circus ring*
Sewall, Marcia. *Ridin' that strawberry roan*
Sewell, Helen Moore. *Peggy and the pony*
Slobodkina, Esphyr. *The wonderful feast*
Sonberg, Lynn. *A horse named Paris*
Thayer, Jane. *Andy and the runaway horse*
The horse with the Easter bonnet
Thompson, Vivian Laubach. *The horse that liked sandwiches*
Tinkelman, Murray. *Cowgirl*
Ward, Lynd. *The silver pony*
Wells, Rosemary. *Abdul*
Wondriska, William. *The stop*
Wright, Dare. *Look at a colt*
Yeoman, John. *The young performing horse*
Young, Miriam Burt. *If I rode a horse*
Zimnik, Reiner. *The proud circus horse*
Zolotow, Charlotte. *I have a horse of my own*

Animals – hyenas

Newberry, Clare Turlay. *Lambert's bargain*
Prelutsky, Jack. *The mean old mean hyena*

Animals – kangaroos

Braun, Kathy. *Kangaroo and kangaroo*
Brown, Margaret Wise. *Young kangaroo*
Cole, Joanna. *Norma Jean, jumping bean*
Du Bois, William Pène. *The forbidden forest*
Hamsa, Bobbie. *Your pet kangaroo*
Harper, Anita. *It's not fair!*
Hurd, Edith Thacher. *The mother kangaroo*
Johnson, Crockett. *Upside down*
Kent, Jack. *Joey*
Joey runs away
Kipling, Rudyard. *The sing-song of old man kangaroo*, ill. by Michael C. Taylor
Pape, Donna Lugg. *Where is my little Joey?*
Payne, Emmy. *Katy no-pocket*
Sanchez, Jose Louis Garcia. *Kangaroo*

Schlein, Miriam. *Big talk*
Selig, Sylvie. *Kangaroo*
Stonehouse, Bernard. *Kangaroos*
Townsend, Anita. *The kangaroo*
Ungerer, Tomi. *Adelaide*
Wiseman, Bernard. *Little new kangaroo*

Animals – kinkajous

Vandivert, William. *Barnaby*

Animals – koala bears

Broome, Errol. *The smallest koala*
Du Bois, William Pène. *Bear circus*
Bear party
Eberle, Irmengarde. *Koalas live here*
Gelman, Rita Golden. *A koala grows up*
Irvine, Georgeanne. *Sydney the koala*
Levens, George. *Kippy the koala*
Quackenbush, Robert M. *I don't want to go, I don't know how to act*
Ruck-Pauquèt, Gina. *Oh, that koala!*
Snyder, Dick. *One day at the zoo*
Walsh, Grahame L. *Didane the koala*

Animals – lemmings

Steig, Jeanne. *Consider the lemming*

Animals – leopards

Aardema, Verna. *Half-a-ball-of-kenki*
Ipcar, Dahlov. *Stripes and spots*
Irvine, Georgeanne. *Lindi the leopard*
Kepes, Juliet. *Run little monkeys, run, run, run*
Kipling, Rudyard. *How the leopard got his spots*, ill. by Caroline Ebborn
Livermore, Elaine. *Looking for Henry*
Maestro, Giulio. *Leopard is sick*

Animals – lions

Adamson, Joy. *Elsa*
Elsa and her cubs
Æsop. *The lion and the mouse*, ill. by Gerald Rose
The lion and the mouse, ill. by Ed Young
Allen, Pamela. *A lion in the night*
Androcles and the lion, ill. by Janusz Grabianski
Balet, Jan B. *Ned and Ed and the lion*
Bannerman, Helen. *The story of the teasing monkey*
Belloc, Hilaire. *Jim, who ran away from his nurse, and was eaten by a lion*
Bible. Old Testament. Daniel. *Daniel in the lions' den*, ill. by Leon Baxter
Bohman, Nils. *Jim, Jock and Jumbo*
Bridges, William. *Lion Island*
Brown, Margaret Wise. *The sleepy little lion*

Daugherty, James Henry. *Andy and the lion*
The picnic
Davis, Douglas F. *The lion's tail*
Delton, Judy. *On a picnic*
Demarest, Chris L. *Clemens' kingdom*
Devlin, Wende. *Aunt Agatha, there's a lion under the couch!*
Du Bois, William Pène. *Lion*
Fatio, Louise. *The happy lion*
The happy lion and the bear
The happy lion in Africa
The happy lion roars
The happy lion's quest
The happy lion's rabbits
The happy lion's treasure
The happy lion's vacation
The three happy lions
Fechner, Amrei. *I am a little lion*
Freeman, Don. *Dandelion*
Galdone, Paul. *Androcles and the lion*
Gay, Zhenya. *I'm tired of lions*
Grimm, Jacob. *The horse, the fox, and the lion*, ill. by Paul Galdone
Hancock, Joy Elizabeth. *The loudest little lion*
Hawkins, Mark. *A lion under her bed*
Hoban, Russell. *The rain door*
Hofer, Angelika. *The lion family book*
Hurd, Edith Thacher. *Johnny Lion's bad day*
Johnny Lion's book
Johnny Lion's rubber boots
Kishida, Eriko. *The lion and the bird's nest*
La Fontaine, Jean de. *The lion and the rat*
Mahy, Margaret. *A lion in the meadow*
Makower, Sylvia. *Samson's breakfast*
Mann, Peggy. *King Laurence, the alarm clock*
Michael, Emory H. *Androcles and the lion*
Michel, Anna. *Little wild lion cub*
Ness, Evaline. *Fierce the lion*
Newberry, Clare Turlay. *Herbert the lion*
Peet, Bill. *Eli*
Hubert's hair-raising adventures
Randy's dandy lions
Pluckrose, Henry. *Lions and tigers*
Presencer, Alain. *Roaring lion tales*
Siddiqui, Ashraf. *Bhombal Dass, the uncle of lion*
Siepmann, Jane. *The lion on Scott Street*
Skorpen, Liesel Moak. *If I had a lion*
Stephenson, Dorothy. *How to scare a lion*
Stewart, Elizabeth Laing. *The lion twins*
Townsend, Kenneth. *Felix, the bald-headed lion*
Varga, Judy. *Miss Lollipop's lion*
Zelinsky, Paul O. *The lion and the stoat*

Animals — llamas

Rockwell, Anne F. *The good llama*

Animals — mice

Æsop. *The country mouse and the city mouse*, ill. by Laura Lydecker
The lion and the mouse, ill. by Gerald Rose
The lion and the mouse, ill. by Ed Young
The town mouse and the country mouse, ill. by Lorinda Bryan Cauley
The town mouse and the country mouse, ill. by Paul Galdone
The town mouse and the country mouse, ill. by Tom Garcia
The town mouse and the country mouse, ill. by Janet Stevens
Alexander, Sue. *Dear Phoebe*
Aliki. *At Mary Bloom's*
Allen, Laura Jean. *Rollo and Tweedy and the case of the missing cheese*
Althea. *Jeremy Mouse and cat*
Angelo, Nancy Carolyn Harrison. *Camembert*
Angelo, Valenti. *The candy basket*
Arnosky, Jim. *Mouse numbers and letters*
Mouse writing
Augarde, Steve. *Barnaby Shrew, Black Dan and...the mighty wedgwood*
Aylesworth, Jim. *Two terrible frights*
Balzano, Jeanne. *The wee moose*
Barbaresi, Nina. *Firemouse*
Barklem, Jill. *Autumn story*
The big book of Brambly Hedge
The high hills
The secret staircase
Spring story
Summer story
Winter story
Barrows, Marjorie Wescott. *The book of favorite Muggins Mouse stories*
Muggins' big balloon
Muggins Mouse
Muggins takes off
Bastin, Marjolein. *Vera dresses up*
Belpré, Pura. *Perez and Martina*
Berson, Harold. *A moose is not a mouse*
Raminagrobis and the mice
Bible. Old Testament. Jonah. *Jonah*, ill. by Kurt Mitchell
Blair, Anne Denton. *Hurrah for Arthur!*
Boegehold, Betty. *Here's Pippa again!*
Pippa Mouse
Pippa pops out!
Bond, Felicia. *The Halloween performance*
Boynton, Sandra. *If at first...*
Brady, Irene. *A mouse named Mus*
Wild mouse
Brady, Susan. *Find my blanket*

Brandenberg, Franz. *Everyone ready?*
It's not my fault
Nice new neighbors
Six new students
What can you make of it?
Brenner, Barbara. *Mr. Tall and Mr. Small*
Bright, Robert. *Georgie and the runaway balloon*
Brook, Judy. *Tim mouse goes down the stream*
Tim mouse visits the farm
Brown, Palmer. *Cheerful*
Hickory
Something for Christmas
Buchanan, Heather S. *Emily Mouse saves the day*
Emily Mouse's beach house
Emily Mouse's first adventure
Emily Mouse's garden
George Mouse learns to fly
George Mouse's covered wagon
George Mouse's first summer
George Mouse's riverboat band
Bunting, Eve. *The Mother's Day mice*
Burningham, John. *Trubloff*
Cameron, John. *If mice could fly*
Cantieni, Benita. *Little Elephant and Big Mouse*
Carle, Eric. *Do you want to be my friend?*
Cartlidge, Michelle. *A mouse's diary*
Pippin and Pod
Castle, Caroline. *Herbert Binns and the flying tricycle*
Charles, Donald. *Calico Cat's exercise book*
Chase, Catherine. *Baby mouse goes shopping*
Baby mouse learns his ABC's
The mouse in my house
Chorao, Kay. *Cathedral mouse*
Christensen, Gardell Dano. *Mrs. Mouse needs a house*
Claret, Maria. *Melissa Mouse*
Coombs, Patricia. *Mouse Café*
Cressey, James. *Max the mouse*
Cunningham, Julia. *A mouse called Junction*
Dauer, Rosamond. *Bullfrog grows up*
Daugherty, James Henry. *The picnic*
Delacre, Lulu. *Nathan and Nicholas Alexander*
Nathan's fishing trip
Delessert, Etienne. *How the mouse was hit on the head by a stone and so discovered the world*
De Paola, Tomie. *Charlie needs a cloak*
De Regniers, Beatrice Schenk. *Picture book theater*
Doty, Roy. *Old-one-eye meets his match*
Durrell, Julie. *Mouse tails*
Elzbieta. *Brave Babette and sly Tom*
Ernst, Lisa Campbell. *The rescue of Aunt Pansy*

Ets, Marie Hall. *Mr. T. W. Anthony Woo*
Felix, Monique. *The further adventures of the little mouse trapped in a book*
The story of a little mouse trapped in a book
Fisher, Aileen. *The house of a mouse*
Sing, little mouse
Freeman, Don. *The guard mouse*
Norman the doorman
Freeman, Lydia. *Pet of the Met*
Freschet, Berniece. *Bear mouse*
Bernard of Scotland Yard
Fuchshuber, Annegert. *Giant story - Mouse tale*
Futamata, Eigorō. *How not to catch a mouse*
Gackenbach, Dick. *The perfect mouse*
Gág, Wanda. *Snippy and Snappy*
Gantz, David. *The genie bear with the light brown hair word book*
Gay, Marie-Louise. *Moonbeam on a cat's ear*
Gili, Phillida. *Fanny and Charles*
Ginsburg, Mirra. *Four brave sailors*
Goodall, John S. *Creepy castle*
Gordon, Margaret. *The supermarket mice*
Goundaud, Karen Jo. *A very mice joke book*
Graham, John. *I love you, mouse*
Greaves, Margaret. *The mice of Nibbling Village*
Greene, Carol. *A computer went a-courting*
Grimm, Jacob. *Godfather Cat and Mousie*, ill. by Ann Schweninger
Little Red Riding Hood, ill. by John S. Goodall
Gundersheimer, Karen. *1 2 3 play with me*
Shapes to show
Gurney, Nancy. *The king, the mice and the cheese*
Hale, Irina. *Chocolate mouse and sugar pig*
Hale, Linda. *The glorious Christmas soup party*
Hall, Malcolm. *And then the mouse...*
Harris, Dorothy Joan. *The school mouse and the hamster*
Harris, Leon A. *The great diamond robbery*
The great picture robbery
Hawkinson, John. *The old stump*
Hazen, Barbara Shook. *The Fat Cats, Cousin Scraggs and the monster mice*
Heathers, Anne. *The thread soldiers*
Henkes, Kevin. *Chester's way*
Sheila Rae, the brave
A weekend with Wendell
Hewett, Joan. *The mouse and the elephant*
Hillman, Priscilla. *A Merry-Mouse book of favorite poems*
A Merry-Mouse book of months
A Merry-Mouse Christmas A B C
The Merry-Mouse schoolhouse
Himmelman, John. *Montigue on the high seas*

Hoban, Lillian. *It's really Christmas*
  The sugar snow spring
Hoban, Russell. *Charlie Meadows*
  Flat cat
Hoff, Carol. *The four friends*
Hoff, Syd. *Mrs. Brice's mice*
Hoffmann, E. T. A. *The nutcracker*, ill. by
  Rachel Isadora
  The nutcracker, ill. by Maurice Sendak
  The nutcracker, ill. by Lisbeth Zwerger
Holabird, Katharine. *Angelina and Alice*
  Angelina and the princess
  Angelina at the fair
  Angelina ballerina
  Angelina on stage
  The little mouse ABC
Holl, Adelaide. *A mouse story*
Hopkins, Margaret. *Sleepytime for baby
  mouse*
Houghton, Eric. *The mouse and the
  magician*
House mouse
Houston, John A. *A mouse in my house*
Howard, Jean G. *Of mice and mice*
Hurd, Edith Thacher. *Come and have fun*
Hurd, Thacher. *The pea patch jig*
Hurford, John. *The dormouse*
Hürlimann, Ruth. *The mouse with the daisy
  hat*
Ivimey, John William. *The complete story of
  the three blind mice*, ill. by Paul Galdone
  The complete version of ye three blind mice
Joerns, Consuelo. *The foggy rescue*
  The lost and found house
  The midnight castle
Keenan, Martha. *The mannerly adventures
  of Little Mouse*
Kellogg, Steven. *The island of the skog*
Koenig, Marion. *The tale of fancy Nancy*
Kraus, Robert. *Another mouse to feed*
  Come out and play, little mouse
  I, Mouse
  Where are you going, little mouse?
  Whose mouse are you?
Kumin, Maxine. *Joey and the birthday
  present*
Kuskin, Karla. *What did you bring me?*
Kwitz, Mary DeBall. *Mouse at home*
Layton, Aviva. *The squeakers*
Lexau, Joan M. *The dog food caper*
Linch, Elizabeth Johanna. *Samson*
Lionni, Leo. *Alexander and the wind-up
  mouse*
  Colors to talk about
  Frederick
  Geraldine, the music mouse
  The greentail mouse
  In the rabbitgarden
  Letters to talk about
  Mouse days
  Nicholas, where have you been?

Numbers to talk about
Theodore and the talking mushroom
Tillie and the wall
What?
When?
Where?
Who?
Words to talk about
Little, Mary E. *Ricardo and the puppets*
Lobel, Arnold. *Martha, the movie mouse*
  Mouse soup
  Mouse tales
  The rose in my garden
Low, Joseph. *The Christmas grump*
  Mice twice
McCully, Emily Arnold. *The Christmas gift*
  First snow
  New baby
  Picnic
  School
McKissack, Patricia C. *Country mouse and
  city mouse*, ill. by Anne Sikorski
McNulty, Faith. *Mouse and Tim*
Majewski, Joe. *A friend for Oscar Mouse*
Mandry, Kathy. *The cat and the mouse and
  the mouse and the cat*
Manushkin, Fran. *Moon dragon*
Martin, Jacqueline Briggs. *Bizzy Bones and
  Moosemouse*
  Bizzy Bones and the lost quilt
  Bizzy Bones and Uncle Ezra
Mayer, Marianna. *Alley oop!*
Mayne, William. *Mousewing*
Mendoza, George. *Henri Mouse*
  Henri Mouse, the juggler
  Need a house? Call Ms. Mouse
Miles, Miska. *Mouse six and the happy
  birthday*
Miller, Alice P. *The mouse family's blueberry
  pie*
Miller, Edna. *Mousekin finds a friend*
  Mousekin takes a trip
  Mousekin's ABC
  Mousekin's Christmas eve
  Mousekin's close call
  Mousekin's Easter basket
  Mousekin's fables
  Mousekin's family
  Mousekin's golden house
  Mousekin's mystery
  Mousekin's Thanksgiving
Miller, Moira. *Oscar Mouse finds a home*
  The proverbial mouse
Moore, Inga. *The vegetable thieves*
Morimoto, Junko. *Mouse's marriage*
Morris, Ann. *Eleanora Mousie catches a
  cold*
  Eleanora Mousie in the dark
  Eleanora Mousie makes a mess
  Eleanora Mousie's gray day
Mouse house

Numeroff, Laura Joffe. *If you give a mouse a cookie*
Oakley, Graham. *The church cat abroad*
  The church mice adrift
  The church mice and the moon
  The church mice at bay
  The church mice at Christmas
  The church mice in action
  The church mice spread their wings
  The church mouse
  The diary of a church mouse
Oechsli, Kelly. *Mice at bat*
Ormondroyd, Edward. *Broderick*
Ostheeren, Ingrid. *Jonathan Mouse*
Peppé, Rodney. *Cat and mouse*
  The kettleship pirates
  The mice and the clockwork bus
  The mice and the flying basket
  The mice who lived in a shoe
Piers, Helen. *The mouse book*
Polushkin, Maria. *Mother, Mother, I want another*
Potter, Beatrix. *The tailor of Gloucester*
  The tale of Johnny Town-Mouse
  The tale of Mrs. Tittlemouse
  The tale of Mrs. Tittlemouse and other mouse stories
  The tale of two bad mice
  The two bad mice pop-up book
Potter, Russell. *The little red ferry boat*
Pryor, Bonnie. *The porcupine mouse*
Quackenbush, Robert M. *Chuck lends a paw*
Roach, Marilynne K. *Two Roman mice*
Roche, P. K. (Patrick K.). *Good-bye, Arnold!*
  Webster and Arnold go camping
Ross, Tony. *Hugo and Oddsock*
  Hugo and the bureau of holidays
  Hugo and the man who stole colors
Schermer, Judith. *Mouse in house*
Schlein, Miriam. *Home, the tale of a mouse*
Schoenherr, John. *The barn*
Scruton, Clive. *Bubble and squeak*
Seidler, Rosalie. *Grumpus and the Venetian cat*
Seignobosc, Françoise. *Small-Trot*
Selden, George. *The mice, the monks and the Christmas tree*
Silverman, Maida. *Mouse's shape book*
Simon, Sidney B. *Henry, the uncatchable mouse*
Slate, Joseph. *Who is coming to our house?*
Smith, Jim. *The frog band and Durrington Dormouse*
Smith, Wendy. *The lonely, only mouse*
Stanley, Diane. *The conversation club*
Steig, William. *Abel's Island*
  Doctor De Soto
Stein, Sara Bonnett. *Mouse*
Steptoe, John. *The story of jumping mouse*

Stevens, Harry. *Fat mouse*
Stevenson, James. *The Sea View Hotel*
Stoddard, Sandol. *Bedtime mouse*
Stone, Bernard. *The charge of the mouse brigade*
  Emergency mouse
Sumiko. *Kittymouse*
Szekeres, Cyndy. *Cyndy Szekeres' counting book, 1 to 10*
Taylor, Judy. *Dudley and the monster*
  Dudley and the strawberry shake
  Dudley goes flying
  Dudley in a jam
Titus, Eve. *Anatole*
  Anatole and the cat
  Anatole and the piano
  Anatole and the Pied Piper
  Anatole and the poodle
  Anatole and the robot
  Anatole and the thirty thieves
  Anatole and the toyshop
  Anatole in Italy
  Anatole over Paris
Tsultim, Yeshe. *The mouse king*
Türk, Hanne. *Goodnight Max*
  Happy birthday Max
  Max packs
  Max the artlover
  Max versus the cube
  Merry Christmas Max
  Rainy day Max
  Raking leaves with Max
  The rope skips Max
  Snapshot Max
  A surprise for Max
Udry, Janice May. *Thump and Plunk*
Vincent, Gabrielle. *Bravo, Ernest and Celestine!*
  Breakfast time, Ernest and Celestine
  Ernest and Celestine
  Ernest and Celestine's patchwork quilt
  Ernest and Celestine's picnic
  Merry Christmas, Ernest and Celestine
  Smile, Ernest and Celestine
  Where are you, Ernest and Celestine?
Vinson, Pauline. *Willie goes to the seashore*
Vreeken, Elizabeth. *Henry*
Waber, Bernard. *Mice on my mind*
Wahl, Jan. *Old Hippo's Easter egg*
  Pleasant Fieldmouse
  The Pleasant Fieldmouse storybook
  Pleasant Fieldmouse's Halloween party
Walsh, Ellen Stoll. *Mouse paint*
Watson, Clyde. *How Brown Mouse kept Christmas*
Wells, Rosemary. *Noisy Nora*
  Shy Charles
  Stanley and Rhoda
Wenning, Elisabeth. *The Christmas mouse*
Wilson, Ron. *Mice*

Wooding, Sharon L. *Arthur's Christmas wish*

Wright, Josephine Lord. *Cotton Cat and Martha Mouse*

Yamashita, Haruo. *Mice at the beach*

Yeoman, John. *Mouse trouble*

Yolen, Jane. *Mice on ice*

Young, Miriam Burt. *The sugar mouse cake*

Zelinsky, Paul O. *The maid and the mouse and the odd-shaped house*

Ziefert, Harriet. *A clean house for Mole and Mouse*
Let's go! Piggety Pig
A new house for Mole and Mouse
No more! Piggety Pig

Animals – minks

Holder, Heidi. *Crows*

Animals – moles

Carter, Anne. *Molly in danger*

Firmin, Peter. *Basil Brush and a dragon*
Basil Brush and the windmills
Basil Brush finds treasure
Basil Brush gets a medal
Basil Brush goes flying

Himmelman, John. *Montigue on the high seas*

Hoban, Lillian. *Silly Tilly and the Easter bunny*

Hoban, Russell. *The mole family's Christmas*

Johnston, Tony. *Mole and Troll trim the tree*

Murschetz, Luis. *Mister Mole*

Obrist, Jürg. *They do things right in Albern*

Quackenbush, Robert M. *Detective Mole*
Detective Mole and the haunted castle mystery
Detective Mole and the secret clues
Detective Mole and the Tip-Top mystery

Takihara, Koji. *Rolli*

Walt Disney Productions. *Walt Disney's The adventures of Mr. Toad*

Ziefert, Harriet. *A clean house for Mole and Mouse*
A new house for Mole and Mouse

Animals – mongooses

Carlson, Natalie Savage. *Marie Louise and Christophe at the carnival*
Marie Louise's heyday
Runaway Marie Louise

Animals – monkeys

Bannerman, Helen. *The story of the teasing monkey*

Browne, Anthony. *Willy the wimp*

Brunhoff, Jean de. *Babar and Zephir*

Brunhoff, Laurent de. *Babar the magician*

Bulette, Sara. *The splendid belt of Mr. Big*

Bunting, Eve. *Monkey in the middle*

Curious George and the dump truck

Curious George and the pizza

Curious George at the fire station

Curious George goes hiking

Curious George goes sledding

Curious George goes to the aquarium

Curious George goes to the circus

Curious George visits the zoo

Drescher, Henrik. *The yellow umbrella*

Elkin, Benjamin. *Such is the way of the world*

Galdone, Paul. *The monkey and the crocodile*

Gelman, Rita Golden. *Professor Coconut and the thief*

Goodall, John S. *Jacko*

Guy, Rosa. *Mother crocodile*

Hoban, Lillian. *Arthur's Christmas cookies*
Arthur's funny money
Arthur's honey bear
Arthur's pen pal
Arthur's prize reader

Hoffman, Mary. *Animals in the wild*

Horio, Seishi. *The monkey and the crab*

Hurd, Edith Thacher. *Last one home is a green pig*
The mother chimpanzee

Irvine, Georgeanne. *Bo the orangutan*

Iwamura, Kazuo. *Tan Tan's hat*
Tan Tan's suspenders

Kaye, Geraldine. *The sea monkey*

Kepes, Juliet. *Five little monkeys*
Run little monkeys, run, run, run

Knight, Hilary. *Where's Wallace?*

Komoda, Beverly. *Simon's soup*

McKissack, Patricia C. *Who is coming?*

Mathiesen, Egon. *Oswald, the monkey*

Meshover, Leonard. *The monkey that went to school*

Moore, Inga. *Fifty red night-caps*

Olds, Helen Diehl. *Miss Hattie and the monkey*

Oxenbury, Helen. *Tom and Pippo go shopping*
Tom and Pippo in the garden
Tom and Pippo see the moon
Tom and Pippo's day

Parish, Peggy. *Jumper goes to school*

Piers, Helen. *A Helen Piers animal book*

Preston, Edna Mitchell. *Monkey in the jungle*

Reitveld, Jane Klatt. *Monkey island*

Rey, Hans Augusto. *Cecily G and the nine monkeys*
Curious George
Curious George gets a medal
Curious George learns the alphabet
Curious George rides a bike
Curious George takes a job

Rey, Margaret Elisabeth Waldstein.
   Curious George flies a kite
   Curious George goes to the hospital
Rockwell, Anne F. *The stolen necklace*
Schubert, Dieter. *Where's my monkey?*
Selsam, Millicent E. *A first look at monkeys*
Shi, Zhang Xiu. *Monkey and the white bone demon*
Slobodkina, Esphyr. *Caps for sale*
Standiford, Natalie. *The best little monkeys in the world*
Suba, Susanne. *The monkeys and the pedlar*
Teleki, Geza. *Aerial apes*
Thaler, Mike. *Moonkey*
Whitehead, Patricia. *Monkeys*
Williamson, Hamilton. *Monkey tale*
Wolkstein, Diane. *The cool ride in the sky*

Animals – moose

Alexander, Martha G. *Even that moose won't listen to me*
Brown, Marc. *Moose and goose*
Foreman, Michael. *Moose*
Freschet, Berniece. *Moose baby*
Hoff, Syd. *Santa's moose*
Latimer, Jim. *Going the moose way home*
McNeer, May Yonge. *My friend Mac*
Marshall, James. *The guest*
Platt, Kin. *Big Max in the mystery of the missing moose*
Seuss, Dr. *Thidwick, the big-hearted moose*
Slobodkin, Louis. *Melvin, the moose child*
Wiseman, Bernard. *Morris and Boris at the circus*
   Morris has a birthday party!

Animals – mules

Beatty, Hetty Burlingame. *Droopy*
Sharmat, Marjorie Weinman. *Hooray for Father's Day!*
Snyder, Anne. *The old man and the mule*
Zemach, Margot. *Jake and Honeybunch go to heaven*

Animals – muskrats

Hoban, Russell. *Harvey's hideout*

Animals – octopuses see Octopuses

Animals – otters

Allen, Laura Jean. *Ottie and the star*
Benchley, Nathaniel. *Oscar Otter*
Burdick, Margaret. *Bobby Otter and the blue boat*
Hall, Derek. *Otter swims*
Harshman, Terry Webb. *Porcupine's pajama party*
Hoban, Russell. *Emmet Otter's jug-band Christmas*

Shaw, Evelyn S. *Sea otters*
Sheehan, Angela. *The otter*
Tompert, Ann. *Little Otter remembers and other stories*
Wisbeski, Dorothy Gross. *Pícaro, a pet otter*

Animals – pack rats

Miller, Edna. *Pebbles, a pack rat*
Quackenbush, Robert M. *Pete Pack Rat*
Van Horn, William. *Harry Hoyle's giant jumping bean*

Animals – pandas

Bonners, Susan. *Panda*
Foreman, Michael. *Panda and the bushfire*
Greaves, Margaret. *Once there were no pandas*
Grosvenor, Donna. *Pandas*
Hall, Derek. *Panda climbs*
Hoban, Tana. *Panda, panda*
Hoffman, Mary. *Animals in the wild*
Jensen, Helen Zane. *When Panda came to our house*
Maestro, Betsy. *The pandas take a vacation*
Pluckrose, Henry. *Bears*
Rigby, Shirley Lincoln. *Smaller than most*

Animals – pigs

Alexander, Lloyd. *Coll and his white pig*
Allard, Harry. *There's a party at Mona's tonight*
Anholt, Catherine. *Truffles in trouble*
   Truffles is sick
Augarde, Steve. *Pig*
Aylesworth, Jim. *Hanna's hog*
Baldner, Gaby. *Joba and the wild boar*
Berson, Harold. *Truffles for lunch*
Bishop, Claire Huchet. *The truffle pig*
Blegvad, Lenore. *This little pig-a-wig and other rhymes about pigs*
Bloom, Suzanne. *We keep a pig in the parlor*
Bond, Felicia. *Mary Betty Lizzie McNutt's birthday*
   Poinsettia and her family
   Poinsettia and the firefighters
Boynton, Sandra. *Hester in the wild*
Brand, Millen. *This little pig named Curly*
Brock, Emma Lillian. *Pig with a front porch*
Brown, Judith Gwyn. *Max and the truffle pig*
Brown, Marc. *Perfect pigs*
Browne, Anthony. *Piggybook*
Bruna, Dick. *Poppy Pig goes to market*
Brunhoff, Laurent de. *The one pig with horns*
Calhoun, Mary. *The witch's pig*

Calmenson, Stephanie. *Never take a pig to lunch and other funny poems about animals*

Carlson, Nancy. *The mysterious Valentine*
The perfect family
Witch lady

Chorao, Kay. *Oink and Pearl*
Ups and downs with Oink and Pearl

Cole, Brock. *Nothing but a pig*

Coontz, Otto. *Starring Rosa*

Corbalis, Judy. *Porcellus, the flying pig*

Craig, Helen. *The night of the paper bag monsters*
Susie and Alfred in the knight, the princess and the dragon
A welcome for Annie

Cushman, Doug. *Once upon a pig*

Dubanevich, Arlene. *Pig William*
The piggest show on earth
Pigs at Christmas
Pigs in hiding

Dunrea, Olivier. *Eddy B, pigboy*

Dyke, John. *Pigwig*
Pigwig and the pirates

Ernst, Lisa Campbell. *The prize pig surprise*

Erskine, Jim. *Bert and Susie's messy tale*

Fremlin, Robert. *Three friends*

Gackenbach, Dick. *Harvey, the foolish pig*
Hurray for Hattie Rabbit!
The pig who saw everything

Galdone, Paul. *The amazing pig*

Geisert, Arthur. *Pa's balloon and other pig tales*
Pigs from A to Z

Getz, Arthur. *Humphrey, the dancing pig*

Goodall, John S. *The adventures of Paddy Pork*
The ballooning adventures of Paddy Pork
Paddy goes traveling
Paddy Pork odd jobs
Paddy Pork's holiday
Paddy to the rescue
Paddy under water
Paddy's evening out
Paddy's new hat

Gretz, Susanna. *It's your turn, Roger*
Roger loses his marbles!
Roger takes charge!

Hale, Irina. *Chocolate mouse and sugar pig*

Hauptmann, Tatjana. *A day in the life of Petronella Pig*

Hawkins, Colin. *Mig the pig*
This little pig

Heine, Helme. *The pigs' wedding*

Hewitt, Kathryn. *The three sillies*

Hoban, Lillian. *Mr. Pig and family*
Mr. Pig and Sonny too

Hoff, Syd. *Happy birthday, Henrietta!*

Hofstrand, Mary. *Albion pig*
Home before midnight

Inkpen, Mick. *If I had a pig*

Jennings, Linda M. *Crispin and the dancing piglet*

Jeschke, Susan. *Perfect the pig*

Johnston, Tony. *Farmer Mack measures his pig*

Kasza, Keiko. *The pigs' picnic*

Keller, Holly. *Geraldine's big snow*
Geraldine's blanket

Kent, Jack. *Piggy Bank Gonzalez*

Korth-Sander, Irmtraut. *Will you be my friend?*

Kroll, Steven. *Pigs in the house*

Laird, Donivee Martin. *The three little Hawaiian pigs and the magic shark*

Lawrence, John. *Rabbit and pork*

Levine, Abby. *You push, I ride*

Lobel, Arnold. *The book of pigericks*
Small pig
A treeful of pigs

Lorenz, Lee. *A weekend in the country*

McClenathan, Louise. *The Easter pig*

McPhail, David. *Pig Pig and the magic photo album*
Pig Pig goes to camp
Pig Pig grows up
Pig Pig rides

Maestro, Betsy. *The guessing game*

Marshall, James. *Portly McSwine*
Yummers!
Yummers too

Mathews, Louise. *The great take-away*

Miles, Miska. *This little pig*

Moon, Cliff. *Pigs on the farm*

Moore, Inga. *The truffle hunter*

Mother Goose. *This little pig*, ill. by Leonard Lubin
This little pig went to market, ill. by L. Leslie Brooke

Newton, Patricia Montgomery. *Vacation surprise*

Oxenbury, Helen. *Pig tale*

Patterson, Geoffrey. *A pig's tale*

Peck, Robert Newton. *Hamilton*

Peet, Bill. *Chester the worldly pig*

Pomerantz, Charlotte. *The piggy in the puddle*

Potter, Beatrix. *The tale of Little Pig Robinson*
The tale of Pigling Bland

Pryor, Bonnie. *Amanda and April*

Rayner, Mary. *Garth Pig and the ice cream lady*
Mr. and Mrs. Pig's evening out
Mrs. Pig gets cross
Mrs. Pig's bulk buy

Ross, Tony. *The enchanted pig*

Scarry, Richard. *Pig Will and Pig Won't*
Richard Scarry's Peasant Pig and the terrible dragon

Schaffer, Libor. *Arthur sets sail*

Schwartz, Mary. *Spiffen*

Scruton, Clive. *Pig in the air*
Sharmat, Mitchell. *The seven sloppy days of Phineas Pig*
Shecter, Ben. *Partouche plants a seed*
Slate, Joseph. *The mean, clean, giant canoe machine*
Steig, William. *The amazing bone*
Farmer Palmer's wagon ride
Roland, the minstrel pig
Stepto, Michele. *Snuggle Piggy and the magic blanket*
Stevens, Carla. *Hooray for pig!*
Pig and the blue flag
Stobbs, William. *This little piggy*
Stolz, Mary Slattery. *Emmett's pig*
The three little pigs. *The story of the three little pigs*, ill. by L. Leslie Brooke
The story of the three little pigs, ill. by William Stobbs
The three little pigs, facsimile ed.
The three little pigs, ill. by Erik Blegvad
The three little pigs, ill. by Caroline Bucknall
The three little pigs, ill. by Lorinda Bryan Cauley
The three little pigs, ill. by William Pène Du Bois
The three little pigs, ill. by Paul Galdone
The three little pigs, ill. by Rodney Peppé
The three little pigs, ill. by Edda Reinl
The three little pigs, ill. by John Wallner
The three little pigs, ill. by Irma Wilde
The three little pigs, ill. by Margot Zemach
The three pigs, ill. by Tony Ross
Tripp, Wallace. *The tale of a pig*
Tyler, Linda Wagner. *The sick-in-bed birthday book*
Ungerer, Tomi. *Christmas eve at the Mellops*
The Mellops go diving for treasure
The Mellops go flying
The Mellops go spelunking
The Mellops strike oil
Van der Meer, Ron. *Pigs at home*
Van Leeuwen, Jean. *Amanda Pig and her big brother Oliver*
More tales of Amanda Pig
More tales of Oliver Pig
Oliver, Amanda and Grandmother
Tales of Amanda Pig
Tales of Oliver Pig
Vernon, Tannis. *Little Pig and the blue-green sea*
Wabbes, Marie. *Rose is hungry*
Rose is muddy
Rose's bath
Rose's picture
Waechter, Friedrich Karl. *Three is company*
Walker, Barbara K. *Pigs and pirates*
Watson, Pauline. *Wriggles, the little wishing pig*

Weiss, Ellen. *Pigs in space*
West, Ian. *Silas, the first pig to fly*
Weston, Martha. *Peony's rainbow*
Wheeler, Cindy. *Rose*
Wild, Robin. *Little Pig and the big bad wolf*
Wilhelm, Hans. *Oh, what a mess*
Winthrop, Elizabeth. *Sloppy kisses*
Wiseman, Bernard. *Don't make fun!*
Wondriska, William. *Mr. Brown and Mr. Gray*
Wood, Audrey. *Three sisters*
Yeoman, John. *The bear's water picnic*
Yolen, Jane. *Picnic with Piggins*
Piggins
Zakhoder, Boris Vladimirovich. *How a piglet crashed the Christmas party*
Zalben, Jane Breskin. *Basil and Hillary*
Ziefert, Harriet. *Let's go! Piggety Pig*
No more! Piggety Pig
Piggety Pig from morn 'til night

Animals – polar bears

Alborough, Jez. *Bare bear*
Running Bear
Dasent, George W. *East o' the sun, west o' the moon*
De Beer, Hans. *Ahoy there, little polar bear*
Little polar bear
Duvoisin, Roger Antoine. *Snowy and Woody*
Hall, Derek. *Polar bear leaps*
Harlow, Joan Hiatt. *Shadow bear*
Heller, Ruth. *How to hide a polar bear*
Lilly, Kenneth. *Animals of the ocean*
Pluckrose, Henry. *Bears*
Rose, Gerald. *PB takes a holiday*
Ylla. *Polar bear brothers*

Animals – porcupines

Annett, Cora. *When the porcupine moved in*
Carrick, Carol. *Ben and the porcupine*
Christian, Mary Blount. *Penrod again*
Penrod's pants
Harshman, Terry Webb. *Porcupine's pajama party*
Lester, Helen. *A porcupine named Fluffy*
Massie, Diane Redfield. *Tiny pin*
Pfister, Marcus. *Where is my friend?*
The porcupine
Scarry, Patsy. *Little Richard and Prickles*
Schlein, Miriam. *Lucky porcupine!*
Stren, Patti. *Hug me*
Weiner, Beth Lee. *Benjamin's perfect solution*

Animals – possums

Berson, Harold. *Henry Possum*
Burch, Robert. *Joey's cat*

Carlson, Natalie Savage. *Marie Louise's heyday*
Conford, Ellen. *Eugene the brave*
Impossible, possum
Just the thing for Geraldine
Degen, Bruce. *Aunt Possum and the pumpkin man*
Fox, Mem. *Possum magic*
Freschet, Berniece. *Possum baby*
Hoban, Russell. *Nothing to do*
Hurd, Thacher. *Mama don't allow*
Keller, Holly. *Henry's Fourth of July*
Taylor, Mark. *Old Blue, you good dog you*
Tether, Graham. *Skunk and possum*
Weiner, Beth Lee. *Benjamin's perfect solution*
Winthrop, Elizabeth. *Potbellied possums*

Animals – prairie dogs

Baylor, Byrd. *Amigo*
Casey, Denise. *The friendly prairie dog*
Luttrell, Ida. *Lonesome Lester*

Animals – rabbits

Adams, Adrienne. *The Christmas party*
The Easter egg artists
The great Valentine's Day balloon race
Adler, David A. *Bunny rabbit rebus*
Æsop. *The hare and the frogs*
The hare and the tortoise, ill. by Paul Galdone
The hare and the tortoise, ill. by Gerald Rose
The hare and the tortoise, ill. by Peter Weevers
The tortoise and the hare, ill. by Janet Stevens
Alexander, Martha G. *The magic hat*
Anderson, Lonzo. *Two hundred rabbits*
Annett, Cora. *When the porcupine moved in*
Baby's first book of colors
Balian, Lorna. *Humbug rabbit*
Barrett, John M. *The Easter bear*
Bartoli, Jennifer. *In a meadow, two hares hide*
Barton, Byron. *Jack and Fred*
Bate, Lucy. *Little rabbit's loose tooth*
Baumann, Hans. *The hare's race*
Becker, John Leonard. *Seven little rabbits*
Benjamin, Alan. *Busy bunnies*
Berson, Harold. *Pop! goes the turnip*
Bianco, Margery Williams. *The velveteen rabbit*, ill. by Allen Atkinson
The velveteen rabbit, ill. by Michael Green
The velveteen rabbit, ill. by Michael Hague
The velveteen rabbit, ill. by David Jorgensen
The velveteen rabbit, ill. by William Nicholson
The velveteen rabbit, ill. by Ilse Plume

The velveteen rabbit, ill. by S. D. Schindler
The velveteen rabbit, ill. by Tien
Bolliger, Max. *The rabbit with the sky blue ears*
Bornstein, Ruth Lercher. *Indian bunny*
Bowden, Joan Chase. *Bouncy baby bunny finds his bed*
Little grey rabbit
Bright, Robert. *My hopping bunny*
Brown, Marc. *The bionic bunny show*
What do you call a dumb bunny? and other rabbit riddles, games, jokes and cartoons
Brown, Marcia. *The neighbors*
Brown, Margaret Wise. *The golden egg book*
Goodnight moon
Little chicken
The runaway bunny
Bruna, Dick. *Miffy*
Miffy at the beach
Miffy at the playground
Miffy at the seaside
Miffy at the zoo
Miffy goes to school
Miffy in the hospital
Miffy in the snow
Miffy's bicycle
Miffy's dream
Brunhoff, Laurent de. *Gregory and Lady Turtle in the valley of the music trees*
Caldwell, Mary. *Morning, rabbit, morning*
Carlson, Nancy. *Bunnies and their hobbies*
Bunnies and their sports
Loudmouth George and the big race
Loudmouth George and the cornet
Loudmouth George and the fishing trip
Loudmouth George and the new neighbors
Loudmouth George and the sixth-grade bully
Carrick, Carol. *A rabbit for Easter*
Carroll, Ruth. *What Whiskers did*
Where's the bunny?
Carter, Anne. *Bella's secret garden*
Cazet, Denys. *Big shoe, little shoe*
Christmas moon
December 24th
You make the angels cry
Chalmers, Mary. *Come for a walk with me*
Kevin
Chandoha, Walter. *A baby bunny for you*
Christelow, Eileen. *Henry and the Dragon*
Henry and the red stripes
Claret, Maria. *The chocolate rabbit*
Cleveland, David. *The April rabbits*
Coatsworth, Elizabeth. *Pika and the roses*
Coldrey, Jennifer. *The world of rabbits*
Cosgrove, Stephen. *Sleepy time bunny*
Cross, Genevieve. *My bunny book*
Darling, Kathy. *The Easter bunny's secret*
DeLage, Ida. *ABC Easter bunny*
Am I a bunny?

Delton, Judy. *Brimhall turns detective*
  Brimhall turns to magic
  Rabbit goes to night school
  Three friends find spring
Demi. *Fleecy bunny*
Dennis, Lynne. *Raymond Rabbit's early morning*
De Paola, Tomie. *Too many Hopkins*
Dorsky, Blanche. *Harry, a true story*
Du Bois, William Pène. *The hare and the tortoise and the tortoise and the hare*
Dunn, Judy. *The little rabbit*
Dutton, Sandra. *The cinnamon hen's autumn day*
Ehrlich, Amy. *Bunnies all day long*
  Bunnies and their grandma
  Bunnies at Christmastime
  Bunnies on their own
Fatio, Louise. *The happy lion's rabbits*
Fisher, Aileen. *Listen, rabbit*
  Rabbits, rabbits
Flory, Jane. *The bear on the doorstep*
Friskey, Margaret. *Mystery of the gate sign*
Gackenbach, Dick. *Hattie be quiet, Hattie be good*
  Hattie rabbit
  Hurray for Hattie Rabbit!
  Mother Rabbit's son Tom
Gág, Wanda. *ABC bunny*
Galdone, Paul. *A strange servant*
Gay, Michel. *Rabbit express*
Gay, Zhenya. *Small one*
Geringer, Laura. *Molly's new washing machine*
Ginsburg, Mirra. *The fox and the hare*
Gordon, Sharon. *Easter Bunny's lost egg*
Greene, Carol. *The insignificant elephant*
Hands, Hargrave. *Bunny sees*
Heine, Helme. *Superhare*
Henkes, Kevin. *Bailey goes camping*
Henrie, Fiona. *Rabbits*
Hess, Lilo. *Rabbits in the meadow*
Heyward, Du Bose. *The country bunny and the little gold shoes*
Hoban, Lillian. *Harry's song*
Hoban, Tana. *Where is it?*
Hogrogian, Nonny. *Carrot cake*
Hooks, William H. *Three rounds with rabbit*
Hynard, Stephen. *Snowy the rabbit*
Jabar, Cynthia. *Party day!*
Jameson, Cynthia. *A day with Whisker Wickles*
Jaquith, Priscilla. *Bo Rabbit smart for true*
Jewell, Nancy. *The snuggle bunny*
Johnston, Mary Anne. *Sing me a song*
Kahl, Virginia. *The habits of rabbits*
Keller, Holly. *Cromwell's glasses*
Keller, Irene. *Benjamin Rabbit and the stranger danger*
Kelley, True. *A valentine for Fuzzboom*

Kirn, Ann. *The tale of a crocodile*
Kraus, Robert. *Big brother*
  Daddy Long Ears
  Good night Richard Rabbit
  The littlest rabbit
Kroll, Steven. *The big bunny and the Easter eggs*
  The big bunny and the magic show
Kuratomi, Chizuko. *Mr. Bear and the robbers*
Kwitz, Mary DeBall. *Rabbits' search for a little house*
La Fontaine, Jean de. *The hare and the tortoise*
Lawrence, John. *Rabbit and pork*
Leach, Michael. *Rabbits*
Leedy, Loreen. *The bunny play*
Le Tord, Bijou. *Rabbit seeds*
Lifton, Betty Jean. *The rice-cake rabbit*
Lionni, Leo. *Let's make rabbits*
Lipkind, William. *The Christmas bunny*
Littlefield, William. *The whiskers of Ho Ho*
Lorian, Nicole. *A birthday present for Mama*
McCormack, John E. *Rabbit tales*
  Rabbit travels
McLenighan, Valjean. *Turtle and rabbit*
McNaughton, Colin. *Walk rabbit walk*
Manushkin, Fran. *Little rabbit's baby brother*
Mariana. *Miss Flora McFlimsey's Easter bonnet*
Maril, Lee. *Mr. Bunny paints the eggs*
Martin, Rafe. *Foolish rabbit's big mistake*
Mathews, Louise. *Bunches and bunches of bunnies*
Mayne, William. *Come, come to my corner*
Meroux, Felix. *The prince of the rabbits*
Michels, Tilde. *Rabbit spring*
Miles, Miska. *Rabbit garden*
  Small rabbit
Miller, J. P. (John Parr). *Good night, little rabbit*
  Learn to count with Little Rabbit
Milne, A. A. (Alan Alexander). *Prince Rabbit*
Moremen, Grace E. *No, no, Natalie*
Newberry, Clare Turlay. *Marshmallow*
Nilsson, Ulf. *Little sister rabbit*
Parish, Peggy. *Too many rabbits*
Parry, Marian. *King of the fish*
Peet, Bill. *Huge Harold*
Peters, Sharon. *Ready, get set, go!*
  Stop that rabbit
Potter, Beatrix. *The complete adventures of Peter Rabbit*
  Peter Rabbit's one two three
  The story of fierce bad rabbit
  The tale of Benjamin Bunny
  The tale of Mr. Tod
  The tale of Peter Rabbit, ill. by Margot Apple

The tale of Peter Rabbit, ill. by Beatrix Potter
The tale of the Flopsy Bunnies
Where's Peter Rabbit?
The pudgy bunny book
Quackenbush, Robert M. *Detective Mole and the haunted castle mystery*
First grade jitters
Funny bunnies
Rey, Margaret Elisabeth Waldstein. *Spotty*
Roberts, Bethany. *Waiting for spring stories*
Sadler, Marilyn. *It's not easy being a bunny*
Scarry, Patsy. *Little Richard and Prickles*
Patsy Scarry's big bedtime storybook
Scarry, Richard. *The adventures of Tinker and Tanker*
Schlein, Miriam. *Little Rabbit, the high jumper*
Schweninger, Ann. *Birthday wishes*
Christmas secrets
Halloween surprises
The hunt for rabbit's galosh
Off to school!
Valentine friends
Seuss, Dr. *The eye book*
Sharmat, Marjorie Weinman. *Thornton, the worrier*
Silverman, Maida. *Bunny's ABC*
Solotareff, Grégoire. *Don't call me little bunny*
Spier, Peter. *Little rabbits*
Steig, William. *Solomon the rusty nail*
Steiner, Charlotte. *My bunny feels soft*
Steiner, Jörg. *Rabbit Island*
Stevenson, James. *Monty*
Stevenson, Suçie. *Christmas eve*
Do I have to take Violet?
Tafuri, Nancy. *Rabbit's morning*
Tarrant, Graham. *Rabbits*
Tompert, Ann. *Nothing sticks like a shadow*
Tresselt, Alvin R. *Rabbit story*
Trez, Denise. *Rabbit country*
Tripp, Wallace. *My Uncle Podger*
Troughton, Joanna. *How rabbit stole the fire*
Van Woerkom, Dorothy. *Harry and Shelburt*
Velthuijs, Max. *Little Man to the rescue*
Wabbes, Marie. *Good night, Little Rabbit*
Happy birthday, Little Rabbit
It's snowing, Little Rabbit
Little Rabbit's garden
Wahl, Jan. *Carrot nose*
Doctor Rabbit's foundling
The five in the forest
Rabbits on roller skates!
Watson, Wendy. *The bunnies' Christmas eve*
Lollipop
Wayland, April Halprin. *To Rabbittown*
Weil, Lisl. *The candy egg bunny*

Weisgard, Leonard. *The funny bunny factory*
Wells, Rosemary. *Hooray for Max*
Max's bath
Max's bedtime
Max's birthday
Max's breakfast
Max's Christmas
Max's first word
Max's new suit
Max's ride
Max's toys
Wiese, Kurt. *Happy Easter*
Wilhelm, Hans. *More bunny trouble*
Williams, Garth. *The rabbits' wedding*
Wolf, Ann. *The rabbit and the turtle*
Wolf, Winfried. *The Easter bunny*
Worth, Bonnie. *Peter Cottontail's surprise*
Zakhoder, Boris Vladimirovich. *Rosachok*
Ziefert, Harriet. *Breakfast time!*
Bye-bye, daddy!
Good morning, sun!
Happy birthday, Grandpa!
Happy Easter, Grandma!
Let's get dressed!
Zolotow, Charlotte. *The bunny who found Easter*
Mr. Rabbit and the lovely present

Animals – raccoons

Arnosky, Jim. *Raccoons and ripe corn*
Bradford, Ann. *The mystery at Misty Falls*
The mystery of the missing raccoon
Brown, Margaret Wise. *Wait till the moon is full*
Duvoisin, Roger Antoine. *Petunia, I love you*
Freschet, Berniece. *Five fat raccoons*
Hess, Lilo. *The curious raccoons*
Hoban, Lillian. *The case of the two masked robbers*
Here come raccoons
Johnson, Donna Kay. *Brighteyes*
McPhail, David. *Something special*
Stanley Henry Bear's friend
Miklowitz, Gloria D. *Save that raccoon!*
Miles, Miska. *The raccoon and Mrs. McGinnis*
Moore, Lilian. *Little Raccoon and no trouble at all*
Little Raccoon and the outside world
Little Raccoon and the thing in the pool
Morgan, Allen. *Molly and Mr. Maloney*
Noguere, Suzanne. *Little raccoon*
St. George, Judith. *The Halloween pumpkin smasher*
Steiner, Barbara. *But not Stanleigh*
Thayer, Jane. *The clever raccoon*
Wells, Rosemary. *Timothy goes to school*
Whelan, Gloria. *A week of raccoons*

Animals – rats

Annixter, Jane. *Brown rats, black rats*
Augarde, Steve. *Barnaby Shrew, Black Dan and...the mighty wedgwood*
Barnaby Shrew goes to sea
Bartos-Hoppner, Barbara. *The Pied Piper of Hamelin*, ill. by Annegert Fuchshuber
Baynton, Martin. *Fifty saves his friend*
Bellows, Cathy. *Four fat rats*
Berson, Harold. *The rats who lived in the delicatessen*
Biro, Val. *The pied piper of Hamelin*
Black, Floyd. *Alphabet cat*
Browning, Robert. *The pied piper of Hamelin*, ill. by Kate Greenaway
The pied piper of Hamelin, ill. by Anatoly Ivanov
The pied piper of Hamelin, ill. by Errol Le Cain
Bryan, Ashley. *The cat's purr*
Cressey, James. *Fourteen rats and a rat-catcher*
Cunningham, Julia. *A mouse called Junction*
Doty, Roy. *Old-one-eye meets his match*
Erickson, Russell E. *Warton and the traders*
Hearn, Michael Patrick. *The porcelain cat*
Hoban, Russell. *Flat cat*
Hurd, Thacher. *Mystery on the docks*
Kouts, Anne. *Kenny's rat*
La Fontaine, Jean de. *The lion and the rat*
McNaughton, Colin. *The rat race*
Mayer, Mercer. *The Pied Piper of Hamelin*
Miles, Miska. *Wharf rat*
Moore, Inga. *Aktil's big swim*
Murdocca, Sal. *Tuttle's shell*
Oakley, Graham. *The church mice adrift*
Peppé, Rodney. *The mice and the clockwork bus*
The mice and the flying basket
Pomerantz, Charlotte. *The ballad of the long-tailed rat*
Potter, Beatrix. *The sly old cat*
Ross, Tony. *The pied piper of Hamelin*
Saunders, Susan. *Charles Rat's picnic*
Schiller, Barbara. *The white rat's tale*
Sharmat, Marjorie Weinman. *Mooch the messy*
Stevenson, James. *Wilfred the rat*
Van Woerkom, Dorothy. *The rat, the ox and the zodiac*
Walt Disney Productions. *Walt Disney's The adventures of Mr. Toad*
Yolen, Jane. *Mice on ice*
Zemach, Kaethe. *The beautiful rat*

Animals – reindeer

Cleaver, Elizabeth. *The enchanted caribou*
Haywood, Carolyn. *How the reindeer saved Santa*
Hoff, Syd. *Where's Prancer?*
May, Robert Lewis. *Rudolph the red-nosed reindeer*
Owens, Mary Beth. *A caribou alphabet*

Animals – rhinoceros

Ardizzone, Edward. *Diana and her rhinoceros*
Bush, John. *The cross-with-us rhinoceros*
Cazet, Denys. *Great-Uncle Felix*
Johnson, Louise. *Malunda*
Kipling, Rudyard. *How the rhinoceros got his skin*
Maestro, Giulio. *Just enough Rosie*
Silverstein, Shel. *Who wants a cheap rhinoceros?*
Sis, Peter. *Rainbow Rhino*
Standon, Anna. *The singing rhinoceros*

Animals – sea lions

Hamsa, Bobbie. *Your pet sea lion*
Olds, Elizabeth. *Plop plop ploppie*
Schreiber, Georges. *Bambino the clown*

Animals – seals

Barr, Cathrine. *Sammy seal ov the sircus*
Cooper, Susan. *The Selkie girl*
Duran, Bonté. *The adventures of Arthur and Edmund*
Freeman, Don. *The seal and the slick*
Gerstein, Mordicai. *The seal mother*
Hoff, Syd. *Sammy the seal*
Lilly, Kenneth. *Animals of the ocean*
The seal

Animals – sheep

Alborough, Jez. *The grass is always greener*
Beskow, Elsa Maartman. *Pelle's new suit*
Brown, Margaret Wise. *Little lost lamb*
Coe, Lloyd. *Charcoal*
Demi. *Fleecy lamb*
De Paola, Tomie. *Charlie needs a cloak*
Haircuts for the Woolseys
Dunn, Judy. *The little lamb*
Ernst, Lisa Campbell. *Nattie Parsons' good-luck lamb*
Galdone, Paul. *Little Bo-Peep*
Ginsburg, Mirra. *The strongest one of all*
Hale, Sara Josepha. *Mary had a little lamb*, ill. by Tomie de Paola
Heck, Elisabeth. *The black sheep*
Hedderwick, Mairi. *Katie Morag and the two grandmothers*
Helldorfer, M. C. *Daniel's gift*
Inkpen, Mick. *If I had a sheep*
Ipcar, Dahlov. *The land of flowers*
Kitamura, Satoshi. *When sheep cannot sleep*
Lewis, Robin Baird. *Friska, the sheep that was too small*

MacGregor, Marilyn. *On top*
Mendoza, George. *Alphabet sheep*
  Silly sheep and other sheepish rhymes
Miller, Jane. *Lambing time*
Patent, Dorothy Hinshaw. *Maggie, a sheep dog*
Peet, Bill. *Buford, the little bighorn*
Rogers, Paul. *Sheepchase*
Russell, Betty. *Run sheep run*
Ryder, Joanne. *Beach party*
Shaw, Nancy. *Sheep in a jeep*
Slobodkin, Louis. *Up high and down low*
Snyder, Zilpha Keatley. *The changing maze*
Steiner, Charlotte. *Red Ridinghood's little lamb*
Sundgaard, Arnold. *The lamb and the butterfly*
Wallace, Barbara Brooks. *Argyle*
Weiss, Ellen. *Clara the fortune-telling chicken*
Wild, Jocelyn. *Florence and Eric take the cake*

Animals – shrews

Augarde, Steve. *Barnaby Shrew, Black Dan and...the mighty wedgwood*
  Barnaby Shrew goes to sea
Carrick, Malcolm. *Today is shrew's day*
Goodall, John S. *Shrewbettina's birthday*

Animals – skunks

De Regniers, Beatrice Schenk. *A special birthday party for someone very special*
Hoban, Brom. *Skunk Lane*
Schlein, Miriam. *What's wrong with being a skunk?*
Schoenherr, John. *The barn*
Tether, Graham. *Skunk and possum*

Animals – sloths

Knight, Hilary. *Sylvia the sloth*
Sharmat, Mitchell. *Sherman is a slowpoke*

Animals – snails

Lord, John Vernon. *Mr. Mead and his garden*
Marshall, James. *The guest*
O'Hagan, Caroline. *It's easy to have a snail visit you*
Oleson, Jens. *Snail*
Rockwell, Anne F. *The story snail*
Ryder, Joanne. *Snail in the woods*
  The snail's spell
Stadler, John. *Hooray for snail!*
  Snail saves the day
Ungerer, Tomi. *Snail, where are you?*

Animals – squirrels

Alexander, Sue. *There's more...much more*
Angelo, Valenti. *The acorn tree*
Bassett, Lisa. *Beany and Scamp*
Buff, Mary. *Hurry, Skurry and Flurry*
Carey, Valerie Scho. *Harriet and William and the terrible creature*
Carter, Anne. *Scurry's treasure*
Coldrey, Jennifer. *The world of squirrels*
Crane, Donn. *Flippy and Skippy*
DeLage, Ida. *The squirrel's tree party*
Drummond, Violet H. *Phewtus the squirrel*
Earle, Olive L. *Squirrels in the garden*
Fremlin, Robert. *Three friends*
Jones, Penelope. *I didn't want to be nice*
Lane, Margaret. *The squirrel*
Oxford Scientific Films. *Grey squirrel*
Palazzo, Tony. *Federico, the flying squirrel*
Peet, Bill. *Merle the high flying squirrel*
Potter, Beatrix. *The tale of Squirrel Nutkin*
  The tale of Timmy Tiptoes
Pratten, Albra. *Winkie, the grey squirrel*
St. Tamara. *Chickaree, a red squirrel*
Schumacher, Claire. *Nutty's birthday*
  Nutty's Christmas
Shannon, George. *The surprise*
Sharmat, Marjorie Weinman. *Attila the angry*
  Sophie and Gussie
  The trip
Stage, Mads. *The lonely squirrel*
Stevenson, James. *Wilfred the rat*
Yeoman, John. *The bear's water picnic*
Young, Miriam Burt. *Miss Suzy's Easter surprise*
Zion, Gene. *The meanest squirrel I ever met*
Zweifel, Frances. *Bony*

Animals – tapirs

Maestro, Giulio. *The tortoise's tug of war*

Animals – tigers

Adams, Richard. *The tyger voyage*
Anderson, Paul S. *Red fox and the hungry tiger*
Bannerman, Helen. *The story of little black Sambo*
Barrows, Marjorie Wescott. *Timothy Tiger*
Blaustein, Muriel. *Bedtime, Zachary!*
Canning, Kate. *A painted tale*
Dines, Glen. *A tiger in the cherry tree*
Dodds, Siobhan. *Charles Tiger*
Domanska, Janina. *Why so much noise?*
Farber, Norma. *How to ride a tiger*
Fenner, Carol. *Tigers in the cellar*
Frankel, Bernice. *Half-As-Big and the tiger*
Hall, Derek. *Tiger runs*
Hoban, Russell. *The dancing tigers*
Hoffman, Mary. *Animals in the wild*

Ipcar, Dahlov. *Stripes and spots*
Justice, Jennifer. *The tiger*
Kepes, Juliet. *Cock-a-doodle-doo*
Kraus, Robert. *Leo the late bloomer*
Paul, Anthony. *The tiger who lost his stripes*
Pluckrose, Henry. *Lions and tigers*
Prelutsky, Jack. *The terrible tiger*
Rockwell, Anne F. *Big boss*
Root, Phyllis. *Moon tiger*
Rose, Gerald. *The tiger-skin rug*
Round, Graham. *Hangdog*
Taylor, Mark. *Henry explores the jungle*
Tworkov, Jack. *The camel who took a walk*
Villarejo, Mary. *The tiger hunt*
Wahl, Jan. *Tiger watch*
Wersba, Barbara. *Do tigers ever bite kings?*
Whitney, Alex. *Once a bright red tiger*
    The tiger that barks
Wolkstein, Diane. *The banza*
Wolski, Slawomir. *Tiger cat*

Animals – walruses

Bonsall, Crosby Newell. *What spot?*
Bridges, William. *Ookie, the walrus who likes people*
Hoff, Syd. *Walpole*
Stevenson, James. *Winston, Newton, Elton, and Ed*

Animals – water buffaloes

Gobhai, Mehlli. *Lakshmi, the water buffalo who wouldn't*

Animals – weasels

Bach, Alice. *Warren Weasel's worse than measles*
Holder, Heidi. *Crows*
Lobel, Arnold. *Mouse soup*
Mathews, Louise. *Cluck one*
Zelinsky, Paul O. *The lion and the stoat*

Animals – whales

Applebaum, Neil. *Is there a hole in your head?*
Armour, Richard Willard. *Sea full of whales*
Baumann, Kurt. *The story of Jonah*
Behrens, June. *Whales of the world Whalewatch!*
Benchley, Nathaniel. *The deep dives of Stanley Whale*
Berger, Gilda. *Whales*
Bible. Old Testament. Jonah. *The Book of Jonah*, ill. by Peter Spier
    Jonah, ill. by Kurt Mitchell
    Jonah and the great fish, ill. by Leon Baxter.
Bulla, Clyde Robert. *Jonah and the great fish*

Clark, Harry. *The first story of the whale*
Climo, Shirley. *The adventure of Walter*
Conklin, Gladys. *Journey of the gray whales*
Duvoisin, Roger Antoine. *The Christmas whale*
Engle, Joanna. *Cap'n kid goes to the South Pole*
Haiz, Danah. *Jonah's journey*
Hudson, Eleanor. *A whale of a rescue*
Hurd, Edith Thacher. *What whale? Where?*
Hutton, Warwick. *Jonah and the great fish*
Johnston, Johanna. *Whale's way*
Johnston, Tony. *Whale song*
King, Patricia. *Mable the whale*
Le Guin, Ursula K. *Solomon Leviathan's nine hundred and thirty-first trip around the world*
Lent, Blair. *John Tabor's ride*
Lilly, Kenneth. *Animals of the ocean*
McCloskey, Robert. *Bert Dow, deep-water man*
Maestro, Giulio. *The tortoise's tug of war*
Phleger, Fred B. *The whales go by*
Pluckrose, Henry. *Whales*
Postgate, Oliver. *Noggin and the whale*
Roy, Ronald. *A thousand pails of water*
Selsam, Millicent E. *A first look at whales*
Siberell, Anne. *Whale in the sky*
Stansfield, Ian. *The legend of the whale*
Steiner, Barbara. *The whale brother*
Strange, Florence. *Rock-a-bye whale*
Tokuda, Wendy. *Humphrey the lost whale*
Watanabe, Yuichi. *Wally the whale who loved balloons*
Wilson, Bob. *Stanley Bagshaw and the twenty-two ton whale*

Animals – wolves

Ambrus, Victor G. *Country wedding*
Baynes, Pauline. *How dog began*
Blades, Ann. *Mary of mile 18*
Bradman, Tony. *Look out, he's behind you*
Brett, Jan. *The first dog*
Damjan, Mischa. *Atuk*
    The wolf and the kid
Daudet, Alphonse. *The brave little goat of Monsieur Séguin*
Delaney, A. *The gunnywolf*
De Marolles, Chantal. *The lonely wolf*
De Regniers, Beatrice Schenk. *Red Riding Hood*
Evans, Katherine. *The boy who cried wolf*
Firmin, Peter. *Chicken stew*
Friskey, Margaret. *Indian Two Feet and the wolf cubs*
Gackenbach, Dick. *Harvey, the foolish pig*
Gay, Michel. *The Christmas wolf*
Goble, Paul. *The friendly wolf*

Grimm, Jacob. *Little red cap*, ill. by Lisbeth Zwerger
Little Red Riding Hood, ill. by Frank Aloise
Little Red Riding Hood, ill. by Gwen Connelly
Little Red Riding Hood, ill. by Paul Galdone
Little Red Riding Hood, ill. by John S. Goodall
Little Red Riding Hood, ill. by Trina Schart Hyman
Little Red Riding Hood, ill. by Bernadette Watts
The wolf and the seven kids, ill. by Kinuko Craft
The wolf and the seven little kids, ill. by Svend Otto S.
The wolf and the seven little kids, ill. by Martin Ursell
Gunthrop, Karen. *Adam and the wolf*
Harper, Wilhelmina. *The gunniwolf*
Hawkins, Colin. *What time is it, Mr. Wolf?*
Kasza, Keiko. *The wolf's chicken stew*
Lester, Helen. *Tacky the penguin*
Lewis, Robin Baird. *Friska, the sheep that was too small*
McClure, Gillian. *What's the time, Rory Wolf?*
McPhail, David *A wolf story*
Marshall, James. *Red Riding Hood*
Morris, Ann. *The Little Red Riding Hood rebus book*
Parish, Peggy. *Granny, the baby and the big gray thing*
Peck, Robert Newton. *Hamilton*
Prokofiev, Sergei Sergeievitch. *Peter and the wolf*, ill. by Reg Cartwright
Peter and the wolf, ill. by Warren Chappell
Peter and the wolf, ill. by Barbara Cooney
Peter and the wolf, ill. by Frans Haacken
Peter and the wolf, ill. by Alan Howard
Peter and the wolf, ill. by Charles Mikolaycak
Peter and the wolf, ill. by Jörg Müller
Peter and the wolf, ill. by Josef Paleček
Peter and the wolf, ill. by Kozo Shimizu
Peter and the wolf, ill. by Erna Voigt
Prusski, Jeffrey. *Bring back the deer*
Rayner, Mary. *Garth Pig and the ice cream lady*
Mr. and Mrs. Pig's evening out
Rockwell, Anne F. *The wolf who had a wonderful dream*
Ross, Tony. *Stone soup*
Roth, Susan L. *Kanahena*
Schick, Alice. *Just this once*
Selsam, Millicent E. *A first look at dogs*
Sharmat, Marjorie Weinman. *Walter the wolf*

Storr, Catherine. *Clever Polly and the stupid wolf*
The three little pigs. *The story of the three little pigs*, ill. by L. Leslie Brooke
The story of the three little pigs, ill. by William Stobbs
The three little pigs, facsimile ed.
The three little pigs, ill. by Erik Blegvad
The three little pigs, ill. by Caroline Bucknall
The three little pigs, ill. by Lorinda Bryan Cauley
The three little pigs, ill. by William Pène Du Bois
The three little pigs, ill. by Paul Galdone
The three little pigs, ill. by Rodney Peppé
The three little pigs, ill. by Edda Reinl
The three little pigs, ill. by John Wallner
The three little pigs, ill. by Irma Wilde
The three little pigs, ill. by Margot Zemach
The three pigs, ill. by Tony Ross
Wild, Robin. *Little Pig and the big bad wolf*

Animals – wombats

Elks, Wendy. *Charles B. Wombat and the very strange thing*

Animals – worms

Ahlberg, Janet. *The little worm book*
Jennings, Terry. *Earthworms*
Lindgren, Barbro. *A worm's tale*
O'Hagan, Caroline. *It's easy to have a worm visit you*
Scarry, Richard. *Richard Scarry's busy houses*
Thayer, Jane. *Andy and the wild worm*
Wong, Herbert H. *Our earthworms*

Animals – yaks

Lawson, Annetta. *The lucky yak*

Animals – zebras

Arnold, Caroline. *Zebra*
Goodall, Daphne Machin. *Zebras*
Hadithi, Mwenye. *Greedy zebra*
Peet, Bill. *Zella, Zack, and Zodiac*

Antarctic *see* Foreign lands – Antarctic

Anteaters *see* Animals – anteaters

Anti-violence *see* Violence, anti-violence

Ants *see* Insects – ants

Apes *see* Animals – gorillas; Animals – monkeys

Appearance see Character traits –
appearance

April Fools' Day see Holidays – April
Fools' Day

Aquariums

Curious George goes to the aquarium

Arabia see Foreign lands – Arabia

Architects see Careers – architects

Arctic see Foreign lands – Arctic

Arguing see Behavior – fighting, arguing

Arithmetic see Counting

Armadillos see Animals – armadillos

Armenia see Foreign lands – Armenia

Art

Agee, Jon. *The incredible painting of Felix
Clousseau*
Anderson, Douglas. *Let's draw a story*
Angelo, Nancy Carolyn Harrison.
Camembert
Baker, Jeannie. *Grandmother*
Baylor, Byrd. *When clay sings*
Bjork, Christina. *Linnea in Monet's garden*
Bond, Michael. *Paddington's art exhibit*
Borten, Helen. *Do you see what I see?*
A picture has a special look
Brandenberg, Franz. *What can you make of
it?*
Brett, Jan. *The first dog*
Bröger, Achim. *Francie's paper puppy*
Bromhall, Winifred. *Mary Ann's first
picture*
Brown, Laurene Krasny. *Visiting the art
museum*
Browne, Anthony. *Bear hunt*
Bulla, Clyde Robert. *Daniel's duck*
Canning, Kate. *A painted tale*
Carrick, Donald. *Morgan and the artist*
Cazet, Denys. *Frosted glass*
Coatsworth, Elizabeth. *Boston Bells*
Cober, Alan E. *Cober's choice*
Cohen, Miriam. *No good in art*
Craig, Helen. *Susie and Alfred in the
knight, the princess and the dragon*
Decker, Dorothy W. *Stripe visits New York*
De Paola, Tomie. *The art lesson*
Dionetti, Michelle. *Thalia Brown and the
blue bug*
Elliott, Dan. *Ernie's little lie*

Emberley, Ed. *Ed Emberley's big green
drawing book*
Ed Emberley's big orange drawing book
Ed Emberley's big purple drawing book
Ed Emberley's crazy mixed-up face game
Ed Emberley's drawing book make a world
Emberley, Michael. *More dinosaurs!*
Emberley, Rebecca. *Drawing with numbers
and letters*
Ernst, Lisa Campbell. *Hamilton's art show*
Fifield, Flora. *Pictures for the palace*
Freeman, Don. *Norman the doorman*
Goffstein, M. B. (Marilyn Brooke). *Artists'
helpers enjoy the evening*
Green, Marion. *The magician who lived on
the mountain*
Harris, Leon A. *The great picture robbery*
Haskins, Jim. *The Statue of Liberty*
Hurd, Edith Thacher. *Wilson's world*
Johnson, Crockett. *Harold and the purple
crayon*
A picture for Harold's room
Kesselman, Wendy. *Emma*
Kilroy, Sally. *Copycat drawing book*
Lionni, Leo. *Let's make rabbits*
McPhail, David. *The magical drawings of
Moony B. Finch*
Maestro, Betsy. *The story of the Statue of
Liberty*
Mayers, Florence Cassen. *Egyptian art from
the Brooklyn Museum ABC*
The Museum of Fine Arts, Boston ABC
*The Museum of Modern Art, New York
ABC*
Mendoza, George. *Henri Mouse*
Menter, Ian. *The Albany Road mural*
Peet, Bill. *Encore for Eleanor*
Pinkwater, Daniel Manus. *The bear's picture*
Rauch, Hans-Georg. *The lines are coming*
Rey, Margaret Elisabeth Waldstein. *Billy's
picture*
Rubin, Cynthia Elyce. *ABC Americana from
the National Gallery of Art*
Rylant, Cynthia. *All I see*
Schick, Eleanor. *Art lessons*
Seuss, Dr. *I can draw it myself*
Sharon, Mary Bruce. *Scenes from childhood*
Steiner, Barbara. *The whale brother*
Türk, Hanne. *Max the artlover*
Tusa, Tricia. *Stay away from the junkyard!*
Villarejo, Mary. *The art fair*
Wabbes, Marie. *Rose's picture*
Williams, Vera B. *Cherries and cherry pits*
Wolf, Janet. *The best present is me*
Zelinsky, Paul O. *The lion and the stoat*

Artists see Careers – artists

Assertiveness see Character traits –
assertiveness

Astrology *see* Zodiac

Astronauts *see* Careers – astronauts; Space and space ships

Astronomers *see* Careers – astronomers

Australia *see* Foreign lands – Australia

Austria *see* Foreign lands – Austria

Authors, children *see* Children as authors

Automobiles

Alexander, Anne. *ABC of cars and trucks*
Aulaire, Ingri Mortenson d'. *The two cars*
Barrett, N. S. *Racing cars*
Baugh, Dolores M. *Trucks and cars to ride*
Biro, Val. *Gumdrop, the adventures of a vintage car*
Brandenberg, Franz. *What's wrong with a van?*
Bridwell, Norman. *Clifford's good deeds*
Broekel, Ray. *I can be an auto mechanic*
Burningham, John. *Mr. Gumpy's motor car*
  Slam bang
Caines, Jeannette. *Just us women*
Cars and trucks
Cave, Ron. *Automobiles*
Cummings, W. T. (Walter Thies). *Miss Esta Maude's secret*
DiFiori, Lawrence. *If I had a little car*
Emberley, Ed. *Cars, boats, and planes*
Ets, Marie Hall. *Little old automobile*
Fowler, Richard. *Mr. Little's noisy car*
Gay, Michel. *Little auto*
Gibbons, Gail. *Fill it up!*
Holl, Adelaide. *The ABC of cars, trucks and machines*
Janosch. *The magic auto*
Lenski, Lois. *The little auto*
Löfgren, Ulf. *The traffic stopper that became a grandmother visitor*
Mitgutsch, Ali. *From rubber tree to tire*
Newton, Laura P. *William the vehicle king*
Oxenbury, Helen. *The car trip*
Peet, Bill. *Jennifer and Josephine*
Peppé, Rodney. *Little wheels*
Petrie, Catherine. *Hot Rod Harry*
Pinkwater, Daniel Manus. *Tooth-gnasher superflash*
Pitcher, Caroline. *Cars and boats*
Robbins, Ken. *Citycountry*
Rockwell, Anne F. *Cars*
Scarry, Huck. *On the road*
Scarry, Richard. *The great big car and truck book*
  Richard Scarry's cars and trucks and things that go
Spier, Peter. *Bill's service station*

Spurr, Elizabeth. *Mrs. Minetta's car pool*
Stobbs, William. *A car called beetle*
Wilkinson, Sylvia. *Automobiles*
  I can be a race car driver
Young, Miriam Burt. *If I drove a car*

Autumn *see* Seasons – fall

Babies

Ahlberg, Janet. *The baby's catalogue*
  Peek-a-boo!
Alexander, Martha G. *Nobody asked me if I wanted a baby sister*
  When the new baby comes, I'm moving out
Aliki. *At Mary Bloom's*
  Welcome, little baby
Allen, Pamela. *A lion in the night*
Allen, Robert. *Ten little babies count*
  Ten little babies dress
  Ten little babies eat
  Ten little babies play
Ancona, George. *It's a baby!*
Andry, Andrew C. *Hi, new baby*
  How babies are made
Arbeit, Eleanor Werner. *Mrs. cat hides something*
Arnstein, Helene S. *Billy and our new baby*
Asch, Frank. *Starbaby*
Baby's words
Baird, Anne. *Baby socks*
  Kiss, kiss
Baker, Charlotte. *Little brother*
Baker, Gayle. *Special delivery*
Banish, Roslyn. *I want to tell you about my baby*
  Let me tell you about my baby
Bendick, Jeanne. *What made you you?*
Bolognese, Don. *A new day*
Brandenberg, Franz. *Aunt Nina and her nephews and nieces*
Brann, Esther. *A book for baby*
Brice, Tony. *Baby animals*
Brooks, Robert B. *So that's how I was born*
Brown, Marc. *Arthur's baby*
Burningham, John. *Avocado baby*
Busy baby
Byars, Betsy Cromer. *Go and hush the baby*
Byrne, David. *Stay up late*
Caseley, Judith. *Silly baby*
Chaffin, Lillie D. *Tommy's big problem*
Chess, Victoria. *Poor Esmé*
Chorao, Kay. *The baby's good morning book*

Christenson, Larry. *The wonderful way that babies are made*

Clifton, Lucille. *Everett Anderson's nine months long*

Cole, Joanna. *A calf is born*
How you were born
The new baby at your house

De Paola, Tomie. *Baby's first Christmas*

Dragonwagon, Crescent. *Wind Rose*

Dunn, Phoebe. *Baby's animal friends*
Busy, busy toddlers
I'm a baby!

Ferguson, Alane. *That new pet!*

Fisher, Iris L. *Katie-Bo*

Flack, Marjorie. *The new pet*

Foreman, Michael. *Ben's baby*

Foulds, Elfrida Vipont. *The elephant and the bad baby*

Galbraith, Kathryn Osebold. *Waiting for Jennifer*

Gill, Joan. *Hush, Jon!*

Girard, Linda Walvoord. *You were born on your very first birthday*

Graham, Bob. *Crusher is coming!*

Greenberg, Barbara. *The bravest babysitter*

Greenberg, Judith E. *Adopted*

Greenfield, Eloise. *She come bringing me that little baby girl*

Gruenberg, Sidonie Matsner. *The wonderful story of how you were born*

Hamilton-Merritt, Jane. *Our new baby*

Hanson, Joan. *I don't like Timmy*

Harper, Anita. *It's not fair!*

Hayes, Sarah. *Eat up, Gemma*

Hazen, Barbara Shook. *Why couldn't I be an only kid like you, Wigger?*

Hedderwick, Mairi. *Katie Morag and the tiresome Ted*

Hello, baby

Helmering, Doris Wild. *We're going to have a baby*

Henderson, Kathy. *The baby's book of babies*

Hendrickson, Karen. *Baby and I can play*
Fun with toddlers

Herter, Jonina. *Eighty-eight kisses*

Hirsh, Marilyn. *Leela and the watermelon*
Where is Yonkela?

Hobson, Laura Z. *"I'm going to have a baby!"*

Hoffman, Phyllis. *Baby's first year*

Hoffman, Rosekrans. *Sister Sweet Ella*

Holland, Viki. *We are having a baby*

Hush little baby. *Hush little baby*, ill. by Aliki
Hush little baby, ill. by Jeanette Winter
Hush little baby, ill. by Margot Zemach

Hutchins, Pat. *Where's the baby?*

Hutton, Warwick. *Moses in the bulrushes*

Isadora, Rachel. *I hear*
I see

Jarrell, Mary. *The knee baby*

Keats, Ezra Jack. *Peter's chair*

Kelley, True. *Look, baby! Listen, baby! Do, baby!*

Kilroy, Sally. *Babies' bodies*
Baby colors
Busy babies

Krasilovsky, Phyllis. *The very little boy*
The very little girl

Kraus, Robert. *Big brother*

Kunhardt, Edith. *Where's Peter?*

Lakin, Patricia. *Don't touch my room*

Langstaff, Nancy. *A tiny baby for you*

Lasky, Kathryn. *A baby for Max*

Levine, Abby. *What did mommy do before you?*

Lexau, Joan M. *Finders keepers, losers weepers*

Lindgren, Astrid. *I want a brother or sister*

MacGregor, Marilyn. *Baby takes a trip*

McMillan, Bruce. *Step by step*

Malecki, Maryann. *Mom and dad and I are having a baby!*

Manushkin, Fran. *Baby*
Baby, come out!
Little rabbit's baby brother

Miller, Margaret. *At my house*
In my room
Me and my clothes
Time to eat

Miranda, Anne. *Baby talk*
Baby walk

Mueller, Virginia. *Monster and the baby*

Naylor, Phyllis Reynolds. *The baby, the bed, and the rose*

Newberry, Clare Turlay. *Cousin Toby*
T-Bone, the baby-sitter

Ormerod, Jan. *Bend and stretch*
Dad's back
Just like me
Making friends
Messy baby
Mom's home
101 things to do with a baby
Our Ollie
Silly goose
Sleeping
This little nose
Young Joe

Oxenbury, Helen. *All fall down*
Clap hands
I can
I hear
I see
I touch
Playing
Say goodnight
Tickle, tickle

Parish, Peggy. *Granny, the baby and the big gray thing*

Patent, Dorothy Hinshaw. *Babies!*

Pearson, Susan. *When baby went to bed*

Petersham, Maud. *The box with red wheels*
Politi, Leo. *Rosa*
Polushkin, Maria. *Baby brother blues*
The pudgy book of babies
Pursell, Margaret Sanford. *A look at birth*
Rice, Eve. *What Sadie sang*
Rigby, Shirley Lincoln. *Smaller than most*
Robins, Joan. *My brother, Will*
Rogers, Fred. *The new baby*
Ross, Katharine. *When you were a baby*
Rushnell, Elaine Evans. *My mom's having a baby*
Schick, Eleanor. *Peggy's new brother*
Schlein, Miriam. *Laurie's new brother*
Sendak, Maurice. *Outside over there*
Shapp, Martha. *Let's find out about babies*
Sheffield, Margaret. *Before you were born*
Where do babies come from?
Showers, Paul. *A baby starts to grow*
Before you were a baby
Smith, Peter. *Jenny's baby brother*
Stein, Sara Bonnett. *Making babies*
That new baby
Steptoe, John. *Baby says*
Stevenson, James. *Worse than Willy!*
Tafuri, Nancy. *My friends*
Thayer, Jane. *Gus and the baby ghost*
Thomas, Iolette. *Janine and the new baby*
Titherington, Jeanne. *A place for Ben*
Van der Beek, Deborah. *Superbabe!*
Vigna, Judith. *Couldn't we have a turtle instead?*
Watts, Bernadette. *David's waiting day*
What do babies do?
What do toddlers do?
Williams, Barbara. *Jeremy isn't hungry*
Young, Ruth. *My blanket*
The new baby
Ziefert, Harriet. *Baby Ben's bow-wow book*
Baby Ben's busy book
Baby Ben's go-go book
Baby Ben's noisy book
Breakfast time!
Bye-bye, daddy!
Good morning, sun!
Let's get dressed!
Zolotow, Charlotte. *But not Billy*
Do you know what I'll do?

Baby-sitting *see* Activities – baby-sitting

Bad day *see* Behavior – bad day

Badgers *see* Animals – badgers

Bakers *see* Careers – bakers

Bali *see* Foreign lands – Bali

Ballooning *see* Activities – ballooning

Balloons *see* Toys – balloons

Balls *see* Toys – balls

Barbers *see* Careers – barbers

Barns

Brown, Margaret Wise. *Big red barn*
Carrick, Carol. *The old barn*
Climo, Lindee. *Chester's barn*
Martin, Bill (William Ivan). *Barn dance!*
Merrill, Jean. *Tell about the cowbarn, Daddy*
Miles, Miska. *The raccoon and Mrs. McGinnis*
Parnall, Peter. *Winter barn*
Schoenherr, John. *The barn*
Sewell, Helen Moore. *Blue barns*

Barons *see* Royalty

Baseball *see* Sports – baseball

Basketball *see* Sports – basketball

Bathing *see* Activities – bathing

Bats *see* Animals – bats

Bavaria *see* Foreign lands – Austria; Foreign lands – Germany; Foreign lands – Tyrol

Beaches *see* Sea and seashore

Bears *see* Animals – bears; Animals – pandas; Animals – polar bears

Bears – toys *see* Toys – teddy bears

Beasts *see* Monsters

Beavers *see* Animals – beavers

Bedtime

Ahlberg, Allan. *The clothes horse*
Allison, Diane Worfolk. *In window eight, the moon is late*
Anderson, Peggy Perry. *Time for bed, the babysitter said*
Arnold, Tedd. *No jumping on the bed!*
Asch, Frank. *Goodnight horsey*
Aylesworth, Jim. *Tonight's the night*
Baird, Anne. *No sheep*
Bang, Molly. *Ten, nine, eight*
Wiley and the hairy man
Barrett, Judi. *I hate to go to bed*
Beckman, Kaj. *Lisa cannot sleep*
Berenstain, Stan. *Bears in the night*
Berridge, Celia. *Grandmother's tales*
Blaustein, Muriel. *Bedtime, Zachary!*

Blocksma, Mary. *Did you hear that?*
Bond, Felicia. *Poinsettia and the firefighters*
Bottner, Barbara. *There was nobody there*
Bowden, Joan Chase. *Bouncy baby bunny finds his bed*
Bowers, Kathleen Rice. *At this very minute*
Boynton, Sandra. *The going to bed book*
 Good night, good night
Brown, Margaret Wise. *A child's good night book*
 Goodnight moon
Callen, Larry. *Dashiel and the night*
Calmenson, Stephanie. *All aboard the goodnight train*
Cameron, Ann. *Harry (the monster)*
Chevalier, Christa. *Spence and the sleepytime monster*
Chorao, Kay. *Lemon moon*
Christelow, Eileen. *Henry and the Dragon*
Coatsworth, Elizabeth. *Good night*
Cole, William. *Frances face-maker*
Corddry, Thomas I. *Kibby's big feat*
Cosgrove, Stephen. *Sleepy time bunny*
Dahl, Roald. *Dirty beasts*
Denton, Kady MacDonald. *Granny is a darling*
De Paola, Tomie. *Fight the night*
 Pajamas for Kit
Duke, Kate. *Bedtime*
Engvick, William. *Lullabies and night songs*
Eriksson, Eva. *Hocus-pocus*
Erskine, Jim. *Bedtime story*
Fox, Siv Cedering. *The blue horse and other night poems*
Freedman, Sally. *Devin's new bed*
Gackenbach, Dick. *Poppy the panda*
Gay, Marie-Louise. *Moonbeam on a cat's ear*
Gerstein, Mordicai. *William, where are you?*
Ginsburg, Mirra. *Which is the best place?*
Goffstein, M. B. (Marilyn Brooke). *Sleepy people*
Goode, Diane. *I hear a noise*
Goodspeed, Peter. *A rhinoceros wakes me up in the morning*
Greenleaf, Ann. *No room for Sarah*
Gretz, Susanna. *Hide-and-seek*
 I'm not sleepy
 Ready for bed
 Too dark!
Grindley, Sally. *Knock, knock! Who's there?*
Hancock, Joy Elizabeth. *The loudest little lion*
Harris, Dorothy Joan. *Goodnight Jeffrey*
Harshman, Terry Webb. *Porcupine's pajama party*
Hawkins, Colin. *Dip, dip, dip*
 I'm not sleepy!
 One finger, one thumb
 Oops-a-Daisy
 Where's bear?

Hawkins, Mark. *A lion under her bed*
Hill, Eric. *Baby Bear's bedtime*
Hoban, Russell. *Bedtime for Frances*
 Goodnight
Holabird, Katharine. *Alexander and the dragon*
Hopkins, Lee Bennett. *Go to bed!*
Hopkins, Margaret. *Sleepytime for baby mouse*
Impey, Rose. *The flat man*
 Scare yourself to sleep
Inkpen, Mick. *One bear at bedtime*
Ipcar, Dahlov. *The calico jungle*
Jeffers, Susan. *All the pretty horses*
Johnson, Jane. *Today I thought I'd run away*
Johnston, Johanna. *Edie changes her mind*
Jonas, Ann. *The quilt*
Joslin, Sesyle. *Brave Baby Elephant*
Kalman, Maira. *Hey Willy, see the pyramids!*
Keller, Holly. *Ten sleepy sheep*
Kent, Jack. *The once-upon-a-time dragon*
Khalsa, Dayal Kaur. *Sleepers*
Kitamura, Satoshi. *When sheep cannot sleep*
Koide, Tan. *May we sleep here tonight?*
Kotzwinkle, William. *The nap master*
Krahn, Fernando. *Sleep tight, Alex Pumpernickel*
Kraus, Robert. *Good night little one*
 Good night Richard Rabbit
Krauss, Ruth. *The bundle book*
Kuskin, Karla. *The Dallas Titans get ready for bed*
 Night again
 A space story
Larrick, Nancy. *When the dark comes dancing*
Leaf, Munro. *Boo, who used to be scared of the dark*
Lesser, Carolyn. *The goodnight circle*
Lester, Alison. *Ruby*
Levine, Joan. *A bedtime story*
Lifton, Betty Jean. *Goodnight orange monster*
Lippman, Peter. *New at the zoo*
Lloyd, Errol. *Nandy's bedtime*
Lobe, Mira. *Valerie and the good-night swing*
Mack, Stanley. *Ten bears in my bed*
McPhail, David. *The dream child*
Mählqvist, Stefan. *I'll take care of the crocodiles*
Marcin, Marietta. *A zoo in her bed*
Maris, Ron. *My book*
Marshall, James. *What's the matter with Carruthers?*
Marshall, Margaret. *Mike*
Marzollo, Jean. *Close your eyes*
Matura, Mustapha. *Moon jump*

Mayer, Mercer. *Little Monster's bedtime book*
There's a nightmare in my closet
There's an alligator under my bed
Mayper, Monica. *After good-night*
Merriam, Eve. *Good night to Annie*
Miles, Sally. *Alfi and the dark*
Miller, J. P. (John Parr). *Good night, little rabbit*
Milne, A. A. (Alan Alexander). *Pooh's bedtime book*
Montresor, Beni. *Bedtime!*
The moon's the north wind's cooky
Morgan, Allen. *Nicole's boat*
Morris, Ann. *Cuddle up*
Kiss time
Night counting
Sleepy, sleepy
Morris, Terry Nell. *Good night, dear monster!*
Mother Goose. *Hush-a-bye baby*, ill. by Nicola Bayley
Mueller, Virginia. *Monster can't sleep*
Murphy, Jill. *What next, baby bear!*
Nichol, B. P. *Once*
Oppenheim, Joanne. *The story book prince*
Orgel, Doris. *Little John*
Ormerod, Jan. *Moonlight*
Oxenbury, Helen. *Good night, good morning*
Pearson, Susan. *When baby went to bed*
Peck, Richard. *Monster night at Grandma's house*
Petersham, Maud. *Off to bed*
Plath, Sylvia. *The bed book*
Plotz, Helen. *A week of lullabies*
Pomerantz, Charlotte. *All asleep*
Posy
Preston, Edna Mitchell. *Monkey in the jungle*
Pryor, Ainslie. *The baby blue cat who said no*
Rees, Mary. *Ten in a bed*
Rice, Eve. *Goodnight, goodnight*
Richter, Mischa. *To bed, to bed!*
Robison, Deborah. *No elephants allowed*
Rockwell, Anne F. *Buster and the bogeyman*
Rogers, Paul. *Somebody's sleepy*
Rosen, Michael. *Under the bed*
Russo, Marisabina. *Why do grownups have all the fun?*
Saltzberg, Barney. *It must have been the wind*
Schertle, Alice. *Goodnight, Hattie, my dearie, my dove*
Schneider, Nina. *While Susie sleeps*
Schubert, Ingrid. *There's a crocodile under my bed!*
Sharmat, Marjorie Weinman. *Go to sleep, Nicholas Joe*
Goodnight, Andrew. Goodnight, Craig

Skorpen, Liesel Moak. *Outside my window*
Smith, Robert Paul *Nothingatall, nothingatall, nothingatall*
Steiner, Charlotte. *The sleepy quilt*
Stevens, Kathleen. *The beast in the bathtub*
Stevenson, James. *We can't sleep*
What's under my bed?
Stock, Catherine. *Alexander's midnight snack*
Stoddard, Sandol. *Bedtime for bear*
Bedtime mouse
Strahl, Rudi. *Sandman in the lighthouse*
Strand, Mark. *The planet of lost things*
Sugita, Yutaka. *Good night 1, 2, 3*
Sussman, Susan. *Hippo thunder*
Sutherland, Harry A. *Dad's car wash*
Swados, Elizabeth. *Lullaby*
Taylor, Livingston. *Pajamas*
Tobias, Tobi. *Chasing the goblins away*
Trez, Denise. *Good night, Veronica*
Türk, Hanne. *Goodnight Max*
Viorst, Judith. *My mama says there aren't any zombies, ghosts, vampires, creatures, demons, monsters, fiends, goblins, or things*
Wabbes, Marie. *Good night, Little Rabbit*
Waber, Bernard. *Ira sleeps over*
Wahl, Jan. *Humphrey's bear*
Watson, Clyde. *Fisherman lullabies*
Midnight moon
Wells, Rosemary. *Max's bedtime*
Westcott, Nadine Bernard. *Going to bed*
Whiteside, Karen. *Lullaby of the wind*
Wiesner, David. *Free fall*
Willis, Jeanne. *The monster bed*
Winthrop, Elizabeth. *Bunk beds*
Maggie and the monster
Wood, Audrey. *Moonflute*
Yolen, Jane. *Dragon night and other lullabies*
The lullaby songbook
Zalben, Jane Breskin. *Norton's nighttime*
Ziefert, Harriet. *Good night everyone!*
I won't go to bed!
Say good night!
Zinnemann-Hope, Pam. *Time for bed, Ned*
Zolotow, Charlotte. *Flocks of birds*
The sleepy book, ill. by Vladimir Bobri
Sleepy book, ill. by Ilse Plume
The summer night
Wake up and good night
When the wind stops

Bees *see* Insects – bees

Beetles *see* Insects – beetles

Behavior

Babbitt, Lorraine. *Pink like the geranium*
Beim, Jerrold. *The swimming hole*

Belloc, Hilaire. *The bad child's book of beasts*
Benchley, Nathaniel. *Oscar Otter*
Blundell, Tony. *Joe on Sunday*
Boegehold, Betty. *Three to get ready*
Bond, Felicia. *Poinsettia and her family*
Carle, Eric. *The grouchy ladybug*
Caudill, Rebecca. *Contrary Jenkins*
Delton, Judy. *I'm telling you now*
Ets, Marie Hall. *Bad boy, good boy*
 Play with me
Gackenbach, Dick. *Hattie be quiet, Hattie be good*
Gaeddert, Lou Ann Bigge. *Noisy Nancy Nora*
Gambill, Henrietta. *Self-control*
Harris, Robie H. *Don't forget to come back*
Hoban, Russell. *Dinner at Alberta's*
Hogrogian, Nonny. *Carrot cake*
Horvath, Betty F. *Be nice to Josephine*
Livingston, Myra Cohn. *Higgledy-Piggledy*
Low, Joseph. *Don't drag your feet...*
 My dog, your dog
Myller, Lois. *No! No!*
Ness, Evaline. *Marcella's guardian angel*
Panek, Dennis. *Matilda Hippo has a big mouth*
Parker, Nancy Winslow. *Puddums, the Cathcarts' orange cat*
Paterson, Diane. *Wretched Rachel*
Quackenbush, Robert M. *I don't want to go, I don't know how to act*
Ringi, Kjell. *The winner*
Scarry, Richard. *Pig Will and Pig Won't*
Sharmat, Marjorie Weinman. *Scarlet Monster lives here*
Stover, Jo Ann. *If everybody did*
Supraner, Robyn. *Would you rather be a tiger?*
Svendsen, Carol. *Hulda*
Thomas, Karen. *The good thing...the bad thing*
Wittels, Harriet. *Things I hate!*

Behavior — aggressiveness *see* Character traits — assertiveness

Behavior — animals, dislike of

Bemelmans, Ludwig. *Madeline and the bad hat*
Kay, Helen. *An egg is for wishing*
Udry, Janice May. *Alfred*

Behavior — bad day

Alborough, Jez. *Running Bear*
Andrews, F. Emerson (Frank Emerson). *Nobody comes to dinner*
Baker, Alan. *Benjamin's portrait*
Balzola, Asun. *Munia and the day things went wrong*

Berenstain, Stan. *The Berenstain bears get in a fight*
Duncan, Jane. *Janet Reachfar and Chickabird*
Fujikawa, Gyo. *Sam's all-wrong day*
Giff, Patricia Reilly. *Today was a terrible day*
Griffith, Helen V. *Nata*
Haywood, Carolyn. *Santa Claus forever!*
Hoban, Russell. *The sorely trying day*
Hurd, Thacher. *Mystery on the docks*
Keith, Eros. *Bedita's bad day*
Kline, Suzy. *Ooops!*
Krahn, Fernando. *Here comes Alex Pumpernickel!*
Lexau, Joan M. *I should have stayed in bed*
Morris, Ann. *Eleanora Mousie's gray day*
Oxenbury, Helen. *The car trip*
Prater, John. *The perfect day*
Sondheimer, Ilse. *The boy who could make his mother stop yelling*
Van Leeuwen, Jean. *Too hot for ice cream*
Viorst, Judith. *Alexander and the terrible, horrible, no good, very bad day*
Vreeken, Elizabeth. *One day everything went wrong*
Wells, Rosemary. *Unfortunately Harriet*

Behavior — boasting

Augarde, Steve. *Barnaby Shrew, Black Dan and...the mighty wedgwood*
Bonsall, Crosby Newell. *The amazing the incredible super dog*
 Mine's the best
Browne, Anthony. *Look what I've got!*
Carlson, Nancy. *Loudmouth George and the big race*
 Loudmouth George and the cornet
 Loudmouth George and the fishing trip
 Loudmouth George and the new neighbors
 Loudmouth George and the sixth-grade bully
Collins, Pat L. *My friend Andrew*
Diot, Alain. *Better, best, bestest*
Duvoisin, Roger Antoine. *See what I am*
Ellentuck, Shan. *A sunflower as big as the sun*
Johnston, Tony. *Farmer Mack measures his pig*
Kepes, Juliet. *The story of a bragging duck*
Knutson, Barbara. *Why the crab has no head*
Lopshire, Robert. *I am better than you*
Lund, Doris Herold. *You ought to see Herbert's house*
Miller, Warren. *The goings on at Little Wishful*
Oppenheim, Joanne. *You can't catch me!*
Osborn, Lois. *My dad is really something*
Parker, Kristy. *My dad the magnificent*
Pavey, Peter. *I'm Taggarty Toad*

Peterson, Esther Allen. *Frederick's alligator*
Raphael, Elaine. *Turnabout*
Schwartz, Amy. *Her Majesty, Aunt Essie*

Behavior – boredom

Alexander, Martha G. *We never get to do anything*
Ayal, Ora. *The adventures of Chester the chest*
Delton, Judy. *My mom hates me in January*
Duvoisin, Roger Antoine. *Veronica's smile*
Eriksson, Eva. *One short week*
Henkes, Kevin. *Once around the block*
Hoban, Russell. *Nothing to do*
Krauss, Ruth. *A good man and his good wife*
McConnachie, Brian. *Lily of the forest*
McGovern, Ann. *Nicholas Bentley Stoningpot III*
McLaughlin, Lissa. *Why won't winter go?*
Meroux, Felix. *The prince of the rabbits*
Noble, Trinka Hakes. *Meanwhile back at the ranch*
Oram, Hiawyn. *In the attic*
Raskin, Ellen. *Nothing ever happens on my block*
Reit, Seymour. *The king who learned to smile*
Spier, Peter. *Bored - nothing to do!*
Stevenson, James. *There's nothing to do!*
Thayer, Jane. *Mr. Turtle's magic glasses*
Watts, Marjorie-Ann. *Crocodile medicine*

Behavior – bullying

Alexander, Martha G. *I sure am glad to see you, Blackboard Bear*
Move over, Twerp
Berquist, Grace. *The boy who couldn't roar*
Bradbury, Bianca. *One kitten too many*
Browne, Anthony. *Willy the champ*
Bryant, Bernice. *Follow the leader*
Carlson, Nancy. *Loudmouth George and the sixth-grade bully*
Cauley, Lorinda Bryan. *The trouble with Tyrannosaurus Rex*
Chapman, Carol. *Herbie's troubles*
Charlton, Elizabeth. *Terrible tyrannosaurus*
Christopher, Matt. *Johnny no hit*
Cohen, Miriam. *Tough Jim*
De Paola, Tomie. *Katie, Kit and cousin Tom*
Dodd, Lynley. *Hairy Maclary Scattercat*
Freschet, Berniece. *Furlie Cat*
Gretz, Susanna. *Roger takes charge!*
Hadithi, Mwenye. *Crafty chameleon*
Tricky tortoise
Henkes, Kevin. *Chester's way*
Isenberg, Barbara. *Albert the running bear gets the jitters*
Janice. *Angélique*

Keats, Ezra Jack. *Goggles*
Kessler, Leonard P. *Last one in is a rotten egg*
Lagercrantz, Rose. *Brave little Pete of Geranium Street*
Laurencin, Geneviève. *I wish I were*
Little, Emily. *David and the giant*
Peet, Bill. *Big bad Bruce*
Rayner, Mary. *Crocodarling*
Roche, P. K. (Patrick K.). *Plaid bear and the rude rabbit gang*
Staunton, Ted. *Taking care of Crumley*
Wilhelm, Hans. *Tyrone the horrible*

Behavior – carelessness

Aliki. *Keep your mouth closed, dear*
Bottner, Barbara. *Messy*
Brown, Marc. *The cloud over Clarence*
Brunhoff, Laurent de. *Babar's little girl*
Buchanan, Joan. *It's a good thing*
Carrick, Carol. *A rabbit for Easter*
Chislett, Gail. *The rude visitors*
Claret, Maria. *The chocolate rabbit*
Cleary, Beverly. *Lucky Chuck*
De Paola, Tomie. *The quicksand book*
Strega Nona's magic lessons
Gackenbach, Dick. *Binky gets a car*
Gantos, Jack. *Aunt Bernice*
Harris, Robie H. *Messy Jessie*
Ilsley, Velma. *The pink hat*
Kline, Suzy. *Ooops!*
Mayer, Mercer. *Oops*
Moskin, Marietta D. *Lysbet and the fire kittens*
Panek, Dennis. *Catastrophe Cat*
Pender, Lydia. *Barnaby and the horses*
Roberts, Sarah. *Ernie's big mess*
Sommers, Tish. *Bert and the broken teapot*

Behavior – collecting things

Bauer, Caroline Feller. *Too many books!*
Beim, Lorraine. *Lucky Pierre*
Bram, Elizabeth. *Woodruff and the clocks*
Braun, Kathy. *Kangaroo and kangaroo*
Carlstrom, Nancy White. *The moon came too*
Cleary, Beverly. *Janet's thingamajigs*
Enderle, Judith A. *Good junk*
Engel, Diana. *Josephina, the great collector*
Evans, Eva Knox. *That lucky Mrs. Plucky*
Fox, Paula. *Maurice's room*
Gans, Roma. *Rock collecting*
Geringer, Laura. *A three hat day*
Heyduck-Huth, Hilde. *The starfish*
The strawflower
Lewis, Naomi. *The butterfly collector*
Tusa, Tricia. *Stay away from the junkyard!*
Van Horn, William. *Harry Hoyle's giant jumping bean*
Weil, Lisl. *To sail a ship of treasures*

Behavior – disbelief

Alexander, Martha G. *Even that moose won't listen to me*
Cole, Brock. *The king at the door*
Gunthrop, Karen. *Adam and the wolf*
Norman, Howard. *The owl-scatterer*
Turner, Ann. *Nettie's trip south*

Behavior – dissatisfaction

Aliki. *The twelve months*
  The wish workers
Allen, Jeffrey. *The secret life of Mr. Weird*
Balet, Jan B. *The king and the broom maker*
Brewster, Patience. *Nobody*
Brock, Emma Lillian. *Pig with a front porch*
Brothers, Aileen. *Sad Mrs. Sam Sack*
Byars, Betsy Cromer. *The groober*
Chapman, Carol. *The tale of Meshka the Kvetch*
Clymer, Ted. *The horse and the bad morning*
Crowley, Arthur. *The boogey man*
Cushman, Doug. *Nasty Kyle the crocodile*
Dale, Ruth Bluestone. *Benjamin – and Sylvester also*
Day, Shirley. *Waldo's back yard*
Duvoisin, Roger Antoine. *Petunia, beware!*
Elborn, Andrew. *Bird Adalbert*
Ets, Marie Hall. *The cow's party*
Fish, Hans. *Pitschi, the kitten who always wanted to do something else*
Gackenbach, Dick. *Mother Rabbit's son Tom*
Gay, Zhenya. *I'm tired of lions*
Getz, Arthur. *Humphrey, the dancing pig*
Hautzig, Deborah. *It's not fair!*
Hazen, Barbara Shook. *The Fat Cats, Cousin Scraggs and the monster mice*
Hest, Amy. *The mommy exchange*
Hille-Brandts, Lene. *The little black hen*
Hoban, Lillian. *Stick-in-the-mud turtle*
Johnson, Evelyne. *The cow in the kitchen*
Keats, Ezra Jack. *Jennie's hat*
McDermott, Gerald. *The stonecutter*
McGinley, Phyllis. *The horse who lived upstairs*
Massie, Diane Redfield. *Walter was a frog*
O'Donnell, Elizabeth Lee. *Maggie doesn't want to move*
Olujic, Grozdana. *Rose of Mother-of-Pearl*
Oram, Hiawyn. *Jenna and the troublemaker*
Palmer, Mary Babcock. *No-sort-of-animal*
Peet, Bill. *The caboose who got loose*
  The luckiest one of all
  The Whingdingdilly
Price, Roger. *The last little dragon*
Russo, Marisabina. *Why do grownups have all the fun?*
Sadler, Marilyn. *It's not easy being a bunny*
Sarnoff, Jane. *That's not fair*

Sharmat, Marjorie Weinman. *Grumley the grouch*
Turnage, Sheila. *Trout the magnificent*
Wiesner, William. *Turnabout*
Yaffe, Alan. *The magic meatballs*
Zakhoder, Boris Vladimirovich. *Rosachok*
Zolotow, Charlotte. *It's not fair*

Behavior – fighting, arguing

Alexander, Lloyd. *The four donkeys*
Alexander, Martha G. *I'll be the horse if you'll play with me*
Beim, Lorraine. *Two is a team*
Berry, Joy Wilt. *Fighting*
Bonsall, Crosby Newell. *Who's a pest?*
Brandenberg, Franz. *It's not my fault*
Burningham, John. *Mr. Gumpy's outing*
Christian, Mary Blount. *The sand lot*
Dayton, Mona. *Earth and sky*
Gekiere, Madeleine. *The frilly lily and the princess*
Gilchrist, Theo E. *Halfway up the mountain*
Hoban, Russell. *Harvey's hideout*
  The sorely trying day
  Tom and the two handles
Holabird, Katharine. *Alexander and the dragon*
Lasker, Joe. *A tournament of knights*
Levitin, Sonia. *Who owns the moon?*
Lionni, Leo. *It's mine!*
McKee, David. *Tusk tusk*
  Two monsters
Minarik, Else Holmelund. *No fighting, no biting!*
Newsham, Ian. *Lost in the jungle*
Rose, Gerald. *Trouble in the ark*
Sharmat, Marjorie Weinman. *I'm not Oscar's friend any more*
  Rollo and Juliet...forever!
  Sometimes mama and papa fight
Shute, Linda. *Momotaro, the peach boy*
Slobodkin, Louis. *Hustle and bustle*
Steadman, Ralph. *The bridge*
Stevenson, James. *Are we almost there?*
Udry, Janice May. *Let's be enemies*
Venable, Alan. *The checker players*
Winthrop, Elizabeth. *That's mine*
Zolotow, Charlotte. *The quarreling book*
  The unfriendly book

Behavior – forgetfulness

Alexander, Sue. *Witch, Goblin and sometimes Ghost*
Aliki. *Use your head, dear*
Arnold, Tedd. *Ollie forgot*
Cole, Joanna. *Aren't you forgetting something, Fiona?*
Copp, James. *Martha Matilda O'Toole*
De Paola, Tomie. *Strega Nona*
Dines, Glen. *A tiger in the cherry tree*

Domanska, Janina. *Palmiero and the ogre*
Fox, Mem. *Wilfrid Gordon McDonald Partridge*
Galdone, Joanna. *Gertrude, the goose who forgot*
Galdone, Paul. *The magic porridge pot*
Guthrie, Donna. *Grandpa doesn't know it's me*
Hale, Irina. *The lost toys*
Hutchins, Pat. *Don't forget the bacon!*
King-Smith, Dick. *Farmer Bungle forgets*
MacGregor, Ellen. *Theodor Turtle*
McNulty, Faith. *The elephant who couldn't forget*
Miles, Miska. *Chicken forgets*
Parish, Peggy. *Be ready at eight*
Patz, Nancy. *Pumpernickel tickle and mean green cheese*
Rogers, Paul. *Forget-me-not*
Schatell, Brian. *The McGoonys have a party*
Schweninger, Ann. *The hunt for rabbit's galosh*
Stevenson, Suçie. *I forgot*
Van Allsburg, Chris. *The stranger*
Weinberg, Lawrence. *The Forgetful Bears*
The Forgetful Bears meet Mr. Memory
Weisgard, Leonard. *Silly Willy Nilly*

Behavior – gossip

Allen, Jeffrey. *Nosey Mrs. Rat*
Andersen, H. C. (Hans Christian). *It's perfectly true!*, ill. by Janet Stevens
Berson, Harold. *The thief who hugged a moonbeam*
Chicken Little. *Chicken Licken*, ill. by Jutta Ash
Chicken Licken, ill. by Gavin Bishop
Henny Penny, ill. by Paul Galdone
Henny Penny, ill. by William Stobbs
The story of Chicken Licken, adapt. and ill. by Jan Ormerod
Holl, Adelaide. *The runaway giant*
Hutchins, Pat. *The surprise party*
Kraus, Robert. *Mert the blurt*
Stevens, Harry. *Parrot told snake*
Varga, Judy. *The monster behind Black Rock*
Zolotow, Charlotte. *The hating book*

Behavior – greed

Alexander, Lloyd. *The four donkeys*
Aliki. *The eggs*
Allen, Pamela. *Hidden treasure*
Andersen, H. C. (Hans Christian). *The woman with the eggs*, ill. by Ray Cruz
Angelo, Valenti. *The candy basket*
Arnold, Caroline. *The terrible Hodag*
Aulaire, Ingri Mortenson d'. *Don't count your chicks*
Aylesworth, Jim. *Mary's mirror*

Barker, Inga-Lil. *Why teddy bears are brown*
Bascom, Joe. *Malcolm Softpaws*
Battles, Edith. *The terrible terrier*
The terrible trick or treat
Bellows, Cathy. *Four fat rats*
Berenstain, Stan. *The Berenstain bears get the gimmies*
Berson, Harold. *The rats who lived in the delicatessen*
Bohdal, Susi. *The magic honey jar*
Bolliger, Max. *The golden apple*
Bonsall, Crosby Newell. *It's mine! A greedy book*
Brenner, Barbara. *Ostrich feathers*
Brown, Marcia. *The bun*
Buckley, Richard. *The greedy python*
Bunting, Eve. *The man who could call down owls*
Carlson, Nancy. *Harriet's Halloween candy*
Carter, Anne. *Bella's secret garden*
Christian, Mary Blount. *The devil take you, Barnabas Beane!*
Coco, Eugene Bradley. *The wishing well*
Cooper, Susan. *The silver cow*
Dauer, Rosamond. *The 300 pound cat*
De Paola, Tomie. *Andy (that's my name)*
Ernst, Lisa Campbell. *The prize pig surprise*
Evans, Katherine. *The maid and her pail of milk*
Ginsburg, Mirra. *Two greedy bears*
Green, Phyllis. *Bagdad ate it*
Grimm, Jacob. *The fisherman and his wife*, ill. by Monika Laimgruber
The fisherman and his wife, ill. by Margot Tomes
The fisherman and his wife, ill. by Margot Zemach
Mother Holly
Hadithi, Mwenye. *Greedy zebra*
Hewitt, Kathryn. *King Midas and the golden touch*
Ishii, Momoko. *The tongue-cut sparrow*
Jacobs, Joseph. *Hudden and Dudden and Donald O'Neary*
Kennedy, Richard. *The lost kingdom of Karnica*
Kismaric, Carole. *The rumor of Pavel and Paali*
Kuskin, Karla. *What did you bring me?*
Lewis, J. Patrick. *The tsar and the amazing cow*
Lionni, Leo. *The biggest house in the world*
Lorenz, Lee. *Pinchpenny John*
Lussert, Anneliese. *The farmer and the moon*
McClenathan, Louise. *My mother sends her wisdom*
McKissack, Patricia C. *King Midas and his gold*, ill. by Tom Dunnington
McLenighan, Valjean. *Three strikes and you're out*

Mahy, Margaret. *Rooms for rent*
Marshall, James. *Yummers too*
Matsutani, Miyoko. *How the withered trees blossomed*
Obrist, Jürg. *The miser who wanted the sun*
Peet, Bill. *Kermit the hermit*
　The kweeks of Kookatumdee
Peppé, Rodney. *The mice and the flying basket*
Perkins, Al. *King Midas and the golden touch*
Porter, David Lord. *Mine!*
Roffey, Maureen. *Look, there's my hat!*
Rohmer, Harriet. *The invisible hunters*
Ross, Tony. *The greedy little cobbler*
San Souci, Robert D. *The enchanted tapestry*
Shibano, Tamizo. *The old man who made the trees bloom*
Solotareff, Grégoire. *Never trust an ogre*
Stadler, John. *Animal cafe*
Stage, Mads. *The greedy blackbird*
Winthrop, Elizabeth. *That's mine*

Behavior – growing up

Alexander, Sue. *Dear Phoebe*
Allison, Alida. *The toddler's potty book*
Appell, Clara. *Now I have a daddy haircut*
Ardizzone, Edward. *Paul, the hero of the fire*
Aseltine, Lorraine. *First grade can wait*
Aulaire, Ingri Mortenson d'. *Too big*
Barrett, Judi. *I hate to take a bath*
　I'm too small, you're too big
Bogot, Howard. *I'm growing*
Bolliger, Max. *The magic bird*
Bonnici, Peter. *The festival*
Bourgeois, Paulette. *Big Sarah's little boots*
Brentano, Clemens. *Schoolmaster Whackwell's wonderful sons*
Brinckloe, Julie. *Fireflies!*
Bromhall, Winifred. *Bridget's growing day*
Brown, Myra Berry. *Benjy's blanket*
Brown, Palmer. *Hickory*
Bruna, Dick. *I can dress myself*
Bryant, Bernice. *Follow the leader*
Buckley, Kate. *Love notes*
Bulla, Clyde Robert. *Dandelion Hill*
Carle, Eric. *My very first book of growth*
Carrier, Lark. *Scout and Cody*
Chaffin, Lillie D. *Tommy's big problem*
Ciardi, John. *Scrappy the pup*
Civardi, Anne. *Potty time*
Cleary, Beverly. *The growing-up feet*
　Janet's thingamajigs
Coats, Laura Jane. *Mr. Jordan in the park*
Cohen, Miriam. *Jim meets the thing*
Cooney, Nancy Evans. *The blanket that had to go*
　Donald says thumbs down
Corey, Dorothy. *Tomorrow you can*

Dauer, Rosamond. *Bullfrog grows up*
Delton, Judy. *The best mom in the world*
De Paola, Tomie. *Katie's good idea*
Drescher, Joan. *I'm in charge!*
Faison, Eleanora. *Becoming*
Fassler, Joan. *Don't worry dear*
　The man of the house
Felt, Sue. *Rosa-too-little*
Freedman, Sally. *Devin's new bed*
Fribourg, Marjorie G. *Ching-Ting and the ducks*
Goennel, Heidi. *When I grow up...*
Graham, Bob. *The red woolen blanket*
Hall, Derek. *Elephant bathes*
　Gorilla builds
　Polar bear leaps
Hanson, Joan. *I won't be afraid*
Harris, Robie H. *I hate kisses*
Hayes, Geoffrey. *Patrick and Ted*
Heitler, Susan M. *David decides about thumbsucking*
Hines, Anna Grossnickle. *All by myself*
Hoban, Brom. *Skunk Lane*
Hoffman, Phyllis. *Baby's first year*
Horner, Althea J. *Little big girl*
Hurwitz, Johanna. *Superduper Teddy*
Iverson, Genie. *I want to be big*
Johnson, Crockett. *We wonder what will Walter be? When he grows up*
Jonas, Ann. *When you were a baby*
Joosse, Barbara M. *Fourth of July*
Khalsa, Dayal Kaur. *I want a dog*
Klinting, Lars. *Regal the golden eagle*
Krasilovsky, Phyllis. *The very little boy*
　The very little girl
Kraus, Robert. *Leo the late bloomer*
Krauss, Ruth. *The growing story*
Levine, Abby. *What did mommy do before you?*
Lexau, Joan M. *I hate red rover*
Lindgren, Barbro. *Sam's potty*
McPhail, David. *Pig Pig grows up*
Marshak, Samuel. *The pup grew up!*
Massie, Diane Redfield. *Tiny pin*
Moers, Hermann. *Camomile heads for home*
Moncure, Jane Belk. *Now I am five!*
　Now I am four!
　Now I am three!
Mordvinoff, Nicolas. *Coral Island*
Munsch, Robert N. *I have to go!*
Newberry, Clare Turlay. *Percy, Polly and Pete*
Nordlicht, Lillian. *I love to laugh*
Otto, Svend. *The giant fish and other stories*
Parish, Peggy. *I can - can you?*
Pellowski, Anne. *Stairstep farm*
Power, Barbara. *I wish Laura's mommy was my mommy*
Reichmeier, Betty. *Potty time!*
Rogers, Fred. *Going to the potty*
Ross, Katharine. *When you were a baby*

Ross, Tony. *I want my potty*
Schlein, Miriam. *Billy, the littlest one*
  Herman McGregor's world
  When will the world be mine?
Schwartz, Amy. *Begin at the beginning*
Sharmat, Marjorie Weinman. *Bartholomew the bossy*
Smith, Robert Paul. *When I am big*
Snyder, Zilpha Keatley. *Come on, Patsy*
Stanley, Diane. *Captain Whiz-Bang*
Stevenson, James. *Higher on the door*
Turkle, Brinton. *Obadiah the Bold*
Van Leeuwen, Jean. *Amanda Pig and her big brother Oliver*
Waber, Bernard. *You're a little kid with a big heart*
Weiss, Nicki. *Barney is big*
Welber, Robert. *Goodbye, hello*
Wells, Rosemary. *Timothy goes to school*
Wittman, Sally. *A special trade*
Young, Helen. *A throne for Sesame*
Young, Ruth. *My potty chair*
Zagone, Theresa. *No nap for me*
Zimelman, Nathan. *If I were strong enough...*
Zolotow, Charlotte. *But not Billy*
  I like to be little
  May I visit?
  Someone new
  When I have a son

Behavior – hiding

Aruego, José. *We hide, you seek*
Asch, Frank. *Moongame*
Chorao, Kay. *Kate's box*
Dubanevich, Arlene. *Pigs in hiding*
Gerstein, Mordicai. *William, where are you?*
Gomi, Taro. *Where's the fish?*
Gretz, Susanna. *Hide-and-seek*
Greydanus, Rose. *My secret hiding place*
Heller, Ruth. *How to hide a butterfly*
  How to hide a polar bear
Hulse, Gillian. *Morris, where are you?*
Kudrna, C. Imbior. *To bathe a boa*
Livermore, Elaine. *Looking for Henry*
McClung, Robert. *How animals hide*
McPhail, David. *Where can an elephant hide?*
Major, Beverly. *Playing sardines*
Matus, Greta. *Where are you, Jason?*
Mintzberg, Yvette. *Sally, where are you?*
Oxford Scientific Films. *Danger colors*
  Hide and seek
Schertle, Alice. *Jeremy Bean's St. Patrick's Day*
  That Olive!
Turpin, Lorna. *The sultan's snakes*
Vigna, Judith. *The hiding house*
Walsh, Ellen Stoll. *Mouse paint*
Warren, Cathy. *Springtime bears*

Wood, John Norris. *Jungles*
  Oceans
Ziefert, Harriet. *Where's the cat?*
  Where's the dog?
  Where's the guinea pig?
  Where's the turtle?
Zion, Gene. *Hide and seek day*

Behavior – hiding things

Adler, David A. *My dog and the green sock mystery*
Allan, Ted. *Willie the squowse*
Allen, Pamela. *Hidden treasure*
Bason, Lillian. *Those foolish Molboes!*
Baylor, Byrd. *Your own best secret place*
Brady, Susan. *Find my blanket*
Croswell, Volney. *How to hide a hippopotamus*
Demi. *Demi's find the animals A B C*
Wood, Leslie. *A dog called Mischief*

Behavior – hurrying

Gomi, Taro. *First comes Harry*
Greydanus, Rose. *Willie the slowpoke*
Hurd, Edith Thacher. *Hurry hurry!*
Steiner, Charlotte. *What's the hurry, Harry?*
Thoreau, Henry D. *What befell at Mrs. Brooks's*

Behavior – imitation

Allamand, Pascale. *The animals who changed their colors*
Aruego, José. *Look what I can do*
Asch, Frank. *Just like daddy*
Barrett, Judi. *Animals should definitely not act like people*
  Animals should definitely not wear clothing
Bendick, Jeanne. *Why can't I?*
Blakeley, Peggy. *What shall I be tomorrow?*
Buckmaster, Henrietta. *Lucy and Loki*
Calhoun, Mary. *The nine lives of Homer C. Cat*
Canning, Kate. *A painted tale*
Cauley, Lorinda Bryan. *The animal kids*
Charlton, Elizabeth. *Terrible tyrannosaurus*
Christian, Mary Blount. *Swamp monsters*
Clewes, Dorothy. *Henry Hare's boxing match*
Cole, Brock. *Nothing but a pig*
Farber, Norma. *There goes feathertop!*
Graham, Amanda. *Who wants Arthur?*
Hallinan, P. K. (Patrick K.). *Where's Michael?*
Heine, Helme. *Mr. Miller the dog*
Jones, Chuck. *William the backwards skunk*
Kellogg, Steven. *A rose for Pinkerton*
Kent, Jack. *The once-upon-a-time dragon*
Moore, Inga. *Fifty red night-caps*

Numeroff, Laura Joffe. *If you give a mouse a cookie*
Riddell, Chris. *Bird's new shoes*
Saltzberg, Barney. *The yawn*
Schwartz, Amy. *Bea and Mr. Jones*

Behavior – indifference

Blos, Joan W. *Old Henry*
Dubanevich, Arlene. *Pig William*
Hogrogian, Nonny. *The hermit and Harry and me*
Roy, Ronald. *Three ducks went wandering*
Sendak, Maurice. *Pierre*
Sharmat, Marjorie Weinman. *I don't care*
Watts, Mabel. *The day it rained watermelons*

Behavior – lateness *see* Behavior – tardiness

Behavior – losing things

Abolafia, Yossi. *A fish for Mrs. Gardenia*
Ardizzone, Edward. *The little girl and the tiny doll*
Ayer, Jacqueline. *Nu Dang and his kite*
Bannon, Laura. *Red mittens*
Barrows, Marjorie Wescott. *The funny hat*
Bassett, Lisa. *Beany and Scamp*
Birdseye, Tom. *Airmail to the moon*
Bond, Michael. *Paddington at the zoo*
Bottner, Barbara. *Big boss! Little boss!*
Bowden, Joan Chase. *Who took the top hat trick?*
Boyle, Constance. *The story of little owl*
Bromhall, Winifred. *Middle Matilda*
Brunhoff, Laurent de. *Babar loses his crown*
Burningham, John. *The blanket*
Chorao, Kay. *Molly's lies*
  Molly's Moe
Coombs, Patricia. *The lost playground*
Craft, Ruth. *The day of the rainbow*
Davidson, Amanda. *Teddy in the garden*
Dodds, Siobhan. *Charles Tiger*
Eriksson, Eva. *The tooth trip*
Gay, Michel. *Little shoe*
Guthrie, Donna. *Grandpa doesn't know it's me*
Haddon, Mark. *Gilbert's gobstopper*
Handford, Martin. *Where's Waldo?*
Havill, Juanita. *Jamaica's find*
Johnson, B. J. *My blanket Burt*
Jonas, Ann. *Where can it be?*
Kay, Helen. *One mitten Lewis*
Keenen, George. *The preposterous week*
Kelley, Anne. *Daisy's discovery*
Kellogg, Steven. *The mystery of the magic green ball*
  The mystery of the missing red mitten
Lexau, Joan M. *Finders keepers, losers weepers*

Livermore, Elaine. *Lost and found*
  Three little kittens lost their mittens
McGinley, Phyllis. *Lucy McLockett*
McNeely, Jeannette. *Where's Izzy?*
Marcus, Susan. *The missing button adventure*
Marks, Alan. *Nowhere to be found*
Marshak, Samuel. *The pup grew up!*
Martin, Jacqueline Briggs. *Bizzy Bones and the lost quilt*
Morgan, Allen. *Matthew and the midnight money van*
Mother Goose. *The three little kittens*, ill. by Lorinda Bryan Cauley
  The three little kittens, ill. by Paul Galdone
  The three little kittens, ill. by Dorothy Stott
  The three little kittens, ill. by Shelley Thornton
Munari, Bruno. *Jimmy has lost his cap*
O'Brien, Anne S. *Where's my truck?*
Precek, Katharine Wilson. *Penny in the road*
Price, Mathew. *Do you see what I see?*
Rabe, Berniece. *Where's Chimpy?*
Rogers, Jean. *Runaway mittens*
Rogers, Paul. *Forget-me-not*
Ryder, Eileen. *Winston's new cap*
Schubert, Dieter. *Where's my monkey?*
Sharmat, Marjorie Weinman. *The trip*
Upham, Elizabeth. *Little brown bear loses his clothes*
Walsh, Jill Paton. *Lost and found*
White, Florence Meiman. *How to lose your lunch money*
Zander, Hans. *My blue chair*
Ziefert, Harriet. *Good night, Jessie!*
Zinnemann-Hope, Pam. *Find your coat, Ned*

Behavior – lost

Alexander, Liza. *Ernie gets lost*
Allen, Laura Jean. *Where is Freddy?*
Anderson, C. W. (Clarence Williams). *Blaze finds forgotten roads*
  Blaze finds the trail
Ayer, Jacqueline. *Little Silk*
Balian, Lorna. *Amelia's nine lives*
Barklem, Jill. *Autumn story*
Bartoli, Jennifer. *Snow on bear's nose*
Barton, Byron. *Where's Al?*
Bassett, Lisa. *Beany and Scamp*
Belting, Natalia Maree. *Verity Mullens and the Indian*
Bemelmans, Ludwig. *Madeline and the gypsies*
Beni, Ruth. *Sir Baldergog the great*
Benjamin, Alan. *Ribtickle Town*
Berson, Harold. *Henry Possum*
Boegehold, Betty. *Pawpaw's run*
Bograd, Larry. *Lost in the store*

Bolliger, Max. *Sandy at the children's zoo*
Bornstein, Ruth Lercher. *Annabelle*
Jim
Bothwell, Jean. *Paddy and Sam*
Brewster, Patience. *Ellsworth and the cats from Mars*
Brown, Judith Gwyn. *Max and the truffle pig*
Brown, Marcia. *Tamarindo!*
Brown, Margaret Wise. *Little lost lamb*
Three little animals
Brunhoff, Laurent de. *Babar's little girl*
Bunting, Eve. *Jane Martin, dog detective*
Calmenson, Stephanie. *Where is Grandma Potamus?*
Carigiet, Alois. *Anton the goatherd*
Carle, Eric. *Have you seen my cat?*
Carrick, Carol. *The highest balloon on the common*
Left behind
Carter, Anne. *Ruff leaves home*
Cartlidge, Michelle. *Pippin and Pod*
Cohen, Miriam. *Lost in the museum*
Cole, Joanna. *The Clown-Arounds go on vacation*
Corddry, Thomas I. *Kibby's big feat*
Cummings, Betty Sue. *Turtle*, ill. by Susan Dodge
De Beer, Hans. *Little polar bear*
Delaney, Ned. *Bad dog!*
Drummond, Violet H. *Phewtus the squirrel*
Erickson, Phoebe. *Just follow me*
Farber, Norma. *Where's Gomer?*
Flack, Marjorie. *Angus lost*
Fletcher, Elizabeth. *The little goat*
Francis, Frank. *The magic wallpaper*
Gay, Michel. *Take me for a ride*
Gay, Zhenya. *Small one*
Goble, Paul. *The friendly wolf*
Goldsmith, Howard. *Little lost dog*
Grimm, Jacob. *Hansel and Gretel*, ill. by Winslow P. Pels
Guilfoile, Elizabeth. *Have you seen my brother?*
Guthrie, Donna. *Grandpa doesn't know it's me*
Hader, Berta Hoerner. *Lost in the zoo*
Hawkins, Colin. *Tog the dog*
Hayes, Sarah. *This is the bear*
Henkes, Kevin. *Sheila Rae, the brave*
Hill, Eric. *Where's Spot?*
Hines, Anna Grossnickle. *Don't worry, I'll find you*
Hirsh, Marilyn. *Where is Yonkela?*
Hoban, Lillian. *The laziest robot in zone one*
Hutchins, Pat. *Where's the baby?*
Irving, Washington. *Rip Van Winkle*, ill. by John Howe
Rip Van Winkle, ill. by Thomas Locker
Rip Van Winkle, ill. by Peter Wingham
Jaques, Faith. *Tilly's rescue*

Joerns, Consuelo. *The foggy rescue*
The forgotten bear
Jonas, Ann. *Two bear cubs*
Keats, Ezra Jack. *My dog is lost!*
Kessler, Leonard P. *Are we lost, daddy?*
Kočí, Marta. *Katie's kitten*
Lisker, Sonia O. *Lost*
Livermore, Elaine. *Follow the fox*
Lobel, Arnold. *Uncle Elephant*
Lubell, Winifred. *Rosalie, the bird market turtle*
McCloskey, Robert. *Blueberries for Sal*
McCully, Emily Arnold. *Picnic*
Maris, Ron. *Are you there, bear?*
Marks, Alan. *Nowhere to be found*
Martin, Jacqueline Briggs. *Bizzy Bones and Moosemouse*
Mendoza, George. *Alphabet sheep*
Miles, Miska. *This little pig*
Modell, Frank. *Tooley! Tooley!*
Mogensen, Jan. *When Teddy woke early*
Moser, Erwin. *Wilma the elephant*
Nakatani, Chiyoko. *The day Chiro was lost*
Nims, Bonnie L. *Where is the bear?*
Olsen, Ib Spang. *Cat alley*
Parenteau, Shirley. *I'll bet you thought I was lost*
Paul, Jan S. *Hortense*
Peet, Bill. *Ella*
Politi, Leo. *The nicest gift*
Rey, Margaret Elisabeth Waldstein. *Curious George goes to the hospital*
Rubel, Nicole. *It came from the swamp*
Rylant, Cynthia. *Henry and Mudge*
Sauer, Julia Lina. *Mike's house*
Saxon, Charles D. *Don't worry about Poopsie*
Schumacher, Claire. *Tim and Jim*
Seignobosc, Françoise. *Minou*
Springtime for Jeanne-Marie
Shortall, Leonard W. *Andy, the dog walker*
Slobodkin, Louis. *Yasu and the strangers*
Sotomayor, Antonio. *Khasa goes to the fiesta*
Standon, Anna. *Little duck lost*
Stevenson, James. *Howard*
Taylor, Mark. *The case of the missing kittens*
Henry the castaway
Henry the explorer
Titherington, Jeanne. *Where are you going, Emma?*
Tokuda, Wendy. *Humphrey the lost whale*
Vincent, Gabrielle. *Where are you, Ernest and Celestine?*
Vreeken, Elizabeth. *The boy who would not say his name*
Watanabe, Shigeo. *Where's my daddy?*
Wold, Jo Anne. *Well! Why didn't you say so?*
Ylla. *Two little bears*
Young, Evelyn. *The tale of Tai*

Behavior – lying

Æsop. *Wolf! wolf!*
Belloc, Hilaire. *Matilda who told lies and was burned to death*
Berenstain, Stan. *The Berenstain bears and the truth*
Brown, Marc. *The true Francine*
Chorao, Kay. *Molly's lies*
Christopher, Matt. *Jackrabbit goalie*
Cohen, Miriam. *Liar, liar, pants on fire!*
Collodi, Carlo. *The adventures of Pinocchio*
Elliott, Dan. *Ernie's little lie*
Elzbieta. *Dikou the little troon who walks at night*
Evans, Katherine. *The boy who cried wolf*
Gackenbach, Dick. *Crackle, Gluck and the sleeping toad*
Helena, Ann. *The lie*
Lexau, Joan M. *Finders keepers, losers weepers*
Lloyd, David. *The ridiculous story of Gammer Gurton's needle*
Sharmat, Marjorie Weinman. *A big fat enormous lie*
Turkle, Brinton. *The adventures of Obadiah*

Behavior – misbehavior

Agard, John. *Dig away two-hole Tim*
Alexander, Martha G. *We're in big trouble, Blackboard Bear*
Allard, Harry. *Miss Nelson is back*
Miss Nelson is missing!
Arnold, Tedd. *No jumping on the bed!*
Ashley, Bernard. *Dinner ladies don't count*
Baba, Noboru. *Eleven cats and a pig*
Eleven cats and albatrosses
Eleven cats in a bag
Eleven hungry cats
Baker, Alan. *Benjamin's book*
Benjamin's dreadful dream
Baker, Margaret. *A puppy called Spinach*
Baumann, Kurt. *The story of Jonah*
Beech, Caroline. *Peas again for lunch*
Beim, Jerrold. *The taming of Toby*
Belloc, Hilaire. *Jim, who ran away from his nurse, and was eaten by a lion*
Matilda who told lies and was burned to death
Bemelmans, Ludwig. *Madeline and the bad hat*
Berenstain, Stan. *The Berenstain bears and the truth*
Berry, Joy Wilt. *Being destructive*
Being selfish
Disobeying
Fighting
Throwing tantrums
Whining

Blaustein, Muriel. *Baby Mabu and Auntie Moose*
Bedtime, Zachary!
Boyd, Lizi. *Half wild and half child*
Bradbury, Bianca. *Muggins*
Bradman, Tony. *The bad babies' book of colors*
The bad babies' counting book
Brown, Margaret Wise. *Sneakers*
Brunhoff, Laurent de. *Babar's cousin, that rascal Arthur*
Calhoun, Mary. *The goblin under the stairs*
Campbell, Rod. *Henry's busy day*
Misty's mischief
Cartlidge, Michelle. *Pippin and Pod*
Chalmers, Audrey. *Fancy be good*
Chapman, Carol. *Herbie's troubles*
Chess, Victoria. *Alfred's alphabet walk*
Christian, Mary Blount. *Go west, swamp monsters*
Claverie, Jean. *The party*
Cohen, Miriam. *Starring first grade*
Cole, William. *That pest Jonathan*
Colette. *The boy and the magic*
Collington, Peter. *Little pickle*
Collins, Pat L. *Taking care of Tucker*
Collodi, Carlo. *The adventures of Pinocchio*
Costa, Nicoletta. *The naughty puppy*
The new puppy
Craig, Helen. *A welcome for Annie*
Crowley, Arthur. *The boogey man*
Dauer, Rosamond. *My friend, Jasper Jones*
Delaney, A. *The gunnywolf*
Delaney, Ned. *Bad dog!*
Rufus the doofus
Douglass, Barbara. *Good as new*
Eastman, P. D. (Philip D.). *Are you my mother?*
Flack, Marjorie. *The story about Ping*
Froment, Eugène. *The story of a round loaf*
Gackenbach, Dick. *Pepper and all the legs*
Gág, Wanda. *The sorcerer's apprentice*
Galbraith, Kathryn Osebold. *Katie did!*
Gantos, Jack. *Rotten Ralph*
Worse than Rotten Ralph
Gerson, Corinne. *Good dog, bad dog*
Goodall, John S. *Naughty Nancy*
Naughty Nancy goes to school
Gordon, Margaret. *Wilberforce goes to a party*
Grindley, Sally. *Four black puppies*
Harper, Wilhelmina. *The gunniwolf*
Hayes, Sarah. *Bad egg*
Hedderwick, Mairi. *Katie Morag and the big boy cousins*
Katie Morag and the tiresome Ted
Katie Morag delivers the mail
Henkes, Kevin. *A weekend with Wendell*
Herz, Irene. *Hey! Don't do that!*
Hill, Eric. *Spot visits the hospital*
Spot's first picnic

Hiller, Catherine. *Argentaybee and the boonie*
Himmelman, John. *Amanda and the witch switch*
Hirsh, Marilyn. *Deborah the dybbuk*
Hoban, Russell. *How Tom beat Captain Najork and his hired sportsmen*
Hodeir, André. *Warwick's three bottles*
Hogan, Inez. *About Nono, the baby elephant*
Hort, Lenny. *The boy who held back the sea*
Hutchins, Pat. *Where's the baby?*
Inkiow, Dimiter. *Me and Clara and Baldwin the pony*
Me and Clara and Snuffy the dog
Me and my sister Clara
Jameson, Cynthia. *The clay pot boy*
Jeffers, Susan. *Wild Robin*
Joosse, Barbara M. *The thinking place*
Keller, Beverly. *When mother got the flu*
Keller, Holly. *A bear for Christmas*
Kellogg, Steven. *Prehistoric Pinkerton*
Kent, Jack. *The scribble monster*
Kent, Lorna. *No, no, Charlie Rascal!*
Kline, Suzy. *Don't touch!*
Koenig, Marion. *The wonderful world of night*
Krasilovsky, Phyllis. *The man who entered a contest*
Kroll, Steven. *Otto*
Pigs in the house
Leaf, Munro. *A flock of watchbirds*
Levinson, Riki. *Touch! Touch!*
Levy, Elizabeth. *Something queer at the library*
Something queer on vacation
Lexau, Joan M. *I'll tell on you*
Lillie, Patricia. *One very, very quiet afternoon*
Lindgren, Barbro. *The wild baby*
Lipkind, William. *Nubber bear*
Lippman, Peter. *The Know-It-Alls go to sea*
The Know-It-Alls help out
The Know-It-Alls mind the store
The Know-It-Alls take a winter vacation
Littlewood, Valerie. *The season clock*
Lobel, Arnold. *Prince Bertram the bad*
Lorimer, Janet. *The biggest bubble in the world*
Luttrell, Ida. *Mattie and the chicken thief*
McPhail, David. *Andrew's bath*
Mahiri, Jabari. *The day they stole the letter J*
Mahy, Margaret. *The boy with two shadows*
Malloy, Judy. *Bad Thad*
Marshall, Edward. *Fox and his friends*
Fox on wheels
Marshall, James. *The Cut-Ups*
The Cut-Ups cut loose
Fox on the job
George and Martha back in town
Marzollo, Jean. *Uproar on Hollercat Hill*
Mayer, Mercer. *Appelard and Liverwurst*

Moremen, Grace E. *No, no, Natalie*
Morgan, Allen. *Molly and Mr. Maloney*
Murphy, Jill. *All in one piece*
Myller, Lois. *No! No!*
Oana, Kay D. *Shasta and the shebang machine*
Obrist, Jürg. *Bear business*
O'Kelley, Mattie Lou. *Circus!*
Oldfield, Pamela. *Melanie Brown climbs a tree*
Olson, Helen Kronberg. *The strange thing that happened to Oliver Wendell Iscovitch*
Oram, Hiawyn. *Ned and the Joybaloo*
Oxenbury, Helen. *The car trip*
The important visitor
Parker, Nancy Winslow. *Cooper, the McNallys' big black dog*
Poofy loves company
Paterson, Diane. *Soap and suds*
Pearson, Tracey Campbell. *Sing a song of sixpence*
Polushkin, Maria. *Kitten in trouble*
Potter, Beatrix. *The complete adventures of Peter Rabbit*
The tale of Benjamin Bunny
The tale of Peter Rabbit, ill. by Margot Apple
The tale of Peter Rabbit, ill. by Beatrix Potter
The tale of two bad mice
The two bad mice pop-up book
Where's Peter Rabbit?
Poulin, Stephane. *Can you catch Josephine?*
Prater, John. *On Friday something funny happened*
You can't catch me!
Preston, Edna Mitchell. *Horrible Hepzibah*
Squawk to the moon, little goose
Quackenbush, Robert M. *Mouse feathers*
Rabinowitz, Sandy. *A colt named mischief*
Rappus, Gerhard. *When the sun was shining*
Rice, Eve. *Benny bakes a cake*
Robison, Deborah. *Your turn, doctor*
Rockwell, Anne F. *Honk honk!*
Ross, Pat. *M and M and the mummy mess*
Ross, Tony. *Oscar got the blame*
Ruck-Pauquèt, Gina. *Oh, that koala!*
Sadler, Marilyn. *Alistair's elephant*
Sandberg, Inger. *Dusty wants to help*
Nicholas' red day
Sarrazin, Johan. *Tootle*
Schatell, Brian. *Farmer Goff and his turkey Sam*
Schroeder, Binette. *Tuffa and the picnic*
Schumacher, Claire. *King of the zoo*
Sendak, Maurice. *Where the wild things are*
Sherrow, Victoria. *There goes the ghost*
Small, David. *Paper John*

Smith, Janice Lee. *The monster in the third dresser drawer and other stories about Adam Joshua*

Solotareff, Grégoire. *Don't call me little bunny*

Standiford, Natalie. *The best little monkeys in the world*

Standon, Anna. *Three little cats*

Stevenson, Suçie. *Jessica the blue streak*

Tierney, Hanne. *Where's your baby brother, Becky Bunting?*

Van Allsburg, Chris. *The garden of Abdul Gasazi*

Vigna, Judith. *Anyhow, I'm glad I tried She's not my real mother*

Vincent, Gabrielle. *Breakfast time, Ernest and Celestine*

Wallace, Ian. *Morgan the magnificent The sparrow's song*

Ward, Cindy. *Cookie's week*

Ward, Nick. *Giant.*

Ward, Sally G. *Charlie and Grandma*

Watanabe, Yuichi. *Wally the whale who loved balloons*

Watson, Wendy. *Lollipop*

We wish you a merry Christmas

Wells, Rosemary. *Good night, Fred Hazel's amazing mother*

White, Florence Meiman. *How to lose your lunch money*

Williams, Barbara. *Whatever happened to Beverly Bigler's birthday?*

Wiseman, Bernard. *Don't make fun!*

Wood, Audrey. *Elbert's bad word*

Yeoman, John. *The wild washerwomen*

Zemach, Margot. *Jake and Honeybunch go to heaven*

Zhitkov, Boris. *How I hunted for the little fellows*

Ziefert, Harriet. *Strike four!*

Behavior – mistakes

Aliki. *Jack and Jake*

Bonsall, Crosby Newell. *The case of the dumb bells*

Boyd, Selma. *The how*

Brandenberg, Franz. *No school today!*

Bridwell, Norman. *Clifford's good deeds*

Chevalier, Christa. *Spence makes circles*

Coombs, Patricia. *Dorrie's play*

Cresswell, Helen. *Two hoots and the king Two hoots in the snow*

Erickson, Karen. *No one is perfect*

Firmin, Peter. *Basil Brush goes flying*

Gág, Wanda. *Gone is gone*

Galdone, Paul. *Obedient Jack*

Geringer, Laura. *Molly's new washing machine*

Hoff, Syd. *Henrietta, the early bird*

Jacobs, Joseph. *Hereafterthis*

Lexau, Joan M. *It all began with a drip, drip, drip*

Martin, Rafe. *Foolish rabbit's big mistake*

Springstubb, Tricia. *The magic guinea pig*

Waber, Bernard. *Nobody is perfick*

Walker, Barbara K. *New patches for old*

Weiner, Beth Lee. *Benjamin's perfect solution*

Wiseman, Bernard. *Tails are not for painting*

Behavior – misunderstanding

Allard, Harry. *The Stupids die*

Berg, Jean Horton. *The O'Learys and friends*

Berson, Harold. *Kassim's shoes*

Boyd, Lizi. *The not-so-wicked stepmother*

Bryant, Sara Cone. *Epaminondas and his auntie*

Bush, John. *The cross-with-us rhinoceros*

Carrick, Carol. *Old Mother Witch*

Demuth, Patricia Brennan. *Max, the bad-talking parrot*

Dickinson, Mike. *My dad doesn't even notice*

Gackenbach, Dick. *Arabella and Mr. Crack King Wacky*

Hopkins, Lee Bennett. *I loved Rose Ann*

Komaiko, Leah. *Earl's too cool for me*

Kraus, Robert. *Ladybug, ladybug!*

Lionni, Leo. *Fish is fish*

McClintock, Marshall. *A fly went by*

Nixon, Joan Lowery. *Bigfoot makes a movie*

Parish, Peggy. *Amelia Bedelia*
   Amelia Bedelia and the surprise shower
   Amelia Bedelia goes camping
   Amelia Bedelia helps out
   Come back, Amelia Bedelia
   Good work, Amelia Bedelia
   Merry Christmas, Amelia Bedelia
   Play ball, Amelia Bedelia
   Teach us, Amelia Bedelia
   Thank you, Amelia Bedelia

Polushkin, Maria. *Mother, Mother, I want another*

Roberts, Sarah. *Bert and the missing mop mix-up*

Schatell, Brian. *The McGoonys have a party*

Sharmat, Marjorie Weinman. *Gila monsters meet you at the airport*

Stoeke, Janet Morgan. *Minerva Louise*

Tusa, Tricia. *Chicken*

Waber, Bernard. *Funny, funny Lyle*

Wild, Jocelyn. *Florence and Eric take the cake*

Wiseman, Bernard. *Morris has a birthday party!*

Wold, Jo Anne. *Well! Why didn't you say so?*

Yorinks, Arthur. *Company's coming*

Zemke, Deborah. *The way it happened*

Behavior – nagging

Dickinson, Mary. *Alex's outing*
Mahy, Margaret. *Mrs. Discombobulous*
Stalder, Valerie. *Even the Devil is afraid of a shrew*

Behavior – needing someone

Asare, Meshack. *Cat... in search of a friend*
Billam, Rosemary. *Fuzzy rabbit*
Bingham, Mindy. *Minou*
Bulla, Clyde Robert. *The stubborn old woman*
Collins, Pat L. *Taking care of Tucker*
Gauch, Patricia Lee. *Christina Katerina and the time she quit the family*
Guilfoile, Elizabeth. *Nobody listens to Andrew*
Hawkins, Colin. *Where's my mommy?*
Herriot, James. *Blossom comes home*
Hess, Lilo. *A cat's nine lives*
Hughes, Richard. *Gertrude's child*
Hughes, Shirley. *Alfie gives a hand*
Jeschke, Susan. *Lucky's choice*
Keats, Ezra Jack. *Louie's search*
Kent, Jack. *There's no such thing as a dragon*
Livermore, Elaine. *Follow the fox*
Lobel, Anita. *A birthday for the princess*
McLerran, Alice. *The mountain that loved a bird*
McPhail, David. *Emma's pet*
Great cat
Mayer, Mercer. *Whinnie the lovesick dragon*
Morris, Terry Nell. *Lucky puppy! Lucky boy!*
Moser, Erwin. *Wilma the elephant*
Oppenheim, Joanne. *On the other side of the river*
Peet, Bill. *Zella, Zack, and Zodiac*
Rayner, Mary. *Crocodarling*
Roberts, Sarah. *I want to go home!*
Schubert, Dieter. *Where's my monkey?*
Scott, Ann Herbert. *On mother's lap*
Sam
Sendak, Maurice. *Very far away*
Singer, Marilyn. *Pickle plan*
Skorpen, Liesel Moak. *Charles*
Stehr, Frédéric. *Quack-quack*
Sugita, Yutaka. *Helena the unhappy hippopotamus*
Tennyson, Noel. *The lady's chair and the ottoman*
Tokuda, Wendy. *Humphrey the lost whale*
Tompert, Ann. *Will you come back for me?*
Vigna, Judith. *Mommy and me by ourselves again*
Wells, Rosemary. *Noisy Nora*
Wolde, Gunilla. *Betsy and the chicken pox*

Behavior – running away

Adoff, Arnold. *Where wild Willie?*
Alexander, Martha G. *And my mean old mother will be sorry, Blackboard Bear*
Baker, Leslie A. *The third-story cat*
Barrett, Lawrence Louis. *Twinkle, the baby colt*
Bates, H. E. *Achilles the donkey*
Belloc, Hilaire. *Jim, who ran away from his nurse, and was eaten by a lion*
Bond, Felicia. *Wake up, Vladimir*
Brown, Margaret Wise. *The runaway bunny*
Brunhoff, Jean de. *The story of Babar, the little elephant*
Burton, Virginia Lee. *Choo choo*
Byrd, Robert. *Marcella was bored*
Carlson, Natalie Savage. *Runaway Marie Louise*
Carroll, Ruth. *What Whiskers did*
Christian, Mary Blount. *Go west, swamp monsters*
Clifton, Lucille. *My brother fine with me*
Coombs, Patricia. *Lisa and the grompet*
Dumas, Philippe. *Lucy, a tale of a donkey*
DuPasquier, Philippe. *The great escape*
Duvoisin, Roger Antoine. *The missing milkman*
Elzbieta. *Dikou and the mysterious moon sheep*
Freeman, Don. *Beady Bear*
Gackenbach, Dick. *Claude and Pepper*
Galbraith, Richard. *Reuben runs away*
Gianni, Peg. *Alex, the amazing juggler*
The gingerbread boy. *The gingerbread boy, ill. by Scott Cook*
The gingerbread boy, ill. by Paul Galdone
The gingerbread boy, ill. by Joan Elizabeth Goodman
The gingerbread boy, ill. by William Curtis Holdsworth
The gingerbread man
The pancake boy
Whiff, sniff, nibble and chew
Goodall, John S. *The adventures of Paddy Pork*
Greene, Graham. *The little train*
Hale, Irina. *Chocolate mouse and sugar pig*
Hamilton, Morse. *My name is Emily*
Hanson, Joan. *I'm going to run away*
Heck, Elisabeth. *The black sheep*
Heller, Wendy. *Clementine and the cage*
Hillert, Margaret. *The little runaway*
Hoban, Russell. *A baby sister for Frances*
Hogrogian, Nonny. *Billy Goat and his well-fed friends*
Hughes, Richard. *Gertrude's child*
Hyman, Robin. *Casper and the rainbow bird*
Isenberg, Barbara. *The adventures of Albert, the running bear*
Jeschke, Susan. *Lucky's choice*

Joerns, Consuelo. *Oliver's escape*
Johnson, Jane. *Today I thought I'd run away*
Kent, Jack. *Joey runs away*
Knight, Hilary. *Where's Wallace?*
Kraus, Robert. *Where are you going, little mouse?*
La Farge, Phyllis. *Joanna runs away*
Langner, Nola. *By the light of the silvery moon*
Lasker, Joe. *The do-something day*
Lisowski, Gabriel. *Roncalli's magnificent circus*
Lobel, Arnold. *The man who took the indoors out*
Small pig
McClure, Gillian. *Fly home McDoo*
McConnachie, Brian. *Lily of the forest*
McKissack, Patricia C. *Who is coming?*
McPhail, David. *Stanley Henry Bear's friend*
Marol, Jean-Claude. *Vagabul escapes*
Miles, Miska. *This little pig*
Oakley, Graham. *Hetty and Harriet*
O'Donnell, Elizabeth Lee. *Maggie doesn't want to move*
Otto, Svend. *Taxi dog*
Parker, Nancy Winslow. *The crocodile under Louis Finneberg's bed*
Patterson, Geoffrey. *A pig's tale*
Paxton, Tom. *Jennifer's rabbit*
Pearson, Susan. *Saturday, I ran away*
Peet, Bill. *Pamela Camel*
Pittaway, Margaret. *The rainforest children*
Poulin, Stephane. *Have you seen Josephine?*
Prater, John. *You can't catch me!*
Ravilious, Robin. *The runaway chick*
Rockwell, Anne F. *Willy runs away*
Rogers, Paul. *Sheepchase*
Seligman, Dorothy Halle. *Run away home*
Sendak, Maurice. *Very far away*
Sharmat, Marjorie Weinman. *Rex*
Singer, Marilyn. *Archer Armadillo's secret room*
Vernon, Tannis. *Little Pig and the blue-green sea*
Waber, Bernard. *Bernard*
Whitmore, Adam. *Max leaves home*
Wildsmith, Brian. *Daisy*
Woolaver, Lance. *From Ben Loman to the sea*
Wright, Dare. *Edith and Mr. Bear*
Yolen, Jane. *The girl who loved the wind*
Yorinks, Arthur. *Hey, Al*
Zimnik, Reiner. *The bear on the motorcycle*
The proud circus horse
Zion, Gene. *Harry, the dirty dog*
Zolotow, Charlotte. *Big sister and little sister*

Behavior – saving things

Brandenberg, Franz. *What can you make of it?*
Calhoun, Mary. *The traveling ball of string*
Ciardi, John. *John J. Plenty and Fiddler Dan*
Delton, Judy. *Penny wise, fun foolish*
Foster, Doris Van Liew. *A pocketful of seasons*
Mayne, William. *The patchwork cat*

Behavior – secrets

Aardema, Verna. *What's so funny, Ketu?*
Allard, Harry. *Miss Nelson has a field day*
Auerbach, Marjorie. *King Lavra and the barber*
Bahr, Amy C. *Sometimes it's ok to tell secrets*
Bang, Molly. *Dawn*
Barklem, Jill. *The secret staircase*
Baylor, Byrd. *Your own best secret place*
Beisner, Monika. *Secret spells and curious charms*
Brandenberg, Franz. *A secret for grandmother's birthday*
Brighton, Catherine. *Five secrets in a box*
Christelow, Eileen. *The robbery at the diamond dog diner*
Coombs, Patricia. *The magician and McTree*
Cummings, W. T. (Walter Thies). *Miss Esta Maude's secret*
Davis, Maggie S. *Grandma's secret letter*
Galbraith, Kathryn Osebold. *Waiting for Jennifer*
Hayes, Sarah. *This is the bear*
Hughes, Shirley. *Sally's secret*
Krahn, Fernando. *The secret in the dungeon*
Lifton, Betty Jean. *The secret seller*
Pevear, Richard. *Our king has horns!*
Russell, Pamela. *Do you have a secret?*
Thomson, Peggy. *The king has horse's ears*
Willis, Val. *The secret in the matchbox*
Zemke, Deborah. *The way it happened*

Behavior – seeking better things

Abolafia, Yossi. *Yanosh's Island*
Alborough, Jez. *The grass is always greener*
Allen, Jeffrey. *The secret life of Mr. Weird*
Anderson, Joy. *Juma and the magic Jinn*
Brandenberg, Franz. *What's wrong with a van?*
Buckley, Richard. *The foolish tortoise*
Climo, Lindee. *Clyde*
Cole, Brock. *Nothing but a pig*
Cummings, W. T. (Walter Thies). *The kid*
Demarest, Chris L. *Benedict finds a home*
Gackenbach, Dick. *Little bug*
Gage, Wilson. *Mrs. Gaddy and the fast-growing vine*

Ganz, Yaffa. *The story of Mimmy and Simmy*

Giff, Patricia Reilly. *Next year I'll be special*

Heilbroner, Joan. *Tom the TV cat*

Ivanov, Anatoly. *Ol' Jake's lucky day*

Jennings, Linda M. *Crispin and the dancing piglet*

Kent, Jack. *Joey runs away*

Kraus, Robert. *Where are you going, little mouse?*

Lasky, Kathryn. *Sea swan*

Le Guin, Ursula K. *Solomon Leviathan's nine hundred and thirty-first trip around the world*

Lindgren, Astrid. *My nightingale is singing*

Lionni, Leo. *Tillie and the wall*

Lopshire, Robert. *I want to be somebody new!*

McCunn, Ruthanne L. *Pie-Biter*

McKee, David. *The hill and the rock*

Mahy, Margaret. *The man whose mother was a pirate*

Marshall, James. *Rapscallion Jones*

Miller, Moira. *Oscar Mouse finds a home*

Moore, Inga. *The truffle hunter*

Nixon, Joan Lowery. *If you say so, Claude*

Pittaway, Margaret. *The rainforest children*

Rose, Anne. *As right as right can be*

Stanley, Diane. *A country tale*

Tobias, Tobi. *The quitting deal*

Watts, Bernadette. *St. Francis and the proud crow*

Williams, Vera B. *A chair for my mother*

Yorinks, Arthur. *Bravo, Minski*

Behavior – sharing

Albert, Burton. *Mine, yours, ours*

Azaad, Meyer. *Half for you*

Beim, Jerrold. *The smallest boy in the class*

Caudill, Rebecca. *A pocketful of cricket*

Cohen, Miriam. *Don't eat too much turkey!*

Corey, Dorothy. *Everybody takes turns*
We all share

Croll, Carolyn. *Too many babas*

Davis, Gibbs. *The other Emily*

Delacre, Lulu. *Nathan and Nicholas Alexander*

De Lynam, Alicia Garcia. *It's mine!*

Demarest, Chris L. *Morton and Sidney*

Devlin, Wende. *Cranberry Christmas*

Ets, Marie Hall. *The cow's party*

Flory, Jane. *The unexpected grandchild*

Gackenbach, Dick. *Claude the dog*

Galdone, Paul. *The magic porridge pot*

Goldin, Barbara Diamond. *Just enough is plenty*

Gould, Deborah. *Brendan's best-timed birthday*

Gretz, Susanna. *It's your turn, Roger*

Heuck, Sigrid. *Who stole the apples?*

Hooker, Ruth. *Sara loves her big brother*

Houston, John A. *The bright yellow rope*

Hutchins, Pat. *The doorbell rang*

Johnston, Tony. *Mole and Troll trim the tree*

Keats, Ezra Jack. *Peter's chair*

Klein, Norma. *Visiting Pamela*

Lakin, Patricia. *Don't touch my room*

Lesikin, Joan. *Down the road*

Lester, Helen. *The wizard, the fairy and the magic chicken*

Lindgren, Barbro. *Sam's car*
Sam's cookie

Littledale, Freya. *The farmer in the soup*

Maiorano, Robert. *A little interlude*

Noble, June. *Two homes for Lynn*

O'Brien, Anne S. *I want that!*

Ormerod, Jan. *101 things to do with a baby*

Parkinson, Kathy. *The enormous turnip*

Paterson, Bettina. *Bun's birthday*

Politi, Leo. *Mr. Fong's toy shop*

Porte, Barbara Ann. *Harry's visit*

Riddell, Chris. *Ben and the bear*

Rylant, Cynthia. *Birthday presents*

Schulman, Janet. *Jack the bum and the Halloween handout*

Sharmat, Marjorie Weinman. *The trip*

Sherman, Ivan. *I do not like it when my friend comes to visit*

Smith, Wendy. *The lonely, only mouse*

Spinelli, Eileen. *Thanksgiving at Tappletons'*

Stadler, John. *Gorman and the treasure chest*

Stage, Mads. *The greedy blackbird*

Stanek, Muriel. *My little foster sister*

Turkle, Brinton. *Rachel and Obadiah*

Vigna, Judith. *The hiding house*

Vincent, Gabrielle. *Bravo, Ernest and Celestine!*
Ernest and Celestine's patchwork quilt

Waber, Bernard. *Bernard*

Watson, Clyde. *Tom Fox and the apple pie*

Watts, Mabel. *Something for you, something for me*

Wezel, Peter. *The good bird*

Wilson, Christopher Bernard. *Hobnob*

Winthrop, Elizabeth. *That's mine*

Wright, Josephine Lord. *Cotton Cat and Martha Mouse*

Yolen, Jane. *Spider Jane*

Ziefert, Harriet. *Me, too! Me, too!*

Zolotow, Charlotte. *The new friend*

Behavior – solitude

Bennett, Rainey. *The secret hiding place*

Bulla, Clyde Robert. *Keep running, Allen!*

Carrick, Carol. *Sleep out*

Dragonwagon, Crescent. *Katie in the morning*
When light turns into night

Ehrlich, Amy. *The everyday train*
Hall, Donald. *The man who lived alone*
Hallinan, P. K. (Patrick K.). *Just being alone*
Hayes, Geoffrey. *Bear by himself*
Henkes, Kevin. *All alone*
Keller, Beverly. *Pimm's place*
Keyser, Marcia. *Roger on his own*
Luttrell, Ida. *Lonesome Lester*
Morris, Jill. *The boy who painted the sun*
Reesink, Marijke. *The princess who always ran away*
Schertle, Alice. *In my treehouse*
Stubbs, Joanna. *Happy Bear's day*
Tresselt, Alvin R. *I saw the sea come in*
Yezback, Steven A. *Pumpkinseeds*

Behavior – stealing

Ahlberg, Janet. *Jeremiah in the dark wood*
Aylesworth, Jim. *Hanna's hog*
Barr, Cathrine. *Hound dog's bone*
Brennan, Patricia D. *Hitchety hatchety up I go!*
Carlson, Nancy. *Loudmouth George and the sixth-grade bully*
Cass, Joan E. *The cat thief*
Cate, Rikki. *A cat's tale*
Christian, Mary Blount. *The doggone mystery*
  J. J. Leggett, secret agent
Cole, Joanna. *The secret box*
Collington, Peter. *The angel and the soldier boy*
Cooper, Jacqueline. *Angus and the Mona Lisa*
De Gerez, Toni. *Louhi, witch of North Farm*
De Paola, Tomie. *Bill and Pete go down the Nile*
Devlin, Wende. *Cranberry Halloween*
Dyke, John. *Pigwig*
The firebird, ill. by Moira Kemp
Foulds, Elfrida Vipont. *The elephant and the bad baby*
Freschet, Berniece. *Owl in the garden*
Ginsburg, Mirra. *Striding slippers*
Goodall, John S. *Paddy to the rescue*
Hare, Norma Q. *Mystery at mouse house*
Hennessy, B. G. *The missing tarts*
Hogrogian, Nonny. *Rooster brother*
Kroll, Steven. *Amanda and the giggling ghost*
Moore, Inga. *Fifty red night-caps*
Ross, Tony. *Hugo and the man who stole colors*
Yolen, Jane. *Piggins*

Behavior – talking to strangers

Bahr, Amy C. *It's ok to say no*

Berenstain, Stan. *The Berenstain bears learn about strangers*
Boegehold, Betty. *Hurray for Pippa!*
Bradman, Tony. *Look out, he's behind you*
Chlad, Dorothy. *Strangers*
De Regniers, Beatrice Schenk. *Red Riding Hood*
Grimm, Jacob. *Little red cap*, ill. by Lisbeth Zwerger
Little Red Riding Hood, ill. by Frank Aloise
Little Red Riding Hood, ill. by Gwen Connelly
Little Red Riding Hood, ill. by Paul Galdone
Little Red Riding Hood, ill. by John S. Goodall
Little Red Riding Hood, ill. by Trina Schart Hyman
Little Red Riding Hood, ill. by Bernadette Watts
Joyce, Irma. *Never talk to strangers*
Keller, Irene. *Benjamin Rabbit and the stranger danger*
Marshall, James. *Red Riding Hood*
Meyer, Linda D. *Safety zone*
Morris, Ann. *The Little Red Riding Hood rebus book*
Petty, Kate. *Being careful with strangers*
Potter, Beatrix. *The tale of Little Pig Robinson*
Vogel, Carole Garbuny. *The dangers of strangers*
Wachter, Oralee. *Close to home*
Wood, Audrey. *Heckedy Peg*

Behavior – tardiness

Boyd, Selma. *I met a polar bear*
Burningham, John. *John Patrick Norman McHennessy - the boy who was always late*

Behavior – thumbsucking *see* Thumbsucking

Behavior – trickery

Aardema, Verna. *Rabbit makes a monkey of lion*
Æsop. *Three fox fables*
  Wolf! wolf!
Allard, Harry. *There's a party at Mona's tonight*
Althea. *Jeremy Mouse and cat*
Annett, Cora. *When the porcupine moved in*
Aylesworth, Jim. *Hanna's hog*
Barth, Edna. *Jack-o'-lantern*
Bartos-Hoppner, Barbara. *The Pied Piper of Hamelin*, ill. by Annegert Fuchshuber
Bingham, Mindy. *My way Sally*
Biro, Val. *The pied piper of Hamelin*
Boegehold, Betty. *Small Deer's magic tricks*

Bowden, Joan Chase. *Strong John*
Brown, Marcia. *The blue jackal*
Browning, Robert. *The pied piper of Hamelin*, ill. by Kate Greenaway
The pied piper of Hamelin, ill. by Anatoly Ivanov
The pied piper of Hamelin, ill. by Errol Le Cain
Calhoun, Mary. *The pixy and the lazy housewife*
Carey, Valerie Scho. *The devil and mother Crump*
Chicken Little. *Chicken Licken*, ill. by Jutta Ash
Chicken Licken, ill. by Gavin Bishop
Henny Penny, ill. by Paul Galdone
Henny Penny, ill. by William Stobbs
The story of Chicken Licken, adapt. and ill. by Jan Ormerod
Christelow, Eileen. *Jerome the babysitter*
Olive and the magic hat
The robbery at the diamond dog diner
Christian, Mary Blount. *The toady and Dr. Miracle*
Cohen, Caron Lee. *Sally Ann Thunder Ann Whirlwind Crockett*
Craig, Helen. *A welcome for Annie*
Dines, Glen. *Gilly and the wicharoo*
Domanska, Janina. *The best of the bargain*
Duff, Maggie. *Dancing turtle*
Duvoisin, Roger Antoine. *Petunia, I love you*
Elkin, Benjamin. *Gillespie and the guards*
Evans, Katherine. *The boy who cried wolf*
Gage, Wilson. *The crow and Mrs. Gaddy*
Galdone, Paul. *A strange servant*
Grimm, Jacob. *The horse, the fox, and the lion*, ill. by Paul Galdone
Hansen, Ron. *The shadowmaker*
Isenberg, Barbara. *Albert the running bear gets the jitters*
Jennings, Michael. *Robin Goodfellow and the giant dwarf*
Joyce, James. *The cat and the devil*
Kellogg, Steven. *Chicken Little*
Kraus, Robert. *Come out and play, little mouse*
The king's trousers
McAfee, Annalena. *The visitors who came to stay*
Magnus, Erica. *The boy and the devil*
Mayer, Marianna. *The black horse*
Mayer, Mercer. *The Pied Piper of Hamelin*
Mirkovic, Irene. *The greedy shopkeeper*
Nordqvist, Sven. *The fox hunt*
Nygren, Tord. *Fiddler and his brothers*
Oppenheim, Joanne. *Mrs. Peloki's substitute*
Parker, Nancy Winslow. *The crocodile under Louis Finneberg's bed*
Potter, Beatrix. *The pie and the patty-pan*
The story of Miss Moppet

Rockwell, Anne F. *The gollywhopper egg*
Snyder, Dianne. *The boy of the three-year nap*
Steig, William. *Solomon the rusty nail*
Stevenson, James. *Emma*
Fried feathers for Thanksgiving
Thayer, Jane. *The clever raccoon*
Turkle, Brinton. *Do not open*
Ungerer, Tomi. *The beast of Monsieur Racine*
Varga, Judy. *The mare's egg*
Wegen, Ron. *Billy Gorilla*
Wild, Robin. *Spot's dogs and the alley cats*
Wildsmith, Brian. *Python's party*
Wood, Audrey. *The horrible holidays*
Wright, Jill. *The old woman and the Willy Nilly Man*
Zemach, Harve. *The tricks of Master Dabble*

Behavior – unnoticed, unseen

Bishop, Bonnie. *No one noticed Ralph*
Hadithi, Mwenye. *Crafty chameleon*
Kroll, Steven. *The candy witch*
Udry, Janice May. *How I faded away*

Behavior – wishing

Aliki. *I wish I was sick, too!*
The wish workers
Allen, Pamela. *A lion in the night*
Anderson, Joy. *Juma and the magic Jinn*
Ayer, Jacqueline. *A wish for little sister*
Baker, Betty. *My sister says*
Turkey girl
Baruch, Dorothy. *I would like to be a pony and other wishes*
Benchley, Nathaniel. *The magic sled*
Benton, Robert. *Don't ever wish for a 7-foot bear*
Beresford, Elisabeth. *Jack and the magic stove*
Berson, Harold. *Truffles for lunch*
Bodsworth, Nan. *Monkey business*
Brett, Jan. *Fritz and the beautiful horses*
Bright, Robert. *Me and the bears*
Butcher, Julia. *The sheep and the rowan tree*
Chapman, Carol. *Barney Bipple's magic dandelions*
Chess, Victoria. *Poor Esmé*
Christensen, Jack. *The forgotten rainbow*
Clifton, Lucille. *Three wishes*
Coco, Eugene Bradley. *The wishing well*
Coopersmith, Jerome. *A Chanukah fable for Christmas*
Daugherty, Charles Michael. *Wisher*
Dragonwagon, Crescent. *Coconut*
Diana, maybe
Fox, Mem. *Possum magic*
Friedrich, Priscilla. *The wishing well in the woods*
Fuchshuber, Annegert. *The wishing hat*

Gackenbach, Dick. *Hattie rabbit*
Greenberg, Polly. *Oh, Lord, I wish I was a buzzard*
Haas, Irene. *The Maggie B*
Haddon, Mark. *Toni and the tomato soup*
Himmelman, John. *Amanda and the witch switch*
Hoban, Lillian. *It's really Christmas*
Howe, James. *I wish I were a butterfly*
Iwasaki, Chihiro. *The birthday wish*
Jaffe, Rona. *Last of the wizards*
Janosch. *Just one apple*
Kay, Helen. *An egg is for wishing*
Kent, Jack. *Knee-high Nina*
Kojima, Naomi. *The flying grandmother*
Krauss, Ruth. *Mama, I wish I was snow. Child, you'd be very cold*
Lasell, Fen. *Michael grows a wish*
Laurencin, Geneviève. *I wish I were*
Littledale, Freya. *The snow child*
McKissack, Patricia C. *King Midas and his gold*, ill. by Tom Dunnington
Maris, Ron. *I wish I could fly*
Munari, Bruno. *The elephant's wish*
Myers, Bernice. *Sidney Rella and the glass sneaker*
Orbach, Ruth. *Please send a panda*
Paterson, Diane. *If I were a toad*
Perkins, Al. *King Midas and the golden touch*
Power, Barbara. *I wish Laura's mommy was my mommy*
Prater, John. *The gift*
Reed, Kit. *When we dream*
Rosen, Winifred. *Henrietta and the day of the iguana*
Sachs, Marilyn. *Fleet-footed Florence*
Schweninger, Ann. *Birthday wishes*
Seignobosc, Françoise. *Jeanne-Marie counts her sheep*
Seuss, Dr. *I wish that I had duck feet*
Please try to remember the first of octember!
Sewell, Helen Moore. *Peggy and the pony*
Shecter, Ben. *The discontented mother*
Shimin, Symeon. *I wish there were two of me*
Simon, Norma. *I wish I had my father*
Stevenson, James. *The wish card ran out!*
Thaler, Mike. *Hippo lemonade*
Tobias, Tobi. *Jane wishing*
Turkle, Brinton. *Do not open*
Varga, Judy. *Janko's wish*
Vigna, Judith. *I wish my daddy didn't drink so much*
Waber, Bernard. *You're a little kid with a big heart*
Watson, Pauline. *Wriggles, the little wishing pig*
Weisgard, Leonard. *Who dreams of cheese?*
Williams, Barbara. *Someday, said Mitchell*
Wolkstein, Diane. *The magic wings*
Wooding, Sharon L. *Arthur's Christmas wish*
Zemach, Margot. *The three wishes*
Zimelman, Nathan. *To sing a song as big as Ireland*
Zolotow, Charlotte. *Someday*

Behavior – worrying

Benedek, Elissa P. *The secret worry*
Delton, Judy. *The elephant in Duck's garden*
On a picnic
Gross, Alan. *Sometimes I worry... What if the teacher calls on me?*
Herman, Charlotte. *My mother didn't kiss me good-night*
Levitin, Sonia. *A single speckled egg*
Marshall, James. *Portly McSwine*
Segal, Lore. *The story of old Mrs. Brubeck and how she looked for trouble and where she found him*
Sewall, Marcia. *The cobbler's song*
Sharmat, Marjorie Weinman. *Lucretia the unbearable*
Thornton, the worrier
Tyler, Linda Wagner. *Waiting for mom*

Being different *see* Character traits – being different

Bicycling *see* Sports – bicycling

Bigotry *see* Prejudice

Birds

Adoff, Arnold. *Birds*
Alexander, Martha G. *Out! Out! Out!*
Aliki. *The wish workers*
Allred, Mary. *Grandmother Poppy and the funny-looking bird*
Anderson, Lonzo. *Mr. Biddle and the birds*
Arnold, Caroline. *Five nests*
Arnosky, Jim. *A kettle of hawks, and other wildlife groups*
Mouse writing
Asch, Frank. *Bear's bargain*
Moon bear
Mooncake
Ash, Jutta. *Wedding birds*
Ayer, Jacqueline. *A wish for little sister*
Azaad, Meyer. *Half for you*
Bailey, Jill. *Eyes*
Feet
Mouths
Baker, Jeffrey J. W. *Patterns of nature*
Bang, Betsy. *Tutuni the tailor bird*
Barber, Antonia. *The enchanter's daughter*
Baskin, Leonard. *Hosie's aviary*
Baum, Willi. *Birds of a feather*
Beisert, Heide Helene. *Poor fish*
Bellville, Cheryl Walsh. *Theater magic*

Borden, Beatrice Brown. *Wild animals of Africa*

Boyle, Constance. *Little Owl and the weed*

Brenner, Barbara. *Baltimore orioles*

Bright, Robert. *Georgie and the baby birds*

Brock, Emma Lillian. *The birds' Christmas tree*

Bruna, Dick. *Little bird tweet*

Brunhoff, Laurent de. *Babar's visit to Bird Island*

Chönz, Selina. *Florina and the wild bird*

Christelow, Eileen. *The robbery at the diamond dog diner*

Climo, Shirley. *King of the birds*

Coatsworth, Elizabeth. *Under the green willow*

Colby, C. B. (Carroll Burleigh). *Who lives there?*
Who went there?

Cole, Joanna. *A bird's body*

Conklin, Gladys. *If I were a bird*

Cortesi, Wendy W. *Explore a spooky swamp*

Cousins, Lucy. *Portly's hat*

Cristini, Ermanno. *In the woods*

Cross, Diana Harding. *Some birds have funny names*

Cross, Genevieve. *A trip to the yard*

Dalmais, Anne-Marie. *The butterfly book of birds*

Damjan, Mischa. *Goodbye little bird*

Darby, Gene. *What is a bird?*

Demarest, Chris L. *Benedict finds a home*

De Paola, Tomie. *Bill and Pete go down the Nile*

Eastman, P. D. (Philip D.). *Are you my mother?*
Flap your wings

Elborn, Andrew. *Bird Adalbert*

Elzbieta. *Brave Babette and sly Tom*

Fender, Kay. *Odette!*

Fisher, Aileen. *We went looking*

Fitzsimons, Cecilia. *My first birds*

Flanders, Michael. *Creatures great and small*

Freeman, Don. *Fly high, fly low*

French, Fiona. *The blue bird*

Freschet, Berniece. *The little woodcock*
Owl in the garden

Friskey, Margaret. *Birds we know*

Fujita, Tamao. *The boy and the bird*

Gans, Roma. *Hummingbirds in the garden*
When birds change their feathers

Givens, Janet Eaton. *Just two wings*

Grimm, Jacob. *The bear and the kingbird*

Hader, Berta Hoerner. *Mister Billy's gun*

Hawkinson, Lucy. *Birds in the sky*

Helweg, Hans. *Farm animals*

Hirschi, Ron. *What is a bird?*
Where do birds live?
Who lives in... the forest?

Hoban, Tana. *A children's zoo*

Hurd, Edith Thacher. *Look for a bird*

Ipcar, Dahlov. *Bright barnyard*
"The song of the day birds" and "The song of the night birds"

John, Naomi. *Roadrunner*

Kantrowitz, Mildred. *When Violet died*

Kaufmann, John. *Birds are flying*
Flying giants of long ago

Kellogg, Steven. *Aster Aardvark's alphabet adventures*

Kishida, Eriko. *The lion and the bird's nest*

Krauss, Ruth. *The happy egg*

Kuchalla, Susan. *Birds*

Kumin, Maxine. *Mittens in May*

Lifton, Betty Jean. *Joji and the Amanojaku*
Joji and the dragon
Joji and the fog

Lionni, Leo. *Inch by inch*
Tico and the golden wings

Lubell, Winifred. *Rosalie, the bird market turtle*

Lyfick, Warren. *The little book of fowl jokes*

McCauley, Jane. *Baby birds and how they grow*

McLerran, Alice. *The mountain that loved a bird*

McPhail, David. *Farm morning*

Marshak, Samuel. *The merry starlings*

Massie, Diane Redfield. *The baby beebee bird*

Mayer, Marianna. *The little jewel box*

Mayer, Mercer. *Two moral tales*

Millhouse, Nicholas. *Blue-footed booby*

Munari, Bruno. *Bruno Munari's zoo*
Tic, Tac and Toc

Nesbit, Edith. *Cockatoucan*

Ness, Evaline. *Pavo and the princess*

Norman, Charles. *The hornbean tree and other poems*

Oana, Kay D. *Robbie and the raggedy scarecrow*

Olds, Elizabeth. *Feather mountain*

Oppenheim, Joanne. *Have you seen birds?*

Parnall, Peter. *Alfalfa Hill*

Pedersen, Judy. *The tiny patient*

Peet, Bill. *The kweeks of Kookatumdee*
The pinkish, purplish, bluish egg

Postgate, Oliver. *Noggin the king*

Potter, Beatrix. *The tale of Jemima Puddle-Duck and other farmyard tales*

Rockwell, Anne F. *Honk honk!*

Rose, Gerald. *The bird garden*

Schumacher, Claire. *Alto and Tango*

Seidler, Rosalie. *Grumpus and the Venetian cat*

Selsam, Millicent E. *A first look at bird nests*
A first look at owls, eagles and other hunters of the sky
Tony's birds

Seuss, Dr. *Horton hatches the egg*
Thidwick, the big-hearted moose

Sis, Peter. *Rainbow Rhino*
Snoopy on wheels
Stage, Mads. *The greedy blackbird*
Stanley, Diane. *Birdsong Lullaby*
Stone, A. Harris. *The last free bird*
Taylor, Sydney. *Mr. Barney's beard*
Troughton, Joanna. *How the birds changed their feathers*
The quail's egg
Tusa, Tricia. *Maebelle's suitcase*
Van Laan, Nancy. *The big fat worm*
Varley, Dimitry. *The whirly bird*
Velthuijs, Max. *The painter and the bird*
Waechter, Friedrich Karl. *Three is company*
Walsh, Grahame L. *The goori goori bird*
Watts, Barrie. *Bird's nest*
Weatherill, Stephen. *The very first Lucy Goose book*
West, Colin. *Have you seen the crocodile?*
Wezel, Peter. *The good bird*
The naughty bird
Wildsmith, Brian. *Brian Wildsmith's birds*
Wolff, Ashley. *A year of birds*
Yolen, Jane. *Spider Jane*
Ziefert, Harriet. *Happy Easter, Grandma!*
Zolotow, Charlotte. *Flocks of birds*

Birds — albatrosses

Hoff, Syd. *Albert the albatross*

Birds — blackbirds

Duff, Maggie. *Rum pum pum*

Birds — bluejays

Angelo, Valenti. *The acorn tree*
Margolis, Richard J. *Big bear, spare that tree*
Newton, Patricia Montgomery. *The frog who drank the waters of the world*

Birds — buzzards

Sandburg, Helga. *Anna and the baby buzzard*
Wolkstein, Diane. *The cool ride in the sky*

Birds — canaries

Foreman, Michael. *Cat and canary*
Freeman, Don. *Quiet! There's a canary in the library*
Heller, Wendy. *Clementine and the cage*

Birds — cardinals

Galinsky, Ellen. *The baby cardinal*

Birds — chickens

Allard, Harry. *I will not go to market today*
Ambrus, Victor G. *The little cockerel*

Aulaire, Ingri Mortenson d'. *Don't count your chicks*
Foxie, the singing dog
Back, Christine. *Chicken and egg*
Belpré, Pura. *Santiago*
Benchley, Nathaniel. *The strange disappearance of Arthur Cluck*
Berquist, Grace. *Speckles goes to school*
Bishop, Ann. *Chicken riddle*
Bond, Felicia. *Christmas in the chicken coop*
Boreman, Jean. *Bantie and her chicks*
Bourke, Linda. *Ethel's exceptional egg*
Boutwell, Edna. *Red rooster*
Brothers, Aileen. *Jiffy, Miss Boo and Mr. Roo*
Brown, Margaret Wise. *Little chicken*
Carle, Eric. *The rooster who set out to see the world*
Rooster's off to see the world
Casey, Patricia. *Quack quack*
Cazet, Denys. *Lucky me*
Chaucer, Geoffrey. *Chanticleer and the fox*, ill. by Barbara Cooney
Chicken Little. *Chicken Licken*, ill. by Jutta Ash
Chicken Licken, ill. by Gavin Bishop
Henny Penny, ill. by Paul Galdone
Henny Penny, ill. by William Stobbs
The story of Chicken Licken, adapt. and ill. by Jan Ormerod
Chukovsky, Korney. *Good morning, chick*
Coerr, Eleanor. *The Josefina story quilt*
Coldrey, Jennifer. *The world of chickens*
Cole, Joanna. *A chick hatches*
Dabcovich, Lydia. *Mrs. Huggins and her hen Hannah*
Delaney, Ned. *Cosmic chickens*
Dodds, Siobhan. *Elizabeth Hen*
Dumas, Philippe. *Caesar, cock of the village*
Dutton, Sandra. *The cinnamon hen's autumn day*
Edwards, Dorothy. *A wet Monday*
Ehrhardt, Reinhold. *Kikeri or, The proud red rooster*
Fatio, Louise. *The red bantam*
Firmin, Peter. *Chicken stew*
Fox, Mem. *Hattie and the fox*
Freschet, Berniece. *Where's Henrietta's hen?*
Ginsburg, Mirra. *Across the stream*
The chick and the duckling
The golden goose, ill. by William Stobbs
Hader, Berta Hoerner. *Cock-a-doodle doo*
Hartelius, Margaret A. *The chicken's child*
Heine, Helme. *The most wonderful egg in the world*
Three little friends: the alarm clock
Three little friends: the racing cart
Three little friends: the visitor
Hewett, Anita. *The little white hen*
Hille-Brandts, Lene. *The little black hen*

Hoff, Syd. *Happy birthday, Henrietta!*
Henrietta, circus star
Henrietta goes to the fair
Henrietta, the early bird
Henrietta's Halloween
Merry Christmas, Henrietta!
Houselander, Caryll. *Petook*
Hutchins, Pat. *Rosie's walk*
Jackson, Jacqueline. *Chicken ten thousand*
Jaynes, Ruth M. *Three baby chicks*
Kasza, Keiko. *The wolf's chicken stew*
Kellogg, Steven. *Chicken Little*
Kent, Jack. *Little Peep*
Kepes, Juliet. *Cock-a-doodle-doo*
Kwitz, Mary DeBall. *Little chick's breakfast*
Little chick's story
Lester, Helen. *The wizard, the fairy and the magic chicken*
Lexau, Joan M. *Crocodile and hen*
Lifton, Betty Jean. *The many lives of Chio and Goro*
Lindman, Maj. *Flicka, Ricka, Dicka and the big red hen*
Lipkind, William. *The little tiny rooster*
The little red hen. *The little red hen*, ill. by Janina Domanska
The little red hen, ill. by Paul Galdone
The little red hen, ill. by Mel Pekarsky
The little red hen, ill. by William Stobbs
The little red hen, ill. by Margot Zemach
Little Tuppen, ill. by Paul Galdone
Littlefield, William. *The whiskers of Ho Ho*
Lloyd, Megan. *Chicken tricks*
Lobel, Anita. *King Rooster, Queen Hen*
Lobel, Arnold. *How the rooster saved the day*
Luttrell, Ida. *Mattie and the chicken thief*
McCrea, Lilian. *Mother hen*
McCue, Lisa. *The little chick*
McKelvey, David. *Bobby the mostly silky*
McKissack, Patricia C. *The little red hen*, ill. by Dennis Hockerman
Marshall, James. *Wings*
Mathews, Louise. *Cluck one*
Miles, Miska. *Chicken forgets*
Murphey, Sara. *The animal hat shop*
Oakley, Graham. *Hetty and Harriet*
O'Neill, Mary. *Big red hen*
Otto, Margaret Glover. *The little brown horse*
Polushkin, Maria. *The little hen and the giant*
Provensen, Alice. *My little hen*
Pursell, Margaret Sanford. *Jessie the chicken*
Ravilious, Robin. *The runaway chick*
Rockwell, Anne F. *The wonderful eggs of Furicchia*
Ross, Tony. *Stone soup*
Scarry, Richard. *Egg in the hole*

Scheffler, Ursel. *Stop your crowing, Kasimir!*
Selsam, Millicent E. *Egg to chick*
Sharmat, Marjorie Weinman. *Hooray for Mother's Day!*
Sherman, Nancy. *Gwendolyn and the weathercock*
Gwendolyn the miracle hen
Sondergaard, Arensa. *Biddy and the ducks*
Stoeke, Janet Morgan. *Minerva Louise*
Tusa, Tricia. *Chicken*
Uchida, Yoshiko. *The rooster who understood Japanese*
Van Horn, Grace. *Little red rooster*
Van Woerkom, Dorothy. *Something to crow about*
Waber, Bernard. *How to go about laying an egg*
Walton, Rick. *Dumb clucks!*
Weil, Lisl. *Gillie and the flattering fox*
Weiss, Ellen. *Clara the fortune-telling chicken*
Williams, Garth. *The chicken book*

Birds – cockatoos

Cummings, W. T. (Walter Thies). *Wickford of Beacon Hill*

Birds – cormorants

Bunting, Eve. *Magic and the night river*

Birds – cranes

Bang, Molly. *Dawn*
The paper crane
Laurin, Anne. *Perfect crane*
The peasant's pea patch
Yagawa, Sumiko. *The crane wife*

Birds – crows

DeLage, Ida. *The old witch and the crows*
Frascino, Edward. *Nanny Noony and the magic spell*
Freeman, Don. *Cyrano the crow*
Gage, Wilson. *The crow and Mrs. Gaddy*
Hazelton, Elizabeth Baldwin. *Sammy, the crow who remembered*
Holder, Heidi. *Crows*
Huxley, Aldous. *The crows of Pearblossom*
Hyman, Robin. *Casper and the rainbow bird*
Lionni, Leo. *Six crows*

Birds – doves

Agostinelli, Maria Enrica. *On wings of love*
Alexander, Martha G. *The magic hat*
Freeman, Don. *The turtle and the dove*
Peet, Bill. *The pinkish, purplish, bluish egg*
Potter, Beatrix. *The tale of the faithful dove*
Sage, James. *The boy and the dove*

Singer, Isaac Bashevis. *Why Noah chose the dove*
Wolff, Ashley. *The bells of London*

Birds – ducks

Allen, Jeffrey. *Mary Alice, operator number 9*
Mary Alice returns
Andersen, H. C. (Hans Christian). *The ugly duckling*, ill. by Adrienne Adams
The ugly duckling, ill. by Lorinda Bryan Cauley
The ugly duckling, ill. by Tadasu Izawa and Shigemi Hijikata
The ugly duckling, ill. by Johannes Larsen
The ugly duckling, ill. by Thomas Locker
The ugly duckling, ill. by Josef Paleček
The ugly duckling, ill. by Maria Ruis
The ugly duckling, ill. by Daniel San Souci
The ugly duckling, ill. by Robert Van Nutt
The ugly little duck, ill. by Peggy Perry Anderson
Barnhart, Peter. *The wounded duck*
Blocksma, Mary. *Where's that duck?*
Bothwell, Jean. *Paddy and Sam*
Boyd, Lizi. *The not-so-wicked stepmother*
Brown, Margaret Wise. *The duck*
The golden egg book
Bunting, Eve. *Happy birthday, dear duck*
Casey, Patricia. *Quack quack*
Cazet, Denys. *The duck with squeaky feet*
Coats, Laura Jane. *Marcella and the moon*
Conover, Chris. *Six little ducks*
Delton, Judy. *Bear and Duck on the run*
Duck goes fishing
The elephant in Duck's garden
A pet for Duck and Bear
Three friends find spring
Dunn, Judy. *The little duck*
Duvoisin, Roger Antoine. *Two lonely ducks*
Ellis, Anne Leo. *Dabble Duck*
Flack, Marjorie. *Angus and the ducks*
The story about Ping
Freschet, Berniece. *Wood duck baby*
Fribourg, Marjorie G. *Ching-Ting and the ducks*
Friskey, Margaret. *Seven diving ducks*
Garland, Sarah. *Having a picnic*
Georgiady, Nicholas P. *Gertie the duck*
Gerstein, Mordicai. *Arnold of the ducks*
Follow me!
Ginsburg, Mirra. *Across the stream*
The chick and the duckling
Goldin, Augusta. *Ducks don't get wet*
Hader, Berta Hoerner. *Cock-a-doodle doo*
Hillert, Margaret. *The funny baby*
Hurd, Edith Thacher. *Last one home is a green pig*
Isenbart, Hans-Heinrich. *A duckling is born*
Janice. *Angélique*

Kepes, Juliet. *The story of a bragging duck*
Leverich, Kathleen. *The hungry fox and the foxy duck*
Lloyd, David. *Duck*
Lorenz, Lee. *A weekend in the country*
McCloskey, Robert. *Make way for ducklings*
Mamin-Sibiryak, D. N. *Grey Neck*
Miles, Miska. *Noisy gander*
Moore, Sheila. *Samson Svenson's baby*
Pomerantz, Charlotte. *One duck, another duck*
Potter, Beatrix. *The tale of Jemima Puddle-Duck*
Quackenbush, Robert M. *Dig to disaster*
Express train to trouble
Henry babysits
Stairway to doom
Richter, Mischa. *Eric and Matilda*
Quack?
Roy, Ronald. *Three ducks went wandering*
Schroeder, Binette. *Tuffa and the ducks*
Scruton, Clive. *Bubble and squeak*
Seignobosc, Françoise. *Springtime for Jeanne-Marie*
Sewell, Helen Moore. *Blue barns*
Shaw, Evelyn S. *Nest of wood ducks*
Sheehan, Angela. *The duck*
Sondergaard, Arensa. *Biddy and the ducks*
Spier, Peter. *Little ducks*
Standon, Anna. *Little duck lost*
Stehr, Frédéric. *Quack-quack*
Stevenson, James. *Howard Monty*
Tafuri, Nancy. *Have you seen my duckling?*
Thiele, Colin. *Farmer Schulz's ducks*
Tudor, Bethany. *Samuel's tree house*
Skiddycock Pond
Turska, Krystyna. *The woodcutter's duck*
Wahl, Jan. *Old Hippo's Easter egg*
Wildsmith, Brian. *The little wood duck*
Winthrop, Elizabeth. *Bear and Mrs. Duck*
Withers, Carl. *The wild ducks and the goose*
Wright, Dare. *Edith and the duckling*

Birds – eagles

Foreman, Michael. *Moose*
Klinting, Lars. *Regal the golden eagle*

Birds – egrets

Carlson, Natalie Savage. *Time for the white egret*

Birds – flamingos

Rossetti, Christina Georgina. *What is pink?*
Zoll, Max Alfred. *A flamingo is born*

Birds – geese

Asch, Frank. *MacGooses's grocery*
Brown, Marc. *Moose and goose*

Bunting, Eve. *Goose dinner*
Burningham, John. *Borka*
Cauley, Lorinda Bryan. *The goose and the golden coins*
Chandoha, Walter. *A baby goose for you*
Delton, Judy. *On a picnic*
Duvoisin, Roger Antoine. *Petunia*
  Petunia and the song
  Petunia, beware!
  Petunia, I love you
  Petunia takes a trip
  Petunia, the silly goose
  Petunia's Christmas
  Petunia's treasure
Freeman, Don. *Will's quill*
Galdone, Joanna. *Gertrude, the goose who forgot*
George, Lindsay Barrett. *William and Boomer*
Holmes, Efner Tudor. *Amy's goose*
Houston, James. *Kiviok's magic journey*
Illyés, Gyula. *Matt the gooseherd*
Kalas, Sybille. *The goose family book*
Kent, Jack. *Silly goose*
Koch, Dorothy Clarke. *Gone is my goose*
Lasell, Fen. *Fly away goose*
Le Tord, Bijou. *Good wood bear*
Low, Joseph. *Benny rabbit and the owl*
  Boo to a goose
Mother Goose. *The golden goose book*, ill. by L. Leslie Brooke
Piers, Helen. *A Helen Piers animal book*
Pizer, Abigail. *Nosey Gilbert*
Polacco, Patricia. *Rechenka's eggs*
Preston, Edna Mitchell. *Squawk to the moon, little goose*
Rockwell, Anne F. *Poor Goose*
Sewell, Helen Moore. *Blue barns*
Weatherill, Stephen. *The very first Lucy Goose book*
Zijlstra, Tjerk. *Benny and his geese*

Birds — hawks

Baylor, Byrd. *Hawk, I'm your brother*

Birds — mockingbirds

Ryder, Joanne. *Mockingbird morning*

Birds — nightingales

Andersen, H. C. (Hans Christian). *The emperor and the nightingale*, ill. by James Watling
  The emperor's nightingale, ill. by Georges Lemoine
  The nightingale, ill. by Harold Berson
  The nightingale, ill. by Nancy Ekholm Burkert
  The nightingale, ill. by Demi
  The nightingale, ill. by Beni Montresor
  The nightingale, ill. by Lisbeth Zwerger
Chase, Catherine. *The nightingale and the fool*

Birds — ostriches

Burton, Marilee Robin. *Oliver's birthday*
Delton, Judy. *Penny wise, fun foolish*
Peet, Bill. *Zella, Zack, and Zodiac*
Ylla. *Look who's talking*

Birds — owls

Benchley, Nathaniel. *The strange disappearance of Arthur Cluck*
Bennett, Rainey. *After the sun goes down*
Boyle, Constance. *The story of little owl*
Bunting, Eve. *The man who could call down owls*
Carey, Mary. *The owl who loved sunshine*
Cresswell, Helen. *Two hoots and the king*
  Two hoots in the snow
DeLage, Ida. *The old witch and the crows*
Delton, Judy. *Duck goes fishing*
Duvoisin, Roger Antoine. *Day and night*
Eastman, P. D. (Philip D.). *Sam and the firefly*
Flower, Phyllis. *Barn owl*
Foster, Doris Van Liew. *Tell me, Mr. Owl*
Freschet, Berniece. *Owl in the garden*
Funazaki, Yasuko. *Baby owl*
Garelick, May. *About owls*
Goodenow, Earle. *The owl who hated the dark*
Harshman, Terry Webb. *Porcupine's pajama party*
Hoban, Russell. *Charlie Meadows*
Hollander, John. *A book of various owls*
Kirn, Ann. *I spy*
Kraus, Robert. *Owliver*
Lane, Carolyn. *The voices of Greenwillow Pond*
Lear, Edward. *The owl and the pussycat*, ill. by Lorinda Bryan Cauley
  The owl and the pussy-cat, ill. by Barbara Cooney
  The owl and the pussycat, ill. by Emma Crosby
  The owl and the pussy-cat, ill. by William Pène Du Bois
  The owl and the pussy-cat, ill. by Lori Farbanish
  The owl and the pussy-cat, ill. by Gwen Fulton
  The owl and the pussy-cat, ill. by Paul Galdone
  The owl and the pussy-cat, ill. by Elaine Muis
  The owl and the pussycat, ill. by Erica Rutherford
  The owl and the pussycat, ill. by Janet Stevens

The owl and the pussycat, ill. by Colin West
The owl and the pussy-cat, ill. by Owen Wood
Leonard, Marcia. *Little owl leaves the nest*
Lionni, Leo. *Six crows*
Lobel, Arnold. *Owl at home*
McKeever, Katherine. *A family for Minerva*
Maschler, Fay. *T. G. and Moonie go shopping*
    T. G. and Moonie have a baby
    T. G. and Moonie move out of town
Nicoll, Helen. *Meg at sea*
    Meg's eggs
Norman, Howard. *The owl-scatterer*
Panek, Dennis. *Detective Whoo*
Pfister, Marcus. *The sleepy owl*
Piatti, Celestino. *The happy owls*
Piers, Helen. *A Helen Piers animal book*
Potter, Beatrix. *The tale of Squirrel Nutkin*
Scarry, Patsy. *Little Richard and Prickles*
Schären, Beatrix. *Tillo*
Schoenherr, John. *The barn*
Shles, Larry. *Moths and mothers, feathers and fathers*
Slobodkin, Louis. *Wide-awake owl*
Smith, Jim. *The frog band and the owlnapper*
Tejima, Keizaburo. *Owl lake*
Thaler, Mike. *Owley*
Tompert, Ann. *Badger on his own*
Wildsmith, Brian. *The owl and the woodpecker*
Yolen, Jane. *Owl moon*

Birds – parakeets, parrots

Augarde, Steve. *Barnaby Shrew, Black Dan and...the mighty wedgwood*
Banchek, Linda. *Snake in, snake out*
Baum, Louis. *JuJu and the pirate*
Bishop, Bonnie. *No one noticed Ralph*
    Ralph rides away
Blegvad, Lenore. *The parrot in the garret and other rhymes about dwellings*
Bradford, Ann. *The mystery of the tree house*
Cressey, James. *Pet parrot*
Demuth, Patricia Brennan. *Max, the bad-talking parrot*
Dragonwagon, Crescent. *Coconut*
Gordon, Sharon. *Pete the parakeet*
Graham, Bob. *Pete and Roland*
Graham, Margaret Bloy. *Benjy and the barking bird*
Hamsa, Bobbie. *Polly wants a cracker*
Holman, Felice. *Victoria's castle*
Hyman, Robin. *Casper and the rainbow bird*
McDermott, Gerald. *Papagayo, the mischief maker*

Potter, Stephen. *Squawky, the adventures of a Clasperchoice*
Woolf, Virginia. *The widow and the parrot*
Zacharias, Thomas. *But where is the green parrot?*
Zusman, Evelyn. *The Passover parrot*

Birds – peacocks, peahens

Alan, Sandy. *The plaid peacock*
Daniel, Doris Temple. *Pauline and the peacock*
Hamberger, John. *The peacock who lost his tail*
Kepes, Juliet. *The seed that peacock planted*
Peet, Bill. *The spooky tail of Prewitt Peacock*
Wittman, Sally. *Pelly and Peak*
    Plenty of Pelly and Peak

Birds – pelicans

Benchley, Nathaniel. *The flying lessons of Gerald Pelican*
Crane, Alan. *Pepita bonita*
Freeman, Don. *Come again, pelican*
Hewett, Joan. *Fly away free*
Lear, Edward. *The pelican chorus*
    The pelican chorus and the quangle wangle's hat
O'Reilly, Edward. *Brown pelican at the pond*
Wildsmith, Brian. *Pelican*
Wise, William. *Nanette, the hungry pelican*
Wittman, Sally. *Pelly and Peak*
    Plenty of Pelly and Peak

Birds – penguins

Bonners, Susan. *A penguin year*
Bright, Robert. *Which is Willy?*
Coldrey, Jennifer. *Penguins*
Cousins, Lucy. *Portly's hat*
Fatio, Louise. *Hector and Christina*
    Hector penguin
Gay, Michel. *Bibi takes flight*
    Bibi's birthday surprise
Hamsa, Bobbie. *Your pet penguin*
Hogan, Paula Z. *The penguin*
Howe, Caroline Walton. *Counting penguins*
Johnston, Johanna. *Penguin's way*
Lester, Helen. *Tacky the penguin*
Lilly, Kenneth. *Animals of the ocean*
Nichols, Cathy. *Tuxedo Sam*
The penguin, ill. by Norman Weaver
Sheehan, Angela. *The penguin*
Somme, Lauritz. *The penguin family book*
Stevenson, James. *Winston, Newton, Elton, and Ed*
Weiss, Leatie. *Funny feet!*
Whitlock, Ralph. *Penguins*
Winteringham, Victoria. *Penguin day*

Birds – pigeons

Baker, Jeannie. *Home in the sky*
  Millicent
Benchley, Nathaniel. *Walter the homing
  pigeon*
Kingman, Lee. *Pierre Pigeon*
McClure, Gillian. *Fly home McDoo*
Peet, Bill. *Fly, Homer, fly*
Selden, George. *Chester Cricket's pigeon ride*
Shulman, Milton. *Prep, the little pigeon of
  Trafalgar Square*
Suben, Eric. *Pigeon takes a trip*

Birds – puffins

Bonsall, Crosby Newell. *What spot?*
Drew, Patricia. *Spotter Puff*
Hall, Pam. *On the edge of the eastern ocean*
Lawson, Annetta. *The lucky yak*
Lewis, Naomi. *Puffin*
Mariana. *Miss Flora McFlimsey's birthday*

Birds – ravens

Æsop. *The raven and the fox*, ill. by Gerald
  Rose
Aiken, Joan. *Arabel and Mortimer*
Grimm, Jacob. *The seven ravens*, ill. by
  Felix Hoffmann
  The seven ravens, ill. by Lisbeth Zwerger

Birds – robins

Cock Robin. *The courtship, merry marriage,
  and feast of Cock Robin and Jenny Wren*
Flack, Marjorie. *The restless robin*
Hawkinson, John. *Robins and rabbits*
Kent, Jack. *Round Robin*
Kraus, Robert. *The first robin*
Rockwell, Anne F. *My spring robin*
Stern, Elsie-Jean. *Wee Robin's Christmas
  song*
Tresselt, Alvin R. *Hi, Mister Robin*

Birds – sandpipers

Hurd, Edith Thacher. *Sandpipers*
Mendoza, George. *The scribbler*

Birds – sea gulls

Armitage, Ronda. *The lighthouse keeper's
  lunch*
Carrick, Carol. *Beach bird*
Duvoisin, Roger Antoine. *Snowy and
  Woody*
Ness, Evaline. *Do you have the time, Lydia?*
Pursell, Margaret Sanford. *Shelley the sea
  gull*
Turkle, Brinton. *Thy friend, Obadiah*

Birds – sparrows

Crabtree, Judith. *The sparrow's story at the
  king's command*
Fregosi, Claudia. *The pumpkin sparrow*
Gerstein, Mordicai. *Prince Sparrow*
Ishii, Momoko. *The tongue-cut sparrow*
Selden, George. *Sparrow socks*
Wallace, Ian. *The sparrow's song*

Birds – storks

Brown, Margaret Wise. *Wheel on the
  chimney*
Gantschev, Ivan. *Journey of the storks*

Birds – swallows

Politi, Leo. *Song of the swallows*

Birds – swans

Andersen, H. C. (Hans Christian). *The
  ugly duckling*, ill. by Adrienne Adams
  The ugly duckling, ill. by Lorinda Bryan
  Cauley
  The ugly duckling, ill. by Tadasu Izawa
  and Shigemi Hijikata
  The ugly duckling, ill. by Johannes Larsen
  The ugly duckling, ill. by Thomas Locker
  The ugly duckling, ill. by Josef Paleček
  The ugly duckling, ill. by Maria Ruis
  The ugly duckling, ill. by Daniel San Souci
  The ugly duckling, ill. by Robert Van Nutt
  The ugly little duck, ill. by Peggy Perry
  Anderson
  The wild swans, ill. by Angela Barrett
  The wild swans, ill. by Susan Jeffers
Bell, Anthea. *Swan Lake*
Canfield, Jane White. *Swan cove*
Clement, Claude. *The painter and the wild
  swans*
Grimm, Jacob. *The six swans*
Hillert, Margaret. *The funny baby*
Hogan, Paula Z. *The black swan*
Lewis, Naomi. *Swan*
Tejima, Keizaburo. *Swan sky*

Birds – toucans

McKee, David. *Two can toucan*

Birds – turkeys

Baker, Betty. *Turkey girl*
Balian, Lorna. *Sometimes it's turkey*
Kroll, Steven. *One tough turkey*
Schatell, Brian. *Farmer Goff and his turkey
  Sam*
  Sam's no dummy, Farmer Goff

Birds – vultures

Duvoisin, Roger Antoine. *Petunia, I love you*
Peet, Bill. *Eli*
Ungerer, Tomi. *Orlando, the brave vulture*
Wolkstein, Diane. *The cool ride in the sky*

Birds – woodpeckers

Wildsmith, Brian. *The owl and the woodpecker*

Birds – wrens

Brock, Emma Lillian. *Mr. Wren's house*
Cock Robin. *The courtship, merry marriage, and feast of Cock Robin and Jenny Wren*

Birthdays

Abrons, Mary. *For Alice a palace*
Adler, David A. *My dog and the birthday mystery*
Alexander, Sue. *World famous Muriel*
Aliki. *June 7!*
Use your head, dear
Amoss, Berthe. *It's not your birthday*
Anderson, C. W. (Clarence Williams). *Billy and Blaze*
Annett, Cora. *The dog who thought he was a boy*
Armitage, Ronda. *The bossing of Josie*
Arnold, Caroline. *Everybody has a birthday*
Arthur, Catherine. *My sister's silent world*
Asch, Frank. *Happy birthday, moon!*
Ashley, Bernard. *Dinner ladies don't count*
Averill, Esther. *Jenny's birthday book*
Ayer, Jacqueline. *A wish for little sister*
Bannon, Laura. *Manuela's birthday*
Barklem, Jill. *Spring story*
Barrett, Judi. *Benjamin's 365 birthdays*
Bassett, Lisa. *A clock for Beany*
Bauer, Helen. *Good times in the park*
Baum, Arline. *Opt*
Bell, Norman. *Linda's airmail letter*
Bemelmans, Ludwig. *Madeline in London*
Benchley, Peter. *Jonathan visits the White House*
Beskow, Elsa Maartman. *Peter in Blueberry Land*
Peter's adventures in Blueberry land
Bible, Charles. *Jennifer's new chair*
Billam, Rosemary. *Fuzzy rabbit*
Blocksma, Mary. *Grandma Dragon's birthday*
Bond, Felicia. *Mary Betty Lizzie McNutt's birthday*
Bradman, Tony. *The bad babies' book of colors*
Brandenberg, Franz. *Aunt Nina and her nephews and nieces*
A secret for grandmother's birthday

Bromhall, Winifred. *Mary Ann's first picture*
Brown, Tricia. *Hello, amigos!*
Browne, Anthony. *Gorilla*
Bruna, Dick. *Tilly and Tess*
Brunhoff, Laurent de. *Babar's birthday surprise*
Serafina the giraffe
Buntain, Ruth Jaeger. *The birthday story*
Bunting, Eve. *Happy birthday, dear duck*
The robot birthday
Burton, Marilee Robin. *Oliver's birthday*
Calmenson, Stephanie. *The birthday hat*
Carle, Eric. *The secret birthday message*
Cazet, Denys. *December 24th*
Chalmers, Audrey. *A birthday for Obash*
Chalmers, Mary. *A hat for Amy Jean*
Charles, Donald. *Shaggy dog's birthday*
Charlip, Remy. *Handtalk birthday*
Chorao, Kay. *Ups and downs with Oink and Pearl*
Clifton, Lucille. *Don't you remember?*
Cole, William. *What's good for a three-year-old?*
Coombs, Patricia. *Dorrie and the birthday eggs*
Corey, Dorothy. *Will it ever be my birthday?*
Corwin, Judith Hoffman. *Birthday fun*
Costa, Nicoletta. *The birthday party*
Cunliffe, John. *The king's birthday cake*
Daly, Maureen. *Patrick visits the library*
Da Rif, Andrea. *The blueberry cake that little fox baked*
Davidson, Amanda. *Teddy's birthday*
Davis, Lavinia. *The wild birthday cake*
Dayton, Laura. *LeRoy's birthday circus*
De Regniers, Beatrice Schenk. *A special birthday party for someone very special*
Duvoisin, Roger Antoine. *Veronica and the birthday present*
Eberstadt, Isabel. *What is for my birthday?*
Elkin, Benjamin. *The loudest noise in the world*
Eriksson, Eva. *One short week*
Fern, Eugene. *Birthday presents*
Fischer, Hans. *The birthday*
Flack, Marjorie. *Ask Mr. Bear*
Fleischman, Paul. *The birthday tree*
Fowler, Richard. *Inspector Smart gets the message!*
Freedman, Sally. *Monster birthday party*
Freeman, Don. *Corduroy's party*
The guard mouse
Mop Top
Gackenbach, Dick. *Binky gets a car*
Gantos, Jack. *Swampy alligator*
Gibbons, Gail. *Happy birthday!*
Giff, Patricia Reilly. *Happy birthday, Ronald Morgan!*
Glovach, Linda. *The Little Witch's birthday book*

Goodall, John S. *Shrewbettina's birthday*
Gordon, Margaret. *Wilberforce goes to a party*
Gordon, Shirley. *Happy birthday, Crystal*
Gould, Deborah. *Brendan's best-timed birthday*
Greene, Carol. *The world's biggest birthday cake*
Gretz, Susanna. *Roger loses his marbles!*
Hawkins, Colin. *Jen the hen*
Heide, Florence Parry. *Treehorn's wish*
Heller, Nicholas. *Happy birthday, Moe dog*
Hertza, Ole. *Tobias has a birthday*
Hill, Eric. *Spot's birthday party*
Hillert, Margaret. *The birthday car*
 Happy birthday, dear dragon
Hoban, Russell. *A birthday for Frances*
Hoff, Syd. *Happy birthday, Henrietta!*
Homme, Bob. *The friendly giant's birthday*
Hughes, Shirley. *Alfie gives a hand*
Hutchins, Pat. *The best train set ever*
 Happy birthday, Sam
 King Henry's palace
Iwasaki, Chihiro. *The birthday wish*
Jabar, Cynthia. *Party day!*
Jaynes, Ruth M. *What is a birthday child?*
Jones, Penelope. *I didn't want to be nice*
Keller, Holly. *Lizzie's invitation*
Kelley, Anne. *Daisy's discovery*
Krauze, Andrzej. *What's so special about today?*
Kumin, Maxine. *Joey and the birthday present*
Lasell, Fen. *Michael grows a wish*
Laurence, Margaret. *The Christmas birthday story*
Lenski, Lois. *A surprise for Davy*
Lewis, Thomas P. *Call for Mr. Sniff*
Lexau, Joan M. *Go away, dog*
 Me day
Lindman, Maj. *Flicka, Ricka, Dicka bake a cake*
 Snipp, Snapp, Snurr and the red shoes
Little, Lessie Jones. *I can do it by myself*
Lobel, Anita. *A birthday for the princess*
Lorian, Nicole. *A birthday present for Mama*
Lowrey, Janette Sebring. *Six silver spoons*
Lundell, Margo. *Teddy bear's birthday*
Lydon, Kerry Raines. *A birthday for Blue*
McKee, David. *King Rollo and the birthday*
McNeill, Janet. *The giant's birthday*
Mariana. *Miss Flora McFlimsey's birthday*
Marie, Geraldine. *The magic box*
Merriam, Eve. *The birthday door*
Miklowitz, Gloria D. *Bearfoot boy*
Miles, Miska. *Mouse six and the happy birthday*
Minarik, Else Holmelund. *Little Bear*
Modell, Frank. *Ice cream soup*
Moon, Grace Purdie. *One little Indian*

Morice, Dave. *The happy birthday handbook*
Munari, Bruno. *The birthday present*
Myers, Bernice. *Charlie's birthday present*
Myller, Rolf. *How big is a foot?*
Myrick, Jean Lockwood. *Ninety-nine pockets*
Ness, Evaline. *Josefina February*
Oxenbury, Helen. *The birthday party*
Parish, Peggy. *Be ready at eight*
 Scruffy
 Snapping turtle's all wrong day
Park, W. B. *Bakery business*
Parker, Nancy Winslow. *Love from Uncle Clyde*
Paterson, Bettina. *Bun's birthday*
Pearson, Susan. *Happy birthday, Grampie*
Peek, Merle. *Mary wore her red dress and Henry wore his green sneakers*
Peppé, Rodney. *The kettleship pirates*
Perkins, Al. *Tubby and the lantern*
Peters, Sharon. *Happy birthday*
Peterson, Esther Allen. *Penelope gets wheels*
Pomerantz, Charlotte. *The half-birthday party*
Prager, Annabelle. *The surprise party*
Quin-Harkin, Janet. *Helpful Hattie*
Radlauer, Ruth Shaw. *Breakfast by Molly*
Rice, Eve. *Benny bakes a cake*
Rockwell, Anne F. *Happy birthday to me*
 Hugo at the window
Root, Phyllis. *Gretchen's grandma*
Russo, Marisabina. *Only six more days*
Rylant, Cynthia. *Birthday presents*
Sandberg, Inger. *Nicholas' favorite pet*
Sawicki, Norma Jean. *Something for mom*
Schumacher, Claire. *Nutty's birthday*
Schweninger, Ann. *Birthday wishes*
Seuss, Dr. *Happy birthday to you!*
 Hooper Humperdink...? Not him!
Sewell, Helen Moore. *Birthdays for Robin*
Shannon, George. *The surprise*
Shimin, Symeon. *A special birthday*
Steiner, Charlotte. *Birthdays are for everyone*
Steptoe, John. *Birthday*
Stevenson, Suçie. *I forgot*
Stolz, Mary Slattery. *Emmett's pig*
Türk, Hanne. *Happy birthday Max*
Tyler, Linda Wagner. *The sick-in-bed birthday book*
Uchida, Yoshiko. *Sumi's special happening*
Van der Beek, Deborah. *Alice's blue cloth*
Van Leeuwen, Jean. *More tales of Amanda Pig*
Vigna, Judith. *Mommy and me by ourselves again*
Wabbes, Marie. *Happy birthday, Little Rabbit*
Waber, Bernard. *Lyle and the birthday party*
Watanabe, Shigeo. *It's my birthday*
Watson, Nancy Dingman. *The birthday goat*
 Tommy's mommy's fish

Weiss, Ellen. *Mokey's birthday present*
Wells, Rosemary. *Max's birthday*
Williams, Barbara. *Whatever happened to Beverly Bigler's birthday?*
Williams, Vera B. *Something special for me*
Worth, Bonnie. *Peter Cottontail's surprise*
Yashima, Tarō. *Umbrella*
Yolen, Jane. *Picnic with Piggins*
Ziefert, Harriet. *Happy birthday, Grandpa! Surprise!*
Zimelman, Nathan. *Once when I was five*
Zolotow, Charlotte. *Mr. Rabbit and the lovely present*

Black Americans see Ethnic groups in the U.S. — Afro-Americans

Blackbirds see Birds — blackbirds

Blackouts see Power failure

Blindness see Handicaps — blindness

Blocks see Toys — blocks

Bluejays see Birds — bluejays

Board books see Format, unusual — board books

Boasting see Behavior — boasting

Boats, ships

Alexander, Anne. *Boats and ships from A to Z*
Allen, Pamela. *Who sank the boat?*
Anderson, Lonzo. *Arion and the dolphins*
Ardizzone, Edward. *Little Tim and the brave sea captain*
 Ship's cook Ginger
 Tim all alone
 Tim and Charlotte
 Tim and Ginger
 Tim and Lucy go to sea
 Tim in danger
 Tim to the rescue
 Tim's friend Towser
 Tim's last voyage
Augarde, Steve. *Barnaby Shrew goes to sea*
Baker, Betty. *My sister says*
Barton, Byron. *Boats*
Bate, Norman. *What a wonderful machine is a submarine*
Benchley, Nathaniel. *Red Fox and his canoe*
Benjamin, Alan. *A change of plans*
Berenstain, Michael. *The ship book*
Bridgman, Elizabeth. *Nanny bear's cruise*
Brown, Judith Gwyn. *The happy voyage*
Brown, Marcia. *Skipper John's cook*
Bruna, Dick. *The sailor*

Buchanan, Heather S. *George Mouse's riverboat band*
Burchard, Peter. *The Carol Moran*
Burningham, John. *Mr. Gumpy's outing*
Bushey, Jerry. *The barge book*
Calhoun, Mary. *Euphonia and the flood*
Campbell, Ann. *Let's find out about boats*
Carrick, Carol. *The washout*
Carryl, Charles Edward. *A capital ship*
Carter, Katharine. *Ships and seaports*
Chalmers, Mary. *Boats finds a house*
Cohen, Peter Zachary. *Authorized autumn charts of the Upper Red Canoe River country*
Crews, Donald. *Harbor*
DeLage, Ida. *Pilgrim children on the Mayflower*
Dennis, Morgan. *The sea dog*
De Paola, Tomie. *Four stories for four seasons*
Devlin, Harry. *The walloping window blind*
Domanska, Janina. *I saw a ship a-sailing*
Dorros, Arthur. *Pretzels*
Du Bois, William Pène. *Otto at sea*
Dunrea, Olivier. *Fergus and Bridey*
Dupasquier, Philippe. *Dear Daddy... Jack at sea*
Elting, Mary. *The big book of real boats and ships*
Emberley, Ed. *Cars, boats, and planes*
Faulkner, Matt. *The amazing voyage of Jackie Grace*
Flack, Marjorie. *The boats on the river*
Flora, James. *Fishing with dad*
Fry, Christopher. *The boat that mooed*
Fussenegger, Gertrud. *Noah's ark*
Gay, Michel. *Little boat*
Gedin, Birgitta. *The little house from the sea*
Gerrard, Roy. *Sir Francis Drake*
Gibbons, Gail. *Boat book*
Ginsburg, Mirra. *Four brave sailors*
Goodall, John S. *Jacko*
Graham, Margaret Bloy. *Benjy's boat trip*
Graham, Thomas. *Mr. Bear's boat*
Gramatky, Hardie. *Little Toot*
 Little Toot on the Mississippi
 Little Toot on the Thames
 Little Toot through the Golden Gate
Haas, Irene. *The Maggie B*
Hansen, Carla. *Barnaby Bear builds a boat*
Hillert, Margaret. *The yellow boat*
Hurd, Edith Thacher. *What whale? Where?*
Isadora, Rachel. *No, Agatha!*
Joerns, Consuelo. *The foggy rescue*
Kellogg, Steven. *The island of the skog*
Kuskin, Karla. *The animals and the ark*
Lenski, Lois. *The little sail boat*
 Mr. and Mrs. Noah
Lewis, Thomas P. *Clipper ship*
Lindman, Maj. *Sailboat time*
Lippman, Peter. *The Know-It-Alls go to sea*

Locker, Thomas. *Sailing with the wind*
Loof, Jan. *Uncle Louie's fantastic sea voyage*
McCloskey, Robert. *Bert Dow, deep-water man*
McGovern, Ann. *Nicholas Bentley Stoningpot III*
McGowan, Alan. *Sailing ships*
Maestro, Betsy. *Big city port Ferryboat*
Mahy, Margaret. *Sailor Jack and the twenty orphans*
Marshall, James. *Speedboat*
Massie, Diane Redfield. *The Komodo dragon's jewels*
Meddaugh, Susan. *Maude and Claude go abroad*
Mendoza, George. *The alphabet boat*
Miles, Miska. *No, no, Rosina*
Morgan, Allen. *Nicole's boat*
Partridge, Jenny. *Hopfellow*
Peppé, Rodney. *The kettleship pirates*
Perkins, Al. *Tubby and the Poo-Bah*
Petersen, David. *Submarines*
Pitcher, Caroline. *Cars and boats*
Potter, Beatrix. *The tale of Little Pig Robinson*
Potter, Russell. *The little red ferry boat*
Rand, Gloria. *Salty dog*
Ransome, Arthur. *The fool of the world and the flying ship*
Reavin, Sam. *Hurray for Captain Jane!*
Reesink, Marijke. *The golden treasure*
Rettich, Margret. *The voyage of the jolly boat*
Rockwell, Anne F. *Boats*
Round, Graham. *Hangdog*
Rubel, Nicole. *Uncle Henry and Aunt Henrietta's honeymoon*
Schaffer, Libor. *Arthur sets sail*
Schulz, Charles M. *Snoopy's facts and fun book about boats*
Shecter, Ben. *If I had a ship*
Shortall, Leonard W. *Tod on the tugboat*
Spier, Peter. *Noah's ark*
Stevenson, Jocelyn. *Jim Henson's Muppets at sea*
Surany, Anico. *Ride the cold wind*
Swift, Hildegarde Hoyt. *The little red lighthouse and the great gray bridge*
Taylor, Mark. *Henry the castaway*
Thomson, Ruth. *Peabody all at sea*
Tudor, Bethany. *Skiddycock Pond*
Van Allsburg, Chris. *The wreck of the Zephyr*
Venable, Alan. *The checker players*
Vernon, Tannis. *Little Pig and the blue-green sea*
Vinton, Iris. *Look out for pirates!*
Willard, Nancy. *The voyage of the Ludgate Hill*

Williams, Vera B. *Three days on a river in a red canoe*
Young, Miriam Burt. *If I sailed a boat*
Zaffo, George J. *The giant nursery book of things that go*
Ziefert, Harriet. *My sister says nothing ever happens when we go sailing*

Bobcats *see* Animals – bobcats

Boogeyman *see* Monsters

Books *see* Activities – reading; Libraries

Boredom *see* Behavior – boredom

Bravery *see* Character traits – bravery

Bridges

Carlisle, Norman. *Bridges*
Lobel, Anita. *Sven's bridge*
Neville, Emily Cheney. *The bridge*
Oppenheim, Joanne. *On the other side of the river*
Steadman, Ralph. *The bridge*
Swift, Hildegarde Hoyt. *The little red lighthouse and the great gray bridge*

Brothers *see* Family life – Brothers

Brownies *see* Elves and little people

Buffaloes *see* Animals – buffaloes

Bugs *see* Insects

Bulls *see* Animals – bulls, cows

Bullying *see* Behavior–bullying

Bumble bees *see* Insects – bees

Burglars *see* Crime

Burros *see* Animals – donkeys

Bus drivers *see* Careers – bus drivers

Buses

Blance, Ellen. *Monster on the bus*
Cossi, Olga. *Gus the bus*
Crews, Donald. *School bus*
Gomi, Taro. *Bus stop*
Hellen, Nancy. *Bus stop*
Jewell, Nancy. *Bus ride*
Kilroy, Sally. *On the road*
Kovalski, Maryann. *The wheels on the bus*
Matthias, Catherine. *Out the door*
Nichols, Paul. *Big Paul's school bus*

Peppé, Rodney. *The mice and the clockwork bus*
Shuttlesworth, Dorothy E. *ABC of buses*
Wolcott, Patty. *Double-decker, double-decker, double-decker bus*
Young, Miriam Burt. *If I drove a bus*
Ziefert, Harriet. *Jason's bus ride*

Butchers *see* Careers – butchers

Butterflies *see* Insects – butterflies, caterpillars

Buzzards *see* Birds – buzzards

Cab drivers *see* Careers – taxi drivers

Cable cars, trolleys

Burton, Virginia Lee. *Maybelle, the cable car*
Chalmers, Mary. *Here comes the trolley*
Gramatky, Hardie. *Sparky*
MacCabe, Naomi. *Cable car Joey*
Taniuchi, Kota. *Trolley*

Cabs *see* Taxis

Caldecott award book

Aardema, Verna. *Why mosquitoes buzz in people's ears*
Ackerman, Karen. *Song and dance man*
Alger, Leclaire. *Always room for one more*
Aulaire, Ingri Mortenson d'. *Abraham Lincoln*
Bemelmans, Ludwig. *Madeline's rescue*
Brown, Marcia. *Once a mouse...*
Brown, Margaret Wise. *The little island*
Burton, Virginia Lee. *The little house*
Cendrars, Blaise. *Shadow*
Chaucer, Geoffrey. *Chanticleer and the fox*, ill. by Barbara Cooney
De Regniers, Beatrice Schenk. *May I bring a friend?*
Emberley, Barbara. *Drummer Hoff*
Ets, Marie Hall. *Nine days to Christmas*
Field, Rachel Lyman. *Prayer for a child*
Fish, Helen Dean. *Animals of the Bible*
A frog he would a-wooing go (folk-song). *Frog went a-courtin'*, ill. by Feodor Rojankovsky
Goble, Paul. *The girl who loved wild horses*
Hader, Berta Hoerner. *The big snow*
Haley, Gail E. *A story, a story*

Hall, Donald. *The ox-cart man*
Handforth, Thomas. *Mei Li*
Hodges, Margaret. *Saint George and the dragon*
Hogrogian, Nonny. *One fine day*
Keats, Ezra Jack. *The snowy day*
Lawson, Robert. *They were strong and good*
Lipkind, William. *Finders keepers*
Lobel, Arnold. *Fables*
McCloskey, Robert. *Make way for ducklings*
Time of wonder
McDermott, Gerald. *Arrow to the sun*
Milhous, Katherine. *The egg tree*
Mosel, Arlene. *The funny little woman*
Musgrove, Margaret. *Ashanti to Zulu.*
Ness, Evaline. *Sam, Bangs, and moonshine*
Perrault, Charles. *Cinderella*, ill. by Marcia Brown
Petersham, Maud. *The rooster crows*
Politi, Leo. *Song of the swallows*
Provensen, Alice. *The glorious flight*
Ransome, Arthur. *The fool of the world and the flying ship*
Robbins, Ruth. *Baboushka and the three kings*
Sendak, Maurice. *Where the wild things are*
Spier, Peter. *Noah's ark*
Steig, William. *Sylvester and the magic pebble*
Thurber, James. *Many moons*
Tresselt, Alvin R. *White snow, bright snow*
Udry, Janice May. *A tree is nice*
Van Allsburg, Chris. *Jumanji*
The polar express
Ward, Lynd. *The biggest bear*
Yolen, Jane. *Owl moon*
Yorinks, Arthur. *Hey, Al*
Zemach, Harve. *Duffy and the devil*

Caldecott award honor book

Alger, Leclaire. *All in the morning early*
Armer, Laura Adams. *The forest pool*
Artzybasheff, Boris. *Seven Simeons*
Baker, Olaf. *Where the buffaloes begin*
Bang, Molly. *The grey lady and the strawberry snatcher*
Ten, nine, eight
Baskin, Leonard. *Hosie's alphabet*
Baylor, Byrd. *The desert is theirs*
Hawk, I'm your brother
The way to start a day
When clay sings
Belting, Natalia Maree. *The sun is a golden earring*
Bemelmans, Ludwig. *Madeline*
Birnbaum, Abe. *Green eyes*
Brown, Marcia. *Henry fisherman*
Skipper John's cook
Stone soup

Preston, Edna Mitchell. *Pop Corn and Ma Goodness*
Reyher, Becky. *My mother is the most beautiful woman in the world*
Ryan, Cheli Durán. *Hildilid's night*
Rylant, Cynthia. *The relatives came*
When I was young in the mountains
Sawyer, Ruth. *The Christmas Anna angel*
Journey cake, ho!
Scheer, Julian. *Rain makes applesauce*
Schick, Eleanor. *The little school at Cottonwood Corners*
Schlein, Miriam. *When will the world be mine?*
Schreiber, Georges. *Bambino the clown*
Sendak, Maurice. *In the night kitchen*
Outside over there
Seuss, Dr. *Bartholomew and the Oobleck*
If I ran the zoo
McElligot's pool
Shulevitz, Uri. *The treasure*
Sleator, William. *The angry moon*
Snyder, Dianne. *The boy of the three-year nap*
Steig, William. *The amazing bone*
Steptoe, John. *Mufaro's beautiful daughters*
The story of jumping mouse
Tafuri, Nancy. *Have you seen my duckling?*
The three bears. *Goldilocks and the three bears*, ill. by James Marshall
Titus, Eve. *Anatole*
Anatole and the cat
Tom Tit Tot. *Tom Tit Tot*
Tresselt, Alvin R. *Hide and seek fog*
Rain drop splash
Tudor, Tasha. *1 is one*
Turkle, Brinton. *Thy friend, Obadiah*
Udry, Janice May. *The moon jumpers*
Van Allsburg, Chris. *The garden of Abdul Gasazi*
Wheeler, Opal. *Sing in praise*
Sing Mother Goose
Wiese, Kurt. *Fish in the air*
You can write Chinese
Wiesner, David. *Free fall*
Willard, Nancy. *A visit to William Blake's inn*
Williams, Vera B. *A chair for my mother*
Wood, Audrey. *King Bidgood's in the bathtub*
Yashima, Tarō. *Crow boy*
Seashore story
Umbrella
Yolen, Jane. *The emperor and the kite*
Zemach, Harve. *The judge*
Zemach, Margot. *It could always be worse*
Zion, Gene. *All falling down*
Zolotow, Charlotte. *Mr. Rabbit and the lovely present*
The storm book

Camels *see* Animals – camels

Camping *see* Sports – camping

Canada *see* Foreign lands – Canada

Canaries *see* Birds – canaries

Cardboard page books *see* Format, unusual – board books

Cardinals *see* Birds – cardinals

Careers

Aitken, Amy. *Ruby!*
Arnold, Caroline. *What is a community?*
Who keeps us safe?
Who works here?
Azaad, Meyer. *Half for you*
Baker, Eugene. *I want to be a computer operator*
Bank Street College of Education. *People read*
Bauer, Caroline Feller. *My mom travels a lot*
Boxer, Deborah. *26 ways to be somebody else*
Brentano, Clemens. *Schoolmaster Whackwell's wonderful sons*
Burnett, Carol. *What I want to be when I grow up*
Civardi, Anne. *Things people do*
Dupasquier, Philippe. *Dear Daddy...*
Florian, Douglas. *People working*
Freeman, Don. *The night the lights went out*
Gibbons, Gail. *Farming*
Fill it up!
The pottery place
Goffstein, M. B. (Marilyn Brooke). *An actor*
Greene, Carol. *I can be a baseball player*
Harper, Anita. *How we work*
Harris, Steven Michael. *This is my trunk*
Klein, Norma. *Girls can be anything*
Kraus, Robert. *Owliver*
Lasker, Joe. *Mothers can do anything*
Lenski, Lois. *Lois Lenski's big book of Mr. Small*
Le-Tan, Pierre. *Timothy's dream book*
Matthias, Catherine. *I can be a computer operator*
Mayer, Mercer. *Little Monster at work*
Merriam, Eve. *Mommies at work*
Miller, Margaret. *Whose hat?*
Mitchell, Joyce Slayton. *My mommy makes money*
Morrison, Bill. *Louis James hates school*
Nichols, Paul. *Big Paul's school bus*
Oliver, Dexter. *I want to be...*

Oppenheim, Joanne. *On the other side of the river*
Portnoy, Mindy Avra. *Ima on the Bima*
Puner, Helen Walker. *Daddys, what they do all day*
Rowan, James P. *I can be a zoo keeper*
Rowe, Jeanne A. *City workers*
Sandberg, Inger. *Come on out, Daddy!*
Scarry, Richard. *Richard Scarry's busiest people ever*
   Richard Scarry's Postman Pig and his busy neighbors
   What do people do all day?
Seignobosc, Françoise. *What do you want to be?*
The Sesame Street book of people and things
Stewart, Robert S. *The daddy book*
Williams, Barbara. *I know a salesperson*
Winn, Marie. *The man who made fine tops*

Careers – airplane pilots

Baker, Donna. *I want to be a pilot*
Barton, Byron. *Airport*
Behrens, June. *I can be a pilot*
Greene, Carla. *Railroad engineers and airplane pilots*
Krementz, Jill. *Jamie goes on an airplane*
Young, Miriam Burt. *If I flew a plane*

Careers – architects

Clinton, Susan. *I can be an architect*

Careers – artists

Adams, Adrienne. *The great Valentine's Day balloon race*
Angelo, Nancy Carolyn Harrison. *Camembert*
Baker, Alan. *Benjamin's portrait*
Baynton, Martin. *Fifty gets the picture*
Carrick, Donald. *Morgan and the artist*
Leaf, Margaret. *Eyes of the dragon*
Miller, Warren. *Pablo paints a picture*
Payne, Joan Balfour. *The stable that stayed*
Pinkwater, Daniel Manus. *The bear's picture*
Sharon, Mary Bruce. *Scenes from childhood*
Sloan, Carolyn. *Carter is a painter's cat*
Velthuijs, Max. *The painter and the bird*
Ventura, Piero. *The painter's trick*
Weisgard, Leonard. *Mr. Peaceable paints*

Careers – astronauts

Barton, Byron. *I want to be an astronaut*
Eco, Umberto. *The three astronauts*

Careers – astronomers

Fitz-Gerald, Christine Maloney. *I can be an astronomer*

Careers – bakers

Caple, Kathy. *Inspector Aardvark and the perfect cake*
Carle, Eric. *Walter the baker*
Craig, M. Jean. *The man whose name was not Thomas*
Forest, Heather. *The baker's dozen*
Green, Melinda. *Bembelman's bakery*
Kessler, Leonard P. *Soup for the king*
Lillegard, Dee. *I can be a baker*
Pinkwater, Daniel Manus. *The Frankenbagel monster*
Westcott, Nadine Bernard. *Peanut butter and jelly*
Worthington, Phoebe. *Teddy bear baker*
Young, Miriam Burt. *The sugar mouse cake*
Ziegler, Sandra. *A visit to the bakery*

Careers – barbers

Appell, Clara. *Now I have a daddy haircut*
Auerbach, Marjorie. *King Lavra and the barber*
Barry, Robert E. *Next please*
Freeman, Don. *Mop Top*
Kunhardt, Dorothy. *Billy the barber*
Mahiri, Jabari. *The day they stole the letter J*
Peet, Bill. *Hubert's hair-raising adventures*
Rockwell, Anne F. *My barber*

Careers – bus drivers

Young, Miriam Burt. *If I drove a bus*

Careers – butchers

Yorinks, Arthur. *Louis the fish*

Careers – cab drivers *see* Careers – taxi drivers

Careers – carpenters

Adkins, Jan. *Toolchest*
Greene, Carla. *I want to be a carpenter*
Lillegard, Dee. *I can be a carpenter*

Careers – chefs

Tomchek, Ann Heinrichs. *I can be a chef*

Careers – clockmakers

Ardizzone, Edward. *Johnny the clockmaker*

Careers – dentists

Barnett, Naomi. *I know a dentist*
Berenstain, Stan. *The Berenstain bears visit the dentist*
Duvoisin, Roger Antoine. *Crocus*
Krementz, Jill. *Taryn goes to the dentist*
Kuklin, Susan. *When I see my dentist*
Lapp, Carolyn. *The dentists' tools*

Linn, Margot. *A trip to the dentist*
Richter, Alice Numeroff. *You can't put braces on spaces*
Rockwell, Harlow. *My dentist*
Watson, Jane Werner. *My friend the dentist*
Wolf, Bernard. *Michael and the dentist*

Careers – detectives

Allen, Laura Jean. *Where is Freddy?*
Berenstain, Stan. *The bear detectives*
Bonsall, Crosby Newell. *The case of the cat's meow*
The case of the dumb bells
The case of the hungry stranger
The case of the scaredy cats
Bunting, Eve. *Jane Martin, dog detective*
Lawrence, James. *Binky Brothers and the fearless four*
Binky Brothers, detectives
Panek, Dennis. *Detective Whoo*
Platt, Kin. *Big Max*
Big Max in the mystery of the missing moose
Quackenbush, Robert M. *Detective Mole*
Detective Mole and the secret clues
Detective Mole and the Tip-Top mystery
Dig to disaster
Express train to trouble
Piet Potter returns
Piet Potter strikes again
Piet Potter to the rescue
Piet Potter's first case
Stairway to doom
Sharmat, Marjorie Weinman. *Nate the Great*
Nate the Great and the lost list
Nate the Great and the phony clue
Nate the Great goes undercover
Thomson, Ruth. *Peabody all at sea*
Peabody's first case

Careers – doctors

Arnold, Caroline. *Who keeps us healthy?*
Berenstain, Stan. *The Berenstain bears go to the doctor*
Breinburg, Petronella. *Doctor Shawn*
Charlip, Remy. *"Mother, mother I feel sick"*
Cobb, Vicki. *How the doctor knows you're fine*
Corey, Dorothy. *A shot for baby bear*
DeSantis, Kenny. *A doctor's tools*
Gilbert, Helen Earle. *Dr. Trotter and his big gold watch*
Goodsell, Jane. *Katie's magic glasses*
Greene, Carla. *Doctors and nurses what do they do?*
Hanklin, Rebecca. *I can be a doctor*
Kuklin, Susan. *When I see my doctor*
Lerner, Marguerite Rush. *Doctors' tools*
Linn, Margot. *A trip to the doctor*
Marcus, Susan. *Casey visits the doctor*

Oxenbury, Helen. *The checkup*
Robison, Deborah. *Your turn, doctor*
Rockwell, Harlow. *My doctor*
Rogers, Fred. *Going to the doctor*
Roop, Peter. *Stick out your tongue!*
Stein, Sara Bonnett. *A hospital story*
Viorst, Judith. *The tenth good thing about Barney*
Wahl, Jan. *Doctor Rabbit's foundling*
Watson, Jane Werner. *My friend the doctor*
Wolde, Gunilla. *Betsy and the doctor*

Careers – electricians

Lillegard, Dee. *I can be an electrician*

Careers – farmers

Kightley, Rosalinda. *The farmer*
Nordqvist, Sven. *The fox hunt*

Careers – firefighters

Averill, Esther. *The fire cat*
Barbaresi, Nina. *Firemouse*
Barr, Jene. *Fire snorkel number 7*
Baumann, Kurt. *Piro and the fire brigade*
Bester, Roger. *Fireman Jim*
Bridwell, Norman. *Clifford's good deeds*
Brown, Margaret Wise. *Five little firemen*
The little fireman
Bundt, Nancy. *The fire station book*
Bushey, Jerry. *Building a fire truck*
Chalmers, Mary. *Throw a kiss, Harry*
Curious George at the fire station
Elliott, Dan. *A visit to the Sesame Street firehouse*
Fast rolling fire trucks
Firehouse
Fisher, Leonard Everett. *Pumpers, boilers, hooks and ladders*
Gibbons, Gail. *Fire! Fire!*
Gramatky, Hardie. *Hercules*
Greene, Carla. *What do they do? Policemen and firemen*
Greydanus, Rose. *Big red fire engine*
Hanklin, Rebecca. *I can be a fire fighter*
Hansen, Jeff. *Being a fire fighter isn't just squirtin' water*
Hill, Mary Lou. *My dad's a smokejumper*
Homme, Bob. *The friendly giant's book of fire engines*
Keeping, Charles. *Willie's fire-engine*
Killingback, Julia. *Busy Bears at the fire station*
Lenski, Lois. *The little fire engine*
Marston, Hope Irvin. *Fire trucks*
Mayer, Mercer. *Fireman critter*
Rey, Hans Augusto. *Curious George*
Robinson, Nancy K. *Firefighters!*
Rockwell, Anne F. *Fire engines*
Spiegel, Doris. *Danny and Company 92*

Spier, Peter. *Firehouse*
Weiss, Harvey. *The sooner hound*
Zaffo, George J. *Big book of real fire engines*

Careers – fishermen

Aldridge, Josephine Haskell. *Fisherman's luck*
Beim, Lorraine. *Lucky Pierre*
Brown, Marcia. *Henry fisherman*
Brown, Margaret Wise. *The little fisherman*
Bunting, Eve. *Magic and the night river*
Flora, James. *Fishing with dad*
Gramatky, Hardie. *Nikos and the sea god*
Le Tord, Bijou. *Joseph and Nellie*
Matsutani, Miyoko. *The fisherman under the sea*
Miles, Miska. *No, no, Rosina*
Moxley, Susan. *Abdul's treasure*
Napoli, Guillier. *Adventure at Mont-Saint-Michel*
Parker, Dorothy D. *Liam's catch*
Rettich, Margret. *The voyage of the jolly boat*
Weil, Lisl. *Gertie and Gus*

Careers – forest rangers *see* Careers – park rangers

Careers – fortune tellers

Coombs, Patricia. *Dorrie and the fortune teller*
Jeschke, Susan. *Firerose*
Weiss, Ellen. *Clara the fortune-telling chicken*

Careers – garbage collectors

Steig, William. *Tiffky Doofky*
Zion, Gene. *Dear garbage man*

Careers – geologists

Sipiera, Paul P. *I can be a geologist*

Careers – handyman

Rockwell, Anne F. *Handy Hank will fix it*

Careers – judges

Mirkovic, Irene. *The greedy shopkeeper*
Zemach, Harve. *The judge*

Careers – librarians

Baker, Donna. *I want to be a librarian*
Pinkwater, Daniel Manus. *Aunt Lulu*
Porte, Barbara Ann. *Harry in trouble*

Careers – maids

Parish, Peggy. *Amelia Bedelia*
　Amelia Bedelia and the surprise shower
　Amelia Bedelia goes camping
　Amelia Bedelia helps out
　Come back, Amelia Bedelia
　Good work, Amelia Bedelia
　Merry Christmas, Amelia Bedelia
　Play ball, Amelia Bedelia
　Teach us, Amelia Bedelia
　Thank you, Amelia Bedelia

Careers – mail carriers

Beim, Jerrold. *Country mailman*
Brandt, Betty. *Special delivery*
Buchheimer, Naomi. *Let's go to a post office*
Drummond, Violet H. *The flying postman*
Gibbons, Gail. *The post office book*
Haley, Gail E. *The post office cat*
Hedderwick, Mairi. *Katie Morag delivers the mail*
Kightley, Rosalinda. *The postman*
Maury, Inez. *My mother the mail carrier*
Rylant, Cynthia. *Mr. Griggs' work*
Scarry, Richard. *Richard Scarry's Postman Pig and his busy neighbors*

Careers – mechanics

Broekel, Ray. *I can be an auto mechanic*

Careers – military

Ambrus, Victor G. *Brave soldier Janosch*
Brown, Marcia. *Stone soup*
Emberley, Barbara. *Drummer Hoff*
Greene, Carla. *Soldiers and sailors what do they do?*
Langstaff, John M. *Soldier, soldier, won't you marry me?*
McGowen, Tom. *The only glupmaker in the U.S. Navy*
Mahy, Margaret. *Sailor Jack and the twenty orphans*
VanRynbach, Iris. *The soup stone*

Careers – miners

Brown, Margaret Wise. *Two little miners*
Nixon, Joan Lowery. *Fat chance, Claude*

Careers – models

Greene, Carol. *I can be a model*

Careers – nuns

Routh, Jonathan. *The Nuns go to Africa*

Careers – nurses

Arnold, Caroline. *Who keeps us healthy?*
Behrens, June. *I can be a nurse*

Greene, Carla. *Doctors and nurses what do they do?*
Kraus, Robert. *Rebecca Hatpin*
Stein, Sara Bonnett. *A hospital story*
Whitney, Alma Marshak. *Just awful*

Careers – park rangers

Hill, Mary Lou. *My dad's a park ranger*

Careers – peddlers

Crossley-Holland, Kevin. *The pedlar of Swaffham*
Jacobs, Joseph. *The crock of gold*
Rockwell, Anne F. *A bear, a bobcat and three ghosts*
Slobodkina, Esphyr. *Caps for sale*
Pezzo the peddler and the circus elephant
Pezzo the peddler and the thirteen silly thieves
Suba, Susanne. *The monkeys and the pedlar*

Careers – physicians *see* Careers – doctors

Careers – pilots *see* Careers – airplane pilots

Careers – police officers

Adelson, Leone. *Who blew that whistle?*
Ahlberg, Allan. *Cops and robbers*
Baker, Donna. *I want to be a police officer*
Brown, David. *Someone always needs a policeman*
Chapin, Cynthia. *Squad car 55*
Erdoes, Richard. *Policemen around the world*
Goodall, John S. *Paddy's new hat*
Greene, Carla. *What do they do? Policemen and firemen*
Guilfoile, Elizabeth. *Have you seen my brother?*
Keats, Ezra Jack. *My dog is lost!*
Lattin, Anne. *Peter's policeman*
Lenski, Lois. *Policeman Small*
McCloskey, Robert. *Make way for ducklings*
Mayer, Mercer. *Policeman critter*
Schlein, Miriam. *The amazing Mr. Pelgrew*
Vreeken, Elizabeth. *The boy who would not say his name*

Careers – race car drivers

Wilkinson, Sylvia. *I can be a race car driver*

Careers – railroad engineers

Greene, Carla. *Railroad engineers and airplane pilots*
Lenski, Lois. *The little train*

Careers – rangers *see* Careers – park rangers

Careers – reporters

Fitz-Gerald, Christine Maloney. *I can be a reporter*

Careers – sailors *see* Careers – military

Careers – seamstresses

Lobel, Anita. *The seamstress of Salzburg*
Olds, Helen Diehl. *Miss Hattie and the monkey*

Careers – shoemakers

Gilbert, Helen Earle. *Mr. Plum and the little green tree*
Grimm, Jacob. *The elves and the shoemaker*, ill. by Paul Galdone
The elves and the shoemaker, ill. by Bernadette Watts
The shoemaker and the elves, ill. by Cynthia and William Birrer
Ross, Tony. *The greedy little cobbler*
Sheldon, Aure. *Of cobblers and kings*

Careers – soldiers *see* Careers – military

Careers – storekeepers

Pearson, Tracey Campbell. *The storekeeper*

Careers – tailors

Ambrus, Victor G. *The three poor tailors*
Galdone, Paul. *The monster and the tailor*
Grimm, Jacob. *The brave little tailor*, ill. by Mark Corcoran
The brave little tailor, ill. by Svend Otto S.
The brave little tailor, ill. by Daniel San Souci
The valiant little tailor, ill. by Victor G. Ambrus
Hest, Amy. *The purple coat*
Potter, Beatrix. *The tailor of Gloucester*
West, Colin. *I brought my love a tabby cat*

Careers – taxi drivers

Moore, Lilian. *Papa Albert*
Otto, Svend. *Taxi dog*
Ross, Jessica. *Ms. Klondike*

Careers – teachers

Allard, Harry. *Miss Nelson is back*
Miss Nelson is missing!
Arnold, Caroline. *Where do you go to school?*
Beckman, Beatrice. *I can be a teacher*

Cummings, W. T. (Walter Thies). *Miss Esta Maude's secret*
Feder, Paula Kurzband. *Where does the teacher live?*
Johnson, Jean. *Teachers A to Z*
Powers, Mary E. *Our teacher's in a wheelchair*
Weiss, Leatie. *My teacher sleeps in school*

Careers – telephone operators

Allen, Jeffrey. *Mary Alice, operator number 9*
Mary Alice returns

Careers – train engineers *see* Careers – railroad engineers

Careers – truck drivers

Behrens, June. *I can be a truck driver*
Cartlidge, Michelle. *Teddy trucks*
Greene, Carla. *Truck drivers what do they do?*
Young, Miriam Burt. *If I drove a truck*

Careers – veterinarians

Bellville, Rod. *Large animal veterinarians*
Greene, Carla. *Animal doctors what do they do?*
Herriot, James. *Moses the kitten*
Only one woof
Hewett, Joan. *Fly away free*
Kuklin, Susan. *Taking my dog to the vet*
Lumley, Katheryn Wentzel. *I can be an animal doctor*
Polhamus, Jean Burt. *Doctor Dinosaur*

Careers – waiters, waitresses

Krementz, Jill. *Benjy goes to a restaurant*
Mooser, Stephen. *Funnyman's first case*
Peters, Sharon. *Happy Jack*

Careers – waitresses *see* Careers – waiters, waitresses

Careers – welders

Lillegard, Dee. *I can be a welder*

Careers – window cleaners

Dahl, Roald. *The giraffe and the pelly and me*
Rey, Hans Augusto. *Curious George takes a job*

Careers – writers

Broekel, Ray. *I can be an author*
Goffstein, M. B. (Marilyn Brooke). *A writer*

Carelessness *see* Behavior – carelessness

Caribbean Islands *see* Foreign lands – Caribbean Islands

Carnivals *see* Fairs

Carousels *see* Merry-go-rounds

Carpenters *see* Careers – carpenters

Cars *see* Automobiles

Caterpillars *see* Insects – butterflies, caterpillars

Cats *see* Animals – cats

Cavemen

Hoff, Syd. *Stanley*
Seyton, Marion. *The hole in the hill*
Slobodkin, Louis. *Dinny and Danny*

Caves

Baynes, Pauline. *How dog began*
Brett, Jan. *The first dog*
Friedman, Estelle. *Boy who lived in a cave*
Tettelbaum, Michael. *The cave of the lost Fraggle*
Ungerer, Tomi. *The Mellops go spelunking*

Chanukah *see* Holidays – Hanukkah

Character traits

Johnson, Crockett. *The emperor's gift*
Seignobosc, Françoise. *Jeanne-Marie in gay Paris*

Character traits – ambition

Balet, Jan B. *Joanjo*
Barton, Byron. *I want to be an astronaut*
Claude-Lafontaine, Pascale. *Monsieur Bussy, the celebrated hamster*
Graham, Al. *Timothy Turtle*, ill. by Tony Palazzo
Gramatky, Hardie. *Little Toot*
Hochman, Sandra. *The magic convention*
Horwitz, Elinor Lander. *Sometimes it happens*
Kumin, Maxine. *Speedy digs downside up*
Ringi, Kjell. *My father and I*
Seignobosc, Françoise. *What do you want to be?*
Shecter, Ben. *Hester the jester*
Turska, Krystyna. *The magician of Cracow*
Uchida, Yoshiko. *Sumi's prize*

Character traits – appearance

Andersen, H. C. (Hans Christian). *The ugly duckling*, ill. by Adrienne Adams
The ugly duckling, ill. by Lorinda Bryan Cauley
The ugly duckling, ill. by Tadasu Izawa and Shigemi Hijikata
The ugly duckling, ill. by Johannes Larsen
The ugly duckling, ill. by Thomas Locker
The ugly duckling, ill. by Josef Paleček
The ugly duckling, ill. by Maria Ruis
The ugly duckling, ill. by Daniel San Souci
The ugly duckling, ill. by Robert Van Nutt
The ugly little duck, ill. by Peggy Perry Anderson
Balestrino, Philip. *Fat and skinny*
Beim, Jerrold. *Freckle face*
Bonsall, Crosby Newell. *Listen, listen!*
Caseley, Judith. *Molly Pink goes hiking*
Charles, Donald. *Shaggy dog's Halloween*
Chevalier, Christa. *Spence isn't Spence anymore*
Cohen, Burton. *Nelson makes a face*
Collins, Judith Graham. *Josh's scary dad*
Crowley, Arthur. *The ugly book*
Dellinger, Annetta. *You are special to Jesus*
De Paola, Tomie. *Big Anthony and the magic ring*
Eco, Umberto. *The three astronauts*
Elborn, Andrew. *Bird Adalbert*
Fatio, Louise. *The happy lion and the bear*
Freeman, Don. *Dandelion*
Ginsburg, Mirra. *The Chinese mirror*
Girion, Barbara. *The boy with the special face*
Goble, Paul. *Star boy*
Greenfield, Eloise. *Grandpa's face*
Hale, Irina. *Brown bear in a brown chair*
Heine, Helme. *The most wonderful egg in the world*
Hillert, Margaret. *The funny baby*
Iké, Jane Hori. *A Japanese fairy tale*
Kasza, Keiko. *The pigs' picnic*
Keller, Irene. *The Thingumajig book of manners*
McDermott, Gerald. *The magic tree*
Maestro, Betsy. *On the town*
Mayer, Marianna. *Beauty and the beast*
Mayer, Mercer. *How the trollusk got his hat*
Moore, Sheila. *Samson Svenson's baby*
Myers, Amy. *I know a monster*
Nesbit, Edith. *Beauty and the beast*, ill. by Julia Christie
Ness, Evaline. *The girl and the goatherd*
Numeroff, Laura Joffe. *Amy for short*
Ormerod, Jan. *Just like me*
Our Ollie
Silly goose
Ormondroyd, Edward. *Theodore*
Park, Ruth. *When the wind changed*

Primavera, Elise. *Basil and Maggie*
Quinsey, Mary Beth. *Why does that man have such a big nose?*
Ring, Elizabeth. *Tiger lilies*
Salus, Naomi Panush. *My daddy's mustache*
Schaffer, Libor. *Arthur sets sail*
Scott, Natalie. *Firebrand, push your hair out of your eyes*
Small, David. *Imogene's antlers*
Stren, Patti. *Mountain Rose*
Thomson, Peggy. *The king has horse's ears*
Yolen, Jane. *Sleeping ugly*

Character traits – assertiveness

Dunbar, Joyce. *A cake for Barney*

Character traits – being different

Andersen, H. C. (Hans Christian). *The ugly duckling*, ill. by Adrienne Adams
The ugly duckling, ill. by Lorinda Bryan Cauley
The ugly duckling, ill. by Tadasu Izawa and Shigemi Hijikata
The ugly duckling, ill. by Johannes Larsen
The ugly duckling, ill. by Thomas Locker
The ugly duckling, ill. by Josef Paleček
The ugly duckling, ill. by Maria Ruis
The ugly duckling, ill. by Daniel San Souci
The ugly duckling, ill. by Robert Van Nutt
The ugly little duck, ill. by Peggy Perry Anderson
Aulaire, Ingri Mortenson d'. *Nils*
Beim, Jerrold. *Freckle face*
Blos, Joan W. *Old Henry*
Blue, Rose. *I am here: Yo estoy aqui*
Brandenberg, Franz. *Otto is different*
Brightman, Alan. *Like me*
Burningham, John. *Borka*
Caple, Kathy. *The biggest nose*
Carle, Eric. *The mixed-up chameleon*
Chapman, Elizabeth. *Suzy*
Cohen, Miriam. *It's George!*
Coombs, Patricia. *The lost playground*
Corbalis, Judy. *Porcellus, the flying pig*
Counsel, June. *But Martin!*
Crossley-Holland, Kevin. *The green children*
Dinan, Carolyn. *Say cheese!*
Dubanevich, Arlene. *Pigs at Christmas*
Duvoisin, Roger Antoine. *Our Veronica goes to Petunia's farm*
Veronica
Emberley, Ed. *Rosebud*
Escudie, René. *Paul and Sebastian*
Fern, Eugene. *Pepito's story*
Heine, Helme. *Superhare*
Hillert, Margaret. *The funny baby*
Hoff, Syd. *Mrs. Brice's mice*
Karlin, Nurit. *The blue frog*
Krasilovsky, Phyllis. *The very tall little girl*

Kuklin, Susan. *Thinking big*
Lerner, Marguerite Rush. *Lefty, the story of left-handedness*
Levine, Rhoda. *Harrison loved his umbrella*
Lionni, Leo. *Cornelius*
McGovern, Ann. *Mr. Skinner's skinny house*
McKelvey, David. *Bobby the mostly silky*
Nordlicht, Lillian. *I love to laugh*
Paek, Min. *Aekyung's dream*
Payne, Sherry Neuwirth. *A contest*
Peet, Bill. *The spooky tail of Prewitt Peacock*
Quinsey, Mary Beth. *Why does that man have such a big nose?*
Reesink, Marijke. *The princess who always ran away*
Rey, Margaret Elisabeth Waldstein. *Spotty*
Riddell, Chris. *Bird's new shoes*
Schertle, Alice. *Jeremy Bean's St. Patrick's Day*
Schotter, Roni. *Captain Snap and the children of Vinegar Lane*
Sharmat, Marjorie Weinman. *Helga high-up*
Shles, Larry. *Moths and mothers, feathers and fathers*
Shub, Elizabeth. *Dragon Franz*
Simon, Norma. *Why am I different?*
Simon, Sidney B. *The armadillo who had no shell*
Wadhams, Margaret. *Anna*
Wallace, Barbara Brooks. *Argyle*
Wells, Rosemary. *Abdul*
Whitmore, Adam. *Max in America*
Max in Australia
Max in India
Max leaves home
Willis, Jeanne. *The long blue blazer*

Character traits – bravery

Aitken, Amy. *Ruby, the red knight*
Aliki. *George and the cherry tree*
Andersen, H. C. (Hans Christian). *The snow queen*, ill. by Angela Barrett
The snow queen, ill. by Toma Bogdanovic
The snow queen, ill. by June Atkin Corwin
The snow queen, ill. by Susan Jeffers
The snow queen, ill. by Errol Le Cain
The snow queen, ill. by Bernadette Watts
The snow queen, ill. by Arieh Zeldich
Anglund, Joan Walsh. *The brave cowboy*
Ardizzone, Edward. *Little Tim and the brave sea captain*
Paul, the hero of the fire
Peter the wanderer
Tim and Charlotte
Tim to the rescue
Aulaire, Ingri Mortenson d'. *Wings for Per*
Averill, Esther. *When Jenny lost her scarf*
Baker, Betty. *Latki and the lightning lizard*
Baldner, Gaby. *Joba and the wild boar*

Bannon, Laura. *Hat for a hero*
Barr, Cathrine. *Little Ben*
Barrows, Marjorie Wescott. *Fraidy cat*
Baumann, Kurt. *Piro and the fire brigade*
Bawden, Nina. *William Tell*
Beim, Jerrold. *Eric on the desert*
Benchley, Nathaniel. *The deep dives of Stanley Whale*
Blegvad, Lenore. *Anna Banana and me*
Bornstein, Ruth Lercher. *Jim*
Brenner, Anita. *A hero by mistake*
Brook, Judy. *Tim mouse goes down the stream*
Brown, Margaret Wise. *Streamlined pig*
Burgert, Hans-Joachim. *Samulo and the giant*
Cameron, Ann. *Harry (the monster)*
Carleton, Barbee Oliver. *Benny and the bear*
Carlson, Nancy. *Harriet and the roller coaster*
Chaffin, Lillie D. *We be warm till springtime comes*
Chapouton, Anne-Marie. *Billy the brave*
Charlton, Elizabeth. *Jeremy and the ghost*
Conford, Ellen. *Eugene the brave*
Coombs, Patricia. *Molly Mullett*
Coville, Bruce. *The foolish giant*
Craft, Ruth. *Carrie Hepple's garden*
De La Mare, Walter. *Molly Whuppie*
De Posadas Mane, Carmen. *Mister North Wind*
Dreifus, Miriam W. *Brave Betsy*
Dyke, John. *Pigwig*
Fatio, Louise. *The red bantam*
Fern, Eugene. *The most frightened hero*
Fuchshuber, Annegert. *Giant story - Mouse tale*
Furchgott, Terry. *Phoebe and the hot water bottles*
Gantschev, Ivan. *The Christmas train*
Ginsburg, Mirra. *The strongest one of all*
Goodall, John S. *Paddy to the rescue*
Grant, Joan. *The monster that grew small*
Grasshopper to the rescue
Greaves, Margaret. *Once there were no pandas*
Grimm, Jacob. *The brave little tailor*, ill. by Mark Corcoran
The brave little tailor, ill. by Svend Otto S.
The brave little tailor, ill. by Daniel San Souci
The valiant little tailor, ill. by Victor G. Ambrus
Haley, Gail E. *Jack and the fire dragon*
Harris, Leon A. *The great diamond robbery*
Hazen, Barbara Shook. *Fang*
Henkes, Kevin. *Sheila Rae, the brave*
Hiser, Berniece T. *The adventure of Charlie and his wheat-straw hat*
Holl, Adelaide. *Sir Kevin of Devon*

Hort, Lenny. *The boy who held back the sea*
Horvath, Betty F. *Jasper and the hero business*
Hürlimann, Bettina. *Barry*
Jaques, Faith. *Tilly's rescue*
Keller, Beverly. *Pimm's place*
Lagercrantz, Rose. *Brave little Pete of Geranium Street*
Lewis, Robin Baird. *Friska, the sheep that was too small*
Lexau, Joan M. *It all began with a drip, drip, drip*
Little, Lessie Jones. *I can do it by myself*
Littlewood, Valerie. *The season clock*
Low, Joseph. *Benny rabbit and the owl*
Boo to a goose
Mariana. *Miss Flora McFlimsey's Halloween*
Marshak, Samuel. *The tale of a hero nobody knows*
Martin, Bill (William Ivan). *Knots on a counting rope*
Matsutani, Miyoko. *The witch's magic cloth*
Mayer, Marianna. *The unicorn and the lake*
Mayer, Mercer. *Liverwurst is missing*
Liza Lou and the Yeller Belly Swamp
Milne, A. A. (Alan Alexander). *Winnie-the-Pooh*
Nash, Ogden. *Custard the dragon*
Nishikawa, Osamu. *Alexander and the blue ghost*
Olson, Arielle North. *The lighthouse keeper's daughter*
Peet, Bill. *Cowardly Clyde*
Polushkin, Maria. *The little hen and the giant*
Pryor, Bonnie. *The porcupine mouse*
San Souci, Robert D. *The enchanted tapestry*
Scarry, Richard. *Richard Scarry's Peasant Pig and the terrible dragon*
Schertle, Alice. *The gorilla in the hall*
Schumacher, Claire. *Brave Lily*
Sewell, Helen Moore. *Jimmy and Jemima*
Shire, Ellen. *The mystery at number seven, Rue Petite*
Shute, Linda. *Momotaro, the peach boy*
Stanek, Muriel. *All alone after school*
Steig, William. *Brave Irene*
Stevenson, Drew. *The ballad of Penelope Lou...and me*
Taylor, Mark. *Henry explores the jungle*
Henry explores the mountains
Henry the explorer
Titus, Eve. *Anatole and the cat*
Van Woerkom, Dorothy. *Becky and the bear*
Wells, H. G. (Herbert George). *The adventures of Tommy*
Wolkstein, Diane. *The banza*
Yolen, Jane. *The acorn quest*

Character traits – cleanliness

Adelborg, Ottilia. *Clean Peter and the children of Grubbylea*
Bowling, David Louis. *Dirty Dingy Daryl*
Bucknall, Caroline. *One bear in the picture*
Burch, Robert. *The jolly witch*
De Paola, Tomie. *Marianna May and Nursey*
Dickinson, Mary. *Alex's bed*
Flot, Jeannette B. *Princess Kalina and the hedgehog*
Gantos, Jack. *Swampy alligator*
Groves-Raines, Antony. *The tidy hen*
Hamsa, Bobbie. *Dirty Larry*
Hare, Lorraine. *Who needs her?*
Haseley, Dennis. *The soap bandit*
Hickman, Martha Whitmore. *Eeps creeps, it's my room!*
Howells, Mildred. *The woman who lived in Holland*
Hurd, Edith Thacher. *Stop, stop*
Hutchins, Pat. *Where's the baby?*
Jackson, Ellen B. *The bear in the bathtub*
Krasilovsky, Phyllis. *The man who did not wash his dishes*
Madden, Don. *The Wartville wizard*
Morris, Ann. *Eleanora Mousie makes a mess*
Nerlove, Miriam. *I meant to clean my room today*
Peters, Sharon. *Messy Mark*
Polushkin, Maria. *Bubba and Babba*
Potter, Beatrix. *The tale of Mrs. Tittlemouse*
Rockwell, Anne F. *Nice and clean*
Rounds, Glen. *Washday on Noah's ark*
Rudolph, Marguerita. *Sharp and shiny*
Schwartz, Mary. *Spiffen*
Sharmat, Marjorie Weinman. *Mooch the messy*
Sharmat, Mitchell. *The seven sloppy days of Phineas Pig*
Stanton, Elizabeth. *The very messy room*
Wabbes, Marie. *Rose is muddy*
Wilhelm, Hans. *Oh, what a mess*
Willis, Jeanne. *The tale of Georgie Grub*
Ziefert, Harriet. *A clean house for Mole and Mouse*
Hurry up, Jessie!

Character traits – cleverness

Alderson, Sue Ann. *Ida and the wool smugglers*
Aliki. *The eggs*
Andersen, H. C. (Hans Christian). *The swineherd*, ill. by Erik Blegvad
The swineherd, ill. by Dorothée Duntze
Anderson, Paul S. *Red fox and the hungry tiger*
Ardizzone, Edward. *Peter the wanderer*

Asbjørnsen, P. C. (Peter Christen). *The three billy goats Gruff*, ill. by Marcia Brown
Three billy goats Gruff, ill. by Tom Dunnington
The three billy goats Gruff, ill. by Paul Galdone
The three billy goats Gruff, ill. by Janet Stevens
The three billy goats Gruff, ill. by William Stobbs
Baker, Betty. *And me, coyote!*
Partners
Bang, Betsy. *The old woman and the red pumpkin*
The old woman and the rice thief
Bang, Molly. *Wiley and the hairy man*
Bannerman, Helen. *The story of little black Sambo*
Bason, Lillian. *Those foolish Molboes!*
Bell, Anthea. *The wise queen*
Bemelmans, Ludwig. *Welcome home*
Benchley, Nathaniel. *The several tricks of Edgar Dolphin*
Berson, Harold. *How the devil got his due*
Joseph and the snake
Why the jackal won't speak to the hedgehog
Bishop, Claire Huchet. *The five Chinese brothers*
Boegehold, Betty. *Pawpaw's run*
Brett, Jan. *Fritz and the beautiful horses*
Brown, Marcia. *The bun*
Stone soup
Brown, Margaret Wise. *Don't frighten the lion*
Buchanan, Heather S. *George Mouse's first summer*
Burningham, John. *Harquin*
The shopping basket
Burton, Virginia Lee. *Calico the wonder horse*
Byfield, Barbara Ninde. *The haunted churchbell*
Calhoun, Mary. *Cross-country cat*
Jack and the whoopee wind
Cameron, John. *If mice could fly*
Caseley, Judith. *Ada potato*
Castle, Caroline. *Herbert Binns and the flying tricycle*
Cauley, Lorinda Bryan. *The cock, the mouse and the little red hen*
The trouble with Tyrannosaurus Rex
Christelow, Eileen. *Jerome the babysitter*
Christian, Mary Blount. *J. J. Leggett, secret agent*
Climo, Shirley. *King of the birds*
Coatsworth, Elizabeth. *Pika and the roses*
Cohen, Caron Lee. *Renata, Whizbrain and the ghost*
Cole, Joanna. *Doctor Change*
Crompton, Anne Eliot. *The lifting stone*
Damjan, Mischa. *The wolf and the kid*

Daniels, Guy. *The Tsar's riddles*
Dee, Ruby. *Two ways to count to ten*
De La Mare, Walter. *Molly Whuppie*
Demi. *Under the shade of the mulberry tree*
De Regniers, Beatrice Schenk. *Catch a little fox*
Dickens, Frank. *Boffo*
Dines, Glen. *Gilly and the wicharoo*
Dodd, Lynley. *Hairy Maclary's bone*
Domanska, Janina. *The best of the bargain*
King Krakus and the dragon
Why so much noise?
Dos Santos, Joyce Audy. *The diviner*
Elkin, Benjamin. *Gillespie and the guards*
Lucky and the giant
Erickson, Russell E. *Warton and the traders*
Ernst, Lisa Campbell. *The prize pig surprise*
Frankel, Bernice. *Half-As-Big and the tiger*
Frascino, Edward. *My cousin the king*
Freschet, Berniece. *Elephant and friends*
Galdone, Paul. *The monkey and the crocodile*
What's in fox's sack?
Ginsburg, Mirra. *The fisherman's son*
Grimm, Jacob. *The four clever brothers*, ill. by Felix Hoffmann
Hazen, Barbara Shook. *The Fat Cats, Cousin Scraggs and the monster mice*
Hillert, Margaret. *The three goats*
Hirsh, Marilyn. *The Rabbi and the twenty-nine witches*
Hogrogian, Nonny. *Rooster brother*
Hooks, William H. *Three rounds with rabbit*
Hutton, Warwick. *The nose tree*
Huxley, Aldous. *The crows of Pearblossom*
Jaffe, Rona. *Last of the wizards*
Jameson, Cynthia. *The house of five bears*
Kennedy, Richard. *The contests at Cowlick*
Laroche, Michel. *The snow rose*
Leverich, Kathleen. *The hungry fox and the foxy duck*
Lobel, Anita. *The straw maid*
Lobel, Arnold. *How the rooster saved the day*
Mouse soup
Logue, Christopher. *The magic circus*
Lorenz, Lee. *The feathered ogre*
McClenathan, Louise. *My mother sends her wisdom*
McCormack, John E. *Rabbit tales*
McCurdy, Michael. *The devils who learned to be good*
Martin, Charles E. *Dunkel takes a walk*
Obrist, Jürg. *The miser who wanted the sun*
Parish, Peggy. *Zed and the monsters*
Parry, Marian. *King of the fish*
Paterson, Andrew Barton. *The man from Ironbark*
Paul, Anthony. *The tiger who lost his stripes*

Perrault, Charles. *Puss in boots*, ill. by Marcia Brown
Puss in boots, ill. by Lorinda Bryan Cauley
Puss in boots, ill. by Jean Claverie
Puss in boots, ill. by Hans Fischer
Puss in boots, ill. by Paul Galdone
Puss in boots, ill. by Julia Noonan
Puss in boots, ill. by Tony Ross
Puss in boots, ill. by William Stobbs
Puss in boots, ill. by Barry Wilkinson
Pittman, Helena Clare. *A grain of rice*
Potter, Beatrix. *The sly old cat*
The tale of the Flopsy Bunnies
Prokofiev, Sergei Sergeievitch. *Peter and the wolf*, ill. by Reg Cartwright
Peter and the wolf, ill. by Warren Chappell
Peter and the wolf, ill. by Barbara Cooney
Peter and the wolf, ill. by Frans Haacken
Peter and the wolf, ill. by Alan Howard
Peter and the wolf, ill. by Charles Mikolaycak
Peter and the wolf, ill. by Jörg Müller
Peter and the wolf, ill. by Josef Paleček
Peter and the wolf, ill. by Kozo Shimizu
Peter and the wolf, ill. by Erna Voigt
Ransome, Arthur. *The fool of the world and the flying ship*
Rockwell, Anne F. *Big boss*
The bump in the night
The stolen necklace
Ross, Tony. *Stone soup*
Schatell, Brian. *Sam's no dummy, Farmer Goff*
Schatz, Letta. *The extraordinary tug-of-war*
Schulman, Janet. *Jack the bum and the UFO*
Sheldon, Aure. *Of cobblers and kings*
Siddiqui, Ashraf. *Bhombal Dass, the uncle of lion*
Simon, Sidney B. *Henry, the uncatchable mouse*
Singh, Jacquelin. *Fat Gopal*
Small, David. *Paper John*
Steig, William. *Doctor De Soto*
Storr, Catherine. *Clever Polly and the stupid wolf*
The three little pigs. *The story of the three little pigs*, ill. by L. Leslie Brooke
The story of the three little pigs, ill. by William Stobbs
Three little pigs, facsimile ed.
The three little pigs, ill. by Erik Blegvad
The three little pigs, ill. by Caroline Bucknall
The three little pigs, ill. by Lorinda Bryan Cauley
The three little pigs, ill. by William Pène Du Bois
The three little pigs, ill. by Paul Galdone

The three little pigs, ill. by Rodney Peppé
The three little pigs, ill. by Edda Reinl
The three little pigs, ill. by John Wallner
The three little pigs, ill. by Irma Wilde
The three little pigs, ill. by Margot Zemach
The three pigs, ill. by Tony Ross
Troughton, Joanna. *Mouse-Deer's market*
VanRynbach, Iris. *The soup stone*
Van Woerkom, Dorothy. *The rat, the ox and the zodiac*
Walker, Barbara K. *Teeny-Tiny and the witch-woman*
Westwood, Jennifer. *Going to Squintum's*
Wetterer, Margaret. *Patrick and the fairy thief*
Wild, Robin. *Little Pig and the big bad wolf*
Williams, Jay. *School for sillies*
Wolkstein, Diane. *The cool ride in the sky*
Wood, Audrey. *Heckedy Peg*
Young, Ed. *The terrible Nung Gwama*
Zemach, Harve. *Nail soup*

Character traits – completing things

Flack, Marjorie. *Angus and the cat*
Ness, Evaline. *Do you have the time, Lydia?*
Petrides, Heidrun. *Hans and Peter*

Character traits – compromising

Hogrogian, Nonny. *Carrot cake*
Wildsmith, Brian. *The owl and the woodpecker*

Character traits – conceit

Bill, Helen. *Shoes fit for a king*
Brenner, Barbara. *Mr. Tall and Mr. Small*
Flack, Marjorie. *Angus and the ducks*
Grimm, Jacob. *King Grisly-Beard*
Peet, Bill. *Ella*
Sharmat, Marjorie Weinman. *I'm terrific*
Williams, Barbara. *So what if I'm a sore loser?*

Character traits – confidence

Adler, David A. *Jeffrey's ghost and the leftover baseball team*

Character traits – cruelty to animals *see* Character traits – kindness to animals

Character traits – curiosity

Adamson, Gareth. *Old man up a tree*
Alden, Laura. *When?*
Allen, Jeffrey. *Nosey Mrs. Rat*
Ames, Mildred. *The wonderful box*
Bang, Molly. *Dawn*
Bograd, Larry. *Egon*
Broome, Errol. *The smallest koala*

Campbell, Rod. *Buster's afternoon*
 Buster's morning
Clark, Roberta. *Why?*
Climo, Shirley. *The adventure of Walter*
Curious George and the dump truck
Curious George and the pizza
Curious George at the fire station
Curious George goes hiking
Curious George goes sledding
Curious George goes to the aquarium
Curious George goes to the circus
Curious George visits the zoo
Demarest, Chris L. *Clemens' kingdom*
Fisher, Aileen. *Anybody home?*
Flack, Marjorie. *Angus and the cat*
 Angus and the ducks
Gackenbach, Dick. *The pig who saw
 everything*
Kanao, Keiko. *Kitten up a tree*
Kipling, Rudyard. *The elephant's child*, ill.
 by Louise Brierley
 The elephant's child, ill. by Lorinda Bryan
 Cauley
 The elephant's child, ill. by Tim Raglin
MacGregor, Marilyn. *Baby takes a trip*
Meeks, Esther K. *The curious cow*
Moncure, Jane Belk. *Where?*
Napoli, Guillier. *Adventure at
 Mont-Saint-Michel*
Pinkwater, Daniel Manus. *Devil in the
 drain*
Ravilious, Robin. *The runaway chick*
Reece, Colleen L. *What?*
Rey, Hans Augusto. *Curious George*
 Curious George gets a medal
 Curious George learns the alphabet
 Curious George rides a bike
 Curious George takes a job
Rey, Margaret Elisabeth Waldstein.
 Curious George flies a kite
 Curious George goes to the hospital
Rylant, Cynthia. *Miss Maggie*
Sandberg, Inger. *Dusty wants to borrow
 everything*
Waber, Bernard. *Lorenzo*
Weil, Lisl. *Pandora's box*
Zhitkov, Boris. *How I hunted for the little
 fellows*

Character traits – envy *see* Emotions –
envy, jealousy

Character traits – flattery

Æsop. *Three fox fables*
Chaucer, Geoffrey. *Chanticleer and the fox*,
 ill. by Barbara Cooney

Character traits – foolishness

Bason, Lillian. *Those foolish Molboes!*
Bradman, Tony. *Not like this, like that*

Gackenbach, Dick. *Harvey, the foolish pig*
Gammell, Stephen. *The story of Mr. and
 Mrs. Vinegar*
Grimm, Jacob. *Hans in luck*, ill. by Paul
 Galdone
 Hans in luck, ill. by Felix Hoffmann
 Lucky Hans, ill. by Eugen Sopko
Hewitt, Kathryn. *The three sillies*
Jacobs, Joseph. *Lazy Jack*, ill. by Barry
 Wilkinson
Johnson, Evelyne. *The cow in the kitchen*
Keenen, George. *The preposterous week*
Maitland, Antony. *Idle Jack*
Phillips, Louis. *The brothers Wrong and
 Wrong Again*
Schwartz, Amy. *Yossel Zissel and the wisdom
 of Chelm*
Scruton, Clive. *Circus cow*
Zemach, Margot. *The three wishes*

Character traits – fortune *see* Character
traits – luck

Character traits – freedom

Andersen, H. C. (Hans Christian). *The
 emperor and the nightingale*, ill. by James
 Watling
 The emperor's nightingale, ill. by Georges
 Lemoine
 The nightingale, ill. by Harold Berson
 The nightingale, ill. by Nancy Ekholm
 Burkert
 The nightingale, ill. by Demi
 The nightingale, ill. by Beni Montresor
 The nightingale, ill. by Lisbeth Zwerger
Bayar, Steven. *Rachel and Mischa*
Baylor, Byrd. *Hawk, I'm your brother*
Bellville, Cheryl Walsh. *Theater magic*
Blaustein, Muriel. *Baby Mabu and Auntie
 Moose*
Bradford, Ann. *The mystery of the missing
 raccoon*
Brady, Irene. *A mouse named Mus*
Bunting, Eve. *How many days to America?*
Dennis, Wesley. *Tumble, the story of a
 mustang*
Fatio, Louise. *Hector and Christina*
Fujita, Tamao. *The boy and the bird*
Hawkinson, John. *Where the wild apples
 grow*
McPhail, David *A wolf story*
Steiner, Jörg. *Rabbit Island*
Stern, Mark. *It's a dog's life*
Sundgaard, Arnold. *The lamb and the
 butterfly*

Character traits – generosity

Ainsworth, Ruth. *The mysterious Baba and
 her magic caravan*
Aliki. *The story of Johnny Appleseed*

Anglund, Joan Walsh. *Christmas is a time of giving*
Bawden, Nina. *St. Francis of Assisi*
Bohanon, Paul. *Golden Kate*
Brown, Palmer. *Something for Christmas*
Chalmers, Mary. *A hat for Amy Jean*
Christian, Mary Blount. *The devil take you, Barnabas Beane!*
Chute, Beatrice Joy. *Joy to Christmas*
Cohen, Barbara. *Even higher*
Cohen, Miriam. *Liar, liar, pants on fire!*
Erickson, Russell E. *Warton and the traders*
Farjeon, Eleanor. *Mrs. Malone*
Fontane, Theodore. *Sir Ribbeck of Ribbeck of Havelland*
Fox, Mem. *With love, at Christmas*
Grimm, Jacob. *The falling stars*, ill. by Eugen Sopko
Henry, O. *The gift of the Magi*
Hoban, Russell. *Emmet Otter's jug-band Christmas*
The mole family's Christmas
Houston, John A. *The bright yellow rope*
Hush little baby. *Hush little baby*, ill. by Aliki
Hush little baby, ill. by Jeanette Winter
Hush little baby, ill. by Margot Zemach
Janice. *Little Bear's Christmas*
Johnson, Crockett. *The emperor's gift*
Kasza, Keiko. *The wolf's chicken stew*
Kunnas, Mauri. *Twelve gifts for Santa Claus*
Lexau, Joan M. *A house so big*
Lindman, Maj. *Snipp, Snapp, Snurr and the red shoes*
Lionni, Leo. *Tico and the golden wings*
McClenathan, Louise. *The Easter pig*
Muntean, Michaela. *Mokey and the festival of the bells*
Ness, Evaline. *Josefina February*
Rockwell, Anne F. *Gogo's pay day*
Rodanas, Kristina. *The story of Wali Dâd*
Schotter, Roni. *Captain Snap and the children of Vinegar Lane*
Shecter, Ben. *If I had a ship*
Silverstein, Shel. *The giving tree*
Testa, Fulvio. *Wolf's favor*
Timmermans, Felix. *A gift from Saint Nicholas*
Tolstoĭ, Alekseĭ Nikolaevich. *Shoemaker Martin*

Character traits – helpfulness

Adelson, Leone. *Who blew that whistle?*
Adshead, Gladys L. *Brownies - hush!*
Brownies - they're moving
Æsop. *The lion and the mouse*, ill. by Gerald Rose
The lion and the mouse, ill. by Ed Young
Aliki. *The two of them*

Ancona, George. *Helping out*
Androcles and the lion, ill. by Janusz Grabianski
Baker, Betty. *Partners*
Bakken, Harold. *The special string*
Beim, Jerrold. *Country mailman*
Blair, Anne Denton. *Hurrah for Arthur!*
Bonsall, Crosby Newell. *Who's a pest?*
Bridwell, Norman. *Clifford's good deeds*
Bright, Robert. *Georgie and the baby birds*
Georgie and the ball of yarn
Georgie and the little dog
Georgie and the runaway balloon
Brown, Myra Berry. *Company's coming for dinner*
Buchanan, Heather S. *Emily Mouse saves the day*
Calhoun, Mary. *Euphonia and the flood*
Jack the wise and the Cornish cuckoos
Carey, Valerie Scho. *Harriet and William and the terrible creature*
Chevalier, Christa. *Spence is small*
Clifton, Lucille. *My friend Jacob*
Cole, William. *Aunt Bella's umbrella*
Collier, Ethel. *Who goes there in my garden?*
Curle, Jock. *The four good friends*
Cuyler, Margery. *Fat Santa*
Daly, Niki. *Thank you Henrietta*
Davis, Alice Vaught. *Timothy turtle*
Day, Alexandra. *Frank and Ernest*
Day, Shirley. *Waldo's back yard*
Devlin, Wende. *Cranberry Christmas*
Du Bois, William Pène. *Bear circus*
Ets, Marie Hall. *Elephant in a well*
Graham, Al. *Timothy Turtle*, ill. by Tony Palazzo
Graham, Margaret Bloy. *Benjy and his friend Fifi*
Gray, Genevieve. *Send Wendell*
Green, Norma B. *The hole in the dike*
Greene, Laura. *Help*
Grimm, Jacob. *The elves and the shoemaker*, ill. by Paul Galdone
The elves and the shoemaker, ill. by Bernadette Watts
Mother Holly
The shoemaker and the elves, ill. by Cynthia and William Birrer
Herold, Ann Bixby. *The helping day*
Hill, Elizabeth Starr. *Evan's corner*
Holmes, Efner Tudor. *Amy's goose*
Houston, John A. *The bright yellow rope*
Hürlimann, Bettina. *Barry*
Kishida, Eriko. *The lion and the bird's nest*
Kraus, Robert. *Herman the helper*
Rebecca Hatpin
La Fontaine, Jean de. *The lion and the rat*
Lewis, Eils Moorhouse. *The snug little house*

Lindman, Maj. *Flicka, Ricka, Dicka and the new dotted dress*
Snipp, Snapp, Snurr and the red shoes
Lloyd, Errol. *Nini at carnival*
McConnachie, Brian. *Flying boy*
Marcus, Susan. *The missing button adventure*
Marshall, James. *What's the matter with Carruthers?*
Mayer, Mercer. *Just for you*
Mayne, William. *The blue book of Hob stories*
The green book of Hob stories
The red book of Hob stories
The yellow book of Hob stories
Michael, Emory H. *Androcles and the lion*
Nakano, Hirotaka. *Elephant blue*
Ness, Evaline. *Pavo and the princess*
Oxenbury, Helen. *Mother's helper*
Parker, Nancy Winslow. *Cooper, the McNallys' big black dog*
Partridge, Jenny. *Peterkin Pollensnuff*
Paul, Sherry. *2-B and the rock 'n roll band*
Peet, Bill. *The ant and the elephant*
Cyrus the unsinkable sea serpent
Porte, Barbara Ann. *Harry in trouble*
Potter, Beatrix. *The tailor of Gloucester*
Quackenbush, Robert M. *Chuck lends a paw*
Rayner, Mary. *The rain cloud*
Rockwell, Anne F. *Big bad goat*
The bump in the night
Can I help?
Handy Hank will fix it
Seuss, Dr. *Horton hatches the egg*
Simon, Norma. *What do I do?*
Slobodkin, Louis. *Dinny and Danny*
Snow, Pegeen. *Mrs. Periwinkle's groceries*
Stevenson, James. *Will you please feed our cat?*
Suhl, Yuri. *The Purim goat*
Udry, Janice May. *Is Susan here?*
Venino, Suzanne. *Animals helping people*
Waber, Bernard. *Lyle, Lyle Crocodile*
Williams, Barbara. *Someday, said Mitchell*
Wolde, Gunilla. *Betsy's fixing day*
Zemach, Margot. *To Hilda for helping*

Character traits – honesty

Alexander, Lloyd. *The truthful harp*
Aliki. *Diogenes*
Ardizzone, Edward. *Peter the wanderer*
Demi. *Chen Ping and his magic axe*
Gallant, Kathryn. *The flute player of Beppu*
Goldsmith, Howard. *Little lost dog*
Havill, Juanita. *Jamaica's find*
Langton, Jane. *The hedgehog boy*
McLenighan, Valjean. *I know you cheated*
Matsuno, Masako. *A pair of red clogs*
Taro and the Tofu

Mayer, Mercer. *How the trollusk got his hat*
Turkle, Brinton. *The adventures of Obadiah*
Wilson, Julia. *Becky*

Character traits – incentive *see* Character traits – ambition

Character traits – individuality

Abolafia, Yossi. *My three uncles*
Alderson, Sue Ann. *Bonnie McSmithers is at it again!*
Aliki. *Jack and Jake*
Allamand, Pascale. *The animals who changed their colors*
Anglund, Joan Walsh. *Look out the window*
Baker, Jeannie. *Millicent*
Beim, Jerrold. *Country train*
Freckle face
Bright, Robert. *Which is Willy?*
Carey, Mary. *The owl who loved sunshine*
Carlson, Nancy. *I like me*
Charlip, Remy. *Hooray for me!*
Conford, Ellen. *Impossible, possum*
Delaney, Ned. *One dragon to another*
Dellinger, Annetta. *You are special to Jesus*
Delton, Judy. *I'm telling you now*
De Paola, Tomie. *Oliver Button is a sissy*
Duvoisin, Roger Antoine. *Jasmine*
Fatio, Louise. *Hector penguin*
Gramatky, Hardie. *Little Toot through the Golden Gate*
Horvath, Betty F. *Will the real Tommy Wilson please stand up?*
Jaynes, Ruth M. *What is a birthday child?*
Jeffery, Graham. *Thomas the tortoise*
Kraus, Robert. *Owliver*
Kuskin, Karla. *Which horse is William?*
Lampert, Emily. *A little touch of monster*
Leaf, Munro. *The story of Ferdinand the bull*
Lester, Alison. *Clive eats alligators*
Lester, Helen. *Tacky the penguin*
Levine, Rhoda. *Harrison loved his umbrella*
Lionni, Leo. *A color of his own*
Pezzettino
Tico and the golden wings
Littledale, Freya. *The magic plum tree*
Lopshire, Robert. *I want to be somebody new!*
Lystad, Mary H. *That new boy*
McConnachie, Brian. *Flying boy*
McCormack, John E. *Rabbit tales*
MacGregor, Marilyn. *On top*
McKee, David. *Elmer, the story of a patchwork elephant*
Manushkin, Fran. *Shirleybird*
Oram, Hiawyn. *Ned and the Joybaloo*
Peet, Bill. *Buford, the little bighorn*
The spooky tail of Prewitt Peacock

Pinkwater, Daniel Manus. *The big orange splot*
Rand, Gloria. *Salty dog*
Redies, Rainer. *The cats' party*
Reeves, James. *Rhyming Will*
Rogers, Fred. *If we were all the same*
Rubel, Nicole. *Sam and Violet are twins*
Sam and Violet go camping
Ruck-Pauquèt, Gina. *Mumble bear*
Sand, George. *The mysterious tale of Gentle Jack and Lord Bumblebee*
Sendak, Maurice. *Pierre*
Seuling, Barbara. *The triplets*
Seuss, Dr. *I can draw it myself*
Sharmat, Marjorie Weinman. *What are we going to do about Andrew?*
Sharmat, Mitchell. *Sherman is a slowpoke*
Silverstein, Shel. *The missing piece*
Simon, Norma. *I know what I like*
Why am I different?
Singer, Marilyn. *The dog who insisted he wasn't*
Pickle plan
Slobodkin, Louis. *Millions and millions and millions*
Tafuri, Nancy. *Have you seen my duckling?*
Tyrrell, Anne. *Mary Ann always can*
Viorst, Judith. *Try it again, Sam*
Waber, Bernard. *"You look ridiculous," said the rhinoceros to the hippopotamus*
Wells, Rosemary. *Shy Charles*

Character traits – jealousy *see* Emotions – envy, jealousy

Character traits – kindness

Aliki. *The story of William Penn*
Bang, Molly. *The paper crane*
Barber, Antonia. *Satchelmouse and the doll's house*
Baumann, Kurt. *The prince and the lute*
Brown, Margaret Wise. *Dr. Squash the doll doctor*
Calhoun, Mary. *The thieving dwarfs*
Cazet, Denys. *A fish in his pocket*
Cole, Brock. *The king at the door*
Coville, Bruce. *The foolish giant*
Sarah and the dragon
Davis, Maggie S. *Grandma's secret letter*
DeArmond, Dale. *The seal oil lamp*
Elzbieta. *Dikou and the baby star*
Dikou the little troon who walks at night
Fatio, Louise. *The happy lion's rabbits*
Fleischman, Sid. *The scarebird*
Fyleman, Rose. *A fairy went a-marketing*
Gannett, Ruth S. *Katie and the sad noise*
Goodsell, Jane. *Toby's toe*
Grimm, Jacob. *The golden goose*, ill. by Dorothée Duntze
The golden goose, ill. by Isadore Seltzer

The golden goose, ill. by Martin Ursell
Hasler, Eveline. *Martin is our friend*
Hastings, Selina. *The singing ringing tree*
Heyward, Du Bose. *The country bunny and the little gold shoes*
Karlin, Nurit. *The tooth witch*
Kent, Jack. *Clotilda*
Kraus, Robert. *The first robin*
La Rochelle, David. *A Christmas guest*
Lee, Jeanne M. *Ba-Nam*
Lipkind, William. *The magic feather duster*
Mayer, Marianna. *The little jewel box*
Meddaugh, Susan. *Beast*
Mizumura, Kazue. *If I built a village*
Munsch, Robert N. *David's father*
Nesbit, Edith. *The last of the dragons*
Newton, Patricia Montgomery. *The five sparrows*
Noble, Trinka Hakes. *Hansy's mermaid*
Ormondroyd, Edward. *Theodore*
Peterson, Hans. *Erik and the Christmas horse*
Postgate, Oliver. *Noggin the king*
Rohmer, Harriet. *Atariba and Niguayona*
Schotter, Roni. *Captain Snap and the children of Vinegar Lane*
Seuss, Dr. *Horton hears a Who!*
Shibano, Tamizo. *The old man who made the trees bloom*
Small, David. *Eulalie and the hopping head*
Steptoe, John. *Mufaro's beautiful daughters*
Stevens, Carla. *Stories from a snowy meadow*
Tolstoĭ, Alekseĭ Nikolaevich. *Shoemaker Martin*
Ungerer, Tomi. *Zeralda's ogre*
Vigna, Judith. *Anyhow, I'm glad I tried*
Warren, Cathy. *Saturday belongs to Sara*
Wells, H. G. (Herbert George). *The adventures of Tommy*
Wilde, Oscar. *The selfish giant*, ill. by Dom Mansell
The selfish giant, ill. by Lisbeth Zwerger
Wittman, Sally. *The boy who hated Valentine's Day*
Zolotow, Charlotte. *I know a lady*

Character traits – kindness to animals

Allred, Mary. *Grandmother Poppy and the funny-looking bird*
Anderson, C. W. (Clarence Williams). *Lonesome little colt*
The rumble seat pony
Androcles and the lion, ill. by Janusz Grabianski
Aragon, Jane Chelsea. *Winter harvest*
Averill, Esther. *Jenny's adopted brothers*
Baker, Jeannie. *Home in the sky*
Barnhart, Peter. *The wounded duck*
Baumann, Hans. *Chip has many brothers*
Beatty, Hetty Burlingame. *Moorland pony*

Berson, Harold. *Joseph and the snake*
Birrer, Cynthia. *The lady and the unicorn*
Bolliger, Max. *The magic bird*
Boon, Emilie. *It's spring, Peterkin*
Brighton, Catherine. *Hope's gift*
Brock, Emma Lillian. *The birds' Christmas tree*
Brunhoff, Laurent de. *Babar's little girl*
Bryan, Ashley. *Sh-ko and his eight wicked brothers*
Buchanan, Heather S. *Emily Mouse's first adventure*
Burch, Robert. *The hunting trip*
Carey, Mary. *The owl who loved sunshine*
Carter, Anne. *Bella's secret garden*
Clewes, Dorothy. *The wild wood*
Curle, Jock. *The four good friends*
Daugherty, James Henry. *Andy and the lion*
De Marolles, Chantal. *The lonely wolf*
Drew, Patricia. *Spotter Puff*
Dunn, Judy. *The little lamb*
Duvoisin, Roger Antoine. *The happy hunter*
Freeman, Don. *The seal and the slick*
Galdone, Paul. *Androcles and the lion*
Gantschev, Ivan. *Otto the bear*
Georgiady, Nicholas P. *Gertie the duck*
Goffstein, M. B. (Marilyn Brooke). *Natural history*
The good-hearted youngest brother
Graham, Bob. *Pete and Roland*
Grant, Joan. *The monster that grew small*
Hader, Berta Hoerner. *Mister Billy's gun*
Harriott, Ted. *Coming home*
Harrison, David Lee. *Little turtle's big adventure*
Herriot, James. *Christmas Day kitten*
Hewett, Joan. *Rosalie*
Hirsh, Marilyn. *Deborah the dybbuk*
Holmes, Efner Tudor. *Amy's goose*
Carrie's gift
Ishii, Momoko. *The tongue-cut sparrow*
Jeffery, Graham. *Thomas the tortoise*
Keats, Ezra Jack. *Jennie's hat*
Kumin, Maxine. *Mittens in May*
Lathrop, Dorothy Pulis. *Who goes there?*
Levitin, Sonia. *All the cats in the world*
Lipkind, William. *The boy and the forest*
McNulty, Faith. *The lady and the spider*
Mouse and Tim
McPhail, David. *The bear's toothache*
A wolf story
Mamin-Sibiryak, D. N. *Grey Neck*
Michael, Emory H. *Androcles and the lion*
Miklowitz, Gloria D. *Save that raccoon!*
Mogensen, Jan. *Teddy's Christmas gift*
Moore, Sheila. *Samson Svenson's baby*
Nakatani, Chiyoko. *Fumio and the dolphins*
Newberry, Clare Turlay. *Percy, Polly and Pete*

Numeroff, Laura Joffe. *If you give a mouse a cookie*
Pedersen, Judy. *The tiny patient*
Peet, Bill. *Huge Harold*
Roy, Ronald. *A thousand pails of water*
Rylant, Cynthia. *Henry and Mudge in puddle trouble*
Sandburg, Helga. *Anna and the baby buzzard*
Turkle, Brinton. *Thy friend, Obadiah*
Turska, Krystyna. *The woodcutter's duck*
Varley, Dimitry. *The whirly bird*
Velthuijs, Max. *Little Man to the rescue*
Wallace, Ian. *The sparrow's song*
Ward, Lynd. *The biggest bear*
Waterton, Betty. *A salmon for Simon*
Wersba, Barbara. *Do tigers ever bite kings?*
Whitney, Alma Marshak. *Leave Herbert alone*
Wildsmith, Brian. *Hunter and his dog*
Wondriska, William. *The stop*
Yagawa, Sumiko. *The crane wife*

Character traits – laziness

Aylesworth, Jim. *Hush up!*
Baker, Betty. *Partners*
Bolognese, Elaine. *The sleepy watchdog*
Bowen, Vernon. *The lazy beaver*
Bright, Robert. *Gregory, the noisiest and strongest boy in Grangers Grove*
Du Bois, William Pène. *Lazy Tommy pumpkinhead*
Grimm, Jacob. *Mother Holly*
Holding, James. *The lazy little Zulu*
Jacobs, Joseph. *Lazy Jack*, ill. by Barry Wilkinson
Krasilovsky, Phyllis. *The man who did not wash his dishes*
The man who tried to save time
Lazy Jack. *Lazy Jack*, ill. by Bert Dodson
Lazy Jack, ill. by Kurt Werth
The little red hen. *The little red hen*, ill. by Janina Domanska
The little red hen, ill. by Paul Galdone
The little red hen, ill. by Mel Pekarsky
The little red hen, ill. by William Stobbs
The little red hen, ill. by Margot Zemach
Lobel, Arnold. *A treeful of pigs*
Lorenz, Lee. *Big Gus and Little Gus*
McKissack, Patricia C. *The little red hen*, ill. by Dennis Hockerman
Mathews, Louise. *The great take-away*
Pack, Robert. *How to catch a crocodile*
Papas, William. *Taresh the tea planter*
Ross, Tony. *Lazy Jack*
Schmidt, Eric von. *The young man who wouldn't hoe corn*
Sharmat, Marjorie Weinman. *Burton and Dudley*

Snyder, Dianne. *The boy of the three-year nap*
Taylor, Sydney. *Mr. Barney's beard*
Wildsmith, Brian. *The lazy bear*

Character traits – littleness *see* Character traits – smallness

Character traits – loyalty

Aliki. *The two of them*
Ardizzone, Edward. *Tim to the rescue*
Boyle, Vere. *Beauty and the beast*
Bridwell, Norman. *Clifford goes to Hollywood*
Calhoun, Mary. *The witch who lost her shadow*
Collodi, Carlo. *The adventures of Pinocchio*
Cooney, Barbara. *Little brother and little sister*
Crompton, Anne Eliot. *The winter wife*
Haywood, Carolyn. *How the reindeer saved Santa*
Hurd, Edith Thacher. *Under the lemon tree*
Hutton, Warwick. *Beauty and the beast*
Lasker, Joe. *He's my brother*
McCrea, James. *The king's procession*
McLerran, Alice. *The mountain that loved a bird*
Nesbit, Edith. *Beauty and the beast*, ill. by Julia Christie
Potter, Beatrix. *The tale of the faithful dove*
Springstubb, Tricia. *My Minnie is a jewel*
Stanovich, Betty Jo. *Hedgehog adventures*
Whittier, John Greenleaf. *Barbara Frietchie*
Wright, Freire. *Beauty and the beast*

Character traits – luck

Aldridge, Josephine Haskell. *Fisherman's luck*
Aliki. *Three gold pieces*
Beim, Lorraine. *Lucky Pierre*
Bond, Michael. *Paddington's lucky day*
Brown, Margaret Wise. *Wheel on the chimney*
Brown, Myra Berry. *Best of luck*
Cazet, Denys. *Lucky me*
Delton, Judy. *I never win!*
 It happened on Thursday
Elkin, Benjamin. *Lucky and the giant*
Gackenbach, Dick. *Harvey, the foolish pig*
Grimm, Jacob. *Hans in luck*, ill. by Paul Galdone
 Hans in luck, ill. by Felix Hoffmann
 Lucky Hans, ill. by Eugen Sopko
Hann, Jacquie. *Up day, down day*
Holland, Janice. *You never can tell*
Mayer, Marianna. *The little jewel box*
Moeri, Louise. *The unicorn and the plow*
Russell, Betty. *Big store, funny door*

Seuss, Dr. *Did I ever tell you how lucky you are?*
Stafford, Kay. *Ling Tang and the lucky cricket*
Stanley, Diane. *The good-luck pencil*
Velthuijs, Max. *Little Man's lucky day*
Walsh, Jill Paton. *Lost and found*

Character traits – meanness

Barth, Edna. *Jack-o'-lantern*
Bellows, Cathy. *Four fat rats*
Bottner, Barbara. *Mean Maxine*
Burningham, John. *Borka*
Carey, Valerie Scho. *The devil and mother Crump*
Carrick, Carol. *Old Mother Witch*
Coville, Bruce. *Sarah's unicorn*
Freeman, Don. *Tilly Witch*
Gantos, Jack. *Rotten Ralph's rotten Christmas*
 Rotten Ralph's trick or treat
 Worse than Rotten Ralph
Glazer, Lee. *Cookie Becker casts a spell*
Goodsell, Jane. *Toby's toe*
Himmelman, John. *Amanda and the witch switch*
Hoban, Russell. *Big John Turkle*
 The little Brute family
Jones, Rebecca C. *The biggest, meanest, ugliest dog in the whole wide world*
Kidd, Bruce. *Hockey showdown*
Kismaric, Carole. *The rumor of Pavel and Paali*
McCrea, James. *The magic tree*
Mahy, Margaret. *The boy with two shadows*
Manushkin, Fran. *Hocus and Pocus at the circus*
Nickl, Peter. *Ra ta ta tam*
Patz, Nancy. *Gina Farina and the Prince of Mintz*
Prelutsky, Jack. *The mean old mean hyena*
Price, Michelle. *Mean Melissa*
Seuss, Dr. *How the Grinch stole Christmas*
Shibano, Tamizo. *The old man who made the trees bloom*
Snyder, Anne. *The old man and the mule*
Steptoe, John. *Mufaro's beautiful daughters*
Stevenson, James. *Fried feathers for Thanksgiving*
 Happy Valentine's Day, Emma!
Udry, Janice May. *The mean mouse and other mean stories*
Zimelman, Nathan. *Mean Murgatroyd and the ten cats*
Zion, Gene. *The meanest squirrel I ever met*

Character traits – optimism

Alexander, Sue. *Marc the Magnificent*
Aliki. *The twelve months*
Atwood, Margaret. *Anna's pet*

Ayer, Jacqueline. *The paper-flower tree*
Chalmers, Audrey. *A kitten's tale*
Delton, Judy. *My mother lost her job today*
Gregory, Valiska. *Sunny side up*
Terribly wonderful
Hall, Malcolm. *The friends of Charlie Ant Bear*
Hoff, Syd. *Oliver*
Krauss, Ruth. *The carrot seed*
Lindgren, Astrid. *Of course Polly can do almost everything*
Lionni, Leo. *Theodore and the talking mushroom*
Peet, Bill. *The Whingdingdilly*
Piatti, Celestino. *The happy owls*
Rice, Inez. *A long long time*
Seuss, Dr. *Would you rather be a bullfrog?*
Tapio, Pat Decker. *The lady who saw the good side of everything*
Wiesner, William. *Happy-Go-Lucky*
Zakhoder, Boris Vladimirovich. *Rosachok*

Character traits – ostracism *see* Character traits – being different

Character traits – patience

Hellen, Nancy. *Bus stop*
Kibbey, Marsha. *My grammy*
Laurin, Anne. *Little things*
Steiner, Charlotte. *What's the hurry, Harry?*
Weiss, Nicki. *Waiting*
Wells, Rosemary. *Max's breakfast*

Character traits – perseverance

Abisch, Roz. *Sweet Betsy from Pike*
Æsop. *The miller, his son and their donkey*, ill. by Roger Antoine Duvoisin
The miller, his son and their donkey, ill. by Eugen Sopko
The tortoise and the hare, ill. by Janet Stevens
Alexander, Martha G. *Move over, Twerp*
We never get to do anything
Aliki. *A weed is a flower*
Ambrus, Victor G. *The little cockerel*
Mishka
Bethell, Jean. *Hooray for Henry*
Blades, Ann. *Mary of mile 18*
Boynton, Sandra. *If at first...*
Brennan, Joseph Killorin. *Gobo and the river*
Brenner, Barbara. *Wagon wheels*
Calhoun, Mary. *Old man Whickutt's donkey*
Conford, Ellen. *Just the thing for Geraldine*
Day, Shirley. *Ruthie's big tree*
Erickson, Karen. *I'll try*
Gray, Genevieve. *How far, Felipe?*
Hoff, Syd. *Slugger Sal's slump*
Jensen, Virginia Allen. *Sara and the door*
Kahl, Virginia. *Maxie*

Keats, Ezra Jack. *John Henry*
Lane, Carolyn. *The voices of Greenwillow Pond*
Lindgren, Astrid. *Of course Polly can do almost everything*
Piper, Watty. *The little engine that could*
Riordan, James. *The three magic gifts*
Shine, Deborah. *The little engine that could pudgy word book*
Skorpen, Liesel Moak. *All the Lassies*
Steig, William. *Brave Irene*
Thomas, Kathy. *The angel's quest*
Ungerer, Tomi. *The Mellops go spelunking*
Watanabe, Shigeo. *I can build a house!*
I can ride it!
Where's my daddy?

Character traits – persistence

Birdseye, Tom. *Airmail to the moon*
Bulla, Clyde Robert. *The stubborn old woman*
Patz, Nancy. *Gina Farina and the Prince of Mintz*
Ward, Sally G. *Molly and Grandpa*
West, Colin. *"Pardon?" said the giraffe*

Character traits – practicality

Evans, Katherine. *The man, the boy and the donkey*
Gág, Wanda. *Millions of cats*
Gretz, Susanna. *Roger loses his marbles!*
La Fontaine, Jean de. *The miller, the boy and the donkey*
Modell, Frank. *One zillion valentines*
Schlein, Miriam. *The pile of junk*

Character traits – pride

Andersen, H. C. (Hans Christian). *The emperor's new clothes*, ill. by Pamela Baldwin-Ford
The emperor's new clothes, ill. by Erik Blegvad
The emperor's new clothes, ill. by Virginia Lee Burton
The emperor's new clothes, ill. by Jack and Irene Delano
The emperor's new clothes, ill. by Héléne Desputeaux
The emperor's new clothes, ill. by Birte Dietz
The emperor's new clothes, ill. by Dorothée Duntze
The emperor's new clothes, ill. by Jack Kent
The emperor's new clothes, ill. by Monika Laimgruber
The emperor's new clothes, ill. by Anne F. Rockwell
The emperor's new clothes, ill. by Janet Stevens

The emperor's new clothes, ill. by Nadine Bernard Westcott
The red shoes, ill. by Chihiro Iwasaki
Bemelmans, Ludwig. *Rosebud*
Birch, David. *The king's chessboard*
Burningham, John. *Humbert, Mister Firkin and the Lord Mayor of London*
Calhoun, Mary. *The runaway brownie*
Clifton, Lucille. *All us come cross the water*
Dionetti, Michelle. *Thalia Brown and the blue bug*
Duvoisin, Roger Antoine. *Crocus Petunia*
Edwards, Dorothy. *A wet Monday*
Ehrhardt, Reinhold. *Kikeri or, The proud red rooster*
Friskey, Margaret. *Indian Two Feet rides alone*
Gackenbach, Dick. *The dog and the deep dark woods*
Hamberger, John. *The peacock who lost his tail*
Hürlimann, Ruth. *The proud white cat*
Keats, Ezra Jack. *John Henry*
McKissack, Patricia C. *The king's new clothes*, ill. by Gwen Connelly
McLenighan, Valjean. *What you see is what you get*
Politi, Leo. *Mieko*
Pomerantz, Charlotte. *The ballad of the long-tailed rat*
Rogasky, Barbara. *The water of life*
Rylant, Cynthia. *Mr. Griggs' work*
Schwartz, Amy. *Annabelle Swift, kindergartner*
Sharmat, Marjorie Weinman. *I'm terrific*
Tettelbaum, Michael. *The cave of the lost Fraggle*
Whitney, Alex. *Once a bright red tiger*
Winthrop, Elizabeth. *Tough Eddie*
Zimnik, Reiner. *The proud circus horse*

Character traits – questioning

Adler, David A. *A little at a time*
Alden, Laura. *When?*
Allard, Harry. *May I stay?*
Brown, Margaret Wise. *Wait till the moon is full*
Clark, Roberta. *Why?*
Deveaux, Alexis. *Na-ni*
Jacobs, Leland B. *Is somewhere always far away?*
Krauze, Andrzej. *What's so special about today?*
Lionni, Leo. *Tico and the golden wings*
Mahood, Kenneth. *Why are there more questions than answers, Grandad?*
Miller, M. L. *Dizzy from fools*
Moncure, Jane Belk. *Where?*
Reece, Colleen L. *What?*

Simont, Marc. *How come elephants?*
Stover, Jo Ann. *Why? Because*
Thaler, Mike. *Owley*
Vance, Eleanor Graham. *Jonathan*
Williams, Barbara. *If he's my brother*
Ziefert, Harriet. *Sarah's questions*

Character traits – selfishness

Andersen, H. C. (Hans Christian). *The swineherd*, ill. by Erik Blegvad
The swineherd, ill. by Dorothée Duntze
Angelo, Valenti. *The acorn tree*
Baba, Noboru. *Eleven cats and a pig*
Eleven cats and albatrosses
Eleven cats in a bag
Eleven hungry cats
Barrett, John M. *Oscar the selfish octopus*
Bascom, Joe. *Malcolm Softpaws*
Berquist, Grace. *The boy who couldn't roar*
Berry, Joy Wilt. *Being selfish*
Bryant, Bernice. *Follow the leader*
Christian, Mary Blount. *The devil take you, Barnabas Beane!*
Coombs, Patricia. *Mouse Café*
Elkin, Benjamin. *Lucky and the giant*
Garrett, Jennifer. *The queen who stole the sky*
Henkes, Kevin. *A weekend with Wendell*
Kahl, Virginia. *The perfect pancake*
Kraus, Robert. *Rebecca Hatpin*
Lipkind, William. *Even Steven*
Finders keepers
Peet, Bill. *The ant and the elephant*
Reesink, Marijke. *The golden treasure*
Rudolph, Marguerita. *I am your misfortune*
Wilde, Oscar. *The selfish giant*, ill. by Dom Mansell
The selfish giant, ill. by Lisbeth Zwerger
Yolen, Jane. *The acorn quest*

Character traits – shyness

Brice, Tony. *The bashful goldfish*
Devlin, Wende. *Cranberry Valentine*
Dines, Glen. *A tiger in the cherry tree*
Goffstein, M. B. (Marilyn Brooke). *Neighbors*
Hamilton, Morse. *How do you do, Mr. Birdsteps?*
Hogrogian, Nonny. *Carrot cake*
Keats, Ezra Jack. *Louie*
Keller, Beverly. *Fiona's bee*
Krasilovsky, Phyllis. *The shy little girl*
Lexau, Joan M. *Benjie*
Richardson, Jean. *Clara's dancing feet*
Udry, Janice May. *What Mary Jo shared*
Wold, Jo Anne. *Tell them my name is Amanda*
Yashima, Tarō. *Crow boy*
The youngest one

Zolotow, Charlotte. *A tiger called Thomas,* ill. by Catherine Stock
A tiger called Thomas, ill. by Kurt Werth

Character traits – smallness

Andersen, H. C. (Hans Christian). *Thumbelina,* ill. by Adrienne Adams
Thumbelina, ill. by Susan Jeffers
Thumbelina, ill. by Christine Willis Nigognossian
Thumbelina, ill. by Gustaf Tenggren
Thumbelina, ill. by Lisbeth Zwerger, tr. by Richard and Clara Winston
Thumbeline, ill. by Lisbeth Zwerger, tr. by Anthea Bell
Bang, Betsy. *The cucumber stem*
Beim, Jerrold. *The smallest boy in the class*
Bromhall, Winifred. *Bridget's growing day*
Burgess, Gelett. *The little father*
Chevalier, Christa. *Spence is small*
Cooper, Susan. *The silver cow*
Cuneo, Mary Louise. *Inside a sandcastle and other secrets*
De Paola, Tomie. *Andy (that's my name)*
Gay, Michel. *Little helicopter*
Glass, Andrew. *Chickpea and the talking cow*
Hoff, Syd. *The littlest leaguer*
Horvath, Betty F. *Hooray for Jasper*
Johnston, Johanna. *Sugarplum*
Kraus, Robert. *The littlest rabbit*
Kumin, Maxine. *Sebastian and the dragon*
Kuskin, Karla. *Herbert hated being small*
Lipkind, William. *The little tiny rooster*
Lurie, Morris. *The story of Imelda, who was small*
Meddaugh, Susan. *Too short Fred*
Miles, Miska. *No, no, Rosina*
Orgel, Doris. *On the sand dune*
Priolo, Pauline. *Piccolina and the Easter bells*
Rigby, Shirley Lincoln. *Smaller than most*
Schlein, Miriam. *Billy, the littlest one*
Stanley, John. *It's nice to be little*
Tresselt, Alvin R. *Smallest elephant in the world*
Williams, Barbara. *Someday, said Mitchell*
Yolen, Jane. *The emperor and the kite*

Character traits – stubbornness

Beatty, Hetty Burlingame. *Droopy*
Bulla, Clyde Robert. *The stubborn old woman*
Garrett, Jennifer. *The queen who stole the sky*
Leaf, Margaret. *Eyes of the dragon*
O'Brien, Anne S. *I'm not tired*
Steig, William. *Spinky sulks*
Tusa, Tricia. *Miranda*

Character traits – vanity

Andersen, H. C. (Hans Christian). *It's perfectly true!,* ill. by Janet Stevens
Brown, Marcia. *Once a mouse...*
Brown, Margaret Wise. *The duck*
Frascino, Edward. *My cousin the king*
Kepes, Juliet. *The story of a bragging duck*
McCormack, John E. *Rabbit tales*
Marshall, James. *George and Martha, tons of fun*
Sharmat, Marjorie Weinman. *Sasha the silly*
Winter, Paula. *Sir Andrew*

Character traits – willfulness

Alexander, Sue. *Nadia the willful*
Boyd, Lizi. *Half wild and half child*
Cox, David. *Bossyboots*
Lattimore, Deborah Nourse. *The prince and the golden ax*
Lester, Helen. *Pookins gets her way*
Quin-Harkin, Janet. *Benjamin's balloon*
Vesey, A. *The princess and the frog*

Cheetahs see Animals – cheetahs

Chefs see Careers – chefs

Chickens see Birds – chickens

Child abuse

Caines, Jeannette. *Chilly stomach*

Children as authors

Baskin, Leonard. *Hosie's alphabet*
Hosie's aviary
Children's prayers from around the world
Krauss, Ruth. *Somebody else's nut tree, and other tales from children*
Lady Eden's School. *Just how stories*
O'Reilly, Edward. *Brown pelican at the pond*
Pasley, L. *The adventures of Madalene and Louisa*
Phumla. *Nomi and the magic fish*
St. Pierre, Wendy. *Henry finds a home*

Children as illustrators

De Paola, Tomie. *Criss-cross applesauce*
Pasley, L. *The adventures of Madalene and Louisa*

China see Foreign lands – China

Chinese-Americans see Ethnic groups in the U.S. – Chinese-Americans

Chinese New Year *see* Holidays – Chinese New Year

Chipmunks *see* Animals – chipmunks

Christmas *see* Holidays – Christmas

Cinco de Mayo *see* Holidays – Cinco de Mayo

Circular tales

Arnold, Tedd. *Ollie forgot*
Coco, Eugene Bradley. *The wishing well*
Numeroff, Laura Joffe. *If you give a mouse a cookie*
Stevens, Harry. *Fat mouse*
Ueno, Noriko. *Elephant buttons*
Van Laan, Nancy. *The big fat worm*

Circus

Adler, David A. *You think it's fun to be a clown!*
Aitken, Amy. *Wanda's circus*
Allen, Jeffrey. *Bonzini! the tattooed man*
Ambrus, Victor G. *Mishka*
Amoit, Pierre. *Bijou the little bear*
Anno, Mitsumasa. *Dr. Anno's midnight circus*
Austin, Margot. *Barney's adventure*
Bach, Alice. *Millicent the magnificent*
Balet, Jan B. *Five Rollatinis*
Baningan, Sharon Stearns. *Circus magic*
Barr, Cathrine. *Sammy seal ov the sircus*
Barton, Byron. *Harry is a scaredy-cat*
Blance, Ellen. *Monster goes to the circus*
Bond, Michael. *Paddington at the circus*
Booth, Eugene. *At the circus*
Bowden, Joan Chase. *Boo and the flying flews*
Brown, Marc. *Lenny and Lola*
Brunhoff, Laurent de. *Babar's little circus star*
Burningham, John. *Cannonball Simp*
Cameron, Polly. *The cat who thought he was a tiger*
Cassidy, Dianne. *Circus animals*
  Circus people
Chardiet, Bernice. *C is for circus*
Come to the circus
Coontz, Otto. *A real class clown*
Coxe, Molly. *Louella and the yellow balloon*
Curious George goes to the circus
Dayton, Laura. *LeRoy's birthday circus*
De Regniers, Beatrice Schenk. *Circus*
Dreamer, Sue. *Circus ABC*
  Circus 1, 2, 3
Dubanevich, Arlene. *The piggest show on earth*
Du Bois, William Pène. *The alligator case*
  Bear circus

Elks, Wendy. *Charles B. Wombat and the very strange thing*
Ets, Marie Hall. *Mister Penny's circus*
Everton, Macduff. *El circo magico modelo*
Farley, Walter. *Little Black goes to the circus*
Flack, Marjorie. *Wait for William*
Fox, Charles Philip. *Come to the circus*
Freeman, Don. *Bearymore*
Fremlin, Robert. *Three friends*
Garbutt, Bernard. *Roger, the rosin back*
Gascoigne, Bamber. *Why the rope went tight*
Gay, Michel. *Night ride*
Goodall, John S. *The adventures of Paddy Pork*
Gramatky, Hardie. *Homer and the circus train*
Greaves, Margaret. *Little Bear and the Papagini circus*
Hale, Irina. *Donkey's dreadful day*
Harris, Steven Michael. *This is my trunk*
Herrmann, Frank. *The giant Alexander and the circus*
Hill, Eric. *Spot goes to the circus*
Hoff, Syd. *Barkley*
  Henrietta, circus star
  Oliver
Holl, Adelaide. *Mrs. McGarrity's peppermint sweater*
Hopkins, Lee Bennett. *Circus! Circus!*
The house that Jack built. The house that Jack built, ill. by Janet Stevens
Johnson, Crockett. *Harold's circus*
Johnson, Jane. *Bertie on the beach*
Karn, George. *Circus big and small*
  Circus colors
Lent, Blair. *Pistachio*
Lipkind, William. *Circus rucus*
Lisowski, Gabriel. *Roncalli's magnificent circus*
Logue, Christopher. *The magic circus*
Lopshire, Robert. *Put me in the zoo*
Maestro, Betsy. *Busy day*
  Harriet goes to the circus
Maley, Anne. *Have you seen my mother?*
Marokvia, Merelle. *A French school for Paul*
Mayer, Mercer. *Liverwurst is missing*
Modell, Frank. *Seen any cats?*
Munari, Bruno. *The circus in the mist*
Myers, Bernice. *Herman and the bears and the giants*
Ness, Evaline. *Fierce the lion*
O'Kelley, Mattie Lou. *Circus!*
Palazzo, Tony. *Bianco and the New World*
Panek, Dennis. *Detective Whoo*
Peet, Bill. *Chester the worldly pig*
  Ella
  Randy's dandy lions
Pellowski, Michael. *Clara joins the circus*
Peppé, Rodney. *Circus numbers*
  Little circus

Petersham, Maud. *The circus baby*
Prelutsky, Jack. *Circus*
Price, Mathew. *Do you see what I see?*
Quackenbush, Robert M. *The man on the flying trapeze*
Rey, Hans Augusto. *Curious George rides a bike*
See the circus
Rounds, Glen. *The day the circus came to Lone Tree*
Saville, Lynn. *Horses in the circus ring*
Schulz, Charles M. *Life is a circus, Charlie Brown*
Seignobosc, Françoise. *Small-Trot*
Seuss, Dr. *If I ran the circus*
Slobodkina, Esphyr. *Pezzo the peddler and the circus elephant*
Slocum, Rosalie. *Breakfast with the clowns*
Taylor, Mark. *Henry explores the jungle*
Tester, Sylvia Root. *Parade!*
Tresselt, Alvin R. *Smallest elephant in the world*
Varga, Judy. *Circus cannonball*
Miss Lollipop's lion
Wahl, Jan. *Sylvester Bear overslept*
The toy circus
Wallace, Ian. *Morgan the magnificent*
Weil, Lisl. *Let's go to the circus*
Wildsmith, Brian. *Brian Wildsmith's circus*
Wiseman, Bernard. *Morris and Boris at the circus*
Zimnik, Reiner. *The bear on the motorcycle*
The proud circus horse

City

Adoff, Arnold. *Where wild Willie?*
Asch, Frank. *City sandwich*
Asch, George. *Linda*
Baker, Jeannie. *Home in the sky*
Millicent
Bank Street College of Education. *Around the city*
Green light, go
In the city
My city
Uptown, downtown
Barrett, Judi. *Old MacDonald had an apartment house*
Baylor, Byrd. *The best town in the world*
Bemelmans, Ludwig. *Sunshine*
Bergere, Thea. *Paris in the rain with Jean and Jacqueline*
Binzen, Bill. *Carmen*
Blance, Ellen. *Monster comes to the city*
Blue, Rose. *How many blocks is the world?*
Bowden, Joan Chase. *Emilio's summer day*
Bozzo, Maxine Zohn. *Toby in the country, Toby in the city*
Bright, Robert. *Georgie to the rescue*
Brock, Emma Lillian. *Nobody's mouse*

Brown, Marcia. *The little carousel*
Brown, Margaret Wise. *Three little animals*
Burton, Virginia Lee. *Katy and the big snow*
The little house
Maybelle, the cable car
Busch, Phyllis S. *City lots*
Carrick, Carol. *Left behind*
Chalmers, Mary. *Kevin*
Chapouton, Anne-Marie. *Ben finds a friend*
Chwast, Seymour. *Tall city, wide country*
City
Clifton, Lucille. *The boy who didn't believe in spring*
Everett Anderson's Christmas coming
Clymer, Eleanor Lowenton. *The big pile of dirt*
Coats, Laura Jane. *City cat*
Colman, Hila. *Peter's brownstone house*
Come out to play
Corcos, Lucille. *The city book*
Craft, Ruth. *The day of the rainbow*
Crews, Donald. *Parade*
Crowell, Maryalicia. *A horse in the house*
Daly, Niki. *Not so fast Songololo*
Decker, Dorothy W. *Stripe visits New York*
Deveaux, Alexis. *Na-ni*
Donnelly, Liza. *Dinosaurs' Halloween*
Duvoisin, Roger Antoine. *Lonely Veronica*
Veronica
Ellis, Anne Leo. *Dabble Duck*
Fife, Dale. *Adam's ABC*
Finsand, Mary Jane. *The town that moved*
Florian, Douglas. *The city*
Fraser, Kathleen. *Adam's world, San Francisco*
Freeman, Don. *Fly high, fly low*
The guard mouse
Gelman, Rita Golden. *Dumb Joey*
Gerstein, Mordicai. *The room*
Gibbons, Gail. *Up goes the skyscraper!*
Goodall, John S. *The story of a main street*
The story of an English village
Gramatky, Hardie. *Little Toot through the Golden Gate*
Grifalconi, Ann. *City rhythms*
Grossbart, Francine. *A big city*
Guilfoile, Elizabeth. *Have you seen my brother?*
Harvey, Brett. *Immigrant girl*
Hawkesworth, Jenny. *The lonely skyscraper*
Himler, Ronald. *The girl on the yellow giraffe*
Hoban, Tana. *Is it red? Is it yellow? Is it blue?*
Holl, Adelaide. *A mouse story*
Hopkins, Lee Bennett. *I think I saw a snail*
Ingle, Annie. *The big city book*
Isadora, Rachel. *City seen from A to Z*
Ivory, Lesley Anne. *A day in London*
A day in New York

Jonas, Ann. *Round trip*
Jordan, June. *Kimako's story*
Kahn, Joan. *Hi, Jock, run around the block*
Kaufman, Curt. *Hotel boy*
Keats, Ezra Jack. *Apartment 3*
   Goggles
   Hi, cat!
Keeping, Charles. *Alfie finds the other side of the world*
   Through the window
Kesselman, Wendy. *Angelita*
Kightley, Rosalinda. *The postman*
Kovalski, Maryann. *Jingle bells*
Krementz, Jill. *A visit to Washington, D.C.*
Kuskin, Karla. *Jerusalem, shining still*
Lenski, Lois. *Policeman Small*
   Sing a song of people
Lent, Blair. *Bayberry Bluff*
Lewin, Hugh. *Jafta - the town*
Lewis, Stephen. *Zoo city*
Lexau, Joan M. *Benjie on his own*
   Come here, cat
   Me day
Low, Alice. *David's windows*
McCloskey, Robert. *Make way for ducklings*
McGinley, Phyllis. *All around the town*
McKissack, Patricia C. *Country mouse and city mouse*, ill. by Anne Sikorski
Maestro, Betsy. *Big city port*
Maestro, Giulio. *The remarkable plant in apartment 4*
Mayer, Mercer. *Little Monster's neighborhood*
Miles, Miska. *No, no, Rosina*
   Rolling the cheese
Mizumura, Kazue. *If I built a village*
Moak, Allan. *A big city ABC*
Morris, Jill. *The boy who painted the sun*
Munro, Roxie. *Christmastime in New York City*
   The inside-outside book of New York City
   The inside-outside book of Washington, D.C.
Nichols, Cathy. *Tuxedo Sam*
Olds, Elizabeth. *Little Una*
Olsen, Ib Spang. *Cat alley*
O'Shell, Marcia. *Alphabet Annie announces an all-American album*
Our house
Peet, Bill. *Fly, Homer, fly*
Perera, Lydia. *Frisky*
Pitt, Valerie. *Let's find out about the city*
Provensen, Alice. *Shaker lane*
   Town and country
Quackenbush, Robert M. *City trucks*
Raskin, Ellen. *Franklin Stein*
   Nothing ever happens on my block
Ressner, Phil. *Dudley Pippin*
Rice, Eve. *City night*
Roach, Marilynne K. *Two Roman mice*

Rockwell, Anne F. *Come to town*
   Hugo at the window
Rogers, Paul. *Tumbledown*
Rosario, Idalia. *Idalia's project ABC*
Roth, Harold. *Let's look all around the town*
Rowe, Jeanne A. *City workers.*
Ryder, Joanne. *The night flight*
Sauer, Julia Lina. *Mike's house*
Scarry, Richard. *Richard Scarry's Postman*
   Pig and his busy neighbors
Schick, Eleanor. *City green*
   City in the winter
   One summer night
   Peter and Mr. Brandon
Scott, Ann Herbert. *Let's catch a monster*
Selden, George. *Chester Cricket's pigeon ride*
Shannon, George. *Beanboy*
Shecter, Ben. *Emily, girl witch of New York*
Simon, Norma. *What do I do?*
Sonneborn, Ruth A. *Friday night is papa night*
   I love Gram
   Lollipop's party
Sopko, Eugen. *Townsfolk and countryfolk*
Stanley, Diane. *A country tale*
Steptoe, John. *Uptown*
Stevenson, James. *Grandpa's great city tour*
Thomas, Ianthe. *Walk home tired, Billy Jenkins*
Tresselt, Alvin R. *It's time now!*
Trimby, Elisa. *Mr. Plum's paradise*
Vasiliu, Mircea. *What's happening?*
Ventura, Piero. *Piero Ventura's book of cities*
Walters, Marguerite. *The city-country ABC*
Williams, Jay. *The city witch and the country witch*
Williamson, Mel. *Walk on!*
Wold, Jo Anne. *Well! Why didn't you say so?*
Yashima, Tarō. *Umbrella*
Yezback, Steven A. *Pumpkinseeds*
Zion, Gene. *Dear garbage man*
   Hide and seek day
Zolotow, Charlotte. *One step, two...*
   The park book

Cleanliness *see* Character traits – cleanliness

Cleverness *see* Character traits – cleverness

Clockmakers *see* Careers – clockmakers

Clocks

Aiken, Conrad. *Tom, Sue and the clock*
Ardizzone, Edward. *Johnny the clockmaker*
Bassett, Lisa. *A clock for Beany*
Berg, Jean Horton. *The noisy clock shop*
Bragdon, Lillian J. *Tell me the time, please*

Bram, Elizabeth. *Woodruff and the clocks*
Cohen, Carol L. *Wake up, groundhog!*
Colman, Hila. *Watch that watch*
Gibbons, Gail. *Clocks and how they go*
Gilbert, Helen Earle. *Dr. Trotter and his big gold watch*
Gordon, Sharon. *Tick tock clock*
Gould, Deborah. *Brendan's best-timed birthday*
Hutchins, Pat. *Clocks and more clocks*
Katz, Bobbi. *Tick-tock, let's read the clock*
Lloyd, David. *The stopwatch*
McGinley, Phyllis. *Wonderful time*
Maestro, Betsy. *Around the clock with Harriet*
Mother Goose. *The real Mother Goose clock book*
Pieńkowski, Jan. *Time*
Slobodkin, Louis. *The late cuckoo*
Steinmetz, Leon. *Clocks in the woods*

Clothing

Alda, Arlene. *Matthew and his dad*
Allen, Robert. *Ten little babies count*
Ten little babies dress
Andersen, H. C. (Hans Christian). *The emperor's new clothes*, ill. by Pamela Baldwin-Ford
The emperor's new clothes, ill. by Erik Blegvad
The emperor's new clothes, ill. by Virginia Lee Burton
The emperor's new clothes, ill. by Jack and Irene Delano
The emperor's new clothes, ill. by Héléne Desputeaux
The emperor's new clothes, ill. by Birte Dietz
The emperor's new clothes, ill. by Dorothée Duntze
The emperor's new clothes, ill. by Jack Kent
The emperor's new clothes, ill. by Monika Laimgruber
The emperor's new clothes, ill. by Anne F. Rockwell
The emperor's new clothes, ill. by Janet Stevens
The emperor's new clothes, ill. by Nadine Bernard Westcott
The red shoes, ill. by Chihiro Iwasaki
Anderson, Leone Castell. *The wonderful shrinking shirt*
Arnold, Tim. *The winter mittens*
Asch, Frank. *Yellow, yellow*
Azaad, Meyer. *Half for you*
Babbitt, Lorraine. *Pink like the geranium*
Baird, Anne. *Baby socks*
Bannon, Laura. *Hat for a hero*
Red mittens

Barrett, Judi. *Animals should definitely not wear clothing*
Peter's pocket
Barrows, Marjorie Wescott. *The funny hat*
Barton, Pat. *A week is a long time*
Bastin, Marjolein. *Vera dresses up*
Beskow, Elsa Maartman. *Pelle's new suit*
Blocksma, Mary. *The best dressed bear*
Blos, Joan W. *Martin's hats*
Bourgeois, Paulette. *Big Sarah's little boots*
Bowden, Joan Chase. *A hat for the queen*
Brandenberg, Franz. *Leo and Emily*
Brenner, Barbara. *Somebody's slippers, somebody's shoes*
Briggs, Raymond. *Dressing up*
Bromhall, Winifred. *Middle Matilda*
Bruna, Dick. *I can dress myself*
Bulette, Sara. *The splendid belt of Mr. Big*
Carlstrom, Nancy White. *Jesse Bear, what will you wear?*
Carrick, Malcolm. *The extraordinary hatmaker*
Chalmers, Mary. *A hat for Amy Jean*
Christelow, Eileen. *Olive and the magic hat*
Cousins, Lucy. *Portly's hat*
Credle, Ellis. *Down, down the mountain*
Daly, Niki. *Joseph's other red sock*
De Paola, Tomie. *Charlie needs a cloak*
Pajamas for Kit
Duvoisin, Roger Antoine. *Jasmine*
Fisher, Leonard Everett. *A head full of hats*
Freeman, Don. *Corduroy*
A pocket for Corduroy
Fremlin, Robert. *Three friends*
Gackenbach, Dick. *Poppy the panda*
Gay, Michel. *Little shoe*
Geringer, Laura. *A three hat day*
Grimm, Jacob. *The falling stars*, ill. by Eugen Sopko
Hadithi, Mwenye. *Greedy zebra*
Harris, Robie H. *Hot Henry*
Hest, Amy. *The purple coat*
Hiser, Berniece T. *The adventure of Charlie and his wheat-straw hat*
Hoberman, Mary Ann. *I like old clothes*
Holland, Isabelle. *Kevin's hat*
Hughes, Shirley. *Two shoes, new shoes*
Hürlimann, Ruth. *The mouse with the daisy hat*
Hutchins, Pat. *You'll soon grow into them, Titch*
Iwamura, Kazuo. *Tan Tan's hat*
Tan Tan's suspenders
Jaynes, Ruth M. *Benny's four hats*
Jensen, Virginia Allen. *Sara and the door*
Johnson, B. J. *A hat like that*
Kay, Helen. *One mitten Lewis*
Keats, Ezra Jack. *Jennie's hat*
Krasilovsky, Phyllis. *The girl who was a cowboy*
Kraus, Robert. *The king's trousers*

Kumin, Maxine. *Mittens in May*
Kuskin, Karla. *The Dallas Titans get ready for bed*
The Philharmonic gets dressed
Lear, Edward. *The quangle wangle's hat*, ill. by Emma Crosby
The quangle wangle's hat, ill. by Helen Oxenbury
The quangle wangle's hat, ill. by Janet Stevens
Two laughable lyrics
LeRoy, Gen. *Billy's shoes*
Lexau, Joan M. *Who took the farmer's hat?*
Lloyd, Errol. *Nini at carnival*
Lobel, Anita. *The seamstress of Salzburg*
Lynn, Sara. *Clothes*
McClintock, Marshall. *What have I got?*
McKee, David. *King Rollo and the new shoes*
McKissack, Patricia C. *The king's new clothes*, ill. by Gwen Connelly
Nettie Jo's friends
McLenighan, Valjean. *What you see is what you get*
Maestro, Betsy. *On the town*
Mariana. *Miss Flora McFlimsey's Easter bonnet*
Matsuno, Masako. *A pair of red clogs*
Mayer, Mercer. *Two moral tales*
Miklowitz, Gloria D. *Bearfoot boy*
Miller, Margaret. *Me and my clothes*
Whose hat?
Monsell, Mary. *Underwear!*
Moore, Inga. *Fifty red night-caps*
Murphey, Sara. *The animal hat shop*
Myrick, Jean Lockwood. *Ninety-nine pockets*
Ormerod, Jan. *Dad's back*
Oxenbury, Helen. *Dressing*
Partridge, Jenny. *Grandma Snuffles*
Payne, Emmy. *Katy no-pocket*
Peppé, Rodney. *Little dolls*
Politi, Leo. *Little Leo*
Potter, Beatrix. *The tale of Mrs. Tiggy-Winkle*
Rice, Eve. *New blue shoes*
Rice, Inez. *The March wind*
Riddell, Chris. *Bird's new shoes*
Rogers, Jean. *Runaway mittens*
Roy, Ronald. *Whose hat is that?*
Whose shoes are these?
Rudolph, Marguerita. *How a shirt grew in the field*
Ryder, Eileen. *Winston's new cap*
Scott, Ann Herbert. *Big Cowboy Western*
Selden, George. *Sparrow socks*
Sharmat, Marjorie Weinman. *The trip*
Shearer, John. *The case of the sneaker snatcher*
Silver, Jody. *Isadora*
Slobodkina, Esphyr. *Caps for sale*
Pezzo the peddler and the circus elephant

Pezzo the peddler and the thirteen silly thieves
Smith, Donald. *Who's wearing my baseball cap?*
Who's wearing my bow tie?
Who's wearing my sneakers?
Sutton, Jane. *What should a hippo wear?*
Taback, Simms. *Joseph had a little overcoat*
Tafuri, Nancy. *One wet jacket*
Two new sneakers
Thayer, Jane. *Gus was a gorgeous ghost*
The horse with the Easter bonnet
Townsend, Kenneth. *Felix, the bald-headed lion*
Tusa, Tricia. *Maebelle's suitcase*
Tyrrell, Anne. *Elizabeth Jane gets dressed*
Ungerer, Tomi. *The hat*
Vigna, Judith. *Boot weather*
Ward, Nanda Weedon. *The black sombrero*
Watanabe, Shigeo. *How do I put it on?*
Watson, Pauline. *The walking coat*
Weiss, Harvey. *My closet full of hats*
Weiss, Leatie. *Funny feet!*
Wells, Rosemary. *Max's new suit*
West, Colin. *I brought my love a tabby cat*
Westerberg, Christine. *The cap that mother made*
Winthrop, Elizabeth. *Shoes*
Wright, Jill. *The old woman and the Willy Nilly Man*
Ziefert, Harriet. *Bear gets dressed*
Let's get dressed!
A new coat for Anna
Zinnemann-Hope, Pam. *Find your coat, Ned*
Zion, Gene. *No roses for Harry*

Clouds *see* Weather – clouds

Clowns, jesters

Adler, David A. *You think it's fun to be a clown!*
Allen, Jeffrey. *Bonzini! the tattooed man*
Amoit, Pierre. *Bijou the little bear*
Anno, Mitsumasa. *Dr. Anno's midnight circus*
Austin, Margot. *Barney's adventure*
Barr, Cathrine. *Sammy seal ov the sircus*
Bradford, Ann. *The mystery of the midget clown*
Burningham, John. *Cannonball Simp*
Cole, Joanna. *The Clown-Arounds go on vacation*
Get well, Clown-Arounds!
Coontz, Otto. *A real class clown*
De Paola, Tomie. *Sing, Pierrot, sing*
Douglass, Barbara. *The chocolate chip cookie contest*
Faulkner, Nancy. *Small clown*
Freeman, Don. *Forever laughter*

Harris, Steven Michael. *This is my trunk*
Krahn, Fernando. *A funny friend from heaven*
Lent, Blair. *Pistachio*
Lynn, Sara. *Colors*
Marceau, Marcel. *The story of Bip*
Mendoza, George. *The Marcel Marceau counting book*
Miller, M. L. *Dizzy from fools*
Olds, Elizabeth. *Plop plop ploppie*
Pellowski, Michael. *Clara joins the circus*
Petersham, Maud. *The circus baby*
Politi, Leo. *Lito and the clown*
Quackenbush, Robert M. *The man on the flying trapeze*
Richardson, Jean. *Tall inside*
Rockwell, Anne F. *Gogo's pay day*
Schreiber, Georges. *Bambino goes home*
 Bambino the clown
Shecter, Ben. *Hester the jester* .
Slocum, Rosalie. *Breakfast with the clowns*
Sobol, Harriet Langsam. *Clowns*
Thurber, James. *Many moons*

Clubs, gangs

Alexander, Sue. *Seymour the prince*
Bonsall, Crosby Newell. *The case of the double cross*
Bradford, Ann. *The mystery at Misty Falls*
 The mystery in the secret club house
 The mystery of the blind writer
 The mystery of the midget clown
 The mystery of the missing dogs
 The mystery of the square footsteps
 The mystery of the tree house
Kotzwinkle, William. *The day the gang got rich*
Myrick, Mildred. *The secret three*
Stanley, Diane. *The conversation club*
Thaler, Mike. *Pack 109*

Cockatoos *see* Birds – cockatoos

Codes *see* Secret codes

Cold *see* Weather – cold

Collecting things *see* Behavior – collecting things

Color *see* Concepts – color

Columbus Day *see* Holidays – Columbus Day

Communication

Arnold, Caroline. *How do we communicate?*
Bohdal, Susi. *Tom cat*
Bonsall, Crosby Newell. *The case of the dumb bells*

Borchers, Elisabeth. *Dear Sarah*
Branley, Franklyn M. *Timmy and the tin-can telephone*
Brown, Margaret Wise. *The big fur secret*
Buchheimer, Naomi. *Let's go to a post office*
Charlip, Remy. *Handtalk*
Chukovsky, Korney. *The telephone*
Clifford, Eth. *A bear before breakfast*
Emberley, Ed. *Green says go*
Engdahl, Sylvia. *Our world is earth*
Gibbons, Gail. *The post office book*
Goor, Ron. *Signs*
Hoban, Tana. *I read signs*
 I read symbols
Joslin, Sesyle. *Dear dragon*
Potter, Beatrix. *Yours affectionately, Peter Rabbit*
Stanley, Diane. *The conversation club*
 Telephones
Tolkien, J. R. R. (John Ronald Reuel). *The Father Christmas letters*
Van Woerkom, Dorothy. *Hidden messages*

Communities, neighborhoods

Arnold, Caroline. *What is a community?*
 Where do you go to school?
 Who works here?
Blakeley, Peggy. *Two little ducks*
Groner, Judyth. *My very own Jewish community*
Henkes, Kevin. *Once around the block*
Rogers, Fred. *Moving*
Scheffler, Ursel. *Stop your crowing, Kasimir!*
Yeoman, John. *Our village*

Competition *see* Sibling rivalry

Completing things *see* Character traits – completing things

Compromising *see* Character traits – compromising

Computers *see* Machines

Conceit *see* Character traits – conceit

Concepts

Albert, Burton. *Mine, yours, ours*
Anno, Mitsumasa. *Anno's math games*
Arvetis, Chris. *Why is it dark?*
Balestrino, Philip. *Hot as an ice cube*
Beisner, Monika. *Topsy turvy*
Berenstain, Stan. *Inside outside upside down*
Berkley, Ethel S. *Ups and down*
Bodger, Joan. *Belinda's ball*
Booth, Eugene. *At the circus*
 At the fair
 In the air

In the garden
In the jungle
Under the ocean
Borten, Helen. *Do you see what I see?*
Brown, Marcia. *Touch will tell*
Walk with your eyes
Browner, Richard. *Look again!*
Carle, Eric. *My very first book of motion*
Charosh, Mannis. *Number ideas through pictures*
Chase, Catherine. *Hot and cold*
Crews, Donald. *Light*
We read A to Z
Cushman, Doug. *Nasty Kyle the crocodile*
Dantzer-Rosenthal, Marya. *Some things are different, some things are the same*
Duke, Kate. *Guinea pigs far and near*
What bounces?
Emberley, Ed. *Ed Emberley's amazing look through book*
Fisher, Leonard Everett. *Boxes! Boxes!*
Freudberg, Judy. *Some, more, most*
Froman, Robert. *Angles are easy as pie*
A game of functions
Seeing things
Gillham, Bill. *Where does it go?*
Green, Mary McBurney. *Is it hard? Is it easy?*
Greene, Laura. *Change*
Hoban, Tana. *Dots, spots, speckles, and stripes*
Is it rough? Is it smooth? Is it shiny?
Look! Look! Look!
Take another look
Hughes, Shirley. *Lucy and Tom's 1, 2, 3*
Jennings, Terry. *Bouncing and rolling*
Floating and sinking
Jensen, Virginia Allen. *What's that?*
Johnson, Ryerson. *Upstairs and downstairs*
Jonas, Ann. *Reflections*
Kuskin, Karla. *All sizes of noises*
Lopshire, Robert. *The biggest, smallest, fastest, tallest things you've ever heard of*
McMillan, Bruce. *Becca backward, Becca forward*
Dry or wet?
Maestro, Betsy. *Where is my friend?*
Matthiesen, Thomas. *Things to see*
Mayer, Mercer. *Mine!*
Peppé, Rodney. *Odd one out*
Rodney Peppé's puzzle book
Rahn, Joan Elma. *Holes*
Ruben, Patricia. *True or false?*
Scarry, Richard. *Richard Scarry's best first book ever*
Richard Scarry's great big schoolhouse
The Sesame Street book of people and things
Supraner, Robyn. *Giggly-wiggly, snickety-snick*
Wallner, John. *Look and find*

Webb, Angela. *Light*
Reflections
Sound
Yektai, Niki. *Bears in pairs*

Concepts – color

Abisch, Roz. *Open your eyes*
Adoff, Arnold. *Greens*
Allamand, Pascale. *The animals who changed their colors*
Allen, Robert. *Ten little babies play*
Asch, Frank. *Yellow, yellow*
Baby's first book of colors
Baker, Alan. *Benjamin's portrait*
Berger, Judith. *Butterflies and rainbows*
Bradman, Tony. *The bad babies' book of colors*
Bright, Robert. *I like red*
Brown, Margaret Wise. *Red light, green light*
Brunhoff, Laurent de. *Babar's book of color*
Burningham, John. *John Burningham's colors*
Campbell, Ann. *Let's find out about color*
Carle, Eric. *The mixed-up chameleon*
Charlip, Remy. *Harlequin and the gift of many colors*
Chermayeff, Ivan. *Tomato and other colors*
Clifford, Eth. *Red is never a mouse*
Dines, Glen. *Pitadoe, the color maker*
Dunham, Meredith. *Colors: how do you say it?*
Duvoisin, Roger Antoine. *The house of four seasons*
See what I am
Emberley, Ed. *Green says go*
Ernst, Lisa Campbell. *A colorful adventure of the bee who left home one Monday morning and what he found along the way*
Feeney, Stephanie. *Hawaii is a rainbow*
Fisher, Leonard Everett. *Boxes! Boxes!*
Freeman, Don. *The chalk box story*
A rainbow of my own
Gillham, Bill. *Let's look for colors*
Goffstein, M. B. (Marilyn Brooke). *Artists' helpers enjoy the evening*
Graham, Amanda. *Picasso, the green tree frog*
Graham, Bob. *The red woolen blanket*
Gundersheimer, Karen. *Colors to know*
Haskins, Ilma. *Color seems*
Hest, Amy. *The purple coat*
Hill, Eric. *Spot looks at colors*
Hoban, Tana. *Dots, spots, speckles, and stripes*
Is it red? Is it yellow? Is it blue?
Red, blue, yellow shoe
Hughes, Shirley. *Colors*
Karn, George. *Circus colors*
Kessler, Leonard P. *Mr. Pine's purple house*

Kilroy, Sally. *Baby colors*
Kirkpatrick, Rena K. *Look at rainbow colors*
Kumin, Maxine. *What color is Caesar?*
Lewis, Naomi. *Once upon a rainbow*
Lionni, Leo. *A color of his own*
  Colors to talk about
  Little blue and little yellow
A little book of colors.
Lobel, Arnold. *The great blueness and other*
  predicaments
Löfgren, Ulf. *The color trumpet*
Lopshire, Robert. *Put me in the zoo*
Lynn, Sara. *Colors*
McMillan, Bruce. *Growing colors*
Maril, Lee. *Mr. Bunny paints the eggs*
Miller, J. P. (John Parr). *Do you know*
  color?
  Learn about colors with Little Rabbit
Ostheeren, Ingrid. *Jonathan Mouse*
Oxford Scientific Films. *Danger colors*
  Hide and seek
Peek, Merle. *Mary wore her red dress and*
  Henry wore his green sneakers
Pieńkowski, Jan. *Colors*
Pinkwater, Daniel Manus. *The bear's picture*
  The big orange splot
Podendorf, Illa. *Color*
Reiss, John J. *Colors*
Rogers, Margaret. *Green is beautiful*
Ross, Tony. *Hugo and the man who stole*
  colors
Rossetti, Christina Georgina. *What is pink?*
Sandberg, Inger. *Nicholas' red day*
Scott, Rochelle. *Colors, colors all around*
Selkowe, Valrie M. *Spring green*
Serfozo, Mary. *Who said red?*
Shub, Elizabeth. *Dragon Franz*
Silverman, Maida. *Ladybug's color book*
Spier, Peter. *Oh, were they ever happy!*
Steiner, Charlotte. *My slippers are red*
Stinson, Kathy. *Red is best*
Tafuri, Nancy. *In a red house*
Testa, Fulvio. *If you take a paintbrush*
Tison, Annette. *The adventures of the three*
  colors
Troughton, Joanna. *How the birds changed*
  their feathers
Wolff, Robert Jay. *Feeling blue*
  Hello, yellow!
  Seeing red
Youldon, Gillian. *Colors*
Youngs, Betty. *Pink pigs in mud*
Zacharias, Thomas. *But where is the green*
  parrot?
Ziefert, Harriet. *No more! Piggety Pig*
Zolotow, Charlotte. *Mr. Rabbit and the*
  lovely present

Concepts – counting *see* Counting

Concepts – distance

Tresselt, Alvin R. *How far is far?*

Concepts – in and out

Banchek, Linda. *Snake in, snake out*
Daughtry, Duanne. *What's inside?*
Ueno, Noriko. *Elephant buttons*

Concepts – left and right

Chase, Catherine. *Feet*
Stanek, Muriel. *Left, right, left, right!*

Concepts – measurement

Adler, David A. *3D, 2D, 1D*
Branley, Franklyn M. *How little and how*
  much
Lionni, Leo. *Inch by inch*
Myller, Rolf. *How big is a foot?*
Thompson, Brenda. *The winds that blow*

Concepts – opposites

Banchek, Linda. *Snake in, snake out*
Barrett, Judi. *I'm too small, you're too big*
Boynton, Sandra. *Opposites*
Butterworth, Nick. *Nice or nasty*
Crowther, Robert. *The most amazing*
  hide-and-seek opposites book
Demi. *Demi's opposites*
Gillham, Bill. *Let's look for opposites*
  What's the difference?
Green, Suzanne. *The little choo-choo*
Hoban, Tana. *Push-pull, empty-full*
Hughes, Shirley. *Bathwater's hot*
Karn, George. *Circus big and small*
Kightley, Rosalinda. *Opposites*
Lippman, Peter. *Peter Lippman's*
  opposites
McKissack, Patricia C. *Big bug book of*
  opposites
McLenighan, Valjean. *Stop-go, fast-slow*
McMillan, Bruce. *Becca backward, Becca*
  forward
  Here a chick, there a chick
McNaughton, Colin. *At home*
  At playschool
  At the park
  At the party
  At the stores
Maestro, Betsy. *Traffic*
Matthias, Catherine. *Over-under*
Mendoza, George. *The Sesame Street book*
  of opposites with Zero Mostel
Provensen, Alice. *Karen's opposites*
Spier, Peter. *Fast-slow, high-low*
Watson, Carol. *Opposites*
Wildsmith, Brian. *What the moon saw*
Ziefert, Harriet. *Let's go! Piggety Pig*

Concepts – perspective

Adler, David A. *3D, 2D, 1D*
Titherington, Jeanne. *Big world, small world*
Wakefield, Joyce. *From where you are*

Concepts – self *see* Self-concept

Concepts – shape

Adler, David A. *3D, 2D, 1D*
Allen, Robert. *Round and square*
Atwood, Ann. *The little circle*
Berenstain, Stan. *Old hat, new hat*
Brown, Marcia. *Listen to a shape*
Budney, Blossom. *A kiss is round*
Charosh, Mannis. *The ellipse*
Craig, M. Jean. *Boxes*
Crews, Donald. *Ten black dots*
Dunham, Meredith. *Shapes: how do you say it?*
Emberley, Ed. *The wing on a flea*
Fisher, Leonard Everett. *Look around!*
Friskey, Margaret. *Three sides and the round one*
Gardner, Beau. *Guess what?*
Gillham, Bill. *Let's look for shapes*
Gundersheimer, Karen. *Shapes to show*
Hatcher, Charles. *What shape is it?*
Hefter, Richard. *The strawberry book of shapes*
Hill, Eric. *Spot looks at shapes*
Hoban, Tana. *Circles, triangles, and squares*
  Dots, spots, speckles, and stripes
  Is it red? Is it yellow? Is it blue?
  Round and round and round
  Shapes and things
  Shapes, shapes, shapes
Hughes, Peter. *The emperor's oblong pancake*
Hughes, Shirley. *All shapes and sizes*
Jensen, Virginia Allen. *Catching*
Kightley, Rosalinda. *Shapes*
Lionni, Leo. *Pezzettino*
McMillan, Bruce. *Fire engine shapes*
Newth, Philip. *Roly goes exploring*
Pieńkowski, Jan. *Shapes*
Pluckrose, Henry. *Shape*
Podendorf, Illa. *Shapes, sides, curves and corners*
Reiss, John J. *Shapes*
Reit, Seymour. *Round things everywhere*
Roberts, Cliff. *The dot*
  Start with a dot
Salazar, Violet. *Squares are not bad*
Santoro, Christopher. *Book of shapes*
Schlein, Miriam. *Shapes*
The Sesame Street book of shapes
Seuss, Dr. *The shape of me and other stuff*
Shaw, Charles Green. *It looked like spilt milk*

Silverman, Maida. *Mouse's shape book*
Silverstein, Shel. *The missing piece*
Stoddard, Sandol. *Curl up small*
Testa, Fulvio. *If you look around*
Watson, Carol. *Shapes*
Wildsmith, Brian. *Animal shapes*
Youldon, Gillian. *Shapes*

Concepts – size

Anno, Mitsumasa. *The king's flower*
Aulaire, Ingri Mortenson d'. *Too big*
Balian, Lorna. *Where in the world is Henry?*
Barrett, Judi. *I hate to take a bath*
Berenstain, Stan. *Old hat, new hat*
Black, Irma Simonton. *Big puppy and little puppy*
Blue, Rose. *How many blocks is the world?*
Brown, Marcia. *Once a mouse...*
Brown, Margaret Wise. *Big dog, little dog*
  Bumble bugs and elephants
Bulette, Sara. *The splendid belt of Mr. Big*
Cantieni, Benita. *Little Elephant and Big Mouse*
Chalmers, Audrey. *Hector and Mr. Murfit*
Craig, M. Jean. *Boxes*
Croswell, Volney. *How to hide a hippopotamus*
Hoban, Tana. *Big ones, little ones*
  Is it larger? Is it smaller?
  Is it red? Is it yellow? Is it blue?
Hughes, Shirley. *All shapes and sizes*
Hutchins, Pat. *Titch*
Ipcar, Dahlov. *The biggest fish in the sea*
  The land of flowers
Joyce, William. *George shrinks*
Kalan, Robert. *Blue sea*
Kraus, Robert. *The little giant*
Krauss, Ruth. *Big and little*
  A bouquet of littles
Kuskin, Karla. *Herbert hated being small*
Lipkind, William. *Chaga*
Long, Earlene. *Gone fishing*
Peet, Bill. *Huge Harold*
Pieńkowski, Jan. *Sizes*
Pluckrose, Henry. *Big and little*
Schwartz, David. *How much is a million?*
Shapp, Charles. *Let's find out what's big and what's small*
Stoddard, Sandol. *Curl up small*
Ueno, Noriko. *Elephant buttons*
Watson, Carol. *Sizes*
Youldon, Gillian. *Sizes*

Concepts – speed

Schlein, Miriam. *Fast is not a ladybug*
Spier, Peter. *Fast-slow, high-low*

Concepts – up and down

Berkley, Ethel S. *Ups and down*

Johnson, Crockett. *Upside down*
Knight, Hilary. *Sylvia the sloth*
Seuss, Dr. *A great day for up*
Slobodkin, Louis. *Up high and down low*
Zion, Gene. *All falling down*

Concepts – weight

Fischer, Vera Kistiakowsky. *One way is down*
MacDonald, George. *The light princess*, ill. by Katie Thamer Treherne
Pluckrose, Henry. *Weight*
Schlein, Miriam. *Heavy is a hippopotamus*

Confidence *see* Character traits – confidence

Conservation *see* Ecology

Cooking *see* Activities – cooking

Cooks *see* Careers – bakers; Careers – chefs

Copying *see* Behavior – imitation

Coral Islands *see* Foreign lands – South Sea Islands

Cormorants *see* Birds – cormorants

Correspondence *see* Pen pals

Cougars *see* Animals – cougars

Counting

Adler, David A. *Base five*
Alexander, Anne. *My daddy and I*
Allbright, Viv. *Ten go hopping*
Allen, Robert. *Numbers: a first counting book*
Ten little babies count
Ten little babies dress
Ten little babies eat
Ten little babies play
Ambler, Christopher Gifford. *Ten little foxhounds.*
Anno, Mitsumasa. *Anno's counting book*
Anno's counting house
Anno's math games
Arnosky, Jim. *Mouse numbers and letters*
Asch, Frank. *Little Devil's 123*
Aylesworth, Jim. *One crow*
Baker, Bonnie Jeanne. *A pear by itself*
Baker, Jeannie. *One hungry spider*
Bang, Molly. *Ten, nine, eight*
Baum, Arline. *One bright Monday morning*
Bayley, Nicola. *One old Oxford ox*
Becker, John Leonard. *Seven little rabbits*
Berenstain, Stan. *Bears on wheels*
The Berenstain bears' counting book

Bishop, Claire Huchet. *Twenty-two bears*
Blegvad, Lenore. *One is for the sun*
Boon, Emilie. *1 2 3 how many animals can you see?*
Boynton, Sandra. *Hippos go berserk*
Bradman, Tony. *The bad babies' counting book*
Not like this, like that
Brenner, Barbara. *The snow parade*
Bridgman, Elizabeth. *All the little bunnies*
Bright, Robert. *My red umbrella*
Bruna, Dick. *I know more about numbers*
Poppy Pig goes to market
Brunhoff, Laurent de. *Babar's counting book*
Bucknall, Caroline. *One bear all alone*
Burningham, John. *Count up*
Five down
Just cats
Pigs plus
Read one
Ride off
The shopping basket
Carle, Eric. *1, 2, 3 to the zoo*
The rooster who set out to see the world
Rooster's off to see the world
Charlip, Remy. *Thirteen*
Charosh, Mannis. *Number ideas through pictures*
Chwast, Seymour. *Still another number book*
Cleveland, David. *The April rabbits*
Cole, Joanna. *Animal sleepyheads*
Conover, Chris. *Six little ducks*
Corbett, Grahame. *What number now?*
Count me in
Counting rhymes
Cretan, Gladys Yessayan. *Ten brothers with camels*
Crews, Donald. *Ten black dots*
Crowther, Robert. *Hide and seek counting book*
Dalmais, Anne-Marie. *In my garden*
Dayton, Laura. *LeRoy's birthday circus*
DeCaprio, Annie. *One, two*
Demi. *Demi's count the animals 1-2-3*
De Regniers, Beatrice Schenk. *So many cats!*
Dodd, Lynley. *The nickle nackle tree*
Dodds, Siobhan. *Elizabeth Hen*
Doolittle, Eileen. *World of wonders*
Dreamer, Sue. *Circus 1, 2, 3*
Dunham, Meredith. *Numbers: how do you say it?*
Duvoisin, Roger Antoine. *Two lonely ducks*
Eichenberg, Fritz. *Dancing in the moon*
Elkin, Benjamin. *Six foolish fishermen*
Ernst, Lisa Campbell. *Up to ten and down again*
Farber, Norma. *Up the down elevator*
Feelings, Muriel. *Moja means one*
Fisher, Leonard Everett. *Boxes! Boxes!*

Florian, Douglas. *A summer day*
Freeman, Lydia. *Corduroy's day*
Freschet, Berniece. *The ants go marching*
  Where's Henrietta's hen?
Friskey, Margaret. *Chicken Little,*
  count-to-ten
  Seven diving ducks
Gantz, David. *Captain Swifty counts to 50*
Gardner, Beau. *Can you imagine...?*
Gerstein, Mordicai. *Roll over!*
Giganti, Paul. *How many snails?*
Gillham, Bill. *Let's look for numbers*
Ginsburg, Mirra. *Kitten from one to ten*
Gregor, Arthur S. *One, two, three, four,*
  five
Gretz, Susanna. *Teddy bears ABC*
  Teddy bears 1 - 10
Grimm, Jacob. *Mrs. Fox's wedding*
Gundersheimer, Karen. *1 2 3 play with me*
Hague, Kathleen. *Numbears*
Hamsa, Bobbie. *Polly wants a cracker*
Harada, Joyce. *It's the 0-1-2-3 book*
Haskins, Jim. *Count your way through*
  China
  Count your way through Japan
  Count your way through Russia
  Count your way through the Arab world
Hawkins, Colin. *Take away monsters*
Hay, Dean. *Now I can count*
Hoban, Russell. *Ten what?*
Hoban, Tana. *Count and see*
  1, 2, 3
  26 letters and 99 cents
Holder, Heidi. *Crows*
Holt, Margaret. *David McCheever's*
  twenty-nine dogs
Hooper, Meredith. *Seven eggs*
Howard, Katherine. *I can count to 100...*
  can you?
Howe, Caroline Walton. *Counting penguins*
Hughes, Shirley. *Lucy and Tom's 1, 2, 3*
  When we went to the park
Hutchins, Pat. *1 hunter*
Inkpen, Mick. *One bear at bedtime*
Ipcar, Dahlov. *Brown cow farm*
  Ten big farms
Jabar, Cynthia. *Party day!*
Johnston, Tony. *Whale song*
Kessler, Ethel. *Two, four, six, eight*
Kitamura, Satoshi. *When sheep cannot sleep*
Kitchen, Bert. *Animal numbers*
Koontz, Robin Michal. *This old man*
Kramer, Anthony Penta. *Numbers on*
  parade
Kraus, Robert. *Good night little one*
  Good night Richard Rabbit
Krüss, James. *3 X 3*
Langstaff, John M. *Over in the meadow*
Lasker, Joe. *Lentil soup*
Leedy, Loreen. *A number of dragons*
Let's count and count out

Lewin, Betsy. *Cat count*
  Hip, hippo, hooray!
Lindberg, Reeve. *Midnight farm*
Lionni, Leo. *Numbers to talk about*
Lippman, Peter. *Peter Lippman's numbers*
A little book of numbers
Livermore, Elaine. *One to ten, count again*
Löfgren, Ulf. *One-two-three*
Lynn, Sara. *1 2 3*
McCrea, Lilian. *Mother hen*
MacDonald, Elizabeth. *My aunt and the*
  animals
MacDonald, Suse. *Numblers*
Mack, Stanley. *Ten bears in my bed*
McKissack, Patricia C. *Big bug book of*
  counting
McLeod, Emilie Warren. *One snail and me*
McMillan, Bruce. *Counting wildflowers*
Maestro, Betsy. *Dollars and cents for*
  Harriet
  Harriet goes to the circus
Maestro, Giulio. *One more and one less*
Magee, Doug. *Trucks you can count on*
Maris, Ron. *In my garden*
Marshall, Ray. *Pop-up numbers #1*
  Pop-up numbers #2
  Pop-up numbers #3
  Pop-up numbers #4
Martin, Bill (William Ivan). *Sounds I*
  remember
  Sounds of numbers
Mathews, Louise. *Bunches and bunches of*
  bunnies
  Cluck one
  The great take-away
Matthias, Catherine. *Too many balloons*
Mayer, Marianna. *Alley oop!*
Mayer, Mercer. *Little Monster's counting*
  book
Meeks, Esther K. *One is the engine*, ill. by
  Ernie King
  One is the engine, ill. by Joe Rogers
Merrill, Jean. *How many kids are hiding on*
  my block?
Miller, J. P. (John Parr). *Learn to count*
  with Little Rabbit
Miller, Jane. *Farm counting book*
Milne, A. A. (Alan Alexander). *Pooh's*
  counting book
Morris, Ann. *Night counting*
Morse, Samuel French. *Sea sums*
Noll, Sally. *Off and counting*
Nordqvist, Sven. *Willie in the big world*
One rubber duckie
One, two, buckle my shoe, ill. by Rowan
  Barnes-Murphy
One, two, buckle my shoe, ill. by Gail E.
  Haley
Ormerod, Jan. *Young Joe*
Over in the meadow, ill. by Paul Galdone
Over in the meadow, ill. by Ezra Jack Keats

Oxenbury, Helen. *Numbers of things*
Pavey, Peter. *One dragon's dream*
Pearson, Susan. *When baby went to bed*
Peek, Merle. *The balancing act*
Peppé, Rodney. *Circus numbers*
  Little numbers
Petie, Haris. *Billions of bugs*
Pieńkowski, Jan. *Numbers*
Pluckrose, Henry. *Counting*
  Numbers
Pomerantz, Charlotte. *One duck, another*
  duck
Potter, Beatrix. *Peter Rabbit's one two three*
Price, Christine. *One is God*
The pudgy fingers counting book
Rand, Ann. *Little 1*
Rees, Mary. *Ten in a bed*
Reiss, John J. *Numbers*
Rockwell, Norman. *Norman Rockwell's*
  counting book
Roll over!
Ross, H. L. *Not counting monsters*
Samton, Sheila White. *The world from my*
  window
Sazer, Nina. *What do you think I saw?*
Scarry, Richard. *Richard Scarry's best*
  counting book ever
  Richard Scarry's great big schoolhouse
Schertle, Alice. *Goodnight, Hattie, my*
  dearie, my dove
Schwartz, David. *How much is a million?*
Seignobosc, Françoise. *Jeanne-Marie counts*
  her sheep
Sendak, Maurice. *One was Johnny*
  Seven little monsters
The Sesame Street book of numbers
Seuss, Dr. *Ten apples up on top*
Shostak, Myra. *Rainbow candles*
Sis, Peter. *Waving*
Sitomer, Mindel. *How did numbers begin?*
Smith, Donald. *Farm numbers 1, 2, 3*
Stanek, Muriel. *One, two, three for fun*
Steiner, Charlotte. *Five little finger*
  playmates
Stobbs, Joanna. *One sun, two eyes, and a*
  million stars
Stobbs, William. *This little piggy*
Sugita, Yutaka. *Good night 1, 2, 3*
Szekeres, Cyndy. *Cyndy Szekeres' counting*
  book, 1 to 10
Tafuri, Nancy. *Who's counting?*
Testa, Fulvio. *If you take a pencil*
Thompson, Susan L. *One more thing, dad*
Trinca, Rod. *One woolly wombat*
Tudor, Tasha. *1 is one*
Wadsworth, Olive A. *Over in the meadow*
Warren, Cathy. *The ten-alarm camp-out*
Watson, Nancy Dingman. *What is one?*
Weihs, Erika. *Count the cats*
Wells, Rosemary. *Max's toys*
Wild, Robin. *The bears' counting book*

Williams, Garth. *The chicken book*
Williams, Jenny. *One, two, buckle my shoe*
Wilson, Barbara. *ABC et/and 123*
Yolen, Jane. *An invitation to the butterfly*
  ball
Youldon, Gillian. *Counting*
  Numbers
Youngs, Betty. *One panda*
Zaslavsky, Claudia. *Count on your fingers*
  African style
Ziefert, Harriet. *A dozen dogs*
Ziner, Feenie. *Counting carnival*
Zirbes, Laura. *How many bears?*
Zolotow, Charlotte. *One step, two...*

Countries, foreign *see* Foreign lands

Country

Asch, Frank. *Country pie*
Atwood, Margaret. *Anna's pet*
Barklem, Jill. *The big book of Brambly*
  Hedge
Barton, Pat. *A week is a long time*
Bozzo, Maxine Zohn. *Toby in the country,*
  Toby in the city
Bröger, Achim. *Francie's paper puppy*
Brown, Margaret Wise. *The country noisy*
  book
Browne, Caroline. *Mrs. Christie's farmhouse*
Burns, Maurice. *Go ducks, go!*
Burton, Virginia Lee. *The little house*
Caudill, Rebecca. *Contrary Jenkins*
Chwast, Seymour. *Tall city, wide country*
Dale, Ruth Bluestone. *Benjamin — and*
  Sylvester also
Dickinson, Mary. *Alex's outing*
Goffstein, M. B. (Marilyn Brooke). *Our*
  prairie home
Griffith, Helen V. *Grandaddy's place*
Hawkesworth, Jenny. *The lonely skyscraper*
Hodeir, André. *Warwick's three bottles*
Holl, Adelaide. *A mouse story*
Kingman, Lee. *Peter's long walk*
Lorenz, Lee. *A weekend in the country*
McKissack, Patricia C. *Country mouse and*
  city mouse, ill. by Anne Sikorski
Martin, Bill (William Ivan). *Barn dance!*
Moore, Elaine. *Grandma's house*
  Grandma's promise
Moore, Inga. *The truffle hunter*
Parnall, Peter. *Apple tree*
Payne, Joan Balfour. *The stable that stayed*
Pender, Lydia. *Barnaby and the horses*
Polacco, Patricia. *Meteor!*
Provensen, Alice. *Town and country*
Roach, Marilynne K. *Two Roman mice*
Rylant, Cynthia. *Night in the country*
Scheffler, Ursel. *Stop your crowing,*
  Kasimir!
Sopko, Eugen. *Townsfolk and countryfolk*

Stanley, Diane. *A country tale*
Teal, Valentine. *The little woman wanted noise*
Van Allsburg, Chris. *The stranger*
Walters, Marguerite. *The city-country ABC*
The weekend
Williams, Jay. *The city witch and the country witch*

Cowboys

Anderson, C. W. (Clarence Williams).
  Blaze and the Indian cave
  Blaze and the lost quarry
  Blaze and the mountain lion
  Blaze and Thunderbolt
  Blaze finds forgotten roads
  Blaze finds the trail
Anglund, Joan Walsh. *The brave cowboy*
  Cowboy and his friend
  The cowboy's Christmas
  Cowboy's secret life
Aulaire, Ingri Mortenson d'. *Nils*
Beatty, Hetty Burlingame. *Bucking horse*
Bellville, Cheryl Walsh. *Rodeo*
Bishop, Ann. *Wild Bill Hiccup's riddle book*
Bright, Robert. *Georgie goes west*
Burton, Virginia Lee. *Calico the wonder horse*
Chandler, Edna Walker. *Cattle drive*
  Cowboy Andy
  Pony rider
  Secret tunnel
Dewey, Ariane. *Pecos Bill*
Doughtie, Charles. *High Henry...the cowboy who was too tall to ride a horse*
Fain, James W. *Rodeos*
Felton, Harold W. *Pecos Bill and the mustang*
Fitzhugh, Louise. *Bang, bang, you're dead*
Greene, Carla. *Cowboys what do they do?*
Hancock, Sibyl. *Old Blue*
Hillert, Margaret. *The little cowboy and the big cowboy*
Kellogg, Steven. *Pecos Bill*
Kennedy, Richard. *The contests at Cowlick*
Krasilovsky, Phyllis. *The girl who was a cowboy*
Lenski, Lois. *Cowboy Small*
Martini, Teri. *Cowboys*
Mayer, Mercer. *Cowboy critter*
Moon, Dolly M. *My very first book of cowboy songs*
Quackenbush, Robert M. *Pete Pack Rat*
Scott, Ann Herbert. *Big Cowboy Western*
Sewall, Marcia. *Ridin' that strawberry roan*
Ward, Nanda Weedon. *The black sombrero*
Wise, William. *The cowboy surprise*
Wood, Nancy C. *Little wrangler*

Cows see Animals – bulls, cows

Coyotes see Animals – coyotes

Crabs see Crustacea

Cranes see Birds – cranes

Creatures see Goblins; Monsters

Creeks see Rivers

Crickets see Insects – crickets

Crime

Adamson, Gareth. *Old man up a tree*
Ahlberg, Allan. *Cops and robbers*
Ahlberg, Janet. *Burglar Bill*
Alderson, Sue Ann. *Ida and the wool smugglers*
Allard, Harry. *It's so nice to have a wolf around the house*
Anderson, C. W. (Clarence Williams).
  Blaze and the gypsies
Berson, Harold. *The thief who hugged a moonbeam*
Blake, Quentin. *Snuff*
Bradford, Ann. *The mystery in the secret club house*
  The mystery of the blind writer
  The mystery of the tree house
Brandenberg, Franz. *A robber! A robber!*
Brenner, Anita. *A hero by mistake*
Bright, Robert. *Georgie and the robbers*
Brunhoff, Laurent de. *Babar's mystery*
Burton, Virginia Lee. *Calico the wonder horse*
Calders, Pere. *Brush*
Cass, Joan E. *The cat thief*
Christelow, Eileen. *The robbery at the diamond dog diner*
Christian, Mary Blount. *The doggone mystery*
  J. J. Leggett, secret agent
Coombs, Patricia. *Dorrie and the haunted house*
Cox, David. *Bossyboots*
Cressey, James. *Max the mouse*
  Pet parrot
Dahl, Roald. *The giraffe and the pelly and me*
Daly, Niki. *Vim, the rag mouse*
Dumas, Philippe. *Laura and the bandits*
Duvoisin, Roger Antoine. *Petunia and the song*
Gage, Wilson. *Down in the boondocks*
Goodall, John S. *Paddy to the rescue*
Harris, Leon A. *The great diamond robbery*
  The great picture robbery
Heller, George. *Hiroshi's wonderful kite*
Heymans, Margriet. *Pippin and Robber Grumblecroak's big baby*

Hickman, Martha Whitmore. *When can daddy come home?*
Hogrogian, Nonny. *The contest*
Rooster brother
Jacobs, Joseph. *Hereafterthis*
Janice. *Mr. and Mrs. Button's wonderful watchdogs*
Kirn, Ann. *I spy*
Krahn, Fernando. *Mr. Top*
Kraus, Robert. *The detective of London*
Kroll, Steven. *Looking for Daniela*
Woof, woof!
Levitin, Sonia. *Nobody stole the pie*
Levy, Elizabeth. *Something queer at the ball park*
Lobel, Anita. *The straw maid*
Lobel, Arnold. *How the rooster saved the day*
McKee, David. *123456789 Benn*
McPhail, David. *Stanley Henry Bear's friend*
Marzollo, Jean. *Jed and the space bandits*
Massie, Diane Redfield. *Chameleon the spy and the terrible toaster trap*
Mathews, Louise. *The great take-away*
Mayer, Mercer. *Liverwurst is missing*
Miles, Miska. *The raccoon and Mrs. McGinnis*
Moore, John. *Granny Stickleback*
Mooser, Stephen. *Funnyman and the penny dodo*
Myller, Rolf. *A very noisy day*
Parish, Peggy. *The cat's burglar*
Granny and the desperadoes
Partch, Virgil Franklin. *The Christmas cookie sprinkle snitcher*
Politi, Leo. *Emmet*
Pryor, Bonnie. *Mr. Munday and the rustlers*
Reidel, Marlene. *Jacob and the robbers*
Rose, Gerald. *The tiger-skin rug*
Rosenbloom, Joseph. *Deputy Dan and the bank robbers*
Ruby-Spears Enterprises. *The puppy's new adventures*
Scarry, Richard. *Richard Scarry's great big mystery book*
Schulman, Janet. *Jack the bum and the haunted house*
Seabrooke, Brenda. *The best burglar alarm*
Shire, Ellen. *The mystery at number seven, Rue Petite*
Slobodkina, Esphyr. *Pezzo the peddler and the thirteen silly thieves*
Solotareff, Grégoire. *Don't call me little bunny*
Thomson, Ruth. *Peabody all at sea*
Peabody's first case
Titus, Eve. *Anatole and the thirty thieves*
Ungerer, Tomi. *The three robbers*
Watson, Nancy Dingman. *The birthday goat*

Criminals *see* Crime; Prisons

Crippled *see* Handicaps

Crocodiles *see* Reptiles – alligators, crocodiles

Crows *see* Birds – crows

Cruelty to animals *see* Character traits – kindness to animals

Crustacea

Amos, William H. *Exploring the seashore*
Carle, Eric. *A house for Hermit Crab*
Carrick, Carol. *The blue lobster*
Coldrey, Jennifer. *The world of crabs*
Heller, Ruth. *How to hide an octopus*
Heyduck-Huth, Hilde. *The starfish*
Horio, Seishi. *The monkey and the crab*
Kipling, Rudyard. *The crab that played with the sea*
Knutson, Barbara. *Why the crab has no head*
Mogensen, Jan. *Teddy in the undersea kingdom*
Morris, Robert A. *Seahorse*
Peet, Bill. *Kermit the hermit*
Yamaguchi, Tohr. *Two crabs and the moonlight*

Cumulative tales

Aardema, Verna. *Bringing the rain to Kapiti Plain*
The riddle of the drum
Adoff, Arnold. *The cabbages are chasing the rabbits*
Alger, Leclaire. *Always room for one more*
Aliki. *June 7!*
Allbright, Viv. *Ten go hopping*
Asbjørnsen, P. C. (Peter Christen). *The three billy goats Gruff*, ill. by Marcia Brown
Three billy goats Gruff, ill. by Tom Dunnington
The three billy goats Gruff, ill. by Paul Galdone
The three billy goats Gruff, ill. by Janet Stevens
The three billy goats Gruff, ill. by William Stobbs
Austin, Margot. *Manuel's kite string*
Baker, Betty. *Little runner of the longhouse*
Rat is dead and ant is sad
Barton, Byron. *Buzz, buzz, buzz*
Berson, Harold. *The boy, the baker, the miller and more*
Bishop, Claire Huchet. *Twenty-two bears*
Blegvad, Erik. *Burnie's hill*
Bonne, Rose. *I know an old lady*, ill. by Abner Graboff
I know an old lady who swallowed a fly, ill. by William Stobbs

Boutwell, Edna. *Red rooster*
Bowden, Joan Chase. *The bean boy*
A boy went out to gather pears
Brand, Oscar. *When I first came to this land*
Brown, Marcia. *The bun*
  The neighbors
Brown, Margaret Wise. *The little brass band*
Brown, Ruth. *A dark, dark tale*
Bryan, Ashley. *Beat the story-drum,*
  pum-pum
Bunting, Eve. *The big cheese*
Burningham, John. *Mr. Gumpy's outing*
Burton, Virginia Lee. *Katy and the big*
  snow
Carle, Eric. *Pancakes, pancakes*
Chicken Little. *Chicken Licken*, ill. by Jutta
  Ash
  Chicken Licken, ill. by Gavin Bishop
  Henny Penny, ill. by Paul Galdone
  Henny Penny, ill. by William Stobbs
  The story of Chicken Licken, adapt. and ill.
  by Jan Ormerod
Christian, Mary Blount. *Nothing much*
  happened today
Clifford, Eth. *Why is an elephant called an*
  elephant?
Cunliffe, John. *The king's birthday cake*
Delaney, A. *The butterfly*
Dodd, Lynley. *Hairy Maclary from*
  Donaldson's dairy
  Hairy Maclary's bone
Domanska, Janina. *The turnip*
Elkin, Benjamin. *The king who could not*
  sleep
  Such is the way of the world
  Why the sun was late
Emberley, Barbara. *Drummer Hoff*
Ets, Marie Hall. *Elephant in a well*
Evans, Eva Knox. *Sleepy time*
The fat cat
Fenton, Edward. *The big yellow balloon*
Fiddle-i-fee
Firmin, Peter. *Basil Brush gets a medal*
Flora, James. *The day the cow sneezed*
Foulds, Elfrida Vipont. *The elephant and*
  the bad baby
Fox, Mem. *Hattie and the fox*
Gág, Wanda. *Millions of cats*
Galdone, Paul. *Cat goes fiddle-i-fee*
  The greedy old fat man
Garrison, Christian. *Little pieces of the west*
  wind
The gingerbread boy. *The gingerbread boy*,
  ill. by Scott Cook
  The gingerbread boy, ill. by Paul Galdone
  The gingerbread boy, ill. by Joan Elizabeth
  Goodman
  The gingerbread boy, ill. by William Curtis
  Holdsworth
  The gingerbread man
  The pancake boy

Whiff, sniff, nibble and chew
The golden goose, ill. by William Stobbs
Grasshopper to the rescue
Grimm, Jacob. *The table, the donkey and the*
  stick
  The wishing table, ill. by Eve Tharlet
Grossman, Bill. *Donna O'Neeshuck was*
  chased by some cows
Hearn, Michael Patrick. *The porcelain cat*
Heilbroner, Joan. *This is the house where*
  Jack lives
Hewett, Anita. *The little white hen*
  The tale of the turnip
Hillert, Margaret. *The three goats*
Hogrogian, Nonny. *The cat who loved to*
  sing
  One fine day
Hoguet, Susan Ramsay. *I unpacked my*
  grandmother's trunk
Home before midnight
Hooper, Meredith. *Seven eggs*
The house that Jack built. *The house that*
  Jack built, ill. by Randolph Caldecott
  The house that Jack built, ill. by Seymour
  Chwast
  The house that Jack built, ill. by Antonio
  Frasconi
  The house that Jack built, ill. by Rodney
  Peppé
  The house that Jack built, ill. by Janet
  Stevens
  This is the house that Jack built, ill. by Liz
  Underhill
Houston, John A. *A mouse in my house*
Hughes, Shirley. *Alfie gets in first*
Hush little baby. *Hush little baby*, ill. by
  Aliki
  Hush little baby, ill. by Jeanette Winter
  Hush little baby, ill. by Margot Zemach
Hutchins, Pat. *Don't forget the bacon!*
  Good night owl
  Titch
Jacobs, Joseph. *Johnny-cake*, ill. by Emma
  Lillian Brock
  Johnny-cake, ill. by William Stobbs
Jameson, Cynthia. *The clay pot boy*
Johnston, Tony. *Yonder*
Kahl, Virginia. *Whose cat is that?*
Kalan, Robert. *Jump, frog, jump!*
Krahn, Fernando. *The mystery of the giant*
  footprints
Krasilovsky, Phyllis. *The cow who fell in the*
  canal
Kroll, Steven. *The tyrannosaurus game*
Kuskin, Karla. *A boy had a mother who*
  bought him a hat
Lazy Jack. *Lazy Jack*, ill. by Bert Dodson
  Lazy Jack, ill. by Kurt Werth
Lear, Edward. *Whizz!*
Lenski, Lois. *Susie Mariar*
Lester, Helen. *It wasn't my fault*

Lexau, Joan M. *Crocodile and hen*
Lindman, Maj. *Snipp, Snapp, Snurr and the buttered bread*
The little red hen. *The little red hen*, ill. by Janina Domanska
The little red hen, ill. by Paul Galdone
The little red hen, ill. by Mel Pekarsky
The little red hen, ill. by William Stobbs
The little red hen, ill. by Margot Zemach
Little Tuppen, ill. by Paul Galdone
Lobel, Anita. *The pancake*
Lobel, Arnold. *The rose in my garden*
Lorenz, Lee. *Big Gus and Little Gus*
McClintock, Marshall. *A fly went by*
McKissack, Patricia C. *The little red hen*, ill. by Dennis Hockerman
Martin, Bill (William Ivan). *Brown bear, brown bear, what do you see?*
Murphey, Sara. *The roly poly cookie*
Noble, Trinka Hakes. *The king's tea*
Nolan, Dennis. *Wizard McBean and his flying machine*
Old MacDonald had a farm. *Old MacDonald had a farm*, ill. by Mel Crawford
Old MacDonald had a farm, ill. by David Frankland
Old MacDonald had a farm, ill. by Abner Graboff
Old MacDonald had a farm, ill. by Tracey Campbell Pearson
Old MacDonald had a farm, ill. by Robert M. Quackenbush
Old MacDonald had a farm, ill. by William Stobbs
The old woman and her pig
Oppenheim, Joanne. *You can't catch me!*
Pack, Robert. *Then what did you do?*
Parkinson, Kathy. *The enormous turnip*
Patrick, Gloria. *This is...*
Peet, Bill. *The ant and the elephant*
Petie, Haris. *The seed the squirrel dropped*
Prelutsky, Jack. *The terrible tiger*
Preston, Edna Mitchell. *One dark night*
Quackenbush, Robert M. *No mouse for me*
Raskin, Ellen. *Ghost in a four-room apartment*
Riddell, Chris. *Bird's new shoes*
Robart, Rose. *The cake that Mack ate*
Rockwell, Anne F. *Honk honk! Poor Goose*
Rose, Anne. *The talking turnip*
Ross, Tony. *Lazy Jack*
Sawyer, Ruth. *Journey cake, ho!*
Scott, William R. *This is the milk that Jack drank*
Seeger, Pete. *The foolish frog*
Segal, Lore. *All the way home*
Seuss, Dr. *Green eggs and ham*
Seymour, Dorothy Z. *The tent*

Shannon, George. *Beanboy* *Oh, I love!*
Silverstein, Shel. *A giraffe and a half*
Skorpen, Liesel Moak. *All the Lassies*
Snow, Pegeen. *Mrs. Periwinkle's groceries*
Steger, Hans-Ulrich. *Traveling to Tripiti*
Stoddard, Sandol. *Bedtime mouse*
Stone, Rosetta. *Because a little bug went ka-choo!*
Suhl, Yuri. *Simon Boom gives a wedding*
Sutton, Eve. *My cat likes to hide in boxes*
Tolstoĭ, Alekseĭ Nikolaevich. *The great big enormous turnip*
Tresselt, Alvin R. *Rain drop splash*
Troughton, Joanna. *The quail's egg*
The twelve days of Christmas. English folk song. *Brian Wildsmith's The twelve days of Christmas*
Jack Kent's twelve days of Christmas
The twelve days of Christmas, ill. by Jan Brett
The twelve days of Christmas, ill. by Ilonka Karasz
The twelve days of Christmas, ill. by Erika Schneider
The twelve days of Christmas, ill. by Sophie Windham
Tworkov, Jack. *The camel who took a walk*
Varga, Judy. *The monster behind Black Rock*
Wahl, Jan. *Follow me cried Bee*
Wallner, John. *Old MacDonald had a farm*
West, Colin. *Have you seen the crocodile?*
The king of Kennelwick castle
The king's toothache
Wiesner, William. *Happy-Go-Lucky*
Wildsmith, Brian. *Goat's trail*
Williams, Linda. *The little old lady who was not afraid of anything*
Wolkstein, Diane. *The magic wings*
Wood, Audrey. *The napping house*
Ziner, Feenie. *Counting carnival*
Zolotow, Charlotte. *The quarreling book*

Curiosity *see* Character traits – curiosity

Currency *see* Money

Cycles *see* Motorcycles; Sports – bicycling

Czechoslovakia *see* Foreign lands – Czechoslovakia

Dancing see Activities – dancing

Dark see Night

Darkness – fear see Emotions – fear

Dawn see Morning

Days of the week, months of the year

Borchers, Elisabeth. *There comes a time*
Carle, Eric. *The very hungry caterpillar*
Charles, Donald. *Calico Cat's year*
Clifton, Lucille. *Some of the days of Everett Anderson*
Coleridge, Sara. *January brings the snow*
De Regniers, Beatrice Schenk. *Little Sister and the Month Brothers*
Gág, Flavia. *Chubby's first year*
Hillman, Priscilla. *A Merry-Mouse book of months*
Hooper, Meredith. *Seven eggs*
Howell, Lynn. *Winifred's new bed*
Keenen, George. *The preposterous week*
Lasker, Joe. *Lentil soup*
Lewis, Robin Baird. *Hello, Mr. Scarecrow*
Lord, Beman. *The days of the week*
MacDonald, Elizabeth. *My aunt and the animals*
Maestro, Betsy. *Through the year with Harriet*
Plotz, Helen. *A week of lullabies*
Prater, John. *On Friday something funny happened*
Provensen, Alice. *The year at Maple Hill Farm*
Scarry, Richard. *Richard Scarry's best first book ever*
Richard Scarry's great big schoolhouse
Sendak, Maurice. *Chicken soup with rice*
Shulevitz, Uri. *One Monday morning*
Tafuri, Nancy. *All year long*
Tudor, Tasha. *Around the year*
Tyrrell, Anne. *Elizabeth Jane gets dressed*
Ward, Cindy. *Cookie's week*
Wolff, Ashley. *A year of beasts*
A year of birds
Wood, Audrey. *Heckedy Peg*
Yolen, Jane. *No bath tonight*

Deafness see Handicaps – deafness

Death

Aliki. *Mummies made in Egypt*
Anders, Rebecca. *A look at death*
Andersen, H. C. (Hans Christian). *It's perfectly true!*, ill. by Janet Stevens
Arnold, Caroline. *What we do when someone dies*
Baker, Betty. *Rat is dead and ant is sad*
Barker, Peggy. *What happened when grandma died*
Barnhart, Peter. *The wounded duck*
Bartoli, Jennifer. *Nonna*
Beim, Jerrold. *With dad alone*
Benchley, Nathaniel. *Snip*
Bernstein, Joanne E. *When people die*
Brown, Margaret Wise. *The dead bird*
Bunting, Eve. *The big red barn*
The happy funeral
Burningham, John. *Grandpa*
Carrick, Carol. *The accident*
Caseley, Judith. *When Grandpa came to stay*
Cazet, Denys. *A fish in his pocket*
Clifton, Lucille. *Everett Anderson's goodbye*
Cock Robin. *The courtship, merry marriage, and feast of Cock Robin and Jenny Wren*
Cohen, Miriam. *Jim's dog Muffins*
Cohn, Janice. *I had a friend named Peter*
Cooney, Barbara. *Island boy*
Coutant, Helen. *First snow*
Dabcovich, Lydia. *Mrs. Huggins and her hen Hannah*
DeArmond, Dale. *The seal oil lamp*
De Paola, Tomie. *Nana upstairs and Nana downstairs*
Fassler, Joan. *My grandpa died today*
Fox, Mem. *With love, at Christmas*
Gerstein, Mordicai. *The mountains of Tibet*
Goble, Paul. *Beyond the ridge*
Gould, Deborah. *Grandpa's slide show*
Grimm, Wilhelm. *Dear Mili*
Harranth, Wolf. *My old grandad*
Harriott, Ted. *Coming home*
Hastings, Selina. *The man who wanted to live forever*
Hazen, Barbara Shook. *Why did Grandpa die?*
Hoffmann, E. T. A. *The strange child*
Hogan, Bernice. *My grandmother died but I won't forget her*
Hoopes, Lyn Littlefield. *Nana*
Horio, Seishi. *The monkey and the crab*
Hurd, Edith Thacher. *The black dog who went into the woods*
Jewell, Nancy. *Time for Uncle Joe*
Joosse, Barbara M. *Better with two*
Kaldhol, Marit. *Goodbye Rune*
Kantrowitz, Mildred. *When Violet died*
Keats, Ezra Jack. *Maggie and the pirate*
Keller, Holly. *Goodbye, Max*
Kübler-Ross, Elisabeth. *Remember the secret*

Le Tord, Bijou. *My Grandma Leonie*
Mattingley, Christobel. *The angel with a mouth-organ*
Mendoza, George. *The hunter I might have been*
Osborn, Lois. *My dad is really something*
Patterson, Francine. *Koko's kitten*
Peavy, Linda. *Allison's grandfather*
Porte, Barbara Ann. *Harry's mom*
Rogers, Fred. *When a pet dies*
Simmonds, Posy. *Fred*
Simon, Norma. *The saddest time*
  We remember Philip
Stein, Sara Bonnett. *About dying*
Stevens, Carla. *Stories from a snowy meadow*
Stevens, Margaret. *When grandpa died*
Stiles, Norman. *I'll miss you, Mr. Hooper*
Stilz, Carol Curtis. *Kirsty's kite*
Taha, Karen T. *A gift for Tia Rose*
Tejima, Keizaburo. *Swan sky*
Thomas, Jane Resh. *Saying good-bye to grandma*
Tobias, Tobi. *Petey*
Townsend, Maryann. *Pop's secret*
Varley, Susan. *Badger's parting gifts*
Viorst, Judith. *The tenth good thing about Barney*
Wahl, Jan. *Tiger watch*
Walker, Alice. *To hell with dying*
Wallace, Ian. *The sparrow's song*
Wilhelm, Hans. *I'll always love you*
Zolotow, Charlotte. *My grandson Lew*

Deer *see* Animals – deer

Demons *see* Devil; Monsters

Denmark *see* Foreign lands – Denmark

Dentists *see* Careers – dentists

Department stores *see* Stores

Desert

Bash, Barbara. *Desert giant*
Baylor, Byrd. *The desert is theirs*
  Desert voices
  I'm in charge of celebrations
  We walk in sandy places
Beim, Jerrold. *Eric on the desert*
Busch, Phyllis S. *Cactus in the desert*
Catchpole, Clive. *Deserts*
Caudill, Rebecca. *Wind, sand and sky*
Clark, Ann Nolan. *The desert people*
  Tia Maria's garden
Cretan, Gladys Yessayan. *Ten brothers with camels*
Holmes, Anita. *The 100-year-old cactus*
John, Naomi. *Roadrunner*
Keats, Ezra Jack. *Clementina's cactus*

McKee, David. *The day the tide went out and out and out*
Siebert, Diane. *Mojave*
Ungerer, Tomi. *Orlando, the brave vulture*
Wondriska, William. *The stop*

Detective stories *see* Problem solving

Detectives *see* Careers – detectives

Devil

Alger, Leclaire. *Kellyburn Braes*
Asch, Frank. *Little Devil's ABC*
  Little Devil's 123
Berson, Harold. *How the devil got his due*
Carey, Valerie Scho. *The devil and mother Crump*
Coombs, Patricia. *The magic pot*
Elwell, Peter. *The king of the pipers*
Galdone, Joanna. *Amber day*
Grimm, Jacob. *The bearskinner*
  The devil with the green hairs
Joyce, James. *The cat and the devil*
McCurdy, Michael. *The devils who learned to be good*
Magnus, Erica. *The boy and the devil*
Pinkwater, Daniel Manus. *Devil in the drain*
Scribner, Charles. *The devil's bridge*
Shute, Linda. *Momotaro, the peach boy*
Stalder, Valerie. *Even the Devil is afraid of a shrew*
Turska, Krystyna. *The magician of Cracow*
Zemach, Harve. *Duffy and the devil*

Dictionaries

A child's picture English-Hebrew dictionary
Daly, Kathleen N. *The Macmillan picture wordbook*
Floyd, Lucy. *Agatha's alphabet, with her very own dictionary*
Halsey, William D. *The magic world of words*
Hayward, Linda. *The Julian Messner picture dictionary of phonics*
  The Sesame Street dictionary
Howard, Katherine. *My first picture dictionary*
Krensky, Stephen. *My first dictionary*
MacBean, Dilla Wittemore. *Picture book dictionary*
McIntire, Alta. *Follett beginning to read picture dictionary*
Parke, Margaret B. *Young reader's color-picture dictionary*
Rand McNally picturebook dictionary
Scarry, Richard. *Richard Scarry's best word book ever*
  Richard Scarry's biggest word book ever!
  Richard Scarry's storybook dictionary

Schulz, Charles M. *The Charlie Brown dictionary*
Seuss, Dr. *The cat in the hat beginner book dictionary*

Digging *see* Activities – digging

Dinosaurs

Aliki. *Dinosaur bones*
   Dinosaurs are different
   Fossils tell of long ago
   My visit to the dinosaurs
Barber, Antonia. *Satchelmouse and the dinosaurs*
Berenstain, Stan. *After the dinosaurs*
Brasch, Kate. *Prehistoric monsters*
Brown, Laurene Krasny. *Dinosaurs travel*
Brown, Marc. *Dinosaurs, beware!*
Carrick, Carol. *The crocodiles still wait*
   Patrick's dinosaurs
   What happened to Patrick's dinosaurs?
Cauley, Lorinda Bryan. *The trouble with Tyrannosaurus Rex*
Charlton, Elizabeth. *Terrible tyrannosaurus*
Cohen, Daniel. *Dinosaurs*
Cole, William. *Dinosaurs and beasts of yore*
Corbett, Scott. *The foolish dinosaur fiasco*
Craig, M. Jean. *Dinosaurs and more dinosaurs*
Cutts, David. *More about dinosaurs*
Daly, Kathleen N. *Dinosaurs*
Dinosaurs and monsters
Donnelly, Liza. *Dinosaurs' Halloween*
Eastman, David. *The story of dinosaurs*
Emberley, Michael. *More dinosaurs!*
Freedman, Russell. *Dinosaurs and their young*
Gibbons, Gail. *Dinosaurs*
Gordon, Sharon. *Dinosaurs in trouble*
Harrison, Sarah. *In granny's garden*
Hennessy, B. G. *The dinosaur who lived in my backyard*
Hodgetts, Blake Christopher. *Dream of the dinosaurs*
Hoff, Syd. *Danny and the dinosaur*
Hurd, Edith Thacher. *Dinosaur, my darling*
Joyce, William. *Dinosaur Bob*
Kellogg, Steven. *Prehistoric Pinkerton*
Klein, Robin. *Thing*
Knight, David C. *Dinosaur days*
Koontz, Robin Michal. *Dinosaur dream*
Kroll, Steven. *The tyrannosaurus game*
Lambert, David. *Dinosaurs*
Milton, Joyce. *Dinosaur days*
Moseley, Keith. *Dinosaurs*
Mosley, Francis. *The dinosaur eggs*
Most, Bernard. *If the dinosaurs came back*
   Whatever happened to the dinosaurs?
Nicoll, Helen. *Meg's eggs*
Parish, Peggy. *Dinosaur time*

Petty, Kate. *Dinosaurs*
Polhamus, Jean Burt. *Dinosaur do's and don'ts*
   Doctor Dinosaur
Prelutsky, Jack. *Tyrannosaurus was a beast* ✕
Riehecky, Janet. *Apatosaurus* ⨍ 567-97
Ross, Wilda S. *What did the dinosaurs eat?*
Rubel, Nicole. *Bruno Brontosaurus*
Sant, Laurent Sauveur. *Dinosaurs*
Schwartz, Henry. *How I captured a dinosaur*
Selsam, Millicent E. *A first look at dinosaurs*
Sharmat, Marjorie Weinman. *Mitchell is moving*
Silverman, Maida. *Dinosaur babies*
Simon, Seymour. *The largest dinosaurs*
   The smallest dinosaurs
Slobodkin, Louis. *Dinny and Danny*
Smith, Jim. *Nimbus the explorer*
Stewart, Frances Todd. *Dinosaurs and other creatures of long ago*
Sundgaard, Arnold. *Jethro's difficult dinosaur*
Thayer, Jane. *Quiet on account of dinosaur*
Wilhelm, Hans. *Tyrone the horrible*
Zallinger, Peter. *Dinosaurs*

Disbelief *see* Behavior – disbelief

Dissatisfaction *see* Behavior – dissatisfaction

Distance *see* Concepts – distance

Diving *see* Sports – skin diving

Divorce

Baum, Louis. *One more time*
Berger, Terry. *How does it feel when your parents get divorced?*
Bienenfeld, Florence. *My mom and dad are getting a divorce*
Boegehold, Betty. *Daddy doesn't live here anymore*
Caines, Jeannette. *Daddy*
Dragonwagon, Crescent. *Always, always*
Girard, Linda Walvoord. *At Daddy's on Saturdays*
Goff, Beth. *Where's daddy?*
Hazen, Barbara Shook. *Two homes to live in*
Jukes, Mavis. *Like Jake and me*
Lexau, Joan M. *Me day*
Lisker, Sonia O. *Two special cards*
Mayle, Peter. *Divorce can happen to the nicest people*
   Why are we getting a divorce?
Noble, June. *Two homes for Lynn*
Paris, Lena. *Mom is single*

Perry, Patricia. *Mommy and daddy are divorced*
Peterson, Jeanne Whitehouse. *That is that*
Pursell, Margaret Sanford. *A look at divorce*
Rogers, Helen Spelman. *Morris and his brave lion*
Roy, Ronald. *Breakfast with my father*
Schuchman, Joan. *Two places to sleep*
Simon, Norma. *The daddy days*
Stein, Sara Bonnett. *On divorce*
Stinson, Kathy. *Mom and dad don't live together any more*
Tangvald, Christine. *Mom and dad don't live together anymore*
Thomas, Ianthe. *Eliza's daddy*
Vigna, Judith. *Daddy's new baby*
Grandma without me
She's not my real mother
Watson, Jane Werner. *Sometimes a family has to split up*

Doctors *see* Careers – doctors

Dogs *see* Animals – Dogs

Dolls *see* Toys – dolls

Dolphins *see* Animals – dolphins

Donkeys *see* Animals – donkeys

Doves *see* Birds – doves

Down and up *see* Concepts – up and down

Dragonflies *see* Insects

Dragons

Aruego, José. *The king and his friends*
Baskin, Hosie. *A book of dragons*
Boswell, Stephen. *King Gorboduc's fabulous zoo*
Bradfield, Roger. *A good night for dragons*
Brandenberg, Franz. *Leo and Emily and the dragon*
Buck, Pearl S. (Pearl Sydenstricker). *The dragon fish*
Buckaway, C. M. *Alfred, the dragon who lost his flame*
Chalmers, Mary. *George Appleton*
Christelow, Eileen. *Henry and the Dragon*
Company González, Mercè. *Killian and the dragons*
Coville, Bruce. *Sarah and the dragon*
Craig, M. Jean. *The dragon in the clock box*
Cressey, James. *The dragon and George*
Cretien, Paul D. *Sir Henry and the dragon*
Davis, Reda. *Martin's dinosaur*
DeLage, Ida. *The old witch and the dragon*

Delaney, Ned. *One dragon to another*
Demi. *Dragon kites and dragonflies*
De Paola, Tomie. *The knight and the dragon*
The wonderful dragon of Timlin
Dewey, Ariane. *Dorin and the dragon*
Domanska, Janina. *King Krakus and the dragon*
Emberley, Ed. *Klippity klop*
Fassler, Joan. *The man of the house*
Firmin, Peter. *Basil Brush and a dragon*
Gág, Wanda. *The funny thing*
Garrison, Christian. *The dream eater*
Goode, Diane. *I hear a noise*
Grimm, Jacob. *The four clever brothers*, ill. by Felix Hoffmann
Haley, Gail E. *Jack and the fire dragon*
Hillert, Margaret. *Happy birthday, dear dragon*
Merry Christmas, dear dragon
Hoban, Russell. *Ace Dragon Ltd.*
Holabird, Katharine. *Alexander and the dragon*
Janosch. *Just one apple*
Jeschke, Susan. *Firerose*
Joerns, Consuelo. *The midnight castle*
Jones, Maurice. *I'm going on a dragon hunt*
Joslin, Sesyle. *Dear dragon*
Kent, Jack. *The once-upon-a-time dragon*
There's no such thing as a dragon
Kimmel, Margaret Mary. *Magic in the mist*
Krahn, Fernando. *The secret in the dungeon*
Kumin, Maxine. *Sebastian and the dragon*
Leaf, Margaret. *Eyes of the dragon*
Leedy, Loreen. *A dragon Christmas*
The dragon Halloween party
A number of dragons
Lifton, Betty Jean. *Joji and the dragon*
Lindgren, Astrid. *The dragon with red eyes*
Lobel, Arnold. *Prince Bertram the bad*
Long, Claudia. *Albert's story*
McCrea, James. *The story of Olaf*
Mahood, Kenneth. *The laughing dragon*
Mahy, Margaret. *The dragon of an ordinary family*
A lion in the meadow
Manushkin, Fran. *Moon dragon*
Martin, C. L. G. *The dragon nanny*
Massie, Diane Redfield. *The Komodo dragon's jewels*
Mayer, Mercer. *Whinnie the lovesick dragon*
Mogensen, Jan. *Teddy and the Chinese dragon*
Murphy, Shirley Rousseau. *Valentine for a dragon*
Nash, Ogden. *Custard and Company*
Custard the dragon
Custard the dragon and the wicked knight
Nesbit, Edith. *The last of the dragons*
Nolan, Dennis. *The castle builder*
Oksner, Robert M. *The incompetent wizard*

Pavey, Peter. *One dragon's dream*
Peet, Bill. *How Droofus the dragon lost his head*
Phillips, Louis. *The brothers Wrong and Wrong Again*
Price, Roger. *The last little dragon*
Rosen, Winifred. *Dragons hate to be discreet*
Rudchenko, Ivan. *Ivanko and the dragon*
Scarry, Richard. *Richard Scarry's Peasant Pig and the terrible dragon*
Scullard, Sue. *Miss Fanshawe and the great dragon adventure*
Sherman, Nancy. *Gwendolyn the miracle hen*
Shub, Elizabeth. *Dragon Franz*
Stern, Simon. *Vasily and the dragon*
Stock, Catherine. *Emma's dragon hunt*
Thayer, Jane. *The popcorn dragon*
Trez, Denise. *The little knight's dragon*
Van Woerkom, Dorothy. *Alexandra the rock-eater*
Varga, Judy. *The dragon who liked to spit fire*
Wiesner, David. *Free fall*
The loathsome dragon
Williams, Jay. *Everyone knows what a dragon looks like*
Willis, Val. *The secret in the matchbox*
Wilson, Sarah. *Beware the dragons!*
Yolen, Jane. *The acorn quest*

Drawing games *see* Games

Dreams

Adoff, Arnold. *Flamboyan*
Alexander, Martha G. *Bobo's dream*
Allison, Diane Worfolk. *In window eight, the moon is late*
Anrooy, Frans van. *The sea horse*
Arnold, Tedd. *No jumping on the bed!*
Axworthy, Anni. *Ben's Wednesday*
Aylesworth, Jim. *The bad dream*
Tonight's the night
Balet, Jan B. *Joanjo*
Balzola, Asun. *Munia and the orange crocodile*
Berenstain, Stan. *The Berenstain bears and the bad dream*
Bohdal, Susi. *The magic honey jar*
Bond, Felicia. *Wake up, Vladimir*
Brown, M. K. *Let's go swimming with Mr. Sillypants*
Brown, Margaret Wise. *Dream book*
The little farmer
Bruna, Dick. *Miffy's dream*
Buckley, Helen Elizabeth. *Someday with my father*
Callen, Larry. *Dashiel and the night*
Carroll, Lewis. *The nursery "Alice"*
Chorao, Kay. *Lemon moon*

Chwast, Seymour. *Still another children's book*
Collington, Peter. *Little pickle*
Coombs, Patricia. *Dorrie and the dreamyard monsters*
Craig, M. Jean. *What did you dream?*
Crowley, Arthur. *The wagon man*
Cuyler, Margery. *Fat Santa*
Dahl, Roald. *Dirty beasts*
Daugherty, Charles Michael. *Wisher*
Dennis, Wesley. *Flip*
Dewey, Ariane. *Dorin and the dragon*
Donaldson, Lois. *Karl's wooden horse*
Dragonwagon, Crescent. *Half a moon and one whole star*
Drescher, Henrik. *Simon's book*
Duncan, Lois. *Horses of dreamland*
Duvoisin, Roger Antoine. *The missing milkman*
Elzbieta. *Dikou and the mysterious moon sheep*
Erskine, Jim. *Bedtime story*
Foreman, Michael. *Land of dreams*
Francis, Anna B. *Pleasant dreams*
Francis, Frank. *The magic wallpaper*
Gantos, Jack. *Greedy Greeny*
Garrison, Christian. *The dream eater*
Gay, Marie-Louise. *Moonbeam on a cat's ear*
Giff, Patricia Reilly. *Next year I'll be special*
Ginsburg, Mirra. *Across the stream*
Four brave sailors
Gould, Deborah. *Grandpa's slide show*
Greenfield, Eloise. *Africa dream*
Greenwood, Ann. *A pack of dreams*
Hague, Kathleen. *Out of the nursery, into the night*
Hale, Irina. *Donkey's dreadful day*
Hansen, Ron. *The shadowmaker*
Hayes, Geoffrey. *The secret inside*
Hill, Susan. *Go away, bad dreams!*
Hodgetts, Blake Christopher. *Dream of the dinosaurs*
Hunter, Mollie. *The knight of the golden plain*
Hurd, Edith Thacher. *Little dog, dreaming*
Jacobs, Joseph. *The crock of gold*
Jennings, Michael. *The bears who came to breakfix*
Johnson, Jane. *Bertie on the beach*
Jonas, Ann. *The quilt*
Karlin, Nurit. *The dream factory*
Keats, Ezra Jack. *Dreams*
Keith, Eros. *Nancy's backyard*
Knotts, Howard. *The lost Christmas*
Koontz, Robin Michal. *Dinosaur dream*
Kotzwinkle, William. *The nap master*
Krahn, Fernando. *Sebastian and the mushroom*
Lester, Alison. *Ruby*
Le-Tan, Pierre. *Visit to the North Pole*

Low, Joseph. *Don't drag your feet...*
McDermott, Gerald. *Daniel O'Rourke*
McPhail, David. *Adam's smile*
  The dream child
  Mistletoe
  The train
Mählqvist, Stefan. *I'll take care of the crocodiles*
Martin, Bill (William Ivan). *Barn dance!*
Mayer, Mercer. *There's something in my attic*
Mayper, Monica. *After good-night*
Moeschlin, Elsa. *The red horse*
Montresor, Beni. *Bedtime!*
Morgan, Allen. *Nicole's boat*
Orgel, Doris. *Little John*
Pavey, Peter. *One dragon's dream*
Paxton, Tom. *Jennifer's rabbit*
Reed, Kit. *When we dream*
Rockwell, Anne F. *Buster and the bogeyman*
  The wolf who had a wonderful dream
Ryder, Joanne. *The night flight*
Say, Allen. *A river dream*
Sendak, Maurice. *In the night kitchen*
Shimin, Symeon. *I wish there were two of me*
Shulevitz, Uri. *The treasure*
Simons, Traute. *Paulino*
Spier, Peter. *Dreams*
Steig, William. *The Zabajaba Jungle*
Stevens, Janet. *Animal fair*
Strand, Mark. *The planet of lost things*
Tafuri, Nancy. *Junglewalk*
Tejima, Keizaburo. *Fox's dream*
Thorne, Jenny. *My uncle*
Tompert, Ann. *Will you come back for me?*
Trez, Denise. *Good night, Veronica*
Troughton, Joanna. *Tortoise's dream*
Tudor, Tasha. *A tale for Easter*
Updike, David. *A winter's journey*
Van Allsburg, Chris. *Ben's dream*
Wahl, Jan. *Humphrey's bear*
  The toy circus
Ward, Lynd. *The silver pony*
Weisgard, Leonard. *Who dreams of cheese?*
Wende, Philip. *Bird boy*
Wersba, Barbara. *Amanda dreaming*
Wiesner, David. *Free fall*
Wildsmith, Brian. *Carousel*
Willard, Nancy. *The mountains of quilt*
  Night story
Yorinks, Arthur. *Hey, Al*
Zemach, Kaethe. *The funny dream*
Zolotow, Charlotte. *I have a horse of my own*
  Someday

Droughts *see* Weather – droughts

Ducks *see* Birds – ducks

Dwarfs *see* Elves and little people

Dying *see* Death

Eagles *see* Birds – eagles

Ears *see* Anatomy

Earth

Asimov, Isaac. *The best new things*
Bernstein, Margery. *Earth namer*
Branley, Franklyn M. *What makes day and night*
Dayton, Mona. *Earth and sky*
Engdahl, Sylvia. *Our world is earth*
Leutscher, Alfred. *Earth*
Lewis, Claudia Louise. *When I go to the moon*
McNulty, Faith. *How to dig a hole to the other side of the world*
Simon, Seymour. *Beneath your feet*
  Earth

Easter *see* Holidays – Easter

Eating *see* Food

Ecology

Arneson, D. J. *Secret places*
Baker, Jeannie. *Where the forest meets the sea*
Baylor, Byrd. *The desert is theirs*
Beisert, Heide Helene. *Poor fish*
Bloome, Enid. *The air we breathe!*
  The water we drink!
Burton, Virginia Lee. *The little house*
Busch, Phyllis S. *Puddles and ponds*
Caputo, Robert. *More than just pets*
Carrick, Carol. *A clearing in the forest*
De Paola, Tomie. *Michael Bird-Boy*
Duvoisin, Roger Antoine. *The happy hunter*
Fife, Dale. *The little park*
Firmin, Peter. *Basil Brush and the windmills*
Freeman, Don. *The seal and the slick*
Hader, Berta Hoerner. *The mighty hunter*
Haley, Gail E. *Noah's ark*
Hamberger, John. *The day the sun disappeared*
Hoff, Syd. *Grizzwold*
Hurd, Edith Thacher. *Wilson's world*
Ichikawa, Satomi. *Suzanne and Nicholas in the garden*

Jewell, Nancy. *Try and catch me*
Kalman, Benjamin. *Animals in danger*
Leutscher, Alfred. *Water*
Lewis, Naomi. *Hare and badger go to town*
Mabey, Richard. *Oak and company*
Margolis, Richard J. *Big bear, spare that tree*
Meyer, Louis A. *The clean air and peaceful contentment dirigible airline*
Miles, Miska. *Rabbit garden*
Mizumura, Kazue. *If I built a village*
Murschetz, Luis. *Mister Mole*
Newton, James R. *Forest log*
Parnall, Peter. *The great fish*
Peet, Bill. *The caboose who got loose*
  Farewell to Shady Glade
  Fly, Homer, fly
  The gnats of knotty pine
  The wump world
Quackenbush, Robert M. *Calling Doctor Quack*
Ricciuti, Edward R. *Donald and the fish that walked*
Roach, Marilynne K. *Dune fox*
Seuss, Dr. *The Lorax*
Short, Mayo. *Andy and the wild ducks*
Shortall, Leonard W. *Just-in-time Joey*
Stone, A. Harris. *The last free bird*
Torgersen, Don Arthur. *The troll who lived in the lake*
Tresselt, Alvin R. *The beaver pond*
  The dead tree
Wegen, Ron. *Where can the animals go?*
Williams, Terry Tempest. *Between cattails*

Ecuador *see* Foreign lands – Ecuador

Education *see* School

Eggs

Andersen, H. C. (Hans Christian). *The woman with the eggs*, ill. by Ray Cruz
Asch, Frank. *MacGooses's grocery*
Back, Christine. *Chicken and egg*
Bourke, Linda. *Ethel's exceptional egg*
Brown, Margaret Wise. *The golden egg book*
Campbell, Rod. *Oh dear!*
Casey, Patricia. *Quack quack*
Claret, Maria. *The chocolate rabbit*
Coombs, Patricia. *Dorrie and the birthday eggs*
Coontz, Otto. *The quiet house*
Dodds, Siobhan. *Elizabeth Hen*
Eastman, P. D. (Philip D.) *Flap your wings*
  Eggs
Gordon, Sharon. *Easter Bunny's lost egg*
Heller, Ruth. *Chickens aren't the only ones*
Hill, Eric. *Spot's first Easter*

Hoban, Lillian. *The case of the two masked robbers*
Hooper, Meredith. *Seven eggs*
Huxley, Aldous. *The crows of Pearblossom*
Kay, Helen. *An egg is for wishing*
Kent, Jack. *The egg book*
Krauss, Ruth. *The happy egg*
Kumin, Maxine. *Eggs of things*
Kwitz, Mary DeBall. *Little chick's story*
Lasell, Fen. *Fly away goose*
Lauber, Patricia. *What's hatching out of that egg?*
Levitin, Sonia. *A single speckled egg*
Lloyd, Megan. *Chicken tricks*
Long, Earlene. *Johnny's egg*
McCrea, Lilian. *Mother hen*
McGovern, Ann. *Eggs on your nose*
Mathews, Louise. *Cluck one*
Milgrom, Harry. *Egg-ventures*
Nicoll, Helen. *Meg's eggs*
O'Neill, Mary. *Big red hen*
Peet, Bill. *The pinkish, purplish, bluish egg*
Polacco, Patricia. *Rechenka's eggs*
Potter, Beatrix. *The tale of Jemima Puddle-Duck*
Pursell, Margaret Sanford. *Jessie the chicken*
  Sprig the tree frog
Rockwell, Anne F. *The gollywhopper egg*
  The wonderful eggs of Furicchia
Scarry, Richard. *Egg in the hole*
Schick, Eleanor. *A surprise in the forest*
Selsam, Millicent E. *The bug that laid the golden eggs*
  Egg to chick
Seuss, Dr. *Horton hatches the egg*
Standon, Anna. *Little duck lost*
Stevenson, James. *The great big especially beautiful Easter egg*
Sundgaard, Arnold. *Jethro's difficult dinosaur*
Tresselt, Alvin R. *The world in the candy egg*
Troughton, Joanna. *The quail's egg*
Waber, Bernard. *How to go about laying an egg*
Wahl, Jan. *The five in the forest*
Wilhelm, Hans. *More bunny trouble*
Wright, Dare. *Edith and the duckling*
Ziefert, Harriet. *Happy Easter, Grandma!*

Egrets *see* Birds – egrets

Egypt *see* Foreign lands – Egypt

Egyptian language *see* Hieroglyphics

Elderly *see* Old age

Electricians *see* Careers – electricians

Elephants *see* Animals – elephants

Elves and little people

Adshead, Gladys L. *Brownies - hush!*
Brownies - it's Christmas
Brownies - they're moving
Alden, Laura. *Learning about fairies*
Balian, Lorna. *Leprechauns never lie*
Barrie, J. M. (James M.). *Peter Pan*, ill. by Diane Goode
Baruch, Dorothy. *Kappa's tug-of-war with the big brown horse*
Bass, Donna. *The tale of the dark crystal*
Berenstain, Michael. *The dwarks*
Berg, Jean Horton. *The wee little man*
Beskow, Elsa Maartman. *Peter in Blueberry Land*
Peter's adventures in Blueberry land
Bolliger, Max. *The magic bird*
Borg, Inga. *Plupp builds a house*
Brennan, Patricia D. *Hitchety hatchety up I go!*
Bulette, Sara. *The elf in the singing tree*
Calhoun, Mary. *The hungry leprechaun*
The pixy and the lazy housewife
The runaway brownie
The thieving dwarfs
Chenault, Nell. *Parsifal the Poddley*
Cox, Palmer. *Another Brownie book*
The Brownies
Davis, Maggie S. *Grandma's secret letter*
De Paola, Tomie. *The Prince of the Dolomites*
De Regniers, Beatrice Schenk. *Penny*
Elves, fairies and gnomes
Fish, Helen Dean. *When the root children wake up*, published by Green Tiger Pr., 1988
When the root children wake up, published by Lippincott, 1930
Fujikawa, Gyo. *Come follow me...to the secret world of elves and fairies and gnomes and trolls*
Funai, Mamoru. *Moke and Poki in the rain forest*
Grimm, Jacob. *The earth gnome*, ill. by Margot Tomes
The elves and the shoemaker, ill. by Paul Galdone
The elves and the shoemaker, ill. by Bernadette Watts
The shoemaker and the elves, ill. by Cynthia and William Birrer
Snow White, ill. by Trina Schart Hyman
Snow White, ill. by Bernadette Watts
Snow White and Rose Red, ill. by Adrienne Adams
Snow-White and Rose-Red, ill. by Barbara Cooney

Snow White and Rose Red, ill. by John Wallner
Snow White and Rose Red, ill. by Bernadette Watts
Snow White and the seven dwarfs, ill. by Chihiro Iwasaki
Hastings, Selina. *The singing ringing tree*
Hawthorne, Julian. *Rumpty-Dudget's tower*
Irving, Washington. *Rip Van Winkle*, ill. by John Howe
Rip Van Winkle, ill. by Thomas Locker
Rip Van Winkle, ill. by Peter Wingham
Kennedy, Richard. *The leprechaun's story*
Koontz, Robin Michal. *This old man*
Korschunow, Irina. *Small fur*
Krauss, Ruth. *Everything under a mushroom*
Kunnas, Mauri. *Santa Claus and his elves*
Twelve gifts for Santa Claus
Lester, Helen. *Pookins gets her way*
McDermott, Gerald. *Daniel O'Rourke*
McLenighan, Valjean. *You can go jump*
Madden, Don. *Lemonade serenade or the thing in the garden*
May, Robert Lewis. *Rudolph the red-nosed reindeer*
Mayer, Marianna. *The little jewel box*
Mayne, William. *The blue book of Hob stories*
The green book of Hob stories
The red book of Hob stories
The yellow book of Hob stories
Minarik, Else Holmelund. *The little giant girl and the elf boys*
Moncure, Jane Belk. *Happy healthkins*
The healthkin food train
Healthkins exercise!
Healthkins help
Morimoto, Junko. *The inch boy*
Norby, Lisa. *The Herself the elf storybook*
Shub, Elizabeth. *Seeing is believing*
Shute, Linda. *Clever Tom and the leprechaun*
Smith, Mary. *Long ago elf*
Steiner, Charlotte. *Red Ridinghood's little lamb*
Tom Thumb. *Grimm Tom Thumb*
Tom Thumb, ill. by L. Leslie Brooke
Tom Thumb, ill. by Dennis Hockerman
Tom Thumb, ill. by Felix Hoffmann
Tom Thumb, ill. by Lidia Postma
Tom Thumb, ill. by Richard Jesse Watson
Tom Thumb, ill. by William Wiesner
Velthuijs, Max. *Little Man finds a home*
Little Man to the rescue
Little Man's lucky day
Walt Disney Productions. *Walt Disney's Snow White and the seven dwarfs*
Zimelman, Nathan. *To sing a song as big as Ireland*

Embarrassment *see* Emotions –
embarrassment

Emergencies *see* Hospitals

Emotions

Allington, Richard L. *Feelings*
Andersen, H. C. (Hans Christian). *The snow queen*, ill. by Bernadette Watts
Andersen, Karen Born. *What's the matter, Sylvie, can't you ride?*
Bach, Alice. *The day after Christmas*
Berger, Terry. *How does it feel when your parents get divorced?*
I have feelings
I have feelings too
Bienenfeld, Florence. *My mom and dad are getting a divorce*
Borten, Helen. *Do you move as I do?*
Brenner, Barbara. *Faces, faces, faces*
Brown, Tricia. *Someone special, just like you*
Calhoun, Mary. *The witch who lost her shadow*
Castle, Sue. *Face talk, hand talk, body talk*
Clifford, Eth. *Your face is a picture*
Clifton, Lucille. *Everett Anderson's goodbye*
Cohen, Miriam. *Jim's dog Muffins*
Cole, William. *Frances face-maker*
Conta, Marcia Maher. *Feelings between brothers and sisters*
Feelings between friends
Feelings between kids and grownups
Feelings between kids and parents
Cunningham, Julia. *A mouse called Junction*
Dabcovich, Lydia. *Mrs. Huggins and her hen Hannah*
DeJong, Meindert. *Nobody plays with a cabbage*
Dragonwagon, Crescent. *Rainy day together*
Galdone, Paul. *The teeny-tiny woman*
Hann, Jacquie. *Crybaby*
Hazen, Barbara Shook. *Happy, sad, silly, mad*
Two homes to live in
Helena, Ann. *The lie*
Hoban, Russell. *La corona and the tin frog*
The stone doll of Sister Brute
Hopkins, Lee Bennett. *I loved Rose Ann*
Horvath, Betty F. *Will the real Tommy Wilson please stand up*
Jewell, Nancy. *Time for Uncle Joe*
Keller, Holly. *Lizzie's invitation*
Kherdian, David. *Right now*
Knox-Wagner, Elaine. *My grandpa retired today*
Krauss, Ruth. *The bundle book*
Lalli, Judy. *Feelings alphabet*
Lewin, Hugh. *Jafta*
Jafta - the journey
Jafta - the town
McCrea, James. *The magic tree*
McGovern, Ann. *Feeling mad, feeling sad, feeling bad, feeling glad*
Mayer, Mercer. *Mine!*
Mayers, Patrick. *Just one more block*
Mendoza, George. *The hunter I might have been*
Mitchell, Cynthia. *Playtime*
Ness, Evaline. *Pavo and the princess*
O'Donnell, Elizabeth Lee. *Maggie doesn't want to move*
Pursell, Margaret Sanford. *A look at divorce*
Rogers, Fred. *Making friends*
Moving
Ross, David. *More hugs!*
The Sesame Street book of people and things
Simon, Norma. *How do I feel?*
Stanton, Elizabeth. *Sometimes I like to cry*
Sussman, Susan. *Hippo thunder*
Tobias, Tobi. *Moving day*
Petey
Tresselt, Alvin R. *What did you leave behind?*
Waber, Bernard. *Ira says goodbye*
Wittels, Harriet. *Things I hate!*
Wolde, Gunilla. *This is Betsy*
Yudell, Lynn Deena. *Make a face*

Emotions – anger

Alexander, Martha G. *And my mean old mother will be sorry, Blackboard Bear*
Aliki. *We are best friends*
Andrews, F. Emerson (Frank Emerson). *Nobody comes to dinner*
Aseltine, Lorraine. *I'm deaf and it's okay*
Boegehold, Betty. *Daddy doesn't live here anymore*
Brunhoff, Laurent de. *The one pig with horns*
Craft, Ruth. *The day of the rainbow*
Du Bois, William Pène. *Bear party*
Erickson, Karen. *I was so mad*
Hapgood, Miranda. *Martha's mad day*
Hautzig, Deborah. *Why are you so mean to me?*
Hoban, Lillian. *Arthur's great big Valentine*
I'm mad at you
Sharmat, Marjorie Weinman. *Attila the angry*
I'm not Oscar's friend any more
Rollo and Juliet...forever!
Simon, Norma. *I was so mad!*
Small, David. *Paper John*
Watson, Jane Werner. *Sometimes I get angry*
Wilhelm, Hans. *Let's be friends again!*
Zolotow, Charlotte. *The quarreling book*

Emotions – embarrassment

Alexander, Martha G. *Sabrina*
Aylesworth, Jim. *Shenandoah Noah*
Boyd, Selma. *The how*
Bulla, Clyde Robert. *Daniel's duck*
Carlson, Nancy. *Loudmouth George and the big race*
Caseley, Judith. *Molly Pink*
Cazet, Denys. *Great-Uncle Felix*
Cooney, Nancy Evans. *Donald says thumbs down*
Davis, Gibbs. *Katy's first haircut*
Freeman, Don. *Quiet! There's a canary in the library*
Hirsh, Marilyn. *The pink suit*
Hoff, Syd. *A walk past Ellen's house*
Lexau, Joan M. *I should have stayed in bed*
Stanek, Muriel. *Left, right, left, right!*
Townsend, Kenneth. *Felix, the bald-headed lion*
Udry, Janice May. *How I faded away*

Emotions – envy, jealousy

Abisch, Roz. *Mai-Ling and the mirror*
Alexander, Martha G. *Nobody asked me if I wanted a baby sister*
When the new baby comes, I'm moving out
Asch, Frank. *Bear's bargain*
Averill, Esther. *Jenny's adopted brothers*
Aylesworth, Jim. *Mary's mirror*
Bach, Alice. *Millicent the magnificent*
Baker, Charlotte. *Little brother*
Beim, Jerrold. *Country mailman*
Buck, Pearl S. (Pearl Sydenstricker). *The Chinese story teller*
Bunting, Eve. *Monkey in the middle*
Burningham, John. *Humbert, Mister Firkin and the Lord Mayor of London*
Caines, Jeannette. *I need a lunch box*
Carlson, Nancy. *Poor Carl*
Castle, Caroline. *Herbert Binns and the flying tricycle*
Cole, Joanna. *The new baby at your house*
Conford, Ellen. *Why can't I be William?*
Corey, Dorothy. *Will it ever be my birthday?*
Cretan, Gladys Yessayan. *Lobo and Brewster*
Doherty, Berlie. *Paddiwak and cozy*
Drescher, Joan. *My mother's getting married*
Eriksson, Eva. *Jealousy*
Ferguson, Alane. *That new pet!*
Gantos, Jack. *Rotten Ralph's rotten Christmas*
Ganz, Yaffa. *The story of Mimmy and Simmy*
Gill, Joan. *Hush, Jon!*
Gordon, Shirley. *Happy birthday, Crystal*
Graham, Margaret Bloy. *Benjy and the barking bird*

Greenfield, Eloise. *She come bringing me that little baby girl*
Grimm, Jacob. *Snow White*, ill. by Trina Schart Hyman
Snow White, ill. by Bernadette Watts
Snow White and the seven dwarfs, ill. by Chihiro Iwasaki
Hathorn, Libby. *Freya's fantastic surprise*
Hazen, Barbara Shook. *Why couldn't I be an only kid like you, Wigger?*
Hedderwick, Mairi. *Katie Morag and the tiresome Ted*
Hoban, Russell. *A baby sister for Frances*
A birthday for Frances
Howe, James. *I wish I were a butterfly*
Jenkin-Pearce, Susie. *Bad Boris and the new kitten*
Kellogg, Steven. *Best friends*
Levine, Abby. *Sometimes I wish I were Mindy*
Lindgren, Astrid. *I want a brother or sister*
Lionni, Leo. *Alexander and the wind-up mouse*
McLenighan, Valjean. *You can go jump*
Manushkin, Fran. *Little rabbit's baby brother*
Mayer, Mercer. *One frog too many*
Miller, Warren. *The goings on at Little Wishful*
O'Connor, Jane. *Lulu goes to witch school*
Ormondroyd, Edward. *Theodore's rival*
Osborn, Lois. *My dad is really something*
Peet, Bill. *The luckiest one of all*
Schick, Eleanor. *Peggy's new brother*
Shyer, Marlene Fanta. *Stepdog*
Skorpen, Liesel Moak. *His mother's dog*
Velthuijs, Max. *Little Man to the rescue*
Vigna, Judith. *Couldn't we have a turtle instead?*
Waber, Bernard. *Lyle and the birthday party*
Walt Disney Productions. *Walt Disney's Snow White and the seven dwarfs*
Watson, Jane Werner. *Sometimes I'm jealous*
Zemach, Margot. *To Hilda for helping*
Zolotow, Charlotte. *It's not fair*

Emotions – fear

Alexander, Anne. *Noise in the night*
Alexander, Martha G. *I'll protect you from the jungle beasts*
Maybe a monster
Alexander, Sue. *Witch, Goblin and sometimes Ghost*
Anrooy, Frans van. *The sea horse*
Aseltine, Lorraine. *I'm deaf and it's okay*
Aylesworth, Jim. *Siren in the night*
Two terrible frights
Babbitt, Natalie. *The something*
Bannon, Laura. *Little people of the night*
The scary thing

Barton, Byron. *Harry is a scaredy-cat*
Benedek, Elissa P. *The secret worry*
Berenstain, Stan. *The Berenstain bears learn about strangers*
Bergström, Gunilla. *Who's scaring Alfie Atkins?*
Blegvad, Lenore. *Anna Banana and me*
Bonsall, Crosby Newell. *Who's afraid of the dark?*
Bourgeois, Paulette. *Franklin in the dark*
Brenner, Anita. *A hero by mistake*
Brown, Margaret Wise. *Night and day*
Bunting, Eve. *Ghost's hour, spook's hour*
  Terrible things
Byfield, Barbara Ninde. *The haunted churchbell*
Caines, Jeannette. *Chilly stomach*
Cameron, Ann. *Harry (the monster)*
Carlson, Nancy. *Harriet's recital*
  Witch lady
Carrick, Carol. *Dark and full of secrets*
Chorao, Kay. *Lester's overnight*
Clifton, Lucille. *Amifika*
Cohen, Miriam. *Jim meets the thing*
Coles, Alison. *Michael and the sea*
  Michael in the dark
  Michael's first day
Company González, Mercè. *Killian and the dragons*
Conford, Ellen. *Eugene the brave*
Credle, Ellis. *Big fraid, little fraid*
Crowe, Robert L. *Clyde monster*
Cunningham, Julia. *A mouse called Junction*
Devlin, Wende. *Aunt Agatha, there's a lion under the couch!*
Dinardo, Jeffrey. *Timothy and the night noises*
Dodd, Lynley. *Hairy Maclary from Donaldson's dairy*
Erickson, Karen. *It's dark*
Freschet, Berniece. *Furlie Cat*
Gackenbach, Dick. *Harry and the terrible whatzit*
Gay, Zhenya. *Who's afraid?*
Gikow, Louise. *Boober Fraggle's ghosts*
Girard, Linda Walvoord. *Jeremy's first haircut*
Goode, Diane. *I hear a noise*
Goodenow, Earle. *The owl who hated the dark*
Graham, Margaret Bloy. *Benjy and his friend Fifi*
Grant, Joan. *The monster that grew small*
Greenberg, Barbara. *The bravest babysitter*
Gretz, Susanna. *Hide-and-seek*
  Too dark!
Grifalconi, Ann. *Darkness and the butterfly*
Hall, Derek. *Otter swims*
  Panda climbs
  Tiger runs

Hamilton, Morse. *Who's afraid of the dark?*
Hanlon, Emily. *What if a lion eats me and I fall into a hippopotamus' mud hole?*
Hanson, Joan. *I won't be afraid*
Harlow, Joan Hiatt. *Shadow bear*
Hawkins, Colin. *Snap! Snap!*
Hazen, Barbara Shook. *Fang*
  The knight who was afraid of the dark
Hill, Susan. *Go away, bad dreams!*
Hoban, Russell. *Goodnight*
Howe, James. *There's a monster under my bed*
Impey, Rose. *The flat man*
  Scare yourself to sleep
Jonas, Ann. *Holes and peeks*
Joosse, Barbara M. *Spiders in the fruit cellar*
Keller, Beverly. *Pimm's place*
Kitamura, Satoshi. *Lily takes a walk*
Klinting, Lars. *Regal the golden eagle*
Kraus, Robert. *Noel the coward*
Lakin, Patricia. *Don't touch my room*
Leaf, Munro. *Boo, who used to be scared of the dark*
Lifton, Betty Jean. *Goodnight orange monster*
Low, Joseph. *Benny rabbit and the owl*
  Boo to a goose
Martin, Jacqueline Briggs. *Bizzy Bones and Uncle Ezra*
Mayer, Mercer. *There's a nightmare in my closet*
  There's an alligator under my bed
  There's something in my attic
  You're the scaredy cat
Moore, Lilian. *Little Raccoon and the thing in the pool*
Nash, Ogden. *The adventures of Isabel*
Pittman, Helena Clare. *Once when I was scared*
Pizer, Abigail. *Nosey Gilbert*
Pryor, Bonnie. *The porcupine mouse*
Reed, Jonathan. *Do armadillos come in houses?*
Robison, Deborah. *No elephants allowed*
Rodgers, Frank. *Who's afraid of the ghost train?*
Ross, Pat. *Your first airplane trip*
Ross, Tony. *I'm coming to get you!*
Schertle, Alice. *The gorilla in the hall*
Scruton, Clive. *Scaredy cat*
Seuss, Dr. *The Sneetches, and other stories*
Sharmat, Marjorie Weinman. *Frizzy the fearful*
Shortall, Leonard W. *Tony's first dive*
Smith, Janice Lee. *The monster in the third dresser drawer and other stories about Adam Joshua*
Stein, Sara Bonnett. *About phobias*
Stevenson, Drew. *The ballad of Penelope Lou...and me*

Stevenson, James. *What's under my bed?*
Strand, Mark. *The night book*
Stubbs, Joanna. *With cat's eyes you'll never be scared of the dark*
Szilagyi, Mary. *Thunderstorm*
Taylor, Anelise. *Lights on, lights off*
Tompert, Ann. *Will you come back for me?*
Townson, Hazel. *Terrible Tuesday*
Trez, Denise. *The royal hiccups*
Turkle, Brinton. *It's only Arnold*
Udry, Janice May. *Alfred*
Vigna, Judith. *Nobody wants a nuclear war*
Viorst, Judith. *My mama says there aren't any zombies, ghosts, vampires, creatures, demons, monsters, fiends, goblins, or things*
Vogel, Ilse-Margaret. *The don't be scared book*
Wallace, Ian. *Chin Chiang and the dragon's dance*
Watson, Jane Werner. *Sometimes I'm afraid*
Williams, Gweneira Maureen. *Timid Timothy, the kitten who learned to be brave*
Williams, Linda. *The little old lady who was not afraid of anything*
Willis, Jeanne. *The monster bed*
Winthrop, Elizabeth. *Potbellied possums*
Wolf, Bernard. *Michael and the dentist*
Wondriska, William. *The stop*
Zolotow, Charlotte. *The storm book*

Emotions – happiness

Asch, George. *Linda*
Bradbury, Bianca. *Mutt*
Corrigan, Kathy. *Emily Umily*
Low, Joseph. *The Christmas grump*
McCrea, James. *The magic tree*
Piatti, Celestino. *The happy owls*
Rice, Eve. *What Sadie sang*
Steig, William. *Spinky sulks*
Tapio, Pat Decker. *The lady who saw the good side of everything*
Tobias, Tobi. *Jane wishing*
Tripp, Paul. *The strawman who smiled by mistake*
Williams, Barbara. *Someday, said Mitchell*
Wondriska, William. *Mr. Brown and Mr. Gray*
Yabuki, Seiji. *I love the morning*

Emotions – hate

Brunhoff, Laurent de. *The one pig with horns*
Udry, Janice May. *Let's be enemies*
Zolotow, Charlotte. *The hating book*

Emotions – jealousy *see* Emotions – envy, jealousy; Sibling rivalry

Emotions – loneliness

Alexander, Sue. *Dear Phoebe*
Aliki. *We are best friends*
Ardizzone, Edward. *Lucy Brown and Mr. Grimes*
Austin, Margot. *Growl Bear*
Battles, Edith. *One to teeter-totter*
Blegvad, Lenore. *Mr. Jensen and cat*
Bolliger, Max. *The lonely prince*
Brett, Jan. *Annie and the wild animals*
Bröger, Achim. *Francie's paper puppy*
Brown, Marcia. *The little carousel*
Buck, Pearl S. (Pearl Sydenstricker). *The little fox in the middle*
Buntain, Ruth Jaeger. *The birthday story*
Chenault, Nell. *Parsifal the Poddley*
Chess, Victoria. *Poor Esmé*
Clewes, Dorothy. *Happiest day*
Coatsworth, Elizabeth. *Lonely Maria*
Conaway, Judith. *I'll get even*
Conger, Marion. *The chipmunk that went to church*
Coontz, Otto. *The quiet house*
Craven, Carolyn. *What the mailman brought*
Cummings, W. T. (Walter Thies). *The kid*
Delton, Judy. *My grandma's in a nursing home*
Duvoisin, Roger Antoine. *Periwinkle*
Ellis, Anne Leo. *Dabble Duck*
Fatio, Louise. *The happy lion roars*
Fujikawa, Gyo. *Shags finds a kitten*
Funazaki, Yasuko. *Baby owl*
Gág, Wanda. *Nothing at all*
Goffstein, M. B. (Marilyn Brooke). *Goldie the dollmaker*
    Neighbors
Harranth, Wolf. *My old grandad*
Hughes, Shirley. *Moving Molly*
Keats, Ezra Jack. *The trip*
Kesselman, Wendy. *Angelita*
    Emma
Lukešová, Milena. *The little girl and the rain*
Luttrell, Ida. *Lonesome Lester*
McClure, Gillian. *What's the time, Rory Wolf?*
McGovern, Ann. *Mr. Skinner's skinny house*
    Nicholas Bentley Stoningpot III
McNeer, May Yonge. *My friend Mac*
Munthe, Adam John. *I believe in unicorns*
Murphy, Shirley Rousseau. *Valentine for a dragon*
Norton, Natalie. *A little old man*
Park, W. B. *The costume party*
Sarton, May. *Punch's secret*
Schick, Eleanor. *Home alone*
Seignobosc, Françoise. *The story of Colette*
Siekkinen, Raija. *Mister King*
Skurzynski, Gloria. *Martin by himself*
Slate, Joseph. *Lonely Lula cat*

Smith, Wendy. *The lonely, only mouse*
Sonneborn, Ruth A. *Lollipop's party*
Spang, Günter. *Clelia and the little mermaid*
Stage, Mads. *The lonely squirrel*
Stanek, Muriel. *All alone after school*
Stevenson, James. *The bear who had no place to go*
Stren, Patti. *Hug me*
Sugita, Yutaka. *Helena the unhappy hippopotamus*
Surany, Anico. *Kati and Kormos*
Titherington, Jeanne. *A place for Ben*
Walter, Mildred Pitts. *My mama needs me*
Yashima, Tarō. *Crow boy*
Zindel, Paul. *I love my mother*
Zolotow, Charlotte. *Janey*
  Three funny friends
  A tiger called Thomas, ill. by Catherine Stock
  A tiger called Thomas, ill. by Kurt Werth

Emotions – love

Agostinelli, Maria Enrica. *On wings of love*
Alexander, Sue. *Dear Phoebe*
  Nadia the willful
Andersen, H. C. (Hans Christian). *The snow queen*, ill. by Angela Barrett
  The snow queen, ill. by Toma Bogdanovic
  The snow queen, ill. by June Atkin Corwin
  The snow queen, ill. by Susan Jeffers
  The snow queen, ill. by Errol Le Cain
  The snow queen, ill. by Arieh Zeldich
Anglund, Joan Walsh. *Love is a special way of feeling*
Bianco, Margery Williams. *The velveteen rabbit*, ill. by Allen Atkinson
  The velveteen rabbit, ill. by Michael Green
  The velveteen rabbit, ill. by Michael Hague
  The velveteen rabbit, ill. by David Jorgensen
  The velveteen rabbit, ill. by William Nicholson
  The velveteen rabbit, ill. by Ilse Plume
  The velveteen rabbit, ill. by S. D. Schindler
  The velveteen rabbit, ill. by Tien
Billam, Rosemary. *Fuzzy rabbit*
Boegehold, Betty. *Pawpaw's run*
Boyle, Vere. *Beauty and the beast*
Brown, Palmer. *Something for Christmas*
Buckley, Helen Elizabeth. *Grandmother and I*
Carter, Anne. *Beauty and the beast*, ill. by Binette Schroeder
Clifton, Lucille. *Everett Anderson's goodbye*
De Paola, Tomie. *Helga's dowry*
Dragonwagon, Crescent. *Wind Rose*
Dyke, John. *Pigwig*
Estes, Eleanor. *A little oven*
Fatio, Louise. *The happy lion's treasure*
Flack, Marjorie. *Ask Mr. Bear*

Freedman, Florence B. *Brothers*
Freeman, Don. *Corduroy*
Gerstein, Mordicai. *Prince Sparrow*
Girard, Linda Walvoord. *At Daddy's on Saturdays*
Glass, Andrew. *Chickpea and the talking cow*
Hazen, Barbara Shook. *Even if I did something awful*
Hoopes, Lyn Littlefield. *When I was little*
Jenkins, Jordan. *Learning about love*
Jewell, Nancy. *The snuggle bunny*
Kočí, Marta. *Sarah's bear*
Krauss, Ruth. *Big and little*
Lasky, Kathryn. *I have four names for my grandfather*
Lexau, Joan M. *A house so big*
McPhail, David. *Sisters*
Marshall, Edward. *Fox in love*
Martin, Bill (William Ivan). *Knots on a counting rope*
Mayer, Marianna. *Beauty and the beast*
Mayer, Mercer. *Just for you*
  Whinnie the lovesick dragon
Mayne, William. *The patchwork cat*
Miles, Betty. *Around and around... love*
Mizumura, Kazue. *If I were a cricket...*
Naylor, Phyllis Reynolds. *The baby, the bed, and the rose*
Nesbit, Edith. *Beauty and the beast*, ill. by Julia Christie
Neumeyer, Peter F. *The phantom of the opera*
Newton, Laura P. *Me and my aunts*
Otsuka, Yuzo. *Suho and the white horse*
Paterson, Diane. *Wretched Rachel*
Reinl, Edda. *The little snake*
Rohmer, Harriet. *Mother scorpion country*
Rowand, Phyllis. *Every day in the year*
Samuels, Barbara. *Faye and Dolores*
Scott, Ann Herbert. *On mother's lap*
Shecter, Ben. *If I had a ship*
Springstubb, Tricia. *My Minnie is a jewel*
Steig, William. *Tiffky Doofky*
Tudor, Tasha. *Miss Kiss and the nasty beast*
Vaës, Alain. *The porcelain pepper pot*
Wahl, Jan. *Old Hippo's Easter egg*
Zalben, Jane Breskin. *A perfect nose for Ralph*
Zindel, Paul. *I love my mother*
Zola, Meguido. *Only the best*
Zolotow, Charlotte. *Do you know what I'll do?*
  May I visit?
  A rose, a bridge, and a wild black horse
  Say it!
  The sky was blue

Emotions – sadness

Alexander, Sue. *Nadia the willful*

Allen, Frances Charlotte. *Little hippo*
Baker, Betty. *Rat is dead and ant is sad*
Bartoli, Jennifer. *Nonna*
Delton, Judy. *I'll never love anything ever again*
De Paola, Tomie. *Nana upstairs and Nana downstairs*
Deveaux, Alexis. *Na-ni*
Kaldhol, Marit. *Goodbye Rune*
Lindgren, Astrid. *My nightingale is singing*
Low, Joseph. *The Christmas grump*
McLerran, Alice. *The mountain that loved a bird*
Sharmat, Marjorie Weinman. *I don't care*
Sugita, Yutaka. *Helena the unhappy hippopotamus*
Wolff, Ashley. *The bells of London*

Emotions – unhappiness *see* Emotions – happiness; Emotions – sadness

Emperors *see* Royalty

Endangered animals *see* Animals – endangered animals

Engineered books *see* Format, unusual – toy and movable books

England *see* Foreign lands – England

Entertainment *see* Theater

Envy *see* Emotions – envy, jealousy; Sibling rivalry

Eskimos

Andrews, Jan. *Very last first time*
Beim, Lorraine. *The little igloo*
Damjan, Mischa. *Atuk*
DeArmond, Dale. *The seal oil lamp*
Harlow, Joan Hiatt. *Shadow bear*
Hopkins, Marjorie. *Three visitors*
Houston, James. *Kiviok's magic journey*
Machetanz, Sara. *A puppy named Gia*
Morrow, Suzanne Stark. *Inatuck's friend*
Parish, Peggy. *Ootah's lucky day*
San Souci, Robert D. *Song of Sedna*
Scott, Ann Herbert. *On mother's lap*
Steiner, Barbara. *The whale brother*
Wiesenthal, Eleanor. *Let's find out about Eskimos*

Ethnic groups in the U.S.

Belpré, Pura. *Santiago*
Bettinger, Craig. *Follow me, everybody*
Blue, Rose. *I am here: Yo estoy aqui*
Brenner, Barbara. *Faces, faces, faces*
Caseley, Judith. *Apple pie and onions*
Clifford, Eth. *Your face is a picture*

Cohen, Miriam. *Will I have a friend?*
Crume, Marion W. *Listen!*
Fisher, Iris L. *Katie-Bo*
Greene, Roberta. *Two and me makes three*
Hogan, Paula Z. *The hospital scares me*
Jaynes, Ruth M. *Benny's four hats*
    Friends! friends! friends!
    Tell me please! What's that?
    That's what it is!
    What is a birthday child?
Keats, Ezra Jack. *My dog is lost!*
Kesselman, Wendy. *Angelita*
Klein, Leonore. *Just like you*
Lansdown, Brenda. *Galumpf*
May, Julian. *Why people are different colors*
Merriam, Eve. *Boys and girls, girls and boys*
Merrill, Jean. *How many kids are hiding on my block?*
Paek, Min. *Aekyung's dream*
Reit, Seymour. *Round things everywhere*
Rosenberg, Maxine B. *Being adopted*
Simon, Norma. *What do I say?*
Sobol, Harriet Langsam. *We don't look like our mom and dad*
Solbert, Ronni. *I wrote my name on the wall*
Stanek, Muriel. *One, two, three for fun*
Udry, Janice May. *What Mary Jo shared*

Ethnic groups in the U.S. – Afro-Americans

Adoff, Arnold. *Big sister tells me that I'm black*
    Where wild Willie?
Alexander, Martha G. *Bobo's dream*
    The story grandmother told
Aliki. *A weed is a flower*
Bang, Molly. *Ten, nine, eight*
    Wiley and the hairy man
Beim, Jerrold. *The swimming hole*
Beim, Lorraine. *Two is a team*
Blue, Rose. *Black, black, beautiful black*
    How many blocks is the world?
Bonsall, Crosby Newell. *The case of the cat's meow*
    The case of the hungry stranger
Breinburg, Petronella. *Doctor Shawn*
    Shawn goes to school
    Shawn's red bike
Brenner, Barbara. *Wagon wheels*
Bryan, Ashley. *I'm going to sing*
Burch, Robert. *Joey's cat*
Caines, Jeannette. *Abby*
    Daddy
    Just us women
Calloway, Northern J. *Northern J. Calloway presents Super-vroomer!*
Carlstrom, Nancy White. *Wild wild sunflower child Anna*
Children go where I send thee

Clifton, Lucille. *All us come cross the water*
Amifika
The black B C's
The boy who didn't believe in spring
Don't you remember?
Everett Anderson's Christmas coming
Everett Anderson's friend
Everett Anderson's goodbye
Everett Anderson's nine months long
Everett Anderson's 1-2-3
Everett Anderson's year
My brother fine with me
My friend Jacob
Some of the days of Everett Anderson
Three wishes
Clymer, Eleanor Lowenton. *Horatio*
Cummings, Pat. *Jimmy Lee did it*
Dale, Penny. *You can't*
Dionetti, Michelle. *Thalia Brown and the blue bug*
Evans, Mari. *Singing black*
Fassler, Joan. *Don't worry dear*
Fife, Dale. *Adam's ABC*
Flournoy, Valerie. *The best time of day*
The patchwork quilt
The twins strike back
Fraser, Kathleen. *Adam's world, San Francisco*
Freeman, Don. *Corduroy*
A pocket for Corduroy
George, Jean Craighead. *The wentletrap trap*
Gill, Joan. *Hush, Jon!*
Giovanni, Nikki. *Spin a soft black song*
Gray, Genevieve. *Send Wendell*
Greenberg, Polly. *Oh, Lord, I wish I was a buzzard*
Greenfield, Eloise. *Daydreamers*
First pink light
Me and Nessie
She come bringing me that little baby girl
Grifalconi, Ann. *City rhythms*
Havill, Juanita. *Jamaica's find*
Hayes, Sarah. *Eat up, Gemma*
Happy Christmas, Gemma
Hill, Elizabeth Starr. *Evan's corner*
Hoffman, Phyllis. *Steffie and me*
Hogan, Paula Z. *The hospital scares me*
Hopkins, Lee Bennett. *I think I saw a snail*
Horvath, Betty F. *Hooray for Jasper*
Jasper and the hero business
Jasper makes music
Jensen, Virginia Allen. *Sara and the door*
Kaufman, Curt. *Hotel boy*
Keats, Ezra Jack. *Apartment 3*
Dreams
Goggles
Hi, cat!
John Henry
A letter to Amy
Louie

Pet show!
Peter's chair
Skates
The snowy day
The trip
Whistle for Willie
Kirn, Ann. *Beeswax catches a thief*
Lansdown, Brenda. *Galumpf*
Lester, Julius. *The knee-high man and other tales*
Lexau, Joan M. *Benjie*
Benjie on his own
I should have stayed in bed
Me day
The rooftop mystery
Lipkind, William. *Four-leaf clover*
Little, Lessie Jones. *Children of long ago*
McGovern, Ann. *Black is beautiful*
McKissack, Patricia C. *Flossie and the fox*
Mirandy and brother wind
Mayer, Mercer. *Liza Lou and the Yeller Belly Swamp*
Merriam, Eve. *Epaminondas*
Monjo, F. N. *The drinking gourd*
Nolan, Madeena Spray. *My daddy don't go to work*
Scott, Ann Herbert. *Big Cowboy Western*
Let's catch a monster
Sam
Selsam, Millicent E. *Tony's birds*
Sharmat, Marjorie Weinman. *I don't care*
Showers, Paul. *Look at your eyes*
Your skin and mine
Steptoe, John. *Birthday*
My special best words
Stevie
Uptown
Stolz, Mary Slattery. *Storm in the night*
Taylor, Sydney. *The dog who came to dinner*
Thomas, Ianthe. *Eliza's daddy*
Lordy, Aunt Hattie
Walk home tired, Billy Jenkins
Turner, Ann. *Nettie's trip south*
Udry, Janice May. *Mary Ann's mud day*
Mary Jo's grandmother
What Mary Jo shared
What Mary Jo wanted
Walker, Alice. *To hell with dying*
Walter, Mildred Pitts. *My mama needs me*
Williams, Vera B. *Cherries and cherry pits*
Williamson, Mel. *Walk on!*
Williamson, Stan. *The no-bark dog*
Wilson, Julia. *Becky*
Winter, Jeanette. *Follow the drinking gourd*
Yezback, Steven A. *Pumpkinseeds*
Zemach, Margot. *Jake and Honeybunch go to heaven*
Ziner, Feenie. *Counting carnival*

Ethnic groups in the U.S. – Black Americans *see* Ethnic groups in the U.S. – Afro-Americans

Ethnic groups in the U.S. – Chinese-Americans

Behrens, June. *Soo Ling finds a way*
Bunting, Eve. *The happy funeral*
Coerr, Eleanor. *Chang's paper pony*
McCunn, Ruthanne L. *Pie-Biter*
Politi, Leo. *Mr. Fong's toy shop*
  Moy Moy
Wallace, Ian. *Chin Chiang and the dragon's dance*

Ethnic groups in the U.S. – Eskimos *see* Eskimos

Ethnic groups in the U.S. – Indians *see* Indians of North America

Ethnic groups in the U.S. – Japanese-Americans

Copeland, Helen. *Meet Miki Takino*
Hawkinson, Lucy. *Dance, dance, Amy-Chan!*
Politi, Leo. *Mieko*
Yashima, Mitsu. *Momo's kitten*
Yashima, Tarō. *Umbrella*
  The youngest one

Ethnic groups in the U.S. – Mexican-Americans

Adams, Ruth Joyce. *Fidelia*
Behrens, June. *Fiesta!*
Bolognese, Don. *A new day*
Brown, Tricia. *Hello, amigos!*
Ets, Marie Hall. *Bad boy, good boy*
  Gilberto and the wind
  Nine days to Christmas
Felt, Sue. *Rosa-too-little*
Fife, Dale. *Rosa's special garden*
Fraser, James Howard. *Los Posadas*
Garrett, Helen. *Angelo the naughty one*
Hitte, Kathryn. *Mexicallie soup*
Jaynes, Ruth M. *Melinda's Christmas stocking*
  Tell me please! What's that?
  That's what it is!
  What is a birthday child?
Molnar, Joe. *Graciela*
Ormsby, Virginia H. *Twenty-one children plus ten*
Politi, Leo. *Juanita*
  The mission bell
  Pedro, the angel of Olvera Street
  Song of the swallows
Serfozo, Mary. *Welcome Roberto!*
  Bienvenido, Roberto!

Taha, Karen T. *A gift for Tia Rose*

Ethnic groups in the U.S. – Puerto Rican-Americans

Belpré, Pura. *Santiago*
Blue, Rose. *I am here: Yo estoy aqui*
Bowden, Joan Chase. *Emilio's summer day*
Keats, Ezra Jack. *My dog is lost!*
Kesselman, Wendy. *Angelita*
Simon, Norma. *What do I do?*
  What do I say?
Sonneborn, Ruth A. *Friday night is papa night*
  Lollipop's party
  Seven in a bed

Ethnic groups in the U.S. – Vietnamese-Americans

Surat, Michele Maria. *Angel child, dragon child*

Etiquette

Ackley, Edith Flack. *Please*
  Thank you
Anastasio, Dina. *Pass the peas, please*
Behrens, June. *The manners book*
Berenstain, Stan. *The Berenstain bears forget their manners*
Betz, Betty. *Manners for moppets*
Brown, Marc. *Perfect pigs*
Brown, Myra Berry. *Company's coming for dinner*
Charles, Donald. *Shaggy dog's birthday*
Cole, Joanna. *Monster manners*
Demuth, Patricia Brennan. *Max, the bad-talking parrot*
Duvoisin, Roger Antoine. *Periwinkle*
Gardner, Martin. *Never make fun of a turtle, my son*
Gordon, Margaret. *Wilberforce goes to a party*
Hawkins, Colin. *Max and the magic word*
Hoban, Russell. *Dinner at Alberta's*
  The little Brute family
Jefferds, Vincent. *Disney's elegant book of manners*
Joslin, Sesyle. *Dear dragon*
  What do you do, dear?
  What do you say, dear?
Keenan, Martha. *The mannerly adventures of Little Mouse*
Keller, Irene. *The Thingumajig book of manners*
Keller, John G. *Krispin's fair*
Leaf, Munro. *A flock of watchbirds*
  How to behave and why
  Manners can be fun
Lexau, Joan M. *Cathy is company*
Myller, Lois. *No! No!*

Parish, Peggy. *Mind your manners*
Petersham, Maud. *The circus baby*
Polhamus, Jean Burt. *Dinosaur do's and don'ts*
Potter, Beatrix. *The sly old cat*
Quackenbush, Robert M. *I don't want to go, I don't know how to act*
Scarry, Richard. *Richard Scarry's please and thank you book*
Seignobosc, Françoise. *The thank-you book*
Sherman, Ivan. *I do not like it when my friend comes to visit*
Slobodkin, Louis. *Thank you - you're welcome*
Smaridge, Norah. *You know better than that*
Stover, Jo Ann. *If everybody did*
Weiss, Ellen. *Telephone time*

Europe *see* Foreign lands – Europe

Evening *see* Twilight

Experiments *see* Science

Eye glasses *see* Glasses

Eyes *see* Anatomy

Fables *see* Folk and fairy tales

Faces *see* Anatomy

Fairies

Alden, Laura. *Learning about fairies*
Anderson, Lonzo. *Two hundred rabbits*
Barker, Cicely Mary. *Berry flower fairies*
  Blossom flower fairies
  Flower fairies of the seasons
  Spring flower fairies
  Summer flower fairies
Bate, Lucy. *Little rabbit's loose tooth*
Beim, Lorraine. *Sasha and the samovar*
Boujon, Claude. *The fairy with the long nose*
Coombs, Patricia. *Lisa and the grompet*
Elves, fairies and gnomes
Enright, Elizabeth. *Zeee*
Fairy poems for the very young
Fujikawa, Gyo. *Come follow me...to the secret world of elves and fairies and gnomes and trolls*
Fyleman, Rose. *A fairy went a-marketing*

Gardner, Mercedes. *Scooter and the magic star*
Griffith, Helen V. *Nata*
Gunther, Louise. *A tooth for the tooth fairy*
Hoffmann, E. T. A. *The nutcracker*, ill. by Rachel Isadora
  The nutcracker, ill. by Maurice Sendak
Hollyn, Lynn. *Lynn Hollyn's Christmas toyland*
Jeschke, Susan. *Mia, Grandma and the genie*
Karlin, Nurit. *The tooth witch*
Kent, Jack. *Clotilda*
Kroll, Steven. *Loose tooth*
Lester, Helen. *The wizard, the fairy and the magic chicken*
MacDonald, George. *Little Daylight*
Mahy, Margaret. *Pillycock's shop*
Manson, Beverlie. *The fairies' alphabet book*
Mayne, William. *The green book of Hob stories*
  The red book of Hob stories
  The yellow book of Hob stories
Myers, Bernice. *Sidney Rella and the glass sneaker*
Newbolt, Henry John, Sir. *Rilloby-rill*
Sand, George. *The mysterious tale of Gentle Jack and Lord Bumblebee*
Waddell, Martin. *The tough princess*
Wallace, Daisy. *Fairy poems*
Wetterer, Margaret. *Patrick and the fairy thief*

Fairs

Baker, Jill. *Basil of Bywater Hollow*
Barker, Melvern J. *Country fair*
Baynton, Martin. *Fifty and the great race*
Bond, Michael. *Paddington at the fair*
Booth, Eugene. *At the fair*
Bourke, Linda. *Ethel's exceptional egg*
Brunhoff, Laurent de. *Babar's fair will be opened next Sunday*
Carrick, Carol. *The highest balloon on the common*
Chiefari, Janet. *Kids are baby goats*
Coombs, Patricia. *Dorrie and the Witchville fair*
Delton, Judy. *Penny wise, fun foolish*
Devlin, Wende. *Old Witch and the polka-dot ribbon*
Ets, Marie Hall. *Mr. Penny's race horse*
Gauch, Patricia Lee. *On to Widecombe Fair*
Hedderwick, Mairi. *Katie Morag and the two grandmothers*
Herriot, James. *Bonny's big day*
Hill, Eric. *Spot at the fair*
Hoff, Syd. *Henrietta goes to the fair*
Holabird, Katharine. *Angelina at the fair*
Leech, Jay. *Bright Fawn and me*
Miles, Miska. *Jump frog jump*

Schatell, Brian. *Farmer Goff and his turkey Sam*

Seignobosc, Françoise. *Jeanne-Marie at the fair*

Stevens, Janet. *Animal fair*

Tudor, Tasha. *Corgiville fair*

Watson, Clyde. *Tom Fox and the apple pie*

Watson, Nancy Dingman. *The birthday goat*
Widdecombe Fair

Wildsmith, Brian. *Carousel*

Fairy tales *see* Folk and fairy tales

Fall *see* Seasons — fall

Families *see* Family life

Family life

Abolafia, Yossi. *My three uncles*

Adoff, Arnold. *Big sister tells me that I'm black*
Black is brown is tan
Ma nDa La
Make a circle, keep us in

Ahlberg, Janet. *The baby's catalogue*
Peek-a-boo!

Aho, Jennifer J. *Learning about sex*

Aitken, Amy. *Wanda's circus*

Alexander, Martha G. *Even that moose won't listen to me*
I'll be the horse if you'll play with me
Marty McGee's space lab, no girls allowed

Alexander, Sue. *Dear Phoebe*
Nadia the willful

Aliki. *Jack and Jake*
June 7!
Keep your mouth closed, dear
Welcome, little baby

Allen, Laura Jean. *Ottie and the star*

Amoss, Berthe. *Tom in the middle*

Anderson, C. W. (Clarence Williams). *Billy and Blaze*

Anderson, Douglas. *Let's draw a story*

Anderson, Lonzo. *The day the hurricane happened*

Arbeit, Eleanor Werner. *Mrs. cat hides something*

Arkin, Alan. *Tony's hard work day*

Armitage, Ronda. *The bossing of Josie*
Don't forget, Matilda
One moonlit night

Arnstein, Helene S. *Billy and our new baby*

Arthur, Catherine. *My sister's silent world*

Asch, Frank. *Goodbye house*

Aulaire, Ingri Mortenson d'. *Children of the northlights*
Nils

Avery, Kay. *Wee willow whistle*

Ayer, Jacqueline. *A wish for little sister*

Aylesworth, Jim. *The bad dream*
Siren in the night

Babbitt, Lorraine. *Pink like the geranium*

Bach, Alice. *Millicent the magnificent*
The smartest bear and his brother Oliver

Baird, Anne. *Kiss, kiss*

Baisch, Cris. *When the lights went out*

Baker, Betty. *Little runner of the longhouse*
Sonny-Boy Sim

Baker, Charlotte. *Little brother*

Balet, Jan B. *The fence*
Five Rollatinis

Balzola, Asun. *Munia and the day things went wrong*

Banish, Roslyn. *I want to tell you about my baby.*
Let me tell you about my baby

Banks, Kate. *Alphabet soup*

Barbato, Juli. *From bed to bus*

Barbour, Karen. *Little Nino's pizzeria*

Bartoli, Jennifer. *Nonna*

Bascom, Joe. *Malcolm's job*

Battles, Edith. *One to teeter-totter*

Bawden, Nina. *Princess Alice*

Beatty, Hetty Burlingame. *Moorland pony*

Beckman, Kaj. *Lisa cannot sleep*

Beim, Jerrold. *Jay's big job*

Beim, Lorraine. *Lucky Pierre*

Bemelmans, Ludwig. *Quito express*
Sunshine

Benjamin, Alan. *A change of plans*

Bennett, Olivia. *A Turkish afternoon*

Benson, Ellen. *Philip's little sister*

Benton, Robert. *Little brother, no more*

Berenstain, Michael. *The dwarks*

Berenstain, Stan. *The Berenstain bears and the truth*
The Berenstain bears and too much TV
The Berenstain bears' Christmas tree
The Berenstain bears forget their manners
The Berenstain bears in the dark
The Berenstain bears learn about strangers
The Berenstain bears' moving day

Berger, Terry. *How does it feel when your parents get divorced?*

Bernheim, Marc. *In Africa*

Bettina (Bettina Ehrlich). *Of uncles and aunts*

Bible, Charles. *Jennifer's new chair*

Bishop, Claire Huchet. *The five Chinese brothers*

Blaine, Marge. *The terrible thing that happened at our house*

Blank, Joani. *A kid's first book about sex*

Blaustein, Muriel. *Bedtime, Zachary!*

Blue, Rose. *How many blocks is the world?*

Blume, Judy. *The one in the middle is the green kangaroo*
The Pain and The Great One

Boegehold, Betty. *Daddy doesn't live here anymore*

Bograd, Larry. *Felix in the attic*
Boholm-Olsson, Eva. *Tuan*
Bolliger, Max. *The fireflies*
  The golden apple
Bolognese, Don. *A new day*
Bond, Felicia. *Poinsettia and her family*
Bond, Michael. *Paddington's garden*
Bonners, Susan. *A penguin year*
Bonsall, Crosby Newell. *The day I had to play with my sister*
Boon, Emilie. *Belinda's balloon*
Bornstein, Ruth Lercher. *Of course a goat*
Bourgeois, Paulette. *Big Sarah's little boots*
Bradman, Tony. *Through my window*
  Wait and see
Brady, Susan. *Find my blanket*
Brandenberg, Franz. *Everyone ready?*
  It's not my fault
  Leo and Emily's zoo
  What's wrong with a van?
Brann, Esther. *A book for baby*
Brennan, Jan. *Born two-gether*
Brenner, Barbara. *The prince and the pink blanket*
Bright, Robert. *Georgie*
Brock, Emma Lillian. *Mr. Wren's house*
  A pet for Barbie
  A present for Auntie
Brooks, Robert B. *So that's how I was born*
Brothers, Aileen. *Sad Mrs. Sam Sack*
Brothers and sisters are like that!
Brown, Jeff. *Flat Stanley*
Brown, Marc. *Arthur's baby*
Brown, Myra Berry. *Pip camps out*
  Pip moves away
Brown, Tricia. *Hello, amigos!*
Bruna, Dick. *Miffy*
Buchanan, Heather S. *Emily Mouse saves the day*
Buck, Pearl S. (Pearl Sydenstricker). *The little fox in the middle*
Bunin, Catherine. *Is that your sister?*
Bunting, Eve. *The big red barn*
  Ghost's hour, spook's hour
Burch, Robert. *The hunting trip*
  Joey's cat
Burningham, John. *Avocado baby*
  Where's Julius?
Burns, Maurice. *Go ducks, go!*
Burstein, Fred. *Rebecca's nap*
Byars, Betsy Cromer. *Go and hush the baby*
Byrd, Robert. *Marcella was bored*
Byrne, David. *Stay up late*
Caines, Jeannette. *Abby*
  Chilly stomach
  I need a lunch box
Cairo, Shelley. *Our brother has Down's syndrome*
Calders, Pere. *Brush*
Cameron, Polly. *"I can't," said the ant*
Campbell, Wayne. *What a catastrophe!*

Caple, Kathy. *The purse*
Carlson, Nancy. *The perfect family*
Carlstrom, Nancy White. *Jesse Bear, what will you wear?*
Carmi, Giora. *And Shira imagined*
Caseley, Judith. *Silly baby*
Castiglia, Julie. *Jill the pill*
Cauley, Lorinda Bryan. *The new house*
Cazet, Denys. *Great-Uncle Felix*
  Sunday
Chaffin, Lillie D. *Tommy's big problem*
Chalmers, Mary. *Mr. Cat's wonderful surprise*
  Take a nap, Harry
Charlip, Remy. *Hooray for me!*
Chase, Catherine. *Pete, the wet pet*
Chevalier, Christa. *The little bear who forgot*
Chorao, Kay. *Lester's overnight*
Christenson, Larry. *The wonderful way that babies are made*
Clark, Ann Nolan. *In my mother's house*
Claverie, Jean. *Shopping*
Cleary, Beverly. *The growing-up feet*
  Janet's thingamajigs
Clifton, Lucille. *Amifika*
  Don't you remember?
  Everett Anderson's goodbye
  Everett Anderson's nine months long
  Everett Anderson's 1-2-3
  My brother fine with me
  Some of the days of Everett Anderson
Cole, Joanna. *How you were born*
  The new baby at your house
Cole, William. *Frances face-maker*
  That pest Jonathan
Collins, Pat L. *Taking care of Tucker*
Conford, Ellen. *Why can't I be William?*
Conta, Marcia Maher. *Feelings between brothers and sisters*
  Feelings between kids and parents
Cook, Bernadine. *Looking for Susie*
Coombs, Patricia. *Lisa and the grompet*
Cooney, Barbara. *Island boy*
Cornish, Sam. *Grandmother's pictures*
Craig, M. Jean. *The dragon in the clock box*
Credle, Ellis. *Down, down the mountain*
Cressey, James. *Fourteen rats and a rat-catcher*
Crompton, Margaret. *The house where Jack lives*
Crowley, Arthur. *The boogey man*
Curry, Nancy. *The littlest house*
Daniel, Doris Temple. *Pauline and the peacock*
De Angeli, Marguerite. *Yonie Wondernose*
Delton, Judy. *Brimhall comes to stay*
  It happened on Thursday
  My Uncle Nikos
Denison, Carol. *A part-time dog for Nick*
Dennis, Lynne. *Raymond Rabbit's early morning*

Denton, Kady MacDonald. *The picnic*
De Paola, Tomie. *The art lesson*
 The family Christmas tree book
 Katie, Kit and cousin Tom
 Too many Hopkins
De Regniers, Beatrice Schenk. *The giant story*
 A little house of your own
Dragonwagon, Crescent. *Diana, maybe*
 Rainy day together
Drescher, Joan. *I'm in charge!*
 The marvelous mess
 Your family, my family
Duke, Kate. *Bedtime*
 Clean-up day
 The playground
 What bounces?
Edwards, Patricia Kier. *Chester and Uncle Willoughby*
Ehrlich, Amy. *Bunnies at Christmastime*
 Bunnies on their own
 Zeek Silver Moon
Elzbieta. *Brave Babette and sly Tom*
 Dikou and the mysterious moon sheep
Escudie, René. *Paul and Sebastian*
Ets, Marie Hall. *Bad boy, good boy*
Factor, Jane. *Summer*
Fassler, Joan. *One little girl*
Felt, Sue. *Rosa-too-little*
Fenton, Edward. *Fierce John*
Fisher, Aileen. *In one door and out the other*
Flack, Marjorie. *The new pet*
 Wait for William
Fleisher, Robbin. *Quilts in the attic*
Florian, Douglas. *A summer day*
Flournoy, Valerie. *The best time of day*
 The twins strike back
Foreman, Michael. *Ben's baby*
Fox, Charles Philip. *Mr. Stripes the gopher*
Fraser, Kathleen. *Adam's world, San Francisco*
Freudberg, Judy. *Susan and Gordon adopt a baby*
Friedman, Estelle. *Boy who lived in a cave*
Friedman, Ina R. *How my parents learned to eat*
Galbraith, Kathryn Osebold. *Katie did!*
 Waiting for Jennifer
Galdone, Paul. *Obedient Jack*
Ganly, Helen. *Jyoti's journey*
Gantos, Jack. *Aunt Bernice*
Garland, Sarah. *Going shopping*
 Having a picnic
Gauch, Patricia Lee. *Christina Katerina and the time she quit the family*
Gay, Marie-Louise. *Rainy day magic*
Gill, Joan. *Hush, Jon!*
Girard, Linda Walvoord. *Adoption is for always*
 At Daddy's on Saturdays

Glass, Andrew. *Chickpea and the talking cow*
Gobhai, Mehlli. *Usha, the mouse-maiden*
Goffstein, M. B. (Marilyn Brooke). *Family scrapbook*
 Our prairie home
 Our snowman
Goldman, Susan. *Cousins are special*
Goudey, Alice E. *The day we saw the sun come up*
Graham, Bob. *First there was Frances*
 The wild
Graham, Thomas. *Mr. Bear's chair*
Graves, Robert. *The big green book*
Gray, Catherine. *Tammy and the gigantic fish*
Gray, Genevieve. *Send Wendell*
Gray, Nigel. *It'll all come out in the wash*
Greaves, Margaret. *Little Bear and the Papagini circus*
Green, Phyllis. *Uncle Roland, the perfect guest*
Greenfield, Eloise. *Me and Nessie*
Griffith, Helen V. *Mine will, said John*
Gruenberg, Sidonie Matsner. *The wonderful story of how you were born*
Hague, Kathleen. *The man who kept house*
Hale, Kathleen. *Orlando and the water cats*
Hall, Derek. *Elephant bathes*
 Gorilla builds
 Polar bear leaps
Hamilton-Merritt, Jane. *Our new baby*
Harper, Anita. *It's not fair!*
Harris, Robie H. *Don't forget to come back*
 Hot Henry
 Messy Jessie
Harvey, Brett. *Immigrant girl*
Hautzig, Esther. *At home*
Hayes, Sarah. *Happy Christmas, Gemma*
Hazelton, Elizabeth Baldwin. *Sammy, the crow who remembered*
Hazen, Barbara Shook. *Even if I did something awful*
 Tight times
Hedderwick, Mairi. *Katie Morag and the big boy cousins*
Heide, Florence Parry. *The shrinking of Treehorn*
 Treehorn's treasure
Heller, Linda. *Lily at the table*
Heller, Nicholas. *The monster in the cave*
Helmering, Doris Wild. *We're going to have a baby*
Hendershot, Judith. *In coal country*
Hendrickson, Karen. *Baby and I can play*
 Fun with toddlers
Henkes, Kevin. *Bailey goes camping*
Hess, Edith. *Peter and Susie find a family*
Hest, Amy. *The purple coat*
Hickman, Martha Whitmore. *When can daddy come home?*

Hill, Elizabeth Starr. *Evan's corner*
Hill, Eric. *At home*
  Spot goes to the beach
Hill, Susan. *Go away, bad dreams!*
Hines, Anna Grossnickle. *Daddy makes the best spaghetti*
Hirsh, Marilyn. *The pink suit*
Hitte, Kathryn. *Mexicallie soup*
Hoban, Julia. *Amy loves the sun*
Hoban, Lillian. *Arthur's prize reader*
  Mr. Pig and family
Hoban, Russell. *A baby sister for Frances*
  Harvey's hideout
  They came from Aargh!
Hobson, Laura Z. *"I'm going to have a baby!"*
Hoff, Syd. *My Aunt Rosie*
Hoffman, Phyllis. *Steffie and me*
Hoffman, Rosekrans. *Sister Sweet Ella*
Hoffmann, E. T. A. *The strange child*
Hoke, Helen L. *The biggest family in the town*
Holland, Viki. *We are having a baby*
Hooker, Ruth. *At Grandma and Grandpa's house*
  Sara loves her big brother
Hoopes, Lyn Littlefield. *Daddy's coming home*
  Mommy, daddy, me
Hopkins, Margaret. *Sleepytime for baby mouse*
Horvath, Betty F. *Be nice to Josephine*
Houston, Gloria. *The year of the perfect Christmas tree*
Hughes, Shirley. *Bathwater's hot*
  David and dog
  Dogger
  An evening at Alfie's
  Lucy and Tom's A.B.C.
  Lucy and Tom's Christmas
  Lucy and Tom's 1, 2, 3
  Moving Molly
  Noisy
  Out and about
  When we went to the park
Hurd, Edith Thacher. *The mother kangaroo*
Hutchins, Pat. *The doorbell rang*
  Titch
  You'll soon grow into them, Titch
Ichikawa, Satomi. *Suzanne and Nicholas at the market*
  Suzette and Nicholas in the garden
Ionesco, Eugene. *Story number 1*
Isadora, Rachel. *I hear*
  I see
Iwasaki, Chihiro. *Staying home alone on a rainy day*
Jack Sprat. *The life of Jack Sprat, his wife and his cat*
Jarrell, Mary. *The knee baby*
Jewell, Nancy. *Time for Uncle Joe*

Johnston, Tony. *The quilt story*
Jones, Penelope. *I'm not moving!*
Joosse, Barbara M. *Jam day*
Jordan, June. *Kimako's story*
Joyce, William. *George shrinks*
Jukes, Mavis. *Like Jake and me*
Kaufman, Curt. *Hotel boy*
Keats, Ezra Jack. *Apartment 3*
  Louie's search
  Peter's chair
Keller, Holly. *A bear for Christmas*
  Cromwell's glasses
  Geraldine's blanket
Kelley, Anne. *Daisy's discovery*
Kellogg, Steven. *Can I keep him?*
Kent, Jack. *Joey runs away*
Kerr, Judith. *Mog and bunny*
Kessler, Leonard P. *Are we lost, daddy?*
Khalsa, Dayal Kaur. *I want a dog*
  My family vacation
Killingback, Julia. *Monday is washing day*
  What time is it, Mrs. Bear?
Kilroy, Sally. *What a week!*
Koch, Dorothy Clarke. *I play at the beach*
Krasilovsky, Phyllis. *The very little boy*
  The very little girl
  The very tall little girl
Kraus, Robert. *Another mouse to feed*
  Big brother
  Phil the ventriloquist
Krauss, Ruth. *The backward day*
Krementz, Jill. *Benjy goes to a restaurant*
  Jack goes to the beach
  Lily goes to the playground
  Taryn goes to the dentist
Krensky, Stephen. *Lionel at large*
Kroll, Steven. *Happy Mother's Day*
Kunhardt, Edith. *Where's Peter?*
Lakin, Patricia. *Don't touch my room*
  Oh, brother!
Lampert, Emily. *A little touch of monster*
Lapsley, Susan. *I am adopted*
Lasker, Joe. *He's my brother*
Lawson, Robert. *They were strong and good*
Layton, Aviva. *The squeakers*
Leiner, Katherine. *Both my parents work*
Lenski, Lois. *At our house*
  Debbie and her family
  The little family
  Papa Small
Levine, Abby. *You push, I ride*
Levinson, Riki. *I go with my family to Grandma's*
  Our home is the sea
  Touch! Touch!
  Watch the stars come out
Levoy, Myron. *The Hanukkah of Great-Uncle Otto*
Lewin, Hugh. *Jafta*
  Jafta and the wedding

Lexau, Joan M. *Benjie*
Every day a dragon
Finders keepers, losers weepers
Me day
Lindman, Maj. *Flicka, Ricka, Dicka and a
little dog*
Flicka, Ricka, Dicka and the big red hen
*Flicka, Ricka, Dicka and the new dotted
dress*
Flicka, Ricka, Dicka and the three kittens
Flicka, Ricka, Dicka bake a cake
Snipp, Snapp, Snurr and the buttered bread
Snipp, Snapp, Snurr and the magic horse
Snipp, Snapp, Snurr and the red shoes
Snipp, Snapp, Snurr and the reindeer
Snipp, Snapp, Snurr and the seven dogs
Snipp, Snapp, Snurr and the yellow sled
Lisker, Sonia O. *Two special cards*
Livingston, Carole. *"Why was I adopted?"*
Lobel, Arnold. *Uncle Elephant*
Lydon, Kerry Raines. *A birthday for Blue*
McCloskey, Robert. *Blueberries for Sal*
One morning in Maine
McConnachie, Brian. *Lily of the forest*
McGinley, Phyllis. *Lucy McLockett*
MacGregor, Marilyn. *Helen the hungry bear*
Mack, Gail. *Yesterday's snowman*
MacKay, Jed. *The big secret*
McKee, David. *Snow woman*
McKissack, Patricia C. *Nettie Jo's friends*
MacLachlan, Patricia. *The sick day*
McPhail, David. *The cereal box*
Emma's pet
Emma's vacation
Mahy, Margaret. *Jam*
Mrs. Discombobulous
Malecki, Maryann. *Mom and dad and I are
having a baby!*
Mallett, Anne. *Here comes Tagalong*
Malloy, Judy. *Bad Thad*
Manes, Esther. *The bananas move to the
ceiling*
Manushkin, Fran. *Baby*
Bubblebath!
Little rabbit's baby brother
The perfect Christmas picture
Martel, Cruz. *Yagua days*
Martin, Bill (William Ivan). *White Dynamite
and Curly Kidd*
Maschler, Fay. *T. G. and Moonie have a
baby*
Mayle, Peter. *Divorce can happen to the
nicest people*
Why are we getting a divorce?
Maynard, Joyce. *Camp-out*
Mayper, Monica. *After good-night*
Merriam, Eve. *The Christmas box*
Merrill, Jean. *Emily Emerson's moon*
Milgram, Mary. *Brothers are all the same*
Miller, Edna. *Mousekin's family*

Miller, J. P. (John Parr). *Good night, little
rabbit*
Miller, Margaret. *At my house*
In my room
Me and my clothes
Time to eat
Milord, Sue. *Maggie and the goodbye gift*
Mintzberg, Yvette. *Sally, where are you?*
Miranda, Anne. *Baby talk*
Monjo, F. N. *Rudi and the distelfink*
Moore, Lilian. *Papa Albert*
Morimoto, Junko. *The inch boy*
Mosley, Francis. *The dinosaur eggs*
Munsch, Robert N. *I have to go!*
Murphy, Jill. *All in one piece*
Five minutes' peace
Myller, Lois. *No! No!*
Naylor, Phyllis Reynolds. *The baby, the bed,
and the rose*
Nelson, Vaunda Micheaux. *Always
Gramma*
Ness, Evaline. *Exactly alike*
Neumeyer, Peter F. *The faithful fish*
Neville, Emily Cheney. *The bridge*
Newton, Laura P. *Me and my aunts*
Nilsson, Ulf. *Little sister rabbit*
Noble, June. *Two homes for Lynn*
Nolan, Madeena Spray. *My daddy don't go
to work*
O'Connor, Jane. *Lulu and the witch baby*
O'Donnell, Elizabeth Lee. *Maggie doesn't
want to move*
O'Kelley, Mattie Lou. *Circus!*
Ormerod, Jan. *Moonlight*
Oxenbury, Helen. *Beach day*
Family
Our dog
Paterson, Diane. *Wretched Rachel*
Pearce, Philippa. *Emily's own elephant*
Pearson, Susan. *Karin's Christmas walk*
Saturday, I ran away
Pellowski, Anne. *Stairstep farm*
Pitt, Valerie. *Let's find out about the family*
Politi, Leo. *Little Leo*
Polushkin, Maria. *Baby brother blues*
Pomerantz, Charlotte. *The mango tooth*
Posy
Porte, Barbara Ann. *Harry's mom*
Price, Mathew. *Peekaboo!*
Provensen, Alice. *An owl and three
pussycats*
Prusski, Jeffrey. *Bring back the deer*
Purdy, Carol. *Iva Dunnit and the big wind*
Least of all
Quackenbush, Robert M. *I don't want to
go, I don't know how to act*
Mouse feathers
Raffi. *One light, one sun*
Raphael, Elaine. *Turnabout*
Raskin, Ellen. *Ghost in a four-room
apartment*

Ray, Deborah Kogan. *Sunday morning we went to the zoo*
Rayner, Mary. *Mrs. Pig gets cross*
Redies, Rainer. *The cats' party*
Rees, Mary. *Ten in a bed*
Rice, Eve. *City night*
  Ebbie
  Papa's lemonade and other stories
Rider, Alex. *Chez nous. At our house*
Rigby, Shirley Lincoln. *Smaller than most*
Riggio, Anita. *Wake up, William!*
Robb, Brian. *My grandmother's djinn*
Roche, P. K. (Patrick K.). *Good-bye, Arnold!*
Rockwell, Anne F. *Blackout*
  In our house
Roffey, Maureen. *Family scramble*
Rogers, Fred. *Moving*
Rogers, Paul. *Somebody's awake*
  Somebody's sleepy
Rosenberg, Maxine B. *Being adopted*
Ross, Katharine. *When you were a baby*
Roy, Ronald. *Breakfast with my father*
Rubel, Nicole. *Uncle Henry and Aunt Henrietta's honeymoon*
Ruffins, Reynold. *My brother never feeds the cat*
Rushnell, Elaine Evans. *My mom's having a baby*
Russo, Marisabina. *The line up book*
  Why do grownups have all the fun?
Ryder, Joanne. *Beach party*
Rylant, Cynthia. *Birthday presents*
  Henry and Mudge in the sparkle days
  The relatives came
  When I was young in the mountains
Sandin, Joan. *The long way to a new land*
Sarnoff, Jane. *That's not fair*
Say, Allen. *A river dream*
Schermer, Judith. *Mouse in house*
Schick, Eleanor. *Peggy's new brother*
  A piano for Julie
Schlein, Miriam. *Billy, the littlest one*
  Laurie's new brother
  My family
  My house
Schuchman, Joan. *Two places to sleep*
Schumacher, Claire. *Brave Lily*
Schwartz, Amy. *Her Majesty, Aunt Essie*
Schweninger, Ann. *Valentine friends*
Scott, Ann Herbert. *On mother's lap*
  Sam
Segal, Lore. *Tell me a Mitzi*
  Tell me a Trudy
Seligman, Dorothy Halle. *Run away home*
Seuling, Barbara. *What kind of family is this?*
Seyton, Marion. *The hole in the hill*
Sharmat, Marjorie Weinman. *Go to sleep, Nicholas Joe*
  Goodnight, Andrew. Goodnight, Craig

Sometimes mama and papa fight
What are we going to do about Andrew?
Sharr, Christine. *Homes*
Sherman, Eileen Bluestone. *The odd potato*
Showers, Paul. *Me and my family tree*
Shyer, Marlene Fanta. *Stepdog*
Simon, Norma. *All kinds of families*
  How do I feel?
  Oh, that cat!
  What do I say?
Skorpen, Liesel Moak. *His mother's dog*
Slobodkin, Louis. *Clear the track*
  Magic Michael
Smith, Lucia B. *A special kind of sister*
Smith, Peter. *Jenny's baby brother*
Sobol, Harriet Langsam. *We don't look like our mom and dad*
Sonneborn, Ruth A. *Seven in a bed*
Spinelli, Eileen. *Thanksgiving at Tappletons'*
Stanton, Elizabeth. *The very messy room*
Steig, William. *Spinky sulks*
  Sylvester and the magic pebble
Stein, Sara Bonnett. *The adopted one*
  Making babies
  On divorce
  That new baby
Steiner, Charlotte. *Daddy comes home*
Stepto, Michele. *Snuggle Piggy and the magic blanket*
Steptoe, John. *My special best words*
Stevenson, James. *"Could be worse!"*
  When I was nine
  Worse than Willy!
Stevenson, Robert Louis. *The moon*
Stock, Catherine. *Sophie's bucket*
  Sophie's knapsack
Stoddard, Sandol. *Curl up small*
  The thinking book
Strathdee, Jean. *The house that grew*
Tafuri, Nancy. *Do not disturb*
Taha, Karen T. *A gift for Tia Rose*
Tallarico, Tony. *At home*
Tax, Meredith. *Families*
Taylor, Judy. *Sophie and Jack*
Tejima, Keizaburo. *Owl lake*
Thomson, Pat. *Rhymes around the day*
Thorne, Jenny. *My uncle*
Thwaites, Lyndsay. *Super Adam and Rosie Wonder*
Tierney, Hanne. *Where's your baby brother, Becky Bunting?*
Tobias, Tobi. *At the beach*
  A day off
  Jane wishing
  The quitting deal
Todd, Kathleen. *Snow*
Townson, Hazel. *Terrible Tuesday*
Tresselt, Alvin R. *Hi, Mister Robin*
Tsow, Ming. *A day with Ling*
Tsutsui, Yoriko. *Anna's secret friend*
  Before the picnic

Tulloch, Richard. *Stories from our house*
Turner, Ann. *Nettie's trip south*
Udry, Janice May. *Theodore's parents*
  What Mary Jo wanted
Updike, David. *A winter's journey*
Van der Beek, Deborah. *Alice's blue cloth*
  Superbabe!
Van Leeuwen, Jean. *More tales of Amanda Pig*
  More tales of Oliver Pig
  Tales of Amanda Pig
  Tales of Oliver Pig
Van Woerkom, Dorothy. *Alexandra the rock-eater*
Vasiliu, Mircea. *A day at the beach*
Vesey, A. *Merry Christmas, Thomas!*
Vevers, Gwynne. *Animal parents*
Vigna, Judith. *Couldn't we have a turtle instead?*
  Nobody wants a nuclear war
  She's not my real mother
Viorst, Judith. *Alexander and the terrible, horrible, no good, very bad day*
  I'll fix Anthony
  Sunday morning
Waber, Bernard. *Funny, funny Lyle*
Wahl, Jan. *Old Hippo's Easter egg*
  Sylvester Bear overslept
Walter, Mildred Pitts. *My mama needs me*
Watson, Clyde. *Catch me and kiss me and say it again*
  Valentine foxes
Watson, Jane Werner. *Sometimes a family has to move*
  Sometimes a family has to split up
Watson, Pauline. *Days with Daddy*
Watts, Bernadette. *David's waiting day*
Wegen, Ron. *The balloon trip*
Weil, Lisl. *Gertie and Gus*
Weiss, Nicki. *Barney is big*
  Weekend at Muskrat Lake
Wells, Rosemary. *Shy Charles*
Westcott, Nadine Bernard. *Getting up*
  Going to bed
  Peanut butter and jelly
Whitney, Alex. *The tiger that barks*
Wild, Jocelyn. *Florence and Eric take the cake*
Wilhelm, Hans. *A new home, a new friend*
Williams, Barbara. *Donna Jean's disaster*
  If he's my brother
  So what if I'm a sore loser?
Williams, Vera B. *A chair for my mother*
  Music, music for everyone
  Something special for me
  Stringbean's trip to the shining sea
Winn, Chris. *My day*
Winthrop, Elizabeth. *Bunk beds*
  I think he likes me

Wolde, Gunilla. *Betsy and Peter are different*
  Betsy and the vacuum cleaner
  Betsy's fixing day
  This is Betsy
Wolff, Ashley. *Only the cat saw*
Wood, Audrey. *Elbert's bad word*
  The horrible holidays
Wyse, Lois. *Two guppies, a turtle and Aunt Edna*
Yaffe, Alan. *The magic meatballs*
Yamashita, Haruo. *Mice at the beach*
Young, Evelyn. *Wu and Lu and Li*
Zalben, Jane Breskin. *Beni's first Chanukah*
Zemach, Kaethe. *The funny dream*
Zemach, Margot. *To Hilda for helping*
Ziefert, Harriet. *Good night, Jessie!*
  Keeping daddy awake on the way home from the beach
  My sister says nothing ever happens when we go sailing
  A new coat for Anna
  Strike four!
Zimelman, Nathan. *If I were strong enough...*
Zinnemann-Hope, Pam. *Let's play ball, Ned*
Zolotow, Charlotte. *Big sister and little sister*
  Do you know what I'll do?
  If it weren't for you
  It's not fair
  May I visit?
  My grandson Lew
  A rose, a bridge, and a wild black horse
  The sky was blue
  Someone new
  The summer night
  When I have a son
  William's doll
Zusman, Evelyn. *The Passover parrot*

Family life – brothers

Cummings, Pat. *Jimmy Lee did it*
Freedman, Florence B. *Brothers*
Robins, Joan. *My brother, Will*
San Souci, Robert D. *The enchanted tapestry*
Titherington, Jeanne. *A place for Ben*

Family life – fathers

Aksakov, Sergei. *The scarlet flower*
Alda, Arlene. *Matthew and his dad*
Alexander, Anne. *My daddy and I*
Asch, Frank. *Goodnight horsey*
  Just like daddy
Ayres, Pam. *When dad cuts down the chestnut tree*
  When dad fills in the garden pond
Baker, Betty. *My sister says*
Barbato, Juli. *Mom's night out*
Barrett, Judi. *I'm too small, you're too big*
Baum, Louis. *One more time*

Beim, Jerrold. *With dad alone*
Bergström, Gunilla. *Who's scaring Alfie Atkins?*
Blaustein, Muriel. *Play ball, Zachary!*
Bradman, Tony. *Not like this, like that*
Browne, Anthony. *Gorilla*
Buckley, Helen Elizabeth. *Someday with my father*
Burgess, Gelett. *The little father*
Caines, Jeannette. *Daddy*
Claverie, Jean. *Working*
Clifton, Lucille. *Amifika*
Cole, Babette. *The trouble with dad*
Diot, Alain. *Better, best, bestest*
Dupasquier, Philippe. *Dear Daddy...*
Fassler, Joan. *All alone with daddy*
Gay, Michel. *Night ride*
Gray, Nigel. *A balloon for grandad*
Greenfield, Eloise. *First pink light*
Grindley, Sally. *Knock, knock! Who's there?*
Haseley, Dennis. *Kite flier*
Hendershot, Judith. *In coal country*
Hillert, Margaret. *The little cowboy and the big cowboy*
Hines, Anna Grossnickle. *Daddy makes the best spaghetti*
Hooks, William H. *Moss gown*
Kauffman, Lois. *What's that noise?*
Kessler, Leonard P. *Are we lost, daddy?*
Kilroy, Sally. *Market day*
Kroll, Steven. *Happy Father's Day*
Lenski, Lois. *Papa Small*
Lewin, Hugh. *Jafta's father*
Lexau, Joan M. *Every day a dragon*
Me day
Long, Earlene. *Gone fishing*
Lubell, Winifred. *Here comes daddy*
McAfee, Annalena. *The visitors who came to stay*
Marzollo, Jean. *Amy goes fishing*
Close your eyes
Mayer, Mercer. *Just me and my dad*
Minarik, Else Holmelund. *Father Bear comes home*
Monjo, F. N. *The one bad thing about father*
Morgan, Allen. *Nicole's boat*
Nolan, Madeena Spray. *My daddy don't go to work*
Ormerod, Jan. *Dad's back*
Messy baby
Reading
Sleeping
Osborn, Lois. *My dad is really something*
Paris, Lena. *Mom is single*
Parker, Kristy. *My dad the magnificent*
Porte, Barbara Ann. *Harry's dog*
Harry's mom
Puner, Helen Walker. *Daddys, what they do all day*
Quinlan, Patricia. *My dad takes care of me*
Rabe, Berniece. *Where's Chimpy?*

Radlauer, Ruth Shaw. *Molly at the library*
Ringi, Kjell. *My father and I*
Sandberg, Inger. *Come on out, Daddy!*
Schwartz, Amy. *Bea and Mr. Jones*
Simmonds, Posy. *Lulu and the flying babies*
Simon, Norma. *The daddy days*
I wish I had my father
Sonneborn, Ruth A. *Friday night is papa night*
Stecher, Miriam B. *Daddy and Ben together*
Stein, Sara Bonnett. *About phobias*
Steiner, Charlotte. *Daddy comes home*
Steptoe, John. *Daddy is a monster...sometimes*
Stewart, Robert S. *The daddy book*
Thomas, Ianthe. *Willie blows a mean horn*
Tyler, Linda Wagner. *When daddy comes home*
Udry, Janice May. *What Mary Jo shared*
Van Leeuwen, Jean. *More tales of Amanda Pig*
Van Woerkom, Dorothy. *Something to crow about*
Vigna, Judith. *Daddy's new baby*
I wish my daddy didn't drink so much
Watanabe, Shigeo. *Daddy, play with me!*
I can take a bath!
Where's my daddy?
Watson, Pauline. *Days with Daddy*
Yolen, Jane. *The emperor and the kite*
Owl moon
Zola, Meguido. *Only the best*
Zolotow, Charlotte. *The summer night*

Family life – grandfathers

Ackerman, Karen. *Song and dance man*
Adler, David A. *A little at a time*
Aliki. *The two of them*
Barrett, Judi. *Cloudy with a chance of meatballs*
Behrens, June. *Soo Ling finds a way*
Borack, Barbara. *Grandpa*
Brooks, Ron. *Timothy and Gramps*
Buckley, Helen Elizabeth. *Grandfather and I*
Bunting, Eve. *The happy funeral*
Magic and the night river
Burningham, John. *Grandpa*
Caseley, Judith. *When Grandpa came to stay*
Cazet, Denys. *December 24th*
Coatsworth, Elizabeth. *Lonely Maria*
De Paola, Tomie. *Now one foot, now the other*
Douglass, Barbara. *Good as new*
Dumas, Philippe. *Laura loses her head*
Fassler, Joan. *My grandpa died today*
Flora, James. *Grandpa's farm*
Grandpa's ghost stories
Gray, Nigel. *A balloon for grandad*
Greenfield, Eloise. *Grandpa's face*

Griffith, Helen V. *Georgia music*
  Grandaddy's place
Guthrie, Donna. *Grandpa doesn't know it's
  me*
Harranth, Wolf. *My old grandad*
Hartley, Deborah. *Up north in the winter*
Hayes, Geoffrey. *Patrick and his grandpa*
Hazen, Barbara Shook. *Why did Grandpa
  die?*
Henkes, Kevin. *Grandpa and Bo*
Hest, Amy. *The crack-of-dawn walkers*
  The purple coat
Hughes, Shirley. *When we went to the park*
Hutchins, Pat. *Happy birthday, Sam*
Isadora, Rachel. *Jesse and Abe*
Kessler, Ethel. *Grandpa Witch and the
  magic doobelator*
Kirk, Barbara. *Grandpa, me and our house
  in the tree*
Knox-Wagner, Elaine. *My grandpa retired
  today*
Langner, Nola. *Freddy my grandfather*
Lapp, Eleanor. *In the morning mist*
Lasky, Kathryn. *I have four names for my
  grandfather*
Locker, Thomas. *The mare on the hill*
  Where the river begins
McCully, Emily Arnold. *The Christmas gift*
Mahood, Kenneth. *Why are there more
  questions than answers, Grandad?*
Marron, Carol A. *No trouble for Grandpa*
Martin, Bill (William Ivan). *Knots on a
  counting rope*
Mayer, Mercer. *Little Monster at work*
Paterson, Diane. *Hey, cowboy!*
Pearson, Susan. *Happy birthday, Grampie*
Peavy, Linda. *Allison's grandfather*
Pomerantz, Charlotte. *Buffy and Albert
  Timothy Tall Feather*
Radin, Ruth Yaffe. *High in the mountains*
Rigby, Shirley Lincoln. *Smaller than most*
Rodgers, Frank. *Who's afraid of the ghost
  train?*
Sandberg, Inger. *Dusty wants to help*
Schlein, Miriam. *Go with the sun*
Shulevitz, Uri. *Dawn*
Stevens, Margaret. *When grandpa died*
Stevenson, James. *"Could be worse!"*
  Grandpa's great city tour
  The great big especially beautiful Easter egg
  No friends
  That dreadful day
  That terrible Halloween night
  There's nothing to do!
  We can't sleep
  What's under my bed?
  Will you please feed our cat?
  Worse than Willy!
Stilz, Carol Curtis. *Kirsty's kite*
Stock, Catherine. *Emma's dragon hunt*
Stolz, Mary Slattery. *Storm in the night*

Titherington, Jeanne. *Where are you going,
  Emma?*
Townsend, Maryann. *Pop's secret*
Wahl, Jan. *The fishermen*
Wallace, Ian. *Chin Chiang and the dragon's
  dance*
Walsh, Jill Paton. *Lost and found*
Ward, Sally G. *Molly and Grandpa*
Ziefert, Harriet. *Happy birthday, Grandpa!*
Zolotow, Charlotte. *My grandson Lew*

Family life – grandmothers

Addy, Sharon Hart. *A visit with
  great-grandma*
Alexander, Martha G. *The story
  grandmother told*
Allen, Linda. *Mr. Simkin's grandma*
Allred, Mary. *Grandmother Poppy and the
  funny-looking bird*
Ambrus, Victor G. *Grandma, Felix, and
  Mustapha Biscuit*
Baker, Jeannie. *Grandmother*
Balian, Lorna. *Humbug rabbit*
Barker, Peggy. *What happened when
  grandma died*
Bartoli, Jennifer. *Nonna*
Base, Graeme. *My grandma lived in
  Gooligulch*
Berridge, Celia. *Grandmother's tales*
Bible, Charles. *Jennifer's new chair*
Brandenberg, Franz. *A secret for
  grandmother's birthday*
Buckley, Helen Elizabeth. *Grandmother and
  I*
Caines, Jeannette. *Window wishing*
Carlstrom, Nancy White. *The moon came
  too*
Caseley, Judith. *Apple pie and onions*
Chorao, Kay. *Lemon moon*
Cole, Babette. *The trouble with Gran*
Cornish, Sam. *Grandmother's pictures*
Coutant, Helen. *First snow*
Daly, Niki. *Not so fast Songololo*
DeJong, David Cornel. *Looking for
  Alexander*
Delton, Judy. *My grandma's in a nursing
  home*
Denton, Kady MacDonald. *Granny is a
  darling*
De Paola, Tomie. *Haircuts for the Woolseys*
  Nana upstairs and Nana downstairs
Ehrlich, Amy. *Bunnies and their grandma*
Eisenberg, Phyllis Rose. *A mitzvah is
  something special*
Finfer, Celentha. *Grandmother dear*
Flournoy, Valerie. *The patchwork quilt*
Goffstein, M. B. (Marilyn Brooke). *Fish for
  supper*
Goldman, Susan. *Grandma is somebody
  special*

Gomi, Taro. *Coco can't wait!*
Gordon, Shirley. *Grandma zoo*
Hamm, Diane Johnston. *Grandma drives a motor bed*
Hayes, Sarah. *Happy Christmas, Gemma*
Hedderwick, Mairi. *Katie Morag and the big boy cousins*
Katie Morag and the two grandmothers
Katie Morag delivers the mail
Henriod, Lorraine. *Grandma's wheelchair*
Hines, Anna Grossnickle. *Come to the meadow*
Grandma gets grumpy
Hiser, Berniece T. *The adventure of Charlie and his wheat-straw hat*
Hogan, Bernice. *My grandmother died but I won't forget her*
Hoopes, Lyn Littlefield. *Nana*
Jarrell, Mary. *The knee baby*
Jeschke, Susan. *Mia, Grandma and the genie*
Kay, Helen. *A stocking for a kitten*
Khalsa, Dayal Kaur. *Tales of a gambling grandma*
Kibbey, Marsha. *My grammy*
Kojima, Naomi. *The flying grandmother*
Kovalski, Maryann. *The wheels on the bus*
Kraus, Robert. *Rebecca Hatpin*
Kroll, Steven. *If I could be my grandmother*
Kunhardt, Edith. *Danny's mystery Valentine*
Lasky, Kathryn. *My island grandma*
Lenski, Lois. *Debbie and her grandma*
Le Tord, Bijou. *My Grandma Leonie*
Levinson, Riki. *I go with my family to Grandma's*
Watch the stars come out
Lexau, Joan M. *Benjie*
Benjie on his own
Lloyd, David. *Duck*
Grandma and the pirate
The stopwatch
Low, Alice. *David's windows*
McCully, Emily Arnold. *The grandma mix-up*
McQueen, John Troy. *A world full of monsters*
Moore, Elaine. *Grandma's house*
Grandma's promise
Mower, Nancy. *I visit my Tūtū and Grandma*
Neasi, Barbara J. *Listen to me*
Nelson, Vaunda Micheaux. *Always Gramma*
Olson, Arielle North. *Hurry home, Grandma!*
Orbach, Ruth. *Please send a panda*
Parish, Peggy. *Granny and the desperadoes*
Granny and the Indians
Granny, the baby and the big gray thing
Peck, Richard. *Monster night at Grandma's house*

Peterson, Jeanne Whitehouse. *Sometimes I dream horses*
Roberts, Sarah. *I want to go home!*
Rockwell, Anne F. *When I go visiting*
Rogers, Paul. *From me to you*
Root, Phyllis. *Gretchen's grandma*
Roth, Susan L. *Patchwork tales*
Scheffler, Ursel. *A walk in the rain*
Schwartz, Amy. *Oma and Bobo*
Sonneborn, Ruth A. *I love Gram*
Stanovich, Betty Jo. *Big boy, little boy*
Steiner, Charlotte. *Kiki and Muffy*
Storr, Catherine. *Hugo and his grandma*
Thomas, Jane Resh. *Saying good-bye to grandma*
Turkle, Brinton. *It's only Arnold*
Udry, Janice May. *Mary Jo's grandmother*
Van Leeuwen, Jean. *Oliver, Amanda and Grandmother*
Vigna, Judith. *Everyone goes as a pumpkin*
Grandma without me
Ward, Sally G. *Charlie and Grandma*
Waterton, Betty. *Pettranella*
Whitlock, Susan Love. *Donovan scares the monsters*
Willard, Nancy. *The mountains of quilt*
Williams, Barbara. *Kevin's grandma*
Williams, Vera B. *Music, music for everyone*
Wolf, Janet. *The best present is me*
Wood, Audrey. *The napping house*
Wood, Joyce. *Grandmother Lucy goes on a picnic*
Grandmother Lucy in her garden
Yolen, Jane. *No bath tonight*
Zhitkov, Boris. *How I hunted for the little fellows*

Family life – grandparents

Allen, Linda. *Mr. Simkin's grandma*
Bate, Lucy. *How Georgina drove the car very carefully from Boston to New York*
Bunting, Eve. *Winter's coming*
Cazet, Denys. *Big shoe, little shoe*
Saturday
Child, Lydia Maria. *Over the river and through the wood*
Copeland, Helen. *Meet Miki Takino*
De Paola, Tomie. *Pajamas for Kit*
Eisenberg, Phyllis Rose. *A mitzvah is something special*
Farber, Norma. *How does it feel to be old?*
Flory, Jane. *The unexpected grandchild*
Gantschev, Ivan. *The train to Grandma's*
Gould, Deborah. *Grandpa's slide show*
Hamm, Diane Johnston. *Grandma drives a motor bed*
Hawes, Judy. *Fireflies in the night*
Haywood, Carolyn. *Hello, star*
Heller, Linda. *The castle on Hester Street*

Hooker, Ruth. *At Grandma and Grandpa's house*
Hurd, Edith Thacher. *I dance in my red pajamas*
Joosse, Barbara M. *Jam day*
Kilroy, Sally. *Grandpa's garden*
Kitamura, Satoshi. *Captain Toby*
Kroll, Steven. *Toot! Toot!*
Maris, Ron. *Is anyone home?*
Minarik, Else Holmelund. *Little Bear's visit*
Morgan, Michaela. *Visitors for Edward*
Newman, Shirlee. *Tell me, grandma; tell me, grandpa*
Oxenbury, Helen. *Grandma and Grandpa*
Porte, Barbara Ann. *Harry's mom*
Raynor, Dorka. *Grandparents around the world*
Rockwell, Anne F. *When I go visiting*
Rosen, Winifred. *Henrietta and the gong from Hong Kong*
Sandberg, Inger. *Dusty wants to borrow everything*
Scheffler, Ursel. *A walk in the rain*
Skofield, James. *Snow country*
Stevenson, James. *Higher on the door*
Watanabe, Shigeo. *It's my birthday*
Ziefert, Harriet. *Chocolate mud cake*
Zolotow, Charlotte. *William's doll*

Family life – great-grandparents

Budd, Lillian. *The people on Long Ago Street*
Herter, Jonina. *Eighty-eight kisses*
Knotts, Howard. *Great-grandfather, the baby and me*
Swayne, Samuel F. *Great-grandfather in the honey tree*

Family life – mothers

Alda, Arlene. *Sonya's mommy works*
Asch, Frank. *Bread and honey*
Baker, Gayle. *Special delivery*
Bauer, Caroline Feller. *My mom travels a lot*
Blaine, Marge. *The terrible thing that happened at our house*
Browne, Anthony. *Piggybook*
Carton, Lonnie Caming. *Mommies*
Cole, Babette. *The trouble with mom*
Delton, Judy. *The best mom in the world*
My mother lost her job today
Dionetti, Michelle. *The day Eli went looking for bear*
Drescher, Joan. *My mother's getting married*
Eastman, P. D. (Philip D.). *Are you my mother?*
English, Jennifer. *My mommy's special*
Fassler, Joan. *The man of the house*

Fisher, Aileen. *Do bears have mothers too?*
My mother and I
Flack, Marjorie. *Ask Mr. Bear*
Gackenbach, Dick. *Hurray for Hattie Rabbit!*
Hawkins, Colin. *Where's my mommy?*
Hest, Amy. *The mommy exchange*
Hines, Anna Grossnickle. *It's just me, Emily*
Maybe a band-aid will help
Hurd, Edith Thacher. *The mother chimpanzee*
Jenkins, Jordan. *Learning about love*
Jennings, Michael. *The bears who came to breakfix*
Johnson, Angela. *Tell me a story, mama*
Jonas, Ann. *Two bear cubs*
Kanao, Keiko. *Kitten up a tree*
Keller, Beverly. *When mother got the flu*
Keller, Holly. *When Francie was sick*
Kent, Jack. *Joey*
Kilroy, Sally. *On the road*
Krauss, Ruth. *The bundle book*
Lasker, Joe. *Mothers can do anything*
Levine, Abby. *What did mommy do before you?*
Lewin, Hugh. *Jafta's mother*
Lexau, Joan M. *A house so big*
Lindgren, Barbro. *The wild baby*
The wild baby goes to sea
MacLachlan, Patricia. *Mama one, Mama two*
Maley, Anne. *Have you seen my mother?*
Mayer, Mercer. *Just for you*
Merriam, Eve. *Mommies at work*
Miles, Miska. *Mouse six and the happy birthday*
Mitchell, Joyce Slayton. *My mommy makes money*
Mizumura, Kazue. *If I were a mother*
Morris, Ann. *Cuddle up*
Ormerod, Jan. *Bend and stretch*
Making friends
Mom's home
This little nose
Oxenbury, Helen. *Mother's helper*
Paris, Lena. *Mom is single*
Polushkin, Maria. *Mother, Mother, I want another*
Porte, Barbara Ann. *Harry's mom*
Portnoy, Mindy Avra. *Ima on the Bima*
Power, Barbara. *I wish Laura's mommy was my mommy*
Quinlan, Patricia. *My dad takes care of me*
Radlauer, Ruth Shaw. *Breakfast by Molly*
Reimold, Mary Gallagher. *My mom is a runner*
Reuter, Margaret. *My mother is blind*
Reyher, Becky. *My mother is the most beautiful woman in the world*
Rice, Eve. *New blue shoes*
Sawicki, Norma Jean. *Something for mom*

Schick, Eleanor. *Home alone*
Scott, Ann Herbert. *On mother's lap*
Sharmat, Marjorie Weinman. *My mother never listens to me*
Skurzynski, Gloria. *Martin by himself*
Sondheimer, Ilse. *The boy who could make his mother stop yelling*
Standon, Anna. *Little duck lost*
Stanek, Muriel. *All alone after school*
Stehr, Frédéric. *Quack-quack*
Stilz, Carol Curtis. *Kirsty's kite*
Thaler, Mike. *Owley*
Titherington, Jeanne. *Big world, small world*
Tompert, Ann. *Little Otter remembers and other stories*
Tyler, Linda Wagner. *Waiting for mom*
Udry, Janice May. *Is Susan here?*
   Thump and Plunk
Ungerer, Tomi. *No kiss for mother*
Vigna, Judith. *Couldn't we have a turtle instead?*
   Mommy and me by ourselves again
Viorst, Judith. *My mama says there aren't any zombies, ghosts, vampires, creatures, demons, monsters, fiends, goblins, or things*
Waber, Bernard. *Lyle finds his mother*
Warren, Cathy. *Saturday belongs to Sara*
Watson, Nancy Dingman. *Tommy's mommy's fish*
Wells, Rosemary. *Hazel's amazing mother*
Wetterer, Margaret. *Patrick and the fairy thief*
Ziefert, Harriet. *Sarah's questions*
   Surprise!
Zindel, Paul. *I love my mother*
Zinnemann-Hope, Pam. *Time for bed, Ned*
Zolotow, Charlotte. *I like to be little*
   Mr. Rabbit and the lovely present
   Say it!
   Some things go together

Family life – only child

Conford, Ellen. *Why can't I be William?*
Dragonwagon, Crescent. *Rainy day together*
Hallinan, P. K. (Patrick K.). *I'm glad to be me*
   Just being alone
Hamberger, John. *Hazel was an only pet*
Hazen, Barbara Shook. *Tight times*
   Why couldn't I be an only kid like you, Wigger?
Iwasaki, Chihiro. *Staying home alone on a rainy day*
Schick, Eleanor. *City in the winter*
   Summer at the sea
Sharmat, Marjorie Weinman. *I want mama*
Shyer, Marlene Fanta. *Here I am, an only child*
Skorpen, Liesel Moak. *All the Lassies*

Smith, Wendy. *The lonely, only mouse*

Family life – sisters

Caseley, Judith. *My sister Celia*
Henkes, Kevin. *Sheila Rae, the brave*
Howard, Elizabeth Fitzgerald. *The train to Lulu's*
Kalman, Maira. *Hey Willy, see the pyramids!*
Porazińska, Janina. *The enchanted book*
Prall, Jo. *My sister's special*
Pryor, Bonnie. *Amanda and April*
Samuels, Barbara. *Duncan and Dolores*
Weiss, Nicki. *A family story*
   Princess Pearl
Wilhelm, Hans. *Let's be friends again!*

Family life – step families

Boyd, Lizi. *The not-so-wicked stepmother*
Helmering, Doris Wild. *I have two families*
Lewis, Naomi. *The stepsister*
Seuling, Barbara. *What kind of family is this?*

Family life – stepchildren *see* Divorce; Family life – step families

Family life – stepparents *see* Divorce; Family life – step families

Farmers *see* Careers – farmers

Farms

Alborough, Jez. *The grass is always greener*
Amery, H. *The farm picture book*
Anholt, Catherine. *Chaos at Cold Custard Farm*
Arnosky, Jim. *Raccoons and ripe corn*
At the farm
Augarde, Steve. *Pig*
Aulaire, Ingri Mortenson d'. *Wings for Per*
Avery, Kay. *Wee willow whistle*
Aylesworth, Jim. *One crow*
Azarian, Mary. *A farmer's alphabet*
Baker, Betty. *Partners*
Balian, Lorna. *A garden for a groundhog*
Balzano, Jeanne. *The wee moose*
Barr, Cathrine. *A horse for Sherry*
Barrett, Judi. *Old MacDonald had an apartment house*
Baruch, Dorothy. *Kappa's tug-of-war with the big brown horse*
Bax, Martin. *Edmond went far away*
Baynton, Martin. *Fifty and the fox*
   Fifty and the great race
   Fifty gets the picture
   Fifty saves his friend
Bellville, Cheryl Walsh. *Round-up*
Benchley, Nathaniel. *The strange disappearance of Arthur Cluck*

Ipcar, Dahlov. *Bright barnyard*
  Brown cow farm
  Hard scrabble harvest
  One horse farm
  Ten big farms
Isenbart, Hans-Heinrich. *Baby animals on the farm*
Israel, Marion Louise. *The tractor on the farm*
Jacobs, Joseph. *Hereafterthis*
Johnston, Tony. *Farmer Mack measures his pig*
Kent, Jack. *Little Peep*
Kessler, Ethel. *Are there hippos on the farm?*
Kightley, Rosalinda. *The farmer*
King-Smith, Dick. *Cuckoobush farm*
  Farmer Bungle forgets
Koch, Dorothy Clarke. *When the cows got out*
Koontz, Robin Michal. *This old man*
Koralek, Jenny. *The friendly fox*
Kwitz, Mary DeBall. *Little chick's breakfast*
Lapp, Eleanor. *The mice came in early this year*
Lasson, Robert. *Orange Oliver*
Lenski, Lois. *The little farm*
Levitin, Sonia. *A single speckled egg*
Lexau, Joan M. *Who took the farmer's hat?*
Lilly, Kenneth. *Animals on the farm*
Lindberg, Reeve. *Midnight farm*
Lindgren, Astrid. *The dragon with red eyes*
  The tomten
Lindman, Maj. *Snipp, Snapp, Snurr and the buttered bread*
Lionni, Leo. *Six crows*
The little red hen. *The little red hen*, ill. by Janina Domanska
  The little red hen, ill. by Paul Galdone
  The little red hen, ill. by Mel Pekarsky
  The little red hen, ill. by William Stobbs
  The little red hen, ill. by Margot Zemach
Littledale, Freya. *The farmer in the soup*
Lobel, Arnold. *Small pig*
  A treeful of pigs
Locker, Thomas. *Family farm*
  The mare on the hill
Lorenz, Lee. *Hugo and the spacedog*
Low, Joseph. *Benny rabbit and the owl*
  Boo to a goose
Lüton, Mildred. *Little chicks' mothers and all the others*
McCrea, Lilian. *Mother hen*
McCue, Lisa. *The little chick*
McKissack, Patricia C. *The little red hen*, ill. by Dennis Hockerman
McNeer, May Yonge. *Little Baptiste*
McPhail, David. *Farm morning*
Maris, Ron. *Is anyone home?*
Mayer, Mercer. *Appelard and Liverwurst*
Mayne, William. *Tibber*
Meeks, Esther K. *Friendly farm animals*

Merrill, Jean. *Tell about the cowbarn, Daddy*
Miles, Miska. *Noisy gander*
  This little pig
Miller, J. P. (John Parr). *Farmer John's animals*
Miller, Jane. *Farm alphabet book*
  Farm counting book
  Seasons on the farm
Moeri, Louise. *The unicorn and the plow*
Moon, Cliff. *Pigs on the farm*
Nakatani, Chiyoko. *My day on the farm*
O'Kelley, Mattie Lou. *Circus!*
Old MacDonald had a farm. *Old MacDonald had a farm*, ill. by Mel Crawford
  Old MacDonald had a farm, ill. by David Frankland
  Old MacDonald had a farm, ill. by Abner Graboff
  Old MacDonald had a farm, ill. by Tracey Campbell Pearson
  Old MacDonald had a farm, ill. by Robert M. Quackenbush
  Old MacDonald had a farm, ill. by William Stobbs
Olney, Ross R. *Farm giants*
Patterson, Geoffrey. *A pig's tale*
Paul, Jan S. *Hortense*
Peck, Robert Newton. *Hamilton*
Pellowski, Anne. *Stairstep farm*
Petersham, Maud. *The box with red wheels*
Pieńkowski, Jan. *Farm*
Polushkin, Maria. *Morning*
Potter, Beatrix. *The tale of Peter Rabbit*, ill. by Beatrix Potter
Provensen, Alice. *Our animal friends*
  An owl and three pussycats
  The year at Maple Hill Farm
Pryor, Bonnie. *Mr. Munday and the rustlers*
The pudgy book of farm animals
Raphael, Elaine. *Donkey and Carlo*
  Donkey, it's snowing
Rider, Alex. *A la ferme. At the farm*
Robart, Rose. *The cake that Mack ate*
Robinson, W. W. (William Wilcox). *On the farm*
Rockwell, Anne F. *The gollywhopper egg*
Rojankovsky, Feodor. *Animals on the farm*
  The great big animal book
Roth, Harold. *Let's look all around the farm*
Russell, Sandra Joanne. *A farmer's dozen*
Schlein, Miriam. *Something for now, something for later*
Schmid, Eleonore. *Farm animals*
Schmidt, Eric von. *The young man who wouldn't hoe corn*
Schoenherr, John. *The barn*
Schulz, Charles M. *Snoopy's facts and fun book about farms*
Seignobosc, Françoise. *The big rain*

Selsam, Millicent E. *Keep looking!*
  More potatoes!
Sewell, Helen Moore. *Blue barns*
Sherman, Nancy. *Gwendolyn and the
  weathercock*
Short, Mayo. *Andy and the wild ducks*
Skofield, James. *Snow country*
Slobodkina, Esphyr. *The wonderful feast*
Smith, Donald. *Farm numbers 1, 2, 3*
Stevenson, James. *"Could be worse!"*
Stolz, Mary Slattery. *Emmett's pig*
Tafuri, Nancy. *Early morning in the barn
  Who's counting?*
Teal, Valentine. *The little woman wanted
  noise*
Thiele, Colin. *Farmer Schulz's ducks*
Tolstoĭ, Alekseĭ Nikolaevich. *The great big
  enormous turnip*
Torgersen, Don Arthur. *The girl who
  tricked the troll*
Tresselt, Alvin R. *Sun up
  Wake up, farm!*
Tripp, Paul. *The strawman who smiled by
  mistake*
Turner, Ann. *Dakota dugout*
Udry, Janice May. *Emily's autumn*
Vaës, Alain. *The porcelain pepper pot*
Van Horn, Grace. *Little red rooster*
Wallner, John. *Old MacDonald had a
  farm*
Watson, Nancy Dingman. *What does A
  begin with?
  What is one?*
Wheeler, Cindy. *Rose*
Wiesner, William. *Happy-Go-Lucky*
Wolff, Ashley. *A year of beasts*
Worthington, Phoebe. *Teddy bear farmer*
Wright, Dare. *Look at a calf
  Look at a colt*
Yolen, Jane. *The giant's farm*
Zalben, Jane Breskin. *Basil and Hillary*
Ziefert, Harriet. *On our way to the barn*

Fathers *see* Family life – fathers

Father's Day *see* Holidays – Father's Day

Fear *see* Emotions – fear

Feeling *see* Senses – touching

Feelings *see* Emotions

Feet *see* Anatomy

Fighting *see* Behavior – fighting, arguing

Fingers *see* Anatomy

Finishing things *see* Character traits –
  completing things

Finland *see* Foreign lands – Finland

Fire

Anderson, C. W. (Clarence Williams).
  Blaze and the forest fire
Augarde, Steve. *Pig*
Averill, Esther. *When Jenny lost her scarf*
Baker, Eugene. *Fire*
Barr, Jene. *Fire snorkel number 7*
Baumann, Kurt. *Piro and the fire brigade*
Beatty, Hetty Burlingame. *Little Owl
  Indian*
Belloc, Hilaire. *Matilda who told lies and
  was burned to death*
Bernstein, Margery. *Coyote goes hunting for
  fire*
Bester, Roger. *Fireman Jim*
Bible, Charles. *Jennifer's new chair*
Bond, Ruskin. *Flames in the forest*
Brenner, Barbara. *Mr. Tall and Mr. Small*
Brown, Margaret Wise. *The little fireman*
De Regniers, Beatrice Schenk. *Willy
  O'Dwyer jumped in the fire*
Du Bois, William Pène. *Otto and the magic
  potatoes*
Elliott, Dan. *A visit to the Sesame Street
  firehouse*
Fire
Firehouse
Foreman, Michael. *Panda and the bushfire*
Gramatky, Hardie. *Hercules*
Greene, Graham. *The little fire engine*
Haines, Gail Kay. *Fire*
Kirn, Ann. *The tale of a crocodile*
Lawrence, John. *Pope Leo's elephant*
Mahood, Kenneth. *The laughing dragon*
Miklowitz, Gloria D. *Save that raccoon!*
Miles, Miska. *The fox and the fire*
Moskin, Marietta D. *Lysbet and the fire
  kittens*
Newton, James R. *A forest is reborn*
Quackenbush, Robert M. *There'll be a hot
  time in the old town tonight*
Roth, Susan L. *Fire came to the earth people*
Spiegel, Doris. *Danny and Company 92*
Taylor, Mark. *Henry explores the mountains*
Troughton, Joanna. *How rabbit stole the
  fire*
Ungerer, Tomi. *Adelaide
  The Mellops strike oil*
Woolf, Virginia. *The widow and the parrot*
Ziefert, Harriet. *Lewis the fire fighter*

Fire engines *see* Careers – firefighters;
  Trucks

Firefighters *see* Careers – firefighters

Fireflies *see* Insects – fireflies

Fish

Aliki. *The long lost coelacanth and other living fossils*
Arnosky, Jim. *A kettle of hawks, and other wildlife groups*
Aruego, José. *Pilyo the piranha*
Balet, Jan B. *Joanjo*
Beisert, Heide Helene. *Poor fish*
Berger, Gilda. *Sharks*
Brice, Tony. *The bashful goldfish*
Broekel, Ray. *Dangerous fish*
Brown, Margaret Wise. *The little fisherman*
Bruna, Dick. *The fish*
Buck, Pearl S. (Pearl Sydenstricker). *The dragon fish*
Coatsworth, Elizabeth. *Under the green willow*
Cole, Joanna. *A fish hatches*
  Hungry, hungry sharks
Cook, Bernadine. *The little fish that got away*
Cooper, Elizabeth K. *The fish from Japan*
Curious George goes to the aquarium
Damjan, Mischa. *The little sea horse*
Darby, Gene. *What is a fish?*
Eastman, David. *What is a fish?*
Friedman, Judi. *The eels' strange journey*
Gomi, Taro. *Where's the fish?*
Hall, Bill. *Fish tale*
Hawes, Judy. *Shrimps*
Hogan, Paula Z. *The salmon*
Ipcar, Dahlov. *The biggest fish in the sea*
Jacobs, Francine. *Barracuda*
Kalan, Robert. *Blue sea*
Laird, Donivee Martin. *The three little Hawaiian pigs and the magic shark*
Lionni, Leo. *Fish is fish*
  Swimmy
Mendoza, George. *The gillygoofang*
Miller, Susanne Santoro. *Whales and sharks and other creatures of the deep*
Oxford Scientific Films. *Jellyfish and other sea creatures*
  The stickleback cycle
Palmer, Helen Marion. *A fish out of water*
Parnall, Peter. *The great fish*
Parry, Marian. *King of the fish*
Phleger, Fred B. *Red Tag comes back*
Ricciuti, Edward R. *Donald and the fish that walked*
Schatell, Brian. *Midge and Fred*
Schumacher, Claire. *Alto and Tango*
Selsam, Millicent E. *A first look at sharks*
  Plenty of fish
Seuss, Dr. *McElligot's pool*
  One fish, two fish, red fish, blue fish
Shaw, Evelyn S. *Fish out of school*
Turnage, Sheila. *Trout the magnificent*
Valens, Evans G. *Wingfin and Topple*
Waber, Bernard. *Lorenzo*

Waechter, Friedrich Karl. *Three is company*
Walton, Rick. *Something's fishy!*
Wezel, Peter. *The good bird*
Wildsmith, Brian. *Brian Wildsmith's fishes*
Wong, Herbert H. *My goldfish*
Wood, John Norris. *Oceans*
Wyse, Lois. *Two guppies, a turtle and Aunt Edna*
Yorinks, Arthur. *Louis the fish*

Fish tanks *see* Aquariums

Fishermen *see* Careers — fishermen

Fishing *see* Sports — fishing

Flamingos *see* Birds — flamingos

Flattery *see* Character traits — flattery

Fleas *see* Insects — fleas

Flies *see* Insects — flies

Floods *see* Weather — floods

Flowers

Aksakov, Sergei. *The scarlet flower*
Anno, Mitsumasa. *The king's flower*
Baker, Jeffrey J. W. *Patterns of nature*
Barker, Cicely Mary. *Berry flower fairies*
  Blossom flower fairies
  Flower fairies of the seasons
  Spring flower fairies
  Summer flower fairies
Bjork, Christina. *Linnea in Monet's garden*
Campbell, Rod. *Buster's afternoon*
Chapman, Carol. *Barney Bipple's magic dandelions*
Cooney, Barbara. *Miss Rumphius*
Delaney, A. *The gunnywolf*
Denver, John. *The children and the flowers*
De Paola, Tomie. *The legend of the bluebonnet*
Ehlert, Lois. *Planting a rainbow*
Ellentuck, Shan. *A sunflower as big as the sun*
Fisher, Aileen. *And a sunflower grew*
  Petals yellow and petals red
Givens, Janet Eaton. *Something wonderful happened*
Harper, Wilhelmina. *The gunniwolf*
Heilbroner, Joan. *Robert the rose horse*
Heller, Ruth. *The reason for a flower*
Heyduck-Huth, Hilde. *The strawflower*
Hidaka, Masako. *Girl from the snow country*
Hoban, Julia. *Amy loves the sun*
Ichikawa, Satomi. *Suzette and Nicholas in the garden*
Ipcar, Dahlov. *The land of flowers*

Kirkpatrick, Rena K. *Look at flowers*
Lerner, Carol. *Flowers of a woodland spring*
Lobel, Arnold. *The rose in my garden*
McMillan, Bruce. *Counting wildflowers*
Maris, Ron. *In my garden*
Olson, Arielle North. *The lighthouse keeper's daughter*
Rockwell, Anne F. *My spring robin*
Selsam, Millicent E. *A first look at flowers*
Slobodkina, Esphyr. *Pinky and the petunias*
Steig, William. *Rotten island*
Sugita, Yutaka. *The flower family*
Williams, Barbara. *Hello, dandelions!*

Flying *see* Activities – flying

Fog *see* Weather – fog

Fold-out books *see* Format, unusual – toy and movable books

Folk and fairy tales

Aardema, Verna. *Bimwili and the Zimwi*
Bringing the rain to Kapiti Plain
Half-a-ball-of-kenki
Ji-nongo-nongo means riddles
Oh, Kojo! How could you!
Princess Gorilla and a new kind of water
The riddle of the drum
The vingananee and the tree toad
Who's in Rabbit's house?
Why mosquitoes buzz in people's ears
Abisch, Roz. *The clever turtle*
Mai-Ling and the mirror
Sweet Betsy from Pike
Adshead, Gladys L. *Brownies - hush!*
Æsop. *The Æsop for children*, ill. by Milo Winter
Æsop's fables, ill. by Gaynor Chapman
Æsop's fables, ill. by Heidi Holder
Æsop's fables, ill. by Claire Littlejohn
Æsop's fables, ill. by Nick Price
Æsop's fables, ill. by Alice and Martin Provensen
Æsop's fables, ill. by Robert Rayevsky
Æsop's fables, ill. by Helen Siegl
The country mouse and the city mouse, ill. by Laura Lydecker
The fables of Æsop, ill. by Frank Baber
The hare and the frogs
The hare and the tortoise, ill. by Paul Galdone
The hare and the tortoise, ill. by Gerald Rose
The hare and the tortoise, ill. by Peter Weevers
The lion and the mouse, ill. by Gerald Rose
The lion and the mouse, ill. by Ed Young

The miller, his son and their donkey, ill. by Roger Antoine Duvoisin
The miller, his son and their donkey, ill. by Eugen Sopko
Once in a wood
The raven and the fox, ill. by Gerald Rose
Seven fables from Æsop, ill. by Robert W. Alley
Tales from Æsop, ill. by Harold Jones
Three fox fables
The tortoise and the hare, ill. by Janet Stevens
The town mouse and the country mouse, ill. by Lorinda Bryan Cauley
The town mouse and the country mouse, ill. by Paul Galdone
The town mouse and the country mouse, ill. by Tom Garcia
The town mouse and the country mouse, ill. by Janet Stevens
Wolf! wolf!
Afanas'ev, Aleksandr. *Russian folk tales*
Ahlberg, Allan. *The Cinderella show*
Alden, Laura. *Learning about fairies*
Aleichem, Sholem. *Hanukah money*
Alexander, Lloyd. *Coll and his white pig*
The king's fountain
The truthful harp
Alger, Leclaire. *All in the morning early*
Always room for one more
Aliki. *Diogenes*
The eggs
George and the cherry tree
The story of Johnny Appleseed
Three gold pieces
The twelve months
The all-amazing ha ha book
Allard, Harry. *May I stay?*
Allen, Linda. *The giant who had no heart*
Ambrus, Victor G. *The little cockerel*
The seven skinny goats
The Sultan's bath
The three poor tailors
Andersen, H. C. (Hans Christian). *The emperor and the nightingale*, ill. by James Watling
The emperor's new clothes, ill. by Pamela Baldwin-Ford
The emperor's new clothes, ill. by Erik Blegvad
The emperor's new clothes, ill. by Virginia Lee Burton
The emperor's new clothes, ill. by Jack and Irene Delano
The emperor's new clothes, ill. by Hélène Desputeaux
The emperor's new clothes, ill. by Birte Dietz
The emperor's new clothes, ill. by Dorothée Duntze
The emperor's new clothes, ill. by Jack Kent

The emperor's new clothes, ill. by Monika Laimgruber

The emperor's new clothes, ill. by Anne F. Rockwell

The emperor's new clothes, ill. by Janet Stevens

The emperor's new clothes, ill. by Nadine Bernard Westcott

The emperor's nightingale, ill. by Georges Lemoine

The fir tree, ill. by Nancy Elkholm Burkert

It's perfectly true!, ill. by Janet Stevens

The little match girl, ill. by Rachel Isadora

The little match girl, ill. by Blair Lent

The little mermaid, ill. by Edward Frascino

The little mermaid, ill. by Chihiro Iwasaki

The little mermaid, ill. by Dorothy Pulis Lathrop

The little mermaid, ill. by Josef Paleček

The little mermaid, ill. by Daniel San Souci

The nightingale, ill. by Harold Berson

The nightingale, ill. by Nancy Ekholm Burkert

The nightingale, ill. by Demi

The nightingale, ill. by Beni Montresor

The nightingale, ill. by Lisbeth Zwerger

The old man is always right, ill. by Feodor Rojankovsky

The princess and the pea, ill. by Dorothée Duntze

The princess and the pea, ill. by Dick Gackenbach

The princess and the pea, ill. by Paul Galdone

The princess and the pea, ill. by Janet Stevens

The princess and the pea, ill. by Eve Tharlet

The snow queen, ill. by Angela Barrett

The snow queen, ill. by Toma Bogdanovic

The snow queen, ill. by June Atkin Corwin

The snow queen, ill. by Susan Jeffers

The snow queen, ill. by Errol Le Cain

The snow queen, ill. by Bernadette Watts

The snow queen, ill. by Arieh Zeldich

The snow queen and other stories from Hans Andersen, ill. by Edmund Dulac

The steadfast tin soldier, ill. by Thomas Di Grazia

The steadfast tin soldier, ill. by Paul Galdone

The steadfast tin soldier, ill. by David Jorgensen

The steadfast tin soldier, ill. by Monika Laimgruber

The steadfast tin soldier, ill. by Alain Vaës

The swineherd, ill. by Erik Blegvad

The swineherd, ill. by Dorothée Duntze

The swineherd, ill. by Lisbeth Zwerger

Thumbelina, ill. by Adrienne Adams

Thumbelina, ill. by Susan Jeffers

Thumbelina, ill. by Christine Willis Nigognossian

Thumbelina, ill. by Gustaf Tenggren

Thumbelina, ill. by Lisbeth Zwerger, tr. by Richard and Clara Winston

Thumbeline, ill. by Lisbeth Zwerger, tr. by Anthea Bell

The tinderbox, ill. by Warwick Hutton

The ugly duckling, ill. by Adrienne Adams

The ugly duckling, ill. by Lorinda Bryan Cauley

The ugly duckling, ill. by Tadasu Izawa and Shigemi Hijikata

The ugly duckling, ill. by Johannes Larsen

The ugly duckling, ill. by Thomas Locker

The ugly duckling, ill. by Josef Paleček

The ugly duckling, ill. by Maria Ruis

The ugly duckling, ill. by Daniel San Souci

The ugly duckling, ill. by Robert Van Nutt

The ugly little duck, ill. by Peggy Perry Anderson

The wild swans, ill. by Angela Barrett

The wild swans, ill. by Susan Jeffers

The woman with the eggs, ill. by Ray Cruz

Anderson, Lonzo. *Arion and the dolphins*

Anderson, Robin. *Sinabouda Lily*

Androcles and the lion, ill. by Janusz Grabianski

Anglund, Joan Walsh. *Nibble nibble mousekin*

Anno, Mitsumasa. *Anno's Æsop*

In shadowland

Arabian Nights. *Arabian Nights entertainments*

The flying carpet

Ariane. *Small Cloud*

Armitage, Marcia. *Lupatelli's favorite nursery tales*

Arnold, Caroline. *The terrible Hodag*

Arnott, Kathleen. *Spiders, crabs and creepy crawlers*

Aronin, Ben. *The secret of the Sabbath fish*

Aruego, José. *A crocodile's tale*

Look what I can do

Asbjørnsen, P. C. (Peter Christen). *The three billy goats Gruff*, ill. by Marcia Brown

Three billy goats Gruff, ill. by Tom Dunnington

The three billy goats Gruff, ill. by Paul Galdone

The three billy goats Gruff, ill. by Janet Stevens

The three billy goats Gruff, ill. by William Stobbs

Auerbach, Marjorie. *King Lavra and the barber*

Aulaire, Ingri Mortenson d'. *Children of the northlights*

Don't count your chicks

East of the sun and west of the moon

Bro, Marguerite H. *The animal friends of Peng-u*

Brown, Abbie Farwell. *Under the rowan tree*

Brown, Marcia. *The blue jackal*
The bun
Once a mouse...
Stone soup

Browning, Robert. *The pied piper of Hamelin*, ill. by Kate Greenaway
The pied piper of Hamelin, ill. by Anatoly Ivanov
The pied piper of Hamelin, ill. by Errol Le Cain

Bryan, Ashley. *Beat the story-drum, pum-pum*
The cat's purr
Lion and the ostrich chicks
Sh-ko and his eight wicked brothers

Bryant, Sara Cone. *Epaminondas and his auntie*

Bryson, Bernarda. *The twenty miracles of Saint Nicolas*

Buck, Pearl S. (Pearl Sydenstricker). *The Chinese story teller*
The dragon fish

Buckley, Richard. *The foolish tortoise*
The greedy python

Burland, Brian. *St. Nicholas and the tub*

Caldecott, Randolph. *The Randolph Caldecott treasury*

Calhoun, Mary. *The goblin under the stairs*
Jack the wise and the Cornish cuckoos
Old man Whickutt's donkey
The pixy and the lazy housewife
The runaway brownie
The thieving dwarfs
The witch's pig

Carey, Valerie Scho. *The devil and mother Crump*

Carle, Eric. *Eric Carle's treasury of classic stories for children*
Twelve tales from Æsop

Carrick, Malcolm. *Happy Jack*
I can squash elephants!

Carter, Angela. *The sleeping beauty and other favourite fairy tales*

Carter, Anne. *Beauty and the beast*, ill. by Binette Schroeder

Cauley, Lorinda Bryan. *The cock, the mouse and the little red hen*
The goose and the golden coins

Cendrars, Blaise. *Shadow*

Chafetz, Henry. *The legend of Befana*

Chapman, Carol. *The tale of Meshka the Kvetch*

Chapman, Gaynor. *The luck child*

Chapman, Jean. *Moon-Eyes*

Charles Prince of Wales. *The old man of Lochnagar*

Charlip, Remy. *Harlequin and the gift of many colors*

Charlot, Martin. *Felisa and the magic tikling bird*

Chase, Catherine. *The nightingale and the fool*

Chase, Richard. *Jack and the three sillies*

Chaucer, Geoffrey. *Chanticleer and the fox*, ill. by Barbara Cooney

Chicken Little. *Chicken Licken*, ill. by Jutta Ash
Chicken Licken, ill. by Gavin Bishop
Henny Penny, ill. by Paul Galdone
Henny Penny, ill. by William Stobbs
The story of Chicken Licken, adapt. and ill. by Jan Ormerod

Chorao, Kay. *The baby's story book*
The child's story book

Christensen, Jack. *The forgotten rainbow*

Christian, Mary Blount. *April fool*

Cleaver, Elizabeth. *The enchanted caribou*

Clement, Claude. *The painter and the wild swans*

Coatsworth, Elizabeth. *The giant golden book of cat stories*

Cocagnac, A. M. (Augustin Maurice). *The three trees of the Samurai*

Cohen, Barbara. *The demon who would not die*
Here come the Purim players!

Cohen, Carol L. *The mud pony*

Cohen, Caron Lee. *Renata, Whizbrain and the ghost*
Sally Ann Thunder Ann Whirlwind Crockett

Cole, Babette. *Prince Cinders*

Cole, Brock. *The giant's toe*

Cole, Joanna. *Bony-legs*
Doctor Change
Golly Gump swallowed a fly

Collodi, Carlo. *The adventures of Pinocchio*

Conger, Lesley. *Tops and bottoms*

Conover, Chris. *The wizard's daughter*

Coombs, Patricia. *The magic pot*
Tilabel

Cooney, Barbara. *Little brother and little sister*

Cooper, Susan. *The Selkie girl*
The silver cow

Cormack, M. Grant. *Animal tales from Ireland*

Costa, Nicoletta. *The mischievous princess*

Coville, Bruce. *Sarah and the dragon*

Credle, Ellis. *Big fraid, little fraid*

Crompton, Anne Eliot. *The lifting stone*
The winter wife

Crossley-Holland, Kevin. *The green children*
The pedlar of Swaffham

Cummings, E. E. *Fairy tales*

Daniels, Guy. *The Tsar's riddles*

Dasent, George W. *East o' the sun, west o' the moon*

Daugherty, Sonia. *Vanka's donkey*

Davis, Douglas F. *The lion's tail*

Dayrell, Elphinstone. *Why the sun and the moon live in the sky*

DeArmond, Dale. *The seal oil lamp*

Dee, Ruby. *Two ways to count to ten*

De Gerez, Toni. *Louhi, witch of North Farm*

Demi. *Chen Ping and his magic axe*
A Chinese zoo
Demi's reflective fables
The hallowed horse
Under the shade of the mulberry tree

De Paola, Tomie. *Favorite nursery tales*
Fin M'Coul
The legend of Old Befana
The legend of the bluebonnet
The legend of the Indian paintbrush
The mysterious giant of Barletta
The Prince of the Dolomites

De Regniers, Beatrice Schenk. *Everyone is good for something*
Little Sister and the Month Brothers
Red Riding Hood

Dewey, Ariane. *Febold Feboldson*
The fish Peri
Laffite, the pirate
Pecos Bill
The thunder god's son

Dick Whittington and his cat. *Dick Whittington*, ill. by Edward Ardizzone
Dick Whittington, ill. by Antony Maitland
Dick Whittington and his cat, ill. by Marcia Brown
Dick Whittington and his cat, ill. by Kurt Werth

Dobbs, Rose. *More once-upon-a-time stories*
Once-upon-a-time story book

Domanska, Janina. *The best of the bargain*
Busy Monday morning
King Krakus and the dragon
Look, there is a turtle flying
Marek, the little fool
Palmiero and the ogre
A scythe, a rooster and a cat
The tortoise and the tree
The turnip
What happens next?
Why so much noise?

Dos Santos, Joyce Audy. *The diviner*
Henri and the Loup-Garou

Du Bois, William Pène. *The hare and the tortoise and the tortoise and the hare*

Duff, Maggie. *Dancing turtle*
The princess and the pumpkin
Rum pum pum

Dukas, P. (Paul Abraham). *The sorcerer's apprentice*, ill. by Ryohei Yanagihara

Elkin, Benjamin. *The big jump and other stories*
The king's wish and other stories
Six foolish fishermen
Such is the way of the world
The wisest man in the world

Elwell, Peter. *The king of the pipers*

Emberley, Barbara. *One wide river to cross*

Esbensen, Barbara Juster. *The star maiden*

Evans, Katherine. *The boy who cried wolf*
A bundle of sticks
The maid and her pail of milk
The man, the boy and the donkey

Felton, Harold W. *Pecos Bill and the mustang*

Fiddle-i-fee

The firebird, ill. by Moira Kemp

The firebird, ill. by Boris Zvorykin

Fisher, Leonard Everett. *The Olympians*
Star signs
Theseus and the minotaur

Fleischman, Paul. *The animal hedge*

Flot, Jeannette B. *Princess Kalina and the hedgehog*

Foley, Bernice Williams. *The gazelle and the hunter*
A walk among clouds

Forest, Heather. *The baker's dozen*

Fournier, Catharine. *The coconut thieves*

The fox went out on a chilly night

Francis, Frank. *Natasha's new doll*

Frasconi, Antonio. *The snow and the sun, la nieve y el sol*

Freedman, Florence B. *Brothers*

Fregosi, Claudia. *The pumpkin sparrow*
Snow maiden

Fritz, Jean. *The good giants and the bad Pukwudgies*

Gackenbach, Dick. *Arabella and Mr. Crack*
The perfect mouse

Gág, Wanda. *The sorcerer's apprentice*

Galdone, Joanna. *Amber day*
The little girl and the big bear

Galdone, Paul. *The amazing pig*
Androcles and the lion
The greedy old fat man
King of the cats
The magic porridge pot
The monkey and the crocodile
Obedient Jack
A strange servant
The teeny-tiny woman
What's in fox's sack?

Gammell, Stephen. *The story of Mr. and Mrs. Vinegar*

Gauch, Patricia Lee. *The little friar who flew*
On to Widecombe Fair

Gerstein, Mordicai. *The seal mother*

Gilleo, Alma. *Learning about monsters*

The gingerbread boy. *The gingerbread boy,*
ill. by Scott Cook
The gingerbread boy, ill. by Paul Galdone
The gingerbread boy, ill. by Joan Elizabeth
Goodman
The gingerbread boy, ill. by William Curtis
Holdsworth
The gingerbread man
The pancake boy
Whiff, sniff, nibble and chew
Ginsburg, Mirra. *The Chinese mirror*
The fisherman's son
The fox and the hare
How the sun was brought back to the sky
Pampalche of the silver teeth
Striding slippers
Go tell Aunt Rhody. *Go tell Aunt Rhody,*
ill. by Aliki
Gobhai, Mehlli. *Usha, the mouse-maiden*
Goble, Paul. *Buffalo woman*
The gift of the sacred dog
Her seven brothers
Iktomi and the boulder
Star boy
The golden goose, ill. by William Stobbs
The good-hearted youngest brother
Gramatky, Hardie. *Nikos and the sea god*
Grant, Joan. *The monster that grew small*
Greene, Ellin. *Princess Rosetta and the
popcorn man*
Grieg, E. H. (Edvard Hagerup). *E. H.
Grieg's Peer Gynt*
Grifalconi, Ann. *The village of round and
square houses*
Grimm, Jacob. *The bear and the kingbird*
The bearskinner
The brave little tailor, ill. by Mark
Corcoran
The brave little tailor, ill. by Svend Otto S.
The brave little tailor, ill. by Daniel San
Souci
The Bremen town musicians, ill. by Donna
Diamond
The Bremen town musicians, ill. by Janina
Domanska
The Bremen town musicians, ill. by Paul
Galdone
Bremen town musicians, ill. by Josef
Paleček
The Bremen town musicians, ill. by Ilse
Plume
Cinderella, ill. by Nonny Hogrogian
Cinderella, ill. by Svend Otto S.
Clever Kate
The devil with the green hairs
The donkey prince, ill. by Barbara Cooney
The earth gnome, ill. by Margot Tomes
The elves and the shoemaker, ill. by Paul
Galdone
The elves and the shoemaker, ill. by
Bernadette Watts

The falling stars, ill. by Eugen Sopko
The fisherman and his wife, ill. by Monika
Laimgruber
The fisherman and his wife, ill. by Margot
Tomes
The fisherman and his wife, ill. by Margot
Zemach
The four clever brothers, ill. by Felix
Hoffmann
The glass mountain, ill. by Nonny
Hogrogian
Godfather Cat and Mousie, ill. by Ann
Schweninger
The golden bird
The golden goose, ill. by Dorothée Duntze
The golden goose, ill. by Isadore Seltzer
The golden goose, ill. by Martin Ursell
The goose girl, ill. by Sabine Bruntjen
Hans in luck, ill. by Paul Galdone
Hans in luck, ill. by Felix Hoffmann
Hansel and Gretel, ill. by Adrienne
Adams
Hansel and Gretel, ill. by Anthony
Browne
Hansel and Gretel, ill. by Susan Jeffers
Hansel and Gretel, ill. by Winslow P. Pels
Hansel and Gretel, ill. by Conxita
Rodriguez
Hansel and Gretel, ill. by John Wallner
Hansel and Gretel, ill. by Paul O. Zelinsky
Hansel and Gretel, ill. by Lisbeth Zwerger
The horse, the fox, and the lion, ill. by Paul
Galdone
Jorinda and Joringel, ill. by Adrienne
Adams
Jorinda and Joringel, ill. by Jutta Ash
Jorinda and Joringel, ill. by Margot
Tomes
King Grisly-Beard
Little red cap, ill. by Lisbeth Zwerger
Little Red Riding Hood, ill. by Frank
Aloise
Little Red Riding Hood, ill. by Gwen
Connelly
Little Red Riding Hood, ill. by Paul
Galdone
Little Red Riding Hood, ill. by John S.
Goodall
Little Red Riding Hood, ill. by Trina
Schart Hyman
Little Red Riding Hood, ill. by Bernadette
Watts
Lucky Hans, ill. by Eugen Sopko
Mother Holly
Mrs. Fox's wedding
The musicians of Bremen, ill. by Svend
Otto S.
The musicians of Bremen, ill. by Martin
Ursell
Rapunzel, ill. by Jutta Ash
Rapunzel, ill. by Bert Dodson

Ichikawa, Satomi. *A child's book of seasons*
Sun through small leaves
Iké, Jane Hori. *A Japanese fairy tale*
Illyés, Gyula. *Matt the gooseherd*
I'm mad at you
Irving, Washington. *The legend of Sleepy Hollow*, ill. by Daniel San Souci
Rip Van Winkle, ill. by John Howe
Rip Van Winkle, ill. by Thomas Locker
Rip Van Winkle, ill. by Peter Wingham
Isele, Elizabeth. *The frog princess*
Ishii, Momoko. *The tongue-cut sparrow*
Ivanov, Anatoly. *Ol' Jake's lucky day*
Jack and the beanstalk. *The history of Mother Twaddle and the marvelous achievements of her son Jack*
Jack and the beanstalk, ill. by Lorinda Bryan Cauley
Jack and the beanstalk, ill. by Ed Parker
Jack and the beanstalk, ill. by Tony Ross
Jack and the beanstalk, ill. by William Stobbs
Jack and the beanstalk, ill. by Anne Wilsdorf
Jack the giantkiller, ill. by Tony Ross
Jack the giant killer, ill. by Anne Wilsdorf
Jacobs, Joseph. *The crock of gold*
Hereafterthis
Hudden and Dudden and Donald O'Neary
Johnny-cake, ill. by Emma Lillian Brock
Johnny-cake, ill. by William Stobbs
Lazy Jack, ill. by Barry Wilkinson
Master of all masters
Old Mother Wiggle-Waggle
The three sillies
Jagendorf, Moritz A. *Kwi-na the eagle*
Jameson, Cynthia. *The clay pot boy*
The house of five bears
A January fog will freeze a hog
Jaquith, Priscilla. *Bo Rabbit smart for true*
Jennings, Linda M. *Coppelia*
The sleeping beauty: the story of the ballet
Johnson, Crockett. *Harold's fairy tale*
Jones, Harold. *Tales to tell*
Jones, Olive. *A treasure box of fairy tales*
Keats, Ezra Jack. *John Henry*
Kellogg, Steven. *Chicken Little*
Johnny Appleseed
Pecos Bill
Kent, Jack. *Jack Kent's happy-ever-after book*
Jack Kent's hokus pokus bedtime book
Kirn, Ann. *The tale of a crocodile*
Kismaric, Carole. *The rumor of Pavel and Paali*
Knight, Hilary. *Hilary Knight's Cinderella*
Knutson, Barbara. *Why the crab has no head*
Koenig, Marion. *The tale of fancy Nancy*
Kurtycz, Marcos. *Tigers and opossums*

La Fontaine, Jean de. *The hare and the tortoise*
The lion and the rat
The miller, the boy and the donkey
The north wind and the sun
Langstaff, John M. *Oh, a-hunting we will go*
Ol' Dan Tucker
On Christmas day in the morning
Over in the meadow
Soldier, soldier, won't you marry me?
The swapping boy
The two magicians
Langton, Jane. *The hedgehog boy*
Laroche, Michel. *The snow rose*
Lattimore, Deborah Nourse. *The prince and the golden ax*
Lazy Jack. *Lazy Jack*, ill. by Bert Dodson
Lazy Jack, ill. by Kurt Werth
Lee, Jeanne M. *Legend of the Li River*
The legend of the milky way
Toad is the uncle of heaven
Lenski, Lois. *Susie Mariar*
Lent, Blair. *John Tabor's ride*
Lester, Julius. *The knee-high man and other tales*
Lewis, J. Patrick. *The tsar and the amazing cow*
Lexau, Joan M. *Crocodile and hen*
It all began with a drip, drip, drip
Lipkind, William. *The magic feather duster*
The little red hen. *The little red hen*, ill. by Janina Domanska
The little red hen, ill. by Paul Galdone
The little red hen, ill. by Mel Pekarsky
The little red hen, ill. by William Stobbs
The little red hen, ill. by Margot Zemach
Little Tuppen, ill. by Paul Galdone
Littledale, Freya. *The farmer in the soup*
Peter and the north wind
Littlefield, William. *The whiskers of Ho Ho*
Lloyd, David. *The ridiculous story of Gammer Gurton's needle*
Löfgren, Ulf. *The boy who ate more than the giant and other Swedish folktales*
Lorenz, Lee. *Big Gus and Little Gus*
The feathered ogre
Pinchpenny John
Scornful Simkin
Luenn, Nancy. *The dragon kite*
MacBeth, George. *Jonah and the Lord*
McCurdy, Michael. *The devils who learned to be good*
McDermott, Beverly Brodsky. *The crystal apple*
The Golem
McDermott, Gerald. *Anansi the spider*
Arrow to the sun
Daniel O'Rourke
Daughter of earth
The stonecutter

The voyage of Osiris
MacDonald, George. *The light princess*, ill. by Maurice Sendak
The light princess, ill. by Katie Thamer Treherne
Little Daylight
McFarland, John. *The exploding frog and other fables from Æsop*
McHale, Ethel Kharasch. *Son of thunder*
McKee, David. *The man who was going to mind the house*
McKissack, Patricia C. *Cinderella*, ill. by Tom Dunnington
Mirandy and brother wind
McLenighan, Valjean. *Turtle and rabbit*
What you see is what you get
You are what you are
You can go jump
Maestro, Giulio. *The tortoise's tug of war*
Magnus, Erica. *The boy and the devil*
Old Lars
Maitland, Antony. *Idle Jack*
Malcolmson, Anne. *The song of Robin Hood*
Mamin-Sibiryak, D. N. *Grey Neck*
Marshall, James. *Red Riding Hood*
Martin, Bill (William Ivan). *Sounds of laughter*
Martin, Rafe. *Foolish rabbit's big mistake*
The hungry tigress
Matsuno, Masako. *Taro and the bamboo shoot*
Matsutani, Miyoko. *The fisherman under the sea*
The witch's magic cloth
Mayer, Marianna. *Beauty and the beast*
The black horse
The little jewel box
My first book of nursery tales
Mayer, Mercer. *The Pied Piper of Hamelin*
Merriam, Eve. *Epaminondas*
Michael, Emory H. *Androcles and the lion*
Miller, Edna. *Mousekin's fables*
Milne, A. A. (Alan Alexander). *Prince Rabbit*
Mirkovic, Irene. *The greedy shopkeeper*
Mobley, Jane. *The star husband*
Moeri, Louise. *Star Mother's youngest child*
Molarsky, Osmond. *The peasant and the fly*
Moncure, Jane Belk. *The talking tabby cat*
Moon, Dolly M. *My very first book of cowboy songs*
Morel, Eve. *Fairy tales*
Fairy tales and fables
Morimoto, Junko. *The inch boy*
Mouse's marriage
Morris, Ann. *The Cinderella rebus book*
The Little Red Riding Hood rebus book
Morris, Winifred. *The magic leaf*
Mosel, Arlene. *Tikki Tikki Tembo*

Mother Goose. *The golden goose book*, ill. by L. Leslie Brooke
London Bridge is falling down, ill. by Ed Emberley
London Bridge is falling down, ill. by Peter Spier
Moxley, Susan. *Abdul's treasure*
Muller, Robin. *The lucky old woman*
The sorcerer's apprentice
Myers, Walter Dean. *The golden serpent*
Neale, J. M. *Good King Wenceslas*
Nesbit, Edith. *Beauty and the beast*, ill. by Julia Christie
The last of the dragons
Ness, Evaline. *The girl and the goatherd*
Newton, Patricia Montgomery. *The five sparrows*
Nikly, Michelle. *The princess on the nut*
Nister, Ernest. *Little tales from long ago*
Nixon, Joan Lowery. *Bigfoot makes a movie*
Norman, Howard. *Who-Paddled-Backward-With-Trout*
Nygren, Tord. *Fiddler and his brothers*
O'Connor, Jane. *The teeny tiny woman*
Odoyevsky, Vladimir. *Old Father Frost*
The old-fashioned children's storybook
The old woman and her pig
Opie, Iona Archibald. *A nursery companion*
Oram, Hiawyn. *Skittlewonder and the wizard*
Over in the meadow, ill. by Ezra Jack Keats
A paper of pins
Parkinson, Kathy. *The enormous turnip*
Parnall, Peter. *The great fish*
Parry, Marian. *King of the fish*
Parsons, Virginia. *Pinocchio and Gepetto*
Pinocchio and the money tree
Pinocchio goes on the stage
Pinocchio plays truant
The peasant's pea patch
Pellowski, Anne. *The nine crying dolls*
Perrault, Charles. *Cinderella*, ill. by Sheilah Beckett
Cinderella, ill. by Marcia Brown
Cinderella, ill. by Paul Galdone
Cinderella, ill. by Diane Goode
Cinderella, ill. by Susan Jeffers
Cinderella, ill. by Emanuele Luzzati
Cinderella, ill. by Phil Smith
Puss in boots, ill. by Marcia Brown
Puss in boots, ill. by Lorinda Bryan Cauley
Puss in boots, ill. by Jean Claverie
Puss in boots, ill. by Hans Fischer
Puss in boots, ill. by Paul Galdone
Puss in boots, ill. by Julia Noonan
Puss in boots, ill. by Tony Ross
Puss in boots, ill. by William Stobbs
Puss in boots, ill. by Barry Wilkinson
The sleeping beauty

Pevear, Richard. *Mister cat-and-a-half*
  Our king has horns!
Phillips, Mildred. *The sign in Mendel's
  window*
Phumla. *Nomi and the magic fish*
Pittman, Helena Clare. *The gift of the
  willows*
  A grain of rice
Plante, Patricia. *The turtle and the two
  ducks*
Plume, Ilse. *The story of Befana*
Polacco, Patricia. *Rechenka's eggs*
Polushkin, Maria. *Bubba and Babba*
  The little hen and the giant
Porazińska, Janina. *The enchanted book*
Prather, Ray. *The ostrich girl*
Presencer, Alain. *Roaring lion tales*
The prince who knew his fate
Prokofiev, Sergei Sergeievitch. *Peter and
  the wolf*, ill. by Reg Cartwright
  Peter and the wolf, ill. by Warren
  Chappell
  Peter and the wolf, ill. by Barbara Cooney
  Peter and the wolf, ill. by Frans Haacken
  Peter and the wolf, ill. by Alan Howard
  Peter and the wolf, ill. by Charles
  Mikolaycak
  Peter and the wolf, ill. by Jörg Müller
  Peter and the wolf, ill. by Josef Paleček
  Peter and the wolf, ill. by Kozo Shimizu
  Peter and the wolf, ill. by Erna Voigt
Quackenbush, Robert M. *Clementine*
  She'll be comin' 'round the mountain
  Skip to my Lou
  *There'll be a hot time in the old town
  tonight*
Quigley, Lillian Fox. *The blind men and the
  elephant*
Raphael, Elaine. *Turnabout*
Reesink, Marijke. *The golden treasure*
  The princess who always ran away
Riordan, James. *The three magic gifts*
Robbins, Ruth. *Baboushka and the three
  kings*
  How the first rainbow was made
Robinson, Adjai. *Femi and old grandaddie*
Rockwell, Anne F. *Bafana*
  *The old woman and her pig and 10 other
  stories*
  Poor Goose
  The three bears and 15 other stories
  Thump thump thump!
  The wolf who had a wonderful dream
  The wonderful eggs of Furicchia
Rogasky, Barbara. *The water of life*
Rogers, Margaret. *Green is beautiful*
Rohmer, Harriet. *How we came to the fifth
  world*
  The invisible hunters
  Mother scorpion country
Ronay, Jadja. *Ginger*

Root, Phyllis. *Soup for supper*
Rose, Anne. *Akimba and the magic cow*
  Pot full of luck
  Spider in the sky
  The talking turnip
  The triumphs of Fuzzy Fogtop
Ross, Tony. *The enchanted pig*
  Lazy Jack
  The pied piper of Hamelin
  Stone soup
Roth, Susan L. *Fire came to the earth people*
  Kanahena
Roughsey, Dick. *The giant devil-dingo*
Rounds, Glen. *The boll weevil*
  Casey Jones
  Sweet Betsy from Pike
Rudchenko, Ivan. *Ivanko and the dragon*
Rudolph, Marguerita. *I am your misfortune*
Sahagun, Bernardino de. *Spirit child*
San Souci, Robert D. *The enchanted tapestry*
  The legend of Scarface
  Song of Sedna
Sawyer, Ruth. *Journey cake, ho!*
Say, Allen. *Once under the cherry blossom
  tree*
Scarry, Richard. *Richard Scarry's animal
  nursery tales*
Schatz, Letta. *The extraordinary tug-of-war*
Schiller, Barbara. *The white rat's tale*
Schwartz, Alvin. *All of our noses are here
  and other stories*
Schwartz, Amy. *Yossel Zissel and the wisdom
  of Chelm*
Scott, Sally. *The magic horse*
  The three wonderful beggars
Scribner, Charles. *The devil's bridge*
Seeger, Pete. *Abiyoyo*
  The foolish frog
Seuling, Barbara. *The teeny tiny woman*
Sewall, Marcia. *Animal song*
  The little wee tyke
  The wee, wee mannie and the big, big coo
Shannon, George. *Oh, I love!*
  The Piney Woods peddler
Sherman, Josepha. *Vassilisa the wise*
Shi, Zhang Xiu. *Monkey and the white bone
  demon*
Showalter, Jean B. *The donkey ride*
Shub, Elizabeth. *Seeing is believing*
Shulevitz, Uri. *The treasure*
Shute, Linda. *Clever Tom and the
  leprechaun*
  Momotaro, the peach boy
Siberell, Anne. *Whale in the sky*
Siddiqui, Ashraf. *Bhombal Dass, the uncle
  of lion*
Simon, Seymour. *Volcanoes*
Sleator, William. *The angry moon*
Slobodkin, Louis. *Colette and the princess*
Snyder, Dianne. *The boy of the three-year
  nap*

Snyder, Zilpha Keatley. *The changing maze*

Spier, Peter. *The Erie Canal*
The legend of New Amsterdam
The squire's bride, ill. by Marcia Sewall

Stalder, Valerie. *Even the Devil is afraid of a shrew*

Stan-Padilla, Viento. *Dream Feather*

Stansfield, Ian. *The legend of the whale*

Steptoe, John. *Mufaro's beautiful daughters*
The story of jumping mouse

Stern, Simon. *Vasily and the dragon*

Stevens, Bryna. *Borrowed feathers and other fables*

Still, James. *Jack and the wonder beans*

Talbot, Toby. *A bucketful of moon*

Tarrant, Margaret. *Fairy tales*

Taylor, Mark. *The bold fisherman*
Old Blue, you good dog you

Tempest, P. *How the cock wrecked the manor*

Thompson, Harwood. *The witch's cat*

The three bears. *Goldilocks and the three bears*, ill. by Jan Brett
Goldilocks and the three bears, ill. by Lorinda Bryan Cauley
Goldilocks and the three bears, ill. by Jane Dyer
Goldilocks and the three bears, ill. by Lynn Bywaters Ferris
Goldilocks and the three bears, ill. by James Marshall
Goldilocks and the three bears, ill. by Janet Stevens
Goldilocks and the three bears, ill. by Bernadette Watts
The story of the three bears, ill. by L. Leslie Brooke
The story of the three bears, ill. by William Stobbs
The three bears, ill. by Paul Galdone
The three bears, ill. by Feodor Rojankovsky
The three bears, ill. by Robin Spowart

The three little pigs. *The story of the three little pigs*, ill. by L. Leslie Brooke
The story of the three little pigs, ill. by William Stobbs
The three-little pigs, facsimile ed.
The three little pigs, ill. by Caroline Bucknall
The three little pigs, ill. by Lorinda Bryan Cauley
The three little pigs, ill. by William Pène Du Bois
The three little pigs, ill. by Paul Galdone
The three little pigs, ill. by Rodney Peppé
The three little pigs, ill. by Edda Reinl
The three little pigs, ill. by John Wallner
The three little pigs, ill. by Irma Wilde
The three little pigs, ill. by Margot Zemach
The three pigs, ill. by Tony Ross

Tolstoĭ, Alekseĭ Nikolaevich. *The great big enormous turnip*

Tom Thumb. *Grimm Tom Thumb*
Tom Thumb, ill. by L. Leslie Brooke
Tom Thumb, ill. by Dennis Hockerman
Tom Thumb, ill. by Felix Hoffmann
Tom Thumb, ill. by Lidia Postma
Tom Thumb, ill. by Richard Jesse Watson
Tom Thumb, ill. by William Wiesner

Tom Tit Tot. *Tom Tit Tot*

Towle, Faith M. *The magic cooking pot*

Toye, William. *Fire stealer*
How summer came to Canada
The loon's necklace
The mountain goats of Temlaham

Tresselt, Alvin R. *The mitten*

Tripp, Wallace. *The tale of a pig*

Troughton, Joanna. *How rabbit stole the fire*
How the birds changed their feathers
Tortoise's dream
What made Tiddalik laugh
Who will be the sun?

Tsultim, Yeshe. *The mouse king*

Tune, Suelyn Ching. *How Maui slowed the sun*

Turkle, Brinton. *Deep in the forest*

Turska, Krystyna. *The magician of Cracow*
The woodcutter's duck

Uchida, Yoshiko. *The two foolish cats*

VanRynbach, Iris. *The soup stone*

Van Woerkom, Dorothy. *Alexandra the rock-eater*
The queen who couldn't bake gingerbread
The rat, the ox and the zodiac
Sea frog, city frog
Tit for tat

Varga, Judy. *The mare's egg*

Vernon, Adele. *The riddle*

Vesey, A. *The princess and the frog*

Waddell, Martin. *The tough princess*

Walker, Barbara K. *New patches for old*

Walsh, Grahame L. *Didane the koala*
The goori goori bird

Walt Disney Productions. *Walt Disney's Snow White and the seven dwarfs*

Walter, Mildred Pitts. *Ty's one-man band*

Watts, Bernadette. *St. Francis and the proud crow*

Weil, Lisl. *Pandora's box*

Weiss, Harvey. *The sooner hound*

Weiss, Nicki. *If you're happy and you know it*

Westerberg, Christine. *The cap that mother made*

Westwood, Jennifer. *Going to Squintum's*
Widdecombe Fair

Wiesner, David. *The loathsome dragon*

Wildsmith, Brian. *The true cross*

Williams, Jay. *Petronella*
The practical princess

The surprising things Maui did
Wilson, Sarah. *Beware the dragons!*
Winter, Jeanette. *The girl and the moon man*
Wolf, Ann. *The rabbit and the turtle*
Wolkstein, Diane. *The banza*
The cool ride in the sky
The legend of Sleepy Hollow
The magic wings
White wave
Wood, Audrey. *Heckedy Peg*
Wright, Freire. *Beauty and the beast*
Wright, Jill. *The old woman and the Willy Nilly Man*
Yagawa, Sumiko. *The crane wife*
Yashima, Tarō. *Seashore story*
Yeoman, John. *The wild washerwomen*
Yolen, Jane. *The hundredth dove and other tales*
Sleeping ugly
The three bears rhyme book
Young, Ed. *The rooster's horns*
The terrible Nung Gwama
Zelinsky, Paul O. *The maid and the mouse and the odd-shaped house*
Zemach, Harve. *Duffy and the devil*
Nail soup
Zemach, Kaethe. *The beautiful rat*
Zemach, Margot. *It could always be worse*
Jake and Honeybunch go to heaven
The little tiny woman
The three wishes
Zijlstra, Tjerk. *Benny and his geese*
Zola, Meguido. *The dream of promise*

Food

Adler, David A. *Bunny rabbit rebus*
Allamand, Pascale. *Cocoa beans and daisies*
Allen, Laura Jean. *Rollo and Tweedy and the case of the missing cheese*
Allen, Robert. *Ten little babies eat*
Ambrus, Victor G. *Country wedding*
Andrews, Jan. *Very last first time*
Armitage, Ronda. *Ice creams for Rosie*
The lighthouse keeper's lunch
Arnosky, Jim. *Raccoons and ripe corn*
Aronin, Ben. *The secret of the Sabbath fish*
Asch, Frank. *Good lemonade*
Moon bear
Popcorn
Azarian, Mary. *The tale of John Barleycorn or, From barley to beer*
Bach, Alice. *The smartest bear and his brother Oliver*
Banks, Kate. *Alphabet soup*
Barbato, Juli. *Mom's night out*
Barbour, Karen. *Little Nino's pizzeria*
Barklem, Jill. *The secret staircase*
Barrett, Judi. *An apple a day*
Cloudy with a chance of meatballs

Basso, Bill. *The top of the pizzas*
Baugh, Dolores M. *Supermarket*
Benchley, Nathaniel. *Walter the homing pigeon*
Benedictus, Roger. *Fifty million sausages*
Benjamin, Alan. *Ribtickle Town*
Berson, Harold. *Pop! goes the turnip*
The rats who lived in the delicatessen
Beskow, Elsa Maartman. *Peter in Blueberry Land*
Peter's adventures in Blueberry land
Bethell, Jean. *Hooray for Henry*
Bishop, Claire Huchet. *Pancakes - Paris*
Black, Irma Simonton. *Is this my dinner?*
Bolliger, Max. *The giants' feast*
The golden apple
Bond, Michael. *Paddington and the knickerbocker rainbow*
Boutell, Clarence Burley. *The fat baron*
Brandenberg, Franz. *Fresh cider and apple pie*
Brierley, Louise. *King Lion and his cooks*
Bright, Robert. *Gregory, the noisiest and strongest boy in Grangers Grove*
Brimner, Larry Dane. *Country Bear's good neighbor*
Broome, Errol. *The smallest koala*
Brown, Judith Gwyn. *Max and the truffle pig*
Brown, Marc. *Pickle things*
Brown, Marcia. *Stone soup*
Bruna, Dick. *The fish*
Budd, Lillian. *The pie wagon*
Burch, Robert. *The hunting trip*
Burningham, John. *Avocado baby*
The cupboard
Where's Julius?
Burt, Olive. *Let's find out about bread*
Calhoun, Mary. *Audubon cat*
The hungry leprechaun
Carle, Eric. *My very first book of food*
Pancakes, pancakes
Walter the baker
Carrick, Donald. *Milk*
Cauley, Lorinda Bryan. *Pease porridge hot*
Cazet, Denys. *Lucky me*
Chalmers, Audrey. *Hundreds and hundreds of pancakes*
Coatsworth, Elizabeth. *Under the green willow*
Coontz, Otto. *Starring Rosa*
Croll, Carolyn. *Too many babas*
Curious George and the pizza
Degen, Bruce. *Jamberry*
Demarest, Chris L. *No peas for Nellie*
De Paola, Tomie. *Pancakes for breakfast*
The popcorn book
De Regniers, Beatrice Schenk. *Sam and the impossible thing*
Devlin, Wende. *Old Witch and the polka-dot ribbon*

Ehlert, Lois. *Growing vegetable soup*
Flory, Jane. *We'll have a friend for lunch*
Fontaine, Jan. *The spaghetti tree*
Fox, Mem. *Possum magic*
Gackenbach, Dick. *Mother Rabbit's son Tom*
Gág, Wanda. *The funny thing*
Galdone, Paul. *The magic porridge pot*
Gantschev, Ivan. *RumpRump*
Gibbons, Gail. *The milk makers*
  The missing maple syrup sap mystery
  The seasons of Arnold's apple tree
The gingerbread boy. *The gingerbread boy*,
  ill. by Paul Galdone
  The gingerbread boy, ill. by Joan Elizabeth
  Goodman
  The gingerbread boy, ill. by William Curtis
  Holdsworth
  The gingerbread man
  The pancake boy
Goodall, John S. *The surprise picnic*
Greene, Carol. *The world's biggest birthday
  cake*
Greene, Ellin. *Princess Rosetta and the
  popcorn man*
  The pumpkin giant
Gretz, Susanna. *It's your turn, Roger*
Gunthrop, Karen. *Adam and the wolf*
Gurney, Nancy. *The king, the mice and the
  cheese*
Haddon, Mark. *Toni and the tomato soup*
Hale, Irina. *Chocolate mouse and sugar pig*
Hale, Linda. *The glorious Christmas soup
  party*
Hayes, Sarah. *Eat up, Gemma*
Heller, Linda. *Lily at the table*
Hellsing, Lennart. *The wonderful pumpkin*
Hirsh, Marilyn. *Leela and the watermelon*
  Potato pancakes all around
Hitte, Kathryn. *Mexicallie soup*
Hoban, Russell. *Bread and jam for Frances*
  Dinner at Alberta's
Holden, Edith. *The hedgehog feast*
Holl, Adelaide. *Small Bear solves a mystery*
Hughes, Peter. *The emperor's oblong
  pancake*
  The king who loved candy
Hutchins, Pat. *Don't forget the bacon!*
Jack Sprat. *The life of Jack Sprat, his wife
  and his cat*
Jacobs, Joseph. *Johnny-cake*, ill. by Emma
  Lillian Brock
  Johnny-cake, ill. by William Stobbs
Janice. *Little Bear's pancake party*
  Little Bear's Sunday breakfast
Kahl, Virginia. *The Duchess bakes a cake*
  The perfect pancake
  Plum pudding for Christmas
Kantor, MacKinlay. *The preposterous week*
Kasza, Keiko. *The wolf's chicken stew*

Kessler, Leonard P. *Do you have any
  carrots?*
  Soup for the king
Komoda, Beverly. *Simon's soup*
Kwitz, Mary DeBall. *Little chick's breakfast*
Lapp, Eleanor. *The blueberry bears*
Lasker, Joe. *Lentil soup*
Lemerise, Bruce. *Sheldon's lunch*
Levitin, Sonia. *Nobody stole the pie*
Lewin, Betsy. *Animal snackers*
Lindsey, Treska. *When Batistine made
  bread*
Lobel, Anita. *The pancake*
Lurie, Morris. *The story of Imelda, who was
  small*
Lynn, Sara. *Food*
McCloskey, Robert. *Blueberries for Sal*
McGovern, Ann. *Eggs on your nose*
MacGregor, Marilyn. *Helen the hungry bear*
McKee, David. *King Rollo and the bread*
Mahy, Margaret. *Jam*
Manushkin, Fran. *Moon dragon*
Marshall, James. *Miss Dog's Christmas*
  Yummers!
  Yummers too
Mayer, Mercer. *Frog goes to dinner*
Miller, Margaret. *Time to eat*
Mitgutsch, Ali. *From lemon to lemonade*
Murphey, Sara. *The roly poly cookie*
Nordqvist, Sven. *Pancake pie*
Orbach, Ruth. *Apple pigs*
Oxenbury, Helen. *Eating out*
Paterson, Diane. *Eat*
Petie, Haris. *The seed the squirrel dropped*
Radlauer, Ruth Shaw. *Breakfast by Molly*
Rayner, Mary. *Mrs. Pig's bulk buy*
Retan, Walter. *The steam shovel that
  wouldn't eat dirt*
Rice, Eve. *Sam who never forgets*
Robart, Rose. *The cake that Mack ate*
Rockwell, Anne F. *The Mother Goose
  cookie-candy book*
  The wolf who had a wonderful dream
Rockwell, Harlow. *My kitchen*
Rogers, Paul. *Somebody's awake*
Rogow, Zak. *Oranges*
Root, Phyllis. *Soup for supper*
Ross, Wilda S. *What did the dinosaurs eat?*
Schwalje, Marjory. *Mr. Angelo*
Seuss, Dr. *Green eggs and ham*
  Scrambled eggs super!
Sharmat, Marjorie Weinman. *Nate the
  Great*
  Nate the Great and the lost list
  Nate the Great and the phony clue
  Nate the Great goes undercover
Sharmat, Mitchell. *Gregory, the terrible eater*
Slobodkina, Esphyr. *The wonderful feast*
Slocum, Rosalie. *Breakfast with the clowns*
Sobol, Harriet Langsam. *A book of
  vegetables*

Spier, Peter. *Food market*
Stadler, John. *Animal cafe*
Stamaty, Mark Alan. *Minnie Maloney and Macaroni*
Stevenson, Jocelyn. *Red and the pumpkins*
Stock, Catherine. *Alexander's midnight snack*
Taylor, Judy. *Dudley and the strawberry shake*
Dudley in a jam
Testa, Fulvio. *The land where the ice cream grows*
Thayer, Jane. *The popcorn dragon*
Thompson, Vivian Laubach. *The horse that liked sandwiches*
Towle, Faith M. *The magic cooking pot*
Uchida, Yoshiko. *The two foolish cats*
VanRynbach, Iris. *The soup stone*
Van Woerkom, Dorothy. *Alexandra the rock-eater*
Vevers, Gwynne. *Animals that store food*
Wabbes, Marie. *Rose is hungry*
Wallner, Alexandra. *Munch*
Ward, Sally G. *Molly and Grandpa*
Wasmuth, Eleanor. *The picnic basket*
Watanabe, Shigeo. *What a good lunch!*
Watson, Clyde. *Tom Fox and the apple pie*
Valentine foxes
Watson, Nancy Dingman. *Sugar on snow*
Westcott, Nadine Bernard. *Peanut butter and jelly*
Wikler, Madeline. *My first seder*
Williams, Gweneira Maureen. *Timid Timothy, the kitten who learned to be brave*
Windham, Sophie. *Noah's ark*
Winthrop, Elizabeth. *Potbellied possums*
Wood, Audrey. *Heckedy Peg*
Wood, Leslie. *A dog called Mischief*
Young, Miriam Burt. *The sugar mouse cake*
Ziefert, Harriet. *Breakfast time!*
Surprise!

Foolishness see Character traits – foolishness

Football see Sports – football

Foreign lands

Aleichem, Sholem. *Hanukah money*
Allen, Thomas B. *Where children live*
Anglund, Joan Walsh. *Love one another*
Anno, Mitsumasa. *All in a day*
Baylor, Byrd. *The way to start a day*
Berg, Leila. *Folk tales for reading and telling*
Borchers, Elisabeth. *Dear Sarah*
Brann, Esther. *'Round the world*
Bridgman, Elizabeth. *How to travel with grownups*

Bryson, Bernarda. *The twenty miracles of Saint Nicolas*
De Regniers, Beatrice Schenk. *Little Sister and the Month Brothers*
Domanska, Janina. *Marek, the little fool*
Douglas, Michael. *Round, round world*
Gerrard, Roy. *Sir Francis Drake*
Goffstein, M. B. (Marilyn Brooke). *Across the sea*
Handford, Martin. *Where's Waldo?*
Mitchell, Cynthia. *Here a little child I stand*
Otto, Svend. *The giant fish and other stories*
Robb, Brian. *My grandmother's djinn*
Sandin, Joan. *The long way to a new land*
Schulz, Charles M. *Bon voyage, Charlie Brown (and don't come back!!)*
Scott, Sally. *The magic horse*
Van Woerkom, Dorothy. *Alexandra the rock-eater*

Foreign lands – Africa

Aardema, Verna. *Bimwili and the Zimwi*
Bringing the rain to Kapiti Plain
Half-a-ball-of-kenki
Ji-nongo-nongo means riddles
Oh, Kojo! How could you!
Princess Gorilla and a new kind of water
Rabbit makes a monkey of lion
The vingananee and the tree toad
Who's in Rabbit's house?
Why mosquitoes buzz in people's ears
Abisch, Roz. *The clever turtle*
Adamson, Joy. *Elsa*
Elsa and her cubs
Pippa the cheetah and her cubs
Adoff, Arnold. *Ma nDa La*
Anderson, Joy. *Juma and the magic Jinn*
Arkin, Alan. *Black and white*
Arnott, Kathleen. *Spiders, crabs and creepy crawlers*
Aruego, José. *We hide, you seek*
Bemelmans, Ludwig. *Rosebud*
Bernheim, Marc. *In Africa*
A week in Aya's world
Bernstein, Margery. *The first morning*
Berson, Harold. *Kassim's shoes*
Why the jackal won't speak to the hedgehog
Bess, Clayton. *The truth about the moon*
Bible, Charles. *Hamdaani*
Bond, Jean Carey. *A is for Africa*
Borden, Beatrice Brown. *Wild animals of Africa*
Bryan, Ashley. *Beat the story-drum, pum-pum*
Lion and the ostrich chicks
Carrick, Malcolm. *I can squash elephants!*
Cendrars, Blaise. *Shadow*
Cole, Babette. *Nungu and the elephant*
Nungu and the hippopotamus
Daly, Niki. *Not so fast Songololo*

Davis, Douglas F. *The lion's tail*
Dayrell, Elphinstone. *Why the sun and the moon live in the sky*
Dee, Ruby. *Two ways to count to ten*
De Paola, Tomie. *Bill and Pete*
Domanska, Janina. *The tortoise and the tree*
Du Bois, William Pène. *Otto in Africa*
Economakis, Olga. *Oasis of the stars*
Elkin, Benjamin. *Such is the way of the world*
Fatio, Louise. *The happy lion in Africa*
Feelings, Muriel. *Jambo means hello*
  Moja means one
Fournier, Catharine. *The coconut thieves*
Graham, Lorenz B. *Song of the boat*
Greenfield, Eloise. *Africa dream*
Grifalconi, Ann. *Darkness and the butterfly*
  The village of round and square houses
Guy, Rosa. *Mother crocodile*
Hadithi, Mwenye. *Greedy zebra*
  Hot hippo
Haley, Gail E. *A story, a story*
Hofer, Angelika. *The lion family book*
Holding, James. *The lazy little Zulu*
Kipling, Rudyard. *The elephant's child*, ill. by Louise Brierley
  The elephant's child, ill. by Tim Raglin
  How the camel got his hump, ill. by Quentin Blake
Kirn, Ann. *The tale of a crocodile*
Knutson, Barbara. *Why the crab has no head*
Laskowski, Jerzy. *Master of the royal cats*
Lewin, Hugh. *An elephant came to swim*
  Jafta
  Jafta and the wedding
  Jafta - the journey
  Jafta - the town
  Jafta's father
  Jafta's mother
Lexau, Joan M. *Crocodile and hen*
McDermott, Gerald. *Anansi the spider*
McKissack, Patricia C. *Who is coming?*
Musgrove, Margaret. *Ashanti to Zulu.*
Phumla. *Nomi and the magic fish*
Prather, Ray. *The ostrich girl*
Purcell, John Wallace. *African animals*
Robinson, Adjai. *Femi and old grandaddie*
Rose, Anne. *Akimba and the magic cow*
  Pot full of luck
Roth, Susan L. *Fire came to the earth people*
Routh, Jonathan. *The Nuns go to Africa*
Schatz, Letta. *The extraordinary tug-of-war*
Steptoe, John. *Mufaro's beautiful daughters*
Troughton, Joanna. *Tortoise's dream*
Walter, Mildred Pitts. *Brother to the wind*
Ward, Leila. *I am eyes, ni macho*
Zaslavsky, Claudia. *Count on your fingers African style*

Foreign lands – Antarctic

Bonners, Susan. *A penguin year*

Foreign lands – Arabia

Alexander, Sue. *Nadia the willful*
Arabian Nights. *Arabian Nights entertainments*
Haskins, Jim. *Count your way through the Arab world*

Foreign lands – Arctic

Bonsall, Crosby Newell. *What spot?*

Foreign lands – Armenia

Hogrogian, Nonny. *The contest*

Foreign lands – Australia

The all-amazing ha ha book
Baker, Jeannie. *Where the forest meets the sea*
Base, Graeme. *My grandma lived in Gooligulch*
Cox, David. *Bossyboots*
  Tin Lizzie and Little Nell
Factor, Jane. *Summer*
Foreman, Michael. *Panda and the bushfire*
Fox, Mem. *Possum magic*
Kipling, Rudyard. *The sing-song of old man kangaroo*, ill. by Michael C. Taylor
Paterson, Andrew Barton. *Mulga Bill's bicycle*
  Waltzing Matilda
Pittaway, Margaret. *The rainforest children*
Powzyk, Joyce. *Tasmania*
Roughsey, Dick. *The giant devil-dingo*
Thiele, Colin. *Farmer Schulz's ducks*
Trinca, Rod. *One woolly wombat*
Troughton, Joanna. *What made Tiddalik laugh*
Vaughan, Marcia K. *Wombat stew*
Wagner, Jenny. *The bunyip of Berkeley's Creek*
Walsh, Grahame L. *Didane the koala*
  The goori goori bird
Whitmore, Adam. *Max in Australia*

Foreign lands – Austria

Kahl, Virginia. *Away went Wolfgang*

Foreign lands – Bali

Cox, David. *Ayu and the perfect moon*

Foreign lands – Bavaria *see* Foreign lands – Austria; Foreign lands – Germany; Foreign lands – Tyrol

Foreign lands – Canada

Andrews, Jan. *Very last first time*
Blades, Ann. *Mary of mile 18*
Bonne, Rose. *I know an old lady*, ill. by
  Abner Graboff
  I know an old lady who swallowed a fly, ill.
  by William Stobbs
Climo, Lindee. *Chester's barn*
Dos Santos, Joyce Audy. *The diviner*
  Henri and the Loup-Garou
Holling, Holling C. (Holling Clancy).
  Paddle-to-the-sea
Moak, Allan. *A big city ABC*
Norman, Howard. *The owl-scatterer*
Poulin, Stephane. *Can you catch Josephine?*
  Have you seen Josephine?
Speare, Jean. *A candle for Christmas*
Ward, Lynd. *The biggest bear*
  Nic of the woods
Waterton, Betty. *Pettranella*
Woolaver, Lance. *Christmas with the rural
  mail*

Foreign lands – Caribbean Islands

Anderson, Lonzo. *The day the hurricane
  happened*
  Izzard
Buffett, Jimmy. *The jolly mon*
Dobrin, Arnold Jack. *Josephine's
  'magination*
George, Jean Craighead. *The wentletrap
  trap*
Greenfield, Eloise. *Under the Sunday tree*
Lessac, Frané. *My little island*
Ness, Evaline. *Josefina February*

Foreign lands – China

Abisch, Roz. *Mai-Ling and the mirror*
Andersen, H. C. (Hans Christian). *The
  emperor and the nightingale*, ill. by James
  Watling
  The emperor's nightingale, ill. by Georges
  Lemoine
  The nightingale, ill. by Harold Berson
  The nightingale, ill. by Nancy Ekholm
  Burkert
  The nightingale, ill. by Demi
  The nightingale, ill. by Beni Montresor
  The nightingale, ill. by Lisbeth Zwerger
Behrens, June. *Soo Ling finds a way*
Bellville, Cheryl Walsh. *Theater magic*
Bishop, Claire Huchet. *The five Chinese
  brothers*
Bright, Robert. *The travels of Ching*
Bro, Marguerite H. *The animal friends of
  Peng-u*
Buck, Pearl S. (Pearl Sydenstricker). *The
  Chinese story teller*
  The dragon fish

Cheng, Hou-Tien. *The Chinese New Year*
Demi. *The adventures of Marco Polo*
  Chen Ping and his magic axe
  A Chinese zoo
  Demi's reflective fables
  Dragon kites and dragonflies
  Under the shade of the mulberry tree
Fairclough, Chris. *Take a trip to China*
Flack, Marjorie. *The story about Ping*
Foley, Bernice Williams. *A walk among
  clouds*
Fribourg, Marjorie G. *Ching-Ting and the
  ducks*
Fyson, Nance Lui. *A family in China*
Handforth, Thomas. *Mei Li*
Haskins, Jim. *Count your way through
  China*
High on a hill
Holland, Janice. *You never can tell*
Jensen, Helen Zane. *When Panda came to
  our house*
Leaf, Margaret. *Eyes of the dragon*
Lee, Jeanne M. *Legend of the Li River*
  The legend of the milky way
Levinson, Riki. *Our home is the sea*
Littlefield, William. *The whiskers of Ho Ho*
Lobel, Arnold. *Ming Lo moves the
  mountain*
Miles, Miska. *The pointed brush...*
Morris, Winifred. *The magic leaf*
Mosel, Arlene. *Tikki Tikki Tembo*
Perkins, Al. *Tubby and the lantern*
Pittman, Helena Clare. *A grain of rice*
San Souci, Robert D. *The enchanted tapestry*
Shi, Zhang Xiu. *Monkey and the white bone
  demon*
Skipper, Mervyn. *The fooling of King
  Alexander*
Slobodkin, Louis. *Moon Blossom and the
  golden penny*
Stafford, Kay. *Ling Tang and the lucky
  cricket*
Stone, Jon. *Big Bird in China*
Van Woerkom, Dorothy. *The rat, the ox
  and the zodiac*
Wiese, Kurt. *Fish in the air*
Williams, Jay. *Everyone knows what a
  dragon looks like*
Wolkstein, Diane. *The magic wings*
  White wave
Yolen, Jane. *The emperor and the kite*
  The seeing stick
Young, Ed. *The rooster's horns*
  The terrible Nung Gwama
Young, Evelyn. *The tale of Tai
  Wu and Lu and Li*

Foreign lands – Czechoslovakia

Bolliger, Max. *The fireflies*

Ginsburg, Mirra. *How the sun was brought back to the sky*
Marshak, Samuel. *The Month-Brothers*

Foreign lands – Denmark

Andersen, H. C. (Hans Christian). *The snow queen*, ill. by Toma Bogdanovic
Bason, Lillian. *Those foolish Molboes!*
Blegvad, Lenore. *Mr. Jensen and cat*
Bodecker, N. M. (Nils Mogens). *"It's raining," said John Twaining*
Brande, Marlie. *Sleepy Nicholas*
A Christmas book
Conover, Chris. *The wizard's daughter*
Coombs, Patricia. *The magic pot*
Kent, Jack. *Hoddy doddy*
Lobel, Anita. *King Rooster, Queen Hen*

Foreign lands – Ecuador

Bemelmans, Ludwig. *Quito express*

Foreign lands – Egypt

Aliki. *Mummies made in Egypt*
De Paola, Tomie. *Bill and Pete go down the Nile*
Goodenow, Earle. *The last camel*
Grant, Joan. *The monster that grew small*
Hutton, Warwick. *Moses in the bulrushes*
Laskowski, Jerzy. *Master of the royal cats*
McDermott, Gerald. *The voyage of Osiris*
Mayers, Florence Cassen. *Egyptian art from the Brooklyn Museum ABC*
The prince who knew his fate
Stolz, Mary Slattery. *Zekmet, the stone carver*

Foreign lands – England

Ahlberg, Allan. *Cops and robbers*
Ambler, Christopher Gifford. *Ten little foxhounds.*
Anno, Mitsumasa. *Anno's Britain*
Ardizzone, Edward. *Lucy Brown and Mr. Grimes*
Armitage, Ronda. *Don't forget, Matilda*
Azarian, Mary. *The tale of John Barleycorn or, From barley to beer*
Beatty, Hetty Burlingame. *Moorland pony*
Belting, Natalia Maree. *Christmas folk*
Summer's coming in
Bemelmans, Ludwig. *Madeline in London*
Bennett, Jill. *Teeny tiny*
Bennett, Olivia. *A Turkish afternoon*
Bentley, Anne. *The Groggs' day out*
The Groggs have a wonderful summer
Bond, Michael. *Paddington and the knickerbocker rainbow*
Paddington at the circus
Paddington at the fair
Paddington at the palace
Paddington at the seaside
Paddington at the tower
Paddington at the zoo
Paddington cleans up
Paddington's art exhibit
Paddington's garden
Paddington's lucky day
Brown, Ruth. *A dark, dark tale*
Burningham, John. *Borka*
Calhoun, Mary. *The pixy and the lazy housewife*
The witch's pig
Carrick, Donald. *Harold and the great stag*
Christian, Mary Blount. *April fool*
Cole, Brock. *The king at the door*
Conger, Lesley. *Tops and bottoms*
Cooper, Susan. *The silver cow*
Cressey, James. *The dragon and George*
Crompton, Margaret. *The house where Jack lives*
Crossley-Holland, Kevin. *The green children*
Davidson, Amanda. *Teddy at the seashore*
Davis, Reda. *Martin's dinosaur*
Dick Whittington and his cat. *Dick Whittington*, ill. by Edward Ardizzone
Dick Whittington, ill. by Antony Maitland
Dick Whittington and his cat, ill. by Marcia Brown
Dick Whittington and his cat, ill. by Kurt Werth
Dines, Glen. *Gilly and the wicharoo*
Drummond, Violet H. *The flying postman*
Emecheta, Buchi. *Nowhere to play*
Fairclough, Chris. *Take a trip to England*
Fisher, Leonard Everett. *The tower of London*
Freeman, Don. *The guard mouse*
Will's quill
Freschet, Berniece. *Bernard of Scotland Yard*
Ganly, Helen. *Jyoti's journey*
Gauch, Patricia Lee. *On to Widecombe Fair*
Gerrard, Jean. *Matilda Jane*
Goodall, John S. *An Edwardian Christmas*
An Edwardian summer
The story of a castle
The story of a farm
The story of an English village
Gramatky, Hardie. *Little Toot on the Thames*
Haley, Gail E. *The post office cat*
Herrmann, Frank. *The giant Alexander*
The giant Alexander and the circus
Hughes, Shirley. *Bathwater's hot*
Lucy and Tom's A.B.C.
Lucy and Tom's Christmas
Noisy
Out and about
When we went to the park
Ivory, Lesley Anne. *A day in London*

Jacobs, Joseph. *The crock of gold*
Keeping, Charles. *Alfie finds the other side of the world*
Through the window
Lawrence, John. *The giant of Grabbist*
Lodge, Bernard. *Door to door*
Menter, Ian. *Carnival*
Mother Goose. *London Bridge is falling down*, ill. by Ed Emberley
London Bridge is falling down, ill. by Peter Spier
Oakley, Graham. *The church cat abroad*
The church mice and the moon
The church mice at bay
The church mice spread their wings
The church mouse
Oldfield, Pamela. *Melanie Brown climbs a tree*
Oxenbury, Helen. *The queen and Rosie Randall*
Petty, Kate. *On a plane*
Ross, Diana. *The story of the little red engine*
Seuling, Barbara. *The teeny tiny woman*
Sewall, Marcia. *The little wee tyke*
Shulman, Milton. *Prep, the little pigeon of Trafalgar Square*
Solomon, Joan. *A present for Mum*
Storr, Catherine. *Robin Hood*
Thompson, Harwood. *The witch's cat*
Widdecombe Fair
Willard, Barbara. *To London! To London!*
Wolff, Ashley. *The bells of London*
Wood, Joyce. *Grandmother Lucy in her garden*
Worthington, Phoebe. *Teddy bear baker*
Teddy bear coalman
Zemach, Harve. *Duffy and the devil*

Foreign lands – Europe

Bornstein, Ruth Lercher. *The dancing man*
Sopko, Eugen. *Townsfolk and countryfolk*

Foreign lands – Finland

De Gerez, Toni. *Louhi, witch of North Farm*

Foreign lands – France

Allen, Laura Jean. *Rollo and Tweedy and the case of the missing cheese*
Angelo, Nancy Carolyn Harrison. *Camembert*
Bemelmans, Ludwig. *Madeline*
Madeline and the bad hat
Madeline and the gypsies
Madeline [pop-up book]
Madeline's rescue
Bergere, Thea. *Paris in the rain with Jean and Jacqueline*

Berson, Harold. *Barrels to the moon*
Charles and Claudine
How the devil got his due
Joseph and the snake
Bingham, Mindy. *Minou*
Bishop, Claire Huchet. *Pancakes - Paris*
The truffle pig
Bjork, Christina. *Linnea in Monet's garden*
Bring a torch, Jeannette, Isabella
Brown, Judith Gwyn. *Max and the truffle pig*
Brunhoff, Jean de. *The story of Babar, the little elephant*
Charlip, Remy. *Harlequin and the gift of many colors*
Daudet, Alphonse. *The brave little goat of Monsieur Séguin*
Dauphin, Francine Legrand. *A French A. B. C.*
Diska, Pat. *Andy says ... Bonjour!*
Dumas, Philippe. *Caesar, cock of the village*
Laura loses her head
The story of Edward
Fatio, Louise. *The happy lion*
The happy lion and the bear
The happy lion in Africa
The happy lion roars
The happy lion's quest
The happy lion's rabbits
The happy lion's treasure
The three happy lions
Fender, Kay. *Odette!*
Froment, Eugène. *The story of a round loaf*
Goffstein, M. B. (Marilyn Brooke). *Artists' helpers enjoy the evening*
Harris, Leon A. *The great picture robbery*
Hautzig, Esther. *At home*
In the park
Ichikawa, Satomi. *Suzanne and Nicholas at the market*
Suzanne and Nicholas in the garden
Joslin, Sesyle. *Baby elephant's trunk*
Klein, Leonore. *Henri's walk to Paris*
Lubell, Winifred. *Rosalie, the bird market turtle*
Marokvia, Merelle. *A French school for Paul*
Meddaugh, Susan. *Maude and Claude go abroad*
Mendoza, George. *Henri Mouse, the juggler*
Moore, Inga. *The truffle hunter*
Moore, Lilian. *Papa Albert*
Napoli, Guillier. *Adventure at Mont-Saint-Michel*
Perrault, Charles. *Puss in boots*, ill. by Julia Noonan
Raffi. *Wheels on the bus*
Rider, Alex. *A la ferme. At the farm*
Chez nous. At our house
Rockwell, Anne F. *Poor Goose*
The wolf who had a wonderful dream

Schiller, Barbara. *The white rat's tale*
Scribner, Charles. *The devil's bridge*
Seignobosc, Françoise. *The big rain*
  Biquette, the white goat
  Chouchou
  Jeanne-Marie at the fair
  Jeanne-Marie counts her sheep
  Jeanne-Marie in gay Paris
  Minou
  Noël for Jeanne-Marie
  Springtime for Jeanne-Marie
Shecter, Ben. *Partouche plants a seed*
Slobodkin, Louis. *Colette and the princess*
Titus, Eve. *Anatole*
  Anatole and the cat
  Anatole and the piano
  Anatole and the Pied Piper
  Anatole and the poodle
  Anatole and the robot
  Anatole and the thirty thieves
  Anatole and the toyshop
  Anatole over Paris
Ungerer, Tomi. *Adelaide*
  The beast of Monsieur Racine
Vacheron, Edith. *Here is Henri!*
Weelen, Guy. *The little red train*

Foreign lands – Germany

Allard, Harry. *May I stay?*
Attenberger, Walburga. *The little man in winter*
  Who knows the little man?
Bartos-Hoppner, Barbara. *The Pied Piper of Hamelin*, ill. by Annegert Fuchshuber
Bechstein, Ludwig. *The rabbit catcher and other fairy tales*
Biro, Val. *The pied piper of Hamelin*
Browning, Robert. *The pied piper of Hamelin*, ill. by Kate Greenaway
  The pied piper of Hamelin, ill. by Anatoly Ivanov
  The pied piper of Hamelin, ill. by Errol Le Cain
Calhoun, Mary. *The thieving dwarfs*
Coombs, Patricia. *Tilabel*
Cooney, Barbara. *Little brother and little sister*
Delaney, A. *The gunnywolf*
Fairclough, Chris. *Take a trip to West Germany*
Grimm, Jacob. *The elves and the shoemaker*, ill. by Paul Galdone
  The elves and the shoemaker, ill. by Bernadette Watts
  The shoemaker and the elves, ill. by Cynthia and William Birrer
Harper, Wilhelmina. *The gunniwolf*
Hürlimann, Ruth. *The proud white cat*
Kahl, Virginia. *Droopsi*
  Maxie

Mayer, Mercer. *The Pied Piper of Hamelin*
Morgenstern, Elizabeth. *The little gardeners*
Ross, Tony. *The pied piper of Hamelin*
Spang, Günter. *Clelia and the little mermaid*
Van Woerkom, Dorothy. *The queen who couldn't bake gingerbread*

Foreign lands – Greece

Aliki. *Diogenes*
  The eggs
  Three gold pieces
  The twelve months
Anderson, Lonzo. *Arion and the dolphins*
Birrer, Cynthia. *Song to Demeter*
Brown, Marcia. *Tamarindo!*
Delton, Judy. *My Uncle Nikos*
Fisher, Leonard Everett. *The Olympians*
Walker, Barbara K. *Pigs and pirates*

Foreign lands – Greenland

Hertza, Ole. *Tobias catches trout*
  Tobias goes ice fishing
  Tobias goes seal hunting
  Tobias has a birthday

Foreign lands – Guyana

Agard, John. *Dig away two-hole Tim*

Foreign lands – Holland

Bouhuys, Mies. *The lady of Stavoren*
Bromhall, Winifred. *Johanna arrives*
Chasek, Judith. *Have you seen Wilhelmina Krumpf?*
Fairclough, Chris. *Take a trip to Holland*
Green, Norma B. *The hole in the dike*
Howells, Mildred. *The woman who lived in Holland*
Krasilovsky, Phyllis. *The cow who fell in the canal*
Reesink, Marijke. *The golden treasure*
Van Stockum, Hilda. *A day on skates*

Foreign lands – Hungary

Ambrus, Victor G. *Brave soldier Janosch*
  The three poor tailors
Brown, Margaret Wise. *Wheel on the chimney*
Ginsburg, Mirra. *Two greedy bears*
  The good-hearted youngest brother
Illyés, Gyula. *Matt the gooseherd*
Surany, Anico. *Kati and Kormos*
Varga, Judy. *Janko's wish*

Foreign lands – India

Alan, Sandy. *The plaid peacock*
Ambrus, Victor G. *The Sultan's bath*
Bang, Betsy. *The cucumber stem*
  The old woman and the red pumpkin

The old woman and the rice thief
Tutuni the tailor bird
Bannerman, Helen. *Sambo and the twins*
The story of little black Sambo
Bond, Ruskin. *Flames in the forest*
Bonnici, Peter. *The festival*
Brown, Marcia. *The blue jackal*
Once a mouse...
Cassedy, Sylvia. *Moon-uncle, moon-uncle*
Cathon, Laura E. *Tot Botot and his little flute*
Chase, Catherine. *The nightingale and the fool*
Demi. *The hallowed horse*
Domanska, Janina. *Why so much noise?*
Duff, Maggie. *Rum pum pum*
Ganly, Helen. *Jyoti's journey*
Gobhai, Mehlli. *Lakshmi, the water buffalo who wouldn't*
Usha, the mouse-maiden
Hirsh, Marilyn. *Leela and the watermelon*
Kipling, Rudyard. *The miracle of the mountain*
Lexau, Joan M. *It all began with a drip, drip, drip*
Myers, Walter Dean. *The golden serpent*
Papas, William. *Taresh the tea planter*
Quigley, Lillian Fox. *The blind men and the elephant*
Rockwell, Anne F. *The stolen necklace*
Rodanas, Kristina. *The story of Wali Dâd*
Singh, Jacquelin. *Fat Gopal*
Slobodkin, Louis. *The polka-dot goat*
Towle, Faith M. *The magic cooking pot*
Trez, Denise. *Maila and the flying carpet*
Villarejo, Mary. *The tiger hunt*
Wahl, Jan. *Tiger watch*
Ward, Nanda Weedon. *The elephant that ga-lumphed*
Whitmore, Adam. *Max in India*

Foreign lands – Ireland

Balian, Lorna. *Leprechauns never lie*
Bromhall, Winifred. *Bridget's growing day*
Bunting, Eve. *Clancy's coat*
Calhoun, Mary. *The hungry leprechaun*
Cooper, Susan. *The Selkie girl*
Cormack, M. Grant. *Animal tales from Ireland*
De Paola, Tomie. *Fin M'Coul*
Haugaard, Erik. *Prince Boghole*
Jacobs, Joseph. *Hudden and Dudden and Donald O'Neary*
Kennedy, Richard. *The leprechaun's story*
McDermott, Gerald. *Daniel O'Rourke*
Parker, Dorothy D. *Liam's catch*
What do you feed your donkey on?
Zimelman, Nathan. *To sing a song as big as Ireland*

Foreign lands – Israel

Adler, David A. *A picture book of Israel*
Allstrom, Elizabeth C. *Songs along the way*
Brin, Ruth F. *David and Goliath*
The story of Esther
Carmi, Giora. *And Shira imagined*
Elkin, Benjamin. *The wisest man in the world*
Fairclough, Chris. *Take a trip to Israel*
Kuskin, Karla. *Jerusalem, shining still*
Segal, Sheila. *Joshua's dream*

Foreign lands – Italy

Androcles and the lion, ill. by Janusz Grabianski
Anno, Mitsumasa. *Anno's Italy*
Atene, Ann. *The golden guitar*
Basile, Giambattista. *Petrosinella*
Bettina (Bettina Ehrlich). *Pantaloni*
Bowden, Joan Chase. *The bean boy*
Brighton, Catherine. *Five secrets in a box*
Brown, Marcia. *Felice*
Cauley, Lorinda Bryan. *The goose and the golden coins*
Chafetz, Henry. *The legend of Befana*
Chapman, Jean. *Moon-Eyes*
De Paola, Tomie. *The clown of God*
The legend of Old Befana
Merry Christmas, Strega Nona
The mysterious giant of Barletta
The Prince of the Dolomites
Fairclough, Chris. *Take a trip to Italy*
Galdone, Paul. *Androcles and the lion*
Kroll, Steven. *Looking for Daniela*
Michael, Emory H. *Androcles and the lion*
Morpurgo, Michael. *Jo-Jo the melon donkey*
Plume, Ilse. *The story of Befana*
Politi, Leo. *Little Leo*
Priolo, Pauline. *Piccolina and the Easter bells*
Rockwell, Anne F. *The wonderful eggs of Furicchia*
Seidler, Rosalie. *Grumpus and the Venetian cat*
Titus, Eve. *Anatole in Italy*
Ungerer, Tomi. *The hat*

Foreign lands – Japan

Ashby, Gwynneth. *Take a trip to Japan*
Bang, Molly. *Dawn*
Bartoli, Jennifer. *Snow on bear's nose*
Baruch, Dorothy. *Kappa's tug-of-war with the big brown horse*
Battles, Edith. *What does the rooster say, Yoshio?*
Bryan, Ashley. *Sh-ko and his eight wicked brothers*
Bunting, Eve. *Magic and the night river*

Cocagnac, A. M. (Augustin Maurice). *The three trees of the Samurai*
Creekmore, Raymond. *Fujio*
Damjan, Mischa. *The little prince and the tiger cat*
DeForest, Charlotte B. *The prancing pony*
Dines, Glen. *A tiger in the cherry tree*
Don't tell the scarecrow
Fifield, Flora. *Pictures for the palace*
Fujita, Tamao. *The boy and the bird*
Gackenbach, Dick. *The perfect mouse*
Garrison, Christian. *The dream eater*
Haskins, Jim. *Count your way through Japan*
Heller, George. *Hiroshi's wonderful kite*
Hidaka, Masako. *Girl from the snow country*
Iké, Jane Hori. *A Japanese fairy tale*
Ishii, Momoko. *The tongue-cut sparrow*
Laurin, Anne. *Perfect crane*
Lifton, Betty Jean. *Joji and the Amanojaku*
Joji and the dragon
The many lives of Chio and Goro
The rice-cake rabbit
Luenn, Nancy. *The dragon kite*
McDermott, Gerald. *The stonecutter*
Matsuno, Masako. *A pair of red clogs*
Taro and the bamboo shoot
Taro and the Tofu
Matsutani, Miyoko. *The fisherman under the sea*
How the withered trees blossomed
The witch's magic cloth
Mosel, Arlene. *The funny little woman*
Nakatani, Chiyoko. *Fumio and the dolphins*
Newton, Patricia Montgomery. *The five sparrows*
Pittman, Helena Clare. *The gift of the willows*
Roy, Ronald. *A thousand pails of water*
Sasaki, Jeannie. *Chōchō is for butterfly*
Say, Allen. *The bicycle man*
Once under the cherry blossom tree
Shute, Linda. *Momotaro, the peach boy*
Slobodkin, Louis. *Yasu and the strangers*
Takeshita, Fumiko. *The park bench*
Uchida, Yoshiko. *Sumi's prize*
Sumi's special happening
Van Woerkom, Dorothy. *Sea frog, city frog*
Yagawa, Sumiko. *The crane wife*
Yashima, Mitsu. *Plenty to watch*
Yashima, Tarō. *Crow boy*
The village tree

Foreign lands – Korea

Fregosi, Claudia. *The pumpkin sparrow*
Ginsburg, Mirra. *The Chinese mirror*
Parry, Marian. *King of the fish*

Foreign lands – Lapland

Aulaire, Ingri Mortenson d'. *Children of the northlights*
Borg, Inga. *Plupp builds a house*
Lindman, Maj. *Snipp, Snapp, Snurr and the red shoes*
McHale, Ethel Kharasch. *Son of thunder*
Stalder, Valerie. *Even the Devil is afraid of a shrew*

Foreign lands – Latvia

Langton, Jane. *The hedgehog boy*

Foreign lands – Lithuania

Rudolph, Marguerita. *I am your misfortune*

Foreign lands – Malaysia

Kaye, Geraldine. *The sea monkey*

Foreign lands – Mexico

Aardema, Verna. *The riddle of the drum*
Balet, Jan B. *The fence*
Bannon, Laura. *Hat for a hero*
Manuela's birthday
Watchdog
Blackmore, Vivien. *Why corn is golden*
Crane, Alan. *Pepita bonita*
De Gerez, Toni. *My song is a piece of jade*
De Paola, Tomie. *The Lady of Guadalupe*
Ets, Marie Hall. *Nine days to Christmas*
Everton, Macduff. *El circo magico modelo*
Fisher, Leonard Everett. *Pyramid of the sun, pyramid of the moon*
Fraser, James Howard. *Los Posadas*
Grifalconi, Ann. *The toy trumpet*
Hader, Berta Hoerner. *The story of Pancho and the bull with the crooked tail*
Hinojosa, Francisco. *The old lady who ate people*
Hitte, Kathryn. *Mexicallie soup*
Kent, Jack. *The Christmas piñata*
Kurtycz, Marcos. *Tigers and opossums*
Lewis, Thomas P. *Hill of fire*
Martin, Bill (William Ivan). *My days are made of butterflies*
Miles, Miska. *Friend of Miguel*
Morrow, Elizabeth Cutter. *The painted pig*
Politi, Leo. *Lito and the clown*
Rosa
Rohmer, Harriet. *How we came to the fifth world*
Sahagun, Bernardino de. *Spirit child*
Tompert, Ann. *The silver whistle*
Ungerer, Tomi. *Orlando, the brave vulture*

Foreign lands – New Guinea

Anderson, Robin. *Sinabouda Lily*

Foreign lands – Nicaragua

Rohmer, Harriet. *The invisible hunters*
  Mother scorpion country

Foreign lands – Norway

Allard, Harry. *May I stay?*
Allen, Linda. *The giant who had no heart*
Aulaire, Ingri Mortenson d'. *Ola*
  The terrible troll-bird
Benchley, Nathaniel. *Snorri and the strangers*
Dasent, George W. *East o' the sun, west o' the moon*
Grieg, E. H. (Edvard Hagerup). *E. H. Grieg's Peer Gynt*
Hague, Kathleen. *The man who kept house*
Magnus, Erica. *The boy and the devil*
  Old Lars
The squire's bride, ill. by Marcia Sewall
Wiesner, William. *Happy-Go-Lucky*
  Turnabout

Foreign lands – Pakistan

Siddiqui, Ashraf. *Bhombal Dass, the uncle of lion*

Foreign lands – Panama

Janosch. *The trip to Panama*

Foreign lands – Persia

Chaikin, Miriam. *Esther*
Foley, Bernice Williams. *The gazelle and the hunter*

Foreign lands – Peru

Dewey, Ariane. *The thunder god's son*

Foreign lands – Philippines

Aruego, José. *A crocodile's tale*
  Look what I can do
Charlot, Martin. *Felisa and the magic tikling bird*

Foreign lands – Poland

Adler, David A. *The children of Chelm*
Bernhard, Josephine Butkowska. *Lullaby*
  Nine cry-baby dolls
Din dan don, it's Christmas
Domanska, Janina. *The best of the bargain*
  Busy Monday morning
  King Krakus and the dragon
  Look, there is a turtle flying
Pellowski, Anne. *The nine crying dolls*
Porazińska, Janina. *The enchanted book*
Turska, Krystyna. *The magician of Cracow*
  The woodcutter's duck

Foreign lands – Portugal

Balet, Jan B. *The gift*
  Joanjo

Foreign lands – Puerto Rico

Belpré, Pura. *Dance of the animals*
  Perez and Martina
Martel, Cruz. *Yagua days*
Rohmer, Harriet. *Atariba and Niguayona*

Foreign lands – Russia

Afanas'ev, Aleksandr. *Russian folk tales*
Aksakov, Sergei. *The scarlet flower*
Beim, Lorraine. *Sasha and the samovar*
Bider, Djemma. *The buried treasure*
Black, Algernon D. *The woman of the wood*
Brown, Marcia. *The neighbors*
  Stone soup
Campbell, M. Rudolph. *The talking crocodile*
Cohen, Barbara. *The demon who would not die*
Cole, Joanna. *Bony-legs*
Daniels, Guy. *The Tsar's riddles*
Daugherty, Sonia. *Vanka's donkey*
De Marolles, Chantal. *The lonely wolf*
De Regniers, Beatrice Schenk. *Everyone is good for something*
Domanska, Janina. *A scythe, a rooster and a cat*
  The turnip
The firebird, ill. by Boris Zvorykin
Francis, Frank. *Natasha's new doll*
Fregosi, Claudia. *Snow maiden*
Galdone, Paul. *A strange servant*
Ginsburg, Mirra. *The fisherman's son*
  The fox and the hare
  Pampalche of the silver teeth
  The strongest one of all
  Which is the best place?
Hall, Amanda. *The gossipy wife*
Haskins, Jim. *Count your way through Russia*
Hautzig, Esther. *At home*
  In the park
Heller, Linda. *Alexis and the golden ring*
Isele, Elizabeth. *The frog princess*
Ivanov, Anatoly. *Ol' Jake's lucky day*
Jameson, Cynthia. *The clay pot boy*
  The house of five bears
McDermott, Beverly Brodsky. *The crystal apple*
Marshak, Samuel. *The tale of a hero nobody knows*
Odoyevsky, Vladimir. *Old Father Frost*
The peasant's pea patch
Pevear, Richard. *Our king has horns!*
Polushkin, Maria. *The little hen and the giant*

Prokofiev, Sergei Sergeievitch. *Peter and the wolf*, ill. by Reg Cartwright
Peter and the wolf, ill. by Warren Chappell
Peter and the wolf, ill. by Barbara Cooney
Peter and the wolf, ill. by Frans Haacken
Peter and the wolf, ill. by Alan Howard
Peter and the wolf, ill. by Charles Mikolaycak
Peter and the wolf, ill. by Jörg Müller
Peter and the wolf, ill. by Josef Paleček
Peter and the wolf, ill. by Kozo Shimizu
Peter and the wolf, ill. by Erna Voigt
Robbins, Ruth. *Baboushka and the three kings*
Sherman, Josepha. *Vassilisa the wise*
Slobodkina, Esphyr. *Boris and his balalaika*
Stern, Simon. *Vasily and the dragon*
Tolstoĭ, Alekseĭ Nikolaevich. *The great big enormous turnip*
Varga, Judy. *The mare's egg*
Winter, Jeanette. *The girl and the moon man*
Wiseman, Bernard. *Little new kangaroo*
Zhitkov, Boris. *How I hunted for the little fellows*
Zimmerman, Andrea Griffing. *Yetta, the trickster*

Foreign lands – Scotland

Alger, Leclaire. *All in the morning early*
Always room for one more
Kellyburn Braes
Blegvad, Erik. *Burnie's hill*
Calhoun, Mary. *The runaway brownie*
Cate, Rikki. *A cat's tale*
Charles Prince of Wales. *The old man of Lochnagar*
Cooper, Susan. *The Selkie girl*
Duncan, Jane. *Janet Reachfar and Chickabird*
Fern, Eugene. *The most frightened hero*
Hedderwick, Mairi. *Katie Morag and the big boy cousins*
Katie Morag and the tiresome Ted
Katie Morag and the two grandmothers
Katie Morag delivers the mail
Jeffers, Susan. *Wild Robin*
Leaf, Munro. *Wee Gillis*
Lewis, Naomi. *Puffin*
Sewall, Marcia. *The wee, wee mannie and the big, big coo*

Foreign lands – Siam *see* Foreign lands – Thailand

Foreign lands – South Africa

Daly, Niki. *Not so fast Songololo*

Foreign lands – South America

Aruego, José. *Pilyo the piranha*
Cowcher, Helen. *Rain forest*
Frasconi, Antonio. *The snow and the sun, la nieve y el sol*
Gramatky, Hardie. *Bolivar*
Maestro, Giulio. *The tortoise's tug of war*
Maiorano, Robert. *Francisco*
Rockwell, Anne F. *The good llama*
Sotomayor, Antonio. *Khasa goes to the fiesta*
Surany, Anico. *Ride the cold wind*
Troughton, Joanna. *How the birds changed their feathers*

Foreign lands – South Sea Islands

Mordvinoff, Nicolas. *Coral Island*

Foreign lands – Spain

Duff, Maggie. *The princess and the pumpkin*
García Lorca, Federico. *The Lieutenant Colonel and the gypsy*
Hautzig, Esther. *At home*
In the park
Leaf, Munro. *The story of Ferdinand the bull*
Oleson, Claire. *For Pipita, an orange tree*
Vernon, Adele. *The riddle*

Foreign lands – Sweden

Beskow, Elsa Maartman. *Children of the forest*
Pelle's new suit
Peter in Blueberry Land
Peter's adventures in Blueberry land
Lindgren, Astrid. *Christmas in noisy village*
Christmas in the stable
The tomten
The tomten and the fox
Lindman, Maj. *Flicka, Ricka, Dicka and a little dog*
Flicka, Ricka, Dicka and the new dotted dress
Flicka, Ricka, Dicka bake a cake
Sailboat time
Snipp, Snapp, Snurr and the buttered bread
Snipp, Snapp, Snurr and the magic horse
Snipp, Snapp, Snurr and the reindeer
Snipp, Snapp, Snurr and the seven dogs
Snipp, Snapp, Snurr and the yellow sled
Peterson, Hans. *Erik and the Christmas horse*
Westerberg, Christine. *The cap that mother made*
Zemach, Harve. *Nail soup*

Foreign lands – Switzerland

Allamand, Pascale. *Cocoa beans and daisies*

Baumann, Kurt. *Piro and the fire brigade*
Bawden, Nina. *William Tell*
Carigiet, Alois. *The pear tree, the birch tree and the barberry bush*
Chönz, Selina. *A bell for Ursli*
  Florina and the wild bird
  The snowstorm
Freeman, Don. *Ski pup*

Foreign lands – Thailand

Ayer, Jacqueline. *Nu Dang and his kite*
  The paper-flower tree
  A wish for little sister
Northrup, Mili. *The watch cat*

Foreign lands – Tibet

Tsultim, Yeshe. *The mouse king*

Foreign lands – Turkey

Bennett, Olivia. *A Turkish afternoon*
Dewey, Ariane. *The fish Peri*
Van Woerkom, Dorothy. *Abu Ali*
  The friends of Abu Ali
Walker, Barbara K. *Teeny-Tiny and the witch-woman*

Foreign lands – Tyrol

Bemelmans, Ludwig. *Hansi*

Foreign lands – Ukraine

Kay, Helen. *An egg is for wishing*
Lisowski, Gabriel. *How Tevye became a milkman*
Rudchenko, Ivan. *Ivanko and the dragon*
Rudolph, Marguerita. *How a shirt grew in the field*
Tresselt, Alvin R. *The mitten*

Foreign lands – Vatican City

Lawrence, John. *Pope Leo's elephant*

Foreign lands – Vietnam

Boholm-Olsson, Eva. *Tuan*
Lee, Jeanne M. *Ba-Nam*
Trân-Khánh-Tuyêt. *The little weaver of Thái-Yên Village*

Foreign lands – Zaire

Knutson, Barbara. *Why the crab has no head*

Foreign lands – Zanzibar

Aardema, Verna. *Bimwili and the Zimwi*

Foreign languages

ABCDEF...

Alger, Leclaire. *Kellyburn Braes*
Anglund, Joan Walsh. *Love one another*
Baldner, Gaby. *Joba and the wild boar*
Blue, Rose. *I am here: Yo estoy aqui*
A child's picture English-Hebrew dictionary
Dauphin, Francine Legrand. *A French A. B. C.*
De Gerez, Toni. *My song is a piece of jade*
Delacre, Lulu. *Arroz con leche*
Diska, Pat. *Andy says ... Bonjour!*
Du Bois, William Pène. *The hare and the tortoise and the tortoise and the hare*
Dunham, Meredith. *Colors: how do you say it?*
  Numbers: how do you say it?
  Picnic: how do you say it?
  Shapes: how do you say it?
Everton, Macduff. *El circo magico modelo*
Feelings, Muriel. *Jambo means hello*
  Moja means one
Frasconi, Antonio. *See again, say again*
  See and say
  The snow and the sun, la nieve y el sol
Gunning, Monica. *The two Georges*
Hautzig, Esther. *At home*
  In the park
The house that Jack built. *The house that Jack built*, ill. by Antonio Frasconi
Jaynes, Ruth M. *Tell me please! What's that?*
Joslin, Sesyle. *Baby elephant goes to China*
  Baby elephant's trunk
  Señor Baby Elephant, the pirate
Kahn, Michèle. *My everyday Spanish word book*
Keats, Ezra Jack. *My dog is lost!*
Matsutani, Miyoko. *How the withered trees blossomed*
Maury, Inez. *My mother the mail carrier*
Moore, Lilian. *Papa Albert*
Mother Goose. *Mother Goose in French*
  Mother Goose in Spanish
  Rimes de la Mere Oie
On the little hearth
Pomerantz, Charlotte. *If I had a Paka*
  The tamarindo puppy and other poems
Rider, Alex. *A la ferme. At the farm*
  Chez nous. At our house
Rosario, Idalia. *Idalia's project ABC*
Rothman, Joel. *This can lick a lollipop*
Sasaki, Jeannie. *Chōchō is for butterfly*
Schaffer, Marion. *I love my cat!*
Serfozo, Mary. *Welcome Roberto!*
  Bienvenido, Roberto!
Simon, Norma. *What do I say?*
Standon, Anna. *Three little cats*
Steiner, Charlotte. *A friend is "Amie"*
Stevens, Cat. *Teaser and the firecat*
Takeshita, Fumiko. *The park bench*

Uchida, Yoshiko. *The rooster who understood Japanese*
Vacheron, Edith. *Here is Henri!*
Wiese, Kurt. *You can write Chinese*
Wilson, Barbara. *ABC et/and 123*
Zola, Meguido. *The dream of promise*

Forest rangers *see* Careers – park rangers

Forest, woods

Adler, David A. *Redwoods are the tallest trees in the world*
Ahlberg, Janet. *Jeremiah in the dark wood*
Allen, Gertrude E. *Everyday animals*
Anglund, Joan Walsh. *Nibble nibble mousekin*
Armer, Laura Adams. *The forest pool*
Arneson, D. J. *Secret places*
Arnold, Caroline. *The terrible Hodag*
Baker, Jeannie. *Where the forest meets the sea*
Bellamy, David. *The forest*
Berenstain, Stan. *The Berenstain bears and the ghost of the forest*
Beskow, Elsa Maartman. *Children of the forest*
Biro, Val. *The wind in the willows the wild wood*
Bond, Ruskin. *Flames in the forest*
Bradman, Tony. *Look out, he's behind you*
Brady, Irene. *A mouse named Mus*
Buff, Mary. *Dash and Dart*
Forest folk
Carrick, Carol. *A clearing in the forest*
Carrick, Donald. *Harold and the great stag*
Cowcher, Helen. *Rain forest*
Cristini, Ermanno. *In the woods*
Ets, Marie Hall. *Another day*
In the forest
Friedman, Judi. *Noises in the woods*
Frost, Robert. *Stopping by woods on a snowy evening*
Greaves, Margaret. *A net to catch the wind*
Grimm, Jacob. *Hansel and Gretel*, ill. by Adrienne Adams
Hansel and Gretel, ill. by Anthony Browne
Hansel and Gretel, ill. by Susan Jeffers
Hansel and Gretel, ill. by Winslow P. Pels
Hansel and Gretel, ill. by Conxita Rodriguez
Hansel and Gretel, ill. by John Wallner
Hansel and Gretel, ill. by Paul O. Zelinsky
Hansel and Gretel, ill. by Lisbeth Zwerger
Hill, Mary Lou. *My dad's a smokejumper*
Hirschi, Ron. *Who lives in... Alligator Swamp?*
Who lives in... the forest?
Hyman, Trina Schart. *The enchanted forest*
Jones, Chuck. *William the backwards skunk*

Latimer, Jim. *Going the moose way home*
Leister, Mary. *The silent concert*
Lerner, Carol. *Flowers of a woodland spring*
Lipkind, William. *The boy and the forest*
Lukešová, Milena. *Julian in the autumn woods*
McConnachie, Brian. *Lily of the forest*
Maris, Ron. *Hold tight, bear!*
Marshall, Edward. *Troll country*
Miklowitz, Gloria D. *Save that raccoon!*
Miles, Miska. *The fox and the fire*
Sylvester Jones and the voice in the forest
Miller, Edna. *Mousekin's ABC*
Mousekin's close call
Mouskin's Thanksgiving
Moore, Inga. *Fifty red night-caps*
Mora, Emma. *Animals of the forest*
Gideon, the little bear cub
Newton, James R. *A forest is reborn*
Forest log
Paul, Anthony. *The tiger who lost his stripes*
Peet, Bill. *Big bad Bruce*
Peyo. *The Smurfs and their woodland friends*
Prather, Ray. *The ostrich girl*
Prusski, Jeffrey. *Bring back the deer*
Schick, Eleanor. *A surprise in the forest*
Slobodkin, Louis. *Melvin, the moose child*
Storr, Catherine. *Robin Hood*
Tejima, Keizaburo. *Fox's dream*
Wahl, Jan. *The five in the forest*
Ward, Lynd. *Nic of the woods*
Yolen, Jane. *All in the woodland early*
Owl moon
Zalben, Jane Breskin. *Norton's nighttime*
Ziefert, Harriet. *On our way to the forest*

Forgetfulness *see* Behavior – forgetfulness

Format, unusual

Ahlberg, Janet. *Peek-a-boo!*
Alexander, Martha G. *The magic box*
The magic hat
The magic picture
Anno, Mitsumasa. *Anno's peekaboo*
Barrows, Marjorie Wescott. *Fraidy cat*
The funny hat
Brown, Margaret Wise. *The little fur family*
Burlson, Joe. *Space colony*
Campbell, Rod. *Henry's busy day*
Misty's mischief
Carle, Eric. *My very first book of growth*
My very first book of homes
My very first book of motion
My very first book of touch
The very hungry caterpillar
Carrier, Lark. *There was a hill...*
Chwast, Seymour. *Tall city, wide country*
De Paola, Tomie. *Country farm*

Emberley, Ed. *Ed Emberley's amazing look through book*
Ernst, Lisa Campbell. *The rescue of Aunt Pansy*
Fort, Patrick. *Redbird*
Fuchshuber, Annegert. *Giant story - Mouse tale*
Gantschev, Ivan. *The train to Grandma's*
Golden tales from long ago
Gomi, Taro. *Hi, butterfly!*
Goodall, John S. *The adventures of Paddy Pork*
 The ballooning adventures of Paddy Pork
 Creepy castle
 An Edwardian Christmas
 An Edwardian summer
 Jacko
 The midnight adventures of Kelly, Dot and Esmeralda
 Naughty Nancy
 Naughty Nancy goes to school
 Paddy goes traveling
 Paddy Pork odd jobs
 Paddy Pork's holiday
 Paddy under water
 Paddy's evening out
 Paddy's new hat
 Shrewbettina's birthday
 The story of a castle
 The story of a farm
 The story of a main street
 The story of an English village
 The surprise picnic
Gorey, Edward. *The tunnel calamity*
Grimm, Jacob. *Little Red Riding Hood*, ill. by John S. Goodall
Hague, Michael. *Michael Hague's world of unicorns*
Hauptmann, Tatjana. *A day in the life of Petronella Pig*
Hawkins, Colin. *Jen the hen*
 Tog the dog
Hellen, Nancy. *Bus stop*
Hoban, Tana. *Look! Look! Look!*
 26 letters and 99 cents
Hooper, Meredith. *Seven eggs*
Howell, Lynn. *Winifred's new bed*
Hyman, Trina Schart. *The enchanted forest*
Jensen, Virginia Allen. *Catching*
Jonas, Ann. *Reflections*
Kent, Lorna. *No, no, Charlie Rascal!*
Ladybug, ladybug, and other nursery rhymes
Lenski, Lois. *Sing a song of people*
Lewis, Stephen. *Zoo city*
Lodge, Bernard. *Door to door*
 Rhyming Nell
Mari, Iela. *Eat and be eaten*
Miranda, Anne. *Baby walk*
Munari, Bruno. *The circus in the mist*
Newell, Peter. *Topsys and turvys*
Newth, Philip. *Roly goes exploring*

Pearson, Tracey Campbell. *A apple pie*
Potter, Beatrix. *Where's Peter Rabbit?*
Price, Mathew. *Do you see what I see?*
Rey, Hans Augusto. *Anybody at home?*
 How do you get there?
 See the circus
 Where's my baby?
Roffey, Maureen. *Family scramble*
 Look, there's my hat!
Russell, Naomi. *The tree*
Scarry, Richard. *Egg in the hole*
 Richard Scarry's biggest word book ever!
Scullard, Sue. *Miss Fanshawe and the great dragon adventure*
Steiner, Charlotte. *The climbing book*
Taback, Simms. *Joseph had a little overcoat*
Tarrant, Graham. *Rabbits*
Tison, Annette. *The adventures of the three colors*
 Animal hide-and-seek
 Animals in color magic
 Inside and outside
The twelve days of Christmas. English folk song. The twelve days of Christmas, ill. by Erika Schneider
Van der Meer, Ron. *Pigs at home*
Waber, Bernard. *The snake*
Walters, Marguerite. *The city-country ABC*
Watson, Wendy. *The bunnies' Christmas eve*
Wildsmith, Brian. *Daisy*
 Give a dog a bone
 Goat's trail
 Pelican
Windham, Sophie. *Noah's ark*
Wood, John Norris. *Jungles*
 Oceans
Youldon, Gillian. *Counting*
 Shapes
 Sizes
Ziefert, Harriet. *Where's the cat?*
 Where's the dog?
 Where's the guinea pig?
 Where's the turtle?

Format, unusual – board books

Aronin, Ben. *The secret of the Sabbath fish*
At the farm
Baby's first book of colors
Baby's words
Bailey, Jill. *Eyes*
 Feet
 Mouths
 Noses
Baird, Anne. *Baby socks*
 Kiss, kiss
 Little tree
 No sheep
Bambi
Bohdal, Susi. *Bobby the bear*
 Harry the hare

Boon, Emilie. *It's spring, Peterkin*
  Peterkin's very own garden
Boynton, Sandra. *But not the hippopotamus*
  Doggies
  The going to bed book
  Horns to toes and in between
  Moo, baa, lalala
  Opposites
Burningham, John. *Count up*
  The dog
  Five down
  Just cats
  Pigs plus
  Read one
  Ride off
Busy baby
Campbell, Rod. *Look inside! All kinds of
  places*
  Look inside! Land, sea, air
Cars and trucks
Cassidy, Dianne. *Circus animals*
  Circus people
The caterpillar who turned into a butterfly
Children's Television Workshop. *Muppets
  in my neighborhood*
City
Come to the circus
Corbett, Grahame. *Guess who?*
  What number now?
  Who is hiding?
  Who is inside?
  Who is next?
Cosgrove, Stephen. *Sleepy time bunny*
Costa, Nicoletta. *The birthday party*
  Dressing up
  A friend comes to play
  The missing cat
Davidson, Amanda. *Teddy goes outside*
Demi. *Fleecy bunny*
  Fleecy lamb
De Paola, Tomie. *Katie and Kit at the beach*
  Katie, Kit and cousin Tom
  Katie's good idea
  Pajamas for Kit
DiFiori, Lawrence. *Baby animals*
  The farm
  If I had a little car
  My first book
  My toys
Domestic animals
Dreamer, Sue. *Circus ABC*
  Circus 1, 2, 3
Dubov, Christine Salac. *Aleksandra, where
  are your toes?*
  Aleksandra, where is your nose?
Duke, Kate. *Bedtime*
  Clean-up day
  The playground
  What bounces?
Dunn, Phoebe. *Baby's animal friends*
  Busy, busy toddlers

I'm a baby!
Edwards, Roberta. *Anna Bear's first winter*
Emberley, Ed. *Animals*
  Cars, boats, and planes
  Home
  Sounds
Farm animals
Farm house
Fast rolling fire trucks
Fast rolling work trucks
Fechner, Amrei. *I am a little dog*
  I am a little elephant
  I am a little lion
Firehouse
Fitzsimons, Cecilia. *My first birds*
  My first butterflies
Fowler, Richard. *Cat's story*
Freeman, Don. *Corduroy's party*
Freeman, Lydia. *Corduroy's day*
Fujikawa, Gyo. *Let's grow a garden*
  Millie's secret
  My favorite thing
  Surprise! Surprise!
Gellman, Ellie. *It's Chanukah!*
  It's Rosh Hashanah!
  Shai's Shabbat walk
Greeley, Valerie. *Farm animals*
  Field animals
  Pets
  Zoo animals
Gretz, Susanna. *Hide-and-seek*
  I'm not sleepy
  Ready for bed
  Too dark!
Groner, Judyth. *Where is the Afikomen?*
Hands, Hargrave. *Bunny sees*
  Duckling sees
  Little lamb sees
Haus, Felice. *Beep! Beep! I'm a jeep*
Hayes, Geoffrey. *Patrick and his grandpa*
Hello, baby
Hill, Eric. *Spot at the fair*
  Spot goes to the circus
  Spot goes to the farm
  Spot looks at colors
  Spot looks at shapes
  Spot on the farm
  Spot's first words
Hoban, Tana. *1, 2, 3*
  Panda, panda
  Red, blue, yellow shoe
  What is it?
Hopkins, Margaret. *Sleepytime for baby
  mouse*
Johnson, John E. *My first book of things*
Karn, George. *Circus big and small*
  Circus colors
Kessler, Ethel. *Are there hippos on the
  farm?*
  Is there an elephant in your kitchen?

Kilroy, Sally. *Animal noises*
  Babies' bodies
  Babies' homes
  Babies' outings
  Babies' zoo
  Baby colors
  Busy babies
  Noisy homes
Koelling, Caryl. *Animal mix and match*
  Mad monsters mix and match
  Silly stories mix and match
Koenner, Alfred. *Be quite quiet beside the lake*
  High flies the ball
Krementz, Jill. *Benjy goes to a restaurant*
  Jack goes to the beach
  Jamie goes on an airplane
  Katherine goes to nursery school
  Lily goes to the playground
  Taryn goes to the dentist
Lilly, Kenneth. *Animal builders*
  Animal climbers
  Animal jumpers
  Animal runners
  Animal swimmers
  Animals at the zoo
  Animals in the country
  Animals in the jungle
  Animals of the ocean
  Animals on the farm
Lionni, Leo. *Colors to talk about*
  Letters to talk about
  Numbers to talk about
  What?
  When?
  Where?
  Who?
  Words to talk about
  A little ABC book
  A little book of colors
  A little book of numbers
Lundell, Margo. *Teddy bear's birthday*
Lynn, Sara. *Big animals*
  Clothes
  Farm animals
  Food
  Garden animals
  Home
  Small animals
  Toys
McCue, Lisa. *Corduroy's toys*
  The little chick
McNaught, Harry. *Baby animals*
McNaughton, Colin. *At home*
  At playschool
  At the park
  At the party
  At the stores
  Autumn
  Spring
  Summer
  Winter
Maestro, Betsy. *Harriet at home*
  Harriet at play
  Harriet at school
  Harriet at work
Mayer, Mercer. *Astronaut critter*
  Cowboy critter
  Fireman critter
  Policeman critter
Miller, J. P. (John Parr). *Good night, little rabbit*
Miller, Margaret. *At my house*
  In my room
  Me and my clothes
  Time to eat
Mother Goose. *ABC rhymes*, ill. by Lulu Delarce
  Baa baa black sheep, ill. by Sue Porter
  Baa baa black sheep, ill. by Ferelith Eccles Williams
  Hey diddle diddle, ill. by Nita Sowter
  Hey diddle diddle, ill. by Eleanor Wasmuth
  Jack and Jill, ill. by Eleanor Wasmuth
  Kate Greenaway's Mother Goose
  Kitten rhymes
  Little boy blue
  Mother Goose house
  The old woman in a shoe, ill. by Eleanor Wasmuth
  Pussy cat, pussy cat, ill. by Ferelith Eccles Williams
  Sing a song of sixpence, ill. by Margaret Chamberlain
  Sing a song of sixpence, ill. by Ferelith Eccles Williams
  This little pig, ill. by Eleanor Wasmuth
  This little pig went to market, ill. by Ferelith Eccles Williams
  The three little kittens, ill. by Dorothy Stott
Mouse house
My body
My day
My first book of baby animals
My toy box
Nickl, Peter. *Ra ta ta tam*
O'Brien, Anne S. *Come play with us*
  I want that!
  I'm not tired
  Where's my truck?
Our house
Oxenbury, Helen. *All fall down*
  Beach day
  Clap hands
  Dressing
  Family
  Friends
  I can
  I hear
  I see

I touch
Playing
Say goodnight
729 curious creatures
729 merry mix-ups
729 puzzle people
The shopping trip
Tickle, tickle
Parish, Peggy. *I can - can you?*
Pearson, Susan. *Baby and the bear*
When baby went to bed
Peppé, Rodney. *Little circus*
Little dolls
Little games
Little numbers
Little wheels
Pfister, Marcus. *Where is my friend?*
Pfloog, Jan. *Kittens*
Puppies
Phillips, Joan. *Peek-a-boo! I see you!*
The pudgy book of babies
The pudgy book of farm animals
The pudgy book of here we go
The pudgy book of make-believe
The pudgy book of Mother Goose
The pudgy book of toys
The pudgy bunny book
The pudgy fingers counting book
The pudgy pals
The pudgy pat-a-cake book
The pudgy peek-a-boo book
The pudgy rock-a-bye book
Puppies and kittens
Roosevelt, Michelle Chopin. *Zoo animals*
Roth, Harold. *Autumn days*
A checkup
Nursery school
Winter days
Scarry, Richard. *My first word book*
Richard Scarry's busy houses
Richard Scarry's Lowly Worm word book
Schmid, Eleonore. *Farm animals*
Schroeder, Binette. *Tuffa and her friends*
Tuffa and the bone
Tuffa and the ducks
Tuffa and the picnic
Tuffa and the snow
Sesame Street. *Ernie and Bert can...can you?*
Shine, Deborah. *The little engine that could pudgy word book*
Shostak, Myra. *Rainbow candles*
Silverman, Maida. *Bunny's ABC*
Ladybug's color book
Mouse's shape book
Smith, Donald. *Who's wearing my baseball cap?*
Who's wearing my bow tie?
Who's wearing my sneakers?
Who's wearing my sunglasses?
Spanner, Helmut. *I am a little cat*

Spier, Peter. *Bill's service station*
Firehouse
Food market
Little cats
Little dogs
Little ducks
Little rabbits
My school
The pet store
The toy shop
Stevens, Harry. *Fat mouse*
Parrot told snake
Struppi
Suben, Eric. *Pigeon takes a trip*
Tabler, Judith. *The new puppy*
Tafuri, Nancy. *In a red house*
My friends
One wet jacket
Two new sneakers
Where we sleep
The three bears. *Goldilocks and the three bears*, ill. by Jane Dyer
A visit to a pond
Wells, Rosemary. *Hooray for Max*
Max's bath
Max's bedtime
Max's birthday
Max's breakfast
Max's first word
Max's new suit
Max's ride
Max's toys
What do babies do?
What do toddlers do?
Wikler, Madeline. *Let's build a Sukkah*
My first seder
The Purim parade
Winn, Chris. *Helping*
Holiday
My day
Playing
Young animals in the zoo
Young domestic animals
Ziefert, Harriet. *Baby Ben's bow-wow book*
Baby Ben's busy book
Baby Ben's go-go book
Baby Ben's noisy book
Nicky's friends
No, no, Nicky!
On our way to the barn
On our way to the forest
On our way to the water
On our way to the zoo
Where's the cat?
Where's the dog?
Where's the guinea pig?
Where's the turtle?
Zoo animals

Format, unusual – cardboard pages *see*
Format, unusual – board books

Format, unusual – toy and movable books

Æsop. *Æsop's fables*, ill. by Claire Littlejohn
Alexander, Martha G. *3 magic flip books*
Anno, Mitsumasa. *Anno's magical ABC*
Belloc, Hilaire. *The bad child's pop-up book of beasts*
Bemelmans, Ludwig. *Madeline [pop-up book]*
Benjamin, Alan. *1000 monsters*
Berger, Melvin. *Early humans*
 Prehistoric mammals
Bradman, Tony. *Look out, he's behind you*
 See you later, alligator
Brown, Marc. *What do you call a dumb bunny? and other rabbit riddles, games, jokes and cartoons*
Campbell, Rod. *Buster's afternoon*
 Buster's morning
 Dear zoo
 It's mine
 Oh dear!
Carle, Eric. *My very first book of food*
 My very first book of heads and tails
 My very first book of sounds
 My very first book of tools
 Papa, please get the moon for me
 The secret birthday message
 Watch out! A giant!
Carter, David A. *How many bugs in a box?*
Cassidy, Dianne. *Circus animals*
 Circus people
Cremins, Robert. *My animal ABC*
 My animal Mother Goose
Crowther, Robert. *Hide and seek counting book*
 The most amazing hide-and-seek alphabet book
 The most amazing hide-and-seek opposites book
 Pop goes the weasel!
Facklam, Margery. *But not like mine*
 So can I
Faulkner, Keith. *Sam at the seaside*
 Sam helps out
Fowler, Richard. *Mr. Little's noisy car*
Gerstein, Mordicai. *William, where are you?*
Grimm, Jacob. *Sleeping Beauty*, ill. by John Wallner
Hawkins, Colin. *The elephant*
 Incy wincy spider
 Round the garden
 Take away monsters
 This little pig
 What time is it, Mr. Wolf?
Hill, Eric. *Spot goes to school*
 Spot goes to the beach
 Spot's birthday party
 Spot's first Christmas
 Spot's first Easter
 Spot's first walk
 Where's Spot?
The house that Jack built. *The house that Jack built*, ill. by Seymour Chwast
Hurd, Thacher. *A night in the swamp*
Johnson, B. J. *A hat like that*
 My blanket Burt
Jonas, Ann. *Where can it be?*
Kunhardt, Edith. *Pat the cat*
Lippman, Peter. *Peter Lippman's numbers*
 Peter Lippman's opposites
Lobel, Arnold. *The frog and toad pop-up book*
McGowan, Alan. *Sailing ships*
Maris, Ron. *Is anyone home?*
Marshall, Ray. *Pop-up numbers #1*
 Pop-up numbers #2
 Pop-up numbers #3
 Pop-up numbers #4
 The train
Martin, Sarah Catherine. *Old Mother Hubbard*, ill. by Colin Hawkins
Meggendorfer, Lothar. *The genius of Lothar Meggendorfer*
Milne, A. A. (Alan Alexander). *House at Pooh corner: a pop-up book*
 Pooh and some bees
 Pooh goes visiting
 Winnie-the-Pooh
Miranda, Anne. *Baby talk*
Moseley, Keith. *Dinosaurs*
Mother Goose. *Sing a song of sixpence*, ill. by Ray Marshall and Korky Paul
Munari, Bruno. *The elephant's wish*
 Jimmy has lost his cap
 Tic, Tac and Toc
 Who's there? Open the door
Oakley, Graham. *Graham Oakley's magical changes*
Pelham, David. *Worms wiggle*
Potter, Beatrix. *The two bad mice pop-up book*
Presencer, Alain. *Roaring lion tales*
Price, Mathew. *Peekaboo!*
Prokofiev, Sergei Sergeievitch. *Peter and the wolf*, ill. by Barbara Cooney
Roffey, Maureen. *Home sweet home*
Roth, Harold. *Let's look all around the farm*
 Let's look all around the house
 Let's look all around the town
 Let's look for surprises all around
Ruby-Spears Enterprises. *The puppy's new adventures*
Scarry, Huck. *Looking into the Middle Ages*
Scarry, Richard. *Richard Scarry's mix or match storybook*
Selberg, Ingrid. *Nature's hidden world*
Seymour, Peter. *Animals in disguise*
 How the weather works
 Insects
 What lives in the sea?

Conford, Ellen. *Why can't I be William?*
Conta, Marcia Maher. *Feelings between friends*
Coontz, Otto. *The quiet house*
Costa, Nicoletta. *A friend comes to play*
Coville, Bruce. *The foolish giant*
Craig, Helen. *The night of the paper bag monsters*
  A welcome for Annie
Cunningham, Julia. *A mouse called Junction*
Cuyler, Margery. *Freckles and Willie*
Dabcovich, Lydia. *Mrs. Huggins and her hen Hannah*
Damjan, Mischa. *Goodbye little bird*
Dauer, Rosamond. *Bullfrog builds a house*
De Beer, Hans. *Little polar bear*
De Bruyn, Monica. *Lauren's secret ring*
Degen, Bruce. *The little witch and the riddle*
Delacre, Lulu. *Nathan's fishing trip*
Delaney, Ned. *Bert and Barney*
Delton, Judy. *Duck goes fishing*
  A pet for Duck and Bear
  Three friends find spring
De Paola, Tomie. *Andy (that's my name)*
De Regniers, Beatrice Schenk. *May I bring a friend?*
Dickinson, Mary. *Alex and Roy*
Drdek, Richard E. *Horace the friendly octopus*
Dunrea, Olivier. *Fergus and Bridey*
Duvoisin, Roger Antoine. *The crocodile in the tree*
  Periwinkle
  Petunia
  Petunia and the song
  Petunia, I love you
  Petunia's treasure
  Snowy and Woody
Ehrlich, Amy. *Leo, Zack and Emmie*
  Leo, Zack, and Emmie together again
Ellis, Anne Leo. *Dabble Duck*
Eriksson, Eva. *Hocus-pocus*
  Jealousy
  One short week
  The tooth trip
Ernst, Lisa Campbell. *The rescue of Aunt Pansy*
Escudie, René. *Paul and Sebastian*
Fassler, Joan. *Boy with a problem*
Fatio, Louise. *The happy lion*
  Hector and Christina
Felt, Sue. *Hello-goodbye*
Fern, Eugene. *What's he been up to now?*
Fink, Dale Borman. *Mr. Silver and Mrs. Gold*
Fleischman, Sid. *The scarebird*
Flory, Jane. *We'll have a friend for lunch*
Fremlin, Robert. *Three friends*
Fuchshuber, Annegert. *Giant story - Mouse tale*

Gantschev, Ivan. *RumpRump*
Gay, Michel. *Rabbit express*
Gelman, Rita Golden. *Dumb Joey*
Giff, Patricia Reilly. *Happy birthday, Ronald Morgan!*
Ginsburg, Mirra. *The fox and the hare*
Goldsmith, Howard. *Little lost dog*
Gordon, Shirley. *Crystal is my friend*
  Crystal is the new girl
Graham, Al. *Timothy Turtle*, ill. by Tony Palazzo
Graham, Bob. *Crusher is coming!*
Hallinan, P. K. (Patrick K.). *That's what a friend is*
Hanson, Joan. *I don't like Timmy*
Heine, Helme. *Friends*
  Three little friends: the alarm clock
  Three little friends: the racing cart
  Three little friends: the visitor
Helena, Ann. *The lie*
Henkes, Kevin. *Jessica*
Hickman, Martha Whitmore. *My friend William moved away*
Hissey, Jane. *Old Bear*
Hoban, Lillian. *Arthur's great big Valentine*
Hoban, Russell. *A bargain for Frances*
  Best friends for Frances
Hoff, Syd. *Who will be my friends?*
Hoffman, Phyllis. *Steffie and me*
Hogrogian, Nonny. *The hermit and Harry and me*
Holabird, Katharine. *Alexander and the dragon*
  Angelina and Alice
Hopkins, Lee Bennett. *Best friends*
Horvath, Betty F. *Will the real Tommy Wilson please stand up?*
Hughes, Shirley. *Moving Molly*
Hutchins, Pat. *The doorbell rang*
Hutton, Warwick. *The nose tree*
Inkpen, Mick. *If I had a pig*
  If I had a sheep
Iwamura, Kazuo. *Ton and Pon*
Iwasaki, Chihiro. *Will you be my friend?*
Jaques, Faith. *Tilly's rescue*
Jaynes, Ruth M. *Friends! friends! friends!*
Jeschke, Susan. *Lucky's choice*
Jewell, Nancy. *Try and catch me*
Joerns, Consuelo. *Oliver's escape*
Jones, Rebecca C. *The biggest, meanest, ugliest dog in the whole wide world*
Kaldhol, Marit. *Goodbye Rune*
Kamen, Gloria. *The ringdoves*
Kantrowitz, Mildred. *I wonder if Herbie's home yet*
Keats, Ezra Jack. *A letter to Amy*
  Peter's chair
Keller, Holly. *Lizzie's invitation*
Keller, John G. *Krispin's fair*
Kellogg, Steven. *Best friends*
Kent, Jack. *Socks for supper*

Saunders, Susan. *Charles Rat's picnic*
Scarry, Patsy. *Little Richard and Prickles*
Schick, Eleanor. *Making friends*
Schreiber, Georges. *Bambino goes home*
Schroeder, Binette. *Tuffa and her friends*
Schulman, Janet. *The big hello*
  The great big dummy
Schumacher, Claire. *Alto and Tango*
  King of the zoo
  Tim and Jim
Schweitzer, Iris. *Hilda's restful chair*
Scruton, Clive. *Bubble and squeak*
Sharmat, Marjorie Weinman. *Bartholomew the bossy*
  Burton and Dudley
  Gladys told me to meet her here
  I'm not Oscar's friend any more
  Mitchell is moving
  Rollo and Juliet...forever!
  Scarlet Monster lives here
  Sophie and Gussie
  Taking care of Melvin
  The trip
Sherman, Ivan. *I do not like it when my friend comes to visit*
Sis, Peter. *Rainbow Rhino*
Slate, Joseph. *Lonely Lula cat*
Slobodkin, Louis. *Dinny and Danny*
Smaridge, Norah. *Peter's tent*
Sommers, Tish. *Bert and the broken teapot*
Spang, Günter. *Clelia and the little mermaid*
Stanley, Diane. *A country tale*
Steadman, Ralph. *The bridge*
Steiner, Charlotte. *A friend is "Amie"*
Steptoe, John. *Stevie*
Stevens, Carla. *Stories from a snowy meadow*
Stevenson, James. *Howard*
  No friends
  Wilfred the rat
  The worst person in the world
  The worst person in the world at Crab Beach
Sugita, Yutaka. *Helena the unhappy hippopotamus*
Tafuri, Nancy. *My friends*
Taha, Karen T. *A gift for Tia Rose*
Taylor, Mark. *Old Blue, you good dog you*
Tether, Graham. *Skunk and possum*
Thaler, Mike. *It's me, hippo!*
  Moonkey
Thayer, Jane. *Gus was a friendly ghost*
  The popcorn dragon
Tibo, Gilles. *Simon and the snowflakes*
Tripp, Paul. *The strawman who smiled by mistake*
Tsutsui, Yoriko. *Anna's secret friend*
Tudor, Bethany. *Samuel's tree house*
Udry, Janice May. *Let's be enemies*
Van Woerkom, Dorothy. *Harry and Shelburt*
Varley, Susan. *Badger's parting gifts*

Venable, Alan. *The checker players*
Vigna, Judith. *The hiding house*
Vincent, Gabrielle. *Breakfast time, Ernest and Celestine*
  Ernest and Celestine's patchwork quilt
  Merry Christmas, Ernest and Celestine
Viorst, Judith. *Rosie and Michael*
Waber, Bernard. *Ira says goodbye*
  Ira sleeps over
  Lovable Lyle
  Nobody is perfick
Wade, Anne. *A promise is for keeping*
Waechter, Friedrich Karl. *Three is company*
Walker, Alice. *To hell with dying*
Warren, Cathy. *Fred's first day*
Weil, Lisl. *Gillie and the flattering fox*
Weiss, Ellen. *Mokey's birthday present*
Weiss, Nicki. *Battle day at Camp Delmont*
  A family story
  Maude and Sally
Wiesner, William. *Tops*
Wildsmith, Brian. *The lazy bear*
Wilhelm, Hans. *Let's be friends again!*
  A new home, a new friend
Williams, Barbara. *Kevin's grandma*
Williams, Vera B. *Stringbean's trip to the shining sea*
Winthrop, Elizabeth. *Katharine's doll*
  Lizzie and Harold
  Sloppy kisses
Wittman, Sally. *The boy who hated Valentine's Day*
  Pelly and Peak
  Plenty of Pelly and Peak
  A special trade
  The wonderful Mrs. Trumbly
Wolcott, Patty. *Double-decker, double-decker, double-decker bus*
Wolde, Gunilla. *Betsy and Peter are different*
Yashima, Tarō. *The youngest one*
Yeoman, John. *Mouse trouble*
Zalben, Jane Breskin. *Beni's first Chanukah*
  Oliver and Alison's week
Zelinsky, Paul O. *The lion and the stoat*
Ziefert, Harriet. *Mike and Tony best friends*
  Nicky's friends
Zion, Gene. *The meanest squirrel I ever met*
Zolotow, Charlotte. *The hating book*
  Hold my hand
  Janey
  My friend John
  The new friend
  Three funny friends
  Timothy too!
  The unfriendly book
  The white marble

Frogs and toads

Æsop. *The hare and the frogs*

Alexander, Martha G. *No ducks in our bathtub*

Anderson, Peggy Perry. *Time for bed, the babysitter said*

Back, Christine. *Tadpole and frog*

Berson, Harold. *Charles and Claudine*

Campbell, Wayne. *What a catastrophe!*

Canfield, Jane White. *The frog prince*

Carrick, Malcolm. *Today is shrew's day*

Charles, Robert Henry. *The roundabout turn*

Chenery, Janet. *The toad hunt*

Coldrey, Jennifer. *The world of frogs*

Cortesi, Wendy W. *Explore a spooky swamp*

Dauer, Rosamond. *Bullfrog builds a house*
Bullfrog grows up

Dinardo, Jeffrey. *Timothy and the night noises*

Duke, Kate. *Seven froggies went to school*

Duvoisin, Roger Antoine. *Periwinkle*

Erickson, Russell E. *Warton and the traders*
Warton's Christmas eve adventure

Flack, Marjorie. *Tim Tadpole and the great bullfrog*

Freschet, Berniece. *The old bullfrog*

A frog he would a-wooing go (folk-song).
Frog went a-courtin', ill. by Feodor Rojankovsky
Froggie went a-courting, ill. by Chris Conover

Gackenbach, Dick. *Crackle, Gluck and the sleeping toad*

Gordon, Margaret. *Frogs' holiday*

Graham, Amanda. *Picasso, the green tree frog*

Greydanus, Rose. *Freddie the frog*

Harrison, David Lee. *The case of Og, the missing frog*

Hawes, Judy. *Spring peepers*
Why frogs are wet

Hellard, Susan. *Froggie goes a-courting*

Himmelman, John. *Amanda and the witch switch*

Hoban, Russell. *Jim Frog*

Hogan, Paula Z. *The frog*

Isele, Elizabeth. *The frog princess*

Kalan, Robert. *Jump, frog, jump!*

Karlin, Nurit. *The blue frog*

Keith, Eros. *Rrra-ah*

Kellogg, Steven. *The mysterious tadpole*

Kent, Jack. *The caterpillar and the polliwog*

Kepes, Juliet. *Frogs, merry*

Kraus, Robert. *Mert the blurt*

Kumin, Maxine. *Eggs of things*

Lane, Carolyn. *The voices of Greenwillow Pond*

Lane, Margaret. *The frog*

Lee, Jeanne M. *Toad is the uncle of heaven*

Lionni, Leo. *Fish is fish*
It's mine!

Lobel, Arnold. *Days with Frog and Toad*
Frog and Toad all year
Frog and Toad are friends
The frog and toad pop-up book
Frog and Toad together

Lucas, Barbara. *Sleeping over*

MacLachlan, Patricia. *Moon, stars, frogs and friends*

McLenighan, Valjean. *You are what you are*

McPhail, David. *Captain Toad and the motorbike*

Maris, Ron. *Better move on, frog!*

Massie, Diane Redfield. *Walter was a frog*

Mayer, Mercer. *A boy, a dog, a frog and a friend*
A boy, a dog and a frog
Frog goes to dinner
Frog on his own
Frog, where are you?
One frog too many

Miles, Miska. *Jump frog jump*

Newton, Patricia Montgomery. *The frog who drank the waters of the world*

Noll, Sally. *Off and counting*

Partridge, Jenny. *Hopfellow*

Pavey, Peter. *I'm Taggarty Toad*

Pendery, Rosemary. *A home for Hopper*

Potter, Beatrix. *The tale of Mr. Jeremy Fisher*

Pursell, Margaret Sanford. *Sprig the tree frog*

Rockwell, Anne F. *Big boss Toad*

Schumacher, Claire. *Brave Lily*

Seeger, Pete. *The foolish frog*

Seuss, Dr. *Would you rather be a bullfrog?*

Small, David. *Eulalie and the hopping head*

Smith, Jim. *The frog band and Durrington Dormouse*
The frog band and the onion seller
The frog band and the owlnapper

Solotareff, Grégoire. *The ogre and the frog king*

Steig, William. *Gorky rises*

Steptoe, John. *The story of jumping mouse*

Stevenson, James. *Monty*

Stratemeyer, Clara Georgeanna. *Frog fun*
Tuggy

Thayer, Mike. *In the middle of the puddle*

Tresselt, Alvin R. *Frog in the well*

Troughton, Joanna. *What made Tiddalik laugh*

Turska, Krystyna. *The woodcutter's duck*

Van Woerkom, Dorothy. *Sea frog, city frog*

Velthuijs, Max. *Little Man to the rescue*

Vesey, A. *The princess and the frog*

Wahl, Jan. *Doctor Rabbit's foundling*

Walt Disney Productions. *Walt Disney's The adventures of Mr. Toad.*

West, Colin. *"Pardon?" said the giraffe*

Yeoman, John. *The bear's water picnic*

Yolen, Jane. *Commander Toad and the big black hole*
Commander Toad and the planet of the grapes
Commander Toad in space
Zakhoder, Boris Vladimirovich. *Rosachok*

Games

Agostinelli, Maria Enrica. *I know something you don't know*
Ahlberg, Janet. *Each peach pear plum*
Peek-a-boo!
Alexander, Martha G. *We never get to do anything*
Allen, Jeffrey. *The secret life of Mr. Weird*
Anderson, Douglas. *Let's draw a story*
Anglund, Joan Walsh. *The brave cowboy*
Cowboy's secret life
Anno, Mitsumasa. *Anno's animals*
Anno's Britain
Anno's counting house
Anno's flea market
Anno's Italy
Anno's journey
Anno's magical ABC
Anno's U.S.A.
Topsy-turvies
Upside-downers
Applebaum, Neil. *Is there a hole in your head?*
Aruego, José. *Look what I can do*
We hide, you seek
Asch, Frank. *Goodnight horsey*
Battles, Edith. *One to teeter-totter*
Baylor, Byrd. *Guess who my favorite person is*
Beach, Stewart. *Good morning, sun's up!*
Behrens, June. *Can you walk the plank?*
The big Peter Rabbit book
Bonsall, Crosby Newell. *The day I had to play with my sister*
Piggle
Booth, Eugene. *At the circus*
At the fair
In the air
In the garden
In the jungle
Under the ocean
Brinckloe, Julie. *Playing marbles*
Brown, Marc. *Finger rhymes*
Hand rhymes
Play rhymes

What do you call a dumb bunny? and other rabbit riddles, games, jokes and cartoons
Brown, Margaret Wise. *The indoor noisy book*
Byars, Betsy Cromer. *Go and hush the baby*
Carroll, Ruth. *Where's the bunny?*
Charlip, Remy. *Arm in arm*
Where is everybody?
Civardi, Anne. *Things people do*
Clark, Harry. *The first story of the whale*
Cohen, Peter Zachary. *Authorized autumn charts of the Upper Red Canoe River country*
Craig, M. Jean. *Boxes*
Dale, Penny. *You can't*
Delacre, Lulu. *Arroz con leche*
Delaney, Ned. *One dragon to another*
Delton, Judy. *I never win!*
Demi. *Demi's opposites*
De Paola, Tomie. *Andy (that's my name)*
Things to make and do for Valentine's Day
De Regniers, Beatrice Schenk. *What can you do with a shoe?*
Dubanevich, Arlene. *Pigs in hiding*
Elting, Mary. *Q is for duck*
Emberley, Ed. *Ed Emberley's crazy mixed-up face game*
Klippity klop
The farmer in the dell. *The farmer in the dell*, ill. by Kathy Parkinson
The farmer in the dell, ill. by Mary Maki Rae
The farmer in the dell, ill. by Diane Stanley
Fisher, Leonard Everett. *Look around!*
Fleisher, Robbin. *Quilts in the attic*
Fox, Dorothea Warren. *Follow me the leader*
French, Fiona. *Hunt the thimble*
Gardner, Beau. *Guess what?*
Gillham, Bill. *Can you see it?*
What can you do?
What's the difference?
Where does it go?
Glazer, Tom. *Do your ears hang low?*
Eye winker, Tom Tinker, chin chopper
Glovach, Linda. *The Little Witch's black magic book of games*
Go tell Aunt Rhody. *Go tell Aunt Rhody*, ill. by Aliki
Go tell Aunt Rhody, ill. by Robert M. Quackenbush
Gretz, Susanna. *Hide-and-seek*
I'm not sleepy
Grindley, Sally. *Knock, knock! Who's there?*
Hahn, Hannelore. *Take a giant step*
Handford, Martin. *Find Waldo now*
Where's Waldo?
Hann, Jacquie. *Follow the leader*
Hawkins, Colin. *Incy wincy spider*
Round the garden

Zion, Gene. *Hide and seek day*
Jeffie's party

Gangs *see* Clubs, gangs

Garage sales

Rockwell, Anne F. *Our garage sale*

Garbage collectors *see* Careers – garbage
collectors

Gardening *see* Activities – gardening

Geese *see* Birds – geese

Generosity *see* Character traits –
generosity

Geologists *see* Careers – geologists

Gerbils *see* Animals – gerbils

Germany *see* Foreign lands – Germany

Ghosts

Adler, David A. *Jeffrey's ghost and the
leftover baseball team*
Ahlberg, Janet. *Funnybones*
Alexander, Sue. *More Witch, Goblin, and
Ghost stories*
*Witch, Goblin, and Ghost in the haunted
woods*
*Witch, Goblin and Ghost's book of things to
do*
Witch, Goblin and sometimes Ghost
Allard, Harry. *Bumps in the night*
Benchley, Nathaniel. *A ghost named Fred*
Bennett, Jill. *Teeny tiny*
Berenstain, Stan. *The Berenstain bears and
the ghost of the forest*
Bergström, Gunilla. *Who's scaring Alfie
Atkins?*
Bright, Robert. *Georgie*
Georgie and the baby birds
Georgie and the ball of yarn
Georgie and the buried treasure
Georgie and the little dog
Georgie and the magician
Georgie and the noisy ghost
Georgie and the robbers
Georgie and the runaway balloon
Georgie goes west
Georgie to the rescue
Georgie's Christmas carol
Georgie's Halloween
Brown, Marc. *Spooky riddles*
Brunhoff, Laurent de. *Babar and the ghost*
Charlton, Elizabeth. *Jeremy and the ghost*
Cohen, Caron Lee. *Renata, Whizbrain and
the ghost*

Coombs, Patricia. *Dorrie and the screebit
ghost*
Cuyler, Margery. *Sir William and the
pumpkin monster*
DeLage, Ida. *The old witch and the ghost
parade*
Du Bois, William Pène. *Elisabeth the cow
ghost*
Eisenberg, Phyllis Rose. *Don't tell me a
ghost story*
Fife, Dale. *Follow that ghost!*
Flora, James. *Grandpa's ghost stories*
Friedrich, Priscilla. *The marshmallow ghosts*
Gage, Wilson. *Mrs. Gaddy and the ghost*
Galdone, Joanna. *The tailypo*
Galdone, Paul. *King of the cats*
The monster and the tailor
The teeny-tiny woman
Gikow, Louise. *Boober Fraggle's ghosts*
Hancock, Sibyl. *Esteban and the ghost*
Hayes, Geoffrey. *The mystery of the pirate
ghost*
Herman, Emily. *Hubknuckles*
Hirsh, Marilyn. *Deborah the dybbuk*
Johnston, Tony. *Four scary stories*
Kroll, Steven. *Amanda and the giggling
ghost*
Kunnas, Mauri. *One spooky night and other
scary stories*
Levy, Elizabeth. *Something queer at the
haunted school*
Lexau, Joan M. *Millicent's ghost*
McMillan, Bruce. *Ghost doll*
Mooser, Stephen. *The ghost with the
Halloween hiccups*
Nishikawa, Osamu. *Alexander and the blue
ghost*
Nixon, Joan Lowery. *The Thanksgiving
mystery*
O'Connor, Jane. *The teeny tiny woman*
Olson, Helen Kronberg. *The strange thing
that happened to Oliver Wendell Iscovitch*
Raskin, Ellen. *Ghost in a four-room
apartment*
Roche, P. K. (Patrick K.). *Webster and
Arnold go camping*
Rockwell, Anne F. *A bear, a bobcat and
three ghosts*
Rodgers, Frank. *Who's afraid of the ghost
train?*
Ross, Pat. *M and M and the haunted house
game*
Sandberg, Inger. *Little ghost Godfry*
Schulman, Janet. *Jack the bum and the
haunted house*
Seuling, Barbara. *The teeny tiny woman*
Sharmat, Marjorie Weinman. *Two ghosts
on a bench*
Sherrow, Victoria. *There goes the ghost*
Thayer, Jane. *Gus and the baby ghost*
Gus was a friendly ghost

Gus was a gorgeous ghost
Gus was a real dumb ghost
What's a ghost going to do?
Wallace, Daisy. *Ghost poems*
Wolkstein, Diane. *The legend of Sleepy Hollow*
Zemach, Margot. *The little tiny woman*

Giants

Allen, Linda. *The giant who had no heart*
Balian, Lorna. *A sweetheart for Valentine*
Benjamin, Alan. *Ribtickle Town*
Bodwell, Gaile. *The long day of the giants*
Bolliger, Max. *The giants' feast*
The magic bird
Bradfield, Roger. *Giants come in different sizes*
Briggs, Raymond. *Jim and the beanstalk*
Carle, Eric. *Watch out! A giant!*
Cole, Brock. *The giant's toe*
Coville, Bruce. *The foolish giant*
Cunliffe, John. *Sara's giant and the upside down house*
Cushman, Doug. *Giants*
De La Mare, Walter. *Molly Whuppie*
De Paola, Tomie. *Fin M'Coul*
The mysterious giant of Barletta
De Regniers, Beatrice Schenk. *The giant story*
Du Bois, William Pène. *Giant Otto*
Otto and the magic potatoes
Otto at sea
Otto in Africa
Otto in Texas
Elkin, Benjamin. *Lucky and the giant*
Foreman, Michael. *The two giants*
Fritz, Jean. *The good giants and the bad Pukwudgies*
Fuchshuber, Annegert. *Giant story - Mouse tale*
Greene, Ellin. *The pumpkin giant*
Grimm, Jacob. *The brave little tailor*, ill. by Mark Corcoran
The brave little tailor, ill. by Svend Otto S.
The brave little tailor, ill. by Daniel San Souci
The glass mountain, ill. by Nonny Hogrogian
The valiant little tailor, ill. by Victor G. Ambrus
Haley, Gail E. *Jack and the bean tree*
Herrmann, Frank. *The giant Alexander*
The giant Alexander and the circus
Hillert, Margaret. *The magic beans*
Homme, Bob. *The friendly giant's birthday*
The friendly giant's book of fire engines

Jack and the beanstalk. The history of Mother Twaddle and the marvelous achievements of her son Jack
Jack and the beanstalk, ill. by Lorinda Bryan Cauley
Jack and the beanstalk, ill. by Ed Parker
Jack and the beanstalk, ill. by Tony Ross
Jack and the beanstalk, ill. by William Stobbs
Jack and the beanstalk, ill. by Anne Wilsdorf
Jack the giantkiller, ill. by Tony Ross
Jack the giant killer, ill. by Anne Wilsdorf
Jennings, Michael. *Robin Goodfellow and the giant dwarf*
Kahl, Virginia. *Giants, indeed!*
Kraus, Robert. *The little giant*
Lawrence, John. *The giant of Grabbist*
Little, Emily. *David and the giant*
Lobel, Arnold. *Giant John*
Löfgren, Ulf. *The boy who ate more than the giant and other Swedish folktales*
McNeill, Janet. *The giant's birthday*
Minarik, Else Holmelund. *The little giant girl and the elf boys*
Munsch, Robert N. *David's father*
Polushkin, Maria. *The little hen and the giant*
Root, Phyllis. *Soup for supper*
Sherman, Ivan. *I am a giant*
Still, James. *Jack and the wonder beans*
Tompert, Ann. *Charlotte and Charles*
Ungerer, Tomi. *Zeralda's ogre*
Wallace, Daisy. *Giant poems*
Ward, Nick. *Giant*
Wiesner, William. *Tops*
Yolen, Jane. *The giant's farm*
The giants go camping

Gilbert Islands *see* Foreign lands – South Sea Islands

Giraffes *see* Animals – giraffes

Glasses

Brown, Marc. *Arthur's eyes*
Giff, Patricia Reilly. *Watch out, Ronald Morgan!*
Goodsell, Jane. *Katie's magic glasses*
Keller, Holly. *Cromwell's glasses*
Kessler, Leonard P. *Mr. Pine's mixed-up signs*
Lasson, Robert. *Orange Oliver*
Raskin, Ellen. *Spectacles*
Smith, Donald. *Who's wearing my sunglasses?*
Thayer, Jane. *Mr. Turtle's magic glasses*
Tusa, Tricia. *Libby's new glasses*
Wise, William. *The cowboy surprise*

Gnats *see* Insects – gnats

Gnomes *see* Elves and little people

Goats *see* Animals – goats

Goblins

Alden, Laura. *Learning about fairies*
Alexander, Sue. *More Witch, Goblin, and Ghost stories*
  Witch, Goblin, and Ghost in the haunted woods
  Witch, Goblin and Ghost's book of things to do
  Witch, Goblin and sometimes Ghost
Bunting, Eve. *Scary, scary Halloween*
Calhoun, Mary. *The goblin under the stairs*
Coombs, Patricia. *Dorrie and the goblin*
Haley, Gail E. *Go away, stay away*
Impey, Rose. *The flat man*
  Scare yourself to sleep
Johnston, Tony. *Four scary stories*
Lifton, Betty Jean. *Joji and the Amanojaku*
Mariana. *Miss Flora McFlimsey's Halloween*
Schertle, Alice. *Bill and the google-eyed goblins*
Sendak, Maurice. *Outside over there*
Tobias, Tobi. *Chasing the goblins away*

Gorillas *see* Animals – gorillas

Gossip *see* Behavior – gossip

Grammar *see* Language

Grandfathers *see* Family life – grandfathers; Family life – grandparents

Grandmothers *see* Family life – grandmothers; Family life – grandparents

Grandparents *see* Family life – grandfathers; Family life – grandmothers; Family life – grandparents

Grasshoppers *see* Insects – grasshoppers

Great-grandparents *see* Family life – great-grandparents

Greece *see* Foreign lands – Greece

Greed *see* Behavior – greed

Greenland *see* Foreign lands – Greenland

Griffins *see* Mythical creatures

Grocery stores *see* Shopping; Stores

Groundhog Day *see* Holidays – Groundhog Day

Groundhogs *see* Animals – groundhogs

Growing up *see* Behavior – growing up

Guinea pigs *see* Animals – guinea pigs

Guns *see* Weapons

Guyana *see* Foreign lands – Guyana

Gymnastics *see* Sports – gymnastics

Gypsies

Anderson, C. W. (Clarence Williams). *Blaze and the gypsies*
Bemelmans, Ludwig. *Madeline and the gypsies*
García Lorca, Federico. *The Lieutenant Colonel and the gypsy*
Kellogg, Steven. *The mystery of the magic green ball*
Mahy, Margaret. *Mrs. Discombobulous*
Oram, Hiawyn. *Skittlewonder and the wizard*

Hair

Abisch, Roz. *The Pumpkin Heads*
Appell, Clara. *Now I have a daddy haircut*
Bright, Robert. *I like red*
Davis, Gibbs. *Katy's first haircut*
Freeman, Don. *Mop Top*
Girard, Linda Walvoord. *Jeremy's first haircut*
Goldin, Augusta. *Straight hair, curly hair*
Grimm, Jacob. *Rapunzel*, ill. by Jutta Ash
  Rapunzel, ill. by Bert Dodson
  Rapunzel, ill. by Trina Schart Hyman
Hair
Kunhardt, Dorothy. *Billy the barber*
Quin-Harkin, Janet. *Helpful Hattie*
Rockwell, Anne F. *My barber*
Scott, Natalie. *Firebrand, push your hair out of your eyes*
Tether, Graham. *The hair book*
Townsend, Kenneth. *Felix, the bald-headed lion*

Halloween *see* Holidays – Halloween

Hamsters *see* Animals – hamsters

Handicaps

Arnold, Katrin. *Anna joins in*
Bradford, Ann. *The mystery of the missing dogs*
Brightman, Alan. *Like me*
Briscoe, Jill. *The innkeeper's daughter*
Brown, Tricia. *Someone special, just like you*
Cairo, Shelley. *Our brother has Down's syndrome*
Charlot, Martin. *Felisa and the magic tikling bird*
Clifton, Lucille. *My friend Jacob*
English, Jennifer. *My mommy's special*
Fanshawe, Elizabeth. *Rachel*
Fassler, Joan. *Howie helps himself*
  One little girl
Gold, Phyllis. *Please don't say hello*
Hamm, Diane Johnston. *Grandma drives a motor bed*
Hasler, Eveline. *Martin is our friend*
Henriod, Lorraine. *Grandma's wheelchair*
Kaufman, Curt. *Rajesh*
Kuklin, Susan. *Thinking big*
Larsen, Hanne. *Don't forget Tom*
Lasker, Joe. *He's my brother*
  Nick joins in
Marron, Carol A. *No trouble for Grandpa*
Payne, Sherry Neuwirth. *A contest*
Powers, Mary E. *Our teacher's in a wheelchair*
Prall, Jo. *My sister's special*
Rabe, Berniece. *The balancing girl*
  Where's Chimpy?
Rosenberg, Maxine B. *My friend Leslie*
Schatell, Brian. *The McGoonys have a party*
Smith, Lucia B. *A special kind of sister*
Sobol, Harriet Langsam. *My brother Steven is retarded*
Stein, Sara Bonnett. *About handicaps*
Wahl, Jan. *Button eye's orange*
White, Paul. *Janet at school*
Wolf, Bernard. *Don't feel sorry for Paul*

Handicaps – blindness

Bradford, Ann. *The mystery of the blind writer*
Brighton, Catherine. *My hands, my world*
Chapman, Elizabeth. *Suzy*
Cohen, Miriam. *See you tomorrow*
DeArmond, Dale. *The seal oil lamp*
Herman, Bill. *Jenny's magic wand*
Jensen, Virginia Allen. *Catching*
  Red thread riddles
  What's that?
Johnson, Donna Kay. *Brighteyes*
Keats, Ezra Jack. *Apartment 3*
Litchfield, Ada B. *A cane in her hand*

Martin, Bill (William Ivan). *Knots on a counting rope*
Newth, Philip. *Roly goes exploring*
Quigley, Lillian Fox. *The blind men and the elephant*
Reuter, Margaret. *My mother is blind*
Sargent, Susan. *My favorite place*
Saxe, John Godfrey. *The blind men and the elephant*
Yolen, Jane. *The seeing stick*

Handicaps – deafness

Arthur, Catherine. *My sister's silent world*
Aseltine, Lorraine. *I'm deaf and it's okay*
Baker, Pamela J. *My first book of sign*
Bove, Linda. *Sign language ABC with Linda Bove*
Chaplin, Susan Gibbons. *I can sign my ABCs*
Charlip, Remy. *Handtalk*
  Handtalk birthday
Gage, Wilson. *Down in the boondocks*
Greenberg, Judith E. *What is the sign for friend?*
Litchfield, Ada B. *A button in her ear*
Mother Goose. *Nursery rhymes from Mother Goose in signed English*
Pace, Elizabeth. *Chris gets ear tubes*
Wahl, Jan. *Jamie's tiger*
Wolf, Bernard. *Anna's silent world*

Hands *see* Anatomy

Handyman *see* Careers – handyman

Hanukkah *see* Holidays – Hanukkah

Happiness *see* Emotions – happiness

Hares *see* Animals – rabbits

Hate *see* Emotions – hate

Hawaii

Funai, Mamoru. *Moke and Poki in the rain forest*
Laird, Donivee Martin. *The three little Hawaiian pigs and the magic shark*
Lewis, Richard. *In the night, still dark*
Mower, Nancy. *I visit my Tūtū and Grandma*
Tune, Suelyn Ching. *How Maui slowed the sun*
Williams, Jay. *The surprising things Maui did*

Hawks *see* Birds – hawks

Health

Berger, Melvin. *Why I cough, sneeze, shiver, hiccup and yawn*
Borten, Helen. *Do you move as I do?*
Burnstein, John. *Slim Goodbody*
Cobb, Vicki. *How the doctor knows you're fine*
Gross, Ruth Belov. *A book about your skeleton*
Isenberg, Barbara. *Albert the running bear's exercise book*
Kuklin, Susan. *When I see my dentist*
Leaf, Munro. *Health can be fun*
Marcus, Susan. *Casey visits the doctor*
Marshall, Lyn. *Yoga for your children*
Moncure, Jane Belk. *Happy healthkins*
  The healthkin food train
  Healthkins exercise!
  Healthkins help
Oxenbury, Helen. *The checkup*
Radlauer, Ruth Shaw. *Of course, you're a horse!*
Rockwell, Harlow. *My doctor*
Roth, Harold. *A checkup*
Seuss, Dr. *The tooth book*
Sharmat, Marjorie Weinman. *Lucretia the unbearable*
Watson, Jane Werner. *My friend the dentist*
  My friend the doctor

Hearing *see* Handicaps – deafness; Senses – hearing

Heavy equipment *see* Machines

Hedgehogs *see* Animals – hedgehogs

Helicopters

Barrett, N. S. *Helicopters*
Drummond, Violet H. *The flying postman*
Firmin, Peter. *Basil Brush goes flying*
Gay, Michel. *Little helicopter*
Ingoglia, Gina. *The big book of real airplanes*
Petersen, David. *Helicopters*
Taylor, Mark. *Henry explores the mountains*
Zaffo, George J. *The big book of real airplanes*

Helpfulness *see* Character traits – helpfulness

Hens *see* Birds – chickens

Hibernation

Barrett, John M. *The bear who slept through Christmas*
Bartoli, Jennifer. *Snow on bear's nose*
Cohen, Carol L. *Wake up, groundhog!*

De Paola, Tomie. *Four stories for four seasons*
Evans, Eva Knox. *Sleepy time*
Fisher, Aileen. *Where does everyone go?*
Freeman, Don. *Bearymore*
Janice. *Little Bear's Christmas*
Kepes, Juliet. *Frogs, merry*
Kesselman, Wendy. *Time for Jody*
Krauss, Ruth. *The happy day*
McClure, Gillian. *Prickly pig*
Marshall, James. *What's the matter with Carruthers?*
Miller, Edna. *Mousekin's golden house*
Parker, Nancy Winslow. *The ordeal of Byron B. Blackbear*
Piers, Helen. *Grasshopper and butterfly*
Stott, Rowena. *The hedgehog feast*
Ward, Andrew. *Baby bear and the long sleep*
Watson, Wendy. *Has winter come?*
Yulya. *Bears are sleeping*

Hiding *see* Behavior – hiding

Hiding things *see* Behavior – hiding things

Hieroglyphics

Mother Goose. *Mother Goose in hieroglyphics*
The prince who knew his fate

Hiking *see* Sports – hiking

Hippopotami *see* Animals – Hippopotami

Hobby horses *see* Toys – rocking horses

Hockey *see* Sports – hockey

Holidays

Adler, David A. *A picture book of Jewish holidays*
Alexander, Sue. *Small plays for special days*
Belting, Natalia Maree. *Summer's coming in*
Berenstain, Stan. *The bears' almanac*
Bonnici, Peter. *The festival*
Cazet, Denys. *December 24th*
Chaikin, Miriam. *Esther*
Cohen, Barbara. *Even higher*
Cone, Molly. *The Jewish Sabbath*
Conger, Marion. *The little golden holiday book*
Corwin, Judith Hoffman. *Jewish holiday fun*
Crespi, Francesca. *Little Bear and the oompah-pah*
Fisher, Aileen. *Arbor day*
  Skip around the year
Forrester, Victoria. *Oddward*
Gellman, Ellie. *Shai's Shabbat walk*

Glovach, Linda. *The Little Witch's spring holiday book*
Groner, Judyth. *Where is the Afikomen?*
Kumin, Maxine. *Follow the fall*
Livingston, Myra Cohn. *Celebrations Poems for Jewish holidays*
Menter, Ian. *Carnival*
Meyer, Elizabeth C. *The blue china pitcher*
Roop, Peter. *Let's celebrate!*
Ross, Tony. *Hugo and the bureau of holidays*
Sotomayor, Antonio. *Khasa goes to the fiesta*
Steele, Philip. *Festivals around the world*
Tudor, Tasha. *A time to keep*
Wikler, Madeline. *Let's build a Sukkah*
Winn, Chris. *Holiday*
Wood, Audrey. *The horrible holidays*
Zolotow, Charlotte. *Over and over*

Holidays – April Fools' Day

Brown, Marc. *Arthur's April fool*
Christian, Mary Blount. *April fool*
Kelley, Emily. *April Fools' Day*
Krahn, Fernando. *April fools*
Modell, Frank. *Look out, it's April Fools' Day*
Rockwell, Norman. *Norman Rockwell's counting book*
Wegen, Ron. *Billy Gorilla*

Holidays – Chanukah *see* Holidays – Hanukkah

Holidays – Chinese New Year

Cheng, Hou-Tien. *The Chinese New Year*
Handforth, Thomas. *Mei Li*
Politi, Leo. *Moy Moy*
Wallace, Ian. *Chin Chiang and the dragon's dance*
Young, Evelyn. *The tale of Tai*

Holidays – Christmas

Adams, Adrienne. *The Christmas party*
Adshead, Gladys L. *Brownies - it's Christmas*
Ahlberg, Allan. *The Cinderella show Cops and robbers*
Aichinger, Helga. *The shepherd*
Andersen, H. C. (Hans Christian). *The fir tree*, ill. by Nancy Elkholm Burkert
Anglund, Joan Walsh. *A Christmas book Christmas is a time of giving The cowboy's Christmas*
Aoki, Hisako. *Santa's favorite story*
Ardizzone, Aingelda. *The night ride*
Armour, Richard Willard. *The year Santa went modern*
Bach, Alice. *The day after Christmas*

Bach, Othello. *Hector McSnector and the mail-order Christmas witch*
Baker, Laura Nelson. *The friendly beasts O children of the wind and pines*
Balet, Jan B. *The gift*
Balian, Lorna. *Bah! Humbug?*
Barrett, John M. *The bear who slept through Christmas*
Barry, Robert E. *Mr. Willowby's Christmas tree*
Belting, Natalia Maree. *Christmas folk*
Bemelmans, Ludwig. *Hansi*
Benchley, Nathaniel. *The magic sled*
Berenstain, Stan. *The Berenstain bears' Christmas tree The Berenstain bears meet Santa Bear*
Bible. New Testament. Gospels. *Christmas The Nativity*
Blough, Glenn O. *Christmas trees and how they grow*
Bolognese, Don. *A new day*
Bond, Felicia. *Christmas in the chicken coop*
Bonsall, Crosby Newell. *Twelve bells for Santa*
Briggs, Raymond. *Father Christmas Father Christmas goes on holiday*
Bright, Robert. *Georgie's Christmas carol Bring a torch, Jeannette, Isabella*
Brock, Emma Lillian. *The birds' Christmas tree*
Bröger, Achim. *The Santa Clauses*
Brown, Abbie Farwell. *The Christmas angel*
Brown, Marc. *Arthur's Christmas*
Brown, Margaret Wise. *Christmas in the barn The little fir tree On Christmas eve Pussycat's Christmas The steamroller*
Brown, Palmer. *Something for Christmas*
Bruna, Dick. *Christmas The Christmas book*
Brunhoff, Jean de. *Babar and Father Christmas*
Bryson, Bernarda. *The twenty miracles of Saint Nicolas*
Budbill, David. *Christmas tree farm*
Burland, Brian. *St. Nicholas and the tub*
Butterworth, Nick. *The Nativity play*
Carlson, Natalie Savage. *Surprise in the mountains*
Carrier, Lark. *A Christmas promise*
Cazet, Denys. *Christmas moon*
Chafetz, Henry. *The legend of Befana*
Chalmers, Mary. *A Christmas story Merry Christmas, Harry*
Chapman, Jean. *Moon-Eyes A Christmas book*
Chute, Beatrice Joy. *Joy to Christmas*
Clifton, Lucille. *Everett Anderson's Christmas coming*

Climo, Shirley. *The cobweb Christmas*
Coatsworth, Elizabeth. *The children come running*
Cooney, Barbara. *The little juggler*
Cummings, E. E. *Little tree*
Cuyler, Margery. *Fat Santa*
Darling, Kathy. *The mystery in Santa's toyshop*
Davidson, Amanda. *Teddy's first Christmas*
De Paola, Tomie. *Baby's first Christmas*
 The cat on the Dovrefell
 The Christmas pageant
 The clown of God
 An early American Christmas
 The family Christmas tree book
 Merry Christmas, Strega Nona
 The story of the three wise kings
Devlin, Wende. *Cranberry Christmas*
Din dan don, it's Christmas
Domanska, Janina. *I saw a ship a-sailing*
Donaldson, Lois. *Karl's wooden horse*
Drescher, Henrik. *Looking for Santa Claus*
Dubanevich, Arlene. *Pigs at Christmas*
Duvoisin, Roger Antoine. *The Christmas whale*
 One thousand Christmas beards
 Petunia's Christmas
Ehrlich, Amy. *Bunnies at Christmastime*
Ephron, Delia. *Santa and Alex*
Erickson, Russell E. *Warton's Christmas eve adventure*
Ets, Marie Hall. *Nine days to Christmas*
Factor, Jane. *Summer*
Farber, Norma. *How the hibernators came to Bethlehem*
Fatio, Louise. *Anna, the horse*
Fenner, Carol. *Christmas tree on the mountain*
Forrester, Victoria. *Poor Gabriella*
Fox, Mem. *With love, at Christmas*
Fraser, James Howard. *Los Posadas*
Freeman, Jean Todd. *Cynthia and the unicorn*
The friendly beasts and A partridge in a pear tree
Gackenbach, Dick. *Claude the dog*
Gannett, Ruth S. *Katie and the sad noise*
Gantos, Jack. *Rotten Ralph's rotten Christmas*
Gantschev, Ivan. *The Christmas train*
Gay, Michel. *The Christmas wolf*
Gikow, Louise. *Sprocket's Christmas tale*
Glovach, Linda. *The Little Witch's Christmas book*
Goodall, John S. *An Edwardian Christmas*
Gordon, Sharon. *Christmas surprise*
Hale, Linda. *The glorious Christmas soup party*
Hayes, Sarah. *Happy Christmas, Gemma*
Haywood, Carolyn. *A Christmas fantasy*
 How the reindeer saved Santa

 Santa Claus forever!
Heck, Elisabeth. *The black sheep*
Helldorfer, M. C. *Daniel's gift*
Heller, Nicholas. *The monster in the cave*
Henry, O. *The gift of the Magi*
Herriot, James. *Christmas Day kitten*
Hill, Eric. *Spot's first Christmas*
Hill, Susan. *Can it be true?*
Hillert, Margaret. *Merry Christmas, dear dragon*
Hillman, Priscilla. *A Merry-Mouse Christmas A B C*
Hoban, Lillian. *Arthur's Christmas cookies*
 It's really Christmas
Hoban, Russell. *Emmet Otter's jug-band Christmas*
 The mole family's Christmas
Hoff, Syd. *Merry Christmas, Henrietta!*
 Santa's moose
 Where's Prancer?
Hoffmann, E. T. A., *The nutcracker*, ill. by Rachel Isadora
 The nutcracker, ill. by Maurice Sendak
 The nutcracker, ill. by Lisbeth Zwerger
Hoffmann, Felix. *The story of Christmas*
Hollyn, Lynn. *Lynn Hollyn's Christmas toyland*
Holm, Mayling Mack. *A forest Christmas*
Holmes, Efner Tudor. *The Christmas cat*
Houston, Gloria. *The year of the perfect Christmas tree*
Howe, James. *The fright before Christmas*
Hughes, Shirley. *Lucy and Tom's Christmas*
Hurd, Edith Thacher. *Christmas eve*
Hutchins, Pat. *The best train set ever*
 King Henry's palace
 The silver Christmas tree
Janice. *Little Bear's Christmas*
Jaques, Faith. *Tilly's rescue*
Jaynes, Ruth M. *Melinda's Christmas stocking*
Johnson, Crockett. *Harold at the North Pole*
Johnston, Tony. *Mole and Troll trim the tree*
Jones, Jessie Mae Orton. *A little child*
Joslin, Sesyle. *Baby elephant and the secret wishes*
Jüchen, Aurel von. *The Holy Night*
Kahl, Virginia. *Gunhilde's Christmas booke*
 Plum pudding for Christmas
Keats, Ezra Jack. *The little drummer boy*
Keller, Holly. *A bear for Christmas*
Kent, Jack. *The Christmas piñata*
Kerr, Judith. *Mog's Christmas*
King, B. A. *The very best Christmas tree*
Knight, Hilary. *Angels and berries and candy canes*
Knotts, Howard. *The lost Christmas*
Krahn, Fernando. *The biggest Christmas tree on earth*

Kraus, Robert. *The tree that stayed up until next Christmas*

Kroll, Steven. *Santa's crash-bang Christmas*

Kunnas, Mauri. *Santa Claus and his elves*
Twelve gifts for Santa Claus

Langstaff, John M. *On Christmas day in the morning*

La Rochelle, David. *A Christmas guest*

Lathrop, Dorothy Pulis. *An angel in the woods*

Laurence, Margaret. *The Christmas birthday story*

Leedy, Loreen. *A dragon Christmas*

Linch, Elizabeth Johanna. *Samson*

Lindgren, Astrid. *Christmas in noisy village*
Christmas in the stable
Of course Polly can do almost everything

Lines, Kathleen. *Once in royal David's city*

Lipkind, William. *The Christmas bunny*

Low, Joseph. *The Christmas grump*

McCully, Emily Arnold. *The Christmas gift*

McGinley, Phyllis. *How Mrs. Santa Claus saved Christmas*

McPhail, David. *Mistletoe*

Manushkin, Fran. *The perfect Christmas picture*

Mariana. *The journey of Bangwell Putt*
Miss Flora McFlimsey's Christmas Eve

Marshall, James. *Merry Christmas, space case*
Miss Dog's Christmas

Martin, Judith. *The tree angel*

Mattingley, Christobel. *The angel with a mouth-organ*

May, Robert Lewis. *Rudolph the red-nosed reindeer*

Merriam, Eve. *The Christmas box*

Miller, Edna. *Mousekin's Christmas eve*

Moeschlin, Elsa. *The red horse*

Mogensen, Jan. *Teddy's Christmas gift*

Mohr, Joseph. *Silent night*

Monsell, Helen Albee. *Paddy's Christmas*

Moore, Clement C. *The night before Christmas*, ill. by Tomie de Paola
The night before Christmas, ill. by Michael Foreman
The night before Christmas, ill. by Gyo Fujikawa
The night before Christmas, ill. by Scott Gustafson
The night before Christmas, ill. by Anita Lobel
The night before Christmas, ill. by Jacqueline Rogers
The night before Christmas, ill. by Robin Spowart
The night before Christmas, ill. by Gustaf Tenggren
The night before Christmas, ill. by Tasha Tudor

The night before Christmas, ill. by Jody Wheeler
A visit from St. Nicholas

Munro, Roxie. *Christmastime in New York City*

Naylor, Phyllis Reynolds. *Old Sadie and the Christmas bear*

Neale, J. M. *Good King Wenceslas*

Newland, Mary Reed. *Good King Wenceslas*

Noble, Trinka Hakes. *Apple tree Christmas*

Nussbaumer, Mares. *Away in a manger*

Oakley, Graham. *The church mice at Christmas*

Olson, Arielle North. *Hurry home, Grandma!*

Parish, Peggy. *Merry Christmas, Amelia Bedelia*

Parker, Nancy Winslow. *The Christmas camel*

Partch, Virgil Franklin. *The Christmas cookie sprinkle snitcher*

Pearson, Susan. *Karin's Christmas walk*

Peet, Bill. *Countdown to Christmas*

Peterson, Hans. *Erik and the Christmas horse*

Play and sing - it's Christmas!

Plume, Ilse. *The story of Befana*

Politi, Leo. *The nicest gift*
Pedro, the angel of Olvera Street
Rosa

Robbins, Ruth. *Baboushka and the three kings*

Rockwell, Anne F. *Bafana*

Rowand, Phyllis. *Every day in the year*

Rylant, Cynthia. *Henry and Mudge in the sparkle days*

Sahagun, Bernardino de. *Spirit child*

Sawyer, Ruth. *The Christmas Anna angel*

Scarry, Richard. *Richard Scarry's best Christmas book ever!*

Schenk, Esther M. *Christmas time*

Schumacher, Claire. *Nutty's Christmas*

Schweninger, Ann. *Christmas secrets*

Seignobosc, Françoise. *Noël for Jeanne-Marie*

Selden, George. *The mice, the monks and the Christmas tree*

Seuss, Dr. *How the Grinch stole Christmas*

Speare, Jean. *A candle for Christmas*

Spier, Peter. *Peter Spier's Christmas!*

Steiner, Charlotte. *The climbing book*

Stephenson, Dorothy. *The night it rained toys*

Stern, Elsie-Jean. *Wee Robin's Christmas song*

Stevenson, Suçie. *Christmas eve*

Stock, Catherine. *Sampson the Christmas cat*

Thayer, Jane. *The puppy who wanted a boy*, ill. by Seymour Fleishman
The puppy who wanted a boy, ill. by Lisa McCue

Timmermans, Felix. *A gift from Saint Nicholas*
Tippett, James Sterling. *Counting the days*
Tolkien, J. R. R. (John Ronald Reuel). *The Father Christmas letters*
Tompert, Ann. *The silver whistle*
Trent, Robbie. *The first Christmas*
Trivas, Irene. *Emma's Christmas*
Tudor, Tasha. *The doll's Christmas*
Snow before Christmas
Türk, Hanne. *Merry Christmas Max*
Tutt, Kay Cunningham. *And now we call him Santa Claus*
The twelve days of Christmas. English folk song. *Brian Wildsmith's The twelve days of Christmas*
Jack Kent's twelve days of Christmas
The twelve days of Christmas, ill. by Jan Brett
The twelve days of Christmas, ill. by Ilonka Karasz
The twelve days of Christmas, ill. by Erika Schneider
The twelve days of Christmas, ill. by Sophie Windham
Ungerer, Tomi. *Christmas eve at the Mellops*
Van Allsburg, Chris. *The polar express*
Vesey, A. *Merry Christmas, Thomas!*
Vincent, Gabrielle. *Ernest and Celestine*
Merry Christmas, Ernest and Celestine
Wahl, Jan. *The Muffletumps' Christmas party*
Watson, Clyde. *How Brown Mouse kept Christmas*
Watson, Wendy. *The bunnies' Christmas eve*
We wish you a merry Christmas
Weil, Lisl. *Santa Claus around the world*
The story of the Wise Men and the Child
Weiss, Ellen. *Things to make and do for Christmas*
Wells, Rosemary. *Max's Christmas*
Wenning, Elisabeth. *The Christmas mouse*
What a morning!
Wheeler, Cindy. *Marmalade's Christmas present*
Wild, Robin. *Little Pig and the big bad wolf*
Williams, Marcia. *The first Christmas*
Wilson, Robina Beckles. *Merry Christmas!*
Winthrop, Elizabeth. *A child is born*
Wooding, Sharon L. *Arthur's Christmas wish*
Woolaver, Lance. *Christmas with the rural mail*
Yeomans, Thomas. *For every child a star*
Zakhoder, Boris Vladimirovich. *How a piglet crashed the Christmas party*
Ziefert, Harriet. *Nicky's Christmas surprise*
Zimelman, Nathan. *The star of Melvin*

Zolotow, Charlotte. *The beautiful Christmas tree*

Holidays – Cinco de Mayo

Bannon, Laura. *Watchdog*
Behrens, June. *Fiesta!*

Holidays – Columbus Day

Showers, Paul. *Columbus Day*

Holidays – Easter

Adams, Adrienne. *The Easter egg artists*
Armour, Richard Willard. *The adventures of Egbert the Easter egg*
Balian, Lorna. *Humbug rabbit*
Barrett, John M. *The Easter bear*
Benchley, Nathaniel. *The strange disappearance of Arthur Cluck*
Brown, Margaret Wise. *The golden egg book*
The runaway bunny
Carrick, Carol. *A rabbit for Easter*
Chalmers, Mary. *Easter parade*
Claret, Maria. *The chocolate rabbit*
Cross, Genevieve. *My bunny book*
Darling, Kathy. *The Easter bunny's secret*
DeLage, Ida. *ABC Easter bunny*
Dunn, Judy. *The little rabbit*
Duvoisin, Roger Antoine. *Easter treat*
Friedrich, Priscilla. *The Easter bunny that overslept*
Gordon, Sharon. *Easter Bunny's lost egg*
Heyward, Du Bose. *The country bunny and the little gold shoes*
Hill, Eric. *Spot's first Easter*
Hoban, Lillian. *Silly Tilly and the Easter bunny*
Hopkins, Lee Bennett. *Easter buds are springing*
Houselander, Caryll. *Petook*
Kay, Helen. *An egg is for wishing*
Kraus, Robert. *Daddy Long Ears*
Kroll, Steven. *The big bunny and the Easter eggs*
The big bunny and the magic show
Littlefield, William. *The whiskers of Ho Ho*
McClenathan, Louise. *The Easter pig*
Mariana. *Miss Flora McFlimsey's Easter bonnet*
Maril, Lee. *Mr. Bunny paints the eggs*
Milhous, Katherine. *The egg tree*
Miller, Edna. *Mouskin's Easter basket*
Pieńkowski, Jan. *Easter*
Priolo, Pauline. *Piccolina and the Easter bells*
Thayer, Jane. *The horse with the Easter bonnet*
Tresselt, Alvin R. *The world in the candy egg*

Tudor, Tasha. *A tale for Easter*
Wahl, Jan. *The five in the forest*
Weil, Lisl. *The candy egg bunny*
Weisgard, Leonard. *The funny bunny factory*
Wells, Rosemary. *Max's chocolate chicken*
Wiese, Kurt. *Happy Easter*
Wilhelm, Hans. *More bunny trouble*
Winthrop, Elizabeth. *He is risen*
Wolf, Winfried. *The Easter bunny*
Young, Miriam Burt. *Miss Suzy's Easter surprise*
Ziefert, Harriet. *Happy Easter, Grandma!*
Zolotow, Charlotte. *The bunny who found Easter*
Mr. Rabbit and the lovely present

Holidays – Father's Day

Kroll, Steven. *Happy Father's Day*
Sharmat, Marjorie Weinman. *Hooray for Father's Day!*
Simon, Norma. *I wish I had my father*

Holidays – Fourth of July

Joosse, Barbara M. *Fourth of July*
Keller, Holly. *Henry's Fourth of July*
Shortall, Leonard W. *One way*
Zion, Gene. *The summer snowman*

Holidays – Groundhog Day

Balian, Lorna. *A garden for a groundhog*
Cohen, Carol L. *Wake up, groundhog!*
Delton, Judy. *Groundhog's Day at the doctor*
Glass, Marvin. *What happened today, Freddy Groundhog?*
Hamberger, John. *This is the day*
Johnson, Crockett. *Will spring be early?*
Kesselman, Wendy. *Time for Jody*
Kroll, Steven. *It's Groundhog Day!*
Palazzo, Tony. *Waldo the woodchuck*

Holidays – Halloween

Adams, Adrienne. *A Halloween happening*
A woggle of witches
Adler, David A. *The twisted witch and other spooky riddles*
Anderson, Lonzo. *The Halloween party*
Asch, Frank. *Popcorn*
Averill, Esther. *Jenny's moonlight adventure*
Balian, Lorna. *Humbug witch*
Barth, Edna. *Jack-o'-lantern*
Battles, Edith. *The terrible trick or treat*
Beim, Jerrold. *Sir Halloween*
Benarde, Anita. *The pumpkin smasher*
Bond, Felicia. *The Halloween performance*
Borten, Helen. *Halloween*
Bradford, Ann. *The mystery of the live ghosts*
Bridwell, Norman. *Clifford's Halloween*

Bright, Robert. *Georgie's Halloween*
Brown, Marc. *Arthur's Halloween*
Bunting, Eve. *Scary, scary Halloween*
Calhoun, Mary. *The witch of Hissing Hill*
Wobble the witch cat
Carlson, Natalie Savage. *Spooky and the ghost cat*
Spooky and the wizard's bats
Spooky night
Carrick, Carol. *Old Mother Witch*
Cavagnaro, David. *The pumpkin people*
Charles, Donald. *Shaggy dog's Halloween*
Charlton, Elizabeth. *Jeremy and the ghost*
Coombs, Patricia. *Dorrie and the Halloween plot*
Cooper, Paulette. *Let's find out about Halloween*
Corey, Dorothy. *Will it ever be my birthday?*
Corwin, Judith Hoffman. *Halloween fun*
Cuyler, Margery. *Sir William and the pumpkin monster*
Davis, Maggie S. *Rickety witch*
Degen, Bruce. *Aunt Possum and the pumpkin man*
DeLage, Ida. *The old witch and her magic basket*
Devlin, Wende. *Cranberry Halloween*
Old Witch rescues Halloween
Donnelly, Liza. *Dinosaurs' Halloween*
Embry, Margaret. *The blue-nosed witch*
Feczko, Kathy. *Halloween party*
Foster, Doris Van Liew. *Tell me, Mr. Owl*
Freeman, Don. *Space witch*
Tilly Witch
Friedrich, Priscilla. *The marshmallow ghosts*
Gantos, Jack. *Rotten Ralph's trick or treat*
Gibbons, Gail. *Halloween*
Glovach, Linda. *The Little Witch's black magic book of disguises*
The Little Witch's Halloween book
Greene, Carol. *The thirteen days of Halloween*
Greene, Ellin. *The pumpkin giant*
Guthrie, Donna. *The witch who lives down the hall*
Hellsing, Lennart. *The wonderful pumpkin*
Herman, Emily. *Hubknuckles*
Hoff, Syd. *Henrietta's Halloween*
Hurd, Edith Thacher. *The so-so cat*
Hutchins, Pat. *The best train set ever*
Irving, Washington. *The legend of Sleepy Hollow*, ill. by Daniel San Souci
Johnson, Hannah Lyons. *From seed to jack-o'-lantern*
Johnston, Tony. *The vanishing pumpkin*
Kahl, Virginia. *Gunhilde and the Halloween spell*
Keats, Ezra Jack. *The trip*
Kellogg, Steven. *The mystery of the flying orange pumpkin*

Kessler, Ethel. *Grandpa Witch and the magic doobelator*
Kessler, Leonard P. *Riddles that rhyme for Halloween time*
Krensky, Stephen. *Lionel in the fall*
Kroll, Steven. *The candy witch*
Kunhardt, Edith. *Trick or treat, Danny!*
Kunnas, Mauri. *One spooky night and other scary stories*
Leedy, Loreen. *The dragon Halloween party*
Low, Alice. *The witch who was afraid of witches*
  Witch's holiday
Maestro, Giulio. *Halloween howls*
Manushkin, Fran. *Hocus and Pocus at the circus*
Mariana. *Miss Flora McFlimsey's Halloween*
Marks, Burton. *The spook book*
Marshall, Edward. *Space case*
Massey, Jeanne. *The littlest witch*
Merriam, Eve. *Halloween ABC*
Miller, Edna. *Mousekin's golden house*
Mooser, Stephen. *The ghost with the Halloween hiccups*
Mueller, Virginia. *A Halloween mask for Monster*
Nicoll, Helen. *Meg and Mog*
Nolan, Dennis. *Witch Bazooza*
Numeroff, Laura Joffe. *Emily's bunch*
Ott, John. *Peter Pumpkin*
Patterson, Lillie. *Haunted houses on Halloween*
Paul, Sherry. *2-B and the space visitor*
Peters, Sharon. *Trick or treat Halloween*
Prager, Annabelle. *The spooky Halloween party*
Prelutsky, Jack. *It's Halloween*
Preston, Edna Mitchell. *One dark night*
Racioppo, Larry. *Halloween*
Rockwell, Anne F. *A bear, a bobcat and three ghosts*
Rose, David S. *It hardly seems like Halloween*
Rylant, Cynthia. *Henry and Mudge under the yellow moon*
St. George, Judith. *The Halloween pumpkin smasher*
Schertle, Alice. *Bill and the google-eyed goblins*
  Hob Goblin and the skeleton
Schulman, Janet. *Jack the bum and the Halloween handout*
Schweninger, Ann. *Halloween surprises*
Scott, Ann Herbert. *Let's catch a monster*
Shaw, Richard. *The kitten in the pumpkin patch*
Slobodkin, Louis. *Trick or treat*
Stevenson, James. *That terrible Halloween night*
Thayer, Jane. *Gus was a gorgeous ghost*
Titherington, Jeanne. *Pumpkin pumpkin*

Vigna, Judith. *Everyone goes as a pumpkin*
Von Hippel, Ursula. *The craziest Halloween*
Wahl, Jan. *Pleasant Fieldmouse's Halloween party*
Watson, Jane Werner. *Which is the witch?*
Wegen, Ron. *The Halloween costume party*
Wolkstein, Diane. *The legend of Sleepy Hollow*
Young, Miriam Burt. *The witch mobile*
Zimmer, Dirk. *The trick-or-treat trap*
Zolotow, Charlotte. *A tiger called Thomas*, ill. by Catherine Stock
  A tiger called Thomas, ill. by Kurt Werth

Holidays – Hanukkah

Adler, David A. *A picture book of Hanukkah*
  A picture book of Jewish holidays
Aleichem, Sholem. *Hanukah money*
Chanover, Hyman. *Happy Hanukah everybody*
Coopersmith, Jerome. *A Chanukah fable for Christmas*
Fisher, Aileen. *My first Hanukkah book*
Gellman, Ellie. *It's Chanukah!*
Goffstein, M. B. (Marilyn Brooke). *Laughing latkes*
Goldin, Barbara Diamond. *Just enough is plenty*
Hirsh, Marilyn. *I love Hanukkah*
  Potato pancakes all around
Levoy, Myron. *The Hanukkah of Great-Uncle Otto*
Sherman, Eileen Bluestone. *The odd potato*
Shostak, Myra. *Rainbow candles*
Zalben, Jane Breskin. *Beni's first Chanukah*

Holidays – Independence Day *see* Holidays – Fourth of July

Holidays – Mardi Gras *see* Mardi Gras

Holidays – May Day

Mariana. *Miss Flora McFlimsey's May Day*

Holidays – Memorial Day

Scott, Geoffrey. *Memorial Day*

Holidays – Mother's Day

Bunting, Eve. *The Mother's Day mice*
Howe, James. *The case of the missing mother*
Kroll, Steven. *Happy Mother's Day*
Livingston, Myra Cohn. *Poems for mothers*
Morgan, Allen. *Matthew and the midnight money van*
Sharmat, Marjorie Weinman. *Hooray for Mother's Day!*

Holidays – New Year's

Andersen, H. C. (Hans Christian). *The little match girl*, ill. by Rachel Isadora
The little match girl, ill. by Blair Lent
Janice. *Little Bear's New Year's party*
Mariana. *Miss Flora McFlimsey and the baby New Year*
Modell, Frank. *Goodbye old year, hello new year*

Holidays – Passover

Adler, David A. *A picture book of Jewish holidays*
A picture book of Passover
Auerbach, Julie Jaslow. *Everything's changing - It's pesach!*
Behrens, June. *Passover*
Hirsh, Marilyn. *I love Passover*
One little goat
Rosen, Anne. *A family Passover*
Wikler, Madeline. *My first seder*
Zusman, Evelyn. *The Passover parrot*

Holidays – Purim

Cohen, Barbara. *Here come the Purim players!*
Suhl, Yuri. *The Purim goat*
Wikler, Madeline. *The Purim parade*

Holidays – Rosh Hashanah

Gellman, Ellie. *It's Rosh Hashanah!*

Holidays – St. Patrick's Day

Bunting, Eve. *St. Patrick's Day in the morning*
Calhoun, Mary. *The hungry leprechaun*
Janice. *Little Bear marches in the St. Patrick's Day parade*
Schertle, Alice. *Jeremy Bean's St. Patrick's Day*
Zimelman, Nathan. *To sing a song as big as Ireland*

Holidays – Thanksgiving

Adler, David A. *The purple turkey and other Thanksgiving riddles*
Balian, Lorna. *Sometimes it's turkey*
Brown, Marc. *Arthur's Thanksgiving*
Bunting, Eve. *How many days to America?*
Child, Lydia Maria. *Over the river and through the wood*
Dalgliesh, Alice. *The Thanksgiving story*
Devlin, Wende. *Cranberry Thanksgiving*
Dragonwagon, Crescent. *Alligator arrived with apples*
Gibbons, Gail. *Thanksgiving Day*
Glovach, Linda. *The Little Witch's Thanksgiving book*

Hopkins, Lee Bennett. *Merrily comes our harvest in*
Ipcar, Dahlov. *Hard scrabble harvest*
Janice. *Little Bear's Thanksgiving*
Kroll, Steven. *One tough turkey*
Lowitz, Sadyebeth. *The pilgrims' party*
Miller, Edna. *Mouskin's Thanksgiving*
Nixon, Joan Lowery. *The Thanksgiving mystery*
Ott, John. *Peter Pumpkin*
Quackenbush, Robert M. *Sheriff Sally Gopher and the Thanksgiving caper*
Rylant, Cynthia. *Henry and Mudge under the yellow moon*
Spinelli, Eileen. *Thanksgiving at Tappletons'*
Tresselt, Alvin R. *Autumn harvest*
Williams, Barbara. *Chester Chipmunk's Thanksgiving*
Zion, Gene. *The meanest squirrel I ever met*

Holidays – Valentine's Day

Adams, Adrienne. *The great Valentine's Day balloon race*
Balian, Lorna. *A sweetheart for Valentine*
Bond, Felicia. *Four Valentines in a rainstorm*
Brown, Marc. *Arthur's Valentine*
Bulla, Clyde Robert. *Valentine cat*
Bunting, Eve. *The Valentine bears*
Carlson, Nancy. *The mysterious Valentine*
Cohen, Miriam. *Bee my Valentine!*
De Paola, Tomie. *Things to make and do for Valentine's Day*
Devlin, Wende. *Cranberry Valentine*
Gibbons, Gail. *Valentine's Day*
Greene, Carol. *A computer went a-courting*
Guilfoile, Elizabeth. *Valentine's Day*
Hoban, Lillian. *Arthur's great big Valentine*
Keeshan, Robert. *She loves me, she loves me not*
Kelley, True. *A valentine for Fuzzboom*
Krahn, Fernando. *Little love story*
Kraus, Robert. *How spider saved Valentine's Day*
Kunhardt, Edith. *Danny's mystery Valentine*
Livingston, Myra Cohn. *Valentine poems*
Mariana. *Miss Flora McFlimsey's Valentine*
Modell, Frank. *One zillion valentines*
Murphy, Shirley Rousseau. *Valentine for a dragon*
Nixon, Joan Lowery. *The Valentine mystery*
Prelutsky, Jack. *It's Valentine's Day*
Schultz, Gwen. *The blue Valentine*
Schweninger, Ann. *The hunt for rabbit's galosh*
Valentine friends
Sharmat, Marjorie Weinman. *The best Valentine in the world*
Stevenson, James. *Happy Valentine's Day, Emma!*

Watson, Clyde. *Valentine foxes*
Wittman, Sally. *The boy who hated Valentine's Day*

Holidays – Washington's Birthday

Blair, Anne Denton. *Hurrah for Arthur!*
Bulla, Clyde Robert. *Washington's birthday*

Holland *see* Foreign lands – Holland

Homes *see* Houses

Honesty *see* Character traits – honesty

Honey bees *see* Insects – bees

Horses *see* Animals – horses

Horses, rocking *see* Toys – rocking horses

Hospitals

Baker, Gayle. *Special delivery*
Bemelmans, Ludwig. *Madeline*
  Madeline [pop-up book]
Blance, Ellen. *Monster goes to the hospital*
Bruna, Dick. *Miffy in the hospital*
Ciliotta, Claire. *"Why am I going to the hospital?"*
Collier, James Lincoln. *Danny goes to the hospital*
Elliott, Ingrid Glatz. *Hospital roadmap*
Hautzig, Deborah. *A visit to the Sesame Street hospital*
Hill, Eric. *Spot visits the hospital*
Hogan, Paula Z. *The hospital scares me*
Marino, Barbara Pavis. *Eric needs stitches*
Martin, Charles E. *Island rescue*
Pace, Elizabeth. *Chris gets ear tubes*
Pope, Billy N. *Your world: let's visit the hospital*
Rey, Margaret Elisabeth Waldstein. *Curious George goes to the hospital*
Rockwell, Anne F. *The emergency room*
Rogers, Fred. *Going to the hospital*
Shay, Arthur. *What happens when you go to the hospital*
Sobol, Harriet Langsam. *Jeff's hospital book*
Sonneborn, Ruth A. *I love Gram*
Stein, Sara Bonnett. *A hospital story*
Stone, Bernard. *Emergency mouse*
Tamburine, Jean. *I think I will go to the hospital*
Watts, Marjorie-Ann. *Crocodile medicine*
  Crocodile plaster
Weber, Alfons. *Elizabeth gets well*
Wolde, Gunilla. *Betsy and the doctor*

Hotels

Mahy, Margaret. *Rooms for rent*

Parkin, Rex. *The red carpet*
Stevenson, James. *The Sea View Hotel*

Houses

Adler, David A. *The house on the roof*
Alger, Leclaire. *Always room for one more*
Arkin, Alan. *Tony's hard work day*
Ayars, James Sterling. *Caboose on the roof*
Bannon, Laura. *The best house in the world*
Barton, Byron. *Building a house*
Becker, Edna. *Nine hundred buckets of paint*
Bemelmans, Ludwig. *Sunshine*
Binzen, Bill. *Alfred goes house hunting*
Biro, Val. *The wind in the willows home sweet home*
Blegvad, Lenore. *The parrot in the garret and other rhymes about dwellings*
Blos, Joan W. *Old Henry*
Borg, Inga. *Plupp builds a house*
Bour, Danièle. *The house from morning to night*
Brown, Marc. *There's no place like home*
Brown, Marcia. *The neighbors*
Brown, Margaret Wise. *House of a hundred windows*
  The wonderful house
Burton, Virginia Lee. *The little house*
Calhoun, Mary. *Mrs. Dog's own house*
Calmenson, Stephanie. *Where will the animals stay?*
Campbell, Rod. *Buster's morning*
Carle, Eric. *My very first book of homes*
Carter, Katharine. *Houses*
Cauley, Lorinda Bryan. *The new house*
Chase, Catherine. *The mouse in my house*
Chorao, Kay. *Cathedral mouse*
Christensen, Gardell Dano. *Mrs. Mouse needs a house*
Clymer, Eleanor Lowenton. *The tiny little house*
Colby, C. B. (Carroll Burleigh). *Who lives there?*
Colman, Hila. *Peter's brownstone house*
Crompton, Margaret. *The house where Jack lives*
Curry, Nancy. *The littlest house*
Cutler, Ivor. *The animal house*
Dauer, Rosamond. *Bullfrog builds a house*
De Regniers, Beatrice Schenk. *A little house of your own*
Emberley, Ed. *Home*
Erickson, Phoebe. *Just follow me*
Farm house
Feder, Paula Kurzband. *Where does the teacher live?*
Firehouse
Fisher, Aileen. *Best little house*
  The house of a mouse
Flory, Jane. *The bear on the doorstep*

Friedman, Estelle. *Boy who lived in a cave*
Gedin, Birgitta. *The little house from the sea*
Green, Mary McBurney. *Everybody has a house and everybody eats*
Greydanus, Rose. *Tree house fun*
Harper, Anita. *How we live*
Hoberman, Mary Ann. *A house is a house for me*
Hoff, Syd. *Stanley*
Högner, Franz. *From blueprint to house*
Holl, Adelaide. *Small Bear builds a playhouse*
Hughes, Shirley. *Alfie gets in first*
Sally's secret
Hunter, Norman. *Professor Branestawn's building bust-up*
Ichikawa, Satomi. *Nora's castle*
Jaques, Faith. *Tilly's house*
Jaynes, Ruth M. *The biggest house*
Joerns, Consuelo. *The lost and found house*
Kaune, Merriman B. *My own little house*
Kessler, Ethel. *Is there an elephant in your kitchen?*
Kilroy, Sally. *Babies' homes*
Kirk, Barbara. *Grandpa, me and our house in the tree*
Krauss, Ruth. *A very special house*
Kroll, Steven. *Pigs in the house*
Kwitz, Mary DeBall. *Rabbits' search for a little house*
Le Tord, Bijou. *Good wood bear*
Lewis, Eils Moorhouse. *The snug little house*
Lippman, Peter. *The Know-It-Alls help out*
Lynn, Sara. *Home*
McGovern, Ann. *Mr. Skinner's skinny house*
McPhail, David. *Lorenzo*
Maestro, Betsy. *Harriet at home*
Malone, Nola Langner. *A home*
Maris, Ron. *Better move on, frog!*
Mayer, Mercer. *Little Monster at home*
Maynard, Joyce. *New house*
Mendoza, George. *Need a house? Call Ms. Mouse*
Merriam, Eve. *The birthday door*
Miles, Betty. *A house for everyone*
Milne, A. A. (Alan Alexander). *House at Pooh corner: a pop-up book*
Mizumura, Kazue. *If I built a village*
Mother Goose. *Mother Goose house*
Mouse house
Muntean, Michaela. *The house that bear built*
Murphy, Shirley Rousseau. *Tattie's river journey*
Nolan, Dennis. *Witch Bazooza*
Nussbaum, Hedda. *Animals build amazing homes*
Our house
Palmer, Helen Marion. *Why I built the boogle house*

Pape, Donna Lugg. *Doghouse for sale*
Patterson, Lillie. *Haunted houses on Halloween*
Peppé, Rodney. *The mice who lived in a shoe*
Pieńkowski, Jan. *Homes*
Pinkwater, Daniel Manus. *The big orange splot*
Rey, Hans Augusto. *Anybody at home?*
Rockwell, Anne F. *Nice and clean*
Roffey, Maureen. *Home sweet home*
Ross, Pat. *M and M and the haunted house game*
Roth, Harold. *Let's look all around the house*
Rusling, Albert. *The mouse and Mrs. Proudfoot*
Sattler, Helen Roney. *No place for a goat*
Scarry, Richard. *Is this the house of Mistress Mouse?*
Richard Scarry's busy houses
Schaaf, Peter. *An apartment house close up*
Schertle, Alice. *In my treehouse*
Schlein, Miriam. *My house*
Schulman, Janet. *Jack the bum and the haunted house*
Schulz, Charles M. *Snoopy's facts and fun book about houses*
Seuss, Dr. *Come over to my house*
In a people house
Shapp, Martha. *Let's find out about houses*
Sharr, Christine. *Homes*
Shecter, Ben. *Emily, girl witch of New York*
Shefelman, Janice. *Victoria House*
Sherrow, Victoria. *There goes the ghost*
Stern, Simon. *Mrs. Vinegar*
Strathdee, Jean. *The house that grew*
Tallarico, Tony. *At home*
Testa, Fulvio. *The ideal home*
Thayer, Jane. *What's a ghost going to do?*
Tison, Annette. *Inside and outside*
Tudor, Bethany. *Samuel's tree house*
Van Allsburg, Chris. *Two bad ants*
Velthuijs, Max. *Little Man finds a home*
Vevers, Gwynne. *Animal homes*
Watanabe, Shigeo. *I can build a house!*
Wildsmith, Brian. *Animal homes*
Woolf, Virginia. *The widow and the parrot*
Zelinsky, Paul O. *The maid and the mouse and the odd-shaped house*
Ziefert, Harriet. *A new house for Mole and Mouse*

Humor

Aardema, Verna. *Oh, Kojo! How could you!*
What's so funny, Ketu?
Who's in Rabbit's house?
Adams, Richard. *The tyger voyage*
Adamson, Gareth. *Old man up a tree*

Adler, David A. *The children of Chelm*
  The purple turkey and other Thanksgiving riddles
  The twisted witch and other spooky riddles
Æsop. *The miller, his son and their donkey*, ill. by Roger Antoine Duvoisin
Ahlberg, Janet. *The little worm book*
Alborough, Jez. *Bare bear*
Alexander, Martha G. *Move over, Twerp*
Alexander, Sue. *World famous Muriel*
Aliki. *Digging up dinosaurs*
  The eggs
The all-amazing ha ha book
Allamand, Pascale. *The animals who changed their colors*
Allan, Ted. *Willie the squowse*
Allard, Harry. *Miss Nelson has a field day*
  The Stupids die
  The Stupids have a ball
  The Stupids step out
  There's a party at Mona's tonight
Allen, Jonathan. *A bad case of animal nonsense*
Allen, Linda. *Mr. Simkin's grandma*
  Mrs. Simkin's bed
Allen, Marjorie N. *One, two, three - ah-choo!*
Allen, Pamela. *Mr. Archimedes' bath*
Ambrus, Victor G. *Grandma, Felix, and Mustapha Biscuit*
  The seven skinny goats
Andersen, H. C. (Hans Christian). *The emperor's new clothes*, ill. by Pamela Baldwin-Ford
The emperor's new clothes, ill. by Erik Blegvad
The emperor's new clothes, ill. by Virginia Lee Burton
The emperor's new clothes, ill. by Jack and Irene Delano
The emperor's new clothes, ill. by Hélène Desputeaux
The emperor's new clothes, ill. by Birte Dietz
The emperor's new clothes, ill. by Dorothée Duntze
The emperor's new clothes, ill. by Jack Kent
The emperor's new clothes, ill. by Monika Laimgruber
The emperor's new clothes, ill. by Anne F. Rockwell
The emperor's new clothes, ill. by Janet Stevens
The emperor's new clothes, ill. by Nadine Bernard Westcott
The old man is always right, ill. by Feodor Rojankovsky
Anderson, Leone Castell. *The wonderful shrinking shirt*
Anno, Mitsumasa. *Anno's Britain*
  Anno's counting house

Anno's flea market
Anno's Italy
Anno's journey
Anno's U.S.A.
Dr. Anno's midnight circus
Topsy-turvies
Upside-downers
Armour, Richard Willard. *Animals on the ceiling*
Arnosky, Jim. *Outdoors on foot*
Asch, Frank. *Sand cake*
  Turtle tale
Aulaire, Ingri Mortenson d'. *Don't count your chicks*
Ayars, James Sterling. *Caboose on the roof*
Aylesworth, Jim. *Hush up!*
  Shenandoah Noah
Baker, Alan. *Benjamin bounces back*
  Benjamin's book
  Benjamin's dreadful dream
  Benjamin's portrait
Baker, Betty. *Sonny-Boy Sim*
  Three fools and a horse
  Worthington Botts and the steam machine
Bakken, Harold. *The special string*
Balian, Lorna. *Leprechauns never lie*
Barr, Cathrine. *Hound dog's bone*
Barrett, John M. *The bear who slept through Christmas*
Behn, Harry. *What a beautiful noise*
Belloc, Hilaire. *The bad child's book of beasts*
Bemelmans, Ludwig. *Rosebud*
  Sunshine
Benchley, Nathaniel. *Walter the homing pigeon*
Benedictus, Roger. *Fifty million sausages*
Benjamin, Alan. *1000 monsters*
Bennett, Jill. *Roger was a razor fish and other poems*
  Tiny Tim
Benton, Robert. *Don't ever wish for a 7-foot bear*
Berenstain, Stan. *Old hat, new hat*
Bishop, Ann. *Chicken riddle*
  The Ella Fannie elephant riddle book
  Hey riddle riddle
  Merry-go-riddle
  Noah riddle?
  Oh, riddlesticks!
  The riddle ages
  Riddle-iculous rid-alphabet book
  Wild Bill Hiccup's riddle book
Bishop, Claire Huchet. *The man who lost his head*
Blake, Quentin. *Mister Magnolia*
  Mrs. Armitage on wheels
  Quentin Blake's nursery rhyme book

Bodecker, N. M. (Nils Mogens). *"It's raining," said John Twaining*
"Let's marry" said the cherry, and other nonsense poems
Snowman Sniffles and other verse
Bohman, Nils. *Jim, Jock and Jumbo*
Bonne, Rose. *I know an old lady*, ill. by Abner Graboff
I know an old lady who swallowed a fly, ill. by William Stobbs
Borten, Helen. *Do you go where I go?*
Bossom, Naomi. *A scale full of fish and other turnabouts*
Bowden, Joan Chase. *The bean boy*
Why the tides ebb and flow
Boynton, Sandra. *If at first...*
Bradfield, Roger. *The flying hockey stick*
Brecht, Bertolt. *Uncle Eddie's moustache*
Brenner, Barbara. *A dog I know*
Bridwell, Norman. *The witch grows up*
Briggs, Raymond. *Jim and the beanstalk*
Bright, Robert. *Georgie and the baby birds*
Georgie and the ball of yarn
Georgie and the buried treasure
Georgie and the little dog
Georgie and the magician
Georgie and the runaway balloon
Brock, Emma Lillian. *Mr. Wren's house*
Nobody's mouse
Skipping Island
Bröger, Achim. *Little Harry*
The Santa Clauses
Brooke, L. Leslie (Leonard Leslie). *Johnny Crow's garden*
Johnny Crow's new garden
Johnny Crow's party
Brothers, Aileen. *Sad Mrs. Sam Sack*
Brown, Jeff. *Flat Stanley*
Brown, Marc. *Spooky riddles*
What do you call a dumb bunny? and other rabbit riddles, games, jokes and cartoons
Brown, Margaret Wise. *Once upon a time in pigpen and three other stories*
Brown, Ruth. *The big sneeze*
Browne, Caroline. *Mrs. Christie's farmhouse*
Bruna, Dick. *Kitten Nell*
Brunhoff, Laurent de. *Serafina the giraffe*
Bryant, Sara Cone. *Epaminondas and his auntie*
Buchanan, Joan. *It's a good thing*
Burningham, John. *The shopping basket*
Burroway, Janet. *The truck on the track*
Burton, Marilee Robin. *The elephant's nest*
Byfield, Barbara Ninde. *The haunted churchbell*
Calhoun, Mary. *The nine lives of Homer C. Cat*
Old man Whickutt's donkey
The traveling ball of string
Cameron, Polly. *A child's book of nonsense*

Carroll, Lewis. *Jabberwocky*
The walrus and the carpenter, ill. by Julian Doyle
The walrus and the carpenter, ill. by Jane Breskin Zalben
Carroll, Ruth. *Old Mrs. Billups and the black cats*
Caudill, Rebecca. *Contrary Jenkins*
Causley, Charles. *"Quack!" said the billy-goat*
Cerf, Bennett Alfred. *Bennett Cerf's book of animal riddles*
Bennett Cerf's book of laughs
Bennett Cerf's book of riddles
More riddles
Chalmers, Audrey. *Hundreds and hundreds of pancakes*
Chalmers, Mary. *Six dogs, twenty-three cats, forty-five mice, and one hundred sixteen spiders*
Charlip, Remy. *Arm in arm*
Fortunately
"Mother, mother I feel sick"
Thirteen
Chevalier, Christa. *Spence makes circles*
Christian, Mary Blount. *Nothing much happened today*
The toady and Dr. Miracle
Chukovsky, Korney. *The telephone*
Ciardi, John. *I met a man*
The man who sang the sillies
You know who
Cole, Joanna. *The Clown-Arounds go on vacation*
Get well, Clown-Arounds!
Golly Gump swallowed a fly
Cole, William. *Dinosaurs and beasts of yore*
I went to the animal fair
Collins, Judith Graham. *Josh's scary dad*
Coontz, Otto. *Starring Rosa*
Copp, James. *Martha Matilda O'Toole*
Craig, M. Jean. *The man whose name was not Thomas*
Daugherty, James Henry. *Andy and the lion*
Davis, Maggie S. *The best way to Ripton*
Delaney, M. C. *The marigold monster*
Delaney, Ned. *Terrible things could happen*
Dennis, Suzanne E. *Answer me that*
De Paola, Tomie. *Bill and Pete*
Flicks
Strega Nona
Strega Nona's magic lessons
De Regniers, Beatrice Schenk. *May I bring a friend?*
Dorros, Arthur. *Pretzels*
Duvoisin, Roger Antoine. *Petunia's Christmas*
Easton, Violet. *Elephants never jump*
Ellentuck, Shan. *Did you see what I said?*
A sunflower as big as the sun

Ets, Marie Hall. *Beasts and nonsense*
Mister Penny
Evans, Katherine. *The maid and her pail of*
milk
The man, the boy and the donkey
Farber, Norma. *There once was a woman*
who married a man
Fenton, Edward. *The big yellow balloon*
Flora, James. *The day the cow sneezed*
Grandpa's farm
My friend Charlie
Folsom, Marcia. *Easy as pie*
Freeman, Don. *Forever laughter*
Frith, Michael K. *I'll teach my dog 100*
words
A frog he would a-wooing go (folk-song).
Frog went a-courtin', ill. by Feodor
Rojankovsky
From King Boggen's hall to nothing-at-all
Fuchshuber, Annegert. *The wishing hat*
Gackenbach, Dick. *The pig who saw*
everything
Gardner, Beau. *Have you ever seen...?*
Gelman, Rita Golden. *Hey, kid*
The golden goose, ill. by William Stobbs
Grimm, Jacob. *Clever Kate*
The golden goose, ill. by Dorothée Duntze
The golden goose, ill. by Isadore Seltzer
The golden goose, ill. by Martin Ursell
Hall, Donald. *Andrew the lion farmer*
Hall, Katy. *Fishy riddles*
Hample, Stoo. *Stoo Hample's silly joke book*
Hart, Jeanne McGahey. *Scareboy*
Heide, Florence Parry. *The shrinking of*
Treehorn
Heilbroner, Joan. *Robert the rose horse*
Hellard, Susan. *Froggie goes a-courting*
Hirsh, Marilyn. *Could anything be worse?*
Hoban, Lillian. *Silly Tilly and the Easter*
bunny
Hoban, Russell. *A near thing for Captain*
Najork
Hoff, Syd. *Syd Hoff's best jokes ever*
Holman, Felice. *Victoria's castle*
Hunter, Norman. *Professor Branestawn's*
building bust-up
Hutchins, Pat. *Clocks and more clocks*
Don't forget the bacon!
Rosie's walk
Jeschke, Susan. *Firerose*
Johnson, Crockett. *Harold and the purple*
crayon
Harold's circus
Upside down
Joslin, Sesyle. *Dear dragon*
What do you do, dear?
What do you say, dear?
Joyce, Irma. *Never talk to strangers*
Kantor, MacKinlay. *The preposterous week*
Keats, Ezra Jack. *Skates*
Keenen, George. *The preposterous week*

Keller, Charles. *Giggle puss*
The nutty joke book
School daze
Kennedy, Richard. *The contests at Cowlick*
Kent, Jack. *Hoddy doddy*
King-Smith, Dick. *Farmer Bungle forgets*
Koelling, Caryl. *Silly stories mix and match*
Krahn, Fernando. *April fools*
Krauss, Ruth. *I'll be you and you be me*
This thumbprint
Kumin, Maxine. *Eggs of things*
Speedy digs downside up
La Fontaine, Jean de. *The miller, the boy*
and the donkey
Laurin, Anne. *Little things*
Lear, Edward. *The dong with the luminous*
nose
Edward Lear's nonsense book
A Learical lexicon
Lear's nonsense verses
The nutcrackers and the sugar-tongs
The pelican chorus
The pelican chorus and the quangle
wangle's hat
The pobble who has no toes, ill. by Emma
Crosby
The pobble who has no toes, ill. by Kevin
W. Maddison
The quangle wangle's hat, ill. by Emma
Crosby
The quangle wangle's hat, ill. by Helen
Oxenbury
The quangle wangle's hat, ill. by Janet
Stevens
Two laughable lyrics
Whizz!
Lent, Blair. *John Tabor's ride*
LeRoy, Gen. *Lucky stiff!*
Lionni, Leo. *Where?*
Lloyd, David. *The ridiculous story of*
Gammer Gurton's needle
Lloyd, Megan. *Chicken tricks*
Lobel, Arnold. *The book of pigericks*
Lucille
Mouse tales
A treeful of pigs
Löfgren, Ulf. *The boy who ate more than the*
giant and other Swedish folktales
Macaulay, David. *Why the chicken crossed*
the road
McGovern, Ann. *Eggs on your nose*
Too much noise
McKié, Roy. *The riddle book*
McKissack, Patricia C. *The king's new*
clothes, ill. by Gwen Connelly
McLenighan, Valjean. *What you see is what*
you get
McPhail, David. *Alligators are awful (and*
they have terrible manners, too)
The cereal box

Rounds, Glen. *The day the circus came to Lone Tree*
Roy, Ronald. *Three ducks went wandering*
Rubel, Nicole. *It came from the swamp*
Rusling, Albert. *The mouse and Mrs. Proudfoot*
Saddler, Allen. *The Archery contest*
 The king gets fit
Sage, Michael. *Dippy dos and don'ts*
 If you talked to a boar
Saltzberg, Barney. *Cromwell*
Samuels, Barbara. *Duncan and Dolores*
Sazer, Nina. *What do you think I saw?*
Scarry, Richard. *Richard Scarry's funniest storybook ever*
Schatell, Brian. *Midge and Fred*
Scheer, Julian. *Rain makes applesauce*
Schmidt, Eric von. *The young man who wouldn't hoe corn*
Schwalje, Marjory. *Mr. Angelo*
Schwartz, Alvin. *All of our noses are here and other stories*
Seligson, Susan. *Amos*
Sendak, Maurice. *Pierre*
Seuss, Dr. *And to think that I saw it on Mulberry Street*
 Bartholomew and the Oobleck
 The cat in the hat
 The cat in the hat beginner book dictionary
 The cat in the hat comes back!
 The cat's quizzer
 Did I ever tell you how lucky you are?
 Dr. Seuss's ABC
 Dr. Seuss's sleep book
 The foot book
 Fox in sox
 A great day for up
 Green eggs and ham
 Happy birthday to you!
 Hooper Humperdink...? Not him!
 Hop on Pop
 Horton hatches the egg
 Horton hears a Who!
 How the Grinch stole Christmas
 I am not going to get up today!
 I can lick 30 tigers today and other stories
 I can read with my eyes shut
 I can write!
 I had trouble getting to Solla Sollew
 If I ran the circus
 If I ran the zoo
 In a people house
 The king's stilts
 The Lorax
 McElligot's pool
 Marvin K. Mooney, will you please go now!
 Mr. Brown can moo! Can you?
 Oh say can you say?
 Oh, the thinks you can think!
 On beyond zebra

 One fish, two fish, red fish, blue fish
 Please try to remember the first of octember!
 Scrambled eggs super!
 The shape of me and other stuff
 The Sneetches, and other stories
 There's a wocket in my pocket
 Thidwick, the big-hearted moose
 Wacky Wednesday
Shannon, George. *Beanboy*
Showalter, Jean B. *The donkey ride*
Silverstein, Shel. *A giraffe and a half*
Singer, Marilyn. *The dog who insisted he wasn't*
Slobodkina, Esphyr. *Caps for sale*
 Pezzo the peddler and the circus elephant
 Pezzo the peddler and the thirteen silly thieves
Smith, Jim. *The frog band and the onion seller*
 The frog band and the owlnapper
Smith, Robert Paul. *Jack Mack*
Smith, William Jay. *Puptents and pebbles*
Spier, Peter. *Bored - nothing to do!*
 Oh, were they ever happy!
Spilka, Arnold. *And the frog went "Blah!"*
 A lion I can do without
 A rumbudgin of nonsense
Spinelli, Eileen. *Thanksgiving at Tappletons'*
Stamaty, Mark Alan. *Minnie Maloney and Macaroni*
Steig, William. *Farmer Palmer's wagon ride*
Stevenson, James. *Happy Valentine's Day, Emma!*
 The worst person in the world at Crab Beach
Stinson, Kathy. *Those green things*
Stone, Rosetta. *Because a little bug went ka-choo!*
Stroyer, Poul. *It's a deal*
Suba, Susanne. *The monkeys and the pedlar*
Suhl, Yuri. *Simon Boom gives a wedding*
Sundgaard, Arnold. *Jethro's difficult dinosaur*
Tapio, Pat Decker. *The lady who saw the good side of everything*
Thaler, Mike. *Pack 109*
 The yellow brick toad
Thomas, Patricia. *"Stand back," said the elephant, "I'm going to sneeze!"*
Tobias, Tobi. *Jane wishing*
Tomkins, Jasper. *The catalog*
Tripp, Wallace. *Marguerite, go wash your feet*
 My Uncle Podger
Tulloch, Richard. *Stories from our house*
The twelve days of Christmas. English folk song. Jack Kent's twelve days of Christmas
Ueno, Noriko. *Elephant buttons*
Ungerer, Tomi. *The beast of Monsieur Racine*
 Crictor

Emile
Van der Meer, Ron. *Oh Lord!*
Van Woerkom, Dorothy. *Abu Ali*
Donkey Ysabel
The friends of Abu Ali
The queen who couldn't bake gingerbread
Viorst, Judith. *Sunday morning*
Waber, Bernard. *How to go about laying an egg*
Nobody is perfick
Wahl, Jan. *Cabbage moon*
Watanabe, Shigeo. *What a good lunch!*
Watson, Clyde. *Hickory stick rag*
Weatherill, Stephen. *The very first Lucy Goose book*
Westcott, Nadine Bernard. *The lady with the alligator purse*
Wiese, Kurt. *Fish in the air*
Wiesner, William. *Happy-Go-Lucky Turnabout*
Willard, Nancy. *Simple pictures are best*
Williams, Barbara. *Jeremy isn't hungry*
Williams, Jay. *School for sillies*
Wiseman, Bernard. *Tails are not for painting*
Wolkstein, Diane. *The legend of Sleepy Hollow*
Wood, Audrey. *King Bidgood's in the bathtub*
Woolf, Virginia. *The widow and the parrot*
Wright, Jill. *The old woman and the Willy Nilly Man*
Yolen, Jane. *The acorn quest*
Yorinks, Arthur. *Company's coming*
Zemach, Harve. *The tricks of Master Dabble*
Zemach, Margot. *It could always be worse*
Zimmerman, Andrea Griffing. *Yetta, the trickster*

Hungary *see* Foreign lands – Hungary

Hunting *see* Sports – hunting

Hurrying *see* Behavior – hurrying

Hyenas *see* Animals – hyenas

Ice skating *see* Sports – ice skating

Iguanas *see* Reptiles – Iguanas

Illness

Aliki. *I wish I was sick, too!*

Anholt, Catherine. *Truffles is sick*
Arnold, Katrin. *Anna joins in*
Bains, Rae. *Hiccups, hiccups*
Barrett, Judi. *An apple a day*
Berger, Melvin. *Germs make me sick!*
Why I cough, sneeze, shiver, hiccup and yawn
Bradman, Tony. *Through my window*
Brown, Margaret Wise. *When the wind blew*
Bruna, Dick. *Miffy in the hospital*
Buckley, Helen Elizabeth. *Someday with my father*
Carrick, Carol. *Old Mother Witch*
Chalmers, Mary. *Come to the doctor, Harry*
Charlip, Remy. *"Mother, mother I feel sick"*
Cherry, Lynne. *Who's sick today?*
Christelow, Eileen. *Henry and the red stripes*
Ciliotta, Claire. *"Why am I going to the hospital?"*
Cole, Joanna. *Get well, Clown-Arounds!*
Craven, Carolyn. *What the mailman brought*
De Groat, Diane. *Alligator's toothache*
Delton, Judy. *Groundhog's Day at the doctor*
It happened on Thursday
De Paola, Tomie. *Now one foot, now the other*
DeWitt, Jamie. *Jamie's turn*
Duff, Maggie. *The princess and the pumpkin*
Duvoisin, Roger Antoine. *The Christmas whale*
Eberstadt, Isabel. *What is for my birthday?*
Elliott, Ingrid Glatz. *Hospital roadmap*
Eriksson, Eva. *Jealousy*
Fern, Eugene. *Pepito's story*
Fleischman, Sid. *Kate's secret riddle*
Gackenbach, Dick. *Hattie be quiet, Hattie be good*
What's Claude doing?
Galbraith, Kathryn Osebold. *Spots are special*
Gay, Marie-Louise. *Rainy day magic*
Goldsmith, Howard. *Little lost dog*
Gomi, Taro. *Toot!*
Gretz, Susanna. *Teddy bears cure a cold*
Hamm, Diane Johnston. *Grandma drives a motor bed*
Hewett, Joan. *Fly away free*
Hogan, Paula Z. *The hospital scares me*
Holl, Adelaide. *Small Bear solves a mystery*
Hurd, Edith Thacher. *Johnny Lion's bad day*
Hutchins, Pat. *The best train set ever*
Jenkins, Jordan. *Learning about love*
Johnson, Louise. *Malunda*
Keller, Beverly. *When mother got the flu*
Keller, Holly. *When Francie was sick*
Kibbey, Marsha. *My grammy*
Knotts, Howard. *The lost Christmas*
Kraus, Robert. *The first robin*

Kroll, Steven. *The big bunny and the Easter eggs*
Kunhardt, Edith. *Trick or treat, Danny!*
Le Guin, Ursula K. *A visit from Dr. Katz*
Lerner, Marguerite Rush. *Dear little mumps child*
Michael gets the measles
Peter gets the chickenpox
Lewin, Betsy. *Hip, hippo, hooray!*
Lexau, Joan M. *Benjie on his own*
Lobel, Arnold. *A holiday for Mister Muster*
MacLachlan, Patricia. *Mama one, Mama two*
The sick day
McPhail, David. *Adam's smile*
The bear's toothache
Maestro, Giulio. *Leopard is sick*
Mann, Peggy. *King Laurence, the alarm clock*
Marshall, James. *Yummers!*
Mayer, Mercer. *Ah-choo*
Hiccup
Morris, Ann. *Eleanora Mousie catches a cold*
Moss, Elaine. *Polar*
Nelson, Vaunda Micheaux. *Always Gramma*
Nourse, Alan Edward. *Lumps, bumps and rashes*
Numeroff, Laura Joffe. *Phoebe Dexter has Harriet Peterson's sniffles*
Ormerod, Jan. *This little nose*
Ostrovsky, Vivian. *Mumps!*
Pace, Elizabeth. *Chris gets ear tubes*
Pedersen, Judy. *The tiny patient*
Polhamus, Jean Burt. *Doctor Dinosaur*
Porte, Barbara Ann. *Harry's dog*
Quackenbush, Robert M. *Calling Doctor Quack*
Rockwell, Anne F. *The emergency room*
Sick in bed
Rogers, Fred. *Going to the hospital*
Rohmer, Harriet. *Atariba and Niguayona*
Sandberg, Inger. *Nicholas' red day*
Say, Allen. *A river dream*
Seignobosc, Françoise. *Biquette, the white goat*
Sharmat, Marjorie Weinman. *I want mama*
Shay, Arthur. *What happens when you go to the hospital*
Showers, Paul. *No measles, no mumps for me*
Sonneborn, Ruth A. *I love Gram*
Stein, Sara Bonnett. *A hospital story*
Stephenson, Dorothy. *How to scare a lion*
Thurber, James. *Many moons*
Tobias, Tobi. *A day off*
Trez, Denise. *The royal hiccups*
Tyler, Linda Wagner. *The sick-in-bed birthday book*
Udry, Janice May. *Mary Jo's grandmother*

Vigna, Judith. *I wish my daddy didn't drink so much*
Wadhams, Margaret. *Anna*
Wahl, Jan. *Jamie's tiger*
Watson, Wendy. *Tales for a winter's eve*
Watts, Marjorie-Ann. *Crocodile medicine*
Crocodile plaster
Weber, Alfons. *Elizabeth gets well*
West, Colin. *The king's toothache*
Whitney, Alma Marshak. *Just awful*
Wildsmith, Brian. *Carousel*
Williams, Barbara. *Albert's toothache*
Williams, Vera B. *Music, music for everyone*
Wolde, Gunilla. *Betsy and the chicken pox*
Betsy and the doctor
Yolen, Jane. *Commander Toad and the planet of the grapes*

Illness – Alzheimer's

Guthrie, Donna. *Grandpa doesn't know it's me*

Illusions, optical *see* Optical illusions

Illustrators, children *see* Children as illustrators

Imaginary friends *see* Imagination – imaginary friends

Imagination

Abisch, Roz. *Open your eyes*
Adam, Barbara. *The big big box*
Adler, David A. *I know I'm a witch*
Agee, Jon. *Ellsworth*
The incredible painting of Felix Clousseau
Aiken, Joan. *Arabel and Mortimer*
Aitken, Amy. *Kate and Mona in the jungle*
Ruby!
Ruby, the red knight
Alexander, Martha G. *Bobo's dream*
Marty McGee's space lab, no girls allowed
Allen, Jeffrey. *The secret life of Mr. Weird*
Allen, Pamela. *A lion in the night*
Andersen, H. C. (Hans Christian). *The emperor's new clothes*, ill. by Pamela Baldwin-Ford
The emperor's new clothes, ill. by Erik Blegvad
The emperor's new clothes, ill. by Virginia Lee Burton
The emperor's new clothes, ill. by Jack and Irene Delano
The emperor's new clothes, ill. by Hélène Desputeaux
The emperor's new clothes, ill. by Birte Dietz
The emperor's new clothes, ill. by Dorothée Duntze
The emperor's new clothes, ill. by Jack Kent

The emperor's new clothes, ill. by Monika Laimgruber

The emperor's new clothes, ill. by Anne F. Rockwell

The emperor's new clothes, ill. by Janet Stevens

The emperor's new clothes, ill. by Nadine Bernard Westcott

Anderson, C. W. (Clarence Williams). *Linda and the Indians*

Anglund, Joan Walsh. *Cowboy's secret life*

Anno, Mitsumasa. *Anno's alphabet*
Anno's animals
Anno's Britain
Anno's counting book
Anno's counting house
Anno's flea market
Anno's Italy
Anno's journey
Anno's magical ABC
Anno's U.S.A.
Dr. Anno's midnight circus
The king's flower
Topsy-turvies
Upside-downers

Armour, Richard Willard. *Animals on the ceiling*

Arnold, Tedd. *No jumping on the bed!*

Asch, Frank. *City sandwich*
Goodnight horsey
Rebecka

Ayal, Ora. *The adventures of Chester the chest*
Ugbu

Bach, Othello. *Lilly, Willy and the mail-order witch*

Baker, Alan. *Benjamin bounces back*

Baker, Betty. *My sister says*

Balet, Jan B. *Ned and Ed and the lion*

Bang, Molly. *The grey lady and the strawberry snatcher*

Banks, Kate. *Alphabet soup*

Bannon, Laura. *The best house in the world*

Barber, Antonia. *Satchelmouse and the dinosaurs*

Barrett, Judi. *Cloudy with a chance of meatballs*
I hate to go to bed

Barry, Katharina. *A bug to hug*

Barthelme, Donald. *The slightly irregular fire engine*

Bate, Lucy. *How Georgina drove the car very carefully from Boston to New York*

Baumann, Kurt. *The paper airplane*

Bayley, Nicola. *Crab cat*
Elephant cat
Parrot cat
Polar bear cat
Spider cat

Beech, Caroline. *Peas again for lunch*

Behrens, June. *Can you walk the plank?*

Beim, Jerrold. *The taming of Toby*

Benedictus, Roger. *Fifty million sausages*

Benjamin, Alan. *Ribtickle Town*

Bennett, Rowena. *The day is dancing and other poems*
Songs from around a toadstool table

Berenstain, Stan. *The Berenstain bears in the dark*

Blakeley, Peggy. *What shall I be tomorrow?*

Blegvad, Lenore. *Anna Banana and me*
Rainy day Kate

Blocksma, Mary. *The pup went up*

Blos, Joan W. *Martin's hats*

Blundell, Tony. *Joe on Sunday*

Bodsworth, Nan. *Monkey business*

Boegehold, Betty. *Hurray for Pippa!*
In the castle of cats

Bonsall, Crosby Newell. *Tell me some more*

Boon, Emilie. *Peterkin meets a star*
Peterkin's wet walk

Bottner, Barbara. *Mean Maxine*
Myra
There was nobody there

Boutell, Clarence Burley. *The fat baron*

Bowers, Kathleen Rice. *At this very minute*

Boyd, Selma. *I met a polar bear*

Brandenberg, Franz. *Leo and Emily and the dragon*

Brenner, Anita. *I want to fly*

Briggs, Raymond. *Walking in the air*

Bröger, Achim. *Francie's paper puppy*
Little Harry

Brooks, Gregory. *Monroe's island*

Brown, Paul. *Merrylegs, the rocking pony*

Browne, Anthony. *Gorilla*
Look what I've got!

Bruce, Sheilah B. *The radish day jubilee*

Brunhoff, Laurent de. *Gregory and Lady Turtle in the valley of the music trees*

Buckaway, C. M. *Alfred, the dragon who lost his flame*

Budd, Lillian. *The people on Long Ago Street*

Bulette, Sara. *The elf in the singing tree*

Burningham, John. *Come away from the water, Shirley*
John Patrick Norman McHennessy - the boy who was always late
Time to get out of the bath, Shirley
Where's Julius?
Would you rather...

Calders, Pere. *Brush*

Callen, Larry. *Dashiel and the night*

Carmi, Giora. *And Shira imagined*

Carrick, Carol. *Patrick's dinosaurs*
What happened to Patrick's dinosaurs?

Carrier, Lark. *Scout and Cody*
There was a hill...

Carroll, Lewis. *The nursery "Alice"*

Chalmers, Mary. *The cat who liked to pretend*

Chapouton, Anne-Marie. *Sebastian is always late*
Charles Prince of Wales. *The old man of Lochnagar*
Chevalier, Christa. *Spence and the sleepytime monster*
Chislett, Gail. *The rude visitors*
Chorao, Kay. *Lester's overnight*
Collins, Pat L. *My friend Andrew*
Cooper, Elizabeth K. *The fish from Japan*
Craig, Helen. *Susie and Alfred in the knight, the princess and the dragon*
Craig, M. Jean. *The dragon in the clock box*
Craven, Carolyn. *What the mailman brought*
Cummings, E. E. *Fairy tales*
Cutler, Ivor. *Herbert*
Davis, Douglas F. *There's an elephant in the garage*
Delaney, A. *Monster tracks?*
Delessert, Etienne. *A long long song*
Demarest, Chris L. *No peas for Nellie*
Orville's odyssey
De Regniers, Beatrice Schenk. *Laura's story*
A little house of your own
Waiting for mama
What can you do with a shoe?
Devlin, Wende. *Aunt Agatha, there's a lion under the couch!*
Dickinson, Mary. *Alex and Roy*
Dickinson, Mike. *My dad doesn't even notice*
DiFiori, Lawrence. *If I had a little car*
D'Ignazio, Fred. *Katie and the computer*
Dobrin, Arnold Jack. *Josephine's 'magination*
Doolittle, Eileen. *World of wonders*
Dorian, Marguerite. *When the snow is blue*
Drescher, Henrik. *Looking for Santa Claus*
Edwards, Patricia Kier. *Chester and Uncle Willoughby*
Ekker, Ernest A. *What is beyond the hill?*
Elzbieta. *Dikou and the mysterious moon sheep*
Etherington, Frank. *The spaghetti word race*
Ets, Marie Hall. *In the forest*
Faulkner, Matt. *The amazing voyage of Jackie Grace*
Felix, Monique. *The further adventures of the little mouse trapped in a book*
The story of a little mouse trapped in a book
Fenner, Carol. *Tigers in the cellar*
Fenton, Edward. *Fierce John*
Firmin, Peter. *Basil Brush and a dragon*
Fleischman, Paul. *Rondo in C*
Fontaine, Jan. *The spaghetti tree*
Francis, Frank. *The magic wallpaper*
Freeman, Don. *The paper party*
Quiet! There's a canary in the library
Furtado, Jo. *Sorry, Miss Folio!*
Gackenbach, Dick. *Harry and the terrible whatzit*
Mag the magnificent

Supposes
Gage, Wilson. *Mrs. Gaddy and the ghost*
Galbraith, Kathryn Osebold. *Spots are special*
Gillham, Bill. *What can you do?*
Glass, Andrew. *My brother tries to make me laugh*
Graves, Robert. *The big green book*
Gwynne, Fred. *A little pigeon toad*
Hamsa, Bobbie. *Your pet bear*
Your pet beaver
Your pet camel
Your pet elephant
Your pet giraffe
Your pet kangaroo
Your pet penguin
Your pet sea lion
Hanlon, Emily. *What if a lion eats me and I fall into a hippopotamus' mud hole?*
Haus, Felice. *Beep! Beep! I'm a jeep*
Heller, Nicholas. *An adventure at sea*
Hennessy, B. G. *The dinosaur who lived in my backyard*
Hillert, Margaret. *What is it?*
Himler, Ronald. *The girl on the yellow giraffe*
Hines, Anna Grossnickle. *Bethany for real*
Hoban, Russell. *The flight of Bembel Rudzuk*
Goodnight
The great gum drop robbery
The rain door
Hoffmann, E. T. A. *The nutcracker*, ill. by Rachel Isadora
The nutcracker, ill. by Maurice Sendak
The nutcracker, ill. by Lisbeth Zwerger
Holl, Adelaide. *Most-of-the-time Maxie*
Holman, Felice. *Victoria's castle*
Horwitz, Elinor Lander. *Sometimes it happens*
Howard, Jane R. *When I'm sleepy*
Hughes, Shirley. *Up and up*
Hunter, Mollie. *The knight of the golden plain*
Hurd, Edith Thacher. *The white horse*
Inkpen, Mick. *If I had a pig*
If I had a sheep
One bear at bedtime
Ionesco, Eugene. *Story number 1*
Isadora, Rachel. *The pirates of Bedford Street*
Ivanov, Anatoly. *Ol' Jake's lucky day*
Janosch. *Hey Presto! You're a bear!*
Jeschke, Susan. *Tamar and the tiger*
Jewell, Nancy. *Try and catch me*
Johnson, Crockett. *The blue ribbon puppies*
Ellen's lion
Harold and the purple crayon
Harold at the North Pole
Harold's ABC
Harold's circus

Rosen, Winifred. *Dragons hate to be discreet*
Rosner, Ruth. *Arabba gah zee, Marissa and Me!*
Russ, Lavinia. *Alec's sand castle*
Russo, Marisabina. *Why do grownups have all the fun?*
Schoberle, Ceile. *Beyond the Milky Way*
Scott, Ann Herbert. *Big Cowboy Western*
Seligson, Susan. *Amos*
Sendak, Maurice. *In the night kitchen*
   The sign on Rosie's door
   Where the wild things are
Seuss, Dr. *And to think that I saw it on Mulberry Street*
   McElligot's pool
   Oh say can you say?
   Oh, the thinks you can think!
Sharmat, Marjorie Weinman. *My mother never listens to me*
Shaw, Charles Green. *It looked like spilt milk*
Shecter, Ben. *Conrad's castle*
   If I had a ship
Sherman, Ivan. *I am a giant*
Shimin, Symeon. *I wish there were two of me*
Shulevitz, Uri. *One Monday morning*
Sicotte, Virginia. *A riot of quiet*
Siepmann, Jane. *The lion on Scott Street*
Simmonds, Posy. *Lulu and the flying babies*
Skorpen, Liesel Moak. *If I had a lion*
Sleator, William. *That's silly*
Slobodkin, Louis. *Clear the track*
   Magic Michael
Smith, Jim. *Nimbus the explorer*
Stanley, Diane. *Birdsong Lullaby*
Steiner, Charlotte. *Look what Tracy found*
Stemp, Robin. *Guy and the flowering plum tree*
Stevens, Cat. *Teaser and the firecat*
Stevenson, James. *Worse than Willy!*
Stevenson, Jocelyn. *Red and the pumpkins*
Stinson, Kathy. *Those green things*
Stoddard, Sandol. *Curl up small*
   The thinking book
Sundgaard, Arnold. *Meet Jack Appleknocker*
Supraner, Robyn. *Would you rather be a tiger?*
Sutherland, Harry A. *Dad's car wash*
Tafuri, Nancy. *Junglewalk*
Taniuchi, Kota. *Trolley*
Testa, Fulvio. *The land where the ice cream grows*
Thayer, Jane. *Andy and the wild worm*
Thomas, Ianthe. *Walk home tired, Billy Jenkins*
Tompert, Ann. *Little Fox goes to the end of the world*
Townson, Hazel. *Terrible Tuesday*
Turkle, Brinton. *The sky dog*

Udry, Janice May. *Is Susan here?*
Updike, David. *An autumn tale*
Van Allsburg, Chris. *The garden of Abdul Gasazi*
   Jumanji
   The mysteries of Harris Burdick
   The polar express
Van Leeuwen, Jean. *Oliver, Amanda and Grandmother*
Velthuijs, Max. *The painter and the bird*
Vigna, Judith. *Boot weather*
Viorst, Judith. *The good-bye book*
   My mama says there aren't any zombies, ghosts, vampires, creatures, demons, monsters, fiends, goblins, or things
Vogel, Ilse-Margaret. *The don't be scared book*
Vreeken, Elizabeth. *The boy who would not say his name*
Watson, Clyde. *Midnight moon*
Watson, Jane Werner. *The tall book of make-believe*
Wayland, April Halprin. *To Rabbittown*
Wells, Rosemary. *Good night, Fred*
   A lion for Lewis
Willard, Nancy. *A visit to William Blake's inn*
Williams, Vera B. *Cherries and cherry pits*
Winthrop, Elizabeth. *Bunk beds*
Yorinks, Arthur. *Hey, Al*
   Louis the fish
Young, Miriam Burt. *Jellybeans for breakfast*
Ziefert, Harriet. *Lewis the fire fighter*
Zimelman, Nathan. *Once when I was five*
Zolotow, Charlotte. *When I have a son*

Imagination – imaginary friends

Alexander, Martha G. *And my mean old mother will be sorry, Blackboard Bear*
   Blackboard Bear
   I sure am glad to see you, Blackboard Bear
   I'll protect you from the jungle beasts
   We're in big trouble, Blackboard Bear
Andrews, F. Emerson (Frank Emerson). *Nobody comes to dinner*
Anglund, Joan Walsh. *Cowboy and his friend*
   The cowboy's Christmas
Berger, Barbara Helen. *When the sun rose*
Bornstein, Ruth Lercher. *The seedling child*
Bram, Elizabeth. *There is someone standing on my head*
Brewster, Patience. *Nobody*
Brighton, Catherine. *My hands, my world*
Brown, Palmer. *The silver nutmeg*
Cummings, Pat. *Jimmy Lee did it*
Dauer, Rosamond. *My friend, Jasper Jones*
Dillon, Barbara. *The beast in the bed*
Dinan, Carolyn. *The lunch box monster*

Greenfield, Eloise. *Me and Nessie*
Hazen, Barbara Shook. *The gorilla did it!*
  Gorilla wants to be the baby
Henkes, Kevin. *Jessica*
Hiller, Catherine. *Argentaybee and the boonie*
Hoff, Syd. *The horse in Harry's room*
Jeschke, Susan. *Angela and Bear*
  The devil did it
Joosse, Barbara M. *The thinking place*
Krahn, Fernando. *The creepy thing*
Krensky, Stephen. *The lion upstairs*
Langner, Nola. *By the light of the silvery moon*
Morris, Terry Nell. *Good night, dear monster!*
Noble, June. *Two homes for Lynn*
Oram, Hiawyn. *Ned and the Joybaloo*
Pinkwater, Daniel Manus. *Pickle creature*
Ross, Tony. *Hugo and Oddsock*
St. George, Judith. *The Halloween pumpkin smasher*
Steiner, Charlotte. *Lulu*
Thaler, Mike. *My puppy*
Thayer, Jane. *Andy and his fine friends*
Watts, Marjorie-Ann. *Zebra goes to school*
Zolotow, Charlotte. *Three funny friends*

Imitation *see* Behavior – imitation

In and out *see* Concepts – in and out

Incentive *see* Character traits – ambition

Independence Day *see* Holidays – Fourth of July

India *see* Foreign lands – India

Indians, American *see* Indians of North America

Indians of North America

Abisch, Roz. *'Twas in the moon of wintertime*
Aliki. *Corn is maize*
Anderson, C. W. (Clarence Williams). *Linda and the Indians*
Aulaire, Ingri Mortenson d'. *Pocahontas*
Baker, Betty. *And me, coyote!*
  Latki and the lightning lizard
  Little runner of the longhouse
  Rat is dead and ant is sad
  Three fools and a horse
  Turkey girl
Baker, Laura Nelson. *O children of the wind and pines*
Baker, Olaf. *Where the buffaloes begin*
Baylor, Byrd. *The desert is theirs*
  A God on every mountain top

Hawk, I'm your brother
Moon song
When clay sings
Beatty, Hetty Burlingame. *Little Owl Indian*
Behrens, June. *Powwow*
Belting, Natalia Maree. *Verity Mullens and the Indian*
Benchley, Nathaniel. *Red Fox and his canoe*
  Running Owl the hunter
  Small Wolf
Bernstein, Margery. *Coyote goes hunting for fire*
  Earth namer
  How the sun made a promise and kept it
Bierhorst, John. *Doctor Coyote*
  The ring in the prairie
Blood, Charles L. *The goat in the rug*
Bornstein, Ruth Lercher. *Indian bunny*
Brock, Emma Lillian. *One little Indian boy*
Clark, Ann Nolan. *The desert people*
  In my mother's house
  The little Indian basket maker
  The little Indian pottery maker
Cleaver, Elizabeth. *The enchanted caribou*
Cohen, Carol L. *The mud pony*
Crompton, Anne Eliot. *The winter wife*
Day, Michael E. *Berry Ripe Moon*
De Paola, Tomie. *The legend of the bluebonnet*
  The legend of the Indian paintbrush
Ehrlich, Amy. *Zeek Silver Moon*
Elting, Mary. *The Hopi way*
Esbensen, Barbara Juster. *The star maiden*
Flöthe, Louise Lee. *The Indian and his pueblo*
Friskey, Margaret. *Indian Two Feet and his eagle feather*
  Indian Two Feet and his horse
  Indian Two Feet and the wolf cubs
  Indian Two Feet rides alone
Fritz, Jean. *The good giants and the bad Pukwudgies*
Goble, Paul. *Beyond the ridge*
  Buffalo woman
  Death of the iron horse
  The friendly wolf
  The gift of the sacred dog
  The girl who loved wild horses
  Her seven brothers
  Iktomi and the boulder
  Star boy
Gorsline, Marie. *North American Indians*
Hader, Berta Hoerner. *The mighty hunter*
Hays, Wilma Pitchford. *Little Yellow Fur*
Hodges, Margaret. *The fire bringer*
Hood, Flora Mae. *Living in Navajoland*
Jagendorf, Moritz A. *Kwi-na the eagle*
Jones, Hettie. *The trees stand shining*
Leech, Jay. *Bright Fawn and me*

Longfellow, Henry Wadsworth. *Hiawatha*
  Hiawatha's childhood
McDermott, Gerald. *Arrow to the sun*
Mariana. *Doki, the lonely papoose*
Martin, Bill (William Ivan). *Brave little*
  Indian
  Knots on a counting rope
Mobley, Jane. *The star husband*
Monjo, F. N. *The drinking gourd*
  Indian summer
Moon, Grace Purdie. *One little Indian*
Norman, Howard. *Who-Paddled-*
  Backward-With-Trout
Ortiz, Simon. *The people shall continue*
Parish, Peggy. *Good hunting, Blue Sky*
  Good hunting, Little Indian
  Granny and the Indians
  Granny, the baby and the big gray thing
  Little Indian
  Snapping turtle's all wrong day
Parnall, Peter. *The great fish*
Perrine, Mary. *Salt boy*
Pomerantz, Charlotte. *Timothy Tall Feather*
Robbins, Ruth. *How the first rainbow was*
  made
Rose, Anne. *Spider in the sky*
Roth, Susan L. *Kanahena*
San Souci, Robert D. *The legend of*
  Scarface
Siberell, Anne. *Whale in the sky*
Sleator, William. *The angry moon*
Speare, Jean. *A candle for Christmas*
Stan-Padilla, Viento. *Dream Feather*
Toye, William. *Fire stealer*
  How summer came to Canada
  The loon's necklace
  The mountain goats of Temlaham
Troughton, Joanna. *How rabbit stole the*
  fire
  Who will be the sun?
Wheeler, M. J. *First came the Indians*
Wondriska, William. *The stop*

Indifference *see* Behavior – indifference

Individuality *see* Character traits –
  individuality

Indonesian Archipelago *see* Foreign lands
  – South Sea Islands

Insects

Adelson, Leone. *Please pass the grass*
Aldis, Dorothy. *Quick as a wink*
Aldridge, Alan. *The butterfly ball and the*
  grasshopper's feast
Arnosky, Jim. *A kettle of hawks, and other*
  wildlife groups
Barrett, Judi. *Snake is totally tail*
Belpré, Pura. *Perez and Martina*

Bernstein, Joanne E. *Creepy crawly critter*
  riddles
Boegehold, Betty. *Bear underground*
Brouillette, Jeanne S. *Moths*
Carter, David A. *How many bugs in a box?*
Colby, C. B. (Carroll Burleigh). *Who lives*
  there?
Cole, Joanna. *Find the hidden insect*
Conklin, Gladys. *I caught a lizard*
  We like bugs
  When insects are babies
Cristini, Ermanno. *In the pond*
Farber, Norma. *Never say ugh to a bug*
Fields, Alice. *Insects*
Fisher, Aileen. *When it comes to bugs*
Gackenbach, Dick. *Little bug*
George, Jean Craighead. *All upon a stone*
Geraghty, Paul. *Over the steamy swamp*
Goudey, Alice E. *Red legs*
Griffen, Elizabeth. *A dog's book of bugs*
Hall, Katy. *Buggy riddles*
Heller, Ruth. *How to hide a butterfly*
Ipcar, Dahlov. *Bug city*
Jaynes, Ruth M. *That's what it is!*
Kaufmann, John. *Flying giants of long ago*
Kraus, Robert. *How spider saved Valentine's*
  Day
Lionni, Leo. *Inch by inch*
Lobel, Arnold. *Grasshopper on the road*
McKissack, Patricia C. *Big bug book of*
  counting
  Big bug book of opposites
  Big bug book of places to go
  Big bug book of the alphabet
Milne, A. A. (Alan Alexander). *Pooh and*
  some bees
Parker, Nancy Winslow. *Bugs*
Pasley, L. *The adventures of Madalene and*
  Louisa
Petie, Haris. *Billions of bugs*
Peyo. *The Smurfs and their woodland*
  friends
Roop, Peter. *Going buggy!*
Rounds, Glen. *The boll weevil*
Selden, George. *Chester Cricket's pigeon ride*
Selsam, Millicent E. *Backyard insects*
  The bug that laid the golden eggs
  Where do they go? Insects in winter
Seymour, Peter. *Insects*
Soya, Kiyoshi. *A house of leaves*
Stone, Rosetta. *Because a little bug went*
  ka-choo!
Tison, Annette. *Animal hide-and-seek*
Van Woerkom, Dorothy. *Hidden messages*

Insects – ants

Cameron, Polly. *"I can't," said the ant*
Ciardi, John. *John J. Plenty and Fiddler*
  Dan
Clay, Pat. *Ants*

Dorros, Arthur. *Ant cities*
Freschet, Berniece. *The ants go marching*
Myrick, Mildred. *Ants are fun*
Peet, Bill. *The ant and the elephant*
Pluckrose, Henry. *Ants*
Van Allsburg, Chris. *Two bad ants*

Insects – bees

Baran, Tancy. *Bees*
Barton, Byron. *Buzz, buzz, buzz*
Ernst, Lisa Campbell. *A colorful adventure of the bee who left home one Monday morning and what he found along the way*
Galdone, Joanna. *Honeybee's party*
Hawes, Judy. *Watch honeybees with me*
Hogan, Paula Z. *The honeybee*
Keller, Beverly. *Fiona's bee*
Lobel, Arnold. *The rose in my garden*
Pizer, Abigail. *Nosey Gilbert*
Pluckrose, Henry. *Bees and wasps*
Rockwell, Anne F. *Big bad goat*
Sand, George. *The mysterious tale of Gentle Jack and Lord Bumblebee*
Wahl, Jan. *Follow me cried Bee*

Insects – beetles

Conklin, Gladys. *I like beetles*
Hoban, Russell. *Jim Frog*

Insects – butterflies, caterpillars

Aardema, Verna. *Who's in Rabbit's house?*
Abisch, Roz. *Let's find out about butterflies*
Aldridge, Alan. *The butterfly ball and the grasshopper's feast*
Carle, Eric. *The very hungry caterpillar*
Carrick, Malcolm. *I can squash elephants!*
The caterpillar who turned into a butterfly
Conklin, Gladys. *I like butterflies*
I like caterpillars
Cutts, David. *Look...a butterfly*
Darby, Gene. *What is a butterfly?*
Delaney, A. *The butterfly*
Delaney, Ned. *One dragon to another*
Fitzsimons, Cecilia. *My first butterflies*
Garelick, May. *Where does the butterfly go when it rains?*
Gomi, Taro. *Hi, butterfly!*
Grifalconi, Ann. *Darkness and the butterfly*
Heller, Ruth. *How to hide a butterfly*
Hogan, Paula Z. *The butterfly*
Kent, Jack. *The caterpillar and the polliwog*
Kipling, Rudyard. *The butterfly that stamped*
Lewis, Naomi. *The butterfly collector*
McClung, Robert. *Sphinx*
O'Hagan, Caroline. *It's easy to have a caterpillar visit you*
Piers, Helen. *Grasshopper and butterfly*
Pluckrose, Henry. *Butterflies and moths*
Roscoe, William. *The butterfly's ball*

Selsam, Millicent E. *A first look at caterpillars*
Terry and the caterpillars
Sundgaard, Arnold. *The lamb and the butterfly*
Thompson, Susan L. *Diary of a monarch butterfly*
Watts, Barrie. *Butterfly and caterpillar*
Wong, Herbert H. *Our caterpillars*

Insects – caterpillars *see* Insects – butterflies, caterpillars

Insects – crickets

Caudill, Rebecca. *A pocketful of cricket*
Kimmel, Eric A. *Why worry?*
Mizumura, Kazue. *If I were a cricket...*

Insects – fireflies

Berends, Polly Berrien. *Ladybug and dog and the night walk*
Bolliger, Max. *The fireflies*
Brinckloe, Julie. *Fireflies!*
Buckley, Paul. *Amy Belligera and the fireflies*
Callen, Larry. *Dashiel and the night*
Eastman, P. D. (Philip D.). *Sam and the firefly*
Harris, Louise Dyer. *Flash, the life of a firefly*
Hawes, Judy. *Fireflies in the night*
Knight, Hilary. *A firefly in a fir tree*
Ryder, Joanne. *Fireflies*

Insects – fleas

Wiese, Kurt. *The dog, the fox and the fleas*

Insects – flies

Aardema, Verna. *Half-a-ball-of-kenki*
Brandenberg, Franz. *Fresh cider and apple pie*
Conklin, Gladys. *I watch flies*
Elkin, Benjamin. *Why the sun was late*
Kraus, Robert. *The trouble with spider*
McClintock, Marshall. *A fly went by*
Oppenheim, Joanne. *You can't catch me!*
Winter, Paula. *The bear and the fly*
Yolen, Jane. *Spider Jane*

Insects – gnats

Peet, Bill. *The gnats of knotty pine*

Insects – grasshoppers

Aldridge, Alan. *The butterfly ball and the grasshopper's feast*
Ciardi, John. *John J. Plenty and Fiddler Dan*
Du Bois, William Pène. *Bear circus*

Grasshopper to the rescue
Kimmel, Eric A. *Why worry?*
Lobel, Arnold. *Grasshopper on the road*
Newbolt, Henry John, Sir. *Rilloby-rill*
Piers, Helen. *Grasshopper and butterfly*

Insects – lady birds *see* Insects – ladybugs

Insects – ladybugs

Berends, Polly Berrien. *Ladybug and dog and the night walk*
Carle, Eric. *The grouchy ladybug*
Conklin, Gladys. *Lucky ladybugs*
Fisher, Aileen. *We went looking*
Hawes, Judy. *Ladybug, ladybug, fly away home*
Kepes, Juliet. *Lady bird, quickly*
Kraus, Robert. *Ladybug, ladybug!*
Schlein, Miriam. *Fast is not a ladybug*
Silverman, Maida. *Ladybug's color book*
Sueyoshi, Akiko. *Ladybird on a bicycle*
Watts, Barrie. *Ladybug*
Wong, Herbert H. *My ladybug*

Insects – lightning bugs *see* Insects – fireflies

Insects – mosquitoes

Aardema, Verna. *Why mosquitoes buzz in people's ears*
Oxford Scientific Films. *Mosquito*

Insects – moths

Pluckrose, Henry. *Butterflies and moths*

Insects – praying mantis

Conklin, Gladys. *Praying mantis*

Insects – wasps

Pluckrose, Henry. *Bees and wasps*

Interracial marriage *see* Marriage, interracial

Ireland *see* Foreign lands – Ireland

Islands

Abolafia, Yossi. *Yanosh's Island*
Adoff, Arnold. *Flamboyan*
Alderson, Sue Ann. *Ida and the wool smugglers*
Armitage, Ronda. *Ice creams for Rosie*
Beni, Ruth. *Sir Baldergog the great*
Brock, Emma Lillian. *Skipping Island*
Brown, Margaret Wise. *The little island*
Brunhoff, Laurent de. *Babar's visit to Bird Island*
Civardi, Anne. *Things people do*

Coatsworth, Elizabeth. *Lonely Maria*
Cooney, Barbara. *Island boy*
Farley, Walter. *Black stallion*
Gantschev, Ivan. *The train to Grandma's*
Greenfield, Eloise. *Under the Sunday tree*
Hedderwick, Mairi. *Katie Morag and the big boy cousins*
Katie Morag and the tiresome Ted
Katie Morag and the two grandmothers
Katie Morag delivers the mail
Hoopes, Lyn Littlefield. *Mommy, daddy, me*
Johnston, Tony. *Pages of music*
Kellogg, Steven. *The island of the skog*
Kessler, Leonard P. *The pirates' adventure on Spooky Island*
King, Deborah. *Sirius and Saba*
Krahn, Fernando. *The great ape*
Lasky, Kathryn. *My island grandma*
Lent, Blair. *Bayberry Bluff*
Lessac, Frané. *My little island*
McCloskey, Robert. *Time of wonder*
McGovern, Ann. *Nicholas Bentley Stoningpot III*
McPhail, David. *Great cat*
Martin, Charles E. *For rent*
Island rescue
Island winter
Millhouse, Nicholas. *Blue-footed booby*
Mordvinoff, Nicolas. *Coral Island*
Olson, Arielle North. *The lighthouse keeper's daughter*
Round, Graham. *Hangdog*
Steig, William. *Abel's Island*
Rotten island

Israel *see* Foreign lands – Israel

Italy *see* Foreign lands – Italy

Jail *see* Prisons

Japan *see* Foreign lands – Japan

Japanese-Americans *see* Ethnic groups in the U.S. – Japanese-Americans

Jealousy *see* Emotions – envy, jealousy; Sibling rivalry

Jesters *see* Clowns, jesters

Jewish culture

Adler, David A. *The children of Chelm*
The house on the roof
A picture book of Hanukkah
A picture book of Israel
A picture book of Jewish holidays
A picture book of Passover
Aleichem, Sholem. *Hanukah money*
Aronin, Ben. *The secret of the Sabbath fish*
Auerbach, Julie Jaslow. *Everything's
changing - It's pesach!*
Bayar, Steven. *Rachel and Mischa*
Behrens, June. *Passover*
Bogot, Howard. *I'm growing*
Burstein, Chaya M. *Joseph and Anna's time
capsule*
Caseley, Judith. *When Grandpa came to stay*
Chaikin, Miriam. *Esther*
Exodus
Chanover, Hyman. *Happy Hanukah
everybody*
Chapman, Carol. *The tale of Meshka the
Kvetch*
A child's picture English-Hebrew dictionary
Cohen, Barbara. *Even higher*
Gooseberries to oranges
Here come the Purim players!
Cone, Molly. *The Jewish Sabbath*
Coopersmith, Jerome. *A Chanukah fable
for Christmas*
Corwin, Judith Hoffman. *Jewish holiday
fun*
Eisenberg, Phyllis Rose. *A mitzvah is
something special*
Fass, David E. *The shofar that lost its voice*
Fassler, Joan. *My grandpa died today*
Fisher, Aileen. *My first Hanukkah book*
Freedman, Florence B. *Brothers*
Ganz, Yaffa. *The story of Mimmy and
Simmy*
Gellman, Ellie. *It's Chanukah!*
It's Rosh Hashanah!
Shai's Shabbat walk
Gershator, Phillis. *Honi and his magic circle*
Goffstein, M. B. (Marilyn Brooke). *Goldie
the dollmaker*
Laughing latkes
Goldin, Barbara Diamond. *Just enough is
plenty*
Greene, Jacqueline Dembar. *Butchers and
bakers, rabbis and kings*
Groner, Judyth. *My very own Jewish
community*
Where is the Afikomen?
Gross, Michael. *The fable of the fig tree*
Harvey, Brett. *Immigrant girl*
Hirsh, Marilyn. *Captain Jiri and Rabbi
Jacob*
Could anything be worse?
I love Hanukkah

I love Passover
Joseph who loved the Sabbath
One little goat
The pink suit
Potato pancakes all around
The Rabbi and the twenty-nine witches
Where is Yonkela?
Hutton, Warwick. *Moses in the bulrushes*
Karlinsky, Ruth Schild. *My first book of
Mitzvos*
Levitin, Sonia. *A sound to remember*
Levoy, Myron. *The Hanukkah of
Great-Uncle Otto*
Levy, Sara G. *Mother Goose rhymes for
Jewish children*
Lisowski, Gabriel. *How Tevye became a
milkman*
Livingston, Myra Cohn. *Poems for Jewish
holidays*
McDermott, Beverly Brodsky. *The Golem*
Margalit, Avishai. *The Hebrew alphabet
book*
On the little hearth
Patterson, José. *Mazal-Tov*
Phillips, Mildred. *The sign in Mendel's
window*
Portnoy, Mindy Avra. *Ima on the Bima*
Rosen, Anne. *A family Passover*
Schwartz, Amy. *Mrs. Moskowitz and the
Sabbath candlesticks*
Yossel Zissel and the wisdom of Chelm
Segal, Lore. *Tell me a Mitzi*
Tell me a Trudy
Segal, Sheila. *Joshua's dream*
Sherman, Eileen Bluestone. *The odd potato*
Shostak, Myra. *Rainbow candles*
Shulevitz, Uri. *The magician*
Sugarman, Joan G. *Inside the Synagogue*
Suhl, Yuri. *Simon Boom gives a wedding*
Weilerstein, Sadie Rose. *The best of
K'tonton*
Wikler, Madeline. *Let's build a Sukkah*
My first seder
The Purim parade
Zalben, Jane Breskin. *Beni's first Chanukah*
Zemach, Margot. *It could always be worse*
Zola, Meguido. *The dream of promise*
Zusman, Evelyn. *The Passover parrot*

Jobs *see* Careers

Jokes *see* Riddles

Judges *see* Careers – judges

Jumping *see* Activities – jumping

Jungle

Aardema, Verna. *Rabbit makes a monkey of
lion*

Aitken, Amy. *Kate and Mona in the jungle*
Booth, Eugene. *In the jungle*
Catchpole, Clive. *Jungles*
Corddry, Thomas I. *Kibby's big feat*
Drescher, Henrik. *The yellow umbrella*
Hadithi, Mwenye. *Tricky tortoise*
Kemp, Anthea. *Mr. Percy's magic greenhouse*
Lilly, Kenneth. *Animals in the jungle*
Mahy, Margaret. *17 kings and 42 elephants*
Newsham, Ian. *Lost in the jungle*
Smith, Jim. *Nimbus the explorer*
Steig, William. *The Zabajaba Jungle*
Tafuri, Nancy. *Junglewalk*
Van Allsburg, Chris. *Jumanji*
Wood, John Norris. *Jungles*

Kangaroos *see* Animals – kangaroos

Kindness *see* Character traits – kindness

Kindness to animals *see* Character traits – kindness to animals

Kings *see* Royalty

Kinkajous *see* Animals – kinkajous

Kites

Ayer, Jacqueline. *Nu Dang and his kite*
Brown, Marcia. *The little carousel*
Cooper, Elizabeth K. *The fish from Japan*
Gerstein, Mordicai. *The mountains of Tibet*
Haseley, Dennis. *Kite flier*
Heller, George. *Hiroshi's wonderful kite*
Luenn, Nancy. *The dragon kite*
Peet, Bill. *Merle the high flying squirrel*
Rey, Margaret Elisabeth Waldstein. *Curious George flies a kite*
Ruthstrom, Dorotha. *The big kite contest*
Stilz, Carol Curtis. *Kirsty's kite*
Titus, Eve. *Anatole over Paris*
Uchida, Yoshiko. *Sumi's prize*
Wiese, Kurt. *Fish in the air*
Yolen, Jane. *The emperor and the kite*

Knights

Blake, Quentin. *Snuff*
Boutell, Clarence Burley. *The fat baron*
Bradfield, Roger. *A good night for dragons*
Carrick, Donald. *Harold and the giant knight*
Cressey, James. *The dragon and George*

Cretien, Paul D. *Sir Henry and the dragon*
De Paola, Tomie. *The knight and the dragon*
  The wonderful dragon of Timlin
Emberley, Ed. *Klippity klop*
Fradon, Dana. *Sir Dana - a knight*
Gerrard, Roy. *Sir Cedric rides again*
Goodall, John S. *Creepy castle*
Haley, Gail E. *The green man*
Hazen, Barbara Shook. *The knight who was afraid of the dark*
Holl, Adelaide. *Sir Kevin of Devon*
Hunter, Mollie. *The knight of the golden plain*
Ipcar, Dahlov. *Sir Addlepate and the unicorn*
Lasker, Joe. *A tournament of knights*
McCrea, James. *The story of Olaf*
Mayer, Mercer. *Terrible troll*
Nolan, Dennis. *The castle builder*
Peet, Bill. *Cowardly Clyde*
  How Droofus the dragon lost his head
Scarry, Huck. *Looking into the Middle Ages*
Trez, Denise. *The little knight's dragon*

Knitting *see* Activities – knitting

Koala bears *see* Animals – koala bears

Korea *see* Foreign lands – Korea

Lady birds *see* Insects – ladybugs

Ladybugs *see* Insects – ladybugs

Language

The all-amazing ha ha book
Baby's words
Baer, Edith. *Words are like faces*
Baker, Pamela J. *My first book of sign*
Battles, Edith. *What does the rooster say, Yoshio?*
Benjamin, Alan. *Rat-a-tat, pitter pat*
Berson, Harold. *A moose is not a mouse*
Bond, Michael. *Paddington and the knickerbocker rainbow*
Bossom, Naomi. *A scale full of fish and other turnabouts*
Bove, Linda. *Sign language ABC with Linda Bove*
Chaplin, Susan Gibbons. *I can sign my ABCs*

Charlip, Remy. *Handtalk*
  Handtalk birthday
Clifford, Eth. *A bear before breakfast*
Cohen, Caron Lee. *Three yellow dogs*
Day, Alexandra. *Frank and Ernest*
Dunham, Meredith. *Colors: how do you say it?*
  Numbers: how do you say it?
  Picnic: how do you say it?
  Shapes: how do you say it?
Ellentuck, Shan. *Did you see what I said?*
Folsom, Marcia. *Easy as pie*
Goodspeed, Peter. *Hugh and Fitzhugh*
Greenberg, Judith E. *What is the sign for friend?*
Gwynne, Fred. *A little pigeon toad*
Hawkins, Colin. *Tog the dog*
Hayward, Linda. *The Julian Messner picture dictionary of phonics*
Heller, Ruth. *Kites sail high*
Hill, Eric. *Spot's big book of words*
  Spot's first words
Hoban, Tana. *More than one*
Hunt, Bernice Kohn. *Your ant is a which*
Johnston, Johanna. *Speak up, Edie*
Krauss, Ruth. *A hole is to dig*
Krupp, Robin Rector. *Get set to wreck!*
Leaf, Munro. *Grammar can be fun*
Leeton, Will C. *The Tower of Babel*
Lionni, Leo. *Words to talk about*
McNaught, Harry. *Words to grow on*
Maestro, Betsy. *Camping out*
  On the go
Marks, Alan. *Nowhere to be found*
Moncure, Jane Belk. *Word Bird's fall words*
  Word Bird's spring words
  Word Bird's summer words
  Word Bird's winter words
Most, Bernard. *There's an ape behind the drape*
Parish, Peggy. *Amelia Bedelia*
  Amelia Bedelia and the surprise shower
  Amelia Bedelia goes camping
  Amelia Bedelia helps out
  Come back, Amelia Bedelia
  Good work, Amelia Bedelia
  Play ball, Amelia Bedelia
  Teach us, Amelia Bedelia
  Thank you, Amelia Bedelia
Preiss, Byron. *The first crazy word book*
Rand, Ann. *Sparkle and spin*
Richardson, Jack E. *Six in a mix*
Riddell, Edwina. *One hundred first words*
Root, Phyllis. *Gretchen's grandma*
Rose, Gerald. *The bird garden*
Sage, Michael. *If you talked to a boar*
Sattler, Helen Roney. *Train whistles*
Scarry, Richard. *Richard Scarry's best story book ever*
  Richard Scarry's biggest word book ever!

Sesame Street. *Sesame Street sign language fun*
  Sesame Street word book
Sherman, Ivan. *Walking talking words*
Simon, Seymour. *Turtle talk*
Snell, Nigel. *A bird in hand...*
Steig, William. *The bad speller*
Steptoe, John. *My special best words*
Terban, Marvin. *I think I thought*
Tester, Sylvia Root. *Never monkey with a monkey*
  What did you say?
Trân-Khánh-Tuyêt.*The little weaver of Thái-Yên Village*
Wells, Rosemary. *Max's first word*
  Max's ride
Wiesner, William. *The Tower of Babel*
Wildsmith, Brian. *What the moon saw*
Wood, Audrey. *Elbert's bad word*

Language, foreign *see* Foreign languages

Lapland *see* Foreign lands – Lapland

Lateness *see* Behavior – tardiness

Latvia *see* Foreign lands – Latvia

Laundry

Behrens, June. *Soo Ling finds a way*
Freeman, Don. *A pocket for Corduroy*
Ormondroyd, Edward. *Theodore*

Law *see* Careers – judges; Careers – police officers; Crime

Laziness *see* Character traits – laziness

Left and right *see* Concepts – left and right

Left-handedness

Lerner, Marguerite Rush. *Lefty, the story of left-handedness*

Legends *see* Folk and fairy tales

Lemmings *see* Animals – lemmings

Leopards *see* Animals – leopards

Leprechauns *see* Elves and little people

Letters

Bell, Norman. *Linda's airmail letter*
Brandt, Betty. *Special delivery*
Keats, Ezra Jack. *A letter to Amy*
Seuss, Dr. *On beyond zebra*

Librarians *see* Careers — librarians

Libraries

Alexander, Martha G. *How my library grew by Dinah*
Aliki. *How a book is made*
Baker, Donna. *I want to be a librarian*
Bartlett, Susan. *A book to begin on libraries*
Bauer, Caroline Feller. *Too many books!*
Baugh, Dolores M. *Let's take a trip*
Bonsall, Crosby Newell. *Tell me some more*
Charles, Donald. *Calico Cat meets bookworm*
Daly, Maureen. *Patrick visits the library*
Daugherty, James Henry. *Andy and the lion*
Demarest, Chris L. *Clemens' kingdom*
De Paola, Tomie. *The knight and the dragon*
Felt, Sue. *Rosa-too-little*
Freeman, Don. *Quiet! There's a canary in the library*
Furtado, Jo. *Sorry, Miss Folio!*
Gay, Zhenya. *Look!*
Gibbons, Gail. *Check it out!*
Levinson, Nancy Smiler. *Clara and the bookwagon*
Levy, Elizabeth. *Something queer at the library*
Lewis, Robin Baird. *Aunt Armadillo*
Little, Mary E. *ABC for the library*
  Ricardo and the puppets
Radlauer, Ruth Shaw. *Molly at the library*
Rockwell, Anne F. *I like the library*
Sadler, Marilyn. *Alistair in outer space*
Sauer, Julia Lina. *Mike's house*
Tudor, Tasha. *Mildred and the mummy*

Lighthouses

Armitage, Ronda. *The lighthouse keeper's lunch*
Barker, Melvern J. *Little island star*
Myrick, Mildred. *The secret three*
Olson, Arielle North. *The lighthouse keeper's daughter*
Strahl, Rudi. *Sandman in the lighthouse*
Swift, Hildegarde Hoyt. *The little red lighthouse and the great gray bridge*

Lightning bugs *see* Insects — fireflies

Lights

Baisch, Cris. *When the lights went out*
Crews, Donald. *Light*

Lions *see* Animals — lions

Lithuania *see* Foreign lands — Lithuania

Little people *see* Elves and little people

Littleness *see* Character traits — smallness

Lizards *see* Reptiles — lizards

Llamas *see* Animals — llamas

Lobsters *see* Crustacea

Loneliness *see* Emotions — loneliness

Losing things *see* Behavior — losing things

Lost *see* Behavior — lost

Love *see* Emotions — love

Loyalty *see* Character traits — loyalty

Luck *see* Character traits — luck

Lying *see* Behavior — lying

Machines

Adkins, Jan. *Heavy equipment*
Baker, Betty. *Worthington Botts and the steam machine*
Baker, Eugene. *I want to be a computer operator*
Barton, Byron. *Machines at work*
Bate, Norman. *Vulcan*
  Who built the bridge?
  Who built the highway?
Baugh, Dolores M. *Let's take a trip*
Baynton, Martin. *Fifty and the fox*
  Fifty and the great race
  Fifty gets the picture
  Fifty saves his friend
Behn, Harry. *All kinds of time*
Benedictus, Roger. *Fifty million sausages*
Bradfield, Roger. *The flying hockey stick*
Brown, Margaret Wise. *The steamroller*
Burton, Virginia Lee. *Katy and the big snow*
  Mike Mulligan and his steam shovel
Calhoun, Mary. *Jack and the whoopee wind*
Climo, Lindee. *Clyde*
Cowcher, Helen. *Rain forest*
Cox, David. *Tin Lizzie and Little Nell*
D'Ignazio, Fred. *Katie and the computer*
Du Bois, William Pène. *Lazy Tommy pumpkinhead*
Fleishman, Seymour. *Too hot in Potzburg*
Gackenbach, Dick. *Dog for a day*

Geringer, Laura. *Molly's new washing machine*
Goor, Ron. *In the driver's seat*
Greene, Carol. *A computer went a-courting*
Henstra, Friso. *Wait and see*
Hill, Eric. *Spot goes to the farm*
Hoban, Tana. *Dig, drill, dump, fill*
Holl, Adelaide. *The ABC of cars, trucks and machines*
Hunter, Norman. *Professor Branestawn's building bust-up*
Hutchings, Tony. *Things that go word book*
Ipcar, Dahlov. *One horse farm*
Israel, Marion Louise. *The tractor on the farm*
Löfgren, Ulf. *The traffic stopper that became a grandmother visitor*
Lyon, David. *The brave little computer*
Matthias, Catherine. *I can be a computer operator*
Modell, Frank. *Skeeter and the computer*
Munsch, Robert N. *Jonathan cleaned up - then he heard a sound*
Neville, Emily Cheney. *The bridge*
Olney, Ross R. *Construction giants*
Farm giants
Retan, Walter. *The snowplow that tried to go south*
The steam shovel that wouldn't eat dirt
Rockwell, Anne F. *Big wheels*
Machines
Sadler, Marilyn. *Alistair's time machine*
Simon, Seymour. *Turtle talk*
Steadman, Ralph. *The little red computer*
Wolde, Gunilla. *Betsy and the vacuum cleaner*
Young, Miriam Burt. *If I drove a tractor*
Zaffo, George J. *The giant nursery book of things that work*

Magic

Alexander, Martha G. *The magic box*
The magic hat
3 magic flip books
Alexander, Sue. *Marc the Magnificent*
Aliki. *The wish workers*
Andersen, H. C. (Hans Christian). *The tinderbox*, ill. by Warwick Hutton
The wild swans, ill. by Angela Barrett
The wild swans, ill. by Susan Jeffers
Anderson, Joy. *Juma and the magic Jinn*
Anderson, Lonzo. *Two hundred rabbits*
Anderson, Robin. *Sinabouda Lily*
Arabian Nights. *The flying carpet*
Armitage, Ronda. *The bossing of Josie*
Arnold, Tim. *The winter mittens*
Babbitt, Samuel F. *The forty-ninth magician*
Bach, Othello. *Hector McSnector and the mail-order Christmas witch*
Lilly, Willy and the mail-order witch

Balian, Lorna. *Humbug potion*
Baningan, Sharon Stearns. *Circus magic*
Barber, Antonia. *The enchanter's daughter*
Satchelmouse and the dinosaurs
Bass, Donna. *The tale of the dark crystal*
Baumann, Hans. *Chip has many brothers*
Beisner, Monika. *Secret spells and curious charms*
Bell, Anthea. *Swan Lake*
Berenstain, Stan. *The Berenstain bears and the sitter*
Berson, Harold. *Charles and Claudine*
The thief who hugged a moonbeam
Beskow, Elsa Maartman. *Peter in Blueberry Land*
Peter's adventures in Blueberry land
Bianco, Margery Williams. *The velveteen rabbit*, ill. by Allen Atkinson
The velveteen rabbit, ill. by Michael Green
The velveteen rabbit, ill. by Michael Hague
The velveteen rabbit, ill. by David Jorgensen
The velveteen rabbit, ill. by William Nicholson
The velveteen rabbit, ill. by Ilse Plume
The velveteen rabbit, ill. by S. D. Schindler
The velveteen rabbit, ill. by Tien
Birrer, Cynthia. *The lady and the unicorn*
Blance, Ellen. *Monster and the magic umbrella*
Boujon, Claude. *The fairy with the long nose*
Bowden, Joan Chase. *Who took the top hat trick?*
Boyle, Vere. *Beauty and the beast*
Brandenberg, Franz. *Leo and Emily*
Brenner, Barbara. *The flying patchwork quilt*
Bridwell, Norman. *The witch grows up*
Bright, Robert. *Georgie and the magician*
Brown, Abbie Farwell. *Under the rowan tree*
Brown, Marcia. *Once a mouse...*
Brunhoff, Laurent de. *Babar the magician*
Buck, Pearl S. (Pearl Sydenstricker). *The dragon fish*
Buckaway, C. M. *Alfred, the dragon who lost his flame*
Buckley, Paul. *Amy Belligera and the fireflies*
Bunting, Eve. *The man who could call down owls*
Carlson, Natalie Savage. *Spooky and the ghost cat*
Spooky and the wizard's bats
Carter, Anne. *Beauty and the beast*, ill. by Binette Schroeder
Chapman, Carol. *Barney Bipple's magic dandelions*
Christelow, Eileen. *Olive and the magic hat*
Cleaver, Elizabeth. *The enchanted caribou*

Climo, Shirley. *The cobweb Christmas*
Coco, Eugene Bradley. *The wishing well*
Cole, Babette. *Nungu and the elephant*
  Prince Cinders
Cole, Joanna. *Bony-legs*
Colette. *The boy and the magic*
Conover, Chris. *The wizard's daughter*
Coombs, Patricia. *Dorrie and the amazing*
  magic elixir
  Dorrie and the blue witch
  Dorrie and the dreamyard monsters
  Dorrie and the museum case
  Dorrie and the weather-box
  Dorrie and the witch doctor
  Dorrie and the witch's imp
  Dorrie and the Witchville fair
  Dorrie and the wizard's spell
  Dorrie's magic
  The magic pot
  The magician and McTree
Cooper, Gale. *Unicorn moon*
Corbett, Scott. *Dr. Merlin's magic shop*
  The foolish dinosaur fiasco
  The great custard pie panic
Coville, Bruce. *The foolish giant*
  Sarah and the dragon
Degen, Bruce. *The little witch and the riddle*
Delton, Judy. *Brimhall turns to magic*
  Rabbit goes to night school
Demi. *Chen Ping and his magic axe*
  Liang and the magic paintbrush
De Paola, Tomie. *Big Anthony and the*
  magic ring
  Merry Christmas, Strega Nona
  Strega Nona
  Strega Nona's magic lessons
Dewey, Ariane. *Dorin and the dragon*
  The fish Peri
  The thunder god's son
Dines, Glen. *A tiger in the cherry tree*
Domanska, Janina. *Palmiero and the ogre*
Dukas, P. (Paul Abraham). *The sorcerer's*
  apprentice, ill. by Ryohei Yanagihara
The firebird, ill. by Moira Kemp
Flot, Jeannette B. *Princess Kalina and the*
  hedgehog
Frascino, Edward. *Nanny Noony and the*
  magic spell
Fuchshuber, Annegert. *The wishing hat*
Gackenbach, Dick. *Ida Fanfanny*
Gág, Wanda. *Nothing at all*
  The sorcerer's apprentice
Galdone, Paul. *The magic porridge pot*
Ginsburg, Mirra. *Striding slippers*
Glazer, Lee. *Cookie Becker casts a spell*
The good-hearted youngest brother
Graves, Robert. *The big green book*
  Two wise children
Greaves, Margaret. *The magic flute*
Green, Marion. *The magician who lived on*
  the mountain

Grimm, Jacob. *The donkey prince*, ill. by
  Barbara Cooney
The earth gnome, ill. by Margot Tomes
Rapunzel, ill. by Bernadette Watts
Rumpelstiltskin, ill. by Jacqueline Ayer
Rumpelstiltskin, ill. by Donna Diamond
Rumpelstiltskin, ill. by Paul Galdone
Rumpelstiltskin, ill. by John Wallner
Rumpelstiltskin, ill. by Paul O. Zelinsky
The seven ravens, ill. by Felix Hoffmann
The seven ravens, ill. by Lisbeth Zwerger
The six swans
Snow White, ill. by Trina Schart Hyman
Snow White, ill. by Bernadette Watts
Snow White and Rose Red, ill. by
  Adrienne Adams
Snow White and Rose Red, ill. by John
  Wallner
Snow White and Rose Red, ill. by
  Bernadette Watts
Snow White and the seven dwarfs, ill. by
  Chihiro Iwasaki
Guthrie, Donna. *The witch who lives down*
  the hall
Haley, Gail E. *Jack and the bean tree*
Haller, Danita Ross. *Not just any ring*
Haseley, Dennis. *The cave of snores*
Hastings, Selina. *The singing ringing tree*
Hazen, Barbara Shook. *The sorcerer's*
  apprentice
Hearn, Michael Patrick. *The porcelain cat*
Heide, Florence Parry. *Treehorn's treasure*
  Treehorn's wish
Heller, Linda. *Alexis and the golden ring*
Hiller, Catherine. *Abracatabby*
Himmelman, John. *Amanda and the magic*
  garden
Hochman, Sandra. *The magic convention*
Hoffman, Rosekrans. *Sister Sweet Ella*
Hoffmann, E. T. A. *The strange child*
Hooks, William H. *Moss gown*
Houghton, Eric. *The mouse and the*
  magician
Hunter, Mollie. *The knight of the golden*
  plain
Hutton, Warwick. *Beauty and the beast*
Isele, Elizabeth. *The frog princess*
Janosch. *Joshua and the magic fiddle*
  The magic auto
Jeschke, Susan. *Angela and Bear*
  Firerose
  Mia, Grandma and the genie
  Rima and Zeppo
Johnston, Tony. *The witch's hat*
Kemp, Anthea. *Mr. Percy's magic*
  greenhouse
Kennedy, Richard. *The porcelain man*
Kepes, Juliet. *The seed that peacock planted*
Kimmel, Margaret Mary. *Magic in the mist*
Knight, Hilary. *Hilary Knight's the owl and*
  the pussy-cat

Krahn, Fernando. *Amanda and the mysterious carpet*
Kroll, Steven. *The big bunny and the magic show*
 The candy witch
 Fat magic
Kumin, Maxine. *The wizard's tears*
Langstaff, John M. *The two magicians*
Laurin, Anne. *Perfect crane*
Leichman, Seymour. *The wicked wizard and the wicked witch*
Lindman, Maj. *Snipp, Snapp, Snurr and the magic horse*
Lipkind, William. *The boy and the forest*
 The magic feather duster
Lobel, Anita. *The troll music*
Lopshire, Robert. *It's magic*
Lorenz, Lee. *The feathered ogre*
Lussert, Anneliese. *The farmer and the moon*
McDermott, Gerald. *The magic tree*
MacDonald, George. *Little Daylight*
McLenighan, Valjean. *Three strikes and you're out*
 You can go jump
McPhail, David. *The magical drawings of Moony B. Finch*
Marie, Geraldine. *The magic box*
Mayer, Marianna. *The black horse*
 The little jewel box
Mayer, Mercer. *Mrs. Beggs and the wizard*
 A special trick
 Whinnie the lovesick dragon
Mendoza, George. *Henri Mouse, the juggler*
Moncure, Jane Belk. *Riddle me a riddle*
Muller, Robin. *The sorcerer's apprentice*
Nicoll, Helen. *Meg and Mog*
 Meg at sea
 Meg on the moon
 Meg's eggs
 Mog's box
Nolan, Dennis. *Wizard McBean and his flying machine*
Norby, Lisa. *The Herself the elf storybook*
Oksner, Robert M. *The incompetent wizard*
Ostheeren, Ingrid. *Jonathan Mouse*
Peet, Bill. *Countdown to Christmas*
 Jethro and Joel were a troll
Phumla. *Nomi and the magic fish*
Postma, Lidia. *The stolen mirror*
 The prince who knew his fate
Rockwell, Anne F. *The story snail*
 The wonderful eggs of Furicchia
Rogasky, Barbara. *The water of life*
Ronay, Jadja. *Ginger*
Rose, Anne. *Akimba and the magic cow*
Ross, Tony. *The enchanted pig*
Sachs, Marilyn. *Fleet-footed Florence*
Saddler, Allen. *The Archery contest*

Saunders, Susan. *A sniff in time*
Scott, Sally. *The magic horse*
Seeger, Pete. *Abiyoyo*
Shecter, Ben. *Emily, girl witch of New York*
Shulevitz, Uri. *The magician*
Sleator, William. *That's silly*
Slobodkin, Louis. *Magic Michael*
Snyder, Zilpha Keatley. *The changing maze*
Stanley, Diane. *The good-luck pencil*
Steig, William. *The amazing bone*
 Caleb and Kate
 Gorky rises
 Solomon the rusty nail
 Sylvester and the magic pebble
 Tiffky Doofky
Steptoe, John. *The story of jumping mouse*
Stevenson, James. *Yuck!*
Stubbs, Joanna. *With cat's eyes you'll never be scared of the dark*
Tempest, P. *How the cock wrecked the manor*
Thaler, Mike. *Madge's magic show*
Thayer, Jane. *Mr. Turtle's magic glasses*
Tom Tit Tot. *Tom Tit Tot*
Towle, Faith M. *The magic cooking pot*
Tresselt, Alvin R. *The world in the candy egg*
Trez, Denise. *Maila and the flying carpet*
Tune, Suelyn Ching. *How Maui slowed the sun*
Turkle, Brinton. *The magic of Millicent Musgrave*
Turska, Krystyna. *The magician of Cracow*
Ungerer, Tomi. *The hat*
Van Allsburg, Chris. *The garden of Abdul Gasazi*
Varga, Judy. *Janko's wish*
Waber, Bernard. *You're a little kid with a big heart*
Walt Disney Productions. *Walt Disney's Snow White and the seven dwarfs*
Wiesner, David. *The loathsome dragon*
Willard, Nancy. *The mountains of quilt*
Wright, Freire. *Beauty and the beast*
Wyler, Rose. *Spooky tricks*
Yaffe, Alan. *The magic meatballs*
Yolen, Jane. *Mice on ice*
 Sleeping ugly

Maids *see* Careers – maids

Mail *see* Letters

Mail carriers *see* Careers – mail carriers

Malaysia *see* Foreign lands – Malaysia

Manners *see* Etiquette

Mardi Gras

Lionni, Leo. *The greentail mouse*

Marionettes *see* Puppets

Markets *see* Stores

Marriage, interracial

Adoff, Arnold. *Black is brown is tan*

Marriages *see* Weddings

Math *see* Counting

May Day *see* Holidays — May Day

Meanness *see* Character traits — meanness

Measurement *see* Concepts — measurement

Mechanical books *see* Format, unusual — toy and movable books

Mechanical men *see* Robots

Mechanics *see* Careers — mechanics

Memorial Day *see* Holidays — Memorial Day

Mermaids *see* Mythical creatures

Merry-go-rounds

Ardizzone, Edward. *Paul, the hero of the fire*
Brown, Marcia. *The little carousel*
Charles, Robert Henry. *The roundabout turn*
Crews, Donald. *Carousel*
Leigh, Oretta. *The merry-go-round*
Martin, Bill (William Ivan). *Up and down on the merry-go-round*
Perera, Lydia. *Frisky*
Schneider, Elisa. *The merry-go-round dog*
Thomas, Art. *Merry-go-rounds*
Wildsmith, Brian. *Carousel*

Mexican-Americans *see* Ethnic groups in the U.S. — Mexican-Americans

Mexico *see* Foreign lands — Mexico

Mice *see* Animals — mice

Middle ages

Alexander, Lloyd. *The four donkeys*
Althea. *Castle life*
Arnold, Tedd. *Ollie forgot*
Azarian, Mary. *The tale of John Barleycorn or, From barley to beer*
Biro, Val. *The pied piper of Hamelin*
Bishop, Ann. *The riddle ages*
Carrick, Donald. *Harold and the great stag*
Cohen, Barbara. *Here come the Purim players!*
Coombs, Patricia. *The magician and McTree*
Cressey, James. *The dragon and George*
Dick Whittington and his cat. *Dick Whittington*, ill. by Edward Ardizzone
Dick Whittington, ill. by Antony Maitland
Dick Whittington and his cat, ill. by Marcia Brown
Dick Whittington and his cat, ill. by Kurt Werth
Fradon, Dana. *Sir Dana - a knight*
Gerrard, Roy. *Sir Cedric rides again*
Hazen, Barbara Shook. *The knight who was afraid of the dark*
Kahl, Virginia. *The Baron's booty*
The Duchess bakes a cake
Gunhilde and the Halloween spell
Gunhilde's Christmas booke
The habits of rabbits
Mayer, Mercer. *Whinnie the lovesick dragon*
Phillips, Louis. *The brothers Wrong and Wrong Again*
Scarry, Huck. *Looking into the Middle Ages*
Scarry, Richard. *Richard Scarry's Peasant Pig and the terrible dragon*
Storr, Catherine. *Robin Hood*
Tompert, Ann. *Charlotte and Charles*

Military *see* Careers — military

Mimes *see* Clowns, jesters

Miners *see* Careers — miners

Minks *see* Animals — minks

Minorities *see* Ethnic groups in the U.S.

Mirages *see* Optical illusions

Misbehavior *see* Behavior — misbehavior

Missions

Politi, Leo. *The mission bell*
Song of the swallows

Mist *see* Weather — fog

Mistakes *see* Behavior — mistakes

Misunderstanding *see* Behavior — misunderstanding

Mockingbirds *see* Birds – mockingbirds

Models *see* Careers – models

Moles *see* Animals – moles

Money

Allan, Ted. *Willie the squowse*
Armstrong, Louise. *How to turn lemons into money*
Arnold, Caroline. *What will we buy?*
Berenstain, Stan. *The Berenstain bears' trouble with money*
Brenner, Barbara. *The five pennies*
Brown, Marcia. *The little carousel*
Caple, Kathy. *The purse*
Heide, Florence Parry. *Treehorn's treasure*
Hoban, Lillian. *Arthur's funny money*
Kent, Jack. *Piggy Bank Gonzalez*
Maestro, Betsy. *Dollars and cents for Harriet*
A paper of pins
Rockwell, Anne F. *Gogo's pay day*
Rose, Anne. *As right as right can be*
Slobodkin, Louis. *Moon Blossom and the golden penny*
Turkle, Brinton. *Rachel and Obadiah*
Vincent, Gabrielle. *Bravo, Ernest and Celestine!*
Viorst, Judith. *Alexander, who used to be rich last Sunday*
Wondriska, William. *Mr. Brown and Mr. Gray*

Mongooses *see* Animals – mongooses

Monkeys *see* Animals – monkeys

Monsters

Alexander, Martha G. *The magic box*
  Maybe a monster
Allen, Martha Dickson. *Real life monsters*
Arnold, Caroline. *The terrible Hodag*
Axworthy, Anni. *Ben's Wednesday*
Babbitt, Natalie. *The something*
Bang, Molly. *Wiley and the hairy man*
Barden, Rosalind. *TV monster*
Bass, Donna. *The tale of the dark crystal*
Basso, Bill. *The top of the pizzas*
Benjamin, Alan. *1000 monsters*
Blance, Ellen. *Lady Monster has a plan*
  Lady Monster helps out
  Monster and the magic umbrella
  Monster and the mural
  Monster and the surprise cookie
  Monster at school
  Monster buys a pet
  Monster cleans his house
  Monster comes to the city
  Monster gets a job

  Monster goes around the town
  Monster goes to school
  Monster goes to the beach
  Monster goes to the circus
  Monster goes to the hospital
  Monster goes to the museum
  Monster goes to the zoo
  Monster has a party
  Monster, Lady Monster and the bike ride
  Monster looks for a friend
  Monster looks for a house
  Monster meets Lady Monster
  Monster on the bus
Brown, Marc. *Marc Brown's full house*
  Spooky riddles
Bunting, Eve. *Scary, scary Halloween*
Cameron, Ann. *Harry (the monster)*
Carey, Valerie Scho. *Harriet and William and the terrible creature*
Carrick, Malcolm. *I can squash elephants!*
Chapouton, Anne-Marie. *Billy the brave*
Chevalier, Christa. *Spence and the sleepytime monster*
Christian, Mary Blount. *Go west, swamp monsters*
  Swamp monsters
Ciardi, John. *The monster den*
Cohen, Barbara. *The demon who would not die*
Cohen, Caron Lee. *Whiffle Squeek*
Cohen, Daniel. *America's very own monsters*
Cohen, Miriam. *Jim meets the thing*
Cole, Joanna. *Monster manners*
Conger, Lesley. *Tops and bottoms*
Coombs, Patricia. *Dorrie and the dreamyard monsters*
  Molly Mullett
Craig, Helen. *The night of the paper bag monsters*
Crowe, Robert L. *Clyde monster*
Crowley, Arthur. *The boogey man*
Dahl, Roald. *Dirty beasts*
Delaney, M. C. *The marigold monster*
Demarest, Chris L. *Morton and Sidney*
Denton, Kady MacDonald. *Granny is a darling*
De Regniers, Beatrice Schenk. *Sam and the impossible thing*
Dillon, Barbara. *The beast in the bed*
Dinan, Carolyn. *The lunch box monster*
Dinosaurs and monsters
Dos Santos, Joyce Audy. *Henri and the Loup-Garou*
Drescher, Henrik. *Simon's book*
Eisenberg, Phyllis Rose. *Don't tell me a ghost story*
Fassler, Joan. *The man of the house*
Flora, James. *Leopold, the see-through crumbpicker*
Francis, Anna B. *Pleasant dreams*
Freedman, Sally. *Monster birthday party*

Gackenbach, Dick. *Harry and the terrible whatzit*
Mag the magnificent
Gág, Wanda. *The funny thing*
Galdone, Paul. *The monster and the tailor*
Gantos, Jack. *Greedy Greeny*
The werewolf family
Gilleo, Alma. *Learning about monsters*
Ginsburg, Mirra. *Ookie-Spooky*
Goodall, John S. *Creepy castle*
Goode, Diane. *I hear a noise*
Gorey, Edward. *The tunnel calamity*
Grant, Joan. *The monster that grew small*
Grindley, Sally. *Knock, knock! Who's there?*
Harshman, Terry Webb. *Porcupine's pajama party*
Hawkins, Colin. *Snap! Snap!*
Take away monsters
Haywood, Carolyn. *The king's monster*
Heide, Florence Parry. *A monster is coming! A monster is coming!*
Heller, Nicholas. *The monster in the cave*
Heyer, Marilee. *The forbidden door*
Howe, James. *There's a monster under my bed*
Hutchins, Pat. *The very worst monster*
Where's the baby?
Impey, Rose. *The flat man*
Scare yourself to sleep
Johnson, Jane. *Today I thought I'd run away*
Johnston, Tony. *Four scary stories*
Kahl, Virginia. *Giants, indeed!*
How do you hide a monster?
Kellogg, Steven. *The island of the skog*
The mysterious tadpole
Kimura, Yasuko. *Fergus and the sea monster*
Koelling, Caryl. *Mad monsters mix and match*
Krahn, Fernando. *The mystery of the giant footprints*
Kunnas, Mauri. *One spooky night and other scary stories*
Lerner, Sharon. *Follow the monsters!*
Lifton, Betty Jean. *Goodnight orange monster*
Logue, Christopher. *The magic circus*
McKee, David. *Two monsters*
McQueen, John Troy. *A world full of monsters*
Marshall, Edward. *Four on the shore*
Marshall, James. *Three up a tree*
Mayer, Mercer. *Little Monster at home*
Little Monster at school
Little Monster at work
Little Monster's alphabet book
Little Monster's bedtime book
Little Monster's counting book
Little Monster's neighborhood
Liza Lou and the Yeller Belly Swamp

Mrs. Beggs and the wizard
Terrible troll
There's a nightmare in my closet
Meddaugh, Susan. *Beast*
Memling, Carl. *What's in the dark?*
Minsberg, David. *The book monster*
Moore, Lilian. *See my lovely poison ivy, and other verses about witches, ghosts and things*
Mooser, Stephen. *Funnyman meets the monster from outer space*
Morris, Ann. *Eleanora Mousie in the dark*
Morris, Terry Nell. *Good night, dear monster!*
Mosel, Arlene. *The funny little woman*
Mueller, Virginia. *A Halloween mask for Monster*
Monster and the baby
Monster can't sleep
A playhouse for Monster
Murphy, Shirley Rousseau. *Valentine for a dragon*
Myers, Amy. *I know a monster*
Newsham, Wendy. *The monster hunt*
Niland, Deborah. *ABC of monsters*
Nixon, Joan Lowery. *Bigfoot makes a movie*
Paige, Rob. *Some of my best friends are monsters*
Parish, Peggy. *No more monsters for me!*
Zed and the monsters
Parker, Nancy Winslow. *Love from Aunt Betty*
Peck, Richard. *Monster night at Grandma's house*
Peet, Bill. *Cyrus the unsinkable sea serpent*
Pinkwater, Daniel Manus. *The Frankenbagel monster*
I was a second grade werewolf
Prelutsky, Jack. *The baby uggs are hatching*
Rockwell, Anne F. *Thump thump thump!*
Ross, David. *Gorp and the space pirates*
Space monster
Space Monster Gorp and the runaway computer
Ross, H. L. *Not counting monsters*
Ross, Tony. *I'm coming to get you!*
Towser and the terrible thing
Rudolph, Marguerita. *I am your misfortune*
Schroder, William. *Pea soup and serpents*
Seeger, Pete. *Abiyoyo*
Selsam, Millicent E. *Sea monsters of long ago*
Sendak, Maurice. *Seven little monsters*
Where the wild things are
Seymour, Peter. *What's at the beach?*
Sharmat, Marjorie Weinman. *Scarlet Monster lives here*
Smith, Janice Lee. *The monster in the third dresser drawer and other stories about Adam Joshua*

Solotareff, Grégoire. *The ogre and the frog king*
Steig, William. *Rotten island*
Steptoe, John. *Daddy is a monster...sometimes*
Stevens, Kathleen. *The beast in the bathtub*
Stevenson, James. *"Could be worse!"*
Taylor, Judy. *Dudley and the monster*
Turkle, Brinton. *Do not open*
Ungerer, Tomi. *The beast of Monsieur Racine*
Zeralda's ogre
Viorst, Judith. *My mama says there aren't any zombies, ghosts, vampires, creatures, demons, monsters, fiends, goblins, or things*
Wagner, Jenny. *The bunyip of Berkeley's Creek*
Wahl, Jan. *Dracula's cat*
Frankenstein's dog
Wallace, Daisy. *Monster poems*
Watson, Pauline. *Wriggles, the little wishing pig*
Whitlock, Susan Love. *Donovan scares the monsters*
Willis, Jeanne. *The monster bed*
Willoughby, Elaine Macmann. *Boris and the monsters*
Winthrop, Elizabeth. *Maggie and the monster*
Young, Ed. *The terrible Nung Gwama*
Zemach, Harve. *The judge*

Months of the year see Days of the week, months of the year

Moon

Alexander, Martha G. *Maggie's moon*
Asch, Frank. *Happy birthday, moon!*
Moon bear
Mooncake
Moongame
Asimov, Isaac. *The moon*
Balet, Jan B. *Amos and the moon*
Baylor, Byrd. *Moon song*
Berenstain, Stan. *The bears' almanac*
The Berenstain bears on the moon
Berger, Barbara Helen. *Grandfather Twilight*
Bess, Clayton. *The truth about the moon*
Branley, Franklyn M. *The moon seems to change*
What the moon is like
Brown, Margaret Wise. *Goodnight moon*
Wait till the moon is full
Carle, Eric. *Papa, please get the moon for me*
Cazet, Denys. *Christmas moon*
Coats, Laura Jane. *Marcella and the moon*
Come out to play

Dayrell, Elphinstone. *Why the sun and the moon live in the sky*
De Gerez, Toni. *Louhi, witch of North Farm*
De Paola, Tomie. *The Prince of the Dolomites*
De Regniers, Beatrice Schenk. *Willy O'Dwyer jumped in the fire*
Freeman, Mae. *The sun, the moon and the stars*
You will go to the moon
Fuchs, Erich. *Journey to the moon*
Gantschev, Ivan. *The moon lake*
Garelick, May. *Look at the moon*
Gay, Marie-Louise. *Moonbeam on a cat's ear*
Griffith, Helen V. *Alex remembers*
Hillert, Margaret. *Up, up and away*
Janosch. *Joshua and the magic fiddle*
King, Christopher. *The boy who ate the moon*
Levitin, Sonia. *Who owns the moon?*
Lewis, Claudia Louise. *When I go to the moon*
Lifton, Betty Jean. *The rice-cake rabbit*
Lussert, Anneliese. *The farmer and the moon*
McDermott, Gerald. *Anansi the spider*
Papagayo, the mischief maker
Manushkin, Fran. *Moon dragon*
Matura, Mustapha. *Moon jump*
Merrill, Jean. *Emily Emerson's moon*
Moche, Dinah L. *The astronauts*
Nicoll, Helen. *Meg on the moon*
Oakley, Graham. *The church mice and the moon*
Olsen, Ib Spang. *The boy in the moon*
Oxenbury, Helen. *Tom and Pippo see the moon*
Preston, Edna Mitchell. *Squawk to the moon, little goose*
Schweninger, Ann. *The man in the moon as he sails the sky and other moon verse*
Simon, Seymour. *The moon*
Sleator, William. *The angry moon*
Stevens, Cat. *Teaser and the firecat*
Stevenson, Robert Louis. *The moon*
Talbot, Toby. *A bucketful of moon*
Thaler, Mike. *Moonkey*
Thurber, James. *Many moons*
Turska, Krystyna. *The magician of Cracow*
Udry, Janice May. *The moon jumpers*
Ungerer, Tomi. *Moon man*
Vaughn, Jenny. *On the moon*
Wahl, Jan. *Cabbage moon*
Watson, Clyde. *Midnight moon*
Wildsmith, Brian. *What the moon saw*
Willard, Nancy. *The nightgown of the sullen moon*
Winter, Jeanette. *The girl and the moon man*

Wood, Audrey. *Moonflute*
Yamaguchi, Tohr. *Two crabs and the moonlight*
Ziegler, Ursina. *Squaps the moonling*

Moose *see* Animals — moose

Mopeds *see* Motorcycles

Morning

Anglund, Joan Walsh. *Morning is a little child*
Barbato, Juli. *From bed to bus*
Beach, Stewart. *Good morning, sun's up!*
Brown, Margaret Wise. *A child's good morning book*
 The quiet noisy book
Caldwell, Mary. *Morning, rabbit, morning*
Chorao, Kay. *The baby's good morning book*
Craig, M. Jean. *Spring is like the morning*
 What did you dream?
Dennis, Lynne. *Raymond Rabbit's early morning*
Dennis, Wesley. *Flip and the morning*
Dragonwagon, Crescent. *Katie in the morning*
Funakoshi, Canna. *One morning*
Harrison, David Lee. *Wake up, sun!*
Hill, Eric. *Good morning, baby bear*
Himler, Ronald. *Wake up, Jeremiah*
Kandoian, Ellen. *Under the sun*
Lapp, Eleanor. *In the morning mist*
McNulty, Faith. *When a boy wakes up in the morning*
Mann, Peggy. *King Laurence, the alarm clock*
Ormerod, Jan. *Sunshine*
Oxenbury, Helen. *Good night, good morning*
Polushkin, Maria. *Morning*
Ray, Deborah Kogan. *Fog drift morning*
Rogers, Paul. *Somebody's awake*
Shulevitz, Uri. *Dawn*
Tafuri, Nancy. *Early morning in the barn*
Tresselt, Alvin R. *Wake up, farm!*
Tworkov, Jack. *The camel who took a walk*
Westcott, Nadine Bernard. *Getting up*
Yabuki, Seiji. *I love the morning*
Ziefert, Harriet. *Good morning, sun! Say good night!*
Zolotow, Charlotte. *Something is going to happen*
 Wake up and good night

Mosquitoes *see* Insects — mosquitoes

Mother Goose *see* Nursery rhymes

Mothers *see* Family life — mothers

Mother's Day *see* Holidays — Mother's Day

Moths *see* Insects — moths

Motorcycles

Barrett, N. S. *Motorcycles*
Cave, Ron. *Motorcycles*
Cleary, Beverly. *Lucky Chuck*
Dickens, Frank. *Boffo*
McPhail, David. *Captain Toad and the motorbike*
Zimnik, Reiner. *The bear on the motorcycle*

Movable books *see* Format, unusual — toy and movable books

Moving

Adshead, Gladys L. *Brownies - they're moving*
Aliki. *We are best friends*
Asch, Frank. *Goodbye house*
Becker, Edna. *Nine hundred buckets of paint*
Berenstain, Stan. *The Berenstain bears' moving day*
Berg, Jean Horton. *The O'Learys and friends*
Bond, Felicia. *Poinsettia and her family*
Bottner, Barbara. *Horrible Hannah*
Brandenberg, Franz. *Nice new neighbors*
 What can you make of it?
Brown, Myra Berry. *Pip moves away*
Carter, Anne. *Molly in danger*
Clymer, Eleanor Lowenton. *A yard for John*
Cohen, Barbara. *Gooseberries to oranges*
DeLage, Ida. *The old witch finds a new house*
Felt, Sue. *Hello-goodbye*
Finsand, Mary Jane. *The town that moved*
Fisher, Aileen. *Best little house*
Graham, Bob. *First there was Frances*
Gretz, Susanna. *Teddy bears' moving day*
Hickman, Martha Whitmore. *My friend William moved away*
Hoff, Syd. *Who will be my friends?*
Hughes, Shirley. *Moving Molly*
Ilsley, Velma. *M is for moving*
Isadora, Rachel. *The Potters' kitchen*
Jennings, Michael. *The bears who came to breakfix*
Johnston, Tony. *The quilt story*
Jones, Penelope. *I'm not moving!*
Keats, Ezra Jack. *The trip*
Keyworth, C. L. *New day*
Komaiko, Leah. *Annie Bananie*
Lexau, Joan M. *The rooftop mystery*
Lobel, Arnold. *Ming Lo moves the mountain*
Lystad, Mary H. *That new boy*

Malone, Nola Langner. *A home*
Marshak, Samuel. *In the van*
Maschler, Fay. *T. G. and Moonie move out of town*
Milord, Sue. *Maggie and the goodbye gift*
Morris, Jill. *The boy who painted the sun*
Obrist, Jürg. *Fluffy*
O'Donnell, Elizabeth Lee. *Maggie doesn't want to move*
Provensen, Alice. *Shaker lane*
Rabe, Berniece. *A smooth move*
Rogers, Fred. *Moving*
Sandin, Joan. *The long way to a new land*
Schlein, Miriam. *My house*
Schulman, Janet. *The big hello*
Sharmat, Marjorie Weinman. *Gila monsters meet you at the airport*
  Mitchell is moving
  Scarlet Monster lives here
Shefelman, Janice. *Victoria House*
Sherrow, Victoria. *There goes the ghost*
Singer, Marilyn. *Archer Armadillo's secret room*
Stevenson, James. *No friends*
Strathdee, Jean. *The house that grew*
Tobias, Tobi. *Moving day*
Tsutsui, Yoriko. *Anna's secret friend*
Waber, Bernard. *Ira says goodbye*
Watson, Jane Werner. *Sometimes a family has to move*
Watson, Wendy. *Moving*
Wilhelm, Hans. *A new home, a new friend*
Ziefert, Harriet. *A new house for Mole and Mouse*
Zolotow, Charlotte. *Janey*

Mules *see* Animals – mules

Multi-ethnic *see* Ethnic groups in the U.S.

Multiple birth childen *see* Triplets; Twins

Muppets *see* Puppets

Museums

Aliki. *My visit to the dinosaurs*
Berenstain, Stan. *The Berenstain bears and the missing dinosaur bone*
Bjork, Christina. *Linnea in Monet's garden*
Blance, Ellen. *Monster goes to the museum*
Brown, Laurene Krasny. *Visiting the art museum*
Cohen, Miriam. *Lost in the museum*
Coombs, Patricia. *Dorrie and the museum case*
De Paola, Tomie. *Bill and Pete go down the Nile*
Fradon, Dana. *Sir Dana - a knight*
Freeman, Don. *Norman the doorman*
Gramatky, Hardie. *Hercules*

Hoff, Syd. *Danny and the dinosaur*
Kellogg, Steven. *Prehistoric Pinkerton*
Krementz, Jill. *A visit to Washington, D.C.*
Mayers, Florence Cassen. *Egyptian art from the Brooklyn Museum ABC*
  The Museum of Fine Arts, Boston ABC
  The Museum of Modern Art, New York ABC
  The National Air and Space Museum ABC
Munro, Roxie. *The inside-outside book of Washington, D.C.*
Papajani, Janet. *Museums*
Ross, Pat. *M and M and the mummy mess*
Simmonds, Posy. *Lulu and the flying babies*
Thayer, Jane. *Gus and the baby ghost*
Vincent, Gabrielle. *Where are you, Ernest and Celestine?*

Music

Abisch, Roz. *Sweet Betsy from Pike*
  'Twas in the moon of wintertime
Alexander, Cecil Frances. *All things bright and beautiful*
Alexander, Lloyd. *The truthful harp*
Alger, Leclaire. *Always room for one more*
  Kellyburn Braes
Ambrus, Victor G. *Mishka*
  The seven skinny goats
Arkin, Alan. *Black and white*
Ash, Jutta. *Wedding birds*
Atene, Ann. *The golden guitar*
Azarian, Mary. *The tale of John Barleycorn or, From barley to beer*
Bach, Othello. *Lilly, Willy and the mail-order witch*
Baker, Laura Nelson. *The friendly beasts*
  O children of the wind and pines
Bascom, Joe. *Malcolm's job*
Behn, Harry. *What a beautiful noise*
Bianco, Margery Williams. *The hurdy-gurdy man*
Boesel, Ann Sterling. *Sing and sing again*
  Singing with Peter and Patsy
Bolliger, Max. *The most beautiful song*
Bonne, Rose. *I know an old lady*, ill. by Abner Graboff
Bottner, Barbara. *Zoo song*
Botwin, Esther. *A treasury of songs for little children*
Boynton, Sandra. *Good night, good night*
Bring a torch, Jeannette, Isabella
Brown, Marc. *Play rhymes*
Brown, Margaret Wise. *The little brass band*
Bruna, Dick. *The orchestra*
Buffett, Jimmy. *The jolly mon*
Bulla, Clyde Robert. *The donkey cart*
Bunting, Eve. *The traveling men of Ballycoo*
Burningham, John. *Jangle twang*
  Trubloff
Carle, Eric. *I see a song*

Carryl, Charles Edward. *A capital ship*
Caseley, Judith. *Ada potato*
Cathon, Laura E. *Tot Botot and his little flute*
Causley, Charles. *Early in the morning*
Chanover, Hyman. *Happy Hanukah everybody*
Children go where I send thee
Clement, Claude. *The voice of the wood*
Coco, Eugene Bradley. *The fiddler's son*
Colette. *The boy and the magic*
Conover, Chris. *Six little ducks*
Count me in
Crespi, Francesca. *Little Bear and the oompah-pah*
Cummings, W. T. (Walter Thies). *The kid*
Dallas-Smith, Peter. *Trumpets in Grumpetland*
Dalton, Alene. *My new picture book of songs*
Delacre, Lulu. *Arroz con leche*
Dillon, Eilis. *The cats' opera*
Domanska, Janina. *Busy Monday morning*
Engvick, William. *Lullabies and night songs*
The farmer in the dell. *The farmer in the dell*, ill. by Kathy Parkinson
The farmer in the dell, ill. by Mary Maki Rae
The farmer in the dell, ill. by Diane Stanley
Flack, Marjorie. *The restless robin*
Fleischman, Paul. *Rondo in C*
Freeman, Lydia. *Pet of the Met*
The friendly beasts and A partridge in a pear tree
A frog he would a-wooing go (folk-song). *Froggie went a-courting*, ill. by Chris Conover
Glazer, Tom. *Do your ears hang low?*
Eye winker, Tom Tinker, chin chopper
On top of spaghetti
Go tell Aunt Rhody. *Go tell Aunt Rhody*, ill. by Robert M. Quackenbush
Goffstein, M. B. (Marilyn Brooke). *A little Schubert*
Gomi, Taro. *Toot!*
Greaves, Margaret. *The magic flute*
Greene, Carol. *A computer went a-courting*
Hinny Winny Bunco
The thirteen days of Halloween
The world's biggest birthday cake
Grifalconi, Ann. *The toy trumpet*
Griffith, Helen V. *Georgia music*
Hale, Sara Josepha. *Mary had a little lamb*, ill. by Tomie de Paola
Haseley, Dennis. *The old banjo*
Hoban, Russell. *Emmet Otter's jug-band Christmas*
Horvath, Betty F. *Jasper makes music*
Hot cross buns, and other old street cries
Howe, Caroline Walton. *Teddy Bear's bird and beast band*

Hurd, Thacher. *Mama don't allow*
The pea patch jig
Hush little baby. *Hush little baby*, ill. by Aliki
Hush little baby, ill. by Jeanette Winter
Hush little baby, ill. by Margot Zemach
I sing a song of the saints of God
Ipcar, Dahlov. *The cat came back*
"The song of the day birds" and "The song of the night birds"
Isele, Elizabeth. *Pooks*
Ivimey, John William. *The complete story of the three blind mice*, ill. by Paul Galdone
The complete version of ye three blind mice
Janosch. *Joshua and the magic fiddle*
Tonight at nine
Johnston, Tony. *Pages of music*
Kahl, Virginia. *Droopsi*
Gunhilde's Christmas booke
Kapp, Paul. *Cock-a-doodle-doo! Cock-a-doodle-dandy!*
Keats, Ezra Jack. *Apartment 3*
The little drummer boy
Kepes, Juliet. *The seed that peacock planted*
Kimmel, Eric A. *Why worry?*
Komaiko, Leah. *I like the music*
Koontz, Robin Michal. *This old man*
Kovalski, Maryann. *Jingle bells*
The wheels on the bus
Krull, Kathleen. *Songs of praise*
Langstaff, John M. *Oh, a-hunting we will go*
Ol' Dan Tucker
On Christmas day in the morning
Soldier, soldier, won't you marry me?
The swapping boy
The two magicians
Lasker, David. *The boy who loved music*
Lear, Edward. *Edward Lear's nonsense book*
The pelican chorus
The pelican chorus and the quangle wangle's hat
Lenski, Lois. *At our house*
Davy and his dog
Davy goes places
Debbie and her grandma
A dog came to school
I like winter
I went for a walk
Levy, Elizabeth. *Something queer in rock 'n' roll*
Lionni, Leo. *Frederick*
Geraldine, the music mouse
Lobel, Anita. *The troll music*
Löfgren, Ulf. *The flying orchestra*
McCarthy, Bobette. *Buffalo girls*
McCloskey, Robert. *Lentil*
McMillan, Bruce. *The alphabet symphony*
Maiorano, Robert. *A little interlude*
Maril, Lee. *Mr. Bunny paints the eggs*

Mayer, Mercer. *The queen always wanted to dance*

Mills, Alan. *The hungry goat*

Mother Goose. *The Mother Goose songbook*, ill. by Jacqueline Sinclair

Mother Goose's rhymes and melodies, ill. by J. L. Webb

Sing hey diddle diddle

Thirty old-time nursery songs

Neale, J. M. *Good King Wenceslas*

Nelson, Esther L. *The funny songbook*

Holiday singing and dancing games

The silly songbook

Neumeyer, Peter F. *The phantom of the opera*

Newbolt, Henry John, Sir. *Rilloby-rill*

Newland, Mary Reed. *Good King Wenceslas*

Nichol, B. P. *Once*

Nussbaumer, Mares. *Away in a manger*

Old MacDonald had a farm. *Old MacDonald had a farm*, ill. by Mel Crawford

Old MacDonald had a farm, ill. by David Frankland

Old MacDonald had a farm, ill. by Abner Graboff

Old MacDonald had a farm, ill. by Tracey Campbell Pearson

Old MacDonald had a farm, ill. by Robert M. Quackenbush

Old MacDonald had a farm, ill. by William Stobbs

On the little hearth

Peek, Merle. *The balancing act*

Perrault, Charles. *Cinderella*, ill. by Emanuele Luzzati

Play and sing - it's Christmas!

Poston, Elizabeth. *Baby's song book*

Prokofiev, Sergei Sergeievitch. *Peter and the wolf*, ill. by Warren Chappell

Peter and the wolf, ill. by Barbara Cooney

Peter and the wolf, ill. by Frans Haacken

Peter and the wolf, ill. by Alan Howard

Peter and the wolf, ill. by Charles Mikolaycak

Peter and the wolf, ill. by Jörg Müller

Peter and the wolf, ill. by Josef Paleček

Peter and the wolf, ill. by Kozo Shimizu

Peter and the wolf, ill. by Erna Voigt

Quackenbush, Robert M. *Clementine*

The man on the flying trapeze

Pop! goes the weasel and Yankee Doodle

She'll be comin' 'round the mountain

Skip to my Lou

There'll be a hot time in the old town tonight

Raffi. *Down by the bay*

One light, one sun

Shake my sillies out

Wheels on the bus

Raposo, Joe. *The Sesame Street song book*

Rey, Hans Augusto. *Humpty Dumpty and other Mother Goose songs*

Robbins, Ruth. *Baboushka and the three kings*

Root, Phyllis. *Soup for supper*

Rounds, Glen. *The boll weevil*

Casey Jones

The strawberry roan

Sweet Betsy from Pike

Schaaf, Peter. *The violin close up*

Schackburg, Richard. *Yankee Doodle*

Schick, Eleanor. *One summer night*

A piano for Julie

Scholey, Arthur. *Baboushka*

Seeger, Pete. *The foolish frog*

Sendak, Maurice. *Maurice Sendak's Really Rosie*

Singer, Marilyn. *Will you take me to town on strawberry day?*

Slobodkin, Louis. *Wide-awake owl*

Spier, Peter. *The Erie Canal*

Stadler, John. *Hector, the accordion-nosed dog*

Stapler, Sarah. *Trilby's trumpet*

Stecher, Miriam B. *Max, the music-maker*

Steig, William. *Roland, the minstrel pig*

Stern, Elsie-Jean. *Wee Robin's Christmas song*

Stevenson, James. *Clams can't sing*

Taylor, Mark. *The bold fisherman*

Old Blue, you good dog you

Thomas, Ianthe. *Willie blows a mean horn*

Titus, Eve. *Anatole and the piano*

Anatole and the Pied Piper

Tudor, Tasha. *Junior's tune*

Tusa, Tricia. *Miranda*

The twelve days of Christmas. English folk song. *Brian Wildsmith's The twelve days of Christmas*

Jack Kent's twelve days of Christmas

The twelve days of Christmas, ill. by Jan Brett

The twelve days of Christmas, ill. by Ilonka Karasz

The twelve days of Christmas, ill. by Erika Schneider

The twelve days of Christmas, ill. by Sophie Windham

Vaughan, Marcia K. *Wombat stew*

Vincent, Gabrielle. *Bravo, Ernest and Celestine!*

Wallner, John. *Old MacDonald had a farm*

Walter, Mildred Pitts. *Ty's one-man band*

Watson, Clyde. *Father Fox's feast of songs*

Fisherman lullabies

Weiss, Nicki. *If you're happy and you know it*

Wenning, Elisabeth. *The Christmas mouse*

What a morning!

Wheeler, Opal. *Sing in praise*
Sing Mother Goose
Widdecombe Fair
Williams, Vera B. *Music, music for everyone*
Winter, Jeanette. *The girl and the moon man*
Wolkstein, Diane. *The banza*
Yolen, Jane. *The lullaby songbook*
Yulya. *Bears are sleeping*
Zemach, Harve. *Mommy, buy me a China doll*
Zimelman, Nathan. *To sing a song as big as Ireland*

Musical instruments *see* Music

Muskrats *see* Animals – muskrats

Mysteries *see* Problem solving

Mythical creatures

Ahlberg, Janet. *Jeremiah in the dark wood*
Andersen, H. C. (Hans Christian). *The little mermaid*, ill. by Edward Frascino
The little mermaid, ill. by Chihiro Iwasaki
The little mermaid, ill. by Dorothy Pulis Lathrop
The little mermaid, ill. by Josef Paleček
The little mermaid, ill. by Daniel San Souci
Aruego, José. *The king and his friends*
Asbjørnsen, P. C. (Peter Christen). *The three billy goats Gruff*, ill. by Marcia Brown
Three billy goats Gruff, ill. by Tom Dunnington
The three billy goats Gruff, ill. by Paul Galdone
The three billy goats Gruff, ill. by Janet Stevens
The three billy goats Gruff, ill. by William Stobbs
Aulaire, Ingri Mortenson d'. *The terrible troll-bird*
Birrer, Cynthia. *The lady and the unicorn*
Cooper, Gale. *Unicorn moon*
Cooper, Susan. *The Selkie girl*
Coville, Bruce. *Sarah and the dragon*
Sarah's unicorn
Dallas-Smith, Peter. *Trumpets in Grumpetland*
Decker, Dorothy W. *Stripe and the merbear*
Elzbieta. *Dikou the little troon who walks at night*
Fisher, Leonard Everett. *Pyramid of the sun, pyramid of the moon*
Theseus and the minotaur
Foreman, Michael. *Panda and the bushfire*
Freeman, Jean Todd. *Cynthia and the unicorn*
Gilleo, Alma. *Learning about monsters*
Gramatky, Hardie. *Nikos and the sea god*

Hague, Michael. *Michael Hague's world of unicorns*
Heyer, Marilee. *The forbidden door*
Hillert, Margaret. *The three goats*
Howe, James. *How the Ewoks saved the trees*
Ipcar, Dahlov. *Sir Addlepate and the unicorn*
Keeshan, Robert. *She loves me, she loves me not*
Lorenz, Lee. *The feathered ogre*
Malnig, Anita. *The big strawberry book of questions and answers and facts and things*
Mayer, Marianna. *The unicorn and the lake*
Mayer, Mercer. *Terrible troll*
Moeri, Louise. *The unicorn and the plow*
Munthe, Adam John. *I believe in unicorns*
Noble, Trinka Hakes. *Hansy's mermaid*
Oram, Hiawyn. *Jenna and the troublemaker*
Peet, Bill. *Cyrus the unsinkable sea serpent*
Jethro and Joel were a troll
No such things
The pinkish, purplish, bluish egg
Robb, Brian. *My grandmother's djinn*
Rockwell, Anne F. *Buster and the bogeyman*
Schroder, William. *Pea soup and serpents*
Small, David. *Paper John*
Solotareff, Grégoire. *Never trust an ogre*
Spang, Günter. *Clelia and the little mermaid*
Todaro, John. *Phillip the flower-eating phoenix*
Wagner, Jenny. *The bunyip of Berkeley's Creek*

Nagging *see* Behavior – nagging

Names

Ackerman, Karen. *Flannery Row*
Alexander, Martha G. *Sabrina*
Bayer, Jane. *A my name is Alice*
Beim, Jerrold. *The smallest boy in the class*
Benton, Robert. *Little brother, no more*
Browner, Richard. *Everyone has a name*
Cross, Diana Harding. *Some birds have funny names*
Some plants have funny names
Davis, Gibbs. *The other Emily*
De Paola, Tomie. *Andy (that's my name)*
Dragonwagon, Crescent. *Wind Rose*
Goffstein, M. B. (Marilyn Brooke). *School of names*
Hogan, Inez. *About Nono, the baby elephant*

Lester, Helen. *A porcupine named Fluffy*
Low, Joseph. *Adam's book of odd creatures*
McKee, David. *Two can toucan*
Mosel, Arlene. *Tikki Tikki Tembo*
Norman, Howard. *Who-Paddled-Backward-With-Trout*
Parish, Peggy. *Little Indian*
Peterson, Scott K. *What's your name?*
Raskin, Ellen. *A & the*
Rice, Eve. *Ebbie*
Tom Tit Tot. *Tom Tit Tot*
Vreeken, Elizabeth. *The boy who would not say his name*
Waber, Bernard. *But names will never hurt me*
Williams, Jay. *I wish I had another name*
Wold, Jo Anne. *Tell them my name is Amanda*
Wolf, Janet. *Adelaide to Zeke*

Napping see Sleep

Native Americans see Eskimos; Indians of North America

Nature

Ayres, Pam. *When dad cuts down the chestnut tree*
When dad fills in the garden pond
Baylor, Byrd. *I'm in charge of celebrations*
The other way to listen
Campbell, Rod. *Buster's afternoon*
Carter, Anne. *Molly in danger*
Scurry's treasure
Clay, Pat. *Ants*
George, William T. *Beaver at Long Pond*
Geraghty, Paul. *Over the steamy swamp*
Graham, Bob. *The wild*
Griffith, Helen V. *Georgia music*
Hands, Hargrave. *Bunny sees*
Hofer, Angelika. *The lion family book*
Hoopes, Lyn Littlefield. *Mommy, daddy, me*
Hurd, Edith Thacher. *Look for a bird*
Leach, Michael. *Rabbits*
Lewis, Naomi. *Swan*
Michels, Tilde. *Rabbit spring*
Neal, Ernest. *Badgers*
Norman, Charles. *The hornbean tree and other poems*
Parnall, Peter. *Apple tree*
Peters, Lisa W. *The sun, the wind and the rain*
Powzyk, Joyce. *Tasmania*
Radin, Ruth Yaffe. *High in the mountains*
Russell, Naomi. *The tree*
Ryder, Joanne. *Mockingbird morning*
Step into the night
Sarton, May. *A walk through the woods*
Schulz, Charles M. *Snoopy's facts and fun book about nature*

Seymour, Peter. *What's at the beach?*
Simon, Seymour. *Icebergs and glaciers*
The song of the Three Holy Children
Stone, Lynn M. *Endangered animals*
Tejima, Keizaburo. *Owl lake*
Ward, Leila. *I am eyes, ni macho*
Watts, Barrie. *Apple tree*
Wells, Rosemary. *Forest of dreams*
Wildsmith, Brian. *Seasons*
Wilson, Ron. *Mice*
Ziefert, Harriet. *Sarah's questions*
Zolotow, Charlotte. *Say it!*
The song
Zweifel, Frances. *Animal baby-sitters*

Needing someone see Behavior – needing someone

Neighborhoods see Communities, neighborhoods

New Guinea see Foreign lands – New Guinea

New Year's see Holidays – New Year's

Nicaragua see Foreign lands – Nicaragua

Night

Adoff, Arnold. *Make a circle, keep us in*
Ahlberg, Janet. *Funnybones*
Alexander, Anne. *Noise in the night*
Alexander, Martha G. *Maggie's moon*
We're in big trouble, Blackboard Bear
Aliki. *Overnight at Mary Bloom's*
Anrooy, Frans van. *The sea horse*
Aragon, Jane Chelsea. *Winter harvest*
Ardizzone, Aingelda. *The night ride*
Armitage, Ronda. *One moonlit night*
Arnosky, Jim. *Raccoons and ripe corn*
Artis, Vicki Kimmel. *Pajama walking*
Asch, Frank. *Moon bear*
Averill, Esther. *Jenny's moonlight adventure*
Axworthy, Anni. *Ben's Wednesday*
Aylesworth, Jim. *Tonight's the night*
Two terrible frights
Babbitt, Natalie. *The something*
Bannon, Laura. *Little people of the night*
Bennett, Rainey. *After the sun goes down*
Berends, Polly Berrien. *Ladybug and dog and the night walk*
Berenstain, Stan. *Bears in the night*
The Berenstain bears in the dark
Berg, Jean Horton. *The wee little man*
Blocksma, Mary. *Did you hear that?*
Bolliger, Max. *The fireflies*
Bond, Felicia. *Poinsettia and the firefighters*
Bonsall, Crosby Newell. *Who's afraid of the dark?*
Bourgeois, Paulette. *Franklin in the dark*

Bradbury, Ray. *Switch on the night*
Brandenberg, Franz. *A robber! A robber!*
Brown, Margaret Wise. *A child's good night book*
Night and day
Wait till the moon is full
Brown, Myra Berry. *Pip camps out*
Buckley, Paul. *Amy Belligera and the fireflies*
Budney, Blossom. *After dark*
Bunting, Eve. *Ghost's hour, spook's hour*
Burningham, John. *The blanket*
Callen, Larry. *Dashiel and the night*
Cass, Joan E. *The cat thief*
Chapouton, Anne-Marie. *Billy the brave*
Cole, Joanna. *Large as life nighttime animals*
Coles, Alison. *Michael in the dark*
Conford, Ellen. *Eugene the brave*
Cosgrove, Stephen. *Sleepy time bunny*
Credle, Ellis. *Big fraid, little fraid*
Crowe, Robert L. *Clyde monster*
DeLage, Ida. *The old witch and the crows*
Delton, Judy. *A walk on a snowy night*
Denton, Kady MacDonald. *Granny is a darling*
Dinardo, Jeffrey. *Timothy and the night noises*
Donaldson, Lois. *Karl's wooden horse*
Dragonwagon, Crescent. *Half a moon and one whole star*
When light turns into night
Duncan, Lois. *Horses of dreamland*
Duvoisin, Roger Antoine. *The missing milkman*
Emberley, Barbara. *Night's nice*
Erickson, Karen. *It's dark*
Erskine, Jim. *Bedtime story*
Fenner, Carol. *Tigers in the cellar*
Fisher, Aileen. *In the middle of the night*
Freeman, Don. *The night the lights went out*
Funakoshi, Canna. *One evening*
Garelick, May. *Sounds of a summer night*
Gay, Michel. *Night ride*
George, William T. *Beaver at Long Pond*
Ginsburg, Mirra. *The sun's asleep behind the hill*
Where does the sun go at night?
Goode, Diane. *I hear a noise*
Goodenow, Earle. *The owl who hated the dark*
Gretz, Susanna. *Hide-and-seek*
Too dark!
Grifalconi, Ann. *Darkness and the butterfly*
Hague, Kathleen. *Out of the nursery, into the night*
Hamilton, Morse. *Who's afraid of the dark?*
Hasler, Eveline. *Winter magic*
Hawkins, Colin. *Snap! Snap!*
Hazen, Barbara Shook. *The knight who was afraid of the dark*

Heine, Helme. *Three little friends: the alarm clock*
Highwater, Jamake. *Moonsong lullaby*
Hill, Susan. *Go away, bad dreams!*
Horwitz, Elinor Lander. *When the sky is like lace*
Howe, James. *There's a monster under my bed*
Hurd, Thacher. *A night in the swamp*
The quiet evening
Impey, Rose. *The flat man*
Scare yourself to sleep
Ipcar, Dahlov. *The cat at night*
"The song of the day birds" and "The song of the night birds"
Kandoian, Ellen. *Under the sun*
Kauffman, Lois. *What's that noise?*
Keats, Ezra Jack. *Dreams*
Kessler, Ethel. *Night story*
Koenig, Marion. *The wonderful world of night*
Kraus, Robert. *Good night little one*
Good night Richard Rabbit
Kunnas, Mauri. *The nighttime book*
Larrick, Nancy. *When the dark comes dancing*
Leaf, Munro. *Boo, who used to be scared of the dark*
Lesser, Carolyn. *The goodnight circle*
Lexau, Joan M. *Millicent's ghost*
Lifton, Betty Jean. *Goodnight orange monster*
Lindberg, Reeve. *Midnight farm*
Lionni, Leo. *When?*
Lloyd, Errol. *Nandy's bedtime*
Lyon, David. *The biggest truck*
McPhail, David. *Adam's smile*
The dream child
McQueen, John Troy. *A world full of monsters*
Martin, Bill (William Ivan). *Barn dance!*
Matus, Greta. *Where are you, Jason?*
Mayer, Mercer. *There's something in my attic*
You're the scaredy cat
Memling, Carl. *What's in the dark?*
Miles, Sally. *Alfi and the dark*
The moon's the north wind's cooky
Morris, Ann. *Cuddle up*
Eleanora Mousie in the dark
Kiss time
Night counting
Sleepy, sleepy
Murphy, Jill. *What next, baby bear!*
Nichol, B. P. *Once*
Peck, Richard. *Monster night at Grandma's house*
Peters, Sharon. *Animals at night*
Pittman, Helena Clare. *Once when I was scared*
Pizer, Abigail. *Harry's night out*

Preston, Edna Mitchell. *Monkey in the jungle*
Reidel, Marlene. *Jacob and the robbers*
Rice, Eve. *City night*
  Goodnight, goodnight
Rockwell, Anne F. *The night we slept outside*
Rowand, Phyllis. *It is night*
Rukeyser, Muriel. *More night*
Ryan, Cheli Durán. *Hildilid's night*
Ryder, Joanne. *The night flight*
  The snail's spell
  Step into the night
Rylant, Cynthia. *Night in the country*
Schlein, Miriam. *Here comes night*
Schneider, Nina. *While Susie sleeps*
Selsam, Millicent E. *Night animals*
Stanley, Diane. *Birdsong Lullaby*
Stepto, Michele. *Snuggle Piggy and the magic blanket*
Stevens, Cat. *Teaser and the firecat*
Stolz, Mary Slattery. *Storm in the night*
Strand, Mark. *The night book*
Stubbs, Joanna. *With cat's eyes you'll never be scared of the dark*
Tafuri, Nancy. *Do not disturb*
Taylor, Anelise. *Lights on, lights off*
Tejima, Keizaburo. *Owl lake*
Tobias, Tobi. *Chasing the goblins away*
Updike, David. *An autumn tale*
Van Allsburg, Chris. *The polar express*
Vevers, Gwynne. *Animals of the dark*
Wallace, Daisy. *Ghost poems*
Westcott, Nadine Bernard. *Going to bed*
Willard, Nancy. *Night story*
  The nightgown of the sullen moon
Winthrop, Elizabeth. *Potbellied possums*
Wolff, Ashley. *Only the cat saw*
Wood, Audrey. *Moonflute*
Yeomans, Thomas. *For every child a star*
Yolen, Jane. *Owl moon*
Zalben, Jane Breskin. *Norton's nighttime*
Ziefert, Harriet. *Hurry up, Jessie!*
  Say good night!
Zolotow, Charlotte. *I have a horse of my own*
  Wake up and good night
  When the wind stops
  The white marble

Nightingales see Birds – nightingales

Nightmares see Bedtime; Goblins; Monsters; Night; Sleep

No text see Wordless

Noah see Religion – Noah

Noise, sounds

Alexander, Anne. *Noise in the night*
Alexander, Martha G. *Pigs say oink*
Allard, Harry. *Bumps in the night*
Allen, Pamela. *Bertie and the bear*
Aylesworth, Jim. *Hush up!*
  Siren in the night
Bassett, Preston R. *Raindrop stories*
Behn, Harry. *What a beautiful noise*
Benjamin, Alan. *Rat-a-tat, pitter pat*
Berenstain, Stan. *Bears in the night*
Berg, Jean Horton. *The noisy clock shop*
  The wee little man
Blocksma, Mary. *Did you hear that?*
Bond, Felicia. *Poinsettia and the firefighters*
Borten, Helen. *Do you hear what I hear?*
Boynton, Sandra. *Moo, baa, lalala*
Brandenberg, Franz. *Cock-a-doodle-doo*
  A robber! A robber!
Branley, Franklyn M. *High sounds, low sounds*
Bright, Robert. *Georgie and the noisy ghost*
  Gregory, the noisiest and strongest boy in Grangers Grove
Brown, Margaret Wise. *The country noisy book*
  Five little firemen
  The indoor noisy book
  Noisy book
  The quiet noisy book
  The seashore noisy book
  SHHhhh . . . Bang
  The summer noisy book
  The winter noisy book
Burningham, John. *Cluck baa*
  Jangle twang
  Skip trip
  Slam bang
  Sniff shout
  Wobble pop
Carle, Eric. *My very first book of sounds*
Causley, Charles. *"Quack!" said the billy-goat*
Chukovsky, Korney. *Good morning, chick*
Cleary, Beverly. *The hullabaloo ABC*
Crowe, Robert L. *Tyler Toad and the thunder*
Dinardo, Jeffrey. *Timothy and the night noises*
Domanska, Janina. *Why so much noise?*
Duvoisin, Roger Antoine. *Petunia and the song*
Elkin, Benjamin. *The loudest noise in the world*
Emberley, Ed. *Sounds*
Evans, Mel. *The tiniest sound*
Farber, Norma. *There once was a woman who married a man*
Forrester, Victoria. *The magnificent moo*
Fowler, Richard. *Mr. Little's noisy car*

Friedman, Judi. *Noises in the woods*
Gaeddert, Lou Ann Bigge. *Noisy Nancy Nora*
Gannett, Ruth S. *Katie and the sad noise*
Garelick, May. *Sounds of a summer night*
Graham, John. *A crowd of cows*
Green, Suzanne. *The little choo-choo*
Hancock, Joy Elizabeth. *The loudest little lion*
Horvath, Betty F. *The cheerful quiet*
Hughes, Shirley. *Noisy*
Hutchins, Pat. *Good night owl*
Jaquith, Priscilla. *Bo Rabbit smart for true*
Kauffman, Lois. *What's that noise?*
Kelley, True. *Look, baby! Listen, baby! Do, baby!*
Kilroy, Sally. *Animal noises*
Noisy homes
Kline, Suzy. *Shhhh!*
Koenner, Alfred. *Be quite quiet beside the lake*
Kuskin, Karla. *All sizes of noises*
Roar and more
Leister, Mary. *The silent concert*
Lemieux, Michèle. *What's that noise?*
McCloskey, Robert. *Lentil*
McGovern, Ann. *Too much noise*
McNulty, Faith. *When a boy wakes up in the morning*
Madden, Don. *Lemonade serenade or the thing in the garden*
Martin, Bill (William Ivan). *Sounds around the clock*
Sounds I remember
Sounds of home
Sounds of laughter
Sounds of numbers
Massie, Diane Redfield. *The baby beebee bird*
Meyer, Louis A. *The clean air and peaceful contentment dirigible airline*
Miles, Miska. *Noisy gander*
Morrison, Sean. *Is that a happy hippopotamus?*
Murphy, Jill. *Peace at last*
Myller, Rolf. *A very noisy day*
Ogle, Lucille. *I hear*
Oxenbury, Helen. *I hear*
Panek, Dennis. *Detective Whoo*
Pickett, Carla. *Calvin Crocodile and the terrible noise*
Polushkin, Maria. *Who said meow?*, ill. by Giulio Maestro
Who said meow?, ill. by Ellen Weiss
Raskin, Ellen. *Who, said Sue, said whoo?*
Richter, Mischa. *Quack?*
Saltzberg, Barney. *It must have been the wind*
Scheffler, Ursel. *Stop your crowing, Kasimir!*
Seuss, Dr. *Mr. Brown can moo! Can you?*

Showers, Paul. *The listening walk*
Sicotte, Virginia. *A riot of quiet*
Skaar, Grace Marion. *What do the animals say?*
Slobodkin, Louis. *Colette and the princess*
Spier, Peter. *Crash! bang! boom!*
Gobble, growl, grunt
Stanley, Diane. *The conversation club*
Stapler, Sarah. *Trilby's trumpet*
Steiner, Charlotte. *Listen to my seashell*
Stevenson, James. *Clams can't sing*
Strand, Mark. *The planet of lost things*
Tafuri, Nancy. *Do not disturb*
Teal, Valentine. *The little woman wanted noise*
Thayer, Jane. *Quiet on account of dinosaur*
Voake, Charlotte. *Tom's cat*
Webb, Angela. *Sound*
Wheeler, Cindy. *Marmalade's nap*
Wildsmith, Brian. *Goat's trail*
Zalben, Jane Breskin. *Norton's nighttime*
Ziefert, Harriet. *Listen! Piggety Pig*
On our way to the barn
On our way to the forest
On our way to the water
On our way to the zoo
Zion, Gene. *Harry and the lady next door*
Zolotow, Charlotte. *The poodle who barked at the wind*

Norway *see* Foreign lands – Norway

Noses *see* Anatomy

Numbers *see* Counting

Nuns *see* Careers – nuns

Nursery rhymes

B. B. Blacksheep and Company
Barchilon, Jacques. *The authentic Mother Goose fairy tales and nursery rhymes*
Bartlett, Robert Merrill. *Jack Horner and song of sixpence*
Baum, L. Frank (Lyman Frank). *Mother Goose in prose*
Bayley, Nicola. *Nicola Bayley's book of nursery rhymes*
Blake, Pamela. *Peep-show*
Blake, Quentin. *Quentin Blake's nursery rhyme book*
Blegvad, Lenore. *Hark! Hark! The dogs do bark, and other poems about dogs*
Mittens for kittens and other rhymes about cats
This little pig-a-wig and other rhymes about pigs
Bodecker, N. M. (Nils Mogens). *"It's raining," said John Twaining*

Brian Wildsmith's Mother Goose
Carolyn Wells' edition of Mother Goose
Cats by Mother Goose, ill. by Carol
  Newsom
The Charles Addams Mother Goose
A child's book of old nursery rhymes
The Chinese Mother Goose rhymes
The city and country Mother Goose
Frank Baber's Mother Goose
The gay Mother Goose
The glorious Mother Goose, sel. by Cooper
  Edens
Grafa' Grig had a pig
*Gray goose and gander and other Mother
  Goose rhymes*
Gregory Griggs
Hey diddle diddle, ill. by Nita Sowter
Hey diddle diddle, ill. by Eleanor
  Wasmuth
Hey diddle diddle, and Baby bunting, ill. by
  Randolph Caldecott
Hey diddle diddle picture book, ill. by
  Randolph Caldecott
Hurrah, we're outward bound!
Hush-a-bye baby, ill. by Nicola Bayley
In a pumpkin shell
Jack and Jill, ill. by Eleanor Wasmuth
Jack Kent's merry Mother Goose
James Marshall's Mother Goose
Kate Greenaway's Mother Goose
Kitten rhymes
The Larousse book of nursery rhymes
Lavender's blue
Little boy blue
The little Mother Goose
London Bridge is falling down, ill. by Ed
  Emberley
London Bridge is falling down, ill. by
  Peter Spier
Mother Goose, ill. by Roger Antoine
  Duvoisin
Mother Goose, ill. by Miss Elliott
Mother Goose, ill. by C. B. Falls
Mother Goose, ill. by Gyo Fujikawa
Mother Goose, ill. by Vernon Grant
Mother Goose, ill. by Kate Greenaway
Mother Goose, ill. by Michael Hague
Mother Goose, ill. by Violet La Mont
Mother Goose, ill. by Arthur Rackham
Mother Goose, ill. by Frederick
  Richardson, 1915
Mother Goose, ill. by Frederick
  Richardson, 1976
Mother Goose, ill. by Gustaf Tenggren
Mother Goose, ill. by Tasha Tudor
Mother Goose and nursery rhymes
The Mother Goose book, ill. by Alice and
  Martin Provensen
The Mother Goose book, ill. by Sonia
  Roetter
Mother Goose house

Mother Goose in French
Mother Goose in hieroglyphics
Mother Goose in Spanish
Mother Goose melodies, facsimile of c.1833
  Muroe and Francis edition
Mother Goose nursery rhymes, ill. by
  Arthur Rackham, 1969
Mother Goose nursery rhymes, ill. by
  Arthur Rackham, 1975
Mother Goose rhymes, ill. by Eulalie M.
  Banks and Lois Lenski
The Mother Goose songbook, ill. by
  Jacqueline Sinclair
The Mother Goose treasury
Mother Goose's melodies, ill. by William A.
  Wheeler
Mother Goose's melody, facsimile of John
  Newbery's 1794 printing
Mother Goose's nursery rhymes, ill. by Allen
  Atkinson
Mother Goose's rhymes and melodies, ill. by
  J. L. Webb
Nursery rhyme book
Nursery rhymes, ill. by Douglas Gorsline
Nursery rhymes, ill. by Eloise Wilkin
*Nursery rhymes from Mother Goose in
  signed English*
The old woman in a shoe, ill. by Eleanor
  Wasmuth
*One I love, two I love, and other loving
  Mother Goose rhymes*
One misty moisty morning
The only true Mother Goose melodies
Over the moon
The piper's son, ill. by Emily N. Barto
A pocket full of posies
Pussy cat, pussy cat, ill. by Ferelith Eccles
  Williams
The rainbow Mother Goose
The real Mother Goose
The real Mother Goose clock book
*Richard Scarry's best Mother Goose
  ever*
*Richard Scarry's favorite Mother Goose
  rhymes*
Rimes de la Mere Oie
Ring o' roses
*The Sesame Street players present Mother
  Goose*
Sing a song of Mother Goose, ill. by
  Barbara Reid
Sing a song of sixpence, ill. by Randolph
  Caldecott; Barron's, 1988
Sing a song of sixpence, ill. by Randolph
  Caldecott; Hart, 1977
Sing a song of sixpence, ill. by Margaret
  Chamberlain
Sing a song of sixpence, ill. by Leonard
  Lubin
Sing a song of sixpence, ill. by Ray
  Marshall and Korky Paul

Sing a song of sixpence, ill. by Ferelith Eccles Williams
Sing hey diddle diddle
Songs for Mother Goose
The tall Mother Goose
Thirty old-time nursery songs
This little pig, ill. by Leonard Lubin
This little pig, ill. by Eleanor Wasmuth
This little pig went to market, ill. by L. Leslie Brooke
This little pig went to market, ill. by Ferelith Eccles Williams
The three jovial huntsmen, ill. by Susan Jeffers
The three little kittens, ill. by Lorinda Bryan Cauley
The three little kittens, ill. by Paul Galdone
The three little kittens, ill. by Dorothy Stott
The three little kittens, ill. by Shelley Thornton
To market! To market! ill. by Emma Lillian Brock
To market! To market! ill. by Peter Spier
Tom, Tom the piper's son, ill. by Paul Galdone
Twenty nursery rhymes
Willy Pogany's Mother Goose
The moving adventures of Old Dame Trot and her comical cat
Namm, Diane. *Favorite nursery rhymes*
Nursery rhymes, ill. by Gertrude Elliott
One, two, buckle my shoe, ill. by Rowan Barnes-Murphy
One, two, buckle my shoe, ill. by Gail E. Haley
Opie, Iona Archibald. *A family book of nursery rhymes*
A nursery companion
The Oxford nursery rhyme book
Puffin book of nursery rhymes
Tail feathers from Mother Goose
Over in the meadow, ill. by Paul Galdone
Palazzo, Tony. *Animals 'round the mulberry bush*
Patterson, Pat. *Hickory dickory duck*
Pearson, Tracey Campbell. *Sing a song of sixpence*
Peppé, Rodney. *Cat and mouse*
Hey riddle diddle
Petersham, Maud. *The rooster crows*
Potter, Beatrix. *Appley Dapply's nursery rhymes*
Beatrix Potter's nursery rhyme book
Cecily Parsley's nursery rhymes
The pudgy book of Mother Goose
Rey, Hans Augusto. *Humpty Dumpty and other Mother Goose songs*
Robbins, Ruth. *The harlequin and Mother Goose*
Scarry, Richard. *Richard Scarry's animal nursery tales*

Sendak, Maurice. *Hector Protector, and As I went over the water*
Simple Simon. *The adventures of Simple Simon*
Simple Simon, ill. by Rodney Peppé
The story of Simple Simon, ill. by Paul Galdone
Stearns, Monroe. *Ring-a-ling*
Stobbs, William. *This little piggy*
Tarrant, Margaret. *The Margaret Tarrant nursery rhyme book*
Nursery rhymes
Thomas, Katherine Elwes. *The real personages of Mother Goose*
Thomson, Pat. *Rhymes around the day*
Tucker, Nicholas. *Mother Goose abroad*
Watson, Clyde. *Father Fox's pennyrhymes*
Weil, Lisl. *Mother Goose picture riddles*
What do you feed your donkey on?
Wheeler, Opal. *Sing Mother Goose*
Williams, Jenny. *Here's a ball for baby*
One, two, buckle my shoe
Ride a cockhorse
Ring around a rosy
Williams, Sarah. *Ride a cock-horse*
Wood, Ray. *The American Mother Goose*
Fun in American folk rhymes

Nursery school *see* School

Nurses *see* Careers – nurses

Oceans *see* Sea and seashore

Octopuses

Barrett, John M. *Oscar the selfish octopus*
Brandenberg, Franz. *Otto is different*
Carrick, Carol. *Octopus*
Drdek, Richard E. *Horace the friendly octopus*
Heller, Ruth. *How to hide an octopus*
Kraus, Robert. *Herman the helper*
Most, Bernard. *My very own octopus*
Shaw, Evelyn S. *Octopus*
Ungerer, Tomi. *Emile*
Waber, Bernard. *I was all thumbs*

Oil

Freeman, Don. *The seal and the slick*
Ungerer, Tomi. *The Mellops strike oil*

Old age

Allard, Harry. *It's so nice to have a wolf around the house*
Ardizzone, Edward. *Lucy Brown and Mr. Grimes*
Benchley, Nathaniel. *Snip*
Briggs, Raymond. *Jim and the beanstalk*
Coats, Laura Jane. *Mr. Jordan in the park*
Delton, Judy. *My grandma's in a nursing home*
Edelman, Elaine. *Boom-de-boom*
Farber, Norma. *How does it feel to be old?*
Fassler, Joan. *My grandpa died today*
Fender, Kay. *Odette!*
Fink, Dale Borman. *Mr. Silver and Mrs. Gold*
Fox, Mem. *Wilfrid Gordon McDonald Partridge*
Gammell, Stephen. *Git along, old Scudder*
Goffstein, M. B. (Marilyn Brooke). *Fish for supper*
Griffith, Helen V. *Georgia music*
Grimm, Jacob. *The Bremen town musicians*, ill. by Donna Diamond
  The Bremen town musicians, ill. by Janina Domanska
  The Bremen town musicians, ill. by Paul Galdone
  Bremen town musicians, ill. by Josef Paleček
  The Bremen town musicians, ill. by Ilse Plume
  The horse, the fox, and the lion, ill. by Paul Galdone
  The musicians of Bremen, ill. by Svend Otto S.
  The musicians of Bremen, ill. by Martin Ursell
Guthrie, Donna. *Grandpa doesn't know it's me*
Hamm, Diane Johnston. *Grandma drives a motor bed*
Hazen, Barbara Shook. *Why did Grandpa die?*
Herriot, James. *Blossom comes home*
Hewett, Joan. *Rosalie*
Hoff, Syd. *Barkley*
Kahl, Virginia. *Maxie*
Keeping, Charles. *Molly o' the moors*
Kibbey, Marsha. *My grammy*
Klein, Leonore. *Old, older, oldest*
Knox-Wagner, Elaine. *My grandpa retired today*
Kunhardt, Dorothy. *Billy the barber*
Lasky, Kathryn. *Sea swan*
Lewis, J. Patrick. *The tsar and the amazing cow*
Littledale, Freya. *The snow child*
Nelson, Vaunda Micheaux. *Always Gramma*

Peet, Bill. *Smokey*
Pomerantz, Charlotte. *Buffy and Albert*
Seligson, Susan. *Amos*
Skorpen, Liesel Moak. *Old Arthur*
Slobodkina, Esphyr. *Billy, the condominium cat*
Snow, Pegeen. *Mrs. Periwinkle's groceries*
Sonneborn, Ruth A. *I love Gram*
Taber, Anthony. *Cats' eyes*
Taylor, Mark. *Old Blue, you good dog you*
Tusa, Tricia. *Maebelle's suitcase*
Uchida, Yoshiko. *Sumi's special happening*
Wittman, Sally. *A special trade*
Zolotow, Charlotte. *I know a lady*

Olympics *see* Sports – Olympics

Only child *see* Family life – only child

Opossums *see* Animals – possums

Opposites *see* Concepts – opposites

Optical illusions

Anno, Mitsumasa. *Anno's alphabet*
  Anno's counting book
  Anno's counting house
  Anno's flea market
  Anno's Italy
  Anno's journey
  Anno's magical ABC
  Dr. Anno's midnight circus
  Topsy-turvies
  Upside-downers
Baum, Arline. *Opt*
Doty, Roy. *Eye fooled you*
Emberley, Ed. *The Wizard of Op*
Gardner, Beau. *The look again...and again, and again, and again book*
  The turn about, think about, look about book

Optimism *see* Character traits – optimism

Orphans

Ardizzone, Edward. *Lucy Brown and Mr. Grimes*
The babes in the woods. *The old ballad of the babes in the woods*
Bemelmans, Ludwig. *Madeline*
  Madeline and the bad hat
  Madeline and the gypsies
  Madeline in London
  Madeline [pop-up book]
  Madeline's rescue
Bulla, Clyde Robert. *Poor boy, rich boy*
Goffstein, M. B. (Marilyn Brooke). *Goldie the dollmaker*
Graves, Robert. *The big green book*

Mahy, Margaret. *Sailor Jack and the twenty orphans*
Moore, Inga. *The vegetable thieves*
Thomas, Kathy. *The angel's quest*
Ungerer, Tomi. *The three robbers*

Ostracism *see* Character traits – being different

Ostriches *see* Birds – ostriches

Otters *see* Animals – otters

Out and in *see* Concepts – in and out

Owls *see* Birds – owls

Pack rats *see* Animals – pack rats

Painters *see* Activities – painting; Careers – artists

Painting *see* Activities – painting

Pakistan *see* Foreign lands – Pakistan

Panama *see* Foreign lands – Panama

Pandas *see* Animals – pandas

Panthers *see* Animals – leopards

Paper

Gibbons, Gail. *Deadline!*
 Paper, paper everywhere
Huff, Vivian. *Let's make paper dolls*
Milgrom, Harry. *Paper science*
Mitgutsch, Ali. *From wood to paper*
Small, David. *Paper John*
Testa, Fulvio. *The paper airplane*

Parades

Anderson, C. W. (Clarence Williams). *The rumble seat pony*
Brenner, Barbara. *The snow parade*
Bright, Robert. *Hurrah for Freddie!*
Chalmers, Audrey. *Parade of Obash*
Chalmers, Mary. *Easter parade*
Crews, Donald. *Parade*
Emberley, Ed. *The parade book*
Ets, Marie Hall. *Another day*
 In the forest
Feczko, Kathy. *Umbrella parade*

Flack, Marjorie. *Wait for William*
Holt, Margaret. *David McCheever's twenty-nine dogs*
Janice. *Little Bear marches in the St. Patrick's Day parade*
Joosse, Barbara M. *Fourth of July*
Kroll, Steven. *The goat parade*
Richter, Mischa. *Eric and Matilda*
Slobodkina, Esphyr. *Pezzo the peddler and the circus elephant*
Spier, Peter. *Crash! bang! boom!*
Ziner, Feenie. *Counting carnival*

Parakeets *see* Birds – parakeets, parrots

Park rangers *see* Careers – park rangers

Parrots *see* Birds – parakeets, parrots

Participation

Agostinelli, Maria Enrica. *I know something you don't know*
Barrett, Judi. *What's left?*
Bendick, Jeanne. *Why can't I?*
Bester, Roger. *Guess what?*
Black, Irma Simonton. *Is this my dinner?*
Booth, Eugene. *At the circus*
 At the fair
 In the air
 In the garden
 In the jungle
 Under the ocean
Brown, Marc. *Finger rhymes*
Brown, Margaret Wise. *The country noisy book*
 The indoor noisy book
 Noisy book
 The quiet noisy book
 The seashore noisy book
 The summer noisy book
 The winter noisy book
Cameron, Polly. *"I can't," said the ant*
Carroll, Ruth. *Where's the bunny?*
Charlip, Remy. *Fortunately*
Cole, William. *Frances face-maker*
Corbett, Grahame. *Guess who?*
 What number now?
 Who is hiding?
 Who is inside?
 Who is next?
Craig, M. Jean. *Boxes*
Crume, Marion W. *Let me see you try*
 Listen!
 What do you say?
De Regniers, Beatrice Schenk. *It does not say meow!*
Elting, Mary. *Q is for duck*
Emberley, Ed. *Ed Emberley's amazing look through book*
 Klippity klop

Ets, Marie Hall. *Just me*
   Talking without words
French, Fiona. *Hunt the thimble*
Garten, Jan. *The alphabet tale*
Glazer, Tom. *Do your ears hang low?*
   Eye winker, Tom Tinker, chin chopper
Heilbroner, Joan. *This is the house where Jack lives*
Hewett, Anita. *The tale of the turnip*
Hoban, Tana. *Look again*
   Where is it?
The house that Jack built. *The house that Jack built,* ill. by Seymour Chwast
Hutchins, Pat. *Good night owl*
Ipcar, Dahlov. *Lost and found*
Jaynes, Ruth M. *Benny's four hats*
Johnson, Ryerson. *Let's walk up the wall*
Kepes, Juliet. *Run little monkeys, run, run, run*
Kuskin, Karla. *Roar and more*
Löfgren, Ulf. *One-two-three*
MacGregor, Ellen. *Theodor Turtle*
Martin, Bill (William Ivan). *Brave little Indian*
Montgomerie, Norah. *This little pig went to market*
Ogle, Lucille. *I hear*
Paterson, Diane. *If I were a toad*
Patrick, Gloria. *This is...*
Seignobosc, Françoise. *The things I like*
Seuss, Dr. *Mr. Brown can moo! Can you?*
   Wacky Wednesday
Shaw, Charles Green. *It looked like spilt milk*
Siewert, Margaret. *Bear hunt*
Simon, Norma. *What do I say?*
Sivulich, Sandra Stroner. *I'm going on a bear hunt*
Skaar, Grace Marion. *What do the animals say?*
Skorpen, Liesel Moak. *All the Lassies*
Slobodkina, Esphyr. *Caps for sale*
   Pezzo the peddler and the circus elephant
   Pezzo the peddler and the thirteen silly thieves
Spier, Peter. *Crash! bang! boom!*
   Gobble, growl, grunt
Steiner, Charlotte. *Five little finger playmates*
Sutton, Eve. *My cat likes to hide in boxes*
Ueno, Noriko. *Elephant buttons*
Watanabe, Shigeo. *How do I put it on?*
Weil, Lisl. *Owl and other scrambles*
Yudell, Lynn Deena. *Make a face*

Parties

Adams, Adrienne. *The Christmas party*
   A Halloween happening
Allard, Harry. *The Stupids have a ball*
   There's a party at Mona's tonight

Anderson, Lonzo. *The Halloween party*
Asch, Frank. *Popcorn*
Averill, Esther. *Jenny's birthday book*
   Jenny's first party
Bible, Charles. *Jennifer's new chair*
Blance, Ellen. *Monster has a party*
Bonsall, Crosby Newell. *Twelve bells for Santa*
Bowden, Joan Chase. *The bear's surprise party*
Brandenberg, Franz. *The hit of the party*
Briggs, Raymond. *The party*
Brooke, L. Leslie (Leonard Leslie). *Johnny Crow's party*
Brown, Myra Berry. *Company's coming for dinner*
Chalmers, Mary. *Six dogs, twenty-three cats, forty-five mice, and one hundred sixteen spiders*
Claverie, Jean. *The party*
Cohen, Miriam. *Tough Jim*
Corey, Dorothy. *Will it ever be my birthday?*
Corwin, Judith Hoffman. *Birthday fun*
Crothers, Samuel McChord. *Miss Muffet's Christmas party*
DeLage, Ida. *The squirrel's tree party*
Du Bois, William Pène. *Bear party*
Ehrlich, Amy. *Bunnies at Christmastime*
Ets, Marie Hall. *The cow's party*
Feczko, Kathy. *Halloween party*
Freedman, Sally. *Monster birthday party*
Freeman, Don. *Corduroy's party*
   Dandelion
   The paper party
Gackenbach, Dick. *Annie and the mud monster*
Galdone, Joanna. *Honeybee's party*
Gay, Michel. *Bibi's birthday surprise*
Gendel, Evelyn. *Tortoise and turtle*
   Tortoise and turtle abroad
Glovach, Linda. *The Little Witch's birthday book*
Gordon, Margaret. *Wilberforce goes to a party*
Gordon, Shirley. *Happy birthday, Crystal*
Gould, Deborah. *Brendan's best-timed birthday*
Goyder, Alice. *Party in Catland*
Harshman, Terry Webb. *Porcupine's pajama party*
Heller, Nicholas. *The monster in the cave*
Hoff, Syd. *Henrietta's Halloween*
Hughes, Shirley. *Alfie gives a hand*
Hutchins, Pat. *The surprise party*
Hynard, Julia. *Percival's party*
Ichikawa, Satomi. *Nora's castle*
Janice. *Little Bear's New Year's party*
   Little Bear's pancake party
Jones, Penelope. *I didn't want to be nice*
Keats, Ezra Jack. *A letter to Amy*
Lazard, Naomi. *What Amanda saw*

Leedy, Loreen. *The dragon Halloween party*
Lenski, Lois. *A surprise for Davy*
Lillie, Patricia. *One very, very quiet afternoon*
Lipkind, William. *The Christmas bunny*
MacKay, Jed. *The big secret*
McNaughton, Colin. *At the party*
Marks, Burton. *The spook book*
Meyer, Elizabeth C. *The blue china pitcher*
Modell, Frank. *Ice cream soup*
O'Connor, Jane. *The Care Bears' party cookbook*
Oxenbury, Helen. *The queen and Rosie Randall*
Parish, Peggy. *Amelia Bedelia and the surprise shower*
Park, W. B. *The costume party*
Paterson, Bettina. *Bun's birthday*
Potter, Beatrix. *The sly old cat*
Prager, Annabelle. *The spooky Halloween party*
  The surprise party
Pryor, Bonnie. *Amanda and April*
Quackenbush, Robert M. *Detective Mole and the haunted castle mystery*
Quin-Harkin, Janet. *Helpful Hattie*
Redies, Rainer. *The cats' party*
Schertle, Alice. *Jeremy Bean's St. Patrick's Day*
Schweninger, Ann. *Birthday wishes*
Selkowe, Valrie M. *Spring green*
Stott, Rowena. *The hedgehog feast*
Vincent, Gabrielle. *Merry Christmas, Ernest and Celestine*
Wegen, Ron. *The Halloween costume party*
Wiseman, Bernard. *Morris has a birthday party!*
Worth, Bonnie. *Peter Cottontail's surprise*
Yolen, Jane. *Piggins*
Zimmer, Dirk. *The trick-or-treat trap*
Zion, Gene. *Jeffie's party*

Passover see Holidays – Passover

Patience see Character traits – patience

Peacocks see Birds – peacocks, peahens

Peahens see Birds – peacocks, peahens

Peddlers see Careers – peddlers

Pelicans see Birds – pelicans

Pen pals

Caple, Kathy. *Harry's smile*

Penguins see Birds – penguins

Perseverance see Character traits – perseverance

Persia see Foreign lands – Persia

Persistence see Character traits – persistence

Perspective see Concepts – perspective

Peru see Foreign lands – Peru

Petroleum see Oil

Pets

Aiken, Joan. *Arabel and Mortimer*
Alexander, Martha G. *No ducks in our bathtub*
Allard, Harry. *It's so nice to have a wolf around the house*
Allen, Jonathan. *My cat*
Allen, Marjorie N. *One, two, three - ah-choo!*
Ardizzone, Edward. *Diana and her rhinoceros*
Arnold, Caroline. *Pets without homes*
Asch, Frank. *The last puppy*
Atwood, Margaret. *Anna's pet*
Baldner, Gaby. *Joba and the wild boar*
Balian, Lorna. *Amelia's nine lives*
Bannon, Laura. *Watchdog*
Bare, Colleen Stanley. *Guinea pigs don't read books*
  To love a cat
  To love a dog
Barton, Byron. *Jack and Fred*
Baylor, Byrd. *Amigo*
Beatty, Hetty Burlingame. *Moorland pony*
Belpré, Pura. *Santiago*
Benchley, Peter. *Jonathan visits the White House*
Bishop, Claire Huchet. *The truffle pig*
Blackwood, Gladys Rourke. *Whistle for Cindy*
Blance, Ellen. *Monster buys a pet*
Blegvad, Lenore. *The great hamster hunt*
Bliss, Corinne Demas. *That dog Melly!*
Boegehold, Betty. *Pawpaw's run*
Brenner, Barbara. *The five pennies*
Brett, Jan. *Annie and the wild animals*
  The first dog
Brice, Tony. *The bashful goldfish*
Brock, Emma Lillian. *A pet for Barbie*
Bröger, Achim. *Bruno takes a trip*
  Francie's paper puppy
Brothers, Aileen. *Jiffy, Miss Boo and Mr. Roo*
Brown, Ruth. *Our puppy's vacation*
Brunhoff, Laurent de. *Babar and the Wully-Wully*

Calders, Pere. *Brush*
Carlson, Natalie Savage. *Spooky night*
Carrick, Carol. *The accident*
  A clearing in the forest
  The foundling
Carroll, Ruth. *Pet tale*
Chalmers, Mary. *Six dogs, twenty-three cats, forty-five mice, and one hundred sixteen spiders*
Chapouton, Anne-Marie. *Ben finds a friend*
Chenery, Janet. *Pickles and Jake*
Chittum, Ida. *The cat's pajamas*
Christian, Mary Blount. *Devin and Goliath*
Coerr, Eleanor. *The Josefina story quilt*
Cohen, Miriam. *Jim's dog Muffins*
Cole, Babette. *Princess Smartypants*
Collington, Peter. *My darling kitten*
Collins, Pat L. *Tumble, tumble, tumbleweed*
Cooper, Elizabeth K. *The fish from Japan*
Crane, Donn. *Flippy and Skippy*
Crowell, Maryalicia. *A horse in the house*
Cummings, Betty Sue. *Turtle*, ill. by Susan Dodge
Daly, Niki. *Just like Archie*
De Hamel, Joan. *Hemi's pet*
Delton, Judy. *I'll never love anything ever again*
  A pet for Duck and Bear
Dunn, Judy. *The little goat*
  The little puppy
  The little rabbit
Ferguson, Alane. *That new pet!*
Foster, Sally. *A pup grows up*
Fujita, Tamao. *The boy and the bird*
Furchgott, Terry. *Phoebe and the hot water bottles*
Gackenbach, Dick. *Mother Rabbit's son Tom*
Gantos, Jack. *The perfect pal*
George, Lindsay Barrett. *William and Boomer*
Gerson, Corinne. *Good dog, bad dog*
Graham, Bob. *The wild*
Greeley, Valerie. *Pets*
Griffith, Helen V. *Mine will, said John*
Hamberger, John. *Hazel was an only pet*
Hausherr, Rosmarie. *My first kitten*
  My first puppy
Henrie, Fiona. *Cats*
  Dogs
  Gerbils
  Rabbits
Hill, Eric. *My pets*
Hoff, Syd. *Mrs. Brice's mice*
Hurd, Edith Thacher. *The black dog who went into the woods*
Joosse, Barbara M. *Better with two*
Jordan, June. *Kimako's story*
Joyce, William. *Dinosaur Bob*
Kahl, Virginia. *The habits of rabbits*
Keats, Ezra Jack. *Maggie and the pirate*
  Pet show!

Keith, Eros. *Rrra-ah*
Keller, Charles. *Giggle puss*
Keller, Holly. *Goodbye, Max*
Kellogg, Steven. *Can I keep him?*
  The mysterious tadpole
Kerr, Judith. *Mog and bunny*
Klein, Robin. *Thing*
Kouts, Anne. *Kenny's rat*
Kuklin, Susan. *Taking my dog to the vet*
Kunhardt, Edith. *Pat the cat*
Kuskin, Karla. *Something sleeping in the hall*
Landshoff, Ursula. *Cats are good company*
Lansdown, Brenda. *Galumpf*
Lathrop, Dorothy Pulis. *Puppies for keeps*
Lindgren, Barbro. *Sam's cookie*
McNeely, Jeannette. *Where's Izzy?*
McNulty, Faith. *Mouse and Tim*
McPhail, David. *Emma's pet*
Marzollo, Jean. *Jed and the space bandits*
Mathers, Petra. *Theodor and Mr. Balbini*
Miles, Miska. *The rice bowl pet*
  Somebody's dog
Morgan, Allen. *Molly and Mr. Maloney*
Morgan, Michaela. *Edward gets a pet*
Most, Bernard. *My very own octopus*
Newberry, Clare Turlay. *April's kittens*
  Barkis
  Herbert the lion
  Percy, Polly and Pete
Newfield, Marcia. *Iggy*
O'Hagan, Caroline. *It's easy to have a caterpillar visit you*
  It's easy to have a snail visit you
  It's easy to have a worm visit you
Orbach, Ruth. *Please send a panda*
Oxenbury, Helen. *Our dog*
Palmer, Helen Marion. *Why I built the boogle house*
Parish, Peggy. *No more monsters for me!*
  Scruffy
Pearce, Philippa. *Emily's own elephant*
Phillips, Joan. *My new boy*
Piecewicz, Ann Thomas. *See what I caught!*
Politi, Leo. *Lito and the clown*
Pollock, Penny. *Emily's tiger*
Pratten, Albra. *Winkie, the grey squirrel*
Provensen, Alice. *An owl and three pussycats*
Pursell, Margaret Sanford. *Polly the guinea pig*
  Shelley the sea gull
Quackenbush, Robert M. *No mouse for me*
Ricciuti, Edward R. *An animal for Alan*
Ridlon, Marcia. *Kittens and more kittens*
Rockwell, Anne F. *I love my pets*
Rogers, Fred. *When a pet dies*
Rosen, Winifred. *Henrietta and the day of the iguana*
Ross, George Maxim. *When Lucy went away*

Rylant, Cynthia. *Henry and Mudge*
Henry and Mudge in puddle trouble
Henry and Mudge in the green time
Henry and Mudge under the yellow moon
Sandberg, Inger. *Nicholas' favorite pet*
Schaffer, Marion. *I love my cat!*
Schick, Alice. *Just this once*
Schmeltz, Susan Alton. *Pets I wouldn't pick*
Schwartz, Henry. *How I captured a
dinosaur*
Seabrooke, Brenda. *The best burglar alarm*
Seignobosc, Françoise. *The story of Colette*
Selsam, Millicent E. *Let's get turtles*
Plenty of fish
Sendak, Maurice. *Some swell pup*
Sharmat, Marjorie Weinman. *Nate the
Great and the fishy prize*
Simon, Norma. *Cats do, dogs don't*
Oh, that cat!
Skorpen, Liesel Moak. *All the Lassies*
Smath, Jerry. *But no elephants*
Smyth, Gwenda. *A pet for Mrs. Arbuckle*
Snow, Pegeen. *A pet for Pat*
Spier, Peter. *The pet store*
Steiner, Charlotte. *Polka Dot*
Stevenson, James. *Will you please feed our
cat?*
Stevenson, Suçie. *Jessica the blue streak*
Stoddard, Sandol. *My very own special
particular private and personal cat*
Szilagyi, Mary. *Thunderstorm*
Tabler, Judith. *The new puppy*
Tallon, Robert. *Latouse my moose*
Thaler, Mike. *My puppy*
Tobias, Tobi. *Petey*
Tusa, Tricia. *Chicken*
Udry, Janice May. *"Oh no, cat!"*
What Mary Jo wanted
Vaës, Alain. *The wild hamster*
Vandivert, William. *Barnaby*
Varga, Judy. *Miss Lollipop's lion*
Viorst, Judith. *The tenth good thing about
Barney*
Vreeken, Elizabeth. *Henry*
Ward, Lynd. *The biggest bear*
Wayland, April Halprin. *To Rabbittown*
Wilhelm, Hans. *I'll always love you*
Wirth, Beverly. *Margie and me*
Wisbeski, Dorothy Gross. *Pícaro, a pet otter*
Wolski, Slawomir. *Tiger cat*
Wong, Herbert H. *My goldfish*
Wright, Dare. *The lonely doll learns a lesson*
Zimelman, Nathan. *Positively no pets
allowed*
Zinnemann-Hope, Pam. *Find your coat,
Ned*
Zolotow, Charlotte. *The poodle who barked
at the wind*
Zweifel, Frances. *Bony*

Philippines *see* Foreign lands – Philippines

Phoenix *see* Mythical creatures

Photography *see* Activities –
photographing

Physicians *see* Careers – doctors

Picnicking *see* Activities – picnicking

Pigeons *see* Birds – pigeons

Pigs *see* Animals – pigs

Pilots *see* Careers – airplane pilots

Pirates

Baum, Louis. *JuJu and the pirate*
Burningham, John. *Come away from the
water, Shirley*
Carryl, Charles Edward. *A capital ship*
Collington, Peter. *The angel and the soldier
boy*
Devlin, Harry. *The walloping window blind*
Dewey, Ariane. *Laffite, the pirate*
Dyke, John. *Pigwig and the pirates*
Faulkner, Matt. *The amazing voyage of
Jackie Grace*
Ginsburg, Mirra. *Four brave sailors*
Graham, Mary Stuart Campbell. *The
pirates' bridge*
Haseley, Dennis. *The pirate who tried to
capture the moon*
Hayes, Geoffrey. *The mystery of the pirate
ghost*
Hutchins, Pat. *One-eyed Jake*
Isadora, Rachel. *The pirates of Bedford
Street*
Joslin, Sesyle. *Señor Baby Elephant, the
pirate*
Keats, Ezra Jack. *Maggie and the pirate*
Kessler, Leonard P. *The pirates' adventure
on Spooky Island*
Kroll, Steven. *Are you pirates?*
Lloyd, David. *Grandma and the pirate*
Mahy, Margaret. *The man whose mother
was a pirate*
Sailor Jack and the twenty orphans
Nash, Ogden. *Custard the dragon*
Peppé, Rodney. *The kettleship pirates*
Perkins, Al. *Tubby and the lantern*
Roberts, Thom. *Pirates in the park*
Ross, David. *Gorp and the space pirates*
Thompson, Brenda. *Pirates*
Vinton, Iris. *Look out for pirates!*
Walker, Barbara K. *Pigs and pirates*
Weiss, Ellen. *The pirates of Tarnoonga*

Pixies *see* Elves and little people; Fairies

Planes *see* Airplanes, airports

Plants

Adelson, Leone. *Please pass the grass*
Aliki. *Corn is maize*
Amos, William H. *Exploring the seashore*
Ayer, Jacqueline. *The paper-flower tree*
Back, Christine. *Bean and plant*
Baker, Jeffrey J. W. *Patterns of nature*
Bash, Barbara. *Desert giant*
Bellamy, David. *The forest*
 The river
Berson, Harold. *Pop! goes the turnip*
Bishop, Gavin. *Mrs. McGinty and the bizarre plant*
Blackmore, Vivien. *Why corn is golden*
Brown, Marc. *Your first garden book*
Bulla, Clyde Robert. *A tree is a plant*
Busch, Phyllis S. *Cactus in the desert*
 Lions in the grass
Carle, Eric. *The tiny seed*
Chapman, Carol. *Barney Bipple's magic dandelions*
Cole, Joanna. *Evolution*
 Plants in winter
Craig, M. Jean. *Spring is like the morning*
Credle, Ellis. *Down, down the mountain*
Cristini, Ermanno. *In the pond*
Cross, Diana Harding. *Some plants have funny names*
Cross, Genevieve. *A trip to the yard*
Darby, Gene. *What is a plant?*
Domanska, Janina. *The turnip*
Ellentuck, Shan. *A sunflower as big as the sun*
Fisher, Aileen. *And a sunflower grew*
 As the leaves fall down
 Mysteries in the garden
 Now that spring is here
 Plant magic
 Prize performance
 Seeds on the go
 Swords and daggers
 We went looking
Gage, Wilson. *Anna's summer songs*
Ginsburg, Mirra. *Mushroom in the rain*
 The green grass grows all around
Greenberg, Polly. *Oh, Lord, I wish I was a buzzard*
Heller, Ruth. *Plants that never ever bloom*
Hewett, Anita. *The tale of the turnip*
Hillert, Margaret. *The magic beans*
Hogan, Paula Z. *The dandelion*
Holmes, Anita. *The 100-year-old cactus*
Hutchins, Pat. *Titch*
Ipcar, Dahlov. *Hard scrabble harvest*
Jack and the beanstalk. *The history of Mother Twaddle and the marvelous achievements of her son Jack*
Jennings, Terry. *Seeds*
Johnson, Hannah Lyons. *From seed to jack-o'-lantern*

Jordan, Helene J. *Seeds of wind and water*
Kepes, Juliet. *The seed that peacock planted*
Kirkpatrick, Rena K. *Look at leaves*
 Look at seeds and weeds
Krauss, Ruth. *The carrot seed*
Kuchalla, Susan. *All about seeds*
Le Tord, Bijou. *Picking and weaving*
Lewis, Naomi. *Leaves*
Little, Lessie Jones. *I can do it by myself*
The little red hen. *The little red hen*, ill. by Janina Domanska
 The little red hen, ill. by Paul Galdone
 The little red hen, ill. by Mel Pekarsky
 The little red hen, ill. by William Stobbs
 The little red hen, ill. by Margot Zemach
Littledale, Freya. *The magic plum tree*
Maestro, Giulio. *The remarkable plant in apartment 4*
Miller, Judith Ransom. *Nabob and the geranium*
Nash, Ogden. *The animal garden*
Oleson, Claire. *For Pipita, an orange tree*
Petie, Haris. *The seed the squirrel dropped*
Pouyanne, Rési. *What I see hidden by the pond*
Rey, Hans Augusto. *Elizabite, adventures of a carnivorous plant*
Ring, Elizabeth. *Tiger lilies*
Ringi, Kjell. *The sun and the cloud*
Rockwell, Harlow. *The compost heap*
Rudolph, Marguerita. *How a shirt grew in the field*
Selberg, Ingrid. *Nature's hidden world*
Selsam, Millicent E. *The amazing dandelion*
 Cotton
 A first look at the world of plants
 More potatoes!
 Seeds and more seeds
Shecter, Ben. *Partouche plants a seed*
Sugita, Yutaka. *The flower family*
Tolstoĭ, Alekseĭ Nikolaevich. *The great big enormous turnip*
Watts, Barrie. *Dandelion*
 Mushrooms
Wexler, Jerome. *Flowers, fruits, seeds*
Williams, Barbara. *Hello, dandelions!*
Wondriska, William. *The tomato patch*
Wong, Herbert H. *My plant*
Zion, Gene. *The plant sitter*
Zolotow, Charlotte. *In my garden*

Playing *see* Activities – playing

Plays *see* Theater

Poetry, rhyme

Aardema, Verna. *Bringing the rain to Kapiti Plain*
 The riddle of the drum
Abrons, Mary. *For Alice a palace*

Ackerman, Karen. *Flannery Row*

Adams, Richard. *The tyger voyage*

Adelborg, Ottilia. *Clean Peter and the children of Grubbylea*

Adelson, Leone. *Please pass the grass*

Adler, David A. *You think it's fun to be a clown!*

Adoff, Arnold. *Big sister tells me that I'm black*
Birds
Black is brown is tan
The cabbages are chasing the rabbits
Greens
Make a circle, keep us in
Tornado!
Where wild Willie?

Æsop. *Æsop's fables*, ill. by Robert Rayevsky
Once in a wood

Ahlberg, Allan. *Cops and robbers*

Ahlberg, Janet. *Each peach pear plum*
Peek-a-boo!

Aiken, Conrad. *Tom, Sue and the clock*

Alborough, Jez. *Bare bear*

Alderson, Sue Ann. *Bonnie McSmithers is at it again!*

Aldis, Dorothy. *All together*
Before things happen
Hello day
Quick as a wink

Aldridge, Alan. *The butterfly ball and the grasshopper's feast*

Alexander, Anne. *ABC of cars and trucks*
Boats and ships from A to Z
I want to whistle
My daddy and I

Alger, Leclaire. *All in the morning early*
Kellyburn Braes

Allen, Jonathan. *A bad case of animal nonsense*

Allen, Pamela. *Who sank the boat?*

Allison, Diane Worfolk. *In window eight, the moon is late*

Allstrom, Elizabeth C. *Songs along the way*

Ambler, Christopher Gifford. *Ten little foxhounds*

Anastasio, Dina. *Pass the peas, please*

Anderson, Joy. *Juma and the magic Jinn*

Andre, Evelyn M. *Places I like to be*

Anglund, Joan Walsh. *A Christmas book*
The Joan Walsh Anglund story book
Morning is a little child

Armour, Richard Willard. *The adventures of Egbert the Easter egg*
Animals on the ceiling
Have you ever wished you were something else?
Sea full of whales
The year Santa went modern

Arnold, Tedd. *Ollie forgot*

Arnosky, Jim. *A kettle of hawks, and other wildlife groups*

Asch, Frank. *City sandwich*
Country pie

Attenberger, Walburga. *The little man in winter*
Who knows the little man?

Atwood, Ann. *The little circle*

Auerbach, Julie Jaslow. *Everything's changing - It's pesach!*

Aylesworth, Jim. *Mary's mirror*
One crow

Ayres, Pam. *Guess what?*
Guess who?
When dad cuts down the chestnut tree
When dad fills in the garden pond

Azarian, Mary. *The tale of John Barleycorn or, From barley to beer*

The babes in the woods. *The old ballad of the babes in the woods*

Bach, Othello. *Lilly, Willy and the mail-order witch*

Baer, Edith. *Words are like faces*

Baker, Sanna Anderson. *Who's a friend of the water-spurting whale*

Bang, Molly. *Ten, nine, eight*

Baningan, Sharon Stearns. *Circus magic*

Barker, Cicely Mary. *Berry flower fairies*
Blossom flower fairies
Flower fairies of the seasons
Spring flower fairies
Summer flower fairies

Barrett, Judi. *Pickles have pimples*

Barry, Katharina. *A is for anything*
A bug to hug

Barry, Robert E. *Animals around the world*
Mr. Willowby's Christmas tree

Barto, Emily N. *Chubby bear*

Baruch, Dorothy. *I would like to be a pony and other wishes*

Base, Graeme. *My grandma lived in Gooligulch*

Baskin, Leonard. *Hosie's zoo*

Bauer, Caroline Feller. *Rainy day*
Snowy day

Baylor, Byrd. *Amigo*
The desert is theirs
Desert voices
Everybody needs a rock
The other way to listen

Behn, Harry. *Crickets and bullfrogs and whispers of thunder*

Beisner, Monika. *Topsy turvy*

Belloc, Hilaire. *The bad child's book of beasts, and more beasts for worse children*
The bad child's pop-up book of beasts
Matilda who told lies and was burned to death
More beasts for worse children

Belting, Natalia Maree. *Christmas folk*
Summer's coming in

Bemelmans, Ludwig. *Madeline*
Madeline and the bad hat

Madeline and the gypsies
Madeline in London
Madeline's rescue
Welcome home
Benét, William Rose. *Angels*
Benjamin, Alan. *A change of plans*
Ribtickle Town
Bennett, Jill. *Days are where we live and other poems*
Roger was a razor fish and other poems
Tiny Tim
Bennett, Rainey. *The secret hiding place*
Bennett, Rowena. *The day is dancing and other poems*
Songs from around a toadstool table
Berenstain, Stan. *The bear detectives*
The bears' almanac
The Berenstain bears and the missing dinosaur bone
The Berenstain bears and the spooky old tree
The Berenstain bears' Christmas tree
He bear, she bear
Berg, Jean Horton. *The wee little man*
Berger, Judith. *Butterflies and rainbows*
Beskow, Elsa Maartman. *Children of the forest*
Peter in Blueberry Land
Peter's adventures in Blueberry land
Betz, Betty. *Manners for moppets*
Billy Boy
Black, Irma Simonton. *Is this my dinner?*
Blake, Quentin. *Mister Magnolia*
Blegvad, Erik. *Burnie's hill*
Blegvad, Lenore. *One is for the sun*
The parrot in the garret and other rhymes about dwellings
Blocksma, Mary. *Where's that duck?*
Bloom, Suzanne. *We keep a pig in the parlor*
Blos, Joan W. *Old Henry*
Bober, Natalie S. *Let's pretend*
Bodecker, N. M. (Nils Mogens). *"Let's marry" said the cherry, and other nonsense poems*
Snowman Sniffles and other verse
Bodwell, Gaile. *The long day of the giants*
Boegehold, Betty. *Pawpaw's run*
Borchers, Elisabeth. *There comes a time*
Bornstein, Ruth Lercher. *The seedling child*
Borten, Helen. *Do you go where I go?*
Do you hear what I hear?
Do you know what I know?
Bottner, Barbara. *There was nobody there*
Bouton, Josephine. *Favorite poems for the children's hour*
A boy went out to gather pears
Boynton, Sandra. *But not the hippopotamus*
The going to bed book
Good night, good night
Hippos go berserk

Moo, baa, lalala
Bradman, Tony. *The bad babies' counting book*
Braun, Kathy. *Kangaroo and kangaroo*
Brecht, Bertolt. *Uncle Eddie's moustache*
Bridgman, Elizabeth. *All the little bunnies*
Bright, Robert. *My hopping bunny*
Brooke, L. Leslie (Leonard Leslie). *Johnny Crow's garden*
Johnny Crow's new garden
Brooks, Gwendolyn. *Bronzeville boys and girls*
Brown, Beatrice Curtis. *Jonathan Bing*, ill. by Judith Gwyn Brown
Jonathan Bing, ill. by Pelagie Doane
Brown, Judith Gwyn. *Alphabet dreams*
Brown, Marc. *Finger rhymes*
Hand rhymes
Pickle things
The silly tail book
Wings on things
Witches four
Brown, Margaret Wise. *Big red barn*
Four fur feet
Nibble nibble
Sleepy ABC
Two little trains
Where have you been?
Whistle for the train
The wonderful story book
Brown, Myra Berry. *Best friends*
Best of luck
Brown, Palmer. *The silver nutmeg*
Browner, Richard. *Everyone has a name*
Browning, Robert. *The pied piper of Hamelin*, ill. by Kate Greenaway
The pied piper of Hamelin, ill. by Anatoly Ivanov
The pied piper of Hamelin, ill. by Errol Le Cain
Bruce, Sheilah B. *The radish day jubilee*
Bruna, Dick. *Christmas*
The fish
Kitten Nell
Little bird tweet
The orchestra
Poppy Pig goes to market
Tilly and Tess
Bryan, Ashley. *Beat the story-drum, pum-pum*
The cat's purr
Buckley, Helen Elizabeth. *Josie and the snow*
Josie's Buttercup
Buckley, Richard. *The foolish tortoise*
The greedy python
Bucknall, Caroline. *One bear all alone*
One bear in the picture
Budney, Blossom. *A kiss is round*
Buell, Ellen Lewis. *Read me a poem*
Buff, Mary. *Hurry, Skurry and Flurry*

Bunting, Eve. *Happy birthday, dear duck*
  Scary, scary Halloween
Burdekin, Harold. *A child's grace*
Burgess, Gelett. *The little father*
Burgunder, Rose. *From summer to summer*
Burnstein, John. *Slim Goodbody*
Burroway, Janet. *The truck on the track*
Bush, John. *The cross-with-us rhinoceros*
Calmenson, Stephanie. *Never take a pig to
  lunch and other funny poems about
  animals*
  Where will the animals stay?
Cameron, John. *If mice could fly*
Cameron, Polly. *A child's book of nonsense*
  "I can't," said the ant
Carlstrom, Nancy White. *Better not get wet,
  Jesse Bear*
  The moon came too
  Wild wild sunflower child Anna
Carroll, Lewis. *Jabberwocky*
  The walrus and the carpenter, ill. by Julian
    Doyle
  The walrus and the carpenter, ill. by Jane
    Breskin Zalben
Carton, Lonnie Caming. *Mommies*
Cassidy, Dianne. *Circus animals*
  Circus people
Cate, Rikki. *A cat's tale*
Caudill, Rebecca. *Wind, sand and sky*
Causley, Charles. *"Quack!" said the
  billy-goat*
Cendrars, Blaise. *Shadow*
Chardiet, Bernice. *C is for circus*
Charles, Donald. *Calico Cat meets bookworm*
  Calico Cat's year
  Shaggy dog's animal alphabet
  Time to rhyme with Calico Cat
Charles, Robert Henry. *The roundabout
  turn*
Cherry, Lynne. *Who's sick today?*
Chönz, Selina. *A bell for Ursli*
  Florina and the wild bird
  The snowstorm
Chorao, Kay. *The baby's bedtime book*
  The baby's good morning book
Chukovsky, Korney. *The telephone*
Ciardi, John. *I met a man*
  John J. Plenty and Fiddler Dan
  The man who sang the sillies
  The monster den
  You know who
  You read to me, I'll read to you
Clark, Leonard. *Drums and trumpets*
Clifford, Eth. *Red is never a mouse*
Clifton, Lucille. *The black B C's*
  Everett Anderson's Christmas coming
  Everett Anderson's friend
  Everett Anderson's goodbye
  Everett Anderson's nine months long
  Everett Anderson's 1-2-3
  Everett Anderson's year

  Some of the days of Everett Anderson
Clithero, Sally. *Beginning-to-read poetry*
Coatsworth, Elizabeth. *The children come
  running*
  The giant golden book of cat stories
  A peaceable kingdom, and other poems
Cohen, Caron Lee. *Whiffle Squeek*
Cole, Joanna. *Animal sleepyheads*
  Golly Gump swallowed a fly
Cole, William. *Frances face-maker*
  That pest Jonathan
  What's good for a four-year-old?
  What's good for a six-year-old?
  What's good for a three-year-old?
Coleridge, Sara. *January brings the snow*
Coletta, Irene. *From A to Z*
Conover, Chris. *Six little ducks*
Cooney, Barbara. *A garland of games and
  other diversions*
Copp, James. *Martha Matilda O'Toole*
Count me in
Counting rhymes
Craft, Ruth. *The day of the rainbow*
  The winter bear
Crowley, Arthur. *Bonzo Beaver*
  The wagon man
Cummings, E. E. *In just-spring*
  Little tree
Cummings, Pat. *Jimmy Lee did it*
Cushman, Doug. *Giants*
  Once upon a pig
Dahl, Roald. *Dirty beasts*
Dalmais, Anne-Marie. *In my garden*
Dayton, Laura. *LeRoy's birthday circus*
Degen, Bruce. *Jamberry*
De Gerez, Toni. *My song is a piece of jade*
Delacre, Lulu. *Arroz con leche*
Delaunay, Sonia. *Sonia Delaunay's alphabet*
Demi. *Demi's count the animals 1-2-3*
Demuth, Patricia Brennan. *Max, the
  bad-talking parrot*
Dennis, Suzanne E. *Answer me that*
De Paola, Tomie. *Songs of the fog maiden*
  Tomie de Paola's book of poems
De Regniers, Beatrice Schenk. *A bunch of
  poems and verses*
  Cats cats cats
  It does not say meow!
  May I bring a friend?
  Red Riding Hood
  Sam and the impossible thing
  So many cats!
  Something special
  Was it a good trade?
Dodd, Lynley. *Hairy Maclary from
  Donaldson's dairy*
  Hairy Maclary Scattercat
  Hairy Maclary's bone
  The nickle nackle tree
Dodge, Mary Mapes. *Mary Anne*

The dog writes on the window with his nose,
   and other poems
Domanska, Janina. *What do you see?*
Don't tell the scarecrow
Doolittle, Eileen. *World of wonders*
Dowers, Patrick. *One day scene through a*
   leaf
Dragonwagon, Crescent. *Half a moon and*
   one whole star
   Jemima remembers
Driz, Ovsei. *The boy and the tree*
Duke, Kate. *Seven froggies went to school*
Eastwick, Ivy O. *Cherry stones! Garden*
   swings!
   Rainbow over all
Eberstadt, Isabel. *What is for my birthday?*
Edelman, Elaine. *Boom-de-boom*
Eichenberg, Fritz. *Dancing in the moon*
Elborn, Andrew. *Bird Adalbert*
Elkin, Benjamin. *The king who could not*
   sleep
Elves, fairies and gnomes
Emberley, Barbara. *Drummer Hoff*
   Night's nice
   One wide river to cross
Emberley, Ed. *The wing on a flea*
Esbensen, Barbara Juster. *The star maiden*
Ets, Marie Hall. *Beasts and nonsense*
Euvremer, Teryl. *After dark*
Evans, Mel. *The tiniest sound*
Fairy poems for the very young
Farber, Norma. *As I was crossing Boston*
   Common
   How the hibernators came to Bethlehem
   How the left-behind beasts built Ararat
   How to ride a tiger
   Never say ugh to a bug
   Small wonders
   There goes feathertop!
   There once was a woman who married a
   man
   Up the down elevator
   Where's Gomer?
Farjeon, Eleanor. *Around the seasons*
   Mrs. Malone
Field, Eugene. *Wynken, Blynken and Nod*
Field, Rachel Lyman. *General store*, ill. by
   Giles Laroche
   General store, ill. by Nancy Winslow
   Parker
Finfer, Celentha. *Grandmother dear*
First graces
First prayers, ill. by Anna Maria Magagna
First prayers, ill. by Tasha Tudor
Fisher, Aileen. *And a sunflower grew*
   Anybody home?
   Best little house
   Cricket in the thicket
   Do bears have mothers too?
   Going barefoot
   The house of a mouse

I like weather
I wonder how, I wonder why
In one door and out the other
In the middle of the night
In the woods, in the meadow, in the sky
Like nothing at all
Listen, rabbit
My first Hanukkah book
My mother and I
Mysteries in the garden
Now that spring is here
Petals yellow and petals red
Plant magic
Prize performance
Rabbits, rabbits
Seeds on the go
Sing, little mouse
Skip around the year
Swords and daggers
A tree with a thousand uses
We went looking
When it comes to bugs
Where does everyone go?
Fisher, Leonard Everett. *Boxes! Boxes!*
Flanders, Michael. *Creatures great and*
   small
Fleischman, Paul. *Rondo in C*
Fontane, Theodore. *Sir Ribbeck of Ribbeck*
   of Havelland
Forrester, Victoria. *Words to keep against*
   the night
Fowler, Richard. *Cat's story*
Fox, Dorothea Warren. *Follow me the*
   leader
Fox, Siv Cedering. *The blue horse and other*
   night poems
Frank, Josette. *More poems to read to the*
   very young
   Poems to read to the very young
Frankenberg, Lloyd. *Wings of rhyme*
Frasconi, Antonio. *The snow and the sun,*
   la nieve y el sol
Freeman, Don. *The day is waiting*
   Mop Top
Freeman, Jean Todd. *Cynthia and the*
   unicorn
Freschet, Berniece. *The ants go marching*
Frith, Michael K. *I'll teach my dog 100*
   words
From morn to midnight
Froman, Robert. *Seeing things*
Frost, Robert. *Stopping by woods on a snowy*
   evening
Fujikawa, Gyo. *Come follow me...to the secret*
   world of elves and fairies and gnomes and
   trolls
Fyleman, Rose. *A fairy went a-marketing*
Gág, Wanda. *ABC bunny*
Gage, Wilson. *Anna's summer songs*
   Down in the boondocks

Galdone, Joanna. *Gertrude, the goose who forgot*
The tailypo
García Lorca, Federico. *The Lieutenant Colonel and the gypsy*
Gardner, Martin. *Never make fun of a turtle, my son*
Garelick, May. *Look at the moon*
Where does the butterfly go when it rains?
Garten, Jan. *The alphabet tale*
Gay, Marie-Louise. *Moonbeam on a cat's ear*
Gay, Zhenya. *Look!*
What's your name?
Gelman, Rita Golden. *Hey, kid*
Gerrard, Roy. *The Favershams*
Sir Cedric rides again
Sir Francis Drake
Gerstein, Mordicai. *Roll over!*
Gibson, Myra Tomback. *What is your favorite thing to touch?*
Gilchrist, Theo E. *Halfway up the mountain*
The gingerbread boy. *The gingerbread boy*, ill. by Paul Galdone
Whiff, sniff, nibble and chew
Ginsburg, Mirra. *Four brave sailors*
Kitten from one to ten
The sun's asleep behind the hill
Giovanni, Nikki. *Spin a soft black song*
Gomi, Taro. *Toot!*
Goodspeed, Peter. *A rhinoceros wakes me up in the morning*
Graham, Al. *Songs for a small guitar*
Graham, Lorenz B. *Song of the boat*
Greaves, Margaret. *The mice of Nibbling Village*
The green grass grows all around
Greenaway, Kate. *Marigold garden*
Under the window
Greenberg, David. *Slugs*
Greene, Carol. *The world's biggest birthday cake*
Greenfield, Eloise. *Daydreamers*
Under the Sunday tree
Greenwood, Ann. *A pack of dreams*
Gregorich, Barbara. *My friend goes left*
Grossman, Bill. *Donna O'Neeshuck was chased by some cows*
Gundersheimer, Karen. *Happy winter*
Gunning, Monica. *The two Georges*
Haas, Irene. *The Maggie B*
Hague, Kathleen. *Alphabears*
Out of the nursery, into the night
Hall, Pam. *On the edge of the eastern ocean*
Hallinan, P. K. (Patrick K.). *Just open a book*
That's what a friend is
Hample, Stoo. *Yet another big fat funny silly book*
Hamsa, Bobbie. *Polly wants a cracker*

Harrison, David Lee. *The case of Og, the missing frog*
Harrison, Sarah. *In granny's garden*
Hawkins, Colin. *Boo! Who?*
Jen the hen
Mig the pig
Snap! Snap!
Take away monsters
Tog the dog
Hayes, Sarah. *Clap your hands*
This is the bear
Hazen, Barbara Shook. *Where do bears sleep?*
Heller, Ruth. *How to hide a butterfly*
How to hide a polar bear
How to hide an octopus
Kites sail high
The reason for a flower
Hennessy, B. G. *The missing tarts*
Highwater, Jamake. *Moonsong lullaby*
Hill, Helen. *Dusk to dawn*
Hill, Susan. *Can it be true?*
Hillert, Margaret. *What is it?*
Hillman, Priscilla. *A Merry-Mouse book of favorite poems*
A Merry-Mouse book of months
Hines, Anna Grossnickle. *It's just me, Emily*
Hoban, Russell. *Goodnight*
Hoban, Tana. *One little kitten*
Where is it?
Hoberman, Mary Ann. *The cozy book*
A house is a house for me
I like old clothes
Nuts to you and nuts to me
Hofstrand, Mary. *Albion pig*
Holder, Heidi. *Crows*
Holl, Adelaide. *Mrs. McGarrity's peppermint sweater*
Sir Kevin of Devon
Holland, Marion. *A big ball of string*
Hollander, John. *A book of various owls*
Hooper, Patricia. *A bundle of beasts*
Hoopes, Lyn Littlefield. *Mommy, daddy, me*
Hopkins, Lee Bennett. *And God bless me*
Best friends
Circus! Circus!
A dog's life
Easter buds are springing
Go to bed!
I think I saw a snail
Merrily comes our harvest in
More surprises
Morning, noon and nighttime, too
The sea is calling me
The sky is full of song
Hot cross buns, and other old street cries
Houston, John A. *The bright yellow rope*
Howells, Mildred. *The woman who lived in Holland*
Hughes, Shirley. *All shapes and sizes*
Bathwater's hot

Colors
Noisy
Out and about
Two shoes, new shoes
When we went to the park
Hurd, Edith Thacher. *Caboose*
Come and have fun
Hutchins, Pat. *The tale of Thomas Mead*
The wind blew
Hymes, Lucia. *Oodles of noodles and other rhymes*
If dragon flies made honey
Ilsley, Velma. *A busy day for Chris*
The pink hat
Ipcar, Dahlov. *Black and white*
The cat came back
Hard scrabble harvest
Jack and the beanstalk. *The history of Mother Twaddle and the marvelous achievements of her son Jack*
Jack and the beanstalk, ill. by Anne Wilsdorf
Jack the giant killer, ill. by Anne Wilsdorf
Jacobs, Leland B. *Is somewhere always far away?*
Janosch. *Tonight at nine*
Jarrell, Randall. *A bat is born*
Jefferds, Vincent. *Disney's elegant book of manners*
Jerome, Judson. *I never saw...*
Jewell, Nancy. *ABC cat*
Johnson, B. J. *A hat like that*
My blanket Burt
Jones, Hettie. *The trees stand shining*
Jones, Jessie Mae Orton. *Small rain*
Kahl, Virginia. *The Baron's booty*
The Duchess bakes a cake
Gunhilde and the Halloween spell
Gunhilde's Christmas booke
The habits of rabbits
How do you hide a monster?
The perfect pancake
Plum pudding for Christmas
Kahn, Joan. *Hi, Jock, run around the block*
Kalman, Benjamin. *Animals in danger*
Katz, Bobbi. *Tick-tock, let's read the clock*
Kavanaugh, James J. *The crooked angel*
Kennedy, Jimmy. *The teddy bears' picnic*, ill. by Prue Theobalds
Kessler, Ethel. *Do baby bears sit in chairs?*
Kessler, Leonard P. *Riddles that rhyme for Halloween time*
Kherdian, David. *Country cat, city cat*
King, Larry L. *Because of Lozo Brown*
Klimowicz, Barbara. *The strawberry thumb*
Knight, Hilary. *Hilary Knight's the owl and the pussy-cat*
Knight, Joan. *Tickle-toe rhymes*
Koenner, Alfred. *High flies the ball*
Komaiko, Leah. *Annie Bananie*
Earl's too cool for me

I like the music
Krauss, Ruth. *Bears*
A bouquet of littles
Everything under a mushroom
Kroll, Steven. *Pigs in the house*
Krüss, James. *3 X 3*
Kudrna, C. Imbior. *To bathe a boa*
Kumin, Maxine. *Follow the fall*
Sebastian and the dragon
Speedy digs downside up
Spring things
A winter friend
Kuskin, Karla. *All sizes of noises*
The animals and the ark
A boy had a mother who bought him a hat
Herbert hated being small
In the flaky frosty morning
James and the rain
Roar and more
Sand and snow
Something sleeping in the hall
Kwitz, Mary DeBall. *When it rains*
Lagercrantz, Rose. *Brave little Pete of Geranium Street*
Lalicki, Barbara. *If there were dreams to sell*
La Rochelle, David. *A Christmas guest*
Larrick, Nancy. *Cats are cats*
When the dark comes dancing
Lawrence, John. *Rabbit and pork*
Lear, Edward. *ABC*
A book of nonsense
The dong with the luminous nose
Edward Lear's ABC
Edward Lear's nonsense book
The jumblies, ill. by Emma Crosby
A Learical lexicon
Lear's nonsense verses
Limericks by Lear
Nonsense alphabets
The nutcrackers and the sugar-tongs
The owl and the pussycat, ill. by Lorinda Bryan Cauley
The owl and the pussy-cat, ill. by Barbara Cooney
The owl and the pussycat, ill. by Emma Crosby
The owl and the pussy-cat, ill. by William Pène Du Bois
The owl and the pussycat, ill. by Lori Farbanish
The owl and the pussy-cat, ill. by Gwen Fulton
The owl and the pussy-cat, ill. by Paul Galdone
The owl and the pussy-cat, ill. by Elaine Muis
The owl and the pussycat, ill. by Erica Rutherford
The owl and the pussycat, ill. by Janet Stevens

Mellings, Joan. *It's fun to go to school*
Mendoza, George. *The hunter I might have been*
The scribbler
Merriam, Eve. *The birthday cow*
Blackberry ink
Halloween ABC
Messenger, Jannat. *Lullabies and baby songs*
Michels, Tilde. *Who's that knocking at my door?*
Miles, Betty. *Around and around... love*
Miles, Miska. *Apricot ABC*
Miller, Edna. *Mousekin's ABC*
Miller, Moira. *The proverbial mouse*
Mitchell, Cynthia. *Halloweena Hecatee*
Here a little child I stand
Playtime
Under the cherry tree
Mizumura, Kazue. *If I were a cricket...*
Moncure, Jane Belk. *Happy healthkins*
The healthkin food train
Healthkins exercise!
Healthkins help
The moon's the north wind's cooky
Moore, Clement C. *The night before Christmas*, ill. by Tomie de Paola
The night before Christmas, ill. by Michael Foreman
The night before Christmas, ill. by Gyo Fujikawa
The night before Christmas, ill. by Scott Gustafson
The night before Christmas, ill. by Anita Lobel
The night before Christmas, ill. by Jacqueline Rogers
The night before Christmas, ill. by Robin Spowart
The night before Christmas, ill. by Gustaf Tenggren
The night before Christmas, ill. by Tasha Tudor
The night before Christmas, ill. by Jody Wheeler
A visit from St. Nicholas
Moore, Lilian. *I feel the same way*
See my lovely poison ivy, and other verses about witches, ghosts and things
Mora, Emma. *Gideon, the little bear cub*
Morice, Dave. *Dot town*
A visit from St. Alphabet
Morrison, Bill. *Squeeze a sneeze*
Morrison, Sean. *Is that a happy hippopotamus?*
Morse, Samuel French. *Sea sums*
Moss, Jeffrey. *The songs of Sesame Street in poems and pictures*
Mullins, Edward S. *Animal limericks*
Muntean, Michaela. *Bicycle bear*
Nash, Ogden. *The adventures of Isabel*
The animal garden

A boy is a boy
Custard and Company
Custard the dragon and the wicked knight
Nerlove, Miriam. *I made a mistake*
I meant to clean my room today
Newberry, Clare Turlay. *The kittens' ABC*
Nims, Bonnie L. *Where is the bear?*
Nolan, Dennis. *Wizard McBean and his flying machine*
Noll, Sally. *Off and counting*
Norman, Charles. *The hornbean tree and other poems*
O'Neill, Mary. *Big red hen*
Opie, Iona Archibald. *Tail feathers from Mother Goose*
Oppenheim, Joanne. *Have you seen roads?*
Have you seen trees?
The story book prince
You can't catch me!
Orbach, Ruth. *Apple pigs*
Orgel, Doris. *Merry merry FIBruary*
Osborne, Valerie. *One big yo to go*
Over in the meadow, ill. by Ezra Jack Keats
Owens, Mary Beth. *A caribou alphabet*
Oxenbury, Helen. *Pig tale*
Pack, Robert. *How to catch a crocodile*
Then what did you do?
Partch, Virgil Franklin. *The Christmas cookie sprinkle snitcher*
Paterson, Andrew Barton. *The man from Ironbark*
Mulga Bill's bicycle
Patrick, Gloria. *This is...*
Patz, Nancy. *Moses supposes his toeses are roses and 7 other silly old rhymes*
Pavey, Peter. *One dragon's dream*
Paxton, Tom. *Jennifer's rabbit*
Peaceable kingdom
Pearson, Tracey Campbell. *A apple pie*
Peck, Robert Newton. *Hamilton*
Peek, Merle. *The balancing act*
Peet, Bill. *Ella*
Hubert's hair-raising adventures
Huge Harold
Kermit the hermit
The kweeks of Kookatumdee
The luckiest one of all
No such things
The pinkish, purplish, bluish egg
Randy's dandy lions
Smokey
Zella, Zack, and Zodiac
Peppé, Rodney. *Cat and mouse*
Hey riddle diddle
Perkins, Al. *The digging-est dog*
The ear book
Hand, hand, fingers, thumb
The nose book
Petie, Haris. *Billions of bugs*
The seed the squirrel dropped
Peyo. *What do smurfs do all day?*

Marvin K. Mooney, will you please go now!
Mr. Brown can moo! Can you?
Oh say can you say?
Oh, the thinks you can think!
On beyond zebra
One fish, two fish, red fish, blue fish
Please try to remember the first of octember!
Scrambled eggs super!
The shape of me and other stuff
The Sneetches, and other stories
There's a wocket in my pocket
Thidwick, the big-hearted moose
The tooth book
Wacky Wednesday
Sewall, Marcia. *Ridin' that strawberry roan*
Sexton, Gwain. *There once was a king*
Shannon, George. *Oh, I love!*
Shaw, Nancy. *Sheep in a jeep*
Sherman, Ivan. *Walking talking words*
Sherman, Nancy. *Gwendolyn and the weathercock*
Gwendolyn the miracle hen
Shortall, Leonard W. *One way*
Shulevitz, Uri. *Rain rain rivers*
Siebert, Diane. *Mojave*
Truck song
Silverstein, Shel. *A giraffe and a half*
The giving tree
Who wants a cheap rhinoceros?
Simon, Mina Lewiton. *Is anyone here?*
Singer, Marilyn. *Will you take me to town on strawberry day?*
Singh, Jacquelin. *Fat Gopal*
Slate, Joseph. *The star rocker*
Who is coming to our house?
Slobodkin, Louis. *Clear the track*
Friendly animals
Millions and millions and millions
One is good, but two are better
The seaweed hat
Up high and down low
Smaridge, Norah. *You know better than that*
Smart, Christopher. *For I will consider my cat Jeoffry*
Smith, William Jay. *Puptents and pebbles*
Typewriter town
Snow, Pegeen. *A pet for Pat*
Snyder, Zilpha Keatley. *Come on, Patsy*
Spier, Peter. *Noah's ark*
Spilka, Arnold. *And the frog went "Blah!"*
A lion I can do without
Little birds don't cry
A rumbudgin of nonsense
Starbird, Kaye. *The covered bridge house and other poems*
Steig, Jeanne. *Consider the lemming*
Steig, William. *An eye for elephants*
Stephenson, Dorothy. *The night it rained toys*
Stevens, Janet. *Animal fair*

Stevenson, Drew. *The ballad of Penelope Lou...and me*
Stevenson, Robert Louis. *Block city*, ill. by Ashley Wolff
A child's garden of verses, ill. by Erik Blegvad
A child's garden of verses, ill. by Pelagie Doane
A child's garden of verses, ill. by Michael Foreman
A child's garden of verses, ill. by Toni Frissell
A child's garden of verses, ill. by Gyo Fujikawa
A child's garden of verses, ill. by Joan Hassall
A child's garden of verses, ill. by Alice and Martin Provensen
A child's garden of verses, ill. by Tasha Tudor
A child's garden of verses, ill. by Brian Wildsmith
The moon
Stobbs, William. *This little piggy*
Stoddard, Sandol. *Bedtime for bear*
Bedtime mouse
My very own special particular private and personal cat
Stone, Rosetta. *Because a little bug went ka-choo!*
Stover, Jo Ann. *If everybody did*
Sundgaard, Arnold. *Jethro's difficult dinosaur*
Supraner, Robyn. *Would you rather be a tiger?*
Sutton, Eve. *My cat likes to hide in boxes*
Svendsen, Carol. *Hulda*
Swann, Brian. *A basket full of white eggs*
Terban, Marvin. *I think I thought*
Tether, Graham. *The hair book*
Thayer, Ernest L. *Casey at the bat*, ill. by Patricia Polacco
Thomas, Gary. *The best of the little books*
Thomas, Patricia. *"Stand back," said the elephant, "I'm going to sneeze!"*
"There are rocks in my socks!" said the ox to the fox
Thomson, Ruth. *My bear I can...can you?*
My bear I like...do you?
The three little pigs. *The three little pigs*, ill. by Erik Blegvad
The three little pigs, ill. by Caroline Bucknall
The three little pigs, ill. by William Pène Du Bois
Tippett, James Sterling. *Counting the days*
Trent, Robbie. *The first Christmas*
Tresselt, Alvin R. *Follow the wind*
Tripp, Wallace. *Marguerite, go wash your feet*
Tudor, Tasha. *Around the year*

Turner, Ann. *Tickle a pickle*
Tyrrell, Anne. *Elizabeth Jane gets dressed*
  Mary Ann always can
Udry, Janice May. *A tree is nice*
Vance, Eleanor Graham. *Jonathan*
Van der Beek, Deborah. *Superbabe!*
Van Vorst, M. L. *A Norse lullaby*
Voake, Charlotte. *First things first*
Vogel, Ilse-Margaret. *The don't be scared book*
Wadsworth, Olive A. *Over in the meadow*
Wahl, Jan. *Follow me cried Bee*
  Rabbits on roller skates!
Wakefield, Joyce. *Ask a silly question*
  From where you are
Wallace, Daisy. *Fairy poems*
  Ghost poems
  Giant poems
  Monster poems
Wallner, Alexandra. *Munch*
Watson, Clyde. *Applebet*
  Catch me and kiss me and say it again
  Father Fox's feast of songs
  Hickory stick rag
Watson, Jane Werner. *The tall book of make-believe*
Welber, Robert. *Goodbye, hello*
Wells, Rosemary. *Don't spill it again, James*
  Noisy Nora
  Shy Charles
Wersba, Barbara. *Do tigers ever bite kings?*
West, Colin. *The king's toothache*
  A moment in rhyme
Westcott, Nadine Bernard. *The lady with the alligator purse*
  Peanut butter and jelly
Weygant, Noemi. *It's autumn!*
  It's summer!
  It's winter!
What do you feed your donkey on?
Wheeling, Lynn. *When you fly*
Wild, Robin. *Little Pig and the big bad wolf*
Wildsmith, Brian. *Animal tricks*
Willard, Nancy. *Night story*
  A visit to William Blake's inn
  The voyage of the Ludgate Hill
Williams, Barbara. *Donna Jean's disaster*
Williams, Garth. *The chicken book*
Williams, Jay. *I wish I had another name*
Williams, Terry Tempest. *Between cattails*
Willis, Jeanne. *The monster bed*
Winthrop, Elizabeth. *Shoes*
Wise, William. *Nanette, the hungry pelican*
Wiseman, Bernard. *Little new kangaroo*
Witch poems
Wittels, Harriet. *Things I hate!*
Wood, Audrey. *The napping house*
Woolaver, Lance. *Christmas with the rural mail*
  From Ben Loman to the sea

Worth, Valerie. *Small poems again*
  Still more small poems
Wright, Josephine Lord. *Cotton Cat and Martha Mouse*
Yektai, Niki. *Bears in pairs*
Yeoman, John. *Our village*
Yolen, Jane. *An invitation to the butterfly ball*
  Ring of earth
  The three bears rhyme book
Yoshi. *Who's hiding here?*
Zemach, Harve. *The judge*
Ziefert, Harriet. *On our way to the barn*
  On our way to the forest
  On our way to the water
  On our way to the zoo
Ziner, Feenie. *Counting carnival*
Zolotow, Charlotte. *River winding*
  Some things go together
  Summer is...

Poland *see* Foreign lands – Poland

Polar bears *see* Animals – polar bears

Police officers *see* Careers – police officers

Poltergeists *see* Ghosts

Poor *see* Poverty

Pop-up books *see* Format, unusual – toy and movable books

Porcupines *see* Animals – porcupines

Porpoise *see* Animals – dolphins

Portugal *see* Foreign lands – Portugal

Possums *see* Animals – possums

Poverty

Alexander, Lloyd. *The king's fountain*
Ambrus, Victor G. *The three poor tailors*
Andersen, H. C. (Hans Christian). *The little match girl*, ill. by Rachel Isadora
  The little match girl, ill. by Blair Lent
Balet, Jan B. *The fence*
Bettina (Bettina Ehrlich). *Pantaloni*
Brand, Oscar. *When I first came to this land*
De Paola, Tomie. *Helga's dowry*
Deveaux, Alexis. *Na-ni*
Hazen, Barbara Shook. *Tight times*
Hoban, Lillian. *Stick-in-the-mud turtle*
Keeping, Charles. *Joseph's yard*
Lindgren, Astrid. *My nightingale is singing*
McCrea, James. *The king's procession*
Maiorano, Robert. *Francisco*

Nolan, Madeena Spray. *My daddy don't go to work*
Provensen, Alice. *Shaker lane*
Rose, Anne. *How does a czar eat potatoes?*
Sawyer, Ruth. *Journey cake, ho!*
Sonneborn, Ruth A. *Friday night is papa night*
  Seven in a bed
Steptoe, John. *Uptown*

Power failure

Baisch, Cris. *When the lights went out*
Freeman, Don. *The night the lights went out*
Rockwell, Anne F. *Blackout*

Practicality *see* Character traits – practicality

Prairie dogs *see* Animals – prairie dogs

Praying mantis *see* Insects – praying mantis

Prejudice

Anders, Rebecca. *A look at prejudice and understanding*
Carlson, Nancy. *Loudmouth George and the new neighbors*
Escudie, René. *Paul and Sebastian*

Pride *see* Character traits – pride

Princes *see* Royalty

Princesses *see* Royalty

Prisons

DuPasquier, Philippe. *The great escape*
Hickman, Martha Whitmore. *When can daddy come home?*
McKee, David. *123456789 Benn*
Solotareff, Grégoire. *Don't call me little bunny*

Problem solving

Adler, David A. *The children of Chelm*
  My dog and the birthday mystery
  My dog and the green sock mystery
  My dog and the key mystery
  My dog and the knock knock mystery
Alexander, Martha G. *I'll protect you from the jungle beasts*
  Move over, Twerp
  Out! Out! Out!
  We never get to do anything
  We're in big trouble, Blackboard Bear
Alexander, Sue. *World famous Muriel*

Allen, Laura Jean. *Rollo and Tweedy and the case of the missing cheese*
  Where is Freddy?
Ames, Mildred. *The wonderful box*
Armitage, Ronda. *Ice creams for Rosie*
  The lighthouse keeper's lunch
Arnosky, Jim. *Mud time and more*
Ashley, Bernard. *Dinner ladies don't count*
Bakken, Harold. *The special string*
Balet, Jan B. *The fence*
Barklem, Jill. *The secret staircase*
Barrett, Judi. *What's left?*
Barry, Katharina. *A bug to hug*
Beim, Lorraine. *Two is a team*
Benarde, Anita. *The pumpkin smasher*
Benchley, Nathaniel. *A ghost named Fred*
Berenstain, Stan. *The bear detectives*
  The Berenstain bears and the messy room
  The Berenstain bears and the missing dinosaur bone
Berg, Jean Horton. *The O'Learys and friends*
Bester, Roger. *Guess what?*
Blaine, Marge. *The terrible thing that happened at our house*
Bonsall, Crosby Newell. *The case of the cat's meow*
  The case of the double cross
  The case of the dumb bells
  The case of the hungry stranger
Booth, Eugene. *At the circus*
  At the fair
  In the air
  In the garden
  In the jungle
  Under the ocean
Bradford, Ann. *The mystery at Misty Falls*
  The mystery of the blind writer
  The mystery of the midget clown
  The mystery of the missing dogs
  The mystery of the square footsteps
  The mystery of the tree house
Brandenberg, Franz. *A picnic, hurrah!*
Branley, Franklyn M. *Big tracks, little tracks*
Bröger, Achim. *Little Harry*
Brown, Jeff. *Flat Stanley*
Brown, Margaret Wise. *They all saw it*
Brown, Palmer. *The silver nutmeg*
Browne, Anthony. *Bear hunt*
Bulette, Sara. *The splendid belt of Mr. Big*
Bunting, Eve. *Jane Martin, dog detective*
Burton, Marilee Robin. *Tail toes eyes ears nose*
Calhoun, Mary. *Audubon cat*
Carlson, Nancy. *Harriet and the garden*
Carrick, Carol. *Ben and the porcupine*
Cauley, Lorinda Bryan. *The new house*
Chaffin, Lillie D. *Tommy's big problem*
Chapman, Carol. *Herbie's troubles*

Christensen, Gardell Dano. *Mrs. Mouse needs a house*

Christian, Mary Blount. *The doggone mystery*
J. J. Leggett, secret agent

Cleary, Beverly. *The real hole*, ill. by DyAnne DiSalvo-Ryan
The real hole, ill. by Mary Stevens

Clymer, Ted. *The horse and the bad morning*

Cole, Babette. *Princess Smartypants*

Coombs, Patricia. *Dorrie and the witches' camp*

Cooney, Nancy Evans. *The blanket that had to go*
Donald says thumbs down

Cooper, Jacqueline. *Angus and the Mona Lisa*

Cressey, James. *Fourteen rats and a rat-catcher*

Cummings, Pat. *Jimmy Lee did it*

Darling, Kathy. *The mystery in Santa's toyshop*

De Paola, Tomie. *Charlie needs a cloak*

Dewey, Ariane. *The fish Peri*

Dickinson, Mary. *Alex's bed*

Domanska, Janina. *The turnip*

Du Bois, William Pène. *The alligator case*

Economakis, Olga. *Oasis of the stars*

Elkin, Benjamin. *Such is the way of the world*

Emberley, Ed. *Rosebud*

Farber, Norma. *How the left-behind beasts built Ararat*

Fassler, Joan. *Boy with a problem*

Feder, Paula Kurzband. *Where does the teacher live?*

Fife, Dale. *Follow that ghost!*

Fowler, Richard. *Inspector Smart gets the message!*

Fremlin, Robert. *Three friends*

Freschet, Berniece. *Bernard of Scotland Yard*

Gelman, Rita Golden. *Professor Coconut and the thief*

Gibbons, Gail. *The missing maple syrup sap mystery*

Gordon, Margaret. *The supermarket mice*

Hancock, Sibyl. *Freaky Francie*

Harber, Frances. *My king has donkey ears*

Hare, Norma Q. *Mystery at mouse house*

Harrison, David Lee. *Detective Bob and the great ape escape*

Heide, Florence Parry. *The shrinking of Treehorn*

Heitler, Susan M. *David decides about thumbsucking*

Hines, Anna Grossnickle. *Maybe a band-aid will help*

Hoban, Lillian. *Arthur's funny money*
The case of the two masked robbers

Holman, Felice. *Elisabeth, the treasure hunter*

Horvath, Betty F. *The cheerful quiet*

Houston, John A. *The bright yellow rope*
A mouse in my house

Hughes, Shirley. *An evening at Alfie's*

Hulse, Gillian. *Morris, where are you?*

Johnston, Johanna. *Edie changes her mind*

Jonas, Ann. *Holes and peeks*

Keats, Ezra Jack. *Goggles*
Whistle for Willie

Keenen, George. *The preposterous week*

Kellogg, Steven. *The mystery of the missing red mitten*
The mystery of the stolen blue paint

Klimowicz, Barbara. *The strawberry thumb*

Krahn, Fernando. *Arthur's adventure in the abandoned house*

Kraus, Robert. *The detective of London*

Kroll, Steven. *Looking for Daniela*

Leonard, Marcia. *Little owl leaves the nest*

Levitin, Sonia. *Who owns the moon?*

Levy, Elizabeth. *Something queer at the ball park*
Something queer at the haunted school
Something queer at the library
Something queer in rock 'n' roll
Something queer is going on
Something queer on vacation

Lewis, Thomas P. *Call for Mr. Sniff*
Mr. Sniff and the motel mystery

Lexau, Joan M. *Benjie*
Benjie on his own
The dog food caper

Lobel, Arnold. *On the day Peter Stuyvesant sailed into town*

Low, Joseph. *What if...?*

Lyon, David. *The brave little computer*

McCloskey, Robert. *Lentil*

McKee, David. *123456789 Benn*

Maestro, Betsy. *The guessing game*

Maiorano, Robert. *Francisco*

Marie, Geraldine. *The magic box*

Maris, Ron. *Hold tight, bear!*

Marshall, James. *Four little troubles*

Marshall, Margaret. *Mike*

Mayer, Mercer. *What do you do with a kangaroo?*

Merriam, Eve. *The birthday door*

Miller, Edna. *Mousekin's mystery*

Molarsky, Osmond. *The peasant and the fly*

Mooser, Stephen. *Funnyman and the penny dodo*
Funnyman's first case

Munsch, Robert N. *Jonathan cleaned up - then he heard a sound*

Musicant, Elke. *The night vegetable eater*

Myers, Walter Dean. *The golden serpent*

Myrick, Jean Lockwood. *Ninety-nine pockets*

Ness, Evaline. *Do you have the time, Lydia?*

Nixon, Joan Lowery. *The Thanksgiving
mystery*
The Valentine mystery
Oakley, Graham. *The church mice in action*
Obrist, Jürg. *They do things right in Albern*
Panek, Dennis. *Detective Whoo*
Pape, Donna Lugg. *Snoino mystery*
Partridge, Jenny. *Hopfellow*
Mr. Squint
Peterkin Pollensnuff
Payne, Emmy. *Katy no-pocket*
Platt, Kin. *Big Max*
Big Max in the mystery of the missing moose
Quackenbush, Robert M. *Detective Mole*
*Detective Mole and the haunted castle
mystery*
Detective Mole and the secret clues
Detective Mole and the Tip-Top mystery
Dig to disaster
Express train to trouble
Piet Potter returns
Piet Potter strikes again
Piet Potter to the rescue
Piet Potter's first case
Stairway to doom
Robb, Brian. *My grandmother's djinn*
Robison, Deborah. *Bye-bye, old buddy*
No elephants allowed
Schermer, Judith. *Mouse in house*
Schurr, Cathleen. *The long and the short of
it*
Segal, Lore. *The story of old Mrs. Brubeck
and how she looked for trouble and where
she found him*
Seuss, Dr. *Did I ever tell you how lucky you
are?*
Hunches in bunches
Sharmat, Marjorie Weinman. *Nate the
Great and the fishy prize*
Nate the Great and the lost list
Nate the Great goes undercover
Shearer, John. *Billy Jo Jive and the case of
the midnight voices*
The case of the sneaker snatcher
Smith, Donald. *Who's wearing my baseball
cap?*
Who's wearing my bow tie?
Who's wearing my sneakers?
Who's wearing my sunglasses?
Smith, Jim. *The frog band and the onion
seller*
Tallon, Robert. *Handella*
Taylor, Mark. *The case of the missing kittens*
Thayer, Jane. *What's a ghost going to do?*
Thomas, Patricia. *"There are rocks in my
socks!" said the ox to the fox*
Thompson, Vivian Laubach.
Camp-in-the-yard
Thomson, Ruth. *Peabody all at sea*
Peabody's first case

Titus, Eve. *Anatole and the cat*
Anatole and the Pied Piper
Anatole and the poodle
Anatole and the robot
Anatole and the thirty thieves
Anatole and the toyshop
Anatole in Italy
Tolstoĭ, Aleksei Nikolaevich. *The great big
enormous turnip*
Türk, Hanne. *Max versus the cube*
A surprise for Max
Van Horn, William. *Twitchtoe, the
beastfinder*
Winthrop, Elizabeth. *Maggie and the
monster*
Wiseman, Bernard. *Doctor Duck and Nurse
Swan*
Wold, Jo Anne. *Tell them my name is
Amanda*
Wood, Audrey. *Detective Valentine*
Wyse, Lois. *Two guppies, a turtle and Aunt
Edna*
Yektai, Niki. *What's missing?*
Yolen, Jane. *Mice on ice*
Piggins
Yorinks, Arthur. *Bravo, Minski*
Zemach, Margot. *It could always be worse*
Zion, Gene. *Harry and the lady next door*

Progress

Barton, Byron. *Wheels*
Burton, Virginia Lee. *The little house*
Coombs, Patricia. *Dorrie and the fortune
teller*
Duvoisin, Roger Antoine. *Lonely Veronica*
Fife, Dale. *The little park*
Goodall, John S. *The story of an English
village*
Greene, Graham. *The little fire engine*
Harrison, David Lee. *Little turtle's big
adventure*
Hoban, Russell. *Arthur's new power*
Ipcar, Dahlov. *One horse farm*
Murschetz, Luis. *Mister Mole*
Peet, Bill. *Countdown to Christmas*
Farewell to Shady Glade
The wump world
Schulman, Janet. *Jack the bum and the
UFO*
Shecter, Ben. *Emily, girl witch of New York*
Steiner, Jörg. *The bear who wanted to be a
bear*

Puerto Rican-Americans *see* Ethnic groups
in the U.S. – Puerto Rican-Americans

Puerto Rico *see* Foreign lands – Puerto
Rico

Puffins *see* Birds – puffins

Pumas *see* Animals – cougars

Puppets

Abelson, Danny. *The Muppets take Manhattan*
Atene, Ann. *The golden guitar*
Brandenberg, Franz. *Aunt Nina's visit*
Brennan, Joseph Killorin. *Gobo and the river*
Bruce, Sheilah B. *The radish day jubilee*
Chernoff, Goldie Taub. *Puppet party*
Children's Television Workshop. *Muppets in my neighborhood*
Cleaver, Elizabeth. *The enchanted caribou*
Collodi, Carlo. *The adventures of Pinocchio*
Eaton, Su. *Punch and Judy in the rain*
Elliott, Dan. *Ernie's little lie*
  A visit to the Sesame Street firehouse
Freeman, Don. *The paper party*
Gikow, Louise. *Boober Fraggle's ghosts*
  Follow that Fraggle!
  Sprocket's Christmas tale
Gilmour, H. B. *Why Wembley Fraggle couldn't sleep*
Hautzig, Deborah. *It's not fair!*
  A visit to the Sesame Street hospital
Heymans, Margriet. *Pippin and Robber Grumblecroak's big baby*
Howe, James. *The case of the missing mother*
Keats, Ezra Jack. *Louie*
Klimowicz, Barbara. *The strawberry thumb*
Lerner, Sharon. *Big Bird's copycat day*
  Follow the monsters!
Little, Mary E. *Ricardo and the puppets*
Marks, Burton. *Puppet plays and puppet-making*
Masks and puppets
Moss, Jeffrey. *The Sesame Street ABC storybook*
  The songs of Sesame Street in poems and pictures
Mother Goose. *The Sesame Street players present Mother Goose*
Muntean, Michaela. *Mokey and the festival of the bells*
  Muppet babies through the year
The Muppet Show book
One rubber duckie
Parsons, Virginia. *Pinocchio and Gepetto*
  Pinocchio and the money tree
  Pinocchio goes on the stage
  Pinocchio plays truant
Peters, Sharon. *Puppet show*
Politi, Leo. *Mr. Fong's toy shop*
Roberts, Sarah. *Bert and the missing mop mix-up*
  Ernie's big mess
  I want to go home!

Sesame Street. *Ernie and Bert can...can you?*
  Sesame Street sign language fun
  Sesame Street word book
Steiner, Charlotte. *Pete's puppets*
Stevenson, Jocelyn. *Jim Henson's Muppets at sea*
  Red and the pumpkins
Stiles, Norman. *I'll miss you, Mr. Hooper*
Stone, Jon. *Big Bird in China*
Tettelbaum, Michael. *The cave of the lost Fraggle*
Tornborg, Pat. *The Sesame Street cookbook*
Weiss, Ellen. *Mokey's birthday present*
  Pigs in space
  You are the star of a Muppet adventure
Young, Ed. *The rooster's horns*

Purim *see* Holidays – Purim

Puzzles *see* Rebuses; Riddles

Queens *see* Royalty

Questioning *see* Character traits – questioning

Quicksand *see* Sand

Rabbits *see* Animals – rabbits

Raccoons *see* Animals – raccoons

Race *see* Ethnic groups in the U.S.

Race car drivers *see* Careers – race car drivers

Racing *see* Sports – racing

Railroad engineers *see* Careers – railroad engineers

Railroads *see* Trains

Rain *see* Weather – rain

Rainbows *see* Weather – rainbows

Rangers *see* Careers – park rangers

Rats *see* Animals – rats

Ravens *see* Birds – ravens

Reading *see* Activities – reading

Rebuses

Adler, David A. *Bunny rabbit rebus*
Coletta, Irene. *From A to Z*
Doolittle, Eileen. *The ark in the attic*
Downie, Jill. *Alphabet puzzle*
Eberle, Irmengarde. *Picture stories for children*
Heuck, Sigrid. *Who stole the apples?*
Marzollo, Jean. *The rebus treasury*
Morris, Ann. *The Cinderella rebus book*
 The Little Red Riding Hood rebus book
Mother Goose. *Mother Goose in hieroglyphics*
Partch, Virgil Franklin. *The Christmas cookie sprinkle snitcher*
 The VIP's mistake book
Weil, Lisl. *Mother Goose picture riddles*

Reindeer *see* Animals – reindeer

Religion

Adler, David A. *A picture book of Hanukkah*
 A picture book of Israel
Aichinger, Helga. *The shepherd*
Alexander, Cecil Frances. *All things bright and beautiful*
Aliki. *Mummies made in Egypt*
Allstrom, Elizabeth C. *Songs along the way*
Androcles and the lion, ill. by Janusz Grabianski
Anglund, Joan Walsh. *A book of good tidings from the Bible*
Aoki, Hisako. *Santa's favorite story*
Baker, Betty. *And me, coyote!*
Baker, Sanna Anderson. *Who's a friend of the water-spurting whale*
Balet, Jan B. *The gift*
Barker, Peggy. *What happened when grandma died*
Bawden, Nina. *St. Francis of Assisi*
Bayar, Steven. *Rachel and Mischa*
Baylor, Byrd. *The way to start a day*
Berger, Barbara Helen. *The donkey's dream*
Bible. *Best-loved Bible verses for children*
Bible. New Testament. *The Lord's prayer*, Catholic version, ill. by Ingri and Edgar Parin d'Aulaire
 The Lord's prayer, Protestant version, ill. by Ingri and Edgar Parin d'Aulaire

 The Lord's prayer, ill. by George Kraus
Bible. New Testament. Gospels. *Christmas*
 The first Christmas, ill. by Barbara Neustadt
 The Nativity
Bible. Old Testament. Daniel. *Daniel in the lions' den*, ill. by Leon Baxter
 Shadrach, Meshack and Abednego
Bible. Old Testament. David. *David and Goliath*, ill. by Leon Baxter
Bible. Old Testament. Jonah. *The Book of Jonah*, ill. by Peter Spier
 Jonah, ill. by Kurt Mitchell
 Jonah and the great fish, ill. by Leon Baxter
Bible. Old Testament. Psalms. *The Lord is my shepherd*, ill. by George Kraus
 The Lord is my shepherd, ill. by Tasha Tudor
Brin, Ruth F. *David and Goliath*
 The story of Esther
Briscoe, Jill. *The innkeeper's daughter*
Brown, Margaret Wise. *On Christmas eve*
Bruna, Dick. *Christmas*
Bulla, Clyde Robert. *Jonah and the great fish*
Burdekin, Harold. *A child's grace*
Chaikin, Miriam. *Exodus*
Chanover, Hyman. *Happy Hanukah everybody*
Chapman, Jean. *Moon-Eyes*
Chase, Catherine. *The miracles at Cana*
Children go where I send thee
Children's prayers from around the world
A child's book of prayers, ill. by Michael Hague
Cohen, Barbara. *The donkey's story*
Cone, Molly. *The Jewish Sabbath*
Cooney, Barbara. *A little prayer*
Dellinger, Annetta. *You are special to Jesus*
De Paola, Tomie. *The clown of God*
 The Lady of Guadalupe
 The legend of Old Befana
 The miracles of Jesus
 The parables of Jesus
 The story of the three wise kings
De Regniers, Beatrice Schenk. *David and Goliath*
Din dan don, it's Christmas
Douglas, Robert W. *John Paul II*
Farber, Norma. *How the hibernators came to Bethlehem*
Fass, David E. *The shofar that lost its voice*
Field, Rachel Lyman. *Prayer for a child*
First graces
First prayers, ill. by Anna Maria Magagna
First prayers, ill. by Tasha Tudor
Fisher, Leonard Everett. *The seven days of creation*
Fitch, Florence Mary. *A book about God*
Forrester, Victoria. *Poor Gabriella*

Fraser, James Howard. *Los Posadas*
The friendly beasts and A partridge in a pear tree
Galdone, Paul. *The first seven days*
Garfield, Leon. *King Nimrod's tower*
The writing on the wall
Goddard, Carrie Lou. *Isn't it a wonder!*
Graham, Lorenz B. *David he no fear*
Every man heart lay down
Hongry catch the foolish boy
A road down in the sea
Gramatky, Hardie. *Nikos and the sea god*
Haas, Dorothy. *My first communion*
Haiz, Danah. *Jonah's journey*
Hamil, Thomas Arthur. *Brother Alonzo*
Heck, Elisabeth. *The black sheep*
Heine, Helme. *One day in paradise*
Hillman, Priscilla. *The Merry-Mouse book of prayers and graces*
Hirsh, Marilyn. *I love Passover*
Joseph who loved the Sabbath
Potato pancakes all around
Hoffmann, Felix. *The story of Christmas*
Hopkins, Lee Bennett. *And God bless me*
Houselander, Caryll. *Petook*
Hughes, Shirley. *Lucy and Tom's Christmas*
Hutton, Warwick. *Adam and Eve*
Jonah and the great fish
Moses in the bulrushes
I sing a song of the saints of God
Ife, Elaine. *The childhood of Jesus*
Moses in the bulrushes
Stories Jesus told
Jones, Jessie Mae Orton. *A little child*
Small rain
This is the way
Jüchen, Aurel von. *The Holy Night*
Karlinsky, Ruth Schild. *My first book of Mitzvos*
Keats, Ezra Jack. *God is in the mountain*
The little drummer boy
Kipling, Rudyard. *The miracle of the mountain*
Knapp, John II. *A pillar of pepper and other Bible nursery rhymes*
Krull, Kathleen. *Songs of praise*
Kuskin, Karla. *Jerusalem, shining still*
Laurence, Margaret. *The Christmas birthday story*
Leeton, Will C. *The Tower of Babel*
Levitin, Sonia. *A sound to remember*
Lexau, Joan M. *More beautiful than flowers*
Lindgren, Astrid. *Christmas in the stable*
Lines, Kathleen. *Once in royal David's city*
Little, Emily. *David and the giant*
MacBeth, George. *Jonah and the Lord*
McDermott, Beverly Brodsky. *Jonah*
McDermott, Gerald. *The voyage of Osiris*
McKissack, Patricia C. *My Bible ABC book*
Marshall, Lyn. *Yoga for your children*
Michael, Emory H. *Androcles and the lion*

Mitchell, Cynthia. *Here a little child I stand*
Miyoshi, Sekiya. *Singing David*
Nussbaumer, Mares. *Away in a manger*
Petersham, Maud. *The Christ Child*
Pieńkowski, Jan. *Easter*
Price, Christine. *One is God*
Reed, Allison. *Genesis*
Sahagun, Bernardino de. *Spirit child*
Scholey, Arthur. *Baboushka*
Schwartz, Amy. *Mrs. Moskowitz and the Sabbath candlesticks*
Seignobosc, Françoise. *The thank-you book*
Shulevitz, Uri. *The magician*
Slate, Joseph. *Who is coming to our house?*
The song of the Three Holy Children
Stan-Padilla, Viento. *Dream Feather*
Sugarman, Joan G. *Inside the Synagogue*
Taylor, Mark. *"Lamb," said the lion, "I am here"*
Thomas, Kathy. *The angel's quest*
Tolstoĭ, Alekseĭ Nikolaevich. *Shoemaker Martin*
Trent, Robbie. *The first Christmas*
Tudor, Tasha. *More prayers*
Van der Meer, Ron. *Oh Lord!*
Vasiliu, Mircea. *Everything is somewhere*
Waddell, Helen. *The story of Saul the king*
Weil, Lisl. *The story of the Wise Men and the Child*
The very first story ever told
What a morning!
Wheeler, Opal. *Sing in praise*
Wiesner, William. *The Tower of Babel*
Wildsmith, Brian. *The true cross*
Williams, Marcia. *The first Christmas*
Winthrop, Elizabeth. *A child is born*
He is risen

Religion – Noah

Bible. Old Testament. *Noah and the ark,* ill. by Pauline Baynes
Bolliger, Max. *Noah and the rainbow*
Chase, Catherine. *Noah's ark*
Delessert, Etienne. *The endless party*
De Paola, Tomie. *Noah and the ark*
Duvoisin, Roger Antoine. *A for the ark*
Elborn, Andrew. *Noah and the ark and the animals*
Farber, Norma. *How the left-behind beasts built Ararat*
Where's Gomer?
Fussenegger, Gertrud. *Noah's ark*
Geisert, Arthur. *The ark*
Goffstein, M. B. (Marilyn Brooke). *My Noah's ark*
Graham, Lorenz B. *God wash the world and start again*
Haubensak-Tellenbach, Margrit. *The story of Noah's ark*
Hewitt, Kathryn. *Two by two*

Hogrogian, Nonny. *Noah's ark*
Hutton, Warwick. *Noah and the great flood*
Ife, Elaine. *Noah and the ark*
Kuskin, Karla. *The animals and the ark*
Lenski, Lois. *Mr. and Mrs. Noah*
MacBeth, George. *Noah's journey*
McKié, Roy. *Noah's ark*
Martin, Charles E. *Noah's ark*
Matias. *Mr. Noah and the animals*
Mee, Charles L. *Noah*
Palazzo, Tony. *Noah's ark*
Rose, Gerald. *Trouble in the ark*
Rounds, Glen. *Washday on Noah's ark*
Singer, Isaac Bashevis. *Why Noah chose the dove*
Smith, Elmer Boyd. *The story of Noah's ark*
Smith, Roger. *How the animals saved the ark and put two and two together*
Spier, Peter. *Noah's ark*
Webb, Clifford. *The story of Noah*
Wiesner, William. *Noah's ark*
Windham, Sophie. *Noah's ark*

Repetitive stories *see* Circular tales; Cumulative tales

Reporters *see* Careers – reporters

Reptiles

Barrett, Judi. *Snake is totally tail*
Colby, C. B. (Carroll Burleigh). *Who went there?*
Cortesi, Wendy W. *Explore a spooky swamp*
Cristini, Ermanno. *In the pond*
Daly, Kathleen N. *A child's book of snakes, lizards and other reptiles*
Harris, Susan. *Reptiles*
Kuchalla, Susan. *What is a reptile?*
Pluckrose, Henry. *Reptiles*

Reptiles – alligators, crocodiles

Aliki. *Keep your mouth closed, dear*
Use your head, dear
Aruego, José. *A crocodile's tale*
Balzola, Asun. *Munia and the orange crocodile*
Bradman, Tony. *See you later, alligator*
Brown, Ruth. *Crazy Charlie*
Campbell, M. Rudolph. *The talking crocodile*
Carrick, Carol. *The crocodiles still wait*
Cazet, Denys. *The duck with squeaky feet*
Christelow, Eileen. *Jerome the babysitter*
Cushman, Doug. *Nasty Kyle the crocodile*
Dahl, Roald. *The enormous crocodile*
De Groat, Diane. *Alligator's toothache*
De Paola, Tomie. *Bill and Pete*
Bill and Pete go down the Nile
Dorros, Arthur. *Alligator shoes*

Dragonwagon, Crescent. *Alligator arrived with apples*
Du Bois, William Pène. *The alligator case*
Duvoisin, Roger Antoine. *The crocodile in the tree*
Crocus
Eastman, P. D. (Philip D.). *Flap your wings*
Galdone, Paul. *The monkey and the crocodile*
Gantos, Jack. *Swampy alligator*
Gross, Ruth Belov. *Alligators and other crocodilians*
Guy, Rosa. *Mother crocodile*
Hartelius, Margaret A. *The chicken's child*
Hirschi, Ron. *Who lives in... Alligator Swamp?*
Hoban, Russell. *Arthur's new power*
Dinner at Alberta's
Hodeir, André. *Warwick's three bottles*
Holland, Isabelle. *Kevin's hat*
Hurd, Thacher. *Mama don't allow*
Kinnell, Galway. *How the alligator missed breakfast*
Kirn, Ann. *The tale of a crocodile*
Kunhardt, Edith. *Danny's mystery Valentine*
Trick or treat, Danny!
Lexau, Joan M. *Crocodile and hen*
Lionni, Leo. *Cornelius*
McPhail, David. *Alligators are awful (and they have terrible manners, too)*
Mayer, Marianna. *Alley oop!*
Mayer, Mercer. *There's an alligator under my bed*
Minarik, Else Holmelund. *No fighting, no biting!*
Muntean, Michaela. *Alligator's garden*
Pack, Robert. *How to catch a crocodile*
Parker, Nancy Winslow. *The crocodile under Louis Finneberg's bed*
Peterson, Esther Allen. *Frederick's alligator*
Pickett, Carla. *Calvin Crocodile and the terrible noise*
Rice, James. *Gaston goes to Texas*
Rubel, Nicole. *It came from the swamp*
Schubert, Ingrid. *There's a crocodile under my bed!*
Sendak, Maurice. *Alligators all around*
Shaw, Evelyn S. *Alligator*
Stevenson, James. *Monty*
No need for Monty
Venable, Alan. *The checker players*
Waber, Bernard. *Funny, funny Lyle*
Lovable Lyle
Lyle and the birthday party
Lyle finds his mother
Lyle, Lyle Crocodile
Wasmuth, Eleanor. *An alligator day*
The picnic basket
Watts, Marjorie-Ann. *Crocodile medicine*
Crocodile plaster
Weiss, Ellen. *Millicent Maybe*
West, Colin. *Have you seen the crocodile?*

Reptiles – crocodiles *see* Reptiles – alligators, crocodiles

Reptiles – iguanas

Newfield, Marcia. *Iggy*
Rosen, Winifred. *Henrietta and the day of the iguana*

Reptiles – lizards

Anderson, Lonzo. *Izzard*
Baker, Betty. *Latki and the lightning lizard*
Carle, Eric. *The mixed-up chameleon*
Conklin, Gladys. *I caught a lizard*
Himmelman, John. *Talester the lizard*
Lionni, Leo. *A color of his own*
Lopshire, Robert. *I am better than you*
McNeely, Jeannette. *Where's Izzy?*
Massie, Diane Redfield. *Chameleon the spy and the terrible toaster trap*
   The Komodo dragon's jewels
Shannon, George. *Lizard's song*

Reptiles – snakes

Aardema, Verna. *What's so funny, Ketu?*
Appleby, Leonard. *Snakes*
Banchek, Linda. *Snake in, snake out*
Berson, Harold. *Joseph and the snake*
Buckley, Richard. *The greedy python*
Carlson, Natalie Savage. *Marie Louise and Christophe at the carnival*
Demi. *The hallowed horse*
Forrester, Victoria. *Oddward*
Freschet, Berniece. *The watersnake*
Hoff, Syd. *Slithers*
Huxley, Aldous. *The crows of Pearblossom*
Kudrna, C. Imbior. *To bathe a boa*
Lauber, Patricia. *Snakes are hunters*
Le Guin, Ursula K. *Solomon Leviathan's nine hundred and thirty-first trip around the world*
Lemerise, Bruce. *Sheldon's lunch*
Lesikin, Joan. *Down the road*
Lionni, Leo. *In the rabbitgarden*
Newton, Patricia Montgomery. *The frog who drank the waters of the world*
Noble, Trinka Hakes. *The day Jimmy's boa ate the wash*
   Jimmy's boa bounces back
Oppenheim, Joanne. *Mrs. Peloki's snake*
Prather, Ray. *The ostrich girl*
Reinl, Edda. *The little snake*
Turpin, Lorna. *The sultan's snakes*
Ungerer, Tomi. *Crictor*
Waber, Bernard. *The snake*
Wildsmith, Brian. *Python's party*

Reptiles – turtles, tortoises

Abisch, Roz. *The clever turtle*
Æsop. *The hare and the tortoise*, ill. by Paul Galdone
   The hare and the tortoise, ill. by Gerald Rose
   The hare and the tortoise, ill. by Peter Weevers
   The tortoise and the hare, ill. by Janet Stevens
Asch, Frank. *Turtle tale*
Augarde, Steve. *Barnaby Shrew, Black Dan and...the mighty wedgwood*
   Barnaby Shrew goes to sea
Baumann, Hans. *The hare's race*
Bourgeois, Paulette. *Franklin in the dark*
Brunhoff, Laurent de. *Gregory and Lady Turtle in the valley of the music trees*
Buckley, Richard. *The foolish tortoise*
Christian, Mary Blount. *Devin and Goliath*
Craig, Janet. *Turtles*
Cromie, William J. *Steven and the green turtle*
Cummings, Betty Sue. *Turtle*, ill. by Susan Dodge
Darby, Gene. *What is a turtle?*
Davis, Alice Vaught. *Timothy turtle*
Dodd, Lynley. *The smallest turtle*
Domanska, Janina. *Look, there is a turtle flying*
   The tortoise and the tree
Du Bois, William Pène. *The hare and the tortoise and the tortoise and the hare*
Elks, Wendy. *Charles B. Wombat and the very strange thing*
Emberley, Ed. *Rosebud*
Freeman, Don. *The turtle and the dove*
Freschet, Berniece. *Turtle pond*
Gendel, Evelyn. *Tortoise and turtle*
   Tortoise and turtle abroad
Goldsmith, Howard. *Toto the timid turtle*
Graham, Al. *Timothy Turtle*, ill. by Tony Palazzo
Harris, Dorothy Joan. *Four seasons for Toby*
Harrison, David Lee. *Little turtle's big adventure*
Hoban, Lillian. *Stick-in-the-mud turtle*
   Turtle spring
Jeffery, Graham. *Thomas the tortoise*
La Fontaine, Jean de. *The hare and the tortoise*
Lesikin, Joan. *Down the road*
Lubell, Winifred. *Rosalie, the bird market turtle*
MacGregor, Ellen. *Theodor Turtle*
McLenighan, Valjean. *Turtle and rabbit*
Maestro, Giulio. *The tortoise's tug of war*
Maris, Ron. *I wish I could fly*
Marshall, James. *Yummers too*
Matsutani, Miyoko. *The fisherman under the sea*

Murdocca, Sal. *Tuttle's shell*
Parry, Marian. *King of the fish*
St. Pierre, Wendy. *Henry finds a home*
Selsam, Millicent E. *Let's get turtles*
Thayer, Jane. *Mr. Turtle's magic glasses*
Thayer, Mike. *In the middle of the puddle*
Troughton, Joanna. *Tortoise's dream*
The turtle, ill. by Charlotte Knox
Van Woerkom, Dorothy. *Harry and Shelburt*
Wiese, Kurt. *The cunning turtle*
Williams, Barbara. *Albert's toothache*
Wolf, Ann. *The rabbit and the turtle*
Wyse, Lois. *Two guppies, a turtle and Aunt Edna*
Yashima, Tarō. *Seashore story*
Ziefert, Harriet. *Where's the turtle?*

Rest *see* Sleep

Rhinoceros *see* Animals – rhinoceros

Rhyming text *see* Poetry, rhyme

Riddles

Aardema, Verna. *Ji-nongo-nongo means riddles*
Adler, David A. *The carsick zebra and other riddles*
The purple turkey and other Thanksgiving riddles
The twisted witch and other spooky riddles
Anno, Mitsumasa. *Anno's math games*
Bell, Anthea. *The wise queen*
Bernstein, Joanne E. *Creepy crawly critter riddles*
More unidentified flying riddles
What was the wicked witch's real name?
The big Peter Rabbit book
Bishop, Ann. *Chicken riddle*
The Ella Fannie elephant riddle book
Hey riddle riddle
Merry-go-riddle
Noah riddle?
Oh, riddlesticks!
The riddle ages
Riddle-iculous rid-alphabet book
Wild Bill Hiccup's riddle book
Brown, Marc. *Spooky riddles*
What do you call a dumb bunny? and other rabbit riddles, games, jokes and cartoons
Burns, Diane L. *Elephants never forget!*
Burton, Marilee Robin. *Tail toes eyes ears nose*
Cerf, Bennett Alfred. *Bennett Cerf's book of animal riddles*
Bennett Cerf's book of laughs
Bennett Cerf's book of riddles
More riddles

Cole, Joanna. *The Clown-Arounds go on vacation*
Get well, Clown-Arounds!
Crowley, Arthur. *The wagon man*
Daniels, Guy. *The Tsar's riddles*
Degen, Bruce. *The little witch and the riddle*
Delaney, M. C. *The marigold monster*
Demi. *Where is it?*
De Regniers, Beatrice Schenk. *It does not say meow!*
Doolittle, Eileen. *The ark in the attic*
Downie, Jill. *Alphabet puzzle*
Duncan, Riana. *A nutcracker in a tree*
Elkin, Benjamin. *The wisest man in the world*
Emberley, Ed. *Ed Emberley's amazing look through book*
Fleischman, Sid. *Kate's secret riddle*
Fletcher, Elizabeth. *What am I?*
Gackenbach, Dick. *Supposes*
Gay, Zhenya. *What's your name?*
Geisert, Arthur. *Pigs from A to Z*
Goundaud, Karen Jo. *A very mice joke book*
Gregorich, Barbara. *My friend goes left*
Grimm, Jacob. *Rapunzel*, ill. by Bernadette Watts
Rumpelstiltskin, ill. by Jacqueline Ayer
Rumpelstiltskin, ill. by Donna Diamond
Rumpelstiltskin, ill. by Paul Galdone
Rumpelstiltskin, ill. by John Wallner
Rumpelstiltskin, ill. by Paul O. Zelinsky
Hall, Katy. *Buggy riddles*
Fishy riddles
Hall, Malcolm. *CariCATures*
Hample, Stoo. *Stoo Hample's silly joke book*
Yet another big fat funny silly book
High on a hill
Hoff, Syd. *Syd Hoff's best jokes ever*
Holman, Felice. *Elisabeth, the treasure hunter*
Jensen, Virginia Allen. *Red thread riddles*
Keller, Charles. *Giggle puss*
The nutty joke book
School daze
Kessler, Leonard P. *Riddles that rhyme for Halloween time*
Lewis, Naomi. *The butterfly collector*
Low, Joseph. *Five men under one umbrella*
A mad wet hen and other riddles
Lyfick, Warren. *Animal tales*
The little book of fowl jokes
McKié, Roy. *The riddle book*
Maestro, Giulio. *Halloween howls*
A raft of riddles
Riddle romp
Modell, Frank. *Look out, it's April Fools' Day*
Moncure, Jane Belk. *Riddle me a riddle*
Mooser, Stephen. *Funnyman's first case*
Peppé, Rodney. *Hey riddle diddle*
Peterson, Scott K. *What's your name?*

Phillips, Louis. *The upside down riddle book*
Potter, Beatrix. *The tale of Squirrel Nutkin*
Romanoli, Robert. *What's so funny?!!*
Roop, Peter. *Going buggy!*
Let's celebrate!
Stick out your tongue!
Rosenbloom, Joseph. *The funniest joke book ever!*
Schwartz, Alvin. *Ten copycats in a boat and other riddles*
Selberg, Ingrid. *Nature's hidden world*
Seuss, Dr. *The cat's quizzer*
Swann, Brian. *A basket full of white eggs*
Thaler, Mike. *The yellow brick toad*
Thomas, Gary. *The best of the little books*
Türk, Hanne. *Max versus the cube*
Wakefield, Joyce. *Ask a silly question*
Walton, Rick. *Dumb clucks!*
Something's fishy!
Zwetchkenbaum, G. *The Peanuts shape circus puzzle book*
The Peanuts sleepy time puzzle book
The Snoopy farm puzzle book
Snoopy safari puzzle book

Right and left *see* Concepts – left and right

Rivers

Bellamy, David. *The river*
Biro, Val. *The wind in the willows the river bank*
Brennan, Joseph Killorin. *Gobo and the river*
Brook, Judy. *Tim mouse goes down the stream*
Bushey, Jerry. *The barge book*
Carrick, Carol. *The brook*
Dabcovich, Lydia. *Follow the river*
Flack, Marjorie. *The boats on the river*
Grahame, Kenneth. *The river bank*
Gramatky, Hardie. *Little Toot on the Mississippi*
Grasshopper to the rescue
Hadithi, Mwenye. *Hot hippo*
Holling, Holling C. (Holling Clancy). *Paddle-to-the-sea*
Keeping, Charles. *Alfie finds the other side of the world*
Locker, Thomas. *Where the river begins*
Michl, Reinhard. *A day on the river*
Murphy, Shirley Rousseau. *Tattie's river journey*
Oakley, Graham. *The church mice adrift*

Roads

Bate, Norman. *Who built the highway?*
Goodall, John S. *The story of a main street*
Kehoe, Michael. *Road closed*
Roennfeldt, Robert. *A day on the avenue*

Robbers *see* Crime

Robins *see* Birds – robins

Robots

Bradford, Ann. *The mystery of the square footsteps*
Bunting, Eve. *The robot birthday*
Cole, Babette. *The trouble with dad*
Greene, Carol. *Robots*
Hoban, Lillian. *The laziest robot in zone one*
Krahn, Fernando. *Robot-bot-bot*
Kroll, Steven. *Otto*
Lauber, Patricia. *Get ready for robots!*
Marshall, Edward. *Space case*
Marzollo, Jean. *Jed and the space bandits*
Jed's junior space patrol
Paul, Sherry. *2-B and the rock 'n roll band*
2-B and the space visitor
Titus, Eve. *Anatole and the robot*

Rockets *see* Space and space ships

Rocking horses *see* Toys – rocking horses

Rocks

Baylor, Byrd. *Everybody needs a rock*
Gans, Roma. *Rock collecting*
Kehoe, Michael. *The rock quarry book*
Lee, Jeanne M. *Legend of the Li River*
Lionni, Leo. *On my beach there are many pebbles*
McKee, David. *The hill and the rock*
Selsam, Millicent E. *A first look at rocks*

Roller skating *see* Sports – Roller skating

Roosters *see* Birds – chickens

Rosh Hashanah *see* Holidays – Rosh Hashanah

Round-robin tales *see* Circular tales

Royalty

Aardema, Verna. *The riddle of the drum*
Abrons, Mary. *For Alice a palace*
Aitken, Amy. *Ruby, the red knight*
Alexander, Lloyd. *The king's fountain*
Allen, Pamela. *Bertie and the bear*
A lion in the night
Ambrus, Victor G. *The Sultan's bath*
Andersen, H. C. (Hans Christian). *The emperor's new clothes*, ill. by Pamela Baldwin-Ford
The emperor's new clothes, ill. by Erik Blegvad
The emperor's new clothes, ill. by Virginia Lee Burton

The emperor's new clothes, ill. by Jack and Irene Delano
The emperor's new clothes, ill. by Hélène Desputeaux
The emperor's new clothes, ill. by Birte Dietz
The emperor's new clothes, ill. by Dorothée Duntze
The emperor's new clothes, ill. by Jack Kent
The emperor's new clothes, ill. by Monika Laimgruber
The emperor's new clothes, ill. by Anne F. Rockwell
The emperor's new clothes, ill. by Janet Stevens
The emperor's new clothes, ill. by Nadine Bernard Westcott
The nightingale, ill. by Demi
The nightingale, ill. by Beni Montresor
The nightingale, ill. by Lisbeth Zwerger
The princess and the pea, ill. by Dorothée Duntze
The princess and the pea, ill. by Dick Gackenbach
The princess and the pea, ill. by Paul Galdone
The princess and the pea, ill. by Janet Stevens
The princess and the pea, ill. by Eve Tharlet
The swineherd, ill. by Dorothée Duntze
Anderson, Lonzo. *Two hundred rabbits*
Anno, Mitsumasa. *The king's flower*
Aruego, José. *The king and his friends*
Auerbach, Marjorie. *King Lavra and the barber*
Babbitt, Samuel F. *The forty-ninth magician*
Balet, Jan B. *The king and the broom maker*
Bang, Betsy. *Tutuni the tailor bird*
Bang, Molly. *Tye May and the magic brush*
Baring, Maurice. *The blue rose*
Basile, Giambattista. *Petrosinella*
Baum, Arline. *Opt*
Baumann, Kurt. *The prince and the lute*
Bawden, Nina. *Princess Alice*
Bell, Anthea. *The wise queen*
Bellville, Cheryl Walsh. *Theater magic*
Beresford, Elisabeth. *Jack and the magic stove*
Berson, Harold. *The thief who hugged a moonbeam*
Bill, Helen. *Shoes fit for a king*
Birch, David. *The king's chessboard*
Birrer, Cynthia. *The lady and the unicorn*
Bohdal, Susi. *The magic honey jar*
Bolliger, Max. *The most beautiful song*
Bond, Michael. *Paddington at the palace*
Boswell, Stephen. *King Gorboduc's fabulous zoo*
Bowden, Joan Chase. *A hat for the queen*
A new home for Snow Ball

Brenner, Barbara. *The prince and the pink blanket*
Brierley, Louise. *King Lion and his cooks*
Bright, Robert. *Hurrah for Freddie!*
Browne, Caroline. *Mrs. Christie's farmhouse*
Brunhoff, Jean de. *Babar the king*
Brunhoff, Laurent de. *Babar's visit to Bird Island*
Buffett, Jimmy. *The jolly mon*
Burningham, John. *Time to get out of the bath, Shirley*
Canfield, Jane White. *The frog prince*
Chapman, Gaynor. *The luck child*
Clifford, Eth. *Why is an elephant called an elephant?*
Climo, Shirley. *King of the birds*
Cole, Babette. *Prince Cinders*
Princess Smartypants
Cole, Brock. *The king at the door*
Company González, Mercè. *Killian and the dragons*
Conover, Chris. *The wizard's daughter*
Coombs, Patricia. *Tilabel*
Cooney, Barbara. *Little brother and little sister*
Cooper, Gale. *Unicorn moon*
Costa, Nicoletta. *The mischievous princess*
Crabtree, Judith. *The sparrow's story at the king's command*
Cretien, Paul D. *Sir Henry and the dragon*
Cunliffe, John. *The king's birthday cake*
Damjan, Mischa. *The little prince and the tiger cat*
Dasent, George W. *East o' the sun, west o' the moon*
De La Mare, Walter. *Molly Whuppie*
De Paola, Tomie. *The wonderful dragon of Timlin*
De Regniers, Beatrice Schenk. *May I bring a friend?*
Dewey, Ariane. *Dorin and the dragon*
Domanska, Janina. *King Krakus and the dragon*
Look, there is a turtle flying
Dos Santos, Joyce Audy. *The diviner*
Elkin, Benjamin. *The big jump and other stories*
Gillespie and the guards
The king who could not sleep
The king's wish and other stories
The loudest noise in the world
The wisest man in the world
Espenscheid, Gertrude E. *The oh ball*
Fern, Eugene. *The king who was too busy*
The firebird, ill. by Moira Kemp
Fisher, Leonard Everett. *Theseus and the minotaur*
The tower of London
Fleischman, Sid. *Longbeard the wizard*
Flot, Jeannette B. *Princess Kalina and the hedgehog*

Foreman, Michael. *War and peas*
Freeman, Don. *Forever laughter*
Gackenbach, Dick. *Harvey, the foolish pig*
  King Wacky
Galdone, Paul. *The amazing pig*
  The monster and the tailor
Garrett, Jennifer. *The queen who stole the sky*
Gay, Michel. *Bibi's birthday surprise*
Gekiere, Madeleine. *The frilly lily and the princess*
Gianni, Peg. *Alex, the amazing juggler*
Glass, Andrew. *Chickpea and the talking cow*
The golden goose, ill. by William Stobbs
Greaves, Margaret. *A net to catch the wind*
Greene, Ellin. *Princess Rosetta and the popcorn man*
Grimm, Jacob. *Cinderella*, ill. by Nonny Hogrogian
  Cinderella, ill. by Svend Otto S.
  The donkey prince, ill. by Barbara Cooney
  The earth gnome, ill. by Margot Tomes
  The golden goose, ill. by Dorothée Duntze
  The golden goose, ill. by Isadore Seltzer
  The golden goose, ill. by Martin Ursell
  The goose girl, ill. by Sabine Bruntjen
  King Grisly-Beard
  Rapunzel, ill. by Jutta Ash
  Rapunzel, ill. by Bert Dodson
  Rapunzel, ill. by Trina Schart Hyman
  Rapunzel, ill. by Bernadette Watts
  Rumpelstiltskin, ill. by Jacqueline Ayer
  Rumpelstiltskin, ill. by Donna Diamond
  Rumpelstiltskin, ill. by Paul Galdone
  Rumpelstiltskin, ill. by John Wallner
  Rumpelstiltskin, ill. by Paul O. Zelinsky
  The twelve dancing princesses, ill. by Dennis Hockerman
  The twelve dancing princesses, ill. by Errol Le Cain
  The twelve dancing princesses, ill. by Gerald McDermott
  The twelve dancing princesses, ill. by Uri Shulevitz
Gurney, Nancy. *The king, the mice and the cheese*
Harber, Frances. *My king has donkey ears*
Hastings, Selina. *The singing ringing tree*
Haugaard, Erik. *Prince Boghole*
Hawthorne, Julian. *Rumpty-Dudget's tower*
Hayes, Sarah. *Bad egg*
Haywood, Carolyn. *The king's monster*
Heine, Helme. *King Bounce the 1st*
  The most wonderful egg in the world
Hewitt, Kathryn. *King Midas and the golden touch*
Hoffmann, E. T. A. *The nutcracker*, ill. by Lisbeth Zwerger

Hughes, Peter. *The emperor's oblong pancake*
  The king who loved candy
Hutchins, Pat. *King Henry's palace*
Isele, Elizabeth. *The frog princess*
Joerns, Consuelo. *The midnight castle*
Johnson, Crockett. *The emperor's gift*
  The frowning prince
Kahl, Virginia. *The Baron's booty*
  The Duchess bakes a cake
  Gunhilde and the Halloween spell
  Gunhilde's Christmas booke
  The habits of rabbits
  Plum pudding for Christmas
Karlin, Nurit. *A train for the king*
Kennedy, Richard. *The lost kingdom of Karnica*
Kessler, Leonard P. *Soup for the king*
Knight, Hilary. *Hilary Knight's Cinderella*
Kraus, Robert. *The king's trousers*
Kroll, Steven. *Fat magic*
Langner, Nola. *By the light of the silvery moon*
Langton, Jane. *The hedgehog boy*
Laroche, Michel. *The snow rose*
Lasker, David. *The boy who loved music*
Laskowski, Jerzy. *Master of the royal cats*
Lattimore, Deborah Nourse. *The prince and the golden ax*
Lee, Jeanne M. *Toad is the uncle of heaven*
Littledale, Freya. *The magic plum tree*
Lobel, Anita. *A birthday for the princess*
  The seamstress of Salzburg
  Sven's bridge
Lobel, Arnold. *Prince Bertram the bad*
Lorenz, Lee. *The feathered ogre*
McCrea, James. *The king's procession*
  The magic tree
McDermott, Gerald. *The voyage of Osiris*
MacDonald, George. *The light princess*, ill. by Katie Thamer Treherne
  Little Daylight
McKee, David. *King Rollo and the birthday*
  King Rollo and the bread
  King Rollo and the new shoes
McKissack, Patricia C. *Cinderella*, ill. by Tom Dunnington
  King Midas and his gold, ill. by Tom Dunnington
  The king's new clothes, ill. by Gwen Connelly
McLenighan, Valjean. *What you see is what you get*
  You are what you are
McNaughton, Colin. *The rat race*
Mahood, Kenneth. *The laughing dragon*
Mahy, Margaret. *17 kings and 42 elephants*
Martin, C. L. G. *The dragon nanny*
Matsutani, Miyoko. *The fisherman under the sea*
Mayer, Marianna. *The black horse*

Mayer, Mercer. *The queen always wanted to dance*

Miller, M. L. *Dizzy from fools*

Milne, A. A. (Alan Alexander). *Prince Rabbit*

Morris, Ann. *The Cinderella rebus book*

Mother Goose. *The golden goose book*, ill. by L. Leslie Brooke

Sing a song of sixpence, ill. by Leonard Lubin

Moxley, Susan. *Abdul's treasure*

Muller, Robin. *The sorcerer's apprentice*

Myers, Walter Dean. *The golden serpent*

Myller, Rolf. *How big is a foot?*

Rolling round

Nesbit, Edith. *The last of the dragons*

Ness, Evaline. *Pavo and the princess*

Nikly, Michelle. *The emperor's plum tree*

The princess on the nut

Nishikawa, Osamu. *Alexander and the blue ghost*

Noble, Trinka Hakes. *The king's tea*

Nygren, Tord. *Fiddler and his brothers*

Oppenheim, Joanne. *The story book prince*

Oram, Hiawyn. *Skittlewonder and the wizard*

Oxenbury, Helen. *The queen and Rosie Randall*

Patz, Nancy. *Gina Farina and the Prince of Mintz*

Peet, Bill. *How Droofus the dragon lost his head*

Perkins, Al. *King Midas and the golden touch*

Perrault, Charles. *Cinderella*, ill. by Sheilah Beckett

Cinderella, ill. by Marcia Brown

Cinderella, ill. by Paul Galdone

Cinderella, ill. by Diane Goode

Cinderella, ill. by Susan Jeffers

Cinderella, ill. by Emanuele Luzzati

Cinderella, ill. by Phil Smith

Puss in boots, ill. by Marcia Brown

Puss in boots, ill. by Lorinda Bryan Cauley

Puss in boots, ill. by Jean Claverie

Puss in boots, ill. by Hans Fischer

Puss in boots, ill. by Paul Galdone

Puss in boots, ill. by Julia Noonan

Puss in boots, ill. by Tony Ross

Puss in boots, ill. by William Stobbs

Puss in boots, ill. by Barry Wilkinson

Pevear, Richard. *Our king has horns!*

Pittman, Helena Clare. *A grain of rice*

Postgate, Oliver. *Noggin the king*

The prince who knew his fate

Reesink, Marijke. *The princess who always ran away*

Reeves, James. *Rhyming Will*

Reit, Seymour. *The king who learned to smile*

Richter, Mischa. *To bed, to bed!*

Rogasky, Barbara. *The water of life*

Rogers, Paul. *Tumbledown*

Rose, Anne. *How does a czar eat potatoes?*

Rose, Gerald. *The bird garden*

Ross, Tony. *Towser and the terrible thing*

Saddler, Allen. *The Archery contest*

The king gets fit

Schiller, Barbara. *The white rat's tale*

Scholey, Arthur. *Baboushka*

Schwartz, Amy. *Her Majesty, Aunt Essie*

Scott, Sally. *The magic horse*

Seuss, Dr. *Bartholomew and the Oobleck*

The king's stilts

Sexton, Gwain. *There once was a king*

Sherman, Josepha. *Vassilisa the wise*

Shulevitz, Uri. *One Monday morning*

Siekkinen, Raija. *Mister King*

Skipper, Mervyn. *The fooling of King Alexander*

Slobodkin, Louis. *Colette and the princess*

Steig, William. *Roland, the minstrel pig*

Stephenson, Dorothy. *The night it rained toys*

Steptoe, John. *Mufaro's beautiful daughters*

Thomson, Peggy. *The king has horse's ears*

Thurber, James. *Many moons*

Trez, Denise. *Maila and the flying carpet*

The royal hiccups

Turpin, Lorna. *The sultan's snakes*

Van Woerkom, Dorothy. *The queen who couldn't bake gingerbread*

Varga, Judy. *The dragon who liked to spit fire*

Vernon, Adele. *The riddle*

Vesey, A. *The princess and the frog*

Waddell, Martin. *The tough princess*

Wahl, Jan. *Cabbage moon*

Wersba, Barbara. *Do tigers ever bite kings?*

West, Colin. *The king of Kennelwick castle*

The king's toothache

Wiesner, David. *The loathsome dragon*

Williams, Jay. *The practical princess*

School for sillies

Wood, Audrey. *King Bidgood's in the bathtub*

Yolen, Jane. *The emperor and the kite*

The seeing stick

Young, Miriam Burt. *The sugar mouse cake*

Zemach, Harve. *The tricks of Master Dabble*

Running *see* Sports – racing

Running away *see* Behavior – running away

Russia *see* Foreign lands – Russia

Sadness *see* Emotions – sadness

Safety

Arnold, Caroline. *Who keeps us safe?*
Bahr, Amy C. *It's ok to say no*
  Sometimes it's ok to tell secrets
  What should you do when...?
  Your body is your own
Baker, Eugene. *Bicycles*
  Fire
  Home
  Outdoors
  School
  Water
Berenstain, Stan. *The Berenstain bears learn about strangers*
Brown, Marc. *Dinosaurs, beware!*
Brown, Margaret Wise. *Red light, green light*
Chlad, Dorothy. *Bicycles are fun to ride*
  Matches, lighters, and firecrackers are not toys
  Poisons make you sick
Cleary, Beverly. *Lucky Chuck*
Emecheta, Buchi. *Nowhere to play*
Girard, Linda Walvoord. *My body is private*
Glovach, Linda. *The Little Witch's black magic book of games*
Joyce, Irma. *Never talk to strangers*
Leaf, Munro. *Safety can be fun*
Lindgren, Barbro. *Sam's lamp*
McKissack, Patricia C. *Who is coming?*
McLeod, Emilie Warren. *The bear's bicycle*
Meyer, Linda D. *Safety zone*
Moss, Elaine. *Polar*
Myller, Lois. *No! No!*
Petty, Kate. *Being careful with strangers*
Russell, Pamela. *Do you have a secret?*
Shortall, Leonard W. *One way*
Smaridge, Norah. *Watch out!*
Viorst, Judith. *Try it again, Sam*
Vogel, Carole Garbuny. *The dangers of strangers*
Wachter, Oralee. *Close to home*
Yamashita, Haruo. *Mice at the beach*
Ziefert, Harriet. *No, no, Nicky!*

Sailors *see* Careers – military

St. Patrick's Day *see* Holidays – St. Patrick's Day

Sand

Bason, Lillian. *Castles and mirrors and cities of sand*
Krementz, Jill. *Jack goes to the beach*
Lloyd, David. *Grandma and the pirate*
Nolan, Dennis. *The castle builder*
Ormondroyd, Edward. *Johnny Castleseed*
Roach, Marilynne K. *Dune fox*
Robbins, Ken. *Beach days*
Vasiliu, Mircea. *A day at the beach*
Watanabe, Shigeo. *I'm the king of the castle!*
Webb, Angela. *Sand*

Sandcastles *see* Sand

Sandman

Strahl, Rudi. *Sandman in the lighthouse*

Sandpipers *see* Birds – sandpipers

Saving things *see* Behavior – saving things

Scarecrows

Bolliger, Max. *The wooden man*
Farber, Norma. *There goes feathertop!*
Fleischman, Sid. *The scarebird*
Gordon, Sharon. *Sam the scarecrow*
Hart, Jeanne McGahey. *Scareboy*
Lewis, Robin Baird. *Hello, Mr. Scarecrow*
Lifton, Betty Jean. *Joji and the Amanojaku*
  Joji and the dragon
  Joji and the fog
Martin, Bill (William Ivan). *Barn dance!*
Miller, Edna. *Pebbles, a pack rat*
Oana, Kay D. *Robbie and the raggedy scarecrow*
Tripp, Paul. *The strawman who smiled by mistake*
Williams, Linda. *The little old lady who was not afraid of anything*

School

Adelson, Leone. *All ready for school*
Ahlberg, Allan. *The Cinderella show*
Ahlberg, Janet. *Starting school*
Alexander, Martha G. *Move over, Twerp*
  Sabrina
Allard, Harry. *Miss Nelson has a field day*
  Miss Nelson is back
  Miss Nelson is missing!
Annett, Cora. *The dog who thought he was a boy*
Arnold, Caroline. *Where do you go to school?*
Arnold, Katrin. *Anna joins in*
Aseltine, Lorraine. *First grade can wait*
Ashley, Bernard. *Dinner ladies don't count*

Aulaire, Ingri Mortenson d'. *Children of the northlights*
Nils
Babbitt, Lorraine. *Pink like the geranium*
Baker, Eugene. *School*
Behrens, June. *Who am I?*
Beim, Jerrold. *The taming of Toby*
Bemelmans, Ludwig. *Madeline*
Berenstain, Stan. *The Berenstain bears go to school*
Berquist, Grace. *Speckles goes to school*
Blance, Ellen. *Monster at school*
Monster goes to school
Blue, Rose. *How many blocks is the world?*
I am here: Yo estoy aqui
Bond, Felicia. *The Halloween performance*
Boon, Emilie. *1 2 3 how many animals can you see?*
Boreman, Jean. *Bantie and her chicks*
Boyd, Selma. *I met a polar bear*
Bram, Elizabeth. *I don't want to go to school*
Brandenberg, Franz. *No school today!*
Six new students
Breinburg, Petronella. *Shawn goes to school*
Brooks, Ron. *Timothy and Gramps*
Brown, Marc. *Arthur's teacher trouble*
Arthur's Valentine
The true Francine
Brown, Tricia. *Hello, amigos!*
Bruna, Dick. *Miffy goes to school*
The school
Buchheimer, Naomi. *Let's go to a school*
Buckley, Kate. *Love notes*
Budney, Blossom. *N is for nursery school*
Burningham, John. *John Patrick Norman McHennessy - the boy who was always late*
Butterworth, Nick. *The Nativity play*
Calmenson, Stephanie. *The kindergarten book*
Caple, Kathy. *The biggest nose*
Carlson, Nancy. *Louanne Pig in making the team*
Carrick, Carol. *Left behind*
Caseley, Judith. *Ada potato*
Molly Pink
Caudill, Rebecca. *A pocketful of cricket*
Cazet, Denys. *A fish in his pocket*
Frosted glass
Chapouton, Anne-Marie. *Sebastian is always late*
Charles, Donald. *Calico Cat at school*
Charmatz, Bill. *The Troy St. bus*
Chorao, Kay. *Molly's lies*
Christian, Mary Blount. *Swamp monsters*
Clewes, Dorothy. *Happiest day*
Clifton, Lucille. *All us come cross the water*
Cohen, Miriam. *Bee my Valentine!*
Best friends
Don't eat too much turkey!
First grade takes a test
It's George!

Jim meets the thing
Liar, liar, pants on fire!
Lost in the museum
The new teacher
No good in art
See you tomorrow
So what?
Starring first grade
Tough Jim
When will I read?
Will I have a friend?
Coker, Gylbert. *Naptime*
Cole, Babette. *The trouble with mom*
Cole, Joanna. *Norma Jean, jumping bean*
Coles, Alison. *Michael's first day*
Cooney, Nancy Evans. *The blanket that had to go*
Coontz, Otto. *A real class clown*
Copp, James. *Martha Matilda O'Toole*
Corrigan, Kathy. *Emily Umily*
Crews, Donald. *School bus*
De Hamel, Joan. *Hemi's pet*
Delaney, Ned. *Rufus the doofus*
Delton, Judy. *The new girl at school*
Rabbit goes to night school
De Paola, Tomie. *The art lesson*
Bill and Pete
Bill and Pete go down the Nile
Dinan, Carolyn. *Say cheese!*
Dorsky, Blanche. *Harry, a true story*
Dreifus, Miriam W. *Brave Betsy*
Duke, Kate. *Seven froggies went to school*
Ehrlich, Amy. *Leo, Zack and Emmie*
Leo, Zack, and Emmie together again
Ets, Marie Hall. *Bad boy, good boy*
Fanshawe, Elizabeth. *Rachel*
Feder, Paula Kurzband. *Where does the teacher live?*
Giff, Patricia Reilly. *The beast in Ms. Rooney's room*
Happy birthday, Ronald Morgan!
Next year I'll be special
Today was a terrible day
Watch out, Ronald Morgan!
Goffstein, M. B. (Marilyn Brooke). *School of names*
Goodall, John S. *Naughty Nancy goes to school*
Gordon, Shirley. *Crystal is my friend*
Crystal is the new girl
Gross, Alan. *What if the teacher calls on me?*
Hader, Berta Hoerner. *The mighty hunter*
Hale, Sara Josepha. *Mary had a little lamb*, ill. by Tomie de Paola
Hamilton-Merritt, Jane. *My first days of school*
Harris, Dorothy Joan. *The school mouse and the hamster*
Hathorn, Libby. *Freya's fantastic surprise*
Henkes, Kevin. *Jessica*

Welber, Robert. *Goodbye, hello*
Wells, Rosemary. *Timothy goes to school*
White, Florence Meiman. *How to lose your lunch money*
White, Paul. *Janet at school*
Whitney, Alma Marshak. *Just awful*
Williams, Barbara. *Donna Jean's disaster*
Willis, Jeanne. *The long blue blazer*
Willis, Val. *The secret in the matchbox*
Winthrop, Elizabeth. *Tough Eddie*
Wiseman, Bernard. *Tails are not for painting*
Wittman, Sally. *The boy who hated Valentine's Day*
  The wonderful Mrs. Trumbly
Wolde, Gunilla. *Betsy's first day at nursery school*
Wolf, Bernard. *Adam Smith goes to school*
Yashima, Tarō. *Crow boy*

Science

Abisch, Roz. *Let's find out about butterflies*
Adler, David A. *Redwoods are the tallest trees in the world*
Aho, Jennifer J. *Learning about sex*
Aldridge, Alan. *The butterfly ball and the grasshopper's feast*
Alexander, Alison. *Science magic*
Aliki. *Corn is maize*
  Digging up dinosaurs
  Dinosaurs are different
  Fossils tell of long ago
  The long lost coelacanth and other living fossils
  My hands
  My visit to the dinosaurs
  A weed is a flower
  Wild and woolly mammoths
Allen, Gertrude E. *Everyday animals*
Allen, Martha Dickson. *Real life monsters*
Allen, Pamela. *Mr. Archimedes' bath*
  Who sank the boat?
Anderson, Lucia. *The smallest life around us*
Andry, Andrew C. *How babies are made*
Annixter, Jane. *Brown rats, black rats*
Applebaum, Stan. *Going my way?*
Appleby, Leonard. *Snakes*
Ariane. *Small Cloud*
Arnold, Caroline. *The biggest living thing*
  Five nests
  Sun fun
Aruego, José. *Symbiosis*
Arvetis, Chris. *Why does it fly?*
  Why is it dark?
Asimov, Isaac. *The best new things*
  The moon
Back, Christine. *Bean and plant*
  Chicken and egg
  Spider's web

Tadpole and frog
Baker, Gayle. *Special delivery*
Baker, Jeannie. *One hungry spider*
Baker, Jeffrey J. W. *Patterns of nature*
Balestrino, Philip. *Hot as an ice cube*
Balian, Lorna. *Where in the world is Henry?*
Baran, Tancy. *Bees*
Barner, Bob. *Elephant facts*
Bartlett, Margaret Farrington. *The clean brook*
  Down the mountain
  Where the brook begins
Bason, Lillian. *Castles and mirrors and cities of sand*
Batherman, Muriel. *Animals live here*
Behrens, June. *Whales of the world*
  Whalewatch!
Bendick, Jeanne. *All around you*
  What made you you?
  Why can't I?
Berenstain, Stan. *The Berenstain bears' science fair*
Berger, Gilda. *Sharks*
  Whales
Berger, Melvin. *Early humans*
  Germs make me sick!
Blank, Joani. *A kid's first book about sex*
Boegehold, Betty. *Bear underground*
Bonners, Susan. *Panda*
  A penguin year
Boreman, Jean. *Bantie and her chicks*
Brady, Irene. *Wild mouse*
Branley, Franklyn M. *Air is all around you*
  The big dipper
  Big tracks, little tracks
  A book of satellites for you
  Comets
  Eclipse darkness in daytime
  Flash, crash, rumble, and roll
  Floating and sinking
  Gravity is a mystery
  High sounds, low sounds
  Hurricane watch
  Is there life in outer space?
  Journey into a black hole
  Light and darkness
  The moon seems to change
  North, south, east and west
  The planets in our solar system
  Rain and hail
  The sky is full of stars
  Snow is falling
  The sun, our nearest star
  Sunshine makes the seasons
  Timmy and the tin-can telephone
  Tornado alert
  Volcanoes
  What makes day and night
  What the moon is like
Brasch, Kate. *Prehistoric monsters*
Brighton, Catherine. *Five secrets in a box*

Brooks, Robert B. *So that's how I was born*
Brouillette, Jeanne S. *Moths*
Budbill, David. *Christmas tree farm*
Burt, Olive. *Let's find out about bread*
Busch, Phyllis S. *Cactus in the desert*
 City lots
 Lions in the grass
 Once there was a tree
 Puddles and ponds
Carrick, Carol. *The blue lobster*
 The crocodiles still wait
 Octopus
 Patrick's dinosaurs
 Two coyotes
Charosh, Mannis. *The ellipse*
Chenery, Janet. *The toad hunt*
Christenson, Larry. *The wonderful way that babies are made*
Clark, Harry. *The first story of the whale*
Clay, Pat. *Ants*
 Beetles
Cobb, Vicki. *Lots of rot*
Colby, C. B. (Carroll Burleigh). *Who lives there?*
 Who went there?
Coldrey, Jennifer. *The world of chickens*
 The world of crabs
 The world of frogs
 The world of rabbits
 The world of squirrels
Cole, Joanna. *A bird's body*
 A calf is born
 A cat's body
 A chick hatches
 A dog's body
 Evolution
 Find the hidden insect
 A fish hatches
 How you were born
 Hungry, hungry sharks
 My puppy is born
 Plants in winter
Conklin, Gladys. *Cheetahs, the swift hunters*
 I caught a lizard
 I like beetles
 I like butterflies
 I like caterpillars
 I watch flies
 If I were a bird
 Journey of the gray whales
 Little apes
 Lucky ladybugs
 Praying mantis
 We like bugs
 When insects are babies
Cooke, Ann. *Giraffes at home*
Cosgrove, Margaret. *Wintertime for animals*
Craig, Janet. *Turtles*
Craig, M. Jean. *Dinosaurs and more dinosaurs*

Cromie, William J. *Steven and the green turtle*
Cutts, David. *Look...a butterfly*
Dabcovich, Lydia. *Busy beavers*
Dallinger, Jane. *Spiders*
Daly, Kathleen N. *A child's book of snakes, lizards and other reptiles*
 Today's biggest animals
 Unusual animals
Daniel, Doris Temple. *Pauline and the peacock*
Darby, Gene. *What is a bird?*
 What is a butterfly?
 What is a fish?
 What is a plant?
 What is a turtle?
David, Eugene. *Crystal magic*
Dodd, Lynley. *The smallest turtle*
Dorros, Arthur. *Ant cities*
Eastman, David. *What is a fish?*
Eastman, Patricia. *Sometimes things change*
Engdahl, Sylvia. *Our world is earth*
Engelbrektson, Sune. *Gravity at work and play*
 The sun is a star
Fischer, Vera Kistiakowsky. *One way is down*
Fischer-Nagel, Heiderose. *A kitten is born*
 A puppy is born
Fisher, Aileen. *And a sunflower grew*
 As the leaves fall down
 Like nothing at all
 Mysteries in the garden
 Now that spring is here
 Petals yellow and petals red
 Plant magic
 Prize performance
 Seeds on the go
 Swords and daggers
 A tree with a thousand uses
Florian, Douglas. *A bird can fly*
Flower, Phyllis. *Barn owl*
Freedman, Russell. *Hanging on*
 Tooth and claw
 When winter comes
Freeman, Mae. *The sun, the moon and the stars*
Freschet, Berniece. *Bear mouse*
 The little woodcock
 Moose baby
 Wood duck baby
Friedman, Judi. *The eels' strange journey*
Friskey, Margaret. *Birds we know*
Frith, Michael K. *Some of us walk, some fly, some swim*
Gans, Roma. *Rock collecting*
 When birds change their feathers
Garelick, May. *About owls*
 The tremendous tree book
Gelman, Rita Golden. *A koala grows up*
George, Jean Craighead. *All upon a stone*

Milgrom, Harry. *Egg-ventures*
 Paper science
Miller, Edna. *Jumping bean*
Miller, Judith Ransom. *Nabob and the geranium*
Miller, Susanne Santoro. *Prehistoric mammals*
Millhouse, Nicholas. *Blue-footed booby*
Mitgutsch, Ali. *From gold to money*
 From graphite to pencil
 From sea to salt
 From swamp to coal
Moche, Dinah L. *The astronauts*
Morris, Robert A. *Dolphin*
 Seahorse
Moseley, Keith. *Dinosaurs*
Myrick, Mildred. *Ants are fun*
Neal, Ernest. *Badgers*
Newton, James R. *A forest is reborn*
 Forest log
Nussbaum, Hedda. *Animals build amazing homes*
Oleson, Jens. *Snail*
Oxford Scientific Films. *Grey squirrel*
 Jellyfish and other sea creatures
 Mosquito
 The stickleback cycle
Palazzo, Janet. *Our friend the sun*
Parish, Peggy. *Dinosaur time*
Parker, Nancy Winslow. *Bugs*
 The ordeal of Byron B. Blackbear
Peters, Lisa W. *The sun, the wind and the rain*
Phleger, Fred B. *Red Tag comes back*
 The whales go by
 You will live under the sea
Pluckrose, Henry. *Ants*
 Bears
 Bees and wasps
 Butterflies and moths
 Elephants
 Floating and sinking
 Horses
 Hot and cold
 Reptiles
 Whales
Polacco, Patricia. *Meteor!*
Pouyanne, Rési. *What I see hidden by the pond*
Powzyk, Joyce. *Tasmania*
Pursell, Margaret Sanford. *A look at birth*
 Polly the guinea pig
 Shelley the sea gull
 Sprig the tree frog
Quackenbush, Robert M. *What has Wild Tom done now?!!!*
Rabinowitz, Sandy. *What's happening to Daisy?*
Ricciuti, Edward R. *An animal for Alan Donald and the fish that walked*
Richard, Jane. *A horse grows up*

Ross, Wilda S. *What did the dinosaurs eat?*
Rushnell, Elaine Evans. *My mom's having a baby*
Russell, Solveig Paulson. *What good is a tail?*
Ryder, Joanne. *Fireflies*
 Snail in the woods
 The spiders dance
Sadler, Marilyn. *Alistair's time machine*
St. Tamara. *Chickaree, a red squirrel*
Scarry, Richard. *Richard Scarry's great big air book*
Schilling, Betty. *Two kittens are born*
Schlein, Miriam. *Lucky porcupine!*
 What's wrong with being a skunk?
Schneider, Herman. *Follow the sunset*
Schoberle, Ceile. *Beyond the Milky Way*
Schulz, Charles M. *Snoopy's facts and fun book about nature*
Selberg, Ingrid. *Nature's hidden world*
Selsam, Millicent E. *All kinds of babies*
 The amazing dandelion
 Backyard insects
 Benny's animals and how he put them in order
 The bug that laid the golden eggs
 Egg to chick
 A first look at bird nests
 A first look at caterpillars
 A first look at cats
 A first look at flowers
 A first look at kangaroos, koalas and other animals with pouches
 A first look at monkeys
 A first look at owls, eagles and other hunters of the sky
 A first look at rocks
 A first look at seashells
 A first look at sharks
 A first look at spiders
 A first look at the world of plants
 A first look at whales
 Greg's microscope
 How kittens grow
 How puppies grow
 Is this a baby dinosaur? and other science picture puzzles
 Let's get turtles
 More potatoes!
 Plenty of fish
 Seeds and more seeds
 Terry and the caterpillars
 Tony's birds
 When an animal grows
 Where do they go? Insects in winter
 You see the world around you
Seymour, Peter. *How the weather works*
Shapp, Martha. *Let's find out about babies*
Shaw, Evelyn S. *Alligator*
 Fish out of school
 Nest of wood ducks

Octopus
Sea otters
Sheehan, Angela. *The beaver*
  The duck
  The otter
  The penguin
Sheffield, Margaret. *Before you were born*
  Where do babies come from?
Showers, Paul. *A baby starts to grow*
  Before you were a baby
  Me and my family tree
  No measles, no mumps for me
  You can't make a move without your
    muscles
Silverman, Maida. *Dinosaur babies*
Simon, Seymour. *Beneath your feet*
  Galaxies
  Icebergs and glaciers
  Jupiter
  Mars
  Saturn
  The stars
  The sun
  Uranus
  Volcanoes
  The spider's web
Stecher, Miriam B. *Max, the music-maker*
Stein, Sara Bonnett. *Cat*
  Mouse
Strange, Florence. *Rock-a-bye whale*
Sugita, Yutaka. *The flower family*
Thompson, Susan L. *Diary of a monarch*
  butterfly
Townsend, Anita. *The kangaroo*
Tresselt, Alvin R. *How far is far?*
  Rain drop splash
Van Woerkom, Dorothy. *Hidden messages*
Vasiliu, Mircea. *A day at the beach*
Wandelmaier, Roy. *Stars*
Watts, Barrie. *Apple tree*
  Bird's nest
  Butterfly and caterpillar
  Dandelion
  Hamster
  Ladybug
  Mushrooms
Webb, Angela. *Air*
  Light
  Reflections
  Sand
  Soil
  Sound
  Water
Wexler, Jerome. *Flowers, fruits, seeds*
White, Laurence B. *Science toys and tricks*
Williams, Gweneira Maureen. *Timid*
  Timothy, the kitten who learned to be
  brave
Wilson, Ron. *Mice*
Wong, Herbert H. *My goldfish*
  My ladybug

My plant
Our caterpillars
Our earthworms
Our tree
Yabuuchi, Masayuki. *Animals sleeping*
Zallinger, Peter. *Dinosaurs*
Zoll, Max Alfred. *A flamingo is born*

Scotland *see* Foreign lands – Scotland

Scuba diving *see* Sports – skin diving

Sea and seashore

Adkins, Jan. *The art and industry of*
  sandcastles
Allen, Laura Jean. *Ottie and the star*
Allen, Pamela. *Hidden treasure*
Amos, William H. *Exploring the seashore*
Andrews, Jan. *Very last first time*
Anrooy, Frans van. *The sea horse*
Ardizzone, Edward. *Little Tim and the*
  brave sea captain
  Peter the wanderer
  Ship's cook Ginger
  Tim all alone
  Tim and Charlotte
  Tim and Ginger
  Tim and Lucy go to sea
  Tim in danger
  Tim to the rescue
  Tim's friend Towser
  Tim's last voyage
Asch, Frank. *Sand cake*
  Starbaby
Bate, Norman. *What a wonderful machine*
  is a submarine
Bennett, Rainey. *The secret hiding place*
Bentley, Anne. *The Groggs have a*
  wonderful summer
Blance, Ellen. *Monster goes to the beach*
Bond, Michael. *Paddington at the seaside*
Bonsall, Crosby Newell. *Mine's the best*
Booth, Eugene. *Under the ocean*
Bowden, Joan Chase. *Why the tides ebb and*
  flow
Bright, Robert. *Georgie and the noisy ghost*
Brown, Marc. *D. W. all wet*
Brown, Margaret Wise. *The seashore noisy*
  book
Bruna, Dick. *Miffy at the beach*
  Miffy at the seaside
Buchanan, Heather S. *Emily Mouse's beach*
  house
  George Mouse's covered wagon
Burningham, John. *Come away from the*
  water, Shirley
Carle, Eric. *A house for Hermit Crab*
Carrick, Carol. *Beach bird*
Carter, Debby L. *Clipper*
Cohen, Caron Lee. *Whiffle Squeek*

Selsam, Millicent E. *A first look at seashells*
  Sea monsters of long ago
Seymour, Peter. *What lives in the sea?*
  What's at the beach?
Shaw, Evelyn S. *Fish out of school*
  Octopus
Simon, Mina Lewiton. *Is anyone here?*
Slobodkin, Louis. *The seaweed hat*
Smith, Raymond Kenneth. *The long dive*
Smith, Theresa Kalab. *The fog is secret*
Steiner, Barbara. *The whale brother*
Steiner, Charlotte. *Listen to my seashell*
Stevenson, James. *Clams can't sing*
Stevenson, Jocelyn. *Jim Henson's Muppets
  at sea*
Stock, Catherine. *Sophie's bucket*
Strahl, Rudi. *Sandman in the lighthouse*
Straker, Joan Ann. *Animals that live in the
  sea*
Taylor, Mark. *The bold fisherman*
Thompson, Brenda. *The winds that blow*
Tobias, Tobi. *At the beach*
Tokuda, Wendy. *Humphrey the lost whale*
Tresselt, Alvin R. *Hide and seek fog*
  I saw the sea come in
Turkle, Brinton. *Do not open*
  Obadiah the Bold
  The sky dog
Ungerer, Tomi. *The Mellops go diving for
  treasure*
Vasiliu, Mircea. *A day at the beach*
Vernon, Tannis. *Little Pig and the
  blue-green sea*
Vinson, Pauline. *Willie goes to the seashore*
Waber, Bernard. *I was all thumbs*
Watson, Nancy Dingman. *When is
  tomorrow?*
The weekend
Wegen, Ron. *Sand castle*
Willard, Nancy. *The voyage of the Ludgate
  Hill*
Wood, John Norris. *Oceans*
Woolaver, Lance. *From Ben Loman to the
  sea*
Yamashita, Haruo. *Mice at the beach*
Yashima, Tarō. *Seashore story*
Ziefert, Harriet. *A dozen dogs*
  Good night, Jessie!
  *Keeping daddy awake on the way home
  from the beach*
Zion, Gene. *Harry by the sea*

Sea gulls *see* Birds – sea gulls

Sea horses *see* Crustacea

Sea lions *see* Animals – sea lions

Sea serpents *see* Monsters; Mythical
  creatures

Seals *see* Animals – seals

Seamstresses *see* Careers – seamstresses

Seashore *see* Sea and seashore

Seasons

Arnosky, Jim. *Outdoors on foot*
Barker, Cicely Mary. *Flower fairies of the
  seasons*
Berenstain, Stan. *The bears' almanac*
Beskow, Elsa Maartman. *Children of the
  forest*
Blegvad, Erik. *Burnie's hill*
Blocksma, Mary. *Apple tree! Apple tree!*
Branley, Franklyn M. *Sunshine makes the
  seasons*
Brown, Margaret Wise. *The little island*
Burningham, John. *Seasons*
Carle, Eric. *The tiny seed*
Carrick, Carol. *The old barn*
Charles, Donald. *Calico Cat's year*
Clifton, Lucille. *Everett Anderson's year*
De Paola, Tomie. *Four stories for four
  seasons*
Don't tell the scarecrow
Dow, Katharine. *My time of year*
Dragonwagon, Crescent. *Jemima remembers*
DuPasquier, Philippe. *Our house on the hill*
Duvoisin, Roger Antoine. *The house of four
  seasons*
Farjeon, Eleanor. *Around the seasons*
Fisher, Aileen. *As the leaves fall down*
  Going barefoot
  I stood upon a mountain
  Like nothing at all
Foster, Doris Van Liew. *A pocketful of
  seasons*
Fox, Charles Philip. *Mr. Stripes the gopher*
Gackenbach, Dick. *Ida Fanfanny*
Gibbons, Gail. *Farming*
  The seasons of Arnold's apple tree
Goennel, Heidi. *Seasons*
Greydanus, Rose. *Changing seasons*
Haley, Gail E. *Go away, stay away*
  The green man
Hall, Bill. *A year in the forest*
Hall, Donald. *The ox-cart man*
Hall, Fergus. *Groundsel*
Harris, Dorothy Joan. *Four seasons for
  Toby*
Heyduck-Huth, Hilde. *The strawflower*
Howell, Ruth. *Everything changes*
Hurd, Edith Thacher. *The day the sun
  danced*
Ichikawa, Satomi. *A child's book of seasons*
Johnston, Tony. *Yonder*
King-Smith, Dick. *Cuckoobush farm*
Kwitz, Mary DeBall. *Mouse at home*
Lambert, David. *The seasons*

Lewis, Naomi. *Leaves*
Lionni, Leo. *Mouse days*
  When?
Littlewood, Valerie. *The season clock*
Lobel, Arnold. *Frog and Toad all year*
McDermott, Gerald. *Daughter of earth*
Maestro, Betsy. *Through the year with Harriet*
Mangin, Marie-France. *Suzette and Nicholas and the seasons clock*
Marshak, Samuel. *The Month-Brothers*
Miller, Edna. *Mousekin's fables*
Miller, Jane. *Seasons on the farm*
Miller, Moira. *The search for spring*
Mora, Emma. *Gideon, the little bear cub*
Muntean, Michaela. *Muppet babies through the year*
Oppenheim, Joanne. *Have you seen trees?*
Pearson, Susan. *My favorite time of year*
Provensen, Alice. *A book of seasons*
  The year at Maple Hill Farm
Roach, Marilynne K. *Dune fox*
Rockwell, Anne F. *First comes spring*
Schulz, Charles M. *Snoopy's facts and fun book about seasons*
Tresselt, Alvin R. *It's time now!*
  Johnny Maple-Leaf
Tudor, Tasha. *Around the year*
Udry, Janice May. *A tree is nice*
Welber, Robert. *Song of the seasons*
Wellington, Anne. *Apple pie*
Wildsmith, Brian. *Seasons*
Wolff, Ashley. *A year of birds*
Wood, Joyce. *Grandmother Lucy in her garden*
Yolen, Jane. *Ring of earth*
Ziefert, Harriet. *Bear all year*
Zolotow, Charlotte. *In my garden*
  The song

Seasons – autumn *see* Seasons – fall

Seasons – fall

Adelson, Leone. *All ready for school*
Allington, Richard L. *Autumn*
Barklem, Jill. *Autumn story*
Cavagnaro, David. *The pumpkin people*
Cohen, Peter Zachary. *Authorized autumn charts of the Upper Red Canoe River country*
Dutton, Sandra. *The cinnamon hen's autumn day*
Fregosi, Claudia. *The happy horse*
Freschet, Berniece. *Owl in the garden*
Griffith, Helen V. *Alex remembers*
Hoban, Julia. *Amy loves the wind*
Hopkins, Lee Bennett. *Merrily comes our harvest in*
Krensky, Stephen. *Lionel in the fall*
Kumin, Maxine. *Follow the fall*

Lapp, Eleanor. *The mice came in early this year*
Lenski, Lois. *Now it's fall*
McNaughton, Colin. *Autumn*
Moncure, Jane Belk. *Word Bird's fall words*
Ott, John. *Peter Pumpkin*
Potter, Beatrix. *The tale of Squirrel Nutkin*
Roth, Harold. *Autumn days*
Rylant, Cynthia. *Henry and Mudge under the yellow moon*
Taylor, Mark. *Henry explores the mountains*
Tejima, Keizaburo. *The bears' autumn*
Tresselt, Alvin R. *Autumn harvest*
  Johnny Maple-Leaf
Udry, Janice May. *Emily's autumn*
Updike, David. *An autumn tale*
Van Allsburg, Chris. *The stranger*
Weygant, Noemi. *It's autumn!*
Wheeler, Cindy. *Marmalade's yellow leaf*
Zolotow, Charlotte. *Say it!*

Seasons – spring

Alexander, Sue. *There's more...much more*
Allington, Richard L. *Spring*
Anglund, Joan Walsh. *Spring is a new beginning*
Barklem, Jill. *Spring story*
Barrett, John M. *The Easter bear*
Baum, Arline. *One bright Monday morning*
Beer, Kathleen Costello. *What happens in the spring*
Belting, Natalia Maree. *Summer's coming in*
Boon, Emilie. *It's spring, Peterkin*
Chönz, Selina. *A bell for Ursli*
Clifton, Lucille. *The boy who didn't believe in spring*
Cohen, Carol L. *Wake up, groundhog!*
Craig, M. Jean. *Spring is like the morning*
Cummings, E. E. *In just-spring*
Dabcovich, Lydia. *Sleepy bear*
Delton, Judy. *Three friends find spring*
De Posadas Mane, Carmen. *Mister North Wind*
Dodd, Lynley. *Wake up, bear*
Fish, Helen Dean. *When the root children wake up*, published by Green Tiger Pr., 1988
  When the root children wake up, published by Lippincott, 1930
Fisher, Aileen. *My mother and I*
  Now that spring is here
Forrester, Victoria. *The touch said hello*
Glovach, Linda. *The Little Witch's spring holiday book*
Hoban, Lillian. *The sugar snow spring*
  Turtle spring
Hurd, Edith Thacher. *The day the sun danced*
Ichikawa, Satomi. *Sun through small leaves*
Janice. *Little Bear's pancake party*

Johnson, Crockett. *Time for spring*
  Will spring be early?
Kesselman, Wendy. *Time for Jody*
Kraus, Robert. *The first robin*
Krauss, Ruth. *The happy day*
Kroll, Steven. *I love spring!*
Kumin, Maxine. *Spring things*
Lenski, Lois. *Spring is here*
Lerner, Carol. *Flowers of a woodland spring*
Levens, George. *Kippy the koala*
McNaughton, Colin. *Spring*
Martin, Charles E. *Island rescue*
Miller, Edna. *Mouskin's Easter basket*
Moncure, Jane Belk. *Word Bird's spring words*
Rockwell, Anne F. *My spring robin*
Rylant, Cynthia. *Henry and Mudge in puddle trouble*
Schlein, Miriam. *Little Red Nose*
Seignobosc, Françoise. *Springtime for Jeanne-Marie*
Selkowe, Valrie M. *Spring green*
Taylor, Judy. *Dudley and the monster*
Taylor, Mark. *Henry the castaway*
Tresselt, Alvin R. *Hi, Mister Robin*
Warren, Cathy. *Springtime bears*
Waterton, Betty. *Pettranella*
Wells, Rosemary. *Forest of dreams*
  Max's chocolate chicken
Wilde, Oscar. *The selfish giant*, ill. by Dom Mansell
  The selfish giant, ill. by Lisbeth Zwerger
Wolkstein, Diane. *The magic wings*
Wood, Joyce. *Grandmother Lucy in her garden*
Woolaver, Lance. *From Ben Loman to the sea*
Worth, Bonnie. *Peter Cottontail's surprise*
Zion, Gene. *Really spring*

Seasons – summer

Adelson, Leone. *All ready for summer*
Allington, Richard L. *Summer*
Barklem, Jill. *Summer story*
Beim, Jerrold. *The swimming hole*
Belting, Natalia Maree. *Summer's coming in*
Bentley, Anne. *The Groggs have a wonderful summer*
Berenstain, Stan. *The Berenstain bears go to camp*
Bowden, Joan Chase. *Emilio's summer day*
Brown, Margaret Wise. *The summer noisy book*
Burgunder, Rose. *From summer to summer*
Burn, Doris. *The summerfolk*
Cavagnaro, David. *The pumpkin people*
Chönz, Selina. *Florina and the wild bird*
Chwast, Seymour. *Still another children's book*
Craft, Ruth. *The day of the rainbow*

Factor, Jane. *Summer*
Farjeon, Eleanor. *Mr. Garden*
Firmin, Peter. *Basil Brush finds treasure*
Gage, Wilson. *Anna's summer songs*
Gans, Roma. *Hummingbirds in the garden*
Garelick, May. *Down to the beach*
Gerstein, Mordicai. *The seal mother*
Goodall, John S. *An Edwardian summer*
Griffith, Helen V. *Georgia music*
Haywood, Carolyn. *Hello, star*
Henkes, Kevin. *Grandpa and Bo*
Knotts, Howard. *The summer cat*
Kuskin, Karla. *Sand and snow*
Lenski, Lois. *On a summer day*
Lund, Doris Herold. *The paint-box sea*
McCloskey, Robert. *Time of wonder*
McNaughton, Colin. *Summer*
Martin, Charles E. *For rent*
  Sam saves the day
Moncure, Jane Belk. *Word Bird's summer words*
Moore, Elaine. *Grandma's house*
Rylant, Cynthia. *Henry and Mudge in the green time*
Schick, Eleanor. *One summer night*
  Summer at the sea
Stobbs, William. *There's a hole in my bucket*
Taylor, Mark. *Henry explores the jungle*
Thomas, Ianthe. *Eliza's daddy*
  Lordy, Aunt Hattie
Weygant, Noemi. *It's summer!*
Yashima, Tarō. *The village tree*
Yolen, Jane. *Milkweed days*
Zion, Gene. *Harry by the sea*
  The summer snowman
Zolotow, Charlotte. *Summer is...*

Seasons – winter

Adelson, Leone. *All ready for winter*
Allington, Richard L. *Winter*
Aragon, Jane Chelsea. *Winter harvest*
Arnold, Tim. *The winter mittens*
Asch, Frank. *Mooncake*
Attenberger, Walburga. *The little man in winter*
Aulaire, Ingri Mortenson d'. *Children of the northlights*
Barklem, Jill. *The secret staircase*
  Winter story
Barnhart, Peter. *The wounded duck*
Bartoli, Jennifer. *In a meadow, two hares hide*
  Snow on bear's nose
Bassett, Lisa. *Beany and Scamp*
Bauer, Caroline Feller. *Midnight snowman*
Brown, Margaret Wise. *The winter noisy book*
Bruna, Dick. *Miffy in the snow*
Buckley, Helen Elizabeth. *Josie and the snow*

Bunting, Eve. *Winter's coming*
Burton, Virginia Lee. *Katy and the big snow*
Carlson, Natalie Savage. *Surprise in the mountains*
Carrick, Carol. *Two coyotes*
Chaffin, Lillie D. *We be warm till springtime comes*
Chönz, Selina. *The snowstorm*
Cole, Joanna. *Plants in winter*
Cosgrove, Margaret. *Wintertime for animals*
Coutant, Helen. *First snow*
Craft, Ruth. *The winter bear*
Dabcovich, Lydia. *Sleepy bear*
Delton, Judy. *My mom hates me in January*
Three friends find spring
Dionetti, Michelle. *The day Eli went looking for bear*
Fisher, Aileen. *Where does everyone go?*
Flack, Marjorie. *Angus lost*
Freedman, Russell. *When winter comes*
Freeman, Don. *The night the lights went out*
Frost, Robert. *Stopping by woods on a snowy evening*
Fujikawa, Gyo. *That's not fair!*
Funakoshi, Canna. *One evening*
Gundersheimer, Karen. *Happy winter*
Hartley, Deborah. *Up north in the winter*
Hasler, Eveline. *Winter magic*
Hertza, Ole. *Tobias goes ice fishing*
Hoban, Russell. *Some snow said hello*
Hoff, Syd. *When will it snow?*
Hoopes, Lyn Littlefield. *When I was little*
Janosch. *Dear snowman*
Johnston, Tony. *Mole and Troll trim the tree*
Keats, Ezra Jack. *The snowy day*
Kessler, Leonard P. *Old Turtle's winter games*
Knotts, Howard. *The winter cat*
Kovalski, Maryann. *Jingle bells*
Krauss, Ruth. *The happy day*
Kumin, Maxine. *A winter friend*
Kuskin, Karla. *In the flaky frosty morning*
Sand and snow
Lapp, Eleanor. *The mice came in early this year*
Lathrop, Dorothy Pulis. *Who goes there?*
Lenski, Lois. *I like winter*
Linch, Elizabeth Johanna. *Samson*
Lindgren, Astrid. *The tomten*
The tomten and the fox
Littledale, Freya. *The snow child*
McCully, Emily Arnold. *First snow*
McLaughlin, Lissa. *Why won't winter go?*
McNaughton, Colin. *Winter*
Mamin-Sibiryak, D. N. *Grey Neck*
Martin, Charles E. *Island winter*
Michels, Tilde. *Who's that knocking at my door?*
Miller, Edna. *Mousekin's golden house*

Moncure, Jane Belk. *Word Bird's winter words*
Moore, Elaine. *Grandma's promise*
Odoyevsky, Vladimir. *Old Father Frost*
Parnall, Peter. *Alfalfa Hill*
Winter barn
Prusski, Jeffrey. *Bring back the deer*
Radin, Ruth Yaffe. *A winter place*
Retan, Walter. *The snowplow that tried to go south*
Roberts, Bethany. *Waiting for spring stories*
Rockwell, Anne F. *The first snowfall*
Roth, Harold. *Winter days*
Schick, Eleanor. *City in the winter*
Schlein, Miriam. *Deer in the snow*
Go with the sun
Selsam, Millicent E. *Keep looking!*
Where do they go? Insects in winter
Steig, William. *Brave Irene*
Taylor, Mark. *Henry the explorer*
Tejima, Keizaburo. *Fox's dream*
Tudor, Tasha. *Snow before Christmas*
Turkle, Brinton. *Thy friend, Obadiah*
Udry, Janice May. *Mary Jo's grandmother*
Van Vorst, M. L. *A Norse lullaby*
Vigna, Judith. *Boot weather*
Wabbes, Marie. *It's snowing, Little Rabbit*
Ward, Andrew. *Baby bear and the long sleep*
Watson, Wendy. *Has winter come?*
Tales for a winter's eve
Weiss, Ellen. *Clara the fortune-telling chicken*
Wells, Rosemary. *Forest of dreams*
Weygant, Noemi. *It's winter!*

Secret codes

Balian, Lorna. *Humbug potion*
Bonsall, Crosby Newell. *The case of the double cross*
Myrick, Mildred. *The secret three*

Secrets *see* Behavior – secrets

Seeds

Back, Christine. *Bean and plant*
Carle, Eric. *The tiny seed*
Petie, Haris. *The seed the squirrel dropped*
Selsam, Millicent E. *The amazing dandelion*
Seeds and more seeds
Shecter, Ben. *Partouche plants a seed*
Takihara, Koji. *Rolli*

Seeing *see* Senses – seeing

Seeking better things *see* Behavior – seeking better things

Self-concept

Appell, Clara. *Now I have a daddy haircut*
Bach, Alice. *Warren Weasel's worse than measles*
Bahr, Amy C. *It's ok to say no*
Sometimes it's ok to tell secrets
What should you do when...?
Your body is your own
Behrens, June. *Who am I?*
Berger, Terry. *I have feelings*
Blume, Judy. *The one in the middle is the green kangaroo*
Bolliger, Max. *The rabbit with the sky blue ears*
Brown, Ruth. *Crazy Charlie*
Browne, Anthony. *Willy the wimp*
Caple, Kathy. *Harry's smile*
Carle, Eric. *The mixed-up chameleon*
Carlson, Nancy. *I like me*
Charlip, Remy. *Hooray for me!*
Charlot, Martin. *Felisa and the magic tikling bird*
Cohen, Miriam. *No good in art*
So what?
DeLage, Ida. *Am I a bunny?*
De Regniers, Beatrice Schenk. *Everyone is good for something*
Fitzhugh, Louise. *I am five*
I am three
Girard, Linda Walvoord. *My body is private*
Hallinan, P. K. (Patrick K.). *I'm glad to be me*
Where's Michael?
Hines, Anna Grossnickle. *All by myself*
Karlin, Nurit. *A train for the king*
Keats, Ezra Jack. *Peter's chair*
Whistle for Willie
Krauss, Ruth. *The carrot seed*
Kuskin, Karla. *What did you bring me?*
Leaf, Munro. *Noodle*
Levitin, Sonia. *A sound to remember*
Lionni, Leo. *Pezzettino*
Lipkind, William. *The little tiny rooster*
Palmer, Mary Babcock. *No-sort-of-animal*
Peet, Bill. *Pamela Camel*
Purdy, Carol. *Least of all*
Richardson, Jean. *Tall inside*
Sadler, Marilyn. *It's not easy being a bunny*
Schick, Eleanor. *Joey on his own*
Sharmat, Marjorie Weinman. *I'm terrific*
Taking care of Melvin
Simon, Norma. *Why am I different?*
Slobodkin, Louis. *Magic Michael*
Stren, Patti. *Mountain Rose*
Supraner, Robyn. *Would you rather be a tiger?*
Titherington, Jeanne. *Big world, small world*
Tobias, Tobi. *Jane wishing*
Turnage, Sheila. *Trout the magnificent*

Tusa, Tricia. *Chicken Libby's new glasses*
Udry, Janice May. *How I faded away*
Waber, Bernard. *"You look ridiculous," said the rhinoceros to the hippopotamus*
Weiner, Beth Lee. *Benjamin's perfect solution*
Wold, Jo Anne. *Tell them my name is Amanda*
Wondriska, William. *Puff*
Zola, Meguido. *The dream of promise*

Self-esteem *see* Self-concept

Self-image *see* Self-concept

Selfishness *see* Character traits – selfishness

Senility *see* Illness – Alzheimer's

Senses – hearing

Aliki. *My five senses*
Allington, Richard L. *Hearing*
Arthur, Catherine. *My sister's silent world*
Aseltine, Lorraine. *I'm deaf and it's okay*
Baker, Pamela J. *My first book of sign*
Borten, Helen. *Do you hear what I hear?*
Do you know what I know?
Bove, Linda. *Sign language ABC with Linda Bove*
Brenner, Barbara. *Faces, faces, faces*
Chaplin, Susan Gibbons. *I can sign my ABCs*
Charlip, Remy. *Handtalk*
Handtalk birthday
Greenberg, Judith E. *What is the sign for friend?*
Isadora, Rachel. *I hear*
Jaynes, Ruth M. *Melinda's Christmas stocking*
Lionni, Leo. *What?*
Litchfield, Ada B. *A button in her ear*
Moncure, Jane Belk. *Sounds all around*
Ogle, Lucille. *I hear*
Oxenbury, Helen. *I hear*
Pace, Elizabeth. *Chris gets ear tubes*
Perkins, Al. *The ear book*
Pluckrose, Henry. *Things we hear*
Think about hearing
Showers, Paul. *The listening walk*
Teal, Valentine. *The little woman wanted noise*
Wahl, Jan. *Jamie's tiger*
Wolf, Bernard. *Anna's silent world*

Senses – seeing

Aliki. *My five senses*
Allington, Richard L. *Looking*

Borten, Helen. *Do you know what I know?*
  Do you see what I see?
Bram, Elizabeth. *One day I closed my eyes*
  and the world disappeared
Brenner, Barbara. *Faces, faces, faces*
Brighton, Catherine. *My hands, my world*
Brown, Marc. *Arthur's eyes*
Brown, Marcia. *Walk with your eyes*
Chapman, Elizabeth. *Suzy*
Cohen, Miriam. *See you tomorrow*
DeArmond, Dale. *The seal oil lamp*
Giff, Patricia Reilly. *Watch out, Ronald*
  Morgan!
Goodsell, Jane. *Katie's magic glasses*
Hay, Dean. *I see a lot of things*
Herman, Bill. *Jenny's magic wand*
Hoban, Tana. *Look again*
Isadora, Rachel. *I see*
Jaynes, Ruth M. *Melinda's Christmas*
  stocking
Jensen, Virginia Allen. *Catching*
  Red thread riddles
  What's that?
Johnson, Donna Kay. *Brighteyes*
Keats, Ezra Jack. *Apartment 3*
Keller, Holly. *Cromwell's glasses*
Kessler, Leonard P. *Mr. Pine's mixed-up*
  signs
Lasson, Robert. *Orange Oliver*
Lionni, Leo. *What?*
Litchfield, Ada B. *A cane in her hand*
Martin, Bill (William Ivan). *Knots on a*
  counting rope
Matthiesen, Thomas. *Things to see*
Moncure, Jane Belk. *The look book*
Newth, Philip. *Roly goes exploring*
Ogle, Lucille. *I spy with my little eye*
Oxenbury, Helen. *I see*
Pluckrose, Henry. *Things we see*
  Think about seeing
Quigley, Lillian Fox. *The blind men and the*
  elephant
Raskin, Ellen. *Spectacles*
Reuter, Margaret. *My mother is blind*
Sargent, Susan. *My favorite place*
Saxe, John Godfrey. *The blind men and the*
  elephant
Shecter, Ben. *The stocking child*
Showers, Paul. *Look at your eyes*
Thayer, Jane. *Mr. Turtle's magic glasses*
Thomson, Ruth. *Eyes*
Tusa, Tricia. *Libby's new glasses*
Wise, William. *The cowboy surprise*
Yolen, Jane. *The seeing stick*

Senses – smelling

Aliki. *My five senses*
Allington, Richard L. *Smelling*
Borten, Helen. *Do you know what I know?*
Brenner, Barbara. *Faces, faces, faces*

Doughtie, Charles. *Gabriel Wrinkles, the*
  bloodhound who couldn't smell
Jaynes, Ruth M. *Melinda's Christmas*
  stocking
Lionni, Leo. *What?*
Moncure, Jane Belk. *What your nose*
  knows!
Perkins, Al. *The nose book*
Pluckrose, Henry. *Think about smelling*
Rose, Gerald. *Scruff*
Saunders, Susan. *A sniff in time*

Senses – tasting

Aliki. *My five senses*
Allington, Richard L. *Tasting*
Borten, Helen. *Do you know what I know?*
Brenner, Barbara. *Faces, faces, faces*
Jaynes, Ruth M. *Melinda's Christmas*
  stocking
Lionni, Leo. *What?*
Moncure, Jane Belk. *A tasting party*
Pluckrose, Henry. *Think about tasting*

Senses – touching

Aliki. *My five senses*
Allington, Richard L. *Touching*
Borten, Helen. *Do you know what I know?*
Brenner, Barbara. *Faces, faces, faces*
Brown, Marcia. *Touch will tell*
Carle, Eric. *My very first book of touch*
Gibson, Myra Tomback. *What is your*
  favorite thing to touch?
Isadora, Rachel. *I touch*
Jaynes, Ruth M. *Melinda's Christmas*
  stocking
Lionni, Leo. *What?*
Moncure, Jane Belk. *The touch book*
Oxenbury, Helen. *I touch*
Pluckrose, Henry. *Things we touch*
  Think about touching

Shadows

Anno, Mitsumasa. *In shadowland*
Asch, Frank. *Bear shadow*
Bond, Felicia. *Wake up, Vladimir*
Cendrars, Blaise. *Shadow*
Christelow, Eileen. *Henry and the Dragon*
De Regniers, Beatrice Schenk. *The shadow*
  book
Gackenbach, Dick. *Mr. Wink and his*
  shadow, Ned
Goor, Ron. *Shadows*
Hansen, Ron. *The shadowmaker*
McHargue, Georgess. *Private zoo*
Mahy, Margaret. *The boy with two shadows*
Marol, Jean-Claude. *Vagabul and his*
  shadow
Narahashi, Keiko. *I have a friend*
Simon, Seymour. *Shadow magic*

Tompert, Ann. *Nothing sticks like a shadow*

Shakespeare

Freeman, Don. *Will's quill*

Shape *see* Concepts – shape

Shaped books *see* Format, unusual

Sharing *see* Behavior – sharing

Sheep *see* Animals – sheep

Ships *see* Boats, ships

Shoemakers *see* Careers – shoemakers

Shopping

Allard, Harry. *I will not go to market today*
Anholt, Catherine. *Truffles in trouble*
Ardizzone, Edward. *The little girl and the tiny doll*
Arnold, Caroline. *What will we buy?*
Baugh, Dolores M. *Supermarket*
Black, Irma Simonton. *The little old man who could not read*
Bond, Michael. *Paddington's lucky day*
Bradman, Tony. *Wait and see*
Brenner, Barbara. *Somebody's slippers, somebody's shoes*
Calmenson, Stephanie. *The birthday hat*
Cass, Joan E. *The cats go to market*
Chase, Catherine. *Baby mouse goes shopping*
Chorao, Kay. *Molly's Moe*
Claverie, Jean. *Shopping*
Daly, Niki. *Not so fast Songololo*
Edwards, Linda Strauss. *The downtown day*
Faulkner, Keith. *Sam helps out*
Fyleman, Rose. *A fairy went a-marketing*
Garland, Sarah. *Going shopping*
Gretz, Susanna. *Teddy bears go shopping*
Greydanus, Rose. *Susie goes shopping*
Guzzo, Sandra E. *Fox and Heggie*
Hastings, Evelyn Beilhart. *The department store*
Hines, Anna Grossnickle. *Don't worry, I'll find you*
Holt, Margaret. *David McCheever's twenty-nine dogs*
Hutchins, Pat. *Don't forget the bacon!*
Ichikawa, Satomi. *Suzanne and Nicholas at the market*
Kilroy, Sally. *Market day*
Lobel, Arnold. *On Market Street*
McPhail, David. *The cereal box*
Maschler, Fay. *T. G. and Moonie go shopping*
Mother Goose. *To market! To market!* ill. by Emma Lillian Brock

Oxenbury, Helen. *The shopping trip*
Tom and Pippo go shopping
Patz, Nancy. *Pumpernickel tickle and mean green cheese*
Potter, Beatrix. *The tale of Little Pig Robinson*
Rice, Eve. *New blue shoes*
Rockwell, Anne F. *The supermarket*
Ross, Pat. *M and M and the big bag*
Russell, Betty. *Big store, funny door*
Schick, Eleanor. *Joey on his own*
Shopping
Solomon, Joan. *A present for Mum*
Spier, Peter. *Food market*
Winn, Chris. *My day*
Ziefert, Harriet. *Bear goes shopping*
Zinnemann-Hope, Pam. *Let's go shopping, Ned*

Shops *see* Stores

Shows *see* Theaters

Shrews *see* Animals – shrews

Shyness *see* Character traits – shyness

Siam *see* Foreign lands – Thailand

Sibling rivalry

Aitken, Amy. *Wanda's circus*
Alexander, Martha G. *I'll be the horse if you'll play with me*
Marty McGee's space lab, no girls allowed
Nobody asked me if I wanted a baby sister
When the new baby comes, I'm moving out
Allen, Pamela. *Hidden treasure*
Amoss, Berthe. *It's not your birthday*
Tom in the middle
Armitage, Ronda. *The bossing of Josie*
Arnstein, Helene S. *Billy and our new baby*
Bach, Alice. *The smartest bear and his brother Oliver*
Baker, Betty. *My sister says*
Baker, Charlotte. *Little brother*
Beecroft, John. *What? Another cat!*
Benson, Ellen. *Philip's little sister*
Berenstain, Stan. *The Berenstain bears and the double dare*
The Berenstain bears get in a fight
Blume, Judy. *The Pain and The Great One*
Bond, Felicia. *Poinsettia and her family*
Bonsall, Crosby Newell. *Who's a pest?*
Bottner, Barbara. *Big boss! Little boss!*
Jungle day
Brandenberg, Franz. *It's not my fault*
Brothers and sisters are like that!
Brown, Marc. *D. W. all wet*
Buchanan, Heather S. *Emily Mouse's garden*

Ray, Deborah Kogan. *Sunday morning we went to the zoo*
Reesink, Marijke. *The princess who always ran away*
Riordan, James. *The three magic gifts*
Robins, Joan. *My brother, Will*
Roche, P. K. (Patrick K.). *Good-bye, Arnold!*
Webster and Arnold and the giant box
Rogasky, Barbara. *The water of life*
Rogers, Fred. *The new baby*
Root, Phyllis. *Moon tiger*
Rosen, Winifred. *Henrietta and the gong from Hong Kong*
Rushnell, Elaine Evans. *My mom's having a baby*
Russo, Marisabina. *Only six more days*
Ruthstrom, Dorotha. *The big kite contest*
Samuels, Barbara. *Faye and Dolores*
Sarnoff, Jane. *That's not fair*
Schick, Eleanor. *Peggy's new brother*
Schlein, Miriam. *Laurie's new brother*
Schwartz, Amy. *Annabelle Swift, kindergartner*
Scott, Ann Herbert. *On mother's lap*
Seuling, Barbara. *What kind of family is this?*
Sewell, Helen Moore. *Jimmy and Jemima*
Skorpen, Liesel Moak. *His mother's dog*
Smith, Lucia B. *A special kind of sister*
Smith, Peter. *Jenny's baby brother*
Stanek, Muriel. *My little foster sister*
Stapler, Sarah. *Trilby's trumpet*
Steptoe, John. *Baby says*
Stevenson, James. *Winston, Newton, Elton, and Ed*
Worse than Willy!
Stevenson, Suçie. *Christmas eve*
Do I have to take Violet?
Thomas, Iolette. *Janine and the new baby*
Tierney, Hanne. *Where's your baby brother, Becky Bunting?*
Tudor, Tasha. *Junior's tune*
Turkle, Brinton. *Rachel and Obadiah*
Tyrrell, Anne. *Mary Ann always can*
Udry, Janice May. *Thump and Plunk*
Van der Beek, Deborah. *Superbabe!*
Van Leeuwen, Jean. *Amanda Pig and her big brother Oliver*
Tales of Amanda Pig
Vigna, Judith. *Daddy's new baby*
Viorst, Judith. *I'll fix Anthony*
Wahl, Jan. *Peter and the troll baby*
Weiss, Nicki. *Princess Pearl*
Wells, Rosemary. *Good night, Fred*
Max's bedtime
Max's breakfast
Max's chocolate chicken
Peabody
Stanley and Rhoda
Williams, Barbara. *Donna Jean's disaster*

Williams, Vera B. *Stringbean's trip to the shining sea*
Winthrop, Elizabeth. *I think he likes me*
That's mine
Wolde, Gunilla. *Betsy and the chicken pox*
Wood, Audrey. *Three sisters*
Young, Ruth. *The new baby*
Zolotow, Charlotte. *If it weren't for you*
Timothy too!

Sickness see Health; Illness

Sight see Handicaps – blindness; Senses – seeing

Signs see Traffic, traffic signs

Sisters see Family life – Sisters

Size see Concepts – size

Skating see Sports – ice skating; Sports – roller skating

Skiing see Sports – skiing

Skin diving see Sports – skin diving

Skunks see Animals – skunks

Sky

Asch, Frank. *Starbaby*
Belting, Natalia Maree. *The sun is a golden earring*
Branley, Franklyn M. *Comets*
The sky is full of stars
Dayrell, Elphinstone. *Why the sun and the moon live in the sky*
Dayton, Mona. *Earth and sky*
Schoberle, Ceile. *Beyond the Milky Way*
Shaw, Charles Green. *It looked like spilt milk*
Spier, Peter. *Dreams*

Sledding see Sports – sledding

Sleep

Alexander, Martha G. *I'll protect you from the jungle beasts*
Andersen, H. C. (Hans Christian). *The princess and the pea*, ill. by Dorothée Duntze
The princess and the pea, ill. by Paul Galdone
The princess and the pea, ill. by Eve Tharlet
Aylesworth, Jim. *The bad dream*
Tonight's the night
Bach, Alice. *The smartest bear and his brother Oliver*

Beckman, Kaj. *Lisa cannot sleep*
Bottner, Barbara. *There was nobody there*
Brande, Marlie. *Sleepy Nicholas*
Bright, Robert. *Me and the bears*
Brown, Margaret Wise. *A child's good night book*
  Sleepy ABC
  The sleepy little lion
Brown, Myra Berry. *First night away from home*
Burstein, Fred. *Rebecca's nap*
Chalmers, Mary. *Take a nap, Harry*
Chorao, Kay. *Lester's overnight*
Ciardi, John. *Scrappy the pup*
Coker, Gylbert. *Naptime*
Collington, Peter. *Little pickle*
De Paola, Tomie. *Fight the night*
  When everyone was fast asleep
Dodd, Lynley. *Wake up, bear*
Edwards, Patricia Kier. *Chester and Uncle Willoughby*
Edwards, Roberta. *Anna Bear's first winter*
Elkin, Benjamin. *The king who could not sleep*
Evans, Eva Knox. *Sleepy time*
Field, Eugene. *Wynken, Blynken and Nod*
Gilmour, H. B. *Why Wembley Fraggle couldn't sleep*
Gretz, Susanna. *I'm not sleepy*
Harshman, Terry Webb. *Porcupine's pajama party*
Haseley, Dennis. *The cave of snores*
Hazen, Barbara Shook. *Where do bears sleep?*
Heine, Helme. *King Bounce the 1st*
Howard, Jane R. *When I'm sleepy*
Hutchins, Pat. *Good night owl*
Irving, Washington. *Rip Van Winkle*, ill. by John Howe
  Rip Van Winkle, ill. by Thomas Locker
  Rip Van Winkle, ill. by Peter Wingham
Jeffers, Susan. *All the pretty horses*
Kantrowitz, Mildred. *Willy Bear*
Karlin, Nurit. *The dream factory*
Keats, Ezra Jack. *Dreams*
Khalsa, Dayal Kaur. *Sleepers*
Kotzwinkle, William. *The nap master*
Krahn, Fernando. *Sleep tight, Alex Pumpernickel*
Kraus, Robert. *Good night little one*
  Good night Richard Rabbit
  Milton the early riser
Lucas, Barbara. *Sleeping over*
McCauley, Jane. *The way animals sleep*
McPhail, David. *The dream child*
Marino, Dorothy. *Edward and the boxes*
Massie, Diane Redfield. *The baby beebee bird*
Mueller, Virginia. *Monster can't sleep*
Murphy, Jill. *Peace at last*
Nichol, B. P. *Once*

Oppenheim, Joanne. *The story book prince*
Ormerod, Jan. *Moonlight*
  Sleeping
Oxenbury, Helen. *Say goodnight*
Panek, Dennis. *Ba ba sheep wouldn't go to sleep*
Pfister, Marcus. *The sleepy owl*
Plath, Sylvia. *The bed book*
Polushkin, Maria. *Mother, Mother, I want another*
Preston, Edna Mitchell. *Monkey in the jungle*
Reidel, Marlene. *Jacob and the robbers*
Riggio, Anita. *Wake up, William!*
Rowand, Phyllis. *It is night*
Saleh, Harold J. *Even tiny ants must sleep*
Schneider, Nina. *While Susie sleeps*
Seuss, Dr. *Dr. Seuss's sleep book*
  I am not going to get up today!
Simon, Norma. *Where does my cat sleep?*
Slobodkin, Louis. *Wide-awake owl*
Sonneborn, Ruth A. *Seven in a bed*
Stanley, Diane. *Birdsong Lullaby*
Stevenson, James. *We can't sleep*
Sugita, Yutaka. *Good night 1, 2, 3*
Tafuri, Nancy. *Where we sleep*
Tobias, Tobi. *Chasing the goblins away*
Trez, Denise. *Good night, Veronica*
Van Vorst, M. L. *A Norse lullaby*
Waber, Bernard. *Ira sleeps over*
Wahl, Jan. *Sylvester Bear overslept*
  The toy circus
Weisgard, Leonard. *Who dreams of cheese?*
Wersba, Barbara. *Amanda dreaming*
Wheeler, Cindy. *Marmalade's nap*
Whiteside, Karen. *Lullaby of the wind*
Wood, Audrey. *Moonflute*
  The napping house
Yabuuchi, Masayuki. *Animals sleeping*
Yolen, Jane. *Dragon night and other lullabies*
Yulya. *Bears are sleeping*
Zagone, Theresa. *No nap for me*
Ziefert, Harriet. *Good night everyone!*
  Say good night!
  Sleepy dog
Zolotow, Charlotte. *The sleepy book*, ill. by Vladimir Bobri
  Sleepy book, ill. by Ilse Plume

Sleight-of-hand *see* Magic

Sloths *see* Animals – sloths

Smallness *see* Character traits – smallness

Smelling *see* Senses – smelling

Snails *see* Animals – snails

Snakes *see* Reptiles – snakes

Snow *see* Weather – snow

Snowmen

Bauer, Caroline Feller. *Midnight snowman*
Briggs, Raymond. *Building the snowman*
  Dressing up
  The party
  The snowman
  Walking in the air
Chorao, Kay. *Kate's snowman*
Erskine, Jim. *The snowman*
Goffstein, M. B. (Marilyn Brooke). *Our snowman*
Gordon, Sharon. *Friendly snowman*
Holl, Adelaide. *The runaway giant*
Janosch. *Dear snowman*
Johnson, Crockett. *Time for spring*
Kellogg, Steven. *The mystery of the missing red mitten*
Kuskin, Karla. *In the flaky frosty morning*
Lobe, Mira. *The snowman who went for a walk*
Mack, Gail. *Yesterday's snowman*
McKee, David. *Snow woman*
Zion, Gene. *The summer snowman*

Snowplows *see* Machines

Soccer *see* Sports – soccer

Society Islands *see* Foreign lands – South Sea Islands

Soldiers *see* Careers – military

Soldiers, toy *see* Toys – soldiers

Solitude *see* Behavior – solitude

Songs

Abisch, Roz. *Sweet Betsy from Pike*
Alexander, Cecil Frances. *All things bright and beautiful*
Alger, Leclaire. *All in the morning early*
  Kellyburn Braes
Arkin, Alan. *Black and white*
Ash, Jutta. *Wedding birds*
Bangs, Edward. *Yankee Doodle*
Billy Boy
Boesel, Ann Sterling. *Sing and sing again*
  Singing with Peter and Patsy
Bonne, Rose. *I know an old lady*, ill. by Abner Graboff
  I know an old lady who swallowed a fly, ill. by William Stobbs
Botwin, Esther. *A treasury of songs for little children*
Boynton, Sandra. *Good night, good night*
Brand, Oscar. *When I first came to this land*
Briggs, Raymond. *The white land*

Bring a torch, Jeannette, Isabella
Brown, Marc. *Play rhymes*
Bryan, Ashley. *I'm going to sing*
  Lion and the ostrich chicks
Buffett, Jimmy. *The jolly mon*
Bulla, Clyde Robert. *The donkey cart*
Byrne, David. *Stay up late*
Calmenson, Stephanie. *All aboard the goodnight train*
Carryl, Charles Edward. *A capital ship*
Caseley, Judith. *Molly Pink*
Child, Lydia Maria. *Over the river and through the wood*
Conover, Chris. *Six little ducks*
Count me in
Dalton, Alene. *My new picture book of songs*
Delacre, Lulu. *Arroz con leche*
Delaney, A. *The gunnywolf*
Delessert, Etienne. *A long long song*
Denver, John. *The children and the flowers*
De Regniers, Beatrice Schenk. *Was it a good trade?*
Devlin, Harry. *The walloping window blind*
Din dan don, it's Christmas
Domanska, Janina. *Busy Monday morning*
Duvoisin, Roger Antoine. *Petunia and the song*
Emberley, Barbara. *One wide river to cross*
  Simon's song
Engvick, William. *Lullabies and night songs*
The farmer in the dell. The farmer in the dell, ill. by Kathy Parkinson
  The farmer in the dell, ill. by Mary Maki Rae
  The farmer in the dell, ill. by Diane Stanley
Fern, Eugene. *Birthday presents*
The fox went out on a chilly night
The friendly beasts and A partridge in a pear tree
A frog he would a-wooing go (folk-song). *Frog went a-courtin'*, ill. by Feodor Rojankovsky
  Froggie went a-courting, ill. by Chris Conover
Glazer, Tom. *Do your ears hang low?*
  Eye winker, Tom Tinker, chin chopper
  On top of spaghetti
Go tell Aunt Rhody. *Go tell Aunt Rhody*, ill. by Aliki
  Go tell Aunt Rhody, ill. by Robert M. Quackenbush
Graham, Al. *Songs for a small guitar*
The green grass grows all around
Greene, Carol. *A computer went a-courting*
  Hinny Winny Bunco
  The thirteen days of Halloween
Harris, Leon A. *The great diamond robbery*
Hirsh, Marilyn. *One little goat*
Hoban, Brom. *Skunk Lane*
Hoban, Lillian. *Harry's song*

Hobzek, Mildred. *We came a-marching...1, 2, 3*
Hogrogian, Nonny. *The cat who loved to sing*
Homme, Bob. *The friendly giant's birthday*
Hopkins, Lee Bennett. *And God bless me*
Hot cross buns, and other old street cries
Houston, John A. *The bright yellow rope*
A mouse in my house
A room full of animals
Hush little baby. *Hush little baby*, ill. by Aliki
Hush little baby, ill. by Jeanette Winter
Hush little baby, ill. by Margot Zemach
I sing a song of the saints of God
Ipcar, Dahlov. *The cat came back*
"The song of the day birds" and "The song of the night birds"
Ivimey, John William. *The complete story of the three blind mice*, ill. by Paul Galdone
The complete version of ye three blind mice
Johnston, Mary Anne. *Sing me a song*
Kapp, Paul. *Cock-a-doodle-doo!*
Cock-a-doodle-dandy!
Keats, Ezra Jack. *The little drummer boy*
Key, Francis Scott. *The Star-Spangled Banner*, ill. by Paul Galdone
The Star-Spangled Banner, ill. by Peter Spier
Kimmel, Eric A. *Why worry?*
Koontz, Robin Michal. *This old man*
Kovalski, Maryann. *Jingle bells*
The wheels on the bus
Krull, Kathleen. *Songs of praise*
Langstaff, John M. *Oh, a-hunting we will go*
Ol' Dan Tucker
On Christmas day in the morning
Over in the meadow
Soldier, soldier, won't you marry me?
The swapping boy
The two magicians
Lear, Edward. *The pelican chorus*
The pelican chorus and the quangle wangle's hat
Lenski, Lois. *At our house*
Davy and his dog
Davy goes places
Debbie and her grandma
A dog came to school
I like winter
I went for a walk
The life I live
Lord, Beman. *The days of the week*
McCarthy, Bobette. *Buffalo girls*
Mack, Stanley. *Ten bears in my bed*
Maril, Lee. *Mr. Bunny paints the eggs*
Messenger, Jannat. *Lullabies and baby songs*
Mills, Alan. *The hungry goat*
Mohr, Joseph. *Silent night*

Moon, Dolly M. *My very first book of cowboy songs*
Moss, Jeffrey. *The songs of Sesame Street in poems and pictures*
Mother Goose. *London Bridge is falling down*, ill. by Ed Emberley
London Bridge is falling down, ill. by Peter Spier
The Mother Goose songbook, ill. by Jacqueline Sinclair
Mother Goose's melodies, ill. by William A. Wheeler
Thirty old-time nursery songs
Neale, J. M. *Good King Wenceslas*
Nelson, Esther L. *The funny songbook*
Holiday singing and dancing games
The silly songbook
Newbolt, Henry John, Sir. *Rilloby-rill*
Newland, Mary Reed. *Good King Wenceslas*
Nichol, B. P. *Once*
Old MacDonald had a farm. *Old MacDonald had a farm*, ill. by Mel Crawford
Old MacDonald had a farm, ill. by David Frankland
Old MacDonald had a farm, ill. by Abner Graboff
Old MacDonald had a farm, ill. by Tracey Campbell Pearson
Old MacDonald had a farm, ill. by Robert M. Quackenbush
Old MacDonald had a farm, ill. by William Stobbs
On the little hearth
Over in the meadow, ill. by Ezra Jack Keats
A paper of pins
Paterson, Andrew Barton. *Waltzing Matilda*
Peek, Merle. *The balancing act*
Mary wore her red dress and Henry wore his green sneakers
Play and sing - it's Christmas!
Pomerantz, Charlotte. *All asleep*
Poston, Elizabeth. *Baby's song book*
Preston, Edna Mitchell. *Pop Corn and Ma Goodness*
Price, Christine. *One is God*
Quackenbush, Robert M. *Clementine*
The man on the flying trapeze
Pop! goes the weasel and Yankee Doodle
She'll be comin' 'round the mountain
Skip to my Lou
There'll be a hot time in the old town tonight
Raebeck, Lois. *Who am I?*
Raffi. *Down by the bay*
One light, one sun
Shake my sillies out
Wheels on the bus
Raposo, Joe. *The Sesame Street song book*

Rey, Hans Augusto. *Humpty Dumpty and other Mother Goose songs*
Robbins, Ruth. *Baboushka and the three kings*
Roll over!
Root, Phyllis. *Soup for supper*
Rounds, Glen. *The boll weevil*
Casey Jones
The strawberry roan
Sweet Betsy from Pike
Schackburg, Richard. *Yankee Doodle*
Seeger, Pete. *The foolish frog*
Sewall, Marcia. *Animal song*
Shannon, George. *Lizard's song*
Oh, I love!
Singer, Marilyn. *Will you take me to town on strawberry day?*
Slobodkin, Louis. *Wide-awake owl*
The song of the Three Holy Children
Spier, Peter. *The Erie Canal*
Stern, Elsie-Jean. *Wee Robin's Christmas song*
Stobbs, William. *There's a hole in my bucket*
Swados, Elizabeth. *Lullaby*
Taylor, Livingston. *Pajamas*
Taylor, Mark. *The bold fisherman*
Old Blue, you good dog you
Trivas, Irene. *Emma's Christmas*
The twelve days of Christmas. English folk song. *Brian Wildsmith's The twelve days of Christmas*
Jack Kent's twelve days of Christmas
The twelve days of Christmas, ill. by Jan Brett
The twelve days of Christmas, ill. by Ilonka Karasz
The twelve days of Christmas, ill. by Erika Schneider
The twelve days of Christmas, ill. by Sophie Windham
Vaughan, Marcia K. *Wombat stew*
Wallner, John. *Old MacDonald had a farm*
Watson, Clyde. *Fisherman lullabies*
We wish you a merry Christmas
Weiss, Nicki. *If you're happy and you know it*
Wenning, Elisabeth. *The Christmas mouse*
What a morning!
Wheeler, Opal. *Sing in praise*
Sing Mother Goose
Whiteside, Karen. *Lullaby of the wind*
Widdecombe Fair
Wolff, Ashley. *The bells of London*
Yolen, Jane. *Dragon night and other lullabies*
The lullaby songbook
Yulya. *Bears are sleeping*
Zemach, Harve. *Mommy, buy me a China doll*

Zolotow, Charlotte. *The song*

Sounds *see* Noise, sounds

South Africa *see* Foreign lands – South Africa

South America *see* Foreign lands – South America

South Sea Islands *see* Foreign lands – South Sea Islands

Space and space ships

Alexander, Martha G. *Marty McGee's space lab, no girls allowed*
Asimov, Isaac. *The best new things*
Barden, Rosalind. *TV monster*
Barton, Byron. *I want to be an astronaut*
Berenstain, Stan. *The Berenstain bears on the moon*
Bernstein, Joanne E. *More unidentified flying riddles*
Blocksma, Mary. *Easy-to-make spaceships that really fly*
Bogart, Bonnie. *The Ewoks join the fight*
Branley, Franklyn M. *A book of satellites for you*
Is there life in outer space?
Journey into a black hole
The planets in our solar system
Brewster, Patience. *Ellsworth and the cats from Mars*
Brunhoff, Laurent de. *Babar visits another planet*
Carey, Valerie Scho. *Harriet and William and the terrible creature*
Cole, Babette. *The trouble with Gran*
Counsel, June. *But Martin!*
Delaney, Ned. *Cosmic chickens*
Eco, Umberto. *The three astronauts*
Freeman, Don. *Space witch*
Freeman, Mae. *You will go to the moon*
Fuchs, Erich. *Journey to the moon*
Glass, Andrew. *My brother tries to make me laugh*
Hillert, Margaret. *Up, up and away*
Johnson, Crockett. *Harold's trip to the sky*
Keats, Ezra Jack. *Regards to the man in the moon*
Kuskin, Karla. *A space story*
Lorenz, Lee. *Hugo and the spacedog*
Marshall, Edward. *Space case*
Marshall, James. *Merry Christmas, space case*
Marzollo, Jean. *Jed and the space bandits*
Jed's junior space patrol
May, Charles Paul. *High-noon rocket*
Mayer, Mercer. *Astronaut critter*

Mayers, Florence Cassen. *The National Air and Space Museum ABC*
Moche, Dinah L. *The astronauts*
Mooser, Stephen. *Funnyman meets the monster from outer space*
Murphy, Jill. *What next, baby bear!*
Oxenbury, Helen. *Tom and Pippo see the moon*
Paul, Sherry. *2-B and the space visitor*
Peet, Bill. *The wump world*
Podendorf, Illa. *Space*
Rey, Hans Augusto. *Curious George gets a medal*
Robison, Nancy. *UFO kidnap*
Ross, David. *Gorp and the space pirates*
Space monster
Space Monster Gorp and the runaway computer
Ross, Tony. *I'm coming to get you!*
Sadler, Marilyn. *Alistair in outer space*
Alistair's time machine
Schoberle, Ceile. *Beyond the Milky Way*
Schulman, Janet. *Jack the bum and the UFO*
Simon, Seymour. *Galaxies*
Jupiter
Mars
Saturn
The stars
Uranus
Star wars
Steadman, Ralph. *The little red computer*
Ungerer, Tomi. *Moon man*
Vaughn, Jenny. *On the moon*
Weiss, Ellen. *Pigs in space*
Wildsmith, Brian. *Professor Noah's spaceship*
Willis, Jeanne. *The long blue blazer*
Yolen, Jane. *Commander Toad and the big black hole*
Commander Toad and the planet of the grapes
Commander Toad in space
Yorinks, Arthur. *Company's coming*
Zaffo, George J. *The giant book of things in space*
Ziegler, Ursina. *Squaps the moonling*

Spain *see* Foreign lands – Spain

Sparrows *see* Birds – sparrows

Spectacles *see* Glasses

Speech *see* Language

Speed *see* Concepts – speed

Spelunking *see* Caves

Spiders

Aardema, Verna. *The vingananee and the tree toad*
Adelson, Leone. *Please pass the grass*
Back, Christine. *Spider's web*
Baker, Jeannie. *One hungry spider*
Brandenberg, Franz. *Fresh cider and apple pie*
Carle, Eric. *The very busy spider*
Chenery, Janet. *Wolfie*
Climo, Shirley. *The cobweb Christmas*
Conklin, Gladys. *I caught a lizard*
Crothers, Samuel McChord. *Miss Muffet's Christmas party*
Dallinger, Jane. *Spiders*
Fisher, Aileen. *When it comes to bugs*
Freschet, Berniece. *The web in the grass*
Galdone, Joanna. *Honeybee's party*
George, Jean Craighead. *All upon a stone*
Goldin, Augusta. *Spider silk*
Graham, Margaret Bloy. *Be nice to spiders*
Hawes, Judy. *My daddy longlegs*
Hawkins, Colin. *Incy wincy spider*
Joosse, Barbara M. *Spiders in the fruit cellar*
Kraus, Robert. *How spider saved Valentine's Day*
The trouble with spider
McDermott, Gerald. *Anansi the spider*
McNulty, Faith. *The lady and the spider*
Rose, Anne. *Spider in the sky*
Ryder, Joanne. *The spiders dance*
Selsam, Millicent E. *A first look at spiders*
The spider's web
Wagner, Jenny. *Aranea*
Yolen, Jane. *Spider Jane*

Split-page books *see* Format, unusual

Spooks *see* Ghosts; Goblins

Sports

Blaustein, Muriel. *Play ball, Zachary!*
Carlson, Nancy. *Bunnies and their sports*
Carrick, Carol. *The climb*
Caseley, Judith. *Molly Pink goes hiking*
Creekmore, Raymond. *Fujio*
Hoberman, Mary Ann. *Mr. and Mrs. Muddle*
Kessler, Leonard P. *Old Turtle's winter games*
Martin, Bill (William Ivan). *White Dynamite and Curly Kidd*
Ormerod, Jan. *Bend and stretch*
Peterson, Esther Allen. *Penelope gets wheels*
Saddler, Allen. *The Archery contest*
Tinkelman, Murray. *Cowgirl*

Sports – baseball

Adler, David A. *Jeffrey's ghost and the leftover baseball team*
Christian, Mary Blount. *The sand lot*
Christopher, Matt. *Johnny no hit*
Downing, Joan. *Baseball is our game*
Giff, Patricia Reilly. *Ronald Morgan goes to bat*
Gordon, Sharon. *Play ball, Kate!*
Greene, Carol. *I can be a baseball player*
Hillert, Margaret. *Play ball*
Hoff, Syd. *The littlest leaguer*
   Slugger Sal's slump
Isadora, Rachel. *Max*
Kessler, Leonard P. *Here comes the strikeout*
   Old Turtle's baseball stories
Lexau, Joan M. *I'll tell on you*
Oechsli, Kelly. *Mice at bat*
Parish, Peggy. *Play ball, Amelia Bedelia*
Perkins, Al. *Don and Donna go to bat*
Rubin, Jeff. *Baseball brothers*
Rudolph, Marguerita. *I am your misfortune*
Sachs, Marilyn. *Fleet-footed Florence*
   Matt's mitt
Schulman, Janet. *Camp Kee Wee's secret weapon*
Stadler, John. *Hooray for snail!*
Thayer, Ernest L. *Casey at the bat*, ill. by Patricia Polacco

Sports – basketball

Porte, Barbara Ann. *Harry's visit*
Shearer, John. *The case of the sneaker snatcher*

Sports – bicycling

Andersen, Karen Born. *What's the matter, Sylvie, can't you ride?*
Baker, Eugene. *Bicycles*
Bang, Molly. *Delphine*
Baugh, Dolores M. *Bikes*
Bentley, Anne. *The Groggs' day out*
Blake, Quentin. *Mrs. Armitage on wheels*
Blance, Ellen. *Monster, Lady Monster and the bike ride*
Breinburg, Petronella. *Shawn's red bike*
Bruna, Dick. *Miffy's bicycle*
Chlad, Dorothy. *Bicycles are fun to ride*
Heine, Helme. *Friends*
McLeod, Emilie Warren. *The bear's bicycle*
Muntean, Michaela. *Bicycle bear*
Myers, Bernice. *Herman and the bears and the giants*
Paterson, Andrew Barton. *Mulga Bill's bicycle*
Phleger, Fred B. *Off to the races*
Rey, Hans Augusto. *Curious George rides a bike*
Rockwell, Anne F. *Bikes*

Say, Allen. *The bicycle man*
Sueyoshi, Akiko. *Ladybird on a bicycle*
Thomas, Jane Resh. *Wheels*

Sports – camping

Armitage, Ronda. *One moonlit night*
Berenstain, Stan. *The Berenstain bears go to camp*
Boynton, Sandra. *Hester in the wild*
Brown, Marc. *Arthur goes to camp*
Brown, Myra Berry. *Pip camps out*
Carrick, Carol. *Sleep out*
Henkes, Kevin. *Bailey goes camping*
McPhail, David. *Pig Pig goes to camp*
Maestro, Betsy. *Camping out*
Marino, Dorothy. *Buzzy Bear goes camping*
Mayer, Mercer. *Just me and my dad*
   You're the scaredy cat
Maynard, Joyce. *Camp-out*
Parish, Peggy. *Amelia Bedelia goes camping*
Peters, Sharon. *Fun at camp*
Price, Dorothy E. *Speedy gets around*
Roche, P. K. (Patrick K.). *Webster and Arnold go camping*
Rockwell, Anne F. *The night we slept outside*
Rubel, Nicole. *Sam and Violet go camping*
Schulman, Janet. *Camp Kee Wee's secret weapon*
Schwartz, Henry. *How I captured a dinosaur*
Shearer, John. *Billy Jo Jive and the case of the midnight voices*
Shulevitz, Uri. *Dawn*
Stock, Catherine. *Sophie's knapsack*
Tafuri, Nancy. *Do not disturb*
Thompson, Vivian Laubach. *Camp-in-the-yard*
Warren, Cathy. *The ten-alarm camp-out*
Weiss, Nicki. *Battle day at Camp Delmont*
Williams, Vera B. *Three days on a river in a red canoe*
Yolen, Jane. *The giants go camping*

Sports – fishing

Aldridge, Josephine Haskell. *Fisherman's luck*
   A peony and a periwinkle
Bettina (Bettina Ehrlich). *Pantaloni*
Cook, Bernadine. *The little fish that got away*
Delacre, Lulu. *Nathan's fishing trip*
Delton, Judy. *Duck goes fishing*
Demarest, Chris L. *Orville's odyssey*
Elkin, Benjamin. *Six foolish fishermen*
Gelman, Rita Golden. *Uncle Hugh*
Goffstein, M. B. (Marilyn Brooke). *Fish for supper*
Gray, Catherine. *Tammy and the gigantic fish*

Griffith, Helen V. *Grandaddy's place*
Hall, Bill. *Fish tale*
Hann, Jacquie. *Up day, down day*
Hertza, Ole. *Tobias catches trout*
  Tobias goes ice fishing
Ipcar, Dahlov. *The biggest fish in the sea*
Lapp, Eleanor. *In the morning mist*
Long, Earlene. *Gone fishing*
Marzollo, Jean. *Amy goes fishing*
Mayer, Mercer. *A boy, a dog, a frog and a friend*
  A boy, a dog and a frog
Miles, Miska. *No, no, Rosina*
Ness, Evaline. *Sam, Bangs, and moonshine*
Neumeyer, Peter F. *The faithful fish*
Parker, Dorothy D. *Liam's catch*
Potter, Beatrix. *The tale of Mr. Jeremy Fisher*
Rey, Margaret Elisabeth Waldstein. *Curious George flies a kite*
Say, Allen. *A river dream*
Stevenson, Robert Louis. *The moon*
Surany, Anico. *Ride the cold wind*
Taylor, Mark. *The bold fisherman*
Thorne, Jenny. *My uncle*
Wahl, Jan. *The fishermen*
Waterton, Betty. *A salmon for Simon*
Watson, Nancy Dingman. *Tommy's mommy's fish*
Wildsmith, Brian. *Pelican*
Wilson, Bob. *Stanley Bagshaw and the twenty-two ton whale*

Sports – football

Carlson, Nancy. *Louanne Pig in making the team*
Kessler, Leonard P. *Kick, pass, and run*
  Super bowl
Kuskin, Karla. *The Dallas Titans get ready for bed*
Myers, Bernice. *Sidney Rella and the glass sneaker*
Stadler, John. *Snail saves the day*

Sports – gymnastics

Brown, Marc. *D. W. flips!*
Schulman, Janet. *Jenny and the tennis nut*
Stevens, Carla. *Pig and the blue flag*

Sports – hiking

Curious George goes hiking

Sports – hockey

Kidd, Bruce. *Hockey showdown*

Sports – hunting

Baker, Betty. *Sonny-Boy Sim*
Bemelmans, Ludwig. *Parsley*

Browne, Anthony. *Bear hunt*
Burch, Robert. *The hunting trip*
Burningham, John. *Harquin*
Calhoun, Mary. *Houn' dog*
Carrick, Donald. *The deer in the pasture*
  Harold and the great stag
De Paola, Tomie. *The hunter and the animals*
De Regniers, Beatrice Schenk. *Catch a little fox*
Dionetti, Michelle. *The day Eli went looking for bear*
Duvoisin, Roger Antoine. *The happy hunter*
Gage, Wilson. *Cully Cully and the bear*
Hader, Berta Hoerner. *The mighty hunter*
Hertza, Ole. *Tobias goes seal hunting*
Hoban, Russell. *The dancing tigers*
Jones, Maurice. *I'm going on a dragon hunt*
Kahl, Virginia. *How do you hide a monster?*
Kamen, Gloria. *The ringdoves*
Kellogg, Steven. *Tallyho, Pinkerton!*
Kilroy, Sally. *The baron's hunting party*
Kroll, Steven. *One tough turkey*
Langstaff, John M. *Oh, a-hunting we will go*
Livermore, Elaine. *Looking for Henry*
Mari, Iela. *Eat and be eaten*
Mendoza, George. *The hunter I might have been*
Michels, Tilde. *Who's that knocking at my door?*
Parish, Peggy. *Good hunting, Blue Sky*
  Ootah's lucky day
Peet, Bill. *Buford, the little bighorn*
  The gnats of knotty pine
Prusski, Jeffrey. *Bring back the deer*
Rohmer, Harriet. *The invisible hunters*
Steiner, Charlotte. *Pete and Peter*
Wahl, Jan. *Tiger watch*
Wildsmith, Brian. *Hunter and his dog*
Withers, Carl. *The wild ducks and the goose*

Sports – ice skating

Hoban, Lillian. *Mr. Pig and Sonny too*
Johnson, Mildred D. *Wait, skates!*
Lindman, Maj. *Snipp, Snapp, Snurr and the yellow sled*
Radin, Ruth Yaffe. *A winter place*
Van Stockum, Hilda. *A day on skates*
Yolen, Jane. *Mice on ice*

Sports – Olympics

Kessler, Leonard P. *On your mark, get set, go!*
Schulz, Charles M. *You're the greatest, Charlie Brown*

Sports – racing

Aarle, Thomas Van. *Don't put your cart before the horse race*
Adams, Adrienne. *The great Valentine's Day balloon race*
Æsop. *The hare and the tortoise*, ill. by Paul Galdone
The hare and the tortoise, ill. by Gerald Rose
The hare and the tortoise, ill. by Peter Weevers
The tortoise and the hare, ill. by Janet Stevens
Alborough, Jez. *Running Bear*
Barrett, N. S. *Racing cars*
Baumann, Hans. *The hare's race*
Baynton, Martin. *Fifty and the great race*
Benchley, Nathaniel. *Walter the homing pigeon*
Calloway, Northern J. *Northern J. Calloway presents Super-vroomer!*
Dickens, Frank. *Boffo*
Hall, Derek. *Tiger runs*
Heine, Helme. *Three little friends: the racing cart*
Hurd, Edith Thacher. *Last one home is a green pig*
Isenberg, Barbara. *The adventures of Albert, the running bear*
Albert the running bear gets the jitters
Kessler, Leonard P. *The big mile race*
La Fontaine, Jean de. *The hare and the tortoise*
McLenighan, Valjean. *Turtle and rabbit*
McNaughton, Colin. *The rat race*
Marshall, Edward. *Fox on wheels*
Moore, John. *Granny Stickleback*
Neuhaus, David. *His finest hour*
Otsuka, Yuzo. *Suho and the white horse*
Phleger, Fred B. *Off to the races*
Reimold, Mary Gallagher. *My mom is a runner*
Van Woerkom, Dorothy. *Harry and Shelburt*
Wilkinson, Sylvia. *I can be a race car driver*

Sports – roller skating

Wahl, Jan. *Rabbits on roller skates!*

Sports – skiing

Calhoun, Mary. *Cross-country cat*
Freeman, Don. *Ski pup*
Lindman, Maj. *Snipp, Snapp, Snurr and the red shoes*
Marol, Jean-Claude. *Vagabul goes skiing*
Peet, Bill. *Buford, the little bighorn*

Sports – skin diving

Carrick, Carol. *Dark and full of secrets*

Ungerer, Tomi. *The Mellops go diving for treasure*

Sports – sledding

Curious George goes sledding

Sports – soccer

Christopher, Matt. *Jackrabbit goalie*

Sports – surfing

Ormondroyd, Edward. *Broderick*

Sports – swimming

Alexander, Martha G. *We never get to do anything*
Beatty, Hetty Burlingame. *Droopy*
Beim, Jerrold. *The swimming hole*
Brown, M. K. *Let's go swimming with Mr. Sillypants*
Cohn, Norma. *Brother and sister*
Coles, Alison. *Michael and the sea*
George, Lindsay Barrett. *William and Boomer*
Ginsburg, Mirra. *The chick and the duckling*
Hall, Derek. *Otter swims*
Kessler, Leonard P. *Last one in is a rotten egg*
Lasky, Kathryn. *Sea swan*
Moore, Inga. *Aktil's big swim*
Shortall, Leonard W. *Tony's first dive*
Stevens, Carla. *Hooray for pig!*
Van Leeuwen, Jean. *Too hot for ice cream*

Sports – T-ball

Gemme, Leila Boyle. *T-ball is our game*

Sports – tennis

Schulman, Janet. *Jenny and the tennis nut*

Sports – wrestling

Stren, Patti. *Mountain Rose*

Spring *see* Seasons – spring

Squirrels *see* Animals – squirrels

Stage *see* Theater

Stars

Allen, Laura Jean. *Ottie and the star*
Asch, Frank. *Starbaby*
Boon, Emilie. *Peterkin meets a star*
Branley, Franklyn M. *The big dipper*
Journey into a black hole
The sky is full of stars
Coatsworth, Elizabeth. *Good night*
Elzbieta. *Dikou and the baby star*

Freeman, Mae. *The sun, the moon and the stars*
Kuskin, Karla. *A space story*
Lee, Jeanne M. *The legend of the milky way*
Mobley, Jane. *The star husband*
Radley, Gail. *The night Stella hid the stars*
Simon, Seymour. *Galaxies*
  The stars
Slate, Joseph. *The star rocker*
Tibo, Gilles. *Simon and the snowflakes*
Wandelmaier, Roy. *Stars*
Winter, Jeanette. *Follow the drinking gourd*
Yeomans, Thomas. *For every child a star*

Stealing *see* Behavior – stealing

Steam shovels *see* Machines

Steamrollers *see* Machines

Step families *see* Divorce; Family life – step families

Stepchildren *see* Divorce; Family life – step families

Stepparents *see* Divorce; Family life – step families

Stones *see* Rocks

Storekeepers *see* Careers – storekeepers

Stores

Alexander, Liza. *Ernie gets lost*
Anholt, Catherine. *Truffles in trouble*
Baugh, Dolores M. *Let's go*
  Supermarket
Bograd, Larry. *Lost in the store*
Cooper, Letice Ulpha. *The bear who was too big*
Field, Rachel Lyman. *General store*, ill. by Giles Laroche
  General store, ill. by Nancy Winslow Parker
Freeman, Don. *Corduroy*
Gibbons, Gail. *Department store*
Gordon, Margaret. *The supermarket mice*
Graham, Amanda. *Who wants Arthur?*
Hale, Kathleen. *Orlando the frisky housewife*
Harris, Leon A. *The great diamond robbery*
Hastings, Evelyn Beilhart. *The department store*
Hoff, Syd. *Merry Christmas, Henrietta!*
Lippman, Peter. *The Know-It-Alls mind the store*
Lobel, Arnold. *On Market Street*
McNaughton, Colin. *At the stores*
Maschler, Fay. *T. G. and Moonie go shopping*

Miller, Alice P. *The little store on the corner*
Pearson, Tracey Campbell. *The storekeeper*
Potter, Beatrix. *Ginger and Pickles*
Rockwell, Anne F. *The supermarket*
Sawyer, Jean. *Our village shop*
Scarry, Richard. *Richard Scarry's great big mystery book*
Solomon, Joan. *A present for Mum*
Spier, Peter. *Food market*
  The pet store
  The toy shop
Steiner, Jörg. *The bear who wanted to be a bear*
Williams, Barbara. *I know a salesperson*

Stories in the round *see* Circular tales

Storks *see* Birds – storks

Storms *see* Weather – storms

Streams *see* Rivers

Street signs *see* Traffic, traffic signs

Streets *see* Roads

String

Bakken, Harold. *The special string*
Calhoun, Mary. *The traveling ball of string*
Heathers, Anne. *The thread soldiers*
Holland, Marion. *A big ball of string*

Stubbornness *see* Character traits – stubbornness

Sucking of thumb *see* Thumbsucking

Sullivan Islands *see* Foreign lands – South Sea Islands

Summer *see* Seasons – summer

Sun

Anno, Mitsumasa. *In shadowland*
Arnold, Caroline. *Sun fun*
Baylor, Byrd. *The way to start a day*
Berenstain, Stan. *The bears' almanac*
Bernstein, Margery. *How the sun made a promise and kept it*
Branley, Franklyn M. *Eclipse darkness in daytime*
  The planets in our solar system
  The sun, our nearest star
  Sunshine makes the seasons
Dayrell, Elphinstone. *Why the sun and the moon live in the sky*
De Gerez, Toni. *Louhi, witch of North Farm*

De Regniers, Beatrice Schenk. *Who likes the sun?*
Elkin, Benjamin. *Why the sun was late*
Engelbrektson, Sune. *The sun is a star*
Euvremer, Teryl. *Sun's up*
Freeman, Mae. *The sun, the moon and the stars*
Gibbons, Gail. *Sun up, sun down*
Ginsburg, Mirra. *How the sun was brought back to the sky*
Where does the sun go at night?
Goudey, Alice E. *The day we saw the sun come up*
Greene, Carol. *Shine, sun!*
Hamberger, John. *The day the sun disappeared*
Harrison, David Lee. *Wake up, sun!*
Hurd, Edith Thacher. *The day the sun danced*
Kandoian, Ellen. *Under the sun*
Kinney, Jean. *What does the sun do?*
La Fontaine, Jean de. *The north wind and the sun*
Novak, Matt. *Claude and Sun*
Obrist, Jürg. *The miser who wanted the sun*
Ormerod, Jan. *Sunshine*
Palazzo, Janet. *Our friend the sun*
Ringi, Kjell. *The sun and the cloud*
Schlein, Miriam. *The sun looks down*
The sun, the wind, the sea and the rain
Schneider, Herman. *Follow the sunset*
Shulevitz, Uri. *Dawn*
Simon, Seymour. *The sun*
Tresselt, Alvin R. *Sun up*
Troughton, Joanna. *Who will be the sun?*
Wildsmith, Brian. *What the moon saw*

Surfing *see* Sports – surfing

Swallows *see* Birds – swallows

Swans *see* Birds – swans

Sweden *see* Foreign lands – Sweden

Swimming *see* Sports – swimming

Swinging *see* Activities – swinging

Switzerland *see* Foreign lands – Switzerland

T-ball *see* Sports – T-ball

Tailors *see* Careers – tailors

Talking to strangers *see* Behavior – talking to strangers; Safety

Tapirs *see* Animals – tapirs

Tardiness *see* Behavior – tardiness

Tasting *see* Senses – tasting

Taxi drivers *see* Careers – taxi drivers

Taxis

Moore, Lilian. *Papa Albert*
Ross, Jessica. *Ms. Klondike*

Teachers *see* Careers – teachers

Teddy bears *see* Toys – teddy bears

Teeth

Austin, Margot. *Trumpet*
Balzola, Asun. *Munia and the orange crocodile*
Barnett, Naomi. *I know a dentist*
Bate, Lucy. *Little rabbit's loose tooth*
Birdseye, Tom. *Airmail to the moon*
Brown, Marc. *Arthur's tooth*
Brown, Ruth. *Crazy Charlie*
Cooney, Nancy Evans. *The wobbly tooth*
De Groat, Diane. *Alligator's toothache*
Dinan, Carolyn. *Say cheese!*
Duvoisin, Roger Antoine. *Crocus*
Eriksson, Eva. *The tooth trip*
Gunther, Louise. *A tooth for the tooth fairy*
Kroll, Steven. *Loose tooth*
McCloskey, Robert. *One morning in Maine*
McGinley, Phyllis. *Lucy McLockett*
McPhail, David. *The bear's toothache*
Pomerantz, Charlotte. *The mango tooth*
Quin-Harkin, Janet. *Helpful Hattie*
Richter, Alice Numeroff. *You can't put braces on spaces*
Ricketts, Michael. *Teeth*
Rockwell, Harlow. *My dentist*
Ross, Pat. *Molly and the slow teeth*
Seuss, Dr. *The tooth book*
West, Colin. *The king's toothache*
Williams, Barbara. *Albert's toothache*
Wolf, Bernard. *Michael and the dentist*

Telephone

Allen, Jeffrey. *Mary Alice, operator number 9*
Mary Alice returns
Telephones
Weiss, Ellen. *Telephone time*

Wyse, Lois. *Two guppies, a turtle and Aunt Edna*

Telephone operators *see* Careers – telephone operators

Television

Barden, Rosalind. *TV monster*
Berenstain, Stan. *The Berenstain bears and too much TV*
Brown, Marc. *The bionic bunny show*
Heilbroner, Joan. *Tom the TV cat*
McPhail, David. *Fix-it*

Telling time *see* Clocks; Time

Temper tantrums *see* Emotions – anger

Tennis *see* Sports – tennis

Textless *see* Wordless

Thailand *see* Foreign lands – Thailand

Thanksgiving *see* Holidays – Thanksgiving

Theater

Ahlberg, Allan. *The Cinderella show*
Alexander, Sue. *Seymour the prince*
Small plays for special days
Small plays for you and a friend
Bellville, Cheryl Walsh. *Theater magic*
Brighton, Catherine. *Hope's gift*
Brown, Marc. *Arthur's Thanksgiving*
Butterworth, Nick. *The Nativity play*
Carlson, Nancy. *The talent show*
Cazet, Denys. *The duck with squeaky feet*
Cohen, Miriam. *Starring first grade*
Coombs, Patricia. *Dorrie's play*
De Paola, Tomie. *The Christmas pageant*
Sing, Pierrot, sing
De Regniers, Beatrice Schenk. *Picture book theater*
Ets, Marie Hall. *Another day*
Freeman, Don. *Hattie the backstage bat*
Will's quill
Freeman, Lydia. *Pet of the Met*
Frye, Dean. *Days of sunshine, days of rain*
Giff, Patricia Reilly. *The almost awful play*
Goffstein, M. B. (Marilyn Brooke). *An actor*
Goodall, John S. *Paddy's evening out*
Greaves, Margaret. *The magic flute*
Grimm, Jacob. *King Grisly-Beard*
Hoffmann, E. T. A. *The nutcracker*, ill. by Maurice Sendak
Holabird, Katharine. *Angelina on stage*
Isadora, Rachel. *Jesse and Abe*
Opening night
Johnston, Johanna. *Speak up, Edie*

Layton, Aviva. *The squeakers*
Leedy, Loreen. *The bunny play*
Lobel, Arnold. *Martha, the movie mouse*
Maiorano, Robert. *Backstage*
Marks, Burton. *Puppet plays and puppet-making*
Martin, Judith. *The tree angel*
Neumeyer, Peter F. *The phantom of the opera*
Oppenheim, Joanne. *Mrs. Peloki's class play*
Patz, Nancy. *Gina Farina and the Prince of Mintz*
Rose, Mitchell. *Norman*
Sage, James. *The boy and the dove*
Sendak, Maurice. *Maurice Sendak's Really Rosie*
Steiner, Charlotte. *Kiki is an actress*
Tallon, Robert. *Handella*
Yeoman, John. *The young performing horse*
Yolen, Jane. *Mice on ice*

Thumbsucking

Cooney, Nancy Evans. *Donald says thumbs down*
Heitler, Susan M. *David decides about thumbsucking*
Klimowicz, Barbara. *The strawberry thumb*

Thunder *see* Weather – storms; Weather – thunder

Tibet *see* Foreign lands – Tibet

Tigers *see* Animals – tigers

Time

Abisch, Roz. *Do you know what time it is?*
Aiken, Conrad. *Tom, Sue and the clock*
Allen, Jeffrey. *Mary Alice, operator number 9*
Behn, Harry. *All kinds of time*
Bodwell, Gaile. *The long day of the giants*
Bragdon, Lillian J. *Tell me the time, please*
Carle, Eric. *The grouchy ladybug*
Colman, Hila. *Watch that watch*
Gibbons, Gail. *Clocks and how they go*
Gordon, Sharon. *Tick tock clock*
Handford, Martin. *Find Waldo now*
Hawkins, Colin. *What time is it, Mr. Wolf?*
Hay, Dean. *Now I can count*
Hoff, Syd. *Henrietta, the early bird*
Hutchins, Pat. *Clocks and more clocks*
Katz, Bobbi. *Tick-tock, let's read the clock*
Killingback, Julia. *What time is it, Mrs. Bear?*
Krasilovsky, Phyllis. *The man who tried to save time*
Littlewood, Valerie. *The season clock*

Lyon, George Ella. *Father Time and the day boxes*
McGinley, Phyllis. *Wonderful time*
Maestro, Betsy. *Around the clock with Harriet*
May, Charles Paul. *High-noon rocket*
Mother Goose. *The real Mother Goose clock book*
Ness, Evaline. *Do you have the time, Lydia?*
Pieńkowski, Jan. *Time*
Pluckrose, Henry. *Time*
Rockwell, Anne F. *Bear Child's book of hours*
Sadler, Marilyn. *Alistair's time machine*
Scarry, Richard. *Richard Scarry's great big schoolhouse*
Schlein, Miriam. *It's about time*
Seignobosc, Françoise. *What time is it, Jeanne-Marie?*
Slobodkin, Louis. *The late cuckoo*
Steinmetz, Leon. *Clocks in the woods*
Watson, Nancy Dingman. *When is tomorrow?*
Ziner, Feenie. *The true book of time*
Zolotow, Charlotte. *Over and over*

Tin soldiers *see* Toys – soldiers

Toads *see* Frogs and toads

Tongue twisters

Bodecker, N. M. (Nils Mogens). *Snowman Sniffles and other verse*
Brown, Marcia. *Peter Piper's alphabet*
Obligado, Lilian. *Faint frogs feeling feverish and other terrifically tantalizing tongue twisters*
Patz, Nancy. *Pumpernickel tickle and mean green cheese*
Pomerantz, Charlotte. *The piggy in the puddle*
Schwartz, Alvin. *Busy buzzing bumblebees*
Smith, Robert Paul. *Jack Mack*
Thomas, Gary. *The best of the little books*

Tools

Adkins, Jan. *Toolchest*
Beim, Jerrold. *Tim and the tool chest*
Carle, Eric. *My very first book of tools*
DeSantis, Kenny. *A doctor's tools*
Gibbons, Gail. *Tool book*
Kesselman, Judi R. *I can use tools*
Lerner, Marguerite Rush. *Doctors' tools*
Pluckrose, Henry. *Things we cut*
Rockwell, Anne F. *The toolbox*
Zaffo, George J. *The giant nursery book of things that work*

Tortoises *see* Reptiles – turtles, tortoises

Toucans *see* Birds – toucans

Touching *see* Senses – touching

Towns *see* City

Toy and movable books *see* Format, unusual – toy and movable books

Toy books *see* Format, unusual – toy and movable books

Toys

Abolafia, Yossi. *Yanosh's Island*
Alexander, Martha G. *The story grandmother told*
Ardizzone, Aingelda. *The night ride*
Avery, Kay. *Wee willow whistle*
Ayer, Jacqueline. *Nu Dang and his kite*
Bambi
Beckman, Kaj. *Lisa cannot sleep*
Bianco, Margery Williams. *The velveteen rabbit*, ill. by Allen Atkinson
The velveteen rabbit, ill. by Michael Green
The velveteen rabbit, ill. by Michael Hague
The velveteen rabbit, ill. by David Jorgensen
The velveteen rabbit, ill. by William Nicholson
The velveteen rabbit, ill. by Ilse Plume
The velveteen rabbit, ill. by S. D. Schindler
The velveteen rabbit, ill. by Tien
Billam, Rosemary. *Fuzzy rabbit*
Binzen, Bill. *Alfred goes house hunting*
Boegehold, Betty. *Hurray for Pippa!*
Bohdal, Susi. *Harry the hare*
Bornstein, Ruth Lercher. *Annabelle*
Brandenberg, Franz. *Aunt Nina and her nephews and nieces*
Bright, Robert. *Hurrah for Freddie!*
Browne, Anthony. *Gorilla*
Bryant, Dean. *See the bear*
Burdick, Margaret. *Bobby Otter and the blue boat*
Burns, Maurice. *Go ducks, go!*
Campbell, Rod. *Buster's morning*
Chorao, Kay. *Kate's car*
Molly's Moe
Coombs, Patricia. *The lost playground*
Corbett, Grahame. *Guess who?*
Who is hiding?
Who is inside?
Who is next?
Craig, M. Jean. *Boxes*
Dale, Penny. *You can't*
Daly, Niki. *Vim, the rag mouse*
De Lynam, Alicia Garcia. *It's mine!*
DiFiori, Lawrence. *My toys*
Dobrin, Arnold Jack. *Josephine's 'magination*

Toys – balloons

Bright, Robert. *Georgie and the runaway balloon*
Brock, Emma Lillian. *Surprise balloon*
Carrick, Carol. *The highest balloon on the common*
Chase, Catherine. *My balloon*
Coxe, Molly. *Louella and the yellow balloon*
Fenton, Edward. *The big yellow balloon*
Goodsell, Jane. *Toby's toe*
Gray, Nigel. *A balloon for grandad*
Mari, Iela. *The magic balloon*
Matthias, Catherine. *Too many balloons*
Sharmat, Marjorie Weinman. *I don't care*
Watanabe, Yuichi. *Wally the whale who loved balloons*

Toys – balls

Espenscheid, Gertrude E. *The oh ball*
Hamberger, John. *The lazy dog*
Holl, Adelaide. *The remarkable egg*
Kellogg, Steven. *The mystery of the magic green ball*
Krahn, Fernando. *The biggest Christmas tree on earth*
Lindgren, Barbro. *Sam's ball*
McClintock, Marshall. *Stop that ball*
Maley, Anne. *Have you seen my mother?*

Toys – bears *see* Toys – teddy bears

Toys – blocks

Hutchins, Pat. *Changes, changes*
Mayers, Patrick. *Just one more block*
Winthrop, Elizabeth. *That's mine*

Toys – dolls

Ainsworth, Ruth. *The mysterious Baba and her magic caravan*
Ardizzone, Aingelda. *The night ride*
Ardizzone, Edward. *The little girl and the tiny doll*
Ayer, Jacqueline. *Little Silk*
Bannon, Laura. *Katy comes next*
  Manuela's birthday
Barber, Antonia. *Satchelmouse and the doll's house*
Bernhard, Josephine Butkowska. *Nine cry-baby dolls*
Blegvad, Lenore. *Rainy day Kate*
Bright, Robert. *The travels of Ching*
Brown, Margaret Wise. *Dr. Squash the doll doctor*
Dodge, Mary Mapes. *Mary Anne*
Dreifus, Miriam W. *Brave Betsy*
Francis, Frank. *Natasha's new doll*
Goffstein, M. B. (Marilyn Brooke). *Goldie the dollmaker*
  Me and my captain
  Our prairie home

Hines, Anna Grossnickle. *Don't worry, I'll find you*
  Keep your old hat
  Maybe a band-aid will help
Hoban, Russell. *The stone doll of Sister Brute*
Huff, Vivian. *Let's make paper dolls*
Jaques, Faith. *Tilly's house*
  Tilly's rescue
Jennings, Linda M. *Coppelia*
Johnston, Johanna. *Sugarplum*
Keller, Holly. *Geraldine's blanket*
Kroll, Steven. *The hand-me-down doll*
Kunhardt, Dorothy. *Kitty's new doll*
Lenski, Lois. *Debbie and her dolls*
  Let's play house
Lexau, Joan M. *The rooftop mystery*
McGinley, Phyllis. *The most wonderful doll in the world*
McKissack, Patricia C. *Nettie Jo's friends*
McMillan, Bruce. *Ghost doll*
Mariana. *The journey of Bangwell Putt*
  Miss Flora McFlimsey and the baby New Year
  Miss Flora McFlimsey's birthday
  Miss Flora McFlimsey's Christmas Eve
  Miss Flora McFlimsey's Easter bonnet
  Miss Flora McFlimsey's Halloween
  Miss Flora McFlimsey's May Day
  Miss Flora McFlimsey's Valentine
Maris, Ron. *Hold tight, bear!*
Ormerod, Jan. *Making friends*
Pellowski, Anne. *The nine crying dolls*
Pincus, Harriet. *Minna and Pippin*
Politi, Leo. *Rosa*
Sandburg, Carl. *The wedding procession of the rag doll and the broom handle and who was in it*, ill. by Harriet Pincus
Schulman, Janet. *The big hello*
  The great big dummy
Shecter, Ben. *The stocking child*
Skorpen, Liesel Moak. *Elizabeth*
Steig, William. *Yellow and pink*
Tudor, Tasha. *The doll's Christmas*
Udry, Janice May. *Emily's autumn*
Wahl, Jan. *The Muffletump storybook*
  The Muffletumps
  The Muffletumps' Christmas party
  The Muffletumps' Halloween scare
Wells, Rosemary. *Peabody*
Wilson, Julia. *Becky*
Winthrop, Elizabeth. *Katharine's doll*
Wiseman, Bernard. *Oscar is a mama*
Wright, Dare. *The doll and the kitten*
  Edith and Midnight
  Edith and Mr. Bear
  Edith and the duckling
  The lonely doll
  The lonely doll learns a lesson
Zemach, Harve. *Mommy, buy me a China doll*

Zolotow, Charlotte. *William's doll*

Toys – hobby horses *see* Toys – rocking horses

Toys – pandas *see* Toys – teddy bears

Toys – rocking horses

Brown, Paul. *Merrylegs, the rocking pony*
Donaldson, Lois. *Karl's wooden horse*
Lindman, Maj. *Snipp, Snapp, Snurr and the magic horse*
Moeschlin, Elsa. *The red horse*
Roberts, Thom. *Pirates in the park*
Robertson, Lilian. *Runaway rocking horse*

Toys – soldiers

Andersen, H. C. (Hans Christian). *The steadfast tin soldier*, ill. by Thomas Di Grazia
The steadfast tin soldier, ill. by Paul Galdone
The steadfast tin soldier, ill. by David Jorgensen
The steadfast tin soldier, ill. by Monika Laimgruber
The steadfast tin soldier, ill. by Alain Vaës
The swineherd, ill. by Lisbeth Zwerger
Brown, Margaret Wise. *Dr. Squash the doll doctor*
Collington, Peter. *The angel and the soldier boy*
Heathers, Anne. *The thread soldiers*
Nicholson, William, Sir. *Clever Bill*

Toys – teddy bears

Alexander, Martha G. *I'll protect you from the jungle beasts*
Ardizzone, Aingelda. *The night ride*
Barker, Inga-Lil. *Why teddy bears are brown*
Behrens, June. *The manners book*
Bohdal, Susi. *Bobby the bear*
Boyle, Constance. *The story of little owl*
Brown, Myra Berry. *First night away from home*
Cooper, Letice Ulpha. *The bear who was too big*
Craft, Ruth. *The winter bear*
Davidson, Amanda. *Teddy at the seashore*
Teddy goes outside
Teddy in the garden
Teddy's birthday
Teddy's first Christmas
Davis, Douglas F. *There's an elephant in the garage*
Decker, Dorothy W. *Stripe and the merbear*
Stripe visits New York
Douglass, Barbara. *Good as new*
Flora, James. *Sherwood walks home*

The fox went out on a chilly night
Freeman, Don. *Beady Bear*
Corduroy
Corduroy's party
A pocket for Corduroy
Freeman, Lydia. *Corduroy's day*
Galbraith, Richard. *Reuben runs away*
Gretz, Susanna. *Hide-and-seek*
I'm not sleepy
Teddy bears ABC
Teddy bears cure a cold
Teddy bears go shopping
Teddy bears' moving day
Teddy bears 1 - 10
Teddy bears stay indoors
Teddy bears take the train
Teddybears cookbook
Too dark!
Grindley, Sally. *Knock, knock! Who's there?*
Hague, Kathleen. *Alphabears*
Numbears
Out of the nursery, into the night
Hale, Irina. *Brown bear in a brown chair*
Hawkins, Colin. *Dip, dip, dip*
One finger, one thumb
Oops-a-Daisy
Where's bear?
Hayes, Geoffrey. *Bear by himself*
Hayes, Sarah. *This is the bear*
Hines, Anna Grossnickle. *I'll tell you what they say*
Hissey, Jane. *Old Bear*
Old Bear tales
Hoban, Lillian. *Arthur's honey bear*
Howe, Caroline Walton. *Teddy Bear's bird and beast band*
Howe, Deborah. *Teddy Bear's scrapbook*
Ingpen, Robert. *The idle bear*
Inkpen, Mick. *One bear at bedtime*
Joerns, Consuelo. *The forgotten bear*
Kantrowitz, Mildred. *Willy Bear*
Keller, Holly. *A bear for Christmas*
Kennedy, Jimmy. *The teddy bears' picnic*, ill. by Alexandra Day
The teddy bears' picnic, ill. by Prue Theobalds
Kočí, Marta. *Sarah's bear*
Le-Tan, Pierre. *Visit to the North Pole*
Lewis, Naomi. *Once upon a rainbow*
Lindgren, Barbro. *Sam's teddy bear*
Lindsay, Elizabeth. *A letter for Maria*
Lundell, Margo. *Teddy bear's birthday*
McCue, Lisa. *Corduroy's toys*
McLeod, Emilie Warren. *The bear's bicycle*
McPhail, David. *The dream child*
First flight
Marcus, Susan. *The missing button adventure*
Maris, Ron. *Are you there, bear?*
Marzollo, Jean. *Jed's junior space patrol*

Milne, A. A. (Alan Alexander). *House at Pooh corner: a pop-up book*
Pooh and some bees
Pooh goes visiting
Pooh's alphabet book
Pooh's bedtime book
Pooh's counting book
Pooh's quiz book
Winnie-the-Pooh
Mogensen, Jan. *Teddy and the Chinese dragon*
Teddy in the undersea kingdom
Teddy's Christmas gift
When Teddy woke early
Moss, Elaine. *Polar*
Nims, Bonnie L. *Where is the bear?*
Ormondroyd, Edward. *Theodore*
Theodore's rival
Pearson, Susan. *Baby and the bear*
Phillips, Joan. *Lucky bear*
Prince, Pamela. *The secret world of teddy bears*
Romanek, Enid Warner. *Teddy*
Siewert, Margaret. *Bear hunt*
Skorpen, Liesel Moak. *Charles*
Steger, Hans-Ulrich. *Traveling to Tripiti*
Thomson, Ruth. *My bear I can...can you?*
My bear I like...do you?
Tobias, Tobi. *Moving day*
Waber, Bernard. *Ira sleeps over*
Wahl, Jan. *Humphrey's bear*
Worthington, Phoebe. *Teddy bear baker*
Teddy bear coalman
Teddy bear farmer
Wright, Dare. *The doll and the kitten*
Edith and Midnight
Edith and Mr. Bear
Edith and the duckling
The lonely doll
The lonely doll learns a lesson
Zalben, Jane Breskin. *A perfect nose for Ralph*

Toys – tin soldiers *see* Toys – soldiers

Toys – trains

Green, Suzanne. *The little choo-choo*
Kroll, Steven. *Toot! Toot!*
McPhail, David. *The train*

Tractors *see* Machines

Trading *see* Activities – trading

Traffic, traffic signs

Bank Street College of Education. *Green light, go*
Baugh, Dolores M. *Bikes*
Brown, Margaret Wise. *Red light, green light*

Krahn, Fernando. *Mr. Top*
Maestro, Betsy. *Traffic*
Shortall, Leonard W. *One way*
Thayer, Jane. *Andy and the runaway horse*

Train engineers *see* Careers – railroad engineers

Trains

Ardizzone, Edward. *Nicholas and the fast-moving diesel*
Ayars, James Sterling. *Caboose on the roof*
Barton, Byron. *Trains*
Beim, Jerrold. *Country train*
Bemelmans, Ludwig. *Quito express*
Bontemps, Arna Wendell. *The fast sooner hound*
Brandenberg, Franz. *Everyone ready?*
Broekel, Ray. *Trains*
Bröger, Achim. *Bruno takes a trip*
Brown, Margaret Wise. *Two little trains*
Whistle for the train
Bunce, William. *Freight trains*
Burton, Virginia Lee. *Choo choo*
Corney, Estelle. *Pa's top hat*
Crews, Donald. *Freight train*
Cushman, Jerome. *Marvella's hobby*
Ehrlich, Amy. *The everyday train*
Emmett, Fredrick Rowland. *New world for Nellie*
Gantschev, Ivan. *The Christmas train*
The train to Grandma's
Gibbons, Gail. *Trains*
Goble, Paul. *Death of the iron horse*
Gramatky, Hardie. *Homer and the circus train*
Greene, Graham. *The little train*
Gretz, Susanna. *Teddy bears take the train*
Hurd, Edith Thacher. *Caboose*
Engine, engine number 9
Hurd, Thacher. *Hobo dog*
Kessler, Ethel. *All aboard the train*
Kroll, Steven. *Toot! Toot!*
Lenski, Lois. *The little train*
Lyon, George Ella. *A regular rolling Noah*
McPhail, David. *The train*
Marshak, Samuel. *The pup grew up!*
Marshall, Ray. *The train*
Martin, Bill (William Ivan). *Smoky Poky*
Meeks, Esther K. *One is the engine*, ill. by Ernie King
One is the engine, ill. by Joe Rogers
Munsch, Robert N. *Jonathan cleaned up - then he heard a sound*
Nickl, Peter. *Ra ta ta tam*
Peet, Bill. *The caboose who got loose*
Smokey
Pierce, Jack. *The freight train book*
Piper, Watty. *The little engine that could*

Rodgers, Frank. *Who's afraid of the ghost train?*
Ross, Diana. *The story of the little red engine*
Rounds, Glen. *Casey Jones*
Sasaki, Isao. *Snow*
Sattler, Helen Roney. *Train whistles*
Scarry, Huck. *Huck Scarry's steam train journey*
Shine, Deborah. *The little engine that could pudgy word book*
Slobodkin, Louis. *Clear the track*
Thayer, Jane. *I like trains*
Van Allsburg, Chris. *The polar express*
Weelen, Guy. *The little red train*
Wells, Rosemary. *Don't spill it again, James*
Wondriska, William. *Puff*
Young, Miriam Burt. *If I drove a train*

Trains, toy *see* Toys – trains

Transportation

Ardizzone, Edward. *Nicholas and the fast-moving diesel*
Arnold, Caroline. *How do we travel?*
Bagwell, Richard. *This is an airport*
Barton, Byron. *Airport*
Baugh, Dolores M. *Trucks and cars to ride*
Billout, Guy. *By camel or by car*
Broekel, Ray. *Trains*
  Trucks
Brown, Richard Eric. *One hundred words about transportation*
Burton, Virginia Lee. *Maybelle, the cable car*
Campbell, Rod. *Look inside! Land, sea, air*
Cars and trucks
Cave, Ron. *Airplanes*
  Automobiles
  Motorcycles
Cleary, Beverly. *Lucky Chuck*
Crews, Donald. *School bus*
  Truck
Emberley, Ed. *Cars, boats, and planes*
Gay, Michel. *Little truck*
Gibbons, Gail. *New road!*
Gomi, Taro. *Bus stop*
Gramatky, Hardie. *Sparky*
Hellen, Nancy. *Bus stop*
Hoberman, Mary Ann. *How do I go?*
Ingoglia, Gina. *The big book of real airplanes*
Koren, Edward. *Behind the wheel*
Lenski, Lois. *Davy goes places*
  Lois Lenski's big book of Mr. Small
Levinson, Riki. *I go with my family to Grandma's*
McNaught, Harry. *The truck book*
Marston, Hope Irvin. *Big rigs*
Munari, Bruno. *The birthday present*
Olschewski, Alfred. *The wheel rolls over*

Oppenheim, Joanne. *Have you seen roads?*
Potter, Russell. *The little red ferry boat*
Rey, Hans Augusto. *How do you get there?*
Rockwell, Anne F. *Planes*
  Things that go
Scarry, Richard. *Richard Scarry's cars and trucks and things that go*
  Richard Scarry's hop aboard! Here we go!
Steele, Philip. *Land transport around the world*
Stevenson, James. *No need for Monty*
Thayer, Jane. *I like trains*
Young, Miriam Burt. *If I drove a bus*
  If I drove a car
  If I drove a train
  If I drove a truck
  If I flew a plane
Zaffo, George J. *The big book of real airplanes*
  The giant nursery book of things that go
  The giant nursery book of things that work

Traveling *see* Activities – traveling

Trees

Adler, David A. *Redwoods are the tallest trees in the world*
Adoff, Arnold. *Flamboyan*
Aliki. *The story of Johnny Appleseed*
Andersen, H. C. (Hans Christian). *The fir tree*, ill. by Nancy Elkholm Burkert
Angelo, Valenti. *The acorn tree*
Arnold, Caroline. *The biggest living thing*
Ayres, Pam. *When dad cuts down the chestnut tree*
Baird, Anne. *Little tree*
Baker, Jeffrey J. W. *Patterns of nature*
Barker, Cicely Mary. *Flower fairies of the seasons*
Barry, Robert E. *Mr. Willowby's Christmas tree*
Bason, Lillian. *Pick a raincoat, pick a whistle*
Bemelmans, Ludwig. *Parsley*
Berenstain, Stan. *The Berenstain bears and the spooky old tree*
  The Berenstain bears' Christmas tree
Blocksma, Mary. *Apple tree! Apple tree!*
Blough, Glenn O. *Christmas trees and how they grow*
Bond, Felicia. *Christmas in the chicken coop*
Brown, Margaret Wise. *The little fir tree*
Budbill, David. *Christmas tree farm*
Bulla, Clyde Robert. *A tree is a plant*
Burns, Diane L. *Arbor Day*
Busch, Phyllis S. *Once there was a tree*
Butcher, Julia. *The sheep and the rowan tree*
Carigiet, Alois. *The pear tree, the birch tree and the barberry bush*
Carrier, Lark. *A Christmas promise*

Chalmers, Mary. *A Christmas story*
Cleary, Beverly. *The real hole*, ill. by
  DyAnne DiSalvo-Ryan
  The real hole, ill. by Mary Stevens
Clement, Claude. *The voice of the wood*
Coats, Laura Jane. *The oak tree*
Cole, Joanna. *Plants in winter*
Cummings, E. E. *Little tree*
Day, Shirley. *Ruthie's big tree*
DeLage, Ida. *The squirrel's tree party*
De Paola, Tomie. *The family Christmas tree
  book*
Fenner, Carol. *Christmas tree on the
  mountain*
Fisher, Aileen. *Arbor day*
  As the leaves fall down
  A tree with a thousand uses
Fleischman, Paul. *The birthday tree*
Garelick, May. *The tremendous tree book*
Gibbons, Gail. *The missing maple syrup sap
  mystery*
  The seasons of Arnold's apple tree
Gilbert, Helen Earle. *Mr. Plum and the
  little green tree*
Gordon, Sharon. *Trees*
Greydanus, Rose. *Tree house fun*
Hall, Derek. *Panda climbs*
Hawkinson, John. *The old stump*
Himmelman, John. *The talking tree*
Hogan, Paula Z. *The oak tree*
Houston, Gloria. *The year of the perfect
  Christmas tree*
Howe, James. *How the Ewoks saved the
  trees*
Hutchins, Pat. *The silver Christmas tree*
Johnston, Tony. *Mole and Troll trim the
  tree*
Kellogg, Steven. *Johnny Appleseed*
King, B. A. *The very best Christmas tree*
Kirk, Barbara. *Grandpa, me and our house
  in the tree*
Kirkpatrick, Rena K. *Look at trees*
Krahn, Fernando. *The biggest Christmas
  tree on earth*
Kraus, Robert. *The tree that stayed up until
  next Christmas*
Lakin, Patricia. *Oh, brother!*
Lewis, Naomi. *Leaves*
Lindgren, Astrid. *Of course Polly can do
  almost everything*
Lloyd, David. *Hello, goodbye*
Löfgren, Ulf. *The wonderful tree*
Lyon, George Ella. *A B Cedar*
Mabey, Richard. *Oak and company*
McCord, David. *Every time I climb a tree*
Margolis, Richard J. *Big bear, spare that
  tree*
Marshall, James. *Three up a tree*
Maynard, Joyce. *New house*
Miles, Miska. *Apricot ABC*
Myers, Bernice. *Charlie's birthday present*

Newton, James R. *Forest log*
Nikly, Michelle. *The emperor's plum tree*
Noble, Trinka Hakes. *Apple tree Christmas*
Oana, Kay D. *Robbie and the raggedy
  scarecrow*
Oppenheim, Joanne. *Have you seen trees?*
Orbach, Ruth. *Apple pigs*
Parnall, Peter. *Apple tree*
Peet, Bill. *Merle the high flying squirrel*
Petie, Haris. *The seed the squirrel dropped*
Pike, Norman. *The peach tree*
Rogow, Zak. *Oranges*
Russell, Naomi. *The tree*
Schertle, Alice. *In my treehouse*
Stemp, Robin. *Guy and the flowering plum
  tree*
Thelen, Gerda. *The toy maker*
Tresselt, Alvin R. *The dead tree*
  Johnny Maple-Leaf
Tudor, Bethany. *Samuel's tree house*
Udry, Janice May. *A tree is nice*
Watts, Barrie. *Apple tree*
Wiese, Kurt. *The thief in the attic*
Wong, Herbert H. *Our tree*
Yashima, Tarō. *The village tree*
Young, Ed. *Up a tree*
Zolotow, Charlotte. *The beautiful Christmas
  tree*

Trickery *see* Behavior – trickery

Tricks *see* Magic

Triplets

Abolafia, Yossi. *My three uncles*
Brunhoff, Jean de. *Babar and his children*
Lindman, Maj. *Flicka, Ricka, Dicka and a
  little dog*
  Flicka, Ricka, Dicka and the big red hen
  *Flicka, Ricka, Dicka and the new dotted
  dress*
  Flicka, Ricka, Dicka and the three kittens
  Flicka, Ricka, Dicka bake a cake
  Snipp, Snapp, Snurr and the buttered bread
  Snipp, Snapp, Snurr and the magic horse
  Snipp, Snapp, Snurr and the red shoes
  Snipp, Snapp, Snurr and the reindeer
  Snipp, Snapp, Snurr and the seven dogs
  Snipp, Snapp, Snurr and the yellow sled
Seuling, Barbara. *The triplets*

Trolleys *see* Cable cars, trolleys

Trolls

Aardema, Verna. *Bimwili and the Zimwi*
Asbjørnsen, P. C. (Peter Christen). *The three
  billy goats Gruff*, ill. by Marcia Brown
  Three billy goats Gruff, ill. by Tom
  Dunnington

The three billy goats Gruff, ill. by Paul Galdone
The three billy goats Gruff, ill. by Janet Stevens
The three billy goats Gruff, ill. by William Stobbs
Aulaire, Ingri Mortenson d'. *The terrible troll-bird*
Berenstain, Michael. *The troll book*
De Paola, Tomie. *The cat on the Dovrefell*
Helga's dowry
Fujikawa, Gyo. *Come follow me...to the secret world of elves and fairies and gnomes and trolls*
Hillert, Margaret. *The three goats*
Johnston, Tony. *Mole and Troll trim the tree*
Lindgren, Astrid. *The tomten*
The tomten and the fox
Lobel, Anita. *The troll music*
Marshall, Edward. *Troll country*
Mayer, Mercer. *Terrible troll*
Peet, Bill. *Jethro and Joel were a troll*
Schertle, Alice. *Hob Goblin and the skeleton*
Svendsen, Carol. *Hulda*
Torgersen, Don Arthur. *The girl who tricked the troll*
The troll who lived in the lake
Tudor, Tasha. *Corgiville fair*
Wahl, Jan. *Peter and the troll baby*

Truck drivers *see* Careers – truck drivers

Trucks

Adkins, Jan. *Heavy equipment*
Alexander, Anne. *ABC of cars and trucks*
Barr, Jene. *Fire snorkel number 7*
Barrett, N. S. *Trucks*
Barton, Byron. *Trucks*
Baugh, Dolores M. *Trucks and cars to ride*
Broekel, Ray. *Trucks*
Burroway, Janet. *The truck on the track*
Bushey, Jerry. *Building a fire truck*
Cars and trucks
Cartlidge, Michelle. *Teddy trucks*
Crews, Donald. *Truck*
Curious George and the dump truck
Fast rolling fire trucks
Fast rolling work trucks
Fisher, Leonard Everett. *Pumpers, boilers, hooks and ladders*
Gay, Michel. *Little truck*
Gibbons, Gail. *Trucks*
Gramatky, Hardie. *Hercules*
Greene, Carla. *Truck drivers what do they do?*
Greydanus, Rose. *Big red fire engine*
Holl, Adelaide. *The ABC of cars, trucks and machines*

Homme, Bob. *The friendly giant's book of fire engines*
Kessler, Ethel. *Night story*
Lyon, David. *The biggest truck*
McNaught, Harry. *The truck book*
Magee, Doug. *Trucks you can count on*
Marston, Hope Irvin. *Big rigs*
Fire trucks
Newton, Laura P. *William the vehicle king*
Peppé, Rodney. *Little wheels*
Petrie, Catherine. *Joshua James likes trucks*
Pomerantz, Charlotte. *How many trucks can a tow truck tow?*
Quackenbush, Robert M. *City trucks*
Robbins, Ken. *Trucks of every sort*
Rockwell, Anne F. *Fire engines*
Trucks
Scarry, Richard. *The great big car and truck book*
Richard Scarry's cars and trucks and things that go
Schulz, Charles M. *Snoopy's facts and fun book about trucks*
Siebert, Diane. *Truck song*
Trucks, ill. by Art Seiden
Wolfe, Robert L. *The truck book*
Young, Miriam Burt. *If I drove a truck*
Zaffo, George J. *The giant nursery book of things that go*

Turkey *see* Foreign lands – Turkey

Turkeys *see* Birds – turkeys

Turtles *see* Reptiles – turtles, tortoises

TV *see* Television

Twilight

Berger, Barbara Helen. *Grandfather Twilight*
Major, Beverly. *Playing sardines*
Udry, Janice May. *The moon jumpers*

Twins

Aliki. *Jack and Jake*
Balet, Jan B. *Ned and Ed and the lion*
Brennan, Jan. *Born two-gether*
Bruna, Dick. *Tilly and Tess*
Cleary, Beverly. *The growing-up feet*
The real hole, ill. by DyAnne DiSalvo-Ryan
The real hole, ill. by Mary Stevens
Two dog biscuits, ill. by DyAnne DiSalvo-Ryan
Two dog biscuits, ill. by Mary Stevens
Clymer, Eleanor Lowenton. *Horatio goes to the country*
Flournoy, Valerie. *The twins strike back*
Hoban, Lillian. *Here come raccoons*

King-Smith, Dick. *Cuckoobush farm*
Kismaric, Carole. *The rumor of Pavel and Paali*
Lawrence, James. *Binky Brothers and the fearless four*
Binky Brothers, detectives
McDermott, Gerald. *The magic tree*
McKissack, Patricia C. *Who is who?*
Moore, Lilian. *Little Raccoon and no trouble at all*
Neasi, Barbara J. *Just like me*
Obrist, Jürg. *Bear business*
Perkins, Al. *Don and Donna go to bat*
Rubel, Nicole. *Sam and Violet are twins*
Sam and Violet go camping
Simon, Norma. *How do I feel?*
Stewart, Elizabeth Laing. *The lion twins*
Thompson, Vivian Laubach. *Camp-in-the-yard*
Yeoman, John. *The young performing horse*

Tyrol *see* Foreign lands – Tyrol

Ukraine *see* Foreign lands – Ukraine

Umbrellas

Blance, Ellen. *Monster and the magic umbrella*
Bright, Robert. *My red umbrella*
Cole, William. *Aunt Bella's umbrella*
Drescher, Henrik. *The yellow umbrella*
Feczko, Kathy. *Umbrella parade*
Levine, Rhoda. *Harrison loved his umbrella*
Lipkind, William. *Professor Bull's umbrella*
Pinkwater, Daniel Manus. *Roger's umbrella*
Yashima, Tarō. *Umbrella*

Unhappiness *see* Emotions – happiness; Emotions – sadness

UNICEF

Coatsworth, Elizabeth. *The children come running*
Schulman, Janet. *Jack the bum and the Halloween handout*

Unicorns *see* Mythical creatures

U.S. history

Abisch, Roz. *The Pumpkin Heads*
Sweet Betsy from Pike

Aliki. *George and the cherry tree*
The many lives of Benjamin Franklin
The story of Johnny Appleseed
The story of William Penn
A weed is a flower
Aulaire, Ingri Mortenson d'. *Abraham Lincoln*
Pocahontas
Austin, Margot. *Willamet way*
Baker, Betty. *The pig war*
Bangs, Edward. *Yankee Doodle*
Belting, Natalia Maree. *Verity Mullens and the Indian*
Benchley, Nathaniel. *George the drummer boy*
Sam the minute man
Small Wolf
Snorri and the strangers
Benchley, Peter. *Jonathan visits the White House*
Bethell, Jean. *Three cheers for Mother Jones!*
Brandt, Betty. *Special delivery*
Brenner, Barbara. *Wagon wheels*
Bulla, Clyde Robert. *Washington's birthday*
Chenault, Nell. *Parsifal the Poddley*
Coatsworth, Elizabeth. *Boston Bells*
Dalgliesh, Alice. *The Thanksgiving story*
DeLage, Ida. *Pilgrim children on the Mayflower*
De Paola, Tomie. *An early American Christmas*
Dewey, Ariane. *Laffite, the pirate*
Gorsline, Marie. *North American Indians*
Grant, Anne. *Danbury's burning!*
Haley, Gail E. *Jack Jouett's ride*
Harvey, Brett. *My prairie year*
Haskins, Jim. *The Statue of Liberty*
Hiser, Berniece T. *The adventure of Charlie and his wheat-straw hat*
Holbrook, Stewart. *America's Ethan Allen*
Jones, Rebecca C. *The biggest (and best) flag that ever flew*
Kellogg, Steven. *Johnny Appleseed*
Pecos Bill
Key, Francis Scott. *The Star-Spangled Banner*, ill. by Paul Galdone
The Star-Spangled Banner, ill. by Peter Spier
Lawson, Robert. *They were strong and good*
Levinson, Riki. *Watch the stars come out*
Lobel, Arnold. *On the day Peter Stuyvesant sailed into town*
Longfellow, Henry Wadsworth. *Paul Revere's ride*, ill. by Paul Galdone
Paul Revere's ride, ill. by Nancy Winslow Parker
Lowitz, Sadyebeth. *The pilgrims' party*
Lowrey, Janette Sebring. *Six silver spoons*
Lydon, Kerry Raines. *A birthday for Blue*

Maestro, Betsy. *The story of the Statue of Liberty*
Monjo, F. N. *The drinking gourd*
Indian summer
The one bad thing about father
Poor Richard in France
Moskin, Marietta D. *Lysbet and the fire kittens*
Nixon, Joan Lowery. *If you say so, Claude*
Ortiz, Simon. *The people shall continue*
Petersham, Maud. *An American ABC*
Precek, Katharine Wilson. *Penny in the road*
Pryor, Bonnie. *The house on Maple Street*
Quackenbush, Robert M. *Clementine*
Pop! goes the weasel and Yankee Doodle
There'll be a hot time in the old town tonight
Rappaport, Doreen. *The Boston coffee party*
Schackburg, Richard. *Yankee Doodle*
Schick, Alice. *The remarkable ride of Israel Bissell... as related to Molly the crow*
Showers, Paul. *Columbus Day*
Spier, Peter. *The Erie Canal*
The legend of New Amsterdam
We the people
Szekeres, Cyndy. *Long ago*
Turkle, Brinton. *The adventures of Obadiah*
Obadiah the Bold
Thy friend, Obadiah
Turner, Ann. *Dakota dugout*
Van Woerkom, Dorothy. *Becky and the bear*
Vaughn, Jenny. *On the moon*
Waber, Bernard. *Just like Abraham Lincoln*
Whittier, John Greenleaf. *Barbara Frietchie*
Winter, Jeanette. *Follow the drinking gourd*

Unnoticed *see* Behavior – unnoticed, unseen

Unseen *see* Behavior – unnoticed, unseen

Unusual format *see* Format, unusual

Up and down *see* Concepts – up and down

Vacationing *see* Activities – vacationing

Vacuum cleaners *see* Machines

Valentine's Day *see* Holidays – Valentine's Day

Values

Mahy, Margaret. *Pillycock's shop*
Schlein, Miriam. *The pile of junk*

Vampires *see* Monsters

Vanity *see* Character traits – vanity

Vatican City *see* Foreign lands – Vatican City

Veterinarians *see* Careers – veterinarians

Vietnam *see* Foreign lands – Vietnam

Vietnamese-Americans *see* Ethnic groups in the U.S. – Vietnamese-Americans

Violence, anti-violence

Charters, Janet. *The general*
Duvoisin, Roger Antoine. *The happy hunter*
Fitzhugh, Louise. *Bang, bang, you're dead*
Foreman, Michael. *Moose*
Hader, Berta Hoerner. *Mister Billy's gun*
Leaf, Munro. *The story of Ferdinand the bull*
Lobel, Anita. *Potatoes, potatoes*
Peet, Bill. *The pinkish, purplish, bluish egg*
Sharmat, Marjorie Weinman. *Walter the wolf*
Wiesner, William. *Tops*
Wondriska, William. *The tomato patch*

Volcanoes

Branley, Franklyn M. *Volcanoes*
Grifalconi, Ann. *The village of round and square houses*
Lewis, Thomas P. *Hill of fire*
Simon, Seymour. *Volcanoes*

Vultures *see* Birds – vultures

Waiters *see* Careers – waiters, waitresses

Waitresses *see* Careers – waiters, waitresses

Walking *see* Activities – walking

Walruses *see* Animals – walruses

War

Abells, Chana Byers. *The children we remember*
Ambrus, Victor G. *Brave soldier Janosch*
Aulaire, Ingri Mortenson d'. *Wings for Per*
Baumann, Kurt. *The prince and the lute*
Benchley, Nathaniel. *George the drummer boy*
  Sam the minute man
Bishop, Claire Huchet. *Pancakes - Paris*
Bogart, Bonnie. *The Ewoks join the fight*
De Paola, Tomie. *The mysterious giant of Barletta*
Du Bois, William Pène. *The forbidden forest*
Dupasquier, Philippe. *Jack at sea*
Eco, Umberto. *The bomb and the general*
Fitzhugh, Louise. *Bang, bang, you're dead*
Foreman, Michael. *War and peas*
Gauch, Patricia Lee. *Once upon a Dinkelsbühl*
Goble, Paul. *Death of the iron horse*
Grimm, Wilhelm. *Dear Mili*
Holbrook, Stewart. *America's Ethan Allen*
Hughes, Peter. *The king who loved candy*
Jones, Rebecca C. *The biggest (and best) flag that ever flew*
Mattingley, Christobel. *The angel with a mouth-organ*
Miller, Edward. *Frederick Ferdinand Fox*
Phillips, Louis. *The brothers Wrong and Wrong Again*
Sand, George. *The mysterious tale of Gentle Jack and Lord Bumblebee*
Schick, Alice. *The remarkable ride of Israel Bissell... as related to Molly the crow*
Seuss, Dr. *The butter battle book*
Stone, Bernard. *The charge of the mouse brigade*
Vigna, Judith. *Nobody wants a nuclear war*
Whittier, John Greenleaf. *Barbara Frietchie*
Ziefert, Harriet. *A new coat for Anna*

Washington's Birthday *see* Holidays – Washington's Birthday

Wasps *see* Insects – wasps

Watches *see* Clocks

Water buffaloes *see* Animals – water buffaloes

Weapons

Bolliger, Max. *The wooden man*
Duvoisin, Roger Antoine. *The happy hunter*
Emberley, Barbara. *Drummer Hoff*
Fitzhugh, Louise. *Bang, bang, you're dead*
Hader, Berta Hoerner. *Mister Billy's gun*
Wondriska, William. *The tomato patch*

Weasels *see* Animals – weasels

Weather

Allington, Richard L. *Autumn*
  Spring
  Summer
  Winter
Ardizzone, Edward. *Tim to the rescue*
Asch, Frank. *Country pie*
Barrett, Judi. *Cloudy with a chance of meatballs*
Baum, Arline. *One bright Monday morning*
Bell, Norman. *Linda's airmail letter*
Berenstain, Stan. *The bears' almanac*
Bolliger, Max. *The wooden man*
Branley, Franklyn M. *Rain and hail*
Brenner, Barbara. *The snow parade*
Brown, Margaret Wise. *The little island*
Burgert, Hans-Joachim. *Samulo and the giant*
Coombs, Patricia. *Dorrie and the weather-box*
Davidson, Amanda. *Teddy goes outside*
Dewey, Ariane. *Febold Feboldson*
Fisher, Aileen. *I like weather*
Frye, Dean. *Days of sunshine, days of rain*
Gackenbach, Dick. *Ida Fanfanny*
Ginsburg, Mirra. *Four brave sailors*
Greenberg, Barbara. *The bravest babysitter*
A January fog will freeze a hog
Jaynes, Ruth M. *Benny's four hats*
Kirkpatrick, Rena K. *Look at weather*
Lewin, Betsy. *Hip, hippo, hooray!*
McCloskey, Robert. *Time of wonder*
Maestro, Betsy. *Through the year with Harriet*
Marshak, Samuel. *The Month-Brothers*
Palazzo, Janet. *What makes the weather*
Peters, Lisa W. *The sun, the wind and the rain*
Pieńkowski, Jan. *Weather*
Rockwell, Anne F. *Blackout*

Schlein, Miriam. *The sun, the wind, the sea and the rain*
Seymour, Peter. *How the weather works*
Tresselt, Alvin R. *Sun up*
Vance, Eleanor Graham. *Jonathan*
Van Leeuwen, Jean. *Too hot for ice cream*
Vigna, Judith. *Boot weather*
Zolotow, Charlotte. *The storm book*

Weather – clouds

Ariane. *Small Cloud*
Cummings, Pat. *C.L.O.U.D.S.*
De Paola, Tomie. *The cloud book*
Greene, Carol. *Hi, clouds*
McFall, Gardner. *Jonathan's cloud*
Manushkin, Fran. *Swinging and swinging*
Marol, Jean-Claude. *Vagabul in the clouds*
Ray, Deborah Kogan. *The cloud*
Rayner, Mary. *The rain cloud*
Renberg, Dalia Hardof. *Hello, clouds!*
Ringi, Kjell. *The sun and the cloud*
Shaw, Charles Green. *It looked like spilt milk*
Spier, Peter. *Dreams*
Turkle, Brinton. *The sky dog*
Wandelmaier, Roy. *Clouds*
Wegen, Ron. *Sky dragon*
Williams, Leslie. *A bear in the air*

Weather – cold

Hoban, Lillian. *The sugar snow spring*

Weather – droughts

Aardema, Verna. *Bringing the rain to Kapiti Plain*

Weather – floods

Cartwright, Ann. *Norah's ark*
Ipcar, Dahlov. *A flood of creatures*
McKié, Roy. *Noah's ark*
Morpurgo, Michael. *Jo-Jo the melon donkey*
Tapio, Pat Decker. *The lady who saw the good side of everything*

Weather – fog

Fry, Christopher. *The boat that mooed*
Keeping, Charles. *Alfie finds the other side of the world*
Lifton, Betty Jean. *Joji and the fog*
May, Robert Lewis. *Rudolph the red-nosed reindeer*
Morse, Samuel French. *Sea sums*
Munari, Bruno. *The circus in the mist*
Ryder, Joanne. *Fog in the meadow*
Schroder, William. *Pea soup and serpents*
Smith, Theresa Kalab. *The fog is secret*
Tresselt, Alvin R. *Hide and seek fog*

Weather – mist *see* Weather – fog

Weather – rain

Aardema, Verna. *Bringing the rain to Kapiti Plain*
Ariane. *Small Cloud*
Baker, Jill. *Basil of Bywater Hollow*
Bassett, Preston R. *Raindrop stories*
Bauer, Caroline Feller. *Rainy day*
Bergere, Thea. *Paris in the rain with Jean and Jacqueline*
Blegvad, Lenore. *Rainy day Kate*
Bonnici, Peter. *The first rains*
Boon, Emilie. *Peterkin's wet walk*
Bourgeois, Paulette. *Big Sarah's little boots*
Brandenberg, Franz. *A picnic, hurrah!*
Branley, Franklyn M. *Rain and hail*
Bright, Robert. *My red umbrella*
Burningham, John. *Mr. Gumpy's motor car*
Calhoun, Mary. *Euphonia and the flood*
Carrick, Carol. *Sleep out*
　The washout
Cartwright, Ann. *Norah's ark*
Cazet, Denys. *You make the angels cry*
Charlip, Remy. *Where is everybody?*
Claverie, Jean. *The picnic*
Cole, William. *Aunt Bella's umbrella*
De Paola, Tomie. *Katie and Kit at the beach*
Dragonwagon, Crescent. *Rainy day together*
Dubanevich, Arlene. *Pig William*
Ferro, Beatriz. *Caught in the rain*
Freeman, Don. *Dandelion*
Garelick, May. *Where does the butterfly go when it rains?*
Gay, Marie-Louise. *Rainy day magic*
Ginsburg, Mirra. *Mushroom in the rain*
Goudey, Alice E. *The good rain*
Greene, Carol. *Rain! Rain!*
Hines, Anna Grossnickle. *Taste the raindrops*
Hoban, Russell. *The rain door*
Holl, Adelaide. *The rain puddle*
Hurd, Edith Thacher. *Johnny Lion's rubber boots*
Iwasaki, Chihiro. *Staying home alone on a rainy day*
Kalan, Robert. *Rain*
Keats, Ezra Jack. *A letter to Amy*
Keith, Eros. *Nancy's backyard*
Keller, Holly. *Will it rain?*
Kishida, Eriko. *The hippo boat*
Kuskin, Karla. *James and the rain*
Kwitz, Mary DeBall. *When it rains*
Lee, Jeanne M. *Toad is the uncle of heaven*
Lloyd, David. *Hello, goodbye*
Lukešová, Milena. *The little girl and the rain*
Marino, Dorothy. *Good-bye thunderstorm*
Martin, Bill (William Ivan). *Listen to the rain*

Murphy, Shirley Rousseau. *Tattie's river journey*
Prelutsky, Jack. *Rainy rainy Saturday*
Preston, Edna Mitchell. *Pop Corn and Ma Goodness*
Raskin, Ellen. *And it rained*
Ricketts, Michael. *Rain*
Robbins, Ruth. *How the first rainbow was made*
Ryder, Joanne. *A wet and sandy day*
Scheer, Julian. *Rain makes applesauce*
Scheffler, Ursel. *A walk in the rain*
Schlein, Miriam. *The sun, the wind, the sea and the rain*
Seignobosc, Françoise. *The big rain*
Sherman, Nancy. *Gwendolyn and the weathercock*
Shulevitz, Uri. *Rain rain rivers*
Simon, Norma. *The wet world*
Skofield, James. *All wet! All wet!*
Soya, Kiyoshi. *A house of leaves*
Spier, Peter. *Peter Spier's rain*
Tapio, Pat Decker. *The lady who saw the good side of everything*
Taylor, Mark. *Henry the castaway*
Thayer, Mike. *In the middle of the puddle*
Tresselt, Alvin R. *Rain drop splash*
Türk, Hanne. *Rainy day Max*
Van Allsburg, Chris. *Ben's dream*
Velthuijs, Max. *Little Man finds a home*
Vincent, Gabrielle. *Ernest and Celestine's picnic*
Wagner, Jenny. *Aranea*
Wahl, Jan. *Follow me cried Bee*
Wandelmaier, Roy. *Clouds*
Wells, Rosemary. *Don't spill it again, James*
Yashima, Tarō. *Umbrella*
Zinnemann-Hope, Pam. *Find your coat, Ned*
Zolotow, Charlotte. *The quarreling book*
The storm book

Weather – rainbows

Asch, Frank. *Skyfire*
Craft, Ruth. *The day of the rainbow*
Freeman, Don. *A rainbow of my own*
Kirkpatrick, Rena K. *Look at rainbow colors*
Kwitz, Mary DeBall. *When it rains*
Marino, Dorothy. *Buzzy Bear and the rainbow*
Weston, Martha. *Peony's rainbow*
Williams, Leslie. *A bear in the air*
Zolotow, Charlotte. *The storm book*

Weather – snow

Arnold, Tim. *The winter mittens*
Bahr, Robert. *Blizzard at the zoo*
Barklem, Jill. *Winter story*
Bartoli, Jennifer. *Snow on bear's nose*

Bauer, Caroline Feller. *Midnight snowman*
Snowy day
Benchley, Nathaniel. *The magic sled*
Branley, Franklyn M. *Snow is falling*
Brown, Margaret Wise. *The winter noisy book*
Bruna, Dick. *Another story to tell*
Miffy in the snow
Buckley, Helen Elizabeth. *Josie and the snow*
Burningham, John. *Trubloff*
Burton, Virginia Lee. *Katy and the big snow*
Chönz, Selina. *The snowstorm*
Claverie, Jean. *Working*
Delaney, A. *Monster tracks?*
Delton, Judy. *Brimhall turns detective*
A walk on a snowy night
Dorian, Marguerite. *When the snow is blue*
Funakoshi, Canna. *One evening*
Greene, Carol. *Snow Joe*
Gunther, Louise. *Anna's snow day*
Hader, Berta Hoerner. *The big snow*
Hidaka, Masako. *Girl from the snow country*
Hoban, Lillian. *The sugar snow spring*
Hoban, Russell. *Some snow said hello*
Hoff, Syd. *When will it snow?*
Iwasaki, Chihiro. *The birthday wish*
Janosch. *Dear snowman*
Keats, Ezra Jack. *The snowy day*
Keller, Holly. *Geraldine's big snow*
Krauss, Ruth. *The happy day*
Kuskin, Karla. *In the flaky frosty morning*
McCully, Emily Arnold. *First snow*
McKié, Roy. *Snow*
McPhail, David. *Snow lion*
Parnall, Peter. *Alfalfa Hill*
Raphael, Elaine. *Donkey, it's snowing*
Retan, Walter. *The snowplow that tried to go south*
Rockwell, Anne F. *The first snowfall*
Sasaki, Isao. *Snow*
Sauer, Julia Lina. *Mike's house*
Schick, Eleanor. *City in the winter*
Schlein, Miriam. *Deer in the snow*
Schroeder, Binette. *Tuffa and the snow*
Simmonds, Posy. *Lulu and the flying babies*
Skofield, James. *Snow country*
Steig, William. *Brave Irene*
Tibo, Gilles. *Simon and the snowflakes*
Todd, Kathleen. *Snow*
Tresselt, Alvin R. *White snow, bright snow*
Tudor, Tasha. *Snow before Christmas*
Udry, Janice May. *Mary Jo's grandmother*
Updike, David. *A winter's journey*
Wabbes, Marie. *It's snowing, Little Rabbit*
Watson, Nancy Dingman. *Sugar on snow*
Wheeler, Cindy. *Marmalade's snowy day*
Wood, Audrey. *Detective Valentine*
Zion, Gene. *The summer snowman*

Zolotow, Charlotte. *Hold my hand
Something is going to happen*

Weather – storms

Adoff, Arnold. *Make a circle, keep us in
Tornado!*
Aldridge, Josephine Haskell. *Fisherman's
luck*
Anderson, Lonzo. *The day the hurricane
happened*
Bahr, Robert. *Blizzard at the zoo*
Branley, Franklyn M. *Hurricane watch
Tornado alert*
Chönz, Selina. *The snowstorm*
Delton, Judy. *A walk on a snowy night*
Dennis, Morgan. *The sea dog*
Faulkner, Matt. *The amazing voyage of
Jackie Grace*
Gedin, Birgitta. *The little house from the sea*
Keats, Ezra Jack. *Clementina's cactus*
Keller, Holly. *Will it rain?*
Kitamura, Satoshi. *Captain Toby*
Lee, Jeanne M. *Ba-Nam*
McNulty, Faith. *Hurricane*
Marino, Dorothy. *Good-bye thunderstorm*
Noble, Trinka Hakes. *Apple tree Christmas*
Olson, Arielle North. *The lighthouse
keeper's daughter*
Rettich, Margret. *The voyage of the jolly
boat*
Steig, William. *Brave Irene*
Stolz, Mary Slattery. *Storm in the night*
Szilagyi, Mary. *Thunderstorm*
Taylor, Judy. *Sophie and Jack help out*
Van Allsburg, Chris. *The wreck of the
Zephyr*
Willard, Nancy. *The voyage of the Ludgate
Hill*
Wilson, Sarah. *Beware the dragons!*

Weather – thunder

Branley, Franklyn M. *Flash, crash, rumble,
and roll*
Crowe, Robert L. *Tyler Toad and the
thunder*
Marino, Dorothy. *Good-bye thunderstorm*
Novak, Matt. *Rolling*
Sussman, Susan. *Hippo thunder*
Szilagyi, Mary. *Thunderstorm*

Weather – wind

Ardizzone, Edward. *Tim's last voyage*
Brown, Margaret Wise. *When the wind blew*
Calhoun, Mary. *Jack and the whoopee wind*
De Posadas Mane, Carmen. *Mister North
Wind*
Ets, Marie Hall. *Gilberto and the wind*
Garrison, Christian. *Little pieces of the west
wind*

Greene, Carol. *Please, wind?*
Hoban, Julia. *Amy loves the wind*
Hutchins, Pat. *The wind blew*
Keats, Ezra Jack. *A letter to Amy*
La Fontaine, Jean de. *The north wind and
the sun*
Lexau, Joan M. *Who took the farmer's hat?*
Littledale, Freya. *Peter and the north wind*
Lobel, Arnold. *The turnaround wind*
McKay, Louise. *Marny's ride with the wind*
Munsch, Robert N. *Millicent and the wind*
Purdy, Carol. *Iva Dunnit and the big wind*
Rice, Inez. *The March wind*
Saltzberg, Barney. *It must have been the
wind*
Schick, Eleanor. *City in the winter*
Schlein, Miriam. *The sun, the wind, the sea
and the rain*
Thompson, Brenda. *The winds that blow*
Tresselt, Alvin R. *Follow the wind
The wind and Peter*
Ungerer, Tomi. *The hat*
Whiteside, Karen. *Lullaby of the wind*
Yolen, Jane. *The girl who loved the wind*
Zolotow, Charlotte. *When the wind stops*

Weaving *see* Activities – weaving

Weddings

Ambrus, Victor G. *Country wedding*
Ash, Jutta. *Wedding birds*
Balian, Lorna. *A sweetheart for Valentine*
Barklem, Jill. *Summer story*
Caseley, Judith. *My sister Celia*
Claret, Maria. *Melissa Mouse*
Cock Robin. *The courtship, merry marriage,
and feast of Cock Robin and Jenny Wren*
Coombs, Patricia. *Mouse Café*
De Paola, Tomie. *Helga's dowry*
Drescher, Joan. *My mother's getting married*
A frog he would a-wooing go (folk-song).
Froggie went a-courting, ill. by Chris
Conover
Ganly, Helen. *Jyoti's journey*
Goodall, John S. *Naughty Nancy*
Grimm, Jacob. *The goose girl*, ill. by Sabine
Bruntjen
Mrs. Fox's wedding
Rapunzel, ill. by Bernadette Watts
Rumpelstiltskin, ill. by Jacqueline Ayer
Rumpelstiltskin, ill. by Donna Diamond
Rumpelstiltskin, ill. by Paul Galdone
Rumpelstiltskin, ill. by John Wallner
Rumpelstiltskin, ill. by Paul O. Zelinsky
Snow White and Rose Red, ill. by
Adrienne Adams
Snow White and Rose Red, ill. by John
Wallner
Gross, Ruth Belov. *The girl who wouldn't
get married*

Heine, Helme. *The pigs' wedding*
Hoban, Lillian. *Mr. Pig and Sonny too*
Hogrogian, Nonny. *Carrot cake*
Hürlimann, Ruth. *The mouse with the daisy hat*
Langton, Jane. *The hedgehog boy*
Lewin, Hugh. *Jafta and the wedding*
Patterson, José. *Mazal-Tov*
Quin-Harkin, Janet. *Peter Penny's dance*
Sandburg, Carl. *The wedding procession of the rag doll and the broom handle and who was in it*, ill. by Harriet Pincus
Seguin-Fontes, Marthe. *A wedding book*
The squire's bride, ill. by Marcia Sewall
Suhl, Yuri. *Simon Boom gives a wedding*
Trivas, Irene. *Emma's Christmas*
Varga, Judy. *Janko's wish*
West, Colin. *I brought my love a tabby cat*
Williams, Barbara. *Whatever happened to Beverly Bigler's birthday?*
Williams, Garth. *The rabbits' wedding*
Wittman, Sally. *The wonderful Mrs. Trumbly*

Weekdays *see* Days of the week, months of the year

Weight *see* Concepts – weight

Welders *see* Careers – welders

Werewolves *see* Monsters

Whales *see* Animals – whales

Wheels

Barton, Byron. *Wheels*
Berenstain, Stan. *Bears on wheels*
Myller, Rolf. *Rolling round*
Olschewski, Alfred. *The wheel rolls over*
Snoopy on wheels

Whistling *see* Activities – whistling

Willfulness *see* Character traits – willfulness

Wind *see* Weather – wind

Windmills

Yeoman, John. *Mouse trouble*

Window cleaners *see* Careers – window cleaners

Winter *see* Seasons – winter

Wishing *see* Behavior – wishing

Witches

Adams, Adrienne. *A Halloween happening*
A woggle of witches
Adler, David A. *I know I'm a witch*
Alexander, Martha G. *The magic box*
Alexander, Sue. *More Witch, Goblin, and Ghost stories*
Witch, Goblin, and Ghost in the haunted woods
Witch, Goblin and Ghost's book of things to do
Witch, Goblin and sometimes Ghost
Andersen, H. C. (Hans Christian). *The tinderbox*, ill. by Warwick Hutton
Anderson, Robin. *Sinabouda Lily*
Anglund, Joan Walsh. *Nibble nibble mousekin*
Armitage, Ronda. *The bossing of Josie*
Bach, Othello. *Hector McSnector and the mail-order Christmas witch*
Lilly, Willy and the mail-order witch
Balian, Lorna. *Humbug potion*
Humbug witch
Basile, Giambattista. *Petrosinella*
Benarde, Anita. *The pumpkin smasher*
Berridge, Celia. *Grandmother's tales*
Berson, Harold. *Charles and Claudine*
Bridwell, Norman. *The witch grows up*
The witch next door
Brown, Marc. *Spooky riddles*
Witches four
Buckley, Paul. *Amy Belligera and the fireflies*
Burch, Robert. *The jolly witch*
Calhoun, Mary. *The witch of Hissing Hill*
The witch who lost her shadow
The witch's pig
Wobble the witch cat
Carlson, Nancy. *Witch lady*
Carlson, Natalie Savage. *Spooky and the bad luck raven*
Spooky and the wizard's bats
Spooky night
Cole, Babette. *The trouble with mom*
Cole, Joanna. *Bony-legs*
Coombs, Patricia. *Dorrie and the amazing magic elixir*
Dorrie and the birthday eggs
Dorrie and the blue witch
Dorrie and the dreamyard monsters
Dorrie and the fortune teller
Dorrie and the goblin
Dorrie and the Halloween plot
Dorrie and the haunted house
Dorrie and the museum case
Dorrie and the screebit ghost
Dorrie and the weather-box
Dorrie and the witch doctor
Dorrie and the witches' camp
Dorrie and the witch's imp

Nicoll, Helen. *Meg and Mog*
 Meg at sea
 Meg on the moon
 Meg's eggs
 Mog's box
Nolan, Dennis. *Witch Bazooza*
Nygren, Tord. *Fiddler and his brothers*
O'Connor, Jane. *Lulu and the witch baby*
 Lulu goes to witch school
Oram, Hiawyn. *Skittlewonder and the wizard*
Peet, Bill. *Big bad Bruce*
 The Whingdingdilly
Prather, Ray. *The ostrich girl*
Ross, Tony. *The enchanted pig*
Serraillier, Ian. *Suppose you met a witch*
Shaw, Richard. *The kitten in the pumpkin patch*
Shecter, Ben. *Emily, girl witch of New York*
Slate, Joseph. *The mean, clean, giant canoe machine*
Springstubb, Tricia. *The magic guinea pig*
Steig, William. *Caleb and Kate*
Stevenson, James. *Emma*
 Fried feathers for Thanksgiving
 Happy Valentine's Day, Emma!
 Yuck!
Thompson, Harwood. *The witch's cat*
Walker, Barbara K. *Teeny-Tiny and the witch-woman*
Walt Disney Productions. *Walt Disney's Snow White and the seven dwarfs*
Watson, Jane Werner. *Which is the witch?*
Weil, Lisl. *The candy egg bunny*
Williams, Jay. *The city witch and the country witch*
Witch poems
Wood, Audrey. *Heckedy Peg*
Young, Miriam Burt. *The witch mobile*
Zimmer, Dirk. *The trick-or-treat trap*

Wizards

Barber, Antonia. *The enchanter's daughter*
Bradfield, Roger. *Giants come in different sizes*
Carlson, Natalie Savage. *Spooky and the wizard's bats*
Coombs, Patricia. *Dorrie and the amazing magic elixir*
 Dorrie and the fortune teller
 Dorrie and the haunted house
 Dorrie and the wizard's spell
De Regniers, Beatrice Schenk. *Picture book theater*
Dines, Glen. *Pitadoe, the color maker*
Emberley, Ed. *The Wizard of Op*
Fleischman, Sid. *Longbeard the wizard*
Grimm, Jacob. *The donkey prince*, ill. by Barbara Cooney
Hansen, Ron. *The shadowmaker*

Haseley, Dennis. *The cave of snores*
Houghton, Eric. *The mouse and the magician*
Kimmel, Margaret Mary. *Magic in the mist*
Kumin, Maxine. *The wizard's tears*
Leichman, Seymour. *The wicked wizard and the wicked witch*
Lester, Helen. *The wizard, the fairy and the magic chicken*
Lobel, Arnold. *The great blueness and other predicaments*
McCrea, James. *The story of Olaf*
Madden, Don. *The Wartville wizard*
Mayer, Mercer. *Mrs. Beggs and the wizard*
Nolan, Dennis. *Wizard McBean and his flying machine*
Oksner, Robert M. *The incompetent wizard*
Oram, Hiawyn. *Skittlewonder and the wizard*
Saunders, Susan. *A sniff in time*
Scott, Sally. *The magic horse*
Snyder, Zilpha Keatley. *The changing maze*
Zijlstra, Tjerk. *Benny and his geese*

Wolves *see* Animals — wolves

Wombats *see* Animals — wombats

Woodchucks *see* Animals — groundhogs

Woodpeckers *see* Birds — woodpeckers

Woods *see* Forest, woods

Word games *see* Language

Wordless

Alexander, Martha G. *Bobo's dream*
 The magic box
 The magic hat
 The magic picture
 Out! Out! Out!
 3 magic flip books
Andersen, H. C. (Hans Christian). *The ugly duckling,* ill. by Maria Ruis
Anno, Mitsumasa. *Anno's animals*
 Anno's Britain
 Anno's counting house
 Anno's flea market
 Anno's Italy
 Anno's journey
 Anno's peekaboo
 Anno's U.S.A.
 Dr. Anno's midnight circus
 Topsy-turvies
Arnosky, Jim. *Mouse numbers and letters*
 Mouse writing
 Mud time and more
Asch, George. *Linda*
Bakken, Harold. *The special string*

Bambi

Banchek, Linda. *Snake in, snake out*

Bang, Molly. *The grey lady and the strawberry snatcher*

Barton, Byron. *Where's Al?*

Baum, Willi. *Birds of a feather*

Briggs, Raymond. *Building the snowman*
  Dressing up
  Father Christmas
  Father Christmas goes on holiday
  The party
  The snowman
  Walking in the air

Bruna, Dick. *Another story to tell*

Burlson, Joe. *Space colony*

Burton, Marilee Robin. *The elephant's nest*

Campbell, Rod. *Look inside! All kinds of places*
  Look inside! Land, sea, air

Carle, Eric. *Do you want to be my friend?*
  I see a song

Carroll, Ruth. *What Whiskers did*
  Where's the bunny?

Charlot, Martin. *Sunnyside up*

Chwast, Seymour. *Still another alphabet book*

City

Collington, Peter. *The angel and the soldier boy*
  Little pickle

Crews, Donald. *Truck*

Cristini, Ermanno. *In my garden*
  In the woods

Daughtry, Duanne. *What's inside?*

Degen, Bruce. *Aunt Possum and the pumpkin man*

De Groat, Diane. *Alligator's toothache*

Demarest, Chris L. *Orville's odyssey*

De Paola, Tomie. *Country farm*
  Flicks
  The hunter and the animals
  Pancakes for breakfast
  Sing, Pierrot, sing

Domestic animals

Drescher, Henrik. *The yellow umbrella*

DuPasquier, Philippe. *The great escape*
  Our house on the hill

Emberley, Ed. *Ed Emberley's big green drawing book*

Euvremer, Teryl. *Sun's up*

Felix, Monique. *The further adventures of the little mouse trapped in a book*
  The story of a little mouse trapped in a book

Florian, Douglas. *The city*

Freeman, Don. *Forever laughter*

Fromm, Lilo. *Muffel and Plums*

Fuchs, Erich. *Journey to the moon*

Fujikawa, Gyo. *Millie's secret*
  My favorite thing

Goodall, John S. *The adventures of Paddy Pork*
  The ballooning adventures of Paddy Pork
  Creepy castle
  An Edwardian Christmas
  An Edwardian summer
  Jacko
  The midnight adventures of Kelly, Dot and Esmeralda
  Naughty Nancy
  Naughty Nancy goes to school
  Paddy goes traveling
  Paddy Pork odd jobs
  Paddy Pork's holiday
  Paddy to the rescue
  Paddy under water
  Paddy's evening out
  Paddy's new hat
  Shrewbettina's birthday
  The story of a castle
  The story of a farm
  The story of a main street
  The story of an English village
  The surprise picnic

Gorey, Edward. *The tunnel calamity*

Greeley, Valerie. *Farm animals*
  Field animals
  Pets
  Zoo animals

Grimm, Jacob. *Hansel and Gretel*, ill. by Conxita Rodriguez
  Little Red Riding Hood, ill. by John S. Goodall
  Sleeping Beauty, ill. by Fina Rifa

Hamberger, John. *The lazy dog*

Hartelius, Margaret A. *The chicken's child*

Hauptmann, Tatjana. *A day in the life of Petronella Pig*

Heller, Linda. *Lily at the table*

Hill, Eric. *At home*
  The park
  Up there

Hoban, Tana. *Big ones, little ones*
  Circles, triangles, and squares
  Dig, drill, dump, fill
  Is it larger? Is it smaller?
  Is it red? Is it yellow? Is it blue?
  Is it rough? Is it smooth? Is it shiny?
  Look again
  Look! Look! Look!
  1, 2, 3
  Shapes and things
  Shapes, shapes, shapes
  Take another look
  What is it?

Hughes, Shirley. *Up and up*

Hutchins, Pat. *Changes, changes*

Hyman, Trina Schart. *The enchanted forest*

Keats, Ezra Jack. *Clementina's cactus*
  Kitten for a day
  Psst, doggie

Skates
Kent, Jack. *The egg book*
Kilroy, Sally. *Animal noises*
Koontz, Robin Michal. *Dinosaur dream*
Krahn, Fernando. *Amanda and the mysterious carpet*
April fools
Arthur's adventure in the abandoned house
The biggest Christmas tree on earth
Catch that cat!
The creepy thing
A funny friend from heaven
The great ape
Here comes Alex Pumpernickel!
How Santa Claus had a long and difficult journey delivering his presents
Little love story
The mystery of the giant footprints
Robot-bot-bot
Sebastian and the mushroom
The secret in the dungeon
Sleep tight, Alex Pumpernickel
Who's seen the scissors?
Lemke, Horst. *Places and faces*
Lewis, Stephen. *Zoo city*
Lilly, Kenneth. *Animals in the country*
Lionni, Leo. *What?*
When?
Where?
Who?
Lisker, Sonia O. *Lost*
McCue, Lisa. *Corduroy's toys*
McCully, Emily Arnold. *The Christmas gift*
First snow
New baby
Picnic
School
MacGregor, Marilyn. *Baby takes a trip*
On top
Mari, Iela. *Eat and be eaten*
The magic balloon
Maris, Ron. *Hold tight, bear!*
Marol, Jean-Claude. *Vagabul and his shadow*
Vagabul escapes
Vagabul goes skiing
Vagabul in the clouds
Mayer, Mercer. *Ah-choo*
A boy, a dog, a frog and a friend
A boy, a dog and a frog
Bubble bubble
Frog goes to dinner
Frog on his own
Frog, where are you?
The great cat chase
Hiccup
One frog too many
Oops
Two moral tales
My body

Nygren, Tord. *The red thread*
Oakley, Graham. *Graham Oakley's magical changes*
Ogle, Lucille. *I spy with my little eye*
Ormerod, Jan. *Moonlight*
Sunshine
Oxenbury, Helen. *Beach day*
Good night, good morning
Monkey see, monkey do
Mother's helper
The shopping trip
Panek, Dennis. *Catastrophe Cat at the zoo*
Pitcher, Caroline. *Animals*
Cars and boats
Ponti, Claude. *Adele's album*
Prater, John. *The gift*
Rappus, Gerhard. *When the sun was shining*
Ringi, Kjell. *The winner*
Roennfeldt, Robert. *A day on the avenue*
Rojankovsky, Feodor. *Animals on the farm*
Saltzberg, Barney. *The yawn*
Sasaki, Isao. *Snow*
Schick, Eleanor. *The little school at Cottonwood Corners*
Making friends
Schubert, Dieter. *Where's my monkey?*
Selig, Sylvie. *Kangaroo*
Shimin, Symeon. *A special birthday*
Shopping
Spier, Peter. *Dreams*
Noah's ark
Peter Spier's rain
Stobbs, William. *Animal pictures*
Struppi
Sugita, Yutaka. *My friend Little John and me*
Tafuri, Nancy. *Do not disturb*
Junglewalk
Rabbit's morning
Türk, Hanne. *Goodnight Max*
Happy birthday Max
Max packs
Max the artlover
Max versus the cube
Merry Christmas Max
Rainy day Max
Raking leaves with Max
The rope skips Max
Snapshot Max
A surprise for Max
Turkle, Brinton. *Deep in the forest*
Ueno, Noriko. *Elephant buttons*
Ungerer, Tomi. *One, two, where's my shoe?*
Snail, where are you?
Vincent, Gabrielle. *Breakfast time, Ernest and Celestine*
Ernest and Celestine's patchwork quilt
A visit to a pond
Ward, Lynd. *The silver pony*
Wegen, Ron. *The balloon trip*

Wezel, Peter. *The good bird*
  The naughty bird
Wiesner, David. *Free fall*
Winter, Paula. *The bear and the fly*
  Sir Andrew
Young animals in the zoo
Young domestic animals
Young, Ed. *Up a tree*
Zoo animals

Words *see* Language

Working *see* Activities – working

World

Anno, Mitsumasa. *All in a day*
Bendick, Jeanne. *All around you*
Branley, Franklyn M. *The planets in our
  solar system*
Brann, Esther. *'Round the world*
Brown, Margaret Wise. *Four fur feet*
Delessert, Etienne. *How the mouse was hit
  on the head by a stone and so discovered
  the world*
Domanska, Janina. *What do you see?*
Douglas, Michael. *Round, round world*
Ekker, Ernest A. *What is beyond the hill?*
Fisher, Aileen. *I stood upon a mountain*
Goffstein, M. B. (Marilyn Brooke). *School
  of names*
Johnson, Crockett. *Upside down*
Nesbit, Edith. *The ice dragon*
Peet, Bill. *Chester the worldly pig*
Quin-Harkin, Janet. *Peter Penny's dance*
Schlein, Miriam. *Herman McGregor's world*
Schneider, Herman. *Follow the sunset*
Spier, Peter. *People*

Worms *see* Animals – worms

Worrying *see* Behavior – worrying

Wrecking machines *see* Machines

Wrens *see* Birds – wrens

Wrestling *see* Sports – wrestling

Writers *see* Careers – writers

Writing *see* Activities – writing

Writing letters *see* Letters

Yaks *see* Animals – yaks

Zaire *see* Foreign lands – Zaire

Zanzibar *see* Foreign lands – Zanzibar

Zebras *see* Animals – zebras

Zodiac

Fisher, Leonard Everett. *Star signs*
Van Woerkom, Dorothy. *The rat, the ox
  and the zodiac*

Zoos

Aitken, Amy. *Kate and Mona in the jungle*
Allen, Robert. *The zoo book*
Arthur, Catherine. *My sister's silent world*
Bahr, Robert. *Blizzard at the zoo*
Barry, Robert E. *Next please*
Baskin, Leonard. *Hosie's zoo*
Bauer, Helen. *Good times in the park*
Belloc, Hilaire. *Jim, who ran away from his
  nurse, and was eaten by a lion*
Bishop, Bonnie. *Ralph rides away*
Blance, Ellen. *Monster goes to the zoo*
Blue, Rose. *Black, black, beautiful black*
Bodsworth, Nan. *Monkey business*
Bolliger, Max. *Sandy at the children's zoo*
Bond, Michael. *Paddington at the zoo*
Boswell, Stephen. *King Gorboduc's fabulous
  zoo*
Bottner, Barbara. *Zoo song*
Brandenberg, Franz. *Leo and Emily's zoo*
Bridges, William. *Lion Island*
Bright, Robert. *Me and the bears*
Brown, Margaret Wise. *The big fur secret*
  Don't frighten the lion
Bruna, Dick. *Miffy at the zoo*
Calmenson, Stephanie. *Where will the
  animals stay?*
Campbell, Rod. *Dear zoo*
Canning, Kate. *A painted tale*
Carle, Eric. *1, 2, 3 to the zoo*
Carrick, Carol. *Patrick's dinosaurs*

Chalmers, Audrey. *Hundreds and hundreds of pancakes*
Parade of Obash
Charles, Donald. *Calico Cat at the zoo*
Colonius, Lillian. *At the zoo*
Curious George visits the zoo
Cutler, Ivor. *The animal house*
DeLage, Ida. *ABC triplets at the zoo*
Drescher, Henrik. *The yellow umbrella*
Fatio, Louise. *The happy lion*
The happy lion and the bear
The happy lion in Africa
The happy lion roars
The happy lion's rabbits
The happy lion's treasure
Hector and Christina
The three happy lions
Fay, Hermann. *My zoo*
Flora, James. *Leopold, the see-through crumbpicker*
Gibbons, Gail. *Zoo*
Gordon, Shirley. *Grandma zoo*
Graham, Margaret Bloy. *Be nice to spiders*
Greeley, Valerie. *Zoo animals*
Greydanus, Rose. *Animals at the zoo*
Grosvenor, Donna. *Zoo babies*
Hader, Berta Hoerner. *Lost in the zoo*
Hanlon, Emily. *What if a lion eats me and I fall into a hippopotamus' mud hole?*
Harrison, David Lee. *Detective Bob and the great ape escape*
Hoban, Tana. *A children's zoo*
Hoff, Syd. *Sammy the seal*
Howe, James. *The day the teacher went bananas*
Irvine, Georgeanne. *Bo the orangutan*
Elmer the elephant
Georgie the giraffe
Lindi the leopard
The nursery babies
Sasha the cheetah
Sydney the koala
Tully the tree kangaroo
Isenberg, Barbara. *The adventures of Albert, the running bear*
Jacobs, Francine. *Sewer Sam*

Johnson, Louise. *Malunda*
Kilroy, Sally. *Babies' zoo*
Kishida, Eriko. *The hippo boat*
Knight, Hilary. *Where's Wallace?*
Lewis, Stephen. *Zoo city*
Lilly, Kenneth. *Animals at the zoo*
Lippman, Peter. *New at the zoo*
Lisker, Sonia O. *Lost*
Lobel, Arnold. *A holiday for Mister Muster*
A zoo for Mister Muster
Loof, Jan. *Uncle Louie's fantastic sea voyage*
McCarthy, Ruth. *Katie and the smallest bear*
McGovern, Ann. *Zoo, where are you?*
Matthias, Catherine. *Too many balloons*
Meeks, Esther K. *Something new at the zoo*
Miklowitz, Gloria D. *The zoo that moved*
Munari, Bruno. *Bruno Munari's zoo*
Oxenbury, Helen. *Monkey see, monkey do*
Palmer, Helen Marion. *I was kissed by a seal at the zoo*
Panek, Dennis. *Catastrophe Cat at the zoo*
Pieńkowski, Jan. *Zoo*
Ray, Deborah Kogan. *Sunday morning we went to the zoo*
Reitveld, Jane Klatt. *Monkey island*
Rey, Hans Augusto. *Curious George takes a job*
Feed the animals
Rice, Eve. *Sam who never forgets*
Roffey, Maureen. *I spy at the zoo*
Rojankovsky, Feodor. *Animals in the zoo*
Roosevelt, Michelle Chopin. *Zoo animals*
Rowan, James P. *I can be a zoo keeper*
San Diego Zoological Society. *Families*
A visit to the zoo
Schumacher, Claire. *King of the zoo*
Seuss, Dr. *If I ran the zoo*
Snyder, Dick. *One day at the zoo*
Talk to me tiger
Tensen, Ruth M. *Come to the zoo!*
Tester, Sylvia Root. *A visit to the zoo*
Ylla. *Look who's talking*
Young, Miriam Burt. *Please don't feed Horace*
Ziefert, Harriet. *On our way to the zoo*

Bibliographic Guide

Arranged alphabetically by author's name in boldface (or by title, if author is unknown), each entry includes title, illustrator, publisher, publication date, and subjects. Joint authors and their titles appear as short entries, with the main author name (in parentheses after the title) citing where the complete entry will be found. Where only an author and title are given, complete information is listed under the *title* as the main entry. ISBNs are included for entries new to this edition.

A is for alphabet by Cathy, Marly and Wendy; ill. by George Suyeoka. Scott, 1968. Subj: ABC books.

Aardema, Verna. *Bimwili and the Zimwi* ill. by Susan Meddaugh. Dial Pr., 1985. ISBN 0-8037-0213-2 Subj: Folk and fairy tales. Foreign lands – Africa. Foreign lands – Zanzibar. Trolls.

Bringing the rain to Kapiti Plain: a Nandi tale ill. by Beatriz Vidal. Dial, 1981. Subj: Cumulative tales. Folk and fairy tales. Foreign lands – Africa. Poetry, rhyme. Weather – droughts. Weather – rain.

Half-a-ball-of-kenki: an Ashanti tale retold by Verna Aardema; ill. by Diane Stanley. Warne, 1979. Subj: Animals – leopards. Folk and fairy tales. Foreign lands – Africa. Insects – flies.

Ji-nongo-nongo means riddles ill. by Jerry Pinkney. Four Winds Pr., 1978. Subj: Folk and fairy tales. Foreign lands – Africa. Riddles.

Oh, Kojo! How could you! an Ashanti tale ill. by Marc Brown. Dial, 1984. Subj: Folk and fairy tales. Foreign lands – Africa. Humor.

Princess Gorilla and a new kind of water ill. by Victoria Chess. Dial Pr., 1988. ISBN 0-8037-0413-5 Subj: Animals. Animals – gorillas. Folk and fairy tales. Foreign lands – Africa.

Rabbit makes a monkey of lion ill. by Jerry Pinkney. Dial Pr., 1988. ISBN 0-8037-0297-3 Subj: Animals. Behavior – trickery. Foreign lands – Africa. Jungle.

The riddle of the drum: a tale from Tizapan, Mexico ill. by Tony Chen. Four Winds Pr., 1978. Subj: Cumulative tales. Folk and fairy tales. Foreign lands – Mexico. Poetry, rhyme. Royalty.

The vingananee and the tree toad: a Liberian tale ill. by Ellen Weiss. Warne, 1983. Subj: Animals. Folk and fairy tales. Foreign lands – Africa. Spiders.

What's so funny, Ketu? a Nuer tale ill. by Marc Brown. Dial, 1982. Subj: Animals. Behavior – secrets. Humor. Reptiles – snakes.

Who's in Rabbit's house? ill. by Leo and Diane Dillon. Dial Pr., 1977. Subj: Animals. Folk and fairy tales. Foreign lands – Africa. Humor. Insects – butterflies, caterpillars.

Why mosquitoes buzz in people's ears: a West African tale ill. by Leo and Diane Dillon. Dial Pr., 1975. Subj: Animals. Caldecott award book. Folk and fairy tales. Foreign lands – Africa. Insects – mosquitoes.

Aarle, Thomas Van. *Don't put your cart before the horse race* ill. by Bob Barner. Houghton, 1980. Subj: Animals – horses. Sports – racing.

ABCDEF... *in English and Spanish* ill. by Robert Tallon. Lion Pr., 1969. Subj: ABC books. Foreign languages.

Abel, Ray. *The new sitter* (Abel, Ruth)

Abel, Ruth. *The new sitter* by Ruth and Ray Abel; ill. by Ray Abel. Oxford Univ. Pr., 1950. Subj: Activities – baby-sitting.

Abells, Chana Byers. *The children we remember* photos. from the Archives of Yad Vashem, the Holocaust Martyrs' and Heroes' Remembrance Authority, Jerusalem, Israel. Greenwillow, 1986. ISBN 0-688-06372-1 Subj: War.

Abelson, Danny. *The Muppets take Manhattan: a movie storybook* adapt. by Danny Abelson; ill. with photos. Random House, 1983. Subj: Activities – working. Puppets.

Abisch, Roslyn Kroop *see* Abisch, Roz

Abisch, Roz. *The clever turtle* ill. by Boche Kaplan. Prentice-Hall, 1969. Subj: Animals. Folk and fairy tales. Foreign lands – Africa. Reptiles – turtles, tortoises.

Do you know what time it is? ill. by Boche Kaplan. Prentice-Hall, 1968. Subj: Time.

Let's find out about butterflies ill. by Boche Kaplan. Subj: Insects – butterflies, caterpillars. Science.

Mai-Ling and the mirror: a Chinese folktale ill. by Boche Kaplan. Prentice-Hall, 1969. Subj: Emotions – envy, jealousy. Folk and fairy tales. Foreign lands – China.

Open your eyes ill. by Boche Kaplan. Parents, 1964. Subj: Concepts – color. Imagination.

The Pumpkin Heads ill. by Boche Kaplan. Prentice-Hall, 1968. Based on an anecdote from general history of Connecticut, by Reverend Samuel Peters. Subj: Hair. U.S. history.

Sweet Betsy from Pike by Roz Abisch and Boche Kaplan; ill. by Boche Kaplan. McCall's, 1970. Subj: Character traits – perseverance. Folk and fairy tales. Music. Songs. U.S. history.

'Twas in the moon of wintertime: the first American Christmas carol adapt. by Roz Abisch; ill. by Boche Kaplan. Prentice-Hall, 1969. Subj: Indians of North America. Music.

Abolafia, Yossi. *A fish for Mrs. Gardenia* ill. by author. Greenwillow, 1988. ISBN 0-688-07468-5 Subj: Activities – cooking. Behavior – losing things.

My three uncles ill. by author. Greenwillow, 1984. ISBN 0-688-04025-X Subj: Character traits – individuality. Family life. Triplets.

Yanosh's Island ill. by author. Greenwillow, 1987. ISBN 0-688-06817-0 Subj: Activities – flying. Behavior – seeking better things. Islands. Toys.

Abrons, Mary. *For Alice a palace* ill. by Gertrude Barrer-Russell. W. R. Scott, 1966. Subj: ABC books. Birthdays. Poetry, rhyme. Royalty.

Ackerman, Karen. *Flannery Row* ill. by Karen Ann Weinhaus. Little, 1986. ISBN 0-87113-054-8 Subj: ABC books. Names. Poetry, rhyme.

Song and dance man ill. by Stephen Gammell. Knopf, 1988. ISBN 0-394-89330-1 Subj: Activities – dancing. Caldecott award book. Family life – grandfathers.

Ackley, Edith Flack. *Please* ill. by Telka Ackley. Stokes, 1941. Subj: Etiquette.

Thank you ill. by Telka Ackley. Stokes, 1942. Subj: Etiquette.

Adair, Towle *see* Jagendorf, Moritz A.

Adam, Barbara. *The big big box* ill. by author. Doubleday, 1960. Subj: Activities – playing. Animals – cats. Imagination.

Adams, Adrienne. *The Christmas party* ill. by author. Scribner's, 1978. Subj: Animals – rabbits. Holidays – Christmas. Parties.

The Easter egg artists ill. by author. Scribner's, 1976. Subj: Activities – painting. Activities – vacationing. Animals – rabbits. Holidays – Easter.

The great Valentine's Day balloon race ill. by author. Scribner's, 1980. Subj: Activities – ballooning. Animals – rabbits. Careers – artists. Holidays – Valentine's Day. Sports – racing.

A Halloween happening ill. by author. Scribner's, 1981. Subj: Holidays – Halloween. Parties. Witches.

Two hundred rabbits (Anderson, Lonzo)

A woggle of witches ill. by author. Scribner's, 1971. Subj: Holidays – Halloween. Witches.

Adams, Richard. *The tyger voyage* ill. by Nicola Bayley. Knopf, 1976. Subj: Animals – tigers. Humor. Poetry, rhyme.

Adams, Richard Newbold *see* Adams, Richard

Adams, Ruth Joyce. *Fidelia* ill. by author. Lothrop, 1970. Subj: Ethnic groups in the U.S. – Mexican-Americans.

Adamson, Gareth. *Old man up a tree* ill. by author. Abelard-Schuman, 1963. Subj: Character traits – curiosity. Crime. Humor.

Adamson, Joy. *Elsa* photos. by author. Pantheon, 1961. Subj: Animals – lions. Foreign lands – Africa.

Elsa and her cubs photos. by author. Harcourt, 1965. Subj: Animals – lions. Foreign lands – Africa.

Pippa the cheetah and her cubs photos. by author. Harcourt, 1971. Subj: Animals – cheetahs. Foreign lands – Africa.

Addy, Sharon Hart. *A visit with great-grandma* ill. by author. Albert Whitman, 1988. ISBN 0-8075-8497-5 Subj: Family life – grandmothers.

Adelberg, Doris *see* Orgel, Doris

Adelborg, Ottilia. *Clean Peter and the children of Grubbylea* tr. by Ada Wallas; ill. by author. Platt, 1968. Subj: Character traits – cleanliness. Poetry, rhyme.

Adelson, Leone. *All ready for school* ill. by Kathleen Elgin. McKay, 1957. Subj: School. Seasons – fall.

All ready for summer ill. by Kathleen Elgin. McKay, 1955. Subj: Seasons – summer.

All ready for winter ill. by Kathleen Elgin. McKay, 1952. Subj: Seasons – winter.

Please pass the grass ill. by Roger Antoine Duvoisin. McKay, 1960. Subj: Insects. Plants. Poetry, rhyme. Spiders.

Who blew that whistle? ill. by Oscar Fabrès. W. R. Scott, 1946. Subj: Careers – police officers. Character traits – helpfulness.

Adkins, Jan. *The art and industry of sandcastles* ill. by author. Walker, 1971. Subj: Sea and seashore.

Heavy equipment ill. by author. Scribner's, 1980. Subj: Machines. Trucks.

Toolchest: a primer of woodcraft ill. by author. Walker, 1973. Subj: Careers – carpenters. Tools.

Adler, David A. *Base five* ill. by Larry Ross. Crowell, 1975. Subj: Counting.

Bunny rabbit rebus ill. by Madelaine Gill Linden. Crowell, 1983. Subj: Animals – rabbits. Food. Rebuses.

The carsick zebra and other riddles ill. by Tomie de Paola. Holiday, 1983. Subj: Animals. Riddles.

The children of Chelm ill. by Arthur Friedman. Bonium Books, 1980. Subj: Foreign lands – Poland. Humor. Jewish culture. Problem solving.

The house on the roof: a Sukkot story ill. by Marilyn Hirsh. Bonim, 1976. Subj: Houses. Jewish culture.

I know I'm a witch ill. by Suçie Stevenson. Holt, 1988. ISBN 0-8050-0427-0 Subj: Imagination. Witches.

Jeffrey's ghost and the leftover baseball team ill. by Jean Jenkins. Holt, 1984. Subj: Character traits – confidence. Ghosts. Sports – baseball.

A little at a time ill. by author. Random House, 1976. Subj: Character traits – questioning. Family life – grandfathers.

My dog and the birthday mystery ill. by Dick Gackenbach. Holiday, 1987. ISBN 0-8234-0632-6 Subj: Animals – dogs. Birthdays. Friendship. Problem solving.

My dog and the green sock mystery ill. by Dick Gackenbach. Holiday, 1986. ISBN 0-8234-0590-7 Subj: Animals – dogs. Behavior – hiding things. Problem solving.

My dog and the key mystery ill. by Byron Barton. Watts, 1982. Subj: Animals – dogs. Problem solving.

My dog and the knock knock mystery ill. by Marsha Winborn. Holiday, 1985. ISBN 0-8234-0551-6 Subj: Animals – dogs. Problem solving.

A picture book of Hanukkah ill. by Linda Heller. Holiday, 1982. Subj: Holidays – Hanukkah. Jewish culture. Religion.

A picture book of Israel ill. with photos. Holiday, 1984. Subj: Foreign lands – Israel. Jewish culture. Religion.

A picture book of Jewish holidays ill. by Linda Heller. Holiday, 1981. Subj: Holidays. Holidays – Hanukkah. Holidays – Passover. Jewish culture.

A picture book of Passover ill. by Linda Heller. Holiday, 1982. Subj: Holidays – Passover. Jewish culture.

The purple turkey and other Thanksgiving riddles ill. by Marylin Hafner. Holiday, 1986. ISBN 0-8234-0613-X Subj: Holidays – Thanksgiving. Humor. Riddles.

Redwoods are the tallest trees in the world ill. by Kazue Mizumura. Crowell, 1978. Subj: Forest, woods. Science. Trees.

3D, 2D, 1D ill. by Harvey Weiss. Crowell, 1975. Subj: Concepts – measurement. Concepts – perspective. Concepts – shape.

The twisted witch and other spooky riddles ill. by Victoria Chess. Holiday, 1985. ISBN 0-8234-0571-0 Subj: Holidays – Halloween. Humor. Riddles.

You think it's fun to be a clown! ill. by Ray Cruz. Doubleday, 1980. Subj: Circus. Clowns, jesters. Poetry, rhyme.

Adler, Irene *see* Storr, Catherine

Adoff, Arnold. *Big sister tells me that I'm black* ill. by Lorenzo Lynch. Holt, 1976. Subj: Ethnic groups in the U.S. – Afro-Americans. Family life. Poetry, rhyme.

Birds ill. by Troy Howell. Lippincott, 1982. Subj: Birds. Poetry, rhyme.

Black is brown is tan ill. by Emily Arnold McCully. Harper, 1973. Subj: Family life. Marriage, interracial. Poetry, rhyme.

The cabbages are chasing the rabbits ill. by Janet Stevens. Harcourt, 1985. ISBN 0-15-213875-7 Subj: Cumulative tales. Poetry, rhyme.

Flamboyan ill. by Karen Barbour. Harcourt, 1988. ISBN 0-15-228404-4 Subj: Activities – flying. Dreams. Islands. Trees.

Greens ill. by Betsy Lewin. Lothrop, 1988. ISBN 0-688-04277-5 Subj: Concepts – color. Poetry, rhyme.

Ma nDa La ill. by Emily Arnold McCully. Harper, 1971. Subj: Family life. Foreign lands – Africa.

Make a circle, keep us in: poems for a good day ill. by Ronald Himler. Delacorte Pr., 1975. Subj: Family life. Night. Poetry, rhyme. Weather – storms.

Tornado! poems ill. by Ronald Himler. Delacorte Pr., 1977. Subj: Poetry, rhyme. Weather – storms.

Where wild Willie? ill. by Emily Arnold McCully. Harper, 1978. Subj: Behavior – running away. City. Ethnic groups in the U.S. – Afro-Americans. Poetry, rhyme.

Adshead, Gladys L. *Brownies - hush!* ill. by Elizabeth Orton Jones. Oxford Univ. Pr., 1938. Subj: Character traits – helpfulness. Elves and little people. Folk and fairy tales.

Brownies - it's Christmas ill. by Velma Ilsley. Oxford Univ. Pr., 1955. Subj: Elves and little people. Holidays – Christmas.

Brownies - they're moving ill. by Richard Lebenson. Walck, 1970. Subj: Character traits – helpfulness. Elves and little people. Moving.

Æsop. *The Æsop for children* ill. by Milo Winter. Rand McNally, 1984. ISBN 0-528-82134-2 Subj: Folk and fairy tales.

Æsop's fables sel. and ill. by Gaynor Chapman. Atheneum, 1972. Subj: Folk and fairy tales.

Æsop's fables ill. by Heidi Holder. Viking, 1981. Subj: Folk and fairy tales.

Æsop's fables: a pull-the-tab-pop-up-book ill. by Claire Littlejohn. Dial Pr., 1988. ISBN 0-8037-0487-9 Subj: Folk and fairy tales. Format, unusual – toy and movable books.

Æsop's fables retold by Carol Watson; ill. by Nick Price. Usborne, 1982. Subj: Folk and fairy tales.

Æsop's fables sel. and adapt. by Louis Untermeyer; ill. by Alice and Martin Provensen. Golden Pr., 1965. Subj: Folk and fairy tales.

Æsop's fables ed. by Tom Paxton; ill. by Robert Rayevsky. Morrow, 1988. ISBN 0-688-07361-1 Subj: Folk and fairy tales. Poetry, rhyme.

Æsop's fables retold by Anne Terry White; ill. by Helen Siegl. Random House, 1964. Subj: Folk and fairy tales.

Anno's Æsop (Anno, Mitsumasa)

The country mouse and the city mouse ill. by Laura Lydecker. Knopf, 1987. ISBN 0-394-99027-7 Subj: Animals – mice. Folk and fairy tales.

Doctor Coyote (Bierhorst, John)

The donkey ride (Showalter, Jean B.)

The fables of Æsop ed. by Ruth Spriggs; ill. by Frank Baber. Rand McNally, 1975. Subj: Folk and fairy tales.

The hare and the frogs adapt. and ill. by William Stobbs. Merrimack, 1979. Subj: Animals – rabbits. Folk and fairy tales. Frogs and toads.

The hare and the tortoise ill. by Paul Galdone. Whittlesey House, 1962. Subj: Animals – rabbits. Folk and fairy tales. Reptiles – turtles, tortoises. Sports – racing.

The hare and the tortoise adapt. and ill. by Gerald Rose. Macmillan, 1988. ISBN 0-689-71197-2 Subj: Animals – rabbits. Folk and fairy tales. Reptiles – turtles, tortoises. Sports – racing.

The hare and the tortoise adapt. by Caroline Castle; ill. by Peter Weevers. Dial Pr., 1985. ISBN 0-8037-0138-1 Subj: Animals – rabbits. Folk and fairy tales. Reptiles – turtles, tortoises. Sports – racing.

The lion and the mouse adapt. and ill. by Gerald Rose. Macmillan, 1988. ISBN 0-689-71196-4 Subj: Animals – lions. Animals – mice. Character traits – helpfulness. Folk and fairy tales.

The lion and the mouse: an Æsop fable ill. by Ed Young. Doubleday, 1980. Subj: Animals – lions. Animals – mice. Character traits – helpfulness. Folk and fairy tales.

The miller, his son and their donkey ill. by Roger Antoine Duvoisin. McGraw-Hill, 1962. Subj: Animals – donkeys. Character traits – perseverance. Humor. Folk and fairy tales.

The miller, his son and their donkey ill. by Eugen Sopko. Holt, 1985. ISBN 0-8050-0475-0 Subj: Animals – donkeys. Character traits – perseverance. Folk and fairy tales.

Once in a wood: ten tales from Æsop adapt. and ill. by Eve Rice. Greenwillow, 1980. Subj: Folk and fairy tales. Poetry, rhyme.

The raven and the fox adapt. and ill. by Gerald Rose. Macmillan, 1988. ISBN 0-689-71194-8 Subj: Animals – foxes. Birds – ravens. Folk and fairy tales.

Seven fables from Æsop retold and ill. by Robert W. Alley. Dodd, 1986. ISBN 0-396-08820-1 Subj: Animals. Folk and fairy tales.

Tales from Æsop retold and ill. by Harold Jones. Watts, 1982. Subj: Folk and fairy tales.

Three fox fables ill. by Paul Galdone. Seabury Pr., 1971. Subj: Animals – foxes. Behavior – trickery. Character traits – flattery. Folk and fairy tales.

The tortoise and the hare: an Æsop fable adapt. and ill. by Janet Stevens. Holiday, 1984. ISBN 0-8234-0510-9 Subj: Animals – rabbits. Character traits – perseverance. Folk and fairy tales. Reptiles, turtles, tortoises. Sports – racing.

The town mouse and the country mouse ill. by Lorinda Bryan Cauley. Putnam's, 1984. Subj: Animals – mice. Folk and fairy tales.

The town mouse and the country mouse ill. by Paul Galdone. McGraw-Hill, 1971. Subj: Animals – mice. Folk and fairy tales.

The town mouse and the country mouse ill. by Tom Garcia. Troll Assoc., 1979. Subj: Animals – mice. Folk and fairy tales.

The town mouse and the country mouse adapt. and ill. by Janet Stevens. Holiday, 1987. ISBN 0-8234-0633-4 Subj: Animals – mice. Folk and fairy tales.

Twelve tales from Æsop (Carle, Eric)

Wolf! wolf! adapt. and ill. by Gerald Rose. Macmillan, 1988. ISBN 0-689-71195-6 Subj: Behavior – lying. Behavior – trickery. Folk and fairy tales.

Afanas'ev, Aleksandr. *Russian folk tales* tr. by Robert Chandler; ill. by Ivan I. Bilibin. Random House, 1980. Subj: Folk and fairy tales. Foreign lands – Russia.

Agard, John. *Dig away two-hole Tim* ill. by Jennifer Northway. Bodley Head, 1982. Subj: Behavior – misbehavior. Foreign lands – Guyana.

Agee, Joel. *The crow in the snow and other bedtime stories* (Moser, Erwin)

Agee, Jon. *Ellsworth* ill. by author. Pantheon, 1983. Subj: Activities – playing. Animals – dogs. Imagination.

The incredible painting of Felix Clousseau ill. by author. Farrar, 1988. ISBN 0-374-33633-4 Subj: Activities – painting. Art. Imagination.

Agostinelli, Maria Enrica. *I know something you don't know* ill. by author. Watts, 1970. Translation of Ich weiss etwas, was du nicht weisst. Subj: Games. Participation.

On wings of love: the United Nations declaration of the rights of the child ill. by author. Collins-World, 1979. Subj: Birds – doves. Emotions – love.

Ahlberg, Allan. *The baby's catalogue* (Ahlberg, Janet)

Burglar Bill (Ahlberg, Janet)

The Cinderella show by Allan and Janet Ahlberg; ill. by authors. Viking, 1987. ISBN 0-670-81037-1 Subj: Folk and fairy tales. Holidays – Christmas. School. Theater.

The clothes horse: and other stories ill. by Janet Ahlberg. Viking, 1988. ISBN 0-670-81267-6 Subj: Bedtime.

Cops and robbers ill. by Janet Ahlberg. Greenwillow, 1979. Subj: Careers – police officers. Crime. Foreign lands – England. Holidays – Christmas. Poetry, rhyme.

Each peach pear plum (Ahlberg, Janet)

Funnybones (Ahlberg, Janet)

Jeremiah in the dark wood (Ahlberg, Janet)

The little worm book (Ahlberg, Janet)

Peek-a-boo! (Ahlberg, Janet)

Starting school (Ahlberg, Janet)

Ahlberg, Janet. *The baby's catalogue* by Janet and Allan Ahlberg; ill. by authors. Little, 1983. Subj: Babies. Family life.

Burglar Bill by Janet and Allan Ahlberg; ill. by authors. Greenwillow, 1977. Subj: Crime.

The Cinderella show (Ahlberg, Allan)

Each peach pear plum: an "I spy" story by Janet and Allan Ahlberg; ill. by authors. Viking, 1978. Subj: Games. Poetry, rhyme.

Funnybones by Janet and Allan Ahlberg; ill. by authors. Greenwillow, 1981. Subj: Activities – playing. Ghosts. Night.

Jeremiah in the dark wood by Janet and Allan Ahlberg; ill. by Janet Ahlberg. Viking, 1987. ISBN 0-670-40637-6 Subj: Behavior – stealing. Forest, woods. Mythical creatures.

The little worm book by Janet and Allan Ahlberg; ill. by authors. Viking, 1980. Subj: Animals – worms. Humor.

Peek-a-boo! by Janet and Allan Ahlberg; ill. by authors. Viking, 1981. Subj: Babies. Family life. Format, unusual. Games. Poetry, rhyme.

Starting school by Janet and Allan Ahlberg; ill. by authors. Viking, 1988. ISBN 0-670-82175-6 Subj: School.

Aho, Jennifer J. *Learning about sex: a guide for children and their parents* by Jennifer J. Aho and John W. Petras; ill. by Jennifer J. Aho. Holt, 1978. Subj: Family life. Science.

Aichinger, Helga. *The shepherd* ill. by author. Crowell, 1967. Subj: Holidays – Christmas. Religion.

Aiello, Susan. *A hat like that* (Johnson, B. J.)

My blanket Burt (Johnson, B. J.)

Aiken, Conrad. *Tom, Sue and the clock* ill. by Julie Maas. Macmillan, 1966. Subj: Clocks. Poetry, rhyme. Time.

Aiken, Conrad Potter *see* Aiken, Conrad

Aiken, Joan. *Arabel and Mortimer* ill. by Quentin Blake. Doubleday, 1981. Subj: Birds – ravens. Imagination. Pets.

Ainsworth, Ruth. *The mysterious Baba and her magic caravan* ill. by Joan Hickson. Deutsch, dist. by Elsevier-Dutton, 1980. Subj: Character traits – generosity. Toys – dolls.

Aitken, Amy. *Kate and Mona in the jungle* ill. by author. Bradbury Pr., 1981. Subj: Animals. Imagination. Jungle. Zoos.

Ruby! ill. by author. Bradbury Pr., 1979. Subj: Careers. Imagination.

Ruby, the red knight ill. by author. Bradbury Pr., 1983. Subj: Character traits – bravery. Imagination. Royalty.

Wanda's circus ill. by author. Bradbury Pr., 1985. ISBN 0-02-700370-1 Subj: Animals. Circus. Family life. Sibling rivalry.

Akens, Floyd *see* Baum, L. Frank (Lyman Frank)

Akers, Floyd *see* Baum, L. Frank (Lyman Frank)

Aksakov, Sergei. *The scarlet flower* tr. by Isadora Levin; ill. by Boris Diodorov. Harcourt, 1989. ISBN 0-15-270487-6 Subj: Activities – traveling. Family life – fathers. Flowers. Foreign lands – Russia.

Alan, Sandy. *The plaid peacock* ill. by Kelly Oechsli. Pantheon, 1965. Subj: Birds – peacocks, peahens. Foreign lands – India.

Albert, Burton. *Mine, yours, ours* ill. by Lois Axeman. Albert Whitman, 1977. Subj: Behavior – sharing. Concepts.

Alborough, Jez. *Bare bear* ill. by author. Knopf, 1984. Subj: Activities – bathing. Animals – polar bears. Humor. Poetry, rhyme.

The grass is always greener ill. by author. Dial Pr., 1987. ISBN 0-8037-0468-2 Subj: Animals – sheep. Behavior – seeking better things. Farms.

Running Bear ill. by author. Knopf, 1985. ISBN 0-394-97963-X Subj: Animals – polar bears. Behavior – bad day. Sports – racing.

Alda, Arlene. *Arlene Alda's ABC* photos. by author. Celestial Arts, 1981. Subj: ABC books.

Matthew and his dad photos. by author. Simon and Schuster, 1983. Subj: Clothing. Family life – fathers.

Sonya's mommy works photos. by author. Messner, 1982. Subj: Activities – working. Family life – mothers.

Alden, Jack *see* Barrows, Marjorie Wescott

Alden, Laura. *Learning about fairies* ill. by Krystyna Stasiak. Childrens Pr., 1982. Subj: Elves and little people. Fairies. Folk and fairy tales. Goblins.

When? ill. by Lois Axeman. Childrens Pr., 1983. Subj: Character traits – curiosity. Character traits – questioning.

Alderson, Brian. *Cakes and custard*

The Helen Oxenbury nursery rhyme book

Alderson, Sue Ann. *Bonnie McSmithers is at it again!* ill. by Fiona Garrick. Tree Frog Pr., 1980. Subj: Activities. Character traits – individuality. Poetry, rhyme.

Ida and the wool smugglers ill. by Ann Blades. Macmillan, 1987. ISBN 0-689-50440-3 Subj: Character traits – cleverness. Crime. Islands.

Aldis, Dorothy. *All together: a child's treasury of verse* ill. by Helen D. Jameson, Marjorie Flack and Margaret Freeman. Putnam's, 1952. Subj: Poetry, rhyme.

Before things happen ill. by Margaret Freeman. Putnam's, 1939. Subj: Poetry, rhyme.

Hello day ill. by Susan Elson. Putnam's, 1959. Subj: Poetry, rhyme.

Quick as a wink ill. by Peggy Westphal. Putnam's, 1960. Subj: Insects. Poetry, rhyme.

Aldrich, Bess Streeter *see* Stevens, Margaret

Aldridge, Alan. *The butterfly ball and the grasshopper's feast* by Alan Aldridge, with verses by William Plomer and nature notes by Richard Fitter; rev. by Edward G. Atkins; ill. by William Mulready. Grossman Pub., 1975. Subj: Animals. Insects. Insects – butterflies, caterpillars. Insects – grasshoppers. Poetry, rhyme. Science.

Aldridge, Josephine Haskell. *The best of friends* ill. by Betty Peterson. Parnassus, 1963. Subj: Animals. Friendship.

Fisherman's luck ill. by Ruth Robbins. Parnassus, 1966. Subj: Careers – fishermen. Character traits – luck. Sports – fishing. Weather – storms.

A peony and a periwinkle ill. by Ruth Robbins. Parnassus, 1961. Subj: Sports – fishing.

Aleichem, Sholem. *Hanukah money* ill. by Uri Shulevitz. Greenwillow, 1978. Subj: Folk and fairy tales. Foreign lands. Holidays – Hanukkah. Jewish culture.

Aleichem, Sholom *see* Aleichem, Sholem

Alexander, Alison. *Science magic: scientific experiments for young children* by Alison Alexander and Susie Bower; ill. by Carolyn Scarce. Prentice-Hall, 1987. ISBN 0-13-795311-9 Subj: Science.

Alexander, Anna Barbara Cooke *see* Alexander, Anne

Alexander, Anne. *ABC of cars and trucks* ill. by Ninon. Doubleday, 1956. Subj: ABC books. Automobiles. Poetry, rhyme. Trucks.

Boats and ships from A to Z ill. by Will Huntington. Rand McNally, 1961. Subj: Boats, ships. Poetry, rhyme.

I want to whistle ill. by Abner Graboff. Abelard-Schuman, 1958. Subj: Activities – whistling. Poetry, rhyme.

My daddy and I ill. by Cyril Satorsky. Abelard-Schuman, 1961. Subj: Counting. Poetry, rhyme. Family life – fathers.

Noise in the night ill. by Abner Graboff. Rand McNally, 1960. Subj: Emotions – fear. Night. Noise, sounds.

Alexander, Cecil Frances. *All things bright and beautiful: a hymn* ill. by Leo Politi. Scribner's, 1962. Subj: Music. Religion. Songs.

Alexander, Janet *see* McNeill, Janet

Alexander, Jocelyn Anne Arundel *see* Arundel, Jocelyn

Alexander, Liza. *Ernie gets lost* ill. by Tom Cooke. Childrens Pr., 1985. ISBN 0-307-62115-4 Subj: Behavior – lost. Stores.

Alexander, Lloyd. *Coll and his white pig* ill. by Evaline Ness. Holt, 1965. Subj: Animals – pigs. Folk and fairy tales.

The four donkeys ill. by Lester Abrams. Holt, 1972. ISBN 0-03-080214-8 Subj: Animals – donkeys. Behavior – fighting, arguing. Behavior – greed. Middle ages.

The king's fountain ill. by Ezra Jack Keats. Dutton, 1971. Subj: Folk and fairy tales. Poverty. Royalty.

The truthful harp ill. by Evaline Ness. Holt, 1967. Subj: Character traits – honesty. Folk and fairy tales. Music.

Alexander, Martha G. *And my mean old mother will be sorry, Blackboard Bear* ill. by author. Dial Pr., 1972. Subj: Animals – bears. Behavior – running away. Emotions – anger. Imagination – imaginary friends.

Blackboard Bear ill. by author. Dial Pr., 1969. Subj: Animals – bears. Imagination – imaginary friends.

Bobo's dream ill. by author. Dial Pr., 1970. Subj: Animals – dogs. Dreams. Ethnic groups in the U.S. – Afro-Americans. Imagination. Wordless.

Even that moose won't listen to me ill. by author. Dial Pr., 1988. ISBN 0-8037-0188-8 Subj: Animals – moose. Behavior – disbelief. Family life.

How my library grew by Dinah ill. by author. H. W. Wilson, 1982. Subj: Libraries.

I sure am glad to see you, Blackboard Bear ill. by author. Dial Pr., 1976. Subj: Animals – bears. Behavior – bullying. Imagination – imaginary friends.

I'll be the horse if you'll play with me ill. by author. Dial Pr., 1975. Subj: Activities – playing. Behavior – fighting, arguing. Sibling rivalry. Family life.

I'll protect you from the jungle beasts ill. by author. Dial Pr., 1973. Subj: Emotions – fear. Imagination – imaginary friends. Problem solving. Sleep. Toys – teddy bears.

Maggie's moon ill. by author. Dial Pr., 1982. Subj: Animals – dogs. Moon. Night.

The magic box ill. by author. Dial Pr., 1984. ISBN 0-8037-0051-2 Subj: Format, unusual. Magic. Monsters. Witches. Wordless.

The magic hat ill. by author. Dial Pr., 1984. ISBN 0-8037-0051-2 Subj: Animals – rabbits. Birds – doves. Format, unusual. Magic. Wordless.

The magic picture ill. by author. Dial Pr., 1984. ISBN 0-8037-0051-2 Subj: Animals – dogs. Format, unusual. Wordless.

Marty McGee's space lab, no girls allowed ill. by author. Dial Pr., 1981. Subj: Family life. Imagination. Sibling rivalry. Space and space ships.

Maybe a monster ill. by author. Dial Pr., 1968. Subj: Emotions – fear. Monsters.

Move over, Twerp ill. by author. Dial Pr., 1981. Subj: Behavior – bullying. Character traits – perseverance. Humor. Problem solving. School.

No ducks in our bathtub ill. by author. Dial Pr., 1973. Subj: Frogs and toads. Pets.

Nobody asked me if I wanted a baby sister ill. by author. Dial Pr., 1971. Subj: Babies. Emotions – envy, jealousy. Sibling rivalry.

Out! Out! Out! ill. by author. Dial Pr., 1968. Subj: Birds. Problem solving. Wordless.

Pigs say oink: a first book of sounds ill. by author. Random House, 1978. Subj: Animals. Noise, sounds.

Sabrina ill. by author. Dial Pr., 1971. Subj: Emotions – embarrassment. Names. School.

The story grandmother told ill. by author. Dial Pr., 1969. Subj: Ethnic groups in the U.S. – Afro-Americans. Family life – grandmothers. Toys.

3 magic flip books: The magic hat; The magic box; The magic picture ill. by author. Dial Pr., 1984. Subj: Format, unusual – toy and movable books. Magic. Wordless.

We never get to do anything ill. by author. Dial Pr., 1970. Subj: Behavior – boredom. Character traits – perseverance. Games. Problem solving. Sports – swimming.

We're in big trouble, Blackboard Bear ill. by author. Dial Pr., 1980. Subj: Animals – bears. Behavior – misbehavior. Imagination – imaginary friends. Night. Problem solving.

When the new baby comes, I'm moving out ill. by author. Dial Pr., 1979. Subj: Babies. Emotions – envy, jealousy. Sibling rivalry.

Alexander, Sue. *Dear Phoebe* ill. by Eileen Christelow. Little, 1984. Subj: Animals – mice. Behavior – growing up. Emotions – loneliness. Emotions – love. Family life.

Marc the Magnificent ill. by Tomie de Paola. Pantheon, 1978. Subj: Character traits – optimism. Magic.

More Witch, Goblin, and Ghost stories ill. by Jeanette Winter. Pantheon, 1978. Subj: Ghosts. Goblins. Witches.

Nadia the willful ill. by Lloyd Bloom. Pantheon, 1983. Subj: Character traits – willfulness. Emotions – love. Emotions – sadness. Family life. Foreign lands – Arabia.

Seymour the prince ill. by Lillian Hoban. Pantheon, 1979. Subj: Clubs, gangs. Theater.

Small plays for special days ill. by Tom Huffman. Seabury Pr., 1977. Subj: Holidays. Theater.

Small plays for you and a friend ill. by Olivia Cole. Houghton, 1974. Subj: Friendship. Theater.

There's more...much more ill. by Patience Brewster. Harcourt, 1987. ISBN 0-15-200605-2 Subj: Animals – squirrels. Seasons – spring.

Witch, Goblin, and Ghost in the haunted woods ill. by Jeanette Winter. Pantheon, 1981. Subj: Ghosts. Goblins. Witches.

Witch, Goblin and Ghost's book of things to do ill. by Jeanette Winter. Pantheon, 1982. Subj: Activities. Ghosts. Goblins. Witches.

Witch, Goblin and sometimes Ghost ill. by Jeanette Winter. Pantheon, 1976. Subj: Behavior – forgetfulness. Emotions – fear. Friendship. Ghosts. Goblins. Witches.

World famous Muriel ill. by Chris L. Demarest. Little, 1984. Subj: Birthdays. Humor. Problem solving.

Alger, Leclaire. *All in the morning early* ill. by Evaline Ness. Holt, 1963. Subj: Caldecott award honor book. Folk and fairy tales. Foreign lands – Scotland. Poetry, rhyme. Songs.

Always room for one more ill. by Nonny Hogrogian. Holt, 1965. Children's story based on the Scottish ballad of the same title. Subj: Caldecott award book. Cumulative tales. Folk and fairy tales. Foreign lands – Scotland. Houses. Music.

Kellyburn Braes ill. by Evaline Ness. Harcourt, 1968. Subj: Devil. Foreign lands – Scotland. Foreign languages. Music. Poetry, rhyme. Songs.

Alger, Leclaire Gowans see Alger, Leclaire

Aliki. *At Mary Bloom's* ill. by author. Greenwillow, 1976. Subj: Animals – mice. Babies.

Corn is maize: the gift of the Indians ill. by author. Crowell, 1976. Subj: Activities – gardening. Indians of North America. Plants. Science.

Digging up dinosaurs ill. by author. Rev. ed. Crowell, 1988. ISBN 0-690-04716-9 Subj: Activities – digging. Humor. Science.

Dinosaur bones ill. by author. Harper, 1988. ISBN 0-690-04550-6 Subj: Dinosaurs.

Dinosaurs are different ill. by author. Crowell, 1985. ISBN 0-690-04458-5 Subj: Dinosaurs. Science.

Diogenes: the story of the Greek philosopher ill. by author. Prentice-Hall, 1969. Subj: Character traits – honesty. Folk and fairy tales. Foreign lands – Greece.

The eggs: a Greek folk tale ill. by adapt. Pantheon, 1969. Subj: Behavior – greed. Character traits – cleverness. Folk and fairy tales. Foreign lands – Greece. Humor.

Fossils tell of long ago ill. by author. Crowell, 1972. Subj: Dinosaurs. Science.

George and the cherry tree ill. by author. Dial Pr., 1964. Subj: Character traits – bravery. Folk and fairy tales. U.S. history.

How a book is made ill. by author. Harper, 1986. ISBN 0-690-04498-4 Subj: Activities – reading. Libraries.

I wish I was sick, too! ill. by author. Greenwillow, 1976. Subj: Behavior – wishing. Illness.

Jack and Jake ill. by author. Greenwillow, 1986. ISBN 0-688-06100-1 Subj: Behavior – mistakes. Character traits – individuality. Family life. Twins.

June 7! ill. by author. Macmillan, 1972. Subj: Birthdays. Cumulative tales. Family life.

Keep your mouth closed, dear ill. by author. Dial Pr., 1966. Subj: Behavior – carelessness. Family life. Reptiles – alligators, crocodiles.

The long lost coelacanth and other living fossils ill. by author. Crowell, 1973. Subj: Fish. Science.

The many lives of Benjamin Franklin ill. by author. Prentice-Hall, 1977. Subj: U.S. history.

Mummies made in Egypt ill. by author. Crowell, 1979. Subj: Death. Foreign lands – Egypt. Religion.

My five senses ill. by author. Crowell, 1962. Subj: Senses – hearing. Senses – seeing. Senses – smelling. Senses – tasting. Senses – touching.

My hands ill. by author. Crowell, 1962. Subj: Anatomy. Science.

My visit to the dinosaurs ill. by author. Rev. ed. Crowell, 1985. ISBN 0-690-04423-2 Subj: Dinosaurs. Museums. Science.

Overnight at Mary Bloom's ill. by author. Greenwillow, 1987. ISBN 0-688-06765-4 Subj: Activities. Activities – playing. Friendship. Night.

The story of Johnny Appleseed ill. by author. Prentice-Hall, 1963. Subj: Activities – gardening. Character traits – generosity. Folk and fairy tales. Trees. U.S. history.

The story of William Penn ill. by author. Prentice-Hall, 1964. Subj: Character traits – kindness. U.S. history.

Three gold pieces: a Greek folk tale ill. by author. Pantheon, 1967. Subj: Character traits – luck. Folk and fairy tales. Foreign lands – Greece.

The twelve months: a Greek folktale ill. by adapt. Greenwillow, 1978. Subj: Behavior – dissatisfaction. Character traits – optimism. Folk and fairy tales. Foreign lands – Greece.

The two of them ill. by author. Greenwillow, 1979. Subj: Character traits – helpfulness. Character traits – loyalty. Family life – grandfathers.

Use your head, dear ill. by author. Greenwillow, 1983. Subj: Behavior – forgetfulness. Birthdays. Reptiles – alligators, crocodiles.

We are best friends ill. by author. Greenwillow, 1982. Subj: Emotions – anger. Emotions – loneliness. Friendship. Moving.

A weed is a flower: the life of George Washington Carver ill. by author. Prentice-Hall, 1965. Subj: Character traits – perseverance. Ethnic groups in the U.S. – Afro-Americans. Science. U.S. history.

Welcome, little baby ill. by author. Greenwillow, 1987. ISBN 0-688-06811-1 Subj: Babies. Family life.

Wild and woolly mammoths ill. by author. Crowell, 1977. Subj: Animals. Science.

The wish workers ill. by author. Dial Pr., 1962. Subj: Behavior – dissatisfaction. Behavior – wishing. Birds. Magic.

The all-amazing ha ha book. Merrimack, 1985. ISBN 0-19-554581-8 Subj: Folk and fairy tales. Foreign lands – Australia. Humor. Language.

Allamand, Pascale. *The animals who changed their colors* ill. by Elizabeth Watson Taylor. Morrow, 1979. Subj: Animals. Behavior – imitation. Character traits – individuality. Concepts – color. Humor.

Cocoa beans and daisies: how chocolate is made photos. by author. Warne, 1978. Subj: Food. Foreign lands – Switzerland.

The little goat in the mountains tr. by Michael Bullock; ill. by author. Warne, 1978. Subj: Animals – goats.

Allan, Ted. *Willie the squowse* ill. by Quentin Blake. Hastings, 1978. Subj: Animals. Behavior – hiding things. Humor. Money.

Allard, Harry. *Bumps in the night* ill. by James Marshall. Doubleday, 1979. Subj: Animals. Ghosts. Noise, sounds.

I will not go to market today ill. by James Marshall. Dial Pr., 1979. Subj: Birds – chickens. Shopping.

It's so nice to have a wolf around the house ill. by James Marshall. Doubleday, 1977. Subj: Crime. Old age. Pets.

May I stay? ill. by F. A. Fitzgerald. Prentice-Hall, 1977. Subj: Character traits – questioning. Folk and fairy tales. Foreign lands – Germany. Foreign lands – Norway.

Miss Nelson has a field day ill. by James Marshall. Houghton, 1985. Subj: Behavior – secrets. Humor. School.

Miss Nelson is back by Harry Allard and James Marshall; ill. by James Marshall. Houghton, 1982. Subj: Behavior – misbehavior. Careers – teachers. School.

Miss Nelson is missing! by Harry Allard and James Marshall; ill. by James Marshall. Houghton, 1977. Subj: Behavior – misbehavior. Careers – teachers. School.

The Stupids die ill. by James Marshall. Houghton, 1981. Subj: Behavior – misunderstanding. Humor.

The Stupids have a ball by Harry Allard and James Marshall; ill. by James Marshall. Houghton, 1978. Subj: Humor. Parties.

The Stupids step out ill. by James Marshall. Houghton, 1974. Subj: Humor.

There's a party at Mona's tonight ill. by James Marshall. Doubleday, 1981. Subj: Animals – pigs. Behavior – trickery. Humor. Parties.

Three is company (Waechter, Friedrich Karl)

Allbright, Viv. *Ten go hopping* ill. by author. Faber, 1985. ISBN 0-571-13473-4 Subj: Counting. Cumulative tales.

Allen, Allyn *see* Eberle, Irmengarde

Allen, Frances Charlotte. *Little hippo* ill. by Laura Jean Allen. Putnam's, 1971. Subj: Animals – hippopotami. Emotions – sadness.

Allen, Gertrude E. *Everyday animals* ill. by author. Houghton, 1961. Subj: Animals. Forest, woods. Science.

Allen, Jeffrey. *Bonzini! the tattooed man* ill. by James Marshall. Little, 1976. Subj: Circus. Clowns, jesters.

Mary Alice, operator number 9 ill. by James Marshall. Little, 1975. Subj: Activities – working. Animals. Birds – ducks. Careers – telephone operators. Telephone. Time.

Mary Alice returns ill. by James Marshall. Little, 1986. ISBN 0-316-03429-0 Subj: Birds – ducks. Careers – telephone operators. Telephone.

Nosey Mrs. Rat ill. by James Marshall. Viking, 1985. ISBN 0-670-80880-6 Subj: Animals. Behavior – gossip. Character traits – curiosity.

The secret life of Mr. Weird ill. by Ned Delaney. Little, 1982. Subj: Animals – dogs. Behavior – dissatisfaction. Behavior – seeking better things. Games. Imagination.

Allen, Jonathan. *A bad case of animal nonsense* ill. by author. Godine, 1981. Subj: Animals. Humor. Poetry, rhyme.

My cat ill. by author. Dial Pr., 1986. ISBN 0-8037-0292-2 Subj: Animals – cats. Pets.

Allen, Laura Jean. *Ottie and the star* ill. by author. Harper, 1979. Subj: Animals – otters. Family life. Sea and seashore. Stars.

Rollo and Tweedy and the case of the missing cheese ill. by author. Harper, 1983. Subj: Animals – mice. Food. Foreign lands – France. Problem solving.

Where is Freddy? ill. by author. Harper, 1986. ISBN 0-06-020099-5 Subj: Activities – flying. Behavior – lost. Careers – detectives. Problem solving.

Allen, Linda. *The giant who had no heart* ill. by author. Philomel, 1988. ISBN 0-399-21446-1 Subj: Folk and fairy tales. Foreign lands – Norway. Giants.

Mr. Simkin's grandma ill. by Loretta Lustig. Morrow, 1979. Subj: Family life – grandmothers. Family life – grandparents. Humor.

Mrs. Simkin's bed ill. by Loretta Lustig. Morrow, 1980. Subj: Animals. Humor.

Allen, Marjorie N. *One, two, three - ah-choo!* ill. by Dick Gackenbach. Coward, 1980. Subj: Animals. Humor. Pets.

The remarkable ride of Israel Bissell... as related to Molly the crow (Schick, Alice)

Allen, Martha Dickson. *Real life monsters* ill. by author. Prentice-Hall, 1979. Subj: Animals. Monsters. Science.

Allen, Pamela. *Bertie and the bear* ill. by author. Coward, 1984. Subj: Activities – dancing. Animals – bears. Animals – dogs. Noise, sounds. Royalty.

Hidden treasure ill. by author. Putnam's, 1987. Orig. published as Herbert and Harry. ISBN 0-399-21427-5 Subj: Behavior – greed. Behavior – hiding things. Sea and seashore. Sibling rivalry.

A lion in the night ill. by author. Putnam's, 1986. ISBN 0-399-21203-5 Subj: Animals – lions. Babies. Behavior – wishing. Imagination. Royalty.

Mr. Archimedes' bath ill. by author. Lothrop, 1980. Subj: Activities – bathing. Animals. Humor. Science.

Who sank the boat? ill. by author. Coward, 1983. Subj: Animals. Boats, ships. Poetry, rhyme. Science.

Allen, Robert. *Numbers: a first counting book* ill. by Mottke Weissman. Platt, 1968. Subj: Counting.

Round and square ill. by Philippe Thomas. Platt, 1965. Subj: Concepts – shape.

Ten little babies count by Janet Martin [pseud.]; photos. by Michael Watson. St. Martin's, 1986. ISBN 0-312-79112-7 Subj: Babies. Clothing. Counting.

Ten little babies dress by Janet Martin [pseud.]; photos. by Michael Watson. St. Martin's, 1986. ISBN 0-312-79113-5 Subj: Babies. Clothing. Counting.

Ten little babies eat by Janet Martin [pseud.]; photos. by Michael Watson. St. Martin's, 1986. ISBN 0-312-79114-3 Subj: Babies. Counting. Food.

Ten little babies play: a book of colors by Janet Martin [pseud.]; photos. by Michael Watson. St. Martin's, 1986. ISBN 0-312-79115-1 Subj: Activities – playing. Babies. Concepts – color. Counting.

The zoo book: a child's world of animals photos. by Peter Sahula. Platt, 1968. Subj: Animals. Zoos.

Allen, Thomas B. *Where children live* ill. by author. Prentice-Hall, 1980. Subj: Foreign lands.

Alley, Robert W. *Seven fables from Æsop* (Æsop)

Allington, Richard L. *Autumn* by Richard L. Allington and Kathleen Krull; ill. by Bruce Bond. Raintree, 1981. Subj: Seasons – fall. Weather.

Feelings by Richard L. Allington and Kathleen Cowles; ill. by Brian Cody. Raintree, 1981. Subj: Activities. Emotions.

Hearing by Richard L. Allington and Kathleen Cowles; ill. by Wayne Dober. Raintree, 1981. Subj: Activities. Senses – hearing.

Looking by Richard L. Allington and Kathleen Cowles; ill. by Bill Bober. Raintree, 1981. Subj: Activities. Senses – seeing.

Smelling by Richard L. Allington and Kathleen Cowles; ill. by Rick Thrun. Raintree, 1981. Subj: Activities. Senses – smelling.

Spring by Richard L. Allington and Kathleen Krull; ill. by Lynn Uhde. Raintree, 1981. Subj: Seasons – spring. Weather.

Summer by Richard L. Allington and Kathleen Krull; ill. by Dennis Hockerman. Raintree, 1981. Subj: Seasons – summer. Weather.

Tasting by Richard L. Allington and Kathleen Cowles; ill. by Noel Spangler. Raintree, 1981. Subj: Activities. Senses – tasting.

Touching by Richard L. Allington and Kathleen Cowles; ill. by Yoshi Miyake. Raintree, 1981. Subj: Activities. Senses – touching.

Winter by Richard L. Allington and Kathleen Krull; ill. by John Wallner. Raintree, 1981. Subj: Seasons – winter. Weather.

Allison, Alida. *The toddler's potty book* by Alida Allison and Paula Sapphire. Price Stern Sloan, 1981, 1979. Subj: Behavior – growing up.

Allison, Diane Worfolk. *In window eight, the moon is late* ill. by author. Little, 1988. ISBN 0-316-03435-5 Subj: Bedtime. Dreams. Poetry, rhyme.

Allred, Mary. *Grandmother Poppy and the funny-looking bird* ill. by Paul Behrens. Broadman Pr., 1981. Subj: Birds. Character traits – kindness to animals. Family life – grandmothers.

Allstrom, Elizabeth C. *Songs along the way* ill. by Mel Silverman. Abingdon Pr., 1961. Subj: Foreign lands – Israel. Poetry, rhyme. Religion.

Althea. *Castle life* ill. by Maureen Galvani. Merrimack, 1980. Subj: Middle ages.

Jeremy Mouse and cat ill. by author. Merrimack, 1980. Subj: Animals – cats. Animals – mice. Behavior – trickery.

Ambler, Christopher Gifford. *Ten little fox-hounds.* Children's Pr., 1968. Subj: Animals – dogs. Counting. Foreign lands – England. Poetry, rhyme.

Ambrus, Gyozo Laszlo *see* Ambrus, Victor G.

Ambrus, Victor G. *Brave soldier Janosch* ill. by author. Harcourt, 1967. Subj: Careers – military. Foreign lands – Hungary. War.

Country wedding ill. by author. Addison-Wesley, 1975. Subj: Animals – foxes. Animals – wolves. Food. Weddings.

Grandma, Felix, and Mustapha Biscuit ill. by author. W. Morrow, 1982. Subj: Animals – cats. Animals – hamsters. Family life – grandmothers. Humor.

The little cockerel ill. by author. Harcourt, 1968. Subj: Birds – chickens. Character traits – perseverance. Folk and fairy tales.

Mishka ill. by author. Warne, 1978. Subj: Animals – elephants. Character traits – perseverance. Circus. Music.

The seven skinny goats ill. by author. Harcourt, 1969. Subj: Activities – dancing. Animals – goats. Folk and fairy tales. Humor. Music.

The Sultan's bath ill. by author. Oxford Univ. Pr., 1971. Subj: Activities – bathing. Folk and fairy tales. Foreign lands – India. Royalty.

The three poor tailors ill. by author. Harcourt, 1966. Subj: Activities – whistling. Animals – goats. Careers – tailors. Folk and fairy tales. Foreign lands – Hungary. Poverty.

Amery, H. *The farm picture book* ill. by author. Educational Development Corp., 1988. ISBN 0-7460-0128-2 Subj: Animals. Farms.

Ames, Gerald. *Spooky tricks* (Wyler, Rose)

Ames, Mildred. *The wonderful box* ill. by Richard Cuffari. Dutton, 1978. Subj: Character traits – curiosity. Problem solving.

Ames, Noel *see* Barrows, Marjorie Wescott

Ames, Rose *see* Wyler, Rose

Amoit, Pierre. *Bijou the little bear.* Coward, 1950. Subj: Animals – bears. Circus. Clowns, jesters.

Amos, William H. *Exploring the seashore* ill. with photos. National Geographic Soc., 1984. ISBN 0-87044-531-6 Subj: Animals. Crustacea. Plants. Sea and seashore.

Amoss, Berthe. *It's not your birthday* ill. by author. Harper, 1966. Subj: Birthdays. Sibling rivalry.

Tom in the middle ill. by author. Harper, 1968. Subj: Family life. Sibling rivalry.

Anastasio, Dina. *Pass the peas, please: a book of manners* ill. by Katy Keck Arnsteen. Warner Brothers, 1988. ISBN 1-55782-021-X Subj: Etiquette. Poetry, rhyme.

Anchondo, Mary. *How we came to the fifth world* (Rohmer, Harriet)

Ancona, George. *Dancing is* ill. by author. Dutton, 1981. Subj: Activities – dancing.

Handtalk (Charlip, Remy)

Helping out photos. by author. Clarion, 1985. ISBN 0-89919-278-5 Subj: Character traits – helpfulness.

It's a baby! ill. by author. Dutton, 1979. Subj: Babies.

Ancona, Mary Beth. *Handtalk* (Charlip, Remy)

Anders, Rebecca. *A look at death* photos. by Maria S. Forrai; foreword by Robert C. Slater. Lerner, 1978. Subj: Death.

A look at prejudice and understanding ill. by Maria S. Forrai. Lerner, 1976. Subj: Prejudice.

Andersen, H. C. (Hans Christian). *The emperor and the nightingale* ill. by James Watling. Troll Assoc., 1979. Subj: Birds – nightingales. Character traits – freedom. Folk and fairy tales. Foreign lands – China.

The emperor's new clothes ill. by Pamela Baldwin-Ford. Troll Assoc., 1979. Translation of Kejserens nye klæder. Subj: Character traits – pride. Clothing. Folk and fairy tales. Humor. Imagination. Royalty.

The emperor's new clothes ill. by Erik Blegvad. Harcourt, 1959. Translation of Kejserens nye klæder by Erik Blegvad. Subj: Character traits – pride. Clothing. Folk and fairy tales. Humor. Imagination. Royalty.

The emperor's new clothes ill. by Virginia Lee Burton. Houghton, 1949. Translation of Kejserens nye klæder. Subj: Character traits – pride. Clothing. Folk and fairy tales. Humor. Imagination. Royalty.

The emperor's new clothes ill. by Jack and Irene Delano. Random House, 1971. Translation of Kejserens nye klæder. Text adapted from Hans Christian Andersen and other sources by Jean Van Leeuwen. Subj: Character traits – pride. Clothing. Folk and fairy tales. Humor. Imagination. Royalty.

The emperor's new clothes ill. by Hélène Desputeaux. Gallery Books, 1984. ISBN 0-8317-2736-5 Subj: Character traits – pride. Clothing. Folk and fairy tales. Humor. Imagination. Royalty.

The emperor's new clothes ill. by Birte Dietz; tr. by M. R. James; adapt. by Jean Van Leeuwen. Van Nostrand, 1972. Translation of Kejserens nye klæder. Subj: Character traits – pride. Clothing. Folk and fairy tales. Humor. Imagination. Royalty.

The emperor's new clothes adapt. by Anthea Bell; ill. by Dorothée Duntze. Holt, 1986. ISBN 0-8050-0010-0 Subj: Character traits – pride. Clothing. Folk and fairy tales. Humor. Imagination. Royalty.

The emperor's new clothes ill. by Jack Kent. Four Winds Pr., 1977. Adaptation of Kejserens nye klæder by Ruth Belov Gross. Subj: Character traits – pride. Clothing. Folk and fairy tales. Humor. Imagination. Royalty.

The emperor's new clothes ill. by Monika Laimgruber. Addison-Wesley, 1973. Translation of Kejserens nye klæder. Subj: Character traits – pride. Clothing. Folk and fairy tales. Humor. Imagination. Royalty.

The emperor's new clothes ill. by Anne F. Rockwell. Crowell, 1982. Translation of Kejserens nye klæder by H. W. Dulcken. Subj: Character traits – pride. Clothing. Folk and fairy tales. Humor. Imagination. Royalty.

The emperor's new clothes adapt. and ill. by Janet Stevens. Holiday, 1985. ISBN 0-8234-0566-4 Subj: Character traits – pride. Clothing. Folk and fairy tales. Humor. Imagination. Royalty.

The emperor's new clothes ill. by Nadine Bernard Westcott. Little, 1984. Subj: Character traits – pride. Clothing. Folk and fairy tales. Humor. Imagination. Royalty.

The emperor's nightingale tr. by Erik Haugaard; ill. by Georges Lemoine. Schocken, 1981. Subj: Birds – nightingales. Character traits – freedom. Folk and fairy tales. Foreign lands – China.

The fir tree ill. by Nancy Ekholm Burkert. Harper, 1970. Translation of Grantræet by H. W. Dulcken. Subj: Folk and fairy tales. Holidays – Christmas. Trees.

It's perfectly true! adapt. and ill. by Janet Stevens. Holiday, 1987. ISBN 0-8234-0672-5 Subj: Behavior – gossip. Character traits – vanity. Death. Folk and fairy tales.

The little match girl ill. by Rachel Isadora. Putnam's, 1987. Translation of Den lille pige med svovlstikkerne. ISBN 0-399-21336-8 Subj: Folk and fairy tales. Holidays – New Year's. Poverty.

The little match girl ill. by Blair Lent. Houghton, 1968. Translation of Den lille pige med svovlstikkerne. Subj: Folk and fairy tales. Holidays – New Year's. Poverty.

The little mermaid tr. by Eva Le Gallienne; ill. by Edward Frascino. Harper, 1971. Subj: Folk and fairy tales. Mythical creatures.

The little mermaid adapt. by Anthea Bell; ill. by Chihiro Iwasaki. Alphabet Pr., 1984. Adaptation of Den lille havfrue. ISBN 0-907234-59-3 Subj: Folk and fairy tales. Mythical creatures.

The little mermaid ill. by Dorothy Pulis Lathrop. Macmillan, 1939. Subj: Folk and fairy tales. Mythical creatures.

The little mermaid ill. by Josef Paleček. Faber, 1981. Translation of Den lille havfrue by M. R. James. Subj: Folk and fairy tales. Mythical creatures.

The little mermaid adapt. by Freya Littledale; ill. by Daniel San Souci. Scholastic, 1986. ISBN 0-590-33590-1 Subj: Folk and fairy tales. Mythical creatures.

The nightingale ill. by Harold Berson. Lippincott, 1962. Subj: Birds – nightingales. Character traits – freedom. Folk and fairy tales. Foreign lands – China.

The nightingale tr. by Eva Le Gallienne; ill. by Nancy Ekholm Burkert. Harper, 1965. Subj: Birds – nightingales. Character traits – freedom. Folk and fairy tales. Foreign lands – China.

The nightingale adapt. by Anna Bier; ill. by Demi. Harcourt, 1985. Adaptation of Nattergalen. ISBN 0-15-257427-1 Subj: Birds – nightingales. Character traits – freedom. Folk and fairy tales. Foreign lands – China. Royalty.

The nightingale adapt. by Alan Benjamin; ill. by Beni Montresor. Crown, 1985. Adaptation of Nattergalen. ISBN 0-517-55211-6 Subj: Birds – nightingales. Character traits – freedom. Folk and fairy tales. Foreign lands – China. Royalty.

The nightingale ill. by Lisbeth Zwerger; tr. from the Danish by Anthea Bell. Alphabet Pr., 1984. Adaptation of Nattergalen. ISBN 0-907234-57-7 Subj: Birds – nightingales. Character traits – freedom. Folk and fairy tales. Foreign lands – China. Royalty.

The old man is always right ill. by Feodor Rojankovsky. Harper, 1940. Subj: Activities – trading. Folk and fairy tales. Humor.

The princess and the pea ill. by Dorothée Duntze. Holt, 1985. ISBN 0-8050-0170-0 Subj: Folk and fairy tales. Royalty. Sleep.

The princess and the pea ill. by Dick Gackenbach. Macmillan, 1983. Subj: Folk and fairy tales. Royalty.

The princess and the pea ill. by Paul Galdone. Seabury Pr., 1978. Translation of Den prindsessen paa aerten. Subj: Folk and fairy tales. Royalty. Sleep.

The princess and the pea adapt. and ill. by Janet Stevens. Holiday, 1982. Subj: Folk and fairy tales. Royalty.

The princess and the pea tr. by Anthea Bell; ill. by Eve Tharlet. Picture Book Studio, 1987. ISBN 0-88708-052-9 Subj: Folk and fairy tales. Royalty. Sleep.

The red shoes tr. from Danish by Anthea Bell; ill. by Chihiro Iwasaki. Alphabet Pr., 1983. Subj: Activities – dancing. Angels. Character traits – pride. Clothing.

The snow queen tr. by Naomi Lewis; ill. by Angela Barrett. Holt, 1988. ISBN 0-8050-00830-6 Subj: Character traits – bravery. Emotions – love. Folk and fairy tales.

The snow queen ill. by Toma Bogdanovic. Scroll Pr., n.d. An adapt. by Naomi Lewis of Sneedrenningen. Subj: Character traits – bravery. Emotions – love. Folk and fairy tales. Foreign lands – Denmark.

The snow queen ill. by June Atkin Corwin. Atheneum, 1968. Subj: Character traits – bravery. Emotions – love. Folk and fairy tales.

The snow queen adapt. by Amy Ehrlich; ill. by Susan Jeffers. Dial Pr., 1982. Subj: Character traits – bravery. Emotions – love. Folk and fairy tales.

The snow queen adapt. by Naomi Lewis; ill. by Errol Le Cain. Viking, 1979. Subj: Character traits – bravery. Emotions – love. Folk and fairy tales.

The snow queen tr. by Eva Le Gallienne; ill. by Arieh Zeldich. Harper, 1985. ISBN 0-06-023695-7 Subj: Character traits – bravery. Emotions – love. Folk and fairy tales.

The snow queen: a fairy tale adapt. by Anthea Bell; ill. by Bernadette Watts. Holt, 1987. First pub. in Sweden under the title Die Schneekönigin. ISBN 0-8050-0485-8 Subj: Character traits – bravery. Emotions. Folk and fairy tales.

The snow queen and other stories from Hans Andersen ill. by Edmund Dulac. Doubleday, 1976. Subj: Folk and fairy tales.

The steadfast tin soldier ill. by Thomas Di Grazia. Prentice-Hall, 1981. Subj: Folk and fairy tales. Toys – soldiers.

The steadfast tin soldier ill. by Paul Galdone. Houghton, 1979. Translation of Den standhaftige tinsoldat. Subj: Folk and fairy tales. Toys – soldiers.

The steadfast tin soldier adapt. by Joel Tuber; ill. by David Jorgensen. Knopf, 1986. ISBN 0-394-88402-7 Subj: Folk and fairy tales. Toys – soldiers.

The steadfast tin soldier ill. by Monika Laimgruber. Atheneum, 1971. Translation of Den standhaftige tinsoldat. Subj: Folk and fairy tales. Toys – soldiers.

The steadfast tin soldier ill. by Alain Vaës. Little, 1983. Translation of Den standhaftige tinsoldat. Subj: Folk and fairy tales. Toys – soldiers.

The swineherd ill. by Erik Blegvad. Harcourt, 1958. Translation of Den svinedrengen by Erik Blegvad. Subj: Character traits – cleverness. Character traits – selfishness. Folk and fairy tales.

The swineherd ill. by Dorothée Duntze. Holt, 1987. Translation of Den svinedrengen by Naomi Lewis. ISBN 0-8050-0232-4 Subj: Character traits – cleverness. Character traits – selfishness. Folk and fairy tales. Royalty.

The swineherd ill. by Lisbeth Zwerger. Morrow, 1982. Translation of Den svinedrengen by Anthea Bell. Subj: Folk and fairy tales. Toys – soldiers.

Thumbelina ill. by Adrienne Adams. Scribner's, 1961. Translation of Tommelise by R. P. Keigwin. Subj: Character traits – smallness. Folk and fairy tales.

Thumbelina ill. by Susan Jeffers; retold by Amy Ehrlich. Dial Pr., 1979. Translation of Tommelise. Subj: Character traits – smallness. Folk and fairy tales.

Thumbelina ill. by Christine Willis Nigognossian. Troll Assoc., 1979. Translation of Tommelise. Subj: Character traits – smallness. Folk and fairy tales.

Thumbelina ill. by Gustaf Tenggren. Simon and Schuster, 1953. Translation of Tommelise. Subj: Character traits – smallness. Folk and fairy tales.

Thumbelina ill. by Lisbeth Zwerger. Morrow, 1980. Translation of Tommelise by Richard and Clara Winston. Subj: Character traits – smallness. Folk and fairy tales.

Thumbeline tr. by Anthea Bell; ill. by Lisbeth Zwerger. Picture Book Studio, 1985. ISBN 0-88708-006-5 Subj: Character traits – smallness. Folk and fairy tales.

The tinderbox ill. by Warwick Hutton Macmillan, 1988. ISBN 0-689-50458-6 Subj: Folk and fairy tales. Magic. Witches.

The ugly duckling ill. by Adrienne Adams. Scribner's, 1965. Translation of Den grimme ælling by R. P. Keigwin. Subj: Birds – ducks. Birds – swans. Character traits – appearance. Character traits – being different. Folk and fairy tales.

The ugly duckling ill. by Lorinda Bryan Cauley. Harcourt, 1979. Subj: Birds – ducks. Birds – swans. Character traits – appearance. Character traits – being different. Folk and fairy tales.

The ugly duckling ill. by Tadasu Izawa and Shigemi Hijikata. Grosset, 1971. Translation of Den grimme ælling by Phyllis Paleček. Subj: Birds – ducks. Birds – swans. Character traits – appearance. Character traits – being different. Folk and fairy tales.

The ugly duckling tr. by Anne Stewart; ill. by Monika Laimgruber. Greenwillow, 1985. ISBN 0-688-04951-6 Subj: Folk and fairy tales.

The ugly duckling ill. by Johannes Larsen. Ward, 1956. Translation of Den grimme ælling by R. P. Keigwin. Subj: Birds – ducks. Birds – swans. Character traits – appearance. Character traits – being different. Folk and fairy tales.

The ugly duckling adapt. by Marianna Mayer; ill. by Thomas Locker. Macmillan, 1987. ISBN 0-02-765130-4 Subj: Birds – ducks. Birds – swans. Character traits – appearance. Character traits – being different. Folk and fairy tales.

The ugly duckling adapt. by Phyllis Hoffman; ill. by Josef Paleček. Abelard-Schuman, 1972. Subj: Birds – ducks. Birds – swans. Character traits – appearance. Character traits – being different. Folk and fairy tales.

The ugly duckling tr. from Spanish by Leland Northam; adapt. by M. Eulalia Valeri; ill. by Maria Ruis. Silver Burdett, 1985. ISBN 0-382-09071-3 Subj: Birds – ducks. Birds – swans. Character traits – appearance. Character traits – being different. Folk and fairy tales. Wordless.

The ugly duckling adapt. by Lilian Moore; ill. by Daniel San Souci. Scholastic, 1987. ISBN 0-590-40957-3 Subj: Birds – ducks. Birds – swans. Character traits – appearance. Character traits – being different. Folk and fairy tales.

The ugly duckling adapt. by Joel Tuber and Clara Stites; ill. by Robert Van Nutt. Knopf, 1986. ISBN 0-394-88403-5 Subj: Birds – ducks. Birds – swans. Character traits – appearance. Character traits – being different. Folk and fairy tales.

The ugly little duck adapt. by Patricia C. and Fredrick McKissack; ill. by Peggy Perry Anderson. Childrens Pr., 1986. Prepared under the direction of Robert Hillerick. ISBN 0-516-03982-2 Subj: Birds – ducks. Birds – swans. Character traits – appearance. Character traits – being different. Folk and fairy tales.

The wild swans tr. from Danish by Naomi Lewis; ill. by Angela Barrett. Harper, 1984. Subj: Birds – swans. Folk and fairy tales. Magic.

The wild swans retold by Amy Ehrlich; ill. by Susan Jeffers. Dial Pr., 1981. Subj: Birds – swans. Folk and fairy tales. Magic.

The woman with the eggs adapt. by Jan Wahl; ill. by Ray Cruz. Crown, 1974. An adaptation of a poem by H. C. Andersen pub. in Den danske bondeven, 1836. Subj: Behavior – greed. Eggs. Folk and fairy tales.

Andersen, Karen Born. *What's the matter, Sylvie, can't you ride?* ill. by author. Dial Pr., 1981. Subj: Emotions. Sports – bicycling.

Anderson, Adrienne Adams *see* Adams, Adrienne

Anderson, C. W. (Clarence Williams). *Billy and Blaze* ill. by author. Macmillan, 1936. Subj: Animals – horses. Birthdays. Family life.

Blaze and the forest fire ill. by author. Macmillan, 1938. Subj: Animals – horses. Fire.

Blaze and the gray spotted pony ill. by author. Macmillan, 1968. Subj: Animals – horses.

Blaze and the gypsies ill. by author. Macmillan, 1937. Subj: Animals – horses. Crime. Gypsies.

Blaze and the Indian cave ill. by author. Macmillan, 1964. Subj: Animals – horses. Cowboys.

Blaze and the lost quarry ill. by author. Macmillan, 1966. Subj: Animals – horses. Cowboys.

Blaze and the mountain lion ill. by author. Macmillan, 1959. Subj: Animals – cougars. Animals – horses. Cowboys.

Blaze and Thunderbolt ill. by author. Macmillan, 1955. Subj: Animals – horses. Cowboys.

Blaze finds forgotten roads ill. by author. Macmillan, 1970. Subj: Animals – horses. Behavior – lost. Cowboys.

Blaze finds the trail ill. by author. Macmillan, 1950. Subj: Animals – horses. Behavior – lost. Cowboys.

Blaze shows the way ill. by author. Macmillan, 1969. Subj: Animals – horses.

The crooked colt ill. by author. Macmillan, 1954. Subj: Animals – horses.

Linda and the Indians ill. by author. Macmillan, 1952. Subj: Animals – horses. Imagination. Indians of North America.

Lonesome little colt ill. by author. Macmillan, 1961. Subj: Animals – horses. Character traits – kindness to animals.

A pony for Linda ill. by author. Macmillan, 1951. Subj: Animals – horses.

A pony for three ill. by author. Macmillan, 1958. Subj: Animals – horses.

The rumble seat pony ill. by author. Macmillan, 1971. Subj: Animals – horses. Character traits – kindness to animals. Parades.

Anderson, Douglas. *Let's draw a story* ill. by author. Sterling, 1959. Subj: Animals – cats. Animals – dogs. Art. Family life. Games.

Anderson, John L. *see* Anderson, Lonzo

Anderson, Joy. *Juma and the magic Jinn* ill. by Charles Mikolaycak. Lothrop, 1986. ISBN 0-688-05444-7 Subj: Behavior – seeking better things. Behavior – wishing. Foreign lands – Africa. Magic. Poetry, rhyme.

Anderson, Leone Castell. *The wonderful shrinking shirt* ill. by Irene Trivas. Albert Whitman, 1983. Subj: Clothing. Humor.

Anderson, Lonzo. *Arion and the dolphins* ill. by Adrienne Adams. Scribner's, 1978. Based on an ancient Greek legend. Subj: Animals – dolphins. Boats, ships. Folk and fairy tales. Foreign lands – Greece.

The day the hurricane happened ill. by Ann Grifalconi. Scribner's, 1974. Subj: Family life. Foreign lands – Caribbean Islands. Weather – storms.

The Halloween party ill. by Adrienne Adams. Scribner's, 1974. Subj: Holidays – Halloween. Parties.

Izzard ill. by Adrienne Adams. Scribner's, 1973. Subj: Foreign lands – Caribbean Islands. Reptiles – lizards.

Mr. Biddle and the birds ill. by Adrienne Adams. Scribner's, 1971. Subj: Activities – flying. Birds.

Two hundred rabbits by Lonzo Anderson and Adrienne Adams; ill. by Adrienne Adams. Viking, 1968. Subj: Animals – rabbits. Fairies. Magic. Royalty.

Anderson, Lucia. *The smallest life around us* ill. by Leigh Grant. Crown, 1978. Subj: Science.

Anderson, Neil *see* Beim, Jerrold

Anderson, Paul S. *Red fox and the hungry tiger* ill. by Robert Kraus. Addison-Wesley, 1962. Subj: Animals – foxes. Animals – tigers. Character traits – cleverness. Friendship.

Anderson, Peggy Perry. *Time for bed, the babysitter said* ill. by author. Houghton, 1987. ISBN 0-395-41851-8 Subj: Activities – baby-sitting. Bedtime. Frogs and toads.

Anderson, Robin. *Sinabouda Lily: a folk tale from Papua New Guinea* ill. by Jennifer Allen. Oxford Univ. Pr., 1979. Subj: Activities – swinging. Folk and fairy tales. Foreign lands – New Guinea. Magic. Witches.

Andre, Evelyn M. *Places I like to be* photos. by author. Abingdon Pr., 1980. Subj: Activities. Poetry, rhyme.

Andrews, F. Emerson (Frank Emerson). *Nobody comes to dinner* ill. by Lydia Dabcovich. Little, 1977. Subj: Behavior – bad day. Emotions – anger. Imagination – imaginary friends.

Andrews, Jan. *Very last first time* ill. by Ian Wallace. Atheneum, 1986. ISBN 0-689-50388-1 Subj: Eskimos. Food. Foreign lands – Canada. Sea and seashore.

Andrews, Wayne. *Snow White and Rose Red* (Grimm, Jacob)

Androcles and the lion ill. by Janusz Grabianski. Watts, 1970. Subj: Animals – lions. Character traits – helpfulness. Character traits – kindness to animals. Folk and fairy tales. Foreign lands – Italy. Religion.

Andry, Andrew C. *Hi, new baby: a book to help your child learn about the new baby* by Andrew C. Andry and Suzanne C. Kratka; ill. by Thomas Di Grazia. Simon and Schuster, 1970. Subj: Babies.

How babies are made by Andrew C. Andry and Steven Schepp; ill. by Blake Hampton. Time-Life, 1968. Subj: Babies. Science.

Angeli, Marguerite De *see* De Angeli, Marguerite

Angelis, Nancy de *see* Angelo, Nancy Carolyn Harrison

Angelo, Nancy Carolyn Harrison. *Camembert* ill. by author. Houghton, 1958. Subj: Animals – mice. Art. Careers – artists. Foreign lands – France.

Angelo, Valenti. *The acorn tree* ill. by author. Viking, 1958. Subj: Animals – chipmunks. Animals – squirrels. Birds – bluejays. Character traits – selfishness. Trees.

The candy basket ill. by author. Viking, 1960. Subj: Animals – mice. Behavior – greed.

Anglund, Joan Walsh. *A is for always: an ABC book* ill. by author. Harcourt, 1968. Subj: ABC books.

A book of good tidings from the Bible ill. by author. Harcourt, 1965. Subj: Religion.

The brave cowboy ill. by author. Harcourt, 1959. Subj: Character traits – bravery. Cowboys. Games.

A Christmas book ill. by author. Random House, 1983. Subj: Holidays – Christmas. Poetry, rhyme.

Christmas is a time of giving ill. by author. Harcourt, 1961. Subj: Character traits – generosity. Holidays – Christmas.

Cowboy and his friend ill. by author. Harcourt, 1961. Subj: Animals – bears. Cowboys. Friendship. Imagination – imaginary friends.

The cowboy's Christmas ill. by author. Atheneum, 1972. Subj: Animals – bears. Cowboys. Holidays – Christmas. Imagination – imaginary friends.

Cowboy's secret life ill. by author. Harcourt, 1963. Subj: Cowboys. Games. Imagination.

A friend is someone who likes you ill. by author. Harcourt, 1958. Subj: Friendship.

The Joan Walsh Anglund story book ill. by author. Random House, 1978. Subj: Poetry, rhyme.

Look out the window ill. by author. Random, 1978. Subj: Character traits – individuality.

Love is a special way of feeling ill. by author. Harcourt, 1960. Subj: Emotions – love.

Love one another ill. by author. Determined Prod., 1981. Subj: Foreign lands. Foreign languages.

Morning is a little child: poems ill. by author. Harcourt, 1969. Subj: Morning. Poetry, rhyme.

Nibble nibble mousekin: a tale of Hansel and Gretel ill. by author. Harcourt, 1962. Subj: Folk and fairy tales. Forest, woods. Witches.

Spring is a new beginning ill. by author. Harcourt, 1963. Subj: Seasons – spring.

Anholt, Catherine. *Chaos at Cold Custard Farm* ill. by author. Oxford Univ. Pr., 1988. ISBN 0-19-520645-2 Subj: Animals. Farms.

Truffles in trouble ill. by author. Little, 1987. ISBN 0-316-04260-9 Subj: Animals – pigs. Shopping. Stores.

Truffles is sick ill. by author. Little, 1987. ISBN 0-316-04259-5 Subj: Animals – pigs. Illness.

Annett, Cora. *The dog who thought he was a boy* ill. by Walter Lorraine. Houghton, 1965. Subj: Animals – dogs. Birthdays. School.

When the porcupine moved in ill. by Peter Parnall. Watts, 1971. Subj: Animals – porcupines. Animals – rabbits. Behavior – trickery.

Annixter, Jane. *Brown rats, black rats* by Jane and Paul Annixter; ill. by Gilbert Riswold. Prentice-Hall, 1977. Subj: Animals – rats. Science.

Annixter, Paul. *Brown rats, black rats* (Annixter, Jane)

Anno, Masaichiro. *Anno's magical ABC* (Anno, Mitsumasa)

Anno, Mitsumasa. *All in a day* by Mitsumasa Anno and others; ill. by Mitsumasa Anno. Putnam's, 1986. ISBN 0-399-21311-2 Subj: Activities. Foreign lands. World.

Anno's Æsop: a book of fables by Æsop and Mr. Fox adapt. and ill. by author. Watts, 1989. ISBN 0-531-08374-8 Subj: Animals – foxes. Folk and fairy tales.

Anno's alphabet: an adventure in imagination ill. by author. Crowell, 1975. Subj: ABC books. Imagination. Optical illusions.

Anno's animals ill. by author. Collins-World, 1979. Subj: Animals. Games. Imagination. Wordless.

Anno's Britain ill. by author. Philomel, 1982. Subj: Foreign lands – England. Games. Humor. Imagination. Wordless.

Anno's counting book ill. by author. Crowell, 1975. Subj: Counting. Imagination. Optical illusions.

Anno's counting house ill. by author. Philomel, 1982. Translation of 10-nin no yukai na hikkoshi. Subj: Counting. Games. Humor. Imagination. Optical illusions. Wordless.

Anno's flea market ill. by author. Philomel, 1984. Translation of Nomi no ichi. Subj: Games. Humor. Imagination. Optical illusions. Wordless.

Anno's Italy ill. by author. Collins-World, 1980. Japanese ed. entitled My journey II, a translation of Tabi no ehon, II. Subj: Foreign lands – Italy. Games. Humor. Imagination. Optical illusions. Wordless.

Anno's journey ill. by author. Collins-World, 1978. Pub. in 1977 under title: My journey, a translation of Tabi no ehon. Subj: Games. Humor. Imagination. Optical illusions. Wordless.

Anno's magical ABC: an anamorphic alphabet by Mitsumasa and Masaichiro Anno; ill. by authors. Putnam's, 1981. Subj: ABC books. Format, unusual – toy and movable books. Games. Imagination. Optical illusions.

Anno's math games ill. by author. Philomel, 1987. ISBN 0-399-21151-9 Subj: Concepts. Counting. Riddles.

Anno's peekaboo ill. by author. Putnam's, 1988. ISBN 0-399-21520-4 Subj: Format, unusual. Wordless.

Anno's U.S.A. ill. by author. Philomel, 1983. Translation of Tabi no ehon, IV. Subj: Games. Humor. Imagination. Wordless.

Dr. Anno's midnight circus ill. by author. Weatherhill, 1972. Subj: Circus. Clowns, jesters. Humor. Imagination. Optical illusions. Wordless.

In shadowland ill. by author. Watts, 1988. ISBN 0-531-08341-1 Subj: Folk and fairy tales. Shadows. Sun.

The king's flower ill. by author. Collins-World, 1979. Subj: Concepts – size. Flowers. Imagination. Royalty.

Topsy-turvies: pictures to stretch the imagination ill. by author. Weatherhill, 1970. Subj: Games. Humor. Imagination. Optical illusions. Wordless.

Upside-downers: more pictures to stretch the imagination adapt. into English by Meredith Weatherby and Susan Trumbull; ill. by author. Weatherhill, 1971. Subj: Games. Humor. Imagination. Optical illusions.

Anrooy, Frans van. *The sea horse* ill. by Jaap Tol. Harcourt, 1968. Originally pub. in Holland under the title of Het Zeepaardje. Subj: Dreams. Emotions – fear. Night. Sea and seashore.

Anthony, Barbara *see* Barber, Antonia

Aoki, Hisako. *Santa's favorite story* by Hisako Aoki and Ivan Gantschev; ill. by authors. Neugebauer, 1982. Subj: Holidays – Christmas. Religion.

Appell, Clara. *Now I have a daddy haircut* by Clara and Morey Appell; photos. by authors. Dodd, 1960. Subj: Behavior – growing up. Careers – barbers. Hair. Self-concept.

Appell, Morey. *Now I have a daddy haircut* (Appell, Clara)

Applebaum, Neil. *Is there a hole in your head?* ill. by author. Ivan Obolensky, 1963. Subj: Animals – whales. Games.

Applebaum, Stan. *Going my way?* by Stan Applebaum and Victoria Cox; ill. by Leonard W. Shortall. Harcourt, 1976. Subj: Animals. Science.

Appleby, Leonard. *Snakes* photos. by author. A & C Black, 1983. Subj: Reptiles – snakes. Science.

Arabian Nights. *Arabian Nights entertainments: the first book of tales of ancient Araby* comp. by Charles Mozley. Watts, 1960. Subj: Folk and fairy tales. Foreign lands – Arabia.

The flying carpet ill. by Marcia Brown. Scribner's, 1956. Subj: Activities – flying. Folk and fairy tales. Magic.

The magic horse (Scott, Sally)

Aragon, Jane Chelsea. *Winter harvest* ill. by Leslie A. Baker. Little, 1989. ISBN 0-316-04937-9 Subj: Animals – deer. Character traits – kindness to animals. Night. Seasons – winter.

Arbeit, Eleanor Werner. *Mrs. cat hides something* ill. by author. Gibbs M. Smith, 1985. ISBN 0-87905-205-8 Subj: Animals – cats. Babies. Family life.

Archambault, John. *Here are my hands* (Martin, Bill (William Ivan))

Knots on a counting rope (Martin, Bill (William Ivan))

Listen to the rain (Martin, Bill (William Ivan))

Up and down on the merry-go-round (Martin, Bill (William Ivan))

White Dynamite and Curly Kidd (Martin, Bill (William Ivan))

Ardizzone, Aingelda. *The night ride* ill. by Edward Ardizzone. Windmill, 1975. Subj: Holidays – Christmas. Night. Toys. Toys – dolls. Toys – teddy bears.

Ardizzone, Edward. *Diana and her rhinoceros* ill. by author. Walck, 1964. Subj: Animals – rhinoceros. Pets.

Johnny the clockmaker ill. by author. Walck, 1960. Subj: Careers – clockmakers. Clocks.

The little girl and the tiny doll ill. by author. Delacorte Pr., 1967. Subj: Behavior – losing things. Shopping. Toys – dolls.

Little Tim and the brave sea captain ill. by author. Walck, 1955. Subj: Boats, ships. Character traits – bravery. Sea and seashore.

Lucy Brown and Mr. Grimes ill. by author. Walck, 1970. A new version of a story published in 1937. Subj: Emotions – loneliness. Foreign lands – England. Old age. Orphans.

Nicholas and the fast-moving diesel ill. by author. Walck, 1959. Subj: Trains. Transportation.

Paul, the hero of the fire ill. by author. Walck, 1963. A new version of a story published in 1949. Subj: Activities – working. Behavior – growing up. Character traits – bravery. Merry-go-rounds.

Peter the wanderer ill. by author. Walck, 1963. Subj: Character traits – bravery. Character traits – cleverness. Character traits – honesty. Sea and seashore.

Ship's cook Ginger ill. by author. Macmillan, 1978. First published in London by Bodley Head, 1977. Subj: Boats, ships. Sea and seashore.

Tim all alone ill. by author. Oxford Univ. Pr., 1957. Subj: Boats, ships. Sea and seashore.

Tim and Charlotte ill. by author. Oxford Univ. Pr., 1951. Subj: Boats, ships. Character traits – bravery. Sea and seashore.

Tim and Ginger ill. by author. Walck, 1965. Subj: Boats, ships. Sea and seashore.

Tim and Lucy go to sea ill. by author. Walck, 1958. Subj: Boats, ships. Friendship. Sea and seashore.

Tim in danger ill. by author. Walck, 1953. Subj: Boats, ships. Sea and seashore.

Tim to the rescue ill. by author. Walck, 1949. Subj: Boats, ships. Character traits – bravery. Character traits – loyalty. Sea and seashore. Weather.

Tim's friend Towser ill. by author. Walck, 1962. Subj: Animals – dogs. Boats, ships. Sea and seashore.

Tim's last voyage ill. by author. Walck, 1972. Subj: Boats, ships. Sea and seashore. Weather – wind.

Argent, Kerry. *One woolly wombat* (Trinca, Rod)

Ariane. *Animal stories* ill. by Feodor Rojankovsky. Western Pub., 1944. Subj: Animals.

Small Cloud ill. by Annie Gusman. Dutton, 1984. ISBN 0-525-44085-2 Subj: Folk and fairy tales. Science. Weather – clouds. Weather – rain.

Arkin, Alan. *Black and white* music by Earl Robinson; ill. by author. Golden Pr., 1966. Subj: Foreign lands – Africa. Music. Songs.

Tony's hard work day ill. by James Stevenson. Harper, 1972. Subj: Activities – working. Family life. Houses.

Armalyte, Olimpija. *How the cock wrecked the manor* (Tempest, P.)

Armer, Laura Adams. *The forest pool* ill. by author. Longman, 1938. Subj: Caldecott award honor book. Forest, woods.

Armitage, David. *Ice creams for Rosie* (Armitage, Ronda)

One moonlit night (Armitage, Ronda)

Armitage, Marcia. *Lupatelli's favorite nursery tales* ill. by Anthony Lupatelli. Grosset, 1977. Subj: Folk and fairy tales.

Armitage, Ronda. *The bossing of Josie* ill. by David Armitage. Elsevier-Dutton, 1980. Subj: Birthdays. Family life. Magic. Sibling rivalry. Witches.

Don't forget, Matilda ill. by David Armitage. Elsevier-Dutton, 1979. Subj: Family life. Foreign lands – England.

Ice creams for Rosie by Ronda and David Armitage; ill. by David Armitage. Elsevier-Dutton, 1981. Subj: Food. Islands. Problem solving.

The lighthouse keeper's lunch ill. by David Armitage. Elsevier-Dutton, 1979. Subj: Birds – sea gulls. Food. Lighthouses. Problem solving.

One moonlit night by Ronda and David Armitage; ill. by David Armitage. Dutton, 1983. Subj: Family life. Night. Sports – camping.

Armour, Richard Willard. *The adventures of Egbert the Easter egg* ill. by Paul Galdone. McGraw-Hill, 1965. Subj: Holidays – Easter. Poetry, rhyme.

Animals on the ceiling ill. by Paul Galdone. McGraw-Hill, 1966. Subj: Animals. Humor. Imagination. Poetry, rhyme.

Have you ever wished you were something else? ill. by Scott Gustafson. Children's Pr., 1983. Subj: Animals. Poetry, rhyme.

Sea full of whales ill. by Paul Galdone. McGraw-Hill, 1974. Subj: Animals – whales. Poetry, rhyme.

The year Santa went modern ill. by Paul Galdone. McGraw-Hill, 1964. Subj: Holidays – Christmas. Poetry, rhyme.

Armstrong, Louise. *How to turn lemons into money: a child's guide to economics* ill. by Bill Basso. Harcourt, 1976. Subj: Activities – working. Money.

Arneson, D. J. *Secret places* ill. by Peter Arnold. Holt, 1971. Subj: Ecology. Forest, woods.

Arnold, Caroline. *The biggest living thing* ill. by author. Carolrhoda Bks., 1983. Subj: Science. Trees.

Everybody has a birthday ill. by Anthony Accardo. Watts, 1987. ISBN 0-531-10094-4 Subj: Birthdays.

Five nests ill. by Ruth Sanderson. Dutton, 1980. Includes index. Subj: Animals. Birds. Science.

Giraffe photos. by Richard Hewett. Morrow, 1987. ISBN 0-688-07070-1 Subj: Animals – giraffes.

How do we communicate? ill. by Ginger Giles. Watts, 1983. Subj: Communication.

How do we have fun? photos. by Ginger Giles. Watts, 1983. Subj: Activities. Activities – playing.

How do we travel? photos. by Ginger Giles. Watts, 1983. Subj: Activities – traveling. Transportation.

Pets without homes ill. by Richard Hewett. Clarion, 1983. Subj: Animals. Pets.

Sun fun ill. by author. Watts, 1981. Subj: Science. Sun.

The terrible Hodag ill. by Lambert Davis. Harcourt, 1989. ISBN 0-15-284750-2 Subj: Behavior – greed. Folk and fairy tales. Forest, woods. Monsters.

What is a community? ill. by Carole Bertole. Watts, 1982. Subj: Careers. Communities, neighborhoods.

What we do when someone dies ill. by Helen K. Davie. Watts, 1987. ISBN 0-531-10095-2 Subj: Death.

What will we buy? photos. by Ginger Giles. Watts, 1983. Subj: Money. Shopping.

Where do you go to school? ill. by Carole Bertole. Watts, 1982. Includes index. Subj: Careers – teachers. Communities, neighborhoods. School.

Who keeps us healthy? ill. by Carole Bertole. Watts, 1982. Subj: Careers – doctors. Careers – nurses.

Who keeps us safe? photos. by Carole Bertole. Watts, 1983. Subj: Careers. Safety.

Who works here? ill. by Carole Bertole. Watts, 1982. Subj: Careers. Communities, neighborhoods.

Zebra photos. by Richard Hewett. Morrow, 1987. ISBN 0-688-07068-X Subj: Animals – zebras.

Arnold, Katrin. *Anna joins in* ill. by Renate Seelig. Abingdon Pr., 1983. Subj: Handicaps. Illness. School.

Arnold, Tedd. *No jumping on the bed!* ill. by author. Dial Pr., 1987. ISBN 0-8037-0039-3 Subj: Bedtime. Behavior – misbehavior. Dreams. Imagination.

Ollie forgot ill. by author. Dial Pr., 1988. ISBN 0-8037-0488-7 Subj: Behavior – forgetfulness. Circular tales. Middle ages. Poetry, rhyme.

Arnold, Tim. *The winter mittens* ill. by author. Macmillan, 1988. ISBN 0-689-50449-7 Subj: Clothing. Magic. Seasons – winter. Weather – snow.

Arnosky, Jim. *Deer at the brook* ill. by author. Lothrop, 1986. ISBN 0-688-04100-0 Subj: Animals – deer.

A kettle of hawks, and other wildlife groups ill. by author. Coward, 1979. Subj: Animals. Birds. Insects. Fish. Poetry, rhyme.

Mouse numbers and letters ill. by author. Harcourt, 1982. Subj: ABC books. Animals – mice. Counting. Wordless.

Mouse writing ill. by author. Harcourt, 1983. Subj: ABC books. Activities – writing. Animals – mice. Birds. Wordless.

Mud time and more: Nathaniel stories ill. by author. Addison-Wesley, 1979. Subj: Problem solving. Wordless.

Outdoors on foot ill. by author. Coward, 1978. Subj: Activities – walking. Humor. Seasons.

Raccoons and ripe corn ill. by author. Lothrop, 1987. ISBN 0-688-05456-0 Subj: Animals – raccoons. Farms. Food. Night.

Watching foxes ill. by author. Lothrop, 1985. ISBN 0-688-04260-0 Subj: Activities – playing. Animals – foxes.

Arnott, Kathleen. *Spiders, crabs and creepy crawlers: two African folktales* ill. by Bette Davis. Garrard, 1978. Subj: Folk and fairy tales. Foreign lands – Africa.

Arnstein, Helene S. *Billy and our new baby* ill. by M. Jane Smyth. Human Sciences Pr., 1973. Subj: Babies. Family life. Sibling rivalry.

Aronin, Ben. *The secret of the Sabbath fish* ill. by Shay Rieger. Jewish Pub. Soc., 1979. Subj: Folk and fairy tales. Food. Format, unusual – board books. Jewish culture.

Arquette, Lois Steinmetz *see* Duncan, Lois

Arthur, Catherine. *My sister's silent world* ill. by Nathan Talbot. Children's Pr., 1979. Subj: Birthdays. Handicaps – deafness. Family life. Senses – hearing. Zoos.

Artis, Vicki Kimmel. *Pajama walking* ill. by Emily Arnold McCully. Houghton, 1981. Subj: Activities – playing. Friendship. Night.

Artzybasheff, Boris. *Seven Simeons* ill. by author. Viking, 1937. Subj: Caldecott award honor book.

Aruego, Ariane *see* Dewey, Ariane

Aruego, José. *A crocodile's tale: a Philippine folk story* by José Aruego and Ariane Dewey; ill. by authors. Scribner's, 1972. Subj: Folk and fairy tales. Foreign lands – Philippines. Reptiles – alligators, crocodiles.

The king and his friends ill. by author. Scribner's, 1969. Subj: Dragons. Friendship. Mythical creatures. Royalty.

Look what I can do ill. by author. Scribner's, 1971. Subj: Animals. Behavior – imitation. Folk and fairy tales. Foreign lands – Philippines. Games.

Pilyo the piranha ill. by author. Macmillan, 1971. Subj: Fish. Foreign lands – South America.

Symbiosis: a book of unusual friendships ill. by author. Scribner's, 1970. Subj: Science.

We hide, you seek by José Aruego and Ariane Dewey; ill. by authors. Greenwillow, 1979. Subj: Animals. Behavior – hiding. Foreign lands – Africa. Games.

Arundel, Anne *see* Arundel, Jocelyn

Arundel, Jocelyn. *Shoes for Punch* ill. by Wesley Dennis. McGraw-Hill, 1964. Subj: Animals – horses.

Arvetis, Chris. *Why does it fly?* by Chris Arvetis and Carole Palmer; ill. by James Buckley. Rand McNally, 1984. ISBN 0-528-82074-5 Subj: Activities – flying. Animals. Science.

Why is it dark? by Chris Arvetis and Carole Palmer; ill. by James Buckley. Rand McNally, 1984. ISBN 0-528-82075-3 Subj: Animals. Concepts. Science.

Asare, Meshack. *Cat... in search of a friend* ill. by author. Kane Miller, 1986. ISBN 0-916291-07-3 Subj: Animals – cats. Behavior – needing someone. Friendship.

Asbjørnsen, P. C. (Peter Christen). *The squire's bride*

The three billy goats Gruff ill. by Marcia Brown. Harcourt, 1957. Subj: Animals – goats. Character traits – cleverness. Cumulative tales. Folk and fairy tales. Mythical creatures. Trolls.

Three billy goats Gruff adapt. by Patricia C. and Fredrick McKissack; ill. by Tom Dunnington. Childrens Pr., 1987. ISBN 0-516-02366-7 Subj: Animals – goats. Character traits – cleverness. Cumulative tales. Folk and fairy tales. Mythical creatures. Trolls.

The three billy goats Gruff ill. by Paul Galdone. Seabury Pr., 1973. Translation of De tre bukkene Bruse. Subj: Animals – goats. Character traits – cleverness. Cumulative tales. Folk and fairy tales. Mythical creatures. Trolls.

The three billy goats Gruff adapt. and ill. by Janet Stevens. Harcourt, 1987. ISBN 0-15-286396-6 Subj: Animals – goats. Character traits – cleverness. Cumulative tales. Folk and fairy tales. Mythical creatures. Trolls.

The three billy goats Gruff ill. by William Stobbs. McGraw-Hill, 1967. Subj: Animals – goats. Character traits – cleverness. Cumulative tales. Folk and fairy tales. Mythical creatures. Trolls.

Asch, Frank. *Bear shadow* ill. by author. Prentice-Hall, 1985. ISBN 0-13-071580-8 Subj: Animals – bears. Shadows.

Bear's bargain ill. by author. Prentice-Hall, 1985. ISBN 0-13-071606-5 Subj: Animals – bears. Birds. Emotions – envy, jealousy.

Bread and honey ill. by author. Parents, 1981. Adapted from the author's Monkey face. Subj: Activities – painting. Animals. Animals – bears. Family life – mothers.

City sandwich ill. by author. Greenwillow, 1978. Subj: City. Imagination. Poetry, rhyme.

Country pie ill. by author. Greenwillow, 1979. Subj: Country. Poetry, rhyme. Weather.

Good lemonade ill. by author. Watts, 1976. Subj: Activities – working. Food.

Goodbye house ill. by author. Prentice-Hall, 1986. ISBN 0-13-360272-9 Subj: Animals – bears. Family life. Moving.

Goodnight horsey ill. by author. Prentice-Hall, 1981. Subj: Animals – horses. Bedtime. Family life – fathers. Games. Imagination.

Happy birthday, moon! ill. by author. Prentice-Hall, 1982. Subj: Animals – bears. Birthdays. Moon.

Just like daddy ill. by author. Prentice-Hall, 1981. Subj: Animals – bears. Behavior – imitation. Family life – fathers.

The last puppy ill. by author. Prentice-Hall, 1980. Subj: Animals – dogs. Pets.

Little Devil's ABC ill. by author. Scribner's, 1979. Subj: ABC books. Devil.

Little Devil's 123 ill. by author. Scribner's, 1979. Subj: Counting. Devil.

MacGoose's grocery ill. by James Marshall. Dial Pr., 1978. Subj: Birds – geese. Eggs.

Moon bear ill. by author. Scribner's, 1978. Subj: Animals – bears. Birds. Food. Moon. Night.

Mooncake ill. by author. Prentice-Hall, 1983. Subj: Animals – bears. Birds. Moon. Seasons – winter.

Moongame ill. by author. Prentice-Hall, 1984. ISBN 0-13-3600503-9 Subj: Activities – dancing. Animals – bears. Behavior – hiding. Moon.

Oats and wild apples ill. by author. Holiday House, 1988. ISBN 0-8234-0677-6 Subj: Animals – bulls, cows. Animals – deer. Friendship.

Popcorn ill. by author. Parents, 1979. Subj: Animals – bears. Food. Holidays – Halloween. Parties.

Rebecka ill. by author. Harper, 1972. Subj: Activities – playing. Animals – dogs. Imagination.

Sand cake ill. by author. Parents, 1979. Subj: Activities – picnicking. Animals – bears. Humor. Sea and seashore.

Skyfire ill. by author. Prentice-Hall, 1984. Subj: Animals – bears. Weather – rainbows.

Starbaby ill. by author. Scribner's, 1980. Subj: Babies. Sea and seashore. Sky. Stars.

Turtle tale ill. by author. Dial Pr., 1978. Subj: Humor. Reptiles – turtles, tortoises.

Yellow, yellow ill. by Mark Alan Stamaty. McGraw-Hill, 1971. Subj: Clothing. Concepts — color.

Asch, George. *Linda* ill. by author. McGraw-Hill, 1969. Subj: City. Emotions — happiness. Wordless.

Aseltine, Lorraine. *First grade can wait* ill. by Virginia Wright-Frierson. Albert Whitman, 1988. ISBN 0-8075-2451-4 Subj: Behavior — growing up. School.

I'm deaf and it's okay by Lorraine Aseltine, Evelyn Mueller and Nancy Tait; ill. by Helen Cogancherry. Albert Whitman, 1986. ISBN 0-8075-3472-2 Subj: Emotions — anger. Emotions — fear. Handicaps — deafness. Senses — hearing.

Ash, Jutta. *Rapunzel* (Grimm, Jacob)

Wedding birds ill. by author. Little, 1987. ISBN 0-87113-122-6 Subj: Birds. Music. Songs. Weddings.

Ashby, Gwynneth. *Take a trip to Japan* ill. by author. Watts, 1980. Subj: Foreign lands — Japan.

Ashey, Bella *see* Breinburg, Petronella

Ashley, Bernard. *Dinner ladies don't count* ill. by Janet Duchesne. Watts, 1981. Subj: Behavior — misbehavior. Birthdays. Problem solving. School.

Asimov, Isaac. *Animals of the Bible* ill. by Howard Berelson. Doubleday, 1978. ISBN 0-385-07215-5 Subj: Animals.

The best new things ill. by Symeon Shimin. Collins-World, 1971. Subj: Earth. Science. Space and space ships.

The moon ill. by Alex Ebel. Follett, 1967. Subj: Moon. Science.

At the farm ill. by Roser Capdevila. Firefly Pr., 1985. ISBN 0-920303-08-0 Subj: Farms. Format, unusual — board books.

Atene, Ann. *The golden guitar* ill. by author. Little, 1967. Subj: Foreign lands — Italy. Music. Puppets.

Atene, Anna *see* Atene, Ann

Attenberger, Walburga. *The little man in winter* ill. by author. Random House, 1972. Translation of Het mannetje in de winter. Subj: Foreign lands — Germany. Poetry, rhyme. Seasons — winter.

Who knows the little man? ill. by author. Random House, 1972. Translation of Wie kent dat kleine mannetje? Subj: Foreign lands — Germany. Poetry, rhyme.

Attenborough, Elizabeth. *Walk rabbit walk* (McNaughton, Colin)

Atwood, Ann. *The little circle* ill. by author. Scribner's, 1967. Subj: Concepts — shape. Poetry, rhyme.

Atwood, Margaret. *Anna's pet* by Margaret Atwood and Joyce Barkhouse; ill. by Ann Blades. Lorimer, 1980. Subj: Animals. Character traits — optimism. Country. Pets.

Auerbach, Julie Jaslow. *Everything's changing - It's pesach!* ill. by Chari Radin. Kar-Ben Copies, 1986. ISBN 0-930494-53-9 Subj: Holidays — Passover. Jewish culture. Poetry, rhyme.

Auerbach, Marjorie. *King Lavra and the barber* ill. by author. Knopf, 1964. Subj: Behavior — secrets. Careers — barbers. Folk and fairy tales. Royalty.

Augarde, Stephen *see* Augarde, Steve

Augarde, Steve. *Barnaby Shrew, Black Dan and... the mighty wedgwood* ill. by author. Elsevier-Dutton, 1980. Subj: Animals — mice. Animals — rats. Animals — shrews. Behavior — boasting. Birds — parakeets, parrots. Reptiles — turtles, tortoises.

Barnaby Shrew goes to sea ill. by author. Elsevier-Dutton, 1979. Subj: Animals — rats. Animals — shrews. Boats, ships. Reptiles — turtles, tortoises.

Pig ill. by author. Bradbury Pr., 1977. Subj: Animals — pigs. Farms. Fire.

Aulaire, Edgar Parin d'. *Abraham Lincoln* (Aulaire, Ingri Mortenson d')

Animals everywhere (Aulaire, Ingri Mortenson d')

Children of the northlights (Aulaire, Ingri Mortenson d')

Don't count your chicks (Aulaire, Ingri Mortenson d')

East of the sun and west of the moon (Aulaire, Ingri Mortenson d')

Foxie, the singing dog (Aulaire, Ingri Mortenson d')

Nils (Aulaire, Ingri Mortenson d')

Ola (Aulaire, Ingri Mortenson d')

Pocahontas (Aulaire, Ingri Mortenson d')

The terrible troll-bird (Aulaire, Ingri Mortenson d')

Too big (Aulaire, Ingri Mortenson d')

The two cars (Aulaire, Ingri Mortenson d')

Wings for Per (Aulaire, Ingri Mortenson d')

Aulaire, Ingri Mortenson d'. *Abraham Lincoln* by Ingri and Edgar Parin d'Aulaire; ill. by authors. Doubleday, 1939, 1957. Subj: Caldecott award book. U.S. history.

Animals everywhere by Ingri and Edgar Parin d'Aulaire; ill. by authors. Doubleday, 1940. Subj: Animals.

Children of the northlights by Ingri and Edgar Parin d'Aulaire; ill. by authors. Viking, 1962. Subj: Activities — bathing. Activities — playing. Animals. Family life. Folk and fairy tales. Foreign lands — Lapland. School. Seasons — winter.

Don't count your chicks by Ingri and Edgar Parin d'Aulaire; ill. by authors. Doubleday, 1943. Subj: Behavior – greed. Birds – chickens. Folk and fairy tales. Humor.

East of the sun and west of the moon ed. by Ingri and Edgar Parin d'Aulaire; ill. by eds. Doubleday, 1969. Subj: Folk and fairy tales.

Foxie, the singing dog by Ingri and Edgar Parin d'Aulaire; ill. by authors. Doubleday, 1949. Subj: Animals – cats. Animals – dogs. Birds – chickens.

Nils by Ingri and Edgar Parin d'Aulaire; ill. by authors. Doubleday, 1948. Subj: Character traits – being different. Cowboys. Family life. School.

Ola by Ingri and Edgar Parin d'Aulaire; ill. by authors. Doubleday, 1932. Subj: Foreign lands – Norway.

Pocahontas by Ingri and Edgar Parin d'Aulaire; ill. by authors. Doubleday, 1946. Subj: Indians of North America. U.S. history.

The terrible troll-bird by Ingri and Edgar Parin d'Aulaire; ill. by authors. Doubleday, 1976. Subj: Foreign lands – Norway. Mythical creatures. Trolls.

Too big by Ingri and Edgar Parin d'Aulaire; ill. by authors. Doubleday, 1945. Subj: Behavior – growing up. Concepts – size.

The two cars by Ingri and Edgar Parin d'Aulaire; ill. by authors. Doubleday, 1955. Subj: Automobiles.

Wings for Per by Ingri and Edgar Parin d'Aulaire; ill. by authors. Doubleday, 1944. Subj: Activities – flying. Character traits – bravery. Farms. War.

Austin, Margot. *Barney's adventure* ill. by author. Dutton, 1941. Subj: Circus. Clowns, jesters.

Growl Bear ill. by author. Dutton, 1951. Subj: Animals – bears. Emotions – loneliness.

Manuel's kite string ill. by author. Scribner's, 1943. Subj: Cumulative tales. Folk and fairy tales.

Trumpet ill. by author. Dutton, 1926. Subj: Animals – dogs. Teeth.

Willamet way ill. by author. Scribner's, 1941. Subj: Activities – traveling. Animals – dogs. U.S. history.

Averill, Esther. *The fire cat* ill. by author. Harper, 1960. Subj: Animals – cats. Careers – firefighters.

Jenny and the cat club ill. by author. Harper, 1973. Subj: Animals – cats.

Jenny's adopted brothers ill. by author. Harper, 1952. Subj: Animals – cats. Character traits – kindness to animals. Emotions – envy, jealousy.

Jenny's birthday book ill. by author. Harper, 1954. Subj: Animals – cats. Birthdays. Parties.

Jenny's first party ill. by author. Harper, 1948. Subj: Animals – cats. Parties.

Jenny's moonlight adventure ill. by author. Harper, 1949. Subj: Animals – cats. Holidays – Halloween. Night.

When Jenny lost her scarf ill. by author. Harper, 1951. Subj: Animals – cats. Character traits – bravery. Fire.

Avery, Kay. *Wee willow whistle* ill. by Winifred Bromhall. Knopf, 1947. Subj: Activities – whistling. Family life. Farms. Toys.

Axworthy, Anni. *Ben's Wednesday* ill. by author. David & Charles, 1986. ISBN 0-340-33289-1 Subj: Dreams. Monsters. Night.

Ayal, Ora. *The adventures of Chester the chest* by Ora Ayal and Naomi Löw Nakao; ill. by Ora Ayal. Harper, 1982. Subj: Activities – flying. Behavior – boredom. Imagination.

Ugbu tr. by Naomi Löw Nakao; ill. by author. Harper, 1979. Subj: Activities – playing. Imagination.

Ayars, James Sterling. *Caboose on the roof* ill. by Bob Hodgell. Abelard-Schuman, 1956. Subj: Houses. Humor. Trains.

Contrary Jenkins (Caudill, Rebecca)

Ayer, Jacqueline. *Little Silk* ill. by author. Harcourt, 1970. Subj: Behavior – lost. Toys – dolls.

Nu Dang and his kite ill. by author. Harcourt, 1959. Subj: Behavior – losing things. Foreign lands – Thailand. Kites. Toys.

The paper-flower tree: a tale from Thailand ill. by author. Harcourt, 1962. Subj: Character traits – optimism. Foreign lands – Thailand. Plants.

A wish for little sister ill. by author. Harcourt, 1962. Subj: Behavior – wishing. Birds. Birthdays. Family life. Foreign lands – Thailand.

Aylesworth, Jim. *The bad dream* ill. by Judith Friedman. Albert Whitman, 1985. ISBN 0-8075-0506-4 Subj: Animals – dogs. Dreams. Family life. Sleep.

Hanna's hog ill. by Glen Rounds. Atheneum, 1988. ISBN 0-689-31367-5 Subj: Animals – pigs. Behavior – stealing. Behavior – trickery.

Hush up! ill. by Glen Rounds. Holt, 1980. Subj: Character traits – laziness. Humor. Noise, sounds.

Mary's mirror ill. by Richard Egielski. Holt, 1982. Subj: Behavior – greed. Emotions – envy, jealousy. Poetry, rhyme.

One crow: a counting rhyme ill. by Ruth Young. Harper, 1988. ISBN 0-397-32175-9 Subj: Animals. Counting. Farms. Poetry, rhyme.

Shenandoah Noah ill. by Glen Rounds. Holt, 1985. ISBN 0-03-003749-2 Subj: Activities – working. Emotions – embarrassment. Humor.

Siren in the night ill. by Tom Centola. Albert Whitman, 1983. Subj: Activities – walking. Emotions – fear. Family life. Noise, sounds.

Tonight's the night ill. by John Wallner. Albert Whitman, 1981. Subj: Bedtime. Dreams. Night. Sleep.

Two terrible frights ill. by Eileen Christelow. Atheneum, 1987. ISBN 0-689-31327-6 Subj: Animals – mice. Emotions – fear. Night.

Ayres, Pam. *Guess what?* ill. by Julie Lacome. Knopf, 1988. ISBN 0-394-99287-3 Subj: Poetry, rhyme.

Guess who? ill. by Julie Lacome. Knopf, 1988. ISBN 0-394-99288-1 Subj: Poetry, rhyme.

When dad cuts down the chestnut tree ill. by Percy Graham. Knopf, 1988. ISBN 0-394-90435-4 Subj: Family life – fathers. Nature. Poetry, rhyme. Trees.

When dad fills in the garden pond ill. by Percy Graham. Knopf, 1988. ISBN 0-394-90441-4 Subj: Activities – digging. Family life – fathers. Nature. Poetry, rhyme.

Azaad, Meyer. *Half for you* ill. by Nāhîd Ḥaqîqāt. Carolrhoda, 1971. Subj: Behavior – sharing. Birds. Careers. Clothing.

Azarian, Mary. *A farmer's alphabet* ill. by author. Godine, 1981. Subj: ABC books. Activities. Farms.

The tale of John Barleycorn or, From barley to beer: a traditional English ballad ill. by author. Godine, 1983. Subj: Folk and fairy tales. Food. Foreign lands – England. Middle ages. Music. Poetry, rhyme.

B. B. Blacksheep and Company: *a collection of favorite nursery rhymes* ill. by Nick Butterworth. Grosset, 1982. Subj: Animals. Nursery rhymes.

Baba, Noboru. *Eleven cats and a pig* ill. by author. Carolrhoda Books, 1988. ISBN 0-87614-338-9 Subj: Animals – cats. Behavior – misbehavior. Character traits – selfishness.

Eleven cats and albatrosses ill. by author. Carolrhoda Books, 1988. ISBN 0-87614-335-4 Subj: Animals – cats. Behavior – misbehavior. Character traits – selfishness.

Eleven cats in a bag ill. by author. Carolrhoda Books, 1988. ISBN 0-87614-336-2 Subj: Animals – cats. Behavior – misbehavior. Character traits – selfishness.

Eleven hungry cats ill. by author. Carolrhoda Books, 1988. ISBN 0-87614-337-0 Subj: Animals – cats. Behavior – misbehavior. Character traits – selfishness.

Babbitt, Lorraine. *Pink like the geranium* ill. by author. Children's Pr., 1973. Subj: Behavior. Clothing. Family life. School.

Babbitt, Natalie. *The something* ill. by author. Farrar, 1970. Subj: Emotions – fear. Monsters. Night.

Babbitt, Samuel F. *The forty-ninth magician* ill. by Natalie Babbitt. Pantheon, 1966. Subj: Magic. Royalty.

The babes in the woods. *The old ballad of the babes in the woods* ed. by Kathleen Lines; ill. by Edward Ardizzone. Walck, 1972. Derived from a Chapbook ed. published in 1640. Subj: Folk and fairy tales. Orphans. Poetry, rhyme.

Baby's first book of colors ill. by Nina Barbaresi. Platt, 1986. ISBN 0-448-10827-5 Subj: Animals – rabbits. Concepts – color. Format, unusual – board books.

Baby's words photos. sel. by Debby Slier. Macmillan, 1988. ISBN 0-02-688751-7 Subj: Babies. Format, unusual – board books. Language.

Bach, Alice. *The day after Christmas* ill. by Mary Chalmers. Harper, 1975. Subj: Emotions. Holidays – Christmas.

Millicent the magnificent ill. by Steven Kellogg. Harper, 1978. Subj: Animals – bears. Circus. Emotions – envy, jealousy. Family life.

The smartest bear and his brother Oliver ill. by Steven Kellogg. Harper, 1975. ISBN 0-06-020335-8 Subj: Animals – bears. Family life. Food. Sibling rivalry. Sleep.

Warren Weasel's worse than measles ill. by Hilary Knight. Harper, 1980. Subj: Animals – bears. Animals – weasels. Self-concept.

Bach, Othello. *Hector McSnector and the mail-order Christmas witch* ill. by Timothy Hildebrandt. Caedmon, 1984. ISBN 0-89845-342-9 Subj: Holidays – Christmas. Magic. Witches.

Lilly, Willy and the mail-order witch ill. by Timothy Hildebrandt. Caedmon, 1983. Subj: Activities – working. Imagination. Magic. Music. Poetry, rhyme. Witches.

Back, Christine. *Bean and plant* photos. by Barrie Watts. Silver Burdett, 1986. ISBN 0-382-09286-4 Subj: Plants. Science. Seeds.

Chicken and egg photos. by Bo Jarner. Silver Burdett, 1986. ISBN 0-382-09284-8 Subj: Birds – chickens. Eggs. Science.

Spider's web photos. by Barrie Watts. Silver Burdett, 1986. ISBN 0-382-09288-8 Subj: Science. Spiders.

Tadpole and frog photos. by Barrie Watts. Silver Burdett, 1986. ISBN 0-382-09285-6 Subj: Frogs and toads. Science.

Bacon, Joan Chase *see* Bowden, Joan Chase

Baer, Edith. *Words are like faces* ill. by Karen Gundersheimer. Pantheon, 1980. Subj: Language. Poetry, rhyme.

Bagwell, Elizabeth. *This is an airport* (Bagwell, Richard)

Bagwell, Richard. *This is an airport* by Richard and Elizabeth Bagwell; photos. by Lee Balterman. Follett, 1967. Subj: Airplanes, airports. Transportation.

Bahlke, Valerie Worth *see* Worth, Valerie

Bahr, Amy C. *It's ok to say no: a book for parents and children to read together* ill. by Frederick Bennett Green. Grosset, 1986. ISBN 0-448-15328-9 Subj: Behavior – talking to strangers. Safety. Self-concept.

Sometimes it's ok to tell secrets: a book for parents and children to read together ill. by Frederick Bennett Green. Grosset, 1986. ISBN 0-448-15325-4 Subj: Behavior – secrets. Safety. Self-concept.

What should you do when...? a book for parents and children to read together ill. by Frederick Bennett Green. Grosset, 1986. ISBN 0-448-15327-0 Subj: Safety. Self-concept.

Your body is your own: a book for parents and children to read together ill. by Frederick Bennett Green. Grosset, 1986. ISBN 0-448-15326-2 Subj: Safety. Self-concept.

Bahr, Robert. *Blizzard at the zoo* ill. by Consuelo Joerns. Lothrop, 1982. Subj: Animals. Weather – snow. Weather – storms. Zoos.

Bailey, Jill. *Eyes* photos. by Jim Bailey. Putnam's, 1984. Subj: Anatomy. Animals. Birds. Format, unusual – board books.

Feet photos. by Jim Bailey. Putnam's, 1984. Subj: Anatomy. Animals. Birds. Format, unusual – board books.

Mouths photos. by Jim Bailey. Putnam's, 1984. Subj: Anatomy. Animals. Birds. Format, unusual – board books.

Noses photos. by Jim Bailey. Putnam's, 1984. Subj: Anatomy. Animals. Format, unusual – board books.

Bains, Rae. *Hiccups, hiccups* ill. by Otto Coontz. Troll Assoc., 1981. Subj: Illness.

Baird, Anne. *Baby socks* ill. by author. Morrow, 1984. ISBN 0-688-02436-X Subj: Babies. Clothing. Format, unusual – board books.

Kiss, kiss ill. by author. Morrow, 1984. ISBN 0-688-02493-9 Subj: Babies. Family life. Format, unusual – board books.

Little tree ill. by author. Morrow, 1984. ISBN 0-688-02421-9 Subj: Format, unusual – board books. Trees.

No sheep ill. by author. Morrow, 1984. ISBN 0-688-02377-0 Subj: Bedtime. Format, unusual – board books.

Baisch, Cris. *When the lights went out* ill. by Ulises Wensell. Putnam's, 1987. ISBN 0-399-21415-1 Subj: Family life. Lights. Power failure.

Baker, Alan. *Benjamin and the box* ill. by author. Lippincott, 1978. Subj: Animals – hamsters. Friendship.

Benjamin bounces back ill. by author. Lippincott, 1978. Subj: Animals – hamsters. Humor. Imagination.

Benjamin's book ill. by author. Lothrop, 1983. Subj: Animals – hamsters. Behavior – misbehavior. Humor.

Benjamin's dreadful dream ill. by author. Lippincott, 1980. Subj: Animals – hamsters. Behavior – misbehavior. Humor.

Benjamin's portrait ill. by author. Lothrop, 1987. ISBN 0-688-06878-2 Subj: Activities – painting. Animals – hamsters. Behavior – bad day. Careers – artists. Concepts – color. Humor.

Baker, Barbara. *Digby and Kate* ill. by Marsha Winborn. Dutton, 1988. ISBN 0-525-44370-3 Subj: Animals – cats. Animals – dogs. Friendship.

Baker, Betty. *And me, coyote!* ill. by Maria Horvath. Macmillan, 1982. Subj: Animals – coyotes. Character traits – cleverness. Folk and fairy tales. Indians of North America. Religion.

Latki and the lightning lizard ill. by Donald Carrick. Macmillan, 1979. Subj: Animals. Character traits – bravery. Folk and fairy tales. Indians of North America. Reptiles – lizards.

Little runner of the longhouse ill. by Arnold Lobel. Harper, 1962. Subj: Cumulative tales. Family life. Indians of North America.

My sister says ill. by Tricia Taggart. Macmillan, 1984. Subj: Behavior – wishing. Boats, ships. Family life – fathers. Imagination. Sibling rivalry.

Partners ill. by Emily Arnold McCully. Greenwillow, 1978. Subj: Animals – badgers. Animals – coyotes. Character traits – cleverness. Character traits – helpfulness. Character traits – laziness. Farms. Friendship.

The pig war ill. by Robert Lopshire. Harper, 1969. Subj: U.S. history.

Rat is dead and ant is sad: based on a Pueblo Indian tale ill. by Mamoru Funai. Harper, 1981. Subj: Cumulative tales. Death. Emotions – sadness. Indians of North America. Folk and fairy tales.

Sonny-Boy Sim ill. by Susanne Suba. Rand McNally, 1948. Subj: Animals. Family life. Humor. Sports – hunting.

Three fools and a horse ill. by Glen Rounds. Macmillan, 1975. Subj: Animals – horses. Humor. Indians of North America.

Turkey girl ill. by Harold Berson. Macmillan, 1983. Based on a traditional Zuni tale. Subj: Activities – working. Behavior – wishing. Birds – turkeys. Folk and fairy tales. Indians of North America.

Worthington Botts and the steam machine ill. by Sal Murdocca. Macmillan, 1981. Subj: Activities – reading. Humor. Machines.

Baker, Bonnie Jeanne. *A pear by itself* ill. by author. Children's Pr., 1982. Subj: Counting.

Baker, Charlotte. *Little brother* ill. by author. McKay, 1959. Subj: Animals – dogs. Babies. Emotions – envy, jealousy. Family life. Sibling rivalry.

Baker, Donna. *I want to be a librarian* ill. by Richard Wahl. Children's Pr., 1978. Subj: Careers – librarians. Libraries.

I want to be a pilot ill. by Richard Wahl. Children's Pr., 1978. Subj: Careers – airplane pilots. Airplanes, airports.

I want to be a police officer ill. by Richard Wahl. Children's Pr., 1978. Subj: Careers – police officers.

Baker, Eugene. *Bicycles* ill. by Tom Dunnington. Creative Ed., 1980. Subj: Animals. Safety. Sports – bicycling.

Fire ill. by Tom Dunnington. Creative Ed., 1980. Subj: Animals. Fire. Safety.

Home ill. by Tom Dunnington. Creative Ed., 1980. Subj: Animals. Safety.

I want to be a computer operator ill. by Tom Dunnington. Children's Pr., 1973. Subj: Careers. Machines.

Outdoors ill. by Tom Dunnington. Creative Ed., 1980. Subj: Animals. Safety.

School ill. by Tom Dunnington. Creative Ed., 1980. Subj: Animals. Safety. School.

Water ill. by Tom Dunnington. Creative Ed., 1980. Subj: Animals. Safety.

Baker, Gayle. *Special delivery: a book for kids about cesarean and vaginal birth* ill. by Debra Hillyer. Chas. Franklin Pr., 1981. Subj: Babies. Family life – mothers. Hospitals. Science.

Baker, Jeannie. *Grandmother* ill. by author. Elsevier-Dutton, 1979. Subj: Art. Family life – grandmothers.

Home in the sky ill. by author. Greenwillow, 1984. Subj: Animals – dogs. Birds – pigeons. Character traits – kindness to animals. City.

Millicent ill. by author. Elsevier-Dutton, 1980. Subj: Birds – pigeons. Character traits – individuality. City.

One hungry spider ill. by author. Elsevier-Dutton, 1983. Subj: Counting. Science. Spiders.

Where the forest meets the sea ill. by author. Greenwillow, 1987. ISBN 0-688-06364-0 Subj: Ecology. Foreign lands – Australia. Forest, woods.

Baker, Jeffrey J. W. *Patterns of nature* photos. by Jaroslav Salek. Doubleday, 1967. Subj: Animals. Birds. Flowers. Plants. Science. Trees.

Baker, Jill. *Basil of Bywater Hollow* ill. by Lynn Bywaters Ferris. Holt, 1987. ISBN 0-8050-0268-5 Subj: Animals – bears. Fairs. Weather – rain.

Baker, Laura Nelson. *The friendly beasts* ill. by Nicolas Sidjakov. Parnassus, 1958. Adapt. from an old English Christmas carol of the same title. Subj: Animals. Holidays – Christmas. Music.

O children of the wind and pines ill. by Inez Storer. Lippincott, 1967. Subj: Holidays – Christmas. Indians of North America. Music.

Baker, Leslie A. *The third-story cat* ill. by author. Little, 1987. ISBN 0-316-07832-8 Subj: Animals – cats. Behavior – running away.

Baker, Margaret. *A puppy called Spinach* by Margaret and Mary Baker; ill. by Mary Baker. Dodd, 1939. Subj: Animals – dogs. Behavior – misbehavior.

Baker, Mary. *A puppy called Spinach* (Baker, Margaret)

Baker, Olaf. *Where the buffaloes begin* ill. by Stephen Gammell. Subj: Animals – buffaloes. Caldecott award honor book. Folk and fairy tales. Indians of North America.

Baker, Pamela J. *My first book of sign* ill. by Patricia Bellan Gillen. Gallaudet Univ. Pr., 1986. ISBN 0-930323-20-3 Subj: Handicaps – deafness. Language. Senses – hearing.

Baker, Sanna Anderson. *Who's a friend of the water-spurting whale* handlettered and ill. by Tomie de Paola. David C. Cook, 1987. ISBN 0-89191-587-7 Subj: Poetry, rhyme. Religion.

Bakken, Harold. *The special string* ill. by Mischa Richter. Prentice-Hall, 1981. Subj: Character traits – helpfulness. Humor. Problem solving. String. Wordless.

Baldner, Gaby. *Joba and the wild boar: Joba und das wildschwein* ill. by Gerhard Oberländer. Hastings, 1961. Text in English and German. Subj: Animals – pigs. Character traits – bravery. Foreign languages. Pets.

Balestrino, Philip. *Fat and skinny* ill. by Pam Makie. Crowell, 1975. Subj: Character traits – appearance.

Hot as an ice cube ill. by Tomie de Paola. Crowell, 1971. Subj: Concepts. Science.

Balet, Jan B. *Amos and the moon* ill. by author. Oxford Univ. Pr., 1948. Subj: Moon.

The fence: a Mexican tale ill. by author. Delacorte Pr., 1969. Translation of Der Zaun. Subj: Family life. Folk and fairy tales. Foreign lands – Mexico. Poverty. Problem solving.

Five Rollatinis ill. by author. Lippincott, 1959. Subj: Animals – horses. Circus. Family life.

The gift: a Portuguese Christmas tale ill. by author. Delacorte, 1967. Subj: Foreign lands – Portugal. Holidays – Christmas. Religion.

Joanjo: a Portuguese tale ill. by author. Delacorte Pr., 1967. Subj: Character traits – ambition. Dreams. Fish. Foreign lands – Portugal.

The king and the broom maker ill. by author. Delacorte, 1968. Translation of König und der Besenbinder. Subj: Behavior – dissatisfaction. Royalty.

Ned and Ed and the lion ill. by author. Oxford Univ. Pr., 1949. Subj: Animals – lions. Imagination. Twins.

Balian, Lorna. *Amelia's nine lives* ill. by author. Abingdon Pr., 1986. ISBN 0-687-01250-3 Subj: Animals – cats. Behavior – lost. Pets.

Bah! Humbug? ill. by author. Abingdon, 1977. Subj: Holidays – Christmas.

A garden for a groundhog ill. by author. Abingdon Pr., 1985. ISBN 0-687-14009-9 Subj: Activities – gardening. Animals – groundhogs. Farms. Holidays – Groundhog Day.

Humbug potion: an A B Cipher ill. by author. Abingdon, 1984. Subj: ABC books. Magic. Secret codes. Witches.

Humbug rabbit ill. by author. Abingdon, 1974. Subj: Animals – rabbits. Family life – grandmothers. Holidays – Easter.

Humbug witch ill. by author. Abingdon, 1965. Subj: Holidays – Halloween. Witches.

Leprechauns never lie ill. by author. Abingdon, 1980. Subj: Animals – cats. Elves and little people. Folk and fairy tales. Foreign lands – Ireland. Humor.

Sometimes it's turkey ill. by author. Abingdon, 1973. Subj: Birds – turkeys. Holidays – Thanksgiving.

A sweetheart for Valentine ill. by author. Abingdon, 1979. Subj: Giants. Holidays – Valentine's Day. Weddings.

Where in the world is Henry? ill. by author. Bradbury Pr., 1972. Subj: Concepts – size. Science.

Balterman, Marcia Ridlon *see* Ridlon, Marcia

Balzano, Jeanne. *The wee moose* ill. by Enrico Arno. Parents, 1964. Subj: Animals – mice. Farms.

Balzola, Asun. *Munia and the day things went wrong* ill. by author. Cambridge Univ. Pr., 1988. ISBN 0-521-35643-1 Subj: Behavior – bad day. Family life.

Munia and the orange crocodile ill. by author. Cambridge Univ. Pr., 1988. ISBN 0-521-35642-3 Subj: Dreams. Reptiles – alligators, crocodiles. Teeth.

Bambi ill. by Christa Stephan. Imported Pubs., 1983. Subj: Format, unusual – board books. Toys. Wordless.

Banbery, Fred. *Paddington at the circus* (Bond, Michael)

Banchek, Linda. *Snake in, snake out* ill. by Elaine Arnold. Crowell, 1978. Subj: Birds – parakeets, parrots. Concepts – in and out. Concepts – opposites. Reptiles – snakes. Wordless.

Bancroft, Laura *see* Baum, L. Frank (Lyman Frank)

Bang, Betsy. *The cucumber stem* ill. by Tony Chen. Greenwillow, 1980. Adapt. from a Bengali folk tale. Subj: Character traits – smallness. Folk and fairy tales. Foreign lands – India.

The old woman and the red pumpkin ill. by Molly Bang. Macmillan, 1975. Adapt. and tr. from a Bengali folk tale by Betsy Bang. Subj: Animals. Character traits – cleverness. Folk and fairy tales. Foreign lands – India.

The old woman and the rice thief ill. by Molly Bang. Greenwillow, 1978. Adapt. and tr. from a Bengali folk tale by Betsy Bang. Subj: Animals. Character traits – cleverness. Folk and fairy tales. Foreign lands – India.

Tutuni the tailor bird ill. by Molly Bang. Greenwillow, 1978. Adapt. and tr. from a Bengali folk tale by Betsy Bang. Subj: Birds. Folk and fairy tales. Foreign lands – India. Royalty.

Bang, Molly. *Dawn* ill. by author. Morrow, 1983. An adaptation of the Japanese folk tale: Tsuru Nyōbō. Also known as The Crane Wife. Subj: Activities – weaving. Behavior – secrets. Birds – cranes. Character traits – curiosity. Folk and fairy tales. Foreign lands – Japan.

Delphine ill. by author. Morrow, 1988. ISBN 0-688-05637-7 Subj: Animals. Sports – bicycling.

The grey lady and the strawberry snatcher ill. by author. Four Winds Pr., 1980. Subj: Caldecott award honor book. Imagination. Wordless.

The paper crane ill. by author. Greenwillow, 1985. ISBN 0-688-04109-4 Subj: Birds – cranes. Character traits – kindness. Folk and fairy tales.

Ten, nine, eight ill. by author. Greenwillow, 1983. ISBN 0-688-00907-7 Subj: Bedtime. Caldecott award honor book. Counting. Ethnic groups in the U.S. – Afro-Americans. Poetry, rhyme.

Tye May and the magic brush ill. by author. Greenwillow, 1981. ISBN 0-688-84290-9 Subj: Activities – painting. Royalty.

Wiley and the hairy man: adapted from an American folk tale ill. by author. Macmillan, 1976. Subj: Bedtime. Character traits – cleverness. Ethnic groups in the U.S. – Afro-Americans. Folk and fairy tales. Monsters.

Bangs, Edward. *Yankee Doodle* ill. by Steven Kellogg. Parents, 1976. Subj: Songs. U.S. history.

Baningan, Sharon Stearns. *Circus magic* ill. by Katharina Maillard. Dutton, 1958. Subj: Circus. Magic. Poetry, rhyme.

Banish, Roslyn. *I want to tell you about my baby.* Wingbow Pr., 1982. Subj: Babies. Family life.

Let me tell you about my baby photos. by author. Harper, 1988. ISBN 0-06-020383-8 Subj: Babies. Family life.

Bank Street College of Education. *Around the city* ill. by Aurelius Battaglia and others. Rev. ed. Macmillan, 1972. Subj: City.

Green light, go ill. by Jack Endewelt and others. Rev. ed. Subj: City. Traffic, traffic signs.

In the city ill. by Dan Dickas. Rev. ed. Macmillan, 1972. Subj: City.

My city ill. by Ron Becker and others. Macmillan, 1965. Subj: City.

People read ill. by Dan Dickas. Rev. ed. Macmillan, 1972. Subj: Activities – reading. Careers.

Uptown, downtown ill. by Ron Becker and others. Macmillan, 1965. Subj: City.

Banks, Kate. *Alphabet soup* ill. by Peter Sis. Knopf, 1988. ISBN 0-394-99151-6 Subj: Family life. Food. Imagination.

Bannerman, Helen. *Sambo and the twins* ill. by author. Lippincott, 1937. Subj: Folk and fairy tales. Foreign lands – India.

The story of little black Sambo ill. by author. Lippincott, 1943. Subj: Animals – tigers. Character traits – cleverness. Foreign lands – India.

The story of the teasing monkey ill. by author. Lippincott, 1907. Subj: Animals – lions. Animals – monkeys.

Bannon, Laura. *The best house in the world* ill. by author. Houghton, 1952. Subj: Animals. Houses. Imagination.

Hat for a hero: a Tarasean boy of Mexico ill. by author. Albert Whitman, 1954. Subj: Character traits – bravery. Clothing. Foreign lands – Mexico.

Katy comes next ill. by author. Albert Whitman, 1959. Subj: Toys – dolls.

Little people of the night ill. by author. Houghton, 1963. Subj: Animals. Emotions – fear. Night.

Manuela's birthday ill. by author. Albert Whitman, 1972. Orig. pub. in 1939. Subj: Birthdays. Foreign lands – Mexico. Toys – dolls.

Red mittens ill. by author. Houghton, 1946. Subj: Animals. Behavior – losing things. Clothing.

The scary thing ill. by author. Houghton, 1956. Subj: Animals. Emotions – fear.

Watchdog ill. by author. Albert Whitman, 1948. Subj: Animals – dogs. Foreign lands – Mexico. Holidays – Cinco de Mayo. Pets.

Baran, Tancy. *Bees* ill. by author. Grosset, 1971. Subj: Insects – bees. Science.

Barbaresi, Nina. *Firemouse* ill. by author. Crown, 1987. ISBN 0-517-56337-1 Subj: Animals – cats. Animals – mice. Careers – firefighters.

Barbato, Juli. *From bed to bus* ill. by Brian Schatell. Macmillan, 1985. ISBN 0-02-708380-2 Subj: Family life. Morning.

Mom's night out ill. by Brian Schatell. Macmillan, 1985. ISBN 0-02-708480-9 Subj: Family life – fathers. Food.

Barber, Antonia. *The enchanter's daughter* ill. by Errol Le Cain. Farrar, 1988. ISBN 0-374-32170-1 Subj: Birds. Magic. Wizards.

Satchelmouse and the dinosaurs ill. by Claudio Muñoz. Barron's, 1988. ISBN 0-8120-5872-0 Subj: Dinosaurs. Imagination. Magic.

Satchelmouse and the doll's house ill. by Claudio Muñoz. Barron's, 1988. ISBN 0-8120-5873-9 Subj: Character traits – kindness. Toys – dolls.

Barbour, Karen. *Little Nino's pizzeria* ill. by author. Harcourt, 1987. ISBN 0-15-247650-4 Subj: Family life. Food.

Barchilon, Jacques. *The authentic Mother Goose fairy tales and nursery rhymes.* Alan Swallow, 1960. Subj: Nursery rhymes.

Barden, Rosalind. *TV monster* ill. by author. Crown, 1989. ISBN 0-517-56934-5 Subj: Monsters. Space and space ships. Television.

Bare, Colleen Stanley. *Guinea pigs don't read books* photos. by author. Dodd, 1985. ISBN 0-396-08538-5 Subj: Animals – guinea pigs. Pets.

To love a cat photos. by author. Dodd, 1986. ISBN 0-396-08834-1 Subj: Animals – cats. Pets.

To love a dog photos. by author. Dodd, 1987. ISBN 0-396-09057-5 Subj: Animals – dogs. Pets.

Baring, Maurice. *The blue rose* ill. by Anne Dalton. Heinemann, 1987. ISBN 0-7182-2100-1 Subj: Folk and fairy tales. Royalty.

Barker, Carol. *Achilles and Diana* (Bates, H. E.)

Achilles the donkey (Bates, H. E.)

Barker, Cicely Mary. *Berry flower fairies* ill. by author. Putnam's, 1981. Subj: Fairies. Flowers. Poetry, rhyme.

Blossom flower fairies ill. by author. Putnam's, 1981. Subj: Fairies. Flowers. Poetry, rhyme.

Flower fairies of the seasons ill. by author. Harper, 1984. First published in 1923. Subj: Fairies. Flowers. Poetry, rhyme. Seasons. Trees.

Spring flower fairies ill. by author. Putnam's, 1981. Subj: Fairies. Flowers. Poetry, rhyme.

Summer flower fairies ill. by author. Putnam's, 1981. Subj: Fairies. Flowers. Poetry, rhyme.

Barker, George. *Why teddy bears are brown* (Barker, Inga-Lil)

Barker, Inga-Lil. *Why teddy bears are brown* by Inga-Lil and George Barker; ill. by authors. Crowell, 1946. Subj: Behavior – greed. Toys – teddy bears.

Barker, Melvern J. *Country fair.* Oxford Univ. Pr., 1955. Subj: Animals – bulls, cows. Fairs.

Little island star. Oxford Univ. Pr., 1954. Subj: Lighthouses.

Barker, Peggy. *What happened when grandma died* ill. by Patricia Mattozzi. Concordia, 1984. Subj: Death. Family life – grandmothers. Religion.

Barkhouse, Joyce. *Anna's pet* (Atwood, Margaret)

Barklem, Jill. *Autumn story* ill. by author. Putnam's, 1980. Subj: Animals – mice. Behavior – lost. Seasons – fall.

The big book of Brambly Hedge ill. by author. Putnam's, 1981. Subj: Animals – mice. Country.

The high hills ill. by author. Philomel, 1986. ISBN 0-399-21361-9 Subj: Activities – traveling. Animals – mice.

The secret staircase ill. by author. Putnam's, 1983. Subj: Animals – mice. Behavior – secrets. Food. Problem solving. Seasons – winter.

Spring story ill. by author. Putnam's, 1980. Subj: Animals – mice. Birthdays. Seasons – spring.

Summer story ill. by author. Putnam's, 1980. Subj: Animals – mice. Seasons – summer. Weddings.

Winter story ill. by author. Putnam's, 1980. Subj: Animals – mice. Seasons – winter. Weather – snow.

Barner, Bob. *Elephant facts* ill. by author. Dutton, 1979. Subj: Animals – elephants. Science.

Barnes-Murphy, Rowan. *One, two, buckle my shoe*

Barnett, Naomi. *I know a dentist* ill. by Linda Boehm. Putnam's, 1977. Subj: Careers – dentists. Teeth.

Barnhart, Peter. *The wounded duck* ill. by Adrienne Adams. Scribner's, 1979. Subj: Birds – ducks. Character traits – kindness to animals. Death. Seasons – winter.

Barr, Cathrine. *A horse for Sherry* ill. by author. Walck, 1963. Subj: Animals – horses. Farms.

Hound dog's bone ill. by author. Walck, 1961. Subj: Animals – dogs. Animals – foxes. Behavior – stealing. Humor.

Little Ben ill. by author. Walck, 1960. Subj: Animals – beavers. Character traits – bravery.

Sammy seal ov the sircus ill. by author. [1st initial teaching alphabet ed.] Walck, 1955, 1964. Subj: Animals – seals. Circus. Clowns, jesters.

Barr, Jene. *Fire snorkel number 7* ill. by Joe Rogers. Albert Whitman, 1965. Subj: Careers – firefighters. Fire. Trucks.

Barrett, John M. *The bear who slept through Christmas.* Ideals, 1980. Subj: Animals – bears. Hibernation. Holidays – Christmas. Humor.

The Easter bear. Children's Pr., 1981. Subj: Animals – bears. Animals – rabbits. Holidays – Easter. Seasons – spring.

Oscar the selfish octopus ill. by Joe Servello. Human Sciences Pr., 1978. Subj: Character traits – selfishness. Octopuses.

Barrett, Judi. *Animals should definitely not act like people* ill. by Ron Barrett. Atheneum, 1980. Subj: Animals. Behavior – imitation.

Animals should definitely not wear clothing ill. by Ron Barrett. Atheneum, 1974. Subj: Animals. Behavior – imitation. Clothing.

An apple a day ill. by Tim Lewis. Atheneum, 1973. Subj: Food. Illness.

Benjamin's 365 birthdays ill. by Ron Barrett. Atheneum, 1974. Subj: Birthdays.

Cloudy with a chance of meatballs ill. by Ron Barrett. Atheneum, 1978. Subj: Family life – grandfathers. Food. Imagination. Weather.

I hate to go to bed ill. by Ray Cruz. Four Winds Pr., 1977. Subj: Bedtime. Imagination.

I hate to take a bath ill. by Charles B. Slackman. Atheneum, 1981. Subj: Behavior – growing up. Concepts – size.

I'm too small, you're too big ill. by David S. Rose. Atheneum, 1981. Subj: Behavior – growing up. Concepts – opposites. Family life – fathers.

Old MacDonald had an apartment house ill. by Ron Barrett. Atheneum, 1969. Subj: Activities – gardening. City. Farms.

Peter's pocket ill. by Julia Noonan. Atheneum, 1974. Subj: Clothing.

Pickles have pimples ill. by Lonni Sue Johnson. Atheneum, 1986. ISBN 0-689-31187-7 Subj: Poetry, rhyme.

Snake is totally tail ill. by L. S. Johnson. Atheneum, 1983. Subj: Animals. Insects. Reptiles.

What's left? ill. by author. Atheneum, 1983. Subj: Participation. Problem solving

Barrett, Lawrence Louis. *Twinkle, the baby colt.* Knopf, 1945. Subj: Animals – horses. Behavior – running away.

Barrett, N. S. *Airliners* ill. by Tony Bryan. Watts, 1985. ISBN 0-531-03720-7 Subj: Airplanes, airports.

Helicopters ill. by Tony Bryan. Watts, 1985. ISBN 0-531-03721-5 Subj: Helicopters.

Motorcycles ill. by Tony Bryan. Watts, 1985. ISBN 0-531-03783-5 Subj: Motorcycles.

Racing cars ill. by Tony Bryan. Watts, 1985. ISBN 0-531-03784-3 Subj: Automobiles. Sports – racing.

Trucks ill. by Tony Bryan. Watts, 1985. ISBN 0-531-03723-1 Subj: Trucks.

Barrie, J. M. (James M.). *Peter Pan* ill. by Diane Goode. Random House, 1983. Subj: Elves and little people. Folk and fairy tales.

Barrie, James M. Ogilvy Gavin Sir *see* Barrie, J. M. (James M.)

Barrows, Marjorie Wescott. *The book of favorite Muggins Mouse stories* ill. by Anne Sellers Leaf. Rand McNally, 1965. Subj: Animals – mice.

Fraidy cat ill. by Barbara Maynard. Rand McNally, 1942. Subj: Animals – cats. Character traits – bravery. Format, unusual.

The funny hat ill. by Norv Mink. Rand McNally, 1943. Subj: Behavior – losing things. Clothing. Format, unusual.

Muggins' big balloon ill. by Anne Sellers Leaf. Rand McNally, 1967. Subj: Animals – mice. Toys – balloons.

Muggins Mouse ill. by Anne Sellers Leaf. Rand McNally, 1965. Subj: Animals – mice.

Muggins takes off ill. by Anne Sellers Leaf. Rand McNally, 1964. Subj: Animals – mice.

Timothy Tiger ill. by Keith Ward. Rand McNally, 1943. Subj: Animals – tigers.

Barrows, R. M. *see* Barrows, Marjorie Wescott

Barry, Katharina. *A is for anything* ill. by author. Harcourt, 1961. Subj: ABC books. Poetry, rhyme.

A bug to hug ill. by author. Harcourt, 1964. Subj: Imagination. Poetry, rhyme. Problem solving.

Barry, Robert E. *Animals around the world* ill. by author. McGraw-Hill, 1967. Subj: ABC books. Animals. Poetry, rhyme.

Mr. Willowby's Christmas tree ill. by Paul Galdone. McGraw-Hill, 1963. Subj: Holidays – Christmas. Poetry, rhyme. Trees.

Next please ill. by author. Houghton, 1961. Subj: Careers – barbers. Zoos.

Barth, Edna. *Jack-o'-lantern* ill. by Paul Galdone. Seabury Pr., 1974. Subj: Behavior – trickery. Character traits – meanness. Folk and fairy tales. Holidays – Halloween.

Barthelme, Donald. *The slightly irregular fire engine: or, The hithering thithering djinn* ill. by author. Farrar, 1971. Collage ill. made from nineteenth-century engravings. Subj: Imagination.

Bartlett, Margaret Farrington. *The clean brook* ill. by Aldren Auld Watson. McGraw-Hill, 1960. Subj: Science.

Down the mountain: a book about the ever-changing soil ill. by Rhys Caparn. Addison-Wesley, 1963. Subj: Science.

Raindrop stories (Bassett, Preston R.)

Where the brook begins ill. by Aldren Auld Watson. Crowell, 1961. Subj: Science.

Bartlett, Robert Merrill. *Jack Horner and song of sixpence* ill. by Emily N. Barto. Longman, 1943. Subj: Nursery rhymes.

Bartlett, Susan. *A book to begin on libraries* ill. by Gioia Fiammenghi. Holt, 1964. Subj: Libraries.

Barto, Emily N. *Chubby bear* ill. by author. Longman, 1941. Subj: Animals – bears. Poetry, rhyme.

Bartoli, Jennifer. *In a meadow, two hares hide* ill. by Takeo Ishida; ed. by Kathy Pacini. Albert Whitman, 1978. Subj: Animals – rabbits. Seasons – winter.

Nonna ill. by Joan Drescher. Harvey House, 1975. Subj: Death. Emotions – sadness. Family life. Family life – grandmothers.

Snow on bear's nose: a story of a Japanese moon bear cub ed. by Caroline Rubin; ill. by Takeo Ishida. Albert Whitman, 1972. Subj: Animals – bears. Behavior – lost. Foreign lands – Japan. Hibernation. Seasons – winter. Weather – snow.

Barton, Byron. *Airplanes* ill. by author. Crowell, 1986. ISBN 0-690-04532-8 Subj: Airplanes, airports.

Airport ill. by author. Crowell, 1982. Subj: Airplanes, airports. Careers – airplane pilots. Transportation.

Boats ill. by author. Crowell, 1986. ISBN 0-690-04563-0 Subj: Boats, ships.

Building a house ill. by author. Greenwillow, 1981. Subj: Houses.

Buzz, buzz, buzz ill. by author. Macmillan, 1973. Subj: Cumulative tales. Insects – bees.

Harry is a scaredy-cat ill. by author. Macmillan, 1974. Subj: Circus. Emotions – fear.

I want to be an astronaut ill. by author. Crowell, 1988. ISBN 0-690-04744-4 Subj: Careers – astronauts. Character traits – ambition. Space and space ships.

Jack and Fred ill. by author. Macmillan, 1974. Subj: Animals – dogs. Animals – rabbits. Pets.

Machines at work ill. by author. Harper, 1987. ISBN 0-690-04573-5 Subj: Activities – working. Machines.

Trains ill. by author. Crowell, 1986. ISBN 0-690-04534-4 Subj: Trains.

Trucks ill. by author. Crowell, 1986. ISBN 0-690-04530-1 Subj: Trucks.

Wheels ill. by author. Crowell, 1979. Subj: Progress. Wheels.

Where's Al? ill. by author. Seabury Pr., 1972. Subj: Animals – dogs. Behavior – lost. Wordless.

Barton, Pat. *A week is a long time* ill. by Jutta Ash. Academy Chicago Ltd., 1980. Subj: Country. Clothing.

Bartos-Hoppner, Barbara. *The Pied Piper of Hamelin* tr. by Anthea Bell; ill. by Annegert Fuchshuber. Lippincott, 1987. Adapt. of the poem The pied piper of Hamelin by Robert Browning. ISBN 0-397-32240-2 Subj: Animals – rats. Behavior – trickery. Folk and fairy tales. Foreign lands – Germany.

Baruch, Dorothy. *I would like to be a pony and other wishes* ill. by Mary Chalmers. Harper, 1959. Subj: Behavior – wishing. Poetry, rhyme.

Kappa's tug-of-war with the big brown horse: the story of a Japanese water imp ill. by Sanryo Sakai. Tuttle, 1962. Subj: Animals. Elves and little people. Farms. Folk and fairy tales. Foreign lands – Japan.

Bascom, Joe. *Malcolm Softpaws* ill. by author. Lippincott, 1958. Subj: Animals – cats. Behavior – greed. Character traits – selfishness.

Malcolm's job ill. by author. Lippincott, 1959. Subj: Animals – cats. Family life. Music.

Base, Graeme. *Animalia* ill. by author. Abrams, 1987. ISBN 0-8109-1868-4 Subj: ABC books. Animals.

My grandma lived in Gooligulch ill. by author. Australian Book Serv., 1988, 1983. ISBN 0-944176-01-1 Subj: Animals. Family life – grandmothers. Foreign lands – Australia. Poetry, rhyme.

Bash, Barbara. *Desert giant: the world of the Saguaro cactus* ill. by author. Little, 1988. ISBN 0-316-08301-1 Subj: Desert. Plants.

Bashevis, Isaac *see* Singer, Isaac Bashevis

Basile, Giambattista. *Petrosinella: a Neapolitan Rapunzel* adapt. by John Edward Taylor; ill. by Diane Stanley. Warne, 1981. Subj: Folk and fairy tales. Foreign lands – Italy. Royalty. Witches.

Basile, Gloria Vitanza *see* Morgan, Michaela

Baskin, Hosie. *A book of dragons* ill. by Leonard Baskin. Knopf, 1985. ISBN 0-394-96298-2 Subj: Dragons.

Baskin, Leonard. *Hosie's alphabet* ill. by author; words by Hosea, Tobias and Lisa Baskin. Viking, 1972. Subj: ABC books. Caldecott award honor book. Children as authors.

Hosie's aviary ill. by author; words mostly by Tobias Baskin and others. Viking, 1979. Subj: Birds. Children as authors.

Hosie's zoo ill. by author; words by Tobias Baskin and others. Viking, 1981. Subj: Animals. Poetry, rhyme. Zoos.

Baskin, Tobias. *Hosie's aviary* (Baskin, Leonard)

Hosie's zoo (Baskin, Leonard)

Bason, Lillian. *Castles and mirrors and cities of sand* ill. by Allan Eitzen. Lothrop, 1968. Subj: Animals. Sand. Science.

Pick a raincoat, pick a whistle ill. by Allan Eitzen. Lothrop, 1966. Subj: Activities – whistling. Trees.

Those foolish Molboes! ill. by Margot Tomes. Coward, 1977. Subj: Behavior – hiding things. Character traits – cleverness. Character traits – foolishness. Folk and fairy tales. Foreign lands – Denmark.

Bass, Donna. *The tale of the dark crystal* ill. by Bruce McNally. Holt, 1982. Subj: Elves and little people. Folk and fairy tales. Magic. Monsters.

Bassett, Lisa. *Beany and Scamp* ill. by Jeni Bassett. Dodd, 1987. ISBN 0-396-08822-8 Subj: Animals – bears. Animals – squirrels. Behavior – losing things. Behavior – lost. Seasons – winter.

A clock for Beany ill. by Jeni Bassett. Dodd, 1985. ISBN 0-396-08484-2 Subj: Animals. Animals – bears. Birthdays. Clocks.

Bassett, Preston R. *Raindrop stories* by Preston R. Bassett and Margaret Farrington Bartlett; ill. by Jim Arnosky. Four Winds Pr., 1981. Subj: Noise, sounds. Weather – rain.

Basso, Bill. *The top of the pizzas* ill. by author. Dodd, 1977. Subj: Activities – working. Food. Monsters.

Bastin, Marjolein. *Vera dresses up* ill. by author. Barron's, 1985. ISBN 0-8120-5691-4 Subj: Animals – mice. Clothing.

Bate, Lucy. *How Georgina drove the car very carefully from Boston to New York* ill. by Tamar Taylor. Crown, 1989. ISBN 0-517-57142-0 Subj: Activities – traveling. Family life – grandparents. Imagination.

Little rabbit's loose tooth ill. by Diane de Groat. Crown, 1975. Subj: Animals – rabbits. Fairies. Teeth.

Bate, Norman. *Vulcan* ill. by author. Scribner's, 1961. Subj: Machines.

What a wonderful machine is a submarine ill. by author. Scribner's, 1961. Subj: Boats, ships. Sea and seashore.

Who built the bridge? ill. by author. Crown, 1975. Subj: Machines.

Who built the highway? ill. by author. Scribner's, 1953. Subj: Machines. Roads.

Bates, H. E. *Achilles and Diana* by H. E. Bates and Carol Barker; ill. by Carol Barker. Dobson, 1963. Subj: Animals – donkeys.

Achilles the donkey by H. E. Bates and Carol Barker; ill. by Carol Barker. Watts, 1963. Subj: Animals – donkeys. Behavior – running away.

Bates, Herbert Ernest *see* Bates, H. E.

Batherman, Muriel. *Animals live here* ill. by author. Greenwillow, 1979. Subj: Animals. Science.

Some things you should know about my dog ill. by author. Prentice-Hall, 1976. Subj: Animals – dogs.

Battles, Edith. *One to teeter-totter* ill. by Rosalind Fry. Albert Whitman, 1973. Subj: Emotions – loneliness. Family life. Friendship. Games.

The terrible terrier ill. by Tom Funk. Addison-Wesley, 1972. Subj: Animals – dogs. Behavior – greed.

The terrible trick or treat ill. by Tom Funk. Addison-Wesley, 1970. Subj: Behavior – greed. Holidays – Halloween.

What does the rooster say, Yoshio? ill. by Toni Hormann. Albert Whitman, 1978. Subj: Animals. Foreign lands – Japan. Language.

Bauer, Caroline Feller. *Midnight snowman* ill. by Catherine Stock. Atheneum, 1987. ISBN 0-689-31294-6 Subj: Seasons – winter. Snowmen. Weather – snow.

My mom travels a lot ill. by Nancy Winslow Parker. Warne, 1981. Subj: Careers. Family life – mothers.

Rainy day: stories and poems ill. by Michele Chessare. Lippincott, 1986. ISBN 0-397-32105-8 Subj: Poetry, rhyme. Weather – rain.

Snowy day: stories and poems ill. by Margot Tomes. Lippincott, 1986. ISBN 0-397-32177-5 Subj: Poetry, rhyme. Weather – snow.

Too many books! ill. by Diane Paterson. Viking, 1986. ISBN 0-670-81130-0 Subj: Activities – reading. Behavior – collecting things. Libraries.

Bauer, Helen. *Good times in the park* photos. by Hubert A. Lowman. Melmont, 1954. Subj: Activities – playing. Birthdays. Zoos.

Baugh, Dolores M. *Bikes* by Dolores M. Baugh and Marjorie P. Pulsifer; ill. by Eve Hoffmann. Rev. ed. Chandler, 1965. Subj: Sports – bicycling. Traffic, traffic signs.

Let's go by Dolores M. Baugh and Marjorie P. Pulsifer; ill. by Eve Hoffmann. Noble, 1970. Subj: Stores.

Let's see the animals by Dolores M. Baugh and Marjorie P. Pulsifer; ill. by Eve Hoffmann. Chandler, 1965. Subj: Animals.

Let's take a trip by Dolores M. Baugh and Marjorie P. Pulsifer; ill. by Richard Szumski and others. Chandler, 1965. Subj: Libraries. Machines.

Slides by Dolores M. Baugh and Marjorie P. Pulsifer; ill. by Eve Hoffmann. Noble, 1970. Subj: Activities – playing.

Supermarket by Dolores M. Baugh and Marjorie P. Pulsifer; ill. by Eve Hoffmann. Noble, 1970. Subj: Food. Shopping. Stores.

Swings by Dolores M. Baugh and Marjorie P. Pulsifer; ill. by Eve Hoffmann. Noble, 1970. Subj: Activities – playing. Activities – swinging.

Trucks and cars to ride by Dolores M. Baugh and Marjorie P. Pulsifer; ill. by Eve Hoffmann. Noble, 1970. Subj: Automobiles. Trucks. Transportation.

Baum, Arline. *One bright Monday morning* by Arline and Joseph Baum; ill. by Joseph Baum. Random House, 1962. Subj: Counting. Seasons – spring. Weather.

Opt: an illusionary tale by Arline and Joseph Baum; ill. by authors. Viking, 1987. ISBN 0-670-80870-9 Subj: Birthdays. Optical illusions. Royalty.

Baum, Joseph. *One bright Monday morning* (Baum, Arline)

Opt (Baum, Arline)

Baum, L. Frank (Lyman Frank). *Mother Goose in prose* ill. by Maxfield Parrish. Bounty Books, 1901. Subj: Nursery rhymes.

Baum, Louis. *JuJu and the pirate* ill. by Philippe Matter. Harper, 1984. Subj: Activities – traveling. Birds – parakeets, parrots. Pirates.

One more time ill. by Paddy Bouma. Morrow, 1986. ISBN 0-688-06587-2 Subj: Divorce. Family life – fathers.

Baum, Willi. *Birds of a feather* ill. by author. Addison-Wesley, 1969. Subj: Birds. Wordless.

Baumann, Hans. *Chip has many brothers* ill. by Eric Carle. Philomel, 1985. ISBN 0-399-21283-3 Subj: Animals. Character traits – kindness to animals. Folk and fairy tales. Magic.

The hare's race ill. by Antoni Boratynski; tr. from the German by Elizabeth D. Crawford. Morrow, 1976. Subj: Animals – rabbits. Folk and fairy tales. Reptiles – turtles, tortoises. Sports – racing.

Baumann, Kurt. *The paper airplane* ill. by Fulvio Testa. Little, 1982. Subj: Airplanes, airports. Imagination.

Piro and the fire brigade ill. by Jiri Bernard. Faber, 1981. Translation of: Piro und die Feuerwehr. Subj: Animals – dogs. Careers – firefighters. Character traits – bravery. Fire. Foreign lands – Switzerland.

The prince and the lute ill. by Jean Claverie. North-South, 1986. First pub. in Switzerland under the title Der Prinz und die Laute. ISBN 0-03-008018-5 Subj: Character traits – kindness. Folk and fairy tales. Royalty. War.

Puss in boots (Perrault, Charles)

The story of Jonah tr. from German by Jock Curle; ill. by Allison Reed. Holt, 1987. ISBN 0-8050-233-2 Subj: Animals – whales. Behavior – misbehavior.

Bawden, Nina. *Princess Alice* ill. by Phillida Gili. Dutton, 1986. ISBN 0-233-97746-5 Subj: Adoption. Family life. Royalty.

St. Francis of Assisi ill. by Pascale Allamand. Lothrop, 1983. Subj: Character traits – generosity. Religion.

William Tell ill. by Pascale Allamand. Lothrop, 1981. Subj: Character traits – bravery. Folk and fairy tales. Foreign lands – Switzerland.

Bax, Martin. *Edmond went far away* ill. by Michael Foreman. Harcourt, 1989. ISBN 0-15-225105-7 Subj: Activities – walking. Animals. Farms.

Bayar, Ilene. *Rachel and Mischa* (Bayar, Steven)

Bayar, Steven. *Rachel and Mischa* by Steven and Ilene Bayar; ill. by Marlene Lobell Ruthen; photos. by Joanne Strauss. Kar-Ben Copies, 1988. ISBN 0-930-49477-6 Subj: Character traits – freedom. Jewish culture. Religion.

Bayer, Jane. *A my name is Alice* ill. by Steven Kellogg. Dial Pr., 1984. Subj: ABC books. Animals. Names.

Bayley, Nicola. *Crab cat* ill. by author. Knopf, 1984. Subj: Animals – cats. Imagination.

Elephant cat ill. by author. Knopf, 1984. Subj: Animals – cats. Imagination.

Nicola Bayley's book of nursery rhymes ill. by author. Knopf, 1975. Subj: Nursery rhymes.

One old Oxford ox ill. by author. Atheneum, 1977. Subj: Animals. Counting.

Parrot cat ill. by author. Knopf, 1984. Subj: Animals – cats. Imagination.

Polar bear cat ill. by author. Knopf, 1984. Subj: Animals – cats. Imagination.

Spider cat ill. by author. Knopf, 1984. Subj: Animals – cats. Imagination.

Baylor, Byrd. *Amigo* ill. by Garth Williams. Macmillan, 1963. Subj: Animals – prairie dogs. Pets. Poetry, rhyme.

The best town in the world ill. by Ronald Himler. Scribner's, 1983. Subj: City.

Coyote cry ill. by Symeon Shimin. Lothrop, 1972. Subj: Animals – coyotes. Animals – dogs.

The desert is theirs ill. by Peter Parnall. Scribner's, 1975. Subj: Caldecott award honor book. Desert. Ecology. Folk and fairy tales. Indians of North America. Poetry, rhyme.

Desert voices ill. by Peter Parnall. Scribner's, 1981. Subj: Animals. Desert. Poetry, rhyme.

Everybody needs a rock ill. by Peter Parnall. Scribner's, 1974. Subj: Poetry, rhyme. Rocks.

A God on every mountain top: stories of southwest Indian sacred mountains ill. by Carol Brown. Scribner's, 1981. Subj: Folk and fairy tales. Indians of North America.

Guess who my favorite person is ill. by Robert Andrew Parker. Scribner's, 1977. Subj: Friendship. Games.

Hawk, I'm your brother ill. by Peter Parnall. Scribner's, 1976. Subj: Birds – hawks. Caldecott award honor book. Character traits – freedom. Indians of North America.

I'm in charge of celebrations ill. by Peter Parnall. Scribner's, 1986. ISBN 0-684-18579-2 Subj: Desert. Nature.

Moon song ill. by Ronald Himler. Scribner's, 1982. Subj: Animals – coyotes. Folk and fairy tales. Indians of North America. Moon.

The other way to listen ill. by Peter Parnall. Scribner's, 1978. Subj: Nature. Poetry, rhyme.

The way to start a day ill. by Peter Parnall. Scribner's, 1978. Subj: Caldecott award honor book. Folk and fairy tales. Foreign lands. Religion. Sun.

We walk in sandy places ill. by Marilyn Schweitzer. Scribner's, 1976. Subj: Animals. Desert.

When clay sings ill. by Tom Bahti. Scribner's, 1972. Subj: Art. Caldecott award honor book. Indians of North America.

Your own best secret place ill. by Peter Parnall. Scribner's, 1979. Subj: Behavior – hiding things. Behavior – secrets.

Baynes, Pauline. *How dog began* ill. by author. Holt, 1987. ISBN 0-8050-0011-9 Subj: Animals – dogs. Animals – wolves. Caves.

Baynton, Martin. *Fifty and the fox* ill. by author. Crown, 1986. ISBN 0-517-56069-0 Subj: Animals – foxes. Farms. Machines.

Fifty and the great race ill. by author. Crown, 1987. ISBN 0-517-56354-1 Subj: Fairs. Farms. Machines. Sports – racing.

Fifty gets the picture ill. by author. Crown, 1987. ISBN 0-517-56355-X Subj: Activities – digging. Careers – artists. Farms. Machines.

Fifty saves his friend ill. by author. Crown, 1986. ISBN 0-517-56022-4 Subj: Animals – rats. Farms. Friendship. Machines.

Beach, Stewart. *Good morning, sun's up!* ill. by Yutaka Sugita. Scroll Pr., 1970. German ed. has title: Guten Morgen, liebe Sonne! Subj: Animals. Games. Morning.

Beatty, Hetty Burlingame. *Bucking horse* ill. by author. Houghton, 1957. Subj: Animals – horses. Cowboys.

Droopy ill. by author. Houghton, 1954. Subj: Animals – mules. Character traits – stubbornness. Sports – swimming.

Little Owl Indian ill. by author. Houghton, 1951. Subj: Animals – horses. Fire. Indians of North America.

Moorland pony ill. by author. Houghton, 1961. Subj: Activities – traveling. Animals – horses. Character traits – kindness to animals. Family life. Foreign lands – England. Pets.

Bechstein, Ludwig. *The rabbit catcher and other fairy tales* tr. and intro. by Randall Jarrell; ill. by Ugo Fontana. Macmillan, 1962. Subj: Folk and fairy tales. Foreign lands – Germany.

Becker, Edna. *Nine hundred buckets of paint* ill. by Margaret Bradfield. Abingdon Pr., 1945. Subj: Activities – painting. Houses. Moving.

Becker, John Leonard. *Seven little rabbits* ill. by Barbara Cooney. Walker, 1973. Subj: Animals – rabbits. Counting.

Becker, May Lamberton. *The rainbow Mother Goose* (Mother Goose)

Beckett, Hilary. *The rooster's horns* (Young, Ed)

Beckman, Beatrice. *I can be a teacher* ill. with photos. Childrens Pr., 1985. ISBN 0-516-01843-4 Subj: Careers – teachers.

Beckman, Kaj. *Lisa cannot sleep* ill. by Per Beckman. Watts, 1970. Subj: Bedtime. Family life. Sleep. Toys.

Bedford, A. N. (Annie North) *see* Watson, Jane Werner

The bedtime book: *a collection of fairy tales* ill. by Daniel San Souci. Messner, 1985. ISBN 0-671-60505-4 Subj: Folk and fairy tales.

Beech, Caroline. *Peas again for lunch* ill. by Gina Calleja. Annick Pr., 1981. Subj: Behavior – misbehavior. Imagination.

Beecroft, John. *What? Another cat!* ill. by Kurt Wiese. Dodd, 1960. Subj: Animals – cats. Sibling rivalry.

Beer, Kathleen Costello. *What happens in the spring.* National Geographic Soc., 1977. Subj: Seasons – spring.

Behn, Harry. *All kinds of time* ill. by author. Harcourt, 1950. Subj: Machines. Time.

Crickets and bullfrogs and whispers of thunder sel. by Lee Bennett Hopkins; ill. by author. Harcourt, 1984. Subj: Poetry, rhyme.

What a beautiful noise ill. by Harold Berson. Collins-World, 1970. Subj: Humor. Music. Noise, sounds.

Behrens, June. *Can you walk the plank?* ill. by Michele and Tom Grimm. Childrens Pr., 1976. Subj: Activities. Games. Imagination.

Fiesta! ill. by Scott Taylor. Childrens Pr., 1978. Subj: Ethnic groups in the U.S. – Mexican-Americans. Holidays – Cinco de Mayo.

I can be a nurse. Childrens Pr., 1986. ISBN 0-516-01893-0 Subj: Careers – nurses.

I can be a pilot. Childrens Pr., 1985. ISBN 0-516-01888-4 Subj: Careers – airplane pilots.

I can be a truck driver ill. with photos. Childrens Pr., 1985. ISBN 0-516-01848-5 Subj: Careers – truck drivers.

The manners book: what's right, Ned? ill. by Michele and Tom Grimm. Childrens Pr., 1980. Subj: Etiquette. Toys – teddy bears.

Passover photos. by Terry Behrens. Childrens Pr., 1987. ISBN 0-516-02389-6 Subj: Holidays – Passover. Jewish culture.

Powwow. Childrens Pr., 1983. ISBN 0-516-02387-X Subj: Indians of North America.

Soo Ling finds a way ill. by Tarō Yashima. Childrens Pr., 1965. Subj: Ethnic groups in the U.S. – Chinese-Americans. Family life – grandfathers. Foreign lands – China. Laundry.

Whales of the world. Childrens Pr., 1987. ISBN 0-516-08877-7 Subj: Animals – whales. Science.

Whalewatch! ill. by John Olguin. Childrens Pr., 1978. Photographs collected by John Olguin. Subj: Animals – whales. Science.

Who am I? ill. by Ray Ambraziunas. Elk Grove Pr., 1968. Subj: School. Self-concept.

Beim, Jerrold. *Country mailman* ill. by Leonard W. Shortall. Morrow, 1958. Subj: Careers – mail carriers. Character traits – helpfulness. Emotions – envy, jealousy.

Country train ill. by Leonard W. Shortall. Morrow, 1950. Subj: Character traits – individuality. Trains.

Eric on the desert ill. by Louis Darling. Morrow, 1953. Subj: Animals. Character traits – bravery. Desert.

Freckle face ill. by Barbara Cooney. Crowell, 1957. Subj: Character traits – appearance. Character traits – being different. Character traits – individuality.

Jay's big job ill. by Tracy Sugarman. Morrow, 1957. Subj: Activities – painting. Activities – working. Family life.

The little igloo (Beim, Lorraine)

Lucky Pierre (Beim, Lorraine)

Sasha and the samovar (Beim, Lorraine)

Sir Halloween ill. by Tracy Sugarman. Morrow, 1959. Subj: Holidays – Halloween.

The smallest boy in the class ill. by Meg Wohlberg. Morrow, 1949. Subj: Behavior – sharing. Character traits – smallness. Names.

The swimming hole ill. by Louis Darling. Morrow, 1950. Subj: Behavior. Ethnic groups in the U.S. – Afro-Americans. Friendship. Seasons – summer. Sports – swimming.

The taming of Toby ill. by Tracy Sugarman. Morrow, 1953. Subj: Behavior – misbehavior. Imagination. School.

Tim and the tool chest ill. by Tracy Sugarman. Morrow, 1951. Subj: Tools.

Two is a team (Beim, Lorraine)

With dad alone ill. by Don Sibley. Harcourt, 1954. Subj: Death. Family life – fathers.

Beim, Lorraine. *The little igloo* by Lorraine and Jerrold Beim; ill. by Howard Simon. Harcourt, 1941. Subj: Animals – dogs. Eskimos.

Lucky Pierre by Lorraine and Jerrold Beim; ill. by Howard Simon. Harcourt, 1940. Subj: Behavior – collecting things. Careers – fishermen. Character traits – luck. Family life.

Sasha and the samovar by Lorraine and Jerrold Beim; ill. by Rafaello Busoni. Harcourt, 1944. Subj: Fairies. Foreign lands – Russia.

Two is a team by Lorraine and Jerrold Beim; ill. by Ernest Crichlow. Harcourt, 1945. Subj: Behavior – fighting, arguing. Ethnic groups in the U.S. – Afro-Americans. Friendship. Problem solving.

Beisert, Heide Helene. *Poor fish* tr. from German by Marion Koenig; ill. by author. Harper, 1982. Subj: Birds. Ecology. Fish.

Beisner, Monika. *Secret spells and curious charms* ill. by author. Farrar, 1986. ISBN 0-374-36692-6 Subj: Behavior – secrets. Magic.

Topsy turvy: the world of upside down ill. by author. Farrar, 1987. ISBN 0-374-37679-4 Subj: Concepts. Poetry, rhyme.

Bell, Anthea. *Billy the brave* (Chapouton, Anne-Marie)

The brave little tailor (Grimm, Jacob)

Bremen town musicians (Grimm, Jacob)

The emperor's new clothes (Andersen, H. C. (Hans Christian))

The farmer and the moon (Lussert, Anneliese)

The golden goose (Grimm, Jacob)

Goodbye little bird (Damjan, Mischa)

The goose girl (Grimm, Jacob)

Grimm Tom Thumb (Tom Thumb)

The little mermaid (Andersen, H. C. (Hans Christian))

The magic honey jar (Bohdal, Susi)

Mumble bear (Ruck-Pauquèt, Gina)

The nightingale (Andersen, H. C. (Hans Christian))

Noah's ark (Fussenegger, Gertrud)

The nutcracker (Hoffmann, E. T. A.)

The Pied Piper of Hamelin (Bartos-Hoppner, Barbara)

The princess and the pea (Andersen, H. C. (Hans Christian))

The proud white cat (Hürlimann, Ruth)

The red shoes (Andersen, H. C. (Hans Christian))

Sandman in the lighthouse (Strahl, Rudi)

The snow queen (Andersen, H. C. (Hans Christian))

Snow White and the seven dwarfs (Grimm, Jacob)

The strange child (Hoffmann, E. T. A.)

Swan Lake: a traditional folktale ill. by Chihiro Iwasaki. Picture Book Studio, 1986. Adaptation of Tchaikovsky's Lebedinoe ozero. ISBN 0-88708-028-6 Subj: Activities – dancing. Birds – swans. Folk and fairy tales. Magic.

The swineherd (Andersen, H. C. (Hans Christian))

Thumbeline (Andersen, H. C. (Hans Christian))

The trip to Panama (Janosch)

The wise queen ill. by Chihiro Iwasaki. Picture Book Studio, 1986. ISBN 0-88708-014-6 Subj: Character traits – cleverness. Folk and fairy tales. Riddles. Royalty.

The wishing table (Grimm, Jacob)

Bell, Gina *see* Balzano, Jeanne

Bell, Janet *see* Clymer, Eleanor Lowenton

Bell, Norman. *Linda's airmail letter* ill. by Patricia Villemain. Follett, 1964. Subj: Birthdays. Friendship. Letters. Weather.

Bell-Zano, Gina *see* Balzano, Jeanne

Bellamy, David. *The forest* ill. by Jill Dow. Crown, 1988. ISBN 0-517-56800-4 Subj: Animals. Forest, woods. Plants.

The river ill. by Jill Dow. Crown, 1988. ISBN 0-517-56801-2 Subj: Animals. Plants. Rivers.

Beller, Janet. *A-B-C-ing: an action alphabet.* Crown, 1984. Subj: ABC books. Activities.

Belling the cat and other stories retold by Leland B. Jacobs; ill. by Harold Berson. Golden Pr., 1960. Subj: Animals. Folk and fairy tales.

Belloc, Hilaire. *The bad child's book of beasts* ill. by Basil T. Blackwood [B.A.T.]. Knopf, 1965. Originally published in 1896. Subj: Animals. Behavior. Humor.

The bad child's book of beasts, and more beasts for worse children ill. by Harold Berson. Grosset, 1966. Subj: Animals. Poetry, rhyme.

The bad child's pop-up book of beasts ill. by Wallace Tripp. Putnam's, 1987. ISBN 0-399-21431-3 Subj: Animals. Format, unusual – toy and movable books. Poetry, rhyme.

Jim, who ran away from his nurse, and was eaten by a lion ill. by Victoria Chess. Little, 1987. ISBN 0-316-13815-0 Subj: Animals – lions. Behavior – misbehavior. Behavior – running away. Zoos.

Matilda who told lies and was burned to death ill. by Steven Kellogg. Dial Pr., 1970. Subj: Behavior – lying. Behavior – misbehavior. Fire. Poetry, rhyme.

More beasts for worse children ill. by Basil T. Blackwood [B.A.T.]. Knopf, 1966. Subj: Animals. Poetry, rhyme.

Bellows, Cathy. *Four fat rats* ill. by author. Macmillan, 1987. ISBN 0-02-708830-8 Subj: Animals – rats. Behavior – greed. Character traits – meanness.

Bellville, Cheryl Walsh. *Large animal veterinarians* (Bellville, Rod)

Rodeo photos. by author. Carolrhoda, 1985. ISBN 0-87614-272-2 Subj: Animals. Cowboys.

Round-up photos. by author. Carolrhoda Books, 1982. Subj: Animals – bulls, cows. Animals – horses. Farms.

Theater magic: behind the scenes at a children's theater photos. by author. Carolrhoda, 1986. ISBN 0-87614-278-1 Subj: Birds. Character traits – freedom. Foreign lands – China. Royalty. Theater.

Bellville, Rod. *Large animal veterinarians* by Rod and Cheryl Walsh Bellville; photos. by authors. Carolrhoda Books, 1983. Subj: Animals. Careers – veterinarians.

Belpré, Pura. *Dance of the animals: a Puerto Rican folk tale* ill. by Paul Galdone. Warne, 1972. Subj: Animals. Folk and fairy tales. Foreign lands – Puerto Rico.

Perez and Martina: a Portorican folk tale ill. by Carlos Sanchez. Rev. ed. Warne, 1961. Originally pub. in 1960. Subj: Animals – mice. Folk and fairy tales. Foreign lands – Puerto Rico. Insects.

Santiago ill. by Symeon Shimin. Warne, 1969. Subj: Birds – chickens. Ethnic groups in the U.S. Ethnic groups in the U.S. – Puerto Rican-Americans. Pets.

Belting, Natalia Maree. *Christmas folk* ill. by Barbara Cooney. Holt, 1969. Subj: Foreign lands – England. Holidays – Christmas. Poetry, rhyme.

Summer's coming in ill. by Adrienne Adams. Holt, 1970. Subj: Foreign lands – England. Holidays – Christmas. Poetry, rhyme. Seasons – spring. Seasons – summer.

The sun is a golden earring ill. by Bernarda Bryson. Holt, 1962. Subj: Caldecott award honor book. Folk and fairy tales. Sky.

Verity Mullens and the Indian ill. by Leonard Everett Fisher. Holt, 1960. Subj: Animals – dogs. Behavior – lost. Indians of North America. U.S. history.

Bemelmans, Ludwig. *Hansi* ill. by author. Viking, 1934. Subj: Activities – vacationing. Foreign lands – Tyrol. Holidays – Christmas.

Madeline ill. by author. Viking, 1939. Subj: Caldecott award honor book. Foreign lands – France. Hospitals. Orphans. Poetry, rhyme. School.

Madeline and the bad hat ill. by author. Viking, 1956. Subj: Behavior – animals, dislike of. Behavior – misbehavior. Foreign lands – France. Orphans. Poetry, rhyme.

Madeline and the gypsies ill. by author. Viking, 1959. Subj: Behavior – lost. Foreign lands – France. Gypsies. Orphans. Poetry, rhyme.

Madeline in London ill. by author. Viking, 1961. Subj: Animals – horses. Birthdays. Foreign lands – England. Orphans. Poetry, rhyme.

Madeline [pop-up book] ill. by author. Viking, 1987. ISBN 0-670-81667-1 Subj: Format, unusual – toy and movable books. Foreign lands – France. Hospitals. Orphans.

Madeline's rescue ill. by author. Viking, 1953. Subj: Animals – dogs. Caldecott Award book. Foreign lands – France. Orphans. Poetry, rhyme.

Parsley ill. by author. Harper, 1955. Subj: Animals – deer. Sports – hunting. Trees.

Quito express ill. by author. Viking, 1938. Subj: Activities – traveling. Family life. Foreign lands – Ecuador. Trains.

Rosebud ill. by author. Random House, 1942. Subj: Animals. Character traits – pride. Folk and fairy tales. Foreign lands – Africa. Humor.

Sunshine ill. by author. Simon and Schuster, 1950. Subj: City. Family life. Houses. Humor.

Welcome home ill. by author. Harper, 1970. Based on a poem by Beverley Bogert. Subj: Animals – foxes. Character traits – cleverness. Poetry, rhyme.

Benarde, Anita. *The pumpkin smasher* ill. by author. Walker, 1972. Subj: Holidays – Halloween. Problem solving. Witches.

Benchley, Nathaniel. *The deep dives of Stanley Whale* ill. by Mischa Richter. Harper, 1973. Subj: Animals – whales. Character traits – bravery.

The flying lessons of Gerald Pelican ill. by Mamoru Funai. Harper, 1970. Subj: Activities – flying. Birds – pelicans.

George the drummer boy ill. by Don Bolognese. Harper, 1977. Subj: U.S. history. War.

A ghost named Fred ill. by Ben Shecter. Harper, 1968. Subj: Ghosts. Problem solving.

The magic sled ill. by Mel Furakawa. Harper, 1972. Subj: Behavior – wishing. Holidays – Christmas. Weather – snow.

Oscar Otter ill. by Arnold Lobel. Harper, 1966. Subj: Animals – otters. Behavior.

Red Fox and his canoe ill. by Arnold Lobel. Harper, 1964. Subj: Animals – bears. Boats, ships. Indians of North America.

Running Owl the hunter ill. by Mamoru Funai. Harper, 1979. Subj: Animals. Indians of North America.

Sam the minute man ill. by Arnold Lobel. Harper, 1969. Subj: U.S. history. War.

The several tricks of Edgar Dolphin ill. by Mamoru Funai. Harper, 1978. Subj: Animals – dolphins. Character traits – cleverness.

Small Wolf ill. by Joan Sandin. Harper, 1972. Subj: Indians of North America. U.S. history.

Snip ill. by Irene Trivas. Doubleday, 1981. Subj: Animals – dogs. Death. Old age.

Snorri and the strangers ill. by Don Bolognese. Harper, 1976. Subj: Foreign lands – Norway. U.S. history.

The strange disappearance of Arthur Cluck ill. by Arnold Lobel. Harper, 1967. Subj: Birds – chickens. Birds – owls. Farms. Holidays – Easter.

Walter the homing pigeon ill. by Whitney Darrow, Jr. Harper, 1981. Subj: Birds – pigeons. Food. Humor. Sports – racing.

Benchley, Peter. *Jonathan visits the White House* ill. by Richard Bergere. McGraw-Hill, 1964. Subj: Animals – dogs. Birthdays. Pets. U.S. history.

Bendick, Jeanne. *All around you* foreword by Glenn O. Blough; ill. by author. McGraw-Hill, 1951. Subj: Science. World.

What made you you? ill. by author. McGraw-Hill, 1971. Subj: Babies. Science.

Why can't I? ill. by author. McGraw-Hill, 1969. Subj: Animals. Behavior – imitation. Participation. Science.

Benedek, Elissa P. *The secret worry* ill. by Patricia Rosamilia. Human Sciences Pr., 1984. ISBN 0-89885-133-5 Subj: Behavior – worrying. Emotions – fear.

Benedictus, Roger. *Fifty million sausages* ill. by Kenneth Mahood. Elsevier-Dutton, 1979. Subj: Food. Humor. Imagination. Machines.

Benét, William Rose. *Angels* ill. by Constantin Alajalov. Crowell, 1947. Subj: Activities – playing. Angels. Poetry, rhyme.

Mother Goose (Mother Goose)

Beni, Ruth. *Sir Baldergog the great* ill. by author. Dutton, 1985. ISBN 0-233-97628-0 Subj: Activities. Behavior – lost. Islands.

Benjamin, Alan. *Busy bunnies* ill. by Christopher Santoro. Simon & Schuster, 1988. ISBN 0-671-64807-1 Subj: Activities. Animals – rabbits.

A change of plans ill. by Steven Kellogg. Four Winds Pr., 1982. Subj: Activities – picnicking. Boats, ships. Family life. Poetry, rhyme.

The nightingale (Andersen, H. C. (Hans Christian))

1000 monsters ill. by Sal Murdocca. Four Winds Pr., 1979. Subj: Format, unusual – toy and movable books. Humor. Monsters.

Rat-a-tat, pitter pat ill. by Margaret Miller. Harper, 1987. ISBN 0-690-04611-1 Subj: Language. Noise, sounds.

Ribtickle Town ill. by Ann Schweninger. Four Winds Pr., 1983. Subj: Behavior – lost. Food. Giants. Imagination. Poetry, rhyme.

Bennett, Jill. *Days are where we live and other poems* ill. by Maureen Roffey. Lothrop, 1982. Subj: Activities. Poetry, rhyme.

Roger was a razor fish and other poems ill. by Maureen Roffey. Lothrop, 1981. Subj: Humor. Poetry, rhyme.

Teeny tiny ill. by Tomie de Paola. Putnam's, 1986. ISBN 0-399-21293-0 Subj: Folk and fairy tales. Foreign lands – England. Ghosts.

Tiny Tim: verses for children ill. by Helen Oxenbury. Delacorte Pr., 1982. Subj: Humor. Poetry, rhyme.

Bennett, Olivia. *A Turkish afternoon* photos. by Christopher Cormack. David and Charles, 1984. Subj: Family life. Foreign lands – England. Foreign lands – Turkey.

Bennett, Rainey. *After the sun goes down* ill. by author. Collins-World, 1961. Subj: Birds – owls. Night.

The secret hiding place ill. by author. Collins-World, 1960. Subj: Animals – hippopotami. Behavior – solitude. Poetry, rhyme. Sea and seashore.

Bennett, Rowena. *The day is dancing and other poems* ill. by Rainey Bennett. Follett, 1968. Subj: Imagination. Poetry, rhyme.

Songs from around a toadstool table ill. by Betty Fraser. Follett, 1967. Subj: Imagination. Poetry, rhyme.

Benson, Ellen. *Philip's little sister* ill. by Rachael Davis. Childrens Pr., 1979. Subj: Family life. Sibling rivalry.

Bentley, Anne. *The Groggs' day out* ill. by Roy Bentley. Elsevier-Dutton, 1981. Subj: Foreign lands – England. Sports – bicycling.

The Groggs have a wonderful summer by Anne and Roy Bentley; ill. by Roy Bentley. Elsevier-Dutton, 1980. Subj: Foreign lands – England. Sea and seashore. Seasons – summer.

Bentley, Roy. *The Groggs have a wonderful summer* (Bentley, Anne)

Benton, Robert. *Don't ever wish for a 7-foot bear* ill. by Sally Benton. Knopf, 1972. Subj: Animals – bears. Behavior – wishing. Humor.

Little brother, no more ill. by author. Knopf, 1960. Subj: Family life. Names.

Berends, Polly Berrien. *Ladybug and dog and the night walk* ill. by Cyndy Szekeres. Random House, 1980. Subj: Animals – dogs. Friendship. Insects – fireflies. Insects – ladybugs. Night.

Berenstain, Jan. *After the dinosaurs* (Berenstain, Stan)

The bear detectives (Berenstain, Stan)

The bears' almanac (Berenstain, Stan)

Bears in the night (Berenstain, Stan)

Bears on wheels (Berenstain, Stan)

The Berenstain bears and the bad dream (Berenstain, Stan)

The Berenstain bears and the double dare (Berenstain, Stan)

The Berenstain bears and the ghost of the forest (Berenstain, Stan)

The Berenstain bears and the messy room (Berenstain, Stan)

The Berenstain bears and the missing dinosaur bone (Berenstain, Stan)

The Berenstain bears and the sitter (Berenstain, Stan)

The Berenstain bears and the spooky old tree (Berenstain, Stan)

The Berenstain bears and the truth (Berenstain, Stan)

The Berenstain bears and too much TV (Berenstain, Stan)

The Berenstain bears' Christmas tree (Berenstain, Stan)

The Berenstain bears' counting book (Berenstain, Stan)

The Berenstain bears forget their manners (Berenstain, Stan)

The Berenstain bears get in a fight (Berenstain, Stan)

The Berenstain bears get the gimmies (Berenstain, Stan)

The Berenstain bears go to camp (Berenstain, Stan)

The Berenstain bears go to school (Berenstain, Stan)

The Berenstain bears go to the doctor (Berenstain, Stan)

The Berenstain bears in the dark (Berenstain, Stan)

The Berenstain bears learn about strangers (Berenstain, Stan)

The Berenstain bears meet Santa Bear (Berenstain, Stan)

The Berenstain bears' moving day (Berenstain, Stan)

The Berenstain bears on the moon (Berenstain, Stan)

The Berenstain bears ready, set, go! (Berenstain, Stan)

The Berenstain bears' science fair (Berenstain, Stan)

The Berenstain bears' trouble with money (Berenstain, Stan)

The Berenstain bears visit the dentist (Berenstain, Stan)

The Berenstains' B book (Berenstain, Stan)

He bear, she bear (Berenstain, Stan)

Inside outside upside down (Berenstain, Stan)

Old hat, new hat (Berenstain, Stan)

Berenstain, Michael. *The dwarks: book 1* ill. by author. Bantam, 1983. Subj: Elves and little people. Family life.

The ship book ill. by author. McKay, 1978. Subj: Boats, ships.

The troll book ill. by author. Random House, 1980. Subj: Folk and fairy tales. Trolls.

Berenstain, Stan. *After the dinosaurs* by Stan and Jan Berenstain; ill. by authors. Random House, 1988. ISBN 0-394-90518-0 Subj: Animals – bears. Dinosaurs.

The bear detectives: the case of the missing pumpkin by Stan and Jan Berenstain; ill. by authors. Random House, 1975. Subj: Animals – bears. Careers – detectives. Poetry, rhyme. Problem solving.

The bears' almanac: a year in bear country; holidays, seasons, weather, actual facts about snow, wind, rain, thunder, lightning, the sun, the moon and lots more by Stan and Jan Berenstain; ill. by authors. Random House, 1973. Subj: Animals – bears. Holidays. Moon. Poetry, rhyme. Seasons. Sun. Weather.

Bears in the night by Stan and Jan Berenstain; ill. by authors. Random House, 1971. Subj: Animals – bears. Bedtime. Night. Noise, sounds.

Bears on wheels by Stan and Jan Berenstain; ill. by authors. Random House, 1969. Subj: Animals – bears. Counting. Wheels.

The Berenstain bears and the bad dream by Stan and Jan Berenstain; ill. by authors. Random House, 1988. ISBN 0-394-97341-0 Subj: Animals – bears. Dreams.

The Berenstain bears and the double dare by Stan and Jan Berenstain; ill. by authors. Random House, 1988. ISBN 0-394-99748-4 Subj: Animals – bears. Sibling rivalry.

The Berenstain bears and the ghost of the forest by Stan and Jan Berenstain; ill. by authors. Random House, 1988. ISBN 0-394-90565-2 Subj: Animals – bears. Forest, woods. Ghosts.

The Berenstain bears and the messy room by Stan and Jan Berenstain; ill. by authors. Random House, 1983. Subj: Animals – bears. Problem solving.

The Berenstain bears and the missing dinosaur bone by Stan and Jan Berenstain; ill. by authors. Random House, 1980. Subj: Animals – bears. Museums. Poetry, rhyme. Problem solving.

The Berenstain bears and the sitter by Stan and Jan Berenstain; ill. by authors. Random House, 1981. Subj: Activities – baby-sitting. Animals – bears. Magic.

The Berenstain bears and the spooky old tree by Stan and Jan Berenstain; ill. by authors. Random House, 1978. Subj: Animals – bears. Poetry, rhyme. Trees.

The Berenstain bears and the truth by Stan and Jan Berenstain; ill. by authors. Random House, 1983. Subj: Animals – bears. Behavior – lying. Behavior – misbehavior. Family life.

The Berenstain bears and too much TV by Stan and Jan Berenstain; ill. by authors. Random House, 1984. Subj: Animals – bears. Family life. Television.

The Berenstain bears' Christmas tree by Stan and Jan Berenstain; ill. by authors. Random House, 1980. Subj: Animals – bears. Family life. Holidays – Christmas. Poetry, rhyme. Trees.

The Berenstain bears' counting book by Stan and Jan Berenstain; ill. by authors. Random House, 1976. Subj: Animals – bears. Counting.

The Berenstain bears forget their manners by Stan and Jan Berenstain; ill. by authors. Random, 1985. ISBN 0-394-97333-X Subj: Animals – bears. Etiquette. Family life.

The Berenstain bears get in a fight by Stan and Jan Berenstain; ill. by authors. Random House, 1982. Subj: Animals – bears. Behavior – bad day. Sibling rivalry.

The Berenstain bears get the gimmies by Stan and Jan Berenstain; ill. by authors. Random House, 1988. ISBN 0-394-90566-0 Subj: Animals – bears. Behavior – greed.

The Berenstain bears go to camp by Stan and Jan Berenstain; ill. by authors. Random House, 1982. Subj: Animals – bears. Seasons – summer. Sports – camping.

The Berenstain bears go to school by Stan and Jan Berenstain; ill. by authors. Random House, 1978. Subj: Animals – bears. School.

The Berenstain bears go to the doctor by Stan and Jan Berenstain; ill. by authors. Random House, 1981. Subj: Animals – bears. Careers – doctors.

The Berenstain bears in the dark by Stan and Jan Berenstain; ill. by authors. Random House, 1982. Subj: Animals – bears. Family life. Imagination. Night.

The Berenstain bears learn about strangers by Stan and Jan Berenstain; ill. by authors. Random, 1985. ISBN 0-394-87334-3 Subj: Animals – bears. Behavior – talking to strangers. Emotions – fear. Family life. Safety.

The Berenstain bears meet Santa Bear by Stan and Jan Berenstain; ill. by authors. Random House, 1988. ISBN 0-394-89797-8 Subj: Animals – bears. Holidays – Christmas.

The Berenstain bears' moving day by Stan and Jan Berenstain; ill. by authors. Random House, 1981. Subj: Animals – bears. Family life. Friendship. Moving.

The Berenstain bears on the moon by Stan and Jan Berenstain; ill. by authors. Random House, 1985. ISBN 0-394-97180-9 Subj: Animals – bears. Animals – dogs. Moon. Space and space ships.

The Berenstain bears ready, set, go! by Stan and Jan Berenstain; ill. by authors. Random House, 1988. ISBN 0-394-90564-4 Subj: Animals – bears.

The Berenstain bears' science fair by Stan and Jan Berenstain; ill. by authors. Random House, 1977. Subj: Animals – bears. Science.

The Berenstain bears' trouble with money by Stan and Jan Berenstain; ill. by authors. Random House, 1983. Subj: Animals – bears. Money.

The Berenstain bears visit the dentist by Stan and Jan Berenstain; ill. by authors. Random House, 1981. Subj: Animals – bears. Careers – dentists.

The Berenstains' B book by Stan and Jan Berenstain; ill. by authors. Random House, 1971. Subj: ABC books. Animals – bears.

He bear, she bear by Stan and Jan Berenstain; ill. by authors. Random House, 1974. Subj: Animals – bears. Poetry, rhyme.

Inside outside upside down by Stan and Jan Berenstain; ill. by authors. Random House, 1968. Subj: Animals – bears. Concepts.

Old hat, new hat by Stan and Jan Berenstain; ill. by authors. Random House, 1970. Subj: Animals – bears. Concepts – shape. Concepts – size. Humor.

Beresford, Elisabeth. *Jack and the magic stove* ill. by Rita van Bilsen. Hutchinson, 1984. Subj: Behavior – wishing. Folk and fairy tales. Royalty.

Snuffle to the rescue ill. by Gunvor Edwards. Penguin, 1975. Subj: Animals – dogs.

Berg, Jean Horton. *The little red hen*

The noisy clock shop ill. by Art Seiden. Grosset, 1950. Subj: Clocks. Noise, sounds.

The O'Learys and friends ill. by Mary Stevens. Follett, 1961. Subj: Animals – cats. Behavior – misunderstanding. Moving. Problem solving.

The wee little man ill. by Charles Geer. Follett, 1963. Subj: Animals – cats. Elves and little people. Night. Noise, sounds. Poetry, rhyme.

Berg, Leila. *Folk tales for reading and telling* ill. by George Him. Collins-World, 1966. Subj: Folk and fairy tales. Foreign lands.

Berger, Barbara Helen. *The donkey's dream* ill. by author. Philomel, 1986. ISBN 0-399-21233-7 Subj: Religion.

Grandfather Twilight ill. by author. Philomel, 1984. ISBN 0-399-20996-4 Subj: Folk and fairy tales. Moon. Twilight.

When the sun rose ill. by author. Philomel, 1986. ISBN 0-399-21360-0 Subj: Friendship. Imagination – imaginary friends.

Berger, Gilda. *Sharks* ill. by Christopher Santoro. Doubleday, 1987. ISBN 0-385-23419-8 Subj: Fish. Science.

Whales ill. by Lisa Bonforte. Doubleday, 1987. ISBN 0-385-23421-X Subj: Animals – dolphins. Animals – whales. Science.

Berger, Judith. *Butterflies and rainbows* by Judith Berger and Terry Landau; ill. by Carmen Lowhar. Bande House, 1982. Subj: Concepts – color. Poetry, rhyme.

Berger, Melvin. *Early humans: a pop-up book* ill. by Michael Welply. Putnam's, 1988. ISBN 0-399-21476-3 Subj: Format, unusual – toy and movable books. Science.

Germs make me sick! ill. by Marylin Hafner. Crowell, 1985. ISBN 0-690-04429-1 Subj: Illness. Science.

Prehistoric mammals: a new world ill. by Robert Cremins. Putnam's, 1986. ISBN 0-399-21312-0 Subj: Animals. Format, unusual – toy and movable books.

Why I cough, sneeze, shiver, hiccup and yawn ill. by Holly Keller. Crowell, 1983. Subj: Health. Illness.

Berger, Terry. *Ben's ABC day* photos. by Alice Kandell. Lothrop, 1982. Subj: ABC books.

Friends photos. by Alice Kandell. Messner, 1981. Subj: Friendship.

How does it feel when your parents get divorced? photos. by Miriam Shapiro. Messner, 1977. Subj: Divorce. Emotions. Family life.

I have feelings ill. by Howard Spivak. Behavioral, 1971. Subj: Emotions. Self-concept.

I have feelings too photos. by Michael E. Ach. Human Sciences Pr., 1979. Subj: Emotions.

The turtles' picnic and other nonsense stories ill. by Erkki Alanen. Crown, 1977. Subj: Activities – picnicking. Animals.

Bergere, Thea. *Paris in the rain with Jean and Jacqueline* ill. by Richard Bergere. McGraw-Hill, 1963. Subj: City. Foreign lands – France. Weather – rain.

Bergman, David. *The turtle and the two ducks* (Plante, Patricia)

Bergstrom, Corinne. *Losing your best friend* ill. by Patricia Rosamilia. Human Sciences Pr., 1980. Subj: Friendship.

Bergström, Gunilla. *Who's scaring Alfie Atkins?* tr. by Joan Sandin; ill. by author. Farrar, 1987. ISBN 91-29-58318-7 Subj: Emotions – fear. Family life – fathers. Ghosts.

Beris, Sandra. *The cat's surprise* (Seguin-Fontes, Marthe)

A wedding book (Seguin-Fontes, Marthe)

Berkley, Ethel S. *Ups and down: a first book of space* ill. by Kathleen Elgin. Addison-Wesley, 1951. Subj: Concepts. Concepts – up and down.

Berman, Linda. *The goodbye painting* ill. by Mark Hannon. Human Sciences Pr., 1983. Subj: Activities – baby-sitting.

Bernadette *see* Watts, Bernadette

Bernhard, Josephine Butkowska. *Lullaby: why the pussy-cat washes himself so often; a folk-tale adapted from the Polish* ill. by Irena Lorentowicz. Roy Pubs., 1944. Subj: Animals – cats. Folk and fairy tales. Foreign lands – Poland.

Nine cry-baby dolls ill. by Irena Lorentowicz. Roy Pubs., 1945. Subj: Folk and fairy tales. Foreign lands – Poland. Toys – dolls.

Bernheim, Evelyne. *In Africa* (Bernheim, Marc)

A week in Aya's world (Bernheim, Marc)

Bernheim, Marc. *In Africa* by Marc and Evelyne Bernheim; photos. by authors. Atheneum, 1973. Subj: Family life. Foreign lands – Africa.

A week in Aya's world: the Ivory Coast by Marc and Evelyne Bernheim; photos. by authors. Macmillan, 1970. Subj: Foreign lands – Africa.

Bernstein, Alan. *Regal the golden eagle* (Klinting, Lars)

Bernstein, Joanne E. *Creepy crawly critter riddles* by Joanne E. Bernstein and Paul Cohen; ill. by Rosekrans Hoffman. Albert Whitman, 1986. ISBN 0-8075-1345-8 Subj: Animals. Insects. Riddles.

More unidentified flying riddles by Joanne E. Bernstein and Paul Cohen; ill. by Meyer Seltzer. Albert Whitman, 1985. ISBN 0-8075-5279-8 Subj: Riddles. Space and space ships.

What was the wicked witch's real name? and other character riddles by Joanne E. Bernstein and Paul Cohen; ill. by Ann Iosa. Albert Whitman, 1986. ISBN 0-8075-8854-7 Subj: Riddles.

When people die by Joanne E. Bernstein and Steven V. Gullo; photos. by Rosmarie Hausherr. Dutton, 1977. Subj: Death.

Bernstein, Margery. *Coyote goes hunting for fire: a California Indian myth* by Margery Bernstein and Janet Kobrin; ill. by Ed Heffernan. Scribner's, 1974. Subj: Animals. Animals – coyotes. Fire. Folk and fairy tales. Indians of North America.

Earth namer: a California Indian myth by Margery Bernstein and Janet Kobrin; ill. by Ed Heffernan. Scribner's, 1974. Subj: Earth. Folk and fairy tales. Indians of North America.

The first morning: an African myth by Margery Bernstein and Janet Kobrin; ill. by Enid Warner Romanek. Scribner's, 1976. Subj: Animals. Folk and fairy tales. Foreign lands – Africa.

How the sun made a promise and kept it: a Canadian Indian myth retold by Margery Bernstein and Janet Kobrin; ill. by Ed Heffernan. Scribner's, 1974. Subj: Folk and fairy tales. Indians of North America. Sun.

Berquist, Grace. *The boy who couldn't roar* ill. by Ruth Van Sciver. Abingdon Pr., 1960. Subj: Behavior – bullying. Character traits – selfishness.

Speckles goes to school ill. by Kathleen Elgin. Abingdon Pr., 1952. Subj: Birds – chickens. School.

Berridge, Celia. *Grandmother's tales* ill. by author. Elsevier-Dutton, 1981. Subj: Bedtime. Family life – grandmothers. Witches.

Berry, Joy Wilt. *Being destructive* ill. by John Costanza. Rev. ed. Childrens Pr., 1984. Subj: Behavior – misbehavior.

Being selfish ill. by John Costanza. Rev. ed. Childrens Pr., 1984. Subj: Behavior – misbehavior. Character traits – selfishness.

Disobeying ill. by John Costanza. Rev. ed. Childrens Pr., 1984. Subj: Behavior – misbehavior.

Fighting ill. by John Costanza. Rev. ed. Childrens Pr., 1984. Subj: Behavior – fighting, arguing. Behavior – misbehavior.

Throwing tantrums ill. by John Costanza. Rev. ed. Childrens Pr., 1984. Subj: Behavior – misbehavior.

Whining ill. by John Costanza. Rev. ed. Childrens Pr., 1984. Subj: Behavior – misbehavior.

Berson, Harold. *Balarin's goat* ill. by author. Crown, 1972. Subj: Animals – goats. Folk and fairy tales.

Barrels to the moon ill. by author. Coward, 1982. Subj: Folk and fairy tales. Foreign lands – France.

The boy, the baker, the miller and more ill. by author. Crown, 1974. "The story is based on a French folk tale called Un Morceau de pain." Subj: Cumulative tales. Folk and fairy tales.

Charles and Claudine ill. by adapt. Macmillan, 1980. Subj: Folk and fairy tales. Foreign lands – France. Frogs and toads. Magic. Witches.

Henry Possum ill. by author. Crown, 1973. Subj: Animals – foxes. Animals – possums. Behavior – lost.

How the devil got his due ill. by adapt. Crown, 1972. Subj: Character traits – cleverness. Devil. Folk and fairy tales. Foreign lands – France.

Joseph and the snake ill. by author. Macmillan, 1979. Subj: Animals – foxes. Character traits – cleverness. Character traits – kindness to animals. Folk and fairy tales. Foreign lands – France. Reptiles – snakes.

Kassim's shoes ill. by adapt. Crown, 1977. Subj: Behavior – misunderstanding. Folk and fairy tales. Foreign lands – Africa.

A moose is not a mouse ill. by author. Crown, 1975. Subj: Animals – mice. Language.

Pop! goes the turnip ill. by author. Grosset, 1966. Subj: Activities – gardening. Animals – rabbits. Food. Plants.

Raminagrobis and the mice ill. by author. Seabury Pr., 1966. Subj: Animals – cats. Animals – mice. Folk and fairy tales.

The rats who lived in the delicatessen ill. by author. Crown, 1976. Subj: Animals – rats. Behavior – greed. Food.

The thief who hugged a moonbeam ill. by author. Seabury Pr., 1972. Subj: Behavior – gossip. Crime. Magic. Royalty.

Truffles for lunch ill. by author. Macmillan, 1980. Subj: Animals – pigs. Behavior – wishing.

Why the jackal won't speak to the hedgehog: a Tunisian folk tale ill. by adapt. Seabury Pr., 1970. Subj: Animals. Animals – hedgehogs. Character traits – cleverness. Folk and fairy tales. Foreign lands – Africa.

Beskow, Elsa Maartman. *Children of the forest* adapt. from the Swedish by William Jay Smith; ill. by author. Delacorte Pr., 1969. Subj: Foreign lands – Sweden. Forest, woods. Poetry, rhyme. Seasons.

Pelle's new suit ill. by author. Harper, 1919. Subj: Animals – sheep. Clothing. Foreign lands – Sweden.

Peter in Blueberry Land ill. by author. Merrimack, 1984. A new ed. of a 100-year-old picture book. Subj: Birthdays. Elves and little people. Food. Foreign lands – Sweden. Magic. Poetry, rhyme.

Peter's adventures in Blueberry land adapt. by Sheila La Farge; ill. by author. Delacorte Pr., 1975. Pub. in Sweden in 1901. Subj: Birthdays. Elves and little people. Food. Foreign lands – Sweden. Magic. Poetry, rhyme.

Bess, Clayton. *The truth about the moon* ill. by Rosekrans Hoffman. Houghton, 1983. Subj: Folk and fairy tales. Foreign lands – Africa. Moon.

Bester, Roger. *Fireman Jim* photos. by author. Crown, 1981. Subj: Careers – firefighters. Fire.

Guess what? photos. by author. Crown, 1980. Subj: Animals. Participation. Problem solving.

Bethell, Jean. *Bathtime.* Holt, 1979. Subj: Activities – bathing. Animals.

Hooray for Henry ill. by Sergio Leone. Grosset, 1966. Subj: Character traits – perseverance. Food.

Playmates photos. by author. Holt, 1981. Subj: Activities – playing. Animals.

Three cheers for Mother Jones! ill. by Kathleen Garry-McCord. Holt, 1980. Subj: Activities – working. U.S. history.

Bettina (Bettina Ehrlich). *Cocolo comes to America* ill. by author. Harper, 1949. Subj: Animals – donkeys.

Cocolo's home ill. by author. Harper, 1950. Subj: Animals – donkeys.

Of uncles and aunts ill. by author. Norton, 1964. Subj: Family life.

Pantaloni ill. by author. Harper, 1957. Subj: Animals – dogs. Foreign lands – Italy. Poverty. Sports – fishing.

Piccolo ill. by author. Harper, 1954. Subj: Animals – donkeys.

Bettinger, Craig. *Follow me, everybody* ill. by Edward S. Hollander. Doubleday, 1968. Subj: Ethnic groups in the U.S.

Betz, Betty. *Manners for moppets* ill. by author. Grosset, 1962. Subj: Etiquette. Poetry, rhyme.

Bianco, Margery Williams. *The hurdy-gurdy man* ill. by Robert Lawson. Gregg, 1980. Subj: Activities – dancing. Music.

The velveteen rabbit ill. by David Jorgensen. Knopf, 1985. ISBN 0-394-87711-X Subj: Animals – rabbits. Emotions – love. Folk and fairy tales. Magic. Toys.

The velveteen rabbit: or, How toys became real ill. by Allen Atkinson. Knopf, 1983. Subj: Animals – rabbits. Emotions – love. Folk and fairy tales. Magic. Toys.

The velveteen rabbit: or, How toys became real ill. by Michael Green. Running Pr., 1984. ISBN 0-89741-291-8 Subj: Animals – rabbits. Emotions – love. Folk and fairy tales. Magic. Toys.

The velveteen rabbit: or, How toys became real ill. by Michael Hague. Holt, 1983. Subj: Animals – rabbits. Emotions – love. Folk and fairy tales. Magic. Toys.

The velveteen rabbit: or, How toys became real ill. by William Nicholson. Doubleday, n.d. Subj: Animals – rabbits. Emotions – love. Folk and fairy tales. Magic. Toys.

The velveteen rabbit: or, How toys became real ill. by Ilse Plume. Godine, 1983. Subj: Animals – rabbits. Emotions – love. Folk and fairy tales. Magic. Toys.

The velveteen rabbit: or, How toys became real ed. by David Eastman; ill. by S. D. Schindler. Troll Assoc., 1987. ISBN 0-8167-1061-9 Subj: Animals – rabbits. Emotions – love. Folk and fairy tales. Magic. Toys.

The velveteen rabbit: or, How toys became real ill. by Tien. Simon and Schuster, 1983. Subj: Animals – rabbits. Emotions – love. Folk and fairy tales. Magic. Toys.

Bible. *Best-loved Bible verses for children* ill. by Anna Maria Magagna. Grosset, 1983. Subj: Religion.

Bible, Charles. *Hamdaani: a traditional tale from Zanzibar* ill. by adapt. Holt, 1977. Subj: Animals. Folk and fairy tales. Foreign lands – Africa.

Jennifer's new chair ill. by author. Holt, 1978. Subj: Birthdays. Family life. Family life – grandmothers. Fire. Parties.

Bible. New Testament. *The Lord's prayer* ill. by Ingri and Edgar Parin d'Aulaire. Catholic version. Doubleday, 1934. Subj: Religion.

The Lord's prayer ill. by Ingri and Edgar Parin d'Aulaire. Protestant version. Doubleday, 1934. Subj: Religion.

The Lord's prayer ill. by George Kraus. Dutton, 1970. Subj: Religion.

Bible. New Testament. Gospels. *Christmas: the King James Version* ill. by Jan Pieńkowski. Knopf, 1984. ISBN 0-394-86923-0 Subj: Holidays – Christmas. Religion.

The first Christmas: from the Gospels according to Saint Luke and Saint Matthew ill. by Barbara Neustadt. Crowell, 1960. Subj: Religion.

The Nativity ill. by Julie Vivas. Harcourt, 1988. Text consists of excerpts from the authorized King James version of the Bible. ISBN 0-15-200535-8 Subj: Holidays – Christmas. Religion.

Bible. Old Testament. *David and the giant* (Little, Emily)

Noah and the ark ill. by Pauline Baynes. Holt, 1988. ISBN 0-8050-0886-1 Subj: Religion – Noah.

Bible. Old Testament. Daniel. *Daniel in the lions' den* adapt. by Belinda Hollyer; ill. by Leon Baxter. Silver Burdett, 1984. ISBN 0-382-067090-8 Subj: Animals – lions. Religion.

Shadrach, Meshack and Abednego ill. by Paul Galdone. McGraw-Hill, 1965. Subj: Religion.

Bible. Old Testament. David. *David and Goliath* adapt. by Belinda Hollyer; ill. by Leon Baxter. Silver Burdett, 1984. ISBN 0-382-06791-6 Subj: Religion.

Bible. Old Testament. Jonah. *The Book of Jonah* adapt. and ill. by Peter Spier. Doubleday, 1985. ISBN 0-385-19335-1 Subj: Animals – whales. Religion.

Jonah: the complete text of Jonah from the Holy Bible, New International version ill. by Kurt Mitchell. Crossway, 1981. Subj: Animals – mice. Animals – cats. Animals – whales. Religion.

Jonah and the great fish adapt. by Belinda Hollyer; ill. by Leon Baxter. Silver Burdett, 1984. ISBN 0-382-06792-4 Subj: Animals – whales. Religion.

Bible. Old Testament. Psalms. *The Lord is my shepherd* ill. by George Kraus. Dutton, 1971. Subj: Religion.

The Lord is my shepherd: the twenty-third Psalm ill. by Tasha Tudor. Putnam, 1980. Subj: Religion.

Bider, Djemma. *The buried treasure* ill. by Debby L. Carter. Dodd, 1982. Subj: Folk and fairy tales. Foreign lands – Russia.

Bienenfeld, Florence. *My mom and dad are getting a divorce* ill. by Art Scott. EMC, 1980. Subj: Divorce. Emotions.

Bier, Anna. *The nightingale* (Andersen, H. C. (Hans Christian))

Bierhorst, John. *Doctor Coyote: a Native American Æsop's fables* ill. by Wendy Watson. Macmillan, 1987. ISBN 0-02-709780-3 Subj: Animals. Animals – coyotes. Folk and fairy tales. Indians of North America.

The ring in the prairie: a Shawnee legend tr. by John Bierhorst; ill. by Leo and Diane Dillon. Dial Pr., 1970. Subj: Folk and fairy tales. Indians of North America.

Spirit child (Sahagun, Bernardino de)

The big Peter Rabbit book: *things to do, games to play, stories, presents to make* ill. by Beatrix Potter. Warne, 1986. ISBN 0-7232-3409-4 Subj: Animals. Games. Riddles.

Bileck, Marvin. *Penny* (De Regniers, Beatrice Schenk)

Rain makes applesauce (Scheer, Julian)

Bill, Helen. *Shoes fit for a king* ill. by Louis Slobodkin. Watts, 1956. Subj: Character traits – conceit. Royalty.

Billam, Rosemary. *Fuzzy rabbit* ill. by Vanessa Julian-Ottie. Random House, 1984. Subj: Behavior – needing someone. Birthdays. Emotions – love. Toys.

Billington, Elizabeth T. *The Randolph Caldecott treasury* (Caldecott, Randolph)

Billout, Guy. *By camel or by car: a look at transportation* ill. by author. Prentice-Hall, 1979. Subj: Activities – traveling. Transportation.

Billy Boy verses sel. by Richard Chase; ill. by Glen Rounds. Children's Pr., 1966. Subj: Folk and fairy tales. Poetry, rhyme. Songs.

Bingham, Mindy. *Minou* ill. by Itoko Maeno. Advocacy Pr., 1987. ISBN 0-911655-36-0 Subj: Animals – cats. Behavior – needing someone. Foreign lands – France.

My way Sally by Mindy Bingham and Penelope Colville Paine; ill. by Itoko Maeno. Advocacy Pr., 1988. ISBN 0-911655-27-1 Subj: Animals – dogs. Animals – foxes. Behavior – trickery.

Binzen, Bill. *Alfred goes house hunting* ill. by author. Doubleday, 1974. Subj: Animals. Houses. Toys.

Carmen photos. by author. Coward, 1970. Subj: City. Friendship.

Birch, David. *The king's chessboard* ill. by Devis Grebu. Dial Pr., 1988. ISBN 0-8037-0367-8 Subj: Character traits – pride. Royalty.

Birdseye, Tom. *Airmail to the moon* ill. by Stephen Gammell. Holiday, 1988. ISBN 0-8234-0683-0 Subj: Behavior – losing things. Character traits – persistence. Teeth.

Birnbaum, Abe. *Green eyes* ill. by author. Western Pr., 1953. Subj: Caldecott award honor book.

Biro, B. S. *see* Biro, Val

Biro, Val. *Gumdrop, the adventures of a vintage car* ill. by author. Follett, 1966. Subj: Automobiles.

The pied piper of Hamelin ill. by reteller. Silver Burdett, 1985. ISBN 0-382-09014-4 Subj: Animals – rats. Behavior – trickery. Folk and fairy tales. Foreign lands – Germany. Middle ages.

The wind in the willows: home sweet home ill. by author. Simon & Schuster, 1985. Subj: Animals. Houses.

The wind in the willows: the open road ill. by author. Simon & Schuster, 1985. ISBN 0-671-63626-X Subj: Activities – traveling. Animals.

The wind in the willows: the river bank ill. by author. Simon & Schuster, 1985. Subj: Animals. Rivers.

The wind in the willows: the wild wood ill. by author. Simon & Schuster, 1985. Subj: Animals. Forest, woods.

Birrer, Cynthia. *The lady and the unicorn* by Cynthia and William Birrer; ill. by authors. Lothrop, 1987. ISBN 0-688-04038-1 Subj: Character traits – kindness to animals. Folk and fairy tales. Magic. Mythical creatures. Royalty.

Song to Demeter by Cynthia and William Birrer; ill. by authors. Lothrop, 1987. ISBN 0-688-04041-1 Subj: Folk and fairy tales. Foreign lands – Greece.

Birrer, William. *The lady and the unicorn* (Birrer, Cynthia)

Song to Demeter (Birrer, Cynthia)

Bishop, Ann. *Chicken riddle* ill. by Jerry Warshaw. Albert Whitman, 1972. Subj: Birds – chickens. Humor. Riddles.

The Ella Fannie elephant riddle book ill. by Jerry Warshaw. Albert Whitman, 1974. Subj: Animals – elephants. Humor. Riddles.

Hey riddle riddle ill. by Jerry Warshaw. Albert Whitman, 1968. Subj: Humor. Riddles.

Merry-go-riddle ill. by Jerry Warshaw. Albert Whitman, 1973. Subj: Humor. Riddles.

Noah riddle? ill. by Jerry Warshaw. Albert Whitman, 1970. Subj: Humor. Riddles.

Oh, riddlesticks! ill. by Jerry Warshaw. Albert Whitman, 1976. Subj: Humor. Riddles.

The riddle ages ill. by Jerry Warshaw. Albert Whitman, 1977. Subj: Humor. Middle ages. Riddles.

Riddle-iculous rid-alphabet book ill. by Jerry Warshaw. Albert Whitman, 1971. Subj: ABC books. Humor. Riddles.

Wild Bill Hiccup's riddle book ed. by Caroline Rubin; ill. by Jerry Warshaw. Albert Whitman, 1969. Subj: Cowboys. Humor. Riddles.

Bishop, Bonnie. *No one noticed Ralph* ill. by Jack Kent. Doubleday, 1979. Subj: Behavior – unnoticed, unseen. Birds – parakeets, parrots.

Ralph rides away ill. by Jack Kent. Doubleday, 1979. Subj: Activities – picnicking. Birds – parakeets, parrots. Zoos.

Bishop, Claire Huchet. *The five Chinese brothers* by Claire Huchet Bishop and Kurt Wiese; ill. by Kurt Wiese. Coward, 1938. Subj: Character traits – cleverness. Family life. Folk and fairy tales. Foreign lands – China.

The man who lost his head ill. by Robert McCloskey. Viking, 1942. Subj: Anatomy. Humor.

Pancakes - Paris ill. by Georges Schreiber. Viking, 1947. Subj: Food. Foreign lands – France. War.

The truffle pig ill. by Kurt Wiese. Coward, 1971. Subj: Animals – pigs. Foreign lands – France. Pets.

Twenty-two bears ill. by Kurt Wiese. Viking, 1964. Subj: Animals – bears. Counting. Cumulative tales.

Bishop, Gavin. *Chicken Licken* (Chicken Little)

Mrs. McGinty and the bizarre plant ill. by author. Oxford Univ. Pr., 1983. Subj: Activities – gardening. Plants.

Bjork, Christina. *Linnea in Monet's garden* ill. by Lena Anderson. Farrar, 1987. ISBN 91-29-58314-4 Subj: Art. Flowers. Foreign lands – France. Museums.

Linnea's windowsill garden ill. by Lena Anderson. Farrar, 1988. ISBN 91-29-59064-7 Subj: Activities – gardening.

Black, Algernon D. *The woman of the wood: a tale from old Russia* ill. by Evaline Ness. Holt, 1973. Subj: Folk and fairy tales. Foreign lands – Russia.

Black, Floyd. *Alphabet cat* ill. by Carol Nicklaus. Elsevier-Dutton, 1979. Subj: ABC books. Animals – cats. Animals – rats.

Black, Irma Simonton. *Big puppy and little puppy* ill. by Theresa Sherman. Holiday, 1960. Subj: Animals – dogs. Concepts – size.

Is this my dinner? ill. by Rosalind Fry. Albert Whitman, 1972. Subj: Food. Participation. Poetry, rhyme.

The little old man who could not read ill. by Seymour Fleishman. Albert Whitman, 1968. Subj: Activities – reading. Shopping.

Blackmore, Vivien. *Why corn is golden: stories about plants* ill. by Susana Martínez-Ostos. Little, 1984. Subj: Folk and fairy tales. Foreign lands – Mexico. Plants.

Blackwood, Gladys Rourke. *Whistle for Cindy* ill. by author. Albert Whitman, 1952. Subj: Activities – whistling. Animals – dogs. Pets.

Blades, Ann. *Mary of mile 18* ill. by author. Scribner's, 1976. Subj: Animals – wolves. Character traits – perseverance. Farms. Foreign lands – Canada.

Blaine, Marge. *The terrible thing that happened at our house* ill. by John Wallner. Parents, 1975. Subj: Family life. Family life – mothers. Problem solving.

Blaine, Margery Kay *see* Blaine, Marge

Blair, Anne Denton. *Hurrah for Arthur! a Mount Vernon birthday party* ill. by Carol Watson. Seven Locks Pr., 1983. Subj: Animals – mice. Character traits – helpfulness. Holidays – Washington's Birthday.

Blake, Alfred *see* Wilson, Barbara

Blake, Andrew *see* Wilson, Barbara

Blake, Pamela. *Peep-show: a little book of rhymes* ill. by author. Macmillan, 1973. Subj: Nursery rhymes.

Blake, Quentin. *Custard and Company* (Nash, Ogden)

Mister Magnolia ill. by author. Jonathan Cape, 1980. Subj: Humor. Poetry, rhyme.

Mrs. Armitage on wheels ill. by author. Knopf, 1988. ISBN 0-394-99498-1 Subj: Humor. Sports – bicycling.

Quentin Blake's nursery rhyme book ill. by author. Harper, 1984. Subj: Humor. Nursery rhymes.

Snuff ill. by author. Lippincott, 1973. Subj: Crime. Knights.

The story of the dancing frog ill. by author. Knopf, 1985. Subj: Folk and fairy tales.

Blakeley, Peggy. *Two little ducks* ill. by Kenzo Kobayashi. Alphabet Pr., 1984. Subj: Communities, neighborhoods.

What shall I be tomorrow? ill. by Helga Aichinger. Alphabet Pr., 1984. Subj: Behavior – imitation. Imagination.

Blance, Ellen. *Lady Monster has a plan* by Ellen Blance and Ann Cook; ill. by Quentin Blake. Bowmar, 1977. Subj: Monsters.

Lady Monster helps out by Ellen Blance and Ann Cook; ill. by Quentin Blake. Bowmar, 1977. Subj: Monsters.

Monster and the magic umbrella by Ellen Blance and Ann Cook; ill. by Quentin Blake. Bowmar, 1973. Subj: Magic. Monsters. Umbrellas.

Monster and the mural by Ellen Blance and Ann Cook; ill. by Quentin Blake. Bowmar, 1977. Subj: Monsters.

Monster and the surprise cookie by Ellen Blance and Ann Cook; ill. by Quentin Blake. Bowmar, 1977. Subj: Monsters.

Monster at school by Ellen Blance and Ann Cook; ill. by Quentin Blake. Bowmar, 1973. Subj: Monsters. School.

Monster buys a pet by Ellen Blance and Ann Cook; ill. by Quentin Blake. Bowmar, 1977. Subj: Monsters. Pets.

Monster cleans his house by Ellen Blance and Ann Cook; ill. by Quentin Blake. Bowmar, 1973. Subj: Monsters.

Monster comes to the city by Ellen Blance and Ann Cook; ill. by Quentin Blake. Bowmar, 1973. Subj: City. Monsters.

Monster gets a job by Ellen Blance and Ann Cook; ill. by Quentin Blake. Bowmar, 1977. Subj: Activities – working. Monsters.

Monster goes around the town by Ellen Blance and Ann Cook; ill. by Quentin Blake. Bowmar, 1977. Subj: Monsters.

Monster goes to school by Ellen Blance and Ann Cook; ill. by Quentin Blake. Bowmar, 1973. Subj: Monsters. School.

Monster goes to the beach by Ellen Blance and Ann Cook; ill. by Quentin Blake. Bowmar, 1977. Subj: Monsters. Sea and seashore.

Monster goes to the circus by Ellen Blance and Ann Cook; ill. by Quentin Blake. Bowmar, 1977. Subj: Circus. Monsters.

Monster goes to the hospital by Ellen Blance and Ann Cook; ill. by Quentin Blake. Bowmar, 1977. Subj: Hospitals. Monsters.

Monster goes to the museum by Ellen Blance and Ann Cook; ill. by Quentin Blake. Bowmar, 1973. Subj: Monsters. Museums.

Monster goes to the zoo by Ellen Blance and Ann Cook; ill. by Quentin Blake. Bowmar, 1973. Subj: Monsters. Zoos.

Monster has a party by Ellen Blance and Ann Cook; ill. by Quentin Blake. Bowmar, 1973. Subj: Monsters. Parties.

Monster, Lady Monster and the bike ride by Ellen Blance and Ann Cook; ill. by Quentin Blake. Bowmar, 1977. Subj: Monsters. Sports – bicycling.

Monster looks for a friend by Ellen Blance and Ann Cook; ill. by Quentin Blake. Bowmar, 1973. Subj: Friendship. Monsters.

Monster looks for a house by Ellen Blance and Ann Cook; ill. by Quentin Blake. Bowmar, 1973. Subj: Monsters.

Monster meets Lady Monster by Ellen Blance and Ann Cook; ill. by Quentin Blake. Bowmar, 1973. Subj: Monsters.

Monster on the bus by Ellen Blance and Ann Cook; ill. by Quentin Blake. Bowmar, 1973. Subj: Buses. Monsters.

Bland, Edith Nesbit *see* Nesbit, Edith

Bland, Fabian *see* Nesbit, Edith

Blank, Joani. *A kid's first book about sex* ill. by Marcia Quackenbush. Rev. ed. Down There Pr., 1983. Subj: Family life. Science.

Blathwayt, Benedict. *Bear's adventure* ill. by author. Knopf, 1988. ISBN 0-394-90568-7 Subj: Animals – bears.

Blaustein, Muriel. *Baby Mabu and Auntie Moose* ill. by author. Four Winds Pr., 1983. Subj: Activities – baby-sitting. Behavior – misbehavior. Character traits – freedom.

Bedtime, Zachary! ill. by author. Harper, 1987. ISBN 0-06-020537-7 Subj: Animals – tigers. Bedtime. Behavior – misbehavior. Family life.

Play ball, Zachary! ill. by author. Harper, 1988. ISBN 0-06-020544-X Subj: Family life – fathers. Sports.

Blech, Dietlind. *Hello Irina* ill. by author. Holt, 1971. Translation of Allo Irina by Yaak Karsunke. Subj: Activities – traveling. Animals – horses.

Blegvad, Erik. *Burnie's hill: a traditional rhyme* ill. by author. Atheneum, 1977. Subj: Cumulative tales. Foreign lands – Scotland. Poetry, rhyme. Seasons.

The emperor's new clothes (Andersen, H. C. (Hans Christian))

One is for the sun (Blegvad, Lenore)

The swineherd (Andersen, H. C. (Hans Christian))

Blegvad, Lenore. *Anna Banana and me* ill. by Erik Blegvad. Atheneum, 1985. ISBN 0-689-50274-5 Subj: Character traits – bravery. Emotions – fear. Imagination.

The great hamster hunt ill. by Erik Blegvad. Harcourt, 1969. Subj: Animals – hamsters. Pets.

Hark! Hark! The dogs do bark, and other poems about dogs ill. by Erik Blegvad. Atheneum, 1975. Subj: Animals – dogs. Nursery rhymes.

Mr. Jensen and cat ill. by Erik Blegvad. Harcourt, 1965. Subj: Animals – cats. Emotions – loneliness. Foreign lands – Denmark.

Mittens for kittens and other rhymes about cats ill. by Erik Blegvad. Atheneum, 1974. Subj: Animals – cats. Nursery rhymes.

One is for the sun by Lenore and Erik Blegvad; ill. by Erik Blegvad. Harcourt, 1968. Subj: Counting. Poetry, rhyme.

The parrot in the garret and other rhymes about dwellings ill. by Erik Blegvad. Atheneum, 1982. Subj: Birds – parakeets, parrots. Houses. Poetry, rhyme.

Rainy day Kate ill. by Erik Blegvad. Macmillan, 1988. ISBN 0-689-50442-X Subj: Activities – playing. Imagination. Toys – dolls. Weather – rain.

This little pig-a-wig and other rhymes about pigs ill. by Erik Blegvad. Atheneum, 1978. Subj: Animals – pigs. Nursery rhymes.

Bliss, Austin. *That dog Melly!* (Bliss, Corinne Demas)

Bliss, Corinne Demas. *That dog Melly!* by Corinne Demas Bliss with Austin Bliss; photos. by Corinne Demas Bliss and Jim Judkis. Hastings, 1981. Subj: Animals – dogs. Friendship. Pets.

Bliss, Reginald see Wells, H. G. (Herbert George)

Bloch, Marie Halun. *Ivanko and the dragon* (Rudchenko, Ivan)

Blocksma, Dewey. *Easy-to-make spaceships that really fly* (Blocksma, Mary)

Blocksma, Mary. *Apple tree! Apple tree!* ill. by Sandra Cox Kalthoff. Childrens Pr., 1983. Subj: Seasons. Trees.

The best dressed bear ill. by Sandra Cox Kalthoff. Childrens Pr., 1984. ISBN 0-516-01585-0 Subj: Activities – dancing. Animals – bears. Clothing.

Did you hear that? ill. by Sandra Cox Kalthoff. Childrens Pr., 1983. Subj: Bedtime. Night. Noise, sounds.

Easy-to-make spaceships that really fly by Mary and Dewey Blocksma; ill. by Marisabina Russo. Prentice-Hall, 1983. Subj: Space and space ships.

Grandma Dragon's birthday ill. by Sandra Cox Kalthoff. Childrens Pr., 1983. Subj: Birthdays.

The pup went up ill. by Sandra Cox Kalthoff. Childrens Pr., 1983. Subj: Animals – dogs. Imagination.

Rub-a-dub-dub: What's in the tub? ill. by Sandra Cox Kalthoff. Childrens Pr., 1984. ISBN 0-516-01586-9 Subj: Activities – bathing. Animals – dogs.

Where's that duck? ill. by Sandra Cox Kalthoff. Childrens Pr., 1985. ISBN 0-516-01587-7 Subj: Birds – ducks. Farms. Poetry, rhyme.

Blood, Charles L. *The goat in the rug* by Charles L. Blood and Martin A. Link; ill. by Nancy Winslow Parker. Parents, 1976. Subj: Activities – weaving. Animals – goats. Indians of North America.

Bloom, Suzanne. *We keep a pig in the parlor* ill. by author. Potter, 1988. ISBN 0-517-56829-2 Subj: Animals – pigs. Farms. Poetry, rhyme.

Bloome, Enid. *The air we breathe!* ill. with photos. Doubleday, 1972. Subj: Ecology.

The water we drink! ill. with photos. Doubleday, 1971. Subj: Ecology.

Blos, Joan W. *Martin's hats* ill. by Marc Simont. Morrow, 1984. Subj: Clothing. Imagination.

Old Henry ill. by Stephen Gammell. Morrow, 1987. ISBN 0-688-06400-0 Subj: Behavior – indifference. Character traits – being different. Houses. Poetry, rhyme.

Blough, Glenn O. *Christmas trees and how they grow* ill. by Jeanne Bendick. McGraw-Hill, 1961. Subj: Holidays – Christmas. Trees.

Who lives in this meadow? ill. by Jeanne Bendick. McGraw-Hill, 1961. Subj: Animals.

Blue, Rose. *Black, black, beautiful black* ill. by Emmett Wigglesworth. Watts, 1969. Subj: Ethnic groups in the U.S. – Afro-Americans. Zoos.

How many blocks is the world? ill. by Harold James. Watts, 1970. Subj: City. Concepts – size. Ethnic groups in the U.S. – Afro-Americans. Family life. School.

I am here: Yo estoy aqui ill. by Moneta Barnett. Watts, 1971. Subj: Character traits – being different. Ethnic groups in the U.S. Ethnic groups in the U.S. – Puerto Rican-Americans. Foreign languages. School.

Bluestone, Rose see Blue, Rose

Blume, Judy. *The one in the middle is the green kangaroo* ill. by Amy Aitken. Bradbury Pr., 1981. Subj: Family life. Self-concept.

The Pain and The Great One ill. by Irene Trivas. Bradbury Pr., 1984. Orig. pub. in Free to be... you and me, McGraw-Hill, 1974. Subj: Family life. Sibling rivalry.

Blundell, Tony. *Joe on Sunday* ill. by author. Dial Pr., 1987. ISBN 0-8037-0446-1 Subj: Behavior. Imagination.

Blutig, Eduard see Gorey, Edward

Blyth, Alan. *Cinderella* (Perrault, Charles)

Bober, Natalie S. *Let's pretend: poems of flight and fancy* ill. by Bill Bell. Viking, 1986. ISBN 0-670-81176-9 Subj: Poetry, rhyme.

Bodecker, N. M. (Nils Mogens). *Good night little one* (Kraus, Robert)

Good night Richard Rabbit (Kraus, Robert)

"It's raining," said John Twaining: Danish nursery rhymes ill. by author. Atheneum, 1973. Subj: Foreign lands – Denmark. Humor. Nursery rhymes.

"Let's marry" said the cherry, and other nonsense poems ill. by author. Atheneum, 1974. Subj: Humor. Poetry, rhyme.

Snowman Sniffles and other verse ill. by author. Atheneum, 1983. Subj: Humor. Poetry rhyme. Tongue twisters.

Bodger, Joan. *Belinda's ball* ill. by Mark Thurman. Atheneum, 1981. Subj: Concepts.

Bodsworth, Nan. *Monkey business* ill. by author. Dial Pr., 1987. ISBN 0-8037-0393-7 Subj: Animals. Behavior – wishing. Imagination. Zoos.

Bodwell, Gaile. *The long day of the giants* ill. by Leon Steinmetz. McGraw-Hill, 1975. Subj: Giants. Poetry, rhyme. Time.

Boegehold, Betty. *Bear underground* ill. by Jim Arnosky. Doubleday, 1980. Subj: Animals – bears. Insects. Science.

Daddy doesn't live here anymore: a book about divorce ill. by Deborah Borgo. Childrens Pr., 1985. ISBN 0-307-62480-3 Subj: Divorce. Emotions – anger. Family life.

Here's Pippa again! ill. by Cyndy Szekeres. Knopf, 1975. Subj: Animals – mice.

Hurray for Pippa! ill. by Cyndy Szekeres. Knopf, 1980. Subj: Behavior – talking to strangers. Imagination. Toys.

In the castle of cats ill. by Jan Brett. Dutton, 1981. Subj: Animals – cats. Imagination.

Pawpaw's run ill. by Christine Price. Dutton, 1968. Subj: Animals – cats. Behavior – lost. Character traits – cleverness. Emotions – love. Pets. Poetry, rhyme.

Pippa Mouse ill. by Cyndy Szekeres. Knopf, 1973. Subj: Animals – mice.

Pippa pops out! ill. by Cyndy Szekeres. Knopf, 1979. Subj: Animals – mice.

Small Deer's magic tricks ill. by Jacqueline Chwast. Coward, 1977. Subj: Animals – deer. Behavior – trickery.

Three to get ready ill. by Mary Chalmers. Harper, 1965. Subj: Animals – cats. Behavior.

Boegehold, Betty Doyle *see* Boegehold, Betty

Boesel, Ann Sterling. *Sing and sing again* ill. by Louise Costello. Oxford Univ. Pr., 1938. Subj: Music. Songs.

Singing with Peter and Patsy ill. by Pelagie Doane. Oxford Univ. Pr., 1944. Subj: Music. Songs.

Bogart, Bonnie. *The Ewoks join the fight* ill. by Diane de Groat. Random House, 1983. Subj: Space and space ships. War.

Bogot, Howard. *I'm growing* by Howard Bogot and Daniel B. Syme; ill. by Janet Compere. Union of American Hebrew Congregations, 1982. Subj: Behavior – growing up. Jewish culture.

Bograd, Larry. *Egon* ill. by Dirk Zimmer. Macmillan, 1980. Subj: Animals. Character traits – curiosity.

Felix in the attic ill. by Dirk Zimmer. Harvey House, 1978. Subj: Family life.

Lost in the store ill. by Victoria Chess. Macmillan, 1981. Subj: Behavior – lost. Stores.

Bohanon, Paul. *Golden Kate* ill. by Gertrude Howe. Oxford Univ. Pr., 1943. Subj: Character traits – generosity. Farms.

Bohdal, Susi. *Bobby the bear* ill. by author. Holt, 1986. ISBN 0-03-008028-2 Subj: Format, unusual – board books. Friendship. Toys – teddy bears.

Harry the hare ill. by author. Holt, 1986. ISBN 0-03-008029-0 Subj: Format, unusual – board books. Toys.

The magic honey jar tr. by Anthea Bell; ill. by author. North-South, 1987. ISBN 0-8050-0491-2 Subj: Behavior – greed. Dreams. Royalty.

Tom cat ill. by author. Doubleday, 1977. Subj: Animals. Animals – cats. Communication.

Bohman, Nils. *Jim, Jock and Jumbo* ill. by Einar Norelius. Dutton, 1946. Subj: Animals – elephants. Animals – hippopotami. Animals – lions. Humor.

Boholm-Olsson, Eva. *Tuan* tr. by Dianne Jonasson; ill. by Pham van Don. Farrar, 1988. ISBN 91-29-58766-2 Subj: Family life. Foreign lands – Vietnam.

Bois, Ivy Du *see* DuBois, Ivy

Bois, William Pène Du *see* Du Bois, William Pène

Bolliger, Max. *The fireflies* ill. by Jiři Trnka. Atheneum, 1970. Based on a Czechoslovakian story: Broučci, by Jan Karafiát, first published in 1875; translated by Roseanna Hoover. Subj: Family life. Folk and fairy tales. Foreign lands – Czechoslovakia. Insects – fireflies. Night.

The giants' feast ill. by Monica Laimgruber. Addison-Wesley, 1976. Translation of Das Reisenfest; English version by Barbara Willard. Subj: Food. Giants.

The golden apple ill. by Celestino Piatti. Atheneum, 1970. Translated by Roseanna Hoover. Subj: Behavior – greed. Family life. Food.

The lonely prince ill. by Jurg Obrist. Atheneum, 1982. Subj: Emotions – loneliness. Friendship.

The magic bird ill. by Jan Lenica. David & Charles, 1988. ISBN 0-86264-146-2 Subj: Behavior – growing up. Character traits – kindness to animals. Elves and little people. Giants.

The most beautiful song ill. by Jindra Capek. Little, 1981. Subj: Music. Royalty.

Noah and the rainbow: an ancient story tr. by Clyde Robert Bulla; ill. by Helga Aichinger. Crowell, 1972. Subj: Religion – Noah.

The rabbit with the sky blue ears ill. by Jürg Obrist. David & Charles, 1989. ISBN 0-86241-204-8 Subj: Anatomy. Animals – rabbits. Self-concept.

Sandy at the children's zoo tr. from German by Elisabeth Gemming; ill. by Klaus Brunner. Crowell, 1967. Subj: Behavior – lost. Zoos.

The wooden man ill. by Fred Bauer. Seabury Pr., 1974. Translation of Der Mann aus Holz. Subj: Scarecrows. Weapons. Weather.

Bolognese, Don. *Donkey and Carlo* (Raphael, Elaine)

Donkey, it's snowing (Raphael, Elaine)

A new day ill. by author. Delacorte Pr., 1970. Subj: Activities – traveling. Babies. Ethnic groups in the U.S. – Mexican-Americans. Family life. Holidays – Christmas.

The sleepy watchdog (Bolognese, Elaine)

Turnabout (Raphael, Elaine)

Bolognese, Elaine. *The sleepy watchdog* by Elaine and Don Bolognese; ill. by Don Bolognese. Lothrop, 1964. Subj: Animals – dogs. Character traits – laziness.

Bolton, Evelyn *see* Bunting, Eve

Bond, Felicia. *Christmas in the chicken coop* ill. by author. Crowell, 1983. Subj: Birds – chickens. Holidays – Christmas. Trees.

Four Valentines in a rainstorm ill. by author. Crowell, 1983. Subj: Friendship. Holidays – Valentine's Day.

The Halloween performance ill. by author. Crowell, 1983. Subj: Animals – mice. Holidays – Halloween. School.

Mary Betty Lizzie McNutt's birthday ill. by author. Crowell, 1983. Subj: Animals – pigs. Birthdays.

Poinsettia and her family ill. by author. Harper, 1981. ISBN 0-690-04145-4 Subj: Animals – pigs. Behavior. Family life. Moving. Sibling rivalry.

Poinsettia and the firefighters ill. by author. Crowell, 1984. Subj: Animals – pigs. Bedtime. Night. Noise, sounds.

Wake up, Vladimir ill. by author. Crowell, 1987. ISBN 0-690-04453-4 Subj: Animals – groundhogs. Behavior – running away. Dreams. Shadows.

Bond, Jean Carey. *A is for Africa* ill. by author. Watts, 1969. Subj: ABC books. Foreign lands – Africa.

Bond, Michael. *Paddington and the knickerbocker rainbow* ill. by David McKee. Putnam's, 1985. ISBN 0-399-21202-7 Subj: Animals – bears. Food. Foreign lands – England. Language.

Paddington at the circus by Michael Bond and Fred Banbery; ill. by Fred Banbery. Random House, 1973. Subj: Animals – bears. Circus. Foreign lands – England.

Paddington at the fair ill. by David McKee. Putnam's, 1986. ISBN 0-399-21271-X Subj: Animals – bears. Fairs. Foreign lands – England.

Paddington at the palace ill. by David McKee. Putnam's, 1986. ISBN 0-399-21340-6 Subj: Animals – bears. Foreign lands – England. Royalty.

Paddington at the seaside ill. by Fred Banbery. Random House, 1975. Subj: Activities – vacationing. Animals – bears. Foreign lands – England. Sea and seashore.

Paddington at the tower ill. by Fred Banbery. Random House, 1975. Subj: Animals – bears. Foreign lands – England.

Paddington at the zoo ill. by David McKee. Putnam's, 1985. ISBN 0-399-21201-9 Subj: Animals – bears. Behavior – losing things. Foreign lands – England. Zoos.

Paddington cleans up ill. by David McKee. Putnam's, 1986. ISBN 0-399-21339-2 Subj: Activities – working. Animals – bears. Foreign lands – England.

Paddington's art exhibit ill. by David McKee. Putnam's, 1986. ISBN 0-399-21270-1 Subj: Activities – painting. Animals – bears. Art. Foreign lands – England.

Paddington's garden ill. by Fred Banbery. Random House, 1973. ISBN 0-394-92643-9 Subj: Activities – gardening. Animals – bears. Family life. Foreign lands – England.

Paddington's lucky day ill. by Fred Banbery. Random House, 1973. Subj: Animals – bears. Character traits – luck. Foreign lands – England. Shopping.

Bond, Ruskin. *Flames in the forest* ill. by Valerie Littlewood. Watts, 1981. Subj: Fire. Foreign lands – India. Forest, woods.

Bonino, Louise. *The cozy little farm* ill. by Angelia. Random House, 1946. Subj: Animals. Farms.

Bonne, Rose. *I know an old lady* ill. by Abner Graboff. Rand McNally, 1961. Music by Alan Mills. Subj: Cumulative tales. Folk and fairy tales. Foreign lands – Canada. Humor. Music. Songs.

I know an old lady who swallowed a fly ill. by William Stobbs. Oxford University Pr., 1987. ISBN 0-19-279837-5 Subj: Cumulative tales. Folk and fairy tales. Foreign lands – Canada. Humor. Songs.

Bonners, Susan. *Panda* ill. by author. Delacorte Pr., 1978. Subj: Animals – pandas. Science.

A penguin year ill. by author. Delacorte Pr., 1981. Subj: Birds – penguins. Family life. Foreign lands – Antarctic. Science.

Bonnici, Peter. *The festival* ill. by Lisa Kopper. Carolrhoda Books, 1985. ISBN 0-87614-229-3 Subj: Behavior – growing up. Foreign lands – India. Holidays.

The first rains ill. by Lisa Kopper. Carolrhoda Books, 1985. ISBN 0-87614-228-5 Subj: Weather – rain.

Bonsall, Crosby Newell. *The amazing the incredible super dog* ill. by author. Harper, 1986. ISBN 0-06-020591-1 Subj: Animals – cats. Animals – dogs. Behavior – boasting.

And I mean it, Stanley ill. by author. Harper, 1974. Subj: Activities – playing. Animals – dogs.

The case of the cat's meow ill. by author. Harper, 1965. Subj: Animals – cats. Careers – detectives. Ethnic groups in the U.S. – Afro-Americans. Problem solving.

The case of the double cross ill. by author. Harper, 1980. Subj: Clubs, gangs. Problem solving. Secret codes.

The case of the dumb bells ill. by author. Harper, 1966. Subj: Behavior – mistakes. Careers – detectives. Communication. Problem solving.

The case of the hungry stranger ill. by author. Harper, 1963. Subj: Careers – detectives. Ethnic groups in the U.S. – Afro-Americans. Problem solving.

The case of the scaredy cats ill. by author. Harper, 1971. Subj: Careers – detectives.

The day I had to play with my sister ill. by author. Harper, 1972. Subj: Family life. Games.

I'll show you cats (Ylla)

It's mine! A greedy book ill. by author. Harper, 1964. Subj: Behavior – greed. Friendship.

Listen, listen! by Crosby Newell Bonsall and Ylla; photos. by Ylla. Harper, 1961. Subj: Animals – cats. Animals – dogs. Character traits – appearance.

Look who's talking (Ylla)

Mine's the best ill. by author. Harper, 1973. Subj: Behavior – boasting. Sea and seashore. Toys – balloons.

Piggle ill. by author. Harper, 1973. Subj: Activities – playing. Friendship. Games.

Polar bear brothers (Ylla)

Tell me some more ill. by Fritz Siebel. Harper, 1961. Subj: Imagination. Libraries.

Twelve bells for Santa ill. by author. Harper, 1977. Subj: Holidays – Christmas. Parties.

What spot? ill. by author. Harper, 1963. Subj: Animals – walruses. Birds – puffins. Foreign lands – Arctic.

Who's a pest? ill. by author. Harper, 1962. Subj: Behavior – fighting, arguing. Character traits – helpfulness. Sibling rivalry.

Who's afraid of the dark? ill. by author. Harper, 1980. Subj: Animals – dogs. Emotions – fear. Night.

Bontemps, Arna Wendell. *The fast sooner hound* by Arna Wendell Bontemps and Jack Conroy; ill. by Virginia Lee Burton. Houghton, 1942. Subj: Animals – dogs. Trains.

Boojum *see* Barrows, Marjorie Wescott

Bookman, Charlotte *see* Zolotow, Charlotte

Boon, Emilie. *Belinda's balloon* ill. by author. Knopf, 1985. ISBN 0-394-97342-0 Subj: Animals – bears. Family life. Toys – balloons.

It's spring, Peterkin ill. by author. Random, 1986. ISBN 0-394-87997-X Subj: Character traits – kindness to animals. Format, unusual – board books. Seasons – spring.

1 2 3 how many animals can you see? ill. by author. Random, 1987. ISBN 0-531-08301-2 Subj: Animals. Counting. School.

Peterkin meets a star ill. by author. Random House, 1984. Subj: Imagination. Stars.

Peterkin's very own garden ill. by author. Random, 1987. ISBN 0-394-88666-6 Subj: Activities – gardening. Animals. Format, unusual – board books.

Peterkin's wet walk ill. by author. Random House, 1984. Subj: Animals. Imagination. Weather – rain.

Booth, Eugene. *At the circus* ill. by Derek Collard. Raintree, 1977. Subj: Circus. Concepts. Games. Participation. Problem solving.

At the fair ill. by Derek Collard. Raintree, 1977. Subj: Concepts. Fairs. Games. Participation. Problem solving.

In the air ill. by Derek Collard. Raintree, 1977. Subj: Concepts. Games. Participation. Problem solving.

In the garden ill. by Derek Collard. Raintree, 1977. Subj: Concepts. Games. Participation. Problem solving.

In the jungle ill. by Derek Collard. Raintree, 1977. Subj: Concepts. Games. Jungle. Participation. Problem solving.

Under the ocean ill. by Derek Collard. Raintree, 1977. Subj: Concepts. Games. Participation. Problem solving. Sea and seashore.

Borack, Barbara. *Grandpa* ill. by Ben Shecter. Harper, 1967. Subj: Family life – grandfathers.

Borchers, Elisabeth. *Dear Sarah* tr. and adapt. from German by Elizabeth Shub; ill. by Wilhelm Schlote. Greenwillow, 1980. Subj: Activities – traveling. Communication. Foreign lands.

There comes a time tr. by Babette Deutsch; ill. by Dietlind Blech. Doubleday, 1969. Subj: Days of the week, months of the year. Poetry, rhyme.

Borden, Beatrice Brown. *Wild animals of Africa* photos. by author. Random House, 1982. Subj: Animals. Birds. Foreign lands – Africa.

Borden, M. *see* Seyton, Marion

Boreman, Jean. *Bantie and her chicks* ill. by June Hendrickson. Melmont, 1959. Subj: Birds – chickens. School. Science.

Borg, Inga. *Plupp builds a house* ill. by author. Warne, 1961. Subj: Animals. Elves and little people. Foreign lands – Lapland. Houses.

Bornstein, Ruth Lercher. *Annabelle* ill. by author. Crowell, 1978. Subj: Behavior – lost. Toys.

The dancing man ill. by author. Seabury Pr., 1978. Subj: Activities – dancing. Foreign lands – Europe.

I'll draw a meadow ill. by author. Harper, 1979. Subj: Activities – vacationing. Animals – dogs.

Indian bunny ill. by author. Childrens Pr., 1973. Subj: Animals – rabbits. Indians of North America.

Jim ill. by author. Seabury Pr., 1978. Subj: Animals – dogs. Behavior – lost. Character traits – bravery.

Of course a goat ill. by author. Harper, 1980. Subj: Animals – goats. Family life.

The seedling child ill. by author. Harcourt, 1987. ISBN 0-15-272459-1 Subj: Friendship. Imagination – imaginary friends. Poetry, rhyme.

Borten, Helen. *Do you go where I go?* ill. by author. Abelard-Schuman, 1972. Subj: Humor. Poetry, rhyme.

Do you hear what I hear? ill. by author. Abelard-Schuman, 1960. Subj: Noise, sounds. Poetry, rhyme. Senses – hearing.

Do you know what I know? ill. by author. Abelard-Schuman, 1970. Subj: Poetry, rhyme. Senses – hearing. Senses – seeing. Senses – smelling. Senses – tasting. Senses – touching.

Do you move as I do? ill. by author. Abelard-Schuman, 1963. Subj: Emotions. Health.

Do you see what I see? ill. by author. Abelard-Schuman, 1959. Subj: Art. Concepts. Senses – seeing.

Halloween ill. by author. Crowell, 1965. Subj: Holidays – Halloween.

A picture has a special look ill. by author. Abelard-Schuman, 1961. Subj: Art.

Bossom, Naomi. *A scale full of fish and other turnabouts* ill. by author. Greenwillow, 1979. Subj: Humor. Language.

Boston. Children's Hospital Medical Center. *Curious George goes to the hospital* (Rey, Margaret Elisabeth Waldstein)

Boswell, Stephen. *King Gorboduc's fabulous zoo* ill. by Beverley Gooding. Dutton, 1986. ISBN 0-525-44267-7 Subj: Dragons. Royalty. Zoos.

Bothwell, Jean. *Paddy and Sam* ill. by Margaret Ayer. Abelard-Schuman, 1952. Subj: Behavior – lost. Birds – ducks.

Bottner, Barbara. *Big boss! Little boss!* ill. by author. Pantheon, 1978. ISBN 0-394-93939-5 Subj: Behavior – losing things. Sibling rivalry.

Horrible Hannah ill. by Joan Drescher. Crown, 1980. Subj: Animals – dogs. Friendship. Moving.

Jungle day: or, How I learned to love my nosey little brother ill. by author. Delacorte Pr., 1978. Subj: Sibling rivalry.

Mean Maxine ill. by author. Pantheon, 1980. Subj: Character traits – meanness. Friendship. Imagination.

Messy ill. by author. Delacorte Pr., 1979. Subj: Activities – dancing. Behavior – carelessness.

Myra ill. by author. Macmillan, 1979. Subj: Activities – dancing. Imagination.

There was nobody there ill. by author. Macmillan, 1978. Subj: Bedtime. Imagination. Poetry, rhyme. Sleep.

Zoo song ill. by Lynn Munsinger. Scholastic, 1987. ISBN 0-590-41005-9 Subj: Animals. Music. Zoos.

Botwin, Esther. *A treasury of songs for little children* ill. by Evelyn Urbanowich. Hart, 1954. Subj: Music. Songs.

Bouhuys, Mies. *The lady of Stavoren: a story from Holland* ill. by Francien Van Westering. Penguin, 1979. Subj: Folk and fairy tales. Foreign lands – Holland.

Boujon, Claude. *The fairy with the long nose* ill. by author. Macmillan, 1987. ISBN 0-689-50424-1 Subj: Anatomy. Fairies. Magic.

Bour, Danièle. *The house from morning to night* ill. by author. Kane, 1985. Subj: Houses.

Bourgeois, Paulette. *Big Sarah's little boots* ill. by Brenda Clark. Kids Can Pr., 1987. ISBN 0-921103-11-5 Subj: Behavior – growing up. Clothing. Family life. Weather – rain.

Franklin in the dark ill. by Brenda Clark. Kids Can Pr., 1986. ISBN 0-919964-93-1 Subj: Emotions – fear. Night. Reptiles – turtles, tortoises.

Bourke, Linda. *Ethel's exceptional egg* ill. by author. Harvey House, 1977. Subj: Birds – chickens. Eggs. Fairs.

Boutell, Clarence Burley. *The fat baron* ill. by Frank Lieberman. Houghton, 1946. Subj: Food. Imagination. Knights.

Bouton, Josephine. *Favorite poems for the children's hour* ill. by Bonnie and Bill Rutherford; foreword by Carolyn Sherwin Bailey. Platt, 1967. Subj: Poetry, rhyme.

Boutwell, Edna. *Red rooster* ill. by Bernard Garbutt. Atheneum, 1950. Subj: Birds – chickens. Cumulative tales. Folk and fairy tales.

Bove, Linda. *Sign language ABC with Linda Bove* ill. by Tom Cooke. Random, 1985. ISBN 0-394-97516-2 Subj: ABC books. Handicaps – deafness. Language. Senses – hearing.

Bowden, Joan Chase. *The bean boy* ill. by Sal Murdocca. Macmillan, 1979. Subj: Cumulative tales. Folk and fairy tales. Foreign lands – Italy. Humor.

The bear's surprise party ill. by Jerry Scott. Golden Pr., 1975. Subj: Animals – bears. Parties.

Boo and the flying flews ill. by Don Leake. Western, 1974. Subj: Animals – dogs. Circus.

Bouncy baby bunny finds his bed ill. by Christine Westerberg. Western, 1977. Subj: Animals – rabbits. Bedtime.

Emilio's summer day ill. by Ben Shecter. Harper, 1966. Subj: City. Ethnic groups in the U.S. – Puerto Rican-Americans. Seasons – summer.

The Ginghams and the backward picnic ill. by Joane Koenig. Western, 1979. Subj: Activities – picnicking.

A hat for the queen ill. by Olindo Giacomini. Golden Pr., 1974. Subj: Clothing. Royalty.

Little grey rabbit ill. by Lorinda Bryan Cauley. Western, 1979. Subj: Animals – rabbits.

A new home for Snow Ball ill. by Jan Pyk. Western, 1979. Subj: Animals – horses. Royalty.

Strong John ill. by Sal Murdocca. Macmillan, 1980. Subj: Behavior – trickery. Folk and fairy tales.

Who took the top hat trick? ill. by Jim Cummins. Golden Pr., 1974. Subj: Behavior – losing things. Magic.

Why the tides ebb and flow ill. by Marc Brown. Houghton, 1979. Subj: Folk and fairy tales. Humor. Sea and seashore.

Bowen, Vernon. *The lazy beaver* ill. by Jim Davis. McKay, 1948. Subj: Animals – beavers. Character traits – laziness.

Bower, Susie. *Science magic* (Alexander, Alison)

Bowers, Kathleen Rice. *At this very minute* ill. by Linda Shute. Little, 1983. Subj: Bedtime. Imagination.

Bowling, David Louis. *Dirty Dingy Daryl* ill. by Patricia Hendy Bowling. Inka Dinka Ink, 1981. Subj: Character traits – cleanliness.

Boxer, Deborah. *26 ways to be somebody else* ill. by author. Pantheon, 1960. Subj: ABC books. Careers.

A boy went out to gather pears: *an old verse* ill. by Felix Hoffmann. Harcourt, 1966. Subj: Cumulative tales. Poetry, rhyme.

Boyd, Lizi. *Half wild and half child* ill. by author. Viking, 1988. ISBN 0-670-82072-5 Subj: Behavior – misbehavior. Character traits – willfulness.

The not-so-wicked stepmother ill. by author. Viking, 1987. ISBN 0-670-81589-6 Subj: Activities. Behavior – misunderstanding. Birds – ducks. Family life – step families.

Boyd, Pauline. *The how* (Boyd, Selma)

I met a polar bear (Boyd, Selma)

Boyd, Selma. *The how: making the best of a mistake* by Selma and Pauline Boyd; ill. by Peggy Luks. Human Sciences Pr., 1981. Subj: Behavior – mistakes. Emotions – embarrassment. Friendship.

I met a polar bear by Selma and Pauline Boyd; ill. by Patience Brewster. Lothrop, 1983. Subj: Animals. Behavior – tardiness. Imagination. School.

Boyle, Constance. *Little Owl and the weed* ill. by author. Barron's, 1985. ISBN 0-8120-5639-6 Subj: Activities – gardening. Birds.

The story of little owl ill. by author. Barron's, 1985. Subj: Behavior – losing things. Birds – owls. Toys – teddy bears.

Boyle, Vere. *Beauty and the beast* ill. by author. Barron's, 1988. ISBN 0-8120-5902-6 Subj: Character traits – loyalty. Emotions -love. Folk and fairy tales. Magic.

Boynton, Sandra. *A is for angry* ill. by author. Workman, 1983. Subj: ABC books. Animals.

But not the hippopotamus ill. by author. Simon and Schuster, 1982. Subj: Animals – hippopotami. Format, unusual – board books. Poetry, rhyme.

Chloë and Maude ill. by author. Little, 1985. ISBN 0-316-10492-2 Subj: Animals – cats. Friendship.

Doggies ill. by author. Simon & Schuster, 1984. ISBN 0-671-49318-3 Subj: Animals – dogs. Format, unusual – board books.

The going to bed book ill. by author. Simon and Schuster, 1982. Subj: Animals. Bedtime. Format unusual – board books. Poetry, rhyme.

Good night, good night ill. by author. Random, 1985. ISBN 0-394-97285-6 Subj: Animals. Bedtime. Music. Poetry, rhyme. Songs.

Hester in the wild ill. by author. Harper, 1979. Subj: Animals – hippopotami. Animals – pigs. Sports – camping.

Hippos go berserk ill. by author. Little, 1979. Subj: Animals – hippopotami. Counting. Poetry, rhyme.

Horns to toes and in between ill. by author. Simon & Schuster, 1984. ISBN 0-671-49319-1 Subj: Anatomy. Format, unusual – board books.

If at first... ill. by author. Little, 1980. Subj: Animals – elephants. Animals – mice. Character traits – perseverance. Humor.

Moo, baa, lalala ill. by author. Simon and Schuster, 1982. Subj: Animals. Format unusual – board books. Noise, sounds. Poetry, rhyme.

Opposites ill. by author. Simon and Schuster, 1982. Subj: Concepts – opposites. Format unusual – board books.

Bozzo, Maxine Zohn. *Toby in the country, Toby in the city* ill. by Frank Modell. Greenwillow, 1982. Subj: City. Country.

Bradbury, Bianca. *The antique cat* ill. by Diana Thorne and Connie Moran. Winston, 1945. Subj: Animals – cats.

Muggins ill. by Diana Thorne. Houghton, 1944. Subj: Animals – cats. Behavior – misbehavior.

Mutt ill. by Mary Stevens. Houghton, 1974. Subj: Animals – dogs. Emotions – happiness.

One kitten too many ill. by Marie C. Nichols. Houghton, 1952. Subj: Animals – cats. Behavior – bullying. Friendship.

Bradbury, Ray. *Switch on the night* ill. by Madeleine Gekiere. Pantheon, 1955. Subj: Night.

Bradbury, Ray Douglas *see* Bradbury, Ray

Bradfield, Jolly Roger *see* Bradfield, Roger

Bradfield, Roger. *The flying hockey stick* ill. by author. Rand McNally, 1966. Subj: Activities – flying. Humor. Machines.

Giants come in different sizes ill. by author. Rand McNally, 1966. Subj: Giants. Wizards.

A good night for dragons ill. by author. Addison-Wesley, 1967. Subj: Dragons. Knights.

Bradford, Ann. *The mystery at Misty Falls* by Ann Bradford and Kal Gezi; ill. by Mina Gow McLean. Children's Pr., 1980. Subj: Animals – raccoons. Clubs, gangs. Problem solving.

The mystery in the secret club house by Ann Bradford and Kal Gezi; ill. by Mina Gow McLean. Children's Pr., 1978. Subj: Clubs, gangs. Crime.

The mystery of the blind writer by Ann Bradford and Kal Gezi; ill. by Mina Gow McLean. Children's Pr., 1980. Subj: Animals – dogs. Clubs, gangs. Crime. Handicaps – blindness. Problem solving.

The mystery of the live ghosts by Ann Bradford and Kal Gezi; ill. by Mina Gow McLean. Children's Pr., 1978. Subj: Holidays – Halloween.

The mystery of the midget clown by Ann Bradford and Kal Gezi; ill. by Mina Gow McLean. Children's Pr., 1980. Subj: Clowns, jesters. Clubs, gangs. Problem solving.

The mystery of the missing dogs by Ann Bradford and Kal Gezi; ill. by Mina Gow McLean. Children's Pr., 1980. Subj: Animals – dogs. Clubs, gangs. Handicaps. Problem solving.

The mystery of the missing raccoon by Ann Bradford and Kal Gezi; ill. by Mina Gow McLean. Children's Pr., 1978. Subj: Animals – raccoons. Character traits – freedom.

The mystery of the square footsteps by Ann Bradford and Kal Gezi; ill. by Mina Gow McLean. Children's Pr., 1980. Subj: Clubs, gangs. Problem solving. Robots.

The mystery of the tree house by Ann Bradford and Kal Gezi; ill. by Mina Gow McLean. Children's Pr., 1980. Subj: Birds – parakeets, parrots. Clubs, gangs. Crime. Problem solving.

Bradman, Tony. *The bad babies' book of colors* ill. by Deborah Van der Beek. Knopf, 1987. ISBN 0-394-99046-3 Subj: Behavior – misbehavior. Birthdays. Concepts – color.

The bad babies' counting book ill. by Deborah Van der Beek. Knopf, 1986. ISBN 0-394-98352-1 Subj: Behavior – misbehavior. Counting. Poetry, rhyme.

Look out, he's behind you ill. by Margaret Chamberlain. Putnam's, 1988. ISBN 0-399-21485-2 Subj: Animals – wolves. Behavior – talking to strangers. Forest, woods. Format, unusual – toy and movable books.

Not like this, like that ill. by Joanna Burroughes. Oxford Univ. Pr., 1988. ISBN 0-19-520712-2 Subj: Character traits – foolishness. Counting. Family life – fathers.

See you later, alligator ill. by Colin Hawkins. Dial Pr., 1986. ISBN 0-8037-0267-1 Subj: Animals. Format, unusual – toy and movable books. Reptiles – alligators, crocodiles.

Through my window ill. by Eileen Browne. Silver Burdett, 1986. ISBN 0-382-09258-9 Subj: Family life. Illness.

Wait and see ill. by Eileen Browne. Oxford University Pr., 1988. ISBN 0-19-520644-4 Subj: Family life. Shopping.

Brady, Irene. *A mouse named Mus* ill. by author. Houghton, 1972. Subj: Animals. Animals – mice. Character traits – freedom. Forest, woods.

Wild mouse ill. by author. Scribner's, 1976. Subj: Animals – mice. Science.

Brady, Susan. *Find my blanket* ill. by author. Harper, 1988. ISBN 0-397-32248-8 Subj: Animals – mice. Behavior – hiding things. Family life.

Bragdon, Lillian J. *Tell me the time, please* ill. by Frank and Margaret Phares. Lippincott, 1937. Subj: Clocks. Time.

Bragg, Michael. *The writing on the wall* (Garfield, Leon)

Braithwaite, Althea *see* Althea

Bram, Elizabeth. *I don't want to go to school* ill. by author. Greenwillow, 1977. Subj: School.

One day I closed my eyes and the world disappeared ill. by author. Dial Pr., 1978. Subj: Senses – seeing.

Saturday morning lasts forever ill. by author. Dial Pr., 1978. Subj: Activities – playing.

There is someone standing on my head ill. by author. Dial Pr., 1979. Subj: Imagination – imaginary friends.

Woodruff and the clocks ill. by author. Dial Pr., 1980. Subj: Behavior – collecting things. Clocks.

Brand, Millen. *This little pig named Curly* ill. by John Hamberger. Crown, 1968. Subj: Animals – pigs. Farms.

Brand, Oscar. *When I first came to this land* ill. by Doris Burn. Putnam's, 1974. Subj: Cumulative tales. Folk and fairy tales. Poverty. Songs.

Brande, Marlie. *Sleepy Nicholas* adapted by Noel Streatfield; ill. by author. Follett, 1970. Subj: Foreign lands – Denmark. Sleep.

Brandenberg, Aliki *see* Aliki

Brandenberg, Alyce Christina *see* Aliki

Brandenberg, Franz. *Aunt Nina and her nephews and nieces* ill. by Aliki. Greenwillow, 1983. Subj: Animals. Animals – cats. Babies. Birthdays. Toys.

Aunt Nina's visit ill. by Aliki. Greenwillow, 1984. Subj: Animals – cats. Puppets.

Cock-a-doodle-doo ill. by Aliki. Greenwillow, 1986. ISBN 0-688-06104-4 Subj: Animals. Farms. Noise, sounds.

Everyone ready? ill. by Aliki. Greenwillow, 1979. Subj: Activities – traveling. Animals – mice. Family life. Trains.

Fresh cider and apple pie ill. by Aliki. Macmillan, 1973. Subj: Food. Insects – flies. Spiders.

The hit of the party ill. by Aliki. Greenwillow, 1985. ISBN 0-688-04241-4 Subj: Animals – hamsters. Parties.

It's not my fault ill. by Aliki. Greenwillow, 1980. Subj: Animals – mice. Behavior – fighting, arguing. Family life. Sibling rivalry.

Leo and Emily ill. by Aliki. Greenwillow, 1981. Subj: Clothing. Friendship. Magic.

Leo and Emily and the dragon ill. by Aliki. Greenwillow, 1984. Subj: Activities – baby-sitting. Dragons. Imagination.

Leo and Emily's zoo ill. by Yossi Abolafia. Greenwillow, 1988. ISBN 0-688-07458-8 Subj: Animals. Family life. Zoos.

Nice new neighbors ill. by Aliki. Greenwillow, 1977. Subj: Animals – mice. Friendship. Moving.

No school today! ill. by Aliki. Subj: Animals – cats. Behavior – mistakes. School.

Otto is different ill. by James Stevenson. Greenwillow, 1985. ISBN 0-688-04254-6 Subj: Activities. Character traits – being different. Octopuses.

A picnic, hurrah! ill. by Aliki. Greenwillow, 1978. Subj: Activities – picnicking. Animals – cats. Problem solving. Weather – rain.

A robber! A robber! ill. by Aliki. Greenwillow, 1975. Subj: Animals – cats. Crime. Night. Noise, sounds.

A secret for grandmother's birthday ill. by Aliki. Greenwillow, 1975. Subj: Behavior – secrets. Birthdays. Family life – grandmothers.

Six new students ill. by Aliki. Greenwillow, 1978. Subj: Animals – mice. School.

What can you make of it? ill. by Aliki. Greenwillow, 1977. Subj: Animals – mice. Art. Behavior – saving things. Moving.

What's wrong with a van? ill. by Aliki. Greenwillow, 1987. ISBN 0-688-06775-1 Subj: Animals – cats. Automobiles. Behavior – seeking better things. Family life.

Brandt, Betty. *Special delivery* ill. by Kathy Haubrich. Carolrhoda Books, 1988. ISBN 0-87614-312-5 Subj: Careers – mail carriers. Letters. U.S. history.

Branley, Franklyn M. *Air is all around you* ill. by Holly Keller. Rev. ed. Crowell, 1986. ISBN 0-690-04503-4 Subj: Science.

The big dipper ill. by Ed Emberley. Crowell, 1962. Subj: Science. Stars.

Big tracks, little tracks ill. by Leonard P. Kessler. Crowell, 1960. Subj: Animals. Problem solving. Science.

A book of satellites for you ill. by Leonard P. Kessler. Rev. ed. Crowell, 1971. Subj: Science. Space and space ships.

Comets ill. by Giulio Maestro. Crowell, 1984. Subj: Science. Sky.

Eclipse: darkness in daytime ill. by Donald Crews. Rev. ed. Harper, 1988. ISBN 0-690-04619-7 Subj: Science. Sun.

Flash, crash, rumble, and roll ill. by Barbara and Ed Emberley. Rev. ed. Crowell, 1985. ISBN 0-690-04425-9 Subj: Science. Weather – thunder.

Floating and sinking ill. by Robert Galster. Crowell, 1967. Subj: Science.

Gravity is a mystery ill. by Don Madden. Rev. ed. Crowell, 1986. ISBN 0-690-04527-1 Subj: Science.

High sounds, low sounds ill. by Paul Showers. Crowell, 1967. Subj: Noise, sounds. Science.

How little and how much: a book about scales ill. by Byron Barton. Crowell, 1976. Subj: Concepts – measurement.

Hurricane watch ill. by Giulio Maestro. Crowell, 1985. ISBN 0-690-04471-2 Subj: Science. Weather – storms.

Is there life in outer space? ill. by Don Madden. Crowell, 1984. ISBN 0-690-04375-9 Subj: Science. Space and space ships.

Journey into a black hole ill. by Marc Simont. Crowell, 1986. ISBN 0-690-04544-1 Subj: Science. Space and space ships. Stars.

Light and darkness ill. by Reynold Ruffins. Crowell, 1975 Subj: Science.

The moon seems to change ill. by Barbara and Ed Emberley. Crowell, 1987. ISBN 0-690-04585-9 Subj: Moon. Science.

North, south, east and west ill. by Robert Galster. Crowell, 1966. Subj: Science.

The planets in our solar system ill. by Don Madden. Crowell, 1981. Subj: Science. Space and space ships. Sun. World.

Rain and hail ill. by Harriett Barton. Rev. ed. Crowell, 1983. Subj: Science. Weather. Weather – rain.

The sky is full of stars ill. by Felicia Bond. Crowell, 1981. Subj: Science. Sky. Stars.

Snow is falling ill. by Holly Keller. Rev. ed. Crowell, 1986. ISBN 0-690-04548-4 Subj: Science. Weather – snow.

The sun, our nearest star ill. by Helen Borten. Crowell, 1961. Subj: Science. Sun.

Sunshine makes the seasons ill. by Giulio Maestro. Rev. ed. Crowell, 1985. ISBN 0-690-04482-8 Subj: Science. Seasons. Sun.

Timmy and the tin-can telephone by Franklyn M. Branley and Eleanor K. Vaughan; ill. by Paul Galdone. Crowell, 1959. Subj: Communication. Science.

Tornado alert ill. by Giulio Maestro. Crowell, 1988. ISBN 0-690-04688-X Subj: Science. Weather – storms.

Volcanoes ill. by Marc Simont. Crowell, 1985. ISBN 0-690-04431-3 Subj: Science. Volcanoes.

What makes day and night ill. by Arthur Dorros. Rev. ed. Crowell, 1986. ISBN 0-690-04524-7 Subj: Earth. Science.

What the moon is like ill. by True Kelley. Rev. ed. Crowell, 1986. ISBN 0-690-04512-3 Subj: Moon. Science.

Brann, Esther. *A book for baby* ill. by author. Macmillan, 1945. Subj: Activities. Babies. Family life.

'Round the world ill. by author. Macmillan, 1935. Subj: Activities – traveling. Foreign lands. World.

Brasch, Kate. *Prehistoric monsters* photos. by Jean-Philippe Varin. Merrimack, 1985. ISBN 0-88162-098-X Subj: Animals. Dinosaurs. Science.

Braun, Kathy. *Kangaroo and kangaroo* ill. by Jim McMullan. Doubleday, 1965. Subj: Animals – kangaroos. Behavior – collecting things. Poetry, rhyme.

Brazos, Waco *see* Jennings, Michael

Brecht, Bertolt. *Uncle Eddie's moustache* ill. by Ursula Kirchberg. Pantheon, 1974. Translation of Onkel Ede hat einen Schnurrbart by Muriel Rukeyser. Subj: Humor. Poetry, rhyme.

Brecht, Eugen Berthold Friedrich *see* Brecht, Bertolt

Breda, Tjalmar *see* DeJong, David Cornel

Breinburg, Petronella. *Doctor Shawn* ill. by Errol Lloyd. Crowell, 1975. Subj: Activities – playing. Careers – doctors. Ethnic groups in the U.S. – Afro-Americans.

Shawn goes to school ill. by Errol Lloyd. Crowell, 1973. Subj: Ethnic groups in the U.S. – Afro-Americans. Friendship. School.

Shawn's red bike ill. by Errol Lloyd. Crowell, 1976. Subj: Ethnic groups in the U.S. – Afro-Americans. Sports – bicycling.

Brennan, Jan. *Born two-gether* photos. by Leo Brennan. J & L Books, 1984. ISBN 0-9613536-1-9 Subj: Family life. Twins.

Brennan, Joseph Killorin. *Gobo and the river* ill. by Diane Dawson. Holt, 1985. ISBN 0-03-004552-5 Subj: Character traits – perseverance. Puppets. Rivers.

Brennan, Patricia D. *Hitchety hatchety up I go!* ill. by Robert Rayevsky. Macmillan, 1985. ISBN 0-02-712300-6 Subj: Behavior – stealing. Elves and little people. Folk and fairy tales.

Brenner, Anita. *A hero by mistake* ill. by Jean Charlot. Addison-Wesley, 1953. Subj: Character traits – bravery. Crime. Emotions – fear.

I want to fly ill. by Lucienne Bloch. Addison-Wesley, 1943. Subj: Airplanes, airports. Imagination.

Brenner, Barbara. *Baltimore orioles* ill. by J. Winslow Higginbottom. Harper, 1974. Subj: Birds.

A dog I know ill. by Fred Brenner. Harper, 1983. Subj: Animals – dogs. Humor.

Faces, faces, faces photos. by George Ancona. Dutton, 1970. Subj: Anatomy. Emotions. Ethnic groups in the U.S. Senses – hearing. Senses – seeing. Senses – smelling. Senses – tasting. Senses – touching.

The five pennies ill. by Erik Blegvad. Knopf, 1964. Subj: Money. Pets.

The flying patchwork quilt ill. by Fred Brenner. Addison-Wesley, 1965. Subj: Activities – flying. Magic.

Mr. Tall and Mr. Small ill. by Tomi Ungerer. Addison-Wesley, 1966. Subj: Animals – giraffes. Animals – mice. Character traits – conceit. Fire.

Ostrich feathers ill. by Vera B. Williams and Evelyn Armstrong. Parents, 1979. Subj: Animals. Behavior – greed.

The prince and the pink blanket ill. by Nola Langner. Four Winds Pr., 1980. Subj: Family life. Royalty.

The snow parade ill. by Mary Tara O'Keefe Crown, 1984. ISBN 0-571-55210-8 Subj: Counting. Parades. Weather.

Somebody's slippers, somebody's shoes ill. by Leslie Jacobs. Addison-Wesley, 1957. Subj: Clothing. Shopping.

The tremendous tree book (Garelick, May)

Wagon wheels ill. by Don Bolognese. Harper, 1978. Subj: Character traits – perseverance. Ethnic groups in the U.S. – Afro-Americans. Farms. U.S. history.

Brentano, Clemens. *Schoolmaster Whackwell's wonderful sons* ill. by Maurice Sendak. Random House, 1962. Subj: Behavior – growing up. Careers. Folk and fairy tales.

Brett, Jan. *Annie and the wild animals* ill. by author. Houghton, 1985. Subj: Animals. Animals – cats. Emotions – loneliness. Pets.

The first dog ill. by author. Harcourt, 1988. ISBN 0-15-227650-5 Subj: Animals – dogs. Animals – wolves. Art. Caves. Pets.

Fritz and the beautiful horses ill. by author. Houghton, 1981. Subj: Animals – horses. Behavior – wishing. Character traits – cleverness. Folk and fairy tales.

Goldilocks and the three bears (The three bears)

Brewster, Benjamin *see* Elting, Mary

Brewster, Patience. *Ellsworth and the cats from Mars* ill. by author. Houghton, 1981. Subj: Animals – cats. Behavior – lost. Space and space ships.

Nobody ill. by author. Houghton, 1982. Subj: Behavior – dissatisfaction. Imagination – imaginary friends.

Brice, Tony. *Baby animals* ill. by author. Rand McNally, 1945. Subj: Animals. Babies.

The bashful goldfish ill. by author. Rand McNally, 1942. Subj: Character traits – shyness. Fish. Pets.

Bridges, William. *Lion Island* photos. by Emmy Haas and Sam Dunton. Morrow, 1965. Subj: Animals – lions. Zoos.

Ookie, the walrus who likes people photos. by Emmy Haas and Sam Dunton. Morrow, 1962. Subj: Animals – walruses.

Bridgman, Elizabeth. *All the little bunnies: a counting book* ill. by author. Atheneum, 1977. Subj: Counting. Poetry, rhyme.

How to travel with grownups ill. by Eleanor Hazard. Crowell, 1980. Subj: Activities – traveling. Foreign lands.

Nanny bear's cruise ill. by author. Harper, 1981. Subj: Activities – traveling. Animals – bears. Boats, ships.

A new dog next door ill. by author. Harper, 1978. Subj: Animals – dogs.

Bridle, Martin. *Punch and Judy in the rain* (Eaton, Su)

Bridwell, Norman. *Clifford goes to Hollywood* ill. by author. Scholastic, 1981. Subj: Animals – dogs. Character traits – loyalty.

Clifford's ABC ill. by author. Scholastic, 1984. ISBN 0-590-33154-X Subj: ABC books. Animals – dogs.

Clifford's good deeds ill. by author. Four Winds Pr., 1975. Subj: Animals – dogs. Automobiles. Behavior – mistakes. Careers – firefighters. Character traits – helpfulness.

Clifford's Halloween ill. by author. Four Winds Pr., 1967. Subj: Animals – dogs. Holidays – Halloween.

The witch grows up ill. by author. Scholastic, 1980. Subj: Humor. Magic. Witches.

The witch next door ill. by author. Four Winds Pr., 1966. Subj: Witches.

Brierley, Louise. *King Lion and his cooks* ill. by author. Holt, 1982. Subj: Animals. Food. Royalty.

Briggs, Raymond. *Building the snowman* ill. by author. Little, 1985. ISBN 0-316-10813-8 Subj: Snowmen. Wordless.

Dressing up ill. by author. Little, 1985. ISBN 0-316-10814-6 Subj: Clothing. Snowmen. Wordless.

Father Christmas ill. by author. Coward, 1973. Subj: Holidays – Christmas. Wordless.

Father Christmas goes on holiday ill. by author. Coward, 1975. Subj: Activities – vacationing. Holidays – Christmas. Wordless.

Fee fi fo fum ill. by author. Coward, 1964. Subj: Nursery rhymes.

Jim and the beanstalk ill. by author. Coward, 1970. Subj: Folk and fairy tales. Giants. Humor. Old age.

The party ill. by author. Little, 1985. ISBN 0-316-10816-2 Subj: Parties. Snowmen. Wordless.

Ring-a-ring o' roses ill. by author. Coward, 1962. Subj: Nursery rhymes.

The snowman ill. by author. Random House, 1978. Subj: Friendship. Snowmen. Wordless.

Walking in the air ill. by author. Little, 1985. ISBN 0-316-10815-4 Subj: Imagination. Snowmen. Wordless.

The white land: a picture book of traditional rhymes and verses ill. by compiler. Coward, 1963. Subj: Nursery rhymes. Songs.

Bright, Robert. *Georgie* ill. by author. Doubleday, 1944. Subj: Family life. Farms. Ghosts.

Georgie and the baby birds ill. by author. Doubleday, 1983. Subj: Birds. Character traits – helpfulness. Ghosts. Humor.

Georgie and the ball of yarn ill. by author. Doubleday, 1983. Subj: Character traits – helpfulness. Ghosts. Humor.

Georgie and the buried treasure ill. by author. Doubleday, 1979. Subj: Ghosts. Humor.

Georgie and the little dog ill. by author. Doubleday, 1983. Subj: Animals – dogs. Character traits – helpfulness. Ghosts. Humor.

Georgie and the magician ill. by author. Doubleday, 1966. Subj: Ghosts. Humor. Magic.

Georgie and the noisy ghost ill. by author. Doubleday, 1971. Subj: Activities – vacationing. Ghosts. Noise, sounds. Sea and seashore.

Georgie and the robbers ill. by author. Doubleday, 1963. Subj: Crime. Ghosts.

Georgie and the runaway balloon ill. by author. Doubleday, 1983. Subj: Animals – mice. Character traits – helpfulness. Ghosts. Humor. Toys – balloons.

Georgie goes west ill. by author. Doubleday, 1973. Subj: Cowboys. Ghosts.

Georgie to the rescue ill. by author. Doubleday, 1956. Subj: City. Ghosts.

Georgie's Christmas carol ill. by author. Doubleday, 1975. Subj: Ghosts. Holidays – Christmas.

Georgie's Halloween ill. by author. Doubleday, 1958. Subj: Ghosts. Holidays – Halloween.

Gregory, the noisiest and strongest boy in Grangers Grove ill. by author. Doubleday, 1969. Subj: Character traits – laziness. Food. Noise, sounds.

Hurrah for Freddie! ill. by author. Doubleday, 1955. Subj: Parades. Royalty. Toys.

I like red ill. by author. Doubleday, 1955. Subj: Concepts – color. Hair.

Me and the bears ill. by author. Doubleday, 1951. Subj: Animals – bears. Behavior – wishing. Friendship. Sleep. Zoos.

Miss Pattie ill. by author. Doubleday, 1954. Subj: Animals – cats.

My hopping bunny ill. by author. Doubleday, 1971. Subj: Activities – jumping. Animals – rabbits. Poetry, rhyme.

My red umbrella ill. by author. Morrow, 1959. Subj: Counting. Umbrellas. Weather – rain.

The travels of Ching ill. by author. Addison-Wesley, 1943. Subj: Foreign lands – China. Toys – dolls.

Which is Willy? ill. by author. Doubleday, 1962. Subj: Birds – penguins. Character traits – individuality.

Brightman, Alan. *Like me* ill. by author. Little, 1976. Subj: Character traits – being different. Handicaps.

Brighton, Catherine. *Five secrets in a box* ill. by author. Dutton, 1987. ISBN 0-525-44318-5 Subj: Behavior – secrets. Foreign lands – Italy. Science.

Hope's gift ill. by author. Doubleday, 1988. ISBN 0-385-24598-X Subj: Character traits – kindness to animals. Theater.

My hands, my world ill. by author. Macmillan, 1984. Subj: Handicaps – blindness. Imagination – imaginary friends. Senses – seeing.

Brimner, Larry Dane. *Country Bear's good neighbor* ill. by Ruth T. Councell. Watts, 1988. ISBN 0-531-08308-X Subj: Animals – bears. Food.

Brin, Ruth F. *David and Goliath* ill. by H. Hechtkopf. Lerner, 1977. Subj: Foreign lands – Israel. Religion.

The story of Esther ill. by H. Hechtkopf. Lerner, 1976. Subj: Foreign lands – Israel. Religion.

Brinckloe, Julie. *Fireflies!* ill. by author. Macmillan, 1985. ISBN 0-02-713310-9 Subj: Behavior – growing up. Insects – fireflies.

Gordon's house ill. by author. Doubleday, 1976. Subj: Animals – bears.

Playing marbles ill. by author. Morrow, 1988. ISBN 0-688-07144-9 Subj: Activities – playing. Games.

Bring a torch, Jeannette, Isabella ill. by Adrienne Adams. Scribner's, 1963. A provincial carol attributed to Nicholas Saboly, seventeenth century. Subj: Foreign lands – France. Holidays – Christmas. Music. Songs.

Briscoe, Jill. *The innkeeper's daughter* ill. by Dennis Hockerman. Childrens Pr., 1984. ISBN 0-516-09484-X Subj: Handicaps. Religion.

Briscoe, Margaret Sutton *see* Hopkins, Margaret

Brister, Hope. *The cunning fox and other tales* ill. by Henry C. Pitz. Knopf, 1943. Subj: Animals. Folk and fairy tales.

Bro, Marguerite H. *The animal friends of Peng-u* ill. by Seong Moy. Doubleday, 1965. Subj: Animals. Folk and fairy tales. Foreign lands – China.

Brock, Emma Lillian. *The birds' Christmas tree* ill. by author. Knopf, 1946. Subj: Birds. Character traits – kindness to animals. Holidays – Christmas.

Mr. Wren's house ill. by author. Knopf, 1944. Subj: Birds – wrens. Family life. Humor.

Nobody's mouse ill. by author. Knopf, 1938. Subj: Animals. City. Humor.

One little Indian boy ill. by author. Hale, 1932. Subj: Indians of North America.

A pet for Barbie ill. by author. Knopf, 1947. Subj: Family life. Pets.

Pig with a front porch ill. by author. Knopf, 1937. Subj: Animals – pigs. Behavior – dissatisfaction.

A present for Auntie ill. by author. Knopf, 1939. Subj: Family life.

Skipping Island ill. by author. Knopf, 1958. Subj: Humor. Islands.

Surprise balloon ill. by author. Knopf, 1949. Subj: Activities – flying. Animals. Toys – balloons.

Brodsky, Beverly *see* McDermott, Beverly Brodsky

Broekel, Ray. *Dangerous fish* ill. with photos. Childrens Pr., 1982. Subj: Fish.

I can be an author ill. by author. Childrens Pr., 1986. ISBN 0-516-01891-4 Subj: Careers – writers.

I can be an auto mechanic. Childrens Pr., 1985. ISBN 0-516-01885-X Subj: Automobiles. Careers – mechanics.

Trains ill. with photos. Children's Pr., 1981. Subj: Trains. Transportation.

Trucks ill. with photos. Childrens Pr., 1983. Subj: Trucks. Transportation.

Brogan, Peggy. *Sounds around the clock* (Martin, Bill (William Ivan))

Sounds I remember (Martin, Bill (William Ivan))

Sounds of home (Martin, Bill (William Ivan))

Sounds of laughter (Martin, Bill (William Ivan))

Sounds of numbers (Martin, Bill (William Ivan))

Bröger, Achim. *Bruno takes a trip* tr. from German by Caroline Gueritz; ill. by Gisela Kalow. Morrow, 1978. Subj: Activities – traveling. Pets. Trains.

Francie's paper puppy ill. by Michele Sambin; tr. from German. Alphabet Pr., 1984. Subj: Animals – dogs. Art. Country. Emotions – loneliness. Imagination. Pets.

Little Harry tr. from German by Elizabeth D. Crawford; ill. by Judy Morgan. Morrow, 1979. Subj: Humor. Imagination. Problem solving.

The Santa Clauses ill. by Ute Krause. Dial Pr., 1986. ISBN 0-8037-0266-3 Subj: Holidays – Christmas. Humor.

Bromhall, Winifred. *Bridget's growing day* ill. by author. Knopf, 1957. Subj: Behavior – growing up. Character traits – smallness. Foreign lands – Ireland.

Johanna arrives ill. by author. Knopf, 1941. Subj: Activities – traveling. Foreign lands – Holland.

Mary Ann's first picture ill. by author. Knopf, 1947. Subj: Activities – painting. Art. Birthdays.

Middle Matilda ill. by author. Knopf, 1962. Subj: Behavior – losing things. Clothing.

Brook, Judy. *Hector and Harriet the night hamsters: two adventures* ill. by author. Dutton, 1985. ISBN 0-233-97625-6 Subj: Animals – hamsters.

Tim mouse goes down the stream ill. by author. Lothrop, 1975. Subj: Animals – hedgehogs. Animals – mice. Character traits – bravery. Rivers.

Tim mouse visits the farm ill. by author. Lothrop, 1977. Subj: Animals – hedgehogs. Animals – mice. Farms.

Brooke, L. Leslie (Leonard Leslie). *The golden goose book* (Mother Goose)

Johnny Crow's garden ill. by author. Warne, 1903. Subj: Animals. Humor. Poetry, rhyme.

Johnny Crow's new garden ill. by author. Warne, 1935. Subj: Animals. Humor. Poetry, rhyme.

Johnny Crow's party ill. by author. Warne, 1907. Subj: Animals. Humor. Parties.

Oranges and lemons ill. by author. Warne, 1913. Subj: Nursery rhymes.

This little pig went to market (Mother Goose)

Brooks, Andrea. *The guinea pigs' adventure* ill. by author. Little, 1980. Subj: Animals – guinea pigs.

Brooks, Ann Tedlock see Carter, Anne

Brooks, Gregory. *Monroe's island* ill. by author. Bradbury Pr., 1979. Subj: Imagination.

Brooks, Gwendolyn. *Bronzeville boys and girls* ill. by Ronni Solbert. Harper, 1956. Subj: Poetry, rhyme.

Brooks, Robert B. *So that's how I was born* ill. by Susan Perl. Simon and Schuster, 1983. Subj: Babies. Family life. Science.

Brooks, Ron. *Timothy and Gramps* ill. by author. Bradbury Pr., 1978. Subj: Family life – grandfathers. School.

Broome, Errol. *The smallest koala* ill. by Gwen Mason. Australian Book Source, 1988. ISBN 0-949447-65-X Subj: Animals – koala bears. Character traits – curiosity. Food.

Brother Graham see Jeffery, Graham

Brothers, Aileen. *Jiffy, Miss Boo and Mr. Roo* ill. by Audean Johnson. Follett, 1966. Subj: Birds – chickens. Pets.

Sad Mrs. Sam Sack ill. by Muriel and Jim Collins. Follett, 1963. Subj: Behavior – dissatisfaction. Family life. Humor.

Brothers and sisters are like that! ill. by Michael Hampshire. Crowell, 1971. Selected by The Child Study Association of America. Subj: Family life. Sibling rivalry.

Brouillette, Jeanne S. *Moths* ill. by Bill Barss. Follett, 1966. Subj: Insects. Science.

Brown, Abbie Farwell. *The Christmas angel* ill. by Reginald Birch. Houghton, 1910. Subj: Angels. Holidays – Christmas.

Under the rowan tree ill. by Maurice Day. Houghton, 1926. Subj: Folk and fairy tales. Magic.

Brown, Beatrice Curtis. *Jonathan Bing* ill. by Judith Gwyn Brown. Lothrop, 1968. Subj: Poetry, rhyme.

Jonathan Bing ill. by Pelagie Doane. Oxford Univ. Pr., 1937. Subj: Poetry, rhyme.

Brown, Daphne Faunce see Faunce-Brown, Daphne

Brown, David. *Someone always needs a policeman* ill. by author. Simon and Schuster, 1972. Subj: Careers – police officers.

Brown, Elinor. *The little story book* ill. by author. Oxford Univ. Pr., 1940. Subj: Activities.

Brown, Jeff. *Flat Stanley* ill. by Tomi Ungerer. Harper, 1961. Subj: Family life. Humor. Problem Solving.

Brown, Judith Gwyn. *Alphabet dreams* ill. by author. Prentice-Hall, 1976. Subj: ABC books. Poetry, rhyme.

The happy voyage ill. by author. Macmillan, 1965. Subj: Boats, ships.

Max and the truffle pig ill. by author. Abingdon Pr., 1963. Subj: Animals – pigs. Behavior – lost. Food. Foreign lands – France.

Brown, Laurene Krasny. *The bionic bunny show* (Brown, Marc)

Dinosaurs travel by Laurie Krasny Brown and Marc Brown; ill. by Marc Brown. Little, 1988. ISBN 0-316-11076-0 Subj: Activities – traveling. Dinosaurs.

Visiting the art museum by Laurene Krasny Brown and Marc Brown; ill. by authors. Dutton, 1986. ISBN 0-525-44233-2 Subj: Art. Museums.

Brown, M. K. *Let's go swimming with Mr. Sillypants* ill. by author. Crown, 1986. ISBN 0-517-56185-9 Subj: Dreams. Sports – swimming.

Brown, Marc. *Arthur goes to camp* ill. by author. Little, 1982. Subj: Animals. Sports – camping.

Arthur's April fool ill. by author. Little, 1983. Subj: Animals. Holidays – April Fools' Day.

Arthur's baby ill. by author. Little, 1987. ISBN 0-316-11123-6 Subj: Animals – aardvarks. Babies. Family life.

Arthur's Christmas ill. by author. Little, 1984. Subj: Animals. Holidays – Christmas.

Arthur's eyes ill. by author. Little, 1979. Subj: Animals. Glasses. Senses – seeing.

Arthur's Halloween ill. by author. Little, 1982. Subj: Animals. Holidays – Halloween.

Arthur's teacher trouble ill. by author. Little, 1986. ISBN 0-87113-091-2 Subj: Animals. School.

Arthur's Thanksgiving ill. by author. Little, 1983. Subj: Animals. Holidays – Thanksgiving. Theater.

Arthur's tooth ill. by author. Little, 1985. ISBN 0-87113-006-8 Subj: Animals. Teeth.

Arthur's Valentine ill. by author. Little, 1980. Subj: Animals. Holidays – Valentine's Day. School.

The bionic bunny show by Marc Brown and Laurene Krasny Brown; ill. by Marc Brown. Little, 1984. Subj: Animals. Animals – rabbits. Television.

The cloud over Clarence ill. by author. Dutton, 1979. Subj: Animals – cats. Behavior – carelessness. Friendship.

D. W. all wet ill. by author. Little, 1988. ISBN 0-316-11077-9 Subj: Animals – anteaters. Sea and seashore. Sibling rivalry.

D. W. flips! ill. by author. Little, 1987. ISBN 0-316-11239-9 Subj: Animals. Sports – gymnastics.

Dinosaurs, beware! a safety guide by Marc Brown and Stephen Krensky; ill. by authors. Little, 1982. Subj: Dinosaurs. Safety.

Dinosaurs travel (Brown, Laurene Krasny)

Finger rhymes ill. by author. Dutton, 1980. Subj: Games. Participation. Poetry, rhyme.

Hand rhymes ill. by selector. Dutton, 1985. ISBN 0-525-44201-4 Subj: Games. Poetry, rhyme.

Lenny and Lola ill. by author. Dutton, 1978. Subj: Circus.

Marc Brown's full house ill. by author. Addison-Wesley, 1977. Subj: Monsters.

Moose and goose ill. by author. Dutton, 1978. Subj: Animals – moose. Birds – geese.

Perfect pigs: an introduction to manners by Marc Brown and Stephen Krensky; ill. by authors. Little, 1983. Subj: Animals – pigs. Etiquette.

Pickle things ill. by author. Parents, 1980. Subj: Food. Poetry, rhyme.

Play rhymes ill. by author. Dutton, 1987. ISBN 0-525-44336-3 Subj: Games. Nursery rhymes. Music. Songs.

The silly tail book ill. by author. Parents, 1983. Subj: Animals. Poetry, rhyme.

Spooky riddles ill. by author. Random House, 1983. Subj: Ghosts. Humor. Monsters. Riddles. Witches.

There's no place like home ill. by author. Parents, 1984. ISBN 0-8193-1125-1 Subj: Houses.

The true Francine ill. by author. Little, 1981. Subj: Animals. Behavior – lying. School.

Visiting the art museum (Brown, Laurene Krasny)

What do you call a dumb bunny? and other rabbit riddles, games, jokes and cartoons ill. by author. Little, 1983. Subj: Animals – rabbits. Format, unusual – toy and movable books. Games. Humor. Riddles.

Wings on things ill. by author. Random House, 1982. Subj: Activities – flying. Poetry, rhyme.

Witches four ill. by author. Parents, 1980. Subj: Poetry, rhyme. Witches.

Your first garden book ill. by author. Little, 1981. Subj: Activities – gardening. Plants.

Brown, Marcia. *All butterflies: an ABC* ill. by author. Scribner's, 1974. Subj: ABC books.

The blue jackal ill. by author. Scribner's, 1977. Subj: Animals. Behavior – trickery. Folk and fairy tales. Foreign lands – India.

The bun: a tale from Russia ill. by author. Harcourt, 1972. Subj: Animals. Behavior – greed. Character traits – cleverness. Cumulative tales. Folk and fairy tales.

Dick Whittington and his cat

Felice ill. by author. Scribner's, 1958. Subj: Animals – cats. Foreign lands – Italy.

Henry fisherman ill. by author. Scribner's, 1949. Subj: Caldecott award honor book. Careers – fishermen.

How, hippo! ill. by author. Scribner's, 1969. Subj: Animals – hippopotami.

Listen to a shape photos. by author. Watts, 1979. Subj: Concepts – shape.

The little carousel ill. by author. Scribner's, 1946. Subj: City. Emotions – loneliness. Kites. Merry-go-rounds. Money.

The neighbors ill. by author. Scribner's, 1967. "Text adapted from Afanas'yev." Subj: Animals – foxes. Animals – rabbits. Cumulative tales. Foreign lands – Russia. Houses.

Once a mouse... adapt. and ill. by author. Scribner's, 1961. An adaption of Hitopadeśa, a tale from ancient India. Subj: Animals. Caldecott award book. Character traits – vanity. Concepts – size. Folk and fairy tales. Foreign lands – India. Magic.

Peter Piper's alphabet ill. by author. Scribner's, 1959. Subj: ABC books. Nursery rhymes. Tongue twisters.

Skipper John's cook ill. by author. Scribner's, 1951. Subj: Activities – cooking. Boats, ships. Caldecott award honor book.

Stone soup ill. by author. Scribner's, 1947. Subj: Caldecott award honor book. Careers – military. Character traits – cleverness. Folk and fairy tales. Food. Foreign lands – Russia.

Tamarindo! ill. by author. Scribner's, 1960. Subj: Animals – donkeys. Behavior – lost. Foreign lands – Greece.

Touch will tell photos. by author. Watts, 1979. Subj: Concepts. Senses – touching.

Walk with your eyes photos. by author. Watts, 1979. Subj: Concepts. Senses – seeing.

Brown, Margaret Wise. *Baby animals* ill. by Mary Cameron. Random House, 1941. Subj: Animals.

Big dog, little dog ill. by Leonard Weisgard. Doubleday, 1943. Subj: Animals – dogs. Concepts – size.

The big fur secret ill. by Robert de Veyrac. Harper, 1944. Subj: Animals. Communication. Zoos.

Big red barn ill. by Rosella Hartman. Addison-Wesley, 1956. Subj: Barns. Farms. Poetry, rhyme.

Bumble bugs and elephants ill. by Clement Hurd. Addison-Wesley, 1941. Subj: Concepts – size.

A child's good morning book ill. by Jean Charlot. Addison-Wesley, 1952. Subj: Morning.

A child's good night book ill. by Jean Charlot. Addison-Wesley, 1950. Subj: Bedtime. Caldecott award honor book. Night. Sleep.

Christmas in the barn ill. by Barbara Cooney. Crowell, 1952. Subj: Holidays – Christmas.

The country noisy book ill. by Leonard Weisgard. Harper, 1940. Subj: Animals – dogs. Country. Noise, sounds. Participation.

The dead bird ill. by Remy Charlip. W. R. Scott, 1958. Subj: Death.

Dr. Squash the doll doctor ill. by J. P. Miller. Simon and Schuster, 1952. Subj: Character traits – kindness. Toys – dolls. Toys – soldiers.

Don't frighten the lion ill. by H. A. Rey. Harper, 1942. Subj: Animals. Animals – dogs. Character traits – cleverness. Zoos.

Dream book ill. by Richard Floethe. Random House, 1950. Subj: Dreams.

The duck photos. by Ylla. Harper, 1953. Subj: Animals. Birds – ducks. Character traits – vanity.

Five little firemen by Margaret Wise Brown and Edith Thacher Hurd; ill. by Tibor Gergely. Simon and Schuster, 1959. Subj: Careers – firefighters. Noise, sounds.

Four fur feet ill. by Remy Charlip. W. R. Scott, 1961. Subj: Activities – walking. Poetry, rhyme. World.

Fox eyes ill. by Garth Williams. Pantheon, 1977, 1951. Subj: Animals. Animals – foxes.

The golden egg book ill. by Leonard Weisgard. Simon and Schuster, 1947. Subj: Animals – rabbits. Birds – ducks. Eggs. Holidays – Easter.

Goodnight moon ill. by Clement Hurd. Harper, 1934. Subj: Animals – rabbits. Bedtime. Moon.

House of a hundred windows Cat and architecture by Robert de Veyrac; ill. by Henri Rousseau and others. Harper, 1945. Subj: Animals – cats. Houses.

The indoor noisy book ill. by Leonard Weisgard. Harper, 1942. Subj: Animals – dogs. Games. Noise, sounds. Participation.

The little brass band ill. by Clement Hurd. Harper, 1948. Subj: Cumulative tales. Music.

Little chicken ill. by Leonard Weisgard. Harper, 1943. Subj: Animals – rabbits. Birds – chickens.

The little farmer ill. by Esphyr Slobodkina. Addison-Wesley, 1948. Subj: Dreams. Farms.

The little fir tree ill. by Barbara Cooney. Crowell, 1954. Subj: Holidays – Christmas. Trees.

The little fireman ill. by Esphyr Slobodkina. Addison-Wesley, 1952. Subj: Careers – firefighters. Fire.

The little fisherman ill. by Dahlov Ipcar. Addison-Wesley, 1945. Subj: Careers – fishermen. Fish.

The little fur family ill. by Garth Williams. Harper, 1946. Subj: Activities. Format, unusual.

The little island ill. by Leonard Weisgard. Doubleday, 1946. Subj: Caldecott award book. Islands. Seasons. Weather.

Little lost lamb ill. by Leonard Weisgard. Doubleday, 1945. Subj: Animals – sheep. Behavior – lost. Caldecott award honor book.

Nibble nibble ill. by Leonard Weisgard. Addison-Wesley, 1959. Subj: Poetry, rhyme.

Night and day ill. by Leonard Weisgard. Harper, 1942. Subj: Animals – cats. Emotions – fear. Night.

Noisy book ill. by Leonard Weisgard. Harper, 1939. Subj: Noise, sounds. Participation.

On Christmas eve ill. by Beni Montresor. W. R. Scott, 1961. Subj: Holidays – Christmas. Religion.

Once upon a time in pigpen and three other stories ill. by Ann Strugnell. Addison-Wesley, 1980. Subj: Animals. Humor.

Pussycat's Christmas ill. by Helen Stone. Harper, 1949. Subj: Animals – cats. Holidays – Christmas.

The quiet noisy book ill. by Leonard Weisgard. Harper, 1950. Subj: Animals – dogs. Morning. Noise, sounds. Participation.

Red light, green light ill. by Leonard Weisgard. Doubleday, 1944. Subj: Concepts – color. Safety. Traffic, traffic signs.

The runaway bunny ill. by Clement Hurd. Harper, 1942. Subj: Animals – rabbits. Behavior – running away. Holidays – Easter.

The seashore noisy book ill. by Leonard Weisgard. Harper, 1941. Subj: Noise, sounds. Participation. Sea and seashore.

SHHhhh...Bang: a whispering book ill. by Robert De Veyrac. Harper, 1943. Subj: Noise, sounds.

Sleepy ABC ill. by Esphyr Slobodkina. Lothrop, 1953. Subj: ABC books. Poetry, rhyme. Sleep.

The sleepy little lion ill. by Ylla. Harper, 1947. Subj: Animals – lions. Sleep.

Sneakers ill. by Jean Charlot. Addison-Wesley, 1979, 1955. Reissue of 1955 ed. published by W. R. Scott under title Seven stories about a cat named Sneakers. Subj: Animals – cats. Behavior – misbehavior.

The steamroller: a fantasy ill. by Evaline Ness. Walker, 1974. Published in 1938 in the author's collection, The fish with the deep sea smile. Subj: Holidays – Christmas. Machines.

Streamlined pig ill. by Kurt Wiese. Harper, 1938. Subj: Activities – flying. Airplanes, airports. Animals. Character traits – bravery.

The summer noisy book ill. by Leonard Weisgard. Harper, 1951. Subj: Farms. Noise, sounds. Participation. Seasons – summer.

They all saw it photos. by Ylla. Harper, 1944. Subj: Animals. Problem solving.

Three little animals ill. by Garth Williams. Harper, 1956. Subj: Activities – traveling. Animals. Behavior – lost. City.

Two little miners ill. by Edith Thacher Hurd. Simon and Schuster, 1949. Subj: Careers – miners.

Two little trains ill. by Jean Charlot. Addison-Wesley, 1949. Subj: Poetry, rhyme. Trains.

Wait till the moon is full ill. by Garth Williams. Harper, 1948. Subj: Animals. Animals – raccoons. Character traits – questioning. Moon. Night.

Wheel on the chimney by Margaret Wise Brown and Tibor Gergely; ill. by Tibor Gergely. Lippincott, 1954. Subj: Birds – storks. Caldecott award honor book. Character traits – luck. Foreign lands – Hungary.

When the wind blew ill. by Geoffrey Hayes. Harper, 1977, 1937. Subj: Animals – cats. Illness. Weather – wind.

Where have you been? ill. by Barbara Cooney. Reissue of Crowell, 1952 ed. Hastings House, 1981. Subj: Animals. Poetry, rhyme.

Whistle for the train ill. by Leonard Weisgard. Doubleday, 1956. Subj: Poetry, rhyme. Trains.

The winter noisy book ill. by Charles Green Shaw. Harper, 1947. Subj: Animals – dogs. Noise, sounds. Participation. Seasons – winter. Weather – snow.

The wonderful house ill. by J. P. Miller. Simon and Schuster, 1950. Subj: Houses.

The wonderful story book ill. by J. P. Miller. Simon and Schuster, 1948. Subj: Poetry, rhyme.

Young kangaroo ill. by Symeon Shimin. Addison-Wesley, 1955. Subj: Animals – kangaroos.

Brown, Myra Berry. *Benjy's blanket* ill. by Dorothy Marino. Watts, 1952. Subj: Animals – cats. Behavior – growing up.

Best friends ill. by Don Freeman. Golden Gate, 1967. Subj: Friendship. Poetry, rhyme.

Best of luck ill. by Don Freeman. Golden Gate, 1969. Subj: Character traits – luck. Poetry, rhyme.

Company's coming for dinner ill. by Dorothy Marino. Watts, 1960. Subj: Character traits – helpfulness. Etiquette. Parties.

First night away from home ill. by Dorothy Marino. Watts, 1960. Subj: Activities – playing. Friendship. Sleep. Toys – teddy bears.

Pip camps out ill. by Phyllis Graham. Golden Gate, 1966. Subj: Family life. Night. Sports – camping.

Pip moves away ill. by Pauline Jackson. Golden Gate, 1967. Subj: Family life. Moving.

Brown, Palmer. *Cheerful* ill. by author. Harper, 1957. Subj: Animals – mice.

Hickory ill. by author. Harper, 1978. Subj: Animals – mice. Behavior – growing up. Friendship.

The silver nutmeg ill. by author. Harper, 1956. Subj: Imagination – imaginary friends. Poetry, rhyme. Problem solving.

Something for Christmas ill. by author. Harper, 1958. Subj: Animals – mice. Character traits – generosity. Emotions – love. Holidays – Christmas.

Brown, Paul. *Merrylegs, the rocking pony* ill. by author. Scribner's, 1946. Subj: Imagination. Toys – rocking horses.

Brown, Richard Eric. *One hundred words about animals* ill. by author. Harcourt, 1987. ISBN 0-15-200550-1 Subj: Animals.

One hundred words about transportation ill. by author. Harcourt, 1987. ISBN 0-15-200551-X Subj: Transportation.

Brown, Ruth. *The big sneeze* ill. by author. Lothrop, 1985. ISBN 0-688-04666-5 Subj: Farms. Humor.

Crazy Charlie ill. by author. Rourke, 1982. Subj: Reptiles – alligators, crocodiles. Self-concept. Teeth.

A dark, dark tale ill. by author. Dial Pr., 1981. Subj: Cumulative tales. Foreign lands – England.

Our cat Flossie ill. by author. Dutton, 1986. ISBN 0-525-44256-1 Subj: Activities. Animals – cats.

Our puppy's vacation ill. by author. Dutton, 1987. ISBN 0-525-44326-6 Subj: Activities – playing. Activities – vacationing. Animals – dogs. Pets.

Brown, Tricia. *Hello, amigos!* photos. by Fran Ortiz. Holt, 1986. ISBN 0-8050-0090-9 Subj: Birthdays. Ethnic groups in the U.S. – Mexican-Americans. Family life. School.

Someone special, just like you photos. by Fran Ortiz. Holt, 1984. Subj: Emotions. Handicaps.

Browne, Anthony. *Bear hunt* ill. by author. Atheneum, 1980. Subj: Animals – bears. Art. Problem solving. Sports – hunting.

Gorilla ill. by author. Knopf, 1985, 1983. ISBN 0-394-97525-1 Subj: Animals – gorillas. Birthdays. Family life – fathers. Imagination. Toys.

Look what I've got! ill. by author. Watts, 1980. Subj: Behavior – boasting. Imagination.

Piggybook ill. by author. Knopf, 1986. ISBN 0-394-98416-1 Subj: Animals – pigs. Family life – mothers.

Willy the champ ill. by author. Knopf, 1986. ISBN 0-394-97907-9 Subj: Animals – gorillas. Behavior – bullying.

Willy the wimp ill. by author. Knopf, 1985. Subj: Animals – gorillas. Animals – monkeys. Self-concept.

Browne, Caroline. *Mrs. Christie's farmhouse* ill. by author. Doubleday, 1977. Subj: Activities – gardening. Country. Farms. Humor. Royalty.

Brownell, Amanda Benjamin Hall *see* Hall, Amanda

Browner, Richard. *Everyone has a name* ill. by Emma Landau. Walck, 1961. Subj: Animals. Names. Poetry, rhyme.

Look again! ill. by Emma Landau. Atheneum, 1962. Subj: Concepts.

Browning, Robert. *The Pied Piper of Hamelin* (Bartos-Hoppner, Barbara)

The Pied Piper of Hamelin (Mayer, Mercer)

The pied piper of Hamelin ill. by Kate Greenaway. Warne, n.d. Subj: Animals – rats. Behavior – trickery. Folk and fairy tales. Foreign lands – Germany. Poetry, rhyme.

The pied piper of Hamelin ill. by Anatoly Ivanov. Lothrop, 1986. ISBN 0-688-03810-1 Subj: Animals – rats. Behavior – trickery. Folk and fairy tales. Foreign lands – Germany. Poetry, rhyme.

The pied piper of Hamelin adapt. by Sara and Stephen Corrin; ill. by Errol Le Cain. Harcourt, 1989. ISBN 0-15-261596-2 Subj: Animals – rats. Behavior – trickery. Folk and fairy tales. Foreign lands – Germany. Poetry, rhyme.

Bruce, Sheilah B. *The radish day jubilee* ill. by Lawrence DiFiori. Holt, 1983. Subj: Imagination. Poetry, rhyme. Puppets.

Bruna, Dick. *Another story to tell* ill. by author. Methuen, 1978. Subj: Weather – snow. Wordless.

B is for bear: an A-B-C ill. by author. Methuen, 1971. Subj: ABC books.

Christmas ill. by author. Doubleday, 1969. Translation of Kerstmis. English verse by Eve Merriam. Subj: Holidays – Christmas. Poetry, rhyme. Religion.

The Christmas book ill. by author. Methuen, 1964. Subj: Holidays – Christmas.

Farmer John ill. by author. Price, Stern, Sloan, 1984. Subj: Farms.

The fish ill. by author. Follett, 1963. English verse translated from the Dutch by Sandra Greifenstein. Subj: Fish. Food. Poetry, rhyme.

I can dress myself ill. by author. Methuen, 1977. Subj: Behavior – growing up. Clothing.

I can read difficult words ill. by author. Methuen, 1978. Subj: Activities – reading.

I know more about numbers ill. by author. Methuen, 1981. Subj: Counting.

Kitten Nell ill. by author. Follett, 1963. Subj: Animals – cats. Humor. Poetry, rhyme.

Little bird tweet ill. by author. Follett, 1963. Subj: Birds. Farms. Poetry, rhyme.

Miffy ill. by author. Follett, 1970. Translation of Nijntje. Subj: Animals – rabbits. Family life.

Miffy at the beach ill. by author. Methuen, 1980. Subj: Animals – rabbits. Sea and seashore.

Miffy at the playground ill. by author. Methuen, 1980. Subj: Activities – playing. Animals – rabbits.

Miffy at the seaside ill. by author. Follett, 1970. Translation of Nijntje aan zee. Subj: Animals – rabbits. Sea and seashore.

Miffy at the zoo ill. by author. Follett, 1970. Translation of Nijntje in de dierentuin. Subj: Animals – rabbits. Zoos.

Miffy goes to school ill. by author. Price, Stern, Sloan, 1984. Subj: Animals – rabbits. School.

Miffy in the hospital ill. by author. Methuen, 1978. Subj: Animals – rabbits. Hospitals. Illness.

Miffy in the snow ill. by author. Follett, 1970. Translation of Nijntje in de sneeuw. Subj: Animals – rabbits. Seasons – winter. Weather – snow.

Miffy's bicycle ill. by author. Price, Stern, Sloan, 1984. Subj: Animals – rabbits. Sports – bicycling.

Miffy's dream ill. by author. Methuen, 1980. Subj: Activities – playing. Animals – rabbits. Dreams.

The orchestra ill. by author. Price, Stern, Sloan, 1984. Subj: Music. Poetry, rhyme.

Poppy Pig goes to market ill. by author. Methuen, 1981. Subj: Animals – pigs. Counting. Poetry, rhyme.

The sailor ill. by author. Methuen, 1980. Subj: Activities – traveling. Boats, ships.

The school ill. by author. Methuen, 1980. Subj: School.

Tilly and Tess ill. by author. Follett, 1963. Subj: Birthdays. Poetry, rhyme. Twins.

Brunhoff, Jean de. *Babar and Father Christmas* tr. by Merle Haas; ill. by author. Random House, 1940. Translation of Babar et le Père Nöel. Subj: Animals – elephants. Holidays – Christmas.

Babar and his children tr. by Merle Haas; ill. by author. Random House, 1938. Subj: Animals – elephants. Triplets.

Babar and Zephir tr. from French by Merle Haas; ill. by author. Reprint of 1937 ed. Random House, 1942. Subj: Animals – elephants. Animals – monkeys.

Babar the king tr. by Merle Haas; ill. by author. Random House, 1935. Subj: Animals – elephants. Royalty.

Babar the king tr. by Merle Haas; ill. by author. Facsimile ed. Random House, 1986. ISBN 0-394-88245-8 Subj: Animals – elephants. Royalty.

Babar's anniversary album: 6 favorite stories by Jean de Brunhoff and Laurent de Brunhoff; ill. by authors. Random House, 1981. Subj: Activities. Animals – elephants.

The story of Babar, the little elephant tr. by Merle Haas; ill. by author. Random House, 1960. Subj: Animals – elephants. Behavior – running away. Foreign lands – France.

The travels of Babar tr. by Merle Haas; ill. by author. Random House, 1934, 1961. Subj: Activities – traveling. Animals – elephants.

Brunhoff, Laurent de. *Babar and the ghost* ill. by author. Random House, 1981. Subj: Animals – elephants. Ghosts.

Babar and the ghost ill. by author. Easy-to-read ed. Random House, 1986. ISBN 0-394-97908-7 Subj: Animals – elephants. Ghosts.

Babar and the Wully-Wully ill. by author. Random House, 1975. Subj: Animals – elephants. Pets.

Babar comes to America tr. by M. Jean Craig; ill. by author. Random House, 1965. Translation of Babar en Amérique. Subj: Animals – elephants.

Babar learns to cook ill. by author. Random House, 1979. Subj: Activities – cooking. Animals – elephants.

Babar loses his crown ill. by author. Random House, 1967. Subj: Animals – elephants. Behavior – losing things.

Babar the magician ill. by author. Random House, 1980. Subj: Animals – elephants. Animals – monkeys. Magic.

Babar visits another planet tr. by Merle Haas; ill. by author. Random House, 1972. Translation of Babar sur la planète molle. Subj: Animals – elephants. Space and space ships.

Babar's ABC ill. by author. Random House, 1983. Subj: ABC books. Animals – elephants.

Babar's anniversary album (Brunhoff, Jean de)

Babar's birthday surprise ill. by author. Random House, 1970. Translation of Anniversaire de Babar. Subj: Animals – elephants. Birthdays.

Babar's book of color ill. by author. Random House, 1984. Subj: Animals – elephants. Concepts – color.

Babar's castle tr. by Merle Haas; ill. by author. Random House, 1962. Subj: Animals – elephants.

Babar's counting book ill. by author. Random House, 1986. ISBN 0-394-97517-0 Subj: Animals. Animals – elephants. Counting.

Babar's cousin, that rascal Arthur tr. by Merle Haas; ill. by author. Random House, 1948. Translation of Babar et ce coquin d'Arthur. A continuation of the Babar stories of Jean de Brunhoff. Subj: Activities – vacationing. Animals – elephants. Behavior – misbehavior.

Babar's fair will be opened next Sunday tr. by Merle Haas; ill. by author. Random House, 1954. Translation of La fête de Célesteville. Subj: Animals – elephants. Fairs.

Babar's little circus star ill. by author. Random House, 1988. ISBN 0-394-98959-7 Subj: Animals. Animals – elephants. Circus.

Babar's little girl ill. by author. Random House, 1987. ISBN 0-394-98689-X Subj: Animals – elephants. Behavior – carelessness. Behavior – lost. Character traits – kindness to animals.

Babar's mystery ill. by author. Random House, 1978. Subj: Activities – vacationing. Animals – elephants. Crime.

Babar's picnic ill. by author. Random House, 1959. Subj: Activities – picnicking. Animals – elephants.

Babar's visit to Bird Island ill. by author. Random House, 1952. Subj: Animals – elephants. Birds. Islands. Royalty.

Gregory and Lady Turtle in the valley of the music trees tr. by Richard Howard; ill. by author. Pantheon, 1971. Subj: Animals – Rabbits. Imagination. Reptiles – turtles, tortoises.

The one pig with horns tr. from French by Richard Howard; ill. by author. Pantheon, 1979. Subj: Animals – pigs. Emotions – anger. Emotions – hate.

Serafina the giraffe ill. by author. Collins-World, 1961. Subj: Animals – giraffes. Birthdays. Humor.

Brustlein, Janice Tworkov *see* Janice

Bryan, Ashley. *Beat the story-drum, pum-pum* ill. by adapt. Atheneum, 1980. Subj: Cumulative tales. Folk and fairy tales. Foreign lands – Africa. Poetry, rhyme.

The cat's purr ill. by author. Atheneum, 1985. ISBN 0-689-31086-2 Subj: Animals – cats. Animals – rats. Folk and fairy tales. Poetry, rhyme.

I'm going to sing: Black American spirituals, Vol. II ill. by author. Atheneum, 1982. ISBN 0-689-30915-5 Subj: Ethnic groups in the U.S. – Afro-Americans. Songs.

Lion and the ostrich chicks: and other African tales ill. by author. Atheneum, 1986. ISBN 0-689-31311-X Subj: Folk and fairy tales. Foreign lands – Africa. Songs.

Sh-ko and his eight wicked brothers ill. by Fumio Yoshimura. Atheneum, 1988. ISBN 0-689-31446-9 Subj: Character traits – kindness to animals. Folk and fairy tales. Foreign lands – Japan.

Bryan, Dorothy. *Friendly little Jonathan* by Dorothy and Marguerite Bryan; ill. by Marguerite Bryan. Dodd, 1939. Subj: Animals – dogs. Friendship.

Just Tammie! by Dorothy and Marguerite Bryan; ill. by Marguerite Bryan. Dodd, 1951. Subj: Animals – dogs.

Bryan, Marguerite. *Friendly little Jonathan* (Bryan, Dorothy)

Just Tammie! (Bryan, Dorothy)

Bryant, Bernice. *Follow the leader* ill. by author. Houghton, 1950. Subj: Behavior – bullying. Behavior – growing up. Character traits – selfishness.

Bryant, Dean. *Here am I* ill. by author. Rand McNally, 1947. Subj: Activities.

See the bear ill. by author. Rand McNally, 1947. Subj: Toys.

Bryant, Sara Cone. *Epaminondas* (Merriam, Eve)

Epaminondas and his auntie ill. by Inez Hogan. Houghton, 1938. Subj: Behavior – misunderstanding. Folk and fairy tales. Humor.

Bryson, Bernarda. *The twenty miracles of Saint Nicolas* ill. by author. Atlantic Monthly Pr., 1960. Subj: Folk and fairy tales. Foreign lands. Holidays – Christmas.

Buchanan, Heather S. *Emily Mouse saves the day* ill. by author. Dial Pr., 1985. ISBN 0-8037-0175-6 Subj: Animals – mice. Character traits – helpfulness. Family life.

Emily Mouse's beach house ill. by author. Dial Pr., 1987. ISBN 0-8037-0263-9 Subj: Animals – mice. Sea and seashore.

Emily Mouse's first adventure ill. by author. Dial Pr., 1985. ISBN 0-8037-0174-8 Subj: Animals – mice. Character traits – kindness to animals.

Emily Mouse's garden ill. by author. Dial Pr., 1987. ISBN 0-8037-0261-2 Subj: Activities – gardening. Animals – mice. Sibling rivalry.

George Mouse learns to fly ill. by author. Dial Pr., 1985. ISBN 0-8037-0172-1 Subj: Activities – flying. Airplanes, airports. Animals – mice.

George Mouse's covered wagon ill. by author. Dial Pr., 1987. ISBN 0-8037-0258-2 Subj: Activities – traveling. Activities – vacationing. Animals – mice. Sea and seashore.

George Mouse's first summer ill. by author. Dial Pr., 1985. ISBN 0-8037-0173-X Subj: Animals – mice. Character traits – cleverness.

George Mouse's riverboat band ill. by author. Dial Pr., 1987. ISBN 0-8037-0260-4 Subj: Animals – mice. Boats, ships.

Buchanan, Joan. *It's a good thing* ill. by Barbara Di Lella. Firefly Pr., 1984. Subj: Activities – walking. Behavior – carelessness. Humor.

Buchheimer, Naomi. *Let's go to a post office* ill. by Ruth Van Sciver. Putnam's, 1957. Subj: Careers – mail carriers. Communication.

Let's go to a school ill. by Ruth Van Sciver. Putnam's, 1957. Subj: School.

Buck, Frank. *Jungle animals* by Frank Buck; text by Ferrin Fraser; ill. by Roger Vernam. Random House, 1945. Subj: Animals.

Buck, Pearl S. (Pearl Sydenstricker). *The Chinese story teller* ill. by Regina Shekerjian. John Day, 1971. Subj: Animals – cats. Animals – dogs. Emotions – envy, jealousy. Folk and fairy tales. Foreign lands – China.

The dragon fish ill. by Esther Broch Bird. John Day, 1944. Subj: Dragons. Fish. Folk and fairy tales. Foreign lands – China. Magic.

The little fox in the middle ill. by Robert Jones. Collier, 1966. Subj: Animals – foxes. Emotions – loneliness. Family life. Friendship.

Stories for little children ill. by Weda Yap. John Day, 1940. Subj: Activities.

Welcome child ill. by Alan D. Haas. John Day, 1963. Subj: Adoption.

Buckaway, C. M. *Alfred, the dragon who lost his flame* ill. by Sarie Jenkins. Firefly Pr., 1982. Subj: Dragons. Imagination. Magic.

Buckley, Helen Elizabeth. *Grandfather and I* ill. by Paul Galdone. Lothrop, 1959. Subj: Activities – walking. Family life – grandfathers.

Grandmother and I ill. by Paul Galdone. Lothrop, 1961. Subj: Emotions – love. Family life – grandmothers.

Josie and the snow ill. by Evaline Ness. Lothrop, 1964. Subj: Poetry, rhyme. Seasons – winter. Weather – snow.

Josie's Buttercup ill. by Evaline Ness. Lothrop, 1967. Subj: Animals – dogs. Poetry, rhyme.

Someday with my father ill. by Ellen Eagle. Harper, 1985. ISBN 0-06-020877-5 Subj: Dreams. Family life – fathers. Illness.

Buckley, Kate. *Love notes* ill. by author. Albert Whitman, 1988. ISBN 0-8075-4780-8 Subj: Behavior – growing up. School.

Buckley, Paul. *Amy Belligera and the fireflies* ill. by Kate Buckley. Albert Whitman, 1987. ISBN 0-8075-0324-X Subj: Insects – fireflies. Magic. Night. Witches.

Buckley, Richard. *The foolish tortoise* ill. by Eric Carle. Picture Book Studio, 1985. ISBN 0-88708-002-2 Subj: Behavior – seeking better things. Folk and fairy tales. Poetry, rhyme. Reptiles – turtles, tortoises.

The greedy python ill. by Eric Carle. Picture Book Studio, 1985. ISBN 0-88708-001-4 Subj: Behavior – greed. Folk and fairy tales. Poetry, rhyme. Reptiles – snakes.

Buckmaster, Henrietta. *Lucy and Loki* ill. by Barbara Cooney. Scribner's, 1958. Subj: Animals – cats. Animals – dogs. Behavior – imitation.

Bucknall, Caroline. *One bear all alone* ill. by author. Dial Pr., 1986. ISBN 0-8037-0238-8 Subj: Animals – bears. Counting. Poetry, rhyme.

One bear in the picture ill. by author. Dial Pr., 1988. ISBN 0-8037-0463-1 Subj: Animals – bears. Character traits – cleanliness. Poetry, rhyme.

The three little pigs

Budbill, David. *Christmas tree farm* ill. by Donald Carrick. Macmillan, 1974. Subj: Farms. Holidays – Christmas. Science. Trees.

Budd, Lillian. *The people on Long Ago Street* ill. by Marilyn Miller. Rand McNally, 1964. Subj: Family life – great-grandparents. Imagination.

The pie wagon ill. by Marilyn Miller. Lothrop, 1960. Subj: ABC books. Food.

Budney, Blossom. *After dark* ill. by Tony Chen. Lothrop, 1975. Subj: Night.

A kiss is round ill. by Vladimir Bobri. Lothrop, 1954. Subj: Concepts – shape. Poetry, rhyme.

N is for nursery school ill. by Vladimir Bobri. Lothrop, 1956. Subj: ABC books. School.

Buell, Ellen Lewis. *Read me a poem: children's favorite poetry* ill. by Anna Maria Magagna. Grosset, 1965. Subj: Poetry, rhyme.

Buff, Conrad. *Dash and Dart* (Buff, Mary)

Forest folk (Buff, Mary)

Hurry, Skurry and Flurry (Buff, Mary)

Buff, Mary. *Dash and Dart* by Mary and Conrad Buff; ill. by authors. Viking, 1942. Subj: Animals – deer. Caldecott award honor book. Forest, woods.

Forest folk by Mary and Conrad Buff; ill. by authors. Viking, 1962. Subj: Animals. Animals – deer. Forest, woods.

Hurry, Skurry and Flurry by Mary and Conrad Buff; ill. by authors. Viking, 1954. Subj: Animals – squirrels. Poetry, rhyme.

Buffett, Jimmy. *The jolly mon* by Jimmy and Savannah Jane Buffett; ill. by Lambert Davis. Harcourt, 1988. ISBN 0-15-240530-5 Subj: Activities – traveling. Foreign lands – Caribbean Islands. Music. Royalty. Songs.

Buffett, Savannah Jane. *The jolly mon* (Buffett, Jimmy)

Bulette, Sara. *The elf in the singing tree* ill. by Tom Dunnington. Follett, 1964. Reading consultant: Morton Botel. Subj: Elves and little people. Imagination.

The splendid belt of Mr. Big ill. by Lou Myers. Follett, 1964. Reading consultant: Morton Botel. Subj: Animals – monkeys. Clothing. Concepts – size. Problem solving.

Bulla, Clyde Robert. *Dandelion Hill* ill. by Bruce Degen. Dutton, 1982. Subj: Animals – bulls, cows. Behavior – growing up. Farms.

Daniel's duck ill. by Joan Sandin. Harper, 1979. Subj: Activities. Art. Emotions – embarrassment.

The donkey cart ill. by Lois Lenski. Harper, 1942. Subj: Animals – donkeys. Music. Songs.

Jonah and the great fish ill. by Helga Aichinger. Crowell, 1970. Subj: Animals – whales. Religion.

Keep running, Allen! ill. by Satomi Ichikawa. Crowell, 1978. Subj: Behavior – solitude. Sibling rivalry.

Noah and the rainbow (Bolliger, Max)

Poor boy, rich boy ill. by Marcia Sewall. Harper, 1982. Subj: Orphans.

The stubborn old woman ill. by Anne F. Rockwell. Crowell, 1980. Subj: Behavior – needing someone. Character traits – persistence. Character traits – stubbornness.

A tree is a plant ill. by Lois Lignell. Crowell, 1960. Subj: Plants. Trees.

Valentine cat ill. by Leonard Weisgard. Crowell, 1959. Subj: Animals – cats. Holidays – Valentine's Day.

Washington's birthday ill. by Don Bolognese. Crowell, 1967. Subj: Holidays – Washington's Birthday. U.S. history.

Bunce, William. *Freight trains* ill. by Lemuel B. Line. Putnam's, 1954. Subj: Trains.

Bundt, Nancy. *The fire station book* text by Jeff Linzer; photos. by Nancy Bundt. Carolrhoda Books, 1981. Subj: Careers – firefighters.

Bunin, Catherine. *Is that your sister? a true story of adoption* by Catherine Bunin and Sherry Bunin; ill. with photos. Pantheon, 1976. Subj: Adoption. Family life.

Bunin, Sherry. *Is that your sister?* (Bunin, Catherine)

Buntain, Ruth Jaeger. *The birthday story* ill. by Eloise Wilkin. Holiday, 1953. Subj: Birthdays. Emotions – loneliness. Friendship.

Bunting, A. E. (Anne Evelyn) *see* Bunting, Eve

Bunting, Eve. *The big cheese* ill. by Sal Murdocca. Macmillan, 1977. Subj: Cumulative tales.

The big red barn ill. by Howard Knotts. Harcourt, 1979. Subj: Death. Family life.

Clancy's coat ill. by Lorinda Bryan Cauley. Warne, 1984. Subj: Foreign lands – Ireland. Friendship.

Ghost's hour, spook's hour ill. by author. Clarion, 1987. ISBN 0-89919-484-2 Subj: Animals – dogs. Emotions – fear. Family life. Night.

Goose dinner ill. by Howard Knotts. Harcourt, 1981. Subj: Birds – geese. Farms.

Happy birthday, dear duck ill. by Jan Brett. Clarion, 1988. ISBN 0-89919-541-5 Subj: Animals. Birds – ducks. Birthdays. Poetry, rhyme.

The happy funeral ill. by Vo-Dinh Mai. Harper, 1982. Subj: Death. Ethnic groups in the U.S. – Chinese-Americans. Family life – grandfathers.

How many days to America? a Thanksgiving story ill. by Beth Peck. Clarion, 1988. ISBN 0-89919-521-0 Subj: Character traits – freedom. Holidays – Thanksgiving.

Jane Martin, dog detective ill. by Amy Schwartz. Harcourt, 1984. ISBN 0-15-239586-5 Subj: Animals – dogs. Behavior – lost. Careers – detectives. Problem solving.

Magic and the night river ill. by Allen Say. Harper, 1978. Subj: Birds – cormorants. Careers – fishermen. Family life – grandfathers. Foreign lands – Japan.

The man who could call down owls ill. by Charles Mikolaycak. Macmillan, 1984. Subj: Behavior – greed. Birds – owls. Magic.

Monkey in the middle ill. by Lynn Munsinger. Harcourt, 1984. Subj: Animals – monkeys. Emotions – envy, jealousy. Friendship.

The Mother's Day mice ill. by Jan Brett. Clarion, 1986. ISBN 0-89919-387-0 Subj: Animals – mice. Holidays – Mother's Day.

The robot birthday ill. by Marie DeJohn. Dutton, 1980. Subj: Birthdays. Robots.

St. Patrick's Day in the morning ill. by Jan Brett. Houghton, 1980. Subj: Holidays – St. Patrick's Day.

Scary, scary Halloween ill. by Jan Brett. Houghton, 1986. ISBN 0-89919-414-1 Subj: Goblins. Holidays – Halloween. Monsters. Poetry, rhyme.

Terrible things ill. by Stephen Gammell. Harper, 1980. Subj: Animals. Emotions – fear.

The traveling men of Ballycoo ill. by Kaethe Zemach. Harcourt, 1983. Subj: Activities – traveling. Music.

The Valentine bears ill. by Jan Brett. Seabury Pr., 1983. Subj: Animals – bears. Holidays – Valentine's Day.

Winter's coming ill. by Howard Knotts. Harcourt, 1977. Subj: Family life – grandparents. Farms. Seasons – winter.

Burch, Robert. *The hunting trip* ill. by Susanne Suba. Scribner's, 1971. Subj: Character traits – kindness to animals. Family life. Food. Sports – hunting.

Joey's cat ill. by Don Freeman. Viking, 1969. Subj: Animals – cats. Animals – possums. Ethnic groups in the U.S. – Afro-Americans. Family life.

The jolly witch ill. by Leigh Grant. Dutton, 1975. Subj: Character traits – cleanliness. Witches.

Burchard, Peter. *The Carol Moran* ill. by author. Macmillan, 1958. Subj: Boats, ships.

Burdekin, Harold. *A child's grace* by Harold Burdekin and Ernest Claxton; the grace by Mrs. E. Rutter Leatham; photos. by Harold Burdekin. Dutton, 1938. Subj: Activities. Poetry, rhyme. Religion.

Burdick, Margaret. *Bobby Otter and the blue boat* ill. by author. Little, 1987. ISBN 0-316-11616-5 Subj: Activities – trading. Animals. Animals – otters. Toys.

Burgert, Hans-Joachim. *Samulo and the giant* ill. by author. Holt, 1970. Subj: Character traits – bravery. Weather.

Burgess, Anthony. *The land where the ice cream grows* (Testa, Fulvio)

Burgess, Gelett. *The little father* ill. by Richard Egielski. Farrar, 1985. ISBN 0-374-34596-1 Subj: Character traits – smallness. Family life – fathers. Poetry, rhyme.

Burgunder, Rose. *From summer to summer* ill. by author. Viking, 1965. Subj: Poetry, rhyme. Seasons – summer.

Burland, Brian. *St. Nicholas and the tub* ill. by Joseph Low. Holiday, 1964. Subj: Folk and fairy tales. Holidays – Christmas.

Burlingham, Mary. *The climbing book* (Steiner, Charlotte)

Burlson, Joe. *Space colony* ill. by author. Putnam's, 1984. Subj: Format, unusual. Wordless.

Burn, Doris. *The summerfolk* ill. by author. Coward, 1968. Subj: Seasons – summer.

Burnett, Carol. *What I want to be when I grow up* ill. by Sheldon Secunda. Simon and Schuster, 1975. Created by George Mendoza and Sheldon Secunda. Subj: Careers.

Burningham, Helen Oxenbury *see* Oxenbury, Helen

Burningham, John. *Avocado baby* ill. by author. Crowell, 1982. Subj: Babies. Family life. Food.

The blanket ill. by author. Crowell, 1976, 1975. Subj: Behavior – losing things. Night.

Borka: the adventures of a goose with no feathers ill. by author. Random House, 1963. Subj: Birds – geese. Character traits – being different. Character traits – meanness. Foreign lands – England.

Cannonball Simp ill. by author. Bobbs-Merrill, 1966. Subj: Animals – dogs. Circus. Clowns, jesters.

Cluck baa ill. by author. Viking, 1985. ISBN 0-670-22580-0 Subj: Animals. Noise, sounds.

Come away from the water, Shirley ill. by author. Crowell, 1977. Subj: Imagination. Pirates. Sea and seashore.

Count up: learning sets ill. by author. Viking, 1983. Subj: Counting. Format, unusual – board books.

The cupboard ill. by author. Crowell, 1977. Subj: Food.

The dog ill. by author. Crowell, 1975. Subj: Animals – dogs. Format, unusual – board books.

Five down: numbers as signs ill. by author. Viking, 1983. Subj: Counting. Format, unusual – board books.

The friend ill. by author. Crowell, 1975. Subj: Friendship.

Grandpa ill. by author. Crown, 1985. ISBN 0-517-55643-X Subj: Death. Family life – grandfathers.

Harquin: the fox who went down to the valley ill. by author. Bobbs-Merrill, 1968. Subj: Animals – foxes. Character traits – cleverness. Sports – hunting.

Humbert, Mister Firkin and the Lord Mayor of London ill. by author. Bobbs-Merrill, 1967. Subj: Animals – horses. Character traits – pride. Emotions – envy, jealousy.

Jangle twang ill. by author. Viking, 1985. ISBN 0-670-40570-5 Subj: Music. Noise, sounds.

John Burningham's ABC ill. by author. Bobbs-Merrill, 1977. Subj: ABC books.

John Burningham's colors ill. by author. Crown, 1986. ISBN 0-517-55961-7 Subj: Concepts – color.

John Patrick Norman McHennessy - the boy who was always late ill. by author. Crown, 1988. ISBN 0-517-56805-5 Subj: Behavior – tardiness. Imagination. School.

Just cats: learning groups ill. by author. Viking, 1983. Subj: Counting. Format, unusual – board books.

Mr. Gumpy's motor car ill. by author. Macmillan, 1975, 1973. Subj: Automobiles. Weather – rain.

Mr. Gumpy's outing ill. by author. Macmillan, 1971. Subj: Animals. Behavior – fighting, arguing. Boats, ships. Cumulative tales.

Pigs plus: learning addition ill. by author. Viking, 1983. Subj: Counting. Format, unusual – board books.

Read one: numbers as words ill. by author. Viking, 1983. Subj: Counting. Format, unusual – board books.

Ride off: learning subtraction ill. by author. Viking, 1983. Subj: Counting. Format, unusual – board books.

Seasons ill. by author. Bobbs-Merrill, 1970. Subj: Seasons.

The shopping basket ill. by author. Crowell, 1980. Subj: Character traits – cleverness. Counting. Humor.

Skip trip ill. by author. Viking, 1984. Subj: Activities. Noise, sounds.

Slam bang ill. by author. Viking, 1985. ISBN 0-670-65076-5 Subj: Automobiles. Noise, sounds.

Sniff shout ill. by author. Viking, 1984. Subj: Activities. Noise, sounds.

Time to get out of the bath, Shirley ill. by author. Crowell, 1978. Subj: Activities – bathing. Imagination. Royalty.

Trubloff: the mouse who wanted to play the balalaika ill. by author. Random House, 1965. Subj: Animals – mice. Music. Weather – snow.

Where's Julius? ill. by author. Crown, 1986. ISBN 0-517-56511-0 Subj: Activities – playing. Family life. Food. Imagination.

Wobble pop ill. by author. Viking, 1984. Subj: Activities. Noise, sounds.

Would you rather... ill. by author. Crowell, 1978. Subj: Imagination.

Burns, Diane L. *Arbor Day* ill. by Kathy Rogers. Carolrhoda Books, 1988. ISBN 0-87614-346-X Subj: Trees.

Elephants never forget! ill. by Joan Hanson. Lerner, 1987. ISBN 0-8225-0992-X Subj: Animals – elephants. Riddles.

Burns, Maurice. *Go ducks, go!* ill. by Ron Brooks. Scholastic, 1988. ISBN 0-590-41544-1 Subj: Activities – playing. Country. Family life. Toys.

Burnstein, John. *Slim Goodbody: what can go wrong and how to be strong* ill. with photos. and drawings. McGraw-Hill, 1978. Subj: Health. Poetry, rhyme.

Burroway, Janet. *The truck on the track* ill. by John Vernon Lord. Bobbs-Merrill, 1970. Subj: Humor. Poetry, rhyme. Trucks.

Burstein, Chaya M. *Joseph and Anna's time capsule* ill. by Nancy Edwards Calder. Simon and Schuster, 1984. Subj: Jewish culture.

Burstein, Fred. *Rebecca's nap* ill. by Helen Cogancherry. Bradbury Pr., 1988. ISBN 0-02-715620-6 Subj: Family life. Sleep.

Burt, Olive. *Let's find out about bread* ill. by Mimi Korach. Watts, 1966. Subj: Food. Science.

Burton, Marilee Robin. *Aaron awoke: an alphabet story* ill. by author. Harper, 1982. Subj: ABC books. Farms.

The elephant's nest ill. by author. Harper, 1979. Subj: Animals. Humor. Wordless.

Oliver's birthday ill. by author. Harper, 1986. ISBN 0-06-020880-5 Subj: Birds – ostriches. Birthdays.

Tail toes eyes ears nose ill. by author. Harper, 1988. ISBN 0-06-020874-0 Subj: Animals. Problem solving. Riddles.

Burton, Virginia Lee. *Calico the wonder horse: or, the saga of Stewy Slinker* ill. by author. Houghton, 1941. Subj: Animals – horses. Character traits – cleverness. Cowboys. Crime.

Choo choo: the story of a little engine who ran away ill. by author. Houghton, 1937. Subj: Behavior – running away. Trains.

Katy and the big snow ill. by author. Houghton, 1943. Subj: City. Cumulative tales. Machines. Seasons – winter. Weather – snow.

The little house ill. by author. Houghton, 1939. Subj: Caldecott award book. City. Country. Ecology. Houses. Progress.

Maybelle, the cable car ill. by author. Houghton, 1939. Subj: Cable cars, trolleys. City. Transportation.

Mike Mulligan and his steam shovel ill. by author. Houghton, 1939. Subj: Activities – working. Machines.

Busch, Phyllis S. *Cactus in the desert* ill. by Harriett Barton. Crowell, 1979. Subj: Desert. Plants. Science.

City lots: living things in vacant spots photos. by Arline Strong. Collins-World, 1970. Subj: City. Science.

Lions in the grass: the story of the dandelion, a green plant photos. by Arline Strong. Collins-World, 1968. Subj: Plants. Science.

Once there was a tree: the story of the tree, a changing home for plants and animals photos. by Arline Strong. Collins-World, 1968. Subj: Science. Trees.

Puddles and ponds: living things in watery places photos. by Arline Strong. Collins-World, 1969. Subj: Ecology. Science.

Bush, John. *The cross-with-us rhinoceros* ill. by Paul Geraghty. Dutton, 1988. ISBN 0-525-44411-4 Subj: Animals – rhinoceros. Behavior – misunderstanding. Poetry, rhyme.

Bushey, Jerry. *The barge book* photos. by author. Carolrhoda Books, 1984. Subj: Activities – trading. Boats, ships. Rivers.

Building a fire truck photos. by author. Carolrhoda Books, 1981. Subj: Careers – firefighters. Trucks.

Busy baby photos. sel. by Debby Slier. Macmillan, 1988. ISBN 0-02-688753-3 Subj: Babies. Format, unusual – board books.

Butcher, Julia. *The sheep and the rowan tree* ill. by author. Holt, 1984. Subj: Behavior – wishing. Trees.

Butterfield-Campbell, Jill. *The queen and Rosie Randall* (Oxenbury, Helen)

Butterworth, Nick. *The Nativity play* by Nick Butterworth and Mick Inkpen; ill. by authors. Little, 1985. ISBN 0-316-11903-2 Subj: Holidays – Christmas. School. Theater.

Nice or nasty by Nick Butterworth and Mick Inkpen; ill. by authors. Little, 1987. ISBN 0-316-11915-6 Subj: Concepts – opposites.

Buxbaum, Susan Kovacs. *Splash! all about baths* by Susan Kovacs Buxbaum and Rita Golden Gelman; ill. by Maryann Cocca-Leffler. Little, 1987. ISBN 0-316-30726-2 Subj: Activities – bathing.

Byars, Betsy Cromer. *Go and hush the baby* ill. by Emily Arnold McCully. Viking, 1971. Subj: Babies. Family life. Games.

The groober ill. by author. Harper, 1967. Subj: Animals. Behavior – dissatisfaction.

Byfield, Barbara Ninde. *The haunted churchbell* ill. by author. Doubleday, 1971. Subj: Character traits – cleverness. Emotions – fear. Humor.

Byrd, Robert. *Marcella was bored* ill. by author. Dutton, 1985. ISBN 0-525-44156-5 Subj: Animals – cats. Behavior – running away. Family life.

Byrne, David. *Stay up late* ill. by Maira Kalman. Viking, 1987. ISBN 0-670-81895-X Subj: Babies. Family life. Sibling rivalry. Songs.

Caines, Jeannette. *Abby* ill. by Steven Kellogg. Harper, 1973. Subj: Adoption. Ethnic groups in the U.S. – Afro-Americans. Family life. Sibling rivalry.

Chilly stomach ill. by Pat Cummings. Harper, 1986. ISBN 0-06-020977-1 Subj: Child abuse. Emotions – fear. Family life.

Daddy ill. by Ronald Himler. Harper, 1977. Subj: Divorce. Ethnic groups in the U.S. – Afro-Americans. Family life – fathers.

I need a lunch box ill. by Pat Cummings. Harper, 1988. ISBN 0-06-020985-2 Subj: Emotions – envy, jealousy. Family life.

Just us women ill. by Pat Cummings. Harper, 1982. Subj: Activities – traveling. Automobiles. Ethnic groups in the U.S. – Afro-Americans.

Window wishing ill. by Kevin Brooks. Harper, 1980. Subj: Family life – grandmothers.

Cairo, Jasmine. *Our brother has Down's syndrome* (Cairo, Shelley)

Cairo, Shelley. *Our brother has Down's syndrome: an introduction for children* by Shelley, Jasmine and Tara Cairo; photos. by Irene McNeil; designed by Helmut W. Weyerstrahs. Firefly Pr., 1985. ISBN 0-920303-30-7 Subj: Family life. Handicaps.

Cairo, Tara. *Our brother has Down's syndrome* (Cairo, Shelley)

Cakes and custard: *children's rhymes* comp. by Brian Alderson; ill. by Helen Oxenbury. Morrow, 1975, 1974. Subj: Nursery rhymes.

Caldecott, Randolph. *Panjandrum picture book* ill. by author. Warne, 1885. Subj: Nursery rhymes.

The Queen of Hearts ill. by author. Warne, 1881. Subj: Nursery rhymes.

The Randolph Caldecott treasury sel. and ed. by Elizabeth T. Billington; ill. by author. Warne, 1978. Subj: Folk and fairy tales.

Randolph Caldecott's favorite nursery rhymes ill. by author. Castle Books, 1980. Subj: Nursery rhymes.

Randolph Caldecott's John Gilpin and other stories ill. by author. Warne, 1977. The diverting history of John Gilpin.—The house that Jack built.—The frog he would a-wooing go.—The milkmaid. Subj: Nursery rhymes.

Randolph Caldecott's picture book, no. 1 ill. by author. Warne, 1879. Subj: Nursery rhymes.

Randolph Caldecott's picture book, no. 2 ill. by author. Warne, 1879. Subj: Nursery rhymes.

Sing a song of sixpence (Mother Goose)

The three jovial huntsmen ill. by author. Warne, 1880. Subj: Nursery rhymes.

Calders, Pere. *Brush* tr. from Spanish by Marguerite Feitlowitz; ill. by Carme Solé Vendrell. Kane Miller, 1986. ISBN 0-916291-05-7 Subj: Crime. Family life. Imagination. Pets.

Caldwell, Mary. *Morning, rabbit, morning* ill. by Ann Schweninger. Harper, 1982. Subj: Animals – rabbits. Morning.

Calhoun, Mary. *Audubon cat* ill. by Susan Bonners. Morrow, 1981. Subj: Animals – cats. Food. Problem solving.

Cross-country cat ill. by Erick Ingraham. Morrow, 1979. Subj: Animals – cats. Character traits – cleverness. Sports – skiing.

Euphonia and the flood ill. by Simms Taback. Parents, 1976. Subj: Animals. Boats, ships. Character traits – helpfulness. Weather – rain.

The goblin under the stairs ill. by Janet McCaffery. Morrow, 1968. Subj: Behavior – misbehavior. Folk and fairy tales. Goblins.

Hot-air Henry ill. by Erick Ingraham. Morrow, 1981. Subj: Activities – ballooning. Animals – cats.

Houn' dog ill. by Roger Antoine Duvoisin. Morrow, 1959. Subj: Animals – dogs. Animals – foxes. Sports – hunting.

The hungry leprechaun ill. by Roger Antoine Duvoisin. Harber, 1962. Subj: Elves and little people. Food. Foreign lands – Ireland. Holidays – St. Patrick's Day.

Jack and the whoopee wind ill. by Dick Gackenbach. Morrow, 1987. ISBN 0-688-06138-9 Subj: Character traits – cleverness. Machines. Weather – wind.

Jack the wise and the Cornish cuckoos ill. by Tasha Tudor. Morrow, 1978. Subj: Character traits – helpfulness. Folk and fairy tales.

Mrs. Dog's own house ill. by Janet McCaffery. Morrow, 1972. Subj: Animals – dogs. Houses.

The nine lives of Homer C. Cat ill. by Roger Antoine Duvoisin. Morrow, 1961. Subj: Animals – cats. Behavior – imitation. Humor.

Old man Whickutt's donkey ill. by Tomie de Paola. Parents, 1975. Subj: Animals – donkeys. Character traits – perseverance. Folk and fairy tales. Humor.

The pixy and the lazy housewife ill. by Janet McCaffery. Morrow, 1969. Subj: Behavior – trickery. Elves and little people. Folk and fairy tales. Foreign lands – England.

The runaway brownie ill. by Janet McCaffery. Morrow, 1967. Subj: Character traits – pride. Elves and little people. Folk and fairy tales. Foreign lands – Scotland.

The thieving dwarfs ill. by Janet McCaffery. Morrow, 1967. Subj: Character traits – kindness. Elves and little people. Folk and fairy tales. Foreign lands – Germany.

The traveling ball of string ill. by Janet McCaffery. Morrow, 1969. Subj: Behavior – saving things. Humor. String.

The witch of Hissing Hill ill. by Janet McCaffery. Morrow, 1964. Subj: Animals – cats. Holidays – Halloween. Witches.

The witch who lost her shadow ill. by Trinka Hakes Noble. Harper, 1979. Subj: Animals – cats. Character traits – loyalty. Emotions. Friendship. Witches.

The witch's pig: a Cornish folktale ill. by Tasha Tudor. Morrow, 1977. Subj: Animals – pigs. Folk and fairy tales. Foreign lands – England. Witches.

Wobble the witch cat ill. by Roger Antoine Duvoisin. Morrow, 1958. Subj: Animals – cats. Holidays – Halloween. Witches.

Callahan, Claire Wallace *see* Cole, Ann

Callen, Larry. *Dashiel and the night* ill. by Leslie Morrill. Dutton, 1981. Subj: Bedtime. Dreams. Imagination. Insects – fireflies. Night.

Calloway, Northern J. *Northern J. Calloway presents Super-vroomer!* ill. by Sammis McLean. Doubleday, 1978. Written by Carol Hall; conceived by Northern J. Calloway. Subj: Ethnic groups in the U.S. – Afro-Americans. Sports – racing.

Calmenson, Stephanie. *All aboard the goodnight train* ill. by Normand Chartier. Grosset, 1984. ISBN 0-448-11226-4 Subj: Animals. Bedtime. Songs.

The birthday hat ill. by Susan Gantner. Grosset, 1983. Subj: Animals – hippopotami. Birthdays. Shopping.

The kindergarten book ill. by Beth Lee Weiner. Grosset, 1983. Subj: Activities. Animals. School.

Never take a pig to lunch and other funny poems about animals ill. by Hilary Knight. Doubleday, 1982. Subj: Animals – pigs. Poetry, rhyme.

Where is Grandma Potamus? ill. by Susan Gantner. Grosset, 1983. Subj: Animals – hippopotami. Behavior – lost.

Where will the animals stay? ill. by Ellen Appleby. Parents, 1983. Subj: Animals. Houses. Poetry, rhyme. Zoos.

Calvert, Elinor H. *see* Lasell, Fen

Calvert, John *see* Leaf, Munro

Cameron, Ann. *Harry (the monster)* ill. by Jeanette Winter. Pantheon, 1980. Subj: Bedtime. Character traits – bravery. Emotions – fear. Monsters.

Cameron, Elizabeth Jane *see* Duncan, Jane

Cameron, John. *If mice could fly* ill. by author. Atheneum, 1979. Subj: Animals – cats. Animals – mice. Character traits – cleverness. Poetry, rhyme.

Cameron, Polly. *The cat who thought he was a tiger* ill. by author. Coward, 1956. Subj: Animals – cats. Circus.

A child's book of nonsense ill. by author. Coward, 1960. Subj: Humor. Poetry, rhyme.

"I can't," said the ant: a second book of nonsense ill. by author. Coward, 1961. Subj: Family life. Insects – ants. Participation. Poetry, rhyme.

Campbell, Ann. *Let's find out about boats* ill. by author. Watts, 1967. Subj: Boats, ships.

Let's find out about color ill. by author. Watts, 1966. Subj: Concepts – color.

Campbell, M. Rudolph. *The talking crocodile* ill. by Judy Piussi-Campbell. Atheneum, 1968. Adapt. from Krokodil by Fyodor Dostoyevsky. Subj: Foreign lands – Russia. Reptiles – alligators, crocodiles.

Campbell, Rod. *Buster's afternoon* ill. by author. Harper, 1984. ISBN 0-911745-74-2 Subj: Character traits – curiosity. Flowers. Format, unusual – toy and movable books. Nature.

Buster's morning ill. by author. Harper, 1984. ISBN 0-911745-73-4 Subj: Character traits – curiosity. Format, unusual – toy and movable books. Houses. Toys.

Dear zoo ill. by author. Four Winds Pr., 1984. ISBN 0-02-716440-3 Subj: Animals. Format, unusual – toy and movable books. Zoos.

Henry's busy day ill. by author. Viking, 1984. ISBN 0-670-80024-4 Subj: Animals – dogs. Behavior – misbehavior. Format, unusual.

It's mine ill. by author. Barron's, 1988. ISBN 0-8120-5921-2 Subj: Anatomy. Animals. Format, unusual – toy and movable books.

Look inside! All kinds of places ill. by author. Harper, 1983. Subj: Format, unusual – board books. Wordless.

Look inside! Land, sea, air ill. by author. Harper, 1983. Subj: Format, unusual – board books. Transportation. Wordless.

Misty's mischief ill. by author. Viking, 1985. ISBN 0-670-80149-6 Subj: Animals – cats. Behavior – misbehavior. Format, unusual.

Oh dear! ill. by author. Four Winds Pr., 1986. ISBN 0-590-07944-1 Subj: Eggs. Farms. Format, unusual – toy and movable books.

Campbell, Wayne. *What a catastrophe!* ill. by Eileen Christelow. Bradbury Pr., 1987. ISBN 0-02-716420-9 Subj: Family life. Frogs and toads.

Canfield, Jane White. *The frog prince: a true story* ill. by Winn Smith. Harper, 1970. Subj: Frogs and toads. Royalty.

Swan cove ill. by Jo Polseno. Harper, 1978. Subj: Birds – swans.

Canning, Kate. *A painted tale* ill. by author. Barron's, 1979. Subj: Animals – tigers. Art. Behavior – imitation. Zoos.

Cantieni, Benita. *Little Elephant and Big Mouse* tr. by Oliver Gadsby; ill. by Fred Gächter. Alphabet Pr., 1981. Orig. title: Der Kleine Elefant und die Grosse Maus. Subj: Animals – elephants. Animals – mice. Concepts – size.

Caple, Kathy. *The biggest nose* ill. by author. Houghton, 1985. ISBN 0-395-36894-4 Subj: Anatomy. Animals – elephants. Character traits – being different. School.

Harry's smile ill. by author. Houghton, 1987. ISBN 0-395-43417-3 Subj: Friendship. Pen pals. Self-concept.

Inspector Aardvark and the perfect cake ill. by author. Windmill, 1980. Subj: Animals – aardvarks. Careers – bakers.

The purse ill. by author. Houghton, 1986. ISBN 0-395-41852-6 Subj: Activities – working. Family life. Money.

Caprio, Annie De *see* DeCaprio, Annie

Caputo, Robert. *More than just pets: why people study animals* photos. by author. Coward, 1980. Subj: Anatomy. Ecology.

Cardoza, Lois S. *see* Duncan, Lois

Carey, Bonnie. *Grasshopper to the rescue*

Carey, Helen H. *Adopted* (Greenberg, Judith E.)

Carey, Mary. *The owl who loved sunshine* ill. by Joe Giordano. Golden Pr., 1977. Subj: Birds – owls. Character traits – individuality. Character traits – kindness to animals.

Carey, Valerie Scho. *The devil and mother Crump* ill. by Arnold Lobel. Harper, 1987. ISBN 0-06-020983-6 Subj: Behavior – trickery. Character traits – meanness. Devil. Folk and fairy tales.

Harriet and William and the terrible creature ill. by Lynne Cherry. Dutton, 1985. ISBN 0-525-44154-9 Subj: Animals – squirrels. Character traits – helpfulness. Monsters. Space and space ships.

Carigiet, Alois. *Anton the goatherd* ill. by author. Walck, 1966. Subj: Animals – goats. Behavior – lost.

The pear tree, the birch tree and the barberry bush ill. by author. Walck, 1967. Subj: Foreign lands – Switzerland. Trees.

Carle, Eric. *Do you want to be my friend?* ill. by author. Crowell, 1971. Subj: Animals – mice. Friendship. Wordless.

Eric Carle's treasury of classic stories for children by Æsop, Hans Christian Andersen and the Brothers Grimm; ill. by adapt. Watts, 1988. ISBN 0-531-05742-9 Subj: Folk and fairy tales.

The grouchy ladybug ill. by author. Crowell, 1977. English title: The bad-tempered ladybird. Subj: Behavior. Insects – ladybugs. Time.

Have you seen my cat? ill. by author. Watts, 1973. Subj: Animals – cats. Behavior – lost.

A house for Hermit Crab ill. by author. Picture Book Studio, 1988. ISBN 0-88708-056-1 Subj: Crustacea. Sea and seashore.

I see a song ill. by author. Crowell, 1973. Subj: Music. Wordless.

The mixed-up chameleon ill. by author. Crowell, 1975; rev. ed. 1984. Subj: Character traits – being different. Concepts – color. Reptiles – lizards. Self-concept.

My very first book of food ill. by author. Crowell, 1986. ISBN 0-694-00130-9 Subj: Food. Format, unusual – toy and movable books.

My very first book of growth ill. by author. Crowell, 1986. ISBN 0-694-00094-9 Subj: Behavior – growing up. Format, unusual.

My very first book of heads and tails ill. by author. Crowell, 1986. ISBN 0-694-00128-7 Subj: Anatomy. Format, unusual – toy and movable books.

My very first book of homes ill. by author. Crowell, 1986. ISBN 0-694-00092-2 Subj: Format, unusual. Houses.

My very first book of motion ill. by author. Crowell, 1986. ISBN 0-694-00093-0 Subj: Concepts. Format, unusual.

My very first book of sounds ill. by author. Crowell, 1986. ISBN 0-694-00131-7 Subj: Format, unusual – toy and movable books. Noise, sounds.

My very first book of tools ill. by author. Crowell, 1986. ISBN 0-694-00129-5 Subj: Format, unusual – toy and movable books. Tools.

My very first book of touch ill. by author. Crowell, 1986. ISBN 0-694-00095-7 Subj: Format, unusual. Senses – touching.

1, 2, 3 to the zoo ill. by author. Collins-World, 1969. Subj: Animals. Counting. Zoos.

Pancakes, pancakes ill. by author. Knopf, 1970. Subj: Cumulative tales. Food.

Papa, please get the moon for me ill. by author. Alphabet Pr., 1986. ISBN 0-88708-026-X Subj: Format, unusual – toy and movable books. Moon.

The rooster who set out to see the world ill. by author. Watts, 1972. Subj: Activities – traveling. Birds – chickens. Counting.

Rooster's off to see the world ill. by author. Picture Book Studio, 1987. ISBN 0-88708-042-1 Subj: Activities – traveling. Birds – chickens. Counting.

The secret birthday message ill. by author. Crowell, 1972. Subj: Birthdays. Format, unusual – toy and movable books.

The tiny seed ill. by author. Rev. ed. Picture Book Studio, 1987. ISBN 0-88708-015-4 Subj: Plants. Seasons. Seeds.

Twelve tales from Æsop ill. by adapt. Putnam's, 1980. Subj: Folk and fairy tales.

The very busy spider ill. by author. Philomel, 1985. ISBN 0-399-21166-7 Subj: Animals. Spiders.

The very hungry caterpillar ill. by author. Collins-World, 1969. Subj: Days of the week, months of the year. Format, unusual. Insects – butterflies, caterpillars.

Walter the baker: an old story ill. by author. Knopf, 1972. Subj: Activities – working. Careers – bakers. Food.

Watch out! A giant! ill. by author. Collins-World, 1978. Subj: Format, unusual – toy and movable books. Giants.

Carleton, Barbee Oliver. *Benny and the bear* ill. by Dagmar Wilson. Follett, 1960. Subj: Animals – bears. Character traits – bravery.

Carlisle, Clark *see* Holding, James

Carlisle, Madelyn. *Bridges* (Carlisle, Norman)

Carlisle, Norman. *Bridges* by Norman and Madelyn Carlisle; ill. with photos. Childrens Pr., 1983. Subj: Bridges.

Carlson, Maria. *Peter and the wolf* (Prokofiev, Sergei Sergeievitch)

Carlson, Nancy. *Bunnies and their hobbies* ill. by author. Carolrhoda Books, 1984. Subj: Activities. Animals – rabbits.

Bunnies and their sports ill. by author. Viking, 1987. ISBN 0-670-81109-2 Subj: Animals – rabbits. Sports.

Harriet and the garden ill. by author. Carolrhoda Books, 1982. Subj: Animals – dogs. Problem solving.

Harriet and the roller coaster ill. by author. Carolrhoda Books, 1982. Subj: Animals – dogs. Character traits – bravery.

Harriet and Walt ill. by author. Carolrhoda Books, 1982. Subj: Animals – dogs. Sibling rivalry.

Harriet's Halloween candy ill. by author. Carolrhoda Books, 1982. Subj: Animals – dogs. Behavior – greed.

Harriet's recital ill. by author. Carolrhoda Books, 1982. Subj: Animals – dogs. Emotions – fear.

I like me ill. by author. Viking, 1988. ISBN 0-670-82062-8 Subj: Character traits – individuality. Self-concept.

Louanne Pig in making the team ill. by author. Carolrhoda Books, 1985. ISBN 0-87614-281-1 Subj: Animals. Friendship. School. Sports — football.

Loudmouth George and the big race ill. by author. Carolrhoda Books, 1983. Subj: Animals — rabbits. Behavior — boasting. Emotions — embarrassment.

Loudmouth George and the cornet ill. by author. Carolrhoda Books, 1983. Subj: Animals — rabbits. Behavior — boasting.

Loudmouth George and the fishing trip ill. by author. Carolrhoda Books, 1983. Subj: Animals — rabbits. Behavior — boasting.

Loudmouth George and the new neighbors ill. by author. Carolrhoda Books, 1983. Subj: Animals — rabbits. Behavior — boasting. Prejudice.

Loudmouth George and the sixth-grade bully ill. by author. Carolrhoda Books, 1983. Subj: Animals — rabbits. Behavior — boasting. Behavior — bullying. Behavior — stealing.

The mysterious Valentine ill. by author. Carolrhoda Books, 1985. ISBN 0-87614-282-X Subj: Animals — pigs. Holidays — Valentine's Day.

The perfect family ill. by author. Carolrhoda Books, 1985. ISBN 0-87614-282-X Subj: Animals — pigs. Family life. Sibling rivalry.

Poor Carl ill. by author. Viking, 1989. ISBN 0-670-81774-0 Subj: Animals — dogs. Emotions — envy, jealousy.

The talent show ill. by author. Carolrhoda Books, 1985. ISBN 0-87614-284-6 Subj: Animals. Theater.

Witch lady ill. by author. Carolrhoda Books, 1985. ISBN 0-87614-283-8 Subj: Animals — pigs. Emotions — fear. Witches.

Carlson, Natalie Savage. *Marie Louise and Christophe at the carnival* ill. by José Aruego and Ariane Dewey. Scribner's, 1981. Subj: Animals — mongooses. Reptiles — snakes.

Marie Louise's heyday ill. by José Aruego and Ariane Dewey. Scribner's, 1975. Subj: Activities — baby-sitting. Animals — mongooses. Animals — possums.

Runaway Marie Louise ill. by José Aruego and Ariane Dewey. Scribner's, 1977. Subj: Animals — mongooses. Behavior — running away.

Spooky and the bad luck raven ill. by Andrew Glass. Lothrop, 1988. ISBN 0-688-07651-3 Subj: Animals — cats. Witches.

Spooky and the ghost cat ill. by Andrew Glass. Lothrop, 1985. ISBN 0-688-04317-8 Subj: Animals — cats. Holidays — Halloween. Magic.

Spooky and the wizard's bats ill. by Andrew Glass. Lothrop, 1986. ISBN 0-688-06281-4 Subj: Animals — bats. Animals — cats. Holidays — Halloween. Magic. Witches. Wizards.

Spooky night ill. by Andrew Glass. Lothrop, 1982. Subj: Animals — cats. Holidays — Halloween. Pets. Witches.

Surprise in the mountains ill. by Elise Primavera. Harper, 1983. Subj: Animals. Holidays — Christmas. Seasons — winter.

Time for the white egret ill. by Charles Robinson. Scribner's, 1978. Subj: Animals — bulls, cows. Birds — egrets. Farms.

Carlstrom, Nancy White. *Better not get wet, Jesse Bear* ill. by Bruce Degen. Macmillan, 1988. ISBN 0-02-717280-5 Subj: Animals — bears. Poetry, rhyme.

Jesse Bear, what will you wear? ill. by Bruce Degen. Macmillan, 1986. ISBN 0-02-717350-X Subj: Animals — bears. Clothing. Family life.

The moon came too ill. by Stella Ormai. Macmillan, 1987. ISBN 0-02-717380-1 Subj: Activities — vacationing. Behavior — collecting things. Family life — grandmothers. Poetry, rhyme.

Wild wild sunflower child Anna ill. by Jerry Pinkney. Macmillan, 1987. ISBN 0-02-717360-7 Subj: Ethnic groups in the U.S. — Afro-Americans. Poetry, rhyme.

Carmi, Giora. *And Shira imagined* ill. by author. Jewish Pub. Soc., 1988. ISBN 0-8276-0288-X Subj: Activities — traveling. Family life. Foreign lands — Israel. Imagination.

Carrick, Carol. *The accident* ill. by Donald Carrick. Seabury Pr., 1976. Subj: Animals — dogs. Death. Pets.

Beach bird by Carol and Donald Carrick; ill. by Donald Carrick. Dial Pr., 1973. Subj: Birds — sea gulls. Sea and seashore.

Ben and the porcupine ill. by Donald Carrick. Houghton, 1981. Subj: Animals — dogs. Animals — porcupines. Problem solving.

The blue lobster: a life cycle by Carol and Donald Carrick; ill. by Donald Carrick. Dial Pr., 1975. Subj: Crustacea. Science.

The brook by Carol and Donald Carrick; ill. by Donald Carrick. Macmillan, 1967. Subj: Rivers.

A clearing in the forest by Carol and Donald Carrick; ill. by Donald Carrick. Dial Pr., 1970. Subj: Ecology. Forest, woods. Pets.

The climb ill. by Donald Carrick. Houghton, 1980. Subj: Activities — baby-sitting. Sports.

The crocodiles still wait ill. by Donald Carrick. Houghton, 1980. Subj: Dinosaurs. Reptiles — alligators, crocodiles. Science.

Dark and full of secrets ill. by Donald Carrick. Houghton, 1984. Subj: Emotions — fear. Sports — skin diving.

The foundling ill. by Donald Carrick. Seabury Pr., 1977. Subj: Animals — dogs. Pets.

The highest balloon on the common by Carol and Donald Carrick; ill. by Donald Carrick. Greenwillow, 1977. Subj: Behavior — lost. Fairs. Toys — balloons.

Left behind ill. by Donald Carrick. Clarion, 1988. ISBN 0-89919-535-0 Subj: Behavior — lost. City. School.

Octopus ill. by Donald Carrick. Seabury Pr., 1978. Subj: Octopuses. Science.

The old barn ill. by Donald Carrick. Bobbs-Merrill, 1966. Subj: Barns. Seasons.

Old Mother Witch ill. by Donald Carrick. Seabury Pr., 1975. Subj: Behavior – misunderstanding. Character traits – meanness. Holidays – Halloween. Illness.

Patrick's dinosaurs ill. by Donald Carrick. Houghton, 1983. Subj: Animals. Dinosaurs. Imagination. Science. Zoos.

A rabbit for Easter ill. by Donald Carrick. Greenwillow, 1979. Subj: Animals – rabbits. Behavior – carelessness. Holidays – Easter.

Sleep out ill. by Donald Carrick. Seabury Pr., 1973. Subj: Behavior – solitude. Sports – camping. Weather – rain.

Two coyotes ill. by Donald Carrick. Houghton, 1982. Subj: Animals – coyotes. Science. Seasons – winter.

The washout ill. by Donald Carrick. Seabury Pr., 1978. Subj: Activities – vacationing. Boats, ships. Weather – rain.

What happened to Patrick's dinosaurs? ill. by Donald Carrick. Houghton, 1986. ISBN 0-89919-406-0 Subj: Dinosaurs. Imagination.

Carrick, Donald. *Beach bird* (Carrick, Carol)

The blue lobster (Carrick, Carol)

The brook (Carrick, Carol)

A clearing in the forest (Carrick, Carol)

The deer in the pasture ill. by author. Greenwillow, 1976. Subj: Animals – bulls, cows. Animals – deer. Farms. Sports – hunting.

Harold and the giant knight ill. by author. Houghton, 1982. Subj: Farms. Knights.

Harold and the great stag ill. by author. Clarion, 1988. ISBN 0-89919-514-8 Subj: Animals – deer. Foreign lands – England. Forest, woods. Middle ages. Sports – hunting.

The highest balloon on the common (Carrick, Carol)

Milk ill. by author. Greenwillow, 1985. ISBN 0-688-04823-4 Subj: Animals – bulls, cows. Farms. Food.

Morgan and the artist ill. by author. Clarion, 1985. ISBN 0-89919-300-5 Subj: Activities – painting. Art. Careers – artists.

Carrick, Malcolm. *The extraordinary hatmaker* ill. by author. Grosset, 1977. Subj: Clothing.

Happy Jack ill. by author. Harper, 1979. Subj: Folk and fairy tales.

I can squash elephants! a Masai tale about monsters ill. by author. Viking, 1978. Subj: Animals. Folk and fairy tales. Foreign lands – Africa. Insects – butterflies, caterpillars. Monsters.

Today is shrew's day ill. by author. Harper, 1978. Subj: Animals – shrews. Friendship. Frogs and toads.

Carrier, Lark. *A Christmas promise* ill. by author. Picture Book Studio, 1986. ISBN 0-88708-032-4 Subj: Animals. Friendship. Holidays – Christmas. Trees.

Scout and Cody ill. by author. Picture Book Studio, 1987. ISBN 0-88708-013-8 Subj: Activities – playing. Animals – dogs. Behavior – growing up. Imagination.

There was a hill... ill. by author. Picture Book Studio, 1985. ISBN 0-907234-70-4 Subj: Format, unusual. Imagination.

Carroll, Latrobe. *Pet tale* (Carroll, Ruth)

Carroll, Lewis. *Jabberwocky* ill. by Jane Breskin Zalben. Warne, 1977. Subj: Humor. Poetry, rhyme.

The nursery "Alice" intro. by Martin Gardner; ill. by Sir John Tenniel. McGraw-Hill, 1966. A facsimile of the 2d ed. (1890) of Carroll's adapt. of Alice's Adventures in Wonderland. Subj: Dreams. Imagination.

The walrus and the carpenter ill. by Julian Doyle. Merrimack, 1986. ISBN 0-88162-218-4 Subj: Humor. Poetry, rhyme.

The walrus and the carpenter ill. by Jane Breskin Zalben. Holt, 1986. ISBN 0-8050-0071-2 Subj: Humor. Poetry, rhyme.

Carroll, Ruth. *Old Mrs. Billups and the black cats* ill. by author. Walck, 1961. Subj: Animals – cats. Humor.

Pet tale by Ruth and Latrobe Carroll; ill. by Ruth Carroll. Oxford Univ. Pr., 1949. Subj: Pets.

What Whiskers did ill. by author. Walck, 1965. Subj: Animals – dogs. Animals – foxes. Animals – rabbits. Behavior – running away. Wordless.

Where's the bunny? ill. by author. Walck, 1950. Subj: Activities – playing. Animals – rabbits. Games. Participation. Wordless.

Carryl, Charles Edward. *A capital ship: or, The walloping window-blind* ill. by Paul Galdone. McGraw-Hill, 1963. Subj: Boats, ships. Music. Pirates. Songs.

Cars and trucks ill. by Daisuke Yokoi. Simon and Schuster, 1984. Subj: Automobiles. Format, unusual – board books. Transportation. Trucks.

Carter, Angela. *The sleeping beauty and other favourite fairy tales* ill. by Michael Foreman. Schocken, 1984. ISBN 0-8052-3921-9 Subj: Folk and fairy tales.

Carter, Anne. *Beauty and the beast* ill. by Binette Schroeder. Potter, 1986. A retelling of Belle et la bête by Madame Leprince de Beaumont. ISBN 0-517-56173-5 Subj: Emotions – love. Folk and fairy tales. Magic.

Bella's secret garden ill. by John Butler. Crown, 1987. ISBN 0-517-56308-8 Subj: Animals – rabbits. Animals – cats. Behavior – greed. Character traits – kindness to animals.

Molly in danger ill. by John Butler. Crown, 1987. ISBN 0-517-56534-X Subj: Animals – moles. Moving. Nature.

Ruff leaves home ill. by John Butler. Crown, 1986. ISBN 0-517-56068-2 Subj: Animals – foxes. Behavior – lost.

Scurry's treasure ill. by John Butler. Crown, 1987. ISBN 0-517-56535-8 Subj: Animals – squirrels. Nature.

Carter, David A. *How many bugs in a box?* ill. by author. Simon & Schuster, 1988. ISBN 0-671-64965-5 Subj: Format, unusual – toy and movable books. Insects.

Carter, Debby L. *Clipper* ill. by author. Harper, 1981. Subj: Animals – dogs. Sea and seashore.

Carter, James *see* Mayne, William

Carter, Katharine. *Houses* ill. with photos. Childrens Pr., 1982. Subj: Houses.

Ships and seaports ill. with photos. Children's Pr., 1982. Subj: Boats, ships.

Carter, Peter. *My old grandad* (Harranth, Wolf)

Carter, Phyllis Ann *see* Eberle, Irmengarde

Cartlidge, Michelle. *The bear's bazaar: a story craft book* ill. by author. Lothrop, 1980. Subj: Activities. Animals – bears.

A mouse's diary ill. by author. Lothrop, 1982. Subj: Activities. Animals – mice.

Pippin and Pod ill. by author. Pantheon, 1978. Subj: Activities – playing. Animals – mice. Behavior – lost. Behavior – misbehavior.

Teddy trucks ill. by author. Lothrop, 1982. Subj: Animals – bears. Careers – truck drivers. Trucks.

Carton, Lonnie Caming. *Mommies* ill. by Leslie Jacobs. Random House, 1960. Subj: Activities. Family life – mothers. Poetry, rhyme.

Cartwright, Ann. *Norah's ark* ill. by Reg Cartwright. Simon & Schuster, 1984. ISBN 0-671-52540-9 Subj: Animals. Farms. Weather – floods. Weather – rain.

Caryder, Teresa *see* Colman, Hila

Caseley, Judith. *Ada potato* ill. by author. Greenwillow, 1988. ISBN 0-688-07843-9 Subj: Character traits – cleverness. Music. School.

Apple pie and onions ill. by author. Greenwillow, 1987. ISBN 0-688-06763-8 Subj: Ethnic groups in the U.S. Family life – grandmothers.

Molly Pink ill. by author. Greenwillow, 1985. ISBN 0-688-04005-5 Subj: Emotions – embarrassment. School. Songs.

Molly Pink goes hiking ill. by author. Greenwillow, 1985. ISBN 0-688-05700-4 Subj: Character traits – appearance. Sports.

My sister Celia ill. by author. Greenwillow, 1986. ISBN 0-688-06484-1 Subj: Family life – sisters. Weddings.

Silly baby ill. by author. Greenwillow, 1988. ISBN 0-688-07356-5 Subj: Babies. Family life. Sibling rivalry.

When Grandpa came to stay ill. by author. Greenwillow, 1986. ISBN 0-688-06129-X Subj: Death. Family life – grandfathers. Jewish culture.

Casey, Denise. *The friendly prairie dog* photos. by Tim W. Clark and others. Dodd, 1987. ISBN 0-396-08901-1 Subj: Animals – prairie dogs.

Casey, Patricia. *Quack quack* ill. by author. Lothrop, 1988. ISBN 0-688-07765-X Subj: Birds – chickens. Birds – ducks. Eggs.

Cass, Joan E. *The cat thief* ill. by William Stobbs. Abelard-Schuman, 1961. Subj: Animals – cats. Behavior – stealing. Crime. Night.

The cats go to market ill. by William Stobbs. Abelard-Schuman, 1969. Subj: Animals – cats. Shopping.

Cassedy, Sylvia. *Moon-uncle, moon-uncle: rhymes from India* sel. and tr. by Sylvia Cassedy and Parvathi Thampi; ill. by Susanne Suba. Doubleday, 1973. Subj: Foreign lands – India. Nursery rhymes.

Cassidy, Dianne. *Circus animals* ill. by author. Little, 1985. ISBN 0-316-13241-1 Subj: Animals. Circus. Format, unusual – board books. Format, unusual – toy and movable books. Poetry, rhyme.

Circus people ill. by author. Little, 1985. ISBN 0-316-13243-8 Subj: Circus. Format, unusual – board books. Format, unusual – toy and movable books. Poetry, rhyme.

Castiglia, Julie. *Jill the pill* ill. by Steven Kellogg. Atheneum, 1979. Subj: Family life. Sibling rivalry.

Castillo, Violetta. *Animal babies* (Zoll, Max Alfred)

Castle, Caroline. *The hare and the tortoise* (Æsop)

Herbert Binns and the flying tricycle ill. by Peter Weevers. Dial Pr., 1987. ISBN 0-8037-0041-5 Subj: Animals. Animals – mice. Character traits – cleverness. Emotions – envy, jealousy.

Castle, Sue. *Face talk, hand talk, body talk* ill. by Frances McLaughlin-Gill. Doubleday, 1977. Subj: Anatomy. Emotions.

Catchpole, Clive. *Deserts* ill. by Brian McIntyre. Dial Pr., 1984. Subj: Animals. Desert.

Grasslands ill. by Peter Snowball. Dial Pr., 1984. Subj: Animals.

Jungles ill. by Denise Finney. Dial Pr., 1984. Subj: Animals. Jungle.

Mountains ill. by Brian McIntyre. Dial Pr., 1984. Subj: Animals.

Cate, Rikki. *A cat's tale* ill. by Shirley Hughes. Harcourt, 1982. Subj: Animals – cats. Behavior – stealing. Foreign lands – Scotland. Poetry, rhyme.

The caterpillar who turned into a butterfly. Simon and Schuster, 1980. Subj: Format, unusual – board books. Insects – butterflies, caterpillars.

Cathon, Laura E. *Tot Botot and his little flute* ill. by Arnold Lobel. Macmillan, 1970. Subj: Animals. Caldecott award honor book. Foreign lands – India. Music.

Caudill, Rebecca. *Contrary Jenkins* by Rebecca Caudill and James Sterling Ayars; ill. by Glen Rounds. Holt, 1969. Subj: Behavior. Country. Humor.

A pocketful of cricket ill. by Evaline Ness. Holt, 1964. Subj: Behavior – sharing. Caldecott award honor book. Farms. Insects – crickets. School.

Wind, sand and sky ill. by Donald Carrick. Dutton, 1976. Subj: Desert. Poetry, rhyme.

Cauley, Lorinda Bryan. *The animal kids* ill. by author. Putnam's, 1979. Subj: Animals. Behavior – imitation.

The bake-off ill. by author. Putnam's, 1978. Subj: Activities – cooking. Animals.

The cock, the mouse and the little red hen ill. by adapt. Putnam's, 1982. Subj: Animals. Character traits – cleverness. Folk and fairy tales.

Goldilocks and the three bears (The three bears)

The goose and the golden coins ill. by adapt. Harcourt, 1981. Subj: Birds – geese. Folk and fairy tales. Foreign lands – Italy.

The new house ill. by author. Harcourt, 1981. Subj: Animals – groundhogs. Family life. Houses. Problem solving.

The pancake boy (The gingerbread boy)

Pease porridge hot: a Mother Goose cookbook ill. by author. Putnam's, 1977. Subj: Activities – cooking. Food. Nursery rhymes.

Puss in boots (Perrault, Charles)

The trouble with Tyrannosaurus Rex ill. by author. Harcourt, 1988. ISBN 0-15-290880-3 Subj: Behavior – bullying. Character traits – cleverness. Dinosaurs.

Causley, Charles. *Dick Whittington* (Dick Whittington and his cat)

Early in the morning ill. by Michael Foreman. Viking, 1987. ISBN 0-670-80810-5 Subj: Music. Nursery rhymes.

"Quack!" said the billy-goat ill. by Barbara Firth. Lippincott, 1986. ISBN 0-397-32192-9 Subj: Animals. Humor. Noise, sounds. Poetry, rhyme.

Cavagnaro, David. *The pumpkin people* by David Cavagnaro and Maggie Cavagnaro; ill. with photos. Scribner's, 1979. Subj: Activities – gardening. Holidays – Halloween. Seasons – fall. Seasons – summer.

Cavagnaro, Maggie. *The pumpkin people* (Cavagnaro, David)

Cave, Joyce. *Airplanes* (Cave, Ron)

Automobiles (Cave, Ron)

Motorcycles (Cave, Ron)

Cave, Ron. *Airplanes* by Ron and Joyce Cave; ill. by David West and others. Watts, 1982. Subj: Airplanes, airports. Transportation.

Automobiles by Ron and Joyce Cave; ill. by David West and others. Watts, 1982. Subj: Automobiles. Transportation.

Motorcycles by Ron and Joyce Cave; ill. by David West and others. Watts, 1982. Subj: Motorcycles. Transportation.

Cazet, Denys. *Big shoe, little shoe* ill. by author. Bradbury Pr., 1984. Subj: Activities – baby-sitting. Animals – rabbits. Family life – grandparents.

Christmas moon ill. by author. Bradbury Pr., 1984. Subj: Animals – rabbits. Holidays – Christmas. Moon.

December 24th ill. by author. Bradbury Pr., 1986. ISBN 0-02-717950-8 Subj: Animals – rabbits. Birthdays. Family life – grandfathers. Holidays.

The duck with squeaky feet ill. by author. Bradbury Pr., 1980. Subj: Animals. Birds – ducks. Reptiles – alligators, crocodiles. Theater.

A fish in his pocket ill. by author. Watts, 1987. ISBN 0-531-08313-6 Subj: Character traits – kindness. Death. School.

Frosted glass ill. by author. Bradbury Pr., 1987. ISBN 0-02-717960-5 Subj: Animals. Animals – dogs. Art. School.

Great-Uncle Felix ill. by author. Watts, 1988. ISBN 0-531-08350-0 Subj: Animals – rhinoceros. Emotions – embarrassment. Family life.

Lucky me ill. by author. Bradbury Pr., 1983. Subj: Animals. Birds – chickens. Character traits – luck. Food.

Saturday ill. by author. Bradbury Pr., 1985. ISBN 0-02-717800-5 Subj: Animals – dogs. Family life – grandparents.

Sunday ill. by author. Bradbury Pr., 1988. ISBN 0-02-717970-2 Subj: Animals. Family life.

You make the angels cry ill. by author. Bradbury Pr., 1982. ISBN 0-02-717830-7 Subj: Animals – rabbits. Weather – rain.

Cendrars, Blaise. *Shadow* tr. and ill. by Marcia Brown. Scribner's, 1982. Subj: Caldecott award book. Folk and fairy tales. Foreign lands – Africa. Poetry, rhyme. Shadows.

Cerf, Bennett Alfred. *Bennett Cerf's book of animal riddles* ill. by Roy McKié. Random House, 1964. Subj: Humor. Riddles.

Bennett Cerf's book of laughs ill. by Carl Rose. Random House, 1959. Subj: Humor. Riddles.

Bennett Cerf's book of riddles ill. by Roy McKié. Random House, 1960. Subj: Humor. Riddles.

More riddles ill. by Roy McKié. Random House, 1961. Subj: Humor. Riddles.

Chafetz, Henry. *The legend of Befana* ill. by Ronni Solbert. Houghton, 1958. Subj: Folk and fairy tales. Foreign lands – Italy. Holidays – Christmas.

Chaffin, Lillie D. *Tommy's big problem* ill. by Haris Petie. Lantern Pr., 1965. Subj: Babies. Behavior – growing up. Family life. Problem solving.

We be warm till springtime comes ill. by Lloyd Bloom. Macmillan, 1980. Subj: Character traits – bravery. Seasons – winter.

Chaikin, Miriam. *Esther* ill. by Vera Rosenberry. Jewish Pub. Soc., 1987. ISBN 0-8276-0272-3 Subj: Foreign lands – Persia. Holidays. Jewish culture.

Exodus ill. by Charles Mikolaycak. Holiday, 1987. ISBN 0-8234-0607-5 Subj: Jewish culture. Religion.

On the little hearth

Chalmers, Audrey. *A birthday for Obash* ill. by author. Viking, 1952. First pub. in 1937. Subj: Birthdays.

Fancy be good ill. by author. Viking, 1941. Subj: Animals – cats. Behavior – misbehavior. Sibling rivalry.

Hector and Mr. Murfit ill. by author. Viking, 1953. Subj: Animals – dogs. Concepts – size.

Hundreds and hundreds of pancakes ill. by author. Viking, 1942. Subj: Animals. Food. Humor. Zoos.

A kitten's tale ill. by author. Viking, 1946. Subj: Animals – cats. Character traits – optimism.

Parade of Obash ill. by author. Oxford Univ. Pr., 1939. Subj: Animals – hippopotami. Parades. Zoos.

Chalmers, Mary. *Be good, Harry* ill. by author. Harper, 1967. Subj: Activities – baby-sitting. Animals – cats.

Boats finds a house ill. by author. Harper, 1958. Subj: Animals – cats. Boats, ships.

The cat who liked to pretend ill. by author. Harper, 1959. Subj: Animals – cats. Imagination.

A Christmas story ill. by author. Rev. ed. Harper, 1987, 1956. ISBN 0-06-021191-1 Subj: Animals. Holidays – Christmas. Trees.

Come for a walk with me ill. by author. Harper, 1955. Subj: Animals – rabbits.

Come to the doctor, Harry ill. by author. Harper, 1981. Subj: Animals – cats. Illness.

Easter parade ill. by author. Harper, 1988. ISBN 0-06-021233-0 Subj: Animals. Holidays – Easter. Parades.

George Appleton ill. by author. Harper, 1957. Subj: Animals – cats. Dragons.

A hat for Amy Jean ill. by author. Harper, 1956. Subj: Birthdays. Character traits – generosity. Clothing.

Here comes the trolley ill. by author. Harper, 1955. Subj: Activities – picnicking. Activities – traveling. Cable cars, trolleys.

Kevin ill. by author. Harper, 1957. Subj: Animals – rabbits. City.

Merry Christmas, Harry ill. by author. Harper, 1977. Subj: Animals – cats. Holidays – Christmas.

Mr. Cat's wonderful surprise ill. by author. Harper, 1961. Subj: Activities – picnicking. Animals – cats. Family life.

Six dogs, twenty-three cats, forty-five mice, and one hundred sixteen spiders ill. by author. Harper, 1986. ISBN 0-06-021189-X Subj: Humor. Parties. Pets.

Take a nap, Harry ill. by author. Harper, 1964. Subj: Animals – cats. Family life. Sleep.

Throw a kiss, Harry ill. by author. Harper, 1958. Subj: Animals – cats. Careers – firefighters.

Chan, Chin-Yi. *Good luck horse* ill. by Plao Chan. Whittlesey House, 1943. Subj: Animals – horses. Caldecott award honor book.

Chandler, Edna Walker. *Cattle drive* ill. by Jack Merryweather. Benefic Pr., 1966. Subj: Cowboys.

Cowboy Andy ill. by Raymond Kinstler. Random House, 1959. Subj: Cowboys.

Pony rider ill. by Jack Merryweather. Benefic Pr., 1966. Subj: Animals – horses. Cowboys.

Secret tunnel ill. by Jack Merryweather. Benefic Pr., 1967. Subj: Cowboys.

Chandler, Robert. *Russian folk tales* (Afanas'ev, Aleksandr)

Chandoha, Walter. *A baby bunny for you* ill. by author. Collins, 1968. Subj: Animals – rabbits.

A baby goat for you ill. by author. Collins, 1968. Subj: Animals – goats.

A baby goose for you ill. by author. Collins, 1968. Subj: Birds – geese.

Chanover, Alice. *Happy Hanukah everybody* (Chanover, Hyman)

Chanover, Hyman. *Happy Hanukah everybody* by Hyman and Alice Chanover; ill. by Maurice Sendak. United Synagogue Books, n.d. ISBN 0-8381-0712-5 Subj: Holidays – Hanukkah. Jewish culture. Music. Religion.

Chapin, Cynthia. *Squad car 55* ill. by Dale Fleming. Albert Whitman, 1966. Educational consultant: Jene Barr. Subj: Careers – police officers.

Chaplin, Susan Gibbons. *I can sign my ABCs* ill. by Laura McCaul. Gallaudet Univ. Pr., 1986. ISBN 0-930323-19-X Subj: ABC books. Handicaps – deafness. Language. Senses – hearing.

Chapman, Carol. *Barney Bipple's magic dandelions* ill. by Steven Kellogg. Dutton, 1988, 1977. ISBN 0-525-44449-1 Subj: Behavior – wishing. Flowers. Magic. Plants.

Herbie's troubles ill. by Kelly Oechsli. Dutton, 1981. Subj: Behavior – bullying. Behavior – misbehavior. Problem solving.

The tale of Meshka the Kvetch ill. by Arnold Lobel. Dutton, 1980. Subj: Behavior – dissatisfaction. Folk and fairy tales. Jewish culture.

Chapman, Elizabeth. *Suzy* ill. by Margery Gill. Salem House, 1987. ISBN 0-370-30375-X Subj: Character traits – being different. Handicaps – blindness. Senses – seeing.

Chapman, Gaynor. *The luck child* ill. by author. Atheneum, 1968. Based on a story of the Brothers Grimm. Subj: Folk and fairy tales. Royalty.

Chapman, Jean. *Moon-Eyes* ill. by Astra Lacis. McGraw-Hill, 1980. Subj: Animals – cats. Folk and fairy tales. Foreign lands – Italy. Holidays – Christmas. Religion.

Chapman, Noralee. *The story of Barbara* ill. by Helen S. Hull. John Knox Pr., 1963. Subj: Adoption.

Chapouton, Anne-Marie. *Ben finds a friend* tr. by Andrea Mernan; ill. by Ulises Wensell. Putnam's, 1986. ISBN 0-399-21268-X Subj: City. Friendship. Pets.

Billy the brave tr. from French by Anthea Bell; ill. by Jean Claverie. Holt, 1986. ISBN 0-03-008019-3 Subj: Character traits – bravery. Monsters. Night.

Sebastian is always late ill. by Chantal van der Berghe. Holt, 1987. ISBN 0-8050-0487-4 Subj: Imagination. School.

Chardiet, Bernice. *C is for circus* ill. by Brinton Turkle. Walker, 1971. Subj: ABC books. Circus. Poetry, rhyme.

Charles Prince of Wales. *The old man of Lochnagar* ill. by Hugh Casson. Farrar, 1980. Subj: Folk and fairy tales. Foreign lands – Scotland. Imagination.

Charles, Donald. *Calico Cat at school* ill. by author. Children's Pr., 1981. Subj: Animals – cats. School.

Calico Cat at the zoo ill. by author. Children's Pr., 1981. Subj: Animals. Animals – cats. Zoos.

Calico Cat meets bookworm ill. by author. Children's Pr., 1978. Subj: Animals – cats. Libraries. Poetry, rhyme.

Calico Cat's exercise book ill. by author. Children's Pr., 1982. Subj: Animals – cats. Animals – mice.

Calico Cat's year ill. by author. Childrens Pr., 1984. ISBN 0-516-03461-8 Subj: Animals – cats. Days of the week, months of the year. Poetry, rhyme. Seasons.

Shaggy dog's animal alphabet ill. by author. Children's Pr., 1979. Subj: ABC books. Animals. Poetry, rhyme.

Shaggy dog's birthday ill. by author. Childrens Pr., 1986. ISBN 0-516-03576-2 Subj: Animals – dogs. Birthdays. Etiquette.

Shaggy dog's Halloween ill. by author. Childrens Pr., 1984. ISBN 0-516-03575-4 Subj: Animals – dogs. Character traits – appearance. Holidays – Halloween.

Shaggy dog's tall tale ill. by author. Children's Pr., 1980. Subj: Animals – dogs.

Time to rhyme with Calico Cat ill. by author. Children's Pr., 1978. Subj: Animals – cats. Animals – dogs. Poetry, rhyme.

Charles, Nicholas see Kuskin, Karla

Charles, R. H. see Charles, Robert Henry

Charles, Robert Henry. *The roundabout turn* ill. by L. Leslie Brooke. Warne, 1930. Subj: Frogs and toads. Merry-go-rounds. Poetry, rhyme.

Charlip, Remy. *Arm in arm* ill. by author. Parents, 1969. Subj: Games. Humor.

Fortunately ill. by author. Parents, 1964. Subj: Humor. Participation.

Handtalk: an ABC of finger spelling and sign language by Remy Charlip, Mary Beth and George Ancona; ill. by George Ancona. Parents, 1974. Subj: ABC books. Communication. Handicaps – deafness. Language. Senses – hearing.

Handtalk birthday: a number and story book in sign language photos. by George Ancona. Four Winds Pr., 1987. ISBN 0-02-718080-8 Subj: Birthdays. Handicaps – deafness. Language. Senses – hearing.

Harlequin and the gift of many colors by Remy Charlip and Burton Supree; ill. by Remy Charlip. Parents, 1973. Subj: Concepts – color. Folk and fairy tales. Foreign lands – France.

Hooray for me! by Remy Charlip and Lilian Moore; ill. by Vera B. Williams. Parents, 1975. Subj: Character traits – individuality. Family life. Self-concept.

"Mother, mother I feel sick" by Remy Charlip and Burton Supree; ill. by Remy Charlip. Parents, 1966. Subj: Careers – doctors. Humor. Illness.

Thirteen by Remy Charlip and Jerry Joyner; ill. by Remy Charlip. Parents, 1975. Subj: Counting. Humor.

The tree angel (Martin, Judith)

Where is everybody? ill. by author. Addison-Wesley, 1957. Subj: Games. Weather – rain.

Charlot, Martin. *Felisa and the magic tikling bird* ill. by Martin Charlot from a story by Jodi Parry Belknap. Island Heritage, 1973. Subj: Activities – dancing. Folk and fairy tales. Foreign lands – Philippines. Handicaps. Self-concept.

Sunnyside up ill. by author. Weatherhill, 1972. Subj: Wordless.

Charlton, Elizabeth. *Jeremy and the ghost* ill. by Celia Reisman. Dandelion, 1979. Subj: Character traits – bravery. Ghosts. Holidays – Halloween.

Terrible tyrannosaurus ill. by Andrew Glass. Elsevier-Nelson, 1981. Subj: Behavior – bullying. Behavior – imitation. Dinosaurs.

Charmatz, Bill. *The Troy St. bus* ill. by author. Macmillan, 1977. Subj: Animals – horses. School.

Charosh, Mannis. *The ellipse* ill. by Leonard P. Kessler. Crowell, 1972. Subj: Concepts – shape. Science.

Number ideas through pictures ill. by Giulio Maestro. Crowell, 1975. Subj: Concepts. Counting.

Charters, Janet. *The general* by Janet Charters and Michael Foreman; ill. by Michael Foreman. Dutton, 1961. Subj: Violence, anti-violence.

Chase, Alice *see* McHargue, Georgess

Chase, Catherine. *An alphabet book* ill. by June Goldsborough. Dandelion, 1979. Subj: ABC books.

Baby mouse goes shopping ill. by Jill Elgin. Elsevier-Nelson, 1981. Subj: Animals – mice. Shopping.

Baby mouse learns his ABC's ill. by Jill Elgin. Dandelion, 1979. Subj: ABC books. Animals – mice.

Feet ill. by Susan Reiss. Dandelion, 1979. Subj: Anatomy. Concepts – left and right.

Hot and cold ill. by Gail Gibbons. Dandelion, 1979. Subj: Concepts.

The miracles at Cana ill. by Wayne Atkinson. Dandelion, 1979. Subj: Religion.

The mouse in my house ill. by Gail Gibbons. Dandelion, 1979. Subj: Animals – mice. Houses.

My balloon ill. by Gail Gibbons. Dandelion, 1979. Subj: Toys – balloons.

The nightingale and the fool ill. by Judith Cheng. Dandelion, 1979. Subj: Birds – nightingales. Folk and fairy tales. Foreign lands – India.

Noah's ark ill. by Elliot Ivenbaum. Dandelion, 1979. Subj: Religion – Noah.

Pete, the wet pet ill. by Gail Gibbons. Elsevier-Nelson, 1981. Subj: Animals – dogs. Family life.

Chase, Richard. *Billy Boy*

Jack and the three sillies ill. by Joshua Tolford. Houghton, 1950. Subj: Folk and fairy tales.

Chasek, Judith. *Have you seen Wilhelmina Krumpf?* ill. by Sal Murdocca. Lothrop, 1973. Subj: Foreign lands – Holland.

Chaucer, Geoffrey. *Chanticleer and the fox* adapt. and ill. by Barbara Cooney. Crowell, 1958. Adapt. of the "Nun's priest's tale" from the Canterbury tales. Subj: Animals – foxes. Birds – chickens. Caldecott award book. Character traits – flattery. Farms. Folk and fairy tales.

Chenault, Nell. *Parsifal the Poddley* ill. by Vee Guthrie. Little, 1960. Subj: Elves and little people. Emotions – loneliness. U.S. history.

Chenery, Janet. *Pickles and Jake* ill. by Lilian Obligado. Viking, 1975. Subj: Animals – cats. Animals – dogs. Pets.

The toad hunt ill. by Ben Shecter. Harper, 1967. Subj: Frogs and toads. Science.

Wolfie ill. by Marc Simont. Harper, 1969. Subj: Sibling rivalry. Spiders.

Cheng, Hou-Tien. *The Chinese New Year* ill. by author. Holt, 1976. Subj: Foreign lands – China. Holidays – Chinese New Year.

Chermayeff, Ivan. *Tomato and other colors* ill. by author. Prentice-Hall, 1981. Subj: Concepts – color.

Chernoff, Goldie Taub. *Clay-dough, play-dough* ill. and photos. by Margaret A. Hartelius. Walker, 1974. Subj: Activities.

Just a box? ill. by Margaret A. Hartelius. Walker, 1973. Subj: Activities.

Pebbles and pods: a book of nature crafts ill. by Margaret A. Hartelius. Walker, 1973. Subj: Activities.

Puppet party ill. by Margaret A. Hartelius. Walker, 1972. Subj: Activities. Puppets.

Cherry, Lynne. *Who's sick today?* ill. by author. Dutton, 1988. ISBN 0-525-44380-0 Subj: Animals. Illness. Poetry, rhyme.

Chess, Victoria. *Alfred's alphabet walk* ill. by author. Greenwillow, 1979. Subj: ABC books. Behavior – misbehavior.

Poor Esmé ill. by author. Holiday, 1982. Subj: Babies. Behavior – wishing. Emotions – loneliness.

Chevalier, Christa. *The little bear who forgot* ed. by Kathleen Tucker; ill. by author. Albert Whitman, 1984. Subj: Animals – bears. Family life.

Spence and the sleepytime monster ill. by author. Albert Whitman, 1984. Subj: Bedtime. Imagination. Monsters.

Spence is small ill. by author. Albert Whitman, 1987. ISBN 0-8075-7567-4 Subj: Character traits – helpfulness. Character traits – smallness.

Spence isn't Spence anymore ill. by author. Albert Whitman, 1985. ISBN 0-8075-7565-8 Subj: Character traits – appearance.

Spence makes circles ill. by author. Albert Whitman, 1982. Subj: Behavior – mistakes. Humor.

Chevalier, Joan. *Suzette and Nicholas and the seasons clock* (Mangin, Marie-France)

Chicken Little. *Chicken Licken* text by Kenneth McLeish; ill. by Jutta Ash. Bradbury Pr., 1973. Subj: Animals. Behavior – gossip. Behavior – trickery. Birds – chickens. Cumulative tales. Folk and fairy tales.

Chicken Licken adapt. and ill. by Gavin Bishop. Oxford University Pr., 1985. ISBN 0-19-558108-3 Subj: Animals. Behavior – gossip. Behavior – trickery. Birds – chickens. Cumulative tales. Folk and fairy tales.

Henny Penny ill. by Paul Galdone. Seabury Pr., 1968. Subj: Animals. Behavior – gossip. Behavior – trickery. Birds – chickens. Cumulative tales. Folk and fairy tales.

Henny Penny ill. by William Stobbs. Follett, 1968. Subj: Animals. Behavior – gossip. Behavior – trickery. Birds – chickens. Cumulative tales. Folk and fairy tales.

The story of Chicken Licken adapt. and ill. by Jan Ormerod. Lothrop, 1986. ISBN 0-688-06058-7 Subj: Animals. Behavior – gossip. Behavior – trickery. Birds – chickens. Cumulative tales. Folk and fairy tales.

Chiefari, Janet. *Kids are baby goats* ill. with photos. Dodd, 1984. Subj: Animals – goats. Fairs.

Child, Lydia Maria. *Over the river and through the wood* ill. by Brinton Turkle. Coward, 1974. First published in 1844 as The boy's Thanksgiving Day in the 2d vol. of the author's Flowers for children. Subj: Family life – grandparents. Farms. Holidays – Thanksgiving. Songs.

Child Study Association of America. *Brothers and sisters are like that!*

Children go where I send thee: *an American spiritual* ill. by Kathryn E. Shoemaker. Winston Pr., 1980. ISBN 0-03-056673-8 Subj: Ethnic groups in the U.S. – Afro-Americans. Music. Religion.

Children's prayers from around the world. Sadlier, 1981. Subj: Children as authors. Religion.

Children's Television Workshop. *Muppets in my neighborhood* ill. by Harry McNaught. Random House, 1977. Subj: Format, unusual – board books. Puppets.

The Sesame Street book of letters

The Sesame Street book of numbers

The Sesame Street book of opposites with Zero Mostel (Mendoza, George)

The Sesame Street book of people and things

The Sesame Street book of shapes

The Sesame Street players present Mother Goose (Mother Goose)

The Sesame Street song book (Raposo, Joe)

A visit to the Sesame Street firehouse (Elliott, Dan)

A child's book of prayers ill. by Michael Hague. Holt, 1985. ISBN 0-03-001412-3 Subj: Religion.

A child's picture English-Hebrew dictionary ill. by Ita Meshi. Adama, 1985. ISBN 0-915361-07-8 Subj: ABC books. Dictionaries. Foreign languages. Jewish culture.

Chimaera see Farjeon, Eleanor

Chislett, Gail. *The rude visitors* ill. by Barbara Di Lella. Firefly Pr., 1984. Subj: Behavior – carelessness. Imagination.

Chittum, Ida. *The cat's pajamas* ill. by Art Cumings. Parents, 1980. ISBN 0-8193-1030-1 Subj: Animals – cats. Pets.

Chlad, Dorothy. *Bicycles are fun to ride* ill. by Lydia Halverson. Children's Pr., 1984. Subj: Safety. Sports – bicycling.

Matches, lighters, and firecrackers are not toys ill. by Lydia Halverson. Children's Pr., 1982. Subj: Safety.

Poisons make you sick ill. by Lydia Halverson. Children's Pr., 1984. Subj: Safety.

Strangers ill. by Lydia Halverson. Children's Pr., 1982. Subj: Behavior – talking to strangers.

Chönz, Selina. *A bell for Ursli* ill. by Alois Carigiet. Walck, 1950. Subj: Foreign lands – Switzerland. Poetry, rhyme. Seasons – spring.

Florina and the wild bird tr. by Anne and Ian Serraillier; ill. by Alois Carigiet. Walck, 1966. Translation of Flurina und das Wildvöglein. Subj: Birds. Foreign lands – Switzerland. Poetry, rhyme. Seasons – summer.

The snowstorm ill. by Alois Carigiet. Walck, 1958. Translated from the German. Subj: Foreign lands – Switzerland. Poetry, rhyme. Seasons – winter. Weather – snow. Weather – storms.

Chorao, Kay. *The baby's bedtime book* ill. by comp. Dutton, 1984. Subj: Nursery rhymes. Poetry, rhyme.

The baby's good morning book ill. by adapt. Dutton, 1986. ISBN 0-525-44257-X Subj: Babies. Morning. Poetry, rhyme.

The baby's story book ill. by author. Dutton, 1985. ISBN 0-525-44200-6 Subj: Folk and fairy tales. Nursery rhymes.

Cathedral mouse ill. by author. Dutton, 1988. ISBN 0-525-44400-9 Subj: Animals – mice. Houses.

The child's story book ill. by adapt. Dutton, 1987. ISBN 0-525-44328-2 Subj: Folk and fairy tales.

George told Kate ill. by author. Dutton, 1987. ISBN 0-525-44293-6 Subj: Animals – elephants. Sibling rivalry.

Kate's box ill. by author. Dutton, 1982. Subj: Animals – elephants. Behavior – hiding.

Kate's car ill. by author. Dutton, 1982. Subj: Animals – elephants. Toys.

Kate's quilt ill. by author. Dutton, 1982. Subj: Animals – elephants.

Kate's snowman ill. by author. Dutton, 1982. Subj: Animals – elephants. Snowmen.

Lemon moon ill. by author. Holiday, 1983. Subj: Animals. Bedtime. Dreams. Family life – grandmothers.

Lester's overnight ill. by author. Dutton, 1977. Subj: Emotions – fear. Family life. Imagination. Sleep.

Molly's lies ill. by author. Seabury Pr., 1979. Subj: Behavior – losing things. Behavior – lying. Friendship. School.

Molly's Moe ill. by author. Seabury Pr., 1976. Subj: Behavior – losing things. Shopping. Toys.

Oink and Pearl ill. by author. Harper, 1981. Subj: Animals – pigs. Sibling rivalry.

Ups and downs with Oink and Pearl ill. by author. Harper, 1986. ISBN 0-06-021275-6 Subj: Animals – pigs. Birthdays. Sibling rivalry.

Chouinard, Mariko. *The amazing animal alphabet book* (Chouinard, Roger)

Chouinard, Roger. *The amazing animal alphabet book* by Roger and Mariko Chouinard; ill. by Roger Chouinard. Doubleday, 1988. ISBN 0-385-24029-5 Subj: ABC books. Animals.

Chow, Octavio. *The invisible hunters* (Rohmer, Harriet)

Christelow, Eileen. *Henry and the Dragon* ill. by author. Houghton, 1984. Subj: Animals – rabbits. Bedtime. Dragons. Shadows.

Henry and the red stripes ill. by author. Houghton, 1982. Subj: Animals – foxes. Animals – rabbits. Illness.

Jerome the babysitter ill. by author. Houghton, 1985. Subj: Activities – baby-sitting. Behavior – trickery. Character traits – cleverness. Reptiles – alligators, crocodiles.

Olive and the magic hat ill. by author. Clarion, 1987. ISBN 0-89919-513-X Subj: Animals. Behavior – trickery. Clothing. Magic.

The robbery at the diamond dog diner ill. by author. Clarion, 1986. ISBN 0-89919-425-7 Subj: Animals. Behavior – secrets. Behavior – trickery. Birds. Crime.

Christensen, Gardell Dano. *Mrs. Mouse needs a house* ill. by author. Holt, 1958. Subj: Animals. Animals – mice. Houses. Problem solving.

Christensen, Jack. *The forgotten rainbow* by Jack and Lee Christensen; ill. by authors. Morrow, 1960. Subj: Behavior – wishing. Folk and fairy tales.

Christensen, Lee. *The forgotten rainbow* (Christensen, Jack)

Christenson, Larry. *The wonderful way that babies are made* ill. by Dwight Walles. Bethany House, 1982. Subj: Babies. Family life. Science.

Christian, Mary Blount. *April fool* ill. by Diane Dawson. Macmillan, 1982. Subj: Folk and fairy tales. Foreign lands – England. Holidays – April Fools' Day.

The devil take you, Barnabas Beane! ill. by Anne Burgess. Crowell, 1980. Subj: Behavior – greed. Character traits – generosity. Character traits – selfishness.

Devin and Goliath ill. by Normand Chartier. Addison-Wesley, 1974. Subj: Pets. Reptiles – turtles, tortoises.

The doggone mystery ill. by Irene Trivas. Albert Whitman, 1980. Subj: Behavior – stealing. Crime. Problem solving.

Go west, swamp monsters ill. by Marc Brown. Dial Pr., 1985. ISBN 0-8037-0144-6 Subj: Activities – picnicking. Behavior – misbehavior. Behavior – running away. Monsters.

J. J. Leggett, secret agent ill. by Jacquie Hann. Lothrop, 1978. Subj: Behavior – stealing. Character traits – cleverness. Crime. Problem solving.

No dogs allowed, Jonathan! ill. by Don Madden. Addison-Wesley, 1973. Subj: Animals – dogs.

Nothing much happened today ill. by Don Madden. Addison-Wesley, 1973. Subj: Cumulative tales. Humor.

Penrod again ill. by Jane Dyer. Macmillan, 1987. ISBN 0-02-718550-8 Subj: Animals – bears. Animals – porcupines. Friendship.

Penrod's pants ill. by Jane Dyer. Macmillan, 1986. ISBN 0-02-718520-6 Subj: Animals – bears. Animals – porcupines. Friendship.

The sand lot ill. by Dennis Kendrick. Harvey House, 1978. Subj: Activities – playing. Behavior – fighting, arguing. Sports – baseball.

Swamp monsters ill. by Marc Brown. Dial Pr., 1983. Subj: Behavior – imitation. Monsters. School.

The toady and Dr. Miracle ill. by Ib Spang Olsen. Macmillan, 1985. ISBN 0-02-718470-6 Subj: Behavior – trickery. Humor.

A Christmas book tr. from Danish by Joan Tate; ill. by Svend Otto S. Larousse, 1982. Subj: Foreign lands – Denmark. Holidays – Christmas.

Christopher, Matt. *Jackrabbit goalie* ill. by Ed Parker. Little, 1978. Subj: Behavior – lying. Sports – soccer.

Johnny no hit ill. by Raymond Burns. Little, 1977. Subj: Behavior – bullying. Sports – baseball.

Christopher, Matthew F. *see* Christopher, Matt

Chukovsky, Korney. *Good morning, chick* adapt. by Mirra Ginsburg; ill. by Byron Barton. Greenwillow, 1980. Subj: Birds – chickens. Noise, sounds.

The telephone adapt. from Russian by William Jay Smith in collaboration with Max Hayward; ill. by Blair Lent. Delacorte Pr., 1977. Subj: Communication. Humor. Poetry, rhyme.

Chute, Beatrice Joy. *Joy to Christmas* ill. by Erik Blegvad. Dutton, 1958. Subj: Character traits – generosity. Holidays – Christmas.

Chwast, Seymour. *Still another alphabet book* by Seymour Chwast and Martin Stephen Moskof; ill. by authors. McGraw-Hill, 1969. Subj: ABC books. Wordless.

Still another children's book by Seymour Chwast and Martin Stephen Moskof; ill. by authors. McGraw-Hill, 1972. Subj: Dreams. Seasons – summer.

Still another number book by Seymour Chwast and Martin Stephen Moskof; ill. by authors. McGraw-Hill, 1971. Subj: Counting.

Tall city, wide country: a book to read forward and backward ill. by author. Viking, 1983. Subj: Activities – traveling. City. Country. Format, unusual.

Ciardi, John. *I met a man* ill. by Robert Osborn. Houghton, 1961. Subj: Humor. Poetry, rhyme.

John J. Plenty and Fiddler Dan: a new fable of the grasshopper and the ant ill. by Madeleine Gekiere. Lippincott, 1963. Subj: Behavior – saving things. Insects – ants. Insects – grasshoppers. Poetry, rhyme.

The man who sang the sillies ill. by Edward Gorey. Lippincott, 1961. ISBN 0-397-30569-9 Subj: Humor. Poetry, rhyme.

The monster den: or, Look what happened at my house - and to it ill. by Edward Gorey. Lippincott, 1966. Subj: Monsters. Poetry, rhyme.

Scrappy the pup ill. by Jane Miller. Lippincott, 1960. Subj: Animals – dogs. Behavior – growing up. Sleep.

You know who ill. by Edward Gorey. Lippincott, 1964. ISBN 0-397-30792-6 Subj: Humor. Poetry, rhyme.

You read to me, I'll read to you ill. by Edward Gorey. Lippincott, 1962. Subj: Poetry, rhyme.

Ciliotta, Claire. *"Why am I going to the hospital?"* by Claire Ciliotta and Carole Livingston; ill. by Dick Wilson. Lyle Stuart, 1982. Subj: Hospitals. Illness.

City ill. by Roser Capdevila. Firefly Pr., 1986. ISBN 0-920303-45-5 Subj: City. Format, unusual – board books. Wordless.

Civardi, Anne. *Potty time* ill. by Jonathan Langley. Simon & Schuster, 1988. ISBN 0-671-65896-4 Subj: Behavior – growing up.

Things people do ill. by Stephen Cartwright; designed by Roger Priddy. Usborne Pub., 1985. ISBN 0-86020-864-8 Subj: Activities – working. Careers. Games. Islands.

Claret, Maria. *The chocolate rabbit* ill. by author. Barron's, 1985. ISBN 0-416-48260-0 Subj: Animals – rabbits. Behavior – carelessness. Eggs. Holidays – Easter.

Melissa Mouse ill. by author. Barron's, 1985. Subj: Animals – mice. Weddings.

Clark, Ann Nolan. *The desert people* ill. by Allan Houser. Viking, 1962. Subj: Desert. Indians of North America.

In my mother's house ill. by Velino Herrera. Viking, 1941. Subj: Caldecott award honor book. Family life. Indians of North America.

The little Indian basket maker ill. by Harrison Begay. Melmont, 1955. Subj: Activities – working. Indians of North America.

The little Indian pottery maker ill. by Don Perceval. Melmont, 1955. Subj: Activities – working. Indians of North America.

Tia Maria's garden ill. by Ezra Jack Keats. Viking, 1963. Subj: Desert.

Clark, Harry. *The first story of the whale* ill. by author. Houghton, 1938. Subj: Animals – whales. Games. Science.

Clark, Irene Haas *see* Haas, Irene

Clark, Leonard. *Drums and trumpets: poetry for the youngest* ill. by Heather Copley. Bodley Head, 1979. Subj: Nursery rhymes. Poetry, rhyme.

Clark, Roberta. *Why?* ill. by Lois Axeman. Children's Pr., 1983. Subj: Character traits – curiosity. Character traits – questioning.

Claude-Lafontaine, Pascale. *Monsieur Bussy, the celebrated hamster* ill. by Annick Delhumeau. McGraw-Hill, 1968. Delhumeau's name appeared first on the title page of the French ed. pub. under title: Bussy, le hamster doré. Subj: Animals – hamsters. Character traits – ambition.

Claverie, Jean. *The party* ill. by author. Crown, 1986. ISBN 0-517-56026-7 Subj: Behavior – misbehavior. Parties.

The picnic ill. by author. Crown, 1986. ISBN 0-517-56025-9 Subj: Activities – picnicking. Weather – rain.

Shopping ill. by author. Crown, 1986. ISBN 0-517-56024-0 Subj: Family life. Shopping.

Working ill. by author. Crown, 1986. ISBN 0-517-56021-6 Subj: Activities – working. Family life – fathers. Weather – snow.

Claxton, Ernest. *A child's grace* (Burdekin, Harold)

Clay, Helen. *Ants* (Clay, Pat)

Beetles (Clay, Pat)

Clay, Pat. *Ants* by Pat and Helen Clay; ill. with photos. Global Lib. Mktg. Serv., 1984. ISBN 0-7136-2386-1 Subj: Insects – ants. Nature. Science.

Beetles by Pat and Helen Clay; photos. by authors. A & C Black, 1983. Subj: Science.

Cleary, Beverly. *The growing-up feet* ill. by DyAnne DiSalvo-Ryan. Morrow, 1987. ISBN 0-688-06620-8 Subj: Behavior – growing up. Family life. Twins.

The hullabaloo ABC ill. by Earl Thollander. Parnassus, 1960. Subj: ABC books. Farms. Noise, sounds.

Janet's thingamajigs ill. by DyAnne DiSalvo-Ryan. Morrow, 1987. ISBN 0-688-06618-6 Subj: Behavior – collecting things. Behavior – growing up. Family life. Sibling rivalry.

Lucky Chuck ill. by J. Winslow Higginbottom. Morrow, 1984. Subj: Behavior – carelessness. Motorcycles. Safety. Transportation.

The real hole ill. by DyAnne DiSalvo-Ryan. Morrow, 1986. ISBN 0-688-05851-5 Subj: Activities – digging. Problem solving. Trees. Twins.

The real hole ill. by Mary Stevens. Morrow, 1960. Subj: Activities – digging. Problem solving. Trees. Twins.

Two dog biscuits ill. by DyAnne DiSalvo-Ryan. Morrow, 1986. ISBN 0-688-05848-5 Subj: Animals – cats. Animals – dogs. Twins.

Two dog biscuits ill. by Mary Stevens. Morrow, 1961. Subj: Twins.

Cleaver, Elizabeth. *ABC* ill. by author. Atheneum, 1985. Subj: ABC books.

The enchanted caribou ill. by author. Atheneum, 1985. ISBN 0-689-31170-2 Subj: Animals – reindeer. Folk and fairy tales. Indians of North America. Magic. Puppets.

Clement, Claude. *The painter and the wild swans* ill. by Frederic Clement. Dial Pr., 1986. ISBN 0-8037-0268-X Subj: Birds – swans. Folk and fairy tales.

The voice of the wood ill. by Frederic Clement. Dial Pr., 1989. ISBN 0-8037-0635-9 Subj: Music. Trees.

Cleveland, David. *The April rabbits* ill. by Nurit Karlin. Coward, 1978. ISBN 0-698-20463-8 Subj: Animals – rabbits. Counting.

Clewes, Dorothy. *Happiest day* ill. by Sofia. Coward, 1959. Subj: Emotions – loneliness. School.

Henry Hare's boxing match ill. by Patricia W. Turner. Coward, 1950. Subj: Animals. Behavior – imitation.

Hide and seek ill. by Sofia. Coward, 1960. Subj: Farms.

The wild wood ill. by Irene Hawkins. Coward, 1948. Subj: Animals. Character traits – kindness to animals.

Clifford, David. *Your face is a picture* (Clifford, Eth)

Clifford, Eth. *A bear before breakfast* ill. by Kelly Oechsli. Putnam's, 1962. Subj: Communication. Language.

Red is never a mouse ill. by Bill Heckler. Bobbs-Merrill, 1960. Subj: Concepts – color. Poetry, rhyme.

Why is an elephant called an elephant? ill. by Jackie Lacy. Bobbs-Merrill, 1966. Subj: Animals – elephants. Cumulative tales. Royalty.

Your face is a picture by Eth and David Clifford; photos. by David Clifford; ed. consultant: Leo Fay. E. C. Seale, 1963. Subj: Emotions. Ethnic groups in the U.S.

Clifton, Lucille. *All us come cross the water* ill. by John Steptoe. Holt, 1973. Subj: Character traits – pride. Ethnic groups in the U.S. – Afro-Americans. School.

Amifika ill. by Thomas Di Grazia. Dutton, 1977. Subj: Emotions – fear. Ethnic groups in the U.S. – Afro-Americans. Family life. Family life – fathers.

The black B C's ill. by Don Miller. Dutton, 1970. Subj: ABC books. Ethnic groups in the U.S. – Afro-Americans. Poetry, rhyme.

The boy who didn't believe in spring ill. by Brinton Turkle. Dutton, 1973. Subj: City. Ethnic groups in the U.S. – Afro-Americans. Seasons – spring.

Don't you remember? ill. by Evaline Ness. Dutton, 1973. Subj: Birthdays. Ethnic groups in the U.S. – Afro-Americans. Family life.

Everett Anderson's Christmas coming ill. by Evaline Ness. Holt, 1971. Subj: City. Ethnic groups in the U.S. – Afro-Americans. Holidays – Christmas. Poetry, rhyme.

Everett Anderson's friend ill. by Ann Grifalconi. Holt, 1976. Subj: Ethnic groups in the U.S. – Afro-Americans. Friendship. Poetry, rhyme.

Everett Anderson's goodbye ill. by Ann Grifalconi. Holt, 1988, 1983. ISBN 0-8050-0800-4 Subj: Death. Emotions. Emotions – love. Ethnic groups in the U.S. – Afro-Americans. Family life. Poetry, rhyme.

Everett Anderson's nine months long ill. by Ann Grifalconi. Holt, 1987, 1970. Subj: Babies. Ethnic groups in the U.S. – Afro-Americans. Family life. Poetry, rhyme.

Everett Anderson's 1-2-3 ill. by Ann Grifalconi. Holt, 1977. Subj: Ethnic groups in the U.S. – Afro-Americans. Family life. Poetry, rhyme.

Everett Anderson's year ill. by Ann Grifalconi. Holt, 1974. Subj: Ethnic groups in the U.S. – Afro-Americans. Poetry, rhyme. Seasons.

My brother fine with me ill. by Moneta Barnett. Holt, 1975. Subj: Behavior – running away. Ethnic groups in the U.S. – Afro-Americans. Family life. Sibling rivalry.

My friend Jacob ill. by Thomas Di Grazia. Dutton, 1980. Subj: Character traits – helpfulness. Ethnic groups in the U.S. – Afro-Americans. Friendship. Handicaps.

Some of the days of Everett Anderson ill. by Evaline Ness. Holt, 1987, 1970. Subj: Days of the week, months of the year. Ethnic groups in the U.S. – Afro-Americans. Family life. Poetry, rhyme.

Three wishes ill. by Stephanie Douglas. Viking, 1976. Subj: Behavior – wishing. Ethnic groups in the U.S. – Afro-Americans. Friendship.

Climo, Lindee. *Chester's barn* ill. by author. Tundra, 1982. Subj: Barns. Farms. Foreign lands – Canada.

Clyde ill. by author. Tundra, 1986. ISBN 0-88776-185-2 Subj: Animals – horses. Behavior – seeking better things. Machines.

Climo, Shirley. *The adventure of Walter* ill. by Ingrid Fetz. Atheneum, 1965. Subj: Animals – whales. Character traits – curiosity.

The cobweb Christmas ill. by Joe Lasker. Crowell, 1982. Subj: Animals. Holidays – Christmas. Magic. Spiders.

King of the birds ill. by Ruth Heller. Harper, 1988. ISBN 0-690-04623-5 Subj: Birds. Character traits – cleverness. Royalty.

Clinton, Susan. *I can be an architect.* Childrens Pr., 1986. ISBN 0-516-01890-6 Subj: Careers – architects.

Clithero, Myrtle Ely see Clithero, Sally

Clithero, Sally. *Beginning-to-read poetry.* Follett, 1967. Subj: Poetry, rhyme.

Clymer, Eleanor Lowenton. *The big pile of dirt* ill. by Robert Shore. Holt, 1968. Subj: Activities – playing. City.

Horatio ill. by Robert M. Quackenbush. Atheneum, 1968. Subj: Animals – cats. Ethnic groups in the U.S. – Afro-Americans.

Horatio goes to the country ill. by Robert M. Quackenbush. Atheneum, 1978. Subj: Animals – cats. Twins.

The tiny little house ill. by Ingrid Fetz. Atheneum, 1964. Subj: Houses.

A yard for John ill. by Mildred Boyle. McBride, 1943. Subj: Moving.

Clymer, Ted. *The horse and the bad morning* by Ted Clymer and Miska Miles; ill. by Leslie Morrill. Dutton, 1982. Subj: Animals. Behavior – dissatisfaction. Problem solving.

Coats, Belle. *Little maverick cow* ill. by George Fulton. Scribner's, 1957. Subj: Animals – bulls, cows. Farms.

Coats, Laura Jane. *City cat* ill. by author. Macmillan, 1987. ISBN 0-02-719051-X Subj: Animals – cats. City.

Marcella and the moon ill. by author. Macmillan, 1986. ISBN 0-02-719050-1 Subj: Activities – painting. Birds – ducks. Moon.

Mr. Jordan in the park ill. by author. Macmillan, 1988. ISBN 0-02-719053-6 Subj: Behavior – growing up. Old age.

The oak tree ill. by author. Macmillan, 1987. ISBN 0-02-719052-8 Subj: Trees.

Coatsworth, Elizabeth. *Boston Bells* ill. by Manning Lee. Macmillan, 1952. Subj: Art. U.S. history.

The children come running: UNICEF greeting cards. Golden Pr., 1961. Subj: Holidays – Christmas. Poetry, rhyme. UNICEF

The giant golden book of cat stories ill. by Feodor Rojankovsky. Simon and Schuster, 1953. Subj: Animals – cats. Folk and fairy tales. Poetry, rhyme.

Good night ill. by José Aruego. Macmillan, 1972. Subj: Bedtime. Stars.

Lonely Maria ill. by Evaline Ness. Pantheon, 1960. Subj: Emotions – loneliness. Family life – grandfathers. Islands.

A peaceable kingdom, and other poems ill. by Fritz Eichenberg. Pantheon, 1958. Subj: Animals. Poetry, rhyme.

Pika and the roses ill. by Kurt Wiese. Pantheon, 1959. Subj: Animals – rabbits. Character traits – cleverness.

Under the green willow ill. by Janina Domanska. Macmillan, 1971. Subj: Birds. Fish. Food.

Cobb, Vicki. *How the doctor knows you're fine* ill. by Anthony Ravielli. Lippincott, 1973. Subj: Careers – doctors. Health.

Lots of rot ill. by Brian Schatell. Lippincott, 1981. Subj: Science.

Cobbett, Richard *see* Pluckrose, Henry

Cober, Alan E. *Cober's choice* ill. by author. Dutton, 1979. Subj: Animals. Art.

Cocagnac, A. M. (Augustin Maurice). *The three trees of the Samurai* adapt. from a Japanese no play; ill. by Alain Le Foll. Dial Pr., 1970. Subj: Folk and fairy tales. Foreign lands – Japan.

Cock Robin. *The courtship, merry marriage, and feast of Cock Robin and Jenny Wren: to which is added the doleful death of Cock Robin* ill. by Barbara Cooney. Scribner's, 1965. Subj: Birds – robins. Birds – wrens. Death. Nursery rhymes. Weddings.

Coco, Eugene Bradley. *The fiddler's son* ill. by Robert James Sabuda. Green Tiger Pr., 1988. ISBN 0-88138-111-X Subj: Music.

The wishing well ill. by Robert James Sabuda. Green Tiger Pr., 1988. ISBN 0-88138-112-8 Subj: Behavior – greed. Behavior – wishing. Circular tales. Magic.

Coe, Lloyd. *Charcoal* ill. by author. Crowell, 1946. Subj: Animals – sheep.

Coerr, Eleanor. *The big balloon race* ill. by Carolyn Croll. Harper, 1981. Subj: Activities – ballooning.

Chang's paper pony ill. by Deborah Kogan Ray. Harper, 1988. ISBN 0-06-021329-9 Subj: Animals – horses. Ethnic groups in the U.S. – Chinese-Americans.

The Josefina story quilt ill. by Bruce Degen. Harper, 1986. ISBN 0-06-021349-3 Subj: Activities – traveling. Birds – chickens. Pets.

Coerr, Eleanor Beatrice *see* Coerr, Eleanor

Cohen, Barbara. *The demon who would not die* ill. by Anatoly Ivanov. Atheneum, 1982. Subj: Folk and fairy tales. Foreign lands – Russia. Monsters.

The donkey's story ill. by Susan Jeanne Cohen. Lothrop, 1988. ISBN 0-688-04105-1 Subj: Animals – donkeys. Religion.

Even higher ill. by Anatoly Ivanov. Lothrop, 1987. ISBN 0-688-06453-1 Subj: Character traits – generosity. Holidays. Jewish culture.

Gooseberries to oranges ill. by Beverly Brodsky McDermott. Lothrop, 1982. Subj: Jewish culture. Moving.

Here come the Purim players! ill. by Beverly Brodsky McDermott. Lothrop, 1984. Subj: Folk and fairy tales. Holidays – Purim. Jewish culture. Middle ages.

Cohen, Burton. *Nelson makes a face* ill. by William Schroder. Lothrop, 1978. Subj: Character traits – appearance.

Cohen, Carol L. *The mud pony: a traditional Skidi Pawnee tale* ill. by Shonto Begay. Scholastic, 1988. ISBN 0-590-41525-5 Subj: Animals – horses. Folk and fairy tales. Indians of North America.

Wake up, groundhog! ill. by author. Crown, 1975. Subj: Animals – groundhogs. Clocks. Hibernation. Holidays – Groundhog Day. Seasons – spring.

Cohen, Caron Lee. *Renata, Whizbrain and the ghost* ill. by Blanche Sims. Atheneum, 1987. ISBN 0-689-31271-1 Subj: Character traits – cleverness. Folk and fairy tales. Ghosts.

Sally Ann Thunder Ann Whirlwind Crockett ill. by Ariane Dewey. Greenwillow, 1985. ISBN 0-688-04007-1 Subj: Behavior – trickery. Folk and fairy tales.

Three yellow dogs ill. by Peter Sis. Greenwillow, 1986. ISBN 0-688-06231-8 Subj: Animals – dogs. Language.

Whiffle Squeek ill. by Ted Rand. Dodd, 1987. ISBN 0-396-08999-2 Subj: Animals – cats. Monsters. Poetry, rhyme. Sea and seashore.

Cohen, Daniel. *America's very own monsters* ill. by Tom Huffman. Dodd, 1982. Subj: Monsters.

Dinosaurs ill. by Jean Zallinger. Doubleday, 1987. ISBN 0-385-23415-5 Subj: Dinosaurs.

Cohen, Miriam. *Bee my Valentine!* ill. by Lillian Hoban. Greenwillow, 1978. Subj: Holidays – Valentine's Day. School.

Best friends ill. by Lillian Hoban. Macmillan, 1971. Subj: Friendship. School.

Don't eat too much turkey! ill. by Lillian Hoban. Greenwillow, 1987. ISBN 0-688-07142-2 Subj: Behavior – sharing. School.

First grade takes a test ill. by Lillian Hoban. Greenwillow, 1980. Subj: Friendship. School.

It's George! ill. by Lillian Hoban. Greenwillow, 1988. ISBN 0-688-06813-8 Subj: Character traits – being different. School.

Jim meets the thing ill. by Lillian Hoban. Greenwillow, 1981. Subj: Behavior – growing up. Emotions – fear. Monsters. School.

Jim's dog Muffins ill. by Lillian Hoban. Greenwillow, 1984. Subj: Animals – dogs. Death. Emotions. Pets.

Liar, liar, pants on fire! ill. by Lillian Hoban. Greenwillow, 1985. ISBN 0-688-04245-7 Subj: Behavior – lying. Character traits – generosity. Friendship. School.

Lost in the museum ill. by Lillian Hoban. Greenwillow, 1979. Subj: Behavior – lost. Museums. School.

The new teacher ill. by Lillian Hoban. Macmillan, 1972. Subj: School.

No good in art ill. by Lillian Hoban. Greenwillow, 1980. Subj: Art. School. Self-concept.

See you tomorrow ill. by Lillian Hoban. Greenwillow, 1983. Subj: Handicaps – blindness. School. Senses – seeing.

So what? ill. by Lillian Hoban. Greenwillow, 1982. Subj: School. Self-concept.

Starring first grade ill. by Lillian Hoban. Greenwillow, 1985. ISBN 0-688-04030-6 Subj: Behavior – misbehavior. School. Theater.

Tough Jim ill. by Lillian Hoban. Macmillan, 1974. Subj: Behavior – bullying. Parties. School.

When will I read? ill. by Lillian Hoban. Greenwillow, 1977. Subj: Activities – reading. School.

Will I have a friend? ill. by Lillian Hoban. Macmillan, 1967. Subj: Ethnic groups in the U.S. Friendship. School.

Cohen, Paul. *Creepy crawly critter riddles* (Bernstein, Joanne E.)

More unidentified flying riddles (Bernstein, Joanne E.)

What was the wicked witch's real name? (Bernstein, Joanne E.)

Cohen, Peter Zachary. *Authorized autumn charts of the Upper Red Canoe River country* ill. by Tomie de Paola. Atheneum, 1972. Subj: ABC books. Boats, ships. Games. Seasons – fall.

Cohn, Janice. *I had a friend named Peter: talking to children about the death of a friend* ill. by Gail Owens. Morrow, 1987. ISBN 0-688-06686-0 Subj: Death. Friendship.

Cohn, Norma. *Brother and sister* ill. by author. Oxford Univ. Pr., 1942. Subj: Animals – cats. Sports – swimming.

Coker, Gylbert. *Naptime* ill. by author. Delacorte, 1978. Subj: School. Sleep.

Colby, C. B. (Carroll Burleigh). *Who lives there?* ill. by author. Atheneum, 1953. Subj: Animals. Birds. Houses. Insects. Science.

Who went there? ill. by author. Atheneum, 1953. Subj: Animals. Birds. Reptiles. Science.

Coldrey, Jennifer. *Danger colors* (Oxford Scientific Films)

Hide and seek (Oxford Scientific Films)

Penguins photos. by Douglas Allan and others. André Deutsch, 1983. Subj: Birds – penguins.

The world of chickens ill. with photos. Gareth Stevens, 1987. ISBN 1-55532-071-6 Subj: Birds – chickens. Science.

The world of crabs photos. by Oxford Scientific Films. Gareth Stevens, 1986. ISBN 1-55532-063-5 Subj: Crustacea. Science.

The world of frogs photos. by Oxford Scientific Films. Gareth Stevens, 1986. ISBN 1-55532-024-4 Subj: Frogs and toads. Science.

The world of rabbits photos. by Oxford Scientific Films. Gareth Stevens, 1986. ISBN 1-55532-064-3 Subj: Animals – rabbits. Science.

The world of squirrels photos. by Oxford Scientific Films. Gareth Stevens, 1986. ISBN 1-55532-065-1 Subj: Animals – squirrels. Science.

Cole, Ann. *I saw a purple cow: and 100 other recipes for learning* by Ann Cole and others; ill. by True Kelley. Little, 1972. Subj: Activities.

Purple cow to the rescue by Ann Cole and Carolyn Haas; ill. by True Kelley. Little, 1982. Subj: Activities.

Cole, Ann Kilborn *see* Cole, Ann

Cole, Annette *see* Steiner, Barbara

Cole, Babette. *Nungu and the elephant* ill. by author. McGraw-Hill, 1980. Subj: Animals – elephants. Foreign lands – Africa. Magic.

Nungu and the hippopotamus ill. by author. McGraw-Hill, 1979. Subj: Animals – hippopotami. Foreign lands – Africa.

Prince Cinders ill. by author. Putnam's, 1988. ISBN 0-399-21502-6 Subj: Folk and fairy tales. Magic. Royalty.

Princess Smartypants ill. by author. Putnam's, 1987. ISBN 0-399-21409-7 Subj: Pets. Problem solving. Royalty.

The trouble with dad ill. by author. Putnam's, 1986. ISBN 0-399-21206-X Subj: Activities – working. Family life – fathers. Robots.

The trouble with Gran ill. by author. Putnam's, 1987. ISBN 0-399-21428-3 Subj: Family life – grandmothers. Space and space ships.

The trouble with mom ill. by author. Coward, 1984. Subj: Family life – mothers. School. Witches.

Cole, Brock. *The giant's toe* ill. by author. Farrar, 1986. ISBN 0-374-32559-6 Subj: Anatomy. Folk and fairy tales. Giants.

The king at the door ill. by author. Doubleday, 1979. Subj: Behavior – disbelief. Character traits – kindness. Foreign lands – England. Royalty.

Nothing but a pig ill. by author. Doubleday, 1981. Subj: Animals – pigs. Behavior – imitation. Behavior – seeking better things. Friendship.

Cole, Davis *see* Elting, Mary

Cole, Joanna. *Animal sleepyheads: one to ten* ill. by Jeni Bassett. Scholastic, 1988. ISBN 0-590-40919-0 Subj: Animals. Counting. Poetry, rhyme.

Aren't you forgetting something, Fiona? ill. by Ned Delaney. Parents, 1984. Subj: Animals – elephants. Behavior – forgetfulness.

A bird's body photos. by Jerome Wexler. Morrow, 1982. Subj: Anatomy. Birds. Science.

Bony-legs ill. by Dirk Zimmer. Four Winds Pr., 1983. Subj: Folk and fairy tales. Foreign lands – Russia. Magic. Witches.

A calf is born photos. by Jerome Wexler. Morrow, 1975. Subj: Animals – bulls, cows. Babies. Science.

A cat's body photos. by Jerome Wexler. Morrow, 1982. Subj: Anatomy. Animals – cats. Science.

A chick hatches photos. by Jerome Wexler. Morrow, 1976. Subj: Birds – chickens. Science.

The Clown-Arounds go on vacation ill. by Jerry Smath. Parents, 1984. Subj: Activities – vacationing. Behavior – lost. Clowns, jesters. Humor. Riddles.

Doctor Change ill. by Donald Carrick. Morrow, 1986. ISBN 0-688-06136-2 Subj: Character traits – cleverness. Folk and fairy tales.

A dog's body photos. by Jim and Ann Monteith. Morrow, 1986. ISBN 0-688-04154-X Subj: Animals – dogs. Anatomy. Science.

Evolution ill. by Aliki. Crowell, 1987. ISBN 0-690-04598-0 Subj: Animals. Plants. Science.

Find the hidden insect by Joanna Cole and Jerome Wexler; photos. by Jerome Wexler. Morrow, 1979. Subj: Insects. Science.

A fish hatches photos. by Jerome Wexler. Morrow, 1978. Subj: Fish. Science.

Get well, Clown-Arounds! ill. by Jerry Smath. Parents, 1983. Subj: Clowns, jesters. Humor. Illness. Riddles.

Golly Gump swallowed a fly ill. by Bari Weissman. Parents, 1982. Subj: Folk and fairy tales. Humor. Poetry, rhyme.

How you were born photos. by Lennart Nilsson. Morrow, 1984. Subj: Babies. Family life. Science.

Hungry, hungry sharks ill. by Patricia Wynne. Random, 1986. ISBN 0-394-97471-9 Subj: Fish. Science.

Large as life daytime animals ill. by Kenneth Lilly. Knopf, 1985. ISBN 0-394-97188-4 Subj: Animals.

Large as life nighttime animals ill. by Kenneth Lilly. Knopf, 1985. ISBN 0-394-97189-2 Subj: Animals. Night.

Monster manners ill. by Jared D. Lee. Scholastic, 1985. ISBN 0-590-33592-8 Subj: Etiquette. Monsters.

My puppy is born photos. by Jerome Wexler. Morrow, 1973. Subj: Animals – dogs. Science.

The new baby at your house photos. by Hella Hammid. Morrow, 1985. ISBN 0-688-05807-8 Subj: Babies. Emotions – envy, jealousy. Family life. Sibling rivalry.

Norma Jean, jumping bean ill. by Lynn Munsinger. Random House, 1987. ISBN 0-394-98668-7 Subj: Activities – jumping. Animals – kangaroos. School.

Plants in winter ill. by Kazue Mizumura. Crowell, 1973. Subj: Plants. Science. Seasons – winter. Trees.

The secret box ill. by Joan Sandin. Morrow, 1971. Subj: Behavior – stealing.

Cole, Sheila. *When the tide is low* ill. by Virginia Wright-Frierson. Lothrop, 1985. ISBN 0-688-04067-5 Subj: Animals. Sea and seashore.

Cole, William. *Aunt Bella's umbrella* ill. by Jacqueline Chwast. Doubleday, 1970. Subj: Character traits – helpfulness. Umbrellas. Weather – rain.

Dinosaurs and beasts of yore ill. by Susanna Natti. Collins-World, 1979. Subj: Dinosaurs. Humor.

Frances face-maker ill. by Tomi Ungerer. Collins-World, 1963. Subj: Bedtime. Emotions. Family life. Participation. Poetry, rhyme.

I went to the animal fair ill. by Colette Rosselli. Collins-World, 1959. Subj: Animals. Humor.

I'm mad at you

That pest Jonathan ill. by Tomi Ungerer. Harper, 1970. Subj: Behavior – misbehavior. Family life. Poetry, rhyme.

What's good for a four-year-old? ill. by Tomi Ungerer. Holt, 1967. Subj: Activities – playing. Poetry, rhyme.

What's good for a six-year-old? ill. by Ingrid Fetz. Holt, 1965. Subj: Activities – playing. Poetry, rhyme.

What's good for a three-year-old? ill. by Lillian Hoban. Holt, 1974. Subj: Activities – baby-sitting. Birthdays. Poetry, rhyme.

Coleridge, Sara. *January brings the snow: a book of months* ill. by Jenni Oliver. Dial Pr., 1986. ISBN 0-8037-0314-7 Subj: Days of the week, months of the year. Poetry, rhyme.

Coles, Alison. *Michael and the sea* ill. by Michael Charlton. EDC, 1985. ISBN 0-88110-268-7 Subj: Emotions – fear. Sea and seashore. Sports – swimming.

Michael in the dark ill. by Michael Charlton. EDC, 1985. ISBN 0-88110-267-9 Subj: Emotions – fear. Night.

Michael's first day ill. by Michael Charlton. EDC, 1985. ISBN 0-88110-266-0 Subj: Emotions – fear. School.

Coletta, Hallie. *From A to Z* (Coletta, Irene)

Coletta, Irene. *From A to Z* by Irene and Hallie Coletta; ill. by Hallie Coletta. Prentice-Hall, 1979. Subj: ABC books. Poetry, rhyme. Rebuses.

Colette. *The boy and the magic* tr. by Christopher Fry; ill. by Gerard Hoffnung. Putnam's, 1965. Subj: Behavior – misbehavior. Magic. Music.

Colette, Sidonie Gabrielle *see* Colette

Collier, Ethel. *I know a farm* ill. by Honoré Guilbeau. Addison-Wesley, 1960. Subj: Farms.

Who goes there in my garden? ill. by Honoré Guilbeau. Abelard-Schuman, 1963. Subj: Activities – gardening. Character traits – helpfulness.

Collier, James Lincoln. *Danny goes to the hospital* ill. by Yale Joel. Norton, 1970. Subj: Hospitals.

Collington, Peter. *The angel and the soldier boy* ill. by author. Knopf, 1987. ISBN 0-394-98626-1 Subj: Angels. Behavior – stealing. Pirates. Toys – soldiers. Wordless.

Little pickle ill. by author. Dutton, 1986. ISBN 0-525-44230-8 Subj: Behavior – misbehavior. Dreams. Sleep. Wordless.

My darling kitten ill. by author. Knopf, 1988. ISBN 0-394-89924-5 Subj: Animals – cats. Pets.

Collins, Judith Graham. *Josh's scary dad* ill. by Diane Paterson. Abingdon Pr., 1983. Subj: Character traits – appearance. Humor.

Collins, Pat L. *My friend Andrew* ill. by Howard Berelson. Prentice-Hall, 1981. Subj: Behavior – boasting. Imagination.

Taking care of Tucker ill. by Maxie Chambliss. Putnam's, 1989. ISBN 0-399-21586-7 Subj: Behavior – misbehavior. Behavior – needing someone. Family life.

Tumble, tumble, tumbleweed ill. by Charles Robinson. Albert Whitman, 1982. Subj: Friendship. Pets.

Collodi, Carlo. *The adventures of Pinocchio* adapt. by Stephanie Spinner; ill. by Diane Goode. Random House, 1983. Subj: Behavior – lying. Behavior – misbehavior. Character traits – loyalty. Folk and fairy tales. Puppets.

Colman, Hila. *Peter's brownstone house* ill. by Leonard Weisgard. Morrow, 1963. Subj: City. Houses.

Watch that watch ill. by Leonard Weisgard. Morrow, 1962. Subj: Animals. Clocks. Time.

Colodny, Helen Kay *see* Kay, Helen

Colonius, Lillian. *At the zoo* by Lillian Colonius and Glen W. Schroeder; ill. by Glen W. Schroeder. Melmont, 1954. Subj: Zoos.

Come out to play ill. by Jeanette Winter. Knopf, 1986. ISBN 0-394-97742-4 Subj: City. Moon. Nursery rhymes.

Come to the circus. Simon and Schuster, 1980. Subj: Circus. Format, unusual – board books.

Company González, Mercè. *Killian and the dragons* adapt. by Paula Franklin; ill. by Agustí Asensio Sauri. Silver Burdett, 1986. ISBN 0-382-09180-9 Subj: Dragons. Emotions – fear. Royalty.

Conaway, Judith. *I'll get even* ill. by Mark Gubin. Raintree Pub., 1977. Subj: Emotions – loneliness. Sibling rivalry.

Cone, Molly. *The Jewish Sabbath* ill. by Ellen Raskin. Crowell, 1966. Subj: Holidays. Jewish culture. Religion.

Cone, Molly Lamken *see* Cone, Molly

Conford, Ellen. *Eugene the brave* ill. by John M. Larrecq. Little, 1978. Subj: Animals – possums. Character traits – bravery. Emotions – fear. Night.

Impossible, possum ill. by Rosemary Wells. Little, 1971. Subj: Animals – possums. Character traits – individuality.

Just the thing for Geraldine ill. by John M. Larrecq. Little, 1974. Subj: Animals – possums. Character traits – perseverance.

Why can't I be William? ill. by Philip Wende. Little, 1972. Subj: Emotions – envy, jealousy. Family life. Family life – only child. Friendship.

Conger, Lesley. *Tops and bottoms* ill. by Imero Gobbato. Four Winds Pr., 1970. Subj: Folk and fairy tales. Foreign lands – England. Monsters.

Conger, Marion. *The chipmunk that went to church* ill. by author. Simon and Schuster, 1952. Subj: Animals – chipmunks. Emotions – loneliness.

The little golden holiday book ill. by author. Simon and Schuster, 1951. Subj: Holidays.

Conklin, Gladys. *Cheetahs, the swift hunters* ill. by Charles Robinson. Holiday, 1976. Subj: Animals – cheetahs. Science.

I caught a lizard ill. by Artur Marokvia. Holiday, 1967. Subj: Animals. Insects. Reptiles – lizards. Science. Spiders.

I like beetles ill. by Jean Zallinger. Holiday, 1975. Subj: Insects – beetles. Science.

I like butterflies ill. by Barbara Latham. Holiday, 1960. Subj: Insects – butterflies, caterpillars. Science.

I like caterpillars ill. by Barbara Latham. Holiday, 1958. Subj: Insects – butterflies, caterpillars. Science.

I watch flies ill. by Jean Zallinger. Holiday, 1977. Subj: Insects – flies. Science.

If I were a bird ill. by Artur Marokvia. Holiday, 1965. Subj: Birds. Science.

Journey of the gray whales ill. by Leonard Everett Fisher. Holiday, 1974. Subj: Animals – whales. Science.

Little apes ill. by Joseph Cellini. Holiday, 1970. Subj: Animals – gorillas. Science.

Lucky ladybugs ill. by Glen Rounds. Holiday, 1968. Subj: Insects – ladybugs. Science.

Praying mantis: the garden dinosaur ill. by Glen Rounds. Holiday, 1978. Subj: Insects – praying mantis. Science.

We like bugs ill. by Artur Marokvia. Holiday, 1962. Subj: Insects. Science.

When insects are babies ill. by Artur Marokvia. Holiday, 1969. Subj: Insects. Science.

Conover, Chris. *Froggie went a-courting* (A frog he would a-wooing go (folk-song))

Six little ducks ill. by author. Crowell, 1976. Subj: Birds – ducks. Counting. Music. Poetry, rhyme. Songs.

The wizard's daughter: a Viking legend ill. by author. Little, 1984. Subj: Folk and fairy tales. Foreign lands – Denmark. Magic. Royalty.

Conran, Sebastian. *My first ABC book* ill. by author. Macmillan, 1988. ISBN 0-689-71198-0 Subj: ABC books.

Conroy, Jack. *The fast sooner hound* (Bontemps, Arna Wendell)

Constant Reader *see* Parker, Dorothy D.

Conta, Marcia Maher. *Feelings between brothers and sisters* ill. by Jules M. Rosenthal. Raintree Pub., 1974. Subj: Emotions. Family life.

Feelings between friends ill. by Jules M. Rosenthal. Raintree Pub., 1974. Subj: Emotions. Friendship.

Feelings between kids and grownups ill. by Jules M. Rosenthal. Raintree Pub., 1974. Subj: Emotions.

Feelings between kids and parents ill. by Jules M. Rosenthal. Raintree Pub., 1974. Subj: Emotions. Family life.

Cook, Ann. *Lady Monster has a plan* (Blance, Ellen)

Lady Monster helps out (Blance, Ellen)

Monster and the magic umbrella (Blance, Ellen)

Monster and the mural (Blance, Ellen)

Monster and the surprise cookie (Blance, Ellen)

Monster at school (Blance, Ellen)

Monster buys a pet (Blance, Ellen)

Monster cleans his house (Blance, Ellen)

Monster comes to the city (Blance, Ellen)

Monster gets a job (Blance, Ellen)

Monster goes around the town (Blance, Ellen)

Monster goes to school (Blance, Ellen)

Monster goes to the beach (Blance, Ellen)

Monster goes to the circus (Blance, Ellen)

Monster goes to the hospital (Blance, Ellen)

Monster goes to the museum (Blance, Ellen)

Monster goes to the zoo (Blance, Ellen)

Monster has a party (Blance, Ellen)

Monster, Lady Monster and the bike ride (Blance, Ellen)

Monster looks for a friend (Blance, Ellen)

Monster looks for a house (Blance, Ellen)

Monster meets Lady Monster (Blance, Ellen)

Monster on the bus (Blance, Ellen)

Cook, Bernadine. *The little fish that got away* ill. by Crockett Johnson. Addison-Wesley, 1956. Subj: Fish. Sports – fishing.

Looking for Susie ill. by Judith Shahn. Addison-Wesley, 1959. Subj: Animals – cats. Family life. Farms.

Cook, John Estes *see* Baum, L. Frank (Lyman Frank)

Cook, Marion B. *Waggles and the dog catcher* ill. by Louis Darling. Morrow, 1951. Subj: Animals – dogs.

Cook, Scott. *The gingerbread boy*

Cooke, Ann. *Giraffes at home* ill. by Robert M. Quackenbush. Harper, 1972. Subj: Animals – giraffes. Science.

Cooke, Barbara *see* Alexander, Anne

Coombs, Patricia. *Dorrie and the amazing magic elixir* ill. by author. Lothrop, 1974. Subj: Magic. Witches. Wizards.

Dorrie and the birthday eggs ill. by author. Lothrop, 1971. Subj: Birthdays. Eggs. Witches.

Dorrie and the blue witch ill. by author. Lothrop, 1964. Subj: Magic. Witches.

Dorrie and the dreamyard monsters ill. by author. Lothrop, 1977. Subj: Dreams. Magic. Monsters. Witches.

Dorrie and the fortune teller ill. by author. Lothrop, 1973. Subj: Careers – fortune tellers. Progress. Witches. Wizards.

Dorrie and the goblin ill. by author. Lothrop, 1972. Subj: Activities – baby-sitting. Goblins. Witches.

Dorrie and the Halloween plot ill. by author. Lothrop, 1976. Subj: Activities – flying. Holidays – Halloween. Witches.

Dorrie and the haunted house ill. by author. Lothrop, 1970. Subj: Crime. Witches. Wizards.

Dorrie and the museum case ill. by author. Lothrop, 1986. ISBN 0-688-04279-1 Subj: Magic. Museums. Witches.

Dorrie and the screebit ghost ill. by author. Lothrop, 1979. Subj: Ghosts. Witches.

Dorrie and the weather-box ill. by author. Lothrop, 1966. Subj: Activities – picnicking. Magic. Weather. Witches.

Dorrie and the witch doctor ill. by author. Lothrop, 1967. Subj: Magic. Witches

Dorrie and the witches' camp ill. by author. Lothrop, 1983. Subj: Problem solving. Witches.

Dorrie and the witch's imp ill. by author. Lothrop, 1975. Subj: Magic. Witches.

Dorrie and the Witchville fair ill. by author. Lothrop, 1980. Subj: Fairs. Magic. Witches.

Dorrie and the wizard's spell ill. by author. Lothrop, 1968. Subj: Magic. Witches. Wizards.

Dorrie's magic ill. by author. Lothrop, 1962. Subj: Magic. Witches.

Dorrie's play ill. by author. Lothrop, 1965. Subj: Behavior – mistakes. Theater. Witches.

Lisa and the grompet ill. by author. Lothrop, 1970. Subj: Behavior – running away. Fairies. Family life.

The lost playground ill. by author. Lothrop, 1963. Subj: Behavior – losing things. Character traits – being different. Toys.

The magic pot ill. by author. Lothrop, 1977. Subj: Devil. Folk and fairy tales. Foreign lands – Denmark. Magic.

The magician and McTree ill. by author. Lothrop, 1984. Subj: Animals – cats. Behavior – secrets. Magic. Middle ages.

Molly Mullett ill. by author. Lothrop, 1975. Subj: Character traits – bravery. Monsters.

Mouse Café ill. by author. Lothrop, 1972. Subj: Animals – mice. Character traits – selfishness. Weddings.

Tilabel ill. by author. Lothrop, 1978. Subj: Activities – weaving. Animals – groundhogs. Folk and fairy tales. Foreign lands – Germany. Royalty.

Cooney, Barbara. *Chanticleer and the fox* (Chaucer, Geoffrey)

A garland of games and other diversions: an alphabet book initial letters by Suzanne R. Morse; ill. by author. Holt, 1969. Subj: ABC books. Poetry, rhyme.

Island boy ill. by author. Viking, 1988. ISBN 0-670-81749-X Subj: Death. Family life. Islands.

Little brother and little sister ill. by author. Doubleday, 1982. Subj: Character traits – loyalty. Folk and fairy tales. Foreign lands – Germany. Royalty. Witches.

The little juggler ill. by author. Hastings, 1982. Reprint of 1961 ed. Subj: Holidays – Christmas.

A little prayer ill. by author. Hastings, 1967. Subj: Religion.

Miss Rumphius ill. by author. Viking, 1982. Subj: Activities – traveling. Flowers.

Snow-White and Rose-Red (Grimm, Jacob)

Cooney, Nancy Evans. *The blanket that had to go* ill. by Diane Dawson. Putnam's, 1981. Subj: Behavior – growing up. Problem solving. School.

Donald says thumbs down ill. by Maxie Chambliss. Putnam's, 1987. ISBN 0-399-21373-2 Subj: Behavior – growing up. Emotions – embarrassment. Problem solving. Thumbsucking.

The wobbly tooth ill. by Marylin Hafner. Putnam's, 1978. Subj: Teeth.

Coontz, Otto. *The quiet house* ill. by author. Little, 1978. Subj: Animals – dogs. Eggs. Emotions – loneliness. Friendship.

A real class clown ill. by author. Little, 1979. Subj: Circus. Clowns, jesters. School.

Starring Rosa ill. by author. Little, 1980. Subj: Animals – pigs. Food. Humor.

Cooper, Elizabeth K. *The fish from Japan* ill. by Beth and Joe Krush. Harcourt, 1969. Subj: Fish. Imagination. Kites. Pets.

Cooper, Gale. *Unicorn moon* ill. by author. Dutton, 1984. Subj: Animals. Magic. Mythical creatures. Royalty.

Cooper, Jacqueline. *Angus and the Mona Lisa* ill. by author. Lothrop, 1981. Subj: Animals – cats. Behavior – stealing. Problem solving.

Cooper, Letice Ulpha. *The bear who was too big* ill. by Ruth Ives. Follett, 1963. Subj: Stores. Toys – teddy bears.

Cooper, Paulette. *Let's find out about Halloween* ill. by Errol Le Cain. Watts, 1972. Subj: Holidays – Halloween.

Cooper, Susan. *The Selkie girl* ill. by Warwick Hutton. McElderry Books, 1986. ISBN 0-689-50390-3 Subj: Animals – seals. Folk and fairy tales. Foreign lands – Ireland. Foreign lands – Scotland. Mythical creatures.

The silver cow: a Welsh tale ill. by Warwick Hutton. Atheneum, 1983. Subj: Behavior – greed. Character traits – smallness. Folk and fairy tales. Foreign lands – England.

Coopersmith, Jerome. *A Chanukah fable for Christmas* ill. by Syd Hoff. Putnam's, 1969. Subj: Behavior – wishing. Holidays – Hanukkah. Jewish culture.

Cope, Dawn. *Humpty Dumpty's favorite nursery rhymes* comp. by Dawn and Peter Cope; ill. by Jessie M. King, Randolph Caldecott and others. Holt, 1981. Subj: Nursery rhymes.

Cope, Peter. *Humpty Dumpty's favorite nursery rhymes* (Cope, Dawn)

Copeland, Helen. *Meet Miki Takino* ill. by Kurt Werth. Lothrop, 1963. Subj: Ethnic groups in the U.S. – Japanese-Americans. Family life – grandparents.

Copp, Andrew James *see* Copp, James

Copp, James. *Martha Matilda O'Toole* ill. by Steven Kellogg. Bradbury Pr., 1969. Originally appeared as a song in the author's phonorecord: Jim Copp tales. Subj: Behavior – forgetfulness. Humor. Poetry, rhyme. School.

Copp, Jim *see* Copp, James

Corbalis, Judy. *Porcellus, the flying pig* ill. by Helen Craig. Dial Pr., 1988. ISBN 0-8037-0486-0 Subj: Activities – flying. Animals – pigs. Character traits – being different.

Corbett, Grahame. *Guess who?* ill. by author. Dial Pr., 1982. Subj: Format, unusual – board books. Participation. Toys.

What number now? ill. by author. Dial Pr., 1982. Subj: Counting. Format, unusual – board books. Participation.

Who is hiding? ill. by author. Dial Pr., 1982. Subj: Format, unusual – board books. Participation. Toys.

Who is inside? ill. by author. Dial Pr., 1982. Subj: Format, unusual – board books. Participation. Toys.

Who is next? ill. by author. Dial Pr., 1982. Subj: Format, unusual – board books. Participation. Toys.

Corbett, Scott. *Dr. Merlin's magic shop* ill. by Joseph Mathieu. Little, 1973. Subj: Magic.

The foolish dinosaur fiasco ill. by Jon McIntosh. Little, 1978. Subj: Dinosaurs. Magic.

The great custard pie panic ill. by Joseph Mathieu. Little, 1974. Subj: Magic.

The mysterious Zetabet ill. by Jon McIntosh. Little, 1979. Subj: ABC books.

Corcos, Lucille. *The city book* ill. by author. Golden Pr., 1972. Subj: City.

Corddry, Thomas I. *Kibby's big feat* ill. by Quentin Blake. Follett, 1971. Subj: Bedtime. Behavior – lost. Jungle.

Corey, Dorothy. *Everybody takes turns* ill. by Lois Axeman. Albert Whitman, 1979. Subj: Behavior – sharing.

A shot for baby bear ill. by Doug Cushman. Albert Whitman, 1988. ISBN 0-8075-7348-5 Subj: Animals. Careers – doctors.

Tomorrow you can ill. by Lois Axeman. Albert Whitman, 1977. Subj: Behavior – growing up.

We all share ill. by Rondi Colette. Albert Whitman, 1980. Subj: Behavior – sharing.

Will it ever be my birthday? ill. by Eileen Christelow. Albert Whitman, 1986. ISBN 0-8075-9106-8 Subj: Animals. Birthdays. Emotions – envy, jealousy. Holidays – Halloween. Parties.

Cormack, M. Grant. *Animal tales from Ireland* ill. by Vana Earle. John Day, 1955. First published in England, 1954. Subj: Animals. Folk and fairy tales. Foreign lands – Ireland.

Corney, Estelle. *Pa's top hat* ill. by Hilary Abrahams. Elsevier-Dutton, 1981. Subj: Sea and seashore. Trains.

Cornish, Sam. *Grandmother's pictures* ill. by Jeanne Johns. Bradbury Pr., 1974. Subj: Family life. Family life – grandmothers.

Corrigan, Kathy. *Emily Umily* ill. by Vlasta van Kampen. Firefly Pr., 1984. ISBN 0-920236-99-5 Subj: Emotions – happiness. School.

Corrin, Sara. *Mrs. Fox's wedding* (Grimm, Jacob)

The pied piper of Hamelin (Browning, Robert)

Corrin, Stephen. *Mrs. Fox's wedding* (Grimm, Jacob)

The pied piper of Hamelin (Browning, Robert)

Cortesi, Wendy W. *Explore a spooky swamp* ill. by Joseph H. Bailey. National Geographic Soc., 1979. Subj: Animals. Birds. Frogs and toads. Reptiles.

Corwin, Judith Hoffman. *Birthday fun* ill. by author. Messner, 1986. ISBN 0-671-55519-7 Subj: Birthdays. Parties.

Halloween fun ill. by author. Messner, 1983. Subj: Holidays – Halloween.

Jewish holiday fun ill. by author. Messner, 1987. ISBN 0-671-60230-6 Subj: Holidays. Jewish culture.

Cosgrove, Margaret. *Wintertime for animals* ill. by author. Dodd, 1975. Subj: Animals. Science. Seasons – winter.

Cosgrove, Stephen. *Sleepy time bunny* by Stephen Cosgrove and Charles Reasoner. Price, Stern, Sloan, 1984. Subj: Animals – rabbits. Bedtime. Format, unusual – board books. Night.

Cosgrove, Stephen Edward *see* Cosgrove, Stephen

Cossi, Olga. *Gus the bus* ill. by Howie Schneider. Scholastic, 1989. ISBN 0-590-41616-2 Subj: Buses.

Costa, Nicoletta. *The birthday party* ill. by author. Grosset, 1984. Subj: Animals – cats. Birthdays. Format, unusual – board books.

Dressing up ill. by author. Grosset, 1984. Subj: Animals – cats. Format, unusual – board books.

A friend comes to play ill. by author. Grosset, 1984. Subj: Animals – cats. Format, unusual – board books. Friendship.

The mischievous princess ill. by author. Silver Burdett, 1986. ISBN 0-382-09179-5 Subj: Folk and fairy tales. Royalty.

The missing cat ill. by author. Grosset, 1984. Subj: Animals – cats. Format, unusual – board books.

The naughty puppy ill. by author. Macmillan, 1985. ISBN 0-02-724660-4 Subj: Animals – dogs. Behavior – misbehavior.

The new puppy ill. by author. Macmillan, 1985. ISBN 0-02-724650-7 Subj: Animals – dogs. Behavior – misbehavior.

Counsel, June. *But Martin!* ill. by Carolyn Dinan. Faber, 1984. ISBN 0-571-13349-5 Subj: Character traits – being different. Space and space ships.

Count me in: *44 songs and rhymes about numbers.* Sterling, 1985. ISBN 0-7136-2622-4 Subj: Counting. Music. Poetry, rhyme. Songs.

Counting rhymes ill. by Corinne Malvern. Simon and Schuster, 1946. Subj: Counting. Poetry, rhyme.

Cousins, Lucy. *Portly's hat* ill. by author. Dutton, 1989. ISBN 0-525-44457-2 Subj: Birds. Birds – penguins. Clothing.

Coutant, Helen. *First snow* ill. by Vo-Dinh Mai. Knopf, 1974. Subj: Death. Family life – grandmothers. Seasons – winter.

Coville, Bruce. *The foolish giant* by Bruce and Katherine Coville; ill. by Katherine Coville. Lippincott, 1978. Subj: Character traits – bravery. Character traits – kindness. Friendship. Giants. Magic.

Sarah and the dragon ill. by Beth Peck. Lippincott, 1984. Subj: Character traits – kindness. Dragons. Folk and fairy tales. Magic. Mythical creatures. Witches.

Sarah's unicorn by Bruce and Katherine Coville; ill. by authors. Lippincott, 1979. Subj: Animals. Character traits – meanness. Mythical creatures. Witches.

Coville, Katherine. *The foolish giant* (Coville, Bruce)

Sarah's unicorn (Coville, Bruce)

Cowcher, Helen. *Rain forest* ill. by author. Farrar, 1988. ISBN 0-374-36167-3 Subj: Animals. Foreign lands – South America. Forest, woods. Machines.

Cowles, Kathleen. *Feelings* (Allington, Richard L.)

Hearing (Allington, Richard L.)

Looking (Allington, Richard L.)

Smelling (Allington, Richard L.)

Tasting (Allington, Richard L.)

Touching (Allington, Richard L.)

Cowper, Francis Henry *see* Roe, Richard

Cox, David. *Ayu and the perfect moon* ill. by author. Subj: Activities – dancing. Foreign lands – Bali.

Bossyboots ill. by author. Crown, 1987. ISBN 0-517-56491-2 Subj: Character traits – willfulness. Crime. Foreign lands – Australia.

Tin Lizzie and Little Nell ill. by author. Merrimack, 1984. ISBN 0-370-30922-7 Subj: Animals – horses. Foreign lands – Australia. Machines.

Cox, Palmer. *Another Brownie book* ill. by author. McGraw-Hill, 1967. Re-publication of the orig. 1890 ed. Subj: Elves and little people.

The Brownies: their book ill. by author. McGraw-Hill, 1967. Re-publication of the orig. 1887 ed. Subj: Elves and little people.

Cox, Victoria. *Going my way?* (Applebaum, Stan)

Coxe, Molly. *Louella and the yellow balloon* ill. by author. Crowell, 1988. ISBN 0-690-04748-7 Subj: Circus. Toys – balloons.

Crabtree, Judith. *The sparrow's story at the king's command* ill. by author. Oxford Univ. Pr., 1983. Subj: Birds – sparrows. Royalty.

Craft, Ruth. *Carrie Hepple's garden* ill. by Irene Haas. Atheneum, 1979. Subj: Activities – gardening. Animals – cats. Character traits – bravery.

The day of the rainbow ill. by Niki Daly. Viking, 1989. ISBN 0-670-82456-9 Subj: City. Behavior – losing things. Emotions – anger. Poetry, rhyme. Seasons – summer. Weather – rainbows.

The winter bear ill. by Erik Blegvad. Atheneum, 1974. Subj: Poetry, rhyme. Seasons – winter. Toys – teddy bears.

Craig, Helen. *The night of the paper bag monsters* ill. by author. Knopf, 1985. ISBN 0-394-97307-0 Subj: Animals – pigs. Friendship. Monsters.

Susie and Alfred in the knight, the princess and the dragon ill. by author. Knopf, 1985. Subj: Animals – pigs. Art. Imagination.

A welcome for Annie ill. by author. Knopf, 1986. ISBN 0-394-97954-0 Subj: Animals – pigs. Behavior – misbehavior. Behavior – trickery. Friendship.

Craig, Janet. *Ballet dancer* ill. by Barbara Todd. Troll Assoc., 1988. ISBN 0-8167-1434-7 Subj: Activities – dancing.

Turtles ill. by Kathie Kelleher. Troll Assoc., 1982. Subj: Reptiles – turtles, tortoises. Science.

What's under the ocean? ill. by Paul Harvey. Troll Assoc., 1982. Subj: Sea and seashore.

Craig, M. Jean. *Babar comes to America* (Brunhoff, Laurent de)

Boxes ill. by Joe Lasker. Norton, 1964. Subj: Concepts – shape. Concepts – size. Games. Participation. Toys.

Dinosaurs and more dinosaurs ill. by George Solonevich. Four Winds Pr., 1968. Subj: Dinosaurs. Science.

The donkey prince (Grimm, Jacob)

The dragon in the clock box ill. by Kelly Oechsli. Norton, 1962. Subj: Dragons. Family life. Imagination.

The man whose name was not Thomas ill. by Diane Stanley. Doubleday, 1981. Subj: Careers – bakers. Humor.

Spring is like the morning ill. by Don Almquist. Putnam's, 1965. Subj: Animals. Morning. Plants. Seasons – spring.

What did you dream? ill. by Margery Gill. Abelard-Schuman, 1964. Subj: Dreams. Morning.

Crampton, Patricia. *The beaver family book* (Kalas, Sybille)

The dragon with red eyes (Lindgren, Astrid)

The goose family book (Kalas, Sybille)

The lion family book (Hofer, Angelika)

My nightingale is singing (Lindgren, Astrid)

The penguin family book (Somme, Lauritz)

Peter and the wolf (Prokofiev, Sergei Sergeievitch)

Crane, Alan. *Pepita bonita* ill. by author. Nelson, 1942. Subj: Birds – pelicans. Foreign lands – Mexico. Sea and seashore.

Crane, Donn. *Flippy and Skippy* ill. by author. Winston, 1940. Subj: Animals – squirrels. Pets.

Craven, Carolyn. *What the mailman brought* ill. by Tomie de Paola. Putnam's, 1987. ISBN 0-399-21290-6 Subj: Activities – painting. Emotions – loneliness. Illness. Imagination.

Crawford, Elizabeth D. *Baby animals on the farm* (Isenbart, Hans-Heinrich)

Blackie and Marie (Koči, Marta)

Hansel and Gretel (Grimm, Jacob)

The hare's race (Baumann, Hans)

Little Harry (Bröger, Achim)

Little red cap (Grimm, Jacob)

The seven ravens (Grimm, Jacob)

Tiger cat (Wolski, Slawomir)

Crawford, Phyllis. *The blot: little city cat* ill. by Holling C. Holling. Cape, 1930. Subj: Animals – cats.

Crayder, Teresa *see* Colman, Hila

Credle, Ellis. *Big fraid, little fraid: a folktale* ill. by author. Macmillan, 1964. Subj: Emotions – fear. Folk and fairy tales. Night.

Down, down the mountain ill. by author. Nelson, 1934, 1961. Subj: Clothing. Family life. Plants.

Creekmore, Raymond. *Fujio* ill. by author. Macmillan, 1951. Subj: Foreign lands – Japan. Sports.

Cremins, Robert. *My animal ABC* ill. by author. Crown, 1983. Subj: ABC books. Animals. Format, unusual – toy and movable books.

My animal Mother Goose ill. by author. Crown, 1983. Subj: Animals. Format, unusual – toy and movable books. Nursery rhymes.

Crespi, Francesca. *Little Bear and the oompah-pah* ill. by author. Dial Pr., 1987. ISBN 0-8037-0394-5 Subj: Animals – bears. Holidays. Music.

Cressey, James. *The dragon and George* ill. by Tamasin Cole. Prentice-Hall, 1979. Subj: Dragons. Foreign lands – England. Knights. Middle ages.

Fourteen rats and a rat-catcher ill. by Tamasin Cole. Prentice-Hall, 1978. Subj: Animals – rats. Family life. Problem solving.

Max the mouse ill. by Tamasin Cole. Prentice-Hall, 1979. Subj: Animals – mice. Crime.

Pet parrot ill. by Tamasin Cole. Prentice-Hall, 1979. Subj: Birds – parakeets, parrots. Crime.

Cresswell, Helen. *Two hoots and the king* ill. by Martine Blanc. Crown, 1978. Subj: Birds – owls. Behavior – mistakes.

Two hoots in the snow ill. by Martine Blanc. Crown, 1978. Subj: Birds – owls. Behavior – mistakes.

Cretan, Gladys Yessayan. *Lobo and Brewster* ill. by Patricia Coombs. Lothrop, 1971. Subj: Animals – cats. Animals – dogs. Emotions – envy, jealousy.

Ten brothers with camels ill. by Piero Ventura. Golden Pr., 1975. Subj: Counting. Desert.

Cretien, Paul D. *Sir Henry and the dragon* ill. by author. Follett, 1958. Subj: Animals – horses. Dragons. Knights. Royalty. Witches.

Crews, Donald. *Carousel* ill. by author. Greenwillow, 1982. Subj: Merry-go-rounds.

Flying ill. by author. Greenwillow, 1986. ISBN 0-688-04319-4 Subj: Activities – flying. Airplanes, airports.

Freight train ill. by author. Greenwillow, 1978. Subj: Caldecott award honor book. Trains.

Harbor ill. by author. Greenwillow, 1982. Subj: Boats, ships.

Light ill. by author. Greenwillow, 1981. Subj: Concepts. Lights.

Parade ill. by author. Greenwillow, 1983. Subj: City. Parades.

School bus ill. by author. Greenwillow, 1984. ISBN 0-688-02808-X Subj: Buses. School. Transportation.

Ten black dots ill. by author. Rev. ed. Greenwillow, 1986. ISBN 0-688-06068-4 Subj: Concepts — shape. Counting.

Truck ill. by author. Greenwillow, 1980. Subj: Caldecott award honor book. Transportation. Trucks. Wordless.

We read: A to Z ill. by author. Harper, 1967. Subj: ABC books. Concepts.

Crichton, Douglas *see* Douglas, Michael

Crichton, Michael *see* Douglas, Michael

Crile, Helga Sandburg *see* Sandburg, Helga

Cristini, Ermanno. *In my garden* by Ermanno Cristini and Luigi Puricelli; ill. by authors. Alphabet Pr., 1981. Orig title: Falter, Blumen, Tierre und Ich. Subj: Wordless.

In the pond by Ermanno Cristini and Luigi Puricelli; ill. by authors. Alphabet Pr., 1984. Subj: Animals. Insects. Plants. Reptiles.

In the woods by Ermanno Cristini and Luigi Puricelli; ill. by authors. Alphabet Pr., 1983. Subj: Animals. Birds. Forest, woods. Wordless.

Croll, Carolyn. *Too many babas* ill. by author. Harper, 1979. Subj: Behavior — sharing. Food.

Cromie, William J. *Steven and the green turtle* ill. by Tom Eaton. Harper, 1970. Subj: Animals — endangered animals. Reptiles — turtles, tortoises. Science.

Crompton, Anne Eliot. *The lifting stone* ill. by Marcia Sewall. Holiday, 1978. Subj: Folk and fairy tales. Character traits — cleverness.

The winter wife: an Abenaki folktale ill. by Robert Andrew Parker. Little, 1975. Subj: Character traits — loyalty. Folk and fairy tales. Indians of North America.

Crompton, Margaret. *The house where Jack lives* ill. by Margery Gill. Merrimack, 1980. Subj: Family life. Foreign lands — England. Houses.

Crosby-Jones, Michael. *Goodbye Rune* (Kaldhol, Marit)

Cross, Diana Harding. *Some birds have funny names* ill. by Jan Brett. Crown, 1981. Subj: Birds. Names.

Some plants have funny names ill. by Jan Brett. Crown, 1983. Subj: Names. Plants.

Cross, Genevieve. *My bunny book* ill. by Charles Clement. Doubleday, 1952. Subj: Animals — rabbits. Holidays — Easter.

A trip to the yard ill. by Marjorie Hartwell and Rachel Dixon. Doubleday, 1952. Subj: Animals. Birds. Plants.

Crossley-Holland, Kevin. *The green children* ill. by Margaret Gordon. Seabury Pr., 1968. Subj: Character traits — being different. Folk and fairy tales. Foreign lands — England.

The pedlar of Swaffham ill. by Margaret Gordon. Seabury Pr., 1971. Subj: Careers — peddlers. Folk and fairy tales.

Croswell, Volney. *How to hide a hippopotamus* ill. by author. Dodd, 1958. Subj: Animals — hippopotami. Behavior — hiding things. Concepts — size.

Crothers, Samuel McChord. *Miss Muffet's Christmas party* ill. by Olive M. Long. Houghton, 1929. Subj: Parties. Spiders.

Crowe, Robert L. *Clyde monster* ill. by Kay Chorao. Dutton, 1976. Subj: Emotions — fear. Monsters. Night.

Tyler Toad and the thunder ill. by Kay Chorao. Dutton, 1980. Subj: Animals. Noise, sounds. Weather — thunder.

Crowell, Maryalicia. *A horse in the house* ill. by Leonard P. Kessler. Addison-Wesley, 1957. Subj: City. Pets.

Crowley, Arthur. *Bonzo Beaver* ill. by Annie Gusman. Houghton, 1980. Subj: Activities — babysitting. Animals — beavers. Poetry, rhyme. Sibling rivalry.

The boogey man ill. by Annie Gusman. Houghton, 1978. Subj: Behavior — dissatisfaction. Behavior — misbehavior. Family life. Monsters.

The ugly book ill. by Annie Gusman. Houghton, 1982. Subj: Character traits — appearance.

The wagon man ill. by Annie Gusman. Houghton, 1981. Subj: Dreams. Poetry, rhyme. Riddles.

Crowther, Robert. *Hide and seek counting book* ill. by author. Viking, 1981. Subj: Counting. Format, unusual — toy and movable books.

The most amazing hide-and-seek alphabet book ill. by author. Viking, 1978. Subj: ABC books. Format, unusual — toy and movable books.

The most amazing hide-and-seek opposites book ill. by author. Viking, 1985. ISBN 0-670-80121-6 Subj: Concepts — opposites. Format, unusual — toy and movable books.

Pop goes the weasel! 25 pop-up nursery rhymes ill. by comp. Viking, 1987. ISBN 0-670-81815-1 Subj: Format, unusual — toy and movable books. Nursery rhymes.

Croxford, Vera. *All kinds of animals* ill. by author. Grosset, 1972. Orig. title: All sorts of animals (Hamlyn Pub. Group, 1968). Subj: Animals.

Crume, Marion W. *Let me see you try* ill. by Jacques Rupp. Bowmar, 1968. Subj: Activities. Participation.

Listen! ill. by Cliff Rowe and Judy Houston. Bowmar, 1968. Subj: Activities. Ethnic groups in the U.S. Participation.

What do you say? ill. by Harvey Mandlin. Bowmar, 1967. Subj: Activities. Participation.

Crump, Donald J. *Creatures small and furry* ill. with photos. National Geographic Soc., 1983. Subj: Animals.

Cummings, Betty Sue. *Turtle* ill. by Susan Dodge. Atheneum, 1981. Subj: Behavior – lost. Pets. Reptiles – turtles, tortoises.

Cummings, E. E. *Fairy tales* ill. by John Eaton. Harcourt, 1965. Subj: Folk and fairy tales. Imagination.

In just-spring ill. by Heidi Goennel. Little, 1988. ISBN 0-316-16390-2 Subj: Poetry, rhyme. Seasons – spring.

Little tree ill. by Deborah Kogan Ray. Crown, 1987. ISBN 0-517-56598-6 Subj: Holidays – Christmas. Poetry, rhyme. Trees.

Cummings, Edward Estlin *see* Cummings, E. E.

Cummings, Pat. *C.L.O.U.D.S.* ill. by author. Lothrop, 1986. ISBN 0-688-04683-5 Subj: Weather – clouds.

Jimmy Lee did it ill. by author. Lothrop, 1985. ISBN 0-688-04633-9 Subj: Ethnic groups in the U.S. – Afro-Americans. Family life – brothers. Imagination – imaginary friends. Poetry, rhyme. Problem solving.

Cummings, W. T. (Walter Thies). *The kid* ill. by author. McGraw-Hill, 1960. Subj: Animals – horses. Behavior – seeking better things. Emotions – loneliness. Music.

Miss Esta Maude's secret ill. by author. McGraw-Hill, 1961. Subj: Automobiles. Behavior – secrets. Careers – teachers.

Wickford of Beacon Hill ill. by author. Subj: Birds – cockatoos.

Cuneo, Mary Louise. *Inside a sandcastle and other secrets* ill. by Jan Brett. Houghton, 1979. Subj: Character traits – smallness.

Cunliffe, John. *The king's birthday cake* ill. by Faith Jaques. Elsevier-Dutton, 1979. Subj: Activities – cooking. Birthdays. Cumulative tales. Royalty.

Sara's giant and the upside down house ill. by Hilary Abrahams. Elsevier-Dutton, 1980. Subj: Giants.

Cunningham, Julia. *A mouse called Junction* ill. by Michael Hague. Pantheon, 1980. Subj: Animals – mice. Animals – rats. Emotions. Emotions – fear. Friendship.

The vision of Francois the fox ill. by Nicholas Angelo. Pantheon, 1969. Subj: Animals – foxes.

Curious George and the dump truck. Houghton, 1984. ISBN 0-395-36635-6 Subj: Animals – monkeys. Character traits – curiosity. Trucks.

Curious George and the pizza. Houghton, 1985. ISBN 0-395-39039-7 Subj: Animals – monkeys. Character traits – curiosity. Food.

Curious George at the fire station. Houghton, 1985. ISBN 0-395-39037-0 Subj: Animals – monkeys. Careers – firefighters. Character traits – curiosity.

Curious George goes hiking. Houghton, 1985. ISBN 0-395-39038-9 Subj: Animals – monkeys. Character traits – curiosity. Sports – hiking.

Curious George goes sledding. Houghton, 1984. ISBN 0-395-36637-2 Subj: Animals – monkeys. Character traits – curiosity. Sports – sledding.

Curious George goes to the aquarium. Houghton, 1984. ISBN 0-395-36634-8 Subj: Animals – monkeys. Aquariums. Character traits – curiosity. Fish.

Curious George goes to the circus. Houghton, 1984. ISBN 0-395-36636-4 Subj: Animals – monkeys. Character traits – curiosity. Circus.

Curious George visits the zoo. Houghton, 1985. ISBN 0-395-39036-2 Subj: Animals – monkeys. Character traits – curiosity. Zoos.

Curle, J. J. *The sleepy owl* (Pfister, Marcus)

Curle, Jock. *The four good friends* ill. by Bernadette Watts. Holt, 1987. ISBN 0-8050-0231-6 Subj: Animals. Character traits – helpfulness. Character traits – kindness to animals.

Lucky Hans (Grimm, Jacob)

The story of Jonah (Baumann, Kurt)

Curry, Nancy. *The littlest house* ill. by Jacques Rupp. Bowmar, 1968. Subj: Family life. Houses.

Curry, Peter. *Animals* ill. by author. Price, Stern, Sloan, 1984. Subj: Animals.

Curtis Brown, Beatrice *see* Brown, Beatrice Curtis

Curtis, Dal *see* Nichols, Paul

Cushman, Doug. *Giants* ill. by comp. Platt, 1980. Subj: Giants. Poetry, rhyme.

Nasty Kyle the crocodile ill. by author. Grosset, 1983. Subj: Behavior – dissatisfaction. Concepts. Reptiles – alligators, crocodiles.

Once upon a pig ill. by comp. Grosset, 1982. Subj: Animals – pigs. Poetry, rhyme.

Cushman, Jerome. *Marvella's hobby* ill. by Prue Theobalds. Abelard-Schuman, 1962. Subj: Animals – bulls, cows. Trains.

Cutler, Ebbitt. *Paulino* (Simons, Traute)

Cutler, Ivor. *The animal house* ill. by Helen Oxenbury. Morrow, 1977, 1976. Subj: Animals. Houses. Zoos.

Herbert: five stories ill. by Patrick Benson. Lothrop, 1988. ISBN 0-688-08148-7 Subj: Animals. Imagination.

Cutts, David. *The gingerbread boy*

Look...a butterfly ill. by Eulala Conner. Troll Assoc., 1982. Subj: Insects – butterflies, caterpillars. Science.

More about dinosaurs ill. by Gregory C. Wenzel. Troll Assoc., 1982. Subj: Dinosaurs.

Cuyler, Margery. *Fat Santa* ill. by Marsha Winborn. Holt, 1987. ISBN 0-8050-0423-8 Subj: Character traits – helpfulness. Dreams. Holidays – Christmas.

Freckles and Willie ill. by Marsha Winborn. Holt, 1986. ISBN 0-03-003772-7 Subj: Animals – dogs. Friendship.

Sir William and the pumpkin monster ill. by Marsha Winborn. Holt, 1984. Subj: Ghosts. Holidays – Halloween.

D'Andrea, Annette Cole *see* Steiner, Barbara

D'Aulaire, Edgar Parin *see* Aulaire, Edgar d'

D'Aulaire, Ingri Mortenson *see* Aulaire, Ingri Mortenson d'

Dabcovich, Lydia. *Busy beavers* ill. by author. Dutton, 1988. ISBN 0-525-44384-3 Subj: Animals – beavers. Science.

Follow the river ill. by author. Dutton, 1980. Subj: Rivers.

Mrs. Huggins and her hen Hannah ill. by author. Dutton, 1985. ISBN 0-525-44203-0 Subj: Birds – chickens. Death. Emotions. Friendship.

Sleepy bear ill. by author. Dutton, 1982. Subj: Animals – bears. Seasons – spring. Seasons – winter.

Dahl, Roald. *Dirty beasts* ill. by Rosemary Fawcett. Farrar, 1983. Subj: Bedtime. Dreams. Monsters. Poetry, rhyme.

The enormous crocodile ill. by Quentin Blake. Knopf, 1978. Subj: Animals. Reptiles – alligators, crocodiles.

The giraffe and the pelly and me ill. by Quentin Blake. Farrar, 1985. ISBN 0-374-32602-9 Subj: Activities – working. Animals. Careers – window cleaners. Crime.

Dale, Margaret Jessy Miller *see* Miller, Margaret

Dale, Penny. *You can't* ill. by author. Harper, 1988. ISBN 0-397-32256-9 Subj: Ethnic groups in the U.S. – Afro-Americans. Games. Toys.

Dale, Ruth Bluestone. *Benjamin — and Sylvester also* ill. by J. B. Handelsman. McGraw-Hill, 1960. Subj: Animals – dogs. Behavior – dissatisfaction. Country.

Dalgliesh, Alice. *The little wooden farmer* ill. by Anita Lobel. Macmillan, 1988, 1930. ISBN 0-02-725590-5 Subj: Farms.

The Thanksgiving story ill. by Helen Moore Sewell. Scribner's, 1954. Subj: Caldecott award honor book. Holidays – Thanksgiving. U.S. history.

Dallas-Smith, Peter. *Trumpets in Grumpetland* ill. by Peter Cross. Random House, 1985. ISBN 0-394-97028-4 Subj: Music. Mythical creatures.

Dallinger, Jane. *Spiders* photos. by Satoshi Kuribayashi. Lerner, 1981. Subj: Science. Spiders.

Dallis, Nicholas Peter *see* Nichols, Paul

Dalmais, Anne-Marie. *The butterfly book of birds* ill. by Guy Michel. Two Continents, 1977. Subj: Birds.

In my garden: learning to count ill. by Genji. Two Continents, 1977. Subj: Counting. Poetry, rhyme.

Dalton, Alene. *My new picture book of songs* scores by Reah Allen; ill. by Gini Bunnell. Osmond Pub., 1979. Subj: Music. Songs.

Daly, Kathleen N. *A child's book of snakes, lizards and other reptiles* ill. by Lilian Obligado. Doubleday, 1980. Subj: Reptiles. Science.

Dinosaurs ill. by Tim and Greg Hildebrandt. Golden Pr., 1977. Subj: Dinosaurs.

The Giant little Golden Book of dogs ill. by Tibor Gergely. Simon and Schuster, 1957. Subj: Animals – dogs.

The Macmillan picture wordbook ill. by John Wallner. Macmillan, 1982. Subj: Dictionaries.

The three bears

Today's biggest animals ill. by Tim and Greg Hildebrandt. Golden Pr., 1977. Subj: Animals. Science.

Unusual animals ill. by Tim and Greg Hildebrandt. Golden Pr., 1977. Subj: Animals. Science.

Daly, Maureen. *Patrick visits the library* ill. by Paul Lantz. Dodd, 1961. Subj: Animals – dogs. Birthdays. Libraries.

Daly, Niki. *Joseph's other red sock* ill. by author. Atheneum, 1982. Subj: Clothing.

Just like Archie ill. by author. Viking, 1986. ISBN 0-670-81253-6 Subj: Pets.

Look at me! ill. by author. Viking, 1986. ISBN 0-670-81252-8 Subj: Sibling rivalry.

Not so fast Songololo ill. by author. Atheneum, 1986. ISBN 0-689-50367-9 Subj: City. Family life – grandmothers. Foreign lands – Africa. Foreign lands – South Africa. Shopping.

Thank you Henrietta ill. by author. Viking, 1986. ISBN 0-670-81254-4 Subj: Character traits – helpfulness.

Vim, the rag mouse ill. by author. Atheneum, 1979. Subj: Crime. Toys.

Dame Wiggins of Lee and her seven wonderful cats ed. by John Ruskin; ill. by Robert Broomfield. McGraw-Hill, 1963. Ascribed to Richard Scrafton Sharpe and Mrs. Pearson. Endpapers: reproduction of Kate Greenaway drawings. Subj: Nursery rhymes.

Damjan, Mischa. *Atuk* ill. by Gian Casty. Pantheon, 1966. Subj: Animals – dogs. Animals – wolves. Eskimos.

Goodbye little bird tr. from German by Anthea Bell; ill. by Dorothée Duntze. Faber, 1983. Subj: Birds. Friendship.

The little prince and the tiger cat ill. by Ralph Steadman. McGraw-Hill, 1967. Subj: Animals – cats. Foreign lands – Japan. Royalty.

The little sea horse ill. by Riccardo Bellettati. Faber, 1983. Subj: Fish. Sea and seashore.

The wolf and the kid ill. by Max Velthuijs. McGraw-Hill, 1967. Subj: Animals – goats. Animals – wolves. Character traits – cleverness.

Dangerfield, Balfour see McCloskey, Robert

Daniel, Anne see Steiner, Barbara

Daniel, Doris Temple. *Pauline and the peacock* ill. by Barbara Brown Schoenewolf. E. C. Temple, 1980. Subj: Birds – peacocks, peahens. Family life. Farms. Science.

Daniels, Guy. *The peasant's pea patch*

The Tsar's riddles: or, the wise little girl ill. by Paul Galdone. McGraw-Hill, 1967. Subj: Character traits – cleverness. Folk and fairy tales. Foreign lands – Russia. Riddles.

Dantzer-Rosenthal, Marya. *Some things are different, some things are the same* ill. by Miriam Nerlove. Albert Whitman, 1986. ISBN 0-8075-7535-6 Subj: Concepts.

Darby, Gene. *What is a bird?* ill. by Lucy and John Hawkinson. Benefic Pr., 1959. Subj: Birds. Science.

What is a butterfly? ill. by Lucy and John Hawkinson. Benefic Pr., 1958. Subj: Insects – butterflies, caterpillars. Science.

What is a fish? ill. by Lucy and John Hawkinson. Benefic Pr., 1958. Subj: Fish. Science.

What is a plant? ill. by Lucy and John Hawkinson. Benefic Pr., 1959. Subj: Plants. Science.

What is a turtle? ill. by Lucy and John Hawkinson. Benefic Pr., 1959. Subj: Reptiles – turtles, tortoises. Science.

Da Rif, Andrea. *The blueberry cake that little fox baked* ill. by author. Atheneum, 1984. Subj: Activities – cooking. Birthdays.

Darling, Kathy. *The Easter bunny's secret* ill. by Kelly Oechsli. Garrard, 1978. Subj: Animals – rabbits. Holidays – Easter.

The mystery in Santa's toyshop ill. by Lori Pierson. Garrard, 1978. Subj: Holidays – Christmas. Problem solving.

Darling, Mary Kathleen see Darling, Kathy

Dasent, George W. *The cat on the Dovrefell* (De Paola, Tomie)

East o' the sun, west o' the moon tr. by George W. Dasent; ill. by Gillian Barlow. Putnam's, 1988. ISBN 0-399-21570-0 Subj: Animals – polar bears. Folk and fairy tales. Foreign lands – Norway. Royalty. Witches.

Daudet, Alphonse. *The brave little goat of Monsieur Séguin: a picture story from Provence* ill. by Chiyoko Nakatani. Collins-World, 1968. Translation and adaptation of La chèvre de M. Séguin. Subj: Animals – goats. Animals – wolves. Foreign lands – France.

Dauer, Rosamond. *Bullfrog builds a house* ill. by Byron Barton. Greenwillow, 1977. Subj: Friendship. Frogs and toads. Houses.

Bullfrog grows up ill. by Byron Barton. Greenwillow, 1976. Subj: Animals – mice. Behavior – growing up. Frogs and toads.

My friend, Jasper Jones ill. by Jerry Joyner. Parents, 1977. Subj: Behavior – misbehavior. Imagination – imaginary friends.

The 300 pound cat ill. by Skip Morrow. Holt, 1981. Subj: Animals – cats. Behavior – greed.

Daugherty, Charles Michael. *Wisher* ill. by James Henry Daugherty. Viking, 1960. Subj: Animals – cats. Behavior – wishing. Dreams.

Daugherty, James Henry. *Andy and the lion* ill. by author. Viking, 1938. Subj: Animals – lions. Caldecott award honor book. Character traits – kindness to animals. Humor. Libraries.

The picnic: a frolic in two colors and three parts ill. by author. Viking, 1958. Subj: Activities – picnicking. Animals – lions. Animals – mice.

Daugherty, Olive Lydia see Earle, Olive L.

Daugherty, Sonia. *Vanka's donkey* ill. by James Henry Daugherty. Stokes, 1940. Subj: Animals – donkeys. Folk and fairy tales. Foreign lands – Russia.

Daughtry, Duanne. *What's inside?* photos. by author. Knopf, 1984. Subj: Concepts – in and out. Wordless.

Dauphin, Francine Legrand. *A French A. B. C.* ill. by author. Coward, 1947. Subj: ABC books. Foreign lands – France. Foreign languages.

David, Eugene. *Crystal magic* ill. by Abner Graboff. Prentice-Hall, 1965. Subj: Science.

Davidson, Amanda. *Teddy at the seashore* ill. by author. Holt, 1984. Originally published under title: Teddy at the seaside. Subj: Foreign lands – England. Sea and seashore. Toys – teddy bears.

Teddy goes outside ill. by author. Holt, 1985. ISBN 0-03-005004-9 Subj: Format, unusual – board books. Toys – teddy bears. Weather.

Teddy in the garden ill. by author. Holt, 1986. ISBN 0-03-008502-0 Subj: Behavior – losing things. Toys – teddy bears.

Teddy's birthday ill. by author. Holt, 1985. ISBN 0-03-002887-6 Subj: Birthdays. Toys – teddy bears.

Teddy's first Christmas ill. by author. Holt, 1982. Subj: Holidays – Christmas. Toys – teddy bears.

Davies, Sumiko *see* Sumiko

Davis, Alice Vaught. *Timothy turtle* ill. by Guy Brown Wiser. Harcourt, 1940. Subj: Character traits – helpfulness. Reptiles – turtles, tortoises.

Davis, Douglas F. *The lion's tail* ill. by Ronald Himler. Atheneum, 1980. Subj: Animals – lions. Folk and fairy tales. Foreign lands – Africa.

There's an elephant in the garage ill. by Steven Kellogg. Dutton, 1979. Subj: Animals. Animals – cats. Imagination. Toys – teddy bears.

Davis, Gibbs. *Katy's first haircut* ill. by Linda Shute. Houghton, 1985. ISBN 0-395-38942-9 Subj: Emotions – embarrassment. Hair.

The other Emily ill. by Linda Shute. Houghton, 1984. Subj: Behavior – sharing. Names.

Davis, Lavinia. *Roger and the fox* ill. by Hildegard Woodward. Doubleday, 1947. Subj: Animals – foxes. Caldecott award honor book.

The wild birthday cake ill. by Hildegard Woodward. Doubleday, 1949. Subj: Birthdays. Caldecott award honor book.

Davis, Lavinia Riker *see* Davis, Lavinia

Davis, Maggie S. *The best way to Ripton* ill. by Stephen Gammell. Holiday, 1982. Subj: Activities – traveling. Humor.

Grandma's secret letter ill. by John Wallner. Holiday, 1982. Subj: Behavior – secrets. Character traits – kindness. Elves and little people.

Rickety witch ill. by Kay Chorao. Holiday, 1984. Subj: Holidays – Halloween. Witches.

Davis, Reda. *Martin's dinosaur* ill. by Louis Slobodkin. Crowell, 1959. Subj: Dragons. Foreign lands – England.

Dawson, Linda. *Phoebe and the hot water bottles* (Furchgott, Terry)

Day, Alexandra. *Frank and Ernest* ill. by author. Scholastic, 1988. ISBN 0-590-41557-3 Subj: Animals – bears. Animals – elephants. Character traits – helpfulness. Language.

Day, Michael E. *Berry Ripe Moon* ill. by Carol Whitmore. Tide Grass Pr., 1977. Subj: Indians of North America.

Day, Shirley. *Ruthie's big tree* ill. by author. Firefly Pr., 1982. Subj: Character traits – perseverance. Trees.

Waldo's back yard ill. by author. Firefly Pr., 1984. Subj: Behavior – dissatisfaction. Character traits – helpfulness.

Dayrell, Elphinstone. *Why the sun and the moon live in the sky: an African folktale* ill. by Blair Lent. Houghton, 1968. First published in 1914 in the author's Folk stories from southern Nigeria, West Africa. Subj: Caldecott award honor book. Folk and fairy tales. Foreign lands – Africa. Moon. Sky. Sun.

Dayton, Laura. *LeRoy's birthday circus* ill. by Susan Huggins. Nelson, 1981. Subj: Birthdays. Circus. Counting. Poetry, rhyme.

Dayton, Mona. *Earth and sky* ill. by Roger Antoine Duvoisin. Harper, 1969. Subj: Behavior – fighting, arguing. Earth. Sky.

Dean, Leigh. *Two special cards* (Lisker, Sonia O.)

De Angeli, Marguerite. *The book of nursery and Mother Goose rhymes* ill. by compiler. Doubleday, 1954. Subj: Caldecott award honor book. Nursery rhymes.

Yonie Wondernose: for three little Wondernoses, Nina, David and Kiki ill. by author. Doubleday, 1944. Subj: Caldecott award honor book. Family life. Farms.

DeArmond, Dale. *The seal oil lamp* ill. by author. Little, 1988. ISBN 0-316-17786-5 Subj: Character traits – kindness. Death. Eskimos. Folk and fairy tales. Handicaps – blindness. Senses – seeing.

De Beer, Hans. *Ahoy there, little polar bear* ill. by author. Holt, 1988. ISBN 3-85539-006-1 Subj: Animals – polar bears.

Little polar bear ill. by author. Holt, 1987. ISBN 0-8050-0486-6 Subj: Animals – polar bears. Behavior – lost. Friendship.

De Brunhoff, Jean *see* Brunhoff, Jean de

De Brunhoff, Laurent *see* Brunhoff, Laurent de

De Bruyn, Monica. *Lauren's secret ring* ill. by author. Albert Whitman, 1980. Subj: Friendship.

DeCaprio, Annie. *One, two* ill. by Seymour Nydorf. Grosset, 1965. Designed by David Krieger. Subj: Counting.

Decker, Dorothy W. *Stripe and the merbear* ill. by author. Dillon, 1986. ISBN 0-87518-329-8 Subj: Mythical creatures. Sea and seashore. Toys – teddy bears.

Stripe visits New York ill. by author. Dillon, 1986. ISBN 0-87518-267-4 Subj: Activities – painting. Art. City. Toys – teddy bears.

Dee, Ruby. *Two ways to count to ten: a Liberian folktale* ill. by Susan Meddaugh. Holt, 1988. ISBN 0-8050-0407-6 Subj: Character traits – cleverness. Folk and fairy tales. Foreign lands – Africa.

DeForest, Charlotte B. *The prancing pony: nursery rhymes from Japan* adapted into English verse for children, with "Kusa-e"; ill. by Keiko Hida. Walker, 1968. Subj: Foreign lands – Japan. Nursery rhymes.

Degen, Bruce. *Aunt Possum and the pumpkin man* ill. by author. Harper, 1977. Subj: Animals – cats. Animals – possums. Holidays – Halloween. Wordless.

Jamberry ill. by author. Harper, 1983. Subj: Animals – bears. Food. Poetry, rhyme.

The little witch and the riddle ill. by author. Harper, 1980. Subj: Friendship. Magic. Riddles. Witches.

De Gerez, Toni. *Louhi, witch of North Farm* ill. by Barbara Cooney. Viking, 1986. A story from Finlands's epic poem The Kalevala. ISBN 0-670-80556-4 Subj: Behavior – stealing. Folk and fairy tales. Foreign lands – Finland. Moon. Sun. Witches.

My song is a piece of jade: poems of ancient Mexico in English and Spanish ill. by William Stark. Little, 1984. Subj: Foreign lands – Mexico. Foreign languages. Poetry, rhyme.

De Groat, Diane. *Alligator's toothache* ill. by author. Crown, 1977. Subj: Illness. Reptiles – alligators, crocodiles. Teeth. Wordless.

De Hamel, Joan. *Hemi's pet* ill. by Christine Ross. Houghton, 1987. ISBN 0-395-43665-6 Subj: Pets. School. Sibling rivalry.

DeJong, David Cornel. *Looking for Alexander* ill. by Harvey Weiss. Little, 1963. Subj: Animals – cats. Family life – grandmothers.

DeJong, Meindert. *Nobody plays with a cabbage* ill. by Thomas B. Allen. Harper, 1962. Subj: Activities – gardening. Emotions.

De Kay, Ormonde. *Rimes de la Mere Oie* (Mother Goose)

Delacre, Lulu. *Arroz con leche: popular songs and rhymes from Latin America* ill. by author. Scholastic, 1989. ISBN 0-590-42442-4 Subj: Foreign languages. Games. Music. Poetry, rhyme. Songs.

Nathan and Nicholas Alexander ill. by author. Scholastic, 1986. ISBN 0-590-33956-7 Subj: Animals – elephants. Animals – mice. Behavior – sharing.

Nathan's fishing trip ill. by author. Scholastic, 1988. ISBN 0-590-41281-7 Subj: Animals – elephants. Animals – mice. Friendship. Sports – fishing.

De La Fontaine, Jean *see* La Fontaine, Jean de

DeLage, Ida. *ABC Easter bunny* ill. by Ellen Sloan. Garrard, 1979. Subj: ABC books. Animals – rabbits. Holidays – Easter.

ABC triplets at the zoo ill. by Lori Pierson. Garrard, 1980. Subj: ABC books. Animals. Zoos.

Am I a bunny? ill. by Ellen Sloan. Garrard, 1978. Subj: Animals – rabbits. Self-concept.

The old witch and her magic basket ill. by Ellen Sloan. Garrard, 1978. Subj: Holidays – Halloween. Witches.

The old witch and the crows ill. by Marianne Smith. Garrard, 1983. Subj: Birds – crows. Birds – owls. Night. Witches.

The old witch and the dragon ill. by Unada. Garrard, 1979. Subj: Dragons. Witches.

The old witch and the ghost parade ill. by Jody Taylor. Garrard, 1978. Subj: Ghosts. Witches.

The old witch finds a new house ill. by Pat Paris. Garrard, 1979. Subj: Moving. Witches.

Pilgrim children on the Mayflower ill. by Bert Dodson. Garrard, 1980. Subj: Boats, ships. U.S. history.

The squirrel's tree party ill. by Tracy McVay. Garrard, 1978. Subj: Animals – squirrels. Parties. Trees.

De La Mare, Walter. *Molly Whuppie* ill. by Errol Le Cain. Farrar, 1983. Subj: Character traits – bravery. Character traits – cleverness. Giants. Royalty.

De La Mare, Walter John *see* De La Mare, Walter

Delaney, A. *The butterfly* ill. by author. Crown, 1977. Subj: Cumulative tales. Insects – butterflies, caterpillars.

The gunnywolf ill. by author. Harper, 1988. ISBN 0-06-021595-X Subj: Animals – wolves. Behavior – misbehavior. Flowers. Foreign lands – Germany. Songs.

Monster tracks? ill. by author. Harper, 1981. Subj: Imagination. Weather – snow.

Delaney, M. C. *The marigold monster* ill. by Ned Delaney. Dutton, 1983. Subj: Humor. Monsters. Riddles.

Delaney, Ned. *Bad dog!* ill. by author. Morrow, 1987. ISBN 0-688-06596-1 Subj: Animals – dogs. Behavior – lost. Behavior – misbehavior.

Bert and Barney ill. by author. Houghton, 1979. Subj: Friendship.

Cosmic chickens ill. by author. Harper, 1988. ISBN 0-06-021584-4 Subj: Birds – chickens. Farms. Space and space ships.

One dragon to another ill. by author. Houghton, 1976. Subj: Character traits – individuality. Dragons. Games. Insects – butterflies, caterpillars.

Rufus the doofus ill. by author. Houghton, 1978. Subj: Behavior – misbehavior. School.

Terrible things could happen ill. by author. Lothrop, 1983. Subj: Activities – working. Humor.

Delaunay, Sonia. *Sonia Delaunay's alphabet* ill. by author. Crowell, 1972. Subj: ABC books. Poetry, rhyme.

Delessert, Etienne. *The endless party* tr. by Jeffrey Tabberner; ill. by author. Oxford Univ. Pr., 1981. Subj: Religion – Noah.

How the mouse was hit on the head by a stone and so discovered the world text and ill. by Etienne Delessert in collaboration with Odie Mosimann; foreword by Jean Piaget; tr. by C. Ross Smith. Doubleday, 1971. Subj: Animals – mice. World.

A long long song ill. by author. Farrar, 1988. ISBN 0-374-34638-0 Subj: Imagination. Nursery rhymes. Songs.

Dellinger, Annetta. *You are special to Jesus* ill. by Jan Brett. Concordia, 1984. Subj: Character traits – appearance. Character traits – individuality. Religion.

Delmar, Roy *see* Wexler, Jerome

Delton, Judy. *Bear and Duck on the run* ill. by Lynn Munsinger. Albert Whitman, 1984. Subj: Animals – bears. Birds – ducks.

The best mom in the world ill. by John Faulkner. Albert Whitman, 1979. Subj: Behavior – growing up. Family life – mothers.

Brimhall comes to stay ill. by Cyndy Szekeres. Lothrop, 1978. Subj: Animals – bears. Family life.

Brimhall turns detective ill. by Cherie R. Wyman. Carolrhoda, 1983. Subj: Animals – bears. Animals – rabbits. Weather – snow.

Brimhall turns to magic ill. by Bruce Degen. Lothrop, 1979. Subj: Animals – bears. Animals – rabbits. Magic.

Duck goes fishing ill. by Lynn Munsinger. Albert Whitman, 1983. Subj: Animals – foxes. Birds – ducks. Birds – owls. Friendship. Sports – fishing.

The elephant in Duck's garden ill. by Lynn Munsinger. Albert Whitman, 1985. ISBN 0-8075-1959-6 Subj: Animals – bears. Animals – elephants. Behavior – worrying. Birds – ducks.

Groundhog's Day at the doctor ill. by Giulio Maestro. Parents, 1981. Subj: Animals – groundhogs. Holidays – Groundhog Day. Illness.

I never win! ill. by Cathy Gilchrist. Carolrhoda, 1981. Subj: Character traits – luck. Games.

I'll never love anything ever again ill. by Rodney Pate. Albert Whitman, 1985. ISBN 0-8075-3521-4 Subj: Animals – dogs. Emotions – sadness. Pets.

I'm telling you now ill. by Lillian Hoban. Dutton, 1983. Subj: Activities. Behavior. Character traits – individuality.

It happened on Thursday ill. by June Goldsborough. Albert Whitman, 1978. Subj: Character traits – luck. Family life. Illness.

My grandma's in a nursing home ill. by Charles Robinson. Albert Whitman, 1986. ISBN 0-8075-5333-6 Subj: Emotions – loneliness. Family life – grandmothers. Old age.

My mom hates me in January ill. by John Faulkner. Albert Whitman, 1977. Subj: Behavior – boredom. Seasons – winter.

My mother lost her job today ill. by Irene Trivas. Albert Whitman, 1980. Subj: Activities – working. Character traits – optimism. Family life – mothers.

My Uncle Nikos ill. by Marc Simont. Crowell, 1983. Subj: Family life. Foreign lands – Greece.

The new girl at school ill. by Lillian Hoban. Dutton, 1979. Subj: School.

On a picnic ill. by Mamoru Funai. Doubleday, 1979. ISBN 0-385-12945-9 Subj: Activities – picnicking. Animals – gorillas. Animals – lions. Behavior – worrying. Birds – geese.

Penny wise, fun foolish ill. by Giulio Maestro. Crown, 1977. Subj: Animals – elephants. Behavior – saving things. Birds – ostriches. Fairs.

A pet for Duck and Bear ill. by Lynn Munsinger. Albert Whitman, 1982. Subj: Animals – bears. Birds – ducks. Friendship. Pets.

Rabbit goes to night school ill. by Lynn Munsinger. Albert Whitman, 1986. ISBN 0-8075-6725-6 Subj: Animals – rabbits. Magic. School.

Three friends find spring ill. by Giulio Maestro. Crown, 1977. Subj: Animals – rabbits. Birds – ducks. Friendship. Seasons – spring. Seasons – winter.

A walk on a snowy night ill. by Ruth Rosner. Harper, 1982. Subj: Night. Weather – snow. Weather – storms.

Del Vecchio, Ellen. *Big city port* (Maestro, Betsy)

Delving, Michael *see* Williams, Jay

De Lynam, Alicia Garcia. *It's mine!* ill. by author. Dial Pr., 1988. ISBN 0-8037-0509-3 Subj: Behavior – sharing. Sibling rivalry. Toys.

Demarest, Chris L. *Benedict finds a home* ill. by author. Lothrop, 1982. Subj: Behavior – seeking better things. Birds.

Clemens' kingdom ill. by author. Lothrop, 1983. Subj: Animals – lions. Character traits – curiosity. Libraries.

Morton and Sidney ill. by author. Macmillan, 1987. ISBN 0-02-728450-6 Subj: Behavior – sharing. Monsters.

No peas for Nellie ill. by author. Macmillan, 1988. ISBN 0-02-728460-3 Subj: Food. Imagination.

Orville's odyssey ill. by author. Prentice-Hall, 1986. ISBN 0-13-642851-7 Subj: Imagination. Sports – fishing. Wordless.

De Marolles, Chantal. *The lonely wolf* ill. by Eleonore Schmid. Holt, 1986. ISBN 0-8050-0006-2 Subj: Animals – wolves. Character traits – kindness to animals. Foreign lands – Russia.

Demi. *The adventures of Marco Polo* ill. by author. Holt, 1982. Subj: Activities – traveling. Foreign lands – China.

Chen Ping and his magic axe ill. by author. Dodd, 1987. ISBN 0-396-08907-0 Subj: Character traits – honesty. Folk and fairy tales. Foreign lands – China. Magic.

A Chinese zoo: fables and proverbs ill. by adapt. Harcourt, 1987. ISBN 0-15-217510-5 Subj: Animals. Folk and fairy tales. Foreign lands – China.

Demi's count the animals 1-2-3 ill. by author. Grosset, 1986. ISBN 0-448-18980-1 Subj: Animals. Counting. Poetry, rhyme.

Demi's find the animals A B C: an alphabet-game book ill. by author. Grosset, 1985. ISBN 0-448-18970-4 Subj: ABC books. Animals. Behavior – hiding things.

Demi's opposites: an animal game book ill. by author. Grosset, 1987. ISBN 0-448-18995-X Subj: Concepts – opposites. Games.

Demi's reflective fables ill. by author. Grosset, 1988. ISBN 0-448-09281-6 Subj: Folk and fairy tales. Foreign lands – China.

Dragon kites and dragonflies: a collection of Chinese nursery rhymes ill. by adapt. Harcourt, 1986. ISBN 0-15-224199-X Subj: Dragons. Foreign lands – China. Nursery, rhymes.

Fleecy bunny ill. by author. Grosset, 1987. ISBN 0-448-19151-2 Subj: Animals – rabbits. Format, unusual – board books.

Fleecy lamb ill. by author. Grosset, 1987. ISBN 0-448-19152-0 Subj: Animals – sheep. Format, unusual – board books.

The hallowed horse ill. by adapt. Dodd, 1987. ISBN 0-396-08908-9 Subj: Animals – horses. Folk and fairy tales. Foreign lands – India. Reptiles – snakes.

Liang and the magic paintbrush ill. by author. Holt, 1988. ISBN 0-8050-0801-2 Subj: Activities – painting. Magic.

Under the shade of the mulberry tree ill. by author. Prentice-Hall, 1979. Subj: Character traits – cleverness. Folk and fairy tales. Foreign lands – China.

Where is it? ill. by author. Doubleday, 1979. Subj: Riddles.

Dempewolff, Richard Frederic *see* Day, Michael E.

Demuth, Patricia Brennan. *Max, the bad-talking parrot* ill. by Bo Zaunders. Dodd, 1986. ISBN 0-396-08767-1 Subj: Behavior – misunderstanding. Birds – parakeets, parrots. Etiquette. Poetry, rhyme.

Denison, Carol. *A part-time dog for Nick* ill. by Jane Miller. Dodd, 1959. Subj: Animals – dogs. Family life.

Denney, Diana *see* Ross, Diana

Dennis, Lynne. *Raymond Rabbit's early morning* ill. by author. Dutton, 1987. ISBN 0-525-44316-9 Subj: Animals – rabbits. Family life. Morning.

Dennis, Morgan. *Burlap* ill. by author. Viking, 1945. Subj: Animals – bears. Animals – dogs.

The pup himself ill. by author. Viking, 1943. Subj: Animals – dogs.

The sea dog ill. by author. Viking, 1958. Subj: Animals – dogs. Boats, ships. Weather – storms.

Skit and Skat ill. by author. Viking, 1952. Subj: Animals – cats. Animals – dogs.

Dennis, Suzanne E. *Answer me that* ill. by Owen Wood. Bobbs-Merrill, 1969. Subj: Animals. Humor. Poetry, rhyme.

Dennis, Wesley. *Flip* ill. by author. Viking, 1941. Subj: Animals. Dreams. Farms.

Flip and the cows ill. by author. Viking, 1942. Subj: Animals – bulls, cows. Animals – horses. Farms.

Flip and the morning ill. by author. Viking, 1951. Subj: Animals – horses. Morning.

Tumble, the story of a mustang ill. by author. Hastings, 1966. Subj: Animals – horses. Character traits – freedom.

Denton, Kady MacDonald. *Granny is a darling* ill. by author. Macmillan, 1988. ISBN 0-689-50452-7 Subj: Bedtime. Family life – grandmothers. Monsters. Night.

The picnic ill. by author. Dutton, 1988. ISBN 0-525-44376-2 Subj: Activities – picnicking. Family life.

Denver, John. *The children and the flowers* ill. by Randi Gullerud. Green Tiger Pr., 1979. Subj: Flowers. Songs.

De Paola, Thomas Anthony *see* De Paola, Tomie

De Paola, Tomie. *Andy (that's my name)* ill. by author. Prentice-Hall, 1973. Subj: Behavior – greed. Character traits – smallness. Friendship. Games. Names.

The art lesson ill. by author. Putnam's, 1989. ISBN 0-399-21688-X Subj: Art. Family life. School.

Baby's first Christmas ill. by author. Putnam's, 1988. ISBN 0-399-21591-3 Subj: Babies. Holidays – Christmas.

Big Anthony and the magic ring ill. by author. Harcourt, 1979. Subj: Character traits – appearance. Magic.

Bill and Pete ill. by author. Putnam's, 1978. Subj: Foreign lands – Africa. Humor. Reptiles – alligators, crocodiles. School.

Bill and Pete go down the Nile ill. by author. Putnam's, 1987. ISBN 0-399-21395-3 Subj: Behavior – stealing. Birds. Foreign lands – Egypt. Museums. Reptiles – alligators, crocodiles. School.

The cat on the Dovrefell: a Christmas tale tr. by George W. Dasent; ill. by author. Putnam's, 1979. Subj: Holidays – Christmas. Trolls.

Charlie needs a cloak ill. by author. Prentice-Hall, 1973. Subj: Animals – mice. Animals – sheep. Clothing. Problem solving.

The Christmas pageant ill. by author. Winston Pr., 1978. Subj: Holidays – Christmas. Theater.

The cloud book ill. by author. Holiday, 1975. Subj: Weather – clouds.

The clown of God: an old story ill. by author. Harcourt, 1978. Subj: Foreign lands – Italy. Holidays – Christmas. Religion.

Country farm ill. by author. Putnam's, 1984. Subj: Animals. Farms. Format, unusual. Wordless.

Criss-cross applesauce photos. by B. A. King; ill. by the B. A. King children. Addison-Wesley, 1979. Subj: Children as illustrators.

An early American Christmas ill. by author. Holiday, 1987. ISBN 0-8234-0617-2 Subj: Holidays – Christmas. U.S. history.

The family Christmas tree book ill. by author. Holiday, 1980. Subj: Family life. Holidays – Christmas. Trees.

Favorite nursery tales ill. by adapt. Putnam's, 1986. ISBN 0-399-21319-8 Subj: Folk and fairy tales. Nursery rhymes.

Fight the night ill. by author. Lippincott, 1968. Subj: Bedtime. Sleep.

Fin M'Coul: the giant of Knockmany Hill ill. by author. Holiday, 1981. Subj: Folk and fairy tales. Foreign lands – Ireland. Giants.

Flicks ill. by author. Harcourt, 1979. Subj: Humor. Wordless.

Four stories for four seasons ill. by author. Prentice-Hall, 1977. Subj: Activities – gardening. Boats, ships. Hibernation. Seasons.

Haircuts for the Woolseys ill. by author. Putnam's, 1989. ISBN 0-399-21662-6 Subj: Animals – sheep. Family life – grandmothers.

Helga's dowry ill. by author. Harcourt, 1977. Subj: Emotions – love. Poverty. Trolls. Weddings.

The hunter and the animals ill. by author. Holiday, 1981. Subj: Animals. Sports – hunting. Wordless.

Katie and Kit at the beach ill. by author. Little, 1987. ISBN 0-671-61722-2 Subj: Format, unusual – board books. Sea and seashore. Weather – rain.

Katie, Kit and cousin Tom ill. by author. Little, 1987. ISBN 0-671-61724-9 Subj: Behavior – bullying. Family life. Format, unusual – board books.

Katie's good idea ill. by author. Little, 1987. ISBN 0-671-61725-7 Subj: Behavior – growing up. Format, unusual – board books.

The knight and the dragon ill. by author. Putnam's, 1980. Subj: Dragons. Knights. Libraries.

The Lady of Guadalupe ill. by author. Holiday, 1980. Subj: Foreign lands – Mexico. Religion.

The legend of Old Befana ill. by author. Harcourt, 1980. Subj: Folk and fairy tales. Foreign lands – Italy. Religion.

The legend of the bluebonnet ill. by author. Putnam's, 1983. Subj: Indians of North America. Flowers. Folk and fairy tales.

The legend of the Indian paintbrush ill. by author. Putnam's, 1987. ISBN 0-399-21534-4 Subj: Activities – painting. Folk and fairy tales. Indians of North America.

Marianna May and Nursey ill. by author. Holiday, 1983. Subj: Character traits – cleanliness.

Merry Christmas, Strega Nona ill. by author. Harcourt, 1986. ISBN 0-15-253183-1 Subj: Foreign lands – Italy. Holidays – Christmas. Magic. Witches.

Michael Bird-Boy ill. by author. Prentice-Hall, 1975. Subj: Ecology.

The miracles of Jesus ill. by author. Holiday, 1987. ISBN 0-8234-0635-0 Subj: Religion.

The mysterious giant of Barletta: an Italian folktale ill. by author. Harcourt, 1984. Subj: Folk and fairy tales. Foreign lands – Italy. Giants. War.

Nana upstairs and Nana downstairs ill. by author. Putnam's, 1973. Subj: Death. Emotions – sadness. Family life – grandmothers.

Noah and the ark ill. by author. Winston, 1983. Subj: Religion – Noah.

Now one foot, now the other ill. by author. Putnam's 1981. Subj: Family life – grandfathers. Illness.

Oliver Button is a sissy ill. by author. Harcourt, 1979. Subj: Activities – dancing. Character traits – individuality.

Pajamas for Kit ill. by author. Little, 1987. ISBN 0-671-61723-0 Subj: Bedtime. Clothing. Family life – grandparents. Format, unusual – board books.

Pancakes for breakfast ill. by author. Harcourt, 1978. Subj: Activities – cooking. Food. Wordless.

The parables of Jesus ill. by author. Holiday, 1987. ISBN 0-8234-0636-9 Subj: Religion.

The popcorn book ill. by author. Holiday, 1978. Subj: Activities – cooking. Food.

The Prince of the Dolomites ill. by author. Harcourt, 1980. Subj: Elves and little people. Folk and fairy tales. Foreign lands – Italy. Moon.

The quicksand book ill. by author. Holiday, 1977. Subj: Behavior – carelessness.

Sing, Pierrot, sing: a picture book in mime ill. by author. Harcourt, 1983. Subj: Clowns, jesters. Theater. Wordless.

Songs of the fog maiden ill. by author. Holiday, 1979. Subj: Poetry, rhyme.

The story of the three wise kings ill. by author. Putnam's, 1983. Subj: Holidays – Christmas. Religion.

Strega Nona: an old tale ill. by author. Prentice-Hall, 1975. Subj: Behavior – forgetfulness. Caldecott award honor book. Humor. Magic. Witches.

Strega Nona's magic lessons ill. by author. Harcourt, 1982. Subj: Behavior – carelessness. Humor. Magic. Witches.

Things to make and do for Valentine's Day ill. by author. Watts, 1976. Subj: Activities – cooking. Games. Holidays – Valentine's Day.

Tomie de Paola's book of poems ill. by author. Putnam's, 1988. ISBN 0-399-21540-9 Subj: Poetry, rhyme.

Tomie de Paola's Mother Goose ill. by selector. Putnam's, 1985. ISBN 0-399-21258-2 Subj: Nursery rhymes.

Too many Hopkins ill. by author. Putnam's, 1989. ISBN 0-399-21661-8 Subj: Activities – gardening. Animals – rabbits. Family life.

When everyone was fast asleep ill. by author. Holiday, 1976. Subj: Sleep.

The wonderful dragon of Timlin ill. by author. Bobbs-Merrill, 1966. Subj: Dragons. Knights. Royalty.

De Posadas Mane, Carmen. *Mister North Wind* adapt. by Joanne Fink; tr. from Spanish by Candido A. Valderrama; ill. by Alfonso Ruano. Silver Burdett, 1986. ISBN 0-382-09191-4 Subj: Animals. Character traits – bravery. Seasons – spring. Weather – wind.

De Regniers, Beatrice Schenk. *A bunch of poems and verses* ill. by Mary Jane Dunton. Seabury Pr., 1977. Subj: Poetry, rhyme.

Catch a little fox: variations on a folk rhyme ill. by Brinton Turkle. Seabury Pr., 1979. Subj: Character traits – cleverness. Nursery rhymes. Sports – hunting.

Cats cats cats ill. by Bill Sokol. Pantheon, 1958. Subj: Animals – cats. Poetry, rhyme.

Circus photos. by Al Giese. Viking, 1966. Subj: Circus.

David and Goliath ill. by Richard M. Powers. Viking, 1965. Subj: Religion.

Everyone is good for something ill. by Margot Tomes. Houghton, 1980. Subj: Animals – cats. Folk and fairy tales. Foreign lands – Russia. Self-concept.

The giant story ill. by Maurice Sendak. Harper, 1953. Subj: Family life. Giants.

Going for a walk ill. by author. Harper, 1982. Orig. title: The little book. Subj: Activities – walking.

It does not say meow! ill. by Paul Galdone. Seabury Pr., 1972. Subj: Animals. Participation. Poetry, rhyme. Riddles.

Jack and the beanstalk

Jack the giant killer (Jack and the beanstalk)

Laura's story ill. by Jack Kent. Atheneum, 1979. Subj: Imagination.

A little house of your own ill. by Irene Haas. Harcourt, 1954. Subj: Family life. Houses. Imagination.

Little Sister and the Month Brothers ill. by Margot Tomes. Seabury Pr., 1976. Subj: Days of the week, months of the year. Folk and fairy tales. Foreign lands.

May I bring a friend? ill. by Beni Montresor. Atheneum, 1964. Subj: Animals. Caldecott award book. Friendship. Humor. Poetry, rhyme. Royalty.

Penny by Beatrice Schenk de Regniers and Marvin Bileck; ill. by Marvin Bileck. Viking, 1966. Subj: Elves and little people.

Picture book theater: the mysterious stranger and the magic spell ill. by William Lahey Cummings. Seabury Pr., 1982. Subj: Animals – cats. Animals – mice. Theater. Wizards.

Red Riding Hood ill. by Edward Gorey. Atheneum, 1972. Retold in verse for boys and girls to read themselves. Subj: Animals – wolves. Behavior – talking to strangers. Folk and fairy tales. Poetry, rhyme.

Sam and the impossible thing ill. by Brinton Turkle. Norton, 1967. Subj: Activities – cooking. Food. Monsters. Poetry, rhyme.

The shadow book ill. by Isabel Gordon. Harcourt, 1960. Subj: Shadows.

So many cats! ill. by Ellen Weiss. Clarion, 1985. ISBN 0-89919-322-6 Subj: Animals – cats. Counting. Poetry, rhyme.

Something special ill. by Irene Haas. Harcourt, 1958. Subj: Poetry, rhyme.

A special birthday party for someone very special ill. by Brinton Turkle. Norton, 1966. Subj: Animals – skunks. Birthdays.

Waiting for mama ill. by Victoria de Larrea. Clarion, 1984. Subj: Imagination.

Was it a good trade? ill. by Irene Haas. Harcourt, 1956. Subj: Activities – trading. Poetry, rhyme. Songs.

What can you do with a shoe? ill. by Maurice Sendak. Harper, 1955. Subj: Games. Imagination.

Who likes the sun? ill. by Leona Pierce. Harcourt, 1961. Subj: Sun.

Willy O'Dwyer jumped in the fire variations on a folk rhyme ill. by Beni Montresor. Atheneum, 1968. Subj: Fire. Moon. Nursery rhymes. Witches.

DeSantis, Kenny. *A doctor's tools* photos. by Patricia Agre. Dodd, 1985. ISBN 0-396-08516-4 Subj: Careers – doctors. Tools.

Detine, Padre *see* Olsen, Ib Spang

Deutsch, Babette. *There comes a time* (Borchers, Elisabeth)

Deutschendorf, Henry John, Jr. *see* Denver, John

Deveaux, Alexis. *Na-ni* ill. by author. Harper, 1973. Subj: Character traits – questioning. City. Emotions – sadness. Poverty.

Devlin, Harry. *Aunt Agatha, there's a lion under the couch!* (Devlin, Wende)

Cranberry Christmas (Devlin, Wende)

Cranberry Thanksgiving (Devlin, Wende)

Cranberry Valentine (Devlin, Wende)

Old Black Witch (Devlin, Wende)

Old Witch and the polka-dot ribbon (Devlin, Wende)

Old Witch rescues Halloween (Devlin, Wende)

The walloping window blind: an old nautical tale ill. by author. Van Nostrand, 1968. Adapted from an old sea tune. Subj: Boats, ships. Pirates. Songs.

Devlin, Wende. *Aunt Agatha, there's a lion under the couch!* by Wende and Harry Devlin; ill. by authors. Van Nostrand, 1968. Subj: Animals – lions. Emotions – fear. Imagination.

Cranberry Christmas by Wende and Harry Devlin; ill. by authors. Parents, 1976. Subj: Behavior – sharing. Character traits – helpfulness. Holidays – Christmas.

Cranberry Halloween ill. by Harry Devlin. Four Winds Pr., 1982. Subj: Behavior – stealing. Holidays – Halloween.

Cranberry Thanksgiving by Wende and Harry Devlin; ill. by Harry Devlin. Parents, 1971. Subj: Holidays – Thanksgiving.

Cranberry Valentine by Wende and Harry Devlin; ill. by authors. Four Winds Pr., 1986. ISBN 0-02-729200-2 Subj: Character traits – shyness. Holidays – Valentine's Day.

Old Black Witch by Wende and Harry Devlin; ill. by Harry Devlin. Encyclopaedia Brit., 1963. Subj: Activities – cooking. Witches.

Old Witch and the polka-dot ribbon by Wende and Harry Devlin; ill. by Harry Devlin. Parents, 1970. Subj: Activities – cooking. Fairs. Food. Witches.

Old Witch rescues Halloween by Wende and Harry Devlin; ill. by Harry Devlin. Parents, 1972. Subj: Activities – cooking. Holidays – Halloween. Witches.

Dewey, Ariane. *A crocodile's tale* (Aruego, José)

Dorin and the dragon ill. by author. Greenwillow, 1982. Subj: Dragons. Dreams. Magic. Royalty.

Febold Feboldson ill. by author. Greenwillow, 1984. Subj: Farms. Folk and fairy tales. Weather.

The fish Peri ill. by author. Macmillan, 1979. Subj: Folk and fairy tales. Foreign lands – Turkey. Magic. Problem solving.

Laffite, the pirate ill. by author. Greenwillow, 1985. ISBN 0-688-04230-9 Subj: Folk and fairy tales. Pirates. U.S. history.

Pecos Bill ill. by author. Greenwillow, 1983. Subj: Cowboys. Folk and fairy tales.

The thunder god's son: a Peruvian folktale ill. by author. Greenwillow, 1981. Subj: Folk and fairy tales. Foreign lands – Peru. Magic.

We hide, you seek (Aruego, José)

DeWitt, Jamie. *Jamie's turn* ill. by Julie Brinckloe. Raintree, 1984. ISBN 0-940742-37-3 Subj: Farms. Illness.

Diamond, Donna. *The Bremen town musicians* (Grimm, Jacob)

Rumpelstiltskin (Grimm, Jacob)

Dick Whittington and his cat. *Dick Whittington* retold by Kathleen Lines; ill. by Edward Ardizzone. Walck, 1970. Subj: Activities – trading. Animals – cats. Folk and fairy tales. Foreign lands – England. Middle ages.

Dick Whittington: a story from England retold by Charles Causley; ill. by Antony Maitland. Penguin, 1979. Subj: Activities – trading. Animals – cats. Folk and fairy tales. Foreign lands – England. Middle ages.

Dick Whittington and his cat retold and ill. by Marcia Brown. Scribner's, 1950. Subj: Activities – trading. Animals – cats. Caldecott award honor book. Folk and fairy tales. Foreign lands – England. Middle ages.

Dick Whittington and his cat retold by Eva Moore; ill. by Kurt Werth. Seabury Pr., 1974. Subj: Activities – trading. Animals – cats. Folk and fairy tales. Foreign lands – England. Middle ages.

Dickens, Frank. *Boffo: the great motorcycle race* ill. by author. Parents, 1978. Subj: Character traits – cleverness. Motorcycles. Sports – racing.

Dickinson, Mary. *Alex and Roy* ill. by Charlotte Firmin. Elsevier-Dutton, 1981. Subj: Friendship. Imagination.

Alex's bed ill. by Charlotte Firmin. Elsevier-Dutton, 1980. Subj: Character traits – cleanliness. Problem solving.

Alex's outing ill. by Charlotte Firmin. Dutton, 1983. Subj: Activities – picnicking. Behavior – nagging. Country.

Dickinson, Mike. *My dad doesn't even notice* ill. by author. Elsevier-Dutton, 1982. Subj: Behavior – misunderstanding. Imagination.

Dietz, Gertrud *see* Fussenegger, Gertrud

DiFiori, Lawrence. *Baby animals* ill. by author. Macmillan, 1983. Subj: Animals. Format, unusual – board books.

The farm ill. by author. Macmillan, 1983. Subj: Farms. Format, unusual – board books.

If I had a little car ill. by author. Golden Pr., 1985. Subj: Automobiles. Format, unusual – board books. Imagination.

My first book ill. by author. Macmillan, 1983. Subj: Activities – reading. Format, unusual – board books.

My toys ill. by author. Macmillan, 1983. Subj: Format, unusual – board books. Toys.

D'Ignazio, Fred. *Katie and the computer* ill. by Stan Gilliam. Creative Computing, 1980. Subj: Imagination. Machines.

Dillon, Barbara. *The beast in the bed* ill. by Chris Conover. Morrow, 1981. Subj: Imagination – imaginary friends. Monsters.

Dillon, Eilis. *The cats' opera* ill. by Kveta Vanecek. Bobbs-Merrill, 1963. Subj: Animals – cats. Music.

Din dan don, it's Christmas ill. by Janina Domanska. Greenwillow, 1975. Text is a rendition of an anonymous Polish Christmas carol. Subj: Foreign lands – Poland. Holidays – Christmas. Religion. Songs.

Dinan, Carolyn. *The lunch box monster* ill. by author. Faber, 1983. Subj: Imagination – imaginary friends. Monsters.

Say cheese! ill. by author. Viking, 1986. ISBN 0-670-80954-3 Subj: Character traits – being different. School. Teeth.

Dinardo, Jeffrey. *Timothy and the night noises* ill. by author. Prentice-Hall, 1986. ISBN 0-13-922048-8 Subj: Emotions – fear. Frogs and toads. Night. Noise, sounds.

Dines, Glen. *Gilly and the wicharoo* ill. by author. Lothrop, 1968. Subj: Behavior – trickery. Character traits – cleverness. Foreign lands – England.

Pitadoe, the color maker ill. by author. Macmillan, 1959. Subj: Concepts – color. Wizards.

A tiger in the cherry tree ill. by author. Macmillan, 1958. Subj: Animals – tigers. Behavior – forgetfulness. Character traits – shyness. Foreign lands – Japan. Magic.

Dinosaurs and monsters ill. by Louise Nevett. Watts, 1984. Subj: Activities. Dinosaurs. Monsters.

Dionetti, Michelle. *The day Eli went looking for bear* ill. by Joyce Audy Dos Santos. Addison-Wesley, 1980. Subj: Animals. Family life – mothers. Seasons – winter. Sports – hunting.

Thalia Brown and the blue bug ill. by James Calvin. Addison-Wesley, 1979. Subj: Art. Character traits – pride. Ethnic groups in the U.S. – Afro-Americans.

Diot, Alain. *Better, best, bestest* ill. by Joel Naprstek. Dial Pr., 1977. Subj: Behavior – boasting. Family life – fathers.

Diska, Pat. *Andy says ... Bonjour!* ill. by Chris Jenkyns. Vanguard, 1954. Subj: Animals – cats. Foreign lands – France. Foreign languages.

Dixon, Ruth *see* Barrows, Marjorie Wescott

Dobbs, Rose. *More once-upon-a-time stories* ill. by Flavia Gág. Random House, 1961. Subj: Folk and fairy tales.

Once-upon-a-time story book ill. by Walter Hodges. Random House, 1958. Subj: Folk and fairy tales.

Dobrin, Arnold Jack. *Josephine's 'magination* ill. by author. Four Winds Pr., 1973. Subj: Foreign lands – Caribbean Islands. Imagination. Toys.

Dr. Seuss *see* Seuss, Dr.

Dodd, Lynley. *Hairy Maclary from Donaldson's dairy* ill. by author. Gareth Stevens, 1985. Subj: Animals – cats. Animals – dogs. Cumulative tales. Emotions – fear. Poetry, rhyme.

Hairy Maclary Scattercat ill. by author. Gareth Stevens, Inc., 1988. ISBN 1-555-32-123-2 Subj: Animals – cats. Animals – dogs. Behavior – bullying. Poetry, rhyme.

Hairy Maclary's bone ill. by author. Gareth Stevens, 1985. ISBN 0-918331-06-7 Subj: Animals – dogs. Character traits – cleverness. Cumulative tales. Poetry, rhyme.

The nickle nackle tree ill. by author. Macmillan, 1976. Subj: Counting. Poetry, rhyme.

The smallest turtle ill. by author. Gareth Stevens, 1985. ISBN 0-918831-07-5 Subj: Reptiles – turtles, tortoises. Science. Sea and seashore.

Wake up, bear ill. by author. Gareth Stevens, Inc., 1988. ISBN 1-555-32-124-0 Subj: Animals. Animals – bears. Seasons – spring. Sleep.

Dodds, Siobhan. *Charles Tiger* ill. by author. Little, 1988. ISBN 0-316-18817-4 Subj: Animals. Animals – tigers. Behavior – losing things.

Elizabeth Hen ill. by author. Little, 1988. ISBN 0-316-18818-2 Subj: Animals. Birds – chickens. Counting. Eggs. Farms.

Dodge, Mary Mapes. *Mary Anne* ill. by June Amos Grammer. Lothrop, 1983. Subj: Poetry, rhyme. Toys – dolls.

Dodgson, Charles Lutwidge *see* Carroll, Lewis

The dog writes on the window with his nose, and other poems collected by David Kherdian; ill. by Nonny Hogrogian. Four Winds Pr., 1977. Subj: Poetry, rhyme.

Doherty, Berlie. *Paddiwak and cozy* ill. by Teresa O'Brien. Dial Pr., 1989. ISBN 0-8037-0483-6 Subj: Animals – cats. Emotions – envy, jealousy.

Domanska, Janina. *The best of the bargain* ill. by author. Greenwillow, 1977. Subj: Activities – gardening. Animals – foxes. Animals – hedgehogs. Behavior – trickery. Character traits – cleverness. Folk and fairy tales. Foreign lands – Poland.

Busy Monday morning ill. by author. Greenwillow, 1985. Subj: Folk and fairy tales. Foreign lands – Poland. Music. Songs.

I saw a ship a-sailing ill. by author. Macmillan, 1972. Subj: Boats, ships. Holidays – Christmas. Nursery rhymes.

If all the seas were one sea ill. by author. Macmillan, 1971. Subj: Caldecott award honor book Nursery rhymes. Sea and seashore.

King Krakus and the dragon ill. by author. Greenwillow, 1979. Subj: Character traits – cleverness. Dragons. Folk and fairy tales. Foreign lands – Poland. Royalty.

Look, there is a turtle flying ill. by author. Macmillan, 1968. Subj: Folk and fairy tales. Foreign lands – Poland. Reptiles – turtles, tortoises. Royalty.

Marek, the little fool ill. by author. Greenwillow, 1982. Subj: Folk and fairy tales. Foreign lands.

Palmiero and the ogre ill. by author. Macmillan, 1967. Subj: Behavior – forgetfulness. Folk and fairy tales. Magic.

A scythe, a rooster and a cat ill. by author. Greenwillow, 1981. Subj: Folk and fairy tales. Foreign lands – Russia.

The tortoise and the tree ill. by author. Greenwillow, 1978. Subj: Folk and fairy tales. Foreign lands – Africa. Reptiles – turtles, tortoises.

The turnip ill. by author. Macmillan, 1969. Subj: Cumulative tales. Farms. Folk and fairy tales. Foreign lands – Russia. Plants. Problem solving.

What do you see? ill. by author. Macmillan, 1974. Subj: Animals. Poetry, rhyme. World.

What happens next? ill. by author. Greenwillow, 1983. Subj: Folk and fairy tales.

Why so much noise? ill. by author. Harper, 1965. "Adaptation of the tale entitled 'The elephant has a bet with the tiger,' [as recorded] by Walter William Skeat." Subj: Animals – elephants. Animals – tigers. Character traits – cleverness. Folk and fairy tales. Foreign lands – India. Noise, sounds.

Domestic animals ill. with photos. Imported Pubs., 1983. Subj: Animals. Format, unusual – board books. Wordless.

Donaldson, Lois. *Karl's wooden horse* ill. by Annie Bergmann. Albert Whitman, 1970. Subj: Dreams. Holidays – Christmas. Night. Toys – rocking horses.

Donnelly, Liza. *Dinosaurs' Halloween* ill. by author. Scholastic, 1987. ISBN 0-590-41025-3 Subj: City. Dinosaurs. Holidays – Halloween.

Don't tell the scarecrow: *and other Japanese poems* by Issa, Yayū, Kikaku and other Japanese poets; ill. by Tālivaldis Stubis. Four Winds Pr., 1970. Subj: Foreign lands – Japan. Poetry, rhyme. Seasons.

Doolittle, Eileen. *The ark in the attic: an alphabet adventure* photos. by Starr Ockenga. Godine, 1987. ISBN 0-87923-648-1 Subj: ABC books. Rebuses. Riddles.

World of wonders: a trip through numbers photos. by Starr Ockenga; ill. by author. Houghton, 1988. ISBN 0-325-48726-9 Subj: Counting. Imagination. Poetry, rhyme.

Dorian, Marguerite. *When the snow is blue* ill. by author. Lothrop, 1960. Subj: Animals – bears. Imagination. Weather – snow.

Dorros, Arthur. *Alligator shoes* ill. by author. Dutton, 1982. Subj: Reptiles – alligators, crocodiles.

Ant cities ill. by author. Crowell, 1987. ISBN 0-690-04570-0 Subj: Insects – ants. Science.

Pretzels ill. by author. Greenwillow, 1981. Subj: Boats, ships. Humor.

Dorsky, Blanche. *Harry, a true story* ill. by Muriel Batherman. Prentice-Hall, 1977. Subj: Animals – rabbits. School.

Dos Santos, Joyce Audy. *The diviner* ill. by author. Lippincott, 1980. Subj: Character traits – cleverness. Folk and fairy tales. Foreign lands – Canada. Royalty.

Henri and the Loup-Garou ill. by author. Pantheon, 1982. Subj: Folk and fairy tales. Foreign lands – Canada. Monsters.

Sand dollar, sand dollar ill. by author. Lippincott, 1980. Subj: Sea and seashore.

Dostoyevsky, Fyodor. *The talking crocodile* (Campbell, M. Rudolph)

Doty, Roy. *Eye fooled you: the big book of optical illusions* ill. by author. Macmillan, 1983. Subj: Optical illusions.

Old-one-eye meets his match ill. by author. Lothrop, 1978. Subj: Animals – mice. Animals – rats.

Doughtie, Charles. *Gabriel Wrinkles, the bloodhound who couldn't smell* ill. by Charles D. Saxon. Dodd, 1959. Subj: Animals – dogs. Senses – smelling.

High Henry...the cowboy who was too tall to ride a horse ill. by Don Gregg. Dodd, 1960. Subj: Animals – giraffes. Cowboys.

Douglas, Michael. *Round, round world* ill. by author. Golden Pr., 1960. Subj: Animals – cats. Foreign lands. World.

Douglas, Robert W. *John Paul II: the Pilgrim Pope* ill., map and photos. Children's Pr., 1979. Subj: Religion.

Douglass, Barbara. *The chocolate chip cookie contest* ill. by Eric Jon Nones. Lothrop, 1985. ISBN 0-688-04044-6 Subj: Activities – cooking. Clowns, jesters.

Good as new ill. by Patiences Brewster. Lothrop, 1982. Subj: Behavior – misbehavior. Family life – grandfathers. Toys – teddy bears.

Dow, Katharine. *My time of year* ill. by Walter Erhard. Walck, 1961. Subj: Seasons.

Dowdy, Mrs. Regera *see* Gorey, Edward

Dowers, Patrick. *One day scene through a leaf* ill. by author. Green Tiger Pr., 1981. Subj: Poetry, rhyme.

Downie, Jill. *Alphabet puzzle* ill. by author. Lothrop, 1988. ISBN 0-688-08044-8 Subj: ABC books. Rebuses. Riddles.

Downing, Joan. *Baseball is our game* ill. by Tony Freeman. Children's Pr., 1982. Subj: Sports – baseball.

Doyle, Donovan *see* Boegehold, Betty

Doyle, John *see* Graves, Robert

Dragonwagon, Crescent. *Alligator arrived with apples: a potluck alphabet feast* ill. by José Aruego and Ariane Dewey. Macmillan, 1987. ISBN 0-02-733090-7 Subj: ABC books. Animals. Holidays – Thanksgiving. Reptiles – alligators, crocodiles.

Always, always ill. by Arieh Zeldich. Macmillan, 1984. Subj: Divorce.

Coconut ill. by Nancy Tafuri. Harper, 1984. Subj: Behavior – wishing. Birds – parakeets, parrots.

Diana, maybe ill. by Deborah Kogan Ray. Macmillan, 1987. ISBN 0-02-733180-6 Subj: Behavior – wishing. Family life.

Half a moon and one whole star ill. by Jerry Pinkney. Macmillan, 1986. ISBN 0-02-733120-2 Subj: Dreams. Night. Poetry, rhyme.

I hate my brother Harry ill. by Dick Gackenbach. Harper, 1983. Subj: Sibling rivalry.

Jemima remembers ill. by Troy Howell. Macmillan, 1984. ISBN 0-02-733070-2 Subj: Farms. Poetry, rhyme. Seasons.

Katie in the morning ill. by Betsy Day. Harper, 1983. Subj: Behavior – solitude. Morning.

Rainy day together ill. by Lillian Hoban. Harper, 1971. Subj: Emotions. Family life. Family life – only child. Weather – rain.

When light turns into night ill. by Robert Andrew Parker. Harper, 1975. Subj: Behavior – solitude. Night.

Wind Rose ill. by Ronald Himler. Harper, 1976. Subj: Babies. Emotions – love. Names.

Drdek, Richard E. *Horace the friendly octopus* ill. by Joseph Veno. Allyn and Bacon, 1965. Reading consultants: William D. Sheldon and Mary C. Austin. Subj: Friendship. Octopuses.

Dreamer, Sue. *Circus ABC* ill. by author. Little, 1985. ISBN 0-316-19196-5 Subj: ABC books. Circus. Format, unusual – board books.

Circus 1, 2, 3 ill. by author. Little, 1985. ISBN 0-316-19195-7 Subj: Circus. Counting. Format, unusual – board books.

Dreifus, Miriam W. *Brave Betsy* ill. by Sheila Greenwald. Putnam's, 1961. Subj: Character traits – bravery. School. Toys – dolls.

Drescher, Henrik. *Looking for Santa Claus* ill. by author. Lothrop, 1984. Subj: Animals – bulls, cows. Holidays – Christmas. Imagination.

Simon's book ill. by author. Lothrop, 1983. Subj: Dreams. Monsters.

The yellow umbrella ill. by author. Bradbury Pr., 1987. ISBN 0-02-733240-3 Subj: Animals – monkeys. Jungle. Umbrellas. Wordless. Zoos.

Drescher, Joan. *I'm in charge!* ill. by author. Little, 1981. Subj: Behavior – growing up. Family life.

The marvelous mess ill. by author. Houghton, 1980. Subj: Family life. Sibling rivalry.

My mother's getting married ill. by author. Dial Pr., 1986. ISBN 0-8037-0176-4 Subj: Emotions – envy, jealousy. Family life – mothers. Weddings.

Your family, my family ill. by author. Walker, 1980. Subj: Family life.

Drew, Patricia. *Spotter Puff* ill. by author. Merrimack Book Serv., 1979. Subj: Birds – puffins. Character traits – kindness to animals.

Driz, Ovsei. *The boy and the tree* tr. by Joachim Neugroschel; ill. by Victor Pivovarov. Prentice-Hall, 1978. Subj: Poetry, rhyme.

Drummond, Violet H. *The flying postman* ill. by author. Walck, 1964. Subj: Careers – mail carriers. Foreign lands – England. Helicopters.

Phewtus the squirrel ill. by author. Lothrop, 1987. ISBN 0-688-07013-2 Subj: Animals – squirrels. Behavior – lost. Toys.

Dubanevich, Arlene. *Pig William* ill. by author. Bradbury Pr., 1985. ISBN 0-02-733200-4 Subj: Activities – picnicking. Animals – pigs. Behavior – indifference. Sibling rivalry. Weather – rain.

The piggest show on earth ill. by author. Watts, 1989. ISBN 0-531-05789-5 Subj: Animals – pigs. Circus.

Pigs at Christmas ill. by author. Bradbury Pr., 1986. ISBN 0-02-733160-1 Subj: Animals – pigs. Character traits – being different. Holidays – Christmas.

Pigs in hiding ill. by author. Four Winds Pr., 1983. Subj: Animals – pigs. Behavior – hiding. Games.

DuBois, Ivy. *Baby Jumbo* ill. by Elsie Wrigley. Grosset, 1977. Subj: Animals – elephants.

Mother fox ill. by Elsie Wrigley. Grosset, 1977. Subj: Animals – foxes.

Du Bois, William Pène. *The alligator case* ill. by author. Harper, 1966. Subj: Circus. Problem solving. Reptiles – alligators, crocodiles.

Bear circus ill. by author. Viking, 1971. Subj: Animals. Animals – koala bears. Character traits – helpfulness. Circus. Insects – grasshoppers.

Bear party ill. by author. Viking, 1951. Subj: Animals. Animals – koala bears. Caldecott award honor book. Emotions – anger. Parties.

Elisabeth the cow ghost ill. by author. Viking, 1964. Subj: Animals – bulls, cows. Ghosts.

The forbidden forest ill. by author. Harper, 1978. Subj: Animals – kangaroos. War.

Giant Otto ill. by author. Viking, n.d. Subj: Animals – dogs. Giants.

The hare and the tortoise and the tortoise and the hare: La liebre y la tortuga and La tortuga y la liebre by William Pène Du Bois and Lee Po; ill. by William Pène Du Bois. Doubleday, 1972. Subj: Animals – rabbits. Folk and fairy tales. Foreign languages. Reptiles – turtles, tortoises.

Lazy Tommy pumpkinhead ill. by author. Harper, 1966. Subj: Character traits – laziness. Machines.

Lion ill. by author. Viking, 1957. Subj: Animals – lions. Caldecott award honor book.

Otto and the magic potatoes ill. by author. Viking, 1970. Subj: Activities – vacationing. Animals – dogs. Fire. Giants.

Otto at sea ill. by author. Viking, 1936. Subj: Animals – dogs. Boats, ships. Giants.

Otto in Africa ill. by author. Viking, 1961. Subj: Animals – dogs. Foreign lands – Africa. Giants.

Otto in Texas ill. by author. Viking, 1959. Subj: Animals – dogs. Giants.

Dubov, Christine Salac. *Aleksandra, where are your toes?* photos. by Josef Schneider. St. Martin's, 1986. ISBN 0-312-01717-0 Subj: Anatomy. Format, unusual – board books.

Aleksandra, where is your nose? photos. by Josef Schneider. St. Martin's, 1986. ISBN 0-312-01719-7 Subj: Anatomy. Format, unusual – board books.

Duff, Maggie. *Dancing turtle* ill. by Maria Horvath. Macmillan, 1981. Subj: Animals. Behavior – trickery. Folk and fairy tales.

The princess and the pumpkin: from a Majorcan tale ill. by Catherine Stock. Macmillan, 1980. Subj: Folk and fairy tales. Foreign lands – Spain. Illness.

Rum pum pum ill. by José Aruego. Macmillan, 1978. Subj: Birds – blackbirds. Folk and fairy tales. Foreign lands – India.

Duff, Margaret K. *see* Duff, Maggie

Dukas, P. (Paul Abraham). *The sorcerer's apprentice* Adapt. by Makoto Oishi; tr. by Ann Brannen; ill. by Ryohei Yanagihara. Gakken, 1971. Subj: Folk and fairy tales. Magic.

Duke, Anita *see* Hewett, Anita

Duke, Kate. *Bedtime* ill. by author. Dutton, 1986. ISBN 0-525-44207-3 Subj: Animals – guinea pigs. Bedtime. Family life. Format, unusual – board books.

Clean-up day ill. by author. Dutton, 1986. ISBN 0-525-44208-1 Subj: Activities – working. Animals – guinea pigs. Family life. Format, unusual – board books.

The guinea pig ABC ill. by author. Dutton, 1983. Subj: ABC books. Animals – guinea pigs.

Guinea pigs far and near ill. by author. Dutton, 1984. Subj: Animals – guinea pigs. Concepts.

The playground ill. by author. Dutton, 1986. ISBN 0-525-44206-5 Subj: Activities – playing. Animals – guinea pigs. Family life. Format, unusual – board books.

Seven froggies went to school ill. by author. Dutton, 1985. ISBN 0-525-44160-3 Subj: Frogs and toads. Poetry, rhyme. School.

What bounces? ill. by author. Dutton, 1986. ISBN 0-525-44209-X Subj: Animals – guinea pigs. Concepts. Family life. Format, unusual – board books.

Dulcken, H. W. *The fir tree* (Andersen, H. C. (Hans Christian))

Dumas, Philippe. *Caesar, cock of the village* ill. by author. Prentice-Hall, 1979. Subj: Birds – chickens. Foreign lands – France.

Laura, Alice's new puppy ill. by author. David and Charles, 1979. Subj: Animals – dogs.

Laura and the bandits ill. by author. David and Charles, 1980. Subj: Animals – dogs. Crime.

Laura loses her head ill. by author. David and Charles, 1982. Subj: Animals – dogs. Family life – grandfathers. Foreign lands – France.

Laura on the road ill. by author. David and Charles, 1979. Subj: Animals – dogs.

Lucy, a tale of a donkey ill. by author. Prentice-Hall, 1980. Subj: Animals – donkeys. Behavior – running away.

The story of Edward ill. by author. Parents, 1977. Subj: Animals – donkeys. Foreign lands – France.

Dunbar, Joyce. *A cake for Barney* ill. by Emilie Boon. Watts, 1988. ISBN 0-531-08335-7 Subj: Animals – bears. Character traits – assertiveness.

Duncan, Gregory *see* McClintock, Marshall

Duncan, Jane. *Janet Reachfar and Chickabird* ill. by Mairi Hedderwick. Seabury Pr., 1978. Subj: Behavior – bad day. Farms. Foreign lands – Scotland.

Duncan, Lois. *Giving away Suzanne* ill. by Leonard Weisgard. Dodd, 1964. Subj: Sibling rivalry.

Horses of dreamland ill. by Donna Diamond. Little, 1985. ISBN 0-316-19554-5 Subj: Animals – horses. Dreams. Night.

Duncan, Riana. *A nutcracker in a tree: a book of riddles* ill. by author. Delacorte, 1981. Subj: Animals. Riddles.

Dunham, Meredith. *Colors: how do you say it?* ill. by author. Lothrop, 1987. ISBN 0-688-06949-5 Subj: Concepts – color. Foreign languages. Language.

Numbers: how do you say it? ill. by author. Lothrop, 1987. ISBN 0-688-06951-7 Subj: Counting. Foreign languages. Language.

Picnic: how do you say it? ill. by author. Lothrop, 1987. ISBN 0-688-07097-3 Subj: Activities – picnicking. Foreign languages. Language.

Shapes: how do you say it? ill. by author. Lothrop, 1987. ISBN 0-688-06953-3 Subj: Concepts – shape. Foreign languages. Language.

Dunn, Judy. *The animals of Buttercup Farm* photos. by Phoebe Dunn. Random House, 1981. Subj: Animals. Farms.

The little duck ill. by Phoebe Dunn. Random House, 1978. Subj: Birds – ducks.

The little goat ill. by Phoebe Dunn. Random House, 1978. Subj: Animals – goats. Pets.

The little lamb ill. by Phoebe Dunn. Random House, 1977. Subj: Animals – sheep. Character traits – kindness to animals. Farms.

The little puppy photos. by Phoebe Dunn. Random House, 1984. Subj: Animals – dogs. Pets.

The little rabbit photos. by Phoebe Dunn. Random House, 1980. Subj: Animals – rabbits. Holidays – Easter. Pets.

Dunn, Phoebe. *Baby's animal friends* photos. by author. Random House, 1988. ISBN 0-394-89583-5 Subj: Animals. Babies. Format, unusual – board books.

Busy, busy toddlers photos. by author. Random House, 1987. ISBN 0-394-88604-6 Subj: Activities. Babies. Format, unusual – board books.

I'm a baby! photos. by author. Random House, 1987. ISBN 0-394-88605-4 Subj: Babies. Format, unusual – board books.

Dunrea, Olivier. *Eddy B, pigboy* ill. by author. Atheneum, 1983. Subj: Animals – pigs. Farms.

Fergus and Bridey ill. by author. Holiday, 1985. ISBN 0-8234-0554-0 Subj: Animals – dogs. Boats, ships. Friendship.

Dupasquier, Philippe. *Dear Daddy...* ill. by author. Bradbury Pr., 1985. ISBN 0-02-733170-9 Subj: Boats, ships. Careers. Family life – fathers. Sea and seashore.

The great escape ill. by author. Houghton, 1988. ISBN 0-395-46806-X Subj: Behavior – running away. Prisons. Wordless.

Jack at sea ill. by author. Prentice-Hall, 1987. ISBN 0-13-509209-4 Subj: Boats, ships. Sea and seashore. War.

Our house on the hill ill. by author. Viking, 1988. ISBN 0-670-81971-9 Subj: Seasons. Wordless.

Duplaix, Georges *see* Ariane

Dupré, Ramona Dorrel. *Too many dogs* ill. by Howard Baer. Follett, 1960. Subj: Animals – dogs.

Duran, Bonté. *The adventures of Arthur and Edmund: a tale of two seals* ill. by Quentin Blake. Atheneum, 1984. Subj: Animals – seals.

Durrell, Julie. *Mouse tails* ill. by author. Crown, 1985. Subj: Animals. Animals – mice.

Dutton, Sandra. *The cinnamon hen's autumn day* ill. by author. Atheneum, 1988. ISBN 0-689-31414-0 Subj: Animals – rabbits. Birds – chickens. Seasons – fall.

Duvoisin, Roger Antoine. *A for the ark* ill. by author. Lothrop, 1952. Subj: ABC books. Animals. Religion – Noah.

The Christmas whale ill. by author. Knopf, 1945. Subj: Animals – whales. Holidays – Christmas. Illness.

The crocodile in the tree ill. by author. Knopf, 1973. Subj: Animals. Farms. Friendship. Reptiles – alligators, crocodiles.

Crocus ill. by author. Knopf, 1977. Subj: Careers – dentists. Character traits – pride. Farms. Reptiles – alligators, crocodiles. Teeth.

Day and night ill. by author. Knopf, 1960. Subj: Animals – dogs. Birds – owls.

Donkey-donkey ill. by author. Parents, 1968. Subj: Animals – donkeys.

Easter treat ill. by author. Knopf, 1954. Subj: Holidays – Easter.

The happy hunter ill. by author. Lothrop, 1961. Subj: Character traits – kindness to animals. Ecology. Sports – hunting. Violence, anti-violence. Weapons.

The house of four seasons ill. by author. Lothrop, 1956. Subj: Activities – painting. Concepts – color. Seasons.

Jasmine ill. by author. Knopf, 1973. Subj: Animals. Character traits – individuality. Clothing. Farms.

Lonely Veronica ill. by author. Knopf, 1963. Subj: Animals – hippopotami. City. Progress.

The missing milkman ill. by author. Knopf, 1967. Subj: Behavior – running away. Dreams. Night.

One thousand Christmas beards ill. by author. Knopf, 1955. Subj: Holidays – Christmas.

Our Veronica goes to Petunia's farm ill. by author. Knopf, 1962. Subj: Animals. Animals – hippopotami. Character traits – being different. Farms.

Periwinkle ill. by author. Knopf, 1976. Subj: Animals – giraffes. Emotions – loneliness. Etiquette. Friendship. Frogs and toads.

Petunia ill. by author. Knopf, 1950. Subj: Activities – reading. Animals. Birds – geese. Character traits – pride. Farms. Friendship.

Petunia and the song ill. by author. Knopf, 1951. Subj: Animals. Birds – geese. Crime. Farms. Friendship. Noise, sounds. Songs.

Petunia, beware! ill. by author. Knopf, 1958. Subj: Animals. Behavior – dissatisfaction. Birds – geese. Farms.

Petunia, I love you ill. by author. Knopf, 1965. Subj: Animals – raccoons. Behavior – trickery. Birds – geese. Birds – vultures. Farms. Friendship.

Petunia takes a trip ill. by author. Knopf, 1953. Subj: Activities – flying. Activities – vacationing. Animals. Birds – geese.

Petunia, the silly goose: stories ill. by author. Knopf, 1987. ISBN 0-394-98292-4 Subj: Animals. Birds – geese. Farms.

Petunia's Christmas ill. by author. Knopf, 1952. Subj: Birds – geese. Holidays – Christmas. Humor.

Petunia's treasure ill. by author. Knopf, 1975. Subj: Animals. Birds – geese. Farms. Friendship.

See what I am ill. by author. Lothrop, 1974. Subj: Behavior – boasting. Concepts – color.

Snowy and Woody ill. by author. Knopf, 1979. ISBN 0-394-94241-8 Subj: Animals – bears. Animals – polar bears. Birds – sea gulls. Friendship.

Two lonely ducks ill. by author. Knopf, 1955. Subj: Birds – ducks. Counting. Farms.

Veronica ill. by author. Knopf, 1961. Subj: Animals – hippopotami. Character traits – being different. City. Farms.

Veronica and the birthday present ill. by author. Knopf, 1971. Subj: Animals – cats. Animals – hippopotami. Birthdays. Farms.

Veronica's smile ill. by author. Knopf, 1964. Subj: Animals – hippopotami. Behavior – boredom.

Dyke, John. *Pigwig* ill. by author. Methuen, 1978. Subj: Animals – pigs. Behavior – stealing. Character traits – bravery. Emotions – love.

Pigwig and the pirates ill. by author. Methuen, 1979. Subj: Animals – pigs. Pirates. Sea and seashore.

Dynely, James *see* Mayne, William

Dyssegaard, Elisabeth. *The little house from the sea* (Gedin, Birgitta)

Earle, Olive L. *Squirrels in the garden* ill. by author. Morrow, 1963. Subj: Animals – squirrels.

Eastman, David. *The story of dinosaurs* ill. by Joel Snyder. Troll Assoc., 1982. Subj: Dinosaurs.

The velveteen rabbit (Bianco, Margery Williams)

What is a fish? ill. by Lynn Sweat. Troll Assoc., 1982. Subj: Fish. Science.

Eastman, P. D. (Philip D.). *Are you my mother?* ill. by author. Random House, 1960. Subj: Behavior – misbehavior. Birds. Family life – mothers.

The cat in the hat beginner book dictionary (Seuss, Dr.)

Flap your wings ill. by author. Random House, 1969. Subj: Birds. Eggs. Reptiles – alligators, crocodiles.

Go, dog, go! ill. by author. Random House, 1961. Subj: Animals – dogs.

Sam and the firefly ill. by author. Random House, 1958. Subj: Birds – owls. Insects – fireflies.

Snow (McKie, Roy)

Eastman, Patricia. *Sometimes things change* ill. by Seymour Fleishman. Children's Pr., 1983. Subj: Science.

Easton, Violet. *Elephants never jump* ill. by Carme Solé Vendrell. Little, 1986. ISBN 0-87113-049-1 Subj: Activities – jumping. Animals. Animals – elephants. Humor.

Eastwick, Ivy O. *Cherry stones! Garden swings! poems* ill. by Robert Jones. Abingdon Pr., 1962. Subj: Poetry, rhyme.

Rainbow over all ill. by Anne Siberell. McKay, 1970. Subj: Poetry, rhyme.

Eaton, Su. *Punch and Judy in the rain* by Su Eaton and Martin Bridle; ill. by authors. Hamish Hamilton, 1985. Subj: Puppets.

Eberle, Irmengarde. *Bears live here* ill. with photos. Doubleday, 1962. Subj: Animals – bears.

A chipmunk lives here ill. by Matthew Kalmenoff. Doubleday, 1966. Subj: Animals – chipmunks.

Fawn in the woods photos. by Lilo Hess. Crowell, 1962. Subj: Animals – deer.

Foxes live here ill. with photos. Doubleday, 1966. Subj: Animals – foxes.

Koalas live here ill. with photos. Doubleday, 1967. Subj: Animals – koala bears.

Picture stories for children: a rebus ill. by author. Delacorte, 1984. ISBN 0-385-29340-2 Subj: Animals. Rebuses.

Eberstadt, Frederick. *What is for my birthday?* (Eberstadt, Isabel)

Eberstadt, Isabel. *What is for my birthday?* by Isabel and Frederick Eberstadt; ill. by Leonard Weisgard. Little, 1961. Subj: Birthdays. Illness. Poetry, rhyme.

Eckert, Horst *see* Janosch

Eco, Umberto. *The bomb and the general* ill. by Eugenio Carmi. Harcourt, 1989. ISBN 0-15-209700-7 Subj: War.

The three astronauts ill. by Eugenio Carmi. Harcourt, 1989. ISBN 0-15-286383-4 Subj: Careers – astronauts. Character traits – appearance. Space and space ships.

Economakis, Olga. *Oasis of the stars* ill. by Blair Lent. Coward, 1965. Subj: Foreign lands – Africa. Problem solving.

Edelman, Elaine. *Boom-de-boom* ill. by Karen Gundersheimer. Pantheon, 1980. Subj: Activities – dancing. Old age. Poetry, rhyme.

I love my baby sister (most of the time) ill. by Wendy Watson. Lothrop, 1984. Subj: Sibling rivalry.

Edens, Cooper. *The glorious Mother Goose* (Mother Goose)

Edman, Polly. *Red thread riddles* (Jensen, Virginia Allen)

Edwards, Al *see* Nourse, Alan Edward

Edwards, Dorothy. *A wet Monday* by Dorothy Edwards and Jenny Williams; ill. by Jenny Williams. Morrow, 1975. Subj: Birds – chickens. Character traits – pride.

Edwards, Linda Strauss. *The downtown day* ill. by author. Pantheon, 1983. Subj: Shopping.

Edwards, Patricia Kier. *Chester and Uncle Willoughby* ill. by Diane Worfolk Allison. Little, 1987. ISBN 0-316-21173-7 Subj: Family life. Imagination. Sleep.

Edwards, Roberta. *Anna Bear's first winter* ill. by Laura Lydecker. Random House, 1986. ISBN 0-3294-88199-0 Subj: Animals – bears. Format, unusual – board books. Sleep.

Eggs ill. by Esmé Eve. Grosset, 1971. Subj: Eggs.

Ehlert, Lois. *Growing vegetable soup* ill. by author. Harcourt, 1987. ISBN 0-15-232575-1 Subj: Activities – gardening. Food.

Planting a rainbow ill. by author. Harcourt, 1988. ISBN 0-15-262609-3 Subj: Activities – gardening. Flowers.

Ehrhardt, Reinhold. *Kikeri or, The proud red rooster* ill. by Bernadette Watts. Collins, 1969. Subj: Birds – chickens. Character traits – pride.

Ehrlich, Amy. *Bunnies all day long* ill. by Marie H. Henry. Dial Pr., 1985. ISBN 0-8037-0185-3 Subj: Activities. Animals – rabbits.

Bunnies and their grandma ill. by Marie H. Henry. Dial Pr., 1985. ISBN 0-8037-0186-1 Subj: Animals – rabbits. Family life – grandmothers.

Bunnies at Christmastime ill. by Marie H. Henry. Dial Pr., 1986. ISBN 0-8037-0321-X Subj: Animals – rabbits. Family life. Holidays – Christmas. Parties. Sibling rivalry.

Bunnies on their own ill. by Marie H. Henry. Dial Pr., 1986. ISBN 0-8037-0256-6 Subj: Animals – rabbits. Family life. Sibling rivalry.

Cinderella (Perrault, Charles)

The everyday train ill. by Martha G. Alexander. Dial Pr., 1977. Subj: Behavior – solitude. Trains.

Leo, Zack and Emmie ill. by Steven Kellogg. Dial Pr., 1981. Subj: Friendship. School.

Leo, Zack, and Emmie together again ill. by Steven Kellogg. Dial Pr., 1987. ISBN 0-8037-0382-1 Subj: Friendship. School.

The snow queen (Andersen, H. C. (Hans Christian))

Thumbelina (Andersen, H. C. (Hans Christian))

The wild swans (Andersen, H. C. (Hans Christian))

Zeek Silver Moon ill. by Robert Andrew Parker. Dial Pr., 1972. Subj: Family life. Indians of North America.

Ehrlich, Bettina Bauer *see* Bettina

Eichenberg, Fritz. *Ape in cape* ill. by author. Harcourt, 1952. Subj: ABC books. Caldecott award honor book.

Dancing in the moon ill. by author. Harcourt, 1955. Subj: Animals. Counting. Poetry, rhyme.

Eisen, Armand. *Goldilocks and the three bears* (The three bears)

Eisenberg, Lisa. *Buggy riddles* (Hall, Katy)

Fishy riddles (Hall, Katy)

Eisenberg, Phyllis Rose. *Don't tell me a ghost story* ill. by Lynn Munsinger. Harcourt, 1982. Subj: Ghosts. Monsters. Sibling rivalry.

A mitzvah is something special ill. by Susan Jeschke. Harper, 1978. Subj: Family life – grandmothers. Family life – grandparents. Jewish culture.

Eisler, Colin. *Cats know best* ill. by Lesley Anne Ivory. Dial Pr., 1988. ISBN 0-8037-0560-3 Subj: Animals – cats.

Ekker, Ernest A. *What is beyond the hill?* ill. by Hilde Heyduck-Huth. Lippincott, 1986. ISBN 0-397-32167-8 Subj: Activities – traveling. Imagination. World.

Elborn, Andrew. *Bird Adalbert* ill. by Susi Bohdal. Alphabet Pr., 1983. Subj: Behavior – dissatisfaction. Birds. Character traits – appearance. Poetry, rhyme.

Noah and the ark and the animals ill. by Ivan Gantschev. Picture Book Studio, 1984. ISBN 0-907234-58-5 Subj: Animals. Animals – horses. Religion – Noah.

Elkin, Benjamin. *The big jump and other stories* ill. by Katherine Evans. Random House, 1958. Subj: Animals – dogs. Folk and fairy tales. Royalty.

Gillespie and the guards ill. by James Henry Daugherty. Viking, 1956. Subj: Anatomy. Behavior – trickery. Caldecott award honor book. Character traits – cleverness. Royalty.

The king who could not sleep ill. by Victoria Chess. Parents, 1975. Subj: Cumulative tales. Poetry, rhyme. Royalty. Sleep.

The king's wish and other stories ill. by Leonard W. Shortall. Random House, 1960. Subj: Folk and fairy tales. Royalty.

The loudest noise in the world ill. by James Henry Daugherty. Viking, 1954. Subj: Birthdays. Noise, sounds. Royalty.

Lucky and the giant ill. by Katherine Evans. Children's Pr., 1962. Subj: Character traits – cleverness. Character traits – luck. Character traits – selfishness. Giants.

Six foolish fishermen ill. by Katherine Evans. Children's Pr., 1957. Based on a folktale in Ashton's Chap-Books of the 18th century. Subj: Counting. Folk and fairy tales. Sports – fishing.

Such is the way of the world ill. by Yōko Mitsuhashi. Parents, 1968. Subj: Animals – monkeys. Cumulative tales. Folk and fairy tales. Foreign lands – Africa. Problem solving.

Why the sun was late ill. by James Snyder. Parents, 1966. Subj: Animals. Cumulative tales. Insects – flies. Sun.

The wisest man in the world: a legend of ancient Israel retold by Benjamin Elkin; ill. by Anita Lobel. Parents, 1968. Subj: Folk and fairy tales. Foreign lands – Israel. Riddles. Royalty.

Elks, Wendy. *Charles B. Wombat and the very strange thing* ill. by author. David & Charles, 1989. ISBN 0-09-168910-4 Subj: Animals – wombats. Circus. Reptiles – turtles, tortoises.

Ellen, Barbara. *Phillip the flower-eating phoenix* (Todaro, John.)

Ellentuck, Shan. *Did you see what I said?* ill. by author. Doubleday, 1967. Subj: Humor. Language.

A sunflower as big as the sun ill. by author. Doubleday, 1968. Subj: Behavior – boasting. Flowers. Humor. Plants.

Elliott, Dan. *Ernie's little lie* ill. by Joseph Mathieu. Random House, 1983. Subj: Art. Behavior – lying. Puppets.

A visit to the Sesame Street firehouse: featuring Jim Henson's Sesame Street Muppets ill. by Joseph Mathieu. Random House, 1983. Subj: Careers – firefighters. Fire. Puppets.

Elliott, Ingrid Glatz. *Hospital roadmap: a book to help explain the hospital experience to young children* ill. by author. Resources for Children in Hospitals, 1982. Subj: Hospitals. Illness.

Elliott, Robert *see* Allen, Robert

Ellis, Anne Leo. *Dabble Duck* ill. by Sue Truesdell. Harper, 1984. Subj: Birds – ducks. City. Emotions – loneliness. Friendship.

Elting, Mary. *The big book of real boats and ships* ill. by George J. Zaffo. Grosset, 1951. Subj: Boats, ships.

The Hopi way ill. by Louis Mofsie. Lippincott, 1970. Subj: Indians of North America.

Q is for duck: an alphabet guessing game by Mary Elting and Michael Folsom; ill. by Jack Kent. Houghton, 1980. Subj: ABC books. Animals. Games. Participation.

Elves, fairies and gnomes: *poems* sel. by Lee Bennett Hopkins; ill. by Rosekrans Hoffman. Knopf, 1980. Subj: Elves and little people. Fairies. Poetry, rhyme.

Elwell, Peter. *The king of the pipers* ill. by author. Macmillan, 1984. Subj: Devil. Folk and fairy tales.

Elzbieta. *Brave Babette and sly Tom* ill. by author. Dial Pr., 1989. ISBN 0-8037-0633-2 Subj: Animals – cats. Animals – mice. Birds. Family life.

Dikou and the baby star ill. by author. Crowell, 1988. ISBN 0-690-04721-5 Subj: Character traits – kindness. Stars.

Dikou and the mysterious moon sheep ill. by author. Crowell, 1988. ISBN 0-690-04694-4 Subj: Behavior – running away. Dreams. Family life. Imagination.

Dikou the little troon who walks at night ill. by author. Barron's, 1985. ISBN 0-8120-5621-3 Subj: Behavior – lying. Character traits – kindness. Mythical creatures.

Emberley, Barbara. *Drummer Hoff* ill. by Ed Emberley. Prentice-Hall, 1967. Adapted from a folk verse. Subj: Caldecott award book. Careers – military. Cumulative tales. Poetry, rhyme. Weapons.

Night's nice by Barbara and Ed Emberley; ill. by Ed Emberley. Doubleday, 1963. Subj: Night. Poetry, rhyme.

One wide river to cross ill. by Ed Emberley. Prentice-Hall, 1966. Includes unacc. melody. Adaptation of the American folk song. Subj: Animals. Caldecott award honor book. Folk and fairy tales. Poetry, rhyme. Songs.

Simon's song ill. by Ed Emberley. Prentice-Hall, 1969. Includes unacc. melody. Adaptation of the folk song Simple Simon. Subj: Nursery rhymes. Songs.

Emberley, Ed. *Animals* ill. by author. Little, 1987. ISBN 0-316-23428-1 Subj: Animals. Format, unusual – board books.

Cars, boats, and planes ill. by author. Little, 1987. ISBN 0-316-23430-3 Subj: Airplanes, airports. Automobiles. Boats, ships. Format, unusual – board books. Transportation.

Ed Emberley's ABC ill. by author. Little, 1978. Subj: ABC books.

Ed Emberley's amazing look through book ill. by author. Little, 1979. Subj: Concepts. Format, unusual. Participation. Riddles.

Ed Emberley's big green drawing book ill. by author. Little, 1979. Subj: Art. Wordless.

Ed Emberley's big orange drawing book ill. by author. Little, 1980. Subj: Art.

Ed Emberley's big purple drawing book ill. by author. Little, 1981. Subj: Art.

Ed Emberley's crazy mixed-up face game ill. by author. Little, 1981. Subj: Anatomy. Art. Games.

Ed Emberley's drawing book: make a world ill. by author. Little, 1972. ISBN 0-316-23598-9 Subj: Art.

Green says go ill. by author. Little, 1968. Subj: Communication. Concepts – color.

Home ill. by author. Little, 1987. ISBN 0-316-23433-8 Subj: Format, unusual – board books. Houses.

Klippity klop ill. by author. Little, 1974. Subj: Dragons. Games. Knights. Participation.

Night's nice (Emberley, Barbara)

The parade book ill. by author. Little, 1962. Subj: Parades.

Rosebud ill. by author. Little, 1966. Subj: Character traits – being different. Problem solving. Reptiles – turtles, tortoises.

Sounds ill. by author. Little, 1987. ISBN 0-316-23431-1 Subj: Format, unusual – board books. Noise, sounds.

The wing on a flea: a book about shapes ill. by author. Little, 1961. Subj: Concepts – shape. Poetry, rhyme.

The Wizard of Op ill. by author. Little, 1975. Subj: Optical illusions. Wizards.

Emberley, Edward Randolph *see* Emberley, Ed

. More dinosaurs! and other pre- *.* by author. Little, 1983. Subj:
s.

..ebecca. Drawing with numbers and *.* by author. Little, 1981. Subj: Art.

., Margaret. The blue-nosed witch ill. by Carl .se. Holiday, 1956. Subj: Holidays — Hal-.oween. Witches.

Emecheta, Buchi. *Nowhere to play* ill. by Peter Archer. Schocken, 1981. Subj: Activities — playing. Foreign lands — England. Safety.

Emerson, Sally. *The nursery treasury* ill. by Moira and Colin Maclean. Doubleday, 1988. ISBN 0-385-24650-1 Subj: Nursery rhymes.

Emmett, Fredrick Rowland. *New world for Nellie* ill. by author. Harcourt, 1952. Subj: Trains.

Emmons, Ramona Ware. *Your world: let's visit the hospital* (Pope, Billy N.)

Encking, Louise F. *The little gardeners* (Morgenstern, Elizabeth)

The toy maker (Thelen, Gerda)

Enderle, Judith A. *Good junk* ill. by Gail Gibbons. Elsevier-Nelson, 1981. Subj: Behavior — collecting things.

Engdahl, Sylvia. *Our world is earth* ill. by Don Sibley. Atheneum, 1979. Subj: Communication. Earth. Science.

Engel, Diana. *Josephina, the great collector* ill. by author. Morrow, 1988. ISBN 0-688-07543-6 Subj: Behavior — collecting things. Sibling rivalry.

Engelbrektson, Sune. *Gravity at work and play* ill. by Eric Carle. Holt, 1963. Subj: Science.

The sun is a star ill. by Eric Carle. Holt, 1963. Subj: Science. Sun.

Engle, Joanna. *Cap'n kid goes to the South Pole* ill. by Pat Paris. Random House, 1983. Subj: Animals — whales.

English, Jennifer. *My mommy's special* ill. with photos. Childrens Pr., 1985. ISBN 0-516-03861-3 Subj: Family life — mothers. Handicaps.

Engvick, William. *Lullabies and night songs* ed. by William Engvick; music by Alec Wilder; ill. by Maurice Sendak. Harper, 1965. Subj: Bedtime. Music. Songs.

Enright, Elizabeth. *Zeee* ill. by Irene Haas. Houghton, 1965. Subj: Fairies.

Ephron, Delia. *Santa and Alex* ill. by Elise Primavera. Little, 1983. Subj: Holidays — Christmas.

Erdoes, Richard. *Policemen around the world* ill. by author. McGraw-Hill, 1968. Subj: Careers — police officers.

Erickson, Karen. *I was so mad* ill. by Maureen Roffey. Viking, 1987. ISBN 0-670-81573-X Subj: Emotions — anger.

I'll try ill. by Maureen Roffey. Viking, 1987. ISBN 0-670-81572-1 Subj: Character traits — perseverance.

It's dark ill. by Maureen Roffey. Viking, 1987. ISBN 0-670-81571-3 Subj: Emotions — fear. Night.

No one is perfect ill. by Maureen Roffey. Viking, 1987. ISBN 0-670-81570-5 Subj: Behavior — mistakes.

Erickson, Phoebe. *Just follow me* ill. by author. Follett, 1960. Subj: Animals — dogs. Behavior — lost. Houses.

Erickson, Russell E. *Warton and the traders* ill. by Lawrence DiFiori. Lothrop, 1979. Subj: Animals — rats. Character traits — cleverness. Character traits — generosity. Frogs and toads.

Warton's Christmas eve adventure ill. by Lawrence DiFiori. Lothrop, 1977. Subj: Animals. Frogs and toads. Holidays — Christmas.

Eriksson, Eva. *Hocus-pocus* ill. by author; tr. from Swedish by Barbro Eriksson Roehrdanz. Carolrhoda Books, 1985. ISBN 0-87614-235-8 Subj: Bedtime. Friendship.

Jealousy ill. by author; tr. from Swedish by Barbro Eriksson Roehrdanz. Carolrhoda Books, 1985. ISBN 0-87614-237-4 Subj: Emotions — envy, jealousy. Friendship. Illness.

One short week ill. by author; tr. from Swedish by Barbro Eriksson Roehrdanz. Carolrhoda Books, 1985. ISBN 0-87614-234-X Subj: Behavior — boredom. Birthdays. Friendship.

The tooth trip ill. by author; tr. from Swedish by Barbro Eriksson Roehrdanz. Carolrhoda Books, 1985. ISBN 0-87614-236-6 Subj: Behavior — losing things. Friendship. Teeth.

Ernst, Lisa Campbell. *A colorful adventure of the bee who left home one Monday morning and what he found along the way* ill. by Lee Ernst. Lothrop, 1986. ISBN 0-688-05564-8 Subj: Concepts — color. Insects — bees.

Hamilton's art show ill. by author. Lothrop, 1986. ISBN 0-688-04121-3 Subj: Activities — gardening. Activities — painting. Animals. Art.

Nattie Parsons' good-luck lamb ill. by author. Viking, 1988. ISBN 0-670-81778-3 Subj: Activities — weaving. Animals — sheep.

The prize pig surprise ill. by author. Lothrop, 1984. Subj: Animals — pigs. Behavior — greed. Character traits — cleverness.

The rescue of Aunt Pansy ill. by author. Viking, 1987. ISBN 0-670-81716-3 Subj: Animals — cats. Animals — mice. Format, unusual. Friendship. Toys.

Sam Johnson and the blue ribbon quilt ill. by author. Lothrop, 1983. Subj: Activities.

Up to ten and down again ill. by author. Lothrop, 1986. ISBN 0-688-04542-1 Subj: Activities – picnicking. Counting.

Erskine, Jim. *Bedtime story* ill. by Ann Schweninger. Crown, 1982. Subj: Bedtime. Dreams. Night.

Bert and Susie's messy tale ill. by author. Crown, 1979. Subj: Activities. Animals – pigs.

The snowman ill. by author. Crown, 1978. Subj: Snowmen.

Esbensen, Barbara Juster. *The star maiden: an Ojibway tale* ill. by Helen K. Davie. Little, 1988. ISBN 0-316-24951-3 Subj: Folk and fairy tales. Indians of North America. Poetry, rhyme.

Escudie, René. *Paul and Sebastian* tr. by Roderick Townley; ill. by Ulises Wensell. Kane Miller, 1988. ISBN 0-916291-19-7 Subj: Character traits – being different. Family life. Friendship. Prejudice.

Espenscheid, Gertrude E. *The oh ball* ill. by author. Crown, 1966. Subj: Royalty. Toys – balls.

Estes, Eleanor. *A little oven* ill. by author. Harper, 1966. Subj: Emotions – love.

Etherington, Frank. *The spaghetti word race* ill. by Gina Calleja. Firefly Pr., 1982. Subj: Imagination. Sibling rivalry.

Ets, Marie Hall. *Another day* ill. by author. Viking, 1953. Subj: Animals. Forest, woods. Parades. Theater.

Bad boy, good boy ill. by author. Crowell, 1967. Subj: Behavior. Ethnic groups in the U.S. – Mexican-Americans. Family life. School.

Beasts and nonsense ill. by author. Viking, 1952. Subj: Animals. Humor. Poetry, rhyme.

The cow's party ill. by author. Viking, 1958. Subj: Animals – bulls, cows. Behavior – dissatisfaction. Behavior – sharing. Parties.

Elephant in a well ill. by author. Viking, 1972. Subj: Animals. Animals – elephants. Character traits – helpfulness. Cumulative tales.

Gilberto and the wind ill. by author. Viking, 1963. Subj: Ethnic groups in the U.S. – Mexican-Americans. Weather – wind.

In the forest ill. by author. Viking, 1944. Subj: Activities – picnicking. Animals. Caldecott award honor book. Forest, woods. Imagination. Parades.

Just me ill. by author. Viking, 1965. Subj: Animals. Caldecott award honor book. Participation.

Little old automobile ill. by author. Viking, 1948. Subj: Automobiles.

Mister Penny ill. by author. Viking, 1935. Subj: Animals. Caldecott award honor book. Farms. Humor.

Mister Penny's circus ill. by author. Viking, 1961. Subj: Animals. Circus.

Mr. Penny's race horse ill. by author. Viking, 1956. Subj: Animals – horses. Caldecott award honor book. Fairs. Farms.

Mr. T. W. Anthony Woo ill. by author. Viking, 1951. Subj: Animals – cats. Animals – dogs. Animals – mice. Caldecott award honor book.

Nine days to Christmas ill. by author. Viking, 1959. Subj: Caldecott award book. Ethnic groups in the U.S. – Mexican-Americans. Foreign lands – Mexico. Holidays – Christmas.

Play with me ill. by author. Viking, 1955. Subj: Activities – playing. Animals. Behavior. Caldecott award honor book.

Talking without words ill. by author. Viking, 1968. Subj: Participation.

Euvremer, Teryl. *After dark* ill. by author. Crown, 1989. ISBN 0-517-57104-8 Subj: Poetry, rhyme.

Sun's up ill. by author. Crown, 1987. ISBN 0-517-56432-7 Subj: Activities – working. Farms. Sun. Wordless.

Evans, Eva Knox. *Sleepy time* ill. by Reed Champion. Houghton, 1962. Subj: Animals. Cumulative tales. Hibernation. Sleep.

That lucky Mrs. Plucky ill. by Jo Ann Stover. McKay, 1961 Subj: Animals – cats. Behavior – collecting things.

Where do you live? ill. by Beatrice Darwin. Golden Pr., 1960. Subj: Animals.

Evans, Katherine. *The boy who cried wolf* ill. by author. Albert Whitman, 1960. Subj: Animals – wolves. Behavior – lying. Behavior – trickery. Folk and fairy tales.

A bundle of sticks ill. by author. Albert Whitman, 1962. A retelling of an Æsop fable. Subj: Folk and fairy tales.

The maid and her pail of milk ill. by author. Albert Whitman, 1959. Subj: Behavior – greed. Folk and fairy tales. Humor.

The man, the boy and the donkey ill. by author. Albert Whitman, 1958. Subj: Animals – donkeys. Character traits – practicality. Folk and fairy tales. Humor.

Evans, Mari. *Singing black* ill. by Ramon Price. Third World Pr., 1978. Subj: Ethnic groups in the U.S. – Afro-Americans. Nursery rhymes.

Evans, Mel. *The tiniest sound* ill. by Ed Young. Doubleday, 1969. Subj: Noise, sounds. Poetry, rhyme.

Everton, Macduff. *El circo magico modelo: Finding the magic circus* ill. by author. Carolrhoda Books, 1979. Subj: Activities – vacationing. Circus. Foreign lands – Mexico. Foreign languages.

Eysselinck, Janet Gay *see* Burroway, Janet

Facklam, Margery. *But not like mine* ill. by Jeni Bassett. Harcourt, 1988. ISBN 015-200585-4 Subj: Anatomy. Animals. Format, unusual – toy and movable books.

So can I ill. by Jeni Bassett. Harcourt, 1988. ISBN 0-15-200419-X Subj: Activities. Animals. Format, unusual – toy and movable books.

Factor, Jane. *Summer* ill. by Alison Lester. Viking, 1988. ISBN 0-670-81157-2 Subj: Family life. Foreign lands – Australia. Holidays – Christmas. Seasons – summer.

Fain, James W. *Rodeos* ill. with photos. Children's Pr., 1983. Subj: Animals – horses. Cowboys.

Fair, Sylvia. *The bedspread* ill. by author. Morrow, 1982. Subj: Activities. Sibling rivalry.

Fairclough, Chris. *Take a trip to China* photos. by author. Watts, 1981. Subj: Activities – traveling. Foreign lands – China.

Take a trip to England photos. by author. Watts, 1982. Subj: Activities – traveling. Foreign lands – England.

Take a trip to Holland photos. by author. Watts, 1982. Subj: Activities – traveling. Foreign lands – Holland.

Take a trip to Israel photos. by author. Watts, 1981. Subj: Activities – traveling. Foreign lands – Israel.

Take a trip to Italy photos. by author. Watts, 1981. Subj: Activities – traveling. Foreign lands – Italy.

Take a trip to West Germany photos. by author. Watts, 1981. Subj: Activities – traveling. Foreign lands – Germany.

Fairy poems for the very young ill. by Beverlie Manson. Doubleday, 1982. Subj: Fairies. Poetry, rhyme.

Faison, Eleanora. *Becoming* ill. by Cecelia Ercin. Patterson Pr., 1981. Subj: Behavior – growing up.

Falls, C. B. (Charles Buckles). *ABC book* ill. by author. Doubleday, 1923. Subj: ABC books.

Fanshawe, Elizabeth. *Rachel* ill. by Michael Charlton. Dutton, 1975. Subj: Handicaps. School.

Farber, Norma. *As I was crossing Boston Common* ill. by Arnold Lobel. Dutton, 1975. Subj: ABC books. Animals. Poetry, rhyme.

How does it feel to be old? ill. by Trina Schart Hyman. Dutton, 1988, 1979. ISBN 0-525-44367-3 Subj: Family life – grandparents. Old age.

How the hibernators came to Bethlehem ill. by Barbara Cooney. Walker, 1980. Subj: Animals. Holidays – Christmas. Poetry, rhyme. Religion.

How the left-behind beasts built Ararat ill. by Antonio Frasconi. Walker, 1978. Subj: Animals. Poetry, rhyme. Problem solving. Religion – Noah.

How to ride a tiger ill. by Claire Schumacher. Houghton, 1983. Subj: Animals. Animals – tigers. Poetry. rhyme.

Never say ugh to a bug ill. by José Aruego. Greenwillow, 1979. Subj: Insects. Poetry, rhyme.

Small wonders ill. by Kazue Mizumura. Coward, 1979. Subj: Poetry, rhyme.

There goes feathertop! ill. by Marc Brown. Unicorn-Dutton, 1979. Subj: Behavior – imitation. Poetry, rhyme. Scarecrows.

There once was a woman who married a man ill. by Lydia Dabcovich. Addison-Wesley, 1978. Subj: Humor. Noise, sounds. Poetry, rhyme.

Up the down elevator ill. by Annie Gusman. Addison-Wesley, 1979. Subj: Counting. Poetry, rhyme.

Where's Gomer? ill. by William Pène Du Bois. Dutton, 1974. Subj: Behavior – lost. Poetry, rhyme. Religion – Noah.

Farge, Phyllis La *see* La Farge, Phyllis

Farge, Sheila La *see* La Farge, Sheila

Farjeon, Eleanor. *Around the seasons: poems* ill. by Jane Paton. Walck, 1969. Subj: Poetry, rhyme. Seasons.

Mr. Garden ill. by Jane Paton. Walck, 1966. Subj: Activities – gardening. Seasons – summer.

Mrs. Malone ill. by Edward Ardizzone. Walck, 1962. Subj: Character traits – generosity. Poetry, rhyme.

Farley, Walter. *Black stallion: an easy-to-read adaptation* ill. by Sandy Rabinowitz. Random House, 1986. ISBN 0-394-96876-X Subj: Animals – horses. Islands.

Little Black, a pony ill. by James Schucker. Random House, 1961. Subj: Animals – horses.

Little Black goes to the circus ill. by James Schucker. Random House, 1963. Subj: Animals – horses. Circus.

Farm animals photos. sel. by Debby Slier. Macmillan, 1988. ISBN 0-02-688752-5 Subj: Animals. Format, unusual – board books.

Farm house ill. by Zokeisha; ed. by Kate Klimo. Simon and Schuster, 1983. Subj: Animals. Farms. Format, unusual – board books. Houses.

The farmer in the dell. *The farmer in the dell* ed. by Ann Fay; ill. by Kathy Parkinson. Albert Whitman, 1988. ISBN 0-8075-2271-6 Subj: Games. Music. Songs.

The farmer in the dell ill. by Mary Maki Rae. Viking, 1988. ISBN 0-670-81853-4 Subj: Games. Music. Songs.

The farmer in the dell ill. by Diane Stanley. Little, 1978. Subj: Games. Music. Songs.

Farmer, Wendell *see* Davis, Lavinia

Fass, David E. *The shofar that lost its voice* ill. by Marlene Lobell Ruthen. Union of American Hebrew Cong., 1982. Subj: Jewish culture. Religion.

Fassler, Joan. *All alone with daddy* ill by Dorothy Lake Gregory. Behavioral, 1969. Subj: Family life – fathers.

Boy with a problem ill. by Stuart [i.e. Stewart] Kranz. Behavioral, 1971. Subj: Friendship. Problem solving.

Don't worry dear ill. by Stuart [i.e. Stewart] Kranz. Behavioral, 1971. Subj: Behavior – growing up. Ethnic groups in the U.S. – Afro-Americans.

Howie helps himself ill. by Joe Lasker. Albert Whitman, 1975. Subj: Handicaps.

The man of the house ill. by Peter Landa. Behavioral, 1969. Subj: Behavior – growing up. Dragons. Family life – mothers. Monsters.

My grandpa died today ill. by Stuart [i.e. Stewart] Kranz. Behavioral, 1971. Subj: Death. Family life – grandfathers. Jewish culture. Old age.

One little girl ill. by M. Jane Smyth. Behavioral, 1969. Subj: Family life. Handicaps.

Fast rolling fire trucks ill. by Carolyn Bracken. Grosset, 1984. Subj: Careers – firefighters. Format unusual – board books. Trucks.

Fast rolling work trucks ill. by Alan Singer. Grosset, 1984. Subj: Format, unusual – board books. Trucks.

The fat cat ill. by Jack Kent. Parents, 1971. Translated from the Danish by Jack Kent. Subj: Animals – cats. Cumulative tales.

Fatio, Louise. *Anna, the horse* ill. by Roger Antoine Duvoisin. Atheneum, 1951. Subj: Animals – horses. Holidays – Christmas.

The happy lion ill. by Roger Antoine Duvoisin. McGraw-Hill, 1954. Subj: Animals – lions. Foreign lands – France. Friendship. Zoos.

The happy lion and the bear ill. by Roger Antoine Duvoisin. McGraw-Hill, 1964. Subj: Animals – bears. Animals – lions. Character traits – appearance. Foreign lands – France. Zoos.

The happy lion in Africa ill. by Roger Antoine Duvoisin. McGraw-Hill, 1955. Subj: Animals – lions. Foreign lands – Africa. Foreign lands – France. Zoos.

The happy lion roars ill. by Roger Antoine Duvoisin. McGraw-Hill, 1957. Subj: Animals – lions. Emotions – loneliness. Foreign lands – France. Zoos.

The happy lion's quest ill. by Roger Antoine Duvoisin. McGraw-Hill, 1961. Subj: Animals – lions. Foreign lands – France.

The happy lion's rabbits ill. by Roger Antoine Duvoisin. McGraw-Hill, 1974. Subj: Animals – lions. Animals – rabbits. Character traits – kindness. Foreign lands – France. Zoos.

The happy lion's treasure ill. by Roger Antoine Duvoisin. McGraw-Hill, 1970. Subj: Animals – lions. Emotions – love. Foreign lands – France. Zoos.

The happy lion's vacation ill. by Roger Antoine Duvoisin. McGraw-Hill, 1967. Subj: Activities – vacationing. Animals – lions.

Hector and Christina ill. by Roger Antoine Duvoisin. McGraw-Hill, 1977. Subj: Birds – penguins. Character traits – freedom. Friendship. Zoos.

Hector penguin ill. by Roger Antoine Duvoisin. McGraw-Hill, 1973. Subj: Birds – penguins. Character traits – individuality.

Marc and Pixie and the walls in Mrs. Jones's garden ill. by Roger Antoine Duvoisin. McGraw-Hill, 1975. Subj: Animals – cats.

The red bantam ill. by Roger Antoine Duvoisin. McGraw-Hill, 1963. Subj: Animals – foxes. Birds – chickens. Character traits – bravery. Farms.

The three happy lions ill. by Roger Antoine Duvoisin. McGraw-Hill, 1959. Subj: Animals – lions. Foreign lands – France. Zoos.

Faulkner, Anne Irvin R. *see* Faulkner, Nancy

Faulkner, Keith. *Sam at the seaside* ill. by Jonathan Lambert. Macmillan, 1988. ISBN 0-689-71183-2 Subj: Format, unusual – toy and movable books. Sea and seashore.

Sam helps out ill. by Jonathan Lambert. Macmillan, 1988. ISBN 0-689-71182-4 Subj: Format, unusual – toy and movable books. Shopping.

Faulkner, Matt. *The amazing voyage of Jackie Grace* ill. by author. Scholastic, 1987. ISBN 0-590-40713-9 Subj: Activities – bathing. Boats, ships. Imagination. Pirates. Weather – storms.

Faulkner, Nancy. *Small clown* ill. by Paul Galdone. Doubleday, 1960. Subj: Clowns, jesters.

Faunce-Brown, Daphne. *Snuffles' house* ill. by Frances Thatcher. Children's Pr., 1983. Subj: Activities. Animals – cats.

Faxon, Lavinia *see* Russ, Lavinia

Fay, Ann. *Boot weather* (Vigna, Judith)
The farmer in the dell
I wish my daddy didn't drink so much (Vigna, Judith)
Ooops! (Kline, Suzy)

Fay, Hermann. *My zoo* ill. by author. Hubbard Sci., 1972. Subj: Animals. Zoos.

Fayon, Lavinia *see* Russ, Lavina

Fechner, Amrei. *I am a little dog* tr. from German by Robert Kimber; ill. by author. Barron's, 1983. Subj: Animals – dogs. Format, unusual – board books.

I am a little elephant ill. by author. Barron's, 1983. Subj: Animals – elephants. Format, unusual – board books.

I am a little lion ill. by author. Barron's, 1983. Subj: Animals – lions. Format, unusual – board books.

Feczko, Kathy. *Halloween party* ill. by Blanche Sims. Troll Assoc., 1985. ISBN 0-8167-0354-X Subj: Holidays – Halloween. Parties.

Umbrella parade ill. by Deborah Borgo. Troll Assoc., 1985. ISBN 0-8167-0356-6 Subj: Animals. Parades. Umbrellas.

Feder, Jane. *Beany* ill. by Karen Gundersheimer. Pantheon, 1979. Subj: Animals – cats.

Feder, Paula Kurzband. *Where does the teacher live?* ill. by Lillian Hoban. Dutton, 1979. Subj: Careers – teachers. Houses. Problem solving. School.

Feelings, Muriel. *Jambo means hello: Swahili alphabet book* ill. by Tom Feelings. Dial Pr., 1974. Subj: ABC books. Caldecott award honor book. Foreign lands – Africa. Foreign languages.

Moja means one: Swahili counting book ill. by Tom Feelings. Dial Pr., 1972. Subj: Caldecott award honor book. Counting. Foreign lands – Africa. Foreign languages.

Feeney, Stephanie. *Hawaii is a rainbow* photos. by Jeff Reese. Kolowalu Books, 1985. ISBN 0-8248-1007-4 Subj: Concepts – color.

Feilen, John *see* May, Julian

Feinberg, Harold S. *Snail in the woods* (Ryder, Joanne)

Feistel, Sally. *The guinea pigs that went to school* (Meshover, Leonard)

The monkey that went to school (Meshover, Leonard)

Feitlowitz, Marguerite. *Brush* (Calders, Pere)

Felix, Monique. *The further adventures of the little mouse trapped in a book* ill. by author. Green Tiger Pr., 1984. ISBN 0-88138-009-1 Subj: Animals – mice. Imagination. Wordless.

The story of a little mouse trapped in a book ill. by author. Green Tiger Pr., 1980. Subj: Animals – mice. Imagination. Wordless.

Felt, Sue. *Hello-goodbye* ill. by author. Doubleday, 1960. Subj: Friendship. Moving.

Rosa-too-little ill. by author. Doubleday, 1950. Subj: Activities – writing. Behavior – growing up. Ethnic groups in the U.S. – Mexican-Americans. Family life. Libraries.

Felton, Harold W. *Pecos Bill and the mustang* ill. by Leonard W. Shortall. Prentice-Hall, 1965. Subj: Animals – horses. Cowboys. Folk and fairy tales.

Fender, Kay. *Odette! a bird in Paris* ill. by Philippe Dumas. Prentice-Hall, 1978. Subj: Birds. Foreign lands – France. Old age.

Fenner, Carol. *Christmas tree on the mountain* ill. by author. Harcourt, 1966. Subj: Holidays – Christmas. Trees.

Tigers in the cellar ill. by author. Harcourt, 1963. Subj: Animals – tigers. Imagination. Night.

Fenton, Edward. *The big yellow balloon* ill. by Ib Spang Olsen. Doubleday, 1967. Subj: Cumulative tales. Humor. Toys – balloons.

Fierce John ill. by William Pène Du Bois. Doubleday, 1959. Subj: Family life. Imagination.

Ferguson, Alane. *That new pet!* ill. by Catherine Stock. Lothrop, 1986. ISBN 0-688-05516-8 Subj: Babies. Emotions – envy, jealousy. Pets.

Fern, Eugene. *Birthday presents* ill. by author. Farrar, 1967. Includes the song Sing me (2 p.) Subj: Birthdays. Songs.

The king who was too busy ill. by author. Ariel, 1966. Subj: Royalty.

The most frightened hero ill. by author. Coward, 1961. Subj: Character traits – bravery. Foreign lands – Scotland.

Pepito's story ill. by author. Ariel, 1960. Subj: Activities – dancing. Character traits – being different. Illness.

What's he been up to now? ill. by author. Dial Pr., 1961. Subj: Animals – elephants. Friendship.

Ferraro, Renato. *Alex, the amazing juggler* (Gianni, Peg)

Ferro, Beatriz. *Caught in the rain* ill. by Michele Sambin. Doubleday, 1980. Subj: Weather – rain.

Fiddle-i-fee: a traditional American chant ill. by Diane Stanley. Little, 1979. Subj: Animals. Cumulative tales. Folk and fairy tales.

Field, Eugene. *Wynken, Blynken and Nod* ill. by Barbara Cooney. Hastings, 1964. Subj: Poetry, rhyme. Sea and seashore. Sleep.

Field, Rachel Lyman. *General store* ill. by Giles Laroche. Little, 1988. ISBN 0-316-28163-8 Subj: Poetry, rhyme. Stores.

General store ill. by Nancy Winslow Parker. Greenwillow, 1988. ISBN 0-688-07354-9 Subj: Poetry, rhyme. Stores.

Prayer for a child ill. by Elizabeth Orton Jones. Macmillan, 1944. Subj: Caldecott award book. Religion.

Fields, Alice. *Insects* ill. by David Hurrell. Watts, 1980. Subj: Insects.

Fife, Dale. *Adam's ABC* ill. by Don Robertson. Coward, 1971. Subj: ABC books. City. Ethnic groups in the U.S. – Afro-Americans.

Follow that ghost! ill. by Joan Drescher. Dutton, 1979. Subj: Ghosts. Problem solving.

The little park ill. by Janet LaSalle. Albert Whitman, 1973. Subj: Animals. Ecology. Progress.

Rosa's special garden ill. by Marie DeJohn. Albert Whitman, 1985. ISBN 0-8075-7115-6 Subj: Activities – gardening. Ethnic groups in the U.S. – Mexican-Americans. Sibling rivalry.

Fifield, Flora. *Pictures for the palace* ill. by Nola Langner. Vanguard, 1957. Subj: Art. Foreign lands – Japan.

Finfer, Celentha. *Grandmother dear* by Celentha Finfer, Esther Wasserberg and Florence Weinberg; ill. by Roy Mathews. Follett, 1966. Subj: Activities – baby-sitting. Family life – grandmothers. Poetry, rhyme.

Fink, Dale Borman. *Mr. Silver and Mrs. Gold* ill. by Shirley Chan. Human Sciences Pr., 1980. Subj: Friendship. Old age.

Fink, Joanne. *Mister North Wind* (De Posadas Mane, Carmen)

Finsand, Mary Jane. *The town that moved* ill. by Reg Sandland. Carolrhoda, 1983. Subj: City. Moving.

Fire ill. by Michael Ricketts. Grosset, 1972. Subj: Fire.

The firebird retold and ill. by Moira Kemp. Godine, 1984. Subj: Behavior – stealing. Folk and fairy tales. Magic. Royalty.

The firebird: *and other Russian fairy tales* ill. by Boris Zvorykin; ed. by Jacqueline Onassis. Viking, 1978. Subj: Folk and fairy tales. Foreign lands – Russia.

Firehouse ill. by Zokeisha; ed. by Kate Klimo. Simon and Schuster, 1983. Subj: Careers – firefighters. Fire. Format, unusual – board books. Houses.

Firmin, Peter. *Basil Brush and a dragon* ill. by author. Prentice-Hall, 1978. Subj: Animals – foxes. Animals – moles. Dragons. Imagination.

Basil Brush and the windmills ill. by author. Prentice-Hall, 1980. Subj: Animals – foxes. Animals – moles. Ecology.

Basil Brush finds treasure ill. by author. Prentice-Hall, 1979. Subj: Animals – foxes. Animals – moles. Seasons – summer.

Basil Brush gets a medal ill. by author. Prentice-Hall, 1978. Subj: Animals – foxes. Animals – moles. Cumulative tales.

Basil Brush goes flying ill. by author. Prentice-Hall, 1977. Subj: Airplanes, airports. Animals – foxes. Animals – moles. Behavior – mistakes. Helicopters.

Chicken stew ill. by author. Merrimack, 1982. Subj: Activities – gardening. Animals – wolves. Birds – chickens.

Noggin and the whale (Postgate, Oliver)

Noggin the king (Postgate, Oliver)

First graces ill. by Tasha Tudor. Walck, 1955. Subj: Poetry, rhyme. Religion.

First prayers ill. by Anna Maria Magagna. Macmillan, 1983. Subj: Poetry, rhyme. Religion.

First prayers ill. by Tasha Tudor. Oxford Univ. Pr., 1952. Subj: Poetry, rhyme. Religion.

Fischer, Hans. *The birthday* ill. by author. Harcourt, 1954. Subj: Animals. Birthdays.

Puss in boots (Perrault, Charles)

Fischer, Vera Kistiakowsky. *One way is down: a book about gravity* ill. by Ward Brackett. Little, 1967. Subj: Concepts – weight. Science.

Fischer-Nagel, Andreas. *A kitten is born* (Fischer-Nagel, Heiderose)

A puppy is born (Fischer-Nagel, Heiderose)

Fischer-Nagel, Heiderose. *A kitten is born* by Heiderose and Andreas Fischer-Nagel; tr. from German by Andrea Mernan; photos. by authors. Putnam's, 1983. Subj: Animals – cats. Science.

A puppy is born by Heiderose and Andreas Fischer-Nagel; tr. from German by Andrea Mernan; photos. by authors. Putnam's, 1985. ISBN 0-399-21234-5 Subj: Animals – dogs. Science.

Fischtrom, Harvey *see* Zemach, Harve

Fischtrom, Margot Zemach *see* Zemach, Margot

Fish, Hans. *Pitschi, the kitten who always wanted to do something else* ill. by author. Harcourt, 1953. Subj: Animals – cats. Behavior – dissatisfaction.

Fish, Helen Dean. *Animals of the Bible* ill. by Dorothy Pulis Lathrop. Lippincott, 1937. Subj: Caldecott award book.

Four and twenty blackbirds ill. by Robert Lawson. Stokes, 1937. Subj: Caldecott award honor book. Nursery rhymes.

When the root children wake up ill. by Sibylle Von Olfers. Green Tiger Pr., 1988. ISBN 0-88138-103-9 Subj: Elves and little people. Seasons – spring.

When the root children wake up ill. by Sibylle Von Olfers. Lippincott, 1930. Subj: Elves and little people. Seasons – spring.

Fisher, Aileen. *And a sunflower grew* ill. by Trina Schart Hyman; lettering by Paul Taylor. Noble, 1977. Subj: Flowers. Plants. Poetry, rhyme. Science.

Anybody home? ill. by Susan Bonners. Crowell, 1980. Subj: Character traits – curiosity. Poetry, rhyme.

Arbor day ill. by Nonny Hogrogian. Crowell, 1965. Subj: Holidays. Trees.

As the leaves fall down ill. by Barbara Smith. Noble, 1977. Subj: Plants. Science. Seasons. Trees.

Best little house ill. by Arnold Spilka. Crowell, 1966. Subj: Houses. Moving. Poetry, rhyme.

Cricket in the thicket ill. by Feodor Rojankovsky. Scribner's, 1963. Subj: Poetry, rhyme.

Do bears have mothers too? ill. by Eric Carle. Crowell, 1973. Subj: Animals. Family life – mothers. Poetry, rhyme.

Going barefoot ill. by Adrienne Adams. Crowell, 1960. Subj: Poetry, rhyme. Seasons.

The house of a mouse ill. by Joan Sandin. Harper, 1988. ISBN 0-06-021849-5 Subj: Animals – mice. Houses. Poetry, rhyme.

I like weather ill. by Janina Domanska. Crowell, 1963. Subj: Animals – dogs. Poetry, rhyme. Weather.

I stood upon a mountain ill. by Blair Lent. Crowell, 1979. Subj: Seasons. World.

I wonder how, I wonder why ill. by Carol Barker. Abelard-Schuman, 1963. Subj: Poetry, rhyme.

In one door and out the other: a book of poems ill. by Lillian Hoban. Crowell, 1969. Subj: Family life. Poetry, rhyme.

In the middle of the night ill. by Adrienne Adams. Crowell, 1965. Subj: Night. Poetry, rhyme.

In the woods, in the meadow, in the sky ill. by Margot Tomes. Scribner's, 1965. Subj: Poetry, rhyme.

Like nothing at all ill. by Leonard Weisgard. Crowell, 1962. Subj: Poetry, rhyme. Science. Seasons.

Listen, rabbit ill. by Symeon Shimin. Crowell, 1964. Subj: Animals – rabbits. Poetry, rhyme.

My first Hanukkah book ill. by Priscilla Kiedrowski. Childrens, 1985. ISBN 0-516-42905-1 Subj: Holidays – Hanukkah. Jewish culture. Poetry, rhyme.

My mother and I ill. by Kazue Mizumura. Crowell, 1967. Subj: Family life – mothers. Poetry, rhyme. Seasons – spring.

Mysteries in the garden ill. by Ati Forberg; lettering by Paul Taylor. Noble, 1977. Subj: Plants. Poetry, rhyme. Science.

Now that spring is here ill. by Symeon Shimin; lettering by Paul Taylor. Noble, 1977. Subj: Plants. Poetry, rhyme. Science. Seasons – spring.

Petals yellow and petals red ill. by Albert John Pucci; lettering by Paul Taylor. Noble, 1977. Subj: Flowers. Poetry, rhyme. Science.

Plant magic ill. by Barbara Cooney; lettering by Paul Taylor. Noble, 1977. Subj: Plants. Poetry, rhyme. Science.

Prize performance ill by Margot Tomes. Noble, 1977. Subj: Plants. Poetry, rhyme. Science.

Rabbits, rabbits ill. by Gail Niemann. Harper, 1983. Subj: Animals – rabbits. Poetry, rhyme.

Seeds on the go ill. by Hans Zander; lettering by Paul Taylor. Noble, 1977. Subj: Plants. Poetry, rhyme. Science.

Sing, little mouse ill. by Symeon Shimin. Crowell, 1969. Subj: Animals – mice. Poetry, rhyme.

Skip around the year ill. by Gioia Fiammenghi. Crowell, 1967. Subj: Holidays. Poetry, rhyme.

Swords and daggers ill. by James Higa; lettering by Paul Taylor. Noble, 1977. Subj: Plants. Poetry, rhyme. Science.

A tree with a thousand uses ill. by James R. Endicott. Noble, 1977. Subj: Poetry, rhyme. Science. Trees.

We went looking ill. by Marie Angel. Crowell, 1968. Subj: Animals. Birds. Insects – ladybugs. Plants. Poetry, rhyme.

When it comes to bugs ill. by Chris and Bruce Degen. Harper, 1986. ISBN 0-06-021822-3 Subj: Insects. Poetry, rhyme. Spiders.

Where does everyone go? ill. by Adrienne Adams. Crowell, 1961. Subj: Animals. Hibernation. Poetry, rhyme. Seasons – winter.

Fisher, Iris L. *Katie-Bo: an adoption story* ill. by Miriam Schaer. Watts, 1988. ISBN 0-915361-91-4 Subj: Adoption. Babies. Ethnic groups in the U.S. Sibling rivalry.

Fisher, Leonard Everett. *Boxes! Boxes!* ill. by author. Viking, 1984. Subj: Concepts. Concepts – color. Counting. Poetry, rhyme.

A head full of hats ill. by author. Dial Pr., 1962. Subj: Clothing.

Look around! a book about shapes ill. by author. Viking, 1987. ISBN 0-670-80869-5 Subj: Concepts – shape. Games.

The Olympians: great gods and goddesses of ancient Greece ill. by author. Holiday, 1984. ISBN 0-8234-0522-2 Subj: Folk and fairy tales. Foreign lands – Greece.

Pumpers, boilers, hooks and ladders: a book of fire engines ill. by author. Dial Pr., 1961. Subj: Careers – firefighters. Trucks.

Pyramid of the sun, pyramid of the moon ill. by author. Macmillan, 1988. ISBN 0-02-735300-1 Subj: Foreign lands – Mexico. Mythical creatures.

The seven days of creation ill. by the author. Holiday, 1981. Adapted from the Bible. Subj: Religion.

Star signs ill. by author. Holiday, 1983. Subj: Folk and fairy tales. Zodiac.

Theseus and the minotaur ill. by author. Holiday, 1988. ISBN 0-8234-0703-9 Subj: Folk and fairy tales. Mythical creatures. Royalty.

The tower of London ill. by author. Macmillan, 1987. ISBN 0-02-735370-2 Subj: Foreign lands – England. Royalty.

Fitch, Florence Mary. *A book about God* ill. by Leonard Weisgard. Lothrop, 1953. Subj: Religion.

Fitter, Richard. *The butterfly ball and the grasshopper's feast* (Aldridge, Alan)

Fitz-Gerald, Christine Maloney. *I can be a reporter* ill. with photos. Childrens Pr., 1986. ISBN 0-516-01899-X Subj: Careers – reporters.

I can be an astronomer ill. with photos. Childrens Pr., 1986. ISBN 0-516-01883-3 Subj: Careers – astronomers.

Fitzgerald, Hugh Captain *see* Baum, L. Frank (Lyman Frank)

Fitzhugh, Louise. *Bang, bang, you're dead* by Louise Fitzhugh and Sandra Scoppetone; ill. by Louise Fitzhugh. Harper, 1969. Subj: Activities – playing. Cowboys. Violence, anti-violence. War. Weapons.

I am five ill. by author. Delacorte, 1978. Subj: Self-concept.

I am three ill. by Susanna Natti. Delacorte, 1982. Subj: Self-concept.

Fitzpatrick, Jean Grasso. *Animals of the forest* (Mora, Emma)

Gideon, the little bear cub (Mora, Emma)

Fitzsimons, Cecilia. *My first birds* ill. by author. Harper, 1985. Subj: Birds. Format, unusual – board books.

My first butterflies ill. by author. Harper, 1985. Subj: Format, unusual – board books. Insects – butterflies, caterpillars.

Flack, Marjorie. *Angus and the cat* ill. by author. Doubleday, 1931. Subj: Animals – cats. Animals – dogs. Character traits – completing things. Character traits – curiosity.

Angus and the ducks ill. by author. Doubleday, 1930. Subj: Animals – dogs. Birds – ducks. Character traits – conceit. Character traits – curiosity.

Angus lost ill. by author. Doubleday, 1932. Subj: Animals – dogs. Behavior – lost. Seasons – winter.

Ask Mr. Bear ill. by author. Macmillan, 1932. Subj: Animals. Animals – bears. Birthdays. Emotions – love. Family life – mothers.

The boats on the river ill. by author. Viking, 1946. Subj: Boats, ships. Caldecott award honor book. Rivers.

The new pet ill. by author. Doubleday, 1943. Subj: Babies. Family life.

The restless robin ill. by author. Houghton, 1937. Subj: Birds – robins. Music.

The story about Ping ill. by Kurt Wiese. Viking, 1933. Subj: Behavior – misbehavior. Birds – ducks. Foreign lands – China.

Tim Tadpole and the great bullfrog ill. by author. Doubleday, 1934. Subj: Frogs and toads.

Wait for William ill. by Marjorie Flack and Richard A. Holberg. Houghton, 1934. Subj: Circus. Family life. Parades.

William and his kitten ill. by author. Houghton, 1938. Subj: Animals – cats.

Flanagan, Ellen *see* Raskin, Ellen

Flanders, Michael. *Creatures great and small* ill. by Marcello Minale. Holt, 1965. Subj: Animals. Birds. Poetry, rhyme.

Fleischman, Paul. *The animal hedge* ill. by Lydia Dabcovich. Dutton, 1983. Subj: Activities – working. Farms. Folk and fairy tales.

The birthday tree ill. by Marcia Sewall. Harper, 1979. Subj: Birthdays. Trees.

Rondo in C ill. by Janet Wentworth. Harper, 1988. ISBN 0-06-021857-6 Subj: Imagination. Music. Poetry, rhyme.

Fleischman, Sid. *Kate's secret riddle* ill. by Barbara Bottner. Watts, 1977. Subj: Illness. Riddles.

Longbeard the wizard ill. by Charles Bragg. Little, 1970. Subj: Royalty. Wizards.

The scarebird ill. by Peter Sis. Greenwillow, 1988. ISBN 0-688-07317-4 Subj: Character traits – kindness. Farms. Friendship. Scarecrows.

Fleisher, Robbin. *Quilts in the attic* ill. by Ati Forberg. Macmillan, 1978. Subj: Family life. Games.

Fleishman, Seymour. *Too hot in Potzburg* ill. by author. Walker, 1981. Subj: Animals – bears. Machines.

Fletcher, Elizabeth. *The little goat* ill. by Deborah and Kilmeny Niland. Grosset, 1977. Subj: Animals – goats. Behavior – lost.

What am I? ill. by Deborah and Kilmeny Niland. Grosset, 1977. Subj: Animals. Riddles.

Flora, James. *The day the cow sneezed* ill. by author. Harcourt, 1957. Subj: Animals. Cumulative tales. Humor.

Fishing with dad ill. by author. Harcourt, 1967. Subj: Boats, ships. Careers – fishermen.

Grandpa's farm: 4 tall tales ill. by author. Harcourt, 1965. Subj: Family life – grandfathers. Farms. Humor.

Grandpa's ghost stories ill. by author. Atheneum. Subj: Family life – grandfathers. Ghosts. Witches.

Leopold, the see-through crumbpicker ill. by author. Harcourt, 1961. Subj: Monsters. Zoos.

My friend Charlie ill. by author. Harcourt, 1964. Subj: Humor.

Sherwood walks home ill. by author. Harcourt, 1966. Subj: Toys – teddy bears.

Florian, Douglas. *Airplane ride* ill. by author. Crowell, 1984. Subj: Activities – flying. Airplanes, airports.

A bird can fly ill. by author. Greenwillow, 1980. Subj: Animals. Science.

The city ill. by author. Crowell, 1982. Subj: City. Wordless.

People working ill. by author. Crowell, 1983. Subj: Activities – working. Careers.

A summer day ill. by author. Greenwillow, 1988. ISBN 0-688-07565-7 Subj: Activities – vacationing. Counting. Family life.

Flory, Jane. *The bear on the doorstep* ill. by Carolyn Croll. Houghton, 1980. Subj: Animals – bears. Animals – rabbits. Houses.

The unexpected grandchild ill. by Carolyn Croll. Houghton, 1977. Subj: Behavior – sharing. Family life – grandparents.

We'll have a friend for lunch ill. by Carolyn Croll. Houghton, 1974. Subj: Animals – cats. Food. Friendship.

Flot, Jeannette B. *Princess Kalina and the hedgehog* adapt. by Frances Marshall; ill. by Dorothée Duntze. Faber, 1981. Subj: Animals – hedgehogs. Character traits – cleanliness. Folk and fairy tales. Magic. Royalty.

Flöthe, Louise Lee. *The Indian and his pueblo* ill. by Richard Floethe. Scribner's, 1960. Subj: Indians of North America.

Flournoy, Valerie. *The best time of day* ill. by George Ford. Random House, 1979. Subj: Activities. Ethnic groups in the U.S. – Afro-Americans. Family life.

The patchwork quilt ill. by Jerry Pinkney. Dial Pr., 1985. ISBN 0-8037-0098-9 Subj: Ethnic groups in the U.S. – Afro-Americans. Family life – grandmothers.

The twins strike back ill. by Diane de Groat. Dial Pr., 1980. Subj: Ethnic groups in the U.S. – Afro-Americans. Family life. Sibling rivalry. Twins.

Flower, Phyllis. *Barn owl* ill. by Cherryl Pape. Harper, 1978. Subj: Birds – owls. Science.

Floyd, Lucy. *Agatha's alphabet, with her very own dictionary* ill. by Dora Leder. Rand McNally, 1975. Subj: ABC books. Dictionaries.

Foley, Bernice Williams. *The gazelle and the hunter: a folk tale from Persia* ill. by Diana Magnuson. Children's Pr., 1980. Subj: Folk and fairy tales. Foreign lands – Persia.

A walk among clouds: a folk tale from China ill. by Mina Gow McLean. Children's Pr., 1980. Subj: Folk and fairy tales. Foreign lands – China.

Folsom, Marcia. *Easy as pie: a guessing game of sayings* by Marcia and Michael Folsom; ill. by Jack Kent. Houghton, 1985. Subj: Humor. Language.

Folsom, Mary Elting *see* Elting, Mary

Folsom, Michael. *Easy as pie* (Folsom, Marcia)

Q is for duck (Elting, Mary)

Fontaine, Jan. *The spaghetti tree* ill. by Anne Marshall Runyon. Talespinner, 1980. Subj: Activities – gardening. Food. Imagination.

Fontaine, Jean de La *see* La Fontaine, Jean de

Fontane, Theodore. *Sir Ribbeck of Ribbeck of Havelland* tr. from German by Elizabeth Shub; ill. by Nonny Hogrogian. Macmillan, 1969. Subj: Character traits – generosity. Poetry, rhyme.

Ford, George. *Walk on!* (Williamson, Mel)

Ford, Lauren. *The ageless story* ill. by author. Dodd, 1940. Subj: Caldecott award honor book.

Foreman, Michael. *Ben's baby* ill. by author. Harper, 1988. ISBN 0-06-021844-4 Subj: Babies. Family life.

Cat and canary ill. by author. Dial Pr., 1985. Subj: Animals – cats. Birds – canaries.

The general (Charters, Janet)

Land of dreams ill. by author. Holt, 1982. Subj: Dreams.

Moose ill. by author. Pantheon, 1972. Subj: Animals – bears. Animals – moose. Birds – eagles. Violence, anti-violence.

Panda and the bushfire ill. by author. Prentice-Hall, 1986. ISBN 0-13-648395-X Subj: Animals. Animals – pandas. Fire. Foreign lands – Australia. Mythical creatures.

The two giants ill. by author. Pantheon, 1967. Subj: Giants.

War and peas ill by author. Crowell, 1974. Subj: Royalty. War.

Forest, Charlotte B. De *see* DeForest, Charlotte B.

Forest, Heather. *The baker's dozen* ill. by Susan Graber. Harcourt, 1988. ISBN 0-15-200412-2 Subj: Careers – bakers. Folk and fairy tales.

Forrester, Victoria. *The magnificent moo* ill. by author. Atheneum, 1983. Subj: Animals – bulls, cows. Animals – cats. Noise, sounds.

Oddward ill. by author. Atheneum, 1982. Subj: Holidays. Reptiles – snakes.

Poor Gabriella: a Christmas story ill. by Susan Boulet. Atheneum, 1986. ISBN 0-689-31266-0 Subj: Holidays – Christmas. Religion.

The touch said hello ill. by author. Atheneum, 1982. Subj: Seasons – spring.

Words to keep against the night ill. by author. Atheneum, 1983. Subj: Poetry, rhyme.

Fort, Patrick. *Redbird* ill. by author. Watts, 1988. ISBN 0-531-05746-1 Subj: Activities – flying. Airplanes, airports. Format, unusual.

Foster, Doris Van Liew. *A pocketful of seasons* ill. by Tälivaldis Stubis. Lothrop, 1961. Subj: Behavior – saving things. Seasons.

Tell me, Mr. Owl ill. by Helen Stone. Lothrop, 1957. Subj: Birds – owls. Holidays – Halloween.

Foster, Margaret Rumer Godden *see* Godden, Rumer

Foster, Marian Curtis *see* Mariana

Foster, Rumer Godden *see* Godden, Rumer

Foster, Sally. *A pup grows up* photos. by author. Dodd, 1984. Subj: Animals – dogs. Pets.

Foulds, Elfrida Vipont. *The elephant and the bad baby* ill. by Raymond Briggs. Coward, 1986, 1969. ISBN 0-698-20039-X Subj: Animals – elephants. Babies. Behavior – stealing. Cumulative tales.

Fournier, Catharine. *The coconut thieves* ill. by Janina Domanska. Scribner's, 1964. Subj: Animals. Folk and fairy tales. Foreign lands – Africa.

Fowler, Mary Jane see Wheeler, M. J.

Fowler, Richard. *Cat's story* ill. by author. Grosset, 1985. Subj: Animals – cats. Format, unusual – board books. Poetry, rhyme.

Inspector Smart gets the message! ill. by author. Little, 1983. Subj: Birthdays. Problem solving.

Mr. Little's noisy car ill. by author. Grosset, 1986. ISBN 0-448-18977-1 Subj: Animals. Automobiles. Format, unusual – toy and movable books. Noise, sounds.

Fowles, John. *Cinderella* (Perrault, Charles)

Fox, Charles Philip. *Come to the circus* photos. by author. Reilly and Lee, 1960. Subj: Circus.

A fox in the house photos. by author. Reilly and Lee, 1960. Subj: Animals – foxes.

Mr. Stripes the gopher photos. by author. Reilly and Lee, 1962. Subj: Animals. Family life. Seasons.

Fox, Dorothea Warren. *Follow me the leader* ill. by author. Parents, 1968. Subj: Games. Poetry, rhyme.

Fox, Mem. *Hattie and the fox* ill. by Patricia Mullins. Bradbury Pr., 1987. ISBN 0-02-735470-9 Subj: Animals. Birds – chickens. Cumulative tales. Farms.

Possum magic ill. by Julie Vivas. Abingdon, 1987. ISBN 0-687-31732-0 Subj: Activities – traveling. Animals – possums. Behavior – wishing. Food. Foreign lands – Australia.

Wilfrid Gordon McDonald Partridge ill. by Julie Vivas. Kane Miller, 1985. ISBN 0-916291-04-9 Subj: Behavior – forgetfulness. Old age.

With love, at Christmas ill. by Gary Lippincott. Abingdon Pr., 1988. ISBN 0-687-45863-3 Subj: Character traits – generosity. Death. Holidays – Christmas.

Fox, Paula. *Maurice's room* ill. by Ingrid Fetz. Macmillan, 1966. Subj: Behavior – collecting things.

Fox, Siv Cedering. *The blue horse and other night poems* ill. by Donald Carrick. Seabury Pr., 1979. Subj: Bedtime. Poetry, rhyme.

The fox went out on a chilly night ill. by Peter Spier. Doubleday, 1961. Subj: Animals – foxes. Caldecott award honor book. Folk and fairy tales. Songs. Toys – teddy bears.

Fradon, Dana. *Sir Dana - a knight: as told by his trusty armor* ill. by author. Dutton, 1988. ISBN 0-525-44424-6 Subj: Knights. Middle ages. Museums.

Frances, Esteban. *The thread soldiers* (Heathers, Anne)

Francis, Anna B. *Pleasant dreams* ill. by author. Holt, 1983. Subj: Dreams. Monsters. Toys.

Francis, Dee see Haas, Dorothy

Francis, Frank. *The magic wallpaper* ill. by author. Abelard-Schuman, 1970. Subj: Animals. Behavior – lost. Dreams. Imagination.

Natasha's new doll ill. by author. O'Hara, 1971. Subj: Folk and fairy tales. Foreign lands – Russia. Toys – dolls. Witches.

Françoise see Seignobosc, Françoise

Frank, Josette. *More poems to read to the very young* ill. by Dagmar Wilson. Random House, 1968. Subj: Poetry, rhyme.

Poems to read to the very young ill. by Dagmar Wilson. Random House, 1988. ISBN 0-394-99768-9 Subj: Poetry, rhyme.

Frankel, Bernice. *Half-As-Big and the tiger* ill. by Leonard Weisgard. Watts, 1961. Subj: Animals – deer. Animals – tigers. Character traits – cleverness.

Frankenberg, Lloyd. *Wings of rhyme* ill. by Alan Benjamin. Funk & Wagnalls, 1967. Subj: Nursery rhymes. Poetry, rhyme.

Franklin, Paula. *Killian and the dragons* (Company González, Mercè)

Franklin, Sheila. *Egyptian art from the Brooklyn Museum: ABC* (Mayers, Florence Cassen)

The Museum of Fine Arts, Boston: ABC (Mayers, Florence Cassen)

The Museum of Modern Art, New York: ABC (Mayers, Florence Cassen)

The National Air and Space Museum: ABC (Mayers, Florence Cassen)

Frascino, Edward. *My cousin the king* ill. by author. Prentice-Hall, 1985. ISBN 0-13-608423-0 Subj: Animals. Animals – cats. Character traits – cleverness. Character traits – vanity.

Nanny Noony and the magic spell ill. by author. Pippin Pr., 1988. ISBN 0-945912-00-5 Subj: Animals – cats. Birds – crows. Farms. Magic. Witches.

Frasconi, Antonio. *See again, say again: a picture book in four languages* ill. by author. Harcourt, 1964. Subj: Foreign languages.

See and say: a picture book in four languages ill. by author. Harcourt, 1955. Subj: Foreign languages.

The snow and the sun, la nieve y el sol: a South American folk rhyme in two languages ill. by author. Harcourt, 1961. Subj: Folk and fairy tales. Foreign lands – South America. Foreign languages. Poetry, rhyme.

Fraser, Ferrin. *Jungle animals* (Buck, Frank)

Fraser, James Howard. *Los Posadas: a Christmas story* ill. by Nick De Grazia. Northland, 1963. Subj: Ethnic groups in the U.S. – Mexican-Americans. Foreign lands – Mexico. Holidays – Christmas. Religion.

Fraser, Kathleen. *Adam's world, San Francisco* ill. by Helen D. Hipshman. Albert Whitman, 1971. Subj: City. Ethnic groups in the U.S. – Afro-Americans. Family life.

Fraser, Phyllis Maurine. *Mother Goose*

Frederick, Dick *see* Day, Michael E.

Freedman, Florence B. *Brothers: a Hebrew legend* ill. by Robert Andrew Parker. Harper, 1985. ISBN 0-06-021872-X Subj: Emotions – love. Family life – brothers. Folk and fairy tales. Jewish culture.

Freedman, Russell. *Dinosaurs and their young* ill. by Leslie Morrill. Holiday, 1983. Subj: Dinosaurs.

Farm babies photos. by author. Holiday, 1981. Subj: Animals. Farms.

Hanging on: how animals carry their young ill. by author. Holiday, 1977. Subj: Animals. Science.

Tooth and claw: a look at animal weapons photos. by author. Holiday, 1980. Subj: Animals. Science.

When winter comes ill. by Pamela Johnson. Dutton, 1981. Subj: Animals. Science. Seasons – winter.

Freedman, Sally. *Devin's new bed* ill. by Robin Oz. Albert Whitman, 1986. ISBN 0-8075-1565-5 Subj: Bedtime. Behavior – growing up.

Monster birthday party ill. by Diane Dawson. Albert Whitman, 1983. Subj: Birthdays. Monsters. Parties.

Freeman, Don. *Add-a-line alphabet* ill. by author. Golden Gate, 1968. Subj: ABC books. Animals.

Beady Bear ill. by author. Viking, 1954. Subj: Behavior – running away. Toys – teddy bears.

Bearymore ill. by author. Viking, 1976. Subj: Animals – bears. Circus. Hibernation.

The chalk box story ill. by author. Lippincott, 1976. Subj: Activities – painting. Concepts – color.

Come again, pelican ill. by author. Viking, 1961. Subj: Birds – pelicans. Sea and seashore.

Corduroy ill. by author. Viking, 1968. Subj: Clothing. Emotions – love. Ethnic groups in the U.S. – Afro-Americans. Stores. Toys – teddy bears.

Corduroy's party ill. by Lisa McCue. Viking, 1985. ISBN 0-670-80520-3 Subj: Birthdays. Format, unusual – board books. Parties. Toys. Toys – teddy bears.

Cyrano the crow ill. by author. Viking, 1960. Subj: Birds – crows.

Dandelion ill. by author. Viking, 1964. Subj: Animals – lions. Character traits – appearance. Parties. Weather – rain.

The day is waiting ill. by author; words by Linda Z. Knab. Viking, 1980. ISBN 0-670-71820-3 Subj: Activities. Poetry, rhyme.

Fly high, fly low ill. by author. Viking, 1957. Subj: Birds. Caldecott award honor book. City.

Forever laughter ill. by author. Golden Gate, 1970. Subj: Clowns, jesters. Humor. Royalty. Wordless.

The guard mouse ill. by author. Viking, 1967. Subj: Animals – mice. Birthdays. City. Foreign lands – England.

Hattie the backstage bat ill. by author. Viking, 1970. Subj: Animals – bats. Theater.

Mop Top ill. by author. Viking, 1955. Subj: Birthdays. Careers – barbers. Hair. Poetry, rhyme.

The night the lights went out ill. by author. Viking, 1958. Subj: Careers. Night. Power failure. Seasons – winter.

Norman the doorman ill. by author. Viking, 1959. Subj: Animals – mice. Art. Museums.

The paper party ill. by author. Viking, 1974. Subj: Imagination. Parties. Puppets.

A pocket for Corduroy ill. by author. Viking, 1978. Subj: Clothing. Ethnic groups in the U.S. – Afro-Americans. Laundry. Toys – teddy bears.

Quiet! There's a canary in the library ill. by author. Golden Gate, 1969. Subj: Birds – canaries. Emotions – embarrassment. Imagination. Libraries.

A rainbow of my own ill. by author. Viking, 1966. Subj: Concepts – color. Weather – rainbows.

The seal and the slick ill. by author. Viking, 1974. Subj: Animals – seals. Character traits – kindness to animals. Ecology. Oil.

Ski pup ill. by author. Viking, 1963. Subj: Animals – dogs. Foreign lands – Switzerland. Sports – skiing.

Space witch ill. by author. Viking, 1959. Subj: Holidays – Halloween. Space and space ships. Witches.

Tilly Witch ill. by author. Viking, 1969. Subj: Character traits – meanness. Holidays – Halloween. Witches.

The turtle and the dove ill. by author. Viking, 1964. Subj: Birds – doves. Reptiles – turtles, tortoises.

Will's quill ill. by author. Viking, 1975. Subj: Birds – geese. Foreign lands – England. Shakespeare. Theater.

Freeman, Grace R. *Inside the Synagogue* (Sugarman, Joan G.)

Freeman, Ira. *The sun, the moon and the stars* (Freeman, Mae)

You will go to the moon (Freeman, Mae)

Freeman, Jean Todd. *Cynthia and the unicorn* ill. by Leonard Weisgard. Norton, 1967. Subj: Holidays – Christmas. Mythical creatures. Poetry, rhyme.

Freeman, Lydia. *Corduroy's day* ill. by Lisa McCue. Viking, 1985. ISBN 0-670-80521-1 Subj: Counting. Format, unusual – board books. Toys – teddy bears.

Pet of the Met ill. by Don Freeman. Viking, 1953. Subj: Animals – mice. Music. Theater.

Freeman, Mae. *The sun, the moon and the stars* by Mae and Ira Freeman; ill. by René Martin. Rev. ed. Random House, 1979. Subj: Moon. Science. Stars. Sun.

You will go to the moon ill. by Lee J. Ames. Rev. ed. Random House, 1971. Subj: Moon. Space and space ships.

Fregosi, Claudia. *The happy horse* ill. by author. Greenwillow, 1977. Subj: Animals – horses. Seasons – fall.

The pumpkin sparrow: adapt. from a Korean folktale ill. by author. Morrow, 1977. Subj: Birds – sparrows. Folk and fairy tales. Foreign lands – Korea.

Snow maiden ill. by author. Prentice-Hall, 1979. Subj: Folk and fairy tales. Foreign lands – Russia.

Fremlin, Robert. *Three friends* ill. by Wallace Tripp. Little, 1975. Subj: Animals – cats. Animals – pigs. Animals – squirrels. Circus. Clothing. Friendship. Problem solving.

French, Fiona. *The blue bird* ill. by author. Walck, 1972. Subj: Birds.

Hunt the thimble ill. by author. Oxford Univ. Pr., 1978. Subj: Games. Participation.

French, Paul *see* Asimov, Isaac

Freschet, Berniece. *The ants go marching* ill. by Stefan Martin. Scribner's, 1973. Subj: Activities – picnicking. Counting. Insects – ants. Poetry, rhyme.

Bear mouse ill. by Donald Carrick. Scribner's, 1973. Subj: Animals – mice. Science.

Bernard of Scotland Yard ill. by Gina Freschet. Scribner's, 1978. Subj: Animals – mice. Foreign lands – England. Problem solving.

Elephant and friends ill. by Glen Rounds. Scribner's, 1978. Subj: Animals – elephants. Character traits – cleverness.

Five fat raccoons ill. by Irene Brady. Scribner's, 1980. Subj: Animals – raccoons.

Furlie Cat ill. by Betsy Lewin. Lothrop, 1986. ISBN 0-688-05918-X Subj: Animals – cats. Behavior – bullying. Emotions – fear.

The little woodcock ill. by Leonard Weisgard. Scribner's, 1967. Subj: Birds. Science.

Moose baby ill. by Jim Arnosky. Putnam's, 1979. Subj: Animals – moose. Science.

The old bullfrog ill. by Roger Antoine Duvoisin. Scribner's, 1968. Subj: Frogs and toads.

Owl in the garden ill. by Carol Newsom. Lothrop, 1985. ISBN 0-688-04048-9 Subj: Animals. Behavior – stealing. Birds. Birds – owls. Seasons – fall.

Possum baby ill. by Jim Arnosky. Putnam's, 1978. Subj: Animals – possums.

Turtle pond ill. by Donald Carrick. Scribner's, 1971. Subj: Reptiles – turtles, tortoises.

The watersnake ill. by Susanne Suba. Scribner's, 1979. Subj: Reptiles – snakes.

The web in the grass ill. by Roger Antoine Duvoisin. Scribner's, 1972. Subj: Spiders.

Where's Henrietta's hen? ill. by Lorinda Bryan Cauley. Putnam's, 1980. Subj: Animals. Birds – chickens. Counting. Farms.

Wood duck baby ill. by Jim Arnosky. Putnam's, 1983. Subj: Birds – ducks. Science.

Freudberg, Judy. *Some, more, most* ill. by Richard Hefter. Larousse, 1976. Subj: Concepts.

Susan and Gordon adopt a baby by Judy Freudberg and Tony Geiss; ill. by Joseph Mathieu. Random House, 1986. ISBN 0-394-98341-6 Subj: Adoption. Family life. Sibling rivalry.

Fribourg, Marjorie G. *Ching-Ting and the ducks* ill. by Artur Marokvia. Sterling, 1957. Subj: Behavior – growing up. Birds – ducks. Foreign lands – China.

Friedman, Estelle. *Boy who lived in a cave* ill. by Theresa Sherman. Putnam's, 1960. Subj: Caves. Family life. Houses.

Friedman, Ina R. *How my parents learned to eat* ill. by Allen Say. Houghton, 1984. Subj: Family life.

Friedman, Judi. *The eels' strange journey* ill. by Gail Owens. Crowell, 1976. Subj: Fish. Science.

Noises in the woods ill. by John Hamberger. Dutton, 1979. Subj: Forest, woods. Noise, sounds.

Friedman, Warner. *Uncle Hugh* (Gelman, Rita Golden)

Friedrich, Otto. *The Easter bunny that overslept* (Friedrich, Priscilla)

The marshmallow ghosts (Friedrich, Priscilla)

The wishing well in the woods (Friedrich, Priscilla)

Friedrich, Priscilla. *The Easter bunny that overslept* by Priscilla and Otto Friedrich; ill. by Adrienne Adams. Lothrop, 1957. Subj: Holidays – Easter.

The marshmallow ghosts by Priscilla and Otto Friedrich; ill. by Louis Slobodkin. Lothrop, 1960. Subj: Ghosts. Holidays – Halloween.

The wishing well in the woods by Priscilla and Otto Friedrich; ill. by Roger Antoine Duvoisin. Lothrop, 1961. Subj: Animals. Behavior – wishing.

The friendly beasts and A partridge in a pear tree ill. by Virginia Parsons; calligraphy by Sheila Waters. Doubleday, 1977. Subj: Holidays – Christmas. Music. Religion. Songs.

Friskey, Margaret. *Birds we know* ill. with photos. Children's Pr., 1981. Subj: Birds. Science.

Chicken Little, count-to-ten ill. by Katherine Evans. Children's Pr., 1946. Subj: Counting.

Indian Two Feet and his eagle feather ill. by John and Lucy Hawkinson. Children's Pr., 1967. Subj: Indians of North America.

Indian Two Feet and his horse ill. by Katherine Evans. Children's Pr., 1959. Subj: Animals – horses. Indians of North America.

Indian Two Feet and the wolf cubs ill. by John Hawkinson. Children's Pr., 1971. Subj: Animals – wolves. Indians of North America.

Indian Two Feet rides alone ill. by John Hawkinson. Children's Pr., 1980. Subj: Character traits – pride. Indians of North America.

Mystery of the gate sign ill. by Katherine Evans. Children's Pr., 1958. Subj: Activities – reading. Animals – rabbits.

Seven diving ducks ill. by Jean Morey. Children's Pr., 1965. Subj: Birds – ducks. Counting.

Three sides and the round one ill. by Mary Gehr. Children's Pr., 1973. Subj: Concepts – shape.

Friskey, Margaret Richards *see* Friskey, Margaret

Frith, Michael K. *I'll teach my dog 100 words* ill. by P. D. Eastman. Random House, 1973. Subj: Animals – dogs. Humor. Poetry, rhyme.

Some of us walk, some fly, some swim ill. by author. Random House, 1971. Subj: Animals. Science.

Fritz, Jean. *The good giants and the bad Pukwudgies* ill. by Tomie de Paola. Putnam's, 1982. Subj: Indians of North America. Folk and fairy tales. Giants.

A frog he would a-wooing go (folk-song). *Frog went a-courtin'* adapt. by John M. Langstaff, ill. by Feodor Rojankovsky. Harcourt, 1955. Subj: Caldecott award book. Frogs and toads. Humor. Songs.

Froggie went a-courting retold and ill. by Chris Conover. Farrar, 1986. ISBN 0-374-32466-2 Subj: Animals. Frogs and toads. Music. Songs. Weddings.

From King Boggen's hall to nothing-at-all: *a collection of improbable houses and unusual places found in traditional rhymes and limericks* ill. by Blair Lent. Little, 1967. Subj: Animals. Humor. Nursery rhymes.

From morn to midnight sel. by Elaine Moss; ill. by Satomi Ichikawa. Crowell, 1977. ISBN 0-690-01394-9 Subj: Poetry, rhyme.

Froman, Robert. *Angles are easy as pie* ill. by Byron Barton. Crowell, 1976. Subj: Concepts.

A game of functions ill. by Enrico Arno. Crowell, 1975. Subj: Concepts.

Seeing things: a book of poems ill. by author; lettering by Ray Barber. Crowell, 1974. Subj: Concepts. Poetry, rhyme.

Froment, Eugène. *The story of a round loaf* adapt. and ill. by Kathleen Rebek. Prentice-Hall, 1979. Subj: Behavior – misbehavior. Foreign lands – France.

Fromm, Lilo. *Muffel and Plums* ill. by author. Macmillan, 1972. Subj: Animals. Wordless.

Frost, Erica *see* Supraner, Robyn

Frost, Robert. *Stopping by woods on a snowy evening* ill. by Susan Jeffers. Dutton, 1978. Subj: Forest, woods. Poetry, rhyme. Seasons – winter.

Fry, Christopher. *The boat that mooed* ill. by Leonard Weisgard. Macmillan, 1965. Subj: Boats, ships. Weather – fog.

The boy and the magic (Colette)

Frye, Dean. *Days of sunshine, days of rain* ill. by Roger Antoine Duvoisin. McGraw-Hill, 1965. Subj: Theater. Weather.

Fuchs, Erich. *Journey to the moon* ill. by author. Delacorte Pr., 1969. Translation of Hier Apollo 11. Subj: Moon. Space and space ships. Wordless.

Fuchshuber, Annegert. *Giant story - Mouse tale: a half picture book* ill. by author. Carolrhoda Books, 1988. ISBN 0-87614-319-2 Subj: Animals – mice. Character traits – bravery. Format, unusual. Friendship. Giants.

The wishing hat ill. by author. Morrow, 1977. Translation of Korbinian mit dem Wunschhut by Elizabeth D. Crawford. Subj: Behavior – wishing. Humor. Magic.

Fujikawa, Gyo. *Come follow me...to the secret world of elves and fairies and gnomes and trolls* ill. by author. Grosset, 1979. Subj: Elves and little people. Fairies. Poetry, rhyme. Trolls.

Gyo Fujikawa's A to Z picture book ill. by author. Grosset, 1974. Subj: ABC books.

Let's grow a garden ill. by author. Grosset, 1978. Subj: Activities – gardening. Format, unusual – board books.

Millie's secret ill. by author. Grosset, 1978. Subj: Animals – dogs. Format, unusual – board books. Wordless.

My favorite thing ill. by author. Grosset, 1978. Subj: Activities. Format, unusual – board books. Wordless.

Sam's all-wrong day ill. by author. Grosset, 1982. Subj: Behavior – bad day.

Shags finds a kitten ill. by author. Grosset, 1983. Subj: Animals – cats. Animals – dogs. Emotions – loneliness.

Surprise! Surprise! ill. by author. Grosset, 1978. Subj: Activities. Format, unusual – board books.

That's not fair! ill. by author. Grosset, 1983. Subj: Activities – playing. Seasons – winter.

Fujita, Tamao. *The boy and the bird* tr. from Japanese by Kiyoko Tucker; ill. by Chiyo Ono. Harper, 1972. Subj: Birds. Character traits – freedom. Foreign lands – Japan. Pets.

Funai, Mamoru. *Moke and Poki in the rain forest* ill. by author. Harper, 1972. Subj: Elves and little people. Hawaii.

Funakoshi, Canna. *One evening* tr. and ill. by Yohji Izawa. Picture Book Studio, 1988. ISBN 0-88708-063-4 Subj: Night. Seasons – winter. Weather – snow.

One morning ill. by Yohji Izawa. Picture Book Studio, 1986. ISBN 0-88707-033-2 Subj: Animals – cats. Morning.

Funazaki, Yasuko. *Baby owl* ill. by Shuji Tateishi. Methune, 1980. Subj: Birds – owls. Emotions – loneliness.

Funk, Thompson *see* Funk, Tom

Funk, Tom. *I read signs* ill. by author. Holiday, 1962. Subj: Activities – reading.

Furchgott, Terry. *Phoebe and the hot water bottles* by Terry Furchgott and Linda Dawson; ill. by Terry Furchgott. Elsevier-Dutton, 1979. Subj: Animals – dogs. Character traits – bravery. Pets.

Furtado, Jo. *Sorry, Miss Folio!* ill. by Frederic Joos. Kane Miller, 1988. ISBN 0-916291-18-9 Subj: Activities – reading. Imagination. Libraries.

Fussenegger, Gertrud. *Noah's ark* ill. by Annegert Fuchshuber. Lippincott, 1987. Tr. of Die Arche Noah by Anthea Bell. ISBN 0-397-32242-9 Subj: Animals. Boats, ships. Religion – Noah.

Futamata, Eigorō. *How not to catch a mouse* ill. by author. Weatherhill, 1972. Translation of Nezumi wa tsukamaru ka. Subj: Animals. Animals – mice.

Fyleman, Rose. *A fairy went a-marketing* ill. by Jamichael Henterly. Dutton, 1986. ISBN 0-525-44258-8 Subj: Character traits – kindness. Fairies. Poetry, rhyme. Shopping.

Fyson, Nance Lui. *A family in China* ill. with photos. Lerner, 1985. Orig. published by A & C Black, dist. by Global Library Mktg. Services, 1982 under the title: Chun Ling in China. Subj: Foreign lands – China.

Gackenbach, Dick. *Annie and the mud monster* ill. by author. Lothrop, 1982. Subj: Parties.

Arabella and Mr. Crack ill. by author. Macmillan, 1982. A retelling of Joseph Jacob's Master of all masters. Subj: Behavior – misunderstanding. Folk and fairy tales.

A bag full of pups ill. by author. Houghton, 1981. Subj: Animals – dogs.

Binky gets a car ill. by author. Houghton, 1983. Subj: Behavior – carelessness. Birthdays.

Claude and Pepper ill. by author. Coward, 1976. Subj: Animals – dogs. Behavior – running away.

Claude the dog ill. by author. Seabury Pr., 1974. Subj: Animals – dogs. Behavior – sharing. Holidays – Christmas.

Crackle, Gluck and the sleeping toad ill. by author. Seabury Pr., 1979. Subj: Behavior – lying. Farms. Frogs and toads.

The dog and the deep dark woods ill. by author. Harper, 1984. Subj: Animals – dogs. Character traits – pride.

Dog for a day ill. by author. Clarion, 1987. ISBN 0-899-19452-4 Subj: Animals – dogs. Machines.

Harry and the terrible whatzit ill. by author. Seabury Pr., 1977. Subj: Emotions – fear. Imagination. Monsters.

Harvey, the foolish pig ill. by author. Clarion, 1988. ISBN 0-89919-540-7 Subj: Animals – pigs. Animals – wolves. Character traits – foolishness. Character traits – luck. Royalty.

Hattie be quiet, Hattie be good ill. by author. Harper, 1977. Subj: Animals – rabbits. Behavior. Illness.

Hattie rabbit ill. by author. Harper, 1971. Subj: Animals – rabbits. Behavior – wishing.

Hurray for Hattie Rabbit! ill. by author. Harper, 1986. ISBN 0-06-021983-1 Subj: Animals – pigs. Animals – rabbits. Family life – mothers.

Ida Fanfanny ill. by author. Harper, 1978. Subj: Magic. Seasons. Weather.

King Wacky ill. by author. Crown, 1984. Subj: Behavior – misunderstanding. Royalty.

Little bug ill. by author. Houghton, 1981. Subj: Behavior – seeking better things. Insects.

Mag the magnificent ill. by author. Clarion, 1985. ISBN 0-89919-339-0 Subj: Imagination. Monsters.

Mr. Wink and his shadow, Ned ill. by author. Harper, 1983. Subj: Shadows.

Mother Rabbit's son Tom ill. by author. Harper, 1978. Subj: Animals – rabbits. Behavior – dissatisfaction. Food. Pets.

Pepper and all the legs ill. by author. Seabury Pr., 1978. Subj: Animals – dogs. Behavior – misbehavior.

The perfect mouse: a Japanese tale ill. by author. Macmillan, 1984. Subj: Animals – mice. Folk and fairy tales. Foreign lands – Japan.

The pig who saw everything ill. by author. Seabury Pr., 1978. Subj: Animals – pigs. Character traits – curiosity. Farms. Humor.

Poppy the panda ill. by author. Houghton, 1984. Subj: Bedtime. Clothing. Toys.

Supposes ill. by author. Harcourt, 1989. ISBN 0-15-200594-3 Subj: Animals. Imagination. Riddles.

What's Claude doing? ill. by author. Houghton, 1984. Subj: Animals – dogs. Illness.

Gadsby, Oliver. *Little Elephant and Big Mouse* (Cantieni, Benita)

Gaeddert, Lou Ann Bigge. *Noisy Nancy Nora* ill. by Gioia Fiammenghi. Doubleday, 1965. Subj: Behavior. Noise, sounds.

Gág, Flavia. *Chubby's first year* ill. by author. Holt, 1960. Subj: Animals – cats. Days of the week, months of the year.

Gág, Wanda. *ABC bunny* ill. by author; hand lettered by Howard Gág. Doubleday, 1965. Subj: ABC books. Animals – rabbits. Poetry, rhyme.

The earth gnome (Grimm, Jacob)

The funny thing ill. by author. Coward, 1929. Subj: Dragons. Food. Monsters.

Gone is gone ill. by author. Coward, 1935. Subj: Activities – working. Behavior – mistakes.

Jorinda and Joringel (Grimm, Jacob)

Millions of cats ill. by author. Coward, 1928. Subj: Animals – cats. Character traits – practicality. Cumulative tales.

Nothing at all ill. by author. Coward, 1941. Subj: Animals – dogs. Caldecott award honor book. Emotions – loneliness. Magic.

The six swans (Grimm, Jacob)

Snippy and Snappy ill. by author. Coward, 1931. Subj: Animals – mice.

The sorcerer's apprentice ill. by Margot Tomes. Coward, 1979. Subj: Behavior – misbehavior. Folk and fairy tales. Magic.

Gage, Wilson. *Anna's summer songs* ill. by Lena Anderson. Greenwillow, 1988. ISBN 0-688-07181-3 Subj: Plants. Poetry, rhyme. Seasons – summer.

The crow and Mrs. Gaddy ill. by Marylin Hafner. Greenwillow, 1984. Subj: Behavior – trickery. Birds – crows.

Cully Cully and the bear ill. by James Stevenson. Greenwillow, 1983. Subj: Animals – bears. Sports – hunting.

Down in the boondocks ill. by Glen Rounds. Greenwillow, 1977. Subj: Crime. Handicaps – deafness. Poetry, rhyme.

Mrs. Gaddy and the fast-growing vine ill. by Marylin Hafner. Greenwillow, 1985. ISBN 0-688-04232-5 Subj: Activities – gardening. Animals – goats. Behavior – seeking better things.

Mrs. Gaddy and the ghost ill. by Marylin Hafner. Greenwillow, 1979. Subj: Ghosts. Imagination.

Galbraith, Kathryn Osebold. *Katie did!* ill. by Ted Ramsey. Atheneum, 1982. Subj: Behavior – misbehavior. Family life. Sibling rivalry.

Spots are special ill. by Diane Dawson. Atheneum, 1976. Subj: Illness. Imagination.

Waiting for Jennifer ill. by Irene Trivas. Macmillan, 1987. ISBN 0-689-50430-6 Subj: Babies. Behavior – secrets. Family life.

Galbraith, Richard. *Reuben runs away* ill. by author. Watts, 1989. ISBN 0-531-08390-X Subj: Behavior – running away. Toys – teddy bears.

Galdone, Joanna. *Amber day* ill. by Paul Galdone. McGraw-Hill, 1978. Subj: Devil. Folk and fairy tales.

Gertrude, the goose who forgot ill. by Paul Galdone. Watts, 1975. Subj: Behavior – forgetfulness. Birds – geese. Poetry, rhyme.

Honeybee's party ill. by Paul Galdone. Watts, 1972. Subj: Insects – bees. Parties. Spiders.

The little girl and the big bear ill. by Paul Galdone. Houghton, 1980. Subj: Animals – bears. Folk and fairy tales.

The tailypo: a ghost story ill. by Paul Galdone. Seabury Pr., 1977. Subj: Ghosts. Poetry, rhyme.

Galdone, Paul. *The amazing pig: an old Hungarian tale* ill. by author. Houghton, 1981. Subj: Animals – pigs. Folk and fairy tales. Royalty.

Androcles and the lion ill. by author. McGraw-Hill, 1970. Subj: Animals – lions. Character traits – kindness to animals. Folk and fairy tales. Foreign lands – Italy.

Cat goes fiddle-i-fee ill. by adapt. Clarion Books, 1985. ISBN 0-89919-336-6 Subj: Animals. Cumulative tales. Nursery rhymes.

Counting carnival (Ziner, Feenie)

The first seven days ill. by Paul Galdone. Crowell, 1962. Subj: Religion.

The greedy old fat man: an American folk tale ill. by author. Houghton, 1983. Subj: Cumulative tales. Folk and fairy tales.

Hans in luck (Grimm, Jacob)

King of the cats: a ghost story by Joseph Jacobs; ill. by adapt. Houghton, 1980. Subj: Animals – cats. Folk and fairy tales. Ghosts.

The life of Jack Sprat, his wife and his cat (Jack Sprat)

Little Bo-Peep ill. by author. Ticknor & Fields, 1986. ISBN 0-89919-395-1 Subj: Animals – sheep. Nursery rhymes.

The magic porridge pot ill. by Paul Galdone. Seabury Pr., 1976. Subj: Behavior – forgetfulness. Behavior – sharing. Folk and fairy tales. Food. Magic.

The monkey and the crocodile: a Jataka tale from India ill. by author. Seabury Pr., 1969. Subj: Animals – monkeys. Character traits – cleverness. Folk and fairy tales. Reptiles – alligators, crocodiles.

The monster and the tailor: a ghost story ill. by author. Houghton, 1982. An adaptation of Joseph Jacobs' The sprightly tailor. Subj: Careers – tailors. Ghosts. Monsters. Royalty.

Obedient Jack ill. by author. Watts, 1971. Subj: Behavior – mistakes. Family life. Folk and fairy tales.

Over in the meadow

Rumpelstiltskin (Grimm, Jacob)

A strange servant: a Russian folktale tr. by Blanche Ross; ill. by author. Knopf, 1977. Subj: Animals – rabbits. Behavior – trickery. Folk and fairy tales. Foreign lands – Russia.

The table, the donkey and the stick (Grimm, Jacob)

The teeny-tiny woman: a ghost story ill. by adapt. Clarion, 1984. ISBN 0-89919-270-X Subj: Emotions. Folk and fairy tales. Ghosts.

What's in fox's sack? ill. by author. Houghton, 1982. Subj: Character traits – cleverness. Folk and fairy tales.

Galinsky, Ellen. *The baby cardinal* photos. by author. Putnam's, 1977. Subj: Birds – cardinals.

Gallant, Kathryn. *The flute player of Beppu* ill. by Kurt Wiese. Coward, 1960. Subj: Character traits – honesty.

Gallaudet Pre-school Signed English Project. *Nursery rhymes from Mother Goose in signed English.* (Mother Goose)

Gallo, Giovanni. *The lazy beaver* ill. by Ermanno Samsa; tr. from Italian by Jane Fior. Putnam's, 1983. Subj: Activities – working. Animals – beavers.

Gambill, Henrietta. *Self-control* ill. by Kathryn Hutton. Rev. ed. Children's Pr., 1982. Subj: Behavior.

Gammell, Stephen. *Git along, old Scudder* ill. by author. Lothrop, 1983. Subj: Old age.

Once upon MacDonald's farm ill. by author. Four Winds Pr., 1981. Subj: Animals. Farms.

The story of Mr. and Mrs. Vinegar ill. by author. Lothrop, 1982. Subj: Character traits – foolishness. Folk and fairy tales.

Ganly, Helen. *Jyoti's journey* ill. by author. Dutton, 1986. ISBN 0-233-97899-2 Subj: Family life. Foreign lands – England. Foreign lands – India. Weddings.

Gannett, Ruth S. *Katie and the sad noise* ill. by Ellie Simmons. Random House, 1961. Subj: Animals – dogs. Character traits – kindness. Holidays – Christmas. Noise, sounds.

Gans, Roma. *Hummingbirds in the garden* ill. by Grambs Miller. Crowell, 1969. Subj: Birds. Seasons – summer.

Rock collecting ill. by Holly Keller. Crowell, 1984. Subj: Behavior – collecting things. Rocks. Science.

When birds change their feathers ill. by Felicia Bond. Crowell, 1980. Subj: Birds. Science.

Gant, Elizabeth. *Little Red Riding Hood* (Grimm, Jacob)

Gant, Katherine. *Little Red Riding Hood* (Grimm, Jacob)

Gantos, Jack. *Aunt Bernice* ill. by Nicole Rubel. Houghton, 1978. Subj: Behavior – carelessness. Family life.

Greedy Greeny ill. by Nicole Rubel. Doubleday, 1979. Subj: Dreams. Monsters.

The perfect pal ill. by Nicole Rubel. Houghton, 1979. Subj: Animals. Pets.

Rotten Ralph ill. by Nicole Rubel. Houghton, 1976. Subj: Animals – cats. Behavior – misbehavior.

Rotten Ralph's rotten Christmas ill. by Nicole Rubel. Houghton, 1984. Subj: Animals – cats. Character traits – meanness. Emotions – envy, jealousy. Holidays – Christmas.

Rotten Ralph's trick or treat ill. by Nicole Rubel. Houghton, 1986. ISBN 0-395-38943-7 Subj: Animals – cats. Character traits – meanness. Holidays – Halloween.

Swampy alligator ill. by Nicole Rubel. Windmill, 1980. Subj: Birthdays. Character traits – cleanliness. Reptiles – alligators, crocodiles.

The werewolf family ill. by Nicole Rubel. Houghton, 1980. Subj: Monsters.

Worse than Rotten Ralph ill. by Nicole Rubel. Houghton, 1978. Subj: Animals – cats. Behavior – misbehavior. Character traits – meanness.

Gantos, John, Jr. see Gantos, Jack

Gantschev, Ivan. *The Christmas train* ill. by author; tr. from German by Karen M. Klockner. Little, 1984. Subj: Character traits – bravery. Holidays – Christmas. Trains.

Journey of the storks ill. by author. Alphabet Pr., 1983. Subj: Birds – storks.

The moon lake tr. by Oliver Gadsby; ill. by author. Alphabet Pr., 1981. Subj: Moon.

Otto the bear tr. from German by Karen M. Klockner; ill. by author. Little, 1986. ISBN 0-316-30348-8 Subj: Animals – bears. Character traits – kindness to animals.

RumpRump ill. by author. Alphabet Pr., 1984. Subj: Animals – bears. Food. Friendship.

Santa's favorite story (Aoki, Hisako)

The train to Grandma's ill. by author. Picture Book Studio, 1987. ISBN 0-88708-053-7 Subj: Activities – traveling. Family life – grandparents. Format, unusual. Islands. Trains.

Gantz, David. *Captain Swifty counts to 50* ill. by author. Doubleday, 1982. Subj: Counting.

The genie bear with the light brown hair word book ill. by author. Doubleday, 1982. Subj: ABC books. Animals – bears. Animals – mice.

Ganz, Yaffa. *The story of Mimmy and Simmy* ill. by Harvey Klineman. Feldheim, 1985. ISBN 0-87306-385-6 Subj: Behavior – seeking better things. Emotions – envy, jealousy. Jewish culture.

Garbutt, Bernard. *Roger, the rosin back* ill. by author. Hastings, 1961. Subj: Animals – horses. circus.

García Lorca, Federico. *The Lieutenant Colonel and the gypsy* tr. and ill. by Marc Simont. Doubleday, 1971. Subj: Foreign lands – Spain. Gypsies. Poetry, rhyme.

Gardner, Beau. *Can you imagine...? a counting book* ill. by author. Dodd, 1987. ISBN 0-396-09001-X Subj: Animals. Counting.

Guess what? ill. by author. Lothrop, 1985. ISBN 0-688-04983-4 Subj: Animals. Concepts – shape. Games.

Have you ever seen...? an ABC book ill. by author. Dodd, 1986. ISBN 0-396-08825-2 Subj: ABC books. Humor.

The look again...and again, and again, and again book ill. by author. Lothrop, 1984. Subj: Optical illusions.

The turn about, think about, look about book ill. by author. Lothrop, 1980. Subj: Optical illusions.

Gardner, Martin. *Never make fun of a turtle, my son* ill. by John Alcorn. Simon & Schuster, 1969. ISBN 0-671-65033-5 Subj: Etiquette. Poetry, rhyme.

Gardner, Mercedes. *Scooter and the magic star* by Mercedes and Jean Shannon Smith; ill. by Bob Johnson. Atheneum, 1980. Subj: Fairies.

Garelick, May. *About owls* ill. by Tony Chen. Four Winds Pr., 1975. Subj: Birds – owls. Science.

Down to the beach ill. by Barbara Cooney. Four Winds Pr., 1973. Subj: Sea and seashore. Seasons – summer.

Look at the moon ill. by Leonard Weisgard. Addison-Wesley, 1969. Subj: Animals. Moon. Poetry, rhyme.

Sounds of a summer night ill. by Beni Montresor. Addison-Wesley, 1963. Subj: Night. Noise, sounds.

The tremendous tree book by May Garelick and Barbara Brenner; ill. by Fred Brenner. Four Winds Pr., 1979. Subj: Science. Trees.

Where does the butterfly go when it rains? ill. by Leonard Weisgard. Addison-Wesley, 1961. Subj: Insects – butterflies, caterpillars. Poetry, rhyme. Weather – rain.

Garfield, Leon. *King Nimrod's tower* ill. by Michael Bragg. Lothrop, 1982. Subj: Religion.

The writing on the wall by Leon Garfield and Michael Bragg; ill. by Michael Bragg. Lothrop, 1983. Subj: Religion.

Garfinkel, Bernard *see* Allen, Robert

Garland, Sarah. *Going shopping* ill. by author. Little, 1985. ISBN 0-87113-001-7 Subj: Family life. Shopping.

Having a picnic ill. by author. Little, 1985. ISBN 0-87113-002-5 Subj: Activities – picnicking. Birds – ducks. Family life.

Garrett, Helen. *Angelo the naughty one* ill. by Leo Politi. Viking, 1944. Subj: Ethnic groups in the U.S. – Mexican-Americans.

Garrett, Jennifer. *The queen who stole the sky* ill. by Linda Hendry. North Winds Pr., 1986. ISBN 0-590-71524-0 Subj: Character traits – selfishness. Character traits – stubbornness. Royalty.

Garrison, Christian. *The dream eater* ill. by Diane Goode. Dutton, 1978. Subj: Dragons. Dreams. Foreign lands – Japan.

Little pieces of the west wind ill. by Diane Goode. Dutton, 1975. Subj: Cumulative tales. Weather – wind.

Garten, Jan. *The alphabet tale* ill. by Muriel Batherman. Random House, 1964. Subj: ABC books. Animals. Participation. Poetry, rhyme.

Gascoigne, Bamber. *Why the rope went tight* ill. by Christina Gascoigne. Lothrop, 1981. Subj: Circus.

Gaston, Susan. *New boots for Salvador* ill. by Lydia Schwartz. Ritchie, 1972. Subj: Animals – horses.

Gauch, Patricia Lee. *Christina Katerina and the time she quit the family* ill. by Elise Primavera. Putnam's, 1987. ISBN 0-399-21408-9 Subj: Behavior – needing someone. Family life. Sibling rivalry.

The little friar who flew ill. by Tomie de Paola. Putnam's, 1980. Subj: Folk and fairy tales.

On to Widecombe Fair ill. by Trina Schart Hyman. Putnam's, 1978. Subj: Fairs. Folk and fairy tales. Foreign lands – England.

Once upon a Dinkelsbühl ill. by Tomie de Paola. Putnam's, 1977. Subj: War.

Gay, Marie-Louise. *Moonbeam on a cat's ear* ill. by author. Silver Burdett, 1986. ISBN 0-385-09162-0 Subj: Animals – cats. Animals – mice. Bedtime. Dreams. Moon. Poetry, rhyme.

Rainy day magic ill. by author. Stoddart, 1987. ISBN 0-7737-2112-6 Subj: Family life. Illness. Weather – rain.

Gay, Michel. *Bibi takes flight* ill. by author. Morrow, 1988. ISBN 0-688-06829-4 Subj: Activities – flying. Airplanes, airports. Birds – penguins.

Bibi's birthday surprise ill. by author. Morrow, 1987. ISBN 0-688-06978-9 Subj: Animals. Birds – penguins. Parties. Royalty. Toys.

The Christmas wolf ill. by author. Greenwillow, 1983. ISBN 0-688-02291-X Subj: Animals – wolves. Holidays – Christmas.

Little auto ill. by author. Macmillan, 1986. ISBN 0-02-737900-0 Subj: Automobiles. Sea and seashore.

Little boat ill. by author. Macmillan, 1985. Subj: Boats, ships.

Little helicopter ill. by author. Macmillan, 1986. ISBN 0-02-737920-5 Subj: Character traits – smallness. Helicopters.

Little plane ill. by author. Macmillan, 1985. Subj: Airplanes, airports.

Little shoe ill. by author. Macmillan, 1986. ISBN 0-02-737890-X Subj: Behavior – losing things. Clothing.

Little truck ill. by author. Macmillan, 1985. Subj: Trucks. Transportation.

Night ride ill. by author. Morrow, 1987. ISBN 0-688-07287-9 Subj: Activities – traveling. Animals. Circus. Family life – fathers. Night.

Rabbit express ill. by author. Morrow, 1985. ISBN 0-688-04648-7 Subj: Animals – cats. Animals – rabbits. Friendship.

Take me for a ride ill. by author. Morrow, 1985. Subj: Behavior – lost.

Gay, Zhenya. *I'm tired of lions* ill. by author. Viking, 1961. Subj: Animals – lions. Behavior – dissatisfaction.

Look! ill. by author. Viking, 1952. Subj: Animals. Libraries. Poetry, rhyme.

Small one ill. by author. Viking, 1958. Subj: Animals – rabbits. Behavior – lost.

What's your name? ill. by author. Viking, 1955. Subj: Animals. Poetry, rhyme. Riddles.

Who's afraid? ill. by author. Viking, 1965. Subj: Emotions – fear.

Wonderful things ill. by author. Viking, 1954. Subj: Animals – horses.

Gebert, Warren. *The old ball and the sea* ill. by author. Bradbury Pr., 1988. ISBN 0-02-735821-6 Subj: Activities – playing. Sea and seashore.

Gedin, Birgitta. *The little house from the sea* tr. by Elisabeth Dyssegaard; ill. by Petter Pettersson. Farrar, 1988. ISBN 91-29-58770-0 Subj: Boats, ships. Houses. Sea and seashore. Weather – storms.

Geisel, Theodor Seuss *see* Seuss, Dr.

Geisert, Arthur. *The ark* ill. by author. Houghton, 1988. ISBN 0-395-43078-X Subj: Religion – Noah.

Pa's balloon and other pig tales ill. by author. Houghton, 1984. Subj: Activities – ballooning. Animals – pigs.

Pigs from A to Z ill. by author. Houghton, 1986. ISBN 0-395-38509-1 Subj: ABC books. Animals – pigs. Riddles.

Geiss, Tony. *Susan and Gordon adopt a baby* (Freudberg, Judy)

Gekiere, Madeleine. *The frilly lily and the princess* ill. by author. Lippincott, 1960. Subj: Behavior – fighting, arguing. Royalty.

Gellman, Ellie. *It's Chanukah!* ill. by Katherine Janus Kahn. Kar-Ben Copies, 1985. ISBN 0-930494-51-2 Subj: Format, unusual – board books. Holidays – Hanukkah. Jewish culture.

It's Rosh Hashanah! ill. by Katherine Janus Kahn. Kar-Ben Copies, 1985. ISBN 0-930494-50-4 Subj: Format, unusual – board books. Holidays – Rosh Hashanah. Jewish culture.

Shai's Shabbat walk ill. by Chari R. McLean. Kar-Ben Copies, 1985. ISBN 0-930494-49-0 Subj: Format, unusual – board books. Holidays. Jewish culture.

Gelman, Rita Golden. *Dumb Joey* ill. by Cheryl Pelavin. Holt, 1973. Subj: Activities – playing. City. Friendship.

Hey, kid ill. by Carol Nicklaus. Watts, 1977. Subj: Humor. Poetry, rhyme.

A koala grows up ill. by Gioia Fiammenghi. Scholastic, 1986. ISBN 0-590-30563-8 Subj: Animals – koala bears. Science.

Professor Coconut and the thief ill. by Emily Arnold McCully. Holt, 1977. Subj: Animals – monkeys. Problem solving.

Splash! (Buxbaum, Susan Kovacs)

Uncle Hugh: a fishing story by Rita Golden Gelman and Warner Friedman; ill. by Eros Keith. Harcourt, 1978. Subj: Sports – fishing.

Gemme, Leila Boyle. *T-ball is our game* photos. by Richard Marshall. Children's Pr., 1978. Subj: Sports – T-ball.

Gemming, Elisabeth. *Sandy at the children's zoo* (Bolliger, Max)

Gendel, Evelyn. *Tortoise and turtle* ill. by Hilary Knight. Simon and Schuster, 1960. Subj: Animals. Parties. Reptiles – turtles, tortoises.

Tortoise and turtle abroad ill. by Hilary Knight. Simon and Schuster, 1963. Subj: Animals. Parties. Reptiles – turtles, tortoises.

George, Jean Craighead. *All upon a stone* ill. by Don Bolognese. Crowell, 1971. Subj: Insects. Science. Spiders.

The grizzly bear with the golden ears ill. by Tom Catania. Harper, 1982. Subj: Animals – bears.

The wentletrap trap ill. by Symeon Shimin. Dutton, 1978. Subj: Ethnic groups in the U.S. – Afro-Americans. Foreign lands – Caribbean Islands. Sea and seashore.

George, Lindsay Barrett. *Beaver at Long Pond* (George, William T.)

William and Boomer ill. by author. Greenwillow, 1987. ISBN 0-688-06641-0 Subj: Birds – geese. Pets. Sports – swimming.

George, William T. *Beaver at Long Pond* by William T. and Lindsay Barrett George; ill. by Lindsay Barrett George. Greenwillow, 1988. ISBN 0-688-07107-4 Subj: Animals – beavers. Nature. Night.

Georgiady, Nicholas P. *Gertie the duck* ill. by Dagmar Wilson. Follett, 1959. Subj: Birds – ducks. Character traits – kindness to animals.

Georgiou, Stephen *see* Stevens, Cat

Geraghty, Paul. *Over the steamy swamp* ill. by author. Harcourt, 1989. ISBN 0-15-200561-7 Subj: Animals. Insects. Nature.

Gerez, Toni De *see* De Gerez, Toni

Gergely, Tibor. *Wheel on the chimney* (Brown, Margaret Wise)

Geringer, Laura. *Molly's new washing machine* ill. by Petra Mathers. Harper, 1986. ISBN 0-06-022151-8 Subj: Activities – dancing. Animals – rabbits. Behavior – mistakes. Machines.

A three hat day ill. by Arnold Lobel. Harper, 1985. ISBN 0-06-021989-0 Subj: Behavior – collecting things. Clothing.

Germano, Margaret *see* Mann, Peggy

Gerrard, Jean. *Matilda Jane* ill. by Roy Gerrard. Farrar, 1983. Subj: Foreign lands – England. Sea and seashore.

Gerrard, Roy. *The Favershams* ill. by author. Farrar, 1983. Subj: Poetry, rhyme.

Sir Cedric rides again ill. by author. Farrar, 1987. ISBN 0-374-36961-5 Subj: Knights. Middle ages. Poetry, rhyme.

Sir Francis Drake: his daring deeds ill. by author. Farrar, 1988. ISBN 0-374-36962-3 Subj: Boats, ships. Foreign lands. Poetry, rhyme. Sea and seashore.

Gershator, Phillis. *Honi and his magic circle* ill. by Shay Rieger. Jewish Publication Society of America, 1980. Subj: Jewish culture.

Gerson, Corinne. *Good dog, bad dog* ill. by Emily Arnold McCully. Atheneum, 1983. Subj: Animals – dogs. Behavior – misbehavior. Pets.

Gerstein, Mordicai. *Arnold of the ducks* ill. by author. Harper, 1983. Subj: Birds – ducks.

Follow me! ill. by author. Morrow, 1983. Subj: Birds – ducks.

The mountains of Tibet ill. by author. Harper, 1987. ISBN 0-06-022149-6 Subj: Death. Kites.

Prince Sparrow ill. by author. Four Winds Pr., 1984. Subj: Birds – sparrows. Emotions – love.

Roll over! ill. by author. Crown, 1984. Subj: Counting. Poetry, rhyme.

The room ill. by author. Harper, 1984. Subj: City.

The seal mother ill. by author. Dial Pr., 1986. ISBN 0-8037-0303-1 Subj: Animals – seals. Folk and fairy tales. Seasons – summer.

William, where are you? ill. by author. Crown, 1985. ISBN 0-517-55644-8 Subj: Animals. Bedtime. Behavior – hiding. Format, unusual – toy and movable books.

Getz, Arthur. *Humphrey, the dancing pig* ill. by author. Dial Pr., 1980. Subj: Activities – dancing. Animals – pigs. Behavior – dissatisfaction.

Gezi, Kal. *The mystery at Misty Falls* (Bradford, Ann)

The mystery in the secret club house (Bradford, Ann)

The mystery of the blind writer (Bradford, Ann)

The mystery of the live ghosts (Bradford, Ann)

The mystery of the midget clown (Bradford, Ann)

The mystery of the missing dogs (Bradford, Ann)

The mystery of the missing raccoon (Bradford, Ann)

The mystery of the square footsteps (Bradford, Ann)

The mystery of the tree house (Bradford, Ann)

Gianni, Peg. *Alex, the amazing juggler* by Peg Gianni and Renato Ferraro; ill. by Peg Gianni. Holt, 1981. Subj: Behavior – running away. Royalty.

Gibbon, David. *Kittens* ill. with photos. Crescent Books, 1979. ISBN 84-499-5052-X Subj: Animals – cats.

Gibbons, Gail. *Boat book* ill. by author. Holiday, 1983. Subj: Boats, ships.

Check it out! the book about libraries ill. by author. Harcourt, 1985. ISBN 0-15-216400-6 Subj: Libraries.

Clocks and how they go ill. by author. Crowell, 1979. Subj: Clocks. Time.

Deadline! from news to newspaper ill. by author. Harper, 1987. ISBN 0-690-04602-2 Subj: Activities – working. Paper.

Department store ill. by author. Crowell, 1984. Subj: Stores.

Dinosaurs ill. by author. Holiday, 1987. ISBN 0-8234-0657-1 Subj: Dinosaurs.

Farming ill. by author. Holiday House, 1988. ISBN 0-8234-0682-2 Subj: Careers. Farms. Seasons.

Fill it up! all about service stations ill. by author. Crowell, 1985. ISBN 0-690-04440-2 Subj: Automobiles. Careers.

Fire! Fire! ill. by author. Crowell, 1984. Subj: Careers – firefighters.

Flying ill. by author. Holiday, 1986. ISBN 0-8234-0599-0 Subj: Activities – ballooning. Activities – flying. Airplanes, airports.

Halloween ill. by author. Holiday, 1984. Subj: Holidays – Halloween.

Happy birthday! ill. by author. Holiday, 1986. ISBN 0-8234-0614-8 Subj: Birthdays.

The milk makers ill. by author. Macmillan, 1985. ISBN 0-02-736640-5 Subj: Farms. Food.

The missing maple syrup sap mystery: or, How maple syrup is made ill. by author. Warne, 1979. Subj: Activities. Food. Problem solving. Trees.

New road! ill. by author. Crowell, 1983. Subj: Transportation.

Paper, paper everywhere ill. by author. Harcourt, 1983. Subj: Paper.

Playgrounds ill. by author. Holiday, 1985. ISBN 0-8234-0553-2 Subj: Activities – playing.

The post office book: mail and how it moves ill. by author. Crowell, 1982. Subj: Careers – mail carriers. Communication.

The pottery place ill. by author. Harcourt, 1987. ISBN 0-15-263265-4 Subj: Careers.

Prehistoric animals ill. by author. Holiday, 1988. ISBN 0-8234-0707-1 Subj: Animals. Science.

The seasons of Arnold's apple tree ill. by author. Harcourt, 1988. ISBN 0-15-271246-1 Subj: Food. Seasons. Trees.

Sun up, sun down ill. by author. Harcourt, 1983. Subj: Science. Sun.

Thanksgiving Day ill. by author. Holiday, 1983. Subj: Holidays – Thanksgiving.

The too-great bread bake book ill. by author. Warne, 1980. Subj: Activities – cooking.

Tool book ill. by author. Holiday, 1982. Subj: Tools.

Trains ill. by author. Holiday, 1987. ISBN 0-8234-0640-7 Subj: Trains.

Trucks ill. by author. Crowell, 1981. Subj: Trucks.

Tunnels ill. by author. Holiday, 1984. ISBN 0-8234-0507-9 Subj: Activities – digging.

Up goes the skyscraper! ill. by author. Four Winds Pr., 1986. ISBN 0-02-736780-0 Subj: City.

Valentine's Day ill. by author. Holiday, 1985. ISBN 0-8234-0572-9 Subj: Holidays – Valentine's Day.

Zoo ill. by author. Crowell, 1987. ISBN 0-690-04633-2 Subj: Activities – working. Animals. Zoos.

Gibson, Josephine *see* Joslin, Sesyle

Gibson, Myra Tomback. *What is your favorite thing to touch?* ill. by author. Grosset, 1965. Subj: Poetry, rhyme. Senses – touching.

Giesen, Rosemary. *Famous planes* (Thompson, Brenda)

Pirates (Thompson, Brenda)

Giff, Patricia Reilly. *The almost awful play* ill. by Susanna Natti. Viking, 1984. Subj: Theater.

The beast in Ms. Rooney's room ill. by Blanche Sims. Dell, 1984. Subj: Activities – reading. School.

Happy birthday, Ronald Morgan! ill. by Susanna Natti. Viking, 1986. ISBN 0-670-80741-9 Subj: Birthdays. Friendship. School.

Next year I'll be special ill. by Marylin Hafner. Dutton, 1980. Subj: Behavior – seeking better things. Dreams. School.

Ronald Morgan goes to bat ill. by Susanna Natti. Viking, 1988. ISBN 0-670-81457-1 Subj: Sports – baseball.

Today was a terrible day ill. by Susanna Natti. Viking, 1980. Subj: Behavior – bad day. School.

Watch out, Ronald Morgan! ill. by Susanna Natti. Viking, 1985. ISBN 0-670-80433-9 Subj: Glasses. School. Senses – seeing.

Giganti, Paul. *How many snails? a counting book* by Paul Giganti, Jr.; ill. by Donald Crews. Greenwillow, 1988. ISBN 0-688-06370-5 Subj: Counting.

Gikow, Louise. *Boober Fraggle's ghosts* ill. by Lawrence DiFiori. Holt, 1985. ISBN 0-03-004549-5 Subj: Emotions – fear. Ghosts. Puppets.

Follow that Fraggle! ill. by Barbara Lanza. Holt, 1985. ISBN 0-03-004558-4 Subj: Activities – traveling. Animals – dogs. Puppets.

Sprocket's Christmas tale ill. by Lisa McCue. Holt, 1984. Subj: Holidays – Christmas. Puppets.

Gilbert, Helen Earle. *Dr. Trotter and his big gold watch* ill. by Margaret Bradfield. Abingdon Pr., 1948. Subj: Careers – doctors. Clocks.

Mr. Plum and the little green tree ill. by Margaret Bradfield. Abingdon Pr., 1946. Subj: Careers – shoemakers. Trees.

Gilbert, Ruth Gallard Ainsworth *see* Ainsworth, Ruth

Gilbreath, Alice. *Making toys that crawl and slide* ill. by Joe Rogers. Follett, 1978. Subj: Toys.

Making toys that swim and float ill. by Joe Rogers. Follett, 1978. Subj: Toys.

Gilchrist, Theo E. *Halfway up the mountain* ill. by Glen Rounds. Lippincott, 1978. Subj: Behavior – fighting, arguing. Poetry, rhyme.

Gili, Phillida. *Fanny and Charles: a regency escapade or, The trick that went wrong* ill. by author. Viking, 1983. Subj: Activities – vacationing. Animals – mice. Sibling rivalry.

Gill, Bob. *A balloon for a blunderbuss* by Bob Gill and Alastair Reid; ill. by Bob Gill. Harper, 1961. Subj: Activities – trading.

Gill, Joan. *Hush, Jon!* ill. by Tracy Sugarman. Doubleday, 1968. Subj: Babies. Emotions – envy, jealousy. Ethnic groups in the U.S. – Afro-Americans. Family life.

Gilleo, Alma. *Learning about monsters* ill. by Joe Van Severen. Children's Pr., 1982. Subj: Folk and fairy tales. Monsters. Mythical creatures.

Gillham, Bill. *Can you see it?* photos. by Fiona Horne. Putnam's, 1986. ISBN 0-399-21323-6 Subj: Games.

The early words picture book photos. by Sam Grainger. Coward, 1983. Subj: Activities – reading.

Let's look for colors by Bill Gillham and Susan Hulme; photos. by Jan Siegieda. Putnam's, 1984. Subj: Concepts – color.

Let's look for numbers by Bill Gillham and Susan Hulme; photos. by Jan Siegieda. Putnam's, 1984. Subj: Counting.

Let's look for opposites by Bill Gillham and Susan Hulme; photos. by Jan Siegieda. Putnam's, 1984. Subj: Concepts – opposites.

Let's look for shapes by Bill Gillham and Susan Hulme; photos. by Jan Siegieda. Putnam's, 1984. Subj: Concepts – shape.

What can you do? photos. by Fiona Horne. Putnam's, 1986. ISBN 0-399-21324-4 Subj: Games. Imagination.

What's the difference? photos. by Fiona Horne. Putnam's, 1986. ISBN 0-399-21321-X Subj: Concepts – opposites. Games.

Where does it go? photos. by Fiona Horne. Putnam's, 1986. ISBN 0-399-21322-8 Subj: Concepts. Games.

Gillham, Elizabeth Wright Enright *see* Enright, Elizabeth

Gilmour, H. B. *Why Wembley Fraggle couldn't sleep* ill. by Barbara McClintock. Holt, 1985. ISBN 0-03-004557-6 Subj: Puppets. Sleep.

The gingerbread boy. *The gingerbread boy* retold and ill. by Scott Cook. Knopf, 1987. ISBN 0-394-98698-9 Subj: Behavior – running away. Cumulative tales. Folk and fairy tales.

The gingerbread boy ill. by Paul Galdone. Seabury Pr., 1975. Subj: Behavior – running away. Cumulative tales. Folk and fairy tales. Food. Poetry, rhyme.

The gingerbread boy retold by David Cutts; ill. by Joan Elizabeth Goodman. Troll Assoc., 1979. Subj: Behavior – running away. Cumulative tales. Folk and fairy tales. Food.

The gingerbread boy ill. by William Curtis Holdsworth. Farrar, 1968. Subj: Behavior – running away. Cumulative tales. Folk and fairy tales. Food.

The gingerbread man retold by Barbara Ireson; ill. by Gerald Rose. Norton, 1963. Subj: Behavior – running away. Cumulative tales. Folk and fairy tales. Food.

The pancake boy adapt. and ill. by Lorinda Bryan Cauley. Putnam's, 1988. ISBN 0-399-21505-0 Subj: Behavior – running away. Cumulative tales. Folk and fairy tales. Food.

Whiff, sniff, nibble and chew: The Gingerbread boy retold by Charlotte Pomerantz; ill. by Monica Incisa. Greenwillow, 1984. ISBN 0-688-02552-8 Subj: Behavior – running away. Cumulative tales. Folk and fairy tales. Poetry, rhyme.

Ginsburg, Mirra. *Across the stream* ill. by Nancy Tafuri. Greenwillow, 1982. Subj: Animals – foxes. Birds – chickens. Birds – ducks. Dreams.

The chick and the duckling ill. by José Aruego and Ariane Dewey, 1972. Translation of Tŝyplenok i utenok by Vladimir Grigorévich Suteyev. Subj: Birds – chickens. Birds – ducks. Sports – swimming.

The Chinese mirror ill. by Margot Zemach. Harcourt, 1988. ISBN 0-15-200420-3 Subj: Character traits – appearance. Folk and fairy tales. Foreign lands – Korea.

The fisherman's son ill. by Tony Chen. Greenwillow, 1979. Subj: Character traits – cleverness. Folk and fairy tales. Foreign lands – Russia.

Four brave sailors ill. by Nancy Tafuri. Greenwillow, 1987. ISBN 0-688-06515-5 Subj: Animals. Animals – mice. Boats, ships. Dreams. Pirates. Poetry, rhyme. Sea and seashore. Toys. Weather.

The fox and the hare ill. by Victor Nolden. Crown, 1969. Subj: Animals. Animals – foxes. Animals – rabbits. Folk and fairy tales. Foreign lands – Russia. Friendship.

Good morning, chick (Chukovsky, Korney)

How the sun was brought back to the sky: adapted from a Slovenian folk tale ill. by José Aruego and Ariane Dewey. Macmillan, 1975. Subj: Folk and fairy tales. Foreign lands – Czechoslovakia. Sun.

Kitten from one to ten ill. by Giulio Maestro. Crown, 1980. Subj: Animals – cats. Counting. Poetry, rhyme.

Mushroom in the rain ill. by José Aruego and Ariane Dewey. Macmillan, 1988, 1974. Adapted from the Russian of Valdimir Grigorévich Suteyev. ISBN 0-02-736241-8 Subj: Animals. Animals – foxes. Plants. Weather – rain.

Ookie-Spooky ill. by Emily Arnold McCully. Crown, 1979. Subj: Monsters.

Pampalche of the silver teeth ill. by Rocco Negri. Crown, 1976. Subj: Folk and fairy tales. Foreign lands – Russia. Witches.

Striding slippers: an Udmurt tale ill. by Sal Murdocca. Macmillan, 1978. Subj: Behavior – stealing. Folk and fairy tales. Magic.

The strongest one of all ill. by José Aruego and Ariane Dewey. Greenwillow, 1977. Subj: Animals – sheep. Character traits – bravery. Foreign lands – Russia.

The sun's asleep behind the hill ill. by Paul O. Zelinsky. Greenwillow, 1982. Subj: Night. Poetry, rhyme.

Two greedy bears ill. by José Aruego and Ariane Dewey. Macmillan, 1976. Subj: Animals – bears. Animals – foxes. Behavior – greed. Foreign lands – Hungary. Sibling rivalry.

Where does the sun go at night? ill. by José Aruego and Ariane Dewey. Greenwillow, 1980. Subj: Night. Sun.

Which is the best place? ill. by Roger Antoine Duvoisin. Macmillan, 1976. Tr. from Gde luchshe by Pyotr Dubochkin. Subj: Bedtime. Foreign lands – Russia.

Giovanni, Nikki. *Spin a soft black song* ill. by George Martins. Rev. ed. Hill & Wang, 1985. ISBN 0-8090-8796-0 Subj: Ethnic groups in the U.S. – Afro-Americans. Poetry, rhyme.

Giovanni, Yolande Cornelia, Jr. *see* Giovanni, Nikki

Gipson, Morrell. *Favorite nursery tales* ill. by S. D. Schindler. Doubleday, 1983. Subj: Nursery rhymes.

Hello, Peter ill. by Clement Hurd. Doubleday, 1948. Subj: Activities.

Girard, Linda Walvoord. *Adoption is for always* ill. by Judi Friedman. Albert Whitman, 1986. ISBN 0-8075-0185-9 Subj: Adoption. Family life.

At Daddy's on Saturdays ill. by Judith Friedman. Albert Whitman, 1987. ISBN 0-8075-0475-0 Subj: Divorce. Emotions – love. Family life.

Jeremy's first haircut ill. by Mary Jane Begin. Albert Whitman, 1986. ISBN 0-8075-3805-1 Subj: Emotions – fear. Hair.

My body is private ill. by Rodney Pate. Albert Whitman, 1984. ISBN 0-8075-5320-4 Subj: Safety. Self-concept.

You were born on your very first birthday ill. by Christa Kieffer. Albert Whitman, 1983. Subj: Babies. Science.

Girion, Barbara. *The boy with the special face* ill. by Heidi Palmer. Abingdon, 1978. Subj: Character traits – appearance.

Givens, Janet Eaton. *Just two wings* ill. by Susan Dodge. Atheneum, 1984. Subj: Birds.

Something wonderful happened ill. by Susan Dodge. Atheneum, 1982. Subj: Flowers.

Glaser, Byron. *Action alphabet* (Neumeier, Marty)

Glass, Andrew. *Chickpea and the talking cow* ill. by author. Lothrop, 1987. ISBN 0-688-06175-3 Subj: Animals – bulls, cows. Character traits – smallness. Emotions – love. Family life. Farms. Royalty.

My brother tries to make me laugh ill. by author. Lothrop, 1984. Subj: Imagination. Space and space ships.

Glass, Marvin. *What happened today, Freddy Groundhog?* ill. by author. Crown, 1989. ISBN 0-517-57140-4 Subj: Animals – groundhogs. Holidays – Groundhog Day.

Glazer, Lee. *Cookie Becker casts a spell* ill. by Margot Apple. Little, 1980. Subj: Character traits – meanness. Magic.

Glazer, Tom. *Do your ears hang low? fifty more musical fingerplays* ill. by Mila Lazarevich. Doubleday, 1980. Subj: Games. Music. Participation. Songs.

Eye winker, Tom Tinker, chin chopper: fifty musical fingerplays ill. by Ronald Himler. Doubleday, 1974. Subj: Games. Music. Participation. Songs.

On top of spaghetti ill. by Tom Garcia. Doubleday, 1982. Subj: Music. Songs.

Glovach, Linda. *The Little Witch's birthday book* ill. by author. Prentice-Hall, 1981. Subj: Birthdays. Parties. Witches.

The Little Witch's black magic book of disguises ill. by author. Prentice-Hall, 1973. Subj: Holidays – Halloween. Witches.

The Little Witch's black magic book of games ill. by author. Prentice-Hall, 1974. Subj: Games. Safety.

The Little Witch's Christmas book ill. by author. Prentice-Hall, 1975. Subj: Holidays – Christmas. Witches.

The Little Witch's Halloween book ill. by author. Prentice-Hall, 1975. Subj: Holidays – Halloween. Witches.

The Little Witch's spring holiday book ill. by author. Prentice-Hall, 1983. Subj: Holidays. Seasons – spring. Witches.

The Little Witch's Thanksgiving book ill. by author. Prentice-Hall, 1976. Subj: Holidays – Thanksgiving. Witches.

Go tell Aunt Rhody. *Go tell Aunt Rhody* ill. by Aliki. Macmillan, 1974. Subj: Folk and fairy tales. Games. Songs.

Go tell Aunt Rhody ill. by Robert M. Quackenbush. Lippincott, 1973. Subj: Games. Music. Songs.

Gobhai, Mehlli. *Lakshmi, the water buffalo who wouldn't* ill. by author. Hawthorn, 1969. Subj: Animals – water buffaloes. Foreign lands – India.

Usha, the mouse-maiden ill. by author. Hawthorn, 1969. Subj: Family life. Folk and fairy tales. Foreign lands – India.

Goble, Paul. *Beyond the ridge* ill. by author. Bradbury Pr., 1988. ISBN 0-02-736581-6 Subj: Death. Indians of North America.

Buffalo woman ill. by author. Bradbury Pr., 1984. Subj: Folk and fairy tales. Indians of North America.

Death of the iron horse ill. by author. Bradbury Pr., 1987. ISBN 0-02-737830-6 Subj: Indians of North America. Trains. War.

The friendly wolf ill. by author. Dutton, 1974. Subj: Animals – wolves. Behavior – lost. Indians of North America.

The gift of the sacred dog ill. by author. Bradbury Pr., 1980. Subj: Animals – horses. Folk and fairy tales. Indians of North America.

The girl who loved wild horses ill. by author. Dutton, 1978. Subj: Animals – horses. Caldecott award book. Indians of North America.

Her seven brothers ill. by author. Bradbury Pr., 1988. ISBN 0-02-737960-4 Subj: Animals – buffaloes. Folk and fairy tales. Indians of North America.

Iktomi and the boulder: a Plains Indian story ed. by Richard Jackson; ill. by author. Watts, 1988. ISBN 0-531-08360-8 Subj: Folk and fairy tales. Indians of North America.

Star boy ill. by author. Bradbury Pr., 1983. ISBN 0-02-722660-3 Subj: Activities – dancing. Character traits – appearance. Folk and fairy tales. Indians of North America.

Goddard, Carrie Lou. *Isn't it a wonder!* ill. by Leigh Grant. Abingdon Pr., 1976. Subj: Religion.

Godden, Rumer. *A kindle of kittens* ill. by Lynne Byrnes. Viking, 1979. Subj: Animals – cats.

Goennel, Heidi. *My day* ill. by author. Little, 1988. ISBN 0-316-31839-6 Subj: Activities.

Seasons ill. by author. Little, 1986. ISBN 0-316-31836-1 Subj: Seasons.

When I grow up... ill. by author. Little, 1987. ISBN 0-316-31838-8 Subj: Behavior – growing up.

Goff, Beth. *Where's daddy?* ill. by Susan Perl. Beacon Pr., 1969. Subj: Divorce.

Goffe, Toni. *Toby's animal rescue service* ill. by author. David and Charles, 1982. Subj: Activities – ballooning. Animals.

Goffstein, M. B. (Marilyn Brooke). *Across the sea* ill. by author. Farrar, 1968. Subj: Foreign lands.

An actor ill. by author. Harper, 1987. ISBN 0-06-022169-0 Subj: Activities – working. Careers. Theater.

Artists' helpers enjoy the evening ill. by author. Harper, 1987. ISBN 0-06-022182-8 Subj: Art. Concepts – color. Foreign lands – France.

Family scrapbook ill. by author. Farrar, 1978. Subj: Family life.

Fish for supper ill. by author. Dial Pr., 1976. Subj: Caldecott award honor book. Family life – grandmothers. Old age. Sports – fishing.

Goldie the dollmaker ill. by author. Farrar, 1969. Subj: Emotions – loneliness. Jewish culture. Orphans. Toys – dolls.

Laughing latkes ill. by author. Farrar, 1981. Subj: Holidays – Hanukkah. Jewish culture.

A little Schubert ill. by author. Harper, 1972. Subj: Music.

Me and my captain ill. by author. Farrar, 1974. Subj: Toys – dolls.

My Noah's ark ill. by author. Harper, 1978. Subj: Religion – Noah.

Natural history ill. by author. Farrar, 1979. Subj: Animals. Character traits – kindness to animals.

Neighbors ill. by author. Harper, 1979. Subj: Character traits – shyness. Emotions – loneliness.

Our prairie home: a picture album ill. by author. Harper, 1988. ISBN 0-06-022291-3 Subj: Country. Toys – dolls. Family life.

Our snowman ill. by author. Harper, 1986. ISBN 0-06-022153-4 Subj: Activities – playing. Family life. Snowmen.

School of names ill. by author. Harper, 1986. ISBN 0-06-021985-8 Subj: Names. School. World.

Sleepy people ill. by author. Farrar, 1966. Subj: Bedtime.

A writer ill. by author. Harper, 1984. Subj: Activities – working. Careers – writers.

Gold, Phyllis. *Please don't say hello* ill. by Carl Baker. Human Sci. Pr., 1975. Subj: Handicaps.

Goldberg, Phyllis *see* Gold, Phyllis

The golden goose ill. by William Stobbs. McGraw-Hill, 1967. Subj: Birds – chickens. Cumulative tales. Folk and fairy tales. Humor. Royalty.

Golden tales from long ago: *Like Grandpa, Only birds, The three kittens.* Delacorte, 1980. Anonymous stories published by Ernest Nister in London near the turn of the century. Subj: Format, unusual.

Goldfrank, Helen Colodny Kay *see* Kay, Helen

Goldie-Morrison, Karen. *Danger colors* (Oxford Scientific Films)

Hide and seek (Oxford Scientific Films)

Goldin, Augusta. *Ducks don't get wet* ill. by Leonard P. Kessler. Crowell, 1965. Subj: Birds – ducks. Science.

Salt ill. by Robert Galster. Crowell, 1966. Subj: Science.

The shape of water ill. by Demi. Doubleday, 1979. Subj: Science.

Spider silk ill. by Joseph Low. Crowell, 1964. Subj: Science. Spiders.

Straight hair, curly hair ill. by Ed Emberley. Crowell, 1966. Subj: Hair. Science.

Where does your garden grow? ill. by Helen Borten. Crowell, 1967. Subj: Activities – gardening. Science.

Goldin, Barbara Diamond. *Just enough is plenty: a Hannukkah tale* ill. by Seymour Chwast. Viking, 1988. ISBN 0-670-81852-6 Subj: Behavior – sharing. Holidays – Hanukkah. Jewish culture.

Goldman, Susan. *Cousins are special* ill. by author. Albert Whitman, 1978. Subj: Family life.

Grandma is somebody special ed. by Caroline Rubin; ill. by author. Albert Whitman, 1976. Subj: Family life – grandmothers.

Goldner, Kathryn Allen. *The dangers of strangers* (Vogel, Carole Garbuny)

Goldsmith, Howard. *Little lost dog* ill. by Ulises Wensell. Santillana, 1983. ISBN 0-88272-179-8 Subj: Animals – dogs. Behavior – lost. Character traits – honesty. Friendship. Illness.

Toto the timid turtle ill. by Shirley Chan. Human Sciences Pr., 1981. Subj: Reptiles – turtles, tortoises.

Gomi, Taro. *Bus stop* ill. by author. Chronicle, 1988. ISBN 0-87701-551-1 Subj: Activities – traveling. Buses. Transportation.

Coco can't wait! ill. by author. Morrow, 1984. Subj: Family life – grandmothers.

First comes Harry ill. by author. Morrow, 1987. ISBN 0-688-06732-8 Subj: Behavior – hurrying.

Hi, butterfly! ill. by author. Morrow, 1985. ISBN 0-688-04138-8 Subj: Format, unusual. Insects – butterflies, caterpillars.

Toot! ill. by author. Morrow, 1986. ISBN 0-688-06421-3 Subj: Illness. Music. Poetry, rhyme.

Where's the fish? ill. by author. Morrow, 1986. ISBN 0-688-06242-3 Subj: Behavior – hiding. Fish.

The good-hearted youngest brother: *an Hungarian folktale* tr. by Emöke de Papp Severo; ill. by Diane Goode. Bradbury Pr., 1981. Subj: Character traits – kindness to animals. Folk and fairy tales. Foreign lands – Hungary. Magic.

Goodall, Daphne Machin. *Zebras* ill. with photos. Raintree, 1978. Subj: Animals – zebras.

Goodall, John S. *The adventures of Paddy Pork* ill. by author. Harcourt, 1968. Subj: Animals – pigs. Behavior – running away. Circus. Format, unusual. Wordless.

The ballooning adventures of Paddy Pork ill. by author. Harcourt, 1969. Subj: Animals – pigs. Format, unusual. Wordless.

Creepy castle ill. by author. Atheneum, 1975. Subj: Animals – mice. Format, unusual. Knights. Monsters. Wordless.

An Edwardian Christmas ill. by author. Atheneum, 1978. Subj: Foreign lands – England. Format, unusual. Holidays – Christmas. Wordless.

An Edwardian summer ill. by author. Atheneum, 1976. Subj: Foreign lands – England. Format, unusual. Seasons – summer. Wordless.

Jacko ill. by author. Harcourt, 1971. Subj: Animals – monkeys. Boats, ships. Format, unusual. Wordless.

The midnight adventures of Kelly, Dot and Esmeralda ill. by author. Atheneum, 1972. Subj: Format, unusual. Wordless.

Naughty Nancy ill. by author. Atheneum, 1975. Subj: Behavior – misbehavior. Format, unusual. Weddings. Wordless.

Naughty Nancy goes to school ill. by author. Atheneum, 1985. ISBN 0-689-50329-6 Subj: Behavior – misbehavior. Format, unusual. School. Wordless.

Paddy goes traveling ill. by author. Atheneum, 1982. Subj: Activities – traveling. Animals – pigs. Format, unusual. Wordless.

Paddy Pork: odd jobs ill. by author. Atheneum, 1983. Subj: Activities – working. Animals – pigs. Format, unusual. Wordless.

Paddy Pork's holiday ill. by author. Atheneum, 1976. Subj: Activities – vacationing. Animals – pigs. Format, unusual. Wordless.

Paddy to the rescue ill. by author. Atheneum, 1986. ISBN 0-689-50330-X Subj: Animals – pigs. Behavior – stealing. Character traits – bravery. Crime. Wordless.

Paddy under water ill. by author. Atheneum, 1984. Subj: Animals – pigs. Format, unusual. Sea and seashore. Wordless.

Paddy's evening out ill. by author. Atheneum, 1973. Subj: Animals – pigs. Format, unusual. Theater. Wordless.

Paddy's new hat ill. by author. Atheneum, 1980. Subj: Animals – pigs. Careers – police officers. Format, unusual. Wordless.

Shrewbettina's birthday ill. by author. Harcourt, 1970. Subj: Animals – shrews. Birthdays. Format, unusual. Wordless.

The story of a castle ill. by author. Macmillan, 1986. ISBN 0-689-50405-5 Subj: Foreign lands – England. Format, unusual. Wordless.

The story of a farm ill. by author. Macmillan, 1988. ISBN 0-689-50479-9 Subj: Farms. Foreign lands – England. Format, unusual. Wordless.

The story of a main street ill. by author. Macmillan, 1987. ISBN 0-233-98070-9 Subj: City. Format, unusual. Roads. Wordless.

The story of an English village ill. by author. Atheneum, 1979. Subj: City. Foreign lands – England. Format, unusual. Progress. Wordless.

The surprise picnic ill. by author. Atheneum, 1977. Subj: Activities – picnicking. Animals – cats. Food. Format, unusual. Wordless.

Goode, Diane. *Cinderella* (Perrault, Charles)

I hear a noise ill. by author. Dutton, 1988. ISBN 0-525-44353-3 Subj: Bedtime. Dragons. Emotions – fear. Monsters. Night.

Rumpty-Dudget's tower (Hawthorne, Julian)

Goodenow, Earle. *The last camel* ill. by author. Walck, 1968. Subj: Animals – camels. Foreign lands – Egypt.

The owl who hated the dark ill. by author. Walck, 1969. Subj: Birds – owls. Emotions – fear. Night.

Goodnow, Elizabeth *see* Cooper, Elizabeth K.

Goodsell, Jane. *Katie's magic glasses* ill. by Barbara Cooney. Subj: Careers – doctors. Glasses. Senses – seeing.

Toby's toe ill. by Gioia Fiammenghi. Morrow, 1986. ISBN 0-688-06162-1 Subj: Character traits – kindness. Character traits – meanness. Toys – balloons.

Goodspeed, Peter. *Hugh and Fitzhugh* ill. by Carol Nicklaus. Platt, 1974. Subj: Animals – dogs. Language.

A rhinoceros wakes me up in the morning: a bedtime tale ill. by Dennis Panek. Bradbury Pr., 1982. Subj: Animals. Bedtime. Poetry, rhyme.

Goor, Nancy. *All kinds of feet* (Goor, Ron)

In the driver's seat (Goor, Ron)

Shadows (Goor, Ron)

Signs (Goor, Ron)

Goor, Ron. *All kinds of feet* by Ron and Nancy Goor; photos. by authors. Crowell, 1984. Subj: Anatomy. Animals.

Backyard insects (Selsam, Millicent E.)

In the driver's seat by Ron and Nancy Goor; photos. by authors. Crowell, 1982. Subj: Activities. Machines.

Shadows: here, there and everywhere by Ron and Nancy Goor; photos. by authors. Crowell, 1981. Subj: Shadows.

Signs by Ron and Nancy Goor; photos. by authors. Crowell, 1983. Subj: Activities – reading. Communication.

Gordon, Margaret. *Frogs' holiday* ill. by author. Viking, 1987. ISBN 0-670-80854-7 Subj: Activities – baby-sitting. Frogs and toads.

The supermarket mice ill. by author. Dutton, 1984. Subj: Animals – cats. Animals – mice. Problem solving. Stores.

Wilberforce goes on a picnic ill. by author. Morrow, 1982. Subj: Activities – picnicking. Animals – bears.

Wilberforce goes to a party ill. by author. Viking, 1985. ISBN 0-670-80148-8 Subj: Animals – bears. Behavior – misbehavior. Birthdays. Etiquette. Parties.

Gordon, Neil *see* Cameron, John

Gordon, Sharon. *Christmas surprise* ill. by John Magine. Troll Assoc., 1980. Subj: Animals – bears. Holidays – Christmas.

Dinosaurs in trouble ill. by Paul Harvey. Troll Assoc., 1980. Subj: Dinosaurs.

Dolphins and porpoises ill. by June Goldsborough. Troll Assoc., 1985. ISBN 0-8167-0340-X Subj: Animals – dolphins. Sea and seashore.

Easter Bunny's lost egg ill. by John Magine. Troll Assoc., 1980. Subj: Animals – rabbits. Eggs. Holidays – Easter.

Friendly snowman ill. by John Magine. Troll Assoc., 1980. Subj: Snowmen.

Pete the parakeet ill. by Paul Harvey. Troll Assoc., 1980. Subj: Birds – parakeets, parrots.

Play ball, Kate! ill. by Don Page. Troll Assoc., 1981. Subj: Sports – baseball.

Sam the scarecrow ill. by Don Silverstein. Troll Assoc., 1980. Subj: Scarecrows.

Three little witches ill. by Deborah Sims. Troll Assoc., 1980. Subj: Witches.

Tick tock clock ill. by Don Page. Troll Assoc., 1982. Subj: Clocks. Time.

Trees ill. by Irene Trivas. Troll Assoc., 1983. Subj: Trees.

What a dog! ill. by Deborah Sims. Troll Assoc., 1980. Subj: Animals – dogs.

Gordon, Shirley. *Crystal is my friend* ill. by Edward Frascino. Harper, 1978. Subj: Friendship. School.

Crystal is the new girl ill. by Edward Frascino. Harper, 1976. Subj: Friendship. School.

Grandma zoo ill. by Whitney Darrow, Jr. Harper, 1978. Subj: Animals. Family life – grandmothers. Zoos.

Happy birthday, Crystal ill. by Edward Frascino. Harper, 1981. Subj: Birthdays. Emotions – envy, jealousy. Parties.

Gorey, Edward. *The tunnel calamity* ill. by author. Putnam's, 1984. Subj: Format, unusual. Monsters. Wordless.

Gorey, Edward St. John *see* Gorey, Edward

Gorham, Michael *see* Elting, Mary

Gorsline, Douglas. *North American Indians* (Gorsline, Marie)

Gorsline, Marie. *North American Indians* by Marie and Douglas Gorsline; ill. by authors. Random House, 1978. Subj: Indians of North America. U.S. history.

Goudey, Alice E. *The day we saw the sun come up* ill. by Adrienne Adams. Scribner's, 1961. Subj: Caldecott award honor book. Family life. Sun.

The good rain ill. by Nora Spicer Unwin. Dutton, 1950. Subj: Weather – rain.

Houses from the sea ill. by Adrienne Adams. Scribner's, 1959. Subj: Caldecott award honor book. Sea and seashore.

Red legs ill. by Marie Nonnast. Scribner's, 1966. Subj: Insects.

Gould, Deborah. *Brendan's best-timed birthday* ill. by Jacqueline Rogers. Bradbury Pr., 1988. ISBN 0-02-737390-8 Subj: Behavior – sharing. Birthdays. Clocks. Parties.

Grandpa's slide show ill. by Cheryl Harness. Lothrop, 1987. ISBN 0-688-06973-8 Subj: Death. Dreams. Family life – grandparents.

Goundaud, Karen Jo. *A very mice joke book* ill. by Lynn Munsinger. Houghton, 1981. Subj: Animals – mice. Riddles.

Goyder, Alice. *Holiday in Catland* ill. by author. Crowell, 1979. Subj: Activities – vacationing. Animals – cats.

Party in Catland ill. by author. Crowell, 1979. Subj: Animals – cats. Parties.

Grabianski, Janusz. *Cats* ill. by author. Watts, 1966. Subj: Animals – cats.

Grabianski's wild animals ill. by author. Watts, 1969. Translation of Tiere der Wildnis. Subj: Animals.

Horses ill. by author. Watts, 1966. Subj: Animals – horses.

Graham, Al. *Songs for a small guitar* ill. by Tony Palazzo. Duell, 1962. Subj: Poetry, rhyme. Songs.

Timothy Turtle ill. by Tony Palazzo. Walck, 1946. Subj: Caldecott award honor book. Character traits – ambition. Character traits – helpfulness. Friendship. Reptiles – turtles, tortoises.

Graham, Amanda. *Picasso, the green tree frog* ill. by John Siow. Gareth Stevens, 1987. ISBN 1-55532-152-6 Subj: Concepts – color. Frogs and toads.

Who wants Arthur? ill. by Donna Gynell. Gareth Stevens, 1987. ISBN 1-55532-153-4 Subj: Animals – dogs. Behavior – imitation. Stores.

Graham, Bob. *Crusher is coming!* ill. by author. Viking, 1987. ISBN 0-670-82081-4 Subj: Babies. Friendship.

First there was Frances ill. by author. Bradbury Pr., 1986. ISBN 0-02-737030-5 Subj: Animals. Family life. Moving.

Libby, Oscar and me ill. by author. Harper, 1985. Subj: Animals – cats. Animals – dogs. Activities – picnicking.

Pete and Roland ill. by author. Viking, 1984. ISBN 0-670-54912-6 Subj: Birds – parakeets, parrots. Character traits – kindness to animals.

The red woolen blanket ill. by author. Little, 1988. ISBN 0-316-32310-1 Subj: Behavior – growing up. Concepts – color.

The wild ill. by author. Harper, 1987. ISBN 0-87226-139-5 Subj: Family life. Nature. Pets.

Graham, Hugh *see* Barrows, Marjorie Wescott

Graham, John. *A crowd of cows* ill. by Feodor Rojankovsky. Harcourt, 1968. Subj: Animals. Noise, sounds.

I love you, mouse ill. by Tomie de Paola. Harcourt, 1976. Subj: Animals. Animals – mice.

Graham, Lorenz B. *David he no fear* ill. by Ann Grifalconi. Crowell, 1971. Subj: Religion.

Every man heart lay down ill. by Colleen Browning. Crowell, 1970. Subj: Religion.

God wash the world and start again ill. by Clare Romano. Crowell, 1971. Subj: Religion – Noah.

Hongry catch the foolish boy ill. by James Brown, Jr. Crowell, 1973. Story first appeared in the author's How God fix Jonah, published in 1946. Subj: Religion.

A road down in the sea ill. by Gregorio Prestopino. Crowell, 1970. Subj: Religion.

Song of the boat ill. by Leo and Diane Dillon. Crowell, 1975. Subj: Foreign lands – Africa. Poetry, rhyme.

Graham, Margaret Bloy. *Be nice to spiders* ill. by author. Harper, 1967. Subj: Spiders. Zoos.

Benjy and his friend Fifi ill. by author. Harper, 1988. ISBN 0-06-022253-0 Subj: Animals – dogs. Character traits – helpfulness. Emotions – fear.

Benjy and the barking bird ill. by author. Harper, 1971. Subj: Animals – dogs. Birds – parakeets, parrots. Emotions – envy, jealousy.

Benjy's boat trip ill. by author. Harper, 1977. Subj: Animals – dogs. Boats, ships.

Benjy's dog house ill. by author. Harper, 1973. Subj: Animals – dogs.

Graham, Mary Stuart Campbell. *The pirates' bridge* ill. by Winifred Lubell. Lothrop, 1960. Subj: Pirates.

Graham, Thomas. *Mr. Bear's boat* ill. by author. Dutton, 1988. ISBN 0-525-44375-4 Subj: Activities – picnicking. Animals – bears. Boats, ships.

Mr. Bear's chair ill. by author. Dutton, 1987. ISBN 0-525-44300-2 Subj: Animals – bears. Family life.

Grahame, Kenneth. *The open road* ill. by Beverley Gooding. Scribner's, 1980. Subj: Activities – traveling. Animals.

The river bank: from The wind in the willows ill. by Adrienne Adams. Scribner's, 1977. Subj: Animals. Rivers.

Gramatky, Hardie. *Bolivar* ill. by author. Putnam's, 1961. Subj: Animals – donkeys. Foreign lands – South America.

Hercules ill. by author. Putnam's, 1940. Subj: Careers – firefighters. Fire. Museums. Trucks.

Homer and the circus train ill. by author. Putnam's, 1957. Subj: Circus. Trains.

Little Toot ill. by author. Putnam's, 1939. Subj: Boats, ships. Character traits – ambition.

Little Toot on the Mississippi ill. by author. Putnam's, 1973. Subj: Boats, ships. Rivers.

Little Toot on the Thames ill. by author. Putnam's, 1964. Subj: Boats, ships. Foreign lands – England.

Little Toot through the Golden Gate ill. by author. Putnam's, 1975. Subj: Boats, ships. City. Character traits – individuality.

Loopy ill. by author. Putnam's, 1941. Subj: Activities – flying. Airplanes, airports.

Nikos and the sea god ill. by author. Putnam's, 1963. Subj: Careers – fishermen. Folk and fairy tales. Mythical creatures. Religion.

Sparky: the story of a little trolley car ill. by author. Putnam's, 1952. Subj: Cable cars, trolleys. Transportation.

Grant, Anne. *Danbury's burning! The story of Sybil Ludington's ride* ill. by Pat Howell. Walck, 1976. Subj: U.S. history.

Grant, Joan. *The monster that grew small* ill. by Jill K. Schwarz. Lothrop, 1987. ISBN 0-688-06809-X Subj: Character traits – bravery. Character traits – kindness to animals. Emotions – fear. Folk and fairy tales. Foreign lands – Egypt. Monsters.

Grant, Matthew G. *see* May, Julian

Grasshopper to the rescue: *a Georgian story* tr. from the Russian by Bonnie Carey; ill. by Tasha Tudor. Morrow, 1979. Subj: Character traits – bravery. Cumulative tales. Insects – grasshoppers. Rivers.

Graves, Robert. *The big green book* ill. by Maurice Sendak. Macmillan, 1985. ISBN 0-02-736810-6 Subj: Family life. Imagination. Magic. Orphans.

Two wise children ill. by Ralph Pinto. Delacorte, 1967. Subj: Magic.

Graves, Robert Von Ranke *see* Graves, Robert

Gray, Catherine. *Tammy and the gigantic fish* by Catherine and James Gray; ill. by William Joyce. Harper, 1983. Subj: Family life. Sports – fishing.

Gray, Genevieve. *How far, Felipe?* ill. by Ann Grifalconi. Harper, 1978. Subj: Activities – traveling. Animals – donkeys. Character traits – perseverance.

Send Wendell ill. by Symeon Shimin. McGraw-Hill, 1974. Subj: Character traits – helpfulness. Ethnic groups in the U.S. – Afro-Americans. Family life.

Gray, James. *Tammy and the gigantic fish* (Gray, Catherine)

Gray, Jenny *see* Gray, Genevieve

Gray, Nigel. *A balloon for grandad* ill. by Jane Ray. Watts, 1988. ISBN 0-531-08355-1 Subj: Family life – fathers. Family life – grandfathers. Toys – balloons.

It'll all come out in the wash ill. by Edward Frascino. Harper, 1979. Subj: Family life.

Grayson, Marion F. *Let's count and count out*

Greaves, Margaret. *Little Bear and the Papagini circus* ill. by Francesca Crespi. Dial Pr., 1986. ISBN 0-8037-0264-7 Subj: Animals – bears. Circus. Family life.

The magic flute: the story of Mozart's opera ill. by Francesca Crespi. Holt, 1988. ISBN 0-8050-0887-X Subj: Magic. Music. Theater.

The mice of Nibbling Village ill. by Jane Pinkney. Dutton, 1986. ISBN 0-525-44277-4 Subj: Animals – mice. Poetry, rhyme.

A net to catch the wind ill. by Stephen Gammell. Harper, 1979. Subj: Animals – horses. Forest, woods. Royalty.

Once there were no pandas ill. by Beverley Gooding. Dutton, 1985. ISBN 0-525-44211-1 Subj: Animals – pandas. Character traits – bravery.

Greeley, Valerie. *Farm animals* ill. by author. Harper, 1984. Subj: Animals. Farms. Format, unusual – board books. Wordless.

Field animals ill. by author. Harper, 1984. Subj: Animals. Format, unusual – board books. Wordless.

Pets ill. by author. Harper, 1984. Subj: Animals. Format, unusual – board books. Pets. Wordless.

Zoo animals ill. by author. Harper, 1984. Subj: Animals. Format, unusual – board books. Wordless. Zoos.

Green, Adam *see* Weisgard, Leonard

The green grass grows all around: *a traditional folk song* ill. by Hilde Hoffmann. Macmillan, 1968. Subj: Plants. Poetry, rhyme. Songs.

Green, Marion. *The magician who lived on the mountain* ill. by John Dyke. Children's Pr., 1978. Subj: Art. Magic.

Green, Mary McBurney. *Everybody has a house and everybody eats* ill. by Louis Klein. Abelard-Schuman, 1944. Subj: Farms. Houses.

Is it hard? Is it easy? ill. by Lucienne Bloch. Abelard-Schuman, 1948. Subj: Concepts.

Green, Melinda. *Bembelman's bakery* ill. by Barbara Seuling. Parents, 1978. Subj: Careers – bakers.

Green, Norma B. *The hole in the dike* ill. by Eric Carle. Crowell, 1974. Subj: Character traits – helpfulness. Foreign lands – Holland.

Green, Phyllis. *Bagdad ate it* ill. by Joel Schick. Watts, 1980. Subj: Animals – dogs. Behavior – greed.

Uncle Roland, the perfect guest ill. by Marybeth Farrell. Four Winds Pr., 1983. Subj: Family life.

Green, Suzanne. *The little choo-choo: sounds, sights and opposites* ill. by Miho Fujita. Doubleday, 1988. ISBN 0-385-24426-6 Subj: Concepts – opposites. Noise, sounds. Toys – trains.

Greenaway, Kate. *A apple pie* ill. by author. Warne, 1886. Subj: ABC books.

Marigold garden ill. by author. Warne, 1885. Subj: Poetry, rhyme.

Under the window ill. by author. Warne, 1879. Subj: Poetry, rhyme.

Greenberg, Barbara. *The bravest babysitter* ill. by Diane Paterson. Dial Pr., 1977. Subj: Activities – baby-sitting. Babies. Emotions – fear. Weather.

Greenberg, David. *Slugs* ill. by Victoria Chess. Little, 1983. Subj: Poetry, rhyme.

Greenberg, Judith E. *Adopted* by Judith E. Greenberg and Helen H. Carey; photos. by Barbara Kirk. Watts, 1987. ISBN 0-531-10290-4 Subj: Adoption. Babies.

What is the sign for friend? photos. by Gayle Rothschild. Watts, 1985. ISBN 0-531-04939-6 Subj: Handicaps – deafness. Language. Senses – hearing.

Greenberg, Polly. *Oh, Lord, I wish I was a buzzard* ill. by Aliki. Macmillan, 1968. Subj: Behavior – wishing. Ethnic groups in the U.S. – Afro-Americans. Farms. Plants.

Greene, Carla. *Animal doctors: what do they do?* ill. by Leonard P. Kessler. Harper, 1967. Subj: Careers – veterinarians.

Cowboys: what do they do? ill. by Leonard P. Kessler. Harper, 1972. Subj: Cowboys.

Doctors and nurses: what do they do? ill. by Leonard P. Kessler. Harper, 1963. Subj: Careers – doctors. Careers – nurses.

I want to be a carpenter ill. by Frances Eckart. Children's Pr., 1959. Subj: Careers – carpenters.

A motor holiday ill. by Harold L. Van Pelt. Melmont, 1956. Subj: Activities – traveling.

Railroad engineers and airplane pilots: what do they do? ill. by Leonard P. Kessler. Harper, 1964. Subj: Careers – airplane pilots. Careers – railroad engineers.

Soldiers and sailors: what do they do? ill. by Leonard P. Kessler. Harper, 1963. Subj: Careers – military.

Truck drivers: what do they do? ill. by Leonard P. Kessler. Harper, 1967. Subj: Careers – truck drivers. Trucks.

What do they do? Policemen and firemen ill. by Leonard P. Kessler. Harper, 1962. Subj: Careers – firefighters. Careers – police officers.

Greene, Carol. *A computer went a-courting: a love song for Valentine's Day* ill. by Tom Dunnington. Children's Pr., 1983. Subj: Animals – mice. Holidays – Valentine's Day. Machines. Music. Songs.

Hi, clouds ill. by Gene Sharp. Children's Pr., 1983. Subj: Weather – clouds.

Hinny Winny Bunco ill. by Jeanette Winter. Harper, 1982. Subj: Music. Sibling rivalry. Songs.

I can be a baseball player ill. with photos. Childrens Pr., 1985. ISBN 0-516-01845-0 Subj: Careers. Sports – baseball.

I can be a model. Childrens Pr., 1985. ISBN 0-516-01887-6 Subj: Careers – models.

The insignificant elephant ill. by Susan Gantner. Harcourt, 1985. Subj: Animals – elephants. Animals – rabbits.

Please, wind? ill. by Gene Sharp. Children's Pr., 1982. Subj: Weather – wind.

Rain! Rain! ill. by Larry Frederick. Children's Pr., 1982. Subj: Weather – rain.

Robots ill. with photos. Children's Pr., 1983. Subj: Robots.

Shine, sun! ill. by Gene Sharp. Children's Pr., 1983. Subj: Sun.

Snow Joe ill. by Paul Sharp. Children's Pr., 1982. Subj: Weather – snow.

The thirteen days of Halloween ill. by Tom Dunnington. Children's Pr., 1983. Subj: Holidays – Halloween. Music. Songs. Witches.

The world's biggest birthday cake ill. by Tom Dunnington. Childrens Pr., 1985. ISBN 0-516-08233-7 Subj: Birthdays. Food. Music. Poetry, rhyme.

Greene, Ellin. *Princess Rosetta and the popcorn man* ill. by Trina Schart Hyman. Lothrop, 1971. From The Pot of Gold by Mary E. Wilkins. Subj: Folk and fairy tales. Food. Royalty.

The pumpkin giant ill. by Trina Schart Hyman. Lothrop, 1970. Orig. story by Mary E. Wilkins. Subj: Food. Giants. Holidays – Halloween.

Greene, Graham. *The little fire engine* ill. by Edward Ardizzone. Doubleday, 1973. Subj: Fire. Progress.

The little train ill. by Edward Ardizzone. Doubleday, 1973. Subj: Behavior – running away. Trains.

Greene, Jacqueline Dembar. *Butchers and bakers, rabbis and kings* ill. by Marilyn Hirsh. Kar-Ben Copies, 1984. Subj: Jewish culture.

Greene, Laura. *Change: getting to know about ebb and flow* ill. by Gretchen Will Mayo. Human Sciences Pr., 1981. Subj: Concepts.

Help: getting to know about needing and giving ill. by Gretchen Will Mayo. Human Sciences Pr., 1981. Subj: Character traits – helpfulness.

Greene, Roberta. *Two and me makes three* ill. by Paul Galdone. Coward, 1970. Subj: Ethnic groups in the U.S.

Greenfield, Eloise. *Africa dream* ill. by Carole Byard. John Day, 1977. Subj: Dreams. Foreign lands – Africa.

Daydreamers ill. by Tom Feelings. Dial Pr., 1981. Subj: Ethnic groups in the U.S. – Afro-Americans. Poetry, rhyme.

First pink light ill. by Moneta Barnett. Crowell, 1976. Subj: Ethnic groups in the U.S. – Afro-Americans. Family life – fathers.

Grandpa's face ill. by Floyd Cooper. Putnam's, 1988. ISBN 0-399-21525-5 Subj: Character traits – appearance. Family life – grandfathers.

I can do it by myself (Little, Lessie Jones)

Me and Nessie ill. by Moneta Barnett. Crowell, 1975. Subj: Ethnic groups in the U.S. – Afro-Americans. Family life. Imagination – imaginary friends.

She come bringing me that little baby girl ill. by John Steptoe. Lippincott, 1974. Subj: Babies. Emotions – envy, jealousy. Ethnic groups in the U.S. – Afro-Americans. Sibling rivalry.

Under the Sunday tree ill. by Amos Ferguson. Harper, 1988. ISBN 0-06-022254-9 Subj: Foreign lands – Caribbean Islands. Islands. Poetry, rhyme.

Greenhill, Richard. *A family in China* (Fyson, Nance Lui)

Greenleaf, Ann. *No room for Sarah* ill. by author. Dodd, 1983. Subj: Bedtime. Toys.

Greenwood, Ann. *A pack of dreams* ill. by Bernard Colonna and Mary Elizabeth Gordon. Prentice-Hall, 1979. Subj: Dreams. Poetry, rhyme.

Gregor, Arthur S. *Animal babies* (Ylla)

The little elephant (Ylla)

One, two, three, four, five ill. by Robert Doisneau. Lippincott, 1956. Subj: Counting.

Gregorich, Barbara. *My friend goes left* ill. by Joyce John; ed. by Joan Hoffman. School Zone Pub., 1984. Subj: Poetry, rhyme. Riddles.

Gregory, Valiska. *Sunny side up* ill. by Jeni Bassett. Four Winds Pr., 1986. ISBN 0-02-738050-5 Subj: Animals – dogs. Character traits – optimism.

Terribly wonderful ill. by Jeni Bassett. Four Winds Pr., 1986. ISBN 0-02-738110-1 Subj: Animals – dogs. Character traits – optimism.

Greifenstein, Sandra. *The fish* (Bruna, Dick)

Greisman, Joan. *Things I hate!* (Wittels, Harriet)

Gretz, Susanna. *Hide-and-seek* ill. by author. Macmillan, 1986. ISBN 0-02-737400-9 Subj: Bedtime. Behavior – hiding. Emotions – fear. Format, unusual – board books. Games. Night. Toys – teddy bears.

I'm not sleepy ill. by author. Macmillan, 1986. ISBN 0-02-737470-X Subj: Bedtime. Format, unusual – board books. Games. Sleep. Toys – teddy bears.

It's your turn, Roger ill. by author. Dial Pr., 1985. ISBN 0-8037-0198-5 Subj: Animals – pigs. Behavior – sharing. Food.

Ready for bed ill. by author. Macmillan, 1986. ISBN 0-02-737460-2 Subj: Bedtime. Format, unusual – board books.

Roger loses his marbles! ill. by author. Dial Pr., 1988. ISBN 0-8037-0565-4 Subj: Animals – pigs. Birthdays. Character traits – practicality.

Roger takes charge! ill. by author. Dial Pr., 1987. ISBN 0-8037-0121-7 Subj: Activities – baby-sitting. Animals – pigs. Behavior – bullying.

Teddy bears ABC ill. by author. Follett, 1975. Subj: ABC books. Counting. Toys – teddy bears.

Teddy bears cure a cold by Susanna Gretz and Alison Sage; ill. by Susanna Gretz. Four Winds Pr., 1985. ISBN 0-590-07949-2 Subj: Illness. Toys – teddy bears.

Teddy bears go shopping ill. by author. Four Winds Pr., 1982. Subj: Shopping. Toys – teddy bears.

Teddy bears' moving day ill. by author. Four Winds Pr., 1981. Subj: Moving. Toys – teddy bears.

Teddy bears 1 - 10 ill. by author. Four Winds Pr., 1986, 1969. ISBN 0-02-738140-4 Subj: Counting. Toys – teddy bears.

Teddy bears stay indoors ill. by author. Four Winds Pr., 1987. ISBN 0-02-738150-1 Subj: Toys – teddy bears.

Teddy bears take the train by Susanna Gretz and Alison Sage; ill. by Susanna Gretz. Four Winds Pr., 1987. ISBN 0-02-738170-6 Subj: Activities – traveling. Toys – teddy bears. Trains.

Teddybears cookbook by Susanna Gretz and Alison Sage; ill. by Susanna Gretz. Doubleday, 1978. Subj: Activities – cooking. Toys – teddy bears.

Too dark! ill. by author. Macmillan, 1986. ISBN 0-02-737410-6 Subj: Bedtime. Emotions – fear. Format, unusual – board books. Night. Toys – teddy bears.

Greydanus, Rose. *Animals at the zoo* ill. by Susan Hall. Troll Assoc., 1980. Subj: Animals. Zoos.

Big red fire engine ill. by Paul Harvey. Troll Assoc., 1980. Subj: Careers – firefighters. Trucks.

Changing seasons ill. by Susan Hall. Troll Assoc., 1983. Subj: Seasons.

Freddie the frog ill. by Tom Garcia. Troll Assoc., 1980. Subj: Frogs and toads.

Horses ill. by Joel Snyder. Troll Assoc., 1983. Subj: Animals – horses.

My secret hiding place ill. by Paul Harvey. Troll Assoc., 1980. Subj: Behavior – hiding.

Susie goes shopping ill. by Margot Apple. Troll Assoc., 1980. Subj: Shopping.

Tree house fun ill. by Chris L. Demarest. Troll Assoc., 1980. Subj: Houses. Trees.

Willie the slowpoke ill. by Andrea Eberbach. Troll Assoc., 1980. Subj: Behavior – hurrying.

Grieg, E. H. (Edvard Hagerup). *E. H. Grieg's Peer Gynt* ill. by Yoshiharu Suzuki. Gakkenk, 1971. Adapt. by Makoto Oishi; tr. by Ann Brannen. Subj: Folk and fairy tales. Foreign lands – Norway.

Grifalconi, Ann. *City rhythms* ill. by author. Bobbs-Merrill, 1965. Subj: City. Ethnic groups in the U.S. – Afro-Americans.

Darkness and the butterfly ill. by author. Little, 1987. ISBN 0-316-32863-4 Subj: Emotions – fear. Foreign lands – Africa. Insects – butterflies, caterpillars. Night.

The toy trumpet ill. by author. Bobbs-Merrill, 1968. Subj: Foreign lands – Mexico. Music. Toys.

The village of round and square houses ill. by author. Little, 1986. ISBN 0-316-32862-6 Subj: Caldecott award honor book. Folk and fairy tales. Foreign lands – Africa. Volcanoes.

Griffen, Elizabeth. *A dog's book of bugs* ill. by Peter Parnall. Atheneum, 1967. Subj: Insects.

Griffith, Helen V. *Alex and the cat* ill. by Joseph Low. Greenwillow, 1982. Subj: Animals – cats. Animals – dogs.

Alex remembers ill. by Donald Carrick. Greenwillow, 1983. Subj: Animals – cats. Animals – dogs. Moon. Seasons – fall.

Georgia music ill. by James Stevenson. Greenwillow, 1986. ISBN 0-688-06072-2 Subj: Activities – gardening. Family life – grandfathers. Music. Nature. Old age. Seasons – summer.

Grandaddy's place ill. by James Stevenson. Greenwillow, 1987. ISBN 0-688-06254-7 Subj: Animals. Country. Family life – grandfathers. Sports – fishing.

Mine will, said John ill. by Muriel Batherman. Greenwillow, 1980. Subj: Animals – dogs. Family life. Pets.

More Alex and the cat ill. by Donald Carrick. Greenwillow, 1983. Subj: Animals – cats. Animals – dogs.

Nata ill. by Nancy Tafuri. Greenwillow, 1985. ISBN 0-688-04977-X Subj: Behavior – bad day. Fairies.

Grimm, Jacob. *The bear and the kingbird* by Jacob and Wilhelm Grimm; tr. by Lore Segal; ill. by Chris Conover. Farrar, 1979. Subj: Animals – bears. Birds. Folk and fairy tales.

The bearskinner by Jacob and Wilhelm Grimm; ill. by Felix Hoffmann. Atheneum, 1978. Translation of Der Bärenhäuter. Subj: Devil. Folk and fairy tales.

The brave little tailor by Jacob and Wilhelm Grimm; ill. by Mark Corcoran. Troll Assoc., 1979. Subj: Careers – tailors. Character traits – bravery. Folk and fairy tales. Giants.

The brave little tailor by Jacob and Wilhelm Grimm; tr. by Anthea Bell; ill. by Svend Otto S. Larousse, 1979. Subj: Careers – tailors. Character traits – bravery. Folk and fairy tales. Giants.

The brave little tailor by Jacob and Wilhelm Grimm; adapt. by Robert D. San Souci; ill. by Daniel San Souci. Doubleday, 1982. Subj: Careers – tailors. Character traits – bravery. Folk and fairy tales. Giants.

The Bremen town musicians by Jacob and Wilhelm Grimm; retold and ill. by Donna Diamond. Delacorte Pr., 1981. Subj: Animals. Folk and fairy tales. Old age.

The Bremen town musicians by Jacob and Wilhelm Grimm; tr. by Elizabeth Shub; ill. by Janina Domanska. Greenwillow, 1980. Subj: Animals. Folk and fairy tales. Old age.

The Bremen town musicians by Jacob and Wilhelm Grimm; ill. by Paul Galdone. McGraw-Hill, 1968. Tr. of Der Bremer Stadtmusikanten. Subj: Animals. Folk and fairy tales. Old age.

Bremen town musicians by Jacob and Wilhelm Grimm; tr. by Anthea Bell; ill. by Josef Paleček. Picture Book Studio, 1988. ISBN 0-88708-071-5 Subj: Animals. Folk and fairy tales. Old age.

The Bremen town musicians by Jacob and Wilhelm Grimm; retold and ill. by Ilse Plume. Doubleday, 1980. Subj: Animals. Caldecott award honor book. Folk and fairy tales. Old age.

Cinderella by Jacob and Wilhelm Grimm; retold and ill. by Nonny Hogrogian. Greenwillow, 1981. Subj: Folk and fairy tales. Royalty. Sibling rivalry.

Cinderella by Jacob and Wilhelm Grimm; tr. by Anne Rogers; ill. by Svend Otto S. Larouse, 1978. Subj: Folk and fairy tales. Royalty. Sibling rivalry.

Clever Kate by Jacob and Wilhelm Grimm; adapt. by Elizabeth Shub; ill. by Anita Lobel. Macmillan, 1973. Subj: Folk and fairy tales. Humor.

The devil with the green hairs by Jacob and Wilhelm Grimm; retold and ill. by Nonny Hogrogian. Knopf, 1983. Subj: Devil. Folk and fairy tales.

The donkey prince by Jacob and Wilhelm Grimm; adapt. by M. Jean Craig; ill. by Barbara Cooney. Doubleday, 1977. Subj: Animals – donkeys. Folk and fairy tales. Magic. Royalty. Wizards.

The earth gnome by Jacob and Wilhelm Grimm; tr. by Wanda Gág; ill. by Margot Tomes. Coward, 1985. ISBN 0-698-20618-5 Subj: Elves and little people. Folk and fairy tales. Magic. Royalty.

The elves and the shoemaker by Jacob and Wilhelm Grimm; ill. by Paul Galdone. Clarion, 1984. Based on Lucy Crane's tr. from the German. Adaption of Wichtelmänner. Subj: Careers – shoemakers. Character traits – helpfulness. Elves and little people. Folk and fairy tales. Foreign lands – Germany.

The elves and the shoemaker by Jacob and Wilhelm Grimm; adapt. and ill. by Bernadette Watts. Holt, 1986. ISBN 0-03-008022-3 Subj: Careers – shoemakers. Character traits – helpfulness. Elves and little people. Folk and fairy tales. Foreign lands – Germany.

The falling stars by Jacob and Wilhelm Grimm; ill. by Eugen Sopko. Holt, 1985. ISBN 0-03-005742-6 Subj: Character traits – generosity. Clothing. Folk and fairy tales.

The fisherman and his wife by Jacob and Wilhelm Grimm; tr. by Elizabeth Shub; ill. by Monika Laimgruber. Greenwillow, 1979. Subj: Behavior – greed. Folk and fairy tales.

The fisherman and his wife by Jacob and Wilhelm Grimm; adapt. by John Warren Stewig; ill. by Margot Tomes. Holiday, 1988. ISBN 0-8234-0714-4 Subj: Behavior – greed. Folk and fairy tales.

The fisherman and his wife by Jacob and Wilhelm Grimm; tr. by Randall Jarrell; ill. by Margot Zemach. Farrar, 1980. Subj: Behavior – greed. Folk and fairy tales.

The four clever brothers by Jacob and Wilhelm Grimm; ill. by Felix Hoffmann. Harcourt, 1967. Subj: Character traits – cleverness. Dragons. Folk and fairy tales.

The glass mountain by Jacob and Wilhelm Grimm; adapt. and ill. by Nonny Hogrogian. Knopf, 1985. Originally titled The raven. ISBN 0-394-96724-0 Subj: Folk and fairy tales. Giants.

Godfather Cat and Mousie by Jacob and Wilhelm Grimm; adapt. by Doris Orgel; ill. by Ann Schweninger. Macmillan, 1986. ISBN 0-02-768690-6 Subj: Animals – cats. Animals – mice. Folk and fairy tales.

The golden bird: and other fairy tales by Jacob and Wilhelm Grimm; tr. by Randall Jarrell; ill. by Sandro Nardini. Macmillan, 1962. Subj: Folk and fairy tales.

The golden goose by Jacob and Wilhelm Grimm; tr. by Anthea Bell; ill. by Dorothée Duntze. Holt, 1988. ISBN 3-85539-004-5 Subj: Character traits – kindness. Folk and fairy tales. Humor. Royalty.

The golden goose by Jacob and Wilhelm Grimm; adapt. by Susan Saunders; ill. by Isadore Seltzer. Scholastic, 1988. ISBN 0-590-41544-1 Subj: Character traits – kindness. Folk and fairy tales. Humor. Royalty.

The golden goose by Jacob and Wilhelm Grimm; ill. by Martin Ursell; text by Linda M. Jennings. Silver Burdett, 1985. ISBN 0-382-09147-7 Subj: Character traits – kindness. Folk and fairy tales. Humor. Royalty.

The goose girl by Jacob and Wilhelm Grimm; tr. by Anthea Bell; ill. by Sabine Bruntjen. Holt, 1988. ISBN 3-85539-003-7 Subj: Folk and fairy tales. Royalty. Weddings.

Grimm Tom Thumb (Tom Thumb)

Hans in luck by Jacob and Wilhelm Grimm; retold and ill. by Paul Galdone. Parents, 1979. Translation of Hans in Glück. Subj: Character traits – foolishness. Character traits – luck. Folk and fairy tales.

Hans in luck by Jacob and Wilhelm Grimm; ed. and ill. by Felix Hoffmann. Atheneum, 1975. Translation of Hans in Glück. Subj: Character traits – foolishness. Character traits – luck. Folk and fairy tales.

Hansel and Gretel by Jacob and Wilhelm Grimm; tr. by Charles Scribner, Jr.; ill. by Adrienne Adams. Scribner's, 1975. Subj: Folk and fairy tales. Forest, woods. Witches.

Hansel and Gretel by Jacob and Wilhelm Grimm; ill. by Anthony Browne. Watts, 1982. Subj: Folk and fairy tales. Forest, woods. Witches.

Hansel and Gretel by Jacob and Wilhelm Grimm; ill. by Susan Jeffers. Dial Pr., 1980. Subj: Folk and fairy tales. Forest, woods. Witches.

Hansel and Gretel by Jacob and Wilhelm Grimm; ill. by Winslow P. Pels. Scholastic, 1988. ISBN 0-590-41793-2 Subj: Behavior – lost. Folk and fairy tales. Forest, woods. Witches.

Hansel and Gretel by Jacob and Wilhelm Grimm; tr. from Spanish by Leland Northam; adapt. by M. Eulalia Valeri; ill. by Conxita Rodriguez. Silver Burdett, 1985. ISBN 0-392-09072-1 Subj: Folk and fairy tales. Forest, woods. Witches. Wordless.

Hansel and Gretel by Jacob and Wilhelm Grimm; ill. by John Wallner. Prentice-Hall, 1985. ISBN 0-13-383654-1 Subj: Folk and fairy tales. Forest, woods. Witches.

Hansel and Gretel by Jacob and Wilhelm Grimm; retold by Rika Lesser; ill. by Paul O. Zelinsky. Dodd, 1984. Subj: Caldecott award honor book. Folk and fairy tales. Forest, woods. Witches.

Hansel and Gretel by Jacob and Wilhelm Grimm; tr. from the German by Elizabeth D. Crawford; ill. by Lisbeth Zwerger. Morrow, 1980. Subj: Folk and fairy tales. Forest, woods. Witches.

The horse, the fox, and the lion by Jacob and Wilhelm Grimm; ill. by Paul Galdone. Seabury Pr., 1968. Adapt. from The fox and the horse [De Fuchs und das Pferd]. Subj: Animals – dogs. Animals – foxes. Animals – horses. Animals – lions. Behavior – trickery. Folk and fairy tales. Old age.

Jorinda and Joringel by Jacob and Wilhelm Grimm; tr. by Elizabeth Shub; ill. by Adrienne Adams. Scribner's, 1968. Subj: Folk and fairy tales. Witches.

Jorinda and Joringel by Jacob and Wilhelm Grimm; adapt. by Naomi Lewis; ill. by Jutta Ash. David & Charles, 1987. ISBN 0-86264-064-4 Subj: Folk and fairy tales. Witches.

Jorinda and Joringel by Jacob and Wilhelm Grimm; retold by Wanda Gág; ill. by Margot Tomes. Coward, 1978. Subj: Folk and fairy tales. Witches.

King Grisly-Beard by Jacob and Wilhelm Grimm; tr. by Edgar Taylor; ill. by Maurice Sendak. Farrar, 1973. 1823 translation. Subj: Character traits – conceit. Folk and fairy tales. Royalty. Theater.

Little red cap by Jacob and Wilhelm Grimm; tr. from German by Elizabeth D. Crawford; ill. by Lisbeth Zwerger. Morrow, 1983. Subj: Animals – wolves. Behavior – talking to strangers. Folk and fairy tales.

Little Red Riding Hood by Jacob and Wilhelm Grimm; adapt. by Elizabeth and Katherine Gant; ill. by Frank Aloise. Abingdon Pr., 1969. Adapt. and music based on retelling of Rotkäppchen. Incl. melodies with texts, with piano acc. Subj: Animals – wolves. Behavior – talking to strangers. Folk and fairy tales.

Little Red Riding Hood by Jacob and Wilhelm Grimm; adapt. by Margaret Hillert; ill. by Gwen Connelly. Follett, 1982. Subj: Animals – wolves. Behavior – talking to strangers. Folk and fairy tales.

Little Red Riding Hood by Jacob and Wilhelm Grimm; ill. by Paul Galdone. McGraw-Hill, 1974. Adapt. from the retelling of Rotkäppchen. Subj: Animals – wolves. Behavior – talking to strangers. Folk and fairy tales.

Little Red Riding Hood by Jacob and Wilhelm Grimm; ill. by John S. Goodall. Macmillan, 1988. ISBN 0-689-50457-8 Subj: Animals. Animals – mice. Animals – wolves. Behavior – talking to strangers. Folk and fairy tales. Format, unusual. Wordless.

Little Red Riding Hood by Jacob and Wilhelm Grimm; retold and ill. by Trina Schart Hyman. Holiday, 1983. Subj: Animals – wolves. Behavior – talking to strangers. Caldecott award honor book. Folk and fairy tales.

Little Red Riding Hood by Jacob and Wilhelm Grimm; ill. by Bernadette Watts. Collins-World, 1969. Subj: Animals – wolves. Behavior – talking to strangers. Folk and fairy tales.

Lucky Hans by Jacob and Wilhelm Grimm; tr. by Jock Curle; ill. by Eugen Sopko. Holt, 1986. ISBN 0-8050-0009-7 Subj: Character traits – foolishness. Character traits – luck. Folk and fairy tales.

Mother Holly by Jacob and Wilhelm Grimm ill. by Bernadette Watts. Crowell, 1972. Based on the Grimm brothers' Frau Holle. Subj: Behavior – greed. Character traits – helpfulness. Character traits – laziness. Folk and fairy tales.

Mrs. Fox's wedding by Jacob and Wilhelm Grimm; retold by Sara and Stephen Corrin; ill. by Errol Le Cain. Doubleday, 1980. Subj: Animals – foxes. Counting. Folk and fairy tales. Weddings.

The musicians of Bremen by Jacob and Wilhelm Grimm; tr. by Anne Rogers; ill. by Svend Otto S. Larousse, 1974. Subj: Animals. Folk and fairy tales. Old age.

The musicians of Bremen by Jacob and Wilhelm Grimm; ill. by Martin Ursell; text by Linda M. Jennings. Silver Burdett, 1985. ISBN 0-382-09155-8 Subj: Animals. Folk and fairy tales. Old age.

Rapunzel by Jacob and Wilhelm Grimm; retold and ill. by Jutta Ash. Holt, 1982. Subj: Folk and fairy tales. Hair. Royalty. Witches.

Rapunzel by Jacob and Wilhelm Grimm; ill. by Bert Dodson. Troll Assoc., 1979. Subj: Folk and fairy tales. Hair. Royalty. Witches.

Rapunzel by Jacob and Wilhelm Grimm; retold by Barbara Rogasky; ill. by Trina Schart Hyman. Holiday, 1982. Subj: Folk and fairy tales. Hair. Royalty. Witches.

Rapunzel by Jacob and Wilhelm Grimm; adapt. and ill. by Bernadette Watts. Harper, 1975. ISBN 0-690-00980-1 Subj: Folk and fairy tales. Magic. Riddles. Royalty. Weddings.

Rumpelstiltskin by Jacob and Wilhelm Grimm; ill. by Jacqueline Ayer. Harcourt, 1967. Subj: Folk and fairy tales. Magic. Riddles. Royalty. Weddings.

Rumpelstiltskin by Jacob and Wilhelm Grimm; retold and ill. by Donna Diamond. Holiday, 1983. Subj: Folk and fairy tales. Magic. Riddles. Royalty. Weddings.

Rumpelstiltskin by Jacob and Wilhelm Grimm; adapt. and ill. by Paul Galdone. Houghton, 1985. ISBN 0-89919-266-1 Subj: Folk and fairy tales. Magic. Riddles. Royalty. Weddings.

Rumpelstiltskin by Jacob and Wilhelm Grimm; ill. by John Wallner. Prentice-Hall, 1984. Subj: Folk and fairy tales. Magic. Riddles. Royalty. Weddings.

Rumpelstiltskin by Jacob and Wilhelm Grimm; adapt. and ill. by Paul O. Zelinsky. Dutton, 1986. ISBN 0-525-44265-0 Subj: Folk and fairy tales. Magic. Riddles. Royalty. Weddings.

The seven ravens by Jacob and Wilhelm Grimm; ill. by Felix Hoffmann. Harcourt, 1963. Subj: Birds – ravens. Folk and fairy tales. Magic.

The seven ravens by Jacob and Wilhelm Grimm; tr. from German by Elizabeth D. Crawford; ill. by Lisbeth Zwerger. Morrow, 1981. Subj: Birds – ravens. Folk and fairy tales. Magic.

The shoemaker and the elves by Jacob and Wilhelm Grimm; ill. by Cynthia and William Birrer. Lothrop, 1983. Adapt. of Wichtelmänner. Subj: Careers – shoemakers. Character traits – helpfulness. Elves and little people. Folk and fairy tales. Foreign lands – Germany.

The six swans by Jacob and Wilhelm Grimm; retold by Wanda Gág; ill. by Margot Tomes. Coward, 1982. Subj: Birds – swans. Folk and fairy tales. Magic.

The sleeping beauty by Jacob and Wilhelm Grimm; retold and ill. by Warwick Hutton. Atheneum, 1979. Subj: Folk and fairy tales.

The sleeping beauty by Jacob and Wilhelm Grimm; retold and ill. by Trina Schart Hyman. Little, 1977. Subj: Folk and fairy tales.

The sleeping beauty by Jacob and Wilhelm Grimm; adapt. and ill. by Mercer Mayer. Macmillan, 1984. ISBN 0-02-765340-4 Subj: Folk and fairy tales.

Sleeping Beauty by Jacob and Wilhelm Grimm; tr. from Spanish by Leland Northam; adapt. by M. Eulalia Valeri; ill. by Fina Rifa. Silver Burdett, 1985. ISBN 0-382-09068-3 Subj: Folk and fairy tales. Wordless.

The sleeping beauty by Jacob and Wilhelm Grimm; adapt. by Jane Yolen; ill. by Ruth Sanderson. Knopf, 1986. ISBN 0-394-55431-0 Subj: Folk and fairy tales.

Sleeping Beauty by Jacob and Wilhelm Grimm; adapt. and ill. by John Wallner. Viking, 1987. ISBN 0-670-81708-2 Subj: Folk and fairy tales. Format, unusual – toy and movable books.

Snow White by Jacob and Wilhelm Grimm; tr. from German by Paul Heins; ill. by Trina Schart Hyman. Little, 1975. Subj: Elves and little people. Emotions – envy, jealousy. Folk and fairy tales. Magic. Witches.

Snow White by Jacob and Wilhelm Grimm; ill. by Bernadette Watts. Faber, 1983. Subj: Elves and little people. Emotions – envy, jealousy. Folk and fairy tales. Magic. Witches.

Snow White and Rose Red by Jacob and Wilhelm Grimm; tr. by Wayne Andrews; ill. by Adrienne Adams. Scribner's, 1964. Subj: Animals – bears. Elves and little people. Folk and fairy tales. Magic. Weddings.

Snow-White and Rose-Red adapt. and ill. by Barbara Cooney. Dial Pr., 1966. Subj: Animals – bears. Elves and little people. Folk and fairy tales.

Snow White and Rose Red by Jacob and Wilhelm Grimm; tr. by Andrew Lang; ill. by John Wallner. Prentice-Hall, 1984. Subj: Animals – bears. Elves and little people. Folk and fairy tales. Magic. Weddings.

Snow White and Rose Red by Jacob and Wilhelm Grimm; adapt. and ill. by Bernadette Watts. Holt, 1988. ISBN 0-8050-0738-5 Subj: Animals – bears. Elves and little people. Folk and fairy tales. Magic.

Snow White and the seven dwarfs by Jacob and Wilhelm Grimm; ill. by Wanda Gág. Coward, 1938. Subj: Caldecott award honor book. Folk and fairy tales.

Snow White and the seven dwarfs by Jacob and Wilhelm Grimm; adapt. by Anthea Bell; ill. by Chihiro Iwasaki. Picture Book Studio, 1985. ISBN 0-88708-012-X Subj: Elves and little people. Emotions – envy, jealousy. Folk and fairy tales. Magic. Witches.

The table, the donkey and the stick adapt. and ill. by Paul Galdone. McGraw-Hill, 1976. Adapt. from a retelling of Das tapfere Schneiderlein. Subj: Cumulative tales. Folk and fairy tales.

Three Grimms' fairy tales: The fox and the geese; The magic porridge pot; The silver pennies by Jacob and Wilhelm Grimm; ill. by Bernadette Watts. Little, 1981. Subj: Folk and fairy tales.

Tom Thumb

The twelve dancing princesses by Jacob and Wilhelm Grimm; ill. by Dennis Hockerman. Troll Assoc., 1979. Subj: Activities – dancing. Folk and fairy tales. Royalty.

The twelve dancing princesses by Jacob and Wilhelm Grimm; ill. by Errol Le Cain. Viking, 1978. Subj: Activities – dancing. Folk and fairy tales. Royalty.

The twelve dancing princesses by Jacob and Wilhelm Grimm; retold by Marianna Mayer; ill. by Gerald McDermott. Morrow, 1988. ISBN 0-688-02026-7 Subj: Activities – dancing. Folk and fairy tales. Royalty.

The twelve dancing princesses by Jacob and Wilhelm Grimm; tr. by Elizabeth Shub; ill. by Uri Shulevitz. Scribner's, 1966. Subj: Activities – dancing. Folk and fairy tales. Royalty.

The valiant little tailor by Jacob and Wilhelm Grimm; ill. by Victor G. Ambrus. Oxford Univ. Pr., 1980. First pub. in 1971. Subj: Careers – tailors. Character traits – bravery. Folk and fairy tales. Giants.

Walt Disney's Snow White and the seven dwarfs (Walt Disney Productions)

The water of life (Rogasky, Barbara)

The wishing table by Jacob and Wilhelm Grimm; tr. by Anthea Bell; ill. by Eve Tharlet. Picture Book Studio, 1988. ISBN 0-88708-064-2 Subj: Cumulative tales. Folk and fairy tales.

The wolf and the seven kids by Jacob and Wilhelm Grimm; ill. by Kinuko Craft. Troll Assoc., 1979. Subj: Animals – goats. Animals – wolves. Folk and fairy tales.

The wolf and the seven little kids by Jacob and Wilhelm Grimm; tr. by Anne Rogers; ill. by Svend Otto S. Larousse, 1977. Subj: Animals – wolves. Folk and fairy tales.

The wolf and the seven little kids by Jacob and Wilhelm Grimm; adapt. by Linda M. Jennings; ill. by Martin Ursell. Silver Burdett, 1986. ISBN 0-382-09306-2 Subj: Animals – goats. Animals – wolves. Folk and fairy tales.

Grimm, Wilhelm. *The bear and the kingbird* (Grimm, Jacob)

The bearskinner (Grimm, Jacob)

The brave little tailor (Grimm, Jacob)

The Bremen town musicians (Grimm, Jacob)

Cinderella (Grimm, Jacob)

Clever Kate (Grimm, Jacob)

Dear Mili tr. by Ralph Manheim; ill. by Maurice Sendak. Farrar, 1988. ISBN 0-374-31762-3 Subj: Death. Folk and fairy tales. War.

The devil with the green hairs (Grimm, Jacob)

The donkey prince (Grimm, Jacob)

The elves and the shoemaker (Grimm, Jacob)

The falling stars (Grimm, Jacob)

The fisherman and his wife (Grimm, Jacob)

The four clever brothers (Grimm, Jacob)

The glass mountain (Grimm, Jacob)

Godfather Cat and Mousie (Grimm, Jacob)

The golden bird (Grimm, Jacob)

The golden goose (Grimm, Jacob)

The goose girl (Grimm, Jacob)

Grimm Tom Thumb (Tom Thumb)

Hans in luck (Grimm, Jacob)

Hansel and Gretel (Grimm, Jacob)

The horse, the fox, and the lion (Grimm, Jacob)

Jorinda and Joringel (Grimm, Jacob)

King Grisly-Beard (Grimm, Jacob)

Little red cap (Grimm, Jacob)

Little Red Riding Hood (Grimm, Jacob)

Lucky Hans (Grimm, Jacob)

Mother Holly (Grimm, Jacob)

Mrs. Fox's wedding (Grimm, Jacob)

The musicians of Bremen (Grimm, Jacob)

Rapunzel (Grimm, Jacob)

Rumpelstiltskin (Grimm, Jacob)

The seven ravens (Grimm, Jacob)

The shoemaker and the elves (Grimm, Jacob)

The six swans (Grimm, Jacob)

The sleeping beauty (Grimm, Jacob)

Snow White (Grimm, Jacob)

Snow White and Rose Red (Grimm, Jacob)

Snow White and the seven dwarfs (Grimm, Jacob)

The table, the donkey and the stick (Grimm, Jacob)

Three Grimms' fairy tales (Grimm, Jacob)

Tom Thumb

The twelve dancing princesses (Grimm, Jacob)

The valiant little tailor (Grimm, Jacob)

Walt Disney's Snow White and the seven dwarfs (Walt Disney Productions)

The water of life (Rogasky, Barbara)

The wishing table (Grimm, Jacob)

The wolf and the seven kids (Grimm, Jacob)

The wolf and the seven little kids (Grimm, Jacob)

Grindley, Sally. *Four black puppies* ill. by Clive Scruton. Lothrop, 1987. ISBN 0-688-07266-6 Subj: Animals – dogs. Behavior – misbehavior.

Knock, knock! Who's there? ill. by Anthony Browne. Knopf, 1986. ISBN 0-394-98400-5 Subj: Bedtime. Family life – fathers. Games. Monsters. Toys – teddy bears.

Groat, Diane *see* De Groat, Diane

Grode, Redway *see* Gorey, Edward

Groner, Judyth. *Let's build a Sukkah* (Wikler, Madeline)

My first seder (Wikler, Madeline)

My very own Jewish community by Judyth Groner and Madeline Wikler; photos. by Madeline Wikler. Kar-Ben Copies, 1984. ISBN 0-930494-32-6 Subj: Communities, neighborhoods. Jewish culture.

The Purim parade (Wikler, Madeline)

Where is the Afikomen? by Judyth Groner and Madeline Wikler; ill. by Chari R. McLean. Kar-Ben Copies, 1985. ISBN 0-930494-52-0 Subj: Format, unusual – board books. Holidays. Jewish culture.

Gross, Alan. *Sometimes I worry...* ill. by Mike Venezia. Children's Pr., 1978. Subj: Behavior – worrying.

What if the teacher calls on me? ill. by Mike Venezia. Children's Pr., 1980. Subj: Behavior – worrying. School.

Gross, Michael. *The fable of the fig tree* ill. by Mila Lazarevich. Walck, 1975. Subj: Folk and fairy tales. Jewish culture.

Gross, Ruth Belov. *Alligators and other crocodilians* ill. with photos. Four Winds Pr., 1978. Subj: Reptiles – alligators, crocodiles. Science.

A book about your skeleton ill. by Deborah Robison. Hastings, 1979. Subj: Anatomy. Health.

The emperor's new clothes (Andersen, H. C. (Hans Christian))

The girl who wouldn't get married ill. by Jack Kent. Four Winds Pr., 1983. Subj: Animals – horses. Folk and fairy tales. Weddings.

Grossbart, Francine. *A big city* ill. by author. Harper, 1966. Subj: ABC books. City.

Grossman, Bill. *Donna O'Neeshuck was chased by some cows* ill. by Sue Truesdell. Harper, 1988. ISBN 0-06-022159-3 Subj: Cumulative tales. Poetry, rhyme.

Grosvenor, Donna. *Pandas* photos. by author; ill. by George Founds. National Geographic Soc., 1973. ISBN 0-87044-143-4 Subj: Animals – pandas. Science.

Zoo babies ill. by author. National Geographical Soc., 1979. Subj: Animals. Zoos.

Grover, Eulalie Osgood. *Mother Goose* (Mother Goose)

Groves-Raines, Antony. *The tidy hen* ill. by author. Harcourt, 1961. Subj: Character traits – cleanliness.

Gruber, Ruth *see* Michaels, Ruth

Gruenberg, Sidonie Matsner. *The wonderful story of how you were born* ill. by Symeon Shimin. Rev. ed. Doubleday, 1970. Subj: Babies. Family life. Science.

Guilfoile, Elizabeth. *Have you seen my brother?* ill. by Mary Stevens. Follett, 1962. Subj: Behavior – lost. Careers – police officers. City.

Nobody listens to Andrew ill. by Mary Stevens. Follett, 1957. Subj: Animals – bears. Behavior – needing someone.

Valentine's Day ill. by Gordon Laite. Garrard, 1965. Subj: Holidays – Valentine's Day.

Gullo, Stephen V. *When people die* (Bernstein, Joanne E.)

Gundersheimer, Karen. *A B C say with me* ill. by author. Harper, 1984. Subj: ABC books.

Colors to know ill. by author. Harper, 1986. ISBN 0-06-022196-8 Subj: Animals. Concepts – color.

Happy winter ill. by author. Harper, 1982. Subj: Poetry, rhyme. Seasons – winter.

1 2 3 play with me ill. by author. Harper, 1984. Subj: Animals – mice. Counting.

Shapes to show ill. by author. Harper, 1986. ISBN 0-06-022197-6 Subj: Animals – mice. Concepts – shape. Toys.

Gunning, Monica. *The two Georges: Los dos Jorges* ill. by Veronica Mary Miracle. Blaine-Ethridge, 1976. Subj: ABC books. Foreign languages. Poetry, rhyme.

Gunther, Louise. *Anna's snow day* ill. by Paul Frame. Garrard, 1979. Subj: Weather – snow.

A tooth for the tooth fairy ill. by Jim Cummins. Garrard, 1978. Subj: Fairies. Teeth.

Gunthrop, Karen. *Adam and the wolf* ill. by Attilio Cassinelli. Doubleday, 1967. Translation of Il pulcino e il lupo. Subj: Animals – wolves. Behavior – disbelief. Food.

Rina at the farm ill. by Attilio Cassinelli. Doubleday, 1968. Subj: Farms.

Gurney, Eric. *The king, the mice and the cheese* (Gurney, Nancy)

Gurney, Nancy. *The king, the mice and the cheese* by Nancy and Eric Gurney; ill. by Jean Vallier. Random House, 1965. Subj: Animals – mice. Food. Royalty.

Guthrie, Donna. *Grandpa doesn't know it's me* ill. by Katy Keck Arnsteen. Human Sciences Pr., 1986. ISBN 0-89885-308-7 Subj: Behavior – forgetfulness. Behavior – losing things. Behavior – lost. Family life – grandfathers. Illness – Alzheimer's. Old age.

The witch who lives down the hall ill. by Amy Schwartz. Harcourt, 1985. ISBN 0-15-298610-3 Subj: Holidays – Halloween. Magic. Witches.

Guy, Rosa. *Mother crocodile* ill. by John Steptoe. Delacorte, 1981. Subj: Animals – monkeys. Folk and fairy tales. Foreign lands – Africa. Reptiles – alligators, crocodiles.

Guzzo, Sandra E. *Fox and Heggie* ill. by Kathy Parkinson. Albert Whitman, 1983. Subj: Animals – foxes. Animals – hedgehogs. Shopping.

Gwynne, Fred. *A little pigeon toad* ill. by author. Simon & Schuster, 1988. ISBN 0-671-66659-2 Subj: Imagination. Language.

Haas, Carolyn. *Purple cow to the rescue* (Cole, Ann)

Haas, Dorothy. *My first communion* photos. by William Franklin McMahon. Albert Whitman, 1987. ISBN 0-8075-5331-X Subj: Religion.

Haas, Irene. *The Maggie B* ill. by author. Atheneum, 1975. Subj: Behavior – wishing. Boats, ships. Poetry, rhyme. Sea and seashore.

Haas, Merle. *Babar and Father Christmas* (Brunhoff, Jean de)

Babar and his children (Brunhoff, Jean de)

Babar and Zephir (Brunhoff, Jean de)

Babar the king (Brunhoff, Jean de)

Babar visits another planet (Brunhoff, Laurent de)

Babar's castle (Brunhoff, Laurent de)

Babar's cousin, that rascal Arthur (Brunhoff, Laurent de)

Babar's fair will be opened next Sunday (Brunhoff, Laurent de)

The story of Babar, the little elephant (Brunhoff, Jean de)

The travels of Babar (Brunhoff, Jean de)

Haddon, Mark. *Gilbert's gobstopper* ill. by author. Dial Pr., 1988. ISBN 0-8037-0506-9 Subj: Behavior – losing things.

Toni and the tomato soup ill. by author. Harcourt, 1989. ISBN 0-15-200610-9 Subj: Behavior – wishing. Food.

Hader, Berta Hoerner. *The big snow* by Berta and Elmer Hader; ill. by authors. Macmillan, 1948. Subj: Caldecott award book. Weather – snow.

Cock-a-doodle doo: the story of a little red rooster by Berta and Elmer Hader; ill. by authors. Macmillan, 1939. Subj: Birds – chickens. Birds – ducks. Caldecott award honor book. Farms.

Lost in the zoo by Berta and Elmer Hader; ill. by authors. Macmillan, 1951. Subj: Behavior – lost. Zoos.

The mighty hunter by Berta and Elmer Hader; ill. by authors. Macmillan, 1943. Subj: Caldecott award honor book. Ecology. Indians of North America. School. Sports – hunting.

Mister Billy's gun by Berta and Elmer Hader; ill. by authors. Macmillan, 1960. Subj: Activities – gardening. Birds. Character traits – kindness to animals. Violence, anti-violence. Weapons.

The story of Pancho and the bull with the crooked tail by Berta and Elmer Hader; ill. by authors. Oxford Univ. Pr., 1933. Subj: Animals – bulls, cows. Foreign lands – Mexico.

Hader, Elmer. *The big snow* (Hader, Berta Hoerner)

Cock-a-doodle doo (Hader, Berta Hoerner)

Lost in the zoo (Hader, Berta Hoerner)

The mighty hunter (Hader, Berta Hoerner)

Mister Billy's gun (Hader, Berta Hoerner)

The story of Pancho and the bull with the crooked tail (Hader, Berta Hoerner)

Hadithi, Mwenye. *Crafty chameleon* ill. by Adrienne Kennaway. Little, 1987. ISBN 0-316-33723-4 Subj: Animals. Behavior – bullying. Behavior – unnoticed, unseen.

Greedy zebra ill. by Adrienne Kennaway. Little, 1984. ISBN 0-316-33721-8 Subj: Animals – zebras. Behavior – greed. Clothing. Folk and fairy tales. Foreign lands – Africa.

Hot hippo ill. by Adrienne Kennaway. Little, 1986. ISBN 0-316-33722-6 Subj: Animals – hippopotami. Foreign lands – Africa. Rivers.

Tricky tortoise ill. by Adrienne Kennaway. Little, 1988. ISBN 0-316-33724-2 Subj: Animals. Behavior – bullying. Jungle.

Hague, Kathleen. *Alphabears: an ABC book* ill. by Michael Hague. Holt, 1984. Subj: ABC books. Poetry, rhyme. Toys – teddy bears.

The man who kept house by Kathleen and Michael Hague; ill. by Michael Hague. Harcourt, 1981. Subj: Family life. Folk and fairy tales. Foreign lands – Norway.

Numbears: a counting book ill. by Michael Hague. Holt, 1986. ISBN 0-03-007194-1 Subj: Counting. Toys – teddy bears.

Out of the nursery, into the night ill. by Michael Hague. Holt, 1986. ISBN 0-8050-0088-7 Subj: Dreams. Night. Poetry, rhyme. Toys – teddy bears.

Hague, Michael. *The man who kept house* (Hague, Kathleen)

Michael Hague's world of unicorns ill. by author. Holt, 1986. ISBN 0-8050-0070-4 Subj: Format, unusual. Mythical creatures.

Mother Goose

Hahn, Hannelore. *Take a giant step* ill. by Margot Zemach. Little, 1960. Subj: Games.

Haines, Gail Kay. *Fire* ill. by Jacqueline Chwast. Morrow, 1975. Subj: Fire. Science.

What makes a lemon sour? ill. by Janet McCaffery. Morrow, 1977. Subj: Science.

Hair ill. by Christine Sharr. Wonder Books, 1971. Subj: Hair.

Haiz, Danah. *Jonah's journey* ill. by H. Hechtkopf. Lerner, 1973. Subj: Animals – whales. Religion.

Haldane-Stevenson, James Patrick *see* Stevenson, James

Hale, Irina. *Brown bear in a brown chair* ill. by author. Atheneum, 1983. Subj: Character traits – appearance. Toys – teddy bears.

Chocolate mouse and sugar pig ill. by author. Atheneum, 1979. Subj: Animals – mice. Animals – pigs. Behavior – running away. Food. Toys.

Donkey's dreadful day ill. by author. Atheneum, 1982. Subj: Animals – donkeys. Circus. Dreams.

The lost toys ill. by author. Atheneum, 1985. ISBN 0-689-50328-8 Subj: Activities – trading. Behavior – forgetfulness. Toys.

Hale, Kathleen. *Orlando and the water cats* ill. by author. Merrimack, 1979. Subj: Activities – vacationing. Animals – cats. Family life.

Orlando buys a farm ill. by author. Merrimack, 1980. Subj: Animals – cats. Farms.

Orlando the frisky housewife ill. by author. Merrimack, 1979. Subj: Animals – cats. Stores.

Hale, Linda. *The glorious Christmas soup party* ill. by author. Viking, 1962. Subj: Animals – mice. Food. Holidays – Christmas.

Hale, Michael. *Shoemaker Martin* (Tolstoĭ, Alekseĭ Nikolaevich)

Hale, Sara Josepha. *Mary had a little lamb* ill. by Tomie de Paola. Holiday, 1984. ISBN 0-8234-0509-5 Subj: Animals – sheep. Music. Nursery rhymes. School.

Haley, Gail E. *Go away, stay away* ill. by author. Scribner's, 1977. Subj: Goblins. Seasons.

The green man ill. by author. Scribner's, 1980. Subj: Knights. Seasons.

Jack and the bean tree ill. by author. Crown, 1986. ISBN 0-517-55717-7 Subj: Folk and fairy tales. Giants. Magic.

Jack and the fire dragon ill. by author. Crown, 1988. ISBN 0-517-56814-4 Subj: Character traits – bravery. Dragons. Folk and fairy tales.

Jack Jouett's ride ill. by author. Viking, 1973. Subj: U.S. history.

Noah's ark ill. by author. Atheneum, 1971. ISBN 0-689-20659-3 Subj: Animals. Ecology.

The post office cat ill. by author. Scribner's, 1976. Subj: Animals – cats. Careers – mail carriers. Foreign lands – England.

A story, a story ill. by author. Atheneum, 1970. Subj: Caldecott award book. Folk and fairy tales. Foreign lands – Africa.

Haley, Patrick. *The little person* ill. by Jonna Kool. East Eagle Pr., 1981. Subj: Activities – traveling.

Hall, Amanda. *The gossipy wife* ill. by author. Harper, 1984. Subj: Folk and fairy tales. Foreign lands – Russia.

Hall, Amanda Benjamin *see* Hall, Amanda

Hall, Bill. *Fish tale* ill. by John E. Johnson. Norton, 1967. Subj: Fish. Sports – fishing.

A year in the forest ill. by Feodor Rojankovsky. McGraw-Hill, 1973. Subj: Animals. Seasons.

Hall, Carol. *Northern J. Calloway presents Supervroomer!* (Calloway, Northern J.)

Hall, Derek. *Elephant bathes* ill. by John Butler. Sierra Club, 1985. ISBN 0-394-96529-9 Subj: Activities – bathing. Animals – elephants. Behavior – growing up. Family life.

Gorilla builds ill. by John Butler. Sierra Club, 1985. ISBN 0-394-96530-2 Subj: Animals – gorillas. Behavior – growing up. Family life.

Otter swims ill. by John Butler. Sierra Club Knopf, 1984. ISBN 0-394-96503-5 Subj: Animals – otters. Emotions – fear. Sports – swimming.

Panda climbs ill. by John Butler. Sierra Club Knopf, 1984. ISBN 0-394-96502-7 Subj: Animals – pandas. Emotions – fear. Trees.

Polar bear leaps ill. by John Butler. Sierra Club, 1985. ISBN 0-394-96531-0 Subj: Animals – polar bears. Behavior – growing up. Family life.

Tiger runs ill. by John Butler. Sierra Club Knopf, 1984. ISBN 0-394-96504-3 Subj: Animals – tigers. Emotions – fear. Sports – racing.

Hall, Donald. *Andrew the lion farmer* ill. by Jane Miller. Watts, 1959. Subj: Humor.

The man who lived alone ill. by Mary Azarian. Godine, 1984. ISBN 0-87923-538-1 Subj: Behavior – solitude.

The ox-cart man ill. by Barbara Cooney. Viking, 1979. Subj: Activities – working. Caldecott award book. Farms. Seasons.

Hall, Fergus. *Groundsel* ill. by author. Merrimack, 1983. Subj: Activities – gardening. Seasons.

Hall, Katy. *Buggy riddles* by Katy Hall and Lisa Eisenberg; ill. by Simms Taback. Dial Pr., 1986. ISBN 0-8037-0140-3 Subj: Insects. Riddles.

Fishy riddles by Katy Hall and Lisa Eisenberg; ill. by Simms Taback. Dial Pr., 1983. Subj: Humor. Riddles. Sea and seashore.

Hall, Malcolm. *And then the mouse...* ill. by Stephen Gammell. Four Winds Pr., 1980. Subj: Animals – mice. Folk and fairy tales.

CariCATures ill. by Bruce Degen. Coward, 1978. Subj: Animals. Riddles.

The friends of Charlie Ant Bear ill. by Alexandra Wallner. Coward, 1980. Subj: Animals – anteaters. Character traits – optimism.

Hall, Pam. *On the edge of the eastern ocean* ill. by author. Silver Burdett, 1982. Subj: Birds – puffins. Poetry, rhyme.

Hall, Richard. *Humphrey the lost whale* (Tokuda, Wendy)

Haller, Danita Ross. *Not just any ring* ill. by Deborah Kogan Ray. Knopf, 1982. Subj: Magic.

Hallinan, P. K. (Patrick K.). *I'm glad to be me* ill. by author. Children's Pr., 1977. Subj: Activities. Family life – only child. Self-concept.

I'm thankful each day! ill. by author. Children's Pr., 1981. Subj: Folk and fairy tales.

Just being alone ill. by author. Children's Pr., 1976. Subj: Activities. Behavior – solitude. Family life – only child.

Just open a book ill. by author. Children's Pr., 1981. Subj: Activities – reading. Poetry, rhyme.

That's what a friend is ill. by author. Children's Pr., 1977. Subj: Friendship. Poetry, rhyme.

Where's Michael? ill. by author. Children's Pr., 1978. Subj: Behavior – imitation. Self-concept.

Halsey, William D. *The magic world of words: a very first dictionary* ed. by William D. Halsey and Christopher G. Morris. Macmillan, 1977. Subj: Dictionaries.

Hamberger, John. *The day the sun disappeared* ill. by author. Norton, 1964. Subj: Animals. Ecology. Science. Sun.

Hazel was an only pet ill. by author. Norton, 1968. Subj: Animals – dogs. Family life – only child. Pets.

The lazy dog ill. by author. Four Winds Pr., 1971. Subj: Animals – dogs. Toys – balls. Wordless.

The peacock who lost his tail ill. by author. Norton, 1967. Subj: Birds – peacocks, peahens. Character traits – pride.

This is the day ill. by author. Grosset, 1971. Subj: Animals – groundhogs. Holidays – Groundhog Day.

Hamil, Thomas Arthur. *Brother Alonzo* ill. by author. Macmillan, 1957. Subj: Religion.

Hamilton, Emily. *My name is Emily* (Hamilton, Morse)

Hamilton, Morse. *Big sisters are bad witches* ill. by Marylin Hafner. Greenwillow, 1981. Subj: Sibling rivalry. Witches.

How do you do, Mr. Birdsteps? ill. by Patience Brewster. Avon, 1983. Subj: Character traits – shyness.

My name is Emily by Morse and Emily Hamilton; ill. by Jenni Oliver. Greenwillow, 1979. Subj: Behavior – running away. Sibling rivalry.

Who's afraid of the dark? ill. by Patience Brewster. Avon, 1983. Subj: Emotions – fear. Night.

Hamilton-Merritt, Jane. *My first days of school* photos. by author. Simon and Schuster, 1982. Subj: School.

Our new baby photos. by author. Simon and Schuster, 1982. Subj: Babies. Family life.

Hamm, Diane Johnston. *Grandma drives a motor bed* ill. by Charles Robinson. Albert Whitman, 1987. ISBN 0-8075-3025-5 Subj: Family life – grandmothers. Family life – grandparents. Handicaps. Illness. Old age.

Hammarberg, Dyan. *Jessie the chicken* (Pursell, Margaret Sanford)

Polly the guinea pig (Pursell, Margaret Sanford)

Rusty the Irish setter (Overbeck, Cynthia)

Shelley the sea gull (Pursell, Margaret Sanford)

Sprig the tree frog (Pursell, Margaret Sanford)

Hample, Stoo. *Stoo Hample's silly joke book* ill. by author. Delacorte, 1978. Subj: Humor. Riddles.

Yet another big fat funny silly book ill. by author. Delacorte, 1980. Subj: Poetry, rhyme. Riddles.

Hamsa, Bobbie. *Dirty Larry* ill. by Paul Sharp. Children's Pr., 1983. Subj: Character traits – cleanliness.

Polly wants a cracker ill. by Jerry Warshaw. Childrens, 1986. ISBN 0-516-02071-4 Subj: Birds – parakeets, parrots. Counting. Poetry, rhyme.

Your pet bear ill. by Tom Dunnington. Children's Pr., 1980. Subj: Animals – bears. Imagination.

Your pet beaver ill. by Tom Dunnington. Children's Pr., 1980. Subj: Animals – beavers. Imagination.

Your pet camel ill. by Tom Dunnington. Children's Pr., 1980. Subj: Animals – camels. Imagination.

Your pet elephant ill. by Tom Dunnington. Children's Pr., 1980. Subj: Animals – elephants. Imagination.

Your pet giraffe ill. by Tom Dunnington. Children's Pr., 1982. Subj: Animals – giraffes. Imagination.

Your pet kangaroo ill. by Tom Dunnington. Children's Pr., 1980. Subj: Animals – kangaroos. Imagination.

Your pet penguin ill. by Tom Dunnington. Children's Pr., 1980. Subj: Birds – penguins. Imagination.

Your pet sea lion ill. by Tom Dunnington. Children's Pr., 1982. Subj: Animals – sea lions. Imagination.

Hancock, Joy Elizabeth. *The loudest little lion* ill. by Eileen Christelow. Albert Whitman, 1988. ISBN 0-8075-4773-5 Subj: Animals – lions. Bedtime. Noise, sounds.

Hancock, Sibyl. *Esteban and the ghost* ill. by Dirk Zimmer. Dial Pr., 1983. Adapted from The tinker and the ghost by Ralph Steele Boggs and Mary Gould Davis. Subj: Ghosts.

Freaky Francie ill. by Leonard W. Shortall. Prentice-Hall, 1979. Subj: Problem solving.

Old Blue ill. by Erick Ingraham. Putnam's, 1980. Subj: Animals – bulls, cows. Cowboys.

Handford, Martin. *Find Waldo now* ill. by author. Little, 1988. ISBN 0-316-34292-0 Subj: Activities – traveling. Games. Time.

Where's Waldo? ill. by author. Little, 1987. ISBN 0-316-34293-9 Subj: Activities – traveling. Behavior – losing things. Foreign lands. Games.

Handforth, Thomas. *Mei Li* ill. by author. Doubleday, 1938. Subj: Caldecott award book. Foreign lands – China. Holidays – Chinese New Year.

Hands, Hargrave. *Bunny sees* ill. by author. Grosset, 1985. ISBN 0-488-10577-2 Subj: Animals – rabbits. Format, unusual – board books. Nature.

Duckling sees ill. by author. Grosset, 1985. ISBN 0-448-10579-9 Subj: Animals. Format, unusual – board books.

Little lamb sees ill. by author. Grosset, 1985. ISBN 0-448-10576-4 Subj: Animals. Format, unusual – board books.

Hanhart, Brigitte. *Shoemaker Martin* (Tolstoĭ, Alekseĭ Nikolaevich)

Hanklin, Rebecca. *I can be a doctor* ill. with photos. Childrens Pr., 1985. ISBN 0-516-01846-9 Subj: Careers – doctors.

I can be a fire fighter ill. with photos. Childrens Pr., 1985. ISBN 0-516-01847-7 Subj: Careers – firefighters.

Hanlon, Emily. *What if a lion eats me and I fall into a hippopotamus' mud hole?* ill. by Leigh Grant. Delacorte Pr., 1975. Subj: Emotions – fear. Imagination. Zoos.

Hann, Jacquie. *Crybaby* ill. by author. Four Winds Pr., 1979. Subj: Emotions.

Follow the leader ill. by author. Crown, 1982. Subj: Activities – playing. Games.

Up day, down day ill. by author. Four Winds Pr., 1978. Subj: Character traits – luck. Sports – fishing.

Hansen, Carla. *Barnaby Bear builds a boat* by Carla and Vilhelm Hansen; ill. by authors. Random House, 1979. Subj: Animals – bears. Boats, ships.

Barnaby Bear visits the farm by Carla and Vilhelm Hansen; ill. by authors. Random House, 1979. Subj: Animals – bears. Farms.

Hansen, Jeff. *Being a fire fighter isn't just squirtin' water* ill. by author. Vantage Pr., 1978. Subj: Careers – firefighters.

Hansen, Ron. *The shadowmaker* ill. by Margot Tomes. Harper, 1987. ISBN 0-06-022203-4 Subj: Behavior – trickery. Dreams. Shadows. Wizards.

Hansen, Vilhelm. *Barnaby Bear builds a boat* (Hansen, Carla)

Barnaby Bear visits the farm (Hansen, Carla)

Hanson, Joan. *I don't like Timmy* ill. by author. Carolrhoda Books, 1972. Subj: Babies. Friendship.

I won't be afraid ill. by author. Carolrhoda Books, 1974. Subj: Behavior – growing up. Emotions – fear.

I'm going to run away ill. by author. Platt, 1978. Subj: Behavior – running away.

Hapgood, Miranda. *Martha's mad day* ill. by Emily Arnold McCully. Crown, 1977. Subj: Emotions – anger.

Harada, Joyce. *It's the ABC book* ill. by author. Heian Intl., 1982. Subj: ABC books.

It's the 0-1-2-3 book ill. by author. Heian, 1985. ISBN 0-89346-252-7 Subj: Counting.

Harber, Frances. *My king has donkey ears* ill. by Maryann Kovalski. North Winds Pr., 1986. ISBN 0-590-71522-4 Subj: Folk and fairy tales. Problem solving. Royalty.

Hardwick, Homer see Rogers, Paul

Hare, Lorraine. *Who needs her?* ill. by author. Atheneum, 1983. Subj: Character traits – cleanliness.

Hare, Norma Q. *Mystery at mouse house* ill. by Stella Ormai. Garrard, 1980. Subj: Behavior – stealing. Problem solving.

Harlow, Joan Hiatt. *Shadow bear* ill. by Jim Arnosky. Doubleday, 1981. Subj: Animals – polar bears. Emotions – fear. Eskimos.

Harms, D. *The merry starlings* (Marshak, Samuel)

Harper, Anita. *How we live* ill. by Christine Roche. Harper, 1977. Subj: Houses.

How we work ill. by Christine Roche. Harper, 1977. Subj: Activities – working. Careers.

It's not fair! ill. by Susan Hellard. Putnam's, 1986. ISBN 0-399-21365-1 Subj: Animals – kangaroos. Babies. Family life. Sibling rivalry.

Harper, Wilhelmina. *The gunniwolf* ill. by William Wiesner. Dutton, 1967. Subj: Animals – wolves. Behavior – misbehavior. Flowers. Foreign lands – Germany.

Harranth, Wolf. *My old grandad* tr. from German by Peter Carter; ill. by Christina Oppermann-Dimow. Merrimack, 1984. ISBN 0-19-279787-5 Subj: Death. Emotions – loneliness. Family life – grandfathers. Farms.

Harriott, Ted. *Coming home: a dog's true story* ill. by Lisa Kopper. David & Charles, 1985. ISBN 0-575-03583-8 Subj: Animals – dogs. Character traits – kindness to animals. Death.

Harris, Christopher Fry *see* Fry, Christopher

Harris, Dorothy Joan. *Four seasons for Toby* ill. by Vlasta van Kampen. North Winds Pr., 1987. ISBN 0-590-71677-8 Subj: Reptiles – turtles, tortoises. Seasons.

Goodnight Jeffrey ill. by Nancy Hannans. Warne, 1983. Subj: Bedtime.

The school mouse and the hamster ill. by Judy Clifford. Warne, 1979. Subj: Animals – hamsters. Animals – mice. School.

Harris, Joel Chandler. *Jump! the adventures of Brer Rabbit* adapt. by Van Dyke Parks and Malcolm Jones; ill. by Barry Moser. Harcourt, 1986. ISBN 0-15-241350-2 Subj: Animals. Folk and fairy tales.

Jump again! more adventures of Brer Rabbit adapt. by Van Dyke Parks; ill. by Barry Moser. Harcourt, 1987. ISBN 0-15-241352-9 Subj: Animals. Folk and fairy tales.

Harris, Larry M. *see* Wilson, Barbara

Harris, Laurence Mark *see* Wilson, Barbara

Harris, Leon A. *The great diamond robbery* ill. by Joseph Schindelman. Atheneum, 1985. ISBN 0-689-31188-5 Subj: Animals – mice. Character traits – bravery. Crime. Songs. Stores.

The great picture robbery ill. by Joseph Schindelman. Atheneum, 1963. Subj: Animals – mice. Art. Crime. Foreign lands – France.

Harris, Louise Dyer. *Flash, the life of a firefly* by Louise Dyer Harris and Norman Dyer Harris; ill. by Henry B. Kane. Little, 1966. Subj: Insects – Fireflies. Science.

Harris, Norman Dyer. *Flash, the life of a firefly* (Harris, Louise Dyer)

Harris, Robie H. *Don't forget to come back* ill. by Tony DeLuna. Atheneum, 1963. Subj: Activities – baby-sitting. Behavior. Family life.

Hot Henry ill. by Nicole Hollander. St. Martin's, 1987. ISBN 0-312-01041-9 Subj: Clothing. Family life.

I hate kisses ill. by Diane Paterson. Knopf, 1981. Subj: Behavior – growing up.

Messy Jessie ill. by Nicole Hollander. St. Martin's, 1987. ISBN 0-312-01067-2 Subj: Behavior – carelessness. Family life.

Harris, Steven Michael. *This is my trunk* ill. by Norma Welliver. Atheneum, 1985. ISBN 0-689-31128-1 Subj: Careers. Circus. Clowns, jesters.

Harris, Susan. *Creatures that look alike* ill. by Don Forrest. Watts, 1980. Subj: Animals. Science.

Reptiles ill. by Jim Robins. Watts, 1978. Subj: Reptiles. Science.

Harrison, David Lee. *The case of Og, the missing frog* ill. by Jerry Warshaw. Rand McNally, 1972. Subj: Frogs and toads. Poetry, rhyme.

Detective Bob and the great ape escape ill. by Ned Delaney. Parents, 1980. Subj: Animals – gorillas. Problem solving. Zoos.

Little turtle's big adventure ill. by J. P. Miller. Random House, 1969. Subj: Character traits – kindness to animals. Progress. Reptiles – turtles, tortoises.

Wake up, sun! ill. by Hans Wilhelm. Random House, 1986. ISBN 0-394-88256-8 Subj: Animals. Morning. Sun.

Harrison, Sarah. *In granny's garden* ill. by Mike Wilks. Holt, 1980. Subj: Animals. Dinosaurs. Poetry, rhyme.

Harrison, Ted. *A northern alphabet: A is for arctic* ill. by author. Tundra Books, 1982. Subj: ABC books.

Harrop, Beatrice. *Sing hey diddle diddle* (Mother Goose)

Harshman, Terry Webb. *Porcupine's pajama party* ill. by Doug Cushman. Harper, 1988. ISBN 0-06-022249-2 Subj: Animals – otters. Animals – porcupines. Bedtime. Birds – owls. Parties. Monsters. Sleep.

Hart, Jeanne McGahey. *Scareboy* ill. by Gerhardt Hurt. Parnassus, 1957. Subj: Humor. Scarecrows.

Hartelius, Margaret A. *The chicken's child* ill. by author. Doubleday, 1975. Subj: Birds – chickens. Reptiles – alligators, crocodiles. Wordless.

Hartley, Deborah. *Up north in the winter* ill. by Lydia Dabcovich. Dutton, 1986. ISBN 0-525-44268-5 Subj: Animals – foxes. Family life – grandfathers. Seasons – winter.

Hartwell, Nancy *see* Cole, Ann

Harvey, Brett. *Immigrant girl: Becky of Eldridge Street* ill. by Deborah Kogan Ray. Holiday, 1987. ISBN 0-8234-0638-5 Subj: City. Family life. Jewish culture.

My prairie year: based on the diary of Elenore Plaisted ill. by Deborah Kogan Ray. Holiday, 1986. ISBN 0-8234-0604-0 Subj: Activities – working. Farms. U.S. history.

Haseley, Dennis. *The cave of snores* ill. by Eric Beddows. Harper, 1987. ISBN 0-06-022215-8 Subj: Animals. Folk and fairy tales. Magic. Sleep. Wizards.

Kite flier ill. by David Wiesner. Four Winds, 1986. ISBN 0-02-743110-X Subj: Family life – fathers. Kites.

The old banjo ill. by Stephen Gammell. Macmillan, 1983. Subj: Farms. Music.

The pirate who tried to capture the moon ill. by Sue Truesdell. Harper, 1983. Subj: Pirates.

The soap bandit ill. by Jane Chambless-Rigie. Warne, 1984. Subj: Character traits – cleanliness.

Haskins, Ilma. *Color seems* ill. by author. Vanguard, 1973. Subj: Concepts – color.

Haskins, Jim. *Count your way through China* ill. by Dennis Hockerman. Carolrhoda Books, 1987. ISBN 0-87614-302-8 Subj: Counting. Foreign lands – China.

Count your way through Japan ill. by Martin Skoro. Carolrhoda Books, 1987. ISBN 0-87614-301-X Subj: Counting. Foreign lands – Japan.

Count your way through Russia ill. by Vera Mednikov. Carolrhoda Books, 1987. ISBN 0-87614-303-6 Subj: Counting. Foreign lands – Russia.

Count your way through the Arab world ill. by Dana Gustafson. Carolrhoda Books, 1987. ISBN 0-87616-304-4 Subj: Counting. Foreign lands – Arabia.

The Statue of Liberty: America's proud lady ill. with photos. Lerner, 1986. ISBN 0-8225-1706-X Subj: Art. U.S. history.

Hasler, Eveline. *Martin is our friend* ill. by Dorothea Desmarowitz. Abingdon Pr., 1981. Subj: Animals – horses. Character traits – kindness. Handicaps.

Winter magic ill. by Michèle Lemieux. Morrow, 1985. ISBN 0-688-05258-4 Subj: Animals – cats. Night. Seasons – winter.

Hastings, Evelyn Beilhart. *The department store* ill. by Lewis A. Ogan. Melmont, 1956. Subj: Shopping. Stores.

Hastings, Selina. *The man who wanted to live forever* ill. by Reg Cartwright. Holt, 1988. ISBN 0-8050-0572-2 Subj: Death. Folk and fairy tales.

Peter and the wolf (Prokofiev, Sergei Sergeievitch)

The singing ringing tree ill. by Louise Brierley. Holt, 1988. ISBN 0-8050-0573-0 Subj: Character traits – kindness. Elves and little people. Folk and fairy tales. Magic. Royalty.

Hatcher, Charles. *What shape is it?* ill. by Gareth Adamson. Duell, 1966. Subj: Concepts – shape.

Hathorn, Libby. *Freya's fantastic surprise* ill. by Sharon Thompson. Scholastic, 1989. ISBN 0-86896-381-X Subj: Emotions – envy, jealousy. School.

Haubensak-Tellenbach, Margrit. *The story of Noah's ark* ill. by Erna Emhardt. Crown, 1983. Subj: Religion – Noah.

Haugaard, Erik. *The emperor's nightingale* (Andersen, H. C. (Hans Christian))

Prince Boghole ill. by Julie Downing. Macmillan, 1987. ISBN 0-02-743440-0 Subj: Folk and fairy tales. Foreign lands – Ireland. Royalty.

Hauptmann, Tatjana. *A day in the life of Petronella Pig* ill. by author. Holt, 1982. Subj: Animals – pigs. Format, unusual. Wordless.

Haus, Felice. *Beep! Beep! I'm a jeep: a toddler's book of "let's pretend"* ill. by Norman Gorbaty. Random, 1986. ISBN 0-394-88000-5 Subj: Activities – playing. Format, unusual – board books. Imagination. Toys.

Hausherr, Rosmarie. *My first kitten* photos. by author. Four Winds, 1985. ISBN 0-02-743420-6 Subj: Animals – cats. Pets.

My first puppy photos. by author. Four Winds, 1986. ISBN 0-02-743410-9 Subj: Animals – dogs. Pets.

Hautzig, Deborah. *It's not fair!* ill. by Tom Leigh. Random House, 1986. ISBN 0-394-98151-0 Subj: Activities – working. Behavior – dissatisfaction. Puppets.

A visit to the Sesame Street hospital ill. by Joseph Mathieu. Random House, 1985. ISBN 0-394-87062-X Subj: Hospitals. Puppets.

Why are you so mean to me? ill. by Tom Cooke. Random House, 1986. ISBN 0-394-98060-3 Subj: Emotions – anger.

Hautzig, Esther. *At home: a visit in four languages* ill. by Aliki. Macmillan, 1969. Subj: Family life. Foreign lands – France. Foreign lands – Russia. Foreign lands – Spain. Foreign languages.

In the park: an excursion in four languages ill. by Ezra Jack Keats. Macmillan, 1968. Subj: Foreign lands – France. Foreign lands – Russia. Foreign lands – Spain. Foreign languages.

Hautzig, Esther Rudomin *see* Hautzig, Esther

Havill, Juanita. *Jamaica's find* ill. by Anne S. O'Brien. Houghton, 1986. ISBN 0-395-39376-0 Subj: Behavior – losing things. Character traits – honesty. Ethnic groups in the U.S. – Afro-Americans.

Hawes, Judy. *Fireflies in the night* ill. by Kazue Mizumura. Coward, 1963. Subj: Family life – grandparents. Farms. Insects – fireflies. Science.

Ladybug, ladybug, fly away home ill. by Ed Emberley. Crowell, 1968. Subj: Insects – ladybugs. Science.

My daddy longlegs ill. by Walter Lorraine. Crowell, 1972. ISBN 0-690-56656-5 Subj: Spiders.

Shrimps ill. by Joseph Low. Crowell, 1967. Subj: Fish. Science.

Spring peepers ill. by Graham Booth. Crowell, 1975. Subj: Frogs and toads. Science.

Watch honeybees with me ill. by Helen Stone. Crowell, 1964. Subj: Insects – bees. Science.

Why frogs are wet ill. by Don Madden. Crowell, 1968. Subj: Frogs and toads. Science.

Hawkesworth, Jenny. *The lonely skyscraper* ill. by Emanuel Schongut. Doubleday, 1980. Subj: City. Country.

Hawkins, Colin. *Boo! Who?* by Colin and Jacqui Hawkins; ill. by authors. Holt, 1984. Subj: Poetry, rhyme.

Busy ABC by Colin and Jacqui Hawkins; ill. by authors. Viking, 1987. ISBN 0-670-81153-X Subj: ABC books. Activities.

Dip, dip, dip ill. by author. Little, 1986. ISBN 0-87113-087-4 Subj: Activities – playing. Animals – bears. Bedtime. Toys – teddy bears.

The elephant by Colin and Jacqui Hawkins; ill. by authors. Viking, 1986. ISBN 0-670-80314-6 Subj: Animals – elephants. Format, unusual – toy and movable books.

I'm not sleepy! by Colin and Jacqui Hawkins; ill. by authors. Crown, 1986. ISBN 0-517-55973-0 Subj: Animals – bears. Bedtime.

Incy wincy spider by Colin and Jacqui Hawkins; ill. by authors. Viking, 1986. ISBN 0-670-80317-0 Subj: Format, unusual – toy and movable books. Games. Spiders.

Jen the hen by Colin and Jacqui Hawkins; ill. by Colin Hawkins. Putnam's, 1985. ISBN 0-399-21207-8 Subj: Birthdays. Format, unusual. Poetry, rhyme.

Max and the magic word by Colin and Jacqui Hawkins; ill. by authors. Viking, 1986. ISBN 0-670-80853-9 Subj: Animals. Etiquette.

Mig the pig by Colin and Jacqui Hawkins; ill. by Colin Hawkins. Putnam's, 1984. Subj: Animals – pigs. Poetry, rhyme.

Old Mother Hubbard (Martin, Sarah Catherine)

One finger, one thumb ill. by author. Little, 1986. ISBN 0-87113-088-2 Subj: Activities – playing. Animals – bears. Bedtime. Toys – teddy bears.

Oops-a-Daisy ill. by author. Little, 1986. ISBN 0-87113-086-6 Subj: Activities – playing. Animals – bears. Bedtime. Toys – teddy bears.

Pat the cat by Colin and Jacqui Hawkins; ill. by Colin Hawkins. Putnam's, 1983. Subj: Animals – cats.

Round the garden by Colin and Jacqui Hawkins; ill. by authors. Viking, 1986. ISBN 0-670-80315-4 Subj: Format, unusual – toy and movable books. Games.

Snap! Snap! by Colin and Jacqui Hawkins; ill. by Colin Hawkins. Putnam's, 1984. ISBN 0-399-21163-2 Subj: Emotions – fear. Monsters. Night. Poetry, rhyme.

Take away monsters ill. by author. Putnam's, 1984. ISBN 0-399-20962-X Subj: Counting. Format, unusual – toy and movable books. Monsters. Poetry, rhyme.

This little pig by Colin and Jacqui Hawkins; ill. by authors. Viking, 1986. ISBN 0-670-80316-2 Subj: Anatomy. Animals – pigs. Format, unusual – toy and movable books. Games.

Tog the dog by Colin and Jacqui Hawkins; ill. by authors. Putnam's, 1986. ISBN 0-399-21338-4 Subj: Animals – dogs. Behavior – lost. Format, unusual. Language. Poetry, rhyme.

What time is it, Mr. Wolf? ill. by author. Putnam's, 1983. Subj: Animals – wolves. Format, unusual – toy and movable books. Time.

Where's bear? ill. by author. Little, 1986. ISBN 0-87113-090-4 Subj: Activities – playing. Animals – bears. Bedtime. Toys – teddy bears.

Where's my mommy? by Colin and Jacqui Hawkins; ill. by authors. Crown, 1986. ISBN 0-517-55974-9 Subj: Animals. Behavior – needing someone. Family life – mothers.

Hawkins, Jacqui. *Boo! Who?* (Hawkins, Colin)

Busy ABC (Hawkins, Colin)

The elephant (Hawkins, Colin)

I'm not sleepy! (Hawkins, Colin)

Incy wincy spider (Hawkins, Colin)

Jen the hen (Hawkins, Colin)

Max and the magic word (Hawkins, Colin)

Mig the pig (Hawkins, Colin)

Old Mother Hubbard (Martin, Sarah Catherine)

Pat the cat (Hawkins, Colin)

Round the garden (Hawkins, Colin)

Snap! Snap! (Hawkins, Colin)

This little pig (Hawkins, Colin)

Tog the dog (Hawkins, Colin)

Where's my mommy? (Hawkins, Colin)

Hawkins, Mark. *A lion under her bed* ill. by Jean Vallario. Holt, 1978. Subj: Animals – lions. Bedtime.

Hawkinson, John. *Birds in the sky* (Hawkinson, Lucy)

The old stump ill. by author. Albert Whitman, 1965. Subj: Animals – mice. Trees.

Robins and rabbits by John and Lucy Hawkinson; ill. by John Hawkinson. Albert Whitman, 1960. Subj: Animals. Birds – robins.

Where the wild apples grow ill. by author. Albert Whitman, 1967. Subj: Animals – horses. Character traits – freedom.

Hawkinson, Lucy. *Birds in the sky* by Lucy and John Hawkinson; ill. by authors. Children's Pr., 1966. Subj: Birds. Science.

Dance, dance, Amy-Chan! ill. by author. Albert Whitman, 1964. Subj: Ethnic groups in the U.S. – Japanese-Americans.

Robins and rabbits (Hawkinson, John)

Hawthorne, Julian. *Rumpty-Dudget's tower* adapt. and ill. by Diane Goode. Knopf, 1987. ISBN 0-394-97862-5 Subj: Animals – cats. Elves and little people. Folk and fairy tales. Royalty.

Hawthorne, Nathaniel. *King Midas and the golden touch* (Hewitt, Kathryn)

Hay, Dean. *I see a lot of things* ill. by author. Lion, 1966. Subj: Senses – seeing.

Now I can count ill. by author. Lion, 1968. Subj: Counting. Time.

Hay, Timothy *see* Brown, Margaret Wise

Hayes, Geoffrey. *Bear by himself* ill. by author. Harper, 1976. Subj: Behavior – solitude. Toys – teddy bears.

Elroy and the witch's child ill. by author. Harper, 1982. Subj: Animals – cats. Witches.

The mystery of the pirate ghost ill. by author. Random House, 1985. ISBN 0-394-97220-1 Subj: Ghosts. Pirates.

Patrick and his grandpa ill. by author. Random, 1986. ISBN 0-394-87287-8 Subj: Animals – bears. Family life – grandfathers. Format, unusual – board books.

Patrick and Ted ill. by author. Four Winds Pr., 1984. Subj: Animals – bears. Behavior – growing up.

The secret inside ill. by author. Harper, 1980. Subj: Animals – bears. Dreams.

Hayes, Sarah. *Bad egg: the true story of Humpty Dumpty* ill. by Charlotte Voake. Little, 1987. ISBN 0-316-35184-9 Subj: Behavior – misbehavior. Nursery rhymes. Royalty.

Clap your hands: finger rhymes ill. by Toni Goffe. Lothrop, 1988. ISBN 0-688-07693-9 Subj: Games. Poetry, rhyme.

Eat up, Gemma ill. by Jan Ormerod. Lothrop, 1988. ISBN 0-688-08149-5 Subj: Babies. Ethnic groups in the U.S. – Afro-Americans. Food.

Happy Christmas, Gemma ill. by Jan Ormerod. Lothrop, 1986. ISBN 0-688-06508-2 Subj: Ethnic groups in the U.S. – Afro-Americans. Family life. Family life – grandmothers. Holidays – Christmas.

This is the bear ill. by Helen Craig. Lippincott, 1986. ISBN 0-397-32171-6 Subj: Behavior – lost. Behavior – secrets. Poetry, rhyme. Toys – teddy bears.

Hayes, William D. (William Dimmity). *Mexicallie soup* (Hitte, Kathryn)

Haynes-Dixon, Margaret Rumer *see* Godden, Rumer

Haynes, Robert. *The elephant that ga-lumphed* (Ward, Nanda Weedon)

Hays, Daniel. *Charley sang a song* (Hays, Hoffman Reynolds)

Hays, Hoffman Reynolds. *Charley sang a song* by Hoffman and Daniel Hays; ill. by Uri Shulevitz. Harper, 1964. Subj: Activities – flying.

Hays, Wilma Pitchford. *Little Yellow Fur* ill. by Richard Cuffari. Coward, 1973. Subj: Indians of North America.

Hayward, Linda. *The Julian Messner picture dictionary of phonics* ill. by Carol Nicklaus. Messner, 1984. ISBN 0-671-53035-6 Subj: Dictionaries. Language.

The Sesame Street dictionary ill. by Joseph Mathieu. Random House, 1980. Subj: Dictionaries.

Hayward, Max. *The telephone* (Chukovsky, Korney)

Haywood, Carolyn. *A Christmas fantasy* ill. by Glenys and Victor G. Ambrus. Morrow, 1972. Subj: Holidays – Christmas.

Hello, star ill. by Julie Durrell. Morrow, 1987. ISBN 0-688-06651-8 Subj: Animals. Family life – grandparents. Farms. Seasons – summer.

How the reindeer saved Santa ill. by Victor G. Ambrus. Morrow, 1986. ISBN 0-688-05904-X Subj: Animals – reindeer. Character traits – loyalty. Holidays – Christmas.

The king's monster ill. by Victor G. Ambrus. Morrow, 1980. Subj: Monsters. Royalty.

Santa Claus forever! ill. by Glenys and Victor G. Ambrus. Morrow, 1983. ISBN 0-688-02345-2 Subj: Behavior – bad day. Holidays – Christmas.

Hazelton, Elizabeth Baldwin. *Sammy, the crow who remembered* ill. by Ann Atwood. Scribner's, 1969. Subj: Birds – crows. Family life.

Hazen, Barbara Shook. *Even if I did something awful* ill. by Nancy Kincade. Atheneum, 1981. Subj: Emotions – love. Family life.

Fang ill. by Leslie Morrill. Atheneum, 1987. ISBN 0-689-31307-1 Subj: Animals – dogs. Character traits – bravery. Emotions – fear.

The Fat Cats, Cousin Scraggs and the monster mice ill. by Lonni Sue Johnson. Atheneum, 1985. ISBN 0-689-31092-7 Subj: Animals – cats. Animals – mice. Behavior – dissatisfaction. Character traits – cleverness.

The gorilla did it! ill. by Ray Cruz. Atheneum, 1974. Subj: Animals – gorillas. Imagination – imaginary friends.

Gorilla wants to be the baby ill. by Jacqueline Bardner Smith. Atheneum, 1978. Subj: Animals – gorillas. Imagination – imaginary friends.

Happy, sad, silly, mad: a beginning book about emotions ill. by Elizabeth Dauber; ed. consultant: Mary Elting. Grosset, 1971. Subj: Emotions.

If it weren't for Benjamin (I'd always get to lick the icing spoon) ill. by Laura Hartman. Human Sciences Pr., 1979. Subj: Sibling rivalry.

The knight who was afraid of the dark ill. by Tony Ross. Dial Pr., 1988. ISBN 0-8037-0668-5 Subj: Emotions – fear. Knights. Middle ages. Night.

The me I see ill. by Ati Forberg. Abingdon, 1978. Subj: Activities – bathing. Anatomy.

The sorcerer's apprentice ill. by Tomi Ungerer. Lancelot Pr., 1969. Subj: Folk and fairy tales. Magic.

Tight times ill. by Trina Schart Hyman. Viking, 1979. Subj: Animals – cats. Family life. Family life – only child. Poverty.

Two homes to live in ill. by Peggy Luks. Human Sciences Pr., 1978. Subj: Divorce. Emotions.

Where do bears sleep? ill. by Ian E. Staunton. Addison-Wesley, 1970. Subj: Animals. Poetry, rhyme. Sleep.

Why couldn't I be an only kid like you, Wigger? ill. by Leigh Grant. Atheneum, 1975. Subj: Babies. Emotions – envy, jealousy. Family life – only child. Sibling rivalry.

Why did Grandpa die? a book about death ill. by Pat Schories. Childrens Pr., 1985. ISBN 0-307-62484-6 Subj: Death. Family life – grandfathers. Old age.

Hearn, Michael Patrick. *The porcelain cat* ill. by Leo and Diane Dillon. Little, 1985. ISBN 0-316-35330-2 Subj: Animals – cats. Animals – rats. Cumulative tales. Folk and fairy tales. Magic.

Heathers, Anne. *The thread soldiers* by Anne Heathers and Esteban Frances; ill. by Esteban Frances. Harcourt, 1960. Subj: Animals – mice. String. Toys – soldiers.

Heck, Elisabeth. *The black sheep* tr. by Karen Klockner; ill. by Sita Jucker. Little, 1986. ISBN 0-316-35402-3 Subj: Animals – sheep. Behavior – running away. Holidays – Christmas. Religion.

Hedderwick, Mairi. *Katie Morag and the big boy cousins* ill. by author. Little, 1987. ISBN 0-316-35403-1 Subj: Behavior – misbehavior. Family life. Family life – grandmothers. Foreign lands – Scotland. Islands.

Katie Morag and the tiresome Ted ill. by author. Little, 1986. ISBN 0-316-35401-5 Subj: Babies. Behavior – misbehavior. Emotions – envy, jealousy. Foreign lands – Scotland. Islands. Sibling rivalry.

Katie Morag and the two grandmothers ill. by author. Little, 1986. ISBN 0-316-35400-7 Subj: Activities – bathing. Animals – sheep. Fairs. Family life – grandmothers. Foreign lands – Scotland. Islands.

Katie Morag delivers the mail ill. by author. Little, 1987, 1984. ISBN 0-316-35405-8 Subj: Behavior – misbehavior. Careers – mail carriers. Family life – grandmothers. Foreign lands – Scotland. Islands.

Heelis, Beatrix *see* Potter, Beatrix

Hefter, Richard. *The strawberry book of shapes* ill. by author. Larousse, 1976. Subj: Concepts – shape.

Heide, Florence Parry. *A monster is coming! A monster is coming!* by Florence Parry Heide and Roxanne Heide; ill. by Rachi Farrow. Watts, 1980. Subj: Monsters.

The shrinking of Treehorn ill. by Edward Gorey. Holiday, 1971. Subj: Family life. Humor. Problem solving.

Treehorn's treasure ill. by Edward Gorey. Holiday House, 1981. Subj: Family life. Magic. Money.

Treehorn's wish ill. by Edward Gorey. Holiday, 1984. Subj: Birthdays. Magic.

Heide, Roxanne. *A monster is coming! A monster is coming!* (Heide, Florence Parry)

Heilbroner, Joan. *Robert the rose horse* ill. by Philip Eastman. Random House, 1962. Subj: Animals – horses. Flowers. Humor.

This is the house where Jack lives ill. by Aliki. Harper, 1962. Subj: Cumulative tales. Participation.

Tom the TV cat ill. by Sal Murdocca. Random House, 1984. ISBN 0-394-96708-9 Subj: Animals – cats. Behavior – seeking better things. Television.

Heine, Helme. *Friends* ill. by author. Atheneum, 1982. Subj: Animals. Friendship. Sports – bicycling.

King Bounce the 1st ill. by author. Alphabet Pr., 1982. Subj: Royalty. Sleep.

Merry-go-round ill. by author. Barron's, 1980. Subj: Activities – working.

Mr. Miller the dog ill. by author. Atheneum, 1980. Subj: Animals – dogs. Behavior – imitation.

The most wonderful egg in the world ill. by author. Atheneum, 1983. Subj: Birds – chickens. Character traits – appearance. Royalty.

One day in paradise ill. by adapt. Atheneum, 1986. ISBN 0-689-50394-6 Subj: Religion.

The pigs' wedding ill. by author. Atheneum, 1979. Subj: Animals – pigs. Weddings.

Superhare ill. by author. Barron's, 1979. Subj: Animals – rabbits. Character traits – being different.

Three little friends: the alarm clock ill. by author. Atheneum, 1985. ISBN 0-689-71043-7 Subj: Animals. Birds – chickens. Friendship. Night.

Three little friends: the racing cart ill. by author. Atheneum, 1985. ISBN 0-689-71045-3 Subj: Animals. Birds – chickens. Friendship. Sports – racing.

Three little friends: the visitor ill. by author. Atheneum, 1985. ISBN 0-689-71044-5 Subj: Animals. Birds – chickens. Friendship.

Heins, Paul. *Snow White* (Grimm, Jacob)

Heitler, Susan M. *David decides about thumbsucking* photos. by Paula Singer. Reading Matters, 1985. ISBN 0-9614780-12 Subj: Behavior – growing up. Problem solving. Thumbsucking.

The Helen Oxenbury nursery rhyme book chosen by Brian Alderson; ill. by Helen Oxenbury. Morrow, 1987. ISBN 0-688-06899-5 Subj: Nursery rhymes.

Helena, Ann. *The lie* ill. by Ellen Pizer. Raintree, 1977. Subj: Behavior – lying. Emotions. Friendship.

Hellard, Susan. *Froggie goes a-courting* ill. by adapt. Putnam's, 1988. ISBN 0-399-21508-5 Subj: Frogs and toads. Humor.

Helldorfer, M. C. *Daniel's gift* ill. by Julie Downing. Bradbury Pr., 1987. ISBN 0-02-743511-3 Subj: Animals – sheep. Holidays – Christmas.

Hellen, Nancy. *Bus stop* ill. by author. Watts, 1988. ISBN 0-531-05765-8 Subj: Buses. Character traits – patience. Format, unusual. Transportation.

Heller, George. *Hiroshi's wonderful kite* ill. by Kyuzo Tsugami. Silver Burdett, 1968. Subj: Crime. Foreign lands – Japan. Kites.

Heller, Linda. *Alexis and the golden ring* ill. by author. Macmillan, 1980. Subj: Folk and fairy tales. Foreign lands – Russia. Magic.

The castle on Hester Street ill. by author. Jewish Pub. Soc., 1982. Subj: Family life – grandparents.

Lily at the table ill. by author. Macmillan, 1979. Subj: Family life. Food. Wordless.

Heller, Nicholas. *An adventure at sea* ill. by author. Greenwillow, 1988. ISBN 0-688-07847-8 Subj: Imagination. Sea and seashore. Sibling rivalry.

Happy birthday, Moe dog ill. by author. Greenwillow, 1988. ISBN 0-688-07671-8 Subj: Animals – dogs. Birthdays.

The monster in the cave ill. by author. Greenwillow, 1987. ISBN 0-688-07314-X Subj: Family life. Holidays – Christmas. Monsters. Parties.

Heller, Ruth. *Animals born alive and well* ill. by author. Grosset, 1982. Subj: Animals.

Chickens aren't the only ones ill. by author. Grosset, 1981. Subj: Eggs. Science.

How to hide a butterfly: and other insects ill. by author. Grosset, 1985. ISBN 0-488-10478-4 Subj: Behavior – hiding. Insects. Insects – butterflies, caterpillars. Poetry, rhyme.

How to hide a polar bear: and other mammals ill. by author. Grosset, 1985. ISBN 0-488-10477-6 Subj: Animals. Animals – polar bears. Behavior – hiding. Poetry, rhyme.

How to hide an octopus: and other sea creatures ill. by author. Grosset, 1985. ISBN 0-488-10476-8 Subj: Animals. Crustacea. Octopuses. Poetry, rhyme.

Kites sail high: a book about verbs ill. by author. Grosset, 1988. ISBN 0-448-10480-6 Subj: Language. Poetry, rhyme.

Plants that never ever bloom ill. by author. Grosset, 1984. Subj: Plants.

The reason for a flower ill. by author. Grosset, 1983. Subj: Flowers. Poetry, rhyme.

Heller, Wendy. *Clementine and the cage* ill. by Rex J. Irvine. Kalimát, 1980. Subj: Behavior – running away. Birds – canaries.

Hello, baby photos. sel. by Debby Slier. Macmillan, 1988. ISBN 0-02-688750-9 Subj: Babies. Format, unusual – board books.

Hellsing, Lennart. *The wonderful pumpkin* ill. by Svend Otto S. Atheneum, 1976, 1975. Translation of Der underbara pumpan. Subj: Animals – bears. Food. Holidays – Halloween.

Helmering, Doris Wild. *I have two families* ill. by Heidi Palmer. Abingdon Pr., 1981. Subj: Family life – step families.

We're going to have a baby by Doris and John William Helmering; ill. by Robert H. Cassell. Abingdon Pr., 1978. Subj: Babies. Family life. Sibling rivalry.

Helmering, John William. *We're going to have a baby* (Helmering, Doris Wild)

Helweg, Hans. *Farm animals* ill. by author. Random House, 1978. ISBN 0-394-93733-3 Subj: Animals. Birds. Farms.

Hendershot, Judith. *In coal country* ill. by Thomas B. Allen. Knopf, 1987. ISBN 0-394-98190-1 Subj: Family life. Family life – fathers.

Henderson, Kathy. *The baby's book of babies* photos. by Anthea Sieveking. Dial Pr., 1989. ISBN 0-837-0634-0 Subj: Babies.

Hendrickson, Karen. *Baby and I can play* ill. by Marina Megale. Parenting Pr., 1986. ISBN 0-943990-13-0 Subj: Activities – playing. Babies. Family life.

Fun with toddlers ill. by Marina Megale. Parenting Pr., 1986. ISBN 0-943990-14-9 Subj: Activities – playing. Babies. Family life.

Henkes, Kevin. *All alone* ill. by author. Greenwillow, 1981. Subj: Behavior – solitude.

Bailey goes camping ill. by author. Greenwillow, 1985. ISBN 0-688-05702-0 Subj: Animals – rabbits. Family life. Sports – camping.

Chester's way ill. by author. Greenwillow, 1988. ISBN 0-688-07608-4 Subj: Animals – mice. Behavior – bullying.

Clean enough ill. by author. Greenwillow, 1982. Subj: Activities – bathing.

Grandpa and Bo ill. by author. Greenwillow, 1986. ISBN 0-688-04957-5 Subj: Family life – grandfathers. Seasons – summer.

Jessica ill. by author. Greenwillow, 1989. ISBN 0-688-07830-3 Subj: Friendship. Imagination – imaginary friends. School.

Once around the block ill. by Victoria Chess. Greenwillow, 1987. ISBN 0-688-04955-9 Subj: Behavior – boredom. Communities, neighborhoods.

Sheila Rae, the brave ill. by author. Greenwillow, 1987. ISBN 0-688-07156-2 Subj: Animals – mice. Behavior – lost. Character traits – bravery. Family life – sisters.

A weekend with Wendell ill. by author. Greenwillow, 1986. ISBN 0-688-06326-8 Subj: Activities – playing. Animals – mice. Behavior – misbehavior. Character traits – selfishness.

Henkle, Henrietta *see* Buckmaster, Henrietta

Henley, Karyn. *Hatch!* ill. by Susan Kennedy. Carolrhoda Books, 1980. Subj: Animals.

Hennessy, B. G. *The dinosaur who lived in my backyard* ill. by Susan Davis. Viking, 1988. ISBN 0-670-81685-X Subj: Dinosaurs. Imagination.

The missing tarts ill. by Tracey Campbell Pearson. Viking, 1989. ISBN 0-670-82039-3 Subj: Behavior – stealing. Nursery rhymes. Poetry, rhyme.

Henrie, Fiona. *Cats* photos. by Marc Henrie. Watts, 1980. Subj: Animals – cats. Pets.

Dogs photos. by Marc Henrie. Watts, 1980. Subj: Animals – dogs. Pets.

Gerbils photos. by Marc Henrie. Watts, 1980. Subj: Animals – gerbils. Pets.

Rabbits photos. by Marc Henrie. Watts, 1980. Subj: Animals – rabbits. Pets.

Henriod, Lorraine. *Grandma's wheelchair* ill. by Christa Chevalier. Albert Whitman, 1982. Subj: Family life – grandmothers. Handicaps. Sibling rivalry.

Henrioud, Charles *see* Matias

Henry, O. *The gift of the Magi* ill. by Lisbeth Zwerger. Picture Book Studio, 1982. ISBN 0-907234-17-8 Subj: Character traits – generosity. Holidays – Christmas.

Henstra, Friso. *Wait and see* ill. by author. Addison-Wesley, 1978. Subj: Machines.

Herman, Alan *see* Allan, Ted

Herman, Bill. *Jenny's magic wand* by Bill and Helen Herman; photos. by Don Perdue. Watts, 1988. ISBN 0-531-10292-0 Subj: Handicaps – blindness. Senses – seeing.

Herman, Charlotte. *My mother didn't kiss me goodnight* ill. by Bruce Degen. Dutton, 1980. Subj: Behavior – worrying.

Herman, Emily. *Hubknuckles* ill. by Deborah Kogan Ray. Crown, 1985. ISBN 0-517-55646-4 Subj: Ghosts. Holidays – Halloween.

Herman, Helen. *Jenny's magic wand* (Herman, Bill)

Herold, Ann Bixby. *The helping day* ill. by Victoria de Larrea. Coward, 1980. Subj: Character traits – helpfulness.

Herring, Ann. *Peter and the wolf* (Prokofiev, Sergei Sergeievitch)

Suho and the white horse (Otsuka, Yuzo)

Herriot, James. *Blossom comes home* ill. by Ruth Brown. St. Martin's, 1988. ISBN 0-312-02169-0 Subj: Animals – bulls, cows. Behavior – needing someone. Farms. Old age.

Bonny's big day ill. by Ruth Brown. St. Martin's, 1987. ISBN 0-312-01000-1 Subj: Animals – horses. Fairs. Farms.

Christmas Day kitten ill. by Ruth Brown. St. Martin's, 1986. ISBN 0-312-13407-X Subj: Animals – cats. Character traits – kindness to animals. Holidays – Christmas.

Moses the kitten ill. by Peter Barrett. St. Martin's, 1984. Subj: Animals – cats. Careers – veterinarians.

Only one woof ill. by Peter Barrett. St. Martin's, 1985. ISBN 0-312-58583-7 Subj: Animals. Animals – dogs. Careers – veterinarians.

Herrmann, Frank. *The giant Alexander* ill. by George Him. McGraw-Hill, 1965. Subj: Foreign lands – England. Giants.

The giant Alexander and the circus ill. by George Him. McGraw-Hill, 1966. Subj: Circus. Foreign lands – England. Giants.

Herter, Jonina. *Eighty-eight kisses* ill. with photos. Boss Books, 1978. Subj: Babies. Family life – great-grandparents.

Hertza, Ole. *Tobias catches trout* tr. from Danish by Tobi Tobias; ill. by author. Carolrhoda Books, 1984. Subj: Foreign lands – Greenland. Sports – fishing.

Tobias goes ice fishing tr. from Danish by Tobi Tobias; ill. by author. Carolrhoda Books, 1984. Subj: Foreign lands – Greenland. Seasons – winter. Sports – fishing.

Tobias goes seal hunting tr. from Danish by Tobi Tobias; ill. by author. Carolrhoda Books, 1984. Subj: Foreign lands – Greenland. Sports – hunting.

Tobias has a birthday tr. from Danish by Tobi Tobias; ill. by author. Carolrhoda Books, 1984. Subj: Birthdays. Foreign lands – Greenland.

Herz, Irene. *Hey! Don't do that!* ill. by Lucinda McQueen. Prentice-Hall, 1978. Subj: Activities – playing. Animals. Behavior – misbehavior.

Hess, Edith. *Peter and Susie find a family* tr. from German by Miriam Moore; ill. by Jacqueline Blass. Abingdon Pr., 1985. ISBN 0-687-30848-8 Subj: Adoption. Family life.

Hess, Lilo. *A cat's nine lives* ill. by author. Scribner's, 1984. Subj: Animals – cats. Behavior – needing someone.

The curious raccoons photos. by author. Scribner's, 1968. Subj: Animals – raccoons. Science.

Foxes in the woodshed photos. by author. Scribner's, 1966. Subj: Animals – foxes. Science.

Rabbits in the meadow photos. by author. Crowell, 1963. Subj: Animals – rabbits.

Hest, Amy. *The crack-of-dawn walkers* ill. by Amy Schwartz. Macmillan, 1984. Subj: Family life – grandfathers.

The mommy exchange ill. by DyAnne DiSalvo-Ryan. Four Winds, 1988. ISBN 0-02-743650-0 Subj: Behavior – dissatisfaction. Family life – mothers.

The purple coat ill. by Amy Schwartz. Four Winds Pr., 1986. ISBN 0-02-743640-3 Subj: Careers – tailors. Clothing. Concepts – color. Family life. Family life – grandfathers.

Heuck, Sigrid. *Who stole the apples?* ill. by author. Knopf, 1986. ISBN 0-394-98371-8 Subj: Activities – traveling. Animals. Behavior – sharing. Rebuses.

Hewett, Anita. *The little white hen* ill. by William Stobbs. McGraw-Hill, 1963. Subj: Birds – chickens. Cumulative tales. Folk and fairy tales.

The tale of the turnip ill. by Margery Gill. McGraw-Hill, 1961. Subj: Cumulative tales. Participation. Plants.

Hewett, Anne *see* Wellington, Anne

Hewett, Joan. *Fly away free* photos. by Richard Hewett. Walker, 1981. Subj: Birds – pelicans. Careers – veterinarians. Illness.

The mouse and the elephant photos. by Richard Hewett. Little, 1977. Subj: Animals – elephants. Animals – mice.

Rosalie ill. by Donald Carrick. Lothrop, 1987. ISBN 0-688-06229-6 Subj: Animals – dogs. Character traits – kindness to animals. Old age.

Hewitt, Kathryn. *King Midas and the golden touch* by Nathaniel Hawthorne; adapt. and ill. by Kathryn Hewitt. Harcourt, 1987. ISBN 0-15-242800-3 Subj: Behavior – greed. Folk and fairy tales. Royalty.

The three sillies ill. by adapt. Harcourt, 1986. ISBN 0-15-286855-0 Subj: Animals. Animals – pigs. Character traits – foolishness. Folk and fairy tales.

Two by two: the untold story ill. by author. Harcourt, 1984. Subj: Religion – Noah.

Heyduck-Huth, Hilde. *The starfish: a treasure chest story* ill. by author. Macmillan, 1987. ISBN 0-689-50434-9 Subj: Behavior – collecting things. Crustacea. Sea and seashore.

The strawflower: a treasure chest story ill. by author. Macmillan, 1987. ISBN 0-689-50435-7 Subj: Behavior – collecting things. Flowers. Seasons.

Heyer, Marilee. *The forbidden door* ill. by author. Viking, 1988. ISBN 0-670-81740-6 Subj: Monsters. Mythical creatures.

Heymans, Margriet. *Pippin and Robber Grumblecroak's big baby* ill. by author. Addison-Wesley, 1973. Subj: Crime. Puppets.

Heyward, Du Bose. *The country bunny and the little gold shoes* ill. by Marjorie Flack. Houghton, 1939. Subj: Animals – rabbits. Character traits – kindness. Holidays – Easter.

Hickman, Martha Whitmore. *Eeps creeps, it's my room!* ill. by Mary Alice Baer. Abingdon Pr., 1984. Subj: Character traits – cleanliness.

My friend William moved away ill. by Bill Myers. Abingdon Pr., 1979. Subj: Friendship. Moving.

When can daddy come home? ill. by Francis Livingston. Abingdon Pr., 1983. Subj: Crime. Family life. Prisons.

Hicks, Eleanor B. *see* Coerr, Eleanor

Hidaka, Masako. *Girl from the snow country* tr. from Japanese by Amanda Mayer Stinchecum; ill. by author. Kane Miller, 1986. ISBN 0-916291-06-5 Subj: Flowers. Folk and fairy tales. Foreign lands – Japan. Weather – snow.

High on a hill: *a book of Chinese riddles* sel. and ill. by Ed Young. Collins-World, 1980. Subj: Folk and fairy tales. Foreign lands – China. Riddles.

Higham, Jon Atlas. *Aardvark's picnic* ill. by author. Little, 1987. ISBN 0-333-42822-6 Subj: Activities – picnicking. Animals. Animals – aardvarks.

Highwater, Jamake. *Moonsong lullaby* photos. by Marcia Keegan. Lothrop, 1981. Subj: Night. Poetry, rhyme.

Hill, Donna. *Ms. Glee was waiting* ill. by Diane Dawson. Atheneum, 1978. Subj: School.

Hill, Elizabeth Starr. *Evan's corner* ill. by Nancy Grossman. Holt, 1967. Subj: Character traits – helpfulness. Ethnic groups in the U.S. – Afro-Americans. Family life.

Hill, Eric. *At home* ill. by author. Random House, 1983. Subj: Animals – bears. Family life. Wordless.

Baby Bear's bedtime ill. by author. Random House, 1984. ISBN 0-394-96572-8 Subj: Animals – bears. Bedtime.

Good morning, baby bear ill. by author. Random House, 1984. Subj: Animals – bears. Morning.

My pets ill. by author. Random House, 1983. Subj: Animals – bears. Pets.

The park ill. by author. Random House, 1983. Subj: Activities – walking. Wordless.

Spot at play ill. by author. Putnam's, 1985. ISBN 0-399-21228-0 Subj: Activities – playing. Animals. Animals – dogs.

Spot at the fair ill. by author. Putnam's, 1985. ISBN 0-399-21229-9 Subj: Animals. Animals – dogs. Fairs. Format, unusual – board books.

Spot goes to school ill. by author. Putnam's, 1984. Subj: Animals – dogs. Format, unusual – toy and movable books. School.

Spot goes to the beach ill. by author. Putnam's, 1985. ISBN 0-399-21247-7 Subj: Activities – playing. Animals – dogs. Family life. Format, unusual – toy and movable books. Sea and seashore.

Spot goes to the circus ill. by author. Putnam's, 1986. ISBN 0-399-21317-1 Subj: Animals – dogs. Circus. Format, unusual – board books.

Spot goes to the farm ill. by author. Putnam's, 1987. ISBN 0-399-21434-8 Subj: Animals. Animals – dogs. Farms. Format, unusual – board books. Machines.

Spot looks at colors ill. by author. Putnam's, 1986. ISBN 0-399-21349-X Subj: Animals – dogs. Concepts – color. Format, unusual – board books.

Spot looks at shapes ill. by author. Putnam's, 1986. ISBN 0-399-21350-3 Subj: Animals – dogs. Concepts – shape. Format, unusual – board books.

Spot on the farm ill. by author. Putnam's, 1985. ISBN 0-399-21230-2 Subj: Animals. Animals – dogs. Farms. Format, unusual – board books.

Spot visits the hospital ill. by author. Putnam's, 1987. ISBN 0-399-21397-X Subj: Animals – dogs. Behavior – misbehavior. Hospitals.

Spot's big book of words ill. by author. Putnam's, 1988. ISBN 0-399-21563-8 Subj: Animals – dogs. Language.

Spot's birthday party ill. by author. Putnam's, 1982. Subj: Birthdays. Folk and fairy tales. Format, unusual – toy and movable books.

Spot's first Christmas ill. by author. Putnam's, 1983. ISBN 0-399-20963-8 Subj: Animals – dogs. Format, unusual – toy and movable books. Holidays – Christmas.

Spot's first Easter ill. by author. Putnam's, 1988. ISBN 0-399-21435-6 Subj: Animals – dogs. Eggs. Format, unusual – toy and movable books. Holidays – Easter.

Spot's first picnic ill. by author. Putnam's, 1987. ISBN 0-399-21398-8 Subj: Activities – picnicking. Animals – dogs. Behavior – misbehavior.

Spot's first walk ill. by author. Putnam's, 1981. Subj: Activities – walking. Animals – dogs. Format, unusual – toy and movable books.

Spot's first words ill. by author. Putnam's, 1986. ISBN 0-399-21348-1 Subj: Animals – dogs. Format, unusual – board books. Language.

Up there ill. by author. Random House, 1983. Subj: Activities – flying. Animals – bears Wordless.

Where's Spot? ill. by author. Putnam's, 1980. Subj: Behavior – lost. Folk and fairy tales. Format, unusual – toy and movable books.

Hill, Helen. *Dusk to dawn: poems of night* sel. by Helen Hill and others; ill. by Anne Burgess. Crowell, 1981. Subj: Poetry, rhyme.

Hill, Mary Lou. *My dad's a park ranger* ill. by Tom De Hart. Children's Pr., 1978. Subj: Careers – park rangers.

My dad's a smokejumper ill. by Don Hendricks. Children's Pr., 1978. Subj: Careers – firefighters. Forest, woods.

Hill, Monica *see* Watson, Jane Werner

Hill, Susan. *Can it be true?* ill. by Angela Barrett. Viking, 1988. ISBN 0-670-82517-4 Subj: Holidays – Christmas. Poetry, rhyme.

Go away, bad dreams! ill. by Vanessa Julian-Ottie. Random House, 1985. ISBN 0-394-97222-8 Subj: Dreams. Emotions – fear. Family life. Night.

Hille-Brandts, Lene. *The little black hen* tr. and adapt. by Marion Koenig; ill. by Sigrid Heuck. Children's Pr., 1968. Translation of Die Henne Gudula. Subj: Behavior – dissatisfaction. Birds – chickens.

Hiller, Catherine. *Abracatabby* ill. by Victoria De Larrea. Coward, 1981. Subj: Animals – cats. Magic.

Argentaybee and the boonie ill. by Cyndy Szekeres. Coward, 1979. Subj: Behavior – misbehavior. Imagination – imaginary friends.

Hillerich, Robert L. *Rand McNally picturebook dictionary*

Hillert, Margaret. *The birthday car* ill. by Kelly Oechsli. Follett, 1966. Subj: Birthdays. Toys.

The funny baby ill. by Hertha Depper. Follett, 1966. The tale of The Ugly Duckling by H. C. Andersen. Subj: Birds – ducks. Birds – swans. Character traits – appearance. Character traits – being different. Folk and fairy tales.

Happy birthday, dear dragon ill. by Carl Kock. Follett, 1977. Subj: Birthdays. Dragons.

The little cowboy and the big cowboy ill. by Dan Siculan. Follett, 1980. Subj: Cowboys. Family life – fathers.

Little Red Riding Hood (Grimm, Jacob)

The little runaway ill. by Irv Anderson. Follett, 1966. Subj: Animals – cats. Behavior – running away.

The magic beans ill. by Mel Pekarsky. Follett, 1966. The tale of Jack and the beanstalk. Subj: Folk and fairy tales. Giants. Plants.

Merry Christmas, dear dragon ill. by Carl Kock. Follett, 1980. Subj: Dragons. Holidays – Christmas.

Play ball ill. by Dick Martin. Follett, 1978. Subj: Activities – playing. Games. Sports – baseball.

The three bears ill. by Irma Wilde. Follett, 1963. Subj: Animals – bears. Folk and fairy tales.

The three goats ill. by Mel Pekarsky. Follett, 1963. The tale of The three billy goats Gruff. Subj: Animals – goats. Character traits – cleverness. Cumulative tales. Folk and fairy tales. Mythical creatures. Trolls.

The three little pigs

Tom Thumb

Up, up and away ill. by Robert Masheris. Modern Curriculum, 1981. ISBN 0-8136-5096-8 Subj: Moon. Space and space ships.

What is it? ill. by Kinuko Craft. Follett, 1978. ISBN 0-695-40882-8 Subj: Activities – playing. Animals – dogs. Imagination. Poetry, rhyme.

The yellow boat ill. by Ed Young. Follett, 1966. Subj: Boats, ships.

Hillman, Priscilla. *A Merry-Mouse book of favorite poems* ill. by author. Doubleday, 1981. Subj: Animals – mice. Poetry, rhyme.

A Merry-Mouse book of months ill. by author. Doubleday, 1980. Subj: Animals – mice. Days of the week, months of the year. Poetry, rhyme.

The Merry-Mouse book of prayers and graces ill. by author. Doubleday, 1983. Subj: Religion.

A Merry-Mouse Christmas A B C ill. by author. Doubleday, 1980. Subj: ABC books. Animals – mice. Holidays – Christmas.

The Merry-Mouse schoolhouse ill. by author. Doubleday, 1982. Subj: Animals – mice. School.

Himler, Ronald. *The girl on the yellow giraffe* ill. by author. Harper, 1976. Subj: City. Imagination.

Wake up, Jeremiah ill. by author. Harper, 1979. Subj: Morning.

Himmelman, John. *Amanda and the magic garden* ill. by author. Viking, 1987. ISBN 0-670-80823-7 Subj: Activities – gardening. Animals. Magic. Witches.

Amanda and the witch switch ill. by author. Viking, 1985. ISBN 0-670-11531-2 Subj: Behavior – misbehavior. Behavior – wishing. Character traits – meanness. Frogs and toads. Witches.

Montigue on the high seas ill. by author. Viking, 1988. ISBN 0-670-81861-5 Subj: Animals. Animals – mice. Animals – moles.

Talester the lizard ill. by author. Dial Pr., 1982. Subj: Reptiles – lizards.

The talking tree: or Don't believe everything you hear ill. by author. Viking, 1986. ISBN 0-670-80775-3 Subj: Animals – dogs. Trees.

Hine, Sesyle Joslin *see* Joslin, Sesyle

Hines, Anna Grossnickle. *All by myself* ill. by author. Clarion, 1985. ISBN 0-89919-293-9 Subj: Behavior – growing up. Self-concept.

Bethany for real ill. by author. Greenwillow, 1985. ISBN 0-688-04009-8 Subj: Activities – playing. Imagination.

Come to the meadow ill. by author. Houghton, 1984. Subj: Activities – picnicking. Family life – grandmothers.

Daddy makes the best spaghetti ill. by author. Clarion, 1986. ISBN 0-89919-388-9 Subj: Family life. Family life – fathers.

Don't worry, I'll find you ill. by author. Dutton, 1986. ISBN 0-525-44228-6 Subj: Behavior – lost. Shopping. Toys – dolls.

Grandma gets grumpy ill. by author. Clarion, 1988. ISBN 0-89919-529-6 Subj: Activities – baby-sitting. Family life – grandmothers.

I'll tell you what they say ill. by author. Greenwillow, 1987. ISBN 0-688-06487-6 Subj: Animals. Animals – dogs. Farms. Toys – teddy bears.

It's just me, Emily ill. by author. Clarion, 1987. ISBN 0-89919-487-7 Subj: Activities – playing. Family life – mothers. Poetry, rhyme.

Keep your old hat ill. by author. Dutton, 1987. ISBN 0-525-44299-5 Subj: Activities – playing. Toys – dolls.

Maybe a band-aid will help ill. by author. Dutton, 1984. ISBN 0-525-44115-8 Subj: Family life – mothers. Problem solving. Toys – dolls.

Taste the raindrops ill. by author. Greenwillow, 1983. Subj: Weather – rain.

Hinojosa, Francisco. *The old lady who ate people: frightening stories* ill. by Leonel Maciel. Little, 1984. Subj: Folk and fairy tales. Foreign lands – Mexico.

Hippel, Ursula Von *see* Von Hippel, Ursula

The hippo ill. by Caroline Binch. Rourke, 1983. Subj: Animals – hippopotami.

Hippopotamus, Eugene H. *see* Kraus, Robert

Hirschberg, J. Cotter. *My friend the babysitter* (Watson, Jane Werner)

My friend the dentist (Watson, Jane Werner)

My friend the doctor (Watson, Jane Werner)

Sometimes a family has to move (Watson, Jane Werner)

Sometimes a family has to split up (Watson, Jane Werner)

Sometimes I get angry (Watson, Jane Werner)

Sometimes I'm afraid (Watson, Jane Werner)

Sometimes I'm jealous (Watson, Jane Werner)

Hirschi, Ron. *What is a bird?* photos. by Galen Burrell. Walker, 1987. ISBN 0-8027-6721-4 Subj: Birds. Science.

Where do birds live? photos. by Galen Burrell. Walker, 1987. ISBN 0-8027-6723-0 Subj: Birds. Science.

Who lives in... Alligator Swamp? photos. by Galen Burrell. Dodd, 1987. ISBN 0-396-09123-7 Subj: Animals. Forest, woods. Reptiles – alligators, crocodiles. Science.

Who lives in... the forest? photos. by Galen Burrell. Dodd, 1987. ISBN 0-396-09121-0 Subj: Animals. Birds. Forest, woods.

Hirschmann, Linda. *In a lick of a flick of a tongue* ill. by Jeni Bassett. Dodd, 1980. Subj: Anatomy. Animals.

Hirsh, Marilyn. *Captain Jiri and Rabbi Jacob: from a Jewish folktale* ill. by author. Holiday, 1976. Subj: Folk and fairy tales. Jewish culture.

Could anything be worse? a Yiddish tale ill. by author. Holiday, 1974. Subj: Humor. Jewish culture.

Deborah the dybbuk: a ghost story ill. by author. Holiday, 1978. ISBN 0-8234-0315-7 Subj: Behavior – misbehavior. Character traits – kindness to animals. Ghosts.

I love Hanukkah ill. by author. Holiday, 1984. ISBN 0-8234-0525-7 Subj: Holidays – Hanukkah. Jewish culture.

I love Passover ill. by author. Holiday, 1985. ISBN 0-8234-0549-4 Subj: Holidays – Passover. Jewish culture. Religion.

Joseph who loved the Sabbath ill. by Devis Grebu. Viking, 1986. ISBN 0-670-81194-7 Subj: Folk and fairy tales. Jewish culture. Religion.

Leela and the watermelon by Marilyn Hirsh and Maya Narayan; ill. by Marilyn Hirsh. Crown, 1971. Subj: Babies. Food. Foreign lands – India.

One little goat: a Passover song ill. by author. Holiday, 1979. Subj: Folk and fairy tales. Jewish culture. Holidays – Passover. Songs.

The pink suit ill. by author. Crown, 1970. Subj: Activities – trading. Emotions – embarrassment. Family life. Jewish culture.

Potato pancakes all around: a Hanukkah tale ill. by author. Bonim Books, 1978. ISBN 0-88482-762-3 Subj: Food. Holidays – Hanukkah. Jewish culture. Religion.

The Rabbi and the twenty-nine witches ill. by author. Holiday, 1976. Subj: Character traits – cleverness. Jewish culture. Witches.

Where is Yonkela? ill. by author. Crown, 1969. Subj: Babies. Behavior – lost. Jewish culture.

Hiser, Berniece T. *The adventure of Charlie and his wheat-straw hat* ill. by Mary Szilagyi. Dodd, 1986. ISBN 0-396-08772-8 Subj: Character traits – bravery. Clothing. Family life – grandmothers. U.S. history.

Hissey, Jane. *Old Bear* ill. by author. Philomel, 1986. ISBN 0-399-21401-1 Subj: Friendship. Toys. Toys – teddy bears.

Old Bear tales ill. by author. Philomel, 1988. ISBN 0-399-21642-1 Subj: Toys – teddy bears.

Hitte, Kathryn. *Mexicallie soup* by Kathryn Hitte and William D. Hayes; ill. by Anne F. Rockwell. Parents, 1970. Subj: Activities – cooking. Ethnic groups in the U.S. – Mexican-Americans. Family life. Food. Foreign lands – Mexico.

Hoban, Brom. *Skunk Lane* ill. by author. Harper, 1983. Subj: Animals – skunks. Behavior – growing up. Songs.

Hoban, Julia. *Amy loves the sun* ill. by Lillian Hoban. Harper, 1988. ISBN 0-06-022397-9 Subj: Family life. Flowers.

Amy loves the wind ill. by Lillian Hoban. Harper, 1988. ISBN 0-06-022403-7 Subj: Seasons – fall. Weather – wind.

Hoban, Lillian. *Arthur's Christmas cookies* ill. by author. Harper, 1972. Subj: Activities – cooking. Animals – monkeys. Holidays – Christmas.

Arthur's funny money ill. by author. Harper, 1981. Subj: Animals – monkeys. Money. Problem solving.

Arthur's great big Valentine ill. by author. Harper, 1989. ISBN 0-06-022407-X Subj: Emotions – anger. Friendship. Holidays – Valentine's Day.

Arthur's honey bear ill. by author. Harper, 1973. Subj: Animals – monkeys. Toys – teddy bears.

Arthur's pen pal ill. by author. Harper, 1976. Subj: Activities – writing. Animals – monkeys. Sibling rivalry.

Arthur's prize reader ill. by author. Harper, 1978. Subj: Activities – reading. Animals – monkeys. Family life.

The case of the two masked robbers ill. by author. Harper, 1986. ISBN 0-06-022299-9 Subj: Animals. Animals – raccoons. Eggs. Problem solving.

Harry's song ill. by author. Greenwillow, 1980. Subj: Animals – rabbits. Songs.

Here come raccoons ill. by author. Holt, 1977. Subj: Animals – raccoons. Twins.

It's really Christmas ill. by author. Greenwillow, 1982. Subj: Animals – mice. Behavior – wishing. Holidays – Christmas.

The laziest robot in zone one by Lillian and Phoebe Hoban; ill. by Lillian Hoban. Harper, 1983. Subj: Animals – dogs. Behavior – lost. Robots.

Mr. Pig and family ill. by author. Harper, 1980. Subj: Animals – pigs. Family life.

Mr. Pig and Sonny too ill. by author. Harper, 1977. Subj: Animals – pigs. Sports – ice skating. Weddings.

Silly Tilly and the Easter bunny ill. by author. Harper, 1987. ISBN 0-06-022693-6 Subj: Animals – moles. Holidays – Easter. Humor.

Stick-in-the-mud turtle ill. by author. Greenwillow, 1977. Subj: Behavior – dissatisfaction. Poverty. Reptiles – turtles, tortoises.

The sugar snow spring ill. by author. Harper, 1973. Subj: Animals – mice. Seasons – spring. Weather – cold. Weather – snow.

Turtle spring ill. by author. Greenwillow, 1978. Subj: Reptiles – turtles, tortoises. Seasons – spring.

Hoban, Phoebe. *The laziest robot in zone one* (Hoban, Lillian)

Hoban, Russell. *Ace Dragon Ltd.* ill. by Quentin Blake. Merrimack, 1981. Subj: Activities – flying. Dragons.

Arthur's new power ill. by Byron Barton. Crowell, 1978. Subj: Progress. Reptiles – alligators, crocodiles.

A baby sister for Frances ill. by Lillian Hoban. Harper, 1964. Subj: Animals – badgers. Behavior – running away. Emotions – envy, jealousy. Family life. Sibling rivalry.

A bargain for Frances ill. by Lillian Hoban. Harper, 1970. Subj: Animals – badgers. Friendship.

The battle of Zormla ill. by Colin McNaughton. Putnam's, 1982. Subj: Sibling rivalry.

Bedtime for Frances ill. by Garth Williams. Harper, 1960. Subj: Animals – badgers. Bedtime.

Best friends for Frances ill. by Lillian Hoban. Harper, 1969. Subj: Animals – badgers. Friendship.

Big John Turkle ill. by Martin Baynton. Holt, 1984. Subj: Character traits – meanness.

A birthday for Frances ill. by Lillian Hoban. Harper, 1968. Subj: Animals – badgers. Birthdays. Emotions – envy, jealousy.

Bread and jam for Frances ill. by Lillian Hoban. Harper, 1964. Subj: Animals – badgers. Food. School.

Charlie Meadows ill. by Martin Baynton. Holt, 1984. ISBN 0-03-069502-3 Subj: Activities – dancing. Animals – mice. Birds – owls.

Charlie the tramp ill. by Lillian Hoban. Four Winds Pr., 1967. Subj: Activities – working. Animals – beavers.

La corona and the tin frog ill. by Nicola Bayley. Merrimack, 1981. Subj: Emotions. Toys.

The dancing tigers ill. by David Gentleman. Merrimack, 1981. Subj: Activities – dancing. Animals – tigers. Sports – hunting.

Dinner at Alberta's ill. by James Marshall. Crowell, 1975. Subj: Behavior. Etiquette. Food. Reptiles – alligators, crocodiles.

Emmet Otter's jug-band Christmas ill. by Lillian Hoban. Parents, 1971. Subj: Animals – otters. Character traits – generosity. Holidays – Christmas. Music.

Flat cat ill. by Clive Scruton. Putnam's, 1980. Subj: Animals – cats. Animals – mice. Animals – rats.

The flight of Bembel Rudzuk ill. by Colin McNaughton. Putnam's, 1982. Subj: Imagination.

Goodnight ill. by Lillian Hoban. Norton, 1966. Subj: Bedtime. Emotions – fear. Imagination. Poetry, rhyme.

The great gum drop robbery ill. by Colin McNaughton. Putnam's, 1982. Subj: Imagination. Sibling rivalry.

Harvey's hideout ill. by Lillian Hoban. Parents, 1969. Subj: Animals – muskrats. Behavior – fighting, arguing. Family life.

How Tom beat Captain Najork and his hired sportsmen ill. by Quentin Blake. Atheneum, 1974. Subj: Behavior – misbehavior. Games.

Jim Frog ill. by Martin Baynton. Holt, 1984. Subj: Frogs and toads. Insects – beetles.

Lavina bat ill. by Martin Baynton. Holt, 1984. Subj: Animals – bats.

The little Brute family ill. by Lillian Hoban. Macmillan, 1966. Subj: Character traits – meanness. Etiquette.

The mole family's Christmas ill. by Lillian Hoban. Parents, 1969. Subj: Animals – moles. Character traits – generosity. Holidays – Christmas.

A near thing for Captain Najork ill. by Quentin Blake. Atheneum, 1976. Subj: Humor.

Nothing to do ill. by Lillian Hoban. Harper, 1964. Subj: Animals – possums. Behavior – boredom.

The rain door ill. by Quentin Blake. Crowell, 1987. ISBN 0-690-04577-8 Subj: Animals – horses. Animals – lions. Imagination. Weather – rain.

Some snow said hello ill. by Lillian Hoban. Harper, 1963. Subj: Seasons – winter. Sibling rivalry. Weather – snow.

The sorely trying day ill. by Lillian Hoban. Harper, 1964. Subj: Behavior – bad day. Behavior – fighting, arguing.

The stone doll of Sister Brute ill. by Lillian Hoban. Macmillan, 1968. Subj: Animals – dogs. Emotions. Toys – dolls.

Ten what? a mystery counting book by Russell Hoban and Sylvie Selig; ill. by authors. Scribner's, 1974. Subj: Counting.

They came from Aargh! ill. by Colin McNaughton. Putnam's, 1981. Subj: Family life. Sibling rivalry.

Tom and the two handles ill. by Lillian Hoban. Harper, 1965. Subj: Behavior – fighting, arguing.

Hoban, Tana. *A B See!* photos. by author. Greenwillow, 1982. Subj: ABC books.

Big ones, little ones ill. by author. Greenwillow, 1976. Subj: Animals. Concepts – size. Wordless.

A children's zoo photos. by author. Greenwillow, 1985. ISBN 0-688-05204-5 Subj: Animals. Birds. Zoos.

Circles, triangles, and squares ill. by author. Macmillan, 1974. Subj: Concepts – shape. Wordless.

Count and see ill. by author. Macmillan, 1972. Subj: Counting.

Dig, drill, dump, fill ill. by author. Greenwillow, 1975. Subj: Machines. Wordless.

Dots, spots, speckles, and stripes photos. by author. Greenwillow, 1987. ISBN 0-688-06863-4 Subj: Concepts. Concepts – color. Concepts – shape.

I read signs photos. by author. Greenwillow, 1983. Subj: Activities – reading. Communication.

I read symbols photos. by author. Greenwillow, 1983. Subj: Activities – reading. Communication.

I walk and read photos. by author. Greenwillow, 1984. Subj: Activities – reading. Activities – walking.

Is it larger? Is it smaller? photos. by author. Greenwillow, 1985. ISBN 0-688-04028-4 Subj: Concepts – size. Wordless.

Is it red? Is it yellow? Is it blue? photos. by author. Greenwillow, 1978. Subj: City. Concepts – color. Concepts – shape. Concepts – size. Wordless.

Is it rough? Is it smooth? Is it shiny? photos. by author. Greenwillow, 1984. Subj: Concepts. Wordless.

Look again ill. by author. Macmillan, 1971. Subj: Participation. Senses – seeing. Wordless.

Look! Look! Look! photos. by author. Greenwillow, 1988. ISBN 0-688-07240-2 Subj: Concepts. Format, unusual. Wordless.

More than one photos. by author. Greenwillow, 1981. Subj: Language.

One little kitten photos. by author. Greenwillow, 1979. Subj: Animals – cats. Poetry, rhyme.

1, 2, 3 photos. by author. Greenwillow, 1985. Subj: Counting. Format, unusual – board books. Wordless.

Panda, panda ill. by author. Greenwillow, 1986. ISBN 0-688-06564-3 Subj: Animals – pandas. Format, unusual – board books.

Push-pull, empty-full ill. by author. Macmillan, 1972. Subj: Concepts – opposites.

Red, blue, yellow shoe photos. by author. Greenwillow, 1986. ISBN 0-688-06563-5 Subj: Concepts – color. Format, unusual – board books.

Round and round and round photos. by author. Greenwillow, 1983. Subj: Concepts – shape.

Shapes and things ill. by author. Macmillan, 1970. Subj: Concepts – shape. Wordless.

Shapes, shapes, shapes photos. by author. Greenwillow, 1985. ISBN 0-688-05833-7 Subj: Concepts – shape. Wordless.

Take another look photos. by author. Greenwillow, 1981. Subj: Concepts. Wordless.

26 letters and 99 cents photos. by author. Greenwillow, 1987. ISBN 0-688-06362-4 Subj: ABC books. Counting. Format, unusual.

What is it? photos. by author. Greenwillow, 1985. Subj: Format, unusual – board books. Wordless.

Where is it? ill. by author. Macmillan, 1974. Subj: Animals – rabbits. Participation. Poetry, rhyme.

Hoberman, Mary Ann. *The cozy book* ill. by Tony Chen. Viking, 1982. Subj: Poetry, rhyme.

A house is a house for me ill. by Betty Fraser. Viking, 1978. Subj: Houses. Poetry, rhyme.

How do I go? by Mary Ann and Norman Hoberman; ill. by authors. Little, 1958. Subj: Transportation.

I like old clothes ill. by Jacqueline Chwast. Knopf, 1976. Subj: Clothing. Poetry, rhyme.

Mr. and Mrs. Muddle ill. by Catharine O'Neill. Little, 1988. ISBN 0-316-36735-4 Subj: Animals – horses. Sports.

Nuts to you and nuts to me: an alphabet of poems ill. by Ronni Solbert. Knopf, 1974. Subj: ABC books. Poetry, rhyme.

Hoberman, Norman. *How do I go?* (Hoberman, Mary Ann)

Hobson, Bruce *see* Hadithi, Mwenye

Hobson, Laura Z. *"I'm going to have a baby!"* ill. by May Kirkham. John Day, 1967. Subj: Babies. Family life.

Hobzek, Mildred. *We came a-marching...1, 2, 3* ill. by William Pène Du Bois. Parents, 1978. Subj: Folk and fairy tales. Songs.

Hochman, Sandra. *The magic convention* ill. by Ben Shecter. Doubleday, 1971. Subj: Character traits – ambition. Magic.

Hodeir, André. *Warwick's three bottles* by André Hodeir and Tomi Ungerer; ill. by Tomi Ungerer. Grove Pr., 1966. Subj: Behavior – misbehavior. Country. Reptiles – alligators, crocodiles.

Hodges, Margaret. *The fire bringer: a Paiute Indian legend* ill. by Peter Parnall. Little, 1972. ISBN 0-316-36783-4 Subj: Folk and fairy tales. Indians of North America.

Saint George and the dragon ill. by Trina Schart Hyman. Little, 1984. Subj: Caldecott award book. Folk and fairy tales.

The wave ill. by Blair Lent. Houghton, 1964. Subj: Caldecott award honor book.

Hodgetts, Blake Christopher. *Dream of the dinosaurs* ill. by Victoria Hodgetts. Doubleday, 1978. Subj: Dinosaurs. Dreams.

Hofer, Angelika. *The lion family book* tr. by Patricia Crampton; photos. by Gunter Ziesler. Picture Book Studio, 1988. ISBN 0-88708-070-7 Subj: Animals – lions. Foreign lands – Africa. Nature.

Hoff, Carol. *The four friends* ill. by Jim Ponter. Follett, 1958. Subj: Animals. Animals – mice.

Hoff, Syd. *Albert the albatross* ill. by author. Harper, 1961. Subj: Birds – albatrosses. Sea and seashore.

Barkley ill. by author. Harper, 1975. Subj: Animals – dogs. Circus. Old age.

Chester ill. by author. Harper, 1961. Subj: Animals – horses.

Danny and the dinosaur ill. by author. Harper, 1958. Subj: Dinosaurs. Museums.

Grizzwold ill. by author. Harper, 1963. Subj: Animals – bears. Ecology.

Happy birthday, Henrietta! ill. by author. Garrard, 1983. Subj: Animals – pigs. Animals – goats. Birds – chickens. Birthdays.

Henrietta, circus star ill. by author. Garrard, 1978. Subj: Birds – chickens. Circus.

Henrietta goes to the fair ill. by author. Garrard, 1979. Subj: Birds – chickens. Fairs.

Henrietta, the early bird ill. by author. Garrard, 1978. Subj: Behavior – mistakes. Birds – chickens. Time.

Henrietta's Halloween ill. by author. Garrard, 1980. Subj: Birds – chickens. Holidays – Halloween. Parties.

The horse in Harry's room ill. by author. Harper, 1970. Subj: Animals – horses. Imagination – imaginary friends.

Julius ill. by author. Harper, 1959. Subj: Animals – gorillas.

Lengthy ill. by author. Putnam's, 1964. Subj: Animals – dogs.

The littlest leaguer ill. by author. Dutton, 1976. Subj: Character traits – smallness. Games. Sports – baseball.

Merry Christmas, Henrietta! ill. by author. Garrard, 1980. Subj: Birds – chickens. Holidays – Christmas. Stores.

Mrs. Brice's mice ill. by author. Harper, 1988. ISBN 0-06-022452-5 Subj: Animals – mice. Character traits – being different. Pets.

My Aunt Rosie ill. by author. Harper, 1972. Subj: Family life.

Oliver ill. by author. Harper, 1960. Subj: Animals – elephants. Character traits – optimism. Circus.

Sammy the seal ill. by author. Harper, 1959. Subj: Animals – seals. Zoos.

Santa's moose ill. by author. Harper, 1988, 1979. ISBN 0-06-022506-8 Subj: Animals – moose. Holidays – Christmas.

Slithers ill. by author. Putnam's, 1968. Subj: Reptiles – snakes.

Slugger Sal's slump ill. by author. Dutton, 1979. Subj: Character traits – perseverance. Sports – baseball.

Stanley ill. by author. Harper, 1962. Subj: Cavemen. Houses.

Syd Hoff's best jokes ever ill. by author. Putnam's, 1978. Subj: Humor. Riddles.

A walk past Ellen's house ill. by author. McGraw-Hill, 1973. ISBN 0-07-029176-4 Subj: Emotions – embarrassment.

Walpole ill. by author. Harper, 1977. Subj: Animals – walruses.

When will it snow? ill. by Mary Chalmers. Harper, 1971. Subj: Seasons – winter. Weather – snow.

Where's Prancer? ill. by author. Harper, 1960. Subj: Animals – reindeer. Holidays – Christmas.

Who will be my friends? ill. by author. Harper, 1960. Subj: Friendship. Moving.

Hoffman, Joan. *My friend goes left* (Gregorich, Barbara)

Hoffman, Mary. *Animals in the wild: elephant* ill. by author. Random House, 1984. Subj: Animals – elephants. Science.

Animals in the wild: monkey ill. by author. Random House, 1984. Subj: Animals – monkeys. Science.

Animals in the wild: panda ill. by author. Random House, 1984. Subj: Animals – pandas. Science.

Animals in the wild: tiger ill. by author. Random House, 1984. Subj: Animals – tigers. Science.

Hoffman, Phyllis. *Baby's first year* ill. by Sarah Wilson. Harper, 1988. ISBN 0-06-022552-1 Subj: Babies. Behavior – growing up.

Steffie and me ill. by Emily Arnold McCully. Harper, 1970. Subj: Ethnic groups in the U.S. – Afro-Americans. Family life. Friendship. School.

The ugly duckling (Andersen, H. C. (Hans Christian))

Hoffman, Rosekrans. *Sister Sweet Ella* ill. by author. Morrow, 1981. Subj: Babies. Family life. Magic.

Hoffmann, E. T. A. *The nutcracker* retold and ill. by Rachel Isadora. Macmillan, 1981. Adapt. of Nussknacker und Mausekönig. ISBN 0-02-747470-4 Subj: Activities – dancing. Animals – mice. Fairies. Folk and fairy tales. Holidays – Christmas. Imagination.

The nutcracker tr. by Ralph Manheim; ill. by Maurice Sendak. Crown, 1984. Subj: Activities – dancing. Animals – mice. Fairies. Folk and fairy tales. Holidays – Christmas. Imagination. Theater.

The nutcracker retold by Anthea Bell; ill. by Lisbeth Zwerger. Picture Book Studio, 1987. ISBN 0-88708-051-0 Subj: Animals – mice. Folk and fairy tales. Holidays – Christmas. Imagination. Royalty.

The strange child tr. and adapt. by Anthea Bell; ill. by Lisbeth Zwerger. Picture Book Studio, 1984. Adapt. of Das fremde Kind. ISBN 0-907234-60-7 Subj: Death. Family life. Folk and fairy tales. Magic.

Hoffmann, Felix. *Hans in luck* (Grimm, Jacob)

The story of Christmas ill. by author. Atheneum, 1975. Subj: Holidays – Christmas. Religion.

Hofstrand, Mary. *Albion pig* ill. by author. Knopf, 1984. Subj: Animals – pigs. Poetry, rhyme.

Hogan, Bernice. *My grandmother died but I won't forget her* ill. by Nancy Munger. Abingdon, 1983. Subj: Death. Family life – grandmothers.

Hogan, Inez. *About Nono, the baby elephant* ill. by author. Dutton, 1947. Subj: Animals – elephants. Behavior – misbehavior. Names.

Hogan, Kirk. *The hospital scares me* (Hogan, Paula Z.)

Hogan, Paula Z. *The black swan* ill. by Kinuko Craft. Raintree, 1979. Subj: Birds – swans. Science.

The butterfly ill. by Geri K. Strigenz. Raintree, 1979. Subj: Insects – butterflies, caterpillars. Science.

The dandelion ill. by Yoshi Miyake. Raintree, 1979. Subj: Plants. Science.

The frog ill. by Geri K. Strigenz. Raintree, 1979. Subj: Frogs and toads. Science.

The honeybee ill. by Geri K. Strigenz. Raintree, 1979. Subj: Insects – bees. Science.

The hospital scares me by Paula Z. Hogan and Kirk Hogan; ill. by Mary Thelen. Raintree, 1980. ISBN 0-8172-1351-1 Subj: Ethnic groups in the U.S. Ethnic groups in the U.S. – Afro-Americans. Hospitals. Illness.

The oak tree ill. by Kinuko Craft. Raintree, 1979. Subj: Science. Trees.

The penguin ill. by Geri K. Strigenz. Raintree, 1979. Subj: Birds – penguins. Science.

The salmon ill. by Yoshi Miyake. Raintree, 1979. Subj: Fish. Science.

Högner, Franz. *From blueprint to house* ill. by author. Carolrhoda Books, 1986. ISBN 0-87614-295-1 Subj: Houses.

Hogrogian, Nonny. *Billy Goat and his well-fed friends* ill. by author. Harper, 1972. Subj: Animals. Animals – goats. Behavior – running away.

Carrot cake ill. by author. Greenwillow, 1977. Subj: Animals – rabbits. Behavior. Character traits – compromising. Character traits – shyness. Weddings.

The cat who loved to sing ill. by author. Knopf, 1988. ISBN 0-394-99004-8 Subj: Animals – cats. Cumulative tales. Folk and fairy tales. Songs.

Cinderella (Grimm, Jacob)

The contest ill. by author. Greenwillow, 1976. Subj: Caldecott award honor book. Crime. Folk and fairy tales. Foreign lands – Armenia.

The devil with the green hairs (Grimm, Jacob)

The hermit and Harry and me ill. by author. Subj: Behavior – indifference. Friendship.

Noah's ark ill. by author. Knopf, 1986. ISBN 0-394-98191-X Subj: Religion – Noah.

One fine day ill. by author. Macmillan, 1971. Subj: Animals – foxes. Caldecott award book. Cumulative tales.

Rooster brother ill. by author. Macmillan, 1974. ISBN 0-02-743990-9 Subj: Behavior – stealing. Character traits – cleverness. Crime. Folk and fairy tales.

Hoguet, Susan Ramsay. *I unpacked my grand-mother's trunk: a picture book game* ill. by author. Dutton, 1983. Subj: ABC books. Cumulative tales. Games.

Hoke, Helen L. *The biggest family in the town* ill. by Vance Locke. McKay, 1947. Subj: Family life.

Holabird, Katharine. *Alexander and the dragon* ill. by Helen Craig. Potter, 1988. ISBN 0-517-56996-5 Subj: Bedtime. Behavior – fighting, arguing. Dragons. Friendship.

Angelina and Alice ill. by Helen Craig. Potter, 1987. ISBN 0-517-56074-7 Subj: Animals – mice. Friendship. School.

Angelina and the princess ill. by Helen Craig. Crown, 1984. Subj: Activities – dancing. Animals – mice.

Angelina at the fair ill. by Helen Craig. Crown, 1985. ISBN 0-517-55744-4 Subj: Animals – mice. Fairs.

Angelina ballerina ill. by Helen Craig. Crown, 1983. Subj: Activities – dancing. Animals – mice.

Angelina on stage ill. by Helen Craig. Crown, 1986. ISBN 0-517-56073-9 Subj: Activities – dancing. Animals – mice. Theater.

The little mouse ABC ill. by Helen Craig. Simon and Schuster, 1983. Subj: ABC books. Animals – mice.

Holbrook, Stewart. *America's Ethan Allen* ill. by Lynd Ward. Houghton, 1949. Subj: Caldecott award honor book. U.S. history. War.

Holden, Edith. *The hedgehog feast* ill. by Edith Holden; words by Rowena Stott. Dutton, 1978. Subj: Animals – hedgehogs. Food.

Holder, Heidi. *Crows: an old rhyme* ill. by author. Farrar, 1987. ISBN 0-374-31660-0 Subj: Animals – minks. Animals – weasels. Birds – crows. Counting. Poetry, rhyme.

Holding, James. *The lazy little Zulu* ill. by Aliki. Morrow, 1962. Subj: Character traits – laziness. Foreign lands – Africa.

Holding, James Clark Carlisle, Jr. *see* Holding, James

Holl, Adelaide. *The ABC of cars, trucks and machines* ill. by William Dugan. American Heritage, 1970. Subj: ABC books. Automobiles. Machines. Trucks.

Most-of-the-time Maxie ill. by Hilary Knight. Xerox Family Education Services, 1974. ISBN 0-88375-202-6 Subj: Activities – reading. Imagination.

A mouse story: Minnikin, Midgie and Moppet ill. by Priscilla Hillman. Golden Pr., 1977. Subj: Animals – mice. City. Country.

Mrs. McGarrity's peppermint sweater ill. by Abner Graboff. Lothrop, 1966. Subj: Activities – knitting. Circus. Poetry, rhyme.

My father and I (Ringi, Kjell)

The rain puddle ill. by Roger Antoine Duvoisin. Lothrop, 1965. Subj: Animals. Weather – rain.

The remarkable egg ill. by Roger Antoine Duvoisin. Lothrop, 1968. Subj: Toys – balls.

The runaway giant ill. by Mamoru Funai. Lothrop, 1967. Subj: Behavior – gossip. Snowmen.

Sir Kevin of Devon ill. by Leonard Weisgard. Lothrop, 1963. Subj: Character traits – bravery. Knights. Poetry, rhyme.

Small Bear builds a playhouse ill. by Cyndy Szekeres. Garrard, 1978. Subj: Animals. Animals – bears. Houses.

Small Bear solves a mystery ill. by Lorinda Bryan Cauley. Garrard, 1979. Subj: Animals – bears. Food. Illness.

Holland, Isabelle. *Kevin's hat* ill. by Leonard Lubin. Lothrop, 1984. Subj: Clothing. Reptiles – alligators, crocodiles.

Holland, Janice. *You never can tell* ill. by adapt. Scribner's, 1963. Adapted from the tr. by Arthur W. Hummel from the book of Hual nan tzu, written before 122 B.C. Subj: Character traits – luck. Folk and fairy tales. Foreign lands – China.

Holland, Kevin Crossley see Crossley-Holland, Kevin

Holland, Marion. *A big ball of string* ill. by author. Random House, 1958. Subj: Poetry, rhyme. String.

Holland, Viki. *We are having a baby* ill. by author. Scribner's, 1972. Subj: Babies. Family life.

Hollander, John. *A book of various owls* ill. by Tomi Ungerer. Norton, 1963. Subj: Birds – owls. Poetry, rhyme.

Holling, Holling C. (Holling Clancy). *Paddle-to-the-sea* ill. by author. Houghton, 1941. Subj: Caldecott award honor book. Foreign lands – Canada. Rivers.

Hollinshed, Judith see Hawthorne, Julian

Hollyer, Belinda. *Daniel in the lions' den* (Bible. Old Testament. Daniel)

David and Goliath (Bible. Old Testament. David)

Jonah and the great fish (Bible. Old Testament. Jonah)

Hollyn, Lynn. *Lynn Hollyn's Christmas toyland* ill. by Lori Anzalone. Knopf, 1985. ISBN 0-394-97631-2 Subj: Fairies. Holidays – Christmas. Toys.

Holm, Mayling Mack. *A forest Christmas* ill. by author. Harper, 1977. Subj: Animals. Holidays – Christmas.

Holman, Felice. *Elisabeth, the treasure hunter* ill. by Erik Blegvad. Macmillan, 1964. Subj: Problem solving. Riddles.

Victoria's castle ill. by Lillian Hoban. Norton, 1966. Subj: Birds – parakeets, parrots. Humor. Imagination.

Holmes, Anita. *The 100-year-old cactus* ill. by Carol Lerner. Four Winds Pr., 1983. Subj: Desert. Plants. Science.

Holmes, Efner Tudor. *Amy's goose* ill. by Tasha Tudor. Crowell, 1977. Subj: Birds – geese. Character traits – helpfulness. Character traits – kindness to animals.

Carrie's gift ill. by Tasha Tudor. Collins-World, 1978. Subj: Animals – dogs. Character traits – kindness to animals.

The Christmas cat ill. by Tasha Tudor. Crowell, 1976. Subj: Animals – cats. Holidays – Christmas.

Holt, Margaret. *David McCheever's twenty-nine dogs* ill. by Walter Lorraine. Houghton, 1963. Subj: Animals – dogs. Counting. Parades. Shopping.

Holzenthaler, Jean. *My feet do* ill. by George Ancona. Dutton, 1979. Subj: Activities. Anatomy.

My hands can ill. by Nancy Tafuri. Dutton, 1978. Subj: Activities. Anatomy.

Home before midnight: *a traditional verse* ill. by Bobby Lewis. Lothrop, 1984. Subj: Animals – pigs. Cumulative tales.

Homme, Bob. *The friendly giant's birthday* ill. by Kim La Fave and Carol Snelling. CBC Merchandising, 1982. Subj: Birthdays. Giants. Songs.

The friendly giant's book of fire engines ill. by Kim La Fave and Carol Snelling. CBC Merchandising, 1981. Subj: Careers – firefighters. Giants. Trucks.

Hood, Flora Mae. *Living in Navajoland* ill. by Mamoru Funai. Putnam's, 1970. Subj: Indians of North America.

Hooker, Ruth. *At Grandma and Grandpa's house* ill. by Ruth Rosner. Albert Whitman, 1986. ISBN 0-8075-0477-7 Subj: Family life. Family life – grandparents.

Sara loves her big brother ill. by Margot Apple. Albert Whitman, 1987. ISBN 0-8075-7244-6 Subj: Behavior – sharing. Family life. Sibling rivalry.

Hooks, William H. *Moss gown* ill. by Donald Carrick. Clarion, 1987. ISBN 0-89919-460-5 Subj: Family life – fathers. Folk and fairy tales. Magic.

Three rounds with rabbit ill. by Lissa McLaughlin. Lothrop, 1984. Subj: Animals – rabbits. Character traits – cleverness.

Hooper, Meredith. *Seven eggs* ill. by Terry McKenna. Harper, 1985. ISBN 0-06-022586-6 Subj: Counting. Cumulative tales. Days of the week, months of the year. Eggs. Format, unusual.

Hooper, Patricia. *A bundle of beasts* ill. by Mark Steele. Houghton, 1987. ISBN 0-395-44259-1 Subj: ABC books. Animals. Poetry, rhyme.

Hoopes, Lyn Littlefield. *Daddy's coming home* ill. by Bruce Degen. Harper, 1984. ISBN 0-06-022569-6 Subj: Family life.

Mommy, daddy, me ill. by Ruth Lercher Bornstein. Harper, 1988. ISBN 0-06-022550-5 Subj: Family life. Islands. Nature. Poetry, rhyme.

Nana ill. by Arieh Zeldich. Harper, 1981. ISBN 0-06-022575-0 Subj: Death. Family life – grandmothers.

When I was little ill. by Marcia Sewall. Dutton, 1983. Subj: Emotions – love. Seasons – winter. Sibling rivalry.

Hoover, Roseanna. *The golden apple* (Bolliger, Max)

Hopkins, Lee Bennett. *And God bless me: prayers, lullabies and dream-poems* ill. by Patricia Henderson Lincoln. Knopf, 1982. Subj: Poetry, rhyme. Religion. Songs.

Best friends ill. by James Watts. Harper, 1986. ISBN 0-06-022562-9 Subj: Friendship. Poetry, rhyme.

Circus! Circus! ill. by John O'Brien. Knopf, 1982. Subj: Circus. Poetry, rhyme.

Crickets and bullfrogs and whispers of thunder (Behn, Harry)

A dog's life ill. by Linda Rochester Richards. Harcourt, 1983. Subj: Animals – dogs. Poetry, rhyme.

Easter buds are springing ill. by Tomie de Paola. Harcourt, 1979. Subj: Holidays – Easter. Poetry, rhyme.

Elves, fairies and gnomes

Go to bed! a book of bedtime poems ill. by Rosekrans Hoffman. Knopf, 1979. Subj: Bedtime. Poetry, rhyme.

I loved Rose Ann ill. by Ingrid Fetz. Knopf, 1976. Subj: Behavior – misunderstanding. Emotions.

I think I saw a snail: young poems for city seasons ill. by Harold James. Crown, 1969. Subj: City. Ethnic groups in the U.S. – Afro-Americans. Poetry, rhyme.

Merrily comes our harvest in: poems for Thanksgiving ill. by Ben Shecter. Harcourt, 1978. Subj: Holidays – Thanksgiving. Poetry, rhyme. Seasons – fall.

More surprises ill. by Megan Lloyd. Harper, 1987. ISBN 0-06-022605-6 Subj: Poetry, rhyme.

Morning, noon and nighttime, too ill. by Nancy Hannans. Harper, 1980. Subj: Poetry, rhyme.

The sea is calling me ill. by Walter Gaffney-Kessell. Harcourt, 1986. ISBN 0-15-271155-4 Subj: Poetry, rhyme. Sea and seashore.

The sky is full of song ill. by Dirk Zimmer. Harper, 1983. Subj: Poetry, rhyme.

Hopkins, Margaret. *Sleepytime for baby mouse* ill. by Karen Lee Schmidt. Platt, 1985. ISBN 0-448-49875-9 Subj: Animals – mice. Bedtime. Family life. Format, unusual – board books.

Hopkins, Marjorie. *Three visitors* ill. by Anne F. Rockwell. Parents, 1967. Subj: Eskimos.

Horio, Seishi. *The monkey and the crab* by Saru Kani; retold by Seishi Horio; tr. by D. T. Ooka; ill. by Tsutomu Murakami. Heian Int., 1985. ISBN 0-89346-246-2 Subj: Animals – monkeys. Crustacea. Death.

Horner, Althea J. *Little big girl* ill. by Patricia Rosamilia. Human Sciences Pr., 1983. Subj: Behavior – growing up.

Hort, Lenny. *The boy who held back the sea* ill. by Thomas Locker. Dial Pr., 1987. Adapt. of Hans Brinker, or The Silver Skates by Mary Mapes Dodge. ISBN 0-8037-0407-0 Subj: Behavior – misbehavior. Character traits – bravery. Folk and fairy tales.

Horvath, Betty F. *Be nice to Josephine* ill. by Pat Grant Porter. Watts, 1970. Subj: Behavior. Family life.

The cheerful quiet ill. by Jo Ann Stover. Watts, 1969. Subj: Noise, sounds. Problem solving.

Hooray for Jasper ill. by Fermin Rocker. Watts, 1966. Subj: Character traits – smallness. Ethnic groups in the U.S. – Afro-Americans.

Jasper and the hero business ill. by Don Bolognese. Watts, 1977. Subj: Character traits – bravery. Ethnic groups in the U.S. – Afro-Americans.

Jasper makes music ill. by Fermin Rocker. Watts, 1967. Subj: Activities – working. Ethnic groups in the U.S. – Afro-Americans. Music.

Will the real Tommy Wilson please stand up? ill. by Charles Robinson. Watts, 1969. Subj: Character traits – individuality. Emotions. Friendship.

Horwitz, Elinor Lander. *Sometimes it happens* ill. by Susan Jeschke. Harper, 1981. Subj: Character traits – ambition. Imagination.

When the sky is like lace ill. by Barbara Cooney. Lippincott, 1975. Subj: Night.

Hot cross buns, and other old street cries sel. by John M. Langstaff; ill. by Nancy Winslow Parker. Atheneum, 1978. Subj: Music. Poetry, rhyme. Songs.

Houghton, Eric. *The mouse and the magician* ill. by Faith Jaques. Elsevier-Dutton, 1979. Subj: Animals – mice. Magic. Wizards.

House mouse photos. by David Thompson. Putnam's, 1978. Subj: Animals – mice. Science.

The house that Jack built. *The house that Jack built* ill. by Randolph Caldecott. Avenel Books, n.d. Subj: Cumulative tales. Nursery rhymes.

The house that Jack built ill. by Seymour Chwast. Random House, 1973. Subj: Cumulative tales. Format, unusual – toy and movable books. Nursery rhymes. Participation.

The house that Jack built ill. by Rodney Peppé. Delacorte Pr., 1970. Subj: Cumulative tales. Nursery rhymes.

The house that Jack built: a Mother Goose nursery rhyme ill. by Janet Stevens. Holiday, 1985. ISBN 0-8234-0548-6 Subj: Circus. Cumulative tales. Nursery rhymes.

The house that Jack built: la maison que Jacques a batie ill. by Antonio Frasconi. Harcourt, 1958. Subj: Caldecott award honor book. Cumulative tales. Foreign languages. Nursery rhymes.

This is the house that Jack built ill. by Liz Underhill. Holt, 1987. ISBN 0-8050-0339-8 Subj: Cumulative tales. Nursery rhymes.

Houselander, Caryll. *Petook: an Easter story* ill. by Tomie de Paola. Holiday, 1988. ISBN 0-8234-0681-4 Subj: Birds – chickens. Holidays – Easter. Religion.

Houston, Gloria. *The year of the perfect Christmas tree: an Appalachian story* ill. by Barbara Cooney. Dial Pr., 1988. ISBN 0-8037-0300-7 Subj: Family life. Holidays – Christmas. Trees.

Houston, James. *Kiviok's magic journey: an Eskimo legend* ill. by author. Atheneum, 1973. Subj: Birds – geese. Eskimos. Folk and fairy tales.

Houston, John A. *The bright yellow rope* ill. by Winnie Fitch. Addison-Wesley, 1973. Subj: Behavior – sharing. Character traits – generosity. Character traits – helpfulness. Poetry, rhyme. Problem solving. Songs.

A mouse in my house ill. by Winnie Fitch. Addison-Wesley, 1973. Subj: Animals – mice. Cumulative tales. Problem solving. Songs.

A room full of animals ill. by Winnie Fitch. Addison-Wesley, 1973. Subj: Animals. Songs.

Howard, Elizabeth Fitzgerald. *The train to Lulu's* ill. by Robert Casilla. Bradbury Pr., 1988. ISBN 0-02-744620-4 Subj: Activities – traveling. Family life – sisters.

Howard, Jane R. *When I'm sleepy* ill. by Lynne Cherry. Dutton, 1985. ISBN 0-525-44204-9 Subj: Imagination. Sleep.

Howard, Jean G. *Of mice and mice* ill. by author. Tidal Pr., 1978. Subj: Animals – mice.

Howard, Katherine. *Do you know color?* (Miller, J. P. (John Parr))

I can count to 100... can you? ill. by Michael Smollin. Random House, 1979. ISBN 0-394-84090-9 Subj: Counting.

My first picture dictionary ill. by Huck Scarry. Random House, 1978. Subj: Dictionaries.

Howard, Richard. *Gregory and Lady Turtle in the valley of the music trees* (Brunhoff, Laurent de)

The one pig with horns (Brunhoff, Laurent de)

Howard-Gibbon, Amelia Frances. *An illustrated comic alphabet* ill. by author. Walck, 1967. Subj: ABC books.

Howe, Caroline Walton. *Counting penguins* ill. by author. Harper, 1983. Subj: Birds – penguins. Counting.

Teddy Bear's bird and beast band ill. by author. Windmill, 1980. Subj: Music. Toys – teddy bears.

Howe, Deborah. *Teddy Bear's scrapbook* by Deborah and James Howe; ill. by David S. Rose. Atheneum, 1980. Subj: Toys – teddy bears.

Howe, James. *The case of the missing mother* ill. by William Cleaver. Random House, 1983. Subj: Holidays – Mother's Day. Puppets.

The day the teacher went bananas ill. by Lillian Hoban. Dutton, 1984. Subj: Animals – gorillas. School. Zoos.

The fright before Christmas ill. by Leslie Morrill. Morrow, 1988. ISBN 0-688-07665-3 Subj: Animals – dogs. Holidays – Christmas.

How the Ewoks saved the trees: an old Ewok legend ill. by Walter Velez. Random House, 1984. Subj: Mythical creatures. Trees.

I wish I were a butterfly ill. by Ed Young. Harcourt, 1987. ISBN 0-15-200470-X Subj: Behavior – wishing. Emotions – envy, jealousy.

Teddy Bear's scrapbook (Howe, Deborah)

There's a monster under my bed ill. by David S. Rose. Atheneum, 1986. ISBN 0-689-31178-8 Subj: Emotions – fear. Monsters. Night.

When you go to kindergarten photos. by Betsy Imershein. Knopf, 1986. ISBN 0-394-87303-3 Subj: School.

Howe, John. *Rip Van Winkle* (Irving, Washington)

Howell, Lynn. *Winifred's new bed* by Lynn and Richard Howell; ill. by authors. Knopf, 1985. ISBN 0-394-87772-1 Subj: Animals – cats. Days of the week, months of the year. Format, unusual. Toys.

Howell, Richard. *Winifred's new bed* (Howell, Lynn)

Howell, Ruth. *Everything changes* photos. by Arline Strong. Atheneum, 1968. Subj: Seasons.

Splash and flow photos. by Arline Strong. Atheneum, 1973. Subj: Science.

Howells, Mildred. *The woman who lived in Holland* ill. by William Curtis Holdsworth. Farrar, 1973. Text originally published in 1898 in St. Nicholas magazine under title: Going too far. Subj: Character traits – cleanliness. Foreign lands – Holland. Poetry, rhyme.

Hudson, Eleanor. *A whale of a rescue* ill. by Pat Paris. Random House, 1983. Subj: Animals – whales.

Huff, Vivian. *Let's make paper dolls* photos. by author. Harper, 1978. Subj: Paper. Toys – dolls.

Hughes, Peter. *The emperor's oblong pancake* ill. by Gerald Rose. Abelard-Schuman, 1961. Subj: Concepts – shape. Food. Royalty.

The king who loved candy ill. by Gerald Rose. Abelard-Schuman, 1964. Subj: Food. Royalty. War.

Hughes, Richard. *Gertrude's child* ill. by Rick Schreiter. Crown, 1966. Subj: Behavior – needing someone. Behavior – running away. Toys.

Hughes, Shirley. *Alfie gets in first* ill. by author. Lothrop, 1982. Subj: Cumulative tales. Houses.

Alfie gives a hand ill. by author. Lothrop, 1984. Subj: Behavior – needing someone. Birthdays. Parties.

Alfie's feet ill. by author. Lothrop, 1983. Subj: Activities – playing.

All shapes and sizes ill. by author. Lothrop, 1986. ISBN 0-688-04205-8 Subj: Concepts – shape. Concepts – size. Poetry, rhyme.

Bathwater's hot ill. by author. Lothrop, 1985. ISBN 0-688-04202-3 Subj: Activities – bathing. Concepts – opposites. Family life. Foreign lands – England. Poetry, rhyme.

Colors ill. by author. Lothrop, 1986. ISBN 0-688-04206-6 Subj: Concepts – color. Poetry, rhyme.

David and dog ill. by author. Prentice-Hall, 1978. Edition of 1977 published under title: Dogger. Subj: Activities – trading. Family life. Toys.

Dogger ill. by author. Lothrop, 1988, 1977. 1978 Prentice-Hall edition published under title David and dog. ISBN 0-688-07981-4 Subj: Activities – trading. Family life. Toys.

An evening at Alfie's ill. by author. Lothrop, 1985. ISBN 0-688-04123-X Subj: Activities – baby-sitting. Family life. Problem solving.

George the babysitter ill. by author. Prentice-Hall, 1978. Subj: Activities – baby-sitting.

Lucy and Tom's A.B.C. ill. by author. Viking, 1986. ISBN 0-670-81256-0 Subj: ABC books. Family life. Foreign lands – England.

Lucy and Tom's Christmas ill. by author. Viking, 1986. ISBN 0-670-81255-2 Subj: Family life. Foreign lands – England. Holidays – Christmas. Religion.

Lucy and Tom's 1, 2, 3 ill. by author. Viking, 1987. ISBN 0-670-81763-5 Subj: Concepts. Counting. Family life.

Moving Molly ill. by author. Prentice-Hall, 1979. ISBN 0-13-604587-1 Subj: Emotions – loneliness. Family life. Friendship. Moving.

Noisy ill. by author. Lothrop, 1985. ISBN 0-688-04203-1 Subj: Family life. Foreign lands – England. Noise, sounds. Poetry, rhyme.

Out and about ill. by author. Lothrop, 1988. ISBN 0-688-07691-2 Subj: Family life. Foreign lands – England. Poetry, rhyme.

Sally's secret ill. by author. Merrimack, 1980. Subj: Behavior – secrets. Houses.

Two shoes, new shoes ill. by author. Lothrop, 1986. ISBN 0-688-04207-4 Subj: Clothing. Poetry, rhyme.

Up and up ill. by author. Lothrop, 1986. First published by Prentice-Hall, 1979. ISBN 0-688-06261-X Subj: Activities – flying. Imagination. Wordless.

When we went to the park ill. by author. Lothrop, 1985. ISBN 0-688-04204-X Subj: Counting. Family life. Family life – grandfathers. Foreign lands – England. Poetry, rhyme.

Hulme, Susan. *Let's look for colors* (Gillham, Bill)

Let's look for numbers (Gillham, Bill)

Let's look for opposites (Gillham, Bill)

Let's look for shapes (Gillham, Bill)

Hulse, Gillian. *Morris, where are you?* ill. by author. Oxford Univ. Pr., 1988. ISBN 0-19-520646-0 Subj: Animals – cats. Behavior – hiding. Problem solving.

Humpty Dumpty and other first rhymes ill. by Betty Youngs. Bodley Head, 1980. Subj: Nursery rhymes.

Hunt, Bernice Kohn. *Your ant is a which* ill. by Jan Pyk. Harcourt, 1975. ISBN 0-15-299880-2 Subj: Language.

Hunt, Francesca *see* Holland, Isabelle

Hunt, Joyce. *A first look at bird nests* (Selsam, Millicent E.)

A first look at caterpillars (Selsam, Millicent E.)

A first look at cats (Selsam, Millicent E.)

A first look at dinosaurs (Selsam, Millicent E.)

A first look at dogs (Selsam, Millicent E.)

A first look at flowers (Selsam, Millicent E.)

A first look at kangaroos, koalas and other animals with pouches (Selsam, Millicent E.)

A first look at monkeys (Selsam, Millicent E.)

A first look at owls, eagles and other hunters of the sky (Selsam, Millicent E.)

A first look at rocks (Selsam, Millicent E.)

A first look at seashells (Selsam, Millicent E.)

A first look at sharks (Selsam, Millicent E.)

A first look at spiders (Selsam, Millicent E.)

A first look at the world of plants (Selsam, Millicent E.)

A first look at whales (Selsam, Millicent E.)

Keep looking! (Selsam, Millicent E.)

Hunter, Mollie. *The knight of the golden plain* ill. by Marc Simont. Harper, 1983. Subj: Dreams. Imagination. Knights. Magic.

Hunter, Norman. *Professor Branestawm's building bust-up* ill. by Gerald Rose. Merrimack, 1982. Subj: Houses. Humor. Machines.

Hurd, Edith Thacher. *The black dog who went into the woods* ill. by Emily Arnold McCully. Harper, 1980. Subj: Animals – dogs. Death. Pets.

Caboose ill. by Clement Hurd. Lothrop, 1950. Subj: Poetry, rhyme. Trains.

Christmas eve ill. by Clement Hurd. Harper, 1962. Subj: Animals. Holidays – Christmas.

Come and have fun ill. by Clement Hurd. Harper, 1962. Subj: Animals – cats. Animals – mice. Poetry, rhyme.

The day the sun danced ill. by Clement Hurd. Harper, 1965. Subj: Seasons. Seasons – spring. Sun.

Dinosaur, my darling ill. by Don Freeman. Harper, 1978. Subj: Dinosaurs.

Engine, engine number 9 ill. by Clement Hurd. Lothrop, 1940. Subj: Trains.

Five little firemen (Brown, Margaret Wise)

Hurry hurry! ill. by Clement Hurd. Harper, 1960. Subj: Activities – baby-sitting. Behavior – hurrying.

I dance in my red pajamas ill. by Emily Arnold McCully. Harper, 1982. Subj: Activities – dancing. Family life – grandparents.

Johnny Lion's bad day ill. by Clement Hurd. Harper, 1970. Subj: Animals – lions. Illness.

Johnny Lion's book ill. by Clement Hurd. Harper, 1965. Subj: Activities – reading. Animals – lions.

Johnny Lion's rubber boots ill. by Clement Hurd. Harper, 1972. Subj: Animals – lions. Weather – rain.

Last one home is a green pig ill. by Clement Hurd. Harper, 1959. Subj: Animals – monkeys. Birds – ducks. Games. Sports – racing.

Little dog, dreaming by Edith Thacher Hurd and Thacher Hurd; ill. by Clement Hurd. Harper, 1967. Subj: Animals – dogs. Dreams.

Look for a bird ill. by Clement Hurd. Harper, 1977. ISBN 0-06-022720-6 Subj: Birds. Nature. Science.

The mother chimpanzee ill. by Clement Hurd. Little, 1978. Subj: Animals – monkeys. Family life – mothers.

The mother kangaroo ill. by Clement Hurd. Little, 1976. Subj: Animals – kangaroos. Family life. Science.

No funny business ill. by Clement Hurd. Harper, 1962. Subj: Activities – picnicking. Animals – cats.

Sandpipers ill. by Lucienne Bloch. Crowell, 1961. Subj: Birds – sandpipers. Science.

The so-so cat ill. by Clement Hurd. Harper, 1964. Subj: Animals – cats. Holidays – Halloween. Witches.

Starfish ill. by Lucienne Bloch. Crowell, 1962. Subj: Sea and seashore. Science.

Stop, stop ill. by Clement Hurd. Harper, 1961. Subj: Activities – baby-sitting. Character traits – cleanliness.

Under the lemon tree ill. by Clement Hurd. Little, 1980. Subj: Animals – donkeys. Animals – foxes. Character traits – loyalty. Farms.

What whale? Where? ill. by Clement Hurd. Harper, 1966. Subj: Animals – whales. Boats, ships.

The white horse ill. by Tony Chen. Harper, 1970. Subj: Imagination.

Wilson's world ill. by Clement Hurd. Harper, 1971. Subj: Art. Ecology.

Hurd, Thacher. *Hobo dog* ill. by author. Scholastic, 1980. Subj: Activities – traveling. Animals – dogs. Trains.

Little dog, dreaming (Hurd, Edith Thacher)

Mama don't allow ill. by author. Harper, 1984. Subj: Animals – possums. Music. Reptiles – alligators, crocodiles.

Mystery on the docks ill. by author. Harper, 1983. Subj: Animals – rats. Behavior – bad day.

A night in the swamp: a movable book ill. by author. Harper, 1987. ISBN 0-694-00177-5 Subj: Animals. Format, unusual – toy and movable books. Night.

The pea patch jig ill. by author. Crown, 1986. ISBN 0-517-56307-X Subj: Activities – gardening. Animals – mice. Music.

The quiet evening ill. by author. Greenwillow, 1978. Subj: Night.

Hurford, John. *The dormouse* ill. by author. Associated Booksellers, 1986. ISBN 0-907349-25-0 Subj: Animals. Animals – mice.

Hürlimann, Bettina. *Barry: the story of a brave St. Bernard* ill. by Paul Nussbaumer; tr. by Elizabeth D. Crawford. Harcourt, 1968. Subj: Animals – dogs. Character traits – bravery. Character traits – helpfulness.

Hürlimann, Ruth. *The mouse with the daisy hat* ill. by author. White, 1971. Subj: Animals – mice. Clothing. Weddings.

The proud white cat tr. by Anthea Bell; ill. by author. Morrow, 1977. Translation of Der stolze weisse Kater. Subj: Animals – cats. Character traits – pride. Folk and fairy tales. Foreign lands – Germany.

Hurwitz, Johanna. *Superduper Teddy* ill. by Susan Jeschke. Morrow, 1980. Subj: Behavior – growing up.

Hush little baby. *Hush little baby: a folk lullaby* ill. by Aliki. Prentice-Hall, 1968. Subj: Babies. Character traits – generosity. Cumulative tales. Music. Songs.

Hush little baby ill. by Jeanette Winter. Pantheon, 1984. Subj: Babies. Character traits – generosity. Cumulative tales. Folk and fairy tales. Music. Songs.

Hush little baby ill. by Margot Zemach. Dutton, 1976. Subj: Babies. Character traits – generosity. Cumulative tales. Music. Songs.

Hutchings, Tony. *Things that go word book* ill. by author. Rand McNally, 1977. Subj: Machines.

Hutchins, Pat. *The best train set ever* ill. by author. Greenwillow, 1978. Subj: Birthdays. Holidays – Christmas. Holidays – Halloween. Illness.

Changes, changes ill. by author. Macmillan, 1971. Subj: Toys – blocks. Wordless.

Clocks and more clocks ill. by author. Macmillan, 1970. Subj: Clocks. Humor. Time.

Don't forget the bacon! ill. by author. Greenwillow, 1975. Subj: Behavior – forgetfulness. Cumulative tales. Food. Humor. Shopping.

The doorbell rang ill. by author. Greenwillow, 1986. ISBN 0-688-05252-5 Subj: Behavior – sharing. Family life. Friendship.

Good night owl ill. by author. Macmillan, 1972. Subj: Cumulative tales. Noise, sounds. Participation. Sleep.

Happy birthday, Sam ill. by author. Greenwillow, 1978. Subj: Birthdays. Family life – grandfathers.

King Henry's palace ill. by author. Greenwillow, 1983. Subj: Birthdays. Holidays – Christmas. Royalty.

One-eyed Jake ill. by author. Greenwillow, 1979. Subj: Pirates.

1 hunter ill. by author. Greenwillow, 1982. Subj: Animals. Counting.

Rosie's walk ill. by author. Macmillan, 1968. Subj: Animals – foxes. Birds – chickens. Farms. Humor.

The silver Christmas tree ill. by author. Macmillan, 1974. Subj: Animals. Holidays – Christmas. Trees.

The surprise party ill. by author. Macmillan, 1986, 1969. ISBN 0-02-745930-6 Subj: Animals. Behavior – gossip. Parties.

The tale of Thomas Mead ill. by author. Greenwillow, 1980. ISBN 0-688-84282-8 Subj: Activities – reading. Poetry, rhyme.

Titch ill. by author. Macmillan, 1971. Subj: Concepts – size. Cumulative tales. Family life. Plants.

The very worst monster ill. by author. Greenwillow, 1985. ISBN 0-688-04011-X Subj: Monsters. Sibling rivalry.

Where's the baby? ill. by author. Greenwillow, 1988. ISBN 0-688-05934-1 Subj: Babies. Behavior – lost. Behavior – misbehavior. Character traits – cleanliness. Monsters.

The wind blew ill. by author. Macmillan, 1974. Subj: Poetry, rhyme. Weather – wind.

You'll soon grow into them, Titch ill. by author. Greenwillow, 1983. Subj: Clothing. Family life.

Hutton, Warwick. *Adam and Eve: the Bible story* ill. by adapt. Macmillan, 1987. ISBN 0-689-50433-0 Subj: Religion.

Beauty and the beast retold and ill. by Warwick Hutton. Atheneum, 1985. Subj: Character traits – loyalty. Folk and fairy tales. Magic.

Jonah and the great fish ill. by adapt. Atheneum, 1984. Subj: Animals – whales. Religion.

Moses in the bulrushes ill. by adapt. Atheneum, 1986. ISBN 0-689-50393-8 Subj: Babies. Foreign lands – Egypt. Jewish culture. Religion.

Noah and the great flood ill. by author. Atheneum, 1977. Subj: Religion – Noah.

The nose tree ill. by adapt. Atheneum, 1981. Subj: Character traits – cleverness. Friendship. Folk and fairy tales. Witches.

The sleeping beauty (Grimm, Jacob)

Huxley, Aldous. *The crows of Pearblossom* ill. by Barbara Cooney. Random House, 1967. [Written in 1944.] Subj: Birds – crows. Character traits – cleverness. Eggs. Reptiles – snakes.

Hyman, Inge. *Casper and the rainbow bird* (Hyman, Robin)

Hyman, Robin. *Casper and the rainbow bird* by Robin and Inge Hyman; ill. by Yutaka Sugita. Barron's, 1979. Subj: Behavior – running away. Birds – crows. Birds – parakeets, parrots.

Hyman, Trina Schart. *The enchanted forest* ill. by author. Putnam's, 1984. Subj: Forest, woods. Format, unusual. Wordless.

A little alphabet ill. by author. Little, 1980. Subj: ABC books.

Little Red Riding Hood (Grimm, Jacob)

The sleeping beauty (Grimm, Jacob)

Hymes, James L. *Oodles of noodles and other rhymes* (Hymes, Lucia)

Hymes, Lucia. *Oodles of noodles and other rhymes* by Lucia and James L. Hymes, Jr.; ill. by authors. Addison-Wesley, 1964. Subj: Poetry, rhyme.

Hynard, Julia. *Percival's party* ill. by Frances Thatcher. Children's Pr., 1983. Subj: Activities. Parties.

Hynard, Stephen. *Snowy the rabbit* ill. by Frances Thatcher. Children's Pr., 1983. Subj: Activities. Animals – rabbits.

I sing a song of the saints of God ill. by Judith Gwyn Brown. Seabury Pr., 1981. An ill. version of Lesbia Scott's hymn, "I sing a song of the saints of God" written in 1929. Subj: Music. Religion. Songs.

Iannone, Jeanne Koppel *see* Balzano, Jeanne

Ichikawa, Satomi. *A child's book of seasons* ill. by author. Parents, 1976. Subj: Folk and fairy tales. Seasons.

Let's play ill. by author. Philomel, 1981. ISBN 0-399-61186-X Subj: Activities – playing.

Nora's castle ill. by author. Philomel, 1986. ISBN 0-399-21302-3 Subj: Animals. Houses. Parties. Toys.

Sun through small leaves: poems of spring ill. by comp. Collins-World, 1980. Subj: Folk and fairy tales. Seasons – spring.

Suzanne and Nicholas at the market ill. by author. Watts, 1977. Translation by Denise Sheldon of Suzette et Nicolas au marché. ISBN 0-85166-669-8 Subj: Family life. Foreign lands – France. Shopping.

Suzanne and Nicholas in the garden tr. by Denise Sheldon; ill. by author. Watts, 1976. Translation of Suzette et Nicolas dans leur jardin. Subj: Activities – gardening. Ecology. Foreign lands – France.

Suzette and Nicholas in the garden ill. by author. St. Martin's, 1978. Translation by Denise Sheldon of Suzette et Nicolas dans leur jardin. ISBN 0-312-77982-8 Subj: Activities – playing. Family life. Flowers.

If dragon flies made honey: *poems* col. by David Kherdian; ill. by José Aruego and Ariane Dewey. Greenwillow, 1977. Subj: Poetry, rhyme.

Ife, Elaine. *The childhood of Jesus* ill. by Eric Rowe. Rourke, 1983. Subj: Religion.

Moses in the bulrushes ill. by Eric Rowe. Rourke, 1983. Subj: Religion.

Noah and the ark ill. by Russell Lee. Rourke, 1983. Subj: Religion – Noah.

Stories Jesus told ill. by Russell Lee. Rourke, 1983. Subj: Religion.

Iké, Jane Hori. *A Japanese fairy tale* by Jane Hori Iké and Baruch Zimmerman; ill. by Jane Hori Iké. Warne, 1982. Subj: Character traits – appearance. Folk and fairy tales. Foreign lands – Japan.

Illyés, Gyula. *Matt the gooseherd: a story from Hungary* ill. by Károly Reich. Penguin, 1979. Subj: Birds – geese. Folk and fairy tales. Foreign lands – Hungary.

Ilsley, Velma. *A busy day for Chris* ill. by author. Lippincott, 1957. Subj: ABC books. Poetry, rhyme.

M is for moving ill. by author. Walck, 1966. Subj: ABC books. Moving.

The pink hat ill. by author. Lippincott, 1956. Subj: Behavior – carelessness. Poetry, rhyme.

I'm mad at you: *verses* sel. by William Cole; ill. by George MacClain. Collins-World, 1978. Subj: Emotions – anger. Folk and fairy tales.

Impey, Rose. *The flat man* ill. by Moira Kemp. Barron's, 1988. ISBN 0-8120-5975-1 Subj: Bedtime. Emotions – fear. Goblins. Monsters. Night.

Scare yourself to sleep ill. by Moira Kemp. Barron's, 1988. ISBN 0-8120-5974-3 Subj: Bedtime. Emotions – fear. Goblins. Monsters. Night.

Infield, Glenn Berton *see* Rodgers, Frank

Ingle, Annie. *The big city book* ill. by Tim and Greg Hildebrandt. Platt, 1976. Subj: City.

Ingoglia, Gina. *The big book of real airplanes* ill. by George Guzzi. Putnam's, 1987. ISBN 0-448-19179-2 Subj: Airplanes, airports. Helicopters. Transportation.

Ingpen, Robert. *The idle bear* ill. by author. Harper, 1987. ISBN 0-87226-159-X Subj: Toys – teddy bears.

Inkiow, Dimiter. *Me and Clara and Baldwin the pony* tr. from German by Paula McGuire; ill. by Traudl and Walter Reiner. Pantheon, 1980. Subj: Animals – horses. Behavior – misbehavior.

Me and Clara and Casimir the cat tr. from German by Paula McGuire; ill. by Traudl and Walter Reiner. Pantheon, 1979. Subj: Animals – cats.

Me and Clara and Snuffy the dog tr. from German by Paula McGuire; ill. by Traudl and Walter Reiner. Pantheon, 1980. Subj: Animals – dogs. Behavior – misbehavior.

Me and my sister Clara tr. from German by Paula McGuire; ill. by Traudl and Walter Reiner. Pantheon, 1979. Subj: Behavior – misbehavior.

Inkpen, Mick. *If I had a pig* ill. by author. Little, 1988. ISBN 0-316-41887-0 Subj: Animals – pigs. Friendship. Imagination.

If I had a sheep ill. by author. Little, 1988. ISBN 0-316-41888-9 Subj: Animals – sheep. Friendship. Imagination.

The Nativity play (Butterworth, Nick)

Nice or nasty (Butterworth, Nick)

One bear at bedtime ill. by author. Little, 1988. ISBN 0-316-41889-7 Subj: Animals. Bedtime. Counting. Imagination. Toys – teddy bears.

Ionesco, Eugene. *Story number 1* ill. by Etienne Delessert; tr. by Calvin K. Towle. Crown, 1969. Subj: Family life. Imagination.

Ipcar, Dahlov. *Animal hide and seek* ill. by author. Addison-Wesley, 1947. Subj: Animals.

The biggest fish in the sea ill. by author. Viking, 1972. Subj: Concepts – size. Fish. Sports – fishing.

Black and white ill. by author. Knopf, 1963. Subj: Animals – dogs. Poetry, rhyme.

Bright barnyard ill. by author. Knopf, 1966. Subj: Animals. Birds. Farms.

Brown cow farm ill. by author. Doubleday, 1959. Subj: Animals. Counting. Farms.

Bug city ill. by author. Holiday, 1975. Subj: Insects.

The calico jungle ill. by author. Knopf, 1965. Subj: Animals. Bedtime.

The cat at night ill. by author. Doubleday, 1969. Subj: Animals – cats. Night.

The cat came back ill. by author. Knopf, 1971. Subj: Animals – cats. Music. Poetry, rhyme. Songs.

A flood of creatures ill. by author. Holiday, 1973. Subj: Animals. Weather – floods.

Hard scrabble harvest ill. by author. Doubleday, 1976. Subj: Farms. Holidays – Thanksgiving. Plants. Poetry, rhyme.

I like animals ill. by author. Knopf, 1960. Subj: Animals.

I love my anteater with an A ill. by author. Knopf, 1964. Subj: ABC books. Animals.

The land of flowers ill. by author. Viking, 1974. Subj: Activities – gardening. Animals – sheep. Concepts – size. Flowers.

Lost and found: a hidden animal book ill. by author. Doubleday, 1981. Subj: Animals. Participation.

One horse farm ill. by author. Doubleday, 1950. Subj: Animals – horses. Farms. Machines. Progress.

Sir Addlepate and the unicorn ill. by author. Doubleday, 1971. Subj: Knights. Mythical creatures.

"The song of the day birds" and "The song of the night birds" ill. by author. Doubleday, 1967. Subj: Birds. Music. Night. Songs.

Stripes and spots ill. by author. Doubleday, 1953. Subj: Animals – leopards. Animals – tigers.

Ten big farms ill. by author. Knopf, 1958. Subj: Counting. Farms.

Wild and tame animals ill. by author. Doubleday, 1962. Subj: Animals.

World full of horses ill. by author. Doubleday, 1955. Subj: Animals – horses.

Ireson, Barbara. *The gingerbread man* (The gingerbread boy)

Irvine, Georgeanne. *Bo the orangutan* photos. by Ron Garrison. Children's Pr., 1983. Subj: Animals – monkeys. Zoos.

Elmer the elephant photos. by Ron Garrison. Children's Pr., 1983. Subj: Animals – elephants. Zoos.

Georgie the giraffe photos. by Ron Garrison. Children's Pr., 1983. Subj: Animals – giraffes. Zoos.

Lindi the leopard photos. by Ron Garrison. Children's Pr., 1983. Subj: Animals – leopards. Zoos.

The nursery babies photos. by Ron Garrison. Children's Pr., 1983. Subj: Animals. Zoos.

Sasha the cheetah photos. by Ron Garrison. Children's Pr., 1982. Subj: Animals – cheetahs. Zoos.

Sydney the koala photos. by Ron Garrison. Childrens Pr., 1982. ISBN 0-516-09304-5 Subj: Animals – koala bears. Zoos.

Tully the tree kangaroo photos. by Ron Garrison. Children's Pr., 1983. Subj: Animals. Zoos.

Irving, Washington. *The legend of Sleepy Hollow* (Wolkstein, Diane)

The legend of Sleepy Hollow adapt. by Robert D. San Souci; ill. by Daniel San Souci. Doubleday, 1986. ISBN 0-385-23397-3 Subj: Folk and fairy tales. Holidays – Halloween.

Rip Van Winkle adapt. and ill. by John Howe. Little, 1988. ISBN 0-316-37578-0 Subj: Behavior – lost. Elves and little people. Folk and fairy tales. Sleep.

Rip Van Winkle adapt. and ill. by Thomas Locker. Little, 1988. ISBN 0-8037-0521-2 Subj: Behavior – lost. Elves and little people. Folk and fairy tales. Sleep.

Rip Van Winkle adapt. by Catherine Storr; ill. by Peter Wingham. Raintree, 1984. ISBN 0-8172-2108-5 Subj: Behavior – lost. Elves and little people. Folk and fairy tales. Sleep.

Isadora, Rachel. *Ben's trumpet* ill. by author. Greenwillow, 1979. Subj: Caldecott award honor book.

City seen from A to Z ill. by author. Greenwillow, 1983. Subj: ABC books. City.

I hear ill. by author. Greenwillow, 1985. ISBN 0-688-04062-4 Subj: Babies. Family life. Senses – hearing.

I see ill. by author. Greenwillow, 1985. ISBN 0-688-04060-8 Subj: Babies. Family life. Senses – seeing.

I touch ill. by author. Greenwillow, 1985. ISBN 0-688-04256-2 Subj: Senses – touching.

Jesse and Abe ill. by author. Greenwillow, 1981. Subj: Family life – grandfathers. Theater.

Max ill. by author. Macmillan, 1976. Subj: Activities – dancing. Sports – baseball.

My ballet class ill. by author. Greenwillow, 1980. Subj: Activities – dancing.

No, Agatha! ill. by author. Greenwillow, 1980. Subj: Activities – traveling. Boats, ships.

The nutcracker (Hoffmann, E. T. A.)

Opening night ill. by author. Greenwillow, 1984. Subj: Activities – dancing. Theater.

The pirates of Bedford Street ill. by author. Greenwillow, 1988. ISBN 0-688-05208-8 Subj: Imagination. Pirates.

The Potters' kitchen ill. by author. Greenwillow, 1977. Subj: Moving.

Willaby ill. by author. Macmillan, 1977. Subj: School.

Isele, Elizabeth. *The frog princess: a Russian tale* retold ill. by Michael Hague. Harper, 1984. ISBN 0-690-04218-3 Subj: Folk and fairy tales. Foreign lands – Russia. Frogs and toads. Magic. Royalty. Witches.

Pooks ill. by Chris L. Demarest. Lippincott, 1983. Subj: Activities – traveling. Animals – dogs. Music.

Isenbart, Hans-Heinrich. *Baby animals on the farm* tr. from German by Elizabeth D. Crawford; photos by Ruth Rau. Putnam's, 1984. Subj: Animals. Farms.

A duckling is born tr. by Catherine Edwards Sadler; photos. by Othmar Baumli. Putnam's, 1981. Subj: Birds – ducks. Science.

Isenberg, Barbara. *The adventures of Albert, the running bear* by Barbara Isenberg and Susan Wolf; ill. by Dick Gackenbach. Houghton, 1982. Subj: Animals – bears. Behavior – running away. Sports – racing. Zoos.

Albert the running bear gets the jitters by Barbara Isenberg and Susan Wolf; ill. by Diane de Groat. Clarion, 1987. ISBN 0-89919-532-6 Subj: Animals – bears. Behavior – bullying. Behavior – trickery. Sports – racing.

Albert the running bear's exercise book by Barbara Isenberg and Marjorie Jaffe; ill. by Diane de Groat. Houghton, 1984. Subj: Animals – bears. Health.

Ishii, Momoko. *The tongue-cut sparrow* tr. from the Japanese by Katherine Paterson; ill. by Suekichi Akaba. Lodestar, 1987. Tr. of Sita-kiri suzume. ISBN 0-525-67199-4 Subj: Behavior – greed. Birds – sparrows. Character traits – kindness to animals. Folk and fairy tales. Foreign lands – Japan.

Israel, Marion Louise. *The tractor on the farm* ill. by Robert Dranko. Melmont, 1958. Subj: Farms. Machines.

Ivanov, Anatoly. *Ol' Jake's lucky day* ill. by author. Lothrop, 1984. ISBN 0-688-02867-5 Subj: Behavior – seeking better things. Folk and fairy tales. Foreign lands – Russia. Imagination.

Iverson, Genie. *I want to be big* ill. by David McPhail. Dutton, 1979. Subj: Behavior – growing up.

Ivimey, John William. *The complete story of the three blind mice* ill. by Paul Galdone. Clarion, 1987. ISBN 0-89919-481-8 Subj: Animals – mice. Music. Nursery rhymes. Songs.

The complete version of ye three blind mice ill. by Walton Corbould. Warne, 1909. Subj: Animals – mice. Music. Nursery rhymes. Songs.

Ivory, Lesley Anne. *A day in London* ill. by author. Burke, 1982. Subj: City. Foreign lands – England.

A day in New York ill. by author. Burke, 1982. Subj: City.

Iwamatsu, Jun Atsushi *see* Yashima, Tarō

Iwamura, Kazuo. *Tan Tan's hat* ill. by author. Bradbury, 1983. Subj: Animals – monkeys. Clothing.

Tan Tan's suspenders ill. by author. Bradbury, 1983. Subj: Animals – monkeys. Clothing.

Ton and Pon: big and little ill. by author. Bradbury, 1984. Subj: Animals – dogs. Friendship.

Ton and Pon: two good friends ill. by author. Bradbury, 1984. Subj: Animals – dogs. Friendship.

Iwasaki, Chihiro. *The birthday wish* ill. by author. McGraw-Hill, 1974, 1972. Subj: Behavior – wishing. Birthdays. Weather – snow.

Staying home alone on a rainy day ill. by author. McGraw-Hill, 1968. Subj: Family life. Family life – only child. Weather – rain.

What's fun without a friend? ill. by author. McGraw-Hill, 1972. Subj: Animals – dogs. Sea and seashore.

Will you be my friend? ill. by author. McGraw-Hill, 1970. Subj: Friendship.

Izawa, Yohji. *One evening* (Funakoshi, Canna)

Jabar, Cynthia. *Party day!* ill. by author. Little, 1987. ISBN 0-316-43456-6 Subj: Animals – rabbits. Birthdays. Counting.

Jack and the beanstalk. *The history of Mother Twaddle and the marvelous achievements of her son Jack* ill. by Paul Galdone. Seabury Pr., 1974. A verse version of Jack and the beanstalk, written by Basil T. Blackwood [B.A.T.] and pub. in 1807 by J. Harris, London. Subj: Folk and fairy tales. Giants. Plants. Poetry, rhyme.

Jack and the beanstalk adapt. and ill. by Lorinda Bryan Cauley. Putnam's, 1983. Subj: Folk and fairy tales. Giants.

Jack and the beanstalk ill. by Ed Parker. Troll Assoc., 1979. Subj: Folk and fairy tales. Giants.

Jack and the beanstalk adapt. and ill. by Tony Ross. Delacorte, 1981. Subj: Folk and fairy tales. Giants.

Jack and the beanstalk ill. by William Stobbs. Dial Pr., 1966. Subj: Folk and fairy tales. Giants.

Jack and the beanstalk retold by Beatrice Schenk De Regniers; ill. by Anne Wilsdorf. Atheneum, 1985. ISBN 0-689-31174-5 Subj: Folk and fairy tales. Giants. Poetry, rhyme.

Jack the giantkiller adapt. and ill. by Tony Ross. David & Charles, 1987. ISBN 0-862-64060-1 Subj: Folk and fairy tales. Giants.

Jack the giant killer: Jack's first and finest adventure retold in verse as well as other useful information about giants including how to shake hands with a giant retold by Beatrice Schenk De Regniers; ill. by Anne Wilsdorf. Atheneum, 1987. ISBN 0-689-31218-0 Subj: Folk and fairy tales. Giants. Poetry, rhyme.

Jack Sprat. *The life of Jack Sprat, his wife and his cat* retold and ill. by Paul Galdone. McGraw-Hill, 1969. Subj: Animals – cats. Family life. Food. Nursery rhymes.

Jackson, Ellen B. *The bear in the bathtub* ill. by Margot Apple. Addison-Wesley, 1981. Subj: Activities – bathing. Animals – bears. Character traits – cleanliness.

Jackson, Jacqueline. *Chicken ten thousand* ill. by Barbara Morrow. Little, 1968. Subj: Birds – chickens. Science.

Jackson, Richard. *Iktomi and the boulder* (Goble, Paul)

Jacobs, Francine. *Barracuda: tiger of the sea* ill. by Harriett Springer. Walker, 1981. Subj: Fish. Science.

Sewer Sam: the sea cow ill. by Harriett Springer. Walker, 1979. Subj: Animals. Science. Sea and seashore. Zoos.

Jacobs, Joseph. *The crock of gold: being "The pedlar of Swaffham"* ill. by William Stobbs. Follett, 1971. Subj: Careers – peddlers. Dreams. Folk and fairy tales. Foreign lands – England.

Hereafterthis ill. by Paul Galdone. McGraw-Hill, 1973. Subj: Animals. Behavior – mistakes. Crime. Farms. Folk and fairy tales.

Hudden and Dudden and Donald O'Neary ill. by Doris Burn. Coward, 1968. Subj: Behavior – greed. Folk and fairy tales. Foreign lands – Ireland.

Johnny-cake ill. by Emma Lillian Brock. Putnam's, 1967. Subj: Cumulative tales. Folk and fairy tales. Food.

Johnny-cake ill. by William Stobbs. Viking, 1972, 1967. Subj: Cumulative tales. Folk and fairy tales. Food.

Lazy Jack ill. by Barry Wilkinson. World, 1969. Subj: Character traits – foolishness. Character traits – laziness. Folk and fairy tales.

Master of all masters ill. by Anne F. Rockwell. Grosset, 1972. Subj: Folk and fairy tales.

Old Mother Wiggle-Waggle ill. by William Stobbs. Bodley Head, 1980. Subj: Folk and fairy tales.

The three sillies ill. by Paul Galdone. Houghton, 1981. Subj: Folk and fairy tales.

Jacobs, Leland B. *Belling the cat and other stories*

Is somewhere always far away? ill. by John E. Johnson. Holt, 1967. Subj: Character traits – questioning. Poetry, rhyme.

Jacobson, Gela. *The mysterious tale of Gentle Jack and Lord Bumblebee* (Sand, George)

Jaffe, Marjorie. *Albert the running bear's exercise book* (Isenberg, Barbara)

Jaffe, Rona. *Last of the wizards* ill. by Erik Blegvad. Simon and Schuster, 1961. Subj: Behavior – wishing. Character traits – cleverness.

Jagendorf, Moritz A. *Kwi-na the eagle and other Indian tales* ill. by Jack Endewelt; consultant: Carolyn W. Field. Silver Burdett, 1968. Subj: Folk and fairy tales. Indians of North America.

Jameson, Cynthia. *The clay pot boy* ill. by Arnold Lobel. Coward, 1973. Subj: Behavior – misbehavior. Cumulative tales. Folk and fairy tales. Foreign lands – Russia.

A day with Whisker Wickles ill. by James Marshall. Coward, 1975. Subj: Animals – rabbits. Games.

The house of five bears ill. by Lorinda Bryan Cauley. Putnam's, 1978. Subj: Character traits – cleverness. Folk and fairy tales. Foreign lands – Russia.

Janice. *Angélique* ill. by Roger Antoine Duvoisin. McGraw-Hill, 1960. Subj: Animals – dogs. Behavior – bullying. Birds – ducks.

Little Bear marches in the St. Patrick's Day parade ill. by Mariana. Subj: Animals – bears. Holidays – St. Patrick's Day. Parades.

Little Bear's Christmas ill. by Mariana. Lothrop, 1964. Subj: Animals – bears. Character traits – generosity. Hibernation. Holidays – Christmas.

Little Bear's New Year's party ill. by Mariana. Lothrop, 1973. Subj: Animals – bears. Holidays – New Year's. Parties.

Little Bear's pancake party ill. by Mariana. Lothrop, 1960. Subj: Animals – bears. Food. Parties. Seasons – spring.

Little Bear's Sunday breakfast ill. by Mariana. Lothrop, 1958. Subj: Animals – bears. Food.

Little Bear's Thanksgiving ill. by Mariana. Lothrop, 1967. Subj: Animals – bears. Holidays – Thanksgiving.

Minette ill. by Alain. McGraw-Hill, 1959. Subj: Animals – cats.

Mr. and Mrs. Button's wonderful watchdogs ill. by Roger Antoine Duvoisin. Lothrop, 1978. Subj: Animals – dogs. Crime.

Janifer, Laurence Mark *see* Wilson, Barbara

Janosch. *Dear snowman* ill. by author. Collins, 1969. Subj: Seasons – winter. Snowmen. Weather – snow.

Hey Presto! You're a bear! tr. by Klauss Flugge; ill. by author. Little, 1980. Subj: Imagination.

Joshua and the magic fiddle ill. by author. Collins, 1967. Subj: Magic. Moon. Music.

Just one apple tr. by Refna Wilkin; ill. by author. Walck, 1965. Subj: Behavior – wishing. Dragons.

The magic auto ill. by author. Crown, 1971. Translation of Das Regenauto. Subj: Automobiles. Magic.

Tonight at nine ill. by author. Walck, 1967. Translation of Heute um neune hinter der Scheune. Subj: Animals. Music. Poetry, rhyme.

The trip to Panama tr. by Anthea Bell; ill. by author. Little, 1978. Translation of Oh, wie schon ist Panama. Subj: Activities – traveling. Foreign lands – Panama.

A January fog will freeze a hog: *and other weather folklore* comp. and ed. by Hubert Davis; ill. by John Wallner. Crown, 1977. Subj: Folk and fairy tales. Weather.

Jaques, Faith. *Tilly's house* ill. by author. Atheneum, 1979. Subj: Houses. Toys – dolls.

Tilly's rescue ill. by author. Atheneum, 1981. ISBN 0-689-50175-7 Subj: Behavior – lost. Character traits – bravery. Friendship. Holidays – Christmas. Toys – dolls.

Jaquith, Priscilla. *Bo Rabbit smart for true: folktales from the Gullah* ill. by Ed Young. Putnam's, 1981. Subj: Animals – rabbits. Folk and fairy tales. Noise, sounds.

Jarrell, Mary. *The knee baby* ill. by Symeon Shimin. Farrar, 1973. Subj: Babies. Family life. Family life – grandmothers.

Jarrell, Randall. *A bat is born* ill. by John Schoenherr. Doubleday, 1978. Subj: Animals – bats. Poetry, rhyme.

The fisherman and his wife (Grimm, Jacob)

The golden bird (Grimm, Jacob)

The rabbit catcher and other fairy tales (Bechstein, Ludwig)

Jaynes, Ruth M. *Benny's four hats* ill. by Harvey Mandlin. Bowmar, 1967. Subj: Clothing. Ethnic groups in the U.S. Participation. Weather.

The biggest house ill. by Jacques Rupp. Bowmar, 1968. Subj: Houses.

Friends! friends! friends! ill. by Harvey Mandlin. Bowmar, 1967. Subj: Ethnic groups in the U.S. Friendship. School.

Melinda's Christmas stocking ill. by Richard George. Bowmar, 1968. Subj: Ethnic groups in the U.S. – Mexican-Americans. Holidays – Christmas. Senses – hearing. Senses – seeing. Senses – smelling. Senses – tasting. Senses – touching.

Tell me please! What's that? ill. by Harvey Mandlin. Bowmar, 1968. Subj: Animals. Ethnic groups in the U.S. Ethnic groups in the U.S. – Mexican-Americans. Foreign languages.

That's what it is! ill. by Harvey Mandlin. Bowmar, 1968. Subj: Ethnic groups in the U.S. Ethnic groups in the U.S. – Mexican-Americans. Insects.

Three baby chicks ill. by Harvey Mandlin. Bowmar, 1967. Subj: Birds – chickens. School.

What is a birthday child? ill. by Harvey Mandlin. Bowmar, 1967. Subj: Birthdays. Character traits – individuality. Ethnic groups in the U.S. Ethnic groups in the U.S. – Mexican-Americans.

Jeake, Samuel, Jr. *see* Aiken, Conrad

Jefferds, Vincent. *Disney's elegant ABC book.* Simon and Schuster, 1983. Subj: ABC books.

Disney's elegant book of manners. Simon & Schuster, 1985. ISBN 0-671-60507-0 Subj: Etiquette. Poetry, rhyme.

Jeffers, Susan. *All the pretty horses* ill. by author. Macmillan, 1974. Subj: Animals – horses. Bedtime. Sleep.

Forest of dreams (Wells, Rosemary)

The three jovial huntsmen (Mother Goose)

Wild Robin ill. by author. Dutton, 1976. Based on a tale in Little Prudy's fairy book by R. S. Clarke. Subj: Behavior – misbehavior. Foreign lands – Scotland.

Jeffery, Graham. *Thomas the tortoise* ill. by author. Crown, 1988. ISBN 0-517-57043-2 Subj: Character traits – individuality. Character traits – kindness to animals. Reptiles – turtles, tortoises.

Jeffrey, Christopher *see* Leach, Michael

Jenkin-Pearce, Susie. *Bad Boris and the new kitten* ill. by author. Macmillan, 1987. ISBN 0-02-747620-0 Subj: Animals – cats. Animals – elephants. Emotions – envy, jealousy.

Jenkins, Christopher N. H. *The little weaver of Thái-Yên Village* (Trân-Khánh-Tuyêt)

Jenkins, Jordan. *Learning about love* ill. by Gene Ruggles. Children's Pr., 1979. Subj: Emotions – love. Family life – mothers. Illness.

Jennings, Linda M. *Coppelia* ill. by Krystyna Turska. Silver Burdett, 1984. ISBN 0-382-09241-4 Subj: Activities – dancing. Folk and fairy tales. Toys – dolls.

Crispin and the dancing piglet ill. by Krystyna Turska. Silver Burdett, 1986. ISBN 0-382-09242-2 Subj: Activities – dancing. Animals – pigs. Behavior – seeking better things.

The golden goose (Grimm, Jacob)

The musicians of Bremen (Grimm, Jacob)

The sleeping beauty: the story of the ballet ill. by Francesca Crespi. David & Charles, 1987. ISBN 0-340-33518-1 Subj: Activities – dancing. Folk and fairy tales.

The wolf and the seven little kids (Grimm, Jacob)

Jennings, Michael. *The bears who came to breakfix* ill. by Tom Dunnington. Children's Pr., 1977. Subj: Animals – bears. Dreams. Family life – mothers. Moving.

Robin Goodfellow and the giant dwarf ill. by Tomie de Paola. McGraw-Hill, 1981. Subj: Behavior – trickery. Giants.

Jennings, Terry. *Bouncing and rolling* ill. by David Anstey. Watts, 1988. ISBN 0-531-17085-3 Subj: Concepts. Science.

Earthworms ill. by David Anstey. Watts, 1988. ISBN 0-531-17097-7 Subj: Animals – worms. Science.

Floating and sinking ill. by David Anstey. Watts, 1988. ISBN 0-531-17086-1 Subj: Concepts. Science.

Seeds ill. by David Anstey. Watts, 1988. ISBN 0-531-17087-X Subj: Plants. Science.

Jennison, C. S. *see* Starbird, Kaye

Jenny, Anne. *The fantastic story of King Brioche the First* ill. by Joycelyne Pache. Lothrop, 1970. Translation by Catherine Barton from La fantastique histoire du roi Brioche Ier. Subj: Activities – flying. School.

Jensen, Helen Zane. *When Panda came to our house* ill. by author. Dial Pr., 1985. ISBN 0-8037-0236-1 Subj: Activities. Animals – pandas. Foreign lands – China.

Jensen, Virginia Allen. *Cat alley* (Olsen, Ib Spang)

Catching: a book for blind and sighted children with pictures to feel as well as to see ill. by author. Putnam's, 1984. Subj: Concepts – shape. Format, unusual. Handicaps – blindness. Senses – seeing.

Red thread riddles by Virginia Allen Jensen and Polly Edman; ill. by authors. Putnam's, 1980. Subj: Handicaps – blindness. Riddles. Senses – seeing.

Sara and the door ill. by Ann Strugnell. Addison-Wesley, 1977. Subj: Character traits – perseverance. Clothing. Ethnic groups in the U.S. – Afro-Americans.

What's that? ill. by Dorcas Woodbury Haller. Collins-World, 1979. Subj: Concepts. Handicaps – blindness. Senses – seeing.

Jeremy, Richard *see* Fox, Charles Philip

Jerome, Judson. *I never saw...* ill. by Helga Aichinger. Albert Whitman, 1974. Subj: Poetry, rhyme.

Jeschke, Susan. *Angela and Bear* ill. by author. Holt, 1979. Subj: Animals – bears. Imagination – imaginary friends. Magic.

The devil did it ill. by author. Holt, 1979. Subj: Animals – bears. Imagination – imaginary friends.

Firerose ill. by author. Holt, 1974. Subj: Careers – fortune tellers. Dragons. Humor. Magic.

Lucky's choice ill. by author. Scholastic, 1987. ISBN 0-590-40520-9 Subj: Animals – cats. Behavior – needing someone. Behavior – running away. Friendship.

Mia, Grandma and the genie ill. by author. Holt, 1978. Subj: Fairies. Family life – grandmothers. Magic.

Perfect the pig ill. by author. Holt, 1981. Subj: Activities – flying. Animals – pigs.

Rima and Zeppo ill. by author. Dutton, 1976. Subj: Magic. Witches.

Tamar and the tiger ill. by author. Holt, 1980. Subj: Imagination.

Jewell, Nancy. *ABC cat* ill. by Ann Schweninger. Harper, 1983. Subj: ABC books. Animals – cats. Poetry, rhyme.

Bus ride ill. by Ronald Himler. Harper, 1978. Subj: Buses.

The snuggle bunny ill. by Mary Chalmers. Harper, 1972. Subj: Animals – rabbits. Emotions – love.

Time for Uncle Joe ill. by Joan Sandin. Harper, 1981. Subj: Death. Emotions. Family life.

Try and catch me ill. by Leonard Weisgard. Harper, 1972. Subj: Activities – playing. Ecology. Friendship. Imagination.

Jijii, Hanasaka. *The old man who made the trees bloom* (Shibano, Tamizo)

Joerns, Consuelo. *The foggy rescue* ill. by author. Four Winds Pr., 1980. Subj: Animals – mice. Boats, ships. Behavior – lost.

The forgotten bear ill. by author. Four Winds Pr., 1978. Subj: Behavior – lost. Toys – teddy bears.

The lost and found house ill. by author. Four Winds Pr., 1979. Subj: Animals – mice. Houses.

The midnight castle ill. by author. Lothrop, 1983. Subj: Animals – mice. Dragons. Royalty.

Oliver's escape ill. by author. Four Winds Pr., 1981. Subj: Animals. Animals – dogs. Behavior – running away. Friendship.

John, Naomi. *Roadrunner* ill. by Peter and Virginia Parnall. Dutton, 1980. Subj: Birds. Desert.

Johnson, A. E. *see* Johnson, Angela

Johnson, Angela. *Tell me a story, mama* ill. by David Soman. Watts, 1989. ISBN 0-531-05794-1 Subj: Family life – mothers.

Johnson, B. J. *A hat like that* by B. J. Johnson and Susan Aiello; ill. by authors. St. Martin's, 1986. ISBN 0-312-36416-4 Subj: Clothing. Format, unusual – toy and movable books. Poetry, rhyme.

My blanket Burt by B. J. Johnson and Susan Aiello; ill. by authors. St. Martin's, 1986. ISBN 0-312-55600-4 Subj: Behavior – losing things. Format, unusual – toy and movable books. Poetry, rhyme.

Johnson, Benjamin F. *see* Riley, James Whitcomb

Johnson, Crockett. *The blue ribbon puppies* ill. by author. Harper, 1958. Subj: Animals – dogs. Imagination. Toys.

Ellen's lion ill. by author. Harper, 1959. Subj: Imagination. Toys.

The emperor's gift ill. by author. Holt, 1965. Subj: Character traits. Character traits – generosity. Royalty.

The frowning prince ill. by author. Harper, 1959. Subj: Royalty.

Harold and the purple crayon ill. by author. Harper, 1955. Subj: Art. Humor. Imagination.

Harold at the North Pole ill. by author. Harper, 1957. Subj: Holidays – Christmas. Imagination.

Harold's ABC: another purple crayon adventure ill. by author. Harper, 1963. Subj: ABC books. Imagination.

Harold's circus ill. by author. Harper, 1959. Subj: Circus. Humor. Imagination.

Harold's fairy tale: further adventures with the purple crayon ill. by author. Harper, 1956. Subj: Folk and fairy tales. Imagination.

Harold's trip to the sky ill. by author. Harper, 1957. Subj: Imagination. Space and space ships.

A picture for Harold's room ill. by author. Harper, 1960. Subj: Art. Imagination.

Terrible terrifying Toby ill. by author. Harper, 1957. Subj: Animals – dogs.

Time for spring ill. by author. Harper, 1957. Subj: Seasons – spring. Snowmen.

Upside down ill. by author. Albert Whitman, 1969. Subj: Animals – kangaroos. Concepts – up and down. Humor. World.

We wonder what will Walter be? When he grows up ill. by author. Holt, 1964. Subj: Animals. Behavior – growing up.

Will spring be early? ill. by author. Crowell, 1959. Subj: Animals – groundhogs. Holidays – Groundhog Day. Seasons – spring.

Johnson, Donna Kay. *Brighteyes* ill. by author. Holt, 1978. Subj: Animals – raccoons. Handicaps – blindness. Senses – seeing.

Johnson, Elizabeth. *All in free but Janey* ill. by Trina Schart Hyman. Little, 1968. Subj: Games. Imagination.

Johnson, Evelyne. *The cow in the kitchen: a folk tale* ill. by Anthony Rao. Simon and Schuster, 1983. Subj: Behavior – dissatisfaction. Character traits – foolishness.

Johnson, Hannah Lyons. *From seed to jack-o'-lantern* photos. by Daniel Dorn. Lothrop, 1974. Subj: Activities – gardening. Holidays – Halloween. Plants. Science.

Johnson, Jane. *Bertie on the beach* ill. by author. Four Winds Pr., 1981. Subj: Circus. Dreams. Sea and seashore.

Sybil and the blue rabbit ill. by author. Doubleday, 1980. Subj: Imagination. Toys.

Today I thought I'd run away ill. by author. Dutton, 1986. ISBN 0-525-44193-X Subj: Bedtime. Behavior – running away. Monsters.

Johnson, Jean. *Teachers A to Z* photos. by author. Walker, 1987. ISBN 0-8027-6677-3 Subj: ABC books. Careers – teachers. School.

Johnson, John E. *My first book of things* ill. by author. Random House, 1979. Subj: Format, unusual – board books.

Johnson, Louise. *Malunda* ill. by Edward Durose. Carolrhoda, 1982. Subj: Animals – rhinoceros. Illness. Zoos.

Johnson, Mildred D. *Wait, skates!* ill. by Tom Dunnington. Children's Pr., 1983. Subj: Activities – playing. Sports – ice skating.

Johnson, Ryerson. *Let's walk up the wall* ill. by Eva Cellini. Holiday, 1967. Subj: Participation.

Upstairs and downstairs ill. by Lisl Weil. Crowell, 1962. Subj: Concepts.

Johnson, Walter Ryerson *see* Johnson, Ryerson

Johnston, Johanna. *Edie changes her mind* ill. by Paul Galdone. Putnam's, 1964. Subj: Bedtime. Problem solving.

Penguin's way ill. by Leonard Weisgard. Doubleday, 1962. Subj: Birds – penguins. Science.

Speak up, Edie ill. by Paul Galdone. Putman's, 1974. Subj: Language. Theater.

Sugarplum ill. by Marvin Bileck. Knopf, 1955. Subj: Character traits – smallness. Toys – dolls.

That's right, Edie ill. by Paul Galdone. Putnam's, 1966. Subj: Activities – writing.

Whale's way ill. by Leonard Weisgard. Doubleday, 1965. Subj: Animals – whales. Science.

Johnston, Mary Anne. *Sing me a song* ill. by John Magine. Children's Pr., 1977. Subj: Animals – rabbits. Songs.

Johnston, Susan T. *see* Johnston, Tony

Johnston, Tony. *Farmer Mack measures his pig* ill. by Megan Lloyd. Harper, 1986. ISBN 0-06-023018-5 Subj: Animals – pigs. Behavior – boasting. Farms.

Four scary stories ill. by Tomie de Paola. Putnam's, 1978. Subj: Ghosts. Goblins. Monsters.

Mole and Troll trim the tree ill. by Wallace Tripp. Putnam's, 1974. ISBN 0-399-60909-1 Subj: Animals – moles. Behavior – sharing. Holidays – Christmas. Seasons – winter. Trees. Trolls.

Pages of music ill. by Tomie de Paola. Putnam's, 1988. ISBN 0-399-21436-4 Subj: Activities – painting. Islands. Music.

The quilt story ill. by Tomie de Paola. Putnam's, 1984. ISBN 0-399-21009-1 Subj: Family life. Moving.

The vanishing pumpkin ill. by Tomie de Paola. Putnam's, 1983. Subj: Holidays – Halloween. Witches.

Whale song ill. by Ed Young. Putnam's, 1987. ISBN 0-399-21402-X Subj: Animals – whales. Counting.

The witch's hat ill. by Margot Tomes. Putnam's, 1984. Subj: Magic. Witches.

Yonder ill. by Lloyd Bloom. Dial Pr., 1988. ISBN 0-8037-0278-7 Subj: Cumulative tales. Seasons.

Jolliffe, Anne. *From pots to plastics* ill. by author. Hawthorn, 1965. Subj: Science.

Water, wind and wheels ill. by author. Hawthorn, 1965. Subj: Science.

Jolly Roger *see* Bradfield, Roger

Jonas, Ann. *Holes and peeks* ill. by author. Greenwillow, 1984. Subj: Caldecott award honor book. Emotions – fear. Problem solving.

Now we can go ill. by author. Greenwillow, 1986. ISBN 0-688-04803-X Subj: Toys.

The quilt ill. by author. Greenwillow, 1984. Subj: Bedtime. Dreams.

Reflections ill. by author. Greenwillow, 1987. ISBN 0-688-06141-9 Subj: Concepts. Format, unusual.

Round trip ill. by author. Greenwillow, 1983. ISBN 0-688-01781-9 Subj: Activities – traveling. City.

The trek ill. by author. Greenwillow, 1985. ISBN 0-688-04799-8 Subj: Activities – walking. Animals. Games. Imagination.

Two bear cubs ill. by author. Greenwillow, 1982. Subj: Animals – bears. Behavior – lost. Family life – mothers.

When you were a baby ill. by author. Greenwillow, 1982. Subj: Activities. Behavior – growing up.

Where can it be? ill. by author. Greenwillow, 1986. ISBN 0-688-05246-0 Subj: Behavior – losing things. Format, unusual – toy and movable books.

Jonasson, Dianne. *Tuan* (Boholm-Olsson, Eva)

Jones, Chuck. *William the backwards skunk* ill. by author. Crown, 1987. ISBN 0-517-56063-1 Subj: Animals. Behavior – imitation. Forest, woods.

Jones, Harold. *Tales from Æsop* (Æsop)

Tales to tell ill. by author. Greenwillow, 1985. ISBN 0-688-04000-4 Subj: Folk and fairy tales.

There and back again ill. by author. Atheneum, 1977. Subj: Toys.

Jones, Hettie. *The trees stand shining: poetry of the North American Indians* ill. by Robert Andrew Parker. Dial Pr., 1971. Subj: Indians of North America. Poetry, rhyme.

Jones, Jessie Mae Orton. *A little child: the Christmas miracle told in Bible verses* ill. by Elizabeth Orton Jones. Viking, 1946. Subj: Holidays – Christmas. Religion.

Small rain: verses from the Bible ill. by Elizabeth Orton Jones. Viking, 1943. Subj: Caldecott award honor book. Poetry, rhyme. Religion.

This is the way: prayers and precepts from world religions ill. by Elizabeth Orton Jones. Viking, 1951. Subj: Religion.

Jones, Malcolm. *Jump!* (Harris, Joel Chandler)

Jones, Maurice. *I'm going on a dragon hunt* ill. by Charlotte Firmin. Four Winds Pr., 1987. ISBN 0-02-748000-3 Subj: Dragons. Sports – hunting.

Jones, Olive. *A treasure box of fairy tales: Hansel and Gretel; Rapunzel; Jack and the bean stalk; and Aladdin* ill. by Francesca Crespi. Dial Pr., 1984. Four books boxed together. Subj: Folk and fairy tales.

Jones, Penelope. *I didn't want to be nice* ill. by Rosalie Orlando. Bradbury Pr., 1977. Subj: Animals – squirrels. Birthdays. Parties.

I'm not moving! ill. by Amy Aitken. Bradbury Pr., 1980. Subj: Family life. Moving.

Jones, Rebecca C. *The biggest (and best) flag that ever flew* ill. by Charles Geer. Cornell Maritime Pr., 1988. ISBN 0-317-67910-4 Subj: U.S. history. War.

The biggest, meanest, ugliest dog in the whole wide world ill. by Wendy Watson. Macmillan, 1982. Subj: Animals – dogs. Character traits – meanness. Friendship.

Jong, David Cornel De see DeJong, David Cornel

Jong, Meindert De see DeJong, Meindert

Joosse, Barbara M. *Better with two* ill. by Catherine Stock. Harper, 1988. ISBN 0-06-023077-0 Subj: Animals – dogs. Death. Pets.

Fourth of July ill. by Emily Arnold McCully. Knopf, 1985. ISBN 0-394-95195-6 Subj: Behavior – growing up. Holidays – Fourth of July. Parades.

Jam day ill. by Emily Arnold McCully. Harper, 1987. ISBN 0-06-023097-5 Subj: Family life. Family life – grandparents.

Spiders in the fruit cellar ill. by Kay Chorao. Knopf, 1983. Subj: Emotions – fear. Spiders.

The thinking place ill. by Kay Chorao. Knopf, 1982. Subj: Behavior – misbehavior. Imagination – imaginary friends.

Jordan, Helene J. *Seeds of wind and water* ill. by Nils Hogner. Crowell, 1962. Subj: Plants.

Jordan, June. *Kimako's story* ill. by Kay Burford. Houghton, 1981. ISBN 0-395-31604-9 Subj: Animals – dogs. City. Family life. Pets.

Joslin, Sesyle. *Baby elephant and the secret wishes* ill. by Leonard Weisgard. Harcourt, 1962. Subj: Animals – elephants. Holidays – Christmas.

Baby elephant goes to China ill. by Leonard Weisgard. Harcourt, 1963. Subj: Animals – elephants. Foreign languages. Sea and seashore.

Baby elephant's trunk ill. by Leonard Weisgard. Harcourt, 1961. Subj: Animals – elephants. Foreign lands – France. Foreign languages.

Brave Baby Elephant ill. by Leonard Weisgard. Harcourt, 1960. Subj: Animals – elephants. Bedtime.

Dear dragon: and other useful letter forms for young ladies and gentlemen engaged in everyday correspondence ill. by Irene Haas. Harcourt, 1962. Subj: Activities – writing. Communication. Dragons. Etiquette. Humor.

Señor Baby Elephant, the pirate ill. by Leonard Weisgard. Harcourt, 1962. Subj: Animals – elephants. Foreign languages. Pirates.

What do you do, dear? ill. by Maurice Sendak. Addison-Wesley, 1961. Subj: Etiquette. Humor.

What do you say, dear? ill. by Maurice Sendak. Addison-Wesley, 1958. Subj: Caldecott award honor book. Etiquette. Humor.

Joyce, Irma. *Never talk to strangers* ill. by George Buckett. Golden Pr., 1967. Subj: Behavior – talking to strangers. Humor. Safety.

Joyce, James. *The cat and the devil* ill. by Richard Erdoes. Dodd, 1965. Subj: Behavior – trickery. Devil.

Joyce, William. *Dinosaur Bob: and his adventures with the family Lazardo* ill. by author. Harper, 1988. ISBN 0-06-023047-9 Subj: Dinosaurs. Pets.

George shrinks ill. by author. Harper, 1985. ISBN 0-06-023071-1 Subj: Activities – baby-sitting. Concepts – size. Family life.

Joyner, Jerry. *Thirteen* (Charlip, Remy)

Jüchen, Aurel von. *The Holy Night: the story of the first Christmas* tr. from German by Cornelia Schaeffer; ill. by Celestino Piatti. Atheneum, 1968. Subj: Holidays – Christmas. Religion.

Jukes, Mavis. *Like Jake and me* ill. by Lloyd Bloom. Knopf, 1984. Subj: Divorce. Family life.

Justice, Jennifer. *The tiger* ill. by Graham Allen. Watts, 1979. Subj: Animals – tigers. Science.

Kahl, Virginia. *Away went Wolfgang* ill. by author. Scribner's, 1954. Subj: Animals – dogs. Foreign lands – Austria.

The Baron's booty ill. by author. Scribner's, 1963. Subj: Middle ages. Poetry, rhyme. Royalty.

Droopsi ill. by author. Scribner's, 1958 Subj: Foreign lands – Germany. Music.

The Duchess bakes a cake ill. by author. Scribner's, 1955. Subj: Activities – cooking. Food. Middle ages. Poetry, rhyme. Royalty.

Giants, indeed! ill. by author. Scribner's, 1974. Subj: Giants. Monsters.

Gunhilde and the Halloween spell ill. by author. Scribner's, 1975. Subj: Holidays – Halloween. Middle ages. Poetry, rhyme. Royalty. Witches.

Gunhilde's Christmas booke ill. by author. Scribner's, 1972. Subj: Holidays – Christmas. Middle ages. Music. Poetry, rhyme. Royalty.

The habits of rabbits ill. by author. Scribner's, 1957. Subj: Animals – rabbits. Middle ages. Pets. Poetry, rhyme. Royalty.

Here is Henri! (Vacheron, Edith)

How do you hide a monster? ill. by author. Scribner's, 1971. Subj: Monsters. Poetry, rhyme. Sports – hunting.

Maxie ill. by author. Scribner's, 1956. Subj: Animals – dogs. Character traits – perseverance. Foreign lands – Germany. Old age.

The perfect pancake ill. by author. Scribner's, 1960. Subj: Character traits – selfishness. Food. Poetry, rhyme.

Plum pudding for Christmas ill. by author. Scribner's, 1956. Subj: Food. Holidays – Christmas. Poetry, rhyme. Royalty.

Whose cat is that? ill. by author. Scribner's, 1979. Subj: Animals – cats. Cumulative tales.

Kahn, Joan. *Hi, Jock, run around the block* ill. by Whitney Darrow, Jr. Harper, 1978. Subj: City. Poetry, rhyme.

Seesaw ill. by Crosby Newell Bonsall. Harper, 1964. Subj: Games. Toys.

Kahn, Michèle. *My everyday Spanish word book* tr. from French by Michael Mahler and Gwen Marsh; ill. by Benvenuti. Barron's, 1982. Subj: Foreign languages.

Kahng, Kim. *The loathsome dragon* (Wiesner, David)

Kalan, Robert. *Blue sea* ill. by Donald Crews. Greenwillow, 1979. Subj: Concepts – size. Fish.

Jump, frog, jump! ill. by Byron Barton. Greenwillow, 1981. Subj: Cumulative tales. Frogs and toads.

Rain ill. by Donald Crews. Greenwillow, 1978. Subj: Weather – rain.

Kalas, Klaus. *The beaver family book* (Kalas, Sybille)

Kalas, Sybille. *The beaver family book* by Sybille and Klaus Kalas; photos. by Sybille Kalas; tr. by Patricia Crampton. Picture Book Studio, 1987. ISBN 0-88708-050-2 Subj: Animals – beavers. Science.

The goose family book tr. by Patricia Crampton; preface by Konrad Lorenz; ill. with photos. Picture Book Studio, 1986. Tr. of Das gänse-kind-er-buch. ISBN 0-88708-019-7 Subj: Birds – geese.

The penguin family book (Somme, Lauritz)

Kaldhol, Marit. *Goodbye Rune* tr. by Michael Crosby-Jones; adapt. by Catherine Maggs; ill. by Wenche Øyen. Kane/Miller, 1987. Tr. of Farvel, Rune. ISBN 0-916291-11-1 Subj: Death. Emotions – sadness. Friendship.

Kalman, Benjamin. *Animals in danger: poems from no man's valley* ill. by Cécile Curtis and Michael Jupp. Random House, 1982. Subj: Animals. Ecology. Poetry, rhyme.

Kalman, Maira. *Hey Willy, see the pyramids!* ill. by author. Viking, 1988. ISBN 0-670-82163-2 Subj: Bedtime. Family life – sisters. Imagination.

Kamen, Gloria. *The ringdoves: from the fables of Bidpai* ill. by adapt. Atheneum, 1988. ISBN 0-689-31312-8 Subj: Animals. Friendship. Sports – hunting.

Kanagy, Ruth A. *The park bench* (Takeshita, Fumiko)

Kanao, Keiko. *Kitten up a tree* ill. by author. Knopf, 1987. ISBN 0-394-88817-0 Subj: Animals – cats. Character traits – curiosity. Family life – mothers.

Kandell, Alice. *Max, the music-maker* (Stecher, Miriam B.)

Kandoian, Ellen. *Under the sun* ill. by author. Dodd, 1987. ISBN 0-396-09059-1 Subj: Morning. Night. Sun.

Kane, Henry B. *Wings, legs, or fins* photos. and ill. by author. Knopf, 1966. Subj: Animals. Science.

Kani, Saru. *The monkey and the crab* (Horio, Seishi)

Kantor, MacKinlay. *The preposterous week* ill. by Kurt Wiese. Putnam's, 1942. Subj: Food. Humor.

Kantrowitz, Mildred. *I wonder if Herbie's home yet* ill. by Tony DeLuna. Parents, 1971. Subj: Friendship.

When Violet died ill. by Emily Arnold McCully. Parents, 1973. Subj: Birds. Death.

Willy Bear ill. by Nancy Winslow Parker. Parents, 1976. Subj: School. Sleep. Toys – teddy bears.

Kaplan, Boche. *Sweet Betsy from Pike* (Abisch, Roz)

Kapp, Paul. *Cock-a-doodle-doo! Cock-a-doodle-dandy!* ill. by Anita Lobel. Harper, 1966. Subj: Music. Songs.

Kark, Nina Mary Maby *see* Bawden, Nina

Karlin, Nurit. *The blue frog* ill. by author. Coward, 1983. Subj: Character traits – being different. Frogs and toads.

The dream factory ill. by author. Lippincott, 1988. ISBN 0-397-32212-7 Subj: Dreams. Sleep.

The tooth witch ill. by author. Lippincott, 1985. ISBN 0-397-32120-1 Subj: Character traits – kindness. Fairies. Witches.

A train for the king ill. by author. Coward, 1983. Subj: Royalty. Self-concept.

Karlinsky, Ruth Schild. *My first book of Mitzvos* photos. by Isaiah Karlinsky. Feldheim, 1986. ISBN 0-87306-388-0 Subj: Jewish culture. Religion.

Karn, George. *Circus big and small* ill. by author. Little, 1986. ISBN 0-316-30342-9 Subj: Circus. Concepts – opposites. Format, unusual – board books.

Circus colors ill. by author. Little, 1986. ISBN 0-316-30343-7 Subj: Circus. Concepts – color. Format, unusual – board books.

Karsunke, Yaak. *Hello Irina* (Blech, Dietlind)

Kasza, Keiko. *The pigs' picnic* ill. by author. Putnam's, 1988. ISBN 0-399-21543-3 Subj: Activities – picnicking. Animals – pigs. Character traits – appearance.

The wolf's chicken stew ill. by author. Putnam's, 1987. ISBN 0-399-21400-3 Subj: Animals – wolves. Birds – chickens. Character traits – generosity. Food.

Katz, Bobbi. *Tick-tock, let's read the clock* ill. by Carol Nicklaus. Random, 1988. ISBN 0-394-89399-9 Subj: Clocks. Poetry, rhyme. Time.

Kauffman, Lois. *What's that noise?* ill. by Allan Eitzen. Lothrop, 1965. Subj: Family life – fathers. Night. Noise, sounds.

Kaufman, Curt. *Hotel boy* by Curt and Gita Kaufman; photos. by Curt Kaufman. Atheneum, 1987. ISBN 0-689-31287-3 Subj: Activities. City. Ethnic groups in the U.S. – Afro-Americans. Family life.

Rajesh by Curt and Gita Kaufman; photos. by Curt Kaufman. Atheneum, 1985. ISBN 0-689-31074-9 Subj: Handicaps. School.

Kaufman, Gita. *Hotel boy* (Kaufman, Curt)

Rajesh (Kaufman, Curt)

Kaufmann, John. *Birds are flying* ill. by author. Crowell, 1979. Subj: Birds. Science.

Flying giants of long ago ill. by author. Crowell, 1984. Subj: Activities – flying. Animals. Birds. Insects. Science.

Kaune, Merriman B. *My own little house* ill. by author. Follett, 1957. Subj: Houses.

Kavanaugh, James J. *The crooked angel* ill. by Elaine Havelock. Nash, 1970. Subj: Angels. Poetry, rhyme.

Kay, Helen. *An egg is for wishing* ill. by Yaroslava. Abelard-Schuman, 1966. Subj: Behavior – animals, dislike of. Behavior – wishing. Eggs. Foreign lands – Ukraine. Holidays – Easter.

One mitten Lewis ill. by Kurt Werth. Lothrop, 1955. Subj: Behavior – losing things. Clothing.

A stocking for a kitten ill. by Yaroslava. Abelard-Schuman, 1965. Subj: Animals – cats. Family life – grandmothers.

Kay, Ormonde De *see* De Kay, Ormonde

Kaye, Geraldine. *The sea monkey: a picture story from Malaysia* ill. by Gay Galsworthy. Collins-World, 1968. Subj: Animals – monkeys. Foreign lands – Malaysia.

Keats, Ezra Jack. *Apartment 3* ill. by author. Macmillan, 1971. Subj: City. Ethnic groups in the U.S. – Afro-Americans. Family life. Handicaps – blindness. Music. Senses – seeing.

Clementina's cactus ill. by author. Viking, 1983. Subj: Desert. Weather – storms. Wordless.

Dreams ill. by author. Macmillan, 1974. Subj: Dreams. Ethnic groups in the U.S. – Afro-Americans. Imagination. Night. Sleep.

God is in the mountain ill. by author. Holt, 1966. Subj: Religion.

Goggles ill. by author. Macmillan, 1969. Subj: Behavior – bullying. Caldecott award honor book. City. Ethnic groups in the U.S. – Afro-Americans. Problem solving.

Hi, cat! ill. by author. Macmillan, 1970. Subj: Animals – cats. City. Ethnic groups in the U.S. – Afro-Americans.

Jennie's hat ill. by author. Harper, 1966. Subj: Behavior – dissatisfaction. Character traits – kindness to animals. Clothing.

John Henry ill. by author. Harper, 1965. Subj: Character traits – perseverance. Character traits – pride. Ethnic groups in the U.S. – Afro-Americans. Folk and fairy tales.

Kitten for a day ill. by author. Watts, 1974. Subj: Animals – cats. Animals – dogs. Wordless.

A letter to Amy ill. by author. Harper, 1968. Subj: Ethnic groups in the U.S. – Afro-Americans. Friendship. Letters. Parties. Weather – rain. Weather – wind.

The little drummer boy ill. by author. Macmillan, 1968. Words and music by Katherine Davis, Henry Onorati and Harry Simeonne. Subj: Holidays – Christmas. Music. Religion. Songs.

Louie ill. by author. Greenwillow, 1975. Subj: Character traits – shyness. Ethnic groups in the U.S. – Afro-Americans. Puppets.

Louie's search ill. by author. Four Winds Pr., 1980. Subj: Behavior – needing someone. Family life.

Maggie and the pirate ill. by author. Four Winds Pr., 1979. Subj: Death. Pets. Pirates.

My dog is lost! ill. by Ezra Jack Keats. Crowell, 1960. Subj: Animals – dogs. Behavior – lost. Careers – police officers. Ethnic groups in the U.S. Ethnic groups in the U.S. – Puerto Rican-Americans. Foreign languages.

Pet show! ill. by author. Macmillan, 1972. Subj: Animals. Ethnic groups in the U.S. – Afro-Americans. Pets.

Peter's chair ill. by author. Harper, 1967. Subj: Babies. Behavior – sharing. Ethnic groups in the U.S. – Afro-Americans. Family life. Friendship. Self-concept.

Psst, doggie ill. by author. Watts, 1973. Subj: Animals – cats. Animals – dogs. Wordless.

Regards to the man in the moon ill. by author. Four Winds Pr., 1981. Subj: Imagination. Space and space ships.

Skates ill. by author. Watts, 1972. Subj: Activities – playing. Animals – dogs. Ethnic groups in the U.S. – Afro-Americans. Humor. Wordless.

The snowy day ill. by author. Viking, 1962. Subj: Activities – playing. Caldecott award book. Ethnic groups in the U.S. – Afro-Americans. Seasons – winter. Weather – snow.

The trip ill. by author. Greenwillow, 1978. Subj: Emotions – loneliness. Ethnic groups in the U.S. – Afro-Americans. Holidays – Halloween. Imagination. Moving.

Whistle for Willie ill. by author. Viking, 1964. Subj: Activities – whistling. Animals – dogs. Ethnic groups in the U.S. – Afro-Americans. Problem solving. Self-concept.

Keenan, Martha. *The mannerly adventures of Little Mouse* ill. by Meri Shardin. Crown, 1977. Subj: Animals – mice. Etiquette.

Keenen, George. *The preposterous week* ill. by Stanley Mack. Dial Pr., 1971. ISBN 0-8037-7072-3 Subj: Behavior – losing things. Character traits – foolishness. Days of the week, months of the year. Humor. Problem solving.

Keeping, Charles. *Alfie finds the other side of the world* ill. by author. Watts, 1968. Subj: City. Foreign lands – England. Rivers. Weather – fog.

Joseph's yard ill. by author. Watts, 1969. Subj: Activities – gardening. Poverty.

Molly o' the moors: the story of a pony ill. by author. Collins, 1966. Subj: Animals – horses. Old age.

Through the window ill. by author. Watts, 1970. Subj: City. Foreign lands – England.

Willie's fire-engine ill. by author. Oxford Univ. Pr., 1980. Subj: Activities – playing. Careers – firefighters. Imagination.

Keeshan, Robert. *She loves me, she loves me not* ill. by Maurice Sendak. Harper, 1963. Subj: Games. Holidays – Valentine's Day. Mythical creatures.

Kehoe, Michael. *Road closed* photos. by author. Carolrhoda, 1982. Subj: Roads.

The rock quarry book photos. by author. Carolrhoda, 1981. Subj: Rocks.

Keigwin, R. P. *Thumbelina* (Andersen, H. C. (Hans Christian))

The ugly duckling (Andersen, H. C. (Hans Christian))

Keith, Eros. *Bedita's bad day* ill. by author. Harper, 1973. Subj: Behavior – bad day. Witches.

Nancy's backyard ill. by author. Harper, 1973. Subj: Dreams. Weather – rain.

Rrra-ah ill. by author. Bradbury Pr., 1969. Subj: Frogs and toads. Pets.

Keller, Beverly. *Fiona's bee* ill. by Diane Paterson. Coward, 1975. Subj: Character traits – shyness. Insects – bees.

Pimm's place ill. by Jacqueline Chwast. Coward, 1978. Subj: Behavior – solitude. Character traits – bravery. Emotions – fear.

When mother got the flu ill. by Maxie Chambliss. Coward, 1984. Subj: Behavior – misbehavior. Family life – mothers. Illness.

Keller, Charles. *Giggle puss: pet jokes for kids* ill. by Paul Coker, Jr. Prentice-Hall, 1977. Subj: Humor. Pets. Riddles.

The nutty joke book ill. by Jean-Claude Suarès. Prentice-Hall, 1978. Subj: Humor. Riddles.

School daze ill. by Sam Q. Weissman. Prentice-Hall, 1979. Subj: Humor. Riddles.

Keller, Holly. *A bear for Christmas* ill. by author. Greenwillow, 1986. ISBN 0-688-05989-9 Subj: Behavior – misbehavior. Family life. Holidays – Christmas. Toys – teddy bears.

Cromwell's glasses ill. by author. Greenwillow, 1982. Subj: Animals – rabbits. Family life. Glasses. Senses – seeing.

Geraldine's big snow ill. by author. Greenwillow, 1988. ISBN 0-688-07514-2 Subj: Animals – pigs. Weather – snow.

Geraldine's blanket ill. by author. Greenwillow, 1984. ISBN 0-688-02540-4 Subj: Animals – pigs. Family life. Toys – dolls.

Goodbye, Max ill. by author. Greenwillow, 1987. ISBN 0-688-06562-7 Subj: Animals – dogs. Death. Pets.

Henry's Fourth of July ill. by author. Greenwillow, 1985. ISBN 0-688-04013-6 Subj: Activities – picnicking. Animals – possums. Holidays – Fourth of July.

Lizzie's invitation ill. by author. Greenwillow, 1987. ISBN 0-688-06125-7 Subj: Birthdays. Emotions. Friendship.

Ten sleepy sheep ill. by author. Greenwillow, 1983. Subj: Bedtime.

Too big ill. by author. Greenwillow, 1983. Subj: Animals. Sibling rivalry.

When Francie was sick ill. by author. Greenwillow, 1985. ISBN 0-688-05434-X Subj: Family life — mothers. Illness.

Will it rain? ill. by author. Greenwillow, 1984. Subj: Animals. Weather — rain. Weather — storms.

Keller, Irene. *Benjamin Rabbit and the stranger danger* ill. by Dick Keller. Dodd, 1985. ISBN 0-396-08655-1 Subj: Animals — rabbits. Behavior — talking to strangers. School.

The Thingumajig book of manners ill. by Dick Keller. Children's Pr., 1981. Subj: Character traits — appearance. Etiquette.

Keller, John G. *Krispin's fair* ill. by Ed Emberley. Little, 1976. Subj: Etiquette. Friendship.

Kelley, Anne. *Daisy's discovery* ill. by Metin Salih. Barron's, 1985. ISBN 0-8120-5676-0 Subj: Animals — dogs. Behavior — losing things. Birthdays. Family life.

Kelley, Emily. *April Fools' Day* ill. by C. A. Nobens. Carolrhoda, 1983. Subj: Holidays — April Fools' Day.

Kelley, True. *Look, baby! Listen, baby! Do, baby!* ill. by author. Dutton, 1987. ISBN 0-525-44320-7 Subj: Activities. Babies. Noise, sounds.

A valentine for Fuzzboom ill. by author. Houghton, 1981. Subj: Animals — rabbits. Holidays — Valentine's Day.

Kellogg, Stephen *see* Kellogg, Steven

Kellogg, Steven. *Aster Aardvark's alphabet adventures* ill. by author. Morrow, 1987. ISBN 0-688-07257-7 Subj: ABC books. Animals. Animals — aardvarks. Birds.

Best friends ill. by author. Dial Pr., 1986. ISBN 0-8037-0101-2 Subj: Animals — dogs. Emotions — envy, jealousy. Friendship.

Can I keep him? ill. by author. Dial Pr., 1971. Subj: Family life. Pets.

Chicken Little ill. by author. Morrow, 1985. ISBN 0-688-05691-1 Subj: Animals. Behavior — trickery. Birds — chickens. Folk and fairy tales.

The island of the skog ill. by author. Dial Pr., 1973. Subj: Animals — mice. Boats, ships. Islands. Monsters.

Johnny Appleseed: a tall tale ill. by author. Morrow, 1988. ISBN 0-688-06417-5 Subj: Activities — traveling. Folk and fairy tales. Trees. U.S. history.

The mysterious tadpole ill. by author. Dial Pr., 1977. Subj: Frogs and toads. Monsters. Pets.

The mystery of the flying orange pumpkin ill. by author. Dial Pr., 1980. Subj: Holidays — Halloween.

The mystery of the magic green ball ill. by author. Dial Pr., 1978. Subj: Behavior — losing things. Gypsies. Toys — balls.

The mystery of the missing red mitten ill. by author. Dial Pr., 1974. Subj: Behavior — losing things. Problem solving. Snowmen.

The mystery of the stolen blue paint ill. by author. Dial Pr., 1982. Subj: Problem solving.

Pecos Bill ill. by adapt. Morrow, 1986. ISBN 0-688-05872-8 Subj: Cowboys. Folk and fairy tales. U.S. history.

Pinkerton, behave! ill. by author. Dial Pr., 1979. Subj: Animals — dogs.

Prehistoric Pinkerton ill. by author. Dial Pr., 1987. ISBN 0-8037-0323-6 Subj: Animals — dogs. Behavior — misbehavior. Dinosaurs. Museums.

Ralph's secret weapon ill. by author. Dial Pr., 1983. Subj: Activities — vacationing. Imagination.

A rose for Pinkerton ill. by author. Dial Pr., 1981. Subj: Animals — cats. Animals — dogs. Behavior — imitation.

Tallyho, Pinkerton! ill. by author. Dial Pr., 1982. Subj: Animals — cats. Animals — dogs. Sports — hunting.

Kelsey, Joan Marshall *see* Grant, Joan

Kemp, Anthea. *Mr. Percy's magic greenhouse* ill. by Penny Metcalfe. David & Charles, 1988. ISBN 0-575-03870-5 Subj: Activities — gardening. Animals. Jungle. Magic.

Kemp, Moira. *The firebird*

Kennedy, Jimmy. *The teddy bears' picnic* ill. by Alexandra Day. Green Tiger Pr., 1983. Subj: Activities — picnicking. Toys — teddy bears.

The teddy bears' picnic ill. by Prue Theobalds. Harper, 1987. ISBN 0-87226-153-0 Subj: Activities — picnicking. Poetry, rhyme. Toys — teddy bears.

Kennedy, Richard. *The contests at Cowlick* ill. by Marc Simont. Little, 1975. Subj: Character traits — cleverness. Cowboys. Humor.

The leprechaun's story ill. by Marcia Sewall. Dutton, 1979. Subj: Elves and little people. Foreign lands — Ireland.

The lost kingdom of Karnica ill. by Uri Shulevitz. Sierra Club, 1979. ISBN 0-684-16164-8 Subj: Behavior — greed. Royalty.

The porcelain man ill. by Marcia Sewall. Little, 1976. Subj: Magic.

Kent, Jack. *The caterpillar and the polliwog* ill. by author. Prentice-Hall, 1982. Subj: Frogs and toads. Insects — butterflies, caterpillars.

The Christmas piñata ill. by author. Parents, 1975. Subj: Foreign lands — Mexico. Holidays — Christmas.

Clotilda ill. by author. Random House, 1978. Subj: Character traits — kindness. Fairies.

The egg book ill. by author. Macmillan, 1975. Subj: Eggs. Wordless.

Hoddy doddy ill. by author. Greenwillow, 1979. Subj: Foreign lands — Denmark. Humor.

Jack Kent's happy-ever-after book ill. by author. Random House, 1976. Subj: Folk and fairy tales.

Jack Kent's hokus pokus bedtime book ill. by author. Random House, 1979. Subj: Folk and fairy tales.

Joey ill. by author. Prentice-Hall, 1984. Subj: Activities – playing. Animals – kangaroos. Family life – mothers.

Joey runs away ill. by author. Prentice-Hall, 1985. ISBN 0-13-510462-9 Subj: Animals. Animals – kangaroos. Behavior – running away. Behavior – seeking better things. Family life.

Knee-high Nina ill. by author. Doubleday, 1981. Subj: Behavior – wishing.

Little Peep ill. by author. Prentice-Hall, 1981. Subj: Animals. Birds – chickens. Farms.

The once-upon-a-time dragon ill. by author. Harcourt, 1982. Subj: Bedtime. Behavior – imitation. Dragons.

Piggy Bank Gonzalez ill. by author. Parents, 1979. Subj: Animals – pigs. Money. Toys.

Round Robin ill. by author. Prentice-Hall, 1982. Subj: Birds – robins.

The scribble monster ill. by author. Harcourt, 1981. Subj: Behavior – misbehavior.

Silly goose ill. by author. Prentice-Hall, 1983. Subj: Animals – foxes. Birds – geese.

Socks for supper ill. by author. Parents, 1978. Subj: Friendship.

There's no such thing as a dragon ill. by author. Golden Pr., 1975. Subj: Behavior – needing someone. Dragons.

Kent, Lorna. *No, no, Charlie Rascal!* ill. by author. Viking, 1989. ISBN 0-670-82512-3 Subj: Animals – cats. Behavior – misbehavior. Format, unusual.

Kepes, Juliet. *Cock-a-doodle-doo* ill. by author. Pantheon, 1978. Subj: Animals – tigers. Birds – chickens.

Five little monkeys ill. by author. Houghton, 1952. Subj: Animals. Animals – monkeys. Caldecott award honor book.

Frogs, merry ill. by author. Pantheon, 1961. Subj: Frogs and toads. Hibernation.

Lady bird, quickly ill. by author. Little, 1964. Subj: Insects – ladybugs. Nursery rhymes.

Run little monkeys, run, run, run ill. by author. Pantheon, 1974. Subj: Animals – leopards. Animals – monkeys. Participation.

The seed that peacock planted ill. by author. Little, 1967. Subj: Birds – peacocks, peahens. Magic. Music. Plants.

The story of a bragging duck ill. by author. Houghton, 1983. Subj: Behavior – boasting. Birds – ducks. Character traits – vanity.

Ker Wilson, Barbara *see* Wilson, Barbara

Kerr, Judith. *Mog and bunny* ill. by author. Knopf, 1989. ISBN 0-394-82249-8 Subj: Animals – cats. Family life. Pets. Toys.

Mog's Christmas ill. by author. Collins-World, 1976. Subj: Animals – cats. Holidays – Christmas.

Kerrigan, Anthony. *Mother Goose in Spanish* (Mother Goose)

Kerry, Lois *see* Duncan, Lois

Kesselman, Judi R. *I can use tools* by Judi R. Kesselman and Franklynn Peterson; ill. by Tomás Gonzales. Elsevier Nelson, 1981. Subj: Tools.

Kesselman, Judi Rosenthal *see* Kesselman, Judi R.

Kesselman, Wendy. *Angelita* ill. by Norma Holt. Hill and Wang, 1970. Subj: City. Emotions – loneliness. Ethnic groups in the U.S. Ethnic groups in the U.S. – Puerto Rican-Americans.

Emma ill. by Barbara Cooney. Doubleday, 1980. Subj: Art. Emotions – loneliness.

There's a train going by my window ill. by Tony Chen. Doubleday, 1982. Subj: Activities – traveling.

Time for Jody ill. by Gerald Dumas. Harper, 1975. Subj: Animals – groundhogs. Hibernation. Holidays – Groundhog Day. Seasons – spring.

Kessler, Ethel. *All aboard the train* by Ethel and Leonard P. Kessler; ill. by authors. Doubleday, 1964. Subj: Trains.

Are there hippos on the farm? by Ethel and Leonard P. Kessler; ill. by authors. Simon & Schuster, 1987. ISBN 0-671-62066-5 Subj: Animals. Farms. Format, unusual – board books.

Do baby bears sit in chairs? by Ethel and Leonard P. Kessler; ill. by authors. Doubleday, 1961. Subj: Animals. Poetry, rhyme.

Grandpa Witch and the magic doobelator by Ethel and Leonard P. Kessler; ill. by Leonard P. Kessler. Macmillan, 1981. Subj: Family life – grandfathers. Holidays – Halloween. Witches.

Is there an elephant in your kitchen? by Ethel and Leonard P. Kessler; ill. by authors. Simon & Schuster, 1987. ISBN 0-671-62065-7 Subj: Animals. Format, unusual – board books. Houses.

Night story by Ethel and Leonard P. Kessler; ill. by Leonard P. Kessler. Macmillan, 1981. Subj: Activities – working. Night. Trucks.

Two, four, six, eight: a book about legs by Ethel and Leonard P. Kessler; ill. by Leonard P. Kessler. Dodd, 1980. Subj: Counting.

What's inside the box? ill. by Leonard P. Kessler. Dodd, 1978. Subj: Animals.

Kessler, Jascha. *Rose of Mother-of-Pearl* (Olujic, Grozdana)

Kessler, Leonard P. *All aboard the train* (Kessler, Ethel)

Are there hippos on the farm? (Kessler, Ethel)

Are we lost, daddy? ill. by author. Grosset, 1967. Subj: Activities – vacationing. Behavior – lost. Family life. Family life – fathers.

The big mile race ill. by author. Greenwillow, 1983. Subj: Animals. Sports – racing.

Do baby bears sit in chairs? (Kessler, Ethel)

Do you have any carrots? ill. by Lori Pierson. Garrard, 1979. Subj: Animals. Food.

Grandpa Witch and the magic doobelator (Kessler, Ethel)

Here comes the strikeout ill. by author. Harper, 1965. Subj: Sports – baseball.

Is there an elephant in your kitchen? (Kessler, Ethel)

Kick, pass, and run ill. by author. Harper, 1966. Subj: Animals. Sports – football.

Last one in is a rotten egg ill. by author. Harper, 1969. Subj: Behavior – bullying. Sports – swimming.

Mr. Pine's mixed-up signs ill. by author. Grosset, 1961. Subj: Glasses. Senses – seeing.

Mr. Pine's purple house ill. by author. Grosset, 1965. Subj: Activities – painting. Concepts – color.

Mrs. Pine takes a trip ill. by author. Grosset, 1966. Subj: Activities – traveling.

Night story (Kessler, Ethel)

Old Turtle's baseball stories ill. by author. Greenwillow, 1982. Subj: Sports – baseball.

Old Turtle's winter games ill. by author. Greenwillow, 1983. Subj: Animals. Seasons – winter. Sports.

On your mark, get set, go! The first all-animal Olympics ill. by author. Harper, 1972. Subj: Animals. Sports – Olympics.

The pirates' adventure on Spooky Island ill. by author. Garrard, 1979. Subj: Islands. Pirates.

Riddles that rhyme for Halloween time ill. by author. Garrard, 1978. Subj: Holidays – Halloween. Poetry, rhyme. Riddles.

The silly Mother Goose ill. by author. Garrard, 1980. Subj: Nursery rhymes.

Soup for the king ill. by author. Grosset, 1969. Subj: Careers – bakers. Food. Royalty.

Super bowl ill. by author. Greenwillow, 1980. Subj: Animals. Sports – football.

Two, four, six, eight (Kessler, Ethel)

Key, Francis Scott. *The Star-Spangled Banner* ill. by Paul Galdone. Crowell, 1966. Subj: Songs. U.S. history.

The Star-Spangled Banner ill. by Peter Spier. Doubleday, 1973. Subj: Songs. U.S. history.

Keyser, Marcia. *Roger on his own* ill. by Diane Dawson. Crown, 1982. Subj: Animals – dogs. Behavior – solitude.

Keyworth, C. L. *New day* ill. by Carolyn Bracken. Morrow, 1986. ISBN 0-688-05922-8 Subj: Moving.

Khalsa, Dayal Kaur. *I want a dog* ill. by author. Crown, 1987. ISBN 0-517-56532-3 Subj: Animals – dogs. Behavior – growing up. Family life.

My family vacation ill. by author. Potter, 1988. ISBN 0-517-56697-4 Subj: Activities – vacationing. Family life.

Sleepers ill. by author. Crown, 1988. ISBN 0-517-56917-5 Subj: Bedtime. Sleep.

Tales of a gambling grandma ill. by author. Crown, 1986. ISBN 0-517-56137-9 Subj: Family life – grandmothers. Games.

Kherdian, David. *The animal* ill. by Nonny Hogrogian. Knopf, 1984. Subj: Animals.

Country cat, city cat ill. by Nonny Hogrogian. Four Winds Pr., 1978. Subj: Animals – cats. Poetry, rhyme.

The dog writes on the window with his nose, and other poems

If dragon flies made honey

Right now ill. by Nonny Hogrogian. Knopf, 1983. Subj: Emotions.

Kherdian, Nonny Hogrogian *see* Hogrogian, Nonny

Kibbey, Marsha. *My grammy* ill. by Karen Ritz. Carolrhoda Books, 1988. ISBN 0-87614-328-1 Subj: Character traits – patience. Family life – grandmothers. Illness. Old Age.

Kidd, Bruce. *Hockey showdown* ill. by Leoung O'Young. Lorimer, 1980. Subj: Character traits – meanness. Sports – hockey.

Kightley, Rosalinda. *ABC* ill. by author. Little, 1986. ISBN 0-316-49930-7 Subj: ABC books.

The farmer ill. by author. Macmillan, 1988. ISBN 0-02-750290-2 Subj: Careers – farmers. Farms.

Opposites ill. by author. Little, 1986. ISBN 0-316-49931-5 Subj: Concepts – opposites.

The postman ill. by author. Macmillan, 1988. ISBN 0-02-750270-8 Subj: City. Careers – mail carriers.

Shapes ill. by author. Little, 1986. ISBN 0-316-54005-6 Subj: Concepts – shape.

Killingback, Julia. *Busy Bears at the fire station* ill. by author. Oxford Univ. Pr., 1988. ISBN 0-19-520653-3 Subj: Animals – bears. Careers – firefighters.

Busy Bears' picnic ill. by author. Oxford Univ. Pr., 1988. ISBN 0-19-520654-1 Subj: Activities – picnicking. Animals – bears.

Monday is washing day ill. by author. Morrow, 1985. ISBN 0-688-04077-2 Subj: Activities – working. Animals – bears. Family life.

What time is it, Mrs. Bear? ill. by author. Morrow, 1985. ISBN 0-688-04076-4 Subj: Animals – bears. Family life. Time.

Kilreon, Beth *see* Walker, Barbara K.

Kilroy, Sally. *Animal noises* ill. by author. Four Winds Pr., 1983. Subj: Animals. Format, unusual – board books. Noise, sounds. Wordless.

Babies' bodies ill. by author. Scholastic, 1983. Subj: Anatomy. Babies. Format, unusual – board books.

Babies' homes ill. by author. Scholastic, 1984. ISBN 0-590-07945-X Subj: Format, unusual – board books. Houses.

Babies' outings ill. by author. Scholastic, 1984. ISBN 0-590-07946-8 Subj: Format, unusual – board books.

Babies' zoo ill. by author. Scholastic, 1984. ISBN 0-590-07947-6 Subj: Animals. Format, unusual – board books. Zoos.

Baby colors ill. by author. Scholastic, 1983. Subj: Babies. Concepts – color. Format, unusual – board books.

The baron's hunting party ill. by author. Viking, 1988. ISBN 0-317-69208-9 Subj: Sports – hunting.

Busy babies ill. by author. Scholastic, 1984. ISBN 0-590-07948-4 Subj: Activities. Babies. Format, unusual – board books.

Copycat drawing book ill. by author. Dial Pr., 1981. Subj: Art.

Grandpa's garden ill. by author. Viking, 1986. ISBN 0-670-80338-3 Subj: Activities – gardening. Family life – grandparents.

Market day ill. by author. Viking, 1986. ISBN 0-670-80339-1 Subj: Family life – fathers. Shopping.

Noisy homes ill. by author. Scholastic, 1983. Subj: Format, unusual – board books. Noise, sounds.

On the road ill. by author. Viking, 1986. ISBN 0-670-80337-5 Subj: Activities – traveling. Buses. Family life – mothers.

What a week! ill. by author. Viking, 1986. ISBN 0-670-80336-7 Subj: Family life.

Kimber, Robert. *I am a little cat* (Spanner, Helmut)

Kimmel, Eric A. *Why worry?* ill. by Beth Cannon. Pantheon, 1979. Subj: Insects – crickets. Insects – grasshoppers. Music. Songs.

Kimmel, Margaret Mary. *Magic in the mist* ill. by Trina Schart Hyman. Atheneum, 1975. Subj: Dragons. Magic. Wizards.

Kimura, Yasuko. *Fergus and the sea monster* ill. by author. McGraw-Hill, 1978. Subj: Animals – dogs. Friendship. Monsters. Sea and seashore.

Kines, Pat Decker *see* Tapio, Pat Decker

King, B. A. *The very best Christmas tree* ill. by Michael McCurdy. Godine, 1984. ISBN 0-87923-539-X Subj: Holidays – Christmas. Trees.

King, Christopher. *The boy who ate the moon* ill. by John Wallner. Putnam's, 1988. ISBN 0-399-21459-3 Subj: Activities – flying. Moon.

King, Deborah. *Sirius and Saba* ill. by author. David and Charles, 1982. Subj: Animals – dogs. Islands.

King, Kathey *see* King, Christopher

King, Larry L. *Because of Lozo Brown* ill. by Amy Schwartz. Viking, 1988. ISBN 0-670-81031-2 Subj: Friendship. Imagination. Poetry, rhyme.

King, Patricia. *Mable the whale* ill. by Katherine Evans. Follett, 1958. Subj: Animals – whales.

King-Smith, Dick. *Cuckoobush farm* ill. by Kazuko. Greenwillow, 1988. ISBN 0-688-07681-5 Subj: Farms. Seasons. Twins.

Farmer Bungle forgets ill. by Martin Honeysett. Atheneum, 1987. ISBN 0-689-31370-5 Subj: Behavior – forgetfulness. Farms. Humor.

Kingman, Lee. *Peter's long walk* ill. by Barbara Cooney. Doubleday, 1953. Subj: Activities – walking. Animals. Country. Friendship.

Pierre Pigeon ill. by Arnold E. Bare. Houghton, 1943. Subj: Birds – pigeons. Caldecott award honor book.

Kinkaid, Wyatt E. *see* Jennings, Michael

Kinnell, Galway. *How the alligator missed breakfast* ill. by Lynn Munsinger. Houghton, 1982. Subj: Reptiles – alligators, crocodiles.

Kinney, Jean. *What does the sun do?* ill. by Cle Kinney. W. R. Scott, 1967. Subj: Sun.

Kinsey, Elizabeth *see* Clymer, Eleanor Lowenton

Kipling, Rudyard. *The beginning of the armadillos* ill. by Lorinda Bryan Cauley. Harcourt, 1985. ISBN 0-15-206380-3 Subj: Animals – armadillos.

The beginning of the armadillos ill. by Charles Keeping. Harper, 1983. Subj: Animals – armadillos.

The butterfly that stamped ill. by Alan Baker. Harper, 1983. Subj: Insects – butterflies, caterpillars.

The cat that walked by himself ill. by William Stobbs. Harper, 1983. Subj: Animals – cats.

The crab that played with the sea ill. by Michael Foreman. Harper, 1983. Subj: Crustacea. Sea and seashore.

The elephant's child ill. by Louise Brierley. Harper, 1985. ISBN 0-87226-030-5 Subj: Animals. Animals – elephants. Character traits – curiosity. Foreign lands – Africa.

The elephant's child ill. by Lorinda Bryan Cauley. Harcourt, 1983. Subj: Animals. Animals – elephants. Character traits – curiosity.

The elephant's child ill. by Tim Raglin. Knopf, 1986. ISBN 0-394-88401-9 Subj: Animals. Animals – elephants. Character traits – curiosity. Foreign lands – Africa.

How the camel got his hump ill. by Quentin Blake. Harper, 1985. ISBN 0-87226-029-1 Subj: Animals. Animals – camels. Foreign lands – Africa.

How the leopard got his spots ill. by Caroline Ebborn. Harper, 1986. ISBN 0-87226-072-0 Subj: Animals – leopards.

How the rhinoceros got his skin ill. by Leonard Weisgard. Walker, 1974. Subj: Animals – rhinoceros.

Just so stories ill. by Meg Rutherford. Silver Burdett, 1987. ISBN 0-382-09299-6 Subj: Animals.

The miracle of the mountain ill. by Willi Baum. Addison-Wesley, 1969. Adapted by Aroline Arnett Beecher Leach from The Miracle of Purun Bhagat, by Rudyard Kipling. Subj: Animals. Foreign lands – India. Religion.

The sing-song of old man kangaroo ill. by Michael C. Taylor. Harper, 1986. ISBN 0-87226-073-9 Subj: Animals – kangaroos. Foreign lands – Australia.

Kirk, Barbara. *Grandpa, me and our house in the tree* ill. by author. Macmillan, 1978. Subj: Family life – grandfathers. Houses. Trees.

Kirkpatrick, Rena K. *Look at flowers* ill. by Annabel Milne and Peter Stebbing. Raintree, 1978. Subj: Flowers. Science.

Look at leaves ill. by Annabel Milne and Peter Stebbing. Raintree, 1978. Subj: Plants. Science.

Look at magnets ill. by Ann Knight. Raintree, 1978. Subj: Science.

Look at pond life ill. by Annabel Milne and Peter Stebbing. Raintree, 1978. Subj: Science.

Look at rainbow colors ill. by Anna Barnard. Raintree, 1978. Subj: Concepts – color. Science. Weather – rainbows.

Look at seeds and weeds ill. by Debbie King. Raintree, 1978. Subj: Plants. Science.

Look at trees ill. by Jo Worth and Ann Knight. Raintree, 1978. Subj: Science. Trees.

Look at weather ill. by Janetta Lewin. Raintree, 1978. Subj: Science. Weather.

Kirn, Ann. *Beeswax catches a thief: from a Congo folktale* ill. by author. Norton, 1968. Subj: Animals. Ethnic groups in the U.S. – Afro-Americans.

I spy ill. by author. Norton, 1965. Subj: Birds – owls. Crime.

The tale of a crocodile: from a Congo folktale ill. by author. Norton, 1968. Subj: Animals – rabbits. Fire. Folk and fairy tales. Foreign lands – Africa. Reptiles – alligators, crocodiles.

Kirtland, G. B. *see* Joslin, Sesyle

Kishida, Eriko. *The hippo boat* ill. by Chiyoko Nakatani. Collins, 1964. Subj: Animals – hippopotami. Weather – rain. Zoos.

The lion and the bird's nest ill. by Chiyoko Nakatani. Crowell, 1972. Subj: Animals – lions. Birds. Character traits – helpfulness. Friendship.

Kismaric, Carole. *A gift from Saint Nicholas* (Timmermans, Felix)

The rumor of Pavel and Paali: a Ukrainian folktale ill. by Charles Mikolaycak. Harper, 1988. ISBN 0-06-023278-1 Subj: Behavior – greed. Character traits – meanness. Folk and fairy tales. Twins.

Kistiakowsky, Vera *see* Fischer, Vera Kistiakowsky

Kitamura, Satoshi. *Captain Toby* ill. by author. Dutton, 1988. ISBN 0-525-44414-9 Subj: Animals – cats. Family life – grandparents. Sea and seashore. Weather – storms.

Lily takes a walk ill. by author. Dutton, 1987. ISBN 0-525-44333-9 Subj: Animals – dogs. Emotions – fear. Imagination.

What's inside? ill. by author. Farrar, 1985. ISBN 0-374-38306-5 Subj: ABC books.

When sheep cannot sleep ill. by author. Farrar, 1986. ISBN 0-374-38311-1 Subj: Animals – sheep. Bedtime. Counting.

Kitchen, Bert. *Animal alphabet* ill. by author. Dial Pr., 1984. Subj: ABC books. Animals.

Animal numbers ill. by author. Dial Pr., 1987. ISBN 0-8037-0459-3 Subj: Animals. Counting.

Kitt, Tamara *see* De Regniers, Beatrice Schenk

Klein, Arthur Luce. *Puss in boots* (Perrault, Charles)

Klein, Leonore. *Henri's walk to Paris* ill. by Saul Bass. Addison-Wesley, 1962. Subj: Activities – walking. Foreign lands – France.

Just like you ill. by Audrey Walters. Harvey House, 1968. Subj: Ethnic groups in the U.S.

Old, older, oldest ill. by Leonard P. Kessler. Hastings, 1983. Subj: Old age.

Klein, Norma. *Girls can be anything* ill. by Roy Doty. Dutton, 1973. Subj: Careers.

Visiting Pamela ill. by Kay Chorao. Dial Pr., 1979. Subj: Behavior – sharing. Friendship.

Klein, Robin. *Thing* ill. by Alison Lester. Oxford Univ. Pr., 1983. Subj: Dinosaurs. Pets.

Klein, Suzanne. *An elephant in my bed* ill. by Sharleen Pederson. Follett, 1974. Subj: Animals – elephants.

Klimo, Kate. *Farm house*

Firehouse

Mother Goose house (Mother Goose)

Mouse house

Sing a song of sixpence (Mother Goose)

Klimowicz, Barbara. *The strawberry thumb* ill. by Gloria Kamen. Abingdon Pr., 1968. Subj: Poetry, rhyme. Problem solving. Puppets. Thumbsucking.

Kline, Suzy. *Don't touch!* ill. by Dora Leder. Albert Whitman, 1985. ISBN 0-8075-1707-0 Subj: Activities – playing. Behavior – misbehavior.

Ooops! ed. by Ann Fay; ill. by Dora Leder. Albert Whitman, 1988. ISBN 0-8075-6122-3 Subj: Behavior – bad day. Behavior – carelessness.

Shhhh! ill. by Dora Leder. Albert Whitman, 1984. ISBN 0-8075-7321-3 Subj: Noise, sounds.

Klinting, Lars. *Regal the golden eagle* tr. by Alan Bernstein; ill. by author. Farrar, 1988. ISBN 91-2958774-3 Subj: Behavior – growing up. Birds – eagles. Emotions – fear.

Klockner, Karen. *The black sheep* (Heck, Elisabeth)

Otto the bear (Gantschev, Ivan)

Knab, Linda Z. *The day is waiting* (Freeman, Don)

Knapp, John II. *A pillar of pepper and other Bible nursery rhymes* ill. by Dianne Turner Deckert. Cook, 1982. Subj: Nursery rhymes. Religion.

Knifesmith *see* Cutler, Ivor

Knight, David C. *Dinosaur days* ill. by Joel Schick. McGraw-Hill, 1977. Subj: Dinosaurs. Science.

Knight, Hilary. *Angels and berries and candy canes* ill. by author. Harper, 1963. Subj: Angels. Holidays – Christmas.

A firefly in a fir tree ill. by author. Harper, 1963. Subj: Insects – fireflies.

Hilary Knight's Cinderella ill. by author. Random House, 1978. ISBN 0-394-93759-7 Subj: Folk and fairy tales. Royalty. Sibling rivalry.

Hilary Knight's the owl and the pussy-cat ill. by author. Macmillan, 1983. Based on The owl and the pussy-cat by Edward Lear. Subj: Imagination. Magic. Poetry, rhyme.

Sylvia the sloth ill. by author. Harper, 1969. Subj: Animals – sloths. Concepts – up and down.

Where's Wallace? ill. by author. Harper, 1964. Subj: Animals – monkeys. Behavior – running away. Zoos.

Knight, Joan. *Tickle-toe rhymes* ill. by John Wallner. Watts, 1988. ISBN 0-531-08373-X Subj: Games. Poetry, rhyme.

Knotts, Howard. *Great-grandfather, the baby and me* ill. by author. Atheneum, 1978. Subj: Family life – great-grandparents.

The lost Christmas ill. by author. Harcourt, 1978. Subj: Dreams. Holidays – Christmas. Illness.

The summer cat ill. by author. Harper, 1981. Subj: Animals – cats. Seasons – summer.

The winter cat ill. by author. Harper, 1972. Subj: Animals – cats. Seasons – winter.

Knox-Wagner, Elaine. *The best mom in the world* (Delton, Judy)

My grandpa retired today ill. by Charles Robinson. Albert Whitman, 1982. Subj: Emotions. Family life – grandfathers. Old age.

The oldest kid ill. by Gail Owens. Albert Whitman, 1981. Subj: Activities – picnicking. Sibling rivalry.

Knutson, Barbara. *Why the crab has no head: an African tale* ill. by author. Carolrhoda Books, 1987. ISBN 0-87614-322-2 Subj: Behavior – boasting. Crustacea. Folk and fairy tales. Foreign lands – Africa. Foreign lands – Zaire.

Kobayashi, Masako Matsuno *see* Matsuno, Masako

Kobeh, Ana García. *Tigers and opossums* (Kurtycz, Marcos)

Kobrin, Janet. *Coyote goes hunting for fire* (Bernstein, Margery)

Earth namer (Bernstein, Margery)

The first morning (Bernstein, Margery)

How the sun made a promise and kept it (Bernstein, Margery)

Koch, Dorothy Clarke. *Gone is my goose* ill. by Doris Lee. Holiday, 1956. Subj: Birds – geese.

I play at the beach ill. by Feodor Rojankovsky. Random House, 1955. Subj: Family life. Games. Sea and seashore.

When the cows got out ill. by Paul Lantz. Holiday, 1958. Subj: Animals – bulls, cows. Farms.

Kočí, Marta. *Blackie and Marie* tr. from German by Elizabeth D. Crawford; ill. by author. Morrow, 1981. Subj: Animals – dogs. Friendship.

Katie's kitten ill. by author. Alphabet Pr., 1982. Subj: Animals – cats. Behavior – lost.

Sarah's bear ill. by author. Picture Book Studio, 1987. ISBN 0-88708-038-3 Subj: Emotions – love. Toys – teddy bears.

Koehler, Irmengarde *see* Eberle, Irmengarde

Koelling, Caryl. *Animal mix and match* ill. by Roger Beerworth. Delacorte, 1980. Subj: Animals. Format, unusual – board books.

Mad monsters mix and match ill. by Linda Griffith. Delacorte, 1980. Subj: Format, unusual – board books. Monsters.

Silly stories mix and match ill. by Carroll Andrus. Delacorte, 1980. Subj: Format, unusual – board books. Humor.

Koenig, Marion. *The little black hen* (Hille-Brandts, Lene)

Poor fish (Beisert, Heide Helene)

The tale of fancy Nancy: a Spanish folktale ill. by Klaus Ensikat. Merrimack, 1979. Subj: Animals – cats. Animals – mice. Folk and fairy tales.

The wonderful world of night ill. by David Parry. Grosset, 1969. Subj: Animals – cats. Behavior – misbehavior. Night.

Koenner, Alfred. *Be quiet quiet beside the lake* tr. from German by Georgia Peet; ill. by Karl-Heinz Appelmann. Imported Pub., 1981. Subj: Format, unusual – board books. Noise, sounds.

High flies the ball by Alfred Koenner and Siegfried Linke; tr. from German by Georgia Peet; ill. by Siegfried Linke. Imported Pub., 1983. Subj: Format, unusual – board books. Poetry, rhyme.

Koffler, Camilla *see* Ylla

Koide, Tan. *May we sleep here tonight?* ill. by Yasuko Koide. Atheneum, 1983. Subj: Animals. Bedtime.

Kojima, Naomi. *The flying grandmother* ill. by author. Crowell, 1981. Subj: Activities – flying. Behavior – wishing. Family life – grandmothers. Imagination.

Komaiko, Leah. *Annie Bananie* ill. by Laura Cornell. Harper, 1987. ISBN 0-06-023261-7 Subj: Friendship. Moving. Poetry, rhyme.

Earl's too cool for me ill. by Laura Cornell. Harper, 1988. ISBN 0-06-023282-X Subj: Behavior – misunderstanding. Friendship. Poetry, rhyme.

I like the music ill. by Barbara Westman. Harper, 1987. ISBN 0-06-023272-2 Subj: Music. Poetry, rhyme.

Komoda, Beverly. *Simon's soup* ill. by author. Parents, 1978. Subj: Animals – cats. Animals – monkeys. Food.

Komori, Atsushi. *Animal mothers* ill. by Masayuki Yabuuchi. Putnam's, 1983. ISBN 0-399-20980-8 Subj: Animals. Science.

Koontz, Robin Michal. *Dinosaur dream* ill. by author. Putnam's, 1988. ISBN 0-399-21669-3 Subj: Dinosaurs. Dreams. Wordless.

Pussycat ate the dumplings: cat rhymes from Mother Goose ill. by author. Dodd, 1987. ISBN 0-396-08899-6 Subj: Animals – cats. Nursery rhymes.

This old man: the counting song ill. by author. Putnam's, 1988. ISBN 0-396-09120-2 Subj: Counting. Elves and little people. Farms. Music. Songs.

Kopczynski, Anna. *Jerry and Ami* ill. by author. Scribner's, 1963. Subj: Animals – dogs. Friendship.

Kopper, Lisa. *An elephant came to swim* (Lewin, Hugh)

Koralek, Jenny. *The friendly fox* ill. by Beverley Gooding. Little, 1988. ISBN 0-316-50179-4 Subj: Animals. Animals – foxes. Farms. Friendship.

Koren, Edward. *Behind the wheel* ill. by author. Holt, 1972. Subj: Transportation.

Korschunow, Irina. *Small fur* tr. by James Skofield; ill. by Reinhard Michl. Harper, 1988. ISBN 0-06-023248-X Subj: Animals. Elves and little people. Friendship.

Korth-Sander, Irmtraut. *Will you be my friend?* tr. from German by Rosemary Lanning; ill. by author. Holt, 1986. ISBN 0-8050-0039-9 Subj: Animals – pigs. Friendship.

Kotzwinkle, William. *The day the gang got rich* ill. by Joe Servello. Viking, 1970. Subj: Clubs, gangs. Friendship.

The nap master ill. by Joe Servello. Harcourt, 1979. Subj: Bedtime. Dreams. Sleep.

Up the alley with Jack and Joe ill. by Joe Servello. Macmillan, 1974. Subj: Friendship.

Kouts, Anne. *Kenny's rat* ill. by Betty Fraser. Viking, 1970. Subj: Animals – rats. Pets.

Kovalski, Maryann. *Jingle bells* ill. by author. Little, 1988. ISBN 0-316-50258-8 Subj: City. Music. Seasons – winter. Songs.

The wheels on the bus ill. by author. Little, 1987. ISBN 0-316-50256-1 Subj: Buses. Family life – grandmothers. Music. Songs.

Krahn, Fernando. *Amanda and the mysterious carpet* ill. by author. Clarion, 1985. ISBN 0-89919-258-0 Subj: Imagination. Magic. Wordless.

April fools ill. by author. Dutton, 1974. Subj: Holidays – April Fools' Day. Humor. Wordless.

Arthur's adventure in the abandoned house ill. by author. Dutton, 1981. ISBN 0-525-25945-7 Subj: Problem solving. Wordless.

The biggest Christmas tree on earth ill. by author. Little, 1978. Subj: Animals. Holidays – Christmas. Toys – balls. Trees. Wordless.

Catch that cat! ill. by author. Dutton, 1978. Subj: Animals – cats. Wordless.

The creepy thing ill. by author. Houghton, 1982. Subj: Imagination – imaginary friends. Wordless.

A funny friend from heaven ill. by author. Lippincott, 1977. Subj: Angels. Clowns, jesters. Wordless.

The great ape: being the true version of the famous saga of adventure and friendship newly discovered ill. by author. Viking, 1978. Subj: Animals – gorillas. Friendship. Islands. Wordless.

Here comes Alex Pumpernickel! ill. by author. Little, 1981. Subj: Behavior – bad day. Wordless.

How Santa Claus had a long and difficult journey delivering his presents ill. by author. Delacorte Pr., 1970. Holidays - Christmas. Subj: Wordless.

Little love story ill. by author. Lippincott, 1976. Subj: Holidays – Valentine's Day. Wordless.

Mr. Top ill. by author. Morrow, 1983. ISBN 0-688-02369-X Subj: Crime. Traffic, traffic signs.

The mystery of the giant footprints ill. by author. Dutton, 1977. Subj: Cumulative tales. Monsters. Wordless.

Robot-bot-bot ill. by author. Dutton, 1979. Subj: Activities – playing. Activities – working. Robots. Wordless.

Sebastian and the mushroom ill. by author. Delacorte Pr., 1976. Subj: Dreams. Wordless.

The secret in the dungeon ill. by author. Houghton, 1983. Subj: Behavior – secrets. Dragons. Wordless.

Sleep tight, Alex Pumpernickel ill. by author. Little, 1982. Subj: Bedtime. Sleep. Wordless.

Who's seen the scissors? ill. by author. Dutton, 1975. Subj: Wordless.

Kramer, Anthony Penta. *Numbers on parade: 0 to 10* ill. by author. Lothrop, 1987. ISBN 0-688-05555-9 Subj: Animals. Counting.

Krasilovsky, Phyllis. *The cow who fell in the canal* ill. by Peter Spier. Doubleday, 1953. Subj: Animals – bulls, cows. Cumulative tales. Foreign lands – Holland.

The girl who was a cowboy ill. by Cyndy Szekeres. Doubleday, 1965. Subj: Clothing. Cowboys.

The man who did not wash his dishes ill. by Barbara Cooney. Doubleday, 1950. Subj: Character traits – cleanliness. Character traits – laziness.

The man who entered a contest ill. by Yuri Salzman. Doubleday, 1980. Subj: Activities – cooking. Behavior – misbehavior.

The man who tried to save time ill. by Marcia Sewall. Doubleday, 1979. ISBN 0-385-12999-8 Subj: Character traits – laziness. Time.

Scaredy cat ill. by Ninon. Macmillan, 1959. Subj: Animals – cats.

The shy little girl ill. by Trina Schart Hyman. Houghton, 1970. Subj: Character traits – shyness. Friendship.

The very little boy ill. by Ninon. Doubleday, 1962. Subj: Babies. Behavior – growing up. Family life.

The very little girl ill. by Ninon. Doubleday, 1953. Subj: Babies. Behavior – growing up. Family life.

The very tall little girl ill. by Olivia Cole. Doubleday, 1969. Subj: Character traits – being different. Family life.

Kratka, Suzanne C. *Hi, new baby* (Andry, Andrew C.)

Kraus, Bruce. *The detective of London* (Kraus, Robert)

Kraus, Robert. *Another mouse to feed* ill. by José Aruego and Ariane Dewey. Windmill, 1980. Subj: Animals – mice. Family life.

Big brother ill. by author. Parents, 1973. Subj: Animals – rabbits. Babies. Family life.

Boris bad enough ill. by José Aruego and Ariane Dewey. Dutton, 1976. Subj: Animals – elephants

Come out and play, little mouse ill. by José Aruego and Ariane Dewey. Greenwillow, 1987. ISBN 0-688-05838-8 Subj: Activities – playing. Animals – cats. Animals – mice. Behavior – trickery.

Daddy Long Ears ill. by author. Simon and Schuster, 1970. Subj: Animals – rabbits. Holidays – Easter.

The detective of London by Robert and Bruce Kraus; ill. by Robert Byrd. Windmill-Dutton, 1978. Subj: Animals – dogs. Crime. Problem solving.

The first robin ill. by author. Windmill, 1965. ISBN 0-671-44565-0 Subj: Birds – robins. Character traits – kindness. Illness. Seasons – spring.

Good night little one by Robert Kraus and N. M. Bodecker; ill. by N. M. Bodecker. Dutton, 1972. Subj: Bedtime. Counting. Night. Sleep.

Good night Richard Rabbit by Robert Kraus and N. M. Bodecker; ill. by N. M. Bodecker. Dutton, 1972. Subj: Animals – rabbits. Bedtime. Counting. Night. Sleep.

Herman the helper ill. by José Aruego and Ariane Dewey. Dutton, 1974. Subj: Character traits – helpfulness. Octopuses. Sea and seashore.

How spider saved Valentine's Day ill. by author. Scholastic, 1986. ISBN 0-590-33743-2 Subj: Friendship. Holidays – Valentine's Day. Insects. Spiders.

I, Mouse ill. by author. Harper, 1958. Subj: Animals – mice.

The king's trousers ill. by Fred Gwynne. Windmill, 1981. ISBN 0-671-42259-6 Subj: Behavior – trickery. Clothing. Royalty.

Ladybug, ladybug! ill. by author. Harper, 1957. Subj: Behavior – misunderstanding. Friendship. Insects – ladybugs.

Leo the late bloomer ill. by José Aruego. Dutton, 1971. Subj: Animals – tigers. Behavior – growing up.

The little giant ill. by author. Harper, 1967. Subj: Concepts – size. Giants.

The littlest rabbit ill. by author. Harper, 1961. Subj: Animals – rabbits. Character traits – smallness.

Mert the blurt ill. by José Aruego and Ariane Dewey. Windmill, 1981. Subj: Behavior – gossip. Frogs and toads.

Milton the early riser ill. by José Aruego and Ariane Dewey. Dutton, 1972. Subj: Animals – bears. Sleep.

Noel the coward ill. by José Aruego and Ariane Dewey. Dutton, 1977. Subj: Emotions – fear.

Owliver ill. by José Aruego and Ariane Dewey. Prentice-Hall, 1987, 1974. ISBN 0-13-647538-8 Subj: Birds – owls. Careers. Character traits – individuality.

Phil the ventriloquist ill. by author. Greenwillow, 1989. ISBN 0-688-07988-1 Subj: Family life.

Rebecca Hatpin ill. by Robert Byrd. Dutton, 1974. Subj: Careers – nurses. Character traits – helpfulness. Character traits – selfishness. Family life – grandmothers.

Springfellow ill. by Sam Savitt. Dutton, 1978. Subj: Animals – horses.

The three friends ill. by José Aruego and Ariane Dewey. Dutton, 1975. Subj: Friendship.

The tree that stayed up until next Christmas ill. by Edna Eicke. Dutton, 1972. ISBN 0-525-61001-4 Subj: Holidays – Christmas. Toys. Trees.

The trouble with spider ill. by author. Harper, 1962. Subj: Friendship. Insects – flies. Spiders.

Where are you going, little mouse? ill. by José Aruego and Arianne Dewey. Greenwillow, 1986. ISBN 0-688-04295-3 Subj: Animals – mice. Behavior – running away. Behavior – seeking better things.

Whose mouse are you? ill. by José Aruego. Macmillan, 1970. Subj: Animals – mice.

Krauss, Ruth. *The backward day* ill. by Marc Simont. Harper, 1950. Subj: Family life.

Bears ill. by Phyllis Rowand. Harper, 1948. Subj: Animals – bears. Poetry, rhyme.

Big and little ill. by Mary Szilagyi. Scholastic, 1988. ISBN 0-590-41707-X Subj: Concepts – size. Emotions – love.

A bouquet of littles ill. by Jane Flora. Harper, 1963. Subj: Concepts – size. Poetry, rhyme.

The bundle book ill. by Helen Stone. Harper, 1951. Subj: Bedtime. Emotions. Family life – mothers. Games.

The carrot seed ill. by Crockett Johnson. Harper, 1945. Subj: Activities – gardening. Character traits – optimism. Plants. Self-concept.

Charlotte and the white horse ill. by Maurice Sendak. Harper, 1955. Subj: Animals – horses.

Everything under a mushroom ill. by Margot Tomes. Four Winds Pr., 1974. Subj: Elves and little people. Poetry, rhyme.

Eyes, nose, fingers, toes ill. by Elizabeth Schneider. Harper, 1964. Subj: Anatomy.

A good man and his good wife ill. by Marc Simont. Harper, 1962. Subj: Behavior – boredom. Friendship.

The growing story ill. by Phyllis Rowand. Harper, 1947. Subj: Behavior – growing up.

The happy day ill. by Marc Simont. Harper, 1949. Subj: Caldecott award honor book. Hibernation. Seasons – spring. Seasons – winter. Weather – snow.

The happy egg ill. by Crockett Johnson. O'Hara, 1967. Subj: Birds. Eggs.

A hole is to dig: a first book of first definitions ill. by Maurice Sendak. Harper, 1952. ISBN 0-06-023406-7 Subj: Language.

I write it ill. by Mary Chalmers. Harper, 1970. Subj: Activities – writing.

I'll be you and you be me ill. by Maurice Sendak. Harper, 1954. Subj: Friendship. Humor.

Mama, I wish I was snow. Child, you'd be very cold ill. by Ellen Raskin. Atheneum, 1962. Subj: Behavior – wishing. Games.

A moon or a button ill. by Remy Charlip. Harper, 1959. Subj: Imagination.

Open house for butterflies ill. by Maurice Sendak. Harper, 1960. Subj: Imagination.

Somebody else's nut tree, and other tales from children ill. by Maurice Sendak. Harper, 1958. Subj: Children as authors. Imagination.

This thumbprint ill. by author. Harper, 1967. Subj: Humor. Imagination.

A very special house ill. by Maurice Sendak. Harper, 1953. Subj: Caldecott award honor book. Houses. Imagination.

Krauze, Andrzej. *What's so special about today?* ill. by author. Lothrop, 1984. Subj: Animals. Birthdays. Character traits – questioning.

Krementz, Jill. *Benjy goes to a restaurant* photos. by author. Crown, 1986. ISBN 0-517-56166-2 Subj: Careers – waiters, waitresses. Family life. Format, unusual – board books.

Jack goes to the beach photos. by author. Random House, 1986. ISBN 0-394-88001-3 Subj: Family life. Format, unusual – board books. Sand. Sea and seashore.

Jamie goes on an airplane photos. by author. Random House, 1986. ISBN 0-394-88196-6 Subj: Activities – traveling. Airplanes, airports. Careers – airplane pilots. Format, unusual – board books.

Katherine goes to nursery school photos. by author. Random House, 1986. ISBN 0-394-88195-8 Subj: Activities. Format, unusual – board books. School.

Lily goes to the playground photos. by author. Random House, 1986. ISBN 0-394-87999-6 Subj: Activities – playing. Family life. Format, unusual – board books.

Taryn goes to the dentist photos. by author. Crown, 1986. ISBN 0-517-56168-9 Subj: Careers – dentists. Family life. Format, unusual – board books.

A visit to Washington, D.C. photos. by author. Scholastic, 1987. ISBN 0-500-40582-9 Subj: Activities – traveling. City. Museums.

Krensky, Stephen. *Dinosaurs, beware!* (Brown, Marc)

The lion upstairs ill. by Leigh Grant. Atheneum, 1983. Subj: Imagination – imaginary friends.

Lionel at large ill. by Susanna Natti. Dial Pr., 1986. ISBN 0-8037-0241-8 Subj: Family life.

Lionel in the fall ill. by Susanna Natti. Dutton, 1987. ISBN 0-8037-0384-8 Subj: Holidays – Halloween. School. Seasons – fall.

My first dictionary ill. by George Ulrich. Houghton, 1980. Subj: Dictionaries.

Perfect pigs (Brown, Marc)

Kroll, Steven. *Amanda and the giggling ghost* ill. by Dick Gackenbach. Holiday, 1980. Subj: Behavior – stealing. Ghosts.

Are you pirates? ill. by Marylin Hafner. Pantheon, 1982. Subj: Imagination. Pirates.

The big bunny and the Easter eggs ill. by Janet Stevens. Holiday, 1982. Subj: Animals – rabbits. Holidays – Easter. Illness.

The big bunny and the magic show ill. by Janet Stevens. Holiday, 1986. ISBN 0-8234-0589-3 Subj: Animals – rabbits. Holidays – Easter. Magic.

The candy witch ill. by Marylin Hafner. Holiday, 1979. Subj: Behavior – unnoticed, unseen. Holidays – Halloween. Magic. Witches.

Don't get me in trouble ill. by Marvin Glass. Crown, 1988. ISBN 0-517-56724-5 Subj: Animals – dogs. Friendship.

Fat magic ill. by Tomie de Paola. Holiday, 1978. Subj: Magic. Royalty.

The goat parade ill. by Tim Kirk. Parents, 1983. Subj: Animals – goats. Parades.

The hand-me-down doll ill. by Evaline Ness. Holiday, 1983. Subj: Toys – dolls.

Happy Father's Day ill. by Marylin Hafner. Holiday, 1987. ISBN 0-5234-0671-7 Subj: Family life – fathers. Holidays – Father's Day.

Happy Mother's Day ill. by Marylin Hafner. Holiday, 1985. ISBN 0-8234-0504-4 Subj: Family life. Holidays – Mother's Day.

I love spring! ill. by Kathryn E. Shoemaker. Holiday, 1987. ISBN 0-8234-0634-2 Subj: Seasons – spring.

If I could be my grandmother ill. by Tasha Tudor. Pantheon, 1977. Subj: Family life – grandmothers.

It's Groundhog Day! ill. by Jeni Bassett. Holiday, 1987. ISBN 0-8234-0643-1 Subj: Activities – picnicking. Animals. Holidays – Groundhog Day.

Looking for Daniela ill. by Anita Lobel. Holiday, 1988. ISBN 0-8234-0695-4 Subj: Crime. Foreign lands – Italy. Problem solving.

Loose tooth ill. by Tricia Tusa. Holiday, 1984. Subj: Fairies. Teeth.

One tough turkey: a Thanksgiving story ill. by John Wallner. Holiday, 1982. Subj: Birds – turkeys. Holidays – Thanksgiving. Sports – hunting.

Otto ill. by Ned Delaney. Parents, 1983. Subj: Behavior – misbehavior. Robots.

Pigs in the house ill. by Tim Kirk. Parents, 1983. Subj: Animals – pigs. Behavior – misbehavior. Houses. Poetry, rhyme.

Santa's crash-bang Christmas ill. by Tomie de Paola. Holiday, 1977. Subj: Holidays – Christmas.

Toot! Toot! ill. by Anne F. Rockwell. Holiday, 1983. Subj: Family life – grandparents. Imagination. Toys – trains. Trains.

The tyrannosaurus game ill. by Tomie de Paola. Holiday, 1976. Subj: Cumulative tales. Dinosaurs. Games. Imagination.

Woof, woof! ill. by Nicole Rubel. Dial Pr., 1983. Subj: Animals – dogs. Crime.

Krull, Kathleen. *Autumn* (Allington, Richard L.)

Songs of praise ill. by Kathryn Hewitt. Harcourt, 1989. ISBN 0-15-277108-5 Subj: Music. Religion. Songs.

Spring (Allington, Richard L.)

Summer (Allington, Richard L.)

Winter (Allington, Richard L.)

Krum, Charlotte. *The four riders* ill. by Katherine Evans. Follett, 1953. Subj: Animals – horses.

Krupp, E. C. *The comet and you* ill. by Robin Rector Krupp. Macmillan, 1985. ISBN 0-02-751250-9 Subj: Science.

Krupp, Robin Rector. *Get set to wreck!* ill. by author. Macmillan, 1988. ISBN 0-02-751140-5 Subj: Activities – playing. Imagination. Language.

Krush, Beth. *The fish from Japan* (Cooper, Elizabeth K.)

Krüss, James. *3 X 3: Three by three* ill. by Eva Johanna Rubin; English text by Geoffrey Strachan. Macmillan, 1963. Subj: Animals. Counting. Poetry, rhyme.

Kubler, Susanne. *The three friends* ill. by author. Macmillan, 1985. ISBN 0-02-751150-2 Subj: Animals. Friendship.

Kübler-Ross, Elisabeth. *Remember the secret* ill. by Heather Preston. Celestial Arts, 1982. Subj: Death.

Kuchalla, Susan. *All about seeds* ill. by Jane McBee. Troll Assoc., 1982. Subj: Plants. Science.

Baby animals ill. by Joel Snyder. Troll Assoc., 1982. Subj: Animals.

Bears ill. by Kathie Kelleher. Troll Assoc., 1982. Subj: Animals – bears.

Birds ill. by Gary Britt. Troll Assoc., 1982. Subj: Birds.

What is a reptile? ill. by Paul Harvey. Troll Assoc., 1982. Subj: Reptiles.

Kudrna, C. Imbior. *To bathe a boa* ill. by author. Carolrhoda Books, 1986. ISBN 0-87614-306-0 Subj: Activities – bathing. Behavior – hiding. Poetry, rhyme. Reptiles – snakes.

Kuklin, Susan. *Taking my dog to the vet* photos. by author. Bradbury Pr., 1988. ISBN 0-02-751234-7 Subj: Animals. Careers – veterinarians. Pets.

Thinking big: the story of a young dwarf photos. by author. Lothrop, 1986. ISBN 0-688-05827-2 Subj: Character traits – being different. Handicaps.

When I see my dentist photos. by author. Bradbury Pr., 1988. ISBN 0-02-751231-2 Subj: Careers – dentists. Health.

When I see my doctor photos. by author. Bradbury Pr., 1988. ISBN 0-02-751232-0 Subj: Careers – doctors.

Kumin, Maxine. *The beach before breakfast* ill. by Leonard Weisgard. Putnam's, 1964. Subj: Sea and seashore.

Eggs of things ill. by Leonard W. Shortall. Putnam's, 1963. Subj: Eggs. Frogs and toads. Humor. Science.

Follow the fall ill. by Artur Marokvia. Putnam's, 1961. Subj: Holidays. Imagination. Poetry, rhyme. Seasons – fall.

Joey and the birthday present by Maxine Kumin and Anne Sexton; ill. by Evaline Ness. McGraw-Hill, 1971. Subj: Animals – mice. Birthdays.

Mittens in May ill. by Eliott Gilbert. Putnam's, 1962. Subj: Birds. Character traits – kindness to animals. Clothing.

Sebastian and the dragon ill. by William D. Hayes. Putnam's, 1960. Subj: Character traits – smallness. Dragons. Poetry, rhyme.

Speedy digs downside up ill. by Ezra Jack Keats. Putnam's, 1964. Subj: Activities – digging. Character traits – ambition. Humor. Poetry, rhyme.

Spring things ill. by Artur Marokvia. Putnam's, 1961. Subj: Poetry, rhyme. Seasons – spring.

What color is Caesar? ill. by Evaline Ness. McGraw-Hill, 1978. Subj: Animals – dogs. Concepts – color.

A winter friend ill. by Artur Marokvia. Putnam's, 1961. Subj: Poetry, rhyme. Seasons – winter.

The wizard's tears by Maxine Kumin and Anne Sexton; ill. by Evaline Ness. McGraw-Hill, 1975. Subj: Magic. Wizards.

Kunhardt, Dorothy. *Billy the barber* ill. by William Pène Du Bois. Harper, 1961. Subj: Careers – barbers. Hair. Old age.

Kitty's new doll ill. by Lucinda McQueen. Golden Pr., 1984. Subj: Animals – cats. Toys – dolls.

Kunhardt, Edith. *Danny's mystery Valentine* ill. by author. Greenwillow, 1987. ISBN 0-688-06854-5 Subj: Family life – grandmothers. Holidays – Valentine's Day. Reptiles – alligators, crocodiles.

Pat the cat ill. by author. Golden Pr., 1984. Subj: Animals – cats. Format, unusual – toy and movable books. Pets.

Trick or treat, Danny! ill. by author. Greenwillow, 1988. ISBN 0-688-07311-5 Subj: Holidays – Halloween. Illness. Reptiles – alligators, crocodiles.

Where's Peter? ill. by author. Greenwillow, 1988. ISBN 0-688-07205-4 Subj: Babies. Family life. Games.

Kunnas, Mauri. *The nighttime book* by Mauri Kunnas with Tarja Kunnas; tr. from the Finnish by Tim Steffa; ill. by author. Crown, 1985. ISBN 0-517-55819-X Subj: Activities. Night.

One spooky night and other scary stories by Mauri Kunnas with Tarja Kunnas; tr. by Tim Steffa; ill. by author. Crown, 1986. ISBN 0-517-56253-7 Subj: Ghosts. Holidays – Halloween. Monsters.

Santa Claus and his elves by Mauri Kunnas; assisted by Tarja Kunnas; ill. by authors. Harmony, 1982. Translation of Joulupukki. Subj: Elves and little people. Holidays – Christmas.

Twelve gifts for Santa Claus by Mauri and Tarja Kunnas; tr. by Tim Steffa; ill. by authors. Crown, 1988. ISBN 0-517-56631-1 Subj: Character traits – generosity. Elves and little people. Holidays – Christmas.

Kunnas, Tarja. *The nighttime book* (Kunnas, Mauri)

One spooky night and other scary stories (Kunnas, Mauri)

Santa Claus and his elves (Kunnas, Mauri)

Twelve gifts for Santa Claus (Kunnas, Mauri)

Kuratomi, Chizuko. *Mr. Bear and the robbers* ill. by Kozo Kakimoto. Dial Pr., 1970. Subj: Animals – bears. Animals – rabbits.

Kurtycz, Marcos. *Tigers and opossums: animal legends* adapt. by Marcos Kurtycz and Ana García Kobeh; ill. by adaptors. Little, 1984. Subj: Folk and fairy tales. Foreign lands – Mexico.

Kuskin, Karla. *ABCDEFGHIJKLMNOPQRSTUVWXYZ* ill. by author. Harper, 1963. Subj: ABC books.

All sizes of noises ill. by author. Harper, 1962. Subj: Concepts. Noise, sounds. Poetry, rhyme.

The animals and the ark ill. by author. Harper, 1958. Subj: Animals. Boats, ships. Poetry, rhyme. Religion – Noah.

A boy had a mother who bought him a hat ill. by author. Houghton, 1976. Subj: Cumulative tales. Poetry, rhyme.

The Dallas Titans get ready for bed ill. by Marc Simont. Harper, 1986. ISBN 0-06-023563-2 Subj: Bedtime. Clothing. Sports – football.

Herbert hated being small ill. by author. Houghton, 1979. Subj: Character traits – smallness. Concepts – size. Poetry, rhyme.

In the flaky frosty morning ill. by author. Harper, 1969. Subj: Poetry, rhyme. Seasons – winter. Snowmen. Weather – snow.

James and the rain ill. by author. Harper, 1957. Subj: Animals. Poetry, rhyme. Weather – rain.

Jerusalem, shining still ill. by David Frampton. Harper, 1987. ISBN 0-06-023549-7 Subj: City. Foreign lands – Israel. Religion.

Just like everyone else ill. by author. Harper, 1959. Subj: Activities – flying.

Night again ill. by author. Little, 1981. Subj: Bedtime.

The Philharmonic gets dressed ill. by Marc Simont. Harper, 1982. Subj: Clothing.

Roar and more ill. by author. Harper, 1956. Subj: Animals. Noise, sounds. Participation. Poetry, rhyme.

Sand and snow ill. by author. Harper, 1965. Subj: Poetry, rhyme. Sea and seashore. Seasons – summer. Seasons – winter.

Something sleeping in the hall ill. by author. Harper, 1985. ISBN 0-06-023634-5 Subj: Animals. Pets. Poetry, rhyme.

A space story ill. by Marc Simont. Harper, 1978. Subj: Bedtime. Space and space ships. Stars.

Watson, the smartest dog in the U.S.A. ill. by author. Harper, 1968. Subj: Activities – reading. Animals – dogs.

What did you bring me? ill. by author. Harper, 1973. Subj: Animals – mice. Behavior – greed. Self-concept. Witches.

Which horse is William? ill. by author. Harper, 1959. Subj: Character traits – individuality. Imagination.

Kuskin, Karla Seidman *see* Kuskin, Karla

Kwitz, Mary DeBall. *Little chick's breakfast* ill. by Bruce Degen. Harper, 1983. Subj: Birds – chickens. Farms. Food.

Little chick's story ill. by Cyndy Szekeres. Harper, 1978. Subj: Birds – chickens. Eggs.

Mouse at home ill. by author. Harper, 1966. Subj: Animals – mice. Seasons.

Rabbits' search for a little house ill. by Lorinda Bryan Cauley. Crown, 1977. Subj: Animals – rabbits. Houses.

When it rains ill. by author. Follett, 1974. Subj: Animals. Poetry, rhyme. Weather – rain. Weather – rainbows.

Kyte, Dennis. *Mattie and Cataragus* ill. by author. Doubleday, 1988. ISBN 0-385-24404-5 Subj: Animals – cats. Friendship.

Lady Eden's School. *Just how stories* ill. by Derek Steele. Merrimack, 1981. Subj: Animals. Children as authors.

Ladybug, ladybug, and other nursery rhymes ill. by Eloise Wilkin. Random House, 1979. Subj: Format, unusual. Nursery rhymes.

La Farge, Phyllis. *Joanna runs away* ill. by Trina Schart Hyman. Holt, 1973. Subj: Animals – horses. Behavior – running away.

La Farge, Sheila. *The boy who ate more than the giant and other Swedish folktales* (Löfgren, Ulf)

Peter's adventures in Blueberry land (Beskow, Elsa Maartman)

La Fontaine, Jean de. *The hare and the tortoise* ill. by Brian Wildsmith. Watts, 1963. Subj: Animals – rabbits. Folk and fairy tales. Reptiles – turtles, tortoises. Sports – racing.

The lion and the rat ill. by Brian Wildsmith. Watts, 1963. Subj: Animals – lions. Animals – rats. Character traits – helpfulness. Folk and fairy tales.

The miller, the boy and the donkey adapt. and ill. by Brian Wildsmith. Watts, 1969. "Based on a fable by La Fontaine." Subj: Animals – donkeys. Character traits – practicality. Folk and fairy tales. Humor.

The north wind and the sun ill. by Brian Wildsmith. Watts, 1964. Subj: Folk and fairy tales. Sun. Weather – wind.

The turtle and the two ducks (Plante, Patricia)

Lafontaine, Pascale Claude *see* Claude-Lafontaine, Pascale

Lage, Ida De *see* DeLage, Ida

Lagercrantz, Rose. *Brave little Pete of Geranium Street* by Rose and Samuel Lagercrantz; tr. by Jack Prelutsky; ill. by Eva Eriksson. Greenwillow, 1986. ISBN 0-688-06181-8 Subj: Behavior – bullying. Character traits – bravery. Poetry, rhyme.

Lagercrantz, Samuel. *Brave little Pete of Geranium Street* (Lagercrantz, Rose)

Laird, Donivee Martin. *The three little Hawaiian pigs and the magic shark* ill. by Carol Jossem. Bess Pr., 1981. Subj: Animals – pigs. Fish. Hawaii.

Lakin, Patricia. *Don't touch my room* ill. by Patience Brewster. Little, 1985. ISBN 0-316-51230-3 Subj: Babies. Behavior – sharing. Emotions – fear. Family life. Sibling rivalry.

Oh, brother! ill. by Patience Brewster. Little, 1987. ISBN 0-316-51231-1 Subj: Family life. Sibling rivalry. Trees.

Lalicki, Barbara. *If there were dreams to sell* ill. by Margot Tomes. Lothrop, 1984. Subj: ABC books. Poetry, rhyme.

Lalli, Judy. *Feelings alphabet: an album of emotions from A to Z* photos. by Douglas L. Mason-Fry. Jalmar Pr., 1984. Subj: ABC books. Emotions.

La Mare, Walter De *see* De La Mare, Walter

Lambert, David. *Dinosaurs* ill. by Christopher Forsey and others. Watts, 1982. Subj: Dinosaurs. Science.

The seasons ill. with photos. Watts, 1983. Subj: Science. Seasons.

Lamont, Priscilla. *The troublesome pig* (The old woman and her pig)

Lampert, Emily. *A little touch of monster* ill. by Victoria Chess. Atlantic Monthly Pr., 1986. ISBN 0-87113-022-X Subj: Character traits – individuality. Family life.

Landau, Terry. *Butterflies and rainbows* (Berger, Judith)

Landgrave of Hesse *see* Rosen, Michael

Landshoff, Ursula. *Cats are good company* ill. by author. Harper, 1983. Subj: Animals – cats. Pets. Science.

Lane, Carolyn. *The voices of Greenwillow Pond* ill. by Wallace Tripp. Houghton, 1972. Subj: Birds – owls. Character traits – perseverance. Frogs and toads.

Lane, Margaret. *The frog* ill. by Grahame Corbett. Dial Pr., 1981. Subj: Frogs and toads. Science.

The squirrel ill. by Kenneth Lilly. Dial Pr., 1981. Subj: Animals – squirrels. Science.

Lang, Andrew. *Nursery rhyme book* (Mother Goose)

Snow White and Rose Red (Grimm, Jacob)

Langner, Nola. *By the light of the silvery moon* ill. by author. Lothrop, 1983. Subj: Behavior – running away. Imagination – imaginary friends. Royalty.

Freddy my grandfather ill. by author. Four Winds Pr., 1979. Subj: Family life – grandfathers.

Langstaff, John M. *Hot cross buns, and other old street cries*

Oh, a-hunting we will go ill. by Nancy Winslow Parker. Atheneum, 1974. Subj: Folk and fairy tales. Music. Songs. Sports – hunting.

Ol' Dan Tucker ill. by Joe Krush. Harcourt, 1963. Subj: Folk and fairy tales. Music. Songs.

On Christmas day in the morning ill. by Antony Groves-Raines. Harcourt, 1959. Piano settings by Marshall Woodbridge. Subj: Folk and fairy tales. Holidays – Christmas. Music. Songs.

Over in the meadow ill. by Feodor Rojankovsky. Harcourt, 1957. Includes Over in the meadow (for voice and piano) by Marshall Woodbridge. Subj: Animals. Counting. Folk and fairy tales. Songs.

Soldier, soldier, won't you marry me? ill. by Anita Lobel. Doubleday, 1972. Subj: Careers – military. Folk and fairy tales. Music. Songs.

The swapping boy ill. by Beth and Joe Krush. Harcourt, 1960. Subj: Activities – trading. Folk and fairy tales. Music. Songs.

The two magicians ill. by Fritz Eichenberg. Atheneum, 1973. Adapt. by John Langstaff from an ancient ballad. Subj: Folk and fairy tales. Magic. Music. Songs. Witches.

What a morning!

Langstaff, Nancy. *A tiny baby for you* ill. by Suzanne Szasz. Harcourt, 1955. Subj: Babies.

Langton, Jane. *The hedgehog boy: a Latvian folktale* ill. by Ilse Plume. Harper, 1985. ISBN 0-06-023697-3 Subj: Character traits – honesty. Folk and fairy tales. Foreign lands – Latvia. Royalty. Weddings.

Lanning, Rosemary. *Camomile heads for home* (Moers, Hermann)

Jonathan Mouse (Ostheeren, Ingrid)

Will you be my friend? (Korth-Sander, Irmtraut)

Lansdown, Brenda. *Galumpf* ill. by Ernest Crichlow. Houghton, 1963. Subj: Animals – cats. Ethnic groups in the U.S. Ethnic groups in the U.S. – Afro-Americans. Pets.

Lapp, Carolyn. *The dentists' tools* ill. by George Overlie. Lerner, 1961. Subj: Careers – dentists.

Lapp, Eleanor. *The blueberry bears* ill. by Margot Apple. Albert Whitman, 1983. Subj: Animals – bears. Food.

In the morning mist ill. by David Cunningham. Albert Whitman, 1978. Subj: Family life – grandfathers. Morning. Sports – fishing.

The mice came in early this year ill. by David Cunningham. Albert Whitman, 1976. Subj: Animals. Farms. Seasons – fall. Seasons – winter.

Lapsley, Susan. *I am adopted* ill. by Michael Charlton. Bradbury Pr., 1974. Subj: Adoption. Family life.

Laroche, Michel. *The snow rose* ill. by Sandra Laroche. Holiday, 1986. ISBN 0-8234-0594-X Subj: Character traits – cleverness. Folk and fairy tales. Royalty.

La Rochelle, David. *A Christmas guest* ill. by Martin Skoro. Carolrhoda Books, 1988. ISBN 0-87614-325-7 Subj: Character traits – kindness. Holidays – Christmas. Poetry, rhyme.

Larrick, Nancy. *Cats are cats* ill. by Ed Young. Putnam's, 1988. ISBN 0-399-21517-4 Subj: Animals – cats. Poetry, rhyme.

When the dark comes dancing: a bedtime poetry book ill. by John Wallner. Putnam's, 1983. Subj: Bedtime. Night. Poetry, rhyme.

Larsen, Hanne. *Don't forget Tom* ill. with photos. Crowell, 1978. Subj: Handicaps.

Lasell, Fen. *Fly away goose* ill. by author. Houghton, 1965. Subj: Birds – geese. Eggs. Imagination.

Michael grows a wish ill. by author. Houghton, 1974. Subj: Animals – horses. Behavior – wishing. Birthdays.

Lasher, Faith B. *Hubert Hippo's world* ill. by Leonard Lee Rue, III. Children's Pr., 1971. Subj: Animals – hippopotami.

Lasker, David. *The boy who loved music* ill. by Joe Lasker. Viking, 1979. Subj: Music. Royalty.

Lasker, Joe. *The do-something day* ill. by author. Viking, 1982. Subj: Behavior – running away.

He's my brother ill. by author. Albert Whitman, 1974. Subj: Character traits – loyalty. Family life. Handicaps.

Lentil soup ill. by author. Albert Whitman, 1977. Subj: Activities – cooking. Counting. Days of the week, months of the year. Food.

Mothers can do anything ill. by author. Albert Whitman, 1972. Subj: Activities – working. Careers. Family life – mothers.

Nick joins in ill. by author. Albert Whitman, 1980. Subj: Handicaps. School.

A tournament of knights ill. by author. Crowell, 1986. ISBN 0-690-04542-5 Subj: Behavior – fighting, arguing. Knights.

Laskowski, Janina Domanska *see* Domanska, Janina

Laskowski, Jerzy. *Master of the royal cats* ill. by Janina Domanska. Seabury Pr., 1965. Subj: Animals – cats. Animals – dogs. Foreign lands – Africa. Foreign lands – Egypt. Royalty.

Lasky, Kathryn. *A baby for Max* photos. by Christopher G. Knight. Scribner's, 1984. Subj: Babies. Sibling rivalry.

I have four names for my grandfather ill. by Christopher G. Knight. Little, 1976. Subj: Emotions – love. Family life – grandfathers.

My island grandma ill. by Emily Arnold McCully. Warne, 1979. Subj: Family life – grandmothers. Islands.

Sea swan ill. by Catherine Stock. Macmillan, 1988. ISBN 0-02-751700-4 Subj: Behavior – seeking better things. Old age. Sports – swimming.

Lasson, Robert. *Orange Oliver: the kitten who wore glasses* ill. by Chuck Hayden. McKay, 1957. Subj: Animals – cats. Farms. Glasses. Senses – seeing.

Latham, Hugh. *Mother Goose in French* (Mother Goose)

Lathrop, Dorothy Pulis. *An angel in the woods* ill. by author. Macmillan, 1947. Subj: Angels. Holidays – Christmas.

Puppies for keeps ill. by author. Macmillan, 1943. Subj: Animals – dogs. Pets.

Who goes there? ill. by author. Macmillan, 1935. Subj: Activities – picnicking. Animals. Character traits – kindness to animals. Seasons – winter.

Latimer, Jim. *Going the moose way home* ill. by Donald Carrick. Scribner's, 1988. ISBN 0-684-18890-2 Subj: Animals – moose. Forest, woods. Friendship.

Lattimore, Deborah Nourse. *The prince and the golden ax: a Minoan tale* ill. by author. Harper, 1988. ISBN 0-06-023716-3 Subj: Character traits – willfulness. Folk and fairy tales. Royalty.

Lattin, Anne. *Peter's policeman* ill. by Gertrude E. Espenscheid. Follett, 1958. Subj: Careers – police officers.

Lauber, Patricia. *Get ready for robots!* ill. by True Kelley. Harper, 1987. ISBN 0-690-04578-6 Subj: Robots.

Snakes are hunters ill. by Holly Keller. Harper, 1988. ISBN 0-690-04630-8 Subj: Reptiles – snakes. Science.

What's hatching out of that egg? ill. with photos. Crown, 1979. Subj: Eggs. Science.

Laurence, Margaret. *The Christmas birthday story* ill. by Helen Lucas. Knopf, 1980. Subj: Birthdays. Holidays – Christmas. Religion.

Laurencin, Geneviève. *I wish I were* tr. from German by Andrea Mernan; ill. by Ulises Wensell. Putnam's, 1987. ISBN 0-399-21416-X Subj: Animals. Behavior – bullying. Behavior – wishing.

Laurin, Anne. *Little things* ill. by Marcia Sewall. Atheneum, 1978. Subj: Activities – knitting. Character traits – patience. Humor.

Perfect crane ill. by Charles Mikolaycak. Harper, 1981. Subj: Birds – cranes. Foreign lands – Japan. Magic.

Lawrence, James. *Binky Brothers and the fearless four* ill. by Leonard P. Kessler. Harper, 1970. Subj: Careers – detectives. Twins.

Binky Brothers, detectives ill. by Leonard P. Kessler. Harper, 1968. Subj: Careers – detectives. Twins.

Lawrence, John. *The giant of Grabbist* ill. by author. White, 1969. Subj: Foreign lands – England. Giants.

Pope Leo's elephant ill. by author. Collins-World, 1970, 1969. Subj: Animals – elephants. Fire. Foreign lands – Vatican City.

Rabbit and pork: rhyming talk ill. by author. Crowell, 1976. Subj: Animals – cats. Animals – pigs. Animals – rabbits. Poetry, rhyme.

Lawson, Annetta. *The lucky yak* ill. by Allen Say. Houghton, 1980. Subj: Activities – baby-sitting. Animals – yaks. Birds – puffins.

Lawson, Robert. *They were strong and good* ill. by author. Viking, 1940. Subj: Caldecott award book. Family life. U.S. history.

Layton, Aviva. *The squeakers* ill. by Louise Scott. Mosaic Pr., 1982. Subj: Animals – mice. Family life. Theater.

Lazard, Naomi. *What Amanda saw* ill. by Paul O. Zelinsky. Greenwillow, 1981. Subj: Activities – vacationing. Animals. Parties.

Lazy Jack. *Lazy Jack* ill. by Bert Dodson. Troll Assoc., 1979. Subj: Character traits – laziness. Cumulative tales. Folk and fairy tales.

Lazy Jack ill. by Kurt Werth. Viking, 1970. Subj: Character traits – laziness. Cumulative tales. Folk and fairy tales.

Leach, Aroline Arnett Beecher. *The miracle of the mountain* (Kipling, Rudyard)

Leach, Michael. *Rabbits* ill. with photos. Global Lib. Mktg. Serv., 1984. ISBN 0-7136-2387-X Subj: Animals – rabbits. Nature. Science.

Leader, Charles *see* Charles, Robert Henry

Leaf, Margaret. *Eyes of the dragon* ill. by Ed Young. Lothrop, 1987. ISBN 0-688-06156-7 Subj: Activities – painting. Careers – artists. Character traits – stubbornness. Dragons. Foreign lands – China.

Leaf, Munro. *Boo, who used to be scared of the dark* ill. by author. Random House, 1948. Subj: Bedtime. Emotions – fear. Night.

A flock of watchbirds ill. by author. Lippincott, 1946. Subj: Behavior – misbehavior. Etiquette.

Gordon, the goat ill. by author. Lippincott, 1944. Subj: Animals – goats.

Grammar can be fun ill. by author. Lippincott, 1934. Subj: Language.

Health can be fun ill. by author. Stokes, 1943. Subj: Health.

How to behave and why ill. by author. Lippincott, 1946. Subj: Etiquette.

Manners can be fun ill. by author. Rev. ed. Lippincott, 1958. Subj: Etiquette.

Noodle ill. by author. Four Winds Pr., 1965. Subj: Animals – dogs. Self-concept.

Robert Francis Weatherbee ill. by author. Lippincott, 1935. Subj: School.

Safety can be fun ill. by author. New, rev. ed. Lippincott, 1961. Subj: Safety.

The story of Ferdinand the bull ill. by Robert Lawson. Viking, 1936. Subj: Animals – bulls, cows. Character traits – individuality. Foreign lands – Spain. Violence, anti-violence.

Wee Gillis ill. by Robert Lawson. Viking, 1938. Subj: Caldecott award honor book. Foreign lands – Scotland.

Leaf, Wilbur Munro see Leaf, Munro

Leander, Ed. *Q is for crazy* ill. by Jözef Sumichrast. Dial-Delacorte, 1977. Subj: ABC books.

Lear, Edward. *ABC* ill. by author. McGraw-Hill, 1965. Subj: ABC books. Poetry, rhyme.

A book of nonsense ill. by author. Metropolitan Museum of Art-Viking, 1980. Subj: Poetry, rhyme.

The dong with the luminous nose ill. by Edward Gorey. Addison-Wesley, 1969. Subj: Humor. Poetry, rhyme.

An Edward Lear alphabet ill. by Carol Newsom. Lothrop, 1983. Subj: ABC books.

Edward Lear's ABC: alphabet rhymes for children ill. by Carol Pike. Merrimack, 1986. ISBN 0-88162-219-2 Subj: ABC books. Poetry, rhyme.

Edward Lear's nonsense book ill. by Tony Palazzo. Doubleday, 1956. Subj: Humor. Music. Poetry, rhyme.

Hilary Knight's the owl and the pussy-cat (Knight, Hilary)

The jumblies ill. by Emma Crosby. Merrimack, 1986. ISBN 0-88162-185-4 Subj: Poetry, rhyme.

A Learical lexicon sel. by Myra Cohn Livingston; ill. by Joseph Low. Atheneum, 1985. Subj: Humor. Poetry, rhyme.

Lear's nonsense verses ill. by Tomi Ungerer. Grosset, 1967. Subj: Humor. Poetry, rhyme.

Limericks by Lear ill. by Lois Ehlert. Collins-World, 1965. Subj: Poetry, rhyme.

Nonsense alphabets ill. by Richard Scarry. Doubleday, 1962. Subj: ABC books. Poetry, rhyme.

The nutcrackers and the sugar-tongs ill. by Marcia Sewall. Little, 1978. Subj: Humor. Poetry, rhyme.

The owl and the pussycat ill. by Lorinda Bryan Cauley. Putnam's, 1986. ISBN 0-399-21254-X Subj: Animals – cats. Birds – owls. Poetry, rhyme.

The owl and the pussy-cat ill. by Barbara Cooney. Little, 1969. First pub. in 1961. Subj: Animals – cats. Birds – owls. Poetry, rhyme.

The owl and the pussycat ill. by Emma Crosby. Merrimack, 1986. ISBN 0-88162-183-8 Subj: Animals – cats. Birds – owls. Poetry, rhyme.

The owl and the pussy-cat ill. by William Pène Du Bois. Doubleday, 1961. Subj: Animals – cats. Birds – owls. Poetry, rhyme.

The owl and the pussycat ill. by Lori Farbanish. Putnam's, 1988. ISBN 0-448-10229-3 Subj: Animals – cats. Birds – owls. Poetry, rhyme.

The owl and the pussy-cat ill. by Gwen Fulton. Atheneum, 1977. Subj: Animals – cats. Birds – owls. Poetry, rhyme.

The owl and the pussycat ill. by Paul Galdone. Houghton, 1987. ISBN 0-89919-505-9 Subj: Animals – cats. Birds – owls. Poetry, rhyme.

The owl and the pussy-cat ill. by Elaine Muis. Grosset, 1977. Subj: Animals – cats. Birds – owls. Poetry, rhyme.

The owl and the pussycat ill. by Erica Rutherford. Tundra, 1986. ISBN 0-88776-181-X Subj: Animals – cats. Birds – owls. Poetry, rhyme.

The owl and the pussycat ill. by Janet Stevens. Holiday, 1983. ISBN 0-8231-0474-9 Subj: Animals – cats. Birds – owls. Poetry, rhyme.

The owl and the pussycat ill. by Colin West. Warne, 1988. ISBN 0-7232-3541-4 Subj: Animals – cats. Birds – owls. Poetry, rhyme.

The owl and the pussy-cat and other nonsense ill. by Owen Wood. Viking, 1979. Subj: Animals – cats. Birds – owls. Poetry, rhyme.

The pelican chorus ill. by Harold Berson. Parents, 1967. Subj: Birds – pelicans. Humor. Music. Poetry, rhyme. Songs.

The pelican chorus and the quangle wangle's hat ill. by Kevin W. Maddison. Viking, 1981. Subj: Birds – pelicans. Humor. Music. Poetry, rhyme. Songs.

The pobble who has no toes ill. by Emma Crosby. Merrimack, 1986. ISBN 0-88162-184-6 Subj: Humor. Poetry, rhyme.

The pobble who has no toes ill. by Kevin W. Maddison. Viking, 1977. Subj: Humor. Poetry, rhyme.

The quangle wangle's hat ill. by Emma Crosby. Merrimack, 1986. ISBN 0-88162-182-X Subj: Clothing. Humor. Poetry, rhyme.

The quangle wangle's hat ill. by Helen Oxenbury. Watts, 1969. Subj: Clothing. Humor. Poetry, rhyme.

The quangle wangle's hat ill. by Janet Stevens. Harcourt, 1988. ISBN 0-15-264450-4 Subj: Clothing. Humor. Poetry, rhyme.

Two laughable lyrics: The pobble who has no toes, [and] The quangle wangle's hat ill. by Paul Galdone. Putnam's, 1966. Subj: Clothing. Humor. Poetry, rhyme.

Whizz! ill. by Janina Domanska. Macmillan, 1973. Completed by Ogden Nash. Subj: Cumulative tales. Humor. Poetry, rhyme.

Lee, Dennis. *Alligator pie* ill. by Frank Newfeld. Houghton, 1975. Subj: Nursery rhymes. Poetry, rhyme.

Lee, Jeanne M. *Ba-Nam* ill. by author. Holt, 1987. ISBN 0-8050-0169-7 Subj: Character traits — kindness. Foreign lands — Vietnam. Weather — storms.

Legend of the Li River: an ancient Chinese tale ill. by author. Holt, 1983. ISBN 0-03-063523-3 Subj: Folk and fairy tales. Foreign lands — China. Rocks.

The legend of the milky way ill. by author. Holt, 1982. Subj: Folk and fairy tales. Foreign lands — China. Stars.

Toad is the uncle of heaven: a Vietnamese folk tale ill. by reteller. Holt, 1985. ISBN 0-03-004652-1 Subj: Animals. Folk and fairy tales. Frogs and toads. Royalty. Weather — rain.

Leech, Jay. *Bright Fawn and me* by Jay Leech and Zane Spencer; ill. by Glo Coalson. Crowell, 1979. Subj: Fairs. Indians of North America. Sibling rivalry.

Leedy, Loreen. *The bunny play* ill. by author. Holiday House, 1988. ISBN 0-8234-0679-2 Subj: Animals — rabbits. Theater.

A dragon Christmas: things to make and do ill. by author. Holiday, 1988. ISBN 0-8234-0716-0 Subj: Activities. Dragons. Holidays — Christmas.

The dragon Halloween party ill. by author. Holiday, 1986. ISBN 0-8234-0611-3 Subj: Dragons. Holidays — Halloween. Parties. Poetry, rhyme.

A number of dragons ill. by author. Holiday, 1985. ISBN 0-8234-0568-0 Subj: Counting. Dragons. Poetry, rhyme.

Leeton, Will C. *The Tower of Babel* ill. by Jeffrey K. Lindberg. Dandelion, 1979. Subj: Language. Religion.

Le Gallienne, Eva. *The little mermaid* (Andersen, H. C. (Hans Christian))

The nightingale (Andersen, H. C. (Hans Christian))

The snow queen (Andersen, H. C. (Hans Christian))

Le Guin, Ursula K. *Catwings* ill. by S. D. Schindler. Watts, 1988. ISBN 0-531-08359-4 Subj: Activities — flying. Animals — cats.

Solomon Leviathan's nine hundred and thirty-first trip around the world ill. by Alicia Austin. Putnam's, 1988. ISBN 0-399-21491-7 Subj: Animals — giraffes. Animals — whales. Behavior — seeking better things. Reptiles — snakes.

A visit from Dr. Katz ill. by Ann Barrow. Atheneum, 1988. ISBN 0-689-31332-2 Subj: Animals — cats. Illness.

Leichman, Seymour. *Shaggy dogs and spotty dogs and shaggy and spotty dogs* ill. by author. Harcourt, 1973. Subj: Animals — dogs. Poetry, rhyme.

The wicked wizard and the wicked witch ill. by author. Harcourt, 1972. Subj: Magic. Poetry, rhyme. Witches. Wizards.

Leigh, Oretta. *The merry-go-round* ill. by Kathryn E. Shoemaker. Holiday, 1985. ISBN 0-8234-0544-3 Subj: Animals. Merry-go-rounds. Poetry, rhyme.

Leiner, Katherine. *Both my parents work* photos. by Steve Sax. Watts, 1986. ISBN 0-531-10101-0 Subj: Activities — working. Family life.

Leisk, David Johnson *see* Johnson, Crockett

Leister, Mary. *The silent concert* ill. by Yōko Mitsuhashi. Bobbs-Merrill, 1970. Subj: Forest, woods. Noise, sounds.

Lemerise, Bruce. *Sheldon's lunch* ill. by author. Parents, 1980. Subj: Activities — cooking. Food. Reptiles — snakes.

Lemieux, Michèle. *What's that noise?* ill. by author. Morrow, 1985. ISBN 0-688-04140-X Subj: Animals — bears. Noise, sounds.

Lemke, Horst. *Places and faces* ill. by author. Scroll Pr., 1971. Translation of Vielerlei aus Stadt und Land. Subj: Wordless.

Lenski, Lois. *Animals for me* ill. by author. Walck, 1941. Subj: Animals.

At our house ill. by author. Walck, 1959. Music by Clyde Robert Bulla. Subj: Family life. Music. Songs.

Big little Davy ill. by author. Walck, 1956. Subj: Animals.

Cowboy Small ill. by author. Oxford Univ. Pr., 1949. Subj: Cowboys.

Davy and his dog ill. by author. Walck, 1957. Subj: Animals — dogs. Music. Songs.

Davy goes places ill. by author. Walck, 1961. Subj: Activities — traveling. Music. Songs. Transportation.

Debbie and her dolls ill. by author. Walck, 1970. Subj: Animals — dogs. Toys — dolls.

Debbie and her family ill. by author. Walck, 1969. Subj: Family life.

Debbie and her grandma ill. by author. Walck, 1967. Subj: Family life — grandmothers. Music. Songs.

Debbie goes to nursery school ill. by author. Walck, 1970. Subj: School.

A dog came to school ill. by author. Oxford Univ. Pr., 1955. Subj: Animals — dogs. Music. School. Songs.

I like winter ill. by author. Walck, 1950. Subj: Music. Poetry, rhyme. Seasons — winter. Songs.

I went for a walk ill. by author. Walck, 1958. Subj: Activities — walking. Music. Songs.

Let's play house ill. by author. Walck, 1944. Subj: Activities — playing. Toys — dolls.

The life I live: collected poems ill. by author. Walck, 1966. Subj: Poetry, rhyme. Songs.

The little airplane ill. by author. Walck, 1938. Subj: Airplanes, airports.

The little auto ill. by author. Oxford Univ. Pr., 1934. Subj: Automobiles.

The little family ill. by author. Doubleday, 1932. Subj: Family life.

The little farm ill. by author. Walck, 1942. Subj: Farms.

The little fire engine ill. by author. Oxford Univ. Pr., 1946. Subj: Careers – firefighters.

The little sail boat ill. by author. Walck, 1937, 1965. Subj: Boats, ships.

The little train ill. by author. Oxford Univ. Pr., 1940. Subj: Careers – railroad engineers. Trains.

Lois Lenski's big book of Mr. Small ill. by author. Walck, 1979. Subj: Careers. Transportation.

Mr. and Mrs. Noah ill. by author. Crowell, 1948. Subj: Boats, ships. Religion – Noah.

Now it's fall ill. by author. Walck, 1948. Subj: Poetry, rhyme. Seasons – fall.

On a summer day ill. by author. Oxford Univ. Pr., 1953. Subj: Poetry, rhyme. Seasons – summer.

Papa Small ill. by author. Walck, 1951. Subj: Family life. Family life – fathers.

Policeman Small ill. by author. Walck, 1962. Subj: Careers – police officers. City.

Sing a song of people ill. by Giles Laroche. Little, 1987. ISBN 0-316-52074-8 Subj: City. Format, unusual. Poetry, rhyme.

Spring is here ill. by author. Walck, 1945. Subj: Poetry, rhyme. Seasons – spring.

A surprise for Davy ill. by author. Walck, 1947. Subj: Birthdays. Parties.

Susie Mariar ill. by author. Walck, 1967. First pub. in 1939. Subj: Cumulative tales. Folk and fairy tales. Poetry, rhyme.

Lent, Blair. *Bayberry Bluff* ill. by author. Houghton, 1987. ISBN 0-395-35384-X Subj: City. Islands.

John Tabor's ride ill. by author. Little, 1966. Subj: Animals – whales. Folk and fairy tales. Humor.

Pistachio ill. by author. Little, 1964. Subj: Animals – bulls, cows. Circus. Clowns, jesters.

Leodhas, Sorche Nic *see* Alger, Leclaire

Leonard, Marcia. *Little owl leaves the nest* ill. by Carol Newsom. Bantam, 1984. Subj: Birds – owls. Problem solving.

Lerner, Carol. *Flowers of a woodland spring* ill. by author. Morrow, 1979. Subj: Flowers. Forest, woods. Seasons – spring.

Lerner, Marguerite Rush. *Dear little mumps child* ill. by George Overlie. Lerner, 1959. Subj: Illness. Poetry, rhyme.

Doctors' tools ill. by George Overlie. Rev. 2nd ed. Lerner, 1960. Subj: Careers – doctors. Tools.

Lefty, the story of left-handedness ill. by Rov André. Lerner, 1960. Subj: Character traits – being different. Left-handedness.

Michael gets the measles ill. by George Overlie. Lerner, 1959. Subj: Illness.

Peter gets the chickenpox ill. by George Overlie. Lerner, 1959. Subj: Illness.

Lerner, Sharon. *Big Bird's copycat day* featuring Jim Henson's Sesame Street Muppets; ill. by Jean-Pierre Jacquet. Random House, 1984. Subj: Puppets.

Follow the monsters! ill. by Tom Cooke. Random House, 1985. ISBN 0-394-97126-4 Subj: Monsters. Poetry, rhyme. Puppets.

LeRoy, Gen. *Billy's shoes* ill. by J. Winslow Higginbottom. McGraw-Hill, 1981. Subj: Clothing. Sibling rivalry.

Lucky stiff! ill. by J. Winslow Higginbottom. McGraw-Hill, 1981. Subj: Humor. Sibling rivalry.

LeSieg, Theo *see* Seuss, Dr.

Lesikin, Joan. *Down the road* ill. by author. Prentice-Hall, 1978. Subj: Behavior – sharing. Reptiles – snakes. Reptiles – turtles, tortoises.

Lessac, Frané. *My little island* ill. by author. Lippincott, 1985. ISBN 0-397-32115-5 Subj: Foreign lands – Caribbean Islands. Islands.

Lesser, Carolyn. *The goodnight circle* ill. by Lorinda Bryan Cauley. Harcourt, 1984. Subj: Animals. Bedtime. Night.

Lesser, Rika. *Hansel and Gretel* (Grimm, Jacob)

Lester, Alison. *Clive eats alligators* ill. by author. Houghton, 1986. ISBN 0-395-40775-3 Subj: Activities. Character traits – individuality.

Ruby ill. by author. Houghton, 1988. ISBN 0-395-46477-3 Subj: Bedtime. Dreams.

Lester, Helen. *It wasn't my fault* ill. by Lynn Munsinger. Houghton, 1985. ISBN 0-395-35629-6 Subj: Animals. Cumulative tales.

Pookins gets her way ill. by Lynn Munsinger. Houghton, 1987. ISBN 0-395-42636-7 Subj: Character traits – willfulness. Elves and little people.

A porcupine named Fluffy ill. by Lynn Munsinger. Houghton, 1986. ISBN 0-395-36895-2 Subj: Animals – porcupines. Names.

Tacky the penguin ill. by Lynn Munsinger. Houghton, 1988. ISBN 0-395-45536-7 Subj: Animals – wolves. Birds – penguins. Character traits – individuality.

The wizard, the fairy and the magic chicken ill. by Lynn Munsinger. Houghton, 1983. Subj: Behavior – sharing. Birds – chickens. Fairies. Friendship. Wizards.

Lester, Julius. *The knee-high man and other tales* ill. by Ralph Pinto. Dial Pr., 1972. ISBN 0-8037-4593-1 Subj: Ethnic groups in the U.S. – Afro-Americans. Folk and fairy tales.

Le-Tan, Pierre. *The afternoon cat* ill. by author. Pantheon, 1977. Subj: Activities. Animals – cats.

Timothy's dream book ill. by author. Farrar, 1978. Subj: Careers. Imagination.

Visit to the North Pole ill. by author. Crown, 1983. Subj: Dreams. Imagination. Toys – teddy bears.

Le Tord, Bijou. *Good wood bear* ill. by author. Bradbury Pr., 1985. ISBN 0-02-756440-1 Subj: Animals – bears. Birds – geese. Houses.

Joseph and Nellie ill. by author. Bradbury Pr., 1986. ISBN 0-02-756450-9 Subj: Careers – fishermen. Sea and seashore.

My Grandma Leonie ill. by author. Bradbury Pr., 1987. ISBN 0-02-756490-8 Subj: Death. Family life – grandmothers.

Picking and weaving ill. by author. Four Winds Pr., 1980. Subj: Activities – weaving. Plants.

Rabbit seeds ill. by author. Four Winds Pr., 1984. Subj: Activities – gardening. Animals – rabbits.

Let's count and count out comp. by Marion F. Grayson; ill. by Deborah Derr McClintock. Luce, 1975. Subj: Counting. Games. Poetry, rhyme.

Leupold, Nancy S. *Little ghost Godfry* (Sandberg, Inger)

Leutscher, Alfred. *Earth* ill. by John Butler. Dial Pr., 1983. Subj: Earth. Science.

Water ill. by Nick Hardcastle. Dial Pr., 1983. Subj: Ecology. Science.

Levens, George. *Kippy the koala* ill. by Crosby Newell Bonsall. Harper, 1960. Subj: Animals – koala bears. Poetry, rhyme. Seasons – spring.

Leverich, Kathleen. *The hungry fox and the foxy duck* ill. by Paul Galdone. Parents, 1979. Subj: Animals – foxes. Birds – ducks. Character traits – cleverness.

Levin, Isadora. *The scarlet flower* (Aksakov, Sergei)

Levine, Abby. *Sometimes I wish I were Mindy* by Abby and Sarah Levine; ill. by Blanche Sims. Albert Whitman, 1986. ISBN 0-8075-7542-9 Subj: Emotions – envy, jealousy.

What did mommy do before you? ill. by DyAnne DiSalvo-Ryan. Albert Whitman, 1988. ISBN 0-8075-8819-9 Subj: Babies. Behavior – growing up. Family life – mothers.

You push, I ride ill. by Margot Apple. Albert Whitman, 1989. ISBN 0-8075-9444-X Subj: Animals – pigs. Family life. Poetry, rhyme.

Levine, Joan. *A bedtime story* ill. by Gail Owens. Dutton, 1975. Subj: Bedtime.

Levine, Rhoda. *Harrison loved his umbrella* ill. by Karla Kuskin. Atheneum, 1964. Subj: Character traits – being different. Character traits – individuality. Umbrellas.

Levine, Sarah. *Sometimes I wish I were Mindy* (Levine, Abby)

Levinson, Nancy Smiler. *Clara and the bookwagon* ill. by Carolyn Croll. Harper, 1988. ISBN 0-06-023838-0 Subj: Activities – reading. Libraries.

Levinson, Riki. *I go with my family to Grandma's* ill. by Diane Goode. Dutton, 1986. ISBN 0-525-44261-8 Subj: Activities – photographing. Family life. Family life – grandmothers. Transportation.

Our home is the sea ill. by Dennis Luzak. Dutton, 1988. ISBN 0-525-44406-8 Subj: Family life. Foreign lands – China.

Touch! Touch! ill. by True Kelley. Dutton, 1987. ISBN 0-525-44309-6 Subj: Behavior – misbehavior. Family life.

Watch the stars come out ill. by Diane Goode. Dutton, 1985. ISBN 0-525-44205-7 Subj: Family life. Family life – grandmothers. U.S. history.

Levitin, Sonia. *All the cats in the world* ill. by Charles Robinson. Harcourt, 1982. Subj: Animals – cats. Character traits – kindness to animals.

Nobody stole the pie ill. by Fernando Krahn. Harcourt, 1980. Subj: Activities – cooking. Crime. Food.

A single speckled egg ill. by John M. Larrecq. Parnassus Pr., 1976. Subj: Behavior – worrying. Eggs. Farms.

A sound to remember ill. by Gabriel Lisowski. Harcourt, 1979. Subj: Jewish culture. Religion. Self-concept.

Who owns the moon? ill. by John M. Larrecq. Parnassus, 1973. ISBN 0-395-27656-X Subj: Behavior – fighting, arguing. Moon. Problem solving.

Levoy, Myron. *The Hanukkah of Great-Uncle Otto* ill. by Donna Ruff. Jewish Pub. Soc., 1984. ISBN 0-8276-0242-1 Subj: Family life. Holidays – Hanukkah. Jewish culture.

Levy, Elizabeth. *Nice little girls* ill. by Mordicai Gerstein. Delacorte Pr., 1974. Subj: School.

Something queer at the ball park ill. by Mordicai Gerstein. Delacorte, 1975. Subj: Crime. Problem solving.

Something queer at the haunted school ill. by Mordicai Gerstein. Delacorte, 1982. Subj: Ghosts. Problem solving. School.

Something queer at the library ill. by Mordicai Gerstein. Delacorte Pr., 1977. ISBN 0-440-08128-9 Subj: Animals – dogs. Behavior – misbehavior. Libraries. Problem solving.

Something queer in rock 'n' roll ill. by Mordicai Gerstein. Delacorte Pr., 1987. ISBN 0-385-29547-2 Subj: Animals – dogs. Music. Problem solving.

Something queer is going on ill. by Mordecai Gerstein. Delacorte Pr., 1973. Subj: Animals – dogs. Problem solving.

Something queer on vacation ill. by Mordecai Gerstein. Delacorte, 1980. Subj: Activities – vacationing. Behavior – misbehavior. Problem solving. Sea and seashore.

Levy, Miriam F. *Adam's world, San Francisco* (Fraser, Kathleen)

Levy, Sara G. *Mother Goose rhymes for Jewish children* ill. by Jessie B. Robinson. Bloch, 1945. Subj: Jewish culture. Nursery rhymes.

Lewin, Betsy. *Animal snackers* ill. by author. Dodd, 1980. Subj: Animals. Food. Poetry, rhyme.

Cat count ill. by author. Dodd, 1981. Subj: Animals – cats. Counting. Poetry, rhyme.

Hip, hippo, hooray! ill. by author. Dodd, 1982. Subj: Animals – hippopotami. Counting. Illness. Weather.

Lewin, Hugh. *An elephant came to swim* by Hugh Lewin and Lisa Kopper; ill. by authors. David & Charles, 1986. ISBN 0-241-11432-2 Subj: Animals – elephants. Foreign lands – Africa.

Jafta ill. by Lisa Kopper. Carolrhoda, 1983. Subj: Emotions. Family life. Foreign lands – Africa.

Jafta and the wedding ill. by Lisa Kopper. Carolrhoda, 1983. Subj: Family life. Foreign lands – Africa. Weddings.

Jafta - the journey ill. by Lisa Kopper. Carolrhoda, 1984. Subj: Activities – traveling. Emotions. Foreign lands – Africa.

Jafta - the town ill. by Lisa Kopper. Carolrhoda, 1984. Subj: City. Emotions. Foreign lands – Africa.

Jafta's father ill. by Lisa Kopper. Carolrhoda, 1983. Subj: Family life – fathers. Foreign lands – Africa.

Jafta's mother ill. by Lisa Kopper. Carolrhoda, 1983. Subj: Family life – mothers. Foreign lands – Africa.

Lewis, Claudia Louise. *When I go to the moon* ill. by Leonard Weisgard. Macmillan, 1961. Subj: Earth. Moon.

Lewis, Eils Moorhouse. *The snug little house* ill. by Elise Primavera. Atheneum, 1981. ISBN 0-689-50177-3 Subj: Character traits – helpfulness. Houses.

Lewis, J. Patrick. *The tsar and the amazing cow* ill. by Friso Henstra. Dial Pr., 1988. ISBN 0-8037-0411-9 Subj: Behavior – greed. Folk and fairy tales. Old age.

Lewis, Lucia Z. *see* Anderson, Lucia

Lewis, Naomi. *The butterfly collector* ill. by Fulvio Testa. Prentice-Hall, 1979. Subj: Behavior – collecting things. Insects – butterflies, caterpillars. Poetry, rhyme. Riddles.

Hare and badger go to town ill. by Tony Ross. David & Charles, 1987. ISBN 0-905478-94-0 Subj: Animals. Ecology.

Jorinda and Joringel (Grimm, Jacob)

Leaves ill. by Fulvio Testa. Harper, 1983. Subj: Plants. Seasons. Trees.

Once upon a rainbow ill. by Gabriele Eichenauer. Jonathan Cape, 1982. Subj: Concepts – color. Poetry, rhyme. Toys – teddy bears.

Puffin ill. by Deborah King. Lothrop, 1984. Subj: Birds – puffins. Foreign lands – Scotland.

The snow queen (Andersen, H. C. (Hans Christian))

The stepsister ill. by Allison Reed. Dial Pr., 1987. ISBN 0-8037-0430-5 Subj: Animals – cats. Family life – step families.

Swan ill. by Deborah King. Lothrop, 1986. ISBN 0-688-05535-4 Subj: Birds – swans. Nature. Science.

The wild swans (Andersen, H. C. (Hans Christian))

Lewis, Richard. *In a spring garden* ill. by Ezra Jack Keats. Dial Pr., 1965. A collection of haiku. Subj: Poetry, rhyme.

In the night, still dark ill. by Ed Young. Atheneum, 1988. ISBN 0-689-31310-1 Subj: Hawaii. Poetry, rhyme.

Lewis, Robin Baird. *Aunt Armadillo* ill. by author. Firefly Pr., 1985. ISBN 0-920303-38-2 Subj: Animals – armadillos. Libraries.

Friska, the sheep that was too small ill. by author. Farrar, 1988. ISBN 0-374-32461-1 Subj: Animals – sheep. Animals – wolves. Character traits – bravery.

Hello, Mr. Scarecrow ill. by author. Farrar, 1987. ISBN 0-374-32947-8 Subj: Days of the week, months of the year. Scarecrows.

Lewis, Stephen. *Zoo city* ill. by author. Greenwillow, 1976. Subj: Animals. City. Format, unusual. Imagination. Wordless. Zoos.

Lewis, Thomas P. *Call for Mr. Sniff* ill. by Beth Lee Weiner. Harper, 1981. Subj: Animals – dogs. Birthdays. Problem solving.

Clipper ship ill. by Joan Sandin. Harper, 1978. ISBN 0-06-023809-7 Subj: Activities – traveling. Boats, ships.

Hill of fire ill. by Joan Sandin. Harper, 1971. Subj: Foreign lands – Mexico. Volcanoes.

Mr. Sniff and the motel mystery ill. by Beth Lee Weiner. Harper, 1984. ISBN 0-06-023825-9 Subj: Animals – dogs. Problem solving.

Lewiton, Mina *see* Simon, Mina Lewiton

Lexau, Joan M. *Benjie* ill. by Don Bolognese. Dial Pr., 1964. Subj: Character traits – shyness. Ethnic groups in the U.S. – Afro-Americans. Family life. Family life – grandmothers. Problem solving.

Benjie on his own ill. by Don Bolognese. Dial Pr., 1970. Subj: City. Ethnic groups in the U.S. – Afro-Americans. Family life – grandmothers. Illness. Problem solving.

Cathy is company ill. by Aliki. Dial Pr., 1961. Subj: Etiquette. Friendship.

Come here, cat ill. by Steven Kellogg. Harper, 1973. Subj: Animals – cats. City.

Crocodile and hen ill. by Joan Sandin. Harper, 1969. Adaptation of Why the crocodile does not eat the hen, from Notes on the folklore of the Fjort (French Congo), by R. E. Dennett. Subj: Birds – chickens. Cumulative tales. Folk and fairy tales. Foreign lands – Africa. Reptiles – alligators, crocodiles.

The dog food caper ill. by Marylin Hafner. Dial Pr., 1985. ISBN 0-8037-0108-X Subj: Animals – dogs. Animals – mice. Problem solving. Witches.

Every day a dragon ill. by Ben Shecter. Harper, 1967. Subj: Family life. Family life – fathers. Games.

Finders keepers, losers weepers ill. by Tomie de Paola. Lippincott, 1967. Subj: Babies. Behavior – losing things. Behavior – lying. Family life.

Go away, dog ill. by Crosby Newell Bonsall. Harper, 1963. Subj: Animals – dogs. Birthdays.

The homework caper ill. by Syd Hoff. Harper, 1966. Subj: Sibling rivalry.

A house so big ill. by Syd Hoff. Harper, 1968. Subj: Character traits – generosity. Emotions – love. Family life – mothers. Imagination.

I hate red rover ill. by Gail Owens. Dutton, 1979. Subj: Behavior – growing up. Games.

I should have stayed in bed ill. by Syd Hoff. Harper, 1965. Subj: Behavior – bad day. Emotions – embarrassment. Ethnic groups in the U.S. – Afro-Americans.

I'll tell on you ill. by Gail Owens. Dutton, 1981. ISBN 0-525-32542-5 Subj: Animals – dogs. Behavior – misbehavior. Sports – baseball.

It all began with a drip, drip, drip ill. by Joan Sandin. McCall, 1970. Subj: Behavior – mistakes. Character traits – bravery. Folk and fairy tales. Foreign lands – India.

Me day ill. by Robert Weaver. Dial Pr., 1971. Subj: Birthdays. City. Divorce. Ethnic groups in the U.S. – Afro-Americans. Family life. Family life – fathers.

Millicent's ghost ill. by Ben Shecter. Dial Pr., 1962. Subj: Ghosts. Night.

More beautiful than flowers ill. by Don Bolognese. Lippincott, 1966. Subj: Poetry, rhyme. Religion.

Olaf reads ill. by Harvey Weiss. Dial Pr., 1961. Subj: Activities – reading.

The rooftop mystery ill. by Syd Hoff. Harper, 1968. Subj: Ethnic groups in the U.S. – Afro-Americans. Moving. Toys – dolls.

Who took the farmer's hat? ill. by Fritz Siebel. Harper, 1963. Subj: Clothing. Farms. Weather – wind.

Lifton, Betty Jean. *Goodnight orange monster* ill. by Cyndy Szekeres. Atheneum, 1972. Subj: Bedtime. Emotions – fear. Monsters. Night.

Joji and the Amanojaku ill. by Eiichi Mitsui. Norton, 1965. Subj: Birds. Foreign lands – Japan. Goblins. Scarecrows.

Joji and the dragon ill. by Eiichi Mitsui. Morrow, 1957. Subj: Birds. Dragons. Foreign lands – Japan. Scarecrows.

Joji and the fog ill. by Eiichi Mitsui. Morrow, 1959. Subj: Birds. Scarecrows. Weather – fog.

The many lives of Chio and Goro ill. by Yasuo Segawa. Norton, 1968. Subj: Animals – foxes. Birds – chickens. Foreign lands – Japan.

The rice-cake rabbit ill. by Eiichi Mitsui. Norton, 1966. Subj: Animals – rabbits. Foreign lands – Japan. Moon.

The secret seller ill. by Etienne Delessert and Norma Holt. Norton, 1967. Subj: Behavior – secrets. Imagination.

Lillegard, Dee. *I can be a baker.* Childrens Pr., 1986. ISBN 0-516-01892-2 Subj: Careers – bakers.

I can be a carpenter ill. with photos. Childrens Pr., 1986. ISBN 0-516-01884-1 Subj: Careers – carpenters.

I can be a welder by Dee Lillegard and Wayne Stoker. Childrens Pr., 1986. ISBN 0-516-01895-7 Subj: Careers – welders.

I can be an electrician ill. with photos. Childrens Pr., 1986. ISBN 0-516-01896-5 Subj: Careers – electricians.

Lillie, Patricia. *One very, very quiet afternoon* ill. by author. Greenwillow, 1986. ISBN 0-688-04323-2 Subj: ABC books. Behavior – misbehavior. Parties.

Lilly, Kenneth. *Animal builders* ill. by author. Random House, 1984. Subj: Activities. Animals. Format, unusual – board books. Science.

Animal climbers ill. by author. Random House, 1984. Subj: Activities. Animals. Format, unusual – board books. Science.

Animal jumpers ill. by author. Random House, 1984. Subj: Activities. Animals. Format, unusual – board books. Science.

Animal runners ill. by author. Random House, 1984. Subj: Activities. Animals. Format, unusual – board books. Science.

Animal swimmers ill. by author. Random House, 1984. Subj: Activities. Animals. Format, unusual – board books. Science.

Animals at the zoo ill. by author. Simon and Schuster, 1982. Subj: Animals. Format, unusual – board books. Zoos.

Animals in the country ill. by author. Simon and Schuster, 1982. Subj: Animals. Format, unusual – board books. Wordless.

Animals in the jungle ill. by author. Simon and Schuster, 1982. Subj: Animals. Format, unusual – board books. Jungle.

Animals of the ocean ill. by author. Simon and Schuster, 1982. Subj: Animals – dolphins. Animals – polar bears. Animals – seals. Animals – whales. Birds – penguins. Format, unusual – board books. Sea and seashore.

Animals on the farm ill. by author. Simon and Schuster, 1982. Subj: Animals. Farms. Format, unusual – board books.

Linch, Elizabeth Johanna. *Samson* ill. by author. Harper, 1964. Subj: Animals – mice. Holidays – Christmas. Seasons – winter.

Lindberg, Reeve. *Midnight farm* ill. by Susan Jeffers. Dial Pr., 1987. ISBN 0-8037-0333-3 Subj: Animals. Counting. Farms. Night.

Lindbloom, Steven. *Let's give kitty a bath!* ill. by True Kelley. Addison-Wesley, 1982. Subj: Activities – bathing. Animals – cats.

Linden, Madelaine Gill. *Under the blanket* ill. by author. Little, 1987. ISBN 0-316-52626-6 Subj: Poetry, rhyme. Toys.

Lindgren, Astrid. *Christmas in noisy village* by Astrid Lindgren and Ilon Wikland. Tr. by Florence Lamborn; ill. by Ilon Wikland. Viking, 1964. Subj: Foreign lands – Sweden. Holidays – Christmas.

Christmas in the stable ill. by Harald Wiberg. Coward, 1962. Subj: Foreign lands – Sweden. Holidays – Christmas. Religion.

The dragon with red eyes ill. by Ilon Wikland; tr. by Patricia Crampton. Viking, 1987. ISBN 0-670-81620-5 Subj: Dragons. Farms.

I want a brother or sister tr. from Swedish by Barbara Lucas; ill. by Ilon Wikland. Harcourt, 1981. Subj: Babies. Emotions – envy, jealousy. Sibling rivalry.

I want to go to school too tr. by Barbara Lucas; ill. by Ilon Wikland. Farrar, 1987. ISBN 91-29-58328-4 Subj: School. Sibling rivalry.

My nightingale is singing ill. by Svend Otto; tr. by Patricia Crampton. Viking, 1986. ISBN 0-670-80997-7 Subj: Behavior – seeking better things. Emotions – sadness. Poverty.

Of course Polly can do almost everything ill. by Ilon Wikland. Follett, 1978. Subj: Character traits – optimism. Character traits – perseverance. Holidays – Christmas. Trees.

The tomten ill. by Harald Wiberg. Coward, 1961. Adapt. from a poem by Victor Rydberg. Subj: Farms. Foreign lands – Sweden. Seasons – winter. Trolls.

The tomten and the fox adapt. from a poem by Karl-Erik Forsslund; ill. by Harald Wiberg. Coward, 1965. Subj: Animals – foxes. Foreign lands – Sweden. Seasons – winter. Trolls.

Lindgren, Barbro. *Sam's ball* ill. by Eva Eriksson. Morrow, 1983. Subj: Animals – cats. Toys – balls.

Sam's bath ill. by Eva Eriksson. Morrow, 1983. Subj: Activities – bathing. Animals – dogs.

Sam's car ill. by Eva Eriksson. Morrow, 1982. Subj: Behavior – sharing. Toys.

Sam's cookie ill. by Eva Eriksson. Morrow, 1982. Subj: Behavior – sharing. Pets.

Sam's lamp ill. by Eva Eriksson. Morrow, 1983. Subj: Safety.

Sam's potty ill. by Eva Eriksson. Morrow, 1986. ISBN 0-688-06603-8 Subj: Behavior – growing up.

Sam's teddy bear ill. by Eva Eriksson. Morrow, 1982. Subj: Toys – teddy bears.

Sam's wagon ill. by Eva Eriksson. Morrow, 1986. ISBN 0-688-05803-5 Subj: Animals – dogs. Toys.

The wild baby adapt. from Swedish by Jack Prelutsky; ill. by Eva Eriksson. Greenwillow, 1981. Subj: Behavior – misbehavior. Family life – mothers. Poetry, rhyme.

The wild baby goes to sea adapt. from Swedish by Jack Prelutsky; ill. by Eva Eriksson. Greenwillow, 1983. Subj: Activities – playing. Family life – mothers. Imagination. Toys.

A worm's tale ill. by Cecilia Torudd. Farrar, 1988. ISBN 91-29-59068-X Subj: Animals – worms. Friendship.

Lindman, Maj. *Flicka, Ricka, Dicka and a little dog* ill. by author. Albert Whitman, 1946. Subj: Animals – dogs. Family life. Foreign lands – Sweden. Triplets.

Flicka, Ricka, Dicka and the big red hen ill. by author. Albert Whitman, 1960. Subj: Birds – chickens. Family life. Triplets.

Flicka, Ricka, Dicka and the new dotted dress ill. by author. Albert Whitman, 1939. Subj: Character traits – helpfulness. Family life. Foreign lands – Sweden. Triplets.

Flicka, Ricka, Dicka and the three kittens ill. by author. Albert Whitman, 1941. Subj: Animals – cats. Family life. Triplets.

Flicka, Ricka, Dicka bake a cake ill. by author. Albert Whitman, 1955. Subj: Activities – cooking. Birthdays. Family life. Foreign lands – Sweden. Triplets.

Sailboat time ill. by author. Albert Whitman, 1951. Subj: Boats, ships. Foreign lands – Sweden.

Snipp, Snapp, Snurr and the buttered bread ill. by author. Albert Whitman, 1934. Subj: Cumulative tales. Family life. Farms. Foreign lands – Sweden. Triplets.

Snipp, Snapp, Snurr and the magic horse ill. by author. Albert Whitman, 1935. Subj: Family life. Foreign lands – Sweden. Magic. Toys – rocking horses. Triplets.

Snipp, Snapp, Snurr and the red shoes ill. by author. Albert Whitman, 1932. Subj: Activities – vacationing. Birthdays. Character traits – generosity. Character traits – helpfulness. Family life. Foreign lands – Lapland. Sports – skiing. Triplets.

Snipp, Snapp, Snurr and the reindeer ill. by author. Albert Whitman, 1957. Subj: Animals – deer. Family life. Foreign lands – Sweden. Triplets.

Snipp, Snapp, Snurr and the seven dogs ill. by author. Albert Whitman, 1959. Subj: Animals – dogs. Family life. Foreign lands – Sweden. Triplets.

Snipp, Snapp, Snurr and the yellow sled ill. by author. Albert Whitman, 1936. Subj: Animals – dogs. Family life. Foreign lands – Sweden. Sports – ice skating. Triplets.

Lindsay, Elizabeth. *A letter for Maria* ill. by Alex de Wolf. Watts, 1988. ISBN 0-531-08375-6 Subj: Activities – painting. Toys – teddy bears.

Lindsey, Treska. *When Batistine made bread* ill. by author. Macmillan, 1985. Subj: Activities – cooking. Activities – working. Food.

Lines, Kathleen. *Dick Whittington* (Dick Whittington and his cat)

Lavender's blue (Mother Goose)

The old ballad of the babes in the woods (The babes in the woods)

Once in royal David's city; a picture book of the Nativity, retold from the Gospels ill. by Harold Jones. Watts, 1956. Subj: Holidays – Christmas. Religion.

Link, Martin A. *The goat in the rug* (Blood, Charles L.)

Linn, Margot. *A trip to the dentist* ill. by Catherine Siracusa. Harper, 1988. ISBN 0-06-025834-9 Subj: Careers – dentists.

A trip to the doctor ill. by Catherine Siracusa. Harper, 1988. ISBN 0-06-025843-8 Subj: Careers – doctors.

Linzer, Jeff. *The fire station book* (Bundt, Nancy)

Lionni, Leo. *Alexander and the wind-up mouse* ill. by author. Pantheon, 1969. Subj: Animals – mice. Caldecott award honor book. Emotions – envy, jealousy. Friendship. Toys.

The biggest house in the world ill. by author. Pantheon, 1968. Subj: Animals. Behavior – greed.

A color of his own ill. by author. Pantheon, 1975. Subj: Character traits – individuality. Concepts – color. Reptiles – lizards.

Colors to talk about ill. by author. Pantheon, 1985. ISBN 0-394-870034 Subj: Animals – mice. Concepts – color. Format, unusual – board books.

Cornelius ill. by author. Pantheon, 1983. Subj: Character traits – being different. Reptiles – alligators, crocodiles.

Fish is fish ill. by author. Pantheon, 1970. Subj: Behavior – misunderstanding. Fish. Friendship. Frogs and toads.

Frederick ill. by author. Pantheon, 1967. Subj: Animals – mice. Caldecott award honor book. Music.

Frederick's fables ill. by author. Pantheon, 1985. ISBN 0-394-87710-1 Subj: Animals.

Geraldine, the music mouse ill. by author. Pantheon, 1979. Subj: Animals – mice. Music.

The greentail mouse ill. by author. Pantheon, 1973. Subj: Animals – mice. Mardi Gras.

In the rabbitgarden ill. by author. Pantheon, 1975. Subj: Animals – foxes. Animals – mice. Reptiles – snakes.

Inch by inch ill. by author. Astor-Honor, 1960. Subj: Birds. Caldecott award honor book. Concepts – measurement. Insects.

It's mine!: a fable ill. by author. Knopf, 1986. ISBN 0-394-97000-X Subj: Behavior – fighting, arguing. Frogs and toads.

Let's make rabbits ill. by author. Pantheon, 1982. Subj: Activities. Animals – rabbits. Art. Imagination.

Letters to talk about ill. by author. Pantheon, 1985. ISBN 0-394-87001-8 Subj: ABC books. Animals – mice. Format, unusual – board books.

Little blue and little yellow ill. by author. Astor-Honor, 1959. Subj: Concepts – color. Friendship.

Mouse days ill. by author. Pantheon, 1981. Subj: Animals – mice. Seasons.

Nicholas, where have you been? ill. by author. Knopf, 1987. ISBN 0-394-98370-X Subj: Animals – mice. Friendship.

Numbers to talk about ill. by author. Pantheon, 1985. ISBN 0-394-87002-6 Subj: Animals – mice. Counting. Format, unusual – board books.

On my beach there are many pebbles ill. by author. Astor-Honor, 1961. Subj: Rocks. Sea and seashore.

Pezzettino ill. by author. Pantheon, 1975. Subj: Character traits – individuality. Concepts – shape. Self-concept.

Six crows ill. by author. Knopf, 1988. ISBN 0-394-99572-4 Subj: Birds – crows. Birds – owls. Farms.

Swimmy ill. by author. Pantheon, 1963. Subj: Caldecott award honor book. Fish. Sea and seashore.

Theodore and the talking mushroom ill. by author. Pantheon, 1971. Subj: Animals – mice. Character traits – optimism.

Tico and the golden wings ill. by author. Pantheon, 1964. Subj: Birds. Character traits – generosity. Character traits – individuality. Character traits – questioning.

Tillie and the wall ill. by author. Knopf, 1989. ISBN 0-394-82155-6 Subj: Animals – mice. Behavior – seeking better things.

What? pictures to talk about ill. by author. Pantheon, 1983. Subj: Animals – mice. Format, unusual – board books. Senses – hearing. Senses – seeing. Senses – smelling. Senses – tasting. Senses – touching. Wordless.

When? ill. by author. Pantheon, 1983. Subj: Animals – mice. Format, unusual – board books. Night. Seasons. Wordless.

Where? pictures to talk about ill. by author. Pantheon, 1983. Subj: Animals – mice. Format, unusual – board books. Humor. Wordless.

Who? pictures to talk about ill. by author. Pantheon Books, 1983. Subj: Animals – mice. Format, unusual – board books. Wordless.

Words to talk about ill. by author. Pantheon, 1985. ISBN 0-394-87004-2 Subj: Animals – mice. Format, unusual – board books. Language.

Lipkind, William. *Billy the kid* by William Lipkind and Nicolas Mordvinoff; ill. by Nicolas Mordvinoff. Harcourt, 1964. Subj: Animals – goats.

The boy and the forest by William Lipkind and Nicolas Mordvinoff; ill. by Nicolas Mordvinoff. Harcourt, 1964. Subj: Animals. Character traits – kindness to animals. Forest, woods. Magic.

Chaga by William Lipkind and Nicolas Mordvinoff; ill. by Nicolas Mordvinoff. Harcourt, 1955. Subj: Animals – elephants. Concepts – size.

The Christmas bunny by William Lipkind and Nicolas Mordvinoff; ill. by Nicolas Mordvinoff. Harcourt, 1953. Subj: Animals – foxes. Animals – rabbits. Holidays – Christmas. Parties.

Circus rucus by William Lipkind and Nicolas Mordvinoff; ill. by Nicolas Mordvinoff. Harcourt, 1954. Subj: Circus.

Even Steven by William Lipkind and Nicolas Mordvinoff; ill. by Nicolas Mordvinoff. Harcourt, 1952. Subj: Animals – dogs. Character traits – selfishness.

Finders keepers by William Lipkind and Nicolas Mordvinoff; ill. by Nicolas Mordvinoff. Harcourt, 1951. Subj: Animals – dogs. Caldecott award book. Character traits – selfishness.

Four-leaf clover by William Lipkind and Nicolas Mordvinoff; ill. by Nicolas Mordvinoff. Harcourt, 1959. Subj: Ethnic groups in the U.S. – Afro-Americans.

The little tiny rooster by William Lipkind and Nicolas Mordvinoff; ill. by Nicolas Mordvinoff. Harcourt, 1960. Subj: Animals – foxes. Birds – chickens. Character traits – smallness. Self-concept.

The magic feather duster by William Lipkind and Nicolas Mordvinoff; ill. by Nicolas Mordvinoff. Harcourt, 1958. Subj: Character traits – kindness. Folk and fairy tales. Magic.

Nubber bear ill. by Roger Antoine Duvoisin. Harcourt, 1966. Subj: Animals – bears. Behavior – misbehavior.

Professor Bull's umbrella by William Lipkind and Georges Schreiber; ill. by Georges Schreiber. Viking, 1954. Subj: Umbrellas.

Russet and the two reds by William Lipkind and Nicolas Mordvinoff; ill. by Nicolas Mordvinoff. Harcourt, 1962. Subj: Animals – cats.

Sleepyhead by William Lipkind and Nicolas Mordvinoff; ill. by Nicolas Mordvinoff. Harcourt, 1957. Subj: Activities – playing. Games. Poetry, rhyme.

The two reds by William Lipkind and Nicolas Mordvinoff; ill. by Nicolas Mordvinoff. Harcourt, 1950. Subj: Animals – cats. Caldecott award honor book. Friendship.

Lippman, Peter. *The Know-It-Alls go to sea* ill. by author. Doubleday, 1982. Subj: Behavior – misbehavior. Boats, ships.

The Know-It-Alls help out ill. by author. Doubleday, 1982. Subj: Behavior – misbehavior. Houses.

The Know-It-Alls mind the store ill. by author. Doubleday, 1982. Subj: Behavior – misbehavior. Stores.

The Know-It-Alls take a winter vacation ill. by author. Doubleday, 1982. Subj: Activities – vacationing. Behavior – misbehavior.

New at the zoo ill. by author. Harper, 1969. Subj: Animals. Bedtime. Zoos.

Peter Lippman's numbers ill. by author. Grosset, 1988. ISBN 0-448-19105-9 Subj: Counting. Format, unusual – toy and movable books.

Peter Lippman's opposites ill. by author. Grosset, 1988. ISBN 0-448-19106-7 Subj: Concepts – opposites. Format, unusual – toy and movable books.

Lisker, Sonia O. *Lost* ill. by author. Harcourt, 1975. Subj: Behavior – lost. Wordless. Zoos.

Two special cards by Sonia O. Lisker and Leigh Dean; ill. by Sonia O. Lisker. Harcourt, 1976. Subj: Divorce. Family life.

Lisowski, Gabriel. *How Tevye became a milkman* ill. by author. Holt, 1976. Subj: Foreign lands – Ukraine. Jewish culture.

Roncalli's magnificent circus ill. by author. Doubleday, 1980. Subj: Animals – bears. Behavior – running away. Circus.

Litchfield, Ada B. *A button in her ear* ill. by Eleanor Mill. Albert Whitman, 1976. Subj: Handicaps – deafness. Senses – hearing.

A cane in her hand ill. by Eleanor Mill. Albert Whitman, 1977. Subj: Handicaps – blindness. Senses – seeing.

A little ABC book. Simon and Schuster, 1980. Subj: ABC books. Format, unusual – board books.

A little book of colors. Simon and Schuster, 1982. Subj: Concepts – color. Format, unusual – board books.

A little book of numbers. Simon and Schuster, 1980. Subj: Counting. Format, unusual – board books.

Little, Emily. *David and the giant* ill. by Hans Wilhelm. Random House, 1987. ISBN 0-394-98867-1 Subj: Behavior – bullying. Giants. Religion.

Little, Lessie Jones. *Children of long ago* ill. by Jan Spivey Gilchrist. Putnam's, 1988. ISBN 0-399-21473-9 Subj: Ethnic groups in the U.S. – Afro-Americans. Poetry, rhyme.

I can do it by myself by Lessie Jones Little and Eloise Greenfield; ill. by Carole Byard. Crowell, 1978. Subj: Birthdays. Character traits – bravery. Plants.

Little, Mary E. *ABC for the library* ill. by author. Atheneum, 1975. Subj: ABC books. Libraries.

Ricardo and the puppets ill. by author. Scribner's, 1958. Subj: Animals – mice. Libraries. Puppets.

The little red hen. *The little red hen* ill. by Janina Domanska. Macmillan, 1973. Subj: Animals. Birds – chickens. Character traits – laziness. Cumulative tales. Farms. Folk and fairy tales. Plants.

The little red hen ill. by Paul Galdone. Seabury Pr., 1973. Subj: Animals. Birds – chickens. Character traits – laziness. Cumulative tales. Farms. Folk and fairy tales. Plants.

The little red hen retold by Jean Horton Berg; reading consultant: Morton Betel; ill. by Mel Pekarsky. Follett, 1963. Subj: Animals. Birds – chickens. Character traits – laziness. Cumulative tales. Farms. Folk and fairy tales. Plants.

The little red hen adapt. and ill. by William Stobbs. Oxford Univ. Pr., 1985. ISBN 0-19-279807-3 Subj: Animals. Birds – chickens. Character traits – laziness. Cumulative tales. Farms. Folk and fairy tales. Plants.

The little red hen: an old story retold and ill. by Margot Zemach. Farrar, 1983. Subj: Animals. Birds – chickens. Character traits – laziness. Cumulative tales. Farms. Folk and fairy tales. Plants.

Little Red Riding Hood. *Little red cap* (Grimm, Jacob)

Little Red Riding Hood (Grimm, Jacob)

Red Riding Hood (De Regniers, Beatrice Schenk)

Little Tommy Tucker. *The history of Little Tom Tucker* ill. by Paul Galdone. McGraw-Hill, 1970. This version was published by J. Kendrew, York, England, ca. 1820. Subj: Nursery rhymes.

Little Tuppen: *an old tale* ill. by Paul Galdone. Seabury Pr., 1967. Subj: Birds – chickens. Cumulative tales. Folk and fairy tales.

Littledale, Freya. *The farmer in the soup* ill. by Molly Delaney. Scholastic, 1987. ISBN 0-590-40194-7 Subj: Behavior – sharing. Farms. Folk and fairy tales.

The little mermaid (Andersen, H. C. (Hans Christian))

The magic plum tree ill. by Enrico Arno. Crown, 1981. Subj: Character traits – individuality. Plants. Royalty.

Peter and the north wind ill. by Troy Howell. Scholastic, 1988. ISBN 0-590-40756-2 Subj: Folk and fairy tales. Weather – wind.

The snow child ill. by Leon Steinmetz. Scholastic, 1978. Subj: Behavior – wishing. Old age. Seasons – winter.

Littlefield, William. *The whiskers of Ho Ho* ill. by Vladimir Bobri. Lothrop, 1958. Subj: Animals – rabbits. Birds – chickens. Folk and fairy tales. Foreign lands – China. Holidays – Easter.

Littlewood, Valerie. *The season clock* ill. by author. Viking, 1987. ISBN 0-670-81433-4 Subj: Behavior – misbehavior. Character traits – bravery. Seasons. Time.

Livermore, Elaine. *Find the cat* ill. by author. Houghton, 1973. Subj: Animals – cats. Games.

Follow the fox ill. by author. Houghton, 1981. Subj: Animals – foxes. Behavior – lost. Behavior – needing someone.

Looking for Henry ill. by author. Houghton, 1988. ISBN 0-395-44240-0 Subj: Animals – leopards. Behavior – hiding. Sports – hunting.

Lost and found ill. by author. Houghton, 1975. Subj: Behavior – losing things. Games.

One to ten, count again ill. by author. Houghton, 1973. Subj: Counting. Games.

Three little kittens lost their mittens ill. by author. Houghton, 1979. Subj: Animals – cats. Behavior – losing things. Games. Nursery rhymes.

Livingston, Carole. *"Why am I going to the hospital?"* (Ciliotta, Claire)

"Why was I adopted?" ill. by Arthur Robins; designed by Paul Walter. Lyle Stuart, 1978. Subj: Adoption. Family life.

Livingston, Myra Cohn. *Cat poems* ill. by Trina Schart Hyman. Holiday, 1987. ISBN 0-8234-0631-8 Subj: Animals – cats. Poetry, rhyme.

Celebrations Leonard Everett Fisher. Holiday, 1985. ISBN 0-8234-0550-8 Subj: Holidays. Poetry, rhyme.

Higgledy-Piggledy: verses and pictures by Myra Cohn Livingston and Peter Sis; ill. by Peter Sis. Macmillan, 1986. ISBN 0-689-50407-1 Subj: Behavior. Poetry, rhyme.

A Learical lexicon (Lear, Edward)

Poems for Jewish holidays ill. by Lloyd Bloom. Holiday, 1986. ISBN 0-8234-0606-7 Subj: Holidays. Jewish culture. Poetry, rhyme.

Poems for mothers ill. by Deborah Kogan Ray. Holiday, 1988. ISBN 0-8234-0678-4 Subj: Holidays – Mother's Day. Poetry, rhyme.

Valentine poems ill. by Patience Brewster. Holiday, 1987. ISBN 0-8234-0587-7 Subj: Animals. Holidays – Valentine's Day. Poetry, rhyme.

Lloyd, David. *Air* ill. by Peter Visscher. Dial Pr., 1982. Subj: Science.

Cat and dog ill. by Clive Scruton. Lothrop, 1987. ISBN 0-688-07268-2 Subj: Animals – cats. Animals – dogs.

Duck ill. by Charlotte Voake. Lippincott, 1988. ISBN 0-397-32275-5 Subj: Animals. Birds – ducks. Family life – grandmothers.

Grandma and the pirate ill. by Gill Tomblin. Crown, 1986. ISBN 0-517-56023-2 Subj: Family life – grandmothers. Imagination. Pirates. Sand. Sea and seashore.

Hello, goodbye ill. by Louise Voce. Lothrop, 1988. ISBN 0-688-07699-8 Subj: Animals. Trees. Weather – rain.

The ridiculous story of Gammer Gurton's needle ill. by Charlotte Voake. Potter, 1987. ISBN 0-517-56513-7 Subj: Behavior – lying. Folk and fairy tales. Humor.

The stopwatch ill. by Penny Dale. Lippincott, 1986. ISBN 0-397-32193-7 Subj: Clocks. Family life – grandmothers. Sibling rivalry.

Lloyd, Errol. *Nandy's bedtime* ill. by author. Merrimack, 1983. Subj: Bedtime. Night.

Nini at carnival ill. by author. Crowell, 1979. Subj: Character traits – helpfulness. Clothing.

Lloyd, Megan. *Chicken tricks* ill. by author. Harper, 1983. Subj: Birds – chickens. Eggs. Humor. Poetry, rhyme.

Lobe, Mira. *The snowman who went for a walk* tr. from German by Peter Carter; ill. by Winfried Opgenoorth. Morrow, 1984. Subj: Activities – walking. Snowmen.

Valerie and the good-night swing tr. from German by Peter Carter; ill. by Winfried Opgenoorth. Oxford Univ. Pr., 1983. Subj: Bedtime. Poetry, rhyme.

Lobel, Anita. *A birthday for the princess* ill. by author. Harper, 1973. Subj: Behavior – needing someone. Birthdays. Royalty.

King Rooster, Queen Hen ill. by author. Greenwillow, 1975. Subj: Animals. Birds – chickens. Foreign lands – Denmark.

The pancake ill. by author. Greenwillow, 1978. Subj: Cumulative tales. Food.

Potatoes, potatoes ill. by author. Greenwillow, 1967. Subj: Violence, anti-violence.

The seamstress of Salzburg ill. by author. Harper, 1970. Subj: Careers – seamstresses. Clothing. Royalty. Sibling rivalry.

The straw maid ill. by author. Greenwillow, 1983. Subj: Character traits – cleverness. Crime.

Sven's bridge ill. by author. Harper, 1965. Subj: Bridges. Royalty.

The troll music ill. by author. Harper, 1966. Subj: Magic. Music. Trolls.

Lobel, Arnold. *The book of pigericks* ill. by author. Harper, 1983. ISBN 0-06-023983-2 Subj: Animals – pigs. Humor. Poetry, rhyme.

Days with Frog and Toad ill. by author. Harper, 1979. Subj: Friendship. Frogs and toads.

Fables ill. by author. Harper, 1980. Subj: Animals. Caldecott award book.

Frog and Toad all year ill. by author. Harper, 1976. Subj: Friendship. Frogs and toads. Seasons.

Frog and Toad are friends ill. by author. Harper, 1970. Subj: Caldecott award honor book. Friendship. Frogs and toads.

The frog and toad pop-up book ill. by author. Harper, 1986. ISBN 0-06-023986-7 Subj: Format, unusual – toy and movable books. Frogs and toads.

Frog and Toad together ill. by author. Harper, 1971. Subj: Friendship. Frogs and toads.

Giant John ill. by author. Harper, 1964. Subj: Giants.

Grasshopper on the road ill. by author. Harper, 1978. Subj: Insects. Insects – grasshoppers.

The great blueness and other predicaments ill. by author. Harper, 1968. Subj: Concepts – color. Wizards.

A holiday for Mister Muster ill. by author. Harper, 1963. Subj: Animals. Illness. Zoos.

How the rooster saved the day ill. by Anita Lobel. Greenwillow, 1977. Subj: Birds – chickens. Character traits – cleverness. Crime.

Lucille ill. by author. Harper, 1964. Subj: Animals – horses. Humor.

The man who took the indoors out ill. by author. Harper, 1974. Subj: Behavior – running away.

Martha, the movie mouse ill. by author. Harper, 1966. Subj: Animals – mice. Poetry, rhyme. Theater.

Ming Lo moves the mountain ill. by author. Greenwillow, 1982. Subj: Foreign lands – China. Moving.

Mouse soup ill. by author. Harper, 1977. Subj: Animals – mice. Animals – weasels. Character traits – cleverness.

Mouse tales ill. by author. Harper, 1972. Subj: Animals – mice. Humor.

On Market Street ill. by Anita Lobel. Greenwillow, 1981. Subj: ABC books. Caldecott award honor book. Poetry, rhyme. Shopping. Stores.

On the day Peter Stuyvesant sailed into town ill. by author. Harper, 1971. Subj: Poetry, rhyme. Problem solving. U.S. history.

Owl at home ill. by author. Harper, 1975. Subj: Birds – owls.

Prince Bertram the bad ill. by author. Harper, 1963. Subj: Behavior – misbehavior. Dragons. Royalty. Witches.

The rose in my garden ill. by Anita Lobel. Greenwillow, 1984. Subj: Animals – cats. Animals – mice. Cumulative tales. Flowers. Insects – bees. Poetry, rhyme.

Small pig ill. by author. Harper, 1969. Subj: Animals – pigs. Behavior – running away. Farms.

A treeful of pigs ill. by Anita Lobel. Greenwillow, 1979. Subj: Animals – pigs. Character traits – laziness. Farms. Humor.

The turnaround wind ill. by author. Harper, 1988. ISBN 0-06-023988-3 Subj: Weather – wind.

Uncle Elephant ill. by author. Harper, 1981. Subj: Animals – elephants. Behavior – lost. Family life. Sea and seashore.

Whiskers and rhymes ill. by author. Greenwillow, 1985. ISBN 0-688-03836-0 Subj: Animals – cats. Poetry, rhyme.

A zoo for Mister Muster ill. by author. Harper, 1962. Subj: Animals. Zoos.

Locker, Thomas. *Family farm* ill. by author. Dial Pr., 1988. ISBN 0-8037-0490-9 Subj: Farms.

The mare on the hill ill. by author. Dial Pr., 1985. ISBN 0-8037-0208-6 Subj: Animals – horses. Family life – grandfathers. Farms.

Rip Van Winkle (Irving, Washington)

Sailing with the wind ill. by author. Dial Pr., 1986. ISBN 0-8037-0312-0 Subj: Activities – traveling. Boats, ships.

Where the river begins ill. by author. Dial Pr., 1984. Subj: Family life – grandfathers. Rivers.

Lodge, Bernard. *Door to door* ill. by Maureen Roffey. Lothrop, 1980. Subj: Foreign lands – England. Format, unusual.

Rhyming Nell ill. by Maureen Roffey. Lothrop, 1979. Subj: Format, unusual. Poetry, rhyme. Witches.

Löfgren, Ulf. *The boy who ate more than the giant and other Swedish folktales* tr. from Swedish by Sheila La Farge; ill. by author. Collins-World, 1978. Subj: Folk and fairy tales. Giants. Humor.

The color trumpet ill. by author. Addison-Wesley, 1973. English text by Alison Winn; adapt. by Ray Broekel. Subj: Concepts – color.

The flying orchestra ill. by author. Addison-Wesley, 1973. English text by Alison Winn; adapt. by Ray Broekel. Subj: Music.

One-two-three ill. by author. Addison-Wesley, 1973. English text by Alison Winn; adapt. by Ray Brockel. Subj: Animals. Counting. Participation.

The traffic stopper that became a grandmother visitor ill. by author. Addison-Wesley, 1973. English text by Alison Winn; adapt. by Ray Broekel. Subj: Animals – elephants. Automobiles. Machines.

The wonderful tree ill. by author. Delacorte Pr., 1969. Subj: Imagination. Trees.

Logue, Christopher. *The magic circus* ill. by Wayne Anderson. Viking, 1979. Subj: Character traits – cleverness. Circus. Monsters.

Lomas, Steve *see* Brennan, Joseph Killorin

Long, Claudia. *Albert's story* ill. by Judy Glasser. Delacorte Pr., 1978. ISBN 0-440-00080-7 Subj: Dragons. Imagination.

Long, Earlene. *Gone fishing* ill. by Richard Eric Brown. Houghton, 1984. Subj: Concepts – size. Family life – fathers. Sports – fishing.

Johnny's egg photos. by Neal Slavin and Charles Mikolaycak. Addison-Wesley, 1980. Subj: Activities – cooking. Eggs.

Longfellow, Henry Wadsworth. *Hiawatha* ill. by Susan Jeffers. Dial Pr., 1983. Subj: Indians of North America. Poetry, rhyme.

Hiawatha's childhood ill. by Errol Le Cain. Farrar, 1984. Subj: Indians of North America. Poetry, rhyme.

Paul Revere's ride ill. by Paul Galdone. Crowell, 1963. ISBN 0-688-04015-2 Subj: Poetry, rhyme. U.S. history.

Paul Revere's ride ill. by Nancy Winslow Parker. Greenwillow, 1985. Subj: Poetry, rhyme. U.S. history.

Loof, Jan. *Uncle Louie's fantastic sea voyage* ill. by author. Random House, 1978. Subj: Activities – traveling. Boats, ships. Zoos.

Lopshire, Robert. *The biggest, smallest, fastest, tallest things you've ever heard of* ill. by author. Crowell, 1980. Subj: Concepts.

How to make snop snappers and other fine things ill. by author. Greenwillow, 1977. Subj: Games.

I am better than you ill. by author. Harper, 1968. Subj: Behavior – boasting. Reptiles – lizards.

I want to be somebody new! ill. by author. Random House, 1986. ISBN 0-394-97616-9 Subj: Behavior – seeking better things. Character traits – individuality. Poetry, rhyme.

It's magic ill. by author. Macmillan, 1969. Subj: Magic.

Put me in the zoo ill. by author. Random House, 1960. Subj: Animals – dogs. Circus. Concepts – color. Poetry, rhyme.

Lorca, Federico García *see* García Lorca, Federico

Lord, Beman. *The days of the week* ill. by Walter Erhard. Walck, 1968. Subj: Days of the week, months of the year. Poetry, rhyme. Songs.

Lord, John Vernon. *Mr. Mead and his garden* ill. by author. Houghton, 1975. Subj: Activities – gardening. Animals – snails. Poetry, rhyme.

Lord, Nancy *see* Titus, Eve

Lorenz, Konrad. *The goose family book* (Kalas, Sybille)

Lorenz, Lee. *Big Gus and Little Gus* ill. by author. Prentice-Hall, 1982. Subj: Character traits – laziness. Cumulative tales. Folk and fairy tales.

The feathered ogre ill. by author. Prentice-Hall, 1983. ISBN 0-13-308296-2 Subj: Character traits – cleverness. Folk and fairy tales. Magic. Mythical creatures. Royalty.

Hugo and the spacedog ill. by author. Prentice-Hall, 1983. ISBN 0-13-444497-3 Subj: Animals. Animals – dogs. Farms. Space and space ships.

Pinchpenny John ill. by author. Prentice-Hall, 1981. Subj: Behavior – greed. Folk and fairy tales.

Scornful Simkin ill. by author. Prentice-Hall, 1980. Subj: Folk and fairy tales.

A weekend in the country ill. by author. Prentice-Hall, 1984. Subj: Animals – pigs. Birds – ducks. Country.

Lorenzini, Carlo *see* Collodi, Carlo

Lorian, Nicole. *A birthday present for Mama* ill. by J. P. Miller. Random House, 1984. ISBN 0-394-96755-0 Subj: Animals. Animals – rabbits. Birthdays.

Lorimer, Janet. *The biggest bubble in the world* ill. by Diane Paterson. Watts, 1982. Subj: Behavior – misbehavior.

Lorimer, Lawrence T. *Noah's ark* (Martin, Charles E.)

Loriot. *Peter and the wolf* (Prokofiev, Sergei Sergeievitch)

Lourie, Helen *see* Storr, Catherine

Low, Alice. *The charge of the mouse brigade* (Stone, Bernard)

David's windows ill. by Tomie de Paola. Putnam's, 1974. Subj: Animals – horses. City. Family life – grandmothers.

Taro and the bamboo shoot (Matsuno, Masako)

The witch who was afraid of witches ill. by Karen Gundersheimer. Pantheon, 1978. Subj: Holidays – Halloween. Sibling rivalry. Witches.

Witch's holiday ill. by Tony Walton. Pantheon, 1971. Subj: Holidays – Halloween. Poetry, rhyme. Witches.

Low, Joseph. *Adam's book of odd creatures* ill. by author. Atheneum, 1962. Subj: ABC books. Animals. Names. Poetry, rhyme.

Benny rabbit and the owl ill. by author. Greenwillow, 1978. Subj: Birds – geese. Character traits – bravery. Emotions – fear. Farms.

Boo to a goose ill. by author. Atheneum, 1975. Subj: Birds – geese. Character traits – bravery. Emotions – fear. Farms.

The Christmas grump ill. by author. Atheneum, 1977. Subj: Animals – mice. Emotions – happiness. Emotions – sadness. Holidays – Christmas.

Don't drag your feet... ill. by author. Atheneum, 1983. Subj: Behavior. Dreams. Toys.

Five men under one umbrella ill. by author. Macmillan, 1975. Subj: Riddles.

A mad wet hen and other riddles ill. by author. Greenwillow, 1977. Subj: Riddles.

Mice twice ill. by author. Atheneum, 1980. Subj: Animals – mice. Caldecott award honor book.

My dog, your dog ill. by author. Macmillan, 1978. ISBN 0-02-761400-X Subj: Animals – dogs. Behavior.

What if...? fourteen encounters - some frightful, some frivolous - that might happen to anyone ill. by author. Atheneum, 1976. Subj: Problem solving.

Lowitz, Anson. *The pilgrims' party* (Lowitz, Sadyebeth)

Lowitz, Sadyebeth. *The pilgrims' party* by Sadyebeth and Anson Lowitz; ill. by Anson Lowitz. Lerner, 1931. Subj: Holidays – Thanksgiving. U.S. history.

Lowrey, Janette Sebring. *Six silver spoons* ill. by Robert M. Quackenbush. Harper, 1971. Subj: Birthdays. U.S. history.

Lubell, Cicil. *Rosalie, the bird market turtle* (Lubell, Winifred)

Lubell, Winifred. *Here comes daddy: a book for twos and threes* ill. by author. Addison-Wesley, 1944. Subj: Family life – fathers.

I wish I had another name (Williams, Jay)

Rosalie, the bird market turtle by Winifred and Cicil Lubell; ill. by Winifred Lubell. Rand McNally, 1962. Subj: Behavior – lost. Birds. Foreign lands – France. Reptiles – turtles, tortoises.

Lucas, Barbara. *Cats by Mother Goose* (Mother Goose)

I want a brother or sister (Lindgren, Astrid)

I want to go to school too (Lindgren, Astrid)

Sleeping over ill. by Stella Ormai. Macmillan, 1986. ISBN 0-02-761360-7 Subj: Animals – bears. Frogs and toads. Sleep.

Lucas, Victoria *see* Plath, Sylvia

Luenn, Nancy. *The dragon kite* ill. by Michael Hague. Harcourt, 1982. Subj: Folk and fairy tales. Foreign lands – Japan. Kites.

Lukešová, Milena. *Julian in the autumn woods* ill. by Jan Kudláček. Holt, 1977. Subj: Forest, woods.

The little girl and the rain ill. by Jan Kudláček. Holt, 1978. Subj: Emotions – loneliness. Weather – rain.

Lumley, Katheryn Wentzel. *I can be an animal doctor.* Childrens Pr., 1985. ISBN 0-516-01836-1 Subj: Careers – veterinarians.

Lund, Doris Herold. *The paint-box sea* ill. by Symeon Shimin. McGraw-Hill, 1971. Subj: Poetry, rhyme. Sea and seashore. Seasons – summer.

You ought to see Herbert's house ill. by Steven Kellogg. McGraw-Hill, 1973. Subj: Behavior – boasting. Friendship.

Lundell, Margo. *Teddy bear's birthday* ill. by Dee deRosa. Platt, 1985. ISBN 0-448-40876-7 Subj: Birthdays. Format, unusual – board books. Toys – teddy bears.

Lurie, Morris. *The story of Imelda, who was small* ill. by Terry Denton. Houghton, 1988. ISBN 0-395-48863-7 Subj: Character traits – smallness. Food.

Lussert, Anneliese. *The farmer and the moon* tr. by Anthea Bell; ill. by Jozef Wilkon. Holt, 1987. ISBN 0-8050-0281-2 Subj: Behavior – greed. Magic. Moon.

Lüton, Mildred. *Little chicks' mothers and all the others* ill. by Mary Maki Rae. Viking, 1983. Subj: Animals. Farms. Poetry, rhyme.

Luttrell, Ida. *Lonesome Lester* ill. by Megan Lloyd. Harper, 1984. Subj: Animals – prairie dogs. Behavior – solitude. Emotions – loneliness.

Mattie and the chicken thief ill. by Thacher Hurd. Putnam's, 1988. ISBN 0-396-09126-1 Subj: Animals. Behavior – misbehavior. Birds – chickens.

Lydon, Kerry Raines. *A birthday for Blue* ill. by Michael Hays. Albert Whitman, 1988. ISBN 0-8075-0774-1 Subj: Activities – traveling. Birthdays. Family life. U.S. history.

Lyfick, Warren. *Animal tales* ill. by Joe Kohl. Harvey House, 1980. Subj: Animals. Riddles.

The little book of fowl jokes ill. by Chris Cummings. Harvey House, 1980. Subj: Birds. Riddles.

Lynch, Marietta. *Mommy and daddy are divorced* (Perry, Patricia)

Lynn, Patricia *see* Watts, Mabel

Lynn, Sara. *Big animals* ill. by author. Aladdin, 1987. ISBN 0-689-71098-4 Subj: Animals. Format, unusual – board books.

Clothes ill. by author. Macmillan, 1986. ISBN 0-689-71095-X Subj: Clothing. Format, unusual – board books.

Colors ill. by author. Little, 1986. ISBN 0-316-54002-1 Subj: Clowns, jesters. Concepts – color.

Farm animals ill. by author. Aladdin, 1987. ISBN 0-689-71100-X Subj: Animals. Format, unusual – board books.

Food ill. by author. Macmillan, 1986. ISBN 0-689-71094-1 Subj: Food. Format, unusual – board books.

Garden animals ill. by author. Aladdin, 1987. ISBN 0-689-71101-8 Subj: Animals. Format, unusual – board books.

Home ill. by author. Macmillan, 1986. ISBN 0-689-71097-6 Subj: Format, unusual – board books. Houses.

1 2 3 ill. by author. Little, 1986. ISBN 0-316-54004-8 Subj: Animals. Counting.

Small animals ill. by author. Aladdin, 1987. ISBN 0-689-71099-2 Subj: Animals. Format, unusual – board books.

Toys ill. by author. Macmillan, 1986. ISBN 0-689-71096-8 Subj: Format, unusual – board books. Toys.

Lyon, David. *The biggest truck* ill. by author. Lothrop, 1988. ISBN 0-688-05514-1 Subj: Activities – working. Night. Trucks.

The brave little computer ill. by Robert W. Alley. Simon & Schuster, 1984. ISBN 0-671-52455-0 Subj: Machines. Problem solving.

The runaway duck ill. by author. Lothrop, 1985. ISBN 0-688-04002-0 Subj: Toys.

Lyon, George Ella. *A B Cedar: an alphabet of trees* designed and ill. by Tom Parker. Watts, 1989. ISBN 0-531-08395-0 Subj: ABC books. Trees.

Father Time and the day boxes ill. by Robert Andrew Parker. Bradbury Pr., 1985. ISBN 0-02-761370-4 Subj: Time.

A regular rolling Noah ill. by Stephen Gammell. Bradbury Pr., 1986. ISBN 0-02-761330-5 Subj: Activities – traveling. Animals. Trains.

Lystad, Mary H. *That new boy* ill. by Emily Arnold McCully. Crown, 1973. Subj: Character traits – individuality. Friendship. Moving.

Mabey, Richard. *Oak and company* ill. by Clare Roberts. Greenwillow, 1983. Subj: Ecology. Science. Trees.

McAfee, Annalena. *The visitors who came to stay* ill. by Anthony Browne. Viking, 1985. ISBN 0-670-74714-9 Subj: Behavior – trickery. Family life – fathers. Sea and seashore.

MacArthur-Onslow, Annette Rosemary. *Minnie* ill. by author. Rand McNally, 1971. Subj: Animals – cats.

Macaulay, David. *Castle* ill. by author. Houghton, 1977. Subj: Caldecott award honor book.

Cathedral ill. by author. Houghton, 1973. Subj: Caldecott award honor book.

Why the chicken crossed the road ill. by author. Houghton, 1987. ISBN 0-395-44241-9 Subj: Humor.

MacBean, Dilla Wittemore. *Picture book dictionary* ill. by Pauline B. Adams. Children's Pr., 1962. Subj: Dictionaries.

MacBeth, George. *Jonah and the Lord* ill. by Margaret Gordon. Holt, 1970. Subj: Folk and fairy tales. Religion.

Noah's journey ill. by Margaret Gordon. Viking, 1966. Subj: Poetry, rhyme. Religion – Noah.

MacCabe, Lorin. *Cable car Joey* (MacCabe, Naomi.)

MacCabe, Naomi. *Cable car Joey* by Naomi and Lorin MacCabe; ill. by authors. Stanford Univ. Pr., 1949. Subj: Cable cars, trolleys.

McCall, Anthony *see* Kane, Henry B.

McCarthy, Bobette. *Buffalo girls* ill. by author. Crown, 1987. ISBN 0-517-65568-4 Subj: Animals – buffaloes. Music. Songs.

McCarthy, Ruth. *Katie and the smallest bear* ill. by Emilie Boon. Knopf, 1986. ISBN 0-394-97855-2 Subj: Activities – playing. Animals – bears. Zoos.

McCauley, Jane. *Baby birds and how they grow* ill. with photos. National Geographic Soc., 1983. Subj: Birds. Science.

The way animals sleep ill. with photos. National Geographic Soc., 1983. Subj: Animals. Sleep.

McClean, Kathleen *see* Hale, Kathleen

McClenathan, Louise. *The Easter pig* ill. by Rosekrans Hoffman. Morrow, 1982. Subj: Animals – pigs. Character traits – generosity. Holidays – Easter.

My mother sends her wisdom ill. by Rosekrans Hoffman. Morrow, 1979. Subj: Behavior – greed. Character traits – cleverness.

McClintock, Marshall. *A fly went by* ill. by Fritz Siebel. Random House, 1958. Subj: Behavior – misunderstanding. Cumulative tales. Insects – flies.

Stop that ball ill. by Fritz Siebel. Random House, 1959. Subj: Toys – balls.

What have I got? ill. by Leonard P. Kessler. Harper, 1961. Subj: Clothing. Imagination. Poetry, rhyme.

McClintock, Mike *see* McClintock, Marshall

McCloskey, John Robert *see* McCloskey, Robert

McCloskey, Robert. *Bert Dow, deep-water man: a tale of the sea in the classic tradition* ill. by author. Viking, 1963. Subj: Animals – whales. Boats, ships. Sea and seashore.

Blueberries for Sal ill. by author. Viking, 1948. Subj: Animals – bears. Behavior – lost. Caldecott award honor book. Family life. Food.

Lentil ill. by author. Viking, 1940. Subj: Music. Noise, sounds. Problem solving.

Make way for ducklings ill. by author. Viking, 1941. Subj: Birds – ducks. Caldecott award book. Careers – police officers. City.

One morning in Maine ill. by author. Viking, 1952. Subj: Caldecott award honor book. Family life. Sea and seashore. Teeth.

Time of wonder ill. by author. Viking, 1957. Subj: Caldecott award book. Islands. Sea and seashore. Seasons – summer. Weather.

McClung, Robert. *How animals hide* ill. with photos. National Geographic Soc., 1973. ISBN 0-87044-144-2 Subj: Animals. Behavior – hiding. Science.

Sphinx: the story of a caterpillar ill. by Carol Lerner. Rev. ed. Morrow, 1981. Subj: Insects – butterflies, caterpillars. Science.

McClure, Gillian. *Fly home McDoo* ill. by author. Dutton, 1980. Subj: Behavior – running away. Birds – pigeons.

Prickly pig ill. by author. Elsevier-Dutton, 1980. Subj: Animals – hedgehogs. Hibernation.

What's the time, Rory Wolf? ill. by author. Dutton, 1982. Subj: Animals – wolves. Emotions – loneliness. Friendship.

McConnachie, Brian. *Flying boy* ill. by Jack Ziegler. Crown, 1988. ISBN 0-517-55980-3 Subj: Activities – flying. Character traits – helpfulness. Character traits – individuality.

Lily of the forest ill. by Jack Ziegler. Crown, 1987. ISBN 0-517-56595-1 Subj: Animals. Behavior – boredom. Behavior – running away. Family life. Forest, woods.

McCord, David. *Every time I climb a tree* ill. by Marc Simont. Little, 1967. ISBN 0-316-55514-2 Subj: Activities – playing. Poetry, rhyme. Trees.

The star in the pail ill. by Marc Simont. Little, 1976. Subj: Poetry, rhyme.

McCormack, John E. *Rabbit tales* ill. by Jenni Oliver. Dutton, 1980. Subj: Animals – rabbits. Character traits – cleverness. Character traits – individuality. Character traits – vanity. Friendship. Imagination.

Rabbit travels ill. by Lynne Cherry. Dutton, 1984. Subj: Activities – traveling. Animals – rabbits. Friendship.

McCrea, James. *The king's procession* by James and Ruth McCrea; ill. by authors. Atheneum, 1963. Subj: Animals – donkeys. Character traits – loyalty. Poverty. Royalty.

The magic tree by James and Ruth McCrea; ill. by authors. Atheneum, 1965. Subj: Character traits – meanness. Emotions. Emotions – happiness. Royalty.

The story of Olaf by James and Ruth McCrea; ill. by authors. Atheneum, 1964. Subj: Dragons. Knights. Wizards.

McCrea, Lilian. *Mother hen* ill. by Edda Reinl. Picture Book Studio, 1987. ISBN 0-88708-037-5 Subj: Animals. Birds – chickens. Counting. Eggs. Farms.

McCrea, Ruth. *The king's procession* (McCrea, James)

The magic tree (McCrea, James)

The story of Olaf (McCrea, James)

McCready, Lady *see* Tudor, Tasha

McCready, Tasha Tudor *see* Tudor, Tasha

McCue, Lisa. *Corduroy's toys* ill. by author. Viking, 1985. Subj: Format, unusual – board books. Toys. Toys – teddy bears. Wordless.

The little chick ill. by author. Random House, 1986. ISBN 0-394-88017-X Subj: Birds – chickens. Farms. Format, unusual – board books.

McCully, Emily Arnold. *The Christmas gift* ill. by author. Harper, 1988. ISBN 0-06-024212-4 Subj: Animals – mice. Family life – grandfathers. Holidays – Christmas. Toys. Wordless.

First snow ill. by author. Harper, 1985. ISBN 0-06-024129-2 Subj: Activities – playing. Animals – mice. Seasons – winter. Weather – snow. Wordless.

The grandma mix-up ill. by author. Harper, 1988. ISBN 0-06-024202-7 Subj: Activities – baby-sitting. Family life – grandmothers. Wordless.

New baby ill. by author. Harper, 1988. ISBN 0-06-024131-4 Subj: Animals – mice. Sibling rivalry. Wordless.

Picnic ill. by author. Harper, 1984. Subj: Activities – picnicking. Animals – mice. Behavior – lost. Wordless.

School ill. by author. Harper, 1987. ISBN 0-06-024133-0 Subj: Animals – mice. School. Wordless.

McCunn, Ruthanne L. *Pie-Biter* ill. by You-Shan Tang. Design Ent., 1983. ISBN 0-932538-09-6 Subj: Activities – working. Behavior – seeking better things. Ethnic groups in the U.S. – Chinese-Americans.

McCurdy, Michael. *The devils who learned to be good* ill. by author. Little, 1987. ISBN 0-316-55527-4 Subj: Character traits – cleverness. Devil. Folk and fairy tales.

McDaniel, Becky Bring. *Katie did it* ill. by Lois Axeman. Children's Pr., 1983. Subj: Sibling rivalry.

McDermott, Beverly Brodsky. *The crystal apple: a Russian tale* ill. by author. Viking, 1974. Subj: Folk and fairy tales. Foreign lands – Russia. Imagination.

The Golem: a Jewish legend ill. by author. Lippincott, 1976. Subj: Caldecott award honor book. Folk and fairy tales. Jewish culture.

Jonah: an Old Testament story ill. by author. Lippincott, 1977. Subj: Religion.

McDermott, Gerald. *Anansi the spider: a tale from the Ashanti* ill. by author. Holt, 1972. Subj: Caldecott award honor book. Folk and fairy tales. Foreign lands – Africa. Moon. Spiders.

Arrow to the sun: a Pueblo Indian tale ill. by author. Viking, 1974. Subj: Caldecott award book. Folk and fairy tales. Indians of North America.

Daniel O'Rourke: an Irish tale ill. by author. Viking, 1986. ISBN 0-670-80924-1 Subj: Dreams. Elves and little people. Folk and fairy tales. Foreign lands – Ireland.

Daughter of earth: a Roman myth ill. by author. Delacorte, 1984. Subj: Folk and fairy tales. Seasons.

The magic tree: a tale from the Congo ill. by author. Holt, 1973. Subj: Character traits – appearance. Magic. Twins.

Papagayo, the mischief maker ill. by author. Windmill, 1980. Subj: Birds – parakeets, parrots. Moon.

The stonecutter: a Japanese folk tale ill. by author. Viking, 1975. Subj: Behavior – dissatisfaction. Folk and fairy tales. Foreign lands – Japan.

The voyage of Osiris: a myth of ancient Egypt ill. by author. Windmill Books, 1977. Subj: Folk and fairy tales. Foreign lands – Egypt. Religion. Royalty.

MacDonald, Elizabeth. *My aunt and the animals* by Elizabeth MacDonald and Annie Owen; ill. by Annie Owen. Barron's, 1985. ISBN 0-8120-5641-8 Subj: Animals. Counting. Days of the week, months of the year.

MacDonald, George. *The light princess* ill. by Maurice Sendak. Farrar, 1969. Subj: Folk and fairy tales.

The light princess adapt. by Robin McKinley; ill. by Katie Thamer Treherne. Harcourt, 1987. ISBN 0-15-245300-8 Subj: Concepts – weight. Folk and fairy tales. Royalty. Witches.

Little Daylight ill. by Dorothée Duntze. Holt, 1987. ISBN 0-8050-0493-9 Subj: Fairies. Folk and fairy tales. Magic. Royalty.

MacDonald, Golden see Brown, Margaret Wise

MacDonald, Greville see MacDonald, George

MacDonald, Suse. *Alphabatics* ill. by author. Bradbury Pr., 1986. ISBN 0-02-761520-0 Subj: ABC books. Caldecott award honor book.

Numblers by Suse MacDonald and Bill Oakes; ill. by authors. Dial Pr., 1988. ISBN 0-8037-0548-4 Subj: Counting.

Macdonell, A. G. (Archibald Gordon) see Cameron, John

McFall, Gardner. *Jonathan's cloud* ill. by Steven Guarnaccia. Harper, 1986. ISBN 0-06-024124-1 Subj: Weather – clouds.

McFarland, John. *The exploding frog and other fables from Æsop* retold by John McFarland; ill. by James Marshall. Little, 1981. Subj: Folk and fairy tales.

McGillicuddy, Mr. see Abisch, Roz

McGinley, Phyllis. *All around the town* ill. by Helen Stone. Lippincott, 1948. Subj: ABC books. Caldecott award honor book. City. Poetry, rhyme.

The horse who lived upstairs ill. by Helen Stone. Lippincott, 1944. Subj: Animals – horses. Behavior – dissatisfaction.

How Mrs. Santa Claus saved Christmas ill. by Kurt Werth. Lippincott, 1963. Subj: Holidays – Christmas. Poetry, rhyme.

Lucy McLockett ill. by Helen Stone. Lippincott, 1958. Subj: Behavior – losing things. Family life. Poetry, rhyme. Teeth.

The most wonderful doll in the world ill. by Helen Stone. Lippincott, 1950. Subj: Caldecott award honor book. Toys – dolls.

Wonderful time ill. by John Alcorn. Lippincott, 1966. Subj: Clocks. Poetry, rhyme. Time.

McGivern, Maureen Daly *see* Daly, Maureen

McGovern, Ann. *Black is beautiful* photos. by Hope Wurmfeld. Four Winds Pr., 1969. Subj: Ethnic groups in the U.S. – Afro-Americans.

Eggs on your nose ill. by Maxie Chambliss. Macmillan, 1987. ISBN 0-02-765750-7 Subj: Eggs. Food. Humor.

Feeling mad, feeling sad, feeling bad, feeling glad photos. by Hope Wurmfeld. Walker, 1977. Subj: Emotions. Poetry, rhyme.

Mr. Skinner's skinny house ill. by Mort Gerberg. Four Winds Pr., 1980. Subj: Character traits – being different. Emotions – loneliness. Houses.

Nicholas Bentley Stoningpot III ill. by Tomie de Paola. Holiday, 1982. Subj: Behavior – boredom. Boats, ships. Emotions – loneliness. Islands.

Too much noise ill. by Simms Taback. Houghton, 1967. Subj: Humor. Noise, sounds.

Zoo, where are you? ill. by Ezra Jack Keats. Harper, 1965. Subj: Zoos.

McGowan, Alan. *Sailing ships* by Alan McGowan and Ron van der Meer; ill. by Borje Svensson. Viking, 1984. Subj: Boats, ships. Format, unusual – toy and movable books.

McGowen, Thomas *see* McGowen, Tom

McGowen, Tom. *The only glupmaker in the U.S. Navy* ill. by author. Albert Whitman, 1966. Subj: Activities – working. Careers – military.

MacGregor, Ellen. *Mr. Pingle and Mr. Buttonhouse* ill. by Paul Galdone. McGraw-Hill, 1957. Subj: Friendship.

Theodor Turtle ill. by Paul Galdone. McGraw-Hill, 1955. Subj: Behavior – forgetfulness. Participation. Reptiles – turtles, tortoises.

MacGregor, Marilyn. *Baby takes a trip* ill. by author. Macmillan, 1985. ISBN 0-02-761940-0 Subj: Babies. Character traits – curiosity. Wordless.

Helen the hungry bear ill. by author. Four Winds Pr., 1987. ISBN 0-02-761950-8 Subj: Activities – picnicking. Animals – bears. Family life. Food.

On top ill. by author. Morrow, 1988. ISBN 0-688-07491-X Subj: Animals – sheep. Character traits – individuality. Wordless.

McGuire, Paula. *Me and Clara and Baldwin the pony* (Inkiow, Dimiter)

Me and Clara and Casimir the cat (Inkiow, Dimiter)

Me and Clara and Snuffy the dog (Inkiow, Dimiter)

Me and my sister Clara (Inkiow, Dimiter)

McHale, Ethel Kharasch. *Son of thunder: an old Lapp tale* ill. by Ruth Lercher Bornstein. Children's Pr., 1974. Subj: Folk and fairy tales. Foreign lands – Lapland.

McHargue, Georgess. *Private zoo* ill. by Michael Foreman. Viking, 1975. Subj: Imagination. Shadows.

Machetanz, Fred. *A puppy named Gia* (Machetanz, Sara)

Machetanz, Sara. *A puppy named Gia* by Sara and Fred Machetanz; ill. by Fred Machetanz. Scribner's, 1957. Subj: Animals – dogs. Eskimos.

McIlwraith, Maureen Mollie Hunter *see* Hunter, Mollie

McIntire, Alta. *Follett beginning to read picture dictionary* ill. by Janet La Salle. Follett, 1959. Subj: Dictionaries.

Mack, Gail. *Yesterday's snowman* ill. by Erik Blegvad. Pantheon, 1979. ISBN 0-394-93662-0 Subj: Family life. Snowmen.

Mack, Stan *see* Mack, Stanley

Mack, Stanley. *Ten bears in my bed: a goodnight countdown* ill. by author. Pantheon, 1974. Subj: Animals – bears. Bedtime. Counting. Songs.

McKay, George. *Marny's ride with the wind* (McKay, Louise)

MacKay, Jed. *The big secret* ill. by Heather Collins. Firefly Pr., 1984. ISBN 0-920236-88-X Subj: Adoption. Family life. Parties.

McKay, Louise. *Marny's ride with the wind* by Louise and George McKay; ill. by Margaret Smetana. New Harbinger, 1979. Subj: Friendship. Weather – wind.

McKee, David. *The day the tide went out and out and out* ill. by author. Abelard-Schuman, 1975. Subj: Animals – camels. Desert. Sea and seashore.

Elmer, the story of a patchwork elephant ill. by author. McGraw-Hill, 1968. Subj: Animals – elephants. Character traits – individuality.

The hill and the rock ill. by author. Ticknor & Fields, 1985. ISBN 0-89919-341-2 Subj: Behavior – seeking better things. Rocks.

King Rollo and the birthday ill. by author. Little, 1979. Subj: Birthdays. Royalty.

King Rollo and the bread ill. by author. Little, 1979. Subj: Food. Royalty.

King Rollo and the new shoes ill. by author. Little, 1979. Subj: Clothing. Royalty.

The man who was going to mind the house: a Norwegian folk-tale ill. by author. Abelard-Schuman, 1973. Subj: Folk and fairy tales.

123456789 Benn ill. by author. McGraw-Hill, 1970. Subj: Crime. Prisons. Problem solving.

Snow woman ill. by author. Lothrop, 1988. ISBN 0-688-07675-0 Subj: Family life. Snowmen.

Tusk tusk ill. by author. Barron's, 1979. Subj: Animals – elephants. Behavior – fighting, arguing.

Two can toucan ill. by author. Abelard-Schuman, 1964. Subj: Birds – toucans. Names.

Two monsters ill. by author. Bradbury Pr., 1986. ISBN 0-02-765760-4 Subj: Behavior – fighting, arguing. Monsters.

McKee, Douglas. *Good night, Veronica* (Trez, Denise)

Maila and the flying carpet (Trez, Denise)

The royal hiccups (Trez, Denise)

McKeever, Katherine. *A family for Minerva* photos. by author. Greey De Pencier Books, 1981. Subj: Birds – owls. Science.

McKelvey, David. *Bobby the mostly silky* ill. by author. Corona, 1984. Subj: Birds – chickens. Character traits – being different.

MacKie, Maron *see* McNeely, Jeannette

McKié, Roy. *Noah's ark* ill. by author. Random House, 1984. ISBN 0-394-96584-1 Subj: Religion – Noah. Weather – floods.

The riddle book ill. by author. Random House, 1978. Subj: Humor. Riddles.

Snow by Roy McKié and P. D. Eastman; ill. by P. D. Eastman. Random House, 1962. Subj: Activities. Poetry, rhyme. Weather – snow.

McKinley, Robin. *The light princess* (MacDonald, George)

McKissack, Fredrick. *Big bug book of counting* (McKissack, Patricia C.)

Big bug book of opposites (McKissack, Patricia C.)

Big bug book of places to go (McKissack, Patricia C.)

Big bug book of the alphabet (McKissack, Patricia C.)

Cinderella (McKissack, Patricia C.)

Country mouse and city mouse (McKissack, Patricia C.)

King Midas and his gold (McKissack, Patricia C.)

The king's new clothes (McKissack, Patricia C.)

The little red hen (McKissack, Patricia C.)

My Bible ABC book (McKissack, Patricia C.)

Three billy goats Gruff (Asbjørnsen, P. C. (Peter Christen))

The ugly little duck (Andersen, H.C. (Hans Christian))

Who is coming? (McKissack, Patricia C.)

McKissack, Patricia C. *Big bug book of counting* by Patricia C. and Fredrick McKissack; ill. by Bartholomew. Milliken, 1987. ISBN 0-88335-762-3 Subj: Counting. Insects.

Big bug book of opposites by Patricia C. and Fredrick McKissack; ill. by Bartholomew. Milliken, 1987. ISBN 0-88335-763-1 Subj: Concepts – opposites. Insects.

Big bug book of places to go by Patricia C. and Fredrick McKissack; ill. by Bartholomew. Milliken, 1987. ISBN 0-88335-765-8 Subj: Activities – traveling. Insects.

Big bug book of the alphabet by Patricia C. and Fredrick McKissack; ill. by Bartholomew. Milliken, 1987. ISBN 0-88335-764-X Subj: ABC books. Insects.

Cinderella by Patricia C. and Fredrick McKissack; ill. by Tom Dunnington. Childrens Pr., 1985. ISBN 0-516-02361-6 Subj: Folk and fairy tales. Royalty. Sibling rivalry.

Country mouse and city mouse by Patricia C. and Fredrick McKissack; ill. by Anne Sikorski. Childrens Pr., 1985. ISBN 0-516-02362-4 Subj: Animals – mice. City. Country.

Flossie and the fox ill. by Rachel Isadora. Dial Pr., 1986. ISBN 0-8037-0251-5 Subj: Animals – foxes. Ethnic groups in the U.S. – Afro-Americans.

King Midas and his gold by Patricia C. and Fredrick McKissack; ill. by Tom Dunnington. Childrens Pr., 1986. ISBN 0-516-03984-9 Subj: Behavior – greed. Behavior – wishing. Royalty.

The king's new clothes by Patricia C. and Fredrick McKissack; ill. by Gwen Connelly. Childrens Pr., 1987. ISBN 0-516-02365-9 Subj: Character traits – pride. Clothing. Humor. Imagination. Royalty.

The little red hen by Patricia C. and Fredrick McKissack; ill. by Dennis Hockerman. Childrens Pr., 1985. ISBN 0-516-02363-2 Subj: Animals. Birds – chickens. Character traits – laziness. Cumulative tales. Farms.

Mirandy and brother wind ill. by Jerry Pinkney. Knopf, 1988. ISBN 0-394-88765-4 Subj: Activities – dancing. Caldecott award honor book. Ethnic groups in the U.S. – Afro-Americans. Folk and fairy tales.

My Bible ABC book by Patricia C. and Fredrick McKissack; ill. by Reed Merrill. Augsburg, 1987. ISBN 0-8066-2271-7 Subj: ABC books. Religion.

Nettie Jo's friends ill. by Scott Cook. Knopf, 1989. ISBN 0-394-89158-9 Subj: Clothing. Family life. Toys – dolls.

Three billy goats Gruff (Asbjørnsen, P. C. (Peter Christen))

The ugly little duck (Andersen, H. C. (Hans Christian))

Who is coming? by Patricia C. and Fredrick McKissack; ill. by Clovis Martin. Childrens Pr., 1986. Prepared under the direction of Robert Hillerick. ISBN 0-516-02073-0 Subj: Animals – monkeys. Behavior – running away. Foreign lands – Africa. Safety.

Who is who? ill. by Elizabeth M. Allen. Children's Pr., 1983. Subj: Twins.

MacLachlan, Patricia. *Mama one, Mama two* ill. by Ruth Lercher Bornstein. Harper, 1982. Subj: Family life — mothers. Illness.

Moon, stars, frogs and friends ill. by Tomie de Paola. Pantheon, 1980. Subj: Friendship. Frogs and toads. Witches.

The sick day ill. by William Pène Du Bois. Pantheon, 1979. Subj: Family life. Illness.

McLaughlin, Lissa. *Why won't winter go?* ill. by author. Lothrop, 1983. Subj: Behavior — boredom. Seasons — winter.

McLeish, Kenneth. *Chicken Licken* (Chicken Little)

McLenighan, Valjean. *I know you cheated* photos. by Brent Jones. Raintree, 1977. ISBN 0-8172-0962-X Subj: Character traits — honesty. School.

One whole doughnut, one doughnut hole ill. by Steven Roger Cole. Childrens Pr., 1982. Subj: Activities — reading.

Stop-go, fast-slow ill. by Margrit Fiddle. Children's Pr., 1982. Subj: Concepts — opposites.

Three strikes and you're out ill. by Laurie Hamilton. Follett, 1980. Subj: Behavior — greed. Magic.

Turtle and rabbit ill. by Vernon McKissack. Follett, 1980. Subj: Animals — rabbits. Folk and fairy tales. Reptiles — turtles, tortoises. Sports — racing.

What you see is what you get ill. by Dev Appleyard. Four Winds Pr., 1980. Subj: Character traits — pride. Clothing. Folk and fairy tales. Humor. Imagination. Royalty.

You are what you are ill. by Jack Reilly. Follett, 1977. Subj: Folk and fairy tales. Frogs and toads. Royalty.

You can go jump ill. by Jared D. Lee. Follett, 1977. Subj: Elves and little people. Emotions — envy, jealousy. Folk and fairy tales. Magic. Witches.

McLeod, Emilie Warren. *The bear's bicycle* ill. by David McPhail. Little, 1975. Subj: Safety. Sports — bicycling. Toys — teddy bears.

One snail and me: a book of numbers and animals and a bathtub ill. by Walter Lorraine. Little, 1961. Subj: Activities — bathing. Animals. Counting. Imagination.

Macleodhas, Sorche Nic *see* Alger, Leclaire

McLerran, Alice. *The mountain that loved a bird* ill. by Eric Carle. Alphabet Pr., 1985. ISBN 0-88708-000-6 Subj: Behavior — needing someone. Birds. Character traits — loyalty. Emotions — sadness.

McMillan, Bruce. *The alphabet symphony: an ABC book* photos. by author. Greenwillow, 1977. Subj: ABC books. Music.

Becca backward, Becca forward photos. by author. Lothrop, 1986. ISBN 0-688-06283-0 Subj: Concepts. Concepts — opposites.

Counting wildflowers ill. by author. Lothrop, 1986. ISBN 0-688-02860-8 Subj: Counting. Flowers. Science.

Dry or wet? photos. by author. Lothrop, 1988. ISBN 0-688-07101-5 Subj: Concepts.

Fire engine shapes photos. by author. Lothrop, 1988. ISBN 0-688-07843-5 Subj: Concepts — shape.

Ghost doll ill. by author. Houghton, 1983. ISBN 0-395-33073-4 Subj: Ghosts. Toys — dolls.

Growing colors photos. by author. Lothrop, 1988. ISBN 0-688-07845-1 Subj: Concepts — color.

Here a chick, there a chick photos. by author. Lothrop, 1983. Subj: Concepts — opposites.

Kitten can... photos. by author. Lothrop, 1984. Subj: Animals — cats.

Step by step photos. by author. Lothrop, 1987. ISBN 0-688-07234-8 Subj: Activities. Babies.

McNaught, Harry. *Baby animals* ill. by author. Random House, 1976. ISBN 0-394-83241-8 Subj: Animals. Format, unusual — board books.

The truck book ill. by author. Random House, 1978. Subj: Transportation. Trucks.

Words to grow on ill. by author. Random House, 1984. ISBN 0-394-96103-X Subj: Language.

McNaughton, Colin. *At home* ill. by author. Putnam's, 1982. Subj: Concepts — opposites. Format, unusual — board books.

At playschool ill. by author. Putnam's, 1982. Subj: Concepts — opposites. Format, unusual — board books. School.

At the park ill. by author. Putnam's, 1982. Subj: Concepts — opposites. Format, unusual — board books.

At the party ill. by author. Putnam's, 1982. Subj: Concepts — opposites. Format, unusual — board books. Parties.

At the stores ill. by author. Putnam's, 1982. Subj: Concepts — opposites. Format, unusual — board books. Stores.

Autumn ill. by author. Dutton, 1983. Subj: Activities. Format, unusual — board books. Seasons — fall.

The rat race: the amazing adventures of Anton B. Stanton ill. by author. Doubleday, 1978. Subj: Animals — rats. Royalty. Sports — racing.

Spring ill. by author. Dial Pr., 1984. Subj: Format, unusual — board books. Seasons — spring.

Summer ill. by author. Dial Pr., 1984. Subj: Format, unusual — board books. Seasons — summer.

Walk rabbit walk by Colin McNaughton and Elizabeth Attenborough; ill. by Colin McNaughton. Viking, 1977. Subj: Activities — walking. Animals — rabbits.

Winter ill. by author. Dutton, 1983. Subj: Activities. Format, unusual — board books. Seasons — winter.

McNeely, Jeannette. *Where's Izzy?* ill. by Bill Morrison. Follett, 1972. Subj: Behavior – losing things. Pets. Reptiles – lizards.

McNeer, May Yonge. *Little Baptiste* ill. by Lynd Ward. Houghton, 1954. Subj: Animals. Farms.

My friend Mac: the story of Little Baptiste and the moose ill. by Lynd Ward. Houghton, 1960. Subj: Animals – moose. Emotions – loneliness.

McNeill, Janet *The giant's birthday* ill. by Walter Erhard. Walck, 1964. Subj: Birthdays. Giants.

McNulty, Faith. *The elephant who couldn't forget* ill. by Marc Simont. Harper, 1980. Subj: Animals – elephants. Behavior – forgetfulness.

How to dig a hole to the other side of the world ill. by Marc Simont. Harper, 1979. Subj: Earth. Imagination. Science.

Hurricane ill. by Gail Owens. Harper, 1983. Subj: Science. Weather – storms.

The lady and the spider ill. by Bob Marstall. Harper, 1986. ISBN 0-06-024192-6 Subj: Character traits – kindness to animals. Spiders.

Mouse and Tim ill. by Marc Simont. Harper, 1978. Subj: Animals – mice. Character traits – kindness to animals. Pets.

When a boy wakes up in the morning ill. by Leonard Weisgard. Knopf, 1962. Subj: Activities – playing. Morning. Noise, sounds.

Woodchuck ill. by Joan Sandin. Harper, 1974. Subj: Animals – groundhogs. Science.

McPhail, David. *Adam's smile* ill. by author. Dutton, 1987. ISBN 0-525-44327-4 Subj: Dreams. Illness. Night.

Alligators are awful (and they have terrible manners, too) ill. by author. Doubleday, 1980. Subj: Humor. Reptiles – alligators, crocodiles.

Andrew's bath ill. by author. Little, 1984. Subj: Activities – bathing. Animals. Behavior – misbehavior.

Animals A to Z ill. by author. Scholastic, 1988. ISBN 0-590-40715-5 Subj: ABC books. Animals.

The bear's toothache ill. by author. Little, 1972. Subj: Animals – bears. Character traits – kindness to animals. Illness. Teeth.

Captain Toad and the motorbike ill. by author. Atheneum, 1978. Subj: Frogs and toads. Motorcycles.

The cereal box ill. by author. Little, 1974. Subj: Family life. Humor. Imagination. Shopping.

The dream child ill. by author. Dutton, 1985. ISBN 0-525-44109-3 Subj: Bedtime. Dreams. Night. Sleep. Toys – teddy bears.

Emma's pet ill. by author. Dutton, 1987. ISBN 0-525-44210-3 Subj: Activities – vacationing. Animals – bears. Behavior – needing someone. Family life. Pets.

Emma's vacation ill. by author. Dutton, 1987. ISBN 0-525-44315-0 Subj: Activities – vacationing. Animals – bears. Family life.

Farm morning ill. by author. Harcourt, 1985. ISBN 0-15-227299-2 Subj: Animals. Birds. Farms.

First flight ill. by author. Little, 1987. ISBN 0-316-56323-4 Subj: Activities – flying. Airplanes, airports. Toys – teddy bears.

Fix-it ill. by author. Dutton, 1984. Subj: Activities – reading. Television.

Great cat ill. by author. Dutton, 1982. Subj: Animals – cats. Behavior – needing someone. Islands.

Henry Bear's park ill. by author. Little, 1976. Subj: Animals – bears.

Lorenzo ill. by author. Doubleday, 1984. ISBN 0-385-15591-3 Subj: Activities – painting. Animals. Houses.

The magical drawings of Moony B. Finch ill. by author. Doubleday, 1978. Subj: Art. Magic.

Mistletoe ill. by author. Dutton, 1978. Subj: Dreams. Holidays – Christmas. Imagination. Toys.

Pig Pig and the magic photo album ill. by author. Dutton, 1986. ISBN 0-525-44238-3 Subj: Activities – photographing. Animals – pigs. Imagination.

Pig Pig goes to camp ill. by author. Dutton, 1983. Subj: Animals – pigs. Sports – camping.

Pig Pig grows up ill. by author. Dutton, 1980. Subj: Animals – pigs. Behavior – growing up.

Pig Pig rides ill. by author. Dutton, 1982. Subj: Activities – playing. Animals – pigs. Imagination.

Sisters ill. by author. Harcourt, 1984. Subj: Emotions – love. Sibling rivalry.

Snow lion ill. by author. Parents, 1983. Subj: Weather – snow.

Something special ill. by author. Little, 1988. ISBN 0-316-56324-2 Subj: Activities – painting. Animals – raccoons.

Stanley: Henry Bear's friend ill. by author. Little, 1979. Subj: Animals – bears. Animals – raccoons. Behavior – running away. Crime.

The train ill. by author. Little, 1977. Subj: Dreams. Imagination. Toys – trains. Trains.

Where can an elephant hide? ill. by author. Doubleday, 1979. ISBN 0-385-12941-6 Subj: Animals. Animals – elephants. Behavior – hiding.

A wolf story ill. by author. Scribner, 1981. Subj: Animals – wolves. Character traits – freedom. Character traits – kindness to animals.

McQueen, John Troy. *A world full of monsters* ill. by Marc Brown. Crowell, 1986. ISBN 0-690-04546-8 Subj: Family life – grandmothers. Monsters. Night.

McToots, Rudi. *The kid's book of games for cars, trains and planes* ill. by author. Bantam, 1980. Subj: Activities – traveling. Games.

Madden, Don. *Lemonade serenade or the thing in the garden* ill. by author. Albert Whitman, 1966. Subj: Elves and little people. Noise, sounds.

The Wartville wizard ill. by author. Macmillan, 1986. ISBN 0-02-762100-6 Subj: Character traits – cleanliness. Wizards.

Maestro, Betsy. *Around the clock with Harriet: a book about telling time* ill. by Giulio Maestro. Crown, 1984. Subj: Animals – elephants. Clocks. Time.

Big city port by Betsy Maestro and Ellen Del Vecchio; ill. by Giulio Maestro. Four Winds Pr., 1983. Subj: Boats, ships. City.

Busy day: a book of action words by Betsy and Giulio Maestro; ill. by Giulio Maestro. Crown, 1978. Subj: Activities. Circus.

Camping out: a book of action words by Betsy and Giulio Maestro; ill. by authors. Crown, 1985. ISBN 0-517-55119-5 Subj: Language. Sports – camping.

Dollars and cents for Harriet ill. by Giulio Maestro. Crown, 1988. ISBN 0-517-56958-2 Subj: Counting. Money.

Fat polka-dot cat and other haiku ill. by Giulio Maestro. Dutton, 1976. Subj: Poetry, rhyme.

Ferryboat by Betsy and Giulio Maestro; ill. by authors. Crowell, 1986. ISBN 0-690-04520-4 Subj: Activities – traveling. Boats, ships.

The guessing game ill. by Giulio Maestro. Grosset, 1983. Subj: Animals – pigs. Problem solving.

Harriet at home ill. by Giulio Maestro. Crown, 1984. Subj: Animals – elephants. Format, unusual – board books. Houses.

Harriet at play ill. by Giulio Maestro. Crown, 1984. Subj: Activities – playing. Animals – elephants. Format, unusual – board books.

Harriet at school ill. by Giulio Maestro. Crown, 1984. Subj: Animals – elephants. Format, unusual – board books. School.

Harriet at work ill. by Giulio Maestro. Crown, 1984. Subj: Activities – working. Animals – elephants. Format, unusual – board books.

Harriet goes to the circus by Betsy and Giulio Maestro; ill. by Giulio Maestro. Crown, 1977. Subj: Animals – Elephants. Circus. Counting.

Harriet reads signs and more signs ill. by Giulio Maestro. Crown, 1981. Subj: Activities – reading. Animals – elephants.

On the go: a book of adjectives by Betsy and Giulio Maestro; ill. by authors. Crown, 1979. Subj: Animals – elephants. Language.

On the town: a book of clothing words by Betsy and Giulio Maestro; ill. by authors. Crown, 1983. Subj: Animals – elephants. Character traits – appearance. Clothing.

The pandas take a vacation ill. by Giulio Maestro. Western, 1986. ISBN 0-307-10258-0 Subj: Activities – vacationing. Animals – pandas.

The perfect picnic ill. by Giulio Maestro. Western, 1986. ISBN 0-307-10266-1 Subj: Activities – picnicking.

The story of the Statue of Liberty by Betsy and Giulio Maestro; ill. by Giulio Maestro. Lothrop, 1986. ISBN 0-688-05773-X Subj: Art. U.S. history.

Through the year with Harriet by Betsy and Giulio Maestro; ill. by authors. Crown, 1985. ISBN 0-517-55613-8 Subj: Animals – elephants. Days of the week, months of the year. Seasons. Weather.

Traffic: a book of opposites by Betsy and Giulio Maestro; ill. by authors. Crown, 1981. ISBN 0-517-54427-X Subj: Concepts – opposites. Traffic, traffic signs.

Where is my friend? ill. by Giulio Maestro. Crown, 1976. Subj: Animals – elephants. Concepts.

Maestro, Giulio. *Busy day* (Maestro, Betsy)

Camping out (Maestro, Betsy)

Ferryboat (Maestro, Betsy)

Halloween howls: riddles that are a scream ill. by author. Dutton, 1983. Subj: Holidays – Halloween. Riddles.

Harriet goes to the circus (Maestro, Betsy)

Just enough Rosie ill. by author. Grosset, 1983. Subj: Animals – rhinoceros. Humor.

Leopard is sick ill. by author. Greenwillow, 1978. Subj: Animals. Animals – leopards. Friendship. Illness.

On the go (Maestro, Betsy)

On the town (Maestro, Betsy)

One more and one less ill. by author. Crown, 1974. Subj: Animals. Counting.

A raft of riddles ill. by author. Dutton, 1982. Subj: Humor. Riddles.

The remarkable plant in apartment 4 ill. by author. Bradbury Pr., 1973. Subj: City. Humor. Plants.

Riddle romp ill. by author. Houghton, 1983. Subj: Riddles.

The story of the Statue of Liberty (Maestro, Betsy)

Through the year with Harriet (Maestro, Betsy)

The tortoise's tug of war ill. by author. Bradbury Pr., 1971. Subj: Animals – tapirs. Animals – whales. Folk and fairy tales. Foreign lands – South America. Games. Reptiles – turtles, tortoises.

Traffic (Maestro, Betsy)

Magee, Doug. *Trucks you can count on* photos. by author. Dodd, 1985. ISBN 0-396-08507-5 Subj: Counting. Trucks.

Maggs, Catherine. *Goodbye Rune* (Kaldhol, Marit)

Magnus, Erica. *The boy and the devil* ill. by author. Carolrhoda Books, 1986. ISBN 0-87614-305-2 Subj: Behavior – trickery. Devil. Folk and fairy tales. Foreign lands – Norway.

Old Lars ill. by author. Carolrhoda, 1984. Subj: Folk and fairy tales. Foreign lands – Norway.

Mahiri, Jabari. *The day they stole the letter J* ill. by Dorothy Carter. Third World Pr., 1981. Subj: Behavior – misbehavior. Careers – barbers.

Mählqvist, Stefan. *I'll take care of the crocodiles* ill. by Tord Nygren. Atheneum, 1979. Subj: Bedtime. Dreams.

Mahony, Elizabeth Winthrop *see* Winthrop, Elizabeth

Mahood, Kenneth. *The laughing dragon* ill. by author. Scribner's, 1970. Subj: Dragons. Fire. Humor. Royalty.

Why are there more questions than answers, Grandad? ill. by author. Bradbury Pr., 1974. Subj: Character traits – questioning. Family life – grandfathers.

Mahy, Margaret. *The boy who was followed home* ill. by Steven Kellogg. Watts, 1975. Subj: Animals – hippopotami. Humor. Witches.

The boy with two shadows ill. by Jenny Williams. Lippincott, 1988, 1971. ISBN 0-397-32271-2 Subj: Behavior – misbehavior. Character traits – meanness. Shadows. Witches.

The dragon of an ordinary family ill. by Helen Oxenbury. Watts, 1969. Subj: Dragons.

Jam: a true story ill. by Helen Craig. Atlantic Monthly Pr., 1986. ISBN 0-87113-048-3 Subj: Family life. Food.

A lion in the meadow ill. by Jenny Williams. Watts, 1969. Subj: Animals – lions. Dragons.

The man whose mother was a pirate ill. by Margaret Chamberlain. Viking, 1986. ISBN 0-670-81070-3 Subj: Behavior – seeking better things. Pirates. Sea and seashore.

Mrs. Discombobulous ill. by Jan Brychta. Watts, 1969. Subj: Behavior – nagging. Family life. Gypsies.

Pillycock's shop ill. by Carol Baker. Watts, 1969. Subj: Fairies. Values.

Rooms for rent ill. by Jenny Williams. Watts, 1974. Subj: Behavior – greed. Hotels.

Sailor Jack and the twenty orphans ill. by Robert Bartelt. Watts, 1970. Subj: Boats, ships. Careers – military. Orphans. Pirates. Sea and seashore.

17 kings and 42 elephants ill. by Patricia MacCarthy. Dial Pr., 1987. ISBN 0-8037-0458-5 Subj: Animals. Jungle. Poetry, rhyme. Royalty.

Maiorano, Robert. *Backstage* ill. by Rachel Isadora. Greenwillow, 1978. Subj: Theater.

Francisco ill. by Rachel Isadora. Macmillan, 1978. Subj: Foreign lands – South America. Poverty. Problem solving.

A little interlude ill. by Rachel Isadora. Coward, 1980. Subj: Activities – dancing. Behavior – sharing. Music.

Mair, Margaret *see* Crompton, Margaret

Maitland, Antony. *Idle Jack* ill. by author. Farrar, 1979. Subj: Character traits – foolishness. Folk and fairy tales.

Majewski, Joe. *A friend for Oscar Mouse* ill. by Maria Majewska. Dial Pr., 1988. ISBN 0-8037-0348-1 Subj: Animals – mice. Friendship.

Major, Beverly. *Playing sardines* ill. by Andrew Glass. Scholastic, 1988. ISBN 0-590-41153-5 Subj: Activities – playing. Behavior – hiding. Games. Twilight.

Makower, Sylvia. *Samson's breakfast* ill. by author. Watts, 1961. Subj: Animals – lions.

Malcolmson, Anne. *The song of Robin Hood* ill. by Virginia Lee Burton. Houghton, 1947. Subj: Caldecott award honor book. Folk and fairy tales.

Malecki, Maryann. *Mom and dad and I are having a baby!* ill. by author. Pennypress, 1982. Subj: Babies. Family life.

Maley, Anne. *Have you seen my mother?* ill. by Yutaka Sugita. Subj: Circus. Family life – mothers. Toys – balls.

Mallett, Anne. *Here comes Tagalong* ill. by Steven Kellogg. Parents, 1971. Subj: Family life. Friendship. Sibling rivalry.

Malloy, Judy. *Bad Thad* ill. by Martha G. Alexander. Dutton, 1980. ISBN 0-525-26148-6 Subj: Behavior – misbehavior. Family life. School.

Malnig, Anita. *The big strawberry book of questions and answers and facts and things* ill. by Sal Murdocca. Larousse, 1977. Subj: Mythical creatures. Science.

Malone, Nola Langner. *A home* ill. by author. Bradbury Pr., 1988. ISBN 0-02-751440-4 Subj: Friendship. Houses. Moving.

Mamin-Sibiryak, D. N. *Grey Neck* adapt. and tr. from the Russian by Marguerita Rudolph; ill. by Leslie Shuman Kronz. Stemmer House, 1988. ISBN 0-88045-068-1 Subj: Birds – ducks. Character traits – kindness to animals. Folk and fairy tales. Seasons – winter.

Mandry, Kathy. *The cat and the mouse and the mouse and the cat* ill. by Joe Toto. Pantheon, 1972. Subj: Animals – cats. Animals – mice. Friendship.

Manes, Esther. *The bananas move to the ceiling* by Esther and Stephen Manes; ill. by Barbara Samuels. Watts, 1983. Subj: Family life. Humor.

Manes, Stephen. *The bananas move to the ceiling* (Manes, Esther)

Life is no fair! ill. by Warren Miller. Dutton, 1985. ISBN 0-525-44192-1 Subj: Humor.

Mangin, Marie-France. *Suzette and Nicholas and the seasons clock* tr. from French by Joan Chevalier; ill. by Satomi Ichikawa. Putnam's, 1982. Subj: Activities. Seasons.

Manheim, Ralph. *Dear Mili* (Grimm, Wilhelm)

The nutcracker (Hoffmann, E. T. A.)

Mann, Peggy. *King Laurence, the alarm clock* ill. by Ray Cruz. Doubleday, 1976. Subj: Animals. Animals – lions. Illness. Morning.

Manners, Miss *see* Martin, Judith

Manson, Beverlie. *The fairies' alphabet book* ill. by author. Doubleday, 1982. Subj: ABC books. Fairies.

Manushkin, Fran. *Baby* ill. by Ronald Himler. Harper, 1972. ISBN 0-06-024064-4 Subj: Babies. Family life.

Baby, come out! ill. by Ronald Himler. Harper, 1972. Orig. entitled Baby. Subj: Babies.

Bubblebath! ill. by Ronald Himler. Harper, 1974. Subj: Activities – bathing. Family life.

Hocus and Pocus at the circus ill. by Geoffrey Hayes. Harper, 1983. Subj: Character traits – meanness. Holidays – Halloween. Witches.

Little rabbit's baby brother ill. by Diane de Groat. Crown, 1986. ISBN 0-517-56251-0 Subj: Animals – rabbits. Babies. Emotions – envy, jealousy. Family life. Sibling rivalry.

Moon dragon ill. by Geoffrey Hayes. Macmillan, 1982. Subj: Animals – mice. Dragons. Food. Moon.

The perfect Christmas picture ill. by Karen Ann Weinhaus. Harper, 1980. Subj: Activities – photographing. Family life. Holidays – Christmas.

Shirleybird ill. by Carl Stuart. Harper, 1975. ISBN 0-06-024064-4 Subj: Character traits – individuality.

Swinging and swinging ill. by Thomas Di Grazia. Harper, 1976. ISBN 0-06-024067-9 Subj: Activities – playing. Activities – swinging. Weather – clouds.

Marceau, Marcel. *The Marcel Marceau counting book* (Mendoza, George)

The story of Bip ill. by author. Harper, 1976. Subj: Clowns, jesters. Imagination.

Marcin, Marietta. *A zoo in her bed* ill. by Sofia. Coward, 1963. Subj: Bedtime. Poetry, rhyme. Toys.

Marcus, Susan. *Casey visits the doctor* ill. by Deborah Drew-Brook. CBC Merchandising, 1982. Subj: Careers – doctors. Health.

The missing button adventure ill. by Hajime Sawada. CBC Merchandising, 1981. Subj: Behavior – losing things. Character traits – helpfulness. Toys – teddy bears.

Mare, Walter De La *see* De La Mare, Walter

Margalit, Avishai. *The Hebrew alphabet book: Me-Alef'ad Tav* ill. by author. Funk and Wagnalls, 1968. Subj: ABC books. Jewish culture.

Margolis, Matthew. *Some swell pup* (Sendak, Maurice)

Margolis, Richard J. *Big bear, spare that tree* ill. by Jack Kent. Greenwillow, 1980. Subj: Animals – bears. Birds – bluejays. Ecology. Trees.

Secrets of a small brother ill. by Donald Carrick. Macmillan, 1984. Subj: Poetry, rhyme. Sibling rivalry.

Mari, Iela. *Eat and be eaten* ill. by author. Barron's 1980. Subj: Animals. Format, unusual. Sports – hunting. Wordless.

The magic balloon ill. by author. S. G. Phillips, 1970. Subj: Toys – balloons. Wordless.

Mariana. *Doki, the lonely papoose* ill. by author. Lothrop, 1955. Subj: Indians of North America.

The journey of Bangwell Putt ill. by author. Lothrop, 1965. Subj: Holidays – Christmas. Toys – dolls.

Miss Flora McFlimsey and the baby New Year ill. by author. Lothrop, 1951. ISBN 0-688-04533-2 Subj: Holidays – New Year's. Toys – dolls.

Miss Flora McFlimsey's birthday ill. by author. Lothrop, 1987. ISBN 0-688-04538-3 Subj: Activities – flying. Birds – puffins. Birthdays. Friendship. Toys – dolls.

Miss Flora McFlimsey's Christmas Eve ill. by author. Rev. ed. Lothrop, 1988. ISBN 0-688-04283-X Subj: Holidays – Christmas. Toys – dolls.

Miss Flora McFlimsey's Easter bonnet ill. by author. Lothrop, 1987. ISBN 0-688-04536-7 Subj: Animals – rabbits. Clothing. Holidays – Easter. Toys – dolls.

Miss Flora McFlimsey's Halloween ill. by author. Lothrop, 1987. ISBN 0-688-04550-2 Subj: Character traits – bravery. Goblins. Holidays – Halloween. Toys – dolls. Witches.

Miss Flora McFlimsey's May Day ill. by author. Lothrop, 1987. ISBN 0-688-04546-4 Subj: Animals. Holidays – May Day. Toys – dolls.

Miss Flora McFlimsey's Valentine ill. by author. Lothrop, 1987. ISBN 0-688-04548-0 Subj: Animals – cats. Holidays – Valentine's Day. Toys – dolls.

Marie. *Nursery rhymes* (Mother Goose)

Marie, Geraldine. *The magic box* ill. by Michele Chessare. Elsevier-Nelson, 1981. Subj: Animals – dogs. Birthdays. Magic. Problem solving.

Maril, Lee. *Mr. Bunny paints the eggs* ill. by Irena Lorentowicz. Roy Pub., 1945. Subj: Animals – rabbits. Concepts – color. Holidays – Easter. Music. Songs.

Marino, Barbara Pavis. *Eric needs stitches* photos. by Richard Rudinski. Addison-Wesley, 1979. Subj: Hospitals.

Marino, Dorothy. *Buzzy Bear and the rainbow* ill. by author. Watts, 1962. Subj: Animals – bears. Weather – rainbows.

Buzzy Bear goes camping ill. by author. Watts, 1964. Subj: Animals – bears. Sports – camping.

Buzzy Bear in the garden ill. by author. Watts, 1963, 1961. Subj: Activities – gardening. Animals – bears.

Buzzy Bear's busy day ill. by author. Watts, 1965. Subj: Animals – bears.

Edward and the boxes ill. by author. Lippincott, 1957. Subj: Activities – playing. Sleep.

Good-bye thunderstorm ill. by author. Lippincott, 1958. Subj: Weather – rain. Weather – storms. Weather – thunder.

Maris, Ron. *Are you there, bear?* ill. by author. Greenwillow, 1984. ISBN 0-688-03998-7 Subj: Behavior – lost. Toys. Toys – teddy bears.

Better move on, frog! ill. by author. Watts, 1982. Subj: Frogs and toads. Houses.

Hold tight, bear! ill. by author. Delacorte Pr., 1989. ISBN 0-440-50152-0 Subj: Animals – bears. Animals – donkeys. Forest, woods. Problem solving. Toys – dolls. Wordless.

I wish I could fly ill. by author. Greenwillow, 1986. ISBN 0-688-06655-0 Subj: Animals. Behavior – wishing. Reptiles – turtles, tortoises.

In my garden ill. by author. Greenwillow, 1988. ISBN 0-688-07631-9 Subj: Activities – picnicking. Animals. Counting. Flowers.

Is anyone home? ill. by author. Greenwillow, 1985. ISBN 0-688-05899-X Subj: Family life – grandparents. Farms. Format, unusual – toy and movable books.

My book ill. by author. Watts, 1983. Subj: Animals – cats. Bedtime.

Marks, Alan. *Nowhere to be found* ill. by author. Picture Book Studio, 1988. ISBN 0-88708-062-6 Subj: Behavior – lost. Behavior – losing things. Language.

Marks, Burton. *Puppet plays and puppet-making: the plays - the puppets - the production* by Burton and Rita Marks; ill. with photos. Plays, 1982. Subj: Puppets. Theater.

The spook book by Burton and Rita Marks; ill. by Lisa Campbell Ernst. Lothrop, 1981. Subj: Holidays – Halloween. Parties.

Marks, J. *see* Highwater, Jamake

Marks, Marcia Bliss. *Swing me, swing tree* ill. by David Berger. Little, 1959. Subj: Activities – swinging. Poetry, rhyme.

Marks, Rita. *Puppet plays and puppet-making* (Marks, Burton)

The spook book (Marks, Burton)

Marokvia, Merelle. *A French school for Paul* ill. by Artur Marokvia. Lippincott, 1963. Subj: Circus. Foreign lands – France. School.

Marol, Jean-Claude. *Vagabul and his shadow* ill. by author. Creative Education, 1983. Subj: Shadows. Wordless.

Vagabul escapes ill. by author. Creative Education, 1983. Subj: Behavior – running away. Wordless.

Vagabul goes skiing ill. by author. Creative Education, 1983. Subj: Sports – skiing. Wordless.

Vagabul in the clouds ill. by author. Creative Education, 1983. Subj: Weather – clouds. Wordless.

Marron, Carol A. *Gretchen's grandma* (Root, Phyllis)

No trouble for Grandpa ill. by Chaya M. Burstein. Raintree, 1983. ISBN 0-940742-27-6 Subj: Family life – grandfathers. Handicaps. Sibling rivalry.

Marsh, Jeri. *Hurrah for Alexander* ill. by Joan Hanson. Carolrhoda Books, 1977. Subj: Humor.

Marshak, Samuel. *In the van* tr. from Russian by Margaret Wettlin; ill. by V. Lebedev. Imported Pub., 1983. Subj: Animals – dogs. Moving. Poetry, rhyme.

The merry starlings by Samuel Marshak with D. Harms; tr. from Russian by Dorian Rottenberg; ill. by Arieh Zeldich. Harper, 1983. Subj: Birds. Nursery rhymes. Poetry, rhyme.

The Month-Brothers: a Slavic tale tr. from Russian by Thomas P. Whitney; ill. by Diane Stanley. Morrow, 1983. Subj: Foreign lands – Czechoslovakia. Poetry, rhyme. Seasons. Weather.

The pup grew up! tr. by Richard Pevear; ill. by Vladimir Radunsky. Holt, 1989. ISBN 0-8050-0952-3 Subj: Activities – traveling. Animals – dogs. Behavior – growing up. Behavior – losing things. Trains.

The tale of a hero nobody knows tr. from Russian by Peter Tempest; ill. by Vassili Shulzhenko. Imported Pub., 1983. Subj: Character traits – bravery. Foreign lands – Russia. Poetry, rhyme.

Marshall, Douglas *see* McClintock, Marshall

Marshall, Edward. *Four on the shore* ill. by James Marshall. Dial Pr., 1985. Subj: Monsters. Sibling rivalry.

Fox all week ill. by James Marshall. Dial Pr., 1984. ISBN 0-8037-0066-0 Subj: Animals. Animals – foxes. Friendship.

Fox and his friends ill. by James Marshall. Dial Pr., 1982. Subj: Animals – foxes. Behavior – misbehavior.

Fox at school ill. by James Marshall. Dial Pr., 1983. Subj: Animals – foxes. Humor. School.

Fox in love ill. by James Marshall. Dial Pr., 1982. Subj: Animals – foxes. Emotions – love.

Fox on wheels ill. by James Marshall. Dial Pr., 1983. Subj: Animals – foxes. Behavior – misbehavior. Sports – racing.

Space case ill. by James Marshall. Dial Pr., 1980. Subj: Holidays – Halloween. Robots. Space and space ships.

Three by the sea ill. by James Marshall. Dial Pr., 1981. Subj: Activities – picnicking. Friendship.

Troll country ill. by James Marshall. Dial Pr., 1980. Subj: Forest, woods. Trolls.

Marshall, Frances. *Princess Kalina and the hedgehog* (Flot, Jeannette B.)

Marshall, James. *The Cut-Ups* ill. by author. Viking, 1984. Subj: Behavior – misbehavior. Toys.

The Cut-Ups cut loose ill. by author. Viking, 1987. ISBN 0-670-80740-0 Subj: Behavior – misbehavior. Friendship. School.

Four little troubles ill. by author. Houghton, 1975. Subj: Animals. Problem solving.

Fox on the job ill. by author. Dial Pr., 1988. ISBN 0-8037-0351-1 Subj: Activities – working. Animals – foxes. Behavior – misbehavior.

George and Martha ill. by author. Houghton, 1972. Subj: Animals – hippopotami. Friendship.

George and Martha back in town ill. by author. Houghton, 1984. Subj: Animals – hippopotami. Behavior – misbehavior. Friendship.

George and Martha encore ill. by author. Houghton, 1973. Subj: Activities – dancing. Animals – hippopotami. Friendship.

George and Martha one fine day ill. by author. Houghton, 1978. Subj: Animals – hippopotami. Friendship.

George and Martha rise and shine ill. by author. Houghton, 1976. Subj: Animals – hippopotami. Friendship.

George and Martha round and round ill. by author. Houghton, 1988. ISBN 0-395-46763-2 Subj: Activities – vacationing. Animals – hippopotami. Friendship. Imagination.

George and Martha, tons of fun ill. by author. Houghton, 1980. Subj: Animals – hippopotami. Character traits – vanity.

Goldilocks and the three bears (The three bears)

The guest ill. by author. Houghton, 1975. Subj: Animals – moose. Animals – snails. Friendship.

Merry Christmas, space case ill. by author. Dial Pr., 1986. ISBN 0-8037-0216-7 Subj: Holidays – Christmas. Space and space ships.

Miss Dog's Christmas ill. by author. Houghton, 1973. Subj: Animals – dogs. Food. Holidays – Christmas.

Miss Nelson is back (Allard, Harry)

Miss Nelson is missing! (Allard, Harry)

Portly McSwine ill. by author. Houghton, 1979. Subj: Animals – pigs. Behavior – worrying.

Rapscallion Jones ill. by author. Viking, 1983. ISBN 0-670-58965-9 Subj: Animals – foxes. Behavior – seeking better things.

Red Riding Hood ill. by adapt. Dial Pr., 1987. ISBN 0-8037-0345-7 Subj: Animals – wolves. Behavior – talking to strangers. Folk and fairy tales.

Speedboat ill. by author. Houghton, 1976. Subj: Animals – dogs. Boats, ships. Friendship.

The Stupids have a ball (Allard, Harry)

Three up a tree ill. by author. Dutton, 1986. ISBN 0-8037-0329-5 Subj: Activities – playing. Imagination. Monsters. Trees.

What's the matter with Carruthers? ill. by author. Houghton, 1972. Subj: Animals – bears. Bedtime. Character traits – helpfulness. Friendship. Hibernation.

Willis ill. by author. Houghton, 1974. Subj: Animals. Friendship.

Wings: a tale of two chickens ill. by author. Viking, 1986. ISBN 0-670-80961-6 Subj: Activities – reading. Animals – foxes. Birds – chickens.

Yummers! ill. by author. Houghton, 1973. Subj: Animals – pigs. Food. Illness.

Yummers too ill. by author. Houghton, 1986. ISBN 0-395-38990-9 Subj: Animals – pigs. Behavior – greed. Food. Reptiles – turtles, tortoises.

Marshall, Lyn. *Yoga for your children* ill. with photos. Schocken, 1979. Subj: Health. Religion.

Marshall, Margaret. *Mike* ill. by Lorraine Spiro. Merrimack, 1983. Subj: Bedtime. Problem solving.

Marshall, Ray. *Pop-up numbers #1* by Ray Marshall and Korky Paul; ill. by authors. Dutton, 1984. Subj: Counting. Format, unusual – toy and movable books.

Pop-up numbers #2 by Ray Marshall and Korky Paul; ill. by authors. Dutton, 1984. Subj: Counting. Format, unusual – toy and movable books.

Pop-up numbers #3 by Ray Marshall and Korky Paul; ill. by authors. Dutton, 1984. Subj: Counting. Format, unusual – toy and movable books.

Pop-up numbers #4 by Ray Marshall and Korky Paul; ill. by authors. Dutton, 1984. Subj: Counting. Format, unusual – toy and movable books.

The train: watch it work by operating the moving diagrams! ill. by John Bradley. Viking, 1986. ISBN 0-670-81134-3 Subj: Format, unusual – toy and movable books. Trains.

Marston, Hope Irvin. *Big rigs* ill. with photos. Dodd, 1979. Subj: Transportation. Trucks.

Fire trucks ill. with photos. Dodd, 1984. Subj: Careers – firefighters. Trucks.

Martel, Cruz. *Yagua days* ill. by Jerry Pinkney. Dial Pr., 1976. Subj: Family life. Foreign lands – Puerto Rico.

Martin, Bernard H. *Brave little Indian* (Martin, Bill (William Ivan))

Smoky Poky (Martin, Bill (William Ivan))

Martin, Bill (William Ivan). *Barn dance!* ill. by Ted Rand. Holt, 1986. ISBN 0-8050-0089-5 Subj: Activities – dancing. Barns. Country. Dreams. Night. Poetry, rhyme. Scarecrows.

Brave little Indian by Bill Martin, Jr. and Bernard H. Martin; ill. by Bernard H. Martin. Tell-Well Pr., 1951. Subj: Indians of North America. Participation.

Brown bear, brown bear, what do you see? ill. by Eric Carle. Holt, 1983. Subj: Animals – bears. Cumulative tales. Poetry, rhyme.

Here are my hands by Bill Martin, Jr. and John Archambault; ill. by Ted Rand. Holt, 1987. ISBN 0-8050-0328-2 Subj: Anatomy.

Knots on a counting rope by Bill Martin, Jr. and John Archambault; ill. by Ted Rand. Holt, 1987. ISBN 0-8050-0571-4 Subj: Character traits — bravery. Emotions — love. Family life — grandfathers. Handicaps — blindness. Indians of North America. Senses — seeing.

Listen to the rain by Bill Martin, Jr. and John Archambault; ill. by James R. Endicott. Holt, 1988. ISBN 0-8050-0682-6 Subj: Poetry, rhyme. Weather — rain.

My days are made of butterflies adapted by William Ivan Martin, Jr.; written by Sano M. Galea'i Fa'apouli; ill. by Vic Herman. Holt, 1970. Subj: Foreign lands — Mexico.

Smoky Poky by Bill Martin, Jr. and Bernard H. Martin; ill. by Bernard H. Martin. Tell-Well Pr., 1947. Subj: Animals — elephants. Trains.

Sounds around the clock comp. by Bill Martin, Jr. in collaboration with Peggy Brogan. Holt, 1966. Subj: Noise, sounds. Poetry, rhyme.

Sounds I remember comp. by Bill Martin, Jr. in collaboration with Peggy Brogan. Holt, 1974. Subj: Counting. Noise, sounds. Nursery rhymes.

Sounds of home comp. by Bill Martin, Jr. in collaboration with Peggy Brogan. Holt, 1972. Subj: Noise, sounds. Poetry, rhyme.

Sounds of laughter comp. by Bill Martin, Jr. in collaboration with Peggy Brogan. Holt, 1972. Subj: Folk and fairy tales. Humor. Noise, sounds. Poetry, rhyme.

Sounds of numbers comp. by Bill Martin, Jr. in collaboration with Peggy Brogan. Holt, 1972. Subj: Counting. Noise, sounds. Poetry, rhyme.

Up and down on the merry-go-round by Bill Martin, Jr. and John Archambault; ill. by Ted Rand. Holt, 1988. ISBN 0-8050-0681-8 Subj: Merry-go-rounds.

White Dynamite and Curly Kidd by Bill Martin, Jr. and John Archambault; ill. by Ted Rand. Holt, 1986. ISBN 0-03-008399-0 Subj: Animals — bulls, cows. Family life. Sports.

Martin, C. L. G. *The dragon nanny* ill. by Robert Rayevsky. Macmillan, 1988. ISBN 0-02-762440-4 Subj: Activities — baby-sitting. Dragons. Royalty.

Martin, Charles E. *Dunkel takes a walk* ill. by author. Greenwillow, 1983. Subj: Animals — dogs. Character traits — cleverness.

For rent ill. by author. Greenwillow, 1986. ISBN 0-688-05717-9 Subj: Activities — painting. Islands. School. Seasons — summer.

Island rescue ill. by author. Greenwillow, 1985. ISBN 0-688-04258-9 Subj: Hospitals. Islands. Seasons — spring.

Island winter ill. by author. Greenwillow, 1984. Subj: Islands. Seasons — winter.

Noah's ark retold by Lawrence T. Lorimer; ill. by Charles E. Martin. Random House, 1978. Subj: Religion — Noah.

Sam saves the day ill. by author. Greenwillow, 1987. ISBN 0-688-06815-4 Subj: Activities — traveling. Activities — vacationing. Seasons — summer.

Martin, Diane. *Mister Mole* (Murschetz, Luis)

Martin, Frederic see Christopher, Matt

Martin, Jacqueline Briggs. *Bizzy Bones and Moosemouse* ill. by Stella Ormai. Lothrop, 1986. ISBN 0-688-05746-2 Subj: Animals — mice. Behavior — lost. Friendship.

Bizzy Bones and the lost quilt ill. by Stella Ormai. Lothrop, 1988. ISBN 0-688-07408-1 Subj: Animals — mice. Behavior — losing things. Friendship.

Bizzy Bones and Uncle Ezra ill. by Stella Ormai. Lothrop, 1984. Subj: Animals — mice. Emotions — fear.

Martin, Janet see Allen, Robert

Martin, Judith. *The tree angel* by Judith Martin and Remy Charlip; ill. by Remy Charlip. Knopf, 1962. Subj: Angels. Holidays — Christmas. Theater.

Martin, Patricia Miles see Miles, Miska

Martin, Rafe. *Foolish rabbit's big mistake* ill. by Ed Young. Putnam's, 1985. ISBN 0-399-21178-0 Subj: Animals — rabbits. Behavior — mistakes. Folk and fairy tales.

The hungry tigress: and other traditional Asian tales ill. by Richard Wehrman. Shambhala, 1984. Subj: Folk and fairy tales.

Martin, Sarah Catherine. *The comic adventures of Old Mother Hubbard and her dog* ill. by Arnold Lobel. Bradbury Pr., 1968. Subj: Animals — dogs. Nursery rhymes.

Old Mother Hubbard adapt. by Colin and Jacqui Hawkins; ill. by Colin Hawkins. Putnam's, 1985. ISBN 0-399-21162-4 Subj: Animals — dogs. Format, unusual — toy and movable books. Nursery rhymes.

Old Mother Hubbard and her dog ill. by Lisa Amoroso. Knopf, 1987. ISBN 0-394-98922-8 Subj: Animals — dogs. Nursery rhymes.

Old Mother Hubbard and her dog ill. by Paul Galdone. McGraw-Hill, 1960. Subj: Animals — dogs. Nursery rhymes.

Old Mother Hubbard and her dog ill. by Evaline Ness. Holt, 1972. Subj: Animals — dogs. Nursery rhymes.

Martini, Teri. *Cowboys* ill. with photos. Rev. ed. Children's Pr., 1981. Subj: Activities — working. Cowboys.

Marzollo, Claudio. *Jed and the space bandits* (Marzollo, Jean)

Jed's junior space patrol (Marzollo, Jean)

Marzollo, Jean. *Amy goes fishing* ill. by Ann Schweninger. Dial Pr., 1980. Subj: Family life — fathers. Sports — fishing.

Close your eyes ill. by Susan Jeffers. Dial Pr., 1978. Subj: Bedtime. Family life – fathers. Poetry, rhyme.

Jed and the space bandits by Jean and Claudio Marzollo; ill. by Peter Sis. Dial Pr., 1987. ISBN 0-8037-0136-5 Subj: Crime. Pets. Robots. Space and space ships.

Jed's junior space patrol by Jean and Claudio Marzollo; ill. by David S. Rose. Dial Pr., 1982. Subj: Robots. Space and space ships. Toys – teddy bears.

The rebus treasury ill. by Carol D. Carson. Dial Pr., 1986. ISBN 0-8037-0255-8 Subj: Nursery rhymes. Rebuses.

The silver bear il. by Susan Meddaugh. Dial Pr., 1987. ISBN 0-8037-0369-4 Subj: Imagination.

The three little kittens (Mother Goose)

Uproar on Hollercat Hill ill. by Steven Kellogg. Dial Pr., 1980. Subj: Animals – cats. Behavior – misbehavior. Poetry, rhyme.

Maschler, Fay. *T. G. and Moonie go shopping* ill. by Sylvie Selig. Doubleday, 1978. Subj: Animals – cats. Birds – owls. Shopping. Stores.

T. G. and Moonie have a baby ill. by Sylvie Selig. Doubleday, 1979. Subj: Animals – cats. Birds – owls. Family life.

T. G. and Moonie move out of town ill. by Sylvia Selig. Doubleday, 1978. Subj: Animals – cats. Birds – owls. Moving.

Masks and puppets ill. by Louise Nevett. Watts, 1984. Subj: Activities. Puppets.

Massey, Jeanne. *The littlest witch* ill. by Adrienne Adams. Knopf, 1959. Subj: Holidays – Halloween. Witches.

Massie, Diane Redfield. *The baby beebee bird* ill. by author. Harper, 1963. Subj: Animals. Birds. Noise, sounds. Sleep.

Chameleon the spy and the terrible toaster trap ill. by author. Crowell, 1982. Subj: Crime. Reptiles – lizards.

Cockle stew and other rhymes ill. by author. Atheneum, 1967. Subj: Poetry, rhyme.

The Komodo dragon's jewels ill. by author. Macmillan, 1975. Subj: Boats, ships. Dragons. Reptiles – lizards.

Tiny pin ill. by author. Harper, 1964. Subj: Animals – porcupines. Behavior – growing up. Poetry, rhyme.

Walter was a frog ill. by author. Simon and Schuster, 1970. Subj: Behavior – dissatisfaction. Frogs and toads.

Mathers, Petra. *Theodor and Mr. Balbini* ill. by author. Harper, 1988. ISBN 0-06-024144-6 Subj: Animals – dogs. Pets.

Mathews, Louise. *Bunches and bunches of bunnies* ill. by Jeni Bassett. Dodd, 1978. Subj: Animals – rabbits. Counting. Poetry, rhyme.

Cluck one ill. by Jeni Bassett. Dodd, 1982. Subj: Animals – weasels. Birds – chickens. Counting. Eggs.

The great take-away ill. by Jeni Bassett. Dodd, 1980. Subj: Animals – pigs. Character traits – laziness. Counting. Crime.

Mathiesen, Egon. *Oswald, the monkey* adapt. from Danish by Nancy and Edward Maze; ill. by author. Astor-Honor, 1959. Subj: Animals – monkeys.

Mathura, Mustapha *see* Matura, Mustapha

Matias. *Mr. Noah and the animals: Monsieur Noe et les animaux* ill. by author. Walck, 1960. Subj: Religion – Noah.

Matsui, Susan. *The bears' autumn* (Tejima, Keizaburo)

Matsuno, Masako. *A pair of red clogs* ill. by Kazue Mizumura. Collins, 1960. Subj: Character traits – honesty. Clothing. Foreign lands – Japan.

Taro and the bamboo shoot: a Japanese tale ill. by Yasuo Segawa. Pantheon, 1964. Adapted from the Japanese by Alice Low. Subj: Folk and fairy tales. Foreign lands – Japan.

Taro and the Tofu ill. by Kazue Mizumura. Collins-World, 1962. Subj: Character traits – honesty. Foreign lands – Japan.

Matsutani, Miyoko. *The fisherman under the sea* English version by Alvin Tresselt; ill. by Chihiro Iwasaki. Parents, 1969. Translation of Urashima Tarō. Subj: Careers – fishermen. Folk and fairy tales. Foreign lands – Japan. Reptiles – turtles, tortoises. Royalty. Sea and seashore.

How the withered trees blossomed ill. by Yasuo Segawa. Lippincott, 1969. Subj: Behavior – greed. Foreign lands – Japan. Foreign languages.

The witch's magic cloth English version by Alvin Tresselt; ill. by Yasuo Segawa. Parents, 1969. Subj: Character traits – bravery. Folk and fairy tales. Foreign lands – Japan. Witches.

Matthias, Catherine. *I can be a computer operator* ill. with photos. Childrens Pr., 1985. ISBN 0-516-01838-8 Subj: Careers. Machines.

I love cats ill. by Tom Dunnington. Children's Pr., 1983. Subj: Animals – cats.

Out the door ill. by Eileen Mueller Neill. Children's Pr., 1982. Subj: Buses. School.

Over-under ill. by Gene Sharp. Children's Pr., 1984. Subj: Concepts – opposites.

Too many balloons ill. by Gene Sharp. Childrens Pr., 1982. ISBN 0-516-03633-5 Subj: Counting. Toys – balloons. Zoos.

Matthiesen, Thomas. *Things to see: a child's world of familiar objects* photos. by author. Platt, 1968. ISBN 0-448-41051-6 Subj: Concepts. Senses – seeing.

Mattingley, Christobel. *The angel with a mouth-organ* ill. by Astra Lacis. Holiday, 1984. ISBN 0-8234-0593-1 Subj: Death. Holidays – Christmas. War.

Matura, Mustapha. *Moon jump* ill. by Jane Gifford. Knopf, 1988. ISBN 0-394-91976-9 Subj: Bedtime. Imagination. Moon.

Matus, Greta. *Where are you, Jason?* ill. by author. Lothrop, 1974. Subj: Behavior – hiding. Imagination. Night.

Maury, Inez. *My mother the mail carrier: Mi mama la cartera* tr. by Norah E. Alemany; ill. by Tasha Tudor. Feminist Pr., 1976. Subj: Careers – mail carriers. Foreign languages.

Mauver, Judy A. *Dusty wants to help* (Sandberg, Inger)

May, Charles Paul. *High-noon rocket* ill. by Brinton Turkle. Holiday, 1966. Subj: Activities – traveling. Science. Space and space ships. Time.

May, Julian. *Why people are different colors* ill. by Symeon Shimin. Holiday, 1971. Subj: Ethnic groups in the U.S.

May, Robert Lewis. *Rudolph the red-nosed reindeer* ill. by Diana Magnuson. Four Winds Pr., 1980. Subj: Animals – reindeer. Elves and little people. Holidays – Christmas. Weather – fog.

Mayer, Marianna. *Alley oop!* ill. by Gerald McDermott. Holt, 1985. Subj: Animals – mice. Counting. Reptiles – alligators, crocodiles.

Beauty and the beast ill. by Mercer Mayer. Four Winds Pr., 1978. Subj: Animals. Character traits – appearance. Emotions – love. Folk and fairy tales.

The black horse ill. by Katie Thamer. Dial Pr., 1984. ISBN 0-8037-0076-8 Subj: Animals – horses. Behavior – trickery. Folk and fairy tales. Magic. Royalty.

The little jewel box ill. by Margot Tomes. Dial Pr., 1986. ISBN 0-8037-0149-7 Subj: Animals. Birds. Character traits – kindness. Character traits – luck. Elves and little people. Folk and fairy tales. Magic.

Mine! (Mayer, Mercer)

My first book of nursery tales: five favorite bedtime tales ill. by William Joyce. Random House, 1983. Subj: Folk and fairy tales.

One frog too many (Mayer, Mercer)

The twelve dancing princesses (Grimm, Jacob)

The ugly duckling (Andersen, H. C. (Hans Christian))

The unicorn and the lake ill. by Michael Hague. Dial Pr., 1982. Subj: Character traits – bravery. Mythical creatures.

Mayer, Mercer. *Ah-choo* ill. by author. Dial Pr., 1976. Subj: Animals – elephants. Illness. Wordless.

Appelard and Liverwurst ill. by Steven Kellogg. Four Winds Pr., 1978. Subj: Animals. Behavior – misbehavior. Farms.

Astronaut critter ill. by author. Simon & Schuster, 1986. ISBN 0-671-61142-9 Subj: Format, unusual – board books. Space and space ships.

A boy, a dog, a frog and a friend ill. by author. Dial Pr., 1971. Subj: Friendship. Frogs and toads. Sports – fishing. Wordless.

A boy, a dog and a frog ill. by author. Dial Pr., 1967. Subj: Friendship. Frogs and toads. Sports – fishing. Wordless.

Bubble bubble ill. by author. Parents, 1973. Subj: Imagination. Wordless.

Cowboy critter ill. by author. Simon & Schuster, 1986. ISBN 0-671-61141-0 Subj: Cowboys. Format, unusual – board books.

Fireman critter ill. by author. Simon & Schuster, 1986. ISBN 0-671-61143-7 Subj: Careers – firefighters. Format, unusual – board books.

Frog goes to dinner ill. by author. Dial Pr., 1974. Subj: Food. Frogs and toads. Wordless.

Frog on his own ill. by author. Dial Pr., 1973. Subj: Frogs and toads. Wordless.

Frog, where are you? ill. by author. Dial Pr., 1969. Subj: Friendship. Frogs and toads. Wordless.

The great cat chase ill. by author. Four Winds Pr., 1974. Subj: Animals – cats. Wordless.

Hiccup ill. by author. Dial Pr., 1976. Subj: Animals – hippopotami. Illness. Wordless.

How the trollusk got his hat ill. by author. Golden Pr., 1979. Subj: Character traits – appearance. Character traits – honesty.

I am a hunter ill. by author. Dial Pr., 1969. Subj: Imagination.

Just for you ill. by author. Golden Pr., 1975. Subj: Character traits – helpfulness. Emotions – love. Family life – mothers.

Just me and my dad ill. by author. Golden Pr., 1977. Subj: Family life – fathers. Sports – camping.

Little Monster at home ill. by author. Golden Pr., 1978. Subj: Houses. Monsters.

Little Monster at school ill. by author. Golden Pr., 1978. Subj: Monsters. School.

Little Monster at work ill. by author. Golden Pr., 1978. Subj: Careers. Family life – grandfathers. Monsters.

Little Monster's alphabet book ill. by author. Golden Pr., 1978. Subj: ABC books. Monsters.

Little Monster's bedtime book ill. by author. Golden Pr., 1978. Subj: Bedtime. Monsters. Poetry, rhyme.

Little Monster's counting book ill. by author. Golden Pr., 1978. Subj: Counting. Monsters.

Little Monster's neighborhood ill. by author. Golden Pr., 1978. Subj: City. Monsters.

Liverwurst is missing ill. by Steven Kellogg. Four Winds Pr., 1981. Subj: Character traits – bravery. Circus. Crime.

Liza Lou and the Yeller Belly Swamp ill. by author. Parents, 1976. Subj: Character traits – bravery. Ethnic groups in the U.S. – Afro-Americans. Monsters.

Mine! by Mercer and Marianna Mayer; ill. by Mercer Mayer. Simon and Schuster, 1970. Subj: Concepts. Emotions.

Mrs. Beggs and the wizard ill. by author. Parents, 1973. Subj: Magic. Monsters. Wizards.

One frog too many by Mercer and Marianna Mayer; ill. by Mercer Mayer. Dial Pr., 1975. Subj: Emotions – envy, jealousy. Frogs and toads. Wordless.

Oops ill. by author. Dial Pr., 1977. Subj: Animals – hippopotami. Behavior – carelessness. Wordless.

The Pied Piper of Hamelin adapt and ill. by Mercer Mayer. Macmillan, 1987. Adapt. of the poem The pied piper of Hamelin by Robert Browning. ISBN 0-02-765361-7 Subj: Animals – rats. Behavior – trickery. Folk and fairy tales. Foreign lands – Germany.

Policeman critter ill. by author. Simon & Schuster, 1986. ISBN 0-671-61140-2 Subj: Careers – police officers. Format, unusual – board books.

The queen always wanted to dance ill. by author. Simon and Schuster, 1971. Subj: Activities – dancing. Humor. Music. Royalty.

The sleeping beauty (Grimm, Jacob)

A special trick ill. by author. Dial Pr., 1976. ISBN 0-8037-8103-2 Subj: Magic.

Terrible troll ill. by author. Dial Pr., 1968. Subj: Imagination. Knights. Monsters. Mythical creatures. Trolls.

There's a nightmare in my closet ill. by author. Dial Pr., 1968. Subj: Bedtime. Emotions – fear. Monsters.

There's an alligator under my bed ill. by author. Dial Pr., 1987. ISBN 0-8037-0375-9 Subj: Bedtime. Emotions – fear. Reptiles – alligators, crocodiles.

There's something in my attic ill. by author. Dial Pr., 1988. ISBN 0-8037-0415-1 Subj: Dreams. Emotions – fear. Night.

Two moral tales ill. by author. Four Winds Pr., 1974. Bear's new clothes—Bird's new hat. Subj: Animals – bears. Birds. Clothing. Wordless.

What do you do with a kangaroo? ill. by author. Four Winds Pr., 1973. Subj: Animals. Humor. Problem solving.

Whinnie the lovesick dragon ill. by Diane Dawson. Macmillan, 1986. ISBN 0-02-765180-0 Subj: Behavior – needing someone. Dragons. Emotions – love. Magic. Middle ages.

You're the scaredy cat ill. by author. Parents, 1974. Subj: Emotions – fear. Night. Sports – camping.

Mayers, Florence Cassen. *Egyptian art from the Brooklyn Museum: ABC* designed by Florence Cassen Mayers; ed. by Sheila Franklin. Abrams, 1988. ISBN 0-8109-1888-3 Subj: ABC books. Art. Foreign lands – Egypt. Museums.

The Museum of Fine Arts, Boston: ABC designed by Florence Cassen Mayers; ed. by Sheila Franklin. Abrams, 1986. ISBN 0-8109-1847-1 Subj: ABC books. Art. Museums.

The Museum of Modern Art, New York: ABC designed by Florence Cassen Mayers; ed. by Sheila Franklin. Abrams, 1986. ISBN 0-8109-1849-8 Subj: ABC books. Art. Museums.

The National Air and Space Museum: ABC designed by Florence Cassen Mayers; ed. by Sheila Franklin. Abrams, 1988. ISBN 0-8109-1859-5 Subj: ABC books. Museums. Space and space ships.

Mayers, Patrick. *Just one more block* ill. by Lucy Hawkinson. Albert Whitman, 1970. Subj: Activities – playing. Emotions. Sibling rivalry. Toys – blocks.

Mayle, Peter. *Divorce can happen to the nicest people* ill. by Arthur Robins. Macmillan, 1980. Subj: Divorce. Family life.

Why are we getting a divorce? ill. by Arthur Robins. Crown, 1988. ISBN 0-517-56527-7 Subj: Divorce. Family life.

Maynard, Joyce. *Camp-out* ill. by Steve Bethel. Harcourt, 1985. ISBN 0-15-214077-8 Subj: Family life. Sports – camping.

New house ill. by Steve Bethel. Harcourt, 1987. ISBN 0-15-257042-X Subj: Activities – working. Houses. Trees.

Mayne, William. *Barnabas walks* ill. by Barbara Firth. Prentice-Hall, 1987. ISBN 0-13-057001-X Subj: Animals – guinea pigs. School.

The blue book of Hob stories ill. by Patrick Benson. Putnam's, 1984. Subj: Character traits – helpfulness. Elves and little people.

Come, come to my corner ill. by Kenneth Lilly. Prentice-Hall, 1987. ISBN 0-13-152497-6 Subj: Animals. Animals – rabbits.

The green book of Hob stories ill. by Patrick Benore. Putnam's, 1984. ISBN 0-399-21039-3 Subj: Character traits – helpfulness. Elves and little people. Fairies.

A house in town ill. by Sarah Fox-Davis. Prentice-Hall, 1988. ISBN 0-13-395880-9 Subj: Animals – foxes.

Mousewing ill. by Martin Baynton. Prentice-Hall, 1988. ISBN 0-13-604240-6 Subj: Animals – mice.

The patchwork cat ill. by Nicola Bayley. Knopf, 1981. Subj: Animals – cats. Behavior – saving things. Emotions – love.

The red book of Hob stories ill. by Patrick Benson. Putnam's, 1984. ISBN 0-399-21047-4 Subj: Character traits – helpfulness. Elves and little people. Fairies.

Tibber ill. by Jonathan Heale. Prentice-Hall, 1987. ISBN 0-13-921214-0 Subj: Animals – cats. Farms.

The yellow book of Hob stories ill. by Patrick Benson. Putnam's, 1984. ISBN 0-399-21050-4 Subj: Character traits – helpfulness. Elves and little people. Fairies.

Mayper, Monica. *After good-night* ill. by Peter Sis. Harper, 1987. ISBN 0-06-024121-7 Subj: Bedtime. Dreams. Family life.

Maze, Edward. *Oswald, the monkey* (Mathiesen, Egon)

Maze, Nancy. *Oswald, the monkey* (Mathiesen, Egon)

M'Bane, Phumla *see* Phumla

Meddaugh, Susan. *Beast* ill. by author. Houghton, 1981. ISBN 0-395-30349-4 Subj: Character traits – kindness. Monsters.

Maude and Claude go abroad ill. by author. Houghton, 1980. Subj: Activities – traveling. Animals – foxes. Boats, ships. Foreign lands – France.

Too short Fred ill. by author. Houghton, 1978. Subj: Animals – cats. Character traits – smallness.

Mee, Charles L. *Noah* by Charles L. Mee, Jr.; ill. by Ken Munowitz. Harper, 1978. Subj: Religion – Noah.

Meeks, Esther K. *The curious cow* ill. by Mel Pekarsky. Follett, 1960. Also published in German as "Die neugierige Kuh"; in French as "La vache curieuse"; and in Spanish as "La Vaca curiosa." Subj: Animals – bulls, cows. Character traits – curiosity.

Friendly farm animals. Follett, 1965. Subj: Animals. Farms.

The hill that grew ill. by Lazlo Roth. Follett, 1959. Subj: Activities – playing.

One is the engine: a counting book ill. by Joe Rogers. Follett, 1947, 1972. Subj: Counting. Trains.

One is the engine ill. by Ernie King. Follett, 1956. Subj: Counting. Trains.

Playland pony ill. by Mary Miller Salem. Follett, 1951. Subj: Animals – horses.

Something new at the zoo ill. by Hazel Hoecker. Follett, 1957. Subj: Animals. Zoos.

Meggendorfer, Lothar. *The genius of Lothar Meggendorfer* ill. by Jim Deesing. Random House, 1985. ISBN 0-394-54690-3 Subj: Format, unusual – toy and movable books. Poetry, rhyme. Toys.

Mellings, Joan. *It's fun to go to school* ill. by Sandra Laroche. Lippincott, 1986. ISBN 0-694-00125-2 Subj: Poetry, rhyme. School.

Melmoth, Sebastian *see* Wilde, Oscar

Memling, Carl. *What's in the dark?* ill. by John E. Johnson. Parent's, 1971. Subj: Monsters. Night.

Mendoza, George. *The alphabet boat: a seagoing alphabet book* ill. by author. American Heritage, 1972. Subj: ABC books. Boats, ships.

Alphabet sheep ill. by Kathleen Reidy. Grosset, 1982. Subj: ABC books. Animals – sheep. Behavior – lost.

The gillygoofang ill. by Mercer Mayer. Dial Pr., 1982. ISBN 0-8037-2875-1 Subj: Fish.

Henri Mouse ill. by Joelle Boucher. Viking, 1985. Subj: Animals – mice. Art.

Henri Mouse, the juggler ill. by Joelle Boucher. Viking, 1986. ISBN 0-670-80945-4 Subj: Animals – mice. Foreign lands – France. Magic.

The hunter I might have been photos. by De Wayne Dalrymple. Astor-Honor, 1968. Subj: Death. Emotions. Poetry, rhyme. Sports – hunting.

The Marcel Marceau counting book photos. by Milton H. Greene. Doubleday, 1971. Subj: Clowns, jesters.

Need a house? Call Ms. Mouse ill. by Doris Susan Smith. Grosset, 1981. Subj: Animals. Animals – mice. Houses.

Norman Rockwell's American ABC ill. by Norman Rockwell. Abrams, 1975. Subj: ABC books.

The scribbler ill. by Robert M. Quackenbush. Holt, 1971. Subj: Birds – sandpipers. Poetry, rhyme. Sea and seashore.

The Sesame Street book of opposites with Zero Mostel photos. by Sheldon Secunda; book design by Nicole Sekora-Mendoza. Platt, 1974. Subj: Concepts – opposites.

Silly sheep and other sheepish rhymes ill. by Kathleen Reidy. Grosset, 1982. Subj: Animals – sheep. Nursery rhymes.

What I want to be when I grow up (Burnett, Carol.)

Menter, Ian. *The Albany Road mural* photos. by Will Guy. David and Charles, 1984. Subj: Activities – painting. Art.

Carnival photos. by Will Guy. David and Charles, 1983. Subj: Foreign lands – England. Holidays.

Meredith, Lucy. *The princess on the nut* (Nikly, Michelle)

Mernan, Andrea. *Ben finds a friend* (Chapouton, Anne-Marie)

I wish I were (Laurencin, Geneviève)

A walk in the rain (Scheffler, Ursel)

Meroux, Felix. *The prince of the rabbits* ill. by Cooper Edens. Green Tiger Pr., 1985. ISBN 0-88138-030-X Subj: Animals – rabbits. Behavior – boredom.

Merriam, Eve. *The birthday cow* ill. by Guy Michel. Knopf, 1978. ISBN 0-394-93808-9 Subj: Animals. Humor. Poetry, rhyme.

The birthday door ill. by Peter J. Thornton. Morrow, 1986. ISBN 0-688-06194-X Subj: Animals – cats. Birthdays. Houses. Problem solving.

Blackberry ink ill. by Hans Wilhelm. Morrow, 1985. ISBN 0-688-04151-5 Subj: Poetry, rhyme.

Boys and girls, girls and boys ill. by Harriet Sherman. Holt, 1972. Subj: Activities – playing. Ethnic groups in the U.S.

Christmas (Bruna, Dick)

The Christmas box ill. by David Small. Morrow, 1985. ISBN 0-688-05256-8 Subj: Family life. Holidays – Christmas.

Epaminondas ill. by Trina Schart Hyman. Follett, 1968. Originally published in 1938 as "Epaminondas and his Aunty" by Sara Cone Bryant. Subj: Ethnic groups in the U.S. – Afro-Americans. Folk and fairy tales.

Good night to Annie ill. by John Wallner. Four Winds Pr., 1980. Subj: ABC books. Bedtime.

Halloween ABC ill. by Lane Smith. Macmillan, 1987. ISBN 0-02-766870-3 Subj: ABC books. Holidays – Halloween. Poetry, rhyme.

Mommies at work ill. by Beni Montresor. Knopf, 1961. Subj: Activities – working. Careers. Family life – mothers.

Merrill, Jean. *Emily Emerson's moon* by Jean Merrill and Ronni Solbert; ill. by Ronni Solbert. Little, 1960. Subj: Family life. Moon.

How many kids are hiding on my block? by Jean Merrill and Frances Gruse Scott; ill. by Frances Gruse Scott. Albert Whitman, 1970. Subj: Counting. Ethnic groups in the U.S. Games.

Tell about the cowbarn, Daddy ill. by Lili Cassel-Wronker. Addison-Wesley, 1963. Subj: Animals – bulls, cows. Barns. Farms.

Merritt, Jane Hamilton *see* Hamilton-Merritt, Jane

Meshover, Leonard. *The guinea pigs that went to school* by Leonard Meshover and Sally Feistel; photos. by Eve Hoffmann. Follett, 1968. Subj: Animals – guinea pigs. School. Science.

The monkey that went to school by Leonard Meshover and Sally Feistel; photos. by Eve Hoffmann. Follett, 1978. Subj: Animals – monkeys. School. Science.

Messenger, Jannat. *Lullabies and baby songs* ill. by author. Dial Pr., 1988. ISBN 0-8037-0491-7 Subj: Poetry, rhyme. Songs.

Metcalf, Suzanne *see* Baum, L. Frank (Lyman Frank)

Meyer, Elizabeth C. *The blue china pitcher* ill. by author. Abingdon Pr., 1974. Subj: Holidays. Parties.

Meyer, June *see* Jordan, June

Meyer, Linda D. *Safety zone* ill. by Marina Megale. Chas. Franklin Pr., 1984. Subj: Behavior – talking to strangers. Safety.

Meyer, Louis A. *The clean air and peaceful contentment dirigible airline* ill. by author. Little, 1972. Subj: Ecology. Humor. Noise, sounds.

Meyers, Susan. *The truth about gorillas* ill. by John Hamberger. Dutton, 1980. Subj: Animals – gorillas. Science.

Michael, Emory H. *Androcles and the lion* ill. by Mia Hatchem. Winston-Derek, 1988. ISBN 1-55523-132-2 Subj: Animals – lions. Character traits – helpfulness. Character traits – kindness to animals. Folk and fairy tales. Foreign lands – Italy. Religion.

Michaels, Ruth. *The family that grew* (Rondell, Florence)

Michel, Anna. *Little wild lion cub* ill. by Tony Chen. Pantheon, 1981. Subj: Animals – lions.

Michels, Tilde. *Rabbit spring* ill. by Käthi Bhend. Harcourt, 1989. ISBN 0-15-200568-4 Subj: Animals – rabbits. Nature.

Who's that knocking at my door? ill. by Reinhard Michl. Barron's, 1986. ISBN 0-8120-5732-5 Subj: Poetry, rhyme. Seasons – winter. Sports – hunting.

Michl, Reinhard. *A day on the river* ill. by author. Barron's, 1986. ISBN 0-8120-5715-5 Subj: Rivers.

Middleton, Maud Barbara *see* Walker, Barbara K.

Miklowitz, Gloria D. *Bearfoot boy* ill. by Jim Collins. Follett, 1964. Subj: Birthdays. Clothing.

Save that raccoon! ill. by St. Tamara. Harcourt, 1978. Subj: Animals – raccoons. Character traits – kindness to animals. Fire. Forest, woods.

The zoo that moved ill. by Don Madden. Follett, 1968. Subj: Animals. Zoos.

Miles, Betty. *Around and around... love* ill. with photos. Knopf, 1975. Subj: Emotions – love. Poetry, rhyme.

Having a friend ill. by Erik Blegvad. Knopf, 1958. Subj: Friendship.

A house for everyone ill. by Jo Lowery. Knopf, 1958. Subj: Houses.

Miles, Miska. *Apricot ABC* ill. by Peter Parnall. Little, 1969. Subj: ABC books. Poetry, rhyme. Trees.

Chicken forgets ill. by Jim Arnosky. Little, 1976. Subj: Behavior – forgetfulness. Birds – chickens. Humor.

The fox and the fire ill. by John Schoenherr. Little, 1966. Subj: Animals – foxes. Fire. Forest, woods.

Friend of Miguel ill. by Genia. Rand McNally, 1967. Subj: Animals – horses. Foreign lands – Mexico.

The horse and the bad morning (Clymer, Ted)

Jump frog jump ill. by Earl Thollander. Putnam's, 1965. Subj: Fairs. Frogs and toads.

Mouse six and the happy birthday ill. by Leslie Morrill. Dutton, 1978. Subj: Animals – mice. Birthdays. Family life – mothers.

No, no, Rosina ill. by Earl Thollander. Putnam's, 1964. Subj: Boats, ships. Careers – fishermen. Character traits – smallness. City. Sports – fishing.

Noisy gander ill. by Leslie Morrill. Dutton, 1978. Subj: Animals. Birds – ducks. Farms. Noise, sounds.

The pointed brush... ill. by Roger Antoine Duvoisin. Lothrop, 1959. Subj: Activities – writing. Foreign lands – China.

Rabbit garden ill. by John Schoenherr. Little, 1967. Subj: Animals – rabbits. Ecology.

The raccoon and Mrs. McGinnis ill. by Leonard Weisgard. Putnam's, 1961. Subj: Animals – raccoons. Barns. Crime.

The rice bowl pet ill. by Ezra Jack Keats. Crowell, 1962. Subj: Pets.

Rolling the cheese ill. by Alton Raible. Atheneum, 1966. Subj: City. Games.

Show and tell... ill. by Thomas Arthur Hamil. Putnam's, 1962. Subj: Animals – dogs. School.

Small rabbit ill. by Jim Arnosky. Little, 1977. Subj: Animals – rabbits.

Somebody's dog ill. by John Schoenherr. Little, 1973. Subj: Animals – dogs. Pets.

Sylvester Jones and the voice in the forest ill. by Leonard Weisgard. Lothrop, 1958. Subj: Animals. Forest, woods.

This little pig ill. by Leslie Morrill. Dutton, 1980. Subj: Animals – pigs. Behavior – lost. Behavior – running away. Farms.

Wharf rat ill. by John Schoenherr. Little, 1972. Subj: Animals – rats.

Miles, Sally. *Alfi and the dark* ill. by Errol Le Cain. Chronicle, 1988. ISBN 0-87701-527-9 Subj: Bedtime. Friendship. Night.

Milgram, Mary. *Brothers are all the same* ill. by Rosmarie Hausherr. Dutton, 1978. Subj: Adoption. Family life. Sibling rivalry.

Milgrom, Harry. *Egg-ventures: first science experiments* ill. by Giulio Maestro. Dutton, 1974. Subj: Eggs. Science.

Paper science ill. by Dan Nevins. Walker, 1978. Subj: Paper. Science.

Milhous, Katherine. *The egg tree* ill. by author. Scribner's, 1950. Subj: Caldecott award book. Holidays – Easter.

Militant *see* Sandburg, Carl

Milius, Winifred *see* Lubell, Winifred

Millburn, Cynthia *see* Carter, Anne

Miller, Albert *see* Mills, Alan

Miller, Alice P. *The little store on the corner* ill. by John Lawrence. Abelard-Schuman, 1961. Subj: Stores.

The mouse family's blueberry pie ill. by Carol Bloch. Elsevier-Nelson, 1981. Subj: Activities – cooking. Animals – mice.

Miller, Edna. *Jumping bean* ill. by author. Prentice-Hall, 1980. Subj: Science.

Mousekin finds a friend ill. by author. Prentice-Hall, 1967. Subj: Animals – mice. Friendship.

Mousekin takes a trip ill. by author. Prentice-Hall, 1976. ISBN 0-13-604363-1 Subj: Activities – traveling. Animals – mice.

Mousekin's ABC ill. by author. Prentice-Hall, 1972. Subj: ABC books. Animals – mice. Forest, woods. Poetry, rhyme.

Mousekin's Christmas eve ill. by author. Prentice-Hall, 1965. Subj: Animals – mice. Holidays – Christmas.

Mousekin's close call ill. by author. Prentice-Hall, 1978. Subj: Animals – mice. Forest, woods.

Mousekin's Easter basket ill. by author. Prentice-Hall, 1987. ISBN 0-13-604141-8 Subj: Animals – mice. Holidays – Easter. Seasons – spring.

Mousekin's fables ill. by author. Prentice-Hall, 1982. Subj: Animals – mice. Folk and fairy tales. Seasons.

Mousekin's family ill. by author. Prentice-Hall, 1969. Subj: Animals – mice. Family life.

Mousekin's golden house ill. by author. Prentice-Hall, 1964. Subj: Animals – mice. Hibernation. Holidays – Halloween. Seasons – winter.

Mousekin's mystery ill. by author. Prentice-Hall, 1983. Subj: Animals – mice. Problem solving.

Mousekin's Thanksgiving ill. by author. Prentice-Hall, 1985. ISBN 0-13-604299-6 Subj: Animals – mice. Forest, woods. Holidays – Thanksgiving.

Pebbles, a pack rat ill. by author. Prentice-Hall, 1976. Subj: Animals – pack rats. Scarecrows.

Miller, Edward. *Frederick Ferdinand Fox* ill. by author. Crown, 1987. ISBN 0-517-56356-8 Subj: Animals – foxes. War.

Miller, Helen Hill *see* Hill, Helen

Miller, J. P. (John Parr). *Do you know color?* by J. P. Miller and Katherine Howard; ill. by J. P. Miller. Random House, 1979. Subj: Concepts – color.

Farmer John's animals ill. by author. Random House, 1979. ISBN 0-394-84270-7 Subj: Animals. Farms.

Good night, little rabbit ill. by author. Random House, 1986. ISBN 0-394-87992-9 Subj: Animals – rabbits. Bedtime. Family life. Format, unusual – board books.

Learn about colors with Little Rabbit ill. by author. Random House, 1984. Subj: Concepts – color.

Learn to count with Little Rabbit ill. by author. Random House, 1984. ISBN 0-394-96149-8 Subj: Animals – rabbits. Counting.

Miller, Jane. *Birth of a foal* ill. by author. Lippincott, 1977. Subj: Animals – horses.

Farm alphabet book photos. by author. Prentice-Hall, 1984. Subj: ABC books. Farms.

Farm counting book photos. by author. Prentice-Hall, 1983. Subj: Counting. Farms.

Lambing time photos. by author. Methuen, 1978. Subj: Animals – sheep.

Seasons on the farm ill. by author. Prentice-Hall, 1986. ISBN 0-13-797275-X Subj: Animals. Farms. Seasons.

Miller, Judith Ransom. *Nabob and the geranium* ill. by Marilyn Neuhart. Golden Gate, 1967. Subj: Plants. Science.

Miller, M. L. *Dizzy from fools* ill. by Eve Tharlet. Alphabet Pr., 1985. ISBN 0-88708-004-9 Subj: Character traits – questioning. Clowns, jesters. Royalty.

Miller, Margaret. *At my house* ill. by author. Crowell, 1989. ISBN 0-694-00276-3 Subj: Babies. Family life. Format, unusual – board books.

In my room ill. by author. Crowell, 1989. ISBN 0-694-00271-2 Subj: Babies. Family life. Format, unusual – board books.

Me and my clothes ill. by author. Crowell, 1989. ISBN 0-694-00272-0 Subj: Babies. Clothing. Family life. Format, unusual – board books.

Time to eat ill. by author. Crowell, 1989. ISBN 0-694-00274-X Subj: Babies. Family life. Food. Format, unusual – board books.

Whose hat? photos. by author. Greenwillow, 1988. ISBN 0-688-06907-X Subj: Careers. Clothing.

Miller, Moira. *Oscar Mouse finds a home* ill. by Maria Majewska. Dial Pr., 1985. ISBN 0-8037-0229-9 Subj: Animals – mice. Behavior – seeking better things.

The proverbial mouse ill. by Ian Deuchar. Dial Pr., 1987. ISBN 0-8037-0195-0 Subj: Animals – mice. Poetry, rhyme. Toys.

The search for spring ill. by Ian Deuchar. Dial Pr., 1988. ISBN 0-8037-0445-3 Subj: Seasons.

Miller, Susanne Santoro. *Prehistoric mammals* ill. by Christopher Santoro. Messner, 1984. Subj: Animals. Science.

Whales and sharks and other creatures of the deep ill. by Lisa Bonforte. Messner, 1982. ISBN 0-671-46006-4 Subj: Animals. Fish. Sea and seashore.

Miller, Warren. *The goings on at Little Wishful* ill. by Edward Sorel. Little, 1959. Subj: Behavior – boasting. Emotions – envy, jealousy.

Pablo paints a picture ill. by Edward Sorel. Little, 1959. Subj: Activities – painting. Careers – artists.

Millhouse, Nicholas. *Blue-footed booby: bird of the Galápagos* ill. by Margret Bowman. Walker, 1986. ISBN 0-8027-6629-3 Subj: Animals. Birds. Islands. Science.

Mills, Alan. *The hungry goat* ill. by Abner Graboff. Rand McNally, 1964. Subj: Animals – goats. Humor. Music. Songs.

Milne, A. A. (Alan Alexander). *House at Pooh corner: a pop-up book.* Dutton, 1986. ISBN 0-525-44245-6 Subj: Format, unusual – toy and movable books. Houses. Toys – teddy bears.

Pooh and some bees ill. by Robert Cremins. Dutton, 1987. ISBN 0-525-44339-8 Subj: Format, unusual – toy and movable books. Insects. Toys – teddy bears.

Pooh goes visiting ill. by Robert Cremins. Dutton, 1987. ISBN 0-525-44337-1 Subj: Format, unusual – toy and movable books. Toys – teddy bears.

Pooh's alphabet book ill. by E. H. Shepard. Dutton, 1976. Subj: ABC books. Toys – teddy bears.

Pooh's bedtime book ill. by E. H. Shepard; colored by Gail Owens. Dutton, 1980. Subj: Bedtime. Toys – teddy bears.

Pooh's counting book ill. by E. H. Shepard. Dutton, 1982. Subj: Counting. Toys – teddy bears.

Pooh's quiz book ill. by E. H. Shepard. Dutton, 1977. Subj: Games. Humor. Toys – teddy bears.

Prince Rabbit: and, The princess who could not laugh ill. by Mary Shepard. Dutton, 1967. Subj: Animals – rabbits. Folk and fairy tales. Royalty.

Winnie-the-Pooh: a pop-up book ill. by Chuck Murphy; engineering by Keith Moseley. Dutton, 1984. ISBN 0-525-44119-0 Subj: Character traits – bravery. Format, unusual – toy and movable books. Toys – teddy bears.

Milord, Jerry. *Maggie and the goodbye gift* (Milord, Sue)

Milord, Sue. *Maggie and the goodbye gift* by Sue and Jerry Milord; ill. by authors. Lothrop, 1979. Subj: Family life. Moving.

Milton, Joyce. *Dinosaur days* ill. by Richard Roe. Random House, 1985. ISBN 0-394-97023-3 Subj: Dinosaurs.

Minarik, Else Holmelund. *Cat and dog* ill. by Fritz Siebel. Harper, 1960. Subj: Animals – cats. Animals – dogs.

Father Bear comes home ill. by Maurice Sendak. Harper, 1959. Subj: Animals – bears. Family life – fathers.

A kiss for Little Bear ill. by Maurice Sendak. Harper, 1959. Subj: Animals – bears.

Little Bear ill. by Maurice Sendak. Harper, 1957. Subj: Animals – bears. Birthdays.

Little Bear's friend ill. by Maurice Sendak. Harper, 1960. Subj: Animals – bears. Friendship.

Little Bear's visit ill. by Maurice Sendak. Harper, 1961. Subj: Animals – bears. Caldecott award honor book. Family life – grandparents.

The little giant girl and the elf boys ill. by Garth Williams. Harper, 1963. Subj: Elves and little people. Giants.

No fighting, no biting! ill. by Maurice Sendak. Harper, 1958. Subj: Behavior – fighting, arguing. Reptiles – alligators, crocodiles.

Minier, Nelson *see* Baker, Laura Nelson

Minsberg, David. *The book monster* ill. by Shelley Matheis. Littlebee Pr., 1982. Subj: Activities – reading. Monsters.

Mintzberg, Yvette. *Sally, where are you?* ill. by author. David & Charles, 1988. ISBN 0-434-95158-7 Subj: Behavior – hiding. Family life.

Miranda, Anne. *Baby talk* ill. by Dorothy Stott. Dutton, 1987. ISBN 0-525-44319-3 Subj: Babies. Family life. Format, unusual – toy and movable books.

Baby walk ill. by Dorothy Stott. Dutton, 1988. ISBN 0-525-44421-1 Subj: Activities – playing. Babies. Format, unusual.

Mirkovic, Irene. *The greedy shopkeeper* ill. by Harold Berson. Harcourt, 1980. Translated and adapt. from a Serbian folk tale. Subj: Behavior – trickery. Careers – judges. Folk and fairy tales.

Mitchell, Adrian. *Our mammoth* ill. by Priscilla Lamont. Harcourt, 1987. ISBN 0-15-258838-8 Subj: Animals. Humor.

Mitchell, Cynthia. *Halloweena Hecatee* ill. by Eileen Browne. Crowell, 1979. Subj: Activities – playing. Games. Poetry, rhyme.

Here a little child I stand: poems of prayer and praise for children ill. by Satomi Ichikawa. Putnam's, 1985. ISBN 0-399-21244-2 Subj: Foreign lands. Poetry, rhyme. Religion.

Playtime ill. by Satomi Ichikawa. Collins-World, 1978. Subj: Activities – playing. Emotions. Poetry, rhyme.

Under the cherry tree ill. by Satomi Ichikawa. Collins-World, 1979. Subj: Poetry, rhyme.

Mitchell, Joyce Slayton. *My mommy makes money* ill. by True Kelley. Little, 1984. Subj: Activities – working. Careers. Family life – mothers.

Mitgutsch, Ali. *From gold to money* ill. by author. Carolrhoda Books, 1985. ISBN 0-87614-230-7 Subj: Science.

From graphite to pencil ill. by author. Carolrhoda Books, 1985. ISBN 0-87614-231-5 Subj: Science.

From lemon to lemonade ill. by author. Carolrhoda Books, 1986. ISBN 0-87614-298-6 Subj: Food.

From rubber tree to tire ill. by author. Carolrhoda Books, 1986. ISBN 0-87614-297-8 Subj: Automobiles.

From sea to salt ill. by author. Carolrhoda Books, 1985. ISBN 0-87614-232-3 Subj: Science.

From swamp to coal ill. by author. Carolrhoda Books, 1985. ISBN 0-87614-233-1 Subj: Science.

From wood to paper ill. by author. Carolrhoda Books, 1986. ISBN 0-87614-296-X Subj: Paper.

Miyoshi, Sekiya. *Singing David* ill. by author. Watts, 1969. Subj: Religion.

Mizner, Elizabeth Howard *see* Howard, Elizabeth Fitzgerald

Mizumura, Kazue. *If I built a village* ill. by author. Crowell, 1971. Subj: Character traits – kindness. City. Ecology. Houses.

If I were a cricket... ill. by author. Crowell, 1973. Subj: Animals. Emotions – love. Insects – crickets. Poetry, rhyme.

If I were a mother ill. by author. Crowell, 1967. Subj: Family life – mothers.

Moak, Allan. *A big city ABC* ill. by author. Tundra (dist. by Scribner's), 1984. Subj: ABC books. City. Foreign lands – Canada.

Mobley, Jane. *The star husband* ill. by Anna Vojtech. Doubleday, 1979. Subj: Folk and fairy tales. Indians of North America. Stars.

Moche, Dinah L. *The astronauts* ill. with photos. from NASA. Random House, 1979. Subj: Moon. Science. Space and space ships.

Modell, Frank. *Goodbye old year, hello new year* ill. by author. Greenwillow, 1984. Subj: Holidays – New Year's.

Ice cream soup ill. by author. Greenwillow, 1988. ISBN 0-688-07771-4 Subj: Birthdays. Parties.

Look out, it's April Fools' Day ill. by author. Greenwillow, 1985. ISBN 0-688-04017-9 Subj: Holidays – April Fools' Day. Riddles.

One zillion valentines ill. by author. Greenwillow, 1981. Subj: Character traits – practicality. Holidays – Valentine's Day.

Seen any cats? ill. by author. Greenwillow, 1979. Subj: Animals – cats. Circus.

Skeeter and the computer ill. by author. Greenwillow, 1988. ISBN 0-688-03706-2 Subj: Animals – dogs. Machines.

Tooley! Tooley! ill. by author. Greenwillow, 1979. Subj: Animals – dogs. Behavior – lost. Humor.

Moeri, Louise. *Star Mother's youngest child* ill. by Trina Schart Hyman. Houghton, 1975. ISBN 0-395-21406-8 Subj: Folk and fairy tales.

The unicorn and the plow ill. by Diane Goode. Dutton, 1982. Subj: Character traits – luck. Farms. Mythical creatures.

Moers, Hermann. *Camomile heads for home* tr. by Rosemary Lanning; ill. by Marcus Pfister. Holt, 1987. ISBN 0-8050-0280-4 Subj: Animals – bulls, cows. Behavior – growing up.

Moeschlin, Elsa. *The red horse* ill. by author. Coward, 1944. Subj: Dreams. Holidays – Christmas. Toys – rocking horses.

Moffett, Martha A. *A flower pot is not a hat* ill. by Susan Perl. Dutton, 1972. Subj: Humor.

Mogensen, Jan. *Teddy and the Chinese dragon* ill. by author. Gareth Stevens, 1985. ISBN 1-55532-002-3 Subj: Dragons. Toys – teddy bears.

Teddy in the undersea kingdom ill. by author. Gareth Stevens, 1985. ISBN 1-55532-000-7 Subj: Crustacea. Sea and seashore. Toys – teddy bears.

Teddy's Christmas gift ill. by author. Gareth Stevens, 1985. ISBN 1-55532-004-X Subj: Character traits – kindness to animals. Holidays – Christmas. Toys – teddy bears.

When Teddy woke early ill. by author. Gareth Stevens, 1985. ISBN 1-55532-006-6 Subj: Behavior – lost. Toys – teddy bears.

Mohr, Joseph. *Silent night* verses by Joseph Mohr; ill. by Susan Jeffers. Dutton, 1984. Orig. title: Stille Nacht, heilige Nacht. Subj: Holidays – Christmas. Songs.

Molarsky, Osmond. *The peasant and the fly* ill. by Katherine Coville. Harcourt, 1980. Subj: Folk and fairy tales. Problem solving.

Molnar, Joe. *Graciela: a Mexican-American child tells her story* photos. by author. Watts, 1972. Subj: Ethnic groups in the U.S. – Mexican-Americans.

Moncure, Jane Belk. *Happy healthkins* ill. by Lois Axeman. Children's Pr., 1982. Subj: Elves and little people. Health. Poetry, rhyme.

The healthkin food train ill. by Lois Axeman. Children's Pr., 1982. Subj: Elves and little people. Health. Poetry, rhyme.

Healthkins exercise! ill. by Lois Axeman. Children's Pr., 1982. Subj: Elves and little people. Health. Poetry, rhyme.

Healthkins help ill. by Lois Axeman. Children's Pr., 1982. Subj: Elves and little people. Health. Poetry, rhyme.

The look book ill. by Lois Axeman. Children's Pr., 1982. Subj: Senses – seeing.

Now I am five! ill. by Helen Endes. Childrens Pr., 1984. ISBN 0-516-01879-5 Subj: Activities. Behavior – growing up.

Now I am four! ill. by Kathryn Hutton. Childrens Pr., 1984. ISBN 0-516-01878-7 Subj: Activities. Behavior – growing up.

Now I am three! ill. by Linda Hohag. Childrens Pr., 1984. ISBN 0-516-01877-9 Subj: Activities. Behavior – growing up.

Riddle me a riddle ill. by Marc Belenchia. Children's Pr., 1977. Subj: Animals. Magic. Riddles.

Sounds all around ill. by Lois Axeman. Children's Pr., 1982. Subj: Senses – hearing.

The talking tabby cat: a folk tale from France ill. by Helen Endes. Children's Pr., 1980. Subj: Animals – cats. Folk and fairy tales.

A tasting party ill. by Lois Axeman. Children's Pr., 1982. Subj: Senses – tasting.

The touch book ill. by Lois Axeman. Children's Pr., 1982. Subj: Senses – touching.

What your nose knows! ill. by Lois Axeman. Children's Pr., 1982. Subj: Anatomy. Senses – smelling.

Where? ill. by Lois Axeman. Children's Pr., 1983. Subj: Character traits – curiosity. Character traits – questioning.

Word Bird's fall words ill. by Linda Hohag. Childrens Pr., 1985. ISBN 0-89565-308-7 Subj: Language. Seasons – fall.

Word Bird's spring words ill. by Vera Gohman. Childrens Pr., 1985. ISBN 0-89565-310-9 Subj: Language. Seasons – spring.

Word Bird's summer words ill. by Linda Hohag. Childrens Pr., 1985. ISBN 0-89565-311-7 Subj: Language. Seasons – summer.

Word Bird's winter words ill. by Vera Gohman. Childrens Pr., 1985. ISBN 0-89565-309-5 Subj: Language. Seasons – winter.

Monjo, F. N. *The drinking gourd* ill. by Fred Brenner. Harper, 1970. Subj: Ethnic groups in the U.S. – Afro-Americans. Indians of North America. U.S. history.

Indian summer ill. by Anita Lobel. Harper, 1968. Subj: Indians of North America. U.S. history.

The one bad thing about father ill. by Rocco Negri. Harper, 1970. Subj: Family life – fathers. U.S. history.

Poor Richard in France ill. by Brinton Turkle. Holt, 1973. Subj: U.S. history.

Rudi and the distelfink ill. by George Kraus. Windmill, 1972. Subj: Family life.

Monsell, Helen Albee. *Paddy's Christmas* ill. by Kurt Wiese. Knopf, 1942. Subj: Animals – bears. Holidays – Christmas.

Monsell, Mary. *Underwear!* ill. by Lynn Munsinger. Albert Whitman, 1988. ISBN 0-8075-8308-1 Subj: Animals. Clothing. Humor.

Montgomerie, Norah. *This little pig went to market: play rhymes* ill. by Margery Gill. Watts, 1967. Subj: Games. Nursery rhymes. Participation.

Montresor, Beni. *A for angel: Beni Montresor's ABC picture-stories* ill. by author. Knopf, 1969. Subj: ABC books.

Bedtime! ill. by author. Harper, 1978. Subj: Bedtime. Dreams.

Moon, Carl. *One little Indian* (Moon, Grace Purdie)

Moon, Cliff. *Pigs on the farm* ill. by Anna Jupp. Watts, 1983. ISBN 0-531-04696-6 Subj: Animals – pigs. Farms.

Moon, Dolly M. *My very first book of cowboy songs: 21 favorite songs in easy piano arrangements* ill. by Frederic Remington. Dover, 1982. Subj: Cowboys. Folk and fairy tales. Songs.

Moon, Grace Purdie. *One little Indian* by Grace and Carl Moon; ill. by Carl Moon. Albert Whitman, 1950. Subj: Birthdays. Indians of North America.

The moon's the north wind's cooky: *night poems* comp. and ill. by Susan Russo. Lothrop, 1979. Subj: Bedtime. Night. Poetry, rhyme.

Moorat, Joseph. *Thirty old-time nursery songs* (Mother Goose)

Moore, Clement C. *The night before Christmas* ill. by Tomie de Paola. Holiday, 1980. Subj: Holidays – Christmas. Poetry, rhyme.

The night before Christmas ill. by Michael Foreman. Viking, 1988. ISBN 0-670-82388-0 Subj: Holidays – Christmas. Poetry, rhyme.

The night before Christmas ill. by Gyo Fujikawa. Grosset, 1961. Subj: Holidays – Christmas. Poetry, rhyme.

The night before Christmas ill. by Scott Gustafson. Knopf, 1985. ISBN 0-394-54809-4 Subj: Holidays – Christmas. Poetry, rhyme.

The night before Christmas ill. by Anita Lobel. Knopf, 1984. Subj: Holidays – Christmas. Poetry, rhyme.

The night before Christmas ill. by Jacqueline Rogers. Platt, 1988. ISBN 0-448-19097-4 Subj: Holidays – Christmas. Poetry, rhyme.

The night before Christmas ill. by Robin Spowart. Dodd, 1986. ISBN 0-396-08798-1 Subj: Holidays – Christmas. Poetry, rhyme.

The night before Christmas ill. by Gustaf Tenggren. Simon and Schuster, 1951. Subj: Holidays – Christmas. Poetry, rhyme.

The night before Christmas ill. by Tasha Tudor. Rand McNally, 1975. Subj: Holidays – Christmas. Poetry, rhyme.

The night before Christmas ill. by Jody Wheeler. Ideals, 1988. ISBN 0-8249-8279-7 Subj: Holidays – Christmas. Poetry, rhyme.

A visit from St. Nicholas: 'Twas the night before Christmas ill. by Paul Galdone. McGraw-Hill, 1968. Subj: Holidays – Christmas. Poetry, rhyme.

Moore, Elaine. *Grandma's house* ill. by Elise Primavera. Lothrop, 1985. ISBN 0-688-04116-7 Subj: Animals. Country. Family life – grandmothers. Seasons – summer.

Grandma's promise ill. by Elise Primavera. Lothrop, 1988. ISBN 0-688-06741-7 Subj: Country. Family life – grandmothers. Seasons – winter.

Moore, Eva. *Dick Whittington and his cat*

Moore, Inga. *Aktil's big swim* ill. by author. Oxford Univ. Pr., 1981. Subj: Animals – rats. Sports – swimming.

Fifty red night-caps ill. by Linda Moore. Chronicle, 1988. ISBN 0-87701-520-1 Subj: Animals – monkeys. Behavior – imitation. Behavior – stealing. Clothing. Forest, woods.

The truffle hunter ill. by author. Kane Miller, 1987. ISBN 0-91629-09-X Subj: Animals – pigs. Behavior – seeking better things. Country. Foreign lands – France.

The vegetable thieves ill. by author. Viking, 1984. Subj: Activities – gardening. Animals – mice. Orphans.

Moore, John. *Granny Stickleback* by John Moore and Martin Wright; ill. by authors. Hamish Hamilton, 1982. Subj: Animals. Crime. Sports – racing.

Moore, Lilian. *Hooray for me!* (Charlip, Remy)

I feel the same way ill. by Robert M. Quackenbush. Atheneum, 1967. Subj: Poetry, rhyme.

Little Raccoon and no trouble at all ill. by Gioia Fiammenghi. McGraw-Hill, 1972. Subj: Activities – baby-sitting. Animals – chipmunks. Animals – raccoons. Twins.

Little Raccoon and the outside world ill. by Gioia Fiammenghi. McGraw-Hill, 1965. Subj: Animals – raccoons.

Little Raccoon and the thing in the pool ill. by Gioia Fiammenghi. McGraw-Hill, 1963. Subj: Animals – raccoons. Emotions – fear.

Papa Albert ill. by Gioia Fiammenghi. Atheneum, 1964. Subj: Careers – taxi drivers. Family life. Foreign lands – France. Foreign languages. Taxis.

See my lovely poison ivy, and other verses about witches, ghosts and things ill. by Diane Dawson. Atheneum, 1975. Subj: Animals – cats. Monsters. Poetry, rhyme. Witches.

The ugly duckling (Andersen, H. C. (Hans Christian))

Moore, Miriam. *Peter and Susie find a family* (Hess, Edith)

Moore, Sheila. *Samson Svenson's baby* ill. by Karen Ann Weinhaus. Harper, 1983. Subj: Birds – ducks. Character traits – appearance. Character traits – kindness to animals.

Mooser, Stephen. *The fat cat* by Stephen Mooser and Lin Oliver; ill. by Susan Day. Warner, 1988. ISBN 1-55782-022-8 Subj: Animals – cats.

Funnyman and the penny dodo ill. by Tomie De Paola. Watts, 1984. ISBN 0-531-04393-2 Subj: Crime. Humor. Problem solving.

Funnyman meets the monster from outer space ill. by Maxie Chambliss. Scholastic, 1987. ISBN 0-590-33959-1 Subj: Monsters. Space and space ships.

Funnyman's first case ill. by Tomie de Paola. Watts, 1981. ISBN 0-531-04300-2 Subj: Careers – waiters, waitresses. Problem solving. Riddles.

The ghost with the Halloween hiccups ill. by Tomie de Paola. Watts, 1977. Subj: Ghosts. Holidays – Halloween.

Mora, Emma. *Animals of the forest* tr. from Italian by Jean Grasso Fitzpatrick; ill. by Kennedy. Barron's, 1986. ISBN 0-8120-5722-8 Subj: Animals. Forest, woods.

Gideon, the little bear cub tr. from Italian by Jean Grasso Fitzpatrick; ill. by Kennedy. Barron's, 1986. ISBN 0-8120-5728-7 Subj: Forest, woods. Poetry, rhyme. Seasons.

Mordvinoff, Nicolas. *Billy the kid* (Lipkind, William)

The boy and the forest (Lipkind, William)

Chaga (Lipkind, William)

The Christmas bunny (Lipkind, William)

Circus ruckus (Lipkind, William)

Coral Island ill. by author. Doubleday, 1957. Subj: Behavior – growing up. Foreign lands – South Sea Islands. Islands.

Even Steven (Lipkind, William)

Finders keepers (Lipkind, William)

Four-leaf clover (Lipkind, William)

The little tiny rooster (Lipkind, William)

The magic feather duster (Lipkind, William)

Russet and the two reds (Lipkind, William)

Sleepyhead (Lipkind, William)

The two reds (Lipkind, William)

More, Caroline *see* Cone, Molly

Morel, Eve. *Fairy tales* ill. by Gyo Fujikawa. Grosset, 1980. Subj: Folk and fairy tales.

Fairy tales and fables ill. by Gyo Fujikawa. Grosset, 1970. Subj: Folk and fairy tales.

Moremen, Grace E. *No, no, Natalie* photos. by Geoffrey P. Fulton. Children's Pr., 1973. Subj: Animals – rabbits. Behavior – misbehavior. School.

Morgan, Allen. *Matthew and the midnight money van* ill. by Michael Martchenko. Firefly Pr., 1987. ISBN 0-920303-75-7 Subj: Behavior – losing things. Holidays – Mother's Day.

Molly and Mr. Maloney ill. by Maryann Kovalski. Kids Can Pr., 1982. Subj: Animals – raccoons. Behavior – misbehavior. Pets.

Nicole's boat ill. by Jirina Marton. Firefly Pr., 1986. ISBN 0-920303-60-9 Subj: Bedtime. Boats, ships. Dreams. Family life – fathers.

Morgan, Michaela. *Edward gets a pet* ill. by Sue Porter. Dutton, 1987. ISBN 0-525-44349-5 Subj: Animals. Imagination. Pets.

Visitors for Edward ill. by Sue Porter. Dutton, 1988. ISBN 0-525-44354-1 Subj: Family life – grandparents. Imagination.

Morgenstern, Elizabeth. *The little gardeners* tr. from German by Elizabeth Morgenstern; retold by Louise F. Encking; ill. by Marigard Bantzer. Albert Whitman, 1933. Subj: Activities – gardening. Foreign lands – Germany.

Morice, Dave. *Dot town* ill. by author. Toothpaste Pr., 1982. Subj: Poetry, rhyme.

The happy birthday handbook ill. by author. Coffee House Pr., 1982. Subj: Birthdays.

A visit from St. Alphabet ill. by author. Coffee House Pr., 1980. Subj: ABC books. Poetry, rhyme.

Morimoto, Junko. *The inch boy* ill. by author. Viking, 1986. ISBN 0-670-80955-1 Subj: Elves and little people. Family life. Folk and fairy tales.

Mouse's marriage ill. by author. Viking, 1986. ISBN 0-670-81071-1 Subj: Animals – mice. Folk and fairy tales.

Morpurgo, Michael. *Jo-Jo the melon donkey* ill. by Chris Molan. Prentice-Hall, 1988. ISBN 0-13-510009-7 Subj: Animals – donkeys. Foreign lands – Italy. Weather – floods.

Morris, Ann. *The Cinderella rebus book* ill. by Ljiljana Rylands. Watts, 1989. ISBN 0-531-08361-6 Subj: Folk and fairy tales. Rebuses. Royalty. Sibling rivalry.

Cuddle up ill. by Maureen Roffey. Harper, 1986. ISBN 0-694-00072-8 Subj: Bedtime. Family life – mothers. Night.

Eleanora Mousie catches a cold ill. by Ruth Young. Macmillan, 1987. ISBN 0-02-767500-9 Subj: Animals – mice. Illness.

Eleanora Mousie in the dark ill. by Ruth Young. Macmillan, 1987. ISBN 0-02-767530-0 Subj: Animals – mice. Monsters. Night.

Eleanora Mousie makes a mess ill. by Ruth Young. Macmillan, 1987. ISBN 0-02-767520-3 Subj: Animals – mice. Character traits – cleanliness.

Eleanora Mousie's gray day ill. by Ruth Young. Macmillan, 1987. ISBN 0-02-767510-6 Subj: Animals – mice. Behavior – bad day. Friendship.

Kiss time ill. by Maureen Roffey. Harper, 1986. ISBN 0-694-00073-6 Subj: Bedtime. Night.

The Little Red Riding Hood rebus book ill. by Ljiljana Rylands. Orchard, 1987. ISBN 0-531-08330-6 Subj: Animals – wolves. Behavior – talking to strangers. Folk and fairy tales. Rebuses.

Night counting ill. by Maureen Roffey. Harper, 1986. ISBN 0-694-00074-4 Subj: Bedtime. Counting. Night.

Sleepy, sleepy ill. by Maureen Roffey. Harper, 1986. ISBN 0-694-00075-2 Subj: Bedtime. Night.

Morris, Christopher G. *The magic world of words* (Halsey, William D.)

Morris, Jill. *The boy who painted the sun* ill. by Geoff Hocking. Viking, 1984. Subj: Activities – painting. Behavior – solitude. City. Moving.

Morris, Neil. *Find the canary* by Neil Morris and Ting; ill. by Anna Clarke. Little, 1983. Subj: Games.

Hide and seek by Neil Morris and Ting; ill. by Anna Clarke. Little, 1983. Subj: Games.

Search for Sam by Neil Morris and Ting; ill. by Anna Clarke. Little, 1983. Subj: Games.

Where's my hat? by Neil Morris and Ting; ill. by Anna Clarke. Little, 1983. Subj: Games.

Morris, Robert A. *Dolphin* ill. by Mamoru Funai. Harper, 1975. Subj: Animals – dolphins. Science.

Seahorse ill. by Arnold Lobel. Harper, 1972. Subj: Crustacea. Science.

Morris, Terry Nell. *Good night, dear monster!* ill. by author. Knopf, 1980. Subj: Bedtime. Imagination – imaginary friends. Monsters.

Lucky puppy! Lucky boy! ill. by author. Knopf, 1980. Subj: Animals – dogs. Behavior – needing someone.

Morris, Winifred. *The magic leaf* ill. by Ju-Hong Chen. Atheneum, 1987. ISBN 0-689-31358-6 Subj: Folk and fairy tales. Foreign lands – China.

Morrison, Bill. *Louis James hates school* ill. by author. Houghton, 1978. Subj: Careers. School.

Squeeze a sneeze ill. by author. Houghton, 1977. Subj: Poetry, rhyme.

Morrison, Sean. *Is that a happy hippopotamus?* ill. by Aliki. Crowell, 1966. Subj: Animals. Humor. Noise, sounds. Poetry, rhyme.

Morrow, Elizabeth Cutter. *The painted pig* ill. by René D'Harnoncourt. Knopf, 1930. Subj: Foreign lands – Mexico.

Morrow, Suzanne Stark. *Inatuck's friend* ill. by Ellen Raskin. Little, 1968. Subj: Eskimos. Friendship.

Morse, Samuel French. *All in a suitcase* ill. by Barbara Cooney. Little, 1966. Subj: ABC books. Animals.

Sea sums ill. by Fuku Akino. Little, 1970. Subj: Counting. Poetry, rhyme. Sea and seashore. Weather – fog.

Mosel, Arlene. *The funny little woman* ill. by Blair Lent. Dutton, 1972. Based on The old woman and her dumpling by Lafcadio Hearn. Subj: Caldecott award book. Foreign lands – Japan. Monsters.

Tikki Tikki Tembo ill. by Blair Lent. Holt, 1968. Subj: Folk and fairy tales. Foreign lands – China. Names.

Moseley, Keith. *Dinosaurs: a lost world* ill. by Robert Cremins. Putnam's, 1984. ISBN 0-399-21063-6 Subj: Dinosaurs. Format, unusual – toy and movable books. Science.

Moser, Erwin. *The crow in the snow and other bedtime stories* tr. from German by Joel Agee; ill. by author. Adama, 1986. ISBN 0-915361-49-3 Subj: Animals. Imagination.

Wilma the elephant ill. by author. Adama, 1986. ISBN 0-915361-45-0 Subj: Animals – elephants. Behavior – lost. Behavior – needing someone.

Mosimann, Odie. *How the mouse was hit on the head by a stone and so discovered the world* (Delessert, Étienne)

Moskin, Marietta D. *Lysbet and the fire kittens* ill. by Margot Tomes. Coward, 1973. Subj: Animals – cats. Behavior – carelessness. Fire. U.S. history.

Moskof, Martin Stephen. *Still another alphabet book* (Chwast, Seymour)

Still another children's book (Chwast, Seymour)

Still another number book (Chwast, Seymour)

Mosley, Francis. *The dinosaur eggs* ill. by author. Barron's, 1988. ISBN 0-8120-5910-7 Subj: Dinosaurs. Family life.

Moss, Elaine. *From morn to midnight*

Polar ill. by Jeannie Baker. Elsevier-Dutton, 1979. Subj: Activities – playing. Illness. Safety. Toys – teddy bears.

The story of Saul the king (Waddell, Helen)

Moss, Jeffrey. *The Sesame Street ABC storybook* featuring Jim Henson's Muppets; by Jeffrey Moss, Norman Stiles and Daniel Wilcox; ill. by Peter Cross and others. Random House, 1974. Subj: ABC books. Puppets.

The songs of Sesame Street in poems and pictures by Jeffrey Moss and others; ill. by Normand Chartier. Random House, 1983. Subj: Poetry, rhyme. Puppets. Songs.

Most, Bernard. *If the dinosaurs came back* ill. by author. Harcourt, 1978. Subj: Dinosaurs. Imagination.

My very own octopus ill. by author. Harcourt, 1980. Subj: Octopuses. Pets.

There's an ant in Anthony ill. by author. Morrow, 1980. Subj: Activities – reading.

There's an ape behind the drape ill. by author. Morrow, 1981. ISBN 0-688-00381-8 Subj: Animals – gorillas. Games. Language.

Whatever happened to the dinosaurs? ill. by author. Harcourt, 1984. ISBN 0-15-295295-0 Subj: Dinosaurs.

Mostel, Zero. *The Sesame Street book of opposites with Zero Mostel* (Mendoza, George)

Mother Goose. *ABC rhymes* ill. by Lulu Delacre. Simon & Schuster, 1984. ISBN 0-671-49685-9 Subj: ABC books. Format, unusual – board books. Nursery rhymes.

The annotated Mother Goose: nursery rhymes old and new arranged and explained by William S. and Ceil Baring-Gould; chapter decorations by E. M. Simon; ill. by Walter Crane and others. Potter, 1962. Subj: Nursery rhymes.

As I was going up and down: and other nonsense rhymes ill. by Nicola Bayley. Lothrop, 1986. ISBN 0-02-708590-2 Subj: Nursery rhymes.

The authentic Mother Goose fairy tales and nursery rhymes. (Barchilon, Jacques)

Baa baa black sheep ill. by Sue Porter. Peter Bedrick Books (dist. by Harper), 1984. Subj: Format, unusual – board books. Nursery rhymes.

Baa baa black sheep ill. by Ferelith Eccles Williams. David & Charles, 1985. ISBN 0-437-86003-5 Subj: Format, unusual – board books. Nursery rhymes.

The baby's lap book ill. by Kay Chorao. Dutton, 1977. Subj: Nursery rhymes.

Beatrix Potter's nursery rhyme book ill. by Beatrix Potter. Warne, 1984. ISBN 0-7232-3254-7 Subj: Nursery rhymes.

Blessed Mother Goose: favorite nursery rhymes for today's children ill. by Kaye Luke. House-Warven, 1951. Subj: Nursery rhymes.

Brian Wildsmith's Mother Goose ill. by Brian Wildsmith. Watts, 1964. Subj: Nursery rhymes.

Carolyn Wells' edition of Mother Goose ill. by Margeria Cooper and others. Doubleday, 1946. Subj: Nursery rhymes.

Cats by Mother Goose sel. by Barbara Lucas; ill. by Carol Newsom. Lothrop, 1986. ISBN 0-688-04635-5 Subj: Animals – cats. Nursery rhymes.

The Charles Addams Mother Goose ill. by Charles Addams. Harper, 1967. Subj: Nursery rhymes.

A child's book of old nursery rhymes ill. by Joan Walsh Anglund. Atheneum, 1973. Subj: Nursery rhymes.

The Chinese Mother Goose rhymes sel. and ed. by Robert Wyndham; ill. by Ed Young. Putnam's, 1982. Orig. pub. by World, 1968. Subj: Nursery rhymes.

The city and country Mother Goose ill. by Hilda Hoffmann. American Heritage, 1969. Subj: Nursery rhymes.

The comic adventures of Old Mother Hubbard and her dog (Martin, Sarah Catherine)

Frank Baber's Mother Goose Sel. by Ruth Spriggs; ill. by Frank Baber. Crown, 1976. Subj: Nursery rhymes.

The gay Mother Goose ill. by Françoise Seignobosc. Scribner's, 1938. Subj: Nursery rhymes.

The glorious Mother Goose sel. by Cooper Edens. Atheneum, 1988. ISBN 0-689-31434-5 Subj: Nursery rhymes.

The golden goose book ill. by L. Leslie Brooke. Warne, 1977, 1905. ISBN 0-7232-1979-6 Subj: Birds – geese. Folk and fairy tales. Humor. Royalty.

Grafa' Grig had a pig, and other rhymes without reason from Mother Goose ill. by Wallace Tripp. Little, 1976. Subj: Nursery rhymes.

Gray goose and gander and other Mother Goose rhymes ill. by Anne F. Rockwell. Crowell, 1980. Subj: Nursery rhymes.

Gregory Griggs, and other nursery rhyme people sel. and ill. by Arnold Lobel. Greenwillow, 1978. Subj: Nursery rhymes.

Here's a ball for baby (Williams, Jenny)

Hey diddle diddle ill. by Nita Sowter. Peter Bedrick Books (dist. by Harper), 1984. Subj: Format, unusual – board books. Nursery rhymes.

Hey diddle diddle ill. by Eleanor Wasmuth. Simon & Schuster, 1986. ISBN 0-671-61726-5 Subj: Format, unusual – board books. Nursery rhymes.

Hey diddle diddle, and Baby bunting ill. by Randolph Caldecott. Warne, 1882. Subj: Nursery rhymes.

Hey diddle diddle picture book ill. by Randolph Caldecott. Warne, 1883. Subj: Nursery rhymes.

Hurrah, we're outward bound! ill. by Peter Spier. Doubleday, 1968. Subj: Nursery rhymes.

Hush-a-bye baby: and other bedtime rhymes ill. by Nicola Bayley. Lothrop, 1986. ISBN 0-02-708610-0 Subj: Bedtime. Nursery rhymes.

In a pumpkin shell ill. by Joan Walsh Anglund. Harcourt, 1960. Subj: ABC books. Nursery rhymes.

Jack and Jill ill. by Eleanor Wasmuth. Simon & Schuster, 1986. ISBN 0-671-61729-X Subj: Format, unusual – board books. Nursery rhymes.

Jack Kent's merry Mother Goose ill. by Jack Kent. Golden Pr., 1977. Subj: Nursery rhymes.

James Marshall's Mother Goose ill. by James Marshall. Farrar, 1979. Subj: Nursery rhymes.

Kate Greenaway's Mother Goose ill. by Kate Greenaway. Dial Pr., 1988. ISBN 0-8037-0479-8 Subj: Format, unusual – board books. Nursery rhymes.

Kitten rhymes ill. by Lulu Delacre. Simon & Schuster, 1984. ISBN 0-671-49687-5 Subj: Animals – cats. Format, unusual – board books. Nursery rhymes.

The Larousse book of nursery rhymes ed. by Robert Owen; ill. with photos. Larousse, 1984. Ill. are full color photos. of tile pictures, painted during the late 19th and early 20th cents., created by the Royal Doulton Co., designed by Margaret Thompson, William Rowe and John H. McLennan. Subj: Nursery rhymes.

Lavender's blue: a book of nursery rhymes comp. by Kathleen Lines; ill. by Harold Jones. Oxford Univ. Pr., 1982. Subj: Nursery rhymes.

Little boy blue ill. by Nita Sowter. Peter Bedrick Books (dist. by Harper), 1984. Subj: Format, unusual – board books. Nursery rhymes.

The little Mother Goose ill. by Jessie Willcox Smith. Dodd, 1918. Subj: Nursery rhymes.

London Bridge is falling down ill. by Ed Emberley. Little, 1967. Subj: Folk and fairy tales. Foreign lands – England. Games. Nursery rhymes. Songs.

London Bridge is falling down ill. by Peter Spier. Doubleday, 1967. Subj: Folk and fairy tales. Foreign lands – England. Games. Nursery rhymes. Songs.

The Margaret Tarrant nursery rhyme book (Tarrant, Margaret)

Mother Goose sel. by Phyllis Maurine Fraser; ill. by Miss Elliott. Simon and Schuster, 1942. Subj: Nursery rhymes.

Mother Goose ill. by C. B. Falls. Doubleday, 1924. Subj: Nursery rhymes.

Mother Goose ill. by Gyo Fujikawa. Grosset, 1967. Subj: Nursery rhymes.

Mother Goose arranged and ed. by Eulalie Osgood Grover; ill. by Frederick Richardson. The Volland ed. Volland, 1915. Subj: Nursery rhymes.

Mother Goose re-arranged and edited in this form by Eulalie Osgood Grover; ill. by Frederick Richardson. The classic Volland ed. Rand McNally, 1976. Reprint of the 1971 ed. published by Hubbard Press, Northbrook, Ill. Subj: Nursery rhymes.

Mother Goose ill. by Gustaf Tenggren. Little, 1940. Subj: Nursery rhymes.

Mother Goose: a collection of classic nursery rhymes sel. and ill. by Michael Hague. Holt, 1984. Subj: Nursery rhymes.

Mother Goose: a comprehensive collection of the rhymes comp. by William Rose Benét; ill. by Roger Antoine Duvoisin. Heritage Pr., 1943. Subj: Nursery rhymes.

Mother Goose abroad (Tucker, Nicholas)

Mother Goose and nursery rhymes ill. by Philip Reed. Atheneum, 1963. Subj: Caldecott award honor book. Nursery rhymes.

Mother Goose: as told by Kellogg's singing lady ill. by Vernon Grant. Kellogg Co., 1933. Subj: Nursery rhymes.

The Mother Goose book ill. by Alice and Martin Provensen. Random House, 1976. Subj: Nursery rhymes.

The Mother Goose book gathered from many sources; ill. by Sonia Roetter. Peter Pauper Pr., 1946. Subj: Nursery rhymes.

Mother Goose house ill. by Zokeisha; ed. by Kate Klimo. Simon and Schuster, 1983. Subj: Format, unusual – board books. Houses. Nursery rhymes.

Mother Goose in French: Poesies de la vraie Mere Oie tr. by Hugh Latham; ill. by Barbara Cooney. Crowell, 1964. Subj: Foreign languages. Nursery rhymes.

Mother Goose in hieroglyphics ill. by George S. Appleton. Houghton, 1962. Reproduction of the 1st ed. published in 1849. Subj: Games. Hieroglyphics. Nursery rhymes. Rebuses.

Mother Goose in prose (Baum, L. Frank (Lyman Frank))

Mother Goose in Spanish: Poesias de la Madre Oca tr. by Alastair Reid and Anthony Kerrigan; ill. by Barbara Cooney. Crowell, 1968. Subj: Foreign languages. Nursery rhymes.

Mother Goose melodies intro. and bib. note by E. F. Bleiler; ill. with engravings. Facsimile ed. of the Munroe and Francis c.1833 version. Dover, 1970. Subj: Nursery rhymes.

Mother Goose nursery rhymes ill. by Arthur Rackham. Watts, 1969. Reprint of the 1913 ed. Subj: Nursery rhymes.

Mother Goose nursery rhymes ill. by Arthur Rackham. Viking, 1975. Subj: Nursery rhymes.

Mother Goose: or, the old nursery rhymes sel. by Phyllis Maurine Fraser; ill. by Kate Greenaway. Routledge, 1881. Illustrated as originally engraved and printed by Edmund Evans. Subj: Nursery rhymes.

Mother Goose rhymes ed. by Watty Piper; ill. by Eulalie M. Banks and Lois Lenski. Platt, 1947, 1956. Subj: Nursery rhymes.

Mother Goose: seventy-seven verses ill. by Tasha Tudor. Walck, 1944. Subj: Caldecott award honor book. Nursery rhymes.

Mother Goose: sixty-seven favorite rhymes ill. by Violet La Mont. Simon and Schuster, 1957. Subj: Nursery rhymes.

The Mother Goose songbook ill. by Jacqueline Sinclair. David & Charles, 1985. ISBN 0-434-92841-0 Subj: Music. Nursery rhymes. Songs.

Mother Goose: the old nursery rhymes ill. by Arthur Rackham. Century, 1913. Subj: Nursery rhymes.

The Mother Goose treasury ill. by Raymond Briggs. Coward, 1966. Subj: Nursery rhymes.

Mother Goose's melodies: or, songs for the nursery ed. by William A. Wheeler. Houghton, 189?. Subj: Nursery rhymes. Songs.

Mother Goose's melody: or, sonnets for the cradle. Facsimile of John Newbery's collection of Mother Goose rhymes, reproduced from the earliest known perfect copy of the 1794 printing. Frederic G. Melcher, 1945. Subj: Nursery rhymes.

Mother Goose's nursery rhymes ill. by Allen Atkinson. Knopf, 1984. ISBN 0-394-53699-1 Subj: Nursery rhymes.

Mother Goose's rhymes and melodies ill. by J. L. Webb; music and melodies by E. I. Lane. Cassell, 1888. Subj: Music. Nursery rhymes.

Nursery rhyme book ill. by L. Leslie Brooke; ed. by Andrew Lang. Warne, 1897. Subj: Nursery rhymes.

Nursery rhymes sel. by Marie; ill. by Douglas Gorsline. Random House, 1977. Subj: Nursery rhymes.

Nursery rhymes ill. by Eloise Wilkin. Random House, 1979. Subj: Nursery rhymes.

Nursery rhymes from Mother Goose in signed English. Prepared under the supervision of the staff of the Pre-School Signed English Project: Barbara M. Kanapell and others. Gallaudet College Pr., 1972. Subj: Handicaps – deafness. Nursery rhymes.

Old Mother Hubbard and her dog (Martin, Sarah Catherine)

The old woman in a shoe ill. by Eleanor Wasmuth. Simon & Schuster, 1986. ISBN 0-671-61728-1 Subj: Format, unusual – board books. Nursery rhymes.

One I love, two I love, and other loving Mother Goose rhymes ill. by Nonny Hogrogian. Dutton, 1972. Subj: Nursery rhymes.

One misty moisty morning: rhymes from Mother Goose ill. by Mitchell Miller. Farrar, 1971. Subj: Nursery rhymes.

One, two, buckle my shoe (Williams, Jenny)

The only true Mother Goose melodies intro. by Edward Everett Hale. Lothrop, 1905. An exact and full-size reproduction of the original edition published and copyrighted in Boston in the year 1833 by Munroe and Francis. Subj: Nursery rhymes.

Over the moon: a book of nursery rhymes ill. by Charlotte Voake. Crown, 1985. ISBN 0-517-55873-4 Subj: Nursery rhymes.

The piper's son ill. by Emily N. Barto. Longmans, 1942. Subj: Nursery rhymes.

A pocket full of posies ill. by Marguerite De Angeli. Doubleday, 1961. First pub. in 1954. Subj: Nursery rhymes.

The pudgy book of Mother Goose

Pussycat ate the dumplings (Koontz, Robin Michal)

Pussy cat, pussy cat ill. by Ferelith Eccles Williams. David & Charles, 1985. ISBN 0-437-86009-4 Subj: Format, unusual – board books. Nursery rhymes.

The rainbow Mother Goose ed. with an intro. by May Lamberton Becker; ill. by Lili Cassel-Wronker. Collins-World, 1947. Subj: Nursery rhymes.

The real Mother Goose ill. by Blanche Fisher Wright. Rand McNally, 1916. Subj: Nursery rhymes.

The real Mother Goose clock book ill. by Jane Chambless-Rigie. Rand McNally, 1984. ISBN 0-528-82329-9 Subj: Clocks. Nursery rhymes. Time.

The real personages of Mother Goose (Thomas, Katherine Elwes)

Richard Scarry's best Mother Goose ever ill. by Richard Scarry. Golden Pr., 1964. Subj: Nursery rhymes.

Richard Scarry's favorite Mother Goose rhymes ill. by Richard Scarry. Golden Pr., 1976. Subj: Nursery rhymes.

Ride a cock-horse (Williams, Sarah)

Ride a cockhorse (Williams, Jenny)

Rimes de la Mere Oie: Mother Goose rhymes rendered into French by Ormonde De Kay, Jr.; ill. by Seymour Chwast, Milton Glaser, and Barry Zaid. Little, 1971. Subj: Foreign languages. Nursery rhymes.

Ring around a rosy (Williams, Jenny)

Ring o' roses ill. by L. Leslie Brooke. Warne, 1923. Subj: Nursery rhymes.

The Sesame Street players present Mother Goose: featuring Jim Henson's Sesame Street Muppets ill. by Michael Smollin. Random House-Children's Television Workshop, 1982. Subj: Nursery rhymes. Puppets.

Sing a song of Mother Goose ill. by Barbara Reid. North Winds Pr., 1987. ISBN 0-590-71781-2 Subj: Nursery rhymes.

Sing a song of sixpence comp. and ill. by Randolph Caldecott. Barron's, 1988. Reprint of 1888 ed. ISBN 0-8120-5900-X Subj: Nursery rhymes.

Sing a song of sixpence ill. by Randolph Caldecott. New ed. Hart, 1977. Reprint of orig. Warne pub. between 1876 and 1886. Subj: Nursery rhymes.

Sing a song of sixpence ill. by Margaret Chamberlain. Peter Bedrick Books (dist. by Harper), 1984. Subj: Format, unusual – board books. Nursery rhymes.

Sing a song of sixpence ill. by Leonard Lubin. Lothrop, 1987. ISBN 0-688-00545-4 Subj: Nursery rhymes. Royalty.

Sing a song of sixpence ed. by Kate Klimo; ill. by Ray Marshall and Korky Paul. Simon & Schuster, 1983. ISBN 0-671-46237-7 Subj: Format, unusual – toy and movable books. Nursery rhymes.

Sing a song of sixpence ill. by Ferelith Eccles Williams. David & Charles, 1985. ISBN 0-437-86002-7 Subj: Format, unusual – board books. Nursery rhymes.

Sing hey diddle diddle: 66 nursery rhymes with their traditional tunes comp. by Beatrice Harrop; ill. by Frank Francis and Bernard Cheese. Sterling, 1983. Subj: Music. Nursery rhymes.

Songs for Mother Goose ill. by Maginel Wright Enright Barney; set to music by Sidney Homer. Macmillan, 1920. Subj: Nursery rhymes.

The tall Mother Goose ill. by Feodor Rojankovsky. Harper, 1942. Subj: Nursery rhymes.

Thirty old-time nursery songs ed. by Joseph Moorat; ill. by Paul Woodroffe. Norton, 1980. Orig. pub. in 1912. Subj: Music. Nursery rhymes. Songs.

This little pig ill. by Eleanor Wasmuth. Simon & Schuster, 1986. ISBN 0-671-61727-3 Subj: Format, unusual – board books. Nursery rhymes.

This little pig: a Mother Goose favorite ill. by Leonard Lubin. Lothrop, 1985. ISBN 0-688-04089-6 Subj: Animals – pigs. Nursery rhymes.

This little pig went to market ill. by L. Leslie Brooke. Warne, 1922. Subj: Animals – pigs. Nursery rhymes.

This little pig went to market ill. by Ferelith Eccles Williams. David & Charles, 1985. ISBN 0-437-86004-3 Subj: Format, unusual – board books. Games. Nursery rhymes.

The three jovial huntsmen ill. by Susan Jeffers. Bradbury Pr., 1973. Subj: Caldecott award honor book. Nursery rhymes.

The three little kittens ill. by Lorinda Bryan Cauley. Putnam's, 1982. Subj: Animals – cats. Behavior – losing things. Games. Nursery rhymes.

The three little kittens ill. by Paul Galdone. Clarion, 1986. ISBN 0-89919-426-5 Subj: Animals – cats. Behavior – losing things. Nursery rhymes.

The three little kittens ill. by Dorothy Stott. Putnam's, 1984. ISBN 0-448-10216-1 Subj: Animals – cats. Behavior – losing things. Format, unusual – board books. Nursery rhymes.

The three little kittens adapt. by Jean Marzollo; ill. by Shelley Thornton. Scholastic, 1986. ISBN 0-590-33370-4 Subj: Animals – cats. Behavior – losing things. Games. Nursery rhymes.

To market! To market! ill. by Emma Lillian Brock. Knopf, 1930. Subj: Nursery rhymes. Shopping.

To market! To market! ill. by Peter Spier. Doubleday, 1967. Subj: Nursery rhymes.

Tom, Tom the piper's son ill. by Paul Galdone. McGraw-Hill, 1964. Subj: Nursery rhymes.

Tomie de Paola's Mother Goose (De Paola, Tomie)

Twenty nursery rhymes ill. by Philip Van Aver. Grabhorn-Hoyem, 1970. Subj: Nursery rhymes.

Willy Pogany's Mother Goose ill. by Willy Pogany. Nelson, 1928. Subj: Nursery rhymes.

Mouse house ill. by Zokeisha; ed. by Kate Klimo. Simon and Schuster, 1983. Subj: Animals – mice. Format, unusual – board books. Houses.

The moving adventures of Old Dame Trot and her comical cat ill. by Paul Galdone. McGraw-Hill, 1973. Subj: Animals – cats. Nursery rhymes.

Mower, Nancy. *I visit my Tūtū and Grandma* ill. by Patricia A. Wozniak. Press Pacifica, 1984. ISBN 0-9166390-41-2 Subj: Family life – grandmothers. Hawaii.

Moxley, Susan. *Abdul's treasure* ill. by author. David & Charles, 1988. ISBN 0-340-38918-4 Subj: Careers – fishermen. Folk and fairy tales. Royalty.

Mozley, Charles. *Arabian Nights entertainments* (Arabian Nights)

Mude, O. *see* Gorey, Edward

Mueller, Evelyn. *I'm deaf and it's okay* (Aseltine, Lorraine)

Mueller, Virginia. *A Halloween mask for Monster* ill. by Lynn Munsinger. Albert Whitman, 1986. ISBN 0-8075-3134-0 Subj: Holidays – Halloween. Monsters.

Monster and the baby ill. by Lynn Munsinger. Albert Whitman, 1985. ISBN 0-8075-5253-4 Subj: Activities – baby-sitting. Babies. Monsters.

Monster can't sleep ill. by Lynn Munsinger. Albert Whitman, 1986. ISBN 0-8075-5261-5 Subj: Bedtime. Monsters. Sleep.

A playhouse for Monster ill. by Lynn Munsinger. Albert Whitman, 1985. ISBN 0-8075-6541-5 Subj: Activities – playing. Monsters.

Muller, Robin. *The lucky old woman.* Kids Can Pr., 1987. ISBN 0-921103-07-7 Subj: Folk and fairy tales.

The sorcerer's apprentice ill. by author. Silver Burdett, 1986. ISBN 0-382-09382-8 Subj: Folk and fairy tales. Magic. Royalty.

Mullins, Edward S. *Animal limericks* ill. by author. Follett, 1966. Subj: Animals. Poetry, rhyme.

Munari, Bruno. *ABC* ill. by author. Collins-World, 1960. Subj: ABC books.

Animals for sale ill. by author. Collins-World, 1957. Subj: Animals.

The birthday present ill. by author. Collins-World, 1959. Subj: Birthdays. Games. Transportation.

Bruno Munari's zoo ill. by author. Collins-World, 1963. Subj: Animals. Birds. Zoos.

The circus in the mist ill. by author. Collins, 1968. Subj: Circus. Format, unusual. Weather – fog.

The elephant's wish ill. by author. Collins, 1959. First pub. in 1945. Subj: Animals. Behavior – wishing. Format, unusual – toy and movable books.

Jimmy has lost his cap ill. by author. Collins, 1959. Subj: Behavior – losing things. Format, unusual – toy and movable books.

Tic, Tac and Toc ill. by author. Collins-World, 1957. Subj: Birds. Format, unusual – toy and movable books.

Who's there? Open the door tr. by Maria Cimino; ill. by author. Collins-World, 1957. Subj: Animals. Format, unusual – toy and movable books.

Munro, Roxie. *Christmastime in New York City* ill. by author. Dodd, 1987. ISBN 0-396-08909-7 Subj: City. Holidays – Christmas.

The inside-outside book of New York City ill. by author. Dodd, 1985. ISBN 0-396-08513-X Subj: City.

The inside-outside book of Washington, D.C. ill. by author. Dutton, 1987. ISBN 0-525-44298-7 Subj: Activities – traveling. City. Museums.

Munsch, Robert N. *David's father* ill. by Michael Martchenko. Firefly Pr., 1983. Subj: Character traits – kindness. Giants.

I have to go! ill. by Michael Martchenko. Firefly Pr., 1987. ISBN 0-920303-77-3 Subj: Behavior – growing up. Family life.

Jonathan cleaned up - then he heard a sound: or, blackberry subway jam ill. by Michael Martchenko. Firefly Pr., 1981. Subj: Machines. Problem solving. Trains.

Millicent and the wind ill. by Suzanne Duranceau. Firefly Pr., 1984. ISBN 0-920236-98-7 Subj: Friendship. Weather – wind.

Muntean, Michaela. *Alligator's garden* ill. by Nicole Rubel. Dial Pr., 1984. Subj: Activities – gardening. Reptiles – alligators, crocodiles.

Bicycle bear ill. by Doug Cushman. Parents, 1983. Subj: Animals – bears. Poetry, rhyme. Sports – bicycling.

The house that bear built ill. by Nicole Rubel. Dial Pr., 1984. Subj: Animals – bears. Houses.

Mokey and the festival of the bells ill. by Michael Adams. Holt, 1985. ISBN 0-03-004553-3 Subj: Character traits – generosity. Puppets.

Muppet babies through the year ill. by Bruce McNally. Random House, 1984. Subj: Puppets. Seasons.

Munthe, Adam John. *I believe in unicorns* ill. by Elizabeth Falconer. Merrimack, 1980. Subj: Emotions – loneliness. Mythical creatures.

The Muppet Show book ill. by Tudor Banus. Abrams, 1978. Subj: Puppets.

Murdocca, Sal. *Tuttle's shell* ill. by author. Lothrop, 1976. Subj: Animals. Animals – rats. Friendship. Reptiles – turtles, tortoises.

Murphey, Sara. *The animal hat shop* reading consultant: Morton Botel; ill. by Mel Pekarsky. Follett, 1964. Subj: Animals – cats. Birds – chickens. Clothing.

The roly poly cookie reading consultant: Morton Botel; ill. by Leonard W. Shortall. Follett, 1963. Subj: Cumulative tales. Food.

Murphy, Jill. *All in one piece* ill. by author. Putnam's, 1987. ISBN 0-399-21433-X Subj: Animals – elephants. Behavior – misbehavior. Family life.

Five minutes' peace ill. by author. Putnam's, 1986. ISBN 0-399-21354-6 Subj: Animals – elephants. Family life.

Peace at last ill. by author. Dial Pr., 1980. Subj: Animals – bears. Noise, sounds. Sleep.

What next, baby bear! ill. by author. Dial Pr., 1984. Subj: Animals – bears. Bedtime. Imagination. Night. Space and space ships.

Murphy, Shirley Rousseau. *Tattie's river journey* ill. by Tomie de Paola. Dial Pr., 1983. Subj: Houses. Rivers. Weather – rain.

Valentine for a dragon ill. by Kay Chorao. Atheneum, 1984. Subj: Dragons. Emotions – loneliness. Holidays – Valentine's Day. Monsters.

Murschetz, Luis. *Mister Mole* tr. by Diane Martin; ill. by author. Prentice-Hall, 1976. Translation of Der Maulwurf Grabowski. Subj: Animals – moles. Ecology. Progress.

Musgrove, Margaret. *Ashanti to Zulu.* Dial Pr., 1976. Subj: ABC books. Caldecott award book. Foreign lands – Africa.

Musicant, Elke. *The night vegetable eater* by Elke and Ted Musicant; ill. by Jeni Bassett. Dodd, 1981. ISBN 0-396-07923-7 Subj: Activities – gardening. Animals. Problem solving.

Musicant, Ted. *The night vegetable eater* (Musicant, Elke)

My body ill. by Sue Porter. Harper, 1985. Subj: Anatomy. Format, unusual – board books. Wordless.

My day. Simon and Schuster, 1980. Subj: Activities. Format, unusual – board books.

My first book of baby animals ill. by Karen Lee Schmidt. Platt, 1986. ISBN 0-448-10826-7 Subj: Animals. Format, unusual – board books.

My toy box. Simon and Schuster, 1980. Subj: Format, unusual – board books. Toys.

Myers, Amy. *I know a monster* ill. by author. Addison-Wesley, 1979. Subj: Character traits – appearance. Games. Monsters.

Myers, Arthur. *Kids do amazing things* ill. by Anthony Rao. Random House, 1980. Subj: Activities.

Myers, Bernice. *Charlie's birthday present* ill. by author. Scholastic, 1981. Subj: Birthdays. Trees.

Herman and the bears and the giants ill. by author. Scholastic, 1978. Subj: Animals – bears. Circus. Sports – bicycling.

Sidney Rella and the glass sneaker ill. by author. Macmillan, 1985. ISBN 0-02-767790-7 Subj: Behavior – wishing. Fairies. Sports – football.

Myers, Walter Dean. *The golden serpent* ill. by Alice and Martin Provensen. Viking, 1980. ISBN 0-670-34445-1 Subj: Folk and fairy tales. Foreign lands – India. Problem solving. Royalty.

Myller, Lois. *No! No!* ill. by Cyndy Szekeres. Simon and Schuster, 1971. Subj: Animals – hedgehogs. Behavior. Behavior – misbehavior. Etiquette. Family life. Safety.

Myller, Rolf. *How big is a foot?* ill. by author. Atheneum, 1962. Subj: Birthdays. Concepts – measurement. Humor. Royalty.

Rolling round ill. by author. Atheneum, 1963. Subj: Royalty. Wheels.

A very noisy day ill. by author. Atheneum, 1981. ISBN 0-689-30853-1 Subj: Animals – dogs. Crime. Noise, sounds.

Myrick, Jean Lockwood. *Ninety-nine pockets* ill. by Haris Petie. Lantern Pr., 1966. Subj: Birthdays. Clothing. Problem solving.

Myrick, Mildred. *Ants are fun* ill. by Arnold Lobel. Harper, 1968. Subj: Insects – ants. Science.

The secret three ill. by Arnold Lobel. Harper, 1963. Subj: Clubs, gangs. Lighthouses. Secret codes.

Nagel, Andreas Fischer *see* Fischer-Nagel, Andreas

Nagel, Heiderose Fischer *see* Fischer-Nagel, Heiderose

Nakano, Hirotaka. *Elephant blue* tr. by Fukuinkan Shoten; ill. by author. Bobbs-Merrill, 1970. Subj: Animals. Animals – elephants. Character traits – helpfulness.

Nakao, Naomi Löw. *The adventures of Chester the chest* (Ayal, Ora)

Ugbu (Ayal, Ora)

Nakatani, Chiyoko. *The day Chiro was lost* ill. by author. Collins-World, 1969. Subj: Animals – dogs. Behavior – lost.

Fumio and the dolphins ill. by author. Addison-Wesley, 1970. First published in Japan by Fukuinkan-Shoten, Tokyo, 1969. Subj: Animals – dolphins. Character traits – kindness to animals. Foreign lands – Japan. Sea and seashore.

My day on the farm ill. by author. Crowell, 1976. Subj: Farms.

The zoo in my garden ill. by author. Crowell, 1973. Translation of Boku no uchi no dōbutsuen. Subj: Animals.

Nake, Noriko *see* Ueno, Noriko

Namm, Diane. *Favorite nursery rhymes* comp. by Diane Namm; ill. by Delana Bettoli. Little, 1986. ISBN 0-671-60264-0 Subj: Nursery rhymes.

Napoli, Guillier. *Adventure at Mont-Saint-Michel* ill. by author. McGraw-Hill, 1966. Subj: Careers – fishermen. Character traits – curiosity. Foreign lands – France. Sea and seashore.

Narahashi, Keiko. *I have a friend* ill. by author. McElderry, 1987. ISBN 0-689-50432-2 Subj: Shadows.

Narayan, Maya. *Leela and the watermelon* (Hirsh, Marilyn)

Nash, Linell *see* Chenault, Nell

Nash, Ogden. *The adventures of Isabel* ill. by Walter Lorraine. Little, 1963. Subj: Emotions – fear. Humor. Poetry, rhyme.

The animal garden ill. by Hilary Knight. Lippincott, 1963. Subj: Humor. Plants. Poetry, rhyme.

A boy is a boy ill. by Arthur Shilstone. Watts, 1960. Subj: Humor. Poetry, rhyme.

Custard and Company sel. and ill. by Quentin Blake. Little, 1980. Subj: Dragons. Humor. Poetry, rhyme.

Custard the dragon ill. by Linell Nash. Little, 1961. ISBN 0-316-59841-0 Subj: Animals. Character traits – bravery. Dragons. Pirates.

Custard the dragon and the wicked knight ill. by Linell Nash. Little, 1959. Subj: Dragons. Poetry, rhyme.

Nast, Elsa Ruth *see* Watson, Jane Werner

Naxt, Elsa Ruth *see* Watson, Jane Werner

Naylor, Phyllis Reynolds. *The baby, the bed, and the rose* ill. by Mary Szilagyi. Clarion, 1987. ISBN 0-899-19459-1 Subj: Babies. Emotions – love. Family life.

Old Sadie and the Christmas bear ill. by Patricia Montgomery Newton. Atheneum, 1984. Subj: Animals – bears. Holidays – Christmas.

Neal, Ernest. *Badgers* ill. with photos. Global Lib. Mktg. Serv., 1984. ISBN 0-7136-2389-6 Subj: Animals – badgers. Nature. Science.

Neale, J. M. *Good King Wenceslas* ill. by Jamichael Henterly. Dutton, 1988. ISBN 0-525-44420-3 Subj: Folk and fairy tales. Holidays – Christmas. Music. Songs.

Neasi, Barbara J. *Just like me* ill. by Lois Axeman. Children's Pr., 1984. Subj: Twins.

Listen to me ill. by Gene Sharp. Childrens Pr., 1986. ISBN 0-516-02072-2 Subj: Family life – grandmothers.

Nelson, Brenda. *Mud for sale* ill. by Richard Brown. Houghton, 1984. Subj: Activities. Friendship.

Nelson, Esther L. *The funny songbook* ill. by Joyce Behr. Sterling, 1984. Subj: Music. Songs.

Holiday singing and dancing games photos. by Shirley Zeiberg. Sterling, 1980. Subj: Activities – dancing. Games. Music. Songs.

The silly songbook ill. by Joyce Behr. Sterling, 1982. Subj: Music. Songs.

Nelson, Vaunda Micheaux. *Always Gramma* ill. by Kimanne Uhler. Putnam's, 1988. ISBN 0-399-21542-5 Subj: Family life. Family life – grandmothers. Illness. Old age.

Nerlove, Miriam. *I made a mistake* ill. by author. Atheneum, 1985. ISBN 0-689-50327-X Subj: Animals. Poetry, rhyme.

I meant to clean my room today ill. by author. Macmillan, 1988. ISBN 0-689-50438-1 Subj: Character traits – cleanliness. Imagination. Poetry, rhyme.

Nesbit, Edith. *Beauty and the beast* ill. by Julia Christie. Warne, 1988. ISBN 0-7232-3540-6 Subj: Character traits – appearance. Character traits – loyalty. Emotions – love. Folk and fairy tales.

Cockatoucan ill. by Elory Hughes. Dial Pr., 1988. ISBN 0-8037-0474-7 Subj: Birds. Imagination.

The ice dragon ill. by Carole Gray. Dial Pr., 1988. ISBN 0-8037-0475-5 Subj: World.

The last of the dragons ill. by Peter Firmin. McGraw-Hill, 1980. ISBN 0-07-046285-2 Subj: Character traits – kindness. Dragons. Folk and fairy tales. Royalty.

Ness, Evaline. *Do you have the time, Lydia?* ill. by author. Dutton, 1971. Subj: Birds – sea gulls. Character traits – completing things. Problem solving. Time.

Exactly alike ill. by author. Scribner's, 1964. Subj: Family life.

Fierce: the lion ill. by author. Holiday, 1980. Subj: Animals – lions. Circus.

The girl and the goatherd: or, this and that and thus and so ill. by author. Dutton, 1970. Subj: Character traits – appearance. Folk and fairy tales.

Josefina February ill. by author. Scribner's, 1963. Subj: Animals – donkeys. Birthdays. Character traits – generosity. Foreign lands – Caribbean Islands.

Marcella's guardian angel ill. by author. Holiday, 1979. Subj: Angels. Behavior.

Pavo and the princess ill. by author. Scribner's, 1964. Subj: Birds. Character traits – helpfulness. Emotions. Royalty.

Sam, Bangs, and moonshine ill. by author. Holt, 1966. Subj: Caldecott award book. Imagination. Sports – fishing.

Neugroschel, Joachim. *The boy and the tree* (Driz, Ovsei)

Neuhaus, David. *His finest hour* ill. by author. Viking, 1984. Subj: Friendship. Sports – racing.

Neumeier, Marty. *Action alphabet* by Marty Neumeier and Byron Glaser; ill. by authors. Greenwillow, 1985. ISBN 0-688-05704-7 Subj: ABC books. Activities.

Neumeyer, Peter F. *The faithful fish* ill. by Arvis L. Stewart. Young Scott, 1971. ISBN 0-8240-0000-5 Subj: Activities – vacationing. Family life. Sports – fishing.

The phantom of the opera ill. by Don Weller. Gibbs M. Smith, 1988. ISBN 0-87905-330-5 Subj: Emotions – love. Music. Theater.

Neville, Emily Cheney. *The bridge* ill. by Ronald Himler. Harper, 1988. ISBN 0-06-024386-4 Subj: Bridges. Family life. Machines.

Newberry, Clare Turlay. *April's kittens* ill. by author. Harper, 1940. Subj: Animals – cats. Caldecott award honor book. Pets.

Barkis ill. by author. Harper, 1938. Subj: Animals – dogs. Caldecott award honor book. Pets.

Cousin Toby ill. by author. Harper, 1939. Subj: Babies.

Herbert the lion ill. by author. Harper, 1956. First pub. in 1931. Subj: Animals – lions. Pets.

The kittens' ABC verse and pictures by Clare Turlay Newberry. New and rev. ed.; completely redrawn. Harper, 1965. Subj: ABC books. Animals – cats. Poetry, rhyme.

Lambert's bargain ill. by author. Harper, 1941. Subj: Animals – hyenas.

Marshmallow ill. by author. Harper, 1942. Subj: Animals – cats. Animals – rabbits. Caldecott award honor book. Friendship.

Mittens ill. by author. Harper, 1937. Subj: Animals – cats.

Pandora ill. by author. Harper, 1944. Subj: Animals – cats.

Percy, Polly and Pete ill. by author. Harper, 1952. Subj: Animals – cats. Behavior – growing up. Character traits – kindness to animals. Pets.

Smudge ill. by author. Harper, 1948. Subj: Animals – cats.

T-Bone, the baby-sitter story and pictures by author. Harper, 1950. Subj: Activities – baby-sitting. Animals – cats. Babies. Caldecott award honor book.

Widget ill. by author. Harper, 1958. Subj: Animals – cats.

Newbold, Stokes *see* Adams, Richard

Newbolt, Henry John, Sir. *Rilloby-rill* ill. by Susanna Gretz. O'Hara, 1973. Subj: Insects – grasshoppers. Fairies. Music. Songs.

Newell, Crosby Barbara *see* Bonsall, Crosby Newell

Newell, Peter. *Topsys and turvys* ill. by author. Dover, 1965. Subj: Format, unusual. Humor.

Newfield, Marcia. *Iggy* ill. by Jacqueline Chwast. Houghton, 1972. Subj: Pets. Reptiles – iguanas.

Newland, Mary Reed. *Good King Wenceslas: a legend in music and pictures* ill. by author. Seabury Pr., 1980. Subj: Holidays – Christmas. Music. Songs.

Newman, Shirlee. *Tell me, grandma; tell me, grandpa* ill. by Joan Drescher. Houghton, 1979. Subj: Family life – grandparents.

Newsham, Ian. *Lost in the jungle* by Ian and Wendy Newsham; ill. by authors. David & Charles, 1985. ISBN 0-7182-4150-9 Subj: Animals. Behavior – fighting, arguing. Jungle.

The monster hunt (Newsham, Wendy)

Newsham, Wendy. *Lost in the jungle* (Newsham, Ian)

The monster hunt by Wendy and Ian Newsham; ill. by authors. Hamish Hamilton, 1983. Subj: Monsters.

Newth, Philip. *Roly goes exploring: a book for blind and sighted children, in Braille and standard type, with pictures to feel as well as see.* Putnam's, 1981. Subj: Concepts – shape. Format, unusual. Handicaps – blindness. Senses – seeing.

Newton, James R. *A forest is reborn* ill. by Susan Bonners. Crowell, 1982. Subj: Fire. Forest, woods. Science.

Forest log ill. by Irene Brady. Crowell, 1980. Subj: Ecology. Forest, woods. Science. Trees.

Newton, Laura P. *Me and my aunts* ill. by Robin Oz. Albert Whitman, 1986. ISBN 0-8075-5029-9 Subj: Emotions – love. Family life.

William the vehicle king ill. by Jacqueline Rogers. Bradbury Pr., 1987. ISBN 0-02-768230-7 Subj: Automobiles. Imagination. Toys. Trucks.

Newton, Patricia Montgomery. *The five sparrows* ill. by author. Atheneum, 1982. Subj: Character traits – kindness. Folk and fairy tales. Foreign lands – Japan.

The frog who drank the waters of the world ill. by author. Atheneum, 1983. ISBN 0-689-30993-7 Subj: Animals. Birds – bluejays. Frogs and toads. Reptiles – snakes.

Vacation surprise ill. by author. Atheneum, 1986. ISBN 0-689-31264-4 Subj: Activities – vacationing. Animals – pigs.

Nic Leodhas, Sorche *see* Alger, Leclaire

Nichol, B. P. *Once: a lullaby* ill. by Anita Lobel. Greenwillow, 1986. ISBN 0-688-04285-6 Subj: Animals. Bedtime. Music. Night. Sleep. Songs.

Nichols, Cathy. *Tuxedo Sam: a penguin of a different color* ill. by Haruo Takahashi. Random House, 1983. Subj: Birds – penguins. City.

Nichols, Paul. *Big Paul's school bus* ill. by William Marshall. Prentice-Hall, 1981. Subj: Buses. Careers. School.

Nicholson, William, Sir. *Clever Bill* ill. by author. Farrar, 1977. Subj: Toys – soldiers.

Nickl, Peter. *Ra ta ta tam* by Peter Nickl and Binette Schroeder; ill. by authors. Merrimack, 1984. Subj: Character traits – meanness. Format, unusual – board books. Trains.

Nicolas *see* Mordvinoff, Nicolas

Nicoll, Helen. *Meg and Mog* by Helen Nicoll and Jan Pieńkowski; ill. by Jan Pieńkowski. Atheneum, 1972. Subj: Animals – cats. Holidays – Halloween. Magic. Witches.

Meg at sea by Helen Nicoll and Jan Pieńkowski; ill. by Jan Pieńkowski. Harvey House, 1974. Subj: Animals – cats. Birds – owls. Magic. Sea and seashore. Witches.

Meg on the moon by Helen Nicoll and Jan Pieńkowski; ill. by Jan Pieńkowski. Harvey House, 1974. Subj: Animals – cats. Magic. Moon. Witches.

Meg's eggs by Helen Nicoll and Jan Pieńkowski; ill. by Jan Pieńkowski. Atheneum, 1972. Subj: Animals – cats. Birds – owls. Dinosaurs. Eggs. Magic. Witches.

Mog's box ill. by Jan Pieńkowski. David & Charles, 1987. ISBN 0-434-95658-9 Subj: Animals – cats. Magic. Witches.

Nikly, Michelle. *The emperor's plum tree* tr. from French by Elizabeth Shub; ill. by author. Greenwillow, 1982. Subj: Friendship. Royalty. Trees.

The princess on the nut: or, the curious courtship of the son of the princess on the pea tr. by Lucy Meredith; ill. by Jean Claverie. Faber, 1981. Subj: Folk and fairy tales. Royalty.

Niland, Deborah. *ABC of monsters* ill. by author. McGraw-Hill, 1978. Subj: ABC books. Monsters.

Nilsson, Ulf. *Little sister rabbit* ill. by Eva Eriksson. Little, 1985. ISBN 0-87113-009-2 Subj: Activities – baby-sitting. Animals – rabbits. Family life.

Nims, Bonnie L. *Where is the bear?* ill. by John Wallner. Albert Whitman, 1988. ISBN 0-8075-8933-0 Subj: Behavior – lost. Poetry, rhyme. Toys – teddy bears.

Nishikawa, Osamu. *Alexander and the blue ghost* ill. by author. Morrow, 1986. ISBN 0-688-06267-9 Subj: Character traits – bravery. Ghosts. Royalty.

Nister, Ernest. *Little tales from long ago: Cat's cradle, The tale of a dog, Three friends, Three little maids* ill. by author. Delacorte Pr., 1979. Subj: Folk and fairy tales.

Nixon, Joan Lowery. *Beats me, Claude* ill. by Tracey Campbell Pearson. Viking, 1986. ISBN 0-670-80781-8 Subj: Activities – cooking. Humor.

Bigfoot makes a movie ill. by Syd Hoff. Putnam's, 1979. ISBN 0-399-20684-1 Subj: Behavior – misunderstanding. Folk and fairy tales. Monsters.

Fat chance, Claude ill. by Tracey Campbell Pearson. Viking, 1987. ISBN 0-670-81459-8 Subj: Careers – miners.

If you say so, Claude ill. by Lorinda Bryan Cauley. Warne, 1980. ISBN 0-7232-6183-0 Subj: Activities – traveling. Behavior – seeking better things. U.S. history.

If you were a writer ill. by Bruce Degen. Four Winds Pr., 1988. ISBN 0-02-768210-2 Subj: Activities – writing.

The Thanksgiving mystery ill. by Jim Cummins. Albert Whitman, 1980. Subj: Ghosts. Holidays – Thanksgiving. Problem solving.

The Valentine mystery ill. by Jim Cummins. Albert Whitman, 1979. Subj: Holidays – Valentine's Day. Problem solving.

Noble, June. *Two homes for Lynn* ill. by Yuri Salzman. Holt, 1979. Subj: Behavior – sharing. Divorce. Family life. Imagination – imaginary friends.

Noble, Trinka Hakes. *Apple tree Christmas* ill. by author. Dial Pr., 1984. Subj: Holidays – Christmas. Trees. Weather – storms.

The day Jimmy's boa ate the wash ill. by Steven Kellogg. Dial Pr., 1980. Subj: Activities. Reptiles – snakes. School.

Hansy's mermaid ill. by author. Dial Pr., 1983. Subj: Character traits – kindness. Mythical creatures.

Jimmy's boa bounces back ill. by Steven Kellogg. Dial Pr., 1984. Subj: Humor. Reptiles – snakes.

The king's tea ill. by author. Dial Pr., 1979. Subj: Cumulative tales. Royalty.

Meanwhile back at the ranch ill. by Tony Ross. Dial Pr., 1987. ISBN 0-8037-0354-6 Subj: Behavior – boredom. Humor.

Nodset, Joan L. *see* Lexau, Joan M.

Noguere, Suzanne. *Little raccoon* ill. by Tony Chen. Holt, 1981. Subj: Animals – raccoons.

Nolan, Dennis. *The castle builder* ill. by author. Macmillan, 1987. ISBN 0-02-768240-4 Subj: Dragons. Imagination. Knights. Sand. Sea and seashore.

Witch Bazooza ill. by author. Prentice-Hall, 1979. Subj: Holidays – Halloween. Houses. Witches.

Wizard McBean and his flying machine ill. by author. Prentice-Hall, 1977. Subj: Airplanes, airports. Cumulative tales. Magic. Poetry, rhyme. Wizards.

Nolan, Madeena Spray. *My daddy don't go to work* ill. by Jim LaMarche. Carolrhoda Books, 1978. Subj: Ethnic groups in the U.S. – Afro-Americans. Family life. Family life – fathers. Poverty.

Noll, Sally. *Jiggle wiggle prance* ill. by author. Greenwillow, 1987. ISBN 0-688-06761-1 Subj: Activities. Animals.

Off and counting ill. by author. Greenwillow, 1984. Subj: Counting. Frogs and toads. Poetry, rhyme. Toys.

Norby, Lisa. *The Herself the elf storybook.* Scholastic, 1983. Subj: Elves and little people. Magic.

Nordlicht, Lillian. *I love to laugh* ill. by Allen Davis. Raintree, 1980. ISBN 0-8172-1364-3 Subj: Behavior – growing up. Character traits – being different.

Nordqvist, Sven. *The fox hunt* ill. by author. Morrow, 1988. ISBN 0-688-06882-0 Subj: Animals – cats. Animals – foxes. Behavior – trickery. Careers – farmers.

Pancake pie ill. by author. Morrow, 1985. Subj: Animals – cats. Food.

Willie in the big world: adventures with numbers ill. by author. Morrow, 1986. ISBN 0-688-06143-5 Subj: Activities – traveling. Counting.

Norman, Charles. *The hornbean tree and other poems* ill. by Ted Rand. Holt, 1988. ISBN 0-8050-0417-3 Subj: Animals. Birds. Nature. Poetry, rhyme.

Norman, Howard. *The owl-scatterer* ill. by Michael McCurdy. Atlantic Monthly Pr., 1986. ISBN 0-87113-058-0 Subj: Behavior – disbelief. Birds – owls. Foreign lands – Canada.

Who-Paddled-Backward-With-Trout ill. by Ed Young. Little, 1987. ISBN 0-316-61182-4 Subj: Folk and fairy tales. Indians of North America. Names.

North, George Captain *see* Stevenson, Robert Louis

North, Robert *see* Withers, Carl

Northam, Leland. *Hansel and Gretel* (Grimm, Jacob)

Sleeping Beauty (Grimm, Jacob)

The ugly duckling (Andersen, H. C. (Hans Christian))

Northrup, Mili. *The watch cat* ill. by Adrina Zanazanian; designed by Kent Salisbury. Bobbs-Merrill, 1968. Subj: Animals – cats. Foreign lands – Thailand.

Norton, Natalie. *A little old man* ill. by Will Huntington. Rand McNally, 1959. Subj: Emotions – loneliness.

Nourse, Alan Edward. *Lumps, bumps and rashes: a look at kids' diseases.* Watts, 1976. Subj: Illness.

Novak, Matt. *Claude and Sun* ill. by author. Bradbury, 1987. ISBN 0-02-768151-3 Subj: Friendship. Sun.

Rolling ill. by author. Bradbury Pr., 1986. ISBN 0-02-768150-5 Subj: Weather – thunder.

Numeroff, Laura Joffe. *Amy for short* ill. by author. Macmillan, 1976. Subj: Character traits – appearance. Friendship.

Emily's bunch by Laura Joffe Numeroff and Alice Numeroff Richter; ill. by Laura Joffe Numeroff. Macmillan, 1978. Subj: Holidays – Halloween.

If you give a mouse a cookie ill. by Felicia Bond. Harper, 1985. ISBN 0-06-024587-5 Subj: Animals – mice. Character traits – kindness to animals. Circular tales. Behavior – imitation.

Phoebe Dexter has Harriet Peterson's sniffles ill. by author. Greenwillow, 1977. Subj: Illness.

You can't put braces on spaces (Richter, Alice Numeroff.)

Nursery rhymes ill. by Gertrude Elliott. Simon and Schuster, 1948. Subj: Nursery rhymes.

Nussbaum, Hedda. *Animals build amazing homes* ill. by Christopher Santoro. Random House, 1979. Subj: Animals. Houses. Science.

Nussbaumer, Mares. *Away in a manger: a story of the Nativity* by Mares and Paul Nussbaumer; ill. by Paul Nussbaumer. Harcourt, 1965. Translation of Ihr Kinderlein kommet. Subj: Holidays – Christmas. Music. Religion.

Nussbaumer, Paul. *Away in a manger* (Nussbaumer, Mares)

Nygren, Tord. *Fiddler and his brothers* ill. by author. Morrow, 1987. ISBN 0-688-07146-5 Subj: Behavior – trickery. Folk and fairy tales. Royalty. Sibling rivalry. Witches.

The red thread ill. by author. Farrar, 1988. ISBN 91-29-59005-1 Subj: Imagination. Wordless.

O'Cuilleanain, Eilis Dillon *see* Dillon, Eilis

Oakes, Bill. *Numblers* (MacDonald, Suse)

Oakley, Graham. *The church cat abroad* ill. by author. Atheneum, 1973. Subj: Animals – cats. Animals – mice. Foreign lands – England.

The church mice adrift ill. by author. Atheneum, 1976. Subj: Animals – mice. Animals – rats. Rivers.

The church mice and the moon ill. by author. Atheneum, 1974. Subj: Animals – cats. Animals – mice. Foreign lands – England. Moon.

The church mice at bay ill. by author. Atheneum, 1978. Subj: Animals – cats. Animals – mice. Foreign lands – England.

The church mice at Christmas ill. by author. Atheneum, 1980. Subj: Animals – mice. Holidays – Christmas.

The church mice in action ill. by author. Atheneum, 1983. Subj: Animals – mice. Problem solving.

The church mice spread their wings ill. by author. Atheneum, 1975. Subj: Animals – cats. Animals – mice. Foreign lands – England.

The church mouse ill. by author. Atheneum, 1972. Subj: Animals – cats. Animals – mice. Foreign lands – England.

The diary of a church mouse ill. by author. Atheneum, 1987. ISBN 0-689-31334-9 Subj: Activities – writing. Animals – cats. Animals – mice.

Graham Oakley's magical changes ill. by author. Atheneum, 1980. Subj: Format, unusual – toy and movable books. Imagination. Wordless.

Hetty and Harriet ill. by author. Atheneum, 1982. Subj: Behavior – running away. Birds – chickens.

Oana, Kay D. *Robbie and the raggedy scarecrow* ill. by Jackie Stephens. Oddo, 1978. Subj: Birds. Scarecrows. Trees.

Shasta and the shebang machine ill. by Jackie Stephens. Oddo, 1978. Subj: Animals – cats. Behavior – misbehavior.

Obligado, Lilian. *Faint frogs feeling feverish and other terrifically tantalizing tongue twisters* ill. by author. Viking, 1983. Subj: ABC books. Animals. Tongue twisters.

O'Brien, Anne S. *Come play with us* ill. by author. Holt, 1985. ISBN 0-03-005008-1 Subj: Activities. Format, unusual – board books. School.

I want that! ill. by author. Holt, 1985. ISBN 0-03-005012-X Subj: Behavior – sharing. Format, unusual – board books.

I'm not tired ill. by author. Holt, 1985. ISBN 0-03-005009-X Subj: Character traits – stubbornness. Format, unusual – board books.

Where's my truck? ill. by author. Holt, 1985. ISBN 0-03-005013-8 Subj: Behavior – losing things. Format, unusual – board books.

Obrist, Jürg. *Bear business* ill. by author. Atheneum, 1986. ISBN 0-689-31149-4 Subj: Animals – bears. Behavior – misbehavior. Twins.

Fluffy: the story of a cat ill. by author. Atheneum, 1981. Subj: Animals – cats. Moving.

The miser who wanted the sun ill. by author. Atheneum, 1984. Subj: Behavior – greed. Character traits – cleverness. Sun.

They do things right in Albern ill. by author. Atheneum, 1978. Subj: Animals – moles. Problem solving.

O'Connor, Jane. *The Care Bears' party cookbook* ill. by Pat Sustendal. Random House, 1985. ISBN 0-394-97305-4 Subj: Activities – cooking. Animals – bears. Parties.

Lulu and the witch baby ill. by Emily Arnold McCully. Harper, 1986. ISBN 0-06-024627-8 Subj: Family life. Sibling rivalry. Witches.

Lulu goes to witch school ill. by Emily Arnold McCully. Harper, 1987. ISBN 0-06-024629-4 Subj: Emotions – envy, jealousy. School. Witches.

The teeny tiny woman ill. by Robert W. Alley. Random House, 1986. ISBN 0-394-98320-3 Subj: Folk and fairy tales. Ghosts.

O'Donnell, Elizabeth Lee. *Maggie doesn't want to move* ill. by Amy Schwartz. Four Winds Pr., 1987. ISBN 0-02-768830-5 Subj: Behavior – dissatisfaction. Behavior – running away. Emotions. Family life. Moving.

Odoyevsky, Vladimir. *Old Father Frost* tr. from Russian by James Riordan; ill. by Vassili Shulzhenko. Imported Pubs., 1983. Subj: Folk and fairy tales. Foreign lands – Russia. Seasons – winter.

Oechsli, Helen. *In my garden: a child's gardening book* by Helen and Kelly Oechsli; ill. by Kelly Oechsli. Macmillan, 1985. ISBN 0-02-768510-1 Subj: Activities – gardening.

Oechsli, Kelly. *In my garden* (Oechsli, Helen)

Mice at bat ill. by author. Harper, 1986. ISBN 0-06-024624-3 Subj: Animals – mice. Sports – baseball.

Ogle, Lucille. *A B See* by Lucille Ogle and Tina Thoburn; ill. by Ralph Stobart. McGraw-Hill, 1973. Subj: ABC books.

I hear by Lucille Ogle and Tina Thoburn; ill. by Eloise Wilkin. American Heritage, 1971. Subj: Noise, sounds. Participation. Senses – hearing.

I spy with my little eye ill. by Joe Kaufman. McGraw-Hill, 1970. Subj: Senses – seeing. Wordless.

O'Hagan, Caroline. *It's easy to have a caterpillar visit you* ill. by Judith Allan. Lothrop, 1980. Subj: Insects – butterflies, caterpillars. Pets.

It's easy to have a snail visit you ill. by Judith Allan. Lothrop, 1980. Subj: Animals – snails. Pets.

It's easy to have a worm visit you ill. by Judith Allan. Lothrop, 1980. Subj: Animals – worms. Pets.

O'Hare, Colette. *What do you feed your donkey on?*

Ohlsson, Ib see Olsen, Ib Spang

Oishi, Makoto. *E. H. Grieg's Peer Gynt* (Grieg, E. H. (Edvard Hagerup))

O'Kelley, Mattie Lou. *Circus!* ill. by author. Atlantic Monthly Pr., 1986. ISBN 0-87113-094-7 Subj: Behavior – misbehavior. Circus. Family life. Farms.

Oksner, Robert M. *The incompetent wizard* ill. by Janet McCaffery. Morrow, 1965. Subj: Dragons. Magic. Wizards.

The old-fashioned children's storybook. Wanderer, 1980. Subj: Folk and fairy tales.

Old MacDonald had a farm. *Old MacDonald had a farm* ill. by Mel Crawford. Golden Pr., 1967. Subj: Animals. Cumulative tales. Farms. Music. Songs.

Old MacDonald had a farm ill. by David Frankland. Merrill, 1980. Subj: Animals. Cumulative tales. Farms. Music. Songs.

Old MacDonald had a farm ill. by Abner Graboff. Four Winds Pr., 1970. Subj: Animals. Cumulative tales. Farms. Music. Songs.

Old MacDonald had a farm ill. by Tracey Campbell Pearson. Dial Pr., 1984. Subj: Animals. Cumulative tales. Farms. Music. Songs.

Old MacDonald had a farm ill. by Robert M. Quackenbush. Lippincott, 1972. Subj: Animals. Cumulative tales. Farms. Music. Songs.

Old MacDonald had a farm ill. by William Stobbs. Oxford Univ. Pr., 1986. ISBN 0-19-279817-0 Subj: Animals. Cumulative tales. Farms. Music. Songs.

The old woman and her pig ill. by Paul Galdone. McGraw-Hill, 1960. Subj: Cumulative tales. Folk and fairy tales. *The troublesome pig* retold and ill. by Priscilla Lamont. Crown, 1985. ISBN 0-517-55546-8 Cumulative tales. Folk and fairy tales.

Oldfield, Pamela. *Melanie Brown climbs a tree* ill. by Carolyn Dinan. Faber, 1980. Subj: Behavior – misbehavior. Foreign lands – England.

Olds, Elizabeth. *Feather mountain* ill. by author. Houghton, 1951. Subj: Birds. Caldecott award honor book.

Little Una ill. by author. Scribner's, 1963. Subj: City.

Plop plop ploppie ill. by author. Scribner's, 1962. Subj: Animals – sea lions. Clowns, jesters.

Olds, Helen Diehl. *Miss Hattie and the monkey* ill. by Dorothy Marino. Follett, 1958. Subj: Animals – monkeys. Careers – seamstresses.

Oleson, Claire. *For Pipita, an orange tree* ill. by Margot Tomes. Doubleday, 1967. Subj: Foreign lands – Spain. Plants.

Oleson, Jens. *Snail* photos. by Bo Jarner. Silver Burdett, 1986. ISBN 0-382-09289-9 Subj: Animals – snails. Science.

Oliver, Dexter. *I want to be...* by Dexter and Patricia Oliver; photos. by Dexter Oliver. Third World Pr., 1974. Subj: ABC books. Careers.

Oliver, Lin. *The fat cat* (Mooser, Stephen)

Oliver, Patricia. *I want to be...* (Oliver, Dexter)

Olney, Ross R. *Construction giants* ill. with photos. Atheneum, 1984. Subj: Machines.

Farm giants ill. with photos. Atheneum, 1982. Subj: Farms. Machines.

Olschewski, Alfred. *We fly* ill. by author. Little, 1967. Subj: Airplanes, airports.

The wheel rolls over ill. by author. Little, 1962. Subj: Transportation. Wheels.

Olsen, Ib Spang. *The boy in the moon* ill. by author. Parents, 1977. Tr. of Dregen i manen from the Danish by Virginia Allen Jensen. ISBN 0-8193-0734-3 Subj: Moon.

Cat alley tr. by Virginia Allen Jensen; ill. by author. Coward, 1971. Translation of Kattehuset. Subj: Behavior – lost. City.

Olson, Arielle North. *Hurry home, Grandma!* ill. by Lydia Dabcovich. Dutton, 1984. ISBN 0-525-44113-1 Subj: Family life – grandmothers. Holidays – Christmas.

The lighthouse keeper's daughter ill. by Elaine Wentworth. Little, 1987. ISBN 0-316-65053-6 Subj: Character traits – bravery. Flowers. Islands. Lighthouses. Weather – storms.

Olson, Helen Kronberg. *The strange thing that happened to Oliver Wendell Iscovitch* ill. by Betsy Lewin. Dodd, 1983. Subj: Behavior – misbehavior. Ghosts. Humor.

Olujic, Grozdana. *Rose of Mother-of-Pearl* tr. from Serbo-Croatian by Grozdana Olujic and Jascha Kessler; ill. by Kathy Jacobi. Toothpaste Pr., 1983. Subj: Behavior – dissatisfaction. Sea and seashore.

On the little hearth tr. by Miriam Chaikin; ill. by Gabriel Lisowski; score by Mark Warshawski. Holt, 1978. Subj: Foreign languages. Jewish culture. Music. Songs.

Onassis, Jacqueline. *The firebird*

One rubber duckie: a Sesame Street counting book photos. by John E. Barrett. Random House, 1982. Subj: Counting. Puppets.

One, two, buckle my shoe: a book of counting rhymes comp. and ill. by Rowan Barnes-Murphy. Simon & Schuster, 1988. ISBN 0-671-63791-6 Subj: Counting. Nursery rhymes.

One, two, buckle my shoe ill. by Gail E. Haley. Doubleday, 1964. Subj: Counting. Nursery rhymes.

O'Neill, Catharine. *Mrs. Dunphy's dog* ill. by author. Viking, 1987. ISBN 0-670-81135-1 Subj: Activities – reading. Animals – dogs.

O'Neill, Mary. *Big red hen* ill. by Judy Piussi-Campbell. Doubleday, 1971. Subj: Birds – chickens. Eggs. Poetry, rhyme.

Ooka, D. T. *The monkey and the crab* (Horio, Seishi)

The old man who made the trees bloom (Shibano, Tamizo)

Opie, Iona Archibald. *A family book of nursery rhymes* comp. by Iona and Peter Opie; ill. by Pauline Baynes. Oxford Univ. Pr., 1964. Subj: Nursery rhymes.

A nursery companion by Iona and Peter Opie. Oxford Univ. Pr., 1980. Subj: Folk and fairy tales. Nursery rhymes.

The Oxford nursery rhyme book comp. by Iona and Peter Opie; ill. by Joan Hassall. Oxford Univ. Pr., 1955. Subj: Nursery rhymes.

Puffin book of nursery rhymes comp. by Iona and Peter Opie; ill. by Pauline Baynes. Penguin, 1963. Subj: Nursery rhymes.

Tail feathers from Mother Goose: the Opie rhyme book ed. by Iona and Peter Opie. Little, 1988. ISBN 0-316-65081-1 Subj: Nursery rhymes. Poetry, rhyme.

Opie, Peter. *A family book of nursery rhymes* (Opie, Iona Archibald)

A nursery companion (Opie, Iona Archibald)

The Oxford nursery rhyme book (Opie, Iona Archibald)

Puffin book of nursery rhymes (Opie, Iona Archibald)

Tail feathers from Mother Goose (Opie, Iona Archibald)

Oppenheim, Joanne. *Have you seen birds?* ill. by Barbara Reid. Scholastic, 1986. ISBN 0-590-40585-3 Subj: Birds.

Have you seen roads? ill. by Gerard Nook. Addison-Wesley, 1969. Subj: Poetry, rhyme. Transportation.

Have you seen trees? ill. by Irwin Rosenhouse. Addison-Wesley, 1967. Subj: Poetry, rhyme, Seasons. Trees.

James will never die ill. by True Kelley. Dodd, 1982. Subj: Activities – playing.

Mrs. Peloki's class play ill. by Joyce Audy dos Santos. Dodd, 1984. Subj: School. Theater.

Mrs. Peloki's snake ill. by Joyce Audy dos Santos. Dodd, 1980. Subj: Reptiles – snakes. School.

Mrs. Peloki's substitute ill. by Joyce Audy Zarins. Dodd, 1987. ISBN 0-396-08918-6 Subj: Behavior – trickery. School.

On the other side of the river ill. by Aliki. Watts, 1972. Subj: Behavior – needing someone. Bridges. Careers.

The story book prince ill. by Rosanne Litzinger. Harcourt, 1987. ISBN 0-15-200590-0 Subj: Bedtime. Poetry, rhyme. Royalty. Sleep.

You can't catch me! ill. by Andrew Shachat. Houghton, 1986. ISBN 0-395-41452-0 Subj: Animals. Behavior – boasting. Cumulative tales. Insects – flies. Poetry, rhyme.

Oram, Hiawyn. *In the attic* ill. by Satoshi Kitamura. Holt, 1985. Subj: Activities – playing. Behavior – boredom. Imagination.

Jenna and the troublemaker ill. by Tony Ross. Holt, 1986. ISBN 0-8050-0025-9 Subj: Behavior – dissatisfaction. Mythical creatures.

Ned and the Joybaloo ill. by Satoshi Kitamura. David & Charles, 1988. ISBN 0-86264-048-2 Subj: Behavior – misbehavior. Character traits – individuality. Imagination – imaginary friends.

Skittlewonder and the wizard ill. by Jenny Rodwell. Dial Pr., 1980. Subj: Folk and fairy tales. Games. Gypsies. Royalty. Witches. Wizards.

Orbach, Ruth. *Apple pigs* ill. by author. Collins-World, 1977. Subj: Food. Poetry, rhyme. Trees.

Please send a panda ill. by author. Collins-World, 1978. Subj: Behavior – wishing. Family life – grandmothers. Pets.

O'Reilly, Edward. *Brown pelican at the pond* ill. by Florence Strange. Manzanita, 1979. Subj: Birds – pelicans. Children as authors.

Orgel, Doris. *Godfather Cat and Mousie* (Grimm, Jacob)

Little John by Theodor Storm; retold from the German by Doris Orgel; ill. by Anita Lobel. Farrar, 1972. Subj: Bedtime. Dreams.

Merry merry FIBruary ill. by Arnold Lobel. Parents, 1978. Subj: Poetry, rhyme.

On the sand dune ill. by Leonard Weisgard. Harper, 1968. Subj: Character traits – smallness. Sea and seashore.

Ormerod, Jan. *Bend and stretch* ill. by author. Lothrop, 1987. ISBN 0-688-07272-0 Subj: Babies. Family life – mothers. Sports.

Dad's back ill. by author. Lothrop, 1985. ISBN 0-688-04126-4 Subj: Babies. Clothing. Family life – fathers.

Just like me ill. by author. Lothrop, 1986. ISBN 0-688-04211-2 Subj: Babies. Character traits – appearance.

Making friends ill. by author. Lothrop, 1987. ISBN 0-688-07270-4 Subj: Babies. Family life – mothers. Toys – dolls.

Messy baby ill. by author. Lothrop, 1985. ISBN 0-688-04128-0 Subj: Babies. Family life – fathers. Toys.

Mom's home ill. by author. Lothrop, 1987. ISBN 0-688-07274-7 Subj: Babies. Family life – mothers.

Moonlight ill. by author. Lothrop, 1982. Subj: Bedtime. Family life. Sleep. Wordless.

101 things to do with a baby ill. by author. Lothrop, 1984. Subj: Babies. Behavior – sharing. Sibling rivalry.

Our Ollie ill. by author. Lothrop, 1986. ISBN 0-688-04208-2 Subj: Babies. Character traits – appearance.

Reading ill. by author. Lothrop, 1985. Subj: Activities – reading. Family life – fathers.

Silly goose ill. by author. Lothrop, 1986. ISBN 0-688-04209-0 Subj: Babies. Character traits – appearance.

Sleeping ill. by author. Lothrop, 1985. ISBN 0-688-04129-9 Subj: Babies. Family life – fathers. Sleep.

The story of Chicken Licken (Chicken Little)

Sunshine ill. by author. Lothrop, 1981. Subj: Morning. Sun. Wordless.

This little nose ill. by author. Lothrop, 1987. ISBN 0-688-07276-3 Subj: Anatomy. Babies. Family life – mothers. Illness.

Young Joe ill. by author. Lothrop, 1986. ISBN 0-688-04210-4 Subj: Babies. Counting.

Ormondroyd, Edward. *Broderick* ill. by John M. Larrecq. Parnassus, 1969. Subj: Activities – reading. Animals – mice. Sports – surfing.

Johnny Castleseed ill. by Diana Thewlis. Houghton, 1985. ISBN 0-395-38355-2 Subj: Sand. Sea and seashore.

Theodore ill. by John M. Larrecq. Parnassus, 1966. Subj: Character traits – appearance. Character traits – kindness. Laundry. Toys – teddy bears.

Theodore's rival ill. by John M. Larrecq. Parnassus, 1971. Subj: Emotions – envy, jealousy. Sibling rivalry. Toys – teddy bears.

Ormsby, Virginia H. *Twenty-one children plus ten* ill. by author. Lippincott, 1971. Subj: Ethnic groups in the U.S. – Mexican-Americans. School.

Ortiz, Simon. *The people shall continue* ill. by Sharol Graves. Childrens Book Pr., 1988. ISBN 0-89239-041-7 Subj: Indians of North America. U.S. history.

Osborn, Lois. *My dad is really something* ill. by Rodney Pate. Albert Whitman, 1983. Subj: Behavior – boasting. Death. Emotions – envy, jealousy. Family life – fathers. Friendship.

Osborne, Valerie. *One big yo to go* ill. by Jiri Tibor Novak. Oxford Univ. Pr., 1981. Subj: Poetry, rhyme.

O'Shell, Marcia. *Alphabet Annie announces an all-American album* by Marcia O'Shell and Susan Purviance; ill. by Ruth Brunner-Strosser. Houghton, 1988. ISBN 0-395-48070-1 Subj: ABC books. City.

Ostheeren, Ingrid. *Jonathan Mouse* ill. by Agnès Mathieu; tr. by Rosemary Lanning. Holt, 1986. ISBN 0-03-005848-1 Subj: Animals – mice. Concepts – color. Magic.

Ostrovsky, Vivian. *Mumps!* ill. by Rose Ostrovsky. Holt, 1978. Subj: Illness.

Otsuka, Yuzo. *Suho and the white horse: a legend of Mongolia* tr. by Ann Herring; ill. by Suekichi Akaba. Viking, 1981. Subj: Animals – horses. Emotions – love. Sports – racing.

Ott, John. *Peter Pumpkin* originated by Peter Coley; ill. by Ivan Chermayeff. Doubleday, 1963. Subj: Holidays – Halloween. Holidays – Thanksgiving. Seasons – fall.

Otto, Margaret Glover. *The little brown horse* ill. by Barbara Cooney. Knopf, 1959. Subj: Animals – cats. Animals – horses. Birds – chickens.

Otto, Svend. *The giant fish and other stories* by Svend Otto S.; tr. from Danish by Joan Tate; ill. by author. Larousse, 1982. Subj: Behavior – growing up. Foreign lands.

Taxi dog by Svend Otto S.; ill. by author. Parents, 1978. Subj: Animals – dogs. Behavior – running away. Careers – taxi drivers.

Our house ill. by Roser Capdevila. Firefly Pr., 1985. ISBN 0-920303-10-2 Subj: City. Format, unusual – board books. Houses.

Over in the meadow: *an old nursery counting rhyme* adapt. and ill. by Paul Galdone. Prentice-Hall, 1986. ISBN 0-13-646654-0 Subj: Animals. Counting. Nursery rhymes.

Over in the meadow ill. by Ezra Jack Keats. Four Winds Pr., 1971. Subj: Animals. Counting. Folk and fairy tales. Poetry, rhyme. Songs.

Overbeck, Cynthia. *Rusty the Irish setter* rev. English text by Cynthia Overbeck; original French text by Anne Marie Pajot; tr. by Dyan Hammarberg; photos. by Antoinette Barrère; ill. by L'Enc Matte. Carolrhoda Books, 1977. Original ed. published under title: Jimmy, le grand chien. Subj: Animals – dogs.

The winds that blow (Thompson, Brenda)

Owen, Annie. *My aunt and the animals* (MacDonald, Elizabeth)

Owens, Mary Beth. *A caribou alphabet* ill. by author. Dog Ear Pr., 1988. ISBN 0-937966-25-8 Subj: ABC books. Animals – reindeer. Poetry, rhyme.

Oxenbury, Helen. *All fall down* ill. by author. Macmillan, 1987. ISBN 0-02-769040-7 Subj: Activities – playing. Babies. Format, unusual – board books. Games.

Beach day ill. by author. Dial Pr., 1982. Subj: Family life. Format, unusual – board books. Sea and seashore. Wordless.

The birthday party ill. by author. Dial Pr., 1983. Subj: Birthdays.

The car trip ill. by author. Dial Pr., 1983. Subj: Automobiles. Behavior – bad day. Behavior – misbehavior.

The checkup ill. by author. Dial Pr., 1983. Subj: Careers – doctors. Health.

Clap hands ill. by author. Macmillan, 1987. ISBN 0-02-769030-X Subj: Activities – playing. Babies. Format, unusual – board books.

The dancing class ill. by author. Dial Pr., 1983. Subj: Activities – dancing.

Dressing ill. by author. Simon & Schuster, 1981. ISBN 0-671-42113-1 Subj: Clothing. Format, unusual – board books.

Eating out ill. by author. Dial Pr., 1983. Subj: Food.

Family ill. by author. Simon and Schuster, 1981. Subj: Family life. Format, unusual – board books.

First day of school ill. by author. Dial Pr., 1983. Subj: Friendship. School.

Friends ill. by author. Simon and Schuster, 1981. Subj: Animals. Format, unusual – board books. Friendship.

Good night, good morning ill. by author. Dial Pr., 1982. Subj: Bedtime. Morning. Wordless.

Grandma and Grandpa ill. by author. Dial Pr., 1984. ISBN 0-8037-0128-4 Subj: Activities – playing. Family life – grandparents.

Helen Oxenbury's ABC of things ill. by author. Watts, 1971. Subj: ABC books.

I can ill. by author. Random House, 1985. ISBN 0-394-87482-X Subj: Activities. Babies. Format, unusual – board books.

I hear ill. by author. Random House, 1985. ISBN 0-394-87481-1 Subj: Babies. Format, unusual – board books. Noise, sounds. Senses – hearing.

I see ill. by author. Random House, 1985. ISBN 0-394-87479-X Subj: Babies. Format, unusual – board books. Senses – seeing.

I touch ill. by author. Random House, 1985. ISBN 0-394-87480-3 Subj: Babies. Format, unusual – board books. Senses – touching.

The important visitor ill. by author. Dial Pr., 1984. ISBN 0-8037-0125-X Subj: Behavior – misbehavior.

Monkey see, monkey do ill. by author. Dial Pr., 1982. Subj: Animals. Wordless. Zoos.

Mother's helper ill. by author. Dial Pr., 1982. Subj: Character traits – helpfulness. Family life – mothers. Wordless.

Numbers of things ill. by author. Watts, 1968. Subj: Counting.

Our dog ill. by author. Dial Pr., 1984. ISBN 0-8037-0127-6 Subj: Activities – walking. Animals – dogs. Family life. Pets.

Pig tale ill. by author. Morrow, 1974. Subj: Animals – pigs. Poetry, rhyme.

Playing ill. by author. Wanderer Books, 1981. Subj: Activities – playing. Babies. Format, unusual – board books. Toys.

The queen and Rosie Randall by Helen Oxenbury from an idea by Jill Butterfield-Campbell; ill. by author. Morrow, 1979. Subj: Foreign lands – England. Games. Parties. Royalty.

Say goodnight ill. by author. Macmillan, 1987. ISBN 0-02-769010-5 Subj: Activities – playing. Babies. Format, unusual – board books. Sleep.

729 curious creatures ill. by author. Harper, 1980. Subj: Animals. Format, unusual – board books. Imagination.

729 merry mix-ups ill. by author. Harper, 1980. Subj: Animals. Format, unusual – board books. Imagination.

729 puzzle people ill. by author. Harper, 1980. Subj: Format, unusual – board books. Imagination.

The shopping trip ill. by author. Dial Pr., 1982. Subj: Format, unusual – board books. Shopping. Wordless.

Tickle, tickle ill. by author. Macmillan, 1987. ISBN 0-02-769020-2 Subj: Activities – playing. Babies. Format, unusual – board books.

Tom and Pippo go shopping ill. by author. Macmillan, 1989. ISBN 0-689-71278-2 Subj: Animals – monkeys. Shopping. Toys.

Tom and Pippo in the garden ill. by author. Macmillan, 1989. ISBN 0-689-71275-8 Subj: Animals – monkeys. Toys.

Tom and Pippo see the moon ill. by author. Macmillan, 1989. ISBN 0-689-71277-4 Subj: Animals – monkeys. Moon. Space and space ships. Toys.

Tom and Pippo's day ill. by author. Macmillan, 1989. ISBN 0-689-71276-6 Subj: Activities. Animals – monkeys. Toys.

Oxford Scientific Films. *Danger colors* ed. by Jennifer Coldrey and Karen Goldie-Morrison. Putnam's, 1986. ISBN 0-399-21341-4 Subj: Behavior – hiding. Concepts – color.

Grey squirrel photos. by George Bernard and John Paling. Putnam's, 1982. Subj: Animals – squirrels. Science.

Hide and seek ed. by Jennifer Coldrey and Karen Goldie-Morrison. Putnam's, 1986. ISBN 0-399-21342-2 Subj: Behavior – hiding. Concepts – color.

Jellyfish and other sea creatures photos. by Peter Parks. Putnam's, 1982. Subj: Animals. Fish. Sea and seashore. Science.

Mosquito photos. by George Bernard and John Cooke. Putnam's, 1982. Subj: Insects – mosquitoes. Science.

The stickleback cycle photos. by David Thompson. Putnam's, 1979. Subj: Fish. Science.

Pace, Elizabeth. *Chris gets ear tubes* ill. by Kathryn Hutton. Gallaudet Univ. Pr., 1987. ISBN 0-930323-36-X Subj: Handicaps – deafness. Hospitals. Illness. Senses – hearing.

Pacheco, Miguel Angel. *Kangaroo* (Sanchez, Jose Louis Garcia)

Pack, Robert. *How to catch a crocodile* ill. by Nola Langner. Knopf, 1964. Subj: Character traits — laziness. Imagination. Poetry, rhyme. Reptiles — alligators, crocodiles.

Then what did you do? ill. by Nola Langner. Macmillan, 1961. Subj: Animals. Cumulative tales. Humor. Poetry, rhyme.

Paek, Min. *Aekyung's dream* ill. by author. Childrens Book Pr., 1989. ISBN 0-89239-042-5 Subj: Character traits — being different. Ethnic groups in the U.S. School.

Page, Eleanor *see* Coerr, Eleanor

Paige, Rob. *Some of my best friends are monsters* ill. by Paul Yalowitz. Bradbury Pr., 1988. ISBN 0-02-769640-5 Subj: Monsters.

Paine, Lauran Bosworth *see* Howard, Elizabeth Fitzgerald

Paine, Penelope Colville. *My way Sally* (Bingham, Mindy)

Pajot, Anne Marie. *Rusty the Irish setter* (Overbeck, Cynthia)

Palacios, Argentina. *This can lick a lollipop* (Rothman, Joel)

Palazzo, Anthony D. *see* Palazzo, Tony

Palazzo, Janet. *Our friend the sun* ill. by Susan Hall. Troll Assoc., 1982. Subj: Science. Sun.

What makes the weather ill. by Paul Harvey. Troll Assoc., 1982. Subj: Weather.

Palazzo, Tony. *Animal babies* ill. by author. Doubleday, 1960. Subj: Animals.

Animals 'round the mulberry bush ill. by author. Doubleday, 1958. Subj: Animals. Nursery rhymes.

Bianco and the New World ill. by author. Viking, 1957. Subj: Animals — donkeys. Circus.

Federico, the flying squirrel ill. by author. Viking, 1951. Subj: Animals — squirrels.

Noah's ark ill. by author. Doubleday, 1955. Subj: Religion — Noah.

Waldo the woodchuck ill. by author. Duell, 1964. Subj: Animals — groundhogs. Holidays — Groundhog Day.

Paleček, Phyllis. *The ugly duckling* (Andersen, H. C. (Hans Christian))

Palmer, Carole. *Why does it fly?* (Arvetis, Chris)

Why is it dark? (Arvetis, Chris)

Palmer, Helen Marion. *A fish out of water* ill. by P. D. Eastman. Random House, 1961. Subj: Fish. Humor.

I was kissed by a seal at the zoo photos. by Lynn Fayman. Random House, 1962. Subj: Animals. Humor. Zoos.

Why I built the boogle house photos. by Lynn Fayman. Random House, 1964. Subj: Animals. Houses. Pets.

Palmer, Mary Babcock. *No-sort-of-animal* ill. by Abner Graboff. Houghton, 1964. Subj: Animals. Behavior — dissatisfaction. Self-concept.

Panek, Dennis. *Ba ba sheep wouldn't go to sleep* ill. by author. Watts, 1988. ISBN 0-531-08376-4 Subj: School. Sleep.

Catastrophe Cat ill. by author. Bradbury Pr., 1978. Subj: Animals — cats. Behavior — carelessness.

Catastrophe Cat at the zoo ill. by author. Bradbury Pr., 1979. Subj: Animals — cats. Wordless. Zoos.

Detective Whoo ill. by author. Bradbury Pr., 1981 ISBN 0-87888-183-2 Subj: Birds — owls. Careers — detectives. Circus. Noise, sounds. Problem solving.

Matilda Hippo has a big mouth ill. by author. Bradbury Pr., 1980. Subj: Animals — hippopotami. Behavior.

Paola, Thomas Anthony *see* De Paola, Tomie

Paola, Tomi De *see* De Paola, Tomie

Papajani, Janet. *Museums* ill. with photos. Children's Pr., 1983. Subj: Museums.

Papas, William. *Taresh the tea planter* ill. by author. Collins-World, 1968. Subj: Character traits — laziness. Foreign lands — India.

Pape, D. L. *see* Pape, Donna Lugg

Pape, Donna Lugg. *Doghouse for sale* ill. by Tom Eaton. Garrard, 1979. Subj: Animals — dogs. Houses.

Snoino mystery ill. by William Hutchinson. Garrard, 1980. Subj: Problem solving.

Where is my little Joey? ill. by Tom Eaton. Garrard, 1978. Subj: Animals — kangaroos.

A paper of pins ill. by Margaret Gordon. Seabury Pr., 1975. Subj: Folk and fairy tales. Money. Songs.

Parenteau, Shirley. *I'll bet you thought I was lost* ill. by Lorna Tomei. Lothrop, 1981. Subj: Behavior — lost.

Paris, Lena. *Mom is single* ill. by Mark Christianson. Childrens Pr., 1980. ISBN 0-516-01477-3 Subj: Divorce. Family life — fathers. Family life — mothers.

Parish, Peggy. *Amelia Bedelia* ill. by Fritz Siebel. Harper, 1963. Subj: Behavior — misunderstanding. Careers — maids. Humor. Language.

Amelia Bedelia and the surprise shower ill. by Fritz Siebel. Harper, 1966. Subj: Behavior — misunderstanding. Careers — maids. Humor. Language. Parties.

Amelia Bedelia goes camping ill. by Lynn Sweat. Greenwillow, 1985. Subj: Behavior – misunderstanding. Careers – maids. Humor. Language. Sports – camping.

Amelia Bedelia helps out ill. by Lynn Sweat. Greenwillow, 1979. Subj: Behavior – misunderstanding. Careers – maids. Humor. Language.

Be ready at eight ill. by Leonard P. Kessler. Macmillan, 1979. Subj: Behavior – forgetfulness. Birthdays.

The cat's burglar ill. by Lynn Sweat. Greenwillow, 1983. Subj: Animals – cats. Crime.

Come back, Amelia Bedelia ill. by Wallace Tripp. Harper, 1971. Subj: Behavior – misunderstanding. Careers – maids. Humor. Language.

Dinosaur time ill. by Arnold Lobel. Harper, 1974. Subj: Dinosaurs. Science.

Good hunting, Blue Sky ill. by James Watts. Harper, 1988. ISBN 0-06-024662-6 Subj: Indians of North America. Sports – hunting.

Good hunting, Little Indian ill. by Leonard Weisgard. Addison-Wesley, 1962. Subj: Indians of North America.

Good work, Amelia Bedelia ill. by Lynn Sweat. Greenwillow, 1976. Subj: Behavior – misunderstanding. Careers – maids. Humor. Language.

Granny and the desperadoes ill. by Steven Kellogg. Macmillan, 1970. Subj: Crime. Family life – grandmothers. Humor.

Granny and the Indians ill. by Brinton Turkle. Macmillan, 1969. Subj: Family life – grandmothers. Humor. Indians of North America.

Granny, the baby and the big gray thing ill. by Lynn Sweat. Macmillan, 1972. Subj: Animals – wolves. Babies. Family life – grandmothers. Humor. Indians of North America.

I can - can you? ill. by Marylin Hafner. Greenwillow, 1984. Set of 4 books: levels 1-4. Subj: Activities. Behavior – growing up. Format, unusual – board books.

Jumper goes to school ill. by Cyndy Szekeres. Simon and Schuster, 1969. Subj: Animals – monkeys. School.

Little Indian ill. by John E. Johnson. Simon and Schuster, 1968. Subj: Indians of North America. Names.

Merry Christmas, Amelia Bedelia ill. by Lynn Sweat. Greenwillow, 1986. ISBN 0-688-06102-8 Subj: Behavior – misunderstanding. Careers – maids. Holidays – Christmas.

Mind your manners ill. by Marylin Hafner. Greenwillow, 1978. Subj: Etiquette.

No more monsters for me! ill. by Marc Simont. Harper, 1981. Subj: Monsters. Pets.

Ootah's lucky day ill. by Mamoru Funai. Harper, 1970. Subj: Eskimos. Sports – hunting.

Play ball, Amelia Bedelia ill. by Wallace Tripp. Harper, 1972. Subj: Behavior – misunderstanding. Careers – maids. Humor. Language. Sports – baseball.

Scruffy ill. by Kelly Oechsli. Harper, 1988. ISBN 0-06-024660-X Subj: Animals – cats. Birthdays. Pets.

Snapping turtle's all wrong day ill. by John E. Johnson. Simon and Schuster, 1970. Subj: Birthdays. Indians of North America.

Teach us, Amelia Bedelia ill. by Lynn Sweat. Greenwillow, 1977. Subj: Behavior – misunderstanding. Careers – maids. Humor. Language. School.

Thank you, Amelia Bedelia ill. by Fritz Siebel. Harper, 1964. Subj: Behavior – misunderstanding. Careers – maids. Humor. Language.

Too many rabbits ill. by Leonard P. Kessler. Macmillan, 1974. Subj: Animals – rabbits.

Zed and the monsters ill. by Paul Galdone. Doubleday, 1979. Subj: Character traits – cleverness. Monsters.

Park, Ruth. *When the wind changed* ill. by Deborah Niland. Coward, 1981. Subj: Character traits – appearance.

Park, W. B. *Bakery business* ill. by author. Little, 1983. Subj: Birthdays. Humor.

The costume party ill. by author. Little, 1983. Subj: Animals. Emotions – loneliness. Parties.

Parke, Margaret B. *Young reader's color-picture dictionary* ill. by Cynthia and Alvin Koehler. Grosset, 1958. Subj: Dictionaries.

Parker, Dorothy D. *Liam's catch* ill. by Robert Andrew Parker. Viking, 1972. Subj: Careers – fishermen. Foreign lands – Ireland. Sports – fishing.

Parker, Kristy. *My dad the magnificent* ill. by Lillian Hoban. Dutton, 1987. ISBN 0-525-44314-2 Subj: Behavior – boasting. Family life – fathers.

Parker, Nancy Winslow. *Bugs* by Nancy Winslow Parker and Joan Richards Wright; ill. by Nancy Winslow Parker. Greenwillow, 1987. ISBN 0-688-06624-0 Subj: Insects. Science.

The Christmas camel ill. by author. Dodd, 1983. Subj: Animals – camels. Holidays – Christmas.

Cooper, the McNallys' big black dog ill. by author. Dodd, 1981. Subj: Animals – dogs. Behavior – misbehavior. Character traits – helpfulness.

The crocodile under Louis Finneberg's bed ill. by author. Dodd, 1978. Subj: Behavior – running away. Behavior – trickery. Reptiles – alligators, crocodiles.

Love from Aunt Betty ill. by author. Dodd, 1983. Subj: Activities – cooking. Monsters.

Love from Uncle Clyde ill. by author. Dodd, 1977. Subj: Animals – hippopotami. Birthdays.

The ordeal of Byron B. Blackbear ill. by author. Dodd, 1979. Subj: Animals – bears. Hibernation. Science.

Poofy loves company ill. by author. Dodd, 1980. Subj: Animals – dogs. Behavior – misbehavior.

Puddums, the Cathcarts' orange cat ill. by author. Atheneum, 1980. Subj: Animals – cats. Behavior.

Parkin, Rex. *The red carpet* ill. by author. Macmillan, 1988, 1948. ISBN 0-02-770010-0 Subj: Hotels. Humor.

Parkinson, Kathy. *The enormous turnip* ill. by adapt. Albert Whitman, 1985. ISBN 0-8075-2062-4 Subj: Behavior – sharing. Cumulative tales. Folk and fairy tales.

Parks, Van Dyke. *Jump!* (Harris, Joel Chandler)

Jump again! (Harris, Joel Chandler)

Parnall, Peter. *Alfalfa Hill* ill. by author. Doubleday, 1975. Subj: Animals. Birds. Seasons – winter. Weather – snow.

Apple tree ill. by author. Macmillan, 1988. ISBN 0-02-770160-3 Subj: Country. Nature. Trees.

The great fish ill. by author. Doubleday, 1973. Subj: Ecology. Fish. Folk and fairy tales. Indians of North America.

Winter barn ill. by author. Macmillan, 1986. ISBN 0-02-770170-0 Subj: Animals. Barns. Seasons – winter.

Parry, Marian. *King of the fish* ill. by author. Macmillan, 1977. Subj: Animals – rabbits. Character traits – cleverness. Fish. Folk and fairy tales. Foreign lands – Korea. Reptiles – turtles, tortoises.

Parsons, Virginia. *Pinocchio and Gepetto* ill. by adapt. McGraw-Hill, 1979. Subj: Folk and fairy tales. Puppets.

Pinocchio and the money tree ill. by adapt. McGraw-Hill, 1979. Subj: Folk and fairy tales. Puppets.

Pinocchio goes on the stage ill. by adapt. McGraw-Hill, 1979. Subj: Folk and fairy tales. Puppets.

Pinocchio plays truant ill. by adapt. McGraw-Hill, 1979. Subj: Folk and fairy tales. Puppets.

Partch, Virgil Franklin. *The Christmas cookie sprinkle snitcher* ill. by author. Windmill Books, 1969. Subj: Crime. Holidays – Christmas. Poetry, rhyme. Rebuses.

The VIP's mistake book ill. by author. Windmill Books, 1970. Subj: Humor. Rebuses.

Partridge, Jenny. *Colonel Grunt* ill. by author. Holt, 1982. Subj: Animals.

Grandma Snuffles ill. by author. Holt, 1983. Subj: Animals. Clothing.

Hopfellow ill. by author. Holt, 1982. Subj: Animals. Boats, ships. Frogs and toads. Problem solving.

Mr. Squint ill. by author. Holt, 1982. Subj: Animals. Problem solving.

Peterkin Pollensnuff ill. by author. Holt, 1982. Subj: Animals. Character traits – helpfulness. Problem solving.

Parvathi, Thampi. *Moon-uncle, moon-uncle* (Cassedy, Sylvia)

Pasley, L. *The adventures of Madalene and Louisa* by L. and M. S. Pasley; ill. by authors. Random House, 1980. Subj: Children as authors. Children as illustrators. Insects.

Pasley, M. S. *The adventures of Madalene and Louisa* (Pasley, L.)

Patent, Dorothy Hinshaw. *Babies!* photos. by author. Holiday House, 1988. ISBN 0-8234-0685-7 Subj: Babies.

Baby horses photos. by William Muñoz. Dodd, 1985. ISBN 0-396-08629-2 Subj: Animals – horses.

Maggie, a sheep dog photos. by William Muñoz. Dodd, 1986. ISBN 0-396-08617-9 Subj: Animals – dogs. Animals – sheep.

Paterson, Andrew Barton. *The man from Ironbark* ill. by Quentin Hole. Collins-World, 1975. Subj: Character traits – cleverness. Poetry, rhyme.

Mulga Bill's bicycle ill. by Kilmeny and Deborah Niland. Parents, 1975. Subj: Animals – horses. Foreign lands – Australia. Poetry, rhyme. Sports – bicycling.

Waltzing Matilda ill. by Desmund Digby. Holt, 1970. Subj: Foreign lands – Australia. Songs.

Paterson, Banjo *see* Paterson, Andrew Barton

Paterson, Bettina. *Bun and Mrs. Tubby* ill. by author. Watts, 1987. ISBN 0-531-08300-4 Subj: Activities – baby-sitting. Animals – elephants.

Bun's birthday ill. by author. Watts, 1988. ISBN 0-531-08336-5 Subj: Animals – elephants. Behavior – sharing. Birthdays. Parties.

Paterson, Diane. *The bathtub ocean* ill. by author. Dial Pr., 1979. Subj: Activities – bathing. Imagination.

Eat ill. by author. Dial Pr., 1975. Subj: Food. Humor.

Hey, cowboy! ill. by author. Knopf, 1983. Subj: Family life – grandfathers. Sibling rivalry.

If I were a toad ill. by author. Dial Pr., 1977. Subj: Animals. Behavior – wishing. Participation.

Smile for auntie ill. by author. Dial Pr., 1976. Subj: Humor.

Soap and suds ill. by author. Knopf, 1984. Subj: Activities – working. Behavior – misbehavior.

Wretched Rachel ill. by author. Dial Pr., 1978. Subj: Behavior. Emotions – love. Family life.

Paterson, Katherine. *The crane wife* (Yagawa, Sumiko)

The tongue-cut sparrow (Ishii, Momoko)

Paton Walsh, Gillian Honoinne Mary *see* Walsh, Jill Paton

Paton Walsh, Jill *see* Walsh, Jill Paton

Patrick, Gloria. *This is...* ill. by Joan Hanson. Carolrhoda Books, 1970. Subj: Cumulative tales. Participation. Poetry, rhyme.

Patterson, Francine. *Koko's kitten* photos. by Ronald H. Cohn. Scholastic, 1985. ISBN 0-590-33811-0 Subj: Animals – cats. Animals – gorillas. Death.

Patterson, Geoffrey. *A pig's tale* ill. by author. Dutton, 1983. ISBN 0-233-97477-6 Subj: Animals – pigs. Behavior – running away. Farms.

Patterson, José. *Mazal-Tov: a Jewish wedding* photos. by Liba Taylor. David & Charles, 1988. ISBN 0-241-12269-4 Subj: Jewish culture. Weddings.

Patterson, Lillie. *Haunted houses on Halloween* ill. by Doug Cushman. Garrard, 1979. Subj: Holidays – Halloween. Houses.

Patterson, Pat. *Hickory dickory duck: a book of very funny rhymes and picture puzzles* by Pat Patterson and Joe Weissmann. Greey de Pencier Books, 1982. Subj: Games. Nursery rhymes.

Patz, Nancy. *Gina Farina and the Prince of Mintz* ill. by author. Harcourt, 1986. ISBN 0-15-230815-6 Subj: Activities – traveling. Character traits – meanness. Character traits – persistence. Royalty. Theater.

Moses supposes his toeses are roses and 7 other silly old rhymes ill. by author. Harcourt, 1983. Subj: Poetry, rhyme.

Pumpernickel tickle and mean green cheese ill. by author. Watts, 1978. Subj: Animals – elephants. Behavior – forgetfulness. Humor. Shopping. Tongue twisters.

Paul, Anthony. *The tiger who lost his stripes* ill. by Michael Foreman. Harcourt, 1982. Subj: Animals – tigers. Character traits – cleverness. Forest, woods.

Paul, Jan S. *Hortense* ill. by Madelaine Gill Linden. Harper, 1984. ISBN 0-690-04371-6 Subj: Animals. Behavior – lost. Farms.

Paul, Korky. *Pop-up numbers #1* (Marshall, Ray)

Pop-up numbers #2 (Marshall, Ray)

Pop-up numbers #3 (Marshall, Ray)

Pop-up numbers #4 (Marshall, Ray)

Paul, Sherry. *2-B and the rock 'n roll band* ill. by Bob Miller. Children's Pr., 1981. Subj: Character traits – helpfulness. Robots.

2-B and the space visitor ill. by Bob Miller. Children's Pr., 1981. Subj: Holidays – Halloween. Robots. Space and space ships.

Pavey, Peter. *I'm Taggarty Toad* ill. by author. Bradbury Pr., 1980. Subj: Behavior – boasting. Frogs and toads. Imagination.

One dragon's dream ill. by author. Bradbury Pr., 1979. Subj: Counting. Dragons. Dreams. Poetry, rhyme.

Paxton, Tom. *Æsop's fables* (Æsop)

Jennifer's rabbit ill. by Donna Ayers. Morrow, 1988. ISBN 0-688-07432-4 Subj: Behavior – running away. Dreams. Poetry, rhyme.

Payne, Emmy. *Katy no-pocket* ill. by Hans Augusto Rey. Houghton, 1944. Subj: Animals – kangaroos. Clothing. Problem solving.

Payne, Joan Balfour. *The stable that stayed* ill. by author. Ariel, 1952. Subj: Animals. Careers – artists. Country.

Payne, Sherry Neuwirth. *A contest* ill. by Jeff Kyle. Carolrhoda, 1982. ISBN 0-87614-176-9 Subj: Character traits – being different. Handicaps. School.

Peaceable kingdom: *the Shaker abecedarius* ill. by Alice and Martin Provensen. Viking, 1978. Subj: ABC books. Animals. Poetry, rhyme.

Pearce, Philippa. *Emily's own elephant* ill. by John Lawrence. Greenwillow, 1988. ISBN 0-688-07679-3 Subj: Animals – elephants. Family life. Pets.

Pearson, Susan. *Baby and the bear* ill. by Nancy Carlson. Viking, 1987. ISBN 0-670-81299-4 Subj: Format, unusual – board books. Toys – teddy bears.

Everybody knows that! ill. by Diane Paterson. Dial Pr., 1978. Subj: Friendship. School.

Happy birthday, Grampie ill. by Ronald Himler. Dial Pr., 1987. ISBN 0-8037-3457-3 Subj: Birthdays. Family life – grandfathers.

Karin's Christmas walk ill. by Trinka Hakes Noble. Dial Pr., 1980. Subj: Family life. Holidays – Christmas.

My favorite time of year ill. by John Wallner. Harper, 1988. ISBN 0-06-024682-0 Subj: Seasons.

Saturday, I ran away ill. by Susan Jeschke. Harper, 1981. ISBN 0-397-31958-4 Subj: Behavior – running away. Family life.

That's enough for one day! ill. by Kay Chorao. Dial Pr., 1977. Subj: Activities – playing. Activities – reading.

When baby went to bed ill. by Nancy Carlson. Viking, 1987. ISBN 0-670-81300-1 Subj: Babies. Bedtime. Counting. Format, unusual – board books.

Pearson, Tracey Campbell. *A apple pie* ill. by author. Dial Pr., 1986. ISBN 0-8037-0252-3 Subj: ABC books. Format, unusual. Poetry, rhyme.

Sing a song of sixpence ill. by author. Dial Pr., 1985. Subj: Behavior – misbehavior. Humor. Nursery rhymes.

The storekeeper ill. by author. Dial Pr., 1988. ISBN 0-8037-0370-8 Subj: Animals – cats. Careers – storekeepers. Stores.

The peasant's pea patch ill. by Robert M. Quackenbush; tr. by Guy Daniels. Delacorte Pr., 1971. Subj: Birds – cranes. Folk and fairy tales. Foreign lands – Russia.

Peavy, Linda. *Allison's grandfather* ill. by Ronald Himler. Scribner's, 1981. Subj: Death. Family life – grandfathers.

Peck, Richard. *Monster night at Grandma's house* ill. by Don Freeman. Viking, 1977. Subj: Bedtime. Family life – grandmothers. Monsters. Night.

Peck, Robert Newton. *Hamilton* ill. by Laura Lydecker. Little, 1976. Subj: Animals – pigs. Animals – wolves. Farms. Poetry, rhyme.

Pedersen, Judy. *The tiny patient* ill. by author. Knopf, 1989. ISBN 0-394-80170-9 Subj: Birds. Character traits – kindness to animals. Illness.

Peek, Merle. *The balancing act: a counting book* ill. by author. Clarion, 1987. ISBN 0-89919-458-3 Subj: Animals. Animals – elephants. Counting. Music. Poetry, rhyme. Songs.

Mary wore her red dress and Henry wore his green sneakers ill. by adapt. Clarion, 1985. ISBN 0-89919-324-2 Subj: Animals. Animals – bears. Birthdays. Concepts – color. Songs.

Peet, Bill. *The ant and the elephant* ill. by author. Little, 1972. Subj: Animals. Animals – elephants. Character traits – helpfulness. Character traits – selfishness. Cumulative tales. Insects – ants.

Big bad Bruce ill. by author. Houghton, 1977. Subj: Animals – bears. Behavior – bullying. Forest, woods. Humor. Witches.

Buford, the little bighorn ill. by author. Houghton, 1967. Subj: Animals – sheep. Character traits – individuality. Humor. Sports – hunting. Sports – skiing.

The caboose who got loose ill. by author. Houghton, 1971. Subj: Behavior – dissatisfaction. Ecology. Trains.

Chester the worldly pig ill. by author. Houghton, 1965. Subj: Animals – pigs. Circus. Humor. World.

Countdown to Christmas ill. by author. Houghton, 1972. Subj: Holidays – Christmas. Humor. Magic. Progress.

Cowardly Clyde ill. by author. Houghton, 1979. Subj: Animals – horses. Character traits – bravery. Humor. Knights.

Cyrus the unsinkable sea serpent ill. by author. Houghton, 1975. Subj: Character traits – helpfulness. Monsters. Mythical creatures. Sea and seashore.

Eli ill. by author. Houghton, 1978. Subj: Animals – lions. Birds – vultures. Friendship. Humor.

Ella ill. by author. Houghton, 1964. Subj: Animals – elephants. Behavior – lost. Character traits – conceit. Circus. Poetry, rhyme.

Encore for Eleanor ill. by author. Houghton, 1981. Subj: Animals – elephants. Art.

Farewell to Shady Glade ill. by author. Houghton, 1966. Subj: Animals. Ecology. Progress.

Fly, Homer, fly ill. by author. Houghton, 1969. Subj: Birds – pigeons. City. Ecology.

The gnats of knotty pine ill. by author. Houghton, 1975. Subj: Animals. Ecology. Insects – gnats. Sports – hunting.

How Droofus the dragon lost his head ill. by author. Houghton, 1971. Subj: Dragons. Knights. Royalty.

Hubert's hair-raising adventures ill. by author. Houghton, 1959. Subj: Animals – lions. Careers – barbers. Humor. Poetry, rhyme.

Huge Harold ill. by author. Houghton, 1961. Subj: Animals – rabbits. Character traits – kindness to animals. Concepts – size. Humor. Poetry, rhyme.

Jennifer and Josephine ill. by author. Houghton, 1967. Subj: Animals – cats. Automobiles. Humor.

Jethro and Joel were a troll ill. by author. Houghton, 1987. ISBN 0-395-43081-X Subj: Humor. Magic. Mythical creatures. Trolls.

Kermit the hermit ill. by author. Houghton, 1965. Subj: Behavior – greed. Crustacea. Humor. Poetry, rhyme. Sea and seashore.

The kweeks of Kookatumdee ill. by author. Houghton, 1985. ISBN 0-395-37902-4 Subj: Activities – flying. Behavior – greed. Birds. Poetry, rhyme.

The luckiest one of all ill. by author. Houghton, 1982. Subj: Behavior – dissatisfaction. Emotions – envy, jealousy. Poetry, rhyme.

Merle the high flying squirrel ill. by author. Houghton, 1974. Subj: Activities – flying. Animals – squirrels. Humor. Kites. Trees.

No such things ill. by author. Houghton, 1983. ISBN 0-395-33888-3 Subj: Animals. Mythical creatures. Poetry, rhyme.

Pamela Camel ill. by author. Houghton, 1984. Subj: Animals – camels. Behavior – running away. Self-concept.

The pinkish, purplish, bluish egg ill. by author. Houghton, 1963. Subj: Birds. Birds – doves. Eggs. Mythical creatures. Poetry, rhyme. Violence, anti-violence.

Randy's dandy lions ill. by author. Houghton, 1964. Subj: Animals – lions. Circus. Humor. Poetry, rhyme.

Smokey ill. by author. Houghton, 1962. Subj: Old age. Poetry, rhyme. Trains.

The spooky tail of Prewitt Peacock ill. by author. Houghton, 1973. Subj: Birds – peacocks, peahens. Character traits – being different. Character traits – individuality.

The Whingdingdilly ill. by author. Houghton, 1970. Subj: Animals – dogs. Behavior – dissatisfaction. Character traits – optimism. Witches.

The wump world ill. by author. Houghton, 1970. Subj: Ecology. Progress. Space and space ships.

Zella, Zack, and Zodiac ill. by author. Houghton, 1986. ISBN 0-395-40567-5 Subj: Animals – zebras. Behavior – needing someone. Birds – ostriches. Poetry, rhyme.

Peet, Georgia. *Be quite quiet beside the lake* (Koenner, Alfred)

High flies the ball (Koenner, Alfred)

Peet, William Bartlett *see* Peet, Bill

Pelham, David. *Worms wiggle* ill. by Michael Foreman. Simon & Schuster, 1989. ISBN 0-671-67218-5 Subj: Activities. Animals. Format, unusual – toy and movable books.

Pellowski, Anne. *The nine crying dolls: a story from Poland* ill. by Charles Mikolaycak. Philomel, 1980. ISBN 0-399-61162-2 Subj: Folk and fairy tales. Foreign lands – Poland. Toys – dolls.

Stairstep farm: Anna Rose's story ill. by Wendy Watson. Putnam's, 1981. Subj: Behavior – growing up. Family life. Farms.

Pellowski, Michael. *Clara joins the circus* ill. by True Kelley. Parents, 1981. Subj: Animals – bulls, cows. Circus. Clowns, jesters.

Pender, Lydia. *Barnaby and the horses* ill. by Alie Evers. Abelard-Schuman, 1961. Subj: Animals – horses. Behavior – carelessness. Country.

Pendery, Rosemary. *A home for Hopper* ill. by Robert M. Quackenbush. Morrow, 1971. Subj: Frogs and toads.

The penguin ill. by Norman Weaver. Rourke, 1983. Subj: Birds – penguins.

Pène Du Bois, William *see* Du Bois, William Pène

Penn, Ruth Bonn *see* Clifford, Eth

Peppé, Rodney. *The alphabet book* ill. by author. Four Winds Pr., 1968. Subj: ABC books.

Cat and mouse: a book of rhymes: comp. and ill. by Rodney Peppé. Holt, 1973. Subj: Animals – cats. Animals – mice. Nursery rhymes. Poetry, rhyme.

Circus numbers: a counting book ill. by author. Delacorte Pr., 1969. Subj: Circus. Counting.

Hey riddle diddle ill. by author. Holt, 1971. Subj: Nursery rhymes. Poetry, rhyme. Riddles.

The kettleship pirates ill. by author. Lothrop, 1983. Subj: Animals – mice. Birthdays. Boats, ships. Imagination. Pirates.

Little circus ill. by author. Viking, 1984. Subj: Animals. Circus. Format, unusual – board books. Toys.

Little dolls ill. by author. Viking, 1984. Subj: Clothing. Format, unusual – board books. Toys.

Little games ill. by author. Viking, 1984. Subj: Format, unusual – board books. Games. Toys.

Little numbers ill. by author. Viking, 1984. Subj: Counting. Format, unusual – board books. Toys.

Little wheels ill. by author. Viking, 1984. Subj: Automobiles. Format, unusual – board books. Toys. Trucks.

The mice and the clockwork bus ill. by author. Lothrop, 1987. ISBN 0-688-06543-0 Subj: Animals – mice. Animals – rats. Buses.

The mice and the flying basket ill. by author. Lothrop, 1985. ISBN 0-688-04252-X Subj: Activities – ballooning. Animals – mice. Animals – rats. Behavior – greed.

The mice who lived in a shoe ill. by author. Lothrop, 1982. Subj: Animals – mice. Houses.

Odd one out ill. by author. Viking, 1974. Subj: Concepts. Games.

Rodney Peppé's puzzle book ill. by author. Viking, 1977. Subj: Concepts. Games.

Perera, Lydia. *Frisky* ill. by Oscar Liebman. Random House, 1966. Subj: City. Merry-go-rounds.

Peretz, Isaac Loeb. *The magician* (Shulevitz, Uri)

Perez, Carla. *Your turn, doctor* (Robison, Deborah)

Perkins, Al. *The digging-est dog* ill. by Eric Gurney. Random House, 1967. Subj: Activities – digging. Animals – dogs. Poetry, rhyme.

Don and Donna go to bat ill. by Barney Tobey. Random House, 1968. Subj: Sports – baseball. Twins.

The ear book ill. by William O'Brian. Random House, 1968. Subj: Anatomy. Poetry, rhyme. Senses – hearing.

Hand, hand, fingers, thumb ill. by Eric Gurney. Random House, 1969. Subj: Anatomy. Poetry, rhyme.

King Midas and the golden touch ill. by Harold Berson. Random House, 1970. Subj: Behavior – greed. Behavior – wishing. Royalty.

The nose book ill. by Roy McKie. Random House, 1970. Subj: Anatomy. Poetry, rhyme. Senses – smelling.

Tubby and the lantern ill. by Rowland B. Wilson. Random House, 1971. Subj: Animals – elephants. Birthdays. Foreign lands – China. Pirates.

Tubby and the Poo-Bah ill. by Rowland B. Wilson. Random House, 1972. Subj: Animals – elephants. Boats, ships.

Perrault, Charles. *Cinderella* adapt. by John Fowles; ill. by Sheilah Beckett. Little, 1974. Adapt. from Perrault's Cendrillon of 1697. Subj: Folk and fairy tales. Royalty. Sibling rivalry.

Cinderella ill. by Paul Galdone. McGraw-Hill, 1978. Subj: Folk and fairy tales. Royalty. Sibling rivalry.

Cinderella tr. and ill. by Diane Goode. Knopf, 1988. ISBN 0-394-99603-8 Subj: Folk and fairy tales. Royalty. Sibling rivalry.

Cinderella retold by Amy Ehrlich; ill. by Susan Jeffers. Dial Pr., 1985. ISBN 0-8037-0206-X Subj: Folk and fairy tales. Royalty. Sibling rivalry.

Cinderella ill. by Phil Smith. Troll Assoc., 1979. Subj: Folk and fairy tales. Royalty. Sibling rivalry.

Cinderella: or, the little glass slipper ill. by Marcia Brown. Scribner's, 1954. Subj: Caldecott award book. Folk and fairy tales. Royalty. Sibling rivalry.

Cinderella: the story of Rossini's opera adapt. by Alan Blyth; ill. by Emanuele Luzzati. Watts, 1982. Subj: Folk and fairy tales. Music. Royalty. Sibling rivalry.

Puss in boots a free translation from the French; ill. by Marcia Brown. Scribner's, 1952. Subj: Animals – cats. Caldecott award honor book. Character traits – cleverness. Folk and fairy tales. Royalty.

Puss in boots adapt. and ill. by Lorinda Bryan Cauley. Harcourt, 1986. ISBN 0-15-264227-7 Subj: Animals – cats. Character traits – cleverness. Folk and fairy tales. Royalty.

Puss in boots retold by Kurt Baumann; ill. by Jean Claverie. Faber, 1982. Subj: Animals – cats. Character traits – cleverness. Folk and fairy tales. Royalty.

Puss in boots adapt. and ill. by Hans Fischer. Harcourt, 1959. Subj: Animals – cats. Character traits – cleverness. Folk and fairy tales. Royalty.

Puss in boots ill. by Paul Galdone. Seabury Pr., 1976. Subj: Animals – cats. Character traits – cleverness. Folk and fairy tales. Royalty.

Puss in boots adapt. by Arthur Luce Klein; ill. by Julia Noonan. Doubleday, 1970. Adaptation of Le Chat botté. Subj: Animals – cats. Character traits – cleverness. Folk and fairy tales. Foreign lands – France. Royalty.

Puss in boots ill. by William Stobbs. McGraw-Hill, 1975. A retelling of Maître Chat. Subj: Animals – cats. Character traits – cleverness. Folk and fairy tales. Royalty.

Puss in boots ill. by Barry Wilkinson. Collins-World, 1969. Subj: Animals – cats. Character traits – cleverness. Folk and fairy tales. Royalty.

Puss in boots: the story of a sneaky cat adapt. and ill. by Tony Ross. Delacorte Pr., 1981. Subj: Animals – cats. Character traits – cleverness. Folk and fairy tales. Royalty.

The sleeping beauty tr. and ill. by David Walker. Crowell, 1977. Subj: Folk and fairy tales.

Tom Thumb

Perrine, Mary. *Salt boy* ill. by Leonard Weisgard. Houghton, 1968. Subj: Indians of North America.

Perry, Patricia. *Mommy and daddy are divorced* by Patricia Perry and Marietta Lynch; ill. by authors. Dial Pr., 1978. Subj: Divorce.

Peters, Lisa W. *The sun, the wind and the rain* ill. by Ted Rand. Holt, 1988. ISBN 0-8050-0699-0 Subj: Nature. Science. Sea and seashore. Weather.

Peters, Sharon. *Animals at night* ill. by Paul Harvey. Troll Assoc., 1983. Subj: Animals. Night.

Fun at camp ill. by Irene Trivas. Troll Assoc., 1980. Subj: Sports – camping.

Happy birthday ill. by Paul Harvey. Troll Assoc., 1980. Subj: Birthdays.

Happy Jack ill. by Paul Harvey. Troll Assoc., 1980. Subj: Careers – waiters, waitresses.

Messy Mark ill. by Bill Morrison. Troll Assoc., 1980. Subj: Character traits – cleanliness.

Puppet show ill. by Alana Lee. Troll Assoc., 1980. Subj: Puppets.

Ready, get set, go! ill. by Irene Trivas. Troll Assoc., 1980. Subj: Animals – rabbits.

Stop that rabbit ill. by Don Silverstein. Troll Assoc., 1980. Subj: Animals – rabbits.

Trick or treat Halloween ill. by Susan Hall. Troll Assoc., 1980. Subj: Holidays – Halloween.

Petersen, David. *Helicopters* ill. with photos. Children's Pr., 1983. Subj: Helicopters.

Submarines ill. with photos. Children's Pr., 1984. Subj: Boats, ships.

Petersham, Maud. *An American ABC* by Maud and Miska Petersham; ill. by authors. Macmillan, 1941. Subj: ABC books. Caldecott award honor book. U.S. history.

The box with red wheels by Maud and Miska Petersham; ill. by authors. Macmillan, 1949. Subj: Animals. Babies. Farms.

The Christ Child by Maud and Miska Petersham; ill. by authors. Doubleday, 1931. Subj: Religion.

The circus baby by Maud and Miska Petersham; ill. by authors. Macmillan, 1950. Subj: Animals – elephants. Circus. Clowns, jesters. Etiquette.

Off to bed by Maud and Miska Petersham; ill. by authors. Macmillan, 1954. Subj: Bedtime.

The rooster crows by Maud and Miska Petersham; ill. by authors. Macmillan, 1945. Subj: Caldecott award book. Nursery rhymes.

Petersham, Miska. *An American ABC* (Petersham, Maud)

The box with red wheels (Petersham, Maud)

The Christ Child (Petersham, Maud)

The circus baby (Petersham, Maud)

Off to bed (Petersham, Maud)

The rooster crows (Petersham, Maud)

Petersham, Petrezselyem Mikaly see Petersham, Miska

Peterson, Esther Allen. *Frederick's alligator* ill. by Susanna Natti. Crown, 1979. Subj: Animals. Behavior – boasting. Reptiles – alligators, crocodiles.

Penelope gets wheels ill. by Susanna Natti. Crown, 1982. ISBN 0-517-54467-9 Subj: Birthdays. Sports.

Peterson, Franklynn. *I can use tools* (Kesselman, Judi R.)

Peterson, Hans. *Erik and the Christmas horse* tr. from the Swedish by Christine Hyatt; ill. by Ilon Wikland. Lothrop, 1970. Translation of Magnus, Lindberg och hästen Mari. Subj: Character traits – kindness. Foreign lands – Sweden. Holidays – Christmas.

Peterson, Jeanne Whitehouse. *Sometimes I dream horses* ill. by Eleanor Schick. Harper, 1987. ISBN 0-06-024713-4 Subj: Animals – horses. Family life – grandmothers.

That is that ill. by Deborah Kogan Ray. Harper, 1979. Subj: Divorce.

Peterson, Scott K. *What's your name? jokes about names* ill. by Joan Hanson. Lerner, 1987. ISBN 0-8225-0994-6 Subj: Names. Riddles.

Petie, Haris. *Billions of bugs* ill. by author. Prentice-Hall, 1975. Subj: Counting. Insects. Poetry, rhyme.

The seed the squirrel dropped ill. by author. Prentice-Hall, 1976. Subj: Activities – cooking. Cumulative tales. Food. Plants. Poetry, rhyme. Seeds. Trees.

Petras, John W. *Learning about sex* (Aho, Jennifer J.)

Petrides, Heidrun. *Hans and Peter* ill. by author. Harcourt, 1962. Subj: Activities – working. Character traits – completing things.

Petrie, Catherine. *Hot Rod Harry* ill. by Paul Sharp. Children's Pr., 1982. Subj: Automobiles.

Joshua James likes trucks ill. by Jerry Warshaw. Childrens Pr., 1982. ISBN 0-516-43525-6 Subj: Toys. Trucks.

Petty, Kate. *Being careful with strangers* ill. by Lisa Kopper. Watts, 1988. ISBN 0-531-17107-8 Subj: Behavior – talking to strangers. Safety.

Dinosaurs ill. by Alan Baker. Watts, 1984. ISBN 0-531-04811-X Subj: Dinosaurs.

On a plane ill. by Aline Riquier. Watts, 1984. ISBN 0-531-04716-4 Subj: Activities – traveling. Airplanes, airports. Foreign lands – England.

Petty, Roberta see Petie, Haris

Pevear, Richard. *Mister cat-and-a-half* ill. by Robert Rayevsky. Macmillan, 1986. ISBN 0-02-773910-4 Subj: Animals. Animals – cats. Animals – foxes. Folk and fairy tales.

Our king has horns! ill. by Robert Rayevsky. Macmillan, 1987. ISBN 0-02-773920-1 Subj: Behavior – secrets. Folk and fairy tales. Foreign lands – Russia. Royalty.

The pup grew up! (Marshak, Samuel)

Peyo. *The Smurfs and their woodland friends* ill. by author. Random House, 1983. Subj: Animals. Forest, woods. Insects.

What do smurfs do all day? ill. by author. Random House, 1983. Subj: Activities. Poetry, rhyme.

Pfister, Marcus. *The sleepy owl* tr. from German by J. J. Curle; ill. by author. Holt, 1986. ISBN 0-03-008023-1 Subj: Birds – owls. Friendship. Sleep.

Where is my friend? ill. by author. Holt, 1986. ISBN 0-03-008033-9 Subj: Animals – porcupines. Format, unusual – board books. Friendship.

Pfloog, Jan. *Kittens* ill. by author. Random House, 1977. Subj: Animals – cats. Format, unusual – board books.

Puppies ill. by author. Random House, 1979. Subj: Animals – dogs. Format, unusual – board books.

Phang, Ruth. *Patchwork tales* (Roth, Susan L.)

Phillips, David Graham see Graham, John

Phillips, Jack see Sandburg, Carl

Phillips, Joan. *Lucky bear* ill. by J. P. Miller. Random House, 1986. ISBN 0-394-97987-7 Subj: Toys – teddy bears.

My new boy ill. by Lynn Munsinger. Random House, 1986. ISBN 0-394-98277-0 Subj: Animals – dogs. Pets.

Peek-a-boo! I see you! ill. by Kathy Wilburn. Putnam's, 1983. ISBN 0-488-03092-6 Subj: Animals – bears. Format, unusual – board books. Poetry, rhyme.

Phillips, Louis. *The brothers Wrong and Wrong Again* ill. by J. Winslow Higginbottom. McGraw-Hill, 1979. Subj: Character traits – foolishness. Dragons. Middle ages. War.

The upside down riddle book ill. by Beau Gardner. Lothrop, 1982. Subj: Poetry, rhyme. Riddles.

Phillips, Mark see Wilson, Barbara

Phillips, Mildred. *The sign in Mendel's window* ill. by Margot Zemach. Macmillan, 1985. ISBN 0-02-774600-3 Subj: Folk and fairy tales. Jewish culture.

Phleger, Fred B. *Ann can fly* ill. by Robert Lopshire. Random House, 1959. Subj: Activities – flying. Airplanes, airports.

Off to the races by Fred B. and Marjorie Phleger; ill. by Leo Summers. Random House, 1968. Subj: Sports – bicycling. Sports – racing.

Red Tag comes back ill. by Arnold Lobel. Harper, 1961. Subj: Fish. Science.

The whales go by ill. by Paul Galdone. Random House, 1959. Subj: Animals – whales. Science.

You will live under the sea by Fred B. and Marjorie Phleger; ill. by Ward Brackett. Random House, 1966. Subj: Science. Sea and seashore.

Phleger, Marjorie. *Off to the races* (Phleger, Fred B.)

You will live under the sea (Phleger, Fred B.)

Phumla. *Nomi and the magic fish: a story from Africa* ill. by Carole Byard. Doubleday, 1973. Subj: Children as authors. Folk and fairy tales. Foreign lands – Africa. Magic.

Piatti, Celestino. *Celestino Piatti's animal ABC* English text by Jon Reid; ill. by author. Atheneum, 1966. Subj: ABC books. Animals. Poetry, rhyme.

The happy owls ill. by author. Atheneum, 1964. Subj: Birds – owls. Character traits – optimism. Emotions – happiness.

Pickett, Carla. *Calvin Crocodile and the terrible noise* ill. by Carroll Dolezal. Steck-Vaughn, 1972. Subj: Noise, sounds. Reptiles – alligators, crocodiles.

Piecewicz, Ann Thomas. *See what I caught!* ill. by Perf Coxeter. Prentice-Hall, 1974. Subj: Pets.

Pieńkowski, Jan. *Colors* ill. by author. Harvey House, 1974. Subj: Concepts – color.

Easter ill. by author. Knopf, 1989. ISBN 0-394-82455-5 Subj: Holidays – Easter. Religion.

Farm ill. by author. David & Charles, 1985. ISBN 0-434-95651-1 Subj: Animals. Farms.

Homes ill. by author. Messner, 1983. Subj: Animals. Houses.

Meg and Mog (Nicoll, Helen)

Meg at sea (Nicoll, Helen)

Meg on the moon (Nicoll, Helen)

Meg's eggs (Nicoll, Helen)

Numbers ill. by author. Harvey House, 1975. Subj: Counting.

Shapes ill. by author. Harvey House, 1975. Subj: Concepts – shape.

Sizes ill. by author. Messner, 1983. Orig. pub. by Harvey House, 1974. Subj: Concepts – size.

Time ill. by author. Messner, 1983. Subj: Clocks. Time.

Weather ill. by author. Messner, 1983. Subj: Weather.

Zoo ill. by author. David & Charles, 1985. ISBN 0-434-95652-X Subj: Animals. Zoos.

Pierce, Jack. *The freight train book* photos. by author. Carolrhoda, 1980. Subj: Trains.

Piers, Helen. *Grasshopper and butterfly* ill. by Pauline Baynes. McGraw-Hill, 1975. Subj: Hibernation. Insects – butterflies, caterpillars. Insects – grasshoppers.

A Helen Piers animal book photos. by author. Watts, 1968. ISBN 0-531-01852-0 Subj: Animals. Animals – monkeys. Birds – geese. Birds – owls.

The mouse book photos. by author. Watts, 1968. Subj: Animals – mice.

Puppy's ABC photos. by author. Oxford Univ. Pr., 1987. ISBN 0-19-520606-1 Subj: ABC books. Animals – dogs.

Pike, Norman. *The peach tree* ill. by Robin and Patricia DeWitt. Stemmer House, 1983. Subj: Activities – gardening. Trees.

Pincus, Harriet. *Minna and Pippin* ill. by author. Farrar, 1972. Subj: Toys – dolls.

Pinkwater, Daniel Manus. *Aunt Lulu* ill. by author. Macmillan, 1988. ISBN 0-02-774661-5 Subj: Animals – dogs. Careers – librarians.

The bear's picture ill. by author. Dutton, 1984. Subj: Animals – bears. Art. Careers – artists. Concepts – color.

The big orange splot ill. by author. Hastings, 1977. Subj: Activities – painting. Character traits – individuality. Concepts – color. Houses.

Devil in the drain ill. by author. Dutton, 1984. Subj: Character traits – curiosity. Devil.

The Frankenbagel monster ill. by author. Dutton, 1986. ISBN 0-525-44260-X Subj: Careers – bakers. Monsters.

I was a second grade werewolf ill. by author. Dutton, 1983. Subj: Imagination. Monsters.

Pickle creature ill. by author. Four Winds Pr., 1979. Subj: Imagination – imaginary friends.

Roger's umbrella ill. by James Marshall. Dutton, 1982. Subj: Animals – cats. Umbrellas.

Tooth-gnasher superflash ill. by author. Four Winds Pr., 1981. Subj: Automobiles. Imagination.

Piper, Watty. *The little engine that could* ill. by George and Doris Hauman. Platt, 1961. Retold from The pony engine, by Mable C. Bragg. This version first pub. in 1955. Subj: Character traits – perseverance. Trains.

Mother Goose rhymes (Mother Goose)

Pitcher, Caroline. *Animals* ill. by Louise Nevett. Watts, 1983. Subj: Activities. Animals. Wordless.

Cars and boats ill. by Louise Nevett. Watts, 1983. Subj: Activities. Automobiles. Boats, ships. Wordless.

Pitt, Valerie. *Let's find out about the city* ill. by Sheila Granda. Watts, 1968. Subj: City.

Let's find out about the family ill. by Gloria Kamen. Watts, 1970. Subj: Family life.

Pittaway, Margaret. *The rainforest children* ill. by Heather Philpott. Oxford Univ. Pr., 1980. Subj: Behavior – running away. Behavior – seeking better things. Foreign lands – Australia.

Pittman, Helena Clare. *The gift of the willows* ill. by author. Carolrhoda Books, 1988. ISBN 0-87614-354-0 Subj: Folk and fairy tales. Foreign lands – Japan.

A grain of rice ill. by author. Hastings, 1986. ISBN 0-8038-9289-6 Subj: Character traits – cleverness. Folk and fairy tales. Foreign lands – China. Royalty.

Once when I was scared ill. by Ted Rand. Dutton, 1988. ISBN 0-525-44407-6 Subj: Animals. Emotions – fear. Imagination. Night.

Pizer, Abigail. *Harry's night out* ill. by author. Dial, 1987. ISBN 0-8037-0055-5 Subj: Activities. Animals – cats. Night.

Nosey Gilbert ill. by author. Dial, 1987. ISBN 0-8037-0081-4 Subj: Animals – cats. Animals – dogs. Birds – geese. Emotions – fear. Insects – bees.

Plante, Patricia. *The turtle and the two ducks: animal fables* retold from La Fontaine by Patricia Plante and David Bergman; ill. by Anne F. Rockwell. Harper, 1981. ISBN 0-690-04147-0 Subj: Animals. Folk and fairy tales.

Plath, Sylvia. *The bed book* ill. by Emily Arnold McCully. Harper, 1976. Subj: Bedtime. Poetry, rhyme. Sleep.

Platt, Kin. *Big Max* ill. by Robert Lopshire. Harper, 1965. Subj: Animals – elephants. Careers – detectives. Problem solving.

Big Max in the mystery of the missing moose ill. by Robert Lopshire. Harper, 1977. Subj: Animals – moose. Careers – detectives. Problem solving.

Play and sing - it's Christmas! *a piano book of easy-to-play carols* comp. by Brooke Minarik Varnum; ill. by Emily Arnold McCully. Macmillan, 1980. Subj: Holidays – Christmas. Music. Songs.

Plomer, William. *The butterfly ball and the grasshopper's feast* (Aldridge, Alan)

Plotz, Helen. *A week of lullabies* comp. and ed. by Helen Plotz; ill. by Marisabina Russo. Greenwillow, 1988. ISBN 0-688-06653-4 Subj: Bedtime. Days of the week, months of the year. Poetry, rhyme.

Pluckrose, Henry. *Ants* ill. by Tony Weaver and David Cook. Watts, 1981. Subj: Insects – ants. Science.

Bears ill. by Richard Orr. Watts, 1979. Subj: Animals – bears. Animals – pandas. Animals – polar bears. Science.

Bees and wasps ill. by Tony Swift and Norman Weaver. Watts, 1981. Subj: Insects – bees. Insects – wasps. Science.

Big and little photos. by Chris Fairclough. Watts, 1987. ISBN 0-531-10373-0 Subj: Concepts – size.

Butterflies and moths ill. by Norman Weaver and others. Watts, 1981. Subj: Insects – butterflies, caterpillars. Insects – moths. Science.

Counting photos. by Chris Fairclough. Watts, 1988. ISBN 0-531-10524-5 Subj: Counting.

Elephants ill. by Peter Barrett. Watts, 1979. Subj: Animals – elephants. Science.

Floating and sinking photos. by Chris Fairclough. Watts, 1987. ISBN 0-531-10294-7 Subj: Science.

Horses ill. by Peter Barrett and Maurice Wilson. Watts, 1979. Subj: Animals – horses. Science.

Hot and cold photos. by Chris Fairclough. Watts, 1987. ISBN 0-531-10295-5 Subj: Science.

Lions and tigers ill. by Eric Tenny and Maurice Wilson. Archon Pr., 1979. Subj: Animals – lions. Animals – tigers.

Numbers photos. by Chris Fairclough. Watts, 1988. ISBN 0-531-10453-2 Subj: Counting.

Reptiles ill. by Gary Hincks and others. Watts, 1981. Subj: Reptiles. Science.

Shape photos. by Chris Fairclough. Watts, 1987. ISBN 0-531-10374-9 Subj: Concepts – shape.

Things we cut ill. by G. W. Hales. Watts, 1976. Subj: Tools.

Things we hear ill. by G. W. Hales. Watts, 1976. Subj: Senses – hearing.

Things we see ill. by G. W. Hales. Watts, 1976. Subj: Senses – seeing.

Things we touch ill. by G. W. Hales. Watts, 1976. Subj: Senses – touching.

Think about hearing photos. by Chris Fairclough. Watts, 1986. ISBN 0-531-10170-3 Subj: Senses – hearing.

Think about seeing photos. by Chris Fairclough. Watts, 1986. ISBN 0-531-10171-1 Subj: Senses – seeing.

Think about smelling photos. by Chris Fairclough. Watts, 1986. ISBN 0-531-10172-X Subj: Senses – smelling.

Think about tasting photos. by Chris Fairclough. Watts, 1986. ISBN 0-531-10173-8 Subj: Senses – tasting.

Think about touching photos. by Chris Fairclough. Watts, 1986. ISBN 0-531-10174-6 Subj: Senses – touching.

Time photos. by Chris Fairclough. Watts, 1988. ISBN 0-531-10452-4 Subj: Time.

Weight photos. by Chris Fairclough. Watts, 1988. ISBN 0-531-10525-3 Subj: Concepts – weight.

Whales ill. by Norman Weaver. Watts, 1979. Subj: Animals – whales. Science.

Plume, Ilse. *The Bremen town musicians* (Grimm, Jacob)

The story of Befana: an Italian Christmas tale ill. by adapt. Godine, 1981. Subj: Folk and fairy tales. Foreign lands – Italy. Holidays – Christmas.

Po, Lee. *The hare and the tortoise and the tortoise and the hare* (Du Bois, William Pène)

Podendorf, Illa. *Color* ill. by Wayne Stuart. Children's Pr., 1971. Subj: Concepts – color.

Shapes, sides, curves and corners ill. by Frank Rakoncay. Children's Pr., 1970. Subj: Concepts – shape.

Space ill. with photos. Children's Pr., 1982. Subj: Space and space ships.

POLA see Watson, Jane Werner

Polacco, Patricia. *Meteor!* ill. by author. Dodd, 1987. ISBN 0-396-08910-0 Subj: Country. Science.

Rechenka's eggs ill. by author. Putnam's, 1988. ISBN 0-399-21501-8 Subj: Birds – geese. Eggs. Folk and fairy tales.

Polhamus, Jean Burt. *Dinosaur do's and don'ts* ill. by Steve O'Neill. Prentice-Hall, 1975. Subj: Dinosaurs. Etiquette.

Doctor Dinosaur ill. by Steve O'Neill. Prentice-Hall, 1981. Subj: Careers – veterinarians. Dinosaurs. Illness.

Politi, Leo. *Emmet* ill. by author. Scribner's, 1971. Subj: Animals – dogs. Crime.

Juanita ill. by author. Scribner's, 1948. Subj: Caldecott award honor book. Ethnic groups in the U.S. – Mexican-Americans.

Lito and the clown ill. by author. Scribner's, 1964. Subj: Animals – cats. Clowns, jesters. Foreign lands – Mexico. Pets.

Little Leo ill. by author. Scribner's, 1951. Subj: Clothing. Family life. Foreign lands – Italy.

Mieko ill. by author. Golden Gate Jr. Books, 1969. Subj: Character traits – pride. Ethnic groups in the U.S. – Japanese-Americans.

The mission bell ill. by author. Scribner's, 1953. Subj: Ethnic groups in the U.S. – Mexican-Americans. Missions.

Mr. Fong's toy shop ill. by author. Scribner's, 1978. Subj: Behavior – sharing. Ethnic groups in the U.S. – Chinese-Americans. Friendship. Puppets. Toys.

Moy Moy ill. by author. Scribner's, 1960. Subj: Ethnic groups in the U.S. – Chinese-Americans. Holidays – Chinese New Year.

The nicest gift ill. by author. Scribner's, 1973. Subj: Animals – dogs. Behavior – lost. Holidays – Christmas.

Pedro, the angel of Olvera Street ill. by author. Scribner's, 1946. Subj: Caldecott award honor book. Ethnic groups in the U.S. – Mexican-Americans. Holidays – Christmas.

Rosa ill. by author. Scribner's, 1963. Subj: Babies. Foreign lands – Mexico. Holidays – Christmas. Sibling rivalry. Toys – dolls.

Song of the swallows ill. by author. Scribner's, 1949. Subj: Birds – swallows. Caldecott award book. Ethnic groups in the U.S. – Mexican-Americans. Missions.

Pollock, Penny. *Emily's tiger* ill. by author. Paulist Pr., 1985. Subj: Pets. Toys.

Water is wet photos. by Barbara Beirne. Putnam's, 1985. ISBN 0-399-21180-2 Subj: Activities – playing.

Polushkin, Maria. *Baby brother blues* ill. by Ellen Weiss. Bradbury Pr., 1987. ISBN 0-02-774780-8 Subj: Babies. Family life. Sibling rivalry.

Bubba and Babba: based on a Russian folktale ill. by Diane de Groat. Crown, 1976. Subj: Animals – bears. Character traits – cleanliness. Folk and fairy tales.

Kitten in trouble ill. by Betsy Lewin. Bradbury Pr., 1988. ISBN 0-02-774740-9 Subj: Animals – cats. Behavior – misbehavior.

The little hen and the giant ill. by Yuri Salzman. Harper, 1977. Subj: Birds – chickens. Character traits – bravery. Folk and fairy tales. Foreign lands – Russia. Giants.

Morning ill. by Bill Morrison. Four Winds Pr., 1983. Subj: Farms. Morning.

Mother, Mother, I want another ill. by Diane Dawson. Crown, 1978. Subj: Animals – mice. Behavior – misunderstanding. Family life – mothers. Sleep.

Who said meow? ill. by Giulio Maestro. Crown, 1975. An adaptation of Vladimir Grigorévich Suteev's Kto skazal "Mīau"? Subj: Animals. Noise, sounds.

Who said meow? ill. by Ellen Weiss. Bradbury Pr., 1988. ISBN 0-02-774770-0 Subj: Animals – cats. Animals – dogs. Noise, sounds.

Pomerantz, Charlotte. *All asleep* ill. by Nancy Tafuri. Greenwillow, 1984. Subj: Bedtime. Poetry, rhyme. Songs.

The ballad of the long-tailed rat ill. by Marian Parry. Macmillan, 1975. Subj: Animals – cats. Animals – rats. Character traits – pride. Poetry, rhyme.

Buffy and Albert ill. by Yossi Abolafia. Greenwillow, 1982. Subj: Animals – cats. Family life – grandfathers. Old age.

The half-birthday party ill. by DyAnne DiSalvo-Ryan. Houghton, 1984. Subj: Birthdays.

How many trucks can a tow truck tow? ill. by Robert W. Alley. Random House, 1987. ISBN 0-394-88775-1 Subj: Poetry, rhyme. Trucks.

If I had a Paka: poems of eleven languages ill. by Nancy Tafuri. Greenwillow, 1982. Subj: Foreign languages. Poetry, rhyme.

The mango tooth ill. by Marylin Hafner. Greenwillow, 1977. Subj: Family life. Teeth.

One duck, another duck ill. by José Aruego and Ariane Dewey. Greenwillow, 1984. Subj: Birds – ducks. Counting.

The piggy in the puddle ill. by James Marshall. Macmillan, 1974. Subj: Animals – pigs. Poetry, rhyme. Tongue twisters.

Posy ill. by Catherine Stock. Greenwillow, 1983. Subj: Bedtime. Family life.

The tamarindo puppy and other poems ill. by Byron Barton. Greenwillow, 1980. Subj: Foreign languages. Poetry, rhyme.

Timothy Tall Feather ill. by Catherine Stock. Greenwillow, 1986. ISBN 0-688-04247-3 Subj: Family life – grandfathers. Imagination. Indians of North America.

Where's the bear? ill. by Byron Barton. Greenwillow, 1984. ISBN 0-688-01753-3 Subj: Animals – bears.

Whiff, sniff, nibble and chew (The gingerbread boy)

Ponti, Claude. *Adele's album* ill. by author. Dutton, 1988. ISBN 0-525-44412-2 Subj: Imagination. Wordless.

Pope, Billy N. *Your world: let's visit the hospital* by Billy N. Pope and Ramona Ware Emmons. Taylor, 1968. Subj: Hospitals.

Porazińska, Janina. *The enchanted book: a tale from Krakow* ill. by Jan Brett; tr. by Bożena Smith. Harcourt, 1987. ISBN 0-15-225950-3 Subj: Activities – reading. Family life – sisters. Folk and fairy tales. Foreign lands – Poland.

The porcupine ill. by Patrick Oxenham. Rourke, 1983. Subj: Animals – porcupines.

Porte, Barbara Ann. *Harry in trouble* ill. by Yossi Abolafia. Greenwillow, 1989. ISBN 0-688-07722-6 Subj: Careers – librarians. Character traits – helpfulness.

Harry's dog ill. by Yossi Abolafia. Greenwillow, 1983. ISBN 0-688-02556-0 Subj: Animals – dogs. Family life – fathers. Illness.

Harry's mom ill. by Yossi Abolafia. Greenwillow, 1985. ISBN 0-688-04818-8 Subj: Death. Family life. Family life – fathers. Family life – mothers. Family life – grandparents. School.

Harry's visit ill. by Yossi Abolafia. Greenwillow, 1983. Subj: Behavior – sharing. Sports – basketball.

Porter, David Lord. *Mine!* ill. by author. Houghton, 1981. Subj: Behavior – greed.

Porter, William Sydney *see* Henry, O.

Portnoy, Mindy Avra. *Ima on the Bima: my mommy is a Rabbi* ill. by Steffi Karen Rubin. Kar-Ben Copies, 1986. ISBN 0-930494-55-5 Subj: Careers. Family life – mothers. Jewish culture.

Postgate, Oliver. *Noggin and the whale* by Oliver Postgate and Peter Firmin; ill. by Peter Firmin. White, 1967. Subj: Animals – whales. Humor.

Noggin the king by Oliver Postgate and Peter Firmin; ill. by Peter Firmin. White, 1965. Subj: Birds. Character traits – kindness. Humor. Royalty.

Postma, Lidia. *The stolen mirror* ill. by author. McGraw-Hill, 1976. Translation of De gestolen Spiegel. Subj: Imagination. Magic. Sibling rivalry.

Tom Thumb

Poston, Elizabeth. *Baby's song book* ill. by William Stobbs. Crowell, 1971. Subj: Music. Songs.

Potter, Beatrix. *Appley Dapply's nursery rhymes* ill. by author. Warne, 1917. Subj: Animals. Nursery rhymes.

Beatrix Potter's nursery rhyme book (Mother Goose)

Beatrix Potter's nursery rhyme book ill. by author. Warne, 1984. ISBN 0-7232-3254-7 Subj: Animals. Nursery rhymes.

Cecily Parsley's nursery rhymes ill. by author. Warne, 1922. Subj: Animals. Nursery rhymes.

The complete adventures of Peter Rabbit ill. by author. Warne, 1982. Subj: Animals – rabbits. Behavior – misbehavior.

Ginger and Pickles ill. by author. Warne, 1937. First pub. in 1909. Subj: Animals. Stores.

More tales from Beatrix Potter ill. by author. Warne, 1987. ISBN 0-7232-3366-7 Subj: Animals.

Peter Rabbit's ABC ill. by author. Warne, 1987. ISBN 0-7232-3423-X Subj: ABC books. Animals.

Peter Rabbit's one two three ill. by author. Warne, 1988. ISBN 0-7232-3424-8 Subj: Animals – rabbits. Counting.

The pie and the patty-pan ill. by author. Warne, 1933. First pub. in 1905. Subj: Animals – cats. Animals – dogs. Behavior – trickery.

Rolly-polly pudding ill. by author. Warne, 1936. First pub. in 1908. Subj: Animals – cats.

The sly old cat ill. by author. Warne, 1971. Subj: Animals – cats. Animals – rats. Character traits – cleverness. Etiquette. Parties.

The story of fierce bad rabbit ill. by author. Warne, 1906. Subj: Animals – rabbits.

The story of Miss Moppet ill. by author. Warne, 1906. Subj: Animals – cats. Behavior – trickery.

The tailor of Gloucester ill. by author. Warne, 1931. Subj: Animals – mice. Careers – tailors. Character traits – helpfulness.

The tale of Benjamin Bunny ill. by author. Warne, 1904. Subj: Animals – rabbits. Behavior – misbehavior.

The tale of Jemima Puddle-Duck ill. by author. Warne, 1936. First pub. in 1910. Subj: Birds – ducks. Eggs.

The tale of Jemima Puddle-Duck and other farmyard tales: The tale of Mr. Jeremy Fisher; The tale of Mrs. Tiggy-Winkle; The tale of Pigling Bland ill. by author. Large format ed. Warne, 1987. ISBN 0-7232-3425-6 Subj: Animals. Birds.

The tale of Johnny Town-Mouse ill. by author. Warne, 1918. Subj: Animals – mice.

The tale of Little Pig Robinson ill. by author. Warne, 1930. Subj: Animals – pigs. Behavior – talking to strangers. Boats, ships. Shopping.

The tale of Mr. Jeremy Fisher ill. by author. Warne, 1934. Subj: Frogs and toads. Sports – fishing.

The tale of Mr. Tod ill. by author. Warne, 1939. First pub. in 1911. Subj: Animals – badgers. Animals – foxes. Animals – rabbits.

The tale of Mrs. Tiggy-Winkle ill. by author. Warne, 1905. Subj: Animals – hedgehogs. Clothing.

The tale of Mrs. Tittlemouse ill. by author. Warne, 1910. Subj: Animals – mice. Character traits – cleanliness.

The tale of Mrs. Tittlemouse and other mouse stories: The tale of Johnny Town-Mouse; The tale of two bad mice; The tailor of Gloucester ill. by author. Large format ed. Warne, 1985. ISBN 0-7232-3324-1 Subj: Animals – mice.

The tale of Peter Rabbit ill. by Margot Apple. Troll Assoc., 1979. Subj: Animals – rabbits. Behavior – misbehavior.

The tale of Peter Rabbit ill. by author. Warne, 1902. Subj: Animals – rabbits. Behavior – misbehavior. Farms.

The tale of Peter Rabbit and other stories ill. by Allen Atkinson. Knopf, 1982. Subj: Animals.

The tale of Pigling Bland ill. by author. Warne, 1913, 1941. Subj: Animals – pigs.

The tale of Squirrel Nutkin ill. by author. Warne, 1903. Subj: Animals – squirrels. Birds – owls. Riddles. Seasons – fall.

The tale of the faithful dove ill. by Marie Angel. Warne, 1970. Subj: Birds – doves. Character traits – loyalty.

The tale of the Flopsy Bunnies ill. by author. Warne, 1909, 1937. Subj: Animals – rabbits. Character traits – cleverness.

The tale of Timmy Tiptoes ill. by author. Warne, 1911, 1939. Subj: Animals – squirrels.

The tale of Tom Kitten ill. by author. Warne, 1907. Subj: Animals – cats. Humor.

The tale of Tuppeny ill. by Marie Angel. Warne, 1971. Subj: Animals – guinea pigs.

The tale of two bad mice ill. by author. Warne, 1904, 1934. Subj: Animals – mice. Behavior – misbehavior. Toys.

A treasury of Peter Rabbit and other stories ill. by author. Watts, 1978. Subj: Animals.

The two bad mice pop-up book ill. by author. Warne, 1986. ISBN 0-7232-3360-8 Subj: Animals – mice. Behavior – misbehavior. Format, unusual – toy and movable books.

Where's Peter Rabbit? ill. by Colin Twinn. Warne, 1988. ISBN 0-7232-3519-8 Subj: Animals – rabbits. Behavior – misbehavior. Format, unusual.

Yours affectionately, Peter Rabbit: miniature letters ill. by author. Warne, 1984. Subj: Animals. Communication.

Potter, Russell. *The little red ferry boat* ill. by Marjorie Hill. Holt, 1947. Subj: Animals – mice. Boats, ships. Transportation.

Potter, Stephen. *Squawky, the adventures of a Clasperchoice* ill. by George Him. Lippincott, 1964. Subj: Birds – parakeets, parrots.

Poulin, Stephane. *Can you catch Josephine?* ill. by author. Tundra, 1987. ISBN 0-88776-198-4 Subj: Animals – cats. Behavior – misbehavior. Foreign lands – Canada. School.

Have you seen Josephine? ill. by author. Tundra, 1986. ISBN 0-88776-180-1 Subj: Animals – cats. Behavior – running away. Foreign lands – Canada.

Pouyanne, Rési. *What I see hidden by the pond* ill. by Gerda Muller. Two Continents, 1977. Subj: Animals. Plants. Science.

Power, Barbara. *I wish Laura's mommy was my mommy* ill. by Marylin Hafner. Lippincott, 1979. Subj: Behavior – growing up. Behavior – wishing. Family life – mothers.

Powers, George *see* Rodgers, Frank

Powers, Mary E. *Our teacher's in a wheelchair* photos. by author. Albert Whitman, 1986. ISBN 0-8075-6240-8 Subj: Careers – teachers. Handicaps. School.

Powzyk, Joyce. *Tasmania: a wildlife journey* ill. by author. Lothrop, 1987. ISBN 0-688-06460-4 Subj: Animals. Foreign lands – Australia. Nature. Science.

Prager, Annabelle. *The spooky Halloween party* ill. by Tomie de Paola. Pantheon, 1981. Subj: Holidays – Halloween. Parties.

The surprise party ill. by Tomie de Paola. Random House, 1988. ISBN 0-394-93235-8 Subj: Birthdays. Parties.

Prall, Jo. *My sister's special* ill. with photos. Childrens Pr., 1985. ISBN 0-516-03862-1 Subj: Family life – sisters. Handicaps.

Prater, John. *The gift* ill. by author. Viking, 1986. ISBN 0-670-80952-7 Subj: Behavior – wishing. Wordless.

On Friday something funny happened ill. by author. Random House, 1988. ISBN 0-370-30449-7 Subj: Behavior – misbehavior. Days of the week, months of the year.

The perfect day ill. by author. Dutton, 1987. ISBN 0-525-44282-0 Subj: Behavior – bad day. Sea and seashore.

You can't catch me! ill. by author. Salem House, 1986. ISBN 0-370-30594-9 Subj: Behavior – misbehavior. Behavior – running away.

Prather, Ray. *Double dog dare* ill. by author. Macmillan, 1975. Subj: Animals – dogs. Humor.

The ostrich girl ill. by author. Scribner's, 1978. Subj: Folk and fairy tales. Foreign lands – Africa. Forest, woods. Reptiles – snakes. Witches.

Prather, Richard *see* Knight, David C.

Pratten, Albra. *Winkie, the grey squirrel* ill. by Ralph S. Thompson. Oxford Univ. Pr., 1950. Subj: Animals – squirrels. Pets.

Precek, Katharine Wilson. *Penny in the road* ill. by Patricia Cullen-Clark. Macmillan, 1989. ISBN 0-02-774970-3 Subj: Behavior – losing things. U.S. history.

Preiss, Byron. *The first crazy word book: verbs* by Byron Preiss and Ralph Reese; ill. by Ralph Reese. Watts, 1982. Subj: Language.

Prelutsky, Jack. *The baby uggs are hatching* ill. by James Stevenson. Greenwillow, 1982. Subj: Humor. Imagination. Monsters. Poetry, rhyme.

Brave little Pete of Geranium Street (Lagercrantz, Rose)

Circus ill. by Arnold Lobel. Macmillan, 1974. Subj: Circus. Poetry, rhyme.

It's Halloween ill. by Marylin Hafner. Greenwillow, 1977. Subj: Holidays – Halloween. Poetry, rhyme.

It's Valentine's Day ill. by Yossi Abolafia. Greenwillow, 1983. Subj: Holidays – Valentine's Day. Poetry, rhyme.

The mean old mean hyena ill. by Arnold Lobel. Greenwillow, 1978. Subj: Animals – hyenas. Character traits – meanness. Poetry, rhyme.

The pack rat's day and other poems ill. by Margaret Bloy Graham. Macmillan, 1974. Subj: Animals. Poetry, rhyme.

The queen of Eene ill. by Victoria Chess. Greenwillow, 1978. Subj: Humor. Poetry, rhyme.

Rainy rainy Saturday ill. by Marylin Hafner. Greenwillow, 1980. Subj: Poetry, rhyme. Weather – rain.

The Random House book of poetry for children ill. by Arnold Lobel. Random House, 1983. Subj: Humor. Poetry, rhyme.

Read-aloud rhymes for the very young ill. by Marc Brown. Knopf, 1986. ISBN 0-394-97218-X Subj: Poetry, rhyme.

Ride a purple pelican ill. by Garth Williams. Greenwillow, 1986. ISBN 0-688-04031-4 Subj: Imagination. Poetry, rhyme.

The snopp on the sidewalk and other poems ill. by Byron Barton. Greenwillow, 1977. ISBN 0-688-84084-1 Subj: Humor. Imagination. Poetry, rhyme.

The terrible tiger ill. by Arnold Lobel. Macmillan, 1970. Subj: Animals – tigers. Cumulative tales. Poetry, rhyme.

Tyrannosaurus was a beast ill. by Arnold Lobel. Greenwillow, 1988. ISBN 0-688-06443-4 Subj: Dinosaurs. Poetry, rhyme.

What I did last summer ill. by Yossi Abolafia. Greenwillow, 1984. Subj: Poetry, rhyme.

The wild baby (Lindgren, Barbro)

The wild baby goes to sea (Lindgren, Barbro)

Presencer, Alain. *Roaring lion tales* ill. by Ron Van der Meer. Harper, 1984. ISBN 0-216-91606-2 Subj: Animals – lions. Folk and fairy tales. Format, unusual – toy and movable books.

Preston, Edna Mitchell. *Horrible Hepzibah* ill. by Ray Cruz. Viking, 1971. Subj: Behavior – misbehavior. Humor.

Monkey in the jungle ill. by Clement Hurd. Viking, 1968. Subj: Animals – monkeys. Bedtime. Night. Sleep.

One dark night ill. by Kurt Werth. Viking, 1969. Subj: Cumulative tales. Holidays – Halloween.

Pop Corn and Ma Goodness ill. by Robert Andrew Parker. Viking, 1969. Subj: Caldecott award honor book. Humor. Poetry, rhyme. Songs. Weather – rain.

Squawk to the moon, little goose ill. by Barbara Cooney. Viking, 1974. Subj: Animals – foxes. Behavior – misbehavior. Birds – geese. Moon.

Price, Christine. *One is God: two old counting songs* ill. by author. Warne, 1970. Subj: Counting. Religion. Songs.

Price, Dorothy E. *Speedy gets around* ill. by Betsy Warren. Steck-Vaughn, 1965. Subj: Animals – chipmunks. Sports – camping.

Price, Mathew. *Do you see what I see?* ill. by Sue Porter. Harper, 1986. ISBN 0-694-00002-7 Subj: Animals. Behavior – losing things. Circus. Format, unusual.

Peekaboo! ill. by Jean Claverie. Knopf, 1985. ISBN 0-394-87142-1 Subj: Family life. Format, unusual – toy and movable books.

Price, Michelle. *Mean Melissa* ill. by author. Bradbury Pr., 1977. Subj: Character traits – meanness. School.

Price, Roger. *The last little dragon* ill. by Mamoru Funai. Harper, 1969. Subj: Behavior – dissatisfaction. Dragons.

Price-Thomas, Brian. *The magic ark* ill. by author. Crown, 1987. ISBN 0-517-56705-9 Subj: Animals. Imagination.

Primavera, Elise. *Basil and Maggie* ill. by author. Lippincott, 1983. Subj: Animals – horses. Character traits – appearance.

Prince, Pamela. *The secret world of teddy bears* photos. by Elaine Faris Keenan. Crown, 1983. Subj: Poetry, rhyme. Toys – teddy bears.

The prince who knew his fate: an ancient Egyptian tale tr. from hieroglyphs and ill. by Lise Manniche. Putnam's, 1982. Subj: Folk and fairy tales. Foreign lands – Egypt. Hieroglyphics. Magic. Royalty.

Priolo, Pauline. *Piccolina and the Easter bells* ill. by Rita Fava. Little, 1962. Subj: Character traits – smallness. Foreign lands – Italy. Holidays – Easter.

Pritchard, John Wallace *see* Wallace, Ian

Prokofiev, Sergei Sergeievitch. *Peter and the wolf* adapt. by Selina Hastings; ill. by Reg Cartwright. Holt, 1987. ISBN 0-8050-0408-4 Subj: Animals – wolves. Character traits – cleverness. Folk and fairy tales. Foreign lands – Russia.

Peter and the wolf ill. by Warren Chappell; foreword by Serge Koussevitsky; calligraphy by Hollis Holland. Knopf, 1940. Subj: Animals – wolves. Character traits – cleverness. Folk and fairy tales. Foreign lands – Russia. Music.

Peter and the wolf ill. by Barbara Cooney. Viking, 1986. ISBN 0-670-80849-0 Subj: Animals – wolves. Character traits – cleverness. Folk and fairy tales. Foreign lands – Russia. Format, unusual – toy and movable books. Music.

Peter and the wolf ill. by Frans Haacken. Watts, 1961. Subj: Animals – wolves. Character traits – cleverness. Folk and fairy tales. Foreign lands – Russia. Music.

Peter and the wolf ill. by Alan Howard. Transatlantic, 1954. Subj: Animals – wolves. Character traits – cleverness. Folk and fairy tales. Foreign lands – Russia. Music.

Peter and the wolf tr. by Maria Carlson; ill. by Charles Mikolaycak. Viking, 1982. Subj: Animals – wolves. Character traits – cleverness. Folk and fairy tales. Foreign lands – Russia. Music.

Peter and the wolf adapt. by Loriot; ill. by Jörg Müller. Knopf, 1986. Book-cassette included. ISBN 0-394-88417-5 Subj: Animals – wolves. Character traits – cleverness. Folk and fairy tales. Foreign lands – Russia. Music.

Peter and the wolf tr. by Patricia Crampton; ill. by Josef Paleček. Picture Book Studio, 1987. ISBN 0-88708-049-9 Subj: Animals – wolves. Character traits – cleverness. Folk and fairy tales. Foreign lands – Russia. Music.

Peter and the wolf retold by Ann Herring; ill. by Kozo Shimizu; photos. by Yasugi Yajima. Gakken, 1971. Subj: Animals – wolves. Character traits – cleverness. Folk and fairy tales. Foreign lands – Russia. Music.

Peter and the wolf ill. by Erna Voigt. Godine, 1980. ISBN 0-87923-331-1 Subj: Animals – wolves. Character traits – cleverness. Folk and fairy tales. Foreign lands – Russia. Music.

Provensen, Alice. *A book of seasons* by Alice and Martin Provensen; ill. by authors. Random House, 1976. Subj: Seasons.

The glorious flight: across the channel with Louis Blériot by Alice and Martin Provensen; ill. by authors. Viking, 1983. Subj: Activities – flying. Airplanes, airports. Caldecott award book.

Karen's opposites by Alice and Martin Provensen; ill. by authors. Golden Pr., 1963. Subj: Concepts – opposites. Poetry, rhyme.

My little hen by Alice and Martin Provensen; ill. by authors. Random House, 1973. Subj: Birds – chickens.

Our animal friends by Alice and Martin Provensen; ill. by authors. Random House, 1974. Subj: Animals. Farms.

An owl and three pussycats by Alice and Martin Provensen; ill. by authors. Atheneum, 1981. Subj: Family life. Farms. Pets.

Shaker lane by Alice and Martin Provensen; ill. by authors. Viking, 1987. ISBN 0-670-81568-3 Subj: City. Moving. Poverty.

Town and country by Alice and Martin Provensen; ill. by authors. Crown, 1984. Subj: City. Country.

The year at Maple Hill Farm by Alice and Martin Provensen; ill. by authors. Atheneum, 1978. Subj: Animals. Days of the week, months of the year. Farms. Seasons.

Provensen, Martin. *A book of seasons* (Provensen, Alice)

The glorious flight (Provensen, Alice)

Karen's opposites (Provensen, Alice)

My little hen (Provensen, Alice)

Our animal friends (Provensen, Alice)

An owl and three pussycats (Provensen, Alice)

Shaker lane (Provensen, Alice)

Town and country (Provensen, Alice)

The year at Maple Hill Farm (Provensen, Alice)

Prusski, Jeffrey. *Bring back the deer* ill. by Neil Waldman. Harcourt, 1988. ISBN 0-15-200418-1 Subj: Animals – deer. Animals – wolves. Family life. Forest, woods. Seasons – winter. Sports – hunting.

Pryor, Ainslie. *The baby blue cat and the dirty dog brothers* ill. by author. Viking, 1987. ISBN 0-670-81781-3 Subj: Activities – bathing. Animals – cats. Animals – dogs.

The baby blue cat who said no ill. by author. Viking, 1988. ISBN 0-670-81780-5 Subj: Animals – cats. Bedtime.

Pryor, Bonnie. *Amanda and April* ill. by Diane de Groat. Morrow, 1986. ISBN 0-688-05870-1 Subj: Animals – pigs. Family life – sisters. Parties. Sibling rivalry.

The house on Maple Street ill. by Beth Peck. Morrow, 1987. ISBN 0-688-06381-0 Subj: U.S. history.

Mr. Munday and the rustlers ill. by Wallop Manyum. Prentice-Hall, 1988. ISBN 0-13-604737-8 Subj: Crime. Farms.

The porcupine mouse ill. by Mary Jane Begin. Morrow, 1988. ISBN 0-688-07154-6 Subj: Animals – mice. Character traits – bravery. Emotions – fear. Sibling rivalry.

The pudgy book of babies ill. by Kathy Wilburn. Putnam's, 1984. ISBN 0-448-10207-2 Subj: Babies. Format, unusual – board books.

The pudgy book of farm animals ill. by Julie Durrell. Putnam's, 1984. ISBN 0-448-10211-0 Subj: Animals. Farms. Format, unusual – board books.

The pudgy book of here we go ill. by Beth Lee Weiner. Putnam's, 1984. ISBN 0-448-10208-0 Subj: Format, unusual – board books.

The pudgy book of make-believe ill. by Andrea Brooks. Putnam's, 1984. ISBN 0-448-10209-9 Subj: Format, unusual – board books. Imagination.

The pudgy book of Mother Goose ill. by Richard Walz. Putnam's, 1984. ISBN 0-448-10212-9 Subj: Format, unusual – board books. Nursery rhymes.

The pudgy book of toys ill. by Julie Durrell. Grosset, 1983. Subj: Format, unusual – board books. Toys.

The pudgy bunny book ill. by Ruth Sanderson. Putnam's, 1984. ISBN 0-448-10210-2 Subj: Animals – rabbits. Format, unusual – board books.

The pudgy fingers counting book ill. by Doug Cushman. Grosset, 1983. Subj: Counting. Format, unusual – board books.

The pudgy pals ill. by Kathy Wilburn. Grosset, 1983. Subj: Format, unusual – board books.

The pudgy pat-a-cake book ill. by Terri Super. Grosset, 1983. Subj: Format, unusual – board books. Games.

The pudgy peek-a-boo book ill. by Amye Rosenberg. Grosset, 1983. Subj: Format, unusual – board books. Games.

The pudgy rock-a-bye book ill. by Kathy Wilburn. Grosset, 1983. Subj: Format, unusual – board books.

Pulsifer, Marjorie P. *Bikes* (Baugh, Dolores M.)

Let's go (Baugh, Dolores M.)

Let's see the animals (Baugh, Dolores M.)

Let's take a trip (Baugh, Dolores M.)

Slides (Baugh, Dolores M.)

Supermarket (Baugh, Dolores M.)

Swings (Baugh, Dolores M.)

Trucks and cars to ride (Baugh, Dolores M.)

Puner, Helen Walker. *Daddys, what they do all day* ill. by Roger Antoine Duvoisin. Lothrop, 1946. Subj: Activities – working. Careers. Family life – fathers. Poetry, rhyme.

The sitter who didn't sit ill. by Roger Antoine Duvoisin. Lothrop, 1949. Subj: Activities – baby-sitting. Humor. Poetry, rhyme.

Puppies and kittens photos. by Walter Chandoha. Platt, 1983. Subj: Animals – cats. Animals – dogs. Format, unusual – board books. Poetry, rhyme.

Purcell, John Wallace. *African animals* ill. with photos. Rev. ed. Children's Pr., 1982. Subj: Animals. Foreign lands – Africa.

Purdy, Carol. *Iva Dunnit and the big wind* ill. by Steven Kellogg. Dial Pr., 1985. ISBN 0-8037-0184-5 Subj: Family life. Weather – wind.

Least of all ill. by Tim Arnold. Macmillan, 1987. ISBN 0-689-50404-7 Subj: Activities – reading. Activities – working. Family life. Self-concept.

Puricelli, Luigi. *In my garden* (Cristini, Ermanno)

In the pond (Cristini, Ermanno)

In the woods (Cristini, Ermanno)

Pursell, Margaret Sanford. *Jessie the chicken* orig. tr. by Dyan Hammarberg; photos. by Claudie Fayn-Rodriguez; ill. by L'Enc Matte. Carolrhoda Books, 1977. Based on Anne Marie Pajot's Picota la poule. Subj: Birds – chickens. Eggs.

A look at birth ill. by Maria S. Forrai. Lerner, 1976. Subj: Babies. Science.

A look at divorce ill. by Maria S. Forrai. Lerner, 1976. Subj: Divorce. Emotions.

Polly the guinea pig orig. tr. by Dyan Hammarberg; photos. by Antoinette Barrére; ill. by L'enc Matte. Carolrhoda Books, 1977. Original ed. published under title: Amilcar le cochon d'Inde. Subj: Animals – guinea pigs. Pets. Science.

Shelley the sea gull tr. by Dyan Hammarberg; photos. by Jean Christian David, Guy Dhuit and Claudie Fayn-Rodriguez. Carolrhoda Books, 1977. Original ed. published under title: Gwelan le goeland. Subj: Birds – sea gulls. Pets. Science.

Sprig the tree frog tr. by Dyan Hammarberg; ill. by Yves Vial. Carolrhoda Books, 1977. Subj: Eggs. Frogs and toads. Science.

Purviance, Susan. *Alphabet Annie announces an all-American album* (O'Shell, Marcia)

Quackenbush, Robert M. *Calling Doctor Quack* ill. by author. Lothrop, 1978. Subj: Animals. Ecology. Illness.

Chuck lends a paw ill. by author. Clarion, 1986. ISBN 0-89919-363-3 Subj: Animals – mice. Character traits – helpfulness.

City trucks ill. by author. Albert Whitman, 1981. Subj: City. Trucks.

Clementine ill. by author. Lippincott, 1974. Subj: Folk and fairy tales. Music. Songs. U.S. history.

Detective Mole ill. by author. Lothrop, 1976. Subj: Animals. Animals – moles. Careers – detectives. Humor. Problem solving.

Detective Mole and the haunted castle mystery ill. by author. Lothrop, 1985. ISBN 0-688-04641-X Subj: Animals. Animals – moles. Animals – rabbits. Parties. Problem solving.

Detective Mole and the secret clues ill. by author. Lothrop, 1977. Subj: Animals. Animals – moles. Careers – detectives. Humor. Problem solving.

Detective Mole and the Tip-Top mystery ill. by author. Lothrop, 1978. Subj: Animals. Animals – moles. Careers – detectives. Humor. Problem solving.

Dig to disaster ill. by author. Prentice-Hall, 1982. Subj: Birds – ducks. Careers – detectives. Problem solving.

Express train to trouble ill. by author. Prentice-Hall, 1981. Subj: Birds – ducks. Careers – detectives. Problem solving.

First grade jitters ill. by author. Lippincott, 1982. Subj: Animals – rabbits. School.

Funny bunnies ill. by author. Houghton, 1984. Subj: Animals – rabbits. Humor.

Henry babysits ill. by author. Parents, 1983. Subj: Activities – baby-sitting. Birds – ducks.

I don't want to go, I don't know how to act ill. by author. Lippincott, 1983. Subj: Animals – koala bears. Behavior. Etiquette. Family life.

The man on the flying trapeze: the circus life of Emmett Kelly, Sr., told with pictures and song! ill. by author. Lippincott, 1975. Subj: Circus. Clowns, jesters. Music. Songs.

Mouse feathers ill. by author. Clarion, 1988. ISBN 0-89919-527-X Subj: Behavior – misbehavior. Family life.

No mouse for me ill. by author. Watts, 1981. Subj: Cumulative tales. Pets.

Pete Pack Rat ill. by author. Lothrop, 1976. Subj: Animals. Animals – pack rats. Cowboys. Humor.

Piet Potter returns ill. by author. McGraw-Hill, 1980. Subj: Careers – detectives. Problem solving.

Piet Potter strikes again ill. by author. McGraw-Hill, 1981. Subj: Careers – detectives. Problem solving.

Piet Potter to the rescue ill. by author. McGraw-Hill, 1981. Subj: Careers – detectives. Problem solving.

Piet Potter's first case ill. by author. McGraw-Hill, 1980. Subj: Careers – detectives. Problem solving.

Pop! goes the weasel and Yankee Doodle: New York in 1776 and today ill. by author. Harper, 1988, 1976. ISBN 0-397-32265-8 Subj: Music. Poetry, rhyme. Songs. U.S. history.

She'll be comin' 'round the mountain ill. by author. Lippincott, 1973. Subj: Folk and fairy tales. Music. Songs.

Sheriff Sally Gopher and the Thanksgiving caper ill. by author. Lothrop, 1982. Subj: Holidays – Thanksgiving.

Skip to my Lou ill. by author. Lippincott, 1975. Subj: Folk and fairy tales. Music. Songs.

Stairway to doom ill. by author. Prentice-Hall, 1983. Subj: Birds – ducks. Careers – detectives. Problem solving.

There'll be a hot time in the old town tonight: the great Chicago fire of 1871 ill. by author. Harper, 1988, 1974. ISBN 0-397-32267-4 Subj: Fire. Folk and fairy tales. Music. Songs. U.S. history.

What has Wild Tom done now?!!! a story of Thomas Alva Edison ill. by author. Prentice-Hall, 1981. Subj: Humor. Science.

Queen, Ellery, Jr. *see* Holding, James

Quigley, Lillian Fox. *The blind men and the elephant* ill. by Janice Holland. Scribner's, 1959. Subj: Animals – elephants. Folk and fairy tales. Foreign lands – India. Handicaps – blindness. Senses – seeing.

Quin-Harkin, Janet. *Benjamin's balloon* ill. by Robert Censoni. Parents, 1979. Subj: Activities – ballooning. Character traits – willfulness.

Helpful Hattie ill. by Susanna Natti. Harcourt, 1983. Subj: Birthdays. Hair. Parties. Teeth.

Peter Penny's dance ill. by Anita Lobel. Dial Pr., 1976. Subj: Activities – dancing. Weddings. World.

Quinlan, Patricia. *My dad takes care of me* ill. by Vlasta van Kampen. Firefly Pr., 1987. ISBN 0-920303-79-X Subj: Activities – working. Family life – fathers. Family life – mothers.

Quinsey, Mary Beth. *Why does that man have such a big nose?* photos. by Wilson Chan. Parenting Pr., 1986. ISBN 0-943990-25-4 Subj: Character traits – appearance. Character traits – being different.

Ra, Carol F. *Trot, trot to Boston: play rhymes for baby* ill. by Catherine Stock. Lothrop, 1987. ISBN 0-688-06191-5 Subj: Games. Poetry, rhyme.

Rabe, Berniece. *The balancing girl* ill. by Lillian Hoban. Dutton, 1981. ISBN 0-525-26160-5 Subj: Handicaps. School.

A smooth move ill. by Linda Shute. Albert Whitman, 1987. ISBN 0-8075-7486-4 Subj: Activities – traveling. Moving.

Where's Chimpy? photos. by Diane Schmidt. Albert Whitman, 1988. ISBN 0-8075-8928-4 Subj: Behavior – losing things. Family life – fathers. Handicaps. Toys.

Rabinowitz, Sandy. *A colt named mischief* ill. by author. Doubleday, 1979. Subj: Animals – horses. Behavior – misbehavior.

What's happening to Daisy? ill. by author. Harper, 1977. Subj: Animals – horses. Science.

Rabinowitz, Solomon J. *see* Aleichem, Sholem

Racioppo, Larry. *Halloween* photos. by author. Scribner's, 1980. Subj: Holidays – Halloween.

Radin, Ruth Yaffe. *High in the mountains* ill. by Ed Young. Macmillan, 1989. ISBN 0-02-775650-5 Subj: Family life – grandfathers. Nature.

A winter place ill. by Mattie Lou O'Kelley. Little, 1982. Subj: Seasons – winter. Sports – ice skating.

Radlauer, Ruth Shaw. *Breakfast by Molly* ill. by Emily Arnold McCully. Prentice-Hall, 1988. ISBN 0-671-66165-5 Subj: Birthdays. Family life – mothers. Food.

Molly ill. by Emily Arnold McCully. Prentice-Hall, 1987. ISBN 0-13-599762-3 Subj: Activities – picnicking. Activities – walking.

Molly at the library ill. by Emily Arnold McCully. Prentice-Hall, 1988. ISBN 0-671-66166-3 Subj: Activities – reading. Family life – fathers. Libraries.

Molly goes hiking ill. by Emily Arnold McCully. Prentice-Hall, 1987. ISBN 0-13-599770-4 Subj: Activities – picnicking. Activities – walking.

Of course, you're a horse! ill. by Abner Graboff and Sheila Greenwald. Abelard-Schuman, 1959. Subj: Health. Imagination.

Radley, Gail. *The night Stella hid the stars* ill. by John Wallner. Crown, 1978. Subj: Imagination. Stars.

Radyr, Tomos *see* Stevenson, James

Raebeck, Lois. *Who am I?* ill. by June Goldsborough. Follett, 1970. Subj: Activities – playing. Games. Songs.

Rael, Rick. *Baseball brothers* (Rubin, Jeff)

Raffi. *Down by the bay* ill. by Nadine Bernard Westcott. Crown, 1987. ISBN 0-517-56644-3 Subj: Music. Songs.

One light, one sun ill. by Eugenie Fernandes. Crown, 1988. ISBN 0-517-56785-7 Subj: Family life. Music. Songs.

Shake my sillies out ill. by David Allender. Crown, 1987. ISBN 0-517-56646-X Subj: Music. Songs.

Wheels on the bus ill. by Sylvie Kantorovitz Wickstrom. Crown, 1988. ISBN 0-517-56784-9 Subj: Foreign lands – France. Music. Songs.

Rahn, Joan Elma. *Holes* photos. by author. Houghton, 1984. Subj: Concepts.

Ramal, Walter *see* De La Mare, Walter

Rand, Ann. *Little 1* ill. by Paul Rand. Harcourt, 1962. Subj: Counting.

Sparkle and spin: a book about words ill. by Paul Rand. Harcourt, 1957. Subj: Language.

Rand, Gloria. *Salty dog* ill. by Ted Rand. Holt, 1989. ISBN 0-8050-0837-3 Subj: Animals – dogs. Boats, ships. Character traits – individuality.

Rand McNally picturebook dictionary: *a thousand words to see and say* comp. by Robert L. Hillerich and others; ill. by Dan Siculan. Rand McNally, 1971. Subj: Dictionaries.

Ransome, Arthur. *The fool of the world and the flying ship* ill. by Uri Shulevitz. Farrar, 1968. Subj: Activities – flying. Boats, ships. Caldecott award book. Character traits – cleverness.

Raphael, Elaine. *Donkey and Carlo* by Elaine Raphael and Don Bolognese; ill. by authors. Harper, 1978. Subj: Animals – donkeys. Farms. Friendship.

Donkey, it's snowing by Elaine Raphael and Don Bolognese; ill. by authors. Harper, 1981. Subj: Animals – donkeys. Farms. Weather – snow.

Turnabout by Elaine Raphael and Don Bolognese; ill. by authors. Viking, 1980. Subj: Animals – bears. Behavior – boasting. Family life. Folk and fairy tales. Poetry, rhyme.

Raposo, Joe. *The Sesame Street song book* words and music by Joe Raposo and Jeffrey Moss; arrangements by Sy Oliver; ill. by Loretta Trezzo. Simon and Schuster, 1971. "Published in conjunction with Children's Television Workshop." Subj: Music. Songs.

Rappaport, Doreen. *The Boston coffee party* ill. by Emily Arnold McCully. Harper, 1988. ISBN 0-06-024825-4 Subj: U.S. history.

Rappus, Gerhard. *When the sun was shining* ill. by author. Imported Pubs., 1983. Subj: Activities – picnicking. Animals – goats. Behavior – misbehavior. Wordless.

Raskin, Ellen. *A & the: or, William T. C. Baumgarten comes to town* ill. by author. Atheneum, 1970. Subj: Friendship. Names.

And it rained ill. by author. Atheneum, 1969. Subj: Animals. Weather – rain.

Franklin Stein ill. by author. Atheneum, 1972. Subj: City. Friendship. Humor. Imagination.

Ghost in a four-room apartment ill. by author. Atheneum, 1969. Subj: Cumulative tales. Family life. Ghosts. Poetry, rhyme.

Nothing ever happens on my block ill. by author. Atheneum, 1966. Subj: Behavior – boredom. City. Humor.

Spectacles ill. by author. Atheneum, 1968. Subj: Glasses. Imagination. Senses – seeing.

Who, said Sue, said whoo? ill. by author. Atheneum, 1973. Subj: Animals. Noise, sounds. Poetry, rhyme.

Rauch, Hans-Georg. *The lines are coming: a book about drawing* ill. by author. Scribner's, 1978. Subj: Art.

Ravilious, Robin. *The runaway chick* ill. by author. Macmillan, 1987. ISBN 0-02-775640-8 Subj: Behavior – running away. Birds – chickens. Character traits – curiosity.

Ray, Deborah Kogan. *The cloud* ill. by author. Harper, 1984. Subj: Activities – walking. Weather – clouds.

Fog drift morning ill. by author. Harper, 1983. Subj: Morning. Sea and seashore.

Sunday morning we went to the zoo ill. by author. Harper, 1981. Subj: Family life. Sibling rivalry. Zoos.

Rayner, Mary. *Crocodarling* ill. by author. Bradbury Pr., 1986. ISBN 0-02-775770-6 Subj: Behavior – bullying. Behavior – needing someone. School. Toys.

Garth Pig and the ice cream lady ill. by author. Atheneum, 1977. Subj: Animals – pigs. Animals – wolves.

Mr. and Mrs. Pig's evening out ill. by author. Atheneum, 1976. Subj: Activities – baby-sitting. Animals – pigs. Animals – wolves.

Mrs. Pig gets cross: and other stories ill. by author. Dutton, 1987. ISBN 0-525-44280-4 Subj: Animals – pigs. Family life.

Mrs. Pig's bulk buy ill. by author. Atheneum, 1981. Subj: Animals – pigs. Food.

The rain cloud ill. by author. Atheneum, 1980. Subj: Character traits – helpfulness. Weather – clouds.

Raynor, Dorka. *Grandparents around the world* ed. by Caroline Rubin; photos. by author. Albert Whitman, 1977. Subj: Family life – grandparents.

Rea, Jesus Guerrero. *Atariba and Niguayona* (Rohmer, Harriet)

Reader, Constant *see* Parker, Dorothy D.

Reardon, Maureen. *Feelings between brothers and sisters* (Conta, Marcia Maher)

Feelings between friends (Conta, Marcia Maher)

Feelings between kids and grownups (Conta, Marcia Maher)

Feelings between kids and parents (Conta, Marcia Maher)

Reasoner, Charles. *Sleepy time bunny* (Cosgrove, Stephen)

Reavin, Sam. *Hurray for Captain Jane!* ill. by Emily Arnold McCully. Parents, 1971. Subj: Activities – bathing. Boats, ships. Imagination.

Redies, Rainer. *The cats' party* ill. by Gerta Melle. Barron's, 1986. ISBN 0-8120-5720-1 Subj: Animals – cats. Character traits – individuality. Family life. Parties.

Reece, Colleen L. *What?* ill. by Lois Axeman. Children's Pr., 1983. Subj: Character traits – curiosity. Character traits – questioning.

Reed, Allison. *Genesis: the story of creation* ill. by author. Schocken, 1981. Subj: Religion.

Reed, Elizabeth *see* Stewart, Elizabeth

Reed, Jonathan. *Do armadillos come in houses?* ill. by Carol Nicklaus. Atheneum, 1981. Subj: Emotions – fear.

Reed, Kit. *When we dream* ill. by Yutaka Sugita. Hawthorn, 1966. Subj: Behavior – wishing. Dreams.

Reed, Lillian Craig *see* Reed, Kit

Reed, Mary M. *Biddy and the ducks* (Sondergaard, Arensa)

Rees, Mary. *Ten in a bed* ill. by adapt. Little, 1988. ISBN 0-316-73708-9 Subj: Bedtime. Counting. Family life.

Reese, Ralph. *The first crazy word book* (Preiss, Byron)

Reesink, Marijke. *The golden treasure* ill. by Jaap Tol. Harcourt, 1968. Translation of Het vrouwtje van Stavoren. Subj: Boats, ships. Character traits – selfishness. Folk and fairy tales. Foreign lands – Holland.

The princess who always ran away ill. by Françoise Trésy. McGraw-Hill, 1981. Subj: Behavior – solitude. Character traits – being different. Folk and fairy tales. Royalty. Sibling rivalry.

Reeves, James. *Rhyming Will* ill. by Edward Ardizzone. McGraw-Hill, 1967. Subj: Character traits – individuality. Humor. Poetry, rhyme. Royalty.

Reeves, John Morris *see* Reeves, James

Regniers, Beatrice De *see* De Regniers, Beatrice Schenk

Reich, Hanns. *Animal babies* (Zoll, Max Alfred)

Reichmeier, Betty. *Potty time!* ill. by author. Random, 1988. ISBN 0-394-89403-0 Subj: Behavior – growing up.

Reid, Alastair. *A balloon for a blunderbuss* (Gill, Bob)

Mother Goose in Spanish (Mother Goose)

Supposing ill. by Abe Birnbaum. Little, 1960. Subj: Humor. Imagination.

Reid, Jon. *Celestino Piatti's animal ABC* (Piatti, Celestino)

Reidel, Marlene. *Jacob and the robbers* ill. by author. Atheneum, 1967. Subj: Crime. Night. Sleep.

Reimold, Mary Gallagher. *My mom is a runner* photos. by Sid Dorris. Abingdon Pr., 1987. ISBN 0-687-27545-8 Subj: Family life – mothers. Sports – racing.

Reinfeld, Fred *see* Young, Ed

Reinl, Edda. *The little snake* ill. by author. Alphabet Pr., 1982. Subj: Emotions – love. Reptiles – snakes.

Reiss, John J. *Colors* ill. by author. Bradbury Pr., 1969. Subj: Concepts – color.

Numbers ill. by author. Bradbury Pr., 1971. Subj: Counting.

Shapes ill. by author. Bradbury Pr., 1974. Subj: Concepts – shape.

Reit, Seymour. *The king who learned to smile* ill. by Gordon Laite. Golden Pr., 1960. Subj: Behavior – boredom. Royalty.

Round things everywhere photos. by Carol Basen. McGraw-Hill, 1969. Subj: Concepts – shape. Ethnic groups in the U.S.

Reitveld, Jane Klatt. *Monkey island* ill. by author. Viking, 1963. Subj: Animals – monkeys. Zoos.

Relonde, Maurice *see* Jagendorf, Moritz A.

Renberg, Dalia Hardof. *Hello, clouds!* ill. by Alona Frankel. Harper, 1985. ISBN 0-06-024839-4 Subj: Imagination. Weather – clouds.

Ressner, Phil. *August explains* ill. by Crosby Newell Bonsall. Harper, 1963. Subj: Animals – bears.

Dudley Pippin ill. by Arnold Lobel. Harper, 1965. Subj: City. Imagination.

Retan, Walter. *The snowplow that tried to go south* by Walter Retan [i.e. George Walters]; ill. by John Resko. Atheneum, 1950. Subj: Machines. Seasons – winter. Weather – snow.

The steam shovel that wouldn't eat dirt ill. by Roger Antoine Duvoisin. Atheneum, 1948. Subj: Food. Machines.

Rettich, Margret. *The voyage of the jolly boat* tr. from German by Joy Backhouse; ill. by author. Methuen, 1981. Subj: Boats, ships. Careers – fishermen. Weather – storms.

Reuter, Margaret. *My mother is blind* ill. by Philip Lanier. Children's Pr., 1979. Subj: Family life – mothers. Handicaps – blindness. Senses – seeing.

Rey, H. A. *see* Rey, Hans Augusto

Rey, Hans Augusto. *Anybody at home?* ill. by author. Houghton, 1942. Subj: Format, unusual. Houses.

Billy's picture (Rey, Margaret Elisabeth Waldstein)

Cecily G and the nine monkeys ill. by author. Houghton, 1942. Subj: Animals – giraffes. Animals – monkeys. Humor.

Curious George ill. by author. Houghton, 1941. Subj: Animals – monkeys. Careers – firefighters. Character traits – curiosity. Humor.

Curious George gets a medal ill. by author. Houghton, 1957. Subj: Animals – monkeys. Character traits – curiosity. Humor. Space and space ships.

Curious George goes to the hospital (Rey, Margaret Elisabeth Waldstein)

Curious George learns the alphabet ill. by author. Houghton, 1963. Subj: ABC books. Animals – monkeys. Character traits – curiosity.

Curious George rides a bike ill. by author. Houghton, 1952. Subj: Animals – monkeys. Character traits – curiosity. Circus. Humor. Sports – bicycling.

Curious George takes a job ill. by author. Houghton, 1947. Subj: Animals – monkeys. Careers – window cleaners. Character traits – curiosity. Humor. Zoos.

Elizabite, adventures of a carnivorous plant ill. by author. Harper, 1942. Subj: Humor. Plants. Poetry, rhyme.

Feed the animals ill. by author. Houghton, 1944. Subj: Poetry, rhyme. Zoos.

How do you get there? ill. by author. Houghton, 1941. Subj: Format, unusual. Transportation.

Humpty Dumpty and other Mother Goose songs ill. by author. Harper, 1943. Subj: Music. Nursery rhymes. Songs.

Look for the letters ill. by author. Harper, 1942. Subj: ABC books.

See the circus ill. by author. Houghton, 1956. Subj: Circus. Format, unusual. Poetry, rhyme.

Tit for tat ill. by author. Harper, 1942. Subj: Animals. Humor.

Where's my baby? ill. by author. Houghton, 1943. Subj: Animals. Format, unusual. Poetry, rhyme.

Rey, Margaret Elisabeth Waldstein. *Billy's picture* by Margaret and Hans Augusto Rey; ill. by Hans Augusto Rey. Harper, 1948. Subj: Animals. Art. Humor.

Curious George flies a kite ill. by Hans Augusto Rey. Houghton, 1958. Subj: Animals – monkeys. Character traits – curiosity. Humor. Kites. Sports – fishing.

Curious George goes to the hospital by Margaret and Hans Augusto Rey in collaboration with the Children's Hospital Medical Center, Boston; ill. by Hans Augusto Rey. Houghton, 1966. Subj: Animals – monkeys. Behavior – lost. Character traits – curiosity. Hospitals. Humor.

Pretzel ill. by Hans Augusto Rey. Harper, 1941. Subj: Animals – dogs.

Pretzel and the puppies ill. by Hans Augusto Rey. Harper, 1946. Subj: Animals – dogs.

Spotty ill. by Hans Augusto Rey. Harper, 1945. Subj: Animals – rabbits. Character traits – being different.

Reyher, Becky. *My mother is the most beautiful woman in the world* ill. by Ruth S. Gannett. Lothrop, 1945. Subj: Caldecott award honor book. Family life – mothers.

Reynolds, John *see* Whitlock, Ralph

Reynolds, Madge *see* Whitlock, Ralph

Ricciuti, Edward R. *An animal for Alan* pictures by Tom Eaton. Harper, 1970. Subj: Pets. Science.

Donald and the fish that walked ill. by Syd Hoff. Harper, 1974. Subj: Ecology. Fish. Science.

Rice, Eve. *Benny bakes a cake* ill. by author. Greenwillow, 1981. Subj: Activities – cooking. Animals – dogs. Behavior – misbehavior. Birthdays.

City night ill. by Peter Sis. Greenwillow, 1987. ISBN 0-688-06857-X Subj: City. Family life. Night.

Ebbie ill. by author. Greenwillow, 1975. Subj: Family life. Names.

Goodnight, goodnight ill. by author. Greenwillow, 1980. Subj: Bedtime. Night.

New blue shoes ill. by author. Macmillan, 1975. Subj: Clothing. Family life – mothers. Shopping.

Papa's lemonade and other stories ill. by author. Greenwillow, 1976. Subj: Animals – dogs. Family life.

Sam who never forgets ill. by author. Greenwillow, 1977. Subj: Animals. Food. Zoos.

What Sadie sang ill. by author. Greenwillow, 1976. Subj: Babies. Emotions – happiness.

Rice, Inez. *A long long time* ill. by Robert M. Quackenbush. Lothrop, 1964. Subj: Character traits – optimism. Imagination.

The March wind ill. by Vladimir Bobri. Lothrop, 1957. Subj: Clothing. Imagination. Weather – wind.

Rice, James. *Gaston goes to Texas* ill. by author. Pelican, 1978. Subj: Poetry, rhyme. Reptiles – alligators, crocodiles.

Richard, Jane. *A horse grows up* ill. by Bert Hardy. Walker, 1972. Subj: Animals – horses. Science.

Richardson, Jack E. *Six in a mix* by Jack E. Richardson, Jr., and others; ill. by Carlos Alfonso and others. Benziger, 1971. Subj: Language.

Richardson, Jean. *Clara's dancing feet* ill. by Joanna Carey. Putnam's, 1987. ISBN 0-399-21388-0 Subj: Activities – dancing. Character traits – shyness.

Tall inside ill. by Alice Englander. Putnam's, 1988. ISBN 0-399-21486-0 Subj: Clowns, jesters. Self-concept.

Richter, Alice Numeroff. *Emily's bunch* (Numeroff, Laura Joffe)

You can't put braces on spaces by Alice Numeroff Richter and Laura Joffe Numeroff; ill. by Laura Joffe Numeroff. Greenwillow, 1979. Subj: Careers – dentists. Teeth.

Richter, Joan. *Professor Coconut and the thief* (Gelman, Rita Golden)

Richter, Mischa. *Eric and Matilda* ill. by author. Harper, 1967. Subj: Birds – ducks. Parades.

Quack? ill. by author. Harper, 1978. Subj: Animals. Birds – ducks. Noise, sounds.

To bed, to bed! ill. by author. Prentice-Hall, 1981. Subj: Bedtime. Royalty.

Ricketts, Michael. *Rain* ill. by author. Wonder Books, 1971. Subj: Weather – rain.

Teeth ill. by author. Grosset, 1971. Subj: Teeth.

Riddell, Chris. *Ben and the bear* ill. by author. Lippincott, 1986. ISBN 0-397-32194-5 Subj: Animals – bears. Behavior – sharing.

Bird's new shoes ill. by author. Holt, 1987. ISBN 0-8050-0326-6 Subj: Animals. Behavior – imitation. Character traits – being different. Clothing. Cumulative tales.

The trouble with elephants ill. by author. Lippincott, 1988. ISBN 0-397-32273-9 Subj: Animals – elephants.

Riddell, Edwina. *One hundred first words* ill. by author. Barron's, 1988. ISBN 0-8120-5786-4 Subj: Language.

Rider, Alex. *A la ferme. At the farm: learn-a-language book in French and English* ill. by Paul Davis. Doubleday, 1962. Subj: Farms. Foreign lands – France. Foreign languages.

Chez nous. At our house: learn-a-language book in French and English ill. by Isadore Seltzer. Doubleday, 1962. Subj: Family life. Foreign lands – France. Foreign languages.

Ridlon, Marcia. *Kittens and more kittens* ill. by Elizabeth Dauber. Follett, 1967. Subj: Animals – cats. Pets.

Riehecky, Janet. *Apatosaurus* ill. by Lydia Halverson. Child's World, 1988. ISBN 0-89565-423-7 Subj: Dinosaurs.

Rigby, Shirley Lincoln. *Smaller than most* ill. by Debby L. Carter. Harper, 1985. ISBN 0-06-025028-3 Subj: Animals – pandas. Babies. Character traits – smallness. Family life. Family life – grandfathers.

Riggio, Anita. *Wake up, William!* ill. by author. Atheneum, 1987. ISBN 0-689-31344-6 Subj: Family life. Sleep.

Riley, James Whitcomb. *Little Orphant Annie* ill. by Diane Stanley. Putnam's, 1983. Subj: Poetry, rhyme.

Ring, Douglas *see* Knight, David C.

Ring, Elizabeth. *Tiger lilies: and other beastly plants* ill. by Barbara Bash. Walker, 1985. Subj: Character traits – appearance. Plants.

Ringi, Kjell. *My father and I* by Kjell Ringi and Adelaide Holl; ill. by Kjell Ringi. Watts, 1972. Subj: Character traits – ambition. Family life – fathers. Imagination.

The sun and the cloud ill. by author. Harper, 1971. Subj: Plants. Sun. Weather – clouds.

The winner ill. by author. Harper, 1969. Subj: Behavior. Wordless.

Ringi, Kjell Arne Sorensen *see* Ringi, Kjell

Riordan, James. *Old Father Frost* (Odoyevsky, Vladimir)

The three magic gifts ill. by Errol le Cain. Oxford Univ. Pr., 1980. Subj: Character traits – perseverance. Folk and fairy tales. Sibling rivalry.

Rister, Claude *see* Marshall, James

Roach, Marilynne K. *Dune fox* ill. by author. Little, 1977. Subj: Animals – foxes. Ecology. Sand. Seasons.

Two Roman mice by Horace; ill. by author. Crowell, 1975. Based on a version of Æsop's fable about the country mouse and the city mouse as it appeared in Horace's Satirae II, 6. Subj: Animals – mice. City. Country.

Robart, Rose. *The cake that Mack ate* ill. by Maryann Kovalski. Little, 1987. ISBN 0-87113-121-8 Subj: Cumulative tales. Farms. Food.

Robb, Brian. *My grandmother's djinn* ill. by author. Parents, 1978. Subj: Family life. Foreign lands. Mythical creatures. Problem solving.

Robbins, Ken. *Beach days* photos. by author. Viking, 1987. ISBN 0-670-80138-0 Subj: Sand. Sea and seashore.

City country: a car trip in photographs photos. by author. Viking, 1985. ISBN 0-670-80743-5 Subj: Activities – traveling. Automobiles.

Trucks of every sort photos. by author. Crown, 1981. Subj: Trucks.

Robbins, Ruth. *Baboushka and the three kings* ill. by Nicolas Sidjakov; verse by Edith R. Thomas; music by Mary Clement Sanks. Parnassus, 1960. Adapted from a Russian folk tale. Subj: Caldecott award book. Folk and fairy tales. Foreign lands – Russia. Holidays – Christmas. Music. Poetry, rhyme. Songs.

The harlequin and Mother Goose: or, The magic stick ill. by Nicolas Sidjakov. Parnassus, 1965. Subj: Nursery rhymes.

How the first rainbow was made ill. by author. Houghton, 1980. Subj: Folk and fairy tales. Indians of North America. Weather – rain.

Roberts, Bethany. *Waiting for spring stories* ill. by William Joyce. Harper, 1984. Subj: Animals – rabbits. Seasons – winter.

Roberts, Cliff. *The dot* ill. by author. Watts, 1960. Subj: Concepts – shape.

Start with a dot ill. by author. Watts, 1960. Subj: Concepts – shape. Poetry, rhyme.

Roberts, Sarah. *Bert and the missing mop mix-up* ill. by Joseph Mathieu. Random House, 1983. Subj: Behavior – misunderstanding. Puppets.

Ernie's big mess ill. by Joseph Mathieu. Random House, 1981. ISBN 0-394-94847-5 Subj: Behavior – carelessness. Puppets.

I want to go home! ill. by Joseph Mathieu. Random House, 1985. ISBN 0-394-97027-6 Subj: Behavior – needing someone. Family life – grandmothers. Puppets. Sea and seashore.

Roberts, Thom. *Pirates in the park* ill. by Harold Berson. Crown, 1973. Subj: Imagination. Pirates. Toys – rocking horses.

Robertson, Lilian. *Picnic woods* ill. by author. Harcourt, 1949. Subj: Activities – picnicking.

Runaway rocking horse ill. by author. Harcourt, 1948. Subj: Toys – rocking horses.

Robins, Joan. *Addie meets Max* ill. by Sue Truesdell. Harper, 1985. Subj: Animals – dogs. Friendship.

My brother, Will ill. by Marylin Hafner. Greenwillow, 1986. ISBN 0-688-05223-1 Subj: Babies. Family life – brothers. Sibling rivalry.

Robinson, Adjai. *Femi and old grandaddie* ill. by Jerry Pinkney. Coward, 1972. Subj: Folk and fairy tales. Foreign lands – Africa.

Robinson, Earl. *Black and white* (Arkin, Alan)

Robinson, Irene Bowen. *Picture book of animal babies* by Irene and W. W. Robinson; ill. by Irene Bowen Robinson. Macmillan, 1947. Subj: Animals.

Robinson, Nancy K. *Firefighters!* ill. with photos. Scholastic, 1979. Subj: Careers – firefighters.

Robinson, Thomas P. *Buttons* ill. by Peggy Bacon. Viking, 1938. Subj: Animals – cats.

Robinson, Tom *see* Robinson, Thomas P.

Robinson, W. W. (William Wilcox). *On the farm* ill. by Irene Bowen Robinson. Macmillan, 1939. Subj: Animals. Farms.

Picture book of animal babies (Robinson, Irene Bowen)

Robison, Deborah. *Bye-bye, old buddy* ill. by author. Houghton, 1983. Subj: Problem solving.

No elephants allowed ill. by author. Houghton, 1981. Subj: Bedtime. Emotions – fear. Problem solving.

Your turn, doctor by Deborah Robison and Carla Perez; ill. by Deborah Robison. Dial Pr., 1982. Subj: Behavior – misbehavior. Careers – doctors.

Robison, Nancy. *UFO kidnap* ill. by Edward Frascino. Lothrop, 1978. Subj: Space and space ships.

Roche, A. K. *see* Abisch, Roz

Roche, P. K. (Patrick K.). *Good-bye, Arnold!* ill. by author. Dial Pr., 1979. Subj: Animals – mice. Family life. Sibling rivalry.

Jump all the morning: a child's day in verses ill. by author. Viking, 1984. Subj: Poetry, rhyme.

Plaid bear and the rude rabbit gang ill. by author. Dial Pr., 1982. Subj: Behavior – bullying. Toys.

Webster and Arnold and the giant box ill. by author. Dial Pr., 1980. Subj: Imagination. Sibling rivalry.

Webster and Arnold go camping ill. by author. Viking, 1988. ISBN 0-670-81993-X Subj: Animals – mice. Ghosts. Sports – camping.

Roche, Patrick K. *see* Roche, P. K.

Rockwell, Anne F. *At the beach* ill. by Harlow Rockwell. Macmillan, 1987. ISBN 0-02-777940-8 Subj: Activities – playing. Sea and seashore.

Bafana: a Christmas story ill. by author. Atheneum, 1974. Subj: Folk and fairy tales. Holidays – Christmas.

A bear, a bobcat and three ghosts ill. by author. Macmillan, 1977. Subj: Animals – bears. Animals – bobcats. Careers – peddlers. Ghosts. Holidays – Halloween.

Bear Child's book of hours ill. by author. Crowell, 1987. ISBN 0-690-04551-4 Subj: Animals – bears. Time.

Big bad goat ill. by author. Dutton, 1982. ISBN 0-525-45100-5 Subj: Animals. Character traits – helpfulness. Insects – bees.

Big boss ill. by author. Macmillan, 1975. Subj: Animals – foxes. Animals – tigers. Character traits – cleverness. Frogs and toads.

Big wheels ill. by author. Dutton, 1986. ISBN 0-525-44226-X Subj: Machines.

Bikes ill. by author. Dutton, 1987. ISBN 0-525-44287-1 Subj: Sports – bicycling.

Blackout by Anne F. and Harlow Rockwell; ill. by authors. Macmillan, 1979. Subj: Family life. Power failure. Weather.

Boats ill. by author. Dutton, 1982. Subj: Animals – bears. Boats, ships.

The bump in the night ill. by author. Greenwillow, 1979. Subj: Character traits – cleverness. Character traits – helpfulness.

Buster and the bogeyman ill. by author. Four Winds Pr., 1978. Subj: Bedtime. Dreams. Mythical creatures.

Can I help? by Anne F. and Harlow Rockwell; ill. by authors. Macmillan, 1982. Subj: Character traits – helpfulness.

Cars ill. by author. Dutton, 1984. Subj: Automobiles.

Come to town ill. by author. Crowell, 1987. ISBN 0-690-04646-4 Subj: Animals – bears. City.

The emergency room by Anne and Harlow Rockwell; ill. by authors. Macmillan, 1985. ISBN 0-02-777300-0 Subj: Hospitals. Illness.

Fire engines ill. by author. Dutton, 1986. ISBN 0-525-44259-6 Subj: Animals – dogs. Careers – firefighters. Trucks.

First comes spring ill. by author. Crowell, 1985. ISBN 0-690-04455-0 Subj: Animals – bears. Seasons.

The first snowfall by Anne and Harlow Rockwell; ill. by authors. Macmillan, 1987. ISBN 0-02-777770-7 Subj: Seasons – winter. Weather – snow.

Gogo's pay day ill. by author. Doubleday, 1978. Subj: Character traits – generosity. Clowns, jesters. Money.

The gollywhopper egg ill. by author. Macmillan, 1974. Subj: Behavior – trickery. Eggs. Farms.

The good llama ill. by author. World, 1963. Subj: Animals. Animals – llamas. Foreign lands – South America.

Handy Hank will fix it ill. by author. Holt, 1988. ISBN 0-8050-0697-4 Subj: Careers – handyman. Character traits – helpfulness.

Happy birthday to me by Anne F. and Harlow Rockwell; ill. by authors. Macmillan, 1981. Subj: Birthdays.

Honk honk! ill. by author. Dutton, 1980. Subj: Animals. Behavior – misbehavior. Birds. Cumulative tales.

How my garden grew by Anne F. and Harlow Rockwell; ill. by authors. Macmillan, 1982. Subj: Activities – gardening.

Hugo at the window ill. by author. Macmillan, 1988. ISBN 0-02-777330-2 Subj: Animals – dogs. Birthdays. City.

I like the library ill. by author. Dutton, 1977. Subj: Libraries.

I love my pets by Anne F. and Harlow Rockwell; ill. by authors. Macmillan, 1982. Subj: Pets.

I play in my room by Anne F. and Harlow Rockwell; ill. by authors. Macmillan, 1981. Subj: Activities – playing.

In our house ill. by author. Crowell, 1985. ISBN 0-690-04488-7 Subj: Activities. Animals – bears. Family life.

Machines by Anne F. and Harlow Rockwell; ill. by Harlow Rockwell. Macmillan, 1972. Subj: Machines.

The Mother Goose cookie-candy book ill. by author. Random House, 1983. Subj: Activities – cooking. Food.

My back yard by Anne F. and Harlow Rockwell; ill. by authors. Macmillan, 1984. Subj: Activities – playing.

My barber by Anne F. and Harlow Rockwell; ill. by authors. Macmillan, 1981. Subj: Careers – barbers. Hair.

My spring robin by Harlow Rockwell and Lizzy Rockwell. Macmillan, 1989. ISBN 0-02-777611- Subj: Birds – robins. Flowers. Seasons – spring.

Nice and clean by Anne F. and Harlow Rockwell; ill. by authors. Macmillan, 1984. Subj: Character traits – cleanliness. Houses.

The night we slept outside by Anne F. and Harlow Rockwell; ill. by authors. Macmillan, 1983. Subj: Night. Sports – camping.

The old woman and her pig and 10 other stories ill. by adapt. Crowell, 1979. Subj: Folk and fairy tales.

Our garage sale ill. by Harlow Rockwell. Greenwillow, 1984. Subj: Garage sales.

Planes by Anne and Harlow Rockwell; ill. by authors. Dutton, 1985. ISBN 0-525-44159-X Subj: Airplanes, airports. Transportation.

Poor Goose: a French folktale ill. by author. Crowell, 1976. Subj: Animals. Birds – geese. Cumulative tales. Folk and fairy tales. Foreign lands – France.

Sick in bed by Anne F. and Harlow Rockwell; ill. by authors. Macmillan, 1982. Subj: Illness.

The stolen necklace: a picture story from India ill. by author. Collins-World, 1968. "Based on a tale from the Jataka." Subj: Animals – monkeys. Character traits – cleverness. Foreign lands – India.

The story snail ill. by author. Macmillan, 1974. Subj: Animals – snails. Magic.

The supermarket by Anne F. and Harlow Rockwell; ill. by authors. Macmillan, 1979. Subj: Shopping. Stores.

Things that go ill. by author. Dutton, 1986. ISBN 0-525-44266-9 Subj: Transportation.

The three bears and 15 other stories ill. by author. Crown, 1975. Subj: Folk and fairy tales.

Thump thump thump! ill. by author. Dutton, 1981. Subj: Folk and fairy tales. Monsters.

Toad by Anne F. and Harlow Rockwell; ill. by authors. Doubleday, 1972. Subj: Frogs and toads.

The toolbox by Anne F. and Harlow Rockwell; ill. by Harlow Rockwell. Macmillan, 1971. Subj: Tools.

Trucks ill. by author. Dutton, 1984. Subj: Trucks.

When I go visiting by Anne F. and Harlow Rockwell; ill. by authors. Macmillan, 1984. Subj: Family life – grandmothers. Family life – grandparents.

Willy runs away ill. by author. Dutton, 1978. ISBN 0-525-42795-3 Subj: Animals – dogs. Behavior – running away.

The wolf who had a wonderful dream ill. by author. Crowell, 1973. Subj: Animals – wolves. Dreams. Folk and fairy tales. Food. Foreign lands – France.

The wonderful eggs of Furicchia: a picture story from Italy ill. by author. Collins-World, 1969. Subj: Birds – chickens. Eggs. Folk and fairy tales. Foreign lands – Italy. Magic.

Rockwell, Harlow. *Blackout* (Rockwell, Anne F.)

Can I help? (Rockwell, Anne F.)

The compost heap ill. by author. Doubleday, 1974. Subj: Activities – gardening. Plants.

The emergency room (Rockwell, Anne F.)

The first snowfall (Rockwell, Anne F.)

Happy birthday to me (Rockwell, Anne F.)

How my garden grew (Rockwell, Anne F.)

I did it ill. by author. Macmillan, 1974. Subj: Activities.

I love my pets (Rockwell, Anne F.)

I play in my room (Rockwell, Anne F.)

Look at this ill. by author. Macmillan, 1978. Subj: Activities.

Machines (Rockwell, Anne F.)

My back yard (Rockwell, Anne F.)

My barber (Rockwell, Anne F.)

My dentist ill. by author. Greenwillow, 1975. Subj: Careers – dentists. Teeth.

My doctor ill. by author. Macmillan, 1973. Subj: Careers – doctors. Health.

My kitchen ill. by author. Greenwillow, 1980. Subj: Food.

My nursery school ill. by author. Greenwillow, 1976. Subj: School.

Nice and clean (Rockwell, Anne F.)

The night we slept outside (Rockwell, Anne F.)

Planes (Rockwell, Anne F.)

Sick in bed (Rockwell, Anne F.)

The supermarket (Rockwell, Anne F.)

Toad (Rockwell, Anne F.)

The toolbox (Rockwell, Anne F.)

When I go visiting (Rockwell, Anne F.)

Rockwell, Norman. *Norman Rockwell's counting book* sel. by Glorina Taborin; ill. by author. Harmony Books, 1977. Subj: Counting. Games. Holidays – April Fools' Day.

Rodanas, Kristina. *The story of Wali Dâd* ill. by author. Lothrop, 1988. ISBN 0-688-07363-1 Subj: Character traits – generosity. Foreign lands – India.

Rodgers, Frank. *Who's afraid of the ghost train?* ill. by author. Harcourt, 1989. ISBN 0-15-200642-7 Subj: Emotions – fear. Family life – grandfathers. Ghosts. Trains.

Roe, Richard. *Animal ABC* ill. by author. Random House, 1984. ISBN 0-394-96864-6 Subj: ABC books. Animals.

Roehrdanz, Barbro Eriksson. *Hocus-pocus* (Eriksson, Eva)

Jealousy (Eriksson, Eva)

One short week (Eriksson, Eva)

The tooth trip (Eriksson, Eva)

Roennfeldt, Robert. *A day on the avenue* ill. by author. Viking, 1984. Subj: Roads. Wordless.

Roffey, Maureen. *Family scramble* ill. by author. Dutton, 1987. ISBN 0-525-44290-1 Subj: Family life. Format, unusual.

Home sweet home ill. by author. Coward, 1983. Subj: Format, unusual – toy and movable books. Houses.

I spy at the zoo ill. by author. Four Winds Pr., 1988. ISBN 0-02-777150-4 Subj: Animals. Zoos.

I spy on vacation ill. by author. Four Winds Pr., 1988. ISBN 0-02-777160-1 Subj: Activities – vacationing. Sea and seashore.

Look, there's my hat! ill. by author. Putnam's, 1985. Subj: Behavior – greed. Format, unusual.

Rogasky, Barbara. *Rapunzel* (Grimm, Jacob)

The water of life ill. by. Trina Schart Hyman. Holiday, 1986. Adapt. of Das Wasser des Lebens by Jacob and Wilhelm Grimm. ISBN 0-8234-0552-4 Subj: Character traits – pride. Folk and fairy tales. Magic. Royalty. Sibling rivalry.

Rogers, Anne. *Cinderella* (Grimm, Jacob)

The musicians of Bremen (Grimm, Jacob)

The wolf and the seven little kids (Grimm, Jacob)

Rogers, Edmund. *Elephants* ill. with photos. Raintree, 1978. Subj: Animals – elephants.

Rogers, Fred. *Going to day care* photos. by Jim Judkis. Putnam's, 1985. ISBN 0-399-21235-3 Subj: School.

Going to the doctor photos. by Jim Judkis. Putnam's, 1986. ISBN 0-399-21298-1 Subj: Careers — doctors.

Going to the hospital photos. by Jim Judkis. Putnam's, 1988. ISBN 0-399-21503-4 Subj: Hospitals. Illness.

Going to the potty photos. by Jim Judkis. Putnam's, 1986. ISBN 0-399-21296-5 Subj: Behavior — growing up.

If we were all the same ill. by Pat Sustendal. Random House, 1988. ISBN 0-394-98778-0 Subj: Character traits — individuality.

Making friends photos. by Jim Judkis. Putnam's, 1987. ISBN 0-399-21382-1 Subj: Activities — playing. Emotions. Friendship.

Moving photos. by Jim Judkis. Putnam's, 1987. ISBN 0-399-21383-X Subj: Communities, neighborhoods. Emotions. Family life. Friendship. Moving.

The new baby photos. by Jim Judkis. Putnam's, 1985. ISBN 0-399-21236-1 Subj: Babies. Sibling rivalry.

When a pet dies photos. by Jim Judkis. Putnam's, 1988. ISBN 0-399-21504-2 Subj: Death. Pets.

Rogers, Helen Spelman. *Morris and his brave lion* ill. by Glo Coalson. McGraw-Hill, 1975. Subj: Divorce.

Rogers, Jean. *Runaway mittens* ill. by Rie Munoz. Greenwillow, 1988. ISBN 0-688-07054-X Subj: Behavior — losing things. Clothing.

Rogers, Margaret. *Green is beautiful* by Margaret Rogers and Bernadette Watts; ill. by Bernadette Watts. State Mutual Books, 1982. Subj: Concepts — color. Folk and fairy tales.

Rogers, Paul. *Forget-me-not* ill. by Celia Berridge. Viking, 1984. Subj: Behavior — forgetfulness. Behavior — losing things.

From me to you ill. by Jane Johnson. Watts, 1988. ISBN 0-531-08332-2 Subj: Family life — grandmothers. Poetry, rhyme.

Sheepchase ill. by Celia Berridge. Viking, 1986. ISBN 0-670-80599-8 Subj: Animals — sheep. Behavior — running away. Poetry, rhyme.

Somebody's awake ill. by Robin Bell Corfield. Atheneum, 1988. ISBN 0-689-31490-6 Subj: Family life. Food. Morning.

Somebody's sleepy ill. by Robin Bell Corfield. Atheneum, 1988. ISBN 0-689-31491-4 Subj: Bedtime. Family life.

Tumbledown ill. by Robin Bell Corfield. Atheneum, 1988. ISBN 0-689-31392-6 Subj: City. Royalty.

Rogers, Paul Patrick *see* Rogers, Paul

Rogow, Zak. *Oranges* ill. by Mary Szilagyi. Watts, 1988. ISBN 0-531-08343-8 Subj: Food. Trees.

Rohmer, Harriet. *Atariba and Niguayona: a story from the Taino people of Puerto Rico* adapt. by Harriet Rohmer and Jesus Guerrero Rea; ill. by Consuelo Mendez. Childrens Book Pr., 1988. ISBN 0-89239-026-3 Subj: Character traits — kindness. Foreign lands — Puerto Rico. Illness.

How we came to the fifth world: a creation story from Ancient Mexico adapt. by Harriet Rohmer and Mary Anchondo; ill. by Graciela Carrillo. Childrens Book Pr., 1988. ISBN 0-89239-024-7 Subj: Folk and fairy tales. Foreign lands — Mexico.

The invisible hunters by Harriet Rohmer, Octavio Chow and Morris Vidaure; ill. by Joe Sam. Childrens Book Pr., 1987. ISBN 0-89239-031-X Subj: Behavior — greed. Folk and fairy tales. Foreign lands — Nicaragua. Sports — hunting.

Mother scorpion country by Harriet Rohmer and Dorminster Wilson; ill. by Virginia Stearns. Childrens Book Pr., 1987. ISBN 0-89239-032-8 Subj: Emotions — love. Folk and fairy tales. Foreign lands — Nicaragua.

Rojankovsky, Feodor. *ABC, an alphabet of many things* ill. by author. Golden Pr., 1970. Subj: ABC books.

Animals in the zoo ill. by author. Knopf, 1962. Subj: ABC books. Animals. Zoos.

Animals on the farm ill. by author. Knopf, 1962. Subj: Animals. Farms. Wordless.

The great big animal book ill. by author. Simon and Schuster, 1950. Subj: Animals. Farms.

The great big wild animal book ill. by author. Western, 1951. Subj: Animals.

Roll over! *a counting song* ill. by Merle Peek. Houghton, 1981. Subj: Counting. Songs.

Romanek, Enid Warner. *Teddy* ill. by author. Scribner's, 1978. Subj: Toys — teddy bears.

Romanoli, Robert. *What's so funny?!!* ill. by Jerry Zimmerman. Grosset, 1978. Subj: Riddles.

Ronay, Jadja. *Ginger* ill. by Anthony Accardo. Magnolia, 1981. Subj: Folk and fairy tales. Magic.

Rondell, Florence. *The family that grew* by Florence Rondell and Ruth Michaels. Crown, 1965. Subj: Adoption.

Roop, Connie. *Going buggy!* (Roop, Peter)

Let's celebrate! (Roop, Peter)

Stick out your tongue! (Roop, Peter)

Roop, Peter. *Going buggy!* by Peter and Connie Roop; ill. by Joan Hanson. Lerner, 1986. ISBN 0-8225-0988-1 Subj: Insects. Riddles.

Let's celebrate! jokes about holidays by Peter and Connie Roop; ill. by Joan Hanson. Lerner, 1986. ISBN 0-8225-0989-X Subj: Holidays. Riddles.

Stick out your tongue! by Peter and Connie Roop; ill. by Joan Hanson. Lerner, 1986. ISBN 0-8225-0990-3 Subj: Careers — doctors. Riddles.

Roosevelt, Michelle Chopin. *Zoo animals* ill. by author. Random House, 1983. Subj: Format, unusual – board books. Zoos.

Root, Phyllis. *Gretchen's grandma* by Phyllis Root and Carol A. Marron; ill. by Deborah Kogan Ray. Raintree, 1983. ISBN 0-940742-16-0 Subj: Birthdays. Family life – grandmothers. Language.

Moon tiger ill. by Ed Young. Holt, 1985. ISBN 0-03-000042-4 Subj: Animals. Animals – tigers. Imagination. Sibling rivalry.

Soup for supper ill. by Sue Truesdell. Harper, 1986. ISBN 0-06-025071-2 Subj: Folk and fairy tales. Food. Friendship. Giants. Music. Songs.

Rosario, Idalia. *Idalia's project ABC: an urban alphabet book in English and Spanish* ill. by author. Holt, 1981. Subj: ABC books. City. Foreign languages.

Roscoe, William. *The butterfly's ball* ill. by Don Bolognese. McGraw-Hill, 1967. Subj: Animals. Insects – butterflies, caterpillars. Poetry, rhyme.

Rose, Anne. *Akimba and the magic cow: a folktale from Africa* ill. by Hope Meryman. Four Winds Pr., 1979. Subj: Folk and fairy tales. Foreign lands – Africa. Magic.

As right as right can be ill. by Arnold Lobel. Dial Pr., 1976. Subj: Behavior – seeking better things. Money.

How does a czar eat potatoes? ill. by Janosch. Lothrop, 1973. Subj: Poetry, rhyme. Poverty. Royalty.

Pot full of luck ill. by Margot Tomes. Lothrop, 1982. Subj: Folk and fairy tales. Foreign lands – Africa.

Spider in the sky ill. by Gail Owens. Harper, 1978. Based on the story How the Sun came from American Indian mythology by Alice Marriott and Carol K. Rachlin. Subj: Animals. Folk and fairy tales. Indians of North America. Spiders.

The talking turnip ill. by Paul Galdone. Parents, 1979. ISBN 0-8193-1006-9 Subj: Cumulative tales. Folk and fairy tales.

The triumphs of Fuzzy Fogtop ill. by Tomie de Paola. Dial Pr., 1979. Subj: Folk and fairy tales.

Rose, David S. *It hardly seems like Halloween* ill. by author. Lothrop, 1983. Subj: Holidays – Halloween.

Rose, Gerald. *The bird garden* ill. by author. Salem House, 1987. ISBN 0-370-30690-2 Subj: Birds. Language. Royalty.

The hare and the tortoise (Æsop)

The lion and the mouse (Æsop)

PB takes a holiday ill. by author. Bodley Head, 1981. Subj: Activities – traveling. Animals – polar bears.

The raven and the fox (Æsop)

Scruff ill. by author. Salem House, 1985. ISBN 0-370-30619-8 Subj: Animals – dogs. Senses – smelling.

The tiger-skin rug ill. by author. Prentice-Hall, 1979. Subj: Animals – tigers. Crime.

Trouble in the ark ill. by author. Merrimack, 1985. ISBN 0-370-30833-6 Subj: Animals. Behavior – fighting, arguing. Religion – Noah.

Rose, Mitchell. *Norman* ill. by author. Simon and Schuster, 1970. Subj: Animals – dogs. Theater.

Rosen, Anne. *A family Passover* by Anne Rosen and others; photos. by Laurence Salzmann. Jewish Pub. Soc., 1980. Subj: Holidays – Passover. Jewish culture.

Rosen, Michael. *Smelly jelly smelly fish* ill. by Quentin Blake. Prentice-Hall, 1987. ISBN 0-13-814567-9 Subj: Humor. Poetry, rhyme.

Under the bed: the bedtime book ill. by Quentin Blake. Prentice-Hall, 1986. ISBN 0-13-935412-3 Subj: Bedtime. Poetry, rhyme.

You can't catch me! ill. by Quentin Blake. Elsevier-Dutton, 1982. Subj: Humor. Poetry, rhyme.

Rosen, Winifred. *Dragons hate to be discreet* ill. by Edward Koren. Knopf, 1978. Subj: Dragons. Imagination.

Henrietta and the day of the iguana ill. by Kay Chorao. Four Winds Pr., 1978. Subj: Behavior – wishing. Pets. Reptiles – iguanas.

Henrietta and the gong from Hong Kong ill. by Kay Chorao. Four Winds Pr., 1981. Subj: Family life – grandparents. Sibling rivalry.

Rosenberg, David *see* Clifford, David

Rosenberg, Ethel Clifford *see* Clifford, Eth

Rosenberg, Maxine B. *Being adopted* photos. by George Ancona. Lothrop, 1984. Subj: Adoption. Ethnic groups in the U.S. Family life.

My friend Leslie: the story of a handicapped child photos. by George Ancona. Lothrop, 1983. Subj: Handicaps. School.

Rosenberg, Nancy Sherman *see* Sherman, Nancy

Rosenbloom, Joseph. *Deputy Dan and the bank robbers* ill. by Tim Raglin. Random House, 1985. ISBN 0-394-97045-4 Subj: Crime.

The funniest joke book ever! ill. by Hans Wilhelm. Sterling, 1986. ISBN 0-8069-4724-1 Subj: Riddles.

Rosner, Ruth. *Arabba gah zee, Marissa and Me!* ill. by author. Albert Whitman, 1987. ISBN 0-8075-0442-4 Subj: Activities – playing. Friendship. Imagination.

Ross, David. *Gorp and the space pirates* ill. by author. Walker, 1983. Subj: Monsters. Pirates. Space and space ships.

More hugs! ill. by author. Crowell, 1984. ISBN 0-694-00147-3 Subj: Emotions.

Space monster ill. by author. Walker, 1981. Subj: Monsters. Space and space ships.

Space Monster Gorp and the runaway computer ill. by author. Walker, 1984. Subj: Monsters. Space and space ships.

Ross, Diana. *The story of the little red engine* ill. by Leslie Wood. Transatlantic, 1947. Subj: Foreign lands – England. Trains.

Ross, Elizabeth *see* Kübler-Ross, Elisabeth

Ross, George Maxim. *When Lucy went away* ill. by Ingrid Fetz. Dutton, 1976. Subj: Animals – cats. Pets.

Ross, H. L. *Not counting monsters* ill. by Doug Cushman. Platt, 1978. Subj: Activities. Counting. Monsters.

Ross, Isaac *see* Ross, George Maxim

Ross, Jessica. *Ms. Klondike* ill. by author. Viking, 1977. Subj: Activities – working. Careers – taxi drivers. Taxis.

Ross, Joel. *Your first airplane trip* (Ross, Pat)

Ross, John Andrew. *What a morning!*

Ross, Katharine. *When you were a baby* photos. by Phoebe Dunn. Random, 1988. ISBN 0-394-89897-4 Subj: Babies. Behavior – growing up. Family life.

Ross, Pat. *M and M and the big bag* ill. by Marylin Hafner. Pantheon, 1981. Subj: Activities – reading. Shopping.

M and M and the haunted house game ill. by Marylin Hafner. Pantheon, 1980. Subj: Ghosts. Houses.

M and M and the mummy mess ill. by Marylin Hafner. Viking, 1985. ISBN 0-670-80548-3 Subj: Behavior – misbehavior. Museums.

Meet M and M ill. by Marylin Hafner. Pantheon, 1980. Subj: Friendship.

Molly and the slow teeth ill. by Jerry Milord. Lothrop, 1980. Subj: School. Teeth.

Your first airplane trip by Pat and Joel Ross; ill. by Lynn Wheeling. Lothrop, 1981. Subj: Activities – flying. Airplanes, airports. Emotions – fear.

Ross, Tony. *The enchanted pig: an old Rumanian tale* ill. by author. Harper, 1983. Subj: Animals – pigs. Folk and fairy tales. Magic. Witches.

The greedy little cobbler ill. by author. Barron's, 1980. Subj: Behavior – greed. Careers – shoemakers.

Hugo and Oddsock ill. by author. Follett, 1978. Subj: Animals – mice. Imagination – imaginary friends.

Hugo and the bureau of holidays ill. by author. Follett, 1982. Subj: Animals – mice. Holidays.

Hugo and the man who stole colors ill. by author. Follett, 1982. Subj: Animals – mice. Behavior – stealing. Concepts – color.

I want my potty ill. by author. Kane Miller, 1986. ISBN 0-916291-08-1 Subj: Behavior – growing up.

I'm coming to get you! ill. by author. Dial Pr., 1984. ISBN 0-8037-0119-5 Subj: Emotions – fear. Monsters. Space and space ships.

Jack the giantkiller (Jack and the beanstalk)

Lazy Jack ill. by author. Dial Pr., 1986. ISBN 0-8037-0275-2 Subj: Character traits – laziness. Cumulative tales. Folk and fairy tales.

Oscar got the blame ill. by author. Dial Pr., 1988. ISBN 0-8037-0499-2 Subj: Behavior – misbehavior.

The pied piper of Hamelin retold and ill. by Tony Ross. Lothrop, 1978. Subj: Animals – rats. Folk and fairy tales. Foreign lands – Germany.

Stone soup ill. by author. Dial Pr., 1987. ISBN 0-8037-0401-1 Subj: Animals – wolves. Birds – chickens. Character traits – cleverness. Folk and fairy tales.

Towser and the terrible thing ill. by author. Pantheon, 1984. Subj: Animals – dogs. Monsters. Royalty.

Ross, Wilda S. *What did the dinosaurs eat?* ill. by Elizabeth Schmidt. Coward, 1972. Subj: Dinosaurs. Food. Science.

Rossetti, Christina Georgina. *What is pink?* ill. by José Aruego. Macmillan, 1971. Subj: Birds – flamingos. Concepts – color. Poetry, rhyme.

Rossner, Judith. *What kind of feet does a bear have?* ill. by Irwin Rosenhouse. Bobbs-Merrill, 1963. Subj: Humor.

Roth, Harold. *Autumn days* photos. by author. Grosset, 1986. ISBN 0-448-10680-9 Subj: Format, unusual – board books. Seasons – fall.

A checkup photos. by author. Grosset, 1986. ISBN 0-448-10683-3 Subj: Format, unusual – board books. Health.

Let's look all around the farm photos. by author. Putnam's, 1988. ISBN 0-448-10687-6 Subj: Farms. Format, unusual – toy and movable books.

Let's look all around the house photos. by author. Putnam's, 1988. ISBN 0-448-10685-X Subj: Format, unusual – toy and movable books. Houses.

Let's look all around the town photos. by author. Putnam's, 1988. ISBN 0-448-10684-1 Subj: City. Format, unusual – toy and movable books.

Let's look for surprises all around photos. by author. Putnam's, 1988. ISBN 0-448-10686-8 Subj: Format, unusual – toy and movable books.

Nursery school photos. by author. Grosset, 1986. ISBN 0-448-10682-5 Subj: Format, unusual – board books. School.

Winter days photos. by author. Grosset, 1986. ISBN 0-448-10681-7 Subj: Format, unusual – board books. Seasons – winter.

Roth, Susan L. *Fire came to the earth people: a Dahomean folktale* ill. by adapt. St. Martin's, 1988. ISBN 0-312-01723-5 Subj: Fire. Folk and fairy tales. Foreign lands – Africa.

Kanahena: a Cherokee story ill. by adapt. St. Martin's, 1988. ISBN 0-312-01722-7 Subj: Animals – wolves. Folk and fairy tales. Indians of North America.

Patchwork tales by Susan L. Roth and Ruth Phang; ill. by authors. Atheneum, 1984. Subj: Family life – grandmothers.

Rothman, Joel. *This can lick a lollipop: body riddles for kids; esto goza chupando un caramelo: las partes del cuerpo en adivinanzas infantiles* English by Joel Rothman, Spanish by Argentina Palacios; photos. by Patricia Ruben. Doubleday, 1979. ISBN 0-385-13072-4 Subj: Anatomy. Foreign languages.

Rothschild, Dorothy *see* Parker, Dorothy D.

Rottenberg, Dorian. *The merry starlings* (Marshak, Samuel)

Roughsey, Dick. *The giant devil-dingo* ill. by author. Macmillan, 1973. Subj: Animals. Folk and fairy tales. Foreign lands – Australia.

Round, Graham. *Hangdog* ill. by author. Dial Pr., 1987. ISBN 0-8037-0448-8 Subj: Animals – dogs. Animals – tigers. Boats, ships. Friendship. Islands. Sea and seashore.

Rounds, Glen. *The boll weevil* Ill. by author. Golden Gate, 1967. Subj: Folk and fairy tales. Insects. Music. Songs.

Casey Jones: the story of a brave engineer ill. by author. Golden Gate, 1968. Subj: Folk and fairy tales. Music. Songs. Trains.

The day the circus came to Lone Tree ill. by author. Holiday, 1973. Subj: Circus. Humor.

Once we had a horse ill. by author. Holiday, 1971. Subj: Animals – horses.

The strawberry roan ill. by comp. Golden Gate, 1970. Subj: Animals – horses. Music. Songs.

Sweet Betsy from Pike ill. by comp. Children's Pr., 1973. Subj: Folk and fairy tales. Music. Songs.

Washday on Noah's ark ill. by author. Holiday, 1985. ISBN 0-8234-0555-9 Subj: Animals. Character traits – cleanliness. Religion – Noah.

Routh, Jonathan. *The Nuns go to Africa* ill. by author. Bobbs-Merrill, 1971. Subj: Careers – nuns. Foreign lands – Africa.

Rowan, James P. *I can be a zoo keeper.* Childrens Pr., 1985. ISBN 0-516-01889-2 Subj: Animals. Careers. Zoos.

Rowand, Phyllis. *Every day in the year* ill. by author. Little, 1959. Subj: Emotions – love. Holidays – Christmas.

George ill. by author. Little, 1956. Subj: Animals – dogs.

George goes to town ill. by author. Little, 1958. Subj: Animals – dogs.

It is night ill. by author. Harper, 1953. Subj: Night. Sleep.

Rowe, Cliff. *Listen!* (Crume, Marion W.)

Rowe, Jeanne A. *City workers.* Watts, 1969. Subj: Careers. City.

A trip through a school. Watts, 1969. Subj: School.

Roy, Ronald. *Breakfast with my father* ill. by Troy Howell. Houghton, 1980. Subj: Divorce. Family life.

A thousand pails of water ill. by Vo-Dinh Mai. Knopf, 1978. Subj: Animals – whales. Character traits – kindness to animals. Foreign lands – Japan.

Three ducks went wandering ill. by Paul Galdone. Seabury Pr., 1979. Subj: Behavior – indifference. Birds – ducks. Humor.

Whose hat is that? ill. by Rosmarie Hausherr. Clarion, 1987. ISBN 0-89919-446-X Subj: Clothing.

Whose shoes are these? photos. by Rosmarie Hausherr. Clarion, 1988. ISBN 0-89919-445-1 Subj: Clothing.

Rubel, Nicole. *Bruno Brontosaurus* ill. by author. Camelot, 1983. Subj: Dinosaurs.

It came from the swamp ill. by author. Dial Pr., 1988. ISBN 0-8037-0515-8 Subj: Behavior – lost. Humor. Reptiles – alligators, crocodiles.

Me and my kitty ill. by author. Macmillan, 1983. Subj: Activities. Animals – cats.

Sam and Violet are twins ill. by author. Camelot, 1981. Subj: Animals – cats. Character traits – individuality. Twins.

Sam and Violet go camping ill. by author. Camelot, 1981. Subj: Animals – cats. Character traits – individuality. Sports – camping. Twins.

Uncle Henry and Aunt Henrietta's honeymoon ill. by author. Dial Pr., 1986. ISBN 0-8037-0247-7 Subj: Activities – baby-sitting. Boats, ships. Family life.

Ruben, Patricia. *Apples to zippers: an alphabet book* ill. by author. Doubleday, 1976. Subj: ABC books.

True or false? ill. by author. Lippincott, 1978. Subj: Concepts.

Rubin, Caroline. *Snow on bear's nose* (Bartoli, Jennifer)

Tell them my name is Amanda (Wold, Jo Anne)

Wild Bill Hiccup's riddle book (Bishop, Ann)

Rubin, Cynthia Elyce. *ABC Americana from the National Gallery of Art.* Harcourt, 1989. ISBN 0-15-200660-5 Subj: ABC books. Art.

Rubin, Jeff. *Baseball brothers* by Jeff Rubin and Rick Rael; ill. by Sandy Kossin. Lothrop, 1976. Subj: Friendship. Sports – baseball.

Ruby-Spears Enterprises. *The puppy's new adventures: hide and seek* ill. by Ruby-Spears Enterprises. Antioch, 1983. Subj: Animals – dogs. Crime. Format, unusual – toy and movable books.

Ruck-Pauquèt, Gina. *Little hedgehog* ill. by Marianne Richter. Hastings, 1959. Subj: Animals – hedgehogs.

Mumble bear tr. by Anthea Bell; ill. by Erika Dietzsch-Capelle. Putnam's, 1980. Subj: Animals – bears. Character traits – individuality.

Oh, that koala! ill. by Anna Mossakowska. McGraw-Hill, 1979. Subj: Animals – koala bears. Behavior – misbehavior.

Rudchenko, Ivan. *Ivanko and the dragon: an old Ukrainian folk tale* tr. by Marie Halun Bloch; ill. by Yaroslava. Atheneum, 1969. Subj: Dragons. Folk and fairy tales. Foreign lands – Ukraine.

Rudolph, Marguerita. *Grey Neck* (Mamin-Sibiryak, D. N.)

How a piglet crashed the Christmas party (Zakhoder, Boris Vladimirovich)

How a shirt grew in the field adapt. from the Russian of K. Ushinsky; ill. by Yaroslava. McGraw-Hill, 1967. Subj: Clothing. Foreign lands – Ukraine. Plants.

I am your misfortune: a Lithuanian folk tale ill. by Imero Gobbato. Seabury Pr., 1968. Subj: Character traits – selfishness. Folk and fairy tales. Foreign lands – Lithuania. Monsters. Sports – baseball.

Rosachok (Zakhoder, Boris Vladimirovich)

Sharp and shiny ill. by Susan Perl. McGraw-Hill, 1971. Subj: Activities – bathing. Activities – playing. Character traits – cleanliness.

Rudomin, Esther *see* Hautzig, Esther

Ruffins, Reynold. *My brother never feeds the cat* ill. by author. Scribner's, 1979. Subj: Family life.

Rukeyser, Muriel. *More night* ill. by Symeon Shimin. Harper, 1981. Subj: Activities. Night.

Uncle Eddie's moustache (Brecht, Bertolt)

Rushnell, Elaine Evans. *My mom's having a baby* ill. with drawings and photos. Grosset, 1978. Subj: Babies. Family life. Science. Sibling rivalry.

Ruskin, John. *Dame Wiggins of Lee and her seven wonderful cats*

Rusling, Albert. *The mouse and Mrs. Proudfoot* ill. by author. Prentice-Hall, 1985. Subj: Animals. Houses. Humor.

Russ, Lavinia. *Alec's sand castle* ill. by James Stevenson. Harper, 1972. Subj: Activities – playing. Imagination. Sea and seashore.

Russell, Betty. *Big store, funny door* ill. by Mary Gehr. Albert Whitman, 1955. Subj: Character traits – luck. Shopping.

Run sheep run ill. by Mary Gehr. Albert Whitman, 1952. Subj: Animals – sheep.

Russell, Naomi. *The tree* ill. by author. Dutton, 1989. ISBN 0-525-44468-8 Subj: Format, unusual. Nature. Trees.

Russell, Pamela. *Do you have a secret? How to get help for scary secrets* by Pamela Russell and Beth Stone; ill. by Mary McKee. CompCare, 1986. ISBN 0-89638-098-X Subj: Behavior – secrets. Safety.

Russell, Sandra Joanne. *A farmer's dozen* ill. by author. Harper, 1982. Subj: Farms. Poetry, rhyme.

Russell, Solveig Paulson. *What good is a tail?* ill. by Ezra Jack Keats. Bobbs-Merrill, 1962. Subj: Animals. Science.

Russo, Marisabina. *The line up book* ill. by author. Greenwillow, 1986. ISBN 0-688-06205-9 Subj: Activities – playing. Family life. Games.

Only six more days ill. by author. Greenwillow, 1988. ISBN 0-688-07072-8 Subj: Birthdays. Sibling rivalry.

Why do grownups have all the fun? ill. by author. Greenwillow, 1987. ISBN 0-688-06626-7 Subj: Bedtime. Behavior – dissatisfaction. Family life. Imagination.

Russo, Susan. *The ice cream ocean and other delectable poems of the sea* ill. by author. Lothrop, 1984. Subj: Poetry, rhyme. Sea and seashore.

The moon's the north wind's cooky

Ruthstrom, Dorotha. *The big kite contest* ill. by Lillian Hoban. Pantheon, 1980. Subj: Kites. Sibling rivalry.

Ryan, Cheli Durán. *Hildilid's night* ill. by Arnold Lobel. Macmillan, 1971. Subj: Caldecott award honor book. Night.

Ryder, Eileen. *Winklet goes to school* ill. by Stephanie Lang. John Godon Burke, 1982. Subj: School.

Winston's new cap ill. by Stephanie Lang. John Godon Burke, 1982. Subj: Behavior – losing things. Clothing.

Ryder, Joanne. *Beach party* ill. by Diane Stanley. Warne, 1982. Subj: Animals – sheep. Family life. Sea and seashore.

Chipmunk song ill. by Lynne Cherry. Dutton, 1987. ISBN 0-525-67191-9 Subj: Animals – chipmunks. Poetry, rhyme.

Fireflies ill. by Don Bolognese. Harper, 1977. Subj: Insects – fireflies. Science.

Fog in the meadow ill. by Gail Owens. Harper, 1979. Subj: Animals. Weather – fog.

Mockingbird morning ill. by Dennis Nolan. Four Winds Pr., 1989. ISBN 0-02-777961-0 Subj: Birds – mockingbirds. Nature. Poetry, rhyme.

The night flight ill. by Amy Schwartz. Four Winds Pr., 1985. ISBN 0-02-778020-1 Subj: Animals. City. Dreams. Night.

Snail in the woods by Joanne Ryder with the assistance of Harold S. Feinberg; ill. by Jo Polseno. Harper, 1979. Subj: Animals – snails. Science.

The snail's spell ill. by Lynne Cherry. Warne, 1982. Subj: Animals – snails. Night.

The spiders dance ill. by Robert J. Blake. Harper, 1981. Subj: Science. Spiders.

Step into the night ill. by Dennis Nolan. Four Winds Pr., 1988. ISBN 0-02-777951-3 Subj: Nature. Night. Poetry, rhyme.

A wet and sandy day ill. by Donald Carrick. Harper, 1977. Subj: Sea and seashore. Weather – rain.

Rylant, Cynthia. *All I see* ill. by Peter Catalanotto. Watts, 1988. ISBN 0-531-08377-2 Subj: Activities – painting. Art. Friendship.

Birthday presents ill. by Suçie Stevenson. Watts, 1987. ISBN 0-531-08305-5 Subj: Behavior – sharing. Birthdays. Family life.

Henry and Mudge ill. by Suçie Stevenson. Bradbury Pr., 1987. ISBN 0-02-778001-5 Subj: Animals – dogs. Behavior – lost. Pets.

Henry and Mudge in puddle trouble ill. by Suçie Stevenson. Bradbury Pr., 1987. ISBN 0-02-778002-3 Subj: Animals – cats. Animals – dogs. Character traits – kindness to animals. Pets. Seasons – spring.

Henry and Mudge in the green time ill. by Suçie Stevenson. Bradbury Pr., 1987. ISBN 0-02-778003-1 Subj: Animals – dogs. Pets. Seasons – summer.

Henry and Mudge in the sparkle days ill. by Suçie Stevenson. Bradbury Pr., 1988. ISBN 0-02-778005-8 Subj: Animals – dogs. Family life. Holidays – Christmas.

Henry and Mudge under the yellow moon ill. by Suçie Stevenson. Bradbury Pr., 1987. ISBN 0-02-778004-X Subj: Animals – dogs. Holidays – Halloween. Holidays – Thanksgiving. Pets. Seasons – fall.

Miss Maggie ill. by Thomas Di Grazia. Dutton, 1983. Subj: Character traits – curiosity. Friendship.

Mr. Griggs' work ill. by Julie Downing. Watts, 1989. ISBN 0-531-05769-0 Subj: Careers – mail carriers. Character traits – pride.

Night in the country ill. by Mary Szilagyi. Bradbury, 1986. ISBN 0-02-777210-1 Subj: Animals. Country. Night.

The relatives came ill. by Stephen Gammell. Bradbury Pr, 1985. ISBN 0-02-777220-9 Subj: Activities – traveling. Caldecott award honor book. Family life.

This year's garden ill. by Mary Szilagyi. Bradbury Pr., 1984. Subj: Activities – gardening.

When I was young in the mountains ill. by Diane Goode. Dutton, 1982. Subj: Caldecott award honor book. Family life.

S-Ringi, Kjell *see* Ringi, Kjell

Sachs, Marilyn. *Fleet-footed Florence* ill. by Charles Robinson. Doubleday, 1981. Subj: Behavior – wishing. Magic. Sports – baseball.

Matt's mitt ill. by Hilary Knight. Doubleday, 1975. Subj: Sports – baseball.

Saddler, Allen. *The Archery contest* ill. by Joe Wright. Oxford Univ. Pr., 1983. Subj: Humor. Magic. Royalty. Sports.

The king gets fit ill. by Joe Wright. Oxford Univ. Pr., 1983. Subj: Humor. Royalty.

Sadler, Catherine Edwards. *A duckling is born* (Isenbart, Hans-Heinrich)

A flamingo is born (Zoll, Max Alfred)

Sadler, Marilyn. *Alistair in outer space* ill. by Roger Bollen. Prentice-Hall, 1984. Subj: Libraries. Space and space ships.

Alistair's elephant ill. by Roger Bollen. Prentice-Hall, 1983. Subj: Animals – elephants. Behavior – misbehavior.

Alistair's time machine ill. by Roger Bollen. Prentice-Hall, 1986. ISBN 0-317-39621-8 Subj: Machines. School. Science. Space and space ships. Time.

It's not easy being a bunny ill. by Roger Bollen. Random House, 1983. Subj: Animals – rabbits. Behavior – dissatisfaction. Self-concept.

Sage, Alison. *Teddy bears cure a cold* (Gretz, Susanna)

Teddy bears take the train (Gretz, Susanna)

Teddybears cookbook (Gretz, Susanna)

Sage, James. *The boy and the dove* photos. by Robert Doisneau. Workman, 1978. Subj: Birds – doves. Theater.

Sage, Juniper *see* Brown, Margaret Wise

Sage, Juniper *see* Hurd, Edith Thacher

Sage, Michael. *Dippy dos and don'ts* by Michael Sage and Arnold Spilka; ill. by Arnold Spilka. Viking, 1967. Subj: Humor. Poetry, rhyme.

If you talked to a boar ill. by Arnold Spilka. Lippincott, 1960. Subj: Humor. Language.

Sahagun, Bernardino de. *Spirit child: a story of the Nativity* tr. from the Aztec by John Bierhorst; ill. by Barbara Cooney. Morrow, 1984. Subj: Folk and fairy tales. Foreign lands – Mexico. Holidays – Christmas. Religion.

St. George, Judith. *The Halloween pumpkin smasher* ill. by Margot Tomes. Putnam's, 1978. Subj: Animals – raccoons. Holidays – Halloween. Imagination – imaginary friends.

St. Pierre, Wendy. *Henry finds a home* ill. by Barbara Eidlitz. Firefly Pr., 1981. Subj: Children as authors. Reptiles – turtles, tortoises.

St. Tamara. *Chickaree, a red squirrel* ill. by author. Harcourt, 1980. Subj: Animals – squirrels. Science.

Salazar, Violet. *Squares are not bad* ill. by Harlow Rockwell. Golden Pr., 1967. Subj: Concepts – shape.

Saleh, Harold J. *Even tiny ants must sleep* ill. by Jerry Pinkney. McGraw-Hill, 1967. Subj: Animals. Poetry, rhyme. Sleep.

Saltzberg, Barney. *Cromwell* ill. by author. Atheneum, 1986. ISBN 0-689-31282-2 Subj: Animals – dogs. Humor.

It must have been the wind ill. by author. Harper, 1982. Subj: Bedtime. Noise, sounds. Weather – wind.

The yawn ill. by author. Atheneum, 1985. ISBN 0-689-31073-0 Subj: Behavior – imitation. Wordless.

Salus, Naomi Panush. *My daddy's mustache* ill. by Tomie de Paola. Doubleday, 1979. Subj: Character traits – appearance.

Samton, Sheila White. *Beside the bay* ill. by author. Putnam's, 1987. ISBN 0-399-21420-8 Subj: Poetry, rhyme. Sea and seashore.

The world from my window ill. by author. Crown, 1985. ISBN 0-517-55645-6 Subj: Counting. Poetry, rhyme.

Samuels, Barbara. *Duncan and Dolores* ill. by author. Bradbury Pr., 1986. ISBN 0-02-778210-7 Subj: Activities. Animals – cats. Family life – sisters. Humor.

Faye and Dolores ill. by author. Bradbury Pr., 1985. Subj: Emotions – love. Sibling rivalry.

San Diego Zoological Society. *Families* photos. by Ron Garrison and F. D. Schmidt of the Zoological Society of San Diego; captions ed. by Georgeanne Irvine. Heian International, 1983. ISBN 0-89346-218-7 Subj: Animals. Zoos.

A visit to the zoo photos. by Ron Garrison and F. D. Schmidt of the Zoological Society of San Diego; captions ed. by Georgeanne Irvine. Heian International, 1983. ISBN 0-89346-219-5 Subj: Animals. Zoos.

Sanchez, Jose Louis Garcia. *Kangaroo* by Jose Louis Garcia Sanchez and Miguel Angel Pacheco; ill. by Nella Bosnia. H P Books, 1983. Subj: Animals – kangaroos.

Sand, George. *The mysterious tale of Gentle Jack and Lord Bumblebee* tr. by Gela Jacobson; ill. by Gennady Spirin. Dial Pr., 1988. ISBN 0-8037-0538-7 Subj: Character traits – individuality. Fairies. Insects – bees. War.

Sandberg, Inger. *Come on out, Daddy!* by Inger and Lasse Sandberg; ill. by Lasse Sandberg. Delacorte Pr., 1971. Translation of Pappa, kom ut. Subj: Activities – working. Careers. Family life – fathers.

Dusty wants to borrow everything ill. by Lasse Sandberg. Farrar, 1988. ISBN 91-29-58782-4 Subj: Character traits – curiosity. Family life – grandparents.

Dusty wants to help tr. from Swedish by Judy A. Mauver; ill. by Lasse Sandberg. Farrar, 1987. ISBN 91-29-58336-5 Subj: Behavior – misbehavior. Family life – grandfathers.

Little Anna saved by Inger and Lasse Sandberg; ill. by Lasse Sandberg. Lothrop, 1966. Subj: Games.

Little ghost Godfry by Inger and Lasse Sandberg; tr. by Nancy S. Leupold; ill. by Lasse Sandberg. Delacorte Pr., 1968. Subj: Ghosts.

Nicholas' favorite pet by Inger and Lasse Sandberg; ill. by Lasse Sandberg. Delacorte Pr., 1969. Translation of Niklas' önskedjur. Subj: Animals. Animals – dogs. Birthdays. Pets.

Nicholas' red day by Inger and Lasse Sandberg; ill. by authors. Delacorte Pr., 1964. Subj: Behavior – misbehavior. Concepts – color. Illness.

Sandberg, Lasse. *Come on out, Daddy!* (Sandberg, Inger)

Little Anna saved (Sandberg, Inger)

Little ghost Godfry (Sandberg, Inger)

Nicholas' favorite pet (Sandberg, Inger)

Nicholas' red day (Sandberg, Inger)

Sandburg, Carl. *The wedding procession of the rag doll and the broom handle and who was in it* ill. by Harriet Pincus. Harcourt, 1978, 1922. ISBN 0-15-294930-5 Subj: Toys. Toys – dolls. Weddings.

Sandburg, Charles August *see* Sandburg, Carl

Sandburg, Helga. *Anna and the baby buzzard* ill. by Brinton Turkle. Dutton, 1970. Subj: Birds – buzzards. Character traits – kindness to animals.

Sandin, Joan. *The long way to a new land* ill. by author. Harper, 1981. Subj: Family life. Foreign lands. Moving.

Who's scaring Alfie Atkins? (Bergström, Gunilla.)

Sandison, Janet *see* Duncan, Jane

San Souci, Robert D. *The brave little tailor* (Grimm, Jacob)

The enchanted tapestry ill. by László Gál. Dial Pr., 1987. ISBN 0-8037-0306-6 Subj: Activities – weaving. Behavior – greed. Character traits – bravery. Family life – brothers. Folk and fairy tales. Foreign lands – China.

The legend of Scarface ill. by Daniel San Souci. Doubleday, 1987. ISBN 0-385-15874-2 Subj: Folk and fairy tales. Indians of North America.

The legend of Sleepy Hollow (Irving, Washington)

Song of Sedna ill. by Daniel San Souci. Doubleday, 1981. Subj: Eskimos. Folk and fairy tales.

Sant, Laurent Sauveur. *Dinosaurs* ill. by author. Wonder Books, 1971. Subj: Dinosaurs.

Santoro, Christopher. *Book of shapes* ill. by author. Dutton, 1979. ISBN 0-525-69406-4 Subj: Concepts – shape.

Santos, Joyce Audy Dos *see* Dos Santos, Joyce Audy

Sapphire, Paula. *The toddler's potty book* (Allison, Alida)

Sargent, Susan. *My favorite place* by Susan Sargent and Donna Aaron Wirt; ill. by Allan Eitzen. Abingdon Pr., 1983. Subj: Handicaps – blindness. Senses – seeing.

Sarnoff, Jane. *That's not fair* ill. by Reynold Ruffins. Scribner's, 1980. Subj: Behavior – dissatisfaction. Family life. Sibling rivalry.

Sarrazin, Johan. *Tootle* ill. by Aislin. Tundra, 1984. ISBN 0-88776-168-2 Subj: Animals – dogs. Behavior – misbehavior.

Sarton, May. *Punch's secret* ill. by Howard Knotts. Harper, 1974. Subj: Emotions – loneliness. Friendship.

A walk through the woods ill. by Kazue Mizumura. Harper, 1976. ISBN 0-06-025190-5 Subj: Activities – walking. Nature. Poetry, rhyme.

Sasaki, Isao. *Snow* ill. by author. Viking, 1982. Subj: Trains. Weather – snow. Wordless.

Sasaki, Jeannie. *Chōchō is for butterfly: a Japanese-English primer* by Jeannie Sasaki and Frances Uyeda; ill. by authors. Uyeda Sasaki Art, 1975. Subj: Foreign lands – Japan. Foreign languages.

Sattler, Helen Roney. *No place for a goat* ill. by Bari Weissman. Elsevier-Nelson, 1981. Subj: Animals – goats. Houses.

Train whistles ill. by Giulio Maestro. Rev. ed. Lothrop, 1985. ISBN 0-688-03980-4 Subj: Language. Trains.

Saucer-Hall, Fredric *see* Cendrars, Blaise

Sauer, Julia Lina. *Mike's house* ill. by Don Freeman. Viking, 1954. Subj: Behavior – lost. City. Libraries. Weather – snow.

Saunders, Susan. *Charles Rat's picnic* ill. by Robert Byrd. Dutton, 1983. Subj: Activities – picnicking. Animals – armadillos. Animals – rats. Friendship.

Fish fry ill. by S. D. Schindler. Viking, 1982. Subj: Activities – picnicking.

The golden goose (Grimm, Jacob)

A sniff in time ill. by Michael Mariano. Macmillan, 1982. ISBN 0-689-30890-6 Subj: Magic. Senses – smelling. Wizards.

Wales' tale ill. by Marilyn Hirsh. Viking, 1980. Subj: Animals – dogs.

Savage, Kathleen. *Bear hunt* (Siewert, Margaret)

Saville, Lynn. *Horses in the circus ring* ill. by author. Dutton, 1989. ISBN 0-525-44417-3 Subj: Animals – horses. Circus.

Sawicki, Norma Jean. *Something for mom* ill. by Martha Weston. Lothrop, 1987. ISBN 0-688-05590-7 Subj: Birthdays. Family life – mothers.

Sawyer, Jean. *Our village shop* ill. by Faith Jaques. Putnam's, 1984. Subj: Stores.

Sawyer, Ruth. *The Christmas Anna angel* ill. by Kate Seredy. Viking, 1944. Subj: Angels. Caldecott award honor book. Holidays – Christmas.

Journey cake, ho! ill. by Robert McCloskey. Viking, 1953. Subj: Caldecott award honor book. Cumulative tales. Folk and fairy tales. Poverty.

Saxe, John Godfrey. *The blind men and the elephant* ill. by Paul Galdone. McGraw-Hill, 1963. Subj: Animals – elephants. Handicaps – blindness. Senses – seeing.

Saxon, Charles D. *Don't worry about Poopsie* ill. by author. Dodd, 1958. Subj: Animals – dogs. Behavior – lost.

Saxon, Gladys Relyea *see* Seyton, Marion

Say, Allen. *The bicycle man* ill. by author. Houghton, 1982. Subj: Foreign lands – Japan. Sports – bicycling.

Once under the cherry blossom tree: an old Japanese tale ill. by author. Harper, 1974. Subj: Folk and fairy tales. Foreign lands – Japan.

A river dream ill. by author. Houghton, 1988. ISBN 0-395-48294-1 Subj: Dreams. Family life. Illness. Sports – fishing.

Sazer, Nina. *What do you think I saw? a nonsense number book* ill. by Lois Ehlert. Pantheon, 1976. Subj: Counting. Humor. Poetry, rhyme.

Scarry, Huck. *Huck Scarry's steam train journey* ill. by author. Collins-World, 1979. Subj: Trains.

Looking into the Middle Ages ill. by author. Harper, 1985. Subj: Format, unusual – toy and movable books. Knights. Middle ages.

On the road ill. by author. Putnam's, 1981. Subj: Automobiles.

Scarry, Patricia *see* Scarry, Patsy

Scarry, Patsy. *Little Richard and Prickles* ill. by Cyndy Szekeres. American Heritage, 1971. Subj: Animals – porcupines. Animals – rabbits. Birds – owls. Friendship.

Patsy Scarry's big bedtime storybook ill. by Cyndy Szekeres. Random House, 1980. Subj: Animals – rabbits.

Scarry, Richard. *The adventures of Tinker and Tanker* ill. by author. Doubleday, 1968. A reissue of Tinker and Tanker, Tinker and Tanker out West, and Tinker and Tanker and their space ship. Subj: Animals – hippopotami. Animals – rabbits.

Egg in the hole ill. by author. Golden Pr., 1967. Subj: Birds – chickens. Eggs. Format, unusual.

The great big car and truck book ill. by author. Golden Pr., 1951. Subj: Automobiles. Trucks.

Is this the house of Mistress Mouse? ill. by author. Golden Pr., 1964. Subj: Animals. Houses.

My first word book ill. by author. Random, 1986. ISBN 0-394-88016-1 Subj: Activities – picnicking. Format, unusual – board books.

Pig Will and Pig Won't: a book of manners ill. by author. Random House, 1984. ISBN 0-394-96585-X Subj: Animals – pigs. Behavior.

Richard Scarry's ABC word book ill. by author. Random House, 1971. Subj: ABC books.

Richard Scarry's animal nursery tales ill. by author. Golden Pr., 1975. Subj: Animals. Folk and fairy tales. Nursery rhymes.

Richard Scarry's best Christmas book ever! ill. by author. Random House, 1981. Subj: Holidays – Christmas.

Richard Scarry's best counting book ever ill. by author. Random House, 1975. Subj: Counting.

Richard Scarry's best first book ever ill. by author. Random House, 1979. Subj: Concepts. Days of the week, months of the year.

Richard Scarry's best story book ever ill. by author. Golden Pr., 1968. Subj: Language.

Richard Scarry's best word book ever ill. by author. Golden Pr., 1963. Subj: Dictionaries.

Richard Scarry's biggest word book ever! ill. by author. Random House, 1985. ISBN 0-394-87374-2 Subj: Dictionaries. Format, unusual. Language.

Richard Scarry's busiest people ever ill. by author. Random House, 1976. Subj: Careers.

Richard Scarry's busy busy world ill. by author. Golden Pr., 1965. Subj: Activities.

Richard Scarry's busy houses ill. by author. Random House, 1981. Subj: Animals – worms. Format, unusual – board books. Houses.

Richard Scarry's cars and trucks and things that go ill. by author. Golden Pr., 1974. Subj: Automobiles. Transportation. Trucks.

Richard Scarry's funniest storybook ever ill. by author. Random House, 1972. Subj: Humor.

Richard Scarry's great big air book ill. by author. Random House, 1971. Subj: Airplanes, airports. Science.

Richard Scarry's great big mystery book ill. by author. Random House, 1969. Subj: Animals. Crime. Stores.

Richard Scarry's great big schoolhouse ill. by author. Random House, 1969. Subj: ABC books. Concepts. Counting. Days of the week, months of the year. School. Time.

Richard Scarry's hop aboard! Here we go! ill. by author. Golden Pr., 1972. Subj: Transportation.

Richard Scarry's Lowly Worm word book ill. by author. Random House, 1981. Subj: Format, unusual – board books.

Richard Scarry's mix or match storybook ill. by author. Random House, 1979. Subj: Animals. Format, unusual – toy and movable books.

Richard Scarry's Peasant Pig and the terrible dragon ill. by author. Random House, 1980. Subj: Animals – pigs. Character traits – bravery. Dragons. Middle ages.

Richard Scarry's please and thank you book ill. by author. Random House, 1973. Subj: Etiquette.

Richard Scarry's Postman Pig and his busy neighbors ill. by author. Random House, 1978. Subj: Animals. Careers. Careers – mail carriers. City.

Richard Scarry's storybook dictionary ill. by author. Golden Pr., 1966. Subj: Dictionaries.

What do people do all day? ill. by author. Random House, 1968. Subj: Careers.

Schaaf, M. B. *see* Goffstein, M. B. (Marilyn Brooke)

Schaaf, Peter. *An apartment house close up* photos. by author. Four Winds Pr., 1980. Subj: Houses.

The violin close up photos. by author. Four Winds Pr., 1980. Subj: Music.

Schackburg, Richard. *Yankee Doodle* ill. by Ed Emberley. Prentice-Hall, 1965. Subj: Music. Songs. U.S. history.

Schaffer, Libor. *Arthur sets sail* ill. by Agnès Mathieu. Holt, 1987. ISBN 0-8050-0489-0 Subj: Animals – aardvarks. Animals – pigs. Boats, ships. Character traits – appearance.

Schaffer, Marion. *I love my cat!* ill. by Kathy Vanderlinden. Kids Can Pr., 1981. Subj: Animals – cats. Foreign languages. Pets.

Schären, Beatrix. *Tillo* Translated by Gwen Marsh. Addison-Wesley, 1974. Subj: Birds – owls.

Schatell, Brian. *Farmer Goff and his turkey Sam* ill. by author. Lippincott, 1982. Subj: Behavior – misbehavior. Birds – turkeys. Fairs.

The McGoonys have a party ill. by author. Lippincott, 1985. ISBN 0-397-32134-4 Subj: Behavior – forgetfulness. Behavior – misunderstanding. Handicaps.

Midge and Fred ill. by author. Lippincott, 1983. Subj: Fish. Humor.

Sam's no dummy, Farmer Goff ill. by author. Lippincott, 1984. Subj: Birds – turkeys. Character traits – cleverness.

Schatz, Letta. *The extraordinary tug-of-war* ill. by John Burningham. Follett, 1968. Subj: Animals. Character traits – cleverness. Folk and fairy tales. Foreign lands – Africa.

Whiskers, my cat ill. by Paul Galdone. McGraw-Hill, 1967. Subj: Animals – cats.

Scheer, Julian. *Rain makes applesauce* by Julian Scheer and Marvin Bileck; ill. by Marvin Bileck. Holiday, 1964. Subj: Caldecott award honor book. Humor. Weather – rain.

Scheffler, Ursel. *Stop your crowing, Kasimir!* ill. by Silke Brix-Henker. Carolrhoda Books, 1988. ISBN 0-87614-323-0 Subj: Birds – chickens. Communities, neighborhoods. Country. Noise, sounds.

A walk in the rain tr. by Andrea Mernan; ill. by Ulises Wensell. Putnam's, 1986. ISBN 0-399-21267-1 Subj: Family life – grandmothers. Family life – grandparents. Weather – rain.

Schein, Ruth Robbins see Robbins, Ruth

Schenk, Esther M. *Christmas time* ill. by Vera Stone Norman. Follett, 1931. Subj: Holidays – Christmas.

Schepp, Steven. *How babies are made* (Andry, Andrew C.)

Schermer, Judith. *Mouse in house* ill. by author. Houghton, 1979. Subj: Animals – mice. Family life. Problem solving.

Schertle, Alice. *Bill and the google-eyed goblins* ill. by Patricia Coombs. Lothrop, 1987. ISBN 0-688-06702-6 Subj: Activities – dancing. Goblins. Holidays – Halloween.

Goodnight, Hattie, my dearie, my dove ill. by Linda Strauss Edwards. Lothrop, 1985. ISBN 0-688-03934-0 Subj: Bedtime. Counting. Toys.

The gorilla in the hall ill. by Paul Galdone. Lothrop, 1977. Subj: Animals – gorillas. Character traits – bravery. Emotions – fear.

Hob Goblin and the skeleton ill. by Katherine Coville. Lothrop, 1982. Subj: Holidays – Halloween. Trolls.

In my treehouse ill. by Meredith Dunham. Lothrop, 1983. Subj: Behavior – solitude. Houses. Trees.

Jeremy Bean's St. Patrick's Day ill. by Linda Shute. Lothrop, 1987. ISBN 0-688-04814-5 Subj: Behavior – hiding. Character traits – being different. Holidays – St. Patrick's Day. Parties. School.

My two feet ill. by Meredith Dunham. Lothrop, 1985. ISBN 0-688-02677-X Subj: Anatomy.

That Olive! ill. by Cindy Wheeler. Lothrop, 1986. ISBN 0-688-04091-8 Subj: Animals – cats. Behavior – hiding.

Schick, Alice. *Just this once* by Alice and Joel Schick; ill. by Joel Schick. Lippincott, 1978. Subj: Animals – wolves. Pets.

The remarkable ride of Israel Bissell... as related to Molly the crow: being the true account of an extraordinary post rider who persevered by Alice Schick and Marjorie N. Allen; ill. by Joel Schick. Lippincott, 1976. Subj: U.S. history. War.

Schick, Eleanor. *Art lessons* ill. by author. Greenwillow, 1987. ISBN 0-688-05121-9 Subj: Art.

City green ill. by author. Macmillan, 1974. Subj: City. Poetry, rhyme.

City in the winter ill. by author. Macmillan, 1970. Subj: City. Family life – only child. Seasons – winter. Weather – snow. Weather – wind.

Home alone ill. by author. Dial Pr., 1980. Subj: Activities – working. Family life – mothers. Emotions – loneliness.

Joey on his own ill. by author. Dial Pr., 1982. Subj: Self-concept. Shopping.

The little school at Cottonwood Corners ill. by author. Harper, 1965. Subj: Caldecott award honor book. School. Wordless.

Making friends ill. by author. Macmillan, 1969. Subj: Friendship. Wordless.

One summer night ill. by author. Greenwillow, 1977. Subj: City. Music. Seasons – summer.

Peggy's new brother ill. by author. Macmillan, 1970. Subj: Babies. Emotions – envy, jealousy. Family life. Sibling rivalry.

Peter and Mr. Brandon ill. by Donald Carrick. Macmillan, 1973. Subj: Activities – baby-sitting. City.

A piano for Julie ill. by author. Greenwillow, 1984. Subj: Family life. Music.

Summer at the sea ill. by author. Greenwillow, 1979. Subj: Activities – vacationing. Family life – only child. Sea and seashore. Seasons – summer.

A surprise in the forest ill. by author. Harper, 1964. Subj: Animals. Eggs. Forest, woods.

Schick, Joel. *Just this once* (Schick, Alice)

Schiller, Barbara. *The white rat's tale* ill. by Adrienne Adams. Holt, 1967. Subj: Animals – rats. Folk and fairy tales. Foreign lands – France. Royalty.

Schilling, Betty. *Two kittens are born: from birth to two months* photos. by author. Holt, 1980. Subj: Animals – cats. Science.

Schlein, Miriam. *The amazing Mr. Pelgrew* ill. by Harvey Weiss. Abelard-Schuman, 1957. Subj: Careers – police officers.

Big talk ill. by Laura Lydecker. Albert Whitman, 1988. ISBN 0-8075-0729-6 Subj: Animals – kangaroos.

Billy, the littlest one ill. by Lucy Hawkinson. Albert Whitman, 1966. Subj: Behavior – growing up. Character traits – smallness. Family life.

Deer in the snow ill. by Leonard P. Kessler. Abelard-Schuman, 1965. Subj: Animals – deer. Seasons – winter. Weather – snow.

Elephant herd ill. by Symeon Shimin. Addison-Wesley, 1954. Subj: Animals – elephants.

Fast is not a ladybug ill. by Leonard P. Kessler. Addison-Wesley, 1953. Subj: Concepts – speed. Insects – ladybugs.

The four little foxes ill. by Louis Quintanilla. Addison-Wesley, 1953. Subj: Animals – foxes.

Go with the sun ill. by Symeon Shimin. Addison-Wesley, 1952. Subj: Family life – grandfathers. Seasons – winter.

Heavy is a hippopotamus ill. by Leonard P. Kessler. Addison-Wesley, 1954. Subj: Concepts – weight.

Here comes night ill. by Harvey Weiss. Albert Whitman, 1957. Subj: Night.

Herman McGregor's world ill. by Harvey Weiss. Albert Whitman, 1959. Subj: Behavior – growing up. World.

Home, the tale of a mouse ill. by E. Harper Johnson. Abelard-Schuman, 1958. Subj: Animals – mice.

It's about time ill. by Leonard P. Kessler. Addison-Wesley, 1955. Subj: Time.

Laurie's new brother ill. by Elizabeth Donald. Abelard-Schuman, 1961. Subj: Babies. Family life. Sibling rivalry.

Little Rabbit, the high jumper ill. by Theresa Sherman. Addison-Wesley, 1957. Subj: Animals – rabbits.

Little Red Nose ill. by Roger Antoine Duvoisin. Abelard-Schuman, 1955. Subj: Seasons – spring.

Lucky porcupine! ill. by Martha Weston. Four Winds Pr., 1980. Subj: Animals – porcupines. Science.

My family ill. by Harvey Weiss. Abelard-Schuman, 1960. Subj: Family life.

My house ill. by Joe Lasker. Albert Whitman, 1971. Subj: Family life. Houses. Moving.

The pile of junk ill. by Harvey Weiss. Abelard-Schuman, 1962. Subj: Character traits – practicality. Values.

Shapes ill. by Sam Berman. Addison-Wesley, 1952. Subj: Concepts – shape.

Something for now, something for later ill. by Leonard Weisgard. Harper, 1956. Subj: Farms.

The sun looks down ill. by Abner Graboff. Abelard-Schuman, 1954. Subj: Sun.

The sun, the wind, the sea and the rain ill. by Joe Lasker. Abelard-Schuman, 1960. Subj: Sea and seashore. Sun. Weather. Weather – rain. Weather – wind.

What's wrong with being a skunk? ill. by Ray Cruz. Four Winds Pr., 1974. Subj: Animals – skunks. Science.

When will the world be mine? The story of a snowshoe rabbit ill. by Jean Charlot. Addison-Wesley, 1953. Subj: Behavior – growing up. Caldecott award honor book.

Schmeltz, Susan Alton. *Pets I wouldn't pick* ill. by Ellen Appleby. Parents, 1982. Subj: Pets. Poetry, rhyme.

Schmid, Eleonore. *Farm animals* ill. by author. Holt, 1986. ISBN 0-03-008032-0 Subj: Animals. Farms. Format, unusual – board books.

Schmidt, Eric von. *The young man who wouldn't hoe corn* ill. by author. Houghton, 1964. Subj: Character traits – laziness. Farms. Humor.

Schneider, Elisa. *The merry-go-round dog* ill. by author. Knopf, 1988. ISBN 0-394-99069-2 Subj: Animals – dogs. Merry-go-rounds.

Schneider, Herman. *Follow the sunset* by Herman and Nina Schneider; ill. by Lucille Corcos. Doubleday, 1952. Subj: Science. Sun. World.

Schneider, Howie. *Amos* (Seligson, Susan)

Schneider, Nina. *Follow the sunset* (Schneider, Herman)

While Susie sleeps ill. by Dagmar Wilson. Addison-Wesley, 1948. Subj: Bedtime. Night. Sleep.

Schoberle, Ceile. *Beyond the Milky Way* ill. by author. Crown, 1986. ISBN 0-517-55716-9 Subj: Imagination. Science. Sky. Space and space ships.

Schoenherr, John. *The barn* ill. by author. Little, 1968. Subj: Animals – mice. Animals – skunks. Barns. Birds – owls. Farms.

Scholey, Arthur. *Baboushka* ill. by Ray Burrows. Good News, 1983. ISBN 0-89107-281-0 Subj: Music. Religion. Royalty. Toys.

Schongut, Emanuel. *Look kitten* ill. by author. Simon and Schuster, 1983. Subj: Animals.

Schotter, Roni. *Captain Snap and the children of Vinegar Lane* ill. by Marcia Sewall. Watts, 1989. ISBN 0-531-08397-7 Subj: Character traits – being different. Character traits – generosity. Character traits – kindness.

Schreiber, Georges. *Bambino goes home* ill. by author. Viking, 1959. Subj: Clowns, jesters. Friendship.

Bambino the clown ill. by author. Viking, 1947. Subj: Animals – sea lions. Caldecott award honor book. Clowns, jesters.

Professor Bull's umbrella (Lipkind, William)

Schroder, William. *Pea soup and serpents* ill. by author. Lothrop, 1977. Subj: Monsters. Mythical creatures. Weather – fog.

Schroeder, Binette. *Ra ta ta tam* (Nickl, Peter)

Tuffa and her friends ill. by author. Dial Pr., 1983. Subj: Animals – dogs. Format, unusual – board books. Friendship.

Tuffa and the bone ill. by author. Dial Pr., 1983. Subj: Animals – dogs. Format, unusual – board books.

Tuffa and the ducks ill. by author. Dial Pr., 1983. Subj: Animals – dogs. Birds – ducks. Format, unusual – board books.

Tuffa and the picnic ill. by author. Dial Pr., 1983. ISBN 0-8037-9896-2 Subj: Activities – picnicking. Animals – dogs. Behavior – misbehavior. Format, unusual – board books.

Tuffa and the snow ill. by author. Dial Pr., 1983. Subj: Animals – dogs. Format, unusual – board books. Weather – snow.

Schroeder, Glen W. *At the zoo* (Colonius, Lillian)

Schubert, Dieter. *There's a crocodile under my bed!* (Schubert, Ingrid)

Where's my monkey? ill. by author. Dial Pr., 1987. ISBN 0-8037-0069-5 Subj: Animals – monkeys. Behavior – losing things. Behavior – needing someone. Wordless.

Schubert, Ingrid. *There's a crocodile under my bed!* by Ingrid and Dieter Schubert; ill. by authors. McGraw-Hill, 1981. Subj: Bedtime. Reptiles – alligators, crocodiles.

Schuchman, Joan. *Two places to sleep* ill. by Jim LaMarche. Carolrhoda, 1979. Subj: Divorce. Family life.

Schulman, Janet. *The big hello* ill. by Lillian Hoban. Greenwillow, 1976. Subj: Friendship. Moving. Toys – dolls.

Camp Kee Wee's secret weapon ill. by Marylin Hafner. Greenwillow, 1979. Subj: Sports – baseball. Sports – camping.

The great big dummy ill. by Lillian Hoban. Greenwillow, 1979. ISBN 0-688-84208-9 Subj: Animals – dogs. Friendship. Toys – dolls.

Jack the bum and the Halloween handout ill. by James Stevenson. Greenwillow, 1977. Subj: Behavior – sharing. Holidays – Halloween. UNICEF

Jack the bum and the haunted house ill. by James Stevenson. Greenwillow, 1977. Subj: Crime. Ghosts. Houses.

Jack the bum and the UFO ill. by James Stevenson. Greenwillow, 1978. Subj: Character traits – cleverness. Progress. Space and space ships.

Jenny and the tennis nut ill. by Marylin Hafner. Greenwillow, 1978. Subj: Sports – gymnastics. Sports – tennis.

Jungles (Wood, John Norris)

Schultz, Gwen. *The blue Valentine* ill. by Elizabeth Coberly. Rev. ed. Morrow, 1979. Orig. pub. in 1965. Subj: Holidays – Valentine's Day.

Schulz, Charles M. *Bon voyage, Charlie Brown (and don't come back!!)* ill. by author. Random House, 1980. Subj: Activities – traveling. Foreign lands.

The Charlie Brown dictionary based on the rainbow dictionary by Wendell W. Wright; asst. by Helene Laird; ill. by author. Random House, 1973. Subj: Dictionaries.

Life is a circus, Charlie Brown ill. by author. Random House, 1981. Subj: Circus.

Snoopy's facts and fun book about boats ill. by author. Random House, 1979. Subj: Animals – dogs. Boats, ships.

Snoopy's facts and fun book about farms ill. by author. Random House, 1980. Subj: Animals – dogs. Farms.

Snoopy's facts and fun book about houses ill. by author. Random House, 1979. Subj: Animals – dogs. Houses.

Snoopy's facts and fun book about nature ill. by author. Random House, 1979. Subj: Animals – dogs. Nature. Science.

Snoopy's facts and fun book about planes ill. by author. Random House, 1979. Subj: Animals – dogs. Airplanes, airports.

Snoopy's facts and fun book about seashores ill. by author. Random House, 1979. Subj: Animals – dogs. Sea and seashore.

Snoopy's facts and fun book about seasons ill. by author. Random House, 1979. Subj: Animals – dogs. Seasons.

Snoopy's facts and fun book about trucks ill. by author. Random House, 1979. Subj: Animals – dogs. Trucks.

You're the greatest, Charlie Brown ill. by author. Random House, 1979. Subj: Sports – Olympics.

Schumacher, Claire. *Alto and Tango* ill. by author. Morrow, 1984. ISBN 0-688-02740-7 Subj: Birds. Fish. Friendship. Sea and seashore.

Brave Lily ill. by author. Morrow, 1985. ISBN 0-688-04963-X Subj: Character traits – bravery. Family life. Frogs and toads.

King of the zoo ill. by author. Morrow, 1985. Subj: Animals. Behavior – misbehavior. Friendship. Zoos.

Nutty's birthday ill. by author. Morrow, 1986. ISBN 0-688-06496-5 Subj: Activities – flying. Animals – squirrels. Birthdays.

Nutty's Christmas ill. by author. Morrow, 1984. Subj: Animals – squirrels. Holidays – Christmas.

Tim and Jim ill. by author. Dodd, 1987. ISBN 0-396-09040-0 Subj: Animals. Behavior – lost. Friendship.

Schurr, Cathleen. *The long and the short of it* ill. by Dorothy Maas. Vanguard, 1950. Subj: Problem solving.

Schwalje, Marjory. *Mr. Angelo* ill. by Abner Graboff. Abelard-Schuman, 1960. Subj: Activities – cooking. Food. Humor.

Schwartz, Alvin. *All of our noses are here and other stories* ill. by Karen Ann Weinhaus. Harper, 1985. ISBN 0-06-025288-X Subj: Folk and fairy tales. Humor.

Busy buzzing bumblebees: and other tongue twisters ill. by Kathie Abrams. Harper, 1982. Subj: Tongue twisters.

Ten copycats in a boat and other riddles ill. by Marc Simont. Harper, 1980. Subj: Riddles.

Schwartz, Amy. *Annabelle Swift, kindergartner* ill. by author. Orchard, 1988. ISBN 0-531-08337-3 Subj: Character traits – pride. School. Sibling rivalry.

Bea and Mr. Jones ill. by author. Bradbury Pr., 1982. Subj: Behavior — imitation. Family life — fathers.

Begin at the beginning ill. by author. Harper, 1983. Subj: Behavior — growing up.

Her Majesty, Aunt Essie ill. by author. Bradbury Pr., 1984. ISBN 0-02-781450-5 Subj: Behavior — boasting. Family life. Royalty.

Mrs. Moskowitz and the Sabbath candlesticks ill. by author. Jewish Pub. Soc., 1985. Subj: Jewish culture. Religion.

Oma and Bobo ill. by author. Bradbury Pr., 1987. ISBN 0-02-781500-5 Subj: Animals — dogs. Family life — grandmothers.

Yossel Zissel and the wisdom of Chelm ill. by author. Jewish Pub. Soc., 1988. ISBN 0-8276-0258-8 Subj: Character traits — foolishness. Folk and fairy tales. Jewish culture.

Schwartz, David. *How much is a million?* ill. by Steven Kellogg. Lothrop, 1985. ISBN 0-688-04050-0 Subj: Concepts — size. Counting.

Schwartz, Delmore. *"I am Cherry Alive," the little girl sang* ill. by Barbara Cooney. Harper, 1979. Subj: Poetry, rhyme.

Schwartz, Henry. *How I captured a dinosaur* ill. by Amy Schwartz. Watts, 1989. ISBN 0-531-08370-5 Subj: Dinosaurs. Pets. Sports — camping.

Schwartz, Mary. *Spiffen: a tale of a tidy pig* ill. by Lynn Munsinger. Albert Whitman, 1988. ISBN 0-8075-7580-1 Subj: Animals — pigs. Character traits — cleanliness.

Schweitzer, Iris. *Hilda's restful chair* ill. by author. Atheneum, 1982. Subj: Animals. Friendship.

Schweninger, Ann. *Birthday wishes* ill. by author. Viking, 1986. ISBN 0-670-80742-7 Subj: Animals — rabbits. Behavior — wishing. Birthdays. Parties.

Christmas secrets ill. by author. Viking, 1984. Subj: Animals — rabbits. Holidays — Christmas.

Halloween surprises ill. by author. Viking, 1984. Subj: Animals — rabbits. Holidays — Halloween.

The hunt for rabbit's galosh ill. by Kay Chorao. Doubleday, 1976. Subj: Animals — rabbits. Behavior — forgetfulness. Holidays — Valentine's Day.

The man in the moon as he sails the sky and other moon verse ill. by author. Dodd, 1979. Subj: Moon. Poetry, rhyme.

Off to school! ill. by author. Viking, 1987. ISBN 0-670-81447-4 Subj: Animals — rabbits. School.

Valentine friends ill. by author. Viking, 1988. ISBN 0-670-81448-2 Subj: Animals — rabbits. Family life. Holidays — Valentine's Day.

Scoppetone, Sandra. *Bang, bang, you're dead* (Fitzhugh, Louise)

Scott, Ann Herbert. *Big Cowboy Western* ill. by Richard Lewis. Lothrop, 1965. Subj: Clothing. Cowboys. Ethnic groups in the U.S. — Afro-Americans. Imagination.

Let's catch a monster ill. by H. Tom Hall. Lothrop, 1967. Subj: City. Ethnic groups in the U.S. — Afro-Americans. Holidays — Halloween.

On mother's lap ill. by Glo Coalson. McGraw-Hill, 1972. Subj: Behavior — needing someone. Emotions — love. Eskimos. Family life. Family life — mothers. Sibling rivalry.

Sam ill. by Symeon Shimin. McGraw-Hill, 1967. Subj: Behavior — needing someone. Ethnic groups in the U.S. — Afro-Americans. Family life.

Scott, Cora Annett *see* Annett, Cora

Scott, Frances Gruse. *How many kids are hiding on my block?* (Merrill, Jean)

Scott, Geoffrey. *Memorial Day* ill. by Peter E. Hanson. Carolrhoda Books, 1983. Subj: Holidays — Memorial Day.

Scott, Lesbia. *I sing a song of the saints of God*

Scott, Natalie. *Firebrand, push your hair out of your eyes* ill. by Sandra Smith. Carolrhoda Books, 1969. Subj: Character traits — appearance. Hair.

Scott, Natalie Anderson *see* Scott, Natalie

Scott, Rochelle. *Colors, colors all around* ill. by Leonard P. Kessler. Grosset, 1965. Subj: Concepts — color.

Scott, Sally. *Little Wiener* ill. by Beth Krush. Harcourt, 1951. Subj: Animals — dogs.

The magic horse ill. by adapt. Greenwillow, 1985. Retold and adapted from "The Ebony Horse," a story from The Arabian Nights tr. by Sir Richard Burton. ISBN 0-688-05898-1 Subj: Folk and fairy tales. Foreign lands. Magic. Royalty. Wizards.

There was Timmy! ill. by Beth Krush. Harcourt, 1957. Subj: Animals — dogs.

The three wonderful beggars ill. by author. Greenwillow, 1988. ISBN 0-688-06657-7 Subj: Folk and fairy tales.

Scott, William R. *This is the milk that Jack drank* adapt. from Mother Goose; ill. by Charles Green Shaw. Addison-Wesley, 1944. Subj: Cumulative tales.

Scribner, Charles. *The devil's bridge: a legend* retold by Charles Scribner, Jr.; ill. by Evaline Ness. Scribner's, 1978. Subj: Folk and fairy tales. Foreign lands — France. Devil.

Hansel and Gretel (Grimm, Jacob)

Scruton, Clive. *Bubble and squeak* ill. by author. Random House, 1985. ISBN 0-394-87101-4 Subj: Animals — mice. Birds — ducks. Friendship.

Circus cow ill. by author. Random House, 1985. Subj: Animals — bulls, cows. Character traits — foolishness.

Pig in the air ill. by author. Random House, 1985. ISBN 0-394-87103-0 Subj: Activities — flying. Animals — pigs.

Scaredy cat ill. by author. Random House, 1985. ISBN 0-394-87014-X Subj: Animals – cats. Emotions – fear.

Scullard, Sue. *Miss Fanshawe and the great dragon adventure* ill. by author. St. Martin's, 1987. ISBN 0-312-00510-5 Subj: Dragons. Format, unusual.

The Sea World alphabet book concept by Sally and Alan Sloan. Sea World Pr., 1979. Subj: ABC books. Sea and seashore.

Seabrooke, Brenda. *The best burglar alarm* ill. by Loretta Lustig. Morrow, 1978. Subj: Crime. Pets.

The seal ill. by Charlotte Knox. Rourke, 1983. Subj: Animals – seals.

Secunda, Sheldon. *What I want to be when I grow up* (Burnett, Carol)

Sedges, John *see* Buck, Pearl S. (Pearl Sydenstricker)

Seeger, Charles. *The foolish frog* (Seeger, Pete)

Seeger, Pete. *Abiyoyo* ill. by Michael Hays. Macmillan, 1986. ISBN 0-02-781490-4 Subj: Folk and fairy tales. Magic. Monsters.

The foolish frog by Pete Seeger and Charles Seeger; ill. by Miloslav Jágr; adapted and designed from Firebird Film by Gene Deitch. Macmillan, 1973. Subj: Cumulative tales. Folk and fairy tales. Frogs and toads. Music. Songs.

Sefton, Catherine *see* Waddell, Martin

Segal, Lore. *All the way home* ill. by James Marshall. Farrar, 1973. Subj: Cumulative tales.

The bear and the kingbird (Grimm, Jacob)

The story of old Mrs. Brubeck and how she looked for trouble and where she found him ill. by Marcia Sewall. Pantheon, 1981. Subj: Behavior – worrying. Problem solving.

Tell me a Mitzi ill. by Harriet Pincus. Farrar, 1970. Subj: Family life. Jewish culture.

Tell me a Trudy ill. by Rosemary Wells. Farrar, 1977. Subj: Family life. Jewish culture.

Segal, Sheila. *Joshua's dream* ill. by Jana Paiss. Union of American Hebrew Congregations, 1985. ISBN 0-8074-0272-9 Subj: Foreign lands – Israel. Jewish culture.

Seguin-Fontes, Marthe. *The cat's surprise* adapt. by Sandra Beris; ill. by author. Larousse, 1983. Subj: Animals – cats.

A wedding book adapt. by Sandra Beris; ill. by author. Larousse, 1983. Subj: Activities – photographing. Weddings.

Seidler, Rosalie. *Grumpus and the Venetian cat* ill. by author. Atheneum, 1964. Subj: Animals – cats. Animals – mice. Birds. Foreign lands – Italy.

Seignobosc, Françoise. *The big rain* ill. by author. Scribner's, 1961. Subj: Animals. Farms. Foreign lands – France. Weather – rain.

Biquette, the white goat ill. by author. Scribner's, 1953. Subj: Animals – goats. Foreign lands – France. Illness.

Chouchou ill. by author. Scribner's, 1958. Subj: Animals – donkeys. Foreign lands – France.

Jeanne-Marie at the fair ill. by author. Scribner's, 1959. Subj: Fairs. Foreign lands – France.

Jeanne-Marie counts her sheep ill. by author. Scribner's, 1951. Subj: Behavior – wishing. Counting. Foreign lands – France.

Jeanne-Marie in gay Paris ill. by author. Scribner's, 1956. Subj: Character traits. Foreign lands – France.

Minou ill. by author. Scribner's, 1962. Subj: Animals – cats. Behavior – lost. Foreign lands – France.

Noël for Jeanne-Marie ill. by author. Scribner's, 1953. Subj: Foreign lands – France. Holidays – Christmas.

Small-Trot ill. by author. Scribner's, 1952. Subj: Animals – mice. Circus.

Springtime for Jeanne-Marie ill. by author. Scribner's, 1955. Subj: Animals – goats. Behavior – lost. Birds – ducks. Foreign lands – France. Seasons – spring.

The story of Colette ill. by author. Hale, 1940. Subj: Animals. Emotions – loneliness. Pets.

The thank-you book ill. by author. Scribner's, 1947. Subj: Etiquette. Religion.

The things I like ill. by author. Scribner's, 1960. Subj: Participation.

What do you want to be? ill. by author. Scribner's, 1957. Subj: Careers. Character traits – ambition.

What time is it, Jeanne-Marie? ill. by author. Scribner's, 1963. Subj: Time.

Selberg, Ingrid. *Nature's hidden world* ill. by Andrew Miller. Putnam's, 1984. Subj: Animals. Format, unusual – toy and movable books. Plants. Riddles. Science.

Selden, George. *Chester Cricket's pigeon ride* ill. by Garth Williams. Farrar, 1981. Subj: Birds – pigeons. City. Insects.

The mice, the monks and the Christmas tree ill. by Jan Balet. Macmillan, 1963. Subj: Animals – mice. Holidays – Christmas.

Sparrow socks ill. by Peter Lippman. Harper, 1965. Subj: Birds – sparrows. Clothing.

Selig, Sylvie. *Kangaroo* ill. by author. Merrimack, 1980. Subj: Animals – kangaroos. Wordless.

Ten what? (Hoban, Russell)

Seligman, Dorothy Halle. *Run away home* ill. by Christine Hoffmann. Golden Gate, 1969. Subj: Behavior – running away. Family life.

Seligson, Susan. *Amos: the story of an old dog and his couch* by Susan Seligson and Howie Schneider; ill. by Howie Schneider. Little, 1987. ISBN 0-316-77404-9 Subj: Animals – dogs. Humor. Imagination. Old age.

Selkowe, Valrie M. *Spring green* ill. by Jeni Bassett. Lothrop, 1985. ISBN 0-688-04056-X Subj: Animals. Concepts – color. Parties. Seasons – spring.

Sellers, Ronnie. *My first day at school* ill. by Patti Stren. Caedmon, 1985. ISBN 0-89845-373-9 Subj: Poetry, rhyme. School.

Selsam, Millicent E. *All kinds of babies* ill. by Symeon Shimin. Four Winds Pr., 1967. Subj: Animals. Science.

The amazing dandelion photos. by Jerome Wexler. Morrow, 1977. Subj: Plants. Science. Seeds.

Backyard insects by Millicent E. Selsam and Ronald Goor; ill. by Ron Goor. Four Winds Pr., 1983. Subj: Insects. Science.

Benny's animals and how he put them in order ill. by Arnold Lobel. Harper, 1966. Subj: Animals. Science.

The bug that laid the golden eggs photos. by Harold Krieger; ill. by John Kaufmann; designed by Lee Epstein. Harper, 1967. Subj: Eggs. Insects. Science.

Cotton photos. by Jerome Wexler and others. Morrow, 1982. Subj: Activities – weaving. Plants.

Egg to chick ill. by Barbara Wolff. Rev. ed. Harper, 1970. Subj: Birds – chickens. Eggs. Science.

A first look at bird nests by Millicent E. Selsam and Joyce Hunt; ill. by Harriett Springer. Walker, 1985. ISBN 0-8027-6565-3 Subj: Birds. Science.

A first look at caterpillars by Millicent E. Selsam and Joyce Hunt; ill. by Harriett Springer. Walker, 1987. ISBN 0-8027-6702-8 Subj: Insects – butterflies, caterpillars. Science.

A first look at cats by Millicent E. Selsam and Joyce Hunt; ill. by Harriett Springer. Walker, 1981. ISBN 0-8027-6399-5 Subj: Animals – cats. Science.

A first look at dinosaurs by Millicent E. Selsam and Joyce Hunt; ill. by Harriett Springer. Walker, 1982. Subj: Dinosaurs.

A first look at dogs by Millicent E. Selsam and Joyce Hunt; ill. by Harriett Springer. Walker, 1981. Subj: Animals – dogs. Animals – foxes. Animals – wolves.

A first look at flowers by Millicent E. Selsam and Joyce Hunt; ill. by Harriett Springer. Walker, 1977. Subj: Flowers. Science.

A first look at kangaroos, koalas and other animals with pouches by Millicent E. Selsam and Joyce Hunt; ill. by Harriett Springer. Walker, 1985. ISBN 0-8027-6579-3 Subj: Animals. Science.

A first look at monkeys by Millicent E. Selsam and Joyce Hunt; ill. by Harriett Springer. Walker, 1979. Subj: Animals – gorillas. Animals – monkeys. Science.

A first look at owls, eagles and other hunters of the sky by Millicent E. Selsam and Joyce Hunt; ill. by Harriett Springer. Walker, 1986. ISBN 0-8027-6642-0 Subj: Birds. Science.

A first look at rocks by Millicent E. Selsam and Joyce Hunt; ill. by Harriett Springer. Walker, 1984. Subj: Rocks. Science.

A first look at seashells by Millicent E. Selsam and Joyce Hunt; ill. by Harriett Springer. Walker, 1983. Subj: Animals. Sea and seashore. Science.

A first look at sharks by Millicent E. Selsam and Joyce Hunt; ill. by Harriett Springer. Walker, 1979. Subj: Fish. Science.

A first look at spiders by Millicent E. Selsam and Joyce Hunt; ill. by Harriett Springer. Walker, 1983. Subj: Science. Spiders.

A first look at the world of plants by Millicent E. Selsam and Joyce Hunt; ill. by Harriett Springer. Walker, 1978. ISBN 0-8027-6299-9 Subj: Plants. Science.

A first look at whales by Millicent E. Selsam and Joyce Hunt; ill. by Harriett Springer. Walker, 1980. Subj: Animals – whales. Science.

Greg's microscope ill. by Arnold Lobel. Harper, 1963. Subj: Science.

Hidden animals ill. by David Shapiro. Harper, 1969. First pub. in 1947. Subj: Animals.

How kittens grow photos. by Esther Bubley. Four Winds Pr., 1975. Subj: Animals – cats. Science.

How puppies grow photos. by Esther Bubley. Four Winds Pr., 1971. Subj: Animals – dogs. Science.

Is this a baby dinosaur? and other science picture puzzles. Harper, 1972. Subj: Games. Science.

Keep looking! by Millicent E. Selsam and Joyce Hunt; ill. by Normand Chartier. Macmillan, 1988. ISBN 0-02-781840-3 Subj: Animals. Farms. Seasons – winter.

Let's get turtles ill. by Arnold Lobel. Harper, 1965. Subj: Pets. Reptiles – turtles, tortoises. Science.

More potatoes! ill. by Ben Shecter. Harper, 1972. Subj: Farms. Plants. School. Science.

Night animals ill. with photos. Four Winds Pr., 1980. Subj: Animals. Night.

Plenty of fish ill. by Erik Blegvad. Harper, 1960. Subj: Fish. Pets. Science.

Sea monsters of long ago ill. by John Hamberger. Four Winds Pr., 1978. Subj: Monsters. Sea and seashore.

Seeds and more seeds ill. by Tomi Ungerer. Harper, 1959. Subj: Plants. Science. Seeds.

Strange creatures that really lived ill. by Jennifer Dewey. Scholastic, 1987. ISBN 0-590-40707-4 Subj: Animals.

Terry and the caterpillars ill. by Arnold Lobel. Harper, 1962. Subj: Insects – butterflies, caterpillars. Science.

Tony's birds ill. by Kurt Werth. Harper, 1961. Subj: Birds. Ethnic groups in the U.S. – Afro-Americans. Science.

When an animal grows ill. by John Kaufmann. Harper, 1966. Subj: Animals. Science.

Where do they go? Insects in winter ill. by Arabelle Wheatley. Scholastic, 1984. ISBN 0-02-778080-5 Subj: Insects. Science. Seasons – winter.

You see the world around you ill. by Greta Elgaard. Doubleday, 1963. Subj: Science.

Sendak, Maurice. *Alligators all around: an alphabet* ill. by author. Harper, 1962. Subj: ABC books. Reptiles – alligators, crocodiles.

Chicken soup with rice ill. by author. Harper, 1962. Subj: Days of the week, months of the year.

Hector Protector, and As I went over the water: two nursery rhymes ill. by author. Harper, 1965. Subj: Nursery rhymes.

In the night kitchen ill. by author. Harper, 1970. Subj: Caldecott award honor book. Dreams. Imagination.

Maurice Sendak's Really Rosie: starring the Nutshell Kids ill. by author; music by Carole King; design by Jane Byers Bierhorst. Harper, 1976. Subj: Activities – playing. Music. Theater.

One was Johnny: a counting book ill. by author. Harper, 1962. Subj: Counting.

Outside over there ill. by author. Harper, 1981. Subj: Activities – baby-sitting. Babies. Caldecott award honor book. Goblins.

Pierre: a cautionary tale in five chapters and a prologue ill. by author. Harper, 1962. Subj: Behavior – indifference. Character traits – individuality. Humor. Poetry, rhyme.

Seven little monsters ill. by author. Harper, 1977. Subj: Counting. Monsters. Poetry, rhyme.

The sign on Rosie's door ill. by author. Harper, 1960. Subj: Activities – playing. Imagination.

Some swell pup: or Are you sure you want a dog? by Maurice Sendak and Matthew Margolis; ill. by Maurice Sendak. Farrar, 1976. ISBN 0-374-46963-6 Subj: Animals – dogs. Pets.

Very far away ill. by author. Harper, 1957. Subj: Animals. Behavior – needing someone. Behavior – running away.

Where the wild things are ill. by author. Harper, 1963. Subj: Behavior – misbehavior. Caldecott award book. Imagination. Monsters.

Serfozo, Mary. *Welcome Roberto! Bienvenido, Roberto!* ill. by John Serfozo. Follett, 1969. Subj: Ethnic groups in the U.S. – Mexican-Americans. Foreign languages.

Who said red? ill. by Keiko Narahashi. Macmillan, 1988. ISBN 0-689-50455-1 Subj: Concepts – color.

Serraillier, Anne. *Florina and the wild bird* (Chönz, Selina)

Serraillier, Ian. *Florina and the wild bird* (Chönz, Selina)

Suppose you met a witch ill. by Ed Emberley. Little, 1973. Subj: Poetry, rhyme. Witches.

Sesame Street. *Ernie and Bert can...can you?* ill. by Michael Smollin. Random House, 1982. Subj: Format, unusual – board books. Puppets.

Sesame Street sign language fun ill. with photos. Random House, 1980. Subj: Language. Puppets.

Sesame Street word book ill. by Tom Leigh. Golden Pr., 1983. Subj: Language. Puppets.

The Sesame Street book of letters created in cooperation with the Children's Television Workshop, producers of Sesame Street. Designed by Charles I. Miller and James J. Harvin. Preschool Pr.; distributed in assoc. with Time-Life Books, 1970. Subj: ABC books.

The Sesame Street book of numbers created in cooperation with the Children's Television Workshop, producers of Sesame Street. Designed by Charles I. Miller and James J. Harvin. Preschool Pr.; distributed in assoc. with Time-Life Books, 1970. Subj: Counting.

The Sesame Street book of people and things created in cooperation with the Children's Television Workshop, producers of Sesame Street. Designed by Charles I. Miller and James J. Harvin. Preschool Pr.; distributed in assoc. with Time-Life Books, 1970. Subj: Careers. Concepts. Emotions.

The Sesame Street book of shapes created in cooperation with the Children's Television Workshop, producers of Sesame Street. Designed by Charles I. Miller and James J. Harvin. Preschool Pr.; distributed in assoc. with Time-Life Books, 1970. Subj: Concepts – shape.

Seuling, Barbara. *The teeny tiny woman: an old English ghost tale* ill. by author. Viking, 1976. Subj: Folk and fairy tales. Foreign lands – England. Ghosts.

The triplets ill. by author. Houghton, 1980. Subj: Character traits – individuality. Triplets.

What kind of family is this? a book about step families ill. by Ellen Dolce. Childrens Pr., 1985. ISBN 0-307-62482-X Subj: Family life. Family life – step families. Sibling rivalry.

Seuss, Dr. *And to think that I saw it on Mulberry Street* ill. by author. Vanguard, 1937. Subj: Humor. Imagination. Poetry, rhyme.

Bartholomew and the Oobleck ill. by author. Random House, 1949. Subj: Caldecott award honor book. Humor. Royalty.

The butter battle book ill. by author. Random House, 1984. Subj: Poetry, rhyme. War.

The cat in the hat ill. by author. Random House, 1957. Subj: Animals – cats. Humor. Poetry, rhyme.

The cat in the hat beginner book dictionary by the Cat himself and P. D. Eastman; ill. by Dr. Seuss Random House, 1964. Subj: Dictionaries. Humor.

The cat in the hat comes back! ill. by author. Random House, 1958. Subj: Animals – cats. Humor. Poetry, rhyme.

The cat's quizzer ill. by author. Random House, 1976. Subj: Humor. Poetry, rhyme. Riddles.

Come over to my house by Theo. LeSeig; ill. by Richard Erdoes. Random House, 1966. ISBN 0-394-90044-8 Subj: Houses. Poetry, rhyme.

Did I ever tell you how lucky you are? ill. by Richard Erdoes. Random House, 1973. Subj: Character traits – luck. Humor. Poetry, rhyme. Problem solving.

Dr. Seuss's ABC ill. by author. Random House, 1963. Subj: ABC books. Humor. Poetry, rhyme.

Dr. Seuss's sleep book ill. by author. Random House, 1962. Subj: Humor. Poetry, rhyme. Sleep.

The eye book ill. by Roy McKié. Random House, 1968. Subj: Anatomy. Animals – rabbits. Poetry, rhyme.

The foot book ill. by author. Random House, 1968. Subj: Anatomy. Humor. Poetry, rhyme.

Fox in sox ill. by author. Random House, 1965. Subj: Humor. Poetry, rhyme.

A great day for up ill. by Quentin Blake. Random House, 1974. Subj: Concepts – up and down. Humor. Poetry, rhyme.

Green eggs and ham ill. by author. Random House, 1960. Subj: Cumulative tales. Food. Humor. Poetry, rhyme.

Happy birthday to you! ill. by author. Random House, 1959. Subj: Birthdays. Humor. Poetry, rhyme.

Hooper Humperdink...? Not him! ill. by Charles E. Martin. Random House, 1976. Subj: ABC books. Birthdays. Humor. Poetry, rhyme.

Hop on Pop ill. by author. Random House, 1963. Subj: Humor. Poetry, rhyme.

Horton hatches the egg ill. by author. Random House, 1940. Subj: Animals – elephants. Birds. Character traits – helpfulness. Eggs. Humor. Poetry, rhyme.

Horton hears a Who! ill. by author. Random House, 1954. Subj: Animals – elephants. Character traits – kindness. Humor. Poetry, rhyme.

How the Grinch stole Christmas ill. by author. Random House, 1957. Subj: Character traits – meanness. Holidays – Christmas. Humor. Poetry, rhyme.

Hunches in bunches ill. by author. Random House, 1982. Subj: Poetry, rhyme. Problem solving.

I am not going to get up today! ill. by James Stevenson. Random House, 1987. ISBN 0-394-99217-2 Subj: Humor. Poetry, rhyme. Sleep.

I can draw it myself: by me, myself, with a little help from my friend Dr. Seuss ill. by author. Random House, 1987. ISBN 0-394-08009-7 Subj: Art. Character traits – individuality.

I can lick 30 tigers today and other stories ill. by author. Random House, 1969. Subj: Humor. Poetry, rhyme.

I can read with my eyes shut ill. by author. Random House, 1978. Subj: Activities – reading. Humor. Poetry, rhyme.

I can write! a book by me, myself, with a little help from Theo. LeSeig and Roy McKié ill. by Roy McKié. Random House, 1971. Subj: Activities – writing. Humor. Poetry, rhyme.

I had trouble getting to Solla Sollew ill. by author. Random House, 1965. Subj: Activities – traveling. Humor. Poetry, rhyme.

I wish that I had duck feet ill. by Barney Tobey. Random House, 1965. Subj: Behavior – wishing. Poetry, rhyme.

If I ran the circus ill. by author. Random House, 1956. Subj: Circus. Humor. Poetry, rhyme.

If I ran the zoo ill. by author. Random House, 1950. Subj: Caldecott award honor book. Humor. Poetry, rhyme. Zoos.

In a people house ill. by Roy McKié. Random House, 1972. Subj: Houses. Humor. Poetry, rhyme.

The king's stilts ill. by author. Random House, 1939. Subj: Humor. Poetry, rhyme. Royalty. Toys.

The Lorax ill. by author. Random House, 1971. Subj: Ecology. Humor. Poetry, rhyme.

McElligot's pool ill. by author. Random House, 1947. Subj: Caldecott award honor book. Fish. Humor. Imagination. Poetry, rhyme.

Marvin K. Mooney, will you please go now! ill. by author. Random House, 1972. Subj: Humor. Poetry, rhyme.

Mr. Brown can moo! Can you? ill. by author. Random House, 1970. Subj: Animals. Humor. Noise, sounds. Participation. Poetry, rhyme.

Oh say can you say? ill. by author. Random House, 1979. Subj: Humor. Imagination. Poetry, rhyme.

Oh, the thinks you can think! ill. by author. Random House, 1975. Subj: Humor. Imagination. Poetry, rhyme.

On beyond zebra ill. by author. Random House, 1955. Subj: Humor. Letters. Poetry, rhyme.

One fish, two fish, red fish, blue fish ill. by author. Random House, 1960. Subj: Fish. Humor. Poetry, rhyme.

Please try to remember the first of october! ill. by author. Random House, 1977. Subj: Behavior – wishing. Humor. Poetry, rhyme.

Scrambled eggs super! ill. by author. Random House, 1953. Subj: Food. Humor. Poetry, rhyme.

The shape of me and other stuff ill. by author. Random House, 1973. Subj: Concepts – shape. Humor. Poetry, rhyme.

The Sneetches, and other stories ill. by author. Random House, 1961. Subj: Emotions – fear. Humor. Poetry, rhyme.

Ten apples up on top by Theo LeSieg; ill. by Roy McKie. Random House, 1961. ISBN 0-394-90019-7 Subj: Counting.

There's a wocket in my pocket ill. by author. Random House, 1974. Subj: Humor. Poetry, rhyme.

Thidwick, the big-hearted moose ill. by author. Random House, 1948. Subj: Animals – moose. Birds. Humor. Poetry, rhyme.

The tooth book ill. by Roy McKie. Random House, 1981. Subj: Health. Poetry, rhyme. Teeth.

Wacky Wednesday ill. by George Booth. Random House, 1974. Subj: Humor. Participation. Poetry, rhyme.

Would you rather be a bullfrog? ill. by Roy McKie. Random House, 1975. Subj: Animals. Character traits – optimism. Frogs and toads.

Severo, Emöke de Papp. *The good-hearted youngest brother*

Sewall, Marcia. *Animal song* ill. by author. Little, 1988. ISBN 0-316-78191-6 Subj: Animals. Folk and fairy tales. Songs.

The cobbler's song ill. by author. Dutton, 1982. Subj: Behavior – worrying.

The little wee tyke: an English folktale ill. by author. Atheneum, 1979. Subj: Animals – dogs. Folk and fairy tales. Foreign lands – England.

Ridin' that strawberry roan ill. by adapt. Viking, 1985. ISBN 0-670-80623-4 Subj: Animals – horses. Cowboys. Poetry, rhyme.

The wee, wee mannie and the big, big coo: a Scottish folk tale ill. by author. Little, 1977. Subj: Animals – bulls, cows. Folk and fairy tales. Foreign lands – Scotland.

Sewell, Helen Moore. *Birthdays for Robin* ill. by author. Macmillan, 1943. Subj: Animals – dogs. Birthdays.

Blue barns ill. by author. Macmillan, 1935. Subj: Barns. Birds – ducks. Birds – geese. Farms.

Jimmy and Jemima ill. by author. Macmillan, 1940. Subj: Character traits – bravery. Sibling rivalry.

Ming and Mehitable ill. by author. Macmillan, 1936. Subj: Animals – dogs.

Peggy and the pony ill. by author. Oxford Univ. Pr., 1936. Subj: Animals – horses. Behavior – wishing.

Sexton, Gwain. *There once was a king* ill. by author. Scribner's, 1959. Subj: Poetry, rhyme. Royalty.

Seymour, Dorothy Z. *The tent* ill. by Nancé Holman. Grosset, 1965. Subj: Cumulative tales.

Seymour, Peter. *Animals in disguise* ill. by Jean Cassels Helmer. Macmillan, 1985. ISBN 0-02-782160-9 Subj: Animals. Format, unusual – toy and movable books.

How the weather works ill. by Sally Springer. Macmillan, 1985. Subj: Format, unusual – toy and movable books. Science. Weather.

Insects: a close-up look ill. by Jean Cassels Helmer. Macmillan, 1985. ISBN 0-02-782120-X Subj: Format, unusual – toy and movable books. Insects.

What lives in the sea? ill. by Pamela Johnson. Macmillan, 1985. ISBN 0-02-782170-6 Subj: Format, unusual – toy and movable books. Sea and seashore.

What's at the beach? ill. by David A. Carter. Holt, 1985. Subj: Monsters. Nature. Sea and seashore.

Seyton, Marion. *The hole in the hill* ill. by Leonard W. Shortall. Follett, 1960. Subj: Cavemen. Family life.

Shahn, Bernarda Bryson *see* Bryson, Bernarda

Shannon, George. *Beanboy* ill. by Peter Sis. Greenwillow, 1984. Subj: City. Cumulative tales. Humor.

Lizard's song ill. by José Aruego and Ariane Dewey. Greenwillow, 1981. Subj: Animals – bears. Reptiles – lizards. Songs.

Oh, I love! ill. by Cheryl Harness. Bradbury Pr., 1988. ISBN 0-02-782180-3 Subj: Cumulative tales. Folk and fairy tales. Poetry, rhyme. Songs.

The Piney Woods peddler ill. by Nancy Tafuri. Greenwillow, 1982. Subj: Activities – trading. Folk and fairy tales.

The surprise ill. by José Aruego and Ariane Dewey. Greenwillow, 1983. Subj: Animals – squirrels. Birthdays.

Shapp, Charles. *Let's find out about babies* (Shapp, Martha)

Let's find out about houses (Shapp, Martha)

Let's find out what's big and what's small by Charles and Martha Shapp; ill. by Vana Earle. Watts, 1959. Subj: Concepts – size.

Shapp, Martha. *Let's find out about babies* by Martha and Charles Shapp and Sylvia Shepard; ill. by Jenny Williams. Watts, 1975. Subj: Babies. Science.

Let's find out about houses by Martha and Charles Shapp; ill. by Tomie de Paola. Watts, 1975. Subj: Houses.

Let's find out what's big and what's small (Shapp, Charles)

Sharmat, Marjorie Weinman. *Attila the angry* ill. by Lillian Hoban. Holiday, 1985. Subj: Animals – squirrels. Emotions – anger.

Bartholomew the bossy ill. by Normand Chartier. Macmillan, 1984. Subj: Animals. Behavior – growing up. Friendship.

The best Valentine in the world ill. by Lilian Obligado. Holiday, 1982. Subj: Animals – foxes. Holidays – Valentine's Day.

A big fat enormous lie ill. by David McPhail. Dutton, 1978. Subj: Behavior – lying.

Burton and Dudley ill. by Barbara Cooney. Holiday, 1975. Subj: Activities – walking. Character traits – laziness. Friendship.

Frizzy the fearful ill. by John Wallner. Holiday, 1983. Subj: Emotions – fear.

Gila monsters meet you at the airport ill. by Byron Barton. Macmillan, 1980. Subj: Behavior – misunderstanding. Moving.

Gladys told me to meet her here ill. by Edward Frascino. Harper, 1970. Subj: Friendship.

Go to sleep, Nicholas Joe ill. by John Himmelman. Harper, 1988. ISBN 0-06-025504-8 Subj: Bedtime. Family life.

Goodnight, Andrew. Goodnight, Craig ill. by Mary Chalmers. Harper, 1969. Subj: Bedtime. Family life.

Grumley the grouch ill. by Kay Chorao. Holiday, 1980. Subj: Behavior – dissatisfaction.

Helga high-up ill. by David Neuhaus. Scholastic, 1988. ISBN 0-590-40692-2 Subj: Anatomy. Animals – giraffes. Character traits – being different.

Hooray for Father's Day! ill. by John Wallner. Holiday, 1987. ISBN 0-8234-0637-7 Subj: Animals – mules. Holidays – Father's Day.

Hooray for Mother's Day! ill. by John Wallner. Holiday, 1986. ISBN 0-8234-0588-5 Subj: Birds – chickens. Holidays – Mother's Day.

I don't care ill. by Lillian Hoban. Macmillan, 1977. Subj: Behavior – indifference. Emotions – sadness. Ethnic groups in the U.S. – Afro-Americans. Toys – balloons.

I want mama ill. by Emily Arnold McCully. Harper, 1974. Subj: Family life – only child. Illness.

I'm not Oscar's friend any more ill. by Tony DeLuna. Dutton, 1975. Subj: Behavior – fighting, arguing. Emotions – anger. Friendship.

I'm terrific ill. by Kay Chorao. Holiday, 1977. Subj: Animals – bears. Character traits – conceit. Character traits – pride. Self-concept.

Lucretia the unbearable ill. by Janet Stevens. Holiday, 1981. ISBN 0-8234-0395-5 Subj: Animals – bears. Behavior – worrying. Health.

Mitchell is moving ill. by José Aruego and Ariane Dewey. Macmillan, 1978. Subj: Dinosaurs. Friendship. Moving.

Mooch the messy ill. by Ben Shecter. Harper, 1976. Subj: Animals – rats. Character traits – cleanliness.

My mother never listens to me ed. by Kathleen Tucker; ill. by Lynn Munsinger. Albert Whitman, 1984. ISBN 0-8075-5347-6 Subj: Activities – reading. Family life – mothers. Imagination.

Nate the Great ill. by Marc Simont. Coward, 1972. Subj: Careers – detectives. Food.

Nate the Great and the fishy prize ill. by Marc Simont. Coward, 1985. ISBN 0-698-30745-3 Subj: Animals – dogs. Pets. Problem solving.

Nate the Great and the lost list ill. by Marc Simont. Coward, 1975. Subj: Careers – detectives. Food. Problem solving.

Nate the Great and the phony clue ill. by Marc Simont. Coward, 1977. Subj: Careers – detectives. Food.

Nate the Great goes undercover ill. by Marc Simont. Coward, 1974. Subj: Careers – detectives. Food. Problem solving.

Rex ill. by Emily Arnold McCully. Harper, 1967. Subj: Behavior – running away.

Rollo and Juliet...forever! ill. by Marylin Hafner. Doubleday, 1981. Subj: Behavior – fighting, arguing. Emotions – anger. Friendship.

Sasha the silly ill. by Janet Stevens. Holiday, 1984. Subj: Animals – dogs. Character traits – vanity.

Scarlet Monster lives here ill. by Dennis Kendrick. Harper, 1979. Subj: Behavior. Friendship. Monsters. Moving.

Sometimes mama and papa fight ill. by Kay Chorao. Harper, 1980. Subj: Behavior – fighting, arguing. Family life.

Sophie and Gussie ill. by Lillian Hoban. Macmillan, 1973. Subj: Animals – squirrels. Friendship.

Taking care of Melvin ill. by Victoria Chess. Holiday, 1980. Subj: Animals. Friendship. Self-concept.

Thornton, the worrier ill. by Kay Chorao. Holiday, 1978. Subj: Animals – rabbits. Behavior – worrying.

The trip: and other Sophie and Gussie stories ill. by Lillian Hoban. Macmillan, 1976. Subj: Animals – squirrels. Behavior – losing things. Behavior – sharing. Clothing. Friendship.

Two ghosts on a bench ill. by Nola Langner. Harper, 1982. Subj: Ghosts.

Walter the wolf ill. by Kelly Oechsli. Holiday, 1975. Subj: Animals. Animals – wolves. Violence, anti-violence.

What are we going to do about Andrew? ill. by Ray Cruz. Macmillan, 1980. Subj: Character traits – individuality. Family life.

Sharmat, Mitchell. *Gregory, the terrible eater* ill. by José Aruego and Ariane Dewey. Four Winds Pr., 1980. Subj: Animals – goats. Food.

The seven sloppy days of Phineas Pig ill. by Sue Truesdell. Harcourt, 1983. Subj: Animals – pigs. Character traits – cleanliness.

Sherman is a slowpoke ill. by David Neuhaus. Scholastic, 1988. ISBN 0-590-40938-7 Subj: Animals – sloths. Character traits – individuality. School.

Sharon, Mary Bruce. *Scenes from childhood* ill. by author. Dutton, 1978. Subj: Art. Careers – artists.

Sharpe, Sara. *Gardener George goes to town* ill. by Susan Moxley. Harper, 1982. Subj: Activities – gardening.

Sharr, Christine. *Homes* ill. by author. Wonder Books, 1971. Subj: Family life. Houses.

Shaw, Charles Green. *The blue guess book* ill. by author. Addison-Wesley, 1942. Subj: Games.

The guess book ill. by author. Addison-Wesley, 1941. Subj: Games.

It looked like spilt milk ill. by author. Harper, 1947. Subj: Concepts – shape. Games. Imagination. Participation. Sky. Weather – clouds.

Shaw, Evelyn S. *Alligator* ill. by Frances Zweifel. Harper, 1972. Subj: Reptiles – alligators, crocodiles. Science.

Fish out of school ill. by Ralph Carpentier. Harper, 1970. Subj: Fish. Science. Sea and seashore.

Nest of wood ducks ill. by Cherryl Pape. Harper, 1976. Subj: Birds – ducks. Science.

Octopus ill. by Ralph Carpentier. Harper, 1971. Subj: Octopuses. Science. Sea and seashore.

Sea otters ill. by Cherryl Pape. Harper, 1980. Subj: Animals – otters. Science.

Shaw, Nancy. *Sheep in a jeep* ill. by Margot Apple. Houghton, 1986. ISBN 0-395-41105-X Subj: Animals – sheep. Poetry, rhyme.

Shaw, Richard. *The kitten in the pumpkin patch* ill. by Jacqueline Kahane. Warne, 1973. Subj: Animals – cats. Holidays – Halloween. Witches.

Shay, Arthur. *What happens when you go to the hospital* ill. by author. Reilly and Lee, 1969. Subj: Hospitals. Illness.

Shearer, John. *Billy Jo Jive and the case of the midnight voices* ill. by Ted Shearer. Delacorte, 1982. Subj: Problem solving. Sports – camping.

The case of the sneaker snatcher ill. by Ted Shearer. Delacorte, 1977. Subj: Clothing. Problem solving. Sports – basketball.

Shecter, Ben. *Conrad's castle* ill. by author. Harper, 1967. Subj: Imagination.

The discontented mother ill. by author. Harcourt, 1980. Subj: Behavior – wishing.

Emily, girl witch of New York ill. by author. Dial Pr., 1963. Subj: City. Houses. Magic. Progress. Witches.

Hester the jester ill. by author. Harper, 1977. Subj: Character traits – ambition. Clowns, Jesters.

If I had a ship ill. by author. Doubleday, 1970. Subj: Boats, ships. Character traits – generosity. Emotions – love. Imagination.

Partouche plants a seed ill. by author. Harper, 1966. Subj: Activities – gardening. Animals – pigs. Foreign lands – France. Plants. Seeds.

The stocking child ill. by author. Harper, 1976. Subj: Senses – seeing. Toys – dolls.

Stone house stories ill. by author. Harper, 1973. Subj: Animals.

Sheehan, Angela. *The beaver* ill. by Graham Allen. Watts, 1979. Subj: Animals – beavers. Science.

The duck ill. by Maurice Pledger and Bernard Robinson. Warwick Pr., 1979. Subj: Birds – ducks. Science.

The otter ill. by Bernard Robinson. Warwick Pr., 1979. Subj: Animals – otters. Science.

The penguin ill. by Trevor Boyer. Watts, 1979. Subj: Birds – penguins. Science.

Shefelman, Janice. *Victoria House* ill. by Tom Shefelman. Harcourt, 1988. ISBN 0-15-200630-3 Subj: Houses. Moving.

Sheffield, Margaret. *Before you were born* ill. by Sheila Bewley. Knopf, 1984. Subj: Babies. Science.

Where do babies come from? ill. by Sheila Bewley. Knopf, 1973. Subj: Babies. Science.

Sheldon, Aure. *Of cobblers and kings* ill. by Don Leake. Parents, 1978. Subj: Careers – shoemakers. Character traits – cleverness.

Sheldon, Denise *Suzanne and Nicholas in the garden* (Ichikawa, Satomi)

Shepard, Sylvia. *Let's find out about babies* (Shapp, Martha)

Sherman, Eileen Bluestone. *The odd potato: a Chanukah story* ill. by Katherine Janus Kahn. Kar-Ben Copies, 1984. ISBN 0-930494-36-9 Subj: Family life. Holidays – Hanukkah. Jewish culture.

Sherman, Elizabeth *see* Friskey, Margaret

Sherman, Ivan. *I am a giant* ill. by author. Harcourt, 1975. Subj: Giants. Imagination.

I do not like it when my friend comes to visit ill. by author. Harcourt, 1973. Subj: Behavior – sharing. Etiquette. Friendship.

Walking talking words ill. by author. Harcourt, 1980. Subj: Language. Poetry, rhyme.

Sherman, Josepha. *Vassilisa the wise: a tale of medieval Russia* ill. by Daniel San Souci. Harcourt, 1988. ISBN 0-15-293240-2 Subj: Folk and fairy tales. Foreign lands – Russia. Royalty.

Sherman, Nancy. *Gwendolyn and the weathercock* ill. by Edward Sorel. Golden Pr., 1961. Subj: Birds – chickens. Farms. Poetry, rhyme. Weather – rain.

Gwendolyn the miracle hen ill. by Edward Sorel. Western Pub., 1961. Subj: Birds – chickens. Dragons. Poetry, rhyme.

Sherrow, Victoria. *There goes the ghost* ill. by Megan Lloyd. Harper, 1985. ISBN 0-06-025510-2 Subj: Behavior – misbehavior. Ghosts. Houses. Moving.

Shi, Zhang Xiu. *Monkey and the white bone demon* tr. by Ye Ping Kuei; rev. by Jill Morris; ill. by Lin Zheng and others. Viking, 1984. Adapted from the 16th century novel, The pilgrimage to the west, by Wu Cheng En. Subj: Animals – monkeys. Folk and fairy tales. Foreign lands – China.

Shibano, Tamizo. *The old man who made the trees bloom* by Hanasaka Jijii; retold by Tamizo Shibano; tr. by D. T. Ooka; ill. by Bunshu Iguchi. Heian Int., 1985. ISBN 0-89346-247-0 Subj: Animals – dogs. Behavior – greed. Character traits – kindness. Character traits – meanness.

Shimin, Symeon. *I wish there were two of me* ill. by author. Warne, 1976. Subj: Behavior – wishing. Dreams. Imagination.

A special birthday ill. by author. McGraw-Hill, 1976. Subj: Birthdays. Wordless.

Shine, Deborah. *The little engine that could pudgy word book* ill. by Christina Ong. Putnam's, 1988. ISBN 0-448-19054-0 Subj: Character traits – perseverance. Format, unusual – board books. Trains.

Shire, Ellen. *The mystery at number seven, Rue Petite* ill. by author. Random House, 1978. Subj: Character traits – bravery. Crime.

Shles, Larry. *Moths and mothers, feathers and fathers: a story about a tiny owl named Squib* ill. by author. Houghton, 1984. ISBN 0-395-36695-X Subj: Birds – owls. Character traits – being different.

Shopping ill. by Roser Capdevila. Firefly Pr., 1986. ISBN 0-920303-43-9 Subj: Shopping. Format, unusual – toy and movable books. Wordless.

Short, Mayo. *Andy and the wild ducks* ill. by Paul M. Souza. Melmont, 1959. Subj: Animals. Ecology. Farms.

Shortall, Leonard W. *Andy, the dog walker* ill. by author. Morrow, 1968. Subj: Animals – dogs. Behavior – lost.

Just-in-time Joey ill. by author. Morrow, 1973. Subj: Ecology.

One way: a trip with traffic signs ill. by author. Prentice-Hall, 1975. Subj: Holidays – Fourth of July. Poetry, rhyme. Safety. Traffic, traffic signs.

Tod on the tugboat ill. by author. Morrow, 1971. Subj: Boats, ships.

Tony's first dive ill. by author. Morrow, 1972. Subj: Emotions – fear. Sports – swimming.

Shostak, Myra. *Rainbow candles: a Chanukah counting book* ill. by Katherine Janus Kahn. Kar-Ben Copies, 1986. ISBN 0-930494-59-8 Subj: Counting. Format, unusual – board books. Holidays – Hanukkah. Jewish culture.

Shoten, Fukuinkan. *Elephant blue* (Nakano, Hirotaka)

Showalter, Jean B. *The donkey ride: an Æsop fable* ill. by Tomi Ungerer. Doubleday, 1967. Subj: Animals – donkeys. Folk and fairy tales. Humor.

Showers, Kay Sperry. *Before you were a baby* (Showers, Paul)

Showers, Paul. *A baby starts to grow* ill. by Rosalind Fray. Crowell, 1969. Subj: Babies. Science.

Before you were a baby by Paul Showers and Kay Sperry Showers; ill. by Ingrid Fetz. Crowell, 1968. Subj: Babies. Science.

Columbus Day ill. by Ed Emberley. Crowell, 1965. Subj: Holidays – Columbus Day. U.S. history.

The listening walk ill. by Aliki. Crowell, 1961. Subj: Activities – walking. Noise, sounds. Senses – hearing.

Look at your eyes ill. by Paul Galdone. Crowell, 1962. Subj: Anatomy. Ethnic groups in the U.S. – Afro-Americans. Senses – seeing.

Me and my family tree ill. by Don Madden. Crowell, 1978. Subj: Family life. Science.

No measles, no mumps for me ill. by Harriett Barton. Crowell, 1980. Subj: Illness. Science.

You can't make a move without your muscles ill. by Harriett Barton. Crowell, 1982. Subj: Anatomy. Science.

Your skin and mine ill. by Paul Galdone. Crowell, 1965. Subj: Anatomy. Ethnic groups in the U.S. – Afro-Americans.

Shub, Elizabeth. *The Bremen town musicians* (Grimm, Jacob)

Clever Kate (Grimm, Jacob)

Dear Sarah (Borchers, Elisabeth)

Dragon Franz text by Josef Guggenmos; adapt. by Elizabeth Shub; ill. by Ursula Konopka. Greenwillow, 1976. Orig. pub. in German under the title Franz, der Drache. Subj: Character traits – being different. Concepts – color. Dragons.

The emperor's plum tree (Nikly, Michelle)

The fisherman and his wife (Grimm, Jacob)

Jorinda and Joringel (Grimm, Jacob)

Seeing is believing ill. by Rachel Isadora. Greenwillow, 1979. Subj: Elves and little people. Folk and fairy tales.

Sir Ribbeck of Ribbeck of Havelland (Fontane, Theodore)

The twelve dancing princesses (Grimm, Jacob)

Why Noah chose the dove (Singer, Isaac Bashevis)

Shulevitz, Uri. *Dawn* ill. by author. Farrar, 1974. Subj: Family life – grandfathers. Morning. Sports – camping. Sun.

The magician adapt. from the Yiddish of Isaac Loeb Peretz by Uri Shulevitz; ill. by adapt. Macmillan, 1973. Subj: Jewish culture. Magic. Religion.

One Monday morning ill. by author. Scribner's, 1967. Subj: Days of the week, months of the year. Imagination. Royalty.

Rain rain rivers ill. by author. Farrar, 1969. Subj: Poetry, rhyme. Weather – rain.

The treasure ill. by author. Farrar, 1978. Subj: Caldecott award honor book. Dreams. Folk and fairy tales.

Shulman, Milton. *Prep, the little pigeon of Trafalgar Square* ill. by Dale Maxey. Random House, 1964. Subj: Birds – pigeons. Foreign lands – England.

Shute, Linda. *Clever Tom and the leprechaun* ill. by author. Lothrop, 1988. ISBN 0-688-07489-8 Subj: Elves and little people. Folk and fairy tales.

Momotaro, the peach boy ill. by author. Lothrop, 1986. ISBN 0-688-05864-7 Subj: Behavior – fighting, arguing. Character traits – bravery. Devil. Folk and fairy tales. Foreign lands – Japan.

Shuttlesworth, Dorothy E. *ABC of buses* ill. by Leonard W. Shortall. Doubleday, 1965. Subj: ABC books. Buses.

Shyer, Marlene Fanta. *Here I am, an only child* ill. by Donald Carrick. Scribner's, 1985. ISBN 0-684-18296-3 Subj: Family life – only child.

Stepdog ill. by Judith Schermer. Scribner's, 1983. Subj: Animals – dogs. Emotions – envy, jealousy. Family life.

Siberell, Anne. *Whale in the sky* ill. by author. Dutton, 1982. Subj: Animals – whales. Folk and fairy tales. Indians of North America.

Sicotte, Virginia. *A riot of quiet* ill. by Edward Ardizzone. Holt, 1969. Subj: Imagination. Noise, sounds.

Siddiqui, Ashraf. *Bhombal Dass, the uncle of lion: a tale from Pakistan* ill. by Thomas Arthur Hamil. Macmillan, 1959. Subj: Animals – goats. Animals – lions. Character traits – cleverness. Folk and fairy tales. Foreign lands – Pakistan.

Siebert, Diane. *Mojave* ill. by Wendell Minor. Harper, 1988. ISBN 0-690-04569-7 Subj: Desert. Poetry, rhyme.

Truck song ill. by Byron Barton. Crowell, 1984. Subj: Poetry, rhyme. Trucks.

Siekkinen, Raija. *Mister King* tr. from Finnish by Tim Steffa; ill. by Hannu Taina. Carolrhoda Books, 1987. ISBN 0-87614-315-X Subj: Animals – cats. Emotions – loneliness. Royalty.

Siepmann, Jane. *The lion on Scott Street* ill. by Clement Hurd. Oxford Univ. Pr., 1952. Subj: Animals – lions. Imagination.

Siewert, Margaret. *Bear hunt* by Margaret Siewert and Kathleen Savage; ill. by Leonard W. Shortall. Prentice-Hall, 1976. Subj: Animals – bears. Games. Participation. Toys – teddy bears.

Sills, Jennifer *see* Lewis, Stephen

Silver, Jody. *Isadora* ill. by author. Doubleday, 1981. Subj: Animals – donkeys. Clothing.

Silverman, Maida. *Bunny's ABC* ill. by Ellen Blonder. Grosset, 1986. ISBN 0-448-01464-5 Subj: ABC books. Animals – rabbits. Format, unusual – board books.

Dinosaur babies ill. by Carol Inouye. Simon & Schuster, 1988. ISBN 0-671-65897-2 Subj: Dinosaurs. Science.

Ladybug's color book ill. by Nancy Duell. Grosset, 1986. ISBN 0-448-01461-0 Subj: Concepts – color. Format, unusual – board books. Insects – ladybugs.

Mouse's shape book ill. by Frederic Marvin. Grosset, 1986. ISBN 0-448-01463-7 Subj: Animals – mice. Concepts – shape. Format, unusual – board books.

Silverstein, Shel. *A giraffe and a half* ill. by author. Harper, 1964. Subj: Cumulative tales. Humor. Poetry, rhyme.

The giving tree ill. by author. Harper, 1964. Subj: Character traits – generosity. Poetry, rhyme.

The missing piece ill. by author. Harper, 1976. Subj: Character traits – individuality. Concepts – shape.

Who wants a cheap rhinoceros? ill. by author. Rev. ed. Macmillan, 1983. Subj: Animals – rhinoceros. Poetry, rhyme.

Simmonds, Posy. *Fred* ill. by author. Knopf, 1988. ISBN 0-394-98627-X Subj: Animals – cats. Death.

Lulu and the flying babies ill. by author. Knopf, 1988. ISBN 0-394-99597-X Subj: Family life – fathers. Imagination. Museums. Weather – snow.

Simon, Howard. *If you were an eel, how would you feel?* (Simon, Mina Lewiton)

Simon, Mina Lewiton. *If you were an eel, how would you feel?* by Mina and Howard Simon; ill. by Howard Simon. Follett, 1963. Subj: Animals.

Is anyone here? ill. by Howard Simon. Atheneum, 1967. Subj: Poetry, rhyme. Sea and seashore.

Simon, Norma. *All kinds of families* ill. by Joe Lasker. Albert Whitman, 1976. Subj: Family life.

Cats do, dogs don't ill. by Dora Leder. Albert Whitman, 1986. ISBN 0-8075-1102-1 Subj: Animals – cats. Animals – dogs. Pets.

The daddy days ill. by Abner Graboff. Abelard-Schuman, 1958. Subj: Divorce. Family life – fathers.

How do I feel? ill. by Joe Lasker. Albert Whitman, 1970. Subj: Emotions. Family life. Twins.

I know what I like ill. by Dora Leder. Albert Whitman, 1971. Subj: Character traits – individuality.

I was so mad! ill. by Dora Leder. Albert Whitman, 1974. Subj: Emotions – anger.

I wish I had my father ill. by Arieh Zeldich. Albert Whitman, 1983. ISBN 0-8075-3522-2 Subj: Behavior – wishing. Family life – fathers. Holidays – Father's Day.

I'm busy, too ill. by Dora Leder. Albert Whitman, 1980. ISBN 0-8075-3464-1 Subj: Activities. Activities – working. School.

Oh, that cat! ill. by Dora Leder. Albert Whitman, 1986. ISBN 0-8075-5919-9 Subj: Animals – cats. Family life. Pets.

The saddest time ill. by Jacqueline Rogers. Albert Whitman, 1986. ISBN 0-8075-7203-9 Subj: Death.

We remember Philip ill. by Ruth Sanderson. Albert Whitman, 1979. Subj: Death.

The wet world ill. by Jane Miller. Lippincott, 1954. Subj: Weather – rain.

What do I do? ill. by Joe Lasker. Albert Whitman, 1969. Subj: Activities. Character traits – helpfulness. City. Ethnic groups in the U.S. – Puerto Rican-Americans. School.

What do I say? ill. by Joe Lasker. Albert Whitman, 1967. Subj: Ethnic groups in the U.S. Ethnic groups in the U.S. – Puerto Rican-Americans. Family life. Foreign languages. Participation. School.

Where does my cat sleep? ill. by Dora Leder. Albert Whitman, 1982. Subj: Animals – cats. Sleep.

Why am I different? ill. by Dora Leder. Albert Whitman, 1976. Subj: Character traits – being different. Character traits – individuality. Self-concept.

Simon, Seymour. *Animal fact - animal fable* ill. by Diane de Groat. Crown, 1979. Subj: Animals.

Beneath your feet ill. by Daniel Nevins. Walker, 1977. Subj: Earth. Science.

Earth: our planet in space ill. with photos. Four Winds Pr., 1984. Subj: Earth.

Galaxies ill. with photos. Morrow, 1988. ISBN 0-688-08004-9 Subj: Science. Space and space ships. Stars.

Icebergs and glaciers ill. with photos. Morrow, 1987. ISBN 0-688-06187-7 Subj: Nature. Science.

Jupiter ill. with photos. Morrow, 1985. ISBN 0-688-05797-7 Subj: Science. Space and space ships.

The largest dinosaurs ill. by Pamela Carroll. Macmillan, 1986. ISBN 0-02-782910-3 Subj: Dinosaurs.

Mars ill. with photos. Morrow, 1987. ISBN 0-688-06584-8 Subj: Science. Space and space ships.

The moon ill. with photos. Four Winds Pr., 1984. Subj: Moon.

Saturn ill. with photos. Morrow, 1985. ISBN 0-688-05799-3 Subj: Science. Space and space ships.

Shadow magic ill. by Stella Ormai. Lothrop, 1985. ISBN 0-688-02682-6 Subj: Shadows.

The smallest dinosaurs ill. by Anthony Rao. Crown, 1982. Subj: Dinosaurs.

The stars ill. with photos. Morrow, 1986. ISBN 0-688-05856-6 Subj: Science. Space and space ships. Stars.

The sun ill. with photos. Morrow, 1986. ISBN 0-688-05858-2 Subj: Science. Sun.

Turtle talk: a beginner's book of Logo ill. by Barbara Emberley and Ed Emberley. Crowell, 1986. ISBN 0-690-04522-0 Subj: Language. Machines.

Uranus ill. with photos. Morrow, 1987. ISBN 0-688-06583-X Subj: Science. Space and space ships.

Volcanoes ill. with photos. Morrow, 1988. ISBN 0-688-07211-1 Subj: Folk and fairy tales. Science. Volcanoes.

Simon, Sidney B. *The armadillo who had no shell* ill. by Walter Lorraine. Norton, 1966. Subj: Animals – armadillos. Character traits – being different.

Henry, the uncatchable mouse ill. by Nola Langner. Norton, 1964. Subj: Animals – mice. Character traits – cleverness.

Simons, Traute. *Paulino* tr. by Ebbitt Cutler; ill. by Susi Bohdal. Tundra (dist. by Scribner's), 1978. Subj: Dreams. Toys.

Simonson, Mary Jane see Wheeler, M. J.

Simont, Marc. *How come elephants?* ill. by author. Harper, 1965. Subj: Animals – elephants. Character traits – questioning.

Simple Simon. *The adventures of Simple Simon* ill. by Chris Conover. Farrar, 1987. ISBN 0-374-36921-6 Subj: Nursery rhymes.

Simple Simon ill. by Rodney Peppé. Holt, 1973. Subj: Nursery rhymes.

The story of Simple Simon ill. by Paul Galdone. McGraw-Hill, 1966. "The version used in this book was published in London in 1840 by A. Park." Subj: Nursery rhymes.

Singer, Bant see Shaw, Charles Green

Singer, Isaac Bashevis. *Why Noah chose the dove* tr. by Elizabeth Shub; ill. by Eric Carle. Farrar, 1974. Subj: Animals. Birds – doves. Religion – Noah.

Singer, Marilyn. *Archer Armadillo's secret room* ill. by Beth Lee Weiner. Macmillan, 1985. Subj: Animals – armadillos. Behavior – running away. Moving.

The dog who insisted he wasn't ill. by Kelly Oechsli. Dutton, 1976. Subj: Animals – dogs. Character traits – individuality. Humor.

Pickle plan ill. by Steven Kellogg. Dutton, 1978. Subj: Behavior – needing someone. Character traits – individuality.

Will you take me to town on strawberry day? ill. by Trinka Hakes Noble. Harper, 1981. Subj: Music. Poetry, rhyme. Songs.

Singh, Jacquelin. *Fat Gopal* ill. by Demi. Harcourt, 1984. Subj: Character traits – cleverness. Poetry, rhyme. Foreign lands – India.

Sipiera, Paul P. *I can be a geologist* ill. with photos. Childrens Pr., 1986. ISBN 0-516-01897-3 Subj: Careers – geologists.

Sis, Peter. *Higgledy-Piggledy* (Livingston, Myra Cohn)

Rainbow Rhino ill. by author. Knopf, 1987. ISBN 0-394-99009-9 Subj: Animals – rhinoceros. Birds. Friendship.

Waving ill. by author. Greenwillow, 1988. ISBN 0-688-07160-0 Subj: Counting.

Sitomer, Harry. *How did numbers begin?* (Sitomer, Mindel)

Sitomer, Mindel. *How did numbers begin?* by Mindel and Harry Sitomer; ill. by Richard Cuffari. Crowell, 1976. Subj: Counting.

Sivulich, Sandra Stroner. *I'm going on a bear hunt* ill. by Glen Rounds. Dutton, 1973. Subj: Animals – bears. Games. Participation.

Skaar, Grace Marion. *Nothing but (cats) and all about (dogs)* ill. by author. Addison-Wesley, 1947. Subj: Animals – cats. Animals – dogs.

The very little dog: and, The smart little kitty by Grace Marion Skaar and Louise Phinney Woodcock; ill. by authors. Addison-Wesley, 1967. Subj: Animals – cats. Animals – dogs.

What do the animals say? ill. by author. Addison-Wesley, 1968. 1950 ed. published under title: What do they say! Subj: Animals. Noise, sounds. Participation.

Skipper, Mervyn. *The fooling of King Alexander* ill. by Gaynor Chapman. Atheneum, 1967. Originally published in The white man's garden, by Mervyn Skipper. London, Mathews, 1931. Subj: Foreign lands – China. Royalty.

Skofield, James. *All wet! All wet!* ill. by Diane Stanley. Harper, 1984. Subj: Weather – rain.

Small fur (Korschunow, Irina)

Snow country ill. by Laura Jean Allen. Harper, 1983. Subj: Family life – grandparents. Farms. Weather – snow.

Skorpen, Liesel Moak. *All the Lassies* ill. by Bruce Martin Scott. Dial Pr., 1970. Subj: Animals. Animals – dogs. Character traits – perseverance. Cumulative tales. Family life – only child. Participation. Pets.

Charles ill. by Martha G. Alexander. Harper, 1971. Subj: Behavior – needing someone. Toys – teddy bears.

Elizabeth ill. by Martha G. Alexander. Harper, 1970. Subj: Toys – dolls.

His mother's dog ill. by M. E. Mullin. Harper, 1978. Subj: Animals – dogs. Emotions – envy, jealousy. Family life. Sibling rivalry.

If I had a lion ill. by Ursula Landshoff. Harper, 1967. Subj: Animals – lions. Imagination.

Old Arthur ill. by Wallace Tripp. Harper, 1972. Subj: Animals – dogs. Old age.

Outside my window ill. by Mercer Mayer. Harper, 1968. Subj: Animals – bears. Bedtime.

Skurzynski, Gloria. *Martin by himself* ill. by Lynn Munsinger. Houghton, 1979. Subj: Activities – working. Emotions – loneliness. Family life – mothers.

Slate, Joseph. *Lonely Lula cat* ill. by Bruce Degen. Harper, 1985. Subj: Animals – cats. Emotions – loneliness. Friendship.

The mean, clean, giant canoe machine ill. by Lynn Munsinger. Crowell, 1983. Subj: Activities – bathing. Animals – pigs. Witches.

The star rocker ill. by Dirk Zimmer. Harper, 1982. Subj: Poetry, rhyme. Stars.

Who is coming to our house? ill. by Ashley Wolff. Putnam's, 1988. ISBN 0-399-21537-9 Subj: Animals. Animals – mice. Poetry, rhyme. Religion.

Sleator, William. *The angry moon* ill. by Blair Lent. Little, 1970. Subj: Caldecott award honor book. Folk and fairy tales. Indians of North America. Moon.

That's silly ill. by Lawrence DiFiori. Dutton, 1981. ISBN 0-525-40981-5 Subj: Imagination. Magic.

Sleep, baby, sleep: *an old cradle song* ill. by Trudi Oberhänsli. Atheneum, 1967. Includes melody with words.

Slier, Debby. *Baby's words*

Busy baby

Farm animals

Hello, baby

Sloan, Carolyn. *Carter is a painter's cat* ill. by Fritz Wegner. Simon and Schuster, 1971. Subj: Animals – cats. Careers – artists.

Slobodkin, Louis. *Clear the track* ill. by author. Macmillan, 1945. Subj: Family life. Imagination. Poetry, rhyme. Trains.

Colette and the princess ill. by author. Dutton, 1965. Subj: Animals – cats. Folk and fairy tales. Foreign lands – France. Noise, sounds. Royalty.

Dinny and Danny ill. by author. Macmillan, 1951. Subj: Cavemen. Character traits – helpfulness. Dinosaurs. Friendship.

Friendly animals ill. by author. Vanguard, 1944. Subj: Animals. Poetry, rhyme.

Hustle and bustle ill. by author. Macmillan, 1962. Subj: Animals – hippopotami. Behavior – fighting, arguing.

The late cuckoo ill. by author. Vanguard, 1962. Subj: Clocks. Time.

Magic Michael ill. by author. Macmillan, 1944. Subj: Family life. Imagination. Magic. Self-concept.

Melvin, the moose child ill. by author. Macmillan, 1957. Subj: Animals. Animals – moose. Forest, woods.

Millions and millions and millions ill. by author. Vanguard, 1955. Subj: Character traits – individuality. Poetry, rhyme.

Moon Blossom and the golden penny ill. by author. Vanguard, 1963. Subj: Foreign lands – China. Money.

One is good, but two are better ill. by author. Vanguard, 1956. Subj: Poetry, rhyme.

Our friendly friends ill. by author. Vanguard, 1951. Subj: Animals.

The polka-dot goat ill. by author. Macmillan, 1964. Subj: Animals – goats. Foreign lands – India.

The seaweed hat ill. by author. Macmillan, 1947. Subj: Poetry, rhyme. Sea and seashore.

Thank you - you're welcome ill. by author. Vanguard, 1957. Subj: Etiquette

Trick or treat ill. by author. Macmillan, 1959. Subj: Holidays – Halloween.

Up high and down low ill. by author. Macmillan, 1960. Subj: Animals – goats. Animals – sheep. Concepts – up and down. Poetry, rhyme.

Wide-awake owl ill. by author. Macmillan, 1958. Subj: Birds – owls. Music. Sleep. Songs.

Yasu and the strangers ill. by author. Macmillan, 1965. Subj: Behavior – lost. Foreign lands – Japan.

Slobodkina, Esphyr. *Billy, the condominium cat* ill. by author. Addison-Wesley, 1980. ISBN 0-201-09204-2 Subj: Animals – cats. Old age.

Boris and his balalaika ill. by Vladimir Bobri. Abelard-Schuman, 1964. Subj: Foreign lands – Russia.

Caps for sale ill. by author. Addison-Wesley, 1940. Subj: Animals – monkeys. Careers – peddlers. Clothing. Humor. Participation.

Pezzo the peddler and the circus elephant ill. by author. Abelard-Schuman, 1967. Subj: Animals – elephants. Careers – peddlers. Circus. Clothing. Humor. Parades. Participation.

Pezzo the peddler and the thirteen silly thieves ill. by author. Abelard-Schuman, 1970. Subj: Careers – peddlers. Clothing. Crime. Humor. Participation.

Pinky and the petunias ill. by author. Abelard-Schuman, 1959. Based on a story by Tamara Schildkraut. Subj: Animals – cats. Flowers.

The wonderful feast ill. by author. Lothrop, 1955. Subj: Animals. Animals – horses. Farms. Food.

Slocum, Rosalie. *Breakfast with the clowns* ill. by author. Viking, 1937. Subj: Circus. Clowns, jesters. Food.

Small, David. *Eulalie and the hopping head* ill. by author. Macmillan, 1982. Subj: Animals – foxes. Character traits – kindness. Frogs and toads.

Imogene's antlers ill. by author. Crown, 1985. Subj: Animals. Character traits – appearance.

Paper John ill. by author. Farrar, 1987. ISBN 0-374-35738-2 Subj: Behavior – misbehavior. Character traits – cleverness. Emotions – anger. Mythical creatures. Paper.

Small, Ernest *see* Lent, Blair

Smallman, Clare. *Outside in* ill. by Edwina Riddell. Barron's, 1986. ISBN 0-8120-5760-0 Subj: Anatomy. Format, unusual – toy and movable books.

Smaridge, Norah. *Peter's tent* ill. by Brinton Turkle. Viking, 1965. Subj: Friendship.

Watch out! ill. by Susan Perl. Abingdon Pr., 1965. Subj: Safety.

You know better than that ill. by Susan Perl. Abingdon Pr., 1973. Subj: Etiquette. Poetry, rhyme.

Smart, Christopher. *For I will consider my cat Jeoffry* ill. by Emily Arnold McCully. Atheneum, 1984. Subj: Animals – cats. Poetry, rhyme.

Smath, Jerry. *But no elephants* ill. by author. Parents, 1979. Subj: Animals – elephants. Pets.

Elephant goes to school ill. by author. Parents, 1984. ISBN 0-8193-1126-X Subj: Animals – elephants. School.

Smith, Bożena. *The enchanted book* (Porazińska, Janina)

Smith, Catriona Mary. *The long dive* (Smith, Raymond Kenneth)

The long slide (Smith, Raymond Kenneth)

Smith, Donald. *Farm numbers 1, 2, 3* ill. by author. Abingdon Pr., 1970. Subj: Counting. Farms.

Who's wearing my baseball cap? ill. by author. Dial Pr., 1987. ISBN 0-8037-0396-1 Subj: Animals. Clothing. Format, unusual – board books. Problem solving.

Who's wearing my bow tie? ill. by author. Dial Pr., 1987. ISBN 0-8037-0395-3 Subj: Animals. Clothing. Format, unusual – board books. Problem solving.

Who's wearing my sneakers? ill. by author. Dial Pr., 1987. ISBN 0-8037-0398-8 Subj: Animals. Clothing. Format, unusual – board books. Problem solving.

Who's wearing my sunglasses? ill. by author. Dial Pr., 1987. ISBN 0-8037-0399-6 Subj: Animals. Format, unusual – board books. Glasses. Problem solving.

Smith, Elmer Boyd. *The story of Noah's ark* ill. by author. Houghton, 1904. Subj: Religion – Noah.

Smith, Elvet *see* Marshall, Margaret

Smith, Henry Lee. *Frog fun* (Stratemeyer, Clara Georgeanna)

Pepper (Stratemeyer, Clara Georgeanna)

Tuggy (Stratemeyer, Clara Georgeanna)

Smith, Janice Lee. *The monster in the third dresser drawer and other stories about Adam Joshua* ill. by Dick Gackenbach. Harper, 1981. Subj: Behavior – misbehavior. Emotions – fear. Monsters.

Smith, Jean Shannon. *Scooter and the magic star* (Gardner, Mercedes)

Smith, Jim. *The frog band and Durrington Dormouse* ill. by author. Little, 1977. Subj: Animals – mice. Frogs and toads.

The frog band and the onion seller ill. by author. Little, 1976. Subj: Animals. Frogs and toads. Humor. Problem solving.

The frog band and the owlnapper ill. by author. Little, 1981. Subj: Animals. Birds – owls. Frogs and toads. Humor.

Nimbus the explorer ill. by author. Little, 1981. ISBN 0-316-80168-2 Subj: Animals. Dinosaurs. Imagination. Jungle.

Smith, Linell Nash *see* Chenault, Nell

Smith, Lucia B. *A special kind of sister* ill. by Chuck Hall. Holt, 1979. Subj: Family life. Handicaps. Sibling rivalry.

Smith, Mary. *Long ago elf* by Mary and Robert Alan Smith; ill. by authors. Follett, 1968. Subj: Elves and little people.

Smith, Peter. *Jenny's baby brother* ill. by Bob Graham. Viking, 1984. ISBN 0-670-40636-8 Subj: Babies. Family life. Sibling rivalry.

Smith, Raymond Kenneth. *The long dive* by Raymond Kenneth and Catriona Mary Smith; ill. by authors. Atheneum, 1978. Subj: Sea and seashore. Toys.

The long slide by Raymond Kenneth and Catriona Mary Smith; ill. by authors. Atheneum, 1977. Subj: Toys.

Smith, Robert Alan. *Long ago elf* (Smith, Mary)

Smith, Robert Paul. *Jack Mack* ill. by Erik Blegvad. Coward, 1960. Subj: Humor. Tongue twisters.

Nothingatall, nothingatall, nothingatall ill. by Alan E. Cober. Harper, 1965. Subj: Bedtime.

When I am big ill. by Lillian Hoban. Harper, 1965. Subj: Behavior – growing up.

Smith, Roger. *How the animals saved the ark and put two and two together* ill. by author. Simon & Schuster, 1989. ISBN 0-671-66560-X Subj: Animals. Religion – Noah.

Smith, Theresa Kalab. *The fog is secret* ill. by author. Prentice-Hall, 1966. Subj: Sea and seashore. Weather – fog.

Smith, Wendy. *The lonely, only mouse* ill. by author. Viking, 1986. ISBN 0-670-81251-X Subj: Animals – mice. Behavior – sharing. Emotions – loneliness. Family life – only child.

Smith, William Jay. *Children of the forest* (Beskow, Elsa Maartman)

Puptents and pebbles: nonsense ABC ill. by Juliet Kepes. Little, 1959. Subj: ABC books. Humor. Poetry, rhyme.

The telephone (Chukovsky, Korney)

Typewriter town ill. by author. Dutton, 1960. Subj: Poetry, rhyme.

Smyth, Gwenda. *A pet for Mrs. Arbuckle* ill. by Ann James. Crown, 1981. ISBN 0-517-55434-8 Subj: Activities – traveling. Animals – cats. Pets.

Snell, Nigel. *A bird in hand...: a child's guide to sayings* ill. by author. David & Charles, 1987. ISBN 0-241-11815-8 Subj: Language.

Sniff, Mr. *see* Abisch, Roz

Snoopy on wheels ill. by Charles M. Schulz. Random House, 1983. Subj: Animals – dogs. Birds. Toys. Wheels.

Snow, Pegeen. *Mrs. Periwinkle's groceries* ill. by Jerry Warshaw. Children's Pr., 1981. Subj: Character traits – helpfulness. Cumulative tales. Old age.

A pet for Pat ill. by Tom Dunnington. Children's Pr., 1984. Subj: Pets. Poetry, rhyme.

Snyder, Anne. *The old man and the mule* ill. by Mila Lazarevich. Holt, 1978. Subj: Animals – mules. Character traits – meanness.

Snyder, Dianne. *The boy of the three-year nap* ill. by Allen Say. Houghton, 1988. ISBN 0-395-44090-4 Subj: Behavior – trickery. Caldecott award honor book. Character traits – laziness. Folk and fairy tales.

Snyder, Dick. *One day at the zoo* photos. by author. Scribner's, 1960. Subj: Animals. Animals – koala bears. Zoos.

Talk to me tiger photos. by author; foreword by George H. Pournelle. Golden Gate, 1965. Subj: Animals. Zoos.

Snyder, Zilpha Keatley. *The changing maze* ill. by Charles Mikolaycak. Macmillan, 1985. ISBN 0-02-785900-2 Subj: Animals – sheep. Folk and fairy tales. Magic. Wizards.

Come on, Patsy ill. by Margot Zemach. Atheneum, 1982. Subj: Activities – playing. Behavior – growing up. Poetry, rhyme.

Sobol, Harriet Langsam. *A book of vegetables* photos. by Patricia Agre. Dodd, 1984. ISBN 0-396-08450-8 Subj: Activities – gardening. Food.

Clowns photos. by Patricia Agre. Coward, 1982. Subj: Clowns, jesters.

Jeff's hospital book photos. by Patricia Agre. Walck, 1975. Subj: Hospitals.

My brother Steven is retarded photos. by Patricia Agre. Macmillan, 1977. Subj: Handicaps.

We don't look like our mom and dad photos. by Patricia Agre. Coward, 1984. Subj: Adoption. Ethnic groups in the U.S. Family life.

Sokoloff, Natalie B. *see* Scott, Natalie

Solbert, Romaine G. *see* Solbert, Ronni

Solbert, Ronni. *Emily Emerson's moon* (Merrill, Jean)

I wrote my name on the wall: sidewalk songs ill. by author. Little, 1971. Subj: Ethnic groups in the U.S.

Solomon, Joan. *A present for Mum* photos. by Joan and Ryan Solomon. Hamish Hamilton, 1982. Subj: Foreign lands – England. Shopping. Stores.

Solotareff, Grégoire. *Don't call me little bunny* ill. by author. Farrar, 1988. ISBN 0-374-35012-4 Subj: Animals – rabbits. Behavior – misbehavior. Crime. Prisons.

Never trust an ogre ill. by author. Greenwillow, 1988. ISBN 0-688-07741-2 Subj: Animals. Behavior – greed. Mythical creatures.

The ogre and the frog king ill. by author. Greenwillow, 1988. ISBN 0-688-07079-5 Subj: Frogs and toads. Monsters.

Somme, Lauritz. *The penguin family book* by Lauritz Somme and Sybille Kalas; tr. by Patricia Crampton; ill. with photos. Picture Book Studio, 1988. ISBN 0-88708-057-X Subj: Birds – penguins.

Sommers, Tish. *Bert and the broken teapot* ill. by Diane Dawson. Childrens Pr., 1985. ISBN 0-307-62114-6 Subj: Behavior – carelessness. Friendship.

Sonberg, Lynn. *A horse named Paris* ill. by Ken Robbins. Bradbury Pr., 1986. ISBN 0-02-786260-7 Subj: Animals – horses.

Sondergaard, Arensa. *Biddy and the ducks* by Arensa Sondergaard and Mary M. Reed; ill. by Doris Henderson and Marion Henderson. Heath, 1941. Subj: Birds – chickens. Birds – ducks.

Sondheimer, Ilse. *The boy who could make his mother stop yelling* ill. by Dee deRosa. Rainbow Pr., 1982. Subj: Behavior – bad day. Family life – mothers.

The song of the Three Holy Children ill. by Pauline Baynes. Holt, 1986. The text of this edition is taken from The Book of Common Prayer, 1662. ISBN 0-8050-0134-4 Subj: Nature. Religion. Songs.

Sonneborn, Ruth A. *Friday night is papa night* ill. by Emily Arnold McCully. Viking, 1970. Subj: City. Ethnic groups in the U.S. – Puerto Rican-Americans. Family life – fathers. Poverty.

I love Gram ill. by Leo Carty. Viking, 1971. Subj: City. Family life – grandmothers. Hospitals. Illness. Old age.

Lollipop's party ill. by Brinton Turkle. Viking, 1967. Subj: City. Emotions – loneliness. Ethnic groups in the U.S. – Puerto Rican-Americans.

Seven in a bed ill. by Don Freeman. Viking, 1968. Subj: Ethnic groups in the U.S. – Puerto Rican-Americans. Family life. Poverty. Sleep.

Sopko, Eugen. *Townsfolk and countryfolk* ill. by author. Faber, 1982. Subj: City. Country. Foreign lands – Europe.

Sorine, Stephanie Riva. *Our ballet class* photos. by Daniel S. Sorine. Knopf, 1981. Subj: Activities – dancing.

Sotomayor, Antonio. *Khasa goes to the fiesta* ill. by author. Doubleday, 1967. Subj: Behavior – lost. Foreign lands – South America. Holidays.

Soya, Kiyoshi. *A house of leaves* ill. by Akiko Hayashi. Putnam's, 1987. ISBN 0-399-21422-4 Subj: Insects. Weather – rain.

Spang, Günter. *Clelia and the little mermaid* ill. by Pepperl Ott. Abelard-Schuman, 1967. Translation of Clelia und die kleine Wassernixe. Subj: Emotions – loneliness. Foreign lands – Germany. Friendship. Mythical creatures.

Spangenberg, Judith Dunn *see* Dunn, Judy

Spangenburg, Judith Dunn *see* Dunn, Judy

Spanner, Helmut. *I am a little cat* tr. from German by Robert Kimber; ill. by author. Barron's, 1983. Subj: Animals – cats. Format, unusual – board books.

Spaulding, Leonard *see* Bradbury, Ray

Speare, Jean. *A candle for Christmas* ill. by Ann Blades. Macmillan, 1987. ISBN 0-689-50417-9 Subj: Foreign lands – Canada. Holidays – Christmas. Indians of North America.

Spencer, Zane. *Bright Fawn and me* (Leech, Jay)

The spider's web photos. by John Cooke. Putnam's, 1978. Subj: Spiders. Science.

Spiegel, Doris. *Danny and Company 92* ill. by author. Coward, 1945. Subj: Careers – firefighters. Fire.

Spier, Peter. *Bill's service station* ill. by author. Doubleday, 1981. Subj: Automobiles. Format, unusual – board books.

The Book of Jonah (Bible. Old Testament. Jonah)

Bored - nothing to do! ill. by author. Doubleday, 1978. Subj: Airplanes, airports. Behavior – boredom. Humor.

Crash! bang! boom! ill. by author. Doubleday, 1972. Subj: Noise, sounds. Parades. Participation.

Dreams ill. by author. Doubleday, 1986. ISBN 0-385-19336-X Subj: Dreams. Sky. Weather – clouds. Wordless.

The Erie Canal ill. by author. Doubleday, 1970. Subj: Folk and fairy tales. Music. Songs. U.S. history.

Fast-slow, high-low: a book of opposites ill. by author. Doubleday, 1972. Subj: Concepts – opposites. Concepts – speed.

Firehouse ill. by author. Doubleday, 1981. Subj: Careers – firefighters. Format, unusual – board books.

Food market ill. by author. Doubleday, 1981. Subj: Food. Format, unusual – board books. Shopping. Stores.

Gobble, growl, grunt ill. by author. Doubleday, 1971. Subj: Animals. Noise, sounds. Participation.

The legend of New Amsterdam ill. by author. Doubleday, 1979. Subj: Folk and fairy tales. U.S. history.

Little cats ill. by author. Doubleday, 1984. Subj: Animals – cats. Format, unusual – board books.

Little dogs ill. by author. Doubleday, 1984. Subj: Animals – dogs. Format, unusual – board books.

Little ducks ill. by author. Doubleday, 1984. Subj: Birds – ducks. Format, unusual – board books.

Little rabbits ill. by author. Doubleday, 1984. Subj: Animals – rabbits. Format, unusual – board books.

My school ill. by author. Doubleday, 1981. Subj: Format, unusual – board books. School.

Noah's ark ill. by author. Doubleday, 1977. Includes P. Spier's translation of The flood, by Jacobus Revius. Subj: Boats, ships. Caldecott award book. Poetry, rhyme. Religion – Noah. Wordless.

Oh, were they ever happy! ill. by author. Doubleday, 1978. Subj: Activities – painting. Concepts – color. Humor.

People ill. by author. Doubleday, 1980. Subj: World.

The pet store ill. by author. Doubleday, 1981. Subj: Animals. Format, unusual – board books. Pets. Stores.

Peter Spier's Christmas! ill. by author. Doubleday, 1983. Subj: Holidays – Christmas.

Peter Spier's rain ill. by author. Doubleday, 1982. Subj: Weather – rain. Wordless.

The toy shop ill. by author. Doubleday, 1981. Subj: Format, unusual – board books. Stores. Toys.

We the people: the Constitution of the United States of America ill. by author. Doubleday, 1987. ISBN 0-385-23789-8 Subj: U.S. history.

Spilka, Arnold. *And the frog went "Blah!"* ill. by author. Scribner's, 1972. Subj: Humor. Poetry, rhyme.

Dippy dos and don'ts (Sage, Michael)

A lion I can do without ill. by author. Walck, 1964. Subj: Humor. Poetry, rhyme.

Little birds don't cry ill. by author. Viking, 1965. Subj: Animals. Poetry, rhyme.

A rumbudgin of nonsense ill. by author. Scribner's, 1970. Subj: Humor. Poetry, rhyme.

Spinelli, Eileen. *Thanksgiving at Tappletons'* ill. by Maryann Cocca-Leffler. Addison-Wesley, 1982. Subj: Behavior – sharing. Family life. Holidays – Thanksgiving. Humor.

Spinner, Stephanie. *The adventures of Pinocchio* (Collodi, Carlo)

The pirates of Tarnoonga (Weiss, Ellen)

Spriggs, Ruth. *The fables of Æsop* (Æsop)

Frank Baber's Mother Goose (Mother Goose)

Springstubb, Tricia. *The magic guinea pig* ill. by Bari Weissman. Morrow, 1982. Subj: Behavior – mistakes. Witches.

My Minnie is a jewel ill. by Jim LaMarche. Carolrhoda, 1980. Subj: Character traits – loyalty. Emotions – love.

Spurr, Elizabeth. *Mrs. Minetta's car pool* ill. by Blanche Sims. Atheneum, 1985. ISBN 0-689-31103-6 Subj: Activities – flying. Automobiles. School.

The squire's bride: a Norwegian folk tale orig. told by P. C. Asbjørnsen; ill. by Marcia Sewall. Atheneum, 1975. Subj: Folk and fairy tales. Foreign lands – Norway. Weddings.

Stadler, John. *Animal cafe* ill. by author. Bradbury Pr., 1980. Subj: Animals. Behavior – greed. Food.

Gorman and the treasure chest ill. by author. Bradbury Pr., 1984. Subj: Animals. Behavior – sharing.

Hector, the accordion-nosed dog ill. by author. Macmillan, 1987. ISBN 0-02-786680-7 Subj: Animals – dogs. Music.

Hooray for snail! ill. by author. Crowell, 1984. ISBN 0-06-443075-8 Subj: Animals – snails. Sports – baseball.

Snail saves the day ill. by author. Crowell, 1985. ISBN 0-690-04469-0 Subj: Animals – snails. Sports – football.

Three cheers for hippo! ill. by author. Crowell, 1987. ISBN 0-690-04670-7 Subj: Activities – flying. Animals – hippopotami.

Stafford, Kay. *Ling Tang and the lucky cricket* ill. by Louise Zibold. McGraw-Hill, 1944. Subj: Character traits – luck. Foreign lands – China.

Stage, Mads. *The greedy blackbird* ill. by author. John Godon Burke, 1981. Subj: Behavior – greed. Behavior – sharing. Birds.

The lonely squirrel ill. by author. John Godon Burke, 1980. Subj: Animals – squirrels. Emotions – loneliness.

Stalder, Valerie. *Even the Devil is afraid of a shrew: a folktale of Lapland* adapt. by Ray Brocket; ill. by Richard Eric Brown. Addison-Wesley, 1972. Subj: Behavior – nagging. Devil. Folk and fairy tales. Foreign lands – Lapland.

Stamaty, Mark Alan. *Minnie Maloney and Macaroni* ill. by author. Dial Pr., 1976. Subj: Food. Humor.

Standiford, Natalie. *The best little monkeys in the world* ill. by Hilary Knight. Random House, 1987. ISBN 0-394-98616-4 Subj: Activities – baby-sitting. Animals – monkeys. Behavior – misbehavior.

Standon, Anna. *Little duck lost* by Anna and Edward Cyril Standon; ill. by Edward Cyril Standon. Delacorte Pr., 1965. Subj: Behavior – lost. Birds – ducks. Eggs. Family life – mothers.

The singing rhinoceros ill. by Edward Cyril Standon. Coward, 1963. Subj: Animals – rhinoceros.

Three little cats by Anna and Edward Cyril Standon; ill. by authors. Delacorte Pr., 1964. ISBN 0-87459-000-3 Subj: Activities – playing. Animals – cats. Behavior – misbehavior. Foreign languages.

Standon, Edward Cyril. *Little duck lost* (Standon, Anna)

Three little cats (Standon, Anna)

Stanek, Muriel. *All alone after school* ill. by Ruth Rosner. Albert Whitman, 1985. ISBN 0-8075-0278-2 Subj: Character traits – bravery. Emotions – loneliness. Family life – mothers.

Left, right, left, right! ill. by Lucy Hawkinson. Albert Whitman, 1969. Subj: Concepts – left and right. Emotions – embarrassment.

My little foster sister ill. by Judith Cheng. Albert Whitman, 1981. Subj: Adoption. Behavior – sharing. Sibling rivalry.

One, two, three for fun ill. by Seymour Fleishman. Albert Whitman, 1967. Subj: Counting. Ethnic groups in the U.S.

Stang, Judit *see* Varga, Judy

Stanley, Diane. *Birdsong Lullaby* ill. by author. Morrow, 1985. ISBN 0-688-05805-1 Subj: Birds. Imagination. Night. Sleep.

Captain Whiz-Bang ill. by author. Morrow, 1987. ISBN 0-688-06227-X Subj: Animals – cats. Behavior – growing up.

The conversation club ill. by author. Macmillan, 1983. Subj: Animals – mice. Clubs, gangs. Communication. Noise, sounds.

A country tale ill. by author. Four Winds Pr., 1985. ISBN 0-02-786780-3 Subj: Animals – cats. Behavior – seeking better things. City. Country. Friendship.

The good-luck pencil ill. by Bruce Degen. Macmillan, 1986. ISBN 0-02-786800-1 Subj: Character traits – luck. Magic. School.

Stanley, John. *It's nice to be little* ill. by Jean Tamburine. Rand McNally, 1965. Subj: Character traits – smallness.

Stanovich, Betty Jo. *Big boy, little boy* ill. by Virginia Wright-Frierson. Lothrop, 1984. Subj: Family life – grandmothers.

Hedgehog adventures ill. by Chris L. Demarest. Lothrop, 1983. Subj: Animals – groundhogs. Animals – hedgehogs. Character traits – loyalty.

Stan-Padilla, Viento. *Dream Feather* ill. by author. Atheneum, 1980. Subj: Folk and fairy tales. Indians of North America. Religion.

Stansfield, Ian. *The legend of the whale* ill. by author. Godine, 1986. ISBN 0-87923-628-0 Subj: Animals – whales. Folk and fairy tales.

Stanton, Elizabeth. *Sometimes I like to cry* by Elizabeth and Henry Stanton; ill. by Richard Leyden. Albert Whitman, 1978. Subj: Emotions.

The very messy room by Elizabeth and Henry Stanton; ill. by Richard Leyden. Albert Whitman, 1978. Subj: Character traits – cleanliness. Family life.

Stanton, Henry. *Sometimes I like to cry* (Stanton, Elizabeth)

The very messy room (Stanton, Elizabeth)

Stanton, Schuyler *see* Baum, L. Frank (Lyman Frank)

Stapler, Sarah. *Trilby's trumpet* ill. by author. Harper, 1988. ISBN 0-06-025827-6 Subj: Animals – bears. Format, unusual – toy and movable books. Music. Noise, sounds. Sibling rivalry.

Star wars: *the maverick moon* ill. by Walter Wright. Random House, 1979. Subj: Space and space ships.

Starbird, Kaye. *The covered bridge house and other poems* ill. by Jim Arnosky. Four Winds Pr., 1979. Subj: Poetry, rhyme.

Starret, William *see* McClintock, Marshall

Staunton, Ted. *Taking care of Crumley* ill. by Tina Holdcroft. Kids Can Pr., 1984. ISBN 0-919964-75-3 Subj: Behavior – bullying. School.

Steadman, Ralph. *The bridge* ill. by author. Subj: Behavior – fighting, arguing. Bridges. Friendship.

The little red computer ill. by author. McGraw-Hill, 1969. Subj: Machines. Space and space ships.

Stearns, Monroe. *Ring-a-ling* ill. by Adolf Zabransky. Lippincott, 1959. Subj: Nursery rhymes.

Stecher, Miriam B. *Daddy and Ben together* photos. by Alice Kandell. Lothrop, 1981. Subj: Family life – fathers.

Max, the music-maker by Miriam B. Stecher and Alice Kandell; photos. by Alice Kandell. Lothrop, 1980. Subj: Music. Science.

Steele, Mary Quintard Govan *see* Gage, Wilson

Steele, Philip. *Festivals around the world* ill. with photos. Dillon, 1986. ISBN 0-87518-332-8 Subj: Holidays.

Land transport around the world ill. with photos. Dillon, 1986. ISBN 0-87518-337-9 Subj: Transportation.

Steffa, Tim. *Mister King* (Siekkinen, Raija)

The nighttime book (Kunnas, Mauri)

One spooky night and other scary stories (Kunnas, Mauri)

Twelve gifts for Santa Claus (Kunnas, Mauri)

Steger, Hans-Ulrich. *Traveling to Tripiti* tr. by Elizabeth D. Crawford; ill. by author. Harcourt, 1967. Subj: Activities – traveling. Cumulative tales. Toys. Toys – teddy bears.

Stehr, Frédéric. *Quack-quack* ill. by author. Farrar, 1987. ISBN 0-374-36161-4 Subj: Animals. Behavior – needing someone. Birds – ducks. Family life – mothers.

Steig, Jeanne. *Consider the lemming* ill. by William Steig. Farrar, 1988. ISBN 0-374-31536-1 Subj: Animals – lemmings. Poetry, rhyme.

Steig, William. *Abel's Island* ill. by author. Farrar, 1976. ISBN 0-374-30010-0 Subj: Animals – mice. Islands.

The amazing bone ill. by author. Farrar, 1976. Subj: Animals – pigs. Caldecott award honor book. Magic.

The bad speller ill. by author. Windmill Books, 1970. Subj: Games. Language.

Brave Irene ill. by author. Farrar, 1986. ISBN 0-374-30947-7 Subj: Character traits – bravery. Character traits – perseverance. Seasons – winter. Weather – snow. Weather – storms.

Caleb and Kate ill. by author. Farrar, 1977. Subj: Animals – dogs. Magic. Witches.

Doctor De Soto ill. by author. Farrar, 1982. Subj: Animals – foxes. Animals – mice. Character traits – cleverness.

An eye for elephants ill. by author. Windmill Books, 1970. Subj: Animals – elephants. Poetry, rhyme.

Farmer Palmer's wagon ride ill. by author. Farrar, 1974. Subj: Animals – donkeys. Animals – pigs. Humor.

Gorky rises ill. by author. Farrar, 1980. Subj: Frogs and toads. Magic.

Roland, the minstrel pig ill. by author. Windmill Books, 1968. Subj: Animals – foxes. Animals – pigs. Music. Royalty.

Rotten island ill. by author. Rev. ed. of The bad island issued in 1969. Godine, 1984. Subj: Flowers. Islands. Monsters.

Solomon the rusty nail ill. by author. Farrar, 1985. ISBN 0-374-37131-8 Subj: Animals – cats. Animals – rabbits. Behavior – trickery. Magic.

Spinky sulks ill. by author. Farrar, 1988. ISBN 0-374-38321-9 Subj: Character traits – stubbornness. Emotions – happiness. Family life.

Sylvester and the magic pebble ill. by author. Windmill Books, 1969. Subj: Animals. Animals – donkeys. Caldecott award book. Family life. Magic.

Tiffky Doofky ill. by author. Farrar, 1987. ISBN 0-374-37542-9 Subj: Animals – dogs. Careers – garbage collectors. Emotions – love. Magic.

Yellow and pink ill. by author. Farrar, 1984. Subj: Toys – dolls.

The Zabajaba Jungle ill. by author. Farrar, 1987. ISBN 0-374-38790-7 Subj: Dreams. Jungle.

Stein, Sara Bonnett. *About dying: an open family book for parents and children together* by Sara Bonnett Stein, in cooperation with Gilbert W. Kliman [et al.]; photos. by Dick Frank; graphic design by Michael Goldberg. Walker, 1974. Subj: Death.

About handicaps: an open family book for parents and children together by Sara Bonnett Stein, in cooperation with Gilbert W. Kliman [et al.]; photos. by Dick Frank; graphic design by Michael Goldberg. Walker, 1974. Subj: Handicaps.

About phobias: an open family book for parents and children together Thomas R. Holman, consultant; photos. by Erika Stone. Walker, 1979. Subj: Emotions – fear. Family life – fathers.

The adopted one: an open family book for parents and children together Thomas R. Holman, consultant; photos. by Erika Stone. Walker, 1979. Subj: Adoption. Family life.

Cat ill. by Manuel Garcia. Harcourt, 1985. Subj: Animals – cats. Science.

A child goes to school photos. by Don Connors. Doubleday, 1978. Subj: School.

A hospital story: an open family book for parents and children together photos. by Doris Pinney; graphic design by Michel Goldberg. Walker, 1974. Subj: Careers – doctors. Careers – nurses. Hospitals. Illness.

Making babies: an open family book for parents and children together by Sara Bonnett Stein, in cooperation with Gilbert W. Kliman [et al.]; photos. by Doris Pinney; graphic design by Michael Goldberg. Walker, 1974. Subj: Babies. Family life.

Mouse ill. by Manuel Garcia. Harcourt, 1985. Subj: Animals – mice. Science.

On divorce: an open family book for parents and children together Thomas R. Holman, consultant; photos. by Erika Stone. Walker, 1979. Subj: Divorce. Family life.

That new baby: an open family book for parents and children together by Sara Bonnett Stein, in cooperation with Gilbert W. Kliman [et al.]; photos by Dick Frank; graphic design by Michael Goldberg. Walker, 1974. Subj: Babies. Family life.

Steiner, Barbara. *But not Stanleigh* photos. by George and Ruth Cloven. Children's Pr., 1980. Subj: Animals – raccoons.

The whale brother ill. by Gretchen Will Mayo. Walker, 1988. ISBN 0-8027-6805-9 Subj: Art. Animals – whales. Eskimos. Sea and seashore.

Steiner, Barbara Annette *see* Steiner, Barbara

Steiner, Charlotte. *Birthdays are for everyone* ill. by author. Doubleday, 1964. Subj: Birthdays.

Charlotte Steiner's ABC ill. by author. Watts, 1946. Subj: ABC books.

The climbing book by Charlotte Steiner and Mary Burlingham; ill. by Charlotte Steiner. Vanguard, 1943. Subj: Format, unusual. Holidays – Christmas.

Daddy comes home ill. by author. Doubleday, 1944. Subj: Family life. Family life – fathers.

Five little finger playmates ill. by author. Grosset, 1951. Subj: Counting. Games. Participation.

A friend is "Amie" ill. by author. Knopf, 1956. Subj: Foreign languages. Friendship.

Kiki and Muffy ill. by author. Doubleday, 1943. Subj: Animals – cats. Family life – grandmothers.

Kiki is an actress ill. by author. Doubleday, 1958. Subj: Theater.

Kiki's play house ill. by author. Doubleday, 1962. Subj: Activities – playing.

Listen to my seashell ill. by author. Knopf, 1959. Subj: Noise, sounds. Sea and seashore.

Look what Tracy found ill. by author. Knopf, 1972. Subj: Activities – playing. Imagination.

Lulu ill. by author. Doubleday, 1939. Subj: Animals – dogs. Imagination – imaginary friends.

My bunny feels soft ill. by author. Knopf, 1958. Subj: Animals – rabbits.

My slippers are red ill. by author. Knopf, 1958. Subj: Concepts – color.

Pete and Peter ill. by author. Doubleday, 1941. Subj: Animals – dogs. Sports – hunting.

Pete's puppets ill. by author. Doubleday, 1952. Subj: Puppets.

Polka Dot ill. by author. Doubleday, 1947. Subj: Pets.

Red Ridinghood's little lamb ill. by author. Knopf, 1964. Subj: Animals – sheep. Elves and little people. Games.

The sleepy quilt ill. by author. Doubleday, 1947. Subj: Bedtime.

What's the hurry, Harry? ill. by author. Lothrop, 1968. Subj: Behavior – hurrying. Character traits – patience.

Steiner, Jörg. *The bear who wanted to be a bear* from an idea by Frank Tashlin; ill. by Jörg Müller. Atheneum, 1977. Subj: Animals – bears. Progress. Stores.

Rabbit Island ill. by Jörg Müller. Harcourt, 1978. Subj: Animals – rabbits. Character traits – freedom.

Steinmetz, Leon. *Clocks in the woods* ill. by author. Harper, 1979. Subj: Animals. Clocks. Time.

Stemp, Robin. *Guy and the flowering plum tree* ill. by Carolyn Dinan. Atheneum, 1981. Subj: Imagination. Trees.

Stephens, Karen. *Jumping* ill. by George Wiggins. Grosset, 1965. Subj: Activities – jumping.

Stephenson, Dorothy. *How to scare a lion* ill. by John E. Johnson. Follett, 1965. Subj: Animals – lions. Illness.

The night it rained toys ill. by John E. Johnson. Follett, 1963. Subj: Holidays – Christmas. Poetry, rhyme. Royalty. Toys.

Stepto, Michele. *Snuggle Piggy and the magic blanket* ill. by John Himmelman. Dutton, 1987. ISBN 0-525-44308-8 Subj: Animals – pigs. Family life. Night.

Steptoe, John. *Baby says* ill. by author. Lothrop, 1988. ISBN 0-688-07424-3 Subj: Activities – playing. Babies. Sibling rivalry.

Birthday ill. by author. Holt, 1972. Subj: Birthdays. Ethnic groups in the U.S. – Afro-Americans.

Daddy is a monster...sometimes ill. by author. Lippincott, 1980. Subj: Family life – fathers. Monsters.

Jeffrey Bear cleans up his act ill. by author. Lothrop, 1983. Subj: Animals – bears. School.

Mufaro's beautiful daughters: an African tale ill. by author. Lothrop, 1987. ISBN 0-688-04046-2 Subj: Caldecott award honor book. Character traits – kindness. Character traits – meanness. Folk and fairy tales. Foreign lands – Africa. Royalty.

My special best words ill. by author. Viking, 1974. Subj: Ethnic groups in the U.S. – Afro-Americans. Family life. Language.

Stevie ill. by author. Harper, 1969. Subj: Ethnic groups in the U.S. – Afro-Americans. Friendship.

The story of jumping mouse: a Native American legend ill. by author. Lothrop, 1984. Subj: Animals – mice. Caldecott award honor book. Folk and fairy tales. Frogs and toads. Magic.

Uptown ill. by author. Harper, 1970. Subj: City. Ethnic groups in the U.S. – Afro-Americans. Poverty.

Sterling, Helen *see* Hoke, Helen L.

Stern, Elsie-Jean. *Wee Robin's Christmas song* ill. by Elsie McKean. Nelson, 1945. Subj: Birds – robins. Holidays – Christmas. Music. Songs.

Stern, Mark. *It's a dog's life* ill. by author. Atheneum, 1978. Subj: Animals – dogs. Character traits – freedom.

Stern, Peter. *Floyd, a cat's story* ill. by author. Harper, 1982. Subj: Animals – cats.

Stern, Ronnie. *Pop's secret* (Townsend, Maryann)

Stern, Simon. *Mrs. Vinegar* ill. by author. Prentice-Hall, 1979. Subj: Houses.

Vasily and the dragon: an epic Russian fairy tale ill. by author. Merrimack, 1983. ISBN 0-7207-1331-5 Subj: Dragons. Folk and fairy tales. Foreign lands – Russia.

Stevens, Bryna. *Borrowed feathers and other fables* ill. by Freire Wright and Michael Foreman. Random House, 1978. Subj: Folk and fairy tales.

Stevens, Carla. *Hooray for pig!* ill. by Rainey Bennett. Seabury Pr., 1974. Subj: Animals. Animals – pigs. Sports – swimming.

Pig and the blue flag ill. by Rainey Bennett. Seabury Pr., 1977. Subj: Animals. Animals – pigs. School. Sports – gymnastics.

Stories from a snowy meadow ill. by Eve Rice. Seabury Pr., 1976. Subj: Animals. Character traits – kindness. Death. Friendship.

Stevens, Cat. *Teaser and the firecat* ill. by author. Four Winds, 1974. ISBN 0-590-07372-9 Subj: Animals – cats. Foreign languages. Imagination. Moon. Night.

Stevens, Edward *see* Cosgrove, Stephen

Stevens, Harry. *Fat mouse* ill. by author. Viking, 1987. ISBN 0-670-80529-7 Subj: Animals. Animals – mice. Circular tales. Format, unusual – board books.

Parrot told snake ill. by author. Viking, 1987. ISBN 0-670-80530-0 Subj: Animals. Behavior – gossip. Format, unusual – board books.

Stevens, Janet. *Animal fair* adapt. and ill. by Janet Stevens. Holiday, 1981. Subj: Animals. Dreams. Fairs. Poetry, rhyme.

The emperor's new clothes (Andersen, H. C. (Hans Christian))

Goldilocks and the three bears (The three bears)

It's perfectly true! (Andersen, H. C. (Hans Christian))

The princess and the pea (Andersen, H. C. (Hans Christian))

The three billy goats Gruff (Asbjørnsen, P. C. (Peter Christen))

The tortoise and the hare (Æsop)

The town mouse and the country mouse (Æsop)

Stevens, Kathleen. *The beast in the bathtub* ill. by Ray Bowler. Gareth Stevens, Inc., 1985. ISBN 0-918831-15-6 Subj: Activities – bathing. Bedtime. Monsters.

Stevens, Margaret. *When grandpa died* ill. by Kenneth U/aland. Children's Pr., 1979. Subj: Death. Family life – grandfathers.

Stevens, Margaret Dean *see* Stevens, Margaret

Stevenson, Drew. *The ballad of Penelope Lou...and me* ill. by Marcia Sewall. Crossing Pr., 1978. Subj: Character traits – bravery. Emotions – fear. Poetry, rhyme.

Stevenson, James. *Are we almost there?* ill. by author. Greenwillow, 1985. ISBN 0-688-04239-2 Subj: Activities – traveling. Animals – dogs. Behavior – fighting, arguing.

The bear who had no place to go ill. by author. Harper, 1972. Subj: Animals – bears. Emotions – loneliness.

Clams can't sing ill. by author. Greenwillow, 1980. Subj: Animals. Music. Noise, sounds. Sea and seashore.

"Could be worse!" ill. by author. Greenwillow, 1977. Subj: Family life. Family life – grandfathers. Farms. Monsters.

Emma ill. by author. Greenwillow, 1985. ISBN 0-688-04021-7 Subj: Behavior – trickery. Witches.

Fried feathers for Thanksgiving ill. by author. Greenwillow, 1986. ISBN 0-688-06676-3 Subj: Behavior – trickery. Character traits – meanness. Witches.

Grandpa's great city tour: an alphabet book ill. by author. Greenwillow, 1983. Subj: ABC books. Activities – flying. City. Family life – grandfathers.

The great big especially beautiful Easter egg ill. by author. Greenwillow, 1983. Subj: Eggs. Family life – grandfathers.

Happy Valentine's Day, Emma! ill. by author. Greenwillow, 1987. ISBN 0-688-07358-1 Subj: Animals. Character traits – meanness. Holidays – Valentine's Day. Humor. Witches.

Higher on the door ill. by author. Greenwillow, 1987. ISBN 0-688-06637-2 Subj: Behavior – growing up. Family life – grandparents.

Howard ill. by author. Greenwillow, 1980. Subj: Behavior – lost. Birds – ducks. Friendship.

Monty ill. by author. Greenwillow, 1979. Subj: Animals – rabbits. Birds – ducks. Frogs and toads. Reptiles – alligators, crocodiles.

No friends ill. by author. Greenwillow, 1986. ISBN 0-688-06507-4 Subj: Family life – grandfathers. Friendship. Moving.

No need for Monty ill. by author. Greenwillow, 1987. ISBN 0-688-07084-1 Subj: Animals. Reptiles – alligators, crocodiles. Transportation.

The Sea View Hotel ill. by author. Greenwillow, 1978. Subj: Activities – vacationing. Animals – mice. Hotels.

That dreadful day ill. by author. Greenwillow, 1985. ISBN 0-688-04036-5 Subj: Family life – grandfathers. School.

That terrible Halloween night ill. by author. Greenwillow, 1980. Subj: Family life – grandfathers. Holidays – Halloween.

There's nothing to do! ill. by author. Greenwillow, 1986. ISBN 0-688-04699-1 Subj: Behavior – boredom. Family life – grandfathers.

We can't sleep ill. by author. Greenwillow, 1982. Subj: Animals. Bedtime. Family life – grandfathers. Sleep.

What's under my bed? ill. by author. Greenwillow, 1983. Subj: Bedtime. Emotions – fear. Family life – grandfathers.

When I was nine ill. by author. Greenwillow, 1986. ISBN 0-688-05943-0 Subj: Family life.

Wilfred the rat ill. by author. Greenwillow, 1977. Subj: Animals – chipmunks. Animals – rats. Animals – squirrels. Friendship.

Will you please feed our cat? ill. by author. Greenwillow, 1987. ISBN 0-688-06848-0 Subj: Character traits – helpfulness. Family life – grandfathers. Pets.

Winston, Newton, Elton, and Ed ill. by author. Greenwillow, 1978. Subj: Animals – walruses. Birds – penguins. Sibling rivalry.

The wish card ran out! ill. by author. Greenwillow, 1981. Subj: Behavior – wishing.

Worse than Willy! ill. by author. Greenwillow, 1984. Subj: Babies. Family life. Family life – grandfathers. Imagination. Sibling rivalry.

The worst person in the world ill. by author. Greenwillow, 1978. Subj: Friendship.

The worst person in the world at Crab Beach ill. by author. Greenwillow, 1988. ISBN 0-688-07299-2 Subj: Friendship. Humor.

Yuck! ill. by author. Greenwillow, 1984. Subj: Magic. Witches.

Stevenson, James Patrick *see* Stevenson, James

Stevenson, Jocelyn. *Jim Henson's Muppets at sea* ill. by Graham Thompson. Random House, 1980. Subj: Boats, ships. Puppets. Sea and seashore.

Red and the pumpkins ill. by Kelly Oechsli. Holt, 1983. Subj: Food. Imagination. Puppets.

Stevenson, Robert Louis. *Block city* ill. by Ashley Wolff. Dutton, 1988. ISBN 0-525-44399-1 Subj: Poetry, rhyme. Toys.

A child's garden of verses ill. by Erik Blegvad. Random House, 1978. Subj: Poetry, rhyme.

A child's garden of verses ill. by Pelagie Doane. Doubleday, 1942. Subj: Poetry, rhyme.

A child's garden of verses ill. by Michael Foreman. Delacorte Pr., 1985. ISBN 0-385-29430-1 Subj: Poetry, rhyme.

A child's garden of verses ill. by Toni Frissell. U.S. Camera, 1944. Subj: Poetry, rhyme.

A child's garden of verses ill. by Gyo Fujikawa. Grosset, 1957. Subj: Poetry, rhyme.

A child's garden of verses ill. by Joan Hassall. Harper, 1986. ISBN 0-87226-051-8 Subj: Poetry, rhyme.

A child's garden of verses ill. by Alice and Martin Provensen. Western Pub., 1951. Subj: Poetry, rhyme.

A child's garden of verses ill. by Tasha Tudor. Oxford Univ. Pr., 1947. Subj: Poetry, rhyme.

A child's garden of verses ill. by Brian Wildsmith. Watts, 1966. Subj: Poetry, rhyme.

The moon ill. by Denise Saldutti. Harper, 1984. Subj: Family life. Moon. Poetry, rhyme. Sports – fishing.

Stevenson, Suçie. *Christmas eve* ill. by author. Putnam's, 1988. ISBN 0-399-21667-7 Subj: Animals – rabbits. Holidays – Christmas. Sibling rivalry.

Do I have to take Violet? ill. by author. Dodd, 1987. ISBN 0-396-08921-6 Subj: Activities – playing. Animals – rabbits. Sibling rivalry.

I forgot ill. by author. Watts, 1988. ISBN 0-531-08344-6 Subj: Animals. Behavior – forgetfulness. Birthdays.

Jessica the blue streak ill. by author. Watts, 1989. ISBN 0-531-08398-5 Subj: Animals – dogs. Behavior – misbehavior. Pets.

Stewart, Anne. *The ugly duckling* (Andersen, H. C. (Hans Christian))

Stewart, Charles P. *Dinosaurs and other creatures of long ago* (Stewart, Frances Todd)

Stewart, Elizabeth Laing. *The lion twins* photos. by Marlin and Carol Morse Perkins. Atheneum, 1964. Subj: Animals – lions. Twins.

Stewart, Frances Todd. *Dinosaurs and other creatures of long ago* by Frances Todd Stewart and Charles P. Stewart, III; ill. by Forest Rogers and Kathy Borland. Harper, 1988. ISBN 0-694-00229-1 Subj: Dinosaurs.

Stewart, Robert S. *The daddy book* ill. by Don Madden. American Heritage, 1972. Subj: Careers. Family life – fathers.

Stewart, Scott *see* Zaffo, George J.

Stewig, John Warren. *The fisherman and his wife* (Grimm, Jacob)

Stiles, Norman. *I'll miss you, Mr. Hooper* ill. by Joseph Mathieu. Random House, 1984. ISBN 0-394-96600-7 Subj: Death. Puppets.

The Sesame Street ABC storybook (Moss, Jeffrey.)

Still, James. *Jack and the wonder beans* ill. by Margot Tomes. Putnam's, 1977. Subj: Folk and fairy tales. Giants.

Stilz, Carol Curtis. *Kirsty's kite* ill. by Gwen Harrison. Albatross, 1988. ISBN 0-86760-089-6 Subj: Death. Family life – mothers. Family life – grandfathers. Kites.

Stinchecum, Amanda Mayer. *Girl from the snow country* (Hidaka, Masako)

Stinson, Kathy. *The bare naked book* ill. by Heather Collins. Firefly Pr., 1986. ISBN 0-920303-52-8 Subj: Anatomy.

Mom and dad don't live together any more ill. by Nancy Lou Reynolds. Firefly Pr., 1984. ISBN 0-920236-92-8 Subj: Divorce.

Red is best ill. by Robin Baird Lewis. Firefly Pr., 1982. Subj: Concepts – color.

Those green things ill. by Mary McLoughlin. Firefly Pr., 1985. ISBN 0-920303-40-4 Subj: Humor. Imagination.

Stites, Clara. *The ugly duckling* (Andersen, H. C. (Hans Christian))

Stobbs, Joanna. *One sun, two eyes, and a million stars* by Joanna and William Stobbs; ill. by authors. Merrimack, 1983. Subj: Counting.

Stobbs, William. *Animal pictures* ill. by author. Bodley Head, 1982. Subj: Animals. Wordless.

A car called beetle ill. by author. Merrimack, 1979. Bodley Head, 1979. Subj: Automobiles.

The hare and the frogs (Æsop)

The little red hen

One sun, two eyes, and a million stars (Stobbs, Joanna)

There's a hole in my bucket ill. by author. Merrimack, 1983. Subj: Seasons – summer. Songs.

This little piggy ill. by author. Bodley Head, 1981. Subj: Animals – pigs. Counting. Nursery rhymes. Poetry, rhyme.

Stock, Catherine. *Alexander's midnight snack: a little elephant's ABC* ill. by author. Clarion, 1988. ISBN 0-89919-512-1 Subj: ABC books. Animals – elephants. Bedtime. Food.

Emma's dragon hunt ill. by author. Lothrop, 1984. ISBN 0-688-02698-2 Subj: Dragons. Family life – grandfathers.

Sampson the Christmas cat ill. by author. Putnam's, 1984. Subj: Animals – cats. Holidays – Christmas.

Sophie's bucket ill. by author. Lothrop, 1985. Subj: Family life. Sea and seashore.

Sophie's knapsack ill. by author. Lothrop, 1988. ISBN 0-688-06458-2 Subj: Family life. Sports – camping.

Stoddard, Sandol. *Bedtime for bear* ill. by Lynn Munsinger. Houghton, 1985. ISBN 0-395-38811-2 Subj: Animals – bears. Bedtime. Poetry, rhyme.

Bedtime mouse ill. by Lynn Munsinger. Houghton, 1981. ISBN 0-395-31609-X Subj: Animals. Animals – mice. Bedtime. Cumulative tales. Poetry, rhyme.

Curl up small ill. by Trina Schart Hyman. Houghton, 1964. Subj: Concepts – shape. Concepts – size. Family life. Imagination.

My very own special particular private and personal cat ill. by Remy Charlip. Houghton, 1963. Subj: Animals – cats. Pets. Poetry, rhyme.

The thinking book ill. by Ivan Chermayeff. Little, 1960. Subj: Family life. Imagination.

Stoeke, Janet Morgan. *Minerva Louise* ill. by author. Dutton, 1988. ISBN 0-525-44374-6 Subj: Behavior – misunderstanding. Birds – chickens.

Stoker, Wayne. *I can be a welder* (Lillegard, Dee)

Stolz, Mary Slattery. *Emmett's pig* ill. by Garth Williams. Harper, 1959. Subj: Animals – pigs. Birthdays. Farms.

Storm in the night ill. by Pat Cummings. Harper, 1988. ISBN 0-06-025912-4 Subj: Ethnic groups in the U.S. – Afro-Americans. Family life – grandfathers. Night. Weather – storms.

Zekmet, the stone carver: a tale of Ancient Egypt ill. by Deborah Nourse Lattimore. Harcourt, 1988. ISBN 0-15-299961-2 Subj: Activities – working. Foreign lands – Egypt.

Stone, A. Harris. *The last free bird* ill. by Sheila Heins. Prentice-Hall, 1967. Subj: Birds. Ecology.

Stone, Bernard. *The charge of the mouse brigade* by Bernard Stone with Alice Low; ill. by Tony Ross. Pantheon, 1980. Subj: Animals – cats. Animals – mice. War.

Emergency mouse ill. by Ralph Steadman. Prentice-Hall, 1978. Subj: Animals – mice. Hospitals.

Stone, Beth. *Do you have a secret?* (Russell, Pamela)

Stone, Jon. *Big Bird in China* photos. by Victor DiNapoli. Random House, 1983. Subj: Foreign lands – China. Puppets.

Stone, Lynn M. *Endangered animals* ill. with photos. Children's Pr., 1984. Subj: Animals. Nature.

Stone, Rosetta. *Because a little bug went ka-choo!* ill. by Michael K. Frith. Random House, 1975. Subj: Cumulative tales. Humor. Insects. Poetry, rhyme.

Stonehouse, Bernard. *Kangaroos* ill. with photos. Raintree, 1978. Subj: Animals – kangaroos.

Storm, Theodor. *Little John* (Orgel, Doris)

Storr, Catherine. *Clever Polly and the stupid wolf* ill. by Marjorie-Ann Watts. Faber, 1979. Subj: Animals – wolves. Character traits – cleverness.

Hugo and his grandma ill. by Nita Sowter. Merrimack, 1980. Subj: Activities – knitting. Family life – grandmothers.

Rip Van Winkle (Irving, Washington)

Robin Hood ill. by Chris Collingwood. Raintree, 1984. ISBN 0-8172-2109-3 Subj: Foreign lands – England. Forest, woods. Middle ages.

Storr, Catherine Cole *see* Storr, Catherine

Stott, Rowena. *The hedgehog feast* ill. by Edith Holden. Dutton, 1978. Subj: Animals – hedgehogs. Hibernation. Parties.

Stover, Jo Ann. *If everybody did* ill. by author. McKay, 1960. Subj: Behavior. Etiquette. Poetry, rhyme.

Why? Because ill. by author. McKay, 1961. Subj: Character traits – questioning.

Strachan, Margaret Pitcairn *see* Cone, Molly

Strahl, Rudi. *Sandman in the lighthouse* tr. and adapt. by Anthea Bell; ill. by Eberhard Binder. Children's Pr., 1967, 1969. Subj: Bedtime. Lighthouses. Sandman. Sea and seashore.

Straker, Joan Ann. *Animals that live in the sea.* National Geographical Soc., 1979. Subj: Sea and seashore.

Strand, Mark. *The night book* ill. by William Pène Du Bois. Crown, 1985. ISBN 0-517-55047-4 Subj: Emotions – fear. Night.

The planet of lost things ill. by William Pène du Bois. Crown, 1983. Subj: Bedtime. Dreams. Noise, sounds.

Strange, Florence. *Rock-a-bye whale, a story of the birth of a humpback whale* ill. by author. Manzanita Pr., 1977. ISBN 0-931644-08-3 Subj: Animals – whales. Science.

Stratemeyer, Clara Georgeanna. *Frog fun* by Clara G. Stratemeyer and Henry Lee Smith, Jr.; ill. by Lucy Hawkinson. Harper, 1963. Subj: Frogs and toads.

Pepper by Clara G. Stratemeyer and Henry Lee Smith, Jr. Benziger, 1971. Subj: Animals. Animals – cats.

Tuggy by Clara Georgeanna Stratemeyer and Henry Lee Smith, Jr. Harper, 1971. Subj: Animals – dogs. Frogs and toads.

Strathdee, Jean. *The house that grew* ill. by Jessica Wallace. Oxford Univ. Pr., 1980. Subj: Family life. Houses. Moving.

Streatfield, Noel. *Sleepy Nicholas* (Brande, Marlie)

Stren, Patti. *Hug me* ill. by author. Harper, 1977. Subj: Animals – porcupines. Emotions – loneliness.

Mountain Rose ill. by author. Dutton, 1982. Subj: Character traits – appearance. Self-concept. Sports – wrestling.

Stroyer, Poul. *It's a deal* ill. by author. Astor-Honor, 1960. Subj: Activities – trading. Humor.

Struppi ill. by Ingrid Graichen. Imported Pubs., 1983. Subj: Animals. Format, unusual – board books. Wordless.

Stuart, Mary *see* Graham, Mary Stuart Campbell

Stubbs, Joanna. *Happy Bear's day* ill. by author. Elsevier-Dutton, 1979. Subj: Animals – bears. Behavior – solitude.

With cat's eyes you'll never be scared of the dark ill. by author. Dutton, 1983. Subj: Emotions – fear. Magic. Night.

Sturgis, Justin *see* Burgess, Gelett

Sturtzel, Howard Allison *see* Annixter, Paul

Sturtzel, Jane Levington *see* Annixter, Jane

Suba, Susanne. *The monkeys and the pedlar* ill. by author. Viking, 1970. Subj: Animals – monkeys. Careers – peddlers. Humor.

Suben, Eric. *Pigeon takes a trip* ill. by Tiziana Zanetti; graphic design by Giorgio Vanetti. Golden Books, 1984. Subj: Activities – traveling. Birds – pigeons. Format, unusual – board books.

Sueyoshi, Akiko. *Ladybird on a bicycle* ill. by Viv Allbright. Faber, 1983. Subj: Insects – ladybugs. Sports – bicycling.

Sugarman, Joan G. *Inside the Synagogue* by Joan G. Sugarman and Grace R. Freeman; photos. by Ronald Mass and others. Union of American Hebrew Congregations, 1984. ISBN 0-8074-0268-0 Subj: Jewish culture. Religion.

Sugita, Yutaka. *The flower family* ill. by author. McGraw-Hill, 1975. Subj: Flowers. Plants. Science.

Good night 1, 2, 3 ill. by author. Scroll Pr., 1971. Subj: Bedtime. Counting. Sleep.

Helena the unhappy hippopotamus ill. by author. McGraw-Hill, 1972. Subj: Animals – hippopotami. Behavior – needing someone. Emotions – loneliness. Emotions – sadness. Friendship.

My friend Little John and me ill. by author. McGraw-Hill, 1972. Subj: Animals – dogs. Wordless.

Suhl, Yuri. *The Purim goat* ill. by Kaethe Zemach. Four Winds Pr., 1980. Subj: Animals – goats. Character traits – helpfulness. Holidays – Purim.

Simon Boom gives a wedding ill. by Margot Zemach. Four Winds Pr., 1972. Subj: Cumulative tales. Humor. Jewish culture. Weddings.

Sumiko. *Kittymouse* ill. by author. Harcourt, 1979. Subj: Animals – cats. Animals – mice.

Sundgaard, Arnold. *Jethro's difficult dinosaur* ill. by Stanley Mack. Pantheon, 1977. Subj: Dinosaurs. Eggs. Humor. Poetry, rhyme.

The lamb and the butterfly ill. by Eric Carle. Watts, 1988. ISBN 0-531-08379-9 Subj: Animals – sheep. Character traits – freedom. Insects – butterflies, caterpillars.

Meet Jack Appleknocker ill. by Sheila White Samton. Putnam's, 1988. ISBN 0-399-21472-0 Subj: Imagination.

The Superman mix or match storybook ill. by Ross Andru and Joe Orlando. Random House, 1979. Subj: Format, unusual – toy and movable books.

Supraner, Robyn. *Giggly-wiggly, snickety-snick* ill. by Stan Tusan. Parents, 1978. Subj: Concepts.

Would you rather be a tiger? ill. by Barbara Cooney. Houghton, 1973. Subj: Behavior. Imagination. Poetry, rhyme. Self-concept.

Supree, Burton. *Harlequin and the gift of many colors* (Charlip, Remy)

"Mother, mother I feel sick" (Charlip, Remy)

Surany, Anico. *Kati and Kormos* ill. by Leonard Everett Fisher. Holiday, 1966. Subj: Animals – dogs. Emotions – loneliness. Foreign lands – Hungary.

Ride the cold wind ill. by Leonard Everett Fisher. Putnam's, 1964. Subj: Boats, ships. Foreign lands – South America. Sports – fishing.

Surat, Michele Maria. *Angel child, dragon child* ill. by Vo-Dinh Mai. Raintree, 1983. ISBN 0-940742-12-8 Subj: Ethnic groups in the U.S. – Vietnamese-Americans. School.

Sussman, Susan. *Hippo thunder* ill. by John C. Wallner. Albert Whitman, 1982. Subj: Bedtime. Emotions. Weather – thunder.

Sutherland, Harry A. *Dad's car wash* ill. by Maxie Chambliss. Atheneum, 1988. ISBN 0-689-31335-7 Subj: Activities – bathing. Bedtime. Imagination.

Sutton, Eve. *My cat likes to hide in boxes* ill. by Lynley Dodd. Parents, 1973. Subj: Animals – cats. Cumulative tales. Participation. Poetry, rhyme.

Sutton, Jane. *What should a hippo wear?* ill. by Lynn Munsinger. Houghton, 1979. ISBN 0-395-27800-7 Subj: Activities – dancing. Animals. Animals – hippopotami. Clothing.

Svendsen, Carol. *Hulda* ill. by Julius Svendsen. Houghton, 1974. Subj: Behavior. Poetry, rhyme. Trolls.

Swados, Elizabeth. *Lullaby* ill. by Faith Hubley. Harper, 1980. Subj: Bedtime. Songs.

Swann, Brian. *A basket full of white eggs: riddle-poems* ill. by Ponder Goembel. Watts, 1988. ISBN 0-531-08334-9 Subj: Poetry, rhyme. Riddles.

Swayne, Samuel F. *Great-grandfather in the honey tree* by Samuel F. and Zoa Swayne; ill. by authors. Viking, 1949. Subj: Family life – great-grandparents.

Swayne, Zoa. *Great-grandfather in the honey tree* (Swayne, Samuel F.)

Swetenham, Violet Hilda *see* Drummond, Violet H.

Swift, Hildegarde Hoyt. *The little red lighthouse and the great gray bridge* by Hildegarde H. Swift and Lynd Ward; ill. by Lynd Ward. Harcourt, 1942. Subj: Boats, ships. Bridges. Lighthouses.

Switzer, Robert E. *My friend the babysitter* (Watson, Jane Werner)

My friend the dentist (Watson, Jane Werner)

My friend the doctor (Watson, Jane Werner)

Sometimes a family has to move (Watson, Jane Werner)

Sometimes a family has to split up (Watson, Jane Werner)

Sometimes I get angry (Watson, Jane Werner)

Sometimes I'm afraid (Watson, Jane Werner)

Sometimes I'm jealous (Watson, Jane Werner)

Syme, Daniel B. *I'm growing* (Bogot, Howard)

Szekeres, Cyndy. *Cyndy Szekeres' counting book, 1 to 10* ill. by author. Golden Pr., 1984. Subj: Animals – mice. Counting.

Long ago ill. by author. McGraw-Hill, 1977. Subj: Animals. U.S. history.

Szilagyi, Mary. *Thunderstorm* ill. by author. Bradbury Pr., 1985. ISBN 0-02-788580-1 Subj: Emotions – fear. Pets. Weather – storms. Weather – thunder.

Taback, Simms. *Joseph had a little overcoat* ill. by author. Random House, 1977. Subj: Clothing. Format, unusual.

On our way to the barn (Ziefert, Harriet)

On our way to the forest (Ziefert, Harriet)

On our way to the water (Ziefert, Harriet)

On our way to the zoo (Ziefert, Harriet)

Tabberner, Jeffrey. *The endless party* (Delessert, Etienne)

Taber, Anthony. *Cats' eyes* ill. by author. Dutton, 1978. Subj: Animals – cats. Old age.

Tabler, Judith. *The new puppy* ill. by Pat Sustendal. Random House, 1986. ISBN 0-394-88038-2 Subj: Animals – dogs. Format, unusual – board books. Pets. Toys.

Taborin, Glorina. *Norman Rockwell's counting book* (Rockwell, Norman)

Tafuri, Nancy. *All year long* ill. by author. Greenwillow, 1983. Subj: Days of the week, months of the year.

Do not disturb ill. by author. Greenwillow, 1987. ISBN 0-688-06542-2 Subj: Activities. Animals. Family life. Night. Noise, sounds. Sports – camping. Wordless.

Early morning in the barn ill. by author. Greenwillow, 1983. Subj: Farms. Morning.

Have you seen my duckling? ill. by author. Greenwillow, 1984. Subj: Birds – ducks. Caldecott award honor book. Character traits – individuality.

In a red house ill. by author. Greenwillow, 1987. ISBN 0-688-07185-6 Subj: Concepts – color. Format, unusual – board books. Toys.

Junglewalk ill. by author. Greenwillow, 1988. ISBN 0-688-07183-X Subj: Animals. Dreams. Imagination. Jungle. Wordless.

My friends ill. by author. Greenwillow, 1987. ISBN 0-688-07187-2 Subj: Animals. Babies. Format, unusual – board books. Friendship.

One wet jacket ill. by author. Greenwillow, 1988. ISBN 0-688-07465-0 Subj: Clothing. Format, unusual – board books.

Rabbit's morning ill. by author. Greenwillow, 1985. ISBN 0-688-04064-0 Subj: Animals. Animals – rabbits. Wordless.

Two new sneakers ill. by author. Greenwillow, 1988. ISBN 0-688-07462-6 Subj: Clothing. Format, unusual – board books.

Where we sleep ill. by author. Greenwillow, 1987. ISBN 0-688-07189-9 Subj: Animals. Format, unusual – board books. Sleep.

Who's counting? ill. by author. Greenwillow, 1986. ISBN 0-688-06131-1 Subj: Animals. Animals – dogs. Counting. Farms.

Taha, Karen T. *A gift for Tia Rose* ill. by Dee deRosa. Dillon Pr., 1986. ISBN 0-87518-306-9 Subj: Death. Ethnic groups in the U.S. – Mexican-Americans. Family life. Friendship.

Tait, Nancy. *I'm deaf and it's okay* (Aseltine, Lorraine)

Takeshita, Fumiko. *The park bench* tr. by Ruth A. Kanagy; ill. by Mamoru Suzuki. Kane Miller, 1988. ISBN 0-916291-15-4 Subj: Activities. Foreign lands – Japan. Foreign languages.

Takihara, Koji. *Rolli* ill. by author. Picture Book Studio, 1988. ISBN 0-88708-058-8 Subj: Animals – moles. Seeds.

Talbot, Toby. *A bucketful of moon* ill. by Imero Gobbato. Lothrop, 1976. ISBN 0-688-51727-7 Subj: Folk and fairy tales. Moon.

Tallarico, Tony. *At home* ill. by author. Tuffy Books, 1984. Subj: Family life. Houses.

Tallon, Robert. *Handella* ill. by author. Bobbs-Merrill, 1972. Subj: Activities – dancing. Problem solving. Theater.

Latouse my moose ill. by author. Knopf, 1983. Subj: Animals – dogs. Pets.

Tamburine, Jean. *I think I will go to the hospital* ill. by author. Abingdon Pr., 1965. Subj: Hospitals.

Tan, Pierre Le *see* Le-Tan, Pierre

Tanaka, Hideyuki. *The happy dog* ill. by author. Atheneum, 1983. Subj: Animals – dogs.

Tangvald, Christine. *Mom and dad don't live together anymore.* Cook, 1988. ISBN 1-55513-502-1 Subj: Divorce.

Taniuchi, Kota. *Trolley* ill. by author. Watts, 1969. Subj: Cable cars, trolleys. Imagination.

Tapio, Pat Decker. *The lady who saw the good side of everything* ill. by Paul Galdone. Seabury Pr., 1975. Subj: Activities – traveling. Animals – cats. Character traits – optimism. Emotions – happiness. Humor. Weather – floods. Weather – rain.

Tarrant, Graham. *Rabbits* ill. by Tony King. Putnam's, 1984. Subj: Animals – rabbits. Format, unusual.

Tarrant, Margaret. *Fairy tales* ill. with photos. Crowell, 1978. Subj: Folk and fairy tales.

The Margaret Tarrant nursery rhyme book ill. by author. Merrimack, 1986. ISBN 0-00-183732-X Subj: Nursery rhymes.

Nursery rhymes ill. with photos. Crowell, 1978. Subj: Nursery rhymes.

Tate, Joan. *A Christmas book*

The giant fish and other stories (Otto, Svend)

Tatham, Campbell *see* Elting, Mary

Tax, Meredith. *Families* ill. by Marylin Hafner. Little, 1981. Subj: Family life.

Taylor, Anelise. *Lights on, lights off* ill. by author. Oxford Univ. Pr., 1988. ISBN 0-19-279843-X Subj: Emotions – fear. Night.

Taylor, Edgar. *King Grisly-Beard* (Grimm, Jacob)

Taylor, John Edward. *Petrosinella* (Basile, Giambattista)

Taylor, Judy. *Dudley and the monster* ill. by Peter Cross. Putnam's, 1986. ISBN 0-399-21329-5 Subj: Animals – mice. Monsters. Seasons – spring.

Dudley and the strawberry shake ill. by Peter Cross. Putnam's, 1987. ISBN 0-399-21330-9 Subj: Animals – mice. Food.

Dudley goes flying ill. by Peter Cross. Putnam's, 1986. ISBN 0-399-21328-7 Subj: Activities – flying. Animals – mice.

Dudley in a jam ill. by Peter Cross. Putnam's, 1987. ISBN 0-399-21331-7 Subj: Animals – mice. Food.

Sophie and Jack ill. by Susan Gantner. Putnam's, 1983. Subj: Activities – picnicking. Animals – hippopotami. Family life.

Sophie and Jack help out ill. by Susan Gantner. Putnam's, 1984. Subj: Activities – gardening. Animals – hippopotami. Weather – storms.

Taylor, Livingston. *Pajamas* by Livingston and Maggie Taylor; ill. by Tim Bowers. Harcourt, 1988. ISBN 0-15-200564-1 Subj: Bedtime. Songs.

Taylor, Maggie. *Pajamas* (Taylor, Livingston)

Taylor, Mark. *The bold fisherman* ill. by Graham Booth. Golden Gate, 1967. Subj: Folk and fairy tales. Music. Sea and seashore. Songs. Sports – fishing.

The case of the missing kittens ill. by Graham Booth. Atheneum, 1978. Subj: Animals – cats. Animals – dogs. Behavior – lost. Problem solving.

Henry explores the jungle ill. by Graham Booth. Atheneum, 1968. Subj: Animals – tigers. Character traits – bravery. Circus. Seasons – summer.

Henry explores the mountains ill. by Graham Booth. Atheneum, 1975. Subj: Character traits – bravery. Fire. Helicopters. Seasons – fall.

Henry the castaway ill. by Graham Booth. Atheneum, 1972. Subj: Behavior – lost. Boats, ships. Seasons – spring. Weather – rain.

Henry the explorer ill. by Graham Booth. Atheneum, 1966. Subj: Animals – bears. Behavior – lost. Character traits – bravery. Seasons – winter.

"Lamb," said the lion, "I am here." ill. by Anne Siberell. Golden Gate, 1971. Subj: Animals. Religion.

Old Blue, you good dog you ill. by Gene Holtan. Golden Gate, 1970. Subj: Animals – dogs. Animals – possums. Folk and fairy tales. Friendship. Games. Music. Songs. Old age.

Taylor, Sydney. *The dog who came to dinner* ill. by John E. Johnson. Follett, 1966. Subj: Animals – dogs. Ethnic groups in the U.S. – Afro-Americans.

Mr. Barney's beard ill. by Charles Geer. Follett, 1961. Subj: Birds. Character traits – laziness.

Taylor, Talus. *The adventures of the three colors* (Tison, Annette)

Animal hide-and-seek (Tison, Annette)

Inside and outside (Tison, Annette)

Teal, Valentine. *The little woman wanted noise* ill. by Robert Lawson. Rand McNally, 1946. Subj: Country. Farms. Noise, sounds. Senses – hearing.

Tejima, Keizaburo. *The bears' autumn* tr. from the Japanese by Susan Matsui; ill. by author. Green Tiger Pr., 1986. ISBN 0-88138-080-6 Subj: Animals – bears. Seasons – fall.

Fox's dream ill. by author. Philomel, 1987. ISBN 0-399-21455-0 Subj: Animals – foxes. Dreams. Forest, woods. Seasons – winter.

Owl lake ill. by author. Philomel, 1987. ISBN 0-399-21426-7 Subj: Birds – owls. Family life. Nature. Night.

Swan sky ill. by author. Putnam's, 1988. ISBN 0-399-21547-6 Subj: Birds – swans. Death.

Teleki, Geza. *Aerial apes: Gibbons of Asia* by Geza Teleki and others; ill. with photos. Coward, 1979. Subj: Animals – monkeys.

Telephones ill. by Christine Sharr. Wonder Books, 1971. Subj: Communication. Telephone.

Tellenbach, Margrit Haubensak *see* Haubensak-Tellenbach, Margrit

Tempest, P. *How the cock wrecked the manor* tr. from Lithuanian by Olimpija Armalyte; ill. by Albina Makūnaite. Imported Pub., 1982. Subj: Folk and fairy tales. Magic.

Tempest, Peter. *The tale of a hero nobody knows* (Marshak, Samuel)

Tennyson, Noel. *The lady's chair and the ottoman* ill. by author. Lothrop, 1987. ISBN 0-688-04098-5 Subj: Behavior – needing someone.

Tensen, Ruth M. *Come to the zoo!* Reilly, 1948. Subj: Animals. Zoos.

Terban, Marvin. *I think I thought: and other tricky verbs* ill. by Giulio Maestro. Houghton, 1984. Subj: Language. Poetry, rhyme.

Testa, Fulvio. *The ideal home* ill. by author. Harper, 1986. ISBN 0-87226-055-0 Subj: Houses.

If you look around ill. by author. Dial Pr., 1983. Subj: Concepts – shape.

If you take a paintbrush: a book of colors ill. by author. Dial Pr., 1983. Subj: Concepts – color.

If you take a pencil ill. by author. Dial Pr., 1982. Subj: Counting.

The land where the ice cream grows story and ill. by Fulvio Testa; told by Anthony Burgess. Doubleday, 1979. Subj: Food. Imagination.

The paper airplane ill. by author. Holt, 1988. ISBN 0-8050-0743-1 Subj: Activities – flying. Airplanes, airports. Paper.

Wolf's favor ill. by author. Dial Pr., 1986. ISBN 0-8037-0244-2 Subj: Animals. Character traits – generosity.

Tester, Sylvia Root. *Chase!* ill. by author. Children's Pr., 1980. Subj: Animals.

Never monkey with a monkey: a book of homographic homophones ill. by John Keely. Children's Pr., 1977. Subj: Language.

Parade! ill. by author. Children's Pr., 1980. Subj: Circus.

A visit to the zoo photos. by author. Children's Pr., 1987. ISBN 0-516-01494-3 Subj: Animals. Zoos.

What did you say? a book of homophones ill. by John Keely. Children's Pr., 1977. Subj: Language.

Tether, Graham. *The hair book* ill. by Roy McKié. Random House, 1979. Subj: Hair. Poetry, rhyme.

Skunk and possum ill. by Lucinda McQueen. Houghton, 1979. Subj: Activities – picnicking. Animals – possums. Animals – skunks. Friendship.

Tettelbaum, Michael. *The cave of the lost Fraggle* ill. by Peter Elwell. Holt, 1985. ISBN 0-03-004554-1 Subj: Caves. Character traits – pride. Puppets.

Thacher, Edith *see* Hurd, Edith Thacher

Thaler, Mike. *Hippo lemonade* ill. by Maxie Chambliss. Harper, 1986. ISBN 0-06-026162-5 Subj: Animals. Animals – hippopotami. Behavior – wishing.

It's me, hippo! ill. by Maxie Chambliss. Harper, 1983. Subj: Animals. Animals – hippopotami. Friendship.

Madge's magic show ill. by Carol Nicklaus. Watts, 1978. Subj: Magic.

Moonkey ill. by Giulio Maestro. Harper, 1981. Subj: Animals – monkeys. Friendship. Moon.

My puppy ill. by Madeleine Fishman. Harper, 1980. Subj: Animals – dogs. Imagination – imaginary friends. Pets.

Owley ill. by David Wiesner. Harper, 1982. ISBN 0-06-026152-8 Subj: Birds – owls. Character traits – questioning. Family life – mothers.

Pack 109 ill. by Normand Chartier. Dutton, 1988. ISBN 0-525-44393-2 Subj: Animals. Clubs, gangs. Humor.

There's a hippopotamus under my bed ill. by Ray Cruz. Watts, 1977. Subj: Animals – hippopotami.

The yellow brick toad: funny frog cartoons, riddles, and silly stories ill. by author. Doubleday, 1978. Subj: Humor. Riddles.

Thayer, Ernest L. *Casey at the bat: a ballad of the Republic, sung in the year 1888* ill. by Patricia Polacco. Putnam's, 1988. ISBN 0-399-21585-9 Subj: Poetry, rhyme. Sports – baseball.

Thayer, Jane. *Andy and his fine friends* ill. by Meg Wohlberg. Morrow, 1960. Subj: Animals. Imagination – imaginary friends.

Andy and the runaway horse ill. by Meg Wohlberg. Morrow, 1963. Subj: Animals – horses. Traffic, traffic signs.

Andy and the wild worm ill. by Beatrice Darwin. Morrow, 1973, 1954. Subj: Animals – worms. Imagination.

The cat that joined the club ill. by Seymour Fleishman. Morrow, 1967. Subj: Animals – cats.

The clever raccoon ill. by Holly Keller. Morrow, 1981. Subj: Animals – raccoons. Behavior – trickery.

Gus and the baby ghost ill. by Seymour Fleishman. Morrow, 1972. Subj: Babies. Ghosts. Museums.

Gus was a friendly ghost ill. by Seymour Fleishman. Morrow, 1962. Subj: Friendship. Ghosts.

Gus was a gorgeous ghost ill. by Seymour Fleishman. Morrow, 1978. Subj: Clothing. Ghosts. Holidays – Halloween.

Gus was a real dumb ghost ill. by Joyce Audy dos Santos. Morrow, 1982. Subj: Ghosts. School.

The horse with the Easter bonnet ill. by Jay Hyde Barnum. Morrow, 1953. Subj: Animals – horses. Clothing. Holidays – Easter.

I like trains ill. by George Fonseca. Harper, 1965. Subj: Trains. Transportation.

Mr. Turtle's magic glasses ill. by Mamoru Funai. Morrow, 1971. Subj: Behavior – boredom. Glasses. Magic. Reptiles – turtles, tortoises. Senses – seeing.

The popcorn dragon ill. by Jay Hyde Barnum. Morrow, 1953. Subj: Dragons. Food. Friendship.

The puppy who wanted a boy ill. by Seymour Fleishman. Morrow, 1958. Subj: Animals – dogs. Holidays – Christmas.

The puppy who wanted a boy ill. by Lisa McCue. Morrow, 1986. ISBN 0-688-05945-7 Subj: Animals – dogs. Holidays – Christmas.

Quiet on account of dinosaur ill. by Seymour Fleishman. Morrow, 1964. Subj: Dinosaurs. Noise, sounds.

What's a ghost going to do? ill. by Seymour Fleishman. Morrow, 1966. Subj: Ghosts. Houses. Problem solving.

Thayer, Mike. *In the middle of the puddle* ill. by Bruce Degen. Harper, 1988. ISBN 0-06-026054-8 Subj: Frogs and toads. Reptiles – turtles, tortoises. Weather – rain.

Thayer, Peter *see* Wyler, Rose

Thelen, Gerda. *The toy maker: how a tree becomes a toy village* retold by Louise F. Encking; ill. by Fritz Kukenthal. Albert Whitman, 1935. Subj: Toys. Trees.

Thiele, Colin. *Farmer Schulz's ducks* ill. by Mary Milton. Harper, 1988. ISBN 0-06-026183-8 Subj: Birds – ducks. Farms. Foreign lands – Australia.

Thoburn, Tina. *A B See* (Ogle, Lucille)

I hear (Ogle, Lucille)

Thomas, Art. *Merry-go-rounds* ill. by George Overlie. Carolrhoda, 1981. Subj: Merry-go-rounds.

Thomas, Gary. *The best of the little books* ill. by Chris Cummings. Harvey House, 1980. Subj: Poetry, rhyme. Riddles. Tongue twisters.

Thomas, Ianthe. *Eliza's daddy* ill. by Moneta Barnett. Harcourt, 1976. Subj: Divorce. Ethnic groups in the U.S. – Afro-Americans. Seasons – summer.

Lordy, Aunt Hattie ill. by Thomas di Grazia. Harper, 1973. Subj: Ethnic groups in the U.S. – Afro-Americans. Seasons – summer.

Walk home tired, Billy Jenkins ill. by Thomas di Grazia. Harper, 1974. Subj: Activities – walking. City. Ethnic groups in the U.S. – Afro-Americans. Imagination.

Willie blows a mean horn ill. by Ann Toulmin-Rothe. Harper, 1981. Subj: Family life – fathers. Music.

Thomas, Iolette. *Janine and the new baby* ill. by Jennifer Northway. Dutton, 1987. ISBN 0-233-97916-6 Subj: Babies. Sibling rivalry.

Thomas, Jane Resh. *Saying good-bye to grandma* ill. by Marcia Sewall. Clarion, 1988. ISBN 0-89919-645-4 Subj: Death. Family life – grandmothers.

Wheels ill. by Emily Arnold McCully. Ticknor & Fields, 1986. ISBN 0-89919-410-9 Subj: Sports – bicycling.

Thomas, Karen. *The good thing...the bad thing* ill. by Yaroslava. Prentice-Hall, 1979. ISBN 0-13-360354-7 Subj: Behavior.

Thomas, Katherine Elwes. *The real personages of Mother Goose.* Lothrop, 1930. Subj: Nursery rhymes.

Thomas, Kathy. *The angel's quest* ill. by Jacqueline Seitz. Living Flame Pr., 1983. Subj: Angels. Character traits – perseverance. Orphans. Religion.

Thomas, Patricia. *"Stand back," said the elephant, "I'm going to sneeze!"* ill. by Wallace Tripp. Lothrop, 1971. Subj: Animals. Humor. Poetry, rhyme.

"There are rocks in my socks!" said the ox to the fox ill. by Mordicai Gerstein. Lothrop, 1979. Subj: Animals – bulls, cows. Animals – foxes. Poetry, rhyme. Problem solving.

Thompson, Brenda. *Famous planes* by Brenda Thompson and Rosemary Giesen; ill. by Andrew Martin and Rosemary Giesen. Lerner, 1977. Subj: Airplanes, airports.

Pirates by Brenda Thompson and Rosemary Giesen; ill. by Simon Stern and Rosemary Giesen. Lerner, 1977. Subj: Pirates.

The winds that blow by Brenda Thompson and Cynthia Overbeck; ill. by Simon Stern and Rosemary Giesen. Lerner, 1977. Subj: Concepts – measurement. Sea and seashore. Weather – wind.

Thompson, Elizabeth. *The true book of time* (Ziner, Feenie)

Thompson, George Selden *see* Selden, George

Thompson, Harwood. *The witch's cat* ill. by Quentin Blake. Addison-Wesley, 1971. Subj: Animals – cats. Folk and fairy tales. Foreign lands – England. Witches.

Thompson, Susan L. *Diary of a monarch butterfly* graphic design by Sas Colby; ill. by Judy LaMotte. Walker, 1976. Subj: Insects – butterflies, caterpillars. Science.

One more thing, dad ill. by Dora Leder. Albert Whitman, 1980. Subj: Counting.

Thompson, Vivian Laubach. *Camp-in-the-yard* ill. by Brinton Turkle. Holiday, 1961. Subj: Problem solving. Sports – camping. Twins.

The horse that liked sandwiches ill. by Aliki. Putnam's, 1962. Subj: Animals – horses. Food.

Thomson, Pat. *Rhymes around the day* ill. by Jan Ormerod. Lothrop, 1983. Subj: Family life. Nursery rhymes.

Thomson, Peggy. *The king has horse's ears* ill. by David Small. Simon & Schuster, 1988. ISBN 0-671-64953-1 Subj: Behavior – secrets. Character traits – appearance. Royalty.

Thomson, Ruth. *Eyes* ill. by Mike Galletly. Watts, 1988. ISBN 0-531-10549-0 Subj: Anatomy. Senses – seeing.

My bear: I can...can you? ill. by Ian Beck. Dial Pr., 1985. ISBN 0-8037-0110-1 Subj: Activities. Poetry, rhyme. Toys – teddy bears.

My bear: I like...do you? ill. by Ian Beck. Dial Pr., 1985. ISBN 0-8037-0105-5 Subj: Poetry, rhyme. Toys – teddy bears.

Peabody all at sea ill. by Ken Kirkwood. Lothrop, 1978. Subj: Activities – vacationing. Animals – dogs. Boats, ships. Careers – detectives. Crime. Problem solving.

Peabody's first case ill. by Ken Kirkwood. Lothrop, 1978. Subj: Animals – dogs. Careers – detectives. Crime. Problem solving.

Thoreau, Henry D. *What befell at Mrs. Brooks's* ill. by George Overlie. Lerner, 1974. ISBN 0-8225-0284-4 Subj: Behavior – hurrying.

Thorne, Ian *see* May, Julian

Thorne, Jenny. *My uncle* ill. by author. Atheneum, 1982. Subj: Activities. Dreams. Family life. Sports – fishing.

The three bears. *Goldilocks and the three bears* retold and ill. by Jan Brett. Dodd, 1987. ISBN 0-396-08925-9 Subj: Animals – bears. Folk and fairy tales.

Goldilocks and the three bears adapt. and ill. by Lorinda Bryan Cauley. Putnam's, 1981. Subj: Animals – bears. Folk and fairy tales.

Goldilocks and the three bears ill. by Jane Dyer. Grosset, 1984. ISBN 0-448-10213-7 Subj: Animals – bears. Folk and fairy tales. Format, unusual – board books.

Goldilocks and the three bears adapt. by Armand Eisen; ill. by Lynn Bywaters Ferris. Knopf, 1987. ISBN 0-394-55882-0 Subj: Animals – bears. Folk and fairy tales.

Goldilocks and the three bears adapt. and ill. by James Marshall. Dial Pr., 1988. ISBN 0-8037-0543-3 Subj: Animals – bears. Caldecott award honor book. Folk and fairy tales.

Goldilocks and the three bears retold and ill. by Janet Stevens. Holiday, 1985. ISBN 0-8234-0608-3 Subj: Animals – bears. Folk and fairy tales.

Goldilocks and the three bears adapt. and ill. by Bernadette Watts. Knopf, 1985. ISBN 0-03-005737-X Subj: Animals – bears. Folk and fairy tales.

The story of the three bears ill. by L. Leslie Brooke. Warne, 1934. Subj: Animals – bears. Folk and fairy tales.

The story of the three bears ill. by William Stobbs. McGraw-Hill, 1964. Subj: Animals – bears. Folk and fairy tales.

The three bears (Hillert, Margaret)

The three bears ill. by Paul Galdone. Seabury Pr., 1972. Subj: Animals – bears. Folk and fairy tales.

The three bears adapted by Kathleen N. Daly; ill. by Feodor Rojankovsky. Golden Pr., 1967. Subj: Animals – bears. Folk and fairy tales.

The three bears ill. by Robin Spowart. Knopf, 1987. ISBN 0-394-98862-0 Subj: Animals – bears. Folk and fairy tales.

The three little pigs. *The story of the three little pigs* ill. by L. Leslie Brooke. Warne, 1934. Subj: Animals – pigs. Animals – wolves. Character traits – cleverness. Folk and fairy tales.

The story of the three little pigs ill. by William Stobbs. McGraw-Hill, 1965. Subj: Animals – pigs. Animals – wolves. Character traits – cleverness. Folk and fairy tales.

Three little pigs. Facsimile ed. Bragdon, 1987. Reprint of 1924 ed. ISBN 0-916410-38-2 Subj: Animals – pigs. Animals – wolves. Character traits – cleverness. Folk and fairy tales.

The three little pigs ill. by Erik Blegvad. Atheneum, 1980. Subj: Animals – pigs. Animals – wolves. Character traits – cleverness. Poetry, rhyme.

The three little pigs adapt. and ill. by Caroline Bucknall. Dial Pr., 1987. ISBN 0-8037-0100-4 Subj: Animals – pigs. Animals – wolves. Character traits – cleverness. Folk and fairy tales. Poetry, rhyme.

The three little pigs ill. by Lorinda Bryan Cauley. Putnam's, 1980. Subj: Animals – pigs. Animals – wolves. Character traits – cleverness. Folk and fairy tales.

The three little pigs ill. by Paul Galdone. Seabury Pr., 1970. Subj: Animals – pigs. Animals – wolves. Character traits – cleverness. Folk and fairy tales.

The three little pigs ill. by Rodney Peppé. Lothrop, 1980. Subj: Animals – pigs. Animals – wolves. Character traits – cleverness. Folk and fairy tales.

The three little pigs ill. by Edda Reinl. Picture Book Studio, 1983. ISBN 0-907234-32-1 Subj: Animals – pigs. Animals – wolves. Character traits – cleverness. Folk and fairy tales.

The three little pigs ill. by John Wallner. Viking, 1987. ISBN 0-670-81707-4 Subj: Animals – pigs. Animals – wolves. Character traits – cleverness. Folk and fairy tales. Format, unusual – toy and movable books.

The three little pigs retold by Margaret Hillert; ill. by Irma Wilde. Follett, 1963. Subj: Animals – pigs. Animals – wolves. Character traits – cleverness. Folk and fairy tales.

The three little pigs: an old story ill. by Margot Zemach. Farrar, 1988. ISBN 0-374-37527-5 Subj: Animals – pigs. Animals – wolves. Character traits – cleverness. Folk and fairy tales.

The three little pigs: in verse ill. by William Pène Du Bois. Viking, 1962. Subj: Animals – pigs. Animals – wolves. Character traits – cleverness. Folk and fairy tales. Poetry, rhyme.

The three pigs ill. by Tony Ross. Pantheon, 1983. Subj: Animals – pigs. Animals – wolves. Character traits – cleverness. Folk and fairy tales.

Thurber, James. *Many moons* ill. by Louis Slobodkin. Harcourt, 1943. Subj: Caldecott award book. Clowns, jesters. Illness. Moon. Royalty.

Thwaite, Ann. *The day with the Duke* ill. by George Him. World, 1969. Subj: Games.

Thwaites, Lyndsay. *Super Adam and Rosie Wonder* ill. by author. André Deutsch, 1983. ISBN 0-233-97532-2 Subj: Activities – playing. Family life.

Tibo, Gilles. *Simon and the snowflakes* ill. by author. Tundra, 1988. ISBN 0-88776-218-2 Subj: Friendship. Stars. Weather – snow.

Tierney, Hanne. *Where's your baby brother, Becky Bunting?* ill. by Paula Winter. Doubleday, 1979. Subj: Behavior – misbehavior. Family life. Sibling rivalry.

Timmermans, Felix. *A gift from Saint Nicholas* adapt. by Carole Kismaric; ill. by Charles Mikolaycak. Holiday, 1988. ISBN 0-8234-0674-1 Subj: Character traits – generosity. Holidays – Christmas.

Ting. *Find the canary* (Morris, Neil)

Hide and seek (Morris, Neil)

Search for Sam (Morris, Neil)

Where's my hat? (Morris, Neil)

Tinkelman, Murray. *Cowgirl* ill. by author. Greenwillow, 1984. ISBN 0-688-02883-7 Subj: Animals – horses. Sports.

Tippett, James Sterling. *Counting the days* ill. by Elizabeth Tyler Wolcott. Harper, 1940. Subj: Holidays – Christmas. Poetry, rhyme.

Tison, Annette. *The adventures of the three colors* by Annette Tison and Talus Taylor. Collins-World, 1971. Subj: Concepts – color. Format, unusual.

Animal hide-and-seek by Annette Tison and Talus Taylor; ill. by authors. Collins-World, 1972. Subj: Activities – photographing. Animals. Format, unusual. Games. Insects.

Animals in color magic ill. by author. Merrill, 1980. Subj: Animals. Format, unusual.

Inside and outside by Annette Tison and Talus Taylor. Collins-World, 1972. Subj: Format, unusual. Houses.

Titherington, Jeanne. *Big world, small world* ill. by author. Greenwillow, 1985. ISBN 0-688-04023-3 Subj: Concepts – perspective. Family life – mothers. Self-concept.

A place for Ben ill. by author. Greenwillow, 1987. ISBN 0-688-06494-9 Subj: Babies. Emotions – loneliness. Family life – brothers.

Pumpkin pumpkin ill. by author. Greenwillow, 1985. ISBN 0-688-50696-1 Subj: Activities – gardening. Holidays – Halloween.

Where are you going, Emma? ill. by author. Greenwillow, 1988. ISBN 0-688-07082-5 Subj: Behavior – lost. Family life – grandfathers.

Titus, Eve. *Anatole* ill. by Paul Galdone. McGraw-Hill, 1957. Subj: Animals – mice. Caldecott award honor book. Foreign lands – France.

Anatole and the cat ill. by Paul Galdone. McGraw-Hill, 1957. Subj: Animals – cats. Animals – mice. Caldecott award honor book. Character traits – bravery. Foreign lands – France. Problem solving.

Anatole and the piano ill. by Paul Galdone. McGraw-Hill, 1966. Subj: Animals – mice. Foreign lands – France. Music.

Anatole and the Pied Piper ill. by Paul Galdone. McGraw-Hill, 1979. Subj: Animals – mice. Foreign lands – France. Music. Problem solving.

Anatole and the poodle ill. by Paul Galdone. McGraw-Hill, 1965. Subj: Animals – dogs. Animals – mice. Foreign lands – France. Problem solving.

Anatole and the robot ill. by Paul Galdone. McGraw-Hill, 1960. Subj: Animals – mice. Foreign lands – France. Problem solving. Robots.

Anatole and the thirty thieves ill. by Paul Galdone. McGraw-Hill, 1969. Subj: Animals – mice. Crime. Foreign lands – France. Problem solving.

Anatole and the toyshop ill. by Paul Galdone. McGraw-Hill, 1970. Subj: Animals – mice. Foreign lands – France. Problem solving. Toys.

Anatole in Italy ill. by Paul Galdone. McGraw-Hill, 1973. Subj: Animals – mice. Foreign lands – Italy. Problem solving.

Anatole over Paris ill. by Paul Galdone. McGraw-Hill, 1961. Subj: Activities – flying. Animals – mice. Foreign lands – France. Kites.

Tobias, Tobi. *At the beach* ill. by Gloria Singer. McKay, 1978. Subj: Activities – vacationing. Family life. Sea and seashore.

Chasing the goblins away ill. by Victor G. Ambrus. Warne, 1977. Subj: Bedtime. Goblins. Night. Sleep.

The dawdlewalk ill. by Jeanette Swofford. Carolrhoda, 1983. Subj: Activities – walking.

A day off ill. by Ray Cruz. Putnam's, 1973. ISBN 0-399-60762-5 Subj: Family life. Illness.

Jane wishing ill. by Trina Schart Hyman. Viking, 1977. Subj: Behavior – wishing. Emotions – happiness. Family life. Humor. Self-concept.

Moving day ill. by William Pène du Bois. Knopf, 1976. Subj: Emotions. Moving. Toys – teddy bears.

Petey ill. by Symeon Shimin. Putnam's, 1978. Subj: Animals – gerbils. Death. Emotions. Pets.

The quitting deal ill. by Trina Schart Hyman. Viking, 1975. ISBN 0-670-58582-3 Subj: Behavior – seeking better things. Family life.

Tobias catches trout (Hertza, Ole)

Tobias goes ice fishing (Hertza, Ole)

Tobias goes seal hunting (Hertza, Ole)

Tobias has a birthday (Hertza, Ole)

Todaro, John. *Phillip the flower-eating phoenix* by John Todaro and Barbara Ellen; ill. by John Todaro. Abelard-Schuman, 1961. Subj: Mythical creatures.

Todd, Kathleen. *Snow* ill. by author. Addison-Wesley, 1982. Subj: Activities – playing. Family life. Weather – snow.

Tokuda, Wendy. *Humphrey the lost whale: a true story* by Wendy Tokuda and Richard Hall; ill. by Hanako Wakiyama. Heian, 1986. 0-89346-270-5 Subj: Animals – whales. Behavior – lost. Behavior – needing someone. Sea and seashore.

Tolby, Arthur *see* Rodgers, Frank

Tolkien, Baillie. *The Father Christmas letters* (Tolkien, J. R. R. (John Ronald Reuel))

Tolkien, J. R. R. (John Ronald Reuel). *The Father Christmas letters* ed. by Baillie Tolkien; ill. by author. Houghton, 1977. Subj: Communication. Holidays – Christmas.

Tolstoĭ, Alekseĭ Nikolaevich. *The great big enormous turnip* ill. by Helen Oxenbury. Watts, 1968. Subj: Cumulative tales. Farms. Folk and fairy tales. Foreign lands – Russia. Plants. Problem solving.

Shoemaker Martin tr. from Russian by Michael Hale; adapt. by Brigitte Hanhart; ill. by Bernadette Watts. Holt, 1986. ISBN 0-8050-0040-2 Subj: Character traits – generosity. Character traits – kindness. Religion.

Tom Thumb. *Grimm Tom Thumb* by Jacob and Wilhelm Grimm; tr. by Anthea Bell; ill. by Svend Otto S. Larousse, 1976. Translation of Tommeliden. Subj: Elves and little people. Folk and fairy tales.

Tom Thumb ill. by L. Leslie Brooke. Warne, 1904. Subj: Elves and little people. Folk and fairy tales.

Tom Thumb adapt. by Margaret Hillert; ill. by Dennis Hockerman. Follett, 1982. Subj: Elves and little people. Folk and fairy tales.

Tom Thumb by the Brothers Grimm; ill. by Felix Hoffmann. Atheneum, 1973. Translation of Der Daumling. Subj: Elves and little people. Folk and fairy tales.

Tom Thumb adapt. and ill. by Richard Jesse Watson. Harcourt, 1989. ISBN 0-15-289280-X Subj: Elves and little people. Folk and fairy tales.

Tom Thumb ill. by William Wiesner. Walck, 1974. Subj: Elves and little people. Folk and fairy tales.

Tom Thumb: a tale adapt. and ill. by Lidia Postma. Schocken, 1983. Based on a tale by Charles Perrault. Subj: Elves and little people. Folk and fairy tales.

Tom Tit Tot. *Tom Tit Tot: an English folk tale* ill. by Evaline Ness. Scribner's, 1965. Subj: Caldecott award honor book. Folk and fairy tales. Magic. Names.

Tomchek, Ann Heinrichs. *I can be a chef.* Childrens Pr., 1985. ISBN 0-516-01886-8 Subj: Activities – cooking. Careers – chefs.

Tomfool *see* Farjeon, Eleanor

Tomkins, Jasper. *The catalog* ill. by author. Green Tiger Pr., 1981. Subj: Animals. Humor.

Tompert, Ann. *Badger on his own* ill. by Diane de Groat. Crown, 1978. Subj: Animals – badgers. Birds – owls.

Charlotte and Charles ill. by John Wallner. Crown, 1979. Subj: Giants. Middle ages.

Little Fox goes to the end of the world ill. by John Wallner. Crown, 1976. Subj: Animals – foxes. Imagination.

Little Otter remembers and other stories ill. by John Wallner. Crown, 1977. Subj: Animals – otters. Family life – mothers.

Nothing sticks like a shadow ill. by Lynn Munsinger. Houghton, 1984. Subj: Animals – groundhogs. Animals – rabbits. Shadows.

The silver whistle ill. by Beth Peck. Macmillan, 1988. ISBN 0-02-789160-7 Subj: Foreign lands – Mexico. Holidays – Christmas.

Will you come back for me? ill. by Robin Kramer. Albert Whitman, 1988. ISBN 0-8075-9112-2 Subj: Behavior – needing someone. Dreams. Emotions – fear. School.

Tord, Bijou Le *see* Le Tord, Bijou

Torgersen, Don Arthur. *The girl who tricked the troll* ill. by Tom Dunnington. Children's Pr., 1978. Subj: Farms. Trolls.

The troll who lived in the lake ill. by Tom Dunnington. Children's Pr., 1978. Subj: Ecology. Trolls.

Tornborg, Pat. *The Sesame Street cookbook* ill. by Robert Dennis. Platt, 1978. Subj: Activities – cooking. Puppets.

Totham, Mary *see* Breinburg, Petronella

Towle, Faith M. *The magic cooking pot: a folktale of India* ill. by author. Houghton, 1975. Subj: Folk and fairy tales. Food. Foreign lands – India. Magic.

Townsend, Anita. *The kangaroo* ill. by Michael Atkinson. Watts, 1979. Subj: Animals – kangaroos. Science.

Townsend, Kenneth. *Felix, the bald-headed lion* ill. by author. Delacorte, 1967. Subj: Animals – lions. Clothing. Emotions – embarrassment. Hair.

Townsend, Maryann. *Pop's secret* by Maryann Townsend and Ronnie Stern; ill. with photos. Addison-Wesley, 1980. Subj: Death. Family life – grandfathers.

Townson, Hazel. *Terrible Tuesday* ill. by Tony Ross. Morrow, 1986. ISBN 0-688-06244-X Subj: Emotions – fear. Family life. Imagination.

Toye, William. *Fire stealer* photos. by Elizabeth Cleaver. Oxford Univ. Pr., 1988. ISBN 0-19-540515-3 Subj: Folk and fairy tales. Indians of North America.

How summer came to Canada photos. by Elizabeth Cleaver. Oxford Univ. Pr., 1988. ISBN 0-19-540290-1 Subj: Folk and fairy tales. Indians of North America.

The loon's necklace photos. by Elizabeth Cleaver. Oxford Univ. Pr., 1988. ISBN 0-19-540278-2 Subj: Folk and fairy tales. Indians of North America.

The mountain goats of Temlaham photos. by Elizabeth Cleaver. Oxford Univ. Pr., 1988. ISBN 0-19-540320-7 Subj: Folk and fairy tales. Indians of North America.

Trân-Khánh-Tuyêt. *The little weaver of Thái-Yên Village* tr. from Vietnamese by Christopher N. H. Jenkins and author; ill. by Nancy Hom. Childrens Book Pr., 1987. ISBN 0-89239-030-1 Subj: Activities – weaving. Foreign lands – Vietnam. Language.

Tredez, Alain *see* Trez, Alain

Tredez, Denise Laugier *see* Trez, Denise

Trent, Robbie. *The first Christmas* ill. by Marc Simont. Harper, 1948. Subj: Holidays – Christmas. Poetry, rhyme. Religion.

Tresselt, Alvin R. *Autumn harvest* ill. by Roger Antoine Duvoisin. Lothrop, 1951. Subj: Holidays – Thanksgiving. Seasons – fall.

The beaver pond ill. by Roger Antoine Duvoisin. Lothrop, 1970. Subj: Animals – beavers. Ecology.

The dead tree ill. by Charles Robinson. Parents, 1972. Subj: Ecology. Trees.

The fisherman under the sea (Matsutani, Miyoko)

Follow the wind ill. by Roger Antoine Duvoisin. Lothrop, 1950. Subj: Poetry, rhyme. Weather – wind.

Frog in the well ill. by Roger Antoine Duvoisin. Lothrop, 1958. Subj: Frogs and toads.

Hi, Mister Robin ill. by Roger Antoine Duvoisin. Lothrop, 1950. ISBN 0-688-51168-6 Subj: Birds – robins. Family life. Seasons – spring.

Hide and seek fog ill. by Roger Antoine Duvoisin. Lothrop, 1965. Subj: Caldecott award honor book. Sea and seashore. Weather – fog.

How far is far? ill. by Ward Brackett. Parents, 1964. Subj: Concepts – distance. Science.

I saw the sea come in ill. by Roger Antoine Duvoisin. Lothrop, 1954. Subj: Behavior – solitude. Sea and seashore.

It's time now! ill. by Roger Antoine Duvoisin. Lothrop, 1969. Subj: City. Seasons.

Johnny Maple-Leaf ill. by Roger Antoine Duvoisin. Lothrop, 1948. Subj: Seasons. Seasons – fall. Trees.

The mitten: an old Ukrainian folktale ill. by Yaroslava. Lothrop, 1964. Adapted by Alvin Tresselt from the version by E. Rachev. Subj: Animals. Folk and fairy tales. Foreign lands – Ukraine.

Rabbit story ill. by Leonard Weisgard. Lothrop, 1957. Subj: Animals – rabbits.

Rain drop splash ill. by Leonard Weisgard. Lothrop, 1946. Subj: Caldecott award honor book. Cumulative tales. Science. Weather – rain.

Smallest elephant in the world ill. by Milton Glaser. Knopf, 1959. Subj: Animals – elephants. Character traits – smallness. Circus.

Sun up ill. by Roger Antoine Duvoisin. Lothrop, 1949. Subj: Farms. Sun. Weather.

Wake up, farm! ill. by Roger Antoine Duvoisin. Lothrop, 1955. ISBN 0-688-51162-7 Subj: Animals. Farms. Morning.

What did you leave behind? ill. by Roger Antoine Duvoisin. Lothrop, 1978. Subj: Emotions.

White snow, bright snow ill. by Roger Antoine Duvoisin. Lothrop, 1947. Subj: Caldecott award book. Weather – snow.

The wind and Peter ill. by Garry McKenzie. Oxford Univ. Pr., 1948. Subj: Weather – wind.

The witch's magic cloth (Matsutani, Miyoko)

The world in the candy egg ill. by Roger Antoine Duvoisin. Lothrop, 1967. Subj: Eggs. Holidays – Easter. Magic.

Trez, Alain. *Good night, Veronica* (Trez, Denise)

The little knight's dragon (Trez, Denise)

Maila and the flying carpet (Trez, Denise)

Rabbit country (Trez, Denise)

The royal hiccups (Trez, Denise)

Trez, Denise. *Good night, Veronica* by Denise and Alain Trez; tr. by Douglas McKee; ill. by authors. Viking, 1968. Subj: Bedtime. Dreams. Sleep.

The little knight's dragon by Denise and Alain Trez; ill. by authors. Collins-World, 1963. Subj: Dragons. Knights.

Maila and the flying carpet by Denise and Alain Trez; tr. by Douglas McKee; ill. by authors. Viking, 1969. Subj: Activities – flying. Foreign lands – India. Magic. Royalty.

Rabbit country by Denise and Alain Trez; ill. by authors. Viking, 1966. Subj: Animals – rabbits.

The royal hiccups by Denise and Alain Trez; tr. by Douglas McKee; ill. by authors. Viking, 1965. Subj: Emotions – fear. Illness. Royalty.

Trimby, Elisa. *Mr. Plum's paradise* ill. by author. Lothrop, 1977. Subj: Activities – gardening. City.

Trinca, Rod. *One woolly wombat* by Rod Trinca and Kerry Argent; ill. by Kerry Argent. Kane Miller, 1985. ISBN 0-916291-00-6 Subj: Animals. Counting. Foreign lands – Australia.

Tripp, Paul. *The strawman who smiled by mistake* ill. by Wendy Watson. Doubleday, 1967. Subj: Emotions – happiness. Farms. Friendship. Scarecrows.

Tripp, Wallace. *Marguerite, go wash your feet* ill. by author. Houghton, 1985. ISBN 0-395-35392-0 Subj: Humor. Poetry, rhyme.

My Uncle Podger ill. by author. Little, 1975. Based on a passage from Three men in a boat (to say nothing of the dog) by Jerome Klapka Jerome. Subj: Animals – rabbits. Humor.

The tale of a pig: a caucasian folktale adapt. and ill. by Wallace Tripp. McGraw-Hill, 1968. Subj: Animals – pigs. Folk and fairy tales.

Trivas, Irene. *Emma's Christmas* ill. by author. Watts, 1988. ISBN 0-531-08380-2 Subj: Holidays – Christmas. Songs. Weddings.

Trotwood, John *see* Moore, John

Troughton, Joanna. *How rabbit stole the fire* ill. by adapt. Harper, 1986. ISBN 0-87226-040-2 Subj: Animals – rabbits. Fire. Folk and fairy tales. Indians of North America.

How the birds changed their feathers: a South American Indian folk tale ill. by adapt. Harper, 1986. ISBN 0-87226-080-1 Subj: Birds. Concepts – color. Folk and fairy tales. Foreign lands – South America.

Mouse-Deer's market ill. by adapt. Harper, 1984. ISBN 0-911745-63-7 Subj: Animals. Animals – deer. Character traits – cleverness.

The quail's egg ill. by author. Bedrick, 1988. ISBN 0-87226-185-9 Subj: Birds. Cumulative tales. Eggs.

Tortoise's dream: an African folk tale ill. by adapt. Harper, 1986. ISBN 0-87226-039-9 Subj: Dreams. Folk and fairy tales. Foreign lands – Africa. Reptiles – turtles, tortoises.

What made Tiddalik laugh: an Australian Aborigine folk tale ill. by adapt. Harper, 1986. ISBN 0-87226-081-X Subj: Folk and fairy tales. Foreign lands – Australia. Frogs and toads.

Who will be the sun? ill. by adapt. Harper, 1986. ISBN 0-87226-038-0 Subj: Folk and fairy tales. Indians of North America. Sun.

Troy, Alan *see* Hoke, Helen L.

Trucks ill. by Art Seiden. Platt, 1983. Subj: Trucks.

Tsow, Ming. *A day with Ling* photos. by Christopher Cormack. Hamish Hamilton, 1983. Subj: Family life.

Tsultim, Yeshe. *The mouse king: a story from Tibet* ill. by Kusho Ralla. Penguin, 1979. Subj: Animals – mice. Folk and fairy tales. Foreign lands – Tibet.

Tsutsui, Yoriko. *Anna's secret friend* ill. by Akiko Hayashi. Viking, 1987. ISBN 0-670-81670-1 Subj: Family life. Friendship. Moving.

Before the picnic ill. by Akiko Hayashi. Putnam's, 1987. ISBN 0-399-21458-5 Subj: Activities – picnicking. Family life.

Tuber, Joel. *The steadfast tin soldier* (Andersen, H. C. (Hans Christian))

The ugly duckling (Andersen, H. C. (Hans Christian))

Tucker, Kathleen. *The little bear who forgot* (Chevalier, Christa)

My mother never listens to me (Sharmat, Marjorie Weinman)

Tucker, Nicholas. *Mother Goose abroad: nursery rhymes* ill. by Trevor Stubley. Crowell, 1974. Subj: Nursery rhymes.

Tudor, Bethany. *Samuel's tree house* ill. by author. Collins-World, 1979. Subj: Birds – ducks. Friendship. Houses. Toys. Trees.

Skiddycock Pond ill. by author. Lippincott, 1965. Subj: Birds – ducks. Boats, ships.

Tudor, Tasha. *Around the year* ill. by author. Walck, 1957. Subj: Days of the week, months of the year. Poetry, rhyme. Seasons.

Corgiville fair ill. by author. Crowell, 1971. Subj: Animals – goats. Fairs. Trolls.

The doll's Christmas ill. by author. Oxford Univ. Pr., 1950. Subj: Holidays – Christmas. Toys – dolls.

Junior's tune ill. by author. Holiday, 1980. Subj: Music. Sibling rivalry.

Mildred and the mummy ill. by author. Holiday, 1980. Subj: Libraries.

Miss Kiss and the nasty beast ill. by author. Holiday, 1979. Subj: Emotions – love.

More prayers ill. by author. McKay, 1967. ISBN 0-8098-1954-6 Subj: Religion.

1 is one ill. by author. Walck, 1956. Subj: Caldecott award honor book. Counting.

Snow before Christmas ill. by author. Oxford Univ. Pr., 1941. Subj: Holidays – Christmas. Seasons – winter. Weather – snow.

A tale for Easter ill. by author. McKay, 1972. ISBN 0-8098-1807-8 Subj: Dreams. Holidays – Easter.

A time to keep: the Tasha Tudor book of holidays ill. by author. Rand McNally, 1978. Subj: Activities. Holidays.

Tulloch, Richard. *Stories from our house* ill. by Julie Vivas. Cambridge Univ. Pr., 1987. ISBN 0-521-33485-3 Subj: Family life. Humor.

Tune, Suelyn Ching. *How Maui slowed the sun* ill. by Robin Yoko Burningham. Univ. of Hawaii, 1988. ISBN 0-8248-1083-X Subj: Folk and fairy tales. Hawaii. Magic.

Türk, Hanne. *Goodnight Max* ill. by author. Firefly Pr., 1983. Subj: Animals – mice. Bedtime. Wordless.

Happy birthday Max ill. by author. Alphabet Pr., 1984. Subj: Animals – mice. Birthdays. Wordless.

Max packs ill. by author. Alphabet Pr., 1984. Subj: Activities – traveling. Animals – mice. Wordless.

Max the artlover ill. by author. Alphabet Pr., 1983. Subj: Animals – mice. Art. Wordless.

Max versus the cube ill. by author. Alphabet Pr., 1982. Subj: Animals – mice. Problem solving. Riddles. Wordless.

Merry Christmas Max ill. by author. Firefly Pr., 1983. Subj: Animals – mice. Holidays – Christmas. Wordless.

Rainy day Max ill. by author. Alphabet Pr., 1983. Subj: Activities – walking. Animals – mice. Weather – rain. Wordless.

Raking leaves with Max ill. by author. Firefly Pr., 1983. Subj: Activities – working. Animals – mice. Wordless.

The rope skips Max ill. by author. Alphabet Pr., 1982. Subj: Activities. Animals – mice. Wordless.

Snapshot Max ill. by author. Alphabet Pr., 1984. Subj: Activities – photographing. Animals – mice. Wordless.

A surprise for Max ill. by author. Alphabet Pr., 1982. Subj: Animals – mice. Problem solving. Wordless.

Turkel, Pauline *see* Kesselman, Judi R.

Turkle, Brinton. *The adventures of Obadiah* ill. by author. Viking, 1977. ISBN 0-670-10614-3 Subj: Behavior – lying. Character traits – honesty. U.S. history.

Deep in the forest ill. by author. Dutton, 1976. Subj: Animals – bears. Folk and fairy tales. Wordless.

Do not open ill. by author. Dutton, 1981. Subj: Animals – cats. Behavior – trickery. Behavior – wishing. Monsters. Sea and seashore.

It's only Arnold ill. by author. Viking, 1973. Subj: Emotions – fear. Family life – grandmothers.

The magic of Millicent Musgrave ill. by author. Viking, 1967. Subj: Magic.

Obadiah the Bold story and pictures by Brinton Turkle. Viking, 1965. Subj: Activities – playing. Behavior – growing up. Sea and seashore. U.S. history.

Rachel and Obadiah ill. by author. Dutton, 1978. Subj: Behavior – sharing. Money. Sibling rivalry.

The sky dog ill. by author. Viking, 1969. Subj: Animals – dogs. Imagination. Sea and seashore. Weather – clouds.

Thy friend, Obadiah ill. by author. Viking, 1969. Subj: Birds – sea gulls. Caldecott award honor book. Character traits – kindness to animals. Seasons – winter. U.S. history.

Turnage, Sheila. *Trout the magnificent* ill. by Janet Stevens. Harcourt, 1984. Subj: Behavior – dissatisfaction. Fish. Self-concept.

Turner, Ann. *Dakota dugout* ill. by Ronald Himler. Macmillan, 1985. ISBN 0-02-789700-1 Subj: Farms. U.S. history.

Nettie's trip south ill. by Ronald Himler. Macmillan, 1987. ISBN 0-02-789240-9 Subj: Activities – traveling. Behavior – disbelief. Ethnic groups in the U.S. – Afro-Americans. Family life.

Tickle a pickle ill. by Karen Ann Weinhaus. Macmillan, 1986. ISBN 0-02-789280-8 Subj: Poetry, rhyme.

Turner, Gwenda. *Playbook* ill. by author. Viking, 1986. ISBN 0-670-80660-9 Subj: School.

Turner, Josie *see* Crawford, Phyllis

Turpin, Lorna. *The sultan's snakes* ill. by author. Greenwillow, 1980. Subj: Behavior – hiding. Reptiles – snakes. Royalty.

Turska, Krystyna. *The magician of Cracow* ill. by author. Greenwillow, 1975. Subj: Character traits – ambition. Devil. Folk and fairy tales. Foreign lands – Poland. Magic. Moon.

The woodcutter's duck ill. by author. Macmillan, 1972. Subj: Birds – ducks. Character traits – kindness to animals. Folk and fairy tales. Foreign lands – Poland. Frogs and toads.

The turtle ill. by Charlotte Knox. Rourke, 1983. Subj: Reptiles – turtles, tortoises.

Tusa, Tricia. *Chicken* ill. by author. Macmillan, 1986. ISBN 0-02-789320-0 Subj: Behavior – misunderstanding. Birds – chickens. Pets. Self-concept.

Libby's new glasses ill. by author. Holiday, 1984. Subj: Glasses. Self-concept. Senses – seeing.

Maebelle's suitcase ill. by author. Macmillan, 1987. ISBN 0-02-789250-6 Subj: Birds. Clothing. Old age.

Miranda ill. by author. Macmillan, 1985. ISBN 0-02-789520-3 Subj: Character traits – stubbornness. Music.

Stay away from the junkyard! ill. by author. Macmillan, 1988. ISBN 0-02-789541-6 Subj: Art. Behavior – collecting things.

Tutt, Kay Cunningham. *And now we call him Santa Claus* ill. by author. Lothrop, 1963. Subj: Holidays – Christmas.

The twelve days of Christmas. English folk song. *Brian Wildsmith's The twelve days of Christmas* ill. by Brian Wildsmith. Watts, 1972. Subj: Cumulative tales. Holidays – Christmas. Music. Songs.

Jack Kent's twelve days of Christmas ill. by Jack Kent. Parents, 1973. Subj: Cumulative tales. Holidays – Christmas. Humor. Music. Songs.

The twelve days of Christmas ill. by Jan Brett. Dodd, 1986. ISBN 0-396-08821-X Subj: Cumulative tales. Holidays – Christmas. Music. Songs.

The twelve days of Christmas ill. by Ilonka Karasz. Harper, 1949. Subj: Cumulative tales. Holidays – Christmas. Music. Songs.

The twelve days of Christmas ill. by Erika Schneider. Alphabet Pr., 1984. Subj: Cumulative tales. Format, unusual. Holidays – Christmas. Music. Songs.

The twelve days of Christmas ill. by Sophie Windham. Putnam's, 1986. ISBN 0-399-21327-9 Subj: Cumulative tales. Holidays – Christmas. Music. Songs.

Tworkov, Jack. *The camel who took a walk* ill. by Roger Antoine Duvoisin. Aladdin Books, 1951. Subj: Activities – walking. Animals. Animals – camels. Animals – tigers. Cumulative tales. Morning.

Tyler, Linda Wagner. *The sick-in-bed birthday book* ill. by Susan Davis. Viking, 1988. ISBN 0-670-81823-2 Subj: Animals – pigs. Birthdays. Illness.

Waiting for mom ill. by Susan Davis. Viking, 1987. ISBN 0-670-81408-3 Subj: Animals – hippopotami. Behavior – worrying. Family life – mothers. School.

When daddy comes home ill. by Susan Davis. Viking, 1986. ISBN 0-670-80301-4 Subj: Animals – hippopotami. Family life – fathers.

Tyrrell, Anne. *Elizabeth Jane gets dressed* ill. by Caroline Castle. Barron's, 1987. ISBN 0-8120-5775-9 Subj: Clothing. Days of the week, months of the year. Poetry, rhyme. Toys.

Mary Ann always can ill. by Caroline Castle. Barron's, 1988. ISBN 0-8120-5939-5 Subj: Character traits – individuality. Poetry, rhyme. Sibling rivalry.

Uchida, Yoshiko. *The rooster who understood Japanese* ill. by Charles Robinson. Scribner's, 1976. Subj: Animals. Birds – chickens. Foreign languages.

Sumi's prize ill. by Kazue Mizumura. Scribner's, 1964. Subj: Character traits – ambition. Foreign lands – Japan. Kites.

Sumi's special happening ill. by Kazue Mizumura. Scribner's, 1966. Subj: Birthdays. Foreign lands – Japan. Old age.

The two foolish cats ill. by Margot Zemach. Macmillan, 1987. ISBN 0-689-50397-0 Subj: Animals – cats. Folk and fairy tales. Food.

Udry, Janice May. *Alfred* ill. by Judith S. Roth. Albert Whitman, 1960. Subj: Animals – dogs. Behavior – animals, dislike of. Emotions – fear.

Emily's autumn ill. by Erik Blegvad. Albert Whitman, 1969. Subj: Farms. Seasons – fall. Toys – dolls.

How I faded away ill. by Monica De Bruyn. Albert Whitman, 1976. Subj: Behavior – unnoticed, unseen. Emotions – embarrassment. Self-concept.

Is Susan here? ill. by Peter Edwards. Abelard-Schuman, 1962. Subj: Animals. Character traits – helpfulness. Family life – mothers. Imagination.

Let's be enemies ill. by Maurice Sendak. Harper, 1961. Subj: Behavior – fighting, arguing. Emotions – hate. Friendship.

Mary Ann's mud day ill. by Martha G. Alexander. Harper, 1967. Subj: Activities – playing. Ethnic groups in the U.S. – Afro-Americans.

Mary Jo's grandmother ill. by Eleanor Mill. Albert Whitman, 1970. Subj: Ethnic groups in the U.S. – Afro-Americans. Family life – grandmothers. Illness. Seasons – winter. Weather – snow.

The mean mouse and other mean stories ill. by Ed Young. Harper, 1962. Subj: Character traits – meanness.

The moon jumpers ill. by Maurice Sendak. Harper, 1959. Subj: Caldecott award honor book. Moon. Twilight.

"Oh no, cat!" ill. by Mary Chalmers. Coward, 1976. Subj: Animals – cats. Pets.

Theodore's parents ill. by Adrienne Adams. Lothrop, 1958. Subj: Adoption. Family life.

Thump and Plunk ill. by Ann Schweninger. Harper, 1981. Subj: Animals – mice. Family life – mothers. Sibling rivalry.

A tree is nice ill. by Marc Simont. Harper, 1956. Subj: Caldecott award book. Poetry, rhyme. Seasons. Trees.

What Mary Jo shared ill. by Eleanor Mill. Albert Whitman, 1966. Subj: Character traits – shyness. Ethnic groups in the U.S. Ethnic groups in the U.S. – Afro-Americans. Family life – fathers. School.

What Mary Jo wanted ill. by Eleanor Mill. Albert Whitman, 1968. Subj: Animals – dogs. Ethnic groups in the U.S. – Afro-Americans. Family life. Pets.

Ueno, Noriko. *Elephant buttons* ill. by author. Harper, 1973. Subj: Animals. Concepts – in and out. Concepts – size. Circular tales. Games. Humor. Participation. Wordless.

Uncle Gus *see* Rey, Hans Augusto

Ungerer, Jean Thomas *see* Ungerer, Tomi

Ungerer, Tomi. *Adelaide* ill. by author. Harper, 1959. Subj: Activities – traveling. Animals – kangaroos. Fire. Foreign lands – France.

The beast of Monsieur Racine ill. by author. Farrar, 1971. Subj: Behavior – trickery. Foreign lands – France. Humor. Monsters.

Christmas eve at the Mellops ill. by author. Harper, 1960. Subj: Animals – pigs. Holidays – Christmas.

Crictor ill. by author. Harper, 1958. Subj: Humor. Reptiles – snakes.

Emile ill. by author. Harper, 1960. Subj: Humor. Octopuses.

The hat ill. by author. Parents, 1970. Subj: Clothing. Foreign lands – Italy. Magic. Weather – wind.

The Mellops go diving for treasure ill. by author. Harper, 1957. Subj: Animals – pigs. Sea and seashore. Sports – skin diving.

The Mellops go flying ill. by author. Harper, 1957. Subj: Activities – flying. Airplanes, airports. Animals – pigs.

The Mellops go spelunking ill. by author. Harper, 1963. Subj: Animals – pigs. Caves. Character traits – perseverance.

The Mellops strike oil ill. by author. Harper, 1958. Subj: Animals – pigs. Fire. Oil.

Moon man ill. by author. Harper, 1967. Subj: Moon. Space and space ships.

No kiss for mother ill. by author. Harper, 1973. Subj: Animals – cats. Family life – mothers.

One, two, where's my shoe? ill. by author. Harper, 1964. Subj: Games. Wordless.

Orlando, the brave vulture ill. by author. Harper, 1966. Subj: Birds – vultures. Desert. Foreign lands – Mexico.

Rufus ill. by author. Harper, 1961. Subj: Animals – bats.

Snail, where are you? ill. by author. Harper, 1962. Subj: Animals – snails. Games. Wordless.

The three robbers ill. by author. Atheneum, 1962. Subj: Crime. Orphans.

Warwick's three bottles (Hodeir, André)

Zeralda's ogre ill. by author. Harper, 1967. Subj: Activities – cooking. Character traits – kindness. Giants. Monsters.

Untermeyer, Louis. *Æsop's fables* (Æsop)

The kitten who barked ill. by Lilian Obligado. Golden Pr., 1962. Subj: Animals – cats. Animals – dogs.

Updike, David. *An autumn tale* ill. by Robert Andrew Parker. Pippin Pr., 1988. ISBN 0-945912-02-1 Subj: Imagination. Night. Seasons – fall.

A winter's journey ill. by Robert Andrew Parker. Prentice-Hall, 1985. ISBN 0-13-961566-0 Subj: Animals – dogs. Dreams. Family life. Weather – snow.

Upham, Elizabeth. *Little brown bear loses his clothes* ill. by Normand Chartier. Platt, 1978. Subj: Animals – bears. Behavior – losing things.

Usher, Margo Scegge *see* McHargue, Georgess

Uyeda, Frances. *Chōchō is for butterfly* (Sasaki, Jeannie)

Uysal, Ahmet E. *New patches for old* (Walker, Barbara K.)

Vacheron, Edith. *Here is Henri!* by Edith Vacheron and Virginia Kahl; ill. by Virginia Kahl. Scribner's, 1959. Subj: Animals – cats. Foreign lands – France. Foreign languages.

Vaës, Alain. *The porcelain pepper pot* ill. by author. Little, 1985. ISBN 0-14-050727-2 Subj: Activities – picnicking. Emotions – love. Farms.

The wild hamster ill. by author. Little, 1985. ISBN 0-316-89504-0 Subj: Animals – hamsters. Pets.

Vail, Amanda *see* Miller, Warren

Valderrama, Candido A. *Mister North Wind* (De Posadas Mane, Carmen)

Valens, Evans G. *Wingfin and Topple* ill. by Clement Hurd. Collins-World, 1962. Subj: Activities – flying. Fish.

Valeri, M. Eulalia. *Hansel and Gretel* (Grimm, Jacob)

Sleeping Beauty (Grimm, Jacob)

The ugly duckling (Andersen, H. C. (Hans Christian))

Van Allsburg, Chris. *Ben's dream* ill. by author. Houghton, 1982. Subj: Dreams. Weather – rain.

The garden of Abdul Gasazi ill. by author. Houghton, 1979. Subj: Animals – dogs. Behavior – misbehavior. Caldecott award honor book. Imagination. Magic.

Jumanji ill. by author. Houghton, 1981. Subj: Caldecott award book. Games. Imagination. Jungle.

The mysteries of Harris Burdick ill. by author. Houghton, 1984. Subj: Imagination.

The polar express ill. by author. Houghton, 1985. ISBN 0-395-38949-6 Subj: Caldecott award book. Holidays – Christmas. Imagination. Night. Trains.

The stranger ill. by author. Houghton, 1986. ISBN 0-395-42331-7 Subj: Behavior – forgetfulness. Country. Seasons – fall.

Two bad ants ill. by author. Houghton, 1988. ISBN 0-395-48668-8 Subj: Houses. Insects – ants.

The wreck of the Zephyr ill. by author. Houghton, 1983. Subj: Boats, ships. Weather – storms.

The Z was zapped ill. by author. Houghton, 1987. ISBN 0-395-44612-0 Subj: ABC books.

Vance, Eleanor Graham. *Jonathan* ill. by Albert John Pucci. Follett, 1966. Subj: Character traits – questioning. Poetry, rhyme. Weather.

Van den Honert, Dorry. *Demi the baby sitter* ill. by Meg Wohlberg. Morrow, 1961. Subj: Activities – baby-sitting. Animals – dogs.

Van der Beek, Deborah. *Alice's blue cloth* ill. by author. Putnam's, 1989. ISBN 0-399-216227 Subj: Birthdays. Family life.

Superbabe! ill. by author. Putnam's, 1988. ISBN 0-399-21507-7 Subj: Babies. Family life. Poetry, rhyme. Sibling rivalry.

Van der Meer, Atie. *Oh Lord!* (Van der Meer, Ron)

Pigs at home (Van der Meer, Ron)

Van der Meer, Ron. *Oh Lord!* by Ron and Atie van der Meer; ill. by authors. Crown, 1980. Subj: Humor. Religion.

Pigs at home by Ron and Atie Van der Meer; ill. by authors. Atheneum, 1988. ISBN 0-689-71232-4 Subj: Animals – pigs. Format, unusual.

Sailing ships (McGowan, Alan)

Vandivert, William. *Barnaby* photos. by author; story by Rita Vandivert. Dodd, 1963. Subj: Animals – kinkajous. Pets.

Van Dyne, Edith *see* Baum, L. Frank (Lyman Frank)

Van Horn, Grace. *Little red rooster* ill. by Sheila Perry. Abelard-Schuman, 1961. Subj: Birds – chickens. Farms.

Van Horn, William. *Harry Hoyle's giant jumping bean* ill. by author. Atheneum, 1978. Subj: Animals – cats. Animals – pack rats. Behavior – collecting things.

Twitchtoe, the beastfinder ill. by author. Atheneum, 1978. Subj: Problem solving.

Van Laan, Nancy. *The big fat worm* ill. by Marisabina Russo. Knopf, 1987. ISBN 0-394-98763-2 Subj: Animals. Birds. Circular tales.

Van Leeuwen, Jean. *Amanda Pig and her big brother Oliver* ill. by Ann Schweninger. Dial Pr., 1982. Subj: Animals – pigs. Behavior – growing up. Sibling rivalry.

The emperor's new clothes (Andersen, H. C. (Hans Christian))

More tales of Amanda Pig ill. by Ann Schweninger. Dial Pr., 1985. ISBN 0-8037-0224-8 Subj: Activities – playing. Animals – pigs. Birthdays. Family life. Family life – fathers.

More tales of Oliver Pig ill. by Arnold Lobel. Dial Pr., 1981. Subj: Animals – pigs. Family life.

Oliver, Amanda and Grandmother ill. by Ann Schweninger. Dial Pr., 1987. ISBN 0-8037-0362-7 Subj: Animals – pigs. Family life – grandmothers. Imagination.

Tales of Amanda Pig ill. by Ann Schweninger. Dial Pr., 1983. Subj: Animals – pigs. Family life. Sibling rivalry.

Tales of Oliver Pig ill. by Arnold Lobel. Dial, 1979. Subj: Animals – pigs. Family life.

Too hot for ice cream ill. by Martha G. Alexander. Dial Pr., 1974. ISBN 0-8037-6077-9 Subj: Behavior – bad day. Sports – swimming. Weather.

Van Liew Foster, Doris *see* Foster, Doris Van Liew

VanRynbach, Iris. *The soup stone* adapt. and ill. by Iris VanRynbach. Greenwillow, 1988. ISBN 0-688-07255-0 Subj: Careers – military. Character traits – cleverness. Folk and fairy tales. Food.

Van Stockum, Hilda. *A day on skates: the story of a Dutch picnic* ill. by author. Hale, 1934. Subj: Activities – picnicking. Foreign lands – Holland. Sports – ice skating.

Van Vorst, M. L. *A Norse lullaby* ill. by Margot Tomes. Lothrop, 1988. ISBN 0-688-05813-2 Subj: Animals. Poetry, rhyme. Seasons – winter. Sleep.

Van Woerkom, Dorothy. *Abu Ali: three tales of the Middle East* ill. by Harold Berson. Macmillan, 1976. Subj: Foreign lands – Turkey. Humor.

Alexandra the rock-eater: an old Rumanian tale retold ill. by Rosekrans Hoffman. Knopf, 1978. Subj: Dragons. Family life. Folk and fairy tales. Food. Foreign lands.

Becky and the bear ill. by Margot Tomes. Putnam's, 1975. Subj: Animals – bears. Character traits – bravery. U.S. history.

Donkey Ysabel ill. by Normand Chartier. Macmillan, 1978. Subj: Animals – donkeys. Humor.

The friends of Abu Ali: three more tales of the Middle East ill. by Harold Berson. Macmillan, 1978. Subj: Foreign lands – Turkey. Humor.

Harry and Shelburt ill. by Erick Ingraham. Macmillan, 1977. Subj: Animals – rabbits. Friendship. Reptiles – turtles, tortoises. Sports – racing.

Hidden messages ill. by Lynne Cherry. Crown, 1980. Subj: Communication. Insects. Science.

The queen who couldn't bake gingerbread ill. by Paul Galdone. Knopf, 1975. Subj: Folk and fairy tales. Foreign lands – Germany. Humor. Royalty.

The rat, the ox and the zodiac: a Chinese legend ill. by Errol Le Cain. Crown, 1976. Subj: Animals. Animals – rats. Character traits – cleverness. Folk and fairy tales. Foreign lands – China. Zodiac.

Sea frog, city frog ill. by José Aruego and Ariane Dewey. Macmillan, 1975. Subj: Folk and fairy tales. Foreign lands – Japan. Frogs and toads.

Something to crow about ill. by Paul Harvey. Albert Whitman, 1982. Subj: Birds – chickens. Family life – fathers.

Tit for tat ill. by Douglas Florian. Greenwillow, 1977. Subj: Folk and fairy tales.

Varga, Judy. *Circus cannonball* ill. by author. Morrow, 1975. Subj: Circus.

The dragon who liked to spit fire ill. by author. Morrow, 1961. Subj: Dragons. Royalty.

Janko's wish ill. by author. Morrow, 1969. Subj: Behavior – wishing. Foreign lands – Hungary. Magic. Weddings.

The mare's egg ill. by author. Morrow, 1972. Subj: Animals – foxes. Behavior – trickery. Folk and fairy tales. Foreign lands – Russia.

Miss Lollipop's lion ill. by author. Morrow, 1963. Subj: Animals – lions. Circus. Pets.

The monster behind Black Rock ill. by author. Morrow, 1971. Subj: Animals. Behavior – gossip. Cumulative tales.

Varley, Dimitry. *The whirly bird* ill. by Feodor Rojankovsky. Knopf, 1961. Subj: Birds. Character traits – kindness to animals.

Varley, Susan. *Badger's parting gifts* ill. by author. Lothrop, 1984. Subj: Animals – badgers. Death. Friendship.

Varnum, Brooke Minarik. *Play and sing - it's Christmas!*

Vasiliu, Mircea. *A day at the beach* ill. by author. Random House, 1978. ISBN 0-394-93475-X Subj: Activities – playing. Family life. Sand. Science. Sea and seashore.

Everything is somewhere ill. by author. John Day, 1970. Subj: Religion.

What's happening? ill. by author. John Day, 1970. Subj: Activities. City.

Vaughan, Eleanor K. *Timmy and the tin-can telephone* (Branley, Franklyn M.)

Vaughan, Marcia K. *Wombat stew* ill. by Pamela Lofts. ISBN 0-382-09211-2 Subj: Animals. Foreign lands – Australia. Music. Songs.

Vaughn, Jenny. *On the moon* ed. by Jenny Vaughn; Angela Grunsell, consultant; ill. by Tessa Barwick and Elsa Godfrey. Watts, 1983. ISBN 0-531-04631-1 Subj: Moon. Space and space ships. U.S. history.

Vecchio, Ellen Del *see* Del Vecchio, Ellen

Velthuijs, Max. *Little Man finds a home* ill. by author. Holt, 1985. ISBN 0-03-005734-5 Subj: Elves and little people. Houses. Weather – rain.

Little Man to the rescue ill. by author. Holt, 1986. ISBN 0-8050-0036-4 Subj: Animals – rabbits. Character traits – kindness to animals. Elves and little people. Emotions – envy, jealousy. Frogs and toads.

Little Man's lucky day tr. from German by Rosemary Lanning; ill. by author. Holt, 1986. ISBN 0-03-005847-3 Subj: Character traits – luck. Elves and little people.

The painter and the bird tr. by Ray Broekel; ill. by author. Addison-Wesley, 1975. Translation of Der Maler und der Vogel. Subj: Birds. Careers – artists. Imagination.

Venable, Alan. *The checker players* ill. by Byron Barton. Lippincott, 1973. Subj: Animals – bears. Behavior – fighting, arguing. Boats, ships. Friendship. Games. Reptiles – alligators, crocodiles.

Venino, Suzanne. *Animals helping people* ill. with photos. National Geographic Soc., 1983. Subj: Animals. Character traits – helpfulness.

Ventura, Marisa. *The painter's trick* (Ventura, Piero)

Ventura, Piero. *The painter's trick* by Piero and Marisa Ventura; ill. by Marisa Ventura. Random House, 1977. Subj: Careers – artists.

Piero Ventura's book of cities ill. by author. Random House, 1976. Subj: City.

Venturo, Betty Lou Baker *see* Baker, Betty

Vernon, Adele. *The riddle* ill. by Robert Rayevsky and Vladimir Radunsky. Dodd, 1987. ISBN 0-396-08920-8 Subj: Folk and fairy tales. Foreign lands – Spain. Royalty.

Vernon, Tannis. *Little Pig and the blue-green sea* ill. by author. Crown, 1986. ISBN 0-517-56118-2 Subj: Animals – pigs. Behavior – running away. Boats, ships. Sea and seashore.

Vesey, A. *Merry Christmas, Thomas!* ill. by author. Little, 1986. ISBN 0-87113-096-3 Subj: Animals – cats. Family life. Holidays – Christmas.

The princess and the frog ill. by author. Little, 1985. ISBN 0-87113-038-6 Subj: Character traits – willfulness. Folk and fairy tales. Frogs and toads. Royalty.

Vessel, Matthew F. *My goldfish* (Wong, Herbert H.)

My ladybug (Wong, Herbert H.)

My plant (Wong, Herbert H.)

Our caterpillars (Wong, Herbert H.)

Our earthworms (Wong, Herbert H.)

Our tree (Wong, Herbert H.)

Vevers, Gwynne. *Animal homes* ill. by Wendy Bramall. Merrimack, 1982. Subj: Animals. Houses.

Animal parents ill. by Colin Threadgall. Merrimack, 1982. Subj: Animals. Family life.

Animals of the dark ill. by Wendy Bramall. Merrimack, 1982. Subj: Animals. Night.

Animals that store food ill. by Joyce Bee. Merrimack, 1982. Subj: Animals. Food.

Animals that travel ill. by Matthew Hillier. Merrimack, 1982. Subj: Activities – traveling. Animals.

Vicarion, Palmiro Count see Logue, Christopher

Vidaure, Morris. *The invisible hunters* (Rohmer, Harriet)

Vigna, Judith. *Anyhow, I'm glad I tried* ill. by author. Albert Whitman, 1978. Subj: Behavior – misbehavior. Character traits – kindness. School.

Boot weather ed. by Ann Fay; ill. by author. Albert Whitman, 1988. ISBN 0-8075-0837-3 Subj: Activities – playing. Clothing. Imagination. Seasons – winter. Weather.

Couldn't we have a turtle instead? ill. by author. Albert Whitman, 1975. Subj: Animals. Babies. Emotions – envy, jealousy. Family life. Family life – mothers.

Daddy's new baby ill. by author. Albert Whitman, 1982. Subj: Divorce. Family life – fathers. Sibling rivalry.

Everyone goes as a pumpkin ill. by author. Albert Whitman, 1977. Subj: Family life – grandmothers. Holidays – Halloween.

Grandma without me ill. by author. Albert Whitman, 1984. Subj: Divorce. Family life – grandmothers.

The hiding house ill. by author. Albert Whitman, 1979. Subj: Behavior – hiding. Behavior – sharing. Friendship.

I wish my daddy didn't drink so much ed. by Ann Fay; ill. by author. Albert Whitman, 1988. ISBN 0-8075-3523-0 Subj: Behavior – wishing. Family life – fathers. Illness.

Mommy and me by ourselves again ill. by author. Albert Whitman, 1987. ISBN 0-8075-5232-1 Subj: Behavior – needing someone. Birthdays. Family life – mothers.

Nobody wants a nuclear war ill. by author. Albert Whitman, 1986. ISBN 0-8075-5739-0 Subj: Emotions – fear. Family life. War.

She's not my real mother ill. by author. Albert Whitman, 1980. Subj: Behavior – misbehavior. Divorce. Family life.

Villarejo, Mary. *The art fair* ill. by author. Knopf, 1960. Subj: Art.

The tiger hunt ill. by author. Knopf, 1959. Subj: Activities – photographing. Animals. Animals – tigers. Foreign lands – India.

Vincent, Gabrielle. *Bravo, Ernest and Celestine!* ill. by author. Greenwillow, 1982. Subj: Animals – bears. Animals – mice. Behavior – sharing. Money. Music.

Breakfast time, Ernest and Celestine ill. by author. Greenwillow, 1985. ISBN 0-688-04555-3 Subj: Animals – bears. Animals – mice. Behavior – misbehavior. Friendship. Wordless.

Ernest and Celestine ill. by author. Greenwillow, 1982. Subj: Animals – bears. Animals – mice. Holidays – Christmas. Toys.

Ernest and Celestine's patchwork quilt ill. by author. Greenwillow, 1985. ISBN 0-688-04577-X Subj: Animals – bears. Animals – mice. Behavior – sharing. Friendship. Wordless.

Ernest and Celestine's picnic ill. by author. Morrow, 1988, 1982. ISBN 0-688-07809-5 Subj: Activities – picnicking. Animals – bears. Animals – mice. Weather – rain.

Merry Christmas, Ernest and Celestine ill. by author. Greenwillow, 1984. ISBN 0-688-02606-0 Subj: Animals – bears. Animals – mice. Friendship. Holidays – Christmas. Parties.

Smile, Ernest and Celestine ill. by author. Greenwillow, 1982. Subj: Activities – photographing. Animals – bears. Animals – mice.

Where are you, Ernest and Celestine? ill. by author. Greenwillow, 1986. ISBN 0-688-06235-0 Subj: Animals – bears. Animals – mice. Behavior – lost. Museums.

Vinson, Pauline. *Willie goes to the seashore* ill. by author. Macmillan, 1954. Subj: Animals – mice. Sea and seashore.

Vinton, Iris. *Look out for pirates!* ill. by Herman B. Vestal. Random House, 1961. Subj: Boats, ships. Pirates.

Viorst, Judith. *Alexander and the terrible, horrible, no good, very bad day* ill. by Ray Cruz. Atheneum, 1972. Subj: Behavior – bad day. Family life.

Alexander, who used to be rich last Sunday ill. by Ray Cruz. Atheneum, 1978. Subj: Money.

The good-bye book ill. by Kay Chorao. Atheneum, 1988. ISBN 0-689-31308-X Subj: Activities – baby-sitting. Activities – reading. Imagination.

I'll fix Anthony ill. by Arnold Lobel. Harper, 1969. Subj: Family life. Sibling rivalry.

My mama says there aren't any zombies, ghosts, vampires, creatures, demons, monsters, fiends, goblins, or things ill. by Kay Chorao. Atheneum, 1973. Subj: Bedtime. Emotions – fear. Family life – mothers. Imagination. Monsters.

Rosie and Michael ill. by Lorna Tomei. Atheneum, 1974. Subj: Friendship.

Sunday morning ill. by Hilary Knight. Harper, 1968. Subj: Activities – playing. Family life. Humor.

The tenth good thing about Barney ill. by Erik Blegvad. Atheneum, 1971. Subj: Animals – cats. Death. Careers – doctors. Pets.

Try it again, Sam: safety when you walk ill. by Paul Galdone. Lothrop, 1970. Subj: Activities – walking. Character traits – individuality. Safety.

Vipont, Charles *see* Foulds, Elfrida Vipont

Vipont, Elfrida *see* Foulds, Elfrida Vipont

A visit to a pond ill. with photos. Imported Pubs., 1983. Subj: Animals. Format, unusual – board books. Wordless.

Voake, Charlotte. *First things first: a baby's companion* ill. by author. Little, 1988. ISBN 0-316-90510-0 Subj: Activities. Poetry, rhyme.

Tom's cat ill. by author. Lippincott, 1986. ISBN 0-397-32195-3 Subj: Animals – cats. Noise, sounds.

Vogel, Carole Garbuny. *The dangers of strangers* by Carole Garbuny Vogel and Kathryn Allen Goldner; ill. by Lynette Schmidt. Dillon, 1983. Subj: Behavior – talking to strangers. Safety.

Vogel, Ilse-Margaret. *The don't be scared book: scares, remedies and pictures* ill. by author. Atheneum, 1964. Subj: Emotions – fear. Imagination. Poetry, rhyme.

Von Jüchen, Aurel *see* Jüchen, Aurel von

Von Storch, Anne B. *see* Malcolmson, Anne

Von Hippel, Ursula. *The craziest Halloween* ill. by author. Coward, 1957. Subj: Holidays – Halloween.

Vreeken, Elizabeth. *The boy who would not say his name* ill. by Leonard W. Shortall. Follett, 1959. Subj: Behavior – lost. Careers – police officers. Imagination. Names.

Henry ill. by Polly Jackson. Follett, 1961. Subj: Animals – mice. Pets.

One day everything went wrong ill. by Leonard W. Shortall. Follett, 1966. Subj: Behavior – bad day.

Wabbes, Marie. *Good night, Little Rabbit* ill. by author. Little, 1987. ISBN 0-871-13127-7 Subj: Animals – rabbits. Bedtime.

Happy birthday, Little Rabbit ill. by author. Little, 1987. ISBN 0-87113-129-3 Subj: Animals – rabbits. Birthdays.

It's snowing, Little Rabbit ill. by author. Little, 1987. ISBN 0-87113-128-5 Subj: Animals – rabbits. Seasons – winter. Weather – snow.

Little Rabbit's garden ill. by author. Little, 1987. ISBN 0-871-13126-9 Subj: Activities – gardening. Animals – rabbits.

Rose is hungry ill. by author. Messner, 1988. ISBN 0-671-66611-8 Subj: Animals – pigs. Food.

Rose is muddy ill. by author. Messner, 1988. ISBN 0-671-66610-X Subj: Animals – pigs. Character traits – cleanliness.

Rose's bath ill. by author. Messner, 1988. ISBN 0-671-66612-6 Subj: Activities – bathing. Animals – pigs. Toys.

Rose's picture ill. by author. Messner, 1988. ISBN 0-671-66611-8 Subj: Activities – painting. Art. Animals – pigs.

Waber, Bernard. *An anteater named Arthur* ill. by author. Houghton, 1967. Subj: ABC books. Animals – anteaters.

Bernard ill. by author. Houghton, 1982. Subj: Animals – dogs. Behavior – running away. Behavior – sharing.

But names will never hurt me ill. by author. Houghton, 1976. Subj: Names.

Funny, funny Lyle ill. by author. Houghton, 1987. ISBN 0-395-43619-2 Subj: Behavior – misunderstanding. Family life. Reptiles – alligators, crocodiles.

How to go about laying an egg ill. by author. Houghton, 1963. Subj: Birds – chickens. Eggs. Humor.

I was all thumbs ill. by author. Houghton, 1975. Subj: Octopuses. Sea and seashore.

Ira says goodbye ill. by author. Houghton, 1988. ISBN 0-395-48315-8 Subj: Emotions. Friendship. Moving.

Ira sleeps over ill. by author. Houghton, 1972. Subj: Activities – playing. Bedtime. Friendship. Sleep. Toys – teddy bears.

Just like Abraham Lincoln ill. by author. Houghton, 1964. Subj: U.S. history.

Lorenzo ill. by author. Houghton, 1961. Subj: Character traits – curiosity. Fish.

Lovable Lyle ill. by author. Houghton, 1969. Subj: Friendship. Reptiles – alligators, crocodiles.

Lyle and the birthday party ill. by author. Houghton, 1966. Subj: Birthdays. Emotions – envy, jealousy. Reptiles – alligators, crocodiles.

Lyle finds his mother ill. by author. Houghton, 1974. Subj: Family life – mothers. Reptiles – alligators, crocodiles.

Lyle, Lyle Crocodile ill. by author. Houghton, 1965. Subj: Character traits – helpfulness. Reptiles – alligators, crocodiles.

Mice on my mind ill. by author. Houghton, 1977. Subj: Animals – cats. Animals – mice.

Nobody is perfick ill. by author. Houghton, 1971. Subj: Behavior – mistakes. Friendship. Humor.

Rich cat, poor cat ill. by author. Houghton, 1963. Subj: Animals – cats.

The snake: a very long story ill. by author. Houghton, 1978. Subj: Format, unusual. Reptiles – snakes.

"You look ridiculous," said the rhinoceros to the hippopotamus ill. by author. Houghton, 1979. ISBN 0-395-07156-9 Subj: Animals. Animals – hippopotami. Character traits – individuality. Self-concept.

You're a little kid with a big heart ill. by author. Houghton, 1980. Subj: Behavior – growing up. Behavior – wishing. Magic.

Wachter, Oralee. *Close to home* ill. by Jane Aaron. Scholastic, 1986. ISBN 0-590-40330-3 Subj: Behavior – talking to strangers. Safety.

Waddell, Helen. *The story of Saul the king* abridged by Elaine Moss from Helen Waddell's Stories from Holy Writ; ill. by Doreen Roberts. White, 1966. Subj: Religion.

Waddell, Martin. *The tough princess* ill. by Patrick Benson. Putnam's, 1987. ISBN 0-399-21380-5 Subj: Fairies. Folk and fairy tales. Royalty.

Wade, Anne. *A promise is for keeping* ill. by Jon Petersson. Children's Pr., 1979. Subj: Friendship.

Wadhams, Margaret. *Anna* ill. by Michael Charlton. Salem House, 1987. ISBN 0-370-30612-0 Subj: Character traits – being different. Illness.

Wadsworth, Olive A. *Over in the meadow: a counting-out rhyme* ill. by Mary Maki Rae. Viking, 1985. Subj: Counting. Poetry, rhyme.

Waechter, Friedrich Karl. *Three is company* tr. by Harry Allard; ill. by author. Doubleday, 1980. Subj: Animals – pigs. Birds. Fish. Friendship.

Wagner, Elaine Knox *see* Knox-Wagner, Elaine

Wagner, Jenny. *Aranea: a story about a spider* ill. by Ron Brooks. Bradbury Pr., 1978. Subj: Spiders. Weather – rain.

The bunyip of Berkeley's Creek ill. by Ron Brooks. Bradbury Pr., 1977. Subj: Foreign lands – Australia. Monsters. Mythical creatures.

John Brown, Rose and the midnight cat ill. by Ron Brooks. Bradbury Pr., 1978. Subj: Animals – cats. Animals – dogs.

Wahl, Jan. *Button eye's orange* ill. by Wendy Watson. Warne, 1980. Subj: Handicaps. Toys.

Cabbage moon ill. by Adrienne Adams. Holt, 1965. Subj: Humor. Moon. Royalty.

Carrot nose ill. by James Marshall. Farrar, 1978. Subj: Animals – rabbits.

Doctor Rabbit's foundling ill. by Cyndy Szekeres. Pantheon, 1977. Subj: Animals – rabbits. Careers – doctors. Frogs and toads.

Dracula's cat ill. by Kay Chorao. Prentice-Hall, 1978. Subj: Animals – cats. Monsters.

The fishermen ill. by Emily Arnold McCully. Norton, 1969. Subj: Family life – grandfathers. Sports – fishing.

The five in the forest ill. by Erik Blegvad. Follett, 1974. Subj: Animals – rabbits. Eggs. Forest, woods. Holidays – Easter.

Follow me cried Bee ill. by John Wallner. Crown, 1976. Subj: Cumulative tales. Insects – bees. Poetry, rhyme. Weather – rain.

Frankenstein's dog ill. by Kay Chorao. Prentice-Hall, 1977. Subj: Animals – dogs. Monsters.

Hello, elephant ill. by Edward Ardizzone. Holt, 1964. Subj: Animals – elephants.

Humphrey's bear ill. by William Joyce. Holt, 1987. ISBN 0-8050-0332-0 Subj: Bedtime. Dreams. Toys – teddy bears.

Jamie's tiger ill. by Tomie de Paola. Harcourt, 1978. Subj: Handicaps – deafness. Illness. Senses – hearing. Toys.

The Muffletump storybook ill. by Cyndy Szekeres. Follett, 1975. Subj: Toys – dolls.

The Muffletumps ill. by Edward Ardizzone. Holt, 1966. Subj: Toys – dolls.

The Muffletumps' Christmas party ill. by Cyndy Szekeres. Follett, 1975. Subj: Holidays – Christmas. Toys – dolls.

The Muffletumps' Halloween scare ill. by Cyndy Szekeres. Follett, 1977. Subj: Toys – dolls.

Old Hippo's Easter egg ill. by Lorinda Bryan Cauley. Harcourt, 1980. Subj: Animals – hippopotami. Animals – mice. Birds – ducks. Emotions – love. Family life.

Peter and the troll baby ill. by Erik Blegvad. Golden Pr., 1984. Subj: Activities – baby-sitting. Sibling rivalry. Trolls.

Pleasant Fieldmouse ill. by Maurice Sendak. Harper, 1964. Subj: Animals. Animals – mice.

The Pleasant Fieldmouse storybook ill. by Erik Blegvad. Prentice-Hall, 1977. Subj: Animals. Animals – mice.

Pleasant Fieldmouse's Halloween party ill. by Wallace Tripp. Putnam, 1974. Subj: Animals. Animals – mice. Holidays – Halloween.

Push Kitty ill. by Garth Williams. Harper, 1968. Subj: Activities – playing. Animals – cats.

Rabbits on roller skates! ill. by David Allender. Crown, 1986. ISBN 0-517-55935-8 Subj: Animals – rabbits. Poetry, rhyme. Sports – roller skating.

Sylvester Bear overslept ill. by Lee Lorenz. Parents, 1979. Subj: Animals – bears. Circus. Family life. Sleep.

Tiger watch ill. by Charles Mikolaycak. Harcourt, 1982. Subj: Animals – tigers. Death. Foreign lands – India. Sports – hunting.

The toy circus ill. by Tim Bowers. Harcourt, 1986. ISBN 0-15-200609-5 Subj: Circus. Dreams. Sleep. Toys.

The woman with the eggs (Andersen, H. C. (Hans Christian))

Wakefield, Joyce. *Ask a silly question* ill. by Mike Venezia. Children's Pr., 1979. Subj: Poetry, rhyme. Riddles.

From where you are ill. by Tom Dunnington. Children's Pr., 1978. Subj: Concepts – perspective. Poetry, rhyme.

Walker, Alice. *To hell with dying* ill. by Catherine Deeter. Harcourt, 1987. ISBN 0-15-289075-0 Subj: Death. Ethnic groups in the U.S. – Afro-Americans. Friendship.

Walker, Barbara K. *New patches for old: a Turkish folktale* retold by Barbara K. Walker and Ahmet E. Uysal; ill. by Harold Berson. Parents, 1974. Subj: Behavior – mistakes. Folk and fairy tales.

Pigs and pirates: a Greek tale ill. by Harold Berson. White, 1969. Subj: Animals – pigs. Foreign lands – Greece. Pirates.

Teeny-Tiny and the witch-woman ill. by Michael Foreman. Pantheon, 1975. Subj: Character traits – cleverness. Foreign lands – Turkey. Witches.

Walker, Barbara Kerlin *see* Walker, Barbara K.

Wallace, Barbara Brooks. *Argyle* ill. by John Sandford. Abingdon, 1987. ISBN 0-687-01724-6 Subj: Animals – sheep. Character traits – being different.

Wallace, Daisy. *Fairy poems* ill. by Trina Schart Hyman. Holiday, 1980. ISBN 0-8234-0371-8 Subj: Fairies. Poetry, rhyme.

Ghost poems ill. by Tomie de Paola. Holiday, 1979. Subj: Ghosts. Night. Poetry, rhyme.

Giant poems ill. by Margot Tomes. Holiday, 1978. ISBN 0-8234-0326-2 Subj: Giants. Poetry, rhyme.

Monster poems ill. by Kay Chorao. Holiday, 1976. ISBN 0-8234-0268-1 Subj: Monsters. Poetry, rhyme.

Witch poems

Wallace, Ian. *Chin Chiang and the dragon's dance* ill. by author. Atheneum, 1984. Subj: Emotions – fear. Ethnic groups in the U.S. – Chinese-Americans. Family life – grandfathers. Holidays – Chinese New Year.

Morgan the magnificent ill. by author. Macmillan, 1988. ISBN 0-689-50441-1 Subj: Angels. Behavior – misbehavior. Circus.

The sparrow's song ill. by author. Viking, 1987. ISBN 0-670-81453-9 Subj: Behavior – misbehavior. Birds – sparrows. Character traits – kindness to animals. Death.

Wallace, Ruby Ann *see* Dee, Ruby

Wallas, Ada. *Clean Peter and the children of Grubbylea* (Adelborg, Ottilia)

Wallner, Alexandra. *Munch* ill. by author. Crown, 1976. Subj: Food. Poetry, rhyme.

Wallner, John. *Look and find* ill. by author. Putnam's, 1988. ISBN 0-448-19068-0 Subj: Concepts.

Old MacDonald had a farm: a musical pop-up book ill. by author. Dutton, 1986. ISBN 0-525-44279-0 Subj: Animals. Cumulative tales. Farms. Format, unusual – toy and movable books. Music. Songs.

Sleeping Beauty (Grimm, Jacob)

Walsh, Ellen Stoll. *Mouse paint* ill. by author. Harcourt, 1989. ISBN 0-15-256025-4 Subj: Activities – painting. Animals – mice. Behavior – hiding.

Walsh, Grahame L. *Didane the koala* ill. by John Morrison. Univ. of Queensland Pr., 1986. ISBN 0-7022-1889-8 Subj: Animals – koala bears. Folk and fairy tales. Foreign lands – Australia.

The goori goori bird ill. by John Morrison. Univ. of Queensland Pr., 1986. ISBN 0-7022-1777-8 Subj: Birds. Folk and fairy tales. Foreign lands – Australia.

Walsh, Jill Paton. *Lost and found* ill. by Mary Rayner. Deutsch (dist. by Dutton), 1985. Subj: Behavior – losing things. Character traits – luck. Family life – grandfathers.

Walt Disney Productions. *Tod and Copper.* Random House, 1981. Subj: Animals – dogs. Animals – foxes.

Tod and Vixey. Random House, 1981. Subj: Animals – dogs. Animals – foxes.

Walt Disney's Snow White and the seven dwarfs. Viking, 1979. Subj: Elves and little people. Emotions – envy, jealousy. Folk and fairy tales. Magic. Witches.

Walt Disney's The adventures of Mr. Toad. Random House, 1981. Subj: Animals – moles. Animals – rats. Frogs and toads.

Walter, Dorothy Blake *see* Ross, Katharine

Walter, Mildred Pitts. *Brother to the wind* ill. by Leo and Diane Dillon. Lothrop, 1985. ISBN 0-688-03811-5 Subj: Activities – flying. Foreign lands – Africa.

My mama needs me ill. by Pat Cummings. Lothrop, 1983. Subj: Emotions – loneliness. Ethnic groups in the U.S. – Afro-Americans. Family life.

Ty's one-man band ill. by Margot Tomes. Four Winds Pr., 1980. ISBN 0-02-792300-2 Subj: Folk and fairy tales. Music.

Walter, Villiam Christian *see* Andersen, H. C. (Hans Christian)

Walters, Marguerite. *The city-country ABC: My alphabet walk in the country, and My alphabet ride in the city* ill. by Ib Spang Olsen. Doubleday, 1966. The two stories are bound dos-á-dos. Subj: ABC books. City. Country. Format, unusual.

Walton, Ann. *Dumb clucks!* (Walton, Rick)

Something's fishy! (Walton, Rick)

Walton, Rick. *Dumb clucks! jokes about chickens* by Rick and Ann Walton; ill. by Joan Hanson. Lerner, 1987. ISBN 0-8225-0991-1 Subj: Birds – chickens. Riddles.

Something's fishy! jokes about sea creatures by Rick and Ann Walton; ill. by Joan Hanson. Lerner, 1987. ISBN 0-8225-0993-8 Subj: Fish. Riddles.

Wandelmaier, Roy. *Clouds* ill. by John Jones. Troll Assoc., 1985. ISBN 0-8167-0338-8 Subj: Weather – clouds. Weather – rain.

Stars ill. by Irene Trivas. Troll Assoc., 1985. ISBN 0-8167-0339-6 Subj: Science. Stars.

Warbler, J. M. *see* Cocagnac, A. M. (Augustin Maurice)

Ward, Andrew. *Baby bear and the long sleep* ill. by John Walsh. Little, 1980. Subj: Animals – bears. Hibernation. Seasons – winter.

Ward, Cindy. *Cookie's week* ill. by Tomie de Paola. Putnam's, 1988. ISBN 0-399-21498-4 Subj: Animals – cats. Behavior – misbehavior. Days of the week, months of the year.

Ward, Leila. *I am eyes, ni macho* ill. by Nonny Hogrogian. Greenwillow, 1978. Subj: Foreign lands – Africa. Nature.

Ward, Lynd. *The biggest bear* ill. by author. Houghton, 1952. Subj: Animals – bears. Caldecott award book. Character traits – kindness to animals. Foreign lands – Canada. Pets.

The little red lighthouse and the great gray bridge (Swift, Hildegarde Hoyt)

Nic of the woods ill. by author. Houghton, 1965. Subj: Animals. Animals – dogs. Foreign lands – Canada. Forest, woods.

The silver pony ill. by author. Houghton, 1973. Subj: Animals – horses. Dreams. Wordless.

Ward, May McNeer *see* McNeer, May Yonge

Ward, Nanda Weedon. *The black sombrero* ill. by Lynd Ward. Ariel, 1952. Subj: Animals. Clothing. Cowboys.

The elephant that ga-lumphed by Nanda Weedon Ward and Robert Haynes; ill. by Robert Haynes. Ariel, 1959. Subj: Animals. Animals – elephants. Foreign lands – India.

Ward, Nick. *Giant.* Oxford Univ. Pr., 1983. Subj: Behavior – misbehavior. Giants. Toys.

Ward, Sally G. *Charlie and Grandma* ill. by author. Scholastic, 1986. ISBN 0-590-33954-0 Subj: Behavior – misbehavior. Family life –.grandmothers.

Molly and Grandpa ill. by author. Scholastic, 1986. ISBN 0-590-33955-9 Subj: Character traits – persistence. Family life – grandfathers. Food.

Warren, Cathy. *Fred's first day* ill. by Pat Cummings. Lothrop, 1984. ISBN 0-688-03814-X Subj: Friendship. School.

Saturday belongs to Sara ill. by DyAnne DiSalvo-Ryan. Bradbury Pr., 1988. ISBN 0-02-792491-2 Subj: Character traits – kindness. Family life – mothers.

Springtime bears ill. by Pat Cummings. Lothrop, 1987. ISBN 0-688-05906-6 Subj: Animals – bears. Behavior – hiding. Seasons – spring.

The ten-alarm camp-out ill. by Steven Kellogg. Lothrop, 1983. Subj: Counting. Sports – camping.

Warren, Elizabeth *see* Supraner, Robyn

Warshofsky, Isaac *see* Singer, Isaac Bashevis

Wasmuth, Eleanor. *An alligator day* ill. by author. Grosset, 1983. Subj: Activities – playing. Reptiles – alligators, crocodiles.

The picnic basket ill. by author. Grosset, 1983. Subj: Activities – picnicking. Food. Reptiles – alligators, crocodiles.

Wasserberg, Esther. *Grandmother dear* (Finfer, Celentha)

Wasson, Valentina Pavlovna. *The chosen baby* ill. by Glo Coalson. 3rd ed. Harper, 1977. ISBN 0-397-31738-7 Subj: Adoption.

Watanabe, Shigeo. *Daddy, play with me!* ill. by Yasuo Ohtomo. Putnam's, 1985. ISBN 0-399-21211-6 Subj: Activities – playing. Animals – bears. Family life – fathers.

How do I put it on? ill. by Yasuo Ohtomo. Putnam's, 1979. Subj: Animals – bears. Clothing. Participation.

I can build a house! ill. by Yasuo Ohtomo. Philomel, 1983. ISBN 0-399-20950-6 Subj: Activities – playing. Animals – bears. Character traits – perseverance. Houses.

I can ride it! ill. by Yasuo Ohtomo. Putnam's, 1982. Subj: Activities – playing. Animals – bears. Character traits – perseverance.

I can take a bath! ill. by Yasuo Ohtomo. Putnam's, 1987. ISBN 0-399-21362-7 Subj: Activities – bathing. Animals – bears. Family life – fathers.

I can take a walk! ill. by Yasuo Ohtomo. Putnam's, 1984. Subj: Activities – walking. Animals – bears.

I'm the king of the castle! ill. by Yasuo Ohtomo. Putnam's, 1982. Subj: Activities – playing. Animals – bears. Sand.

It's my birthday ill. by Yasuo Ohtomo. Putnam's, 1988. ISBN 0-399-21492-5 Subj: Animals – bears. Birthdays. Family life – grandparents.

What a good lunch! ill. by Yasuo Ohtomo. Collins-World, 1980. Subj: Animals – bears. Food. Humor.

Where's my daddy? ill. by Yasuo Ohtomo. Philomel, 1982. ISBN 0-399-20899-2 Subj: Animals – bears. Behavior – lost. Character traits – perseverance. Family life – fathers.

Watanabe, Yuichi. *Wally the whale who loved balloons* tr. from Japanese by D. T. Ooka; ill. by author. Heian, 1982. Subj: Animals – whales. Behavior – misbehavior. Toys – balloons.

Waterton, Betty. *Pettranella* ill. by Ann Blades. Vanguard, 1981. ISBN 0-8149-0844-6 Subj: Family life – grandmothers. Foreign lands – Canada. Seasons – spring.

A salmon for Simon ill. by Ann Blades. Atheneum, 1980. Subj: Character traits – kindness to animals. Sports – fishing.

Watson, Carol. *Æsop's fables* (Æsop)

Opposites ill. by David Higham. Usborne, 1983. Subj: Concepts – opposites.

Shapes ill. by David Higham. Usborne, 1983. Subj: Concepts – shape.

Sizes ill. by David Higham. Usborne, 1983. Subj: Concepts – size.

Watson, Clyde. *Applebet: an ABC* ill. by Wendy Watson. Farrar, 1982. Subj: ABC books. Poetry, rhyme.

Catch me and kiss me and say it again ill. by Wendy Watson. Collins-World, 1978. Subj: Family life. Poetry, rhyme.

Father Fox's feast of songs ill. by Wendy Watson. Putnam's, 1983. Subj: Animals – foxes. Music. Poetry, rhyme.

Father Fox's pennyrhymes ill. by Wendy Watson. Crowell, 1971. Subj: Nursery rhymes.

Fisherman lullabies ed. and ill. by Wendy Watson; music by Clyde Watson. Collins-World, 1968. Subj: Bedtime. Music. Songs.

Hickory stick rag ill. by Wendy Watson. Crowell, 1976. Subj: Activities – picnicking. Humor. Poetry, rhyme. School.

How Brown Mouse kept Christmas ill. by Wendy Watson. Farrar, 1980. Subj: Animals – mice. Holidays – Christmas.

Midnight moon ill. by Susanna Natti. Collins-World, 1979. Subj: Activities – flying. Bedtime. Imagination. Moon.

Tom Fox and the apple pie ill. by Wendy Watson. Crowell, 1972. Subj: Animals – foxes. Behavior – sharing. Fairs. Food.

Valentine foxes ill. by Wendy Watson. Watts, 1988. ISBN 0-531-08400-0 Subj: Animals – foxes. Family life. Food. Holidays – Valentine's Day.

Watson, Jane Werner. *My friend the babysitter* by Jane Werner Watson, Robert E. Switzer and J. Cotter Hirschberg; ill. by Hilde Hoffmann. Golden Pr., 1971. Subj: Activities – baby-sitting.

My friend the dentist by Jane Werner Watson, Robert E. Switzer and J. Cotter Hirschberg; ill. by Cat Bowman Smith. Crown, 1987. ISBN 0-517-56485-X Subj: Careers – dentists. Health.

My friend the doctor by Jane Werner Watson, Robert E. Switzer and J. Cotter Hirschberg; ill. by Cat Bowman Smith. Crown, 1987. ISBN 0-517-56485-8 Subj: Careers – doctors. Health.

Sometimes a family has to move by Jane Werner Watson, Robert E. Switzer and J. Cotter Hirschberg; ill. by Cat Bowman Smith. Crown, 1988. ISBN 0-517-56593-5 Subj: Family life. Moving.

Sometimes a family has to split up by Jane Werner Watson, Robert E. Switzer and J. Cotter Hirschberg; ill. by Cat Bowman Smith. Crown, 1988. ISBN 0-517-56811-X Subj: Divorce. Family life.

Sometimes I get angry by Jane Werner Watson, Robert E. Switzer and J. Cotter Hirschberg; ill. by Hilde Hoffmann. Golden Pr., 1971. Subj: Emotions – anger.

Sometimes I'm afraid by Jane Werner Watson, Robert E. Switzer and J. Cotter Hirschberg; ill. by Hilde Hoffmann. Golden Pr., 1971. Subj: Emotions – fear.

Sometimes I'm jealous by Jane Werner Watson, Robert E. Switzer and J. Cotter Hirschberg; ill. by Irene Trivas. Crown, 1986. ISBN 0-517-56062-3 Subj: Emotions – envy, jealousy.

The tall book of make-believe ill. by Garth Williams. Harper, 1950. Subj: Imagination. Poetry, rhyme.

Which is the witch? ill. by Victoria Chess. Pantheon, 1979. Subj: Holidays – Halloween. Witches.

Watson, Nancy Dingman. *The birthday goat* ill. by Wendy Watson. Crowell, 1974. Subj: Animals – goats. Birthdays. Crime. Fairs.

Sugar on snow ill. by Aldren Auld Watson. Viking, 1964. Subj: Food. Weather – snow.

Tommy's mommy's fish ill. by Aldren Auld Watson. Viking, 1971. Subj: Birthdays. Family life – mothers. Sports – fishing.

What does A begin with? ill. by Aldren Auld Watson. Knopf, 1956. Subj: ABC books. Farms.

What is one? ill. by Aldren Auld Watson. Knopf, 1954. Subj: Counting. Farms.

When is tomorrow? ill. by Aldren Auld Watson. Knopf, 1955. Subj: Sea and seashore. Time.

Watson, Pauline. *Curley Cat baby-sits* ill. by Lorinda Bryan Cauley. Harcourt, 1977. Subj: Activities – baby-sitting. Animals – cats.

Days with Daddy ill. by Joanne Scribner. Prentice-Hall, 1977. Subj: Family life. Family life – fathers.

The walking coat ill. by Tomie de Paola. Walker, 1980. ISBN 0-8027-6351-0 Subj: Clothing.

Wriggles, the little wishing pig ill. by Paul Galdone. Seabury Pr., 1978. Subj: Animals – pigs. Behavior – wishing. Monsters.

Watson, Richard Jesse. *Tom Thumb* (Tom Thumb)

Watson, Wendy. *The bunnies' Christmas eve* ill. by author. Putnam's, 1983. Subj: Animals – rabbits. Format, unusual. Holidays – Christmas.

Fisherman lullabies (Watson, Clyde)

Has winter come? ill. by author. Collins-World, 1978. Subj: Animals – groundhogs. Hibernation. Seasons – winter.

Lollipop ill. by author. Crowell, 1976. Subj: Animals – rabbits. Behavior – misbehavior.

Moving ill. by author. Crowell, 1978. Subj: Moving.

Tales for a winter's eve ill. by author. Farrar, 1988. ISBN 0-374-37373-6 Subj: Animals – foxes. Illness. Seasons – winter.

Watts, Barrie. *Apple tree* photos. by author. Silver Burdett, 1987. ISBN 0-382-09436-0 Subj: Nature. Science. Trees.

Bird's nest photos. by author. Silver Burdett, 1987. ISBN 0-382-09439-5 Subj: Animals. Birds. Science.

Butterfly and caterpillar photos. by author. Silver Burdett, 1986. ISBN 0-382-09282-1 Subj: Insects – butterflies, caterpillars. Science.

Dandelion photos. by author. Silver Burdett, 1987. ISBN 0-382-09438-7 Subj: Plants. Science.

Hamster photos. by author. Silver Burdett, 1986. ISBN 0-382-09281-3 Subj: Animals – hamsters. Science.

Ladybug photos. by author. Silver Burdett, 1987. ISBN 0-382-09437-9 Subj: Insects – ladybugs. Science.

Mushrooms photos. by author. Silver Burdett, 1986. ISBN 0-382-09287-2 Subj: Plants. Science.

Watts, Bernadette. *David's waiting day* ill. by author. Prentice-Hall, 1978. Subj: Babies. Family life.

Goldilocks and the three bears (The three bears)

Green is beautiful (Rogers, Margaret)

Rapunzel (Grimm, Jacob)

St. Francis and the proud crow ill. by author. Watts, 1988. ISBN 0-531-08358-6 Subj: Behavior – seeking better things. Folk and fairy tales.

Snow White and Rose Red (Grimm, Jacob)

Watts, Helen Hoke see Hoke, Helen L.

Watts, Mabel. *The day it rained watermelons* ill. by Lee Albertson. Lantern Pr., 1964. Subj: Behavior – indifference.

Something for you, something for me ill. by Abner Graboff. Abelard-Schuman, 1960. Subj: Activities – trading. Behavior – sharing.

Weeks and weeks ill. by Abner Graboff. Abelard-Schuman, 1962. Subj: Activities – photographing.

Watts, Mabel Pizzey see Watts, Mabel

Watts, Marjorie-Ann. *Crocodile medicine* ill. by author. Warne, 1978. Subj: Behavior – boredom. Hospitals. Illness. Reptiles – alligators, crocodiles.

Crocodile plaster ill. by author. Dutton, 1984. ISBN 0-233-96962-4 Subj: Hospitals. Illness. Reptiles – alligators, crocodiles.

Zebra goes to school ill. by author. Elsevier-Dutton, 1981. Subj: Imagination – imaginary friends. School.

Wayland, April Halprin. *To Rabbittown* ill. by Robin Spowart. Scholastic, 1989. ISBN 0-590-40852-6 Subj: Animals – rabbits. Imagination. Pets.

We wish you a merry Christmas: *a traditional Christmas carol* ill. by Tracey Campbell Pearson. Dial Pr., 1983. ISBN 0-8037-9400-2 Subj: Behavior – misbehavior. Holidays – Christmas. Songs.

Weary, Ogdred see Gorey, Edward

Weatherill, Stephen. *The very first Lucy Goose book* ill. by author. Prentice-Hall, 1987. ISBN 0-13-941410-X Subj: Birds. Birds – geese. Humor.

Weaver, Harriet Shaw see Wright, Josephine Lord

Webb, Angela. *Air* photos. by Chris Fairclough. Watts, 1987. ISBN 0-531-10369-2 Subj: Science.

Light photos. by Chris Fairclough. Watts, 1988. ISBN 0-531-10455-9 Subj: Concepts. Science.

Reflections photos. by Chris Fairclough. Watts, 1988. ISBN 0-531-10457-5 Subj: Concepts. Science.

Sand photos. by Chris Fairclough. Watts, 1987. ISBN 0-531-10370-6 Subj: Sand. Science.

Soil photos. by Chris Fairclough. Watts, 1987. ISBN 0-531-10371-4 Subj: Science.

Sound photos. by Chris Fairclough. Watts, 1988. ISBN 0-531-10456-7 Subj: Concepts. Noise, sounds. Science.

Water photos. by Chris Fairclough. Watts, 1987. ISBN 0-531-10372-2 Subj: Science.

Webb, Clifford. *The story of Noah* ill. by author. Warne, 1949. Subj: Religion – Noah.

Weber, Alfons. *Elizabeth gets well* ill. by Jacqueline Blass. Crowell, 1970. Translation of Elisabeth wird gesund. Subj: Hospitals. Illness.

The weekend ill. by Roser Capdevila. Firefly Pr., 1986. ISBN 0-920303-44-7 Subj: Activities – picnicking. Country. Sea and seashore.

Weelen, Guy. *The little red train* ill. by Mamoru Funai. Lothrop, 1966. Subj: Foreign lands – France. Trains.

Wegen, Ron. *The balloon trip* ill. by author. Houghton, 1981. Subj: Activities – ballooning. Family life. Wordless.

Billy Gorilla ill. by author. Lothrop, 1983. Subj: Behavior – trickery. Holidays – April Fools' Day.

The Halloween costume party ill. by author. Houghton, 1983. Subj: Holidays – Halloween. Parties.

Sand castle ill. by author. Greenwillow, 1977. Subj: Sea and seashore.

Sky dragon ill. by author. Greenwillow, 1982. Subj: Weather – clouds.

Where can the animals go? ill. by author. Greenwillow, 1978. Subj: Animals. Ecology.

Weihs, Erika. *Count the cats* ill. by author. Doubleday, 1976. Subj: Animals – cats. Counting.

Weil, Ann. *Animal families* ill. by Roger Vernam. Children's Pr., 1956. Subj: Animals.

Weil, Lisl. *The candy egg bunny* ill. by author. Holiday, 1975. Subj: Animals – rabbits. Holidays – Easter. Witches.

Gertie and Gus ill. by author. Parents, 1977. Subj: Careers – fishermen. Family life.

Gillie and the flattering fox ill. by author. Atheneum, 1978. Subj: Animals – foxes. Birds – chickens. Friendship.

Let's go to the circus ill. by author. Holiday, 1988. ISBN 0-8234-0693-8 Subj: Circus.

Mother Goose picture riddles: a book of rebuses ill. by author. Holiday, 1981. Subj: Nursery rhymes. Rebuses.

Owl and other scrambles ill. by author. Dutton, 1980. Subj: Games. Participation.

Pandora's box ill. by adapt. Atheneum, 1986. ISBN 0-689-31216-4 Subj: Character traits – curiosity. Folk and fairy tales.

Santa Claus around the world ill. by author. Holiday, 1987. ISBN 0-8234-0665-2 Subj: Holidays – Christmas.

The story of the Wise Men and the Child ill. by author. Atheneum, 1981. Subj: Holidays – Christmas. Religion.

To sail a ship of treasures ill. by author. Atheneum, 1984. Subj: Behavior – collecting things.

The very first story ever told ill. by author. Atheneum, 1976. Subj: Religion.

Weilerstein, Sadie Rose. *The best of K'tonton* ill. by Marilyn Hirsh. Jewish Pub. Soc., 1980. Subj: Jewish culture.

Weinberg, Florence. *Grandmother dear* (Finfer, Celentha)

Weinberg, Lawrence. *The Forgetful Bears* ill. by Paula Winter. Houghton, 1982. ISBN 0-89919-068-5 Subj: Animals – bears. Behavior – forgetfulness.

The Forgetful Bears meet Mr. Memory ill. by author. Scholastic, 1987. ISBN 0-590-40781-3 Subj: Animals – bears. Animals – elephants. Behavior – forgetfulness.

Weiner, Beth Lee. *Benjamin's perfect solution* ill. by author. Warner, 1979. Subj: Animals – porcupines. Animals – possums. Behavior – mistakes. Self-concept.

Weisgard, Leonard. *The funny bunny factory* ill. by author. Grosset, 1950. Subj: Animals – rabbits. Holidays – Easter.

Mr. Peaceable paints ill. by author. Scribner's, 1956. Subj: Activities – painting. Careers – artists.

Silly Willy Nilly ill. by author. Scribner's, 1953. Subj: Animals – elephants. Behavior – forgetfulness.

Who dreams of cheese? ill. by author. Scribner's, 1950. Subj: Behavior – wishing. Dreams. Sleep.

Weiss, Edna *see* Barth, Edna

Weiss, Ellen. *Clara the fortune-telling chicken* ill. by author. Dutton, 1978. Subj: Animals – sheep. Birds – chickens. Careers – fortune tellers. Seasons – winter.

Millicent Maybe ill. by author. Watts, 1979. Subj: Reptiles – alligators, crocodiles.

Mokey's birthday present ill. by Elizabeth Miles. Holt, 1985. ISBN 0-03-004559-2 Subj: Birthdays. Friendship. Puppets.

Pigs in space ill. by Alastair Graham. Random House, 1983. Subj: Animals – pigs. Puppets. Space and space ships.

The pirates of Tarnoonga ed. by Stephanie Spinner; ill. by Bunny Carter. Random House, 1986. ISBN 0-394-87926-0 Subj: Pirates.

Telephone time: a first book of telephone do's and don'ts ill. by Hilary Knight. Random House, 1986. ISBN 0-394-98252-5 Subj: Etiquette. Telephone.

Things to make and do for Christmas ill. by author. Watts, 1980. Subj: Holidays – Christmas.

You are the star of a Muppet adventure ill. by Benjamin Alexander. Random House, 1983. Subj: Puppets.

Weiss, Harvey. *My closet full of hats* ill. by author. Abelard-Schuman, 1962. Subj: Clothing.

The sooner hound: a tale from American folklore ill. by author. Putnam's, 1959. Subj: Animals – dogs. Careers – firefighters. Folk and fairy tales.

Weiss, Leatie. *Funny feet!* ill. by Ellen Weiss. Watts, 1978. Subj: Anatomy. Birds – penguins. Clothing.

My teacher sleeps in school ill. by Ellen Weiss. Warne, 1984. ISBN 0-7232-6253-5 Subj: Animals – elephants. Careers – teachers. School.

Weiss, Miriam *see* Schlein, Miriam

Weiss, Nicki. *Barney is big* ill. by author. Greenwillow, 1988. ISBN 0-688-07587-8 Subj: Behavior – growing up. Family life. School.

Battle day at Camp Delmont ill. by author. Greenwillow, 1985. ISBN 0-688-04307-0 Subj: Friendship. Sports – camping.

A family story ill. by author. Greenwillow, 1987. ISBN 0-688-06505-8 Subj: Family life – sisters. Friendship.

If you're happy and you know it ill. by author. Greenwillow, 1987. ISBN 0-688-06444-2 Subj: Folk and fairy tales. Music. Songs.

Maude and Sally ill. by author. Greenwillow, 1983. Subj: Friendship.

Princess Pearl ill. by author. Greenwillow, 1986. ISBN 0-688-05895-7 Subj: Family life – sisters. Sibling rivalry.

Waiting ill. by author. Greenwillow, 1981. Subj: Character traits – patience.

Weekend at Muskrat Lake ill. by author. Greenwillow, 1984. Subj: Activities – vacationing. Family life.

Weissmann, Joe. *Hickory dickory duck* (Patterson, Pat)

Welber, Robert. *Goodbye, hello* ill. by Cyndy Szekeres. Pantheon, 1974. Subj: Animals. Behavior – growing up. Poetry, rhyme. School.

Song of the seasons ill. by Deborah Kogan Ray. Pantheon, 1973. Subj: Seasons.

Welch, Martha McKeen. *Will that wake mother?* photos. by author. Dodd, 1982. Subj: Animals – cats.

Wellington, Anne. *Apple pie* ill. by Nita Sowter. Prentice-Hall, 1978. Subj: Seasons.

Wells, H. G. (Herbert George). *The adventures of Tommy* ill. by author. Knopf, 1967. Subj: Animals – elephants. Character traits – bravery. Character traits – kindness.

Wells, Rosemary. *Abdul* ill. by author. Dial Pr., 1986. ISBN 0-8037-4462-5 Subj: Animals – camels. Animals – horses. Character traits – being different.

Don't spill it again, James ill. by author. Dial Pr., 1977. Subj: Animals – foxes. Poetry, rhyme. Trains. Weather – rain.

Forest of dreams by Rosemary Wells and Susan Jeffers; ill. by Susan Jeffers. Dial Pr., 1988. ISBN 0-8037-0570-0 Subj: Nature. Seasons – spring. Seasons – winter.

Good night, Fred ill. by author. Dial Pr., 1981. Subj: Behavior – misbehavior. Imagination. Sibling rivalry.

Hazel's amazing mother ill. by author. Dial Pr., 1985. ISBN 0-8037-0210-8 Subj: Animals. Animals – badgers. Behavior – misbehavior. Family life – mothers.

Hooray for Max ill. by author. Dial Pr., 1986. ISBN 0-8037-0202-7 Subj: Animals – rabbits. Format, unusual – board books.

A lion for Lewis ill. by author. Dial Pr., 1982. Subj: Activities – playing. Imagination.

Max's bath ill. by author. Dial Pr., 1985. ISBN 0-8037-0162-4 Subj: Activities – bathing. Animals – rabbits. Format, unusual – board books.

Max's bedtime ill. by author. Dial Pr., 1985. ISBN 0-8037-0160-8 Subj: Animals – rabbits. Bedtime. Format, unusual – board books. Sibling rivalry. Toys.

Max's birthday ill. by author. Dial Pr., 1985. ISBN 0-8037-0163-2 Subj: Animals – rabbits. Birthdays. Format, unusual – board books. Toys.

Max's breakfast ill. by author. Dial Pr., 1985. Subj: Animals – rabbits. Character traits – patience. Format, unusual – board books. Sibling rivalry.

Max's chocolate chicken ill. by author. Dial Pr., 1988. ISBN 0-8037-0585-9 Subj: Holidays – Easter. Seasons – spring. Sibling rivalry.

Max's Christmas ill. by author. Dial Pr., 1986. ISBN 0-8037-0290-6 Subj: Animals – rabbits. Holidays – Christmas.

Max's first word ill. by author. Dial Pr., 1979. ISBN 0-8037-6066-3 Subj: Animals – rabbits. Format, unusual – board books. Language.

Max's new suit ill. by author. Dial Pr., 1979. Subj: Animals – rabbits. Clothing. Format, unusual – board books.

Max's ride ill. by author. Dial Pr., 1979. ISBN 0-8037-6069-8 Subj: Animals – rabbits. Format, unusual – board books. Language.

Max's toys: a counting book ill. by author. Dial Pr., 1979. ISBN 0-8037-6068-X Subj: Animals – rabbits. Counting. Format, unusual – board books. Toys.

Noisy Nora ill. by author. Dial Pr., 1973. Subj: Animals – mice. Behavior – needing someone. Poetry, rhyme.

Peabody ill. by author. Dial Pr., 1983. Subj: Sibling rivalry. Toys – dolls.

Shy Charles ill. by author. Dial Pr., 1988. ISBN 0-8037-0564-6 Subj: Activities – baby-sitting. Animals – mice. Character traits – individuality. Family life. Poetry, rhyme.

Stanley and Rhoda ill. by author. Dial Pr., 1978. Subj: Activities – baby-sitting. Animals – mice. Sibling rivalry.

Timothy goes to school ill. by author. Dial Pr., 1981. Subj: Animals – raccoons. Behavior – growing up. School.

Unfortunately Harriet ill. by author. Dial Pr., 1972. Subj: Behavior – bad day.

Wende, Philip. *Bird boy* ill. by author. Cowles, 1970. Subj: Activities – flying. Dreams.

Wenning, Elisabeth. *The Christmas mouse* ill. by Barbara Remington. Holt, 1959. Subj: Animals – mice. Holidays – Christmas. Music. Songs.

Werner, Jane *see* Watson, Jane Werner

Wersba, Barbara. *Amanda dreaming* ill. by Mercer Mayer. Atheneum, 1973. Subj: Dreams. Sleep.

Do tigers ever bite kings? ill. by Mario Rivoli. Atheneum, 1966. Subj: Animals – tigers. Character traits – kindness to animals. Poetry, rhyme. Royalty.

West, Colin. *Have you seen the crocodile?* ill. by author. Lippincott, 1986. ISBN 0-397-32172-4 Subj: Birds. Cumulative tales. Reptiles – alligators, crocodiles.

I brought my love a tabby cat ill. by Caroline Anstey. Chronicle, 1988. ISBN 0-87701-518-X Subj: Animals. Careers – tailors. Clothing. Weddings.

The king of Kennelwick castle ill. by Anne Dalton. Lippincott, 1987. ISBN 0-397-32197-X Subj: Cumulative tales. Royalty.

The king's toothache ill. by Anne Dalton. Lippincott, 1988. ISBN 0-397-32252-6 Subj: Cumulative tales. Illness. Poetry, rhyme. Royalty. Teeth.

A moment in rhyme ill. by Julie Banyard. Dial Pr., 1987. ISBN 0-8037-0259-0 Subj: Poetry, rhyme.

"Pardon?" said the giraffe ill. by author. Lippincott, 1986. ISBN 0-397-32173-2 Subj: Animals. Character traits – persistence. Frogs and toads.

West, Emily *see* Payne, Emmy

West, Ian. *Silas, the first pig to fly* ill. by author. Grosset, 1977. Subj: Activities – flying. Animals – pigs.

West, James *see* Withers, Carl

Westcott, Nadine Bernard. *Getting up* ill. by author. Little, 1987. ISBN 0-316-93131-4 Subj: Family life. Morning.

The giant vegetable garden ill. by author. Little, 1981. Subj: Activities – gardening. Activities – picnicking.

Going to bed ill. by author. Little, 1987. ISBN 0-316-93132-2 Subj: Bedtime. Family life. Night. Toys.

The lady with the alligator purse ill. by author. Little, 1988. ISBN 0-316-93135-7 Subj: Games. Humor. Poetry, rhyme.

Peanut butter and jelly: a play rhyme ill. by author. Dutton, 1987. ISBN 0-525-44317-7 Subj: Animals – elephants. Careers – bakers. Family life. Food. Poetry, rhyme.

Westerberg, Christine. *The cap that mother made* ill. by adapt. Prentice-Hall, 1977. Subj: Clothing. Folk and fairy tales. Foreign lands – Sweden.

Weston, Martha. *Peony's rainbow* ill. by author. Lothrop, 1981. Subj: Animals – pigs. Weather – rainbows.

Westwood, Jennifer. *Going to Squintum's: a foxy folktale* ill. by Fiona French. Dial Pr., 1985. ISBN 0-8037-0015-6 Subj: Animals – foxes. Character traits – cleverness. Folk and fairy tales.

Wetterer, Margaret. *Patrick and the fairy thief* ill. by Enrico Arno. Atheneum, 1980. Subj: Character traits – cleverness. Fairies. Family life – mothers.

Wexler, Jerome. *Find the hidden insect* (Cole, Joanna)

Flowers, fruits, seeds photos. by author. Prentice-Hall, 1988. ISBN 0-13-322397-3 Subj: Plants. Science.

Wexler, Jerome LeRoy *see* Wexler, Jerome

Weygant, Noemi. *It's autumn!* photos. by author. Westminster Pr., 1968. Subj: Poetry, rhyme. Seasons – fall.

It's summer! photos. by author. Westminster Pr., 1970. Subj: Poetry, rhyme. Seasons – summer.

It's winter! photos. by author. Westminster Pr., 1969. Subj: Poetry, rhyme. Seasons – winter.

Wezel, Peter. *The good bird* ill. by author. Harper, 1964. Subj: Behavior – sharing. Birds. Fish. Wordless.

The naughty bird ill. by author. Follett, 1967. Translation of Der freche Vogel Figaro. Subj: Animals – cats. Birds. Wordless.

What a morning! *the Christmas story in Black spirituals* sel. and ed. by John M. Langstaff; ill. by Ashley Bryan; musical arrangements by John Andrew Ross. McElderry, 1987. ISBN 0-689-50422-5 Subj: Holidays – Christmas. Music. Religion. Songs.

What do babies do? ill. with photos. Random House, 1985. ISBN 0-394-87279-7 Subj: Babies. Format, unusual – board books.

What do toddlers do? ill. with photos. Random House, 1985. ISBN 0-394-87280-0 Subj: Babies. Format, unusual – board books.

What do you feed your donkey on? *Rhymes from a Belfast childhood* col. by Colette O'Hare; ill. by Jenny Rodwell. Collins-World, 1978. Subj: Foreign lands – Ireland. Nursery rhymes. Poetry, rhyme.

What we do ill. by Roser Capdevila. Firefly Pr., 1986. ISBN 0-920303-46-3 Subj: Activities.

Wheeler, Cindy. *Marmalade's Christmas present* ill. by author. Knopf, 1984. ISBN 0-394-96794-1 Subj: Animals – cats. Holidays – Christmas.

Marmalade's nap ill. by author. Knopf, 1983. Subj: Animals – cats. Noise, sounds. Sleep.

Marmalade's picnic ill. by author. Knopf, 1983. Subj: Activities – picnicking. Animals – cats.

Marmalade's snowy day ill. by author. Knopf, 1982. Subj: Animals – cats. Weather – snow.

Marmalade's yellow leaf ill. by author. Knopf, 1982. Subj: Animals – cats. Seasons – fall.

Rose ill. by author. Knopf, 1985. ISBN 0-394-96233-8 Subj: Animals – pigs. Farms.

Wheeler, M. J. *First came the Indians* ill. by James Houston. Atheneum, 1983. Subj: Indians of North America.

Wheeler, Mary Jane *see* Wheeler, M. J.

Wheeler, Opal. *Sing in praise: a collection of the best loved hymns* ill. by Marjorie Torrey. Dutton, 1946. Subj: Caldecott award honor book. Music. Religion. Songs.

Sing Mother Goose ill. by Marjorie Torrey; music by Opal Wheeler. Dutton, 1945. Subj: Caldecott award honor book. Music. Nursery rhymes. Songs.

Wheeler, William A. *Mother Goose's melodies* (Mother Goose)

Wheeling, Lynn. *When you fly* ill. by author. Little, 1967. Subj: Activities – flying. Airplanes, airports. Poetry, rhyme.

Whelan, Gloria. *A week of raccoons* ill. by Lynn Munsinger. Knopf, 1988. ISBN 0-394-88396-9 Subj: Animals – raccoons.

White, Alan *see* Fraser, James Howard

White, Anne Terry. *Æsop's fables* (Æsop)

White, Florence Meiman. *How to lose your lunch money* ill. by Chris Jenkyns. Ritchie, 1970. Subj: Behavior – losing things. Behavior – misbehavior. School.

White, Laurence B. *Science toys and tricks* by Laurence B. White, Jr.; ill. by Marc Brown. Addison-Wesley, 1981. Subj: Science. Toys.

White, Paul. *Janet at school* photos. by Jeremy Finlay. Crowell, 1978. Subj: Handicaps. School.

Whitehead, Patricia. *Monkeys* ill. by Bert Dodson. Troll Assoc., 1982. Subj: Animals – monkeys.

Whiteside, Karen. *Lullaby of the wind* ill. by Kazue Mizumura. Harper, 1984. ISBN 0-06-026412-8 Subj: Bedtime. Sleep. Songs. Weather – wind.

Whitlock, Ralph. *Penguins* ill. with photos. Raintree, 1978. Subj: Birds – penguins.

Whitlock, Susan Love. *Donovan scares the monsters* ill. by Yossi Abolafia. Greenwillow, 1987. ISBN 0-688-06439-6 Subj: Family life – grandmothers. Monsters.

Whitmore, Adam. *Max in America* ill. by Janice Poltrick Donato. Silver Burdett, 1986. ISBN 0-382-09244-9 Subj: Animals – cats. Character traits – being different.

Max in Australia ill. by Janice Poltrick Donato. Silver Burdett, 1986. ISBN 0-382-09246-5 Subj: Animals – cats. Character traits – being different. Foreign lands – Australia.

Max in India ill. by Janice Poltrick Donato. Silver Burdett, 1986. ISBN 0-382-09245-7 Subj: Animals – cats. Character traits – being different. Foreign lands – India.

Max leaves home ill. by Janice Poltrick Donato. Silver Burdett, 1986. ISBN 0-382-09243-0 Subj: Animals – cats. Behavior – running away. Character traits – being different.

Whitney, Alex. *Once a bright red tiger* ill. by Charles Robinson. Walck, 1973. Subj: Animals – tigers. Character traits – pride.

The tiger that barks: the true picture story of Mohan and his friends photos. by Beverly Ecker. McKay, 1978. Subj: Animals – dogs. Animals – tigers. Family life.

Whitney, Alma Marshak. *Just awful* ill. by Lillian Hoban. Addison-Wesley, 1971. Subj: Careers – nurses. Illness. School.

Leave Herbert alone ill. by David McPhail. Addison-Wesley, 1972. Subj: Animals – cats. Character traits – kindness to animals.

Whitney, Julie *see* Yulya

Whittier, John Greenleaf. *Barbara Frietchie* ill. by Paul Galdone. Crowell, 1965. ISBN 0-690-11532-6 Subj: Character traits – loyalty. U.S. history. War.

Widdecombe Fair: an old English folk song ill. by Christine Price. Warne, 1968. Subj: Fairs. Folk and fairy tales. Foreign lands – England. Music. Songs.

Wiese, Kurt. *The cunning turtle* ill. by author. Viking, 1956. Subj: Reptiles – turtles, tortoises.

The dog, the fox and the fleas ill. by author. McKay, 1953. Subj: Animals – dogs. Animals – foxes. Insects – fleas.

Fish in the air ill. by author. Viking, 1948. Subj: Caldecott award honor book. Foreign lands – China. Humor. Kites.

The five Chinese brothers (Bishop, Claire Huchet)

Happy Easter ill. by author. Viking, 1952. Subj: Animals – rabbits. Holidays – Easter.

The story about Ping (Flack, Marjorie)

The thief in the attic ill. by author. Viking, 1965. Subj: Animals. Trees.

You can write Chinese ill. by author. Viking, 1945. Subj: Caldecott award honor book. Foreign languages.

Wiesenthal, Eleanor. *Let's find out about Eskimos* by Eleanor and Ted Wiesenthal; ill. by Allan Eitzen. Watts, 1969. Subj: Eskimos.

Wiesner, David. *Free fall* ill. by author. Lothrop, 1988. ISBN 0-688-05584-2 Subj: Activities – reading. Bedtime. Caldecott award honor book. Dragons. Dreams. Wordless.

The loathsome dragon by David Wiesner and Kim Kahng; ill. by David Wiesner. Putnam's, 1987. ISBN 0-399-21407-0 Subj: Dragons. Folk and fairy tales. Magic. Royalty.

Wiesner, William. *Happy-Go-Lucky: a Norwegian tale* ill. by author. Seabury Pr., 1970. Subj: Character traits – optimism. Cumulative tales. Farms. Foreign lands – Norway. Humor.

Noah's ark ill. by author. Dutton, 1966. Subj: Religion – Noah.

Tops ill. by author. Viking, 1969. Subj: Friendship. Giants. Violence, anti-violence.

The Tower of Babel ill. by author. Viking, 1968. "Based on the book of Genesis and on commentaries ... in the book Hebrew myths by Robert Graves and Raphael Patai." Subj: Language. Religion.

Turnabout: a Norwegian tale ill. by author. Seabury Pr., 1972. "This text has been adapted from the version of Edouard Laboulaye." Subj: Behavior – dissatisfaction. Foreign lands – Norway. Humor.

Wight, J. A. (James Alfred) *see* Herriot, James

Wikland, Ilon. *Christmas in noisy village* (Lindgren, Astrid)

Wikler, Madeline. *Let's build a Sukkah* by Madeline Wikler and Judyth Groner; ill. by Katherine Janus Kahn. Kar-Ben Copies, 1986. ISBN 0-930494-58-X Subj: Format, unusual – board books. Holidays. Jewish culture.

My first seder by Madeline Wikler and Judyth Groner; ill. by Katherine Janus Kahn. Kar-Ben Copies, 1986. ISBN 0-930494-61-X Subj: Food. Format, unusual – board books. Holidays – Passover. Jewish culture.

My very own Jewish community (Groner, Judyth)

The Purim parade by Madeline Wikler and Judyth Groner; ill. by Katherine Janus Kahn. Kar-Ben Copies, 1986. ISBN 0-930494-60-1 Subj: Format, unusual – board books. Holidays – Purim. Jewish culture.

Where is the Afikomen? (Groner, Judyth)

Wilcox, Daniel. *The Sesame Street ABC storybook* (Moss, Jeffrey)

Wild, Jocelyn. *The bears' ABC book* (Wild, Robin)

The bears' counting book (Wild, Robin)

Florence and Eric take the cake ill. by author. Dial Pr., 1987. ISBN 0-8037-0305-8 Subj: Animals – sheep. Behavior – misunderstanding. Family life.

Little Pig and the big bad wolf (Wild, Robin)

Spot's dogs and the alley cats (Wild, Robin)

Wild, Robin. *The bears' ABC book* by Robin and Jocelyn Wild; ill. by authors. Lippincott, 1978. Subj: ABC books. Animals – bears.

The bears' counting book by Robin and Jocelyn Wild; ill. by authors. Lippincott, 1978. Subj: Animals – bears. Counting.

Little Pig and the big bad wolf by Robin and Jocelyn Wild; ill. by authors. Coward, 1972. Subj: Animals – pigs. Animals – wolves. Character traits – cleverness. Holidays – Christmas. Poetry, rhyme.

Spot's dogs and the alley cats by Robin and Jocelyn Wild; ill. by authors. Lippincott, 1979. Subj: Animals – cats. Animals – dogs. Behavior – trickery.

Wilde, Kathey *see* King, Patricia

Wilde, Oscar. *The selfish giant* ill. by Dom Mansell. Prentice-Hall, 1986. ISBN 0-13-803586-5 Subj: Character traits – kindness. Character traits – selfishness. Seasons – spring.

The selfish giant ill. by Lisbeth Zwerger. Alphabet Pr., 1984. ISBN 0-907234-30-5 Subj: Character traits – kindness. Character traits – selfishness. Seasons – spring.

Wilde, Oscar Fingal O'Flahertie Wills *see* Wilde, Oscar

Wildsmith, Brian. *Animal games* ill. by author. Oxford Univ. Pr., 1980. Subj: Animals. Games.

Animal homes ill. by author. Oxford Univ. Pr., 1980. Subj: Animals. Houses.

Animal shapes ill. by author. Oxford Univ. Pr., 1980. Subj: Animals. Concepts – shape.

Animal tricks ill. by author. Oxford Univ. Pr., 1980. Subj: Animals. Poetry, rhyme.

Bear's adventure ill. by author. Pantheon, 1982. Subj: Activities – ballooning. Animals – bears.

Brian Wildsmith's birds ill. by author. Watts, 1967. Subj: Birds.

Brian Wildsmith's circus ill. by author. Watts, 1970. Subj: Circus.

Brian Wildsmith's fishes ill. by author. Watts, 1968. Subj: Fish.

Brian Wildsmith's puzzles ill. by author. Watts, 1970. Subj: Games.

Brian Wildsmith's wild animals ill. by author. Watts, 1967. Subj: Animals.

Carousel ill. by author. Knopf, 1988. ISBN 0-394-91937-8 Subj: Dreams. Fairs. Illness. Merry-go-rounds.

Daisy ill. by author. Pantheon, 1984. Subj: Animals – bulls, cows. Behavior – running away. Format, unusual.

Give a dog a bone ill. by author. Pantheon, 1985. ISBN 0-394-97709-2 Subj: Animals – dogs. Format, unusual.

Goat's trail ill. by author. Knopf, 1986. ISBN 0-394-98276-2 Subj: Animals. Animals – goats. Cumulative tales. Format, unusual. Noise, sounds.

Hunter and his dog ill. by author. Oxford Univ. Pr., 1979. Subj: Animals – dogs. Character traits – kindness to animals. Sports – hunting.

The lazy bear ill. by author. Watts, 1974. Subj: Animals – bears. Character traits – laziness. Friendship.

The little wood duck ill. by author. Watts, 1972. Subj: Birds – ducks.

The miller, the boy and the donkey (La Fontaine, Jean de)

The owl and the woodpecker ill. by author. Watts, 1971. Subj: Birds – owls. Birds – woodpeckers. Character traits – compromising.

Pelican ill. by author. Pantheon, 1983. Subj: Birds – pelicans. Format, unusual. Sports – fishing.

Professor Noah's spaceship ill. by author. Oxford Univ. Pr., 1980. ISBN 0-19-279741-7 Subj: Space and space ships.

Python's party ill. by author. Watts, 1975. Subj: Animals. Behavior – trickery. Reptiles – snakes.

Seasons ill. by author. Oxford Univ. Pr., 1980. Subj: Nature. Seasons.

The true cross ill. by author. Oxford Univ. Pr., 1985, 1977. ISBN 0-19-279718-2 Subj: Folk and fairy tales. Religion.

What the moon saw ill. by author. Oxford Univ. Pr., 1978. Subj: Animals. Concepts – opposites. Language. Moon. Sun.

Wilhelm, Hans. *I'll always love you* ill. by author. Crown, 1985. ISBN 0-517-55648-0 Subj: Animals – dogs. Death. Pets.

Let's be friends again! ill. by author. ISBN 0-517-56252-9 Subj: Emotions – anger. Family life – sisters. Friendship.

More bunny trouble ill. by author. Scholastic, 1989. ISBN 0-590-41589-1 Subj: Animals – foxes. Animals – rabbits. Eggs. Holidays – Easter.

A new home, a new friend ill. by author. Random House, 1985. Subj: Animals – dogs. Family life. Friendship. Moving.

Oh, what a mess ill. by author. Crown, 1988. ISBN 0-517-56909-4 Subj: Animals – pigs. Character traits – cleanliness.

Tyrone the horrible ill. by author. Scholastic, 1988. ISBN 0-590-41471-2 Subj: Behavior – bullying. Dinosaurs.

Wilkins, Mary Huiskamp Calhoun *see* Calhoun, Mary

Wilkins, Mary Louise *see* Calhoun, Mary

Wilkinson, Sylvia. *Automobiles* ill. with photos. Children's Pr., 1982. Subj: Automobiles.

I can be a race car driver ill. with photos. Childrens Pr., 1986. ISBN 0-516-01898-1 Subj: Automobiles. Careers – race car drivers. Sports – racing.

Will *see* Lipkind, William

Willard, Barbara. *To London! To London!* ill. by Antony Maitland. Weybright and Talley, 1968. Subj: Foreign lands – England.

Willard, Nancy. *The mountains of quilt* ill. by Tomie de Paola. Harcourt, 1987. ISBN 0-15-256010-6 Subj: Dreams. Family life – grandmothers. Magic.

Night story ill. by Ilse Plume. Harcourt, 1986. ISBN 0-15-257348-8 Subj: Dreams. Night. Poetry, rhyme.

The nightgown of the sullen moon ill. by David McPhail. Harcourt, 1983. Subj: Moon. Night.

Simple pictures are best ill. by Tomie de Paola. Harcourt, 1977. Subj: Activities – photographing. Humor.

A visit to William Blake's inn: poems for innocent and experienced travelers ill. by Alice and Martin Provensen. Harcourt, 1981. Subj: Caldecott award honor book. Imagination. Poetry, rhyme.

The voyage of the Ludgate Hill: travels with Robert Louis Stevenson ill. by Alice and Martin Provensen. Harcourt, 1987. ISBN 0-15-294464-8 Subj: Activities – traveling. Animals. Boats, ships. Poetry, rhyme. Sea and seashore. Weather – storms.

Williams, Barbara. *Albert's toothache* ill. by Kay Chorao. Dutton, 1974. Subj: Illness. Reptiles – turtles, tortoises. Teeth.

Chester Chipmunk's Thanksgiving ill. by Kay Chorao. Dutton, 1974. Subj: Animals – chipmunks. Holidays – Thanksgiving.

Donna Jean's disaster ill. by Margot Apple. Albert Whitman, 1986. ISBN 0-8075-1682-1 Subj: Family life. Poetry, rhyme. School. Sibling rivalry.

Hello, dandelions! photos. by author. Holt, 1979. Subj: Flowers. Plants.

I know a salesperson ill. by Frank Aloise. Putnam's, 1978. Subj: Careers. Stores.

If he's my brother ill. by Tomie de Paola. Harvey House, 1976. Subj: Character traits – questioning. Family life.

Jeremy isn't hungry ill. by Martha G. Alexander. Dutton, 1978. Subj: Activities – baby-sitting. Babies. Humor.

Kevin's grandma ill. by Kay Chorao. Dutton, 1975. Subj: Family life – grandmothers. Friendship.

So what if I'm a sore loser? ill. by Linda Strauss Edwards. Harcourt, 1981. Subj: Character traits – conceit. Family life.

Someday, said Mitchell ill. by Kay Chorao. Dutton, 1976. Subj: Behavior – wishing. Character traits – helpfulness. Character traits – smallness. Emotions – happiness.

Whatever happened to Beverly Bigler's birthday? ill. by Emily Arnold McCully. Harcourt, 1979. Subj: Behavior – misbehavior. Birthdays. Weddings.

Williams, Carol Elizabeth Fenner *see* Fenner, Carol

Williams, Charles *see* Collier, James Lincoln

Williams, Garth. *The big golden animal ABC* ill. by author. Simon & Schuster, 1957. First published under the title: The golden animal A.B.C. Subj: ABC books. Animals.

The chicken book ill. by author. Delacorte Pr., 1970. Subj: Birds – chickens. Counting. Poetry, rhyme.

The rabbits' wedding ill. by author. Harper, 1958. Subj: Animals – rabbits. Weddings.

Williams, Gweneira Maureen. *Timid Timothy, the kitten who learned to be brave* ill. by Leonard Weisgard. Addison-Wesley, 1944. Subj: Food. Science. Emotions – fear.

Williams, Jay. *The city witch and the country witch* ill. by Ed Renfro. Macmillan, 1979. Subj: Activities – vacationing. City. Country. Witches.

Everyone knows what a dragon looks like ill. by Mercer Mayer. Four Winds Pr., 1976. Subj: Dragons. Foreign lands – China.

I wish I had another name by Jay Williams and Winifred Lubell; ill. by authors. Atheneum, 1962. Subj: Names. Poetry, rhyme.

Petronella ill. by Friso Henstra. Parents, 1973. Subj: Folk and fairy tales.

The practical princess ill. by Friso Henstra. Parents, 1969. Subj: Folk and fairy tales. Royalty.

School for sillies ill. by Friso Henstra. Parents, 1969. Subj: Character traits – cleverness. Humor. Royalty.

The surprising things Maui did ill. by Charles Mikolaycak. Four Winds Pr., 1980. Subj: Folk and fairy tales. Hawaii.

Williams, Jenny. *Here's a ball for baby: finger rhymes for young children* ill. by author. Dial Pr., 1987. ISBN 0-8037-0388-0 Subj: Nursery rhymes.

One, two, buckle my shoe: counting rhymes for young children ill. by author. Dial Pr., 1987. ISBN 0-8037-0390-2 Subj: Counting. Nursery rhymes.

Ride a cockhorse: animal rhymes for young children ill. by author. Dial Pr., 1987. ISBN 0-8037-0389-9 Subj: Animals. Nursery rhymes.

Ring around a rosy: action rhymes for young children ill. by author. Dial Pr., 1987. ISBN 0-8037-0391-0 Subj: Games. Nursery rhymes.

A wet Monday (Edwards, Dorothy)

Williams, Leslie. *A bear in the air* ill. by Carme Solé Vendrell. Stemmer House, 1980. Subj: Animals – bears. Weather – clouds. Weather – rainbows.

Williams, Linda. *The little old lady who was not afraid of anything* ill. by Megan Lloyd. Crowell, 1986. ISBN 0-690-04586-7 Subj: Cumulative tales. Emotions – fear. Scarecrows.

Williams, Marcia. *The first Christmas* ill. by author. Random House, 1988. ISBN 0-394-80434-1 Subj: Holidays – Christmas. Religion.

Williams, Margery see Bianco, Margery Williams

Williams, Sarah. *Ride a cock-horse* ill. by Ian Beck. Oxford Univ. Pr., 1987. ISBN 0-19-279831-6 Subj: Nursery rhymes.

Williams, Terry Tempest. *Between cattails* ill. by Peter Parnall. Scribner's, 1985. ISBN 0-684-18309-9 Subj: Ecology. Poetry, rhyme.

Williams, Vera B. *A chair for my mother* ill. by author. Greenwillow, 1982. Subj: Behavior – seeking better things. Caldecott award honor book. Family life.

Cherries and cherry pits ill. by author. Greenwillow, 1986. ISBN 0-688-05146-4 Subj: Art. Ethnic groups in the U.S. – Afro-Americans. Imagination.

Music, music for everyone ill. by author. Greenwillow, 1984. Subj: Family life. Family life – grandmothers. Illness. Music.

Something special for me ill. by author. Greenwillow, 1983. Subj: Birthdays. Family life.

Stringbean's trip to the shining sea ill. by Vera B. Williams and Jennifer Williams. Greenwillow, 1988. ISBN 0-688-07162-7 Subj: Activities – traveling. Family life. Friendship. Sibling rivalry.

Three days on a river in a red canoe ill. by author. Greenwillow, 1981. Subj: Boats, ships. Sports – camping.

Williamson, Hamilton. *Little elephant* ill. by Berta and Elmer Hader. Doubleday, 1930. Subj: Animals – elephants.

Monkey tale ill. by Berta and Elmer Hader. Doubleday, 1929. Subj: Animals – monkeys.

Williamson, Mel. *Walk on!* by Mel Williamson and George Ford; ill. by authors. Third Pr., 1972. Subj: City. Ethnic groups in the U.S. – Afro-Americans.

Williamson, Stan. *The no-bark dog* ill. by Tom O'Sullivan. Follett, 1962. Subj: Animals – dogs. Ethnic groups in the U.S. – Afro-Americans.

Willis, Jeanne. *The long blue blazer* ill. by Susan Varley. Dutton, 1988. ISBN 0-525-44381-9 Subj: Character traits – being different. School. Space and space ships.

The monster bed ill. by Susan Varley. Lothrop, 1987. ISBN 0-688-06805-7 Subj: Bedtime. Emotions – fear. Monsters. Poetry, rhyme.

The tale of Georgie Grub ill. by Margaret Chamberlain. Holt, 1982. Subj: Activities – bathing. Character traits – cleanliness.

Willis, Val. *The secret in the matchbox* ill. by John Shelley. Farrar, 1988. ISBN 0-374-36603-9 Subj: Behavior – secrets. Dragons. School.

Willoughby, Elaine Macmann. *Boris and the monsters* ill. by Lynn Munsinger. Houghton, 1980. Subj: Animals – dogs. Monsters.

Willy, Colette see Colette

Wilson, Barbara. *ABC et/and 123* ill. by Gisèle Daigle. Fitzhenry and Whiteside, 1981. Subj: ABC books. Counting. Foreign languages.

Wilson, Bob. *Stanley Bagshaw and the twenty-two ton whale* ill. by author. David & Charles, 1984. ISBN 0-241-10812-8 Subj: Animals — whales. Sports — fishing.

Wilson, Christopher Bernard. *Hobnob* ill. by William Wiesner. Viking, 1968. Subj: Behavior — sharing.

Wilson, Dorminster. *Mother scorpion country* (Rohmer, Harriet)

Wilson, Joyce Lancaster. *Tobi* ill. by Anne Thiess. Funk and Wagnalls, 1968. Subj: Animals – cats.

Wilson, Julia. *Becky* ill. by John Wilson. Crowell, 1966. Subj: Character traits — honesty. Ethnic groups in the U.S. — Afro-Americans. Toys — dolls.

Wilson, Robina Beckles. *Merry Christmas! children at Christmastime around the world* ill. by Satomi Ichikawa. Putnam's, 1983. ISBN 0-399-20921-2 Subj: Holidays — Christmas.

Wilson, Ron. *Mice* ill. with photos. Global Lib. Mktg. Serv., 1984. ISBN 0-7136-2388-8 Subj: Animals — mice. Nature. Science.

Wilson, Sarah. *Beware the dragons!* ill. by author. Harper, 1985. ISBN 0-06-026509-4 Subj: Dragons. Folk and fairy tales. Weather — storms.

Windham, Sophie. *Noah's ark* ill. by author. Putnam's, 1989. ISBN 0-399-21564-6 Subj: Animals. Food. Format, unusual. Religion — Noah.

Winn, Chris. *Helping* ill. by author. Holt, 1986. ISBN 0-8050-0064-X Subj: Activities. Format, unusual — board books.

Holiday ill. by author. Holt, 1986. ISBN 0-8050-0067-4 Subj: Format, unusual – board books. Holidays.

My day ill. by author. Holt, 1986. ISBN 0-8050-0066-6 Subj: Family life. Format, unusual — board books. Shopping.

Playing ill. by author. Holt, 1986. ISBN 0-8050-0065-8 Subj: Activities — playing. Format, unusual — board books.

Winn, Marie. *The man who made fine tops* ill. by John E. Johnson; educational consultant: Helen F. Robison. Simon and Schuster, 1970. Subj: Careers.

Winston, Clara. *Thumbelina* (Andersen, H. C. (Hans Christian))

Winston, Richard. *Thumbelina* (Andersen, H. C. (Hans Christian))

Winter, Jeanette. *Follow the drinking gourd* ill. by author. Knopf, 1988. ISBN 0-394-89694-7 Subj: Ethnic groups in the U.S. — Afro-Americans. Stars. U.S. history.

The girl and the moon man: a Siberian folktale ill. by author. Pantheon, 1984. Subj: Animals. Folk and fairy tales. Foreign lands — Russia. Moon. Music.

Winter, Paula. *The bear and the fly* ill. by author. Crown, 1976. Subj: Animals — bears. Insects — flies. Wordless.

Sir Andrew ill. by author. Crown, 1980. Subj: Animals — donkeys. Character traits — vanity. Wordless.

Winteringham, Victoria. *Penguin day* ill. by author. Harper, 1982. Subj: Activities. Birds – penguins.

Winthrop, Elizabeth. *Bear and Mrs. Duck* ill. by Patience Brewster. Holiday, 1988. ISBN 0-8234-0687-3 Subj: Activities — baby-sitting. Animals — bears. Birds — ducks.

Bunk beds ill. by Ronald Himler. Harper, 1972. ISBN 0-06-026532-9 Subj: Activities — playing. Bedtime. Family life. Imagination.

A child is born: the Christmas story adapt. from the New Testament; ill. by Charles Mikolaycak. Holiday, 1983. Subj: Holidays – Christmas. Religion.

He is risen: the Easter story ill. by Charles Mikolaycak. Holiday, 1985. ISBN 0-8234-0547-8 Subj: Holidays — Easter. Religion.

I think he likes me ill. by Denise Saldutti. Harper, 1980. Subj: Family life. Sibling rivalry.

Katharine's doll ill. by Marylin Hafner. Dutton, 1983. ISBN 0-525-44061-5 Subj: Friendship. Toys — dolls.

Lizzie and Harold ill. by Martha Weston. Lothrop, 1986. ISBN 0-688-02712-1 Subj: Friendship.

Maggie and the monster ill. by Tomie de Paola. Holiday, 1987. ISBN 0-8234-0639-2 Subj: Bedtime. Monsters. Problem solving.

Potbellied possums ill. by Barbara McClintock. Holiday, 1977. ISBN 0-8234-0289-4 Subj: Animals — possums. Emotions — fear. Food. Night.

Shoes ill. by William Joyce. Harper, 1986. ISBN 0-06-026592-2 Subj: Clothing. Poetry, rhyme.

Sloppy kisses ill. by Anne Burgess. Macmillan, 1980. Subj: Animals — pigs. Friendship.

That's mine ill. by Emily Arnold McCully. Holiday House, 1977. Subj: Activities — playing. Behavior — fighting, arguing. Behavior — greed. Behavior — sharing. Sibling rivalry. Toys — blocks.

Tough Eddie ill. by Lillian Hoban. Dutton, 1985. Subj: Character traits — pride. School.

Wirt, Donna Aaron. *My favorite place* (Sargent, Susan)

Wirth, Beverly. *Margie and me* ill. by Karen Ann Weinhaus. Four Winds Pr., 1983. Subj: Animals — dogs. Pets.

Wisbeski, Dorothy Gross. *Pícaro, a pet otter* ill. by Edna Miller. Hawthorn, 1971. Subj: Animals – otters. Pets.

Wise, William. *The cowboy surprise* ill. by Paul Galdone. Putnam's, 1961. Subj: Cowboys. Glasses. Senses – seeing.

Nanette, the hungry pelican ill. by Winifred Lubell. Rand McNally, 1969. Subj: Birds – pelicans. Poetry, rhyme.

Wiseman, Bernard. *Doctor Duck and Nurse Swan* ill. by author. Dutton, 1984. Subj: Animals. Problem solving.

Don't make fun! ill. by author. Houghton, 1982. Subj: Animals – pigs. Behavior – misbehavior.

Little new kangaroo ill. by Robert Lopshire. Macmillan, 1973. Subj: Animals. Animals – kangaroos. Foreign lands – Russia. Poetry, rhyme.

Morris and Boris at the circus ill. by author. Harper, 1988. ISBN 0-06-026478-0 Subj: Animals – bears. Animals – moose. Circus.

Morris has a birthday party! ill. by author. Little, 1983. Subj: Animals – bears. Animals – moose. Behavior – misunderstanding. Parties.

Oscar is a mama ill. by author. Garrard, 1980. Subj: Animals – bulls, cows. Toys – dolls.

Tails are not for painting ill. by author. Garrard, 1980. Subj: Animals. Behavior – mistakes. Humor. School.

Witch poems ed. by Daisy Wallace; ill. by Trina Schart Hyman. Holiday, 1976. ISBN 0-8234-0281-9 Subj: Poetry, rhyme. Witches.

Withers, Carl. *The tale of a black cat* ill. by Alan E. Cober. Holt, 1966. Subj: Animals – cats. Games.

The wild ducks and the goose ill. by Alan E. Cober. Holt, 1968. Subj: Birds – ducks. Games. Sports – hunting.

Wittels, Harriet. *Things I hate!* by Harriet Wittels and Joan Greisman; ill. by Jerry McConnel. Behavioral Pub., 1973. Subj: Behavior. Emotions. Poetry, rhyme.

Wittman, Sally. *The boy who hated Valentine's Day* ill. by Chaya M. Burstein. Harper, 1987. ISBN 0-06-026594-9 Subj: Character traits – kindness. Friendship. Holidays – Valentine's Day. School.

Pelly and Peak ill. by author. Harper, 1978. ISBN 0-06-026560-4 Subj: Birds – peacocks, peahens. Birds – pelicans. Friendship.

Plenty of Pelly and Peak ill. by author. Harper, 1980. Subj: Birds – peacocks, peahens. Birds – pelicans. Friendship.

A special trade ill. by Karen Gundersheimer. Harper, 1978. Subj: Behavior – growing up. Friendship. Old age.

The wonderful Mrs. Trumbly ill. by Margot Apple. Harper, 1982. Subj: Friendship. School. Weddings.

Wodge, Dreary *see* Gorey, Edward

Wolcott, Patty. *Double-decker, double-decker, double-decker bus* ill. by Bob Barner. Addison-Wesley, 1980. Subj: Friendship. Buses.

Wold, Jo Anne. *Tell them my name is Amanda* ed. by Caroline Rubin; ill. by Dennis Hockerman. Albert Whitman, 1977. Subj: Character traits – shyness. Names. Problem solving. Self-concept.

Well! Why didn't you say so? ill. by Unada. Albert Whitman, 1975. Subj: Animals – dogs. Behavior – lost. Behavior – misunderstanding. City.

Wolde, Gunilla. *Betsy and Peter are different* ill. by author. Random House, 1979. Translation of Annorlunda Emma och Per. Subj: Family life. Friendship.

Betsy and the chicken pox ill. by author. Random House, 1976. Translation of Emmas lillebror ar sjuk. ISBN 0-394-83328-7 Subj: Behavior – needing someone. Illness. Sibling rivalry.

Betsy and the doctor ill. by author. Random House, 1978. Translation of Emma hos doktorn. ISBN 0-394-95382-7 Subj: Careers – doctors. Hospitals. Illness.

Betsy and the vacuum cleaner ill. by author. Random House, 1979. Subj: Family life. Machines.

Betsy's first day at nursery school ill. by author. Random House, 1976. Translation of Emmas första dag på dagis. ISBN 0-394-95381-9 Subj: School.

Betsy's fixing day ill. by author. Random House, 1978. Subj: Character traits – helpfulness. Family life.

This is Betsy ill. by author. Random House, 1975. Translation of Emma tvärtimot. ISBN 0-394-93161-0 Subj: Emotions. Family life.

Wolf, Ann. *The rabbit and the turtle* ill. by author. Wonder Books, 1965. Subj: Animals – rabbits. Folk and fairy tales. Reptiles – turtles, tortoises.

Wolf, Bernard. *Adam Smith goes to school* photos. by author. Lippincott, 1978. Subj: School.

Anna's silent world photos. by author. Lippincott, 1977. Subj: Handicaps – deafness. Senses – hearing.

Don't feel sorry for Paul photos. by author. Lippincott, 1974. Subj: Handicaps.

Michael and the dentist photos. by author. Four Winds Pr., 1980. Subj: Careers – dentists. Emotions – fear. Teeth.

Wolf, Frederick *see* Day, Michael E.

Wolf, Janet. *Adelaide to Zeke* ill. by author. Harper, 1987. ISBN 0-06-026598-1 Subj: ABC books. Names.

The best present is me ill. by author. Harper, 1984. Subj: Art. Family life – grandmothers.

Wolf, Susan. *The adventures of Albert, the running bear* (Isenberg, Barbara)

Albert the running bear gets the jitters (Isenberg, Barbara)

Wolf, Winfried. *The Easter bunny* ill. by Agnès Mathieu. Dial Pr., 1986. ISBN 0-8037-0239-6 Subj: Animals – rabbits. Holidays – Easter.

Wolfe, Robert L. *The truck book* photos. by author. Carolrhoda, 1981. Subj: Trucks.

Wolff, Ashley. *The bells of London* ill. by author. Dodd, 1985. Subj: Birds – doves. Emotions – sadness. Foreign lands – England. Songs.

Only the cat saw ill. by author. Dodd, 1985. ISBN 0-396-08727-2 Subj: Animals – cats. Family life. Night.

A year of beasts ill. by author. Dutton, 1986. ISBN 0-525-44240-5 Subj: Animals. Days of the week, months of the year. Farms.

A year of birds ill. by author. Dodd, 1984. Subj: Birds. Days of the week, months of the year. Seasons.

Wolff, Robert Jay. *Feeling blue* ill. by author. Scribner's, 1968. Subj: Concepts – color.

Hello, yellow! ill. by author. Scribner's, 1968. Subj: Concepts – color.

Seeing red ill. by author. Scribner's, 1968. Subj: Concepts – color.

Wolkstein, Diane. *The banza: a Haitian story* ill. by Marc Brown. Dial Pr., 1981. Subj: Animals – goats. Animals – tigers. Character traits – bravery. Folk and fairy tales. Music.

The cool ride in the sky ill. by Paul Galdone. Knopf, 1973. Subj: Activities – flying. Animals – monkeys. Birds – buzzards. Birds – vultures. Character traits – cleverness. Folk and fairy tales.

The legend of Sleepy Hollow ill. by Robert W. Alley. Morrow, 1987. Based on the story by Washington Irving. ISBN 0-688-06533-3 Subj: Ghosts. Folk and fairy tales. Holidays – Halloween. Humor.

The magic wings: a tale from China ill. by Robert Andrew Parker. Dutton, 1983. Subj: Activities – flying. Behavior – wishing. Cumulative tales. Folk and fairy tales. Foreign lands – China. Seasons – spring.

White wave: a Chinese tale ill. by Ed Young. Crowell, 1979. Subj: Folk and fairy tales. Foreign lands – China.

Wolski, Slawomir. *Tiger cat* tr. by Elizabeth D. Crawford; ill. by Jozef Wilkon. Holt, 1988. ISBN 0-8050-0741-5 Subj: Animals – tigers. Pets.

Wondriska, William. *Mr. Brown and Mr. Gray* ill. by author. Holt, 1968. Subj: Animals – pigs. Emotions – happiness. Money.

Puff ill. by author. Pantheon, 1960. Subj: Self-concept. Trains.

The stop ill. by author. Holt, 1972. Subj: Animals – horses. Character traits – kindness to animals. Desert. Emotions – fear. Indians of North America.

The tomato patch ill. by author. Holt, 1964. Subj: Plants. Violence, anti-violence. Weapons.

Wong, Herbert H. *My goldfish* by Herbert H. Wong and Matthew F. Vessel; ill. by Arvis L. Stewart. Addison-Wesley, 1969. Subj: Fish. Pets. Science.

My ladybug by Herbert H. Wong and Matthew F. Vessel; ill. by Marie Nonast Bohlen. Addison-Wesley, 1969. Subj: Insects – ladybugs. Science.

My plant by Herbert H. Wong and Matthew F. Vessel; ill. by Richard Cuffari. Addison-Wesley, 1976. Subj: Plants. Science.

Our caterpillars by Herbert H. Wong and Matthew F. Vessel; ill. by Arvis L. Stewart. Addison-Wesley, 1977. Subj: Insects – Butterflies, caterpillars. Science.

Our earthworms by Herbert H. Wong and Matthew F. Vessel; ill. by Bill Davis. Addison-Wesley, 1977. Subj: Animals – worms. Science.

Our tree by Herbert H. Wong and Matthew F. Vessel; ill. by Kenneth Longtemps. Addison-Wesley, 1969. Subj: Science. Trees.

Wood, Audrey. *Detective Valentine* ill. by author. Harper, 1987. ISBN 0-06-026600-7 Subj: Problem solving. Weather – snow.

Elbert's bad word ill. by author. Harcourt, 1988. ISBN 0-15-225320-3 Subj: Behavior – misbehavior. Family life. Language.

Heckedy Peg ill. by Don Wood. Harcourt, 1987. ISBN 0-15-233678-8 Subj: Behavior – talking to strangers. Character traits – cleverness. Days of the week, months of the year. Folk and fairy tales. Food. Witches.

The horrible holidays ill. by Rosekrans Hoffman. Dial Pr., 1988. ISBN 0-8037-0546-8 Subj: Behavior – trickery. Family life. Holidays.

King Bidgood's in the bathtub ill. by Don Wood. Harcourt, 1985. ISBN 0-15-242730-9 Subj: Activities. Activities – bathing. Caldecott award honor book. Humor. Royalty.

Moonflute ill. by Don Wood. Harcourt, 1986. ISBN 0-15-255337-1 Subj: Bedtime. Moon. Night. Sleep.

The napping house ill. by Don Wood. Harcourt, 1984. ISBN 0-15-256708-9 Subj: Animals. Cumulative tales. Family life – grandmothers. Poetry, rhyme. Sleep.

Three sisters ill. by Rosekrans Hoffman. Dial Pr., 1986. ISBN 0-8037-0280-9 Subj: Activities – dancing. Animals – pigs. Sibling rivalry.

Wood, John Norris. *Jungles* ed. by Janet Schulman; ill. by Kevin Dean. Knopf, 1987. ISBN 0-394-87802-7 Subj: Animals. Behavior – hiding. Format, unusual. Jungle.

Oceans ill. by Mark Harrison. Knopf, 1985. ISBN 0-394-87583-4 Subj: Behavior – hiding. Fish. Format, unusual. Sea and seashore.

Wood, Joyce. *Grandmother Lucy goes on a picnic* ill. by Frank Francis. Collins-World, 1976. Subj: Activities – picnicking. Activities – walking. Family life – grandmothers.

Grandmother Lucy in her garden ill. by Frank Francis. Collins-World, 1975. Subj: Family life – grandmothers. Foreign lands – England. Seasons. Seasons – spring.

Wood, Leslie. *A dog called Mischief* ill. by author. Oxford Univ. Pr., 1984. ISBN 0-19-272155-0 Subj: Animals – dogs. Behavior – hiding things. Food.

Wood, Nancy C. *Little wrangler* ill. by Myron Wood. Doubleday, 1966. Subj: Cowboys.

Wood, Ray. *The American Mother Goose* ill. by Ed Hargis. Lippincott, 1940. Subj: Nursery rhymes.

Fun in American folk rhymes ill. by Ed Hargis; intro. by Carl Carmer. Lippincott, 1952. Subj: Nursery rhymes.

Woodcock, Louise Phinney. *The very little dog* (Skaar, Grace Marion)

Wooding, Sharon L. *Arthur's Christmas wish* ill. by author. Atheneum, 1986. ISBN 0-689-31211-3 Subj: Animals – mice. Behavior – wishing. Holidays – Christmas.

Woolaver, Lance. *Christmas with the rural mail* ill. by Maud Lewis. Nimbus Pub., 1981. Subj: Foreign lands – Canada. Holidays – Christmas. Poetry, rhyme.

From Ben Loman to the sea ill. by Maud Lewis. Nimbus Pub., 1981. Subj: Behavior – running away. Poetry, rhyme. Sea and seashore. Seasons – spring.

Woolf, Virginia. *The widow and the parrot* ill. by Julian Bell. Harcourt, 1988. ISBN 0-15-296783-4 Subj: Birds – parakeets, parrots. Fire. Houses. Humor.

Woolley, Catherine *see* Thayer, Jane

Worth, Bonnie. *Peter Cottontail's surprise* ill. by Greg Hildebrandt. Unicorn Publishing House, 1985. ISBN 0-88101-015-4 Subj: Animals – rabbits. Birthdays. Parties. Seasons – spring.

Worth, Valerie. *Small poems again* ill. by Natalie Babbitt. Farrar, 1985. ISBN 0-374-37074-5 Subj: Poetry, rhyme.

Still more small poems ill. by Natalie Babbitt. Farrar, 1978. ISBN 0-374-37258-6 Subj: Poetry, rhyme.

Worthington, Joan. *Teddy bear farmer* (Worthington, Phoebe)

Worthington, Phoebe. *Teddy bear baker* by Phoebe and Selby Worthington; ill. by authors. Warne, 1980. Subj: Careers – bakers. Foreign lands – England. Toys – teddy bears.

Teddy bear coalman: a story for the very young by Phoebe and Selby Worthington; ill. by authors. Warne, 1980. Subj: Foreign lands – England. Toys – teddy bears.

Teddy bear farmer by Phoebe and Joan Worthington; ill. by authors. Viking, 1985. ISBN 0-670-80342-1 Subj: Animals. Farms. Toys – teddy bears.

Worthington, Selby. *Teddy bear baker* (Worthington, Phoebe)

Teddy bear coalman (Worthington, Phoebe)

Wright, Dare. *The doll and the kitten* photos. by author. Doubleday, 1960. Subj: Animals – cats. Toys – dolls. Toys – teddy bears.

Edith and Midnight photos. by author. Doubleday, 1978. Subj: Toys – dolls. Toys – teddy bears.

Edith and Mr. Bear photos. by author. Random House, 1964. Subj: Behavior – running away. Toys – dolls. Toys – teddy bears.

Edith and the duckling photos. by author. Doubleday, 1981. Subj: Birds – ducks. Eggs. Toys – dolls. Toys – teddy bears.

The lonely doll photos. by author. Doubleday, 1957. Subj: Toys – dolls. Toys – teddy bears.

The lonely doll learns a lesson photos. by author. Random House, 1961. Subj: Animals – cats. Pets. Toys – dolls. Toys – teddy bears.

Look at a calf photos. by author. Random House, 1974. Subj: Animals – bulls, cows. Farms.

Look at a colt photos. by author. Random House, 1969. Subj: Animals – horses. Farms.

Look at a kitten photos. by author. Random House, 1975. Subj: Animals – cats.

Wright, Freire. *Beauty and the beast* ill. by adapt. David & Charles, 1985. ISBN 0-7182-6091-0 Subj: Character traits – loyalty. Folk and fairy tales. Magic.

Wright, Jill. *The old woman and the Willy Nilly Man* ill. by Glen Rounds. Putnam's, 1987. ISBN 0-399-21355-4 Subj: Activities – dancing. Behavior – trickery. Clothing. Folk and fairy tales. Humor.

Wright, Joan Richards. *Bugs* (Parker, Nancy Winslow)

Wright, Josephine Lord. *Cotton Cat and Martha Mouse* ill. by John E. Johnson. Dutton, 1966. Subj: Animals – cats. Animals – mice. Behavior – sharing. Poetry, rhyme.

Wright, Martin. *Granny Stickleback* (Moore, John)

Wyler, Rose. *Spooky tricks* by Rose Wyler and Gerald Ames; ill. by Tālivaldis Stubis. Harper, 1968. Subj: Magic.

Wyndham, Robert. *The Chinese Mother Goose rhymes* (Mother Goose)

Wyse, Lois. *Two guppies, a turtle and Aunt Edna* ill. by Roger Coast. Collins-World, 1966. Subj: Family life. Fish. Problem solving. Reptiles – turtles, tortoises. Telephone.

Yabuki, Seiji. *I love the morning* ill. by author. Collins-World, 1969 Subj: Emotions – happiness. Morning

Yabuuchi, Masayuki. *Animals sleeping* ill. by author. Putnam's, 1983. ISBN 0-399-20983-2 Subj: Animals. Sleep. Science.

Whose baby? ill. by author. Putnam's, 1985. ISBN 0-399-21210-8 Subj: Animals.

Whose footprints? ill. by author. Putnam's, 1985. ISBN 0-399-21209-4 Subj: Animals.

Yaffe, Alan. *The magic meatballs* ill. by Karen Born Andersen. Dial Pr., 1979. Subj: Behavior – dissatisfaction. Family life. Magic.

Yagawa, Sumiko. *The crane wife* tr. from Japanese by Katherine Paterson; ill. by Suekichi Akaba. Morrow, 1982. ISBN 0-688-00496-2 Subj: Activities – weaving. Birds – cranes. Character traits – kindness to animals. Folk and fairy tales. Foreign lands – Japan.

Yamaguchi, Tohr. *Two crabs and the moonlight* ill. by Marianne Yamaguchi. Holt, 1965. Subj: Crustacea. Moon.

Yamashita, Haruo. *Mice at the beach* ill. by Kazuo Iwamura. Morrow, 1987. ISBN 0-688-07064-7 Subj: Animals – mice. Family life. Safety. Sea and seashore.

Yashima, Mitsu. *Momo's kitten* ill. by Tarō Yashima. Viking, 1961. Subj: Animals – cats. Ethnic groups in the U.S. – Japanese-Americans.

Plenty to watch ill. by Tarō Yashima. Viking, 1954. Subj: Foreign lands – Japan.

Yashima, Tarō. *Crow boy* ill. by author. Viking, 1955. ISBN 0-670-24931-9 Subj: Caldecott award honor book. Character traits – shyness. Emotions – loneliness. Foreign lands – Japan. School.

Momo's kitten (Yashima, Mitsu)

Seashore story ill. by author. Viking, 1967. Subj: Caldecott award honor book. Folk and fairy tales. Reptiles – turtles, tortoises. Sea and seashore.

Umbrella ill. by author. Viking, 1958. Subj: Birthdays. Caldecott award honor book. City. Ethnic groups in the U.S. – Japanese-Americans. Umbrellas. Weather – rain.

The village tree ill. by author. Viking, 1953. Subj: Foreign lands – Japan. Seasons – summer. Trees.

The youngest one ill. by author. Viking, 1962. Subj: Character traits – shyness. Ethnic groups in the U.S. – Japanese-Americans. Friendship.

Yektai, Niki. *Bears in pairs* ill. by Diane de Groat. Bradbury Pr., 1987. ISBN 0-02-793691-0 Subj: Animals – bears. Concepts. Poetry, rhyme.

What's missing? ill. by Susannah Ryan. Clarion, 1987. ISBN 0-89919-510-5 Subj: Games. Problem solving.

Yeoman, John. *The bear's water picnic* ill. by Quentin Blake. Atheneum, 1987, 1970. ISBN 0-689-31386-1 Subj: Activities – picnicking. Animals – bears. Animals – hedgehogs. Animals – pigs. Animals – squirrels. Frogs and toads.

Mouse trouble ill. by Quentin Blake. Macmillan, 1972. Subj: Animals – cats. Animals – mice. Friendship. Windmills.

Our village ill. by Quentin Blake. Atheneum, 1988. ISBN 0-689-31451-5 Subj: Communities, neighborhoods. Poetry, rhyme.

The wild washerwomen: a new folk tale ill. by Quentin Blake. Crown, 1986. ISBN 0-517-56255-3 Subj: Activities – working. Behavior – misbehavior. Folk and fairy tales.

The young performing horse ill. by Quentin Blake. Parents, 1979. Subj: Animals – horses. Theater. Twins.

Yeomans, Thomas. *For every child a star: a Christmas story* ill. by Tomie de Paola. Holiday, 1986. ISBN 0-8234-0526-5 Subj: Holidays – Christmas. Night. Stars.

Yezback, Steven A. *Pumpkinseeds* ill. by Mozelle Thompson. Bobbs-Merrill, 1969. Subj: Behavior – solitude. City. Ethnic groups in the U.S. – Afro-Americans.

Ylla. *Animal babies* by Ylla and Arthur S. Gregor; ill. by Ylla. Harper, 1959. Designed by Luc Bouchage. Subj: Animals.

I'll show you cats by Ylla and Crosby Newell Bonsall; ill. by Ylla. Harper, 1964. Planned by Charles Rado; designed by Luc Bouchage. Subj: Animals – cats.

Listen, listen! (Bonsall, Crosby Newell)

The little elephant by Ylla and Arthur S. Gregor; ill. by Ylla. Harper, 1956. Designed by Luc Bouchage. Subj: Animals – elephants.

Look who's talking by Ylla and Crosby Newell Bonsall; ill. by Ylla. Harper, 1962. Planned by Charles Rado; designed by Luc Bouchage. Subj: Birds – ostriches. Zoos.

Polar bear brothers by Ylla and Crosby Newell Bonsall; ill. by Ylla. Harper, 1960. Designed by Luc Bouchage. Subj: Animals – polar bears.

Two little bears ill. by author. Harper, 1954. Subj: Animals – bears. Behavior – lost.

Yolen, Jane. *The acorn quest* ill. by Susanna Natti. Crowell, 1981. Subj: Animals. Character traits – bravery. Character traits – selfishness. Dragons. Humor.

All in the woodland early: an ABC book ill. by Jane Breskin Zalben; music and lyrics by author. Collins-World, 1980. Subj: ABC books. Forest, woods.

Commander Toad and the big black hole ill. by Bruce Degen. Coward, 1983. Subj: Frogs and toads. Space and space ships.

Commander Toad and the planet of the grapes ill. by Bruce Degen. Coward, 1982. Subj: Frogs and toads. Illness. Space and space ships.

Commander Toad in space ill. by Bruce Degen. Coward, 1980. Subj: Frogs and toads. Space and space ships.

Dragon night and other lullabies ill. by Demi. Methuen, 1980. Subj: Animals. Bedtime. Sleep. Songs.

The emperor and the kite ill. by Ed Young. Collins-World, 1967. Subj: Caldecott award honor book. Character traits – smallness. Family life – fathers. Foreign lands – China. Kites. Royalty.

The emperor and the kite ill. by Ed Young. Rev. ed. Putnam's, 1988. ISBN 0-399-21499-2 Subj: Character traits – smallness. Family life – fathers. Foreign lands – China. Kites. Royalty.

The giant's farm ill. by Tomie de Paola. Seabury Pr., 1977. Subj: Farms. Giants.

The giants go camping ill. by Tomie de Paola. Seabury Pr., 1979. Subj: Giants. Sports – camping.

The girl who loved the wind ill. by Ed Young. Crowell, 1972. Subj: Behavior – running away. Weather – wind.

The hundredth dove and other tales ill. by David Paladini. Crowell, 1977. Subj: Folk and fairy tales.

An invitation to the butterfly ball: a counting rhyme ill. by Jane Breskin Zalben. Parents, 1976. Subj: Animals. Counting. Poetry, rhyme.

The lullaby songbook ill. by Charles Mikolaycak; scores by Adam Stemple. Harcourt, 1986. ISBN 0-15-249903-2 Subj: Bedtime. Music. Songs.

Mice on ice ill. by Lawrence DiFiori. Dutton, 1980. Subj: Animals – mice. Animals – rats. Magic. Problem solving. Sports – ice skating. Theater.

Milkweed days photos. by Gabriel Amadeus Cooney. Crowell, 1976. Subj: Seasons – summer.

No bath tonight ill. by Nancy Winslow Parker. Crowell, 1978. Subj: Activities – bathing. Days of the week, months of the year. Family life – grandmothers.

Owl moon ill. by John Schoenherr. Philomel, 1987. ISBN 0-399-21457-7 Subj: Birds – owls. Caldecott award book. Family life – fathers. Forest, woods. Night.

Picnic with Piggins ill. by Jane Dyer. Harcourt, 1988. ISBN 0-15-261534-2 Subj: Activities – picnicking. Animals. Animals – pigs. Birthdays.

Piggins ill. by Jane Dyer. Harcourt, 1987. ISBN 0-15-261685-3 Subj: Animals. Animals – pigs. Behavior – stealing. Parties. Problem solving.

Ring of earth: a child's book of seasons ill. by John Wallner. Harcourt, 1986. ISBN 0-15-267140-4 Subj: Poetry, rhyme. Seasons.

The seeing stick ill. by Remy Charlip and Demetra Maraslis. Crowell, 1977. Subj: Foreign lands – China. Handicaps – blindness. Royalty. Senses – seeing.

The sleeping beauty (Grimm, Jacob)

Sleeping ugly ill. by Diane Stanley. Coward, 1981. Subj: Character traits – appearance. Folk and fairy tales. Magic.

Spider Jane ill. by Stefen Bernath. Coward, 1978. Subj: Behavior – sharing. Birds. Insects – flies. Spiders.

The three bears rhyme book ill. by Jane Dyer. Harcourt, 1987. ISBN 0-15-286-386-9 Subj: Animals – bears. Folk and fairy tales. Poetry, rhyme.

Yorinks, Arthur. *Bravo, Minski* ill. by Richard Egielski. Farrar, 1988. ISBN 0-374-30951-5 Subj: Behavior – seeking better things. Problem solving.

Company's coming ill. by David Small. Crown, 1988. ISBN 0-517-56751-2 Subj: Behavior – misunderstanding. Humor. Space and space ships.

Hey, Al ill. by Richard Egielski. Farrar, 1986. ISBN 0-374-33060-3 Subj: Animals – dogs. Behavior – running away. Caldecott award book. Dreams. Imagination.

Louis the fish ill. by Richard Egielski. Farrar, 1980. Subj: Careers – butchers. Fish. Imagination.

Yoshi. *Who's hiding here?* ill. by author. Picture Book Studio, 1987. ISBN 0-88708-041-3 Subj: Animals. Format, unusual – toy and movable books. Poetry, rhyme.

Youldon, Gillian. *Colors* ill. by author. Watts, 1979. Subj: Concepts – color. Format, unusual – toy and movable books.

Counting ill. by James Hodgson. Watts, 1980. Subj: Counting. Format, unusual.

Numbers ill. by author. Watts, 1979. Subj: Counting. Format, unusual – toy and movable books.

Shapes ill. by author. Watts, 1979. Subj: Concepts – shape. Format, unusual.

Sizes ill. by author. Watts, 1979. Subj: Concepts – size. Format, unusual.

Young animals in the zoo ill. with photos. Imported Pubs., 1983. Subj: Animals. Format, unusual – board books. Wordless.

Young domestic animals ill. with photos. Imported Pubs., 1983. Subj: Animals. Format, unusual – board books. Wordless.

Young, Ed. *The rooster's horns: a Chinese puppet play to make and perform* by Ed Young and Hilary Beckett; ill. by Ed Young. Collins-World, 1978. Subj: Folk and fairy tales. Foreign lands – China. Puppets.

The terrible Nung Gwama: a Chinese folktale ill. by author. Collins-World, 1978. Subj: Character traits – cleverness. Folk and fairy tales. Foreign lands – China. Monsters.

Up a tree ill. by author. Harper, 1983. Subj: Animals – cats. Trees. Wordless.

Young, Edward *see* Young, Ed

Young, Evelyn. *The tale of Tai* ill. by author. Oxford Univ. Pr., 1940. Subj: Behavior – lost. Foreign lands – China. Holidays – Chinese New Year.

Wu and Lu and Li ill. by author. Oxford Univ. Pr., 1939. Subj: Family life. Foreign lands – China.

Young, Helen. *A throne for Sesame* ill. by Shirley Hughes. Elsevier-Dutton, 1979. Subj: Behavior – growing up.

Young, Miriam Burt. *If I drove a bus* ill. by Robert M. Quackenbush. Lothrop, 1973. Subj: Buses. Careers – bus drivers. Transportation.

If I drove a car ill. by Robert M. Quackenbush. Lothrop, 1971. Subj: Automobiles. Transportation.

If I drove a tractor ill. by Robert M. Quackenbush. Lothrop, 1973. Subj: Machines.

If I drove a train ill. by Robert M. Quackenbush. Lothrop, 1972. Subj: Trains. Transportation.

If I drove a truck ill. by Robert M. Quackenbush. Lothrop, 1967. Subj: Careers – truck drivers. Transportation. Trucks.

If I flew a plane ill. by Robert M. Quackenbush. Lothrop, 1970. Subj: Activities – flying. Airplanes, airports. Careers – airplane pilots. Transportation.

If I rode a horse ill. by Robert M. Quackenbush. Lothrop, 1973. Subj: Animals – horses.

If I rode an elephant ill. by Robert M. Quackenbush. Lothrop, 1974. Subj: Animals – elephants.

If I sailed a boat ill. by Robert M. Quackenbush. Lothrop, 1971. Subj: Boats, ships.

Jellybeans for breakfast ill. by Beverly Komoda. Parents, 1968. Subj: Activities – playing. Imagination.

Miss Suzy's Easter surprise ill. by Arnold Lobel. Parents, 1972. Subj: Animals – squirrels. Holidays – Easter.

Please don't feed Horace ill. by Abner Graboff. Dial Pr., 1961. Subj: Animals – hippopotami. Zoos.

The sugar mouse cake ill. by Margaret Bloy Graham. Scribner's, 1964. Subj: Activities – cooking. Animals – mice. Careers – bakers. Food. Royalty.

The witch mobile ill. by Victoria Chess. Lothrop, 1969. Subj: Holidays – Halloween. Witches.

Young, Ruth. *My baby-sitter* ill. by author. Viking, 1987. ISBN 0-670-81305-2 Subj: Activities – baby-sitting.

My blanket ill. by author. Viking, 1987. ISBN 0-670-81306-0 Subj: Babies.

My potty chair ill. by author. Viking, 1987. ISBN 0-670-81307-9 Subj: Behavior – growing up.

The new baby ill. by author. Viking, 1987. ISBN 0-670-81304-4 Subj: Babies. Sibling rivalry.

Youngs, Betty. *One panda: an animal counting book* ill. by author. Merrimack, 1985. ISBN 0-370-30150-1 Subj: Animals. Counting.

Pink pigs in mud: a color book ill. by author. Merrimack, 1985. ISBN 0-370-30344-X Subj: Animals. Concepts – color.

Yudell, Lynn Deena. *Make a face* ill. by author. Little, 1970. Subj: Anatomy. Emotions. Games. Participation.

Yulya. *Bears are sleeping* ill. by Nonny Hogrogian. Scribner's, 1967. Subj: Animals – bears. Hibernation. Music. Sleep. Songs.

Zacharias, Thomas. *But where is the green parrot?* by Thomas and Wanda Zacharias; ill. by Wanda Zacharias. Delacorte Pr., 1968. Translation of Und wo ist der grüne Papagei? Subj: Birds – parakeets, parrots. Concepts – color. Games.

Zacharias, Wanda. *But where is the green parrot?* (Zacharias, Thomas)

Zaffo, George J. *The big book of real airplanes* ill. by author. Grosset, 1951. Subj: Airplanes, airports. Helicopters. Transportation.

Big book of real fire engines text by Elizabeth Cameron; ill. by author. Grosset, 1950. Subj: Careers – firefighters.

The giant book of things in space ill. by author. Doubleday, 1969. Subj: Space and space ships.

The giant nursery book of things that go: fire engines, trains, boats, trucks, airplanes ill. by author. Doubleday, 1959. Subj: Airplanes, airports. Boats, ships. Transportation. Trucks.

The giant nursery book of things that work ill. by author. Doubleday, 1967. Subj: Machines. Tools. Transportation.

Zagone, Theresa. *No nap for me* ill. by Lillian Hoban. Dutton, 1978. Subj: Behavior – growing up. Sleep.

Zakhoder, Boris Vladimirovich. *How a piglet crashed the Christmas party* tr. by Marguerita Rudolph; ill. by Kurt Werth. Lothrop, 1971. Subj: Animals – pigs. Holidays – Christmas.

Rosachok tr. by Marguerita Rudolph; ill. by Yaroslava. Lothrop, 1970. Translation of Rusachok. Subj: Animals – rabbits. Behavior – dissatisfaction. Character traits – optimism. Frogs and toads.

Zalben, Jane Breskin. *Basil and Hillary* ill. by author. Macmillan, 1975. Subj: Animals. Animals – pigs. Farms.

Beni's first Chanukah ill. by author. Holt, 1988. ISBN 0-8050-0479-3 Subj: Animals – bears. Family life. Friendship. Holidays – Hanukkah. Jewish culture.

Norton's nighttime ill. by author. Collins-World, 1979. Subj: Animals. Bedtime. Forest, woods. Night. Noise, sounds.

Oliver and Alison's week ill. by Emily Arnold McCully. Farrar, 1980. Subj: Activities. Friendship.

A perfect nose for Ralph ill. by John Wallner. Putnam's, 1980. Subj: Emotions – love. Toys – teddy bears.

Zallinger, Peter. *Dinosaurs* ill. by author. Random House, 1977. Subj: Dinosaurs. Science.

Zametkin, Laura K. *see* Hobson, Laura Z.

Zander, Hans. *My blue chair* ill. by author. Firefly Pr., 1985. ISBN 0-920303-16-1 Subj: Behavior – losing things.

Zano, Gina Bell *see* Balzano, Jeanne

Zaslavsky, Claudia. *Count on your fingers African style* ill. by Jerry Pinkney. Crowell, 1980. Subj: Counting. Foreign lands – Africa.

Zelinsky, Paul O. *The lion and the stoat* ill. by author. Greenwillow, 1984. Subj: Animals – lions. Animals – weasels. Art. Friendship.

The maid and the mouse and the odd-shaped house ill. by author. Dodd, 1981. Subj: Animals – mice. Folk and fairy tales. Houses.

Rumpelstiltskin (Grimm, Jacob)

Zemach, Harve. *Duffy and the devil: a Cornish tale* ill. by Margot Zemach. Farrar, 1973. Subj: Caldecott award book. Devil. Folk and fairy tales. Foreign lands – England.

The judge: an untrue tale ill. by Margot Zemach. Farrar, 1969. Subj: Caldecott award honor book. Careers – judges. Monsters. Poetry, rhyme.

Mommy, buy me a China doll: adapted from an Ozark children's song ill. by Margot Zemach. Follett, 1966. Subj: Music. Songs. Toys – dolls.

Nail soup: a Swedish folk tale ill. by Margot Zemach. Follett, 1964. Subj: Character traits – cleverness. Folk and fairy tales. Foreign lands – Sweden.

The tricks of Master Dabble ill. by Margot Zemach. Holt, 1965. Subj: Behavior – trickery. Humor. Royalty.

Zemach, Kaethe. *The beautiful rat* ill. by author. Four Winds Pr., 1979. Subj: Animals – rats. Folk and fairy tales.

The funny dream ill. by author. Greenwillow, 1988. ISBN 0-688-07501-0 Subj: Dreams. Family life.

Zemach, Margot. *It could always be worse: a Yiddish folk tale* ill. by author. Farrar, 1976. Subj: Caldecott award honor book. Folk and fairy tales. Humor. Jewish culture. Problem solving.

Jake and Honeybunch go to heaven ill. by author. Farrar, 1982. ISBN 0-374-33652-0 Subj: Animals – mules. Behavior – misbehavior. Ethnic groups in the U.S. – Afro-Americans. Folk and fairy tales.

The little tiny woman ill. by author. Bobbs-Merrill, 1965. Subj: Folk and fairy tales. Ghosts.

The three wishes: an old story adapt. and ill. by Margot Zemach. Farrar, 1986. ISBN 0-374-37529-1 Subj: Behavior – wishing. Character traits – foolishness. Folk and fairy tales.

To Hilda for helping ill. by author. Farrar, 1977. Subj: Character traits – helpfulness. Emotions – envy, jealousy. Family life.

Zemach-Bersin, Kaethe *see* Zemach, Kaethe

Zemke, Deborah. *The way it happened* ill. by author. Houghton, 1988. ISBN 0-395-47984-3 Subj: Behavior – misunderstanding. Behavior – secrets.

Zhitkov, Boris. *How I hunted for the little fellows* tr. from Russian by Djemma Bider; ill. by Paul O. Zelinsky. Dodd, 1979. Subj: Behavior – misbehavior. Character traits – curiosity. Foreign lands – Russia. Family life – grandmothers.

Ziefert, Harriet. *All clean!* ill. by Henrik Drescher. Harper, 1986. ISBN 0-694-00100-7 Subj: Animals.

All gone! ill. by Henrik Drescher. Harper, 1986. ISBN 0-694-00098-1 Subj: Animals.

Baby Ben's bow-wow book ill. by Norman Gorbaty. Random House, 1984. ISBN 0-394-86821-8 Subj: Animals. Babies. Format, unusual – board books.

Baby Ben's busy book ill. by Norman Gorbaty. Random House, 1984. ISBN 0-394-86819-6 Subj: Activities. Babies. Format, unusual – board books.

Baby Ben's go-go book ill. by Norman Gorbaty. Random House, 1984. ISBN 0-394-86820-X Subj: Activities – playing. Babies. Format, unusual – board books. Toys.

Baby Ben's noisy book ill. by Norman Gorbaty. Random House, 1984. ISBN 0-394-86822-6 Subj: Activities. Babies. Format, unusual – board books.

Bear all year ill. by Arnold Lobel. Harper, 1986. ISBN 0-694-0087-6 Subj: Animals – bears. Format, unusual – toy and movable books. Games. Seasons.

Bear gets dressed ill. by Arnold Lobel. Harper, 1986. ISBN 0-694-0086-8 Subj: Animals – bears. Clothing. Format, unusual – toy and movable books. Games.

Bear goes shopping ill. by Arnold Lobel. Harper, 1986. ISBN 0-694-00085-X Subj: Animals – bears. Format, unusual – toy and movable books. Games. Shopping.

Bear's busy morning ill. by Arnold Lobel. Harper, 1986. ISBN 0-694-00084-1 Subj: Activities. Animals – bears. Format, unusual – toy and movable books. Games.

Breakfast time! ill. by author. Viking, 1988. ISBN 0-670-81579-9 Subj: Animals – rabbits. Babies. Food.

Bye-bye, daddy! ill. by author. Viking, 1988. ISBN 0-670-81581-0 Subj: Animals – rabbits. Babies.

Chocolate mud cake ill. by Karen Gundersheimer. Harper, 1988. ISBN 0-06-026892-1 Subj: Family life – grandparents.

A clean house for Mole and Mouse ill. by David Prebenna. Penguin, 1988. ISBN 0-670-82032-6 Subj: Animals – mice. Animals – moles. Character traits – cleanliness.

Cock-a-doodle-doo! ill. by Henrik Drescher. Harper, 1986. ISBN 0-694-00099-X Subj: Animals.

A dozen dogs: a read-and-count story ill. by Carol Nicklaus. Random House, 1985. ISBN 0-394-96935-9 Subj: Animals – dogs. Counting. Sea and seashore.

Good morning, sun! ill. by author. Viking, 1988. ISBN 0-670-81578-0 Subj: Animals – rabbits. Babies. Morning.

Good night everyone! ill. by author. Little, 1988. ISBN 0-316-98756-5 Subj: Bedtime. Sleep. Toys.

Good night, Jessie! ill. by Mavis Smith. Random House, 1987. ISBN 0-394-89193-7 Subj: Behavior – losing things. Family life. Sea and seashore.

Happy birthday, Grandpa! ill. by Sidney Levitt. Harper, 1988. ISBN 0-694-00242-9 Subj: Animals. Animals – rabbits. Birthdays. Family life – grandfathers.

Happy Easter, Grandma! ill. by Sidney Levitt. Harper, 1988. ISBN 0-694-00225-9 Subj: Animals – rabbits. Birds. Eggs. Holidays – Easter.

Harry takes a bath ill. by Mavis Smith. Viking, 1987. ISBN 0-670-81721-X Subj: Activities – bathing. Animals – hippopotami.

Hurry up, Jessie! ill. by Mavis Smith. Random House, 1987. ISBN 0-394-89194-5 Subj: Character traits – cleanliness. Night.

I won't go to bed! ill. by Andrea Baruffi. Little, 1987. ISBN 0-316-98768-9 Subj: Bedtime.

Jason's bus ride ill. by Simms Taback. Viking, 1987. ISBN 0-670-81718-X Subj: Buses.

Keeping daddy awake on the way home from the beach ill. by Seymour Chwast. Harper, 1986. ISBN 0-694-00080-9 Subj: Activities – traveling. Family life. Sea and seashore.

Let's get dressed! ill. by author. Viking, 1988. ISBN 0-670-81580-2 Subj: Animals – rabbits. Babies. Clothing.

Let's go! Piggety Pig ill. by David Prebenna. Little, 1986. ISBN 0-316-98760-3 Subj: Animals – mice. Animals – pigs. Concepts – opposites.

Lewis the fire fighter ill. by Carol Nicklaus. Random House, 1986. ISBN 0-394-97618-5 Subj: Activities – playing. Fire. Imagination.

Listen! Piggety Pig ill. by David Prebenna. Little, 1986. ISBN 0-316-98761-1 Subj: Animals. Noise, sounds.

Me, too! Me, too! ill. by Karen Gundersheimer. Harper, 1988. ISBN 0-06-026893-X Subj: Behavior – sharing.

Mike and Tony: best friends ill. by Catherine Siracusa. Viking, 1987. ISBN 0-670-81719-8 Subj: Friendship.

My sister says nothing ever happens when we go sailing ill. by Seymour Chwast. Harper, 1986. ISBN 0-694-00081-7 Subj: Boats, ships. Family life.

A new coat for Anna ill. by Anita Lobel. Knopf, 1988. ISBN 0-394-97426-3 Subj: Clothing. Family life. War.

A new house for Mole and Mouse ill. by Mavis Smith. Viking, 1987. ISBN 0-670-81720-1 Subj: Animals – mice. Animals – moles. Houses. Moving.

Nicky upstairs and down ill. by Richard Eric Brown. Viking, 1987. ISBN 0-670-81717-1 Subj: Animals – cats.

Nicky's Christmas surprise ill. by Richard Eric Brown. Penguin, 1985. ISBN 0-14-050555-5 Subj: Animals – cats. Holidays – Christmas.

Nicky's friends ill. by Richard Eric Brown. Viking, 1986. ISBN 0-670-81298-6 Subj: Animals – cats. Friendship. Format, unusual – board books.

No more! Piggety Pig ill. by David Prebenna. Little, 1986. ISBN 0-316-98763-8 Subj: Animals – mice. Animals – pigs. Concepts – color.

No, no, Nicky! ill. by Richard Eric Brown. Viking, 1986. ISBN 0-670-81297-8 Subj: Animals – cats. Format, unusual – board books. Safety.

On our way to the barn by Harriet Ziefert and Simms Taback; ill. by Simms Taback. Harper, 1985. ISBN 0-06-026877-8 Subj: Animals. Farms. Format, unusual – board books. Noise, sounds. Poetry, rhyme.

On our way to the forest by Harriet Ziefert and Simms Taback; ill. by Simms Taback. Harper, 1985. ISBN 0-06-026878-6 Subj: Forest, woods. Format, unusual – board books. Noise, sounds. Poetry, rhyme.

On our way to the water by Harriet Ziefert and Simms Taback; ill. by Simms Taback. Harper, 1985. ISBN 0-06-026879-4 Subj: Format, unusual – board books. Noise, sounds. Poetry, rhyme.

On our way to the zoo by Harriet Ziefert and Simms Taback; ill. by Simms Taback. Harper, 1985. ISBN 0-06-026880-8 Subj: Animals. Format, unusual – board books. Noise, sounds. Poetry, rhyme. Zoos.

Piggety Pig from morn 'til night ill. by David Prebenna. Little, 1986. ISBN 0-316-98764-6 Subj: Activities. Animals – pigs.

Run! Run! ill. by Henrik Drescher. Harper, 1986. ISBN 0-694-00097-3 Subj: Animals.

Sarah's questions ill. by Susan Bonners. Lothrop, 1986. ISBN 0-688-05615-6 Subj: Character traits – questioning. Family life – mothers. Nature.

Say good night! ill. by Catherine Siracusa. Viking, 1987. ISBN 0-670-81722-8 Subj: Bedtime. Morning. Night. Sleep.

Sleepy dog ill. by Norman Gorbaty. Random House, 1984. Subj: Animals – dogs. Sleep.

Strike four! ill. by Mavis Smith. Viking, 1988. ISBN 0-670-82033-4 Subj: Activities – playing. Behavior – misbehavior. Family life.

Surprise! ill. by Mary Morgan. Viking, 1988. ISBN 0-670-82036-9 Subj: Birthdays. Family life – mothers. Food.

Where's the cat? ill. by Arnold Lobel. Harper, 1987. ISBN 0-694-00185-6 Subj: Animals – cats. Behavior – hiding. Format, unusual. Format, unusual – board books.

Where's the dog? ill. by Arnold Lobel. Harper, 1987. ISBN 0-694-00184-8 Subj: Animals – dogs. Behavior – hiding. Format, unusual. Format, unusual – board books.

Where's the guinea pig? ill. by Arnold Lobel. Harper, 1987. ISBN 0-694-00182-1 Subj: Animals – guinea pigs. Behavior – hiding. Format, unusual. Format, unusual – board books.

Where's the turtle? ill. by Arnold Lobel. Harper, 1987. ISBN 0-694-00183-X Subj: Behavior – hiding. Format, unusual. Format, unusual – board books. Reptiles – turtles, tortoises.

Ziegler, Sandra. *A visit to the bakery* photos. by author. Childrens Pr., 1987. ISBN 0-516-01495-1 Subj: Careers – bakers.

Ziegler, Ursina. *Squaps the moonling* tr. by Barbara Kowall Gollob; ill. by Sita Jucker. Atheneum, 1969. Translation of Squaps, der Mondling. Subj: Moon. Space and space ships.

Zijlstra, Tjerk. *Benny and his geese* ill. by Ivo de Weerd. McGraw-Hill, 1975. Translation of Bennie en zijn ganzen. Subj: Birds – geese. Folk and fairy tales. Wizards.

Zimelman, Nathan. *If I were strong enough...* ill. by Diane Paterson. Abingdon Pr., 1982. Subj: Behavior – growing up. Family life.

Mean Murgatroyd and the ten cats ill. by Tony Auth. Dutton, 1984. Subj: Animals – cats. Animals – dogs. Character traits – meanness.

Once when I was five ill. by Carol Rogers. Steck-Vaughn, 1967. Subj: Birthdays. Imagination.

Positively no pets allowed ill. by Pamela Johnson. Dutton, 1980. Subj: Animals – gorillas. Pets.

The star of Melvin ill. by Olivier Dunrea. Macmillan, 1987. ISBN 0-02-793750-X Subj: Angels. Holidays – Christmas.

To sing a song as big as Ireland ill. by Joseph Low. Follett, 1967. Subj: Behavior – wishing. Foreign lands – Ireland. Elves and little people. Holidays – St. Patrick's Day. Music.

Walls are to be walked ill. by Donald Carrick. Dutton, 1977. ISBN 0-525-42175-0 Subj: Activities – playing.

Zimmer, Dirk. *The trick-or-treat trap* ill. by author. Harper, 1982. Subj: Holidays – Halloween. Parties. Witches.

Zimmerman, Andrea Griffing. *Yetta, the trickster* ill. by Harold Berson. Seabury Pr., 1978. Subj: Foreign lands – Russia. Humor.

Zimmerman, Baruch. *A Japanese fairy tale* (Iké, Jane Hori)

Zimnik, Reiner. *The bear on the motorcycle* tr. by Cornelia Schaeffer; ill. by author. Atheneum, 1963. Translation of Der bär auf dem motorrad. Subj: Animals – bears. Behavior – running away. Circus. Motorcycles.

The proud circus horse ill. by author. Pantheon, 1957. Subj: Animals – horses. Behavior – running away. Character traits – pride. Circus.

Zindel, Paul. *I love my mother* ill. by John Melo. Harper, 1975. Subj: Emotions – loneliness. Emotions – love. Family life – mothers.

Ziner, Feenie. *Counting carnival* by Feenie Ziner and Paul Galdone; ill. by Paul Galdone. Coward, 1962. Subj: Activities – playing. Counting. Cumulative tales. Ethnic groups in the U.S. – Afro-Americans. Parades. Poetry, rhyme.

The true book of time by Feenie Ziner and Elizabeth Thompson; ill. by Katherine Evans. Children's Pr., 1956. Subj: Time.

Zinnemann-Hope, Pam. *Find your coat, Ned* ill. by Kady MacDonald Denton. Macmillan, 1988. ISBN 0-689-50426-9 Subj: Behavior – losing things. Clothing. Pets. Weather – rain.

Let's go shopping, Ned ill. by Kady MacDonald Denton. Macmillan, 1987. ISBN 0-689-50416-0 Subj: Shopping.

Let's play ball, Ned ill. by Kady MacDonald Denton. Macmillan, 1988. ISBN 0-689-50427-6 Subj: Activities – playing. Family life.

Time for bed, Ned ill. by Kady MacDonald Denton. Macmillan, 1987. ISBN 0-689-50415-2 Subj: Bedtime. Family life – mothers.

Zion, Gene. *All falling down* ill. by Margaret Bloy Graham. Harper, 1951. Subj: Caldecott award honor book. Concepts – up and down.

Dear garbage man ill. by Margaret Bloy Graham. Harper, 1957. Subj: Careers – garbage collectors. City.

Harry and the lady next door ill. by Margaret Bloy Graham. Harper, 1960. Subj: Animals – dogs. Noise, sounds. Problem solving.

Harry by the sea ill. by Margaret Bloy Graham. Harper, 1965. Subj: Animals – dogs. Sea and seashore. Seasons – summer.

Harry, the dirty dog ill. by Margaret Bloy Graham. Harper, 1956. Subj: Activities – bathing. Animals – dogs. Behavior – running away.

Hide and seek day ill. by Margaret Bloy Graham. Harper, 1954. Subj: Behavior – hiding. City. Games.

Jeffie's party ill. by Margaret Bloy Graham. Harper, 1957. Subj: Games. Parties.

The meanest squirrel I ever met ill. by Margaret Bloy Graham. Scribner's, 1962. Subj: Animals – squirrels. Character traits – meanness. Friendship. Holidays – Thanksgiving.

No roses for Harry ill. by Margaret Bloy Graham. Harper, 1958. Subj: Animals – dogs. Clothing.

The plant sitter ill. by Margaret Bloy Graham. Harper, 1959. Subj: Plants.

Really spring ill. by Margaret Bloy Graham. Harper, 1956. Subj: Seasons – spring.

The summer snowman ill. by Margaret Bloy Graham. Harper, 1955. Subj: Holidays – Fourth of July. Seasons – summer. Snowmen. Weather – snow.

Zirbes, Laura. *How many bears?* ill. by E. Harper Johnson. Putnam's, 1960. Subj: Animals – bears. Counting.

Zola, Meguido. *The dream of promise: a folktale in Hebrew and English* ill. by Ruben Zellermayer. Kids Can Pr., 1981. Subj: Folk and fairy tales. Foreign languages. Jewish culture. Self-concept.

Only the best ill. by Valerie Littlewood. Watts, 1982. Subj: Emotions – love. Family life – fathers.

Zoll, Max Alfred. *Animal babies* tr. by Violetta Castillo; ed. by Hanns Reich; ill. by author. Hill and Wang, 1971. Translation of Tierkinder. Subj: Animals.

A flamingo is born tr. by Catherine Edwards Sadler; photos. by Winifried Noack. Putnam's, 1978. Subj: Birds – flamingos. Science.

Zolotow, Charlotte. *The beautiful Christmas tree* ill. by Ruth Robbins. Parnassus Pr., 1972. Subj: Holidays – Christmas. Trees.

Big sister and little sister ill. by Martha G. Alexander. Harper, 1966. Subj: Behavior – running away. Family life.

The bunny who found Easter ill. by Betty Peterson. Parnassus Pr., 1959. Subj: Animals – rabbits. Holidays – Easter.

But not Billy ill. by Kay Chorao. Harper, 1983. Subj: Babies. Behavior – growing up.

Do you know what I'll do? ill. by Garth Williams. Harper, 1958. Subj: Babies. Emotions – love. Family life.

Flocks of birds ill. by Ruth Lercher Bornstein. Crowell, 1981. Subj: Bedtime. Birds.

The hating book ill. by Ben Shecter. Harper, 1969. Subj: Behavior – gossip. Emotions – hate. Friendship.

Hold my hand ill. by Thomas di Grazia. Harper, 1972. Subj: Friendship. Weather – snow.

I have a horse of my own ill. by Yōko Mitsuhashi. Crowell, 1980. Subj: Animals – horses. Dreams. Night.

I know a lady ill. by James Stevenson. Greenwillow, 1984. Subj: Character traits – kindness. Old age.

I like to be little ill. by Erik Blegvad. Harper, 1987. ISBN 0-690-04674-X Subj: Behavior – growing up. Family life – mothers.

If it weren't for you ill. by Ben Shecter. Harper, 1966. Subj: Family life. Sibling rivalry.

In my garden ill. by Roger Antoine Duvoisin. Lothrop, 1960. Subj: Plants. Seasons.

It's not fair ill. by William Pène Du Bois. Harper, 1976. Subj: Behavior – dissatisfaction. Emotions – envy, jealousy. Family life.

Janey ill. by Ronald Himler. Harper, 1973. Subj: Emotions – loneliness. Friendship. Moving.

May I visit? ill. by Erik Blegvad. Harper, 1976. Subj: Behavior – growing up. Emotions – love. Family life.

Mr. Rabbit and the lovely present ill. by Maurice Sendak. Harper, 1962. Subj: Animals – rabbits. Birthdays. Caldecott award honor book. Concepts – color. Family life – mothers. Holidays – Easter.

My friend John ill. by Ben Shecter. Harper, 1968. Subj: Friendship.

My grandson Lew ill. by William Pène Du Bois. Harper, 1974. Subj: Death. Family life. Family life – grandfathers.

The new friend ill. by Emily Arnold McCully. Crowell, 1981. Subj: Behavior – sharing. Friendship.

One step, two... ill. by Roger Antoine Duvoisin. Lothrop, 1955. Subj: Activities – walking. City. Counting.

Over and over ill. by Garth Williams. Harper, 1957. Subj: Holidays. Time.

The park book ill. by Hans Augusto Rey. Harper, 1944. Subj: Activities – playing. City.

The poodle who barked at the wind ill. by Roger Antoine Duvoisin. Lothrop, 1964. Subj: Animals – dogs. Noise, sounds. Pets.

The quarreling book ill. by Arnold Lobel. Harper, 1963. Subj: Behavior – fighting, arguing. Cumulative tales. Emotions – anger. Weather – rain.

River winding ill. by Kazue Mizumura. Crowell, 1978. Subj: Poetry, rhyme.

A rose, a bridge, and a wild black horse ill. by Robin Spowart. Harper, 1987. ISBN 0-06-026939-1 Subj: Emotions – love. Family life.

Say it! ill. by James Stevenson. Greenwillow, 1980. Subj: Activities – walking. Emotions – love. Family life – mothers. Nature. Seasons – fall.

The sky was blue ill. by Garth Williams. Harper, 1963. Subj: Emotions – love. Family life.

Sleepy book ill. by Ilse Plume. Rev. ed. Harper, 1988. ISBN 0-06-026968-5 Subj: Animals. Bedtime. Sleep.

The sleepy book ill. by Vladimir Bobri. Lothrop, 1958. Subj: Bedtime. Sleep.

Some things go together ill. by Karen Gundersheimer. Rev. ed. Crowell, 1983. Subj: Family life – mothers. Poetry, rhyme.

Someday ill. by Arnold Lobel. Harper, 1965. Subj: Behavior – wishing. Dreams.

Someone new ill. by Erik Blegvad. Harper, 1978. ISBN 0-06-027018-7 Subj: Behavior – growing up. Family life.

Something is going to happen ill. by Catherine Stock. Harper, 1988. ISBN 0-06-027029-2 Subj: Morning. Weather – snow.

The song ill. by Nancy Tafuri. Greenwillow, 1982. Subj: Nature. Seasons. Songs.

The storm book ill. by Margaret Bloy Graham. Harper, 1952. Subj: Caldecott award honor book. Emotions – fear. Weather. Weather – rain. Weather – rainbows.

Summer is... ill. by Ruth Lercher Bornstein. Crowell, 1983. Subj: Poetry, rhyme. Seasons – summer.

The summer night ill. by Ben Shecter. Harper, 1974. Published in 1958 under the title The night when mother was away. ISBN 0-06-026960-X Subj: Activities – walking. Bedtime. Family life. Family life – fathers.

Three funny friends ill. by Mary Chalmers. Harper, 1961. Subj: Emotions – loneliness. Friendship. Imagination – imaginary friends.

A tiger called Thomas ill. by Catherine Stock. Lothrop, 1988. ISBN 0-688-06697-6 Subj: Character traits – shyness. Emotions – loneliness. Holidays – Halloween.

A tiger called Thomas ill. by Kurt Werth. Lothrop, 1963. Subj: Character traits – shyness. Emotions – loneliness. Holidays – Halloween.

Timothy too! ill. by Ruth Robbins. Houghton, 1986. ISBN 0-395-39378-7 Subj: Friendship. Sibling rivalry.

The unfriendly book ill. by William Pène Du Bois. Harper, 1975. ISBN 0-06-026931-6 Subj: Behavior – fighting, arguing. Friendship.

Wake up and good night ill. by Leonard Weisgard. Harper, 1971. Subj: Bedtime. Morning. Night.

When I have a son ill. by Hilary Knight. Harper, 1967. Subj: Behavior – growing up. Family life. Imagination.

When the wind stops ill. by Joe Lasker. Abelard-Schuman, 1962. Subj: Bedtime. Night. Weather – wind.

The white marble ill. by Lilian Obligado. Abelard-Schuman, 1963. Subj: Activities – playing. Friendship. Night.

William's doll ill. by William Pène Du Bois. Harper, 1972. Subj: Family life. Family life – grandparents. Toys – dolls.

Zolotow, Charlotte Shapiro *see* Zolotow, Charlotte

Zoo animals ill. with photos. Imported Pubs., 1983. Subj: Animals. Format, unusual – board books. Wordless.

Zusman, Evelyn. *The Passover parrot* ill. by Katherine Janus Kahn. Kar-Ben Copies, 1984. Subj: Birds – parakeets, parrots. Family life. Holidays – Passover. Jewish culture.

Zweifel, Frances. *Animal baby-sitters* ill. by Irene Brady. Morrow, 1981. Subj: Activities – babysitting. Animals. Nature.

Bony ill. by Whitney Darrow, Jr. Harper, 1977. ISBN 0-06-027071-3 Subj: Animals – squirrels. Pets.

Zwetchkenbaum, G. *The Peanuts shape circus puzzle book* ill. by author. Scholastic, 1983. Subj: Riddles.

The Peanuts sleepy time puzzle book ill. by author. Scholastic, 1983. Subj: Riddles.

The Snoopy farm puzzle book ill. by author. Scholastic, 1983. Subj: Riddles.

Snoopy safari puzzle book ill. by author. Scholastic, 1983. Subj: Riddles.

Title Index

Titles appear in alphabetical sequence with the author's name in parentheses, followed by the page number of the Bibliographic Guide. For identical title listings, the illustrator's name is given to further identify the version. In the case of variant titles, both the original and differing titles are listed.

A

C

F

G

L

M

O

P

Q

R

S

T

W

Z

Illustrator Index

Illustrators appear alphabetically in boldface followed by their titles. Names in parentheses are authors of the titles when different than the illustrator. Page numbers refer to the full listing in the Bibliographic Guide.

B

Dance, dance, Amy-Chan!, 494
Frog fun (Stratemeyer, Clara Georgeanna), 648
Indian Two Feet and his eagle feather (Friskey, Margaret), 466
Just one more block (Mayers, Patrick), 566
Left, right, left, right! (Stanek, Muriel), 642
What is a bird? (Darby, Gene), 438
What is a butterfly? (Darby, Gene), 438
What is a fish? (Darby, Gene), 438
What is a plant? (Darby, Gene), 438
What is a turtle? (Darby, Gene), 438

Hay, Dean. *I see a lot of things*, 495
Now I can count, 495

Hayashi, Akiko. *Anna's secret friend* (Tsutsui, Yoriko), 657
Before the picnic (Tsutsui, Yoriko), 657
A house of leaves (Soya, Kiyoshi), 640

Hayden, Chuck. *Orange Oliver* (Lasson, Robert), 537

Hayes, Geoffrey. *Bear by himself*, 495
Elroy and the witch's child, 495
Hocus and Pocus at the circus (Manushkin, Fran), 560
Moon dragon (Manushkin, Fran), 560
The mystery of the pirate ghost, 495
Patrick and his grandpa, 495
Patrick and Ted, 495
The secret inside, 495
When the wind blew (Brown, Margaret Wise), 404

Hayes, William D. (William Dimmity). *Sebastian and the dragon* (Kumin, Maxine), 534

Haynes, Robert. *The elephant that ga-lumphed* (Ward, Nanda Weedon), 667

Hays, Michael. *Abiyoyo* (Seeger, Pete), 627
A birthday for Blue (Lydon, Kerry Raines), 551

Hazard, Eleanor. *How to travel with grownups* (Bridgman, Elizabeth), 399

Heale, Jonathan. *Tibber* (Mayne, William), 566

Hearn, Diane Dawson *see* Dawson, Diane

Hearn, Lafcadio. *The funny little woman* (Mosel, Arlene), 575

Hechtkopf, H. *David and Goliath* (Brin, Ruth F.), 400
Jonah's journey (Haiz, Danah), 489
The story of Esther (Brin, Ruth F.), 400

Heckler, Bill. *Red is never a mouse* (Clifford, Eth), 425

Hedderwick, Mairi. *Janet Reachfar and Chickabird* (Duncan, Jane), 449
Katie Morag and the big boy cousins, 496
Katie Morag and the tiresome Ted, 496
Katie Morag and the two grandmothers, 496
Katie Morag delivers the mail, 496

Heelis, Beatrix *see* Potter, Beatrix

Heffernan, Ed. *Coyote goes hunting for fire* (Bernstein, Margery), 385
Earth namer (Bernstein, Margery), 385
How the sun made a promise and kept it (Bernstein, Margery), 385

Hefter, Richard. *Some, more, most* (Freudberg, Judy), 465
The strawberry book of shapes, 496

Heine, Helme. *Friends*, 496
King Bounce the 1st, 496
Merry-go-round, 496
Mr. Miller the dog, 496
The most wonderful egg in the world, 496
One day in paradise, 496
The pigs' wedding, 496
Superhare, 496
Three little friends the alarm clock, 496
Three little friends the racing cart, 496
Three little friends the visitor, 496

Heins, Sheila. *The last free bird* (Stone, A. Harris), 647

Hellard, Susan. *Froggie goes a-courting*, 497
It's not fair! (Harper, Anita), 491

Hellen, Nancy. *Bus stop*, 497

Heller, Linda. *Alexis and the golden ring*, 497
The castle on Hester Street, 497
Lily at the table, 497
A picture book of Hanukkah (Adler, David A.), 351
A picture book of Jewish holidays (Adler, David A.), 351
A picture book of Passover (Adler, David A.), 351

Heller, Nicholas. *An adventure at sea*, 497
Happy birthday, Moe dog, 497
The monster in the cave, 497

Heller, Ruth. *Animals born alive and well*, 497
Chickens aren't the only ones, 497
How to hide a butterfly, 497
How to hide a polar bear, 497
How to hide an octopus, 497
King of the birds (Climo, Shirley), 425
Kites sail high, 497
Plants that never ever bloom, 497
The reason for a flower, 497

Helmer, Jean Cassels. *Animals in disguise* (Seymour, Peter), 631
Insects (Seymour, Peter), 631

Helweg, Hans. *Farm animals*, 497

Henderson, Doris. *Biddy and the ducks* (Sondergaard, Arensa), 640

Henderson, Marion. *Biddy and the ducks* (Sondergaard, Arensa), 640

Hendricks, Don. *My dad's a smokejumper* (Hill, Mary Lou), 500

Hendrickson, June. *Bantie and her chicks* (Boreman, Jean), 394

Hendry, Linda. *The queen who stole the sky* (Garrett, Jennifer), 470

Henkes, Kevin. *All alone*, 497
Bailey goes camping, 497
Chester's way, 497
Clean enough, 497
Grandpa and Bo, 497
Jessica, 497
Sheila Rae, the brave, 497
A weekend with Wendell, 498

Henrie, Marc. *Cats* (Henrie, Fiona), 498
Dogs (Henrie, Fiona), 498
Gerbils (Henrie, Fiona), 498
Rabbits (Henrie, Fiona), 498

Henrioud, Charles *see* Matias

Henry, Marie H. *Bunnies all day long* (Ehrlich, Amy), 452

J

Russell, Naomi. *The tree*, 618
Russell, Sandra Joanne. *A farmer's dozen*, 618
Russo, Marisabina. *The big fat worm* (Van Laan, Nancy), 661
Easy-to-make spaceships that really fly (Blocksma, Mary), 390
The line up book, 618
Only six more days, 618
A week of lullabies (Plotz, Helen), 599
Why do grownups have all the fun?, 618
Russo, Susan. *The ice cream ocean and other delectable poems of the sea*, 618
The moon's the north wind's cooky, 573
Ruthen, Marlene Lobell. *Rachel and Mischa* (Bayar, Steven), 377
The shofar that lost its voice (Fass, David E.), 457
Rutherford, Bill. *Favorite poems for the children's hour* (Bouton, Josephine), 394
Rutherford, Bonnie. *Favorite poems for the children's hour* (Bouton, Josephine), 394
Rutherford, Erica. *The owl and the pussycat* (Lear, Edward), 538
Rutherford, Meg. *Just so stories* (Kipling, Rudyard), 528
Ryan, DyAnne DiSalvo *see* DiSalvo-Ryan, DyAnne
Ryan, Susannah. *What's missing?* (Yektai, Niki), 681
Rylands, Ljiljana. *The Cinderella rebus book* (Morris, Ann), 574
The Little Red Riding Hood rebus book (Morris, Ann), 574

S

Sabuda, Robert James. *The fiddler's son* (Coco, Eugene Bradley), 426
The wishing well (Coco, Eugene Bradley), 426
Sage, Juniper *see* Hurd, Edith Thacher
Sahula, Peter. *The zoo book* (Allen, Robert), 357
St. Tamara. *Chickaree, a red squirrel*, 620
Save that raccoon! (Miklowitz, Gloria D.), 568
Sakai, Sanryo. *Kappa's tug-of-war with the big brown horse* (Baruch, Dorothy), 375
Saldutti, Denise. *I think he likes me* (Winthrop, Elizabeth), 677
The moon (Stevenson, Robert Louis), 646
Salek, Jaroslav. *Patterns of nature* (Baker, Jeffrey J. W.), 371
Salem, Mary Miller. *Playland pony* (Meeks, Esther K.), 567
Salih, Metin. *Daisy's discovery* (Kelley, Anne), 524
Salle, Janet La *see* La Salle, Janet
Saltzberg, Barney. *Cromwell*, 620
It must have been the wind, 620
The yawn, 620
Salvo-Ryan, DyAnne Di *see* DiSalvo-Ryan, DyAnne
Salzman, Yuri. *The little hen and the giant* (Polushkin, Maria), 600

The man who entered a contest (Krasilovsky, Phyllis), 531
Two homes for Lynn (Noble, June), 583
Salzmann, Laurence. *A family Passover* (Rosen, Anne), 615
Sam, Joe. *The invisible hunters* (Rohmer, Harriet), 614
Sambin, Michele. *Caught in the rain* (Ferro, Beatriz), 458
Francie's paper puppy (Bröger, Achim), 401
Samsa, Ermanno. *The lazy beaver* (Gallo, Giovanni), 469
Samton, Sheila White. *Beside the bay*, 620
Meet Jack Appleknocker (Sundgaard, Arnold), 648
The world from my window, 620
Samuels, Barbara. *The bananas move to the ceiling* (Manes, Esther), 559
Duncan and Dolores, 620
Faye and Dolores, 620
Sanchez, Carlos. *Perez and Martina* (Belpré, Pura), 380
Sandberg, Inger. *Nicholas' red day*, 620
Sandberg, Lasse. *Come on out, Daddy!* (Sandberg, Inger), 620
Dusty wants to borrow everything (Sandberg, Inger), 620
Dusty wants to help (Sandberg, Inger), 620
Little Anna saved (Sandberg, Inger), 620
Little ghost Godfry (Sandberg, Inger), 620
Nicholas' favorite pet (Sandberg, Inger), 620
Nicholas' red day (Sandberg, Inger), 620
Sanderson, Ruth. *Five nests* (Arnold, Caroline), 365
The pudgy bunny book, 604
The sleeping beauty (Grimm, Jacob), 485
We remember Philip (Simon, Norma), 636
Sandford, John. *Argyle* (Wallace, Barbara Brooks), 666
Sandin, Joan. *Clipper ship* (Lewis, Thomas P.), 542
Crocodile and hen (Lexau, Joan M.), 543
Daniel's duck (Bulla, Clyde Robert), 408
Hill of fire (Lewis, Thomas P.), 542
The house of a mouse (Fisher, Aileen), 460
It all began with a drip, drip, drip (Lexau, Joan M.), 543
The long way to a new land, 620
The secret box (Cole, Joanna), 428
Small Wolf (Benchley, Nathaniel), 381
Time for Uncle Joe (Jewell, Nancy), 518
Woodchuck (McNulty, Faith), 557
Sandland, Reg. *The town that moved* (Finsand, Mary Jane), 459
San Souci, Daniel. *The bedtime book*, 378
The brave little tailor (Grimm, Jacob), 483
The legend of Scarface (San Souci, Robert D.), 621
The legend of Sleepy Hollow (Irving, Washington), 514
The little mermaid (Andersen, H. C. (Hans Christian)), 359
Song of Sedna (San Souci, Robert D.), 621
The ugly duckling (Andersen, H. C. (Hans Christian)), 361
Vassilisa the wise (Sherman, Josepha), 633

Szumski, Richard. *Let's take a trip* (Baugh, Dolores M.), 377

T

Taback, Simms. *Buggy riddles* (Hall, Katy), 490
Euphonia and the flood (Calhoun, Mary), 412
Fishy riddles (Hall, Katy), 490
Jason's bus ride (Ziefert, Harriet), 685
Joseph had a little overcoat, 649
On our way to the barn (Ziefert, Harriet), 685
On our way to the forest (Ziefert, Harriet), 685
On our way to the water (Ziefert, Harriet), 685
On our way to the zoo (Ziefert, Harriet), 685
Too much noise (McGovern, Ann), 554

Taber, Anthony. *Cats' eyes*, 649

Tafuri, Nancy. *Across the stream* (Ginsburg, Mirra), 474
All asleep (Pomerantz, Charlotte), 600
All year long, 649
Coconut (Dragonwagon, Crescent), 448
Do not disturb, 649
Early morning in the barn, 649
Four brave sailors (Ginsburg, Mirra), 474
Have you seen my duckling?, 649
If I had a Paka (Pomerantz, Charlotte), 600
In a red house, 649
Junglewalk, 649
My friends, 649
My hands can (Holzenthaler, Jean), 507
Nata (Griffith, Helen V.), 483
One wet jacket, 649
The Piney Woods peddler (Shannon, George), 631
Rabbit's morning, 650
The song (Zolotow, Charlotte), 688
Two new sneakers, 650
Where we sleep, 650
Who's counting?, 650

Taggart, Tricia. *My sister says* (Baker, Betty), 370

Taina, Hannu. *Mister King* (Siekkinen, Raija), 635

Takahashi, Haruo. *Tuxedo Sam* (Nichols, Cathy), 583

Takihara, Koji. *Rolli*, 650

Talbot, Nathan. *My sister's silent world* (Arthur, Catherine), 365

Tallarico, Tony. *At home*, 650

Tallon, Robert. *ABCDEF...*, 349
Handella, 650
Latouse my moose, 650

Tamburine, Jean. *I think I will go to the hospital*, 650
It's nice to be little (Stanley, John), 642

Tan, Pierre Le *see* Le-Tan, Pierre

Tanaka, Hideyuki. *The happy dog*, 650

Tang, You-Shah. *Pie-Biter* (McCunn, Ruthanne L.), 553

Taniuchi, Kota. *Trolley*, 650

Tarrant, Margaret. *The Margaret Tarrant nursery rhyme book*, 650

Tateishi, Shuji. *Baby owl* (Funazaki, Yasuko), 467

Taylor, Anelise. *Lights on, lights off*, 650

Taylor, Elizabeth Watson. *The animals who changed their colors* (Allamand, Pascale), 356

Taylor, Jody. *The old witch and the ghost parade* (DeLage, Ida), 440

Taylor, Liba. *Mazal-Tov* (Patterson, José), 593

Taylor, Michael C. *The sing-song of old man kangaroo* (Kipling, Rudyard), 528

Taylor, Scott. *Fiesta!* (Behrens, June), 379

Taylor, Talus. *The adventures of the three colors* (Tison, Annette), 654
Animal hide-and-seek (Tison, Annette), 654

Taylor, Tamar. *How Georgina drove the car very carefully from Boston to New York* (Bate, Lucy), 376

Tejima, Keizaburo. *The bears' autumn*, 651
Fox's dream, 651
Owl lake, 651
Swan sky, 651

Tenggren, Gustaf. *Mother Goose*, 577
The night before Christmas (Moore, Clement C.), 573
Thumbelina (Andersen, H. C. (Hans Christian)), 360

Tenniel, John. *The nursery "Alice"* (Carroll, Lewis), 416

Tenny, Eric. *Lions and tigers* (Pluckrose, Henry), 599

Tennyson, Noel. *The lady's chair and the ottoman*, 651

Testa, Fulvio. *The butterfly collector* (Lewis, Naomi), 542
The ideal home, 651
If you look around, 651
If you take a paintbrush, 651
If you take a pencil, 651
The land where the ice cream grows, 651
Leaves (Lewis, Naomi), 542
The paper airplane (Baumann, Kurt), 377
The paper airplane, 651
Wolf's favor, 651

Tester, Sylvia Root. *Chase!*, 651
Parade!, 651
A visit to the zoo, 651

Thaler, Mike. *The yellow brick toad*, 652

Thamer, Katie. *The black horse* (Mayer, Marianna), 565

Tharlet, Eve. *Dizzy from fools* (Miller, M. L.), 570
The princess and the pea (Andersen, H. C. (Hans Christian)), 360
The wishing table (Grimm, Jacob), 486

Thatcher, Frances. *Percival's party* (Hynard, Julia), 512
Snowy the rabbit (Hynard, Stephen), 512
Snuffles' house (Faunce-Brown, Daphne), 457

Thelen, Mary. *The hospital scares me* (Hogan, Paula Z.), 506

Theobalds, Prue. *Marvella's hobby* (Cushman, Jerome), 436
The teddy bears' picnic (Kennedy, Jimmy), 524

Thewlis, Diana. *Johnny Castleseed* (Ormondroyd, Edward), 588

MT